D0003888

Familiar Quotations

Familiar Quotations

*A collection of passages, phrases and
proverbs traced to their sources in
ancient and modern literature*

by JOHN BARTLETT

Fourteenth Edition
REVISED AND ENLARGED

EMILY MORISON BECK, *Editor*

Little, Brown and Company · Boston · Toronto

COPYRIGHT 1882, 1891 BY JOHN BARTLETT
COPYRIGHT 1910, 1914, 1919, 1942 BY
ANNA SPRAGUE DEWOLF AND LOUISA BARTLETT DONALDSON
COPYRIGHT 1937, 1948, © 1955, 1965, 1968 BY
LITTLE, BROWN AND COMPANY (INC.)

ALL RIGHTS RESERVED. NO PART OF THIS BOOK MAY BE
REPRODUCED IN ANY FORM OR BY ANY ELECTRONIC
OR MECHANICAL MEANS INCLUDING INFORMATION
STORAGE AND RETRIEVAL SYSTEMS WITHOUT PERMIS-
SION IN WRITING FROM THE PUBLISHER, EXCEPT BY A
REVIEWER WHO MAY QUOTE BRIEF PASSAGES IN A
REVIEW.

LIBRARY OF CONGRESS CATALOGUE CARD NO. 68-15664

00004

First Edition Published 1855
Fourteenth Edition Published 1968

Eleventh Printing

Published simultaneously in Canada
by Little, Brown & Company (Canada) Limited

PRINTED IN THE UNITED STATES OF AMERICA

Preface

TO THE FOURTEENTH EDITION

"BARTLETT" has now entered into our language, itself a "familiar quotation," not associated with either pears or trees, but a source book nearly as indispensable as the dictionary: "Look it up in *Bartlett!*" Sir Winston Churchill thought it an "admirable work" and studied it intently, he tells us in *My Early Life.* "The quotations when engraved upon the memory give you good thoughts. They also make you anxious to read the authors and look for more." Readers and editors of *Bartlett* have done just this—and found more. In more than a century of life *Bartlett* has grown prodigiously and its sales increase steadily each year. So, why now a new edition?

The most obvious reason, of course, is the number of quotations that have become memorable since the last edition in 1955. Historical events, the growth of philosophy and science, the eminence of certain statesmen, writers, poets, and others who use words effectively, strongly influence our use of language and choice of expressions. An appendix to *Bartlett* might have taken care of these addenda; this had been done in some earlier editions. But today there are important additional reasons for a thorough revision—if, like a dictionary, this collection of historical and living sayings is to keep abreast of the times.

Literary tastes and popular expressions change from one generation to another, and the facility of communication has accelerated this process. Figures of the past emerge from the shadow of neglect and begin to be quoted; others fade from fashion, or their words lose their relevance to the times. Fads create catchy phrases, some of them lasting. And all the while there is an accretion of sayings which, one supposes, will provide a ballast for civilization for as long as men continue to communicate with one another.

As the two postwar editions of *Bartlett*, the twelfth and thirteenth, record the advent of the atomic age, so the fourteenth bears the particular imprint of the last decade. Since the publication of the last edition, a large number of world-renowned figures now "belong to the ages," leaving their mark upon our culture—men like Churchill, Kennedy, Adlai Stevenson, Pope John XXIII, Nehru, Oppenheimer, Hammarskjöld, Albert Schweitzer; distinguished men of letters like Robert Frost, Hemingway, T. S. Eliot, Faulkner, Aldous Huxley, E. E. Cummings, Roethke, Pasternak, Thurber, Carl Sandburg, Camus. It is interesting to speculate, furthermore, whether this edition that bears their death dates for the first time will carry more of their quotations than will future editions, affected as they will be by historical perspective.

Some phenomena of recent years are crystallized in a word or phrase: beat generation, brinkmanship, the Great Society, the affluent society, the multiversity, cybernetics, racism, the revolution of rising expectations, the American Establishment, poverty—the other America.

The nature and the size of the *Bartlett* audience provide another reason for a new edition. The vastly increased number of students, the expanding interests of the intellectually curious, as evidenced by the tremendous variety of paperbacks and inexpensive editions on every subject, demand a broader reach into other fields of literature and an amplification of authors hitherto inadequately represented.

Outdated translation is another reason for revision. The classics for the most part have been heretofore represented by translations unchanged since the nineteenth century, some of them clearly archaic. Until now Homer has appeared in Pope's translation, of which even his contemporary, the classicist Richard Bentley, remarked, "It is a pretty poem, Mr. Pope, but you must not call it Homer." True enough; those "familiar quotations" like "Welcome the coming, speed the parting guest" are more Pope than Homer. They now appear appropriately under Pope, while well-known Homeric lines, like "All strangers and beggars are from Zeus, and a gift, though small, is precious," are here included for the first time.

As our range of reference expands inversely with the shrinkage of space on this earth, expressions and sayings from the cultures and literatures of Asia, Europe and South America are assimilated into our common heritage. Increasing interest in science, and the recognition that

Freud, for example, in Auden's phrase is now "a whole climate of opinion," insist on greater representation from scientists and psychiatrists.

A number of figures besides Freud and Jung have never appeared in *Bartlett* before, perhaps because they were not thought to have said anything actually "familiar," or perhaps because they have not occurred to the editors as natural sources of quotations. But it was astonishing to find among the missing Confucius, Columbus, Chekhov, Bolívar, Brandeis, Bergson, Sir Thomas Malory, Cotton Mather, John Marshall, Pushkin, Flaubert, Gandhi, Lao Tzu, Kant, Kierkegaard. . . . Other important figures like St. Augustine or Julius Caesar formerly were credited with a single quote, not necessarily the most famous one.

An amazing number of famous quotations have been overlooked in previous editions. Here are a few: Man is the measure of all things (Protagoras); The greatest reverence is due the young (Juvenal); There is always something new out of Africa (Pliny); But it does move (Galileo); There go the ships (Psalm 104); When I am dead and opened, you shall find "Calais" lying in my heart (Mary Tudor); But that was in another country; and besides, the wench is dead (Marlowe); One man with courage makes a majority (Andrew Jackson); Surprised by joy (Wordsworth); Not Angles, but Angels (Gregory I); Praise the sea, on shore remain (John Florio); $E = mc^2$ (Einstein); Q.E.D. (Euclid); War is much too serious a matter to be entrusted to the military (Clemenceau); Hypocrite lecteur—mon semblable—mon frère (Baudelaire); A journey of a thousand miles must begin with a single step (Lao Tzu); I beseech you, in the bowels of Christ, think it possible you may be mistaken (Cromwell), a saying which Judge Learned Hand would like to have "written over the portals of every church, every school, every courthouse, and . . . of every legislative body in the United States."

Errors persist—one for over a hundred years: the misquotation of the title of Gray's *Elegy* in omitting the word *Written* before *in a Country Churchyard*.

The inescapable conclusion is that a collection of this kind must be thoroughly overhauled from time to time. Today a single editor, or a brace of editors, is no longer adequate for what to John Bartlett in 1891 was still "this very agreeable pursuit." It is one thing to carry on the tradition of "familiar" and "worthy of perpetuation," to recognize in the sifting of hoary sayings the line that still persists as vital or pertinent. But to assume authority on the well-known quotations in all the fields and among all the authors now represented in this edition would be presumptuous. Thus, for the first time, the editor of *Familiar Quotations* has had a staff of consulting scholars who have spent many hours helping to compile well-known material from the classics, from Chinese, Japanese, Sanskrit, Russian, German, French, and Spanish sources, from Latin America, and from the sciences, psychology, medicine, American history, political science, American and English literature. They have also scanned the existing text for errors, and recommended what to eliminate as "dead wood" or no longer relevant. At least a fourth of these experts are under thirty, to give proper representation to the younger generation.

The editor of the fourteenth edition gratefully acknowledges the contributions of the following: Elizabeth Perkins Aldrich, Peter Anastas, George Basalla, William J. Courtenay, Bernard De Voto (for Mark Twain in the thirteenth and fourteenth editions), Admiral E. M. Eller USN, Dudley Fitts, Arthur Freeman, Paul Freund, Richard Gombrich, Stanley Kunitz, Elena Levin, Louis Lyons, David McCord, Robert Minshall, Samuel Eliot Morison, Henry A. Murray, Gregory Rabassa, John Paul Russo, Alain Seznec, Zeph Stewart, Maurice B. Strauss, M.D., John L. Sweeney, Prescott B. Wintersteen, Jr., Philip Young.

In addition to the countless friends and the faithful readers of *Bartlett* who write in to point out errors and omissions, the following are to be especially thanked for help and advice: Judge Bailey Aldrich, Catharine Cooper, John Kenneth Galbraith, Donald Gallup, Seymour Harris, James Laughlin, Robert Lescher, Henry F. Pommer, Arthur Schlesinger, Jr., Robert Sussman, Michael des Tombe, Alexander Williams, the Reverend Prescott B. Wintersteen, D.D.

It is impossible to exaggerate what the thirteenth and fourteenth editions of *Familiar Quotations* owe to Mary Rackliffe, head of the copyediting department at Little, Brown and Company. Her mastery of complex styling problems is matched by her exceptional memory and ear for the elusive line. In judgment and taste she is without peer. Moreover, she is responsible for the index, which is the largest and most thorough that *Bartlett* has ever had.

* * *

"We come too late to say anything which has not been said already," observed La Bruyère in 1688. But anyone looking at the quotations after that date will know that there will always be new ways to bring home old truths. "Poetry reminds man of his limitations . . . of the richness and diversity of his existence," John F. Kennedy remarked. It has always been evident too that, as he said, "Art establishes the basic human truths which must serve as the touchstone of our judgment." The great lines and passages from the ancients make us recognize, with reassurance—or resignation—how little man changes down the ages. Seneca, in the first century, could be speaking of us at this very hour when he writes, "We are mad, not only individually, but nationally. We check manslaughter and isolated murders; but what of war and the much vaunted crime of slaughtering whole peoples?" We can take comfort from Solon in the sixth century B.C.—"I grow old ever learning many things."

Books "are the voices of the distant and the dead," William Ellery Channing tells us, "and make us heirs of the spiritual life of past ages." Quotations, like books, "are true levelers. They give to all, who will faithfully use them, the society, the spiritual presence, of the best and greatest of our race."

Bartlett provides a distillation of this heritage, a guide to the manifold ways in which man has tried to express the basic human truths.

EMILY MORISON BECK, *Editor*

Canton, Massachusetts

Historical Note

THE University Book Store in Cambridge, Massachusetts, was college for John Bartlett. He went to work there at the age of sixteen after attending the Plymouth public schools, and in 1849 when he was twenty-nine he bought the store. It had become a meeting place for book-loving Harvard professors and students, and through them developed John Bartlett's reputation for knowing a quotation, author and source. From his commonplace book of the most popular passages evolved *Familiar Quotations*, which he published himself and had printed in an edition of a thousand copies by the "printers to the university" in 1855.

It was a modest brown paperbound volume of two hundred and fifty-eight pages, representing a hundred and sixty-nine authors, many by a single quotation or, like his friend James Russell Lowell, by two. The Bible and Shakespeare took up about a third of the book; the balance was chiefly English poetry—Milton, Pope, Byron, and Wordsworth claiming the greatest number of entries. There was a small selection of prose from Milton, Bacon, Ben Franklin, Tom Paine, Macaulay, and one maxim from La Rochefoucauld, "Hypocrisy is the homage that vice pays to virtue." No Chaucer, Blake, Shelley, nor several other authors who could not have been much upon the tongue in the mid-nineteenth century. A mere handful of Americans were included: Longfellow, Irving, Bryant, Lowell, and a line each from "Hail Columbia," "The Star-Spangled Banner," and "The Old Oaken Bucket." People then, it seems, were not given to quoting Washington, Adams, Jefferson, Patrick Henry, Daniel Webster, or even Emerson (who made *Bartlett* by the third edition in 1858).

The Gettysburg Address had not yet been delivered. Walt Whitman published *Leaves of Grass* that same year, and Thoreau *Walden* the year before. Both writers were so in advance of their time, it seems, that neither was to be included in *Familiar Quotations* until the tenth edition in 1914, nine years after Bartlett's death.

The little book, one of the earliest collections of quotations, was a success, and in 1863 Little, Brown and Company became the publisher of the fourth edition. John Bartlett joined the firm that same year, becoming senior partner fifteen years later. He continued to edit *Familiar Quotations* until his death at the age of eighty-five in 1905, having also published *The Shakespeare Phrase Book*, a *Catalogue of Books on Angling*, and a *Complete Concordance to Shakespeare's Dramatic Works and Poems*.

In 1914 Nathan Haskell Dole, poet, editor, and translator from the French and Russian, edited the tenth edition, now grown twice the size and three times the thickness of the first. Dole's purpose, as he put it, was "to incorporate in the work quotations from those writers whose place in literature has been achieved since the issue of the ninth edition in 1891," and to add selections from other "best writers of their day." His criterion was that passages should have "the seal of popular approval" and be "distinctly worthy of perpetuation." He paid respectful homage to John Bartlett's "impeccable judgment," declaring, "It is not always easy for Elisha to wear the mantle of Elijah; but it is Elisha's business to carry on his predecessor's work in the same spirit."

Either because of contemporary tastes in literature or oversight, there were some rather surprising omissions in the tenth edition. No Blake, Pindar, Hawthorne, William or Henry James, or Emily Dickinson, to pick at random, but William Butler Yeats made it with, oddly enough, the one poem he himself refused to include in his *Collected Poems*, "The Land of Heart's Desire." There was a large section of "miscellaneous, translations, appendix," and the Bible, for some reason, now appeared at the end of the book. In the present edition it has been restored once more to the front, a fitting opening to quotations from our Judaeo-Christian culture.

No new edition appeared until 1937, a few years after Dole's death. Elijah's mantle passed to Christopher Morley, author, poet, editor, dubbed an "angloliterophile" for his love of the English language for its own sake. Louella D. Everett joined forces as associate editor.

Morley's preface to the eleventh edition is a lively essay which at the outset asks the question which every *Bartlett* editor, we feel, must try to answer: "What makes words memorable?" His broad literary background made him an ideal editor, and Miss Everett's ear for the popular line or verse gave that edition a more topical quality than the book had had hitherto.

For the first time the editors weeded out quotations no longer in currency. Some of the quainter lines by Miss Fannie Steers, Sir Samuel Tuke, and Captain Charles Morris ("Solid men of Boston, make no long orations; Solid men of Boston, drink no deep potations") had seen their day. The flowery descriptive verse and the sugary sentiments of the last half of the nineteenth century were sharply cut, though a great deal still remained. Furthermore, Miss Everett combed over the favorite poetry of the Nineties, and added such versifiers as Mary Artemisia Lathbury, "the Chatauqua Laureate"; and Julia Moore, "the Sweet Singer of Michigan," of whom Mark Twain wrote: "The one and unfailing great quality which distinguishes her poetry from Shakespeare's and makes it precious to us is its stern and simple irrelevancy." They still persevere into this edition of the 1960's.

Morley not only added to the twentieth-century quotations, he culled every period from ancient times on, reflecting perhaps a broadening cultural outlook on the part of the average American. The chronological order of authors remained, but otherwise the change in the eleventh edition was more striking than in any other, and the innovation of the two-column page allowed a vast increment of new quotations within a single volume.

Morley's theory of selection was broader than John Bartlett's. "Previous editions adhered, almost with pedantry, to the touchstone of familiarity," he wrote. "Only phrases or quotations that had gained wide recognition, become hypodermic, were admitted. . . . In the matter of new inclusions this edition is not so stringent: we have tried to make literary power the criterion rather than width and vulgarity of fame."

"Literary power" is so much more a matter of personal opinion than "familiarity" that this new approach opened up for future *Bartlett* editors the temptation to exploit their literary passions. Restraint has been necessary to keep the volume from becoming idiosyncratic or growing into an anthology.

World War II and the atomic age required an updating of *Bartlett*, and in 1948 Morley and Everett published the twelfth edition with quotations from Churchill, Hitler, Einstein, the Charter of the United Nations, William Laurence, Douglas MacArthur, Truman, Lippmann, and others. There was also a catchall section for quotations omitted in previous editions, like "I have not yet begun to fight" (John Paul Jones); Article III, section 3 on treason from the Constitution of the United States; Donne's "No man is an island," famous as the source of the title of Hemingway's novel *For Whom the Bell Tolls*; Lord Acton's "Power tends to corrupt"; Emerson's "Four snakes gliding up and down . . . not to eat, not for love . . ."

The year 1955 marked the centennial of *Familiar Quotations*, and it was altogether appropriate for a new revised edition to appear, this time issued by the Little, Brown editors themselves. They continued the tradition of adding new quotations throughout and of eliminating the no-longer familiar, thus improving the work, which increases steadily in popularity.

The fourteenth edition is discussed in the Preface.

EMILY MORISON BECK, *Editor*

Guide to the Use
of FAMILIAR QUOTATIONS

For the sections of the book see the *Contents*, page xix.
The *Preface*, p. v, discusses the fourteenth edition.
The *Historical Note*, p. xi, tells of the different editions of
Familiar Quotations from the first edition of 1855 on.

The Quotations

The arrangement is not by topics or subject matter, nor is it by authors alphabetically, as in some collections. It is by authors chronologically with selections from their works in chronological order. Birth and death dates as well as pseudonyms accompany the author's name, and each work is dated wherever possible. Quotations give chapter and verse of their sources, or similarly, act, scene and line from dramatic works.

The chronological arrangement lends historical value to the collection of authors and quotations. One becomes quickly aware that Pericles, Sophocles, Euripides, Thucydides and Plato were contemporaries, as were Confucius, Lao Tzu, Aesop, Heraclitus, and the *Suttapitaka* a century earlier. The great poets of the Middle Ages—Dante, Petrarch, and Chaucer—follow one upon another. One discovers that Columbus, Sir Thomas Malory, and Machiavelli were contemporaries. Shakespeare appropriately is in the midst of the Elizabethans. Ben Franklin, Samuel Johnson, William Pitt, and John Adams were contemporaries; so were Jefferson, Goethe, and Talleyrand, while Kipling and Yeats were born in the same year and lived, actively writing, into their seventies.

The chronological selections of an author show his development, and in some instances provide a distillation of his work. Students have found this helpful in studying an author, both as a review and as an incentive to read more of the work quoted.

Footnotes and Cross-References

When the quotation is a translation the original language if familiar in itself appears in a footnote. For example, "The people are a many-headed beast," from Horace, on page 123a, has a footnote quoting the Latin, with cross-references to variations, and examples of derivative versions.

In cases where the familiar quotation differs from the original whence it derives, as in the case of the Latin mottoes of the Great Seal of the United States from Virgil, footnotes (on pages 116b, 117a, and 119b) provide full information. The footnotes also cross-reference. For example, a quotation from Horace's *Epode XIV* has a footnote cross-referring to Keats's *Ode to a Nightingale*, which it inspired. Under Keats we find a footnote to the *Ode* which cross-refers back to Horace.

Suppose you wish to find out who first used the expression "iron curtain." You look up either "iron" or "curtain" in the index, which sends you to page 924b. Here, under Churchill, you find the quotation that made the expression famous, in his speech at Fulton, Missouri, on March 5, 1946, together with a lengthy footnote which relates the other ways people used it before he did.

Franklin D. Roosevelt is usually credited with having first expressed the idea that "The only thing we have to fear is fear itself." Both the index and the footnote for the Roosevelt quotation indicate its derivation from earlier writers, some in languages other than English.

Index of Authors (page 1107)

Authors are listed alphabetically with their birth and death dates. Page numbers are given for both the author's main entry and for his quotations in footnotes throughout the text.

Index (page 1155)

In this edition we have continued and expanded the *Bartlett* tradition of thorough indexing of the quotations. The result is voluminous —more than 117,000 entries.

This thoroughness is aimed first of all at facilitating the location of remembered or half-remembered or almost forgotten or topical

("Let's see what *Bartlett* has about morning") quotations. The index plays another role as a browsing book of unusual proportions. The pursuit of an evocative index entry noticed almost at random may lead to renewed pleasures or to the discovery of hitherto unsuspected sources of illumination and enjoyment.

Keep the following in mind when using the index:

(1) Spelling follows American (Webster) forms, but there are occasional exceptions; for example, *burnt* (not *burned*) *offerings*.

(2) Hyphenation also occasionally varies from Webster; for example, we index *drop-scenes* (in Webster *drop scenes*) to isolate it from other *drop* entries.

(3) Dialect and other significantly variant spellings are generally indexed in Webster forms as well as in the original (*'ammer/hammer*).

(4) Alphabetization is (we hope) strict, which means that entries for inflected forms of a word may be widely separated from entries for the word itself; for example, *nightcap, nightingale, nightmare* and other entries separate *night* from *night's*. The standard order of plural and possessive forms is: *lover's, lovers, lovers'*.

(5) When an important word in a very familiar phrase is in a contracted form (*Beauty's* but skin deep; An honest *man's* the noblest work of God) it is indexed also in the singular (*Beauty* skin deep; Honest *man* noblest work). But most such contractions are indexed only in the original form (What *cat's* averse to fish).

(6) When entries under one keyword continue to another column of the index, the keyword is repeated at the top of the new column. If you find your keyword at the top of a column, check the foot of the previous column—or page if necessary—to be sure of covering all the entries under the keyword.

(7) The words of each entry are in the same order as in the quotation, with the keyword abbreviated in the correct position except when it starts the quotation (*a* and *b* with the page number indicate left and right columns on the page):

> Hope, all h. abandon who enter here, 159b
> beautiful Evelyn H., 663b
> deferred maketh the heart sick, 24a
> feed on h., 201a
> is the thing with feathers, 735a

When the keyword occurs both at the start and in the body of the entry it is not abbreviated:

Alps, beyond A. lies Italy, 125a
on Alps arise, 403a

(8) There are so many familiar ways of indexing one familiar phrase under one keyword (Love, *one* jot of former l.; Love, *jot* of former l.; Intellect, *monuments* of unaging i.; Intellect, *unaging* i.), that you should look for your quotation in all possible alphabetical locations under the keyword. Several columns of entries may come between one possibility and another (as in the first example above).

(9) In checking a two-word term of which one word is the keyword (for example, *old age*), note that retention of the quotation's original order means that all entries about the term will not necessarily appear grouped together:

Age, dance attention upon old a., 885a
green old a., 367b
old a. and experience, 382b
old a. should burn, 1070b
'tis well an old a. is out, 372a

(10) If you don't find your quotation under one keyword, try another. The first word of a quotation, moreover, is not necessarily a keyword. If you think Milton said *fresh fields and pastures new*, you will not find it under *fields* but you will (with its original *fresh woods*) under *fresh, pastures,* and *new*. We have, however, tried to include in footnotes and in the index such popular misquotations as A *poor thing but mine own* as well as the originals—in this case *An ill-favored thing, sir, but mine own*, from Shakespeare's *As You Like It*.

(11) If your quotation does not emerge under any of the remembered keywords, try synonyms or related words. A quotation about *valor* is often remembered as about *courage; dullness* as *boredom; approbation* as *praise*; and so on.

(12) If you are using the index as a topical source (looking for all the quotations you can find about *nature* or *bravery* or *wisdom* or *love* or whatever), think of all the synonyms and related words you can —and then, in addition, browse, eat, enjoy. You'll find more.

Emily Morison Beck
Mary Rackliffe

Contents

Familiar Quotations

ANCIENT EGYPT[1]

Mine is yesterday, I know tomorrow.
*Book of the Dead [c. 3500 B.C.
and after]*

Be a craftsman in speech that thou mayest be strong, for the strength of one is the tongue, and speech is mightier than all fighting.[2]
*Maxims of Ptahhotep
[c. 3400 B.C.]*

More acceptable is the virtue of the upright man than the ox of him that doeth iniquity.
Instruction to Prince Merikere from his father, a pharaoh of Heracleopolis [c. 2200 B.C.]

A man's virtue is his monument, but forgotten is the man of evil repute.
*Egyptian tombstone inscription
[c. 2100 B.C.]*

None cometh from thence
That he may tell us how they fare.
Lo, no man taketh his goods with him.
Yea, none returneth again that is gone thither.[3]
*The Song of the Harp-Player
[c. 2100 B.C.]*

To whom do I speak today?
Brothers are evil,
Friends of today are not of love. . . .
To whom do I speak today?
There are no righteous,
The land is left to those who do iniquity.
*Papyrus[4] by an unknown author
[c. 2000 B.C.]. Second Poem*

Death is before me today
As a man longs to see his house
When he has spent many years in captivity.
*Papyrus by an unknown author.
Third Poem*

Creator of all and giver of their sustenance.
Hymn to the Sun by Suti and Hor, architects to Amenhotep III [c. 1400 B.C.]

Valiant herdman who drives his cattle,
Their refuge and giver of their sustenance. **Ib.**

Sole lord taking captive all lands every day,
As one beholding them that walk therein;
Shining in the sky, a being as the sun.
He makes the seasons by the months,
Heat when he desires,
Cold when he desires. **Ib.**

Every land is in rejoicing
At his rising every day, in order to praise him. **Ib.**

IKHNATON
c. 1385 – 1358 B.C.

Thou dawnest beautifully in the horizon of the sky,
O living Aton who wast the Beginning of life! *Hymn to the Sun*

When thou settest in the western horizon of the sky,
The earth is in darkness like death.[1]
Ib.

Every lion cometh forth from his den,
All serpents, they sting.

[1] See *Psalm 104:20*, p. 21b.

---

[1] From JAMES HENRY BREASTED, *The Dawn of Civilization* [1933].
[2] The pen is mightier than the sword. — EDWARD BULWER-LYTTON, *Richelieu*, act II, sc. 2
[3] See *Ecclesiastes 5:15*, p. 28a; *I Timothy 6:7*, p. 55a; Theognis, p. 77a; and Shakespeare, p. 262a.
[4] Preserved in the Berlin Museum.

Darkness broods,
The world is in silence,
He that made them resteth in his
horizon.[1]   *Hymn to the Sun*

Bright is the earth when thou risest in
the horizon;
When thou shinest as Aton by day
Thou drivest away the darkness. . . .
Men waken and stand upon their
feet
When thou hast raised them up. . . .
Then in all the world they do their
work.[2]   *Ib.*

The barks sail upstream and down-
stream alike.
Every highway is open because thou
dawnest.
The fish in the river leap up before
thee.
Thy rays are in the midst of the great
green sea.[3]   *Ib.*

How manifold are thy works!
They are hidden before men,
O sole God, beside whom there is no
other.
Thou didst create the earth according
to thy heart.[4]   *Ib.*

AMENEMOPE[5]
Tenth century B.C.

In order to return a report to the one
that sent him.[6]
The Wisdom of Amenemope, I

Incline thine ears to hear my sayings,

[1] See *Psalm 104:21*, p. 21b.
[2] See *Psalm 104:22, 23*, p. 21b.
[3] See *Psalm 104:25, 26*, p. 21b.
[4] See *Psalm 104:24*, p. 21b.
[5] The Wisdom of Amenemope was translated
into Hebrew, it was read by Hebrews, and an
important part of it found its way into the
Old Testament. . . . This whole section of
about a chapter and a half of the Book of
Proverbs (22:17–23:11) is largely drawn verba-
tim from The Wisdom of Amenemope; that is,
the Hebrew version is practically a literal translation from the Egyptian. — JAMES HENRY
BREASTED, *The Dawn of Civilization* [1933]
[6] See *Proverbs 22:21*, p. 25b.

And apply thine heart to their compre-
hension.
For it is a profitable thing to put them
in thy heart.[1]
The Wisdom of Amenemope, III

The truly prudent man, who putteth
himself aside,
Is like a tree growing in a garden,
He flourisheth and multiplieth his
fruit,
He abideth in the presence of his
lord,
His fruit is sweet, his shade is pleasant,
And he findeth his end in the garden.[2]
     Ib. VI

Remove not the landmark on the
boundary of the fields.[3]   *Ib. VII*

Better is poverty in the hand of
God
Than riches in the storehouse.
Better are loaves when the heart is
joyous
Than riches in unhappiness.[4]   *Ib. IX*

Weary not thyself to seek for more.[5]
     Ib.

They [riches] have made themselves
wings like geese,
And they have flown to heaven.[6]
     Ib. X

Consider for thyself these thirty chapters,
That they are satisfaction and instruction.[7]   *Ib. XXVII*

A scribe skillful in his office,
He shall find himself worthy of being a
courtier.[8]   *Ib.*

[1] See *Proverbs 22:17–18*, p. 25b.
[2] See *Psalm 1*, p. 166, and *Jeremiah 17:5–8*,
p. 34b.
[3] See *Proverbs 22:28*, p. 25b.
[4] See *Proverbs 15:16–17*, p. 24b.
[5] See *Proverbs 23:4*, p. 25b.
[6] See *Proverbs 23:5*, p. 25b.
[7] See *Proverbs 22:20*, p. 25b, the direct reference to Amenemope and his sayings.
[8] See *Proverbs 22:29*, p. 25b.

THE HOLY BIBLE
THE KING JAMES VERSION[1]
1611

THE OLD TESTAMENT

In the beginning God created the heaven and the earth.

And the earth was without form, and void; and darkness was upon the face of the deep. And the Spirit of God moved upon the face of the waters.

And God said, Let there be light:[2] and there was light.

Genesis[3] 1:1–3[4]

And the evening and the morning were the first day. 1:5

And God saw that it was good. 1:10

And God said, Let us make man in our image, after our likeness. 1:26

Male and female created he them. 1:27

Be fruitful, and multiply, and replenish the earth, and subdue it: and have dominion over the fish of the sea, and over the fowl of the air, and over every living thing that moveth upon the earth. 1:28

And on the seventh day God ended his work which he had made. 2:2

And the Lord God formed man of the dust of the ground, and breathed into his nostrils the breath of life; and man became a living soul.

Genesis 2:7

And the Lord God planted a garden eastward in Eden. 2:8

The tree of life also in the midst of the garden. 2:9

But of the tree of the knowledge of good and evil, thou shalt not eat of it: for in the day that thou eatest thereof thou shalt surely die. 2:17

It is not good that the man should be alone; I will make him an help meet for him. 2:18

And the Lord God caused a deep sleep to fall upon Adam, and he slept: and he took one of his ribs, and closed up the flesh instead thereof.

And the rib, which the Lord God had taken from man, made he a woman. 2:21–22

Bone of my bones, and flesh of my flesh. 2:23

Therefore shall a man leave his father and his mother, and shall cleave unto his wife: and they shall be one flesh.

And they were both naked, the man and his wife, and were not ashamed. 2:24–25

Now the serpent was more subtile than any beast of the field. 3:1

Your eyes shall be opened, and ye shall be as gods, knowing good and evil. 3:5

And they sewed fig leaves together, and made themselves aprons.[1]

And they heard the voice of the Lord God walking in the garden in the cool of the day. 3:7–8

---

[1] Among all our joys, there was no one that more filled our hearts, than the blessed continuance of the preaching of God's sacred Word among us; which is that inestimable treasure, which excelleth all the riches of the earth; because the fruit thereof extendeth itself, not only to the time spent in this transitory world, but directeth and disposeth men unto that eternal happiness which is above in heaven. — *The Translators' Dedication to James I*

[2] Fiat lux. — *The Vulgate*

[3] The First Book of Moses, first of the five books of the Pentateuch.

[4] Numbers in Bible citations represent chapter and verse.

[1] The Geneva Bible of 1557–1560 was known sometimes as the Breeches Bible because in this passage "aprons" is rendered as "breeches."

The woman whom thou gavest to be with me, she gave me of the tree, and I did eat.   *Genesis 3:12*

What is this that thou hast done? And the woman said, The serpent beguiled me, and I did eat.

And the Lord God said unto the serpent, Because thou hast done this, thou art cursed above all cattle, and above every beast of the field; upon thy belly shalt thou go, and dust shalt thou eat all the days of thy life.   3:13-14

It shall bruise thy head, and thou shalt bruise his heel.   3:15

In sorrow thou shalt bring forth children.   3:16

In the sweat of thy face shalt thou eat bread, till thou return unto the ground; for out of it wast thou taken: for dust thou art, and unto dust shalt thou return.

And Adam called his wife's name Eve; because she was the mother of all living.   3:19-20

So he drove out the man: and he placed at the east of the garden of Eden cherubims, and a flaming sword which turned every way, to keep the way of the tree of life.   3:24

And Abel was a keeper of sheep, but Cain was a tiller of the ground.   4:2

Am I my brother's keeper?   4:9

The voice of thy brother's blood crieth unto me from the ground.   4:10

A fugitive and a vagabond shalt thou be in the earth.   4:12

My punishment is greater than I can bear.   4:13

And the Lord set a mark upon Cain.   4:15

And Cain went out from the presence of the Lord, and dwelt in the land of Nod.   4:16

Jabal: he was the father of such as dwell in tents.   4:20

Jubal: he was the father of all such as handle the harp and organ.   *Genesis 4:21*

And Enoch walked with God.   5:24

And all the days of Methuselah were nine hundred sixty and nine years.   5:27

And Noah begat Shem, Ham, and Japheth.   5:32

There were giants in the earth in those days . . . mighty men which were of old, men of renown.   6:4

Make thee an ark of gopher wood.   6:14

And of every living thing of all flesh, two of every sort shalt thou bring into the ark.   6:19

And the rain was upon the earth forty days and forty nights.   7:12

But the dove found no rest for the sole of her foot.   8:9

And, lo, in her mouth was an olive leaf pluckt off.   8:11

For the imagination of man's heart is evil from his youth.   8:21

While the earth remaineth, seedtime and harvest, and cold and heat, and summer and winter, and day and night shall not cease.   8:22

Whoso sheddeth man's blood, by man shall his blood be shed: for in the image of God made he man.   9:6

I do set my bow in the cloud, and it shall be for a token of a covenant between me and the earth.   9:13

Even as Nimrod the mighty hunter before the Lord.   10:9

Therefore is the name of it called Babel; because the Lord did there confound the language of all the earth.   11:9

Let there be no strife, I pray thee, between me and thee . . . for we be brethren.   13:8

Abram dwelled in the land of Canaan, and Lot dwelled in the cities of the plain, and pitched his tent toward Sodom.   *Genesis 13:12*

In a good old age.   *15:15*

His [Ishmael's] hand will be against every man, and every man's hand against him.   *16:12*

Thy name shall be Abraham; for a father of many nations have I made thee.   *17:5*

My Lord, if now I have found favour in thy sight, pass not away, I pray thee, from thy servant.   *18:3*

But his [Lot's] wife looked back from behind him, and she became a pillar of salt.   *19:26*

My son, God will provide himself a lamb for a burnt offering.   *22:8*

Behold behind him a ram caught in a thicket by his horns.   *22:13*

Esau was a cunning hunter, a man of the field; and Jacob was a plain man, dwelling in tents.   *25:27*

And he [Esau] sold his birthright unto Jacob.

Then Jacob gave Esau bread and pottage of lentiles.   *25:33–34*

The voice is Jacob's voice, but the hands are the hands of Esau.   *27:22*

Thy brother came with subtilty, and hath taken away thy blessing.   *27:35*

He [Jacob] dreamed, and behold a ladder set up on the earth, and the top of it reached to heaven: and behold the angels of God ascending and descending on it.   *28:12*

Surely the Lord is in this place; and I knew it not.   *28:16*

This is none other but the house of God, and this is the gate of heaven.   *28:17*

Jacob served seven years for Rachel; and they seemed unto him but a few days, for the love he had to her.   *29:20*

Mizpah; for he said, The Lord watch between me and thee, when we are absent one from another.

Genesis 31:49

And Jacob was left alone; and there wrestled a man with him until the breaking of the day.   *32:24*

I will not let thee go, except thou bless me.   *32:26*

And Jacob called the name of the place Peniel: for I have seen God face to face, and my life is preserved.[1]

32:30

Behold, this dreamer cometh.   *37:19*

They stript Joseph out of his coat, his coat of many colours.   *37:23*

The Lord made all that he did to prosper in his hand.   *39:3*

And she caught him by his garment, saying, Lie with me: and he left his garment in her hand, and fled, and got him out.   *39:12*

And the seven thin and ill favoured kine that came up after them are seven years; and the seven empty ears blasted with the east wind shall be seven years of famine.   *41:27*

Then shall ye bring down my gray hairs with sorrow to the grave.   *42:38*

But Benjamin's mess was five times so much as any of theirs.   *43:34*

Wherefore have ye rewarded evil for good?   *44:4*

The man in whose hand the cup is found, he shall be my servant.   *44:17*

And he fell upon his brother Benjamin's neck, and wept; and Benjamin wept upon his neck.   *45:14*

And ye shall eat the fat of the land.   *45:18*

And they came into the land of Goshen.   *46:28*

But I will lie with my fathers, and thou shalt carry me out of Egypt, and bury me in their buryingplace. And he said, I will do as thou hast said.

47:30

[1] See *1 Corinthians 13:12*, p. 52b.

Unstable as water, thou shalt not excel.   *Genesis* 49:4

I have waited for thy salvation, O Lord.   49:18

Unto the utmost bound of the everlasting hills.   49:26

Now there arose up a new king over Egypt, which knew not Joseph.   *Exodus* [1] 1:8

She took for him an ark of bulrushes, and daubed it with slime and with pitch.   2:3

I have been a stranger in a strange land.[2]   2:22

Behold, the bush burned with fire, and the bush was not consumed.   3:2

Put off thy shoes from off thy feet, for the place whereon thou standest is holy ground.   3:5

And Moses hid his face; for he was afraid to look upon God.   3:6

A land flowing with milk and honey.[3]   3:8

And God said unto Moses, I AM THAT I AM.   3:14

I am slow of speech, and of a slow tongue.   4:10

Let my people go.   5:1

Ye shall no more give the people straw to make brick.   5:7

Thou shalt say unto Aaron, Take thy rod, and cast it before Pharaoh, and it shall become a serpent.   7:9

And he hardened Pharaoh's heart.   7:13

This is the finger of God.   8:19

Darkness which may be felt.   10:21

Yet will I bring one plague more upon Pharaoh, and upon Egypt.   11:1

Your lamb shall be without blemish.   12:5

---

[1] The Second Book of Moses, second of the five books of the Pentateuch.
[2] See Sophocles, p. 82b.
[3] Also in *Exodus* 33:3 and *Jeremiah* 11:5.

And thus shall ye eat it; with your loins girded, your shoes on your feet, and your staff in your hand; and ye shall eat it in haste: it is the Lord's passover.

For I will pass through the land of Egypt this night, and will smite all the firstborn in the land of Egypt, both man and beast; and against all the gods of Egypt I will execute judgment: I am the Lord.   *Exodus* 12:11–12

This day [Passover] shall be unto you for a memorial; and ye shall keep it a feast to the Lord throughout your generations.   12:14

Seven days shall ye eat unleavened bread.   12:15

There was a great cry in Egypt; for there was not a house where there was not one dead.   12:30

Remember this day, in which ye came out from Egypt, out of the house of bondage.   13:3

And the Lord went before them by day in a pillar of a cloud, to lead them the way; and by night in a pillar of fire, to give them light.   13:21

And the children of Israel went into the midst of the sea upon the dry ground: and the waters were a wall unto them on their right hand, and on their left.   14:22

I will sing unto the Lord, for he hath triumphed gloriously: the horse and his rider hath he thrown into the sea.

The Lord is my strength and song, and he is become my salvation.   15:1–2

The Lord is a man of war.   15:3

Thy right hand, O Lord, is become glorious in power: thy right hand, O Lord, hath dashed in pieces the enemy.   15:6

Thou sentest forth thy wrath, which consumed them as stubble.   15:7

Would to God we had died by the hand of the Lord in the land of Egypt, when we sat by the fleshpots, and when we did eat bread to the full.   16:3

It is manna. *Exodus 16:15*

Thou shalt have no other gods before me.

Thou shalt not make unto thee any graven image. 20:3–4

For I the Lord thy God am a jealous God, visiting the iniquity of the fathers upon the children unto the third and fourth generation of them that hate me.[1] 20:5

Thou shalt not take the name of the Lord thy God in vain. 20:7

Remember the sabbath day, to keep it holy.
Six days shalt thou labour, and do all thy work:
But the seventh day . . . thou shalt not do any work. 20:8–10

Honour thy father and thy mother: that thy days may be long upon the land which the Lord thy God giveth thee.[2]
Thou shalt not kill.
Thou shalt not commit adultery.
Thou shalt not steal.
Thou shalt not bear false witness against thy neighbour.
Thou shalt not covet thy neighbour's house, thou shalt not covet thy neighbour's wife, nor his manservant, nor his maidservant, nor his ox, nor his ass, nor any thing that is thy neighbour's.
20:12–17

But let not God speak with us, lest we die. 20:19

He that smiteth a man, so that he die, shall be surely put to death.
21:12

Eye for eye, tooth for tooth,[3] hand for hand, foot for foot. 21:24

Behold, I send an Angel before thee, to keep thee in the way. 23:20

A stiffnecked people. 32:9

Who is on the Lord's side? let him come unto me. 32:26

[1] See Euripides, p. 86a.
[2] See Aeschylus, p. 78a.
[3] Also in *Matthew 5:38*.

Thou canst not see my face: for there shall no man see me, and live. *Exodus 33:20*

And he [Moses] was there with the Lord forty days and forty nights; he did neither eat bread, nor drink water. And he wrote upon the tables the words of the covenant, the ten commandments.
34:28

Whatsoever parteth the hoof, and is clovenfooted, and cheweth the cud, among the beasts, that shall ye eat.
Leviticus [1] 11:3

And the swine . . . is unclean to you.
Of their flesh shall ye not eat.
11:7–8

Let him go for a scapegoat into the wilderness. 16:10

And when ye reap the harvest of your land, thou shalt not wholly reap the corners of thy field, neither shalt thou gather the gleanings of thy harvest.
And thou shalt not glean thy vineyard, neither shalt thou gather every grape of thy vineyard; thou shalt leave them for the poor and stranger: I am the Lord your God. 19:9–10

Thou shalt not go up and down as a talebearer among thy people. 19:16

Thou shalt love thy neighbour as thyself.[2] 19:18

The Lord bless thee, and keep thee:
The Lord make his face shine upon thee, and be gracious unto thee:
The Lord lift up his countenance upon thee, and give thee peace.
Numbers [3] 6:24–26

Sent to spy out the land. 13:16

And your children shall wander in the wilderness forty years. 14:33

He whom thou blessest is blessed.
22:6

[1] The Third Book of Moses, third of the five books of the Pentateuch.
[2] Also in *Matthew 19:19* and *22:39*, *Mark 12:31* and *33*, *Romans 13:9*, *Galatians 5:14*, *James 2:8*.
[3] The Fourth Book of Moses, fourth of the five books of the Pentateuch.

The Lord opened the mouth of the ass, and she said unto Balaam, What have I done unto thee?

Numbers 22:28

Let me die the death of the righteous, and let my last end be like his!   23:10

God is not a man, that he should lie.[1]   23:19

What hath God wrought! [2]   23:23

How goodly are thy tents, O Jacob, and thy tabernacles, O Israel!   24:5

Be sure your sin will find you out.   32:23

Thou shalt love the Lord thy God with all thine heart, and with all thy soul, and with all thy might.
And these words, which I command thee this day, shall be in thine heart:
And thou shalt teach them diligently unto thy children.

Deuteronomy [3] 6:5–7

Ye shall not tempt the Lord your God.[4]   6:16

The Lord thy God hath chosen thee to be a special people unto himself.
7:6

Man doth not live by bread only,[5] but by every word that proceedeth out of the mouth of the Lord doth man live.   8:3

For the Lord thy God bringeth thee into a good land.   8:7

A land of wheat, and barley, and vines, and fig trees, and pomegranates; a land of oil olive, and honey;
A land wherein thou shalt eat bread without scarceness, thou shalt not lack any thing in it; a land whose stones are iron, and out of whose hills thou mayest dig brass.   8:8–9

[1] See Aeschylus, p. 78b.
[2] Quoted by Samuel F. B. Morse in the first telegraph message he sent to his partner, Alfred Vail, from Washington to Baltimore, May 24, 1844.
[3] The Fifth Book of Moses, last of the five books of the Pentateuch.
[4] Also in *Matthew 4:7.*
[5] Man shall not live by bread alone. — *Matthew 4:4*

A dreamer of dreams.

Deuteronomy 13:1

The wife of thy bosom.   13:6

The poor shall never cease out of the land.[1]   15:11

And thou shalt become an astonishment, a proverb, and a byword, among all nations.   28:37

In the morning thou shalt say, Would God it were even! and at even thou shalt say, Would God it were morning!   28:67

The secret things belong unto the Lord our God.   29:29

I have set before you life and death, blessing and cursing: therefore choose life, that both thou and thy seed may live.   30:19

He is the Rock, his work is perfect: for all his ways are judgment: a God of truth.   32:4

He kept him as the apple of his eye.   32:10

Jeshurun waxed fat, and kicked.
32:15

As thy days, so shall thy strength be.   33:25

The eternal God is thy refuge, and underneath are the everlasting arms.
33:27

No man knoweth of his [Moses'] sepulchre unto this day.   34:6

Be strong and of a good courage; [2] be not afraid, neither be thou dismayed: for the Lord thy God is with thee whithersoever thou goest.

The Book of Joshua 1:9

And the priests that bare the ark of the covenant of the Lord stood firm on dry ground in the midst of Jordan, and all the Israelites passed over on dry ground, until all the people were passed clean over Jordan.   3:17

Mighty men of valour.   6:2

And it came to pass, when the people heard the sound of the trumpet, and

[1] See *Matthew 26:11,* p. 44a.
[2] Also in *Deuteronomy 31:6, 7, 23.*

the people shouted with a great shout, that the wall fell down flat, so that the people went up into the city [Jericho].
Joshua 6:20

His fame was noised throughout all the country.　　　　　　6:27

Hewers of wood and drawers of water.　　　　　　　　　　9:21

Sun, stand thou still upon Gibeon; and thou, Moon, in the valley of Ajalon.　　　　　　　　10:12

Old and stricken in years.[1]　　　13:1

I am going the way of all the earth.　　　　　　　　23:14

They shall be as thorns in your sides.[2]　　*The Book of Judges 2:3*

Then Jael, Heber's wife, took a nail of the tent, and took an hammer in her hand, and went softly unto him, and smote the nail into his temples, and fastened it into the ground; for he was fast asleep, and weary: so he died.
　　　　　　　　　　　　4:21

I Deborah arose . . . I arose a mother in Israel.　　　　　5:7

The stars in their courses fought against Sisera.　　　　　5:20

She brought forth butter in a lordly dish.　　　　　　　　5:25

At her feet he bowed, he fell, he lay down: at her feet he bowed, he fell: where he bowed, there he fell down dead.　　　　　　　　　5:27

Why tarry the wheels of his chariots?
　　　　　　　　　　　　5:28

Have they not divided the prey; to every man a damsel or two?　　5:30

The sword of the Lord, and of Gideon.　　　　　　　　7:18

Is not the gleaning of the grapes of Ephraim better than the vintage of Abiezer?　　　　　　　　8:2

Say now Shibboleth: and he said Sibboleth: for he could not frame to pronounce it right.　　　　　12:6

---

[1] Also in *I Kings 1:1*.
[2] See *II Corinthians 12:7*, p. 53b.

There was a swarm of bees and honey in the carcase of the lion.
Judges 14:8

Out of the eater came forth meat, and out of the strong came forth sweetness.　　　　　　　14:14

If ye had not plowed with my heifer, ye had not found out my riddle.
　　　　　　　　　　　14:18

He smote them hip and thigh.
　　　　　　　　　　　15:8

With the jawbone of an ass . . . have I slain a thousand men.　15:16

The Philistines be upon thee, Samson.　　　　　　　　16:9

Strengthen me, I pray thee, only this once, O God, that I may be . . . avenged of the Philistines for my two eyes.　　　　　　　　16:28

So the dead which he slew at his death were more than they which he slew in his life.　　　　16:30

From Dan even to Beersheba.
　　　　　　　　　　　20:1

All the people arose as one man.
　　　　　　　　　　　20:8

In those days there was no king in Israel: every man did that which was right in his own eyes.　　　21:25

Entreat me not to leave thee, or to return from following after thee: for whither thou goest, I will go; and where thou lodgest, I will lodge: thy people shall be my people, and thy God my God.　　　*The Book of Ruth 1:16*

Let me glean and gather after the reapers among the sheaves.　2:7

Go not empty unto thy mother in law.　　　　　　　　3:17

In the flower of their age.
The First Book of Samuel 2:33

The Lord called Samuel: and he answered, Here am I.　　　3:4

Speak, Lord; for thy servant heareth.
　　　　　　　　　　　3:9

Be strong, and quit yourselves like men.[1]   *I Samuel 4:9*

The glory is departed from Israel: for the ark of God is taken.   *4:22*

Is Saul also among the prophets?   *10:11*

God save the king.   *10:24*

A man after his own heart.   *13:14*

Every man's sword was against his fellow.   *14:20*

But Jonathan heard not when his father charged the people with the oath: wherefore he put forth the end of the rod that was in his hand, and dipped it in an honeycomb, and put his hand to his mouth; and his eyes were enlightened.   *14:27*

For the Lord seeth not as man seeth; for man looketh on the outward appearance, but the Lord looketh on the heart.   *16:7*

I know thy pride, and the naughtiness of thine heart.   *17:28*

Let no man's heart fail because of him [Goliath].   *17:32*

Go, and the Lord be with thee.   *17:37*

And he [David] . . . chose him five smooth stones out of the brook.   *17:40*

So David prevailed over the Philistine with a sling and with a stone.   *17:50*

Saul hath slain his thousands, and David his ten thousands.   *18:7*

And Jonathan . . . loved him [David] as he loved his own soul.   *20:17*

Wickedness proceedeth from the wicked.   *24:13*

I have played the fool.   *26:21*

Tell it not in Gath, publish it not in the streets of Askelon.
    The Second Book of Samuel 1:20

Saul and Jonathan were lovely and

[1] See *I Corinthians 16:13*, p. 53a.

pleasant in their lives, and in their death they were not divided: they were swifter than eagles, they were stronger than lions.   *II Samuel 1:23*

How are the mighty fallen in the midst of the battle!   *1:25*

Thy love to me was wonderful, passing the love of women.

How are the mighty fallen, and the weapons of war perished!   *1:26-27*

Abner . . . smote him under the fifth rib.   *2:23*

Know ye not that there is a prince and a great man fallen this day in Israel?   *3:38*

And David and all the house of Israel played before the Lord on all manner of instruments made of fir wood, even on harps, and on psalteries, and on timbrels, and on cornets, and on cymbals.   *6:5*

David danced before the Lord.   *6:14*

Tarry at Jericho until your beards be grown.[1]   *10:5*

Set ye Uriah in the forefront of the hottest battle.   *11:15*

The poor man had nothing, save one little ewe lamb.   *12:3*

Thou art the man.   *12:7*

Now he is dead, wherefore should I fast? Can I bring him back again? I shall go to him, but he shall not return to me.   *12:23*

For we must needs die, and are as water spilt on the ground, which cannot be gathered up again.   *14:14*

Would God I had died for thee, O Absalom, my son, my son!   *18:33*

The Lord is my rock, and my fortress, and my deliverer.   *22:2*

David the son of Jesse . . . the sweet psalmist of Israel.   *23:1*

Went in jeopardy of their lives.   *23:17*

[1] Also in *I Chronicles 19:5*.

A wise and an understanding heart.
The First Book of the Kings 3:12

Many, as the sand which is by the sea in multitude. 4:20

Judah and Israel dwelt safely, every man under his vine and under his fig tree. 4:25

He [Solomon] spake three thousand proverbs: and his songs were a thousand and five. 4:32

The wisdom of Solomon. 4:34

A proverb and a byword among all people. 9:7

When the queen of Sheba heard of the fame of Solomon . . . she came to prove him with hard questions. 10:1

The half was not told me: thy wisdom and prosperity exceedeth the fame which I heard. 10:7

Once in three years came the navy of Tharshish, bringing gold, and silver, ivory, and apes, and peacocks. 10:22

King Solomon loved many strange women. 11:1

My father hath chastised you with whips, but I will chastise you with scorpions. 12:11

To your tents, O Israel. 12:16

He went and dwelt by the brook Cherith, that is before Jordan. 17:5

And the ravens brought him bread and flesh in the morning, and bread and flesh in the evening; and he drank of the brook. 17:6

An handful of meal in a barrel, and a little oil in a cruse. 17:12

And the barrel of meal wasted not, neither did the cruse of oil fail. 17:16

How long halt ye between two opinions? 18:21

Either he is talking, or he is pursuing, or he is in a journey, or peradventure he sleepeth, and must be awaked. 18:27

There ariseth a little cloud out of the sea, like a man's hand. *I Kings* 18:44

And he girded up his loins, and ran before Ahab. 18:46

But the Lord was not in the wind: and after the wind an earthquake; but the Lord was not in the earthquake:
And after the earthquake a fire; but the Lord was not in the fire: and after the fire a still small voice. 19:11–12

Let not him that girdeth on his harness boast himself as he that putteth it off. 20:11

Hast thou found me, O mine enemy? 21:20

The dogs shall eat Jezebel by the wall of Jezreel. 21:23

But there was none like unto Ahab, which did sell himself to work wickedness in the sight of the Lord, whom Jezebel his wife stirred up. 21:25

I saw all Israel scattered upon the hills, as sheep that have not a shepherd. 22:17

Feed him with bread of affliction, and with water of affliction, until I come in peace. 22:27

There appeared a chariot of fire, and horses of fire, and parted them both asunder; and Elijah went up by a whirlwind into heaven.
The Second Book of the Kings 2:11

The chariot of Israel, and the horsemen thereof. And he saw him no more. 2:12

There is death in the pot. 4:40

Is thy servant a dog, that he should do this great thing? 8:13

What hast thou to do with peace? turn thee behind me. 9:18

The driving is like the driving of Jehu the son of Nimshi; for he driveth furiously. 9:20

Jezebel heard of it; and she painted her face, and tired her head, and looked out at a window. 9:30

Set thine house in order.

II Kings 20:1

I will wipe Jerusalem as a man wipeth a dish, wiping it, and turning it upside down. 21:13

His mercy endureth for ever.

The First Book of the Chronicles 16:41

The Lord searcheth all hearts, and understandeth all the imaginations of the thoughts. 28:9

For all things come of thee, and of thine own have we given thee.[1] 29:14

Our days on the earth are as a shadow. 29:15

He [David] died in a good old age, full of days, riches, and honour.

29:28

Thou art a God ready to pardon, gracious and merciful, slow to anger, and of great kindness.

The Book of Nehemiah 9:17

Mordecai rent his clothes, and put on sackcloth with ashes.

The Book of Esther 4:1

The man whom the king delighteth to honour. 6:6

They hanged Haman on the gallows.

7:10

One that feared God, and eschewed evil. *The Book of Job* 1:1

Satan came also. 1:6

And the Lord said unto Satan, Whence comest thou? Then Satan answered the Lord, and said, From going to and fro in the earth, and from walking up and down in it. 1:7

Doth Job fear God for nought?

1:9

Naked came I out of my mother's womb, and naked shall I return thither: the Lord gave, and the Lord hath taken away; blessed be the name of the Lord. 1:21

Skin for skin, yea, all that a man hath will he give for his life. 2:4

Curse God, and die. 2:9

[1] See Marcus Aurelius, p. 142a.

Let the day perish wherein I was born, and the night in which it was said, There is a man child conceived.[1]

Job 3:3

For now should I have lain still and been quiet, I should have slept: then had I been at rest,

With kings and counsellors of the earth, which built desolate places for themselves. 3:13–14

There the wicked cease from troubling; and there the weary be at rest. 3:17

Who ever perished, being innocent? or where were the righteous cut off?

4:7

Fear came upon me, and trembling.

4:14

Then a spirit passed before my face; the hair of my flesh stood up. 4:15

Shall mortal man be more just than God? shall a man be more pure than his maker? 4:17

Wrath killeth the foolish man, and envy slayeth the silly one. 5:2

Man is born unto trouble, as the sparks fly upward. 5:7

He taketh the wise in their own craftiness. 5:13

For thou shalt be in league with the stones of the field: and the beasts of the field shall be at peace with thee.

5:23

Thou shalt come to thy grave in a full age, like as a shock of corn cometh in in his season. 5:26

How forcible are right words!

6:25

My days are swifter than a weaver's shuttle, and are spent without hope.

7:6

He shall return no more to his house, neither shall his place know him any more.[2] 7:10

[1] See Euripides, p. 84a.

[2] When a few years are come, then I shall go the way whence I shall not return. — *Job* 16:22

The place thereof shall know it no more. — *Psalm* 103:16

I would not live alway: let me alone; for my days are vanity. *Job 7:16*

But how should man be just with God? 9:2

The land of darkness and the shadow of death. 10:21

Canst thou by searching find out God? 11:7

And thine age shall be clearer than the noonday. 11:17

No doubt but ye are the people, and wisdom shall die with you. 12:2

The just upright man is laughed to scorn. 12:4

But now ask the beasts, and they shall teach thee; and the fowls of the air, and they shall tell thee:
Or speak to the earth, and it shall teach thee; and the fishes of the sea shall declare unto thee. 12:7–8

With the ancient is wisdom; and in length of days understanding. 12:12

He discovereth deep things out of darkness, and bringeth out to light the shadow of death. 12:22

Man that is born of a woman is of few days, and full of trouble.
He cometh forth like a flower, and is cut down: he fleeth also as a shadow, and continueth not. 14:1–2

But man dieth, and wasteth away: yea, man giveth up the ghost, and where is he? 14:10

If a man die, shall he live again? 14:14

Should a wise man utter vain knowledge, and fill his belly with the east wind? 15:2

Miserable comforters are ye all. 16:2

My days are past. 17:11

I have said to corruption, Thou art my father: to the worm, Thou art my mother, and my sister. 17:14

The king of terrors. 18:14

I am escaped with the skin of my teeth. 19:20

Oh that my words were now written! oh that they were printed in a book! *Job 19:23*

I know that my redeemer liveth, and that he shall stand at the latter day upon the earth: [1]
And though, after my skin, worms destroy this body, yet in my flesh shall I see God. 19:25–26

Seeing the root of the matter is found in me. 19:28

Though wickedness be sweet in his mouth, though he hide it under his tongue. 20:12

Suffer me that I may speak; and after that I have spoken, mock on. 21:3

Shall any teach God knowledge? 21:22

They are of those that rebel against the light. 24:13

The womb shall forget him; the worm shall feed sweetly on him; he shall be no more remembered. 24:20

Yea, the stars are not pure in his sight.
How much less man, that is a worm? and the son of man, which is a worm? 25:5–6

But where shall wisdom be found? and where is the place of understanding? 28:12

The land of the living. 28:13

The price of wisdom is above rubies.[2] 28:18

Behold, the fear of the Lord, that is wisdom; and to depart from evil is understanding. 28:28

I caused the widow's heart to sing for joy. 29:13

I was eyes to the blind, and feet was I to the lame. 29:15

The house appointed for all living. 30:23

[1] Also in *Book of Common Prayer, Burial of the Dead.*

[2] [Wisdom] is more precious than rubies. — *Proverbs 3:15*

See Sophocles, p. 82b.

I am a brother to dragons, and a companion to owls.   *Job* 30:29

My desire is, that the Almighty would answer me, and that mine adversary had written a book.   31:35

Great men are not always wise.   32:9

For I am full of matter, the spirit within me constraineth me.   32:18

One among a thousand.   33:23

Far be it from God, that he should do wickedness.   34:10

He multiplieth words without knowledge.   35:16

Fair weather cometh out of the north.   37:22

Then the Lord answered Job out of the whirlwind, and said,
Who is this that darkeneth counsel by words without knowledge?
Gird up now thy loins like a man.   38:1–3

Where wast thou when I laid the foundations of the earth? declare, if thou hast understanding.   38:4

The morning stars sang together, and all the sons of God shouted for joy.   38:7

Hitherto shalt thou come, but no further: and here shall thy proud waves be stayed?   38:11

Hast thou entered into the springs of the sea? or hast thou walked in the search of the depth?   38:16

Hath the rain a father? or who hath begotten the drops of dew?   38:28

Canst thou bind the sweet influences of Pleiades, or loose the bands of Orion?   38:31

Canst thou guide Arcturus with his sons?   38:32

Who can number the clouds in wisdom? or who can stay the bottles of heaven?   38:37

Hast thou given the horse strength?

hast thou clothed his neck with thunder?   *Job* 39:19

He paweth in the valley, and rejoiceth in his strength: he goeth on to meet the armed men.   39:21

He swalloweth the ground with fierceness and rage; neither believeth he that it is the sound of the trumpet.
He saith among the trumpets, Ha, ha; and he smelleth the battle afar off, the thunder of the captains, and the shouting.   39:24–25

Behold, I am vile; what shall I answer thee?   40:4

Behold now behemoth, which I made with thee; he eateth grass as an ox.   40:15

Canst thou draw out leviathan with a hook?   41:1

Hard as a piece of the nether millstone.   41:24

He maketh the deep to boil like a pot.   41:31

Upon earth there is not his like, who is made without fear.   41:33

He is a king over all the children of pride.   41:34

I have heard of thee by the hearing of the ear: but now mine eye seeth thee.   42:5

So the Lord blessed the latter end of Job more than his beginning.   42:12

Blessed is the man that walketh not in the counsel of the ungodly, nor standeth in the way of sinners, nor sitteth in the seat of the scornful.
But his delight is in the law of the Lord; and in his law doth he meditate day and night.
And he shall be like a tree planted by the rivers of water, that bringeth forth his fruit in his season; his leaf also shall not wither; and whatsoever he doeth shall prosper.
The ungodly are not so: but are like the chaff which the wind driveth away.
The Book of Psalms 1:1–4 [1]

[1] See Amenemope, VI, p. 4b, and *Jeremiah* 17:5–8, p. 34 a–b.

Why do the heathen rage, and the people imagine a vain thing?

Psalms 2:1

Blessed are all they that put their trust in him.　　　　*2:12*

Lord, lift thou up the light of thy countenance upon us.　　　　*4:6*

I will both lay me down in peace, and sleep.[1]　　　　*4:8*

Out of the mouth of babes and sucklings hast thou ordained strength, because of thine enemies; that thou mightest still the enemy and the avenger.　　　　*8:2*

What is man, that thou art mindful of him? and the son of man, that thou visitest him?　　　　*8:4*

Thou hast made him a little lower than the angels.　　　　*8:5*

How excellent is thy name in all the earth.　　　　*8:9*

Flee as a bird to your mountain.

11:1

How long wilt thou forget me, O Lord?　　　　*13:1*

The fool hath said in his heart, There is no God.　　　*14:1 and 53:1*

Lord, who shall abide in thy tabernacle? who shall dwell in thy holy hill?　　　　*15:1*

He that sweareth to his own hurt, and changeth not.　　　　*15:4*

The lines are fallen unto me in pleasant places;[2] yea, I have a goodly heritage.　　　　*16:6*

Keep me as the apple of the eye,[3] hide me under the shadow of thy wings.　　　　*17:8*

He rode upon a cherub, and did fly: yea, he did fly upon the wings of the wind.　　　　*18:10*

The heavens declare the glory of God; and the firmament showeth his handiwork.　　　　*Psalms 19:1*

Day unto day uttereth speech, and night unto night showeth knowledge.　　　　*19:2*

Their line is gone out through all the earth, and their words to the end of the world. In them hath he set a tabernacle for the sun,

Which is as a bridegroom coming out of his chamber, and rejoiceth as a strong man to run a race.

His going forth is from the end of the heaven, and his circuit unto the ends of it: and there is nothing hid from the heat thereof.　　　　*19:4–6*

The judgments of the Lord are true and righteous altogether.

More to be desired are they than gold, yea, than much fine gold: sweeter also than honey and the honeycomb.　　　　*19:9–10*

Cleanse thou me from secret faults.　　　　*19:12*

Let the words of my mouth, and the meditation of my heart, be acceptable in thy sight, O Lord, my strength, and my redeemer.　　　　*19:14*

Thou hast given him his heart's desire.　　　　*21:2*

My God, my God, why hast thou forsaken me?[1] why art thou so far from helping me, and from the words of my roaring?　　　　*22:1*

They part my garments among them, and cast lots upon my vesture.　　　*22:18*

The Lord is my shepherd; I shall not want.

He maketh me to lie down in green pastures: he leadeth me beside the still waters.

He restoreth my soul: he leadeth me in the paths of righteousness for his name's sake.

Yea, though I walk through the valley of the shadow of death, I will

---

[1] I will lay me down in peace, and take my rest. — *Book of Common Prayer, Psalm 4:9*
[2] The lot is fallen unto me in a fair ground. — *Book of Common Prayer, Psalm 16:7*
[3] Also in *Deuteronomy 32:10* and *Proverbs 7:2.*

[1] This was the psalm Christ recited on the cross. See *Matthew 27:46*, p. 45a.

fear no evil: for thou art with me; thy rod and thy staff they comfort me.

Thou preparest a table before me in the presence of mine enemies: thou anointest my head with oil; my cup runneth over.

Surely goodness and mercy shall follow me all the days of my life: and I will dwell in the house of the Lord for ever. *Psalms* 23

The earth is the Lord's, and the fulness thereof; the world, and they that dwell therein.

For he hath founded it upon the seas, and established it upon the floods.

Who shall ascend into the hill of the Lord? or who shall stand in his holy place?

He that hath clean hands, and a pure heart; who hath not lifted up his soul unto vanity, nor sworn deceitfully.
24:1–4

Lift up your heads, O ye gates; and be ye lift up, ye everlasting doors; and the King of glory shall come in.
24:7

Who is this King of glory? The Lord of hosts, he is the King of glory.
24:10

The Lord is my light[1] and my salvation; whom shall I fear? the Lord is the strength of my life; of whom shall I be afraid? 27:1

Though an host should encamp against me, my heart shall not fear: though war should rise against me, in this will I be confident. 27:3

The Lord is my strength and my shield. 28:7

Worship the Lord in the beauty of holiness. 29:2

Weeping may endure for a night, but joy cometh in the morning.
30:5

I am forgotten as a dead man out of mind: I am like a broken vessel.
31:12

[1] **Dominus illuminatio mea.** — *The Vulgate.* Motto of Oxford University.

My times are in thy hand.
Psalms 31:15
From the strife of tongues. 31:20

Sing unto him a new song; play skilfully with a loud noise. 33:3

O taste and see that the Lord is good. 34:8

Keep thy tongue from evil, and thy lips from speaking guile.

Depart from evil, and do good; seek peace, and pursue it. 34:13–14

Rescue my soul from their destructions, my darling from the lions.
35:17

How excellent is thy lovingkindness, O God! 36:7

The meek shall inherit the earth.[1]
37:11

I have been young, and now am old; yet have I not seen the righteous forsaken, nor his seed begging bread.
37:25

I have seen the wicked in great power, and spreading himself[2] like a green bay tree. 37:35

Mark the perfect man, and behold the upright: for the end of that man is peace.[3] 37:37

For thine arrows stick fast in me, and thy hand presseth me sore. 38:2

I said, I will take heed to my ways, that I sin not with my tongue. 39:1

My heart was hot within me, while I was musing the fire burned. 39:3

Lord, make me to know mine end, and the measure of my days, what it is; that I may know how frail I am.
39:4

Every man at his best state is altogether vanity. 39:5

Surely every man walketh in a vain show: surely they are disquieted in

[1] See *Matthew* 5:5, p. 40a.
[2] Flourishing. — *Book of Common Prayer, Psalm 37:36*
[3] For that shall bring a man peace at the last. — *Book of Common Prayer, Psalm 37:38*

18

vain: he heapeth up riches, and knoweth not who shall gather them.
Psalms 39:6

For I am a stranger with thee, and a sojourner, as all my fathers were.

O spare me, that I may recover strength, before I go hence, and be no more. 39:12–13

As the hart panteth after the water brooks, so panteth my soul after thee, O God.

My soul thirsteth for God, for the living God. 42:1–2

Why art thou cast down, O my soul? and why art thou disquieted in me?
42:5, 11 *and* 43:5

Deep calleth unto deep. 42:7

My tongue is the pen of a ready writer. 45:1

The king's daughter is all glorious within. 45:13

God is our refuge and strength, a very present help in trouble.
Therefore will we not fear, though the earth be removed, and though the mountains be carried into the midst of the sea. 46:1–2

Be still, and know that I am God.
46:10

Every beast of the forest is mine, and the cattle upon a thousand hills.
50:10

I was shapen in iniquity; and in sin did my mother conceive me. 51 [1]:5

Purge me with hyssop, and I shall be clean: wash me, and I shall be whiter than snow. 51:7

Create in me a clean heart, O God; and renew a right spirit within me.
51:10

And take not thy holy spirit from me. 51:11

Open thou my lips; and my mouth shall show forth thy praise. 51:15

A broken and a contrite heart, O God, thou wilt not despise.
Psalms 51:17

Oh that I had wings like a dove! for then would I fly away, and be at rest.[1] 55:6

We took sweet counsel together.
55:14

The words of his mouth were smoother than butter, but war was in his heart: [2] his words were softer than oil, yet were they drawn swords.
55:21

They are like the deaf adder that stoppeth her ear;
Which will not hearken to the voice of charmers, charming never so wisely.
58:4–5

Moab is my washpot; over Edom will I cast out my shoe: Philistia, triumph thou because of me. 60:8

Lead me to the rock that is higher than I. 61:2

He only is my rock and my salvation: he is my defence; I shall not be moved. 62:6

Thou renderest to every man according to his work. 62:12

My soul thirsteth for thee, my flesh longeth for thee in a dry and thirsty land, where no water is. 63:1

Thou crownest the year with thy goodness. 65:11

Make a joyful noise unto God, all ye lands. 66:1

We went through fire and through water. 66:12

God setteth the solitary in families.
68:6

Cast me not off in the time of old age; forsake me not when my strength faileth. 71:9

He shall come down like rain upon

---

[1] This Psalm is known as the Miserere from its opening word in the Vulgate. The first line is: Have mercy upon me, O God.

[1] See Euripides, p. 84b.
[2] The words of his mouth were softer than butter, having war in his heart. — *Book of Common Prayer, Psalm 50:22*

the mown grass: as showers that water the earth.   *Psalms 72:6*

His enemies shall lick the dust.
72:9

His name shall endure for ever.
72:17

A stubborn and rebellious generation.
78:8

But ye shall die like men, and fall like one of the princes.   82:7

How amiable are thy tabernacles, O Lord of hosts!   84:1

They go from strength to strength.
84:7

A day in thy courts is better than a thousand. I had rather be a doorkeeper in the house of my God, than to dwell in the tents of wickedness.   84:10

Mercy and truth are met together; righteousness and peace have kissed each other.   85:10

Lord, why castest thou off my soul? why hidest thou thy face from me?
88:14

Lord, thou hast been our dwelling place in all generations.

Before the mountains were brought forth, or ever thou hadst formed the earth and the world, even from everlasting to everlasting, thou art God.

Thou turnest man to destruction; and sayest, Return, ye children of men.

For a thousand years in thy sight are but as yesterday when it is past, and as a watch in the night.

Thou carriest them away as with a flood; they are as a sleep: in the morning they are like grass which groweth up.

In the morning it flourisheth, and groweth up; in the evening it is cut down, and withereth.[1]   90:1–6

We spend our years as a tale that is told.[2]   90:9

[1] See *Isaiah 40:6, 8,* p. 32b, and *1 Peter 1:24,* p. 56b.

[2] We bring our years to an end, as it were a tale that is told. — *Book of Common Prayer, Psalm 90:9*

The days of our years are threescore years and ten; and if by reason of strength they be fourscore years, yet is their strength labour and sorrow; for it is soon cut off, and we fly away.[1]
Psalms 90:–10

So teach us to number our days, that we may apply our hearts unto wisdom.
90:12

Establish thou the work of our hands upon us; yea, the work of our hands establish thou it.   90:17

He that dwelleth in the secret place of the most High shall abide under the shadow of the Almighty.

I will say of the Lord, He is my refuge and my fortress: my God; in him will I trust.

Surely he shall deliver thee from the snare of the fowler, and from the noisome pestilence.

He shall cover thee with his feathers, and under his wings shalt thou trust: his truth shall be thy shield and buckler.

Thou shalt not be afraid for the terror by night; nor for the arrow that flieth by day.

Nor for the pestilence that walketh in darkness; nor for the destruction that wasteth at noonday.

A thousand shall fall at thy side, and ten thousand at thy right hand; but it shall not come nigh thee.   91:1–7

He shall give his angels charge over thee, to keep thee in all thy ways.

They shall bear thee up in their hands, lest thou dash thy foot against a stone.[2]

Thou shalt tread upon the lion and adder: the young lion and the dragon shalt thou trample under feet.

91:11–13

The righteous shall flourish like the

[1] The days of our age are threescore and ten; and though men be so strong that they come to fourscore years, yet is their strength then but labour and sorrow; so soon passeth it away, and we are gone. — *Book of Common Prayer, Psalm 90:10*

[2] Also in *Matthew 4:6.*

palm tree: he shall grow like a cedar in Lebanon. *Psalms 92:12*

Mightier than the noise of many waters. 93:4

In his hand are the deep places of the earth: the strength of the hills is his also.
The sea is his, and he made it: and his hands formed the dry land.
95:4–5

We are the people of his pasture, and the sheep of his hand. 95:7

O sing unto the Lord a new song. 96:1

The Lord reigneth; let the earth rejoice. 97:1

Make a joyful noise unto the Lord, all ye lands.
Serve the Lord with gladness: come before his presence with singing.
Know ye that the Lord he is God: it is he that hath made us, and not we ourselves; we are his people, and the sheep of his pasture.
Enter into his gates with thanksgiving, and into his courts with praise: be thankful unto him, and bless his name.
For the Lord is good; his mercy is everlasting; and his truth endureth to all generations. 100

My days are consumed like smoke. 102:3

I watch, and am as a sparrow alone upon the house top. 102:7

As the heaven is high above the earth, so great is his mercy toward them that fear him. 103:11

As for man, his days are as grass: as a flower of the field, so he flourisheth.
For the wind passeth over it, and it is gone; and the place thereof shall know it no more.[1] 103:15–16

Who layeth the beams of his chambers in the waters: who maketh the clouds his chariot: who walketh upon the wings of the wind. 104:3

[1] See Homer, p. 67a.

Wine that maketh glad the heart of man. *Psalms 104:15*

The cedars of Lebanon. 104:16

He appointeth the moon for seasons: the sun knoweth his going down.
Thou makest darkness, and it is night: wherein all the beasts of the forest do creep forth.
The young lions roar after their prey, and seek their meat from God.
The sun ariseth, they gather themselves together, and lay them down in their dens.
Man goeth forth unto his work and to his labor until the evening.
O Lord, how manifold are thy works! in wisdom hast thou made them all: the earth is full of thy riches.
So is this great and wide sea, wherein are things creeping innumerable, both small and great beasts.
There go the ships: there is that leviathan, whom thou hast made to play therein.
These wait all upon thee; that thou mayest give them their meat in due season. 104:19–27 [1]

Such as sit in darkness and in the shadow of death. 107:10

They that go down to the sea in ships, that do business in great waters. 107:23

They mount up to the heaven, they go down again to the depths. 107:26

They reel to and fro, and stagger like a drunken man, and are at their wit's end. 107:27

For I am poor and needy, and my heart is wounded within me.
I am gone like the shadow when it declineth: I am tossed up and down as the locust. 109:22–23

Thou hast the dew of thy youth. 110:3

The fear of the Lord is the beginning of wisdom. 111:10

From the rising of the sun unto the

[1] See Ikhnaton, p. 3b.

going down of the same the Lord's name is to be praised.   *Psalms* 113:3

The mountains skipped like rams, and the little hills like lambs.   114:4

They have mouths, but they speak not: eyes have they, but they see not.
They have ears, but they hear not.[1]
          115:5–6

I said in my haste, All men are liars.   116:11

Precious in the sight of the Lord is the death of his saints.   116:15

The stone which the builders refused is become the head stone of the corner.[2]   118:22

This is the day which the Lord hath made.   118:24

Blessed be he that cometh in the name of the Lord.[3]   118:26

Thy word is a lamp unto my feet, and a light unto my path.   119:105

I am for peace: but when I speak, they are for war.   120:7

I will lift up mine eyes unto the hills, from whence cometh my help.[4]
My help cometh from the Lord, which made heaven and earth.
He will not suffer thy foot to be moved: he that keepeth thee will not slumber.
Behold, he that keepeth Israel shall neither slumber nor sleep.
The Lord is thy keeper: the Lord is thy shade upon thy right hand.
The sun shall not smite thee by day, nor the moon by night.
The Lord shall preserve thee from all evil: he shall preserve thy soul.
The Lord shall preserve thy going out and thy coming in from this time forth, and even for evermore.   121

I was glad when they said unto me,

Let us go into the house of the Lord.   *Psalms* 122:1

Peace be within thy walls, and prosperity within thy palaces.   122:7

They that sow in tears shall reap in joy.
He that goeth forth and weepeth, bearing precious seed, shall doubtless come again with rejoicing, bringing his sheaves with him.   126:5–6

Except the Lord build the house, they labour in vain that build it: except the Lord keep the city, the watchman waketh but in vain.   127:1

He giveth his beloved sleep.   127:2

As arrows are in the hand of a mighty man; so are children of the youth.
Happy is the man that hath his quiver full of them.   127:4–5

Out of the depths have I cried unto thee, O Lord.   130:1

My soul waiteth for the Lord more than they that watch for the morning.   130:6

I will not give sleep to mine eyes, or slumber to mine eyelids.[1]   132:4

Behold, how good and how pleasant it is for brethren to dwell together in unity!   133:1

By the rivers of Babylon, there we sat down, yea, we wept, when we remembered Zion.[2]
We hanged our harps upon the willows in the midst thereof.
For there they that carried us away captive required of us a song; and they that wasted us required of us mirth, saying, Sing us one of the songs of Zion.
How shall we sing the Lord's song in a strange land?
If I forget thee, O Jerusalem, let my right hand forget her cunning.
If I do not remember thee, let my

---

[1] Also in *Psalm 135:16–17.*
[2] Also in *Matthew 21:42.*
[3] Also in *Matthew 21:9, 23:39, Mark 11:9,* and *Luke 13:35.*
[4] I lift up my eyes to the hills. From whence does my help come? — *Revised Standard Version*

[1] Also in *Proverbs 6:4.*
[2] By the waters of Babylon we sat down and wept: when we remembered thee, O Sion. — *Book of Common Prayer, Psalm 137:1*

tongue cleave to the roof of my mouth.   *Psalms 137:1–6*

O Lord, thou hast searched me, and known me.

Thou knowest my downsitting and mine uprising, thou understandest my thought afar off.   *139:1–2*

Whither shall I go from thy spirit? or whither shall I flee from thy presence?

If I ascend up into heaven, thou art there: if I make my bed in hell, behold, thou art there.

If I take the wings of the morning, and dwell in the uttermost parts of the sea;

Even there shall thy hand lead me, and thy right hand shall hold me.   *139:7–10*

The darkness and the light are both alike to thee.   *139:12*

I am fearfully and wonderfully made.   *139:14*

They have sharpened their tongues like a serpent.   *140:3*

Thou openest thine hand, and satisfiest the desire of every living thing.   *145:16*

The Lord is nigh unto all them that call upon him, to all that call upon him in truth.   *145:18*

Put not your trust in princes.   *146:3*

He telleth the number of the stars; he calleth them all by their names.   *147:4*

Let every thing that hath breath praise the Lord.   *150:6*

To give subtilty to the simple, to the young man knowledge and discretion.   *The Proverbs 1:4*

My son, if sinners entice thee, consent thou not.   *1:10*

Wisdom crieth without; she uttereth her voice in the streets.   *1:20*

Length of days is in her right hand; and in her left hand riches and honor.   *3:16*

Her ways are ways of pleasantness, and all her paths are peace.   *Proverbs 3:17*

Be not afraid of sudden fear.   *3:25*

Wisdom is the principal thing; therefore get wisdom: and with all thy getting get understanding.   *4:7*

The path of the just is as the shining light, that shineth more and more unto the perfect day.   *4:18*

Keep thy heart with all diligence; for out of it are the issues of life.   *4:23*

For the lips of a strange woman drop as an honeycomb, and her mouth is smoother than oil:

But her end is bitter as wormwood, sharp as a two-edged sword.   *5:3–4*

Go to the ant, thou sluggard; consider her ways, and be wise:

Which having no guide, overseer, or ruler,

Provideth her meat in the summer, and gathereth her food in the harvest.   *6:6–8*

Yet a little sleep, a little slumber, a little folding of the hands to sleep: [1]

So shall thy poverty come as one that travelleth, and thy want as an armed man.   *6:10–11*

Lust not after her beauty in thine heart; neither let her take thee with her eyelids.   *6:25*

Can a man take fire in his bosom, and his clothes not be burned?

Can one go upon hot coals, and his feet not be burned?   *6:27–28*

Jealousy is the rage of a man: therefore he will not spare in the day of vengeance.   *6:34*

He goeth after her straightway, as an ox goeth to the slaughter.   *7:22*

I love them that love me; and those that seek me early shall find me.   *8:17*

Wisdom hath builded her house, she hath hewn out her seven pillars.   *9:1*

[1] Also in *Proverbs 24:33.*

Reprove not a scorner, lest he hate thee: rebuke a wise man, and he will love thee. *Proverbs* 9:8

Stolen waters are sweet, and bread eaten in secret is pleasant. 9:17

A wise son maketh a glad father: but a foolish son is the heaviness of his mother. 10:1

Blessings are upon the head of the just: but violence covereth the mouth of the wicked.

The memory of the just is blessed: but the name of the wicked shall rot. 10:6–7

Hatred stirreth up strifes: but love covereth all sins. 10:12

In the multitude of counsellors there is safety.[1]

He that is surety for a stranger shall smart for it. 11:14–15

As a jewel of gold in a swine's snout, so is a fair woman which is without discretion. 11:22

He that trusteth in his riches shall fall. 11:28

A virtuous woman is a crown to her husband. 12:4

A righteous man regardeth the life of his beast: but the tender mercies of the wicked are cruel. 12:10

The way of a fool is right in his own eyes. 12:15

Hope deferred maketh the heart sick. 13:12

The way of transgressors is hard. 13:15

The desire accomplished is sweet to the soul. 13:19

He that spareth his rod hateth his son: but he that loveth him chasteneth him betimes.[2] 13:24

Fools make a mock at sin. 14:9

The heart knoweth his own bitterness; and a stranger doth not intermeddle with his joy. *Proverbs* 14:10

Even in laughter the heart is sorrowful. 14:13

The prudent man looketh well to his going. 14:15

In all labor there is profit: but the talk of the lips tendeth only to penury. 14:23

Righteousness exalteth a nation. 14:34

A soft answer turneth away wrath. 15:1

A merry heart maketh a cheerful countenance: but by sorrow of the heart the spirit is broken. 15:13

He that is of a merry heart hath a continual feast.

Better is little with the fear of the Lord than great treasure and trouble therewith.

Better is a dinner of herbs where love is, than a stalled ox and hatred therewith.[1] 15:15–17

A wrathful man stirreth up strife: but he that is slow to anger appeaseth strife. 15:18

A word spoken in due season, how good is it! 15:23

Before honour is humility. 15:33 *and* 18:12

A man's heart deviseth his way: but the Lord directeth his steps. 16:9

Pride goeth before destruction, and an haughty spirit before a fall.[2] 16:18

The hoary head is a crown of glory, if it be found in the way of righteousness.

He that is slow to anger is better than the mighty; and he that ruleth his spirit than he that taketh a city. 16:31–32

Whoso mocketh the poor reproacheth his Maker. 17:5

---

[1] Also in *Proverbs* 24:6.
[2] See Menander, p. 102a, and note.

[1] See Amenemope, IX, p. 4b.
[2] See Sophocles, p. 81b, and note.

He that repeateth a matter separateth very friends.   *Proverbs* 17:9

Whoso rewardeth evil for good, evil shall not depart from his house.   17:13

A merry heart doeth good like a medicine.   17:22

He that hath knowledge spareth his words: and a man of understanding is of an excellent spirit.
Even a fool, when he holdeth his peace, is counted wise.   17:27–28

A fool's mouth is his destruction.   18:7

A wounded spirit who can bear?   18:14

A brother offended is harder to be won than a strong city: and their contentions are like the bars of a castle.   18:19

Whoso findeth a wife findeth a good thing.   18:22

A man that hath friends must show himself friendly: and there is a friend that sticketh closer than a brother.   18:24

Wealth maketh many friends.   19:4

A foolish son is the calamity of his father: and the contentions of a wife are a continual dropping.   19:13

He that hath pity upon the poor lendeth unto the Lord.   19:17

Wine is a mocker, strong drink is raging.   20:1

It is an honour for a man to cease from strife: but every fool will be meddling.   20:3

Even a child is known by his doings, whether his work be pure, and whether it be right.
The hearing ear, and the seeing eye, the Lord hath made even both of them.   20:11–12

It is naught, it is naught, saith the buyer: but when he is gone his way, then he boasteth.   20:14

Bread of deceit is sweet to a man; but afterwards his mouth shall be filled with gravel.   *Proverbs* 20:17

Meddle not with him that flattereth with his lips.   20:19

It is better to dwell in a corner of the housetop, than with a brawling woman in a wide house.   21:9 *and* 25:24

A good name is rather to be chosen than great riches.   22:1

Train up a child in the way he should go: and when he is old, he will not depart from it.   22:6

The borrower is servant to the lender.   22:7

Bow down thine ear, and hear the words of the wise, and apply thine heart unto my knowledge.
For it is a pleasant thing if thou keep them within thee; they shall withal be fitted in thy lips.[1]   22:17–18

Have I not written to thee excellent things in counsels and knowledge,[2]
That I might make thee know the certainty of the words of truth; that thou mightest answer the words of truth to them that send unto thee?[3]   22:20–21

Remove not the ancient landmark.[4]   22:28

Seest thou a man diligent in his business? He shall stand before kings.[5]   22:29

Put a knife to thy throat, if thou be a man given to appetite.   23:2

Labor not to be rich: cease from thine own wisdom.[6]   23:4

Riches certainly make themselves wings.[7]   23:5

As he thinketh in his heart, so is he.   23:7

[1] See Amenemope, III, p. 4b.
[2] See Amenemope, XXVII, p. 4b.
[3] See Amenemope, I, p. 4a.
[4] Also in *Proverbs 23:10.* See Amenemope, VII, p. 4b.
[5] See Amenemope, XXVII, p. 4b.
[6] See Amenemope, IX, p. 4b.
[7] See Amenemope, X, p. 4b.

The drunkard and the glutton shall come to poverty: and drowsiness shall clothe a man with rags.

Proverbs 23:21

Despise not thy mother when she is old.   23:22

Look not thou upon the wine when it is red, when it giveth his colour in the cup, when it moveth itself aright.
At the last it biteth like a serpent, and stingeth like an adder.   23:31–32

A wise man is strong; yea, a man of knowledge increaseth strength.   24:5

If thou faint in the day of adversity, thy strength is small.   24:10

A word fitly spoken is like apples of gold in pictures of silver.   25:11

If thine enemy be hungry, give him bread to eat; and if he be thirsty, give him water to drink:
For thou shalt heap coals of fire upon his head.[1]   25:21–22

As cold waters to a thirsty soul, so is good news from a far country.   25:25

For men to search their own glory is not glory.   25:27

Answer a fool according to his folly.
26:5

As a dog returneth to his vomit, so a fool returneth to his folly.
Seest thou a man wise in his own conceit? There is more hope of a fool than of him.
The slothful man saith, There is a lion in the way; a lion is in the streets.   26:11–13

Whoso diggeth a pit shall fall therein: and he that rolleth a stone, it will return upon him.   26:27

Boast not thyself of tomorrow; for thou knowest not what a day may bring forth.[2]   27:1

Let another man praise thee, and not thine own mouth.   27:2

[1] See *Romans* 12:20 and Marcus Aurelius, p. 142b.
[2] See Sophocles, p. 82b.

Open rebuke is better than secret love.
Faithful are the wounds of a friend; but the kisses of an enemy are deceitful.

Proverbs 27:5–6

To the hungry soul every bitter thing is sweet.   27:7

Better is a neighbour that is near than a brother far off.   27:10

Iron sharpeneth iron; so a man sharpeneth the countenance of his friend.   27:17

The wicked flee when no man pursueth: but the righteous are bold as a lion.   28:1

He that maketh haste to be rich shall not be innocent.   28:20

He that trusteth in his own heart is a fool.   28:26

He that giveth unto the poor shall not lack.   28:27

A fool uttereth all his mind.
29:11

Where there is no vision, the people perish.   29:18

A man's pride shall bring him low: but honour shall uphold the humble in spirit.   29:23

Give me neither poverty nor riches.
30:8

Accuse not a servant unto his master.
30:10

The horseleach hath two daughters, crying, Give, give.   30:15

There be three things which are too wonderful for me, yea, four which I know not:
The way of an eagle in the air; the way of a serpent upon a rock; the way of a ship in the midst of the sea; and the way of a man with a maid.
30:18–19

Give strong drink unto him that is ready to perish, and wine unto those that be of heavy hearts.   31:6

Who can find a virtuous woman? for her price is far above rubies.

The heart of her husband doth safely trust in her.   *Proverbs* 31:10–11

Her husband is known in the gates, when he sitteth among the elders of the land.   31:23

Strength and honour are her clothing.   31:25

In her tongue is the law of kindness. She looketh well to the ways of her household, and eateth not the bread of idleness.

Her children arise up, and call her blessed.   31:26–28

Many daughters have done virtuously, but thou excellest them all.

Favour is deceitful, and beauty is vain: but a woman that feareth the Lord, she shall be praised.

Give her of the fruit of her hands; and let her own works praise her in the gates.   31:29–31

Vanity of vanities, saith the Preacher, vanity of vanities; all is vanity.

What profit hath a man of all his labour which he taketh under the sun?

One generation passeth away, and another generation cometh: but the earth abideth for ever.

The sun also ariseth.   *Ecclesiastes* 1:2–5

All the rivers run into the sea; yet the sea is not full.   1:7

The eye is not satisfied with seeing, nor the ear filled with hearing.   1:8

There is no new thing under the sun.   1:9

There is no remembrance of former things; neither shall there be any remembrance of things that are to come with those that shall come after.   1:11

I have seen all the works that are done under the sun; and, behold, all is vanity and vexation of spirit.

That which is crooked cannot be made straight: and that which is wanting cannot be numbered.
     Ecclesiastes 1:14–15

In much wisdom is much grief: and he that increaseth knowledge increaseth sorrow.   1:18

Wisdom excelleth folly, as far as light excelleth darkness.   2:13

One event happeneth to them all.   2:14

How dieth the wise man? as the fool.   2:16

To every thing there is a season, and a time to every purpose under the heaven.

A time to be born, and a time to die; a time to plant, and a time to pluck up that which is planted;

A time to kill, and a time to heal; a time to break down, and a time to build up;

A time to weep, and a time to laugh; a time to mourn, and a time to dance;

A time to cast away stones, and a time to gather stones together; a time to embrace, and a time to refrain from embracing;

A time to get, and a time to lose; a time to keep, and a time to cast away;

A time to rend, and a time to sew; a time to keep silence, and a time to speak; [1]

A time to love, and a time to hate; a time of war, and a time of peace.
     3:1–8

Wherefore I praised the dead which are already dead more than the living which are yet alive.   4:2

Better is an handful with quietness, than both the hands full with travail and vexation of spirit.   4:6

A threefold cord is not quickly broken.   4:12

Better is a poor and a wise child than an old and foolish king.   4:13

[1] See Homer, p. 66a.

God is in heaven, and thou upon earth: therefore let thy words be few.
Ecclesiastes 5:2

Better is it that thou shouldest not vow, than that thou shouldest vow and not pay. 5:5

The sleep of a labouring man is sweet . . . but the abundance of the rich will not suffer him to sleep.
5:12

As he came forth of his mother's womb, naked shall he return to go as he came,[1] and shall take nothing of his labour, which he may carry away in his hand.[2] 5:15

A good name is better than precious ointment; and the day of death than the day of one's birth.[3] 7:1

It is better to go to the house of mourning, than to go to the house of feasting. 7:2

As the crackling of thorns under a pot, so is the laughter of the fool.
7:6

Better is the end of a thing than the beginning thereof. 7:8

In the day of prosperity be joyful, but in the day of adversity consider.
7:14

Be not righteous over much. 7:16

There is not a just man upon earth, that doeth good, and sinneth not.
7:20

And I find more bitter than death the woman, whose heart is snares and nets, and her hands as bands. 7:26

One man among a thousand have I found; but a woman among all those have I not found. 7:28

God hath made man upright; but they have sought out many inventions.
7:29

There is no discharge in that war.
8:8

[1] See *Job 1:21*, p. 14a.
[2] See *The Song of the Harp-Player*, p. 3a.
[3] See Publilius Syrus, p. 125a.

A man hath no better thing under the sun, than to eat, and to drink, and to be merry.[1] *Ecclesiastes* 8:15

A living dog is better than a dead lion.

For the living know that they shall die: but the dead know not any thing, neither have they any more a reward; for the memory of them is forgotten.
9:4–5

Whatsoever thy hand findeth to do, do it with thy might; for there is no work, nor device, nor knowledge, nor wisdom, in the grave, whither thou goest. 9:10

The race is not to the swift, nor the battle to the strong. 9:11

A feast is made for laughter, and wine maketh merry: but money answereth all things. 10:19

A bird of the air shall carry the voice, and that which hath wings shall tell the matter. 10:20

Cast thy bread upon the waters: for thou shalt find it after many days.
11:1

He that observeth the wind shall not sow; and he that regardeth the clouds shall not reap. 11:4

In the morning sow thy seed, and in the evening withhold not thine hand.
11:6

Rejoice, O young man, in thy youth.
11:9

Remember now thy Creator in the days of thy youth, while the evil days come not, nor the years draw nigh, when thou shalt say, I have no pleasure in them.

While the sun, or the light, or the moon, or the stars, be not darkened, nor the clouds return after the rain:

In the day when the keepers of the house shall tremble, and the strong men shall bow themselves, and the grinders cease because they are few, and those that look out of the windows be darkened,

[1] See *Luke 12:19*, p. 46b.

And the doors shall be shut in the streets, when the sound of the grinding is low, and he shall rise up at the voice of the bird, and all the daughters of music shall be brought low.

Ecclesiastes 12:1–4

The almond tree shall flourish, and the grasshopper shall be a burden, and desire shall fail; because man goeth to his long home, and the mourners go about the streets:

Or ever the silver cord be loosed, or the golden bowl be broken, or the pitcher be broken at the fountain, or the wheel broken at the cistern.

Then shall the dust return to the earth as it was: and the spirit shall return unto God who gave it.   *12:5–7*

The words of the wise are as goads, and as nails fastened by the masters of assemblies.   *12:11*

Of making many books there is no end; and much study is a weariness of the flesh.

Let us hear the conclusion of the whole matter: Fear God, and keep his commandments: for this is the whole duty of man.

For God shall bring every work into judgment, with every secret thing, whether it be good, or whether it be evil.   *12:12–14*

The song of songs, which is Solomon's.   *The Song of Solomon 1:1*

I am black, but comely, O ye daughters of Jerusalem, as the tents of Kedar, as the curtains of Solomon.

1:5

O thou fairest among women.

1:8

I am the rose of Sharon, and the lily of the valleys.   *2:1*

As the apple tree among the trees of the wood, so is my beloved among the sons.   *2:3*

His banner over me was love.

Stay me with flagons, comfort me with apples: for I am sick of love.

2:4–5

Rise up, my love, my fair one, and come away.

For, lo, the winter is past, the rain is over and gone;

The flowers appear on the earth; the time of the singing of birds is come, and the voice of the turtle is heard in our land.   *Song of Solomon 2:10–12*

The little foxes, that spoil the vines.

2:15

Until the day break, and the shadows flee away.   *2:17 and 4:6*

By night on my bed I sought him whom my soul loveth: I sought him, but I found him not.   *3:1*

Thy two breasts are like two young roes that are twins, which feed among the lilies.   *4:5*

Thou art all fair, my love; there is no spot in thee.   *4:7*

How much better is thy love than wine!   *4:10*

Awake, O north wind; and come, thou south; blow upon my garden, that the spices thereof may flow out. Let my beloved come into his garden, and eat his pleasant fruits.   *4:16*

My beloved put in his hand by the hole of the door, and my bowels were moved for him.   *5:4*

His mouth is most sweet: yea, he is altogether lovely. This is my beloved, and this is my friend, O daughters of Jerusalem.   *5:16*

Who is she that looketh forth as the morning, fair as the moon, clear as the sun, and terrible as an army with banners?   *6:10*

Return, return, O Shulamite.

6:13

Thy belly is like a heap of wheat set about with lilies.   *7:2*

Thy neck is as a tower of ivory.

7:4

Like the best wine . . . that goeth down sweetly, causing the lips of those that are asleep to speak.   *7:9*

I am my beloved's, and his desire is toward me.　　*Song of Solomon* 7:10

Set me as a seal upon thine heart, as a seal upon thine arm: for love is strong as death; jealousy is cruel as the grave.　　8:6

Many waters cannot quench love, neither can the floods drown it.
　　8:7

Make haste, my beloved, and be thou like to a roe or to a young hart upon the mountains of spices.　　8:14

The ox knoweth his owner, and the ass his master's crib.
The Book of the Prophet Isaiah 1:3

The whole head is sick, and the whole heart faint.　　1:5

As a lodge in a garden of cucumbers.
　　1:8

Bring no more vain oblations.
　　1:13

Learn to do well; seek judgment, relieve the oppressed, judge the fatherless, plead for the widow.

Come now, and let us reason together . . . though your sins be as scarlet, they shall be as white as snow.
　　1:17–18

They shall beat their swords into plowshares, and their spears into pruninghooks: nation shall not lift up sword against nation, neither shall they learn war any more.[1]　　2:4

In that day a man shall cast his idols . . . to the moles and to the bats.　　2:20

Cease ye from man, whose breath is in his nostrils.　　2:22

The stay and the staff, the whole stay of bread, and the whole stay of water.　　3:1

What mean ye that ye beat my people to pieces and grind the faces of the poor?　　3:15

[1] Also in *Joel 3:10* and *Micah 4:3*.

Walk with stretched forth necks and wanton eyes, walking and mincing as they go, and making a tinkling with their feet.　　*Isaiah* 3:16

In that day seven women shall take hold of one man.　　4:1

My wellbeloved hath a vineyard in a very fruitful hill.　　5:1

And he looked for judgment, but behold oppression; for righteousness, but behold a cry.

Woe unto them that join house to house, that lay field to field, till there be no place, that they may be placed alone in the midst of the earth!
　　5:7–8

Woe unto them that rise up early in the morning, that they may follow strong drink.　　5:11

Woe unto them that draw iniquity with cords of vanity, and sin as it were with a cart rope.　　5:18

Woe unto them that call evil good, and good evil.　　5:20

I saw also the Lord sitting upon a throne, high and lifted up, and his train filled the temple.

Above it stood the seraphims: each one had six wings; with twain he covered his face, and with twain he covered his feet, and with twain he did fly.　　6:1–2

Holy, holy, holy, is the Lord of hosts: the whole earth is full of his glory.　　6:3

Woe is me! for I am undone; because I am a man of unclean lips, and I dwell in the midst of a people of unclean lips: for mine eyes have seen the King, the Lord of hosts.　　6:5

I heard the voice of the Lord, saying, Whom shall I send, and who will go for us? Then said I, Here am I; send me.　　6:8

Then said I, Lord, how long?
　　6:11

Behold, a virgin shall conceive, and

bear a son, and shall call his name Immanuel.　　　　*Isaiah 7:14*

For a stone of stumbling and for a rock of offence.　　　　8:14

The people that walked in darkness have seen a great light: they that dwell in the land of the shadow of death, upon them hath the light shined.
9:2

For unto us a child is born, unto us a son is given: and the government shall be upon his shoulder: and his name shall be called Wonderful, Counsellor, The mighty God, The everlasting Father, The Prince of Peace.
Of the increase of his government and peace there shall be no end.
9:6-7

The ancient and honorable, he is the head.　　　　9:15

And there shall come forth a rod out of the stem of Jesse, and a Branch shall grow out of his roots:
And the Spirit of the Lord shall rest upon him, the spirit of wisdom and understanding, the spirit of counsel and might, the spirit of knowledge and of the fear of the Lord.　　　　11:1-2

The wolf also shall dwell with the lamb, and the leopard shall lie down with the kid; and the calf and the young lion and the fatling together; and a little child shall lead them.
And the cow and the bear shall feed; their young ones shall lie down together: and the lion shall eat straw like the ox.
And the suckling child shall play on the hole of the asp, and the weaned child shall put his hand on the cockatrice' den.
They shall not hurt nor destroy in all my holy mountain: for the earth shall be full of the knowledge of the Lord, as the waters cover the sea.　　　　11:6-9

For the Lord JEHOVAH is my strength and my song; he also is become my salvation.　　　　12:2

And I will punish the world for their evil, and the wicked for their iniquity; and I will cause the arrogancy of the proud to cease, and will lay low the haughtiness of the terrible.
Isaiah 13:11

How art thou fallen from heaven, O Lucifer, son of the morning!　　14:12

Is this the man that made the earth to tremble, that did shake kingdoms.
14:16

The nations shall rush like the rushing of many waters.　　　　17:13

And they shall fight every one against his brother.　　　　19:2

The burden of the desert of the sea. As whirlwinds in the south pass through; so it cometh from the desert, from a terrible land.　　　　21:1

Babylon is fallen, is fallen; [1] and all the graven images of her gods he hath broken unto the ground.　　　　21:9

Watchman, what of the night?
21:11

Let us eat and drink; for tomorrow we shall die.　　　　22:13

I will fasten him as a nail in a sure place.　　　　22:23

Whose merchants are princes.
23:8

As with the maid, so with her mistress.　　　　24:2

For thou hast been a strength to the poor, a strength to the needy in his distress.　　　　25:4

A feast of fat things, a feast of wines on the lees.　　　　25:6

He will swallow up death in victory;[2] and the Lord God will wipe away tears from off all faces.[3]　　　　25:8

Open ye the gates, that the righteous nation which keepeth the truth may enter in.
Thou wilt keep him in perfect peace, whose mind is stayed on thee.
26:2-3

[1] See *Revelation 14:8*, p. 58b.
[2] See *I Corinthians 15:54*, p. 53a.
[3] See *Revelation 21:4*, p. 58b.

Awake and sing.   *Isaiah 26:19*

Hide thyself as it were for a little moment, until the indignation be overpast.   26:20

Leviathan, that crooked serpent . . . the dragon that is in the sea.
        27:1

For precept must be upon precept, precept upon precept; line upon line, line upon line; here a little, and there a little.   28:10

We have made a covenant with death, and with hell are we at agreement.   28:15

It shall be a vexation only to understand the report.   28:19

They are drunken, but not with wine; they stagger, but not with strong drink.   29:9

Their strength is to sit still.

Now go, write it before them in a table, and note it in a book, that it may be for the time to come for ever and ever.   30:7–8

The bread of adversity, and the water of affliction.   30:20

This is the way, walk ye in it.
        30:21

Behold, a king shall reign in righteousness.   32:1

And a man shall be as an hiding place from the wind, and a covert from the tempest; as rivers of water in a dry place, as the shadows of a great rock in a weary land.   32:2

An habitation of dragons, and a court for owls.   34:13

The desert shall rejoice, and blossom as the rose.   35:1

Then the eyes of the blind shall be opened, and the ears of the deaf shall be unstopped.

Then shall the lame man leap as an hart, and the tongue of the dumb sing.   35:5–6

Sorrow and sighing shall flee away.
        35:10

Thou trustest in the staff of this broken reed.   *Isaiah 36:6*

Incline thine ear, O Lord, and hear.   37:17

I shall go softly all my years in the bitterness of my soul.   38:15

Comfort ye, comfort ye my people.
        40:1

Speak ye comfortably to Jerusalem, and cry unto her, that her warfare is accomplished, that her iniquity is pardoned: for she hath received of the Lord's hand double for all her sins.

The voice of him that crieth in the wilderness, Prepare ye the way of the Lord, make straight in the desert a highway for our God.[1]   40:2–3

Every valley shall be exalted, and every mountain and hill shall be made low: and the crooked shall be made straight, and the rough places plain.
        40:4

All flesh is grass, and all the goodliness thereof is as the flower of the field.   40:6

The grass withereth, the flower fadeth:[2] but the word of our God shall stand for ever.   40:8

Get thee up into the high mountain . . . say unto the cities of Judah, Behold your God!   40:9

He shall feed his flock like a shepherd: he shall gather the lambs with his arm, and carry them in his bosom, and shall gently lead those that are with young.   40:11

The nations are as a drop of a bucket, and are counted as the small dust of the balance.   40:15

Have ye not known? have ye not heard? hath it not been told you from the beginning?   40:21

They that wait upon the Lord shall

[1] See *Matthew 3:3*, p. 39b. Also in *Mark 1:3*, *Luke 3:4* and *John 1:23*.
[2] See *Psalm 90:5–6*, p. 20a, and note.

renew their strength; they shall mount up with wings as eagles; they shall run, and not be weary; and they shall walk, and not faint.   *Isaiah* 40:31

They helped every one his neighbour; and every one said to his brother, Be of good courage.   41:6

A bruised reed shall he not break, and the smoking flax shall he not quench.   42:3

Shall the clay say to him that fashioneth it, What makest thou?   45:9

O that thou hadst hearkened to my commandments! then had thy peace been as a river, and thy righteousness as the waves of the sea.   48:18

There is no peace, saith the Lord, unto the wicked.   48:22

Therefore the redeemed of the Lord shall return, and come with singing unto Zion.   51:11

Thou hast drunken the dregs of the cup of trembling.   51:17

Therefore hear now this.   51:21

How beautiful upon the mountains are the feet of him that bringeth good tidings, that publisheth peace.   52:7

They shall see eye to eye.   52:8

He is despised and rejected of men; a man of sorrows, and acquainted with grief.   53:3

Surely he hath borne our griefs, and carried our sorrows.   53:4

All we like sheep have gone astray.   53:6

He is brought as a lamb to the slaughter.[1]   53:7

Ho, everyone that thirsteth, come ye to the waters.   55:1

Behold, I have given him for a witness to the people, a leader and commander to the people.   55:4

[1] Also in *Acts 8:32.*

Let the wicked forsake his way, and the unrighteous man his thoughts.   *Isaiah* 55:7

For my thoughts are not your thoughts, neither are your ways my ways, saith the Lord.   55:8

Peace to him that is far off, and to him that is near.   57:19

Arise, shine; for thy light is come, and the glory of the Lord is risen upon thee.   60:1

A little one shall become a thousand, and a small one a strong nation.   60:22

Give unto them beauty for ashes, the oil of joy for mourning, the garment of praise for the spirit of heaviness.   61:3

I have trodden the winepress alone; and of the people there was none with me: for I will tread them in mine anger, and trample them in my fury; and their blood shall be sprinkled upon my garments, and I will stain all my raiment.   63:3

All our righteousnesses are as filthy rags; and we all do fade as a leaf.   64:6

We all are the work of thy hand.   64:8

I am holier than thou.   65:5

For, behold, I create new heavens and a new earth.[1]   65:17

And they shall build houses, and inhabit them; and they shall plant vineyards, and eat the fruit of them. They shall not build, and another inhabit; they shall not plant, and another eat.   65:21–22

As one whom his mother comforteth, so will I comfort you.   66:13

They were as fed horses in the morning: every one neighed after his neighbour's wife.
       The Book of the Prophet Jeremiah 5:8

[1] See *Revelation 21:1,* p. 58b.

Hear now this, foolish people, and without understanding; which have eyes, and see not; which have ears, and hear not.   *Jeremiah* 5:21

But this people hath a revolting and a rebellious heart.   5:23

Saying, Peace, peace; when there is no peace.   6:14 *and* 8:11

Stand ye in the ways, and see, and ask for the old paths, where is the good way, and walk therein.[1]   6:16

Amend your ways and your doings.
                    7:3 *and* 26:13

The harvest is past, the summer is ended, and we are not saved.   8:20

Is there no balm in Gilead?   8:22

Oh that I had in the wilderness a lodging place of wayfaring men!
                    9:6

I will feed them . . . with wormwood, and give them water of gall to drink.[2]   9:15

Can the Ethiopian change his skin, or the leopard his spots?   13:23

Her sun is gone down while it was yet day.   15:9

A man of strife and a man of contention.   15:10

The sin of Judah is written with a pen of iron, and with the point of a diamond.   17:1

Cursed be the man that trusteth in man, and maketh flesh his arm, and whose heart departeth from the Lord.

For he shall be like the heath in the desert, and shall not see when good cometh; but shall inhabit the parched places in the wilderness, in a salt land and not inhabited.

Blessed is the man that trusteth in the Lord, and whose hope the Lord is.

For he shall be as a tree planted by the waters, and that spreadeth out her roots by the river, and shall not see

when heat cometh, but her leaf shall be green; and shall not be careful in the year of drought, neither shall cease from yielding fruit.[1]   *Jeremiah* 17:5–8

The heart is deceitful above all things, and desperately wicked: who can know it?   17:9

As the partridge sitteth on eggs, and hatcheth them not; so he that getteth riches, and not by right, shall leave them in the midst of his days, and at his end shall be a fool.   17:11

Thou art my hope in the day of evil.   17:17

O earth, earth, earth, hear the word of the Lord.   22:29

The fathers have eaten a sour grape, and the children's teeth are set on edge.[2]   31:29

With my whole heart and with my whole soul.   32:41

And seekest thou great things for thyself? seek them not.   45:5

How doth the city sit solitary, that was full of people! how is she become as a widow!
                    *The Lamentations of
                    Jeremiah* 1:1

She weepeth sore in the night, and her tears are on her cheeks: among all her lovers she hath none to comfort her.   1:2

Is it nothing to you, all ye that pass by? behold, and see if there be any sorrow like unto my sorrow.   1:12

It is good for a man that he bear the yoke in his youth.   3:27

As it were a wheel in the middle of a wheel.
                    *The Book of the Prophet
                    Ezekiel* 1:16

As is the mother, so is her daughter.
                    16:44

---

[1] Stare super vias antiquas. — *The Vulgate*
[2] I will feed them with wormwood, and make them drink the water of gall. — *Jeremiah* 23:15

[1] See Amenemope, VI, p. 4b; see also *Psalm 1*, p. 16b.
[2] Also in *Ezekiel 18:2*.

The king of Babylon stood at the parting of the way. *Ezekiel 21:21*

Can these bones live? 37:3

O ye dry bones, hear the word of the Lord. 37:4

Every man's sword shall be against his brother. 38:21

His legs of iron, his feet part of iron and part of clay.
The Book of Daniel 2:33

Shadrach, Meshach, and Abednego, fell down bound into the midst of the burning fiery furnace. 3:23

Nebuchadnezzar . . . was driven from men, and did eat grass as oxen.
4:33

Belshazzar the king made a great feast to a thousand of his lords.
5:1

And this is the writing that was written, MENE, MENE, TEKEL, UPHARSIN.
This is the interpretation of the thing: MENE; God hath numbered thy kingdom, and finished it.
TEKEL; Thou art weighed in the balances, and art found wanting.
PERES; Thy kingdom is divided, and given to the Medes and Persians.
5:25–28

According to the law of the Medes and Persians, which altereth not.
6:12

They brought Daniel, and cast him into the den of lions. 6:16

So Daniel was taken up out of the den, and no manner of hurt was found upon him, because he believed in his God. 6:23

The Ancient of days. 7:9 *and* 7:13

Many shall run to and fro, and knowledge shall be increased. 12:4

Ye are the sons of the living God. *Hosea 1:10*

Like people, like priest. 4:9

After two days will he revive us: in the third day he will raise us up, and we shall live in his sight. *Hosea 6:2*

He shall come unto us as the rain, as the latter and former rain unto the earth. 6:3

For I desired mercy, and not sacrifice; and the knowledge of God more than burnt offerings. 6:6

They have sown the wind, and they shall reap the whirlwind. 8:7

Ye have plowed wickedness, ye have reaped iniquity. 10:13

I drew them with . . . bands of love. 11:4

I have multiplied visions, and used similitudes, by the ministry of the prophets. 12:10

I will ransom them from the power of the grave; I will redeem them from death: O death, I will be thy plagues; O grave, I will be thy destruction.[1]
13:14

Your old men shall dream dreams, your young men shall see visions.
Joel 2:28

Multitudes in the valley of decision.
3:14

They sold the righteous for silver, and the poor for a pair of shoes.
Amos 2:6

Can two walk together, except they be agreed? 3:3

And Jonah was in the belly of the fish three days and three nights.
Jonah 1:17

What doth the Lord require of thee, but to do justly, and to love mercy, and to walk humbly with thy God?
Micah 6:8

The faces of them all gather blackness.[2] *Nahum 2:10*

Write the vision, and make it plain

[1] See *I Corinthians 15:54–55*, p. 53a.
[2] The faces of them all are as the blackness of a kettle. — *Douay Bible* [1609], *Nahum 2:10*. The English version of the Roman Catholic Bible was first printed in Douay, France.

upon tables, that he may run that readeth it. *Habakkuk* 2:2

The Lord is in his holy temple: let all the earth keep silence before him. 2:20

Your fathers, where are they? And the prophets, do they live forever? *Zechariah* 1:5

I have spread you abroad as the four winds of the heaven. 2:6

Not by might, nor by power, but by my spirit, saith the Lord of hosts. 4:6

For who hath despised the day of small things? 4:10

Behold, thy King cometh unto thee . . . lowly, and riding upon an ass. 9:9

Prisoners of hope. 9:12

So they weighed for my price thirty pieces of silver.[1] 11:12

What are these wounds in thine hands? . . . Those with which I was wounded in the house of my friends. 13:6

Have we not all one father? hath not one God created us? *Malachi* 2:10

Behold, I will send my messenger, and he shall prepare the way before me. 3:1

Behold, the day cometh. 4:1

Healing in his wings. 4:2

Behold, I will send you Elijah the prophet before the coming of the great and dreadful day of the Lord. 4:5

THE APOCRYPHA[2]

And when they are in their cups, they forget their love both to friends

---

[1] See *Matthew* 26:15, p. 44b.
[2] These books form part of the sacred literature of the Alexandrian Jews, and with the exception of *II Esdras* are found interspersed with the Hebrew Scriptures in the ancient copies of the Septuagint, or Greek Version of the Old Testament. — *The Apocrypha According to the Authorized Version, Preface* (Oxford University Press)

---

and brethren, and a little after draw out swords. *I Esdras* 3:22

Great is Truth, and mighty above all things.[1] 4:41

What is past I know, but what is for to come I know not. *II Esdras* 4:46

Now therefore keep thy sorrow to thyself, and bear with a good courage that which hath befallen thee. 10:15

I shall light a candle of understanding in thine heart, which shall not be put out. 14:25

If thou hast abundance, give alms accordingly: if thou have but a little, be not afraid to give according to that little. *Tobit* 4:8

Put on her garments of gladness. *Judith* 10:3

The ear of jealousy heareth all things. *The Wisdom of Solomon* 1:10

Our time is a very shadow that passeth away. 2:5

Let us crown ourselves with rosebuds, before they be withered. 2:8

For God created man to be immortal, and made him to be an image of his own eternity.
Nevertheless through envy of the devil came death into the world. 2:23–24

The souls of the righteous are in the hand of God, and there shall no torment touch them.
In the sight of the unwise they seemed to die: and their departure is taken for misery,
And their going from us to be utter destruction: but they are in peace.
For though they be punished in the sight of men, yet is their hope full of immortality.
And having been a little chastised, they shall be greatly rewarded: for God proved them, and found them worthy for himself. 3:1–5

---

[1] *Magna est veritas et praevalet.* — *The Vulgate, Book III* (uncanonical)

They that put their trust in him shall understand the truth.

The Wisdom of Solomon 3:9

Even so we in like manner, as soon as we were born, began to draw to our end. 5:13

For the hope of the ungodly is like dust that is blown away with the wind . . . and passeth away as the remembrance of a guest that tarrieth but a day. 5:14

For the very true beginning of her [wisdom] is the desire of discipline; and the care of discipline is love.

6:17

And when I was born, I drew in the common air, and fell upon the earth, which is of like nature; and the first voice which I uttered was crying, as all others do. 7:3

All men have one entrance into life, and the like going out. 7:6

The light that cometh from her [wisdom] never goeth out. 7:10

Who can number the sand of the sea, and the drops of rain, and the days of eternity?

The Wisdom of Jesus the Son of Sirach, or Ecclesiasticus, 1:2

To whom hath the root of wisdom been revealed? 1:6

For the Lord is full of compassion and mercy, longsuffering, and very pitiful, and forgiveth sins, and saveth in time of affliction. 2:11

The greater thou art, the more humble thyself. 3:18

Many are in high place, and of renown: but mysteries are revealed unto the meek. 3:19

Seek not out the things that are too hard for thee, neither search the things that are above thy strength. 3:21

Be not curious in unnecessary matters: for more things are shewed unto thee than men understand. 3:23

Profess not the knowledge . . . that thou hast not.

A stubborn heart shall fare evil at the last. *Ecclesiasticus* 3:25–26

Wisdom exalteth her children, and layeth hold of them that seek her.

He that loveth her loveth life.

4:11–12

Observe the opportunity. 4:20

Be not as a lion in thy house, nor frantick among thy servants.

Let not thine hand be stretched out to receive, and shut when thou shouldest repay. 4:30–31

Set not thy heart upon thy goods; and say not, I have enough for my life. 5:1

Winnow not with every wind, and go not into every way. 5:9

Let thy life be sincere. 5:11

Be not ignorant of any thing in a great matter or a small. 5:15

If thou wouldest get a friend, prove him first. 6:7

A faithful friend is a strong defence: and he that hath found such an one hath found a treasure. 6:14

A faithful friend is the medicine of life. 6:16

If thou seest a man of understanding, get thee betimes unto him, and let thy foot wear the steps of his door.

6:36

Whatsoever thou takest in hand, remember the end, and thou shalt never do amiss. 7:36

Rejoice not over thy greatest enemy being dead, but remember that we die all. 8:7

Miss not the discourse of the elders.

8:9

Forsake not an old friend; for the new is not comparable to him: a new friend is as new wine; when it is old, thou shalt drink it with pleasure.

9:10

Pride is hateful before God and man. *Ecclesiasticus* 10:7

He that is to day a king to morrow shall die. 10:10

Pride was not made for men, nor furious anger for them that are born of a woman. 10:18

Be not overwise in doing thy business. 10:26

Many kings have sat down upon the ground; and one that was never thought of hath worn the crown. 11:5

In the day of prosperity there is a forgetfulness of affliction: and in the day of affliction there is no more remembrance of prosperity. 11:25

Judge none blessed before his death.[1] 11:28

A friend cannot be known in prosperity: and an enemy cannot be hidden in adversity. 12:8

How agree the kettle and the earthen pot together? 13:2

A rich man beginning to fall is held up of his friends: but a poor man being down is thrust also away by his friends. 13:21

The heart of a man changeth his countenance, whether it be for good or evil. 13:25

So is a word better than a gift. 18:16

Be not made a beggar by banqueting upon borrowing. 18:33

He that contemneth small things shall fall by little and little. 19:1

Whether it be to friend or foe, talk not of other men's lives. 19:8

A man's attire, and excessive laughter, and gait, shew what he is. 19:30

A tale out of season [is as] musick in mourning. 22:6

I will not be ashamed to defend a friend. 22:25

[1] See Solon, p. 69a, and note.

All wickedness is but little to the wickedness of a woman.

Ecclesiasticus 25:19

The discourse of fools is irksome. 27:13

Many have fallen by the edge of the sword: but not so many as have fallen by the tongue. 28:18

Better is the life of a poor man in a mean cottage, than delicate fare in another man's house. 29:22

There is no riches above a sound body. 30:16

Gladness of the heart is the life of a man, and the joyfulness of a man prolongeth his days. 30:22

Envy and wrath shorten the life, and carefulness bringeth age before the time. 30:24

Watching for riches consumeth the flesh, and the care thereof driveth away sleep. 31:1

Let thy speech be short, comprehending much in few words. 32:8

Consider that I laboured not for myself only, but for all them that seek learning. 33:17

Leave not a stain in thine honour. 33:22

Let the counsel of thine own heart stand. 37:13

Honour a physician with the honour due unto him for the uses which ye may have of him: for the Lord hath created him. 38:1

When the dead is at rest, let his remembrance rest; and be comforted for him, when his spirit is departed from him. 38:23

How can he get wisdom . . . whose talk is of bullocks? 38:25

Let us now praise famous men, and our fathers that begat us. 44:1

All these were honoured in their generations, and were the glory of their times.

There be of them, that have left a name behind them, that their praises might be reported.

And some there be, which have no memorial; who are perished, as though they had never been; and are become as though they had never been born; and their children after them.
Ecclesiasticus 44:7–9

Their bodies are buried in peace; but their name liveth for evermore.
44:14

His word burned like a lamp.
48:1

O all ye works of the Lord, bless ye the Lord: praise him and exalt him above all [1] for ever.
· *The Song of the Three Holy Children* 35

Daniel had convicted them of false witness by their own mouth.
The History of Susanna 61

It is a foolish thing to make a long prologue, and to be short in the story itself. *The Second Book of the Maccabees* 2:32

When he was at the last gasp.
7:9

Speech finely framed delighteth the ears. 15:39

THE NEW TESTAMENT

Behold, a virgin shall be with child, and shall bring forth a son, and they shall call his name Emmanuel, which being interpreted is, God with us.
The Gospel According to St. Matthew 1:23

Now when Jesus was born in Bethlehem of Judaea in the days of Herod the king, behold, there came wise men from the east to Jerusalem,

Saying, Where is he that is born King of the Jews? for we have seen his star in the east, and are come to worship him. 2:1–2

[1] In the Book of Common Prayer (The Benedicite): "magnify him."

They saw the young child with Mary his mother, and fell down, and worshipped him: and . . . they presented unto him gifts; gold, and frankincense, and myrrh.

And being warned of God in a dream that they should not return to Herod, they departed into their own country another way. *Matthew* 2:11–12

Out of Egypt have I called my son. 2:15

Rachel weeping for her children, and would not be comforted, because they are not.[1] 2:18

He shall be called a Nazarene.
2:23

Repent ye: for the kingdom of heaven is at hand. 3:2

The voice of one crying in the wilderness, Prepare ye the way of the Lord, make his paths straight.[2]
3:3

And his meat was locusts and wild honey. 3:4

O generation of vipers, who hath warned you to flee from the wrath to come? 3:7

Now also the axe is laid unto the root of the trees: therefore every tree which bringeth not forth good fruit is hewn down, and cast into the fire. 3:10

The Spirit of God descending like a dove. 3:16

This is my beloved Son, in whom I am well pleased. 3:17

And when he had fasted forty days and forty nights, he was afterward an hungred. 4:2

Follow me, and I will make you fishers of men. 4:19

Blessed are the poor in spirit: for theirs is the kingdom of heaven. 5:3

[1] Rahel weeping for her children refused to be comforted . . . because they were not. — *Jeremiah 31:15*
[2] See *Isaiah 40:3*, p. 32b.

Blessed are they that mourn: for they shall be comforted.

Blessed are the meek: for they shall inherit the earth.[1]

Blessed are they which do hunger and thirst after righteousness: for they shall be filled.

Blessed are the merciful: for they shall obtain mercy.

Blessed are the pure in heart: for they shall see God.

Blessed are the peacemakers: for they shall be called the children of God.

Blessed are they which are persecuted for righteousness' sake: for theirs is the kingdom of heaven.[2]

Matthew 5:4–10

Ye are the salt of the earth: but if the salt have lost his savour, wherewith shall it be salted? 5:13

Ye are the light of the world. A city that is set on an hill cannot be hid.

Neither do men light a candle, and put it under a bushel, but on a candlestick; and it giveth light unto all that are in the house.

Let your light so shine before men, that they may see your good works, and glorify your Father which is in heaven.

Think not that I am come to destroy the law, or the prophets: I am not come to destroy, but to fulfil.

5:14–17

Till heaven and earth pass, one jot or one tittle shall in no wise pass from the law, till all be fulfilled. 5:18

Whosoever looketh on a woman to lust after her hath committed adultery with her already in his heart.

And if thy right eye offend thee, pluck it out, and cast it from thee: for it is profitable for thee that one of thy members should perish, and not that thy whole body should be cast into hell.

And if thy right hand offend thee, cut it off. 5:28–30

[1] See *Psalm 37:11*, p. 18b.
[2] The Sermon on the Mount.
See Lao-Tzu, p. 74a.

Swear not at all; neither by heaven; for it is God's throne:

Nor by the earth; for it is his footstool. *Matthew 5:34–35*

Resist not evil: but whosoever shall smite thee on thy right cheek, turn to him the other also. 5:39

Love your enemies, bless them that curse you, do good to them that hate you, and pray for them which despitefully use you, and persecute you.

5:44

He maketh his sun to rise on the evil and on the good, and sendeth rain on the just and on the unjust. 5:45

Be ye therefore perfect, even as your Father which is in heaven is perfect.

5:48

When thou doest alms, let not thy left hand know what thy right hand doeth. 6:3

After this manner therefore pray ye: Our Father which art in heaven,[1] Hallowed be thy name.

Thy kingdom come. Thy will be done in earth, as it is in heaven.

Give us this day our daily bread.

And forgive us our debts, as we forgive our debtors.[2]

And lead us not into temptation, but deliver us from evil: For thine is the kingdom, and the power, and the glory, for ever. Amen. 6:9–13

Lay not up for yourselves treasures upon earth, where moth and rust doth corrupt, and where thieves break through and steal:

But lay up for yourselves treasures in heaven. 6:19–20

For where your treasure is, there will your heart be also. 6:21

The light of the body is the eye.

6:22

If therefore the light that is in thee

[1] Our Father, who art in heaven. — *Book of Common Prayer, Morning Prayer*
[2] And forgive us our trespasses, As we forgive those who trespass against us. — *Book of Common Prayer, Morning Prayer*

be darkness, how great is that darkness! *Matthew* 6:23

No man can serve two masters: for either he will hate the one, and love the other; or else he will hold to the one, and despise the other. Ye cannot serve God and mammon. 6:24

Is not the life more than meat, and the body than raiment?
Behold the fowls of the air: for they sow not, neither do they reap, nor gather into barns. 6:25–26

Which of you by taking thought can add one cubit unto his stature? 6:27

Consider the lilies of the field, how they grow; they toil not, neither do they spin. 6:28

Even Solomon in all his glory was not arrayed like one of these. 6:29

Take therefore no thought for the morrow: for the morrow shall take thought for the things of itself. Sufficient unto the day is the evil thereof. 6:34

Judge not, that ye be not judged. 7:1

With what measure ye mete, it shall be measured to you again.
And why beholdest thou the mote that is in thy brother's eye, but considerest not the beam that is in thine own eye? 7:2–3

Thou hypocrite, first cast out the beam out of thine own eye. 7:5

Neither cast ye your pearls before swine. 7:6

Ask, and it shall be given you; seek, and ye shall find; knock, and it shall be opened unto you. 7:7

Or what man is there of you, whom if his son ask bread, will he give him a stone? 7:9

Therefore all things whatsoever ye would that men should do to you, do ye even so to them: for this is the law and the prophets.[1] 7:12

[1] See Confucius, p. 72b.

Wide is the gate, and broad is the way, that leadeth to destruction. *Matthew* 7:13

Strait is the gate, and narrow is the way, which leadeth unto life, and few there be that find it. 7:14

Beware of false prophets, which come to you in sheep's clothing, but inwardly they are ravening wolves. 7:15

By their fruits ye shall know them. 7:20

Not every one that saith unto me, Lord, Lord, shall enter into the kingdom of heaven; but he that doeth the will of my Father which is in heaven. 7:21

[The house] fell not: for it was founded upon a rock. 7:25

But the children of the kingdom shall be cast out into outer darkness: there shall be weeping and gnashing of teeth. 8:12

The foxes have holes, and the birds of the air have nests; but the Son of man hath not where to lay his head. 8:20

Follow me; and let the dead bury their dead. 8:22

Why are ye fearful, O ye of little faith? 8:26

The whole herd of swine ran violently down a steep place into the sea, and perished in the waters. 8:32

He saw a man, named Matthew, sitting at the receipt of custom. 9:9

They that be whole need not a physician, but they that are sick. 9:12

I am not come to call the righteous, but sinners to repentance. 9:13

Can the children of the bridechamber mourn, as long as the bridegroom is with them? 9:15

Neither do men put new wine into old bottles. *Matthew* 9:17

The maid is not dead, but sleepeth. 9:24

The harvest truly is plenteous, but the labourers are few. 9:37

Go rather to the lost sheep of the house of Israel. 10:6

Freely ye have received, freely give. 10:8

Whosoever shall not receive you, nor hear your words, when ye depart out of that house or city, shake off the dust of your feet. 10:14

Be ye therefore wise as serpents, and harmless as doves. 10:16

Ye shall be hated of all men for my name's sake. 10:22

The disciple is not above his master, nor the servant above his lord. 10:24

Are not two sparrows sold for a farthing? and one of them shall not fall on the ground without your Father. But the very hairs of your head are all numbered. 10:29-30

I came not to send peace, but a sword. 10:34

He that findeth his life shall lose it: and he that loseth his life for my sake shall find it.[1] 10:39

He that hath ears to hear, let him hear. 11:15

The Son of man came eating and drinking, and they say, Behold a man gluttonous, and a winebibber, a friend of publicans and sinners. But wisdom is justified of her children. 11:19

Come unto me, all ye that labour and are heavy laden, and I will give you rest.

Take my yoke upon you, and learn of me; for I am meek and lowly in heart: and ye shall find rest unto your souls.

For my yoke is easy, and my burden is light. 11:28-30

[1] See *Matthew 16:25*, p. 43a.

He that is not with me is against me. *Matthew* 12:30

The tree is known by his fruit. 12:33

Out of the abundance of the heart the mouth speaketh. 12:34

Behold, a greater than Solomon is here. 12:42

Some seeds fell by the way side. 13:4

Because they had no root, they withered away. 13:6

But other fell into good ground, and brought forth fruit, some an hundredfold, some sixtyfold, some thirtyfold. 13:8

The care of this world, and the deceitfulness of riches. 13:22

The kingdom of heaven is like to a grain of mustard seed. 13:31

Pearl of great price. 13:46

Is not this the carpenter's son? 13:55

A prophet is not without honour, save in his own country. 13:57

The daughter of Herodias danced before them, and pleased Herod. 14:6

Give me here John Baptist's head in a charger. 14:8

We have here but five loaves, and two fishes. 14:17

And they did all eat, and were filled: and they took up of the fragments that remained twelve baskets full. 14:20

And in the fourth watch of the night Jesus went unto them, walking on the sea. 14:25

Be of good cheer; it is I; be not afraid. 14:27

O thou of little faith, wherefore didst thou doubt? 14:31

Of a truth thou art the Son of God. 14:33

Not that which goeth into the mouth defileth a man; but that which cometh out of the mouth, this defileth a man. *Matthew 15:11*

They be blind leaders of the blind. And if the blind lead the blind, both shall fall into the ditch. *15:14*

The dogs eat of the crumbs which fall from their masters' table. *15:27*

When it is evening, ye say, It will be fair weather: for the sky is red. *16:2*

The signs of the times. *16:3*

Thou art the Christ, the Son of the living God. *16:16*

Thou art Peter, and upon this rock I will build my church; and the gates of hell shall not prevail against it.
And I will give unto thee the keys of the kingdom of heaven. *16:18–19*

Get thee behind me, Satan. *16:23*

Whosoever will save his life shall lose it: and whosoever will lose his life for my sake shall find it.[1]
For what is a man profited, if he shall gain the whole world, and lose his own soul? *16:25–26*

Except ye be converted, and become as little children, ye shall not enter into the kingdom of heaven. *18:3*

He rejoiceth more of that sheep, than of the ninety and nine which went not astray. *18:13*

Where two or three are gathered together in my name, there am I in the midst of them.[2] *18:20*

Until seventy times seven. *18:22*

What therefore God hath joined together, let not man put asunder.[3] *19:6*

If thou wilt be perfect, go and sell that thou hast, and give to the poor, and thou shalt have treasure in heaven. *19:21*

[1] See *Matthew 10:39*, p. 42a.
[2] See *Book of Common Prayer, A Prayer of St. Chrysostom*, p. 60b.
[3] See *Book of Common Prayer, Solemnization of Matrimony*, p. 61b.

It is easier for a camel to go through the eye of a needle, than for a rich man to enter into the kingdom of God. *Matthew 19:24*

Many that are first shall be last; and the last shall be first. *19:30*

Borne the burden and heat of the day. *20:12*

Is it not lawful for me to do what I will with mine own? *20:15*

Overthrew the tables of the money-changers. *21:12*

My house shall be called the house of prayer; but ye have made it a den of thieves. *21:13*

They made light of it. *22:5*

Many are called, but few are chosen. *22:14*

Render therefore unto Caesar the things which are Caesar's; and unto God the things that are God's. *22:21*

Whosoever shall exalt himself shall be abased; and he that shall humble himself shall be exalted. *23:12*

Woe unto you, scribes and Pharisees, hypocrites! for ye pay tithe of mint and anise and cummin. *23:23*

Blind guides, which strain at a gnat, and swallow a camel. *23:24*

Whited sepulchres, which indeed appear beautiful outward, but are within full of dead men's bones. *23:27*

O Jerusalem, Jerusalem, thou that killest the prophets, and stonest them which are sent unto thee, how often would I have gathered thy children together, even as a hen gathereth her chickens under her wings, and ye would not! *23:37*

Ye shall hear of wars and rumours of wars: see that ye be not troubled: for all these things must come to pass, but the end is not yet.

For nation shall rise against nation. *24:6–7*

Abomination of desolation.
                    Matthew 24:15

Wheresoever the carcase is, there will the eagles be gathered together.
                                    24:28

Heaven and earth shall pass away, but my words shall not pass away.
                                    24:35

The one shall be taken, and the other left.   24:40

Then shall the kingdom of heaven be likened unto ten virgins, which took their lamps, and went forth to meet the bridegroom.
And five of them were wise, and five were foolish.   25:1–2

Well done, thou good and faithful servant . . . Enter thou into the joy of thy lord.   25:21

Unto every one that hath shall be given, and he shall have abundance: but from him that hath not shall be taken away even that which he hath.
                                    25:29

And before him shall be gathered all nations: and he shall separate them one from another, as a shepherd divideth his sheep from the goats.   25:32

For I was an hungred, and ye gave me meat: I was thirsty, and ye gave me drink: I was a stranger, and ye took me in:
Naked, and ye clothed me: I was sick, and ye visited me: I was in prison, and ye came unto me.   25:35–36

Inasmuch as ye have done it unto one of the least of these my brethren, ye have done it unto me.   25:40

An alabaster box of very precious ointment.   26:7

To what purpose is this waste?
                                    26:8

For ye have the poor always with you; but me ye have not always.[1]
                                    26:11

What will ye give me, and I will deliver him unto you? And they covenanted with him for thirty pieces of silver.[1]   *Matthew 26:15*

My time is at hand.   26:18

Verily I say unto you, that one of you shall betray me.   26:21

Lord, is it I?   26:22

It had been good for that man if he had not been born.   26:24

Jesus took bread, and blessed it, and brake it, and gave it to the disciples, and said, Take, eat; this is my body.
And he took the cup, and gave thanks, and gave it to them, saying, Drink ye all of it;
For this is my blood of the new testament, which is shed for many for the remission of sins.   26:26–28

This night, before the cock crow, thou shalt deny me thrice.   26:34

O my Father, if it be possible, let this cup pass from me: nevertheless, not as I will, but as thou wilt.   26:39

Could ye not watch with me one hour?
Watch and pray, that ye enter not into temptation: the spirit indeed is willing, but the flesh is weak.
                                    26:40–41

He came to Jesus, and said, Hail, Master; and kissed him.   26:49

All they that take the sword shall perish with the sword.   26:52

Thy speech bewrayeth thee.   26:73

Then began he to curse and to swear, saying, I know not the man. And immediately the cock crew.   26:74

The potter's field, to bury strangers in.   27:7

Have thou nothing to do with that just man.   27:19

Let him be crucified.   27:22

[Pilate] took water, and washed his hands before the multitude, saying, I

[1] See *Deuteronomy 15:11*, p. 10b.

[1] See *Zechariah 11:12*, p. 36a.

am innocent of the blood of this just person: see ye to it.   *Matthew* 27:24

His blood be on us, and on our children.   27:25

A place called Golgotha, that is to say, a place of a skull.   27:33

This is Jesus the King of the Jews.   27:37

He saved others; himself he cannot save.   27:42

Eli, Eli, lama sabachthani? that is to say, My God, my God, why hast thou forsaken me? [1]   27:46

And, behold, the veil of the temple was rent in twain from the top to the bottom; and the earth did quake, and the rocks rent.   27:51

His countenance was like lightning, and his raiment white as snow.   28:3

Go ye therefore, and teach all nations, baptizing them in the name of the Father, and of the Son, and of the Holy Ghost.   28:19

Lo, I am with you alway, even unto the end of the world.   28:20

There cometh one mightier than I after me, the latchet of whose shoes I am not worthy to stoop down and unloose.
The Gospel According to St. Mark 1:7

Arise, and take up thy bed, and walk.   2:9

The sabbath was made for man, and not man for the sabbath.   2:27

If a house be divided against itself, that house cannot stand.   3:25

The earth bringeth forth fruit of herself; first the blade, then the ear, after that the full corn in the ear.   4:28

What manner of man is this?   4:41

My name is Legion: for we are many.   5:9

[1] See *Psalm 22:1*, p. 17b.

Clothed, and in his right mind.   *Mark* 5:15

My little daughter lieth at the point of death.   5:23

Knowing in himself that virtue had gone out of him.   5:30

I see men as trees, walking.   8:24

Lord, I believe; help thou mine unbelief.   9:24

Suffer the little children to come unto me, and forbid them not: for of such is the kingdom of God.   10:14

Which devour widows' houses, and for a pretense make long prayers.   12:40

And there came a certain poor widow, and she threw in two mites.   12:42

Watch ye therefore: for ye know not when the master of the house cometh, at even, or at midnight, or at the cockcrowing, or in the morning:
Lest coming suddenly he find you sleeping.   13:35-36

Go ye into all the world, and preach the gospel to every creature.   16:15

Hail, thou that art highly favoured, the Lord is with thee: blessed art thou among women.
The Gospel According to St. Luke 1:28

For with God nothing shall be impossible.   1:37

Blessed is the fruit of thy womb.   1:42

My soul doth magnify the Lord.   1:46

For he hath regarded the low estate of his handmaiden: for, behold, from henceforth all generations shall call me blessed.   1:48

He hath scattered the proud in the imagination of their hearts.
He hath put down the mighty from their seats, and exalted them of low degree.   1:51-52

He hath filled the hungry with good things; and the rich he hath sent empty away. *Luke 1:53*

Blessed be the Lord God of Israel; for he hath visited and redeemed his people. 1:68

As he spake by the mouth of his holy prophets, which have been since the world began:
That we should be saved from our enemies, and from the hand of all that hate us. 1:70–71

Through the tender mercy of our God; whereby the dayspring from on high hath visited us,
To give light to them that sit in darkness and in the shadow of death. 1:78–79

And she brought forth her firstborn son, and wrapped him in swaddling clothes, and laid him in a manger; because there was no room for them in the inn. 2:7

There were in the same country shepherds abiding in the field, keeping watch over their flock by night.
And, lo, the angel of the Lord came upon them, and the glory of the Lord shone round about them: and they were sore afraid.
And the angel said unto them, Fear not: for, behold, I bring you good tidings of great joy, which shall be to all people.
For unto you is born this day in the city of David a Saviour, which is Christ the Lord. 2:8–11

Glory to God in the highest, and on earth peace, good will toward men.[1] 2:14

Lord, now lettest thou thy servant depart in peace. 2:29

A light to lighten the Gentiles, and the glory of thy people Israel. 2:32

Wist ye not that I must be about my Father's business? 2:49

[1] The Douay Bible has "peace to men of good will."

Jesus increased in wisdom and stature, and in favour with God and man. *Luke 2:52*

[The devil] shewed unto him all the kingdoms of the world in a moment of time. 4:5

Physician, heal thyself. 4:23

Woe unto you, when all men shall speak well of you! 6:26

Her sins, which are many, are forgiven; for she loved much. 7:47

Nothing is secret, that shall not be made manifest. 8:17

No man, having put his hand to the plow, and looking back, is fit for the kingdom of God. 9:62

Nor scrip, nor shoes. 10:4

Peace be to this house. 10:5

The labourer is worthy of his hire. 10:7

I beheld Satan as lightning fall from heaven. 10:18

Many prophets and kings have desired to see those things which ye see, and have not seen them; and to hear those things which ye hear, and have not heard them. 10:24

A certain man went down from Jerusalem to Jericho, and fell among thieves. 10:30

A certain Samaritan . . . had compassion on him. 10:33

Go, and do thou likewise. 10:37

But Martha was cumbered about much serving. 10:40

But one thing is needful: and Mary hath chosen that good part, which shall not be taken away from her. 10:42

This is an evil generation: they seek a sign. 11:29

Soul, thou hast much goods laid up for many years; take thine ease, eat, drink, and be merry.[1] 12:19

Thou fool, this night thy soul shall be required of thee. 12:20

[1] See *Ecclesiastes 8:15,* p. 28b.

Let your loins be girded about, and your lights burning.   *Luke 12:35*

For unto whomsoever much is given, of him shall be much required: and to whom men have committed much, of him they will ask the more.   12:48

The poor, and the maimed, and the halt, and the blind.   14:21

Which of you, intending to build a tower, sitteth not down first, and counteth the cost, whether he have sufficient to finish it?   14:28

Rejoice with me; for I have found my sheep which was lost.   15:6

Wasted his substance with riotous living.   15:13

Bring hither the fatted calf, and kill it.   15:23

For this my son was dead, and is alive again; he was lost, and is found.   15:24

Son, thou art ever with me, and all that I have is thine.   15:31

The children of this world are in their generation wiser than the children of light.   16:8

He that is faithful in that which is least is faithful also in much: and he that is unjust in the least is unjust also in much.   16:10

The beggar died, and was carried by the angels into Abraham's bosom.   16:22

Between us and you there is a great gulf fixed.   16:26

It were better for him that a mill-stone were hanged about his neck, and he cast into the sea.   17:2

Remember Lot's wife.   17:32

God, I thank thee, that I am not as other men are.   18:11

God be merciful to me a sinner.   18:13

Out of thine own mouth will I judge thee.   19:22

If these should hold their peace, the stones would immediately cry out.   *Luke 19:40*

God forbid.   20:16

He is not a God of the dead, but of the living.   20:38

In your patience possess ye your souls.   21:19

The Son of man coming in a cloud with power and great glory.   21:27

This do in remembrance of me.   22:19

Not my will, but thine, be done.   22:42

For if they do these things in a green tree, what shall be done in the dry?   23:31

The place, which is called Calvary.   23:33

Father, forgive them; for they know not what they do.   23:34

Lord, remember me when thou comest into thy kingdom.   23:42

To day shalt thou be with me in paradise.   23:43

Father, into thy hands I commend my spirit.   23:46

He gave up the ghost.   *Ib.*

He was a good man, and a just.   23:50

Why seek ye the living among the dead?   24:5

Their words seemed to them as idle tales.   24:11

Did not our heart burn within us, while he talked with us?   24:32

In the beginning was the Word, and the Word was with God, and the Word was God.
          The Gospel According to
          St. John 1:1

And the light shineth in darkness; and the darkness comprehended it not.   1:5

There was a man sent from God, whose name was John.　　*John* 1:6

The true Light, which lighteth every man that cometh into the world.

1:9

The Word was made flesh, and dwelt among us . . . full of grace and truth.　　1:14

No man hath seen God at any time.　　1:18

Behold the Lamb of God, which taketh away the sin of the world.

1:29

Can there any good thing come out of Nazareth?　　1:46

Hereafter ye shall see heaven open, and the angels of God ascending and descending upon the Son of man.

1:51

Woman, what have I to do with thee? mine hour is not yet come.

2:4

The water that was made wine.

2:9

When he had made a scourge of small cords, he drove them all out of the temple.　　2:15

Make not my Father's house an house of merchandise.　　2:16

Except a man be born again, he cannot see the kingdom of God.

3:3

The wind bloweth where it listeth, and thou hearest the sound thereof, but canst not tell whence it cometh, and whither it goeth: so is every one that is born of the Spirit.　　3:8

How can these things be?　　3:9

God so loved the world, that he gave his only begotten Son, that whosoever believeth in him should not perish, but have everlasting life.　　3:16

The hour cometh, and now is, when the true worshippers shall worship the Father in spirit and in truth.　　4:23

He was a burning and a shining light.　　*John* 5:35

Search the scriptures.　　5:39

What are they among so many?

6:9

Gather up the fragments that remain, that nothing be lost.　　6:12

I am the bread of life.　　6:35

It is the spirit that quickeneth.

6:63

Judge not according to the appearance.　　7:24

Never man spake like this man.

7:46

He that is without sin among you, let him first cast a stone at her.　　8:7

Neither do I condemn thee: go, and sin no more.　　8:11

I am the light of the world: he that followeth me shall not walk in darkness, but shall have the light of life.　　8:12

The truth shall make you free.

8:32

Ye are of your father the devil . . . there is no truth in him. . . . he is a liar, and the father of it.　　8:44

I must work the works of him that sent me, while it is day: the night cometh, when no man can work.

9:4

Whether he be a sinner or no, I know not: one thing I know, that, whereas I was blind, now I see.　　9:25

I am the door.　　10:9

I am come that they might have life, and that they might have it more abundantly.　　10:10

I am the good shepherd: the good shepherd giveth his life for the sheep.

10:11

Other sheep I have, which are not of this fold.　　10:16

I am the resurrection, and the life: he that believeth in me, though he were dead, yet shall he live:

And whosoever liveth and believeth in me shall never die.[1]

John 11:25–26

Jesus wept. 11:35

It is expedient for us, that one man should die for the people. 11:50

Yet a little while is the light with you. Walk while ye have the light, lest darkness come upon you. 12:35

That thou doest, do quickly.

13:27

A new commandment I give unto you, That ye love one another.

13:34

Let not your heart be troubled: ye believe in God, believe also in me.
In my Father's house are many mansions: if it were not so, I would have told you. I go to prepare a place for you. 14:1–2

I will come again, and receive you unto myself; that where I am, there ye may be also. 14:3

I am the way, the truth, and the life. 14:6

I will not leave you comfortless.

14:18

Peace I leave with you, my peace I give unto you: not as the world giveth, give I unto you. Let not your heart be troubled, neither let it be afraid.

14:27

Greater love hath no man than this, that a man lay down his life for his friends. 15:13

Ye have not chosen me, but I have chosen you. 15:16

Whither goest thou? [2] 16:5

Ask, and ye shall receive, that your joy may be full. 16:24

Be of good cheer; I have overcome the world. 16:33

Pilate saith unto him, What is truth? *John* 18:38

Now Barabbas was a robber.

18:40

Behold the man! [1] 19:5

Woman, behold thy son! 19:26

It is finished. 19:30

Touch me not.[2] 20:17

Then saith he to Thomas . . . be not faithless, but believing. 20:27

Blessed are they that have not seen, and yet have believed. 20:29

Suddenly there came a sound from heaven as of a rushing mighty wind.
The Acts of the Apostles 2:2

There appeared unto them cloven tongues like as of fire, and it sat upon each of them.
And they were all filled with the Holy Ghost, and began to speak with other tongues. 2:3–4

Silver and gold have I none; but such as I have give I thee. 3:6

If this counsel or this work be of men, it will come to nought:
But if it be of God, ye cannot overthrow it. 5:38–39

Thy money perish with thee.

8:20

In the gall of bitterness, and in the bond of iniquity. 8:23

Saul, yet breathing out threatenings and slaughter against the disciples of the Lord. 9:1

Saul, Saul, why persecutest thou me? 9:4

It is hard for thee to kick against the pricks. 9:5

He is a chosen vessel unto me.

9:15

Immediately there fell from his eyes as it had been scales. 9:18

[1] Also in *Book of Common Prayer, Burial of the Dead.*
[2] Quo vadis? — *The Vulgate*

[1] Ecce homo. — *The Vulgate*
[2] Noli me tangere. — *The Vulgate*

What God hath cleansed, that call not thou common.   *Acts* 10:15

God is no respecter of persons.[1]
                                        10:34

The gods are come down to us in the likeness of men.   14:11

We also are men of like passions with you.   14:15

Come over into Macedonia, and help us.   16:9

Certain lewd fellows of the baser sort.   17:5

Ye men of Athens, I perceive that in all things ye are too superstitious.

For as I passed by, and beheld your devotions, I found an altar with this inscription, TO THE UNKNOWN GOD.   17:22–23

God that made the world, and all things therein, seeing that he is Lord of heaven and earth, dwelleth not in temples made with hands;

Neither is worshipped with men's hands, as though he needed any thing, seeing he giveth to all life, and breath, and all things;

And hath made of one blood all nations of men for to dwell on all the face of the earth.   17:24–26

For in him we live, and move, and have our being; as certain also of your own poets have said, For we are also his offspring.[2]   17:28

Your blood be upon your own heads.   18:6

Mighty in the Scriptures.   18:24

We have not so much as heard whether there be any Holy Ghost.
                                        19:2

All with one voice about the space of two hours cried out, Great is Diana of the Ephesians.   19:34

It is more blessed to give than to receive.   20:35

[1] For there is no respect of persons with God. — *Romans 2:11*

[2] See Aeschylus, p. 78b; Cleanthes, p. 103b; Aratus, p. 104a; and Dante, p. 161b.

I am . . . a Jew of Tarsus, a city in Cilicia, a citizen of no mean city.
                                        Acts 21:39

Brought up in this city at the feet of Gamaliel.   22:3

And the chief captain answered, With a great sum obtained I this freedom. And Paul said, But I was free born.   22:28

God shall smite thee, thou whited wall.   23:3

Revilest thou God's high priest?
                                        23:4

I am a Pharisee, the son of a Pharisee.   23:6

A conscience void of offence toward God, and toward men.   24:16

When I have a convenient season, I will call for thee.   24:25

I appeal unto Caesar.   25:11

Paul, thou art beside thyself; much learning doth make thee mad.
                                        26:24

I am not mad . . . but speak forth the words of truth and soberness.
                                        26:25

For this thing was not done in a corner.   26:26

Almost thou persuadest me to be a Christian.   26:28

Wherein thou judgest another, thou condemnest thyself.

The Epistle of Paul the Apostle to the Romans 2:1

These, having not the law, are a law unto themselves.   2:14

Where no law is, there is no transgression.   4:15

Who against hope believed in hope.
                                        4:18

Where sin abounded, grace did much more abound.   5:20

Death hath no more dominion over him.   6:9

I speak after the manner of men.
Romans 6:19

The wages of sin is death; but the gift of God is eternal life. 6:23

The good that I would I do not: but the evil which I would not, that I do.[1] 7:19

Who shall deliver me from the body of this death? 7:24

Heirs of God, and joint-heirs with Christ. 8:17

For we know that the whole creation groaneth and travaileth in pain together until now. 8:22

All things work together for good to them that love God. 8:28

If God be for us, who can be against us? 8:31

Who shall separate us from the love of Christ? 8:35

Neither death, nor life, nor angels, nor principalities, nor powers, nor things present, nor things to come,
Nor height, nor depth, nor any other creature, shall be able to separate us from the love of God, which is in Christ Jesus our Lord. 8:38–39

Hath not the potter power over the clay, of the same lump to make one vessel unto honour, and another unto dishonour? 9:21

For who hath known the mind of the Lord? 11:34

Let love be without dissimulation. 12:9

Be kindly affectioned one to another with brotherly love. 12:10

Given to hospitality. 12:13

Be not wise in your own conceits. Recompense to no man evil for evil. 12:16–17

If it be possible, as much as lieth in you, live peaceably with all men. 12:18

Vengeance is mine; I will repay, saith the Lord. *Romans* 12:19

Be not overcome of evil, but overcome evil with good. 12:21

The powers that be are ordained of God. 13:1

Render therefore to all their dues: tribute to whom tribute is due; custom to whom custom; fear to whom fear; honour to whom honour.
Owe no man anything, but to love one another. 13:7–8

Love is the fulfilling of the law. 13:10

The night is far spent, the day is at hand: let us therefore cast off the works of darkness, and let us put on the armour of light.
Let us walk honestly, as in the day; not in rioting and drunkenness, not in chambering and wantonness, not in strife and envying.
But put ye on the Lord Jesus Christ, and make not provision for the flesh, to fulfil the lusts thereof.[1] 13:12–14

Doubtful disputations. 14:1

Let every man be fully persuaded in his own mind. 14:5

For none of us liveth to himself, and no man dieth to himself.
For whether we live, we live unto the Lord; and whether we die, we die unto the Lord: whether we live therefore, or die, we are the Lord's. 14:7–8

Let us therefore follow after the things which make for peace. 14:19

We then that are strong ought to bear the infirmities of the weak, and not to please ourselves. 15:1

God hath chosen the foolish things of the world to confound the wise; and God hath chosen the weak things of the world to confound the things which are mighty.
The First Epistle of Paul the Apostle to the Corinthians 1:27

---

[1] See Euripides, p. 84b, and Ovid, p. 129a.

[1] See St. Augustine, p. 147a, note 1.

As it is written,[1] Eye hath not seen, nor ear heard.   *I Corinthians* 2:9

I have planted, Apollos watered; but God gave the increase.   3:6

We are labourers together with God: ye are God's husbandry.   3:9

Every man's work shall be made manifest: for the day shall declare it, because it shall be revealed by fire; and the fire shall try every man's work of what sort it is.   3:13

For the temple of God is holy, which temple ye are.   3:17

We are made a spectacle unto the world, and to angels, and to men.   4:9

Absent in body, but present in spirit.   5:3

A little leaven leaveneth the whole lump.   5:6

It is better to marry than to burn.   7:9

The fashion of this world passeth away.   7:31

Knowledge puffeth up, but charity edifieth.   8:1

I am made all things to all men.   9:22

Know ye not that they which run in a race run all, but one receiveth the prize?   9:24

Let him that thinketh he standeth take heed lest he fall.   10:12

All things are lawful for me, but all things are not expedient.   10:23

The earth is the Lord's, and the fulness thereof.   10:26

If a woman have long hair, it is a glory to her.   11:15

Though I speak with the tongues of men and of angels, and have not

[1] Men have not heard, nor perceived by the ear, neither hath the eye seen. — *Isaiah 64:4*

charity,[1] I am become as sounding brass, or a tinkling cymbal.
     I Corinthians 13:1

Though I have all faith, so that I could remove mountains, and have not charity, I am nothing.

And though I bestow all my goods to feed the poor, and though I give my body to be burned, and have not charity, it profiteth me nothing.

Charity suffereth long, and is kind; charity envieth not; charity vaunteth not itself, is not puffed up.   13:2–4

Beareth all things, believeth all things, hopeth all things, endureth all things.

Charity never faileth.   13:7–8

We know in part, and we prophesy in part.

But when that which is perfect is come, then that which is in part shall be done away.

When I was a child, I spake as a child, I understood as a child, I thought as a child: but when I became a man, I put away childish things.[2]

For now we see through a glass, darkly; but then face to face:[3] now I know in part; but then shall I know even as also I am known.

And now abideth faith, hope, charity, these three; but the greatest of these is charity.   13:9–13

If the trumpet give an uncertain sound, who shall prepare himself to the battle?   14:8

Let all things be done decently and in order.   14:40

And last of all he was seen of me also, as of one born out of due time.

For I am the least of the apostles, that am not meet to be called an apostle, because I persecuted the church of God.

[1] In the Revised Standard Version *charity* throughout this chapter is translated as *love* — the love of mankind in the sense of the Greek *agapé* and the Latin *caritas*.
[2] See Homer, p. 65a.
[3] See *Genesis 32:30*, p. 7b.

But by the grace of God I am what I am. *I Corinthians* 15:8–10

But now is Christ risen from the dead, and become the firstfruits of them that slept.

For since by man came death, by man came also the resurrection of the dead.

For as in Adam all die, even so in Christ shall all be made alive.

15:20–22

The last enemy that shall be destroyed is death. 15:26

Evil communications corrupt good manners. 15:33

Thou fool, that which thou sowest is not quickened, except it die. 15:36

One star differeth from another star in glory. 15:41

It is sown in corruption; it is raised in incorruption. 15:42

The first man is of the earth, earthy.

15:47

Behold, I show you a mystery; We shall not all sleep, but we shall all be changed,

In a moment, in the twinkling of an eye, at the last trump: for the trumpet shall sound, and the dead shall be raised incorruptible, and we shall be changed.

For this corruptible must put on incorruption, and this mortal must put on immortality. 15:51–53

Death is swallowed up in victory.[1]

O death, where is thy sting? O grave, where is thy victory? 15:54–55

Watch ye, stand fast in the faith, quit you like men, be strong.[2] 16:13

If any man love not the Lord Jesus Christ, let him be Anathema Maranatha. 16:22

Not of the letter, but of the spirit: for the letter killeth, but the spirit giveth life.

The Second Epistle of Paul the Apostle to the Corinthians 3:6

[1] See *Isaiah 25:8*, p. 31b, and *Hosea 13:14*, p. 35b.

[2] See *I Samuel 4:9*, p. 12a.

Seeing then that we have such hope, we use great plainness of speech.

II Corinthians 3:12

The things which are seen are temporal; but the things which are not seen are eternal. 4:18

We walk by faith, not by sight.

5:7

Now is the accepted time. 6:2

By honour and dishonour, by evil report and good report. 6:8

As having nothing, and yet possessing all things.[1] 6:10

God loveth a cheerful giver. 9:7

Though I be rude in speech. 11:6

For ye suffer fools gladly, seeing ye yourselves are wise. 11:19

Forty stripes save one. 11:24

A thorn in the flesh.[2] 12:7

My strength is made perfect in weakness. 12:9

The grace of the Lord Jesus Christ, and the love of God, and the communion of the Holy Ghost, be with you all.[3] 13:14

The right hands of fellowship.

The Epistle of Paul the Apostle to the Galatians 2:9

Weak and beggarly elements.

4:9

It is good to be zealously affected always in a good thing. 4:18

Ye are fallen from grace. 5:4

For the flesh lusteth against the Spirit, and the Spirit against the flesh: and these are contrary the one to the other: so that ye cannot do the things that ye would. 5:17

The fruit of the Spirit is love, joy, peace, longsuffering, gentleness, goodness, faith,

Meekness, temperance. 5:22–23

[1] Terence, p. 109a, and Wotton, p. 300b.

[2] See *Judges 2:3*, p. 11a.

[3] Also in *Book of Common Prayer, Morning Prayer* [end].

Every man shall bear his own burden. *Galatians 6:5*

Be not deceived; God is not mocked: for whatsoever a man soweth, that shall he also reap. 6:7

Let us not be weary in well doing. 6:9

To be strengthened with might by his Spirit in the inner man.
The Epistle of Paul the Apostle to the Ephesians 3:16

Carried about with every wind of doctrine. 4:14

We are members one of another. Be ye angry, and sin not: let not the sun go down upon your wrath. 4:25–26

Speaking to yourselves in psalms and hymns and spiritual songs, singing and making melody in your heart to the Lord.[1] 5:19

Put on the whole armour of God. 6:11

For we wrestle not against flesh and blood, but against principalities, against powers, against the rulers of the darkness of this world, against spiritual wickedness in high places.
Wherefore take unto you the whole armour of God, that ye may be able to withstand in the evil day, and having done all, to stand. 6:12–13

To live is Christ, and to die is gain.
The Epistle of Paul the Apostle to the Philippians 1:21

Work out your own salvation with fear and trembling. 2:12

For it is God which worketh in you both to will and to do of his good pleasure. 2:13

This one thing I do, forgetting those things which are behind, and reaching forth unto those things which are before,
I press toward the mark. 3:13–14

[1] See *Book of Common Prayer, Morning Prayer (Venite)*, p. 59b.

Whose end is destruction, whose God is their belly, and whose glory is in their shame, who mind earthly things.
Philippians 3:19

The peace of God, which passeth all understanding, shall keep your hearts and minds through Christ Jesus.[1] 4:7

Whatsoever things are true, whatsoever things are honest, whatsoever things are just, whatsoever things are pure, whatsoever things are lovely, whatsoever things are of good report; if there be any virtue, and if there be any praise, think on these things. 4:8

I have learned, in whatsoever state I am, therewith to be content. 4:11

By him were all things created, that are in heaven, and that are in earth, visible and invisible . . . all things were created by him, and for him:
And he is before all things, and by him all things consist.
The Epistle of Paul the Apostle to the Colossians 1:16–17

Touch not; taste not; handle not. 2:21

Set your affection on things above, not on things on the earth. 3:2

Where there is neither Greek nor Jew, circumcision nor uncircumcision, Barbarian, Scythian, bond nor free: but Christ is all, and in all. 3:11

Fathers, provoke not your children to anger, lest they be discouraged. 3:21

Let your speech be alway with grace, seasoned with salt. 4:6

Luke, the beloved physician. 4:14

Labour of love.
The First Epistle of Paul the Apostle to the Thessalonians 1:3

Study to be quiet, and to do your own business. 4:11

The day of the Lord so cometh as a thief in the night. 5:2

[1] Also in *Book of Common Prayer, Holy Communion (Blessing)*.

Ye are all the children of light, and the children of the day: we are not of the night, nor of darkness.
I Thessalonians 5:5

Putting on the breastplate of faith and love; and for an helmet, the hope of salvation.   5:8

Pray without ceasing.   5:17

Prove all things; hold fast that which is good.   5:21

The law is good, if a man use it lawfully.
The First Epistle of Paul the Apostle to Timothy 1:8

Christ Jesus came into the world to save sinners; of whom I am chief.
1:15

For if a man know not how to rule his own house, how shall he take care of the church of God? [1]   3:5

Not greedy of filthy lucre.   3:8

Speaking lies in hypocrisy; having their conscience seared with a hot iron.   4:2

Every creature of God is good, and nothing to be refused, if it be received with thanksgiving.   4:4

Refuse profane and old wives' fables.   4:7

But if any provide not for his own, and specially for those of his own house, he hath denied the faith, and is worse than an infidel.   5:8

They learn to be idle, wandering about from house to house; and not only idle, but tattlers also and busy-bodies, speaking things which they ought not.   5:13

Drink no longer water, but use a little wine for thy stomach's sake.
5:23

We brought nothing into this world, and it is certain we can carry nothing out.[2]   6:7

The love of money is the root of all evil.[1]   *I Timothy* 6:10

Fight the good fight of faith, lay hold on eternal life.   6:12

Rich in good works.   6:18

Science falsely so called.   6:20

For God hath not given us the spirit of fear; but of power, and of love, and of a sound mind.
The Second Epistle of Paul the Apostle to Timothy 1:7

A workman that needeth not to be ashamed.   2:15

Be instant in season, out of season.
4:2

I have fought a good fight, I have finished my course, I have kept the faith.   4:7

The Lord reward him according to his works.   4:14

Unto the pure all things are pure.
The Epistle of Paul to Titus 1:15

Making mention of thee always in my prayers.
The Epistle of Paul to Philemon 1:4

Who maketh his angels spirits, and his ministers a flame of fire.
The Epistle of Paul the Apostle to the Hebrews 1:7

The word of God is quick, and powerful, and sharper than any two-edged sword, piercing even to the dividing asunder of soul and spirit, and of the joints and marrow, and is a discerner of the thoughts and intents of the heart.   4:12

Strong meat belongeth to them that are of full age.   5:14

They crucify to themselves the Son of God afresh, and put him to an open shame.   6:6

[1] See Sophocles, p. 82a.
[2] Also in *Book of Common Prayer, Burial of the Dead*. See also *The Song of the Harp-Player*, p. 3a, and *Ecclesiastes 5:15*, p. 28a.

[1] See Sophocles, p. 82a, and Plato, p. 94a.
Radix malorum est cupiditas. — CHAUCER, *The Canterbury Tales* [c. 1387], *The Pardoner's Prologue, l. 6*

Without shedding of blood is no remission. *Hebrews* 9:22

Faith is the substance of things hoped for, the evidence of things not seen. 11:1

Wherefore seeing we also are compassed about with so great a cloud of witnesses . . . let us run with patience the race that is set before us,
Looking unto Jesus the author and finisher of our faith. 12:1–2

Whom the Lord loveth he chasteneth. 12:6

The spirits of just men made perfect. 12:23

Let brotherly love continue.
Be not forgetful to entertain strangers: for thereby some have entertained angels unawares. 13:1–2

The Lord is my helper, and I will not fear what man shall do unto me. 13:6

Jesus Christ the same yesterday, and to day, and for ever. 13:8

For here have we no continuing city, but we seek one to come. 13:14

To do good and to communicate forget not: for with such sacrifices God is well pleased. 13:16

Let patience have her perfect work, that ye may be perfect and entire, wanting nothing.
If any of you lack wisdom, let him ask of God.
The General Epistle of James 1:4–5

Blessed is the man that endureth temptation: for when he is tried, he shall receive the crown of life. 1:12

Every good gift and every perfect gift is from above, and cometh down from the Father of lights, with whom is no variableness, neither shadow of turning. 1:17

Be swift to hear, slow to speak, slow to wrath:

For the wrath of man worketh not the righteousness of God.
James 1:19–20

Be ye doers of the word, and not hearers only. 1:22

Unspotted from the world. 1:27

As the body without the spirit is dead, so faith without works is dead also. 2:26

How great a matter a little fire kindleth! 3:5

The tongue can no man tame; it is an unruly evil. 3:8

This wisdom descendeth not from above, but is earthly, sensual, devilish. 3:15

Resist the devil, and he will flee from you. 4:7

What is your life? It is even a vapour, that appeareth for a little time, and then vanisheth away. 4:14

Be patient therefore, brethren, unto the coming of the Lord. Behold, the husbandman waiteth for the precious fruit of the earth, and hath long patience for it, until he receive the early and latter rain. 5:7

Ye have heard of the patience of Job. 5:11

The effectual fervent prayer of a righteous man availeth much. 5:16

Hope to the end.
The First Epistle General of Peter 1:13

All flesh is as grass, and all the glory of man as the flower of grass. The grass withereth, and the flower thereof falleth away:
But the word of the Lord endureth for ever.[1] 1:24–25

Abstain from fleshly lusts, which war against the soul. 2:11

Honour all men. Love the brotherhood. Fear God. Honour the king. 2:17

[1] See *Isaiah 40:6, 8*, p. 32b.

Ornament of a meek and quiet spirit.   *I Peter* 3:4

Giving honour unto the wife, as unto the weaker vessel.   3:7

Charity shall cover the multitude of sins.   4:8

A crown of glory that fadeth not away.   5:4

Be sober, be vigilant; because your adversary the devil, as a roaring lion, walketh about, seeking whom he may devour.   5:8

And the day star arise in your hearts.   *The Second Epistle General of Peter* 1:19

The dog is turned to his own vomit again.   2:22

God is light, and in him is no darkness at all.   *The First Epistle General of John* 1:5

If we say that we have no sin, we deceive ourselves, and the truth is not in us.   1:8

He is antichrist, that denieth the Father and the Son.   2:22

Whoso hath this world's good, and seeth his brother have need, and shutteth up his bowels of compassion from him, how dwelleth the love of God in him?   3:17

He that loveth not knoweth not God; for God is love.   4:8

There is no fear in love; but perfect love casteth out fear.   4:18

Raging waves of the sea, foaming out their own shame; wandering stars, to whom is reserved the blackness of darkness for ever.   *The General Epistle of Jude* 13

I John, who also am your brother, and companion in tribulation, and in the kingdom and patience of Jesus Christ, was in the isle that is called Patmos, for the word of God, and for the testimony of Jesus Christ.   *The Revelation of St. John the Divine* 1:9

What thou seest, write in a book, and send it unto the seven churches which are in Asia.   1:11

And being turned, I saw seven golden candlesticks.   1:12

His feet like unto fine brass, as if they burned in a furnace; and his voice as the sound of many waters.   1:15

When I saw him, I fell at his feet as dead.   1:17

I am he that liveth, and was dead; and, behold, I am alive for evermore, Amen; and have the keys of hell and of death.   1:18

I have somewhat against thee, because thou hast left thy first love.   2:4

To him that overcometh will I give to eat of the tree of life.   2:7

Be thou faithful unto death, and I will give thee a crown of life.   2:10

He shall rule them with a rod of iron.   2:27

I will give him the morning star.   2:28

I will not blot out his name out of the book of life.   3:5

I know thy works, that thou art neither cold nor hot: I would thou wert cold or hot.
So then because thou art lukewarm, and neither cold nor hot, I will spew thee out of my mouth.   3:15–16

Behold, I stand at the door, and knock.   3:20

The first beast was like a lion, and the second beast like a calf, and the third beast had a face as a man, and the fourth beast was like a flying eagle.
And the four beasts had each of them six wings about him; and they were full of eyes within: and they rest

not day and night, saying, Holy, holy, holy, Lord God Almighty, which was, and is, and is to come.

Revelation 4:7–8

Thou hast created all things, and for thy pleasure they are and were created.

4:11

A book . . . sealed with seven seals.

5:1

He went forth conquering, and to conquer.

6:2

Behold a pale horse: and his name that sat on him was Death, and Hell followed with him.

6:8

Four angels standing on the four corners of the earth, holding the four winds of the earth.

7:1

Hurt not the earth, neither the sea, nor the trees.

7:3

All nations, and kindreds, and people, and tongues.

7:9

These are they which came out of great tribulation, and have washed their robes, and made them white in the blood of the lamb.

7:14

They shall hunger no more, neither thirst any more; neither shall the sun light on them, nor any heat.

7:16

The name of the star is called Wormwood.

8:11

The kingdoms of this world are become the kingdoms of our Lord and of his Christ.

11:15

There was war in heaven: Michael and his angels fought against the dragon; and the dragon fought and his angels,

And prevailed not.

12:7–8

The great dragon was cast out, that old serpent, called the Devil, and Satan, which deceiveth the whole world.

12:9

No man might buy or sell, save that he had the mark, or the name of the beast.

Revelation 13:17

Babylon is fallen, is fallen, that great city.[1]

14:8

Blessed are the dead which die in the Lord . . . that they may rest from their labours.[2]

14:13

And he gathered them together into a place called in the Hebrew tongue Armageddon.

16:16

He is Lord of lords, and King of kings.

17:14

Another book was opened, which is the book of life.

20:12

I saw a new heaven and a new earth:[3] for the first heaven and the first earth were passed away; and there was no more sea.

And I John saw the holy city, new Jerusalem, coming down from God out of heaven, prepared as a bride adorned for her husband.

21:1–2

God shall wipe away all tears[4] from their eyes; and there shall be no more death, neither sorrow, nor crying, neither shall there be any more pain: for the former things are passed away.

21:4

There shall be no night there.

22:5

He that is unjust, let him be unjust still: and he which is filthy, let him be filthy still: and he that is righteous, let him be righteous still: and he that is holy, let him be holy still.

And, behold, I come quickly.

22:11–12

I am Alpha and Omega, the beginning and the end, the first and the last.

22:13

[1] See *Isaiah 21:9*, p. 31b.
[2] Also in *Book of Common Prayer, Burial of the Dead.*
[3] See *Isaiah 65:17*, p. 33b.
[4] See *Isaiah 25:8*, p. 31b.

THE MISSAL

Dominus vobiscum.
The Lord be with you.
Blessing

Mea culpa, mea culpa, mea maxima culpa.
Through my fault, through my fault, through my most grievous fault.
The Confiteor

Kyrie, eleison.
Lord, have mercy on us.
The Kyrie

Gloria in excelsis Deo. Et in terra pax hominibus bonae voluntatis.
Glory to God in the highest. And on earth peace to men of good will.[1]
The Gloria

Agnus Dei, qui tollis peccata mundi, miserere nobis.
O Lamb of God, who takest away the sins of the world, have mercy on us.[2]
Prayer

O felix culpa, quae talem ac tantum meruit habere Redemptorem.
O happy fault, which has deserved to have such and so mighty a Redeemer.[3]
Exsultet on Holy Saturday

THE BOOK OF COMMON PRAYER[4]

Movable feasts.
Tables and Rules, p. xxxi

[1] See *Luke 2:14,* and note p. 46a.
[2] See *John 1:29,* p. 48a.
[3] This dates from the seventh century at the latest, and may be much older. It has been attributed to St. Augustine and St. Ambrose.
[4] It is a most invaluable part of that blessed "liberty wherewith Christ hath made us free," that in his worship different forms and usages may without offence be allowed, provided the substance of the Faith be kept entire; and that, in every Church, what cannot be clearly determined to belong to Doctrine must be referred to Discipline; and therefore, by common consent and authority, may be altered, abridged, enlarged, amended, or otherwise disposed of, as may seem most convenient for the edification

He is risen. The Lord is risen indeed.[1]
Morning Prayer, Easter, p. 5

The Scripture moveth us, in sundry places, to acknowledge and confess our manifold sins and wickedness.
Ib. Minister's Opening Words, p. 5

We have erred, and strayed from thy ways like lost sheep.
Ib. A General Confession, p. 6

We have left undone those things which we ought to have done; And we have done those things which we ought not to have done.   *Ib.*

Have mercy upon us, miserable offenders.   *Ib.*

Who desireth not the death of a sinner, but rather that he may turn from his wickedness and live.
Ib. The Declaration of Absolution, p. 7

Let us come before his presence with thanksgiving; and show ourselves glad in him with psalms.[2]
Ib. Venite, p. 9

In his hand are all the corners of the earth; and the strength of the hills is his also.
The sea is his, and he made it; and his hands prepared the dry land.
Ib.

Glory be to the Father, and to the Son, and to the Holy Ghost;
As it was in the beginning, is now, and ever shall be, world without end.
Amen.   *Ib. Gloria Patri, p. 9*

of the people, "according to the various exigency of times and occasions." — *Preface to the edition for the Protestant Episcopal Church in the United States of America* [1789]
Also in *The Book of Common Prayer* is the prayer by Cardinal Newman on p. 598a.
Page numbers cited are for any printing of *The Book of Common Prayer.*
[1] He is risen. — *Mark 16:6*
The Lord is risen indeed. — *Luke 24:34*
[2] See *Ephesians 5:19,* p. 54a.

The noble army of Martyrs.
Morning Prayer, Te Deum, p. 10

I believe in God the Father Almighty, Maker of Heaven and earth:
And in Jesus Christ his only Son our Lord: Who was conceived by the Holy Ghost, Born of the Virgin Mary: Suffered under Pontius Pilate, Was crucified, dead, and buried: He descended into hell; The third day he rose again from the dead: He ascended into heaven, And sitteth on the right hand of God the Father Almighty: From thence he shall come to judge the quick and the dead.
I believe in the Holy Ghost: The holy Catholic Church; The Communion of Saints: The Forgiveness of sins: The Resurrection of the body: And the Life everlasting.
Ib. Apostles' Creed, p. 15

Begotten of his Father before all worlds, God of God, Light of Light, Very God of very God; Begotten, not made; Being of one substance with the Father; By whom all things were made: Who for us men and for our salvation came down from heaven, And was incarnate by the Holy Ghost of the Virgin Mary, And was made man.
Ib. Nicene Creed, p. 16

O God, who art the author of peace and lover of concord, in knowledge of whom standeth our eternal life, whose service is perfect freedom; Defend us thy humble servants in all assaults of our enemies.
Ib. A Collect for Peace, p. 17

O God, the Creator and Preserver of all mankind, we humbly beseech thee for all sorts and conditions of men; that thou wouldest be pleased to make thy ways known unto them, thy saving health unto all nations.
Ib. A Prayer for All Conditions of Men, p. 18

We commend to thy fatherly goodness all those who are any ways afflicted, or distressed, in mind, body, or estate.
Ib. p. 19

We, thine unworthy servants, do give thee most humble and hearty thanks for all thy goodness and loving-kindness to us, and to all men; We bless thee for our creation, preservation, and all the blessings of this life; but above all, for thine inestimable love in the redemption of the world by our Lord Jesus Christ; for the means of grace, and for the hope of glory.
Morning Prayer, A General Thanksgiving, p. 19

Almighty God, who . . . dost promise that when two or three are gathered together in thy Name [1] thou wilt grant their requests; Fulfil now, O Lord, the desires and petitions of thy servants, as may be most expedient for them.
Ib. A Prayer of St. Chrysostom, p. 20

Lighten our darkness, we beseech thee, O Lord; and by thy great mercy defend us from all perils and dangers of this night.
Evening Prayer, A Collect for Aid against Perils, p. 31

From pride, vainglory, and hypocrisy; from envy, hatred, and malice, and all uncharitableness,
Good Lord, deliver us.
The Litany, p. 54

From all the deceits of the world, the flesh, and the devil. *Ib.*

From battle and murder, and from sudden death. *Ib.*

Give to all nations unity, peace, and concord. *Ib. p. 56*

The kindly fruits of the earth.
Ib. p. 57

Almighty God, unto whom all hearts are open, all desires known, and from whom no secrets are hid; Cleanse the thoughts of our hearts by the inspiration of thy Holy Spirit, that we may perfectly love thee, and worthily magnify thy holy Name.
Holy Communion, Collect, p. 67

[1] See *Matthew 18:20,* p. 43a.

We acknowledge and bewail our manifold sins and wickedness, Which we, from time to time, most grievously have committed, By thought, word, and deed, Against thy Divine Majesty, Provoking most justly thy wrath and indignation against us. We do earnestly repent, And are heartily sorry for these our misdoings; The remembrance of them is grievous unto us; The burden of them is intolerable.

Holy Communion, General
Confession, p. 75

Therefore with Angels and Archangels, and with all the company of heaven, we laud and magnify thy glorious Name; evermore praising thee.
Ib. Proper Preface, p. 77

Miserable sinners.
Ib. The Exhortations, p. 86

Read, mark, learn, and inwardly digest [the Scriptures].
Collect for the Second Sunday
in Advent, p. 92

Dost thou . . . renounce the devil and all his works, the vain pomp and glory of the world, with all covetous desires of the same, and the sinful desires of the flesh, so that thou wilt not follow, nor be led by them?
Holy Baptism, p. 276

An outward and visible sign of an inward and spiritual grace.
Offices of Instruction, Questions
on the Sacraments, p. 292

Is not by any to be entered into unadvisedly or lightly; but reverently, discreetly, advisedly, soberly, and in the fear of God.
Solemnization of Matrimony,
p. 300

If any man can show just cause, why they may not lawfully be joined together, let him now speak, or else hereafter for ever hold his peace.
Ib.

Wilt thou . . . forsaking all others, keep thee only unto her, so long as ye both shall live?   *Ib. p. 301*

To have and to hold from this day forward, for better for worse, for richer for poorer, in sickness and in health, to love and to cherish, till death us do part.
Solemnization of Matrimony,
p. 301

With this Ring I thee wed.
Ib. p. 302

Those whom God hath joined together let no man put asunder.[1]
Ib. p. 303

In the midst of life we are in death.[2]   *Burial of the Dead, p. 332*

Earth to earth, ashes to ashes, dust to dust; in sure and certain hope of the Resurrection unto eternal life.
Ib. p. 333

The iron entered into his soul.
The Psalter, Psalm 105:18, p. 471

THE BOOK OF COMMON PRAYER, ENGLISH

Grant that the old Adam in this Child may be so buried, that the new man may be raised up in him.
Public Baptism of Infants,
Blessing on the Child

To love, cherish, and to obey.
Solemnization of Matrimony

With all my worldly goods I thee endow.   *Ib.*

THE UPANISHADS
800–500 B.C. [3]

Thou art that.[4]
Chandogya Upanishad 6.8.7, etc.

[1] See *Matthew 19:6*, p. 43a.
[2] This is derived from a Latin antiphon, said to have been composed by Notker, a monk of St. Gall, in 911, while watching some workmen building a bridge at Martinsbrücke, in peril of their lives. It forms the groundwork of Luther's antiphon *De Morte*.
[3] Ancient Indian literary chronology is conjectural. The dates given are approximate.
[4] Tat tvam asi (Sanskrit). The context: That which is that subtle essence is the self of this All; it is the true; it is the Self. "Thou art that, O Svetaketu."

Lead me from the unreal to the real!

Lead me from darkness to light!

Lead me from death to immortality![1]
Brihadaranyaka Upanishad 1.3.28

Not thus, not thus.[2]   *Ib.* 2.3.6

This Self is the honey of all beings, and all beings are the honey of this Self.   *Ib.* 2.5.14

The gods love the obscure and hate the obvious.[3]   *Ib.* 4.2.2

Da da da[4] (that is) Be subdued, Give, Be merciful.[5]

If the slayer thinks he slays,
If the slain thinks he is slain,
Both these do not understand:
He slays not, is not slain.[6]
Kaṭha Upanishad 2.19

Om.[7]   *Passim*

Santi.[8]   *Passim*

HOMER
C. 700 B.C.

Sing, goddess, the wrath of Peleus' son Achilles, a destroying wrath which brought upon the Achaeans myriad woes, and sent forth to Hades many valiant souls of heroes.
The Iliad, bk. I, l. 1

And the plan of Zeus was being accomplished.   *I, 5*

---

[1] Translated by F. MAX MÜLLER.
[2] Neti neti. The only possible description of the world soul self. The context: Not thus, not thus; for there is nothing else higher than this "not thus."
[3] Translated by R. C. ZAEHNER.
[4] The voice of the thunder. The full Sanskrit is: Da da da iti. Damyata datta dayadhvamiti. See T. S. Eliot, *The Waste Land*, lines 400–433, and note.
[5] Translated by F. MAX MÜLLER.
[6] See Emerson, *Brahma*, p. 604a. *Bhagavad-Gītā* 2.19 is almost identical.
[7] Om is a sacred syllable used especially to begin and end a scriptural recitation.
[8] Santi means "peace." T. S. Eliot, in his note to line 434 of *The Waste Land*, says, " 'The Peace which passeth understanding' is our equivalent to this word."

A dream, too, is from Zeus.
The Iliad, bk. I, l. 63

He knew the things that were and the things that would be and the things that had been before.   *I, 70*

If you are very valiant, it is a god, I think, who gave you this gift.   *I, 178*

Speaking, he addressed her winged words.   *I, 201 and elsewhere*

Whoever obeys the gods, to him they particularly listen.   *I, 218*

From his tongue flowed speech sweeter than honey.   *I, 249*

Rosy-fingered dawn appeared, the early-born.   *I, 477 and elsewhere*

The son of Kronos [Zeus] spoke, and nodded with his darkish brows, and immortal locks fell forward from the lord's deathless head, and he made great Olympus tremble.   *I, 528*

The Olympian is a difficult foe to oppose.   *I, 589*

Uncontrollable laughter arose among the blessed gods.[1]   *I, 599*

A councilor ought not to sleep the whole night through, a man to whom the populace is entrusted, and who has many responsibilities.   *II, 24*

Proud is the spirit of Zeus-fostered kings — their honor comes from Zeus, and Zeus, god of council, loves them.
II, 196

A multitude of rulers is not a good thing. Let there be one ruler, one king.   *II, 204*

He [Thersites] was the ugliest man who came to Ilium.   *II, 216*

Yet with his powers of augury he [Chromis] did not save himself from dark death.   *II, 859*

The glorious gifts of the gods are not to be cast aside.   *III, 65*

Young men's minds are always changeable, but when an old man is

[1] Also in *Odyssey VIII: 326.*

concerned in a matter, he looks both before and after.
The Iliad, bk. III, l. 108

Like cicadas, which sit upon a tree in the forest and pour out their piping voices, so the leaders of Trojans were sitting on the tower.　　*III, 151*

There is no reason to blame the Trojans and the well-greaved Achaeans that for such a woman they long suffer woes.　　*III, 156*

Words like winter snowflakes.
III, 222

The sun, which sees all things and hears all things.　　*III, 277*

Son of Atreus, what manner of speech has escaped the barrier of your teeth?　　*IV, 350*

Far away in the mountains a shepherd hears their thundering.
IV, 455

He lives not long who battles with the immortals, nor do his children prattle about his knees when he has come back from battle and the dread fray.[1]　　*V, 407*

Not at all similar are the race of the immortal gods and the race of men who walk upon the earth.[2]　　*V, 441*

Great-hearted Stentor with brazen voice, who could shout as loud as fifty other men.　　*V, 785*

He was a wealthy man, and kindly to his fellow men; for dwelling in a house by the side of the road, he used to entertain all comers.　　*VI, 14*

A generation of men is like a generation of leaves: the wind scatters some leaves upon the ground, while others the burgeoning wood brings forth — and the season of spring comes on. So of men one generation springs forth and another ceases.[3]　　*VI, 146*

Always to be bravest and to be preeminent above others.　　*VI, 208*

[1] See Thomas Gray, p. 440a.
[2] See Xenophanes, p. 70b.
[3] See Pindar, p. 79b, and Aristophanes, p. 91b.

Victory shifts from man to man.
The Iliad, bk. VI, l. 339

May men say, "He is far greater than his father," when he returns from battle.　　*VI, 479*

Smiling through tears.　　*VI, 484*

Attach a golden chain from heaven, and all of you take hold of it, you gods and goddesses, yet would you not be able to drag Zeus the most high from heaven to earth.　　*VIII, 19*

Hades is relentless and unyielding.
IX, 158

Hateful to me as the gates of Hades is that man who hides one thing in his heart and speaks another.　　*IX, 312*

Even when someone battles hard, there is an equal portion for one who lingers behind, and in the same honor are held both the coward and the brave man; the idle man and he who has done much meet death alike.
IX, 318

To be both a speaker of words and a doer of deeds.[1]　　*IX, 443*

Prayers are the daughters of mighty Zeus, lame and wrinkled and slanting-eyed.　　*IX, 502*

A companion's words of persuasion are effective.　　*XI, 793*

It was built against the will of the immortal gods, and so it did not last for long.　　*XII, 8*

The single best augury is to fight for one's country.　　*XII, 243*

There is a strength in the union even of very sorry men.　　*XIII, 237*

There is a fullness of all things, even of sleep and of love.　　*XIII, 636*

You will certainly not be able to take the lead in all things yourself, for to one man a god has given deeds of war, and to another the dance, to another the lyre and song, and in another widesounding Zeus puts a good mind.
XIII, 729

[1] See *James 1:22*, p. 56b.

It is not possible to fight beyond your strength, even if you strive.

The Iliad, bk. XIII, l. 787

She [Aphrodite] spoke and loosened from her bosom the embroidered girdle of many colors into which all her allurements were fashioned. In it was love and in it desire and in it blandishing persuasion which steals the mind even of the wise. XIV, 214

There she met sleep, the brother of death.[1] XIV, 231 *and* XVI, 672

Ocean, who is the source of all.
XIV, 246

The hearts of the noble may be turned [by entreaty]. XV, 203

It is not unseemly for a man to die fighting in defense of his country.[2]
XV, 496

Of men who have a sense of honor, more come through alive than are slain, but from those who flee comes neither glory nor any help. XV, 563

The outcome of the war is in our hands; the outcome of words is in the council. XVI, 630

But he, mighty man, lay mightily in the whirl of dust, forgetful of his horsemanship. XVI, 775

Once harm has been done, even a fool understands it. XVII, 32

The most preferable of evils.[3]
XVII, 105

Surely there is nothing more wretched than a man, of all the things

---

[1] Sleep, the brother of Death. — HESIOD [c. 700 B.C.], *The Theogony, l. 756*

See Virgil, p. 119a; Daniel, p. 210b; Shakespeare, p. 284a; and Shelley, p. 568a.

Sleep, Death's twin brother. — TENNYSON, *In Memoriam* [1850], *pt. LXVIII*

[2] See Horace, p. 121b.

[3] See Aristotle, p. 97b.

Of two evils, the least should be chosen. — CICERO [106-43 B.C.], *De Officiis III, 1*

Of harmes two, the lesse is for to chese. — CHAUCER, *Troilus and Criseyde* [1372-1386], *bk. II, l. 470*

Of two evils the less is always to be chosen. — THOMAS À KEMPIS [1380-1471], *Imitation of Christ, bk. III, ch. 12*

---

which breathe and move upon the earth.[1] *The Iliad, bk. XVII, l. 446*

Sweeter it [wrath] is by far than the honeycomb dripping with sweetness, and spreads through the hearts of men. XVIII, 109

I too shall lie in the dust when I am dead, but now let me win noble renown. XVIII, 120

Zeus does not bring all men's plans to fulfillment. XVIII, 328

The Erinyes, who exact punishment of men underground if one swears a false oath. XIX, 259

Not even Achilles will bring all his words to fulfillment. XX, 369

Miserable mortals who, like leaves, at one moment flame with life, eating the produce of the land, and at another moment weakly perish. XXI, 463

It is entirely seemly for a young man killed in battle to lie mangled by the bronze spear. In his death all things appear fair. But when dogs shame the gray head and gray chin and nakedness of an old man killed, it is the most piteous thing that happens among wretched mortals. XXII, 71

Then the father held out the golden scales, and in them he placed two fates of dread death. XXII, 209

There are no compacts between lions and men, and wolves and lambs have no concord. XXII, 262

By the ships there lies a dead man, unwept, unburied: Patroclus.[2]
XXII, 386

Remembering this, he wept bitterly, lying now on his side, now on his back, now on his face. XXIV, 9

The fates have given mankind a patient soul. XXIV, 49

Thus have the gods spun the thread for wretched mortals: that they live in

---

[1] See Aristophanes, p. 91b.

[2] See Horace, p. 122b; Chaucer, p. 164b; Shakespeare, p. 260a; Milton, p. 343b; Scott, p. 519a; and Byron, p. 557b.

grief while they themselves are without cares; for two jars stand on the floor of Zeus of the gifts which he gives, one of evils and another of blessings.

The Iliad, bk. XXIV, l. 525

Tell me, muse, of the man of many resources who wandered far and wide after he sacked the holy citadel of Troy, and he saw the cities and learned the thoughts of many men, and on the sea he suffered in his heart many woes.

The Odyssey, bk. I, l. 1

By their own follies they perished, the fools.   I, 7

Look now how mortals are blaming the gods, for they say that evils come from us, but in fact they themselves have woes beyond their share because of their own follies.   I, 32

Surely these things lie on the knees of the gods.   I, 267

You ought not to practice childish ways, since you are no longer that age.[1]   I, 296

For rarely are sons similar to their fathers: most are worse, and a few are better than their fathers.   II, 276

Gray-eyed Athena sent them a favorable breeze, a fresh west wind, singing over the wine-dark sea.   II, 420

A young man is embarrassed to question an older one.   III, 24

All men have need of the gods.

III, 48

The minds of the everlasting gods are not changed suddenly.   III, 147

A small rock holds back a great wave.   III, 296

No mortal could vie with Zeus, for his mansions and his possessions are deathless.   IV, 78

She [Helen] threw into the wine which they were drinking a drug which takes away grief and passion and brings forgetfulness of all ills.   IV, 220

[1] See *I Corinthians 13:11*, p. 52b.

The immortals will send you to the Elysian plain at the ends of the earth, where fair-haired Rhadamanthys is. There life is supremely easy for men. No snow is there, nor ever heavy winter storm, nor rain, and Ocean is ever sending gusts of the clear-blowing west wind to bring coolness to men.

The Odyssey, bk. IV, l. 563

Olympus, where they say there is an abode of the gods, ever unchanging: it is neither shaken by winds nor ever wet with rain, nor does snow come near it, but clear weather spreads cloudless about it, and a white radiance stretches above it.[1]   VI, 42

May the gods grant you all things which your heart desires, and may they give you a husband and a home and gracious concord, for there is nothing greater and better than this — when a husband and wife keep a household in oneness of mind, a great woe to their enemies and joy to their friends, and win high renown.   VI, 180

All strangers and beggars are from Zeus, and a gift, though small, is precious.[2]   VI, 207

Their ships are swift as a bird or a thought.   VII, 36

We are quick to flare up, we races of men on the earth.   VII, 307

So it is that the gods do not give all men gifts of grace — neither good looks nor intelligence nor eloquence.

VIII, 167

Evil deeds do not prosper; the slow man catches up with the swift.

VIII, 329

Even if you gods, and all the goddesses too, should be looking on, yet

[1] The majesty of the gods is revealed, and their peaceful abodes, which neither the winds shake nor clouds soak with showers, nor does the snow congealed with biting frost besmirch them with its white fall, but an ever cloudless sky vaults them over, and smiles with light bounteously spread abroad. — Lucretius [95–55 B.C.], *De Rerum Natura III, 18*

[2] See Theocritus, p. 104a.

would I be glad to sleep with golden Aphrodite.

The Odyssey, bk. VIII, l. 341

Among all men on the earth bards have a share of honor and reverence, because the muse has taught them songs and loves the race of bards.

VIII, 479

Thus she spoke; and I longed to embrace my dead mother's ghost. Thrice I tried to clasp her image, and thrice it slipped through my hands, like a shadow, like a dream.[1] *XI, 204*

They strove to pile Ossa on Olympus, and on Ossa Pelion with its leafy forests, that they might scale the heavens.[2] *XI, 315*

There is a time for many words, and there is also a time for sleep.[3]

XI, 379

There is nothing more dread and more shameless than a woman who plans such deeds in her heart as the foul deed which she plotted when she contrived her husband's murder.

XI, 427

In the extravagance of her evil she has brought shame both on herself and on all women who will come after her, even on one who is virtuous.

XI, 432

Therefore don't you be gentle to your wife either. Don't tell her everything you know, but tell her one thing and keep another thing hidden.

XI, 441

There is no more trusting in women. *XI, 456*

I should rather labor as another's serf, in the home of a man without for-

[1] See Virgil, p. 118b.

[2] See Virgil, p. 117a.

Then the omnipotent Father with his thunder made Olympus tremble, and from Ossa hurled Pelion. — Ovid [43 B.C.–A.D. 17], *Metamorphoses I, l. 154*

I would have you call to mind the strength of the ancient giants, that undertook to lay the high mountain Pelion on the top of Ossa, and set among those the shady Olympus. — RABELAIS, *Works, bk. IV* [1548], *ch. 38*

[3] See *Ecclesiastes 3:7*, p. 27b.

tune, one whose livelihood was meager, than rule over all the departed dead.

The Odyssey, bk. XI, l. 489

Friends, we have not till now been unacquainted with misfortunes.

XII, 208

It is tedious to tell again tales already plainly told.[1] *XII, 452*

The wine urges me on, the bewitching wine, which sets even a wise man to singing and to laughing gently and rouses him up to dance and brings forth words which were better unspoken.

XIV, 463

It is equally wrong to speed a guest who does not want to go, and to keep one back who is eager. You ought to make welcome the present guest, and send forth the one who wishes to go.[2]

XV, 72

Even his griefs are a joy long after to one that remembers all that he wrought and endured.[3] *XV, 400*

God always pairs off like with like.[4]

XVII, 218

Bad herdsmen ruin their flocks.

XVII, 246

Wide-sounding Zeus takes away half a man's worth on the day when slavery comes upon him. *XVII, 322*

Then dark death seized Argus, as soon as he had seen Odysseus in the twentieth year. *XVII, 326*

The gods, likening themselves to all kinds of strangers, go in various disguises from city to city, observing the wrongdoing and the righteousness of men. *XVII, 485*

Nothing feebler than a man does the earth raise up, of all the things which breathe and move on the earth, for he believes that he will never suffer evil in the future, as long as the gods give him success and he flourishes in his

[1] See Shakespeare, p. 236b.

[2] See Pope, p. 405b.

[3] See Virgil, p. 117b.

[4] See Heywood, p. 183a.

strength; but when the blessed gods bring sorrows too to pass, even these he bears, against his will, with steadfast spirit, for the thoughts of earthly men are like the day which the father of gods and men brings upon them.

The Odyssey, bk. XVIII, l. 130

Men flourish only for a moment.[1]

XIX, 328

Dreams surely are difficult, confusing, and not everything in them is brought to pass for mankind. For fleeting dreams have two gates: one is fashioned of horn and one of ivory. Those which pass through the one of sawn ivory are deceptive, bringing tidings which come to nought, but those which issue from the one of polished horn bring true results when a mortal sees them.[2]   *XIX,* 560

Endure, my heart: you once endured something even more dreadful.

XX, 18

Your heart is always harder than a stone.   *XXIII,* 103

Therefore the fame of her excellence will never perish, and the immortals will fashion among earthly men a gracious song in honor of faithful Penelope.   *XXIV,* 196

HESIOD
c. 700 B.C.

With the muses of Helicon let us begin our singing.

The Theogony, l. 1

They once taught Hesiod beauteous song, when he was shepherding his sheep below holy Helicon.   *Ib.* 22

We know how to speak many falsehoods which resemble real things, but we know, when we will, how to speak true things.   *Ib.* 27

On his tongue they pour sweet dew, and from his mouth flow gentle words.

Ib. 83

[1] See *Psalm 103:15,* p. 21a.
[2] See Virgil, p. 119a.

Love, who is most beautiful among the immortal gods, the melter of limbs, overwhelms in their hearts the intelligence and wise counsel of all gods and all men.   *The Theogony, l.* 120

From their eyelids as they glanced dripped love.   *Ib.* 910

There was not after all a single kind of strife, but on the earth there are two kinds: one of them a man might praise when he recognized her, but the other is blameworthy.

Works and Days, l. 11

Potter bears a grudge against potter, and craftsman against craftsman, and beggar is envious of beggar, and bard of bard.[1]   *Ib.* 25

Fools, they do not even know how much more is the half than the whole.[2]

Ib. 40

Often an entire city has suffered because of an evil man.   *Ib.* 240

He harms himself who does harm to another, and the evil plan is most harmful to the planner.   *Ib.* 265

Badness you can get easily, in quantity: the road is smooth, and it lies close by. But in front of excellence the immortal gods have put sweat, and long and steep is the way to it, and rough at first. But when you come to the top, then it is easy, even though it is hard.[3]

Ib. 287

A bad neighbor is a misfortune, as much as a good one is a great blessing.

Ib. 346

Do not seek evil gains; evil gains are the equivalent of disaster.   *Ib.* 352

If you should put even a little on a little, and should do this often, soon this too would become big.[4]   *Ib.* 361

At the beginning of a cask and at the end take your fill; in the middle be sparing.   *Ib.* 368

[1] See Gay, p. 401b, and Meredith, p. 730a.
[2] See Browning, p. 664b, and note.
[3] See *Matthew 7:13–14,* p. 41b.
[4] See Chaucer, p. 169b.

The dawn speeds a man on his journey, and speeds him too in his work.
Works and Days, l. 579

Observe due measure, for right timing is in all things the most important factor.   *Ib.* 694

Gossip is mischievous, light and easy to raise, but grievous to bear and hard to get rid of. No gossip ever dies away entirely, if many people voice it: it too is a kind of divinity.   *Ib.* 761

ARCHILOCHUS
c. 680 B.C.

Some Saian glories in the shield which I left beside a bush, poor blameless weapon, against my will. But I have saved myself — what care I for that shield? Away with it! I'll get another one no worse.   *Fragment 6*

Old women should not seek to be perfumed.   *Fragment 27*

The fox knows many things, but the hedgehog knows one great thing.[1]
Fragment 103

THE SEVEN SAGES[2]
c. 650 – c. 600 B.C.

Know thyself.
Inscription at the Delphic Oracle. From PLUTARCH, *Morals*

Hesiod might as well have kept his breath to cool his pottage.[3]
PERIANDER. *From* PLUTARCH, *The Banquet of the Seven Wise Men, sec.* 14

Every one of you hath his particular

plague, and my wife is mine; and he is very happy who hath this only.
PITTACUS. *From* PLUTARCH, *Morals, On the Tranquillity of the Mind*

Nothing too much.[1]
From DIOGENES LAERTIUS, *bk. I, sec. 63*

Do not speak ill of the dead.[2]
Ib. 70

Not even the gods fight against necessity.   *Ib.* 77

Know the right timing.   *Ib.* 79

Rule will show the man.
BIAS. *From* ARISTOTLE, *Nichomachean Ethics* V, 1

MIMNERMUS
c. 650 – c. 590 B.C.

What life is there, what delight, without golden Aphrodite?
Fragment 1

SOLON
c. 638 – c. 559 B.C.

Many evil men are rich, and good men poor, but we shall not exchange with them our excellence for riches.
Fragment 4

Poets tell many lies.
Fragment 21

I grow old ever learning many things.   *Fragment 22*

Speech is the image of actions.
From DIOGENES LAERTIUS, *bk. I, sec. 58*

Laws are like spiders' webs, which stand firm when any light, yielding object falls upon them, while a larger

---

[1] The fox has many tricks, and the hedgehog has only one, but that is the best of all. — ERASMUS, *Adagia* [1500]
[2] Sayings throughout antiquity were variously attributed to the figures known as the "seven sages." The list is commonly given as Thales, Solon, Periander, Cleobulus, Chilon, Bias, Pittacus. (See Solon, column *b*.)
[3] Spare your breath to cool your porridge. — RABELAIS, *Works, bk. V* [1552], *ch. 28*

[1] See Terence, p. 108a; Horace, p. 120a; and Anonymous, p. 151a.
[2] The Latin form: De mortuis nil nisi bonum [Of the dead, nothing but good].
See Propertius, p. 128a.

thing breaks through them and escapes.[1]

From PLUTARCH, *The Banquet of the Seven Wise Men*

Let us sacrifice to the Muses.   *Ib.*

Until he is dead, do not yet call a man happy, but only lucky.[2]

From HERODOTUS [3] *I, 32*

STESICHORUS
c. 630 – c. 555 B.C.

This tale is not true: you [Helen] did not even board the well-benched ships, and you did not go to the citadel of Troy.   *Fragment 11*

ALCAEUS
c. 625 – c. 575 B.C.

Wine, dear boy, and truth.[4]
                  Fragment 66

Wine is a peep-hole on a man.[4]
                Fragment 104

Let us run into a safe harbor.[5]
                Fragment 120

ANACHARSIS
fl. c. 600 B.C.

[On learning that the sides of a ship were four fingers thick] The passengers are just that distance from death.[6]

From DIOGENES LAERTIUS, *Anacharsis 5*

---

[1] See Zincgref, p. 321a, and Swift, p. 388b.

[2] See *Ecclesiasticus 11:28*, p. 38a; Aeschylus, p. 78b; Sophocles p. 81b; and Horace, p. 120a.

[3] Herodotus attributed these words to Solon.

[4] Earliest references to what became the proverb *In vino veritas* (In wine is truth) which was known to Plato (*Symposium 217*) and to Pliny the Elder [A.D. 23–79], *Natural History XIV, 141.*

[5] Part of what is probably the oldest poem using the image of the "ship of state." See Sophocles, p. 81b.

[6] "How thick do you judge the planks of our ship to be?" "Some two good inches and upward," returned the pilot. "It seems, then, we are within two fingers' breadth of damnation."
— RABELAIS, *Works, bk. IV* [1548], *ch. 23*

SAPPHO
c. 612 B.C.

Deathless Aphrodite on your rich-wrought throne.[1]   *Fragment 1*

Equal to the gods seems to me that man who sits facing you and hears you nearby sweetly speaking and softly laughing. This sets my heart to fluttering in my breast, for when I look on you a moment, then can I speak no more, but my tongue falls silent, and at once a delicate flame courses beneath my skin, and with my eyes I see nothing, and my ears hum, and a cold sweat bathes me, and a trembling seizes me all over, and I am paler than grass, and I feel that I am near to death.[2]

                 Fragment 2

The stars about the lovely moon hide their shining forms when it lights up the earth at its fullest.   *Fragment 4*

I loved you once long ago, Athis . . . you seemed to me a small, ungainly child.   *Fragments 40–41*

The moon has set, and the Pleiades; it is midnight, and time passes, and I sleep alone.[3]   *Fragment 94*

Sweet mother, I cannot ply the loom, vanquished by desire for a youth through the work of soft Aphrodite.
                Fragment 114

As an apple reddens on the high bough; high atop the highest bough the apple pickers passed it by — no, not passed it by, but they could not reach it.   *Fragment 116*

As shepherds trample underfoot a hyacinth on the mountainside, and on the ground the purple flower.
                Fragment 117

Evening star, you bring all things which the bright dawn has scattered: you bring the sheep, you bring the goat, you bring the child back to its mother.[4]
                Fragment 120

---

[1] Or "with your intricate charms."

[2] See Catullus, p. 115a.

[3] See Housman, p. 854b.

[4] See Meleager, p. 110a, and Housman, p. 854a.

IBYCUS[1]
c. 580 B.C.

There is no medicine to be found for a life which has fled.   *Fragment 23*

An argument needs no reason, nor a friendship.   *Fragment 40*

PHEIDIPPIDES
d. 490 B.C.

Rejoice, we are victorious.

From LUCIAN, *Pro Lapsu in Salutando 3*

ANACREON
c. 570 – c. 480 B.C.

Bring water, bring wine, boy! Bring flowering garlands to me! Yes, bring them, so that I may try a bout with love.   *Fragment 27*

I both love and do not love, and am mad and am not mad.[2]

Fragment 79

War spares not the brave, but the cowardly.[3]

Fragment 101. From The Palatine Anthology VII, 160

HIPPONAX
c. 570 – 520 B.C.

There are two days when a woman is a pleasure: the day one marries her and the day one buries her.   *Fragment*

XENOPHANES
c. 570 – c. 475 B.C.

Homer and Hesiod attributed to the gods everything that is a shame and a reproach among men.   *Fragment 11*

---

[1] Associated with Ibycus is the phrase "the cranes of Ibycus." It derives from the legend that Ibycus was murdered at sea and his murderers were discovered through cranes that followed the ship. Hence, "the cranes of Ibycus" became a proverb for the agency of the gods in revealing crime.
[2] See Catullus, p. 115a.
[3] See Sophocles, p. 82b.

If cattle and horses, or lions, had hands, or were able to draw with their feet and produce the works which men do, horses would draw the forms of gods like horses, and cattle like cattle, and they would make the gods' bodies the same shape as their own.[1]

Fragment 15

One god, greatest among gods and men, similar to mortals neither in shape nor even in thought.[2]

Fragment 23

It takes a wise man to recognize a wise man.

From DIOGENES LAERTIUS, *Xenophanes IX*

SIMONIDES
c. 556 – 468 B.C.

It is hard to be truly excellent, four-square in hand and foot and mind, formed without blemish.   *Fragment 4*

The city is the teacher of the man.

Fragment 53

Fighting in the forefront of the Greeks, the Athenians crushed at Marathon the might of the gold-bearing Medes.   *Fragment 88*

Go tell the Spartans, thou who passest by,
That here, obedient to their laws, we lie.[3]   *Fragment 92*

If the greatest part of excellence is nobly to die, this to us of all men has fortune given: for struggling to clothe Greece in freedom, we lie in unaging glory.[4]   *Fragment 118*

Painting is silent poetry, and poetry painting that speaks.

From PLUTARCH, *De Gloria Atheniensium III, 346*

---

[1] See Montesquieu, p. 414b.
[2] See Homer, p. 63a.
[3] Translated by W. L. BOWLES.
Ruskin said of this epitaph that it was the noblest group of words uttered by man.
[4] See Thucydides, p. 90a.

CONFUCIUS[1]
551–479 B.C.

Fine words and an insinuating appearance are seldom associated with true virtue.

The Confucian Analects, bk. 1:3

A youth, when at home, should be filial, and, abroad, respectful to his elders.   *1:6*

If a man withdraws his mind from the love of beauty, and applies it as sincerely to the love of the virtuous; if, in serving his parents, he can exert his utmost strength; if, in serving his prince, he can devote his life; if, in his intercourse with his friends, his words are sincere — although men say that he has not learned, I will certainly say that he has.   *1:7*

Hold faithfulness and sincerity as first principles.   *1:8, ii*

Have no friends not equal to yourself.   *1:8, iii*

When you have faults, do not fear to abandon them.   *1:8, iv*

He who exercises government by means of his virtue may be compared to the north polar star, which keeps its place and all the stars turn towards it.   *2:1*

[The superior man] acts before he speaks, and afterwards speaks according to his actions.   *2:13*

Learning without thought is labor lost; thought without learning is perilous.[2]   *2:15*

When you know a thing, to hold that you know it; and when you do not know a thing, to allow that you do not know it — this is knowledge.[3]
    2:17

Things that are done, it is needless to speak about . . . things that are past, it is needless to blame.   *3:21, ii*

[1] Sayings attributed to Confucius and his followers from *The Chinese Classics, Vol. I: The Confucian Analects,* translated by JAMES LEGGE.

[2] See Lao Tzu, p. 75b; Heraclitus, p. 77b; and Cardinal Newman, p. 598a.

[3] See Lao Tzu, p. 75a.

I have not seen a person who loved virtue, or one who hated what was not virtuous. He who loved virtue would esteem nothing above it.

The Confucian Analects,
bk. 4:6, i

If a man in the morning hear the right way, he may die in the evening without regret.   *4:8*

The superior man . . . does not set his mind either for anything, or against anything; what is right he will follow.
    4:10

When we see men of worth, we should think of equaling them; when we see men of a contrary character, we should turn inwards and examine ourselves.   *4:17*

The cautious seldom err.   *4:23*

Virtue is not left to stand alone. He who practices it will have neighbors.
    4:25

Man is born for uprightness. If a man lose his uprightness, and yet live, his escape from death is the effect of mere good fortune.   *6:16*

The man of virtue makes the difficulty to be overcome his first business, and success only a subsequent consideration.   *6:20*

With coarse rice to eat, with water to drink, and my bended arm for a pillow — I have still joy in the midst of these things. Riches and honors acquired by unrighteousness are to me as a floating cloud.   *7:15*

I am not one who was born in the possession of knowledge; I am one who is fond of antiquity, and earnest in seeking it there.   *7:19*

Is virtue a thing remote? I wish to be virtuous, and lo! virtue is at hand.
    7:29

The superior man is satisfied and composed; the mean man is always full of distress.   *7:36*

The people may be made to follow a path of action, but they may not be made to understand it.   *8:9*

If a superior man dwelt among [barbarians], what rudeness would there be?

The Confucian Analects,
bk. 9:13, ii

While you are not able to serve men, how can you serve spirits [of the dead]? . . . While you do not know life, how can you know about death?
11:11

To go beyond is as wrong as to fall short. 11:15, *iii*

He with whom neither slander that gradually soaks into the mind, nor statements that startle like a wound in the flesh, are successful may be called intelligent indeed. 12:6

In carrying on your government, why should you use killing [the unprincipled for the good of the unprincipled] at all? Let your evinced desires be for what is good, and the people will be good. The relation between superiors and inferiors is like that between the wind and the grass. The grass must bend when the wind blows across it.
12:19

Good government obtains when those who are near are made happy, and those who are far off are attracted.
13:16, *ii*

The firm, the enduring, the simple, and the modest are near to virtue.
13:27

The scholar who cherishes the love of comfort is not fit to be deemed a scholar. 14:3

The man who in the view of gain thinks of righteousness; who in the view of danger is prepared to give up his life; and who does not forget an old agreement however far back it extends — such a man may be reckoned a complete man. 14:13, *ii*

He who speaks without modesty will find it difficult to make his words good. 14:21

In ancient times, men learned with a view to their own improvement. Nowadays, men learn with a view to the approbation of others.

The Confucian Analects,
bk. 14:25

The superior man is modest in his speech, but exceeds in his actions.
14:29

Recompense injury with justice, and recompense kindness with kindness.
14:36, *iii*

The determined scholar and the man of virtue will not seek to live at the expense of injuring their virtue. They will even sacrifice their lives to preserve their virtue complete. 15:8

If a man take no thought about what is distant, he will find sorrow near at hand. 15:11

The superior man is distressed by his want of ability. 15:18

What the superior man seeks is in himself. What the mean man seeks is in others. 15:20

What you do not want done to yourself, do not do to others.[1] 15:23

When a man's knowledge is sufficient to attain, and his virtue is not sufficient to enable him to hold, whatever he may have gained, he will lose again. 15:32, *i*

The superior man cannot be known in little matters, but he may be entrusted with great concerns. The small man may not be entrusted with great concerns, but he may be known in little matters. 15:33

Virtue is more to man than either water or fire. I have seen men die from treading on water and fire, but I have never seen a man die from treading the course of virtue. 15:34

By nature, men are nearly alike; by practice, they get to be wide apart.
17:2

To be able to practice five things everywhere under heaven constitutes perfect virtue. . . . [They are] gravity,

[1] The Golden Rule. See *Matthew 7:12*, p. 41a.

generosity of soul, sincerity, earnestness, and kindness.

The Confucian Analects,
bk. 17:6

There are three things which the superior man guards against. In youth . . . lust. When he is strong . . . quarrelsomeness. When he is old . . . covetousness. 17:8

Without recognizing the ordinances of Heaven, it is impossible to be a superior man. 20:3, *i*

Without an acquaintance with the rules of propriety, it is impossible for the character to be established.

20:3, *ii*

Without knowing the force of words, it is impossible to know men.

20:3, *iii*

LAO TZU[1]
Sixth century[?] B.C.

The Tao [Way] that can be told of is
    not the eternal Tao;
The name that can be named is not the
    eternal name.
The Nameless is the origin of Heaven
    and Earth;
The Named is the mother of all
    things.
Therefore let there always be non-
    being, so we may see their sub-
    tlety,
And let there always be being, so we
    may see their outcome.
The two are the same,
But after they are produced, they have
    different names.
They both may be called deep and pro-
    found.
Deeper and more profound,
The door of all subtleties!
    The Way of Lao Tzu 1

When the people of the world all know
    beauty as beauty,
    There arises the recognition of ugli-
    ness.
When they all know the good as good,

There arises the recognition of evil.
    The Way of Lao Tzu 2

In the government of the sage,
He keeps their hearts vacuous,
Fills their bellies,
Weakens their ambitions,
And strengthens their bones,
He always causes his people to be with-
    out knowledge [cunning] or de-
    sire,
And the crafty to be afraid to act.
    Ib. 3

Heaven and Earth are not humane.[1]
They regard all things as straw dogs.[2]
    Ib. 5

The spirit of the valley never dies.
    It is called the subtle and profound
    female.
The gate of the subtle and profound
    female
    Is the root of Heaven and Earth.
It is continuous, and seems to be always
    existing.
Use it and you will never wear it out.
    Ib. 6

The best [man] is like water.
Water is good; it benefits all things and
    does not compete with them.
It dwells in [lowly] places that all dis-
    dain.
This is why it is so near to Tao.
    Ib. 8

To produce things and to rear them,
To produce, but not to take possession
    of them,
To act, but not to rely on one's own
    ability,
To lead them, but not to master
    them —
This is called profound and secret vir-
    tue. *Ib.* 10

He who loves the world as his body may
    be entrusted with the empire.
    Ib. 13

We look at it [Tao] and do not see
    it;

[1] I.e., they are impartial.
[2] Straw dogs were used in sacrifices and then discarded.

[1] From *The Way of Lao Tzu,* translated by
WING-TSIT CHAN.

Its name is The Invisible.
We listen to it and do not hear it;
Its name is The Inaudible.
We touch it and do not find it;
Its name is The Subtle [formless].
The Way of Lao Tzu 14

It is The Vague and Elusive.
Meet it and you will not see its head.
Follow it and you will not see its back.
Ib.

Manifest plainness,
Embrace simplicity,
Reduce selfishness,
Have few desires. *Ib. 19*

Abandon learning and there will be no
sorrow. *Ib. 20*

To yield is to be preserved whole.
To be bent is to become straight.
To be empty is to be full.
To be worn out is to be renewed.
To have little is to possess.
To have plenty is to be perplexed.[1]
Ib. 22

He who knows others is wise;
He who knows himself is enlightened.
Ib. 33

[The sage] never strives himself for the
great, and thereby the great is
achieved. *Ib. 34*

Tao invariably takes no action, and yet
there is nothing left undone.
Reversion is the action of Tao.
Weakness is the function of Tao.
All things in the world come from be-
ing.
And being comes from non-being.
Ib. 40

When the highest type of men hear
Tao,
  They diligently practice it.
When the average type of men hear
Tao,
  They half believe in it.
When the lowest type of men hear
Tao,
  They laugh heartily at it. *Ib. 41*

The softest things in the world over-

come the hardest things in the
world.
Non-being penetrates that in which
there is no space.
Through this I know the advantage of
taking no action.
The Way of Lao Tzu 43

There is no calamity greater than lavish
desires.
There is no greater guilt than discon-
tentment.
And there is no greater disaster than
greed. *Ib. 46*

One may know the world without going
out of doors.
One may see the Way of Heaven with-
out looking through the windows.
The further one goes, the less one
knows.[1]
Therefore the sage knows without going
about,
Understands without seeing,
And accomplishes without any action.
Ib. 47

He who possesses virtue in abundance
May be compared to an infant.
Ib. 55

He who knows does not speak.
He who speaks does not know.
Ib. 56

The more laws and order are made
prominent,
The more thieves and robbers there will
be. *Ib. 57*

Ruling a big country is like cooking a
small fish.[2] *Ib. 60*

Tao is the storehouse of all things.
It is the good man's treasure and the
bad man's refuge. *Ib. 62*

A journey of a thousand miles must
begin with a single step.[3] *Ib. 64*

People are difficult to govern because
they have too much knowledge.
Ib. 65

I have three treasures. Guard and keep
them:

[1] I.e., the more one studies, the further one
is from the Tao.
[2] I.e., too much handling will spoil it.
[3] Traditional translation.

[1] See the Sermon on the Mount, *Matthew 5*,
p. 40a.

The first is deep love,
The second is frugality,
And the third is not to dare to be
　ahead of the world.
Because of deep love, one is coura-
　geous.
Because of frugality, one is generous.
Because of not daring to be ahead of
　the world, one becomes the leader
　of the world.
　　　　　　The Way of Lao Tzu 67

When armies are mobilized and issues
　joined,
The man who is sorry over the fact will
　win.　　　　　　　　　*Ib.* 69

To know that you do not know is the
　best.
To pretend to know when you do not
　know is a disease. [1]　　　*Ib.* 71

Heaven's net is indeed vast.
Though its meshes are wide, it misses
　nothing.[2]　　　　　　　*Ib.* 73

To undertake executions for the master
　executioner [Heaven] is like hew-
　ing wood for the master carpen-
　ter.
Whoever undertakes to hew wood for
　the master carpenter rarely escapes
　injuring his own hands.　　*Ib.* 74

The Way of Heaven has no favorites.
It is always with the good man.
　　　　　　　　　　　　Ib. 79

Let there be a small country with few
　people. . . .
Though neighboring communities over-
　look one another and the crowing
　of cocks and barking of dogs can
　be heard,
Yet the people there may grow old and
　die without ever visiting one an-
　other.　　　　　　　　*Ib.* 80

True words are not beautiful; [3]
Beautiful words are not true.
A good man does not argue;
He who argues is not a good man.

[1] See Confucius, p. 71a.
[2] The kingdom of heaven is like unto a net,
that was cast into the sea, and gathered of
every kind. — *Matthew 13:47*
[3] I.e., they are not "fine-sounding."

A wise man has no extensive knowl-
　edge;
He who has extensive knowledge is not
　a wise man.[1]
The sage does not accumulate for him-
　self.
The more he uses for others, the more
　he has himself.
The more he gives to others, the more
　he possesses of his own.
The Way of Heaven is to benefit others
　and not to injure.
The Way of the sage is to act but not
　to compete.
　　　　　　The Way of Lao Tzu 81

AESOP[2]
fl. c. 550 B.C.

The lamb . . . began to follow the
wolf in sheep's clothing.
　　　　　The Wolf in Sheep's Clothing

Appearances often are deceiving.
　　　　　　　　　　　　　Ib.

Do not count your chickens before
they are hatched.[3]
　　　　　The Milkmaid and Her Pail

I am sure the grapes are sour.[4]
　　　　　　The Fox and the Grapes

No act of kindness, no matter how
small, is ever wasted.
　　　　　　The Lion and the Mouse

Slow and steady wins the race.
　　　　　The Hare and the Tortoise

[1] See Confucius, p. 71a; Heraclitus, p. 77b; and
Cardinal Newman, p. 598a.
[2] Animal fables from before Aesop's time and
after were attributed to him. The first collection
was made two hundred years after his death.
See also La Fontaine, p. 359a.
[3] To swallow gudgeons ere they're catch'd,
　And count their chickens ere they're
　hatched.
　　　　　SAMUEL BUTLER, *Hudibras,
　　　　　pt. II* [1664], *canto 3, l. 923*
[4] The fox, when he cannot reach the grapes,
says they are not ripe. — GEORGE HERBERT,
Jacula Prudentum [1640]
　"They are too green," he said, "and only
good for fools." — LA FONTAINE, *bk. III* [*1668*],
fable 11, The Fox and the Grapes

Familiarity breeds contempt.[1]
The Fox and the Lion

The boy cried "Wolf, wolf!" and the villagers came out to help him.
The Shepherd Boy and the Wolf

A crust eaten in peace is better than a banquet partaken in anxiety.
The Town Mouse and the Country Mouse

Borrowed plumes.
The Jay and the Peacock

It is not only fine feathers that make fine birds.　　　　　　*Ib.*

Self-conceit may lead to self-destruction.　　*The Frog and the Ox*

People often grudge others what they cannot enjoy themselves.
The Dog in the Manger

It is thrifty to prepare today for the wants of tomorrow.
The Ant and the Grasshopper

Be content with your lot; one cannot be first in everything.
Juno and the Peacock [2]

A huge gap appeared in the side of the mountain. At last a tiny mouse came forth.[3]
The Mountain in Labor

Any excuse will serve a tyrant.
The Wolf and the Lamb

Beware lest you lose the substance by grasping at the shadow.
The Dog and the Shadow

Who shall bell the cat?
The Rats and the Cat

I will have nought to do with a man who can blow hot and cold with the same breath.
The Man and the Satyr

Thinking to get at once all the gold

the goose could give, he killed it and opened it only to find — nothing.
The Goose with the Golden Eggs

Put your shoulder to the wheel.
Hercules and the Wagoner

The gods help them that help themselves.[1]　　　　　　　*Ib.*

We would often be sorry if our wishes were gratified.[2]
The Old Man and Death

Union gives strength.[3]
The Bundle of Sticks

While I see many hoof marks going in, I see none coming out. It is easier to get into the enemy's toils than out again.
The Lion, the Fox, and the Beasts

The haft of the arrow had been feathered with one of the eagle's own plumes. We often give our enemies the means of our own destruction.[4]
The Eagle and the Arrow

[1] God loves to help him who strives to help himself. — AESCHYLUS [525–456 B.C.], *Fragment 223*

Heaven helps not the men who will not act. — SOPHOCLES [495–405 B.C.]. *Fragment 288*

　Try first thyself, and after call in God;
　For to the worker God himself lends aid.
　　EURIPIDES [485–406 B.C.], *Hippolytus, frag. 435*

Help thyself, and God will help thee. — GEORGE HERBERT, *Jacula Prudentum* [1640]

God helps those who help themselves. — ALGERNON SIDNEY, *Discourses on Government* [1698], *sec. 23*, and BENJAMIN FRANKLIN, *Poor Richard's Almanac* [1733–1758]

[2] Granting our wish one of Fate's saddest jokes is! — J. R. LOWELL [1819–1891], *Two Scenes from the Life of Blondel, sc. II, st. 2*

Beware, my lord! Beware lest stern Heaven hate you enough to hear your prayers! — ANATOLE FRANCE, *The Crime of Sylvestre Bonnard* [1881], *pt. II, ch. 4*

When the gods wish to punish us they answer our prayers. — OSCAR WILDE, *An Ideal Husband* [1895], *act II*

[3] See John Dickinson, p. 460b, and G. P. Morris, p. 600a.

[4] So in the Libyan fable it is told
　That once an eagle, stricken with a dart,
　Said, when he saw the fashion of the shaft,
　"With our own feathers, not by others' hands,
　Are we now smitten."
　　AESCHYLUS [525–456 B.C.], *Fragment 135*
　　　　　(Plumptre's translation)

[1] See Mark Twain, p. 764b.

[2] See Sean O'Casey, p. 981a.

[3] A mountain was in labor, sending forth dreadful groans, and there was in the region the highest expectation. After all, it brought forth a mouse. — PHAEDRUS [c. A.D. 8] *IV, 22:1*
See Horace, p. 124a.

THEOGNIS
fl. c. 545 B.C.

One finds many companions for food and drink, but in a serious business a man's companions are very few.
Elegies, l. 115

Even to a wicked man a divinity gives wealth, Cyrnus, but to few men comes the gift of excellence.
Ib. 149

Surfeit begets insolence, when prosperity comes to a bad man.   *Ib. 153*

Adopt the character of the twisting octopus, which takes on the appearance of the nearby rock. Now follow in this direction, now turn a different hue.
Ib. 215

The best of all things for earthly men is not to be born and not to see the beams of the bright sun; but if born, then as quickly as possible to pass the gates of Hades, and to lie deep buried.[1]
Ib. 425

No man takes with him to Hades all his exceeding wealth.[2]   *Ib. 725*

Bright youth passes swiftly as a thought.   *Ib. 985*

HERACLITUS
c. 540 – c. 480 B.C.

All is flux, nothing stays still.
From DIOGENES LAERTIUS, *bk. IX, sec. 8, and* PLATO, *Cratylus,* 402A

That eagle's fate and mine are one,
  Which on the shaft that made him die
Espied a feather of his own,
  Wherewith he wont to soar so high.
    EDMUND WALLER [1605–1687], *To a Lady Singing a Song of His Composing*
Like a young eagle, who has lent his plume
To fledge the shaft by which he meets his
  doom,
See their own feathers pluck'd to wing the dart
Which rank corruption destines for their heart.
    THOMAS MOORE [1780–1852], *Corruption*
See Byron, p. 555a.
[1] See Sophocles, p. 83a; Bacon, p. 210a; Heine, p. 588b; and Yeats, p. 883b.
[2] See *The Song of the Harp-Player,* p. 3a; *Ecclesiastes 5:15,* p. 28a; and *I Timothy 6:7,* p. 55a.

Nothing endures but change.[1]
From DIOGENES LAERTIUS, *bk. IX, sec. 8, and* PLATO, *Cratylus,* 402A

Although the logos is common to all, the many live as if they had private understanding.   *Fragment 2*

Much learning does not teach a man to have intelligence.[2]   *Fragment 40*

Strife is the source and the master of all things.   *Fragment 53*

The path up and down is one and the same.   *Fragment 60*

Everything comes about by way of strife and necessity.   *Fragment 80*

It is not possible to step twice into the same river.   *Fragment 91*

Character is a man's guiding destiny.   *Fragment 119*

THEMISTOCLES
c. 528 – c. 462 B.C.

Tuning the lyre and handling the harp are no accomplishments of mine, but rather taking in hand a city that was small and inglorious and making it glorious and great.
From PLUTARCH, *Lives, Themistocles, sec. 2*

The wooden wall is your ships.[3]
Ib. 10

Strike, but hear me.[4]   *Ib. 11*

[Of his son] The boy is the most powerful of all the Hellenes; for the Hellenes are commanded by the Athenians, the Athenians by myself, myself by the boy's mother, and the mother by her boy.   *Ib. 18*

[1] See Honorat de Bueil, p. 318b; Swift, p. 388b; and Shelley, p. 568a.
[2] See Confucius, p. 71a; Lao Tzu, p. 75b; and Cardinal Newman, p. 598a.
[3] This was Themistocles' interpretation to the Athenians in 480 B.C. of the second oracle at Delphi: "Safe shall the wooden wall continue for thee and thy children." The account appears in full in Herodotus, Book VII, sec. 141–143.
[4] Said in reply to Eurybiades, commander of the Spartan fleet, when he raised his staff as though to strike.

[Of two suitors for his daughter's hand] I choose the likely man in preference to the rich man; I want a man without money rather than money without a man.

From PLUTARCH, *Lives, Themistocles, sec. 18*

I have with me two gods, Persuasion and Compulsion.[1]   *Ib. 21*

The speech of man is like embroidered tapestries, since like them this too has to be extended in order to display its patterns, but when it is rolled up it conceals and distorts them.   *Ib. 29*

He who commands the sea has command of everything.[2]

From CICERO, *Ad Atticum X, 8*

[Upon being asked whether he would rather be Achilles or Homer] Which would you rather be — a victor in the Olympic games, or the announcer of the victor?

From PLUTARCH, *Apothegms, Themistocles*

AESCHYLUS
525–456 B.C.

I would far rather be ignorant than knowledgeable of evils.

The Suppliants, l. 453

"Reverence for parents" stands written among the three laws of most revered righteousness.[3]   *Ib. 707*

Myriad laughter of the ocean waves.
Prometheus Bound, l. 89

For somehow this is tyranny's disease, to trust no friends.   *Ib. 224*

Words are the physicians of a mind diseased.[4]   *Ib. 378*

Time as he grows old teaches all things.   *Ib. 981*

God's mouth knows not how to speak falsehood, but he brings to pass every word.[1]

Prometheus Bound, l. 1030

On me the tempest falls. It does not make me tremble. O holy Mother Earth, O air and sun, behold me. I am wronged.[2]   *Ib. 1089*

I pray the gods some respite from the weary task of this long year's watch that lying on the Atreidae's roof on bended arm, dog-like, I have kept, marking the conclave of all the night's stars, those potentates blazing in the heavens that bring winter and summer to mortal men, the constellations, when they wane, when they rise.

Agamemnon, l. 1

A great ox stands on my tongue.[3]
Ib. 36

Wisdom comes through suffering.
Ib. 177

She [Helen] brought to Ilium her dowry, destruction.   *Ib. 406*

It is in the character of very few men to honor without envy a friend who has prospered.   *Ib. 832*

Only when man's life comes to its end in prosperity can one call that man happy.[4]   *Ib. 928*

Alas, I am struck a deep mortal blow!
Ib. 1343

Death is better, a milder fate than tyranny.[5]   *Ib. 1364*

Zeus, first cause, prime mover; for what thing without Zeus is done among mortals? [6]   *Ib. 1485*

Do not kick against the pricks.[7]
Ib. 1624

---

[1] Said to the Andrians, when demanding money from them, to which they replied that they already had two great gods, Penury and Powerlessness, who hindered them from giving him money.

[2] See Bacon, p. 209b; Mahan, p. 785b; and Morison, p. 998a.

[3] See *Exodus 20:12*, p. 9a.

[4] See Milton, p. 349a.

[1] See *Numbers 23:19*, p. 10a.

[2] Translated by EDITH HAMILTON.

[3] A proverbial expression of uncertain origin for enforced silence.

[4] See Solon, p. 69a, and note.

[5] See Patrick Henry, p. 465b.

[6] See *Acts 17:28*, p. 50a; Cleanthes, p. 103b; and Aratus, p. 104a.

[7] Also in PINDAR, *Pythian Odes II, l. 174*, and EURIPIDES, *Bacchae, l. 795*. See *Acts 9:5*, p. 49b.

I know how men in exile feed on dreams of hope.

Agamemnon, l. 1668

Good fortune is a god among men, and more than a god.

The Libation Bearers, l. 59

Destiny waits alike for the free man as well as for him enslaved by another's might. *Ib. 103*

For a deadly blow let him pay with a deadly blow: it is for him who has done a deed to suffer. *Ib. 312*

What is pleasanter than the tie of host and guest? *Ib. 702*

His resolve is not to seem, but to be, the best.

The Seven Against Thebes, l. 592

PINDAR
c. 518 – c. 438 B.C.

Water is best. But gold shines like fire blazing in the night, supreme of lordly wealth.

Olympian Odes I, l. 1

The days that are still to come are the wisest witnesses. *Ib. 51*

If any man hopes to do a deed without God's knowledge, he errs.

Ib. 104

Do not peer too far.[1] *Ib. 184*

I have many swift arrows in my quiver which speak to the wise, but for the crowd they need interpreters. The skilled poet is one who knows much through natural gift, but those who have learned their art chatter turbulently, vainly, against the divine bird of Zeus. *Ib. II, 150*

I will not steep my speech in lies; the test of any man lies in action.[2]

Ib. IV, 27

The issue is in God's hands.

Ib. XIII, 147

Zeus, accomplisher, to all grant grave restraint and attainment of sweet delight.[1] *Olympian Odes XIII, last line*

Seek not, my soul, the life of the immortals; but enjoy to the full the resources that are within thy reach.[2]

Pythian Odes III, l. 109

They say that this lot is bitterest: to recognize the good but by necessity to be barred from it.[3] *Ib. IV, 510*

Creatures of a day, what is a man? What is he not? Mankind is a dream of a shadow. But when a god-given brightness comes, a radiant light rests on men, and a gentle life.[4]

Ib. VIII, 135

When toilsome contests have been decided, good cheer is the best physician, and songs, the sage daughters of the Muses, soothe with their touch.

Nemean Odes IV, l. 1

Words have a longer life than deeds. *Ib. 10*

Not every truth is the better for showing its face undisguised; and often silence is the wisest thing for a man to heed. *Ib. V, 30*

One race there is of men, one of gods, but from one mother we both draw our breath. *Ib. VI, 1*

If one but tell a thing well, it moves on with undying voice, and over the fruitful earth and across the sea goes the bright gleam of noble deeds ever unquenchable.

Isthmian Odes IV, l. 67

It is not possible with mortal mind to search out the purposes of the gods.

Fragment 61

O bright and violet-crowned and famed in song, bulwark of Greece, famous Athens, divine city!

Fragment 76

---

[1] Do not set your eyes on things far off. — *Pythian Odes III, 39*
  See Euripides, p. 84a.
[2] Translated by RICHMOND LATTIMORE.

[1] Translated by RICHMOND LATTIMORE.
[2] See Euripides, p. 84a.
[3] See Boethius, p. 148a; Dante, p. 160a; Chaucer, p. 165a; and Tennyson, p. 647a.
[4] See Homer, pp. 63a and 64b, and Aristophanes, p. 91b.

Unsung, the noblest deed will die.
Fragment 120

What is God? Everything.
Fragment 140d

Convention is the ruler of all.
Fragment 169

Hope, which most of all guides the changeful mind of mortals.
Fragment 214

ANAXAGORAS
c. 500 – 428 B.C.

The descent to Hades is the same from every place.
From DIOGENES LAERTIUS, *Anaxagoras 2*

SUTTAPITAKA[1]
c. 500 – c. 250 B.C.[2]

All that is is the result of what we have thought.   *Dhammapada 1.1*

Hatreds never cease by hatred; they cease by non-hatred; this is the primeval law.   *Ib. 1.5*

The scent of flowers does not go against the wind, not sandal, rosebay or jasmine; but the scent of the good goes against the wind; a good man is wafted to all quarters.   *Ib. 4.54*

If one conquer a thousand thousand men in battle, and if one conquer himself alone, he is in battle supreme.
Ib. 8.103

If one live a hundred years idle, without energy, better to live one day of steadfast energy.   *Ib. 8.112*

Think not lightly of evil, "It will not come to me." A waterpot is filled by the fall of waterdrops; a fool is filled with evil, amassing it bit by bit.
Ib. 9.121

If in the hand there be no wound one may hold poison in the hand. No poison follows where there is no wound;

[1] Means "basket of discourses." It is one of the three "baskets" which form the Pali canon, the sacred scriptures of Theravada Buddhists.
[2] Ancient Indian literary chronology is conjectural.

there is no evil for one who commits none.   *Dhammapada 9.124*

All tremble at the rod, all fear death; making yourself the exemplar, do not kill or cause to kill.   *Ib. 10.129*

This man of little learning grows old like an ox: his flesh increases, but not his wisdom.   *Ib. 11.152*

Who have not lived a holy life, have not acquired wealth in their youth, brood like decrepit herons in a pond where the fish have died.   *Ib. 11.155*

Extract yourself from bad ways like an elephant stuck in the mud.
Ib. 23.327

Better to live alone; with a fool there is no companionship. With few desires live alone and do no evil, like an elephant in the forest roaming at will.
Ib. 23.330

Decay is inherent in all component things! Work out your salvation with diligence! [1]

Mahaparinibbanasutta 6.7 [2]

I go for refuge to the Buddha.
I go for refuge to the Doctrine.
I go for refuge to the Order [of monks].
Traditional (liturgical), passim

PERICLES[3]
c. 495 – 429 B.C.

Wait for that wisest of all counselors, Time.

From PLUTARCH, *Lives,*
PERICLES, *sec. 18*

Trees, though they are cut and lopped, grow up again quickly,[4] but if men are destroyed, it is not easy to get them again.   *Ib. 33*

[1] Translated by T. RHYS DAVIDS. The last words of the Buddha. Quoted by T. S. ELIOT, *The Cocktail Party* [1950], *act II,* by Sir Henry Harcourt-Reilly.
[2] Pali Text Society, *Digh Nikaya,* vol. 2, p. 156, and *Samyutta Nikaya,* vol. 1, p. 158.
[3] See THUCYDIDES, *Funeral Speech of Pericles,* p. 89b.
[4] The lopped tree in time may grow again. — ROBERT SOUTHWELL [1561–1595], *Times Go by Turns*

SOPHOCLES[1]
c. 495 – 405 B.C.

Silence gives the proper grace to women. *Ajax, l. 293*

Nobly to live, or else nobly to die,
Befits proud birth.[2] *Ib. 480*

Of all human ills, greatest is fortune's wayward tyranny. *Ib. 486*

For kindness begets kindness evermore,
But he from whose mind fades the memory
Of benefits, noble is he no more.
  Ib. 522

Sleep that masters all. *Ib. 675*

I, whom proof hath taught of late
How so far only should we hate our foes
As though we soon might love them, and so far
Do a friend service as to one most like
Some day to prove our foe, since oftenest men
In friendship but a faithless haven find.[3] *Ib. 678*

Men of ill judgment oft ignore the good
That lies within their hands, till they have lost it. *Ib. 964*

It is not righteousness to outrage
A brave man dead, not even though you hate him. *Ib. 1344*

Ships are only hulls, high walls are nothing,
When no life moves in the empty passageways.[4]
  Oedipus Rex,[5] l. 56

How dreadful knowledge of the truth can be
When there's no help in truth!
  Oedipus Rex, l. 316

The tyrant is a child of Pride
Who drinks from his great sickening cup
Recklessness and vanity,
Until from his high crest headlong
He plummets to the dust of hope.[1]
  Ib. 872

The greatest griefs are those we cause ourselves. *Ib. 1230*

Let every man in mankind's frailty
Consider his last day; and let none
Presume on his good fortune until he find
Life, at his death, a memory without pain.[2] *Ib. 1529*

For God hates utterly
The bray of bragging tongues.
  Antigone[3] [c. 442 B.C.], l. 123

Our ship of State, which recent storms have threatened to destroy, has come safely to harbor at last.[4]
  Ib. 163

I have nothing but contempt for the kind of governor who is afraid, for whatever reason, to follow the course that he knows is best for the State; and as for the man who sets private friendship above the public welfare — I have no use for him, either. *Ib. 181*

---

[1] Sophocles said he drew men as they ought to be, and Euripides as they were. — ARISTOTLE, *Poetics, ch. 25*

[2] See Euripides, p. 85b, and note.

[3] They love as though they will some day hate and hate as though they will some day love. — ARISTOTLE quoting BIAS [c. 650 B.C.], *Rhetoric II, 13*
See Publilius Syrus, p. 126a.

[4] See Thucydides, p. 90b, and Shakespeare, *Coriolanus III, i, 198,* p. 289b.

[5] Translated by DUDLEY FITTS and ROBERT FITZGERALD.

[1] See *Proverbs 16:18,* p. 24b.
Pride will have a fall. — *English proverb* [c. 1509]. A variant is "Pride goeth before a fall."
Pride goeth before, and shame cometh behynde. — *Treatise of a Gallant* [c. 1510]
  Pryde will have a fall;
For pryde goeth before and shame cometh after.
  JOHN HEYWOOD, *Proverbs* [1546], *pt. I, ch. 10*

[2] See Solon, p. 69a, and note.
There is a saying among men, put forth of old, that you cannot rightly judge whether a mortal's lot is good or evil, until he dies. — SOPHOCLES, *Trachiniae, l. 1*

[3] Translated by DUDLEY FITTS and ROBERT FITZGERALD.

[4] See Alcaeus, p. 69a.

Nobody likes the man who brings bad news.[1]   *Antigone, l. 277*

Money: There's nothing in the world so demoralizing as money.[2]   *Ib. 295*

How dreadful it is when the right judge judges wrong!   *Ib. 323*

Numberless are the world's wonders, but none
More wonderful than man.
          Ib. 333 (Ode I)

    It is a good thing
To escape from death, but it is not great pleasure
To bring death to a friend.   *Ib. 437*

Grief teaches the steadiest minds to waver.   *Ib. 563*

All that is and shall be,
And all the past, is his [Zeus's].
          Ib. 611 (Ode II)

Show me the man who keeps his house in hand,
He's fit for public authority.[3]
          Ib. 660

Anarchy, anarchy! Show me a greater evil!
This is why cities tumble and the great houses rain down,
This is what scatters armies!
          Ib. 672

Reason is God's crowning gift to man.
          Ib. 684

The ideal condition
Would be, I admit, that men should be right by instinct;
But since we are all likely to go astray,
The reasonable thing is to learn from those who can teach.   *Ib. 720*

Love, unconquerable [4]
Waster of rich men, keeper
Of warm lights and all-night vigil
In the soft face of a girl:
Sea-wanderer, forest-visitor!

Even the pure immortals cannot escape you,
And mortal man, in his one day's dusk,
Trembles before your glory.
          Antigone, l. 781 (Ode III)

Wisdom outweighs any wealth.[1]
          Ib. 1050

There is no happiness where there is no wisdom; [2]
No wisdom but in submission to the gods.
Big words are always punished,
And proud men in old age learn to be wise.   *Ib. 1347, closing lines*

Death is not the worst; rather, in vain
To wish for death, and not to compass it.   *Electra, l. 1008*

A prudent mind can see room for misgiving, lest he who prospers should one day suffer reverse.[3]
          Trachiniae, l. 296

They are not wise, then, who stand forth to buffet against Love; for Love rules the gods as he will, and me.[4]
          Ib. 441

Knowledge must come through action; you can have no test which is not fanciful, save by trial.   *Ib. 592*

Rash indeed is he who reckons on the morrow, or haply on days beyond it; for tomorrow is not, until today is past.[5]   *Ib. 943*

War never slays a bad man in its course,
But the good always! [6]
          Philoctetes, l. 436

Stranger in a strange country.[7]
     Oedipus at Colonus [8] [406 B.C.],
          l. 184

---

[1] See Shakespeare, pp. 241b and 288a.
[2] See *I Timothy 6:10*, p. 55b, and Plato, p. 94a.
[3] See *I Timothy 3:5*, p. 55a.
[4] See Sophocles, *Trachiniae*, p. 82b; Virgil, p. 117a; and Chaucer, p. 166a.

[1] See *Job 28:18*, p. 15b.
[2] See Epicurus, p. 103a.
[3] See *Proverbs 16:18*, p. 24b.
[4] See Sophocles, *Antigone*, p. 82a.
[5] See *Proverbs 27:1*, p. 26a.
[6] Translated by SIR GEORGE YOUNG. See Anacreon, p. 70a.
[7] See *Exodus 2:22*, p. 8a.
[8] Translated by ROBERT FITZGERALD.

The good befriend themselves.
Oedipus at Colonus, l. 309

The immortal
Gods alone have neither age nor death!
All other things almighty Time dis-
quiets.   *Ib.* 607

Athens, nurse of men.   *Ib.* 701

Not to be born surpasses thought and
speech.
The second best is to have seen the
light
And then to go back quickly whence we
came.[1]   *Ib.* 1224

One word
Frees us of all the weight and pain of
life:
That word is love.   *Ib.* 1616

It made our hair stand up in panic
fear.[2]   *Ib.* 1625

A remedy too strong for the disease.
Tereus, frag. 514 [3]

Truly, to tell lies is not honorable;
But when the truth entails tremendous
ruin,
To speak dishonorably is pardonable.
Creusa, frag. 323

Sons are the anchors of a mother's life.
Phaedra, frag. 612

To him who is in fear everything rus-
tles.   *Acrisius, frag.* 58

No falsehood lingers on into old age.
Ib. frag. 59

No man loves life like him that's growing old.[4]   *Ib. frag.* 64

A woman's vows I write upon the
wave.[5]
Unknown Dramas, frag. 694

---

[1] See Theognis, p. 77a, and note.
[2] See Robert Graves, p. 1034b.
[3] The fragments are from the Everyman Edition of *The Dramas of Sophocles.*
[4] See Euripides, p. 83b.
[5] See Catullus, p. 115a; More, p. 178b; Bacon,
p. 210a; Shakespeare, p. 299a; and Keats,
p. 586a.

EMPEDOCLES
c. 490 – c. 430 B.C.

At one time through love all things
come together into one, at another time
through strife's hatred they are borne
each of them apart.   *Fragment* 17

The blood around men's heart is
their thinking.   *Fragment* 105

EURIPIDES[1]
c. 485 – 406 B.C.

Never say that marriage has more of
joy than pain.
Alcestis [2] [438 B.C.], *l.* 238

A second wife
is hateful to the children of the first;
a viper is not more hateful.   *Ib.* 309

A sweet thing, for whatever time,
to revisit in dreams the dear dead we
have lost.   *Ib.* 355

Oh, if I had Orpheus' voice and poetry
with which to move the Dark Maid and
her Lord,
I'd call you back, dear love, from the
world below.
I'd go down there for you. Charon or
the grim
King's dog could not prevent me
then
from carrying you up into the fields of
light.   *Ib.* 358

Light be the earth upon you, lightly
rest.[3]   *Ib.* 462

God, these old men!
How they pray for death! How heavy
they find this life in the slow drag of
days!
And yet, when Death comes near
them,
You will not find one who will rise and
walk with him,

---

[1] Sophocles said he drew men as they ought
to be, and Euripides as they were. — ARISTOTLE,
Poetics, ch 25
[2] Translated by DUDLEY FITTS and ROBERT
FITZGERALD.
[3] See Anonymous, p. 151b; Beaumont and
Fletcher, p. 316b; and Robert Richardson,
p. 822a.

not one whose years are still a burden
to him.[1]   *Alcestis, l. 669*

You love the daylight: do you think
your
father does not?   *Ib. 691*

Dishonor will not trouble me, once I
am dead.   *Ib. 726*

Today's today. Tomorrow, we may be
ourselves gone down the drain of Eternity.[2]   *Ib. 788*

O mortal man, think mortal thoughts! [3]
Ib. 799

My mother was accursed the night she
bore me,
and I am faint with envy of all the
dead.[4]   *Ib. 865*

You were a stranger to sorrow: therefore Fate
has cursed you.   *Ib. 927*

I have found power in the mysteries of
thought,
exaltation in the chanting of the
Muses;
I have been versed in the reasonings of
men;
but Fate is stronger than anything I
have known.   *Ib. 962*

Time cancels young pain.   *Ib. 1085*

Slight not what's near through aiming
at
what's far.[5]
Rhesus [c. 435 B.C.], *l* 482

There is no benefit in the gifts of a bad
man.
Medea [431 B.C.], *l. 618*

When love is in excess it brings a man
nor honor
nor any worthiness.   *Ib. 627*

What greater grief than the loss of
one's
native land.   *Ib. 650*

I know indeed what evil I intend to
do,
but stronger than all my afterthoughts
is my fury,
fury that brings upon mortals the greatest evils.   *Medea, l. 1078*

We know the good, we apprehend it
clearly,
but we can't bring it to achievement.[1]
Hippolytus [2] [428 B.C.], *l. 380*

There is one thing alone
that stands the brunt of life throughout
its course:
a quiet conscience.   *Ib. 426*

In this world second thoughts, it seems,
are best.[3]   *Ib. 435*

Love distills desire upon the eyes,
love brings bewitching grace into the
heart
of those he would destroy.
I pray that love may never come to me
with murderous intent,
in rhythms measureless and wild.
Not fire nor stars have stronger bolts
than those of Aphrodite sent
by the hand of Eros, Zeus's child.
Ib. 525

My tongue swore, but my mind was
still unpledged.[4]   *Ib. 612*

Would that I were under the cliffs, in
the secret
hiding-places of the rocks,
that Zeus might change me to a winged
bird.[5]   *Ib. 732*

I would win my way to the coast,
apple-bearing Hesperian coast
of which the minstrels sing,
where the Lord of the Ocean
denies the voyager further sailing,
and fixes the solemn limit of Heaven
which giant Atlas upholds.

---

[1] See Sophocles, p. 83a.
[2] See Edward Fitzgerald, p. 630a.
[3] See Pindar, p. 79b.
[4] See *Job 3:3*, p. 14a.
[5] See Pindar, p. 79a, and note.

---

[1] See *Romans 7:19*, p. 51a, and Ovid, p. 129a.
[2] Translated by DAVID GRENE.
[3] Second thoughts, they say, are best. —
DRYDEN, *The Spanish Friar* [1681], act II, sc. 2
    Is it so true that second thoughts are best?
— TENNYSON, *Sea Dreams* [1864]
[4] See Sallust, p. 115b.
[5] See *Psalm 55:6*, p. 19b.

There the streams flow with am-
brosia
by Zeus's bed of love,
and holy Earth, the giver of life,
yields to the Gods rich blessedness.[1]
Hippolytus, l. 742

I care for riches, to make gifts
To friends, or lead a sick man back to
health
With ease and plenty. Else small aid is
wealth
For daily gladness; once a man be
done
With hunger, rich and poor are all as
one.
Electra[1] *[413 B.C.], l. 427*

A coward turns away, but a brave
man's choice is danger.
*Iphigenia in Tauris [c. 412
B.C.], l. 114*

The day is for honest men, the night
for thieves. *Ib. 1026*

Mankind . . . possesses two supreme blessings. First of these is the
goddess Demeter, or Earth — which-
ever name you choose to call her by.
It was she who gave to man his nourishment of grain. But after her there came
the son of Semele, who matched her
present by inventing liquid wine as
his gift to man. For filled with that
good gift, suffering mankind forgets its
grief; from it comes sleep; with it
oblivion of the troubles of the day.
There is no other medicine for misery.[2]
The Bacchae [c. 407 B.C.], l. 274

Talk sense to a fool and he calls
you foolish. *Ib. 480*

Slow but sure moves the might of
the gods.[3] *Ib. 882*

What is wisdom? What gift of the
gods
is held in glory like this:

[1] Translated by GILBERT MURRAY.
[2] Translated by WILLIAM ARROWSMITH.
[3] See George Herbert, p. 325a, and von Logau,
p. 329a.

to hold your hand victorious
over the heads of those you hate?
Glory is precious forever.
The Bacchae, l. 877

Humility, a sense of reverence before
the sons of heaven —
of all the prizes that a mortal man
might win,
these, I say, are wisest; these are best.
Ib. 1150

Yet do I hold that mortal foolish
who strives against the stress of necessity. *Mad Heracles, l. 281*

The company of just and righteous
men is better than wealth and a rich
estate. *Aegeus,*[1] *frag. 7*

A bad beginning makes a bad ending. *Aeolus,*[1] *frag. 32*

Time will explain it all. He is a
talker, and needs no questioning before
he speaks. *Ib. frag. 38*

Waste not fresh tears over old griefs.
Alexander,[1] *frag. 44*

The nobly born must nobly meet his
fate.[2] *Alcymene,*[3] *frag. 100*

Man's best possession is a sympathetic wife. *Antigone,*[3] *frag. 164*

When good men die their goodness
does not perish,
But lives though they are gone. As for
the bad,
All that was theirs dies and is buried
with them.[4]
Temenidae,[5] *frag. 734*

[1] Translated by MORRIS HICKEY MORGAN.
[2] See Sophocles, p. 81a.
If there be any good in nobility, I trow it
to be only this, that it imposeth a necessity
upon those which are noble, that they should
not suffer their nobility to degenerate from
the virtues of their ancestors. — BOETHIUS
[A.D. 470–525], *De Consolatione Philosophiae III,
6:25*
Noblesse oblige. — DUC DE LEVIS [1764–1830]
[3] Translated by MORRIS HICKEY MORGAN.
[4] See Shakespeare, *Julius Caesar III, ii, 79,*
p. 255b.
[5] Translated by MORRIS HICKEY MORGAN.

An old man weds a tyrant, not a wife.
Phoenix (quoted by ARISTOPH-
ANES,   *Thesmophoriazusae)*,
frag. 413

Every man is like the company he is
wont to keep.   *Ib.*[1] *frag. 809*

Who knows but life be that which men
call death,
And death what men call life? [2]
Phrixus,[3] *frag. 830*

Whoso neglects learning in his youth,
Loses the past and is dead for the future.   *Ib. frag. 927*

The gods
Visit the sins of the fathers upon the
children.[4]   *Ib. frag. 970*

In a case of dissension, never dare to
judge till you've heard the other side.
Heracleidae [5] *(quoted by* ARIS-
TOPHANES, *The Wasps)*

Those whom God wishes to destroy,
he first makes mad.[6]   *Fragment*

These men won eight victories over

---

[1] Translated by MORRIS HICKEY MORGAN.
[2] See Aristophanes, p. 92a, and Montaigne,
p. 190b.
[3] Translated by MORRIS HICKEY MORGAN.
[4] See *Exodus 20:5*, p. 9a.
For the sins of your fathers you, though
guiltless, must suffer. — HORACE, *Odes III, 6:1*
The sins of the fathers are to be laid upon
the children. — SHAKESPEARE, *Merchant of Venice* [1596–1597], *III, v, 1*
[5] Translated by MORRIS HICKEY MORGAN.
[6] The anonymous Latin version is: Quos [or
Quem] deus vult perdere prius dementat.
In Boswell's *Life of Dr. Johnson* [1791]
(Everyman ed.), *vol. 2, pp. 442–443*, this is
quoted as a saying which everybody repeats but
nobody knows where to find.
Whom Fortune wishes to destroy she first
makes mad. — PUBLILIUS SYRUS [c. 42 B.C.],
Maxim 911
When falls on man the anger of the gods,
First from his mind they banish under-
standing.   LYCURGUS [fl. 820 B.C.]
For those whom God to ruin has designed,
He fits for fate, and first destroys their mind.
DRYDEN, *The Hind and the Panther*
[1687], *pt. III, l. 1093*
Whom the Gods would destroy they first
make mad. — LONGFELLOW, *The Masque of
Pandora* [1875], *VI*

---

the Syracusans when the favor of the
gods was equal for both sides.
*Epitaph for the Athenians Slain
in Sicily*

HERODOTUS
c. 485 – c. 425 B.C.

Men trust their ears less than their
eyes.   *Book I, ch. 8*

A woman takes off her claim to respect along with her garments.[1]   *Ib.*

In peace, children inter their parents;
war violates the order of nature and
causes parents to inter their children.
I, 87

[The Persians] are accustomed to
deliberate about the most important
matters when they are drunk.   *I, 133*

It was a kind of Cadmean victory.[2]
I, 166

For great wrongdoing there are great
punishments from the gods.
II, 120

If a man insisted always on being
serious, and never allowed himself a bit
of fun and relaxation, he would go mad
or become unstable without knowing
it.   *II, 173*

It is better to be envied than pitied.[3]
III, 52

Envy is born in a man from the
start.   *III, 80*

Force has no place where there is
need of skill.   *III, 127*

From the foot, Hercules.[4]   *IV, 82*

---

[1] See Chaucer, p. 168a.
[2] Polyneices and Eteocles, sons of Oedipus
and descendants of Cadmus, fought for the
possession of Thebes and killed each other.
Hence, a Cadmean victory means one where
victor and vanquished suffer alike.
See also Pyrrhus, p. 103b ("Pyrrhic victory").
[3] Also in PINDAR, *Pythian Odes I, 164.*
[4] Ex pede, Herculem. From AULUS GELLIUS
(*Noctes Atticae I, 1*), who tells how Pythagoras
deduced the stature of Hercules from the
length of his foot.
See Anonymous, p. 150b.

It is the gods' custom to bring low all things of surpassing greatness.[1]
Book VII, ch. 10

Haste in every business brings failures.   *VII,* 10

When life is so burdensome, death has become for man a sought-after refuge.   *VII,* 46

Circumstances rule men; men do not rule circumstances.   *VII,* 49

Great deeds are usually wrought at great risks.   *VII,* 50

Not snow, no, nor rain, nor heat, nor night keeps them from accomplishing their appointed courses with all speed.[2]
VIII, 98

The king's might is greater than human, and his arm is very long.
VIII, 140

This is the bitterest pain among men, to have much knowledge but no power.   *IX,* 16

In soft regions are born soft men.
IX, 122

PROTAGORAS
c. 485 – c. 410 B.C.

Man is the measure of all things.
Fragment 1

There are two sides to every question.
From DIOGENES LAERTIUS,
Protagoras IX, 51

[1] It is the lofty pine that by the storm
  Is oftener tossed; towers fall with heavier
    crash
  Which higher soar.
    Horace [65–8 B.C.], *Odes II,* 10:9
The bigger they come, the harder they fall.
— ROBERT FITZSIMMONS [1862–1917] before his bout with James J. Jeffries, a heavier man, in San Francisco [June 9, 1899]
[2] Neither snow, nor rain, nor heat, nor gloom of night stays these couriers from the swift completion of their appointed rounds. — *Inscription on the Main Post Office, New York City, adapted from Herodotus*

AGIS
fifth century B.C.

The Lacedemonians are not wont to ask how many the enemy are, but where they are.
From PLUTARCH, *Apothegms, Agis*

SOCRATES[1]
469–399 B.C.

Often when looking at a mass of things for sale, he would say to himself, "How many things I have no need of!"
From DIOGENES LAERTIUS,
bk. 2, *sec.* 25

Having the fewest wants, I am nearest to the gods.
Ib. 27

There is only one good, knowledge, and one evil, ignorance.   *Ib.* 31

My divine sign indicates the future to me.   *Ib.* 32

I know nothing except the fact of my ignorance.   *Ib.*

Bad men live that they may eat and drink, whereas good men eat and drink that they may live.[2]
From PLUTARCH, *How a Young Man Ought to Hear Poems,* 4

I am not an Athenian or a Greek, but a citizen of the world.[3]
From PLUTARCH, *Of Banishment*

[1] Much of Plato, especially in the *Apology* and *Phaedo,* is thought to be direct quotation from Socrates. See Plato, p. 93b.
[2] He used to say that other men lived to eat, but that he ate to live. — DIOGENES LAERTIUS [c. A.D. 200], *Socrates* 14
See Molière, p. 361a.
We must eat to live and live to eat. — FIELDING [1707–1754], *The Miser, act III, sc. iii*
[3] See Bacon, p. 208b; Thomas Paine, p. 467b; and William Lloyd Garrison, p. 615b.
Diogenes, when asked from what country he came, replied, "I am a citizen of the world." — DIOGENES LAERTIUS [c. A.D. 200], *Diogenes* 6
Citizen of the world, as I hold myself to be. — BOSWELL, *Life of Dr. Johnson* [1791], *Everyman Edition, vol. I, p. 521*

Crito, I owe a cock to Asclepius; will you remember to pay the debt?
From PLATO, *Phaedo* (*Socrates'
last words*)

DEMOCRITUS
c. 460 – c. 400 B.C.

Whatever a poet writes with enthusiasm and a divine inspiration is very fine.[1]
Fragment 18

In truth we know nothing, for truth lies in the depth.
Fragment 117

By convention there is color, by convention sweetness, by convention bitterness, but in reality there are atoms and space.
Fragment 125

Word is a shadow of deed.
Fragment 145

HIPPOCRATES
c. 460 – 400 B.C.

I swear by Apollo Physician, by Asclepius, by Health, by Panacea, and by all the gods and goddesses, making them my witnesses, that I will carry out, according to my ability and judgment, this oath and this indenture. To hold my teacher in this art equal to my own parents; to make him partner in my livelihood; when he is in need of money to share mine with him; to consider his family as my own brothers, and to teach them this art, if they want to learn it, without fee or indenture . . . I will use treatment to help the sick according to my ability and judgment, but never with a view to injury and wrongdoing . . . I will keep pure and holy both my life and my art . . . In whatsoever houses I enter, I will enter to help the sick, and I will abstain from all intentional wrongdoing and harm, especially from abusing the bodies of man or woman, bond or free. And whatsoever I shall see or hear in the course of my profession in my intercourse with men, if it be what should not be published abroad, I will never

[1] Apparently the earliest reference to the madness or divine inspiration of poets.

divulge, holding such things to be holy secrets. Now if I carry out this oath, and break it not, may I gain forever reputation among all men for my life and for my art; but if I transgress it and forswear myself, may the opposite befall me.
The Physician's Oath [1]

Healing is a matter of time, but it is sometimes also a matter of opportunity.
Precepts,[1] *ch.* 1

Sometimes give your services for nothing, calling to mind a previous benefaction or present satisfaction. And if there be an opportunity of serving one who is a stranger in financial straits, give full assistance to all such. For where there is love of man, there is also love of the art. For some patients, though conscious that their condition is perilous, recover their health simply through their contentment with the goodness of the physician. And it is well to superintend the sick to make them well, to care for the healthy to keep them well, also to care for one's own self, so as to observe what is seemly.
Ib. ch. 6

In all abundance there is lack.
Ib. ch. 8

If for the sake of a crowded audience you do wish to hold a lecture, your ambition is no laudable one, and at least avoid all citations from the poets, for to quote them argues feeble industry.
Ib. ch. 12

Life is short, the art long, timing is exact, experience treacherous, judgment difficult.[2]
Aphorisms, sec. I, 1

For extreme illnesses extreme treatments are most fitting.[3]
Ib. 6

[1] Translated by W. H. S. JONES.
[2] Vita brevis est, ars longa. — SENECA, *De Brevitate Vitae I, 1*
The lyf so short, the craft so long to lerne. — CHAUCER, *The Parliament of Fowls* [1380–1386], *l. 1*
Art's long, though time is short. — BROWNING, *The Ring and the Book* [1868–1869], *IX, Juris Doctor Johannes-Baptista Bottinius*
See Goethe, p. 477b, and Longfellow, p. 620b.
[3] See Shakespeare, *Hamlet IV, iii, 9,* p. 264b.

THUCYDIDES[1]
c. 460 – 400 B.C.

Thucydides, an Athenian, wrote the history of the war between the Peloponnesians and the Athenians; he began at the moment that it broke out, believing that it would be a great war, and more memorable than any that had preceded it.

The History of the Peloponnesian War [431–413 B.C.], bk. I, sec. 1

With reference to the narrative of events, far from permitting myself to derive it from the first source that came to hand, I did not even trust my own impressions, but it rests partly on what I saw myself, partly on what others saw for me, the accuracy of the report being always tried by the most severe and detailed tests possible. My conclusions have cost me some labor from the want of coincidence between accounts of the same occurrences by different eyewitnesses, arising sometimes from imperfect memory, sometimes from undue partiality for one side or the other. The absence of romance in my history will, I fear, detract somewhat from its interest; but I shall be content if it is judged useful by those inquirers who desire an exact knowledge of the past as an aid to the interpretation of the future, which in the course of human things must resemble if it does not reflect it. My history has been composed to be an everlasting possession, not the showpiece of an hour.[2] *Ib.* 22

The great wish of some is to avenge themselves on some particular enemy, the great wish of others to save their own pocket. Slow in assembling, they devote a very small fraction of the time to the consideration of any public object, most of it to the prosecution of their own objects. Meanwhile each fancies that no harm will come of his neglect, that it is the business of somebody else to look after this or that for him; and so, by the same notion being entertained by all separately, the common cause imperceptibly decays.[1]

The History of the Peloponnesian War, bk. I, sec. 141

Our constitution is named a democracy, because it is in the hands not of the few but of the many. But our laws secure equal justice for all in their private disputes, and our public opinion welcomes and honors talent in every branch of achievement, not for any sectional reason but on grounds of excellence alone. And as we give free play to all in our public life, so we carry the same spirit into our daily relations with one another. We have no black looks or angry words for our neighbor if he enjoys himself in his own way, and we abstain from the little acts of churlishness which, though they leave no mark, yet cause annoyance to whoso notes them. Open and friendly in our private intercourse, in our public acts we keep strictly within the control of law. We acknowledge the restraint of reverence; we are obedient to whomsoever is set in authority, and to the laws, more especially to those which offer protection to the oppressed and those unwritten ordinances whose transgression brings admitted shame.

Ib. II (Funeral Oration of Pericles), 37

We are lovers of beauty without extravagance, and lovers of wisdom without unmanliness. Wealth to us is not mere material for vainglory but an opportunity for achievement; and poverty we think it no disgrace to acknowledge but a real degradation to make no effort to overcome. *Ib.* 40

But the bravest are surely those who have the clearest vision of what is before them, glory and danger alike, and yet notwithstanding go out to meet it. *Ib.*

---

[1] Translated by SIR RICHARD LIVINGSTONE.
[2] See Ranke, p. 586a.

[1] Quoted by President John F. Kennedy in Frankfurt [June 25, 1963].

We secure our friends not by accepting favors but by doing them.[1]

> *The History of the Peloponnesian War*, bk. II (*Funeral Oration of Pericles*), sec. 40

In a word I claim that our city as a whole is an education to Greece.

Ib. 41

Fix your eyes on the greatness of Athens as you have it before you day by day, fall in love with her, and when you feel her great, remember that this greatness was won by men with courage, with knowledge of their duty, and with a sense of honor in action . . . So they gave their bodies to the commonwealth and received, each for his own memory, praise that will never die, and with it the grandest of all sepulchers, not that in which their mortal bones are laid, but a home in the minds of men, where their glory remains fresh to stir to speech or action as the occasion comes by. For the whole earth is the sepulcher of famous men; and their story is not graven only on stone over their native earth, but lives on far away, without visible symbol, woven into the stuff of other men's lives. For you now it remains to rival what they have done and, knowing the secret of happiness to be freedom and the secret of freedom a brave heart, not idly to stand aside from the enemy's onset.[2]   *Ib*. 43

Great is the glory of the woman who occasions the least talk among men, whether of praise or of blame.

Ib. 45

For human nature is as surely made arrogant by consideration as it is awed by firmness.   *Ib*. III, 39

---

[1] Rather by conferring than by accepting favors, they [the Romans] established friendly relations. — SALLUST, *The War with Catiline* [c. 40 B.C.], *6*

[2] See Simonides, p. 70b, and Brandeis, p. 832b.

Men make the city, and not walls or ships without men in them.[1]

> *The History of the Peloponnesian War*, bk. VII, 77 (*Address of Nicias to the Athenians at Syracuse*)

This or the like was the cause of the death of a man [Nicias] who, of all the Greeks in my time, least deserved such a fate, for he had lived in the practice of every virtue.   *Ib. VII, 86*

This was the greatest event in the war, or, in my opinion, in Greek history; at once most glorious to the victors and most calamitous to the conquered. They were beaten at all points and altogether; their sufferings in every way were great. They were totally destroyed — their fleet, their army, everything — and few out of many returned home. So ended the Sicilian expedition.   *Ib. VII, 87*

All Hellas is the monument of Euripides, but the Macedonian land holds his bones, for it sheltered the end of his life. His country was Athens, the Hellas of Hellas, and as by his verse he gave exceeding delight, so for many he receiveth praise.

> *Epitaph. Greek Anthology* [*Loeb Classical Library*], bk. VII, no. 45

ARISTOPHANES
c. 450 – 385 B.C.

For then, in wrath, the Olympian Pericles
Thundered and lightened, and confounded Hellas
Enacting laws which ran like drinking songs.[2]

> *Acharnians* [425 B.C.], l. 530

When men drink, then they are rich and successful and win lawsuits and are happy and help their friends.
Quickly, bring me a beaker of wine, so

---

[1] See Sophocles, p. 81a.
[2] Translated by B. B. ROGERS.

that I may wet my mind and say something clever.
Knights [424 *B.C.*], *l. 92*

You have all the characteristics of a popular politician: a horrible voice, bad breeding, and a vulgar manner. *Ib. 217*

To make the worse appear the better reason.[1]
Clouds [423 *B.C.*], *l. 114 and elsewhere*

Haven't you sometimes seen a cloud that looked like a centaur?
Or a leopard perhaps? Or a wolf? Or a bull?[2] *Ib. 346*

Old men are children for a second time.[3] *Ib. 1417*

This is what extremely grieves us, that a man who never fought
Should contrive our fees to pilfer, one who for his native land
Never to this day had oar, or lance, or blister in his hand.
Wasps[4] [422 *B.C.*], *l. 1117*

Let each man exercise the art he knows. *Ib. 1431*

You cannot teach a crab to walk straight.
Peace [421 *B.C.*], *l. 1083*

[On the nightingale] Lord Zeus, listen to the little bird's voice; he has filled the whole thicket with honeyed song.
Birds [414 *B.C.*], *l. 223*

Bringing owls to Athens.[5] *Ib. 301*

The wise learn many things from their enemies. *Ib. 375*

Full of wiles, full of guile, at all times, in all ways,
Are the children of Men.[6] *Ib. 451*

¹ See Milton, p. 343b.
² Translated by DUDLEY FITTS.
See Shakespeare, *Hamlet III, ii, 400,* p. 263b, and *Antony and Cleopatra IV, xii, 2,* p. 288b.
³ See Shakespeare, p. 261a.
⁴ Translated by B. B. ROGERS.
⁵ See Horace, p. 120a.
⁶ Translated by B. B. ROGERS.

Mankind, fleet of life, like tree leaves, weak creatures of clay, unsubstantial as shadows, wingless, ephemeral, wretched, mortal and dreamlike.[1] *Birds, l. 685*

Somewhere, what with all these clouds, and all this air,
There must be a rare name, somewhere . . . How do you like "Cloud-Cuckoo-Land"?[2]
Ib. 817

Halcyon days.[3] *Ib. 1594*

A woman's time of opportunity is short, and if she doesn't seize it, no one wants to marry her, and she sits watching for omens.
Lysistrata [411 *B.C.*], *l. 596*

There is no animal more invincible than a woman, nor fire either, nor any wildcat so ruthless.
Ib. 1014

These impossible women! How they do get around us!
The poet was right: can't live with them, or without them![4]
Ib. 1038

Under every stone lurks a politician.[5]
Thesmophoriazusae [410 *B.C.*], *l. 530*

There's nothing worse in the world than shameless woman — save some other woman. *Ib. l. 531*

Shall I crack any of those old jokes, master,
At which the audience never fail to laugh? *Frogs*[6] [405 *B.C.*], *l. 1*

¹ See Homer, p. 64b, and Pindar, p. 79b.
² Translated by DUDLEY FITTS.
³ See Shakespeare, *Henry VI, Pt. I, I, ii, 131,* p. 214a.
The appellation of Halcyon days, which was applied to a rare and bloodless week of repose.
—GIBBON: *Decline and Fall of the Roman Empire* [1776–1788], *ch. 48*
⁴ Translated by DUDLEY FITTS.
Imitated by Martial (see p. 135b).
⁵ A play on the proverb "Under every stone lurks a scorpion."
⁶ Translated by B. B. ROGERS.

Brekekekex, ko-ax, ko-ax.[1]
> *Frogs, l. 209 and elsewhere*

A savage-creating stubborn-pulling fellow,
Uncurbed, unfettered, uncontrolled of
speech,
Unperiphrastic, bombastiloquent.[2]
> *Ib. 837*

High thoughts must have high language.[3]   *Ib. 1058*

Who knows whether living is dying,
and breathing
Is eating, and sleeping is a wool blanket?[4]   *Ib. 1477*

Blest the man who possesses a
Keen intelligent mind.   *Ib. 1482*

I am amazed that anyone who has
made a fortune should send for his
friends.
> *Plutus [c. 388 B.C.], l. 340*

We say that poverty is the sister of
beggary.   *Ib. 549*

Even if you persuade me, you won't
persuade me.   *Ib. 600*

A man's homeland is wherever he prospers.   *Ib. 1151*

AGATHON
c. 448 – 400 B.C.

This only is denied to God: the
power to undo the past.
> *From* ARISTOTLE, *Nicomachean
> Ethics, bk. VI, ch. 2*

AGESILAUS
444–400 B.C.

If all men were just, there would be
no need of valor.
> *From* PLUTARCH, *Lives,
> Agesilaus, sec. 23*

It is circumstance and proper timing
that give an action its character and
make it either good or bad.   *Ib. 36*

[1] Adopted as a Yale College cheer.
[2] Refers to Aeschylus.
[3] Translated by DUDLEY FITTS.
[4] See Euripides, p. 86a, and Montaigne, p. 190b.

XENOPHON
c. 430 – 355 B.C.

Apollo said that everyone's true worship was that which he found in use in
the place where he chanced to be.
> *Recollections of Socrates, bk. I,
> ch. 3, sec. 1*

The sea! The sea! [1]
> *Anabasis IV, 7, 24*

I knew my son was mortal.[2]
> *From* DIOGENES LAERTIUS,
> *Xenophon II, 55*

ZEUXIS
fl. 400 B.C.

Criticism comes easier than craftsmanship.
> *From* PLINY THE ELDER,
> *Natural History*

PLATO[3]
c. 428 – 348 B.C.

We who of old left the booming
surge of the Aegean lie here in the mid-
plain of Ecbatana: farewell, renowned
Eretria once our country; farewell,
Athens nigh to Euboea; farewell, dear
sea.[4]   *Greek Anthology III, 10* [5]

Beloved Pan, and all ye other gods
who haunt this place, give me beauty in
the inward soul; and may the outward
and inward man be at one. May I
reckon the wise to be the wealthy, and
may I have such a quantity of gold as
none but the temperate can carry.
> *Dialogues, Phaedrus, sec. 279*

Friends have all things in common.[6]
> *Ib.*

[1] Thalatta! Thalatta!
Hail to thee, O Sea, ageless and eternal!
     HEINRICH HEINE [1797–1856], *Thalatta!
Thalatta!, st. 1*
[2] When his son was killed in battle.
[3] Translated by BENJAMIN JOWETT.
[4] On the Eretrian exiles settled in Persia by
Darius.
[5] Edited by J. W. MACKAIL.
[6] According to Timaios, he [Pythagoras, 582–
500 B.C.] originated the saying "Friends share
all things." — DIOGENES LAERTIUS VIII, 10
Also in Euripides, *Orestes, l. 735.*
See Sallust, p. 115b.

And the true order of going, or being led by another, to the things of love, is to begin from the beauties of earth and mount upwards for the sake of that other beauty, using these steps only, and from one going on to two, and from two to all fair forms to fair practices, and from fair practices to fair notions, until from fair notions he arrives at the notion of absolute beauty, and at last knows what the essence of beauty is.

Dialogues, Symposium 211

Beholding beauty with the eye of the mind, he will be enabled to bring forth, not images of beauty, but realities (for he has hold not of an image but of a reality), and bringing forth and nourishing true virtue to become the friend of God and be immortal, if mortal man may. *Ib. 212*

Socrates is a doer of evil, who corrupts the youth; and who does not believe in the gods of the state, but has other new divinities of his own. Such is the charge. *Ib. Apology 24*

The life which is unexamined is not worth living. *Ib. 38*

Either death is a state of nothingness and utter unconsciousness, or, as men say, there is a change and migration of the soul from this world to another.[1] . . . Now if death be of such a nature, I say that to die is to gain; for eternity is then only a single night. *Ib. 40*

No evil can happen to a good man, either in life or after death. *Ib. 41*

The hour of departure has arrived, and we go our ways — I to die, and you to live. Which is better God only knows. *Ib. 42*

Man is a prisoner who has no right to open the door of his prison and run

[1] Either the soul is immortal and we shall not die, or it perishes with the flesh and we shall not know that we are dead. Live, then, as if you were eternal. — ANDRÉ MAUROIS [1885–1967]. From WILL DURANT, *On the Meaning of Life* [1932]. *p. 53.*

away. . . . A man should wait, and not take his own life until God summons him.

Dialogues, Phaedo.[1] 62

Must not all things at the last be swallowed up in death? *Ib. 72*

Will you not allow that I have as much of the spirit of prophecy in me as the swans? For they, when they perceive that they must die, having sung all their life long, do then sing more lustily than ever, rejoicing in the thought that they are going to the god they serve.[2] *Ib. 85*

The partisan, when he is engaged in a dispute, cares nothing about the rights of the question, but is anxious only to convince his hearers of his own assertions. *Ib. 91*

False words are not only evil in themselves, but they infect the soul with evil. *Ib.*

The soul takes nothing with her to the other world but her education and culture; and these, it is said, are of the greatest service or of the greatest injury to the dead man, at the very beginning of his journey thither. *Ib. 107*

He who is of a calm and happy nature will hardly feel the pressure of age, but to him who is of an opposite disposition youth and age are equally a burden. *The Republic, bk. I, 329-D*

No physician, insofar as he is a physician, considers his own good in what he prescribes, but the good of his patient; for the true physician is also a ruler having the human body as a sub-

[1] See Socrates, p. 87b.
[2] The jalous swan, ayens his deth that singeth. — CHAUCER, *The Parliament of Fowls* [1380–1386], *l. 342*
   Makes a swan-like end,
Fading in music.
   SHAKESPEARE, *The Merchant of Venice* [1596–1597], *III, 2, 44*
I will play the swan and die in music. — *Othello* [1604–1605] *V, 2, 245*
See Shakespeare, p. 237a, and Byron, p. 561a.
See Socrates, p. 88a, for his last words.

ject, and is not a mere moneymaker.[1]
The Republic, bk. I, 342–D

When there is an income tax, the just man will pay more and the unjust less on the same amount of income.
Ib. 343–D

Mankind censure injustice fearing that they may be the victims of it, and not because they shrink from committing it.   *Ib. 344–C*

The beginning is the most important part of the work.[2]   *Ib. 377–B*

The judge should not be young; he should have learned to know evil, not from his own soul, but from late and long observation of the nature of evil in others: knowledge should be his guide, not personal experience.
Ib. III, 409–B

Everything that deceives may be said to enchant.   *Ib. 413–C*

How, then, might we contrive . . . one noble lie to persuade if possible the rulers themselves, but failing that the rest of the city?[3]   *Ib. 414–C*

Wealth is the parent of luxury and indolence, and poverty of meanness and viciousness, and both of discontent.[4]
Ib. IV, 422–A

The direction in which education starts a man will determine his future life.   *Ib. 425–B*

What is the prime of life? May it not be defined as a period of about twenty years in a woman's life, and thirty in a man's?   *Ib. V, 460–E*

Until philosophers are kings, or the kings and princes of this world have the spirit and power of philosophy, and political greatness and wisdom meet in one, and those commoner natures who pursue either to the exclusion of the other are compelled to stand aside, cities will never have rest from their

[1] See Hippocrates, p. 88b.
[2] Proverbial. Also in *Laws VI, 2.* See Aristotle, p. 98b; Horace, p. 123a; and Heywood, p. 183b.
[3] *Loeb Classical Library* translation.
[4] See *I Timothy 6:10, p.* 55b, and Sophocles, p. 82a.

evils — no, nor the human race, as I believe — and then only will this our State have a possibility of life and behold the light of day.
The Republic, bk. V, 473–C

Let there be one man who has a city obedient to his will, and he might bring into existence the ideal polity about which the world is so incredulous.
Ib. 502–B

Behold! human beings living in an underground den . . . Like ourselves . . . they see only their own shadows, or the shadows of one another, which the fire throws on the opposite wall of the cave.   *Ib. VII, 515–B*

Astronomy compels the soul to look upwards and leads us from this world to another.   *Ib. 529*

I have hardly ever known a mathematician who was capable of reasoning.   *Ib. 531–E*

Solon was under a delusion when he said that a man when he grows old may learn many things[1] — for he can no more learn much than he can run much; youth is the time for any extraordinary toil.   *Ib. 536–D*

Bodily exercise, when compulsory, does no harm to the body; but knowledge which is acquired under compulsion obtains no hold on the mind.
Ib. 536–E

Let early education be a sort of amusement; you will then be better able to find out the natural bent.
Ib. 537

Oligarchy: A government resting on a valuation of property, in which the rich have power and the poor man is deprived of it.   *Ib. VIII, 550–C*

Democracy, which is a charming form of government, full of variety and disorder, and dispensing a sort of equality to equals and unequals alike.[2]
Ib. 558–C

[1] See Solon, p. 68b.
[2] See Aristotle, p. 98b.

Democracy passes into despotism.[1]
The Republic, bk. VIII,
562–A

The people have always some champion whom they set over them and nurse into greatness. . . . This and no other is the root from which a tyrant springs; when he first appears he is a protector. *Ib. 565–C*

In the early days of his power, he is full of smiles, and he salutes everyone whom he meets. *Ib. 566–D*

When the tyrant has disposed of foreign enemies by conquest or treaty, and there is nothing to fear from them, then he is always stirring up some war or other, in order that the people may require a leader. *Ib. 566–E*

There are three arts which are concerned with all things: one which uses, another which makes, a third which imitates them. *Ib. X, 601–D*

No human thing is of serious importance. *Ib. 604–C*

The soul of man is immortal and imperishable. *Ib. 608–D*

If a person shows that such things as wood, stones, and the like, being many are also one, we admit that he shows the coexistence of the one and many, but he does not show that the many are one or the one many; he is uttering not a paradox but a truism.
Dialogues, Parmenides 129

The absolute natures or kinds are known severally by the absolute idea of knowledge. *Ib. 134*

If a man, fixing his attention on these and the like difficulties, does away with ideas of things and will not admit that every individual thing has its own determinate idea which is always one and the same, he will have nothing on which his mind can rest; and so he will utterly destroy the power of reasoning.
Ib. 135

You cannot conceive the many without the one. *Ib. 166*

[1] Translated by F. M. CORNFORD.

Let us affirm what seems to be the truth, that, whether one is or is not, one and the others in relation to themselves and one another, all of them, in every way, are and are not, and appear to be and appear not to be.
Dialogues, Parmenides 166

Well, my art of midwifery is in most respects like theirs; but differs, in that I attend men and not women, and I look after their souls when they are in labor, and not after their bodies: and the triumph of my art is in thoroughly examining whether the thought which the mind of the young man brings forth is a false idol or a noble and true birth.
Ib. Theaetetus 150

He [the philosopher] does not hold aloof in order that he may gain a reputation; but the truth is, that the outer form of him only is in the city: his mind, disdaining the littlenesses and nothingnesses of human beings, is "flying all abroad" as Pindar says, measuring earth and heaven and the things which are under and on the earth and above the heaven, interrogating the whole nature of each and all in their entirety, but not condescending to anything which is within reach.

Ib. 173

I would have you imagine, then, that there exists in the mind of man a block of wax, which is of different sizes in different men; harder, moister, and having more or less of purity in one than another, and in some of an intermediate quality. . . . Let us say that this tablet is a gift of Memory, the mother of the Muses; and that when we wish to remember anything which we have seen, or heard, or thought in our own minds, we hold the wax to the perceptions and thoughts, and in that material receive the impression of them as from the seal of a ring; and that we remember and know what is imprinted as long as the image lasts; but when the image is effaced, or cannot be taken, then we forget and do not know.
Ib. 191

Let us now suppose that in the mind of each man there is an aviary of all sorts of birds — some flocking together apart from the rest, others in small groups, others solitary, flying anywhere and everywhere. . . . We may suppose that the birds are kinds of knowledge, and that when we were children, this receptacle was empty; whenever a man has gotten and detained in the enclosure a kind of knowledge, he may be said to have learned or discovered the thing which is the subject of the knowledge: and this is to know.

Dialogues, Theaetetus 197

The greatest penalty of evildoing — namely, to grow into the likeness of bad men.   *Laws* 728

Of all the animals, the boy is the most unmanageable.   *Ib.* 808

You are young, my son, and, as the years go by, time will change and even reverse many of your present opinions. Refrain therefore awhile from setting yourself up as a judge of the highest matters.   *Ib.* 888

And this which you deem of no moment is the very highest of all: that is whether you have a right idea of the gods, whereby you may live your life well or ill.   *Ib.*

Not one of them who took up in his youth with this opinion that there are no gods ever continued until old age faithful to his conviction.   *Ib.*

IPHICRATES
419–348 B.C.

My family history begins with me, but yours ends with you.[1]

From PLUTARCH, *Apothegms, Iphicrates*

[1] Iphicrates, a shoemaker's son who became a famous general, said this to Harmodius of distinguished ancestry when he reviled him for his mean birth.

Curtius Rufus seems to be descended from himself. — TIBERIUS. From TACITUS, *Annals XI, 21*

I am my own ancestor [Moi, je suis mon ancêtre.] — ANDOCHE JUNOT [1771–1813]

PHOCION
c. 402 – 317 B.C.

Have I inadvertently said some evil thing?[1]

From PLUTARCH, *Apothegms, Phocion, sec.* 10

The good have no need of an advocate.   *Ib.*

DIOGENES THE CYNIC
c. 400 – c. 325 B.C.

[When asked by Alexander if he wanted anything] Stand a little out of my sun.

From PLUTARCH, *Lives, Alexander, sec.* 14

Plato having defined man to be a two-legged animal without feathers, Diogenes plucked a cock and brought it into the Academy, and said, "This is Plato's man."[2] On which account this addition was made to the definition: "With broad flat nails."

From DIOGENES LAERTIUS, *Diogenes* 6

[When asked what was the proper time for supper] If you are a rich man, whenever you please; and if you are a poor man, whenever you can.[3]

Ib.

I am looking for an honest man.[4]

Ib.

The sun too penetrates into privies, but is not polluted by them.[5]   *Ib.*

[1] Said when an opinion he delivered pleased the people.
[2] Seeing that the human race falls into the same classification as the feathered creatures, we must divide the biped class into featherless and feathered. — PLATO [c. 428 – c. 348 B.C.], *The Statesman 266–E*
[3] The rich when he is hungry, the poor when he has anything to eat. — RABELAIS, *Works, bk. IV* [1548], *ch. 64*
[4] Attributed also to Aesop.
[5] The spiritual virtue of a sacrament is like light: although it passes among the impure, it is not polluted. — ST. AUGUSTINE [A.D. 354–430], *Tract on St. John, ch. 5:15*
The sun shineth upon the dunghill, and is not corrupted. — LYLY, *Euphues* [1579]
The sun, which passeth through pollutions and itself remains as pure as before. — BACON,

ANTIPHANES
c. 388 – c. 311 B.C.

We must have richness of soul.
Greek Comic Fragments, no. 570

ARISTOTLE[1]
384–322 B.C.

Liars when they speak the truth are not believed.
From DIOGENES LAERTIUS, *bk. V, sec. 17*

Hope is a waking dream.   *Ib. 18*

What soon grows old? Gratitude.
Ib.

Beauty is the gift of God.   *Ib. 19*

Educated men are as much superior to uneducated men as the living are to the dead.[2]   *Ib.*

What is a friend? A single soul dwelling in two bodies.[3]   *Ib. 20*

I have gained this by philosophy: that I do without being commanded what others do only from fear of the law.[4]   *Ib. 21*

We should behave to our friends as we would wish our friends to behave to us.[5]   *Ib.*

Education is the best provision for old age.   *Ib.*

Time wastes things away, and all things grow old through time.
Physics, bk. IV, ch. 12

The least initial deviation from the truth is multiplied later a thousandfold.   *On the Heavens, bk. I, ch. 5*

In all things of nature there is something of the marvelous.
Parts of Animals, bk. I, ch. 5

All men by nature desire knowledge.
Metaphysics, bk. I, ch. 1

The final cause, then, produces motion through being loved.[1]   *Ib. ch. 7*

The actuality of thought is life.
Ib. XII, ch. 7

It is of itself that the divine thought thinks (since it is the most excellent of things), and its thinking is a thinking on thinking.   *Ib. ch. 9*

Every science and every inquiry, and similarly every activity and pursuit, is thought to aim at some good.
Nicomachean Ethics, bk. I, ch. 1

While both [Plato and truth] are dear, piety requires us to honor truth above our friends.[2]   *Ib. ch. 6*

One swallow does not make a summer.[3]   *Ib. ch. 7*

For the things we have to learn before we can do them, we learn by doing them.   *Ib. II, ch. 1*

It is possible to fail in many ways . . . while to succeed is possible only in one way (for which reason also one is easy and the other difficult — to miss the mark easy, to hit it difficult).
Ib. ch. 6

We must as second best . . . take the least of the evils.[4]   *Ib. ch. 9*

Advancement of Learning [1605], *bk. II*
Truth is as impossible to be soiled by any outward touch as the sunbeam. — MILTON, *The Doctrine and Discipline of Divorce* [1643]
[1] Chiefly from *The Basic Works of Aristotle,* edited by RICHARD McKEON.
[2] This used to be quoted "with great warmth" by Dr. Johnson, according to BOSWELL in his *Life of Johnson* [1791].
[3] Andrágathos, my soul's half. — MELEAGER [fl. 80 B.C.]. From *The Greek Anthology XII, 52* See Zeno, p. 103a; Cicero, p. 111b; Horace, p. 120b; and Donne, p. 306a.
[4] Also attributed to Xenocrates [396–314 B.C.] by Cicero.
[5] See *Matthew 7:12,* p. 41a, and Lord Chesterfield, p. 415a.

[1] See Dante, p. 162a.
[2] Amicus Plato, sed magis amica veritas [Plato is dear to me, but dearer still is truth]. Adapted from a medieval life of Aristotle.
[3] One swallow maketh not summer. — JOHN HEYWOOD, *Proverbs* [1546], *pt. II, ch. 5*
One swallow proveth not that summer is near. — NORTHBROOKE, *Treatise Against Dancing* [1577]
One swallow never makes a summer. — CERVANTES, *Don Quixote, pt. I* [1605], *bk. II, ch. 4.*
One swallow makes a summer. — ROBERT LOWELL, *Fall, 1961*
[4] See Homer, p. 64a, and note.

A man is the origin of his action.[1]
Nicomachean Ethics,
bk. III, ch. 3

Without friends no one would choose to live, though he had all other goods. *Ib. VIII, ch. 1*

To enjoy the things we ought and to hate the things we ought has the greatest bearing on excellence of character. *Ib. X, ch. 1*

If happiness is activity in accordance with excellence, it is reasonable that it should be in accordance with the highest excellence. *Ib. ch. 7*

We make war that we may live in peace. *Ib.*

With regard to excellence, it is not enough to know, but we must try to have and use it. *Ib. ch. 9*

Man is by nature a political animal. *Politics, bk. I, ch. 2*

Nature does nothing uselessly.[2]
Ib.

He who is unable to live in society, or who has no need because he is sufficient for himself, must be either a beast or a god. *Ib.*

The two qualities which chiefly inspire regard and affection [are] that a thing is your own and that it is your only one. *Ib. II, ch. 4*

It is the nature of desire not to be satisfied, and most men live only for the gratification of it. The beginning of reform is not so much to equalize property as to train the noble sort of natures not to desire more, and to prevent the lower from getting more. *Ib. ch. 7*

Even when laws have been written down, they ought not always to remain unaltered. *Ib. ch. 8*

Again, men in general desire the good, and not merely what their fathers had. *Ib.*

They should rule who are able to rule best. *Ib. ch. 11*

[1] See Sallust, p. 116a.
[2] God and nature do nothing uselessly. —
On the Heavens, bk. I, ch. 4

A state is not a mere society, having a common place, established for the prevention of mutual crime and for the sake of exchange. . . . Political society exists for the sake of noble actions, and not of mere companionship.
Politics, bk. III, ch. 9

If liberty and equality, as is thought by some, are chiefly to be found in democracy, they will be best attained when all persons alike share in the government to the utmost.[1]
Ib. IV, ch. 4

The best political community is formed by citizens of the middle class. *Ib. ch. 11*

Democracy arises out of the notion that those who are equal in any respect are equal in all respects; because men are equally free, they claim to be absolutely equal. *Ib. V, ch. 1*

Inferiors revolt in order that they may be equal, and equals that they may be superior. Such is the state of mind which creates revolutions. *Ib. ch. 2*

In revolutions the occasions may be trifling but great interests are at stake. *Ib. ch. 3*

Well begun is half done.[2] *Ib. ch. 4*

The basis of a democratic state is liberty. *Ib. VI, ch. 2*

Law is order, and good law is good order. *Ib. VII, ch. 4*

Evils draw men together.[3]
Rhetoric, bk. I, ch. 6

It is this simplicity that makes the uneducated more effective than the educated when addressing popular audiences. *Ib. II, ch. 22*

A tragedy is the imitation of an action that is serious and also, as having magnitude, complete in itself . . . with incidents arousing pity and fear,

[1] See Plato, p. 94b.
[2] Aristotle is quoting a proverb.
See Plato, p. 94a, and note.
[3] Aristotle is quoting a proverb.

wherewith to accomplish its catharsis of such emotions.　　*Poetics, ch. 6*

A whole is that which has beginning, middle, and end.　　*Ib. ch. 7*

Poetry is something more philosophic and of graver import than history, since its statements are of the nature of universals, whereas those of history are singulars.　　*Ib. ch. 9*

A likely impossibility is always preferable to an unconvincing possibility.　　*Ib. ch. 24*

Misfortune shows those who are not really friends.[1]
Eudemian Ethics, bk. VII, ch. 2

DEMOSTHENES
c. 384 – 322 B.C.

Every advantage in the past is judged in the light of the final issue.
First Olynthiac, sec. 11

Nothing is easier than self-deceit. For what each man wishes, that he also believes to be true.[2]
Third Olynthiac, sec. 19

You cannot have a proud and chivalrous spirit if your conduct is mean and paltry; for whatever a man's actions are, such must be his spirit.　　*Ib. 33*

I decline to buy repentance at the cost of ten thousand drachmas.[3]
From AULUS GELLIUS, *Noctes Atticae, bk. I, ch. 8*

ANTIGONUS
c. 382 – 301 B.C.

But how many ships do you reckon my presence to be worth?[4]
From PLUTARCH, *Apothegms, Antigonus*

[1] In prosperity it is very easy to find a friend, but in adversity it is the most difficult of all things. — EPICTETUS, *Fragment 127*

See Cicero, p. 111b; Publilius Syrus, p. 127a; Ovid, p. 129a; and John Heywood, p. 184b.

[2] See Caesar, p. 112a.

[3] In reply to the courtesan Laïs.

[4] His pilot had told him that the enemy outnumbered him in ships.

[When described by Hermodotus as "Son of the Sun"] My valet is not aware of this.[1]
From PLUTARCH, *Apothegms, Antigonus*

MENCIUS[2]
372–289 B.C.

When one by force subdues men, they do not submit to him in heart. They submit, because their strength is not adequate to resist.　　*Book II, 1:3.2*

There is no attribute of the superior man greater than his helping men to practice virtue.　　*II, 1:8.5*

The superior man will not manifest either narrow-mindedness or the want of self-respect.　　*II, 1:9.3*

To give the throne to another man would be easy; to find a man who shall benefit the kingdom is difficult.
III, 1:4.10

Never has a man who has bent himself been able to make others straight.
III, 2:1.5

If you know that [a] thing is unrighteous, then use all dispatch in putting an end to it — why wait till next year?　　*III, 2:8.3*

The compass and square produce perfect circles and squares. By the sages, the human relations are perfectly exhibited.　　*IV, 1:2.1*

The root of the kingdom is in the state. The root of the state is in the family. The root of the family is in the person of its head.　　*IV, 1:5*

[1] See Montaigne, p. 190b.

The phrase "No man is a hero to his valet" has often been attributed to Madame de Sévigné, but on the authority of MADAME AÏSSÉ (*Letters*, edited by Jules Ravenal, 1853) it belongs to Madame Cornuel [1614–1694].

It is said that no man is a hero to his valet. That is because a hero can be recognized only by a hero. The valet will probably be able to appreciate his like — that is, his fellow-valet. — GOETHE [1749–1832], *Sprüche in Prosa, vol. III, p. 204*

[2] From *The Chinese Classics, Vol. II: The Works of Mencius*, translated by JAMES LEGGE.

The people turn to a benevolent rule as water flows downwards, and as wild beasts fly to the wilderness.

Book IV, 1:9.2

Benevolence is the tranquil habitation of man, and righteousness is his straight path.   IV, 1:10.2

The path of duty lies in what is near, and man seeks for it in what is remote.

IV, 1:11

Sincerity is the way of Heaven.

IV, 1:12.2

There are three things which are unfilial, and to have no posterity is the greatest of them.[1]   IV, 1:26.1

Men must be decided on what they will not do, and then they are able to act with vigor in what they ought to do.   IV, 2:8

The great man does not think beforehand of his words that they may be sincere, nor of his actions that they may be resolute — he simply speaks and does what is right.   IV, 2:11

The great man is he who does not lose his child's-heart.[2]   IV, 2:12

Friendship with a man is friendship with his virtue, and does not admit of assumptions of superiority.

IV, 2:13.1

If you must do violence and injury to the willow in order to make cups and bowls with it . . . you must in the same way do violence and injury to humanity in order to fashion from it benevolence and righteousness! [This,] alas! would certainly lead all men on to reckon benevolence and righteousness to be calamities.   VI, 1:1.2

[1] To be without posterity . . . is an offense against the whole line of ancestors, and terminates the sacrifices to them. — MENCIUS, *Ib*.

[2] "Except ye be converted, and become as little children, ye shall not enter into the kingdom of heaven." But Christ speaks of the child's-heart as a thing to be regained; Mencius speaks of it as a thing not to be lost. — JAMES LEGGE

See *Book VI, 1:11.4.*

Water indeed will flow indifferently to the east or west, but will it flow indifferently up or down? The tendency of man's nature to good is like the tendency of water to flow downwards. There are none but have this tendency to good, just as all water flows downwards.   *Book VI*, 1:2.2

From the feelings proper to it, [man's nature] is constituted for the practice of what is good.

VI, 1:6.5–6

Benevolence, righteousness, propriety, and knowledge are not infused into us from without.   VI, 1:6.7

Benevolence is man's mind, and righteousness is man's path.

VI, 1:11.1

The great end of learning is nothing else but to seek for the lost mind.[1]

VI, 1:11.4

All men have in themselves that which is truly honorable. Only they do not think of it.   VI, 1:17.1

If a scholar have not faith [in his principles], how shall he take a firm hold of things?   VI, 2:12

When Heaven is about to confer a great office on any man, it first exercises his mind with suffering, and his sinews and bones with toil.   VI, 2:15.2

There is no greater delight than to be conscious of sincerity on self-examination.   VII, 1:4.2

Kindly words do not enter so deeply into men as a reputation for kindness.

VII, 1:14.1

Is it only the mouth and belly which are injured by hunger and thirst? Men's minds are also injured by them.

VII, 1:27.1

The people are the most important element in a nation; the spirits of the land and grain are next; the sovereign is the lightest.   VII, 2:14.1

[1] The Chinese sages always end with the recovery of "the old heart"; the idea of "a new heart" is unknown to them. — JAMES LEGGE

See *Book IV*, 2:12.

CHUANG TZU [1]
369–286 B.C.

Great wisdom is generous; petty wisdom is contentious. Great speech is impassioned, small speech cantankerous.
On Leveling All Things

Take, for instance, a twig and a pillar, or the ugly person and the great beauty, and all the strange and monstrous transformations. These are all leveled together by Tao. Division is the same as creation; creation is the same as destruction.
Ib.

I do not know whether I was then a man dreaming I was a butterfly, or whether I am now a butterfly dreaming I am a man.
Ib.

All men know the utility of useful things; but they do not know the utility of futility.
This Human World

He who pursues fame at the risk of losing his self is not a scholar.
The Great Supreme

Those who seek to satisfy the mind of man by hampering it with ceremonies and music and affecting charity and devotion have lost their original nature.
Joined Toes

In the days of perfect nature, man lived together with birds and beasts, and there was no distinction of their kind. Who could know of the distinctions between gentlemen and common people? Being all equally without knowledge, their virtue could not go astray. Being all equally without desires, they were in a state of natural integrity, the people did not lose their [original] nature.

And then when Sages appeared, crawling for charity and limping with duty, doubt and confusion entered men's minds. They said they must make merry by means of music and enforce distinctions by means of ceremony, and the empire became divided

against itself. . . . Were Tao and virtue not destroyed, what use would there be for charity and duty? Were men's natural instincts not lost, what need would there be for music and ceremonies? . . . Destruction of the natural integrity of these things for the production of articles of various kinds — this is the fault of the artisan. Destruction of Tao and virtue in order to introduce charity and duty — this is the error of the Sages.
Horses' Hoofs

Banish wisdom, discard knowledge, and gangsters will stop!
Opening Trunks, or A Protest Against Civilization

For all men strive to grasp what they do not know, while none strive to grasp what they already know; and all strive to discredit what they do not excel in, while none strive to discredit what they do excel in. This is why there is chaos.
Ib.

Cherish that which is within you, and shut off that which is without; for much knowledge is a curse.
On Tolerance

"The prince keeps [a] tortoise carefully enclosed in a chest in his ancestral temple. Now would this tortoise rather be dead and have its remains venerated, or would it rather be alive and wagging its tail in the mud?"
"It would rather be alive . . . and wagging its tail in the mud."
"Begone!" cried Chuangtse. "I too will wag my tail in the mud."
Autumn Floods

PYTHEAS [1]
fl. 330 B.C.

They smell of the lamp.[2]
From PLUTARCH, *Lives, Demosthenes*

[1] See Virgil, p. 117a, and note.
[2] Pytheas refers to the orations of Demosthenes, who worked in an underground cave lighted only by a lamp.
See Cardozo, p. 902b.

101

A P E L L E S
fl. 325 B.C.

Not a day without a line.[1]
> Proverbial from PLINY THE
> ELDER, *Natural History*
> XXXV, 36

A cobbler should not judge above his last.[2]   *Ib. 85*

A L E X A N D E R
T H E G R E A T
356–323 B.C.

[At Achilles' tomb] O fortunate youth, to have found Homer as the herald of your glory!
> From CICERO, *Pro Archia* 24

If I were not Alexander, I would be Diogenes.
> From PLUTARCH, *Lives,*
> *Alexander* 14

M E N A N D E R[3]
c. 342 – 292 B.C.

We live, not as we wish to, but as we can.   *Lady of Andros, frag. 50*

Riches cover a multitude of woes.
> *The Boeotian Girl, frag. 90*

Whom the gods love dies young.[4]
> *The Double Deceiver, frag. 125*

At times discretion should be thrown aside, and with the foolish we should play the fool.[5]
> *Those Offered for Sale, frag. 421*

The man who has never been flogged has never been taught.[6]
> *The Girl Who Gets Flogged,*
> *frag. 422*

[1] Nulla dies sine linea.
[2] Ne supra crepidam sutor iudicaret.
The more common rendering is: Cobbler, stick to your last.
[3] *Loeb Classical Library* translation.
[4] Also in PLAUTUS, *Bacchides IV, 7:18.*
Those that God loves do not live long. — GEORGE HERBERT, *Jacula Prudentum* [2nd ed. 1651]
See Wordsworth, p. 516a.
Heaven gives its favorites — early death. — BYRON, *Childe Harold, canto IV* [1818], st. *102*
[5] See Horace, p. 122b, and note.
[6] See *Proverbs 13:24,* p. 24a, and Samuel Butler, p. 353a.

The truth sometimes not sought for comes forth to the light.
> *The Girl Who Gets*
> *Flogged, frag. 433*

This is living, not to live unto oneself alone.
> *The Brothers in Love, frag. 508*

A god from the machine.[1]
> *The Woman Possessed with a*
> *Divinity, frag. 227*

I call a fig a fig, a spade a spade.[2]
> *Unidentified fragment 545*

Even God lends a hand to honest boldness.[3]   *Ib. 572*

Marriage, if one will face the truth, is an evil, but a necessary evil.[4]
> *Ib. 651*

It is not white hair that engenders wisdom.   *Ib. 639*

Health and intellect are the two blessings of life.
> *Monostikoi [Single Lines]*

The man who runs may fight again.[5]
> *Ib.*

They spare the rod and spoil the child. — RALPH VENNING, *Mysteries and Revelations* [1649]
[1] The Latin form is usually quoted: Deus ex machina.
Also in LUCIAN, *Hermotimus, sec. 86.*
[2] Also attributed to Aristophanes by LUCIAN, *De Conscribend. Hist. 41.*
The Macedonians are a rude and clownish people that call a spade a spade. — PLUTARCH, *Apothegms, Philip of Macedon*
I think it good plain English, without fraud, To call a spade a spade, a bawd a bawd.
> JOHN TAYLOR, The Water Poet
> [1580–1653], *A Kicksey Winsey*
[3] See Terence, p. 109a and Propertius, p. 127b.
[4] Marriage is an evil that most men welcome. — *Monostikoi [Single Lines] Motto of The Spectator, December 29, 1711*
[5] He who flees will fight again. — TERTULLIAN [c. 155–225], *De Fuga in Persecutione 10*
> That same man that runnith awaie
> Maie again fight an other daie.
> ERASMUS, *Apothegms* [1542], translated by NICHOLAS UDALL [1505–1556]
> Celuy qui fuit de bonne heure
> Peut combattre derechef.
> (Who flies in good time
> Can fight anew.)
> *Satyre Menippée* [1594]

Conscience is a God to all mortals.
Monostikoi [Single Lines]

EPICURUS
341–270 B.C.

Death is nothing to us, since when we are, death has not come, and when death has come, we are not.
From DIOGENES LAERTIUS, *bk. X, sec. 125*

Pleasure is the beginning and the end of living happily.   *Ib. 128*

It is impossible to live pleasurably without living wisely, well, and justly, and impossible to live wisely, well, and justly without living pleasurably.[1]
Ib. 140

ZENO
335–263 B.C.

[When asked, "What is a friend?"] Another I.[2]
From DIOGENES LAERTIUS, *bk. VII, sec. 23*

Qui fuit peut revenir aussi;
Qui meurt, il n'en est pas ainsi.
(Who flies can also return;
Not so with him who dies.)
     PAUL SCARRON [1610–1660]
For those that fly may fight again,
Which he can never do that's slain.
     SAMUEL BUTLER, *Hudibras, pt. III*
     [1678], *canto 3, l. 243*
He that fights and runs away
May turn and fight another day;
But he that is in battle slain
Will never rise to fight again.
     JAMES RAY, *History of the*
     Rebellion [1752]
For he who fights and runs away
May live to fight another day;
But he who is in battle slain
Can never rise and fight again.
     GOLDSMITH, *The Art of Poetry*
     on a New Plan [1761]
But since the man that runs away
Lives to die another day,
And cowards' funerals, when they come,
Are not wept so well at home,
Therefore, though the best is bad,
Stand and do the best, my lad.
     A. E. HOUSMAN [1859–1936],
     The Day of Battle

[1] See Sophocles, p. 82b.
[2] In Latin: Alter ego. See Aristotle p. 97a.

The goal of life is living in agreement with nature.
From DIOGENES LAERTIUS, *bk. VII, sec. 87*

CLEANTHES
c. 330–232 B.C.

For we are your offspring.[1]
Hymn to Zeus, l. 4

Lead me, Zeus, and you, Fate, wherever you have assigned me. I shall follow without hesitation; but even if I am disobedient and do not wish to, I shall follow no less surely.
From EPICTETUS, *Enchiridion, sec. 53*

EUCLID
fl. 300 B.C.

Q.E.D. [Which it was necessary to demonstrate.] [2]
Elements, bk. I, proposition 5

The bridge of asses.[3]   *Ib.*

[To Ptolemy I] There is no royal road to geometry.[4]
From PROCLUS, *Commentary on Euclid, Prologue*

PYRRHUS
c. 318 – 272 B.C.

Another such victory over the Romans, and we are undone.[5]
From PLUTARCH, *Lives, Pyrrhus, sec. 21*

ARATUS
c. 315 – 240 B.C.

From Zeus let us begin, whom we mortals never leave unnamed: full of

[1] Possibly the source of *Acts 17:28*, p. 50a. See also Aratus, p. 104a.
[2] Translated into Latin as: Quod erat demonstrandum.
[3] Pons asinorum (i.e., too difficult for asses, or stupid boys, to get over).
[4] Often misquoted as "learning" rather than "geometry."
[5] Pyrrhus, king of Epirus, refers to the dearly bought victory at Asculum, 280 B.C. Hence the phrase "Pyrrhic victory." See also Herodotus, p. 86b ("Cadmean victory").

Zeus are all streets and all gathering places of men, and full are the sea and harbors. Everywhere we all have need of Zeus. For we are also his offspring.[1]

Phaenomena, sec. 1

THEOPHRASTUS
d. 278 B.C.

Time is the most valuable thing a man can spend.[2]

From DIOGENES LAERTIUS, *Theophrastus V, sec. 40*

LACYDES
fl. c. 241 B.C.

[When asked late in life why he was studying geometry] If I should not be learning now, when should I be?

From DIOGENES LAERTIUS, *Lacydes, sec. V*

THEOCRITUS[3]
c. 310 – 250 B.C.

'Tis peace of mind, lad, we must find, and have a beldame nigh
To sit for us and spit for us and bid all ill go by.

The Harvest Home, l. 126

Oh cricket is to cricket dear, and ant for ant doth long,
The hawk's the darling of his fere, and o' me the Muse and her song.

The Third Country Singing Match, l. 31

Oh to be a frog, my lads, and live aloof from care.   *The Reapers, l. 52*

Thou'lt cut thy finger, niggard, a-splitting caraway.   *Ib. l. 55*

A great love goes here with a little gift.[4]

The Distaff, l. 24

---

[1] Probably the source of *Acts 17:28*, p. 50a. See also Aeschylus, p. 78b; Cleanthes, p. 103b; and Dante, p. 161b.

[2] Nothing is so dear and precious as time. — RABELAIS, *Works, bk. V* [1564], *ch. 5*

Remember that time is money. — BENJAMIN FRANKLIN, *Advice to a Young Tradesman* [1748] See Hemingway, p. 1045a.

[3] Translated by J. M. EDMONDS.

[4] See Homer, p. 65b.

CALLIMACHUS
c. 305 – 240 B.C.

Great book, great evil.

Fragment 359

One told me of thy fate, Heraclitus, and wrung me to tears.[1]

Greek Anthology, J. W. MAC-KAIL, *ed.* [1906], *sec. 4, no. 31*

This is the tomb of Callimachus that thou art passing. He could sing well, and laugh well at the right time over the wine.

His Own Epitaph. Greek Anthology [Loeb Classical Library], bk. VII, no. 415

BION
fl. 280 B.C.

Old age is the harbor of all ills.

From DIOGENES LAERTIUS, *bk. IV, sec. 47*

Wealth is the sinews of affairs.[2]

Ib. 48

The road to Hades is easy to travel.[3]

Ib. 49

He has not acquired a fortune; the fortune has acquired him.[4]   *Ib. 50*

Though boys throw stones at frogs in sport, the frogs do not die in sport, but in earnest.[5]

From PLUTARCH, *Water and Land Animals 7*

---

[1] See W. J. Cory, p. 719b.

[2] Endless money forms the sinews of war. — CICERO, *Philippics V, 2:5*

He who first called money the sinews of affairs seems to have spoken with special reference to the affairs of war. — PLUTARCH, *Lives, Cleomenes 27*

Neither is money the sinews of war (as it is trivially said). — FRANCIS BACON, *Essays* [1625], *Of the True Greatness of Kingdoms*

Money is the sinew of love as well as of war. — THOMAS FULLER, *Gnomologia, no. 3442*

See Rabelais, p. 181a.

[3] See Virgil p. 118b; *Matthew 7:13, 14*, p. 41b; Shakespeare, pp. 258b and 283b.

     A passage broad,
Smooth, easy, inoffensive, down to Hell.

           MILTON, *Paradise Lost II, 432*

[4] See Robert Burton, p. 310b, and Ingersoll, p. 749a.

[5] See L'Estrange, p. 357a.

LEONIDAS OF TARENTUM
fl. 274 B.C.

Now is the season of sailing; for already the chattering swallow is come and the pleasant west wind; the meadows flower, and the sea tossed up with waves and rough blasts has sunk to silence. Weigh thine anchors and unloose thy hawsers, O mariner, and sail with all thy canvas set: this I Priapus of the harbor bid thee, O man, that thou mayest sail forth to all thy trafficking.
Greek Anthology, J. W. MAC-KAIL, *ed.* [1906], *sec. 6, no. 26*

ARCHIMEDES
c. 287 – 212 B.C.

I have found it! [1]
From VITRUVIUS POLLIO, *De Architectura, bk. IX, 215*

Give me where to stand, and I will move the earth.[2]
From PAPPUS OF ALEXANDRIA, *Collectio, bk. VIII, prop. 10, sec. 11*

FABIUS MAXIMUS
c. 275–203 B.C.

To be turned from one's course by men's opinions, by blame, and by misrepresentation shows a man unfit to hold an office.[3]
From PLUTARCH, *Lives, Fabius Maximus, sec. 5*

TITUS MACCIUS PLAUTUS
254–184 B.C.

What is yours is mine, and all mine is yours.[4]
Trinummus, act II, sc. ii, l. 48

---

[1] Eureka! (Said when he found the principle of specific gravity.)
[2] Said with reference to the lever.
[3] See Horace, p. 122a.
[4] See Shakespeare, *Measure for Measure V, i, 529*, p. 272a.

Not by age but by capacity is wisdom acquired.
Trinummus, act II, sc. ii, l. 88

You are seeking a knot in a bulrush.[1]
Menaechmi, act II, sc. i, l. 22

In the one hand he is carrying a stone, while he shows the bread in the other.[2]
Aulularia, act II, sc. ii, l. 18

There are occasions when it is undoubtedly better to incur loss than to make gain.
Captivi, act II, sc. ii, l. 77

Patience is the best remedy for every trouble.   *Rudens, act II, sc. v, l. 71*

Consider the little mouse, how sagacious an animal it is which never entrusts its life to one hole only.[3]
Truculentus, act IV, sc. iv, l. 15

No guest is so welcome in a friend's house that he will not become a nuisance after three days.[4]
Miles Gloriosus, act III, sc. i

No man is wise enough by himself.
Ib. iii

Nothing is there more friendly to a man than a friend in need.[5]
Epidicus, act III, sc. iii, l. 44

---

[1] A proverbial expression implying a desire to create doubts and difficulties where there really are none. It occurs in TERENCE, *Andria V, 4:38;* also in ENNIUS, *Saturae 46.*
[2] See *Matthew 7:9*, p. 41a.
[3] I holde a mouses herte nat worth a leek,
That hath but oon hole for to sterte to,
And if that faille, thanne is al y-do.
    CHAUCER, *The Canterbury Tales* [c. 1387], *The Wife of Bath's Prologue, l. 572*
The mouse that hath but one hole is quickly taken. — GEORGE HERBERT, *Jacula Prudentum* [1640]
    The mouse that always trusts to one poor hole
    Can never be a mouse of any soul.
        POPE, *Paraphrase of the Prologue* [1714], *l. 298*
[4] Fish and guests in three days are stale. — JOHN LYLY, *Euphues* [1579]
Fish and visitors smell in three days. — BENJAMIN FRANKLIN, *Poor Richard's Almanac for 1735*
[5] A friend in need is a friend indeed. — HAZLITT, *English Proverbs*

Things which you do not hope happen more frequently than things which you do hope.[1]
Mostellaria, act I, sc. iii, l. 40

To blow and swallow at the same moment is not easy.   *Ib. III, ii, 104*

Practice yourself what you preach.[2]
Asinaria, act III, sc. iii, l. 644

MAHARBAL
[BARCA
THE CARTHAGINIAN]
fl. 210 B.C.

You know how to win a victory, Hannibal, but not how to use it.[3]
From Livy, *History XXII, 51*

BHAGAVAD GITA[4]
250 B.C. — A.D. 250[5]

For certain is death for the born
And certain is birth for the dead;
Therefore over the inevitable
Thou shouldst not grieve.[6]
Gita, ch. 2, sec. 27

Let not the fruit of action be thy motive,
Nor be thy attachment to inaction.[7]
Ib. 2, 47

Better one's own duty, [though] imperfect,

---

[1] The unexpected always happens. — *Common saying*
[2] Facias ipse quod faciamus suades.
See St. Jerome, p. 145b.
[3] Vincere scis, Hannibal, victoria uti nescis.
See Polybius, p. 107b.
[4] Sanskrit: The Lord's Song.
[5] Ancient Indian literary chronology is conjectural. The dates given are approximate.
[6] Translated by Annie Besant.
[7] Translated by F. Edgerton.
At the moment which is not of action or inaction
You can receive this: "on whatever sphere of being
The mind of a man may be intent
At the time of death" — that is the one action
(And the time of death is every moment)
Which shall fructify in the lives of others:
And do not think of the fruit of action,
Fare forward.
                    T. S. Eliot, *Four Quartets* [*1943*].
                    The Dry Salvages, pt. III

Than another's duty well performed.[1]
Gita 3, 35 and 18, 47

In whatsoever way any come to Me,
In that same way I grant them favor.[1]
Ib. 4, 11

Who sees Me in all,
And sees all in Me,
For him I am not lost,
And he is not lost for Me.[1]   *Ib. 6, 30*

Whatsoever state [of being] meditating upon
He leaves the body at death,[2]
To just that he goes, son of Kunti,
Always being made to be in the condition of that.[3]   *Ib. 8, 6*

If the radiance of a thousand suns
were to burst forth at once in the sky,
that would be like the splendor of the Mighty One.[4]   *Ib. 11, 12*

QUINTUS ENNIUS
239–169 B.C.

No sooner said than done — so acts your man of worth.
Annals, bk. 9 (quoted by Priscianus)

I never indulge in poetics
Unless I am down with rheumatics.
Fragment of a satire (quoted by Priscianus)

By delaying he preserved the state.[5]
From Cicero, *De Senectute IV*

Let no one pay me honor with tears, nor celebrate my funeral rites with weeping.[6]   *Ib. XX*

---

[1] Translated by F. Edgerton.
[2] See Eliot's lines from *The Dry Salvages* quoted in the note to *Gita* 2:47 above.
[3] Translated by F. Edgerton.
[4] Translated by Swami Nikhilananda.
Quoted by J. Robert Oppenheimer when the first atomic bomb exploded on July 16, 1945, near Alamogordo, New Mexico.
[5] This refers to Quintus Fabius Maximus, "Cunctator." Hence the "Fabian policy" of waiting.
[6] See Tennyson, p. 655a.
No funeral gloom, my dears, when I am gone,

The ape, vilest of beasts, how like to us.[1]

> From CICERO, *De Natura Deorum, bk. I, ch. 35*

No one regards what is before his feet; we all gaze at the stars.

> *Iphigenia. From* CICERO, *De Divinatione, bk. II, ch. 13*

The idle mind knows not what it is it wants.   *Ib.*

Whom they fear they hate.

> *Thyestes. From* CICERO, *De Officiis II, 7*

MARCUS PORCIUS CATO, THE ELDER
234–149 B.C.

It is a hard matter, my fellow citizens, to argue with the belly, since it has no ears.[2]

> From PLUTARCH, *Lives, Cato, sec. 8*

Wise men profit more from fools than fools from wise men; for the wise men shun the mistakes of fools, but fools do not imitate the successes of the wise.   *Ib. 9*

I would much rather have men ask why I have no statue, than why I have one.   *Ib. 19*

Carthage must be destroyed.[3]

           Ib. 27

Grasp the subject, the words will follow.[4]

> *From* CAIUS JULIUS VICTOR, *Ars Rhetorica I [4th century A.D.]*

Corpse-gazings, tears, black raiment, graveyard grimness.
    WILLIAM ALLINGHAM [1828–1889],
                        Diary

[1] Simia quam similis, turpissima bestia, nobis!
[2] The belly has no ears nor is it to be filled with fair words. — RABELAIS, *Works IV [1548], 67*
See LaFontaine, p. 359b, and Adlai Stevenson, p. 1048b.
[3] Delenda est Carthago. These words were added to everything Cato said or wrote on any question whatsoever, and were always preceded by "ceterum censeo" (in my opinion).
[4] Rem tene; verba sequentur.

An orator is a good man who is skilled in speaking.

> From SENECA THE ELDER [c. 45 B.C. – A.D. 40], *Controversiae I, Preface, and elsewhere*

CAECILIUS STATIUS
220–168 B.C.

He plants trees to benefit another generation.[1]

> *Synephebi. Quoted by* CICERO *in De Senectute VII*

POLYBIUS
c. 208 – c. 126 B.C.

For peace, with justice and honor, is the fairest and most profitable of possessions, but with disgrace and shameful cowardice it is the most infamous and harmful of all.

> *History, bk. IV, sec. 31*

Those who know how to win are much more numerous than those who know how to make proper use of their victories.[2]   *Ib. X, 36*

That historians should give their own country a break, I grant you; but not so as to state things contrary to fact. For there are plenty of mistakes made by writers out of ignorance, and which any man finds it difficult to avoid. But if we knowingly write what is false, whether for the sake of our country or our friends or just to be pleasant, what difference is there between us and hack-writers? Readers should be very attentive to and critical of historians, and they in turn should be constantly on their guard.[3]   *Ib. XVI*

[1] Serit arbores quae alteri seculo prosint. John Quincy Adams used *Alteri seculo* for his seal [c. 1830].
He that plants trees loves others beside himself. — THOMAS FULLER, *Gnomologia* [1732]
A man does not plant a tree for himself; he plants it for posterity. — ALEXANDER SMITH, *Dreamthorp* [1863], ch. 11
[2] See Maharbal, p. 106a.
[3] Translated by S. E. MORISON.
See Cicero, p. 110b.

There is no witness so dreadful, no accuser so terrible as the conscience that dwells in the heart of every man.

History, bk. XVIII, sec. 43

MARCUS LICINIUS CRASSUS

fl. 70 B.C.

Those who aim at great deeds must also suffer greatly.

From PLUTARCH, *Lives, Crassus, ch. 26*

TERENCE[1]

[PUBLIUS TERENTIUS AFER]

C. 190 – 159 B.C.

Moderation in all things.[2]

Andria (The Lady of Andros), l. 61

Obsequiousness begets friends, truth hatred.[3]   *Ib. 68*

Hence these tears.[4]   *Ib. 126*

I am Davos, not Oedipus.[5]

      Ib. 194

Lovers' quarrels are the renewal of love.[6]   *Ib. 555*

---

[1] Loeb Classical Library edition, with occasional changes in the translation.

[2] Ne quid nimis.
See The Seven Sages, p. 68b, Horace, p. 120a, and note.

[3] Obsequium amicos, veritas odium parit.

[4] Hinc illae lacrimae. The phrase is proverbial for "That's the cause of it," and was often quoted, by Horace in *Epistles I, xix, 41* and others.
Hence rage and tears [Inde irae et lacrimae].
— JUVENAL, *Satires, bk. I, l. 168*

[5] Davos sum, non Oedipus.

[6] Amantium irae amoris integratio est. This was quoted by Winston Churchill in a message to Roosevelt.
The anger of lovers renews the strength of love. — PUBLILIUS SYRUS [c. 42 B.C.], *Maxim 24*
The fallyng out of faithful friends renuyng is of love. — RICHARD EDWARDS, *The Paradise of Dainty Devices* [1576]
Let the falling out of friends be a renewing of affection. — LYLY, *Euphues* [1579]
The falling out of lovers is the renewing of love. — ROBERT BURTON, *Anatomy of Melancholy* [1621–1651], *pt. III, sec. 2*

Charity begins at home.[1]

Andria (The Lady of Andros), l. 635

I am a man: nothing human is alien to me.[2]

Heauton Timoroumenos (The Self-Tormentor), l. 77

Draw from others the lesson that may profit yourself.[3]   *Ib. 221*

Time removes distress.[4]   *Ib. 421*

Nothing is so difficult but that it may be found out by seeking.[5]

      Ib. 675

Some people ask, "What if the sky were to fall?"[6]   *Ib. 719*

Extreme law is often extreme injustice.[7]   *Ib. 796*

There is nothing so easy but that it becomes difficult when you do it reluctantly.   *Ib. 805*

While there's life, there's hope.[8]

      Ib. 981

---

[1] Proximus sum egomet mihi.
Let them learn first to show piety at home. — *I Timothy 5:4*
See Sir Thomas Browne, p. 330a.

[2] Homo sum: humani nil a me alienum puto.
Quoted by CICERO in *De Officiis I, 30*.

[3] Periculum ex aliis facito tibi quod ex usu siet. (A saying.)
Profit by the folly of others. — PLINY THE ELDER [A.D. 23–79], *Natural History XVIII, 31*

[4] Diem adimere aegritudinem hominibus. (A saying: Time heals all wounds.)

[5] Nil tam difficile est quin quaerendo investigari possiet.

[6] Quid si nunc caelum ruat?
Some ambassadors from the Celtae, being asked by Alexander what in the world they dreaded most, answered, that they feared lest the sky should fall upon them. — ARRIANUS [c. A.D. 100–170], *bk. I, 4*

[7] Ius summum saepe summa est malitia. See Anonymous Latin, p. 151b.
Extreme law, extreme injustice, is now become a stale proverb in discourse. — CICERO [106–43 B.C.], *De Officiis I, 33*
Extreme justice is often injustice. — RACINE, *La Thébaïde* [1664], *act IV, sc. 3*
Mais l'extrême justice est une extrême injure. — VOLTAIRE, *Oedipe* [1718], *act III, sc. 3*

[8] Modo liceat vivere, est spes.
See Cicero, p. 111a, Gay, p. 401b, and Goldsmith, p. 447a.

In fact, nothing is said that has not been said before.[1]

Eunuchus, l. 41 (Prologue)

I have everything, yet have nothing; and although I possess nothing, still of nothing am I in want.[2]　　*Ib. 243*

There are vicissitudes in all things.
Ib. 276

I don't care one straw.[3]　　*Ib. 411*

Take care and say this with presence of mind.[4]　　*Ib. 769*

He is wise who tries everything before arms.　　*Ib. 789*

I know the disposition of women: when you will, they won't; when you won't, they set their hearts upon you of their own inclination.　　*Ib. 812*

I took to my heels as fast as I could.
Ib. 844

Many a time . . . from a bad beginning great friendships have sprung up.　　*Ib. 873*

Fortune helps the brave.[5]
Phormio, l. 203

So many men, so many opinions; every one his own way.[6]　　*Ib. 454*

As they say, I have got a wolf by the ears.[7]　　*Ib. 506*

---

[1] See *Ecclesiates 1:9*, p. 27a, and Robert Burton, p. 310a.

[2] See *II Corinthians 6:10*, p. 53b, and Wotton, p. 300b.

[3] Ego non flocci pendere.
Nor do they care a straw. — CERVANTES, *Don Quixote, pt. I* [1605], *bk. III, ch. 9*

[4] Fac animo haec praesenti dicas. Literally, "with a present mind" — equivalent to CAESAR's *praesentia animi (De Bello Gallico V, 43, 4).*

[5] See Menander, p. 102b, and Virgil, p. 119b.
PLINY THE YOUNGER says *(bk. VI, letter 16)* that PLINY THE ELDER said this during the eruption of Vesuvius: "Fortune favors the brave."

[6] Quot homines tot sententiae: suo quoque mos.
So many heads so many wits. — JOHN HEYWOOD, *Proverbs* [1546], *pt. I, ch. 2*
So many men so many minds. — GEORGE GASCOIGNE, *The Glass of Government* [1575]

[7] A proverbial expression which, according to SUETONIUS, was frequently in the mouth of Tiberius Caesar.

I bid him look into the lives of men as though into a mirror, and from others to take an example for himself.

Adelphoe (The Brothers), l. 415

According as the man is, so must you humor him.　　*Ib. 431*

It is the common vice of all, in old age, to be too intent upon our interests.[1]　　*Ib. 833*

TUNG CHUNG-SHU[2]
C. 179 – C. 104 B.C.

He who is the ruler of men takes non-action as his way and considers impartiality as his treasure. He sits upon the throne of non-action and rides upon the perfection of his officials.

Ch'un-ch'iu fan-lu

When the first indications of error begin to appear in the state, Heaven sends forth ominous portents and calamities to warn men and announce the fact.　　*Ib.*

LUCIUS ACCIUS
170–86 B.C.

Let them hate, so long as they fear.[3]

LUCIUS ANNAEUS FLORUS
fl. A.D. 125

Each year new consuls and proconsuls are made; but not every year is a king or a poet born.[4]

De Qualitate Vitae, frag. 8

---

[1] CICERO quotes this in *Tusculan Disputations, bk. III*. The maxim was a favorite with the Stoic philosophers.

[2] From *Sources of Chinese Tradition*, edited by WILLIAM THEODORE DE BARY.

[3] Oderint dum metuant.
From a lost tragedy. Frequently cited by Cicero and others. SUETONIUS (*Gaius Caligula 30*) says that the Emperor Caligula was fond of quoting it.
See Machiavelli, p. 177a.

[4] From this derived the proverb: Poeta nascitur, non fit (The poet is born, not made).
See Ben Jonson, p. 303b.

HAN WU-TI[1]
157–87 B.C.

The sound of her silk skirt has
stopped.
On the marble pavement dust grows.
Her empty room is cold and still.
Fallen leaves are piled against the
doors.
Longing for that lovely lady
How can I bring my aching heart to
rest?
On the death of his mistress [2]

HUAI-NAN TZU[3]
Second century B.C.

Before heaven and earth had taken
form all was vague and amorphous.
Therefore it was called the Great Beginning. The Great Beginning produced
emptiness and emptiness produced the
universe. . . . The combined essences
of heaven and earth became the yin
and yang, the concentrated essences of
the yin and yang became the four seasons, and the scattered essences of the
four seasons became the myriad creatures of the world.

MELEAGER
fl. 95 B.C.

Farewell, Morning Star, herald of
dawn, and quickly come as the Evening
Star, bringing again in secret her whom
thou takest away.[4]
Greek Anthology, J. W. MAC-
KAIL, *ed.* [1906], *sec. 1, no. 21*

MARCUS TERENTIUS VARRO
116–27 B.C.

A sick man dreams nothing so dreadful that some philosopher isn't saying
it.[5]   *Satires, frag. 122*

[1] Sixth emperor of the Han dynasty.
[2] From *Chinese Poems*, ARTHUR WALEY, translator.
[3] An anonymous work compiled at the court
of Liu An (d. 122 B.C.).
From *Sources of Chinese Tradition*, edited by
WILLIAM THEODORE DE BARY.
[4] See Sappho, p. 69b, and Housman, p. 854a.
[5] See Cicero, p. 111a; and Descartes, p. 327b.

MARCUS TULLIUS CICERO
106–43 B.C.

How long, Catiline, will you abuse
our patience? [1]   *In Catilinam I, 1*

Oh what times! Oh what standards! [2]   *Ib.*

He has departed, withdrawn, gone
away, broken out.[3]   *Ib, II, 1*

I am a Roman citizen.[4]
In Verrem V, 57

Law stands mute in the midst of
arms.[5]   *Pro Milone IV, 11*

Who gained by it? [6]
Ib. XII, 32

These studies are a spur to the
young, a delight to the old; an ornament in prosperity, a consoling refuge
in adversity; they are pleasure for us at
home, and no burden abroad; they stay
up with us at night, they accompany us
when we travel, they are with us in our
country visits.
Pro Archia Poeta I, 2

Leisure with dignity.[7]
De Oratore II, 62

History is the witness that testifies to
the passing of time; it illumines reality,
vitalizes memory, provides guidance in
daily life, and brings us tidings of antiquity.   *Ib. II, 36*

The first law for the historian is that
he shall never dare utter an untruth.
The second is that he shall suppress
nothing that is true. Moreover, there

[1] Quo usque, Catilina, abutere patientia nostra?
[2] O tempora! O mores!
[3] Abiit, excessit, evasit, erupit.
Me wretched! Let me curr to quercine shades!
Effund your albid hausts, lactiferous maids!
Oh, might I vole to some umbrageous clump, —
Depart, — be off, — excede, — evade, — erump!
OLIVER WENDELL HOLMES, *The Autocrat of the Breakfast Table* [1858]
Aestivation, ch. II
[4] Civis Romanus sum.
[5] Silent enim leges inter arma.
[6] Cui bono [fuerit]?
[7] Otium cum dignitate.

shall be no suspicion of partiality in his writing, or of malice.[1]

De Oratore II, 62

The freedom of poetic license.[2]

Ib. III, 153

If a man aspires to the highest place, it is no dishonor to him to halt at the second, or even at the third.

Orator ad M. Brutum 4

For just as some women are said to be handsome though without adornment, so this subtle manner of speech, though lacking in artificial graces, delights us.[3]

Ib. 78

Nothing quite new is perfect.

Brutus 71

There were poets before Homer.

Ib.

The aim of forensic oratory is to teach, to delight, to move.

De Optimo Genere Oratorum 16

The dregs of Romulus.[4]

Ad Atticum II, 1

While there's life, there's hope.[5]

Ib. IX, 10

What is more agreeable than one's home? [6] *Ad Familiares IV, 8*

I like myself, but I won't say I'm as handsome as the bull that kidnapped Europa.

De Natura Deorum I, 78

It was ordained at the beginning of the world that certain signs should prefigure certain events.[7]

De Divinatione I, 118

There is nothing so ridiculous but some philosopher has said it.[8]

Ib. II, 119

---

[1] See Polybius, p. 107b.
[2] Poetarum licentiae liberiora.
[3] See Milton, p. 345b, and Thomson, p. 419b.
[4] In Romuli faece. That is, the lowest order of society.
[5] Dum anima est, spes est.
See Terence, p. 108b; Gay, p. 401b; and Goldsmith, p. 447a.
[6] Quae est domestica sede iucundior?
[7] See Thomas Campbell, p. 538a, and note.
[8] See Varro, p. 110a, and Descartes, p. 327b.

I would rather be wrong with Plato than right with such men as these [the Pythagoreans].

Tusculanae Disputationes I, 17

O philosophy, you leader of life.[1]

Ib. V, 2

Socrates was the first to call philosophy down from the heavens and to place it in cities, and even to introduce it into homes and compel it to inquire about life and standards and goods and evils. *Ib. V, 4*

The highest good.[2]

De Officiis I, 2

Let arms yield to the toga, the laurel crown to praise.[3] *Ib. I, 22*

Never less idle than when wholly idle, nor less alone than when wholly alone.[4] *Ib. III, 1*

Rome, fortunately natal 'neath my consulship! [5] *De Consultatu Suo*

The people's good is the highest law.[6] *De Legibus III, 3*

He used to raise a storm in a teapot.[7]

Ib. 16

The shifts of Fortune test the reliability of friends.[8]

De Amicitia XVII

A friend is, as it were, a second self.[9]

Ib. XXI

Give me a young man in whom there is something of the old, and an old man

---

[1] O vitae philosophia dux.
Adapted [1776] as the motto of Phi Beta Kappa, rendered in Greek as: Philosophia biou Kybernetes (Philosophy the guide to life).
[2] Summum bonum.
See Lucretius, p. 114a.
The nature of the good and the highest good.
— HORACE, *Satires II, 6, 76*
[3] Cedant arma togae, concedat laurea laudi.
He is quoting from his own poem *De suis temporibus, bk. III.*
[4] See Samuel Rogers, p. 500b.
[5] O fortunatam natam me consule Romam!
The verse is quoted disparagingly by Juvenal (*X, 122*), Quintilian (*XI, 1, 24*), and others.
[6] Salus populi suprema est lex.
[7] Excitabat enim fluctus in simpulo.
A tempest in a teapot. — *Proverb*
[8] See Aristotle, p. 99a, and note.
[9] See Aristotle, p. 97a.

with something of the young: guided so, a man may grow old in body, but never in mind. *De Senectute XI*

Old men are garrulous by nature. *Ib. XVI*

Old age: the crown of life, our play's last act. *Ib. XXIII*

POMPEY
[CNEIUS POMPEIUS]
106–48 B.C.

More worship the rising than the setting sun.[1]
From PLUTARCH, *Lives, Pompey, sec. 14*

A dead man cannot bite. *Ib. 77*

JULIUS CAESAR
100–44 B.C.

All Gaul is divided into three parts.[2]
De Bello Gallico I, 1

Men willingly believe what they wish.[3] *Ib. III, 18*

I love treason but hate a traitor.[4]
From PLUTARCH, *Lives, Romulus, sec. 17*

I wished my wife to be not so much as suspected.[5] *Ib. Caesar, sec. 10*

I had rather be the first man among these fellows than the second man in Rome. *Ib. 11*

---

[1] Addressed to Sulla.
See David Garrick, p. 439a.
[2] Gallia est omnis divisa in partes tres.
[3] Fere libenter homines id quod volunt credunt.
See Demosthenes, p. 99a.
[4] Princes in this case do hate the traitor, though they love the treason. — SAMUEL DANIEL, *Tragedy of Cleopatra* [1594], *act IV, sc. i*
This principle is old, but true as fate, Kings may love treason, but the traitor hate. DEKKER, *The Honest Whore* [1604], *pt. I, act IV, sc. iv*
Though I love the treason, I hate the traitor. — PEPYS, *Diary* [March 7, 1667]
See Dryden, p. 370b.
[5] Caesar's wife must be above suspicion. — *Traditional saying*

The die is cast.[1]
From PLUTARCH, *Lives, Caesar, sec. 32*

Go on, my friend, and fear nothing; you carry Caesar and his fortune in your boat. *Ib. 38*

The Ides of March have come.[2]
Ib. 63

[In answer to a question as to what sort of death was the best] A sudden death. *Ib.*

I came, I saw, I conquered.[3]
From SUETONIUS, *Lives of the Caesars, Julius, sec. 37*

You also, Brutus my son.[4] *Ib. 82*

It is not these well-fed long-haired men that I fear, but the pale and the hungry-looking.[5]
From PLUTARCH, *Lives, Antony, sec. 11*

LUCRETIUS[6]
[TITUS LUCRETIUS CARUS]
99–55 B.C.

Mother of Aeneas and his race, darling of men and gods, nurturing Venus.
De Rerum Natura (On the Nature of Things), bk. I, l. 1 (Invocation)

For thee the wonder-working earth puts forth sweet flowers. *Ib. 7*

So potent was religion in persuading to evil deeds.[7] *Ib. 101*

---

[1] Iacta alea est. Proverb quoted by Caesar as he crossed the Rubicon.
Also in SUETONIUS, *Lives of the Caesars, Julius.*
[2] See Shakespeare, *Julius Caesar I, ii, 18,* p. 253a.
[3] Veni, vidi, vici. Inscription displayed in Caesar's Pontic triumph.
Also in PLUTARCH, *Apothegms, Caesar.*
[4] Et tu, Brute. Suetonius reports that Caesar said this in Greek.
See Shakespeare, p. 255a.
[5] The reference is to Brutus and Cassius.
See Shakespeare, p. 253b.
[6] Translated by W. H. D. ROUSE.
[7] Tantum religio potuit suadere malorum. (He is referring to Agamemnon's sacrifice of his daughter Iphigenia.)

Nothing can be created from nothing.[1]

De Rerum Natura, bk. I, l. 155

The ring on the finger becomes thin beneath by wearing, the fall of dripping water hollows the stone.[2]   *Ib.* 314

Material objects are of two kinds, atoms and compounds of atoms. The atoms themselves cannot be swamped by any force, for they are preserved indefinitely by their absolute solidity.[3]
                                    Ib. 518

On a dark theme I trace verses full of light, touching all the muses' charm.[4]
                                    Ib. 933

Pleasant it is, when over a great sea the winds trouble the waters, to gaze from shore upon another's tribulation: not because any man's troubles are a delectable joy, but because to perceive from what ills you are free yourself is pleasant.[5]   *Ib. II,* 1

O miserable minds of men! O blind hearts! In what darkness of life, in what great dangers ye spend this little span of years! [1]

De Rerum Natura, bk. II, l. 14

Thus the sum of things is ever being renewed, and mortals live dependent one upon another. Some races increase, others diminish, and in a short space the generations of living creatures are changed and like runners hand on the torch of life.[2]   *Ib.* 75

Never trust her at any time, when the calm sea shows her false alluring smile.   *Ib.* 558

That fear of Acheron be sent packing which troubles the life of man from its deepest depths, suffuses all with the blackness of death, and leaves no delight clean and pure.   *Ib. III,* 37

For as children tremble and fear everything in the blind darkness, so we in the light sometimes fear what is no more to be feared than the things children in the dark hold in terror and imagine will come true.[3]   *Ib.* 87

Therefore death is nothing to us, it matters not one jot, since the nature of the mind is understood to be mortal.[4]
                                    Ib. 831

When immortal Death has taken mortal life.[5]   *Ib.* 869

Why dost thou not retire like a guest sated with the banquet of life, and with calm mind embrace, thou fool, a rest that knows no care? [6]   *Ib.* 938

---

[1] Nil posse creari de nilo.
See Shakespeare, p. 276b.
[2] Anulus in digito subter tenuatur habendo,
Stilicidi casus lapidem cavat.
See also the concluding lines of *Book IV:*
Nonne vides etiam guttas in saxa cadentis
Umoris longo in spatio pertundere saxa?
(Do you not see that even drops of water falling upon a stone in the long run beat a way through the stone?)
Drops of water hollow out a stone, a ring is worn thin by use. — OVID, *Ex Ponto IV, 10:5*
Also in PLUTARCH, *Of the Training of Children.*
The drop of rain maketh a hole in the stone, not by violence, but by oft falling. — HUGH LATIMER, *Seventh Sermon Before Edward VI* [1549]
The soft droppes of rain perce the hard marble. — JOHN LYLY, *Euphues* [1579]
And drizling drops that often doe redound,
The firmest flint doth in continuance wear.
    EDMUND SPENSER, *Amoretti* [1595],
                                  sonnet 18
[3] Translated by R. E. LATHAM.
[4] Translated by CYRIL BAILEY.
[5] It is a pleasure to stand upon the shore, and to see ships tost upon the sea: a pleasure to stand in the window of a castle, and to see a battle and the adventures thereof below: but no pleasure is comparable to the standing upon the vantage ground of truth . . . and to see the errors, and wanderings, and mists, and tempests, in the vale below. — FRANCIS BACON, *Essays* [1625], *Of Truth*

[1] Translated by CYRIL BAILEY.
Insensate care of mortals! Oh how false the argument which makes thee downward beat thy wings. — DANTE, *Divine Comedy* [c. 1300], *Paradiso XI, 1*
[2] Et quasi cursores vitae lampada tradunt.
[3] See Bacon, p. 208a.
[4] Nil igitur mors est ad nos neque pertinet hilum,
Quandoquidem natura animi mortalis habetur.
[5] Translated by CYRIL BAILEY.
Mortalem vitam mors cum immortalis ademit.
[6] Translated by CYRIL BAILEY.
See Horace, p. 120a, and Bryant, p. 574b.

No less long a time will he be no more, who has made an end of life with today's light.

De Rerum Natura, bk. III, l. 1092

What is food to one, is to others bitter poison.[1] *Ib. IV, 637*

From the heart of this fountain of delights wells up some bitter taste to choke them even amid the flowers.[2] *Ib. 1133*

But if one should guide his life by true principles, man's greatest wealth is to live on a little with contented mind; for a little is never lacking.

Ib. V, 1117

[Epicurus] set forth what is the highest good, towards which we all strive, and pointed out the past, whereby along a narrow track we may strain on towards it in a straight course.[3] *Ib. VI, 26*

GAIUS VALERIUS CATULLUS[4]
87 – c. 54 B.C.

To whom am I to present my pretty new book, freshly smoothed off with dry pumice stone? To you, Cornelius: for you used to think that my trifles were worth something, long ago.

Carmina I, l. 1

May it live and last for more than one century. *Ib. 10*

Mourn, ye Graces and Loves, and all you whom the Graces love. My lady's sparrow is dead, the sparrow, my lady's pet.[5] *III, 1*

---

[1] Ut quod ali cibus est aliis fuat acre venenum.
  What's one man's poison, signor,
  Is another's meat or drink.
    BEAUMONT AND FLETCHER, *Love's Cure* [1647], *act III, sc. ii*
[2] Translated by CYRIL BAILEY.
See Byron, p. 555a.
[3] Translated by CYRIL BAILEY.
The highest good [summum bonum]. See Cicero, p. 111b.
[4] Translated by F. W. CORNISH.
[5] Passer, deliciae meae puellae.
This is also the opening line of *Carmina II.*

Now he goes along the dark road, thither whence they say no one returns. *Carmina III, l. 11*

But these things are past and gone.[1] *IV, 25*

Let us live and love, my Lesbia, and value at a penny all the talk of crabbed old men. Suns may set and rise again: for us, when our brief light has set, there's the sleep of one everlasting night. Give me a thousand kisses.[2]

V, 1

Poor Catullus, you should cease your folly. *VIII, 1*

But you, Catullus, be resolved and firm. *Ib. 19*

And let her not look to find my love, as before; my love, which by her fault has dropped like a flower on the meadow's edge, when it has been touched by the plow passing by. *XI, 21*

Over head and heels.[3] *XX, 9*

Ah, what is more blessed than to put cares away! *XXXI, 7*

Whatever it is, wherever he is, whatever he is doing, he smiles: it is a malady he has, neither an elegant one as I think, nor in good taste. *XXXIX, 6*

There is nothing more silly than a silly laugh. *Ib. 16*

Oh this age! How tasteless and illbred it is! *XLIII, 8*

Now spring brings back balmy warmth.[4] *XLVI, 1*

Catullus, the worst of all poets, gives you [Marcus Tullius] his warmest thanks; he being as much the worst of all poets as you are the best of all patrons. *XLIX, 4*

---

[1] Sed haec prius fuere.
[2] Vivamus, mea Lesbia, atque amemus . . .
  Soles occidere et redire possunt:
  Nobis cum semel occidit brevis lux
  Nox est perpetua una dormienda.
  Da mi basia mille.
See Campion, p. 300a; Jonson, p. 302b; Herrick, p. 320a and 321a; and Fouché, p. 500a.
[3] Per caputque pedesque.
[4] Iam ver egelidos refert tepores.

He seems to me to be equal to a god, he, if it may be, seems to surpass the very gods, who sitting opposite you again gazes at you and hears you sweetly laughing.[1]   *Carmina LI, 1*

What an eloquent manikin! [2]
                              LIII, 5

I would see a little Torquatus, stretching his baby hands from his mother's lap, smile a sweet smile at his father with lips half parted.
                              LXI, 209

The evening is come; rise up, ye youths. Vesper from Olympus now at last is just raising his long-looked-for light.   *LXII, 1*

What is given by the gods more desirable than the fortunate hour? [3]
                              Ib. 30

Not unknown am I to the goddess [Venus] who mingles with her cares a sweet bitterness.   *LXVIII, 17*

It is not fit that men should be compared with gods.   *Ib. 141*

What a woman says to her ardent lover should be written in wind and running water.[4]   *LXX*

Leave off wishing to deserve any thanks from anyone, or thinking that anyone can ever become grateful.
                              LXXIII, 1

If a man can take any pleasure in recalling the thought of kindnesses done.   *LXXVI, 1*

It is difficult suddenly to lay aside a long-cherished love.   *Ib. 13*

O ye gods, grant me this in return for my piety.   *Ib. 26*

I hate and I love. Why I do so, perhaps you ask. I know not, but I feel it and I am in torment.[5]   *LXXXV, 1*

[1] See Sappho, p. 69b.
[2] Salaputtium disertum!
[3] Quid datur a divis felici optatius hora?
[4] See Sophocles, p. 83a.
[5] Odi et amo. Quare id faciam, fortasse requiris.
   Nescio, sed fieri sentio et excrucior.
   See Anacreon, p. 70a.

Wandering through many countries and over many seas, I come, my brother, to these sorrowful obsequies, to present you with the last guerdon of death, and speak, though in vain, to your silent ashes.   *Carmina CI, 1*

And forever, O my brother, hail and farewell! [1]   *Ib. 10*

But you shall not escape my iambics.[2]   *Fragment*

SALLUST
[GAIUS SALLUSTIUS CRISPUS]
86–34 B.C.

All our power lies in both mind and body; we employ the mind to rule, the body rather to serve; the one we have in common with the Gods, the other with the brutes.

The War with Catiline [c. 40 B.C.], sec. 1

The renown which riches or beauty confer is fleeting and frail; mental excellence is a splendid and lasting possession.   *Ib.*

Covetous of others' possessions, he [Catiline] was prodigal of his own.[3]
                              Ib. 5

Ambition drove many men to become false; to have one thought locked in the breast, another ready on the tongue.[4]   *Ib. 10*

In truth, prosperity tries the souls even of the wise.[5]   *Ib. 11*

To like and dislike the same things, that is indeed true friendship.[6]
                              Ib. 20

Thus in the highest position there is the least freedom of action.[7]   *Ib. 51*

[1] Atque in perpetuum, frater, ave atque vale.
[2] At non effugies meos iambos.
[3] Alieni appetens, sui profusus.
[4] See Euripides, p. 84b.
[5] Quippe secundae res sapientium animos fatigant.
[6] Idem velle atque idem nolle, ea demum firma amicitia est.
   See Plato, p. 92b.
[7] Ita in maxima fortuna minima licentia est.

On behalf of their country, their children, their altars, and their hearths.[1]

The War with Catiline
[c. 40 B.C.], sec. 59

The soul is the captain and ruler of the life of mortals.[2]

The War with Jugurtha
[c. 41 B.C.], sec 1

The splendid achievements of the intellect, like the soul, are everlasting.
Ib. 2

A city for sale and soon to perish if it finds a buyer![3]   *Ib. 35*

Punic faith.[4]   *Ib. 108*

Experience has shown that to be true which Appius[5] says in his verses, that every man is the architect of his own fortune.[6]

Speech to Caesar on the State, sec. 1

VIRGIL
[PUBLIUS VIRGILIUS MARO]
70–19 B.C.

A god has brought us this peace.
Eclogues I, l. 6

To compare great things with small.
Ib. 23

Happy old man![7]   *Ib. 46*

[1] Pro patria, pro liberis, pro aris atque focis suis.

[2] Dux atque imperator vitae mortalium animus est.

See *Speech to Caesar on the State* (below). See also Shakespeare, p. 253b; Tennyson, p. 653a; and Henley, p. 816a.

Be the proud captain still of thine own fate. — J. B. KENYON [1858–1924], *The Black Camel*

[3] Jugurtha's remark as he looked back at Rome upon being ordered by the senate to leave Italy.

[4] Punica fide (treachery).

[5] Appius Claudius Caecus, consul in 307 B.C., the earliest Roman writer known to us.

[6] See *The War with Jugurtha 1* (above) and Aristotle, p. 98a.

His own character is the arbiter of everyone's fortune. — PUBLILIUS SYRUS [c. 42 B.C.], *Maxim 283*

The brave man carves out his fortune, and every man is the son of his own works. — CERVANTES, *Don Quixote, pt. I* [1605], bk. I, ch. 4

See Bacon, p. 209a.

[7] Fortunate senex!

Ah Corydon, Corydon, what madness has caught you?

Eclogues II, 69

With Jove I begin.[1]   *Ib. III, 60*

A sad thing is a wolf in the fold, rain on ripe corn, wind in the trees, the anger of Amaryllis.   *Ib. 80*

A snake lurks in the grass.   *Ib. 93*

Let us raise a somewhat loftier strain.[2]   *Ib. IV, 1*

The great cycle of the ages is renewed. Now the Maiden returns, returns the Golden Age; a new generation now descends from heaven.[3]   *Ib. 5*

We have made you [Priapus] of marble for the time being.
Ib. VII, 35

We are not all capable of everything.[4]   *Ib. VIII, 63*

Draw Daphnis from the town, my songs, draw Daphnis home.   *Ib. 68*

Hylax barks in the doorway.
Ib. 107

Your descendants shall gather your fruits.[5]   *Ib. IX, 50*

Time bears away all things, even our minds.   *Ib. 51*

Let us go singing as far as we go: the road will be less tedious.   *Ib. 64*

This last labor grant me, O Arethusa.   *Ib. X, 1*

What if Amyntas is dark? Violets are dark, too, and hyacinths.   *Ib. 38*

[1] Ab Iove principium.

[2] Paulo maiora canamus!

[3] Magnus ab integro saeculorum nascitur ordo.
Iam redit et Virgo, redeunt Saturnia regna;
Iam nova progenies caelo demittitur alto.

Interpreted by the Middle Ages as a prophecy of the birth of Christ. DANTE cites the lines in *Purgatorio, canto 22, l. 70.*

A phrase altered from the first line (Novus ordo seclorum) appears on the reverse of the Great Seal of the United States of America (first used on the silver dollar certificates, series of 1935). Virgil supplied the Latin for other phrases of the Great Seal. See p. 117a and p. 119b.

See Shelley, p. 570b.

[4] Non omnia possumus omnes.

[5] Carpent tua poma nepotes.

Love conquers all things; let us too surrender to Love.[1]   *Ib.* 69

Utmost [farthest] Thule.[2]
Georgics I, l. 30

Look with favor upon a bold beginning.[3]   *Ib.* 40

O farmers, pray that your summers be wet and your winters clear.
Ib. 100

Practice and thought might gradually forge many an art.   *Ib.* 133

Thrice they tried to pile Ossa on Pelion, yes, and roll up leafy Olympus upon Ossa; thrice the Father of Heaven split the mountains apart with his thunderbolt.[4]   *Ib.* 281

Frogs in the marsh mud drone their old lament.   *Ib.* 378

Not every soil can bear all things.
Ib. II, 109

Ah too fortunate farmers, if they knew their own good fortune!
Ib. 458

May the countryside and the gliding valley streams content me. Lost to fame, let me love river and woodland.
Ib. 485

Happy the man who could search out the causes of things.[5]   *Ib.* 490

And no less happy he who knows the

rural gods — Pan, and old Sylvanus, and the sisterhood of Nymphs.
Georgics II, l. 493

This life the old Sabines knew long ago; Remus knew it, and his brother.
Ib. 532

Years grow cold to love.
Ib. III, 97

Time is flying never to return.[1]
Ib. 284

All aglow is the work.[2]
Ib. IV, 169

A sudden madness came down upon the unwary lover [Orpheus] — forgivable, surely, if Death knew how to forgive.   *Ib.* 488

I who once played shepherds' songs and in my brash youth sang of you, O Tityrus, beneath the spreading beech.[3]
Ib. 565

Arms and the man I sing.[4]
Aeneid, bk. I, l. 1

Can heavenly minds yield to such rage?   *Ib.* 11

So vast was the struggle to found the Roman state.   *Ib.* 33

Night, pitch-black, lies upon the deep.[5]   *Ib.* 89

O thrice four times blessed! [6]
Ib. 94

Fury provides arms.   *Ib.* 150

You have suffered worse things; God will put an end to these also.
Ib. 199

Perhaps some day it will be pleasant to remember even this.[7]   *Ib.* 203

The organizer a woman.[8]   *Ib.* 364

---

[1] Omnia vincit amor: et nos cedamus amori. See Sophocles, pp. 82a and 82b, and Chaucer, p. 166a.

[2] Ultima Thule.
The phrase, designating a far-off land, has been in use since the Greek mariner Pytheas discovered in the fourth century B.C. an island he named Thule six days north of England, thought to be Iceland. See Seneca, p. 131a, and Thomson, p. 419b.

[3] Audacibus annue coeptis.
This phrase also (see note p. 116b) was adapted for use on the reverse of the Great Seal of the United States of America: Annuit coeptis. See p. 119b for the Latin on the face of the Great Seal.

[4] See Homer, p. 66a.

[5] Felix qui potuit rerum cognoscere causas.
The reference is apparently to the scientist-philosopher-poet Lucretius.

[1] Fugit inreparabile tempus.

[2] Fervet opus.

[3] Tityrus is also referred to in *Eclogues I, 1.*

[4] Arma virumque cano.

[5] See *Genesis 1:2,* p. 5a.

[6] O terque quaterque beati!

[7] Forsan et haec olim meminisse iuvabit. See Homer, p. 66b.

[8] Dux femina facti.

Her walk revealed her as a true goddess. *Aeneid, bk. I, l. 405*

How happy those whose walls already rise! *Ib. 437*

Here are the tears of things; mortality touches the heart.[1] *Ib. 462*

I make no distinction between Trojan and Tyrian. *Ib. 574*

A mind aware of its own rectitude.[2] *Ib. 604*

As long as rivers shall run down to the sea, or shadows touch the mountain slopes, or stars graze in the vault of heaven, so long shall your honor, your name, your praises endure. *Ib. 607*

I have known sorrow and learned to aid the wretched. *Ib. 630*

Unspeakable, O Queen, is the sorrow you bid me renew. *Ib. II, 3*

Whatever it is, I fear Greeks even when they bring gifts.[3] *Ib. 49*

From a single crime know the nation. *Ib. 65*

I shudder to say it.[4] *Ib. 204*

O fatherland, O Ilium home of the gods, O Troy walls famed in battle! *Ib. 241*

Ucalegon's afire next door.[5] *Ib. 311*

We have been Trojans; Troy has been. *Ib. 325*

There is but one safety to the vanquished — to hope not safety. *Ib. 354*

Our foes will provide us with arms. *Ib. 391*

[1] Sunt lacrimae rerum et mentem mortalia tangunt.
[2] The mind, conscious of rectitude, laughed to scorn the falsehood of report. — OVID [43 B.C.–A.D. 18], *Fasti, bk. IV, l. 311*
[3] Quidquid id est, timeo Danaos et dona ferentis.
[4] Horresco referens.
[5] Iam proximus ardet Ucalegon.

The gods thought otherwise.[1] *Aeneid, bk. II, l. 428*

Thrice would I have thrown my arms about her neck, and thrice the ghost embraced fled from my grasp: like a fluttering breeze, like a fleeting dream.[2] *Ib. 793*

O accurst craving for gold! *Ib. III, 57*

Rumor flies.[3] *Ib. 121*

I feel again a spark of that ancient flame.[4] *Ib. IV, 23*

Deep in her breast lives the silent wound. *Ib. 67*

A woman is always a fickle, unstable thing.[5] *Ib. 569*

Arise from my bones, avenger of these wrongs! *Ib. 625*

Thus, thus, it is joy to pass to the world below.[6] *Ib. 660*

Naked in death upon an unknown shore. *Ib. V, 871*

Yield not to evils, but attack all the more boldly. *Ib. VI, 95*

It is easy to go down into Hell; night and day, the gates of dark Death stand wide; but to climb back again, to retrace one's steps to the upper air — there's the rub, the task.[7] *Ib. 126*

[1] Dis aliter visum.
[2] Virgil here translates HOMER, *Odyssey, bk. XI, l. 204.* See p. 66a.
[3] Fama volat.
[4] Agnosco veteris vestigia flammae. See Dante, p. 161b.
[5] Varium et mutabile semper femina.
Woman often changes; foolish the man who trusts her. — FRANCIS I OF FRANCE [1494–1547], written by him with his ring on a window of the château of Chambord (BRANTÔME, *Œuvres VII, 395*)
La donna è mobile. — PIAVE, *Libretto of* VERDI's *Rigoletto,* Duke's song
See Scott, p. 519b.
[6] Sic, sic, iuvat ire sub umbras.
[7]   Facilis descensus Averni:
Noctes atque dies patet atri ianua Ditis;
Sed revocare gradum superasque evadere ad auras,
Hoc opus, hic labor est.
See Bion, p. 104b, and note.

Faithful Achates.[1]
>*Aeneid, bk. VI, l. 158*
>*and elsewhere*

Death's brother, Sleep.[2]   *Ib. 278*

Had I a hundred tongues, a hundred lips, a throat of iron and a chest of brass, I could not tell men's countless sufferings.   *Ib. 298*

The swamp of Styx, by which the gods take oath.   *Ib. 323*

Unwillingly I left your land, O Queen.[3]   *Ib. 460*

That happy place, the green groves of the dwelling of the blest.   *Ib. 638*

The spirit within nourishes, and the mind, diffused through all the members, sways the mass and mingles with the whole frame.   *Ib. 726*

Each of us bears his own Hell.[4]
>*Ib. 743*

Others, I take it, will work better with breathing bronze and draw living faces from marble; others will plead at law with greater eloquence, or measure the pathways of the sky, or forecast the rising stars. Be it your concern, Roman, to rule the nations under law (this is your proper skill) and establish the way of peace; to spare the conquered and put down the mighty from their seat.[5]
>*Ib. 847*

Give me handfuls of lilies to scatter.[6]
>*Ib. 883*

There are two gates of Sleep. One is of horn, easy of passage for the shades of truth; the other, of gleaming white ivory, permits false dreams to ascend to the upper air.[7]   *Ib. 893*

Prayed to the Genius of the place.
>*Ib. VII, 136*

---

[1] Fidus Achates. Proverbial for a trusty friend; Achates was the faithful comrade of Aeneas.
[2] See Homer, p. 64a.
[3] Aeneas to the ghost of Dido, who had killed herself when he left her.
[4] See Marlowe, p. 213a, and note.
[5] See Milton, p. 339b.
[6] Quoted by DANTE in *The Divine Comedy, Purgatorio, canto 30, l. 21.*
[7] See Homer, p. 67a.

We descend from Jove; in ancestral Jove Troy's sons rejoice.
>*Aeneid, bk. VII, l. 219*

If I cannot bend Heaven, I shall move Hell.   *Ib. 312*

An old story, but the glory of it is forever.   *Ib. IX, 79*

To have died once is enough.
>*Ib. 140*

I cannot bear a mother's tears.
>*Ib. 289*

Good speed to your youthful valor, boy! So shall you scale the stars! [1]
>*Ib. 641*

Fortune favors the brave.[2]
>*Ib. X, 284*

Dying dreams of his sweet Argos.[3]
>*Ib. 782*

Believe one who has proved it. Believe an expert.[4]   *Ib. XI, 283*

His limbs were cold in death; his spirit fled with a groan, indignant, to the shades below.   *Ib. XII, 951*

One composed of many.[5]
>*Minor Poems, Moretum, l. 104*

Death twitches my ear. "Live," he says; "I am coming." [6]
>*Minor Poems, Copa, l. 38*

---

[1] Macte nova virtute, puer, sic itur ad astra.
See Dante, p. 161b.
[2] Audentes fortuna iuvat.
See Menander, p. 102b, and Terence, p. 109a.
[3] Dulces moriens reminiscitur Argos.
[4] Experto credite.
Believe an expert; believe one who has had experience. — ST. BERNARD, *Epistle 106*
Believe the experienced Robert. Believe Robert, who has tried it. — ROBERT BURTON, *Anatomy of Melancholy* [1621–1651], *Introduction*
[5] E pluribus unum.
Adapted (E pluribus unum) for the motto on the face of the Great Seal of the United States, adopted June 20, 1782. For the Latin Virgil supplied for the reverse of the Great Seal, see p. 116b and p. 117a.
[6] Quoted by Justice Oliver Wendell Holmes in a radio address on his ninetieth birthday, March 8, 1931.

HORACE
[QUINTUS HORATIUS FLACCUS]
65 – 8 B.C.

How comes it, Maecenas, that no man living is content with the lot that either his choice has given him, or chance has thrown in his way, but each has praise for those who follow other paths?

> *Satires, bk. I* [35 B.C.], *satire i, l. 1*

The story's about you.[1]   *Ib. 69*

There is measure in all things.[2]

> *Ib. 106*

We rarely find anyone who can say he has lived a happy life, and who, content with his life, can retire from the world like a satisfied guest.[3]   *Ib. 117*

And all that tribe.[4]   *Ib. ii, 2*

The limbs of a dismembered poet.[5]

> *Ib. iv, 62*

A man without a flaw.[6]   *Ib. v, 32*

Life grants nothing to us mortals without hard work.   *Ib. ix, 59*

As crazy as hauling timber into the woods.[7]   *Ib. x, 34*

Simplicity and charm.[8]   *Ib. 44*

This used to be among my prayers.[9] — a piece of land not so very large, which would contain a garden, and near the house a spring of ever-flowing water, and beyond these a bit of wood.

> *Ib. bk. II* [30 B.C.], *satire vi, l. 1*

O nights and suppers of the gods![10]

> *Ib. 65*

---

[1] De te fabula.

[2] Est modus in rebus. See The Seven Sages, p. 68b.

[3] See Solon, p. 69a; Aeschylus, p. 78b; Sophocles, p. 81b; Lucretius, p. 113b; and Bryant, p. 574b.

[4] Hoc genus omne.

[5] Disiecti membra poetae. The reference is to Orpheus torn apart by the Maenads.

[6] Ad unguem factus homo.

[7] Carrying coals to Newcastle. — *Proverb*
Bringing owls to Athens. — ARISTOPHANES, *Birds, l. 301*

[8] Molle atque facetum. This refers to Virgil's poetry.

[9] Hoc erat in votis.

[10] O noctes cenaeque deum!

In Rome you long for the country; in the country — oh inconstant! — you praise the distant city to the stars.

> *Satires, bk. II, satire vii, l. 28*

Happy the man who far from schemes of business, like the early generations of mankind, works his ancestral acres with oxen of his own breeding, from all usury free.[1]

> *Epodes* [c. 29 B.C.], *II, st. 1*

You ask me why a soft numbness diffuses all my inmost senses with deep oblivion, as though with thirsty throat I'd drained the cup that brings the sleep of Lethe.[2]   *Ib. XIV, 1*

But if you name me among the lyric bards, I shall strike the stars with my exalted head.

> *Odes, bk. I* [23 B.C.], *ode i, last lines*

The half of my own soul.[3]

> *Ib. iii, 8*

No ascent is too steep for mortals. Heaven itself we seek in our folly.

> *Ib. 37*

Pale Death with impartial tread beats at the poor man's cottage door and at the palaces of kings.   *Ib. iv, 13*

Life's brief span forbids us to enter on far-reaching hopes.[4]   *Ib. 15*

What slender youth, bedewed with liquid odors,
Courts thee on roses in some pleasant cave,
Pyrrha? For whom bind'st thou
In wreaths thy golden hair,
Plain in thy neatness?[5]   *Ib. v, 1*

Never despair.[6]   *Ib. vii, 27*

---

[1] See Pope, p. 402a.

[2] See Keats, p. 582a.

[3] Animae dimidium meae. The reference is to Virgil.
See Aristotle, p. 97a, and note.

[4] Vitae summa brevis spem nos vetat incohare longam.
See Dowson, p. 890a.

[5] Translated by JOHN MILTON [1608–1674].

[6] Nil desperandum.

Tomorrow once again we sail the Ocean Sea.[1]

Odes, bk. I, ode vii, last line

Leave all else to the gods.[2]

Ib. ix, 9

Cease to ask what the morrow will bring forth, and set down as gain each day that Fortune grants.[3]   *Ib. 13*

Seize the day, put no trust in the morrow![4]

Ib. xi, last line

Happy, thrice happy and more, are they whom an unbroken bond unites and whose love shall know no sundering quarrels so long as they shall live.

Ib. xiii, 17

O fairer daughter of a fair mother![5]

Ib. xvi, 1

The pure in life and free from sin.[6]

Ib. xxii, 1

What restraint or limit should there be to grief for one so dear?

Ib. xxiv, 1

Grant me, sound of body and of mind, to pass an old age lacking neither honor nor the lyre.[7]

Ib. xxxi, last lines

A grudging and infrequent worshipper of the gods.[8]   *Ib. xxxiv, 1*

Now is the time for drinking, now the time to beat the earth with unfettered foot.[9]   *Ib. xxxvii, 1*

Persian luxury, boy, I hate.[10]

Ib. xxxviii, 1

Cease your efforts to find where the last rose lingers.[1]

Odes, bk. I, ode xxxviii, l. 3

In adversity remember to keep an even mind.[2]

Ib. bk. II [23 B.C.], ode iii, l. 1

We are all driven into the same fold.[3]   *Ib. 25*

Whoever cultivates the golden mean [4] avoids both the poverty of a hovel and the envy of a palace.   *Ib. x, 5*

It is the mountaintop that the lightning strikes.   *Ib. 11*

Nor does Apollo always stretch the bow.[5]   *Ib. 19*

Alas, Postumus, Postumus, the fleeting years slip by.[6]   *Ib. xiv, 1*

No lot is altogether happy.[7]

Ib. xvi, 27

I hate the common herd of men and keep them afar. Let there be sacred silence: I, the Muses' priest, sing for girls and boys songs not heard before.

Ib. bk. III [23 B.C.], ode i, l. 1

Dark Care sits enthroned behind the Knight.[8]   *Ib. 40*

It is sweet and honorable to die for one's country.[9]   *Ib. ii, 13*

The man who is tenacious of purpose in a rightful cause is not shaken from his firm resolve by the frenzy of his fel-

---

[1] Cras ingens iterabimus aequor.
Translated by S. E. MORISON.
[2] Permitte divis cetera.
[3] See *Matthew 6:34*, p. 41a, and Publilius Syrus, p. 126b.
[4] Carpe diem, quam minimum credula postero. See Ronsard, p. 188a; Spenser, p. 200a; and Herrick, p. 320b.
[5] O matre pulchra filia pulchrior.
[6] Integer vitae scelerisque purus.
[7] Not to be tuneless in old age! — DOBSON [1840–1921], *Henry Wadsworth Longfellow*
[8] Parcus deorum cultor et infrequens.
[9] Nunc est bibendum, nunc pede libero puisanda tellus. Ode on the death of Cleopatra.
[10] Persicos odi, puer, apparatus.

[1] Mitte sectari, rosa quo locorum
Sera moretur.
[2] Aequam memento rebus in arduis
Servare mentem.
[3] Omnes eodem cogimur.
[4] Auream quisquis mediocritatem
Diliget.
Keep the golden mean. — PUBLILIUS SYRUS [c. 42 B.C.], *Maxim 1072*
See The Seven Sages, p. 68b; Terence, p. 108a; and Voltaire, p. 417b.
[5] Neque semper arcum
Tendit Apollo.
[6] Eheu fugaces, Postume, Postume,
Labuntur anni.
[7] Nihil est ab omni
Parte beatum.
[8] Post equitem sedet atra cura.
[9] Dulce et decorum est pro patria mori.
See Homer, p. 64a.

low citizens clamoring for what is wrong, or by the tyrant's threatening countenance.[1]

    Odes, bk. III, ode iii, l. 1

Force without wisdom falls of its own weight.   *Ib. iv, 65*

Our sires' age was worse than our grandsires'. We their sons are more worthless than they: so in our turn we shall give the world a progeny yet more corrupt.   *Ib. vi, 46*

Skilled in the works of both languages.   *Ib. viii, 5*

With you I should love to live, with you be ready to die.[2]

    Ib. ix, last line

Gloriously perjured, a maiden famous to all time.[3]   *Ib. xi, 35*

O fount Bandusian, more sparkling than glass.[4]   *Ib. xiii, 1*

I would not have borne this in my hot youth when Plancus was consul.[5]

    Ib. xiv, 27

A pauper in the midst of wealth.[6]

    Ib. xvi, 28

He will through life be master of himself and a happy man who from day to day can have said, "I have lived: tomorrow the Father may fill the sky with black clouds or with cloudless sunshine." [7]   *Ib. xxix, 41*

---

[1] See Fabius Maximus, p. 105a.

[2] Tecum vivere amem, tecum obeam libens.

[3] Hypermnestra.

Swift chose Splendide mendax (Gloriously perjured) as Gulliver's motto.

[4] O fons Bandusiae splendidior vitro.

[5] In my hot youth, when George the Third was king. — Byron, *Don Juan* [1819–1824], *canto 1, st. 212*

[6] Magnus inter opes inops.

[7]   Ille potens sui

Laetusque deget, cui licet in diem

Dixisse "Vixi: cras vel atra

Nube polum pater occupato

Vel sole puro."

Tomorrow let my sun his beams display

Or in clouds hide them; I have lived my day.

    Cowley, *Discourse XI, Of Myself*
        [1661], *st. 11*

See Dryden, p. 369b, and Sydney Smith, p. 523b.

I have built a monument more lasting than bronze.

    Odes, bk. III, ode xxx, l. 1

I shall not wholly die.[1]   *Ib. 6*

I am not what I was in the reign of the good Cinara. Forbear, cruel mother of sweet loves.[2]

    Odes, bk. IV [13 B.C.], *ode i, l. 3*

The centuries roll back to the ancient age of gold.[3]   *Ib. ii, 39*

We are but dust and shadow.

    Ib. vii, 16

Many brave men lived before Agamemnon; but all are overwhelmed in eternal night, unwept, unknown, because they lack a sacred poet.[4]

    Ib. ix, 25

It is not the rich man you should properly call happy, but him who knows how to use with wisdom the blessings of the gods, to endure hard poverty, and who fears dishonor worse than death, and is not afraid to die for cherished friends or fatherland.

    Ib. 45

It is sweet to let the mind unbend on occasion.[5]   *Ib. xii, 27*

---

[1] Non omnis moriar.

[2] Non sum qualis eram bonae

Sub regno Cinarae. Desine, dulcium

Mater saeva Cupidinum.

Mater saeva Cupidinum. — *Odes, bk. I, xix, l. 1*

See Dowson, p. 890a.

[3] See Milton, p. 334a, and Macaulay, p. 596b.

The golden age, which a blind tradition has hitherto placed in the past, is before us. — C. H. Saint-Simon [1760–1825], quoted by Carlyle in *Sartor Resartus, bk. III, ch. 5*

[4] How many, famous while they lived, utterly forgotten for want of writers! — Boethius [A.D. c. 480–524], *De Consolatione Philosophiae II, 7*

See Homer, p. 64b; Scott, p. 519a; and Byron, p. 557b.

Brave men were living before Agamemnon

And since, exceeding valorous and sage,

A good deal like him too, but quite the same none;

But then they shone not on the poet's page.

    Byron, *Don Juan, canto I, st. 5*

[5] See Menander, p. 102a; Montaigne, p. 191a; and Bacon, p. 209a.

I am not bound over to swear allegiance to any master; where the storm drives me I turn in for shelter.
Epistles, bk. I, epistle i, l. 14

To flee vice is the beginning of virtue, and to have got rid of folly is the beginning of wisdom.   *Ib. 41*

Make money, money by fair means if you can, if not, by any means money.[1]
Ib. 66

The people are a many-headed beast.[2]   *Ib. 76*

He who has begun has half done. Dare to be wise; begin![3]   *Ib. ii. 40*

The covetous man is ever in want.
Ib. 56

Anger is a short madness.   *Ib. 62*

Think to yourself that every day is your last; the hour to which you do not look forward will come as a welcome surprise. As for me, when you want a good laugh, you will find me, in a fine state, fat and sleek, a true hog of Epicurus' herd.[4]   *Ib. iv, 13*

You may drive out Nature with a pitchfork, yet she still will hurry back.
Epistles, bk. I, epistle x, l. 24

They change their clime, not their disposition, who run across the sea.
Ib. xi, 27

He is not poor who has enough of things to use. If it is well with your belly, chest and feet, the wealth of kings can give you nothing more.
Ib. xii, 4

Harmony in discord.[1]   *Ib. 19*

For joys fall not to the rich alone, nor has he lived ill, who from birth to death has passed unknown.
Ib. xvii, 9

It is not everyone that can get to Corinth.[2]   *Ib. 36*

Once a word has been allowed to escape, it cannot be recalled.[3]
Ib. xviii, 71

It is your concern when your neighbor's wall is on fire.   *Ib. 84*

No poems can please for long or live that are written by water-drinkers.
Ib. xix, 2

O imitators, you slavish herd!
Ib. 19

---

[1] Get money; still get money, boy, no matter by what means. — BEN JONSON, *Every Man in His Humor* [1598], *act II, sc. iii*

[2] Belua multorum es capitum.

PLATO [c. 429–347 B.C.] describes the multitude as a "great strong beast." — *The Republic, bk. VI, 493–B*

The multitude of the gross people, being a beast of many heads. — ERASMUS [1465–1536], *Adagia, no. 122*

O weak trust of the many-headed multitude. — SIR PHILIP SIDNEY, *Arcadia* [1590], *bk. II*

See Machiavelli, p. 177b, and Shakespeare, pp. 241a, and 289b.

The beast of many heads, the staggering multitude. — MARSTON AND WEBSTER, *The Malcontent* [1604], *act III, sc. iii*

If there be any among those common objects of hatred I do contemn and laugh at, it is that great enemy of reason, virtue, and religion, the multitude . . . one great beast and a monstrosity more prodigious than Hydra. — SIR THOMAS BROWNE, *Religio Medici* [1643], *II, 1*

Sir, your people is a great beast. — *Attributed to* ALEXANDER HAMILTON [1757–1804]

[3] See Plato, p. 94a, and note.

[4] See Chaucer, p. 166b.

[1] Concordia discors.

[2] A rendering of a Greek proverb, "It's not everyone that can make the voyage to Corinth," which referred to the expense of the life there.

There is but one road that leads to Corinth. — WALTER PATER, *Marius the Epicurean* [1885], *ch. 24*

[3] Semel emissum volat irrevocabile verbum.

The written word, unpublished, can be destroyed, but the spoken word can never be recalled. — HORACE, *Ars Poetica* [c. 8 B.C.], *l. 389*

It is as easy to recall a stone thrown violently from the hand as a word which has left your tongue. — MENANDER [343–292 B.C.], *Fragment 1092K*

Four things come not back: the spoken word; the sped arrow; time past; the neglected opportunity. — OMAR IBN AL-HALIF, *Aphorism*

A word once spoken revoked cannot be. — ALEXANDER BARCLAY, *Shyp of Folys* [1509], *p. 108*

Thoughts unexpressed may sometimes fall
    back dead;
But God Himself can't kill them when
    they're said.
       WILL CARLETON [1845–1912], *The First Settler's Story, st. 21*

And seek for truth in the groves of Academe.[1]

Epistles, bk. II [14 B.C.], *epistle ii, l. 45*

Barefaced poverty drove me to writing verses. *Ib. 51*

The years as they pass plunder us of one thing after another. *Ib. 55*

I have to submit to much in order to pacify the touchy tribe of poets.[2] *Ib. 102*

"Painters and poets," you say, "have always had an equal license in bold invention." We know; we claim the liberty for ourselves and in turn we give it to others.

Ib. bk. III (Ars Poetica) [*c.* 8 B.C.], *l. 9*

It was a wine jar when the molding began: as the wheel runs round why does it turn out a water pitcher? *Ib. 21*

It is when I struggle to be brief that I become obscure. *Ib. 25*

Scholars dispute and the case is still before the courts.[3] *Ib. 78*

Foot and a half long words.[4] *Ib. 97*

Taught or untaught, we all scribble poetry. *Ib. 117*

The mountains will be in labor, and a ridiculous mouse will be brought forth.[5] *Ib. 139*

From the egg.[6] *Ib. 147*

In the midst of things.[7] *Ib. 148*

A praiser of past time.[8] *Ib. 173*

Let a play have five acts, neither more nor less.

Epistles, bk. III (Ars Poetica), l. 189

Turn the pages of your Greek models night and day.[1] *Ib. 268*

He wins every hand who mingles profit with pleasure, by delighting and instructing the reader at the same time. *Ib. 343*

Sometimes even good old Homer nods.[2] *Ib. 359*

As in painting, so in poetry.[3] *Ib. 361*

He has defiled his father's grave. *Ib. 471*

AUGUSTUS CAESAR
63 B.C. – A.D. 14

Quintilius Varus, give me back my legions![4]

From SUETONIUS, *Augustus, sec. 23*

More haste, less speed.[5] *Ib. 25*

Well done is quickly done.[6] *Ib.*

I found Rome a city of bricks and left it a city of marble. *Ib. 28*

After this time I surpassed all others in authority, but I had no more power than the others who were also my colleagues in office. *Res Gestae 34*

Young men, hear an old man to whom old men hearkened when he was young.

From PLUTARCH, *Apothegms, Caesar Augustus*

---

[1] Atque inter silvas Academi quaerere verum.
[2] Genus irritabile vatum.
[3] Grammatici certant et adhuc sub iudice lis est.
[4] Sesquipedalia verba.
[5] Parturient montes, nascetur ridiculus mus. See Aesop, p. 76a, and note.
[6] Ab ovo.
Helen, the cause of the Trojan War, sprang from an egg engendered by Leda and the Swan (Zeus).
[7] In medias res.
[8] Laudator temporis acti.

[1] See Hsieh Ho, p. 148a.
[2] Quandoque bonus dormitat Homerus.
Homer himself, in a long work, may sleep. — ROBERT HERRICK, *Hesperides* [1648], *no. 95*
See Pope, p. 402b.
[3] Ut pictura poesis.
[4] Quintili Vare, legiones redde!
[5] A Greek proverb, a familiar rendering of which is: Festina lente.
[6] A Latin proverb: Sat celeriter fieri quidquid fiat satis bene, See Publilius Syrus, p. 125a, and Anonymous, p. 150a.

LIVY
[TITUS LIVIUS]
59 B.C. — A.D. 17

We can endure neither our evils nor their cures.[1]   *History, Prologue*

Better late than never.[2]
Ib. bk. IV, sec. 23

Woe to the vanquished.[3]
Ib. V, 48

Beyond the Alps lies Italy.[4]
Ib. XXI, 30

PUBLILIUS SYRUS[5]
fl. first century B.C.

As men, we are all equal in the presence of death.   *Maxim 1*

He doubly benefits the needy who gives quickly.[6]   *Maxim 6*

To do two things at once is to do neither.   *Maxim 7*

A god could hardly love and be wise.[7]   *Maxim 25*

The loss which is unknown is no loss at all.[8]   *Maxim 38*

A good reputation is more valuable than money.[9]   *Maxim 108*

It is well to moor your bark with two anchors.   *Maxim 119*

---

[1] The two reasons for writing a history.
[2] Potius sero quam numquam.
It is better to learn late than never. — PUBLILIUS SYRUS, *Maxim 864*
[3] Vae victis.
[4] In conspectu Alpes habeant, quarum alterum latus Italiae sit.
Au-delà des Alpes est l'Italie. — NAPOLEON [1797]
[5] Commonly called Publius, but spelled Publilius by PLINY in his *Natural History, 35, sec. 199.* Translated mainly by DARIUS LYMAN. The numbers are those of the translator.
[6] See Augustus Caesar, p. 124b, and Anonymous, p. 150a.
[7] It is impossible to love and be wise. — FRANCIS BACON, *Essays* [1597–1625], *Of Love*
[8] See Shakespeare, p. 274b.
[9] See *Ecclesiastes 7:1*, p. 28a, and Bacon, p. 208b.
A good name is better than riches. — CERVANTES, *Don Quixote, pt. II* [1615], *bk. II, ch. 33*

Many receive advice, few profit by it.   *Maxim 149*

While we stop to think, we often miss our opportunity.   *Maxim 185*

Whatever you can lose, you should reckon of no account.   *Maxim 191*

For a good cause, wrongdoing is virtuous.[1]   *Maxim 244*

You should hammer your iron when it is glowing hot.[2]   *Maxim 262*

What is left when honor is lost?
Maxim 265

A fair exterior is a silent recommendation.   *Maxim 267*

Fortune is not satisfied with inflicting one calamity.   *Maxim 274*

When Fortune is on our side, popular favor bears her company.
Maxim 275

When Fortune flatters, she does it to betray.[3]   *Maxim 277*

Fortune is like glass — the brighter the glitter, the more easily broken.
Maxim 280

It is more easy to get a favor from Fortune than to keep it.
Maxim 282

There are some remedies worse than the disease.[4]   *Maxim 301*

A cock has great influence on his own dunghill.[5]   *Maxim 357*

---

[1] Honesta turpitudo est pro causa bona.
[2] When the iron is hot, strike. — JOHN HEYWOOD, *Proverbs* [1546], *pt. I, ch. 2*
Strike whilst the iron is hot. — RABELAIS, *bk. II* [1534], *ch. 31*
Nothing like striking while the iron is hot. — CERVANTES, *Don Quixote, pt. II* [1615], *bk. IV, ch. 71*
[3] See Shakespeare, p. 236b.
[4] Marius said, "I see the cure is not worth the pain." — PLUTARCH [A.D. 46–120], *Lives, Caius Marius*
The remedy is worse than the disease. — FRANCIS BACON, *Essays* [1597–1625], *Of Seditions*
I find the medicine worse than the malady. — BEAUMONT AND FLETCHER, *Love's Cure* [1647], *act III, sc. ii*
[5] Every cocke is proud on his owne dunghill. — JOHN HEYWOOD, *Proverbs* [1546], *pt. I, ch. 11*

Anyone can hold the helm when the sea is calm.[1] *Maxim 358*

The bow too tensely strung is easily broken. *Maxim 388*

Treat your friend as if he might become an enemy.[2] *Maxim 402*

No pleasure endures unseasoned by variety.[3] *Maxim 406*

The judge is condemned when the criminal is absolved.[4] *Maxim 407*

Practice is the best of all instructors.[5] *Maxim 439*

He who is bent on doing evil can never want occasion. *Maxim 459*

Never find your delight in another's misfortune. *Maxim 467*

It is a bad plan that admits of no modification. *Maxim 469*

It is an unhappy lot which finds no enemies. *Maxim 499*

The fear of death is more to be dreaded than death itself.[6] *Maxim 511*

A rolling stone gathers no moss.[7] *Maxim 524*

Never promise more than you can perform. *Maxim 528*

No one should be judge in his own case.[8] *Maxim 545*

Necessity knows no law except to prevail.[1] *Maxim 553*

Nothing can be done at once hastily and prudently.[2] *Maxim 557*

We desire nothing so much as what we ought not to have. *Maxim 559*

It is only the ignorant who despise education. *Maxim 571*

Do not turn back when you are just at the goal.[3] *Maxim 580*

It is not every question that deserves an answer. *Maxim 581*

No man is happy who does not think himself so.[4] *Maxim 584*

Never thrust your own sickle into another's corn.[5] *Maxim 593*

You cannot put the same shoe on every foot. *Maxim 596*

Every day should be passed as if it were to be our last.[6] *Maxim 633*

Money alone sets all the world in motion. *Maxim 656*

You should go to a pear tree for pears, not to an elm.[7] *Maxim 674*

[1] See Shakespeare, p. 267b.
[2] Treat your friend as if he will one day be your enemy, and your enemy as if he will one day be your friend. — LABERIUS [105–43 B.C.], *Fragment*
See Sophocles, p. 81a.
[3] See Cowper, p. 458a.
[4] Iudex damnatur ubi nocens absolvitur — motto adopted for the *Edinburgh Review*.
[5] Practice makes perfect. — *Proverb*
The saying "Practice is everything" is Periander's. — DIOGENES LAERTIUS [c. 200 A.D.], *Periander 6*
[6] See Shakespeare, p. 271a.
[7] The rolling stone never gathereth mosse. — JOHN HEYWOOD, *Proverbs* [1546], *pt. I, ch. 11*
The stone that is rolling can gather no moss. — THOMAS TUSSER, *Five Hundred Points of Good Husbandry* [1557]
[8] It is not permitted to the most equitable of men to be a judge in his own cause. — PASCAL [1623–1662], *Pensées, ch. 4, 1*

[1] Proverbial — attributed to Syrus.
Necessity gives the law and does not itself receive it. — *Maxim 399*
See St. Augustine, p. 147a, and note.
And with necessity,
The tyrant's plea, excused his devilish deeds.
MILTON, *Paradise Lost* [1667], *bk. IV, l. 393*
See William Pitt, p. 496b.
[2] See Chaucer, p. 168b.
[3] When men are arrived at the goal, they should not turn back. — PLUTARCH [A.D. 46–120], *Of the Training of Children*
[4] No man can enjoy happiness without thinking that he enjoys it. — SAMUEL JOHNSON [1709–1784], *The Rambler*
[5] Did thrust as now in others' corn his sickle. — DU BARTAS, *Divine Weeks and Works* [1578], *pt. II, Second Week*
Not presuming to put my sickle in another man's corn. — NICHOLAS YONGE, *Musica Transalpina, Epistle Dedicatory* [1588]
[6] See Horace, p. 121a, and Marcus Aurelius, p. 141b.
[7] You may as well expect pears from an elm. — CERVANTES, *Don Quixote, pt. II* [1615], *bk. IV, ch. 40*

It is a very hard undertaking to seek to please everybody.   *Maxim 675*

Look for a tough wedge for a tough log.   *Maxim 723*

Pardon one offense, and you encourage the commission of many.
Maxim 750

In every enterprise consider where you would come out.[1]   *Maxim 777*

It takes a long time to bring excellence to maturity.   *Maxim 780*

No one knows what he can do till he tries.   *Maxim 786*

It is vain to look for a defense against lightning.   *Maxim 835*

Everything is worth what its purchaser will pay for it.[2]   *Maxim 847*

Better be ignorant of a matter than half know it.[3]   *Maxim 865*

Prosperity makes friends, adversity tries them.[4]   *Maxim 872*

Let a fool hold his tongue and he will pass for a sage.   *Maxim 914*

You need not hang up the ivy branch over the wine that will sell.[5]
Maxim 968

It is a consolation to the wretched to have companions in misery.[6]
Maxim 995

[1] In every affair, consider what precedes and what follows and then undertake it. — EPICTETUS [c. A.D. 60]: *That Everything Is to be Undertaken with Circumspection, ch. 15*
[2] What is worth in anything
But so much money as 'twill bring?
BUTLER, *Hudibras, pt. I* [1663], canto *1, l. 465*
[3] See Pope, p. 402b.
[4] See Aristotle, p. 99a, and note.
[5] Good wine needs no bush. — SHAKESPEARE, *As You Like It* [1598–1600], *Epilogue, l. 4*
Good wine needs neither bush nor preface
To make it welcome.
SIR WALTER SCOTT, *Peveril of the Peak* [1822], *ch. 4*
Bush: a shrub or branch, especially of ivy (perhaps as sacred to Bacchus) hung out at vintners' doors, or as a tavern sign. — WEBSTER, *New International Dictionary, 2nd ed.* [1945]. I.e., good wine needs no advertising.
[6] 'Tis the only comfort of the miserable to have partners in their woes. — CERVANTES, *Don Quixote, pt. I* [1605], *bk. III, ch. 10*

Unless degree is preserved, the first place is safe for no one.[1]
Maxim 1042

Confession of our faults is the next thing to innocence.   *Maxim 1060*

I have often regretted my speech, never my silence.[2]   *Maxim 1070*

Speech is a mirror of the soul: as a man speaks, so is he.   *Maxim 1073*

DIONYSIUS OF HALICARNASSUS
c. 54 – c. 7 B.C.

The contact with manners then is education; and this Thucydides appears to assert when he says history is philosophy learned from examples.
Ars Rhetorica XI, 2

SEXTUS AURELIUS PROPERTIUS
54 B.C. – A.D. 2

Never change when love has found its home.   *Elegies I, i, 36*

The seaman's story is of tempest, the plowman's of his team of bulls; the soldier tells his wounds, the shepherd his tale of sheep.   *Ib. II, i, 43*

Let each man pass his days in that wherein his skill is greatest.   *Ib. 46*

What though strength fails? Boldness is certain to win praise. In mighty enterprises, it is enough to have had the determination.[3]   *Ib. x, 5*

Misery loves company. — JOHN RAY, *English Proverbs* [1670]
It is a comfort to the unhappy to have companions in misery. — SPINOZA, *Ethics* [1677], *pt. 4, proposition 57, note*
[1] See Shakespeare, p. 267b.
[2] Simonides said that "he never repented that he held his tongue, but often that he had spoken." — PLUTARCH [A.D. 46–120], *Rules for the Preservation of Health*
[3] Quod si deficiant vires, audacia certe
Laus erit: in magnis et voluisse sat est.
See Menander, p. 102b.

Let no one be willing to speak ill of the absent.[1]   *Elegies II, xix, 32*

Let each man have the wit to go his own way.[2]   *Ib. xxv, 38*

Absence makes the heart grow fonder.[3]   *Ib. xxxiii, 43*

There is something beyond the grave; death does not end all, and the pale ghost escapes from the vanquished pyre.[4]   *Ib. IV, vii, 1*

ALBIUS TIBULLUS
c. 54 – c. 19 B.C.

May I look on you when my last hour comes; may I hold you, as I sink, with my failing hand.[5]
          Elegies I, i, 59

Jupiter laughs at the perjuries of lovers.[6]   *Ib. III, vi, 49*

Jove the Rain-giver.   *Ib. vii, 26*

OVID
[PUBLIUS OVIDIUS NASO]
43 B.C. – A.D. c. 18

Mine is good faith that will yield to none, and ways without reproach, and unadorned simplicity, and blushing modesty.   *Amores I, iii, 13*

The rest who does not know?[7]
          Ib. v, 25

Every lover is a warrior, and Cupid has his camps.[1]   *Amores I, ix, 1*

Stay far hence, far hence, you prudes![2]   *Ib. II, i, 3*

They come to see; they come that they themselves may be seen.[3]
          Ars Amatoria I, 99

It is convenient that there be gods, and, as it is convenient, let us believe there are.[4]   *Ib. 637*

To be loved, be lovable.
          Ib. II, 107

Nothing is stronger than habit.
          Ib. 345

Perhaps too my name will be joined to theirs[5] [the names of famous poets].   *Ib. III, 339*

Now are fields of corn where Troy once was.   *Heroides I, i, 2*

[Chaos] A rough, unordered mass of things.[6]   *Metamorphoses I, 7*

Your lot is mortal: not mortal is what you desire.   *Ib. II, 56*

You will be safest in the middle.[7]
          Ib. 137

I am Actaeon: recognize your master![8]   *Ib. III, 230*

The cause is hidden, but the result is well known.[9]   *Ib. IV, 287*

---

[1] Absenti nemo non nocuisse velit.
See The Seven Sages, p. 68b.
[2] Paddle your own canoe. — ANONYMOUS, *Harper's Monthly* [May 1854]
[3] Semper in absentes felicior aestus amantes.
[4] Our souls survive this death. — OVID, *Metamorphoses XV, l. 158*
[5] Te spectem, suprema mihi cum venerit hora,
Te teneam moriens deficiente manu.
[6] Periuria ridet amantum Iupiter.
Also in OVID [43 B.C.–A.D. c. 18], *Ars Amatoria I, 633*
See Shakespeare, p. 223b.
And Jove but laughs at lovers' perjury. — DRYDEN, *Palamon and Arcite* [*1680*], bk. II, l. 758, and *Amphitryon* [*1690*], act I, sc. ii
[7] Cetera quis nescit?

[1] Love is a kind of warfare. — OVID, *Ars Amatoria II, 233*
A batallas de amor campo de pluma [A field of feathers for the strife of love]. — LUIS DE GÓNGORA [*1571–1627*], *Soledad I*
[2] Procul hinc, procul este, severi!
[3] Spectatum veniunt, veniunt spectentur ut ipsae.
And for to se, and eek for to be seye. — CHAUCER, *The Canterbury Tales* [c. *1387*], *The Wife of Bath's Prologue*, l. 552
To see and to be seen. — BEN JONSON [*1572–1637*], *Epithalamion III, 4*
[4] See Tillotson, p. 366b, and Voltaire, p. 418a.
[5] Forsitan et nostrum nomen miscebitur istis.
[6] Rudis indigestaque moles.
[7] Medio tutissimus ibis.
[8] Actaeon ego sum, dominum cognoscite vestrum!
[9] Causa latet, vis est notissima.

We can learn even from our enemies.[1]　　　*Metamorphoses IV, 428*

I see and approve better things, but
follow worse.[2]　　　*Ib. VII, 20*

The gods have their own rules.[3]
　　　　　　　　　Ib. IX, 500

Time the devourer of all things.[4]
　　　　　　　　　Ib. XV, 234

And now I have finished a work that
neither the wrath of love, nor fire, nor
the sword, nor devouring age shall be
able to destroy.　　　*Ib. 871*

Resist beginnings; the prescription
comes too late when the disease has
gained strength by long delays.[5]
　　　　　　　Remedia Amoris 91

Love yields to business. If you seek a
way out of love, be busy; you'll be safe
then.[6]　　　　　　*Ib. 143*

Poetry comes fine-spun from a mind
at peace.　　　*Tristia I, i, 39*

So long as you are secure you will
count many friends; if your life becomes clouded you will be alone.[7]
　　　　　　　　　Ib. ix, 5

Whatever I tried to write was verse.
　　　　　　　　Ib. IV, x, 26

It is annoying to be honest to no
purpose.　　　*Ex Ponto II, iii, 14*

Note too that a faithful study of
the liberal arts humanizes character
and permits it not to be cruel.
　　　　　　　　　Ib. ix, 47

---

[1] Fas est et ab hoste doceri. Imitated from
ARISTOPHANES, *The Birds, l. 370*: People before
this have learned from their enemies.
[2] Video meliora, proboque, deteriora sequor.
See *Romans 7:19*, p. 51a, and Euripides,
p. 84b.
I know and love the good, yet, ah! the worst
pursue. — PETRARCH, *Sonnet 225, Canzone 21,
To Laura in Life* [c. 1327]
[3] Sunt superis sua iura.
[4] Tempus edax rerum.
[5] See Persius, p. 133b.
[6] Qui finem quaeris amoris
　　Cedit amor rebus; res age, tutus eris.
[7] See Aristotle, p. 99a, and note.

PHAEDRUS[1]
fl. c. A.D. 8

Submit to the present evil, lest a
greater one befall you.
　　　Fables, bk. I, fable 2, l. 31

He was the author, our hand finished
it.　　　　　　　*Ib. 6, 20*

That it is unwise to be heedless ourselves while we are giving advice to others, I will show in a few lines.
　　　　　　　　　Ib. 9, 1

No one returns with good will to the
place which has done him a mischief.
　　　　　　　　　Ib. 18, 1

It has been related that dogs drink at
the river Nile running along, that they
may not be seized by the crocodiles.[2]
　　　　　　　　　Ib. 25, 3

Everyone is bound to bear patiently
the results of his own example.
　　　　　　　　　Ib. 26, 12

Come of it what may, as Sinon said.
　　　　Ib. III, prologue, l. 27

Things are not always what they
seem.[3]　　　　*Ib. IV, 2, 5*

To add insult to injury.　*Ib. V, 3*

LUCIUS ANNAEUS
SENECA[4]
8 B.C. — A.D. 65

What fools these mortals be.[5]
　　　　　　　　Epistles 1, 3

It is not the man who has too little,
but the man who craves more, that is
poor.　　　　　　*Ib. 2, 2*

---

[1] Translated by HENRY THOMAS RILEY [1816–
1878].
[2] PLINY THE ELDER in his *Natural History*
(*bk. VIII, sec. 148*) and AELIAN in his *Various
Histories* relate the same fact as to the dogs
drinking from the Nile. "To treat a thing as the
dogs do the Nile" was a common proverb,
signifying superficial treatment.
[3] Non semper ea sunt quae videntur.
See Longfellow, p. 620b, and W. S. Gilbert,
p. 766a.
[4] Loeb Classical Library.
[5] Tanta stultitia mortalium est.
See Shakespeare, p. 230a.

Love of bustle is not industry.
Epistles 3, 5

Live among men as if God beheld you; speak to God as if men were listening. *Ib. 10, 5*

The best ideas are common property. *Ib. 12, 11*

Men do not care how nobly they live, but only how long, although it is within the reach of every man to live nobly, but within no man's power to live long. *Ib. 22, 17*

A great pilot can sail even when his canvas is rent. *Ib. 30, 3*

Man is a reasoning animal. *Ib. 41, 8*

That most knowing of persons — gossip. *Ib. 43, 1*

It is quality rather than quantity that matters.[1] *Ib. 45, 1*

You can tell the character of every man when you see how he receives praise. *Ib. 52, 12*

Nothing is so certain as that the evils of idleness can be shaken off by hard work. *Ib. 56, 9*

Not lost, but gone before.[2] *Ib. 63, 16*

All art is but imitation of nature. *Ib. 65, 3*

It is a rough road that leads to the heights of greatness. *Ib. 84, 13*

The pilot . . . who has been able to say, "Neptune, you shall never sink this ship except on an even keel," has fulfilled the requirements of his art.[3] *Ib. 85, 33*

I was shipwrecked before I got aboard. *Epistles 87, 1*

It is better, of course, to know useless things than to know nothing. *Ib. 88, 45*

Do not ask for what you will wish you had not got. *Ib. 95, 1*

We are mad, not only individually, but nationally. We check manslaughter and isolated murders; but what of war and the much vaunted crime of slaughtering whole peoples? *Ib. 95, 30*

A great step towards independence is a good-humored stomach, one that is willing to endure rough treatment. *Ib. 123, 3*

Fire is the test of gold; adversity, of strong men.[1]
Moral Essays. On Providence 5, 9

Time discovers truth.[2]
Ib. On Anger 2, 22

Whom they have injured they also hate.[3] *Ib. 33*

I do not distinguish by the eye, but by the mind, which is the proper judge of the man.
Ib. On the Happy Life 2, 2

There is no great genius without some touch of madness.[4]
Ib. On Tranquillity of the Mind 17, 10

---

[1] See Beaumont and Fletcher, p. 316b.
[2] Veritatem dies aperit. Omnia tempus revelat [Time reveals all]. — TERTULLIAN [A.D. c. 155–c. 225], *Apologeticus 7*
Time reveals all things. — ERASMUS [1465–1536], *Adagia*
[3] It is human nature to hate those whom you have injured. — TACITUS [A.D. 54–119], *Agricola 42, 15*
Chi fa ingiuria non perdona mai [He never pardons those he injures]. — *Italian proverb*
The offender never pardons. — GEORGE HERBERT, *Jacula Prudentum* [1640]
Forgiveness to the injured does belong;
But they ne'er pardon who have done the wrong.
DRYDEN, *The Conquest of Granada* [1670], *pt. II, act I, sc. ii*
[4] An ancient commonplace, which Seneca says he quotes from ARISTOTLE, *Problemata 30, 1*: "No excellent soul is exempt from a mixture of madness." It is also in PLATO, *Phaedrus 245A*.

[1] See Anonymous, p. 151a.
[2] Non amittuntur, sed praemittuntur.
Not dead, but gone before. — SAMUEL ROGERS, *Human Life* [1819]
See Masefield, p. 947b–948a.
[3] The mariner of old said thus to Neptune in a great tempest, "O God! thou mayest save me if thou wilt, and if thou wilt, thou mayest destroy me; but whether or no, I will steer my rudder true." — MONTAIGNE, *Essays* [1580–1595], *bk. II, ch. 16*

A great fortune is a great slavery.
*Moral Essays. To Polybius on
Consolation 6, 5*

Wherever the Roman conquers, there
he dwells.
Ib. To Helvia on Consolation 7, 7

He who receives a benefit with gratitude repays the first installment on his
debt.   *On Benefits, bk. II, 22, 1*

You roll my log, and I will roll
yours.   *Apocolocyntosis, sec. 9*

Do you seek Alcides' equal? None is,
except himself.[1]
Hercules Furens 1, 1, 84

Successful and fortunate crime is
called virtue.[2]   *Ibid. 255*

An age will come after many years
when the Ocean will loose the chains of
things, and a huge land lie revealed;
when Tiphys[3] will disclose new worlds
and Thule[4] no more be the ultimate.[5]
Medea, l. 374

Good sense travels on the well-worn paths;
genius, never. And that is why the crowd, not
altogether without reason, is so ready to treat
great men as lunatics. — CESARE LOMBROSO
[1836–1909], *The Man of Genius, preface*
    See Dryden, p. 368a.
[1] None but himself can be his parallel. —
LEWIS THEOBALD [1688–1744], *The Double Falsehood*
    And but herself admits no parallel. — MAS-
SINGER [1583–1640], *Duke of Milan, act IV, sc. iii*
[2] See Harington, p. 210a.
[3] Jason's pilot.
[4] See Virgil, p. 117a, and Thomson, p. 419b.
[5] Venient annis
      Saecula seris, quibus Oceanus
      Vincula rerum laxet, et ingens
      Pateat tellus, Tiphysque novos
      Detegat orbes nec sit terris
      Ultima Thule.
Translated by S. E. MORISON.
As one much addicted to prophesies, and who
had already voyaged beyond Thule (Iceland),
Columbus was much impressed by the passage in
Seneca's *Medea*. — S. E. MORISON, *Admiral of
the Ocean Sea* [1942], *vol. I, ch. 6.*
Next to these lines from *Medea* in an early
edition of Seneca's tragedies that belonged to
Columbus's son Ferdinand, there is this anno-
tation in the son's hand: Haec profetia impleta
est per patrem meum . . . almirantem anno
1492 [The prophecy was fulfilled by my father
the Admiral in the year 1492]. *Ib. I, 5*

A good mind possesses a kingdom.[1]
Thyestes 380

Light griefs are loquacious, but the
great are dumb.[2]
Hippolytus II, 3, 607

CALIGULA
[GAIUS CAESAR]
A.D. 12–41

Would that the Roman people had a
single neck [to cut off their head].
From SUETONIUS, *Gaius
Caligula, sec. 30*

MANILIUS
fl. first century A.D.

He snatched the thunderbolt from
heaven, then the scepter from tyrants.[3]
Astronomica I, l. 104

As soon as we are born we begin to
die, and the end depends upon the beginning.[4]   *Ib. IV, 16*

ONASANDER
fl. A.D. 49

Vigor is found in the man who has
not yet grown old, and discretion in the
man who is not too young.
The General, ch. 1, sec. 10

Envy is a pain of mind that successful men cause their neighbors.
Ib. ch. 42, par. 25

PLINY THE ELDER[5]
A.D. 23–79

In comparing various authors with
one another, I have discovered that

[1] See Dyer, p. 192a.
[2] See Raleigh, p. 199a.
[3] Eripuit Jovi fulmen viresque tonandi.
Adapted by A. R. J. TURGOT for the inscription on the Houdon bust of Franklin [1778] as:
Eripuit coelo fulmen, mox sceptra tyrannis.
See Franklin, p. 421a, note 3.
[4] See *The Wisdom of Solomon 5:13*, p. 37a.
[5] With some alterations, translated by JOHN
BOSTOCK [1773–1846] and HENRY THOMAS RILEY
[1816–1878].
See also Pliny the Younger, p. 140b.

some of the gravest and latest writers have transcribed, word for word, from former works, without making acknowledgment.

Natural History, bk. I, dedication, sec. 22

Everything is soothed by oil, and this is the reason why divers send out small quantities of it from their mouths, because it smooths every part which is rough.[1]   *Ib. II, 234*

It is far from easy to determine whether she [Nature] has proved to man a kind parent or a merciless stepmother.[2]   *Ib. VII, 1*

Man alone at the very moment of his birth, cast naked upon the naked earth, does she abandon to cries and lamentations.[3]   *Ib. 2*

To laugh, if but for an instant only, has never been granted to man before the fortieth day from his birth, and then it is looked upon as a miracle of precocity.[4]   *Ib.*

Man is the only one that knows nothing, that can learn nothing without being taught. He can neither speak nor

[1] Why does pouring oil on the sea make it clear and calm? Is it for that the winds, slipping the smooth oil, have no force, nor cause any waves? — PLUTARCH [A.D. 46–120], *Natural Questions IX*

Bishop Adain [A.D. 651] gave to a company about to take a journey by sea "some holy oil, saying, 'I know that when you go abroad you will meet with a storm and contrary wind; but do you remember to cast this oil I give you into the sea, and the wind shall cease immediately.' " — BEDE [673–735], *Eccesiastical History, bk. III, ch. 14*

In JARED SPARKS's edition of BENJAMIN FRANKLIN's *Works, vol. VI, p. 354*, there are letters between Franklin, Brownrigg, and Parish on the stilling of waves by means of oil.

[2] To man the earth seems altogether
   No more a mother, but a step-dame rather.
       DU BARTAS [1544–1590], *Divine Weeks and Works, First Week, Third Day*

[3] See *The Wisdom of Solomon 7:3, p. 37a.*
He is born naked, and falls a-whining at the first. — ROBERT BURTON, *Anatomy of Melancholy* [1621–1651], *pt. I, sec. 2, member 3, subsec. 10*

[4] This term of forty days is mentioned by ARISTOTLE in his *Natural History.*

walk nor eat, and in short he can do nothing at the prompting of nature only, but weep.[1]

Natural History, bk. VII, sec. 4

With man, most of his misfortunes are occasioned by man.[2]   *Ib. 5*

Indeed, what is there that does not appear marvelous when it comes to our knowledge for the first time?[3] How many things, too, are looked upon as quite impossible until they have been actually effected?   *Ib. 6*

The human features and countenance, although composed of but some ten parts or little more, are so fashioned that among so many thousands of men there are no two in existence who cannot be distinguished from one another.[4]   *Ib. 8*

All men possess in their bodies a poison which acts upon serpents; and the human saliva, it is said, makes them take to flight, as though they had been touched with boiling water. The same substance, it is said, destroys them the moment it enters their throat.[5]

Ib. 15

It has been observed that the height of a man from the crown of the head to the sole of the foot is equal to the distance between the tips of the middle

[1] See Tennyson, p. 650b.
[2] See Burns, p. 492b.
[3] See Tacitus, *Agricola 30, p. 140a.*
[4] It is the common wonder of all men, how among so many millions of faces there should be none alike. — SIR THOMAS BROWNE, *Religio Medici* [1642], *pt. II, sec. 2*
Of a thousand shavers. two do not shave so much alike as not to be distinguished. — SAMUEL JOHNSON [1777]; from BOSWELL, *Life of Dr. Johnson* [1791], *vol. II, p. 120* [Everyman ed.]
See Montaigne, p. 190b.
[5] MADAME D'ABRANTES relates that when Bonaparte was in Cairo he sent for a serpent-detector (Psylli) to remove two serpents that had been seen in his house. He, having enticed one of them from his hiding place, caught it in one hand, just below the jawbone, in such a manner as to oblige the mouth to open, when, spitting into it, the effect was like magic: the reptile appeared struck with instant death. — *Memoirs, vol. I, ch. 59*

fingers of the two hands when extended in a straight line.
Natural History, bk. VII, *sec.* 77

There is always something new out of Africa.[1]   *Ib.* VIII, 17

When a building is about to fall down, all the mice desert it.[2]
Ib. 103

Bears when first born are shapeless masses of white flesh a little larger than mice, their claws alone being prominent. The mother then licks them gradually into proper shape.[3]
Ib. 126

The agricultural population, says Cato, produces the bravest men, the most valiant soldiers, and a class of citizens the least given of all to evil designs.   *Ib.* XVIII, 26

The best plan is to profit by the folly of others.   *Ib.* 31

A grain of salt being added.[4]
Ib. XXIII, 8

Why is it that we entertain the belief that for every purpose odd numbers are the most effectual? [5]
Ib. XXVIII, 23

---

[1] Ex Africa semper aliquid novi.
Quoted as a Greek proverb.
[2] This is alluded to by CICERO in his letters to Atticus, and is mentioned by AELIAN (*Animated Nature, bk.* VI, *ch. 41*). Compare the modern proverb: Rats desert a sinking ship.
[3] Not unlike the bear which bringeth forth
In the end of thirty days a shapeless birth;
But after licking, it in shape she draws,
And by degrees she fashions out the paws,
The head, and neck, and finally doth bring
To a perfect beast that first deformed thing.
DU BARTAS, *Divine Weeks and Works* [1578], *First Week, First Day*
I had not time to lick it into form, as a bear doth her young ones. — ROBERT BURTON, *Anatomy of Melancholy* [1621–1651], *Democritus to the Reader*
[4] Cum grano salis [With a grain of salt].
Pompey's antidote against poison was "to be taken fasting, a grain of salt being added."
[5] The god delights in an odd number. — VIRGIL [70–19 B.C.], *Eclogues* VIII, 75
See Shakespeare, p. 267b, and Samuel Lover, p. 589a.

PERSIUS
[AULUS PERSIUS FLACCUS]
A.D. 34–62

The stomach is the teacher of the arts and the dispenser of invention.[1]
Satires, prologue, l. 10

Tell, priests, what is gold doing in a holy place?   *Ib.* II, 69

Let them look upon virtue and pine because they have lost her.
Ib. III, 38

Meet the disease at its first stage.[2]
Ib. 64

GAIUS PETRONIUS
[PETRONIUS ARBITER[3]]
d. A.D. c. 66

He has joined the great majority.[4]
Satyricon, sec. 42

A man who is always ready to believe what is told him will never do well.
Ib. 43

One good turn deserves another.
Ib. 45

A man must have his faults.   *Ib.*

Not worth his salt.   *Ib.* 57

My heart was in my mouth.
Ib. 62

Beauty and wisdom are rarely conjoined.[5]   *Ib.* 94

---

[1] Magister artis ingenique largitor venter.
See Anonymous Latin, p. 151a.
Necessity, mother of invention. — WYCHERLEY, *Love in a Wood* [1671], act III, sc. iii
Art imitates Nature, and necessity is the mother of invention. — RICHARD FRANCK, *Northern Memoirs* [written 1658, published 1694]
Sheer necessity — the proper parent of an art so nearly allied to invention. — SHERIDAN, *The Critic* [1779], *act I, sc. ii*
[2] Venienti occurrite morbo.
A stitch in time saves nine. — *Proverb*
See Ovid, p. 129a.
Also in Publilius Syrus, *Maxim 866.*
[3] Pliny calls Petronius Titus in *Natural History* XXXVII, 8.
See Tacitus, p. 140a.
[4] Abiit ad plures.
[5] See Petrarch, p. 163a.

The studied spontaneity of Horace.[1]
Satyricon, sec. 118

Natural curls.[2] *Ib.* 126

NERO
A.D. 37–68

What an artist dies with me! [3]
From SUETONIUS, *Nero, sec.* 49

LUCAN
A.D. 39–65

If the victor had the gods on his side,
the vanquished had Cato.[4]
The Civil War, bk. I, 128

There stands the shadow of a glorious name.[5] *Ib.* 135

Pigmies placed on the shoulders of
giants see more than the giants themselves.[6] *Ib.* II, 10 (*Didacus Stella*)

Thinking nothing done while anything remained to be done.[7]
Ib. 657

More was lost than mere life and existence.[8] *Ib.* VII, 639

We all praise fidelity; but the true
friend pays the penalty when he supports those whom Fortune crushes.[9]
Ib. VIII, 485

---

[1] Horatii curiosa felicitas.
[2] Crines ingenio suo flexi.
[3] Qualis artifex pereo!
[4] Victrix causa deis placuit, sed victa Catoni.
[5] Stat magni nominis umbra.
[6] Pigmei gigantum humeris impositi plusquam
ipsi gigantes vident.
See Robert Burton, p. 310a, and Sir Isaac
Newton, p. 379b.
The dwarf sees farther than the giant, when
he has the giant's shoulder to mount on. —
COLERIDGE, *The Friend* [1828]
[7] The reference is to Caesar.
[8] Plus est quam vita salusque
Quod perit.
[9] "Dat poenas laudata fides, dum sustinet,"
inquit,
"Quos fortuna premit."
A praised faith
Is her own scourge, when it sustains their
states
Whom fortune hath depressed.
BEN JONSON, *Anglia 39, 247*

A name illustrious and revered by nations.[1]
The Civil War, bk. IX, 203

Is the dwelling place of God anywhere but in the earth and sea, the air
and sky, and virtue? Why seek we further for deities? Whatever you see,
whatever you touch, that is Jupiter.
Ib. 578

The very ruins have been destroyed.[2]
Ib. 969

DIO CHRYSOSTOM [3]
A.D. C. 40 – C. 120

Diogenes: The man I know not, for
I am not acquainted with his mind.
*Fourth Discourse, On Kingship,
ch.* 17

Idleness and lack of occupation are
the best things in the world to ruin the
foolish.
*Tenth Discourse, On Servants,
ch.* 7

Most men are so completely corrupted by opinion that they would
rather be notorious for the greatest calamities than suffer no ill and be unknown. *Ib. ch.* 6

MARTIAL [4]
[MARCUS VALERIUS MARTIALIS]
A.D. C. 40 – C. 104

My poems are naughty, but my life is
pure.[5] *Epigrams I, 4*

"I'll live." — Yes, but no sensible
man would say so. Tomorrow's life is
too late. Live today. *Ib.* 15

And faith though prais'd, is punish'd, that
supports
Such as good fate forsakes.
FLETCHER, *The False One* [1647], *act I,
sc. i, l. 303*

[1] Clarum et venerabile nomen
Gentibus.
Cato's tribute to the fallen Pompey.
[2] Etiam periere ruinae.
The reference is to Troy.
[3] Translated by J. W. COHOON.
[4] Translated by DUDLEY FITTS.
[5] Lasciva est nobis pagina, vita proba.

Some good, some so-so, and lots plain bad: that's how a book of poems is made, my friend. *Epigrams* I, 16

I don't like you, Sabidius, I can't say why; But I can say this: I don't like you, Sabidius.[1] *Ib.* 32

Stop abusing my verses, or publish some of your own. *Ib.* 91

You complain, friend Swift, of the length of my epigrams, but you yourself write nothing. Yours are shorter.
Ib. 110

Conceal a flaw, and the world will imagine the worst. *Ib.* III, 42

The bee is enclosed, and shines preserved in amber, so that it seems enshrined in its own nectar.[2]
Ib. IV, 32

They praise those verses, yes, but read something else. *Ib.* 49

You ask what a nice girl will do? She won't give an inch, but she won't say no. *Ib.* 71

Our days pass by, and are scored against us.[3] *Ib.* V, 20

What's a wretched man? A man whom no man pleases. *Ib.* 28

A man who lives everywhere lives nowhere. *Ib.* 73

You puff the poets of other days,
  The living you deplore.
Spare me the accolade: your praise
  Is not worth dying for.[4]
Ib. VIII, 69

Virtue extends our days: he lives two lives who relives his past with pleasure.[1]
Epigrams X, 23

Neither fear your death's day nor long for it.[2] *Ib.* 47

Lucretia blushed, and put my book aside. Brutus was there. — Exit Brutus. — Now she'll read. *Ib.* XI, 16

You'll get no laurel crown for outrunning a burro. *Ib.* XII, 36

You're obstinate, pliant, merry, morose, all at once. For me there's no living with you, or without you.[3]
Ib. 47

The country in town.[4] *Ib.* 57

I know these are nothing.[5]
Ib. XIII, 2

TITUS VESPASIANUS
A.D. C. 41 – 81

Friends, I have lost a day.[6]
From SUETONIUS, *Titus, sec.* 8

QUINTILIAN
[MARCUS FABIUS QUINTILIANUS]
A.D. 42 – 118

We give to necessity the praise of virtue.[7]

De Institutione Oratoria,
bk. I, 8, 14

---

[1] See Tom Brown, p. 386b.
[2] Whence we see spiders, flies, or ants entombed preserved forever in amber, a more than royal tomb. — FRANCIS BACON, *Historia Vitae et Mortis* [1623], *Sylva Sylvarum, cent.* I, *exper.* 100
    I saw a flie within a beade
    Of amber cleanly buried.
        HERRICK [1591–1674], *On a Fly*
                        Buried in Amber
See Pope, p. 410b.
[3] Nobis pereunt et imputantur.
[4] See Louis Edwin Thayer, p. 949a.

[1] Thus would I double my life's fading space;
For he that runs it well, runs twice his race.
    COWLEY [1618–1667], *Discourse XI, Of Myself, st. 11*
For he lives twice who can at once employ
The present well, and ev'n the past enjoy.
    POPE [1688–1744], *Imitation of Martial*
[2] See Milton, p. 348a.
[3] Difficilis facilis fucundus acerbus es idem:
Nec tecum possum vivere nec sine te.
See Aristophanes, p. 91b.
[4] Rus in urbe.
[5] Nos haec novimus esse nihil.
Said of his own poems. The phrase was used by John Gay as epigraph for *The Beggar's Opera* [1728].
[6] Amici, diem perdidi.
[7] In the additions of Hadrianus Julius to the *Adages* of ERASMUS, he remarks, under the head of *Necessitatem edere,* that a very familiar proverb was current among his countrymen: Necessitatem in virtutem commutare [To make necessity a virtue].

A liar should have a good memory.[1]
De Institutione Oratoria,
bk. IV, 2, 91

Vain hopes are often like the dreams of those who wake.   *Ib. VI, 2, 30*

For it is feeling and force of imagination that make us eloquent.[2]
Ib. X, 7, 15

Those who wish to appear wise among fools, among the wise seem foolish.[3]   *Ib. 21*

PLUTARCH
A.D. 46–120

As geographers, Sosius, crowd into the edges of their maps parts of the world which they do not know about, adding notes in the margin to the effect that beyond this lies nothing but sandy deserts full of wild beasts, and unapproachable bogs.[4]
Lives, Aemilius Paulus, sec. 5

About Theseus began the saying, "He is a second Hercules."   *Ib. 29*

Thus maketh vertue of necessitee. — CHAUCER, *Troilus and Criseyde* [1372–1386], *bk. IV, l. 1586*
Others made a virtue of necessity. — RABELAIS, *Works, bk. V* [1552], *ch. 23*
See Shakespeare, p. 226a.
Make a virtue of necessity. — ROBERT BURTON, *Anatomy of Melancholy* [1621–1651], *pt. III, sec. 3, member 4, subsec. I*
[1] He who has not a good memory should never take upon him the trade of lying. — MONTAIGNE, *Essays* [1580–1595], *bk. I, ch. 9, Of Liars*
Il faut bonne mémoire, après qu'on a menti. — CORNEILLE, *Le Menteur* [1642], *act IV, sc. v*
Liars ought to have good memories. — ALGERNON SIDNEY, *Discourses on Government* [1698], *ch. 2, sec. 15*
[2] Pectus est enim, quod disertos facit.
[3] A wit with dunces, and a dunce wit.. wits. — POPE, *Dunciad* [1728], *bk. IV, l. 90*
A fool with judges, amongst fools a judge. — COWPER, *Conversation* [1782], *l. 298*
This man [Chesterfield], I thought, had been a lord among wits; but I find he is only a wit among lords. — SAMUEL JOHNSON; from BOSWELL, *Life of Dr. Johnson* [1791], *vol. II, p. 159* [Everyman ed.]
[4] So geographers, in Afric maps,
    With savage pictures fill their gaps,
    And o'er unhabitable downs
    Place elephants for want of towns.
SWIFT, *On Poetry, A Rhapsody* [1733]

A Roman divorced from his wife, being highly blamed by his friends, who demanded, "Was she not chaste? Was she not fair? Was she not fruitful?" holding out his shoe, asked them whether it was not new and well made. "Yet," added he, "none of you can tell where it pinches me."[1]
Lives, Aemilius Paulus, sec. 5

Where the lion's skin will not reach, you must patch it out with the fox's.[2]
Ib. Lysander, sec. 7

Moral habits, induced by public practices, are far quicker in making their way into men's private lives, than the failings and faults of individuals are in infecting the city at large.   *Ib. 17*

As it is in the proverb, played Cretan against Cretan.[3]   *Ib. 20*

Perseverance is more prevailing than violence; and many things which cannot be overcome when they are together, yield themselves up when taken little by little.   *Ib. Sertorius, sec. 16*

Good fortune will elevate even petty minds, and give them the appearance of a certain greatness and stateliness, as from their high place they look down upon the world; but the truly noble and resolved spirit raises itself, and becomes more conspicuous in times of disaster and ill fortune.   *Ib. Eumenes, sec. 9*

Authority and place demonstrate and try the tempers of men, by moving every passion and discovering every frailty.
Ib. Demosthenes and Cicero, sec. 3

Medicine, to produce health, has to

---

[1] The wearer knows where the shoe wrings. — GEORGE HERBERT, *Jacula Prudentum* [1640]
I can tell where my own shoe pinches me. — CERVANTES, *Don Quixote, pt. I* [1605], *bk. IV, ch. 5*
[2] The prince must be a lion, but he must also know how to play the fox. — NICCOLÒ MACHIAVELLI, *The Prince* [1532]
[3] Cheat against cheat. The Cretans were considered notorious liars.

examine disease; and music, to create harmony, must investigate discord.
Lives, Demetrius, sec. 1

It is a true proverb, that if you live with a lame man you will learn to limp.
Morals. Of the Training of Children

The very spring and root of honesty and virtue lie in good education.
Ib.

It is indeed desirable to be well descended, but the glory belongs to our ancestors.
Ib.

Nothing made the horse so fat as the king's eye.
Ib.

It is wise to be silent when occasion requires, and better than to speak, though never so well.[1]
Ib.

An old doting fool, with one foot already in the grave.
Ib.

He is a fool who leaves things close at hand to follow what is out of reach.[2]
Ib. Of Garrulity

All men whilst they are awake are in one common world; but each of them, when he is asleep, is in a world of his own.[3]
Ib. Of Superstition

That proverbial saying, "Bad news travels fast and far."[4]
Ib. Of Inquisitiveness

Spintharus, speaking in commendation of Epaminondas, says he scarce ever met with any man who knew more and spoke less.
Ib. Of Hearing, sec. 6

[1] Closed lips hurt no one, speaking may. — CATO THE CENSOR [234–149 B.C.], *bk. I, distich 12*
[2] Better one bird in hand than ten in the wood. — JOHN HEYWOOD, *Proverbs* [1546], *pt. I, ch. 11*
One bird in the hand is worth two in the wood. — THOMAS LODGE, *Rosalyne* [1590]
A bird in hand is worth two in the bush. — CERVANTES, *Don Quixote, pt. I* [1605], *bk. IV, ch. 4*
A feather in hand is better than a bird in the air. — GEORGE HERBERT, *Jacula Prudentum* [1640]
[3] A saying attributed to Heraclitus.
[4] Evil news fly faster still than good. — THOMAS KYD, *Spanish Tragedy* [1594], *act I*
See Milton, p. 350a.

Antiphanes said merrily that in a certain city the cold was so intense that words were congealed as soon as spoken, but that after some time they thawed and became audible; so that the words spoken in winter were articulated next summer.[1]
Morals. Of Man's Progress in Virtue

When the candles are out all women are fair.[2]
Ib. Conjugal Precepts

Like watermen, who look astern while they row the boat ahead.[3]
Ib. Whether 'Twas Rightfully Said, Live Concealed

The great god Pan is dead.[4]
Ib. Why the Oracles Cease to Give Answers

I am whatever was, or is, or will be; and my veil no mortal ever took up.[5]
Ib. Of Isis and Osiris

For to err in opinion, though it be not the part of wise men, is at least human.[6]
Ib. Against Colotes

Pythagoras, when he was asked what time was, answered that it was the soul of this world.
Ib. Platonic Questions

[1] Rabelais gives a somewhat similar account, referring to Antiphanes, in *Works, bk. IV* [1548], *chs. 55–56.*
See Raspe (Baron Munchausen), p. 468a.
[2] When all candles be out, all cats be gray. — JOHN HEYWOOD, *Proverbs* [1546], *pt. I, ch. 5*
[3] Like rowers, who advance backward. — MONTAIGNE, *Essays* [1580–1595], *Of Profit and Honor, bk. III, ch. 1*
Like the watermen that row one way and look another. — ROBERT BURTON, *Anatomy of Melancholy* [1621–1651], *Democritus to the Reader*
[4] PLUTARCH says in *Of Isis and Osiris* that a ship well laden with passengers drove with the tide near the Isles of Paxi, when a loud voice was heard by most of the passengers calling one Thanus. The voice then said aloud to him, "When you are arrived at Palodes, take care to make it known that the great god Pan is dead."
Great Pan is dead. — ELIZABETH BARRETT BROWNING [1806–1861], *The Dead Pan, st. 26*
[5] I am the things that are, and those that are to be, and those that have been. No one ever lifted my skirts; the fruit which I bore was the sun. — PROCLUS [A.D. c. 411–485], *On Plato's Timaeus* (inscription in the temple of Neith at Sais, in Egypt)
[6] See Anonymous, p. 150b, and Pope, p. 403b.

EPICTETUS[1]
A.D. C. 50 – 120

To the rational being only the irrational is unendurable, but the rational is endurable. *Discourses, bk. I, ch. 2*

When you close your doors, and make darkness within, remember never to say that you are alone, for you are not alone;[2] nay, God is within, and your genius is within. And what need have they of light to see what you are doing? *Ib. 14*

No thing great is created suddenly, any more than a bunch of grapes or a fig. If you tell me that you desire a fig, I answer you that there must be time. Let it first blossom, then bear fruit, then ripen. *Ib. 15*

Any one thing in the creation is sufficient to demonstrate a Providence to a humble and grateful mind. *Ib. 16*

Were I a nightingale, I would sing like a nightingale; were I a swan, like a swan. But as it is, I am a rational being, therefore I must sing hymns of praise to God. *Ib.*

Practice yourself, for heaven's sake, in little things; and thence proceed to greater. *Ib. 18*

It is difficulties that show what men are. *Ib. 24*

The good or ill of man lies within his own will. *Ib. 25*

In theory there is nothing to hinder our following what we are taught; but in life there are many things to draw us aside. *Ib. 26*

Appearances to the mind are of four kinds. Things either are what they appear to be; or they neither are, nor appear to be; or they are, and do not appear to be; or they are not, and yet appear to be. Rightly to aim in all these cases is the wise man's task. *Ib. 27*

[1] Loeb Classical Library.
[2] Though in a wilderness, a man is never alone. — SIR THOMAS BROWNE, *Religio Medici* [1642], *Everyman ed, p. 82*

Only the educated are free. *Discourses, bk. II, ch. 1*

The materials are indifferent, but the use we make of them is not a matter of indifference. *Ib. 5*

Shall I show you the sinews of a philosopher? "What sinews are those?" — A will undisappointed; evils avoided; powers daily exercised; careful resolutions; unerring decisions. *Ib. 8*

What is the first business of one who practices philosophy? To get rid of self-conceit. For it is impossible for anyone to begin to learn that which he thinks he already knows. *Ib. 17*

Whatever you would make habitual, practice it; and if you would not make a thing habitual, do not practice it, but accustom yourself to something else. *Ib. 18*

Be not swept off your feet by the vividness of the impression, but say, "Impression, wait for me a little. Let me see what you are and what you represent. Let me try you." *Ib.*

There are some faults which men readily admit, but others not so readily. *Ib. 21*

Two principles we should always have ready — that there is nothing good or evil save in the will; and that we are not to lead events, but to follow them. *Ib. III, 10*

First say to yourself what you would be; and then do what you have to do. *Ib. 23*

Remember that you ought to behave in life as you would at a banquet. As something is being passed around it comes to you; stretch out your hand, take a portion of it politely. It passes on; do not detain it. Or it has not come to you yet; do not project your desire to meet it, but wait until it comes in front of you. So act toward children, so toward a wife, so toward office, so toward wealth. *The Encheiridion, 15*

Where do you suppose he got that high brow? *The Encheiridion, 22*

Everything has two handles — by one of which it ought to be carried and by the other not.[1] *Ib. 43*

DECIMUS JUNIUS JUVENAL

A.D. C. 50 – C. 130

Honesty is praised and starves.[2] *Satires I, l. 74*

If nature refuses, indignation will produce verses.[3] *Ib. 79*

All the doings of mankind, their wishes, fears, anger, pleasures, joys, and varied pursuits, form the motley subject of my book. *Ib. 85*

Censure pardons the raven, but is visited upon the dove.[4] *Ib. II, 63*

No one becomes depraved in a moment.[5] *Ib. 83*

Grammarian, rhetorician, geometrician, painter, trainer, soothsayer, ropedancer, physician, magician — he knows everything. Tell the hungry little Greek to go to heaven; he'll go.[6] *Ib. III, 76*

Bitter poverty has no harder pang than that it makes men ridiculous.[7] *Ib. 152*

It is not easy for men to rise whose qualities are thwarted by poverty. *Ib. 164*

We all live in a state of ambitious poverty. *Ib. 182*

A rare bird on earth, comparable to a black swan.[8] *Ib. VI, 165*

I wish it, I command it. Let my will take the place of reason.[1] *Satires VI, l. 223*

We are now suffering the evils of a long peace. Luxury, more deadly than war, broods over the city, and avenges a conquered world.[2] *Ib. 292*

But who is to guard the guards themselves?[3] *Ib. 347*

An inveterate and incurable itch for writing besets many, and grows old in their sick hearts. *Ib. VII, 51*

Nobility is the one and only virtue.[4] *Ib. VIII, 20*

Count it the greatest sin to prefer life to honor, and for the sake of living to lose what makes life worth having.[5] *Ib. 83*

The people that once bestowed commands, consulships, legions, and all else, now concerns itself no more, and longs eagerly for just two things — bread and circuses![6] *Ib. X, 79*

Put Hannibal in the scales.[7] *Ib. 147*

You should pray for a sound mind in a sound body.[8] *Ib. 356*

For revenge is always the delight of a mean spirit, of a weak and petty mind! You may immediately draw proof of this — that no one rejoices more in revenge than a woman. *Ib. XIII, 189*

---

[1] There is a right and wrong handle to everything. — RASPE, *Travels of Baron Munchausen* [1785], *ch. 30*

[2] Probitas laudatur et alget.
A favorite quotation of Linnaeus.

[3] Si natura negat, facit indignatio versum.

[4] Dat veniam corvis, vexat censura columbas.

[5] Nemo repente fuit turpissimus.
Translated by GILBERT HIGHET. See Racine, p. 378b.

[6] See Dryden, p. 368b.

[7] Nil habet infelix paupertas durius in se, quam quod ridiculos homines facit.

[8] Rara avis in terris nigroque simillima cycno.

[1] Hoc volo, sic iubeo, sit pro ratione voluntas.

[2] Nunc patimur longae pacis mala, saevior armis
Luxuria incubuit victumque ulciscitur orbem.

[3] Sed quis custodiet ipsos
Custodes?
What an absurd idea — a guardian to need a guardian! — PLATO [c. 429–347 B.C.], *The Republic, bk. III, 403–E*

[4] Nobilitas sola est atque unica virtus.

[5] Summum crede nefas animam praeferre pudori,
Et propter vitam vivendi perdere causas.

[6] Panem et circenses.

[7] Expende Hannibalem.

[8] Mens sana in corpore sano.
See John Locke, p. 373a.

The greatest reverence is due the young.[1]　　　*Satires XIV, l. 47*

CAIUS CORNELIUS TACITUS
A.D. C. 55 – C. 117

The images of the most illustrious families . . . were carried before it [the bier of Julia]. Those of Brutus and Cassius were not displayed; but for that reason they shone with preeminent luster.[2]　　　*Annals, bk. III, 76*

He had talents equal to business, and aspired no higher.　　　*Ib. VI, 39*

What is this day supported by precedents will hereafter become a precedent.[3]　　　*Ib. XI, 24*

[Of Petronius] Arbiter of taste.[4]
　　　Ib. XVI, 18

It is the rare fortune of these days that a man may think what he likes and say what he thinks.
　　　Histories, bk. I, 1

[Of Servius Galba] He seemed more important than a private citizen while he was a private citizen, and in the opinion of all he was capable of rule — if he had not ruled.　　　*Ib. 49*

The desire for glory clings even to the best men longer than any other passion.[5]　　　*Ib. IV, 6*

The gods are on the side of the stronger.[6]　　　*Ib. 17*

Whatever is unknown is taken for marvelous;[7] but now the limits of Britain are laid bare.
　　　Agricola, sec. 30

Where they make a desert, they call it peace.[1]　　　*Agricola, sec. 30*

Fortune favored him . . . in the opportune moment of his death.
　　　Ib. 45

PLINY THE YOUNGER[2]
A.D. 61–105

Modestus said of Regulus that he was "the biggest rascal that walks upon two legs."　　　*Letters,[3] bk. I, letter 5*

There is nothing to write about, you say. Well then, write and let me know just this — that there *is* nothing to write about; or tell me in the good old style if you are well. That's right. I am quite well.[4]　　　*Ib. 11*

An object in possession seldom retains the same charm that it had in pursuit.[5]　　　*Ib. II, 15*

He [Pliny the Elder] used to say that "no book was so bad but some good might be got out of it."[6]
　　　Ib. III, 5

This expression of ours, "Father of a family."[7]　　　*Ib. V, 19*

That indolent but agreeable condition of doing nothing.[8]　　　*Ib. VIII, 9*

---

[1] Calgacus, addressing the Britons at the Battle of the Grampians, referring to the Romans.

See Byron, p. 558b.

[2] Translated [1746] by WILLIAM MELMOTH.

[3] *Book VI, letter 16*, contains the description of the eruption of Vesuvius, A.D. 79, as witnessed by Pliny the Elder.

[4] This comes to inform you that I am in a perfect state of health, hoping you are in the same. Ay, that's the old beginning. — GEORGE COLMAN THE YOUNGER, *The Heir at Law* [1797], act III, sc. ii

[5] It has been a thousand times observed, and I must observe it once more, that the hours we pass with happy prospects in view are more pleasing than those crowned with fruition. — GOLDSMITH, *The Vicar of Wakefield* [1766], ch. 10

[6] "There is no book so bad," said the bachelor, "but something good may be found in it." — CERVANTES, *Don Quixote, pt. II* [1615], ch. 3

[7] Paterfamilias.

[8] Dolce far niente [Sweet doing-nothing]. — *Italian proverb*

---

[1] Maxima debetur puero reverentia.

See Locke, p. 373a.

[2] See Lord John Russell, p. 567b.

[3] One precedent creates another. They soon accumulate and become law. — JUNIUS, *Letters* [1769–1771], *Dedication*

[4] Elegantiae arbiter.

[5] See Milton, p. 338a.

[6] Deos fortioribus adesse.

See Bussy-Rabutin, p. 357a; Boileau, p. 377b; Frederick the Great, p. 435a; and Gibbon, p. 466a.

[7] Omne ignotum pro magnifico.

Objects which are usually the motives of our travels by land and by sea are often overlooked and neglected if they lie under our eye. . . . We put off from time to time going and seeing what we know we have an opportunity of seeing when we please.

Letters, bk. VIII, letter 20

His only fault is that he has no fault.[1] *Ib. IX, 26*

SUETONIUS
A.D. C. 70 – C. 140

Hail, Emperor, we who are about to die salute you.[2] *Life of Claudius 21*

HADRIAN
[PUBLIUS AELIUS HADRIANUS]
A.D. 76–138

Little soul, wandering, gentle guest and companion of the body, into what places will you now go, pale, stiff, and naked, no longer sporting as you did![3]

Ad Animam Suam

CHANG HENG[4]
A.D. 78–139

Heaven is like an egg, and the earth is like the yolk of the egg.

Saying

[1] The greatest of faults, I should say, is to be conscious of none. — CARLYLE, *Heroes and Hero-Worship* [1841], *The Hero as Prophet*
[2] Ave, Caesar, morituri te salutamus.
Also rendered "te salutant": those about to die salute you.
[3] Animula vagula blandula,
Hospes comesque corporis,
Quae nunc abibis in loca
Pallidula rigida nudula,
Nec ut soles dabis iocos!

Amelette Ronsardelette,
mignonelette doucelette,
trèschère hostesse de mon corps,
tu descens là bas foibelette,
pasle, maigrelette, seulette,
dans le froid Royaulme des mors.
RONSARD, *A son âme* [dictated on his deathbed, December 27, 1585]
See Pope, p. 404a.
[4] From *Sources of Chinese Tradition*, edited by WILLIAM THEODORE DE BARY.

MARCUS AURELIUS ANTONINUS[1]
A.D. 121–180

This Being of mine, whatever it really is, consists of a little flesh, a little breath, and the part which governs.

Meditations II, 2

Thou wilt find rest from vain fancies if thou doest every act in life as though it were thy last.[2] *Ib. 5*

Remember that no man loseth other life than that which he liveth, nor liveth other than that which he loseth.

Ib. 14

Each thing is of like form from everlasting and comes round again in its cycle. *Ib.*

The longest-lived and the shortest-lived man, when they come to die, lose one and the same thing. *Ib.*

As for life, it is a battle and a sojourning in a strange land; but the fame that comes after is oblivion. *Ib. 17*

Waste not the remnant of thy life in those imaginations touching other folk, whereby thou contributest not to the common weal. *Ib. III, 4*

A man should *be* upright, not be *kept* upright. *Ib. 5*

Never esteem anything as of advantage to thee that shall make thee break thy word or lose thy self-respect.

Ib. 7

By a tranquil mind I mean nothing else than a mind well ordered.

Ib. IV, 3

The universe is change; our life is what our thoughts make it. *Ib.*

Death, like birth, is a secret of Nature. *Ib. 5*

Whatever happens at all happens as it should; thou wilt find this true, if thou shouldst watch narrowly.

Ib. 10

[1] Translated by MORRIS HICKEY MORGAN [1859–1910].
[2] See Horace, p. 121a, and Publilius Syrus, p. 126b.

How much time he gains who does not look to see what his neighbor says or does or thinks, but only at what he does himself, to make it just and holy.
                    Meditations IV, 18

Whatever is in any way beautiful hath its source of beauty in itself, and is complete in itself; praise forms no part of it. So it is none the worse nor the better for being praised.   *Ib. 20*

All that is harmony for thee, O Universe, is in harmony with me as well. Nothing that comes at the right time for thee is too early or too late for me. Everything is fruit to me that thy seasons bring, O Nature. All things come of thee, have their being in thee, and return to thee.[1]   *Ib. 23*

"Let thine occupations be few," saith the sage,[2] "if thou wouldst lead a tranquil life."   *Ib. 24*

Love the little trade which thou hast learned, and be content therewith.
                    Ib. 31

There is a proper dignity and proportion to be observed in the performance of every act of life.   *Ib. 32*

All is ephemeral — fame and the famous as well.   *Ib. 35*

Search men's governing principles, and consider the wise, what they shun and what they cleave to.   *Ib. 38*

Time is a sort of river of passing events, and strong is its current; no sooner is a thing brought to sight than it is swept by and another takes its place, and this too will be swept away.[3]
                    Ib. 43

All that happens is as usual and familiar as the rose in spring and the crop in summer.   *Ib. 44*

Mark how fleeting and paltry is the estate of man — yesterday in embryo, tomorrow a mummy or ashes. So for the hairsbreadth of time assigned to

[1] See *I Chronicles 29:14*, p. 14a.
[2] Seneca, *De Ira III, 6; De Animi Tranquillitate 13.*
[3] See Isaac Watts, p. 397a.

thee, live rationally, and part with life cheerfully, as drops the ripe olive, extolling the season that bore it and the tree that matured it.
                    Meditations IV, 48

In the morning, when thou art sluggish at rousing thee, let this thought be present: "I am rising to a man's work."   *Ib. V, 1*

A man makes no noise over a good deed, but passes on to another as a vine to bear grapes again in season.[1]
                    Ib. 6

Nothing happens to anybody which he is not fitted by nature to bear.
                    Ib. 18

Live with the gods.   *Ib. 27*

Look beneath the surface; let not the several quality of a thing nor its worth escape thee.   *Ib. VI, 3*

The controlling intelligence understands its own nature, and what it does, and whereon it works.   *Ib. 5*

Do not think that what is hard for thee to master is impossible for man; but if a thing is possible and proper to man, deem it attainable by thee.
                    Ib. 19

What is not good for the swarm is not good for the bee.   *Ib. 54*

One universe made up of all that is; and one God in it all, and one principle of being, and one law, the reason, shared by all thinking creatures, and one truth.   *Ib. VII, 9*

It is man's peculiar duty to love even those who wrong him.[2]   *Ib. 22*

Very little is needed to make a happy life.   *Ib. 67*

To change thy mind and to follow him that sets thee right is to be none the less the free agent that thou wast before.   *Ib. VIII, 16*

Look to the essence of a thing,

[1] See *Matthew 6:3*, p. 40a.
[2] See *Proverbs 25:21*, p. 26a.

whether it be a point of doctrine, of practice, or of interpretation.
Meditations VIII, 22

Be not careless in deeds, nor confused in words, nor rambling in thought. *Ib. 51*

Think not disdainfully of death, but look on it with favor; for even death is one of the things that Nature wills.
Ib. IX, 3

A wrongdoer is often a man that has left something undone, not always he that has done something.[1] *Ib. 5*

Blot out vain pomp; check impulse; quench appetite; keep reason under its own control. *Ib. 7*

All things are the same — familiar in enterprise, momentary in endurance, coarse in substance. All things now are as they were in the day of those whom we have buried. *Ib. 14*

Whatever may befall thee, it was preordained for thee from everlasting.
Ib. X, 5

DIOGENES LAERTIUS
fl. A.D. C. 200

Ignorance plays the chief part among men, and the multitude of words.[2]
Cleobulus 4

Time is the image of eternity.
Plato 41

There is a written and an unwritten law. The one by which we regulate our constitutions in our cities is the written law; that which arises from custom is the unwritten law. *Ib. 51*

QUINTUS SEPTIMIUS TERTULLIAN
A.D. C. 155 – 225

O witness of the soul naturally Christian. *Apologeticus 17*

[1] See *Book of Common Prayer*, p. 59b.
[2] In the multitude of words there wanteth not sin. — *Proverbs 10:19*

See how these Christians love one another.[1] *Apologeticus 39*

We multiply whenever we are mown down by you; the blood of Christians is seed.[2] *Ib. 50*

Man is one name belonging to every nation upon earth. In them all is one soul though many tongues. Every country has its own language, yet the subjects of which the untutored soul speaks are the same everywhere.
Testimony of the Soul

Mother Church.[3] *Ad Martyrās 1*

Truth persuades by teaching, but does not teach by persuading.
Adversus Valentinianos 1

Truth does not blush.[4] *Ib. 3*

The virtues of the heathen, being devoid of grace, can only be looked upon as splendid vices.
De Carne Christi 1

It is to be believed because it is absurd.[5] *Ib. 5*

It is certain because it is impossible.[6]
Ib.

[1] Tertullian is sarcastically repeating what the enemies of Christianity are saying.
See Emerson, p. 606b.
[2] Plures efficimur, quoties metimur a vobis; semen est sanguis christianorum.
This is often rendered as: The blood of the martyrs is the seed of the Church.
The Church of Christ has been founded by shedding its own blood, not that of others; by enduring outrage, not by inflicting it. Persecutions have made it grow; martyrdoms have crowned it. — ST. JEROME [A.D. C. 340–420], *letter 82*
The blood of martyrs is the seed of Christians. — BEYERLINCK, *Magnum Theatrum Vitae Humanorum* [1665]
The seed of the Church, I mean the blood of primitive martyrs. — THOMAS FULLER, *Church History of Britain* [1665], *pt. IV, bk. I*
[3] Domina mater ecclesia.
See St. Cyprian, p. 144a.
[4] Veritas non erubescit.
[5] Prorsus credibile est, quia ineptum est.
[6] Certum est, quia impossibile est.
This is called "Tertullian's rule of faith." It is sometimes rendered as: Credo quia impossibile [I believe because it is impossible]. St. Augustine expresses the same idea in *Confessions VI, 5, 7*.

Out of the frying pan into the fire.[1]
De Carne Christi 6

One man's religion neither harms nor helps another man.
Ad Scapulam 2

It is certainly no part of religion to compel religion. *Ib.*

I must dispel vanity with vanity.
Adversus Marcionem IV, 30

ST. CYPRIAN
d. A.D. 258

He cannot have God for his father who has not the Church for his Mother.[2]
De Unitate Ecclesiae [251], *ch.* 6

There is no salvation outside the Church.[3] *Letter* 73 [*c.* 256]

LONGINUS
A.D. C. 210 — 273

It frequently happens that where the second line is sublime, the third, in which he meant to rise still higher, is perfect bombast.[4]
On the Sublime, sec. 3

Sublimity is the echo of a noble mind. *Ib.* 9

In the Odyssey one may liken Homer to the setting sun, of which the grandeur remains without the intensity.
Ib.

CONSTANTINE
A.D. C. 288 — 337

In this sign shalt thou conquer.[5]
From EUSEBIUS, *Life of Constantine I*, 28

[1] De calcaria in carbonarium.
Leap out of the frying pan into the fire. — JOHN HEYWOOD, *Proverbs* [1546], *pt. II, ch.* 5
[2] Habere non potest deum patrem qui ecclesiam non habet matrem.
See Tertullian, p. 143b.
[3] Salus extra ecclesiam non est.
Quoted by St. Augustine in *De Baptismo*, hence sometimes attributed to him.
[4] The reference is to Lucan's style.
[5] In hoc signo vinces.
The alleged words of Constantine's vision be-

ST. JOHN CHRYSOSTOM
A.D. 327 — 407

No one can harm the man who does himself no wrong.[1]
Letter to Olympia

AMMIANUS MARCELLINUS
A.D. C. 330 — 395

Rose among thorns.
History, bk. XVI, ch. 17

JULIAN
[THE APOSTATE]
A.D. 332 — 363

You have conquered, Galilean.[2]
From THEODORET, *Church History III*, 20

ST. AMBROSE
A.D. C. 340 — 397

When you are at Rome live in the Roman style; when you are elsewhere live as they live elsewhere.[3]
Advice to St. Augustine. From JEREMY TAYLOR, *Ductor Dubitantium* [1660] *I*, 1, 5

fore his battle with Maxentius at Saxa Rubra, near Rome, A.D. 312.
[1] No one is injured save by himself. — ERASMUS [1465–1536], *Adagia*
[2] Vicisti, Galilaee.
The Latin translation of the alleged dying words of the Emperor.
See Swinburne, p. 774a.
[3] Si fueris Romae, Romano vivito more; Si fueris alibi, vivito sicut ibi.
My mother, having joined me at Milan, found that the church there did not fast on Saturdays as at Rome, and was at a loss what to do. I consulted St. Ambrose, of holy memory, who replied, "When I am at Rome, I fast on a Saturday; when I am at Milan, I do not. Follow the custom of the church where you are." — ST. AUGUSTINE [A.D. 354–430], *Epistle to Januarius* (*Epistle* 2), *sec. 18.* Also *Epistle to Casualanus* (*Epistle* 36), *sec.* 32
When in Rome, do as the Romans do.— *Proverb*

ST. JEROME[1]
A.D. C. 342 – 420

A friend is long sought, hardly found, and with difficulty kept.
Letter 1

Love is not to be purchased, and affection has no price. *Letter 3*

The friendship that can cease has never been real. *Ib.*

It is easier to mend neglect than to quicken love. *Letter 7*

Love knows nothing of order. *Ib.*

The fact is that my native land is a prey to barbarism, that in it men's only God is their belly,[2] that they live only for the present, and that the richer a man is the holier he is held to be. *Ib.*

An unstable pilot steers a leaking ship, and the blind is leading the blind straight to the pit.[3] The ruler is like the ruled. *Ib.*

No athlete is crowned but in the sweat of his brow. *Letter 14*

If there is but little water in the stream, it is the fault, not of the channel, but of the source. *Letter 17*

You are a Ciceronian, not a Christian.[4] *Letter 22*

It is idle to play the lyre for an ass.[5] *Letter 27*

Everything must have in it a sharp seasoning of truth. *Letter 31*

While truth is always bitter, pleasantness waits upon evildoing.
Letter 40

The line, often adopted by strong men in controversy, of justifying the means by the end.[6] *Letter 48*

Do not let your deeds belie your words, lest when you speak in church someone may say to himself, "Why do you not practice what you preach?"[1]
Letter 48

Avoid, as you would the plague, a clergyman who is also a man of business. *Letter 52*[2]

A fat paunch never breeds fine thoughts.[3] *Ib.*

No one cares to speak to an unwilling listener. An arrow never lodges in a stone: often it recoils upon the sender of it. *Ib.*

That clergyman soon becomes an object of contempt who being often asked out to dinner never refuses to go. *Ib.*

The best almoner is he who keeps back nothing for himself. *Ib.*

It is worse still to be ignorant of your ignorance. *Letter 53*

Even brute beasts and wandering birds do not fall into the same traps or nets twice.[4] *Letter 54*

Sometimes the character of the mistress is inferred from the dress of her maids. *Ib.*

The face is the mirror of the mind, and eyes without speaking confess the secrets of the heart. *Ib.*

The scars of others should teach us caution. *Ib.*

When the stomach is full, it is easy to talk of fasting. *Letter 58*

Small minds can never handle great themes.[5] *Letter 60*

The Roman world is falling, yet we

---

[1] Translated by W. H. FREMANTLE.
[2] See *Philippians 3:19*, p. 54b.
[3] See *Matthew 15:14*, p. 43a.
[4] This was addressed to Jerome in a dream by Christ the Judge, censuring him for loving the classics more than the Fathers.
[5] A Greek proverb frequently quoted by Jerome.
[6] See Matthew Prior, p. 387b.

[1] Cur ergo haec ipse non facis?
See Plautus, p. 106a.
[2] Translated by F. A. WRIGHT.
[3] This is a Greek proverb.
Fat paunches have lean pates, and dainty bits
Make rich the ribs, but bankrupt quite the wits.
SHAKESPEARE, *Love's Labour's Lost, act I, sc. i, l. 26*
[4] Translated by F. A. WRIGHT.
[5] Translated by W. J. COURTENAY.

hold our heads erect instead of bowing our necks.[1] *Letter 60*

Every day we are changing, every day we are dying, and yet we fancy ourselves eternal. *Ib.*

Early impressions are hard to eradicate from the mind. When once wool has been dyed purple, who can restore it to its previous whiteness? *Letter 107*

The tired ox treads with a firmer step.[2] *Letter 112*

Athletes as a rule are stronger than their backers; yet the weaker presses the stronger to put forth all his efforts. *Letter 118*

For they wished to fill the winepress of eloquence not with the tendrils of mere words but with the rich grape juice of good sense. *Letter 125*

It is no fault of Christianity that a hypocrite falls into sin. *Ib.*

The charges we bring against others often come home to ourselves; we inveigh against faults which are as much ours as theirs; and so our eloquence ends by telling against ourselves. *Ib.*

Preferring to store her money in the stomachs of the needy rather than hide it in a purse.[3] *Letter 127*

The privileges of a few do not make common law.[4] *Exposition on Jona*

Never look a gift horse in the mouth.[5]
On the Epistle to the Ephesians

[1] Romanus orbis ruit.
[2] An old Roman proverb quoted by St. Jerome to St. Augustine after the latter criticized the elder Jerome.
[3] Translated by F. A. WRIGHT.
[4] Privilegia paucorum non faciunt legem.
The exception proves the rule.
[5] Noli equi dentes inspicere donati.
No man ought to look a given horse in the mouth. — JOHN HEYWOOD, *Proverbs* [1546], *pt. I, ch. 5*
A gift horse should not be looked in the mouth. — CERVANTES, *Don Quixote, pt. II* [1615], *bk. IV, ch. 62*

KU K'AI-CHIH[1]
A.D. c. 344 – 406

Of all kinds of painting, figure painting is the most difficult; then comes landscape painting, and next dogs and horses. High towers and pavilions are definite things; they are difficult to execute, but easy to handle since they do not demand insight.
Discussion of Painting

**VEGETIUS
[FLAVIUS VEGETIUS RENATUS]**
fl. A.D. c. 375

Let him who desires peace prepare for war.[2]

De Rei Militari III, prologue

ST. AUGUSTINE
A.D. 354–430

Will is to grace as the horse is to the rider.[3]

De Libero Arbitrio [388–395]

The weakness of little children's limbs is innocent, not their souls.
Confessions [397–401] I, 7

To Carthage I came, where all about me resounded a caldron of dissolute loves.[4] *Ib. III, 1*

I was in love with loving. *Ib.*

He ne'er considered it, as loth
To look a gift horse in the mouth.
SAMUEL BUTLER, *Hudibras, pt. I* [1663], *canto 1, l. 489*
[1] From *The Spirit of the Brush,* translated by SHIO SAKANISHI [*Wisdom of the East Series,* 1957].
[2] Qui desiderat pacem, praeparet bellum.
In peace, like a wise man, he has provided for the needs of war. — HORACE, *Satires, bk. II* [30 B.C.], *ii, 111*
We should provide in peace what we need in war. — PUBLILIUS SYRUS [1st century B.C.], *Maxim 709*
See Robert Burton, p. 311b; Fénélon, p. 383a; and George Washington, p. 461b.
[3] This is considered the most important definition of the relation of grace to free will in the Middle Ages.
[4] To Carthage then I came. — T. S. ELIOT, *The Waste Land* [1922], *III, l. 307 and note.*

In the usual course of study I had come to a book of a certain Cicero.
Confessions III, 4

Give me chastity and continence, but not just now.   *Ib. VIII,* 7

Take up, read! Take up, read! [1]
Ib. 12

Too late I loved you, O Beauty so ancient yet ever new! Too late I loved you! And, behold, you were within me, and I out of myself, and there I searched for you.   *Ib. X,* 27

Give what you command, and command what you will.   *Ib.* 29

Hear the other side.[2]
De Duabus Animabus XIV, 2

I would not have believed the gospel had not the authority of the Church moved me.
Contra Epistulam Fundamenti [c. 410], ch. 5

Necessity has no law.[3]
Soliloquiorum. Animae ad Deum [c. 410], 2

We make a ladder of our vices, if we trample those same vices underfoot.
Sermons 3

Anger is a weed; hate is the tree.
Ib. 58

The dove loves when it quarrels; the wolf hates when it flatters.   *Ib.* 64

Rome has spoken; the case is concluded.[4]   *Ib.* 131

He who created you without you will not justify you without you.   *Ib.* 169

The most glorious city of God.
City of God [415], I, preface

---

[1] Tolle lege, tolle lege. What the bell seemed to say to Augustine at the moment of his conversion. When he opened the Bible, his eyes fell on *Romans 13:12–14* (p. 51b).
[2] Audi partem alteram.
[3] See Publilius Syrus, p. 126b, and note, and Oliver Cromwell, p. 328a.
[4] Roma locuta est; causa finita est.

ST. VINCENT OF LERINS
d. A.D. c. 450

[That faith is catholic] which has been believed always, everywhere, and by all.[1]   *Commonitorium, ch.* 2

Every word almost was a sentence; every sentence a victory.[2]   *Ib.* 18

TSUNG PING[3]
A.D. 375–443

The virtuous man follows the Way by spiritual insight; the wise man takes this same approach. But the lovers of landscapes are led into the Way by a sense of form. The virtuous man also takes pleasure in this. Then, are not the pleasures of the virtuous and the wise similar to those of the lovers of landscapes?
Introduction to Landscape Painting

LONGUS
A.D. third century

There was never any yet that wholly could escape love, and never shall there be any, never so long as beauty shall be, never so long as eyes can see.
Daphnis and Chloe, proem, ch. 2

He is so poor that he could not keep a dog.   *Ib.* 15

CLOVIS
A.D. 465–511

God of Clotilda,[4] if you grant me victory I shall become a Christian.
Legendary vow before battle

---

[1] Quod semper, quod ubique, quod ab omnibus creditum est.
The definition of the traditional articles of faith.
[2] This refers to Tertullian.
[3] From *The Spirit of the Brush,* translated by SHIO SAKANISHI [*Wisdom of the East Series* 1957].
[4] St. Clotilda, wife of Clovis.

BOETHIUS
A.D. C. 470 – 525

In every adversity of fortune, to have been happy is the most unhappy kind of misfortune.[1]

*De Consolatione Philosophiae,
bk. II, 4, 4*

Who hath so entire happiness that he is not in some part offended with the condition of his estate?   *Ib. 41*

Nothing is miserable but what is thought so, and contrariwise, every estate is happy if he that bears it be content.   *Ib. 64*

From thee, great God, we spring, to thee we tend —
Path, motive, guide, original and end.[2]

Ib. III, 9, 27

Who can give law to lovers? Love is a greater law to itself.   *Ib. 12, 47*

HSIEH HO[3]
fl. A.D. 500

[Concerning the Six Principles of painting]

The first is, that through a vitalizing spirit, a painting should possess the movement of life.

The second is, that by means of the brush, the structural basis should be established.

The third is, that the representation should so conform with the objects as to give their likenesses.

The fourth is, that the coloring should be applied according to their characteristics.

The fifth is, that through organization, place and position should be determined.

The sixth is, that by copying the ancient models should be perpetuated.[4]

Notes Concerning the Classification of Old Paintings

[1] See Pindar, p. 79b; Dante, p. 160a; Chaucer, p. 165a; and Tennyson, p. 647a.
[2] Translated by SAMUEL JOHNSON, and used as motto to *The Rambler*, no. 7 [1750].
[3] From *The Spirit of the Brush*, translated by SHIO SAKANISHI [*Wisdom of the East Series*, 1957].
[4] See Horace, p. 124b; Ching Hao, p. 153a; and Fujiwara no Teika, p. 156b.

ST. BENEDICT[1]
A.D. 480–543

We are therefore about to establish a school of the Lord's service in which we hope to introduce nothing harsh or burdensome.

Rule of St. Benedict, prologue

MAGNUS AURELIUS CASSIODORUS
A.D. C. 487 – 583

He receives hope in future benefits who recognizes a benefit that has already taken place.   *Institutiones*

He is invited to great things who receives small things greatly.   *Ib.*

GREGORY I
A.D. 540–604

[They answered that they were called Angles.] It is well, for they have the faces of angels, and such should be the co-heirs of the angels in heaven.[2]

From BEDE, *Ecclesiastical History of the English People II, 1*

ALI IBN-ABU-TALIB[3]
A.D. C. 602 – 661

He who has a thousand friends has
not a friend to spare,
And he who has one enemy will meet
him everywhere.[4]

A Hundred Sayings

THE KORAN[5]
A.D. C. 610 – 632

Turn, therefore, thy face towards the holy temple of Mecca; and wherever ye

[1] Founder of Western monasticism.
[2] Traditionally quoted "Non Angli sed Angeli" (Not Angles but angels), these were the words of the Pope when he beheld two English slaves in a Roman slave market.
[3] Ali ibn-abu-Talib, son-in-law of Mohammed and fourth caliph, who was for his courage called the Lion of God, was murdered A.D. 661.
[4] Translated by EMERSON.
[5] Translated [1734] by GEORGE SALE [1697–1736].

be, turn your faces towards that place.
Ch. 2

Wherever ye be, God will bring you all back at the resurrection.   *Ib.*

As for him who voluntarily performeth a good work, verily God is grateful and knowing.   *Ib.*

Your God is one God; there is no God but He, the most merciful.
Ib.

O true believers, take your necessary precautions against your enemies, and either go forth to war in separate parties, or go forth all together in a body.
Ch. 4

Fight for the religion of God.
Ib.

O men, respect women who have borne you.   *Ib.*

Wheresoever ye be, death will overtake you, although ye be in lofty towers.   *Ib.*

God loveth not the speaking ill of anyone in public.   *Ib.*

Of his mercy he hath made for you the night and the day, that ye may rest in the one, and may seek to obtain provision for yourself of his abundance, by your industry, in the other.   *Ch. 28*

If God should punish men according to what they deserve, he would not leave on the back of the earth so much as a beast.   *Ch. 35*

God obligeth no man to more than he hath given him ability to perform.
Ch. 65

Woe be unto those who pray, and who are negligent at their prayer: who play the hypocrites, and deny necessaries to the needy.   *Ch. 107*

O unbelievers, I will not worship that which ye worship; nor will ye worship that which I worship. . . . Ye have your religion, and I my religion.
Ch. 109

ANONYMOUS MISCELLANEOUS [EARLY]

Whatever kind of word thou speakest the like shalt thou hear.
Greek Anthology [Loeb Classical Library], bk. IX, 382

Envy slays itself by its own arrows.
Ib. X, 111

Give me today, and take tomorrow.
Quoted, and condemned, by St. Chrysostom

One picture is worth more than ten thousand words.[1]   *Chinese proverb*

On the day of victory no one is tired.
Arab proverb

Death is afraid of him because he has the heart of a lion.   *Arab proverb*

I came to the place of my birth, and cried, "'The friends of my youth, where are they?" And echo answered, "Where are they?"   *Arab saying*

If only, when one heard
That Old Age was coming
One could bolt the door,
Answer "Not at home"
And refuse to meet him!
Kokinshu (Collection of Ancient and Modern Poems) [905] [2]

Can this world
From of old
Always have been so sad,
Or did it become so for the sake
Of me alone?   *Ib.[2]*

ANONYMOUS LATIN

Ab urbe condita.
Since the founding of the city [Rome].   *Saying*

Absit omen.
May it not be an omen.   *Saying*

---

[1] See Turgenev, p. 688a.
[2] Translated by ARTHUR WALEY in *Anthology of Japanese Literature*, edited by Donald Keene [1955].

Acta est fabula.
The play is over.
> *Said at ancient dramatic per-*
> *formances and quoted by*
> *Augustus on his deathbed*

Actus non facit reum, nisi mens sit rea.
The act is not criminal unless the intent is criminal.   *Legal maxim*

Ad astra per aspera.
To the stars through hardships.
                    Motto of Kansas

Adeste, fideles,
Laeti triumphantes;
Venite, venite in Bethlehem.

O come, all ye faithful,
Joyful and triumphant,
O come ye, O come ye to Bethlehem.
                    Hymn, eighteenth century

Anno aetatis suae . . .
In the year of his age . . .   *Phrase*

Bis dat qui cito dat.
He gives twice who gives promptly.[1]
                    Saying

Caveat emptor.
Let the buyer beware.   *Proverb*

Cave canem.
Beware of the dog.   *Proverb*

Cras amet qui nunquam amavit quique amavit cras amet.
Tomorrow let him love who has never loved and tomorrow let him who has loved love.[2]
> *Pervigilium Veneris* [A.D. *c.* 350],
> *refrain*

Cucullus non facit monachum.
The cowl does not make a monk.[3]
                    Medieval proverb

Cuius regio eius religio.
He who controls the area controls the religion.   *Proverb*

De gustibus non disputandum.

---

[1] See Publilius Syrus, p. 125a, and Augustus Caesar, p. 124b.
[2] See Parnell, p. 398a.
[3] It takes more than a hood and sad eyes to make a monk. — *Albanian proverb*

There is no accounting for tastes.
                    Proverb

De minimis non curat lex.
The law is not concerned with trifles.   *Legal maxim*

Deus vult.
God wills it.
          Motto of the Crusades [1095]

Dis manibus sacrum [abbreviation DMS].
Sacred to the departed spirit(s).
          Inscription on tombstones

Divide et impera.
Divide and rule.
> *Ancient political maxim cited by*
> MACHIAVELLI

Errare humanum est.
To err is human.[1]   *Saying*

Et in Arcadia ego.
I too have lived in Arcadia.[2]
> *Inscription on a tomb in*
> *a painting by* GUERCINO
> [*c.* 1623]

Ex ungue leonem.
From his toenail [one can tell] a lion.[3]   *Saying*

Finis coronat opus.
The ending crowns the work [in a good or bad sense].   *Saying*

Flagrante delicto.
"Red-handed."   *Saying*

Fluctuat nec mergitur.
It tosses but doesn't sink.
                    Motto of Paris

Gaudeamus igitur,
Iuvenes dum sumus.

---

[1] See Plutarch, p. 137b, and Pope, p. 403b.
[2] This translation is now usually considered erroneous. The accepted translation is: I too am in Arcadia — that is, Even in Arcadia there am I [Death].
SCHIDONI [1560–1616] wrote: "Et ego in Arcadia vixi," which Poussin, Reynolds, and others used in their paintings. E. PANOFSKY discusses the phrase in *Philosophy and History: Essays Presented to E. Cassirer* [1936].
[3] See Herodotus, p. 86b.

Let us live then and be glad
While young life is before us.

       Students' song [c. 1267]

Habeas corpus.
You are to produce the person [of
the accused].   *Legal maxim*

Hannibal ad portas!
Hannibal is at the gates!   *Saying*

In vino veritas.
In wine is truth.[1]

      Proverb quoted by PLATO,
            Symposium 217

Ipse dixit.
He himself [the Master] said it.

           Saying

Ius est ars boni et aequi.
Legal justice is the art of the good
and the fair.   *Saying*

Mater artium necessitas.
Necessity is the mother of invention.[2]

           Saying

Mors ultima ratio.
Death is the final accounting.

           Saying

Nemo me impune lacessit.
No one provokes me with impunity.
    Motto of the Crown of Scotland

Nihil [or Ne quid] nimis.
Nothing in excess.[3]   *Saying*

Non multa sed multum.
Not quantity but quality [Not many
but much].[4]   *Proverb*

Orare est laborare, laborare est
orare.
To pray is to work, to work is to
pray.

      *Ancient motto of the
        Benedictine Monks*

Parvis e glandibus quercus.
Tall oaks from little acorns grow.[5]

Pereant qui nostra ante nos dixerunt.
May they perish who have used our
words before us.   *Saying*

1 See Alcaeus, p. 69a.
2 See Persius, p. 133b, and note.
3 See The Seven Sages, p. 68b.
4 See Seneca, p. 130a.
5 See David Everett, p. 507a.

Piscem natare doces.
You're teaching a fish to swim.

           Saying

Post hoc, ergo propter hoc.
After this, therefore because of this.
      Definition of fallacy in logic

Primus inter pares.
The first among equals.   *Saying*

Pro bono publico.
For the public good.   *Saying*

Requiescat in pace [abbreviation
RIP].
May he rest in peace.   *Saying*

Res iudicata pro veritate habetur.
A matter which has been [legally]
decided is considered true.

         Legal maxim

Salus populi suprema lex.
The people's safety is the highest law.
      Legal and political maxim.

Semper fidelis.
Ever faithful.
      Motto of the U.S. Marine Corps

Sic semper tyrannis.[1]
Thus always to tyrants.

         Motto of Virginia

Sit tibi terra levis [abbreviation
STTL].
May the earth rest lightly on you.[2]
      Inscription on tombstones

Summum ius summa iniuria.
Extreme [legal] justice is extreme injustice.[3]

      *Legal maxim cited by Cicero,
           De Officiis 1. 10. 33*

Testis unus testis nullus.
A single witness is no witness.

         Legal maxim

Ubi bene ibi patria.
Where one is happy, there's one's
homeland.   *Saying*

1 See John Wilkes Booth, p. 778a.
2 See Euripides, p. 83b; Beaumont and
Fletcher, p. 316b; and Richardson, p. 822a.
3 See Terence, p. 108b, and note.

Urbi et orbi.
To the city [Rome] and to the
world.   *Apostolic blessing*

Vade in pace.
Go in peace.
         End of confessional absolution

Vae victis!
Woe to the conquered!
         Quoted by LIVY, *5, 48, as said
         by Brennus to the Romans*

Volenti non fit iniuria.
To a person who consents no injustice is done.   *Legal maxim*

CAEDMON
fl. 670

Light was first
Through the Lord's word
Named day:
Beauteous, bright creation!
         Creation.[1] *The First Day*

The fiend with all his comrades
Fell then from heaven above,
Through as long as three nights and
     days,
The angels from heaven into hell;
And them all the Lord transformed to
     devils,
Because they his deed and word
Would not revere.
         Ib. The Fall of the Rebel Angels

BEDE
[VENERABLE BEDE]
c. 672 – c. 735

It is better never to begin a good
work than, having begun it, to stop.
         *Ecclesiastical History of the
         English People, bk. I, ch. 23*

ST. JOHN OF DAMASCUS
c. 700 – c. 760

God is a sea of infinite substance.[2]
         De Fide Orthodoxa, bk. I, ch. 9

[1] From the text of BENJAMIN THORPE [1782–
1870].
[2] This is the most frequently quoted definition
of God in the Middle Ages. It is based on ST.
GREGORY OF NAZIANZUS [c. 330–390], *Oration 38.*

ALCUIN
735–804

The voice of the people is the voice
of God.[1]
         Letter to Charlemagne
                        [A.D. 800]

Here halt, I pray you, make a little
     stay,
O wayfarer, to read what I have writ,
And know by my fate what thy fate
     shall be.
What thou art now, wayfarer, world-
     renowned,
I was: what I am now, so shall thou
     be.
The world's delight I followed with a
     heart
Unsatisfied: ashes am I, and dust.
         His Own Epitaph [2]

Alcuin was my name: learning I
loved.   *Ib.*

LOTHAIR I
795–855

The times change and we change
with them.[3]
         From OWEN's *Epigrammata*
                        [1615]

ONO NO KOMACHI
Ninth century

The flowers withered,
Their color faded away,
While meaninglessly
I spent my days in the world
And the long rains were falling.
                    Kokinshu [905] [4]

This night of no moon
There is no way to meet him.
I rise in longing —

[1] Vox populi, vox Dei.
See Pope, p. 412a.
[2] Translated by HELEN WADDELL.
[3] Tempora mutantur, nos et mutamur in illis.
Also quoted in HOLINSHED, *Chronicles of
England* [1577].
See Spenser, p. 200b.
[4] Translated by DONALD KEENE. From *Anthology of Japanese Literature,* edited by Donald Keene.

My breast pounds, a leaping flame,
My heart is consumed in fire.

Kokinshu

So lonely am I
My body is a floating weed
Severed at the roots.
Were there water to entice me,
I would follow it, I think.   *Ib.*

CHANG YEN-YUAN
fl. c. 850

The painters of today mix their
brushes and ink with dust and dirt, and
their colors with mud, and in vain
smear the silk. How can this be called
painting?

*Discussion of the Six Principles
of Painting* [1]

CHING HAO
fl. 925

A youth who likes to study will in the
end succeed. To begin with he should
know that there are Six Essentials in
painting. The first is called *spirit*; the
second, *rhythm*; the third, *thought*; the
fourth, *scenery*; the fifth, the *brush*,
and the last is the *ink*.

Notes on Brushwork [1,2]

Resemblance reproduces the formal
aspect of objects, but neglects their
spirit; truth shows the spirit and substance in like perfection. He who tries
to transmit the spirit by means of the
formal aspect and ends by merely obtaining the outward appearance, will
produce a dead thing.   *Ib.*

SEI SHONAGON
b. 966

One writes a letter, taking particular
trouble to get it up as prettily as possible; then waits for the answer, making
sure every moment that it cannot be
much longer before something comes.
At last, frightfully late, is brought in
— one's own note, still folded or tied
exactly as one sent it, but so finger-
marked and smudged that even the address is barely legible. "The family is
not in residence," the messenger says,
giving one back the note.

Makura no Soshi [c. 1002] [1]

If someone with whom one is having
an affair keeps on mentioning some
woman whom he knew in the past,
however long ago it is since they separated, one is always irritated.   *Ib.*

MURASAKI SHIKIBU
c. 978 – 1031

[The art of the novel] does not simply consist in the author's telling a story
about the adventures of some other person. . . . It happens because the
storyteller's own experience of men and
things, whether for good or ill — not
only what he has passed through himself, but even events which he has only
witnessed or been told of — has moved
him to an emotion so passionate that
he can no longer keep it shut up in his
heart. . . . There must never come a
time, he feels, when men do not know
about it. . . .

Clearly then, it is no part of the
storyteller's craft to describe only what
is good or beautiful. Sometimes, of
course, virtue will be his theme, and he
may then make such play with it as he
will. But he is just as likely to have been
struck by numerous examples of vice
and folly in the world around him, and
about them he has exactly the same
feelings as about the preeminently good
deeds which he encounters: they are
important and must all be garnered in.
Thus anything whatsoever may become
the subject of a novel, provided only
that it happens in this mundane life

---

[1] From *The Spirit of the Brush*, translated by
SHIO SAKANISHI [*Wisdom of the East Series*,
1957].
[2] See Hsieh Ho, p. 148a.

[1] Translated by DONALD KEENE. From *Anthology of Japanese Literature*, edited by Donald Keene.

and not in some fairyland beyond our human ken.

The Tale of Genji [*c.* 1000] [1]

ST. ANSELM
c. 1033 – 1109

God is that, the greater than which cannot be conceived.[2]

Proslogion, ch. 3

ABU MOHAMMED KASIM BEN ALI HARIRI
1054–1122

We praise Thee, O God,
For whatever perspicuity of language
    Thou hast taught us
And whatever eloquence Thou hast in-
    spired us with.

Makamat. Prayer

PETER ABELARD
1079–1142

O what their joy and their glory must
    be,
Those endless sabbaths the blessed ones
    see! [3]   *Hymnus Paraclitensis*

Against the disease of writing one must take special precautions, since it is a dangerous and contagious disease.

Letter 8, Abelard to Héloise [4]

ST. BERNARD
1091–1153

You will find something more in woods than in books. Trees and stones will teach you that which you can never learn from masters.[5]   *Epistle 106*

I have liberated my soul.[6]   *Ib. 371*

¹ Translated by ARTHUR WALEY. See Motoori, p. 455b.
² This is commonly referred to as the onto-logical argument for the existence of God, and derives from ST. AUGUSTINE, *De Doctrina Christiana*, bk. I, ch. 7. It is also to be found in DESCARTES, *Third Meditation*.
³ O quanta qualia sunt illa sabbata,
    Quae semper celebrat superna curia.
Translated by JOHN MASON NEALE [1884].
⁴ See Héloise, p. 154b.
⁵ See Shakespeare, *As You Like It*, pp. 247b and 249b, and Wordsworth, p. 509a.
⁶ Liberavi animam meam.

Hell is full of good intentions or de-sires.[1]

Attributed. From ST. FRANCIS DE SALES, *Letter 74*

SONG OF ROLAND
Eleventh century

Friend Roland, sound your oli-phant.[2]

La Chanson de Roland, l. 1070

Roland is valorous and Oliver is wise.[3]   *Ib. 1093*

HÉLOISE[4]
c. 1101 – c. 1164

Riches and power are but gifts of blind fate, whereas goodness is the re-sult of one's own merits.

Letter 2, Héloise to Abelard

ARCHPOET[5]
Twelfth century

When the hour is nigh me,
Let me in the tavern die,
With a tankard by me.[6]   *Confessio*

Sweeter tastes the wine to me in a tav-
    ern tankard
Than the watered stuff my Lord Bishop
    hath decanted.   *Ib.*

¹ Hell is full of good meanings and wishings. — GEORGE HERBERT, *Jacula Prudentum* [1651], *no. 170*
Hell is paved with good intentions. — JOHN RAY, *English Proverbs* [1670]
Quoted by SAMUEL JOHNSON [1775]; from BOSWELL, *Life of Dr. Johnson* [1791], vol. I, p. 555 [*Everyman ed.*]
Hell is paved with good intentions, not with bad ones. — GEORGE BERNARD SHAW [1856–1950], *Maxims for Revolutionists*
² Compagnon Roland sonnez de votre oliphant.
³ Roland est preux et Oliver est sage.
A Roland for an Oliver. I.e., a blow for a blow, tit for tat, referring to the drawn combat between Roland and Oliver.
⁴ See Peter Abelard, p. 154a.
⁵ Translated by HELEN WADDELL.
⁶ In taberna mori
    ut sint vina proxima
    morientis ori.
See Walter Map, p. 155b.

Down the broad way do I go,
Young and unregretting,
Wrap me in my vices up,
Virtue all forgetting,
Greedier for all delight
Than heaven to enter in:
Since the soul in me is dead,
Better save the skin.
Estuans Intrinsecus

GRATIAN
Twelfth century

Paintings are the Bible of the laity.[1]
Decretum, pt. III

POEM OF THE CID[2]
Twelfth century

Were his lord but worthy, God, how
fine a vassal. *l. 20*

Thus parted the one from the others
as the nail from the flesh. *l. 375*

Who serves a good lord lives always
in luxury. *l. 850*

One would grow poor staying in one
place always. *l. 948*

FREDERICK I
[BARBAROSSA]
1122–1190

An emperor is subject to no one but
God and Justice.
From ZINCGREF,
*Apophthegmata,
bk. I* [1626]

AVERROËS
1126–1198

Knowledge is the conformity of the
object and the intellect.[3]
Destructio Destructionum

[1] Also attributed by Gratian to GREGORY
SERENO, Bishop of Massilio, *Letter 9.*
[2] Translated by W. S. MERWIN.
[3] The classic definition of epistemology, still
commented on today and used by the Neo-
Thomists.

HENRY II
1133–1189

Who will free me from this turbulent priest? [1] *Attributed*

MOSES BEN MAIMON
[MAIMONIDES]
1135–1204

Anticipate charity by preventing poverty; assist the reduced fellowman, either by a considerable gift, or a sum of
money, or by teaching him a trade, or
by putting him in the way of business,
so that he may earn an honest livelihood, and not be forced to the dreadful
alternative of holding out his hand for
charity. This is the highest step and the
summit of charity's golden ladder.[2]
Charity's Eight Degrees

WALTER MAP [MAPES]
c. 1140 – c. 1210

I intend to die in a tavern; let the
wine be placed near my dying mouth,[3]
so that when the choirs of angels come,
they may say, "God be merciful to this
drinker!" *De Nugis Curialium*

ALAIN DE LILLE
[ALANUS DE INSULIS]
d. 1202

Do not hold as gold all that shines as
gold.[4] *Parabolae*

[1] Thomas à Becket.
[2] See Andrew Carnegie, p. 757a.
[3] Meum est propositum in taberna mori;
Vinum sit appositum morientis ori.
See Archpoet, p. 154b.
[4] Non teneas aurum totum quod splendet ut
aurum [All that glitters is not gold].
This was considered a common proverb which
had its roots in a Latin translation from ARIS-
TOTLE: Yellow-colored objects appear to be gold.
— *Elenchi, bk. I, ch. 1*
Hyt is not al gold that glareth. — CHAUCER,
The House of Fame [1374–1385], *bk. I, l. 272*
But al thyng which that shineth as the
gold
Nis nat gold, as that I have herd it told.
The Canterbury Tales [c. 1387]. *The
Canon's Yeoman's Tale, l. 962*
All is not golde that outward shewith bright.
— LYDGATE [c. 1370–c. 1451], *On the Mutability
of Human Affairs*
(note continues p. 156)

KAMO NO CHOMEI
1153–1216

The flow of the river is ceaseless and its water is never the same. The bubbles that float in the pools, now vanishing, now forming, are not of long duration: so in the world are man and his dwellings. . . . [People] die in the morning, they are born in the evening, like foam on the water.

Hojoki (An Account of My Hut) [1] [1212]

He who complies with the ways of the world may be impoverished thereby; he who does not, appears deranged. Wherever one may live, whatever work one may do, is it possible even for a moment to find a haven for the body or peace for the mind?   *Ib.*

Only in a hut built for the moment can one live without fears.   *Ib.*

My body is like a drifting cloud — I ask for nothing, I want nothing.
    Ib.

WALTHER VON DER VOGELWEIDE
c. 1160 – 1230

Now the summer came to pass
And flowers through the grass
Joyously sprang,

Non omne quod fulget est aurum. — GABRIEL BIEL [d. 1495], *Expositio Canonis Messe, lecture 77,* derived from WILLIAM OF AUVERGNE [d. 1249]. This is the Latin version closest to the proverb as commonly known.

Gold all is not that doth golden seem. — SPENSER, *Faerie Queene, bk. II* [1590], *canto 8, st. 14*

All that glisters is not gold —
Often have you heard that told.
    SHAKESPEARE, *Merchant of Venice* [1596–1597], *act II, sc. vii, l. 65*

All is not gold that glisters. — CERVANTES, *Don Quixote, pt. II* [1615], *bk. III, ch. 33*

All is not gold that glisteneth. — MIDDLETON, *A Fair Quarrel* [1617], *act V, sc. i*

All, as they say, that glitters is not gold. — DRYDEN, *The Hind and the Panther* [1687], *l. 215*

[1] Translated by DONALD KEENE. From *Anthology of Japanese Literature,* edited by Donald Keene.

While all the tribes of birds sang.[1]
    Dream Song, st. 1 [2]

This was ever the world's distempered will:
Fools have always mocked and spurned the wise.
These shall be judged according to their lies.[3]   *Lament, st.* 2

The sun no longer shows
His face; and treason sows
His secret seeds that no man can detect;
Fathers by their children are undone;
The brother would the brother cheat;
And the cowled monk is a deceit . . .
Might is right, and justice there is none.[4]   *Millennium*

FUJIWARA NO TEIKA
1162–1241

In the expression of the emotions originality merits the first consideration. . . . The words used, however, should be old ones. . . .

The style should imitate the great poems of the masters of former times. One must discard every last phrase of the sentiments and expressions written by men of recent times. . . .

One should impregnate one's mind with a constant study of the forms of expression of ancient poetry.[5]

There are no teachers of Japanese poetry. But they who take the old poems as their teachers, steep their minds in the old style, and learn their words from the masters of former time —who of them will fail to write poetry?
    Guide to the Composition of Poetry [6]

[1] Dô der sumer komen was,
    Und die blumen dur daz gras
    Wünneclâchen sprungen,
    Aedâ die vogele sungen.
[2] See *Sumer is icumen in*, p. 1083a.
[3] Translated by MARGARET F. RICHEY.
[4] Translated by JETHRO BITHELL.
[5] See Horace, p. 124b, and Hsieh Ho, p. 148a.
[6] From *Sources of Japanese Tradition,* edited by WILLIAM THEODORE DE BARY [1958].

HARTMANN VON AUE
c. 1170 – 1215

He who helps in the saving of others,
Saves himself as well.   *Poor Henry*

HERBERT VON FRITZLAR
fl. c. 1210

The cart has no place where a fifth wheel could be used.   *Saying*

EIKE VON REPKOW
fl. c. 1220

He who comes first, eats first.
Sachsenspiegel [1219–1233]

ST. FRANCIS OF ASSISI[1]
c. 1181 – 1226

Praise to thee, my Lord, for all thy
    creatures,
Above all Brother Sun
Who brings us the day and lends us his
    light.
        *The Song of Brother Sun and of
        All His Creatures* [1225]

Love is he, radiant with great splen-
    dor,
And speaks to us of Thee, O Most
High.   *Ib.*

Where there is charity and wisdom,
there is neither fear nor ignorance.
Where there is patience and humility,
there is neither anger nor vexation.
Where there is poverty and joy, there is
neither greed nor avarice. Where there
is peace and meditation, there is neither
anxiety nor doubt.
        *The Counsels of the Holy Father
        St. Francis. Admonition* 27

Lord,
    make me an instrument of Your
    peace.
Where there is hatred let me sow
    love;
Where there is injury, pardon;
Where there is doubt, faith;
Where there is despair, hope;

[1] Translated by Leo Sherley-Price.

Where there is darkness, light; and
Where there is sadness, joy.
O divine Master,
    grant that I may not so much
Seek to be consoled as to console;
To be understood as to understand;
To be loved as to love;
For it is in giving that we receive;
It is in pardoning that we are par-
    doned; and
It is in dying that we are born to
    eternal life.   *Attributed*

I have sinned against my brother the
ass.   *Dying words*

MAGNA CARTA
1215

No freeman shall be taken, or imprisoned, or outlawed, or exiled, or in
any way harmed, nor will we go upon
him nor will we send upon him, except
by the legal judgment of his peers or by
the law of the land.   *Clause* 39

To none will we sell, to none deny or
delay, right or justice.   *Clause* 40

TOMMASO DI CELANO
c. 1185 – c. 1255

Day of wrath and doom impending,
David's word with Sibyl's blending,
Heaven and earth in ashes ending![1]
        Dies Irae

ALFONSO X
[ALFONSO THE WISE]
1221–1284

Had I been present at the creation, I
would have given some useful hints for
the better ordering of the universe.[2]
        Attributed

[1] Dies irae, dies illa
    Solvet saeclum in favilla,
    Teste David cum Sibylla.
Translated by W. J. Irons. This has been attributed also to St. Gregory and St. Bernard.
[2] Carlyle says, in his *History of Frederick
the Great, bk. II, ch. 7,* that this saying of
Alfonso about Ptolemy's astronomy, "that it
seemed a crank machine; that it was pity the
Creator had not taken advice," is still remembered by mankind — this and no other of his
many sayings.

RUTEBEUF
d. 1280

What became of the friends I had
With whom I was always so close
And loved so dearly?
La Complainte Rutebeuf

Friendship is dead:
They were friends who go with the
wind,[1]
And the wind was blowing at my door.
Ib.

ST. THOMAS AQUINAS
1227–1274

Sing, my tongue, the Savior's glory,
Of His Flesh the mystery sing;
Of the Blood, all price exceeding,
Shed by our immortal King.[2]
Pange, Lingua (hymn for Ves-
pers on the Feast of Corpus
Christi), st. 1

Down in adoration falling,
Lo! the sacred Host we hail;
Lo! o'er ancient forms departing,
Newer rites of grace prevail;
Faith for all defects supplying,
Where the feeble senses fail.
Ib. st. 5 (Tantum Ergo)

Thus Angels' Bread is made
The Bread of man today:
The Living Bread from Heaven
With figures doth away:
O wondrous gift indeed!
The poor and lowly may

---

[1] See Dowson, p. 890a.
[2] Pange, lingua, gloriosi
Corporis mysterium
Sanguinisque pretiosi,
Quem in mundi pretium
Fructus ventris generosi
Rex effudit gentium.
Translated by EDWARD CASWALL [1814–1878].
Now, my tongue, the mystery telling
Of the glorious Body sing.
The Hymnal of the Protestant
Episcopal Church
Pange, lingua, gloriosi proelium certaminis
[Sing, my tongue, the glorious battle]. — VE-
NANTIUS HONORIUS CLEMENTIANUS FORTUNATUS,
Bishop of Poitiers [fl. c. 600].

Upon their Lord and Master feed.[1]
Sacris Solemniis Juncta Sint
Gaudia (Matins hymn for
Corpus Christi), st. 6 (Panis
Angelicus)

O saving Victim, opening wide
The gate of heaven to man below,
Our foes press on from every side,
Thine aid supply, Thy strength be-
stow.[2]
Verbum Supernum Prodiens
(hymn for Lauds on Corpus
Christi), st. 5 (O Salutaris
Hostia)

Lord Jesu, blessed Pelican.
Adoro Te Devote (hymn ap-
pointed for the Thanksgiving
after Mass), st. 6 (Pie Pellicane
Jesu Domine)

Three things are necessary for the
salvation of man: to know what he
ought to believe; to know what he ought
to desire; and to know what he ought
to do.
Two Precepts of Charity [1273]

Law: an ordinance of reason for the
common good, made by him who has
care of the community.
Summa Theologica [1273]

Concerning perfect blessedness
which consists in a vision of God.[3]
Ib.

Reason in man is rather like God in
the world.
Opuscule 11, De Regno

Beware the man of one book.[4]
Quoted by ISAAC D'ISRAEL *in*
Curiosities of Literature [1791–
1793]

FREIDANK
fl. c. 1250

New brooms sweep well.   *Saying*

---

[1] Translated by J. D. CHAMBERS [1805–1893].
Man did eat angels' food. — *Psalm 78:25*
[2] Translated by EDWARD CASWALL.
[3] Probably the origin of the phrase "beatific
vision."
[4] Cave ab homine unius libri.

MEISTER ECKHART
c. 1260 – 1327

In silence man can most readily preserve his integrity.

> *Directions for the*
> *Contemplative Life*

The more wise and powerful a master, the more directly is his work created, and the simpler it is.

> *Of the Eternal Birth*

One must not always think so much about what one should do, but rather what one should be. Our works do not ennoble us; but we must ennoble our works.   *Work and Being*

DANTE ALIGHIERI
1265–1321

In that part of the book of my memory before which is little that can be read, there is a rubric, saying, "Incipit Vita Nova."

> *La Vita Nuova* [1293] [1]

Love hath so long possess'd me for his
    own
And made his lordship so familiar.
                                    Ib.

Love with delight discourses in my
    mind
Upon my lady's admirable gifts . . .
Beyond the range of human intellect.
  Il Convito. [2] *Trattato Terzo, l.* 1

In the middle of the journey of our life I came to myself within a dark wood where the straight way was lost. [3]
  The Divine Comedy [c. 1310–
  1320]. *Inferno,* [4] canto I, l. 1

And as he, who with laboring breath has escaped from the deep to the shore, turns to the perilous waters and gazes.
                                    Ib. 22

Thou [1] art my master and my author; thou art he from whom alone I took the style whose beauty has done me honor.
      The Divine Comedy. Inferno,
                        canto I, l. 85

All hope abandon, ye who enter here! [2]   *Ib. III,* 9

Here must all distrust be left behind; all cowardice must be ended.   *Ib.* 14

There sighs, lamentations and loud wailings resounded through the starless air, so that at first it made me weep; strange tongues, horrible language, words of pain, tones of anger, voices loud and hoarse, and with these the sound of hands, made a tumult which is whirling through that air forever dark, as sand eddies in a whirlwind.
                                    Ib. 22

This miserable state is borne by the wretched souls of those who lived without disgrace and without praise.
                                    Ib. 34

Let us not speak of them; but look, and pass on. [3]   *Ib.* 51

These wretches, who never were alive.   *Ib.* 64

Into the eternal darkness, into fire and into ice. [3, 4]   *Ib.* 87

Without hope we live in desire.
                                  Ib. IV, 42

I came into a place void of all light, which bellows like the sea in tempest, when it is combated by warring winds. [5]
                                  Ib. V, 28

As in the cold season their wings bear the starlings along in a broad, dense flock, so does that blast the wicked spir-

---

[1] Translated by DANTE GABRIEL ROSSETTI.
[2] Translated by CHARLES LYELL. The first line is also in *The Divine Comedy, Purgatorio II, 112.*
[3] Nel mezzo del cammin di nostra vita
  Mi ritrovai per una selva oscura,
  Che la diritta via era smarrita.
[4] Translated by JOHN D. SINCLAIR [1958], unless otherwise noted.

[1] Virgil.
[2] Lasciate ogni speranza, voi ch'entrate.
Traditional translation.
[3] Translated by JOHN AITKEN CARLYLE, *The Temple Classics* [1900].
[4] See Housman, p. 853a, and Frost, p. 927a.
[5] Translated by JOHN AITKEN CARLYLE, *The Temple Classics* [1900].

its. Hither, thither, downward, upward, it drives them.[1]

> The Divine Comedy. Inferno,
> canto V, *l. 40*

Love, which is quickly kindled in the gentle heart, seized this man for the fair form that was taken from me, and the manner still hurts me. Love, which absolves no beloved one from loving, seized me so strongly with his charm that, as thou seest, it does not leave me yet.[2]   *Ib. 100*

What sweet thoughts, what longing led them to the woeful pass.[3]
     Ib. 113

There is no greater sorrow
    Than to be mindful of the happy time
In misery.[4]   *Ib. 121*

A Galeotto was the book and he that wrote it; that day we read in it no farther.[5]   *Ib. 137*

I fell as a dead body falls.
     Ib. Last line

Pride, Envy, and Avarice are the three sparks that have set these hearts on fire.   *Ib. VI, 74*

But when thou shalt be in the sweet world, I pray thee bring me to men's memory.[6]   *Ib. 88*

Ye that are of good understanding, note the doctrine that is hidden under the veil of the strange verses!
     Ib. IX, 61

Already I had fixed my look on his; and he rose upright with breast and countenance, as if he entertained great scorn of Hell.[1]

> The Divine Comedy. Inferno,
> canto X, *l. 34*

Necessity brings him [Dante] here, not pleasure.   *Ib. XII, 87*

If thou follow thy star, thou canst not fail of a glorious haven.
     Ib. XV, 55

So my conscience chide me not, I am ready for Fortune as she wills.
     Ib. 91

He listens well who takes notes.
     Ib. 99

A fair request should be followed by the deed in silence.   *Ib. XXIV, 77*

Consider your origin; you were not born to live like brutes, but to follow virtue and knowledge.
     Ib. XXVI, 118

If I thought my answer were to one who would ever return to the world, this flame should stay without another movement; but since none ever returned alive from this depth, if what I hear is true, I answer thee without fear of infamy.[2]   *Ib. XXVII, 60*

And thence we came forth, to see again the stars.[3]   *Ib. XXXIV, 139*

To run over better waters the little vessel of my genius now hoists her sails, as she leaves behind her a sea so cruel.
     Ib. Purgatorio,[4] canto I, *l. 1*

He goes seeking liberty, which is so dear, as he knows who for it renounces life.   *Ib. 71*

---

[1] Di qua, di là, di giù, di su li mena.
[2] Francesca of Rimini tells of the love she and Paolo, her brother-in-law, bore one another and of its tragic end when her husband surprised and stabbed them.
[3] Translated by JOHN AITKEN CARLYLE, *The Temple Classics* [1900].
[4] Translated by LONGFELLOW.
> Nessun maggior dolore
> Che ricordarsi del tempo felice
> Nella miseria.
See Pindar, p. 79b; Boethius, p. 148a; Chaucer, p. 165a; and Tennyson, p. 647a.
[5] Galeotto fu il libro e chi lo scrisse:
> Quel giorno più non vi leggemmo avante.
[6] Ciacco (Hog), noted for his gluttony, entreats Dante.

[1] Translated by JOHN AITKEN CARLYLE, *The Temple Classics* [1901]
Dante speaks of Farinata, head of the Uberti family, leaders of the Ghibelline faction in Florence.
[2] Count Guido da Montefeltro, the famous Ghibelline warrior, addresses Dante.
This passage in Italian is the epigraph for T. S. ELIOT, *The Love Song of J. Alfred Prufrock* [1917].
[3] E quindi uscimmo a riveder le stelle.
[4] Translated by CHARLES ELIOT NORTON [1902], unless otherwise noted.

O conscience, upright and stainless, how bitter a sting to thee is a little fault!
The Divine Comedy. Purgatorio, canto III, l. 8

For to lose time is most displeasing to him who knows most. *Ib. 78*

The Infinite Goodness has such wide arms that it takes whatever turns to it. *Ib. 121*

Unless, before then, the prayer assist me which rises from a heart that lives in grace: what avails the other, which is not heard in heaven? *Ib. IV, 133*

"Why is thy mind so entangled," said the Master,[1] "that thou slackenest thy pace? What is it to thee what they whisper there? Come after me and let the people talk. Stand like a firm tower that never shakes its top for blast of wind." *Ib. V,[2] 10*

Go right on and listen as thou goest. *Ib. 45*

[Beatrice] who shall be a light between truth and intellect.
Ib. VI, 45

It was now the hour that turns back the longing of seafarers and melts their hearts, the day they have bidden dear friends farewell, and pierces the new traveler with love if he hears in the distance the bell that seems to mourn the dying day.[2] *Ib. VIII, 1*

Give us this day the daily manna,[3] without which, in this rough desert, he backward goes, who toils most to go on. *Ib. XI, 13*

Worldly renown is naught but a breath of wind, which now comes this way and now comes that, and changes name because it changes quarter.
Ib. 100

O human race, born to fly upward, wherefore at a little wind dost thou so fall? *Ib. XII, 95*

[1] Virgil.
[2] Translated by JOHN D. SINCLAIR.
[3] See *Matthew, 6:11*, p. 40b.

To a greater force, and to a better nature, you, free, are subject, and that creates the mind in you, which the heavens have not in their charge. Therefore if the present world go astray, the cause is in you, in you it is to be sought.
The Divine Comedy. Purgatorio, canto XVI, l. 79

Everyone confusedly conceives of a good in which the mind may be at rest, and desires it; wherefore everyone strives to attain to it. *Ib. XVII, 127*

Love kindled by virtue always kindles another, provided that its flame appear outwardly. *Ib. XXII, 10*

Less than a drop of blood remains in me that does not tremble; I recognize the signals of the ancient flame.[1]
Ib. XXX, 46

But so much the more malign and wild does the ground become with bad seed and untilled, as it has the more of good earthly vigor. *Ib. 118*

Pure and disposed to mount unto the stars.[2] *Ib. XXXIII, 145*

The glory of Him who moves everything penetrates through the universe, and is resplendent in one part more and in another less.[3]
Ib. Paradiso,[4] canto I, l. 1

A great flame follows a little spark.
Ib. 34

And in His will is our peace.[5]
Ib. III, 85

The greatest gift that God in His bounty made in creation, and the most conformable to His goodness, and that which He prizes the most, was the freedom of the will, with which the crea-

[1] Men che dramma
  Di sangue m'è rimaso, che no tremi;
  Conosco i segni dell' antica fiamma.
See Virgil, p. 118b.
[2] Puro e disposto a salire alle stelle.
See Virgil, p. 119b.
[3] See *Acts 17:28*, p. 50a, and Aratus, p. 104a.
[4] Translated by JOHN D. SINCLAIR.
[5] E'n la sua volontade e nostra pace.
See T. S. Eliot, p. 1004a.

tures with intelligence, they all and they alone, were and are endowed.
The Divine Comedy. Paradiso, canto V, l. 19

Thou shalt prove how salt is the taste of another's bread and how hard is the way up and down another man's stairs.
Ib. XVII, 58

Overcoming me with the light of a smile, she [Beatrice] said to me: "Turn and listen, for not only in my eyes is Paradise." [1]
Ib. XVIII, 19

Therefore the sight that is granted to your world penetrates within the Eternal Justice as the eye into the sea; for though from the shore it sees the bottom, in the open sea it does not, and yet the bottom is there but the depth conceals it.   *Ib. XIX, 73*

The experience of this sweet life. [2]
Ib. XX, 47

Like the lark that soars in the air, first singing, then silent, content with the last sweetness that satiates it, such seemed to me that image, the imprint of the Eternal Pleasure.   *Ib. 73*

The night that hides things from us.
Ib. XXIII, 3

With the color that paints the morning and evening clouds that face the sun I saw then the whole heaven suffused.   *Ib. XXVII, 28*

The Love that moves the sun and the other stars. [3]   *Ib. XXXIII, 145*

YOSHIDA KENKO
1283–1350

To while away the idle hours, seated the livelong day before the ink slab, by jotting down without order or purpose whatever trifling thoughts pass through

my mind, verily this is a queer and crazy thing to do!
Tsurezure-Gusa (Essays in Idleness) [c. 1340] [1]

One should write not unskillfully in the running hand, be able to sing in a pleasing voice and keep good time to music; and, lastly, a man should not refuse a little wine when it is pressed upon him.   *Ib.*

However gifted and accomplished a young man may be, if he has no fondness for women, one has a feeling of something lacking, as of a precious wine cup without a bottom.   *Ib.*

To sit alone in the lamplight with a book spread out before you, and hold intimate converse with men of unseen generations — such is a pleasure beyond compare.   *Ib.*

A certain recluse, I know not who, once said that no bonds attached him to this life, and the only thing he would regret leaving was the sky.   *Ib.*

PHILIP VI
[PHILIP OF VALOIS]
1293–1350

He who loves me, let him follow me. [2]

WILLIAM OF OCKHAM
1300–1348

A plurality must not be asserted without necessity. [3]
Quodlibeta Septem [c. 1320]

---

[1] See Chaucer, p. 165a.
[2] L'esperienza di questa dolce vita.
[3] L'amor che muove il sole e l'altre stelle. See Aristotle, p. 97b.

[1] Translated by DONALD KEENE. From *Anthology of Japanese Literature*, edited by Donald Keene.
[2] Qui m'aime me suive.
[3] Translated by A. C. CROMBIE. This is the original statement of "Ockham's razor." The more familiar form, "Entities should not be multiplied beyond necessity," was introduced in the seventeenth century by John Ponce of Cork.

PETRARCH[1]
[FRANCESCO PETRARCA]
1304–1374

Who overrefines his argument brings himself to grief.
> *To Laura in Life, canzone 11*

A good death does honor to a whole life.
> *To Laura in Death, canzone 16*

To be able to say how much you love is to love but little.   *Ib. 137*

Rarely do great beauty and great virtue dwell together.[2]
> *De Remedies, bk. II*

EDWARD III
1312–1377

Honi soit qui mal y pense.[3]
> *Motto of the Order of the Garter* [1349]

Let the boy win his spurs.
> *Said of the Black Prince at the Battle of Crécy* [1345]

JOHN BARBOUR
c. 1316 – 1395

Ah! Freedom is a noble thing!
Freedom makes man to have liking.
Freedom all solace to man gives;
He lives at ease that freely lives.
> *The Bruce* [c. 1375], *l. 225*

JOHN WYCLIFFE
c. 1320 – 1384

I believe that in the end the truth will conquer.
> *To the Duke of Lancaster* [1381]. *From* J. R. GREEN, *A Short History of the English People, ch. 5*

By hook or by crook.[1]
> *Controversial Tracts* [c. 1380]

This Bible is for the government of the People, by the People, and for the People.[2]   *Attributed* [1382]

WILLIAM OF WYKEHAM
1324–1404

Manners maketh man.
> *Motto of his two foundations, Winchester College and New College, Oxford*

CHARLES V OF FRANCE
1337–1380

I speak Spanish to God, Italian to women, French to men, and German to my horse.[3]   *Attributed*

GEOFFREY CHAUCER[4]
c. 1343 – 1400

To rede, and drive the night away.
> *The Book of the Duchess* [1369], *l. 49*

Soun ys noght but eyr ybroken,
And every speche that ys spoken,

---

[1] The phrase has been said to derive from the custom of some manors where tenants were authorized to take firebote *by hook or by crook;* that is, so much of the underwood as may be cut with a crook, and so much of the loose timber as may be collected from the boughs by means of a hook. Quoted by Skelton, Heywood, Spenser, and others.

[2] Supposedly, Wycliffe used this phrase in the general prologue of his translation of the Bible [1382]. However, this editor could not find it in the 1850 edition collated from all the Wycliffe MSS. by Josiah Forshall and Sir Frederick Madden. The closest sentence is: If this book be wel understanden, it is profitable bothe to goostly governours and bodily lordis, and iustisis and comyns also.
See Webster, p. 547a; Garrison, p. 616a; Lincoln, p. 639a; and Parker, p. 657b.

[3] Je parle espagnol à Dieu, italien aux femmes, français aux hommes, et allemand à mon cheval.

[4] From the text of F. N. ROBINSON, *The Works of Geoffrey Chaucer,* 2nd ed. [1957].

---

[1] Chaucer translated *Sonnet 88* [*In Vita*], *S'amor non è.* See p. 164b.
[2] See Petronius, p. 133b.
[3] Evil to him who evil thinks.

Lowd or pryvee, foul or fair,
In his substaunce ys but air.
The House of Fame [1374–
1385], *bk. II, l. 765*

Venus clerk, Ovide,
That hath ysowen wonder wide
The grete god of Loves name.
Ib. III, 1487

Hard is the herte that loveth nought
In May.
The Romaunt of the Rose[1]
[*c.* 1380], *l. 85*

The tyme, that may not sojourne,
But goth, and may never retourne,
As watir that doun renneth ay,
But never drope retourne may.
Ib. 381

Nakid as a worm was she.   *Ib. 454*

As round as appil was his face.
Ib. 819

So that the more she yaf awey,
The more, ywis, she hadde alwey.
Ib. 1159

A ful gret fool is he, ywis,
That bothe riche and nygard is.
Ib. 1171

The lyf so short, the craft so long to
lerne,[2]
Th' assay so hard, so sharp the con-
queryinge.
The Parliament of Fowls
[1380–1386], *l. 1*

For out of olde feldes, as men seyth,
Cometh al this newe corn fro yer to
yere;[3]
And out of olde bokes, in good feyth,
Cometh al this newe science that men
lere.   *Ib. 22*

Nature, the vicaire of the almyghty
lorde.   *Ib. 379*

[1] Chaucer, and probably others, translated the French *Roman de la Rose* by Guillaume de Lorris (begun in 1237) and Jean de Meun (continued c. 1277).
[2] See Hippocrates, p. 88b, and note.
[3] John Bartlett quoted this line at the head of his preface to the Ninth Edition of *Familiar Quotations* [1891].

A fol can not be stille.[1]
The Parliament of Fowls,
l. 574

Now welcome, somer, with thy sonne
softe,[2]
That hast this wintres weders overshake.
Ib. 680

But the Troian gestes, as they felle,
In Omer, or in Dares, or in Dite,
Whoso that kan may rede hem as they
write.
Troilus and Criseyde [*c.* 1385],
bk. I, l. 145

If no love is, O God, what fele I so?
And if love is, what thing and which is
he?
If love be good, from whennes cometh
my woo?[3]
Ib. 400 (Canticus Troili)

A fool may ek a wys-man ofte gide.
Ib. 630

Ek som tyme it is craft to seme fle
Fro thyng whych in effect men hunte
faste.   *Ib. 747*

Unknowe, unkist, and lost, that is unsought.[4]   *Ib. 809*

O wynd, o wynd, the weder gynneth
clere.   *Ib. II, 2*

Til crowes feet be growen under youre
yë.   *Ib. 403*

Lord, this is an huge rayn!
This were a weder for to slepen inne!
Ib. III, 656

It is nought good a slepyng hound to
wake.[5]   *Ib. 764*

For I have seyn, of a ful misty morwe
Folowen ful often a myrie someris day.
Ib. 1060

Right as an aspes leef she gan to
quake.   *Ib. 1200*

[1] See *Proverbs 29:11*, p. 26b.
[2] In a somer sesun, whan softe was the sonne.
— WILLIAM LANGLAND [c. 1330–c. 1400], *The Vision of Piers Plowman, prologue*
[3] The *Canticus Troili* (*Song of Troilus*) is a fairly close rendering of Petrarch's *Sonnet 88* (*In Vita*), *S'amor non è*.
[4] See Homer, p. 64b, and note.
[5] See Dickens, p. 672a.

For of fortunes sharpe adversitee
The worste kynde of infortune is this,
A man to han ben in prosperitee,
And it remembren, whan it passed is.[1]
    Troilus and Criseyde,
        bk. III, l. 1625

Oon ere it herde, at tothir out it
    wente.[2]   *Ib. IV, 434*

Ek wonder last but nyne nyght nevere
    in towne.   *Ib. 588*

But manly sette the world on six and
    sevene;[3]
And if thow deye a martyr, go to
    hevene!   *Ib. 622*

For tyme ylost may nought recovered
    be.   *Ib. 1283*

They take it wisly, faire, and softe.[4]
          Ib. V, 347

For he that naught n' assaieth, naught
    n' acheveth.[5]   *Ib. 784*

Paradis stood formed in her yën.[6]
          Ib. 817

Trewe as stiel.   *Ib. 831*

This sodeyn Diomede.   *Ib. 1024*

Ye, fare wel al the snow of ferne yere! [7]
          Ib. 1176

Ek gret effect men write in place lite;
Th' entente is al, and nat the lettres
    space.   *Ib. 1629*

Go, litel bok, go, litel myn tragedye.[1]
    Troilus and Criseyde,
        bk. V, l. 1786

O yonge, fresshe folkes, he or she,
In which that love up groweth with
    youre age,
Repeyreth hom fro worldly vanyte.
          Ib. 1835

O moral Gower, this book I directe
To the.   *Ib. 1856*

    Whan that the month of May
Is comen, and that I here the foules
    synge,
And that the floures gynnen for to
    sprynge,
Farewel my bok, and my devocioun!
    The Legend of Good Women
        [c. 1386], l. 36

That, of al the floures in the mede,
Thanne love I most thise floures white
    and rede,
Swiche as men callen daysyes in our
    toun.   *Ib. 41*

Whan that Aprill with his shoures
    soote

---

[1] See Pindar, p. 79b; Boethius, p. 148a;
Dante, p. 160a; and Tennyson, p. 647a.

[2] Went in at the tone eare and ont at tother.
— JOHN HEYWOOD, *Proverbs* [1546], *pt. II, ch. 9*

[3]   All is uneven,
    And everything is left at six and seven.
    SHAKESPEARE, *Richard II* [1595–1596],
        act II, sc. ii, l. 120
    Let things go at sixes and sevens. — CERVANTES,
Don Quixote, pt. I [1605], *bk. IV, ch. 3*
    Things going on at sixes and sevens. — GOLD-
SMITH, *The Good-Natured Man* [1768], *act I*
        Say, why is everything
        Either at sixes or at sevens?
        W.S. GILBERT, *H.M.S. Pinafore*
        [1878], *act II, Fair Moon*

[4] The proverb is: Fair and softly goes far.
See Shakespeare, p. 224b.

[5] See Heywood, p. 184b, and note.

[6] See Dante, p. 162a.

[7] See Villon, p. 171a.

[1] Off with you down where you want to go. —
HORACE [65–8 B.C.], *Epistles I, xx, 5*
    Little book, you will go without me — I
don't mind — to the city. — OVID [43 B.C.–A.D.
18], *Tristia I, i, 1*
    Vade salutatem pro me, liber [Go forth, my
book, to bear my greetings]. — MARTIAL [A.D. c.
40–c. 104], *Epigrams I, 70*
    Go now, my little book, to every place
    Where my first pilgrim has but shown his face.
        JOHN BUNYAN, *Pilgrim's Progress* [1678],
          Apology

    Go, little Book! From this my solitude
    I cast thee on the Waters — go thy ways.
        ROBERT SOUTHEY, *Lay of the Laureate*
          [1815], *L'Envoi*
    These lines of Southey's and the next two
were quoted by BYRON in *Don Juan* [1818],
canto I, stanza 222, which ends: The four first
rhymes are Southey's, every line:/ For God's sake,
reader! take them not for mine!
    Go forth, my little book! pursue thy way;
    Go forth, and please the gentle and the good.
        WORDSWORTH, *Memorials of a Tour on*
        the Continent [1820]
    Go, little book, and wish to all
    Flowers in the garden, meat in the hall.
        R. L. STEVENSON, *Underwoods* [1887],
          Envoy

The droghte of March hath perced to the roote.
The Canterbury Tales [*c.* 1387].
Prologue, l. 1

And smale foweles maken melodye,
That slepen al the nyght with open yë,
(So priketh hem nature in hir corages);
Thanne longen folk to goon on pilgrimages. *Ib.* 9

He was a verray, parfit gentil knight.
Ib. 72

He was as fressh as is the month of May. *Ib.* 92

He koude songes make, and wel endyte. *Ib.* 95

Curteis he was, lowely, and servysable,
And carf beforn his fader at the table.
Ib. 99

Ful weel she soong the service dyvyne,
Entuned in hir nose ful semely;
And Frenssh she spak ful faire and fetisly,
After the scole of Stratford atte Bowe
For Frenssh of Parys was to hir unknowe. *Ib.* 122

She wolde wepe, if that she saugh a mous
Kaught in a trappe, if it were deed or bledde. *Ib.* 144

And theron heng a brooch of gold ful sheene,
On which ther was first write a crowned A,
And after *Amor vincit omnia.*[1]
Ib. 160

His palfrey was as broun as is a berye.
Ib. 207

A Frere ther was, a wantowne and a merye. *Ib.* 208

He knew the tavernes wel in every toun. *Ib.* 240

Somwhat he lipsed, for his wantownesse,
To make his Englissh sweete upon his tonge. *Ib.* 264

[1] See Virgil, p. 117a.

A Clerk ther was of Oxenford also.
The Canterbury Tales.
Prologue, l. 285

As leene was his hors as is a rake.
Ib. 287

For hym was levere have at his beddes heed
Twenty bookes, clad in blak or reed,
Of Aristotle and his philosophie,
Than robes riche, or fithele, or gay sautrie,
But al be that he was a philosophre,
Yet hadde he but litel gold in cofre.
Ib. 293

And gladly wolde he lerne, and gladly teche.[1] *Ib.* 308

Nowher so bisy a man as he ther nas,
And yet he semed bisier than he was.
Ib. 321

For he was Epicurus owene sone.[2]
Ib. 336

It snewed in his hous of mete and drynke. *Ib.* 345

He was a good felawe.[3] *Ib.* 395

His studie was but litel on the Bible.
Ib. 438

For gold in phisik is a cordial,
Therefore he lovede gold in special.
Ib. 443

She was a worthy womman al hir lyve,
Housbondes at chirche dore she hadde fyve. *Ib.* 459

This noble ensample to his sheep he yaf,
That first he wroghte, and afterward he taughte. *Ib.* 496

If gold ruste, what shal iren do?
Ib. 500

But Cristes loore and his apostles twelve
He taughte, but first he folwed it hymselve. *Ib.* 527

[1] See Pope, p. 404a.
[2] See Horace, *Epistles iv, 13,* p. 123a.
[3] If he be not fellow with the best king, thou shalt find him the best king of good fellows. — SHAKESPEARE, *King Henry V* [1598–1600], *act V, sc. ii, l.* 259

And yet he hadde a thombe of gold.[1]
The Canterbury Tales.
Prologue, l. 563

That hadde a fyr-reed cherubynnes
face. *Ib. 624*

Wel loved he garleek, oynons, and eek
lekes,
And for to drynken strong wyn, reed as
blood. *Ib. 634*

And whan that he wel dronken hadde
the wyn,
Than wolde he speke no word but
Latyn. *Ib. 637*

Whoso shal telle a tale after a man,
He moot reherce as ny as evere he kan
Everich a word, if it be in his charge,
Al speke he never so rudeliche and
large,
Or ellis he moot telle his tale untrewe,
Or feyne thyng, or fynde wordes new.
Ib. 731

For May wol have no slogardie anyght.
The sesoun priketh every gentil herte,
And maketh hym out of his slep to
sterte.
Ib. The Knight's Tale, l. 1042

Ech man for hymself. *Ib. 1182*

The bisy larke, messager of day.
Ib. 1491

May, with alle thy floures and thy
grene,
Welcome be thou, faire, fresshe May.
Ib. 1510

That "feeld hath eyen, and the wode
hath eres." [2] *Ib. 1522*

---

[1] In allusion to the proverb: An honest miller
hath a golden thumb.

[2] The proverb also occurs in the Latin form:
Campus habet lumen, et habet nemus auris
acumen.
  Fieldes have eies and woodes have eares. —
JOHN HEYWOOD, *Proverbs* [1546], *pt. II, ch. 5*
  Wode has erys, felde has sigt. — *King Edward
and the Shepherd, MS* [c. 1300]
  Walls have ears. — CERVANTES, *Don Quixote,
pt. II* [1615], *ch. 48*
  Woods have tongues
  As walls have ears.
    TENNYSON, *Idylls of the King.
    Balin and Balan* [1885], *l. 522*

Now up, now doun, as boket in a
welle.
*The Canterbury Tales. The
Knight's Tale, l. 1533*

For pitee renneth soone in gentil
herte. *Ib. 1761*

Cupido,
Upon his shuldres wynges hadde he
two;
And blynd he was, as it is often seene;
A bowe he bar and arwes brighte and
kene. *Ib. 1963*

The smylere with the knyf under the
cloke. *Ib. 1999*

Up roos the sonne, and up roose
Emelye. *Ib. 2273*

Myn be the travaille, and thyn be the
glorie! *Ib. 2406*

And was al his chiere, as in his herte.
Ib. 2683

What is this world? what asketh men
to have?
Now with his love, now in his colde
grave
Allone, withouten any compaignye.
Ib. 2777

This world nys but a thurghfare ful of
wo,
And we been pilgrymes, passing to and
fro.
Deeth is an ende of every worldly
soore. *Ib. 2847*

Jhesu Crist, and seiynte Benedight,
Blesse this hous from every wikked
wight.
Ib. The Miller's Tale, l. 3483

And broghte of myghty ale a large
quart. *Ib. 3497*

"Tehee!" quod she, and clapte the
wyndow to. *Ib. 3740*

Yet in our asshen olde is fyr yreke.[1]
Ib. The Reeve's Prologue, l. 3882

The gretteste clerkes been noght the
wisest men.[2]
Ib. The Reeve's Tale, l. 4054

---

[1] See Thomas Gray, p. 441a.

[2] This proverb goes back to Heraclitus.
  The greatest Clerkes be not the wisest men.
— JOHN HEYWOOD, *Proverbs* [1546], *pt. II, ch. 5*

Thurgh thikke and thurgh thenne.[1]
*The Canterbury Tales. The
Reeve's Tale. l. 4066*

So was hir joly whistle wel ywet.
Ib. 4155

She is mirour of alle curteisye.[2]
Ib. The Man of Law's Tale, l. 166

For in the sterres, clerer than is glas,
Is writen, God woot, whoso koude it
rede,
The deeth of every man.   *Ib. 194*

Sathan, that evere us waiteth to bigile.
Ib. 582

In his owene grece I made hym frye.[3]
*Ib. The Wife of Bath's
Prologue, l. 487*

What thyng we may nat lightly have,
Therafter wol we crie alday and crave.
Ib. 517

Greet prees at market maketh deere
ware,
And to greet cheep is holde at litel
prys.   *Ib. 522*

And for to se, and eek for be seye.[4]
Ib. 552

But yet I hadde alwey a coltes tooth.
Gat-toothed I was, and that bicam me
weel.   *Ib. 601*

A womman cast hir shame away,
Whan she cast of hir smok.[5]   *Ib. 782*

As thikke as motes in the sonne-beem.
Ib. The Wife of Bath's Tale, l. 868

"My lige lady, generally," quod he,
"Wommen desiren have sovereynetee

As well over hir housbond as hir love."
*The Canterbury Tales. The
Wife of Bath's Tale, l. 1037*

Looke who that is moost vertuous
alway,
Pryvee and apert, and most entendeth
ay
To do the gentil dedes that he kan;
Taak hym for the grettest gentil man.
Ib. 1113

That he is gentil that dooth gentil
dedis.[1]   *Ib. 1170*

For thogh we slepe or wake, or rome, or
ryde,
Ay fleeth the tyme, it nyl no man
abyde.[2]
Ib. The Clerk's Tale, l. 118

Love is noght oold as whan that it is
newe.   *Ib. 857*

This flour of wyfly pacience.   *Ib. 919*

O stormy peple! unsad and evere untrewe!   *Ib. 995*

No wedded man so hardy be t'assaille
His wyves pacience, in trust to fynde
Grisildis, for in certein he shal faille!
Ib. 1180

It is no childes pley
To take a wyf withoute avysement.
Ib. The Merchant's Tale, l. 1530

Love is blynd.[3]   *Ib. 1598*

My wit is thynne.   *Ib. 1682*

Ther nys no werkman, whatsoevere he
be,
That may bothe werke wel and hast-
ily;[4]
This wol be doon at leyser parfitly.[5]
Ib. 1832

Therfore bihoveth hire a ful long
spoon

---

[1] Through thicke and thin. — DU BARTAS,
Divine Weeks and Works [1578], *Second Week,
Fourth Day*

[2]   Call him bounteous Buckingham,
The mirror of all courtesy.
SHAKESPEARE, *Henry VIII* [1613], *act II,
sc. i, l. 53*

[3] Proverbial.
Frieth in her own grease. — JOHN HEYWOOD,
Proverbs [1546], *pt. I, ch. 11*
The best way were to entertain him with hope,
till the wicked fire of lust have melted him in
his own grease. — SHAKESPEARE, *Merry Wives of
Windsor* [1601], *act II, sc. i, l. 60*

[4] See Ovid, p. 128b.

[5] See Herodotus *I, 8,* p. 86b.

[1] See Goldsmith, p. 448a.

[2] See John Heywood, p. 182b, and note.

[3] Proverbial. See Shakespeare, p. 228b, and
note.

[4] See Publilius Syrus, p. 126b, and John Heywood, p. 182a.

[5] Ease and speed in doing a thing do not give
the work lasting solidity or exactness of beauty.
— PLUTARCH [A.D. 46–120], *Life of Pericles*

That shal ete with a feend.[1]
> *The Canterbury Tales. The
> Squire's Tale, l. 602*

Men loven of propre kynde newefan-
gelnesse.　　　　　　　*Ib. 610*

Fy on possessioun
But if a man be vertuous withal.
　　　　　　　　　　Ib. 686

Pacience is an heigh vertu, certeyn.
> *Ib. The Franklin's Tale, l. 773*

Servant in love, and lord in mariage.
　　　　　　　　　　Ib. 793

It is agayns the proces of nature.
　　　　　　　　　Ib. 1345

Trouthe is the hyeste thyng that men
may kepe.　　　　　*Ib. 1479*

For dronkenesse is verray sepulture
Of mannes wit and his discrecioun.
> *Ib. The Pardoner's Tale, l. 558*

Mordre wol out, certeyn, it wol nat
faille.[2]
> *Ib. The Prioress's Tale, l. 1776*

This may wel be rym dogerel.
> *Ib. Chaucer's Tale of
> Sir Thopas, l. 2115*

---

[1] Proverbial.
Hee must have a long spoon, shall eat with
the devill. — JOHN HEYWOOD, *Proverbs* [1546],
pt. II, ch. 5
He must have a long spoon that must eat
with the devil. — SHAKESPEARE, *Comedy of Errors*
[1592–1593], *act IV, sc. iii, l. 64*
[2] Proverbial. Also in *The Nun's Priest's Tale,
ll. 4242 and 4247.*
How easily murder is discovered! — SHAKE-
SPEARE, *Titus Andronicus* [1593–1594], *act II,
sc. iii, l. 28*
Truth will come to light; murder cannot be
hid long. — SHAKESPEARE: *Merchant of Venice*
[1596–1597], *act II, sc. ii, l. 86*
Murder, though it have no tongue, will speak
With most miraculous organ.
　　SHAKESPEARE, *Hamlet* [1600–1601],
　　　　　　act II, sc. ii, l. 630
Murder will out. — CERVANTES, *Don Quixote,
pt. I* [1605], *bk. III, ch. 8*
Carcasses bleed at the sight of the murder-
er. — ROBERT BURTON, *Anatomy of Melancholy*
[1621–1651], *pt. I, sec. I member 2, subsec. 5*
Other sins only speak; murder shrieks out.
— JOHN WEBSTER, *Duchess of Malfi* [1623],
act IV, sc. ii

Ful wys is he that kan hymselven
knowe! [1]
> *The Canterbury Tales. The
> Monk's Tale, l. 3329*

He was of knyghthod and of fredom
flour.　　　　　　*Ib. 3832*

For whan a man hath over-greet a wit,
Ful oft hym happeth to mysusen it.
> *Ib. The Canon Yeoman's
> Prologue, l. 648*

My sone, keep wel thy tonge, and keep
thy freend.
> *Ib. The Manciple's Tale, l. 319*

Thing that is seyd, is seyd; and forth it
gooth.　　　　　　*Ib. 355*

For the proverbe seith that "manye
smale maken a greet." [2]
> *Ib. The Parson's Tale, l. 361*

Reule wel thyself, that other folk canst
rede.
And trouthe thee shal delivere, it is no
drede.　　　*Truth [c. 1390], l. 6*
The wrastling for this world axeth a
fal.　　　　　　*Ib. 16*

EUSTACHE DESCHAMPS
c. 1345 – c. 1406

Who will bell the cat? [3]
> *Ballad refrain*

Better honor than shameful wealth.[4]
> *Ib.*

JOHN HUSS
1373–1415

O holy simplicity! [5]
> *Last words, at the stake*

---

[1] See The Seven Sages, p. 68a.
[2] The proverb goes back to St. Augustine. See
also Hesiod, p. 67b.
Many small make a great. — JOHN HEYWOOD,
Proverbs [1546], *pt. I, ch. 11*
[3] Qui pendra la sonnette au chat?
Copied by La Fontaine.
[4] Mieux vaut honneur que honteuse richesse.
[5] O sancta simplicitas!

THE PRIMARY CHRONICLE[1]

1377

The Chuds, the Slavs and the Krivchians then said to the peoples of Rus: "Our whole land is great and rich, but there is no order in it. Come to rule and reign over us."

Annal for the years 860–862: Invitation of the Varangians to Novgorod

Then we went to Greece, and the Greeks led us to the edifices where they worship their God, and we knew not whether we were in heaven or on earth. For on earth there is no such splendor or such beauty, and we are at a loss how to describe it. We only know that God dwells there among men, and their service is fairer than the ceremonies of other nations.

Annal for the year 987: Vladimir's Christianization of Russia

It is the Russians' joy to drink; we cannot do without it.   *Ib.*

THOMAS À KEMPIS

1380–1471

How swiftly passes the glory of the world.[2]

Imitation of Christ [c. 1420], bk. I, ch. 3

Be not angry that you cannot make others as you wish them to be, since you cannot make yourself as you wish to be.   *Ib. 16*

Man proposes, but God disposes.[3]

Ib. 19

What canst thou see elsewhere which thou canst not see here? Behold the heaven and the earth and all the elements; for of these are all things created.

Imitation of Christ, bk. I, ch. 20

No man ruleth safely but he that is willingly ruled.   *Ib.*

And when he is out of sight, quickly also is he out of mind.[1]   *Ib. 23*

First keep the peace within yourself, then you can also bring peace to others.   *Ib. II, 3*

Love is swift, sincere, pious, pleasant, gentle, strong, patient, faithful, prudent, long-suffering, manly and never seeking her own; for wheresoever a man seeketh his own, there he falleth from love.[2]   *Ib. III, 5*

CHARLES D'ORLÉANS

1394–1465

I am dying of thirst by the side of the fountain.[3]   *Ballades, 2*

The season has shed its mantle of wind and chill and rain.[4]

Rondeaux, 63

All by myself, wrapped in my thoughts,

---

[1] The earliest of the Russian chronicles or annals, begun in 1040 and continued through 1118 by various annalists, gives the record of Russian history since A.D. 852. It was copied several times and incorporated into later chronicles as the beginning. These quotations are from the Laurentian version, copied in 1377, translated by Samuel Cross.

[2] O quam cito transit [usual form: sic transit] gloria mundi.

The words addressed to the Pope in the ceremony of his elevation.

[3] This expression appears earlier in *The Chronicle of Battel Abbey, p. 27* (Lower's translation), and in *The Vision of Piers Plowman, l. 13994, ed. 1550.*

Man appoints, and God disappoints. — CERVANTES, *Don Quixote, pt. II [1615], bk. IV, ch. 55*

See *Proverbs 16:9, p. 24b.*

[1] Out of syght, out of mynd. — GOOGE, *Eglogs* [1563]

And out of mind as soon as out of sight. — FULKE GREVILLE [1554–1628], *Sonnet 56*

Fer from eze, fer from herte,
Quoth Hendyng.

HENDYNG, *Proverbs, MS [c. 1320]*

I do perceive that the old proverbis be not alwaies trew, for I do finde that the absence of my Nath. doth breede in me the more continuall remembrance of him. — LADY ANN BACON, *letter to Lady Jane Cornwallis [1613]*

[2] See *I Corinthians 13:4* and 7, p. 52b.

[3] Je meurs de soif en cousté la fontaine. See Wilbur, p. 1080a.

[4] Le temps a laissé son manteau
De vent, de froidure et de pluie.

And building castles in Spain and in France.[1]　　*Rondeaux, 109*

JOHN FORTESCUE
c. 1395 – 1476

Moche crye and no wull.[2]
*De Laudibus Legum Angliae
[1471], ch. 10*

Comparisons are odious.[3]　　*Ib. 19*

HENRY VI
1421–1471

Kingdoms are but cares,
State is devoid of stay;
Riches are ready snares,
And hasten to decay.
From SIR JOHN HARINGTON,
*Nugae Antiquae [published
1769]*

FRANÇOIS VILLON
1431 – c. 1465

Ah God! Had I but studied
In the days of my foolish youth.[4]
Le Grand Testament, 26

But where are the snows of yester-year? [5]
*Ib. Ballade des Dames du
Temps Jadis*

In this faith I will to live and die.
*Ib. Ballade de l'Homage à
Notre Dame*

There's no good speech save in Paris.[1]
*Le Grand Testament, Ballade
des Femmes de Paris*

But pray God that he absolve us all! [2]
Codicile

I know all except myself.[3]
Ballade des Menus Propres

GABRIEL BIEL
d. 1495

To be crushed in the winepress of passion.
*Expositio Canonis Missae,
lectio 52*

Always in these matters desiring rather to be taught than to teach.
Ib. 53

No one conquers who doesn't fight.
Ib. 78

You get what you pay for.[4]
Ib. 86

ALDUS MANUTIUS
1450–1515

Talk of nothing but business, and dispatch that business quickly.
*Placard on the door of the
Aldine Press, Venice, es-
tablished about 1490 [5]*

CHRISTOPHER COLUMBUS
1451–1506

The Admiral [Columbus] says here that today and ever thereafter they had very mild breezes, that the savor of the mornings was a great delight, that the only thing wanting was to hear night-

---

[1] Translated by NORBERT GUTERMAN.
　Thou shalt make castels thanne in Spayne,
　And dreme of joye, all but in vayne.
　　JEAN DE MEUN, *The Romaunt of the
　Rose* [c. 1277], *frag. B, l. 2573*, trans-
　lated by CHAUCER
[2] A great cry, but little wool. — CERVANTES,
Don Quixote, pt. II [1615], *bk. III, ch. 13*
All cry and no wool. — SAMUEL BUTLER,
Hudibras, pt. I [1663], *canto 1, l. 852*
[3] This was a well-known phrase in the four-
teenth century, and has been repeated by many,
including Lydgate, Shakespeare, and Swift.
[4] Hé Dieu! si j'eusse étudié
　Au temps de ma jeunesse folle.
[5] Mais où sont les neiges d'antan?
　See Chaucer, p. 165a.

---

[1] Il n'est bon bec que de Paris.
[2] Mais priez Dieu que tous nous veuille ab-
　soudre.
[3] Je connais tout, fors moi-même.
[4] Pro tali numismate tales merces.
[5] Quoted by THOMAS FROGNALL DIBDIN [1776–
1847] in *Introduction to the Knowledge of Rare
and Valuable Editions of the Greek and Latin
Classics* [1802], *vol. I, p. 436.*

ingales. Says he, "The weather was like April in Andalusia."

Journal of the First Voyage,[1]
September 16, 1492

"Thanks be to God," says the Admiral; "the air is soft as in April in Seville, and it is a pleasure to be in it, so fragrant it is."

Ib. October 8, 1492

Here the people could stand it no longer and complained of the long voyage; but the Admiral cheered them as best he could, holding out good hope of the advantages they would have. He added that it was useless to complain, he had come [to go] to the Indies, and so had to continue it until he found them, with the help of Our Lord.

Ib. October 10, 1492

At two hours after midnight appeared the land, at a distance of 2 leagues. They handed all sails and set the *treo,* which is the mainsail without bonnets, and lay-to waiting for daylight Friday, when they arrived at an island of the Bahamas that was called in the Indians' tongue Guanahaní.

Ib. October 12, 1492

The Admiral says that he never beheld so fair a thing: trees all along the river, beautiful and green, and different from ours, with flowers and fruits each according to their kind, many birds and little birds which sing very sweetly.

Ib. October 28, 1492

The two Christians met on the way many people who were going to their towns, women and men, with a firebrand in the hand, [and] herbs to drink the smoke thereof, as they are accustomed.[2] *Ib. November 6, 1492*

It is certain, Lord Princes, that when there are such lands there should be profitable things without number; but I tarried not in any harbor, because I sought to see the most countries that I could, to give the story of them to Your Highnesses.

Journal of the First Voyage,
November 27, 1492

And I say that Your Highnesses ought not to consent that any foreigner does business or sets foot here, except Christian Catholics, since this was the end and the beginning of the enterprise, that it should be for the enhancement and glory of the Christian religion, nor should anyone who is not a good Christian come to these parts.[1]
Ib.

The Admiral ordered the lord to be given some things, and he and all his folk rested in great contentment, believing truly that they had come from the sky, and to see the Christians they held themselves very fortunate.

Ib. December 22, 1492

I declared to Your Highnesses that all the gain of this my Enterprise should be spent in the conquest of Jerusalem; and Your Highnesses smiled and said that it pleased you, and that even without this you had that strong desire. *Ib. December 26, 1492*

The eternal God had given him [Columbus] strength and courage against all, and other things of much wonder which God had showed forth

---

[1] BARTOLOMÉ DE LAS CASAS [1474–1566] made an abstract of Columbus's Journal of the First Voyage (*El Libro de la Primera Navegación*) which is the nearest thing to an original journal that we have. The quotations have been selected by SAMUEL ELIOT MORISON from his translation and edition of *Journals and Other Documents on the Life and Voyages of Christopher Columbus* [1963].

[2] The first certain reference in history to smoking tobacco. Las Casas, *Historia* ch. 46 (1951

ed. I 231) describes the process. The Indians made cigars which they called *tobacos,* and inhaled the smoke. He says that the Spaniards are taking it up in Hispaniola, "though I don't know what taste or profit they find in it." Esquemeling's *Buccaneers,* chap. xxvii (on Cuba) says "with uncut tobacco leaves they make little bullets that the Spaniards call *gigarros,* and which are smoked without a pipe." — SAMUEL ELIOT MORISON, *Journals and Other Documents on the Life and Voyages of Christopher Columbus*

[1] Here may be found the first suggestion of the exclusive colonial policy that Spain and other nations followed. — SAMUEL ELIOT MORISON, *Journals and Other Documents on the Life and Voyages of Christopher Columbus*

towards him and for him on that voyage.

Journal of the First Voyage, February 14, 1493

"Of this voyage, I observe," says the Admiral, "that it has miraculously been shown, as may be understood by this writing, by the many signal miracles that He has shown on the voyage, and for me, who for so great a time was in the court of Your Highnesses with the opposition and against the opinion of so many high personages of your household, who were all against me, alleging this undertaking to be folly, which I hope in Our Lord will be to the greater glory of Christianity, which to some slight extent already has happened."

Ib. March 15, 1493

All are most beautiful, of a thousand shapes, and all accessible, and filled with trees of a thousand kinds and tall, and they seem to touch the sky; and I am told that they never lose their foliage, which I can believe, for I saw them as green and beautiful as they are in Spain.

Letter to the Sovereigns on the First Voyage, February 15–March 4, 1493 [1]

It is true that after they have been reassured and have lost this fear, they are so artless and so free with all they possess, that no one would believe it without having seen it. Of anything they have, if you ask them for it, they never say no; rather they invite the person to share it, and show as much love as if they were giving their hearts.

Ib.

And they know neither sect nor idolatry, with the exception that all believe that the source of all power and goodness is in the sky, and they believe very firmly that I, with these ships and people, came from the sky, and in this belief they everywhere received me, after they had overcome their fear.

Ib.

Your Highnesses will leave no greater memorial; and may they ponder this, that no prince of Castile is to be found, nor have I found one in word or writing, who has ever gained any land outside of Spain; and Your Highnesses have won these vast lands.

Journal of the Third Voyage, May 30–August 31, 1498 [1]

I have come to believe that this is a mighty continent which was hitherto unknown. I am greatly supported in this view by reason of this great river [Ozama], and by this sea which is fresh.

Ib.

I have always read that the world, both land and water, was spherical, as the authority and researches of Ptolemy and all the others who have written on this subject demonstrate and prove, as do the eclipses of the moon and other experiments that are made from east to west, and the elevation of the North Star from north to south.

Letter to the Sovereigns on the Third Voyage, October 18, 1498

Your Highnesses have an Other World here, by which our holy faith can be so greatly advanced and from which such great wealth can be drawn.

Ib.

I should be judged as a captain who went from Spain to the Indies to conquer a people numerous and warlike, whose manners and religion are very different from ours, who live in sierras and mountains, without fixed settlements, and where by divine will I have placed under the sovereignty of the King and Queen our Lords, an Other World, whereby Spain, which was reckoned poor, is become the richest of countries.

Letter to Doña Juana de Torres, October 1500 [2]

[1] This letter, the first and rarest of all printed Americana, describes the scenery and the natives of Hispaniola.

[1] The abstract of the Third Voyage by Bartolomé de Las Casas is less detailed than that of the First. Translated by SAMUEL ELIOT MORISON and MILTON ANASTOS.

[2] Columbus is coming from the Indies as a prisoner to Cadiz.

The tempest was terrible and separated me from my [other] vessels that night, putting every one of them in desperate straits, with nothing to look forward to but death. Each was certain the others had been destroyed. What man ever born, not excepting Job, who would not have died of despair, when in such weather seeking safety for my son, my brother, shipmates, and myself, we were forbidden [access to] the land and the harbors which I, by God's will and sweating blood, had won for Spain?

> *Lettera Rarissima to the Sovereigns, July 7, 1503 (Fourth Voyage)*[1]

I came to serve you at the age of 28 and now I have not a hair on me that is not white, and my body is infirm and exhausted. All that was left to me and my brothers has been taken away and sold, even to the cloak that I wore, without hearing or trial, to my great dishonor.　　　　*Ib.*

Weep for me, whoever has charity, truth and justice! I did not come on this voyage for gain, honor or wealth, that is certain; for then the hope of all such things was dead. I came to Your Highnesses with honest purpose and sincere zeal; and I do not lie. I humbly beseech Your Highnesses that, if it please God to remove me hence, you will help me to go to Rome and on other pilgrimages.　　　*Ib.*

LEONARDO DA VINCI
1452–1519

Iron rusts from disuse, stagnant water loses its purity, and in cold weather becomes frozen: even so does inaction sap the vigors of the mind.

> *Notebooks* [c. 1500]

Whoever in discussion adduces authority uses not intellect but memory.　　*Ib.*

Intellectual passion drives out sensuality.　　*Ib.*

Let the street be as wide as the height of the houses.　　*Notebooks*

No member needs so great a number of muscles as the tongue; this exceeds all the rest in the number of its movements.　　*Ib.*

As a well-spent day brings happy sleep, so life well used brings happy death.　　*Ib.*

SEBASTIAN BRANT
1457–1521

The world wants to be deceived.
> *Ship of Fools* [*Narrenschiff; 1494*]

SIR THOMAS MALORY
fl. 1470

The noble history of the Sangreal,[1] and of the most renowned Christian king, first and chief of the three best Christian and worthy, King Arthur, which ought most to be remembered among us English men tofore all other Christian kings. For it is notoriously known through the universal world that there be nine worthy and the best that ever were. That is to wit three paynims, three Jews, and three Christian men. As for the paynims they were . . . the first Hector of Troy . . . the second Alexander the Great; and the third Julius Caesar. . . . And as for the three Jews . . . the first was Duke Joshua . . . the second David . . . and the third Judas Maccabaeus . . . And sith the said Incarnation have been three noble Christian men . . . of whom was first the noble Arthur. . . . The second was Charlemagne . . . and the third and last was Godfrey of Bouillon.

> *Le Morte d'Arthur. Preface* [1485] by WILLIAM CAXTON [*c.* 1422–1491], *the first English printer*

For herein may be seen noble chivalry, courtesy, humanity, friendliness,

---

[1] Translated by MILTON ANASTOS.

[1] The Holy Grail.

hardiness, love, friendship, cowardice, murder, hate, virtue, and sin. Do after the good and leave the evil, and it shall bring you to good fame and renown.
Le Morte d' Arthur, preface

Whoso pulleth out this sword of this stone and anvil, is rightwise king born of all England.   *Ib. bk. I, ch. 5*

And with that the king saw coming toward him the strangest beast that ever he saw or heard of; so the beast went to the well and drank, and the noise was in the beast's belly like unto the questing of thirty couple hounds; but all the while the beast drank there was no noise in the beast's belly: and therewith the beast departed with a great noise, whereof the king had great marvel. . . . Pellinore, that time king, followed the questing beast.   *Ib. 19*

In the midst of the lake Arthur was ware of an arm clothed in white samite, that held a fair sword in that hand.
Ib. 25

Always Sir Arthur lost so much blood that it was marvel he stood on his feet, but he was so full of knighthood that knightly he endured the pain.
Ib. IV, 9

What, nephew, said the king, is the wind in that door? [1]   *Ib. VII, 34*

The joy of love is too short, and the sorrow thereof, and what cometh thereof, dureth over long.   *Ib. X, 56*

It is his day.   *Ib. 70*

The month of May was come, when every lusty heart beginneth to blossom, and to bring forth fruit; for like as herbs and trees bring forth fruit and flourish in May, in likewise every lusty heart that is in any manner a lover, springeth and flourisheth in lusty deeds. For it giveth unto all lovers courage, that lusty month of May.
Ib. XVIII, 25

[1] See Shakespeare, p. 246a.

Wherefore I liken love nowadays unto summer and winter; for like as the one is hot and the other cold, so fareth love nowadays; therefore all ye that be lovers call unto your remembrance the month of May, like as did Queen Guenever, for whom I make here a little mention, that while she lived she was a true lover, and therefore she had a good end.
Le Morte d' Arthur,
bk. XVIII, ch. 25

And therefore, said the king, wit you well my heart was never so heavy as it is now, and much more I am sorrier for my good knights' loss than for the loss of my fair queen; for queens I might have enow, but such a fellowship of good knights shall never be together in no company.   *Ib. XX, 9*

I shall curse you with book and bell and candle.[1]   *Ib. XXI, 1*

Through this man [Launcelot] and me [Guenever] hath all this war been wrought, and the death of the most noblest knights of the world; for through our love that we have loved together is my most noble lord slain.
Ib. 9

For as well as I have loved thee, mine heart will not serve me to see thee, for through thee and me is the flower of kings and knights destroyed.   *Ib.*

Then Sir Launcelot saw her visage, but he wept not greatly, but sighed.
Ib. 11

Thou Sir Launcelot, there thou liest, that thou were never matched of earthly knight's hand. And thou were the courteoust knight that ever bare shield. And thou were the truest friend to thy lover that ever bestrad horse. And thou were the truest lover of a sinful man that ever loved woman. And thou were the kindest man that ever struck with sword. And thou were the

[1] The reference is to the ceremony of excommunication, current since the eighth century. performed with bell, book, and candle.
See Shakespeare, p. 236b.

goodliest person that ever came among press of knights. And thou were the meekest man and the gentlest that ever ate in hall among ladies. And thou were the sternest knight to thy mortal foe that ever put spear in the rest.

*Le Morte d' Arthur,
bk. XXI, ch. 13*

JOHN SKELTON
c. 1460 – 1529

I say, thou mad March hare.[1]
*Replication Against Certain
Young Scholars*

He ruleth all the roost.[2]
*Why Come Ye Not to Court,
l. 198*

The wolf from the door.[3]   *Ib.* 1531

Old proverb says,
That bird is not honest
That filleth his own nest.[4]
Poems Against Garnesche

Maid, widow, or wife.
Philip Sparrow

WILLIAM DUNBAR
c. 1465 – c. 1530

London, thou art the flower of Cities all.   *London, refrain*

Gem of all joy, jasper of jocundity.
Ib. st. 3

Timor Mortis conturbat me.[5]
Lament for the Makers[6]
(Makaris) [c. 1508] refrain

Our plesance here is all vain glory,
This false world is but transitory.
Lament for the Makers, st. 2

DESIDERIUS ERASMUS
1465–1536

It is folly alone that stays the fugue of Youth and beats off louring Old Age.   *The Praise of Folly* [1509]

They may attack me with an army of six hundred syllogisms; and if I do not recant, they will proclaim me a heretic.
Ib.

A peck of troubles.
Apothegms [1542]

FERNANDO DE ROJAS
c. 1465 – c. 1538

Goods which are not shared are not goods.   *La Celestina, act I*

The use of riches is better than their possession.   *Ib. II*

The first step towards madness is to think oneself wise.   *Ib.*

Riches do not make one rich but busy.   *Ib. IV*

No one is so old that he cannot live yet another year, nor so young that he cannot die today.   *Ib.*

When God wounds from on high he will follow with the remedy.   *Ib. X*

When one door closes, fortune will usually open another.   *Ib. XV*

NICCOLÓ MACHIAVELLI[1]
1469–1527

There is nothing more difficult to take in hand, more perilous to conduct,

---

[1] Mad as a March hare. — JOHN HEYWOOD, *Proverbs* [1546], *pt. II, ch. 5*
[2] Rule the rost. — JOHN HEYWOOD, *Proverbs* [1546], *pt. I, ch. 5*
Her that ruled the rost. — THOMAS HEYWOOD, *History of Women* [ed. 1624]
Rules the roast. — JONSON, CHAPMAN, MARSTON, *Eastward Ho* [1605], *act II, sc. ii*
[3] To Keepe the woolfe from the durre. — JOHN HEYWOOD, *Proverbs* [1546], *pt. II, ch. 7*
[4] It is a foul bird that filleth his own nest. — JOHN HEYWOOD, *Proverbs* [1546], *pt. II, ch. 5*
[5] Fear of Death hath me in thrall.
[6] Makers: poets.

[1] Every Country hath its Machiavel. — SIR THOMAS BROWNE, *Religio Medici* [1642], *p. 24* [Everyman ed.]
Out of his surname they have coined an epithet for a knave, and out of his Christian name a synonym for the Devil. — MACAULAY, *Machiavelli* [1827]
See Butler, p. 353a.

or more uncertain in its success, than to take the lead in the introduction of a new order of things.

The Prince,[1] ch. 6

From this arises the question whether it is better to be loved rather than feared, or feared rather than loved. It might perhaps be answered that we should wish to be both: but since love and fear can hardly exist together, if we must choose between them, it is far safer to be feared than loved.[2]   *Ib. 8*

The chief foundations of all states, new as well as old or composite, are good laws and good arms; and as there cannot be good laws where the state is not well armed, it follows that where they are well armed they have good laws.   *Ib. 12*

A prince should therefore have no other aim or thought, nor take up any other thing for his study, but war and its organization and discipline, for that is the only art that is necessary to one who commands.   *Ib. 14*

Among other evils which being unarmed brings you, it causes you to be despised.   *Ib.*

But my intention being to write something of use to those who understand, it appears to me more proper to go to the real truth of the matter than to its imagination; and many have imagined republics and principalities which have never been seen or known to exist in reality; for how we live is so far removed from how we ought to live, that he who abandons what is done for what ought to be done, will rather bring about his own ruin than his preservation.   *Ib. 15*

The prince who relies upon their words, without having otherwise provided for his security, is ruined; for friendships that are won by awards, and not by greatness and nobility of soul, although deserved, yet are not real, and

[1] Translated by W. K. MARRIOTT.
[2] See Accius, p. 109b.

cannot be depended upon in time of adversity.   *The Prince, ch. 17*

A prince being thus obliged to know well how to act as a beast must imitate the fox and the lion, for the lion cannot protect himself from traps, and the fox cannot defend himself from wolves. One must therefore be a fox to recognize traps, and a lion to frighten wolves.   *Ib.*

When neither their property nor their honor is touched, the majority of men live content.   *Ib. 19*

There are three classes of intellects: one which comprehends by itself; another which appreciates what others comprehend; and a third which neither comprehends by itself nor by the showing of others; the first is the most excellent, the second is good, the third is useless.   *Ib. 22*

There is no other way of guarding oneself against flattery than by letting men understand that they will not offend you by speaking the truth; but when everyone can tell you the truth, you lose their respect.   *Ib. 23*

Where the willingness is great, the difficulties cannot be great.   *Ib. 26*

God is not willing to do everything, and thus take away our free will and that share of glory which belongs to us.   *Ib.*

Whoever desires to found a state and give it laws, must start with assuming that all men are bad and ever ready to display their vicious nature, whenever they may find occasion for it.

Discourse Upon the First Ten Books of Livy, bk. I, ch. 3

The people resemble a wild beast,[1] which, naturally fierce and accustomed to live in the woods, has been brought up, as it were, in a prison and in servitude, and having by accident got its liberty, not being accustomed to search for its food, and not knowing where to

[1] See Horace, p. 123a, and note.

conceal itself, easily becomes the prey of the first who seeks to incarcerate it again.

> *Discourse Upon the First Ten Books of Livy, bk. I, ch. 16*

CHARLES VIII
1470–1498

This is our gracious will.[1]

> *Royal Order of March 12, 1497*

NICHOLAS COPERNICUS
1473–1543

Finally we shall place the Sun himself at the center of the Universe. All this is suggested by the systematic procession of events and the harmony of the whole Universe, if only we face the facts, as they say, "with both eyes open."

> *De Revolutionibus Orbium Coelestium* [1543][2]

LUDOVICO ARIOSTO
1474–1533

Nature made him, and then broke the mold.[3]

> *Orlando Furioso* [1532], *canto X, st. 84*

MICHELANGELO (BUONARROTI)
1474–1564

The more the marble wastes, the more the statue grows. *Sonnet*

If it be true that any beautiful thing raises the pure and just desire of man from earth to God, the eternal fount of all, such I believe my love. *Sonnet*

The power of one fair face makes my love sublime, for it has weaned my heart from low desires. *Sonnet*

I live and love in God's peculiar light. *Ib.*

---

[1] Tel est notre bon plaisir.
[2] Translated by JOHN F. DOBSON.
[3] Natura il fece, e poi ruppe la stampa.
See Byron, p. 559a.

SIR THOMAS MORE[1]
1478–1535

They wonder much to hear that gold, which in itself is so useless a thing, should be everywhere so much esteemed, that even men for whom it was made, and by whom it has its value, should yet be thought of less value than it is.

> *Utopia* [1516]. *Of Jewels and Wealth*

They have no lawyers among them, for they consider them as a sort of people whose profession it is to disguise matters.

> *Ib. Of Law and Magistrates*

Plato by a goodly similitude declareth, why wise men refrain to meddle in the commonwealth. For when they see the people swarm into the streets, and daily wet to the skin with rain, and yet cannot persuade them to go out of the rain, they do keep themselves within their houses, seeing they cannot remedy the folly of the people.[2]

> *Ib. Concerning the Best State of a Commonwealth*

A little wanton money, which burned out the bottom of his purse.

> *Works* [c. 1530], *p. 195*

This is a fair tale of a tub told of his election.[3]

> *Confutation of Tyndale's Answers* (1532)

For men use, if they have an evil turn, to write it in marble: and whoso doth us a good turn we write it in dust.[4]

> *Richard III and His Miserable End* [1543]

---

[1] Canonized by Pope Pius XI [1935].
See Robert Whittinton, p. 179a.
[2] In the modern phrase, "not sense enough to come in out of the rain."
[3] A tale of a tub is a cock-and-bull story. Jonson used it as the title of a comedy [1633], and Swift as the title of a satire [1696].
[4] See Sophocles, p. 83a, and note.
Words writ in waters. — GEORGE CHAPMAN [c. 1559–c. 1634], *Revenge for Honor, act. V, sc. ii*
L'injure se grave en métal; et le bienfait

See me safe up: for my coming down, I can shift for myself.

On ascending the scaffold. From Froude, *History of England* [1856–1870]

This hath not offended the king.
As he drew his beard aside upon placing his head on the block. From Bacon, *Apothegms, no. 22*

ROBERT WHITTINTON
c. 1480 – c. 1530

More [1] is a man of angel's wit and singular learning; I know not his fellow. For where is the man of that gentleness, lowliness and affability? And as time requireth, a man of marvelous mirth and pastimes; and sometimes of as sad a gravity; a man for all seasons.[2]

Passage composed for schoolboys to put into Latin

MARTIN LUTHER
1483–1546

If it were an art to overcome heresy with fire, the executioners would be the most learned doctors on earth.

To the Christian Nobility of the German States [1520]

Here I stand, I cannot do otherwise.[3]
Speech at the Diet of Worms, April 18, 1521

The mad mob does not ask how it could be better, only that it be different. And when it then becomes worse, it must change again. Thus they get bees for flies, and at last hornets for bees.

Whether Soldiers Can Also Be in a State of Grace [1526]

A mighty fortress is our God,
A bulwark never failing.
Our helper He amid the flood
Of mortal ills prevailing.[1]

Hymn, Ein' Feste Burg [1529]

What can only be taught by the rod and with blows will not lead to much good; they will not remain pious any longer than the rod is behind them.

The Great Catechism. Second Command [1529]

Peace is more important than all justice; and peace was not made for the sake of justice, but justice for the sake of peace.   *On Marriage* [1530]

Justice is a temporary thing that must at last come to an end; but the conscience is eternal and will never die.   *Ib.*

Superstition, idolatry, and hypocrisy have ample wages, but truth goes a-begging.   *Table Talk* [1569], 53

For where God built a church, there the Devil would also build a chapel [2] . . . Thus is the Devil ever God's ape.   *Ib. 67*

The Mass is the greatest blasphemy of God, and the highest idolatry upon earth, an abomination the like of which has never been in Christendom since the time of the Apostles.   *Ib. 171*

There is no more lovely, friendly and charming relationship, communion or company than a good marriage.

       Ib. 292

[1] Ein' feste burg is unser Gott,
    ein gute wehr und waffen.
    Er hilft uns frei aus aller not,
    die uns itzt hat betroffen.
Translated by Frederick Henry Hedge [1853].
Great God! there is no safety here below;
Thou art my fortress, thou that seem'st my foe.
       Francis Quarles [1592–1644],
              Divine Poems

See *Psalm 46:1,* p. 19a.
[2] Where God hath a temple, the Devil will have a chapel. — Robert Burton, *Anatomy of Melancholy* [1621–1651], *pt. III, sec. 4, member 1, subsec. 1*
No sooner is a temple built to God but the Devil builds a chapel hard by. — George Herbert, *Jacula Prudentum* [1640]
See Defoe, p. 385a.

s'escrit en l'onde [An injury is engraved in metal, but a benefit is written in water]. — Jean Bertaut [c. 1611]
All your better deeds shall be in water writ, but this in marble. — Beaumont and Fletcher, *Philaster* [1620], *act V, sc. iii*
[1] Sir Thomas More.
[2] See Ben Jonson, p. 303b.
[3] Hier steh' ich, ich kann nicht anders.
Inscribed on his monument at Worms.

A theologian is born by living, nay dying and being damned, not by thinking, reading, or speculating.
Table Talk, 352

Reason is the greatest enemy that faith has: it never comes to the aid of spiritual things, but — more frequently than not — struggles against the divine Word, treating with contempt all that emanates from God.   *Ib. 353*

If I had heard that as many devils would set on me in Worms as there are tiles on the roofs, I should none the less have ridden there.
Luthers Sammtliche Schriften [1745], XVI, 14

He remains a fool his whole life long
Who loves not women, wine, and
    song.   *Attributed* [1]

It makes a difference whose ox is gored.[2]
Works [1854 ed.], vol. LXII, p. 449

HUGH LATIMER
1485–1555

Play the man, Master Ridley; we shall this day light such a candle, by God's grace, in England, as I trust shall never be put out.[3]
Addressed to Nicholas Ridley [1500–1555] as they were being burned alive at Oxford for heresy, October 16, 1555.[4] From J. R. GREEN, A Short History of the English People, ch. 7

---

[1] First mentioned in *Wandsbecker Bothen*, no. 75 [1775].
[2] This is the moral of the fable of the lawyer, the farmer, and the farmer's ox, which was included in NOAH WEBSTER, *American Spelling Book* [1802], entitled *The Partial Judge*.
[3] See *II Esdras 14:25*, p. 36b, and note 1, p. 981b.
[4] See Latimer and Ridley in the might
    Of Faith stand coupled for a common flight!
      WORDSWORTH [1770–1850], *Ecclesiastical Sonnets, pt. II, no. 34, Latimer and Ridley*

ST. IGNATIUS LOYOLA[1]
1491–1556

Teach us, good Lord, to serve Thee as
    Thou deservest:
To give and not to count the cost;
To fight and not to heed the wounds;
To toil and not to seek for rest;
To labor and not ask for any reward
Save that of knowing that we do Thy
    will.   *Prayer for Generosity [1548]*

PHILIPPUS AUREOLUS PARACELSUS
c. 1493–1541

Every experiment is like a weapon which must be used in its particular way — a spear to thrust, a club to strike. Experimenting requires a man who knows when to thrust and when to strike, each according to need and fashion.[2]   *Chirurgische Bucher [1605]*

FRANCIS I OF FRANCE
1494–1547

All is lost save honor.[3]
Letter to his mother after defeat at Pavia, February 23, 1525

FRANÇOIS RABELAIS
c. 1494–1553

Break the bone and suck out the substantific marrow.
Gargantua and Pantagruel,[4] bk. I [1532], prologue

To laugh is proper to man.[5]
Ib. Rabelais to the Reader

Appetite comes with eating [6] . . . but the thirst goes away with drinking.
Ib. ch. 5

---

[1] Founder of the Society of Jesus.
[2] Translated by HENRY M. PACHTER.
[3] Tout est perdu fors l'honneur.
The actual words written were: De toutes choses ne m'est demeuré que l'honneur et la vie qui est saulvé. The letter is in DULAURE, *Histoire Civile, Physique et Morale de Paris [1821–1825]*.
[4] Translated by SIR THOMAS URQUHART and PETER ANTHONY MOTTEUX [1653–1694].
[5] Pour ce que rire est le propre de l'homme.
[6] My appetite comes to me while eating. — MONTAIGNE, *Essays [1580–1595], III, 9*

War begun without good provision of money beforehand for going through with it is but as a breathing of strength and blast that will quickly pass away. Coin is the sinews of war.[1]

       Gargantua and Pantagruel bk. I, Rableais to the Reader, ch. 46

How shall I be able to rule over others, that have not full power and command of myself?[2]   *Ib. 52*

Do what thou wilt.[3]   *Ib. 57*

Wisdom entereth not into a malicious mind, and science without conscience is but the ruin of the soul.

         Ib. II [1534], 8

Subject to a kind of disease, which at that time they called lack of money.[4]

          Ib. II, 16

So much is a man worth as he esteems himself.   *Ib. 29*

A good crier of green sauce.   *Ib. 31*

Then I began to think that it is very true which is commonly said, that the one half of the world knoweth not how the other half liveth.[5]   *Ib. 32*

This flea which I have in mine ear.

         Ib. III [1545], 31

Oh thrice and four times happy those who plant cabbages![6]

         Ib. IV [1548], 18

Which was performed to a T.[7]

          Ib. 41

[1] See Bion, p. 104b, and note.
[2] He is most powerful who has power over himself. — SENECA [8 B.C.–A.D. 65] *Epistles 90, 34* See Massinger, p. 315b.
[3] Fais ce que voudras.
[4] See Shakespeare, p. 241b.
     Or that eternal want of pence,
     Which vexes public men.
       TENNYSON, *Will Waterproof's Lyrical Monologue* [1842], *st. 6*
[5] See Herbert, p. 325a.
[6] See Montaigne, p. 189b, and Voltaire, p. 417a.
[7] We could manage this matter to a T. — STERNE, *Tristram Shandy, bk. II* [1760], *ch. 5*
You see they'd have fitted him to a T. — SAMUEL JOHNSON; from BOSWELL, *Life* [1791]
You will find it shall echo my speech to a T. — THOMAS MOORE [1779–1852], *Address for the Opening of the New Theatre of St. Stephen*

He that has patience may compass anything.

       Gargantua and Pantagruel bk. IV, Rabelais to the Reader, ch. 48

We will take the good will for the deed.[1]   *Ib. 49*

Speak the truth and shame the Devil.[2]

      Ib. V [1552], *author's prologue*

Plain as a nose in a man's face.[3]

                Ib.

Like hearts of oak.[4]   *Ib.*

Go hang yourselves [critics] . . . you shall never want rope enough.[5]

                Ib.

Looking as like . . . as one pea does like another.[6]   *Ib. ch. 2*

And thereby hangs a tale.[7]   *Ib. 4*

It is meat, drink, and cloth to us.

          Ib. 7

[1] The will for deed I do accept. — DU BARTAS, *Divine Weeks and Works* [1578], *Second Week, Third Day, pt. II*
You must take the will for the deed. — SWIFT, *Polite Conversation* [1738], *Dialogue 2*
[2] While you live, tell truth and shame the devil! — SHAKESPEARE, *Henry IV, pt. I, act III, sc. i, l. 58*
I'd tell the truth, and shame the devil. — SAMUEL JOHNSON; from BOSWELL, *Boswell's Life of Johnson* [1791], *vol. I, p. 460* [Everyman ed.]
     Truth being truth,
     Tell it and shame the devil.
       BROWNING, *The Ring and the Book* [1868–1869], *III, The Other Half-Rome*
[3] See Shakespeare, p. 220b.
As clear and as manifest as the nose in a man's face. — ROBERT BURTON, *Anatomy of Melancholy* [1621–1651], *pt. III, sec. 3, member 4, subsec. 1*
[4] See Garrick, p. 439a.
[5] They were suffered to have rope enough till they had haltered themselves. — THOMAS FULLER, *The Historie of the Holy Warre* [1639], *bk. 5, ch. 7*
Give a man enough rope and he'll hang himself.   *Proverb*
[6] As lyke as one pease is to another. — LYLY, *Euphues* [1579]
       They say we are
       Almost as like as eggs.
         SHAKESPEARE, *The Winter's Tale* [1608–1611], *act I, sc. ii, l. 130*
As one egg is like another. — CERVANTES, *Don Quixote, pt. II* [1615], *bk. III, ch. 14*
[7] Also in Shakespeare, *Taming of the Shrew IV, i, 60, p. 219b.*

I am going to seek a grand perhaps;
draw the curtain, the farce is played.[1]
Alleged last words. From
Motteux, *Life of Rabelais*

JOHN HEYWOOD[2]
c. 1497 – c. 1580

All a green willow, willow, willow,
All a green willow is my garland.[3]
The Green Willow

The loss of wealth is loss of dirt,
As sages in all times assert;
The happy man's without a shirt.[4]
Be Merry Friends

Let the world slide,[5] let the world go;
A fig for care, and a fig for woe!
If I can't pay, why I can owe,
And death makes equal the high and
    low.   *Ib.*

Haste maketh waste.[6]
Proverbs [1546], *pt. I, ch. 2*

Good to be merry and wise.   *Ib.*

Beaten with his own rod.   *Ib.*

Look ere ye leap.[7]   *Ib.*

[1] Je m'en vais chercher un grand peut-être;
tirez le rideau, la farce est jouée.
His religion, at best, is an anxious wish; like
that of Rabelais, "a great Perhaps." — Carlyle,
Essays, Burns.
The grand perhaps. — Browning, *Bishop
Blougram's Apology*
[2] John Heywood's *Proverbs,* first printed in
1546, is the earliest collection of English col-
loquial sayings. The selection here given is
from the edition of 1874 (a reprint of 1598),
edited by Julian Sharman. See also *Oxford
Dictionary of English Proverbs,* compiled by
William G. Smith and revised by Paul Harvey
[2nd ed., 1948], and *A Dictionary of the Proverbs
in English in the 16th and 17th Centuries,* compiled by Morris Palmer Tilley [1950].
[3] The earliest known of the "willow" songs.
See Shakespeare, p. 276a.
[4] This line is the theme of many poems.
[5] Let the world slide. — *Towneley Mysteries*
[1420].
Let the world slide. — Shakespeare, *Taming
of the Shrew* [1593–1594], *Induction, sc. i, l. 6*
[6] In wikked haste is no profit. — Chaucer,
Canterbury Tales [c. 1387], *Melibee, 2240*
[7] Thou shouldst have looked before thou hadst
leapt. — Jonson, Chapman, Marston, *Eastward
Ho* [1605], *act V, sc. i*
See Samuel Butler, p. 353a.

While between two stools my tail go
to the ground.[1]
Proverbs, pt. I, ch. 2

He that will not when he may,
When he would he shall have nay.[2]
                    Ib. 3

The fat is in the fire.   *Ib.*

When the sun shineth, make hay.
                       Ib.

The tide tarrieth no man.[3]   *Ib.*

Fast bind, fast find.[4]   *Ib.*

And while I at length debate and beat
    the bush,
There shall step in other men and catch
    the birds.[5]   *Ib.*

Wedding is destiny,
And hanging likewise.[6]   *Ib.*

Happy man, happy dole.[7]   *Ib.*

[1] Between two stools one sits on the ground.
— *Les Proverbes del Vilain,* MS Bodleian [c.
1303]
[2] He that will not when he may,
   When he will he shall have nay.
       Robert Burton, *Anatomy of Melan-
       choly* [1621–1651], *pt. III, sec. 2, mem-
       ber 5, subsec. 5*
[3] See Chaucer, p. 168b.
Time nor tide tarrieth no man. — Robert
Greene, *Disputations* [1592]
   Hoist up sail while gale doth last,
   Tide and wind stay no man's pleasure.
       Robert Southwell, *St. Peter's
                     Complaint* [1595]
Nae man can tether time or tide. — Burns,
Tam O'Shanter [1787]
[4] Dry sun, dry wind;
   Safe bind, safe find.
       Thomas Tusser, *A Hundred Points
       of Good Husbandry* [1557] *October's
       Abstract, Washing*
   Fast bind, fast find;
   A proverb never stale in thrifty mind.
       Shakespeare, *Merchant of Venice*
              [1596–1597], *act II, sc. v, l. 54*
[5] It is this proverb which Henry V is reported
to have uttered at the siege of Orleans: Shall
I beat the bush and another take the bird?
[6] Hanging and wiving go by destiny. — *The
Schole-hous for Women* [1541]
Marriage and hanging go by destiny; matches
are made in heaven. — Robert Burton, *Anatomy of Melancholy* [1621–1651], *pt. III, sec. 2,
member 5, subsec. 5*
[7] Happy man be his dole. — Shakespeare,
Merry Wives of Windsor [1600–1601], *act III,
sc. iv, l. 68* and *Winter's Tale* [1609–1611], *act I,
sc. ii, l. 163*

God never send'th mouth but he sendeth meat.[1]

Proverbs, pt. I, ch. 4

A hard beginning maketh a good ending. *Ib.*

Like will to like.[2] *Ib.*

When the sky falleth we shall have larks. *Ib.*

More frayd then hurt. *Ib.*

Nothing is impossible to a willing heart. *Ib.*

Let the world wag, and take mine ease in mine inn.[3] *Ib. 5*

Hold their noses to grindstone.[4]

Ib.

A sleeveless errand.[5] *Ib. 7*

Reckoners without their host must reckon twice.[6] *Ib. 8*

Cut my coat after my cloth.[7] *Ib.*

The nearer to the church, the further from God.[8] *Ib. 9*

Now for good luck, cast an old shoe after me. *Proverbs, pt. I, ch. 9*

Better is to bow than break.[1] *Ib.*

It hurteth not the tongue to give fair words.[2] *Ib.*

Two heads are better than one.

Ib.

A short horse is soon curried.

Ib. 10

To tell tales out of school. *Ib.*

To hold with the hare and run with the hound. *Ib.*

Neither fish nor flesh, nor good red herring. *Ib.*

All is well that ends well.[3] *Ib.*

Of a good beginning cometh a good end.[4] *Ib.*

When the steed is stolen, shut the stable door.[5] *Ib.*

She looketh as butter would not melt in her mouth. *Ib.*

Ill weed groweth fast.[6] *Ib.*

---

[1] God sendeth and giveth both mouth and the meat. — THOMAS TUSSER, *Five Hundred Points of Good Husbandry* [1557]
God sends meat, and the Devil sends cooks. — JOHN TAYLOR, *Works* [1630], *vol. II, p. 85*
The holy prophet Zoroaster said,
The Lord who made thy teeth shall give
thee bread. *Persian couplet*

[2] See Homer, p. 66b.
"Like to like" is quoted by Aristotle in *Rhetoric I, 11, 25.*
See Robert Burton, p. 311b.

[3] Shall I not take mine ease in mine inn? — SHAKESPEARE, *Henry IV, pt. I* [1597–1598], *act III, sc. iii, l. 91*

[4] And hold one another's noses to the grindstone hard. — ROBERT BURTON, *Anatomy of Melancholy* [1621–1651], *pt. III, sec. 1, member 3*

[5] Chaucer and Shakespeare use the phrase.
Sending every one of her children upon some sleeveless errand, as she terms it. — JOSEPH ADDISON, *The Spectator, no. 47* [April 24, 1711] (referring to April Fool errands)

[6] He reckoneth without his Hostesse. Love knoweth no lawes. — LYLY, *Euphues* [1579]

[7] A relic of the Sumptuary Laws. One of the earliest [1530] instances occurs in the interlude of *Godly Queene Hester.*

[8] Qui est près de l'église est souvent loin de Dieu [He who is near the Church is often far from God]. — *Les Proverbes Communs* [c. 1500]
To Kerke the narre, from God more farre,
Has bene an old sayd sawe.

And he that strives to touch the starre,
Oft stombles at a strawe.
SPENSER, *The Shepheardes Calender* [1579], *July, l. 97*

[1] Rather to bow than break is profitable; Humility is a thing commendable.
The Moral Proverbs of Cristyne [1390]

[2] Fair words never hurt the tongue. — JONSON, CHAPMAN, MARSTON, *Eastward Ho* [1605], *act IV, sc. i*

[3] Si finis bonus est, totum bonum erit [If the end is good, all will be good]. — *Gesta Romanorum* [1472], *tale 67*
See Shakespeare, *Troilus and Cressida, act IV, sc. v, l. 223, p. 269b,* and *All's Well That Ends Well, act IV, sc. iv, l. 35, p. 270a,* and note.

[4] See Plato, p. 94a; Aristotle, p. 98b; and Horace, p. 123a.
Who that well his warke beginneth,
The rather a good ende he winneth.
GOWER, *Confessio Amantis* [c. 1386–1390]

[5] Quant le cheval est emblé dounke ferme fols l'estable [When the horse has been stolen, the fool shuts the stable]. — *Les Proverbes del Vilain* [c. 1303]

[6] Ewyl weed ys sone y-growe. — *MS Harleian* [c. 1490]

(*note continues p. 184*)

It is a dear collop
That is cut out of th' own flesh.[1]
Proverbs, pt. I, ch. 10

Beggars should be no choosers.
Ib.

Merry as a cricket.   *Ib.* 11

To rob Peter and pay Paul.[2]   *Ib.*

A man may well bring a horse to the water,
But he cannot make him drink without he will.[3]   *Ib.*

Kinde will creep where it may not go.[4]   *Ib.*

The cat would eat fish, and would not wet her feet.[5]   *Ib.*

Rome was not built in one day.
Ib.

Ye have many strings to your bow.[6]
Ib.

Children learn to creep ere they can learn to go.   *Ib.*

Great weeds do grow apace. — SHAKESPEARE, *Richard III* [1592–1593], *act II, sc. iv, l. 13*
An ill weed grows apace. — GEORGE CHAPMAN, *An Humorous Day's Mirth* [1599]
[1] God knows thou art a collop of my flesh. — SHAKESPEARE, *Henry VI* [1591], *pt. I, act V, sc. iv, l. 18*
[2] Rob Peter, and pay Paul. — ROBERT BURTON, *Anatomy of Melancholy* [1621–1651], *Democritus to the Reader*
Give not Saint Peter so much, to leave Saint Paul nothing. — GEORGE HERBERT, *Jacula Prudentum* [1640]
"To rob Peter and pay Paul" is said to have had its origin in the reign of Edward VI when the lands of St. Peter at Westminster were appropriated to raise money for the repair of St. Paul's in London.
The French form of the proverb is: Découvrir saint Pierre pour couvrir saint Paul.
[3] You may bring a horse to the river, but he will drink when and what he pleaseth. — GEORGE HERBERT, *Jacula Prudentum* [1640]
[4]   You know that love
Will creep in service when it cannot go.
     SHAKESPEARE, *Two Gentlemen of Verona* [1594–1595], *act IV, sc. ii, l. 19*
[5] Cat lufat visch, ac he nele his feth wete. — *MS Trinity College, Cambridge* [c. 1250]
See Shakespeare, *Macbeth I, vii, 44,* p. 282b.
[6] Two strings to his bow. — RICHARD HOOKER, *Laws of Ecclesiastical Polity, bk. V* [1597], *ch. 80*

Better is half a loaf than no bread.
Proverbs, pt. I, ch. 11

Nought venture nought have.[1]
Ib.

Children and fools cannot lie.[2]
Ib.

All is fish that cometh to net.[3]
Ib.

Who is worse shod than the shoemaker's wife? [4]   *Ib.*

One good turn asketh another.
Ib.

A dog hath a day.   *Ib.*

A hair of the dog that bit us.[5]
Ib.

But in deed,
A friend is never known till a man have need.[6]   *Ib.*

New broom sweepeth clean.
Ib. II, 1

Burnt child fire dreadeth.[7]   *Ib.* 2

There is no fool to the old fool.[8]
Ib.

All is not gospel that thou dost speak.   *Ib.*

A fool's bolt is soon shot.[9]   *Ib.* 3

---

[1] See Chaucer, p. 165a and W. S. Gilbert, p. 768a.
[2] 'Tis an old saw, Children and fooles speake true. — LYLY, *Endymion* [1591]
[3] All's fish they get that cometh to net. — TUSSER, *Five Hundred Points of Good Husbandry* [1557], *February Abstract*
[4] Him that makes shoes go barefoot himself. — ROBERT BURTON, *Anatomy of Melancholy* [1621–1651], *Democritus to the Reader*
[5] Old receipt books advised that an inebriate should drink sparingly in the morning some of the same kind of liquor which he had drunk to excess the night before.
[6] See Aristotle, p. 99a.
[7] Brend child fur dredth,
Quoth Hendyng.
     Proverbs of Hendyng, MS [c. 1320]
[8] There is no fool like an old fool. — JOHN LYLY, *Mother Bombie* [1592], *act IV, sc. ii,* and in frequent use thereafter.
[9] Sottes bolt is sone shote. — *Proverbs of Hendyng, MS* [c. 1320]

A woman hath nine lives like a cat.
Proverbs, pt. II, ch. 4

A penny for your thought.   *Ib.*

You cannot see the wood for the trees.   *Ib.*

You stand in your own light.   *Ib.*

Tit for tat.[1]   *Ib.*

Three may keep counsel, if two be away.[2]   *Ib. 5*

Small pitchers have wide ears.[3]
Ib.

Many hands make light work.   *Ib.*

Out of God's blessing into the warm sun.[4]   *Ib.*

There is no fire without some smoke.[5]   *Ib.*

A cat may look on a king.   *Ib.*

Have ye him on the hip.[6]   *Ib.*

Much water goeth by the mill
That the miller knoweth not of.[7]
Ib.

He must needs go whom the devil doth drive.   *Ib. 7*

Set the cart before the horse.   *Ib.*

The more the merrier.
Proverbs, pt. II, ch. 7

It is better to be
An old man's darling than a young man's warling.   *Ib.*

Be the day never so long,
Evermore at last they ring to evensong.[1]   *Ib.*

The moon is made of a green cheese.[2]   *Ib.*

I know on which side my bread is buttered.   *Ib.*

The wrong sow by th' ear.   *Ib. 9*

An ill wind that bloweth no man to good.[3]   *Ib.*

For when I gave you an inch, you took an ell.[4]   *Ib.*

Would ye both eat your cake and have your cake?[5]   *Ib.*

Every man for himself and God for us all.[6]   *Ib.*

Though he love not to buy the pig in the poke.[7]   *Ib.*

---

[1] This is a corruption of *Tant pour tant.*
[2] Two may keep counsel when the third's away. — SHAKESPEARE, *Titus Andronicus* [1593–1594], *act IV, sc. ii, l. 145*
Three can hold their peace if two be away. — GEORGE HERBERT, *Jacula Prudentum* [1640]
[3] Pitchers have ears. — SHAKESPEARE, *The Taming of the Shrew* [1593–1594], *act IV, sc. iv, l. 52*, and *Richard III* [1592–1593], *II, iv, 37*
Little pitchers have wide ears. — GEORGE HERBERT, *Jacula Prudentum* [1640]
[4] Thou shalt come out of a warme sunne into Gods blessing. — LYLY, *Euphues* [1579]
Thou out of Heaven's benediction comest
To the warm sun.
SHAKESPEARE, *King Lear* [1605–1606], *act II, sc. ii, l. 168*
[5] There can no great smoke arise, but there must be some fire. — LYLY, *Euphues* [1579]
[6] See Shakespeare, p. 232a.
[7]   More water glideth by the mill
Than wots the miller of.
SHAKESPEARE, *Titus Andronicus* [1593–1594], *act II, sc. i, l. 85*
The miller sees not all the water that goes by his mill. — ROBERT BURTON, *Anatomy of Melancholy* [1621–1651], *pt. III, sec. 3, member 4, subsec. 1*

[1] Be the day short or never so long,
At length it ringeth to evensong.
Quoted at the stake by George Tankerfield [1555] (FOXE, *Book of Martyrs* [1563], *ch. 7*)
[2] They wold make me believe that the moon was made of greene cheese. — JOHN FRITH, *A Pistle to the Christian Reader* [1529]
[3] Except wind stands as never it stood,
It is an ill wind turns none to good.
THOMAS TUSSER [1524–1580], *A Description of the Properties of Winds*
Ill blows the wind that profits nobody. — SHAKESPEARE, *King Henry VI* [1591], *pt. III, act II, sc. v, l. 55*
Falstaff. What wind blew you hither, Pistol?
Pistol. Not the ill wind which blows no man to good.
SHAKESPEARE, *Henry IV* [1597–1598], *pt. II, act V, sc. iii, l. 87*
[4] Give an inch, he'll take an ell. — JOHN WEBSTER [1580–1625], *Sir Thomas Wyatt*
[5] Wouldst thou both eat thy cake and have it? — GEORGE HERBERT, *The Size* [1633]
[6] Every man for himself, his own ends, the Devil for all. — ROBERT BURTON, *Anatomy of Melancholy* [1621–1651], *pt. III, sec. 1, member 3*
[7] For buying or selling of pig in a poke. — TUSSER, *Five Hundred Points of Good Husbandry* [1557], *September Abstract*

This hitteth the nail on the head.
Proverbs, pt. II, ch. 11

Enough is as good as a feast.   *Ib.*

JULIUS III[1]
d. 1555

Do you not know, my son, with what little understanding the world is ruled?[2]

> *To a Portuguese monk who sympathized with the Pope's burdens of office*

CHARLES V[3]
1500–1558

Fortune hath somewhat the nature of a woman; if she be too much wooed, she is the farther off.

> *From* FRANCIS BACON, *Advancement of Learning, bk. II*

Iron hand in a velvet glove.

> *Attributed to Charles V by* THOMAS CARLYLE, *Latter-Day Pamphlets, 11*

I make war on the living, not on the dead.

> *Said when advised to hang Luther's corpse on the gallows* [1546]

GREGORY XIII[4]
1502–1585

To the greater glory of God.[5]

> *Quoted in The Canons and Decrees of the Council of Trent* [1542–1560]

FERDINAND I
1503–1564

Let justice be done, though the world perish.[6]

> *From* MANLIUS, *Loci Communes, II, 290*

[1] Pope from 1550 to 1555.
[2] An nescis, mi fili, quantilla prudentia mundus regatur?
[3] See Lomonosov, p. 434b.
[4] Pope from 1572 to 1585.
[5] Ad maiorem Dei gloriam. Motto of the Society of Jesus.
[6] Fiat iustitia, et pereat mundus.
See Sir Thomas Browne, p. 330b.

SIR THOMAS WYATT
c. 1503–1542

Forget not yet the tried intent
Of such a truth as I have meant;
My great travail so gladly spent,
Forget not yet!

> *Forget Not Yet*

And wilt thou leave me thus?
Say nay, say nay, for shame!

> *The Appeal*

My lute, awake! perform the last
Labor that thou and I shall waste,
  And end that I have now begun;
For when this song is sung and past,
  My lute, be still, for I have done.

> *The Lover Complaineth the Unkindness of His Love*

They flee from me that sometime did me seek.

> *The Lover Showeth How He Is Forsaken of Such as He Sometime Enjoyed*

JOHN KNOX
1505–1572

A man with God is always in the majority.[1]

> *Inscription on Reformation Monument, Geneva, Switzerland*

JOHN BRADFORD
1510–1555

The familiar story, that, on seeing evildoers taken to the place of execution, he was wont to exclaim: "But for the grace of God there goes John Bradford," is a universal tradition, which has overcome the lapse of time.[2]

> *Biographical notice, Parker Society edition, The Writings of John Bradford* [1853]

[1] Un homme avec Dieu est toujours dans la majorité.
See Phillips, p. 659a.
[2] There but for the grace of God goes God.
—*Anonymous saying, attributed to* ORSON WELLES, *among others*

SIR THOMAS VAUX
1510–1556

Companion none is like
Unto the mind alone;
For many have been harmed by
　speech,
Through thinking, few or none.
Of a Contented Mind [1557]

I loathe that I did love,
In youth that I thought sweet,
As time requires for my behove,
Methinks they are not meet.
The Aged Lover Renounceth
Love, st. 1

But age, with his stealing steps,
Hath claw'd me in his clutch.[1]
Ib. 3

RICHARD GRAFTON
d. 1572

Thirty days hath November,
April, June, and September,
February hath twenty-eight alone,
And all the rest have thirty-one.[2]
Chronicles of England [1562]

---

[1] Quoted by First Clown in SHAKESPEARE, *Hamlet*, act V, sc. i, l. 77
[2] Junius, Aprilis, Septémq; Nouemq; tricenos, Unum plus reliqui, Februs tenet octo vicenos, At si bissextus fuerit superadditur unus.
　　WILLIAM HARRISON, *Description of Britain, prefixed to* HOLINSHED'S *Chronicles* [1577]
Thirty days hath September,
April, June, and November,
February has twenty-eight alone,
All the rest have thirty-one;
Excepting leap year — that's the time
When February's days are twenty-nine.
　　The Return from Parnassus [1606]
Thirty days hath September,
April, June, and November;
All the rest have thirty-one,
Excepting February alone,
Which hath but twenty-eight, in fine,
Till leap year gives it twenty-nine.
　　Common in the New England states
Fourth, eleventh, ninth, and sixth,
Thirty days to each affix;
Every other thirty-one
Except the second month alone.
　　Common in Chester County, Pennsylvania, among the Friends
Compare the old Latin class mnemonic:
In March, July, October, May,

MARY TUDOR
1516–1558

When I am dead and opened, you
shall find "Calais" lying in my heart.[1]
From HOLINSHED, *Chronicles*
[1577], III, 1160

AMBROISE PARÉ
1517–1590

I treated him, God cured him.[2]
His favorite saying

JOACHIM DU BELLAY
1522–1560

France, mother of the arts, of arms,
and of laws.[3]
Les Regrets [1559], IX

Happy he who like Ulysses a glorious
voyage made.[4]　　*Ib.* XXXI

PIERRE DE RONSARD
1524–1585

When you are old, at evening candle-
　lit,
Beside the fire bending to your wool,
Read out my verse and murmur, "Ron-
　sard writ
This praise for me when I was beau-
　tiful." [5]
Sonnets pour Hélène, I, 43

The Ides are on the fifteenth day,
The Nones the seventh: all other months
　besides
Have two days less for Nones and Ides.
[1] See Browning, p. 663b.
[2] Je le soignay, Dieu le guérit.
[3] France, mère des arts, des armes et des lois.
[4] Heureux qui, comme Ulysse, a fait un beau voyage.
[5] Quand vous serez bien vieille, au soir à la
　chandelle,
Assise auprès du feu, devidant et filant,
Direz, chantant mes vers, en vous émerveil-
　lant:
"Ronsard me célébrait du temps que j'étais
　belle."
Translated by HUMBERT WOLFE.
See the adaptation by YEATS: When you are old and gray and full of sleep (p. 879b).

Live now, believe me, wait not till tomorrow;
Gather the roses of life today.[1]
>> *Sonnets pour Hélène, I, 43*

Gather, gather your youth:
Just like this flower, old age
Your beauty will wither.[2]
>> *Odes I, 17. À Cassandre*

THOMAS TUSSER
c. 1524 – 1580

At Christmas play and make good
cheer,
For Christmas comes but once a year.
>> *A Hundred Points of Good
Husbandry* [1557], *The Farmer's Daily Diet*

Such mistress, such Nan,
Such master, such man.[3]
>> *Ib. April's Abstract*

Sweet April showers
Do spring May flowers.
>> *Ib. April's Husbandry*

Who goeth a-borrowing
Goeth a-sorrowing.
>> *Ib. June's Abstract*

'Tis merry in hall
Where beards wag all.[4]
>> *Ib. August's Abstract*

PIETER BRUEGEL
c. 1525 – 1569

Because the world is so faithless,
I go my way in mourning.[5]
>> *Inscription in* MOLIÈRE, *The
Misanthrope* [1568]

[1] Vivez, si m'en croyez, n'attendez à demain:
Cueillez des aujourd'hui les roses de la vie.
See Horace, p. 121a; Spenser, p. 200a; and
Herrick, p. 320b.
[2] Cueillez, cueillez votre jeunesse:
Comme à cette fleur, la vieillesse
Fera ternir votre beauté.
[3] Tel maître, tel valet. Attributed to CHEVA-
LIER BAYARD by Cimber.
[4] Merry swithe it is in halle,
When the beards 'waveth alle.
>> *Life of Alexander* [1312]
[5] Om dat de werelt is soe ongetru
Daer om gha ic in den ru.

GABRIEL MEURIER
1530–1601

He who excuses himself accuses himself.[1]
>> *Trésor des Sentences*

WILLIAM STEVENSON
c. 1530 – 1575

I cannot eat but little meat,
My stomach is not good;
But sure I think that I can drink
With him that wears a hood.
>> *Gammer Gurton's Needle
[c. 1573], drinking song,
act II*

Back and side go bare, go bare,
Both foot and hand go cold;
But, belly, God send thee good ale
enough,
Whether it be new or old.
>> *Ib. refrain*

HENRI ESTIENNE
1531–1598

If youth but knew, and old age only
could.[2]
>> *Les Prémices* [1594]

God tempers the wind to the shorn
lamb.[3]
>> *Ib.*

ELIZABETH I
1533–1603

The use of the sea and air is common
to all; neither can a title to the ocean
belong to any people or private persons,
forasmuch as neither nature nor public
use and custom permit any possession
thereof.
>> *To the Spanish Ambassador* [1580]

My care is like my shadow in the
sun —
Follows me flying — flies when I pursue
it.
>> *On the departure of Alençon
[1582]*

[1] Qui s'excuse, s'accuse.
See Shakespeare, pp. 231a and 237a.
[2] Si jeunesse savait, si vieillesse pouvait.
Translated by NORBERT GUTERMAN.
[3] Dieu mesure le froid à la brebis tondue.
See Laurence Sterne, p. 438b.

I know I have the body of a weak and feeble woman, but I have the heart and stomach of a king, and of a king of England too; and think foul scorn that Parma or Spain, or any prince of Europe, should dare to invade the borders of my realm.

Speech to the troops at Tilbury on the approach of the Armada [1588]

I am your anointed Queen. I will never be by violence constrained to do anything. I thank God I am endued with such qualities that if I were turned out of the Realm in my petticoat I were able to live in any place in Christendom.

From CHAMBERLIN, Sayings of Queen Elizabeth

I will make you shorter by the head.
Ib.

The daughter of debate, that eke discord doth sow.[1]   Ib.

[To the Countess of Nottingham] God may forgive you, but I never can.
From HUME, History of England Under the House of Tudor, vol. II, ch. 7

Though God hath raised me high, yet this I count the glory of my crown: that I have reigned with your loves.
The Golden Speech [1601]

Semper eadem [Ever the same].
Motto

I am no lover of pompous title, but only desire that my name may be recorded in a line or two, which shall briefly express my name, my virginity, the years of my reign, the reformation of religion under it, and my preservation of peace.

To her ladies, discussing her epitaph

'Twas God the word that spake it,
He took the Bread and brake it;

[1] Mary Queen of Scots.

And what the word did make it,
That I believe, and take it.[1]

From S. CLARKE, Marrow of Ecclesiastical History [ed. 1675], pt. II, Life of Queen Elizabeth

MICHEL EYQUEM DE MONTAIGNE[2]
1533–1592

Man in sooth is a marvelous vain, fickle, and unstable subject.
Essays,[3] bk. I [1580], ch. 1

The thing of which I have most fear is fear.[4]   Ib. 17

He who should teach men to die would at the same time teach them to live.[5]   Ib. 19

I would let death seize upon me whilst I am setting my cabbages.[6]
Ib. 20

The value of life lies not in the length of days, but in the use we make of them: a man may live long, yet get little from life. Whether you find satisfaction in life depends not on your tale of years, but on your will.   Ib.

My desire is therefore that the parent be very circumspect in choosing a direc-

[1] Answer on being asked her opinion of Christ's presence in the Sacrament.
[2] Translated by CHARLES COTTON [1636–1687], revised by HAZLITT and WIGHT.
[3] This book of Montaigne the world has endorsed by translating it into all tongues. — EMERSON, Representative Men [1850], Montaigne
[4] C'est de quoy j'ay le plus de peur que la peur.
See Proverbs 3:25, p. 23b; Bacon, p. 207b; Wellington, p. 506a; Thoreau, p. 681b; and Roosevelt, p. 971a.
[5] I have taught you, my dear flock, for above thirty years how to live, and I will show you in a very short time how to die. — SIR EDWIN SANDYS [1561–1629], Anglorum Speculum
See Tickell, p. 400b.
    Teach him how to live,
And, oh still harder lesson! how to die.
    BEILBY PORTEUS [1731–1808], Death, l. 316
    In teaching me the way to live
    It taught me how to die.
      GEORGE POPE MORRIS [1802–1864],
          My Mother's Bible, st. 4
[6] Je veux que la mort me trouve plantant mes choux.
Translated by FLORIO [1603].
See Rabelais, p. 181a, and Voltaire, p. 417a.

tor whom I would rather commend for having a well-composed and temperate brain than a full-stuffed head.[1]

Essays, bk. I, ch. 25

If you press me to say why I loved him, I can say no more than it was because he was he and I was I.[2]

Ib. 27

Nothing is so firmly believed as what we least know. *Ib. 31*

A wise man never loses anything if he have himself. *Ib. 38*

We should reserve a storehouse for ourselves, altogether ours,[3] and wholly free, wherein we may hoard up and establish our true liberty, and principal retreat and solitude. *Ib. 39*

The greatest thing in the world is to know how to be sufficient unto oneself.[4] *Ib.*

To know how to live is all my calling and all my art.[5] *Ib. II [1580], 6*

Virtue can have naught to do with ease . . . It craves a steep and thorny path. *Ib. 11*

When I play with my cat, who knows whether I do not make her more sport than she makes me? *Ib. 12*

The souls of emperors and cobblers are cast in the same mold. . . . The same reason that makes us wrangle with a neighbor causes a war betwixt princes. *Ib.*

This idea is more clearly conceived by a question, "What do I know?"[6] which I employ, with the device of a pair of scales. *Ib.*

Man is certainly stark mad; he cannot make a worm, and yet he will be making gods by dozens. *Ib.*

What truth is that, which these mountains bound, and is a lie in the world beyond them? [1]

Essays, bk. II, ch. 12

Life is a dream . . . we sleeping wake and waking sleep.[2] *Ib.*

How many worthy men have we known to survive their own reputation! [3] *Ib. 16*

One may be humble out of pride.

Ib. 17

I find that the best virtue I have has in it some tincture of vice. *Ib. 20*

Saying is one thing, and doing is another. *Ib. 31*

There never were in the world two opinions alike, no more than two hairs or two grains; the most universal quality is diversity.[4] *Ib. 37*

I will follow the right side even to the fire, but excluding the fire if I can.

Ib. III [1595], 1

I speak truth, not so much as I would, but as much as I dare; and I dare a little the more, as I grow older.

Ib. 2

Few men have been admired by their own domestics.[5] *Ib.*

Every man bears the whole stamp of the human condition.[6] *Ib.*

It [marriage] happens as with cages: the birds without despair to get in, and those within despair of getting out.[7]

Ib. 5

---

[1] Plutôt la tête bien faite que bien pleine. Translated by FLORIO.
[2] Parce que c'était lui; parce que c'était moi.
[3] Il se faut réserver une arrière boutique toute notre.
[4] La plus grande chose du monde, c'est de savoir être à soi.
[5] Mon métier et mon art, c'est vivre.
[6] Que sais-je?

[1] Quelle vérité que ces montagnes bornent, qui est mensonge qui se tient au delà?
[2] La vie est un songe . . . nous veillons dormants et veillants dormons.
See Euripides, p. 86b, and Aristophanes, p. 92a.
[3] See Bentley, p. 386a.
[4] See Pliny, p. 132b.
[5] See Antigonus, p. 99b.
[6] Chaque homme porte la form entière de l'humaîne condition.
[7] I myself have loved a lady and pursued her with a great deal of under-age protestation, whom some three or four gallants that have en-

All the world knows me in my book, and my book in me.

Essays, bk. III, ch. 5

'Tis so much to be a king, that he only is so by being so. The strange luster that surrounds him conceals and shrouds him from us; our sight is there broken and dissipated, being stopped and filled by the prevailing light.[1]

Ib. 7

I moreover affirm that our wisdom itself, and wisest consultations, for the most part commit themselves to the conduct of chance.[2]

Ib. 8

Not because Socrates said so,[3] but because it is in truth my own disposition — and perchance to some excess — I look upon all men as my compatriots, and embrace a Pole as a Frenchman, making less account of the national than of the universal and common bond.[4]

Ib. 9

There is no man so good, who, were he to submit all his thoughts and actions to the laws, would not deserve hanging ten times in his life.

Ib.

A little folly is desirable in him that will not be guilty of stupidity.[5]

Ib.

I have never seen a greater monster or miracle in the world than myself.

Essays, bk. III, ch. 11

Men are most apt to believe what they least understand.

Ib.

I have here only made a nosegay of culled flowers, and have brought nothing of my own but the thread that ties them together.[1]

Ib. 12

There is more ado to interpret interpretations than to interpret the things, and more books upon books than upon all other subjects; we do nothing but comment upon one another.

Ib. 13

For truth itself has not the privilege to be spoken at all times and in all sorts.

Ib.

Sits he on never so high a throne, a man still sits on his bottom.

Ib.

Let us a little permit Nature to take her own way; she better understands her own affairs than we.

Ib.

I have ever loved to repose myself, whether sitting or lying, with my heels as high or higher than my head.

Ib.

I do not understand; I pause; I examine.

Inscription for his library

joyed would with all their hearts have been glad to have been rid of. 'Tis just like a summer bird-cage in a garden: the birds that are without despair to get in, and the birds that are within despair and are in a consumption for fear they shall never get out. — JOHN WEBSTER, *The White Devil* [1612], *act I, sc. ii*

Wedlock, indeed, hath oft compared been
To public feasts, where meet a public rout —
Where they that are without would fain go in,
And they that are within would fain go out.
　　SIR JOHN DAVIES [1569–1626], *Contention Betwixt a Wife, etc.*

See Emerson, p. 608a.

[1] See Shakespeare, p. 265a, and Tennyson, p. 653a.

[2] Although men flatter themselves with their great actions, they are not so often the result of great design as of chance. — LA ROCHEFOUCAULD [1613–1680], *Maxim 57*

[3] See Socrates, p. 87b.

[4] See de Montesquieu, p. 414b.

[5] See Menander, p. 102b, Horace, p. 122b, and note.

WILLIAM I
[WILLIAM THE SILENT]
1533–1584

My God, have mercy on my soul and on my poor people.[2]

Last words as he fell under an assassin's bullets

[1] I am but a gatherer and disposer of other men's stuff, at my best value. — SIR HENRY WOTTON, *preface to The Elements of Architecture* [1624]

John Bartlett used this passage as an epigraph for the fourth edition of *Familiar Quotations* [1864]. It was the only quotation from Montaigne in that edition.

[2] Mon Dieu, ayez pitié de mon âme et de mon pauvre peuple.

SIR HUMPHREY GILBERT
c. 1539–1583

We are as near to heaven by sea as by land! [1]

From HAKLUYT, *Voyages, vol. III* [1600], *p. 159*

SIR EDWARD DYER
c. 1540–1607

My mind to me a kingdom is;
Such present joys therein I find
That it excels all other bliss
That earth affords or grows by kind:
Though much I want which most
would have,
Yet still my mind forbids to crave.

*Rawlinson Poetry
MS 85, p. 17* [2]

Some have too much, yet still do
crave;
I little have, and seek no more:
They are but poor, though much they
have,
And I am rich with little store:
They poor, I rich; they beg, I give;
They lack, I have; they pine, I live.

Ib.

[1] The way to heaven out of all places is of like length and distance. — SIR THOMAS MORE, *Utopia* [1516]
Gilbert, on the last day of his life, was seen in his tiny pinnace *Squirrel* with a book in hand, probably More's *Utopia* which inspired his last utterance. He was homeward bound from Newfoundland, which he had just taken possession of in the name of the Queen [August 1583].
"Do not fear! Heaven is as near,"
He said, "by water as by land!"
LONGFELLOW, *Sir Humphrey Gilbert* [1849], *st. 6*
See James T. Fields, p. 679b.
[2] This poem became popular as a song, altered thus:
My mind to me a kingdom is;
Such perfect joy therein I find,
As far exceeds all earthly bliss
That God and Nature hath assigned.
Though much I want that most would have,
Yet still my mind forbids to crave.
BYRD, *Psalms, Sonnets, etc.* [1588]
My mind to me an empire is,
While grace affordeth health.
ROBERT SOUTHWELL [c. 1561–1595],
Content and Rich
See Seneca, p. 131b.

Fain would I, but I dare not; I dare,
and yet I may not;
I may, although I care not, for pleasure
when I play not.

Fain Would I [*attributed*]

WILLIAM GILBERT
1540–1603

In the discovery of secret things and in the investigation of hidden causes, stronger reasons are obtained from sure experiments and demonstrated arguments than from probable conjectures and the opinions of philosophical speculators of the common sort.[1]

De Magnete [1600]

JAN ZAMOYSKI
1541–1605

The king reigns, but does not govern.[2]

Speech in the Polish Parliament [1605], *referring to King Sigismund III*

MARY STUART
[MARY QUEEN OF SCOTS]
1542–1587

In my end is my beginning.

Motto

O Lord my God, I have trusted in
thee;
O Jesu my dearest one, now set me
free.
In prison's oppression, in sorrow's obsession,
I weary for thee.
With sighing and crying bowed down
as dying,
I adore thee, I implore thee, set me
free! [3]

Prayer written in her Book of Devotion before her execution

[1] Translated by P. F. MOTTELAY.
[2] Thiers adopted the epigram as the motto for his journal *Nationale*, which he established with Mignet and Carrel in 1830.
[3] Translated by SWINBURNE.
O Domine Deus! speravi in te;

GUILLAUME DE SALLUSTE, SEIGNEUR DU BARTAS
1544–1590

Oft seen in forehead of the frowning skies.[1]
Divine Weeks and Works [1578], First Week, Second Day

For where's the state beneath the firmament
That doth excel the bees for government?[2]   *Ib. Fifth Day, pt. 1*

These lovely lamps, these windows of the soul.[3]   *Ib. Sixth Day*

Or almost like a spider, who, confin'd
In her web's center, shakt with every wind,
Moves in an instant if the buzzing fly
Stir but a string of her lawn canapie.[4]
          Ib.

Living from hand to mouth.
          Ib. Second Week, First Day, pt. 4

In the jaws of death.[5]   *Ib.*

O care mi Jesu! nunc libera me.
In dura catena, in misera poena,
Disidero te.
Languendo, gemendo, et genuflectendo,
Adore, imploro, ut liberes me!
[1] See Milton, p. 339a.
[2]   So work the honeybees,
Creatures that by a rule in Nature teach
The act of order to a peopled kingdom.
          SHAKESPEARE, *King Henry V* [1598–1600], act I, sc. ii, l. 187
[3] The windows of mine eyes. — SHAKESPEARE, *King Richard III* [1592–1593], act V, sc. iii, l. 117
[4] Much like a subtle spider which doth sit
In middle of her web, which spreadeth wide;
If aught do touch the utmost thread of it
She feels it instantly on every side.
          SIR JOHN DAVIES, *The Immortality of the Soul* [1599]
Our souls sit close and silently within,
And their own webs from their own entrails spin;
And when eyes meet far off, our sense is such
That, spider-like, we feel the tenderest touch.
          DRYDEN, *Marriage à la Mode* [1673], act II, sc. i
The spider's touch, how exquisitely fine!
Feels at each thread, and lives along the line.
          POPE, *An Essay on Man* [1733–1734], epistle I, l. 217
[5] Out of the jaws of death. — SHAKESPEARE, *Twelfth Night* [1598–1600], act III, sc. iv, l. 396
See Tennyson, p. 652a.

Only that he may conform
To tyrant custom.
          Divine Weeks and Works, Second Week, Third Day, pt. 2

Who breaks his faith, no faith is held with him.
          Ib. Fourth Day, bk. 2

Who well lives, long lives; for this age of ours
Should not be numbered by years, days, and hours.   *Ib.*

My lovely living boy,
My hope, my hap, my love, my life, my joy.[1]   *Ib.*

Out of the book of Nature's learned breast.[2]   *Ib.*

Flesh of thy flesh, nor yet bone of thy bone.   *Ib.*

MIGUEL DE CERVANTES
1547–1616

You are a King by your own Fireside, as much as any Monarch in his Throne.
          Don Quixote de la Mancha[3] *[1605–1615] author's preface, p. xix*

I was so free with him as not to mince the matter.[4]   *p. xx*

They can expect nothing but their labor for their pains.[5]   *p. xxiii*

---

[1]   My fair son!
My life, my joy, my food, my all the world.
          SHAKESPEARE, *King John* [1596–1597], act III, sc. iv, l. 103
[2] The book of Nature is that which the physician must read; and to do so he must walk over the leaves. — PARACELSUS [1493–1541]. From *Encyclopaedia Britannica* (*11th ed.*), *vol. XX*, p. 749
[3] Translated in 1700–1703 by PETER ANTHONY MOTTEUX [1660–1718]. Page numbers are those of the Modern Library Giant edition.
[4] See Shakespeare, p. 273b.
You mince matters. — MOLIÈRE, *Tartuffe* [1667], act I, sc. i
[5] Nothing is to be gotten without pains (labor). — Old Proverb
See Shakespeare, p. 267b.

Time out of mind.[1]
> *Don Quixote, pt. I* [1605],
> *bk. I, ch.* 1, *p.* 4

Which I have earned with the sweat of my brows.[2]   *I, 4, p.* 22

By a small sample we may judge of the whole piece.   *p.* 25

Put you in this pickle.[3]
> *I, 5, p.* 30

Can we ever have too much of a good thing?   *I, 6, p.* 37

The charging of his enemy was but the work of a moment.   *I, 8, p.* 50

I don't know that ever I saw one in my born days.   *II, 2, p.* 57

Those two fatal words, Mine and Thine.[4]   *II, 3, p.* 63

The eyes those silent tongues of Love.   *p.* 65

And had a face like a benediction.[5]
> *II, 4, p.* 69

There's not the least thing can be said or done, but people will talk and find fault.[6]   *p.* 70

Without a wink of sleep.[7]   *p.* 72

It is a true saying, that a man must eat a peck of salt with his friend, before he knows him.   *III, 1, p.* 92

Thank you for nothing.   *p.* 94

No limits but the sky.[8]
> *III, 3, p.* 110

To give the devil his due.   *p.* 111

You're leaping over the hedge before you come to the stile.
> *Don Quixote, pt. I, bk. III,*
> *ch.* 4, *p.* 117

Paid him in his own coin.   *p.* 119

The famous Don Quixote de la Mancha, otherwise called The Knight of the Woeful Figure.[1]
> *III, 5, p.* 126

You are come off now with a whole skin.   *p.* 127

Fear is sharp-sighted, and can see things underground, and much more in the skies.   *III, 6, p.* 131

A finger in every pie.[2]   *p.* 133

No better than she should be.[3]
> *Ib.*

That's the nature of women . . . not to love when we love them, and to love when we love them not.[4]   *Ib.*

You may go whistle for the rest.
> *p.* 134

Ill luck, you know, seldom comes alone.[5]   *p.* 135

Why do you lead me a wild-goose chase?   *p.* 136

Experience, the universal Mother of Sciences.   *III, 7, p.* 140

Give me but that, and let the world rub, there I'll stick.   *p.* 148

Sing away sorrow, cast away care.
> *III, 8, p.* 153

Of good natural parts, and of a liberal education.   *p.* 154

---

[1] Time out o' mind. — SHAKESPEARE, *Romeo and Juliet* [1594–1595], *act I, sc. iv, l. 70*
[2] See *Genesis 3:19*, p. 6a.
[3] How cam'st thou in this pickle? — SHAKE-SPEARE, *The Tempest* [1611], *act V, sc. i, l. 281*
[4] See Boileau, p. 377b.
[5] The more familiar translation.
[6] Take wife, or cowl; ride you, or walk:
Doubt not but tongues will have their talk.
     LA FONTAINE, *The Miller, His Son, and the Donkey* [1694]
Do you think you could keep people from talking? — MOLIÈRE, *Tartuffe* [1667], *act I, sc.* 1
[7] See Shakespeare, *Cymbeline III, iv, 103,* p. 291a.
[8] Modern saying: The sky's the limit.

[1] El Caballero de la Triste Figura. More accurately translated by TOBIAS SMOLLETT as The Knight of the Sorrowful Countenance.
[2] No pie was baked at Castlewood but her little finger was in it. — THACKERAY, *The Virginians* [1857–1859], *ch.* 5
[3] An old proverb.
You are no better than you should be.
     BEAUMONT AND FLETCHER, *The Coxcomb* [1647], *act IV, sc.* 3
[4] See George Bernard Shaw, p. 836a.
[5] See Shakespeare, p. 265a.

Let every man mind his own business. *Don Quixote, pt. I, bk. III, ch. 8, p. 157*

Those who'll play with cats must expect to be scratched. *p. 159*

Raise a hue and cry. *Ib.*

'Tis the part of a wise man to keep himself today for tomorrow, and not venture all his eggs in one basket. *III, 9, p. 162*

The ease of my burdens, the staff of my life. *p. 163*

Within a stone's throw of it. *p. 170*

The very remembrance of my former misfortune proves a new one to me. *III, 10, p. 174*

Absence, that common cure of love. *p. 177*

From pro's and con's they fell to a warmer way of disputing. *p. 181*

Little said is soon amended.[1] *p. 184*

A close mouth catches no flies. *Ib.*

Thou hast seen nothing yet. *III, 11, p. 190*

Between jest and earnest. *Ib.*

My love and hers have always been purely Platonic. *p. 192*

'Tis ill talking of halters in the house of a man that was hanged. *p. 195*

My memory is so bad that many times I forget my own name! *Ib.*

'Twill grieve me so to the heart that I shall cry my eyes out. *p. 197*

Ready to split his sides with laughing. *III, 13, p. 208*

My honor is dearer to me than my life. *IV, 1, p. 226*

On the word of a gentleman, and a Christian. *p. 236*

Think before thou speakest. *IV, 3, p. 252*

---

[1] Often rendered: Least said soonest mended.

Let us forget and forgive injuries. *Don Quixote, pt. I, bk. IV, ch. 3, p. 254*

I must speak the truth, and nothing but the truth. *p. 255*

More knave than fool. *IV, 4, p. 261*

Here's the devil-and-all to pay. *IV, 10, p. 319*

I begin to smell a rat. *Ib.*

The proof of the pudding is in the eating. *p. 322*

Let none presume to tell me that the pen is preferable to the sword.[1] *p. 325*

There's no striving against the stream; and the weakest still goes to the wall. *IV, 20, p. 404*

The bow cannot always stand bent, nor can human frailty subsist without some lawful recreation. *IV, 21, p. 412*

It is not the hand but the understanding of a man that may be said to write.[2] *Pt. II [1615], bk. III, author's preface, p. 441*

When the head aches, all the members partake of the pains.[3] *III, 2, p. 455*

Youngsters read it, grown men understand it, and old people applaud it. *III, 3, p. 464*

History is in a manner a sacred thing, so far as it contains truth; for where truth is, the supreme Father of it may

---

[1] See Edward Bulwer-Lytton, p. 601b.
Scholars' pens carry farther, and give a louder report than thunder. — SIR THOMAS BROWNE, *Religio Medici* [1642], Everyman ed., p. 70
[2] Cervantes's left hand was maimed for life by gunshot wounds in the battle of Lepanto.
[3] When the head is not sound, the rest cannot be well. — DU BARTAS, *Divine Weeks and Works* [1578]
For let our finger ache, and it indues
Our other healthful members even to that sense
Of pain.
    SHAKESPEARE, *Othello* [1604–1605], *act III, sc. iv, l. 145*

also be said to be, at least, in as much as concerns truth.

Don Quixote, pt. II, bk. III, ch. 3, p. 465

Every man is as Heaven made him, and sometimes a great deal worse.

III, 4, p. 468

There's no sauce in the world like hunger. *III, 5, p. 473*

He casts a sheep's eye at the wench.

p. 474

I ever loved to see everything upon the square. *p. 475*

Neither will I make myself anybody's laughingstock. *Ib.*

Journey over all the universe in a map, without the expense and fatigue of traveling, without suffering the inconveniences of heat, cold, hunger, and thirst. *III, 6, p. 479*

Presume to put in her oar. *p. 480*

The fair sex.[1] *Ib.*

A little in one's own pocket is better than much in another man's purse. 'Tis good to keep a nest egg. Every little makes a mickle.[2] *III, 7, p. 486*

Remember the old saying, "Faint heart ne'er won fair lady."

III, 10, p. 501

Forewarned forearmed. *p. 502*

As well look for a needle in a bottle of hay.[3] *Ib.*

Are we to mark this day with a white or a black stone? [4] *p. 503*

The very pink of courtesy.

III, 13, p. 521

I'll turn over a new leaf. *p. 524*

He's [5] a muddled fool, full of lucid intervals. *III, 18, p. 556*

---

[1] That sex which is therefore called fair. — STEELE, *The Spectator, no. 302*, February 15, 1712
[2] See Hesiod p. 67b, and note.
[3] A needle in a haystack.
[4] A red-letter day.
[5] Don Quixote.

Marriage is a noose.

Don Quixote, pt. II, bk. III, ch. 19, p. 564

There are only two families in the world, the Haves and the Have-Nots.

III, 20, p. 574

He preaches well that lives well, quoth Sancho; that's all the divinity I understand. *p. 575*

Love and War are the same thing, and stratagems and policy are as allowable in the one as in the other.

III, 21, p. 580

A private sin is not so prejudicial in this world as a public indecency.

III, 22, p. 582

There is no love lost, sir.[1] *Ib.*

Come back sound, wind and limb.

p. 587

Patience, and shuffle the cards.[2]

III, 23, p. 592

Tell me thy company, and I'll tell thee what thou art.[3] *p. 594*

Tomorrow will be a new day.

III, 26, p. 618

I can see with half an eye.

III, 29, p. 632

Great persons are able to do great kindnesses. *III, 32, p. 662*

---

[1] There is no hate lost between us. — MIDDLETON [1580–1627], *The Witch, act IV, sc. ii.*
[2] But patience, cousin, and shuffle the cards, till our hand is a stronger one. — SIR WALTER SCOTT, *Quentin Durward* [1823], *ch. 8*
Cut the fiercest quarrels short
With "Patience, gentlemen, and shuffle."
W. M. PRAED [1802–1839], *Quince, st. 5*
Men disappoint me so, I disappoint myself so, yet courage, patience, shuffle the cards. — MARGARET FULLER OSSOLI [1810–1850], *letter to the Reverend W. H. Channing*
[3] Tell me what you eat, and I will tell you what you are. — ANTHELME BRILLAT-SAVARIN [1755–1826], *La Physiologie du Goût, aphorism 4*
Show me your garden and I shall tell you what you are. — ALFRED AUSTIN, *The Garden That I Love* [1905]

Honesty's the best policy.[1]
> *Don Quixote, pt. II, bk. III,*
> *ch. 33, p. 666*

An honest man's word is as good as his bond.　　　*IV, 34, p. 674*

A blot in thy scutcheon to all futurity.　　　*IV, 35, p. 681*

They had best not stir the rice, though it sticks to the pot.
> *IV, 37, p. 691*

Good wits jump;[2] a word to the wise is enough.　　　*p. 692*

Diligence is the mother of good fortune.　　　*IV, 38, p. 724*

What a man has, so much he's sure of.　　　*p. 725*

The pot calls the kettle black.
> *Ib. p. 727*

Mum's the word.[3]　　　*IV, 44, p. 729*

I shall be as secret as the grave.
> *IV, 62, p. 862*

Now blessings light on him that first invented this same sleep! It covers a man all over, thoughts and all, like a cloak; 'tis meat for the hungry, drink for the thirsty, heat for the cold, and cold for the hot. 'Tis the current coin that purchases all the pleasures of the world cheap; and the balance that sets the king and the shepherd, the fool and the wise man even.　　　*IV, 68, p. 898*

The ass will carry his load, but not a double load; ride not a free horse to death.　　　*IV, 71, p. 917*

I thought it working for a dead horse, because I am paid beforehand.[4]
> *Ib.*

He . . . got the better of himself, and that's the best kind of victory one can wish for.
> *Don Quixote, pt. II, bk. IV,*
> *ch. 72, p. 924*

Every man was not born with a silver spoon in his mouth.　　　*IV, 73, p. 926*

Ne'er look for birds of this year in the nests of the last.[1]　　　*IV, 74, p. 933*

There is a strange charm in the thoughts of a good legacy, or the hopes of an estate, which wondrously alleviates the sorrow that men would otherwise feel for the death of friends.
> *p. 934*

For if he like a madman lived,
At least he like a wise one died.
> *p. 935 (Don Quixote's epitaph)*

Don't put too fine a point to your wit for fear it should get blunted.
> *The Little Gypsy (La Gitanilla)*

My heart is wax molded as she pleases, but enduring as marble to retain.[2]　　　*Ib.*

CHARLES IX
1550–1574

Horses and poets should be fed, not overfed.[3]　　　*Saying*

WILLIAM CAMDEN
1551–1623

My friend, judge not me,
Thou seest I judge not thee.
Betwixt the stirrup and the ground
Mercy I asked, and mercy found.
> *Remains Concerning Britain.*
> *Epitaph for a man killed by*
> *falling from his horse*

---

[1] I hold the maxim no less applicable to public than to private affairs, that honesty is always the best policy. — GEORGE WASHINGTON, *Farewell Address* [1796]

[2] Great wits jump. — LAURENCE STERNE, *Tristram Shandy, vol. III* [1761–1762], ch. 9

[3] Cry "mum." — SHAKESPEARE, *The Merry Wives of Windsor* [1600–1601], act V, sc. ii, l. 6

[4] It is a heartrending delusion and a cruel snare to be paid for your work before you accomplish it. As soon as once your work is finished you ought to be promptly paid; but to receive your lucre one minute before it is due is to tempt Providence to make a Micawber of you. — EDMUND GOSSE, *Gossip in a Library* [1891], *Beau Nash*

[1] For Time will teach thee soon the truth,
　There are no birds in last year's nest!
　　　LONGFELLOW [1807–1882], *It Is Not Always May*, st. 6

[2] See Byron, p. 559b.

[3] Equi et poetae alendi, non saginandi.

THÉODORE AGRIPPA D'AUBIGNÉ
1552–1630

Each of us aspires to worth,
Each of us desires it
And desires it for himself.[1]
Pièces Épigrammatiques 49

More exquisite than any other is the autumn rose.[2]
Les Tragiques. Les Feux

SIR EDWARD COKE
1552–1634

Reason is the life of the law; nay, the common law itself is nothing else but reason. . . . The law, which is perfection of reason.[3]
First Institute [1628]

The gladsome light of jurisprudence. *Ib. epilogue*

For a man's house is his castle, *et domus sua cuique tutissimum refugium.*[4] *Third Institute [1644]*

The house of everyone is to him as his castle and fortress, as well for his defense against injury and violence as for his repose.
Semayne's Case. 5 Report 91

They [corporations] cannot commit treason, nor be outlawed nor excommunicate, for they have no souls.
Case of Sutton's Hospital.
10 Report 32

[1] Chacun au bien aspire,
   Chacun le bien désire,
   Et le désire sien.
[2] Une rose d'automne est plus qu'une autre exquise.
[3] Let us consider the reason of the case. For nothing is law that is not reason. — SIR JOHN POWELL, *Coggs v. Bernard*, 2 Ld. Raym. Rep. p. 911
[4] One's home is the safest refuge to everyone. — *Pandects* [6th century], *lib. II, tit. IV, De in Ius Vocando*
   I in mine own house am an emperor
   And will defend what's mine.
   MASSINGER, *The Roman Actor* [1629], act I, sc. ii

Magna Carta is such a fellow that he will have no sovereign.
Debate in the Commons
[May 17, 1628]

Six hours in sleep, in law's grave study six,
Four spend in prayer, the rest on Nature fix.[1]
Translation quoted by COKE; *from The Pandects (Digests of Roman Civil Law, sixth century). De in Ius Vocando*

SIR WALTER RALEGH
c. 1552 – 1618

Like to an hermit poor in place obscure,
I mean to spend my days of endless doubt,
To wail such woes as time cannot recure,
Where none but Love shall ever find me out.
The Phoenix Nest [1593]. Sonnet

As you came from the holy land
   Of Walsinghame,
Met you not with my true Love
   By the way as you came?
As You Came from the Holy Land [c. 1599], st. 1

But true love is a durable fire,
   In the mind ever burning,
Never sick, never old, never dead,
   From itself never turning.

Ib. st. 11

If all the world and love were young,
And truth in every shepherd's tongue,
These pretty pleasures might me move
To live with thee, and be thy love.
The Nymph's Reply to the Passionate Shepherd[2] *(printed in England's Helicon, 1600), st. 1*

[1] Seven hours to law, to soothing slumber seven;
   Ten to the world allot, and all to heaven.
   SIR WILLIAM JONES [1746–1794]
[2] An answer to CHRISTOPHER MARLOWE, *The Passionate Shepherd to His Love* (see p. 212a).

Fain would I climb, yet fear I to fall.
　　　　Written on a windowpane [1]

Our passions are most like to floods and
　　streams,
The shallow murmur, but the deep are
　　dumb.[2]
　　Sir Walter Ralegh to the Queen
　　　　[c. 1599], st. 1

Silence in love bewrays more woe
Than words, though ne'er so witty;
A beggar that is dumb, you know,
Deserveth double pity. *Ib. st. 5*

Go, Soul, the body's quest,
　　Upon a thankless arrant:
Fear not to touch the best,
　　The truth shall be thy warrant:
Go, since I needs must die,
And give the world the lie.
　　The Lie (printed in FRANCIS
　　DAVISON, *Poetical Rhapsody,*
　　1608; manuscript copy traced
　　to 1595), st. 1

Give me my scallop shell of quiet,
　　My staff of faith to walk upon,
My scrip of joy, immortal diet,
　　My bottle of salvation,
My gown of glory, hope's true gage
And thus I'll take my pilgrimage.
　　Diaphantus [1604]. The Pas-
　　sionate Man's Pilgrimage

Methought I saw the grave where
　　Laura lay.
　　Verses to Edmund Spenser

Shall I, like a hermit, dwell
On a rock or in a cell? *Poem*

What is our life? a play of passion,

---

[1] Under this Queen Elizabeth wrote, "If thy
heart fails thee, climb not at all." — THOMAS
FULLER, *Worthies of England* [1662]

[2] See Sencca, p. 131b.
Altissima quaeque flumina minimo sono labi
[The deepest rivers flow with the least sound].
— QUINTUS CURTIUS [1st century A.D.], *VII, 4, 13*
　Where the stream runneth smoothest, the
water is deepest. — LYLY, *Euphues and his Eng-*
land [1580]
　Smooth runs the water where the brook is
deep. — SHAKESPEARE, *Henry VI* [1591], *pt. II,*
act III, sc. i, l. 53
　Take heed of still waters, the quick pass
away. — GEORGE HERBERT, *Jacula Prudentum*
[1640]

Our mirth the music of division,
Our mothers' wombs the tiring houses
　be
Where we are dressed for this short
　comedy.
　From ORLANDO GIBBONS, *The*
　First Set of Madrigals and Mo-
　tets [1612]. On the Life of Man

[History] hath triumphed over time,
which besides it nothing but eternity
hath triumphed over.
　History of the World [1614],
　preface

Whosoever, in writing a modern history, shall follow truth too near the
heels, it may haply strike out his teeth.
　Ib.

O eloquent, just, and mighty Death!
whom none could advise, thou hast persuaded; what none hath dared, thou
hast done; and whom all the world hath
flattered, thou only hast cast out of the
world and despised. Thou hast drawn
together all the far-stretched greatness,
all the pride, cruelty, and ambition of
man, and covered it all over with these
two narrow words, *Hic jacet!*
　Ib. bk. V, pt. I, ch. 6, conclusion

Even such is time, that takes in trust
Our youth, our joys, our all we have,
And pays us but with age and dust;
Who in the dark and silent grave,
When we have wandered all our ways,
Shuts up the story of our days.
And from which earth, and grave, and
　dust,
The Lord shall raise me up, I trust.
　A version of one of his earlier
　poems, found at his death in his
　Bible in the Gatehouse at West-
　minster.

EDMUND SPENSER

1552–1599

He that strives to touch the stars
Oft stumbles at a straw.
　The Shepheardes Calender
　　[1579]. July, l. 99

Fierce wars and faithful loves shall moralize my song.[1]

> *The Faerie Queene* [1590],
> introduction, st. 1

A gentle knight was pricking on the plain. *Ib. bk. I, canto 1, st. 1*

A bold bad man. *Ib. 37*

Her angel's face
As the great eye of heaven shined bright,
And made a sunshine in the shady place. *Ib. 3, 4*

Ay me, how many perils do enfold
The righteous man, to make him daily fall.[2] *Ib. 8, 1*

Sleep after toil, port after stormy seas,
Ease after war, death after life does greatly please.[3] *Ib. 9, 40*

All for love, and nothing for reward. *Ib. II, 8, 2*

Gather therefore the Rose, whilst yet is prime,
For soon comes age, that will her pride deflower:
Gather the Rose of love, whilst yet is time.[4] *Ib. 12, 75*

Her birth was of the womb of morning dew.[5] *Ib. III, 6, 3*

Roses red and violets blew,
And all the sweetest flowers, that in the forest grew. *Ib. 6*

All that in this delightful garden grows,
Should happy be, and have immortal bliss. *Ib. 41*

That Squire of Dames. *Ib. 8, 44*

And painful pleasure turns to pleasing pain.

> *The Faerie Queene, bk. III,*
> *canto 10, st. 60*

How over that same door was likewise writ,
Be bold, be bold, and everywhere *Be bold.*[1] *Ib. 11, 54*

Another iron door, on which was writ,
Be not too bold.[2] *Ib.*

Dan Chaucer, well of English undefiled,
On Fame's eternal beadroll worthy to be filed. *Ib. IV* [1596], *2, 32*

For all that nature by her mother wit
Could frame in earth. *Ib. 10, 21*

Ill can he rule the great, that cannot reach the small. *Ib. V, 2, 43*

Who will not mercy unto others show,
How can he mercy ever hope to have?[3]
Ib. VI, 1, 42

The gentle mind by gentle deeds is known.
For a man by nothing is so well bewrayed,
As by his manners. *Ib. 3, 1*

That here on earth is no sure happiness. *Ib. 11, 1*

The ever-whirling wheel
Of Change; the which all mortal things doth sway. *Ib. VII, 6, 1*

Wars and alarums unto nations wide.
Ib. 3

But times do change and move continually.[4] *Ib. 47*

For deeds do die, however nobly done,

---

[1] And moralized his song. — POPE, *Epistle to Dr. Arbuthnot* [1735], *l. 340*

[2] Ay me! what perils do environ
The man that meddles with cold iron!
SAMUEL BUTLER: *Hudibras, pt. I* [1663], *canto III, l. 1*

[3] These lines are cut on Joseph Conrad's gravestone at Canterbury.

[4] See Horace, p. 121a; Ronsard, p. 188a; and Herrick, p. 320b.

[5] The dew of thy birth is of the womb of the morning. — *Book of Common Prayer, Psalter, Psalm 110:3*

[1] See Danton, p. 496b, and Channing, p. 544a.

[2] Jockey of Norfolk, be not too bold,
For Dickon thy master is bought and sold.
SHAKESPEARE, *Richard III, act V, sc. iii, l. 305*

Forbear, said I; be not too bold.
Your fleece is white but 'tis too cold.
CRASHAW, *Hymn of the Nativity, l. 50*
Write on your doors the saying wise and old,
"Be bold! be bold!" and everywhere — "Be bold;
Be not too bold!"
LONGFELLOW, *Morituri Salutamus* [1875]

[3] See *Matthew 5:7*, p. 40a, and Pope, p. 412b.

[4] See Lothair I, p. 152b.

And thoughts of men do as themselves
   decay,
But wise words taught in numbers for
   to run,
Recorded by the Muses, live for ay.
   The Ruines of Time [1591], *l. 400*

Full little knowest thou that hast not
   tried,
What hell it is, in suing long to bide:
To lose good days, that might be bet-
   ter spent;
To waste long nights in pensive discon-
   tent;
To speed today, to be put back tomor-
   row;
To feed on hope, to pine with fear and
   sorrow.
   Mother Hubberds Tale [1591],
      l. 895

To fret thy soul with crosses and with
   cares;
To eat thy heart through comfortless
   despairs;
To fawn, to crouch, to wait, to ride, to
   run,
To spend, to give, to want, to be undone.
Unhappy wight, born to disastrous
   end,
That doth his life in so long tendance
   spend.   *Ib. 903*

What more felicity can fall to creature,
Than to enjoy delight with liberty.
   *Muiopotmos; or, The Fate of
   the Butterflie* [1591], *l. 209*

I hate the day, because it lendeth light
To see all things, and not my love to
   see.   *Daphnaida* [1591], *l. 407*

Death slew not him, but he made death
   his ladder to the skies.
   *An Epitaph upon Sir Philip
   Sidney* [1591], *l. 20*

Though last not least.[1]
   Colin Clouts Come Home Again
      [1595], *l. 144*

[1] See Shakespeare, pp. 255a and 276b.
  The last, not least in honor or applause. —
Pope, *The Dunciad* [1728], *bk. IV, l. 577*

Tell her the joyous time will not be
   stayed
Unlesse she do him by the forelock
   take.[1]
   Amoretti [1595]. *Sonnet 70*

The woods shall to me answer, and my
   Echo ring.
   Epithalamion [1595], *l. 18*

Behold whiles she before the altar
   stands
Hearing the holy priest that to her
   speaks
And blesseth her with his two happy
   hands.   *Ib. 223*

Ah! when will this long weary day have
   end,
And lend me leave to come unto my
   love?   *Ib. 278*

For of the soul the body form doth
   take:
For soul is form, and doth the body
   make.
   An Hymne in Honour of Beautie
      [1596], *l. 132*

For all that fair is, is by nature good; [2]
That is a sign to know the gentle
   blood.   *Ib. 139*

Sweet Thames! run softly, till I end my
   Song.[3]
   Prothalamion [1596], *refrain*

I was promised on a time
To have reason for my rhyme;
From that time unto this season,
I received nor rhyme nor reason.
   *Lines on his promised pension.
   From* Thomas Fuller, *Wor-
   thies of England* [1662]

JOHN FLORIO
c. 1553 – 1625

England is the paradise of women,
the purgatory of men, and the hell of
horses.[4]   *Second Frutes* [1591]

[1] Take Time by the forelock. — Thales [c. 636–
c. 546 b.c.]
[2] See Shakespeare, p. 271b.
[3] Sweet Thames, run softly till I end my song,
  Sweet Thames, run softly, for I speak not
    loud or long.
    T. S. Eliot, *The Waste Land* [1922], *pt. III*
[4] See Robert Burton, p. 312a.

Praise the sea; on shore remain.
Second Frutes

HENRI IV OF FRANCE
1553–1610

I want there to be no peasant in my realm so poor that he will not have a chicken in his pot every Sunday.
Attributed

Paris is well worth a Mass.[1]
Attributed

Let my white panache be your rallying point.[2]   *Attributed battle cry*

The wisest fool in Christendom.
Of James I of England; attributed to HENRI IV *or* SULLY

GEORGE KEITH, FIFTH EARL MARISCHAL
1553–1623

Thai half said. Quhat say thai? Let thame say.[3]
Family motto, Mitchell Tower, Marischal College, Aberdeen, Scotland, founded in 1593

FULKE GREVILLE, LORD BROOKE
1554–1628

Oh wearisome condition of humanity! Born under one law, to another bound.
Mustapha [1609], V, 4

RICHARD HOOKER
1554–1600

Of Law there can be no less acknowledged than that her seat is the bosom of God, her voice the harmony of the world. All things in heaven and earth do her homage — the very least

as feeling her care, and the greatest as not exempted from her power.
Laws of Ecclesiastical Polity [1594], *bk.* 1

That to live by one man's will became the cause of all men's misery.
Ib.

JOHN LYLY
c. 1554–1606

Be valiant, but not too venturous. Let thy attire be comely, but not costly.[1]
Euphues: The Anatomy of Wit [1579], *Arber's reprint, p.* 39

The finest edge is made with the blunt whetstone.   *Ib. p.* 47

Delays breed dangers.[2]   *Ib. p.* 65

It seems to me (said she) that you are in some brown study.   *Ib. p.* 80

Many strokes overthrow the tallest oaks.[3]   *Ib. p.* 81

Let me stand to the main chance.[4]
Ib. p. 104

It is a world to see.   *Ib. p.* 116

A clear conscience is a sure card.
Ib. p. 207

Go to bed with the lamb, and rise with the lark.[5]
Euphues and His England, [1580], *p.* 229

A comely old man as busy as a bee.
Ib. p. 252

---

[1] Paris vaut bien une messe.
Attributed also to Henri's minister Sully.
[2] Ralliez-vous à mon panache blanc.
[3] They say. What say they? Let them say. — *Motto over the fireplace in George Bernard Shaw's home*

[1] See Shakespeare, p. 258b.
[2] Periculum in mora. — *Latin proverb*
See Shakespeare, p. 214a.
All delays are dangerous in war. — DRYDEN, *Tyrannic Love* [1669], act I, sc. i
[3] Many strokes, though with a little axe,
Hew down and fell the hardest-timber'd oak.
SHAKESPEARE, *Henry VI* [1591], *pt. III, act II, sc. i, l. 54*
See Franklin, p. 422a.
[4] See Butler, p. 353a.
[5] To rise with the lark and go to bed with the lamb. — BRETON, *Court and Country* [1618]
Rise with the lark, and with the lark to bed.
— JAMES HURDIS [1763–1801], *The Village Curate*

Maidens, be they never so foolish, yet being fair they are commonly fortunate.

> *Euphues and His England*
> *p. 279*

Your eyes are so sharp that you cannot only look through a millstone, but clean through the mind.   *Ib. p. 289*

I am glad that my Adonis hath a sweet tooth in his head.   *Ib. p. 308*

A rose is sweeter in the bud than full-blown.[1]   *Ib. p. 314*

Cupid and my Campaspe play'd
At cards for kisses: Cupid paid.

> *Alexander and Campaspe*
> *[1584], act III, sc. v*

How at heaven's gates she claps her wings,
The morn not waking till she sings.[2]

> *Ib. V, i*

Night hath a thousand eyes.[3]

> *Maides Metamorphosis III, 1*

Marriages are made in heaven and consummated on earth.[4]

> *Mother Bombie* [1590], *act IV, sc. i*

SIR PHILIP SIDNEY
1554–1586

High-erected thoughts seated in the heart of courtesy.[5]

> *The Arcadia* [written 1580], *bk. I*

They are never alone that are accompanied with noble thoughts.[6]   *Ib.*

---

[1] The rose is fairest when 'tis budding new. — SCOTT, *Lady of the Lake* [1810], *canto III, st. 1*

[2] See Shakespeare, p. 290b.

[3] On the stars thou gazest, my star; would I were heaven to look at thee with many eyes. — *Greek Anthology*, edited by J. W. MACKAIL, 8, 7

See Bourdillon, p. 826a.

[4] Les mariages se font au ciel, et se consomment sur la terre. — *French proverb*

See Heywood, p. 182b.

If marriages
Are made in heaven, they should be happier,

THOMAS SOUTHERNE, *The Fatal Marriage* [1694]

[5] Great thoughts come from the heart. — VAUVENARGUES [1715–1747], *Maxim 127*

[6] He never is alone that is accompanied with noble thoughts. — BEAUMONT AND FLETCHER, *Love's Cure* [1647], *act III, sc. iii*

My dear, my better half.

> *The Arcadia, bk. III*

My true-love hath my heart, and I have his,
By just exchange one for the other given:
I hold his dear, and mine he cannot miss,
There never was a better bargain driven.   *Ib. Sonnet*

Ring out your bells! Let mourning shows be spread!
For Love is dead.   *Ib. Song*

Leave me, O Love, which reachest but to dust,
And thou, my mind, aspire to higher things;
Grow rich in that which never taketh rust:
Whatever fades, but fading pleasure brings.   *Ib. Sonnet*

Sweet food of sweetly uttered knowledge.

> *The Defense of Poesy* [*written c. 1580*]

He cometh unto you with a tale which holdeth children from play, and old men from the chimney corner.

> *Ib.*

I never heard the old song of Percy and Douglas that I found not my heart moved more than with a trumpet.

> *Ib.*

"Fool!" said my muse to me, "look in thy heart, and write."[1]

> *Astrophel and Stella* [1591]

With how sad steps, O Moon, thou climb'st the skies!
How silently, and with how wan a face![2]   *Ib.*

Have I caught my heav'nly jewel.[3]

> *Ib. Second Song*

---

[1] Look, then, into thine heart and write. — LONGFELLOW, *Voices of the Night* [1839], *prelude*

[2] Wordsworth begins a sonnet with these two lines [1802].

[3] Quoted by SHAKESPEARE in *Merry Wives of Windsor, act III, sc. iii, l. 45*

Thy necessity [1] is yet greater than mine.

> *Said on the battlefield of Zutphen [September 22, 1586] on giving his water bottle to a dying soldier*

FRANÇOIS DE MALHERBE [2]
1555–1628

And a rose, she lived as roses do, the space of a morn.[3]

> *Consolation à Monsieur du Périer* [1599]

And the fruits will outdo what the flowers have promised.[4]

> *Prière pour le roi Henri le Grand* [1605]

What Malherbe writes will endure forever.   *Sonnet à Louis XIII* [1624]

THOMAS KYD
1558–1594

What outcries call me from my naked bed?

> *The Spanish Tragedy* [5] [1594], act II, sc. v, l. 1

O eyes, no eyes, but fountains fraught with tears;
O life, no life, but lively form of death;
O world, no world, but mass of public wrongs,
Confused and filled with murder and misdeeds.   *Ib. III, ii, 1*

Hieronymo, beware: go by, go by.
> *Ib. III, xii, 31*

Why then I'll fit you,[6] say no more.
When I was young, I gave my mind
And plied myself to fruitless poetry:

---

[1] More often quoted as "Thy need."

[2] See Boileau, p. 377a.

[3] Et rose, elle a vécu ce que vivent les roses, L'espace d'un matin.

[4] Et les fruits passeront la promesse des fleurs.

[5] This play was undoubtedly the most popular drama of its time, outstripping Shakespeare and the other Elizabethans.

[6] Quoted by T. S. ELIOT in *The Waste Land*, *l. 431*, followed by "Hieronymo's mad againe."

Which though it profit the professor naught
Yet it is passing pleasing to the world.
> *The Spanish Tragedy, act IV, sc. ii, l. 70*

THOMAS LODGE
c. 1558–1625

Love in my bosom like a bee
Doth suck his sweet.
> *Rosalind* [1590]

GEORGE PEELE
c. 1558 – c. 1597

Fair and fair, and twice so fair,
As fair as any may be.
> *The Arraignment of Paris* [1584]

My merry, merry, merry roundelay
Concludes with Cupid's curse:
They that do change old love for new,
Pray gods, they change for worse!
> *Ib.*

His golden locks time hath to silver turned;
O time too swift, O swiftness never ceasing!
His youth 'gainst time and age hath ever spurned,
But spurned in vain; youth waneth by increasing.
> *Polyhymnia* [1590]. *The Aged Man-at-Arms, st. 1*

His helmet now shall make a hive for bees,
And lovers' sonnets turned to holy psalms,
A man-at-arms must now serve on his knees,
And feed on prayers, which are age his alms.   *Ib. 2*

CHIDIOCK TICHBORNE [1]
c. 1558 – 1586

My prime of youth is but a frost of cares;
My feast of joy is but a dish of pain;
My crop of corn is but a field of tares;

---

[1] He was executed for an attempt on Queen Elizabeth's life.

And all my good is but vain hope of
    gain:
The day is past, and yet I saw no sun;
And now I live, and now my life is
    done.
          Tichborne's Elegy [1586]

GEORGE CHAPMAN
c. 1559 – 1634

Promise is most given when the least is
said.
          Hero and Leander [1598]

Love calls to war;
  Sighs his alarms,
Lips his swords are,
  The field his arms.
    Ib. Epithalamion Teratos, refrain

Young men think old men are fools;
but old men know young men are
fools.
        All Fools [1605], *act V, sc. i*

Keep thy shop, and thy shop will
keep thee. Light gains make heavy
purses.[1]
    Eastward Ho [2] [1605], *act I, sc. i*

Why, do nothing, be like a gentleman, be idle . . . Make ducks and
drakes with shillings.   *Ib.*

Only a few industrious Scots perhaps, who indeed are dispersed over the
face of the whole earth. But as for
them, there are no greater friends to
Englishmen and England, when they
are out on't, in the world, than they
are. And for my own part, I would a
hundred thousand of them were there
[Virginia]; for we are all one countrymen now, ye know, and we should find
ten times more comfort of them there
than we do here.[3]   *Ib. III, ii*

---

[1] Quoted by BENJAMIN FRANKLIN in *Poor
Richard's Almanac* [1735].

[2] By Chapman, Jonson, and Marston.

[3] This is the famous passage that gave offense
to James I and caused the imprisonment of the
authors. The leaves containing it were canceled
and reprinted, and it only occurs in a few of
the original copies. — RICHARD HERNE SHEPHERD

I will neither yield to the song of the
siren nor the voice of the hyena, the
tears of the crocodile [1] nor the howling
of the wolf.
        Eastward Ho, act V, sc. i

For one heat, all know, doth drive out
    another,
One passion doth expel another still.[2]
        Monsieur d'Olive [1606],
                act V, sc. i

To put a girdle round about the
world.[3]
      Bussy d'Ambois [1607],
             act I, sc. i

Speed his plow.   *Ib.*

  So our lives
In acts exemplary, not only win
Ourselves good names, but doth to oth-
  ers give
Matter for virtuous deeds, by which we
  live.   *Ib.*

Who to himself is law no law doth
  need,
Offends no law, and is a king indeed.
                  Ib. II, i

Give me a spirit that on this life's
  rough sea
Loves t' have his sails fill'd with a lusty
  wind,
Even till his sail-yards tremble, his
  masts crack,
And his rapt ship run on her side so
  low
That she drinks water, and her keel
  plows air.
    *Conspiracy of Charles, Duke of
        Byron* [1608], *act III, sc. i*

We have watered our horses in Helicon.
    May-Day [1611], *act III, sc. iii*

---

[1] These crocodile tears. — ROBERT BURTON,
Anatomy of Melancholy [1621–1651], *pt. III,
sec. 2, member 2, subsec. 4*

She's false, false as the tears of crocodiles. —
SIR JOHN SUCKLING [1609–1642], *The Sad One,
act IV, sc. v*

[2] See Shakespeare, p. 223a.

[3] See Shakespeare, p. 229b.

MAXIMILIEN DUC DE SULLY[1]
1559–1641

Tilling and grazing are the two breasts that feed France.[2]
Economies Royales, III

ROBERT GREENE
1560–1592

Sweet are the thoughts that savor of content;
The quiet mind is richer than a crown.
Farewell to Folly [1591], *st. 1*

A mind content both crown and kingdom is.   *Ib. 2*

For there is an upstart crow, beautified with our feathers, that with his tiger's heart wrapped in a player's hide,[3] supposes he is as well able to bumbast out a blank verse as the best of you; and being an absolute *Johannes fac totum*, is in his own conceit the only Shake-scene in a country.[4]
The Croatsworth of Wit [1592]

Hangs in the uncertain balance of proud time.
Friar Bacon and Friar Bungay
[acted 1594], act III

Hell's broken loose.[5]   *Ib. IV*

FRANCIS BACON[6]
1561–1626

I have taken all knowledge to be my province.
Letter to Lord Burleigh [1592]

The monuments of wit survive the monuments of power.
Essex's Device [1595]

---

[1] See Henri IV of France, p. 202a.
[2] Labourage et pâturage sont les deux mamelles dont la France est alimentée.
[3] See Shakespeare, p. 215b.
[4] First known literary reference to Shakespeare.
[5] See Milton, p. 346a.
[6] If parts allure thee, think how Bacon shined,
    The wisest, brightest, meanest of mankind.
         POPE, *Essay on Man, epistle IV, l. 281*
See Walton, p. 326b.

Knowledge is power [Nam et ipsa scientia potestas est].[1]
Meditationes Sacrae [1597].
De Haeresibus

For all knowledge and wonder (which is the seed of knowledge) is an impression of pleasure in itself.
The Advancement of Learning
[1605], bk. I, i, 3

Time, which is the author of authors.   *Ib. iv, 12*

If a man will begin with certainties, he shall end in doubts; but if he will be content to begin with doubts he shall end in certainties.   *Ib. v, 8*

Antiquitas saeculi juventus mundi. These times are the ancient times, when the world is ancient, and not those which we account ancient *ordine retrogrado*, by a computation backward from ourselves.[2]   *Ib.*

[Knowledge] is a rich storehouse for the glory of the Creator and the relief of man's estate.   *Ib., 11*

It [Poesy] was ever thought to have

---

[1] See *Proverbs 24:5,* p. 26a.
Knowledge is more than equivalent to force.
— SAMUEL JOHNSON, *Rasselas* [1759], *ch. 13*
[2] As in the little, so in the great world, reason will tell you that old age or antiquity is to be accounted by the farther distance from the beginning and the nearer approach to the end — the times wherein we now live being in propriety of speech the most ancient since the world's creation. — GEORGE HAKEWILL, *An Apologie or Declaration of the Power and Providence of God in the Government of the World* [1627]
For as old age is that period of life most remote from infancy, who does not see that old age in this universal man ought not to be sought in the times nearest his birth, but in those most remote from it? — PASCAL [1623–1662], *Preface to the Treatise on Vacuum*
It is worthy of remark that a thought which is often quoted from Francis Bacon occurs in [Giordano] Bruno's *Cena di Cenere,* published in 1584: I mean the notion that the later times are more aged than the earlier. — WHEWELL, *Philosophy of the Inductive Sciences* [1847], *vol. II, p. 198*
    We are Ancients of the earth,
    And in the morning of the times.
         TENNYSON, *The Day Dream* [1842],
                                        L'Envoi

some participation of divineness, because it doth raise and erect the mind by submitting the shews of things to the desires of the mind.

> *The Advancement of Learning,*
> *bk. II, iv, 2*

They are ill discoverers that think there is no land, when they can see nothing but sea. *Ib. vii, 5*

But men must know that in this theatre of man's life it is reserved only for God and angels to be lookers on.
> *Ib. xx, 8*

We are much beholden to Machiavel and others, that write what men do, and not what they ought to do.
> *Ib. xxi, 9*

All good moral philosophy is but the handmaid to religion. *Ib. xxii, 14*

There are and can be only two ways of searching into and discovering truth. The one flies from the senses and particulars to the most general axioms . . . this way is now in fashion. The other derives axioms from the senses and particulars, rising by a gradual and unbroken ascent, so that it arrives at the most general axioms last of all. This is the true way, but as yet untried.
> *Novum Organum* [1620]

There are four classes of Idols which beset men's minds. To these for distinction's sake I have assigned names — calling the first class, Idols of the Tribe; the second, Idols of the Cave; the third, Idols of the Market-Place; the fourth, Idols of the Theatre.
> *Ib. Aphorism* 39

Nature, to be commanded, must be obeyed. *Ib. 129*

I do plainly and ingenuously confess that I am guilty of corruption, and do renounce all defense. I beseech your Lordships to be merciful to a broken reed.[1]

> *On being charged by Parliament*
> *with corruption in the exercise of*
> *his office* [1621]

[1] See *Isaiah 36:6*, p. 32b.

Lucid intervals and happy pauses.
> *History of King Henry VII*
> [1622], *III*

Nothing is terrible except fear itself.[1]
> *De Augmentis Scientiarum,*
> *bk. II, Fortitudo* [1623]

Riches are a good handmaid, but the worst mistress. *Ib. Antitheta*

Hope is a good breakfast, but it is a bad supper.
> *Apothegms* [1624], *no. 36*

Like strawberry wives, that laid two or three great strawberries at the mouth of their pot, and all the rest were little ones. *Ib. 54*

Sir Amice Pawlet, when he saw too much haste made in any matter, was wont to say, "Stay a while, that we may make an end the sooner." *Ib. 76*

Alonso of Aragon was wont to say in commendation of age, that age appears to be best in four things — old wood best to burn, old wine to drink, old friends to trust, and old authors to read.[2] *Ib. 97*

Cosmus, Duke of Florence, was wont to say of perfidious friends, that "We read that we ought to forgive our enemies; but we do not read that we ought to forgive our friends." *Ib. 206*

Cato said the best way to keep good acts in memory was to refresh them with new. *Ib. 247*

My essays . . . come home to men's business and bosoms.
> *Essays, dedication* [1625 edition]

What is truth? said jesting Pilate,[3] and would not stay for an answer.
> *Ib. Of Truth*

[1] Nil terribile nisi ipse timor.
See Montaigne, p. 189b and note.
[2] See Webster, p. 314b.
Old friends are best. King James used to call for his old shoes; they were easiest for his feet.
— SELDEN, *Table Talk* [1689], *Friends*
See Goldsmith, p. 450b.
Old books, old wine, old Nankin blue. —
HENRY AUSTIN DOBSON [1840–1921], *Rondeau,*
To Richard Watson Gilder
[3] See *John 18:38*, p. 49b.

No pleasure is comparable to the standing upon the vantage-ground of truth.

Essays, Of Truth

Men fear death as children fear to go in the dark; and as that natural fear in children is increased with tales, so is the other.[1] *Ib. Of Death*

Revenge is a kind of wild justice, which the more man's nature runs to, the more ought law to weed it out.

Ib. Of Revenge

It was a high speech of Seneca (after the manner of the Stoics), that "The good things which belong to prosperity are to be wished, but the good things that belong to adversity are to be admired." *Ib. Of Adversity*

Prosperity is the blessing of the Old Testament; adversity is the blessing of the New. *Ib.*

Prosperity is not without many fears and distastes; and adversity is not without comforts and hopes. *Ib.*

Prosperity doth best discover vice, but adversity doth best discover virtue. *Ib.*

Virtue is like precious odors — most fragrant when they are incensed or crushed.[2] *Ib.*

He that hath wife and children hath given hostages to fortune; for they are impediments to great enterprises, either of virtue or mischief.

Ib. Of Marriage and Single Life

Wives are young men's mistresses, companions for middle age, and old men's nurses. *Ib.*

A good name is like a precious ointment; it filleth all around about, and will not easily away; for the odors of

ointments are more durable than those of flowers.[1]

Essays, Of Praise

In charity there is no excess.
Ib. Of Goodness and Goodness of Nature

If a man be gracious and courteous to strangers, it shows he is a citizen of the world,[2] and that his heart is no island cut off from other lands, but a continent that joins to them.[3] *Ib.*

The desire of power in excess caused the angels to fall; the desire of knowledge in excess caused man to fall.[4]
Ib.

I had rather believe all the fables in the legends and the Talmud and the Alcoran, than that this universal frame is without a mind. *Ib. Of Atheism*

A little philosophy inclineth man's mind to atheism, but depth in philosophy bringeth men's minds about to religion.[5] *Ib.*

Travel, in the younger sort, is a part of education; in the elder, a part of experience. He that traveleth into a country before he hath some entrance into the language, goeth to school, and not to travel. *Ib. Of Travel*

Princes are like to heavenly bodies, which cause good or evil times, and which have much veneration but no rest.[6] *Ib. Of Empire*

---

[1] See Lucretius, p. 113b.
[2] As aromatic plants bestow
No spicy fragrance while they grow;
But crushed or trodden to the ground,
Diffuse their balmy sweets around.
GOLDSMITH, *The Captivity* [1764], *act I*
The good are better made by ill,
As odors crushed are sweeter still.
SAMUEL ROGERS, *Jacqueline* [1814]. *st. 3*

[1] See *Ecclesiastes 7:1*, p. 28a, and Publilius Syrus, p. 125a.
[2] See Socrates, p. 87b.
[3] See Donne, p. 308b.
[4] Pride still is aiming at the blest abodes;
Men would be angels, angels would be gods.
Aspiring to be gods if angels fell,
Aspiring to be angels men rebel.
ALEXANDER POPE, *Essay on Man, epistle I* [1733]. *l. 125*
[5] A little skill in antiquity inclines a man to Popery; but depth in that study brings him about again to our religion. — THOMAS FULLER, *The Holy State and the Profane State* [1642], *The True Church Antiquary*
[6] See Shelley, p. 570b.

Fortune is like the market, where many times, if you can stay a little, the price will fall.

Essays, Of Delays

Nothing doth more hurt in a state than that cunning men pass for wise.

Ib. Of Cunning

Be so true to thyself, as thou be not false to others.[1]

Ib. Of Wisdom for a Man's Self

It is the nature of extreme self-lovers, as they will set an house on fire, and it were but to roast their eggs. *Ib.*

Cure the disease and kill the patient. *Ib. Of Friendship*

Riches are for spending.

Ib. Of Expense

There is a wisdom in this beyond the rules of physic. A man's own observation, what he finds good of and what he finds hurt of, is the best physic to preserve health.

Ib. Of Regimen of Health

Intermingle . . . jest with earnest.[2]

Ib. Of Discourse

Nature is often hidden; sometimes overcome; seldom extinguished.

Ib. Of Nature in Men

If a man look sharply and attentively, he shall see Fortune; for though she is blind, she is not invisible.[3]

Ib. Of Fortune

Chiefly the mold of a man's fortune is in his own hands.[4] *Ib.*

Young men are fitter to invent than to judge, fitter for execution than for counsel, and fitter for new projects than for settled business.

Ib. Of Youth and Age

Virtue is like a rich stone — best plain set. *Ib. Of Beauty*

[1] See Shakespeare, p. 259a.

[2] See Menander, p. 102a, Horace, p. 122b, and note.

[3] Fortune is painted blind, with a muffler afore her eyes, to signify to you that Fortune is blind. — SHAKESPEARE, *Henry V* [1598–1600], act III, sc. vi, l. 31

[4] See Sallust, p. 116a, and note.

There is no excellent beauty that hath not some strangeness in the proportion.

Essays, Of Beauty

God Almighty first planted a garden.[1] *Ib. Of Gardens*

He that commands the sea is at great liberty, and may take as much and as little of the war as he will.[2]

Ib. Of the True Greatness of Kingdoms

Some books are to be tasted, others to be swallowed, and some few to be chewed and digested. *Ib. Of Studies*

Reading maketh a full man, conference a ready man, and writing an exact man. *Ib.*

Histories make men wise; poets, witty; the mathematics, subtile; natural philosophy, deep; moral, grave; logic and rhetoric, able to contend. *Ib.*

The greatest vicissitude of things amongst men is the vicissitude of sects and religions.

Ib. Of Vicissitude of Things

I bequeath my soul to God. . . . My body to be buried obscurely. For my name and memory, I leave it to men's charitable speeches, and to foreign nations, and the next age.

From his will [1626]

The world's a bubble, and the life of man

[1] See *Genesis 2:8*, p. 5b.

Divina natura dedit agros, ars humana aedificavit urbes [Divine Nature gave the fields, human art built the cities]. — VARRO [116–27 B.C.], *De Re Rustica III, 1*

See Shakespeare, p. 265b.

Gardens were before gardeners, and but some hours after the earth. — SIR THOMAS BROWNE, *The Garden of Cyrus* [1658], ch. I

See Cowley, p. 358a, and Cowper, p. 457b.

[2] See Themistocles, p. 78a; Mahan, p. 785b; and Morison, p. 998a.

He that is master of the sea, may, in some sort, be said to be Master of every country; at least such as are bordering on the sea. For he is at liberty to begin and end War, where, when, and on what terms he pleaseth, and extend his conquests even to the Antipodes. — JOSEPH GANDER, *The Glory of Her Sacred Majesty Queen Anne in the Royal Navy* [1703]

Less than a span.[1]
The World [1629]

Who then to frail mortality shall trust
But limns on water, or but writes in
dust.[2]   *Ib.*

What then remains but that we still
should cry
For being born, and, being born, to
die? [3]   *Ib.*

Books must follow sciences, and not
sciences books.
*Proposition touching amend-
ment of laws*

SIR JOHN HARINGTON
1561–1612

Treason doth never prosper: what's the
reason?
For if it prosper, none dare call it treason.[4]   *Epigrams. Of Treason*

The readers and the hearers like my
books,
But yet some writers cannot them
digest;
But what care I? for when I make a
feast
I would my guests should praise it, not
the cooks.
*Ib. Of Writers Who Carp at
Other Men's Books*

ROBERT SOUTHWELL
c. 1561 – 1595

Times go by turns, and chances change
by course,

From foul to fair, from better hap to
worse.
Times Go by Turns [c. 1595],
st. 1

May never was the month of love,
For May is full of flowers;
But rather April, wet by kind,
For love is full of showers.
Love's Servile Lot

As I in hoary winter night stood shivering in the snow,
Surprised was I with sudden heat which
made my heart to glow;
And lifting up a fearful eye to view
what fire was near
A pretty Babe all burning bright did in
the air appear.
The Burning Babe [written
c. 1595]

With this he vanished out of sight, and
swiftly shrunk away,
And straight I called unto mind that it
was Christmas Day.   *Ib.*

SAMUEL DANIEL
1562–1619

Care-charmer Sleep, son of the sable
Night,
Brother to Death, in silent darkness
born.[1]
Sonnets to Delia [1592]

Make me to say, when all my griefs are
gone,
"Happy the heart that sighed for such a
one!"
Ib. Sonnet: I Must Not Grieve

Let others sing of knights and paladins
In aged accents and untimely words,
Paint shadows in imaginary lines

---

[1] Whose life is a bubble, and in length a
span. — WILLIAM BROWNE, *Britannia's Pastorals*
[1613], *bk. I, song*
    See Sir John Davies, p. 301a, and *The New
England Primer*, p. 1089b.
[2] See Sophocles, p. 83a; Catullus, p. 115a;
More, p. 178b; Shakespeare, p. 299a; and Keats,
p. 586a.
[3] This line frequently occurs in almost exactly the same shape among the minor poems
of the time: "Not to be born, or, being born, to
die." — WILLIAM DRUMMOND, *Poems* [1656]
    See Theognis, p. 77a, and note.
[4] See Seneca, p. 131a.

[1] Care-charmer sleep, sweet ease in restless
misery,
   The captive's liberty, and his freedom's
song,
   Balm of the bruised heart, man's chief
felicity,
   Brother of quiet death, when life is too,
too long!
    BARTHOLOMEW GRIFFIN, *Fidessa More
Chaste Than Kind* [1596]
    See Homer, p. 64a; Virgil, p. 119a; Shakes-
peare, p. 284a; and Shelley, p. 568a.

Which well the reach of their high wits
record.
> *Sonnets to Delia. Sonnet:*
> *I Must Not Grieve*

These are the arks, the trophies, I
erect,
That fortify thy name against old age.
> *Ib.*

And for the few that only lend their
ear,
That few is all the world.
> *Musophilus* [1599], *st.* 97

This is the thing that I was born to
do. *Ib. st. 100*

Unless above himself he can
Erect himself, how poor a thing is man!
> *To the Countess of Cumberland*
> [*c. 1600*], *st. 12*

Love is a sickness full of woes,
All remedies refusing.
> *Hymen's Triumph* [1615]

LOPE DE VEGA
1562–1632

Harmony is pure love, for love is
complete agreement.
> *Fuente Ovejuna,* [1] *act I, l.* 381

Except for God, the King's our only
lord. *Ib.* 1701

MICHAEL DRAYTON
1563–1631

Fair stood the wind for France.
> *The Ballad of Agincourt* [1606],
> *st. 1*

O, when shall Englishmen
With such acts fill a pen,
Or England breed again
Such a King Harry? *Ib. 15*

Since there's no help, come let us kiss
and part —
Nay, I have done: you get no more of
me,
And I am glad, yea glad with all my
heart,
That thus so cleanly I myself can free.

[1] Translated by ANGEL FORES and MURIEL KIT-
TEL. From *Spanish Drama* [1962].

Shake hands forever, cancel all our
vows,
And when we meet at any time again,
Be it not seen in either of our brows
That we one jot of former love retain.
Now at the last gasp of love's latest
breath,
When his pulse failing, Passion speech-
less lies,
When Faith is kneeling by his bed of
death,
And Innocence is closing up his eyes,
Now if thou wouldst, when all have
given him over,
From death to life thou might'st him
yet recover.
> *Poems* [1619]. *Idea*

The coast was clear.
> *Nymphidia* [1627]

Had in him those brave translunary
things
That the first poets had.
> *Said of* MARLOWE. *To Henry*
> *Reynolds, Of Poets and Poesy*
> [1627]

For that fine madness still he did retain
Which rightly should possess a poet's
brain. *Ib.*

GALILEO GALILEI
1564–1642

Philosophy is written in this grand
book — I mean the universe — which
stands continually open to our gaze, but
it cannot be understood unless one first
learns to comprehend the language and
interpret the characters in which it is
written. It is written in the language of
mathematics, and its characters are triangles, circles, and other geometrical
figures, without which it is humanly
impossible to understand a single word
of it; without these, one is wandering
about in a dark labyrinth.
> *Il Saggiatore* [1623] [1]

[1] *The Assayer* in *The Controversy on the
Comets of 1618* [1960], translated by STILLMAN
DRAKE and C. D. O'MALLEY.

But it does move! [1]
> From ABBÉ IRAILH, *Querelles
> litteraires* [1761], *vol. III, p.* 49

CHRISTOPHER
MARLOWE
1564–1593

Our swords shall play the orators for
us.
> *Tamburlaine the Great* [c. 1587],
> *pt. I, l.* 328

Accurst be he that first invented war.
> *Ib.* 664

And ride in triumph through Persepolis.
> *Ib.* 759

Nature that framed us of our ele-
ments,
Warring within our breasts for regi-
ment,
Doth teach us all to have aspiring
minds:
Our souls, whose faculties can compre-
hend
The wondrous Architecture of the
world:
And measure every wandering planet's
course,
Still climbing after knowledge infinite,
And always moving as the restless
Spheres,
Will us to wear ourselves and never
rest,
Until we reach the ripest fruit of all,
That perfect bliss and sole felicity,
The sweet fruition of an earthly crown.
> *Ib.* 869

Tamburlaine, the Scourge of God,
must die.   *Ib.* 4641

Come live with me, and be my love;
And we will all the pleasures prove
That valleys, groves, hills, and fields,
Woods or steepy mountain yields.[2]
> *The Passionate Shepherd to his
> Love* [c. 1589]

---

[1] E pur si muove!
The remark attributed to Galileo immediately
after he was forced to recant his views on the
earth's motion before the Inquisition in 1633.
[2] See Ralegh, p. 198b, and Donne, p. 306a.

By shallow rivers, to whose falls
Melodious birds sing madrigals.[1]
> *The Passionate Shepherd
> to his Love*

And I will make thee beds of roses
And a thousand fragrant posies.[1]
> *Ib.*

I count religion but a childish toy,
And hold there is no sin but ignorance.[2]
> *The Jew of Malta* [c. 1589],
> *prologue*

Infinite riches in a little room.[3]
> *Ib. act I, sc.* 1

Excess of wealth is cause of covetousness.   *Ib.* 2

Now will I show myself to have more
of the serpent than the dove; [4] that is,
more knave than fool.   *Ib. II,* 3

Friar Barnadine: Thou hast committed—
Barabas: Fornication—but that was in
another country;
And besides, the wench is dead.
> *Ib. IV,* 1

My men, like satyrs grazing on the
lawns,
Shall with their goat feet dance the
antic hay.
> *Edward II* [1593], *act I, sc. i*

Who ever loved that loved not at first
sight? [5]
> *Hero and Leander* [1598]

---

[1] To shallow rivers, to whose falls
Melodious birds sing madrigals;
There will we make our peds of roses,
And a thousand fragrant posies.
  SHAKESPEARE, *Merry Wives of Windsor*
  [1600–1601], *act III, sc. i, l. 17* [sung
  by Evans]
[2] See Wilde, p. 839a.
[3] Here lyeth muche rychnesse in lytell space.
— JOHN HEYWOOD, *The Foure PP* [1521–1525]
[4] See *Matthew 10:16*, p. 42a.
[5] Quoted in SHAKESPEARE, *As You Like It,*
act III, sc. v, l. 82
None ever loved but at first sight they loved.
— GEORGE CHAPMAN, *The Blind Beggar of
Alexandria* [1598]
I saw and loved. — GIBBON, *Memoirs* [1796]

Like untuned golden strings all women
   are,
Which long time lie untoucht, will
   harshly jar.
Vessels of brass oft handled brightly
   shine.
                        Hero and Leander

Live and die in Aristotle's works.
   *The Tragical History of Doctor
   Faustus [published 1604], sc. i*

Unhappy spirits that fell with Lucifer,
Conspired against our God with Luci-
   fer,
And are forever damned with Lucifer.
                              Ib. iii

Why this is hell, nor am I out of it:[1]
Think'st thou that I who saw the face
   of God,
And tasted the eternal joys of Heaven,
Am not tormented with ten thousand
   hells,
In being deprived of everlasting bliss?
                                 Ib.

Hell hath no limits, nor is circum-
   scribed
In one self place; for where we are is
   hell,
And where hell is there must we ever
   be.[1]   *Ib. v*

         When all the world dissolves,
And every creature shall be purified,
All places shall be hell that is not
   Heaven.   *Ib.*

Have not I made blind Homer sing to
   me?   *Ib. vi*

Was this the face that launched a thousand ships,
And burnt the topless towers of Ilium?[2]
Sweet Helen, make me immortal with a
   kiss.

[1] See Virgil, p. 119a; Browne, p. 330a; Milton,
p. 342a and p. 345a; Eliot, p. 1007a; Sartre, p.
1058b; and Robert Lowell, p. 1076b.
[2] Was this fair face the cause, quoth she,
   Why the Grecians sacked Troy?
      SHAKESPEARE, *All's Well that Ends Well*
                  [1601–1603], *act I, sc. iii, l. 75*

Her lips suck forth my soul;[1] see,
   where it flies!
      *The Tragical History of Doctor
                        Faustus, sc. xiv*

Oh, thou art fairer than the evening
   air
Clad in the beauty of a thousand stars.
                                 Ib.

Pray for me! and what noise soever
ye hear, come not unto me, for nothing
can rescue me.   *Ib. xvi*

Now hast thou but one bare hour to
   live,
And then thou must be damned per-
   petually!
Stand still, you ever-moving spheres of
   Heaven,
That time may cease, and midnight
   never come.   *Ib.*

O lente, lente currite noctis equi:[2]
The stars move still, time runs, the
   clock will strike,
The Devil will come, and Faustus must
   be damned.
O, I'll leap up to my God! Who pulls
   me down?
See, see where Christ's blood streams
   in the firmament!
One drop would save my soul—half a
   drop: ah, my Christ!   *Ib.*

O soul, be changed into little waterdrops,
And fall into the ocean—ne'er to be
   found.
My God! my God! look not so fierce on
   me!   *Ib.*

I'll burn my books!   *Ib.*

Cut is the branch that might have
   grown full straight,
And burnèd is Apollo's laurel bough,[3]
That sometime grew within this
   learnèd man.   *Ib.*

[1]   Once he drew
With one long kiss my whole soul through
My lips.
         TENNYSON, *Fatima* [1833], *st. 3*
[2] Run slowly, slowly, horses of the night.
At si, quem malis, Cephalum complexa
   teneres,
Clamares "lente currite noctis equi."
      OVID [43 B.C.–A.D. 18], *Amores I, xiii, 39*
[3] See Shakespeare, p. 288b.

WILLIAM
SHAKESPEARE[1]
1564–1616

Hung be the heavens with black, yield
day to night!
> *King Henry VI* [1591], *Part I,*
> *act I, sc. i, l. 1*

Fight till the last gasp.   *I, ii, 127*

Expect Saint Martin's summer, halcyon
days.[2]   *I, ii, 131*

Glory is like a circle in the water,
Which never ceaseth to enlarge itself,
Till by broad spreading it disperse to
nought.   *I, ii, 133*

> Unbidden guests
Are often welcomest when they are
gone.   *II, ii, 55*

Between two hawks, which flies the
higher pitch;
Between two dogs, which hath the
deeper mouth;
Between two blades, which bears the
better temper;
Between two horses, which doth bear
him best;
Between two girls, which hath the merriest eye;
I have, perhaps, some shallow spirit of
judgment;
But in these nice sharp quillets of the
law,
Good faith, I am no wiser than a daw.
> *II, iv, 12*

I'll note you in my book of memory.
> *II, iv, 101*

Just death, kind umpire of men's miseries.   *II, v, 29*

Chok'd with ambition of the meaner
sort.   *II, v, 123*

Delays have dangerous ends.[3]
> *III, ii, 33*

---

[1] From the text of W. J. CRAIG, Oxford University Press. The dates and order, about which there is much conjecture, are those which Sir Edmund Chambers (*William Shakespeare*, 1930) thinks most probable.

[2] See Aristophanes, p. 91b.

[3] See Lyly, p. 202b.

All delays are dangerous in war. — DRYDEN, *Tyrannic Love* [1669], *act I, sc. i*

Of all base passions, fear is most
accurs'd.
> *Henry VI, Part I, V, ii, 18*

She's beautiful and therefore to be
woo'd,
She is a woman, therefore to be won.[1]
> *V, iii, 78*

For what is wedlock forced, but a hell,
An age of discord and continual strife?
Whereas the contrary bringeth bliss,
And is a pattern of celestial peace.
> *V, v, 62*

> Whose large style
Agrees not with the leanness of his
purse.
> *King Henry VI, Part II, act I,*
> *sc. i, l. 112*

'Tis not my speeches that you do mislike,
But 'tis my presence that doth trouble
ye.
Rancor will out.   *I, i, 141*

Could I come near your beauty with
my nails
I'd set my ten commandments in your
face.   *I, iii, 144*

Blessed are the peacemakers on earth.[2]
> *II, i, 34*

Now, God be prais'd, that to believing souls
Gives light in darkness, comfort in despair!   *II, i, 66*

God defend the right!   *II, iii, 55*

> Sometimes hath the brightest day a
cloud;
And after summer evermore succeeds
Barren winter, with his wrathful nip-
ping cold:
So cares and joys abound, as seasons
fleet.   *II, iv, 1*

Now 'tis the spring, and weeds are
shallow-rooted;
Suffer them now and they'll o'ergrow
the garden.   *III, i, 31*

---

[1] See *Titus Andronicus*, p. 218b.

[2] See *Matthew 5:9*, p. 40a.

In thy face I see
The map of honor, truth, and loyalty.
Henry VI, Part II, III, i, 202

What stronger breastplate than a heart
    untainted!
Thrice is he arm'd that hath his quar-
    rel just,
And he but naked, though locked up in
    steel,
Whose conscience with injustice is cor-
    rupted.[1]   *III, ii, 232*

He dies, and makes no sign.
                                III, iii, 29

Forbear to judge, for we are sinners
    all.[2]
Close up his eyes and draw the curtain
    close;
And let us all to meditation.
                                III, iii, 31

The gaudy, blabbing, and remorseful
    day
Is crept into the bosom of the sea.
                                IV, i, 1

Small things make base men proud.
                                IV, i, 106

True nobility is exempt from fear.
                                IV, i, 129

I will make it felony to drink small
beer.[3]   *IV, ii, 75*

The first thing we do, let's kill all the
lawyers.   *IV, ii, 86*

Is not this a lamentable thing, that
of the skin of an innocent lamb should
be made parchment? that parchment,
being scribbled o'er, should undo a
man?   *IV, ii, 88*

And Adam was a gardener.[4]
                                IV, ii, 146

Sir, he made a chimney in my father's house, and the bricks are alive at
this day to testify it.
                Henry VI, Part II, IV, ii, 160

Thou hast most traitorously corrupted the youth of the realm in erecting a grammar-school; and whereas, before, our forefathers had no other books
but the score and the tally, thou hast
caused printing to be used; and, contrary to the king, his crown, and dignity, thou hast built a paper-mill.
                                IV, vii, 35

Beggars mounted run their horse to
    death.[1]
        King Henry VI, Part III, act I,
                            sc. iv, l. 127

O tiger's heart wrapp'd in a woman's
    hide! [2]   *I, iv, 137*

To weep is to make less the depth of
    grief.   *II, i, 85*

The smallest worm will turn being
    trodden on.   *II, ii, 17*

    Didst thou never hear
That things ill got had ever bad suc-
    cess?
And happy always was it for that son
Whose father for his hoarding went to
    hell?   *II, ii, 45*

Thou setter up and plucker down of
    kings.[3]   *II, iii, 37*

And what makes robbers bold but too
    much lenity?   *II, vi, 22*

My crown is in my heart, not on my
    head;
Not deck'd with diamonds and Indian
    stones,
Nor to be seen: my crown is call'd con-
    tent;
A crown it is that seldom kings enjoy.
                                III, i, 62

---

[1] See Milton, p. 337a.

[2] See *Matthew 7:1*, p. 41a.

[3] Doth it not show vilely in me to desire small
beer? — *King Henry IV* [1597–1598], *pt. II, I, ii, 7*
See *Othello*, p. 273b.
    That questionable superfluity — small beer.
— DOUGLAS JERROLD [1803–1857], *The Tragedy
of the Till*

[4] See *Hamlet V, i, 32*, p. 265b; Bacon, p. 209b;
and Kipling, p. 877b.

[1] Set a beggar on horseback and he will ride
a gallop. — ROBERT BURTON, *Anatomy of Melancholy* [1621–1651], *pt. II, sec. 2, member 2*
    Set a beggar on horseback, and he'll outride
the Devil. — BOHN, *Foreign Proverbs, German*
[1855]

[2] See Robert Greene, p. 206a.

[3] Proud setter up and puller down of kings.
—*Ib. III, iii, 157*

'Tis a happy thing
To be the father unto many sons.
　　Henry VI, Part III, III, ii, 104

Like one that stands upon a promontory,
And spies a far-off shore where he would tread,
Wishing his foot were equal with his eye.　　　*III, ii, 135*

　　Yield not thy neck
To fortune's yoke, but let thy dauntless mind
Still ride in triumph over all mischance.　　　*III, iii, 16*

For how can tyrants safely govern home,
Unless abroad they purchase great alliance?　　　*III, iii, 69*

Having nothing, nothing can he lose.
　　　III, iii, 152

Lives like a drunken sailor on a mast,
Ready with every nod to tumble down.
　　　III, iv, 98

Hasty marriage seldom proveth well.
　　　IV, i, 18

Let us be back'd with God and with the seas
Which he hath given for fence impregnable,
And with their helps only defend ourselves:
In them and in ourselves our safety lies.　　　*IV, i, 43*

What fates impose, that men must needs abide;
It boots not to resist both wind and tide.　　　*IV, iii, 57*

Now join your hands, and with your hands your hearts.　　*IV, vi, 39*

For many men that stumble at the threshold
Are well foretold that danger lurks within.　　　*IV, vii, 11*

A little fire is quickly trodden out,
Which, being suffer'd, rivers cannot quench.　　　*IV, viii, 7*

When the lion fawns upon the lamb,
The lamb will never cease to follow him.
　　Henry VI, Part III, IV, viii, 49

What is pomp, rule, reign, but earth and dust?
And, live we how we can, yet die we must.　　　*V, ii, 27*

Every cloud engenders not a storm.
　　　V, iii, 13

What though the mast be now blown overboard,
The cable broke, the holding anchor lost,
And half our sailors swallow'd in the flood?
Yet lives our pilot still.　　　*V, iv, 3*

So part we sadly in this troublous world
To meet with joy in sweet Jerusalem.
　　　V, v, 7

Men ne'er spend their fury on a child.
　　　V, v, 57

He's sudden if a thing comes in his head.　　　*V, v, 86*

Suspicion always haunts the guilty mind;
The thief doth fear each bush an officer.　　　*V, vi, 11*

This word "love," which greybeards call divine.　　　*V, vi, 81*

Now is the winter of our discontent
Made glorious summer by this sun of York.
　　King Richard III [1592–1593],
　　　act I, sc. i, l. 1

Grim-visaged war hath smoothed his wrinkled front.　　　*I, i, 9*

He capers nimbly in a lady's chamber
To the lascivious pleasing of a lute.
　　　I, i, 12

This weak piping time of peace.
　　　I, i, 24

No beast so fierce but knows some touch of pity.　　　*I, ii, 71*

Look, how my ring encompasseth thy finger,

Even so thy breast encloseth my poor
heart;
Wear both of them, for both of them
are thine.
　　　　Richard III, I, ii, 204

Was ever woman in this humor
woo'd?
Was ever woman in this humor won?
　　　　　　　　　I, ii, 229

Fram'd in the prodigality of nature.
　　　　　　　　　I, ii, 245

　　The world is grown so bad,
That wrens make prey where eagles
dare not perch.[1]　　*I, iii, 70*

And thus I clothe my naked villany
With odd old ends stol'n forth of holy
writ,
And seem a saint when most I play the
devil.　　　　　　*I, iii, 336*

Talkers are no good doers.
　　　　　　　　　I, iii, 351

O, I have passed a miserable night,
So full of ugly sights, of ghastly
dreams,
That, as I am a Christian faithful
man,
I would not spend another such a
night,
Though 'twere to buy a world of happy
days.　　　　　　　*I, iv, 2*

Lord, Lord! methought, what pain it
was to drown:
What dreadful noise of waters in mine
ears!
What ugly sights of death within mine
eyes!
Methought I saw a thousand fearful
wracks;
A thousand men that fishes gnaw
upon.　　　　　　　*I, iv, 21*

The kingdom of perpetual night.
　　　　　　　　　I, iv, 47

Sorrow breaks seasons and reposing
hours,
Makes the night morning, and the
noontide night.　　　*I, iv, 76*

A parlous boy.　　　　*II, iv, 35*

[1] See Pope, p. 404a.

So wise so young, they say, do never live
long.[1]
　　　　Richard III, III, i, 79

Off with his head![2]　　*III, iv, 75*

I am not in the giving vein today.
　　　　　　　　　IV, ii, 115

The sons of Edward sleep in Abraham's
bosom.[3]　　　　*IV, iii, 38*

A grievous burden was thy birth to
me;
Tetchy and wayward was thy infancy.
　　　　　　　　　IV, iv, 168

An honest tale speeds best being plainly
told.　　　　　　*IV, iv, 359*

Harp not on that string.　*IV, iv, 365*

Relenting fool, and shallow changing
woman!　　　　　*IV, iv, 432*

Is the chair empty? is the sword un-
sway'd?
Is the king dead? the empire unpos-
sess'd?　　　　　*IV, iv, 470*

Thus far into the bowels of the land
Have we march'd on without impedi-
ment.　　　　　　*V, ii, 3*

True hope is swift, and flies with swallow's wings;
Kings it makes gods, and meaner creatures kings.　　　　*V, ii, 23*

The king's name is a tower of strength.
　　　　　　　　　V, iii, 12

Give me another horse! bind up my
wounds!　　　　*V, iii, 178*

O coward conscience, how dost thou
afflict me!　　　　*V, iii, 180*

My conscience hath a thousand several
tongues,
And every tongue brings in a several
tale,
And every tale condemns me for a villain.　　　　　　*V, iii, 194*

[1] A little too wise, they say, do ne'er live long.
— Middleton [1580–1627], *The Phoenix*, act I,
sc. i
[2] See Colley Cibber, p. 392b, and Lewis Carroll, p. 744a.
[3] See *Luke 16:22*, p. 47a.

By the apostle Paul, shadows tonight
Have struck more terror to the soul of
　　Richard
Than can the substance of ten thou-
　　sand soldiers.
　　　　　　Richard III, V, iii, 217

Conscience is but a word that cowards
　　use,
Devis'd at first to keep the strong in
　　awe.　　　　　*V, iii, 310*

A horse! a horse! my kingdom for a
　　horse!　　　　　*V, iv, 7*

　　I have set my life upon a cast,
And I will stand the hazard of the die.
I think there be six Richmonds in the
　　field.　　　　　*V, iv, 9*

The pleasing punishment that women
　　bear.
　　　The Comedy of Errors [1592–
　　　1593], *act I, sc. i, l. 46*

We may pity, though not pardon thee.
　　　　　　　　I, i, 97

Why, headstrong liberty is lash'd with
　　woe.
There's nothing situate under heaven's
　　eye
But hath his bound, in earth, in sea, in
　　sky.　　　　　*II, i, 15*

Every why hath a wherefore.[1]
　　　　　　　　II, ii, 45

　　There's no time for a man to recover
his hair that grows bald by nature.
　　　　　　　　II, ii, 74

　　What he hath scanted men in hair,
he hath given them in wit.　*II, ii, 83*

Small cheer and great welcome makes a
　　merry feast.　　　*III, i, 26*

There is something in the wind.
　　　　　　　　III, i, 69

We'll pluck a crow together.
　　　　　　　　III, i, 83

For slander lives upon succession,
Forever housed where it gets posses-
　　sion.　　　　　*III, i, 105*

Be not thy tongue thy own shame's
　　orator.
　　The Comedy of Errors III, ii, 10

Ill deeds are doubled with an evil
　　word.　　　　　*III, ii, 20*

A back-friend, a shoulder-clapper.
　　　　　　　　IV, ii, 37

Give me your hand and let me feel your
　　pulse.　　　　　*IV, iv, 54*

The venom clamors of a jealous
　　woman
Poison more deadly than a mad dog's
　　tooth.　　　　　*V, i, 69*

Unquiet meals make ill digestions.
　　　　　　　　V, i, 74

　　One Pinch, a hungry lean-fac'd vil-
　　lain,
A mere anatomy, a mountebank,
A threadbare juggler, and a fortune-
　　teller,
A needy, hollow-ey'd, sharp-looking
　　wretch,
A living-dead man.　　*V, i, 238*

Sweet mercy is nobility's true badge.
　　　Titus Andronicus [1593–1594],
　　　　　　act I, sc. i, l. 119

These words are razors to my wounded
　　heart.　　　　　*I, i, 314*

He lives in fame that died in virtue's
　　cause.　　　　　*I, i, 390*

These dreary dumps.[1]　　*I, i, 391*

She is a woman, therefore may be
　　woo'd;
She is a woman, therefore may be
　　won.[2]　　　　　*II, i, 82*

　　What you cannot as you would
　　achieve,
You must perforce accomplish as you
　　may.　　　　　*II, i, 106*

The eagle suffers little birds to sing,
And is not careful what they mean
　　thereby.　　　　　*IV, iv, 82*

Tut! I have done a thousand dreadful
　　things

---

[1] See *King Henry V*, p. 245a.
For every why he had a wherefore. — SAMUEL
BUTLER, *Hudibras, pt. I* [1663], *canto 1, l. 132*

[1] And doleful dumps the mind oppress. —
Romeo and Juliet, act IV, sc. v, l. 129
[2] See *King Henry VI, Part I*, p. 214b.

As willingly as one would kill a fly.
Titus Andronicus V, i, 141

I'll not budge an inch.
The Taming of the Shrew
[1593–1594], *Induction, i,*
13

And if the boy have not a woman's
gift
To rain a shower of commanded tears,
An onion will do well for such a shift.
Ib. 124

No profit grows where is no pleasure
ta'en;
In brief, sir, study what you most
affect. *Act I, sc. i, l. 39*

There's small choice in rotten apples. *I, i, 137*

To seek their fortunes further than at
home,
Where small experience grows.
I, ii, 51

Nothing comes amiss, so money
comes withal. *I, ii, 82*

And do as adversaries do in law,
Strive mightily, but eat and drink as
friends. *I, ii, 281*

I must dance barefoot on her wedding
day,
And, for your love to her, lead apes in
hell. *II, i, 33*

Asses are made to bear, and so are you.
II, i, 200

Kiss me, Kate, we will be married o'
Sunday. *II, i, 318*

Old fashions please me best.
III, i, 81

Who woo'd in haste and means to wed
at leisure.[1] *III, ii, 11*

Such an injury would vex a saint.
III, ii, 28

A little pot and soon hot.[2]
IV, i, 6

And thereby hangs a tale.[1]
The Taming of the Shrew
IV, i, 60

It was the friar of orders grey,
As he forth walked on his way.[2]
IV, i, 148

Sits as one new-risen from a dream.
IV, i, 189

This is a way to kill a wife with kindness. *IV, i, 211*

Kindness in women, not their beauteous looks,
Shall win my love. *IV, ii, 41*

Our purses shall be proud, our garments poor:
For 'tis the mind that makes the body
rich;
And as the sun breaks through the
darkest clouds,
So honor peereth in the meanest
habit. *IV, iii, 173*

Forward, I pray, since we have come so
far,
And be it moon, or sun, or what you
please:
An if you please to call it a rush-
candle,
Henceforth I vow it shall be so for
me. *IV, v, 12*

He that is giddy thinks the world turns
round. *V, ii, 20*

A woman mov'd is like a fountain troubled,
Muddy, ill-seeming, thick, bereft of
beauty. *V, ii, 143*

Such duty as the subject owes the
prince,
Even such a woman oweth to her husband. *V, ii, 156*

Bid me discourse, I will enchant thine
ear.
Venus and Adonis [1593], *l. 145*

Love is a spirit all compact of fire,

---

[1] See Congreve, p. 391b, and Cabell, p. 949b.
[2] He is a little chimney, and heated hot in a
moment. — LONGFELLOW, *The Courtship of Miles
Standish* [1858]

[1] See Rabelais, p. 181b. Elsewhere in Shakespeare.
[2] THOMAS PERCY [1728-1811] composed *The
Friar of Orders Grey* of various fragments of
ancient ballads found in Shakespeare's plays.
See Anonymous, p. 1084b.

Not gross to sink, but light, and will
aspire.
                 Venus and Adonis, l. 149

O! What a war of looks was then between them.   *l.* 355

Like a red morn, that ever yet be-
token'd
Wrack to the seaman, tempest to the
field.   *l.* 453

The owl, night's herald.   *l.* 531

Love comforteth like sunshine after
rain.   *l.* 799

The text is old, the orator too green.
                                   l. 806

For he being dead, with him is beauty
slain,
And, beauty dead, black chaos comes
again.[1]   *l. 1019*

The grass stoops not, she treads on it so
light.   *l. 1028*

Beauty itself doth of itself persuade
The eyes of men without an orator.
        The Rape of Lucrece [1594], *l.* 29

This silent war of lilies and of roses,
Which Tarquin view'd in her fair face's
field.   *l. 71*

Those that much covet are with gain so
fond,
For what they have not, that which
they possess
They scatter and unloose it from their
bond,
And so, by hoping more, they have but
less.   *l. 134*

One for all, or all for one we gage.[2]
                                   l. 144

Who buys a minute's mirth to wail a
week?
Or sells eternity to get a toy?
For one sweet grape who will the vine
destroy?   *l. 213*

Extreme fear can neither fight nor fly.
                                   l. 230

All orators are dumb when beauty
pleadeth.   *l. 268*

[1] See *Othello*, p. 274a.
[2] See Dumas, p. 598b.

Time's glory is to calm contending
kings,
To unmask falsehood, and bring truth
to light.
             The Rape of Lucrece, l. 939

For greatest scandal waits on greatest
state.   *l. 1006*

To see sad sights moves more than hear
them told.   *l. 1324*

Cloud-kissing Ilion.   *l. 1370*

Lucrece swears he did her wrong.[1]
                                  l. 1462

Home-keeping youth have ever homely
wits.
      The Two Gentlemen of Verona
        [1594–1595], *act* I, *sc.* i, *l.* 2

I have no other but a woman's reason:
I think him so, because I think him
so.   *I, ii,* 23

Julia: They do not love that do not
show their love.
Lucetta: O! they love least that let men
know their love.   *I, ii,* 31

Since maids, in modesty, say "No" to
that
Which they would have the profferer
construe "Ay."   *I, ii,* 53

O! how this spring of love resembleth
The uncertain glory of an April day!
                                  I, iii, 84

O jest unseen, inscrutable, invisible,
As a nose on a man's face,[2] or a weathercock on a steeple!   *II, i,* 145

He makes sweet music with th' enam-
ell'd stones.   *II, vii,* 28

That man that hath a tongue, I say, is
no man,
If with his tongue he cannot win a
woman.   *III, i,* 104

Except I be by Silvia in the night,
There is no music in the nightingale.
                                  III, i, 178

[1] Some villain hath done me wrong. — *King
Lear* [1605–1606], *I, ii, 186*
    See *Frankie and Johnny*, p. 1101b.
[2] See Rabelais, p. 181b.

Much is the force of heaven-bred poesy.
    The Two Gentlemen of Verona
                III, ii, 72

Who is Silvia? what is she,
That all our swains commend her?
Holy, fair, and wise is she;
The heaven such grace did lend her,
That she might admired be.
                  IV, ii, 40

Alas, how love can trifle with itself!
                  IV, iv, 190

Black men are pearls in beauteous
ladies' eyes.   *V, ii, 12*

How use doth breed a habit in a man! [1]
                  V, iv, 1

Spite of cormorant devouring Time.
    Love's Labour's Lost [1594–
    1595], *act I, sc. i, l. 4*

Make us heirs of all eternity.   *I, i, 7*

Why, all delights are vain; but that
    most vain
Which, with pain purchas'd doth in-
    herit pain.   *I, i, 72*

Light seeking light doth light of light
beguile.   *I, i, 77*

Study is like the heaven's glorious sun,
That will not be deep-search'd with
    saucy looks;
Small have continual plodders ever
    won,
Save base authority from others'
    books.
These earthly godfathers of heaven's
    lights
That give a name to every fixed star,
Have no more profit of their shining
    nights
Than those that walk and wot not what
    they are.   *I, i, 84*

At Christmas I no more desire a rose
Than wish a snow in May's newfangled
    mirth;
But like of each thing that in season
    grows.   *I, i, 105*

[1] Custom is almost second nature. — PLUTARCH
[A.D. 46–120], *Rules for the Preservation of
Health, 18*

And men sit down to that nourishment which is called supper.
    Love's Labour's Lost I, i, 237

That unlettered small-knowing soul.
                I, i, 251

A child of our grandmother Eve, a
female; or, for thy more sweet understanding, a woman.   *I, i, 263*

Affliction may one day smile again;
and till then, sit thee down, sorrow!
                I, i, 312

Devise, wit; write, pen; for I am for
whole volumes in folio.   *I, ii, 194*

Beauty is bought by judgment of the
    eye,
Not utter'd by base sale of chapmen's
    tongues.   *II, i, 15*

A man of sovereign parts he is es-
    teem'd;
Well fitted in arts, glorious in arms:
Nothing becomes him ill that he would
    well.   *II, i, 44*

    A merrier man,
Within the limit of becoming mirth,
I never spent an hour's talk withal.
                II, i, 66

Your wit's too hot, it speeds too fast,
    'twill tire.   *II, i, 119*

Warble, child; make passionate my
sense of hearing.   *III, i, 1*

Remuneration! O! that's the Latin
word for three farthings.   *III, i, 143*

A very beadle to a humorous sigh.
                III, i, 185

This wimpled, whining, purblind, way-
    ward boy,
This senior-junior, giant-dwarf, Dan
    Cupid;
Regent of love-rimes, lord of folded
    arms,
The anointed sovereign of sighs and
    groans,
Liege of all loiterers and malcontents.
                III, i, 189

He hath not fed of the dainties that
are bred of a book; he hath not eat

paper, as it were; he hath not drunk ink.
　　Love's Labour's Lost IV, ii, 25

Many can brook the weather that love not the wind.　　　*IV, ii, 34*

You two are book-men.　　*IV, ii, 35*

These are begot in the ventricle of memory, nourished in the womb of pia mater, and delivered upon the mellowing of occasion.　　　*IV, ii, 70*

By heaven, I do love, and it hath taught me to rime, and to be melancholy.　　　*IV, iii, 13*

The heavenly rhetoric of thine eye.
　　　IV, iii, 60

Young blood doth not obey an old decree:
We cannot cross the cause why we were born.　　　*IV, iii, 217*

For where is any author in the world
Teaches such beauty as a woman's eye?
Learning is but an adjunct to ourself.
　　　IV, iii, 312

But love, first learned in a lady's eyes,
Lives not alone immured in the brain.
　　　IV, iii, 327

It adds a precious seeing to the eye.
　　　IV, iii, 333

　　　As sweet and musical
As bright Apollo's lute, strung with his hair;
And when Love speaks, the voice of all the gods
Makes heaven drowsy with the harmony.　　　*IV, iii, 342*

From women's eyes this doctrine I derive:
They sparkle still the right Promethean fire;
They are the books, the arts, the academes,
That show, contain, and nourish all the world.　　　*IV, iii, 350*

He draweth out the thread of his verbosity finer than the staple of his argument.　　　*V, i, 18*

Moth: They have been at a great feast of languages, and stolen the scraps.
Costard: O! they have lived long on the alms-basket of words. I marvel thy master hath not eaten thee for a word; for thou art not so long by the head as *honorificabilitudinitatibus;* thou art easier swallowed than a flap-dragon.
　　Love's Labour's Lost V, i, 39

In the posteriors of this day, which the rude multitude call the afternoon.
　　　V, i, 96

Taffeta phrases, silken terms precise,
Three-pil'd hyperboles, spruce affectation,
Figures pedantical.　　*V, ii, 407*

Let me take you a button-hole lower.　　　*V, ii, 705*

The naked truth of it is, I have no shirt.　　　*V, ii, 715*

A jest's prosperity lies in the ear
Of him that hears it, never in the tongue
Of him that makes it.　　*V, ii, 869*

When daisies pied and violets blue,
And lady-smocks all silver-white,
And cuckoo-buds of yellow hue
Do paint the meadows with delight,
The cuckoo then, on every tree,
Mocks married men; for thus sings he,
　　　　　　　　Cuckoo;
Cuckoo, cuckoo: O word of fear,
Unpleasing to a married ear.
　　　V, ii, 902

When icicles hang by the wall,
And Dick, the shepherd, blows his nail,
And Tom bears logs into the hall,
And milk comes frozen home in pail,
When blood is nipp'd and ways be foul,
Then nightly sings the staring owl,
　　　　　　　　Tu-who;
Tu-whit, tu-who — a merry note,
While greasy Joan doth keel the pot.
　　　V, ii, 920

When all aloud the wind doth blow,
And coughing drowns the parson's
saw,
And birds sit brooding in the snow,
And Marian's nose looks red and raw,
When roasted crabs hiss in the bowl.
　　　Love's Labour's Lost V, *ii*, 929

　The words of Mercury are harsh after
the songs of Apollo.　　　V, *ii*, 938

A pair of star-cross'd lovers.
　　　Romeo and Juliet [1594–1595],
　　　prologue, l. 6

Saint-seducing gold.
　　　act I, *sc. i, l.* 220

One fire burns out another's burning,[1]
One pain is lessen'd by another's anguish.　　　I, *ii*, 47

I will make thee think thy swan a
crow.　　　I, *ii*, 92

For I am proverb'd with a grandsire
phrase.　　　I, *iv*, 37

We burn daylight.　　　I, *iv*, 43

Mercutio: O! then, I see Queen Mab
hath been with you! . . .
She is the fairies' midwife, and she
comes
In shape no bigger than an agate-stone
On the forefinger of an alderman,
Drawn with a team of little atomies
Athwart men's noses as they lie asleep.
　　　I, *iv*, 53

　　　True, I talk of dreams,
Which are the children of an idle
brain,
Begot of nothing but vain fantasy.
　　　I, *iv*, 97

For you and I are past our dancing
days.[2]　　　I, *v*, 35

It seems she hangs upon the cheek of
night
Like a rich jewel in an Ethiop's ear;
Beauty too rich for use, for earth too
dear!　　　I, *v*, 49

[1] See Chapman, p. 205b.
[2] My dancing days are done. — BEAUMONT
AND FLETCHER, *The Scornful Lady* [1616], act V,
sc. iii

My only love sprung from my only
hate!
Too early seen unknown, and known
too late!
　　　Romeo and Juliet I, *v*, 142

Young Adam Cupid, he that shot so
trim
When King Cophetua lov'd the beggar-
maid.[1]　　　II, *i*, 13

He jests at scars, that never felt a
wound.
But, soft! what light through yonder
window breaks?
It is the east, and Juliet is the sun!
　　　II, *ii*, 1

She speaks, yet she says nothing.
　　　II, *ii*, 12

See! how she leans her cheek upon her
hand:
O! that I were a glove upon that hand,
That I might touch that cheek.
　　　II, *ii*, 23

O Romeo, Romeo! wherefore art thou
Romeo? [2]
Deny thy father, and refuse thy name;
Or, if thou wilt not, be but sworn my
love,
And I'll no longer be a Capulet.
　　　II, *ii*, 33

What's in a name? That which we call
a rose
By any other name would smell as
sweet.　　　II, *ii*, 43

For stony limits cannot hold love out.
　　　II, *ii*, 67

　　　At lovers' perjuries,
They say, Jove laughs.[3]　　　II, *ii*, 92

In truth, fair Montague, I am too
fond.　　　II, *ii*, 98

[1] See *Ballads*, p. 1087b, and Tennyson, p. 648a.
[2] HENRY FIELDING burlesqued this in Life and
Death of Tom Thumb the Great [1730] as follows:
　Huncamunca: O Tom Thumb! Tom Thumb!
wherefore art thou Tom Thumb? — *Act II, sc. iii*
[3] See Tibullus, p. 128a.
　And Jove but laughs at lovers' perjury. —
DRYDEN, *Palamon and Arcite* [1680], bk. II,
l. 758, and *Amphitryon* [1690], act I, sc. ii

I'll prove more true
Than those that have more cunning to
be strange.
　　　Romeo and Juliet II, ii, 100

Romeo: Lady, by yonder blessed moon
I swear
That tips with silver all these fruit-tree
tops —
Juliet: O! swear not by the moon, the
inconstant moon,
That monthly changes in her circled
orb,
Lest that thy love prove likewise vari-
able.　　　　　　　　　II, ii, 107

　　　Do not swear at all;
Or, if thou wilt, swear by thy gracious
self,
Which is the god of my idolatry.
　　　　　　　　　　　　II, ii, 112

It is too rash, too unadvis'd, too sud-
den;
Too like the lightning, which doth
cease to be
Ere one can say it lightens.
　　　　　　　　　　　　II, ii, 118

This bud of love, by summer's ripening
breath,
May prove a beauteous flower when
next we meet.　　　　　II, ii, 121

Love goes toward love, as schoolboys
from their books;
But love from love, toward school with
heavy looks.　　　　　II, ii, 156

　　　O! for a falconer's voice,
To lure this tassel-gentle back again.
　　　　　　　　　　　　II, ii, 158

How silver-sweet sound lovers' tongues
by night,
Like softest music to attending ears!
　　　　　　　　　　　　II, ii, 165

　　　I would have thee gone;
And yet no further than a wanton's
bird,
Who lets it hop a little from her hand,
Like a poor prisoner in his twisted
gyves,
And with a silk thread plucks it back
again,

So loving-jealous of his liberty.
　　　Romeo and Juliet II, ii, 176

Good night, good night! parting is such
sweet sorrow,
That I shall say good night till it be
morrow.　　　　　　　II, ii, 184

Virtue itself turns vice, being misap-
plied;
And vice sometime's by action dignified.　　　　　　　　　II, iii, 21

Care keeps his watch in every old man's
eye,
And where care lodges, sleep will never
lie.　　　　　　　　　II, iii, 35

Wisely and slow; they stumble that run
fast.[1]　　　　　　　II, iii, 94

　　One, two, and the third in your
bosom.　　　　　　　II, iv, 24

O flesh, flesh, how art thou fishified!
　　　　　　　　　　　　II, iv, 41

　　The very pink of courtesy.
　　　　　　　　　　　　II, iv, 63

　　A gentleman, nurse, that loves to
hear himself talk, and will speak more
in a minute than he will stand to in a
month.　　　　　　　II, iv, 156

These violent delights have violent
ends.　　　　　　　　II, vi, 9

Therefore love moderately; long love
doth so;[2]
Too swift arrives as tardy as too slow.
　　　　　　　　　　　　II, vi, 14

Here comes the lady: O! so light a
foot
Will ne'er wear out the everlasting
flint.　　　　　　　　II, vi, 16

Thy head is as full of quarrels as an
egg is full of meat.[3]　　　III, i, 23

A word and a blow.[4]　　III, i, 44

　　No, 'tis not so deep as a well, nor so

---

[1] See Chaucer, p. 165a.
[2] See Anonymous, p. 1084b, and Herrick, p. 320a.
[3] It's as full of good-nature as an egg's full of meat. — RICHARD BRINSLEY SHERIDAN, *A Trip to Scarborough* [1777], *act III, sc. iv*
[4] Word and a blow. — BUNYAN, *Pilgrim's Progress* [1678], *pt. I*

wide as a church-door; but 'tis enough, 'twill serve: ask for me tomorrow, and you shall find me a grave man.
Romeo and Juliet III, i, 101

A plague o' both your houses! They have made worms' meat of me.
III, i, 112

O! I am Fortune's fool.   *III, i, 142*

Gallop apace, you fiery-footed steeds, Towards Phoebus' lodging.   *III, ii, 1*

When he shall die, Take him and cut him out in little stars, And he will make the face of heaven so fine That all the world will be in love with night, And pay no worship to the garish sun.
III, ii, 21

He was not born to shame: Upon his brow shame is asham'd to sit.   *III, ii, 91*

Romeo, come forth; come forth, thou fearful man: Affliction is enamor'd of thy parts, And thou art wedded to calamity.
III, iii, 1

Adversity's sweet milk, philosophy.
III, iii, 54

Hang up philosophy! Unless philosophy can make a Juliet.
III, iii, 56

The lark, the herald of the morn.
III, v, 6

Night's candles are burnt out, and jocund day Stands tiptoe on the misty mountain-tops.   *III, v, 9*

Villain and he be many miles asunder.
III, v, 82

Thank me no thankings, nor proud me no prouds.   *III, v, 153*

Is there no pity sitting in the clouds, That sees into the bottom of my grief?
III, v, 198

Past hope, past cure, past help!
Romeo and Juliet IV, i, 45

'Tis an ill cook that cannot lick his own fingers.   *IV, ii, 6*

Apothecary: My poverty, but not my will, consents.
Romeo: I pay thy poverty, and not thy will.   *V, i, 75*

The strength Of twenty men.   *V, i, 78*

The time and my intents are savage-wild, More fierce and more inexorable far Than empty tigers or the roaring sea.
V, iii, 39

Tempt not a desperate man.
V, iii, 59

One writ with me in sour misfortune's book.   *V, iii, 82*

How oft when men are at the point of death Have they been merry!   *V, iii, 88*

Beauty's ensign yet Is crimson in thy lips and in thy cheeks, And death's pale flag is not advanced there.   *V, iii, 94*

O! here Will I set up my everlasting rest, And shake the yoke of inauspicious stars From this world-wearied flesh. Eyes, look your last! Arms, take your last embrace!
V, iii, 109

O true apothecary! Thy drugs are quick.   *V, iii, 119*

See what a scourge is laid upon your hate, That heaven finds means to kill your joys with love.   *V, iii, 292*

For never was a story of more woe Than this of Juliet and her Romeo.
V, iii, 309

The purest treasure mortal times afford
Is spotless reputation.
King Richard II [1595–1596], act I, sc. i, l. 177

Mine honor is my life; both grow in one;
Take honor from me, and my life is done. I, i, 182

We were not born to sue, but to command. I, i, 196

The daintiest last, to make the end most sweet. I, iii, 68

Truth hath a quiet breast. I, iii, 96

How long a time lies in one little word! I, iii, 213

Things sweet to taste prove in digestion sour. I, iii, 236

Must I not serve a long apprenticehood
To foreign passages, and in the end,
Having my freedom, boast of nothing else
But that I was a journeyman to grief? I, iii, 271

All places that the eye of heaven visits
Are to a wise man ports and happy havens.
Teach thy necessity to reason thus;
There is no virtue like necessity.[1]
Think not the king did banish thee,
But thou the king. I, iii, 275

For gnarling sorrow hath less power to bite
The man that mocks at it and sets it light. I, iii, 292

O! who can hold a fire in his hand
By thinking on the frosty Caucasus?
Or cloy the hungry edge of appetite
By bare imagination of a feast?
Or wallow naked in December snow
By thinking on fantastic summer's heat?
O, no! the apprehension of the good
Gives but the greater feeling to the worse. I, iii, 294

[1] See Quintilian, p. 1356, and note.

Where'er I wander, boast of this I can,
Though banish'd, yet a true-born Englishman.[1]
Richard II, I, iii, 308

The tongues of dying men
Enforce attention like deep harmony.
II, i, 5

The setting sun, and music at the close,
As the last taste of sweets, is sweetest last,
Writ in remembrance more than things long past. II, i, 12

Report of fashions in proud Italy,
Whose manners still our tardy apish nation
Limps after in base imitation.
II, i, 21

For violent fires soon burn out themselves;
Small showers last long, but sudden storms are short. II, i, 34

This royal throne of kings, this scepter'd isle,
This earth of majesty, this seat of Mars,
This other Eden, demi-paradise,
This fortress built by Nature for herself
Against infection and the hand of war,
This happy breed of men, this little world,
This precious stone set in the silver sea,
Which serves it in the office of a wall,
Or as a moat defensive to a house,
Against the envy of less happier lands,
This blessed plot, this earth, this realm, this England,
This nurse, this teeming womb of royal kings,
Fear'd by their breed and famous by their birth. II, i, 40

[1] A stern, a true-born Englishman. — SAMUEL JOHNSON; from BOSWELL, *Life of Dr. Johnson* [1791]
The True-born Englishman [1701]. Title of satire by Daniel Defoe.

England, bound in with the triumphant sea,
Whose rocky shore beats back the envious siege
Of watery Neptune.
                 Richard II, II, i, 61

That England, that was wont to conquer others,
Hath made a shameful conquest of itself.   *II, i, 65*

A lunatic lean-witted fool,
Presuming on an ague's privilege.
                        II, i, 115

The ripest fruit first falls.   *II, i, 154*

Each substance of a grief hath twenty
shadows.   *II, ii, 14*

I count myself in nothing else so
happy
As in a soul remembering my good
friends.   *II, iii, 46*

Evermore thanks, the exchequer of the
poor.   *II, iii, 65*

Grace me no grace, nor uncle me no
uncle.   *II, iii, 87*

The caterpillars of the commonwealth,
Which I have sworn to weed and pluck
away.   *II, iii, 166*

Things past redress are now with me
past care.   *II, iii, 171*

I see thy glory like a shooting star
Fall to the base earth from the firmament.   *II, iv, 19*

Eating the bitter bread of banishment.[1]
                        III, i, 21

Not all the water in the rough rude
sea
Can wash the balm from an anointed
king.   *III, ii, 54*

O! call back yesterday, bid time return.[2]   *III, ii, 69*

The worst is death, and death will have
his day.   *III, ii, 103*

Of comfort no man speak:

[1] See *Isaiah 30:20*, p. 32a.
[2] See Thomas Heywood, p. 301b.

Let's talk of graves, of worms, and epitaphs;
Make dust our paper, and with rainy
eyes
Write sorrow on the bosom of the
earth;
Let's choose executors and talk of
wills.   *Richard II, III, ii, 144*

And nothing can we call our own but
death,
And that small model of the barren
earth
Which serves as paste and cover to our
bones.
For God's sake, let us sit upon the
ground
And tell sad stories of the death of
kings:
How some have been depos'd, some
slain in war,
Some haunted by the ghosts they have
depos'd,
Some poison'd by their wives, some
sleeping kill'd;
All murder'd: for within the hollow
crown
That rounds the mortal temples of a
king
Keeps Death his court.   *III, ii, 152*

Comes at the last, and with a little pin
Bores through his castle wall, and farewell king!   *III, ii, 169*

He is come to open
The purple testament of bleeding war.
                        III, iii, 93

O! that I were as great
As is my grief, or lesser than my name,
Or that I could forget what I have
been,
Or not remember what I must be now.
                        III, iii, 136

And my large kingdom for a little
grave,
A little little grave, an obscure grave.
                        III, iii, 153

And there at Venice gave
His body to that pleasant country's
earth,

And his pure soul unto his captain
　　Christ,
Under whose colors he had fought so
　　long.　　　　*Richard II, IV, i, 97*

Peace shall go sleep with Turks and in-
　　fidels.　　　　　　　*IV, i, 139*

So Judas did to Christ: but he, in
　　twelve,
Found truth in all but one; I, in twelve
　　thousand, none.

God save the king! Will no man say,
　　amen?　　　　　　　*IV, i, 170*

Now is this golden crown like a deep
　　well
That owes two buckets filling one an-
　　other;
The emptier ever dancing in the
　　air,
The other down, unseen and full of
　　water:
That bucket down and full of tears am
　　I,
Drinking my griefs, whilst you mount
　　up on high.　　　　　*IV, i, 184*

You may my glories and my state de-
　　pose,
But not my griefs; still am I king of
　　those.　　　　　　　*IV, i, 192*

　　Some of you with Pilate wash your
　　hands,
Showing an outward pity.[1]
　　　　　　　　　　　　IV, i, 239

A mockery king of snow.　　*IV, i, 260*

As in a theatre, the eyes of men,
After a well-grac'd actor leaves the
　　stage,
Are idly bent on him that enters next,
Thinking his prattle to be tedious.
　　　　　　　　　　　　V, ii, 23

　　How sour sweet music is
When time is broke and no proportion
　　kept!
So is it in the music of men's lives.
　　　　　　　　　　　　V, v, 42

I wasted time, and now doth time
　　waste me;

[1] See *Matthew 27:24*, p. 44b.

For now hath time made me his num-
　　bering clock;
My thoughts are minutes.
　　　　　　　　Richard II, V, v, 49

This music mads me: let it sound no
　　more.　　　　　　　*V, v, 61*

Mount, mount, my soul! thy seat is
　　up on high,
Whilst my gross flesh sinks downward,
　　here to die.　　　　　*V, v, 112*

To live a barren sister all your life,
Chanting faint hymns to the cold fruit-
　　less moon.
　　　A Midsummer-Night's Dream
　　　[1595–1596], *act I, sc. i, l. 72*

But earthlier happy is the rose distill'd,
Than that which withering on the vir-
　　gin thorn [1]
Grows, lives and dies, in single blessed-
　　ness.　　　　　　　*I, i, 76*

　　For aught that I could ever read,
Could ever hear by tale or history,
The course of true love never did run
　　smooth.　　　　　　*I, i, 132*

Swift as a shadow, short as any dream,
Brief as the lightning in the collied
　　night,
That, in a spleen, unfolds both heaven
　　and earth,
And ere a man hath power to say, "Be-
　　hold!"
The jaws of darkness do devour it up:
So quick bright things come to confu-
　　sion.　　　　　　　*I, i, 144*

Love looks not with the eyes, but with
　　the mind,
And therefore is wing'd Cupid painted
　　blind.[2]　　　　　　*I, i, 234*

　　The most lamentable comedy, and
most cruel death of Pyramus and
Thisby.　　　　　　　*I, ii, 11*

[1] See Wordsworth, p. 515b.
[2] See Chaucer, p. 168b, and *Merchant of Venice*, p. 233a.
　　I have heard of reasons manifold
　　　Why Love must needs be blind,
　　But this the best of all I hold —
　　　His eyes are in his mind.
　　　　　COLERIDGE, *Reason for Love's Blindness* [1828]

Masters, spread yourselves.
A *Midsummer-Night's Dream*
I, ii, 16

This is Ercles' vein, a tyrant's vein.
I, ii, 43

I'll speak in a monstrous little voice.
I, ii, 55

I am slow of study. I, ii, 70

That would hang us, every mother's son. I, ii, 81

I will aggravate my voice so that I will roar you as gently as any sucking dove; I will roar you as 'twere any nightingale. I, ii, 85

A proper man, as one shall see in a summer's day; a most lovely, gentle-man-like man. I, ii, 89

Over hill, over dale,[1]
Thorough bush, thorough brier,
Over park, over pale,
Thorough flood, thorough fire.
II, i, 2

I must go seek some dew drops here,
And hang a pearl in every cowslip's ear. II, i, 14

I am that merry wanderer of the night.
I jest to Oberon, and make him smile
When I a fat and bean-fed horse beguile,
Neighing in likeness of a filly foal:
And sometimes lurk I in a gossip's bowl,
In very likeness of a roasted crab.
II, i, 43

Since once I sat upon a promontory,
And heard a mermaid on a dolphin's back
Uttering such dulcet and harmonious breath,
That the rude sea grew civil at her song,
And certain stars shot madly from their spheres
To hear the sea-maid's music.
II, i, 149

And the imperial votaress passed on,
In maiden meditation, fancy-free.

[1] See Gruber, p. 952a.

Yet mark'd I where the bolt of Cupid fell:
It fell upon a little western flower,
Before milk-white, now purple with love's wound,
And maidens call it, Love-in-idleness.
A *Midsummer-Night's Dream*
II, i, 163

I'll put a girdle round about the earth
In forty minutes.[1] II, i, 175

For you in my respect are all the world:
Then how can it be said I am alone,
When all the world is here to look on me? II, i, 224

I know a bank whereon the wild thyme blows,
Where oxlips and the nodding violet grows
Quite over-canopied with luscious woodbine,
With sweet musk-roses, and with eglantine:
There sleeps Titania some time of the night,
Lull'd in these flowers with dances and delight;
And there the snake throws her enamell'd skin,
Weed wide enough to wrap a fairy in.
II, i, 249

Some to kill cankers in the musk-rose buds,
Some war with rere-mice for their leathern wings,
To make my small elves coats.
II, ii, 3

The clamorous owl, that nightly hoots, and wonders
At our quaint spirits. II, ii, 6

You spotted snakes with double tongue,
Thorny hedge-hogs, be not seen;
Newts, and blind-worms, do no wrong;
Come not near our fairy queen.
II, ii, 9

Night and silence! who is here?
Weeds of Athens he doth wear.
II, ii, 70

[1] See Chapman, p. 205b.

As a surfeit of the sweetest things
The deepest loathing to the stomach
brings.[1]
  A Midsummer-Night's Dream
    II, ii, 137

To bring in — God shield us! — a
lion among ladies, is a most dreadful
thing, for there is not a more fearful
wild-fowl than your lion living.
      III, i, 32

A calendar, a calendar! look in the
almanack; find out moonshine.
      III, i, 55

Bless thee, Bottom! bless thee! thou
art translated.   III, i, 124

Lord, what fools these mortals be! [2]
      III, ii, 115

  So we grew together,
Like to a double cherry, seeming
  parted,
But yet an union in partition;
Two lovely berries molded on one
  stem.   III, ii, 208

Though she be but little, she is fierce.
      III, ii, 325

I have a reasonable good ear in music: let us have the tongs and the
bones.   IV, i, 32

Truly, a peck of provender: I could
munch your good dry oats. Methinks I
have a great desire to a bottle of hay:
good hay, sweet hay, hath no fellow.
      IV, i, 36

I have an exposition of sleep come
upon me.   IV, i, 44

My Oberon! what visions have I seen!
Methought I was enamor'd of an ass.
      IV, i, 82

  I never heard
So musical a discord, such sweet thunder.   IV, i, 123

I have had a dream, past the wit of
man to say what dream it was.
      IV, i, 211

The eye of man hath not heard, the

ear of man hath not seen,[1] man's hand
is not able to taste, his tongue to conceive, nor his heart to report, what my
dream was.
  A Midsummer-Night's Dream
    IV, i, 218

Eat no onions nor garlic, for we are
to utter sweet breath.   IV, ii, 44

The lunatic, the lover, and the poet,
Are of imagination all compact:
One sees more devils than vast hell can
  hold,
That is, the madman; the lover, all as
  frantic,
Sees Helen's beauty in a brow of
  Egypt:
The poet's eye, in a fine frenzy rolling,
Doth glance from heaven to earth,
  from earth to heaven;
And, as imagination bodies forth
The forms of things unknown, the
  poet's pen
Turns them to shapes, and gives to airy
  nothing
A local habitation and a name.
Such tricks hath strong imagination,
That, if it would but apprehend some
  joy,
It comprehends some bringer of that
  joy;
Or in the night, imagining some fear,
How easy is a bush suppos'd a bear!
      V, i, 7

Very tragical mirth.   V, i, 57
The true beginning of our end.[2]
      V, i, 111

The best in this kind are but shadows.   V, i, 215

A very gentle beast, and of a good
conscience.   V, i, 232

All that I have to say, is, to tell you
that the lanthorn is the moon; I, the
man in the moon; this thorn-bush, my
thorn-bush; and this dog, my dog.
      V, i, 263

Well roared, Lion!   V, i, 272

This passion, and the death of a dear

---

[1] See *King Henry IV*, p. 240a.
[2] See Seneca, p. 129b.

[1] See *I Corinthians* 2:9, p. 52a.
[2] I see the beginning of my end. — MASSINGER,
The Virgin Martyr [1622], act III, sc. iii

friend, would go near to make a man look sad.

> *A Midsummer-Night's Dream*
> V, i, 295

With the help of a surgeon, he might yet recover, and prove an ass.
> V, i, 318

No epilogue, I pray you, for your play needs no excuse. Never excuse.[1]
> V, i, 363

The iron tongue of midnight hath told twelve;
Lovers, to bed; 'tis almost fairy time.
> V, i, 372

If we shadows have offended,
Think but this, and all is mended,
That you have but slumber'd here
While these visions did appear.
> V, ii, 54

Your mind is tossing on the ocean.
> *The Merchant of Venice* [1596–1597], act I, sc. i, l. 8

My ventures are not in one bottom trusted,
Nor to one place.   I, i, 42

Nature hath fram'd strange fellows in her time.   I, i, 51

You have too much respect upon the world:
They lose it that do buy it with much care.   I, i, 74

I hold the world but as the world, Gratiano;
A stage, where every man must play a part,[2]
And mine a sad one.   I, i, 77

Let me play the fool.   I, i, 79

Why should a man, whose blood is warm within,
Sit like his grandsire cut in alabaster?
> I, i, 83

There are a sort of men whose visages
Do cream and mantle like a standing pond.   I, i, 88

[1] See Meurier, p. 188b, and *King John*, p. 237a.
[2] See *As You Like It*, p. 248b.

I am Sir Oracle,
And when I ope my lips let no dog bark!
> *The Merchant of Venice* I, i, 93

I do know of these,
That therefore only are reputed wise
For saying nothing.   I, i, 95

Fish not, with this melancholy bait,
For this fool-gudgeon, this opinion.
> I, i, 101

Gratiano speaks an infinite deal of nothing, more than any man in all Venice. His reasons are as two grains of wheat hid in two bushels of chaff: you shall seek all day ere you find them, and, when you have them, they are not worth the search.   I, i, 114

In my school-days, when I had lost one shaft,
I shot his fellow of the selfsame flight
The selfsame way with more advised watch,
To find the other forth, and by adventuring both,
I oft found both.   I, i, 141

They are as sick that surfeit with too much as they that starve with nothing.
> I, ii, 5

Superfluity comes sooner by white hairs, but competency lives longer.
> I, ii, 9

If to do were as easy as to know what were good to do, chapels had been churches, and poor men's cottages princes' palaces.   I, ii, 13

The brain may devise laws for the blood, but a hot temper leaps o'er a cold decree.   I, ii, 19

He doth nothing but talk of his horse.   I, ii, 43

I fear he will prove the weeping philosopher when he grows old, being so full of unmannerly sadness in his youth.   I, ii, 51

God made him, and therefore let him pass for a man.   I, ii, 59

When he is best, he is a little worse than a man, and when he is worst, he is little better than a beast.

The Merchant of Venice I, ii, 93

I dote on his very absence.

I, ii, 118

My meaning in saying he is a good man is to have you understand me that he is sufficient. I, iii, 15

Ships are but boards, sailors but men: there be land-rats and water-rats, land-thieves and water-thieves.

I, iii, 22

Yes, to smell pork; to eat of the habitation which your prophet the Nazarite [1] conjured the devil into. I will buy with you, sell with you, talk with you, walk with you, and so following; but I will not eat with you, drink with you, nor pray with you. What news on the Rialto? I, iii, 34

How like a fawning publican he looks! I hate him for he is a Christian.

I, iii, 42

If I can catch him once upon the hip,[2] I will feed fat the ancient grudge I bear him. I, iii, 47

Cursed be my tribe,
If I forgive him. I, iii, 52

The devil can cite Scripture for his purpose. I, iii, 99

A goodly apple rotten at the heart.
O, what a goodly outside falsehood hath! I, iii, 102

For sufferance is the badge of all our tribe.
You call me misbeliever, cut-throat dog,
And spit upon my Jewish gaberdine.
I, iii, 111

Shall I bend low, and in a bondman's key,

<hr>

[1] That hee shall be called a Nazarite. — *The Geneva Bible* [1557–1560], *Matthew 2:23*
The Geneva version of the Bible is the one Shakespeare was familiar with.
[2] See Heywood, p. 185a, and *The Merchant of Venice IV, i, 334*, p. 235a.

With bated breath and whispering humbleness,
Say this.

The Merchant of Venice I, iii, 124

I'll seal to such a bond,
And say there is much kindness in the Jew. I, iii, 153

O father Abram! what these Christians are,
Whose own hard dealing teaches them suspect
The thoughts of others. I, iii, 161

I like not fair terms and a villain's mind. I, iii, 180

Mislike me not for my complexion,
The shadow'd livery of the burnish'd sun. II, i, 1

If Hercules and Lichas play at dice
Which is the better man, the greater throw
May turn by fortune from the weaker hand. II, i, 32

O heavens! this is my true-begotten father. II, ii, 36

An honest, exceeding poor man.
II, ii, 54

The very staff of my age, my very prop. II, ii, 71

It is a wise father that knows his own child. II, ii, 83

And the vile squealing of the wry-neck'd fife. II, v, 30

Who riseth from a feast
With that keen appetite that he sits down? II, vi, 8

All things that are,
Are with more spirit chased than enjoy'd.
How like a younker or a prodigal
The scarfed bark puts from her native bay,
Hugg'd and embraced by the strumpet wind!
How like the prodigal doth she return,
With over-weather'd ribs and ragged sails,

Lean, rent, and beggar'd by the strumpet wind!
The Merchant of Venice II, vi, 12

But love is blind,[1] and lovers cannot see
The pretty follies that themselves commit.   *II, vi, 36*

Must I hold a candle to my shames?   *II, vi, 41*

Men that hazard all
Do it in hope of fair advantages:
A golden mind stoops not to show of dross.   *II, vii, 18*

Young in limbs, in judgment old.   *II, vii, 71*

My daughter! O my ducats! O my daughter!
Fled with a Christian! O my Christian ducats!
Justice! the law! my ducats, and my daughter!
A sealed bag, two sealed bags of ducats,
Of double ducats, stol'n from me by my daughter!   *II, viii, 15*

The fool multitude, that choose by show.   *II, ix, 26*

I will not jump with common spirits
And rank me with the barbarous multitude.   *II, ix, 32*

Let none presume
To wear an undeserved dignity.
O! that estates, degrees, and offices
Were not deriv'd corruptly, and that clear honor
Were purchas'd by the merit of the wearer.   *II, ix, 39*

Some there be that shadows kiss;
Such have but a shadow's bliss.
   II, ix, 66

Let him look to his bond.
   III, i, 49

I am a Jew. Hath not a Jew eyes?

hath not a Jew hands, organs, dimensions, senses, affections, passions?
The Merchant of Venice III, i, 62

If you prick us, do we not bleed? if you tickle us, do we not laugh? if you poison us, do we not die? and if you wrong us, shall we not revenge?
   III, i, 65

The villainy you teach me I will execute, and it shall go hard but I will better the instruction.   *III, i, 76*

I would not have given it for a wilderness of monkeys.   *III, i, 130*

There's something tells me, but it is not love,
I would not lose you; and you know yourself,
Hate counsels not in such a quality.
   III, ii, 4

Makes a swan-like end,
Fading in music.[1]   *III, ii, 44*

Tell me where is fancy bred,
Or in the heart or in the head?
How begot, how nourished?
   Reply, reply.   *III, ii, 63*

In law, what plea so tainted and corrupt
But, being season'd with a gracious voice,
Obscures the show of evil?
   III, ii, 75

There is no vice so simple but assumes
Some mark of virtue on his outward parts.   *III, ii, 81*

Thus ornament is but the guiled shore
To a most dangerous sea.   *III, ii, 97*

The seeming truth which cunning times put on
To entrap the wisest.   *III, ii, 100*

How all the other passions fleet to air,
As doubtful thoughts, and rash-embrac'd despair,
And shuddering fear, and green-ey'd jealousy.   *III, ii, 108*

[1] See Chaucer, p. 168b; *Midsummer-Night's Dream*, p. 228b, and note.

[1] See Plato, p. 93b, and note.

An unlesson'd girl, unschool'd, unprac-
tis'd;
Happy in this, she is not yet so old
But she may learn.
           The Merchant of Venice
                 III, ii, 160

Here are a few of the unpleasant'st
words
That ever blotted paper.   *III, ii, 252*

Thou call'dst me dog before thou hadst
a cause,
But, since I am a dog, beware my
  fangs.   *III, iii, 6*

    Thus when I shun Scylla, your fa-
ther, I fall into Charybdis, your
mother.[1]   *III, v, 17*

Some men there are love not a gaping
pig;
Some, that are mad if they behold a
cat.   *IV, i, 47*

A harmless necessary cat.   *IV, i, 55*

Bassanio: Do all men kill the things
they do not love? [2]
Shylock: Hates any man the thing he
would not kill?   *IV, i, 66*

What! wouldst thou have a serpent
sting thee twice?   *IV, i, 69*

    The weakest kind of fruit
Drops earliest to the ground.
                  IV, i, 115

To hold opinion with Pythagoras
That souls of animals infuse them-
selves
Into the trunks of men.[3]   *IV, i, 131*

    I never knew so young a body with so
old a head.[4]   *IV, i, 163*

[1] Scylla to port, and on our starboard beam
Charybdis, dire gorge of the salt sea tide. —
HOMER, *Odyssey*, bk. XII, l. 232
  Scylla guards the right side; implacable Charybdis the left. — VIRGIL, *Aeneid*, bk. III, l. 420
  Incidis in Scyllam cupiens vitare Charybdim
[You fall into Scylla in seeking to avoid Charyb-
dis]. — PHILIPPE GUALTIER, *Alexandreis* [c. 1300],
bk. V, l. 301
  [2] See Oscar Wilde, p. 840b.
  [3] *Clown:* What is the opinion of Pythagoras
concerning wild-fowl?
  Malvolio: That the soul of our grandam
might haply inhabit a bird.
       Twelfth-Night [1598–1600], *IV, ii, 55*
  [4] He is young, but take it from me, a very
staid head. — THOMAS WENTWORTH, EARL OF

The quality of mercy is not strain'd,
It droppeth as the gentle rain from
heaven
Upon the place beneath: it is twice
bless'd;
It blesseth him that gives and him that
takes:
'Tis mightiest in the mightiest; it be-
comes
The throned monarch better than his
crown;
His scepter shows the force of temporal
power,
The attribute to awe and majesty,
Wherein doth sit the dread and fear of
kings;[1]
But mercy is above this scepter'd sway,
It is enthroned in the hearts of kings,
It is an attribute to God himself,
And earthly power doth then show
likest God's
When mercy seasons justice. Therefore,
Jew,
Though justice be thy plea, consider
this,
That in the course of justice, none of
us
Should see salvation: we do pray for
mercy,
And that same prayer doth teach us all
to render
The deeds of mercy.
           The Merchant of Venice
                 IV, i, 184

To do a great right, do a little wrong.
                  IV, i, 216

A Daniel come to judgment! yea, a
Daniel!   *IV, i, 223*

How much more elder art thou than
thy looks!   *IV, i, 251*

Is it so nominated in the bond?
                  IV, i, 260

'Tis not in the bond.   *IV, i, 263*

For herein Fortune shows herself more
kind
Than is her custom: it is still her use

STRAFFORD [1593–1641], *letter commending the
Earl of Ormond to Charles I for appointment as
councilor*
  [1] See *Measure for Measure II, ii, 59*, p. 270b.

To let the wretched man outlive his wealth,
To view with hollow eye and wrinkled brow
An age of poverty.
                    The Merchant of Venice
                              IV, i, 268

I have a daughter;
Would any of the stock of Barabbas
Had been her husband rather than a Christian!   IV, i, 296

An upright judge, a learned judge!
                              IV, i, 324

A second Daniel, a Daniel, Jew!
Now, infidel, I have thee on the hip.[1]
                              IV, i, 334

A Daniel, still say I; a second Daniel!
I thank thee, Jew, for teaching me that word.   IV, i, 341

You take my house when you do take the prop
That doth sustain my house; you take my life
When you do take the means whereby I live.   IV, i, 376

He is well paid that is well satisfied.
                              IV, i, 416

Lorenzo: The moon shines bright: in such a night as this . . .
Troilus methinks mounted the Troyan walls,
And sigh'd his soul toward the Grecian tents,
Where Cressid lay that night.
Jessica: In such a night
Did Thisbe fearfully o'ertrip the dew,
And saw the lion's shadow ere himself,
And ran dismay'd away.
Lorenzo: In such a night
Stood Dido with a willow in her hand
Upon the wild sea-banks, and waft her love
To come again to Carthage.
Jessica: In such a night
Medea gather'd the enchanted herbs
That did renew old Aeson.   V, i, 1

How sweet the moonlight sleeps upon this bank!

Here we will sit, and let the sounds of music
Creep in our ears: soft stillness and the night
Become the touches of sweet harmony.
Sit, Jessica: look, how the floor of heaven
Is thick inlaid with patines of bright gold:
There's not the smallest orb which thou behold'st
But in his motion like an angel sings,
Still quiring to the young-eyed cherubins.
Such harmony is in immortal souls;
But, whilst this muddy vesture of decay
Doth grossly close it in, we cannot hear it.
                    The Merchant of Venice
                              V, i, 54

I am never merry when I hear sweet music.   V, i, 69

The man that hath no music in himself,
Nor is not mov'd with concord of sweet sounds,
Is fit for treasons, stratagems, and spoils;
The motions of his spirit are dull as night,
And his affections dark as Erebus:
Let no such man be trusted.
                              V, i, 83

How far that little candle throws his beams!
So shines a good deed in a naughty world.[1]   V, i, 90

How many things by season season'd are
To their right praise and true perfection!   V, i, 107

This night methinks is but the daylight sick.   V, i, 124

A light wife doth make a heavy husband.   V, i, 130

These blessed candles of the night.
                              V, i, 220

---

[1] See Heywood, p. 185a, and *The Merchant of Venice* I, iii, 47, p. 232a.

[1] See *Matthew 5:15*, p. 40a, and William Bradford, p. 319a.

For new-made honor doth forget men's names.
King John [1596–1597], *act I, sc. i, l. 187*

Sweet, sweet, sweet poison for the age's tooth. *I, i, 213*

Bearing their birthrights proudly on their backs,
To make a hazard of new fortunes here. *II, i, 70*

For courage mounteth with occasion. *II, i, 82*

The hare of whom the proverb goes,
Whose valor plucks dead lions by the beard.[1] *II, i, 137*

A woman's will. *II, i, 194*

Saint George, that swing'd the dragon, and e'er since
Sits on his horse back at mine hostess' door. *II, i, 288*

He is the half part of a blessed man,
Left to be finished by such a she;
And she a fair divided excellence,
Whose fullness of perfection lies in him. *II, i, 437*

'Zounds! I was never so bethump'd with words
Since I first call'd my brother's father dad. *II, i, 466*

Mad world! mad kings! mad composition! *II, i, 561*

That smooth-fac'd gentleman, tickling Commodity,
Commodity, the bias of the world. *II, i, 573*

I will instruct my sorrows to be proud;
For grief is proud and makes his owner stoop. *III, i, 68*

Thou wear a lion's hide! doff it for shame,
And hang a calf's-skin on those recreant limbs. *III, i, 128*

The sun's o'ercast with blood: fair day, adieu!

Which is the side that I must go withal?
I am with both: each army hath a hand;
And in their rage, I having hold of both,
They whirl asunder and dismember me. *King John III, i, 326*

Bell, book and candle shall not drive me back.[1] *III, iii, 12*

Look, who comes here! a grave unto a soul. *III, iv, 17*

Death, death: O, amiable lovely death! [2] *III, iv, 25*

Grief fills the room up of my absent child,
Lies in his bed, walks up and down with me,
Puts on his pretty looks, repeats his words,
Remembers me of all his gracious parts,
Stuffs out his vacant garments with his form. *III, iv, 93*

Life is as tedious as a twice-told tale,[3]
Vexing the dull ear of a drowsy man. *III, iv, 108*

When Fortune means to men most good,
She looks upon them with a threatening eye.[4] *III, iv, 119*

A scepter snatch'd with an unruly hand
Must be as boisterously maintain'd as gain'd;
And he that stands upon a slippery place
Makes nice of no vile hold to stay him up. *III, iv, 135*

As quiet as a lamb. *IV, i, 80*

To gild refined gold, to paint the lily,
To throw a perfume on the violet,
To smooth the ice, or add another hue
Unto the rainbow, or with taper-light

[1] So hares may pull dead lions by the beard.
— KYD, *The Spanish Tragedy* [1594] *I. ii, 172*

[1] See Malory, p. 175b, and note.
[2] See Whitman, p. 702a.
[3] See Homer, p. 66b.
[4] See Publilius Syrus, p. 125b.

To seek the beauteous eye of heaven to
garnish,
Is wasteful and ridiculous excess.
King John IV, *ii,* 11

And oftentimes excusing of a fault
Doth make the fault the worse by the
excuse.[1] IV, *ii, 30*

We cannot hold mortality's strong
hand. IV, *ii, 82*

There is no sure foundation set on
blood,
No certain life achiev'd by others'
death. IV, *ii, 104*

Make haste; the better foot before.[2]
IV, *ii, 170*

Another lean unwash'd artificer.
IV, *ii, 201*

How oft the sight of means to do ill
deeds
Makes ill deeds done! IV, *ii, 219*

Heaven take my soul, and England
keep my bones! IV, *iii, 10*

I am amaz'd, methinks, and lose my
way
Among the thorns and dangers of this
world. IV, *iii, 140*

Unthread the rude eye of rebellion,
And welcome home again discarded
faith. V, *iv, 11*

The day shall not be up so soon as I,
To try the fair adventure of tomorrow.
V, *v, 21*

'Tis strange that death should
sing.
I am the cygnet to this pale faint
swan,
Who chants a doleful hymn to his own
death.[3] V, *vii, 20*

Now my soul hath elbow-room.
V, *vii, 28*

I do not ask you much:
I beg cold comfort.[1]
King John V, *vii,* 41

This England never did, nor never
shall,
Lie at the proud foot of a conqueror.
V, *vii,* 112

Come the three corners of the world in
arms,
And we shall shock them. Nought shall
make us rue,
If England to itself do rest but true.
V, *vii,* 116

So shaken as we are, so wan with care.
King Henry IV [1597–1598],
Part I, act I, sc. i, l. 1

In those holy fields
Over whose acres walk'd those blessed
feet
Which fourteen hundred years ago
were nail'd
For our advantage on the bitter cross.
I, i, 24

Unless hours were cups of sack, and
minutes capons, and clocks the tongues
of bawds, and dials the signs of leaping
houses, and the blessed sun himself a
fair hot wench in flame-color'd taffeta, I
see no reason why thou shouldst be so
superfluous to demand the time of the
day. *I, ii, 7*

Diana's foresters, gentlemen of the
shade, minions of the moon.
I, ii, 29

A purse of gold most resolutely
snatched on Monday night and most
dissolutely spent on Tuesday morning.
I, ii, 38

Thy quips and thy quiddities.
I, ii, 51

So far as my coin would stretch; and
where it would not, I have used my
credit. *I, ii, 61*

Old father antick the law. *I, ii, 69*

I am as melancholy as a gib cat, or a
lugged bear. *I, ii, 82*

---

[1] See Meurier, p. 188b, and *A Midsummer-
Night's Dream,* p. 231a.
[2] Put forward your best foot! — BROWNING,
Respectability [1855], *st. 3*
[3] See Plato, p. 93b, and note.

[1] See *The Tempest, II, i, 10,* p. 296b, and
William Bradford, p. 319a.

I would to God thou and I knew
where a commodity of good names were
to be bought.
Henry IV, Part I, I, ii, 92

O! thou hast damnable iteration, and
art indeed able to corrupt a saint.
I, ii, 101

Now am I, if a man should speak
truly, little better than one of the
wicked. *I, ii, 105*

'Tis my vocation, Hal; 'tis no sin for
a man to labor in his vocation.
I, ii, 116

There's neither honesty, manhood,
nor good fellowship in thee.
I, ii, 154

I know you all, and will a while uphold
The unyok'd humor of your idleness:
Yet herein will I imitate the sun,
Who doth permit the base contagious
clouds
To smother up his beauty from the
world,
That when he please again to be him-
self,
Being wanted, he may be more won-
der'd at,
By breaking through the foul and ugly
mists
Of vapors that did seem to strangle
him.
If all the year were playing holidays,
To sport would be as tedious as to
work. *I, ii, 217*

You tread upon my patience.
I, iii, 4

Came there a certain lord, neat, and
trimly dress'd,
Fresh as a bridegroom; and his chin
new-reap'd,
Show'd like a stubble-land at harvest-
home.
He was perfumed like a milliner,
And 'twixt his finger and his thumb he
held
A pouncet-box, which ever and anon
He gave his nose and took 't away
again. *I, iii, 33*

And as the soldiers bore dead bodies
by.
He call'd them untaught knaves, un-
mannerly,
To bring a slovenly unhandsome corpse
Betwixt the wind and his nobility.
Henry IV, Part I, I, iii, 42

So pester'd with a popinjay.
I, iii, 50

God save the mark! *I, iii, 56*

And but for these vile guns,
He would himself have been a soldier.
I, iii, 63

To put down Richard, that sweet lovely
rose,
And plant this thorn, this canker,
Bolingbroke. *I, iii, 176*

Sink or swim. *I, iii, 194*

O! the blood more stirs
To rouse a lion than to start a hare!
I, iii, 197

By heaven methinks it were an easy
leap
To pluck bright honor from the pale-
fac'd moon,
Or dive into the bottom of the deep,
Where fathom-line could never touch
the ground,
And pluck up drowned honor by the
locks. *I, iii, 201*

Why, what a candy deal of courtesy
This fawning greyhound then did
proffer me! *I, iii, 251*

I know a trick worth two of that.
II, i, 40

If the rascal have not given me medicines to make me love him, I'll be
hanged. *II, ii, 20*

I'll starve ere I'll rob a foot further.
II, ii, 24

It would be argument for a week,
laughter for a month, and a good jest
forever. *II, ii, 104*

Falstaff sweats to death
And lards the lean earth as he walks
along. *II, ii, 119*

Out of this nettle, danger, we pluck this flower, safety.
Henry IV, Part I, II, iii, 11

I could brain him with his lady's fan.
II, iii, 26

Constant you are,
But yet a woman: and for secrecy,
No lady closer; for I well believe
Thou wilt not utter what thou dost not know;
And so far will I trust thee, gentle Kate.
II, iii, 113

A Corinthian, a lad of mettle, a good boy.
II, iv, 13

I am not yet of Percy's mind, the Hotspur of the North; he that kills me some six or seven dozen of Scots at a breakfast, washes his hands, and says to his wife, "Fie upon this quiet life! I want work."
II, iv, 116

A plague of all cowards, I say.
II, iv, 129

There live not three good men unhanged in England, and one of them is fat and grows old.
II, iv, 146

You care not who sees your back: call you that backing of your friends? A plague upon such backing!
II, iv, 168

I have peppered two of them. . . . I tell thee what, Hal, if I tell thee a lie, spit in my face; call me horse.
II, iv, 216

Give you a reason on compulsion! If reasons were as plenty as blackberries, I would give no man a reason upon compulsion, I.
II, iv, 267

Mark now, how a plain tale shall put you down.
II, iv, 285

What doth gravity out of his bed at midnight?
II, iv, 328

A plague of sighing and grief! It blows a man up like a bladder.
II, iv, 370

I must speak in passion, and I will do it in King Cambyses' vein.
II, iv, 429

That reverend vice, that grey iniquity, that father ruffian, that vanity in years.
Henry IV, Part I, II, iv, 505

If sack and sugar be a fault, God help the wicked! If to be old and merry be a sin, then many an old host that I know is damned: if to be fat be to be hated, then Pharaoh's lean kine are to be loved.
II, iv, 524

Banish plump Jack, and banish all the world.
II, iv, 534

Play out the play.
II, iv, 539

O, monstrous! but one half-pennyworth of bread to this intolerable deal of sack!
II, iv, 597

Diseased nature oftentimes breaks forth
In strange eruptions.
III, i, 27

I am not in the roll of common men.
III, i, 43

Glendower: I can call spirits from the vasty deep.
Hotspur: Why, so can I, or so can any man;
But will they come when you do call for them?
III, i, 53

I had rather be a kitten and cry mew,
Than one of these same metre balladmongers.
III, i, 128

Mincing poetry:
'Tis like the forc'd gait of a shuffling nag.
III, i, 133

But in the way of bargain, mark you me,
I'll cavil on the ninth part of a hair.
III, i, 138

A deal of skimble-skamble stuff.
III, i, 153

I understand thy kisses and thou mine,
And that's a feeling disputation.
III, i, 204

Lady Percy: . . . Lie still, ye thief, and hear the lady sing in Welsh.
Hotspur: I had rather hear Lady, my brach, howl in Irish.
III, i, 238

A good mouth-filling oath.
    Henry IV, Part I, III, i, 258

They surfeited with honey and began
To loathe the taste of sweetness,
    whereof a little
More than a little is by much too
    much.[1]   *III, ii, 71*

He was but as the cuckoo is in June,
Heard, not regarded.   *III, ii, 75*

My near'st and dearest enemy.[2]
    III, ii, 123

The end of life cancels all bands.
    III, ii, 157

    An I have not forgotten what the in-
side of a church is made of, I am a
peppercorn, a brewer's horse.
    III, iii, 8

Company, villanous company, hath
been the spoil of me.   *III, iii, 10*

    I have more flesh than another man,
and therefore more frailty.
    III, iii, 187

The very life-blood of our enterprise.
    IV, i, 28

    Were it good
To set the exact wealth of all our
    states
All at one cast? to set so rich a main
On the nice hazard of one doubtful
    hour?   *IV, i, 45*

Baited like eagles having lately
    bath'd; . . .
As full of spirit as the month of May,
And gorgeous as the sun at midsum-
    mer.   *IV, i, 99*

I saw young Harry, with his beaver on.
    IV, i, 104

    Worse than the sun in March
This praise doth nourish agues.
    IV, i, 110

Doomsday is near; die all, die merrily.
    IV, i, 134

The cankers of a calm world and a long
    peace.   *IV, ii, 32*

[1] See *A Midsummer-Night's Dream*, p. 230a.
[2] See *Hamlet I, ii, 180*, p. 258a.

To the latter end of a fray and the be-
    ginning of a feast
Fits a dull fighter and a keen guest.
    Henry IV, Part I, IV, ii, 86

Greatness knows itself.   *IV, iii, 74*

    I could be well content
To entertain the lag-end of my life
With quiet hours.   *V, i, 23*

Rebellion lay in his way, and he found
    it.   *V, i, 28*

    Never yet did insurrection want
Such water-colors to impaint his cause.
    V, i, 79

    I would it were bed-time, Hal, and
all well.   *V, i, 126*

    Honor pricks me on. Yea, but how if
honor prick me off when I come on?
how then? Can honor set to a leg? No.
Or an arm? No. Or take away the grief
of a wound? No. Honor hath no skill in
surgery, then? No. What is honor? a
word. What is that word, honor? Air. A
trim reckoning! Who hath it? he that
died o' Wednesday. Doth he feel it?
No. Doth he hear it? No. It is insensible then? Yea, to the dead. But will it
not live with the living? No. Why? Detraction will not suffer it. Therefore I'll
none of it: honor is a mere scutcheon;
and so ends my catechism.   *V, i, 131*

Suspicion all our lives shall be stuck full
    of eyes;
For treason is but trusted like the fox.
    V, ii, 8

Let me tell the world.[1]   *V, ii, 65*

    The time of life is short;
To spend that shortness basely were too
    long.   *V, ii, 81*

Two stars keep not their motion in one
    sphere.   *V, iv, 65*

But thought's the slave of life, and life
    time's fool;
And time, that takes survey of all the
    world,

[1] I'll tell the world. — SHAKESPEARE, *Measure
for Measure* [1604–1605], *II, iv, 154*
    Ay, tell the world! — BROWNING, *Paracelsus*
[1835], *pt. II*

Must have a stop. O! I could prophesy,
But that the earthy and cold hand of
  death
Lies on my tongue.
              Henry IV, Part I, V, iv, 81

This earth, that bears thee dead,
Bears not alive so stout a gentleman.
                            V, iv, 92

Thy ignominy sleep with thee in the
  grave,
But not remember'd in thy epitaph!
                            V, iv, 100

I could have better spar'd a better man.
                            V, iv, 104

The better part of valor is discretion.[1]   *V, iv, 120*

    Full bravely hast thou flesh'd
Thy maiden sword.   *V, iv, 132*

Lord, Lord, how this world is given
to lying!   *V, iv, 148*

I'll purge, and leave sack, and live
cleanly.   *V, iv, 168*

    Rumor is a pipe
Blown by surmises, jealousies, conjec-
  tures,
And of so easy and so plain a stop
That the blunt monster with un-
  counted heads,
The still-discordant wavering multi-
  tude,[2]
Can play upon it.
        King Henry IV [1597–1598],
              Part II, induction, l. 15

Even such a man, so faint, so spiritless,
So dull, so dead in look, so woe-begone,
Drew Priam's curtain in the dead of
  night,
And would have told him half his Troy
  was burn'd.   *Act I, sc. i, l. 70*

Yet the first bringer of unwelcome
  news
Hath but a losing office, and his
  tongue
Sounds ever after as a sullen bell,

Remember'd knolling a departing
  friend.[1]
              Henry IV, Part II, I, i, 100

I am not only witty in myself, but
the cause that wit is in other men.[2]
                            I, ii, 10

A rascally yea-forsooth knave.
                            I, ii, 40

You lie in your throat.   *I, ii, 97*

Your lordship, though not clean past
your youth, hath yet some smack of age
in you, some relish of the saltness of
time.   *I, ii, 112*

It is the disease of not listening, the
malady of not marking, that I am troubled withal.   *I, ii, 139*

I am as poor as Job, my lord, but not
so patient.   *I, ii, 145*

We that are in the vaward of our
youth.   *I, ii, 201*

Have you not a moist eye, a dry
hand, a yellow cheek, a white beard, a
decreasing leg, an increasing belly?
                            I, ii, 206

Every part about you blasted with
antiquity.   *I, ii, 210*

For my voice, I have lost it with hollaing and singing of anthems.
                            I, ii, 215

It was always yet the trick of our
English nation, if they have a good
thing, to make it too common.
                            I, ii, 244

I were better to be eaten to death
with rust than to be scoured to nothing
with perpetual motion.   *I, ii, 249*

I can get no remedy against this consumption of the purse: borrowing only
lingers and lingers it out, but the disease is incurable.[3]   *I, ii, 267*

    Who lin'd himself with hope,
Eating the air on promise of supply.
                            I, iii, 27

---

[1] It show'd discretion the best part of valor.
— BEAUMONT AND FLETCHER, *A King and No
King* [1619], *act II, sc. iii*
[2] See Horace, p. 123a, and note.

[1] See Sophocles, p. 82a, and *Antony and
Cleopatra II, v, 85,* p. 288a.
[2] See Samuel Johnson, p. 433b.
[3] See Rabelais, p. 181a.

A habitation giddy and unsure
Hath he that buildeth on the vulgar
    heart.
    Henry IV, Part II, I, iii, 89

Past and to come seem best; things
    present worst.   *I, iii, 108*

A poor lone woman.   *II, i, 37*

Away, you scullion! you rampallian!
you fustilarian! I'll tickle your catastrophe.   *II, i, 67*

He hath eaten me out of house and
home.   *II, i, 82*

Let the end try the man.
    II, ii, 52

Thus we play the fools with the time,
and the spirits of the wise sit in the
clouds and mock us.   *II, ii, 155*

He was indeed the glass
Wherein the noble youth did dress
    themselves.   *II, iii, 21*

And let the welkin roar.   *II, iv, 181*

Is it not strange that desire should so
many years outlive performance?
    II, iv, 283

O sleep! O gentle sleep! [1]
Nature's soft nurse, how have I frighted
    thee,
That thou no more wilt weigh my eye-
    lids down
And steep my senses in forgetfulness?
    III, i, 5

With all appliances and means to
    boot.   *III, i, 29*

Uneasy lies the head that wears a
    crown.   *III, i, 31*

O God! that one might read the book
    of fate.   *III, i, 45*

There is a history in all men's lives.
    III, i, 80

Death, as the Psalmist saith, is certain to all; all shall die.   *III, ii, 41*

Most forcible Feeble.   *III, ii, 181*

We have heard the chimes at midnight.   *III, ii, 231*

  [1] Sleep, most gentle sleep. — Ovid [43 B.C.–A.D.
18], *Metamorphoses, bk. II, l. 624*

A man can die but once; we owe God
a death.
    Henry IV, Part II, III, ii, 253

We see which way the stream of time
    doth run
And are enforc'd from our most quiet
    sphere
By the rough torrent of occasion.
    IV, i, 70

We ready are to try our fortunes
To the last man.   *IV, ii, 43*

I may justly say, with the hook-nosed
fellow of Rome, "I came, saw, and
overcame." [1]   *IV, iii, 44*

O polish'd perturbation! golden care!
That keep'st the ports of slumber open
    wide
To many a watchful night!
    IV, v, 22

See, sons, what things you are!
How quickly nature falls into revolt
When gold becomes her object!
    IV, v, 63

Thy wish was father, Harry, to that
    thought.[2]   *IV, v, 91*

Before thy hour be ripe.[3]   *IV, v, 95*

Commit
The oldest sins the newest kind of
    ways.   *IV, v, 124*

His cares are now all ended.   *V, ii, 3*

This is the English, not the Turkish
    court;
Not Amurath an Amurath succeeds,
But Harry Harry.   *V, ii, 47*

How ill white hairs become a fool and
    jester!   *V, v, 53*

Master Shallow, I owe you a thousand pound.   *V, v, 78*

O! for a Muse of fire, that would ascend

  [1] See Julius Caesar, p. 112b.
  [2] Men's thoughts are much according to their
inclination, their discourse and speeches according to their learning and infused opinions. —
Francis Bacon, *Essays* [1597–1625], *Of Custom
and Education*
  [3] See Blake, p. 488b.

The brightest heaven of invention!
> *King Henry* V [1598–1600],
> *Chorus, l. 1*

    Or may we cram
Within this wooden O the very casques
That did affright the air at Agincourt?
> *l. 12*

Consideration like an angel came,
And whipp'd the offending Adam out
of him.   *act I, sc. i, l. 28*

Hear him debate of commonwealth affairs,
You would say it hath been all in all his
study.   *I, i, 41*

Turn him to any cause of policy,
The Gordian knot of it he will unloose,
Familiar as his garter; that, when he speaks,
The air, a charter'd libertine, is still.
> *I, i, 45*

    Therefore doth heaven divide
The state of man in divers functions,
Setting endeavor in continual motion;
To which is fixed, as an aim or butt,
Obedience: for so work the honey-bees,
Creatures that by a rule in nature teach
The act of order to a peopled kingdom.   *I, ii, 183*

The singing masons building roofs of
gold.   *I, ii, 198*

    Many things, having full reference
To one consent, may work contrariously;
As many arrows, loosed several ways,
Fly to one mark; as many ways meet
in one town;
As many fresh streams meet in one salt
sea;
As many lines close in the dial's center;
So may a thousand actions, once afoot,
End in one purpose, and be all well borne
Without defeat.   *I, ii, 205*

    'Tis ever common
That men are merriest when they are
from home.
> *Henry V, I, ii, 271*

Now all the youth of England are on
fire,
And silken dalliance in the wardrobe
lies.   *II, Chorus, 1*

O England! model to thy inward greatness,
Like little body with a mighty heart,
What mightst thou do, that honor
would thee do,
Were all thy children kind and natural!
> *II, Chorus, 16*

That's the humor of it.   *II, i, 63*

    He's in Arthur's bosom, if ever man
went to Arthur's bosom. A' made a
finer end and went away an it had been
any christom child; a' parted even just
between twelve and one, even at the
turning o' the tide: for after I saw him
fumble with the sheets and play with
flowers and smile upon his fingers' ends,
I knew there was but one way; for his
nose was as sharp as a pen, and a' babbled of green fields.   *II, iii, 11*

    As cold as any stone.   *II, iii, 26*

Trust none;
For oaths are straws, men's faiths are
wafer-cakes,
And hold-fast is the only dog, my
duck.   *II, iii, 53*

Once more unto the breach, dear
friends, once more;
Or close the wall up with our English
dead!
In peace there's nothing so becomes a
man
As modest stillness and humility:
But when the blast of war blows in our
ears,
Then imitate the action of the tiger;
Stiffen the sinews, summon up the
blood,
Disguise fair nature with hard-favor'd
rage;
Then lend the eye a terrible aspect.
> *III, i, 1*

And sheath'd their swords for lack of argument. *Henry V, III, i, 21*

I see you stand like greyhounds in the slips,
Straining upon the start. The game's afoot:
Follow your spirit; and upon this charge
Cry "God for Harry! England and Saint George!" *III, i, 31*

I would give all my fame for a pot of ale, and safety. *III, ii, 14*

Men of few words are the best men. *III, ii, 40*

He will maintain his argument as well as any military man in the world. *III, ii, 89*

I know the disciplines of wars. *III, ii, 156*

I thought upon one pair of English legs
Did march three Frenchmen. *III, vi, 161*

We are in God's hand. *III, vi, 181*

That island of England breeds very valiant creatures: their mastiffs are of unmatchable courage. *III, vii, 155*

Give them great meals of beef and iron and steel, they will eat like wolves and fight like devils. *III, vii, 166*

The hum of either army stilly sounds,
That the fix'd sentinels almost receive
The secret whispers of each other's watch:
Fire answers fire, and through their paly flames
Each battle sees the other's umber'd face:
Steed threatens steed, in high and boastful neighs
Piercing the night's dull ear; and from the tents
The armorers, accomplishing the knights,
With busy hammers closing rivets up,
Give dreadful note of preparation. *IV, Chorus, 5*

A little touch of Harry in the night. *Henry V, IV, Chorus, 47*

There is some soul of goodness in things evil,
Would men observingly distill it out. *IV, i, 4*

When blood is their argument. *IV, i, 151*

Every subject's duty is the king's; but every subject's soul is his own. *IV, i, 189*

What infinite heart's ease
Must kings neglect that private men enjoy!
And what have kings that privates have not too,
Save ceremony, save general ceremony?
And what art thou, thou idol [1] ceremony?
What kind of god art thou, that suffer'st more
Of mortal griefs than do thy worshippers?
What are thy rents? what are thy comings-in?
O ceremony! show me but thy worth. *IV, i, 256*

'Tis not the balm, the scepter and the ball,
The sword, the mace, the crown imperial,
The intertissued robe of gold and pearl,
The farced title running 'fore the king,
The throne he sits on, nor the tide of pomp
That beats upon the high shore of this world,
No, not all these, thrice-gorgeous ceremony,
Not all these, laid in bed majestical,
Can sleep so soundly as the wretched slave,
Who with a body fill'd and vacant mind
Gets him to rest, cramm'd with distressful bread. *IV, i, 280*

[1] Sometimes rendered: idle.

O God of battles! steel my soldiers'
    hearts;
Possess them not with fear; take from
    them now
The sense of reckoning, if the opposed
    numbers
Pluck their hearts from them.
                    Henry V, IV, i, 309

But if it be a sin to covet honor,
I am the most offending soul alive.
                    IV, iii, 28

This day is call'd the feast of Crispian:
He that outlives this day, and comes
    safe home,
Will stand a-tip-toe when this day is
    nam'd.
And rouse him at the name of Crisp-
    ian.   *IV, iii, 40*

We few, we happy few, we band of
    brothers;
For he today that sheds his blood with
    me
Shall be my brother.   *IV, iii, 60*

   The saying is true, "The empty vessel makes the greatest sound."
                    IV, iv, 72

   There is occasions and causes why
and wherefore [1] in all things.
                    V, i, 3

   By this leek, I will most horribly revenge. I eat and eat, I swear.
                    V, i, 49

All hell shall stir for this.   *V, i, 72*

The naked, poor, and mangled Peace,
Dear nurse of arts, plenties, and joyful
    births.   *V, ii, 34*

Grow like savages — as soldiers will,
That nothing do but meditate on
    blood.   *V, ii, 59*

For these fellows of infinite tongue,
that can rime themselves into ladies' favors, they do always reason themselves
out again.   *V, ii, 162*

   My comfort is, that old age, that ill
layer-up of beauty, can do no more
spoil upon my face.   *V, ii, 246*

[1] See *The Comedy of Errors*, p. 218a.

Nice customs curtsy to great kings.
                    Henry V, V, ii, 291

   He hath indeed better bettered expectation than you must expect of me
to tell you how.
          Much Ado About Nothing
          [*1598–1600*], *act I, sc. i, l. 15*

How much better is it to weep at joy
than to joy at weeping.   *I, i, 28*

A very valiant trencher-man.
                    I, i, 52

There's a skirmish of wit between
them.   *I, i, 64*

He wears his faith but as the fashion
of his hat.   *I, i, 76*

I see, lady, the gentleman is not in
your books.   *I, i, 79*

What! my dear Lady Disdain, are
you yet living?   *I, i, 123*

Shall I never see a bachelor of threescore again?   *I, i, 209*

In time the savage bull doth bear the
yoke.   *I, i, 271*

Benedick the married man.
                    I, i, 278

   I could not endure a husband with a
beard on his face: I had rather lie in
the woollen.   *II, i, 31*

As merry as the day is long.
                    II, i, 52

   Would it not grieve a woman to be
over-mastered with a piece of valiant
dust? to make an account of her life to
a clod of wayward marl?   *II, i, 64*

I have a good eye, uncle: I can see a
church by daylight.   *II, i, 86*

Speak low, if you speak love.
                    II, i, 104

Friendship is constant in all other
    things
Save in the office and affairs of love:
Therefore all hearts in love use their
    own tongues;

Let every eye negotiate for itself
And trust no agent.[1]

Much Ado About Nothing
II, i, 184

She speaks poniards, and every word
stabs: if her breath were as terrible as
her terminations, there were no living
near her; she would infect to the north
star. II, i, 257

Silence is the perfectest herald of joy:
I were but little happy, if I could say
how much. II, i, 319

It keeps on the windy side of care.[2]
II, i, 328

There was a star danced, and under
that was I born. II, i, 351

I will tell you my drift.[3] II, i, 406

He was wont to speak plain and to
the purpose. II, iii, 19

Sigh no more, ladies, sigh no more,
Men were deceivers ever;
One foot in sea, and one on shore;
To one thing constant never.
II, iii, 65

Sits the wind in that corner? [4]
II, iii, 108

Bait the hook well: this fish will
bite. II, iii, 121

Shall quips and sentences and these
paper bullets of the brain awe a man
from the career of his humor? No; the
world must be peopled. When I said I
would die a bachelor, I did not think I
should live till I were married.
II, iii, 260

From the crown of his head to the
sole of his foot, he is all mirth.
III, ii, 9

He hath a heart as sound as a bell,
and his tongue is the clapper; for what
his heart thinks his tongue speaks.
III, ii, 12

Everyone can master a grief but he
that has it.

Much Ado About Nothing
III, ii, 28

Are you good men and true?
III, iii, 1

To be a well-favored man is the gift
of fortune; but to write and read comes
by nature. III, iii, 14

If they make you not then the better
answer, you may say they are not the
men you took them for. III, iii, 49

They that touch pitch will be defiled.[1] III, iii, 61

The fashion wears out more apparel
than the man. III, iii, 147

A good old man, sir; he will be talking: as they say, When the age is in,
the wit is out. III, v, 36

O! what men dare do! what men
may do! what men daily do, not knowing what they do! IV, i, 19

O! what authority and show of truth
Can cunning sin cover itself withal.
IV, i, 35

For it so falls out
That what we have we prize not to the
worth
Whiles we enjoy it, but being lack'd
and lost,
Why, then we rack the value, then we
find
The virtue that possession would not
show us
Whiles it was ours. IV, i, 219

Masters, it is proved already that you
are little better than false knaves, and it
will go near to be thought so shortly.
IV, ii, 23

Flat burglary as ever was committed.
IV, ii, 54

Thou wilt be condemned into everlasting redemption for this.
IV, ii, 60

---

[1] See Longfellow, p. 623a.
[2] The windy side of the law. — *Twelfth-Night*
[1598–1600], *III, iv, 183*
[3] We know your drift. — *Coriolanus* [1607–
1608], *III, iii, 114*
[4] See Malory, p. 175a.

[1] He that toucheth pitch shall be defiled therewith. — *Apocrypha: Ecclesiasticus 13:1*
This pitch, as ancient writers do report, doth
defile; so doth the company thou keepest. —
King Henry IV [1597–1598], *pt. I, II, iv, 460*

O that he were here to write me down an ass!

Much Ado About Nothing
IV, ii, 80

Patch griefs with proverbs. V, i, 17

Charm ache with air, and agony with words. V, i, 26

For there was never yet philosopher
That could endure the toothache patiently. V, i, 35

Some of us will smart for it.
V, i, 108

What though care killed a cat,[1] thou hast mettle enough in thee to kill care.
V, i, 135

I was not born under a riming planet. V, ii, 40

The trumpet of his own virtues.
V, ii, 91

Done to death by slanderous tongues.
V, iii, 3

Fleet the time carelessly, as they did in the golden world.
As You Like It [1598–1600],
act I, sc. i, l. 126

Always the dullness of the fool is the whetstone of the wits. I, ii, 59

The little foolery that wise men have makes a great show. I, ii, 97

Well said: that was laid on with a trowel. I, ii, 113

Your heart's desires be with you!
I, ii, 214

One out of suits with fortune.
I, ii, 263

My pride fell with my fortunes.
I, ii, 269

Hereafter, in a better world than this,
I shall desire more love and knowledge of you. I, ii, 301

Heavenly Rosalind! I, ii, 306

O, how full of briers is this working-day world!
As You Like It I, iii, 12

Beauty provoketh thieves sooner than gold. I, iii, 113

We'll have a swashing and a martial outside,
As many other mannish cowards have.
I, iii, 123

Hath not old custom made this life more sweet
Than that of painted pomp? Are not these woods
More free from peril than the envious court? II, i, 2

Sweet are the uses of adversity,
Which, like the toad, ugly and venomous,
Wears yet a precious jewel in his head;
And this our life, exempt from public haunt,
Finds tongues in trees, books in the running brooks,
Sermons in stones, and good in every thing.[1] II, i, 12

The big round tears
Cours'd one another down his innocent nose
In piteous chase. II, i, 38

"Poor deer," quoth he, "thou mak'st a testament
As worldlings do, giving thy sum of more
To that which had too much."
II, i, 47

Sweep on, you fat and greasy citizens.
II, i, 55

And He that doth the ravens feed,
Yea, providently caters for the sparrow,
Be comfort to my age! II, iii, 43

Though I look old, yet I am strong and lusty;
For in my youth I never did apply
Hot and rebellious liquors in my blood. II, iii, 47

---

[1] Let care kill a cat,
 We'll laugh and grow fat.
  Shirburn Ballads [1585], *91*
Hang sorrow, care'll kill a cat. — JONSON:
Every Man in His Humour [1598], I, i

[1] See St. Bernard, p. 154a, *As You Like It* III, ii, 5; and Wordsworth, p. 509a.

Therefore my age is as a lusty winter,
Frosty, but kindly.

As You Like It II, iii, 52

Thou art not for the fashion of these
times,
Where none will sweat but for promo-
tion. *II, iii, 59*

Ay, now am I in Arden; the more
fool I: when I was at home, I was in a
better place: but travelers must be content. *II, iv, 16*

If you remember'st not the slightest
folly
That ever love did make thee run into,
Thou hast not lov'd. *II, iv, 34*

We that are true lovers run into
strange capers. *II, iv, 53*

Thou speakest wiser than thou art
ware of. *II, iv, 57*

I shall ne'er be ware of mine own
wit, till I break my shins against it.
II, iv, 59

Under the greenwood tree
Who loves to lie with me,
And turn his merry note
Unto the sweet bird's throat,
Come hither, come hither, come hither:
Here shall he see
No enemy
But winter and rough weather.
II, v, 1

I can suck melancholy out of a song
as a weasel sucks eggs. *II, v, 12*

Who doth ambition shun,
And loves to live i' the sun,
Seeking the food he eats,
And pleas'd with what he gets.
II, v, 38

I met a fool i' the forest,
A motley fool. *II, vii, 12*

And then he drew a dial from his
poke,
And looking on it with lack-luster eye,
Says, very wisely, "It is ten o'clock;
Thus may we see," quoth he, "how the
world wags." [1] *II, vii, 20*

---

[1] So wags the world. — SIR WALTER SCOTT,
Ivanhoe [1819], *ch. 37*

And so, from hour to hour we ripe and
ripe,
And then from hour to hour we rot and
rot;
And thereby hangs a tale.[1]
As You Like It II, vii, 26

My lungs began to crow like chanti-
cleer,
That fools should be so deep-contem-
plative,
And I did laugh sans intermission
An hour by his dial. *II, vii, 30*

Motley's the only wear. *II, vii, 34*

If ladies be but young and fair,
They have the gift to know it.
II, vii, 37

I must have liberty
Withal, as large a charter as the wind,
To blow on whom I please.
II, vii, 47

The "why" is plain as way to parish
church. *II, vii, 52*

But whate'er you are
That in this desert inaccessible,
Under the shade of melancholy
boughs,
Lose and neglect the creeping hours of
time;
If ever you have look'd on better days,
If ever been where bells have knoll'd to
church,
If ever sat at any good man's feast,
If ever from your eyelids wip'd a tear,
And know what 'tis to pity, and be
pitied,
Let gentleness my strong enforcement
be. *II, vii, 109*

True is it that we have seen better
days. *II, vii, 120*

Oppress'd with two weak evils, age and
hunger. *II, vii, 132*

All the world's a stage,
And all the men and women merely
players: [2]

---

[1] See Rabelais, p. 181b.
[2] See *The Merchant of Venice*, p. 231a.
The world's a theatre, the earth a stage,
Which God and Nature do with actors fill.
THOMAS HEYWOOD, *Apology for Actors*
[1612]

They have their exits and their en-
trances;
And one man in his time plays many
parts,
His acts being seven ages. At first the
infant,
Mewling and puking in the nurse's
arms.
And then the whining school-boy, with
his satchel,
And shining morning face, creeping like
snail
Unwillingly to school. And then the
lover,
Sighing like furnace, with a woful bal-
lad
Made to his mistress' eyebrow. Then a
soldier,
Full of strange oaths, and bearded like
the pard,
Jealous in honor, sudden and quick in
quarrel,
Seeking the bubble reputation
Even in the cannon's mouth. And then
the justice,
In fair round belly with good capon
lin'd,
With eyes severe and beard of formal
cut,
Full of wise saws and modern in-
stances;
And so he plays his part. The sixth age
shifts
Into the lean and slipper'd pantaloon,
With spectacles on nose and pouch on
side,
His youthful hose well sav'd, a world
too wide
For his shrunk shank; and his big
manly voice,
Turning again toward childish treble,
pipes
And whistles in his sound. Last scene of
all,
That ends this strange eventful history,
Is second childishness, and mere oblivion,

The world's a stage on which all the parts
are played. — MIDDLETON, *A Game of Chess*
[1624], *V, i*

Sans teeth, sans eyes, sans taste, sans
everything.
As You Like It II, vii, 139

Blow, blow, thou winter wind!
Thou art not so unkind
As man's ingratitude. *II, vii, 174*

These trees shall be my books.[1]
III, ii, 5

The fair, the chaste, and unexpressive
she. *III, ii, 10*

It goes much against my stomach.
Hast any philosophy in thee, shepherd? *III, ii, 21*

He that wants money, means, and
content, is without three good friends.
III, ii, 25

I am a true laborer: I earn that I eat,
get that I wear, owe no man hate, envy
no man's happiness, glad of other
men's good, content with my harm.
III, ii, 78

From the east to western Ind,
No jewel is like Rosalind. *III, ii, 94*

This is the very false gallop of
verses. *III, ii, 120*

Let us make an honorable retreat;
though not with bag and baggage, yet
with scrip and scrippage. *III, ii, 170*

O, wonderful, wonderful, and most
wonderful, wonderful! and yet again
wonderful! and after that out of all
whooping. *III, ii, 202*

Answer me in one word.
III, ii, 238

Do you not know I am a woman?
when I think, I must speak.
III, ii, 265

I do desire we may be better strangers. *III, ii, 276*

Jacques: What stature is she of?
Orlando: Just as high as my heart.
III, ii, 286

Time travels in divers paces with
divers persons. I'll tell you who Time

---

[1] See St. Bernard, p. 154a; *As You Like It II,
i, 12;* and Wordsworth, p. 509a.

ambles withal, who Time trots withal, who Time gallops withal, and who he stands still withal.
As You Like It III, ii, 328

Every one fault seeming monstrous till his fellow fault came to match it.
III, ii, 377

Everything about you demonstrating a careless desolation.　　III, ii, 405

Truly, I would the gods had made thee poetical.　　III, iii, 16

The wounds invisible
That love's keen arrows make.
III, v, 30

Down on your knees,
And thank heaven, fasting, for a good
　man's love.　　III, v, 57

I am falser than vows made in wine.
III, v, 73

It is a melancholy of mine own, compounded of many simples, extracted from many objects, and indeed the sundry contemplation of my travels, which, by often rumination, wraps me in a most humorous sadness.
IV, i, 16

I had rather have a fool to make me merry than experience to make me sad.　　IV, i, 28

Farewell, Monsieur Traveler: look you lisp and wear strange suits, disable all the benefits of your own country, be out of love with your nativity, and almost chide God for making you that countenance you are; or I will scarce think you have swam in a gondola.
IV, i, 35

I'll warrant him heart-whole.
IV, i, 51

Very good orators, when they are out, they will spit; and for lovers lacking — God warn us! — matter, the cleanliest shift is to kiss.　　IV, i, 77

Men have died from time to time, and worms have eaten them, but not for love.　　IV, i, 110

Forever and a day.　　IV, i, 151

Men are April when they woo, December when they wed: maids are May when they are maids, but the sky changes when they are wives.
As You Like It IV, i, 153

My affection hath an unknown bottom, like the bay of Portugal.
IV, i, 219

The horn, the horn, the lusty horn
Is not a thing to laugh to scorn.
IV, ii, 17

Chewing the food of sweet and bitter fancy.　　IV, iii, 103

"So so" is good, very good, very excellent good: and yet it is not; it is but so so.　　V, i, 30

The fool doth think he is wise, but the wise man knows himself to be a fool.　　V, i, 35

No sooner met, but they looked; no sooner looked but they loved; no sooner loved but they sighed; no sooner sighed but they asked one another the reason; no sooner knew the reason but they sought the remedy.　　V, ii, 37

But, O! how bitter a thing it is to look into happiness through another man's eyes!　　V, ii, 48

It was a lover and his lass,
　With a hey, and a ho, and a hey
　　nonino,
That o'er the green corn-field did pass,
　In the spring time, the only pretty
　　ring time,
When birds do sing, hey ding a ding,
　ding;
Sweet lovers love the spring.
V, iii, 18

Here comes a pair of very strange beasts, which in all tongues are called fools.　　V, iv, 36

An ill-favored thing, sir, but mine own.[1]　　V, iv, 60

Rich honesty dwells like a miser, sir, in a poor house, as your pearl in your foul oyster.　　V, iv, 62

[1] "A poor thing but mine own" is the popular version.

"The retort courteous." . . . "the quip modest." . . . "the reply churlish." . . . "the reproof valiant" . . . "the countercheck quarrelsome." . . . "the lie circumstantial," and "the lie direct."　　*As You Like It* V, *iv*, 75

Your "if" is the only peacemaker; much virtue in "if."　　V, *iv*, 108

He uses his folly like a stalking horse, and under the presentation of that he shoots his wit.　　V, *iv*, 112

If music be the food of love,[1] play on;
Give me excess of it, that, surfeiting,
The appetite may sicken, and so die.
That strain again! it had a dying fall:
O! it came o'er my ear like the sweet
　　sound
That breathes upon a bank of violets,
Stealing and giving odor!
　　Twelfth-Night [1598–1600],
　　　　act I, sc. i, l. 1

O spirit of love! how quick and fresh
　　art thou,
That, notwithstanding thy capacity
Receiveth as the sea, nought enters
　　there,
Of what validity and pitch soe'er,
But falls into abatement and low
　　price,
Even in a minute: so full of shapes is
　　fancy,
That it alone is high fantastical.
　　　　I, *i*, 9

When my tongue blabs, then let mine
　　eyes not see.　　I, *ii*, 61

I am sure care's an enemy to life.
　　　　I, *iii*, 2

Let them hang themselves in their own straps.[2]　　I, *iii*, 13

I am a great eater of beef, and I believe that does harm to my wit.
　　　　I, *iii*, 92

Wherefore are these things hid?
　　　　I, *iii*, 135

---

[1] See *Antony and Cleopatra* II, *v*, 1, p. 288a. Is not music the food of love? — RICHARD BRINSLEY SHERIDAN, *The Rivals* [1775], II, *i*
[2] See Rabelais, p. 181b, and note.

Is it a world to hide virtues in?
　　Twelfth-Night I, *iii*, 142

God give them wisdom that have it; and those that are fools, let them use their talents.　　I, *v*, 14

One draught above heat makes him a fool, the second mads him, and a third drowns him.　　I, *v*, 139

'Tis beauty truly blent, whose red and
　　white
Nature's own sweet and cunning hand
　　laid on:
Lady, you are the cruel'st she alive,
If you will lead these graces to the
　　grave
And leave the world no copy.
　　　　I, *v*, 259

Make me a willow cabin at your gate,
And call upon my soul within the
　　house.　　I, *v*, 289

Holla your name to the reverberate
　　hills,
And make the babbling gossip of the
　　air
Cry out, "Olivia!"　　I, *v*, 293

Farewell, fair cruelty.　　I, *v*, 309

O mistress mine! where are you roaming?　　II, *iii*, 42

Journeys end in lovers meeting,
Every wise man's son doth know.
　　　　II, *iii*, 46

What is love? 'tis not hereafter;
Present mirth hath present laughter.
　　What's to come is still unsure:
In delay there lies no plenty;
Then come kiss me, sweet and twenty,
　　Youth's a stuff will not endure.
　　　　II, *iii*, 50

He does it with a better grace, but I do it more natural.　　II, *iii*, 91

Is there no respect of place, persons, nor time, in you?[1]　　II, *iii*, 100

Sir Toby: Dost thou think, because thou art virtuous, there shall be no more cakes and ale?

---

[1] See *Acts 10:34*, p. 50a, and note.

Clown: Yes, by Saint Anne; and ginger shall be hot i' the mouth too.
Twelfth-Night II, iii, 124

My purpose is, indeed, a horse of that color. II, iii, 184

These most brisk and giddy-paced times. II, iv, 6

If ever thou shalt love,
In the sweet pangs of it remember me;
For such as I am all true lovers are:
Unstaid and skittish in all motions else
Save in the constant image of the creature
That is belov'd. II, iv, 15

Let still the woman take
An elder than herself, so wears she to him,
So sways she level in her husband's heart:
For, boy, however we do praise ourselves,
Our fancies are more giddy and unfirm,
More longing, wavering, sooner lost and worn,
Than women's are. II, iv, 29

Then, let thy love be younger than thyself,
Or thy affection cannot hold the bent;
For women are as roses, whose fair flower
Being once display'd, doth fall that very hour. II, iv, 36

The spinsters and the knitters in the sun,
And the free maids that weave their thread with bones,
Do use to chant it: it is silly sooth,
And dallies with the innocence of love,
Like the old age. II, iv, 44

Come away, come away, death,
And in sad cypress let me be laid;
Fly away, fly away, breath;
I am slain by a fair cruel maid.
II, iv, 51

Duke: And what's her history?
Viola: A blank, my lord. She never told her love,

But let concealment, like a worm i' the bud,
Feed on her damask cheek: she pin'd in thought,
And with a green and yellow melancholy,
She sat like Patience on a monument,
Smiling at grief.
Twelfth-Night II, iv, 112

I am all the daughters of my father's house,
And all the brothers too. II, iv, 122

Here comes the trout that must be caught with tickling. II, v, 25

I may command where I adore.
II, v, 116

Be not afraid of greatness: some are born great, some achieve greatness, and some have greatness thrust upon them.
II, v, 159

Remember who commended thy yellow stockings, and wished to see thee ever cross-gartered. II, v, 168

Foolery, sir, does walk about the orb like the sun; it shines everywhere.
III, i, 44

This fellow's wise enough to play the fool,
And to do that well craves a kind of wit. III, i, 68

Music from the spheres.[1] III, i, 122

How apt the poor are to be proud.
III, i, 141

Then westward-ho! III, i, 148

O! what a deal of scorn looks beautiful
In the contempt and anger of his lip.
III, i, 159

Love sought is good, but giv'n unsought is better. III, i, 170

You will hang like an icicle on a Dutchman's beard. III, ii, 30

[1] The music of the spheres. — *Pericles V, i, 231.*
A phrase that stems from the Pythagorean Theory (sixth century B.C.) of the music or harmony of the spheres.
See Sir Thomas Browne, p. 330a.

Let there be gall enough in thy ink.
Twelfth-Night III, *ii*, 54

Laugh yourselves into stitches.
III, *ii*, 75

I think we do know the sweet Roman
hand. III, *iv*, 31

This is very midsummer madness.
III, *iv*, 62

More matter for a May morning.
III, *iv*, 158

He's a very devil. III, *iv*, 304

Out of my lean and low ability
I'll lend you something. III, *iv*, 380

I hate ingratitude more in a man
Than lying, vainness, babbling drunk-
enness,
Or any taint of vice whose strong cor-
ruption
Inhabits our frail blood. III, *iv*, 390

As the old hermit of Prague, that
never saw pen and ink, very wittily said
to a niece of King Gorboduc, "That
that is, is." IV, *ii*, 14

Thus the whirligig of time brings in
his revenges. V, *i*, 388

When that I was and a little tiny boy,
With hey, ho, the wind and the
rain;
A foolish thing was but a toy,
For the rain it raineth every day.[1]
V, *i*, 404

A surgeon to old shoes.
Julius Caesar [1598–1600],
act I, sc. i, l. 26

As proper men as ever trod upon
neat's leather. I, *i*, 27

Have you not made a universal shout,
That Tiber trembled underneath her
banks,
To hear the replication of your sounds
Made in her concave shores?
I, *i*, 48

Beware the ides of March.[2] I, *ii*, 18

Set honor in one eye and death i' the
other,
And I will look on both indifferently.
Julius Caesar I, *ii*, 86

Well, honor is the subject of my story.
I cannot tell what you and other men
Think of this life; but, for my single
self,
I had as lief not be as live to be
In awe of such a thing as I myself.
I, *ii*, 92

Stemming it with hearts of controversy. I, *ii*, 109

Why, man, he doth bestride the narrow
world
Like a Colossus; and we petty men
Walk under his huge legs, and peep
about
To find ourselves dishonorable graves.
Men at some time are masters of their
fates: [1]
The fault, dear Brutus, is not in our
stars,
But in ourselves, that we are under-
lings. I, *ii*, 134

Upon what meat doth this our Caesar
feed,
That he is grown so great? I, *ii*, 148

Let me have men about me that are
fat;
Sleek-headed men, and such as sleep o'
nights.
Yond Cassius has a lean and hungry
look; [2]
He thinks too much: such men are
dangerous. I, *ii*, 191

He reads much;
He is a great observer, and he looks
Quite through the deeds of men.
I, *ii*, 200

Seldom he smiles, and smiles in such a
sort
As if he mock'd himself, and scorn'd
his spirit
That could be moved to smile at anything. I, *ii*, 204

[1] Parodied by the Fool in *King Lear*, p. 278a.
[2] See Julius Caesar, p. 112a.

[1] See Sallust, p. 116a.
[2] See Julius Caesar, p. 112b.

But, for my own part, it was Greek to me.[1]

Julius Caesar I, ii, 288

Yesterday the bird of night did sit,
Even at noonday, upon the market-
place,
Hooting and shrieking.   *I, iii, 26*

So every bondman in his own hand
bears
The power to cancel his captivity.
I, iii, 101

O! he sits high in all the people's
hearts:
And that which would appear offense in
us,
His countenance, like richest alchemy,
Will change to virtue and to worthiness.   *I, iii, 157*

The abuse of greatness is when it disjoins
Remorse from power.   *II, i, 18*

'Tis a common proof,
That lowliness is young ambition's lad-
der,
Whereto the climber-upward turns his
face;
But when he once attains the upmost
round,
He then unto the ladder turns his
back,
Looks in the clouds, scorning the base
degrees
By which he did ascend.   *II, i, 21*

Therefore think him as a serpent's egg
Which, hatch'd, would, as his kind,
grow mischievous,
And kill him in the shell.   *II, i, 32*

Between the acting of a dreadful thing
And the first motion, all the interim
is
Like a phantasma, or a hideous dream:
The genius and the mortal instru-
ments
Are then in council; and the state of
man,
Like to a little kingdom, suffers then
The nature of an insurrection.
II, i, 63

[1] This geare is Greeke to me. — GASCOIGNE,
Supposes I [1573]

O conspiracy!
Sham'st thou to show thy dangerous
brow by night,
When evils are most free?
Julius Caesar II, i, 77

Let's carve him as a dish fit for the
gods,
Not hew him as a carcass fit for
hounds.   *II, i, 173*

But when I tell him he hates flatterers,
He says he does, being then most flattered.   *II, i, 207*

Enjoy the honey-heavy dew of slumber.   *II, i, 230*

You are my true and honorable wife,
As dear to me as are the ruddy drops
That visit my sad heart.[1]   *II, i, 288*

Think you I am no stronger than my
sex,
Being so father'd and so husbanded?
II, i, 296

When beggars die, there are no comets
seen;
The heavens themselves blaze forth the
death of princes.   *II, ii, 30*

Cowards die many times before their
deaths;
The valiant never taste of death but
once.
Of all the wonders that I yet have
heard,
It seems to me most strange that men
should fear;
Seeing that death, a necessary end,
Will come when it will come.
II, ii, 32

Antony, that revels long o' nights.
II, ii, 116

How hard it is for women to keep
counsel!   *II, iv, 9*

But I am constant as the northern
star,
Of whose true-fix'd and resting quality
There is no fellow in the firmament.
III, i, 60

Speak, hands, for me!   *III, i, 76*

[1] Dear as the ruddy drops that warm my heart.
— THOMAS GRAY, *The Bard* [1757], *I, iii, 12*

Et tu, Brute! [1]
Julius Caesar III, i, 77

Some to the common pulpits, and cry out,
"Liberty, freedom, and enfranchisement." III, i, 79

How many ages hence
Shall this our lofty scene be acted o'er,
In states unborn and accents yet unknown! III, i, 111

O mighty Caesar! dost thou lie so low?
Are all thy conquests, glories, triumphs, spoils,
Shrunk to this little measure? III, i, 148

The choice and master spirits of this age. III, i, 163

Though last, not least in love.[2] III, i, 189

O! pardon me, thou bleeding piece of earth,
That I am meek and gentle with these butchers;
Thou art the ruins of the noblest man
That ever lived in the tide of times. III, i, 254

Cry "Havoc!" and let slip the dogs of war. III, i, 273

Romans, countrymen, and lovers! hear me for my cause; and be silent, that you may hear. III, ii, 13

Not that I loved Caesar less, but that I loved Rome more. III, ii, 22

As he was valiant, I honor him; but, as he was ambitious, I slew him. III, ii, 27

If any, speak; for him have I offended. I pause for a reply. III, ii, 36

Friends, Romans, countrymen, lend me your ears;
I come to bury Caesar, not to praise him.
The evil that men do lives after them,

The good is oft interred with their bones.[1]
Julius Caesar III, ii, 79

For Brutus is an honorable man;
So are they all, all honorable men. III, ii, 88

When that the poor have cried, Caesar hath wept;
Ambition should be made of sterner stuff. III, ii, 97

O judgment! thou art fled to brutish beasts,
And men have lost their reason. III, ii, 110

But yesterday the word of Caesar might
Have stood against the world; now lies he there,
And none so poor to do him reverence. III, ii, 124

If you have tears, prepare to shed them now. III, ii, 174

See what a rent the envious Casca made. III, ii, 180

This was the most unkindest cut of all. III, ii, 188

Great Caesar fell.
O! what a fall was there, my countrymen;
Then I, and you, and all of us fell down,
Whilst bloody treason flourish'd over us. III, ii, 194

What private griefs they have, alas! I know not. III, ii, 217

I come not, friends, to steal away your hearts:
I am no orator, as Brutus is;
But, as you know me all, a plain blunt man. III, ii, 220

For I have neither wit, nor words, nor worth,
Action, nor utterance, nor the power of speech,
To stir men's blood: I only speak right on. III, ii, 225

---

[1] See *Julius Caesar*, p. 112b.
[2] See Spenser, p. 201a, and *King Lear*, p. 276b.

[1] See Euripides, p. 85b.

Put a tongue
In every wound of Caesar, that should
move
The stones of Rome to rise and
mutiny.
                Julius Caesar III, ii, 232

When love begins to sicken and decay,
It useth an enforced ceremony.
There are no tricks in plain and simple
faith.   IV, ii, 20

An itching palm.   IV, iii, 10

I had rather be a dog, and bay the
moon,
Than such a Roman.   IV, iii, 27

I'll use you for my mirth, yea, for my
laughter,
When you are waspish.   IV, iii, 49

There is no terror, Cassius, in your
threats;
For I am arm'd so strong in honesty
That they pass by me as the idle wind,
Which I respect not.   IV, iii, 66

A friend should bear his friend's infirmities,
But Brutus makes mine greater than
they are.   IV, iii, 85

All his faults observ'd,
Set in a notebook, learn'd, and conn'd
by rote.   IV, iii, 96

There is a tide in the affairs of men,
Which, taken at the flood, leads on to
fortune;
Omitted, all the voyage of their life
Is bound in shallows and in miseries.
                               IV, iii, 217

We must take the current when it
serves,
Or lose our ventures.   IV, iii, 222

The deep of night is crept upon our
talk,
And nature must obey necessity.
                               IV, iii, 225

But for your words, they rob the Hybla
bees,
And leave them honeyless.   V, i, 34

Forever, and forever, farewell, Cassius!
If we do meet again, why, we shall
smile;

If not, why then, this parting was well
made.   *Julius Caesar* V, i, 117

O! that a man might know
The end of this day's business, ere it
come.   V, i, 123

O Julius Caesar! thou art mighty yet!
Thy spirit walks abroad, and turns our
swords
In our own proper entrails.
                               V, iii, 94

The last of all the Romans, fare thee
well!   V, iii, 99

This was the noblest Roman of them
all.   V, v, 68

His life was gentle, and the elements
So mix'd in him that Nature might
stand up
And say to all the world, "This was a
man!" [1]   V, v, 73

For this relief much thanks; 'tis bitter
cold,
And I am sick at heart.
                Hamlet [1600–1601], *act* I,
                               sc. i, l. 8

Not a mouse stirring.[2]   I, i, 10

Thou art a scholar; speak to it, Horatio.   I, i, 42

But in the gross and scope of my opinion,
This bodes some strange eruption to
our state.   I, i, 68

Whose sore task
Does not divide the Sunday from the
week.   I, i, 75

This sweaty haste
Doth make the night joint-laborer with
the day.   I, i, 77

In the most high and palmy state of
Rome,
A little ere the mightiest Julius fell,
The graves stood tenantless and the
sheeted dead
Did squeak and gibber in the Roman
streets.   I, i, 113

[1] See *Hamlet* I, ii, *187*, p. 258a.
[2] See Clement Clarke Moore, p. 541a.

The moist star
Upon whose influence Neptune's empire stands
Was sick almost to doomsday with eclipse.　　*Hamlet* I, i, 118

And then it started like a guilty thing
Upon a fearful summons.　　I, i, 148

The cock, that is the trumpet to the morn.　　I, i, 150

Whether in sea or fire, in earth or air,
The extravagant and erring spirit hies
To his confine.　　I, i, 153

It faded on the crowing of the cock.
Some say that ever 'gainst that season comes
Wherein our Saviour's birth is celebrated,
The bird of dawning singeth all night long;
And then, they say, no spirit can walk abroad;
The nights are wholesome; then no planets strike,
No fairy takes, nor witch hath power to charm,
So hallow'd and so gracious is the time.　　I, i, 157

But, look, the morn in russet mantle clad,
Walks o'er the dew of yon high eastern hill.　　I, i, 166

The memory be green.[1]　　I, ii, 2

With one auspicious and one dropping eye,
With mirth in funeral and with dirge in marriage,
In equal scale weighing delight and dole.　　I, ii, 11

So much for him.　　I, ii, 25

A little more than kin, and less than kind.　　I, ii, 65

Thou know'st 'tis common; all that live must die,
Passing through nature to eternity.　　I, ii, 72

Seems, madam! Nay, it is; I know not "seems."

[1] See Thomas Moore, p. 541b.

'Tis not alone my inky cloak, good mother,
Nor customary suits of solemn black.　　*Hamlet* I, ii, 76

But I have that within which passeth show;
These but the trappings and the suits of woe.　　I, ii, 85

To persever
In obstinate condolement is a course
Of impious stubbornness; 'tis unmanly grief:
It shows a will most incorrect to heaven,
A heart unfortified, a mind impatient.
　　I, ii, 92

O! that this too too solid [1] flesh would melt,
Thaw and resolve itself into a dew;
Or that the Everlasting had not fix'd
His canon 'gainst self-slaughter! O God! O God!
How weary, stale, flat, and unprofitable
Seem to me all the uses of this world.
　　I, ii, 129

Things rank and gross in nature
Possess it merely. That it should come to this!　　I, ii, 136

So excellent a king; that was, to this,
Hyperion to a satyr; so loving to my mother
That he might not beteem the winds of heaven
Visit her face too roughly.　　I, ii, 139

Why, she would hang on him,
As if increase of appetite had grown
By what it fed on.　　I, ii, 143

Frailty, thy name is woman!
　　I, ii, 146

Like Niobe, all tears.　　I, ii, 149

A beast, that wants discourse of reason.　　I, ii, 150

It is not nor it cannot come to good.
　　I, ii, 158

[1] Alternative readings are "sallied" and "sullied."

A truant disposition.
> *Hamlet I, ii, 169*

Thrift, thrift, Horatio! the funeral bak'd meats
Did coldly furnish forth the marriage tables.

Would I had met my dearest foe [1] in heaven
Ere I had ever seen that day.
> *I, ii, 180*

In my mind's eye, Horatio.　　*I, ii, 185*

He was a man, take him for all in all,[2]
I shall not look upon his like again.
> *I, ii, 187*

Season your admiration for a while.
> *I, ii, 192*

In the dead vast and middle of the night.　　*I, ii, 198*

Arm'd at points exactly, cap-a-pe.
> *I, ii, 200*

Distill'd
Almost to jelly with the act of fear.
> *I, ii, 204*

A countenance more in sorrow than in anger.　　*I, ii, 231*

While one with moderate haste might tell a hundred.　　*I, ii, 237*

Hamlet: His beard was grizzled, no?
Horatio: It was, as I have seen it in his life,
A sable silver'd.　　*I, ii, 239*

Give it an understanding, but no tongue.　　*I, ii, 249*

All is not well;
I doubt some foul play.　　*I, ii, 254*

Foul deeds will rise,
Though all the earth o'erwhelm them, to men's eyes.　　*I, ii, 256*

The chariest maid is prodigal enough
If she unmask her beauty to the moon;
Virtue itself 'scapes not calumnious strokes;
The canker galls the infants of the spring

---

[1] See *Henry IV, pt. I, III, ii, 123,* p. 240a.
[2] See *Julius Caesar V, v, 73,* p. 256b.

Too oft before their buttons be disclos'd,
And in the morn and liquid dew of youth
Contagious blastments are most imminent.　　*Hamlet I, iii, 36*

Do not, as some ungracious pastors do,
Show me the steep and thorny way to heaven,
Whiles, like a puff'd and reckless libertine,
Himself the primrose path of dalliance treads,[1]
And recks not his own rede.[2]
> *I, iii, 47*

Give thy thoughts no tongue.
> *I, iii, 59*

Be thou familiar, but by no means vulgar;
Those friends thou hast, and their adoption tried,
Grapple them to thy soul with hoops of steel.　　*I, iii, 61*

Beware
Of entrance to a quarrel, but, being in,
Bear 't that th' opposed may beware of thee.
Give every man thy ear, but few thy voice;
Take each man's censure, but reserve thy judgment.
Costly thy habit as thy purse can buy,
But not express'd in fancy; rich, not gaudy; [3]
For the apparel oft proclaims the man.
> *I, iii, 65*

Neither a borrower, nor a lender be;
For loan oft loses both itself and friend,

---

[1] See Bion, p. 104b, and *Macbeth II, iii, 22,* p. 283b.
[2] Wel oghte a preest ensample for to yive,
By his clennesse, how that his sheep shold live.
> CHAUCER, *Canterbury Tales* [c. 1387].
> *prologue, l. 504*
And may you better reck the rede,
Than ever did the adviser.
> ROBERT BURNS [1759–1796], *Epistle to a Young Friend*
[2] See Lyly, p. 202b.
Neat, not gaudy. — CHARLES LAMB, *letter to Wordsworth* [1806]

And borrowing dulls the edge of husbandry.

This above all: to thine own self be
true,
And it must follow, as the night the
day,
Thou canst not then be false to any
man.[1]   *Hamlet* I, iii, 75

'Tis in my memory lock'd,
And you yourself shall keep the key of
it.   I, iii, 85

You speak like a green girl,
Unsifted in such perilous circumstance.   I, iii, 101

Springes to catch woodcocks.
I, iii, 115

When the blood burns, how prodigal
the soul
Lends the tongue vows.   I, iii, 116

Be somewhat scanter of your maiden
presence.   I, iii, 121

The air bites shrewdly.   I, iv, 1

But to my mind — though I am native
here
And to the manner born — it is a custom
More honor'd in the breach than the
observance.   I, iv, 14

Angels and ministers of grace defend
us!   I, iv, 39

Be thy intents wicked or charitable,
Thou com'st in such a questionable
shape
That I will speak to thee.   I, iv, 42

What may this mean,
That thou, dead corse, again in com-
plete steel
Revisit'st thus the glimpses of the
moon,
Making night hideous;[2] and we fools
of nature
So horridly to shake our disposition
With thoughts beyond the reaches of
our souls?   I, iv, 51

[1] See Bacon, p. 209a.
[2] And makes night hideous. — ALEXANDER
POPE, *The Dunciad, bk. III* [1728], *l. 166*

I do not set my life at a pin's fee.
Hamlet I, iv, 65

The dreadful summit of the cliff
That beetles o'er his base into the sea.
I, iv, 70

My fate cries out,
And makes each petty artery in this
body
As hardy as the Nemean lion's nerve.
I, iv, 81

Unhand me, gentlemen,
By heaven! I'll make a ghost of him
that lets me.   I, iv, 84

Something is rotten in the state of
Denmark.   I, iv, 90

I could a tale unfold whose lightest
word
Would harrow up thy soul, freeze thy
young blood,
Make thy two eyes, like stars, start from
their spheres,
Thy knotted and combined locks to
part,
And each particular hair to stand an
end,
Like quills upon the fretful porpen-
tine.   I, v, 15

And duller shouldst thou be than the
fat weed
That rots itself in ease on Lethe wharf.
I, v, 32

O my prophetic soul!
My uncle!
I, v, 40

O Hamlet! what a falling-off was there.
I, v, 47

But virtue, as it never will be mov'd,
Though lewdness court it in a shape of
heaven,
So lust, though to a radiant angel
link'd,
Will sate itself in a celestial bed,
And prey on garbage.   I, v, 53

In the porches of mine ears.
I, v, 63

Cut off even in the blossoms of my
sin,
Unhousel'd, disappointed, unanel'd,

No reckoning made, but sent to my account
With all my imperfections on my head.[1]   *Hamlet I, v, 76*

    Leave her to heaven,
And to those thorns that in her bosom lodge,
To prick and sting her.   *I, v, 86*

The glowworm shows the matin to be near,
And 'gins to pale his uneffectual fire.
                    I, v, 89

    While memory holds a seat
In this distracted globe. Remember thee!
Yea, from the table of my memory
I'll wipe away all trivial fond records.
                    I, v, 96

Within the book and volume of my brain.   *I, v, 103*

O villain, villain, smiling, damned villain!
My tables — meet it is I set it down,
That one may smile, and smile, and be a villain;
At least I'm sure it may be so in Denmark.   *I, v, 106*

There's ne'er a villain dwelling in all Denmark,
But he's an arrant knave.   *I, v, 123*

There are more things in heaven and earth, Horatio,
Than are dreamt of in your philosophy.   *I, v, 166*

To put an antic disposition on.
                    I, v, 172

Rest, rest, perturbed spirit!   *I, v, 182*

The time is out of joint; O cursed spite,
That ever I was born to set it right!
                    I, v, 188

Your bait of falsehood takes this carp of truth;
And thus do we of wisdom and of reach,
With windlasses and with assays of bias,

[1] See Homer, p. 64b, and note.

By indirections find directions out.
             Hamlet II, i, 63

Ungarter'd, and down-gyved to his ankle.   *II, i, 80*

This is the very ecstasy of love.
                  II, i, 102

Brevity is the soul of wit.   *II, ii, 90*

More matter, with less art.   *II, ii, 95*

That he is mad, 'tis true; 'tis true 'tis pity;
And pity 'tis 'tis true.   *II, ii, 97*

Find out the cause of this effect,
Or rather say, the cause of this defect,
For this effect defective comes by cause.   *II, ii, 101*

Doubt thou the stars are fire;
  Doubt that the sun doth move;
Doubt truth to be a liar;
  But never doubt I love.
                  II, ii, 115

Polonius: Do you know me, my lord?
Hamlet: Excellent well; you are a fishmonger.   *II, ii, 173*

To be honest, as this world goes, is to be one man picked out of ten thousand.   *II, ii, 179*

Hamlet: For if the sun breed maggots in a dead dog, being a god[1] kissing carrion — Have you a daughter?
Polonius: I have, my lord.
Hamlet: Let her not walk i' the sun.   *II, ii, 183*

Still harping on my daughter.
                  II, ii, 190

Polonius: What do you read, my lord?
Hamlet: Words, words, words.
                  II, ii, 195

They have a plentiful lack of wit.
                  II, ii, 204

Though this be madness, yet there is method in 't.   *II, ii, 211*

These tedious old fools!
                  II, ii, 227

[1] In some editions, good.

The indifferent children of the earth.   *Hamlet II, ii, 235*

Happy in that we are not over happy.   *II, ii, 236*

There is nothing either good or bad, but thinking makes it so.   *II, ii, 259*

O God! I could be bounded in a nutshell, and count myself a king of infinite space, were it not that I have bad dreams.   *II, ii, 263*

Beggar that I am, I am even poor in thanks.   *II, ii, 286*

This goodly frame, the earth, seems to me a sterile promontory; this most excellent canopy, the air, look you, this brave o'erhanging firmament, this majestical roof fretted with golden fire, why, it appears no other thing to me but a foul and pestilent congregation of vapors. What a piece of work is a man! How noble in reason! how infinite in faculty! in form, in moving, how express and admirable! in action how like an angel! in apprehension how like a god!   *II, ii, 317*

And yet, to me, what is this quintessence of dust? man delights not me; no, nor woman neither.   *II, ii, 328*

There is something in this more than natural, if philosophy could find it out.   *II, ii, 392*

I am but mad north-northwest: when the wind is southerly I know a hawk from a handsaw.[1]   *II, ii, 405*

They say an old man is twice a child.[2]   *II, ii, 413*

One fair daughter and no more,
The which he loved passing well.
        II, ii, 435

Come, give us a taste of your quality.   *II, ii, 460*

The play, I remember, pleased not the million; 'twas caviare to the general.   *II, ii, 465*

[1] A heron.
[2] See Aristophanes, p. 91a.

They are the abstracts and brief chronicles of the time: after your death you were better have a bad epitaph than their ill report while you live.
        Hamlet II, ii, 555

Use every man after his desert, and who should 'scape whipping?
        II, ii, 561

O! what a rogue and peasant slave am I.   *II, ii, 584*

What's Hecuba to him or he to Hecuba,
That he should weep for her?
        II, ii, 593

Who calls me villain? breaks my pate across?
Plucks off my beard and blows it in my face?   *II, ii, 607*

But I am pigeon-liver'd, and lack gall
To make oppression bitter.
        II, ii, 613

    The play's the thing
Wherein I'll catch the conscience of
    the king.   *II, ii, 641*

    With devotion's visage
And pious action we do sugar o'er
The devil himself.   *III, i, 47*

To be, or not to be: that is the question:
Whether 'tis nobler in the mind to suffer
The slings and arrows of outrageous fortune,
Or to take arms against a sea of troubles,
And by opposing end them? To die: to sleep;
No more; and, by a sleep to say we end
The heartache and the thousand natural shocks
That flesh is heir to, 'tis a consummation
Devoutly to be wish'd. To die, to sleep;
To sleep: perchance to dream: ay, there's the rub;
For in that sleep of death what dreams may come,

When we have shuffled off this mortal
coil,
Must give us pause. There's the re-
spect
That makes calamity of so long life;
For who would bear the whips and
scorns of time,
The oppressor's wrong, the proud
man's contumely,
The pangs of dispriz'd love, the law's
delay,
The insolence of office, and the spurns
That patient merit of the unworthy
takes,
When he himself might his quietus
make
With a bare bodkin? who would fardels
bear,
To grunt and sweat under a weary life,
But that the dread of something after
death,
The undiscover'd country from whose
bourn
No traveler returns,[1] puzzles the will,
And makes us rather bear those ills we
have
Than fly to others that we know not
of?
Thus conscience does make cowards of
us all;
And thus the native hue of resolution
Is sicklied o'er with the pale cast of
thought,
And enterprises of great pith and mo-
ment
With this regard their currents turn
awry,
And lose the name of action.
Hamlet III, i, 56

Nymph, in thy orisons
Be all my sins remember'd.
III, i, 89

To the noble mind
Rich gifts wax poor when givers prove
unkind.   *III, i, 100*

Get thee to a nunnery.   *III, i, 124*

What should such fellows as I do
crawling between heaven and earth?
We are arrant knaves, all.   *III, i, 128*

[1] See *Song of The Harp-Player,* p. 3a, and
note.

Be thou as chaste as ice, as pure as
snow, thou shalt not escape calumny.
Hamlet III, i, 142

I have heard of your paintings too,
well enough; God has given you one
face, and you make yourselves another.
III, i, 150

O! what a noble mind is here o'erthrown:
The courtier's, soldier's, scholar's, eye,
tongue, sword.   *III, i, 159*

The glass of fashion and the mould of
form,
The observ'd of all observers!
    III, i, 162

Now see that noble and most sovereign
reason,
Like sweet bells jangled, out of tune
and harsh.   *III, i, 166*

O! woe is me,
To have seen what I have seen, see
what I see!   *III, i, 169*

Speak the speech, I pray you, as I
pronounced it to you, trippingly on the
tongue; but if you mouth it, as many of
your players do, I had as lief the town-
crier spoke my lines. Nor do not saw
the air too much with your hand, thus;
but use all gently: for in the very torrent, tempest, and — as I may say —
whirlwind of passion, you must acquire
and beget a temperance, that may give
it smoothness. O! it offends me to the
soul to hear a robustious periwig-pated
fellow tear a passion to tatters, to very
rags, to split the ears of the ground-
lings, who for the most part are capable
of nothing but inexplicable dumb-
shows and noise: I would have such a
fellow whipped for o'erdoing Termagant; it out-herods Herod.   *III, ii, 1*

Suit the action to the word, the word
to the action; with this special observance, that you o'erstep not the modesty
of nature.   *III, ii, 20*

To hold, as 'twere, the mirror up to
nature; to show virtue her own feature,
scorn her own image, and the very age

and body of the time his form and pressure. *Hamlet III, ii, 25*

I have thought some of nature's journeymen had made men and not made them well, they imitated humanity so abominably. *III, ii, 38*

No; let the candied tongue lick absurd pomp,
And crook the pregnant hinges of the knee
Where thrift may follow fawning.
III, ii, 65

A man that fortune's buffets and rewards
Hast ta'en with equal thanks.
III, ii, 72

They are not a pipe for fortune's finger
To sound what stop she please. Give me that man
That is not passion's slave, and I will wear him
In my heart's core, ay, in my heart of heart,
As I do thee. Something too much of this. *III, ii, 75*

My imaginations are as foul
As Vulcan's stithy. *III, ii, 88*

The chameleon's dish: I eat the air, promise-crammed; you cannot feed capons so. *III, ii, 98*

Nay, then, let the devil wear black, for I'll have a suit of sables.
III, ii, 138

There's hope a great man's memory may outlive his life half a year.
III, ii, 141

Marry, this is miching mallecho; it means mischief. *III, ii, 148*

Ophelia: 'Tis brief, my lord.
Hamlet: As woman's love.
III, ii, 165

Where love is great, the littlest doubts are fear;
When little fears grow great, great love grows there. *III, ii, 183*

Wormwood, wormwood.
III, ii, 193

The lady doth protest too much, methinks. *Hamlet III, ii, 242*

Let the galled jade wince, our withers are unwrung. *III, ii, 256*

Why, let the stricken deer go weep,[1]
The hart ungalled play;
For some must watch, while some must sleep:
So runs the world away.
III, ii, 287

You would pluck out the heart of my mystery. *III, ii, 389*

Do you think I am easier to be played on than a pipe? *III, ii, 393*

Hamlet: Do you see yonder cloud that's almost in shape of a camel?
Polonius: By the mass, and 'tis like a camel, indeed.
Hamlet: Methinks it is like a weasel.
Polonius: It is backed like a weasel.
Hamlet: Or like a whale?
Polonius: Very like a whale.[2]
III, ii, 400

They fool me to the top of my bent.
III, ii, 408

By and by is easily said.
III, ii, 411

'Tis now the very witching time of night,
When churchyards yawn and hell itself breathes out
Contagion to this world. *III, ii, 413*

I will speak daggers to her, but use none. *III, ii, 421*

O! my offense is rank, it smells to heaven;
It hath the primal eldest curse upon 't,
A brother's murder! *III, iii, 36*

Now might I do it pat, now he is praying;
And now I'll do 't: and so he goes to heaven;
And so I am reveng'd. *III, iii, 73*

---

[1] See Cowper, p. 458a.
[2] See Aristophanes, p. 91a, and *Antony and Cleopatra IV, xii, 2*, p. 288b.

With all his crimes broad blown, as
flush as May.
Hamlet III, iii, 81

My words fly up, my thoughts remain
below:
Words without thoughts never to
heaven go.   *III, iii, 97*

How now! a rat? Dead, for a ducat,
dead!   *III, iv, 23*

False as dicers' oaths.   *III, iv, 45*

A rhapsody of words.   *III, iv, 48*

See, what a grace was seated on this
brow;
Hyperion's curls; the front of Jove him-
self,
An eye like Mars, to threaten and com-
mand,
A station like the herald Mercury
New-lighted on a heaven-kissing hill.
A combination and a form indeed,
Where every god did seem to set his
seal,
To give the world assurance of a man.
     III, iv, 55

     At your age
The heyday in the blood is tame, it's
humble.   *III, iv, 68*

O shame! where is thy blush? Rebel-
lious hell,
If thou canst mutine in a matron's
bones,
To flaming youth let virtue be as wax,
And melt in her own fire: proclaim no
shame
When the compulsive ardor gives the
charge,
Since frost itself as actively doth burn,
And reason panders will.   *III, iv, 82*

A king of shreds and patches.[1]
     III, iv, 102

Lay not that flattering unction to your
soul.   *III, iv, 145*

     Confess yourself to heaven;
Repent what's past; avoid what is to
come.   *III, iv, 149*

[1] A wandering minstrel I —
     A thing of shreds and patches.
     W. S. GILBERT, *The Mikado* [1885], act I

For in the fatness of these pursy times
Virtue itself of vice must pardon beg.
     Hamlet III, iv, 153

Assume a virtue, if you have it not.
     III, iv, 160

     Refrain tonight;
And that shall lend a kind of easiness
To the next abstinence: the next more
easy;
For use almost can change the stamp of
nature.   *III, iv, 165*

I must be cruel, only to be kind.
     III, iv, 178

For 'tis the sport to have the enginer
Hoist with his own petar.
     III, iv, 206

     Diseases desperate grown
By desperate appliance are reliev'd,
Or not at all.[1]   *IV, iii, 9*

A man may fish with the worm that
hath eat of a king, and eat of the fish
that hath fed of that worm.
     IV, iii, 29

We go to gain a little patch of ground,
That hath in it no profit but the
name.   *IV, iv, 18*

How all occasions do inform against
me,
And spur my dull revenge! What is a
man,
If his chief good and market of his
time
Be but to sleep and feed? a beast, no
more.[2]
Sure he that made us with such large
discourse,
Looking before and after, gave us not
That capability and godlike reason
To fust in us unus'd.   *IV, iv, 32*

     Some craven scruple
Of thinking too precisely on the event.
     IV, iv, 40

     Rightly to be great
Is not to stir without great argument,

[1] See Hippocrates, p. 88b.
[2] The unmotived herd that only sleep and
feed. — JAMES RUSSELL LOWELL [1819–1891],
Under the Old Elm, pt. VII, st. 3

But greatly to find quarrel in a straw
When honor's at the stake.
Hamlet IV, iv, 53

So full of artless jealousy is guilt,
It spills itself in fearing to be spilt.
IV, v, 19

How should I your true love know
From another one?
By his cockle hat and staff,
And his sandal shoon.[1] *IV, v, 23*

He is dead and gone, lady,
He is dead and gone;
At his head a grass-green turf,
At his heels a stone. *IV, v, 29*

We know what we are, but know not
what we may be. *IV, v, 43*

Come, my coach! Good night, ladies;
good night, sweet ladies; good night,
good night. *IV, v, 72*

When sorrows come, they come not
single spies,
But in battalions.[2] *IV, v, 78*

We have done but greenly,
In hugger-mugger to inter him.
IV, v, 84

There's such divinity doth hedge a
king,
That treason can but peep to what it
would.[3]
IV, v, 123

There's rosemary, that's for remembrance . . . and there is pansies, that's
for thoughts. *IV, v, 174*

O! you must wear your rue with a
difference. There's a daisy; I would give
you some violets, but they withered all
when my father died. *IV, v, 181*

[1] Ophelia is quoting a version of a poem by
Sir Walter Ralegh.

[2] See Cervantes, p. 194b.
One woe doth tread upon another's heel,
So fast they follow.
Hamlet IV, vii, 164
Thus woe succeeds a woe, as wave a wave. —
HERRICK, *Sorrows Succeed* [1648]

Woes cluster; rare are solitary woes;
They love a train, they tread each other's heel.
EDWARD YOUNG, *Night Thoughts* [1742–
1745], *Night III, l. 63*

[3] See Montaigne, p. 191a, and Tennyson,
p. 653a.

A very riband in the cap of youth.
Hamlet IV, vii, 77

Nature her custom holds,
Let shame say what it will.
IV, vii, 188

There is no ancient gentlemen but
gardeners, ditchers, and grave-makers;
they hold up Adam's profession.[1]
V, i, 32

Cudgel thy brains no more about it.
V, i, 61

Has this fellow no feeling of his business, that he sings at grave-making?
V, i, 71

Custom hath made it in him a property of easiness. *V, i, 73*

A politician . . . one that would
circumvent God. *V, i, 84*

Why may not that be the skull of a
lawyer? Where be his quiddities now,
his quillets, his cases, his tenures, and
his tricks? *V, i, 104*

One that was a woman, sir; but, rest
her soul, she's dead. *V, i, 145*

How absolute the knave is! we must
speak by the card, or equivocation will
undo us. *V, i, 147*

The age is grown so picked that the
toe of the peasant comes so near the
heel of the courtier, he galls his kibe.
V, i, 150

Alas! poor Yorick. I knew him, Horatio; a fellow of infinite jest, of most
excellent fancy; he hath borne me on
his back a thousand times; and now,
how abhorred in my imagination it is!
my gorge rises at it. Here hung those
lips that I have kissed I know not how
oft. Where be your gibes now? your
gambols? your songs? your flashes of
merriment, that were wont to set the
table on a roar? Not one now, to mock
your own grinning? quite chapfallen?
Now get you to my lady's chamber, and
tell her, let her paint an inch thick, to

[1] See Francis Bacon, p. 209b, and *King Henry
VI, pt. II, IV, ii, 146*, and note, p. 215a.

this favor she must come; make her
laugh at that.   *Hamlet* V, i, 201

To what base uses we may return,
Horatio! Why may not imagination
trace the noble dust of Alexander, till
he find it stopping a bung-hole?
        V, i, 222

Imperious Caesar, dead and turn'd to
    clay,
Might stop a hole to keep the wind
    away.   V, i, 235

    Lay her i' the earth;
And from her fair and unpolluted flesh
May violets spring! [1]   V, i, 260

A ministering angel shall my sister be.[2]
        V, i, 263

Sweets to the sweet: farewell!
        V, i, 265

I thought thy bride-bed to have deck'd,
    sweet maid,
And not have strew'd thy grave.
        V, i, 267

Though I am not splenetive and rash
Yet have I in me something danger-
    ous.   V, i, 283

I lov'd Ophelia: forty thousand broth-
    ers
Could not, with all their quantity of
    love,
Make up my sum.   V, i, 291

    Nay, an thou'lt mouth,
I'll rant as well as thou.   V, i, 305

Let Hercules himself do what he may,
The cat will mew and dog will have his
    day.   V, i, 313

There's a divinity that shapes our
    ends,
Rough-hew them how we will.
        V, ii, 10

I once did hold it, as our statists do,
A baseness to write fair.   V, ii, 33

It did me yeoman's service.
        V, ii, 36

[1] See FitzGerald, p. 629b, and Tennyson,
p. 650a.
[2] See Sir Walter Scott, p. 519b.

Not a whit, we defy augury; there's a
special providence in the fall of a sparrow.[1] If it be now, 'tis not to come; if it
be not to come, it will be now; if it be
not now, yet it will come: the readiness
is all.
        Hamlet V, ii, 232

A hit, a very palpable hit.   V, ii, 295

    This fell sergeant, death,
Is strict in his arrest.   V, ii, 350

Report me and my cause aright.
        V, ii, 353

I am more an antique Roman than a
    Dane.   V, ii, 355

O God! Horatio, what a wounded
    name,
Things standing thus unknown, shall
    live behind me.
If thou didst ever hold me in thy heart,
Absent thee from felicity awhile,
And in this harsh world draw thy
    breath in pain,
To tell my story.   V, ii, 358

The rest is silence.   V, ii, 372

Now cracks a noble heart. Good night,
    sweet prince,
And flights of angels sing thee to thy
    rest!   V, ii, 373

    O proud death! [2]
What feast is toward in thine eternal
    cell?   V, ii, 378

I will make a Star Chamber matter
of it.
    The Merry Wives of Windsor
    [*1600–1601*], act I, sc. i, l. 2

She has brown hair, and speaks small
like a woman.   I, i, 48

Seven hundred pounds and possibilities is goot gifts.   I, i, 65

I had rather than forty shillings I had
my Book of Songs and Sonnets here.
        I, i, 205

"Convey," the wise it call. "Steal!"
foh! a fico for the phrase!   I, iii, 30

[1] See *Matthew 10:29*, p. 42a, and Alexander
Pope, p. 408a.
[2] See Donne, p. 308a.

I am almost out at heels.
The Merry Wives of Windsor
I, *iii*, 32

Thou art the Mars of malcontents.
I, *iii*, 111

Here will be an old abusing of God's patience and the king's English.
I, *iv*, 5

Dispense with trifles. II, *i*, 47

Faith, thou hast some crotchets in thy head now. II, *i*, 158

Why, then the world's mine oyster,
Which I with sword will open.
II, *ii*, 2

This is the short and the long of it.
II, *ii*, 62

Like a fair house built upon another man's ground. II, *ii*, 229

Better three hours too soon than a minute too late. II, *ii*, 332

I cannot tell what the dickens his name is. III, *ii*, 20

He capers, he dances, he has eyes of youth, he writes verses, he speaks holiday, he smells April and May.
III, *ii*, 71

O, what a world of vile ill-favor'd faults
Looks handsome in three hundred pounds a year! III, *iv*, 32

A woman would run through fire and water for such a kind heart.
III, *iv*, 106

I have a kind of alacrity in sinking.
III, *v*, 13

As good luck would have it.[1]
III, *v*, 86

A man of my kidney. III, *v*, 119

[He] curses all Eve's daughters, of what complexion soever. IV, *ii*, 24

Wives may be merry, and yet honest too. IV, *ii*, 110

This is the third time; I hope good

[1] As ill luck would have it. — CERVANTES, *Don Quixote, pt. I* [1605], *bk. I, ch.* 2

luck lies in odd numbers. . . . There is divinity in odd numbers, either in nativity, chance, or death.[1]
The Merry Wives of Windsor
V, *i*, 2

Better a little chiding than a great deal of heartbreak. V, *iii*, 10

Property was thus appall'd,
That the self was not the same;
Single nature's double name
Neither two nor one was call'd.
The Phoenix and the Turtle
[1601], *l.* 37

Reason, in itself confounded,
Saw division grow together. *l.* 41

The chance of war.
Troilus and Cressida [1601–1603], *prologue, l.* 31

I have had my labor for my travail.[2]
Act I, sc. i, l. 73

Women are angels, wooing:
Things won are done; joy's soul lies in the doing. I, *ii*, 310

Men prize the thing ungain'd more than it is. I, *ii*, 313

The sea being smooth,
How many shallow bauble boats dare sail
Upon her patient breast.[3] I, *iii*, 34

The heavens themselves, the planets, and this center,
Observe degree, priority, and place,
Insisture, course, proportion, season, form,
Office, and custom, in all line of order.
I, *iii*, 85

O! when degree is shak'd,
Which is the ladder to all high designs,
The enterprise is sick.[4] I, *iii*, 101

Take but degree away, untune that string,
And, hark! what discord follows; each thing meets

[1] See Pliny, p. 133a, and Samuel Lover, p. 589a.
[2] See Cervantes, p. 193b.
[3] See Publilius Syrus, p. 126a.
[4] See Publilius Syrus, p. 127b.

In mere oppugnancy: the bounded waters
Should lift their bosoms higher than the shores
And make a sop of all this solid globe.
  Troilus and Cressida I, iii, 109

Then everything includes itself in power,
Power into will, will into appetite;
And appetite, an universal wolf,
So doubly seconded with will and power,
Must make perforce a universal prey,
And last eat up himself.   *I, iii, 119*

Like a strutting player, whose conceit
Lies in his hamstring, and doth think it rich
To hear the wooden dialogue and sound
'Twixt his stretch'd footing and the scaffoldage.   *I, iii, 153*

And in such indexes, although small pricks
To their subsequent volumes, there is seen
The baby figure of the giant mass
Of things to come.[1]   *I, iii, 343*

Who wears his wit in his belly, and his guts in his head.   *II, i, 78*

Modest doubt is call'd
The beacon of the wise, the tent that searches
To the bottom of the worst.
    II, ii, 15

'Tis mad idolatry
To make the service greater than the god.   *II, ii, 56*

He that is proud eats up himself; pride is his own glass, his own trumpet, his own chronicle.   *II, iii, 165*

I am giddy, expectation whirls me round.
The imaginary relish is so sweet
That it enchants my sense.
    III, ii, 17

Words pay no debts.   *III, ii, 56*

[1] See Cicero, p. 111a, and Thomas Campbell, p. 538a, and note.

To fear the worst oft cures the worse.
    Troilus and Cressida III, ii, 77

All lovers swear more performance than they are able, and yet reserve an ability that they never perform; vowing more than the perfection of ten, and discharging less than the tenth part of one.   *III, ii, 89*

For to be wise, and love,
Exceeds man's might; that dwells with gods above.   *III, ii, 163*

If I be false, or swerve a hair from truth,
When time is old and hath forgot itself,
When waterdrops have worn the stones of Troy,
And blind oblivion swallow'd cities up,
And mighty states characterless are grated
To dusty nothing, yet let memory,
From false to false, among false maids in love
Upbraid my falsehood! when they have said "as false
As air, as water, wind, or sandy earth,
As fox to lamb, as wolf to heifer's calf,
Pard to the hind, or stepdame to her son";
Yea, let them say, to stick the heart of falsehood,
"As false as Cressid."   *III, ii, 191*

Time hath, my lord, a wallet at his back,
Wherein he puts alms for oblivion.
    III, iii, 145

Perseverance, dear my lord,
Keeps honor bright: to have done, is to hang
Quite out of fashion, like a rusty mail
In monumental mockery.
    III, iii, 150

For honor travels in a strait so narrow
Where one but goes abreast.
    III, iii, 154

Time is like a fashionable host,
That slightly shakes his parting guest by the hand,

And with his arms outstretch'd, as he
would fly,
Grasps in the comer: welcome ever
smiles,
And farewell goes out sighing.
Troilus and Cressida III, iii, 168

Beauty, wit,
High birth, vigor of bone, desert in
service,
Love, friendship, charity, are subjects
all
To envious and calumniating time.
One touch of nature makes the whole
world kin.   *III, iii, 171*

And give to dust that is a little gilt
More laud than gilt o'er-dusted.
III, iii, 178

My mind is troubled, like a fountain
stirr'd;
And I myself see not the bottom of
it.   *III, iii, 314*

You do as chapmen do,
Dispraise the thing that you desire to
buy.   *IV, i, 75*

As many farewells as be stars in heaven.
IV, iv, 44

And sometimes we are devils to our-
selves
When we will tempt the frailty of our
powers,
Presuming on their changeful potency.
IV, iv, 95

The kiss you take is better than you
give.   *IV, v, 38*

Fie, fie upon her!
There's language in her eye, her cheek,
her lip,
Nay, her foot speaks; her wanton spirits
look out
At every joint and motive of her body.
IV, v, 54

What's past and what's to come is
strew'd with husks
And formless ruin of oblivion.
IV, v, 165

The end crowns all,[1]
And that old common arbitrator,
Time,
Will one day end it.
Troilus and Cressida IV, v, 223

Words, words, mere words, no matter
from the heart.   *V, iii, 109*

Hector is dead; there is no more to
say.   *V, x, 22*

O world! world! world! thus is the
poor agent despised.   *V, x, 36*

Love all, trust a few,
Do wrong to none: be able for thine
enemy
Rather in power than use, and keep thy
friend
Under thy own life's key: be check'd
for silence,
But never tax'd for speech.
All's Well That Ends Well [2]
[1601–1603], *act I, sc. i, l. 74*

It were all one
That I should love a bright particular
star
And think to wed it, he is so above
me.   *I, i, 97*

The hind that would be mated by the
lion
Must die for love.   *I, i, 103*

My friends were poor, but honest.[3]
I, iii, 203

Oft expectation fails, and most oft
there
Where most it promises.   *II, i, 145*

They say miracles are past.
II, iii, 1

A young man married is a man that's
marr'd.   *II, iii, 315*

The web of our life is of a mingled
yarn, good and ill together.
IV, iii, 83

[1] See Anonymous, p. 150b; *All's Well That
Ends Well IV, iv, 35* and note, p. 270a; and
Herrick, p. 320a.
[2] See *IV, iv, 35*, p. 270a.
[3] Though I be poor, I'm honest. — THOMAS
MIDDLETON, *The Witch* [c. 1627], *III, 2*
See Anonymous, p. 1103a.

There's place and means for every man alive.
　　　All's Well That Ends Well
　　　　　　　IV, iii, 379

All's well that end's well: still the fine's the crown;
Whate'er the course, the end is the renown.[1]　　　IV, iv, 35

I am a man whom Fortune hath cruelly scratched.　　　V, ii, 28

　　Praising what is lost
Makes the remembrance dear.
　　　　　　　V, iii, 19

The inaudible and noiseless foot of time.[2]　　　V, iii, 41

Love that comes too late,
Like a remorseful pardon slowly carried.　　　V, iii, 57

All impediments in fancy's course
Are motives of more fancy.　V, iii, 216

　　Spirits are not finely touch'd
But to fine issues.
　　Measure for Measure [1604–
　　　1605], act I, sc. i, l. 35

Good counselors lack no clients.
　　　　　　　I, ii, 115

And liberty plucks justice by the nose.　　　I, iii, 29

I hold you as a thing ensky'd and sainted.　　　I, iv, 34

　　A man whose blood
Is very snow-broth; one who never feels
The wanton stings and motions of the sense.　　　I, iv, 57

　　Our doubts are traitors,
And make us lose the good we oft might win,
By fearing to attempt.[3]　　I, iv, 78
We must not make a scarecrow of the law,

[1] See Anonymous, p. 150b; Heywood, p. 183b; and *Troilus and Cressida IV, v, 223, 269b.*
　All's well that ends well yet.— *All's Well That Ends Well V, i, 25*
[2] How noiseless falls the foot of time! — W. R. SPENCER [1769–1834], *Lines to Lady A. Hamilton*
[3] See *Macbeth I, vii, 44,* p. 282b.

Setting it up to fear the birds of prey,
And let it keep one shape, till custom make it
Their perch, and not their terror.
　　Measure for Measure II, i, 1

The jury, passing on the prisoner's life,
May in the sworn twelve have a thief or two
Guiltier than him they try.　II, i, 19

Some rise by sin, and some by virtue fall.　　　II, i, 38

　　Great with child, and longing . . .
for stewed prunes.　　　II, i, 94

This will last out a night in Russia,
When nights are longest there.
　　　　　　　II, i, 144

　　His face is the worst thing about him.　　　II, i, 167

Condemn the fault, and not the act of it?　　　II, ii, 37

No ceremony that to great ones 'longs,
Not the king's crown, nor the deputed sword,
The marshal's truncheon, nor the judge's robe,
Become them with one half so good a grace
As mercy does.[1]　　　II, ii, 59

Why, all the souls that were were forfeit once;
And He that might the vantage best have took,
Found out the remedy. How would you be,
If He, which is the top of judgment, should
But judge you as you are?　II, ii, 73

The law hath not been dead, though it hath slept.　　　II, ii, 90

　　O! it is excellent
To have a giant's strength; but it is tyrannous
To use it like a giant.　　II, ii, 107

　　But man, proud man,
Drest in a little brief authority,
Most ignorant of what he's most assur'd,

[1] See *The Merchant of Venice IV, i, 184,* p. 234b.

His glassy essence, like an angry ape,
Plays such fantastic tricks before high
heaven
As make the angels weep.
Measure for Measure II, ii, 117

That in the captain's but a choleric
word,
Which in the soldier is flat blasphemy.
II, ii, 130

It oft falls out,
To have what we would have, we speak
not what we mean.   *II, iv, 118*

The miserable have no other medicine
But only hope.   *III, i, 2*

Be absolute for death.   *III, i, 5*

A breath thou art,
Servile to all the skyey influences.
III, i, 8

Thou hast nor youth nor age;
But, as it were, an after-dinner's sleep,
Dreaming on both; for all thy blessed
youth
Becomes as aged, and doth beg the
alms
Of palsied eld; and when thou art old
and rich,
Thou hast neither heat, affection, limb,
nor beauty,
To make thy riches pleasant.
III, i, 32

The sense of death is most in apprehen-
sion,[1]
And the poor beetle, that we tread upon,
In corporal sufferance finds a pang as
great
As when a giant dies.   *III, i, 76*

If I must die,
I will encounter darkness as a bride,
And hug it in my arms.   *III, i, 81*

The cunning livery of hell.
III, i, 93

Ay, but to die, and go we know not
where;
To lie in cold obstruction and to rot;
This sensible warm motion to become

[1] See Publilius Syrus, p. 126a.

A kneaded clod; and the delighted
spirit
To bathe in fiery floods, or to reside
In thrilling region of thick-ribbed ice;
To be imprison'd in the viewless
winds,
And blown with restless violence round
about
The pendant world.
Measure for Measure III, i, 116

The weariest and most loathed worldly
life
That age, ache, penury, and imprison-
ment
Can lay on nature, is a paradise
To what we fear of death.   *III, i, 127*

The hand that hath made you fair
hath made you good.[1]   *III, i, 182*

Virtue is bold, and goodness never
fearful.   *III, i, 214*

There, at the moated grange, resides
this dejected Mariana.[2]   *III, i, 279*

This news is old enough, yet it is
every day's news.   *III, ii, 249*

He who the sword of heaven will bear
Should be as holy as severe.
III, ii, 283

O, what may man within him hide,
Though angel on the outward side!
III, ii, 293

Take, O take those lips away,
That so sweetly were forsworn;
And those eyes, the break of day,
Lights that do mislead the morn:
But my kisses bring again, bring again;
Seals of love, but seal'd in vain, seal'd
in vain [3]   *IV, i, 1*

[1] See Spenser, p. 201b.
[2] "Mariana in the moated grange" — motto
used by TENNYSON for the poem *Mariana* [1830].
[3] This song occurs in *act V, sc. ii, of* FLETCH-
ER's *Bloody Brother* [c. 1616], with an additional
stanza:
Hide, O hide those hills of snow,
  Which thy frozen bosom bears,
On whose tops the pinks that grow
  Are of those that April wears!
But first set my poor heart free,
Bound in those icy chains by thee.

Music oft hath such a charm
To make bad good, and good provoke
　to harm.[1]
　　　Measure for Measure IV, i, 16

Every true man's apparel fits your
thief.　　　　　　　　IV, ii, 46

I am a kind of burr; I shall stick.
　　　　　　　　　　　IV, iii, 193

We would, and we would not.
　　　　　　　　　　　IV, iv, 37

A forted residence 'gainst the tooth of
　time
And razure of oblivion.　V, i, 12

　　　Truth is truth
To the end of reckoning.　V, i, 45

Neither maid, widow, nor wife.
　　　　　　　　　　　V, i, 173

They say best men are molded out of
　faults,
And, for the most, become much more
　the better
For being a little bad.　　V, i, 440

What's mine is yours, and what is yours
　is mine.[2]　　　　　　V, i, 539

Horribly stuff'd with epithets of war.
　　Othello [1604–1605], act I, sc. i,
　　　　　　　　　　　　l. 14

A fellow almost damn'd in a fair wife.
　　　　　　　　　　　I, i, 21

The bookish theoric.　　I, i, 24

We cannot all be masters.　I, i, 43

And when he's old, cashier'd.
　　　　　　　　　　　I, i, 48

In following him, I follow but myself.
　　　　　　　　　　　I, i, 58

But I will wear my heart upon my
　sleeve
For daws to peck at.　　I, i, 64

　　An old black ram
Is tupping your white ewe.　I, i, 88

You are one of those that will not
serve God if the devil bid you.
　　　　　　　　　　　I, i, 108

[1] See Congreve, p. 391b, and note.
[2] See Plautus, p. 105a.

Your daughter and the Moor are now
making the beast with two backs.
　　　　　　　　Othello I, i, 117

Keep up your bright swords, for the
　dew will rust them.　I, ii, 59

The wealthy curled darlings of our na-
　tion.　　　　　　　　I, ii, 68

　　The bloody book of law
You shall yourself read in the bitter let-
　ter
After your own sense.　I, iii, 67

　　Rude am I in my speech,
And little bless'd with the soft phrase
　of peace.　　　　　　I, iii, 81

　　Little shall I grace my cause
In speaking for myself. Yet, by your
　gracious patience,
I will a round unvarnish'd tale deliver
Of my whole course of love.
　　　　　　　　　　　I, iii, 88

　　A maiden never bold;
Of spirit so still and quiet, that her mo-
　tion
Blush'd at herself.　　I, iii, 94

Still question'd me the story of my
　life
From year to year, the battles, sieges,
　fortunes
That I have pass'd.　　I, iii, 129

Wherein I spake of most disastrous
　chances,
Of moving accidents by flood and
　field,
Of hair-breadth 'scapes i' the imminent
　deadly breach.　　　I, iii, 134

Hills whose heads touch heaven.
　　　　　　　　　　　I, iii, 141

And of the Cannibals that each other
　eat,
The Anthropophagi, and men whose
　heads
Do grow beneath their shoulders.
　　　　　　　　　　　I, iii, 143

　　My story being done,
She gave me for my pains a world of
　sighs:
She swore, in faith, 'twas strange, 'twas
　passing strange,

'Twas pitiful, 'twas wondrous pitiful:
She wish'd she had not heard it, yet she
    wish'd
That heaven had made her such a man;
    she thank'd me,
And bade me, if I had a friend that
    lov'd her,
I should but teach him how to tell my
    story,
And that would woo her. Upon this
    hint I spake:
She lov'd me for the dangers I had
    pass'd,
And I loved her that she did pity
    them.
This only is the witchcraft I have us'd.
    Othello I, iii, 158

I do perceive here a divided duty.
    I, iii, 181

To mourn a mischief that is past and
    gone
Is the next way to draw new mischief
    on.   *I, iii, 204*

The robb'd that smiles steals something
    from the thief.   *I, iii, 208*

Our bodies are our gardens, to the
which our wills are gardeners.
    I, iii, 324

Put money in thy purse.
    I, iii, 345

The food that to him now is as luscious as locusts, shall be to him shortly
as bitter at coloquintida.   *I, iii, 354*

Framed to make women false.
    I, iii, 404

The enchafed flood.   *II, i, 17*

One that excels the quirks of blazoning
    pens.   *II, i, 63*

    You are pictures out of doors,
Bells in your parlors, wildcats in your
    kitchens,
Saints in your injuries, devils being
    offended,
Players in your housewifery, and house-
    wives in your beds.   *II, i, 109*

For I am nothing if not critical.
    II, i, 119

I am not merry, but I do beguile
The thing I am, by seeming otherwisc.
    Othello II, i, 122

She that was ever fair and never
    proud,
Had tongue at will and yet was never
    loud.   *II, i, 148*

Iago: To suckle fools and chronicle
    small beer.[1]
Desdemona: O most lame and impo-
    tent conclusion!   *II, i, 160*

You may relish him more in the soldier than in the scholar.   *II, i, 165*

    If it were now to die,
'Twere now to be most happy.
    II, i, 192
Base men being in love have then a
nobility in their natures more than is
native to them.   *II, i, 218*

Egregiously an ass.   *II, i, 321*

I have very poor and unhappy brains
for drinking.   *II, iii, 34*

Potations pottle deep.   *II, iii, 57*

Well, God's above all; and there be
souls must be saved, and there be souls
must not be saved.   *II, iii, 106*

Silence that dreadful bell! it frights the
    isle
From her propriety.   *II, iii, 177*

But men are men; the best sometimes
    forget.   *II, iii, 243*

Thy honesty and love doth mince this
    matter.[2]   *II, iii, 249*

Reputation, reputation, reputation!
O! I have lost my reputation. I have
lost the immortal part of myself, and
what remains is bestial.   *II, iii, 264*

Reputation is an idle and most false
imposition; oft got without merit, and
lost without deserving.   *II, iii, 270*

O thou invisible spirit of wine! if
thou hast no name to be known by, let
us call thee devil!   *II, iii, 285*

[1] See *King Henry VI, pt. II, IV, ii, 75,* p. 215a.
[2] See Cervantes, p. 193b.

O God! that men should put an enemy in their mouths to steal away their brains; that we should, with joy, pleasance, revel, and applause, transform ourselves into beasts.

Othello II, iii, 293

Good wine is a good familiar creature if it be well used. *II, iii, 315*

Play the villain. *II, iii, 345*

How poor are they that have not patience!

What wound did ever heal but by degrees? *II, iii, 379*

Excellent wretch! Perdition catch my soul
But I do love thee! and when I love thee not,
Chaos is come again.[1] *III, iii, 99*

Men should be what they seem.

III, iii, 126

Speak to me as to thy thinkings,
As thou dost ruminate, and give thy worst of thoughts
The worst of words. *III, iii, 131*

Good name in man and woman, dear my lord,
Is the immediate jewel of their souls:
Who steals my purse steals trash; 'tis something, nothing;
'Twas mine, 'tis his, and has been slave to thousands;
But he that filches from me my good name
Robs me of that which not enriches him,
And makes me poor indeed.

III, iii, 155

O! beware, my lord, of jealousy;
It is the green-ey'd monster which doth mock
The meat it feeds on; that cuckold lives in bliss
Who, certain of his fate, loves not his wronger;
But, O! what damned minutes tells he o'er
Who dotes, yet doubts; suspects, yet soundly loves! *III, iii, 165*

[1] See *Venus and Adonis*, p. 220a.

Poor and content is rich, and rich enough. *Othello III, iii, 172*

Think'st thou I'd make a life of jealousy,
To follow still the changes of the moon
With fresh suspicions? No; to be once in doubt
Is once to be resolved. *III, iii, 177*

I humbly do beseech you of your pardon
For too much loving you.

III, iii, 212

If I do prove her haggard,
Though that her jesses were my dear heart-strings,
I'd whistle her off and let her down the wind,
To prey at fortune. *III, iii, 260*

I am declin'd
Into the vale of years. *III, iii, 265*

O curse of marriage!
That we can call these delicate creatures ours,
And not their appetites. I had rather be a toad,
And live upon the vapor of a dungeon,
Than keep a corner in the thing I love
For others' uses. *III, iii, 268*

Trifles light as air
Are to the jealous confirmations strong
As proofs of holy writ. *III, iii, 323*

Not poppy, nor mandragora,[1]
Nor all the drowsy syrups of the world,
Shall ever medicine thee to that sweet sleep
Which thou ow'dst yesterday.

III, iii, 331

I swear 'tis better to be much abus'd
Than but to know 't a little.

III, iii, 337

He that is robb'd, not wanting what is stol'n,
Let him not know 't and he's not robb'd at all.[2] *III, iii, 343*

[1] See *Antony and Cleopatra I, v, 4*, p. 287a.
[2] See Publilius Syrus, p. 125a.

O! now, forever
Farewell the tranquil mind; farewell
content!
Farewell the plumed troop and the big
wars
That make ambition virtue! O, farewell!
Farewell the neighing steed, and the
shrill trump,
The spirit-stirring drum, the ear-piercing
fife,
The royal banner, and all quality,
Pride, pomp, and circumstance of glori-
ous war!
And, O you mortal engines, whose rude
throats
The immortal Jove's dread clamors
counterfeit,
Farewell! Othello's occupation's gone!
Othello III, iii, 348

Be sure of it; give me the ocular proof.
III, iii, 361

No hinge nor loop
To hang a doubt on. *III, iii, 366*

On horror's head horrors accumulate.
III, iii, 371

Take note, take note, O world!
To be direct and honest is not safe.
III, iii, 378

But this denoted a foregone conclusion. *III, iii, 429*

Swell, bosom, with thy fraught,
For 'tis of aspics' tongues!
III, iii, 450

Like to the Pontick sea,
Whose icy current and compulsive
course
Ne'er feels retiring ebb, but keeps due
on
To the Propontic and the Hellespont,
Even so my bloody thoughts, with vi-
olent pace,
Shall ne'er look back, ne'er ebb to
humble love,
Till that a capable and wide revenge
Swallow them up. *III, iii, 454*

Our new heraldry is hands not hearts.
III, iv, 48

But jealous souls will not be answer'd
so;
They are not ever jealous for the
cause,
But jealous for they are jealous; 'tis a
monster
Begot upon itself, born on itself.
Othello III, iv, 158

'Tis the strumpet's plague
To beguile many and be beguil'd by
one. *IV, i, 97*

They laugh that win. *IV, i, 123*

My heart is turn'd to stone; I strike
it, and it hurts my hand. O! the world
hath not a sweeter creature; she might
lie by an emperor's side and command
him tasks. *IV, i, 190*

O, she will sing the savageness out of
a bear. *IV, i, 198*

But yet the pity of it, Iago! O! Iago,
the pity of it, Iago! *IV, i, 205*

Is this the noble nature
Whom passion could not shake? whose
solid virtue
The shot of accident nor dart of chance,
Could neither graze nor pierce?
IV, i, 276

I understand a fury in your words,
But not the words. *IV, ii, 31*

Steep'd me in poverty to the very lips.
IV, ii, 49

But, alas! to make me
A fixed figure for the time of scorn
To point his slow and moving finger
at. *IV, ii, 52*

Patience, thou young and rose-lipp'd
cherubin. *IV, ii, 62*

O thou weed!
Who art so lovely fair and smell'st so
sweet
That the sense aches at thee, would
thou hadst ne'er been born.
IV, ii, 66

O heaven! that such companions
thou'dst unfold,
And put in every honest hand a whip

To lash the rascals naked through the world.   *Othello* IV, *ii*, 141

  Unkindness may do much;
And his unkindness may defeat my life,
But never taint my love.   IV, *ii*, 159

The poor soul sat sighing by a sycamore tree,
Sing all a green willow; [1]
Her hand on her bosom, her head on her knee,
Sing willow, willow, willow.
     IV, *iii*, 41

It makes us, or it mars us.   V, *i*, 4

Every way makes my gain.   V, *i*, 14

He hath a daily beauty in his life.
     V, *i*, 19

  This is the night
That either makes me or fordoes me quite.   V, *i*, 128

And smooth as monumental alabaster.
     V, *ii*, 5

Put out the light, and then put out the light:
If I quench thee, thou flaming minister,
I can again thy former light restore,
Should I repent me; but once put out thy light,
Thou cunning'st pattern of excelling nature,
I know not where is that Promethean heat
That can thy light relume.   V, *ii*, 7

It is the very error of the moon;
She comes more near the earth than she was wont,
And makes men mad.   V *ii*, 107

She was as false as water.[2]   V, *ii*, 132

Curse his better angel from his side,
And fall to reprobation.   V, *ii*, 206

Here is my journey's end, here is my butt,
And very sea-mark of my utmost sail.
     V, *ii*, 266

An honorable murderer, if you will;
For naught I did in hate, but all in honor.   *Othello* V, *ii*, 293

I have done the state some service, and they know 't;
No more of that. I pray you, in your letters,
When you shall these unlucky deeds relate,
Speak of me as I am; nothing extenuate,
Nor set down aught in malice: then, must you speak
Of one that lov'd not wisely but too well;
Of one not easily jealous, but, being wrought,
Perplex'd in the extreme; of one whose hand,
Like the base Indian, threw a pearl away
Richer than all his tribe; of one whose subdu'd eyes
Albeit unused to the melting mood,
Drop tears as fast as the Arabian trees
Their med'cinable gum.   V, *ii*, 338

  In Aleppo once,
Where a malignant and a turban'd Turk
Beat a Venetian and traduc'd the state,
I took by the throat the circumcised dog,
And smote him thus.   V, *ii*, 354

  My love's
More richer than my tongue.
  King Lear [1605–1606], *act* I,
    sc. 1, *l.* 79

  Now, our joy,
Although our last, not least.[1]   I, *i*, 84

Nothing will come of nothing.[2]
     I, *i*, 92

  Mend your speech a little,
Lest you may mar your fortunes.
     I, *i*, 96

---

[1] See John Heywood, p. 182a.
[2] See *Troilus and Cressida* III, *ii*, *191*, p. 268b.

[1] See Spenser, p. 201a, and *Julius Caesar* III, *i*, *189*, p. 255a.
[2] See Lucretius, p. 113a.

Lear: So young, and so untender?
Cordelia: So young, my lord, and
　　true.　　　　*King Lear I, i, 108*

Come not between the dragon and his
　　wrath.　　　　*I, i, 124*

Kill thy physician, and the fee bestow
Upon the foul disease.　　*I, i, 166*

　　　I want that glib and oily art,
To speak and purpose not.　*I, i, 227*

A still-soliciting eye.　　*I, i, 234*

Time shall unfold what plighted cun-
　　ning hides;
Who covers faults, at last shame them
　　derides.　　　　*I, i, 282*

　The infirmity of his age.　*I, i, 296*

Who in the lusty stealth of nature
　　take
More composition and fierce quality
Than doth, within a dull, stale, tired
　　bed,
Go to the creating a whole tribe of
　　fops.　　　　*I, ii, 11*

　We have seen the best of our time:
machinations, hollowness, treachery,
and all ruinous disorders, follow us dis-
quietly to our graves.　　*I, ii, 125*

　This is the excellent foppery of the
world, that, when we are sick in fortune — often the surfeit of our own
behavior — we make guilty of our disasters the sun, the moon, and the stars;
as if we were villains by necessity, fools
by heavenly compulsion, knaves,
thieves, and teachers by spherical pre-
dominance, drunkards, liars, and adul-
terers by an enforced obedience of planetary influence.　　　*I, ii, 129*

　Edgar —
　　　[Enter Edgar]
and pat he comes, like the catastrophe
of the old comedy: my cue is villainous
melancholy, with a sigh like Tom o'
Bedlam.　　　　*I, ii, 149*

　That which ordinary men are fit for,
I am qualified in, and the best of me is
diligence.　　　　*I, iv, 36*

　Truth's a dog must to kennel; he
must be whipped out, when Lady the
brach may stand by the fire and stink.
　　　　King Lear I, iv, 125

Have more than thou showest,
Speak less than thou knowest,
Lend less than thou owest.
　　　　I, iv, 132

Ingratitude, thou marble-hearted fiend,
More hideous, when thou show'st thee
　　in a child,
Than the sea-monster.　*I, iv, 283*

How sharper than a serpent's tooth it
　　is
To have a thankless child!
　　　　I, iv, 312

Striving to better, oft we mar what's
　　well.　　　　*I, iv, 371*

　The son and heir of a mongrel
bitch.　　　　*II, ii, 23*

I have seen better faces in my time
Than stands on any shoulder that I see
Before me at this instant.　*II, ii, 99*

A good man's fortune may grow out at
　　heels.　　　　*II, ii, 164*

Fortune, good night, smile once more;
　　turn thy wheel!　　*II, ii, 180*

Hysterica passio! down, thou climbing
　　sorrow!
Thy element's below.　　*II, iv, 57*

That sir which serves and seeks for
　　gain,
　　And follows but for form,
Will pack when it begins to rain,
　　And leave thee in the storm.
　　　　II, iv, 79

Nature in you stands on the very verge
Of her confine.　　　*II, iv, 149*

Necessity's sharp pinch!　*II, iv, 214*

　　　Our basest beggars
Are in the poorest thing superfluous:
Allow not nature more than nature
　　needs,
Man's life is cheap as beast's.
　　　　II, iv, 267

Let not women's weapons, waterdrops,
Stain my man's cheeks!
                King Lear II, iv, 280

I have full cause of weeping, but this
  heart
Shall break into a hundred thousand
  flaws
Or e'er I'll weep. O fool! I shall go
  mad.   *II, iv, 287*

Blow, winds, and crack your cheeks!
  rage! blow!
You cataracts and hurricanoes, spout
Till you have drench'd our steeples,
  drown'd the cocks!
You sulphurous and thought-executing
  fires,
Vaunt-couriers to oak-cleaving thunder-
  bolts,
Singe my white head! And thou, all-
  shaking thunder,
Strike flat the thick rotundity o' the
  world!
Crack nature's molds, all germens spill
  at once
That make ingrateful man!
                       III, ii, 1

I tax not you, you elements, with unkindness.   *III, ii, 16*

A poor, infirm, weak, and despis'd old
  man.   *III, ii, 20*

    There was never yet fair woman but
she made mouths in a glass.
                       III, ii, 35

I will be the pattern of all patience.
                       III, ii, 37

      I am a man
More sinn'd against than sinning.
                       III, ii, 59

The art of our necessities is strange,
That can make vile things precious.
                       III, ii, 70

He that has and a little tiny wit,
  With hey, ho, the wind and the
    rain.
Must make content with his fortunes
  fit,
  Though the rain it raineth every
    day.[1]   *III, ii, 76*

[1] See *Twelfth-Night V, i, 404,* p. 253a.

O! that way madness lies; let me shun
  that.   *King Lear III, iv, 21*

Poor naked wretches, wheresoe'er you
  are,
That bide the pelting of this pitiless
  storm,
How shall your houseless heads and un-
  fed sides,
Your loop'd and window'd raggedness,
  defend you
From seasons such as these?
                       III, iv, 28

      Take physic, pomp;
Expose thyself to feel what wretches
  feel.   *III, iv, 33*

Pillicock sat on Pillicock-hill:
Halloo, halloo, loo, loo!   *III, iv, 75*

      Out-paramoured the Turk.
                       III, iv, 91

    Is man no more than this? Consider
him well. Thou owest the worm no silk,
the beast no hide, the sheep no wool,
the cat no perfume. Ha! here's three
on 's are sophisticated; thou art the
thing itself; unaccommodated man is
no more but such a poor, bare, forked
animal as thou art. Off, off, you
lendings! Come; unbutton here.
                       III, iv, 105

'Tis a naughty night to swim in.
                       III, iv, 113

    The green mantle of the standing
pool.   *III, iv, 137*

But mice and rats and such small deer
Have been Tom's food for seven long
  year.   *III, iv, 142*

The prince of darkness is a gentleman.[1]
                       III, iv, 147

Poor Tom's a-cold.   *III, iv, 151*

Child Rowland to the dark tower came,[2]

[1] The Devil is a gentleman. — SHELLEY, *Peter Bell the Third* [1819], *pt. II, st. 2*
[2] Child Roland to the dark tower came. — SIR WALTER SCOTT, *The Bridal of Triermain* [1813]
    Dauntless the slug-horn to my lips I set,
    And blew. "*Childe Roland to the Dark Tower came.*"
        BROWNING, *Childe Roland to the Dark Tower Came* [1855], *st. 34*

His word was still, Fie, foh, and fum,
I smell the blood of a British man.
   King Lear III, *iv*, 185

He's mad that trusts in the tameness
of a wolf, a horse's health, a boy's love,
or a whore's oath. III, *vi*, 20

 The little dogs and all,
Tray, Blanch, and Sweetheart, see, they
 bark at me. III, *vi*, 65

Is there any cause in nature that
makes these hard hearts? III, *vi*, 81

I am tied to the stake, and I must stand
 the course. III, *vii*, 54

Out, vile jelly! III, *vii*, 83

The lowest and most dejected thing of
 fortune. IV, *i*, 3

 The worst is not,
So long as we can say, "This is the
 worst." IV, *i*, 27

As flies to wanton boys, are we to the
 gods;
They kill us for their sport.
   IV, *i*, 36

You are not worth the dust which the
 rude wind
Blows in your face. IV, *ii*, 30

She that herself will sliver and dis-
 branch
From her material sap, perforce must
 wither
And come to deadly use. IV, *ii*, 34

Wisdom and goodness to the vile seem
 vile;
Filths savor but themselves.
   IV, *ii*, 38

Tigers, not daughters. IV, *ii*, 39

 It is the stars,
The stars above us, govern our conditions. IV, *iii*, 34

Our foster-nurse of nature is repose.
   IV, *iv*, 12

 How fearful
And dizzy 'tis to cast one's eyes so low!
The crows and choughs that wing the
 midway air

Show scarce so gross as beetles; halfway
 down
Hangs one that gathers samphire,
 dreadful trade!
Methinks he seems no bigger than his
 head.
The fishermen that walk upon the
 beach
Appear like mice, and yond tall anchor-
 ing bark
Diminish'd to her cock, her cock a
 buoy
Almost too small for sight. The mur-
 muring surge,
That on the unnumber'd idle pebbles
 chafes,
Cannot be heard so high.
   King Lear IV, *vi*, 12

Nature's above art in that respect.
   IV, *vi*, 87

Ay, every inch a king. IV, *vi*, 110

The wren goes to 't, and the small
 gilded fly
Does lecher in my sight.
Let copulation thrive. IV, *vi*, 115

Give me an ounce of civet, good
apothecary, to sweeten my imagination. IV, *vi*, 133

A man may see how this world goes
with no eyes. Look with thine ears: see
how yond justice rails upon yon simple
thief. Hark, in thine ear: change places;
and, handy-dandy, which is the justice,
which is the thief? IV, *vi*, 154

Through tatter'd clothes small vices do
 appear;
Robes and furr'd gowns hide all. Plate
 sin with gold,
And the strong lance of justice hurtless
 breaks;
Arm it in rags, a pigmy's straw does
 pierce it. IV, *vi*, 169

 Get thee glass eyes;
And, like a scurvy politician, seem
To see the things thou dost not.
   IV, *vi*, 175

When we are born, we cry that we are
 come

To this great stage of fools.
> *King Lear* IV, *vi*, 187

Then, kill, kill, kill, kill, kill, kill!
> IV, *vi*, 192

Mine enemy's dog,
Though he had bit me, should have
stood that night
Against my fire.   IV, *vii*, 36

Thou art a soul in bliss; but I am
bound
Upon a wheel of fire, that mine own
tears
Do scald like molten lead.
> IV, *vii*, 46

I am a very foolish fond old man,
Fourscore and upward, not an hour
more or less;
And, to deal plainly,
I fear I am not in my perfect mind.
> IV, *vii*, 60

Pray you now, forget and forgive.[1]
> IV, *vii*, 84

Men must endure
Their going hence, even as their coming
hither:
Ripeness is all.   V, *ii*, 9

Come, let's away to prison;
We two alone will sing like birds i' the
cage:
When thou dost ask me blessing, I'll
kneel down,
And ask of thee forgiveness: so we'll
live,
And pray, and sing, and tell old tales,
and laugh
At gilded butterflies, and hear poor
rogues
Talk of court news; and we'll talk with
them too,
Who loses and who wins; who's in,
who's out;
And take upon's the mystery of things,
As if we were God's spies: and we'll
wear out,
In a wall'd prison, packs and sets of
great ones

---

[1] All our great fray . . . is forgiven and forgotten between us quite. — HEYWOOD, *Proverbs*
[1546], *pt. II, ch. 3*

That ebb and flow by the moon.
> *King Lear* V, *iii*, 8

Upon such sacrifices, my Cordelia,
The gods themselves throw incense.
> V, *iii*, 20

The gods are just, and of our pleasant
vices
Make instruments to plague us.
> V, *iii*, 172

The wheel is come full circle.
> V, *iii*, 176

Howl, howl, howl, howl! O! you are
men of stones:
Had I your tongues and eyes, I'd use
them so
That heaven's vaults should crack.
She's gone forever.   V, *iii*, 259

Her voice was ever soft,
Gentle, and low, an excellent thing in
woman.   V, *iii*, 274

And my poor fool is hang'd! No, no, no
life!
Why should a dog, a horse, a rat, have
life,
And thou no breath at all? Thou'lt
come no more,
Never, never, never, never, never!
Pray you, undo this button.
> V, *iii*, 307

Vex not his ghost: O! let him pass; he
hates him
That would upon the rack of this tough
world
Stretch him out longer.   V, *iii*, 315

The weight of this sad time we must
obey;
Speak what we feel, not what we ought
to say.
The oldest hath borne most: we that
are young,
Shall never see so much, nor live so
long.   V, *iii*, 325

First Witch: When shall we three
meet again
In thunder, lightning, or in rain?
Second Witch: When the hurlyburly's
done,

When the battle's lost and won.
Macbeth [1605–1606], *act* I,
sc. i, l. 1

Fair is foul, and foul is fair:
Hover through the fog and filthy air.
I, i, 12

Banners flout the sky.   I, ii, 50

A sailor's wife had chestnuts in her
lap,
And munch'd, and munch'd, and
munch'd: "Give me," quoth I:
"Aroint thee, witch!" the rump-fed
ronyon cries.   I, iii, 4

Sleep shall neither night nor day
Hang upon his pent-house lid.
I, iii, 19

Dwindle, peak, and pine.   I, iii, 23

So foul and fair a day I have not seen.
I, iii, 38

If you can look into the seeds of time,
And say which grain will grow and
which will not,
Speak.   I, iii, 58

And to be king
Stands not within the prospect of belief.   I, iii, 73

The earth hath bubbles, as the water
has,
And these are of them.   I, iii, 79

Or have we eaten on the insane root
That takes the reason prisoner?
I, iii, 84

And oftentimes, to win us to our
harm,
The instruments of darkness tell us
truths,
Win us with honest trifles, to betray 's
In deepest consequence.   I, iii, 123

As happy prologues to the swelling act
Of the imperial theme.   I, iii, 128

I am Thane of Cawdor:
If good, why do I yield to that suggestion
Whose horrid image doth unfix my
hair

And make my seated heart knock at my
ribs,
Against the use of nature? Present
fears
Are less than horrible imaginings.
Macbeth I, iii, 134

If chance will have me king, why,
chance may crown me,
Without my stir.   I, iii, 143

Come what come may,
Time and the hour runs through the
roughest day.   I, iii, 146

Nothing in his life
Became him like the leaving it; he died
As one that had been studied in his
death
To throw away the dearest thing he
ow'd,
As 'twere a careless trifle.   I, iv, 7

There's no art
To find the mind's construction in the
face:
He was a gentleman on whom I built
An absolute trust.   I, iv, 11

Glamis thou art, and Cawdor; and shalt
be
What thou art promis'd. Yet do I fear
thy nature;
It is too full o' the milk of human
kindness [1]
To catch the nearest way.   I, v, 16

The raven himself is hoarse
That croaks the fatal entrance of Duncan
Under my battlements. Come, you spirits
That tend on mortal thoughts! unsex
me here,
And fill me from the crown to the toe
top full
Of direst cruelty; make thick my
blood,
Stop up the access and passage to remorse,
That no compunctious visitings of nature

---

[1] The thunder of your words has soured the milk of human kindness in my heart. — RICHARD BRINSLEY SHERIDAN, *The Rivals* [1775], *act* III, sc. iv

Shake my fell purpose, nor keep peace
between
The effect and it! Come to my
woman's breasts,
And take my milk for gall, you murder-
ing ministers.
         Macbeth I, *v*, 38

Nor heaven peep through the blanket
of the dark,
To cry, "Hold, hold!"   I, *v*, 54

Your face, my thane, is as a book where
men
May read strange matters.   I, *v*, 63

     Look like the innocent flower,
But be the serpent under 't.
               I, *v*, 66

Duncan: This castle hath a pleasant
seat; the air
Nimbly and sweetly recommends itself
Unto our gentle senses.
Banquo: This guest of summer,
The temple-haunting martlet, does ap-
prove
By his lov'd mansionry that the
heaven's breath
Smells wooingly here: no jutty, frieze,
Buttress, nor coign of vantage, but this
bird
Hath made his pendent bed and pro-
creant cradle:
Where they most breed and haunt, I
have observed
The air is delicate.   I, *vi*, 1

If it were done when 'tis done, then
'twere well
It were done quickly; if the assassination
Could trammel up the consequence,
and catch
With his surcease success; that but this
blow
Might be the be-all and the end-all
here,
But here, upon this bank and shoal of
time,
We'd jump the life to come.
               I, *vii*, 1

This even-handed justice.   I, *vii*, 10

Besides, this Duncan
Hath borne his faculties so meek, hath
been
So clear in his great office, that his vir-
tues
Will plead like angels trumpet-tongu'd [1]
against
The deep damnation of his taking-off;
And pity, like a naked new-born babe,
Striding the blast, or heaven's cherubin,
hors'd
Upon the sightless couriers of the air,
Shall blow the horrid deed in every
eye,
That tears shall drown the wind. I have
no spur
To prick the sides of my intent, but
only
Vaulting ambition, which o'erleaps it-
self
And falls on the other.
         Macbeth I, *vii*, 16

     I have bought
Golden opinions from all sorts of people.   I, *vii*, 32

Letting "I dare not" wait upon "I
would,"
Like the poor cat i' the adage.[2]
               I, *vii*, 44

I dare do all that may become a man;
Who dares do more is none.   I, *vii*, 46

     Nor time nor place
Did then adhere.   I, *vii*, 51

     I have given suck, and know
How tender 'tis to love the babe that
milks me:
I would, while it was smiling in my
face,
Have pluck'd my nipple from his bone-
less gums,
And dash'd the brains out, had I so
sworn as you
Have done to this.   I, *vii*, 54

Macbeth: If we should fail —
Lady Macbeth: We fail!

[1] And he shall send his angels with a great
sound of a trumpet. — *Matthew 24:31*
[2] See John Heywood, p. 184a, and *Measure
for Measure I, iv, 78*, p. 270a.

But screw your courage to the sticking-place,
And we'll not fail.
Macbeth I, *vii*, 59

Memory, the warder of the brain.
I, *vii*, 65

Away, and mock the time with fairest show:
False face must hide what the false heart doth know. I, *vii*, 81

The moon is down. II, *i*, 2

There's husbandry in heaven;
Their candles are all out. II, *i*, 4

Merciful powers!
Restrain in me the cursed thoughts that nature
Gives way to in repose. II, *i*, 7

Shut up
In measureless content. II, *i*, 16

Is this a dagger which I see before me,
The handle toward my hand? Come, let me clutch thee:
I have thee not, and yet I see thee still.
Art thou not, fatal vision, sensible
To feeling as to sight? or art thou but
A dagger of the mind, a false creation,
Proceeding from the heat-oppressed brain? II, *i*, 33

Now o'er the one half-world
Nature seems dead; and wicked dreams abuse
The curtain'd sleep; witchcraft celebrates
Pale Hecate's offerings. II, *i*, 49

Thou sure and firm-set earth,
Hear not my steps, which way they walk, for fear
The very stones prate of my whereabout.[1] II, *i*, 56

The bell invites me.
Hear it not, Duncan; for it is a knell
That summons thee to heaven or to hell. II, *i*, 62

It was the owl that shriek'd, the fatal bellman,

---

[1] For the stone shall cry out of the wall. — *Habakkuk 2:11*
See *Luke 19:40*, p. 47b.

Which gives the stern'st good-night.
Macbeth II, *ii*, 4

The attempt and not the deed
Confounds us. II, *ii*, 12

Had he not resembled
My father as he slept I had done 't.
II, *ii*, 14

I had most need of blessing, and "Amen"
Stuck in my throat. II, *ii*, 33

Methought I heard a voice cry, "Sleep no more!
Macbeth does murder sleep!" the innocent sleep,
Sleep that knits up the ravel'd sleave of care,
The death of each day's life, sore labor's bath,
Balm of hurt minds, great nature's second course,
Chief nourisher in life's feast.
II, *ii*, 36

Glamis hath murder'd sleep, and therefore Cawdor
Shall sleep no more, Macbeth shall sleep no more! II, *ii*, 43

Infirm of purpose!
Give me the daggers. The sleeping and the dead
Are but as pictures; 'tis the eye of childhood
That fears a painted devil. II, *ii*, 53

Will all great Neptune's ocean wash this blood
Clean from my hand? No, this my hand will rather
The multitudinous seas incarnadine,
Making the green one red.
II, *ii*, 61

The primrose way to the everlasting bonfire.[1] II, *iii*, 22

It [drink] provokes the desire, but it takes away the performance.
II, *iii*, 34

The labor we delight in physics pain.
II, *iii*, 56

---

[1] See **Bion**, p. 104b, and *Hamlet* I, *iii*, 47, p. 258b.

Confusion now hath made his masterpiece!
Most sacrilegious murder hath broke
ope
The Lord's anointed temple, and stole
thence
The life o' the building!
                    Macbeth II, iii, 72

Shake off this downy sleep, death's
counterfeit.[1]   *II, iii,* 83

Had I but died an hour before this
chance
I had liv'd a blessed time; for, from this
instant,
There's nothing serious in mortality,
All is but toys; renown and grace is
dead,
The wine of life is drawn, and the mere
lees
Is left this vault to brag of.
                              II, iii, 98

Who can be wise, amaz'd, temperate
and furious,
Loyal and neutral, in a moment? No
man.   *II, iii,* 115

In the great hand of God I stand, and
thence
Against the undivulg'd pretense I fight
Of treasonous malice.   *II, iii,* 137

To show an unfelt sorrow is an office
Which the false man does easy.
                              II, iii, 143

A falcon, towering in her pride of
place,
Was by a mousing owl hawk'd at and
kill'd.   *II, iv,* 12

I must become a borrower of the night
For a dark hour or twain.   *III, i,* 27

        To be thus is nothing;
But to be safely thus.   *III, i,* 48

Murderer: We are men, my liege.
Macbeth: Ay, in the catalogue ye go
for men.   *III, i,* 91

        I am one, my liege,
Whom the vile blows and buffets of the
world

[1] See Homer, p. 64a, and note.

Have so incens'd that I am reckless
what
I do to spite the world.
                    Macbeth III, i, 108

So weary with disasters, tugg'd with
fortune,
That I would set my life on any
chance,
To mend it or be rid on 't.
                              III, i, 112

    Things without all remedy
Should be without regard: what's done
is done.   *III, ii,* 11

We have scotch'd the snake, not kill'd
it.   *III, ii,* 13

    Duncan is in his grave;
After life's fitful fever he sleeps well;
Treason has done his worst: nor steel,
nor poison,
Malice domestic, foreign levy, nothing
Can touch him further.   *III, ii,* 22

Then be thou jocund. Ere the bat hath
flown
His cloister'd flight, ere, to black Hecate's summons
The shard-borne beetle with his drowsy
hums
Hath rung night's yawning peal, there
shall be done
A deed of dreadful note.   *III, ii,* 40

        Come, seeling night,
Scarf up the tender eye of pitiful day,
And with thy bloody and invisible
hand
Cancel and tear to pieces that great
bond
Which keeps me pale! Light thickens,
and the crow
Makes wing to the rooky wood.
                              III, ii, 46

Now spurs the lated traveler apace
To gain the timely inn.   *III, iii,* 6

But now I am cabin'd, cribb'd, confined, bound in
To saucy doubts and fears.
                              III, iv, 24

Now good digestion wait on appetite,
And health on both!   *III, iv,* 38

Thou canst not say I did it: never shake
Thy gory locks at me.
Macbeth III, *iv,* 50

The air-drawn dagger.   III, *iv,* 62

I drink to the general joy of the whole
table.   III, *iv,* 89

What man dare, I dare:
Approach thou like the rugged Russian
bear,
The arm'd rhinoceros, or the Hyrcan
tiger,
Take any shape but that, and my firm
nerves
Shall never tremble.   III, *iv,* 99

Hence, horrible shadow!
Unreal mockery, hence!   III, *iv,* 106

Stand not upon the order of your
going,
But go at once.   III, *iv,* 119

It will have blood, they say; blood will
have blood:
Stones have been known to move and
trees to speak.   III, *iv,* 122

Macbeth: What is the night?
Lady Macbeth: Almost at odds with
morning, which is which.
     III, *iv,* 126

I am in blood
Stepp'd in so far, that, should I wade
no more,
Returning were as tedious as go o'er.
     III, *iv,* 136

Double, double toil and trouble;
Fire burn and cauldron bubble.
     IV, *i,* 10

Eye of newt, and toe of frog,
Wool of bat, and tongue of dog.
     IV, *i,* 14

Finger of birth-strangled babe,
Ditch-deliver'd by a drab.   IV, *i,* 30

By the pricking of my thumbs,
Something wicked this way comes.
Open, locks,
Whoever knocks!   IV, *i,* 44

How now, you secret, black, and midnight hags!   IV, *i,* 48

A deed without a name.[1]
     Macbeth IV, *i,* 49

Be bloody, bold, and resolute; laugh to
scorn
The power of man, for none of woman
born
Shall harm Macbeth.   IV, *i,* 79

But yet I'll make assurance double
sure,
And take a bond of fate.   IV, *i,* 83

Macbeth shall never vanquish'd be until
Great Birnam wood to high Dunsinane
hill
Shall come against him.[2]   IV, *i,* 92

Show his eyes, and grieve his heart;
Come like shadows, so depart.
     IV, *i,* 110

What! will the line stretch out to the
crack of doom?   IV, *i,* 117

The weird sisters.   IV, *i,* 136

When our actions do not,
Our fears do make us traitors.
     IV, *ii,* 3

He wants the natural touch.
     IV, *ii,* 9

Angels are bright still, though the
brightest fell.   IV, *iii,* 22

Pour the sweet milk of concord into
hell,
Uproar the universal peace, confound
All unity on earth.   IV, *iii,* 98

Give sorrow words; the grief that does
not speak
Whispers the o'er-fraught heart and
bids it break.   IV, *iii,* 209

All my pretty ones?
Did you say all? O hell-kite! All?
What! all my pretty chickens and their
dam
At one fell swoop?   IV, *iii,* 216

Malcolm: Dispute it like a man.
Macbeth: I shall do so;
But I must also feel it as a man:

[1] See Ann Radcliffe, p. 501a.
[2] Till Birnam wood remove to Dunsinane
I cannot taint with fear.
     Macbeth V, *iii,* 2

I cannot but remember such things were

That were most precious to me.
　　　　　　　Macbeth IV, iii, 219

Out, damned spot! out, I say!
　　　　　　　　　　　V, i, 38

Fie, my lord, fie! a soldier, and afeard?　　　　　　V, i, 40

Who would have thought the old man to have had so much blood in him?　　　　　　V, i, 42

The Thane of Fife had a wife: where is she now?　　　　V, i, 46

All the perfumes of Arabia will not sweeten this little hand.　　V, i, 56

Those he commands move only in command,
Nothing in love; now does he feel his title
Hang loose about him, like a giant's robe
Upon a dwarfish thief.　　V, ii, 19

The devil damn thee black, thou cream-fac'd loon
Where gott'st thou that goose look?
　　　　　　　　　　　V, iii, 11

Thou lily-liver'd boy.　　V, iii, 15

I have liv'd long enough: my way of life
Is fall'n into the sere, the yellow leaf; [1]
And that which should accompany old age,
As honor, love, obedience, troops of friends,
I must not look to have; but, in their stead,
Curses, not loud but deep, mouth-honor, breath,
Which the poor heart would fain deny, and dare not.　　V, iii, 22

Macbeth: Canst thou not minister to a mind diseas'd,
Pluck from the memory a rooted sorrow,
Raze out the written troubles of the brain,

[1] See Byron, p. 563a.

And with some sweet oblivious antidote
Cleanse the stuff'd bosom of that perilous stuff
Which weighs upon the heart?
Doctor:　　　　　Therein the patient
Must minister to himself.
Macbeth: Throw physic to the dogs; I'll none of it.
　　　　　　　Macbeth V, iii, 40

I would applaud thee to the very echo,
That should applaud again.　V, iii, 53

Hang out our banners on the outward walls;
The cry is still, "They come"; our castle's strength
Will laugh a siege to scorn.　　V, v, 1

My fell of hair
Would at a dismal treatise rouse and stir
As life were in 't. I have supp'd full with horrors.　　　V, v, 11

She should have died hereafter;
There would have been a time for such a word.
Tomorrow, and tomorrow, and tomorrow,
Creeps in this petty pace from day to day,
To the last syllable of recorded time;
And all our yesterdays have lighted fools
The way to dusty death. Out, out, brief candle!
Life's but a walking shadow, a poor player
That struts and frets his hour upon the stage,
And then is heard no more; it is a tale
Told by an idiot, full of sound and fury,
Signifying nothing.　　　V, v, 17

I 'gin to be aweary of the sun,
And wish the estate o' the world were now undone.　　　　V, v, 49

Blow, wind! come, wrack!
At least we'll die with harness on our back.　　　　　V, v, 51

Why should I play the Roman fool,
and die
On mine own sword?
Macbeth V, *vii*, 30

I bear a charmed life.   V, *vii*, 41

And be these juggling fiends no more
believ'd,
That palter with us in a double sense;
That keep the word of promise to our
ear
And break it to our hope.   V, *vii*, 48

Live to be the show and gaze o' the
time.   V, *vii*, 53

    Lay on, Macduff,
And damn'd be him that first cries,
"Hold, enough!"   V, *vii*, 62

    You shall see in him
The triple pillar of the world trans-
form'd
Into a strumpet's fool.
Antony and Cleopatra [1606–
1607], *act* I, *sc. i, l.* 12

There's beggary in the love that can be
reckon'd.   I, *i*, 15

Let Rome in Tiber melt, and the wide
arch
Of the rang'd empire fall! Here is my
space.
Kingdoms are clay.   I, *i*, 33

In nature's infinite book of secrecy
A little I can read.   I, *ii*, 11

I love long life better than figs.
        I, *ii*, 34

    On the sudden
A Roman thought hath struck him.
        I, *ii*, 90

Eternity was in our lips and eyes,
Bliss in our brows bent.   I, *iii*, 35

O! my oblivion is a very Antony,
And I am all forgotten.   I, *iii*, 90

Give me to drink mandragora.[1] . . .
That I might sleep out this great gap of
time
My Antony is away.   I, *v*, 4

O happy horse, to bear the weight of
Antony!   I, *v*, 21

[1] See *Othello III, iii, 331,* p. 274b.

The demi-Atlas of this earth, the
arm
And burgonet of men.
Antony and Cleopatra I, *v*, 23

Where's my serpent of old Nile?
        I, *v*, 25

A morsel for a monarch.   I, *v*, 31

    My salad days,
When I was green in judgment.
        I, *v*, 73

    We, ignorant of ourselves,
Beg often our own harms, which the
wise powers
Deny us for our good; so find we profit
By losing of our prayers.   II, *i*, 5

    Epicurean cooks
Sharpen with cloyless sauce his appetite.   II, *i*, 24

No worse a husband than the best of
men.   II, *ii*, 135

The barge she sat in, like a burnish'd
throne,
Burn'd on the water; the poop was
beaten gold,
Purple the sails, and so perfumed, that
The winds were love-sick with them;
the oars were silver,
Which to the tune of flutes kept
stroke, and made
The water which they beat to follow
faster,
As amorous of their strokes. For her
own person,
It beggar'd all description.
        II, *ii*, 199

Age cannot wither her, nor custom
stale
Her infinite variety; other women cloy
The appetites they feed, but she makes
hungry
Where most she satisfies; for vilest
things
Become themselves in her, that the
holy priests
Bless her when she is riggish.
        II, *ii*, 243

I have not kept my square; but that to
come

Shall all be done by the rule.
　　　Antony and Cleopatra II, iii, 6

　　Music, moody food
Of us that trade in love.[1]　　*II, v, 1*

Though it be honest, it is never good
To bring bad news.[2]　　*II, v, 85*

Come, thou monarch of the vine,
Plumpy Bacchus, with pink eyne!
　　　　　II, vii, 120

　　Ambition,
The soldier's virtue.　　*III, i, 22*

Celerity is never more admir'd
Than by the negligent.　　*III, vii, 24*

　　We have kiss'd away
Kingdoms and provinces.
　　　　　III, viii, 17

　　He wears the rose
Of youth upon him.　　*III, xi, 20*

　　Men's judgments are
A parcel of their fortunes, and things
　　outward
Do draw the inward quality after
　　them,
To suffer all alike.　　*III, xi, 31*

I found you as a morsel, cold upon
Dead Caesar's Trencher.
　　　　　III, xi, 116

Let's have one other gaudy night.
　　　　　III, xi, 182

Now he'll outstare the lightning. To be
　　furious
Is to be frightened out of fear.
　　　　　III, xi, 194

To business that we love we rise be-
　　time,
And go to 't with delight.
　　　　　IV, iv, 20

O infinite virtue! com'st thou smiling
　　from
The world's great snare uncaught?
　　　　　IV, viii, 17

The shirt of Nessus is upon me.
　　　　　IV, x, 56

Sometimes we see a cloud that's drag-
　　onish;
A vapor sometime like a bear or lion,
A tower'd citadel, a pendant rock,
A forked mountain, or blue promon-
　　tory
With trees upon 't.[1]
　　　Antony and Cleopatra IV, xii, 2

Unarm, Eros; the long day's task is
　　done,
And we must sleep.　　*IV, xii, 35*

　　But I will be
A bridegroom in my death, and run
　　into 't
As to a lover's bed.　　*IV, xii, 99*

　　O sun!
Burn the great sphere thou mov'st in;
　　darkling stand
The varying shore [2] o' the world.
　　　　　IV, xiii, 10

I am dying, Egypt, dying; only
I here importune death awhile, until
Of many thousand kisses the poor last
I lay upon thy lips.　　*IV, xiii, 18*

O! wither'd is the garland of the war,
The soldier's pole is fall'n; young boys
　　and girls
Are level now with men; the odds is
　　gone,
And there is nothing left remarkable
Beneath the visiting moon.
　　　　　IV, xiii, 64

Let's do it after the high Roman fash-
　　ion,
And make death proud to take us.
　　　　　IV, xiii, 87

　　　And it is great
To do that thing that ends all other
　　deeds,
Which shackles accidents, and bolts up
　　change.　　*V, ii, 4*

His legs bestrid the ocean; his rear'd
　　arm
Crested the world; his voice was proper-
　　tied
As all the tuned spheres, and that to
　　friends;

[1] See *Twelfth-Night, I, i, 1,* p. 251a.
[2] See Sophocles, p. 82a, and *King Henry IV,
pt. II, I, i, 100,* p. 241b.

[1] See Aristophanes, p. 91a, and *Hamlet III,
ii, 400,* p. 263b.
[2] In some editions, star.

But when he meant to quail and shake
the orb,
He was as rattling thunder. For his
bounty,
There was no winter in 't, an autumn
'twas
That grew the more by reaping; his de-
lights
Were dolphin-like, they show'd his
back above
The element they liv'd in; in his livery
Walk'd crowns and crownets, realms
and islands were
As plates dropp'd from his pocket.
Antony and Cleopatra V, *ii*, 82

The bright day is done,
And we are for the dark.   V, *ii*, 192

Antony
Shall be brought drunken forth, and I
shall see
Some squeaking Cleopatra boy my
greatness
I' the posture of a whore.   V, *ii*, 217

  A woman is a dish for the gods, if
the devil dress her not.   V, *ii*, 274

I have
Immortal longings in me.   V, *ii*, 282

If thou and nature can so gently part,
The stroke of death is as a lover's
pinch,
Which hurts, and is desir'd.
                         V, *ii*, 296

Dost thou not see my baby at my
breast,
That sucks the nurse asleep?
                         V, *ii*, 311

Now boast thee, death, in thy possession lies
A lass unparallel'd.   V, *ii*, 317

First Guard: . . . Charmian, is this
well done?
Charmian: It is well done, and fitting
for a princess
Descended of so many royal kings.[1]
                         V, *ii*, 327

---

[1] One of the soldiers seeing her, angrily said
unto her: Is that well done Charmian? Very well
said she again, and meet for a princess descended
of so many noble kings. — Sir Thomas North,
Plutarch's "Lives" [1579]

As she would catch another Antony
In her strong toil of grace.
        Antony and Cleopatra V, *ii*, 348

The gods sent not
Corn for the rich men only.
        Coriolanus [1607–1608], *act* I,
                         sc. i, l. 213

They threw their caps
As they would hang them on the horns
o' the moon,
Shouting their emulation.   I, *i*, 218

All the yarn she spun in Ulysses' absence did but fill Ithaca full of moths.
                         I, *iii*, 93

Nature teaches beasts to know their
friends.   II, *i*, 6

A cup of hot wine with not a drop of
allaying Tiber in 't.[1]   II, *i*, 52

My gracious silence, hail!   II, *i*, 194

He himself stuck not to call us the
many-headed multitude.[2]   II, *iii*, 18

Bid them wash their faces,
And keep their teeth clean.
                         II, *iii*, 65

I thank you for your voices, thank you,
Your most sweet voices.   II, *iii*, 179

The mutable, rank-scented many.
                         III, *i*, 65

Hear you this Triton of the minnows?
mark you
His absolute "shall"?   III, *i*, 88

What is the city but the people?[3]
                         III, *i*, 198

His nature is too noble for the world:
He would not flatter Neptune for his
trident,
Or Jove for 's power to thunder. His
heart's his mouth:
What his breast forges, that his tongue
must vent.   III, *i*, 254

The beast
With many heads butts me away.[4]
                         IV, *i*, 1

---

[1] See Lovelace, p. 358b.
[2] See Horace, p. 123a, and note.
[3] See Sophocles, p. 81a.
[4] See Horace, p. 123a, and note.

O! a kiss
Long as my exile, sweet as my revenge! [1]   *Coriolanus V, iii, 44*

Chaste as the icicle
That's curdied by the frost from purest
snow,
And hangs on Dian's temple.
V, iii, 65

He wants nothing of a god but eternity and a heaven to throne in.
V, iv, 25

They'll give him death by inches.
V, iv, 43

If you have writ your annals true, 'tis
there,
That, like an eagle in a dovecote, I
Flutter'd your Volscians in Corioli:
Alone I did it.   *V, v, 114*

Thou hast done a deed whereat valor
will weep.   *V, v, 135*

He shall have a noble memory.
V, v, 155

'Tis not enough to help the feeble up,
But to support him after.
Timon of Athens [1607–1608],
act I, sc. i, l. 108

I call the gods to witness.[2]
I, i, 138

I wonder men dare trust themselves
with men.   *I, ii, 45*

Here's that which is too weak to be a
sinner,
Honest water, which ne'er left man i'
the mire.[3]   *I, ii, 60*

Immortal gods, I crave no pelf;
I pray for no man but myself:
Grant I may never prove so fond,
To trust man on his oath or bond.
I, ii, 64

Men shut their doors against a setting
sun.   *I, ii, 152*

Every man has his fault, and honesty
is his.   *III, i, 30*

Nothing emboldens sin so much as
mercy.
Timon of Athens III, v, 3

You fools of fortune, trencher-friends,
time's flies.   *III, vi, 107*

We have seen better days.   *IV, ii, 27*

O! the fierce wretchedness that glory
brings us.   *IV, ii, 30*

I am Misanthropos, and hate mankind.[1]   *IV, iii, 53*

Life's uncertain voyage.   *V, i, 207*

See, where she comes apparel'd like the
spring.
Pericles [1608–1609], *act I,
sc. i, l. 12*

Few love to hear the sins they love to
act.   *I, i, 92*

The sad companion, dull-eyed melancholy.   *I, ii, 2*

Third Fisherman: . . . Master, I
marvel how the fishes live in the sea.
First Fisherman: Why, as men do a-
land; the great ones eat up the little
ones.[2]   *II, i, 29*

Lest the bargain should catch cold
and starve.
Cymbeline [1609–1610], *act I,
sc. iv, l. 186*

Hath his bellyful of fighting.
II, i, 24

Hark! hark! the lark at heaven's gate
sings,
And Phoebus 'gins arise,[3]
His steeds to water at those springs
On chalic'd flowers that lies;
And winking Mary-buds begin
To ope their golden eyes:
With everything that pretty is,
My lady sweet, arise.   *II, iii, 22*

As chaste as unsunn'd snow.   *II, v, 13*

Some griefs are med'cinable.
III, ii, 33

---

[1] See Byron, p. 560a.
[2] I call heaven and earth to witness. —
Deuteronomy 4:26
[3] Inscribed on the drinking fountain in the
market square of Stratford-on-Avon.

[1] See Molière, p. 361a.
[2] Men lived like fishes; the great ones devoured
the small. — ALGERNON SIDNEY, *Discourses on
Government* [1698], ch. 2, sec. 18
[3] See Lyly, p. 203a.

O! for a horse with wings!
Cymbeline III, ii, 49

The game is up.   *III, iii, 107*

> Slander,
> Whose edge is sharper than the sword, whose tongue
> Outvenoms all the worms of Nile, whose breath
> Rides on the posting winds and doth belie
> All corners of the world.   *III, iv, 35*

I have not slept one wink.[1]
III, iv, 103

> Weariness
> Can snore upon the flint when resty sloth
> Finds the down pillow hard.
> *III, vi, 33*

> An angel! or, if not,
> An earthly paragon!   *III, vi, 42*

> Society is no comfort
> To one not sociable.   *IV, ii, 12*

> I wear not
> My dagger in my mouth.   *IV, ii, 78*

> Fear no more the heat o' the sun,
> Nor the furious winter's rages;
> Thou thy worldly task hast done,
> Home art gone, and ta'en thy wages.
> Golden lads and girls all must,
> As chimney-sweepers, come to dust.
> *IV, ii, 258*

> Quiet consummation have;
> And renowned be thy grave!
> *IV, ii, 280*

Fortune brings in some boats that are not steer'd.   *IV, iii, 46*

> Hang there like fruit, my soul,
> Till the tree die!   *V, v, 264*

From fairest creatures we desire increase,
That thereby beauty's rose might never die.
Sonnets[2] *[published 1609], 1, l. 1*

---

[1] See Cervantes, p. 194a.

[2] The sonnets were written definitely before 1598, according to Meres's *Palladis Tamia*, and according to Leslie Hotson in *Mr. W. H.* [1964]

When forty winters shall besiege thy brow,
And dig deep trenches in thy beauty's field.   *Sonnet 2, l. 1*

Thou art thy mother's glass, and she in thee
Calls back the lovely April of her prime.   *Sonnet 3, l. 9*

Music to hear, why hear'st thou music sadly?
Sweets with sweet war not, joy delights in joy.   *Sonnet 8, l. 1*

> Everything that grows
Holds in perfection but a little moment.   *Sonnet 15, l. 1*

Shall I compare thee to a summer's day?
Thou art more lovely and more temperate:
Rough winds do shake the darling buds of May,
And summer's lease hath all too short a date.   *Sonnet 18, l. 1*

But thy eternal summer shall not fade.
l. 9

The painful warrior famoused for fight,
After a thousand victories, once foil'd,
Is from the books of honor razed quite,
And all the rest forgot for which he toil'd.   *Sonnet 25, l. 9*

When in disgrace with fortune and men's eyes
I all alone beweep my outcast state,
And trouble deaf heaven with my bootless cries.   *Sonnet 29, l. 1*

---

they bear strong evidence of all being written in 1588–1589. They were published [1609] by Thomas Thorpe, who wrote the dedication:

TO THE ONLIE BEGETTER OF
THESE INSUING SONNETS
MR. W. H., ALL HAPPINESSE
AND THAT ETERNITIE
PROMISED
BY
OUR EVER-LIVING POET
WISHETH
THE WELL-WISHING
ADVENTURER IN
SETTING
FORTH
T. T.

Desiring this man's art, and that man's scope,
With what I most enjoy contented least;
Yet in these thoughts myself almost despising,
Haply I think on thee.
                                    Sonnet 29, l. 7

For thy sweet love remember'd such wealth brings
That then I scorn to change my state with kings.   *l. 13*

When to the sessions of sweet silent thought
I summon up remembrance of things past,
I sigh the lack of many a thing I sought,
And with old woes new wail my dear times' waste.   *Sonnet 30, l. 1*

But if the while I think on thee, dear friend,
All losses are restor'd and sorrows end.
                                              l. 13

Full many a glorious morning have I seen.   *Sonnet 33, l. 1*

Roses have thorns, and silver fountains mud;
Clouds and eclipses stain both moon and sun,
And loathsome canker lives in sweetest bud.
All men make faults.
                                    Sonnet 35, l. 2

Be thou the tenth Muse.
                                    Sonnet 38, l. 9

For nimble thought can jump both sea and land.   *Sonnet 44, l. 7*

Against that time when thou shalt strangely pass,
And scarcely greet me with that sun, thine eye,
When love, converted from the thing it was,
Shall reasons find of settled gravity.
                                    Sonnet 49, l. 5

Not marble, nor the gilded monuments

Of princes, shall outlive this powerful rime.   *Sonnet 55, l. i.*

Like as the waves make towards the pebbled shore,
So do our minutes hasten to their end.
                                    Sonnet 60, l. 1

Time doth transfix the flourish set on youth
And delves the parallels in beauty's brow.   *l. 9*

When I have seen by Time's fell hand defac'd
The rich-proud cost of outworn buried age.   *Sonnet 64, l. 1*

When I have seen the hungry ocean gain
Advantage on the kingdom of the shore,
And the firm soil win of the watery main,
Increasing store with loss, and loss with store.   *l. 5*

Tir'd with all these, for restful death I cry.   *Sonnet 66, l. 1*

And art made tongue-tied by authority.
                                              l. 9

And simple truth miscall'd simplicity,
And captive good attending captain ill.
                                              l. 11

No longer mourn for me when I am dead
Than you shall hear the surly sullen bell
Give warning to the world that I am fled
From this vile world, with vilest worms to dwell.   *Sonnet 71, l. 1*

That time of year thou mayst in me behold
When yellow leaves, or none, or few, do hang
Upon those boughs which shake against the cold,[1]
Bare ruin'd choirs, where late the sweet birds sang.   *Sonnet 73, l. 1*

Clean starved for a look.
                                    Sonnet 75, l. 10

[1] See Byron, p. 563a.

Who is it that says most? which can say more

Than this rich praise — that you alone are you?   *Sonnet 84, l. 1*

Farewell! thou art too dear for my possessing,

And like enough thou know'st thy estimate.   *Sonnet 87, l. 1*

In sleep a king, but, waking, no such matter.   *l. 14*

Ah! do not, when my heart hath 'scap'd this sorrow,

Come in the rearward of a conquer'd woe;

Give not a windy night a rainy morrow,

To linger out a purpos'd overthrow.   *Sonnet 90, l. 5*

They that have power to hurt and will do none,

That do not do the thing they most do show,

Who, moving others, are themselves as stone,

Unmoved, cold, and to temptation slow.   *Sonnet 94, l. 1*

They are the lords and owners of their faces,

Others but stewards of their excellence.

The summer's flower is to the summer sweet,

Though to itself it only live and die.   *l. 7*

Lilies that fester smell far worse than weeds.[1]   *l. 14*

The hardest knife ill-used doth lose his edge.   *Sonnet 95, l. 14*

How like a winter hath my absence been.   *Sonnet 97, l. 1*

From you have I been absent in the spring,

---

[1] As in the nature of things, those which most admirably flourish, most swiftly fester or putrefy, as roses, lilies, violets, while others last: so in the lives of men, those that are most blooming, are soonest turned into the opposite. — PLINY [A.D. 23–79], *Natural History, bk. XVI, ch. 15*

When proud-pied April, dress'd in all his trim,

Hath put a spirit of youth in everything.   *Sonnet 98, l. 1*

Sweets grown common lose their dear delight.   *Sonnet 102, l. 12*

To me, fair friend, you never can be old,

For as you were when first your eye I ey'd,

Such seems your beauty still.   *Sonnet 104, l. 1*

When in the chronicle of wasted time
I see descriptions of the fairest wights,
And beauty making beautiful old rime,
In praise of ladies dead and lovely knights,
Then, in the blazon of sweet beauty's best,
Of hand, of foot, of lip, of eye, of brow,
I see their antique pen would have express'd
Even such a beauty as you master now.   *Sonnet 106, l. 1*

Not mine own fears, nor the prophetic soul
Of the wide world dreaming on things to come,
Can yet the lease of my true love control,
Suppos'd as forfeit to a confin'd doom.
The mortal moon hath her eclipse endur'd,
And the sad augurs mock their own presage;
Incertainties now crown themselves assur'd,
And peace proclaims olives of endless age.   *Sonnet 107, l. 1*

O! never say that I was false of heart,
Though absence seem'd my flame to qualify.   *Sonnet 109, l. 1*

That is my home of love: if I have rang'd,
Like him that travels, I return again.   *l. 5*

Alas! 'tis true I have gone here and there,

And made myself a motley to the view,
Gor'd mine own thoughts, sold cheap
   what is most dear,
Made old offenses of affections new.
                 Sonnet 110, l. 1

My nature is subdu'd
To what it works in, like the dyer's
   hand.   *Sonnet 111, l. 6*

Let me not to the marriage of true
   minds
Admit impediments. Love is not love
Which alters when it alteration finds,
Or bends with the remover to remove:
O, no! it is an ever-fixed mark,
That looks on tempests and is never
   shaken;
It is the star to every wandering bark,
Whose worth's unknown, although his
   height be taken.
Love's not Time's fool, though rosy lips
   and cheeks
Within his bending sickle's compass
   come;
Love alters not with his brief hours and
   weeks,
But bears it out even to the edge of
   doom.
If this be error, and upon me prov'd,
I never writ, nor no man ever lov'd.
                     Sonnet 116

What potions have I drunk of Siren
   tears,
Distill'd from limbecks foul as hell
   within.   *Sonnet 119, l. 1*

O benefit of ill!   *l. 9*

And ruin'd love, when it is built anew,
Grows fairer than at first, more strong,
   far greater.   *l. 11*

'Tis better to be vile than vile esteem'd,
When not to be receives reproach of
   being.   *Sonnet 121, l. 1*

The expense of spirit in a waste of
   shame
Is lust in action; and till action, lust
Is perjur'd, murderous, bloody, full of
   blame,
Savage, extreme, rude, cruel, not to
   trust;

Enjoy'd no sooner but despised
   straight;
Past reason hunted; and no sooner
   had,
Past reason hated, as a swallow'd bait,
On purpose laid to make the taker
   mad:
Mad in pursuit, and in possession so;
Had, having, and in quest to have, ex-
   treme;
A bliss in proof — and prov'd, a very
   woe;
Before, a joy propos'd; behind, a
   dream.
All this the world well knows; yet none
   knows well
To shun the heaven that leads men to
   this hell.   *Sonnet 129*

My mistress' eyes are nothing like the
   sun;
Coral is far more red than her lips'
   red:
If snow be white, why then her breasts
   are dun;
If hairs be wires, black wires grow on
   her head.   *Sonnet 130, l. 1*

When my love swears that she is made
   of truth,
I do believe her, though I know she
   lies.   *Sonnet 138, l. 1*

Two loves I have of comfort and despair,
Which like two spirits do suggest me
   still.   *Sonnet 144, l. 1*

Poor soul, the center of my sinful
   earth.   *Sonnet 146, l. 1*

So shalt thou feed on Death, that feeds
   on men,
And Death once dead, there's no more
   dying then.   *l. 13*

Past cure I am, now Reason is past
   care,
And frantic-mad with evermore unrest.
                 Sonnet 147, l. 9

For I have sworn thee fair, and thought
   thee bright,
Who art as black as hell, as dark as
   night.   *l. 13*

You pay a great deal too dear for what's given freely.
The Winter's Tale [1610–1611], act I, sc. i, l. 18

Two lads that thought there was no more behind
But such a day tomorrow as today,
And to be boy eternal.   I, ii, 63

We were as twinn'd lambs that did frisk i' the sun,
And bleat the one at the other: what we chang'd
Was innocence for innocence.
I, ii, 67

Paddling palms and pinching fingers.
I, ii, 116

Affection! thy intention stabs the center:
Thou dost make possible things not so held,
Communicat'st with dreams.
I, ii, 139

He makes a July's day short as December.   I, ii, 169

A sad tale's best for winter.
I have one of sprites and goblins.
II, i, 24

The silence often of pure innocence
Persuades when speaking fails.
II, ii, 41

It is a heretic that makes the fire,
Not she which burns in 't.
II, iii, 115

I am a feather for each wind that blows.   II, iii, 153

What's gone and what's past help
Should be past grief.   III, ii, 223

Exit, pursued by a bear.[1]
III, iii, 57

This is fairy gold, boy, and 'twill prove so.   III, iii, 127

Then comes in the sweet o' the year.
IV, ii, 3

A snapper-up of unconsidered trifles.   IV, ii, 26

---

[1] This is perhaps the most famous stage direction in English.

For the life to come, I sleep out the thought of it.
The Winter's Tale IV, ii, 30

Jog on, jog on, the footpath way,
And merrily hent the stile-a:
A merry heart goes all the day,
Your sad tires in a mile-a.
IV, ii, 133

For you there's rosemary and rue; these keep
Seeming and savor all the winter long.   IV, iii, 74

Daffodils,
That come before the swallow dares, and take
The winds of March with beauty.
IV, iii, 118

What you do
Still betters what is done.
IV, iii, 135

When you do dance, I wish you
A wave o' the sea, that you might ever do
Nothing but that.   IV, iii, 140

Lawn as white as driven snow.
IV, iii, 220

I love a ballad in print, a-life, for then we are sure they are true.
IV, iii, 262

The self-same sun that shines upon his court
Hides not his visage from our cottage, but
Looks on alike.   IV, iii, 457

I'll queen it no inch further,
But milk my ewes and weep.
IV, iii, 462

Prosperity's the very bond of love,
Whose fresh complexion and whose heart together
Affliction alters.   IV, iii, 586

Let me have no lying; it becomes none but tradesmen.   IV, iii, 747

To purge melancholy.
IV, iii, 792

There's time enough for that.
V, iii, 128

He hath no drowning mark upon him; his complexion is perfect gallows.
> *The Tempest* [1611–1612],
> *act I, sc. i, l. 33*

Now would I give a thousand furlongs of sea for an acre of barren ground.   *I, i, 70*

I would fain die a dry death.
> *I, i, 73*

What seest thou else
In the dark backward and abysm of
    time?   *I, ii, 49*

By telling of it,
Made such a sinner of his memory,
To credit his own lie.   *I, ii, 100*

Your tale, sir, would cure deafness.
> *I, ii, 106*

My library
Was dukedom large enough.
> *I, ii, 109*

The very rats
Instinctively have quit it.   *I, ii, 147*

Knowing I lov'd my books, he furnish'd me,
From mine own library with volumes that
I prize above my dukedom.
> *I, ii, 166*

From the still-vexed Bermoothes.
> *I, ii, 229*

I will be correspondent to command,
And do my spiriting gently.
> *I, ii, 297*

You taught me language; and my profit on 't
Is, I know how to curse: the red plague rid you,
For learning me your language!
> *I, ii, 363*

Come unto these yellow sands,
   And then take hands:
Curtsied when you have, and kiss'd —
   The wild waves whist —
Foot it featly here and there.
> *I, ii, 375*

This music crept by me upon the waters,

Allaying both their fury, and my passion,
With its sweet air.
> *The Tempest I, ii, 389*

Full fathom five thy father lies;
   Of his bones are coral made:
Those are pearls that were his eyes:
   Nothing of him that doth fade,
But doth suffer a sea-change
Into something rich and strange.[1]
> *I, ii, 394*

The fringed curtains of thine eye advance.   *I, ii, 405*

Lest too light winning
Make the prize light.   *I, ii, 448*

There's nothing ill can dwell in such a temple:
If the ill spirit have so fair a house,
Good things will strive to dwell with 't.
> *I, ii, 454*

He receives comfort like cold porridge.[2]   *II, i, 10*

I' the commonwealth I would by contraries
Execute all things; for no kind of traffic
Would I admit; no name of magistrate;
Letters should not be known; riches, poverty,
And use of service, none; contract, succession,
Bourn, bound of land, tilth, vineyard, none;
No use of metal, corn, or wine, or oil;
No occupation; all men idle, all;
And women too, but innocent and pure.[3]   *II, i, 154*

---

[1] The last three lines are inscribed on Shelley's gravestone.

[2] See *King John, V, vii, 41*, p. 237b, and William Bradford, p. 319a.

[3] It is a nation, would I answer Plato, that hath no kinde of traffike, no knowledge of Letters, no intelligence of numbers, no name of magistrate, nor of politike superioritie; no use of service, of riches or povertie; no contracts, no successions, no partitions, no occupation but idle; no respect of kindred, but common, no apparel but naturall, no manuring of lands, no use of wine, corne, or mettle. — MONTAIGNE, *Essays, bk. I* [1580], *ch. 30, Of the Canniballes*

What's past is prologue.
>　　　*The Tempest* II, i, 261

Open-eyed Conspiracy
His time doth take.　　　II, i, 309

A very ancient and fish-like smell.
>　　　II, ii, 27

Misery acquaints a man with strange
bedfellows.　　　II, ii, 42

I shall laugh myself to death.
>　　　II, ii, 167

'Ban, 'Ban, Ca — Caliban,
Has a new master — Get a new man.
>　　　II, ii, 197

>　　For several virtues
Have I lik'd several women.
>　　　III, i, 42

Ferdinand: . . . Here's my hand.
Miranda: And mine, with my heart
>　in't.　　　III, i, 89

Moon-calf.　　　III, ii, 25

Thou deboshed fish thou.
>　　　III, ii, 30

Keep a good tongue in your head.
>　　　III, ii, 41

Flout 'em, and scout 'em; and scout
>'em, and flout 'em;
Thought is free.[1]　　　III, ii, 133

He that dies pays all debts.
>　　　III, ii, 143

>　　The isle is full of noises,
Sounds and sweet airs, that give de-
light, and hurt not.
Sometimes a thousand twangling in-
struments
Will hum about mine ears; and some-
times voices,
That, if I then had wak'd after long
sleep,
Will make me sleep again.
>　　　III, ii, 146

>　　A kind
Of excellent dumb discourse.
>　　　III, iii, 38

>　　Do not give dalliance
Too much the rein.　　　IV, i, 51

---

[1] Thought is free. — *Twelfth-Night I, iii, 73*

Our revels now are ended. These our
actors,
As I foretold you, were all spirits and
Are melted into air, into thin air;
And, like the baseless fabric of this vi-
sion,
The cloud-capp'd towers, the gorgeous
palaces,
The solemn temples, the great globe it-
self,
Yea, all which it inherit, shall dissolve;
And, like this insubstantial pageant
faded,
Leave not a rack behind. We are such
stuff
As dreams are made on, and our little
life
Is rounded with a sleep.
>　　　*The Tempest* IV, i, 148

With foreheads villainous low.
>　　　IV, i, 252

>　　I'll break my staff,
Bury it certain fathoms in the earth,
And, deeper than did ever plummet
sound,
I'll drown my book.　　　V, i, 54

Where the bee sucks, there suck I
In a cowslip's bell I lie;
There I couch when owls do cry.
On the bat's back I do fly
After summer merrily:
Merrily, merrily shall I live now
Under the blossom that hangs on the
>bough.　　　V, i, 88

>　　O brave new world,
That has such people in't!
>　　　V, i, 183

Let us not burden our remembrances
With a heaviness that's gone.
>　　　V, i, 199

My ending is despair.
>　　　*Epilogue, l.* 15

>　　No man's pie is freed
From his ambitious finger.
>　　*King Henry VIII* [1] [1613], *act* I,
>　　　*sc. i, l.* 52

The force of his own merit makes his
way.　　　I, i, 64

---

[1] Written by Shakespeare and Fletcher.

Heat not a furnace for your foe so hot
That it do singe yourself.

Henry VIII, I, i, 140

If I chance to talk a little wild, forgive
me;
I had it from my father. *I, iv, 26*

The mirror of all courtesy. *II, i, 53*

Go with me, like good angels, to my
end;
And, as the long divorce of steel falls on
me,
Make of your prayers one sweet sacrifice,
And lift my soul to heaven. *II, i, 75*

This bold bad man. *II, ii, 44*

'Tis better to be lowly born,
And range with humble livers in con-
tent,
Than to be perk'd up in a glist'ring
grief
And wear a golden sorrow.

II, iii, 19

I would not be a queen
For all the world. *II, iii, 45*

Orpheus with his lute made trees,
And the mountain-tops that freeze,
Bow themselves when he did sing.

III, i, 3

Heaven is above all yet; there sits a
judge
That no king can corrupt. *III, i, 99*

'Tis well said again;
And 'tis a kind of good deed to say
well:
And yet words are no deeds.

III, ii, 153

And then to breakfast with
What appetite you have. *III, ii, 203*

I have touch'd the highest point of all
my greatness;
And from that full meridian of my
glory,
I haste now to my setting: I shall fall
Like a bright exhalation in the eve-
ning,
And no man see me more.

III, ii, 224

Press not a falling man too far.[1]

Henry VIII, III, ii, 334

Farewell! a long farewell, to all my
greatness!
This is the state of man: today he puts
forth
The tender leaves of hopes; tomorrow
blossoms,
And bears his blushing honors thick
upon him;
The third day comes a frost, a killing
frost;
And, when he thinks, good easy man,
full surely
His greatness is a-ripening, nips his
root,
And then he falls, as I do. I have ven-
tur'd,
Like little wanton boys that swim on
bladders,
This many summers in a sea of glory,
But far beyond my depth: my high-
blown pride
At length broke under me, and now has
left me,
Weary and old with service, to the
mercy
Of a rude stream, that must forever
hide me.
Vain pomp and glory of this world, I
hate ye:
I feel my heart new open'd. O! how
wretched
Is that poor man that hangs on princes'
favors!
There is, betwixt that smile we would
aspire to,
That sweet aspect of princes, and their
ruin,
More pangs and fears than wars or
women have;
And when he falls, he falls like Luci-
fer,
Never to hope again. *III, ii, 352*

A peace above all earthly dignities,
A still and quiet conscience.

III, ii, 380

A load would sink a navy. *III, ii, 384*

[1] 'Tis a cruelty
To load a falling man.

Henry VIII, V, iii, 76

And sleep in dull cold marble.
Henry VIII, III, ii, 434

Cromwell, I charge thee, fling away
ambition:
By that sin fell the angels.
III, ii, 441

Love thyself last: cherish those hearts
that hate thee;
Corruption wins not more than hon-
esty.
Still in thy right hand carry gentle
peace,
To silence envious tongues: be just, and
fear not.
Let all the ends thou aim'st at be thy
country's,
Thy God's, and truth's; then if thou
fall'st, O Cromwell!
Thou fall'st a blessed martyr!
III, ii, 444

Had I but serv'd my God with half the
zeal [1]
I serv'd my king, he would not in mine
age
Have left me naked to mine enemies.
III, ii, 456

An old man, broken with the storms of
state,
Is come to lay his weary bones among
ye;
Give him a little earth for charity.
IV, ii, 21

He gave his honors to the world again,
His blessed part to heaven, and slept in
peace.   *IV, ii, 29*

So may he rest; his faults lie gently on
him!   *IV, ii, 31*

    He was a man
Of an unbounded stomach.
IV, ii, 33

Men's evil manners live in brass; their
virtues
We write in water.[2]   *IV, ii, 45*

[1] Had I served God as well in every part
As I did serve my king and master still,
My scope had not this season been so short,
Nor would have had the power to do me ill.
    THOMAS CHURCHYARD, *Death of Morton*
                         [1593]
[2] See Sophocles, p. 83a; Sir Thomas More,
p. 178b; Bacon, p. 210a; and Keats, p. 586a.

He was a scholar, and a ripe and good
one;
Exceeding wise, fair-spoken, and persuading;
Lofty and sour to them that lov'd him
not;
But, to those men that sought him
sweet as summer.
Henry VIII, IV, ii, 51

To dance attendance on their lordships'
pleasures.   *V, ii, 30*

Nor shall this peace sleep with her; but
as when
The bird of wonder dies, the maiden
phoenix,
Her ashes new-create another heir
As great in admiration as herself.
V, v, 40

Wherever the bright sun of heaven
shall shine,
His honor and the greatness of his
name
Shall be, and make new nations.
V, v, 51

    Some come to take their ease
And sleep an act or two.
Epilogue, l. 2

Good friend, for Jesus' sake forbear
To dig the dust enclosed here;
Blest be the man that spares these
stones,
And curst be he that moves my bones.
Shakespeare's epitaph

JOHN DAVIES OF HEREFORD
c. 1565 – 1618

Beauty's but skin deep.[1]
*A Select Second Husband for
Sir Thomas Overburie's Wife*
[1616], VI

[1] All the beauty of the world, 'tis but skin
deep. — RALPH VENNING, *Orthodox Paradoxes*
[3d ed., 1650], *The Triumph of Assurance*, p. 41
    Many a dangerous temptation comes to us
in fine gay colors that are but skin-deep. —
MATHEW HENRY [1662–1714], *Commentaries,
Genesis, III*

THOMAS CAMPION
1567–1620

My sweetest Lesbia let us live and
   love,
And though the sager sort our deeds
   reprove,
Let us not weigh them. Heaven's great
   lamps do dive
Into their west, and straight again revive,
But soon as once set is our little light,
Then must we sleep one ever-during
   night.[1]
> *From* Rosseter's *A Book of Airs*
> [1601]. *My Sweetest Lesbia,*
> *st. 1*

Never love unless you can
Bear with all the faults of man.
> *Never Love* [c. 1617], *st. 1*

There is a garden in her face
   Where roses and white lilies grow;
A heavenly paradise is that place
   Wherein all pleasant fruits do flow.
There cherries grow which none may
   buy,
Till "cherry-ripe" themselves do cry.
> *Cherry-Ripe* [2] [c. 1617], *st. 1*

Those cherries fairly do enclose
   Of orient pearl a double row,[3]
Which when her lovely laughter
   shows,
   They look like rosebuds fill'd with
   snow.   *Ib. st. 2*

The summer hath his joys,
   And winter his delights;
Though love and all his pleasures are
   but toys,
   They shorten tedious nights.
> *Winter Nights* [c. 1617], *st. 2*

THOMAS NASHE
1567–1601

Spring, the sweet spring, is the year's
   pleasant king;

Then blooms each thing, then maids
   dance in a ring,
Cold doth not sting, the pretty birds do
   sing.
Cuckoo, jug-jug, pu-we, to-witta-woo!
> *Summer's Last Will and Testa-*
> *ment* [1600]. *Spring, st. 1*

From winter, plague and pestilence,
   good Lord, deliver us!
> *Ib. Autumn, refrain*

Brightness falls from the air;
Queens have died young and fair;
Dust hath closed Helen's eye.
I am sick, I must die.
   Lord, have mercy on us!
> *Ib. Adieu! Farewell Earth's Bliss!*

SIR HENRY WOTTON
1568–1639

Love lodged in a woman's breast
Is but a guest.
> *A Woman's Heart* [1651]

How happy is he born and taught,
   That serveth not another's will;
Whose armour is his honest thought,
   And simple truth his utmost skill!
> *The Character of a Happy Life*
> [1614], *st. 1*

Who God doth late and early pray,
   More of his grace than gifts to send,
And entertains the harmless day
   With a well-chosen book or friend.
> *Ib. st. 5*

Lord of himself, though not of lands;
And having nothing, yet hath all.[1]
> *Ib. st. 6*

You meaner beauties of the night,
   That poorly satisfy our eyes
More by your number than your light;
   You common people of the skies,
   What are you when the sun shall
   rise?
> *On His Mistress, the Queen of*
> *Bohemia,* [2] *st. 1*

---

[1] See Catullus, p. 114b, and note.
[2] "Cherry-ripe" was a familiar street cry of
the time.
   See Herrick, p. 320a.
[3] See Herrick, p. 320a.

[1] See *II Corinthians 6:10,* p. 53b, and Terence, p. 109a.
[2] This was printed with music as early as 1624,
in East's *Sixth Set of Books,* and is found
in many manuscripts.

He first deceased; she for a little tried
To live without him, liked it not, and
died.
> *Upon the Death of Sir Albert
> Morton's Wife* [1651]

Hanging was the worst use a man
could be put to.
> *The Disparity Between Buck-
> ingham and Essex* [1651]

An ambassador is an honest man sent
to lie abroad for the commonwealth.[1]
> *Reliquiae Wottonianae* [1651]

The itch of disputing will prove the
scab of churches.[2]
> *A Panegyric to King Charles* [1651]

SIR JOHN DAVIES
1569–1626

What can we know? or what can we
discern,
When error chokes the windows of the
mind?
> *Nosce Teipsum* [1599], *st. 15*

I know my soul hath power to know all
things,
Yet is she blind and ignorant in all:
I know I'm one of Nature's little
kings,
Yet to the least and vilest things am
thrall.   *Ib. st. 44*

I know my life's a pain, and but a
span; [3]
I know my sense is mock'd in ev'ry
thing:
And to conclude, I know myself a
man,
Which is a proud, and yet a wretched
thing.   *Ib. st. 45*

[1] In a letter to Velserus [1612] Wotton says
that this "merry definition of an ambassador
. . . I had chanced to set down at my friend's,
Mr. Christopher Fleckmore, in his Album."

[2] He directed that the stone over his grave be
inscribed: Hic jacet hujus sententiae primus auc-
tor: DISPUTANDI PRURITUS ECCLESIARUM SCABIES.
Nomen alias quaere [Here lies the author of this
phrase: "The itch for disputing is the sore of
churches." Seek his name elsewhere]. — IZAAK
WALTON, *Life of Wotton* [1651]

[3] See Bacon, p. 210a, and note.

THOMAS HEYWOOD
c. 1570 – 1641

Within the red-leaved table of my
heart.
> *A Woman Killed with Kindness*
> [1607], *act II, sc. 3*

I will walk on eggs.   *Ib. IV, 6*

O God! O God! that it were possible
To undo things done; to call back yesterday! [1]
That Time could turn up his swift
sandy glass,
To untell the days, and to redeem these
hours.   *Ib.*

Pack clouds away, and welcome day,
With night we banish sorrow.
> *Pack Clouds Away* [1630], *st. 1*

I hold he loves me best that calls me
Tom.
> *Hierarchie of the Blessed Angels*
> [1635]

Seven cities warred for Homer being
dead,
Who living had no roof to shroud his
head.[2]   *Ib.*

THOMAS DEKKER
1572–1632

This age thinks better of a gilded fool
Than of a threadbare saint in wisdom's
school.   *Old Fortunatus* [1600]

Honest labor bears a lovely face.
> *Patient Grissell* [1603], *act I, sc. 1*

> The best of men
That e'er wore earth about him, was a
sufferer,
A soft, meek, patient, humble, tranquil spirit,

[1] See Shakespeare, p. 227a.
[2] Seven cities strive for the learned root of
Homer:
> Smyrna, Chios, Colophon, Ithaca, Pylos,
> Argos, Athens.
> UNKNOWN (*Greek Anthology, bk. VI,*
> *epigram 298*)
Seven wealthy towns contend for Homer dead,
Through which the living Homer begged his
bread.
> THOMAS SEWARD [1708–1790], *On Homer*

The first true gentleman that ever breathed.

> *The Honest Whore, pt. I [1604] (in collaboration with* THOMAS MIDDLETON)*, act I, sc. 2*

We are ne'er like angels till our passion dies. *Ib. pt. II [1630], I, 2*

Cast away care, he that loves sorrow
Lengthens not a day, nor can buy to-morrow;
Money is trash, and he that will spend it,
Let him drink merrily, fortune will send it.

> *The Sun's Darling [1656] (in collaboration with* JOHN FORD)

BEN JONSON[1]
1572–1637

As sure as death.

> *Every Man in his Humour [1598], act II, sc. 1*

As he brews, so shall he drink. *Ib.*

It must be done like lightning. *Ib. IV, 5*

Art hath an enemy called Ignorance.

> *Every Man Out of His Humour [1599], act I, sc. 1*

There shall be no love lost. *Ib. II, 1*

True happiness
Consists not in the multitude of friends,
But in the worth and choice.

> *Cynthia's Revels [1600], act III, sc. 2*

Queen and huntress, chaste and fair,
Now the sun is laid to sleep,
Seated in thy silver chair,
State in wonted manner keep:
  Hesperus entreats thy light,
  Goddess, excellently bright.

> *Ib. V, 3*

[1] O rare Ben Jonson! — SIR JOHN YOUNG, *Epitaph.* (Which was done at the charge of Jack Young, who, walking there when the grave was covering, gave the fellow 18 pence to cut it. — JOHN AUBREY [1626–1697], *Brief Lives*)

That old bald cheater, Time.

> *The Poetaster [1601], act I, sc. 1*

Farewell, thou child of my right hand, and joy!
My sin was too much hope of thee, lov'd boy.

> *On My First Son [written c. 1603]; in Epigrams [1616]*

Rest in soft peace, and, ask'd, say here doth lie
Ben Jonson his best piece of poetry:
For whose sake, henceforth, all his vows be such,
As what he loves may never like too much. *Ib.*

Of all wild beasts preserve me from a tyrant; and of all tame, a flatterer.

> *Sejanus [1603], act I*

Calumnies are answered best with silence.

> *Volpone [1606], act II, sc. 2*

Come my Celia, let us prove,
While we can, the sports of love;
Time will not be ours forever,
He at length our good will sever.
Spend not then his gifts in vain;
Suns that set may rise again,
But if once we lose this light,
'Tis with us perpetual night.[1]

> *Song, To Celia [1607]*

Still to be neat, still to be drest,
As you were going to a feast.

> *Epicene; or, The Silent Woman [1609], act I, sc. 1*

Give me a look, give me a face,
That makes simplicity a grace;
Robes loosely flowing, hair as free,
Such sweet neglect more taketh me
Than all the adulteries of art:
They strike mine eyes, but not my heart.[2] *Ib.*

The dignity of truth is lost with much protesting.

> *Catiline's Conspiracy [1611], act III, sc. 2*

[1] See Catullus, p. 114b, and note.
[2] See Herrick, p. 320a.

Truth is the trial of itself
  And needs no other touch,
And purer than the purest gold,
  Refine it ne'er so much.
          On Truth [1616], *st. 1*

Preserving the sweetness of proportion and expressing itself beyond expression.
          The Masque of Hymen [1616]

Underneath this stone doth lie
As much beauty as could die;
Which in life did harbor give
To more virtue than doth live.
          Epitaph on Elizabeth, Lady
          H——, Epigrams [1616]

Follow a shadow, it still flies you;
  Seem to fly it, it will pursue:
So court a mistress, she denies you;
  Let her alone, she will court you.
          The Forest [1616]. *Follow a*
          Shadow, st. 1

Whilst that for which all virtue now is
    sold,
And almost every vice — almighty
    gold.[1]
          Ib. Epistle to Elizabeth,
          Countess of Rutland

God wisheth none should wreck on a
    strange shelf:
To him man's dearer than to himself.
          Ib. To Sir Robert Wroth

Drink to me only with thine eyes,
  And I will pledge with mine;
Or leave a kiss but in the cup
  And I'll not look for wine.[2]
The thirst that from the soul doth rise
  Doth ask a drink divine;
But might I of Jove's nectar sup,
  I would not change for thine.
          Ib. To Celia, st. 1

I sent thee late a rosy wreath,
  Not so much honoring thee
As giving it a hope that there

It could not wither'd be.
But thou thereon didst only breathe,
  And sent'st it back to me;
Since when it grows and smells, I
    swear,
  Not of itself, but thee.
          The Forest. To Celia, st. 2

Reader, look,
Not at his picture, but his book.
          On the portrait of Shakespeare
          prefixed to the First Folio
          [1623]

Soul of the age!
The applause, delight, the wonder of
    our stage!
My Shakespeare, rise; I will not lodge
    thee by
Chaucer or Spenser, or bid Beaumont
    lie
A little further, to make thee a room;
Thou art a monument, without a
    tomb,
And art alive still, while thy book doth
    live,
And we have wits to read, and praise to
    give.[1]
          To the Memory of My Beloved,
          the Author, Mr. William Shake-
          speare [1623]

Marlowe's mighty line.   *Ib.*

And though thou hadst small Latin and
    less Greek.   *Ib.*

Call forth thundering Aeschylus.   *Ib.*

He was not of an age but for all time.[2]
          Ib.

Who casts to write a living line, must
    sweat.   *Ib.*

For a good poet's made, as well as
    born.[3]   *Ib.*

Sweet Swan of Avon!   *Ib.*

Those that merely talk and never
    think,

---

[1] The flattering, mighty, nay, almighty gold.
— WOLCOT, *To Kien Long* [1782–1785], *ode IV*
    See Irving, p. 550b.
[2] Drink to me with your eyes alone. . . . And
if you will, take the cup to your lips and fill
it with kisses, and give it so to me. — PHILO-
STRATUS [C. A.D. 181–250], *letter 24*

[1] See William Basse, p. 319b.
[2] See Robert Whittinton, p. 179a.
[3] See Florus, p. 109b.

That live in the wild anarchy of drink.[1]
Underwoods [1640]. *An Epistle,*
answering to One that asked to
be sealed of the Tribe of Ben

In small proportions we just beauties
see,
And in short measures life may perfect
be.

> *Ib. To the Immortal Memory of*
> *Sir Lucius Cary and Sir Henry*
> *Morison*

The players have often mentioned it
as an honor to Shakespeare that in his
writing (whatsoever he penned) he
never blotted out a line. My answer
hath been, "Would he had blotted a
thousand."

> *Timber; or, Discoveries Made*
> *Upon Men and Matter* [1640]

I loved the man [Shakespeare] and
do honor his memory, on this side idolatry, as much as any.   *Ib.*

Greatness of name in the father oft-
times overwhelms the son; they stand
too near one another. The shadow kills
the growth: so much, that we see the
grandchild come more and oftener to
be heir of the first.   *Ib.*

Though the most be players, some
must be spectators.   *Ib.*

Talking and eloquence are not the
same: to speak, and to speak well, are
two things. A fool may talk, but a wise
man speaks.   *Ib.*

JOHN DONNE[2]
1572–1631

I wonder by my troth, what thou,
and I
Did, till we lov'd? were we not wean'd
till then?
But suck'd on country pleasures, childishly?

---

[1] See Dryden, p. 368b.
> They never taste who always drink;
> They always talk who never think.
> MATTHEW PRIOR [1664–1721], *Upon a*
> *Passage in the Scaligerana*
[2] See Izaak Walton, p. 325b, and Carew, p.
326b.

Or snorted we in the seven sleepers'
den?

> *The Good Morrow, st.* 1 [1]

And now good morrow to our waking
souls,
Which watch not one another out of
fear;
For love, all love of other sights controls,
And makes one little room, an everywhere.
Let sea-discoverers to new worlds have
gone,
Let maps to other, worlds on worlds
have shown,
Let us possess one world, each hath
one, and is one.   *Ib. st.* 2

My face in thine eye, thine in mine
appears,
And true plain hearts do in the faces
rest,
Where can we find two better hemi-
spheres
Without sharp North, without declin-
ing West?   *Ib. st.* 3

Go, and catch a falling star,
  Get with child a mandrake root,
Tell me, where all past years are,
  Or who cleft the Devil's foot.
Teach me to hear mermaids singing.[2]

> *Song, st.* 1

> And swear
> No where
Lives a woman true, and fair.

> *Ib. st.* 2

Though she were true, when you met
her,
And last, till you write your letter,
  Yet she
  Will be
False, ere I come, to two, or three.

> *Ib. st.* 3

---

[1] Quotations through *Farewell to Love* (p.
307a) are from *Songs and Sonnets*, composed
c. 1590–1601, published posthumously.
The *Songs and Sonnets* were written by
Donne before the turn of the century, according
to Ben Jonson "ere he was twenty-five years
old," but there is no evidence to show the exact
date of their composition. — JOHN HAYWARD,
John Donne, Complete Poetry and Selected Prose
[1936]
[2] See T. S. Eliot, p. 1001a.

I have done one braver thing
   Than all the Worthies did;
And yet a braver thence doth spring,
   Which is, to keep that hid.
      The Undertaking, st. 1

But he who loveliness within
   Hath found, all outward loathes,
For he who color loves, and skin,
   Loves but their oldest clothes.
      Ib. st. 4

And dare love that, and say so too,
And forget the He and She.   *Ib. st. 5*

    Busy old fool, unruly Sun,
     Why dost thou thus,
Through windows, and through curtains call on us?
Must to thy motions lovers' seasons
   run?   *The Sun Rising, st. 1*

Love, all alike, no season knows, nor
   clime,
Nor hours, days, months, which are the
   rags of time.   *Ib.*

She is all states, and all princes, I,
Nothing else is.   *Ib. st. 3*

For God sake hold your tongue, and let
me love.
      The Canonization, st. 1

The Phoenix riddle hath more wit
By us, we two being one, are it.
So to one neutral thing both sexes fit,
We die and rise the same, and prove
Mysterious by this love.   *Ib. st. 3*

As well a well-wrought urn becomes
The greatest ashes, as half-acre tombs.
      Ib. st. 4

I am two fools, I know,
For loving, and for saying so
In whining poetry.
      The Triple Fool, st. 1

Who are a little wise, the best fools
   be.   *Ib. st. 2*

Sweetest love, I do not go,
   For weariness of thee,
Nor in hope the world can show
   A fitter love for me;
     But since that I

Must die at last, 'tis best,
To use my self in jest
   Thus by feign'd deaths to die.
      Song, st. 1

Yesternight the sun went hence,
And yet is here today.   *Ib. st. 2*

But think that we
Are but turn'd aside to sleep.
      Ib. st. 5

When I died last, and dear, I die
As often as from thee I go.
      The Legacy, st. 1

Oh do not die, for I shall hate
All women so, when thou art gone.
      The Fever, st. 1

Twice or thrice had I loved thee,
Before I knew thy face or name.
      Air and Angels, st. 1

'Tis true, 'tis day; what though it be?
O wilt thou therefore rise from me?
Why should we rise, because 'tis light?
Did we lie down, because 'twas night?
Love which in spite of darkness brought
   us hether
Should in despite of light keep us together.
      Break of Day, st. 1

All Kings, and all their favorites,
All glory of honors, beauties, wits,
The sun itself, which makes times, as
   they pass,
Is elder by a year, now, than it was
When thou and I first one another
   saw:
All other things, to their destruction
   draw,
Only our love hath no decay;
This, no tomorrow hath, nor yesterday,
Running, it never runs from us away,
But truly keeps his first, last, everlasting
   day.
      The Anniversary, st. 1

Send home my long strayed eyes to
   me,
Which (Oh) too long have dwelt on
   thee.   *The Message, st. 1*

'Tis the year's midnight, and it is the day's.
> *A Nocturnal Upon St. Lucy's Day, being the shortest day,* st. 1

The world's whole sap is sunk:
The general balm th' hydroptic earth hath drunk,
Whither, as to the bed's-feet, life is shrunk,
Dead and enterr'd; yet all these seem to laugh,
Compared with me, who am their epitaph.   *Ib.*

For I am every dead thing,
In whom love wrought new alchemy.
For his art did express
A quintessence even from nothingness,
From dull privations, and lean emptiness
He ruin'd me, and I am re-begot
Of absence, darkness, death; things which are not.   *Ib. st.* 2

Come live with me, and be my love,
And we will some new pleasures prove
Of golden sands, and crystal brooks,
With silken lines, and silver hooks.
> *The Bait,*[1] st. 1

Dull sublunary lovers' love
    (Whose soul is sense) cannot admit
Absence, because it doth remove
    Those things which elemented it.
> *A Valediction Forbidding Mourning,* st. 4

Our two souls therefore which are one,[2]
    Though I must go, endure not yet
A breach, but an expansion,
    Like gold to airy thinness beat.
> *Ib. st.* 6

If they be two, they are two so
    As stiff twin compasses are two,
Thy soul the fixt foot, makes no show
To move, but doth, if the other do.
> *Ib. st.* 7

---

[1] Included by Izaak Walton in *The Compleat Angler* [1653], *ch.* 9, as "made by Dr. Donne, and made to shew the world that he could make soft verses, when he thought them fit and worth his labor."
See Marlowe, p. 212a, and Ralegh, p. 198b.
[2] See Aristotle, p. 97a.

Our eye-beams twisted, and did thread
    Our eyes, upon one double string;
So to entergraft our hands, as yet
    Was all the means to make us one,
And pictures in our eyes to get
    Was all our propagation.
> *The Extasy, l.* 7

That subtle knot, which makes us man.   *Ib. l.* 64

Else a great Prince in prison lies.
> *Ib. l.* 68

Love's mysteries in souls do grow,
    But yet the body is his book.
> *Ib. l.* 71

I long to talk with some old lover's ghost,
Who died before the god of love was born.   *Love's Deity, st.* 1

To rage, to lust, to write to, to commend,
All is the purlieu of the god of love.
> *Ib. st.* 3

Who ever comes to shroud me, do not harm
    Nor question much
That subtle wreath of hair, which crowns my arm;
The mystery, the sign you must not touch,
    For 'tis my outward soul,
Viceroy to that, which then to heaven being gone,
    Will leave this to control,
And keep these limbs, her provinces, from dissolution.
> *The Funeral, st.* 1

A bracelet of bright hair about the bone.   *The Relic, st.* 1

Take heed of loving me.
> *The Prohibition, st.* 1

So, so, break off this last lamenting kiss,
Which sucks two souls, and vapors both away.
> *The Expiration, st.* 1

Ah cannot we
As well as cocks and lions jocund be,

After such pleasures? [1]
>*Farewell to Love, st. 3*

Love built on beauty, soon as beauty,
dies.
>*Elegy II, The Anagram, l. 27*

Nature's lay idiot, I taught thee to
love.
>*Elegy VII, Nature's Lay
Idiot, l. 1*

The Alphabet
Of flowers.   *Ib. l. 9*

She, and comparisons are odious.[2]
>*Elegy VIII, The Comparison,
l. 54*

Sir, more than kisses, letters mingle
souls;
For, thus friends absent speak.
>*Verse Letter to Sir Henry
Wotton, l. 1*

John Donne, Anne Donne, Un-done.
>*Letter to His Wife* [1602]

No spring, nor summer beauty hath
such grace,
As I have seen in one autumnal face.
>*Elegy IX, The Autumnal, l. 1*

The heavens rejoice in motion, why
should I
Abjure my so much lov'd variety.
>*Elegy XVII, Variety, l. 1*

Who ever loves, if he do not propose
The right true end of love, he's one
that goes
To sea for nothing but to make him
sick.
>*Elegy XVIII, Love's
Progress, l. 1*

The Sestos and Abydos of her breasts
Not of two lovers, but two loves the
nests.   *Ib. l. 61*

Those set our hairs, but these our flesh
upright.
>*Elegy XIX, To His Mistress
Going to Bed, l. 24*

O my America! my new-found land.
>*Ib. l. 27*

Full nakedness! All joys are due to
thee,

As souls unbodied, bodies unclothed
must be,
To taste whole joys.
>*Elegy XIX, To His Mistress
Going to Bed l. 33*

And new philosophy calls all in doubt,
The element of fire is quite put out;
The sun is lost, and the earth, and no
man's wit
Can well direct him where to look for
it.
And freely men confess that this
world's spent,
When in the planets, and the firma-
ment
They seek so many new; then see that
this
Is crumbled out again to his atomies.
'Tis all in pieces, all coherence gone;
All just supply, and all relation:
Prince, subject, Father, Son, are things
forgot.
>*An Anatomy of the World. The
First Anniversary of the Death of
Mistress Elizabeth Drury* [1611],
l. 205

Her pure, and eloquent blood
Spoke in her cheeks, and so distinctly
wrought,
That one might almost say, her body
thought.
>*The Progress of the Soul. The
Second Anniversary of the
Death of Mistress Elizabeth
Drury* [1612], *l. 244*

I am a little world made cunningly
Of elements, and an angelic sprite.
>*Holy Sonnets* [*written after
1610*], *V, l. 1*

At the round earth's imagin'd corners,
blow
Your trumpets, angels, and arise, arise
From death, you numberless infinities
Of souls.   *Ib. VII, l. 1*

All whom war, dearth, age, agues,
tyrannies,
Despair, law, chance, hath slain.
>*Ib. l. 6*

If poisonous minerals, and if that tree,

---

[1] See Gogarty, p. 945a.
[2] See Fortescue, p. 171a.

Whose fruit threw death on else immortal us,
If lecherous goats, if serpents envious
Cannot be damn'd; alas; why should I
be?   *Holy Sonnets IX, l. 1*

Death be not proud, though some have
called thee
Mighty and dreadful, for thou art not
so,
For those whom thou think'st thou
dost overthrow,
Die not, poor death, nor yet canst thou
kill me.   *Ib. X, l. 1*

Thou art slave to fate, chance, kings,
and desperate men.   *Ib. l. 9*

One short sleep past, we wake eternally,
And death shall be no more; death,
thou shalt die.   *Ib. l. 13*

What if this present were the world's
last night?   *Ib. XIII, l. 1*

Batter my heart, three-person'd God;
for you
As yet but knock, breathe, shine, and
seek to mend.   *Ib. XIV, l. 1*

Show me, dear Christ, Thy spouse, so
bright and clear.
       Ib. XVIII, l. 1

Since I am coming to that holy room,
Where, with thy choir of saints forever-
more,
I shall be made thy music; as I come
I tune the instrument here at the door,
And what I must do then, think here
before.
       *Hymn to God My God, in My
Sickness [written after 1610],
st. 1*

Whilst my physicians by their love are
grown
Cosmographers, and I their map, who
lie
Flat on this bed.   *Ib. st. 2*

I observe the physician with the same
diligence as he the disease.
       Devotions [written 1623], VI

I do nothing upon myself, and yet
am mine own executioner.
       Devotions XII

The flea, though he kill none, he
does all the harm he can.   *Ib.*

No man is an island, entire of itself;
every man is a piece of the continent,[1] a
part of the main; if a clod be washed
away by the sea, Europe is the less, as
well as if a promontory were, as well as
if a manor of thy friends or of thine
own were; any man's death diminishes
me, because I am involved in mankind;
and therefore never send to know for
whom the bell tolls; it tolls for thee.
       Ib. XVII

Now God comes to thee, not as in
the dawning of the day, not as in the
bud of the spring, but as the sun at
noon to illustrate all shadows, as the
sheaves in harvest, to fill all penuries,
all occasions invite his mercies, and all
times are his seasons.
       Sermon III [1625]

Poor intricated soul! Riddling, perplexed, labyrinthical soul!
       Sermon XLVIII [1628/9]

And what is so intricate, so entangling as death? Who ever got out of a
winding sheet?   *Sermon LIV [1628]*

What gnashing is not a comfort,
what gnawing of the worm is not a tickling, what torment is not a marriage
bed to this damnation, to be secluded
eternally, eternally, eternally from the
sight of God?
       Sermon LXXVI [after 1622]

I throw myself down in my chamber,
and I call in and invite God and his
angels thither, and when they are there,
I neglect God and his angels, for the
noise of a fly, for the rattling of a
coach, for the whining of a door.
       *Sermon LXXX, At the Funeral
of Sir William Cokayne [1626]*

When my mouth shall be filled with

[1] See Bacon, p. 208b.

dust, and the worm shall feed, and feed sweetly upon me, when the ambitious man shall have no satisfaction if the poorest alive tread upon him, nor the poorest receive any contentment in being made equal to princes, for they shall be equal but in dust.

Death's Duel (last sermon) [1]
[1630]

RICHARD BARNFIELD
1574–1627

The waters were his winding sheet, the
   sea was made for his tomb;
Yet for his fame the ocean sea, was not
   sufficient room.

Epitaph on Hawkins [1595]

As it fell upon a day
In the merry month of May,
Sitting in a pleasant shade
Which a grove of myrtles made.

Poems: In Divers Humours
[1598], *Ode*

King Pandion he is dead,
All thy friends are lapp'd in lead.

Ib.

Every one that flatters thee
Is no friend in misery.
Words are easy, like the wind;
Faithful friends are hard to find.
Every man will be thy friend
Whilst thou hast wherewith to spend;
But if store of crowns be scant,
No man will supply thy want.   *Ib.*

He that is thy friend indeed,
He will help thee in thy need.   *Ib.*

If music and sweet poetry agree.
Ib. To His Friend, Mr. R. L.

JOSEPH HALL,
BISHOP OF NORWICH
1574–1656

So little in his purse, so much upon his
   back.

Portrait of a Poor Gallant

---

[1] Called by his Majesty's household the Doctor's Own Funeral Sermon. — *Preface to the first edition* [1632]

'Mongst all these stirs of discontented
   strife,
O, let me lead an academic life;
To know much, and to think for nothing, know
Nothing to have, yet think we have
   enow.

*Discontent of Men with Their
Condition*

Moderation is the silken string running through the pearl chain of all virtues.

*Christian Moderation,
introduction*

Death borders upon our birth, and our cradle stands in the grave.[1]

Epistles. Decade III, epistle 2

There is many a rich stone laid up in the bowels of the earth, many a fair pearl laid up in the bosom of the sea, that never was seen, nor never shall be.[2]

*Contemplations, bk. IV, The
Veil of Moses*

JOHN MARSTON
c. 1575 – c. 1634

Oblivioni sacrum.[3]

Epitaph

HENRY PEACHAM
c. 1576 – c. 1643

Affect not as some do that bookish ambition to be stored with books and have well-furnished libraries, yet keep their heads empty of knowledge; to desire to have many books, and never to use them, is like a child that will have a candle burning by him all the while he is sleeping.

The Compleat Gentleman
[1622]

---

[1] See *The Wisdom of Solomon 5:13*, p. 37a.
They give birth astride a grave, the light gleams an instant, then it's night once more. —
SAMUEL BECKETT, *Waiting for Godot* [1952]
[2] See Thomas Gray, p. 440b.
[3] Sacred to oblivion.

ROBERT BURTON
1577–1640

All my joys to this are folly,
Naught so sweet as melancholy.[1]
Anatomy of Melancholy [2] *[1621–
1651]. The Author's Abstract*

I would help others, out of a fellow-feeling.[3]
Ib. Democritus to the Reader

They lard their lean books with the fat of others' works.[4]   *Ib.*

We can say nothing but what hath been said.[5] Our poets steal from Homer. . . . Our story-dressers do as much; he that comes last is commonly best.   *Ib.*

I say with Didacus Stella, a dwarf standing on the shoulders of a giant may see farther than a giant himself.[6]
Ib.

It is most true, *stylus virum arguit,* — our style bewrays us.[7]   *Ib.*

Old friends become bitter enemies on a sudden for toys and small offenses.[8]
Ib.

Penny wise, pound foolish.   *Ib.*

[1] See Fletcher, p. 313b.
  There's not a string attuned to mirth
  But has its chord in melancholy.
      HOOD [1799–1845], *Ode to Melancholy*
[2] Burton's *Anatomy of Melancholy*, he said, was the only book that ever took him out of bed two hours sooner than he wished to rise. — SAMUEL JOHNSON; from BOSWELL, *Life of Dr. Johnson* [1791]
  If the reader has patience to go through his volumes, he will be more improved for literary conversation than by the perusal of any twenty other works with which I am acquainted. — BYRON [1807], in MOORE'S *Life.*
[3] A fellow-feeling makes one wondrous kind. — GARRICK, *Prologue on Quitting the Stage* [1776]
[4] See Shakespeare, *King Henry IV, pt. I, II, ii, 119,* p. 238b.
[5] See Terence, p. 109a.
[6] See Lucan, p. 134a, and Newton, p. 379b.
[7] Le style c'est l'homme même [The style is the man himself]. — GEORGE-LOUIS LECLERC DE BUFFON, *Discours sur le Style*, on admission to the French Academy [1753]
[8] See Pope, p. 404a.

Women wear the breeches . . . in a word, the world turned upside downward.
Anatomy of Melancholy. Democritus to the Reader

Like Aesop's fox, when he had lost his tail, would have all his fellow foxes cut off theirs.   *Ib.*

All poets are mad.   *Ib.*

Every man hath a good and a bad angel attending on him in particular, all his life long.
Ib. pt. I, sec. 2, member 1, subsec. 2

That which Pythagoras said to his scholars of old, may be forever applied to melancholy men, *A fabis abstinete,* eat no beans.
Ib. member 2, subsec. 1

Cookery is become an art, a noble science; cooks are gentlemen.
Ib. subsec. 2

No rule is so general, which admits not some exception.   *Ib. subsec. 3*

Idleness is an appendix to nobility.
Ib. subsec. 6

Why doth one man's yawning make another yawn?
Ib. member 3, subsec. 2

They do not live but linger.
Ib. subsec. 10

[Desire] is a perpetual rack, or horsemill, according to Austin [St. Augustine], still going round as in a ring.
Ib. subsec. 11

[The rich] are indeed rather possessed by their money than possessors.[1]
Ib. subsec. 12

Were it not that they are loath to lay out money on a rope, they would be hanged forthwith, and sometimes die to save charges.   *Ib.*

A mere madness, to live like a wretch and die rich.   *Ib.*

[1] See Bion, p. 104b.

I may not here omit those two main plagues and common dotages of human kind, wine and women, which have infatuated and besotted myriads of people; they go commonly together.

Anatomy of Melancholy, pt. I, sec. 2, member 3, subsec. 13

All our geese are swans.[1]

Ib. subsec. 14

They are proud in humility; proud in that they are not proud.[2] *Ib.*

We can make majors and officers every year, but not scholars.

Ib. subsec. 15

Hinc quam sic calamus saevior ense, patet. The pen worse than the sword.[3]

Ib. member 4, subsec. 4

See one promontory (said Socrates of old), one mountain, one sea, one river, and see all.[4] *Ib. subsec. 7*

One was never married, and that's his hell; another is, and that's his plague. *Ib.*

Aristotle said melancholy men of all others are most witty.

Ib. sec. 3, member 1, subsec. 3

Seneca thinks the gods are well pleased when they see great men contending with adversity.

Ib. pt. II, sec. 2, member 1, subsec. 1

Machiavel says virtue and riches seldom settle on one man.

Ib. member 2

As he said in Machiavel, *omnes eodem patre nati,* Adam's sons, conceived all and born in sin, etc. "We are by nature all as one, all alike, if you see us naked; let us wear theirs and they our clothes, and what is the difference?"

Anatomy of Melancholy, pt. II, sec. 2, member 2

Who cannot give good counsel? 'Tis cheap, it costs them nothing.

Ib. member 3

Many things happen between the cup and the lip.[1] *Ib.*

All places are distant from heaven alike.[2] *Ib. member 4*

The commonwealth of Venice in their armory have this inscription: "Happy is that city which in time of peace thinks of war." [3]

Ib. member 6

Every man, as the saying is, can tame a shrew but he that hath her. *Ib.*

Tobacco, divine, rare, superexcellent tobacco, which goes far beyond all the panaceas, potable gold, and philosopher's stones, a sovereign remedy to all diseases . . . but as it is commonly abused by most men, which take it as tinkers do ale, 'tis a plague, a mischief, a violent purger of goods, lands, health, hellish, devilish and damned tobacco, the ruin and overthrow of body and soul.

Ib. sec. 4, member 2, subsec. 2

"Let me not live," said Aretine's Antonia, "if I had not rather hear thy discourse than see a play."

Ib. pt. III, sec. 1, member 1, subsec. 1

Birds of a feather will gather together.[4] *Ib. subsec. 2*

---

[1] Every man thinks his own geese swans. — DICKENS, *The Cricket on the Hearth* [1845], *Chirp the Second*

See Matthew Arnold, p. 715a.

[2] See Coleridge, p. 526a.

[3] See Bulwer-Lytton, p. 601b.

Pyrrhus was used to say that Cineas had taken more towns with his words than he with his arms. — PLUTARCH [A.D. 46–120], *Pyrrhus*

[4] See Sir Thomas Browne, p. 330a.

A blade of grass is always a blade of grass, whether in one country or another. — SAMUEL JOHNSON, in MRS. PIOZZI's *Anecdotes of Johnson* [1786]

[1] There is many a slip 'twixt the cup and the lip. — PALLADAS [fl. A.D. 400], *Greek Anthology,* bk. X, epigram 32. A very ancient proverb, sometimes attributed to Homer.

Though men determine, the gods do dispose; and ofttimes many things fall out between the cup and the lip. — ROBERT GREENE, *Perimedes the Blacksmith* [1588]

[2] See Gilbert, p. 192a, and note.

[3] See Vegetius, p. 146b, and note.

[4] See Homer, p. 66b.

Birds of a feather flock together. — GEORGE WITHER, *Abuses* [1613], 72

No cord nor cable can so forcibly draw, or hold so fast, as love can do with a twined thread.[1]
> *Anatomy of Melancholy, pt. III,*
> *sec. 2, member 1, subsec. 2*

To enlarge or illustrate this power and effect of love is to set a candle in the sun.[2]   *Ib.*

[Quoting Seneca] Cornelia kept her in talk till her children came from school, "and these," said she, "are my jewels."   *Ib.*

Diogenes struck the father when the son swore.   *Ib. subsec. 5*

England is a paradise for women and hell for horses; Italy a paradise for horses, hell for women, as the diverb goes.[3]
> *Ib. sec. 3, member 1, subsec. 2*

For "ignorance is the mother of devotion," as all the world knows.   *Ib.*

The fear of some divine and supreme powers keeps men in obedience.[4]
     Ib.

One religion is as true as another.
     Ib.

Be not solitary, be not idle.[5]
> *Last Words*

---

[1] One hair of a woman can draw more than a hundred pair of oxen. — JAMES HOWELL, *Letters* [1621], *bk. II, 4*
She knows her man, and when you rant and swear,
Can draw you to her with a single hair.
     DRYDEN, *Persius* [1693], *satire V, l. 246*
See Pope, p. 404b.

[2] Like his that lights a candle to the sun. — ANDREW FLETCHER [1655–1716], *Letter to Sir Walter Aston*
And hold their farthing candle to the sun. — EDWARD YOUNG, *Satire VII* [1725–1728], *l. 56*
And hold their glimmering tapers to the sun. — GEORGE CRABBE, *The Parish Register* [1807], *pt. I, Introduction*
See Algernon Sidney, p. 362a.

[3] See Florio, p. 201b.

[4] The fear o' hell's a hangman's whip
To haud the wretch in order.
     ROBERT BURNS [1759–1796], *Epistle to*
           a Young Friend

[5] See Johnson, p. 433a.

THOMAS WARD
1577–1639

Where to elect there is but one,
'Tis Hobson's choice — take that or none.[1]
> *England's Reformation* [1630],
> *ch. 4*

WILLIAM HARVEY
1578–1657

I profess both to learn and to teach anatomy, not from books but from dissections; not from positions of philosophers but from the fabric of nature.
> *De Motu Cordis et Sanguinis*
> [1628] [2]

JOHN FLETCHER[3]
1579–1625

Drink today, and drown all sorrow;
You shall perhaps not do't tomorrow.
> *Rollo, Duke of Normandy* [1639]
> (*in collaboration with* JONSON
> *and others*), *act II, sc. 2*

And he that will to bed go sober
Falls with the leaf in October.[4]   *Ib.*

---

[1] Thomas Hobson [1544–1631], of whom Steele wrote in *The Spectator, no. 509* [October 14, 1712]:
Mr. Tobias Hobson, from whom we have the expression . . . was a carrier . . . the first in this Island who let out hackney-horses. He lived in Cambridge, and observing that the scholars rid hard, his manner was to keep a large stable of horses, with boots, bridles, and whips. . . . When a man came for an horse, he was led into the stable, where there was great choice, but he obliged him to take the horse which stood next to the stable-door; so that every customer was alike well served according to his chance, and every horse ridden with the same justice. From whence it became a proverb, when what ought to be your election was forced upon you, to say Hobson's Choice.

[2] *An Anatomical Disquisition on the Motion of the Heart and Blood in Animals,* translated from the Latin by ROBERT WILLIS [1847].

[3] See also BEAUMONT AND FLETCHER, p. 316a.

[4] The following well-known catch, or glee, is formed on this song:
He who goes to bed, and goes to bed sober,
Falls as the leaves do, and dies in October;
But he who goes to bed, and goes to bed mellow,
Lives as he ought to do, and dies an honest fellow.

Three merry boys, and three merry
    boys,
And three merry boys are we.[1]
As ever did sing in a hempen string
Under the gallows tree.
            Rollo, Duke of Normandy,
                act III, sc. 3

O woman, perfect woman! what dis-
    traction
Was meant to mankind when thou
    wast made a devil!
            Monsieur Thomas [1639],
                act III, sc. 1

Man is his own star, and the soul that
    can
Render an honest and a perfect man
Commands all light, all influence, all
    fate.
Nothing to him falls early, or too late.
Our acts our angels are, or good or ill,
Our fatal shadows that walk by us still.
        The Honest Man's Fortune
        [1647] (*in collaboration with
        three other authors*), *epilogue*

    That soul that can
Be honest is the only perfect man.[2]
                Ib.

Weep no more, nor sigh, nor groan,
Sorrow calls no time that's gone;
Violets plucked, the sweetest rain
Makes not fresh nor grow again.[3]
        The Queen of Corinth [1647]
        (*in collaboration with* MASSINGER
        and a third author), *act III, sc. 2*

Of all the paths lead to a woman's
    love
Pity's the straightest.[4]
        The Knight of Malta [1647] (*in
        collaboration with* MASSINGER),
        act I, sc. 1

---

[1] Three merry men be we. — PEELE, *Old
Wives' Tale* [1595]
[2] See Pope, p. 409b.
[3] See *The Friar of Orders Gray*, p. 1085a.
[4] Pity's akin to love. — THOMAS SOUTHERNE,
Oroonoko [1696], *act II, sc. 1*
    For pity melts the mind to love. — DRYDEN,
Alexander's Feast [1697], *l. 96*
    Pity swells the tide of love. — EDWARD YOUNG,
Night Thoughts [1742–1745], *Night III, l. 107*

Go to grass.
        The Little French Lawyer [1647]
        (*in collaboration with* MASSIN-
        GER), *act IV, sc. 7*

There is no jesting with edge tools.
                Ib.

Let's meet, and either do or die.[1]
        The Island Princess [1647],
                act II, sc. 4

Hence, all you vain delights,
As short as are the nights
Wherein you spend your folly!
There's naught in this life sweet
But only melancholy;
O sweetest melancholy!
        Melancholy [2] [*The Nice Valour,*
                1647]

THOMAS MIDDLETON
1580–1627

Better the day, better the deed.[3]
        Michaelmas Term [1607],
                act III, sc. 1

Since the worst comes to the worst.[4]
                Ib. III, 4

What is got over the Devil's back
(that's by knavery), is spent under the
belly (that's by lechery).[5] *Ib. IV, 1*

---

[1] See Burns, p. 496a.
    This expression is a kind of common property,
being the motto, we believe, of a Scottish family.
— SIR WALTER SCOTT [1771–1832], review of
THOMAS CAMPBELL'S *Gertrude of Wyoming,*
where it appears (*pt. III, l. 37*): Tomorrow let
us do or die!
[2] This poem is frequently and with some
likelihood attributed to WILLIAM STRODE [1602–
1645].
    See Robert Burton, p. 310a, and Milton,
p. 334b.
[3] The better the day, the worse deed. —
MATHEW HENRY [1662–1714], *Commentaries,
Genesis, III*
    The better the day the better the deed. —
DICKENS, *Edwin Drood* [1870], *ch. 10*
[4] If the worst comes to the worst. — *Discovery
of the Knights of the Poste* [1597]
[5] What is got over the Devil's back is spent
under the belly. — RABELAIS, *Works, bk. V* [1552],
ch. 11
    Isocrates was in the right to insinuate that
what is got over the Devil's back is spent under
his belly. — LE SAGE, *Gil Blas* [1715–1735],
bk. 8, ch. 9

As true as I live.
> *The Family of Love* [1608],
> act V, sc. 3

Have you summoned your wits from woolgathering? [1] *Ib.* V, 5

By my faith the fool has feathered his nest well. [2]
> *The Roaring Girl* [1611], act I,
> sc. 1

That disease of which all old men sicken — avarice. [3] *Ib.*

Beat all your feathers as flat down as pancakes. *Ib.*

As the case stands.
> *The Old Law* [1656], act II, sc. 1

On his last legs. *Ib.* V, 1

As old Chaucer was wont to say, that broad famous English poet.
> *More Dissemblers Besides
> Women* [1657], act I, sc. 4

'Tis a stinger. [4] *Ib.* III, 2

How many honest words have suffered corruption since Chaucer's days!
> *No Wit, No Help, Like a
> Woman's* [1657], act II, sc. 1

By many a happy accident.
> *Ib.* IV, 1

Anything for a Quiet Life.
> *Title of play* [1662]

This was a good week's labor.
> *Anything for a Quiet Life, act V,
> sc. 3

There's no hate lost between us.
> *The Witch* [written c. 1627],
> act IV, sc. 2

Black spirits and white, red spirits and gray,

---

[1] My understanding has forsook me, and is gone a-woolgathering. — CERVANTES, *Don Quixote,* pt. II [1605–1615], bk. IV, ch. 38

[2] We will feather oure nestes ere tyme may us espie. — *A Merye Enterlude Entitled Respublica* [1553], III, 6

[3] So for a good old-gentlemanly vice
I think I must take up with avarice.
> BYRON, *Don Juan* [1819–1824],
> canto 1, st. 216

[4] He 'as had a stinger. — FLETCHER, *Wit Without Money* [1639], act IV, sc. 1

Mingle, mingle, mingle, you that mingle may. [1]
> *The Witch, act V, sc. 2

MATTHEW ROYDON
c. 1580 – 1622

You knew — who knew not Astrophil?
(That I should live to say I knew,
And have not in possession still!)
Things known permit me to renew;
Of him you know his merit such,
I cannot say, you hear, too much.
> *The Phoenix Nest* [1593]; *An
> Elegy, or Friend's Passion for His
> Astrophil* (on the death of Sir
> Philip Sidney)

A sweet attractive kind of grace,
A full assurance given by looks,
Continual comfort in a face,
The lineaments of Gospel books;
I trow that countenance cannot lie.
Whose thoughts are legible in the eye.
> *Ib.*

Was never eye, did see that face,
Was never ear, did hear that tongue,
Was never mind, did mind his grace,
That ever thought the travel long,
But eyes, and ears, and ev'ry thought,
Were with his sweet perfections caught.
> *Ib.*

JOHN WEBSTER
1580–1625

Is not old wine wholesomest, old pippins toothsomest, old wood burn brightest, old linen wash whitest? Old soldiers, sweethearts, are surest, and old lovers are soundest. [2]
> *Westward Hoe* [1607], *in colla-
> boration with* DEKKER, *act II,
> sc. 2

I saw him now going the way of all flesh. [3] *Ib.*

Call for the robin redbreast and the wren,

---

[1] These lines are introduced into *Macbeth,* act IV, sc. 1. According to Steevens, "the song was, in all probability, a traditional one."

[2] See Bacon, p. 207b.

[3] See Samuel Butler, p. 755b.

Since o'er shady groves they hover,
And with leaves and flowers do cover
The friendless bodies of unburied
   men.
> *The White Devil* [1612], *act* V,
> *sc. 4*

But keep the wolf far thence, that's foe
   to men,
For with his nails he'll dig them up
   again.   *Ib.*

Prosperity doth bewitch men, seeming
   clear;
But seas do laugh, show white, when
   rocks are near.   *Ib.* V, 6

Glories, like glowworms, afar off shine
   bright,
But look'd to near have neither heat
   nor light.
> *Duchess of Malfi* [1623], *act* IV,
> *sc. 2*

Of what is't fools make such vain keep-
   ing?
Sin their conception, their birth, weep-
   ing:
Their life, a general mist of error,
Their death, a hideous storm of terror.
> *Ib.*

I know death hath ten thousand several
   doors
For men to take their exits.[1]   *Ib.*

Heaven-gates are not so highly arch'd
As princes' palaces; they that enter
   there
Must go upon their knees.   *Ib.*

Ferdinand: Cover her face; mine eyes
   dazzle; she died young.
Bosola: I think not so; her infelicity
Seem'd to have years too many.   *Ib.*

Vain the ambition of kings
Who seek by trophies and dead things
To leave a living name behind,

---

[1] Death hath a thousand doors to let out life.
—MASSINGER, *A Very Woman* [1655], *act* V,
sc. 4

  Death hath so many doors to let out life.
— FLETCHER AND MASSINGER, *The Custom of the
Country* [1647], *act* II, *sc. 2*

  The thousand doors that lead to death. —
SIR THOMAS BROWNE, *Religio Medici* [1642],
pt. I, sec. 44

And weave but nets to catch the wind.[1]
> *The Devil's Law Case* [1623],
> *song*

SIR THOMAS OVERBURY
1581–1613

Give me, next good, an understanding
   wife,
By nature wise, not learned much by
   art.   *A Wife* [1614]

  He disdains all things above his
reach, and preferreth all countries before his own.[2]
> *An Affectate Traveller* [1614]

BISHOP RICHARD CORBET
1582–1635

Farewell, rewards and fairies,[3]
Good housewives now may say.
> *Farewell to the Fairies, st. 1*

  Who of late for cleanliness,
Finds sixpence in her shoe?   *Ib.*

Nor too much wealth nor wit come to
   thee,
So much of either may undo thee.
> *To His Son, Vincent Corbet*

PHILIP MASSINGER
1583–1640

  Be wise;
Soar not too high to fall; but stoop to
   rise.[4]
> *Duke of Milan* [1623], *act* I, *sc. 2*

He that would govern others, first
   should be
Master of himself.[5]
> *The Bondman* [1624], *act* I, *sc. 3*

  To be nobly born
Is now a crime.
> *The Roman Actor* [1629], *act* I,
> *sc. 1*

---

[1] Since in a net I seek to hold the wind. —
WYATT, *Sonnet, Whoso List to Hunt* [c. 1557]
[2] See Shakespeare, *As You Like It* IV, i, 35,
p. 250a; Canning, p. 506b; and W.S. Gilbert,
p. 768a.
[3] See Kipling, p. 877a.
[4] See Mather, p. 387a.
[5] See Rabelais, p. 181a, and note.

Whose wealth
Arithmetic cannot number.
The Roman Actor, act I, sc. 3

Grim death.[1]   *Ib. IV, 2*

A New Way to Pay Old Debts.
Title of Play [1632]

JACQUES DU LAURENS
1583–1650

I do not attack fools, but foolishness.   *Satires [1624]*

FRANCIS BEAUMONT[2]
1584–1616

What things have we seen
Done at the Mermaid! heard words
that have been
So nimble, and so full of subtle flame,
As if that everyone from whence they
came,
Had meant to put his whole wit in a
jest,
And resolv'd to live a fool, the rest
Of his dull life.
Letter to Ben Jonson [1640]

BEAUMONT AND FLETCHER[3]
FRANCIS BEAUMONT 1584–1616
JOHN FLETCHER 1579–1625[4]

It is always good
When a man has two irons in the fire.
*The Faithful Friends [c. 1608],
act I, sc. 2*

As cold as cucumbers.
*Cupid's Revenge [1615], act I,
sc. 1*

Kiss till the cow comes home.
*Scornful Lady [1616], act III,
sc. 1*

There is a method in man's wickedness —
It grows up by degrees.[1]
*A King and No King [1619],
act V, sc. 4*

Upon my buried body lie lightly, gentle
earth.[2]
*The Maid's Tragedy [1619],
act I, sc. 2*

The devil take the hindmost!
Philaster [1620], act V

Whistle, and she'll come to you.[3]
*Wit Without Money [1639],
act IV, sc. 4*

Calamity is man's true touchstone.[4]
*Four Plays in One. The Triumph
of Honour [1647], sc. 1*

Though I say it that should not say
it.
*Wit at Several Weapons (probably in collaboration with
WILLIAM ROWLEY [c. 1585–
c. 1642]), act II, sc. 2*

TIRSO DE MOLINA
[FRAY GABRIEL TÉLLEZ]
1584–1648

Through his honor I conquered him.
For these peasants carry their honor in
their hands so that they may constantly
consult it; this same honor that once
felt so much at home in the city but
now has taken refuge in a more rural
setting.
*El Burlador de Sevilla (The
Rogue of Seville) act III,
sc. 3[5]*

---

[1] See Milton, p. 344a.
[2] See also Beaumont and Fletcher below.
[3] Of whose partnership JOHN AUBREY [1626–1697] said, "There was a wonderful consimility of fancy. They lived together not far from the playhouse, had one wench in the house between them, the same clothes and cloak, &c."
[4] Also on p. 312b.

[1] See Juvenal, p. 139a, and Racine, p. 378b.
[2] See Euripides, p. 83b, and note.
[3] Whistle, and I'll come to ye. — ROBERT BURNS [1759–1796], *Whistle, etc.*
[4] See Seneca, p. 130b.
[5] Translated by ROBERT O'BRIEN in *Spanish Drama* [1962]. This is the original Don Juan play.

JOHN SELDEN
1584–1654

Equity is a roguish thing. For Law we have a measure, know what to trust to; Equity is according to the conscience of him that is Chancellor, and as that is larger or narrower, so is Equity. 'Tis all one as if they should make the standard for the measure we call a "foot" a Chancellor's foot; what an uncertain measure would this be! One Chancellor has a long foot, another a short foot, a third an indifferent foot. 'Tis the same thing in the Chancellor's conscience.

       Table Talk [1689]. *Equity*

Humility is a virtue all preach, none practice; and yet everybody is content to hear.   *Ib. Humility*

'Tis not the drinking that is to be blamed, but the excess.   *Ib.*

Commonly we say a judgment falls upon a man for something in him we cannot abide.   *Ib. Judgments*

Ignorance of the law excuses no man; not that all men know the law, but because 'tis an excuse every man will plead, and no man can tell how to refute him.   *Ib. Law*

No man is the wiser for his learning.
       Ib. Learning

Wit and wisdom are born with a man.   *Ib.*

Few men make themselves masters of the things they write or speak.   *Ib.*

Take a straw and throw it up into the air — you may see by that which way the wind is.   *Ib. Libels*

Philosophy is nothing but discretion.   *Ib. Philosophy*

Marriage is a desperate thing.
       Ib. Marriage

Thou little thinkest what a little foolery governs the world.[1]
       Ib. Pope

[1] Behold, my son, with how little wisdom the world is governed. — AXEL OXENSTIERN [1583–1654]

They that govern the most make the least noise.
       Table Talk. Power

Syllables govern the world.   *Ib.*

Never tell your resolution beforehand.   *Ib. Wisdom*

Wise men say nothing in dangerous times.   *Ib.*

Pleasure is nothing else but the intermission of pain.   *Ib. Pleasure*

Preachers say, Do as I say, not as I do.   *Ib. Preaching*

A king is a thing men have made for their own sakes, for quietness' sake. Just as in a family one man is appointed to buy the meat.   *Ib. Of a King*

JOHN FORD
1586–1639

Diamond cut diamond.
       The Lover's Melancholy [1629],
       act I, sc. 1

'Tis Pity She's a Whore.
       Title of Play [1633]

THOMAS RAINBOROUGH
d. 1648

The poorest he that is in England hath a life to live as the greatest he.
       In the Army debates at Putney
       [October 29, 1647]

THOMAS HOBBES
1588–1679

The condition of man . . . is a condition of war of everyone against everyone.
       Leviathan [1651], *pt. I, ch. 4*

Words are wise men's counters, they do but reckon with them, but they are the money of fools.   *Ib.*

The privilege of absurdity; to which no living creature is subject but man only.   *Ib. 5*

Sudden glory is the passion which maketh those grimaces called laughter.
Leviathan, pt. I, ch. 6

The secret thoughts of a man run over all things, holy, profane, clean, obscene, grave, and light, without shame or blame.   *Ib. 8*

[In a state of nature] No arts; no letters; no society; and which is worst of all, continual fear and danger of violent death; and the life of man, solitary, poor, nasty, brutish, and short.
Ib. 13

The Papacy is not other than the Ghost of the deceased Roman Empire, sitting crowned upon the grave thereof.
Ib. pt. IV, ch. 47

The praise of ancient authors proceeds not from the reverence of the dead, but from the competition and mutual envy of the living.
Ib. Review and Conclusion

Such truth as opposeth no man's profit nor pleasure is to all men welcome.   *Ib.*

I am about to take my last voyage, a great leap in the dark.   *Last words*

JOHN WINTHROP
1588–1649

For we must consider that we shall be a city upon a hill.[1] The eyes of all people are upon us, so that if we shall deal falsely with our God in this work we have undertaken, and so cause Him to withdraw His present help from us, we shall be made a story and a byword through the world.
A Model of Christian Charity [1630], a sermon delivered on board the Arbella

GEORGE WITHER
1588–1667

Shall I wasting in despair
Die because a woman's fair?

[1] See *Matthew 5:14*, p. 40a.

Or make pale my cheeks with care
'Cause another's rosy are?
Be she fairer than the day,
Or the flow'ry meads in May,
    If she be not so to me,
    What care I how fair she be?
Fair Virtue [1622]. Sonnet 4, st. 1

If she love me, this believe,
I will die ere she shall grieve;
If she slight me when I woo,
I can scorn and let her go;
    For if she be not for me,
    What care I for whom she be?
Ib. st. 5

'Twas I that beat the bush,
The bird to others flew.
A Love Sonnet [1622], st. 11

Though I am young, I scorn to flit
On the wings of borrowed wit.
The Shepherd's Hunting [1622]

HONORAT DE BUEIL, MARQUIS DE RACAN
1589–1650

Nothing in the world lasts
Save eternal change.[1]
Odes. The Coming of Spring

The good effect of Fortune may be short-lived. To build on it is to build on sand.[2]   *Poésies Diverses*

WILLIAM BRADFORD
1590–1657

They knew they were pilgrims.[3]
Of Plymouth Plantation [1620–1647], ch. 7

So they committed themselves to the will of God and resolved to proceed.
Ib. 9

Being thus arrived in a good harbor, and brought safe to land, they fell upon

[1] Rien au monde ne dure
Qu'un éternel changement.
See Heraclitus, p. 77b, and note.
[2] Le bien de la fortune est un bien périssable: quand on bâtit sur elle, on bâtit sur le sable.
[3] It was owing to this passage, first printed in 1669, that the *Mayflower's* company came eventually to be called the Pilgrim Fathers.

their knees and blessed the God of Heaven who had brought them over the vast and furious ocean, and delivered them from all the perils and miseries thereof, again to set their feet on the firm and stable earth, their proper element.

Of Plymouth Plantation, ch. 9

Our fathers were Englishmen which came over this great ocean, and were ready to perish in this wilderness.

Ib.

The loss of . . . honest and industrious men's lives cannot be valued at any price. *Ib.* 12

But it pleased God to visit us then with death daily, and with so general a disease that the living were scarce able to bury the dead. *Ib.*

Cold comfort to fill their hungry bellies.[1] *Ib.* 13

Behold, now, another providence of God. A ship comes into the harbor.

Ib.

Thus out of small beginnings greater things have been produced by His hand that made all things of nothing,[2] and gives being to all things that are; and, as one small candle may light a thousand, so the light here kindled hath shone unto many, yea in some sort to our whole nation.[3] *Ib.* 21

WILLIAM BASSE
died c. 1653

Renowned Spenser, lie a thought more nigh
To learned Chaucer; and rare Beaumont, lie
A little nearer Spenser; to make room
For Shakespeare in your three-fold fourfold tomb.
To lodge all four in one bed make a shift
Until Doomsday; for hardly will a fift,

[1] See Shakespeare, pp. 237b and 296b.
[2] See Dryden, p. 367a.
[3] See *Matthew 5:15*, p. 40a, and Shakespeare, *Merchant of Venice V, i, 90*, p. 235b.

Betwixt this day and that, by fate be slain,
For whom your curtains may be drawn again.[1]
On Mr. Wm. Shakespeare
[c. 1616]

WILLIAM BROWNE
1591–1643

Underneath this sable hearse
Lies the subject of all verse:
Sidney's sister, Pembroke's mother.
Death, ere thou hast slain another
Fair and learn'd and good as she,
Time shall throw a dart at thee.
Epitaph on the Countess of
Pembroke [1621]

There is no season such delight can bring,
As summer, autumn, winter, and the spring. *Variety*

ROBERT HERRICK
1591–1674

I sing of brooks, of blossoms, birds, and bowers:
Of April, May, of June, and July flowers.
I sing of Maypoles, Hock-carts, wassails, wakes,
Of bridegrooms, brides, and of their bridal cakes.
Hesperides [1648]. Argument of
His Book

What is a kiss? Why this, as some approve:
The sure, sweet cement, glue, and lime of love. *Ib. A Kiss*

Bid me to live, and I will live
Thy Protestant to be,
Or bid me love, and I will give
A loving heart to thee.
Ib. To Anthea

Cherry ripe, ripe, ripe, I cry,
Full and fair ones; come and buy!
If so be you ask me where

[1] See Ben Jonson, p. 303b.

They do grow, I answer, there,
Where my Julia's lips do smile;
There's the land, or cherry-isle.
      Hesperides. Cherry Ripe [1]

It is the end that crowns us, not the
fight.[2]   *Ib. The End*

Some asked how pearls did grow, and
where?
Then spoke I to my girl
To part her lips, and showed them
there
The quarelets of pearl.[3]
      *Ib. The Rock of Rubies, and the
      Quarrie of Pearls*

A sweet disorder in the dress
Kindles in clothes a wantonness.
      Ib. Delight in Disorder

A winning wave, deserving note,
In the tempestuous petticoat,
A careless shoestring, in whose tie
I see a wild civility,
Do more bewitch me than when art
Is too precise in every part.[4]   *Ib.*

You say to me-wards your affection's
strong;
Pray love me little, so you love me
long.[5]
      Ib. Love Me Little, Love Me Long

Night makes no difference 'twixt the
Priest and Clerk;
Joan as my Lady is as good i' the dark.[6]
      Ib. No Difference i' th' Dark

Give me a kiss, and to that kiss a
score;
Then to that twenty, add a hundred
more:
A thousand to that hundred: so kiss
on,[7]
To make that thousand up a million.
Treble that million, and when that is
done,

Let's kiss afresh, as when we first begun.
      *Hesperides. To Anthea: Ah,
      My Anthea!*

Gather ye rosebuds while ye may,
Old Time is still a-flying,
And this same flower that smiles today
Tomorrow will be dying.[1]
      *Ib. To the Virgins to Make
      Much of Time*

Fair daffodils, we weep to see
You haste away so soon.
      Ib. To Daffodils

Her pretty feet, like snails, did creep
A little out, and then,[2]
As if they played at bo-peep,
Did soon draw in again.
      Ib. To Mistress Susanna Southwell

Her eyes the glowworm lend thee,
The shooting stars attend thee;
   And the elves also,
   Whose little eyes glow
Like the sparks of fire, befriend thee.
      Ib. The Night Piece to Julia

Thus times do shift, each thing his turn
does hold;
New things succeed, as former things
grow old.
      Ib. Ceremonies for Candlemas Eve

Made us nobly wild, not mad.
      Ib. Ode for Ben Jonson

Outdid the meat, outdid the frolic
wine.   *Ib.*

Attempt the end, and never stand to
doubt;
Nothing's so hard but search will find it
out.   *Ib. Seek and Find*

Get up, sweet Slug-a-bed, and see
The dew bespangling herb and tree.
      Ib. Corinna's Going a-Maying

   'Tis sin,
Nay, profanation to keep in.   *Ib.*

So when or you or I are made
A fable, song, or fleeting shade,
All love, all liking, all delight

---

[1] See Campion, p. 300a.
[2] See Shakespeare, *Troilus and Cressida IV,*
v, 223, p. 269b, and note.
  See Anonymous, p. 150b.
[3] See Campion, p. 300a.
[4] See Jonson, p. 302b.
[5] See Anonymous, p. 1084b.
[6] See Plutarch, p. 137b.
[7] See Catullus, p. 114b.

[1] See *Wisdom of Solomon,* p. 36b; Horace,
p. 121a; Spenser, p. 200a; and Ronsard, p. 188a.
[2] See Suckling, p. 350b.

Lies drowned with us in endless night.[1]
>　　*Hesperides. Corinna's Going*
>　　　　　　　　*a-Maying*

Whenas in silks my Julia goes,
Then, then (methinks) how sweetly
　flows
That liquefaction of her clothes.
>　　*Ib. Upon Julia's Clothes*

Here a little child I stand
Heaving up my either hand.
Cold as paddocks though they be,
Here I lift them up to Thee,
For a benison to fall
On our meat, and on us all.
>　　*Noble Numbers* [1648]. *A Child's*
>　　　　　　　*Grace*

JULIUS WILHELM ZINCGREF
1591–1635

One who longs for death is miserable, but more miserable is he who fears it.　　*Apophthegmata* [1628], *bk. II*

Laws and police regulations can be compared to a spider's web that lets the big mosquitoes through and catches the small ones.[2]　　　　　　　*Ib.*

HENRY KING, BISHOP OF CHICHESTER
1592–1669

Thou art the book,
The library whereon I look.
>　　　　*The Exequy* [1657]

Then we shall rise
And view ourselves with clearer eyes
In that calm region where no night
Can hide us from each other's sight.
>　　　　　　　　　　*Ib.*

Sleep on, my Love, in thy cold bed,
Never to be disquieted!
My last good-night! Thou wilt not
　wake,
Till I thy fate shall overtake;
Till age, or grief, or sickness, must
Marry my body to that dust
It so much loves, and fill the room

---

[1] See Catullus, p. 114b, and note.
[2] See Solon, p. 68b, and Swift, p. 388b.

My heart keeps empty in thy tomb.
Stay for me there; I will not fail
To meet thee in that hollow vale.
>　　　　　　*The Exequy*

I am content to live
Divided, with but half a heart.　　*Ib.*

FRANCIS QUARLES
1592–1644

Death aims with fouler spite
At fairer marks.[1]
>　　　*Divine Fancies* [1632]

We spend our midday sweat, our mid-
　night oil;
We tire the night in thought, the day
　in toil.
>　　*Emblems* [1635], *bk. II, no. 2*

Be wisely worldly, be not worldly wise.
>　　　　　　　　　　*Ib.*

This house is to be let for life or years;
Her rent is sorrow, and her income
　tears.
Cupid, 't has long stood void; her bills
　make known,
She must be dearly let, or let alone.
>　　　　*Ib. 10, Epigram*

The slender debt to Nature's quickly
　paid,[2]
Discharged, perchance, with greater
　ease than made.　　　*Ib. 13*

The road to resolution lies by doubt:
The next way home's the farthest way
　about.[3]
>　　　*Ib. IV, 2, Epigram*

It is the lot of man but once to die.
>　　　　　　　　*Ib. V, 7*

My soul, sit thou a patient looker-on;
Judge not the play before the play is
　done:
Her plot hath many changes; every day

---

[1] See Edward Young, p. 399b.
[2] To die is a debt we must all of us discharge. — EURIPIDES, *Alcestis, l. 418*
[3] The longest way round is the shortest way home. — BOHN, *Foreign Proverbs, Italian*

Speaks a new scene; the last act crowns
   the play.[1]
                    Epigram. Respice Finem

And what's a life? — a weary pilgrimage,
Whose glory in one day doth fill the
   stage
With childhood, manhood, and decrepit age.   *What Is Life?*

Let all thy joys be as the month of
   May,
And all thy days be as a marriage day:
Let sorrow, sickness, and a troubled
   mind
Be stranger to thee.   *To a Bride*

No man is born unto himself alone; [2]
Who lives unto himself, he lives to
   none.
         Esther, sec. 1, Meditation 1

The way to bliss lies not on beds of
   down,
And he that has no cross deserves no
   crown.[3] *Ib. sec. 9, Meditation 9*

THOMAS RAVENSCROFT
c. 1592 – 1635

Nose, nose, nose, nose!
And who gave thee this jolly red nose?
Nutmegs and ginger, cinnamon and
   cloves,
And they gave me this jolly red nose.
   Deuteromelia [1609]. *Song no. 7* [4]

GEORGE HERBERT
1593–1633

A verse may find him who a sermon
   flies.[5]
      The Temple [1633]. *The Church
                          Porch, st. 1*

---

[1] See Herrick, p. 320a, and Shakespeare,
Troilus and Cressida IV, v, 223, p. 269b, and
note.
[2] See *Romans 14:8,* p. 51b, and Donne, p.
308b.
[3] See William Penn, p. 380b.
[4] Quoted by Beaumont and Fletcher, *The
Knight of the Burning Pestle* [1613], *act I, sc. 3.*
Ravenscroft's *Deuteromelia* was a supplement to
his *Pammelia,* which was the earliest collection
of rounds, catches, and canons printed in
England.
[5] That many people read a song

Drink not the third glass,[1] which thou
   canst not tame
When once it is within thee.
         *The Temple. The Church
                          Porch, st. 5*

Dare to be true: nothing can need a
   lie:
A fault, which needs it most, grows two
   thereby.[2]   *Ib. st. 13*

By all means use sometimes to be
   alone.   *Ib. st. 25*

By no means run in debt: take thine
   own measure.
Who cannot live on twenty pound a
   year,
Cannot on forty.   *Ib. st. 30*

Wit's an unruly engine, wildly striking
Sometimes a friend, sometimes the engineer.   *Ib. st. 41*

Be useful where thou livest.
                             Ib. st. 55

Man is God's image; but a poor man
   is
Christ's stamp to boot: both images regard.   *Ib. st. 64*

Was ever grief like mine?
      *Ib. The Church. The Sacrifice,
                             refrain*

For thirty pence he did my death devise,[3]
Who at three hundred did the ointment prize.[4]   *Ib. st. 5*

Man stole the fruit, but I must climb
   the tree.   *Ib. st. 51*

I got me flowers to strew Thy way,
I got me boughs off many a tree:

Who will not read a sermon.
      WINTHROP MACKWORTH PRAED [1802–
      1839], *The Chant of the Brazenhead,
      st. 1*
[1] See Victor Hugo, p. 599a.
[2] And he that does one fault at first,
   And lies to hide it, makes it two.
      ISAAC WATTS [1674–1748], *Song 15*
[3] See *King John and the Abbott of Canterbury,* p. 1088a.
[4] Then saith one of his disciples, Judas Iscariot,
Simon's son, which should betray him, Why
was not this ointment sold for three hundred
pence, and given to the poor? — *John 12:4*

But Thou wast up by break of day,
And brought'st Thy sweets along with
Thee.
The Temple. Easter, st. 4

Who says that fictions only and false
hair
Become a verse? Is there in truth no
beauty? [1] *Ib. Jordan, st. 1*

Sweet day, so cool, so calm, so bright,
The bridal of the earth and sky.
Ib. Virtue, st. 1

Sweet spring, full of sweet days and
roses,
A box where sweets compacted lie.
Ib. st. 3

Only a sweet and virtuous soul,
Like season'd timber, never gives.
Ib. st. 4

Who goes to bed and does not pray,
Maketh two nights to every day.
Ib. Charms and Knots, st. 4

Nothing wears clothes, but Man; noth-
ing doth need
But he to wear them.
Ib. Providence, st. 28

Most things move th' under-jaw, the
crocodile not.[2]
Most things sleep lying, th' elephant
leans or stands.[3] *Ib. st. 35*

I struck the board, and cried, No
more:
I will abroad.
What? shall I ever sigh and pine?
My lines and life are free; free as the
road,
Loose as the wind, as large as store.
Shall I be still in suit?
Have I no harvest but a thorn
To let me blood, and not restore
What I have lost with cordial fruit?
Sure there was wine
Before my sighs did dry it; there was
corn

[1] See Keats, p. 583b.
[2] The crocodile does not move the lower jaw,
but is the only animal that brings down its
upper jaw to the under one. — HERODOTUS [484–
424 B.C.], *Customs of the Egyptians*
[3] Leans the huge elephant. — JAMES THOM-
SON, *The Seasons, Summer* [1727], *l. 725*

Before my tears did drown it;
Is the year only lost to me?
Have I no bays to crown it?
The Temple. The Collar

Call in thy death's head there: tie up
thy fears. *Ib.*

But as I raved and grew more fierce and
wild
At every word,
Methought I heard one calling, *Child!*
And I replied, *My Lord.*
Ib.

He would adore my gifts instead of
me,
And rest in Nature, not the God of
Nature:
So both should losers be.
Ib. The Pulley, st. 3

Let him be rich and weary, that at
least,
If goodness lead him not, yet weariness
May toss him to my breast.
Ib. st. 4

Grief melts away
Like snow in May,
As if there were no such cold thing.
Ib. The Flower, st. 1

Who would have thought my shrivel'd
heart
Could have recover'd greenness?
Ib. st. 2

And now in age I bud again,
After so many deaths I live and write;
I once more smell the dew and rain,
And relish versing: O my only light,
It cannot be
That I am he
On whom thy tempests fell all night.
Ib. st. 6

The harbingers are come. See, see their
mark;
White is their color, and behold my
head.
Ib. The Forerunners, st. 1

Teach me, my God and King,
In all things thee to see.

And what I do in any thing,
To do it as for thee.
The Temple. The Elixir,
st. 1

A servant with this clause
Makes drudgery divine:
Who sweeps a room, as for thy laws,
Makes that and th' action fine.
Ib. st. 5

Love bade me welcome: yet my soul
drew back,
Guilty of dust and sin.
But quick-ey'd Love, observing me grow
slack
From my first entrance in,
Drew nearer to me, sweetly question-
ing,
If I lack'd anything.
Ib. Love, st. 1

You must sit down, says Love, and taste
my meat:
So I did sit and eat. *Ib. st. 3*

Religion stands on tiptoe in our land,
Ready to pass to the American strand.
The Church Militant [1633], *l. 235*

Love, and a cough, cannot be hid.
Jacula Prudentum [1651], 49

Ill ware is never cheap. Pleasing ware
is half sold. *Ib. 61*

When a dog is drowning, everyone
offers him drink. *Ib. 77*

Deceive not thy physician, confessor,
nor lawyer. *Ib. 105*

Who would do ill ne'er wants occasion. *Ib. 116*

A snow year, a rich year. *Ib. 125*

Well may he smell fire, whose gown
burns. *Ib. 138*

Love your neighbor, yet pull not
down your hedge.[1] *Ib. 141*

Marry your son when you will; your
daughter when you can. *Ib. 149*

The mill cannot grind with the water
that's past. *Ib. 153*

Good words are worth much, and
cost little. *Ib. 155*

[1] See Robert Frost, p. 926a.

Hell is full of good meanings and
wishings.[1]
Jacula Prudentum, 170

Where the drink goes in, there the
wit goes out. *Ib. 187*

Whose house is of glass, must not
throw stones at another. *Ib. 196*

By suppers more have been killed
than Galen ever cured. *Ib. 272*

The lion is not so fierce as they paint
him.[2] *Ib. 289*

Go not for every grief to the physician, nor for every quarrel to the lawyer, nor for every thirst to the pot.
Ib. 290

The best mirror is an old friend.
Ib. 296

When you are an anvil, hold you
still; when you are a hammer, strike
your fill.[3] *Ib. 338*

He that lies with the dogs, riseth
with fleas. *Ib. 343*

He that is not handsome at twenty,
nor strong at thirty, nor rich at forty,
nor wise at fifty, will never be handsome, strong, rich, or wise. *Ib. 349*

The buyer needs a hundred eyes, the
seller not one.[4] *Ib. 390*

My house, my house, though thou
art small, thou art to me the Escurial.
Ib. 413

Trust not one night's ice. *Ib. 453*

For want of a nail the shoe is lost,

[1] Sir, Hell is paved with good intentions.
— SAMUEL JOHNSON [1775]; from BOSWELL, *Life
of Dr. Johnson* [1791], *vol. I, p. 555* [Everyman
ed.]
[2] The lion is not so fierce as painted. —
THOMAS FULLER [1608–1661], *Expecting Prefer-
ment*
[3] Stand like an anvil when it is beaten upon.
— ST. IGNATIUS THEOPHORUS, Bishop of Antioch
[A.D. 104]
When you are the anvil, bear —
When you are the hammer, strike.
EDWIN MARKHAM [1852–1940],
Preparedness
[4] Caveat emptor [Buyer, beware]. — *Proverb*

for want of a shoe the horse is lost, for want of a horse the rider is lost.[1]

> *Jacula Prudentum,* 499

Pension never enriched young man.

> *Ib.* 515

One enemy is too much.[2]   *Ib.* 523

Thursday come, and the week is gone.   *Ib.* 587

Time is the rider that breaks youth.

> *Ib.* 615

Show me a liar, and I'll show thee a thief.   *Ib.* 652

One father is more than a hundred schoolmasters.   *Ib.* 686

Reason lies between the spur and the bridle.   *Ib.* 711

One sword keeps another in the sheath.   *Ib.* 725

God's mill grinds slow, but sure.[3]

> *Ib.* 747

He that lends, gives.   *Ib.* 787

Words are women, deeds are men.[4]

> *Ib.* 842

Poverty is no sin.   *Ib.* 844

None knows the weight of another's burthen.   *Ib.* 880

One hour's sleep before midnight is worth three after.   *Ib.* 882

He hath no leisure who useth it not.

> *Ib.* 897

Half the world knows not how the other half lives.[5]   *Ib.* 907

Life is half spent before we know what it is.   *Ib.* 917

Every mile is two in winter.

> *Ib.* 949

----

[1] See Benjamin Franklin, p. 422a.
[2] See Ali Ibn-abu-Taleb, p. 148b.
[3] See Euripides, p. 85a, and von Logau, p. 329a.
[4] See Samuel Johnson, p. 427b.
Fatti maschii parole femine [Deeds are masculine, words are feminine]. — *State motto of Maryland*
[5] See Rabelais, p. 181a.

The eye is bigger than the belly.

> *Jacula Prudentum,* 1018

His bark is worse than his bite.

> *Ib.* 1090

There is an hour wherein a man might be happy all his life, could he find it.   *Ib.* 1143

Woe be to him that reads but one book.   *Ib.* 1146

IZAAK WALTON
1593–1683

But God, who is able to prevail, wrestled with him, as the Angel did with Jacob, and marked him; marked him for his own.[1]

> *Life of Donne* [1640]

I have laid aside business, and gone a-fishing.

> *The Compleat Angler* [1653–1655]. *Epistle to the Reader*

Angling may be said to be so like the mathematics that it can never be fully learnt.   *Ib.*

As no man is born an artist, so no man is born an angler.   *Ib.*

I shall stay him no longer than to wish him a rainy evening to read this following discourse; and that if he be an honest angler, the east wind may never blow when he goes a-fishing.

> *Ib.*

I am, Sir, a brother of the Angle.

> *Ib. pt. I, ch.* 1

Doubt not but angling will prove to be so pleasant that it will prove to be, like virtue, a reward to itself.[2]

[1] See *Genesis 32:24,* p. 7b, and Thomas Gray, p. 441a.
[2] Ipsa quidem virtus sibimet pulcherrima merces [Virtue herself is her own fairest reward]. — SILIUS ITALICUS [A.D. c. 25–99], *Punica, bk. XIII, l. 663*
Virtue was sufficient of herself for happiness. — DIOGENES LAERTIUS [c. A.D. 200], *Plato XLII*
That virtue is her own reward, is but a cold principle. — SIR THOMAS BROWNE, *Religio Medici* [1642], *pt. I, sec. 47*
Virtue is its own reward. — PRIOR [1664–1721], *Imitations of Horace, bk. III, ode 2*

Sir Henry Wotton . . . was a most dear lover, and a frequent practicer of the art of angling; of which he would say, "it was an employment for his idle time, which was then not idly spent . . . a rest to his mind, a cheerer of his spirits, a diverter of sadness, a calmer of unquiet thoughts, a moderator of passions, a procurer of contentedness; and that it begat habits of peace and patience in those that professed and practiced it."

The Compleat Angler, pt. I, ch. 1

You will find angling to be like the virtue of humility, which has a calmness of spirit and a world of other blessings attending upon it.[1]   *Ib.*

I remember that a wise friend of mine did usually say, "That which is everybody's business is nobody's business."   *Ib. 2*

An honest ale-house where we shall find a cleanly room, lavender in the windows, and twenty ballads stuck about the wall.   *Ib.*

Good company and good discourse are the very sinews of virtue.   *Ib.*

The Chavender or Chub.   *Ib. 3*

An excellent angler, and now with God.   *Ib. 4*

Old-fashioned poetry, but choicely good.   *Ib.*

I love such mirth as does not make friends ashamed to look upon one another next morning.   *Ib. 5*

No man can lose what he never had.   *Ib.*

We may say of angling as Dr. Boteler[2] said of strawberries: "Doubtless God could have made a better berry,

but doubtless God never did"; and so, if I might be judge, God never did make a more calm, quiet, innocent recreation than angling.

The Compleat Angler, pt. I, ch. 5

Thus use your frog. . . . Put your hook through his mouth, and out at his gills; . . . and then with a fine needle and silk sew the upper part of his leg, with only one stitch, to the arming-wire of your hook; or tie the frog's leg, above the upper joint, to the armed-wire; and in so doing use him as though you loved him.[1]   *Ib. 8*

This dish of meat is too good for any but anglers, or very honest men.

Ib.

Look to your health; and if you have it, praise God, and value it next to a good conscience; for health is the second blessing that we mortals are capable of; a blessing that money cannot buy.   *Ib. 21*

Let the blessing of St. Peter's Master be . . . upon all that are lovers of virtue, and dare trust in his Providence, and be quiet and go a-angling.   *Ib.*

The great secretary of Nature and all learning, Sir Francis Bacon.[2]

Life of Herbert [1670]

THOMAS CAREW
c. 1595 – c. 1639

Here lies a King that rul'd, as he
    thought fit
The universal monarchy of wit;
Here lies two flamens, and both those
    the best:
Apollo's first, at last the true God's
    priest.

Elegy on the Death of Donne [1633]

Ask me no more where Jove bestows,
When June is past, the fading rose;

---

[1] There is certainly something in angling . . . that tends to produce a gentleness of spirit, and a pure serenity of mind. — WASHINGTON IRVING, *The Sketch-Book, The Angler*

[2] William Butler [1535–1618], styled by THOMAS FULLER in his *Worthies of England* the "Aesculapius of our age." This praise of the strawberry first appeared in the second edition of *The Angler*, 1655.

[1] See Blunden, p. 1036a.

[2] Plato, Aristotle, and Socrates are secretaries of Nature. — JAMES HOWELL [1594–1666], *Letters, bk. II, letter 11*

For in your beauty's orient deep
These flowers, as in their causes, sleep.
> *Poems* [1640]. *To Celia, st. 1*

Ask me no more whither doth haste
The nightingale when May is past;
For in your sweet dividing throat
She winters and keeps warm her note.
> *Ib. st. 3*

Ask me no more if east or west
The Phoenix builds her spicy nest;
For unto you at last she flies,
And in your fragrant bosom dies.
> *Ib. st. 5*

Give me more love or more disdain;
The torrid or the frozen zone:
Bring equal ease unto my pain;
The temperate affords me none.
> *Ib. Mediocrity in Love Rejected, st. 1*

Thou shalt confess the vain pursuit
Of human glory yields no fruit
But an untimely grave.
> *Ib. On the Duke of Buckingham*

He that loves a rosy cheek,
Or a coral lip admires,
Or, from star-like eyes, doth seek
Fuel to maintain his fires;
As old Time makes these decay,
So his flames must waste away.
> *Ib. Disdain Returned, st. 1*

The firstling of the infant year.
> *Ib. The Primrose*

Then fly betimes, for only they
Conquer Love that run away.
> *Ib. Conquest by Flight*

The magic of a face.
> *Ib. Epitaph on the Lady S——*

RENÉ DESCARTES
1596–1650

Good sense is of all things in the world the most equally distributed, for everybody thinks he is so well supplied with it, that even those most difficult to please in all other matters never desire more of it than they already possess.
> *Le Discours de la Méthode* [1637], *I*

It is not enough to have a good mind. The main thing is to use it well.
> *Le Discours de la Méthode, I*

The greatest minds are capable of the greatest vices as well as of the greatest virtues.
> *Ib.*

The first precept was never to accept a thing as true until I knew it as such without a single doubt.
> *Ib.*

One cannot conceive anything so strange and so implausible that it has not already been said by one philosopher or another.[1]
> *Ib. II*

I think, therefore I am.[2]
> *Ib. IV*

JAMES SHIRLEY
1596–1666

How little room
Do we take up in death that, living, know
No bounds! *The Wedding* [1626]

I presume you're mortal, and may err.[3]
> *The Lady of Pleasure* [1635]

Only the actions of the just
Smell sweet and blossom in their dust.[4]
> *Ib.*

Death calls ye to the crowd of common men. *Cupid and Death* [1653]

The glories of our blood and state
Are shadows, not substantial things;
There is no armor against fate;
Death lays his icy hand on kings.[5]
> *Contention of Ajax and Ulysses* [1659], *sc. 3*

OLIVER CROMWELL
1599–1658

A few honest men are better than numbers.
> *Letter to Sir W. Spring* [September 1643]

---

[1] See Varro, p. 110a, and Cicero, p. 111a.
[2] Cogito, ergo sum.
  Je pense, donc je suis.
[3] See Pope, p. 403b, and note.
[4] The sweet remembrance of the just
  Shall flourish when he sleeps in dust.
    Nahum Tate and Nicholas Brady,
      Psalm 132 [1696], *st. 6*
[5] See Horace, p. 120b.

The State, in choosing men to serve it, takes no notice of their opinions. If they be willing faithfully to serve it, that satisfies.
Before the Battle of Marston Moor [July 2, 1644]

I beseech you, in the bowels of Christ, think it possible you may be mistaken.[1]
Letter to the Church of Scotland [August 3, 1650]

It is not fit that you sit here any longer! . . . you shall now give place to better men.
To the Rump Parliament [January 22, 1654]

Necessity hath no law.[2] Feigned necessities, imaginary necessities . . . are the greatest cozenage that men can put upon the Providence of God, and make pretenses to break known rules by.
To Parliament [September 12, 1654]

I would have been glad to have lived under my woodside, and to have kept a flock of sheep, rather than to have undertaken this government.
To Parliament [1658]

Mr. Lely, I desire you would use all your skill to paint my picture truly like me, and not flatter me at all; but remark all these roughnesses, pimples, warts, and everything as you see me, otherwise I will never pay a farthing for it.[3]
From HORACE WALPOLE, *Anecdotes of Painting in England [1762–1771]*

It is not my design to drink or to sleep, but my design is to make what haste I can to be gone.
Dying words

PEDRO CALDERÓN DE LA BARCA
1600–1681

What is life? A madness. What is life? An illusion, a shadow, a story. And the greatest good is little enough: for all life is a dream, and dreams themselves are only dreams.
Life Is a Dream,[1] act II, l. 1195

But whether it be dream or truth, to do well is what matters. If it be truth, for truth's sake. If not, then to gain friends for the time when we awaken.
Ib. III, 236

The treason past, the traitor is no longer needed.   *Ib. III, 1109*

What surprises you, if a dream taught me this wisdom, and if I still fear I may wake up and find myself once more confined in prison? And even if this should not happen, merely to dream it is enough. For this I have come to know, that all human happiness finally ceases, like a dream.
Ib. III, 1114

MARTIN PARKER
1600–1656

Ye gentlemen of England
That live at home at ease,
Ah! little do you think upon
The dangers of the seas.   *Song*

When the stormy winds do blow.[2]
Ib.

JULES, CARDINAL MAZARIN
1602–1661

I must leave all that! Farewell, dear paintings that I have loved so much and which have cost me so much.[3]
Remark shortly before his death.

SIR KENELM DIGBY
1603–1665

The hot water is to remain upon it [the tea] no longer than whiles you can

---

[1] See Hand, p. 912a.
[2] See Publilius Syrus, p. 126b, and St. Augustine, p. 147a.
[3] Warts and all. — *Saying*

[1] Translated by EDWARD and ELIZABETH HUBERMAN in *Spanish Drama* [1962].
[2] When the battle rages loud and long,
And the stormy winds do blow.
THOMAS CAMPBELL [1777–1884],
Ye Mariners of England
[3] Il faut quitter tout cela! Adieu, chers tableaux que j'ai tant aimés et qui m'ont tant coûté.

say the Miserere Psalm [1] very leisurely.
The Closet Opened. Tea with Eggs

All matter is indifferent to form.
Of the Vegetation of Plants

ROGER WILLIAMS
c. 1603 – 1683

There goes many a ship to sea, with many hundred souls in one ship, whose weal and woe is common, and is a true picture of a commonwealth or a human combination or society. It hath fallen out sometimes that both papists and Protestants, Jews and Turks may be embarked in one ship; upon which supposal I affirm that all the liberty of conscience that ever I pleaded for turns upon these two hinges — that none of the papists, Protestants, Jews or Turks be forced to come to the ship's prayers or worship, nor compelled from their own particular prayers or worship, if they practice any. I further add that I never denied that, notwithstanding this liberty, the commander of this ship ought to command the ship's course, yea, and also command that justice, peace, and also sobriety be kept and practiced, both among the seamen and all the passengers.
Letter to the Town of Providence
[January 1655]

FRIEDRICH VON LOGAU
1604–1655

Armed peace.
Poetic Aphorisms [2] *[1654]*

This month is a kiss
Which heaven gives the earth
That she now become a bride
And then a future mother.
Ib. Characteristics of May

Though the mills of God grind slowly,
    yet they grind exceeding small.[3]
Ib. Retribution

---

[1] Psalm 51.
[2] Sinngedichten
[3] Translated by LONGFELLOW.
See Euripides, p. 85a, and Herbert, p. 325a.

SIR THOMAS BROWNE
1605–1682

I dare, without usurpation, assume the honorable style of a Christian.
Religio Medici [1642], *pt. I, sec. 1*

I could never divide myself from any man upon the difference of an opinion, or be angry with his judgment for not agreeing with me in that from which perhaps within a few days I should dissent myself.   *Ib. 6*

Many . . . have too rashly charged the troops of error, and remain as trophies unto the enemies of truth.
Ib.

A man may be in as just possession of truth as of a city, and yet be forced to surrender.[1]   *Ib.*

As for those wingy mysteries in divinity, and airy subtleties in religion, which have unhinged the brains of better heads, they never stretched the pia mater of mine.   *Ib. 9*

I love to lose myself in a mystery, to pursue my Reason to an *O altitudo!*
Ib.

Rich with the spoils of Nature.[2]
Ib. 13

We carry with us the wonders we seek without us: There is all Africa and her prodigies in us.   *Ib. 15*

All things are artificial, for nature is the art of God.[3]   *Ib. 16*

Obstinacy in a bad cause is but constancy in a good.   *Ib. 25*

Persecution is a bad and indirect way to plant religion.   *Ib.*

Not picked from the leaves of any author, but bred amongst the weeds and tares of mine own brain.   *Ib. 35*

This reasonable moderator, and equal piece of justice, Death.   *Ib. 38*

I am not so much afraid of death, as ashamed thereof. 'Tis the very disgrace

---

[1] See Euripides, p. 84b, and Ovid, p. 129a.
[2] See Thomas Gray, p. 440b.
[3] The course of Nature is the art of God. —
EDWARD YOUNG, *Night Thoughts* [1742–1745],
Night IX, l. 1267

and ignominy of our natures, that in a moment can so disfigure us, that our nearest friends, wife, and children, stand afraid and start at us.

Religio Medici, pt. I, sec. 40

Whosoever enjoys not this life, I count him but an apparition, though he wear about him the sensible affections of flesh. In these moral acceptions, the way to be immortal is to die daily.

Ib. 45

How shall the dead arise, is no question of my faith; to believe only possibilities, is not faith, but mere philosophy. *Ib. 48*

The heart of man is the place the devils dwell in: I feel sometimes a hell within myself.[1] *Ib. 51*

There is no road or ready way to virtue. *Ib. 54*

All places, all airs make unto me one country; I am in England, everywhere, and under any meridian.[2] *Ib. II, 1*

They that endeavor to abolish vice, destroy also virtue; for contraries, though they destroy one another, are yet the life of one another. *Ib. 4*

But how shall we expect charity towards others, when we are uncharitable to ourselves? *Charity begins at home,*[3] is the voice of the world; yet is every man his greatest enemy, and, as it were, his own executioner. *Ib.*

Sure there is music even in the beauty, and the silent note which Cupid strikes, far sweeter than the sound of an instrument. For there is a music wherever there is a harmony, order proportion; and thus far we may maintain the music of the spheres. *Ib. 9*

For the world, I count it not an inn, but an hospital; and a place not to live, but to die in. *Ib. 11*

[1] See Virgil, p. 199a, Marlowe, p. 213a, and note.
[2] See Burton, p. 311a.
[3] See Terence, p. 108b.

There is surely a piece of divinity in us, something that was before the elements, and owes no homage unto the sun.

Religio Medici, pt. II, sec. 11

Ruat coelum, fiat voluntas tua [Though the heaven falls, let Thy will be done].[1] *Ib.*

Sleep is a death; O, make me try,
By sleeping what it is to die,
And as gently lay my head
On my grave, as now my bed.[2]

Ib. 12

When we desire to confine our words, we commonly say they are spoken under the rose.[3]

Vulgar Errors [1645]

An old and gray-headed error. **Ib.**

Times before you, when even living men were antiquities; when the living might exceed the dead, and to depart this world could not be properly said to go unto the greater number.[4]

Urn-Burial; or Hydriotaphia [1658]. Dedication

With rich flames, and hired tears, they solemnized their obsequies.

Ib. ch. 3

Were the happiness of the next world as closely apprehended as the felicities of this, it were a martyrdom to live. *Ib. 4*

These dead bones have . . . quietly rested under the drums and tramplings of three conquests. *Ib. 5*

[1] Fiat iustitia et ruant coeli [Let justice be done though the heavens fall]. — WILLIAM WATSON, *Ten Quodlibetical Questions Concerning Religion and State* [1601]
  See Ferdinand I, p. 186a.
[2] See Thomas Ken, p. 377b.
[3] Sub rosa. This phrase, meaning secretly, is of unknown origin. With the ancients the rose was emblematic of secrecy, and when a host hung a rose above his tables, his guests understood that all words spoken under it were to remain secret. Later, roses were carved as decorations on the ceilings of council chambers and confessionals, with the same significance.
[4] 'Tis long since Death had the majority. — ROBERT BLAIR, *The Grave* [1743], *pt. II, l. 449*

Time which antiquates antiquities, and hath an art to make dust of all things.
> *Urn-Burial; or Hydriotaphia, ch. 5*

What song the Sirens sang, or what name Achilles assumed when he hid himself among women, though puzzling questions, are not beyond all conjecture.   *Ib.*

The long habit of living indisposeth us for dying.   *Ib.*

The iniquity of oblivion blindly scattereth her poppy, and deals with the memory of men without distinction to merit of perpetuity.   *Ib.*

Herostratus lives that burnt the Temple of Diana — he is almost lost that built it.[1]   *Ib.*

Oblivion is not to be hired: the greater part must be content to be as though they had not been, to be found in the register of God, not in the record of man.   *Ib.*

The night of time far surpasseth the day, and who knows when was the equinox?   *Ib.*

Man is a noble animal, splendid in ashes, and pompous in the grave.
          Ib.

That unextinguishable laugh in heaven.
> *Garden of Cyrus [1658], ch. 2*

Life itself is but the shadow of death, and souls departed but the shadows of the living. All things fall under this name. The sun itself is but the dark simulacrum, and light but the shadow of God.   *Ib. 4*

To keep our eyes open longer were but to act our Antipodes. The huntsmen are up in America, and they are already past their first sleep in Persia. But who can be drowsy at that hour which freed us from everlasting sleep?

---

[1] The aspiring youth that fired the Ephesian dome
Outlives in fame the pious fool that raised it.
COLLEY CIBBER [1671–1757], *Richard III, act III, sc. ɪ*

or have slumbering thoughts at that time, when sleep itself must end, and, as some conjecture, all shall awake again?
> *Garden of Cyrus, ch. 5*

The created world is but a small parenthesis in eternity.
> *Christian Morals, III, 29*
> *[1716]*

PIERRE CORNEILLE
1606–1684

To conquer without risk is to triumph without glory.
> *Le Cid [1636], act II, sc. 2*

Brave men are brave from the very first.   *Ib. II, 3*

And the combat ceased for want of combatants.   *Ib. IV, 3*

Do your duty, and leave the rest to heaven.   *Horace [1639], act II, sc. 8*

All evils are equal when they are extreme.   *Ib. III, 4*

The worst of all states is the people's state.   *Cinna [1640], act II, sc. 1*

Who is all-powerful should fear everything.   *Ib. IV, 2*

By speaking of our misfortunes we often relieve them.
> *Polyeucte [1640], act I, sc. 3*

The manner of giving is worth more than the gift.
> *Le Menteur [1642], act I, sc. 1*

A liar is always lavish of oaths.
          Ib. III, 5

A good memory is needed after one has lied.[1]   *Ib. IV, 5*

The fire which seems extinguished often slumbers beneath the ashes.
> *Rodogune [1644], act III, sc. 4*

Guess if you can, choose if you dare.
> *Héraclius [1646], act IV, sc. 4*

---

[1] Liars ought to have good memories. — ALGERNON SIDNEY, *Discourses on Government* [1698], *ch. 2, sec. 15*

A service beyond all recompense
Weighs so heavy that it almost gives
offense.

Suréna [1674], *act III, sc. 1*

I owe my fame only to myself.

Poésies Diverses, 23

SIR WILLIAM
DAVENANT
1606–1668

The lark now leaves his wat'ry nest
And, climbing, shakes his dewy wings.

Song [1637], *st. 1*

For angling-rod he took a sturdy oak;
For line, a cable that in storm ne'er
broke.

Britannia Triumphans [1637]

The hook was baited with a dragon's
tail —
And then on rock he stood to bob for
whale.   *Ib.*

I shall ask leave to desist, when I am
interrupted by so great an experiment
as dying.

*His apology, in illness, for not
having finished Gondibert*

How much pleasure they lose (and
even the pleasures of heroic poesy are
not unprofitable) who take away the
liberty of a poet, and fetter his feet in
the shackles of a historian.

*Prefatory letter to Thomas
Hobbes. From* S. T. COLE-
RIDGE, *Biographia Literaria*
[1817], *ch. 22*

EDMUND WALLER
1606–1687

Illustrious acts high raptures do infuse,
And every conqueror creates a muse.

Panegyric to My Lord Protector

Under the tropic is our language
spoke,
And part of Flanders hath receiv'd our
yoke.

*Upon the Death of the Lord
Protector* [1658]

Guarded with ships, and all our sea our
own.[1]   *To My Lord of Falkland*

The yielding marble of her snowy
breast.

*On a Lady Passing Through a
Crowd of People* [1664]

To man, that was in th' evening made,
   Stars gave the first delight;
Admiring, in the gloomy shade,
   Those little drops of light.

*An Apology for Having Loved
Before* [1664]

That which her slender waist confin'd
Shall now my joyful temples bind;
No monarch but would give his crown
His arms might do what this has done.

On a Girdle [1664], *st. 1*

My joy, my grief, my hope, my love,
Did all within this circle move!

Ib. st. 2

A narrow compass! and yet there
Dwelt all that's good, and all that's
   fair;
Give me but what this riband bound,
Take all the rest the sun goes round!

Ib. st. 3

   Go, lovely rose![2]
Tell her that wastes her time and me
   That now she knows,
When I resemble her to thee,
How sweet and fair she seems to be.

Go, Lovely Rose [1664], *st. 1*

   So all we know
Of what they do above
Is that they happy are, and that they
   love.

*Upon the Death of
My Lady Rich* [1664]

Poets that lasting marble seek
Must come in Latin or in Greek.

Of English Verse [1668]

[1] See Sir Francis Bacon, p. 209b, and note.
[2] Most of all I envy the octogenarian poet
who joined three words — "Go, lovely Rose"
—so happily together, that he left his name
to float down through Time on the wings of a
phrase and a flower. — LOGAN PEARSALL SMITH,
Afterthoughts [1931]

And keeps the palace of the soul.[1]
Of Tea

Poets lose half the praise they should
have got,
Could it be known what they discreetly
blot.
*Upon Roscommon's Translation
of* HORACE, *De Arte Poetica*

The soul's dark cottage, batter'd and
decay'd,
Lets in new light through chinks that
Time has made; [2]
Stronger by weakness, wiser, men be-
come
As they draw near to their eternal
home.
Leaving the old, both worlds at once
they view,
That stand upon the threshold of the
new.
On the Divine Poems [1686]

PAUL GERHARDT
1607–1676

O sacred head, now wounded,
With grief and shame bowed down;
Now scornfully surrounded
With thorns, thy only crown.[3]
*Passion Chorale, based on
twelfth-century Latin hymn,
st.* 1

THOMAS FULLER
1608–1661

Drawing near her death, she sent
most pious thoughts as harbingers to
heaven; and her soul saw a glimpse of
happiness through the chinks of her
sickness-broken body.
Life of Monica [1642]

He was one of a lean body and vis-

---

[1] See Byron, p. 555b.
[2] To vanish in the chinks that Time has made.
— SAMUEL ROGERS, *Italy* [1822], *Paestum*
[3] O Haupt vol Blut und Wunden
Vol Schmerz und voller Hohn!
O Haupt zum Spott gebunden
Mit einer Dornen Krohn!
Translated by JAMES WADDELL ALEXANDER
[1861].

---

age, as if his eager soul, biting for anger
at the clog of his body, desired to fret a
passage through it.[1]
Life of the Duke of Alva [1642]

He knows little who will tell his wife
all he knows.[2]
*The Holy State and the Profane
State* [1642]. *The Good Husband*

One that will not plead that cause
wherein his tongue must be confuted
by his conscience.
Ib. The Good Advocate

Their heads sometimes so little that
there is no room for wit; sometimes so
long that there is no wit for so much
room.   *Ib. Of Natural Fools*

Light, God's eldest daughter, is a
principal beauty in a building.
Ib. Of Building

Learning hath gained most by those
books by which the printers have lost.
Ib. Of Books

Deceive not thyself by overexpecting
happiness in the married estate. Remember the nightingales which sing
only some months in the spring, but
commonly are silent when they have
hatched their eggs.   *Ib. Of Marriage*

They that marry ancient people,
merely in expectation to bury them,
hang themselves in hope that one will
come and cut the halter.   *Ib.*

Fame sometimes hath created something of nothing.   *Ib. Fame*

Anger is one of the sinews of the
soul; he that wants it hath a maimed
mind.   *Ib. Of Anger*

It is always darkest just before the
day dawneth.
Pisgah Sight [1650], *bk. II, ch* 2

JOHN MILTON[3]
1608–1674

This is the month, and this the happy
morn,

---

[1] See Dryden, p. 368a.
[2] See *Odyssey XI, 441*, p. 66a.
[3] See Wordsworth, *London*, p. 512b.

Wherein the Son of Heav'n's eternal
   King,
Of wedded maid and virgin mother
   born,
Our great redemption from above did
   bring;
For so the holy sages once did sing,
That He our deadly forfeit should re-
   lease,
And with His Father work us a perpet-
   ual peace.
     On the Morning of Christ's Na-
       tivity [1629], *st. 1, l. 1*

It was the winter wild
While the Heav'n-born child
All meanly wrapt in the rude manger
   lies.   *Ib. Hymn, st. 1, l. 29*

No war, or battle's sound
Was heard the world around.
The idle spear and shield were high up
   hung.   *Ib. st. 4, l. 53*

Time will run back and fetch the Age
   of Gold.[1]   *Ib. st. 14, l. 135*

The Oracles are dumb.
          Ib. st. 19, l. 173

From haunted spring and dale
Edg'd with poplar pale
The parting genius is with sighing
   sent.   *Ib. st. 20, l. 184*

Peor and Baalim
Forsake their temples dim.
          Ib. st. 22, l. 197

What needs my Shakespeare for his
   honor'd bones
The labor of an age in piled stones?
Or that his hallow'd relics should be
   hid
Under a star-y-pointing pyramid?
Dear son of memory, great heir of
   fame,
What need'st thou such weak witness
   of thy name?
       On Shakespeare [1630]

How soon hath Time, the subtle thief
   of youth,

[1] See Horace, p. 122b.

Stol'n on his wing my three-and-twenti-
   eth year.
     On His Having Arrived at the
       Age of Twenty-three [1631]

As ever in my great Taskmaster's eye.
                Ib.

Such sweet compulsion doth in music
   lie.
      Arcades [1630–1634], *l. 68*

Hence, loathed Melancholy,
Of Cerberus and blackest Midnight
   born,
In Stygian cave forlorn,
'Mongst horrid shapes, and shrieks, and
   sights unholy.
        L'Allegro [1631], *l. 1*

So buxom, blithe, and debonair.
              Ib. l. 24

Haste thee, Nymph, and bring with
   thee
Jest, and youthful jollity,
Quips and cranks and wanton wiles,
Nods and becks and wreathed smiles.
              Ib. l. 25

Sport, that wrinkled Care derides,
And Laughter, holding both his sides.
Come, and trip it, as you go,
On the light fantastic toe.   *Ib. l. 31*

The mountain nymph, sweet liberty.
              Ib. l. 36

Mirth, admit me of thy crew,
To live with her, and live with thee,
In unreproved pleasures free.
              Ib. l. 38

While the cock with lively din
Scatters the rear of darkness thin,
And to the stack, or the barn door,
Stoutly struts his dames before,
Oft list'ning how the hounds and horn
Cheerly rouse the slumb'ring morn.
              Ib. l. 49

And every shepherd tells his tale
Under the hawthorn in the dale.
              Ib. l. 67

Meadows trim, with daisies pied,
Shallow brooks, and rivers wide;
Towers and battlements it sees

Bosom'd high in tufted trees,
Where perhaps some beauty lies,
The cynosure of neighboring eyes.
L'Allegro, l. 75

And the jocund rebecks sound
To many a youth, and many a maid,
Dancing in the checkered shade.
And young and old come forth to play
On a sunshine holiday. *Ib. l.* 94

Then to the spicy nut-brown ale.
Ib. l. 100

Then lies him down the lubber fiend,
And stretch'd out all the chimney's
length,
Basks at the fire his hairy strength.
Ib. l. 110

Tower'd cities please us then,
And the busy hum of men.
Ib. l. 117

Ladies, whose bright eyes
Rain influence, and judge the prize.
Ib. l. 121

And pomp, and feast, and revelry,
With mask, and antique pageantry,
Such sights as youthful poets dream
On summer eves by haunted stream.
Then to the well-trod stage anon,
If Jonson's learned sock be on,
Or sweetest Shakespeare, Fancy's
child,
Warble his native wood-notes wild,
And ever, against eating cares,
Lap me in soft Lydian airs,
Married to immortal verse [1]
Such as the meeting soul may pierce,
In notes with many a winding bout
Of linked sweetness long drawn out.
Ib. l. 127

Untwisting all the chains that tie
The hidden soul of harmony.
Ib. l. 143

Such strains as would have won the ear
Of Pluto, to have quite set free
His half-regain'd Eurydice.
These delights, if thou canst give,
Mirth, with thee, I mean to live.
Ib. l. 148

[1] Wisdom married to immortal verse. —
WORDSWORTH, *The Excursion* [1814], *bk. VII*

Hence vain deluding Joys,
The brood of Folly without father
bred!
Il Penseroso [1631], *l.* 1

The gay motes that people the sunbeams. *Ib. l.* 8

Hail divinest Melancholy. *Ib. l.* 12

Sober, steadfast, and demure.
Ib. l. 32

And looks commercing with the skies,
Thy rapt soul sitting in thine eyes.
Ib. l. 39

Forget thyself to marble. *Ib. l.* 42

And join with thee, calm Peace and
Quiet,
Spare Fast, that oft with gods doth
diet. *Ib. l.* 45

And add to these retired Leisure,
That in trim gardens takes his pleasure. *Ib. l.* 49

Sweet bird, that shunn'st the noise of
folly,
Most musical, most melancholy!
Ib. l. 61

I walk unseen
On the dry smooth-shaven green,
To behold the wandering moon,
Riding near her highest noon,
Like one that had been led astray
Through the heav'n's wide pathless
way,
And oft, as if her head she bow'd,
Stooping through a fleecy cloud.
Ib. l. 65

Oft, on a plat of rising ground,
I hear the far-off curfew sound
Over some wide-watered shore,
Swinging low with sullen roar.
Ib. l. 73

Where glowing embers through the
room
Teach light to counterfeit a gloom,
Far from all resort of mirth,
Save the cricket on the hearth.
Ib. l. 79

Sometime let gorgeous Tragedy
In sceptered pall come sweeping by,

Presenting Thebes, or Pelops' line,
Or the tale of Troy divine.
Il Penseroso, l. 97

Or bid the soul of Orpheus sing
Such notes as, warbled to the string,
Drew iron tears down Pluto's cheek.
Ib. l. 105

Or call up him that left half told
The story of Cambuscan bold.
Ib. l. 109

Where more is meant than meets the
ear. *Ib. l.* 120

Hide me from day's garish eye,
While the bee with honied thigh,
That at her flowery work doth sing,
And the waters murmuring
With such consort as they keep,
Entice the dewy-feather'd sleep.
Ib. l. 141

And storied windows richly dight,
Casting a dim religious light.
There let the pealing organ blow,
To the full-voiced choir below,
In service high, and anthems clear
As may, with sweetness, through mine
ear
Dissolve me into ecstasies,
And bring all Heaven before mine
eyes. *Ib. l.* 159

Till old experience do attain
To something like prophetic strain.
Ib. l. 173

Before the starry threshold of Jove's
Court [1]
My mansion is. *Comus* [1634], *l.* 1

Above the smoke and stir of this dim
spot
Which men call earth. *Ib. l.* 5

Yet some there be that by due steps
aspire
To lay their just hands on that golden
key
That opes the palace of Eternity.
Ib. l. 12

An old, and haughty nation proud in
arms. *Ib. l.* 33

[1] See William Blake, p. 488b.

What never yet was heard in tale or
song,
From old or modern bard, in hall or
bower.
Comus, l. 44

Bacchus, that first from out the purple
grape
Crush'd the sweet poison of misused
wine. *Ib. l.* 46

These my sky-robes, spun out of Iris'
woof. *Ib. l.* 83

The star that bids the shepherd fold.
Ib. l. 93

And the gilded car of day,
His glowing axle doth allay
In the steep Atlantic stream.
Ib. l. 95

Midnight shout and revelry,
Tipsy dance and jollity. *Ib. l.* 103

What hath night to do with sleep?
Ib. l. 122

Ere the blabbing eastern scout,
The nice morn on th' Indian steep,
From her cabin'd loop-hole peep.
Ib. l. 138

Come, knit hands, and beat the
ground,
In a light fantastic round. *Ib. l.* 143

When the gray-hooded Even,
Like a sad votarist in palmer's weed,
Rose from the hindmost wheels of
Phoebus' wain. *Ib. l.* 188

A thousand fantasies
Begin to throng into my memory,
Of calling shapes, and beck'ning shadows dire,
And airy tongues that syllable men's
names
On sands and shores and desert wildernesses. *Ib. l.* 205

Was I deceiv'd or did a sable cloud
Turn forth her silver lining on the
night? *Ib. l.* 221

Sweet Echo, sweetest nymph, that liv'st
unseen
Within thy airy shell

By slow Meander's margent green,
And in the violet-embroider'd vale.
Comus, l. 230

How sweetly did they float upon the wings
Of silence, through the empty-vaulted night,
At every fall smoothing the raven down
Of darkness till it smil'd! *Ib. l.* 249

Such sober certainty of waking bliss.
Ib. l. 263

With thy long level'd rule of streaming light. *Ib. l.* 340

Virtue could see to do what Virtue would
By her own radiant light, though sun and moon
Were in the flat sea sunk. And Wisdom's self
Oft seeks to sweet retired solitude,
Where, with her best nurse Contemplation,
She plumes her feathers, and lets grow her wings. *Ib. l.* 373

The unsunn'd heaps
Of miser's treasure. *Ib. l.* 398

'Tis Chastity, my brother, Chastity:
She that has that, is clad in complete steel.[1] *Ib. l.* 420

How charming is divine philosophy!
Not harsh and crabbed, as dull fools suppose,
But musical as is Apollo's lute,[2]
And a perpetual feast of nectar'd sweets
Where no crude surfeit reigns.
Ib. l. 476

Fill'd the air with barbarous dissonance. *Ib. l.* 550

I was all ear,
And took in strains that might create a soul
Under the ribs of Death. *Ib. l.* 560

[1] See Shakespeare, p. 215a.
[2]   As sweet and musical
As bright Apollo's lute.
SHAKESPEARE, *Love's Labour's Lost*
[1594–1595], *act IV, sc. 3, l. 342*

That power
Which erring men call Chance.
Comus, l. 587

Thou canst not touch the freedom of my mind. *Ib. l.* 663

Praising the lean and sallow abstinence. *Ib. l.* 709

Beauty is Nature's coin, must not be hoarded,
But must be current, and the good thereof
Consists in mutual and partaken bliss.
Ib. l. 739

Beauty is Nature's brag, and must be shown
In courts, at feasts, and high solemnities,
Where most may wonder at the workmanship;
It is for homely features to keep home —
They had their name thence; coarse complexions
And cheeks of sorry grain will serve to ply
The sampler, and to tease the huswife's wool.
What need a vermeil-tinctur'd lip for that,
Love-darting eyes, or tresses like the morn? *Ib. l.* 745

Enjoy your dear wit, and gay rhetoric,
That hath so well been taught her dazzling fence. *Ib. l.* 790

Sabrina fair,
Listen where thou art sitting
Under the glassy, cool, translucent wave,
In twisted braids of lilies knitting
The loose train of thy amber-dropping hair;
Listen for dear honor's sake,
Goddess of the silver lake,
Listen and save. *Ib. l.* 859

But now my task is smoothly done:
I can fly, or I can run. *Ib. l.* 1012

Love Virtue, she alone is free,
She can teach ye how to climb

Higher than the sphery chime;
Or, if Virtue feeble were,
Heav'n itself would stoop to her.
Comus, l. 1019

Yet once more, O ye laurels, and once
 more
Ye myrtles brown, with ivy never sere,
I come to pluck your berries harsh and
 crude,
And with forc'd fingers rude
Shatter your leaves before the mellow-
 ing year. *Lycidas* [1637], *l. 1*

He knew
Himself to sing, and build the lofty
 rhyme. *Ib. l. 10*

Without the meed of some melodious
 tear. *Ib. l. 14*

Hence with denial vain, and coy excuse. *Ib. l. 18*

Under the opening eyelids of the
 morn,
We drove afield; and both together
 heard
What time the gray-fly winds her sultry
 horn,
Batt'ning our flocks with the fresh dews
 of night. *Ib. l. 26*

But O the heavy change, now thou art
 gone,
Now thou art gone and never must return! *Ib. l. 37*

The gadding vine. *Ib. l. 40*

As killing as the canker to the rose.
Ib. l. 45

Whom universal Nature did lament.
Ib. l. 60

Alas! what boots it with incessant
 care
To tend the homely slighted shepherd's
 trade,
And strictly meditate the thankless
 Muse?
Were it not better done as others use,
To sport with Amaryllis in the shade,
Or with the tangles of Neaera's hair?
Fame is the spur that the clear spirit
 doth raise [1]

[1] See Tacitus, p. 140a.

(That last infirmity of noble mind) [1]
To scorn delights, and live laborious
 days;
But the fair guerdon when we hope to
 find,
And think to burst out into sudden
 blaze,
Comes the blind Fury with th' ab-
 horred shears,
And slits the thin-spun life.
Lycidas, l. 64

Fame is no plant that grows on mortal
 soil. *Ib. l. 78*

That strain I heard was of a higher
 mood. *Ib. l. 87*

It was that fatal and perfidious bark,
Built in th' eclipse, and rigg'd with
 curses dark,
That sunk so low that sacred head of
 thine. *Ib. l. 100*

Last came, and last did go,
The Pilot of the Galilean lake;
Two massy keys he bore of metals
 twain,
(The golden opes, the iron shuts
 amain). *Ib. l. 108*

Such as for their bellies' sake,
Creep and intrude, and climb into the
 fold. *Ib. l. 114*

Blind mouths! That scarce themselves
 know how to hold
A sheep-hook. *Ib. l. 119*

The hungry sheep look up, and are not
 fed,
But swoln with wind and the rank mist
 they draw,
Rot inwardly, and foul contagion
 spread:
Besides what the grim wolf with privy
 paw
Daily devours apace, and nothing said;
But that two-handed engine at the
 door

[1] That thirst [for applause], if the last infirmity of noble minds, is also the first infirmity
of weak ones; and on the whole, the strongest
impulsive influence of average humanity. —
RUSKIN, *Sesame and Lilies* [1865], *Of Kings'
Treasuries, sec. 3*

Stands ready to smite once, and smite
no more.

> *Lycidas, l. 123*

Throw hither all your quaint enamel'd
eyes,
That on the green turf suck the honied
showers,
And purple all the ground with vernal
flowers.
Bring the rathe primrose that forsaken
dies.   *Ib. l. 139*

Whether beyond the stormy Hebrides,[1]
Where thou perhaps under the whelm-
ing tide
Visit'st the bottom of the monstrous
world.   *Ib. l. 156*

Look homeward, Angel, now, and melt
with ruth.   *Ib. l. 163*

For Lycidas your sorrow is not dead,
Sunk though he be beneath the watery
floor;
So sinks the day-star in the ocean bed;
And yet anon repairs his drooping
head,
And tricks his beams, and with new-
spangled ore
Flames in the forehead of the morning
sky.
So Lycidas sunk low, but mounted
high,
Through the dear might of him that
walk'd the waves.   *Ib. l. 166*

He touch'd the tender stops of various
quills,
With eager thought warbling his Doric
lay.   *Ib. l. 188*

At last he rose, and twitch'd his mantle
blue:
Tomorrow to fresh woods and pastures
new.   *Ib. l. 192*

    The lazy leaden-stepping Hours,
Whose speed is but the heavy plummet's pace.   *On Time [c. 1637]*

O nightingale, that on yon bloomy
spray

---

[1] See Thomson, p. 420a.

Warbl'st at eve, when all the woods are
still.

> *Sonnet, To the Nightingale*
> *[c. 1637]*

Thy liquid notes that close the eye of
day.   *Ib.*

Where the bright seraphim in burning
row
Their loud up-lifted angel trumpets
blow.

> *At a Solemn Music [c. 1637]*

A poet soaring in the high reason of
his fancies, with his garland and singing
robes about him.

> *The Reason of Church Govern-*
> *ment [1641], bk. II, introduc-*
> *tion*

By labor and intent study (which I
take to be my portion in this life),
joined with the strong propensity of nature, I might perhaps leave something
so written to after-times, as they should
not willingly let it die.   *Ib.*

Beholding the bright countenance of
truth in the quiet and still air of delightful studies.   *Ib.*

He who would not be frustrate of his
hope to write well hereafter in laudable
things ought himself to be a true
poem.

> *Apology for Smectymnuus [1642]*

His words . . . like so many nimble
and airy servitors trip about him at
command.   *Ib.*

Truth . . . never comes into the
world but like a bastard, to the ignominy of him that brought her forth.[1]

> *The Doctrine and Discipline of*
> *Divorce [1643], introduction*

Let not England forget her precedence of teaching nations how to live.[2]

>   *Ib.*

---

[1] Still rule those minds on earth
At whom sage Milton's wormwood words
    were hurled:
"Truth like a bastard comes into the world
Never without ill-fame to him who gives
    her birth"?
         THOMAS HARDY, *Lausanne* [1897]

[2] See Virgil, p. 119a.

Litigious terms, fat contentions, and flowing fees.
Tractate of Education [1644]

Inflamed with the study of learning and the admiration of virtue; stirred up with high hopes of living to be brave men and worthy patriots, dear to God, and famous to all ages. *Ib.*

Ornate rhetoric taught out of the rule of Plato. . . . To which poetry would be made subsequent, or indeed rather precedent, as being less subtle and fine, but more simple, sensuous, and passionate. *Ib.*

In those vernal seasons of the year, when the air is calm and pleasant, it were an injury and sullenness against Nature not to go out, and see her riches, and partake in her rejoicing with heaven and earth. *Ib.*

Books are not absolutely dead things, but do contain a potency of life in them to be as active as that soul was whose progeny they are; nay they do preserve as in a vial the purest efficacy and extraction of that living intellect that bred them. *Areopagitica* [1644]

As good almost kill a man as kill a good book: who kills a man kills a reasonable creature, God's image; but he who destroys a good book kills reason itself. *Ib.*

A good book is the precious lifeblood of a master spirit, embalmed and treasured up on purpose to a life beyond life. *Ib.*

I cannot praise a fugitive and cloistered virtue, unexercised and unbreathed, that never sallies out and sees her adversary, but slinks out of the race, where that immortal garland is to be run for, not without dust and heat. *Ib.*

Where there is much desire to learn, there of necessity will be much arguing, much writing, many opinions; for opinion in good men is but knowledge in the making. *Ib.*

Methinks I see in my mind a noble and puissant nation rousing herself like a strong man after sleep, and shaking her invincible locks. Methinks I see her as an eagle mewing her mighty youth, and kindling her undazzled eyes at the full midday beam.
Areopagitica

Give me the liberty to know, to utter, and to argue freely according to conscience, above all liberties. *Ib.*

Though all the winds of doctrine [1] were let loose to play upon the earth, so Truth be in the field, we do injuriously, by licensing and prohibiting, to misdoubt her strength. Let her and Falsehood grapple; who ever knew Truth put to the worse, in a free and open encounter? [2] *Ib.*

Men of most renowned virtue have sometimes by transgressing most truly kept the law.
Tetrachordon [1644–1645]

That old man eloquent.
To the Lady Margaret Ley
[*c. 1644*]

That would have made Quintilian stare and gasp.
On the Detraction Which Followed Upon My Writing Certain Treatises [1645]

In mirth, that after no repenting draws.
To Cyriack Skinner [1646–1647?]

For other things mild Heav'n a time ordains,
And disapproves that care, though wise in show,
That with superfluous burden loads the day,
And, when God sends a cheerful hour, refrains. *Ib.*

For such kind of borrowing as this, if it be not bettered by the borrower, among good authors is accounted Plagiarè. *Eikonoklastes* [1649], 23

[1] See *Ephesians 4:14*, p. 54a.
[2] Error of opinion may be tolerated where reason is left free to combat it. — JEFFERSON, *Inaugural Address* [March 4, 1801]

None can love freedom heartily, but good men; the rest love not freedom, but license.
Tenure of Kings and Magistrates
[1649]

No man who knows aught, can be so stupid to deny that all men naturally were born free.   *Ib.*

Peace hath her victories
No less renown'd than war.
To the Lord General Cromwell
[1652]

When I consider how my light is spent,
Ere half my days, in this dark world and wide,
And that one talent which is death to hide
Lodg'd with me useless.
On His Blindness [1652]

Doth God exact day-labor, light denied?   *Ib.*

Who best
Bear his mild yoke, they serve him best: his state
Is kingly; thousands at his bidding speed,
And post o'er land and ocean without rest;
They also serve who only stand and wait.   *Ib.*

Avenge, O Lord, thy slaughter'd saints, whose bones
Lie scatter'd on the Alpine mountains cold;
Ev'n them who kept thy truth so pure of old
When all our fathers worship'd stocks and stones
Forget not.
On the Late Massacre in Piedmont [1655]

Yet I argue not
Against Heav'n's hand or will, nor bate one jot
Of heart or hope; but still bear up, and steer
Right onward.
To Cyriack Skinner, Upon his Blindness [c. 1655]

Methought I saw my late espoused saint
Brought to me like Alcestis from the grave.
On his Deceased Wife [c. 1658]

But oh! as to embrace me she inclin'd,
I wak'd, she fled, and day brought back my night.   *Ib.*

Of Man's first disobedience, and the fruit
Of that forbidden tree whose mortal taste
Brought death into the world, and all our woe,
With loss of Eden.
Paradise Lost [1667], *bk. I, l.* 1

Things unattempted yet in prose or rhyme.   *Ib. l.* 16

What in me is dark
Illumine, what is low raise and support;
That to the highth of this great argument
I may assert eternal Providence,
And justify the ways of God to men.[1]
Ib. l. 22

The infernal serpent; he it was, whose guile,
Stirr'd up with envy and revenge, deceiv'd
The mother of mankind.   *Ib. l.* 34

Him the Almighty Power
Hurl'd headlong flaming from th' ethereal sky [2]
With hideous ruin and combustion down
To bottomless perdition, there to dwell
In adamantine chains and penal fire,
Who durst defy th' Omnipotent to arms.   *Ib. l.* 44

As far as angels ken.   *Ib. l.* 59

No light, but rather darkness visible.
Ib. l. 63

Regions of sorrow, doleful shades, where peace

[1] See *Samson Agonistes,* p. 349a; Pope, p. 407b; and A. E. Housman, p. 853b.
[2] See *Luke 10:18,* p. 46b.

And rest can never dwell, hope never
comes
That comes to all.
Paradise Lost, bk. I, l. 65

What though the field be lost?
All is not lost; th' unconquerable will,
And study of revenge, immortal hate,
And courage never to submit or yield.
Ib. l. 105

Vaunting aloud, but rack'd with deep
despair. *Ib. l. 126*

To be weak is miserable,
Doing or suffering. *Ib. l. 157*

And out of good still to find means of
evil. *Ib. l. 165*

The seat of desolation, void of light.
Ib. l. 181

A mind not to be chang'd by place or
time.
The mind is its own place, and in itself
Can make a heav'n of hell, a hell of
heav'n.[1] *Ib. l. 253*

To reign is worth ambition though in
hell:
Better to reign in hell than serve in
heav'n. *Ib. l. 262*

His spear, to equal which the tallest
pine
Hewn on Norwegian hills, to be the
mast
Of some great ammiral, were but a
wand,
He walk'd with, to support uneasy
steps
Over the burning marle. *Ib. l. 292*

Thick as autumnal leaves that strow the
brooks
In Vallombrosa. *Ib. l. 302*

Awake, arise, or be forever fallen!
Ib. l. 330

Spirits, when they please,
Can either sex assume, or both.
Ib. l. 423

[1] See Virgil, p. 199a, Marlowe, p. 213a, and
note.

When night
Darkens the streets, then wander forth
the sons
Of Belial, flown with insolence and
wine.
Paradise Lost, bk. I, l. 500

Th' imperial ensign, which, full high
advanc'd,
Shone like a meteor, streaming to the
wind.[1] *Ib. l. 536*
Sonorous metal blowing martial sounds:
At which the universal host up sent
A shout that tore hell's concave, and
beyond
Frighted the reign of Chaos and old
Night. *Ib. l. 540*

Anon they move
In perfect phalanx, to the Dorian
mood
Of flutes and soft recorders.
Ib. l. 549

His form had yet not lost
All her original brightness, nor ap-
pear'd
Less than archangel ruin'd, and th' ex-
cess
Of glory obscur'd. *Ib. l. 591*

The sun . . .
In dim eclipse, disastrous twilight
sheds
On half the nations, and with fear of
change
Perplexes monarchs. *Ib. l. 594*

Care
Sat on his faded cheek, but under
brows
Of dauntless courage. *Ib. l. 601*

Thrice he assay'd, and thrice, in spite
of scorn,
Tears, such as angels weep, burst
forth. *Ib. l. 619*

Who overcomes
By force hath overcome but half his
foe. *Ib. l. 648*

Mammon, the least erected spirit that
fell

[1] Stream'd like a meteor to the troubled air.
— THOMAS GRAY, *The Bard* [1757], sec. I, st. 2,
l. 6

From heaven; for ev'n in heaven his
  looks and thoughts
Were always downward bent, admiring
  more
The riches of heaven's pavement, trod-
  den gold,
Than aught divine or holy else enjoy'd
In vision beatific.
>   *Paradise Lost, bk. I, l. 679*

>   Let none admire
That riches grow in hell; that soil may
  best
Deserve the precious bane.
>   *Ib. l. 690*

>   From morn
To noon he fell, from noon to dewy
  eve,
A summer's day; and with the setting
  sun
Dropp'd from the zenith like a falling
  star.   *Ib. l. 742*

High on a throne of royal state, which
  far
Outshone the wealth of Ormus and of
  Ind,
Or where the gorgeous East with rich-
  est hand
Showers on her kings barbaric pearl and
  gold,
Satan exalted sat, by merit rais'd
To that bad eminence; and from de-
  spair
Thus high uplifted beyond hope, as-
  pires
Beyond thus high, insatiate to pursue
Vain war with heav'n.   *Ib. II, l. 1*

>   Moloch, scepter'd king,
Stood up, the strongest and the fiercest
  spirit
That fought in heav'n; now fiercer by
  despair.   *Ib. l. 44*

>   Rather than be less
Car'd not to be at all.   *Ib. l. 47*

My sentence is for open war.
>   *Ib. l. 51*

Which if not victory is yet revenge.
>   *Ib. l. 105*

But all was false and hollow; though his
  tongue
Dropp'd manna, and could make the
  worse appear
The better reason.[1]
>   *Paradise Lost, bk. II, l. 112*

>   For who would lose,
Though full of pain, this intellectual
  being,
Those thoughts that wander through
  eternity,
To perish rather, swallow'd up and lost
In the wide womb of uncreated night,
Devoid of sense and motion?
>   *Ib. l. 146*

His red right hand.[2]   *Ib. l. 174*

Unrespited, unpitied, unrepriev'd.[3]
>   *Ib. l. 185*

>   The never-ending flight
Of future days.   *Ib. l. 221*

Thus Belial with words cloth'd in reason's garb
Counsel'd ignoble ease, and peaceful
  sloth,
Not peace.   *Ib. l. 226*

>   With grave
Aspect he rose, and in his rising
  seem'd
A pillar of state; deep on his front en-
  graven
Deliberation sat and public care;
And princely counsel in his face yet
  shone,
Majestic though in ruin.   *Ib. l. 300*

>   To sit in darkness here
Hatching vain empires.   *Ib. l. 377*

The palpable obscure.   *Ib. l. 406*

>   Long is the way
And hard, that out of hell leads up to
  light.[4]   *Ib. l. 432*

Their rising all at once was as the
  sound
Of thunder heard remote.   *Ib. l. 476*

---

[1] See Aristophanes, p. 91a.
[2] Rubente dextera. — HORACE [65–8 B.C.].
Odes I, ii, 2, To Caesar Augustus
[3] See Homer, p. 64b, and note.
[4] See Virgil, p. 118b.

Others apart sat on a hill retir'd,
In thoughts more elevate, and reason'd
  high
Of Providence, foreknowledge, will, and
  fate,
Fix'd fate, free will, foreknowledge absolute,
And found no end, in wand'ring mazes
  lost.
          Paradise Lost, bk. II, l. 557

Vain wisdom all, and false philosophy.
                    Ib. l. 565

    Arm th' obdur'd breast
With stubborn patience as with triple
  steel.[1]   *Ib. l.* 568

Far off from these a slow and silent
  stream,
Lethe the river of oblivion rolls.
                    Ib. l. 582

At certain revolutions all the damn'd
Are brought: and feel by turns the bitter change
Of fierce extremes, extremes by change
  more fierce.   *Ib. l.* 597

    The other shape,
If shape it might be call'd.
                    Ib. l. 666

Whence and what art thou, execrable
  shape?   *Ib. l.* 681

Before mine eyes in opposition sits
Grim Death [2] my son and foe.
                    Ib. l. 803

Hot, cold, moist, and dry, four champions fierce,[3]
Strive here for mast'ry.   *Ib. l.* 898

    To compare
Great things with small.   *Ib. l.* 921

With ruin upon ruin, rout on rout,
Confusion worse confounded.
                    Ib. l. 995

And fast by hanging in a golden chain,
This pendent world, in bigness as a
  star

  [1] See Shakespeare, p. 215a.
  [2] See Massinger, p. 316a.
  [3] Hot and cold, and moist and dry. — Du
Bartas, *Divine Weeks and Works* [1578], *Second Day*
    See Dryden, p. 369b.

Of smallest magnitude close by the
  moon.
          Paradise Lost, bk. II, l. 1051

Hail, holy light! offspring of heav'n firstborn.[1]   *Ib. III, l.* 1

    Thus with the year
Seasons return; but not to me returns
Day, or the sweet approach of ev'n or
  morn,
Or sight of vernal bloom, or summer's
  rose,
Or flocks, or herds, or human face di-
  vine; [2]
But cloud instead, and ever-during
  dark
Surrounds me, from the cheerful ways
  of men
Cut off, and for the book of knowledge
  fair
Presented with a universal blank
Of Nature's works to me expung'd and
  raz'd,
And wisdom at one entrance quite shut
  out.   *Ib. l.* 40

See golden days, fruitful of golden
  deeds,
With Joy and Love triumphing.
                    Ib. l. 337

Dark with excessive bright.
                    Ib. l. 380

Into a limbo large and broad, since
  called
The Paradise of Fools, to few unknown.   *Ib. l.* 495

The hell within him.   *Ib. IV, l.* 20

    At whose sight all the stars
Hide their diminish'd heads.[3]
                    Ib. l. 34

    A grateful mind
By owing owes not, but still pays, at
  once
Indebted and discharg'd.   *Ib. l.* 55

  [1] God's first creature, which was light. —
Bacon, *The New Atlantis* [1626]
    Light, the prime work of God. — Milton,
Samson Agonistes (1671), l. 70
  [2] See Blake, pp. 487a and 489b.
  [3] Ye little stars! hide your diminished rays.
— Pope: *Moral Essays* [1731–1735], *Epistle III,
l.* 282

Me miserable! which way shall I fly
Infinite wrath, and infinite despair?
Which way I fly is hell; myself am
  hell; [1]
And in the lowest deep a lower deep,
Still threat'ning to devour me, opens
  wide,
To which the hell I suffer seems a
  heaven.
  Paradise Lost, bk. IV, l. 73

So farewell hope, and with hope farewell fear,
Farewell remorse: all good to me is
  lost;
Evil, be thou my good. *Ib. l.* 108

  And on the Tree of Life,
The middle tree and highest there that
  grew,
Sat like a cormorant. *Ib. l.* 194

A heaven on earth. *Ib. l.* 208

Flowers of all hue, and without thorn
  the rose. *Ib. l.* 256

Two of far nobler shape erect and tall,
Godlike erect, with native honor clad
In naked majesty seem'd lords of all.
  Ib. l. 288

For contemplation he and valor.
  form'd,
For softness she and sweet attractive
  grace;
He for God only, she for God in him.
  Ib. l. 297

  Implied
Subjection, but requir'd with gentle
  sway,
And by her yielded, by him best re-
  ceiv'd,
Yielded with coy submission, modest
  pride,
And sweet reluctant amorous delay.
  Ib. l. 307

Adam the goodliest man of men since
  born
His sons, the fairest of her daughters
  Eve. *Ib. l.* 323

So spake the Fiend, and with necessity,

[1] See Virgil, p. 199a, Marlowe, p. 213a, and note.

The tyrant's plea,[1] excus'd his devilish
  deeds.
  Paradise Lost, bk. IV, l. 393

Imparadis'd in one another's arms.
  Ib. l. 506

  Live while ye may,
Yet happy pair. *Ib. l.* 533

Now came still evening on, and twilight
  gray
Had in her sober livery all things clad.
  Ib. l. 598

  The wakeful nightingale,
She all night long her amorous descant
  sung;
Silence was pleas'd: now glow'd the
  firmament
With living sapphires: Hesperus, that
  led
The starry host, rode brightest, till the
  moon,
Rising in clouded majesty, at length
Apparent queen unveil'd her peerless
  light,
And o'er the dark her silver mantle
  threw. *Ib. l.* 602

The timely dew of sleep. *Ib. l.* 614

With thee conversing I forget all time,
All seasons, and their change; all please
  alike.
Sweet is the breath of morn, her rising
  sweet,
With charm of earliest birds.
  Ib. l. 639

  Sweet the coming on
Of grateful ev'ning mild, then silent
  night
With this her solemn bird, and this fair
  moon,
And these the gems of heaven, her
  starry train. *Ib. l.* 646

Millions of spiritual creatures walk the
  earth
Unseen, both when we wake, and when
  we sleep. *Ib. l.* 677

  In naked beauty more adorn'd,

[1] See William Pitt, p. 496b.

More lovely, than Pandora.[1]
> *Paradise Lost, bk. IV, l. 713*

Eas'd the putting off
These troublesome disguises which we
wear.   *Ib. l. 739*

Hail wedded love, mysterious law, true
source
Of human offspring.   *Ib. l. 750*

Squat like a toad, close at the ear of
Eve.   *Ib. l. 800*

Not to know me argues yourselves unknown.   *Ib. l. 830*

Abash'd the Devil stood,
And felt how awful goodness is, and
saw
Virtue in her shape how lovely.
         Ib. l. 846

All hell broke loose.[2]   *Ib. l. 918*

Like Teneriff or Atlas unremoved.
         Ib. l. 987

The starry cope
Of heaven.   *Ib. l. 992*

His sleep
Was airy light from pure digestion
bred.   *Ib. V, l. 3*

My latest found,
Heaven's last, best gift, my ever new
delight!   *Ib. l. 18*

Good, the more
Communicated, more abundant grows.
         Ib. l. 71

These are thy glorious works, Parent of
good.   *Ib. l. 153*

Him first, him last, him midst, and
without end.   *Ib. l. 165*

A wilderness of sweets.   *Ib. l. 294*

So saying, with dispatchful looks in
haste
She turns, on hospitable thoughts intent.   *Ib. l. 331*

Nor jealousy
Was understood, the injur'd lover's
hell.   *Ib. l. 449*

[1] See Cicero, p. 111a, and James Thomson,
p. 419b.
[2] See Robert Greene, p. 206a.

Freely we serve,
Because we freely love, as in our will
To love or not; in this we stand or fall.
> *Paradise Lost, bk. V, l. 538*

What if earth
Be but the shadow of heaven, and
things therein
Each to other like, more than on earth
is thought?   *Ib. l. 574*

Hear all ye Angels, progeny of light,
Thrones, Dominations, Princedoms,
Virtues, Powers.   *Ib. l. 600*

All seem'd well pleas'd, all seem'd but
were not all.   *Ib. l. 617*

Among the faithless, faithful only he.
         Ib. l. 897

Morn,
Wak'd by the circling hours, with rosy
hand [1]
Unbarr'd the gates of light.
         Ib. VI, l. 2

Servant of God, well done,[2] well hast
thou fought
The better fight, who single hast maintained
Against revolted multitudes the cause
Of truth, in word mightier than they in
arms.   *Ib. l. 29*

He onward came; far off his coming
shone.   *Ib. l. 768*

More safe I sing with mortal voice, un-
chang'd
To hoarse or mute, though fall'n on
evil days,
On evil days though fall'n, and evil
tongues;
In darkness, and with dangers compass'd round,
And solitude.   *Ib. VII, l. 24*

Out of one man a race
Of men innumerable.   *Ib. l. 155*

There Leviathan
Hugest of living creatures, on the deep
Stretch'd like a promontory sleeps or
swims,

[1] See Homer, p. 62b.
[2] See *Matthew 25:21*, p. 44a.

And seems a moving land, and at his
    gills
Draws in, and at his trunk spouts out a
    sea.
        Paradise Lost, bk. VII, *l. 412*

       Endued
With sanctity of reason.   *Ib. l. 507*

The planets in their stations list'ning
    stood,
While the bright pomp ascended jubi-
    lant.
Open, ye everlasting gates, they sung,
Open, ye heavens, your living doors; [1]
    let in
The great Creator from his work re-
    turn'd
Magnificent, his six days' work, a
    world.   *Ib. l. 563*

The angel ended, and in Adam's ear
So charming left his voice that he
    awhile
Thought him still speaking, still stood
    fix'd to hear.   *Ib.* VIII, *l. 1*

       To know
That which before us lies in daily life
Is the prime wisdom.   *Ib. l. 192*

Liquid lapse of murmuring streams.
                    Ib. l. 263

And feel that I am happier than I
    know.   *Ib. l. 282*

Her virtue and the conscience of her
    worth,
That would be woo'd, and not un-
    sought be won.   *Ib. l. 502*

The sum of earthly bliss.   *Ib. l. 522*

     So absolute she seems
And in herself complete, so well to
    know
Her own, that what she wills to do or
    say,
Seems wisest, virtuousest, discreetest,
    best.   *Ib. l. 547*

Accuse not Nature, she hath done her
    part;
Do thou but thine.   *Ib. l. 561*

[1] See *Psalm 24:7*, p. 18a.

Ofttimes nothing profits more
Than self-esteem, grounded on just and
    right
Well manag'd.
        Paradise Lost, bk. VIII, *l. 571*

My unpremeditated verse.
                Ib. IX, *l. 24*

Pleas'd me long choosing, and begin-
    ning late.   *Ib. l. 26*

    Unless an age too late, or cold
Climate, or years damp my intended
    wing.   *Ib. l. 44*

The serpent subtlest beast of all the
    field.[1]   *Ib. l. 86*

For solitude sometimes is best society,
And short retirement urges sweet re-
    turn.   *Ib. l. 249*

At shut of evening flowers.
                Ib. l. 278

As one who long in populous city
    pent.[2]   *Ib. l. 445*

God so commanded, and left that com-
    mand
Sole daughter of his voice; [3] the rest,
    we live
Law to ourselves, our reason is our law.
                Ib. l. 652

    Her rash hand in evil hour
Forth reaching to the fruit, she pluck'd,
    she eat:
Earth felt the wound, and Nature from
    her seat,
Sighing through all her works, gave
    signs of woe
That all was lost.   *Ib. l. 780*

So dear I love him, that with him all
    deaths
I could endure, without him live no
    life.   *Ib. l. 832*

    In her face excuse
Came prologue, and apology too
    prompt.   *Ib. l. 853*

O fairest of creation! last and best
Of all God's works! creature in whom
    excell'd

[1] See *Genesis 3:1*, p. 5b.
[2] See Keats, p. 579a.
[3] See Wordsworth, p. 514b.

Whatever can to sight or thought be
  form'd,
Holy, divine, good, amiable, or sweet!
How art thou lost, how on a sudden
  lost,
Defac'd, deflower'd, and now to Death
  devote?
          Paradise Lost, bk. IX, l. 896

          I feel
The link of nature draw me: flesh of
  flesh,
Bone of my bone thou art,[1] and from
  thy state
Mine never shall be parted, bliss or
  woe.   *Ib. l. 913*

Our state cannot be sever'd; we are
  one,
One flesh; to lose thee were to lose myself.   *Ib. l. 958*

      I shall temper so
Justice with mercy.   *Ib. X, l. 77*

Pandemonium, city and proud seat
Of Lucifer.   *Ib. l. 424*

A dismal universal hiss, the sound
Of public scorn.   *Ib. l. 508*

Death . . . on his pale horse.[2]
                          Ib. l. 588

Demoniac frenzy, moping melancholy,
And moon-struck madness.
                      Ib. XI, l. 485

Nor love thy life, nor hate; but what
  thou liv'st
Live well; how long or short permit to
  Heaven.[3]   *Ib. l. 553*

A bevy of fair women.   *Ib. l. 582*

      The evening star,
Love's harbinger.   *Ib. l. 588*

The brazen throat of war.
                          Ib. l. 713

      For now I see
Peace to corrupt no less than war to
  waste.   *Ib. l. 783*

An olive leaf he brings, pacific sign.
                          Ib. l. 860

[1] See *Genesis 2:23*, p. 5b.
[2] See *Revelation 6:8*, p. 58a.
[3] See Martial, p. 134b.

In me is no delay; with thee to go,
Is to stay here; without thee here to
  stay,
Is to go hence unwilling; thou to me
Art all things under heaven, all places
  thou,
Who for my willful crime art banished
  hence.
        Paradise Lost, bk. XII, l. 615

The world was all before them, where
  to choose
Their place of rest, and Providence
  their guide:
They hand in hand with wand'ring
  steps and slow
Through Eden took their solitary way.
                          Ib. l. 646

      Most men admire
Virtue who follow not her lore.
        Paradise Regained [1671], *bk. I,
                            l. 482*

Skill'd to retire, and in retiring draw
Hearts after them tangled in amorous
  nets.   *Ib. II, l. 161*

      Beauty stands
In the admiration only of weak minds
Led captive.   *Ib. l. 220*

Rocks whereon greatest men have oftest
  wreck'd.   *Ib. l. 228*

Of whom to be disprais'd were no small
  praise.   *Ib. III, l. 56*

Elephants endorsed with towers.
                          Ib. l. 329

Dusk faces with white silken turbans
  wreath'd.   *Ib. IV, l. 76*

      The childhood shows the man,
As morning shows the day.[1]
                          Ib. l. 220

Athens, the eye of Greece, mother of
  arts
And eloquence.   *Ib. l. 240*

      The olive grove of Academe,[2]
Plato's retirement, where the Attic
  bird
Trills her thick-warbled notes the summer long.   *Ib. l. 244*

[1] See Wordsworth, p. 511b.
[2] See Horace, p. 124a.

Socrates . . .
Whom well inspir'd the oracle pro-
nounc'd
Wisest of men.
> *Paradise Regained,*
> *bk. IV, l. 274*

The first and wisest of them all professed
To know this only, that he nothing
knew.[1]   *Ib. l. 293*

Deep vers'd in books and shallow in
himself.   *Ib. l. 327*

Till morning fair
Came forth with pilgrim steps, in amice
gray.   *Ib. l. 426*

Eyeless in Gaza, at the mill with
slaves.
> *Samson Agonistes* [1671], *l. 41*

O dark, dark, dark, amid the blaze of
noon,
Irrecoverably dark, total eclipse
Without all hope of day!   *Ib. l. 80*

The sun to me is dark
And silent as the moon,
When she deserts the night,
Hid in her vacant interlunar cave.
> *Ib. l. 86*

To live a life half dead, a living death.
> *Ib. l. 100*

Ran on embattled armies clad in iron,
And, weaponless himself,
Made arms ridiculous.   *Ib. l. 129*

Apt words have power to suage
The tumors of a troubled mind.[2]
> *Ib. l. 184*

Wisest men
Have err'd, and by bad women been deceiv'd.   *Ib. l. 210*

Just are the ways of God,
And justifiable to men;[3]
Unless there be who think not God at
all.   *Ib. l. 293*

A grain of manhood.   *Ib. l. 408*

What boots it at one gate to make defense,

[1] See Socrates, p. 87b.
[2] See Aeschylus, p. 78a.
[3] See *Paradise Lost, bk. I, l. 22,* p. 341b.

And at another to let in the foe?
> *Samson Agonistes, l. 560*

My race of glory run, and race of
shame,
And I shall shortly be with them at
rest.   *Ib. l. 597*

But who is this, what thing of sea or
land?
Female of sex it seems,
That so bedeck'd, ornate, and gay,
Comes this way sailing
Like a stately ship
Of Tarsus, bound for th' isles
Of Javan or Gadire,
With all her bravery on, and tackle
trim,
Sails fill'd, and streamers waving,
Courted by all the winds that hold
them play;
An amber scent of odorous perfume
Her harbinger?   *Ib. l. 710*

Dalila: In argument with men a woman
ever
Goes by the worse, whatever be her
cause.
Samson: For want of words, no doubt,
or lack of breath!   *Ib. l. 903*

Fame, if not double-faced, is double-
mouthed,
And with contrary blast proclaims most
deeds;
On both his wings, one black, the other
white,
Bears greatest names in his wild airy
flight.   *Ib. l. 971*

Yet beauty, though injurious, hath
strange power,
After offense returning, to regain
Love once possess'd.   *Ib. l. 1003*

Love-quarrels oft in pleasing concord
end;
Not wedlock-treachery.   *Ib. l. 1008*

Boast not of what thou would'st have
done, but do
What then thou would'st.
> *Ib. l. 1104*

He's gone; and who knows how he may
report

Thy words by adding fuel to the flame?
　　　　　Samson Agonistes, l. 1350

For evil news rides post, while good
　　news baits.[1]　　　　*Ib. l. 1538*

Suspense in news is torture.
　　　　　　　　Ib. l. 1569

Nothing is here for tears, nothing to
　　wail
Or knock the breast, no weakness, no
　　contempt,
Dispraise, or blame, nothing but well
　　and fair,
And what may quiet us in a death so
　　noble.　　　　*Ib. l. 1721*

All is best, though we oft doubt,
What the unsearchable dispose
Of highest Wisdom brings about.
　　　　　　　　Ib. l. 1745

Calm of mind, all passion spent.
　　　　　　　　Ib. l. 1758

Such bickerings to recount, met
often in these our writers, what more
worth is it than to chronicle the wars of
kites or crows flocking and fighting in
the air?
　　　The History of England [1670],
　　　　　　　　　　　　　bk. IV

SIR JOHN SUCKLING
1609–1642

Why so pale and wan, fond lover?
　　Prithee, why so pale?
Will, when looking well can't move
　　her,
　　Looking ill prevail?
　　　　Aglaura [1638]. *Song, st. 1*

Quit, quit, for shame, this will not
　　move,
　　This cannot take her.
If of herself she will not love,
　　Nothing can make her.
The devil take her!　　　*Ib. st. 3*

But as when an authentic watch is
　　shown,
Each man winds up and rectifies his
　　own,

[1] See Plutarch, p. 137a.

So in our very judgments.[1]
　　　　　Aglaura, epilogue

High characters (cries one), and he
　　would see
Things that ne'er were, nor are, nor
　　ne'er will be.[2]
　　　The Goblins [1639], *epilogue*

Her feet beneath her petticoat
Like little mice, stole in and out,[3]
　　As if they feared the light;
But oh, she dances such a way!
No sun upon an Easter-day
　　Is half so fine a sight.
　　　A Ballad Upon a Wedding
　　　　　　　　[1641], *st. 8*

Her lips were red, and one was thin,
Compared with that was next her chin,
　　Some bee had stung it newly.
　　　　　　　　Ib. st. 11

I prithee send me back my heart,
　　Since I cannot have thine;
For if from yours you will not part,
　　Why then shouldst thou have mine?
　　Fragmenta Aurea [1646]. *Song,*
　　　　　　　　　　　　　st. 1

'Tis not the meat, but 'tis the appetite
Makes eating a delight.
　　　Ib. Of Thee, Kind Boy, st. 3

Out upon it, I have loved
　　Three whole days together;
And am like to love three more,
　　If it prove fair weather.
　　　Ib. A Poem with the Answer,
　　　　　　　　　　　　　st. 1

'Tis expectation makes a blessing dear,
Heaven were not heaven, if we knew
　　what it were.
　　　Ib. Against Fruition, st. 4

[1] See Pope, p. 402b.
[2] See Pope, p. 403a.
There's no such thing in Nature, and you'll
　　draw
A faultless monster which the world ne'er saw.
　　JOHN SHEFFIELD, DUKE OF BUCKING-
　　HAM AND NORMANBY [1648–1721], *Es-
　　say on Poetry*
[3] See Herrick, p. 320b.

NAKAE TOJU[1]
1608–1648

Filial piety is the root of man. When it is lost from one's heart, then one's life becomes like a rootless plant, and if one does not expire instantly, it is nothing but sheer luck.

> *Toju Sensei Zenshu (Collected Works), vol. 1*

SIR MATTHEW HALE[2]
1609–1676

Be not biased with compassion to the poor, or favor to the rich, in point of justice.

> *Things Necessary to Be Continually Had in Remembrance*

Not to be solicitous what men will say or think.   *Ib.*

WILLIAM CARTWRIGHT
1611–1643

Love makes those young whom age doth chill,
And whom he finds young, keeps young still.   *To Chloe* [1651]

ARCHBISHOP ROBERT LEIGHTON
1611–1684

Deliver me, O Lord, from the errors of wise men, yea, and of good men.
                                        Saying

ISAAC DE BENSERADE
1612–1691

In bed we laugh, in bed we cry;
And, born in bed, in bed we die.
The near approach a bed may show
Of human bliss to human woe.

> À Son Lit (*Translated by* SAMUEL JOHNSON)

---

[1] From *Sources of Japanese Tradition,* edited by William Theodore de Bary [1958].
[2] Lord Chief Justice of England.

ANNE BRADSTREET
c. 1612 – 1672

Youth is the time of getting, middle age of improving, and old age of spending; a negligent youth is usually attended by an ignorant middle age, and both by an empty old age. He that hath nothing to feed on but vanity and lies must needs lie down in the bed of sorrow.   *Thirty-three Meditations,* 3

Authority without wisdom is like a heavy axe without an edge, fitter to bruise than polish.   *Ib. 12*

If we had no winter, the spring would not be so pleasant: if we did not sometimes taste of adversity, prosperity would not be so welcome.   *Ib. 14*

Iron till it be thoroughly heated is uncapable to be wrought; so God sees good to cast some men into the furnace of affliction, and then beats them on his anvil into what frame he pleases.
                                        Ib. 31

If ever two were one, then surely we.
If ever man were lov'd by wife, then thee;
If ever wife was happy in a man,
Compare with me ye women if you can.

> *To My Dear and Loving Husband* [1678]

SAMUEL BUTLER
1612–1680

When civil fury first grew high,
And men fell out they knew not why.
> *Hudibras, pt. I* [1663], *canto I, l. 1*

And pulpit, drum ecclesiastic,[1]
Was beat with fist, instead of a stick.
                                        Ib. l. 11

Beside, 'tis known he could speak Greek

---

[1] This is the first we hear of the "drum ecclesiastic" beating up for recruits in worldly warfare in our country. — WASHINGTON IRVING, *Knickerbocker's History of New York* [1809], *bk. V, ch. 7*

As naturally as pigs squeak: [1]
That Latin was no more difficile
Than to a blackbird 'tis to whistle.
Hudibras, pt. I, canto I, l. 51

He could distinguish and divide
A hair 'twixt south and southwest side,
On either which he would dispute,
Confute, change hands, and still confute.   *Ib. l.* 67

He'd run in debt by disputation,
And pay with ratiocination.
                          Ib. l. 77

For rhetoric, he could not ope
His mouth, but out there flew a trope.
                          Ib. l. 81

For all a rhetorician's rules
Teach nothing but to name his tools.
                          Ib. l. 89

A Babylonish dialect
Which learned pedants much affect.
                          Ib. l. 93

For he by geometric scale,
Could take the size of pots of ale.
                          Ib. l. 121

And wisely tell what hour o' th' day
The clock doth strike, by algebra.
                          Ib. l. 125

Where entity and quiddity,
The ghosts of defunct bodies, fly.
                          Ib. l. 145

'Twas Presbyterian true blue.
                          Ib. l. 189

Such as do build their faith upon
The holy text of pike and gun.
                          Ib. l. 193

And prove their doctrine orthodox,
By apostolic blows and knocks.
                          Ib. l. 197

Compound for sins they are inclined to,
By damning those they have no mind
to.   *Ib. l.* 213

[1] He Greek and Latin speaks with greater ease
Than hogs eat acorns, and tame pigeons peas.
LIONEL CRANFIELD, EARL OF MIDDLESEX [1575–1645], *Panegyric on Tom Coriate*

The trenchant blade, Toledo trusty,
For want of fighting was grown rusty,
And ate into itself, for lack
Of somebody to hew and hack.
Hudibras, pt. I, canto I, l. 357

For rhyme the rudder is of verses,
With which like ships they steer their courses.   *Ib. l.* 457

And force them, though it was in spite
Of Nature and their stars, to write.
                          Ib. l. 647

Great actions are not always true sons
Of great and mighty resolutions.
                          Ib. l. 885

    I'll make the fur
Fly 'bout the ears of the old cur.
                          Ib. canto III, l. 277

These reasons made his mouth to water.   *Ib. l.* 379

I am not now in fortune's power:
He that is down can fall no lower.[1]
                          Ib. l. 871

Cheer'd up himself with ends of verse,
And sayings of philosophers.
                          Ib. l. 1011

Cleric before, and Lay behind;
A lawless linsey-woolsey brother,
Half of one order, half another.
                          Ib. l. 1226

Some have been beaten till they know
What wood a cudgel's of by th' blow;
Some kick'd, until they can feel whether
A shoe be Spanish or neat's leather.
Ib. pt. II [1664], *canto I, l.* 221

Such great achievements cannot fail,
To cast salt on a woman's tail.
                          Ib. l. 277

For what is worth in anything
But so much money as 'twill bring?
                          Ib. l. 465

She that with poetry is won
Is but a desk to write upon.
                          Ib. l. 591

[1] He that is down needs fear no fall. —
BUNYAN, *Pilgrim's Progress* [1678], *pt. II*

Love is a boy by poets styl'd;
Then spare the rod, and spoil the child.[1]

> *Hudibras, pt. II,*
> *canto I, l. 843*

The sun had long since in the lap
Of Thetis, taken out his nap,
And like a lobster boil'd, the morn
From black to red began to turn.

> *Ib. canto II, l. 29*

Oaths are but words, and words but wind. *Ib. l. 107*

For truth is precious and divine —
Too rich a pearl for carnal swine.

> *Ib. l. 257*

He that imposes an oath makes it,
Not he that for convenience takes it;
Then how can any man be said
To break an oath he never made?

> *Ib. l. 377*

　　　As the ancients
Say wisely, have a care o' th' main chance,[2]
And look before you ere you leap;[3]
For as you sow, ye are like to reap.[4]

> *Ib. l. 501*

Doubtless the pleasure is as great
Of being cheated as to cheat.

> *Ib. canto III, l. 1*

He made an instrument to know
If the moon shine at full or no.

> *Ib. l. 261*

As men of inward light are wont
To turn their optics in upon 't.

> *Ib. pt. III [1678], canto I, l. 481*

What makes all doctrines plain and clear?
About two hundred pounds a year.
And that which was prov'd true before,
Prove false again? Two hundred more.

> *Ib. l. 1277*

Nick Machiavel had ne'er a trick,

Though he gave his name to our Old Nick.

> *Hudibras, pt. III,*
> *canto I, l. 1313*

With crosses, relics, crucifixes,
Beads, pictures, rosaries, and pixes —
The tools of working our salvation
By mere mechanic operation.

> *Ib. l. 1495*

The saints engage in fierce contests
About their carnal interests.

> *Ib. canto II, introduction*

True as the dial to the sun,[1]
Although it be not shin'd upon.

> *Ib. l. 175*

He that complies against his will
Is of his own opinion still.

> *Ib. canto III, l. 547*

Neither have the hearts to stay,
Nor wit enough to run away.

> *Ib. l. 569*

And poets by their sufferings grow,[2]
As if there were no more to do,
To make a poet excellent,
But only want and discontent.

> *Fragments*

JAMES GRAHAM
FIRST MARQUESS OF
MONTROSE
1612–1650

He either fears his fate too much,
　Or his deserts are small,
That puts it not unto the touch
　To win or lose it all.

> *My Dear and Only Love, st. 2*

I'll make thee glorious by my pen,
And famous by my sword.[3]

> *Ib. st. 5*

---

[1] See *Proverbs, 13:24,* p. 24a, and Menander, p. 102a.
[2] See Lyly, p. 202b.
[3] See Heywood, p. 182a.
[4] See *Galatians 6:7,* p. 54a.

[1] True as the needle to the pole,
　Or as the dial to the sun.
　　BARTON BOOTH [1681–1733], *Song*
[2] See Shelley, p. 569b.
[3] I'll make thee famous by my pen,
　And glorious by my sword.
　　SCOTT, *Legend of Montrose* [1819], *ch. 15*

RICHARD CRASHAW
c. 1613 – 1649

The conscious water saw its God, and blushed.[1]
> *Epigrammata Sacra* [1634].
> *Aquae in Vinum Versae*

Two went to pray? Oh, rather say
One went to brag, the other to pray.
> *Steps to the Temple* [1648].
> *Two Went Up into the Temple to Pray* [2]

Whoe'er she be,
That not impossible she
That shall command my heart and me.
> *Ib. Wishes to His Supposed Mistress, l. 1*

Where'er she lie,
Locked up from mortal eye,
In shady leaves of destiny.   *Ib. l. 4*

Life that dares send
A challenge to his end,
And when it comes, say, Welcome, friend!   *Ib. l. 85*

Sidnaeian showers
Of sweet discourse, whose powers
Can crown old Winter's head with flowers.   *Ib. l. 88*

I would be married, but I'd have no wife,
I would be married to a single life.
> *Ib. On Marriage*

All is Caesar's, and what odds
So long as Caesar's self is God's?
> *Ib. Mark XII*

All those fair and flagrant things.
> *The Flaming Heart Upon the Book of Saint Teresa* [1652], *l. 34*

Love's passives are his activ'st part.
The wounded is the wounding heart.
> *Ib. l. 73*

O thou undaunted daughter of desires!
> *Ib. l. 93*

By all the eagle in thee, all the dove.
> *Ib. l. 95*

Poor world (said I) what wilt thou do
To entertain this starry stranger?
Is this the best thou canst bestow?
A cold, and not too cleanly, manger?
Contend, ye powers of heav'n and earth,
To fit a bed for this huge birth.
> *Hymn of the Nativity* [1652], *st. 6*

Proud world, said I, cease your contest,
And let the mighty babe alone.
The phoenix builds the phoenix' nest.
Love's architecture is his own.
The babe whose birth embraves this morn,
Made his own bed ere he was born.
> *Ib. st. 7*

Welcome, all wonders in one sight!
Eternity shut in a span.
> *Ib. Full Chorus*

The modest front of this small floor,
Believe me, reader, can say more
Than many a braver marble can —
"Here lies a truly honest man!"
> *Epitaph Upon Mr. Ashton*

---

[1] Nympha pudica Deum vidit, et erubuit. — Quoted by SAMUEL JOHNSON [1778]; from BOSWELL, *Life of Dr. Johnson* [1791], *vol. II, p. 218* [Everyman ed.]. A footnote states that this line has frequently been attributed to Dryden, but appeared in Crashaw's *Epigrammata Sacra* [1634].
> The bashful stream hath seen its God and blushed. — AARON HILL [1685–1750]
>> The water hears thy faintest word,
>> And blushes into wine.
>>> JOHN SAMUEL BEWLEY MONSELL [1811–1875], *Mysterious Is Thy Presence, Lord, st. 1*

[2] Two men went up into the temple to pray, the one a Pharisee, and the other a publican. — *Luke 18:10*

FRANÇOIS, DUC DE LA ROCHEFOUCAULD[1]
1613–1680

Our virtues are most frequently but vices in disguise.[2]
> *Reflections; or, Sentences and Moral Maxims. Epigraph*

---

[1] The fifth edition [1678] is the standard one.
[2] This epigraph, which is the key to the system of La Rochefoucauld, is found in another form as no. 179 of the Maxims of the first edition, 1665; it is omitted from the second and

Self-love is the greatest of all flatterers.

Reflections 2

We all have strength enough to endure the misfortunes of others.[1]

Ib. 19

Philosophy triumphs easily over past evils and future evils; but present evils triumph over it.[2]

Ib. 22

We need greater virtues to sustain good fortune than bad.

Ib. 25

If we had no faults of our own, we would not take so much pleasure in noticing those of others.

Ib. 31

Jealousy feeds upon suspicion, and it turns into fury or it ends as soon as we pass from suspicion to certainty.

Ib. 32

Self-interest speaks all sorts of tongues, and plays all sorts of roles, even that of disinterestedness.

Ib. 39

We are never so happy nor so unhappy as we imagine.

Ib. 49

To succeed in the world, we do everything we can to appear successful.

Ib. 56

There is no disguise which can for long conceal love where it exists or simulate it where it does not.

Ib. 70

There are very few people who are not ashamed of having been in love when they no longer love each other.

Ib. 71

True love is like ghosts, which everybody talks about and few have seen.

Ib. 76

The love of justice in most men is simply the fear of suffering injustice.

Ib. 78

Silence is the best tactic for him who distrusts himself.

Ib. 79

It is more ignominious to mistrust our friends than to be deceived by them.

Reflections 84

Everyone complains of his memory, and no one complains of his judgment.

Ib. 89

Old people like to give good advice, as solace for no longer being able to provide bad examples.

Ib. 93

A man who is ungrateful is sometimes less to blame for it than his benefactor.

Ib. 96

The mind is always the dupe of the heart.[1]

Ib. 102

Nothing is given so profusely as advice.

Ib. 110

The true way to be deceived is to think oneself more clever than others.

Ib. 127

We would rather speak ill of ourselves than not talk about ourselves at all.

Ib. 138

Usually we praise only to be praised.

Ib. 146

Our repentance is not so much regret for the ill we have done as fear of the ill that may happen to us in consequence.

Ib. 180

Who lives without folly is not so wise as he thinks.

Ib. 209

Most people judge men only by their success or their good fortune.

Ib. 212

Hypocrisy is the homage that vice pays to virtue.

Ib. 218

Too great haste in paying off an obligation is a kind of ingratitude.

Ib. 226

There is great skill in knowing how to conceal one's skill.

Ib. 245

The pleasure of love is in loving. We

---

third, and reappears for the first time in the fourth edition at the head of the Reflections. — AIMÉ MARTIN

[1] See Pope, p. 413a.
[2] See Goldsmith, p. 448b.

[1] The mind lives on the heart
Like any parasite.
EMILY DICKINSON, *The Mind Lives on the Heart* [c. 1876]

are happier in the passion we feel than in that we arouse.[1]

Reflections 259

Absence diminishes mediocre passions and increases great ones, as the wind blows out candles and fans fire.
Ib. 276

We always like those who admire us; we do not always like those whom we admire.   *Ib. 294*

The gratitude of most men is merely a secret desire to receive greater benefits.[2]   *Ib. 298*

We frequently forgive those who bore us, but cannot forgive those whom we bore.   *Ib. 304*

Lovers never get tired of each other, because they are always talking about themselves.   *Ib. 312*

In jealousy there is more self-love than love.   *Ib. 324*

We confess to little faults only to persuade ourselves that we have no great ones.   *Ib. 327*

We pardon to the extent that we love.   *Ib. 330*

We rarely find that people have good sense unless they agree with us.[3]
Ib. 347

Jealousy is always born together with love, but it does not always die when love dies.   *Ib. 361*

Mediocre minds usually dismiss anything which reaches beyond their own understanding.[4]   *Ib. 375*

The greatest fault of a penetrating wit is to go beyond the mark.

Reflections 377
We may give advice, but we do not inspire conduct.   *Ib. 378*

The veracity which increases with old age is not far from folly.   *Ib. 416*

Few people know how to be old.
Ib. 423

Nothing prevents our being natural so much as the desire to appear so.
Ib. 431

In their first passion women love their lovers, in the others they love love.[1]   *Ib. 471*

Quarrels would not last long if the fault were only on one side.   *Ib. 496*

In the misfortune of our best friends we often find something that is not displeasing.[2]   *Ib. 583*

BISHOP JEREMY TAYLOR
1613–1667

Desperate by too quick a sense of constant infelicity.
Holy Dying [1650–1651]

Every schoolboy knows it.
On the Real Presence, V

The union of hands and hearts.
Sermons [1653], *The Marriage Ring, pt. I*

No man ever repented that he arose from the table sober, healthful, and with his wits about him.   *Ib.*

---

[1] See Shelley, p. 569a.
[2] Sir Robert Walpole's [1676–1745] definition of the gratitude of place-expectants, "That it is a lively sense of *future* favors." — WILLIAM HAZLITT, *English Comic Writers* [1819], *Wit and Humor*
[3] "That was excellently observed," say I when I read a passage in another where his opinion agrees with mine. When we differ, then I pronounce him to be mistaken. — SWIFT [1667–1745], *Thoughts on Various Subjects*
[4] See Schopenhauer, p. 564a.

[1] See Byron, p. 560b.
[2] In all distresses of our friends
We first consult our private ends;
While Nature, kindly bent to ease us,
Points out some circumstance to please us.
SWIFT [1667–1745], *A Paraphrase of Rochefoucauld's Maxim*
See Burke, p. 451b.
Maxim 583 is one of the "maximes supprimées" discarded before the 1678 edition.

THOMAS ADY
fl. 1655

Matthew, Mark, Luke, and John,
The bed be blest that I lie on.
Four angels to my bed,
Four angels round my head,
One to watch, and one to pray,
And two to bear my soul away.
A Candle in the Dark [1655]

RICHARD BAXTER
1615–1691

I preached as never sure to preach
again,
And as a dying man to dying men.
*Love Breathing Thanks and
Praise*

SIR JOHN DENHAM
1615–1669

Oh, could I flow like thee,[1] and make
thy stream
My great example, as it is my theme!
Though deep yet clear, though gentle
yet not dull;
Strong without rage, without o'erflow-
ing full.
Cooper's Hill [1642], *l. 189*

SIR ROGER L'ESTRANGE
1616–1704

Though this may be play to you,
'Tis death to us.[2]
*Fables from Several Authors,
Fable 398*

ROGER DE BUSSY-RABUTIN
1618–1693

God is usually on the side of the big
squadrons and against the small ones.[3]
*Letter to the Comte de Limoges
[October 18, 1677]*

---

[1] The river Thames.
[2] See Bion, p. 104b.
[3] It is said that God is always for the big
battalions. — VOLTAIRE, *letter to M. le Riche,
February 6, 1770*

ABRAHAM COWLEY
1618–1667

What shall I do to be forever known,
And make the age to come my own?
The Motto

This only grant me, that my means
may lie
Too low for envy, for contempt too
high.   *The Vote* [1636]

Well then; I now do plainly see
This busy world and I shall ne'er
agree;
The very honey of all earthly joy
Does of all meats the soonest cloy,
  And they (methinks) deserve my
  pity,
Who for it can endure the stings,
The crowd, and buzz and murmurings,
  Of this great hive, the city.
The Wish [1647]

Ah yet, ere I descend to the grave
May I a small house and large garden
have;
And a few friends, and many books,
both true,
Both wise, and both delightful too!
Ib.

A mistress moderately fair.   *Ib.*

The world's a scene of changes, and to
be
Constant, in Nature were inconstancy.
Inconstancy [1647]

The thirsty earth soaks up the rain,
And drinks, and gapes for drink again.
The plants suck in the earth, and are
With constant drinking fresh and fair.
Anacreon [1656], *II, Drinking*

Fill all the glasses there, for why
Should every creature drink but I,
Why, man of morals, tell me why?
Ib.

A mighty pain to love it is,
And 'tis a pain that pain to miss;

Providence is always on the side of the last
reserve. — *Attributed to* NAPOLEON
  See Tacitus, p. 140a; Boileau, p. 377b; Frederick the Great, p. 435a; and Gibbon, p. 466a.

But of all pains, the greatest pain
It is to love, but love in vain.
Anacreon VII, Gold

His time is forever, everywhere his
place.   *Friendship in Absence*

Nothing is there to come, and nothing
past,
But an eternal now does always last.[1]
Davideis [1656], *bk. I, l. 25*

Life is an incurable disease.
To Dr. Scarborough [1656]

Ye fields of Cambridge, our dear Cam-
bridge, say,
Have ye not seen us walking every
day?
Was there a tree about which did not
know
   The love betwixt us two?
On the Death of Mr. William
Harvey [1657] [2]

Let but thy wicked men from out thee
go,
And all the fools that crowd thee so,
Even thou, who dost thy millions
boast,
A village less than Islington wilt grow,
A solitude almost.
Of Solitude, XII

God the first garden made, and the first
city [3]
The Garden [1664], *essay 5*

Hence ye profane! I hate ye all,
Both the great vulgar and the small.[4]
Horace, bk. III, ode 1

Charm'd with the foolish whistling of a
name.[5]
Virgil, Georgics, bk. II, l. 72

Words that weep and tears that speak.[6]
The Prophet

---

[1] One of our poets (which is it?) speaks of an
everlasting now. — ROBERT SOUTHEY, *The Doctor* [1834–1847], *ch. 25*
[2] See William Harvey, p. 312b.
[3] See Bacon, p. 209b, and note.
[4] Odi profanum vulgus.
[5] See Pope, p. 410a.
[6] Thoughts that breathe, and words that burn.
— THOMAS GRAY, *Progress of Poesy* [1754], *III,
3, 4*

Poet and Saint! to thee alone are given
The two most sacred names of earth
and Heaven.
On the Death of Mr. Crashaw [1]
[1668]

His faith, perhaps, in some nice tenets
might
Be wrong; his life, I'm sure, was in the
right.[2]   *Ib.*

RICHARD LOVELACE
1618–1658

Oh, could you view the melody
   Of every grace
   And music of her face,[3]
You'd drop a tear;
   Seeing more harmony
   In her bright eye
Than now you hear.
Lucasta [1649]. *Orpheus to*
Beasts

Tell me not, sweet, I am unkind,
   That from the nunnery
Of thy chaste breast and quiet mind,
   To war and arms I fly.
Ib. To Lucasta: Going to the
Wars, st. 1

I could not love thee, dear, so much,
Lov'd I not honor more.   *Ib. st. 3*

When I lie tangled in her hair,
   And fettered to her eye,
The gods that wanton in the air
   Know no such liberty.
Ib. To Althea: From Prison, st. 1

When flowing cups pass swiftly round
With no allaying Thames.[4]
Ib. st. 2

Stone walls do not a prison make,[5]
   Nor iron bars a cage;
Minds innocent and quiet take
   That for an hermitage;
If I have freedom in my love,

---

[1] See Crashaw, p. 354a.
[2] See Pope, p. 409b.
[3] The mind, the music breathing from her
face. — BYRON, *Bride of Abydos* [1813], *canto 1,
st. 6*
[4] See Shakespeare, p. 289b.
[5] Stone walls a prisoner make, but not a slave.
— WORDSWORTH [1770–1850], *Humanity*

And in my soul am free,
Angels alone that soar above
Enjoy such liberty.[1]
> *Lucasta. To Althea:*
> *From Prison, st. 4*

If to be absent were to be
  Away from thee;
Or that when I am gone,
  You and I were alone;
Then, my Lucasta, might I crave
Pity from blust'ring wind, or swallow-
  ing wave.
> *Ib. To Lucasta: Going Beyond*
> *the Seas, st. 1*

NINON DE L'ENCLOS
1620–1705

Old age is woman's hell.[2]
> *Attributed saying*

JEAN DE LA FONTAINE
1621–1695

We believe no evil till the evil's
done. *Fables, bk. I* [*1668*], *fable 8*

We heed no instincts but our own.
> *Ib.*

The opinion of the strongest is always the best. *Ib. 10*

Better to suffer than to die: that is
mankind's motto. *Ib. 16*

By the work one knows the workman. *Ib. 21*

I bend but do not break. *Ib. 22*

It is a double pleasure to deceive the
deceiver. *Ib. II* [*1668*], *fable 15*

It is impossible to please all the
world and one's father.
> *Ib. III* [*1668*], *fable 1*

In everything one must consider the
end.[1]
> *Fables, bk. III, fable 5*

Beware, as long as you live, of judging people by appearances.
> *Ib. VI* [*1668*], *fable 5*

On the wings of Time grief flies
away. *Ib. 21*

The sign brings customers.
> *Ib. VII* [*1678–1679*], *fable 15*

People who make no noise are dangerous.
> *Ib. VIII* [*1678–1679*], *fable 23*

He knows the universe, and himself
he does not know. *Ib. 26*

A hungry stomach cannot hear.[2]
> *Ib. IX* [*1678–1679*], *fable 17*

ANDREW MARVELL
1621–1678

The inglorious arts of peace.
> *Upon Cromwell's Return from*
> *Ireland* [*1650*]

He [3] nothing common did or mean
Upon that memorable scene,
But with his keener eye
The axe's edge did try. *Ib.*

But bowed his comely head
Down as upon a bed. *Ib.*

So much one man can do,
That does both act and know. *Ib.*

Had we but world enough, and time,
This coyness, lady, were no crime.
> *To His Coy Mistress* [*1650–1652*]

  I would
Love you ten years before the Flood,
And you should, if you please, refuse
Till the conversion of the Jews.
My vegetable love should grow
Vaster than empires, and more slow.
> *Ib.*

---

[1] But though my wing is closely bound,
My heart's at liberty;
My prison walls cannot control
The flight, the freedom of the soul.
  JEANNE GUYON [1648–1717], *A Prison-
  er's Song, Castle of Vincennes, France,
  st. 4*
[2] La vieillesse est l'enfer des femmes.

[1] Whatsoever thou takest in hand, remember
the end, and thou shalt never do amiss. — *Apocrypha, Ecclesiasticus 3:36*
[2] Ventre affamé n'a point d'oreilles.
See Cato the Elder, p. 107a, and note, and
Adlai Stevenson, p. 1048b.
[3] King Charles I.

But at my back I always hear
Time's winged chariot hurrying near;
And yonder all before us lie
Deserts of vast eternity.
> *To His Coy Mistress*

Then worms shall try
That long preserved virginity,
And your quaint honor turn to dust,
And into ashes all my lust.
The grave's a fine and private place,[1]
But none, I think, do there embrace.
> *Ib.*

Though we cannot make our sun
Stand still, yet we will make him run.
> *Ib.*

Annihilating all that's made
To a green thought in a green shade.[2]
> *The Garden* [1650–1652]

Casting the body's vest aside,
My soul into the boughs does glide.
> *Ib.*

The world in all doth but two nations
    bear —
The good, the bad; and these mixed
    everywhere.
> *The Loyal Scot* [1650–1652]

My love is of a birth as rare
  As 'tis for object strange and high;
It was begotten by despair
  Upon impossibility.
> *The Definition of Love* [1650–
> 1652], *st. 1*

As lines, so loves oblique, may well
  Themselves in every angle greet;
But ours, so truly parallel,
  Though infinite, can never meet.
> *Ib. st. 7*

Where the remote Bermudas ride,
In th' ocean's bosom unespied.
> *Bermudas* [1657]

Orange bright,
Like golden lamps in a green light.
> *Ib.*

And all the way, to guide their chime,
With falling oars they kept the time.[1]
> *Bermudas*

MOLIÈRE
[JEAN BAPTISTE POQUELIN]
1622–1673

To pull the chestnuts out of the fire
with the cat's paw.[2]
> *L'Étourdi* [1655], *act III, sc. 6*

We die only once, and for such a
long time!
> *Le Dépit Amoureux* [1656], *act V,*
> *sc. 3*

I always make the first verse well, but
I have trouble making the others.
> *Les Précieuses Ridicules* [1659],
> *act I, sc. 11*

The world, dear Agnes, is a strange
affair.
> *L'École des Femmes* [1662], *act II,*
> *sc. 6*

There is no rampart that will hold
out against malice.
> *Tartuffe* [1664], *act I, sc. 1*

Those whose conduct gives room for
talk are always the first to attack their
neighbors.
> *Ib.*

You are a fool in four letters, my
son.[3]
> *Ib.*

She is laughing up her sleeve at you.
> *Ib. 6*

A woman always has her revenge
ready.
> *Ib. II, 2*

Cover that bosom that I must not
see.[4]
> *Ib. III, 2*

Although I am a pious man, I am
not the less a man.
> *Ib. III, 3*

To create a public scandal is what's
wicked; to sin in private is not a sin.
> *Ib. IV, 5*

---

[1] A grave is such a quiet place. — EDNA ST.
VINCENT MILLAY, *Renascence* [1912]
[2] The same phrase is in VIRGIL, *Eclogues, IX,*
20

[1] See Thomas Moore, p. 541b.
[2] Tirer les marrons du feu avec la patte du
chat. — *Proverb in many languages*
  See Becker, p. 913b.
[3] Vous êtes un sot en trois lettres, mon fils.
[4] Couvrez ce sein que je ne saurais voir.

I saw him, I say, saw him with my own eyes.

Tartuffe, act V, sc. 3

There are fagots and fagots.

Le Médecin Malgré Lui [1666], *act I, sc. 6*

We have changed all that.[1]

Ib. II, 6

On some preference esteem is based; to esteem everything is to esteem nothing.

Le Misanthrope [1666], *act I, sc. 1*

He's a wonderful talker, who has the art of telling you nothing in a great harangue. *Ib. II, 5*

He makes his cook his merit, and the world visits his dinners and not him. *Ib.*

You see him laboring to produce *bons mots*. *Ib.*

The more we love our friends, the less we flatter them; it is by excusing nothing that pure love shows itself. *Ib.*

Doubts are more cruel than the worst of truths. *Ib. III, 7*

Anyone may be an honorable man, and yet write verse badly. *Ib. IV, 1*

If everyone were clothed with integrity, if every heart were just, frank, kindly, the other virtues would be wellnigh useless, since their chief purpose is to make us bear with patience the injustice of our fellows. *Ib. V, 1*

It is a wonderful seasoning of all enjoyments to think of those we love. *Ib. 4*

I prefer an accommodating vice to an obstinate virtue.

Amphitryon [1666], *act I, sc. 4*

One must eat to live, and not live to eat.[2] *Ib. III, 1*

[1] Nous avons changé tout cela.
[2] See Socrates, p. 87b, and note.

The true Amphitryon is the Amphitryon who gives dinners.[1]

Amphitryon, act III, sc. 5

My Lord Jupiter knows how to sugarcoat the pill. *Ib. III, 10*

You've asked for it, Georges Dandin, you've asked for it.[2]

Georges Dandin [1668], *act I, sc. 9*

Good Heavens! For more than forty years I have been speaking prose without knowing it.

Le Bourgeois Gentilhomme [1670], *act II, sc. 4*

All that is not prose is verse; and all that is not verse is prose. *Ib.*

My fair one, let us swear an eternal friendship.[3] *Ib. IV, 1*

I will maintain it before the whole world. *Ib. IV, 5*

What the devil was he doing in that galley? [4]

Les Fourberies de Scapin [1671], *act II, sc. 11*

Grammar, which knows how to control even kings.[5]

Les Femmes Savantes [1672], *act II, sc. 6*

[1] Le véritable Amphitryon est l'Amphitryon où l'on dine.
See Dryden, p. 371a.
[2] Vous l'avez voulu, Georges Dandin, vous l'avez voulu.
[3] A sudden thought strikes me — let us swear an eternal friendship. — FRERE, *The Rovers* [1798]
Madam, I have been looking for a person who disliked gravy all my life; let us swear eternal friendship. — SYDNEY SMITH [1771–1845], *Lady Holland's Memoir, vol. I, ch. 9*
[4] Que diable allait-il faire dans cette galère? Que diable aller faire aussi dans la galère d'un Turc? d'un Turc! [What the deuce did he want on board a Turk's galley? A Turk!] — CYRANO DE BERGERAC, *Le Pédant Joué* [1654], *act II, sc. 4*
The saying of Molière came into his head: "But what the devil was he doing in that galley?" and he laughed at himself. — TOLSTOI, *War and Peace* [1865–1872], *pt. IV, ch. 6*
Often misquoted "in that gallery," as in DICKENS, *A Tale of Two Cities* [1859], *bk. I, ch. 5*: What the devil do you do in that gallery there!
[5] Sigismund [1361–1437], Emperor of the Holy Roman Empire, at the Council of Constance

It is seasoned throughout with Attic salt.
Les Femmes Savantes,
act III, sc. 2

A learned fool is more foolish than an ignorant one. *Ib. IV, 3*

Ah, there are no longer any children!
Le Malade Imaginaire [1673],
act II, sc. 11

Nearly all men die of their remedies, and not of their illnesses.
Ib. III, 3

RICHARD RUMBOLD
1622–1685

I never could believe that Providence had sent a few men into the world, ready booted and spurred to ride, and millions ready saddled and bridled to be ridden.
On the scaffold [1685]. *From* MACAULAY, *History of England, ch. 1*

ALGERNON SIDNEY
1622–1683

This hand, unfriendly to tyrants,
Seeks with the sword placid repose
under liberty.[1]
Life and Memoirs of Algernon Sidney

It is not necessary to light a candle to the sun.[2]
Discourses on Government
[1698], *sec. 23*

HENRY VAUGHAN
1622–1695

Dear Night! this world's defeat;
The stop to busy fools; care's check and curb;

[1414], said to a prelate who had objected to his Majesty's grammar: Ego sum rex Romanus, et supra grammaticam [I am the Roman king, and am above grammar].

[1]   Manus haec, inimica tyrannis,
Ense petit placidam sub libertate quietem.
The second line is the motto of the Commonwealth of Massachusetts.

[2] See Robert Burton, p. 312a.

The day of spirits; my soul's calm retreat
Which none disturb!
Christ's progress, and His prayer-time;
The hours to which high Heaven doth chime.
Silex Scintillans [1655].
The Night, l. 25

There is in God, some say,
A deep but dazzling darkness.
Ib. l. 49

Happy those early days, when I
Shin'd in my angel-infancy! [1]
Before I understood this place
Appointed for my second race.
Ib. The Retreat, l. 1

But felt through all this fleshly dress
Bright shoots of everlastingness.
Ib. l. 19

Some men a forward motion love,
But I by backward steps would move.
Ib. l. 29

I cannot reach it, and my striving eye
Dazzles at it, as at eternity.
Ib. Childhood

I saw Eternity the other night
Like a great ring of pure and endless light.
All calm, as it was bright;
And round beneath it, Time in hours, days, years,
Driv'n by the spheres
Like a vast shadow mov'd; in which the world
And all her train were hurl'd.
Ib. The World

They are all gone into the world of light!
And I alone sit lingering here;
Their very memory is fair and bright,
And my sad thoughts doth clear.
Ib. They Are All Gone, st. 1

I see them walking in an air of glory
Whose light doth trample on my days,
My days, which are at best but dull and hoary,

---

[1] See Traherne, p. 378a, and Wordsworth, p. 513b.

Mere glimmering and decays.
> *Silex Scintillans. They Are*
> *All Gone, st. 3*

Dear, beauteous death, the jewel of the
just!
Shining nowhere but in the dark;
What mysteries do lie beyond thy
dust,
Could man outlook that mark!
> *Ib. st. 5*

My soul, there is a country
Far beyond the stars
Where stands a winged sentry
All skillful in the wars:
There, above noise and danger,
Sweet Peace is crown'd with smiles,
And One born in a manger
Commands the beauteous files.
> *Ib. Peace, st. 1*

YAMAGA SOKO[1]
1622–1685

The business of the samurai consists
in reflecting on his own station in life,
in discharging loyal service to his master if he has one, in deepening his fidelity in associations with friends, and,
with due consideration of his own position, in devoting himself to duty above
all. *The Way of the Samurai*

BLAISE PASCAL
1623–1662

Things are always at their best in
their beginning.
> *Lettres Provinciales* [1656–
> 1657], *no. 4*

True eloquence takes no heed of eloquence, true morality takes no heed of
morality. . . . To take no heed of philosophy is truly to philosophize.
> *Pensées* [1670], *no. 4*

Do you wish people to think well of
you? Don't speak well of yourself.
> *Ib. 44*

What is man in nature? Nothing in
relation to the infinite, everything in relation to nothing, a mean between
nothing and everything.[1]
> *Pensées, no. 72*

I lay it down as a fact that if all men
knew what others say of them, there
would not be four friends in the world.
> *Ib. 101*

The state of man: inconstancy, boredom, anxiety.[2] *Ib. 127*

I have discovered that all human evil
comes from this, man's being unable to
sit still in a room.[3] *Ib. 139*

Cleopatra's nose, had it been shorter,
the whole face of the world would have
been changed. *Ib. 162*

The eternal silence of these infinite
spaces terrifies me. *Ib. 206*

We shall die alone.[4] *Ib. 211*

The heart has its reasons which reason knows nothing of.[5] *Ib. 277*

We know the truth, not only by the
reason, but by the heart. *Ib. 282*

Justice without strength is helpless,
strength without justice is tyrannical. . . . Unable to make what is just
strong, we have made what is strong
just. *Ib. 298*

Man is but a reed, the weakest in
nature, but he is a thinking reed.[6]
> *Ib. 347*

Man is neither angel nor beast; and
the misfortune is that he who would act
the angel acts the beast.[7] *Ib. 358*

Evil is easy, and has infinite forms.
> *Ib. 408*

---

[1] From *Sources of Japanese Tradition* edited
by William Theodore de Bary [1958].

[1] Qu'est-ce que l'homme dans la nature? Un
néant a l'égard de l'infini, un tout a l'égard du
néant, un milieu entre rien et tout.
[2] Condition de l'homme: inconstance, ennui,
inquiétude.
[3] See Walter Bagehot, p. 726b.
[4] On mourra seul.
[5] Le coeur a ses raisons que la raison ne con-
naît point.
[6] L'homme n'est qu'un roseau, le plus faible
de la nature, mais c'est un roseau pensant.
[7] L'homme n'est ni ange ni bête; et le malheur veut que qui veut faire l'ange fait la bête.

To ridicule philosophy is really to philosophize.[1]

Pensées, no. 430

What a chimera then is man! What a novelty! What a monster, what a chaos, what a contradiction, what a prodigy! Judge of all things, feeble earthworm, depository of truth, a sink of uncertainty and error, the glory and the shame of the universe.[2] *Ib.* 434

Self is hateful.[3] *Ib.* 455

Men never do evil so completely and cheerfully as when they do it from religious conviction. *Ib.* 894

"The God of Abraham, the God of Isaac, the God of Jacob," not of philosophers and scholars.

Writing found in Pascal's effects after his death

WILLIAM WALKER
1623–1684

Learn to read slow: all other graces
Will follow in their proper places.[4]

The Art of Reading

GEORGE FOX[5]
1624–1691

The Lord showed me, so that I did see clearly, that he did not dwell in these temples which men had commanded and set up, but in people's hearts . . . his people were his temple, and he dwelt in them.[6]

Journal [1694]

When the Lord sent me forth into the world, He forbade me to put off my hat to any, high or low. *Ib.*

Justice Bennet of Derby, was the first that called us Quakers, because I bid

them tremble at the word of the Lord. This was in the year 1650.

Journal

He [Oliver Cromwell] said: "I see there is a people risen, that I cannot win either with gifts, honors, offices or places; but all other sects and people I can." *Ib.*

ANGELUS SILESIUS [JOHANN SCHEFFLER]
1624–1677

God lives not without me.
I know that without me God cannot
live at all;
Were I to go, he also to his death must
fall.

The Cherubic Wanderer [1657–1675]

I am like God, and God like me.
I am as large as God, he is as small as
I:
He cannot above me, nor I beneath
him be. *Ib.*

Everyone to his own.
The bird is in the sky, the stone rests
on the land,
In water lives the fish, my spirit in
God's hand. *Ib.*

THOMAS SYDENHAM
1624–1689

Fever itself is Nature's instrument.
Quoted in Bulletin of the New York Academy of Medicine, vol. IV [1928], *p.* 922

Gout, unlike any other disease, kills more rich men than poor, more wise men than simple. Great kings, emperors, generals, admirals and philosophers have all died of gout. *Ib.* 993

A man is as old as his arteries. *Ib.*

JOHN AUBREY
1626–1697

He [Hobbes] had read much, but his contemplation was much more than

---

[1] Se moquer de la philosophie, c'est vraiment philosopher.

[2] See Pope, p. 408b–409a.

[3] Le moi est haïssable.

[4] Take time enough; all other graces
Will soon fill up their proper places.
JOHN BYROM [1692–1763], *Advice to Preach Slow*

[5] Founder of the Society of Friends (Quakers).

[6] See *I Corinthians 3:17*, p. 52a.

his reading. He was wont to say that if he had read as much as other men, he should have known no more than other men.   *Brief Lives [ed. 1898], I, 349*

He [John Milton] was so fair that they called him *the lady of* Christ's College.   *Ib.*

Mr. William Shakespeare was born at Stratford upon Avon in the county of Warwick. His father was a butcher, and I have been told heretofore by some of the neighbors, that when he was a boy he exercised his father's trade, but when he killed a calf he would do it in a high style and make a speech.
Ben Johnson and he did gather humors of men daily wherever they came.
                     Ib. II, 225

MARIE DE RABUTIN-CHANTAL, MARQUISE DE SÉVIGNÉ
1626–1696

True friendship is never serene.
            Lettres. À Madame de Grignan
                [September 10, 1671]

Racine will go out of style like coffee.   *Attributed saying*

JACQUES BÉNIGNE BOSSUET
1627–1704

The greatest weakness of all weaknesses is to fear too much to appear weak.
    Politique Tirée de l'Écriture Sainte

The inexorable boredom that is at the core of life.
                From M. A. Couturier,
                    Se Garder Libre

JOHN BUNYAN
1628–1688

Some said, "John, print it"; others said, "Not so."

Some said, "It might do good"; others said, "No."
        Pilgrim's Progress [1678].
            Apology for His Book

As I walked through the wilderness of this world.   *Ib. pt. I*

I saw a man clothed with rags . . . a book in his hand, and a great burden upon his back.   *Ib.*

The name of the one was Obstinate and the name of the other was Pliable.
                         Ib.

The name of the slough was Despond.   *Ib.*

Every fat [vat] must stand upon his bottom.[1]   *Ib.*

The gentleman's name was Mr. Worldly-Wise-Man.   *Ib.*

Set down my name, Sir.   *Ib.*

A very stately palace before him, the name of which was Beautiful.   *Ib.*

The valley of Humiliation.   *Ib.*

A foul Fiend coming over the field to meet him; his name is Apollyon.
                         Ib.

I will talk of things heavenly, or things earthly; things moral, or things evangelical; things sacred, or things profane; things past, or things to come; things foreign, or things at home; things more essential, or things circumstantial.   *Ib.*

It beareth the name of Vanity Fair, because the town where 'tis kept is lighter than vanity.   *Ib.*

Hanging is too good for him, said Mr. Cruelty.   *Ib.*

My great-grandfather was but a water-man, looking one way, and rowing another.[2]   *Ib.*

A castle called Doubting Castle, the owner whereof was Giant Despair.
                         Ib.

---

[1] Every tub must stand upon its bottom. — CHARLES MACKLIN, *The Man of the World* [1781], act I, sc. 2
[2] See Plutarch, p. 137b, and note.

They came to the Delectable Mountains.
Pilgrim's Progress, pt. I

A great horror and darkness fell upon Christian. *Ib.*

So I awoke, and behold it was a dream. *Ib.*

A man that could look no way but downwards with a muckrake in his hand. *Ib. pt. II*

He that is down needs fear no fall,
He that is low no pride.
Ib. Shepherd Boy's Song

Who would true valor see,
Let him come hither;
One here will constant be,
Come wind, come weather.
There's no discouragement
Shall make him once relent
His first avow'd intent
To be a pilgrim. *Ib.*

My sword I give to him that shall succeed me in my pilgrimage, and my courage and skill to him that can get it. My marks and scars I carry with me, to be a witness for me, that I have fought His battle who now will be my rewarder. *Ib.*

So he passed over, and all the trumpets sounded for him on the other side. *Ib.*

The captain of all these men of death that came against him to take him away, was the Consumption, for it was that that brought him down to the grave.
The Life and Death of Mr. Badman [1680]

JOHN RAY
1628–1705

In a calm sea every man is a pilot.
English Proverbs [1670]

If wishes were horses, beggars might ride. *Ib.*

SIR WILLIAM TEMPLE
1628–1699

Books, like proverbs, receive their chief value from the stamp and esteem of ages through which they have passed.
Miscellanea, pt. II [1690]. *Ancient and Modern Learning*

When all is done, human life is, at the greatest and the best, but like a froward child, that must be played with and humored a little to keep it quiet till it falls asleep, and then the care is over. *Ib. Of Poetry*

CHARLES II
1630–1685

This is very true: for my words are my own, and my actions are my ministers'. *Reply to Lord Rochester* [1]

Let not poor Nelly starve.
On his deathbed. From BURNET, *History of My Own Times, vol. I, bk. 2, ch. 17*

He had been, he said, an unconscionable time dying; he hoped that they would excuse it.
From MACAULAY, *History of England* [1849], *vol. I, ch. 4*

JOHN TILLOTSON
1630–1694

If God were not a necessary Being of Himself, He might almost seem to be made for the use and benefit of men.[2]
Sermon

They who are in highest places, and have the most power, have the least liberty, because they are most observed.
Reflections

WALTER POPE
c. 1630 – 1714

May I govern my passions with absolute sway,

[1] See Rochester, p. 382a.
[2] See Ovid, p. 128b, and Voltaire, p. 418a.

And grow wiser and better, as strength
   wears away,
Without gout or stone, by a gentle decay.
          The Old Man's Wish [1685]

BISHOP RICHARD CUMBERLAND
1631–1718

It is better to wear out than to rust
out.
          From BISHOP GEORGE HORNE
          [1730–1792], *Sermon on the
          Duty of Contending for the
          Truth*

JOHN DRYDEN
1631–1700

By viewing Nature, Nature's handmaid
   Art,
Makes mighty things from small begin-
   nings grow.[1]
          Annus Mirabilis [1667], *st.* 155

He [Shakespeare] was the man who
of all modern, and perhaps ancient
poets, had the largest and most comprehensive soul.
          Essay of Dramatic Poesy [1668]

He was naturally learned; he needed
not the spectacles of books to read Nature; he looked inwards, and found her
there.   *Ib.*

Pains of love be sweeter far
Than all other pleasures are.
          Tyrannic Love [1669], *act* IV, *sc.* 1

I am as free as Nature first made man,
Ere the base laws of servitude began,
When wild in woods the noble savage
   ran.
          The Conquest of Granada
          [1669–1670], *pt.* I, *act* I,
          sc. 1

Death in itself is nothing; but we fear
To be we know not what, we know not
   where.
          Aureng-Zebe [1676], *act* IV, *sc.* 1

[1] See William Bradford, p. 319a.

When I consider life, 'tis all a cheat;
Yet, fool'd with hope, men favor the
   deceit;
Trust on, and think tomorrow will repay.
Tomorrow's falser than the former
   day;
Lies worse, and while it says we shall be
   blest
With some new joys, cuts off what we
   possest.
Strange cozenage! None would live past
   years again,
Yet all hope pleasure in what yet remain;
And from the dregs of life think to receive
What the first sprightly running could
   not give.
          Aureng-Zebe, *act* IV, *sc.* 1

The wretched have no friends.
          All for Love [1678], *act* III, *sc.* 1

Your Cleopatra; Dolabella's Cleopatra;
every man's Cleopatra.
                              Ib. IV, 1

With how much ease believe we what
   we wish! [1]
Whatever is, is in its causes just.[2]
          Oedipus [1679] (*with* NATHANIEL
                    LEE), *act* III, *sc.* 1

          His hair just grizzled,
As in a green old age.[3]   *Ib.*

Of no distemper, of no blast he died,
But fell like autumn fruit that mellow'd
   long —
Even wonder'd at, because he dropp'd
   no sooner.
Fate seem'd to wind him up for fourscore years,
Yet freshly ran he on ten winters
   more;
Till like a clock worn out with eating
   time,
The wheels of weary life at last stood
   still.   *Ib.* IV, 1

[1] Men freely believe that which they desire. —
CAESAR [c. 102–44 B.C.], *De Bello Gallico, bk. III,
sec. 18*

[2] See Pope, p. 408b.

[3] A green old age, unconscious of decays. —
POPE, *Translation of the Iliad, XXIII, 929*

In pious times, ere priestcraft did
  begin,
Before polygamy was made a sin.
         Absalom and Achitophel, pt. I
                        [1680], *l. 1*

Whate'er he did was done with so
  much ease,
In him alone, 'twas natural to please.
                              Ib. l. 27

Plots, true or false, are necessary
  things,
To raise up commonwealths and ruin
  kings.   *Ib. l. 83*

Of these the false Achitophel was first,
A name to all succeeding ages curs'd.
For close designs and crooked counsels
  fit,
Sagacious, bold, and turbulent of wit,
Restless, unfix'd in principles and place,
In power unpleas'd, impatient of dis-
  grace;
A fiery soul, which working out its
  way,
Fretted the pygmy-body to decay:
And o'er-inform'd the tenement of
  clay.[1]
A daring pilot in extremity;
Pleas'd with the danger, when the
  waves went high
He sought the storms; but for a calm
  unfit,
Would steer too nigh the sands to
  boast his wit.
Great wits are sure to madness near al-
  lied,
And thin partitions do their bounds di-
  vide.[2]   *Ib. l. 150*

Bankrupt of life, yet prodigal of ease.
                             Ib. l. 168

And all to leave what with his toil he
  won
To that unfeather'd two-legg'd thing,[3] a
  son.   *Ib. l. 169*

[1] See Thomas Fuller, p. 333b.
[2] Remembrance and reflection how allied!
  **What thin partitions sense from thought
  divide!**
        POPE, *Essay on Man* [1733–1734],
                        epistle I, l. 225
See Seneca, p. 130b, and note.
[3] See Diogenes the Cynic, p. 96b.

In friendship false, implacable in hate,
Resolv'd to ruin or to rule the state.
              Absalom and Achitophel,
                          pt. I, l. 173

And Heaven had wanted one immortal
  song.   *Ib. l. 197*

The people's prayer, the glad diviner's
  theme,
The young men's vision, and the old
  men's dream! [1]   *Ib. l. 238*

His courage foes, his friends his truth
  proclaim.   *Ib. l. 357*

All empire is no more than power in
  trust.   *Ib. l. 411*

Better one suffer, than a nation grieve.
                             Ib. l. 416

Who think too little, and who talk too
  much.[2]   *Ib. l. 534*

A man so various that he seem'd to be
Not one, but all mankind's epitome:
Stiff in opinions, always in the wrong;
Was everything by starts, and nothing
  long:
But, in the course of one revolving
  moon,
Was chemist, fiddler, statesman, and
  buffoon.[3]   *Ib. l. 545*

So over violent, or over civil,
That every man with him was God or
  Devil.   *Ib. l. 557*

His tribe were God Almighty's gentlemen.   *Ib. l. 645*

Nor is the people's judgement always
  true:
The most may err as grossly as the
  few.   *Ib. l. 781*

Large was his wealth, but larger was his
  heart.   *Ib. l. 826*

Of ancient race by birth, but nobler
  yet
In his own worth.   *Ib. l. 900*

Beware the fury of a patient man.
                            Ib. l. 1005

[1] See *Joel 2:28*, p. 35b.
[2] See Jonson, p. 304a.
[3] See Juvenal, p. 139a.

Made still a blund'ring kind of melody;
Spurr'd boldly on, and dashed through thick and thin,
Through sense and nonsense, never out nor in.
Free from all meaning, whether good or bad,
And in one word, heroically mad.
　　　　Absalom and Achitophel,
　　　　pt. II [1] [1682], *l. 413*

For every inch that is not fool is rogue.
　　　　Ib. l. 463

There is a pleasure sure
In being mad which none but madmen know.[2]
　　　　The Spanish Friar [1681],
　　　　act II, sc. 1

And, dying, bless the hand that gave the blow.[3]　　　　*Ib.*

He's a sure card.　　　　*Ib.*

They say everything in the world is good for something.　　*Ib. III, 2*

Or break the eternal Sabbath of his rest.　　　　*Ib. V, 2*

All human things are subject to decay,
And, when fate summons, monarchs must obey.
　　　　Mac Flecknoe [1682], *l. 1*

The rest to some faint meaning make pretense,
But Shadwell [4] never deviates into sense.
Some beams of wit on other souls may fall,
Strike through and make a lucid interval;
But Shadwell's genuine night admits no ray,
His rising fogs prevail upon the day.
　　　　Ib. l. 19

And torture one poor word ten thousand ways.
　　　　Mac Flecknoe, l. 208

Wit will shine
Through the harsh cadence of a rugged line.
　　　　To the Memory of Mr. Oldham
　　　　[1684], *l. 15*

Happy the man, and happy he alone,
He who can call today his own;
He who, secure within, can say,
Tomorrow, do thy worst, for I have liv'd today.[1]
　　　　Imitation of Horace, bk. III,
　　　　ode 29 [1685], *l. 65*

Not heaven itself upon the past has power;
But what has been, has been, and I have had my hour.　　*Ib. l. 71*

I can enjoy her [Fortune] while she's kind;
But when she dances in the wind,
And shakes the wings and will not stay,
I puff the prostitute away.　　*Ib. l. 81*

And virtue, though in rags, will keep me warm.　　　　*Ib. l. 87*

Men met each other with erected look,
The steps were higher that they took;
Friends to congratulate their friends made haste,
And long inveterate foes saluted as they pass'd.
　　　　Threnodia Augustalis [1685], *l. 124*

Since heaven's eternal year is thine.
　　　　To the Pious Memory of Mrs.
　　　　Anne Killegrew [1686], *l. 15*

O gracious God! how far have we
Profan'd thy heavenly gift of poesy!
　　　　Ib. l. 56

Her wit was more than man, her innocence a child.[2]　　*Ib. l. 70*

Then cold, and hot, and moist, and dry,[3]

---

[1] In collaboration with NAHUM TATE. See p. 383b.
[2] There is a pleasure in poetic pains
　Which only poets know.
　　COWPER [1731–1800], *The Timepiece, l. 285*
[3] Adore the hand that gives the blow. —
JOHN POMFRET [1667–1702], *Verses to His Friend*
[4] See Shadwell, p. 380a.

[1] See Horace, p. 122a.
[2] Of manners gentle, of affections mild,
　In wit a man; simplicity a child.
　　POPE, *Epitaph on Gay* [1730]
[3] See Milton, *Paradise Lost,* bk. II, *l. 898,*
p. 344a.

In order to their stations leap,
　And Music's power obey.
From harmony, from heavenly har-
　mony,
　This universal frame began:
From harmony to harmony
Through all the compass of the notes it
　ran,
The diapason closing full in Man.
　　　　　A Song for St. Cecilia's Day
　　　　　　　　　　[1687], *st. 1*

What passion cannot Music raise and
　quell?　　　　　　　　　*Ib. st. 2*

The trumpet's loud clangor
　Excites us to arms.　　　　*Ib. st. 3*

The soft complaining flute,
　In dying notes, discovers
　The woes of hopeless lovers.
　　　　　　　　　　　　　Ib. st. 4

The trumpet shall be heard on high
The dead shall live, the living die,
And Music shall untune the sky!
　　　　　　　　Ib. Grand Chorus

She fear'd no danger, for she knew no
　sin.
　　　　　The Hind and the Panther
　　　　　　　　　[1687], *pt. I, l. 4*

And doom'd to death, though fated not
　to die.　　　　　　　　　*Ib. l. 8*

For truth has such a face and such a
　mien
As to be lov'd needs only to be seen.[1]
　　　　　　　　　　　　　Ib. l. 33

Of all the tyrannies on human kind
The worst is that which persecutes the
　mind.　　　　　　　　　*Ib. l. 239*

Reason to rule, mercy to forgive:
The first is law, the last prerogative.
　　　　　　　　　　　　Ib. l. 261

And kind as kings upon their corona-
　tion day.　　　　　　　*Ib. l. 271*

And leaves the private conscience for
　the guide.　　　　　　　*Ib. l. 478*

All have not the gift of martyrdom.
　　　　　　　　　　　Ib. II, l. 59

[1] See Pope, p. 409a.

War seldom enters but where wealth
　allures.[1]
　　　　　The Hind and the Panther,
　　　　　　　　　　pt. II, l. 706

Much malice mingled with a little wit.
　　　　　　　　　　Ib. III, l. 1

Jealousy, the jaundice of the soul.
　　　　　　　　　　　Ib. l. 73

For present joys are more to flesh and
　blood
Than a dull prospect of a distant good.
　　　　　　　　　　　Ib. l. 364

T' abhor the makers, and their laws ap-
　prove,
Is to hate traitors and the treason love.[2]
　　　　　　　　　　　Ib. l. 706

Secret guilt by silence is betrayed.
　　　　　　　　　　　Ib. l. 763

Possess your soul with patience.[3]
　　　　　　　　　　　Ib. l. 839

Our vows are heard betimes! and
　Heaven takes care
To grant, before we can conclude the
　prayer:
Preventing angels met it half the way,
And sent us back to praise, who came
　to pray.[4]
　　　　Britannia Rediviva [1688], *l. 1*

Three poets, in three distant ages born,
Greece, Italy, and England did adorn.
The first in loftiness of thought sur-
　pass'd;
The next, in majesty; in both the last.
The force of Nature could no further
　go.
To make a third, she join'd the former
　two.
　　　Under Mr. Milton's Picture [1688]

This is the porcelain clay of human-
　kind.[5]
　　　Don Sebastian [1690], *act I, sc. 1*

A knockdown argument: 'tis but a
word and a blow.
　　　Amphitryon [1690], *act I, sc. 1*

[1] See Bion, p. 1046, and note.
[2] See Caesar, p. 112a.
[3] See *Luke 21:19*, p. 47b.
[4] See Goldsmith, p. 449b.
[5] The precious porcelain of human clay. —
BYRON, *Don Juan* [1819–1824], *canto 4, st. 11*

Whistling to keep myself from being afraid.[1]

> *Amphitryon, act III, sc. III, 1*

I am the true Amphitryon.[2]

> *Ib. V, 1*

Fairest Isle, all isles excelling,
Seat of pleasures, and of loves;
Venus here will choose her dwelling,
And forsake her Cyprian groves.

> *King Arthur* [1691], *act II, sc. 5,*
> *Song of Venus*

Theirs was the giant race, before the flood.[3]

> *Epistle to Congreve* [1693], *l. 5*

Genius must be born, and never can be taught. *Ib. l. 60*

Be kind to my remains; and oh defend,
Against your judgment, your departed friend! *Ib. l. 72*

Look round the habitable world: how few
Know their own good, or knowing it, pursue.

> *Juvenal, Satire X* [1693]

Arms, and the man I sing, who, forced by fate,
And haughty Juno's unrelenting hate.

> *Virgil, Aeneid, bk. I, l. 1* [1697]

None but the brave deserves the fair.

> *Alexander's Feast* [1697], *l. 15*

With ravish'd ears
The monarch hears;
Assumes the god,
Affects to nod,
And seems to shake the spheres.

> *Ib. l. 37*

Sound the trumpets; beat the drums . . .
Now give the hautboys breath; he comes, he comes.[4] *Ib. l. 50*

Bacchus, ever fair and ever young.

> *Ib. l. 54*

---

[1] Whistling aloud to bear his courage up. —
BLAIR, *The Grave* [1743], *l. 58*
[2] See Molière, p. 361b.
[3] See *Genesis 6:4*, p. 6b.
[4] See Morell, p. 420b.

Rich the treasure,
Sweet the pleasure —
Sweet is pleasure after pain.

> *Alexander's Feast, l. 58*

The king grew vain;
Fought all his battles o'er again;
And thrice he routed all his foes, and thrice he slew the slain.

> *Ib. l. 68*

Fallen from his high estate,
And welt'ring in his blood;
Deserted, at his utmost need,
By those his former bounty fed,
On the bare earth expos'd he lies,
With not a friend to close his eyes.

> *Ib. l. 78*

Softly sweet, in Lydian measures,
Soon he sooth'd his soul to pleasures.
War, he sung, is toil and trouble;
Honor but an empty bubble;
Never ending, still beginning,
Fighting still, and still destroying.
If all the world be worth thy winning,
Think, oh think it worth enjoying:
Lovely Thaïs sits beside thee,
Take the good the gods provide thee. *Ib. l. 97*

Sigh'd and look'd, and sigh'd again.

> *Ib. l. 120*

And, like another Helen, fir'd another Troy. *Ib. l. 154*

Could swell the soul to rage, or kindle soft desire. *Ib. l. 160*

He rais'd a mortal to the skies,
She drew an angel down. *Ib. l. 169*

Words, once my stock, are wanting to commend
So great a poet and so good a friend.

> *Epistle to Peter Antony Motteux*
> [1698], *l. 54*

Lord of yourself, uncumber'd with a wife.

> *Epistle to John Driden of Chesterton* [1700], *l. 18*

Better to hunt in fields, for health unbought,

Than fee the doctor for a nauseous
    draught.
The wise, for cure, on exercise depend;
God never made his work for man to
    mend.
> *Epistle to John Driden
> of Chesterton, l. 92*

A very merry, dancing, drinking,
Laughing, quaffing, and unthinking
    time.
> *The Secular Masque* [1700], *l. 38*

The sword within the scabbard keep,
And let mankind agree.   *Ib. l. 61*

All, all of a piece throughout:
    Thy chase had a beast in view;
Thy wars brought nothing about;
    Thy lovers were all untrue.
'Tis well an old age is out,
    And time to begin a new.[1]
> *Ib. l. 86*

Ill habits gather by unseen degrees —
As brooks make rivers, rivers run to
    seas.
> *Ovid, Metamorphoses* [1700],
> *bk. XV, The Worship of Aes-
> culapius, l. 155*

[Of Chaucer's *Canterbury Tales*]
Here is God's plenty.
> *Fables Ancient and Modern*
> [1700], *preface*

For Art may err, but Nature cannot
    miss.
> *Ib. The Cock and the Fox, l. 452*

Old as I am, for ladies' love unfit,
The power of beauty I remember yet.
> *Ib. Cymon and Iphigenia, l. 1*

He trudg'd along unknowing what he
    sought,
And whistled as he went, for want of
    thought.   *Ib. l. 84*

She hugg'd the offender, and forgave
    the offense:
Sex to the last.[2]   *Ib. l. 367*

Of seeming arms to make a short es-
    say,
Then hasten to be drunk — the busi-
    ness of the day.   *Ib. l. 407*

[1] See Tennyson, p. 651a.
[2] And love the offender, yet detest the offense.
— POPE, *Eloisa to Abelard* [1717], *l. 192*

He was exhal'd; his great Creator drew
His spirit, as the sun the morning
    dew.[1]
> *On the Death of a Very Young
> Gentleman* [1700]

Here lies my wife: here let her lie!
Now she's at rest, and so am I.
> *Epitaph intended for his wife*

WILLIAM STOUGHTON
1631–1701

God hath sifted a nation that he
might send choice grain into this wilderness.[2]
> *Election Sermon at Boston*
> [*April 29, 1669*]

JOHN LOCKE
1632–1704

New opinions are always suspected,
and usually opposed, without any other
reason but because they are not already
common.
> *Essay Concerning Human
> Understanding* [1690], *dedi-
> catory epistle*

No man's knowledge here can go beyond his experience.
> *Ib. bk. II, ch. 1, sec. 19*

It is one thing to show a man that he
is in error, and another to put him in
possession of truth.   *Ib. IV, 7, 11*

All men are liable to error; and most
men are, in many points, by passion or
interest, under temptation to it.
> *Ib. 20, 17*

Wherever Law ends, Tyranny begins.[3]
> *Second Treatise of Government*
> [1690], *sec. 202*

[1] Early, bright, transient, chaste as morning
    dew,
  She sparkled, was exhal'd, and went to
    heaven.
    EDWARD YOUNG, *Night Thoughts* [1742–
    1745], *Night V, l. 600*
[2] God had sifted three kingdoms to find the
wheat for this planting. — LONGFELLOW, *Courtship of Miles Standish* [1858], *IV*
[3] See William Pitt, p. 426a.

A sound mind in a sound body,[1] is a short but full description of a happy state in this world.

Some Thoughts on Education
[1693], sec. 1

Virtue is harder to be got than knowledge of the world; and, if lost in a young man, is seldom recovered.

Ib. 64

He that will have his son have a respect for him and his orders, must himself have a great reverence for his son.[2]

Ib. 65

The only fence against the world is a thorough knowledge of it.   *Ib. 88*

BENEDICT [BARUCH] SPINOZA[3]
1632–1677

Peace is not an absence of war, it is a virtue, a state of mind, a disposition for benevolence, confidence, justice.

Theological-Political Treatise
[1670]

Nature abhors a vacuum.

Ethics [1677],[4] *pt. I, proposition 15: note*

God and all the attributes of God are eternal.   *Ib. 19*

Nothing exists from whose nature some effect does not follow.   *Ib. 36*

He who would distinguish the true from the false must have an adequate idea of what is true and false.

Ib. II, 42: proof

[1] See Juvenal, p. 139b.
[2] See Juvenal, p. 140a.
[3] Ein Gottbetrunkener Mensch [A God-intoxicated man]. — NOVALIS (FRIEDRICH VON HARDENBERG) [1772–1801]
The Lord blot out his name under heaven. The Lord set him apart for destruction from all the tribes of Israel, with all the curses of the firmament which are written in the Book of the Law. . . . There shall no man speak to him, no man write to him, no man show him any kindness, no man stay under the same roof with him, no man come nigh him. — *Amsterdam Synagogue's curse on Spinoza* [1656]
[4] Everyman edition, translated by ANDREW BOYLE.

Will and Intellect are one and the same thing.

Ethics, pt. II, proposition 49: corollary

He that can carp in the most eloquent or acute manner at the weakness of the human mind is held by his fellows as almost divine.

Ib. III: preface

Surely human affairs would be far happier if the power in men to be silent were the same as that to speak. But experience more than sufficiently teaches that men govern nothing with more difficulty than their tongues.

Ib. 2: note

Pride is therefore pleasure arising from a man's thinking too highly of himself.   *Ib. 26: note*

It may easily come to pass that a vain man may become proud and imagine himself pleasing to all when he is in reality a universal nuisance.

Ib. 30: note

Self-complacency is pleasure accompanied by the idea of oneself as cause.

Ib. 51: note

It therefore comes to pass that everyone is fond of relating his own exploits and displaying the strength both of his body and his mind, and that men are on this account a nuisance one to the other.   *Ib. 54: note*

I refer those actions which work out the good of the agent to courage, and those which work out the good of others to nobility. Therefore temperance, sobriety, and presence of mind in danger, etc., are species of courage; but modesty, clemency, etc., are species of nobility.   *Ib. 59: note*

Fear cannot be without hope nor hope without fear.

Ib. definition 13: explanation

So long as a man imagines that he cannot do this or that, so long is he determined not to do it: and consequently, so long it is impossible to him that he should do it.

Ib. 28: explanation

Those who are believed to be most abject and humble are usually most ambitious and envious.

*Ethics, pt. III, proposition
29: explanation*

One and the same thing can at the same time be good, bad, and indifferent, e.g., music is good to the melancholy, bad to those who mourn, and neither good nor bad to the deaf.

Ib. IV: preface

Man is a social animal.[1]

Ib. proposition 35: note

Men will find that they can prepare with mutual aid far more easily what they need, and avoid far more easily the perils which beset them on all sides, by united forces.   *Ib.*

Avarice, ambition, lust, etc., are nothing but species of madness.[2]

Ib. 44: note

He whose honor depends on the opinion of the mob must day by day strive with the greatest anxiety, act and scheme in order to retain his reputation. For the mob is varied and inconstant, and therefore if a reputation is not carefully preserved it dies quickly.

Ib. 58: note

In refusing benefits caution must be used lest we seem to despise or to refuse them for fear of having to repay them in kind.   *Ib. 70: note*

To give aid to every poor man is far beyond the reach and power of every man. . . . Care of the poor is incumbent on society as a whole.[3]

Ib. appendix, 17

None are more taken in by flattery than the proud, who wish to be the first and are not.   *Ib. 21*

Those are most desirous of honor

and glory who cry out the loudest of its abuse and the vanity of the world.

*Ethics, pt. V, proposition
10: note*

We feel and know that we are eternal.   *Ib. 23: note*

All excellent things are as difficult as they are rare.   *Ib. 42: note*

The things which . . . are esteemed as the greatest good of all . . . can be reduced to these three headings: to wit, Riches, Fame, and Pleasure. With these three the mind is so engrossed that it cannot scarcely think of any other good.

*Tractatus de Intellectus
Emendatione* [1677], I, 3

SIR CHRISTOPHER WREN
1632–1723

Si monumentum requiris circumspice [If you would see the man's monument, look around].

Inscription in St. Paul's Cathedral, London. Written by Wren's son

WENTWORTH DILLON, EARL OF ROSCOMMON
1633–1685

Choose an author as you choose a friend.

*Essay on Translated Verse
[1684], l. 96*

Immodest words admit of no defense, For want of decency is want of sense.
Ib. l. 113

The multitude is always in the wrong.
Ib. l. 183

My God, my Father, and my Friend, Do not forsake me in my end.
Translation of Dies Irae

SAMUEL PEPYS
1633–1703

I pray God to keep me from being proud.   *Diary, March 22, 1660*

---

[1] See Blackstone, p. 444b.
[2] To me, avarice seems not so much a vice, as a deplorable piece of madness. — SIR THOMAS BROWNE, *Religio Medici* [1642]
[3] See Samuel Johnson, p. 431a, and Andrew Carnegie, p. 757b.

This morning came home my fine camlet cloak, with gold buttons, and a silk suit, which cost me much money, and I pray God to make me able to pay for it. *Diary, July 1, 1660*

And so to bed. *July 22, 1660, etc.*

I am unwilling to mix my fortune with him that is going down the wind. *September 6, 1660*

A good honest and painful sermon. *March 17, 1661*

One, by his own confession to me, that can put on two several faces, and look his enemies in the face with as much love as his friends. But, good God! what an age is this, and what a world is this! that a man cannot live without playing the knave and dissimulation. *September 1, 1661*

Though he be a fool, yet he keeps much company, and will tell all he sees or hears, so a man may understand what the common talk of the town is. *September 2, 1661*

My wife, poor wretch. *September 18, 1661, etc.*

Thanks be to God, since my leaving drinking of wine, I do find myself much better, and do mind my business better, and do spend less money, and less time lost in idle company. *January 26, 1662*

As happy a man as any in the world, for the whole world seems to smile upon me. *October 31, 1662*

Bought Hudibras again, it being certainly some ill humor to be so against that which all the world cries up to be the example of wit; for which I am resolved once more to read him, and see whether I can find it or no.[1] *February 6, 1663*

To the Trinity House, where a very good dinner among the old soakers. *February 15, 1665*

[1] Pepys had bought *Hudibras* December 26, 1662, but thought it "so silly an abuse of the Presbyter Knight going to the wars" that he sold it the same day.

But Lord! how everybody's looks, and discourse in the street, is of death, and nothing else; and few people going up and down, that the town is like a place distressed and forsaken.[1] *Diary, August 30, 1665*

Strange to see how a good dinner and feasting reconciles everybody. *November 9, 1665*

Saw a wedding in the church; and strange to see what delight we married people have to see these poor fools decoyed into our condition. *December 25, 1665*

Musick and women I cannot but give way to, whatever my business is. *March 9, 1666*

The truth is, I do indulge myself a little the more in pleasure, knowing that this is the proper age of my life to do it; and, out of my observation that most men that do thrive in the world do forget to take pleasure during the time that they are getting their estate, but reserve that till they have got one, and then it is too late for them to enjoy it. *March 10, 1666*

Home, and, being washing-day, dined upon cold meat. *April 4, 1666*

Musick is the thing of the world that I love most. *July 30, 1666*

Busy till night, pleasing myself mightily to see what a deal of business goes off a man's hands when he stays by it. *January 14, 1667*

Did satisfy myself mighty fair in the truth of the saying that the world do not grow old at all, but is in as good condition in all respects as ever it was. *February 3, 1667*

This day I am, by the blessing of God, 34 years old, in very good health and mind's content, and in condition of estate much beyond whatever my friends could expect of a child of theirs, this day 34 years. The Lord's

[1] The time of the Great Plague.

name be praised! and may I be thankful for it.   *Diary, February 23, 1667*

But it is pretty to see what money will do.   *March 21, 1667*

To church; and with my mourning, very handsome, and new periwig, make a great show.   *March 31, 1667*

But to think of the clatter they make with his coach, and their own fine clothes, and yet how meanly they live within doors, and nastily, and borrowing everything of neighbors.
April 1, 1667

Whose red nose makes me ashamed to be seen with him.   *May 3, 1667*

Gives me some kind of content to remember how painful it is sometimes to keep money, as well as to get it.
October 11, 1667

I find my wife hath something in her gizzard, that only waits an opportunity of being provoked to bring up; but I will not, for my content-sake, give it.
June 17, 1668

In appearance, at least, he being on all occasions glad to be at friendship with me, though we hate one another, and know it on both sides.
September 22, 1668

I do hate to be unquiet at home.
January 22, 1669

And so I betake myself to that course, which is almost as much as to see myself go into my grave; for which, and all the discomforts that will accompany my being blind, the good God prepare me!
May 31, 1669 (final entry)

GEORGE SAVILE, MARQUESS OF HALIFAX
1633–1695

Children and fools want everything, because they want wit to distinguish; there is no stronger evidence of a crazy

understanding than the making too large a catalogue of things necessary.
Advice to a Daughter [1688]

Popularity is a crime from the moment it is sought; it is only a virtue where men have it whether they will or no.
Political, Moral, and Miscellaneous Reflections [1750]

Misspending a man's time is a kind of self-homicide.   *Ib.*

Men are not hanged for stealing horses, but that horses may not be stolen.   *Ib.*

ROBERT SOUTH
1634–1716

Speech was given to the ordinary sort of men whereby to communicate their mind; but to wise men, whereby to conceal it.[1]   *Sermon* [1676]

ROBERT HOOKE
1635–1703

The truth is, the science of Nature has been already too long made only a work of the brain and the fancy: It is now high time that it should return to the plainness and soundness of observations on material and obvious things.
Micrographia [1665]

NICOLAS BOILEAU-DESPRÉAUX
1636–1711

Happy who in his verse can gently steer

[1] Speech was made to open man to man, and not to hide him; to promote commerce, and not to betray it. — DAVID LLOYD [1635–1692], *The Statesmen and Favorites of England Since the Reformation* [1665, edited by Whitworth], vol. I, *p. 503*
Men talk only to conceal the mind. — EDWARD YOUNG, *Love of Fame* [1725–1728], satire II, l. 208
The true use of speech is not so much to express our wants as to conceal them. — GOLDSMITH, *The Bee, no. 3* [October 20, 1759]
See Voltaire, p. 417b.

From grave to light, from pleasant to
severe.[1]
The Art of Poetry [1674],
canto I, l. 75

At last comes Malherbe [2] and, the
first to do so in France, brings to his
verse a smooth cadence. *Ib. l. 131*

Whate'er is well conceived is clearly
said,
And the words to say it flow with ease.
Ib. l. 153

Every age has its pleasures, its style
of wit, and its own ways.
Ib. III, l. 374

The wisest man is he who does not
fancy that he is so at all.
Satire 1, l. 46

A Cat's a cat, and Rolet is a knave.
Ib. l. 52

He [Molière] pleases all the world,
but cannot please himself. *Ib. l. 94*

In spite of every sage whom Greece can
show,
Unerring wisdom never dwelt below;
Folly in all of every age we see,
The only difference lies in the degree.
Satire 4, l. 37

Greatest fools are oft most satisfied.
Ib. l. 128

If your descent is from heroic sires,
Show in your life a remnant of their
fires. *Satire 5, l. 43*

Of all the creatures that creep, swim, or
fly,
Peopling the earth, the waters, and the
sky,
From Rome to Iceland, Paris to Japan,
I really think the greatest fool is man.
Satire 8, l. 1

But satire, ever moral, ever new,
Delights the reader and instructs him,
too.
She, if good sense refine her sterling
page,

Oft shakes some rooted folly of the
age. *Satire 8, l. 257*

Honor is like an island, rugged and
without a beach; once we have left it,
we can never return.
Satire 10, l. 167

Now two punctilious envoys, Thine and
Mine,
Embroil the earth about a fancied
line;
And, dwelling much on right and much
on wrong,
Prove how the right is chiefly with
the strong.[1] *Satire 11, l. 141*

Nothing but truth is lovely, nothing
fair. *Epistle 9*

The terrible burden of having nothing
to do. *Epistle 11*

BISHOP THOMAS KEN
1637–1711

Teach me to live, that I may dread
The grave as little as my bed.[2]
Morning and Evening Hymn,
st. 3

Praise God, from whom all blessings
flow!
Praise Him, all creatures here below!
Praise Him above, ye heavenly host!
Praise Father, Son, and Holy Ghost!
Ib. st. 10 (Doxology)

THOMAS TRAHERNE
c. 1637 – 1674

You never enjoy the world aright, till
the sea itself floweth in your veins, till
you are clothed with the heavens, and
crowned with the stars: and perceive
yourself to be the sole heir of the whole
world.
Centuries of Meditations [1908],
Century I, sec. 29

The corn was orient and immortal
wheat, which never should be reaped,

[1] See Pope, p. 410a.
Translated by DRYDEN.
[2] Enfin Malherbe vint.

[1] See Tacitus, p. 140a; Bussy-Rabutin, p.
357a; Frederick the Great, p. 435a; and Gibbon,
p. 466a.
[2] See Browne, p. 330b.

nor was ever sown. I thought it had stood from everlasting to everlasting.[1]
Centuries of Meditations, Century III, sec. 3

How like an angel came I down! [2]
Wonder [1910], *st. 1*

I within did flow
With seas of life like wine.
Ib. st. 3

LOUIS XIV
1638–1715

I am the state.[3]
Attributed remark before the parliament in 1651

Has God forgotten all I have done for him? [4]
Attributed remark upon hearing the news of the French defeat at Malplaquet [1709]

I almost had to wait.[5]
Attributed remark when a coach he had ordered arrived just in time.

JEAN RACINE
1639–1699

I loved him too much not to hate him at all!
Andromaque [1667], *act II*

You are Emperor, my lord, and yet you weep?
Bérénice [1670], *act IV, sc. 5*

My only hope lies in my despair.
Bajazet [1672], *act I, sc. 4*

You have named him, not I.[6]
Phèdre [1677], *act I, sc. 3*

It is no longer a passion hidden in my heart: it is Venus herself fastened to her prey.[1]
Phèdre, act I, sc. 3

Innocence has nothing to dread.
Ib. III, 6

Crime like virtue has its degrees; and timid innocence was never known to blossom suddenly into extreme license.[2]
Ib. IV, 2

To repair the irreparable ravages of time.
Athalie [1691], *act II, sc. 5*

SIR CHARLES SEDLEY
c. 1639 – 1701

When change itself can give no more,
'Tis easy to be true.
Reasons for Constancy, st. 4

Phyllis is my only joy,
Faithless as the winds or seas;
Sometimes coming, sometimes coy,
Yet she never fails to please.
Song [1702], *st. 1*

IHARA SAIKAKU
1642–1693

Heaven says nothing, and the whole earth grows rich beneath its silent rule. Men, too, are touched by heaven's virtue; yet, in their greater part, they are creatures of deceit. They are born, it seems, with an emptiness of soul, and must take their qualities wholly from things without. To be born thus empty into this modern age, this mixture of good and ill, and yet to steer through life on an honest course to the splendors of success — this is a feat reserved for paragons of our kind, a task beyond the nature of the normal man.
The Japanese Family Storehouse; or, The Millionaires' Gospel,[3] *bk. I, 1*

The first consideration for all, throughout life, is the earning of a living.
Ib.

---

[1] See *Psalm 90:2,* p. 20a.
[2] See Vaughan, p. 362b, and Wordsworth, p. 513b.
[3] L'état c'est moi.
See Napoleon Bonaparte, p. 504a.
[4] Dieu a donc oublié tout ce que j'ai fait pour lui?
[5] J'ai failli attendre.
[6] C'est toi qui l'a nommé.

[1] Ce n'est plus une ardeur dans mes veines cachée:
C'est Vénus toute entière à sa proie attachée.
[2] See Juvenal, p. 139a.
[3] Edited and translated by G. W. SARGENT.

Though mothers and fathers give us life, it is money alone which preserves it.

> *The Japanese Family Storehouse; or, The Millionaires' Gospel, bk. I, 1*

In life it is training rather than birth which counts. *Ib. 3*

Ancient simplicity is gone . . . the people of today are satisfied with nothing but finery. *Ib. 4*

Take care! Kingdoms are destroyed by bandits, houses by rats, and widows by suitors.[1] *Ib. 5*

There is always something to upset the most careful of human calculations.[2] *Ib. II, 2*

When you send a clerk on business to a distant province, a man of rigid morals is not your best choice. *Ib. 5*

To think twice in every matter and follow the lead of others is no way to make money. *Ib.*

For each of the four hundred and four bodily ailments celebrated physicians have produced infallible remedies, but the malady which brings the greatest distress to mankind — to even the wisest and cleverest of us — is the plague of poverty. *Ib. III, 1*

To make a fortune some assistance from fate is essential. Ability alone is insufficient. *Ib. 4*

If we live by subhuman means we might as well never have had the good fortune to be born human. *Ib.*

Like ice beneath the sun's rays — to such poverty did he fall . . . his fortune melted to water. *Ib. 5*

If making money is a slow process, losing it is quickly done. *Ib.*

Harshness is for the good of a boy, softheartedness will ruin him.[3] *Ib. V, 5*

[1] See *Matthew 6:19*, p. 40b.
[2] See Robert Burns, p. 492b.
[3] See *Proverbs 13:24*, p. 24a.

SIR ISAAC NEWTON
1642–1727

If I have seen further (than you and Descartes) it is by standing upon the shoulders of Giants.[1]

> *Letter to Robert Hooke, February 5, 1675/6*

I frame no hypotheses; for whatever is not deduced from the phenomena is to be called an hypothesis; and hypotheses, whether metaphysical or physical, whether of occult qualities or mechanical, have no place in experimental philosophy. *Ib.*

Every body continues in its state of rest, or of uniform motion in a right line, unless it is compelled to change that state by forces impressed upon it.

> *Philosophiae Naturalis Principia Mathematica* [1687].[2] *Laws of Motion, I*

The change of motion is proportional to the motive force impressed; and is made in the direction of the right line in which that force is impressed.[3]

> *Ib. II*

To every action there is always opposed an equal reaction: or, the mutual actions of two bodies upon each other are always equal, and directed to contrary parts. *Ib. III*

God in the beginning formed matter in solid, massy, hard, impenetrable, movable particles, of such sizes and figures, and with such other properties, and in such proportion to space, as most conduced to the end for which he formed them. *Optics* [1704]

I do not know what I may appear to the world; but to myself I seem to have been only like a boy playing on the seashore, and diverting myself in now and then finding a smoother pebble or a prettier shell than ordinary, whilst the

[1] See Lucan, p. 134a, and Robert Burton, p. 310a.
[2] *Mathematical Principles of Natural Philosophy.* Translated by ANDREW MOTTE [1729].
[3] In modern terms, acceleration is directly proportional to applied force.

great ocean of truth lay all undiscovered before me.

> From BREWSTER, *Memoirs of Newton* [1855], vol. II, ch. 27

O Diamond! Diamond! thou little knowest the mischief done!

> *Said to a pet dog who knocked over a candle and set fire to his papers*

THOMAS SHADWELL[1]
c. 1642 – 1692

And wit's the noblest frailty of the mind. 　A *True Widow*, act II, sc. 1

The haste of a fool is the slowest thing in the world. 　*Ib. III, 1*

I am, out of the ladies' company, like a fish out of the water. 　*Ib.*

Every man loves what he is good at. 　*Ib. V, 1*

MATSUO BASHO
1644–1694

The months and days are the travelers of eternity. The years that come and go are also voyagers. . . . I too for years past have been stirred by the sight of a solitary cloud drifting with the wind to ceaseless thoughts of roaming.

> *The Narrow Road of Oku (Oku no Hosomichi)* [2]

Such stillness —
The cries of the cicadas
Sink into the rocks. 　*Ib.*

My body, now close to fifty years of age, has become an old tree that bears bitter peaches, a snail which has lost its shell, a bagworm separated from its bag; it drifts with the winds and clouds that know no destination. Morning and

night I have eaten traveler's fare, and have held out for alms a pilgrim's wallet.

> *Prose Poem on The Unreal Dwelling (Genjuan no Fu)* [1]

My poetry is like a stove in the summer or a fan in the winter. It runs against the popular tastes and has no practical use.[2]

> *The Rustic Gate. From the collection titled Basho Bunshu*

Do not seek to follow in the footsteps of the men of old; seek what they sought. 　*Ib.*

The white chrysanthemum
Even when lifted to the eye
Remains immaculate.[2]

> *Conversations with Basho. From the collection Kyoraisho Hyokai*

Clear cascades!
Into the waves scatter
Blue pine needles. 　*Ib.*

An old pond —
A frog leaping in —
The sound of water.[3] 　*Poem*

A rough sea!
Stretched out over Sado
The Milky Way.[3] 　*Poem*

WILLIAM PENN
1644–1718

No cross, no crown.[4]

> *Title of Pamphlet* [1669]

Any government is free to the people under it where the laws rule and the people are a party to the laws.

> *Frame of Government* [1682]

Truth often suffers more by the heat of its defenders than from the arguments of its opposers.

> *Some Fruits of Solitude* [5] [1693]

---

[1] Shadwell was at open feud with Dryden from 1682, and the two poets repeatedly attacked one another in satires, the most famous of which is Dryden's *Mac Flecknoe*. See Dryden, p. 369a.

[2] From *Anthology of Japanese Literature*, edited by Donald Keene [1955].

[1] From *Anthology of Japanese Literature*, edited by Donald Keene [1955].

[2] From *Sources of Japanese Tradition*, edited by William Theodore de Bary [1960].

[3] Translated by DANA B. YOUNG.

[4] See Quarles, p. 322a.

[5] A copy of this little book, wrote ROBERT LOUIS STEVENSON, "I carried in my pocket all

It is a reproach to religion and government to suffer so much poverty and excess.
Some Fruits of Solitude

They that love beyond the world cannot be separated by it. Death is but crossing the world, as friends do the seas; they live in one another still.
Ib.

Men are generally more careful of the breed of their horses and dogs than of their children. *Ib.*

It were endless to dispute upon everything that is disputable. *Ib.*

Have a care where there is more sail than ballast. *Ib.*

Passion is a sort of fever in the mind, which ever leaves us weaker than it found us. *Ib.*

The public must and will be served.
Ib.

Much reading is an oppression of the mind, and extinguishes the natural candle, which is the reason of so many senseless scholars in the world.
Advice to His Children [1699]

EDWARD TAYLOR
c. 1644 – 1729

Who spread its canopy? Or curtains spun?
Who in this bowling alley bowled the sun?
Poetical Works [1939]. *God's Determinations Touching His Elect, preface*

For in Christ's coach saints sweetly sing
As they to glory ride therein.
Ib. The Joy of Church Fellowship Rightly Attended

Make me, O Lord, Thy spinning-wheel complete. *Ib. Housewifery*

about the San Francisco streets, read in street-cars and ferry-boats when I was sick unto death, and found in all times and places a peaceful and sweet companion."

Its food too fine for angels; yet come, take
And eat thy fill! It's Heaven's sugar cake.
Poetical Works. Preparatory Meditations, 8

This bread of life dropt in thy mouth doth cry:
Eat, eat me, soul, and thou shalt never die. *Ib.*

Is Christ thy advocate to plead thy cause?
Art thou his client? Such shall never slide.
He never lost his case. *Ib. 38*

My case is bad. Lord, be my advocate.
My sin is red: I'm under God's arrest.
Ib.

JEAN DE LA BRUYÈRE
1645–1696

We come too late to say anything which has not been said already.
Les Caractères [1688]. *Des Ouvrages de l'Esprit*

Liberality consists less in giving a great deal than in gifts well timed.
Ib. Du Coeur

Time, which strengthens friendship, weakens love. *Ib.*

We must laugh before we are happy, for fear we die before we laugh at all.[1]
Ib.

To laugh at men of sense is the privilege of fools. *Ib. De la Société*

There are but three events in a man's life: birth, life and death. He is not conscious of being born, he dies in pain, and he forgets to live.
Ib. De l'Homme

Most men make use of the first part of their life to render the last part miserable. *Ib.*

[1] See Beaumarchais, p. 460a, and note.

Women run to extremes; they are either better or worse than men.
Les Caractères. Des Femmes

BARON GOTTFRIED WILHELM VON LEIBNITZ
1646–1716

I often say a great doctor kills more people than a great general.[1]
Quoted in Bulletin of The New York Academy of Medicine, vol. V [1929], p. 152

HENRY ALDRICH
1647–1710

If all be true that I do think,
There are five reasons we should drink:
Good wine — a friend — or being dry —
Or lest we should be by and by —
Or any other reason why.
Five Reasons for Drinking

JOHN WILMOT, EARL OF ROCHESTER
1647–1680

Here lies our sovereign lord the King,
Whose promise none relies on;
He never said a foolish thing,
Nor ever did a wise one.
Written on the bedchamber door of Charles II [2]

For pointed satire I would Buckhurst choose,
The best good man with the worst-natured muse.[3]
An Allusion to Horace. Satire X, bk. I

A merry monarch, scandalous and poor.
A Satire on King Charles II

The world appears like a great family,

Whose lord, oppressed with pride and poverty,
(That to the few great bounty he may show)
Is fain to starve the numerous train below.
Like a Great Family

There's not a thing on earth that I can name,
So foolish, and so false, as common fame.
Did E'er This Saucy World

Reason, which fifty times to one does err,
Reason, an ignis fatuus of the mind.
A Satire Against Mankind [1675], l. 11

Books bear him up a while, and make him try
To swim with bladders of philosophy.
Ib. l. 20

Then Old Age and Experience, hand in hand,
Lead him to death, and make him understand,
After a search so painful and so long,
That all his life he has been in the wrong.
Ib. l. 25

Dead, we become the lumber of the world.
After Death

JOHN SHEFFIELD, DUKE OF BUCKINGHAM AND NORMANBY
1648–1721

Of all those arts in which the wise excel,
Nature's chief masterpiece is writing well.
Essay on Poetry [1682]

Read Homer once, and you can read no more;
For all books else appear so mean, so poor,
Verse will seem prose; but still persist to read,
And Homer will be all the books you need.
Ib.

---

[1] See Prior, p. 387b.
[2] See Charles II, p. 366b.
[3] Thou best-humor'd man with the worst-humor'd muse! — GOLDSMITH, *Retaliation* [1774], *Postscript*

And when I feigned an angry look,
Alas! I loved you best.
The Reconcilement [1701]

SIR THOMAS POPE BLOUNT
1649–1697

Every flower of the field, every fiber
of a plant, every particle of an insect,
carries with it the impress of its Maker,
and can — if duly considered — read
us lectures of ethics or divinity.[1]
A Natural History [1693]

WILLIAM III, PRINCE OF ORANGE
1650–1702

There is one certain means by which
I can be sure never to see my country's
ruin: I will die in the last ditch.
From HUME, *History of England*
[1754–1757], *ch.* 65

Every bullet has its billet.
From JOHN WESLEY, *Journal*
[*June 6, 1765*]

FRANÇOIS DE SALIGNAC DE LA MOTHE FÉNELON
1651–1715

Do not men die fast enough without
being destroyed by each other? Can any
man be insensible of the brevity of life?
and can he who knows it, think life too
long!   *Télémaque* [1699], *bk.* VII

To be always ready for war, said
Mentor, is the surest way to avoid it.[2]
Ib. X

Some of the most dreadful mischiefs
that afflict mankind proceed from wine;
it is the cause of disease, quarrels, sedi-
tion, idleness, aversion to labor, and
every species of domestic disorder.
Ib.

The blood of a nation ought never to

be shed except for its own preservation
in the utmost extremity.
Télémaque, bk. XIII

Mankind, by the perverse depravity
of their nature, esteem that which they
have most desired as of no value the
moment it is possessed, and torment
themselves with fruitless wishes for that
which is beyond their reach.
Ib. XVIII

THOMAS OTWAY
1651–1685

What mighty ills have not been done
   by woman!
Who was 't betrayed the Capitol? — A
   woman!
Who lost Mark Antony the world? —
   A woman!
Who was the cause of a long ten years'
   war,
And laid at last old Troy in ashes? —
   Woman!
Destructive, damnable, deceitful wo-
   man!
The Orphan [1680], *act* III, *sc.* 1

Let us embrace, and from this very
moment vow an eternal misery together.   *Ib.* IV, 2

O woman! lovely woman! Nature made
   thee
To temper man: we had been brutes
   without you;
Angels are painted fair, to look like
   you.
Venice Preserved [1682], *act* I,
     sc. 1

NAHUM TATE
1652–1715
AND
NICHOLAS BRADY
1659–1726

When I am laid in earth.
Dido and Aeneas [*c.* 1690] [1]

---

[1] See Tennyson, p. 654b.
[2] See Vegetius, p. 146b, and note.

[1] Tate wrote the libretto for the famous opera
by Henry Purcell.

As pants the hart for cooling streams
When heated in the chase.
Version of Psalm 42 [1696]

Through all the changing scenes of
life.   *Hymn*

While shepherds watch'd their flocks
by night,
All seated on the ground,
The Angel of the Lord came down,
And glory shone around.
Christmas Hymn [1700]

CHIKAMATSU MONZAEMON[1]
1653–1725

In writing *joruri*,[2] one attempts first
to describe facts as they really are, but
in so doing one writes things which are
not true, in the interest of art.
Preface to Hozumi Ikan,
Naniwa Miyage

I take pathos to be entirely a matter
of restraint. . . . . When one says of
something which is sad that it is sad,
one loses the implications, and in the
end, even the impression of sadness is
slight. It is essential that one not say of
a thing that 'it is sad,' but that it be sad
of itself.   *Ib.*

[Literary composition] should have
stylization; this makes it art, and is
what delights men's minds.   *Ib.*

THOMAS D'URFEY
1653–1723

O'er the hills and far away.[3]
Pills to Purge Melancholy

RANSETSU
1653–1708

Against the blue stands
A pine tree etched
By tonight's moon.[4]   *Harvest Moon*

[1] From *Sources of Japanese Tradition,* edited
by William Theodore de Bary [1960].
[2] Plays for life-size puppets.
[3] See Gay, p. 401b.
[4] Translated by Prescott B. Wintersteen, Jr.

ANDREW FLETCHER OF SALTOUN
1655–1716

If a man were permitted to make all
the ballads, he need not care who
should make the laws of a nation.
*Conversation Concerning a
Right Regulation of Governments for the Common Good
of Mankind* [1704]

NATHANIEL LEE[1]
1655–1692

Then he will talk — good gods! how he
will talk!
*The Rival Queens; or, The
Death of Alexander the Great*
[1677], *act I, sc. 3*

When Greeks joined Greeks, then was
the tug of war.   *Ib. IV, 2*

'Tis beauty calls, and glory shows the
way.   *Ib.*

Man, false man, smiling, destructive
man!
Theodosius [1680], *act III, sc. 2*

JOHN DENNIS
1657–1734

A man who could make so vile a pun
would not scruple to pick a pocket.
*The Gentleman's Magazine,
vol. LI* [1781], *p. 324*

They will not let my play run; and
yet they steal my thunder.[2]   *Remark*

[1] Lee collaborated with Dryden on *Oedipus*
(see p. 367b).
[2] For his play *Appius and Virginia* [1709],
Dennis had invented a new species of thunder.
"The tragedy however was coldly received, notwithstanding such assistance, and was acted
but a short time. Some nights after, Mr. Dennis,
being in the pit at the representation of
Macbeth, heard his own thunder made use of;
upon which he rose in a violent passion, and
exclaimed, with an oath, that it was his thunder.
'See,' said he, 'how the rascals use me! They
will not let my play run, and yet they steal my
thunder!' " — *Biographia Britannica, vol. V,
p. 103*

BERNARD LE BOVIER DE FONTENELLE
1657–1757

The geometrical mind is not so closely bound to geometry that it cannot be drawn aside and transferred to other departments of knowledge. A work of morality, politics, criticism, perhaps even eloquence will be more elegant, other things being equal, if it is shaped by the hand of geometry.[1]

Préface sur l'Utilité des Mathé-
matiques et la Physique [1729]

JOHN NORRIS
1657–1711

How fading are the joys we dote upon!
Like apparitions seen and gone.
But those which soonest take their flight
Are the most exquisite and strong —
Like angels' visits, short and bright;[2]
Mortality's too weak to bear them long.   *The Parting* [1678]

DANIEL DEFOE
c. 1661 – 1731

Wherever God erects a house of prayer,
The Devil always builds a chapel there;[3]
And 'twill be found, upon examination,
The latter has the largest congregation.

The True-Born Englishman
[1701], *pt. I, l. 1*

From this amphibious ill-born mob began
That vain, ill-natur'd thing, an Englishman.   *Ib. l. 132*

Great families of yesterday we show,
And lords whose parents were the Lord knows who.   *Ib. l. 374*

[1] Translated by F. CAJORI.
[2] Like those of angels, short and far between. — ROBERT BLAIR, *The Grave* [1743], *l. 588*
   See Campbell, p. 537b.
[3] See Luther, p. 179b, and note.

In their religion they are so uneven,
That each man goes his own byway to heaven.
The True-Born Englishman,
pt. II, l. 104

And of all plagues with which mankind are curs'd,
Ecclesiastic tyranny's the worst.
Ib. l. 299

When kings the sword of justice first lay down,
They are no kings, though they possess the crown.
Titles are shadows, crowns are empty things,
The good of subjects is the end of kings.   *Ib. l. 313*

All men would be tyrants if they could.
The Kentish Petition [1712–1713]

The best of men cannot suspend their fate:
The good die early, and the bad die late.
Character of the Late
Dr. S. Annesley [1715]

He bade me observe it, and I should always find that the calamities of life were shared among the upper and lower part of mankind; but that the middle station had the fewest disasters.
Robinson Crusoe [1719]

One day, about noon, going towards my boat, I was exceedingly surprised with the print of a man's naked foot on the shore, which was very plain to be seen on the sand.   *Ib.*

I takes my man Friday with me.
Ib.

SIR SAMUEL GARTH
1661–1719

A barren superfluity of words.
The Dispensary [1699], *canto II,*
l. 95

Hard was their lodging, homely was their food;

For all their luxury was doing good.[1]
Claremont, l. 148

KIKAKU
1661–1707

A harvest moon!
And on the mats —
Shadows of pine boughs.
Harvest Moon [2]

RICHARD BENTLEY
1662–1742

No man was ever written out of reputation but by himself.[3]
From J. H. MONK, *Life of Bentley* [1831]

It is a pretty poem, Mr. Pope, but you must not call it Homer. [4]
From JOHNSON, *Life of Pope*

MATHEW HENRY
1662–1714

He rolls it under his tongue as a sweet morsel.
Commentaries [1708–1710], *Psalm 36*

Our creature comforts.
Ib. Psalm 37

They that die by famine die by inches.   *Ib. Psalm 59*

To fish in troubled waters.
Ib. Psalm 60

Here is bread, which strengthens man's heart, and therefore called the staff of life.[5]   *Ib. Psalm 104*

---

[1] And learn the luxury of doing good. — GOLDSMITH, *The Traveller* [1764], *l.* 22
[2] Translated by PRESCOTT B. WINTERSTEEN, JR.
[3] See Montaigne, p. 190b.
[4] The reference is to Pope's translation of the *Iliad*. See Pope, p. 405a.
[5] For, behold, the Lord, the Lord of hosts, doth take away from Jerusalem and from Judah the stay and the staff, the whole stay of bread, and the whole stay of water. — *Isaiah 3:1*
Bread is the staff of life. — SWIFT, *Tale of a Tub* [1704]
Corn, which is the staff of life. — EDWARD WINSLOW, *Good News from New England* [1624]

Hearkeners, we say, seldom hear good of themselves.
Commentaries, Ecclesiastes 7

It was a common saying among the Puritans, "Brown bread and the Gospel is good fare."   *Ib. Isaiah 30*

None so blind as those that will not see.[1]   *Ib. Jeremiah 20*

Judas had given them the slip.
Ib. Matthew 22

After a storm comes a calm.
Ib. Acts 9

Men of polite learning and a liberal education.   *Ib. 10*

It is good news, worthy of all acceptation! and yet not too good to be true.   *Ib. Timothy 1*

It is not fit the public trusts should be lodged in the hands of any, till they are first proved and found fit for the business they are to be entrusted with.[2]
Ib. 3

All this and heaven too.
Life of Philip Henry

THOMAS (TOM) BROWN
1663–1704

I do not love thee, Doctor Fell.
The reason why I cannot tell;
But this alone I know full well,
I do not love thee, Doctor Fell.[3]
Written while a student at Christ Church, Oxford

To treat a poor wretch with a bottle of Burgundy, and fill his snuffbox, is like giving a pair of laced ruffles to a man that has never a shirt on his back.[4]
Laconics [1707]

---

[1] See *Jeremiah 5:21*, p. 34a.
[2] See Burke, p. 454b; Jefferson, p. 472b; Clay, p. 538b; Calhoun, p. 545b; Sumner, p. 659b; and Cleveland, p. 771a.
[3] See Martial, p. 135a.
> Je ne vous aime pas, Hylas;
> Je n'en saurois dire la cause,
> Je sais seulement une chose;
> C'est que je ne vous aime pas.
COMTE DE BUSSY-RABUTIN [1618–1693]
[4] See Goldsmith, p. 451b.

COTTON MATHER
1663–1728

I write the wonders of the Christian religion, flying from the depravations of Europe, to the American strand: and, assisted by the Holy Author of that religion, I do, with all conscience of truth, required therein by Him, who is the Truth itself, report the wonderful displays of His infinite power, wisdom, goodness, and faithfulness, wherewith his Divine Providence hath irradiated an Indian wilderness.

Magnalia Christi Americana
[1702], introduction

You are young and have the world before you; stoop as you go through it, and you will miss many hard bumps.

Advice to Benjamin Franklin
upon approaching a low-hang-
ing beam in his parsonage [1]

WILLIAM WALSH
1663–1708

Of all the plagues a lover bears,
Sure rivals are the worst.   *Song, st. 1*

I can endure my own despair,
But not another's hope.   *Ib. st. 2*

MATTHEW PRIOR
1664–1721

All jargon of the schools. [2]
I Am That I Am, An Ode [1688]

Our hopes, like towering falcons, aim
At objects in an airy height;
The little pleasure of the game
Is from afar to view the flight.
To the Honorable Charles
Montague

Odds life! must one swear to the truth
of a song?   *A Better Answer*

Be to her virtues very kind;
Be to her faults a little blind;

[1] From S. E. MORISON, *Vistas of History* [*1964*], *ch. 4*
  See Massinger, p. 315b.
[2] Noisy jargon of the schools. — JOHN POM-FRET [1667–1702], *Reason*
  The sounding jargon of the schools. — COWPER, *Truth* [1782], *l. 367*

Let all her ways be unconfin'd;
And clap your padlock — on her mind!
An English Padlock [1707]

The end must justify the means.[1]
Hans Carvel

And thought the nation ne'er would thrive
Till all the whores were burnt alive.
Paulo Purganti

He rang'd his tropes, and preach'd up patience;
Back'd his opinion with quotations.
Ib.

Cured yesterday of my disease,
I died last night of my physician.[2]
The Remedy Worse Than the
Disease

And often took leave, but was loth to depart.[3]
The Thief and the Cordelier

Nobles and heralds, by your leave,
  Here lies what once was Matthew Prior;
The son of Adam and of Eve:
  Can Bourbon or Nassau claim higher? [4]   *Epitaph*

Lays the rough paths of peevish Nature even,
And opens in each heart a little heaven.   *Charity*

His noble negligences teach
What others' toils despair to reach.
Alma, canto II, l. 7

Till their own dreams at length deceive 'em,
And oft repeating, they believe 'em.
Ib. III, 13

[1] See St. Jerome, p. 145a.
[2] See Leibnitz, p. 382a.
[3] As men that be lothe to departe do often take their leff [JOHN CLERK TO WOLSEY]. — HENRY ELLIS [1777–1869], *Letters, Third Series,* vol. I, p. 262
  "A loth to depart" was the common term for a song, or a tune played, on taking leave of friends.
[4] The following epitaph was written long before the time of Prior:
    Johnnie Carnegie lais heer.
    Descendit of Adam and Eve.
    Gif ony con gang hieher,
    Ise willing give him leve.

Abra was ready ere I called her name;
And though I called another, Abra
came.
> *Solomon on the Vanity of the*
> *World* [1718], *bk. II, l. 364*

To John I ow'd great obligation;
But John, unhappily, thought fit
To publish it to all the nation:
Sure John and I are more than quit.
> *Epigram* [1718]

Venus, take my votive glass;
Since I am not what I was,
What from this day I shall be,
Venus, let me never see.
> *The Lady Who Offers Her*
> *Looking-Glass to Venus. From*
> *The Greek Anthology*

SIR JOHN VANBRUGH
1664–1726

Once a woman has given you her
heart you can never get rid of the rest
of her.
> *The Relapse* [1697], *act II, sc. 1*

No man worth having is true to his
wife, or can be true to his wife, or ever
was, or ever will be so.   *Ib. III, 2*

Belinda: Ay, but you know we must
return good for evil.
Lady Brute: That may be a mistake
in the translation.
> *The Provoked Wife* [1698],
> *act I, sc. 1*

He laughs best who laughs last.[1]
> *The Country House* [1706],
> *act II, sc. 5*

Much of a muchness.
> *The Provoked Husband* [1728]
> (*completed by* COLLEY CIBBER)
> *act I, sc. 1*

JOHN POMFRET
1667–1702

We live and learn, but not the wiser
grow.[2]   *Reason, l. 112*

---

[1] Better the last smile than the first laughter.
— JOHN RAY, *Proverbs* [1670]

[2] It is good to live and learn. — CERVANTES,
Don Quixote, pt. II [1615], *ch. 32*

JONATHAN SWIFT
1667–1745

Books, like men their authors, have
no more than one way of coming into
the world, but there are ten thousand
to go out of it, and return no more.
> *A Tale of a Tub* [1704], *dedication*

Books, the children of the brain.
> *Ib. sec. 1*

As boys do sparrows, with flinging
salt upon their tails.   *Ib. 7*

Satire is a sort of glass, wherein beholders do generally discover everybody's face but their own.
> *The Battle of the Books* [1704],
> *preface*

The two noblest of things, which are
sweetness and light.[1]   *Ib.*

Laws are like cobwebs, which may
catch small flies, but let wasps and hornets break through.[2]
> *A Critical Essay Upon the Fac-*
> *ulties of the Mind* [1707]

There is nothing in this world constant, but inconstancy.[3]   *Ib.*

'Tis very warm weather when one's
in bed.
> *Journal to Stella* [November 8,
> 1710]

With my own fair hands.
> *Ib.* [January 4, 1711]

We are so fond of one another, because our ailments are the same.
> *Ib.* [February 1, 1711]

I love good creditable acquaintance; I
love to be the worst of the company.
> *Ib.* [May 17, 1711]

We were to do more business after
dinner; but after dinner is after din-

Live and learn,
Not first learn and then live.
> BROWNING, *Parleyings with Certain*
> *People. With Christopher Smart*
> [1887], *IX*

[1] See Matthew Arnold, p. 716a.

[2] See Solon, p. 68b, and Zincgref, p. 321a.

[3] See Heraclitus, p. 77b, and note.

ner — an old saying and a true, "much drinking, little thinking." [1]

Journal to Stella
[February 26, 1712]

We have just enough religion to make us hate, but not enough to make us love one another.

Thoughts on Various Subjects
[1711]

Censure is the tax a man pays to the public for being eminent. *Ib.*

Every man desires to live long, but no man would be old. *Ib.*

A nice man is a man of nasty ideas. *Ib.*

Party is the madness of many, for the gain of a few.[2] *Ib.*

'Tis an old maxim in the schools,
That flattery's the food of fools;
Yet now and then your men of wit
Will condescend to take a bit.

Cadenus and Vanessa [3] *[1713]*

Proper words in proper places, make the true definition of a style.

Letter to a Young Clergyman
[January 9, 1720]

If Heaven had looked upon riches to be a valuable thing, it would not have given them to such a scoundrel.

Letter to Miss Vanhomrigh
[August 12, 1720]

He [the Emperor] is taller by almost the breadth of my nail, than any of his court, which alone is enough to strike an awe into the beholders.

Gulliver's Travels [1726].
Voyage to Lilliput, ch. 2

[1] See Addison, p. 394b.
[2] See Pope, p. 405a.
[3] When the poem of "Cadenus and Vanessa" was the general topic of conversation, someone said, "Surely that Vanessa must be an extraordinary woman that could inspire the Dean to write so finely upon her." Mrs. Johnson smiled, and answered that "she thought that point not quite so clear; for it was well known the Dean could write finely upon a broomstick." — SAMUEL JOHNSON, *Lives of the Poets* [1779–1781], *Life of Swift*

I cannot but conclude the bulk of your natives to be the most pernicious race of little odious vermin that nature ever suffered to crawl upon the surface of the earth.

Gulliver's Travels. Voyage to Brobdingnag, ch. 6

And he gave it for his opinion, that whoever could make two ears of corn or two blades of grass to grow upon a spot of ground where only one grew before, would deserve better of mankind, and do more essential service to his country, than the whole race of politicians put together.[1] *Ib.*

He had been eight years upon a project for extracting sunbeams out of cucumbers, which were to be put in vials hermetically sealed, and let out to warm the air in raw inclement summers.

Ib. Voyage to Laputa, ch. 5

I said the thing which was not.
Ib. Voyage to the Houyhnhnms, ch. 3

I told him . . . that we ate when we were not hungry, and drank without the provocation of thirst. *Ib. 6*

A set of phrases learnt by rote;
A passion for a scarlet coat;
When at a play to laugh, or cry,
Yet cannot tell the reason why:
Never to hold her tongue a minute;
While all she prates has nothing in it.

The Furniture of a Woman's Mind [1727]

For conversation well endu'd;
She calls it witty to be rude;
And, placing raillery in railing,
Will tell aloud your greatest failing.
Ib.

In party, furious to her pow'r;
A bitter Whig, or Tory sour;
Her arguments directly tend

[1] He who makes two blades of grass grow in place of one renders a service to the state. — VOLTAIRE, *Letter to M. Moreau* [1765]

Against the side she would defend.
> *The Furniture of a*
> *Woman's Mind*

Not die here in a rage, like a poisoned rat in a hole.
> *Letter to Bolingbroke*
> [*March 21, 1729*]

Yet malice never was his aim;
He lash'd the vice but spar'd the name.
No individual could resent,
Where thousands equally were meant.
His satire points at no defect
But what all mortals may correct;
For he abhorr'd that senseless tribe
Who call it humor when they gibe.
> *Verses on the Death of Dr. Swift*
> [*1731*], *l.* 459

Hobbes clearly proves that every creature
Lives in a state of war by nature.[1]
> *On Poetry. A Rhapsody* [1733]

So, naturalists observe, a flea
Hath smaller fleas that on him prey;
And these have smaller still to bite 'em;
And so proceed *ad infinitum.*
Thus every poet, in his kind,
Is bit by him that comes behind.
> *Ib.*

Conversation is but carving!
Give no more to every guest
Than he's able to digest.
Give him always of the prime,
And but little at a time.
Carve to all but just enough,
Let them neither starve nor stuff,
And that you may have your due,
Let your neighbor carve for you.
> *Conversation*

Under this window in stormy weather
I marry this man and woman together;
Let none but Him who rules the thunder
Put this man and woman asunder.
> *Marriage Service from His*
> *Chamber Window*

[1] See Hobbes, p. 317b.

The sight of you is good for sore eyes.[1]
> *Polite Conversation* [1738?],
> *dialogue 1*

'Tis as cheap sitting as standing.
> *Ib.*

I hate nobody: I am in charity with the world.
> *Ib.*

You were half seas over.
> *Ib.*

I won't quarrel with my bread and butter.
> *Ib.*

She's no chicken; she's on the wrong side of thirty, if she be a day.
> *Ib.*

She wears her clothes, as if they were thrown on her with a pitchfork.
> *Ib.*

He was a bold man that first eat an oyster.
> *Ib.* 2

That's as well said, as if I had said it myself.
> *Ib.*

Fingers were made before forks, and hands before knives.
> *Ib.*

She has more goodness in her little finger, than he has in his whole body.
> *Ib.*

Lord, I wonder what fool it was that first invented kissing!
> *Ib.*

The best doctors in the world are Doctor Diet, Doctor Quiet, and Doctor Merryman.[2]
> *Ib.*

I'll give you leave to call me anything, if you don't call me spade.
> *Ib.*

May you live all the days of your life.
> *Ib.*

I always love to begin a journey on Sundays, because I shall have the prayers of the church to preserve all that travel by land, or by water.
> *Ib.*

[1] What a sight for sore eyes that would be!
— WILLIAM HAZLITT [1778–1830], *Of Persons One Would Have Seen*

[2] Use three physicians —
First, Dr. Quiet;
Next, Dr. Merryman,
And Dr. Dyet.
> *Regimen Sanitatis Salernitanum* [1607]

I know Sir John will go, though he was sure it would rain cats and dogs.
Polite Conversation, dialogue 2

I thought you and he were hand-in-glove. *Ib.*

She watches him, as a cat would watch a mouse. *Ib. dialogue* 3

She pays him in his own coin. *Ib.*

There was all the world and his wife. *Ib.*

Hail, fellow, well met,
All dirty and wet:
Find out if you can,
Who's master, who's man.
My Lady's Lamentation [1765],
l. 171

I shall be like that tree, I shall die at the top.
From Sir Walter Scott, *Life of Swift* [1814]

Ubi saeva indignatio ulterius cor lacerare nequit.[1]
Epitaph. Inscribed on Swift's Grave, St. Patrick's, Dublin

SUSANNAH CENTLIVRE
c. 1667 – 1723

The real Simon Pure.
A Bold Stroke for a Wife [1718],
act V, *sc. 1*

ALAIN RENÉ LE SAGE
1668–1747

It may be said that his wit shines at the expense of his memory.[2]
Gil Blas [1715–1735], *bk. III,
ch. 11*

A flatterer can risk everything with great personages. *Ib.* IV, 7

Pride and conceit were the original sin of man. *Ib.* VII, 3

I wish you all sorts of prosperity with a little more taste. *Ib.* 4

[1] Where savage indignation can no longer tear the heart. See Yeats, p. 884a.
[2] See Sheridan, p. 482a.

The pleasure of talking is the inextinguishable passion of a woman, coeval with the act of breathing.
Gil Blas, bk. VII, *ch.* 7

Facts are stubborn things.[1]
Ib. X, 1

WILLIAM CONGREVE
1670–1729

Eternity was in that moment.
The Old Bachelor [1693],
act IV, *sc.* 7

Marry'd in haste, we may repent at leisure.[2] *Ib.* V, 8

It is the business of a comic poet to paint the vices and follies of human kind.
The Double Dealer [1694],
epistle dedicatory

Retired to their tea and scandal, according to their ancient custom.[3]
Ib. act I, *sc.* 1

Though marriage makes man and wife one flesh, it leaves 'em still two fools. *Ib.* II, 3

No mask like open truth to cover lies,
As to go naked is the best disguise.
Ib. V, 4

Thou liar of the first magnitude.
Love for Love [1695], *act* II, *sc.* 2

I warrant you, if he danced till doomsday, he thought I was to pay the piper. *Ib.*

O fie, miss, you must not kiss and tell. *Ib.* 10

Women are like tricks by sleight of hand,
Which, to admire, we should not understand. *Ib.* IV, 3

Music has charms to soothe a savage breast,[4]

[1] Facts are contrary 'z mules. — James Russell Lowell, *Biglow Papers, ser. II* [1862], *no. 4*
[2] See Shakespeare, p. 219a, and Cabell, p. 949b.
[3] See Fielding, p. 424b.
[4] Music hath charms, we all may find,
Ingratiate deeply with the mind.
Matthew Green [1696–1737], *The Spleen, l. 141*

To soften rocks, or bend a knotted
oak.
The Mourning Bride [1697],
act I, sc. 1

By magic numbers and persuasive
sound. *Ib.*

Heaven has no rage like love to hatred
turned,
Nor hell a fury like a woman scorned.[1]
Ib. III, 8

Love's but a frailty of the mind,
When 'tis not with ambition joined.
The Way of the World [1700],
act III, sc. 12

I nauseate walking; 'tis a country diversion, I loathe the country.
Ib. IV, 5

Let us be very strange and well-bred:
Let us be as strange as if we had been
married a great while; and as well-bred
as if we were not married at all.
Ib.

Thou art a retailer of phrases, and
dost deal in remnants of remnants.
Ib. 9

O, she is the antidote to desire.
Ib. 14

Careless she is with artful care,
Affecting to seem unaffected.
Amoret

Defer not till tomorrow to be wise,
Tomorrow's sun to thee may never
rise.[2] *Letter to Cobham*

RICHARD LEVERIDGE
1670–1758

When mighty roast beef was the Englishman's food,
It ennobled our hearts, and enriched
our blood,

Our soldiers were brave and our courtiers were good.
Oh! the roast beef of old England! [1]
The Roast Beef of Old England,
st. 1

COLLEY CIBBER
1671–1757

As good be out of the world as out of
the fashion.
Love's Last Shift [1696], *act II*

Possession is eleven points in the
law. *Woman's Wit* [1697], *act I*

Words are but empty thanks.
Ib. V

Off with his head [2] — so much for
Buckingham.
Richard III (*altered*) [1700],
act IV, sc. 3

Perish the thought! *Ib. V, 5*

This business will never hold water.
She Wou'd and She Wou'd Not
[1703], *act IV*

Old houses mended,
Cost little less than new before they're
ended.
The Double Gallant [1707],
prologue

Oh, how many torments lie in the
small circle of a wedding ring!
Ib. act I, sc. 2

Stolen sweets are best.
The Rival Fools [1709], *act I*

JOSEPH ADDISON
1672–1719

For wheresoe'er I turn my ravish'd
eyes,
Gay gilded scenes and shining prospects
rise,
Poetic fields encompass me around,

See Shakespeare, *Measure for Measure IV,*
i, 16, p. 372a.
[1] We shall find no fiend in hell can match
the fury of a disappointed woman. — COLLEY
CIBBER, *Love's Last Shift* [1696], *act IV*
[2] See Euripides, p. 84a, and Edward Young.
p. 399a.

[1] Oh, the roast beef of England,
And old England's roast beef!
FIELDING [1707–1754], *The Grub Street*
Opera, act III, sc. 2
[2] See Shakespeare, p. 217b, and Lewis Carroll,
p. 744a.

And still I seem to tread on classic ground.
> *A Letter from Italy* [1703]

And, pleas'd the Almighty's orders to perform,
Rides in the whirlwind and directs the storm.[1]
> *The Campaign* [1704], *l. 91*

The spacious firmament on high,
With all the blue ethereal sky,
And spangled heavens, a shining frame,
Their great Original proclaim.[2]
> *Ode* [*in The Spectator, no. 465,*
> *August 23, 1712*]

Soon as the evening shades prevail,
The moon takes up the wondrous tale,
And nightly to the listening earth
Repeats the story of her birth;
While all the stars that round her burn,
And all the planets in their turn,
Confirm the tidings as they roll,
And spread the truth from pole to pole.
> *Ib.*

Forever singing as they shine,
"The Hand that made us is divine."
> *Ib.*

Should the whole frame of Nature round him break,
In ruin and confusion hurled,
He, unconcerned, would hear the mighty crack,
And stand secure amidst a falling world.
> *Horace, ode 3, bk. III*

'Tis not in mortals to command success,
But we'll do more, Sempronius; we'll deserve it.
> *Cato*[3] [1713], *act I, sc. 2*

Blesses his stars and thinks it luxury.
> *Ib. 4*

---

[1] This line is frequently ascribed to Pope, as it is repeated in his *Dunciad, bk. III* [1728], *l. 264.*

[2] See *Psalm 19*, p. 17a-b.

[3] The *Massachusetts Spy* used the following lines from *Cato* as its motto from November 22, 1771 to April 6, 1775:

Do thou Great Liberty inspire our Souls —
And make our Lives in thy Possession happy —
Or, our Deaths glorious in thy just Defense.

'Tis pride, rank pride, and haughtiness of soul;
I think the Romans call it stoicism.
> *Cato, act I, sc. 4*

Were you with these, my prince, you'd soon forget
The pale, unripened beauties of the north.
> *Ib.*

Beauty soon grows familiar to the lover,
Fades in his eye, and palls upon the sense.
> *Ib.*

My voice is still for war.
Gods! can a Roman senate long debate
Which of the two to choose, slavery or death?
> *Ib. II, 1*

The woman that deliberates is lost.
> *Ib. IV, 1*

Curse on his virtues! they've undone his country.
> *Ib. 4*

What pity is it
That we can die but once to serve our country![1]
> *Ib.*

When vice prevails, and impious men bear sway,
The post of honor is a private station.[2]
> *Ib.*

It must be so — Plato, thou reasonest well!
Else whence this pleasing hope, this fond desire,
This longing after immortality?
Or whence this secret dread, and inward horror,
Of falling into naught? Why shrinks the soul
Back on herself, and startles at destruction?
'Tis the divinity that stirs within us;
'Tis heaven itself, that points out an hereafter,
And intimates eternity to man.

---

[1] See Nathan Hale, p. 484b.

[2] Give me, kind Heaven, a private station,
A mind serene for contemplation!
Title and profit I resign;
The post of honor shall be mine.
> GAY, *Fables, pt. II* [1738], *The Vulture,*
> *The Sparrow, and Other Birds*

Eternity! thou pleasing, dreadful thought!
Cato, act V, sc. 1

Sweet are the slumbers of the virtuous man.   *Ib. 4*

From hence, let fierce contending nations know
What dire effects from civil discord flow.   *Ib.*

Round-heads and Wooden-shoes are standing jokes.
The Drummer, prologue, l. 8

If I can any way contribute to the diversion or improvement of the country in which I live, I shall leave it, when I am summoned out of it, with the secret satisfaction of thinking that I have not lived in vain.[1]
The Spectator, no. 1
[March 1, 1711]

Thus I live in the world rather as a spectator of mankind than as one of the species.   *Ib.*

I shall endeavor to enliven morality with wit, and to temper wit with morality.   *Ib. 10 [March 11, 1711]*

True happiness is of a retired nature, and an enemy to pomp and noise; it arises, in the first place, from the enjoyment of one's self; and, in the next, from the friendship and conversation of a few select companions.
Ib. 15 [March 17, 1711]

In all thy humors, whether grave or mellow,
Thou'rt such a touchy, testy, pleasant fellow;
Hast so much wit, and mirth, and spleen about thee,
There is no living with thee, nor without thee. [2]
Ib. 68 [May 18, 1711]

There is not a more unhappy being than a superannuated idol.
Ib. 73 [May 24, 1711]

[1] See Étienne de Grellet, p. 531a.
[2] A translation of MARTIAL [A.D. 40–102] *XII, 47,* who imitated OVID [43 B.C.–A.D. 18], *Amores III, 11, 39.*

A man that has a taste of music, painting, or architecture, is like one that has another sense, when compared with such as have no relish of those arts.   *The Spectator, no. 93*
[June 16, 1711]

There is no defense against reproach but obscurity.
Ib. 101 [June 26, 1711]

Much might be said on both sides.
Ib. 122 [July 20, 1711]

Authors have established it as a kind of rule, that a man ought to be dull sometimes; as the most severe reader makes allowances for many rests and nodding-places in a voluminous writer.
Ib. 124 [July 23, 1711]

Books are the legacies that a great genius leaves to mankind, which are delivered down from generation to generation, as presents to the posterity of those who are yet unborn.
Ib. 166 [September 10, 1711]

Good nature is more agreeable in conversation than wit, and gives a certain air to the countenance which is more amiable than beauty.
Ib. 169 [September 13, 1711]

Were I to prescribe a rule for drinking, it should be formed upon a saying quoted by Sir William Temple: the first glass for myself, the second for my friends, the third for good humor, and the fourth for mine enemies.[1]
Ib. 195 [October 13, 1711]

A true critic ought to dwell rather upon excellencies than imperfections, to discover the concealed beauties of a writer, and communicate to the world such things as are worth their observation.   *Ib. 291 [February 2, 1712]*

These widows, sir, are the most perverse creatures in the world.
Ib. 335 [March 25, 1712]

Mirth is like a flash of lightning, that breaks through a gloom of clouds, and glitters for a moment; cheerfulness keeps up a kind of daylight in the

[1] See Swift, p. 389a.

mind, and fills it with a steady and perpetual serenity.

> *The Spectator, no. 381*
> *[May 17, 1712]*

Sir Roger made several reflections on the greatness of the British Nation; as, that one Englishman could beat three Frenchmen; that we could never be in danger of Popery so long as we took care of our fleet; that the Thames was the noblest river in Europe . . . with many other honest prejudices which naturally cleave to the heart of a true Englishman.

> *Ib. 383 [May 20, 1712]*

Our disputants put me in mind of the skuttle fish, that when he is unable to extricate himself, blackens all the water about him, till he becomes invisible. *Ib. 476 [September 5, 1712]*

The fraternity of the henpecked.[1]

> *Ib. 482 [September 12, 1712]*

A man should always consider how much he has more than he wants, and how much more unhappy he might be than he really is.

> *Ib. 574 [July 30, 1714]*

We are always doing something for Posterity, but I would fain see Posterity do something for us.

> *Ib. 587 [August 20, 1714]*

See in what peace a Christian can die.

> *Dying words [1719]. From* YOUNG, *Conjectures on Original Composition [1759]*

SIR RICHARD STEELE
1672–1729

I am come to a tavern alone to eat a steak, after which I shall return to the office.

> *Letters to His Wife*
> *[October 28, 1707]*

I was going home two hours ago, but was met by Mr. Griffith, who has kept

[1] See Byron, p. 560a.

me ever since. I will come within a pint of wine.

> *Letters to His Wife [Eleven*
> *at night, January 5, 1708]*

A little in drink, but at all times yr faithful husband.

> *Ib. [September 27, 1708]*

The finest woman in nature should not detain me an hour from you; but you must sometimes suffer the rivalship of the wisest men.

> *Ib. [September 17, 1712]*

Though her mien carries much more invitation than command, to behold her is an immediate check to loose behavior; to love her is a liberal education.[1] *Tatler [1709–1711], no. 49*

Reading is to the mind what exercise is to the body. *Ib. no. 147*

When you fall into a man's conversation, the first thing you should consider is, whether he has a greater inclination to hear you, or that you should hear him.

> *The Spectator, no. 49*
> *[April 26, 1711]*

Of all the affections which attend human life, the love of glory is the most ardent. *Ib. 139 [August 9, 1711]*

Age in a virtuous person, of either sex, carries in it an authority which makes it preferable to all the pleasures of youth.

> *Ib. 153 [August 25, 1711]*

Among all the diseases of the mind there is not one more epidemical or more pernicious than the love of flattery. *Ib. 238 [December 3, 1711]*

Will Honeycomb calls these over-offended ladies the outrageously virtuous. *Ib. 266 [January 4, 1712]*

A favor well bestowed is almost as great an honor to him who confers it as to him who receives it.

> *Ib. 497 [September 30, 1712]*

[1] Lady Elizabeth Hastings [1682–1739].

EDMOND HOYLE[1]
1672–1769

When in doubt, win the trick.
> *Twenty-four Rules for Learners,*
> *rule 12*

FRANÇOIS GOYOT DE PITAVALS
1673–1743

Causes Célèbres.
> *Title of book recounting famous*
> *trials and judgments*

NICHOLAS ROWE
1673–1718

As if Misfortune made the throne her
    seat,
And none could be unhappy but the
    great.[2]
> *The Fair Penitent* [1703], *prologue*

At length the morn and cold indiffer-
    ence came.   *Ib. act I, sc. 1*

Is this that haughty gallant, gay Lo-
    thario?   *Ib. V, 1*

ISAAC WATTS
1674–1748

Were I so tall to reach the pole,
    Or grasp the ocean with my span,
I must be measured by my soul;
    The mind's the standard of the man.
> *Horae Lyricae* [1706], *bk. II,*
> *False Greatness*

Let dogs delight to bark and bite,
    For God hath made them so;
Let bears and lions growl and fight,
    For 'tis their nature too.
> *Divine Songs* [1715], *16,*
> *Against Quarreling and*
> *Fighting*

---

[1] Hoyle published [1742] a *Short Treatise on Whist,* which in subsequent editions added rules for playing piquet, backgammon, chess, and other games. His *Laws* [1760] ruled whist playing until 1864, hence the saying, "according to Hoyle."

[2] None think the great unhappy, but the great. — EDWARD YOUNG, *The Love of Fame* [1725–1728], *satire 1, l. 238*

But, children, you should never let
    Such angry passions rise;
Your little hands were never made
    To tear each other's eyes.
> *Divine Songs. Against*
> *Quarreling and Fighting*

Birds in their little nests agree;
    And 'tis a shameful sight,
When children of one family
    Fall out, and chide, and fight.
> *Ib. 17, Love Between Brothers*
> *and Sisters*

How doth the little busy bee
    Improve each shining hour,[1]
And gather honey all the day
    From every opening flower!
> *Ib. 20, Against Idleness and*
> *Mischief*

For Satan finds some mischief still
    For idle hands to do.   *Ib.*

Let me be dress'd fine as I will,
Flies, worms, and flowers, exceed me
    still.
> *Ib. 22, Against Pride in Clothes*

Hush! my dear, lie still and slumber,
    Holy angels guard thy bed!
Heavenly blessings without number
    Gently falling on thy head.
> *Ib. 35, A Cradle Hymn*

'Tis the voice of the sluggard; I heard
    him complain,
"You have wak'd me too soon, I must
    slumber again." [2]
> *Ib. The Sluggard*

Lord, in the morning thou shalt hear
My voice ascending high.
> *Psalm 5* [1719]

O God, our help in ages past,
    Our hope for years to come,
Our shelter from the stormy blast,
    And our eternal home.
> *Psalm 90* [1719], *st. 1*

A thousand ages in Thy sight
    Are like an evening gone;
Short as the watch that ends the night
    Before the rising sun.   *Ib. st. 4*

---

[1] See Lewis Carroll, p. 743a.
[2] See Lewis Carroll, p. 744b.

Time, like an ever-rolling stream,
  Bears all its sons away;
They fly forgotten, as a dream
  Dies at the opening day.[1]
          Psalm 90, st. 5

Joy to the world! the Lord is come;
  Let earth receive her King.
Let ev'ry heart prepare Him room,
  And heav'n and nature sing.
         Psalm 98 [1719], st. 1

When I can read my title clear
  To mansions in the skies,
I'll bid farewell to every fear,
  And wipe my weeping eyes.
       Hymns and Spiritual Songs,
          bk. II, hymn 65

There is a land of pure delight,
  Where saints immortal reign;
Infinite day excludes the night,
  And pleasures banish pain.   *Ib. 66*

WILLIAM SOMERVILLE[2]
1675-1742

Let all the learned say what they can,
'Tis ready money makes the man.
         Ready Money [1727]

There is something in a face,
An air, and a peculiar grace,
Which boldest painters cannot trace.
         The Lucky Hit [1727]

  The chase, the sport of kings;
Image of war, without its guilt.
         The Chase [1735], I, 13

JOHN PHILIPS
1676-1709

Happy the man who, void of care and
  strife,
In silken or in leathern purse retains
A Splendid Shilling.
    The Splendid Shilling [1701], l. 1

---

[1] See Marcus Aurelius, p. 142a.
[2] Of whom SAMUEL JOHNSON, in his *Lives of the Poets,* made the famous remark, "He writes very well for a gentleman." See Johnson, p. 433b.

SIR ROBERT WALPOLE
1676-1745

The balance of power.
    Speech in the House of Com-
    mons [February 13, 1741]

All those men have their price.
    From WILLIAM COXE, *Memoirs*
    of Walpole [1798], vol. IV,
    p. 369

Anything but history, for history
must be false.   *Walpoliana, no. 141*

HENRY ST. JOHN, VISCOUNT BOLINGBROKE
1678-1751

Truth lies within a little and certain
compass, but error is immense.
    Reflections Upon Exile [1716]

Nations, like men, have their infancy.
    On the Study and Use of History
        [1752], letter 4

They [Thucydides and Xenophon]
maintained the dignity of history.
         Ib. 5

It is the modest, not the presumptuous, inquirer who makes a real and safe
progress in the discovery of divine
truths. One follows Nature and Nature's God; that is, he follows God in
his works and in his word.[1]
       Letter to Alexander Pope

GEORGE FARQUHAR
1678-1707

Reason still keeps its throne, but it
nods a little, that's all.
    The Recruiting Officer [1706],
        act III, sc. 2

I have fed purely upon ale; I have eat
my ale, and I always sleep upon ale.
    The Beaux' Stratagem [1707],
        act I, sc. 1

My Lady Bountiful.   *Ib.*

---

[1] See Pope, p. 410a, and Jefferson, p. 470b.

I believe they talked of me, for they laughed consumedly.
The Beaux' Stratagem,
act III, sc. 1

'Twas for the good of my country that I should be abroad.[1] — Anything for the good of one's country — I'm a Roman for that. *Ib. III, 2*

How a little love and good company improves a woman! *Ib. IV, 1*

Spare all I have, and take my life.
Ib. V, 2

THOMAS PARNELL
1679–1718

My days have been so wondrous free,
The little birds that fly
With careless ease from tree to tree,
Were but as bless'd as I.
Song[2] *[1714], st. 1*

Still an angel appear to each lover beside,
But still be a woman to you.
When Thy Beauty Appears
[1722], st. 3

We call it only pretty Fanny's way.
An Elegy to an Old Beauty
[1722], st. 4

Let those love now who never loved before;
Let those who always loved, now love the more.
Translation of the Pervigilium
Veneris[3]

---

[1] Leaving his country for his country's sake. — CHARLES FITZ-GEFFREY, *The Life and Death of Sir Francis Drake* [1596], *st. 213*
  True patriots all; for, be it understood,
  We left our country for our country's good.
    GEORGE BARRINGTON, *Prologue written for the opening of the playhouse at New South Wales* [*January 16, 1796*]
  (According to *The Oxford Companion to English Literature,* Barrington was the adopted name of a notorious pickpocket who was transported to the penal settlement at Botany Bay.)
[2] Set to music by Francis Hopkinson; one of the earliest American songs.
[3] See Anonymous Latin, p. 150a.

DESTOUCHES
[PHILIPPE NÉRICAULT]
1680–1754

Those not present are always wrong.[1]
L'Obstacle Imprévu [1717],
act I, sc. 6

Criticism is easy, art is difficult.
Le Glorieux [1732], *act II, sc. 5*

EDWARD YOUNG
1683–1765

The love of praise, howe'er conceal'd by art,
Reigns more or less, and glows in ev'ry heart.
Love of Fame [1725–1728],
satire I, l. 51

Some for renown, on scraps of learning dote,
And think they grow immortal as they quote. *Ib. l. 89*

Be wise with speed;
A fool at forty is a fool indeed.
Ib. II, l. 282

Forever most divinely in the wrong.
Ib. VI, l. 105

For her own breakfast she'll project a scheme,
Nor take her tea without a stratagem.
Ib. l. 187

One to destroy, is murder by the law;
And gibbets keep the lifted hand in awe;
To murder thousands takes a specious name,
War's glorious art, and gives immortal fame.[2] *Ib. VII, l. 55*

The man that makes a character makes foes.
To Mr. Pope, epistle I, l. 28

In records that defy the tooth of time.
The Statesman's Creed

Tired nature's sweet restorer, balmy sleep!
Night Thoughts [1742–1745].
Night I, l. 1

---

[1] Les absents ont toujours tort.
[2] See Porteus, p. 460a.

Night, sable goddess! from her ebon throne,
In rayless majesty, now stretches forth
Her leaden scepter o'er a slumbering world.
Night Thoughts. Night I,
l. 18

Creation sleeps! 'Tis as the general pulse
Of life stood still, and Nature made a pause;
An awful pause! prophetic of her end.
Ib. l. 23

The bell strikes one. We take no note of time
But from its loss.   *Ib. l. 55*

Be wise today; 'tis madness to defer.[1]
Ib. l. 390

Procrastination is the thief of time.
Ib. l. 393

At thirty, man suspects himself a fool;
Knows it at forty, and reforms his plan;
At fifty chides his infamous delay,
Pushes his prudent purpose to resolve;
In all the magnanimity of thought
Resolves, and re-resolves; then dies the same.   *Ib. l. 417*

All men think all men mortal but themselves.   *Ib. l. 424*

"I've lost a day!" — the prince who nobly cried,
Had been an emperor without his crown.[2]   *Ib. II, l. 99*

Man wants but little, nor that little long.[3]   *Ib. IV, l. 118*

A God all mercy is a God unjust.
Ib. l. 233

By night an atheist half believes a God.[4]   *Ib. V, l. 177*

Like our shadows,

Our wishes lengthen as our sun declines.
Night Thoughts. Night V,
l. 661

Death loves a shining mark, a signal blow.[1]   *Ib. l. 1011*

Too low they build, who build beneath the stars.   *Ib. VIII, l. 215*

Final Ruin fiercely drives
Her plowshare o'er creation.[2]
Ib. IX, l. 167

An undevout astronomer is mad.
Ib. l. 771

SIR WILLIAM PULTENEY,[3] EARL OF BATH
1684–1764

Since twelve honest men have decided the cause,
And were judges of facts, though not judges of laws.
The Honest Jury [1731], III

GEORGE BERKELEY, BISHOP OF CLOYNE
1685–1753

And what are these fluxions? The velocities of evanescent increments. And what are these same evanescent increments? They are neither finite quantities, nor quantities infinitely small, nor yet nothing. May we not call them ghosts of departed quantities?
The Analyst [1734], *sec. 4*

[Tar water] is of a nature so mild and benign and proportioned to the human constitution, as to warm without heating, to cheer but not inebriate.[4]   *Siris* [1744], *par. 217*

Truth is the cry of all, but the game of the few.   *Ib. par. 368*

---

[1] See Quarles, p. 321b.
[2] See Burns, p. 493a.
[3] One of "the three grand allies," the others being Stanhope and Walpole. Walpole said that he feared Pulteney's tongue more than another man's sword.
[4] See Cowper, p. 458a.

---

[1] See Congreve, p. 392a.
[2] See Anonymous, p. 1090a.
See Vespasian, p. 135b.
[3] See Goldsmith, p. 448a.
[4] See W. T. Cummings, p. 1053a.

He who says there is no such thing as an honest man, you may be sure is himself a knave.

> *Maxims Concerning Patriotism*

Westward the course of empire takes its way;[1]
The four first acts already past,
A fifth shall close the drama with the day:
Time's noblest offspring is the last.

> *On the Prospect of Planting Arts and Learning in America* [1752], *st. 6*

JANE BRERETON
1685–1740

The picture placed the busts between,
  Adds to the thought much strength,
Wisdom, and Wit are little seen,
  But Folly's at full length.

> *On Beau Nash's Picture at Full Length between the Busts of Sir Isaac Newton and Mr. Pope*[2]

AARON HILL
1685–1750

First, then, a woman will or won't, depend on 't;
If she will do 't she will; and there's an end on 't.
But if she won't, since safe and sound your trust is,
Fear is affront, and jealousy injustice.

> *Zara, epilogue*

Tender-handed stroke a nettle,
  And it stings you for your pains;
Grasp it like a man of mettle,
  And it soft as silk remains.[3]

> *Verses Written on a Window in Scotland*

---

[1] Westward the star of empire takes its way.
— JOHN QUINCY ADAMS, *Oration at Plymouth* [1802]

[2] In ALEXANDER DYCE [1798–1869], *Specimens of British Poetesses*. This epigram is generally ascribed to Chesterfield.

[3] The world's a nettle; disturb it, it stings:
  Grasp it firmly, it stings not.
    OWEN MEREDITH [E. R. BULWER-LYTTON],
    Lucile [1860], *pt. I, canto 3, st. 2*

SAMUEL MADDEN
1686–1765

In an orchard there should be enough to eat, enough to lay up, enough to be stolen, and enough to rot upon the ground.

> *Quoted by* SAMUEL JOHNSON [1783]. *From* BOSWELL, *Life of Dr. Johnson, vol. II, p. 457* [Everyman edition]

ALLAN RAMSAY
1686–1758

Farewell to Lochaber, farewell to my Jean.

> *Lochaber No More* [1724], *st. 1*

THOMAS TICKELL
1686–1740

There taught us how to live; and (oh! too high
The price for knowledge) taught us how to die.[1]

> *On the Death of Mr. Addison* [1719], *l. 81*

HENRY CAREY
c. 1687 – 1743

Namby Pamby's little rhymes,
Little jingle, little chimes.

> *Namby Pamby*[2]

Aldiborontiphoscophornio!
Where left you Chrononhotonthologos?

> *Chrononhotonthologos, act I, sc. 1*

His cogitative faculties immersed
In cogibundity of cogitation. *Ib.*

Of all the girls that are so smart,
  There's none like pretty Sally.
She is the darling of my heart,
  And she lives in our alley.

> *Sally in Our Alley* [1729], *st. 1*

---

[1] See Montaigne, p. 189b, and note.

[2] Ambrose Phillips . . . who had the honor of bringing into fashion a species of composition which has been called, after his name, Namby Pamby. — MACAULAY, *Review of Aikin's Life of Addison* [1843]

Of all the days that's in the week
　I dearly love but one day,
And that's the day that comes betwixt
　A Saturday and Monday.
　　　　Sally in Our Alley, st. 4

God save our gracious king!
Long live our noble king!
　God save the king!
　　　God Save the King [*c.* 1740]

JOHN GAY[1]
1688–1732

'Twas when the seas were roaring
With hollow blasts of wind,
A damsel lay deploring,
All on a rock reclin'd.
　　　The What D'ye Call It [1715],
　　　　　　　　act II, sc. 8

All in the Downs the fleet was moor'd.
　Sweet William's Farewell to
　　Black-eyed Susan [1720]

Adieu! she cries; and wav'd her lily
　hand.　　　　　　　　　　*Ib.*

My lodging is on the cold ground,
　And hard, very hard, is my fare,
But that which grieves me more
　Is the coldness of my dear.
　　　My Lodging Is on the Cold
　　　　Ground [1720], *st.* 1

Whence is thy learning? Hath thy toil
O'er books consum'd the midnight oil?
　Fables, pt. I [1727]. *The Shep-*
　　herd and the Philosopher

Where yet was ever found a mother
Who'd give her booby for another?
　Ib. The Mother, the Nurse, and
　　　　　　　　　　the Fairy

When we risk no contradiction,
It prompts the tongue to deal in fic-
　tion.
　　　Ib. The Elephant and the
　　　　　　　　　　Bookseller

Is there no hope? the sick man said;
The silent doctor shook his head.
　　　Ib. The Sick Man and the Angel

[1] See Pope's *Epitaph on Gay,* p. 407b.

While there is life there's hope, he
　cried.[1]
　　　Fables, pt. I. The Sick Man
　　　　　　　and the Angel

Those who in quarrels interpose
Must often wipe a bloody nose.
　　　　　　Ib. The Mastiffs

I hate the man who builds his name
On ruins of another's fame.
　　　　Ib. The Poet and the Rose

And when a lady's in the case,
You know all other things give place.
　Ib. The Hare and Many Friends

In every age and clime we see
Two of a trade can never agree.[2]
　　Ib. The Rat-catcher and Cat

From wine what sudden friendship
　springs!
　　　Ib. II [1738]. *The Squire and*
　　　　　　　　　　His Cur

O Polly, you might have toy'd and
　kiss'd,
By keeping men off, you keep them
　on.
　　　The Beggar's Opera [1728],
　　　　　　act I, sc. 4, *air* 9

If with me you'd fondly stray.
Over the hills and far away.[3]
　　　　　　　Ib. 13, *air* 16

Fill ev'ry glass, for wine inspires us,
　And fires us
With courage, love and joy.
Women and wine should life employ.
Is there ought else on earth desirous?
　　　　　　Ib. II, 1, *air* 19

If the heart of a man is depress'd with
　cares,
The mist is dispell'd when a woman
　appears.　　　　*Ib.* 3, *air* 21

Youth's the season made for joys,
Love is then our duty.　*Ib.* 4, *air* 22

Man may escape from rope and gun;
Nay, some have outliv'd the doctor's
　pill:

[1] See Terence, p. 108b; Cicero, p. 111a; and
Goldsmith, p. 447a.
[2] See Hesiod, p. 67b, and Meredith, p. 730a.
[3] See D'Urfey, p. 384a.

Who takes a woman must be undone,
That basilisk is sure to kill.
The fly that sips treacle is lost in the
  sweets,
So he that tastes woman, woman,
  woman,
He that tastes woman, ruin meets.
    The Beggar's Opera,
    act II, sc. 8, air 26

How happy could I be with either,
Were t'other dear charmer away!
    Ib. 13, air 35

The charge is prepar'd; the lawyers are
  met;
The Judges all ranged (a terrible
  show!)   *Ib. III, 11, air 57*

Life is a jest; and all things show it.
I thought so once; but now I know it.[1]
    My Own Epitaph

PIERRE CARLET DE CHAMBLAIN DE MARIVAUX
1688–1763

In this world, you must be a bit too
kind in order to be kind enough.
    Le Jeu de l'Amour et du Hasard
    [1730], act I, sc. 2

ALEXANDER POPE[2]
1688–1744

Happy the man whose wish and care
A few paternal acres bound,
Content to breathe his native air
  In his own ground.[3]
    Ode on Solitude [c. 1700], st. 1

Thus let me live, unseen, unknown,
Thus unlamented let me die,
Steal from the world, and not a stone
  Tell where I lie.   *Ib. st. 5*

[1] Life is an empty dream. — BROWNING, *Paracelsus II* [1835]
Life seems a jest of Fate's contriving. — J. R. LOWELL, *Harvard Commemoration Ode* [1865], *IV*
[2] A thousand years may elapse before there shall appear another man with a power of versification equal to that of Pope. — SAMUEL JOHNSON [1781]; *from* BOSWELL, *Life of Dr. Johnson* [1791]
[3] See Horace, p. 120b.

Where'er you walk, cool gales shall fan
  the glade,
Trees, where you sit, shall crowd into a
  shade:
Where'er you tread, the blushing flow'rs
  shall rise,
And all things flourish where you turn
  your eyes.
    Pastorals [written 1704]. Sum-
    mer, l. 73

Nor Fame I slight, nor for her favors
  call;
She comes unlook'd for, if she comes at
  all.
    The Temple of Fame [1711],
    l. 513

How vast a memory has Love!
    Sappho to Phaon [1712], l. 52

'Tis with our judgments as our watches,
  none
Go just alike, yet each believes his
  own.[1]
    An Essay on Criticism [1711],
    pt. I, l. 9

Let such teach others who themselves
  excel,
And censure freely who have written
  well.   *Ib. l. 15*

Some are bewilder'd in the maze of
  schools,
And some made coxcombs nature
  meant but fools.   *Ib. l. 26*

Those oft are stratagems which errors
  seem,
Nor is it Homer nods, but we that
  dream.[2]   *Ib. l. 177*

Of all the causes which conspire to
  blind
Man's erring judgment, and misguide
  the mind,
What the weak head with strongest
  bias rules,
Is pride, the never-failing vice of fools.
    Ib. II, l. 1

A little learning is a dangerous thing;[3]

[1] See Suckling, p. 350a.
[2] See Horace, p. 124b.
[3] See Publilius Syrus, p. 127a.

Drink deep, or taste not the Pierian
   spring:
There shallow draughts intoxicate the
   brain,
And drinking largely sobers us again.
         An Essay on Criticism,
               pt. II, l. 15

Hills peep o'er hills, and Alps on Alps
   arise!   *Ib. l. 32*

'Tis not a lip, or eye, we beauty call,
But the joint force and full result of
   all.   *Ib. l. 45*

Whoever thinks a faultless piece to see,
Thinks what ne'er was, nor is, nor e'er
   shall be.[1]   *Ib. l. 53*

True wit is nature to advantage
   dress'd,
What oft was thought, but ne'er so
   well express'd.   *Ib. l. 97*

Words are like leaves; and where they
   most abound,
Much fruit of sense beneath is rarely
   found.   *Ib. l. 109*

Such labor'd nothings, in so strange a
   style,
Amaze th' unlearn'd, and make the
   learned smile.   *Ib. l. 126*

Be not the first by whom the new are
   tried,
Nor yet the last to lay the old aside.
                Ib. l. 135

     As some to church repair,
Not for the doctrine, but the music
   there.
These equal syllables alone require,
Though oft the ear the open vowels
   tire;
While expletives their feeble aid do
   join,
And ten low words oft creep in one dull
   line.   *Ib. l. 142*

Then, at the last and only couplet
   fraught
With some unmeaning thing they call a
   thought,
A needless Alexandrine ends the song,
That, like a wounded snake, drags its
   slow length along.   *Ib. l. 156*

[1] See Suckling, p. 350b, and note.

True ease in writing comes from art,
   not chance,
As those move easiest who have learn'd
   to dance.[1]
'Tis not enough no harshness gives
   offense;
The sound must seem an echo to the
   sense.
         An Essay on Criticism,
               pt. II, l. 162

At ev'ry trifle scorn to take offense.
                Ib. l. 186

Yet let not each gay turn thy rapture
   move;
For fools admire, but men of sense
   approve.   *Ib. l. 190*

Some judge of authors' names, not
   works, and then
Nor praise nor blame the writings, but
   the men.   *Ib. l. 212*

What woeful stuff this madrigal would
   be,
In some starv'd hackney sonneteer, or
   me!
But let a lord once own the happy
   lines,
How the wit brightens! how the style
   refines!   *Ib. l. 218*

Some praise at morning what they
   blame at night,
But always think the last opinion
   right.   *Ib. l. 230*

To err is human, to forgive divine.[2]
                Ib. l. 325

All seems infected that th' infected
   spy,
As all looks yellow to the jaundic'd
   eye.   *Ib. l. 358*

Be silent always when you doubt your
   sense.   *Ib. III, l. 6*

Men must be taught as if you taught
   them not,

[1] Also in *Imitations of Horace* [1737], *Epistle
II, bk. II, l. 178.*
[2] See Plutarch, p. 137b, and Shirley, p. 327b.
   Then gently scan your brother man,
     Still gentler sister woman;
   Though they may gang a kennin' wrang,
   To step aside is human.
     ROBERT BURNS, *Address to the Unco
                Guid* [1787]

And things unknown proposed as things forgot.
> An Essay on Criticism,
> pt. III, l. 15

The bookful blockhead ignorantly read,
With loads of learned lumber in his head,
With his own tongue still edifies his ears,
And always list'ning to himself appears.
All books he reads, and all he reads assails.
Ib. l. 53

For fools rush in where angels fear to tread.[1]
Ib. l. 66

But where's the man who counsel can bestow,
Still pleas'd to teach, and yet not proud to know?[2]
Ib. l. 72

Careless of censure, nor too fond of fame,
Still pleas'd to praise, yet not afraid to blame,
Averse alike to flatter or offend,
Not free from faults, nor yet too vain to mend.
Ib. l. 182

Vital spark of heav'nly flame!
Quit, oh quit, this mortal frame:
Trembling, hoping, ling'ring, flying,
Oh the pain, the bliss of dying![3]
> The Dying Christian to His Soul
> [1712], st. 1

What dire offense from amorous causes springs,
What mighty contests rise from trivial things![4]
> The Rape of the Lock [1712],
> canto I, l. 1

On her white breast a sparkling cross she wore,
Which Jews might kiss, and infidels adore.
Ib. II, l. 7

If to her share some female errors fall,
Look on her face, and you'll forget 'em all.
Ib. l. 17

[1] See Shakespeare, *Richard III, I, iii, 70,* p. 217a.
[2] See Chaucer, p. 166b.
[3] See Hadrian, p. 141a.
[4] See Robert Burton, p. 310a.

Fair tresses man's imperial race ensnare,
And beauty draws us with a single hair.[1]
> The Rape of the Lock,
> canto II, l. 27

Here thou, great Anna![2] whom three realms obey,
Dost sometimes counsel take — and sometimes tea.
Ib. III, l. 7

At every word a reputation dies.
Ib. l. 16

The hungry judges soon the sentence sign,
And wretches hang that jurymen may dine.
Ib. l. 21

Let spades be trumps! she said, and trumps they were.
Ib. l. 46

Coffee, which makes the politician wise.
Ib. l. 117

But when to mischief mortals bend their will,
How soon they find fit instruments of ill!
Ib. l. 125

The meeting points the sacred hair dissever
From the fair head, forever, and forever!
Then flash'd the living lightning from her eyes,
And screams of horror rend th' affrighted skies.
Ib. l. 153

Charms strike the sight, but merit wins the soul.
Ib. V, l. 34

To wake the soul by tender strokes of art,
To raise the genius, and to mend the heart;
To make mankind, in conscious virtue bold,
Live o'er each scene, and be what they behold:
For this the Tragic Muse first trod the stage.
> Prologue to Mr. Addison's Cato
> [1713], l. 1

A brave man struggling in the storms of fate,

[1] See Robert Burton, p. 312a.
[2] Queen Anne [1665–1714].

And greatly falling with a falling state.
*Prologue to Mr. Addison's
Cato, l. 21*

Ignobly vain, and impotently great.
Ib. l. 29

Here hills and vales, the woodland and
the plain,
Here earth and water seem to strive
again,
Not chaos-like together crush'd and
bruis'd,
But, as the world, harmoniously con-
fus'd:
Where order in variety we see,
And where, though all things differ, all
agree.
Windsor Forest [1713], l. 11

Oft, as in airy rings they skim the
heath,
The clam'rous lapwings feel the leaden
death;
Oft, as the mounting larks their notes
prepare,
They fall, and leave their little lives in
air.   *Ib. l. 131*

Party-spirit, which at best is but the
madness of many for the gain of a
few.[1]
*Letter to E. Blount [August 27,
1714]*

The wrath of Peleus' son, the direful
spring
Of all the Grecian woes, O goddess
sing![2]
Translation of Iliad[3] *[1715] I, 1*

She moves a goddess, and she looks a
queen.   *Ib. III, 1*

Tell me, Muse, of the man of many
wiles.
*Translation of Odyssey [1725–
1756] I, 1*

So perish all who do the like again.
Ib. I, 37

True friendship's laws are by this rule
express'd,
Welcome the coming, speed the parting guest.[1]
Translation of Odyssey XV, 83

Dear, damn'd, distracting town, fare-
well!
Thy fools no more I'll tease:
This year in peace, ye critics, dwell,
Ye harlots, sleep at ease!
A Farewell to London [1715], st. 1

Luxurious lobster-nights, farewell,
For sober, studious days!   *Ib. st. 12*

Oh name forever sad! forever dear!
Still breath'd in sighs, still usher'd with
a tear.
Eloisa to Abelard [1717], l. 31

Now warm in love, now with'ring in my
bloom,
Lost in a convent's solitary gloom!
Ib. l. 37

Speed the soft intercourse from soul to
soul,
And waft a sigh from Indus to the
Pole.   *Ib. l. 57*

No, make me mistress to the man I
love;
If there be yet another name more
free,
More fond than mistress, make me that
to thee!   *Ib. l. 88*

And if I lose thy love, I lose my all.
Ib. l. 118

How happy is the blameless vestal's lot!
The world forgetting, by the world forgot.   *Ib. l. 207*

One thought of thee puts all the pomp
to flight,
Priests, tapers, temples, swim before my
sight.[2]   *Ib. l. 273*

He best can paint them who shall feel
them most.   *Ib. l. 366*

What beck'ning ghost, along the moonlight shade

---

[1] See Swift, p. 389a.
[2] Another version is:
Achilles' wrath, to Greece the direful spring
Of woes unnumber'd, heavenly goddess, sing!
[3] See Bentley, p. 386a.

[1] See Pope, *Epistle to Dr. Arbuthnot*, p. 411b.
[2] Priests, altars, victims, swam before my
sight. — EDMUND SMITH, *Phaedra and Hippolytus, adapted from* RACINE [1707], *act I, sc. 1.*

Invites my steps, and points to yonder
   glade?
      Elegy to the Memory of an
      Unfortunate Lady [1717], *l. 1*

Is it, in Heav'n, a crime to love too
   well?
To bear too tender, or too firm a
   heart,
To act a lover's or a Roman's part?
Is there no bright reversion in the sky,
For those who greatly think, or bravely
   die?   *Ib. l. 6*

Ambition first sprung from your blest
   abodes;
The glorious fault of Angels and of
   Gods.   *Ib. l. 13*

By foreign hands thy dying eyes were
   clos'd,
By foreign hands thy decent limbs
   compos'd,
By foreign hands thy humble grave
   adorn'd,
By strangers honor'd, and by strangers
   mourn'd!   *Ib. l. 51*

How lov'd, how honor'd once, avails
   thee not,
To whom related, or by whom begot;
A heap of dust alone remains of thee;
'Tis all thou art, and all the proud shall
   be!   *Ib. l. 71*

  The fate of all extremes is such,
Men may be read, as well as books, too
   much.
To observations which ourselves we
   make,
We grow more partial for th' observer's
   sake.
      Moral Essays [1720–1735].
      Epistle I, To Lord Cobham
      [1734], *l. 9*

Like following life through creatures
   you dissect,
You lose it in the moment you detect.
          Ib. l. 29

Not always actions show the man: we
   find
Who does a kindness is not therefore
   kind.   *Ib. l. 109*

'Tis education forms the common
   mind:
Just as the twig is bent, the tree's inclined.
      Moral Essays. Epistle I,
      To Lord Cobham, l. 149

Give this cheek a little red.
          Ib. l. 251

And you, brave Cobham! to the latest
   breath
Shall feel your ruling passion strong in
   death.   *Ib. l. 262*

Most women have no characters at all.
      Ib. II, To Mrs. M. Blount
      [1735], *l. 2*

Choose a firm cloud before it fall, and
   in it
Catch, ere she change, the Cynthia of
   this minute.   *Ib. l. 19*

Chaste to her husband, frank to all beside,
A teeming mistress, but a barren bride.
          Ib. l. 71

Wise wretch! with pleasures too refin'd
   to please;
With too much spirit to be e'er at
   ease;
With too much quickness ever to be
   taught;
With too much thinking to have common thought.
You purchase pain with all that joy can
   give,
And die of nothing but a rage to live.
          Ib. l. 95

"With ev'ry pleasing, ev'ry prudent part,
Say, what can Chloe want?" — She
   wants a heart.   *Ib. l. 159*

In men, we various ruling passions
   find;
In women, two almost divide the
   kind;
Those, only fixed, they first or last
   obey,
The love of pleasure, and the love of
   sway.   *Ib. l. 207*

Men, some to business, some to pleasure take;

But every woman is at heart a rake.
> *Moral Essays. Epistle II, To
> Mrs. M. Blount, l. 215*

She who ne'er answers till a husband
cools,
Or, if she rules him, never shows she
rules;
Charms by accepting, by submitting,
sways,
Yet has her humor most, when she
obeys.   *Ib. l. 261*

And mistress of herself, though china
fall.   *Ib. l. 268*

Woman's at best a contradiction still.
> *Ib. l. 270*

Who shall decide when doctors disagree? [1]
> *Ib. III, To Lord Bathurst
> [1732], l. 1*

But thousands die, without or this or
that,
Die, and endow a college, or a cat.
> *Ib. l. 95*

The ruling passion, be it what it will,
The ruling passion conquers reason
still.   *Ib. l. 153*

Satan now is wiser than of yore,
And tempts by making rich, not making poor.   *Ib. l. 351*

Good sense, which only is the gift of
Heaven,
And though no science, fairly worth the
seven.
> *Ib. IV, To Lord Burling-
> ton [1731], l. 43*

Statesman, yet friend to truth! of soul
sincere,
In action faithful, and in honor clear;
Who broke no promise, serv'd no private end,
Who gain'd no title, and who lost no
friend.
> *Ib. VII, To Mr. Addison [1720],
> l. 67*

---

[1] When doctors differ who decides amid the
milliard-headed throng? — Sir Richard Francis
Burton [1821–1890], *The Kasidah of Haji Abdu
El-Yazdi VIII, 29*

Blessed is he who expects nothing,
for he shall never be disappointed.[1]
> *Letter to Gay [October 6, 1727]*

You beat your pate, and fancy wit will
come:
Knock as you please, there's nobody at
home.[2]
> *Epigram: An Empty House [1727]*

Ye Gods! annihilate but space and
time,
And make two lovers happy.
> *Martinus Scriblerus on the Art
> of Sinking in Poetry [1728],
> ch. 11*

In wit a man, simplicity a child.
> *Epitaph on Gay [1732]* [3]

Awake, my St. John! leave all meaner
things
To low ambition, and the pride of
kings.
Let us, since life can little more supply
Than just to look about us, and to
die,
Expatiate free o'er all this scene of
man;
A mighty maze! but not without a
plan.
> *An Essay on Man [1733–1734].
> Epistle I, l. 1*

Eye Nature's walks, shoot folly as it
flies,
And catch the manners living as they
rise:
Laugh where we must, be candid where
we can;
But vindicate the ways of God to
man.[4]   *Ib. l. 13*

Say first, of God above or man below,
What can we reason but from what we
know?   *Ib. l. 17*

---

[1] Pope calls this the eighth beatitude (Ros-
coe's edition of Pope, *vol. X, p. 184*).
> Blessed are those that nought expect,
> For they shall not be disappointed.
>> John Wolcot ("Peter Pindar") [1738–
>> 1819], *Ode to Pitt*

[2] His wit invites you by his looks to come,
> But when you knock, it never is at home.
>> Cowper, *Conversation* [1782], *l. 303*

[3] See Gay, p. 401a.

[4] See Milton, p. 341b.

Pleased to the last, he crops the flowery food,
And licks the hand just raised to shed his blood.
An Essay on Man.
Epistle I, l. 83

Who sees with equal eye, as God of all,
A hero perish or a sparrow fall,[1]
Atoms or systems into ruin hurl'd,
And now a bubble burst, and now a world.
Ib. l. 87

Hope springs eternal in the human breast:
Man never is, but always to be blest.
Ib. l. 95

Lo, the poor Indian! whose untutor'd mind
Sees God in clouds, or hears him in the wind;
His soul proud Science never taught to stray
Far as the solar walk or milky way;
Yet simple nature to his hope has giv'n,
Behind the cloud-topped hill, an humbler heav'n.
Ib. l. 99

But thinks, admitted to that equal sky,
His faithful dog shall bear him company.
Ib. l. 111

In pride, in reas'ning pride, our error lies;
All quit their sphere, and rush into the skies!
Pride still is aiming at the bless'd abodes,
Men would be Angels, Angels would be Gods.
Aspiring to be Gods if Angels fell,
Aspiring to be Angels men rebel.
Ib. l. 123

Seas roll to waft me, suns to light me rise;
My footstool earth, my canopy the skies.[2]
Ib. l. 139

Die of a rose in aromatic pain?
Ib. l. 200

[1] See Shakespeare, *Hamlet V, ii, 232*, p. 266b, and note.
[2] See *Matthew 5:35*, p. 40b; H. G. Wells, p. 888b; and Clarence Day, p. 925b.

All are but parts of one stupendous whole,
Whose body Nature is, and God the soul.
An Essay on Man.
Epistle I, l. 267

As full, as perfect, in vile man that mourns
As the rapt seraph that adores and burns.
To Him no high, no low, no great, no small; [1]
He fills, he bounds, connects, and equals all!
Ib. l. 277

All nature is but art unknown to thee,
All chance, direction which thou canst not see;
All discord, harmony not understood;
All partial evil, universal good;
And, spite of pride, in erring reason's spite,
One truth is clear, Whatever is, is right.[2]
Ib. l. 289

Know then thyself, presume not God to scan;
The proper study of mankind is man.[3]
Placed on this isthmus of a middle state,
A being darkly wise and rudely great:
With too much knowledge for the sceptic side,
With too much weakness for the stoic's pride,
He hangs between; in doubt to act or rest;
In doubt to deem himself a god, or beast;
In doubt his mind or body to prefer;
Born but to die, and reas'ning but to err;
Alike in ignorance, his reason such,

[1] There is no great and no small
To the Soul that maketh all.
EMERSON [1803–1882], *Epigraph to History*

[2] See Dryden, p. 367b.
[3] See The Seven Sages, p. 68a.
La vraie science et la vraie étude de l'homme, c'est l'homme [The true science and the true study of man is man]. — PIERRE CHARRON, *Traité de la Sagesse* [1601], *bk. I, preface*
Trees and fields tell me nothing: men are my teachers. — PLATO [427–347 B.C.], *Phaedrus*

Whether he thinks too little or too
    much;
Chaos of thought and passion, all con-
    fused;
Still by himself abused, or disabused;
Created half to rise, and half to fall;
Great lord of all things, yet a prey to
    all;
Sole judge of truth, in endless error
    hurled;
The glory, jest, and riddle of the world! [1]
          An Essay on Man.
          Epistle II, l. 1

Fix'd like a plant on his peculiar spot,
To draw nutrition, propagate, and rot.
          Ib. l. 63

And hence one master-passion in the
    breast,
Like Aaron's serpent, swallows up the
    rest. [2]   *Ib. l. 131*

Vice is a monster of so frightful mien,
As to be hated needs but to be seen; [3]
Yet seen too oft, familiar with her
    face,
We first endure, then pity, then em-
    brace.   *Ib. l. 217*

The learn'd is happy Nature to ex-
    plore,
The fool is happy that he knows no
    more;
The rich is happy in the plenty giv'n,
The poor contents him with the care of
    Heav'n.   *Ib. l. 263*

Behold the child, by Nature's kindly
    law,
Pleased with a rattle, tickled with a
    straw:
Some livelier plaything gives his youth
    delight,
A little louder, but as empty quite:
Scarfs, garters, gold, amuse his riper
    stage,
And beads and prayer-books are the
    toys of age!
Pleased with this bauble still, as that
    before;

Till tired he sleeps, and life's poor play
    is o'er.
          An Essay on Man.
          Epistle II, l. 274

Learn of the little nautilus to sail,
Spread the thin oar, and catch the driv-
    ing gale.   *Ib. III, l. 177*

For forms of government let fools con-
    test;
Whate'er is best administer'd is best:
For modes of faith let graceless zealots
    fight;
His can't be wrong whose life is in the
    right. [1]
In faith and hope the world will dis-
    agree,
But all mankind's concern is charity.
          Ib. l. 303

O happiness! our being's end and aim!
Good, pleasure, ease, content! whate'er
    thy name:
That something still which prompts the
    eternal sigh,
For which we bear to live, or dare to
    die.   *Ib. IV, l. 1*

Worth makes the man, and want of it
    the fellow;
The rest is all but leather or prunella.
          Ib. l. 203

What's Fame? a fancy'd life in others'
    breath,
A thing beyond us, ev'n before our
    death.   *Ib. l. 237*

A wit's a feather, and a chief a rod;
An honest man's the noblest work of
    God. [2]   *Ib. l. 247*

One self-approving hour whole years
    outweighs
Of stupid starers and of loud huzzas:
And more true joy Marcellus exil'd
    feels
Than Caesar with a senate at his heels.
          Ib. l. 255

If parts allure thee, think how Bacon
    shin'd,
The wisest, brightest, meanest of man-
    kind!

---

[1] See Pascal, p. 364a.
[2] For they cast down every man his rod, and
they became serpents: but Aaron's rod swallowed
up their rods. — *Exodus 7:12*
[3] See Dryden, p. 370a.

[1] See Cowley, p. 358b.
[2] See Fletcher, p. 313a, and Burns, p. 492b.

Or ravish'd with the whistling of a
  name,[1]
See Cromwell, damn'd to everlasting
  fame!
An Essay on Man.
Epistle IV, l. 281

Slave to no sect, who takes no private
  road,
But looks through Nature up to Nature's God.[2]   *Ib. l. 331*

Form'd by thy converse, happily to
  steer
From grave to gay, from lively to
  severe.[3]   *Ib. l. 379*

Say, shall my little bark attendant sail,
Pursue the triumph and partake the
  gale? [4]   *Ib. l. 385*

Thou wert my guide, philosopher, and
  friend.[5]   *Ib. l. 390*

That true self-love and social are the
  same.   *Ib. l. 396*

Shut, shut the door, good John! fatigued, I said;
Tie up the knocker! say I'm sick, I'm
  dead.
    The Dog-star rages!
    Epistle to Dr. Arbuthnot [1735].
    Prologue to Imitations of Hor-
    ace, l. 1

Fire in each eye, and papers in each
  hand,
They rave, recite, and madden round
  the land.   *Ib. l. 5*

Is there a parson, much bemused in
  beer,
A maudlin poetess, a rhyming peer,
A clerk foredoom'd his father's soul to
  cross,
Who pens a stanza when he should en-
  gross?
           Ib. l. 15

Fired that the house [1] reject him,
  " 'Sdeath, I'll print it,
And shame the fools."
     Epistle to Dr. Arbuthnot, l. 61

No creature smarts so little as a fool.
     Ib. l. 84

Destroy his fib, or sophistry — in vain!
The creature's at his dirty work again.
     Ib. l. 91

As yet a child, nor yet a fool to fame,
I lisp'd in numbers, for the numbers
  came.   *Ib. l. 127*

This long disease, my life.   *Ib. l. 132*

Pretty! in amber to observe the forms
Of hairs, or straws, or dirt, or grubs, or
  worms! [2]
The things, we know, are neither rich
  nor rare,
But wonder how the devil they got
  there.   *Ib. l. 169*

Means not, but blunders round about a
  meaning;
And he whose fustian's so sublimely
  bad,
It is not poetry, but prose run mad.
     Ib. l. 186

    Were there one whose fires
True Genius kindles, and fair Fame inspires,
Bless'd with each talent, and each art
  to please,
And born to write, converse, and live
  with ease;
Should such a man, too fond to rule
  alone,
Bear, like the Turk, no brother near the
  throne; [3]
View him with scornful, yet with jealous eyes,
And hate for arts that caus'd himself to
  rise;

---

[1] See Cowley, p. 358a.
[2] See Bolingbroke, p. 397b.
[3] See Boileau, p. 377a.
[4] See Dante, *Purgatorio, canto I, l. 1*, p. 160b.
[5] Is this my guide, philosopher, and friend?
— POPE, *Imitations of Horace* [1733–1738], *Epistle I, bk. I, l. 177*

[1] The theater.
[2] See Martial, p. 135a.
[3] Nor is thy fame on lesser ruins built;
  Nor needs thy juster title the foul guilt
  Of Eastern kings, who, to secure their reign,
  Must have their brothers, sons, and kindred
  slain.
    SIR JOHN DENHAM, *On Mr. John*
    Fletcher's Works [1668]

Damn with faint praise, assent with
    civil leer,
And, without sneering, teach the rest to
    sneer; [1]
Willing to wound, and yet afraid to
    strike,
Just hint a fault, and hesitate dislike;
Alike reserv'd to blame or to com-
    mend,
A tim'rous foe, and a suspicious friend;
Dreading e'en fools, by flatterers be-
    sieged,
And so obliging that he ne'er obliged;
Like Cato, give his little Senate laws,[2]
And sit attentive to his own applause.
    Epistle to Dr. Arbuthnot, l. 193

Who but must laugh, if such a man
    there be?
Who would not weep, if Atticus were
    he!   *Ib. l. 213*

Oh let me live my own, and die so too
(To live and die is all I have to do)!
Maintain a poet's dignity and ease,
And see what friends, and read what
    books I please.   *Ib. l. 261*

Curs'd be the verse, how well soe'er it
    flow,
That tends to make one worthy man
    my foe.   *Ib. l. 283*

Let Sporus tremble — "What? that
    thing of silk,
Sporus, that mere white curd of ass's
    milk?
Satire or sense, alas! can Sporus feel?
Who breaks a butterfly upon a wheel?"
    Ib. l. 305

Yet let me flap this bug with gilded
    wings,
This painted child of dirt, that stinks
    and stings;
Whose buzz the witty and the fair
    annoys,

[1] When needs he must, yet faintly then he
    praises;
    Somewhat the deed, much more the means he
    raises:
    So marreth what he makes, and praising
    most, dispraises.
    PHINEAS FLETCHER, *The Purple Island*
    [1633], *canto 7*
[2] While Cato gives his little senate laws. —
Prologue to Mr. Addison's Cato [1713], *l. 23*

Yet wit ne'er tastes, and beauty ne'er
    enjoys.
    Epistle to Dr. Arbuthnot, l. 309

Eternal smiles his emptiness betray,
As shallow streams run dimpling all the
    way.   *Ib. l. 315*

And he himself one vile antithesis.
    Ib. l. 325

Wit that can creep, and pride that licks
    the dust.   *Ib. l. 333*

Unlearn'd, he knew no schoolman's
    subtle art,
No language, but the language of the
    heart.   *Ib. l. 398*

I cannot sleep a wink.[1]
    Imitations of Horace [1733–
    1738], *satire I, bk. II, l. 12*

Satire's my weapon, but I'm too dis-
    creet
To run amuck, and tilt at all I meet.
    Ib. l. 69

But touch me, and no minister so sore.
    Ib. l. 76

There St. John mingles with my
    friendly bowl
The feast of reason and the flow of
    soul.   *Ib. l. 127*

For I, who hold sage Homer's rule the
    best,
Welcome the coming, speed the going
    guest.[2]   *Ib. II, II, l. 159*

I've often wish'd that I had clear,
For life, six hundred pounds a year;
A handsome house to lodge a friend,
A river at my garden's end,
A terrace walk, and half a rood
Of land set out to plant a wood.[3]
    Ib. VI, II, l. 1

Give me again my hollow tree,
A crust of bread, and liberty.
    Ib. l. 220

A patriot is a fool in ev'ry age.
    *Ib. Epilogue to the Satires,
    Dialogue I, l. 41*

[1] See Cervantes, p. 194a.
[2] See Pope, *Odyssey XV, 83*, p. 405b.
[3] See Horace, p. 120a.

Laugh then at any but at fools or foes;
These you but anger, and you mend
not those.
Laugh at your friends, and if your
friends are sore,
So much the better, you may laugh the
more.
> *Imitations of Horace, Epilogue
> to the Satires, Dialogue I, l. 53*

Let humble Allen, with an awkward
shame,
Do good by stealth, and blush to find it
fame. *Ib. l. 135*

Never gallop Pegasus to death.
> *Ib. Epistle I, bk. I, l. 14*

When the brisk minor pants for twenty-
one. *Ib. l. 38*

Not to go back is somewhat to advance,
And men must walk, at least, before
they dance. *Ib. l. 53*

He's arm'd without that's innocent
within. *Ib. l. 94*

Get place and wealth, if possible with
grace;
If not, by any means get wealth and
place.[1] *Ib. l. 103*

Above all Greek, above all Roman
fame. *Ib. II, l. 26*

The people's voice is odd,
It is, and it is not, the voice of God.[2]
> *Ib. l. 89*

In quibbles angel and archangel join,
And God the Father turns a school-
divine.
> *Ib. l. 101 [on Paradise Lost]*

The mob of gentlemen who wrote with
ease. *Ib. l. 108*

One simile that solitary shines
In the dry desert of a thousand lines.
> *Ib. l. 111*

Who says in verse what others say in
prose. *Ib. l. 202*

What will a child learn sooner than a
song? *Ib. l. 205*

Ev'n copious Dryden wanted, or forgot,

[1] See Horace, p. 123a.
[2] See Alcuin, p. 152b.

The last and greatest art — the art to
blot.
> *Imitations of Horace,
> Epistle I, bk. II, l. 280*

There still remains, to mortify a wit,
The many-headed monster of the pit.[1]
> *Ib. l. 304*

We poets are (upon a poet's word)
Of all mankind the creatures most absurd:
The season when to come, and when to
go,
To sing, or cease to sing, we never
know.[2] *Ib. l. 358*

Call, if you will, bad rhyming a
disease,
It gives men happiness, or leaves them
ease. *Ib. II, II, l. 182*

The worst of madmen is a saint run
mad. *Ib. VI, I, l. 27*

Vain was the chief's, the sage's pride!
They had no poet, and they died.
> *Ib. Odes, bk. IV, ode 9, st. 4*

Father of all! in every age,
In every clime ador'd,
By saint, by savage, and by sage,
Jehovah, Jove, or Lord!
> *The Universal Prayer* [1738], *st. 1*

And binding Nature fast in fate,
Left free the human will. *Ib. st. 3*

And deal damnation round the land.
> *Ib. st. 7*

Teach me to feel another's woe,
To hide the fault I see;
That mercy I to others show,
That mercy show to me.[3]
> *Ib. st. 10*

I am his Highness'[4] dog at Kew;
Pray tell me, sir, whose dog are you?
> *On the collar of a dog*

Nature and Nature's laws lay hid in
night:
God said, Let Newton be! and all was
light.
> *Epitaph intended for Sir Isaac
> Newton*

[1] See Horace, p. 123a, and note.
[2] See Robert Frost, p. 926a.
[3] See Spenser, p. 200b.
[4] Frederick, Prince of Wales.

Who dare to love their country, and be poor.
> *On his grotto at Twickenham* [1740]

This is the Jew
That Shakespeare drew.
> *Of Macklin's performance in 1741 of Shylock in The Merchant of Venice. (Attributed to Pope)*

I never knew any man in my life who could not bear another's misfortunes perfectly like a Christian.[1]
> *Thoughts on Various Subjects* [1741]

A man should never be ashamed to own he has been in the wrong, which is but saying, in other words, that he is wiser today than he was yesterday.
> *Ib.*

It is with narrow-souled people as with narrow-necked bottles; the less they have in them the more noise they make in pouring out. *Ib.*

When men grow virtuous in their old age, they only make a sacrifice to God of the devil's leavings.[2] *Ib.*

True disputants are like true sportsmen, their whole delight is in the pursuit. *Ib.*

There, take (says Justice), take ye each a shell:
We thrive at Westminster on fools like you;
'Twas a fat oyster — live in peace — adieu.[3]
> *Verbatim from Boileau*

Whether thou choose Cervantes' serious air,

---

[1] See La Rochefoucauld, p. 355a.
[2] See La Rochefoucauld, p. 355b.
[3] "Tenez voilà," dit-elle, "à chacun une écaille,
Des sottises d'autrui nous vivons au Palais;
Messieurs, l'huître étoit bonne. Adieu. Vivez en paix."
> BOILEAU [1636–1711], *Epître II (à M. l'Abbé des Roches)*

Or laugh and shake in Rabelais' easy chair.
> *The Dunciad* [1728–1743], *bk. I, l. 21*

Poetic Justice, with her lifted scale,
Where, in nice balance, truth with gold she weighs,
And solid pudding against empty praise. *Ib. l. 52*

While pensive poets painful vigils keep,
Sleepless themselves to give their readers sleep. *Ib. l. 93*

Next o'er his books his eyes begin to roll,
In pleasing memory of all he stole.
> *Ib. l. 127*

Or where the pictures for the page atone,
And Quarles is sav'd by beauties not his own. *Ib. l. 139*

And gentle Dullness ever loves a joke.
> *Ib. II, l. 34*

A brain of feathers, and a heart of lead.
> *Ib. l. 44*

Peel'd, patch'd, and piebald, linsey-woolsey brothers,
Grave mummers! sleeveless some, and shirtless others.
That once was Britain.
> *Ib. III, l. 115*

And proud his mistress' order to perform,
Rides in the whirlwind and directs the storm.[1] *Ib. l. 263*

A wit with dunces, and a dunce with wits.[2] *Ib. IV, l. 90*

The Right Divine of Kings to govern wrong. *Ib. l. 188*

Stuff the head
With all such reading as was never read:
For thee explain a thing till all men doubt it,
And write about it, Goddess, and about it. *Ib. l. 249*

---

[1] See Addison, p. 393a.
[2] See Quintilian, p. 136a, and note.

To happy convents, bosom'd deep in
vines,
Where slumber abbots, purple as their
wines.   *The Dunciad, bk. IV, l. 301*

Led by my hand, he saunter'd Europe
round,
And gather'd every vice on Christian
ground.   *Ib. l. 311*

Religion blushing veils her sacred fires,
And unawares Morality expires.
Nor public flame, nor private, dares to
shine;
Nor human spark is left, nor glimpse
divine!
Lo! thy dread empire Chaos! is restor'd:
Light dies before thy uncreating word;
Thy hand, great Anarch! lets the cur-
tain fall,
And universal darkness buries all.
                      Ib. l. 649

LADY MARY WORTLEY MONTAGU
1689–1762

And we meet, with champagne and a
chicken, at last.
                The Lover [1748]

Be plain in dress, and sober in your
diet;
In short, my deary, kiss me, and be
quiet.
        *A Summary of Lord Lyttelton's
                            Advice*

Satire should, like a polished razor
keen,
Wound with a touch that's scarcely felt
or seen.
        *To the Imitator of the First
                Satire of Horace, bk. II*

This world consists of men, women,
and Herveys.[1]
                Letters [1763], vol. I

But the fruit that can fall without shaking
Indeed is too mellow for me.
        *Letters and Works [1837]. The
                                    Answer*

[1] See Sydney Smith, p. 523a.

CHARLES DE SECONDAT, BARON DE MONTESQUIEU[1]
1689–1755

How can anyone be Persian?
        Lettres Persanes [1721], no. 30

A man should be mourned at his
birth, not at his death.   *Ib. 40*

If triangles had a god, he would have
three sides.[2]   *Ib. 59*

Liberty is the right of doing whatever
the laws permit.
        *De l'Esprit des Lois [1748],
                                XI, 3*

Useless laws weaken the necessary
laws.   *Ib. XXIX, 16*

If I knew of something that could
serve my nation but would ruin another, I would not propose it to my
prince, for I am first a man and only
then a Frenchman . . . because I am
necessarily a man, and only accidentally
am I French.[3]
            Pensées et Jugements

You have to study a great deal to
know a little.   *Ib.*

CHARLES MACKLIN
1690–1797

The law is a sort of hocus-pocus science.[4]
        Love à la Mode [1759], act II, sc. 1

JOHN BYROM
1692–1763

God bless the King, I mean the Faith's
Defender;
God bless — no harm in blessing — the
Pretender;

[1] See Carlyle, p. 578a, note 3.
[2] See Xenophanes, p. 70b.
[3] See Montaigne, p. 191a.
[4] Hocus was an old cunning attorney. — DR.
JOHN ARBUTHNOT, *Law Is a Bottomless Pit; or,
History of John Bull* [1712], ch. 5
    The words of consecration, "Hoc est corpus,"
were travestied into a nickname for jugglery, as
"Hocus-pocus." — JOHN RICHARD GREEN, *A Short
History of the English People* [1874], ch. 7.

But who Pretender is, or who is King,
God bless us all — that's quite another
  thing.[1]
     Miscellaneous Poems [1773]. *To
     an officer of the Army, extempore*

Some say, that Signor Bononcini,
Compar'd to Handel's a mere ninny;
Others aver, to him, that Handel
Is scarcely fit to hold a candle.[2]
Strange! that such high dispute should
  be
'Twixt Tweedledum and Tweedledee.
     *Ib. On the Feuds between
       Handel and Bononcini*

As clear as a whistle.
     Epistle to Lloyd

PHILIP DORMER
STANHOPE,
EARL OF CHESTERFIELD
1694–1773

Measures not men.[3]
     Letters [*March 6, 1742*]

Whatever is worth doing at all, is
worth doing well.
     Ib. [*March 10, 1746*]

The knowledge of the world is only
to be acquired in the world, and not in
a closet.   *Ib.* [*October 4, 1746*]

An injury is much sooner forgotten
than an insult.
     Ib. [*October 9, 1746*]

Do as you would be done by, is the
surest method of pleasing.[4]
     Ib. [*October 9, 1747*]

Take the tone of the company that
you are in.   *Ib.*

I knew once a very covetous, sordid
fellow,[5] who used to say, "Take care of

the pence, for the pounds will take care
of themselves."
     Letters [*November 6, 1747*]

Advice is seldom welcome; and those
who want it most always like it least.
     Ib. [*January 29, 1748*]

Speak of the moderns without contempt, and of the ancients without
idolatry.   *Ib.* [*February 22, 1748*]

Wear your learning, like your watch,
in a private pocket: and do not pull it
out and strike it, merely to show that
you have one.   *Ib.*

Manners must adorn knowledge, and
smooth its way through the world. Like
a great rough diamond, it may do very
well in a closet by way of curiosity, and
also for its intrinsic value.
     Ib. [*July 1, 1748*]

Women, then, are only children of a
larger growth.
     Ib. [*September 5, 1748*]

Women who are either indisputably
beautiful, or indisputably ugly, are best
flattered upon the score of their under-
standings; but those who are in a state
of mediocrity are best flattered upon
their beauty, or at least their graces; for
every woman who is not absolutely ugly
thinks herself handsome.   *Ib.*

Without some dissimulation no business can be carried on at all.
     Ib. [*May 22, 1749*]

Idleness is only the refuge of weak
minds.   *Ib.* [*July 20, 1749*]

Style is the dress of thoughts.
     Ib. [*November 24, 1749*]

Dispatch is the soul of business.
     Ib. [*February 5, 1750*]

Knowledge may give weight, but
accomplishments give luster, and many
more people see than weigh.
     Ib. [*May 8, 1750*]

---

[1] Quoted by SIR WALTER SCOTT in *Redgauntlet,*
vol. II, ch. *1* [Edinburgh edition, 1832].
[2] See Lamb, p. 535b.
[3] See Goldsmith, p. 449a, and Burke, p. 452a.
[4] See Kingsley, p. 691b.
[5] William Lowndes [1652–1724], Secretary of
the Treasury in the reigns of William III,
Queen Anne, and George I.

Let blockheads read what blockheads write. *Letters [November 1, 1750]*

Is it possible to love such a man? [1] No. The utmost I can do for him is to consider him as a respectable Hottentot. *Ib. [February 28, 1751]*

It is commonly said, and more particularly by Lord Shaftesbury,[2] that ridicule is the best test of truth. *Ib. [February 6, 1752]*

Every woman is infallibly to be gained by every sort of flattery, and every man by one sort or other. *Ib. [March 16, 1752]*

A chapter of accidents.[3] *Ib. [February 16, 1753]*

I assisted at the birth of that most significant word "flirtation," which dropped from the most beautiful mouth in the world. *The World, no. 101*

Unlike my subject will I frame my song, It shall be witty, and it shan't be long. *Epigram on ["Long"] Sir Thomas Robinson*

The dews of the evening most carefully shun — Those tears of the sky for the loss of the sun. *Advice to a Lady in Autumn*

He adorned whatever subject he either spoke or wrote upon, by the most splendid eloquence.[4] *Character of Bolingbroke*

Give Dayrolles a chair. *Last words*

FRANCIS HUTCHESON
1694–1746

That action is best which procures the greatest happiness for the greatest numbers.[1] *Inquiry Concerning Moral Good and Evil [1720], sec. 3*

FRANÇOIS QUESNAY
1694–1774

Laissez faire, laissez passer.[2] *Attributed*

VOLTAIRE
[FRANÇOIS MARIE AROUET]
1694–1778

Virtue debases itself in justifying itself. *Oedipe [1718], act I, sc. 4*

O what fine times, this age of iron! *Le Mondain [1736]*

Paradise is where I am. *Ib.*

The superfluous, a very necessary thing.[3] *Ib.*

The secret of being a bore is to tell everything. *Sept Discours en Vers sur l'Homme [1738]*

Love truth, but pardon error. *Ib.*

He who is merely just is severe. *Letter to Frederick the Great [1740]*

---

[1] Lord Lyttelton.
[2] Truth, 'tis supposed, may bear all lights; and one of those principal lights or natural mediums by which things are to be viewed in order to a thorough recognition is ridicule itself. — ANTHONY ASHLEY COOPER, LORD SHAFTESBURY, *Essay on the Freedom of Wit and Humor* [1709], *pt. I, sec. 1*
[3] The Chapter of Accidents is the longest chapter in the book. — *Attributed to* JOHN WILKES by SOUTHEY in *The Doctor* [1837], *ch. 118*
[4] See Johnson, p. 430a.
Il embellit tout ce qu'il touche [He adorns whatever he touches]. — FÉNELON [1651–1715]. *Lettre sur les Occupations de l'Académie Française, sec. 4*

[1] Priestley was the first (unless it was Beccaria) who taught my lips to pronounce this sacred truth — that the greatest happiness of the greatest number is the foundation of morals and legislation. — JEREMY BENTHAM [1748–1832], *Works, vol. X, p. 142*
[2] Let it be, let it pass. The phrase is not readily translatable, and also appears as "Laissez faire, laissez aller." It has also been attributed to PIERRE LE PESANT BOISGUILBERT [1676–1714] and JEAN CLAUDE GOURNAY [1712–1759]. It was widely used by the Physiocrats in urging freedom from government interference, and was adopted by ADAM SMITH [1723–1790].
[3] See Holmes, p. 788b.

The first who was king was a fortunate soldier:

Who serves his country well has no need of ancestors.[1]

> *Mérope* [1743], *act I, sc. 3*

It is better to risk saving a guilty person than to condemn an innocent one.[2]

> *Zadig* [1747], *ch. 6*

They squeeze the orange and throw away the skin.

> *Letter to Madame Denis* [September 2, 1751] *referring to his quarrel with Frederick the Great*

This agglomeration which was called and which still calls itself the Holy Roman Empire is neither holy, nor Roman, nor an Empire.

> *Essai sur les Moeurs* [1756]

All is for the best in the best of possible worlds.[3] *Candide* [1759], *ch. 1*

If this is the best of possible worlds, what then are the others? *Ib. 6*

Optimism, said Candide, is a mania for maintaining that all is well when things are going badly. *Ib. 19*

In this country [England] it is good to kill an admiral from time to time, to encourage the others.[4] *Ib. 23*

This is the happiest of mortals, for he is above everything he possesses.

> *Ib. 26*

Work helps to preserve us from three great evils — weariness, vice, and want.

> *Ib. 30*

We must cultivate our garden.[5]

> *Ib.*

There are truths which are not for all men, nor for all times.

> *Letter to Cardinal de Bernis* [April 23, 1761]

One feels like crawling on all fours after reading your work.

> *Letter to Rousseau* [August 31, 1761]

Whatever you do, crush the infamous thing [superstition], and love those who love you.[1]

> *Letter to d'Alembert* [November 28, 1762]

Common sense is not so common.

> *Dictionnaire Philosophique* [1764]. *Self-Love*

In general, the art of government consists in taking as much money as possible from one class of citizens to give to the other. *Ib. Money*

The best is the enemy of the good.[2]

> *Ib. Dramatic Art*

Very learned women are to be found, in the same manner as female warriors; but they are seldom or never inventors.

> *Ib. Women*

The proper mean.[3]

> *Letter to Count d'Argental* [November 28, 1765]

Men use thought only to justify their wrongdoings, and speech only to conceal their thoughts.[4]

> *Dialogue 14. Le Chapon et la Poularde* [1766]

I have never made but one prayer to God, a very short one: "O Lord, make my enemies ridiculous." And God granted it.

> *Letter to M. Damiliville* [May 16, 1767]

History is little else than a picture of human crimes and misfortunes.[5]

> *L'Ingénu* [1767], *ch. 10*

---

[1] What can they see in the longest kingly line in Europe, save that it runs back to a successful soldier? — SIR WALTER SCOTT, *Woodstock* [1826], *ch. 37*

[2] See Blackstone, p. 444b.

[3] Tout est pour le mieux dans le meilleur des mondes possibles (referring to the philosophy of Leibnitz and his followers).

[4] Pour encourager les autres.

The reference is to Admiral Byng, who was executed in 1756 for failing to relieve Minorca.

[5] Il faut cultiver notre jardin.

See Rabelais, p. 181a, and Montaigne, p. 189b.

---

[1] Quoi que vous fassiez, écrasez l'infâme, et aimez qui vous aime.

[2] Le mieux est l'ennemi du bien.

[3] Le juste milieu. See Horace, p. 121b, and note.

[4] See Robert South, p. 376b.

[5] See Gibbon, p. 465b.

Thought depends absolutely on the stomach, but in spite of that, those who have the best stomachs are not the best thinkers.
Letter to d'Alembert
[August 20, 1770]

If God did not exist, it would be necessary to invent him.[1]
Épître á l'Auteur du Livre des Trois Imposteurs [November 10, 1770]

Change everything, except your loves.   *Sur l'Usage de la Vie*

I am very fond of truth, but not at all of martyrdom.
Letter to d'Alembert [February 1776]

The embarrassment of riches.
Le Droit du Seigneur, act II, sc. 6

He who thinks himself wise, O heavens! is a great fool.   *Ib. IV, 1*

Who has not the spirit of his age,
Of his age has all the unhappiness.[2]
Letter to Madame du Châtelet

I advise you to go on living solely to enrage those who are paying your annuities. It is the only pleasure I have left.
Letter to Madame du Deffand

Liberty of thought is the life of the soul.
Essay on Epic Poetry (written in English)

Whoe'er thou art, behold thy master, He is, or was, or has to be.[3]
On a statuette of Cupid in the Cirey Gardens

I disapprove of what you say, but I will defend to the death your right to say it.   *Attributed* [4]

[1] See Ovid, p. 128b, and Tillotson, p. 366b.
[2] Qui n'a pas l'esprit de son âge,
De son âge a tout le malheur.
[3] Qui que tu sois, voici ton maître;
Il l'est — le fut — ou le doit être.
[4] This sentence is not Voltaire's, but was first used in quoting a letter from Voltaire to

MATTHEW GREEN
1696–1737

They politics like ours profess,
The greater prey upon the less.
The Grotto, l. 69

Fling but a stone, the giant dies.
Laugh and be well.
The Spleen [1737], l. 92

By happy alchemy of mind
They turn to pleasure all they find.
Ib. l. 610

WILLIAM OLDYS
1696–1761

Busy, curious, thirsty fly,
Drink with me, and drink as I.
On a Fly Drinking Out of a Cup of Ale, st. 1

MARIE DE VICHY-CHAMROND, MARQUISE DU DEFFAND
1697 – 1780

[Of Voltaire] He has invented history.
From FOURNIER, *L'Esprit dans l' Histoire [1857]*

The first step is the hardest.[1]
Letter to d'Alembert [July 7, 1763]

Helvétius in *The Friends of Voltaire* [1906] by S. G. TALLENTYRE (E. Beatrice Hall). She claims it was a paraphrase of Voltaire's words in the *Essay on Tolerance:* "Think for yourselves and let others enjoy the privilege to do so too."
Norbert Guterman, in *A Book of French Quotations* [1963], suggests that the probable source for the quotation is from a line in a letter to M. le Riche [*February 6, 1770*]: "Monsieur l'abbé, I detest what you write, but I would give my life to make it possible for you to continue to write."

[1] This remark refers to the legend that Saint Denis, carrying his head in his hands, walked from Montmartre to St. Denis, a few miles north of Paris. Voltaire wrote to Madame du Deffand [January 1764] that one of her bon mots was quoted in the notes of *La Pucelle*, canto 1: Il n'y a que le premier pas qui coûte.

a   *b*

KAMO MABUCHI[1]
1697–1769

Japanese poetry has as its subject the human heart. It may seem to be of no practical use and just as well left uncomposed, but when one knows poetry well, one understands also without explanation the reasons governing order and disorder in the world. *Writings*

I need not recite again how troublesome, evil, turbulent a country China is. To mention just one instance — there is the matter of their picture-writing. *Ib.*

RICHARD SAVAGE
1698–1743

No tenth transmitter of a foolish face.
The Bastard [1728], *l. 8*

May see thee now, though late, redeem thy name,
And glorify what else is damn'd to fame.
Character of the Reverend James Foster

WILLIAM WARBURTON, BISHOP OF GLOUCESTER
1698–1779

Orthodoxy is my doxy; heterodoxy is another man's doxy.[2]
From JOSEPH PRIESTLEY [1733–1804], *Memoirs, vol. I, p. 572*

JOHN DYER
c. 1700 – 1758

A little rule, a little sway,
A sunbeam in a winter's day,
Is all the proud and mighty have
Between the cradle and the grave.
Grongar Hill [1726], *l. 89*

[1] From *Sources of Japanese Tradition,* edited by William Theodore de Bary [1960].
[2] Priestley relates that in a debate on the Test Laws, Lord Sandwich said: "I have heard frequent use of the words 'orthodoxy' and 'heterodoxy' but I confess myself at a loss to know precisely what they mean." Bishop Warburton whispered his definition to him.
See Carlyle, p. 577a.

JAMES THOMSON
1700–1748

See, Winter comes to rule the varied year,[1]
Sullen and sad.
The Seasons. Winter [1726], *l. 1*

Welcome, kindred glooms!
Congenial horrors, hail! *Ib. l. 5*

Cruel as death, and hungry as the grave. *Ib. l. 393*

There studious let me sit,
And hold high converse with the mighty dead. *Ib. l. 431*

Ships dim-discover'd dropping from the clouds.
Ib. Summer [1727], *l. 946*

Sigh'd and look'd unutterable things.
Ib. l. 1188

Come, gentle Spring! ethereal mildness, come.
Ib. Spring [1728], *l. 1*

Delightful task! to rear the tender thought,
To teach the young idea how to shoot.
Ib. l. 1149

An elegant sufficiency, content,
Retirement, rural quiet, friendship, books. *Ib. l. 1158*

Crown'd with the sickle, and the wheaten sheaf,
While Autumn, nodding o'er the yellow plain,
Comes jovial on.
Ib. Autumn [1730], *l. 1*

For loveliness
Needs not the foreign aid of ornament,
But is when unadorn'd adorn'd the most.[2] *Ib. l. 208*

Or where the Northern ocean, in vast whirls,
Boils round the naked melancholy isles
Of farthest Thulè,[3] and th' Atlantic surge

[1] See Cowper, p. 458b.
[2] See Cicero, p. 111a, and Milton, p. 346a.
[3] See Virgil, p. 117a, and Seneca, p. 131a.

Pours in among the stormy Hebrides.[1]
The Seasons. Autumn, l. 871

Come then, expressive silence, muse
His praise.
Hymn [1730], *l. 118*

O Sophonisba! Sophonisba, O! [2]
Sophonisba [1730], *act III, sc. 2*

Forever, Fortune, wilt thou prove
An unrelenting foe to love,
And, when we meet a mutual heart,
Come in between and bid us part?
To Fortune

When Britain first, at Heaven's command,
  Arose from out of the azure main,
This was the charter of the land,
  And guardian angels sung this strain:
Rule, Britannia, rule the waves;
Britons never will be slaves.
Alfred [1740], *act II, sc. 5*

A pleasing land of drowsyhead it was.
The Castle of Indolence [1748],
canto I, st. 6

A bard here dwelt, more fat than bard
  beseems,
Who, void of envy, guile, and lust of
  gain,
On virtue still, and nature's pleasing
  themes,
Pour'd forth his unpremeditated strain.
Ib. st. 68

A little round, fat, oily man of God.
Ib. st. 69

PHILIP DODDRIDGE
1702–1751

Awake my soul! stretch every nerve,
  And press with vigor on;
A heavenly race demands thy zeal,
  And an immortal crown.
Hymns [1755]. *Zeal and Vigor
in the Christian Race, st. 1*

---

[1] See Milton, p. 339a.
[2] This line was parodied by Fielding in his *Tom Thumb* [acted 1730]: O Huncamunca, Huncamunca, O.

JONATHAN EDWARDS
1703–1758

Resolved, never to do anything which
I should be afraid to do if it were the
last hour of my life.[1]
Seventy Resolutions

Intend to live in continual mortification, and never to expect or desire any
worldly ease or pleasure.
Diary [1723]

A little, wretched, despicable creature; a worm, a mere nothing, and less
than nothing; a vile insect that has
risen up in contempt against the majesty of Heaven and earth.
The Justice of God in the Damnation of Sinners [1734]

I assert that nothing ever comes to
pass without a cause.
The Freedom of the Will [1754]

This dictate of common sense.
Ib.

THOMAS MORELL
1703–1784

See, the conquering hero comes!
Sound the trumpet, beat the drums! [2]
Joshua [1748], *pt. III*

JOHN WESLEY
1703–1791

I look upon the world as my parish.
Journal [*June 11, 1739*]

That execrable sum of all villainies,
commonly called the Slave Trade.
Ib. [*February 12, 1772*]

Though I am always in haste, I am
never in a hurry.
Letters [*December 10, 1777*]

Let it be observed, that slovenliness
is no part of religion; that neither this
nor any text of Scripture, condemns

---

[1] See Gellert, p. 438b.
[2] Handel used this in his oratorios *Judas Maccabaeus* [April 1, 1747] and *Joshua* [March 9, 1748], the libretti of which were written by Morell.
See Dryden, p. 371a.

neatness of apparel. Certainly this is a duty, not a sin. "Cleanliness is, indeed, next to godliness."[1]

> *Sermon 93, On Dress*

Do all the good you can,
By all the means you can,
In all the ways you can,
In all the places you can,
At all the times you can,
To all the people you can,
As long as ever you can.

> *John Wesley's Rule*

NATHANIEL COTTON
1705-1788

Yet still we hug the dear deceit.

> *Content. Vision IV*

Hold the fleet angel fast until he bless thee.[2]   *Tomorrow*

BENJAMIN FRANKLIN[3]
1706-1790

The body of Benjamin Franklin, Printer (like the cover of an old book, its contents torn out and stripped of its

---

[1] According to Rabbi A. S. Bettelheim, this is found in the Hebrew fathers. He cites PHINEHAS BEN YAIR as follows: "The doctrines of religion are resolved into carefulness; carefulness into vigorousness; vigorousness into guiltlessness; guiltlessness into abstemiousness; abstemiousness into cleanliness; cleanliness into godliness" — literally, next to godliness.

[2] See *Genesis 32:26*, p. 7b, and Whittier, p. 625b.

[3] Eripuit coelo fulmen mox sceptra tyrannis [He snatched the thunderbolt from heaven, then the scepter from tyrants]. — *Attributed to* TURGOT
This line was inscribed on Houdon's bust of Franklin in 1778. FREDERICK VON DER TRENCK [1726-1794] asserted in 1794 that he was the author of the line.
See Manilius, p. 131b.
Antiquity would have raised altars to this mighty genius, who, to the advantage of mankind, compassing in his mind the heavens and the earth, was able to restrain alike thunderbolts and tyrants. — MIRABEAU, *Address Upon the Death of Franklin*
I succeed him; no one could replace him. — THOMAS JEFFERSON [to the Comte de Vergennes, who had remarked, "You replace Mr. Franklin" as envoy to France]
See Byron, p. 563a.

---

lettering and gilding), lies here, food for worms; but the work shall not be lost, for it will (as he believed) appear once more in a new and more elegant edition, revised and corrected by the Author.[1]

> *Epitaph on Himself [composed in 1728]*

Eat to live, and not live to eat.[2]

> *Poor Richard's Almanac [for 1733]*

Where there's marriage without love, there will be love without marriage.

> *Ib. [1734]*

Avarice and happiness never saw each other, how then should they become acquainted.   *Ib.*

A little house well filled, a little field well tilled, and a little wife well willed, are great riches.   *Ib. [1735]*

Some are weatherwise, some are otherwise.   *Ib.*

Necessity never made a good bargain.

> *Ib.*

Three may keep a secret, if two of them are dead.   *Ib.*

Opportunity is the great bawd.

> *Ib.*

Early to bed and early to rise, makes a man healthy, wealthy, and wise.

> *Ib.*

God helps them that help themselves.[3]   *Ib.*

Don't throw stones at your neighbors', if your own windows are glass.

> *Ib.*

There are three faithful friends — an old wife, an old dog, and ready money.

> *Ib. [1738]*

If you would not be forgotten, as soon as you are dead and rotten, either write things worth reading, or do things worth the writing.   *Ib.*

---

[1] See Clare, p. 573b.
[2] See Socrates, p. 87b, and note.
[3] See Aesop, p. 76b, and note.

Keep your eyes wide open before marriage, half shut afterwards.
Poor Richard's Almanac [1738]

None but the well-bred man knows how to confess a fault, or acknowledge himself in an error. *Ib.*

An empty bag cannot stand upright.
Ib. [1740]

He that riseth late must trot all day.
Ib. [1742]

Experience keeps a dear school, but fools will learn in no other.[1]
Ib. [1743]

The used key is always bright.
Ib. [1744]

When the well's dry, we know the worth of water.[2] *Ib.* [1746]

Dost thou love Life? Then do not squander Time; for that's the stuff Life is made of. *Ib.*

Lost time is never found again.
Ib. [1748]

Little strokes fell great oaks.[3]
Ib. [1750]

The cat in gloves catches no mice.
Ib. [1754]

Work as if you were to live a hundred years, pray as if you were to die tomorrow. *Ib.* [1757]

A word to the wise is enough, and many words won't fill a bushel.
Ib. [1758]

He that lives upon hope will die fasting. *Ib.*

Three removes is as bad as a fire.
Ib.

A little neglect may breed great mischief . . . for want of a nail the shoe was lost; for want of a shoe the horse

was lost; and for want of a horse the rider was lost.[1]
Poor Richard's Almanac [1758]

We are a kind of posterity in respect to them.
Letter to William Strahan [1745]

Eighth and lastly. They are so grateful!!
Reasons for Preferring an Elderly Mistress [1745]

Remember that time is money.[2]
Advice to a Young Tradesman
[1748]

They that can give up essential liberty to obtain a little temporary safety deserve neither liberty nor safety.
Historical Review of Pennsylvania [1759]

Idleness and pride tax with a heavier hand than kings and parliaments. If we can get rid of the former, we may easily bear the latter.
Letter on the Stamp Act
[July 11, 1765]

The grand leap of the whale up the Fall of Niagara is esteemed, by all who have seen it, as one of the finest spectacles in nature.
To the editor of a London newspaper [1765], *intended to chaff the English for their ignorance of America*

Here Skugg lies snug
As a bug in a rug.
Letter to Miss Georgiana Shipley [September 1772]

There never was a good war or a bad peace.[3]
Letter to Josiah Quincy
[September 11, 1773]

---

[1] See Burke, p. 455a.
[2] Do not let your chances like sunbeams pass you by,
For you never miss the water till the well runs dry.
ROWLAND HOWARD, *You Never Miss the Water* [1876]
[3] See Lyly, p. 202b.

[1] See Herbert, pp. 324b–325a.
[2] We reckon hours and minutes to be dollars and cents. — T. C. HALIBURTON [1796–1865], *The Clockmaker*
[3] I cease not to advocate peace; even though unjust it is better than the most just war. — CICERO [106–43 B.C.], *Epistolae ad Atticum, bk. VII, epistle 14*
It hath been said that an unjust peace is to be preferred before a just war. — SAMUEL BUTLER, *Butler's Remains* [1759]. *Speeches in the Rump Parliament*

You and I were long friends: you are now my enemy, and I am
Yours,
B. Franklin
Letter to William Strahan
[*July 5, 1775*]

We must all hang together, or assuredly we shall all hang separately.
At the signing of the Declaration of Independence [*July 4, 1776*]

Poor man, said I, you pay too much for your whistle.   *The Whistle* [1779]

Here you would know and enjoy what posterity will say of Washington. For a thousand leagues have nearly the same effect with a thousand years.
Letter to Washington
[*March 5, 1780*]

George Washington, Commander of the American armies, who, like Joshua of old, commanded the sun and the moon to stand still, and they obeyed him.
A toast at a dinner in Versailles [1]

No nation was ever ruined by trade.
Thoughts on Commercial Subjects

I wish the bald eagle had not been chosen as the representative of our country; he is a bird of bad moral character; like those among men who live by sharping and robbing, he is generally poor, and often very lousy.
The turkey is a much more respectable bird, and withal a true original native of America.
Letter to Sarah Bache
[*January 26, 1784*]

He [the sun] gives light as soon as he rises.
An Economical Project [2] [1784]

Our Constitution is in actual operation; everything appears to promise that it will last; but in this world nothing is certain but death and taxes.
Letter to M. Leroy [1789]

The next thing most like living one's life over again seems to be a recollection of that life, and to make that recollection as durable as possible by putting it down in writing.
Autobiography [1771–1867],[1]
ch. 1

Eat not to dullness; drink not to elevation.   *Ib. 6*

I shall never ask, never refuse, nor ever resign an office.   *Ib. 8*

Human felicity is produced not so much by great pieces of good fortune that seldom happen, as by little advantages that occur every day.
Ib. 9

When men are employed, they are best contented; for on the days they worked they were good-natured and cheerful, and, with the consciousness of having done a good day's work, they spent the evening jollily; but on our idle days they were mutinous and quarrelsome.   *Ib. 10*

GEORGES LOUIS LECLERC DE BUFFON
1707–1788

[Of the horse] The noblest conquest man has ever made.
L'Histoire des Mammifères.
Le Cheval

The style is the man himself.[2]
Discourse [*on his admission to the French Academy, 1753*]

Genius is nothing but a greater aptitude for patience.

Attributed [3]

[1] The *Autobiography*, begun in 1771, was published in complete and accurate form in 1867.
[2] Le style c'est l'homme même.
[3] Le génie n'est qu'une plus grande aptitude à la patience.
Hérault de Séchelles, in *Voyage à Montbard*, first attributed this to Buffon. It is quoted by Matthew Arnold in *Essays in Criticism, A French Coleridge* [1865]. There is also a popular proverb: Genius is patience. LORD SYDENHAM [1799–1841] defined genius as a consummate sense of proportion.
See Carlyle, p. 578a; Butler, p. 756b; and Jane Ellice Hopkins, p. 770a.
(*note continued p. 424*)

[1] The British Minister had proposed a toast to George III, in which he likened him to the sun, and the French Minister had toasted Louis XVI, comparing him with the moon.
[2] Letter to the *Journal de Paris* advocating daylight saving.

HENRY FIELDING
1707–1754

All Nature wears one universal grin.
Tom Thumb the Great [1730],
act I, sc. 1

Today it is our pleasure to be drunk;
And this our queen shall be as drunk as
we. *Ib. 2*

When I'm not thank'd at all, I'm
thank'd enough;
I've done my duty, and I've done no
more. *Ib. 3*

I am as sober as a judge.
Don Quixote in England [1734],
act III, sc. 14

This story will never go down.
Tumble-Down Dick

The dusky night rides down the sky,
And ushers in the morn;
The hounds all join in glorious cry,
The huntsman winds his horn,
And a-hunting we will go.[1]
A-Hunting We Will Go [1734],
st. 1

To whom nothing is given, of him
can nothing be required.[2]
Joseph Andrews [1742], *bk. II,*
ch. 8

I describe not men, but manners; not
an individual, but a species.
Ib. III, 1

They are the affectation of affectation. *Ib. 3*

Public schools are the nurseries of all
vice and immorality. *Ib. 5*

Patience is a necessary ingredient of genius.
— DISRAELI, *The Young Duke* [1831]
Genius is capacity for taking trouble. —
LESLIE STEPHEN [1832–1904]
Genius is an intuitive talent for labor. —
JAN WALAEUS
[1] It's of three jovial huntsmen, and a-hunting
they did go;
And they hunted, and they hollo'd, and they
blew their horns also;
Look ye there!
The Three Jovial Huntsmen (old
English ballad), *st. 1*
[2] See *Luke 12:48,* p. 47a.

Some folks rail against other folks,
because other folks have what some
folks would be glad of.
Joseph Andrews, bk. IV, ch. 6

Love and scandal are the best sweeteners of tea.[1]
Love in Several Masques [1743]

Every physician almost hath his favorite disease.
Tom Jones [2] [1749], *bk. II, ch. 9*

Thwackum was for doing justice, and
leaving mercy to heaven. *Ib. III, 10*

Can any man have a higher notion of
the rule of right and the eternal fitness
of things? *Ib. IV, 4*

Distinction without a difference.
Ib. VI, 13

O! more than Gothic ignorance.
Ib. VII, 3

An amiable weakness.[3] *Ib. X, 8*

His designs were strictly honorable,
as the phrase is; that is, to rob a lady of
her fortune by way of marriage.
Ib. XI, 4

Hairbreadth missings of happiness
look like the insults of Fortune.
Ib. XIII, 2

The republic of letters.
Ib. XIV, 1

It hath been often said, that it is not
death, but dying which is terrible.
Amelia [1751], *bk. III, ch. 4*

These are called the pious frauds of
friendship. *Ib. VI, 6*

When widows exclaim loudly against
second marriages, I would always lay a
wager that the man, if not the wedding
day, is absolutely fixed on. *Ib. 8*

---

[1] See Congreve, p. 391b.
[2] See Gibbon, p. 466a.
[3] Amiable weaknesses of human nature. —
GIBBON, *Decline and Fall of the Roman Empire*
[1776–1788], *ch. 14*
It was an amiable weakness. — SHERIDAN,
The School for Scandal [1777]

There is not in the universe a more ridiculous, nor a more contemptible animal, than a proud clergyman.
Amelia, bk. VI, ch. 10

One of my illustrious predecessors.[1]
Covent Garden Journal
[*January* 11, 1752]

LINNAEUS
[CARL VON LINNÉ]
1707–1778

To live by medicine is to live horribly.   *Diaeta Naturalis, introduction*

Nature does not proceed by leaps.[2]
Philosophia Botanica, sec. 77

Mingle your joys sometimes with your earnest occupation.[3]
From biography of Linnaeus by
BENJAMIN DAYDON JONES, *ch.* 9

A professor can never better distinguish himself in his work than by encouraging a clever pupil, for the true discoverers are among them, as comets amongst the stars.   *Ib.*

Live innocently; God is here.
Ib. 15 (*inscribed over the door of Linnaeus's bedchamber*)

If a tree dies, plant another in its place.   *Ib.*

CHARLES WESLEY
1707–1788

"Christ, the Lord, is risen today,"
Sons of men and angels say,
Raise your joys and triumphs high,
Sing, ye heavens, and earth reply.
Hymns and Sacred Poems
[1739]. *Christ, the Lord, Is Risen Today*

Jesus, lover of my soul,
    Let me to Thy bosom fly,
While the waters nearer roll,
    While the tempest still is high;
Hide me, O my Savior, hide,
    Till the storm of life is past;
Safe into the haven glide,
    O receive my soul at last.
Hymns and Sacred Poems.
[1740]. *Jesus, Lover of My Soul*

Gentle Jesus, meek and mild,
Look upon a little child;
Pity my simplicity,
Suffer me to come to thee.
Ib. [1742]. *Gentle Jesus, Meek and Mild*

Soldiers of Christ, arise,
And put your armor on.
Ib. [1749]. *Soldiers of Christ, Arise*

Hark! the herald angels sing
Glory to the newborn King;
Peace on earth, and mercy mild,
God and sinners reconciled!
Joyful all ye nations rise,
Join the triumph of the skies;
With th' angelic host proclaim
Christ is born in Bethlehem.[1]
Ib. [1753]. *Christmas Hymn: Hark! the Herald Angels Sing*

WILLIAM PITT, EARL OF CHATHAM
1708–1778

The atrocious crime of being a young man, which the honorable gentleman [Walpole] has with such spirit and decency charged upon me, I shall neither attempt to palliate nor deny; but content myself with wishing that I may be one of those whose follies may cease with their youth, and not of that num-

---

[1] Illustrious predecessor. — BURKE, *The Present Discontents* [1770]
  I tread in the footsteps of illustrious men. . . . In receiving from the people the sacred trust twice confined to my illustrious predecessor [Andrew Jackson]. — MARTIN VAN BUREN, *Inaugural Address* [March 4, 1837]
[2] Natura non facit saltus.
[3] See Horace, p. 122b, and note.

[1] George Whitefield [1714–1770] altered lines 1 and 2, 7 and 8 from Wesley's original:
  Hark, how all the welkin rings,
    "Glory to the King of kings." . . .
  Universal nature say,
    "Christ the Lord is born today."

ber who are ignorant in spite of experience.
Speech in the House of Commons [1] [*March 6, 1741*]

I rejoice that America has resisted. Three millions of people, so dead to all the feelings of liberty, as voluntarily to submit to be slaves, would have been fit instruments to make slaves of the rest.
Ib. [*January 14, 1766*]

Confidence is a plant of slow growth in an aged bosom; youth is the season of credulity.
Speech in the House of Commons [*January 14, 1766*]

Unlimited power is apt to corrupt the minds of those who possess it; [2] and this I know, my lords, that where laws end, tyranny begins. [3]
Case of Wilkes. Speech [*January 9, 1770*]

There is something behind the throne greater than the King himself.
Speech in the House of Lords [*March 2, 1770*]

I love the Americans because they love liberty, and I love them for the noble efforts they made in the last war.
Ib.

Reparation for our rights at home, and security against the like future violations. [4]
Letter to the Earl of Shelburne [*September 29, 1770*]

If I were an American, as I am an Englishman, while a foreign troop was landed in my country, I never would

---

[1] This is the composition of Johnson, founded on some note or statement of the actual speech. Johnson said, "That speech I wrote in a garret, in Exeter Street." — BOSWELL, *Life of Johnson* [1791]
[2] See Lord Acton, p. 750a.
[3] See John Locke, p. 372b.
[4] Indemnity for the past and security for the future. — LORD JOHN RUSSELL, *Life and Times of Charles James Fox* [1859–1860], *vol. III, p. 345, letter to the Hon. T. Maitland*

lay down my arms, — never — never — never! You cannot conquer America.
Speech [*November 18, 1777*]

I invoke the genius of the Constitution.
Ib.

The poorest man may in his cottage bid defiance to all the forces of the Crown. It may be frail — its roof may shake — the wind may blow through it — the storm may enter — the rain may enter — but the King of England cannot enter — all his force dares not cross the threshold of the ruined tenement!
Speech on the Excise Bill

SAMUEL JOHNSON
1709–1784

Of all the griefs that harass the distrest,
Sure the most bitter is a scornful jest.
London [1738] (*An imitation of the Third Satire of Juvenal*), *l. 166*

This mournful truth is ev'rywhere confess'd —
Slow rises worth, by poverty depress'd. [1]
Ib. l. 176

When learning's triumph o'er her barb'rous foes
First rear'd the stage, immortal Shakespeare rose;
Each change of many-color'd life he drew,
Exhausted worlds, and then imagin'd new:
Existence saw him spurn her bounded reign,
And panting Time toil'd after him in vain.
Prologue at the Opening of Drury Lane Theatre [1747]

Cold approbation gave the ling'ring bays,
For those who durst not censure, scarce could praise.
Ib.

Declamation roar'd, while Passion slept.
Ib.

---

[1] Three years later Johnson wrote, "Mere unassisted merit advances slowly, if — what is not very common — it advances at all."

The wild vicissitudes of taste.
Prologue at the Opening of
Drury Lane Theatre

For we that live to please must please
to live.   *Ib.*

Studious to please, yet not ashamed to
fail.
Prologue to the Tragedy of Irene
[1749]

Let observation with extensive view
Survey mankind, from China to Peru.[1]
Vanity of Human Wishes
[1749], *l. 1*

Deign on the passing world to turn
thine eyes,
And pause a while from learning to be
wise.
There mark what ills the scholar's life
assail —
Toil, envy, want, the patron, and the
jail.   *Ib. l. 157*

A frame of adamant, a soul of fire,
No dangers fright him, and no labors
tire.   *Ib. l. 191*

He left the name at which the world
grew pale,
To point a moral, or adorn a tale.
Ib. l. 221

"Enlarge my life with multitude of
days!"
In health, in sickness, thus the sup-
pliant prays:
Hides from himself his state, and shuns
to know
That life protracted is protracted woe.
Ib. l. 255

Superfluous lags the vet'ran on the
stage.   *Ib. l. 308*

Must helpless man, in ignorance sedate,
Roll darkling down the torrent of his
fate?   *Ib. l. 345*

Secure, whate'er he gives, he gives the
best.   *Ib. l. 356*

[1] DE QUINCEY quotes with approval, but
without naming him, the criticism of a writer
who contends that this couplet amounts in
effect to this: "Let observation with extensive
observation observe mankind extensively." —
Rhetoric [1828]

With these celestial Wisdom calms the
mind,
And makes the happiness she does not
find.
Vanity of Human Wishes,
l. 367

Curiosity is one of the permanent
and certain characteristics of a vigorous
mind.
The Rambler [1] [*March 12, 1751*]

No place affords a more striking conviction of the vanity of human hopes
than a public library.
Ib. [*March 23, 1751*]

I am not so lost in lexicography as to
forget that *words are the daughters of*
earth, and that things are the sons of
heaven.[2]
Dictionary [1755], *preface*

CLUB — An assembly of good fellows, meeting under certain conditions.
Ib.

ESSAY — A loose sally of the mind;
an irregular indigested piece; not a regular and orderly composition.   *Ib.*

EXCISE — A hateful tax levied upon
commodities, and adjudged not by the
common judges of property, but
wretches hired by those to whom excise
is paid.   *Ib.*

GRUBSTREET — The name of a
street near Moorsfield, London, much
inhabited by writers of small histories,
dictionaries, and temporary poems.
Ib.

LEXICOGRAPHER — A writer of dictionaries, a harmless drudge.   *Ib.*

OATS — A grain which in England is
generally given to horses, but in Scotland supports the people.[3]   *Ib.*

[1] For the *Rambler* motto, see Johnson's translation of BOETHIUS, *De Consolatione Philoso-*
phiae III, 9, 27, p. 148a.
[2] See Herbert, p. 325a.
[3] It was pleasant to me to find, that "oats,"
the "food of horses," were so much used as
the food of the people in Dr. Johnson's own
town. — BOSWELL, *Life of Dr. Johnson* [1791],
vol. I, p. 628 [Everyman ed.]
I own that by my definition of *oats* I meant
to vex them [the Scotch]. — SAMUEL JOHNSON;
from Ib. II, 434

The joy of life is variety; the tenderest love requires to be renewed by intervals of absence.
The Idler [1758–1760], *no. 39*

He is no wise man that will quit a certainty for an uncertainty. *Ib. 57*

Ye who listen with credulity to the whispers of fancy, and pursue with eagerness the phantoms of hope; who expect that age will perform the promises of youth, and that the deficiencies of the present day will be supplied by the morrow; attend to the history of Rasselas, Prince of Abyssinia.
Rasselas [1759], *ch. 1*

To a poet nothing can be useless.
Ib. 10

Human life is everywhere a state in which much is to be endured and little to be enjoyed. *Ib. 11*

Marriage has many pains, but celibacy has no pleasures. *Ib. 26*

Example is always more efficacious than precept. *Ib. 29*

The endearing elegance of female friendship. *Ib. 45*

How small, of all that human hearts endure,
That part which laws or kings can cause or cure!
Still to ourselves in every place consign'd,
Our own felicity we make or find.
Lines added to GOLDSMITH's *Traveller* [1763–1764]

That man is little to be envied whose patriotism would not gain force upon the plain of Marathon, or whose piety would not grow warmer among the ruins of Iona.
Journey to the Western Islands [1775]. *Inch Kenneth*

Whoever wishes to attain an English style, familiar but not coarse, and elegant but not ostentatious, must give his days and nights to the volumes of Addison.
Lives of the Poets [1779–1781]. *Addison*

To be of no church is dangerous. Religion, of which the rewards are distant, and which is animated only by faith and hope, will glide by degrees out of the mind unless it be invigorated and reimpressed by external ordinances, by stated calls to worship, and the salutary influence of example. *Ib. Milton*

The father of English criticism.
Ib. Dryden

He delighted to tread upon the brink of meaning. *Ib.*

The *Churchyard* abounds with images which find a mirror in every mind, and with sentiments to which every bosom returns an echo. *Ib. Gray* [1]

His [Garrick's] death has eclipsed the gaiety of nations, and impoverished the public stock of harmless pleasure.
Ib. Edmund Smith

New things are made familiar, and familiar things are made new.
Ib. Pope

Tomorrow I purpose to regulate my room.
Prayers and Meditations [*published 1785*]. [1764]

Preserve me from unseasonable and immoderate sleep. *Ib.* [1767]

Every man naturally persuades himself that he can keep his resolutions, nor is he convinced of his imbecility but by length of time and frequency of experiment. *Ib.* [1770]

This world, where much is to be done and little to be known.
Ib. Against Inquisitive and Perplexing Thoughts

I have, all my life long, been lying till noon; yet I tell all young men, and tell them with great sincerity, that nobody

[1] See Gray, p. 440a.

who does not rise early will ever do any good.

> From BOSWELL, *Journal of a Tour to the Hebrides* [*published 1785*], [*September 14, 1773*]

Wickedness is always easier than virtue; for it takes the short cut to everything.　　*Ib.* [*September 17, 1773*]

Gratitude is a fruit of great cultivation; you do not find it among gross people.　　*Ib.* [*September 20, 1773*]

Here closed in death th' attentive eyes
That saw the manners in the face.
> *Epitaph on Hogarth* [1786]

When the hoary Sage replied,
"Come, my lad, and drink some beer."
> *From* MRS. PIOZZI, *Anecdotes of Samuel Johnson* [1786]

If the man who turnips cries,
Cry not when his father dies,
'Tis a proof that he had rather
Have a turnip than his father.[1]　　*Ib.*

He was a very good hater.　　*Ib.*

The law is the last result of human wisdom acting upon human experience for the benefit of the public.　　*Ib.*

The use of traveling is to regulate imagination by reality, and instead of thinking how things may be, to see them as they are.　　*Ib.*

Dictionaries are like watches; the worst is better than none, and the best cannot be expected to go quite true.
　　Ib.

Books that you may carry to the fire, and hold readily in your hand, are the most useful after all.
> *Apothegms from* HAWKINS, *Life of Johnson* [1787]

As with my hat [2] upon my head
I walk'd along the Strand,

---

[1] Burlesque of Lope de Vega's lines, "Se acquien los leones vence," etc.
[2] Elsewhere found, "I put my hat."

I there did meet another man
With his hat in his hand.[1]
> *Anecdotes of Johnson by* GEORGE STEEVENS

Abstinence is as easy to me as temperance would be difficult.
> *Anecdotes of Johnson by* HANNAH MORE

Boswell: That, sir, was great fortitude of mind.
Johnson: No, sir; stark insensibility.
> *From* BOSWELL, *Life of Johnson* [2] [*published 1791*], [*November 5, 1728*]

Sir, we are a nest of singing birds.[3]
　　Ib. [1730]

Tom Birch is as brisk as a bee in conversation; but no sooner does he take a pen in his hand than it becomes a torpedo to him, and benumbs all his faculties.　　*Ib.* [1743]

I'll come no more behind your scenes, David; [4] for the silk stockings and white bosoms of your actresses excite my amorous propensities.　　*Ib.* [1750]

A man may write at any time, if he will set himself doggedly to it.
　　Ib. [*March 1750*]

Wretched un-idea'd girls.
　　Ib. [1753]

Is not a patron, my lord, one who looks with unconcern on a man struggling for life in the water, and when he has reached ground encumbers him with help? The notice which you have been pleased to take of my labors, had it been early, had been kind; but it has been delayed till I am indifferent, and

---

[1] A parody on the ballad *The Hermit of Warkworth.*
[2] Edited by G. B. Hill and revised by L. F. Powell [1934].
　The *Life of Johnson* is assuredly a great, a very great work. Homer is not more decidedly the first of heroic poets, Shakespeare is not more decidedly the first of dramatists, Demosthenes is not more decidedly the first of orators, than Boswell is the first of biographers. He has no second. — MACAULAY, *Samuel Johnson* [1831]
[3] Of Pembroke College.
[4] David Garrick.

cannot enjoy it; till I am solitary, and cannot impart it; till I am known, and do not want it.[1]

> From BOSWELL, *Life of Johnson* [*Letter to Lord Chesterfield, February 7, 1754*]

[Of Lord Chesterfield] This man, I thought, had been a Lord among wits; but, I find, he is only a wit among Lords!　　　　　　　　*Ib.* [1754]

Sir, he [Bolingbroke] was a scoundrel, and a coward: a scoundrel, for charging a blunderbuss against religion and morality; a coward, because he had not resolution to fire it off himself, but left half a crown to a beggarly Scotchman to draw the trigger at his death.
> *Ib.* [*March 6, 1754*]

Ignorance, madame, pure ignorance.[2]
> *Ib.* [1755]

If a man does not make new acquaintances as he advances through life, he will soon find himself left alone. A man, sir, should keep his friendship in a constant repair.[3]　　*Ib.* [1755]

Towering in the confidence of twenty-one.　　　　*Ib.* [*January 9, 1758*]

Being in a ship is being in a jail, with the chance of being drowned.
> *Ib.* [*March 1759*]

Nothing is little to him that feels it with great sensibility.
> *Ib.* [*July 20, 1762*]

A man of genius has been seldom ruined but by himself.
> *Ib.* [*December 21, 1762*]

Sir, I think all Christians, whether Papists or Protestants, agree in the essential articles, and that their differences are trivial, and rather political than religious.[1]

> From BOSWELL, *Life of Johnson* [1763]

The noblest prospect which a Scotchman ever sees is the high-road that leads him to England!
> *Ib.* [*July 6, 1763*]

A man ought to read just as inclination leads him; for what he reads as a task will do him little good.[2]
> *Ib.* [*July 14, 1763*]

If he does really think that there is no distinction between virtue and vice, why, sir, when he leaves our houses let us count our spoons.　　　*Ib.*

Sir, your levelers wish to level *down* as far as themselves; but they cannot bear leveling *up* to themselves.
> *Ib.* [*July 21, 1763*]

Sherry[3] is dull, naturally dull; but it must have taken him a great deal of pains to become what we now see him. Such an excess of stupidity, sir, is not in Nature.　　　*Ib.* [*July 28, 1763*]

Sir, a woman preaching is like a dog's walking on his hind legs. It is not done well; but you are surprised to find it done at all.　*Ib.* [*July 31, 1763*]

I look upon it, that he who does not mind his belly will hardly mind anything else.　　*Ib.* [*August 5, 1763*]

---

[1] What is a Patron? Johnson knew,
And well that lifelike portrait drew.
He is a Patron who looks down
With careless eye on men who drown;
But if they chance to reach the land,
Encumbers them with helping hand.
　　　AUSTIN DOBSON [1840–1921], *The Noble Patron*

[2] When asked by a lady why he defined "pastern" as the "knee" of a horse in his Dictionary.

[3] Keep your friendships in repair. — EMERSON, *Uncollected Lectures: Table Talk*

[1] See first excerpt for 1772.
I do not find that the age or country makes the least difference; no, nor the language the actor spoke, nor the religion which they professed — whether Arab in the desert, or Frenchman in the Academy. I see that sensible men and conscientious men all over the world were of one religion of well-doing and daring. — EMERSON, *Lectures and Biographical Sketches* [1884]. *The Preacher*
See Disraeli, p. 613a.

[2] The book which you read from a sense of duty, or because for any reason you must, does not commonly make friends with you. — WILLIAM DEAN HOWELLS, *My Literary Passions* [1895], ch. 7

[3] Thomas Sheridan [1719–1788], actor, lecturer, and author.

This was a good dinner enough, to be sure, but it was not a dinner to *ask* a man to.

From BOSWELL, *Life of Johnson* [*August 5, 1763*]

The gloomy calm of idle vacancy.[1]

Ib. [*December 8, 1763*]

[Of Sir John Hawkins] A very unclubable man. *Ib.* [*1764*]

It matters not how a man dies, but how he lives.

Ib. [*October 26, 1769*]

That fellow seems to me to possess but one idea, and that is a wrong one.[2]

Ib. [*1770*]

A gentleman who had been very unhappy in marriage, married immediately after his wife died: Johnson said, it was the triumph of hope over experience. *Ib.*

A decent provision for the poor is the true test of civilization.[3] *Ib.*

All denominations of Christians have really little difference in point of doctrine, though they may differ widely in external forms.[4] *Ib.* [*1772*]

Nobody can write the life of a man, but those who have eat and drunk and lived in social intercourse with him.[5]

Ib. [*March 31, 1772*]

I am a great friend to public amusements; for they keep people from vice.

Ib.

A cow is a very good animal in the field; but we turn her out of a garden.

Ib. [*April 15, 1772*]

Much may be made of a Scotchman if he be caught young.[1]

From BOSWELL, *Life of Johnson* [*Spring 1772*]

It is a foolish thing well done.[2]

Ib. [*April 3, 1773*]

No, sir, do *you* read books *through*? [3]

Ib. [*April 19, 1773*]

An old tutor of a college said to one of his pupils: Read over your compositions, and wherever you meet with a passage which you think is particularly fine, strike it out.[4]

Ib. [*April 30, 1773*]

You are the most unscottified of your countrymen. *Ib.* [*May 1, 1773*]

The woman's a whore, and there's an end on 't.[5] *Ib.* [*May 7, 1773*]

Was ever poet so trusted before? [6]

Ib. [*July 4, 1774*]

Attack is the re-action; I never think I have hit hard unless it rebounds.

Ib. [*April 2, 1775*]

Most vices may be committed very genteelly: a man may debauch his friend's wife genteelly: he may cheat at cards genteelly. *Ib.* [*April 6, 1775*]

A man will turn over half a library to make one book. *Ib.*

Patriotism is the last refuge of a scoundrel. *Ib.* [*April 7, 1775*]

That is the happiest conversation where there is no competition, no vanity, but a calm quiet interchange of sentiments. *Ib.* [*April 14, 1775*]

Knowledge is of two kinds. We know a subject ourselves, or we know where we can find information upon it.

Ib. [*April 18, 1775*]

In lapidary inscriptions a man is not upon oath. *Ib.* [*1775*]

---

[1] See Cowper, p. 458b.
[2] See Disraeli, p. 612a.
[3] See Spinoza, p. 374a, and Andrew Carnegie, p. 757b.
[4] See first entry for 1763.
[5] They only who live with a man can write his life with any genuine exactness and discrimination; and few people who have lived with a man know what to remark about him. — *vol. I, 617* (Everyman ed.)

[1] Of Lord Mansfield, educated in England.
[2] Of Goldsmith's apology in the *London Chronicle* for beating Evans the bookseller.
[3] Upon being asked by Elphinstone if he had read a new book through.
[4] See Sydney Smith, p. 523b.
[5] Of Lady Diana Beauclerk, divorced.
[6] Of Oliver Goldsmith.

There is nothing which has yet been contrived by man by which so much happiness is produced as by a good tavern or inn.[1]

> *From* BOSWELL, *Life of Johnson* [*March 21, 1776*]

No man but a blockhead ever wrote except for money. *Ib.* [*April 5, 1776*]

Life is a progress from want to want, not from enjoyment to enjoyment.
> *Ib.* [*May 1776*]

Sir, you have but two topics, yourself and me. I am sick of both. *Ib.*

Olivarii Goldsmith, Poetae, Physici, Historici, qui nullum fere scribendi genus non tetigit, Nullum quod tetigit non ornavit [To Oliver Goldsmith, Poet, Naturalist, Historian, who left scarcely any style of writing untouched, and touched nothing that he did not adorn].
> *Ib. Epitaph on Goldsmith* [*June 22, 1776*]

Life admits not of delays; when pleasure can be had, it is fit to catch it. Every hour takes away part of the things that please us, and perhaps part of our disposition to be pleased.
> *Ib.* [*September 1, 1777*]

Depend upon it, sir, when a man knows he is to be hanged in a fortnight, it concentrates his mind wonderfully.
> *Ib.* [*September 19, 1777*]

When a man is tired of London, he is tired of life; for there is in London all that life can afford.
> *Ib.* [*September 20, 1777*]

[1] Whoe'er has travel'd life's dull round,
Whate'er his various tour has been,
May sigh to think how oft he found
His warmest welcome at an inn.
WILLIAM SHENSTONE [1714–1763]; *written on a window of an inn at Henley.* Quoted not quite correctly by Johnson following his remark. ROBERT LEIGHTON [1611–1684], Archbishop of Glasgow, often said that if he were to choose

It is a man's own fault, it is from want of use, if his mind grows torpid in old age.
> *From* BOSWELL, *Life of Johnson* [*April 9, 1778*]

Johnson had said that he could repeat a complete chapter of *The Natural History of Iceland*, from the Danish of Horrebow, the whole of which was exactly thus: "Ch. LXXII. *Concerning snakes.* There are no snakes to be met with throughout the whole island." [1]
> *Ib.* [*April 13, 1778*]

Every state of society is as luxurious as it can be. Men always take the best they can get. *Ib.* [*April 14, 1778*]

A country governed by a despot is an inverted cone. *Ib.*

I am willing to love all mankind, except an American.
> *Ib.* [*April 15, 1778*]

Pleasure of itself is not a vice.
> *Ib.*

As the Spanish proverb says, "He, who would bring home the wealth of the Indies, must carry the wealth of the Indies with him," so it is in traveling, a man must carry knowledge with him if he would bring home knowledge.
> *Ib.* [*April 17, 1778*]

It is better to live rich, than to die rich.[2] *Ib.*

Were it not for imagination, sir, a man would be as happy in the arms of a chambermaid as a duchess.
> *Ib.* [*May 9, 1778*]

I would rather be attacked than unnoticed. For the worst thing you can do to an author is to be silent as to his works. *Ib.* [*March 26, 1779*]

a place to die in, it should be an inn. — *Works, vol. I, p. 76*
See the Archpoet, p. 154b.
[1] Chapter XLII is still shorter: "There are no owls of any kind in the whole island."
[2] See Robert Frost, p. 928b.

I remember a passage in Goldsmith's *Vicar of Wakefield*, which he was afterwards a fool enough to expunge: "I do not love a man who is zealous for nothing."

From BOSWELL, *Life of Johnson* [*March 26, 1779*]

Claret is the liquor for boys; port for men; but he who aspires to be a hero must drink brandy.

Ib. [*April 7, 1779*]

Worth seeing? yes; but not worth going to see. *Ib.* [*October 12, 1779*]

If you are idle, be not solitary; if you are solitary, be not idle.[1]

Ib. [*October 27, 1779*]

A Frenchman must be always talking, whether he knows anything of the matter or not; an Englishman is content to say nothing, when he has nothing to say. *Ib.* [*1780*]

Greek, sir, is like lace; every man gets as much of it as he can. *Ib.*

[Of Oliver Goldsmith] No man was more foolish when he had not a pen in his hand, or more wise when he had.

Ib.

The applause of a single human being is of great consequence. *Ib.*

Come to me, my dear Bozzy, and let us be as happy as we can.

Ib. [*March 14, 1781*]

There are people whom one should like very well to drop, but would not wish to be dropped by.

Ib. [*March 1781*]

We are not here to sell a parcel of boilers and vats, but the potentiality of growing rich beyond the dreams of avarice.[2] *Ib.* [*April 4, 1781*]

Classical quotation is the *parole* of literary men all over the world.

From BOSWELL, *Life of Johnson* [*May 8, 1781*]

My friend was of opinion that when a man of rank appeared in that character [as an author], he deserved to have his merit handsomely allowed.[1]

Ib. [*May 1781*]

A jest breaks no bones.

Ib. [*June 4, 1781*]

Officious, innocent, sincere,
Of every friendless name the friend.

Ib. [*January 20, 1782; on the death of Robert Levett*]

To let friendship die away by negligence and silence, is certainly not wise. It is voluntarily to throw away one of the greatest comforts of this weary pilgrimage. *Ib.* [*March 20, 1782*]

Whatever you have, spend less.

Ib. [*December 7, 1782*]

I never have sought the world; the world was not to seek me.[2]

Ib. [*March 23, 1783*]

He is not only dull himself, but the cause of dullness in others.[3] *Ib.* [*1783*]

Clear your mind of cant.[4]

Ib. [*May 15, 1783*]

Who drives fat oxen should himself be fat.[5] *Ib.* [*June 1784*]

I have found you an argument; I am not obliged to find you an understanding. *Ib.*

Blown about by every wind of criticism.[6] *Ib.*

Don't attitudenize. *Ib.*

---

[1] "The great direction which Burton has left to men disordered like you, is this: Be not solitary, be not idle." — *Ib.*
See Burton, p. 312a.
[2] See Edward Moore, p. 435b.

[1] Usually quoted as: When a nobleman writes a book, he ought to be encouraged.
See Somerville, p. 397a.
[2] See Byron, p. 556b, and Emerson, p. 601b.
[3] See Shakespeare, p. 241b.
[4] See Carlyle, p. 576b.
[5] Parody on: Who rules o'er freemen should himself be free. — BROOKE, *Gustavus Vasa* [1739]
[6] See *Ephesians 4:14*, p. 54a.

I look upon every day to be lost, in
which I do not make a new acquaintance.

> *From* BOSWELL, *Life of
> Johnson* [*November 1784*]

God bless you, my dear!

> *Ib.* [*December 13, 1784; his last
> words*]

JULIEN OFFRAY DE
LA METTRIE
1709–1751

The human body is a watch, a large
watch constructed with . . . skill and
ingenuity.

> *L'Homme Machine* [1748] [1]

GEORGE, LORD
LYTTELTON
1709–1773

Women, like princes, find few real
friends.

> *Advice to a Lady*

What is your sex's earliest, latest care,
Your heart's supreme ambition? To be
fair.   *Ib.*

The lover in the husband may be lost.
                                         Ib.

Where none admire, 'tis useless to excel;
Where none are beaux, 'tis vain to be a
belle.

> *Soliloquy on a Beauty in the
> Country*

THEODORE TRONCHIN
1709–1781

In medicine, sins of commission are
mortal, sins of omission venial.

> *Quoted in Bulletin of New York
> Academy of Medicine*, V [1929],
> *151*

[1] *Man a Machine.* Translated by M. W.
CALKINS, 1912.

OLIVER EDWARDS
1711–1791

I have tried too in my time to be a
philosopher; but I don't know how,
cheerfulness was always breaking in.

> [*April 17, 1778*] *From* BOSWELL,
> *Life of Johnson* [1791]

DAVID HUME
1711–1776

Avarice, the spur of industry.

> *Essays* [1741–1742]. *Of Civil
> Liberty*

Beauty in things exists in the mind
which contemplates them.[1]

> *Ib. Of Tragedy*

Custom, then, is the great guide of
human life.

> *An Enquiry Concerning Human
> Understanding* [1748], *pt.* 1

No testimony is sufficient to establish
a miracle, unless the testimony be of
such a kind that its falsehood would be
more miraculous than the fact which it
endeavors to establish.

> *Ib. Of Miracles*

Opposing one species of superstition
to another, set them a-quarreling; while
we ourselves, during their fury and contention, happily make our escape into
the calm, though obscure, regions of
philosophy.

> *The Natural History of Religion*
> [1757]

Never literary attempt was more unfortunate than my Treatise of Human
Nature. It fell dead-born from the
press.   *My Own Life* [1777], *ch.* 1

MIKHAIL LOMONOSOV[2]
1711–1765

Carolus V,[3] Emperor of Rome, was
wont to say that the Hispanic tongue
was seemly for converse with God, the

[1] See Wallace, p. 729b, and Hungerford, p.
831b.
[2] Lomonosov created our first university. To
put it better, he himself was our first university. — ALEXANDER PUSHKIN, *The Trip from
Moscow to Petersburg* [1834]
[3] See Charles V, p. 186a.

French with friends, the German with enemies, the Italian with the feminine sex. Had he been versed in the Russian tongue, however, he would of a certainty have added to this that it is appropriate to converse with all of the above, inasmuch as he would have found in it the magnificence of the Hispanic tongue, the sprightliness of the French, the sturdiness of the German, the tenderness of the Italian and, over and above all that, the richness and conciseness of powerful imagery, of the Greek and Latin tongues.

Russian Grammar [1] [1755]

FREDERICK THE GREAT
1712–1786

By push of bayonets, no firing till you see the whites of their eyes.[2]

At Prague [May 6, 1757]

Rascals, would you live forever? [3]

When the Guards hesitated at Kolin [June 18, 1757]

The prince is the first servant of his state.

Memoirs of the House of Brandenburg [1758]

God is always with the strongest battalions.[4]

Letter to the Duchess Luise Dorothea von Gotha [May 8, 1760]

I am tired of ruling over slaves.

Last words [April 1, 1786]

GEORGE GRENVILLE
1712–1770

A wise government knows how to enforce with temper or to conciliate with dignity.

Speech against expulsion of John Wilkes, in Parliament [1769]

---

[1] Translated by B. G. GUERNEY.
[2] See William Prescott, p. 446b.
[3] Ihr Racker, wollt ihr ewig leben?
　That sergeant at Belleau Woods . . .
　"Come on, you . . . Do you want to live forever?"
　　　　　SANDBURG, *Losers* [*1921*]
[4] See Bussy-Rabutin, p. 357a, and note.

EDWARD MOORE
1712–1757

This is adding insult to injury.[1]

The Foundling [1748], act V, sc. 2

I am rich beyond the dreams of avarice.[2]

The Gamester [1753], act II, sc. 2

JEAN JACQUES ROUSSEAU
1712–1778

The first man who, having fenced in a piece of land, said, "This is mine," and found people naïve enough to believe him, that man was the true founder of civil society.

Discours sur l'Origine et le Fondement de l'Inégalité parmi les Hommes [1754]

Never exceed your rights, and they will soon become unlimited. *Ib.*

Money is the seed of money, and the first guinea is sometimes more difficult to acquire than the second million. *Ib.*

Man is born free, and everywhere he is in chains.[3]

Du Contrat Social [1762], I, ch. 1

The strongest is never strong enough to be always the master, unless he transforms his strength into right, and obedience into duty. *Ib. 3*

The right of conquest has no foundation other than the right of the strongest. *Ib. 4*

In the strict sense of the term, a true democracy has never existed, and never will exist. *Ib. III, 4*

The body politic, like the human body, begins to die from its birth, and bears in itself the causes of its destruction. *Ib. 11*

---

[1] See Phaedrus, p. 129b.
[2] See Johnson, p. 433a.
[3] L'homme est né libre, et partout il est dans les fers.
See Bliss, p. 468b, and Schiller, p. 497b.

Good laws lead to the making of better ones; bad ones bring about worse.
                    Du Contrat Social, III, 15

Everything is good when it leaves the hands of the Creator; everything degenerates in the hands of man.
                    Émile, ou de l'education [1762], I

I shall always maintain that whoso says in his heart, "There is no God," while he takes the name of God upon his lips, is either a liar or a madman.
                    Ib.

People who know little are usually great talkers, while men who know much say little.   *Ib.*

What wisdom can you find that is greater than kindness?   *Ib. II*

Nature never deceives us; it is always we who deceive ourselves.   *Ib. III*

There exists one book, which, to my taste, furnishes the happiest treatise of natural education. What then is this marvelous book? Is it Aristotle? Is it Pliny, is it Buffon? No — it is *Robinson Crusoe*.   *Ib.*

Self-love makes more libertines than love.   *Ib. IV*

Provided a man is not mad, he can be cured of every folly but vanity.
                    Ib.

A man says what he knows, a woman says what will please.   *Ib. V*

Where is the man who owes nothing to the land in which he lives? Whatever that land may be, he owes to it the most precious thing possessed by man, the morality of his actions and the love of virtue.[1]   *Ib.*

I have entered on an enterprise which is without precedent, and will have no imitator. I propose to show my

[1] See John F. Kennedy, p. 1073a, and note.

fellows a man as nature made him, and this man shall be myself.
                    Les Confessions [1781–1788], I

Remorse sleeps during a prosperous period but wakes up in adversity.
                    Ib. II

It is too difficult to think nobly when one only thinks to get a living.
                    Ib. II

Hatred, as well as love, renders its votaries credulous.   **Ib. V**

At length I recollected the thoughtless saying of a great princess, who, on being informed that the country people had no bread, replied, "Let them eat cake." [1]   **Ib. VI**

The thirst after happiness is never extinguished in the heart of man.
                    Ib. IX

He [2] thinks like a philosopher, but governs like a King.   *Ib. XII*

JOSIAH TUCKER, DEAN OF GLOUCESTER
1712–1799

What is true of a shopkeeper is true of a shopkeeping nation.[3]
                    *Tract Against Going to War for
                    the Sake of Trade* [1763]

ALISON COCKBURN
1713–1794

I've seen the smiling of Fortune beguiling,

[1] *Qu'ils mangent de la brioche.*
This remark is usually attributed to Marie Antoinette, after her arrival in France in 1770, but the sixth book of the *Confessions* was written two or three years before that date.
[2] Frederick the Great, King of Prussia [1740–1786]
[3] See Adam Smith, p. 445a.
Let Pitt then boast of his victory to his nation of shopkeepers. — BERTRAND BARÈRE, *Speech* [June 11, 1794]
But it may be said as a rule, that every Englishman in the Duke of Wellington's army paid his way. The remembrance of such a fact surely becomes a nation of shopkeepers. — THACKERAY, *Vanity Fair* [1847–1848], *vol. I, ch. 28*

I've felt all its favors and found its decay.
>   *The Flowers of the Forest*

The flowers of the forest are withered away.[1]
>   *Ib.*

DENIS DIDEROT
1713–1784

My thoughts are my trollops.[2]
>   *Le Neveu de Rameau, ch. 1*

I can be expected to look for truth but not to find it.
>   *Pensées Philosophiques* [1746],
>   *no. 29*

L'esprit de l'escalier [staircase wit].[3]
>   *Paradoxe sur le Comédien*

From fanaticism to barbarism is only one step.
>   *Essai sur le Mérite de la Vertu*

LAURENCE STERNE
1713–1768

Only the brave know how to forgive.
. . . A coward never forgave; it is not in his nature.
>   *Sermons, vol. I* [1760], *no. 12*

This sad vicissitude of things.[4]
>   *Ib. 15*

I wish either my father or my mother, or indeed both of them, as they were in duty both equally bound to it, had minded what they were about when they begot me.
>   *Tristram Shandy, bk. I* [1760],
>   *ch. 1*

"Pray, my dear," quoth my mother, "have you not forgot to wind up the clock?" — "Good G—!" cried my father, making an exclamation, but taking care to moderate his voice at the same time — "Did ever woman, since the creation of the world, interrupt a man with such a silly question?"
>   *Tristram Shandy, bk. I, ch. 1*

So long as a man rides his hobby-horse peaceably and quietly along the king's highway, and neither compels you or me to get up behind him — pray, sir, what have either you or I to do with it?
>   *Ib. 7*

For every ten jokes, thou hast got an hundred enemies.
>   *Ib. 12*

He was within a few hours of giving his enemies the slip forever.
>   *Ib.*

Whistled up to London, upon a Tom Fool's errand.
>   *Ib. 16*

'Tis known by the name of perseverance in a good cause — and of obstinacy in a bad one.
>   *Ib. 17*

Persuasion hung upon his lips.
>   *Ib. 19*

Digressions, incontestably, are the sunshine — they are the life, the soul of reading; take them out of this book for instance — you might as well take the book along with them.
>   *Ib. 22*

The history of a soldier's wound beguiles the pain of it.
>   *Ib. 25*

The desire of knowledge, like the thirst of riches, increases ever with the acquisition of it.   *Ib. II* [1760], *ch. 3*

Writing, when properly managed (as you may be sure I think mine is), is but a different name for conversation.
>   *Ib. 11*

Go, poor devil, get thee gone! Why should I hurt thee? This world surely is wide enough to hold both thee and me.[1]
>   *Ib. 12*

That's another story,[2] replied my father.
>   *Ib. 17*

---

[1] See Jane Elliott, p. 446b.
[2] Mes pensées sont mes catins.
[3] The witty retort thought up after the conversation is finished and one is on one's way downstairs.
[4] See Bacon, p. 209b.
Revolves the sad vicissitude of things. — REV. RICHARD GIFFORD [1725-1807], *Contemplation*

[1] Uncle Toby to the fly.
[2] But that is another story. — KIPLING, *Plain Tales from the Hills* [1888], *Three and — An Extra*

Trust that man in nothing who has not a conscience in everything.
Tristram Shandy, bk. II, ch. 17

Good — bad — indifferent.
Ib. III [1761–1762], *ch.* 2

"Our armies swore terribly in Flanders," cried my uncle Toby — "but nothing to this." *Ib.* 11

Of all the cants which are canted in this canting world, though the cant of hypocrites may be the worst, the cant of criticism is the most tormenting!
Ib. 12

'Twould be as much as my life was worth. *Ib.* 20

One of the two horns of my dilemma. *Ib. IV* [1761–1762], *ch.* 26

The feather put into his cap of having been abroad. *Ib.* 31

Now or never was the time. *Ib.*

There is a Northwest Passage to the intellectual world.
Ib. V [1761–1762], *ch.* 42

The Accusing Spirit, which flew up to heaven's chancery with the oath, blushed as he gave it in; and the Recording Angel, as he wrote it down, dropped a tear upon the word and blotted it out forever.[1]
Ib. VI [1761–1762], *ch.* 8

A man should know something of his own country, too, before he goes abroad. *Ib. VII* [1765], *ch.* 2

Ho! 'tis the time of salads. *Ib.* 17

L — d! said my mother, what is all this story about? — A Cock and a Bull, said Yorick. *Ib. IX* [1767], *ch.* 33

They order, said I, this matter better in France.
A Sentimental Journey [1768], *l.* 1

I pity the man who can travel from

Dan to Beersheba and cry, 'Tis all barren!
A Sentimental Journey. In the Street, Calais

Tant pis and *tant mieux*, being two of the great hinges in French conversation, a stranger would do well to set himself right in the use of them before he gets to Paris. *Ib. Montreuil*

Hail, ye small, sweet courtesies of life! for smooth do ye make the road of it. *Ib. The Pulse, Paris*

God tempers the wind, said Maria, to the shorn lamb.[1] *Ib. Maria*

CHRISTIAN FÜRCHTEGOTT GELLERT
1715–1769

Live as you will have wished to have lived when you are dying.[2]
Of Death, st. 2

CLAUDE ADRIEN HELVÉTIUS
1715–1771

Truth is a torch that gleams through the fog without dispelling it.
De l'Esprit [1758],[3] *preface*

What makes men happy is liking what they have to do. This is a principle on which society is not founded.
Ib.

We don't call a man mad who believes that he eats God, but we do the one who says he is Jesus Christ. *Ib.*

LUC DE CLAPIERS, MARQUIS DE VAUVENARGUES
1715–1747

Great thoughts come from the heart.
Réflexions et Maximes, [c. 1747] *no.* 127

[1] But sad as angels for the good man's sin, Weep to record, and blush to give it in.
CAMPBELL, *Pleasures of Hope* [1799], *pt. II, l. 357*

[2] See Henri Estienne, p. 188b.
[2] See Jonathan Edwards, p. 420b.
[3] Voltaire, when he read *De l'Esprit*, wrote the author: "Your book is dictated by the soundest reason. You had better get out of France as quickly as you can." The book was condemned by the *parlement* and burned.

Lazy people are always looking for something to do.
Réflexions et Maximes, no. 458

The things we know best are those we have not learned. *Ib. 479*

WILLIAM WHITEHEAD
1715–1785

Yes, I'm in love, I feel it now
And Caelia has undone me;
And yet I swear I can't tell how
The pleasing plague stole on me.
The Je ne sçay quoi song

An old tale which every schoolboy knows.
The Roman Father, prologue

DAVID GARRICK
1716–1779

Let others hail the rising sun:
I bow to that whose course is run.[1]
On the Death of Mr. Pelham

Heart of oak are our ships,
Heart of oak are our men:
We always are ready;
Steady, boys, steady;
We'll fight, and we'll conquer again and again.
Heart of Oak [c. 1770]

Here lies Nolly Goldsmith, for shortness called Noll,
Who wrote like an angel, but talk'd like poor Poll.
Impromptu epitaph on Goldsmith

THOMAS GRAY
1716–1771

Ye distant spires, ye antique towers,
That crown the wat'ry glade.
On a Distant Prospect of Eton College [1742], st. 1

Still as they run they look behind,
They hear a voice in every wind,
And snatch a fearful joy. *Ib. st. 4*

Alas, regardless of their doom,
The little victims play!

[1] See Pompey, p. 112a.

No sense have they of ills to come,
Nor care beyond today.
On a Distant Prospect of Eton College, st. 6

Grim-visag'd comfortless Despair.
Ib. st. 7

To each his suff'rings: all are men,
Condemn'd alike to groan,
The tender for another's pain,
Th' unfeeling for his own.
Yet ah! why should they know their fate,
Since sorrow never comes too late,
And happiness too swiftly flies?
Thought would destroy their paradise.
No more; where ignorance is bliss,
'Tis folly to be wise.[1] *Ib. st. 10*

Daughter of Jove, relentless power,
Thou tamer of the human breast,
Whose iron scourge and tort'ring hour
The bad affright, afflict the best!
Hymn to Adversity [1742], st. 1

What sorrow was, thou bad'st her know,
And from her own she learn'd to melt at others' woe. *Ib. st. 2*

What female heart can gold despise?
What cat's averse to fish?
On the Death of a Favorite Cat [1747], st. 4

A fav'rite has no friend! *Ib. st. 6*

As sickly plants betray a niggard earth,
Whose barren bosom starves her gen'rous birth.
The Alliance of Education and Government [c. 1748], l. 1

The social smile, the sympathetic tear.
Ib. l. 37

When love could teach a monarch to be wise,
And gospel-light first dawn'd from Bullen's eyes.[2] *Ib. l. 108*

The curfew tolls the knell of parting day,

[1] See *Ecclesiastes 1:18*, p. 27b.
[2] The monarch is Henry VIII; Anne Boleyn's name is here spelled (as it is in Shakespeare's *Henry VIII*) as it is pronounced.

The lowing herd wind slowly o'er the
    lea,
The plowman homeward plods his
    weary way,
And leaves the world to darkness and to
    me.
        Elegy Written in a Country
           Churchyard [1750], *st. 1*

Now fades the glimmering landscape on
    the sight,
And all the air a solemn stillness holds,
Save where the beetle wheels his dron-
    ing flight,
And drowsy tinklings lull the distant
    folds.   *Ib. st. 2*

Save that from yonder ivy-mantled
    tow'r
The moping owl does to the moon
    complain.   *Ib. st. 3*

Each in his narrow cell forever laid,
The rude forefathers of the hamlet
    sleep.   *Ib. st. 4*

The breezy call of incense-breathing
    Morn.   *Ib. st. 5*

For them no more the blazing hearth
    shall burn,
Or busy housewife ply her evening
    care.[1]   *Ib. st. 6*

Let not ambition mock their useful toil,
Their homely joys, and destiny obscure;
Nor grandeur hear with a disdainful
    smile,
The short and simple annals of the
    poor.   *Ib. st. 8*

The boast of heraldry, the pomp of
    pow'r,
And all that beauty, all that wealth e'er
    gave,
Awaits alike the inevitable hour:
The paths of glory lead but to the
    grave.   *Ib. st. 9*

Where thro' the long-drawn aisle and
    fretted vault
The pealing anthem swells the note of
    praise.   *Ib. st. 10*

Can storied urn, or animated bust
Back to its mansion call the fleeting
    breath?

[1] See Homer, p. 63a.

Can honor's voice provoke the silent
    dust,
Or flatt'ry soothe the dull cold ear of
    death?
        Elegy Written in a Country
           Churchyard, st. 11

Hands, that the rod of empire might
    have sway'd,
Or wak'd to ecstasy the living lyre.
              Ib. st. 12

But knowledge to their eyes her ample
    page
Rich with the spoils of time did ne'er
    unroll; [1]
Chill penury repress'd their noble rage,
And froze the genial current of the
    soul.   *Ib. st. 13*

Full many a gem of purest ray serene,[2]
The dark unfathom'd caves of ocean
    bear:
Full many a flower is born to blush un-
    seen,
And waste its sweetness on the desert
    air.   *Ib. st. 14*

Some village Hampden, that with
    dauntless breast
The little tyrant of his fields withstood;
Some mute inglorious Milton here may
    rest,
Some Cromwell guiltless of his coun-
    try's blood.   *Ib. st. 15*

To scatter plenty o'er a smiling land,
And read their hist'ry in a nation's eyes.
             Ib. st. 16

Forbade to wade through slaughter to a
    throne,
And shut the gates of mercy on man-
    kind.   *Ib. st. 17*

Far from the madding crowd's ignoble
    strife,
Their sober wishes never learn'd to
    stray;
Along the cool sequester'd vale of life

[1] See Sir Thomas Browne, p. 329b.
[2] Every single phrase is a string of perfect
gems, of purest ray serene, strung together on a
loose golden thread. — GEORGE DU MAURIER,
Trilby, pt. VI [1894]
  See Joseph Hall, p. 309b.

They kept the noiseless tenor of their
way.[1]
> *Elegy Written in a Country
> Churchyard, st. 19*

Implores the passing tribute of a sigh.
> *Ib. st. 20*

For who to dumb forgetfulness a prey,
This pleasing anxious being e'er resign'd,
Left the warm precincts of the cheerful
day,
Nor cast one longing ling'ring look behind?   *Ib. st. 22*

E'en from the tomb the voice of nature
cries,
E'en in our ashes live their wonted
fires.[2]   *Ib. st. 23*

Mindful of th' unhonor'd dead.
> *Ib. st. 24*

Here rests his head upon the lap of
Earth
A youth to fortune and to fame un-
known.
Fair Science frown'd not on his humble
birth,
And Melancholy mark'd him for her
own.[3]   *Ib. The Epitaph, st. 1*

Large was his bounty, and his soul sincere,
Heav'n did a recompense as largely
send:
He gave to mis'ry all he had, a tear,
He gained from Heav'n ('twas all he
wish'd) a friend.   *Ib. st. 2*

No farther seek his merits to disclose,
Or draw his frailties from their dread
abode,
(There they alike in trembling hope re-
pose,)
The bosom of his Father and his God.
> *Ib. st. 3*

The meanest floweret of the vale,
The simplest note that swells the gale,
The common sun, the air, the skies,

To him are opening paradise.
> *Ode on the Pleasure Arising
> from Vicissitude [1754], l. 49*

O'er her warm cheek and rising bosom
move
The bloom of young Desire and purple
light of Love.
> *The Progress of Poesy [1754],
> I. 3, l. 16*

Far from the sun and summer-gale,
In thy green lap was Nature's Darling [1]
laid.   *Ib. III. 1, l. 1*

Or ope the sacred source of sympathetic
tears.   *Ib. l. 12*

He [2] pass'd the flaming bounds of place
and time:
The living throne, the sapphire-blaze,
Where angels tremble, while they gaze,
He saw; but blasted with excess of
light,
Closed his eyes in endless night.
> *Ib. 2, l. 4*

Thoughts that breathe, and words that
burn.   *Ib. 3, l. 4*

Ruin seize thee, ruthless King!
Confusion on thy banners wait,
Though fann'd by Conquest's crimson
wing
They mock the air with idle state.
> *The Bard [1757], I. 1, l. 1*

Weave the warp, and weave the woof,
The winding-sheet of Edward's race.
Give ample room and verge enough,
The characters of hell to trace.
> *Ib. II. 1, l. 1*

Fair laughs the morn, and soft the
zephyr blows,
While proudly riding o'er the azure
realm
In gallant trim the gilded vessel goes;
Youth on the prow, and Pleasure at the
helm;
Regardless of the sweeping whirlwind's
sway,
That, hush'd in grim repose, expects his
evening prey.   *Ib. 2, l. 9*

---

[1]   In sober state,
Through the sequestered vale of rural life,
The venerable patriarch guileless held
The tenor of his way.
> PORTEUS [1731–1808], *Death, l. 108*
[2] See Chaucer, p. 167b.
[3] See Walton, p. 325b.

[1] Shakespeare.
[2] Milton.

Visions of glory, spare my aching sight,
Ye unborn ages, crowd not on my soul!
         The Bard III. 1, *l.* 11

And truth severe, by fairy fiction drest.
         Ib. 3, *l.* 3

Now my weary lips I close;
Leave me, leave me to repose!
         Descent of Odin [1761], *l.* 71

Iron sleet of arrowy shower
Hurtles in the darken'd air.
         The Fatal Sisters [1761]

Too poor for a bribe, and too proud to
    importune,
He had not the method of making a
    fortune.
         On His Own Character [1761]

I shall be but a shrimp of an author.
         Letter to Horace Walpole
         [*February 25, 1768*]

Sweet is the breath of vernal shower,
The bee's collected treasures sweet,
Sweet music's melting fall, but sweeter
    yet
The still small voice [1] of gratitude.
         Ode for Music [1769]

HORACE WALPOLE
1717–1797

Our supreme governors, the mob.
         Letters. To Horace Mann
         [*September 7, 1743*]

Every drop of ink in my pen ran
cold.
         Ib. To George Montagu
         [*July 3, 1752*]

It is charming to totter into vogue.
         Ib. To G. A. Selwyn
         [*December 2, 1765*]

The next Augustan age will dawn on
the other side of the Atlantic. There
will, perhaps, be a Thucydides at Boston, a Xenophon at New York, and, in
time, a Virgil at Mexico, and a Newton
at Peru. At last, some curious traveler
from Lima will visit England and give a
description of the ruins of St. Paul's,

---

[1] See *I Kings 19:12,* p. 13b.

like the editions of Balbec and Palmyra.[1]
         Ib. To Mann [*November 24,*
         1774]

This world is a comedy to those that
think, a tragedy to those that feel.
         Ib. To the Countess of Upper
         Ossory [*August 16, 1776*]

Prognostics do not always prove
prophecies — at least the wisest prophets make sure of the event first.
         Ib. To Thomas Walpole
         [*February 19, 1785*]

All his [Sir Joshua Reynolds's] own
geese are swans, as the swans of others
are geese.   *Ib.* [*December 1, 1786*]

JOHANN ELIAS SCHLEGEL
1719–1749

Busy leisure.
         Der Geschäftige Müssiggänger
         [1743]

SAMUEL FOOTE
1720–1777

Born in a cellar . . . and living in a
garret.[2]   *The Author, act II*

Matt Minikin won't set fire to the
Thames though he lives near the
Bridge.
         Trip to Calais [1776]

So she went into the garden to cut a
cabbage leaf to make an apple pie; and
at the same time a great she-bear, coming up the street, pops its head into the
shop. "What! no soap?" So he died,
and she very imprudently married the
barber; and there were present the Pic-
ninnies, and the Joblillies, and the
Garyalies, and the grand Panjandrum
himself, with the little round button at
top, and they all fell to playing the
game of catch as catch can, till the

---

[1] See Macaulay, p. 595b.
[2] Born in the garret, in the kitchen bred. —
BYRON, *A Sketch* [1816]

gunpowder ran out at the heels of their boots.

> *Nonsense written to test the boasted memory of Charles Macklin, The Quarterly Review [1854]. Credited to Foote by* MARIA EDGEWORTH, *Harry and Lucy Concluded, vol. II*

DENNIS O'KELLY
1720–1787

It will be Eclipse first, the rest no-where.

> *Declaration at Epsom [May 3, 1769] when the great race horse Eclipse was to run his first race. Annals of Sporting, vol. II, p. 271*

JOHN WOOLMAN
1720–1772

Though I felt uneasy at the thought of writing an instrument of slavery . . . through weakness I gave way and wrote it; but . . . said before my master and the Friend that I believed slave-keeping to be a practice inconsistent with the Christian religion. This, in some degree, abated my uneasiness; yet . . . I should have been clearer if I had desired to be excused from it, as a thing against my conscience.

> *Journal [published 1774]*

WILLIAM COLLINS
1721–1759

How sleep the brave, who sink to rest,
By all their country's wishes bless'd!
> *Ode Written in the Year 1746, st. 1*

By fairy hands their knell is rung,
By forms unseen their dirge is sung;
There Honor comes, a pilgrim gray,
To bless the turf that wraps their clay,
And Freedom shall awhile repair,
To dwell a weeping hermit there!
> *Ib. st. 2*

In numbers warmly pure and sweetly strong.
> *Ode to Simplicity [1747], st. 1*

If aught of oaten stop or pastoral song
May hope, O pensive Eve, to soothe thine ear.
> *Ode to Evening [1747], l. 1*

Now air is hush'd, save where the weak-ey'd bat,
With short shrill shriek flits by on leathern wing,
   Or where the beetle winds
   His small but sullen horn.   *Ib. l. 9*

'Twas sad by fits, by starts 'twas wild.
> *The Passions [1747], l. 28*

With eyes uprais'd, as one inspir'd,
Pale Melancholy sate retir'd,
And from her wild sequester'd seat,
In notes by distance made more sweet,
Pour'd through the mellow horn her pensive soul   *Ib. l. 57*

In hollow murmurs died away.
>   *Ib. l. 68*

O Music, sphere-descended maid,
Friend of Pleasure, Wisdom's aid!
>   *Ib. l. 95*

JEANNE, MARQUISE DE POMPADOUR
1721–1764

Après nous le déluge [After us the deluge].[1]

> *Reputed reply to Louis XV [November 5, 1757] after the defeat of the French and Austrian armies by Frederick the Great in the battle of Rossbach*

TOBIAS SMOLLETT
1721–1771

He was formed for the ruin of our sex.
> *Roderick Random [1748], ch. 22*

[1] The attribution to Mme. de Pompadour is made by DESPRÉS, *Mémoires de Madame de Hausset;* also by SAINTE-BEUVE and LA TOUR. LAROUSSE, *Fleurs Historiques,* attributes the saying to the King. It was original with neither, for it is an old French proverb.

SAMUEL ADAMS
1722–1803

Let us contemplate our forefathers, and posterity, and resolve to maintain the rights bequeathed to us from the former, for the sake of the latter. The necessity of the times, more than ever, calls for our utmost circumspection, deliberation, fortitude and perseverance. Let us remember that "if we suffer tamely a lawless attack upon our liberty, we encourage it, and involve others in our doom." It is a very serious consideration . . . that millions yet unborn may be the miserable sharers of the event.   *Speech* [1771]

What a glorious morning for America! [1]
Upon hearing the gunfire at Lexington [April 19, 1775]

Driven from every other corner of the earth, freedom of thought and the right of private judgment in matters of conscience direct their course to this happy country as their last asylum. [2]
Speech, Philadelphia [August 1, 1776]

CHRISTOPHER SMART
1722–1771

Tell them I Am, Jehovah said
To Moses; while earth heard in dread,
  And smitten to the heart,
At once above, beneath, around,
All nature, without voice or sound,
  Replied, O Lord, Thou art.
    A Song to David [1763], *st. 40*

For adoration all the ranks
Of angels yield eternal thanks,
  And David in the midst.
      Ib. st. 51

Where ask is have, where seek is find,
Where knock is open wide. [3]
      Ib. st. 77

---

[1] The phrase was adopted by the town of Lexington as a legend for the town seal.
[2] See Thomas Paine, p. 466b.
[3] See *Matthew* 7:7, p. 41a.

And now the matchless deed's achiev'd,
Determin'd, dar'd, and done.
    A Song to David, st. 86

For I bless God in the libraries of the learned and for all the booksellers in the world.
    Jubilate Agno, frag. B1, l. 79

Let James rejoice with the Skuttle-Fish who foils his foe by the effusion of his ink.   *Ib. l. 125*

For the Mouse (mus) prevails in Latin.
For Edi-mus, bibi-mus, vivi-mus, oremus.   *Ib. frag. B2, l. 638*

For I will consider my Cat Jeoffrey,
For he is the servant of the Living God, duly and daily serving him.
      Ib. l. 697

For he counteracts the Devil, who is Death, by brisking about the life.
      Ib. l. 722

SIR WILLIAM BLACKSTONE
1723–1780

Man was formed for society. [1]
Commentaries [1765–1769], introduction

The royal navy of England hath ever been its greatest defense and ornament; it is its ancient and natural strength; the floating bulwark of our island.
      Ib. bk. I, ch. 13

Time whereof the memory of man runneth not to the contrary. [2]   *Ib. 18*

That the king can do no wrong is a necessary and fundamental principle of the English constitution.   *Ib. III, 17*

It is better that ten guilty persons escape than one innocent suffer. [3]
      Ib. IV, 27

---

[1] See Spinoza, p. 374a.
[2] The favorite phrase of their law is "a custom whereof the memory of man runneth not back to the contrary." — EMERSON, *English Traits* [1856]
[3] See Voltaire, p. 417a.

ADAM SMITH
1723–1790

To found a great empire for the sole purpose of raising up a people of customers, may at first sight appear a project fit only for a nation of shopkeepers. It is, however, a project altogether unfit for a nation of shopkeepers; but extremely fit for a nation whose Government is influenced by shopkeepers.[1]

> *Wealth of Nations* [1776],
> *vol. II, bk. IV, ch. 7, pt. 3*

JOHN HOME
1724–1808

In the first days
Of my distracting grief, I found myself
As women wish to be who love their
    lords.

> *Douglas* [1756], *act I, sc. 1*

I'll woo her as the lion woos his brides.
> *Ib.*

My name is Norval; on the Grampian
    hills
My father feeds his flocks; a frugal
    swain,
Whose constant cares were to increase
    his store,
And keep his only son, myself, at home.
> *Ib. III, 1*

Like Douglas conquer, or like Douglas
die.   *Ib. V, 1*

IMMANUEL KANT
1724–1804

Two things fill the mind with ever-increasing wonder and awe, the more often and the more intensely the mind of thought is drawn to them: the starry heavens above me and the moral law within me.

> *Critique of Pure Reason* [1781],
> *conclusion*

Morality is not properly the doctrine of how we may make ourselves happy,

but how we may make ourselves worthy of happiness.

> *Critique of Practical Reason* [1788]

There is . . . only a single categorical imperative and it is this: Act only on that maxim through which you can at the same time will that it should become a universal law.

> *The Metaphysic of Morals*[1]
> [1797], *ch. 11*

FRIEDRICH GOTTLIEB KLOPSTOCK
1724–1803

Worth the sweat of noblemen.
> *Lake Zurich* [1750]

ROBERT, LORD CLIVE
1725–1774

By God, Mr. Chairman, at this moment I stand astonished at my own moderation!

> *Reply During Parliamentary Inquiry* [1773]

LOGAN, MINGO CHIEF
1725–1780

I appeal to any white man to say if he ever entered Logan's cabin hungry and he gave him not meat; if ever he came cold and naked and he clothed him not?[2]

> *Message to Lord Dunmore, Governor of Virginia* [November 11, 1774]. *From* THOMAS JEFFERSON, *Notes on Virginia*

GEORGE MASON
1725–1792

That all men are by nature equally free and independent, and have certain inherent rights, of which, when they enter into a state of society, they can-

---

[1] See Josiah Tucker, p. 436b.

[1] Translated by A. D. LINDSAY.
Categorical imperative. — KANT, *Fundamental Principles of Ethics* [1785], *Part 2*
[2] See *Matthew 25:35-36*, p. 44a.

not by any compact deprive or divest their posterity; namely, the enjoyment of life and liberty, with the means of acquiring and possessing property, and pursuing and obtaining happiness and safety.

Virginia Bill of Rights [1] *[June 12, 1776], art. 1*

Government is, or ought to be instituted for the common benefit, protection, and security of the people, nation, or community; of all the various modes and forms of government, that is best which is capable of producing the greatest degree of happiness and safety, and is most effectually secured against the danger of maladministration.[2]

Ib. 3

The freedom of the press is one of the great bulwarks of liberty, and can never be restrained but by despotic governments. *Ib. 12*

JOHN NEWTON
1725–1807

Glorious things of thee are spoken,
Zion, city of our God.

Olney Hymns [1779], *Glorious Things*

JAMES OTIS
1725–1783

An act against the Constitution is void; an act against natural equity is void.

Argument Against the Writs of Assistance [3] *[1761]*

Taxation without representation is tyranny.[4] *Attributed* [1763]

Ubi libertas ibi patria [Where liberty is, there is my country]. *His motto*

JAMES HUTTON
1726–1797

The result, therefore, of this physical inquiry [into the age of the earth] is, that we find no vestige of a beginning — no prospect of an end.

The Theory of the Earth [1795]

WILLIAM PRESCOTT
1726–1795

Don't one of you fire until you see the whites of their eyes.[1]

At Bunker Hill [June 17, 1775]

JANE ELLIOT
1727–1805

I've heard them lilting, at the ewe milking,
Lasses a' lilting, before dawn of day;
But now they are moaning, on ilka
green loaning;
The flowers of the forest are a' wede
away.

The Flowers of the Forest [2]

ANNE ROBERT JACQUES TURGOT, BARON DE L'AULNE
1727–1781

They [the Americans] are the hope of this world. They may become its model.[3]

Letter to Dr. Richard Price [March 22, 1778]

---

[1] The parent of all American bills of rights. — SAMUEL ELIOT MORISON, *The Oxford History of the American People* [1965]
See Patrick Henry, p. 465b. Henry drafted Article 16 on religious freedom.
[2] See Jefferson, p. 472b–473a.
[3] [Otis arguing] was a flame of fire . . . the seeds of patriots and heroes were then and there sown. — JOHN ADAMS, *Works* [1850–1856], *vol. II, p. 522*
[4] This maxim was the guide and watchword of all the friends of liberty. Otis actually said: No parts of His Majesty's dominions can be

taxed without their consent. — *Rights of the Colonies* [1764], *p. 64.*
[1] Also attributed to ISRAEL PUTNAM [1718–1790].
See Frederick the Great, p. 435a.
Silent till you see the whites of their eyes. — PRINCE CHARLES OF PRUSSIA, at Jagerndorf, May 23, 1745
[2] Sir Walter Scott in *Minstrelsy of the Scottish Border* says that *The Flowers of the Forest* was written to an ancient tune and that the last line, the refrain, is indisputably ancient. The air was also used for verses by Alison Cockburn. See p. 437a.
[3] This is the origin of "America the hope of the world."

JOHN WILKES
1727–1797

Earl of Sandwich: 'Pon my honor, Wilkes, I don't know whether you'll die on the gallows or of the pox.

Wilkes: That must depend, my Lord, upon whether I first embrace your Lordship's principles, or your Lordship's mistresses.

> *From* SIR CHARLES PETRIE, *The Four Georges* [1935]

OLIVER GOLDSMITH
1728–1774

One writer, for instance, excels at a plan or a title page, another works away the body of the book, and a third is a dab at an index.

> *The Bee* [1759], *no.* 1

As writers become more numerous, it is natural for readers to become more indolent.

> *Ib.* 175. *Upon Unfortunate Merit*

Good people all, with one accord,
Lament for Madame Blaize,
Who never wanted a good word —
From those who spoke her praise.

> *Ib. Elegy on Mrs. Mary Blaize* [1759], *st.* 1

A nightcap deck'd his brows instead of bay,
A cap by night — a stocking all the day!

> *Description of an Author's Bedchamber* [1760]

That strain once more; it bids remembrance rise.

> *The Captivity, An Oratorio* [1764], *act I*

O Memory! thou fond deceiver. *Ib.*

To the last moment of his breath
On hope the wretch relies;
And e'en the pang preceding death
Bids expectation rise.[1] *Ib. II*

Hope, like the gleaming taper's light,
Adorns and cheers our way;

[1] See Terence, p. 108b; Cicero, p. 111a; and Gay, p. 401b.

And still, as darker grows the night,
Emits a brighter ray.

> *The Captivity, An Oratorio,*
> *act II*

Remote, unfriended, melancholy, slow,
Or by the lazy Scheldt, or wandering Po. *The Traveller* [1764], *l.* 1

Where'er I roam, whatever realms to see,
My heart untravel'd fondly turns to thee;
Still to my brother turns with ceaseless pain,
And drags at each remove a lengthening chain. *Ib. l.* 7

Such is the patriot's boast, where'er we roam,
His first, best country ever is, at home. *Ib. l.* 73

Where wealth and freedom reign contentment fails,
And honor sinks where commerce long prevails. *Ib. l.* 91

Man seems the only growth that dwindles here.[1] *Ib. l.* 126

But winter ling'ring chills the lap of May. *Ib. l.* 172

They please, are pleas'd, they give to get esteem,
Till, seeming blest, they grow to what they seem.[2] *Ib. l.* 265

To men of other minds my fancy flies,
Embosom'd in the deep where Holland lies.
Methinks her patient sons before me stand,
Where the broad ocean leans against the land. *Ib. l.* 281

Pride in their port, defiance in their eye,
I see the lords of human kind [3] pass by. *Ib. l.* 327

The land of scholars, and the nurse of arms.[4] *Ib. l.* 356

[1] Italy.
[2] The character of the French.
[3] The British.
[4] England.

For just experience tells; in every soil,
That those that think must govern
those that toil.
The Traveller, l. 371

Laws grind the poor,[1] and rich men rule
the law.   *Ib. l. 386*

Vain, very vain, my weary search to
find
That bliss which only centers in the
mind.   *Ib. l. 423*

A book may be very amusing with
numerous errors, or it may be very dull
without a single absurdity.
The Vicar of Wakefield [1766],
preface

I . . . chose my wife, as she did her
wedding gown, not for a fine glossy surface, but such qualities as would wear
well.   *Ib. ch. 1*

We sometimes had those little rubs
which Providence sends to enhance the
value of its favors.   *Ib.*

Handsome is that handsome does.[2]
Ib.

That virtue which requires to be ever
guarded is scarce worth the sentinel.
Ib. 5

I find you want me to furnish you
with argument and intellects too.
Ib. 7

Man wants but little here below,
Nor wants that little long.[3]
*Ib. 8 [The Hermit (Edwin and
Angelina), st. 8]*

She was all of a muck of sweat.
Ib. 9

They would talk of nothing but high
life, and high-lived company, with
other fashionable topics, such as pictures, taste, Shakespeare, and the musical glasses.[4]   *Ib.*

[1] See *Isaiah 3:15*, p. 30a.
[2] See Chaucer, p. 168b.
[3] See Edward Young, p. 339a, and Oliver
Wendell Holmes, p. 634a.
[4] "Shall we talk about Shakespeare?" he
asked sarcastically. "Or the musical glasses?"
— ALDOUS HUXLEY, *Point Counter Point* [1928],
ch. 21

Conscience is a coward, and those
faults it has not strength enough to
prevent it seldom has justice enough to
accuse.
The Vicar of Wakefield, ch. 13

The naked every day he clad
When he put on his clothes.
*Ib. 17. An Elegy on the Death
of a Mad Dog, st. 3*

And in that town a dog was found,
As many dogs there be,
Both mongrel, puppy, whelp, and
hound,
And curs of low degree.   *Ib. st. 4*

The dog, to gain some private ends,
Went mad, and bit the man.
Ib. st. 5

The man recovered of the bite,
The dog it was that died.   *Ib. st. 8*

When lovely woman stoops to folly,
And finds too late that men betray,
What charm can soothe her melan-
choly?
What art can wash her guilt away?[1]
Ib. 29. Song, st. 1

The only art her guilt to cover,
To hide her shame from every eye,
To give repentance to her lover,
And wring his bosom, is — to die.
Ib. st. 2

This same philosophy is a good horse
in the stable, but an arrant jade on a
journey.[2]
The Good-Natur'd Man [1768],
act I

He calls his extravagance, generosity;
and his trusting everybody, universal
benevolence.   *Ib.*

All his faults are such that one loves
him still the better for them.   *Ib.*

Friendship is a disinterested commerce between equals; love, an abject
intercourse between tyrants and slaves.
Ib.

Silence gives consent.   *Ib. II*

[1] See T. S. Eliot, p. 1002b.
[2] See La Rochefoucauld, p. 355a.

Measures, not men, have always been my mark.[1]

> *The Good-Natur'd Man,*
> *act II*

Sweet Auburn! loveliest village of the plain.

> *The Deserted Village* [1770], *l. 1*

The bashful virgin's sidelong looks of love,
The matron's glance that would those looks reprove.   *Ib. l. 29*

Ill fares the land, to hastening ills a prey,
Where wealth accumulates, and men decay;
Princes and lords may flourish, or may fade;
A breath can make them, as a breath has made;
But a bold peasantry, their country's pride,
When once destroy'd, can never be supplied.   *Ib. l. 51*

His best companions, innocence and health;
And his best riches, ignorance of wealth.   *Ib. l. 61*

How happy he who crowns in shades like these,
A youth of labor with an age of ease.
    Ib. l. 99

Bends to the grave with unperceiv'd decay,
While resignation gently slopes the way;
And, all his prospects brightening to the last,
His heaven commences ere the world be past.   *Ib. l. 109*

The watchdog's voice that bay'd the whispering wind,
And the loud laugh that spoke the vacant mind.[2]   *Ib. l. 121*

A man he was to all the country dear,
And passing rich with forty pounds a year.

> *The Deserted Village, l. 141*

Careless their merits or their faults to scan,
His pity gave ere charity began.
Thus to relieve the wretched was his pride,
And e'en his failings lean'd to Virtue's side.   *Ib. l. 161*

And, as a bird each fond endearment tries
To tempt its new-fledg'd offspring to the skies,
He tried each art, reprov'd each dull delay,
Allur'd to brighter worlds, and led the way.   *Ib. l. 167*

Truth from his lips prevail'd with double sway,
And fools, who came to scoff, remain'd to pray.[1]   *Ib. l. 179*

Even children follow'd with endearing wile,
And pluck'd his gown, to share the good man's smile.   *Ib. l. 183*

A man severe he was, and stern to view;
I knew him well, and every truant knew:
Well had the boding tremblers learn'd to trace
The day's disasters in his morning face;
Full well they laugh'd with counterfeited glee,
At all his jokes, for many a joke had he;
Full well the busy whisper, circling round,
Convey'd the dismal tidings when he frown'd;
Yet he was kind; or if severe in aught,
The love he bore to learning was in fault;
The village all declar'd how much he knew;

---

[1] See Chesterfield, p. 415a, and Burke, p. 452a.

[2] Frequent and loud laughter is the characteristic of folly and ill manners: it is the manner in which the mob express their silly joy at silly things, and they call it being merry. In my mind there is nothing so illiberal and so ill-bred as audible laughter. — Lord CHESTERFIELD, *Letters* [March 9, 1748]
    See *Ecclesiastes 7:6*, p. 28a.

[1] See Dryden, p. 470b.

'Twas certain he could write, and cipher too.
> *The Deserted Village, l.* 197

In arguing too, the parson own'd his skill,
For e'en though vanquish'd, he could argue still;
While words of learned length, and thundering sound
Amaz'd the gazing rustics rang'd around;
And still they gaz'd, and still the wonder grew,
That one small head could carry all he knew.   *Ib. l.* 211

Where village statesmen talk'd with looks profound,
And news much older than their ale went round.   *Ib. l.* 223

The whitewash'd wall, the nicely sanded floor,
The varnish'd clock that click'd behind the door;
The chest contriv'd a double debt to pay,
A bed by night, a chest of drawers by day.[1]   *Ib. l.* 227

The twelve good rules, the royal game of goose.[2]   *Ib. l.* 232

To me more dear, congenial to my heart,
One native charm, than all the gloss of art.   *Ib. l.* 253

And, ev'n while fashion's brightest arts decoy,
The heart distrusting asks, if this be joy.   *Ib. l.* 263

---

[1] See *Description of an Author's Bedchamber,* p. 447a.
[2] The twelve good rules were ascribed to Charles I: (1) Urge no healths; (2) profane no divine ordinances; (3) touch no state matters; (4) reveal no secrets; (5) pick no quarrels; (6) make no comparisons; (7) maintain no ill opinions; (8) keep no bad company; (9) encourage no vice; (10) make no long meals; (11) repeat no grievances; (12) lay no wagers.

Goose. A game played with counters on a board divided into compartments, in some of which a goose was depicted. — *Oxford English Dictionary*

Her modest looks the cottage might adorn,
Sweet as the primrose peeps beneath the thorn.
> *The Deserted Village, l.* 329

In all the silent manliness of grief.
> *Ib. l.* 384

Thou source of all my bliss, and all my woe,
That found'st me poor at first, and keep'st me so.   *Ib. l.* 413

In my time, the follies of the town crept slowly among us, but now they travel faster than a stagecoach.
> *She Stoops to Conquer* [1775], *act I*

I love everything that's old: old friends, old times, old manners, old books, old wines.[1]   *Ib.*

The very pink of perfection.   *Ib.*

Let schoolmasters puzzle their brain,
With grammar, and nonsense, and learning;
Good liquor, I stoutly maintain,
Gives genius a better discerning.
> *Ib.*

I'll be with you in the squeezing of a lemon.   *Ib.*

A modest woman, dressed out in all her finery, is the most tremendous object of the whole creation.   *Ib. II*

This is Liberty Hall, gentlemen.
> *Ib.*

The first blow is half the battle.
> *Ib.*

We are the boys
That fear no noise
Where the thundering cannons roar.
> *Ib.*

They liked the book the better the more it made them cry.   *Ib.*

Ask me no questions, and I'll tell you no fibs.[2]   *Ib. III*

---

[1] See Bacon, p. 207b, and note.
[2] Them that asks no questions isn't told a lie. — KIPLING [1865–1936], *A Smuggler's Song, st.* 6

Our Garrick's a salad; for in him we
    see
Oil, vinegar, sugar, and saltness agree!
    Retaliation [1774], *l. 11*

Here lies our good Edmund,[1] whose
    genius was such,
We scarcely can praise it, or blame it
    too much;
Who, born for the universe, narrow'd
    his mind,
And to party gave up what was meant
    for mankind . . .
Who, too deep for his hearers, still
    went on refining,
And thought of convincing, while they
    thought of dining;
Though equal to all things, for all
    things unfit;
Too nice for a statesman, too proud for a
    wit. *Ib. l. 29*

His conduct still right, with his argu-
    ment wrong. *Ib. l. 46*

Here lies David Garrick, describe me,
    who can,
An abridgment of all that was pleasant
    in man. *Ib. l. 93*

As a wit, if not first, in the very first
    line. *Ib. l. 96*

On the stage he was natural, simple,
    affecting;
'Twas only that when he was off he was
    acting. *Ib. l. 101*

He cast off his friends as a huntsman
    his pack,
For he knew when he pleas'd he could
    whistle them back. *Ib. l. 107*

Who pepper'd the highest was surest to
    please. *Ib. l. 112*

When they talk'd of their Raphaels,
    Correggios, and stuff,
He shifted his trumpet and only took
    snuff.[2] *Ib. l. 145*

Such dainties to them, their health it
    might hurt;

[1] Edmund Burke.
[2] Sir Joshua Reynolds, who was exceedingly
deaf.

It's like sending them ruffles, when
    wanting a shirt.[1]
    The Haunch of Venison [1776]

There is no arguing with Johnson:
for if his pistol misses fire, he knocks
you down with the butt end of it.
    From BOSWELL, *Life of Johnson*
    [1791] [*October 26, 1769*]

[To Dr. Johnson] If you were to
make little fishes talk, they would talk
like whales. *Ib.* [*April 27, 1773*]

You may all go to pot.
    Verses in reply to an invitation
    to dine at Dr. Baker's

JOHN STARK
1728–1822

My men, yonder are the Hessians.
They were bought for seven pounds
and ten pence a man. Are you worth
more? Prove it. Tonight, the American
flag floats from yonder hill or Molly
Stark sleeps a widow!
    Before the Battle of Bennington
    [*August 16, 1777*]

EDMUND BURKE[2]
1729–1797

The writers against religion, whilst
they oppose every system, are wisely
careful never to set up any of their own.
    A Vindication of Natural
    Society [1756]

I am convinced that we have a degree of delight, and that no small one,
in the real misfortunes and pains of
others.[3]
    On the Sublime and Beautiful
    [1756], *sec. 14*

[1] See Tom Brown, p. 386b.
[2] You could not stand five minutes with
that man [Burke] beneath a shed while it
rained, but you must be convinced you had
been standing with the greatest man you had
ever seen. — SAMUEL JOHNSON, *Johnsonian
Miscellanies, edited by G. B. Hill* [1897], *vol. I,*
p. 290
[3] See La Rochefoucauld, p. 356b.

Custom reconciles us to everything.[1]
> *On the Sublime and Beautiful, sec. 18*

There is, however, a limit at which forbearance ceases to be a virtue.
> *Observations on a Late Publication on the Present State of the Nation* [1769]

The wisdom of our ancestors.[2]
> *Ib.*

When bad men combine, the good must associate; else they will fall one by one, an unpitied sacrifice in a contemptible struggle.
> *Thoughts on the Cause of the Present Discontents* [April 23, 1770]

Of this stamp is the cant of, Not men, but measures;[3] a sort of charm by which many people get loose from every honorable engagement.   *Ib.*

So to be patriots as not to forget we are gentlemen.   *Ib.*

Public life is a situation of power and energy; he trespasses against his duty who sleeps upon his watch, as well as he that goes over to the enemy.   *Ib.*

Reflect how you are to govern a people who think they ought to be free, and think they are not. Your scheme yields no revenue; it yields nothing but discontent, disorder, disobedience; and such is the state of America, that after wading up to your eyes in blood, you could only end just where you begun; that is, to tax where no revenue is to be found, to — my voice fails me; my inclination indeed carries me no farther — all is confusion beyond it.
> *First Speech on Conciliation with America. American Taxation* [April 19, 1774]

---

[1] See Pushkin, p. 593b.
[2] *De Sapienta Veterum* [The Wisdom of the Ancients]. — *Title of work by* FRANCIS BACON [1609]. The phrase is also in Burke's *Discussion on the Traitorous Correspondence Bill* [1793].
[3] See Chesterfield, p. 415a, and Goldsmith, p. 449a.

Your representative owes you, not his industry only, but his judgment; and he betrays instead of serving you if he sacrifices it to your opinion.
> *Speech to the Electors of Bristol* [November 3, 1774]

I have in general no very exalted opinion of the virtue of paper government.
> *Second Speech on Conciliation with America. The Thirteen Resolutions* [March 22, 1775]

The concessions of the weak are the concessions of fear.   *Ib.*

Young man, there is America — which at this day serves for little more than to amuse you with stories of savage men and uncouth manners; yet shall, before you taste of death, show itself equal to the whole of that commerce which now attracts the envy of the world.   *Ib.*

When we speak of the commerce with our colonies, fiction lags after truth; invention is unfruitful, and imagination cold and barren.   *Ib.*

A people who are still, as it were, but in the gristle, and not yet hardened into the bone of manhood.   *Ib.*

Through a wise and salutary neglect [of the colonies], a generous nature has been suffered to take her own way to perfection; when I reflect upon these effects, when I see how profitable they have been to us, I feel all the pride of power sink and all presumption in the wisdom of human contrivances melt and die away within me. My rigor relents. I pardon something to the spirit of liberty.   *Ib.*

The use of force alone is but *temporary*. It may subdue for a moment; but it does not remove the necessity of subduing again: and a nation is not governed, which is perpetually to be conquered.   *Ib.*

Nothing less will content me, than *whole America*.   *Ib.*

Abstract liberty, like other mere abstractions, is not to be found.

Second Speech on Conciliation with America. The Thirteen Resolutions

The religion most prevalent in our northern colonies is a refinement on the principles of resistance: it is the dissidence of dissent, and the protestantism of the Protestant religion. **Ib.**

In no country perhaps in the world is law so general a study [as in America]. . . . This study renders men acute, inquisitive, dexterous, prompt in attack, ready in defense, full of resources. . . . They augur misgovernment at a distance, and snuff the approach of tyranny in every tainted breeze. **Ib.**

I do not know the method of drawing up an indictment against an whole people. **Ib.**

It is not, what a lawyer tells me I *may* do; but what humanity, reason, and justice, tell me I ought to do. **Ib.**

The march of the human mind is slow. **Ib.**

Freedom and not servitude is the cure of anarchy; as religion, and not atheism, is the true remedy for superstition. **Ib.**

All government — indeed, every human benefit and enjoyment, every virtue and every prudent act — is founded on compromise and barter. **Ib.**

Instead of a standing revenue, you will have therefore a perpetual quarrel. **Ib.**

Slavery they can have anywhere. It is a weed that grows in every soil. **Ib.**

Deny them this participation of freedom, and you break that sole bond, which originally made, and must still preserve the unity of the empire. **Ib.**

It is the love of the [British] people; it is their attachment to their government, from the sense of the deep stake they have in such a glorious institution, which gives you both your army and your navy, and infuses into both that liberal obedience, without which your army would be a base rabble, and your navy nothing but rotten timber.

Second Speech on Conciliation with America. The Thirteen Resolutions

Magnanimity in politics is not seldom the truest wisdom; and a great empire and little minds go ill together. **Ib.**

By adverting to the dignity of this high calling our ancestors have turned a savage wilderness into a glorious empire: and have made the most extensive, and the only honorable conquests, not by destroying, but by promoting the wealth, the number, the happiness of the human race. **Ib.**

Corrupt influence, which is itself the perennial spring of all prodigality, and of all disorder; which loads us, more than millions of debt; which takes away vigor from our arms, wisdom from our councils, and every shadow of authority and credit from the most venerable parts of our constitution.

Speech on the Economical Reform [1780]

He was not merely a chip of the old block, but the old block itself.

On Pitt's first speech [February 26, 1781]

A rapacious and licentious soldiery.

Speech on Fox's East India Bill [1783]

The people never give up their liberties but under some delusion.

Speech at County Meeting of Buckinghamshire [1784]

There never was a bad man that had ability for good service.

Impeachment of Warren Hastings [February 15, 1788]

Religious persecution may shield itself under the guise of a mistaken and over-zealous piety.

Impeachment of Warren Hastings [*February 17, 1788*]

An event has happened, upon which it is difficult to speak, and impossible to be silent.   *Ib.* [*May 5, 1789*]

Resolved to die in the last dike of prevarication.   *Ib.* [*May 7, 1789*]

There is but one law for all, namely, that law which governs all law, the law of our Creator, the law of humanity, justice, equity — the law of nature, and of nations.   *Ib.* [*May 28, 1794*]

They made and recorded a sort of institute and digest of anarchy, called the Rights of Man.

On the Army Estimates [*1790*]

People will not look forward to posterity who never look backward to their ancestors.[1]

Reflections on the Revolution in France [*1790*]

Government is a contrivance of human wisdom to provide for human wants. Men have a right that these wants should be provided for by this wisdom.   *Ib.*

The unbought grace of life, the cheap defense of nations, the nurse of manly sentiment and heroic enterprise is gone!   *Ib.*

That chastity of honor, which felt a stain like a wound.   *Ib.*

Vice itself lost half its evil, by losing all its grossness.   *Ib.*

Kings will be tyrants from policy, when subjects are rebels from principle.   *Ib.*

Learning will be cast into the mire, and trodden down under the hoofs of a swinish multitude.   *Ib.*

Because half-a-dozen grasshoppers under a fern make the field ring with their importunate chink, whilst thousands of great cattle, reposed beneath the shadow of the British oak, chew the cud and are silent, pray do not imagine that those who make the noise are the only inhabitants of the field; that, of course, they are many in number; or that, after all, they are other than the little shriveled, meager, hopping, though loud and troublesome *insects* of the hour.

Reflections on the Revolution in France

Superstition is the religion of feeble minds.   *Ib.*

He that wrestles with us strengthens our nerves, and sharpens our skill. Our antagonist is our helper.   *Ib.*

To execute laws is a royal office; to execute orders is not to be a king. However, a political executive magistracy, though merely such, is a great trust.[1]   *Ib.*

You can never plan the future by the past.[2]

Letter to a member of the National Assembly [*1791*]

Old religious factions are volcanoes burnt out.

Speech on the Petition of the Unitarians [*1792*]

The cold neutrality of an impartial judge.

Preface to Brissot's Address [*1794*]

The only thing necessary for the triumph of evil is for good men to do nothing.

Letter to William Smith [*January 9, 1795*]

All men that are ruined, are ruined on the side of their natural propensities.

Letters on a Regicide Peace [*1796*], *no. 1*

---

[1] The Democratic Party is like a mule — without pride of ancestry or hope of posterity. — IGNATIUS DONNELLY [1831–1901], *Speech in the Minnesota Legislature*

[1] See Matthew Henry, p. 386b; Jefferson, p. 472b; Clay, p. 538b; and Calhoun, p. 545b, and note.

[2] See Patrick Henry, p. 465a.

Example is the school of mankind, and they will learn at no other.[1]

> *Letters on a Regicide Peace, no. 1*

Mere parsimony is not economy. . . . Expense, and great expense, may be an essential part of true economy.

> *Letter to a Noble Lord* [1796]

Economy is a distributive virtue, and consists not in saving but selection. Parsimony requires no providence, no sagacity, no powers of combination, no comparison, no judgment.   *Ib.*

And having looked to Government for bread, on the very first scarcity they will turn and bite the hand that fed them.

> *Thoughts and Details on Scarcity* [1800]

GOTTHOLD EPHRAIM LESSING
1729–1781

He who doesn't lose his wits over certain things has no wits to lose.

> *Emilia Galotti* [1772], *act IV, sc. 7*

No person must have to.

> *Nathan der Weise* [1779], *act I, sc. 3*

People are not always what they seem.   *Ib. 6*

The true beggar is the true king.

> *Ib. II, end*

Not all are free who scorn their chains.   *Ib. IV, 4*

One can drink too much, but one never drinks enough.   *Lieder*

Who will not praise a Klopstock? But will anyone read him? No!

> *Sinngedichte an den Leser*

JOHN PARKER
1729–1775

Stand your ground. Don't fire unless fired upon, but if they mean to have a war let it begin here!

> *To his Minute Men at Lexington* [April 19, 1775]

[1] See Franklin, p. 422a.

JOHANN GEORG HAMANN
1730–1788

Poetry is the mother tongue of mankind.   *Aesthetica in Nuce* [1762]

THOMAS OSBERT MORDAUNT
1730–1809

Sound, sound the clarion, fill the fife,
Throughout the sensual world proclaim,
One crowded hour of glorious life
Is worth an age without a name.[1]

> *From The Bee (October 12, 1791). Verses Written During the War* [1756–1763]

MOTOORI NORINAGA[2]
1730–1801

Thus our country is the source and fountainhead of all other countries, and in all matters it excels all the others.

> *Precious Comb-box*

Sages are superior to other people only in their cleverness. The fact is that they were all impostors. Among them the least blameworthy was Confucius.   *Arrowroot*

The Tale of Genji[3] is simply a tale of human life which leaves aside and does not profess to take up at all the question of good and bad, and which dwells only upon the goodness of those who are aware of the sorrow of human existence.   *Tama no Ogushi*

JOHN SCOTT
1730–1783

I Hate That Drum's Discordant Sound.

> *Title of Poem*

[1] Quoted by Sir Walter Scott in *Old Mortality* [1816], ch. 34.
See Scott, p. 522a.
[2] From *Sources of Japanese Tradition*, edited by William Theodore de Bary [1960].
[3] See Murasaki Shikibu, pp. 153b-154a.

JOSIAH WEDGWOOD
1730–1795

Am I not a man and a brother?
On a Medallion[1] [1787]

CHARLES CHURCHILL
1731–1764

Genius is of no country.
The Rosciad [1761], *l. 207*

He mouths a sentence as curs mouth a
bone. *Ib. l. 322*

So loud each tongue, so empty was each
head,
So much they talked, so very little said.
Ib. l. 549

Learn'd without sense, and venerably
dull. *Ib. l. 591*

Those who would make us feel — must
feel themselves.[2] *Ib. l. 962*

Apt alliteration's artful aid.
The Prophecy of Famine [1763],
l. 86

With curious art the brain, too finely
wrought,
Preys on herself, and is destroyed by
thought.
Epistle to William Hogarth
[1763], *l. 645*

Just to the windward of the law.
The Ghost [1763], *pt. III, l. 56*

Though by whim, envy, or resentment
led,
They damn those authors whom they
never read.
The Candidate [1764], *l. 57*

Be England what she will,
With all her faults she is my country
still.[3] *The Farewell, l. 27*

---

[1] Representing a Negro in chains, with one knee on the ground and both hands lifted up to heaven. This was adopted as a seal by the Anti-Slavery Society of London.
[2] Si vis me flere, dolendum est
Primum ipsi tibi
[If you wish me to weep, you yourself Must first feel grief].
HORACE [65–8 B.C.], *Ars Poetica, l. 102*
See Frost, p. 929b.
[3] England, with all thy faults I love thee still,

WILLIAM COWPER
1731–1800

Oh! for a closer walk with God.
Olney Hymns [1779], *no. 1*

What peaceful hours I once enjoy'd!
How sweet their memory still!
But they have left an aching void
The world can never fill. *Ib.*

God moves in a mysterious way
His wonders to perform;
He plants his footsteps in the sea
And rides upon the storm. *Ib. 35*

Behind a frowning providence
He hides a smiling face. *Ib.*

Happiness depends, as Nature shows,
Less on exterior things than most sup-
pose.
Table Talk [1782], *l. 246*

Freedom has a thousand charms to
show,
That slaves, howe'er contented, never
know. *Ib. l. 260*

Manner is all in all, whate'er is writ,
The substitute for genius, sense, and
wit. *Ib. l. 542*

Low ambition and the thirst of praise.[1]
Ib. l. 591

[Pope] Made poetry a mere mechanic
art. *Ib. l. 656*

Lights of the world, and stars of human
race.
The Progress of Error [1782], *l. 97*

How much a dunce that has been sent
to roam
Excels a dunce that has been kept at
home! *Ib. l. 415*

My country!
COWPER, *The Task* [1784], *bk. II, The Timepiece, l. 206*
Our country! In her intercourse with foreign nations may she always be in the right; but our country, right or wrong. — STEPHEN DECATUR, *Toast given at Norfolk* [April 1816]
I hope to find my country in the right: however, I will stand by her, right or wrong. — JOHN JORDAN CRITTENDEN [1787–1863], *On the Mexican War*
See Carl Schurz, p. 733a.
[1] See Pope, p. 407b.

A fool must now and then be right, by chance.
> *Conversation* [1782], *l.* 96

He would not, with a peremptory tone,
Assert the nose upon his face his own.
> *Ib. l. 121*

A moral, sensible, and well-bred man
Will not affront me, and no other can.
> *Ib. l. 193*

Pernicious weed! [1] whose scent the fair annoys,
Unfriendly to society's chief joys,
Thy worst effect is banishing for hours
The sex whose presence civilizes ours.
> *Ib. l. 251*

I cannot talk with civet in the room,
A fine puss-gentleman that's all perfume.   *Ib. l. 283*

Our wasted oil unprofitably burns,
Like hidden lamps in old sepulchral urns.   *Ib. l. 357*

A business with an income at its heels
Furnishes always oil for its own wheels.
> *Retirement* [1782], *l.* 615

Absence of occupation is not rest,
A mind quite vacant is a mind distress'd.   *Ib. l. 623*

Built God a church, and laugh'd His word to scorn.[2]   *Ib. l. 688*

> Philologists, who chase
A panting syllable through time and space,
Start it at home, and hunt it in the dark
To Gaul, to Greece, and into Noah's ark.   *Ib. l. 691*

I praise the Frenchman,[3] his remark was shrewd —
How sweet, how passing sweet, is solitude!
But grant me still a friend in my retreat
Whom I may whisper — solitude is sweet.   *Ib. l. 739*

[1] Tobacco.
[2] Voltaire, who built a church at Ferney [1760–1761], with the inscription *Deo erexit Voltaire.*
[3] La Bruyère.

I am monarch of all I survey,
My right there is none to dispute.
> *Verses Supposed to be Written by Alexander Selkirk* [1782], *st.* 1

O Solitude! where are the charms
That sages have seen in thy face?
> *Ib.*

There goes the parson, O illustrious spark!
And there, scarce less illustrious, goes the clerk.
> *On Observing Some Names of Little Note* [1782]

> Though on pleasure she was bent,
She had a frugal mind.
> *History of John Gilpin* [1785], *st.* 8

A hat not much the worse for wear.
> *Ib. st. 46*

Now let us sing — Long live the king,
And Gilpin, long live he;
And, when he next doth ride abroad,
May I be there to see!   *Ib. st. 63*

God made the country, and man made the town.[1]
> *The Task* [1785], *bk.* I, *The Sofa, l.* 749

Oh for a lodge in some vast wilderness,[2]
Some boundless contiguity of shade,
Where rumor of oppression and deceit,
Of unsuccessful or successful war,
Might never reach me more.
> *Ib.* II, *The Timepiece, l.* 1

> Mountains interpos'd
Make enemies of nations, who had else
Like kindred drops, been mingled into one.   *Ib. l. 17*

Slaves cannot breathe in England; if their lungs
Receive our air, that moment they are free!
They touch our country, and their shackles fall.   *Ib. l. 40*

[1] See Bacon, p. 209b, and note.
[2] See *Jeremiah 9:2*, p. 34a, and Byron, p. 557b.

Presume to lay their hand upon the ark [1]
Of her magnificent and awful cause.

The Task, bk. II, The Timepiece, l. 231

Variety's the very spice of life.[2]

Ib. l. 606

His head,
Not yet by time completely silver'd o'er,
Bespoke him past the bounds of freakish youth,
But strong for service still, and unimpair'd.

Ib. l. 702

Guilty splendor.

Ib. III, The Garden, l. 70

I was a stricken deer [3] that left the herd
Long since.

Ib. l. 108

Great contest follows, and much learned dust
Involves the combatants.

Ib. l. 161

From reveries so airy, from the toil
Of dropping buckets into empty wells,
And growing old in drawing nothing up.[4]

Ib. l. 188

Riches have wings,[5] and grandeur is a dream.

Ib. l. 265

Who loves a garden loves a greenhouse too.

Ib. l. 566

Now stir the fire, and close the shutters fast,
Let fall the curtains, wheel the sofa round,
And, while the bubbling and loud-hissing urn
Throws up a steamy column, and the cups,
That cheer but not inebriate,[6] wait on each,

So let us welcome peaceful evening in.

The Task, bk. IV, The Winter Evening, l. 36

'Tis pleasant, through the loopholes of retreat,
To peep at such a world; to see the stir
Of the great Babel, and not feel the crowd.

Ib. l. 88

O Winter, ruler of the inverted year! [1]

Ib. l. 120

With spots quadrangular of diamond form,
Ensanguin'd hearts, clubs typical of strife,
And spades, the emblems of untimely graves.

Ib. l. 217

In indolent vacuity of thought.[2]

Ib. l. 297

It seems the part of wisdom.

Ib. l. 336

All learned, and all drunk!   *Ib. l. 478*

Gloriously drunk, obey th' important call.

Ib. l. 510

Silently as a dream the fabric rose —
No sound of hammer or of saw was there.[3]

Ib. V, The Winter Morning Walk, l. 144

But war's a game, which, were their subjects wise,
Kings would not play at.   *Ib. l. 187*

There is in souls a sympathy with sounds;
And as the mind is pitch'd the ear is pleased
With melting airs or martial, brisk, or grave:
Some chord in unison with what we hear

---

[1] Uzzah put forth his hand to the ark of God, and took hold of it . . . and the anger of the Lord was kindled against Uzzah. — *II Samuel 6:6*

  [2] See Publilius Syrus, p. 126a.

  [3] See Shakespeare, p. 263b.

  [4] See Sydney Smith, p. 523a.

  [5] See *Proverbs 23:5*, p. 25b.

  [6] See Berkeley, p. 399b.

[1] See Thomson, p. 419b.

[2] See Samuel Johnson, p. 431a.

[3] So that there was neither hammer nor axe, nor any tool of iron heard in the house while it was in building. — *I Kings 6:7*

No hammers fell, no ponderous axes rung,
Like some tall palm the mystic fabric sprung,
Majestic silence!

  REGINALD HEBER [1783–1826], *Palestine*

Is touch'd within us, and the heart replies.
> *The Task, bk. VI, Winter Walk
> at Noon, l. 1*

Here the heart
May give a useful lesson to the head,
And Learning wiser grow without his
books.   *Ib. l. 85*

Knowledge is proud that he has learn'd
so much;
Wisdom is humble that he knows no
more.   *Ib. l. 96*

Nature is but a name for an effect,
Whose cause is God.   *Ib. l. 223*

An honest man, close-button'd to the
chin,
Broadcloth without, and a warm heart
within.
> *Epistle to Joseph Hill* [1785], *l. 62*

Shine by the side of every path we tread
With such a luster, he that runs may
read.[1]
> *Tirocinium* [1785], *l. 79*

Toll for the brave —
The brave! that are no more;
All sunk beneath the wave,
Fast by their native shore!
> *On the Loss of the Royal
> George* [2] [1791], *st. 1*

And still to love, though prest with ill,
In wintry age to feel no chill,
With me is to be lovely still,
My Mary!
> *To Mary* [1791], *st. 11*

Beware of desp'rate steps! The darkest
day
(Live till tomorrow) will have pass'd
away.
> *The Needless Alarm* [1794].
> *Moral*

The British warrior queen,
Bleeding from the Roman rods.
> *Boadicea* [1782]

---

[1] See *Habakkuk* 2:2, p. 36a.
[2] The *Royal George* was an English man-of-
war of 108 guns, which suddenly heeled over,
under the strain caused by the shifting of her
guns, while being refitted at Spithead, August
29, 1782. The commander, Admiral Kempen-
feldt, and eight hundred of the sailors, marines,
and visitors on board were drowned.

I shall not ask Jean Jacques Rousseau
If birds confabulate or no.
> *Pairing Time Anticipated* [c. 1794]

Misses! the tale that I relate
This lesson seems to carry —
Choose not alone a proper mate,
But proper time to marry.
> *Ib. Moral*

Oh that those lips had language! Life
has pass'd
With me but roughly since I heard
thee last.
> *On the Receipt of My Mother's
> Picture* [1798]

Misery still delights to trace
Its semblance in another's case.
> *The Castaway* [1799]

ERASMUS DARWIN
1731–1802

Soon shall thy arm, unconquer'd steam!
afar
Drag the slow barge, or drive the rapid
car;
Or on wide-waving wings expanded
bear
The flying-chariot through the fields of
air.
> *The Botanic Garden, pt. I,*
> [1789], *l. 289*

Would it be too bold to imagine,
that in the great length of time, since
the earth began to exist, perhaps millions of ages before the commencement
of the history of mankind, would it be
too bold to imagine, that all warm-blooded animals have arisen from one living
filament which the Great First Cause
endued with animality . . . and thus
possessing the faculty of continuing to
improve by its own inherent activity,
and of delivering down those improvements by generation to its posterity,
world without end! [1]
> *Zoonomia* [1794]

---

[1] Here the grandfather of Charles Robert
Darwin announces *his* early theory of organic
evolution.

CHARLES LEE
1731–1782

Beware that your Northern laurels do not change to Southern willows.[1]
To General Horatio Gates after the surrender of Burgoyne at Saratoga [October 17, 1777]

BEILBY PORTEUS
1731–1808

One murder made a villain, Millions, a hero. Princes were privileged To kill, and numbers sanctified the crime.[2] *Death, l. 154*

War its thousands slays, Peace, its ten thousands.[3] *Ib. l. 178*

PIERRE DE BEAUMARCHAIS
1732–1799

Judging by the virtues expected of a servant, does your Excellency know many masters who would be worthy valets?
Le Barbier de Séville [1775], *act I, sc. 2*

I quickly laugh at everything, for fear of having to cry.[4] *Ib.*

If you assure me that your intentions are honorable. *Ib. IV, 6*

If you are mediocre and you grovel, you shall succeed.
Le Mariage de Figaro [1784], *act III, sc. 3*

You went to some trouble to be born, and that's all.[5] *Ib. V, 3*

If censorship reigns there cannot be sincere flattery, and only small men are afraid of small writings.
Le Mariage de Figaro, act V, sc. 3

JOHN DICKINSON
1732–1808

Then join hand in hand, brave Americans all!
By uniting we stand, by dividing we fall.[1] *The Liberty Song* [1768]

RICHARD HENRY LEE
1732–1794

That these united colonies are, and of right ought to be, free and independent states; that they are absolved from all allegiance to the British crown; and that all political connection between them and the State of Great Britain is, and ought to be, totally dissolved.
Resolution moved at the Continental Congress [June 7, 1776; adopted July 2] [2]

JULIE DE LESPINASSE
1732–1776

The logic of the heart is absurd.
Lettres à M. Guibert [August 27, 1774]

GEORGE WASHINGTON[3]
1732–1799

Discipline is the soul of an army. It makes small numbers formidable; procures success to the weak, and esteem to all.
Letter of Instructions to the Captains of the Virginia Regiments [July 29, 1759]

Let us therefore animate and encourage each other, and show the whole world that a Freeman, contending for

---

[1] Gates was later defeated by Cornwallis at Camden, South Carolina [August 16, 1780], and was relieved of his command.
[2] See Young, p. 398b.
[3] See *I Samuel 18:7*, p. 12a.
[4] Je me presse de rire de tout, de peur d'être obligé d'en pleurer.
See La Bruyère, p. 381b; Byron, p. 561a; and Lincoln, p. 638a.
[5] Vous vous êtes donné la peine de naître, et rien de plus.

[1] See Aesop, p. 76b, and George Pope Morris, p. 600a.
[2] See John Adams, p. 463a-b.
[3] The Father of your Country. — HENRY KNOX, *Letter to Washington* [March 19, 1787]
See Henry (Light-Horse Harry) Lee, p. 486a.

liberty on his own ground, is superior to any slavish mercenary on earth.

> *General Orders, Headquarters,*
> *New York [July 2, 1776]*

The time is now near at hand which must probably determine whether Americans are to be freemen or slaves; whether they are to have any property they can call their own; whether their houses and farms are to be pillaged and destroyed, and themselves consigned to a state of wretchedness from which no human efforts will deliver them. The fate of unborn millions will now depend, under God, on the courage and conduct of this army. Our cruel and unrelenting enemy leaves us only the choice of brave resistance, or the most abject submission. We have, therefore, to resolve to conquer or die.

> *Address to the Continental*
> *Army before the Battle of*
> *Long Island [August 27,*
> *1776]*

There is nothing that gives a man consequence, and renders him fit for command, like a support that renders him independent of everybody but the State he serves.

> *Letter to the President of Con-*
> *gress, Heights of Harlem [Sep-*
> *tember 24, 1776]*

To place any dependence upon militia, is, assuredly, resting upon a broken staff.   *Ib.*

Without a decisive Naval force we can do nothing definitive. And with it, everything honorable and glorious.

> *To Lafayette [November 15, 1781]*

If men are to be precluded from offering their sentiments on a matter which may involve the most serious and alarming consequences that can invite the consideration of mankind, reason is of no use to us; the freedom of speech may be taken away, and dumb and silent we may be led, like sheep to the slaughter.

> *Address to Officers of the Army*
> *[March 15, 1783]*

The preservation of the sacred fire of liberty, and the destiny of the republican model of government, are justly considered as deeply, perhaps as finally staked, on the experiment entrusted to the hands of the American people.

> *First Inaugural Address [April*
> *30, 1789]*

Happily the Government of the United States, which gives to bigotry no sanction, to persecution no assistance, requires only that they who live under its protection should demean themselves as good citizens in giving it on all occasions their effectual support.

> *Letter to the Jewish Congrega-*
> *tion of Newport, Rhode Island*
> *[1790]*

To be prepared for war is one of the most effectual means of preserving peace.[1]

> *First Annual Address [to both*
> *Houses of Congress, January 8,*
> *1790]*

The basis of our political system is the right of the people to make and to alter their constitutions of government.

> *Farewell Address [September 17,*
> *1796]*

Let me now . . . warn you in the most solemn manner against the baneful effects of the spirit of party.   *Ib.*

Observe good faith and justice toward all nations. Cultivate peace and harmony with all. . . . The Nation which indulges toward another an habitual hatred or an habitual fondness is in some degree a slave. It is a slave to its animosity or to its affection, either of which is sufficient to lead it astray from its duty and its interest.   *Ib.*

'Tis our true policy to steer clear of permanent alliances, with any portion of the foreign world.   *Ib.*

There can be no greater error than to expect or calculate upon real favors from nation to nation.   *Ib.*

[1] See Vegetius, p. 146b, and note.

It is well, I die hard, but I am not afraid to go.
Last words [December 14, 1799]

Father, I cannot tell a lie, I did it with my little hatchet.[1]
Attributed remark from MARK TWAIN, Mark Twain as Washington

JOSEPH PRIESTLEY
1733–1804

It was ill policy in Leo the Tenth to patronize polite literature. He was cherishing an enemy in disguise. And the English hierarchy (if there be anything unsound in its constitution) has equal reason to tremble even at an air pump or an electrical machine.
Experiments and Observations on Different Kinds of Air [1775–1786]

In completing one discovery we never fail to get an imperfect knowledge of others of which we could have no idea before, so that we cannot solve one doubt without creating several new ones.   Ib.

CHRISTOPH MARTIN WIELAND
1733–1813

To be not as eloquent would be more eloquent.
The Journal Merkur [January 1774]

An illusion which makes me happy is worth a verity which drags me to the ground.
Idris und Zenide [1768], canto III

Too much light often blinds gentlemen of this sort. They cannot see the forest for the trees.
Musarion [1768], canto II

[1] See Weems, p. 499a.

JOHN ADAMS[1]
1735–1826

Facts are stubborn things; and whatever may be our wishes, our inclinations, or the dictates of our passions, they cannot alter the state of facts and evidence.
Defense of the British soldiers on trial for the Boston Massacre [1770]

The law, in all vicissitudes of government, fluctuations of the passions, or flights of enthusiasm, will preserve a steady undeviating course; it will not bend to the uncertain wishes, imaginations and wanton tempers of men. . . . It does not enjoin that which pleases a weak, frail man, but without any regard to persons, commands that which is good and punishes evil in all, whether rich or poor, high or low — 'tis deaf, inexorable, inflexible. On the one hand it is inexorable to the cries and lamentations of the prisoners; on the other it is deaf, deaf as an adder,[2] to the clamors of the populace.   Ib.

This is the most magnificent movement of all! There is a dignity, a majesty, a sublimity, in this last effort of the patriots that I greatly admire. The people should never rise without doing something to be remembered — something notable and striking. This destruction of the tea is so bold, so daring, so firm, intrepid and inflexible, and it must have so important consequences, and so lasting, that I can't but consider it as an epoch in history!
Diary [on the Boston Tea Party, December 17, 1773]

I have passed the Rubicon;[3] swim or

[1] He is as disinterested as the being who made him: he is profound in his view; and accurate in his judgment, except where knowledge of the world is necessary to form a judgment. — THOMAS JEFFERSON [January 30, 1787]
See Webster, p. 547a, note 2.
[2] See Psalms 58:4-5, p. 19b.
[3] See p. 112b, note 1.

sink, live or die, survive or perish with my country — that is my unalterable determination.[1]

> *In conversation with Jonathan Sewall, Falmouth, Maine [July 1774]*

I must study politics and war, that my sons may have liberty to study mathematics and philosophy, geography, natural history and naval architecture, navigation, commerce, and agriculture, in order to give their children a right to study painting, poetry, music, architecture, statuary, tapestry, and porcelain.

> *Letters of John Adams Addressed to his Wife, edited by Charles Francis Adams [1841], vol. II, letter 78 [1780]*

If it be the pleasure of Heaven that my country shall require the poor offering of my life, the victim shall be ready, at the appointed hour of sacrifice, come when that hour may. But while I do live, let me have a country, and that a free country. . . .

Sir, before God, I believe the hour is come. My judgment approves this measure, and my whole heart is in it. All I have, and all that I am, and all that I hope, in this life, I am now ready to stake upon it; and I leave off as I began, that live or die, survive or perish, I am for the Declaration.

> *Speech [1776]*

All great changes are irksome to the human mind, especially those which are attended with great dangers and uncertain effects.

> *Letter to James Warren [April 22, 1776]*

Yesterday, the greatest question was decided which ever was debated in America, and a greater perhaps never was nor will be decided among men. A resolution was passed without one dissenting colony, "that these United Colonies are, and of right ought to be, free and independent States." [1]

> *Letter to Abigail Adams [July 3, 1776]*

The second day of July, 1776,[2] will be the most memorable epoch in the history of America. I am apt to believe that it will be celebrated by succeeding generations as the great anniversary festival. It ought to be commemorated as the day of deliverance, by solemn acts of devotion to God Almighty. It ought to be solemnized with pomp and parade, with shows, games, sports, guns, bells, bonfires, and illuminations, from one end of this continent to the other, from this time forward forevermore.   *Ib.*

The happiness of society is the end of government.

> *Thoughts on Government [1776]*

Fear is the foundation of most governments.   *Ib.*

When annual elections end, there slavery begins.   *Ib.*

The judicial power ought to be distinct from both the legislative and executive, and independent upon both, that so it may be a check upon both.   *Ib.*

A government of laws, and not of men.[3]

> *Original draft of Massachusetts Constitution [1779]*

I pray Heaven to bestow the best of blessings on this house and all that shall hereafter inhabit it. May none but honest and wise men ever rule under this roof.[4]

> *Letter to Abigail Adams [November 2, 1800]*

---

[1] See Daniel Webster, p. 546b-547a.

[1] See Richard Henry Lee, p. 460b.

[2] On July 2, 1776, the resolution for independence, drafted by Richard Henry Lee of Virginia, was adopted by a committee including John Adams. On July 4 the Declaration of Independence was agreed to, engrossed, signed by John Hancock, and sent to the legislatures of the States.

[3] See Burke, p. 452, and note.

[4] Written the day after Adams moved into the new White House. President Franklin D.

Thomas Jefferson still lives [or: . . . surv —].[1] *Last words [July 4, 1826]*

ISAAC BICKERSTAFFE
c. 1735 – c. 1812

There was a jolly miller once
  Lived on the River Dee;
He worked and sang from morn till
    night
  No lark more blithe than he.
> *Love in a Village [1762], act I,
  sc. 2*

And this the burthen of his song
  Forever used to be,
"I care for nobody, not I,
  If no one cares for me."[2] *Ib.*

CHARLES JOSEPH, PRINCE DE LIGNE
1735–1814

The Congress doesn't run — it waltzes.[3]
> *Comment to La Garde–
  Chambonacs [1814]*

WILLIAM JULIUS MICKLE
1735–1788

The dews of summer nights did fall,
  The moon (sweet regent of the
    sky)[4]
Silvered the walls of Cumnor Hall
  And many an oak that grew
    thereby.
> *Cumnor Hall [1784], st. 1*

For there's nae luck about the house,
  There's nae luck at a';
There's little pleasure in the house
  When our gudeman's awa.
> *The Mariner's Wife, st. 1*

Roosevelt had it inscribed on the mantelpiece of the State Dining Room.
[1] Jefferson at Monticello died the same day — the fiftieth anniversary of the adoption of the Declaration of Independence — murmuring "This is the Fourth?"
[2] Naebody cares for me,
  I care for naebody.
      ROBERT BURNS [1759–1796], *I Hae a
          Wife o' My Ain, st. 4*
[3] Le Congrès ne marche pas, il danse [said of the Congress of Vienna].
[4] Now Cynthia, named fair regent of the night. — GAY, *Trivia* [1716], *bk. III*

PAUL REVERE
1735–1818

To the memory of the glorious Ninety-two: members of the Honorable House of Representatives of the Massachusetts Bay who, undaunted by the insolent menaces of villains in power, from a strict regard to conscience and the liberties of their constituents on the 30th of June 1768 voted NOT TO RESCIND.
> *Inscription on Revere's silver
  "Liberty" bowl [1768]*

If the British went out by water, to show two lanterns in the North Church steeple; and if by land, one as a signal, for we were apprehensive it would be difficult to cross the Charles River or get over Boston Neck.[1]
> *Signal code arranged with Colonel Conant of the Charlestown Committee of Safety [April 16, 1775]. Letter to Dr. Jeremy Belknap*

PATRICK HENRY
1736–1799

Caesar had his Brutus; Charles the First his Cromwell; and George the Third ["Treason!" cried the Speaker] — *may profit by their example. If this* be treason, make the most of it.
> *Speech on the Stamp Act, House of Burgesses, Williamsburg, Virginia [May 29, 1765]*

I am not a Virginian, but an American.[2]
> *Speech in First Continental Congress, Philadelphia [October 14, 1774]*

It is natural for man to indulge in the illusions of hope. We are apt to shut our eyes against a painful truth, and listen to the song of that siren till she transforms us into beasts. Is this the part of wise men, engaged in a great and arduous struggle for liberty? Are we disposed to be the number of those who, having eyes, see not, and having

---

[1] See Longfellow, p. 624a.
[2] See Socrates, p. 87b, and note.

ears, hear not,[1] the things which so nearly concern their temporal salvation? For my part, whatever anguish of spirit it may cost, I am willing to know the whole truth; to know the worst, and to provide for it.

> *Speech in Virginia Convention, Richmond [March 23, 1775]. From* WILLIAM WIRT, *Patrick Henry [1818]*

I have but one lamp by which my feet are guided, and that is the lamp of experience. I know no way of judging of the future but by the past.[2]   *Ib.*

We are not weak if we make a proper use of those means which the God of Nature has placed in our power. . . . The battle, sir, is not to the strong alone;[3] it is to the vigilant, the active, the brave.   *Ib.*

If we wish to be free; if we mean to preserve inviolate those inestimable privileges for which we have been so long contending; if we mean not basely to abandon the noble struggle in which we have been so long engaged, and which we have pledged ourselves never to abandon until the glorious object of our contest shall be obtained — we must fight! I repeat it, sir, we must fight! An appeal to arms, and to the God of hosts, is all that is left us.   *Ib.*

It is vain, sir, to extenuate the matter. The gentlemen may cry, Peace, peace! but there is no peace.[4] The war has actually begun! The next gale that sweeps from the north will bring to our ears the clash of resounding arms! Our brethren are already in the field! Why stand we here idle? What is it that the gentlemen wish? What would they have? Is life so dear or peace so sweet as to be purchased at the price of chains and slavery? Forbid it, Almighty God. I know not what course others may take,

but as for me, give me liberty or give me death![1]

> *Speech in Virginia Convention, Richmond [March 23, 1775]*

That religion, or the duty which we owe to our Creator, and the manner of discharging it, can be directed only by reason and conviction, not by force or violence; and therefore all men are equally entitled to the free exercise of religion, according to the dictates of conscience; and that it is the mutual duty of all to practice Christian forbearance, love, and charity towards each other.

> *Virginia Bill of Rights*[2] *[June 12, 1776], art. 16*

EDWARD GIBBON
1737–1794

The various modes of worship, which prevailed in the Roman world, were all considered by the people as equally true; by the philosopher, as equally false; and by the magistrate, as equally useful.

> *Decline and Fall of the Roman Empire [1776–1788], ch. 2*

The principles of a free constitution are irrevocably lost, when the legislative power is nominated by the executive.   *Ib. 3*

His [Antoninus'] reign is marked by the rare advantage of furnishing very few materials for history; which is indeed little more than the register of the crimes, follies, and misfortunes of mankind.[3]   *Ib.*

It has been calculated by the ablest politicians that no State, without being soon exhausted, can maintain above the hundredth part of its members in arms and idleness.   *Ib. 5*

All taxes must, at last, fall upon agriculture.   *Ib. 8*

---

[1] See *Jeremiah 5:21*, p. 34a.
[2] See Burke, p. 454b.
[3] See *Ecclesiastes 9:11*, p. 28b.
[4] See *Jeremiah 6:14*, p. 34a.

[1] See Aeschylus, p. 78b.
[2] See George Mason, p. 446a. Mason drafted Articles 1, 3, and 12.
[3] See Voltaire, p. 417b.

Corruption, the most infallible symptom of constitutional liberty.
Decline and Fall of the Roman Empire, ch. 21

In every deed of mischief he [Comenus] had a heart to resolve, a head to contrive, and a hand to execute.[1] *Ib. 48*

Our sympathy is cold to the relation of distant misery. *Ib. 49*

The winds and waves are always on the side of the ablest navigators.[2] *Ib. 68*

Vicissitudes of fortune, which spares neither man nor the proudest of his works, which buries empires and cities in a common grave. *Ib. 71*

All that is human must retrograde if it does not advance. *Ib.*

The successors of Charles the Fifth may disdain their brethren of England; but the romance of *Tom Jones*,[3] that exquisite picture of human manners, will outlive the palace of the Escurial and the imperial eagle of the house of Austria. *Memoirs* [1796]

Decent easy men, who supinely enjoyed the gifts of the founder. *Ib.*

It was here [at the age of seventeen] that I suspended my religious inquiries. *Ib.*

I saw and loved. *Ib.*

I sighed as a lover, I obeyed as a son. *Ib.*

[Of London] Crowds without company, and dissipation without pleasure. *Ib.*

The captain of the Hampshire grenadiers [4] . . . has not been useless

[1] He [Hampden] had a head to contrive, a tongue to persuade, and a hand to execute any mischief. — EDWARD HYDE, EARL OF CLARENDON [1609–1674], *History of the Rebellion* [1702–1704], *vol. III, bk. VII, sec. 84*
See Junius, p. 1091b.
[2] See Bussy-Rabutin, p. 357a, and note.
[3] See Fielding, p. 424b.
[4] Gibbon was a captain in the Hampshire militia from June 12, 1759, to December 23, 1762.

to the historian of the Roman Empire.
Memoirs

THOMAS PAINE
1737–1809

From the east to the west blow the trumpet to arms!
Through the land let the sound of it flee;
Let the far and the near all unite, with a cheer,
In defense of our Liberty Tree.
The Liberty Tree [July 1775], *st. 4*

Society in every state is a blessing, but Government, even in its best state, is but a necessary evil; in its worst state, an intolerable one.
Common Sense [1776]

Suspicion is the companion of mean souls, and the bane of all good society. *Ib.*

When we are planning for posterity, we ought to remember that virtue is not hereditary. *Ib.*

O! ye that love mankind! Ye that dare oppose not only the tyranny but the tyrant, stand forth! Every spot of the Old World is overrun with oppression. Freedom hath been hunted round the globe. Asia and Africa have long expelled her. Europe regards her as a stranger and England hath given her warning to depart. O! receive the fugitive and prepare in time an asylum for mankind.[1] *Ib.*

These are the times that try men's souls. The summer soldier and the sunshine patriot will, in this crisis, shrink from the service of his country; but he that stands it *now*, deserves the love and thanks of man and woman. Tyranny, like hell, is not easily conquered; yet we have this consolation with us, that the harder the conflict, the more glorious the triumph. What we obtain too cheap, we esteem too lightly; 'tis dearness only that gives everything its value. Heaven knows how to put a proper price upon its goods;

[1] See Samuel Adams, p. 444a.

and it would be strange indeed, if so celestial an article as *Freedom* should not be highly rated.

> *The American Crisis, no. 1*
> *[December 23, 1776]*

Panics, in some cases, have their uses; they produce as much good as hurt. Their duration is always short; the mind soon grows through them and acquires a firmer habit than before. But their peculiar advantage is, that they are the touchstone of sincerity and hypocrisy, and bring things and men to light, which might otherwise have lain forever undiscovered. ***Ib.***

Not a place upon earth might be so happy as America. Her situation is remote from all the wrangling world, and she has nothing to do but to trade with them. ***Ib.***

A bad cause will ever be supported by bad means and bad men.

> ***Ib.** 2 [January 13, 1777]*

Those who expect to reap the blessings of freedom must, like men, undergo the fatigue of supporting it.

> ***Ib.** 4 [September 12, 1777]*

It is not a field of a few acres of ground, but a cause, that we are defending, and whether we defeat the enemy in one battle, or by degrees, the consequences will be the same. ***Ib.***

We fight not to enslave, but to set a country free, and to make room upon the earth for honest men to live in.

> ***Ib.***

It is the object only of war that makes it honorable. And if there was ever a *just* war since the world began, it is this in which America is now engaged.

> ***Ib.** 5 [March 21, 1778]*

Character is much easier kept than recovered. ***Ib.** 13 [April 19, 1783]*

War involves in its progress such a train of unforeseen and unsupposed circumstances that no human wisdom can calculate the end. It has but one thing certain, and that is to increase taxes.

> *Prospects on the Rubicon [1787]*

[Burke] is not affected by the reality of distress touching his heart, but by the showy resemblance of it striking his imagination. He pities the plumage, but forgets the dying bird.

> *Rights of Man, pt. I [1791]*

My country is the world and my religion is to do good.[1]

> *Ib. II [1792], ch. 5*

Every religion is good that teaches man to be good. ***Ib.***

A thing moderately good is not so good as it ought to be. Moderation in temper is always a virtue; but moderation in principle is always a vice.[2]

> ***Ib.***

And the final event to himself [Burke] has been, that, as he rose like a rocket, he fell like a stick.

> *Letter to the Addressers on the*
> *Late Proclamation [1792]*

I believe in one God and no more, and I hope for happiness beyond this life. I believe in the equality of man; and I believe that religious duties consist in doing justice, loving mercy, and endeavoring to make our fellow-creatures happy.

> *The Age of Reason [1793], pt. I*

It is with a pious fraud as with a bad action; it begets a calamitous necessity of going on. ***Ib.***

When authors and critics talk of the sublime, they see not how nearly it borders on the ridiculous.[3]

> *Ib. II, note*

RUDOLF ERICH RASPE
1737–1794

What in the dark I had taken to be a stump of a little tree appearing above the snow, to which I had tied my horse,

---

[1] See Socrates, p. 87b, and note.

[2] See W. L. Garrison, p. 615b.

Extremism in the defense of liberty is no vice. And . . . moderation in the pursuit of justice is no virtue. — BARRY GOLDWATER, *Acceptance speech, Republican Presidential nomination [July 16, 1964]*

[3] See Napoleon, p. 504a.

proved to have been the weathercock of the church steeple.

> *Travels of Baron Munchausen*
> [1785], *ch. 2*

We all did our duty, which, in the patriot's, soldier's, and gentleman's language, is a very comprehensive word, of great honor, meaning, and import.

> *Ib. 5*

The sprigs took root in my horse's body, grew up, and formed a bower over me. *Ib.*

His tunes were frozen up in the horn, and came out now by thawing.

> *Ib. 6*

If any of the company entertain a doubt of my veracity, I shall only say to such, I pity their want of faith. *Ib.*

A traveler has a right to relate and embellish his adventures as he pleases, and it is very impolite to refuse that deference and applause they deserve.

> *Ib. 21*

ETHAN ALLEN
1738–1789

[Captain Delaplace [1]] gazed at Allen in bewildered astonishment. "By whose authority do you act?" exclaimed he. "In the name of the great Jehovah, and the Continental Congress!" replied Allen.

> *From* WASHINGTON IRVING,
> *Life of Washington* [1855–
> 1859], *vol. I, ch. 38*

JACQUES DELILLE
1738–1813

Fate chooses our relatives, we choose our friends.[2]

> *Malheur et Pitié* [1803], *canto 1*

---

[1] Commandant at Fort Ticonderoga, New York, May 10, 1775.
[2] Le sort fait les parents, le choix fait les amis.

PETER PINDAR
[JOHN WOLCOT]
1738–1819

What rage for fame attends both great and small!
Better be damned than mentioned not at all!

> *To the Royal Academicians*

Care to our coffin adds a nail, no doubt;
And every grin so merry, draws one out.

> *Expostulatory Odes, 15*

HESTER LYNCH
THRALE [PIOZZI]
1739–1821

The tree of deepest root is found
Least willing still to quit the ground:
'Twas therefore said by ancient sages,
   That love of life increased with years
So much, that in our latter stages,
When pain grows sharp and sickness rages,
   The greatest love of life appears.

> *Three Warnings*

Johnson's conversation was by much too strong for a person accustomed to obsequiousness and flattery; it was *mustard in a young child's mouth!*

> [*May* 1781] *From* BOSWELL, *Life
> of Johnson* [1791]

DANIEL BLISS
1740–1806

God wills us free, man wills us slaves,
I will as God wills, God's will be done.

> *Epitaph on gravestone of John
> Jack, "A Native of Africa, who
> died March* 1773, *aged about
> 60 years. Tho' born in a land of
> slavery he was born free."* [1]

JAMES BOSWELL[2]
1740–1795

That favorite subject, Myself.

> *Letter to Temple* [*July* 26, 1763]

---

[1] See Rousseau, p. 435b, and Schiller, p. 497b.
[2] See also excerpts from BOSWELL'S JOHNSON, pp. 429–434.

He who praises everybody, praises nobody.

> *Life of Johnson* [1791], footnote [*March 30, 1778*]

We cannot tell the precise moment when friendship is formed. As in filling a vessel drop by drop, there is at last a drop which makes it run over; so in a series of kindnesses there is at last one which makes the heart run over.

> *Ib.* [*September 1777*]

I think no innocent species of wit or pleasantry should be suppressed; and that a good pun may be admitted among the smaller excellencies of lively conversation. *Ib.* [*June 1784*]

LOUIS SÉBASTIEN MERCIER
1740–1814

Extremes meet.[1]

> *Tableaux de Paris* [1782], *vol. IV, ch. 348, title*

AUGUSTUS MONTAGUE TOPLADY
1740–1778

Rock of Ages, cleft for me,
Let me hide myself in thee.

> *Rock of Ages* [1775], *st. 1*

SÉBASTIEN R. N. CHAMFORT
1741–1794

The most wasted day of all is that on which we have not laughed.

> *Maxims and Thoughts, 1*

Chance is a nickname for Providence. *Ib.* 62

Be my brother, or I will kill you.[2]

> *From* CARLYLE, *French Revolution* [1837], *vol. II, pt. 1, ch. 12*

---

[1] "Extremes meet," as the whiting said with its tail in its mouth. — THOMAS HOOD [1799–1845], *The Doves and the Crows*
[2] Sois mon frère ou je te tue.
A paraphrase of the revolutionary watchword: Fraternity or death.

JOHANN KASPAR LAVATER
1741–1801

Say not you know another entirely, till you have divided an inheritance with him.

> *Aphorisms on Man* [1] [*c. 1788*], *no. 157*

He who, when called upon to speak a disagreeable truth, tells it boldly and has done is both bolder and milder than he who nibbles in a low voice and never ceases nibbling.[2] *Ib.* 302

Trust not him with your secrets, who, when left alone in your room, turns over your papers. *Ib.* 449

The public seldom forgive twice.

> *Ib.* 606

Venerate four characters: the sanguine who has checked volatility and the rage for pleasure; the choleric who has subdued passion and pride; the phlegmatic emerged from indolence; and the melancholy who has dismissed avarice, suspicion and asperity.

> *Ib.* 609

If you mean to know yourself, interline such of these aphorisms as affect you agreeably in reading, and set a mark to such as left a sense of uneasiness with you; and then shew your copy to whom you please. *Ib.* 643

GEBHARD LEBERECHT VON BLÜCHER
1742–1819

Ever forward, but slowly.

> *While leading the Russians at Leipzig* [*October 19, 1813*]

May the pens of the diplomats not ruin again what the people have attained with such exertions.

> *After the Battle of Waterloo* [1813]

---

[1] These Aphorisms were much admired and privately annotated by William Blake. See the one-volume edition of Blake's *Poetry and Prose*, edited by Geoffrey Keynes [*1927*].
[2] Blake's marginal comment on this was "Damn such!"

GEORG CHRISTOPH LICHTENBERG
1742–1799

A knife without a blade, for which the handle is missing.

> Göttingen Pocket Calendar [1798], describing an impossible existence

ANNA LETITIA BARBAULD
1743–1825

Life! we've been long together,
Through pleasant and through cloudy weather;
'Tis hard to part when friends are dear,
Perhaps 'twill cost a sigh, a tear;
Then steal away, give little warning,
    Choose thine own time;
Say not "Good night"; but in some brighter clime
    Bid me "Good morning."

> Ode to Life, st. 3

This dead of midnight is the noon of thought.

> A Summer's Evening Meditation

GAVRIIL DERZHAVIN
1743–1816

I am a czar — a slave, I am a worm — a god.   God [1784]

WILLIAM HENRY, DUKE OF GLOUCESTER
1743–1805

Another damned, thick, square book! Always scribble, scribble, scribble! Eh! Mr. Gibbon?

> Upon receiving from EDWARD GIBBON volume II of the Decline and Fall of the Roman Empire [1781]. From Best's Literary Memorials

THOMAS JEFFERSON
1743–1826

A lively and lasting sense of filial duty is more effectually impressed on the mind of a son or daughter by reading King Lear, than by all the dry volumes of ethics, and divinity, that ever were written.

> Letter to Robert Skipwith [August 3, 1771]

The God who gave us life, gave us liberty at the same time.[1]

> Summary View of the Rights of British America [1774]

When, in the course of human events, it becomes necessary for one people to dissolve the political bands which have connected them with another, and to assume among the powers of the earth the separate and equal station to which the laws of nature and of nature's God [2] entitle them, a decent respect to the opinions of mankind requires that they should declare the causes which impel them to the separation. We hold these truths to be self-evident; that all men are created equal; that they are endowed by their creator with certain unalienable rights; [3] that among these are life, liberty, and the pursuit of happiness; that to secure these rights, governments are instituted among men, deriving their just powers from the consent of the governed; that whenever any form of government becomes destructive to these ends, it is the right of the people to alter or to abolish it, and to institute new government, laying its foundation on such principles, and organizing its powers in such form, as to them shall seem most likely to effect their safety and happiness.

> Declaration of Independence [July 4, 1776]

We must therefore . . . hold them [the British] as we hold the rest of mankind, enemies in war, in peace friends.   Ib.

[1] See Patrick Henry, p. 465b.
[2] See Bolingbroke, p. 397b, and Pope, p. 410a.
[3] The phrase is frequently misquoted "inalienable."
    All men are born free and equal, and have certain natural, essential and unalienable rights. — *Constitution of Massachusetts* [1778]

And for the support of this declaration, with a firm reliance on the protection of divine providence, we mutually pledge to each other our lives, our fortunes, and our sacred honor.

Declaration of Independence

Ignorance is preferable to error; and he is less remote from the truth who believes nothing, than he who believes what is wrong.

Notes on the State of Virginia
[1781–1785]. Query 6

A single zealot may commence persecutor, and better men be his victims.

Ib. 17

Indeed, I tremble for my country when I reflect that God is just.

Ib. 18

Those who labor in the earth are the chosen people of God, if ever he had a chosen people, whose breasts He has made His peculiar deposit for substantial and genuine virtue. *Ib. 19*

He who permits himself to tell a lie once, finds it much easier to do it a second and third time, till at length it becomes habitual; he tells lies without attending to it, and truths without the world's believing him. This falsehood of the tongue leads to that of the heart, and in time depraves all its good dispositions.

Letter to Peter Carr [August 19,
1785]

The basis of our government being the opinion of the people, the very first object should be to keep that right; and were it left to me to decide whether we should have a government without newspapers, or newspapers without a government, I should not hesitate a moment to prefer the latter.

Letter to Colonel Edward Car-
rington [January 16, 1787]

Experience declares that man is the only animal which devours his own kind; for I can apply no milder term to the governments of Europe, and to the general prey of the rich on the poor.

Letter to Colonel Edward
Carrington

I hold it, that a little rebellion, now and then, is a good thing, and as necessary in the political world as storms in the physical.

Letter to James Madison
[January 30, 1787]

What country before ever existed a century and a half without a rebellion? . . . The tree of liberty must be refreshed from time to time with the blood of patriots and tyrants.[1] It is its natural manure.

Letter to William Stevens Smith
[November 13, 1787]

The republican is the only form of government which is not eternally at open or secret war with the rights of mankind.

Letter to William Hunter
[March 11, 1790]

We are not to expect to be translated from despotism to liberty in a featherbed.

Letter to Lafayette [April 2, 1790]

Let what will be said or done, preserve your *sang froid* immovably, and to every obstacle, oppose patience, perseverance, and soothing language.

Letter to William Short
[March 18, 1792]

Delay is preferable to error.

Letter to George Washington
[May 16, 1792]

We confide in our strength, without boasting of it; we respect that of others, without fearing it.

Letter to William Carmichael
and William Short [1793]

Offices are as acceptable here as elsewhere, and whenever a man has cast a longing eye on them, a rottenness begins in his conduct.

Letter to Tench Coxe
[May 21, 1799]

[1] See Tertullian, p. 143b, and Barère, p. 484a.

I have sworn upon the altar of God, eternal hostility against every form of tyranny over the mind of man.

Letter to Dr. Benjamin Rush
[September 23, 1800]

We are all Republicans — we are all Federalists. If there be any among us who would wish to dissolve this Union or to change its republican form, let them stand undisturbed as monuments of the safety with which error of opinion may be tolerated where reason is left free to combat it.

First Inaugural Address
[March 4, 1801]

But would the honest patriot, in the full tide of successful experiment, abandon a government which has so far kept us free and firm, on the theoretic and visionary fear that this government, the world's best hope, may by possibility want energy to preserve itself? *Ib.*

Sometimes it is said that man cannot be trusted with the government of himself. Can he, then, be trusted with the government of others? Or have we found angels in the forms of kings to govern him? Let history answer this question. *Ib.*

Still one thing more, fellow citizens — a wise and frugal government, which shall restrain men from injuring one another, which shall leave them otherwise free to regulate their own pursuits of industry and improvement, and shall not take from the mouth of labor the bread it has earned. This is the sum of good government, and this is necessary to close the circle of our felicities. *Ib.*

Equal and exact justice to all men, of whatever state or persuasion, religious or political; peace, commerce, and honest friendship with all nations, entangling alliances with none. . . . Freedom of religion; freedom of the press, and freedom of person under the protection of the *habeas corpus*, and trial by juries impartially selected. These principles form the bright constellation which

has gone before us, and guided our steps through an age of revolution and reformation. The wisdom of our sages and the blood of our heroes have been devoted to their attainment. They should be the creed of our political faith, the text of civil instruction, the touchstone by which we try the services of those we trust; and should we wander from them in moments of error or alarm, let us hasten to retrace our steps and to regain the road which alone leads to peace, liberty, and safety.

First Inaugural Address

Of the various executive abilities, no one excited more anxious concern than that of placing the interests of our fellow-citizens in the hands of honest men, with understanding sufficient for their stations.

Letter to Elias Shipman and Others of New Haven [July 12, 1801]

If a due participation of office is a matter of right, how are vacancies to be obtained? Those by death are few; by resignation, none. *Ib.*

Whensoever hostile aggressions . . . require a resort to war, we must meet our duty and convince the world that we are just friends and brave enemies.

Letter to Andrew Jackson
[December 3, 1806]

When a man assumes a public trust, he should consider himself as public property.[1]

Remark to Baron von Humboldt
[1807]

If, in my retirement to the humble station of a private citizen, I am accompanied with the esteem and approbation of my fellow citizens, trophies obtained by the blood-stained steel, or the tattered flags of the tented field, will never be envied. The care of human life and happiness, and not

[1] See Mathew Henry, p. 386b, and note.

their destruction, is the first and only legitimate object of good government.[1]

To the Republican Citizens of Washington County, Maryland [March 31, 1809]

Politics, like religion, hold up the torches of martyrdom to the reformers of error.

Letter to James Ogilvie [August 4, 1811]

The earth belongs to the living, not to the dead.

Letter to John W. Eppes [June 24, 1813]

I agree with you that there is a natural aristocracy among men. The grounds of this are virtue and talents.

Letter to John Adams [October 28, 1813]

Merchants have no country. The mere spot they stand on does not constitute so strong an attachment as that from which they draw their gains.

Letter to Horatio G. Spafford [March 17, 1814]

If a nation expects to be ignorant and free, in a state of civilization, it expects what never was and never will be.

Letter to Colonel Charles Yancey [January 6, 1816]

Enlighten the people generally, and tyranny and oppressions of body and mind will vanish like evil spirits at the dawn of day.

Letter to Du Pont de Nemours [April 24, 1816]

I have the consolation to reflect that during the period of my administration not a drop of the blood of a single fellow citizen was shed by the sword of war or of the law.

Letter to Count Dugnani, Papal Nuncio [February 14, 1818]

But this momentous question [the Missouri Compromise], like a firebell in the night awakened and filled me with

[1] See George Mason, p. 446a.

terror. I considered it the knell of the Union.

Letter to John Holmes [April 22, 1820]

I know no safe depository of the ultimate powers of the society but the people themselves; and if we think them not enlightened enough to exercise their control with a wholesome discretion, the remedy is not to take it from them, but to inform their discretion.

Letter to William Charles Jarvis [September 28, 1820]

And even should the cloud of barbarism and despotism again obscure the science and libraries of Europe, this country remains to preserve and restore light and liberty to them. In short, the flames kindled on the 4th of July, 1776, have spread over too much of the globe to be extinguished by the feeble engines of despotism; on the contrary, they will consume these engines and all who work them.

Letter to John Adams [September 12, 1821]

Amplification is the vice of modern oratory. It is an insult to an assembly of reasonable men, disgusting and revolting instead of persuading. Speeches measured by the hour, die by the hour.

Letter to David Harding, president of the Jefferson Debating Society of Hingham [April 20, 1824]

Men by their constitutions are naturally divided into two parties: (1) Those who fear and distrust the people, and wish to draw all powers from them into the hands of the higher classes. (2) Those who identify themselves with the people, have confidence in them, cherish and consider them as the most honest and safe, although not the most wise depository of the public interests. In every country these two parties exist; and in every one where they are free to think, speak, and write, they will declare themselves.

Letter to Henry Lee [August 10, 1824]

Never buy what you do not want, because it is cheap; it will be dear to you.

> *A Decalogue of Canons for Observation in Practical Life [February 21, 1825]*

When angry, count ten before you speak; if very angry, an hundred.[1]

> *Ib.*

The good old Dominion, the blessed mother of us all.

> *Thoughts on Lotteries [1826]*

This is the Fourth?

> *Last words [July 4, 1826]* [2]

WILLIAM PALEY
1743–1805

Who can refute a sneer?

> *Moral Philosophy [1785], vol. II, bk. V, ch. 9*

CONSTITUTION
OF THE
UNITED STATES
1787

We the people of the United States, in order to form a more perfect Union, establish justice, insure domestic tranquillity, provide for the common defense, promote the general welfare, and secure the blessings of liberty to ourselves and our posterity, do ordain and establish this Constitution for the United States of America.   *Preamble*

Treason against the United States, shall consist only in levying war against them, or in adhering to their enemies, giving them aid and comfort. No person shall be convicted of treason unless on the testimony of two witnesses to the same overt act, or on confession in open court.   *Art. III, sec. 3*

This Constitution, and the laws of the United States, which shall be made in pursuance thereof; and all treaties made, or which shall be made, under the authority of the United States, shall be the Supreme Law of the land; and the judges in every State shall be bound thereby, any thing in the Constitution or laws of any State to the contrary notwithstanding.   *Art. VI, sec. 2*

Congress shall make no law respecting an establishment of religion, or prohibiting the free exercise thereof; or abridging the freedom of speech, or of the press; or the right of the people peaceably to assemble, and to petition the government for a redress of grievances.   *First Amendment [1791]*

ANTOINE LAURENT
LAVOISIER
1743–1794

It is impossible to dissociate language from science or science from language, because every natural science always involves three things: the sequence of phenomena on which the science is based; the abstract concepts which call these phenomena to mind; and the words in which the concepts are expressed. To call forth a concept a word is needed; to portray a phenomenon, a concept is needed. All three mirror one and the same reality.[1]

> *Traité Élémentaire de Chimie [1789]*

I shall therefore content myself with saying that if, by the term *elements*, we mean to express the simple and indivisible molecules that compose bodies, it is probable that we know nothing about them; but if, on the contrary, we express by the term *elements* or *principles of bodies* the idea of the last point reached by analysis, all substances that we have not yet been able to decompose by any means are elements to us.[2]

> *Ib.*

---

[1] See Mark Twain, p. 762a.
[2] John Adams died the same day. See his last words, p. 464a.

[1] Translated by J. LIPETZ, D. E. GERSHENSON, and D. A. GREENBERG.
[2] Translated by D. McKIE.

JOHANN GOTTFRIED HERDER
1744–1803

A gain it is to find a beautiful human soul.

Der gerettete Jungling [1797]

Light, love, life.

Herder's Epitaph [1803]

ROWLAND HILL
1744–1833

He did not see any reason why the devil should have all the good tunes.

Sermons. From E. W. BROOME, *the Reverend Rowland Hill, p. 93*

JEAN BAPTISTE LAMARCK
1744–1829

FIRST LAW. In every animal . . . a more frequent and continuous use of any organ gradually strengthens, develops and enlarges that organ . . . while the permanent disuse of any organ imperceptibly weakens and deteriorates it, and progressively diminishes its functional capacity, until it finally disappears.

SECOND LAW. All the acquisitions or losses wrought by nature in individuals . . . are preserved by reproduction to the new individuals which arise.

Philosophie Zoologique [1809] [1]

JOSIAH QUINCY
1744–1775

Blandishments will not fascinate us, nor will threats of a "halter" intimidate. For, under God, we are determined that wheresoever, whensoever, or howsoever we shall be called to make our exit, we will die free men.

Observations on the Boston Port Bill [1774]

[1] Translated by HUGH ELLIOT.

CHARLES DIBDIN
1745–1814

Did you ever hear of Captain Wattle? He was all for love, and a little for the bottle.

Captain Wattle and Miss Roe

Here, a sheer hulk, lies poor Tom Bowling,
The darling of our crew;
No more he'll hear the tempest howling,
For death has broach'd him to.

Tom Bowling

Faithful below he did his duty,
But now he's gone aloft.   *Ib.*

Spanking Jack was so comely, so pleasant, so jolly,
Though winds blew great guns, still he'd whistle and sing.

The Sailor's Consolation

HANNAH MORE
1745–1833

Since trifles make the sum of human things,
And half our misery from our foibles springs.

Sensibility

Small habits well pursued betimes
May reach the dignity of crimes.

Florio and His Friend

WILLIAM SCOTT, LORD STOWELL
1745–1836

A dinner lubricates business.

From BOSWELL, *Life of Johnson* [1791]

The elegant simplicity of the three per cents.[1]

From CAMPBELL, *Lives of the Lord Chancellors* [1857], *vol. X, ch. 212*

[1] The sweet simplicity of the three per cents. — DISRAELI, *Endymion* [1880], *ch. 96*

SIR WILLIAM JONES
1746–1794

On parent knees, a naked new-born
   child,
Weeping thou sat'st while all around
   thee smiled;
So live, that sinking in thy last long
   sleep,
Calm thou mayst smile, while all
   around thee weep.

      From the Persian [1786]

GOTTFRIED AUGUST BÜRGER
1747–1794

The dead ride swiftly.

      Lenore [1773]

JOHN PAUL JONES
1747–1792

I have not yet begun to fight.
   Aboard the Bonhomme Richard [1]
      [*September 23, 1779*]

JOHN O'KEEFFE
1747–1833

Amo, amas,
I love a lass,
As a cedar tall and slender;
Sweet cowslip's grace
Is her nominative case,
And she's of the feminine gender!

   Agreeable Surprise, act II, sc. 2,
      Song

Fat, fair and forty [2] were all the toasts
of the young men.   *Irish Minnie*

And why I'm so plump the reason I
   tell —
Who leads a good life is sure to live
   well.
   Merry Sherwood. A Friar of
      Orders Gray, st. 1

You should always except the present
company.   *London Hermit*

---

[1] Engaged with the British frigate *Serapis,* off
Flamborough Head, England.
[2] I am resolved to grow fat, and look young
till forty! — DRYDEN, *Secret Love; or, The
Maiden Queen* [1667], *act III, sc. 1.*

SAMUEL PARR [1]
1747–1825

Now that the old lion is dead, every
ass thinks he may kick at him.
   [1784] *While dining with Sir*
   Joshua Reynolds, after the death
   of Dr. Johnson. From BOSWELL,
   Life of Johnson [1791]

FRANÇOIS ALEXANDRE FRÉDÉRIC, DUC DE LA ROCHEFOUCAULD–LIANCOURT
1747–1827

Louis XVI: Is it a revolt?
La Rochefoucauld-Liancourt: No,
Sire, it is a revolution.
   Upon learning at Versailles of
   the fall of the Bastille [1789]

JOHN LOGAN
1748–1788

Thou hast no sorrow in thy song,
No winter in thy year.
   To the Cuckoo [Attributed][2]

EMMANUEL JOSEPH SIEYÈS
1748–1836

I survived.[3]
   Upon being asked what he had
   done during the Terror

CHARLES JAMES FOX
1749–1806

[On the fall of the Bastille] How
much the greatest event it is that ever
happened in the world! and how much
the best!
   Letter to Richard Fitzpatrick
   [*July 30, 1789*]. *From* LORD
   JOHN RUSSELL, *Life and Times*
   of C. J. Fox [1859–1866],
   vol. II, p. 361

---

[1] Dr. Parr composed the Latin epitaph for the
monument to Dr. Johnson, placed in St. Paul's
Cathedral, London, February 1796.
[2] Also attributed to MICHAEL BRUCE [1746–
1767].
[3] J'ai vécu.

JOHANN WOLFGANG VON GOETHE
1749–1832

There is strong shadow where there is much light.
> *Götz von Berlichingen* [1773], *act I*

One lives but once in the world.
> *Clavigo* [1774], *act I, sc. 1*

If you inquire what the people are like here,
I must answer, "The same as everywhere!"
> *Die Leiden des jungen Werthers* [1774–1787], *May 17*

Radiant misery. *Ib.* [*December 24*]

The history of science is science itself; the history of the individual, the individual. *Mineralogy and Geology*

Getting along with women,
Knocking around with men,
Having more credit than money,
Thus one goes through the world.
> *Claudine von Villa Bella* [1776]

Who never ate his bread with tears,
Who never sat weeping on his bed
During care-ridden nights
Knows you not, you heavenly powers.[1]
> *Wilhelm Meisters Lehrjahre* [1786–1830], *bk. II, ch. 13*

All guilt is punished upon earth. *Ib.*

Who longs in solitude to live,
Ah! soon his wish will gain:
Men hope and love, men get and give,
And leave him to his pain.
> *Ib. III, 1*

Knowst thou the land where the lemon trees bloom,[2]
Where the gold orange glows in the deep thicket's gloom,
Where a wind ever soft from the blue heaven blows,
And the groves are of laurel and myrtle and rose?[3] *Ib.*

If I love you, what business is it of yours?
> *Wilhelm Meisters Lehrjahre,* *bk. IV, ch. 9*

One ought, every day at least, to hear a little song, read a good poem, see a fine picture, and, if it were possible, to speak a few reasonable words.[1]
> *Ib. V, 1*

To know of someone here and there whom we accord with, who is living on with us, even in silence — this makes our earthly ball a peopled garden.
> *Ib. VII, 5*

Art is long, life short;[2] judgment difficult, opportunity transient.
> *Ib. 9*

Seeking with the soul the land of the Greeks.
> *Iphigenie auf Tauris* [1787], *act I, sc. 1*

A useless life is an early death. *Ib. 2*

One says a lot in vain, refusing;
The other mainly hears the "No."
> *Ib. 3*

Pleasure and love are the pinions of great deeds. *Ib. II, 1*

The best is good enough.[3]
> *Italian Journey* [*March 3, 1787*]

A noble person attracts noble people, and knows how to hold on to them.
> *Torquato Tasso* [1790], *act I, sc. 1*

A talent is formed in stillness, a character in the world's torrent.
> *Ib. 2*

Three things are to be looked to in a building: that it stand on the right spot; that it be securely founded; that it be successfully executed.
> *Elective Affinities* [4] [1808], *bk. I, ch. 9*

The sum which two married people owe to one another defies calculation. It

---

[1] See Longfellow, p. 621a.
[2] Kennst du das Land, wo die Zitronen blühn?
[3] See Byron, p. 558a.

[1] See Charles Eliot Norton, p. 728b.
[2] See Hippocrates, p. 88b, and note.
[3] In der Kunst ist das Beste gut genug.
[4] Translated by JAMES ANTHONY FROUDE [1818–1894].

is an infinite debt, which can only be discharged through all eternity.

Elective Affinities, bk. I, ch. 9

A pretty foot is a great gift of nature.

Ib. 11

One is never satisfied with a portrait of a person that one knows.

Ib. II, 2

The fate of the architect is the strangest of all. How often he expends his whole soul, his whole heart and passion, to produce buildings into which he himself may never enter.

Ib. 3

Let us live in as small a circle as we will, we are either debtors or creditors before we have had time to look round.

Ib. 4

Mediocrity has no greater consolation than in the thought that genius is not immortal.   *Ib. 5*

A teacher who can arouse a feeling for one single good action, for one single good poem, accomplishes more than he who fills our memory with rows on rows of natural objects, classified with name and form.   *Ib. 7*

Who wants to understand the poem
Must go to the land of poetry;
Who wishes to understand the poet
Must go to the poet's land.

*West-östlicher Diwan
[1819], motto*

For I have been a man, and that means to have been a fighter.

Ib. Buch des Paradies

If I work incessantly to the last, nature owes me another form of existence when the present one collapses.

*Letter to Eckermann
[February 4, 1829]*

I call architecture frozen music.[1]

Ib. [March 23, 1829]

[1] Ich die Baukunst eine erstarrte Musik nenne. Since it [architecture] is music in space, as it were a frozen music. — FRIEDRICH VON SCHELLING [1775–1854], *Philosophie der Kunst, p. 576*
See Madame de Staël, p. 502b.

The artist may be well advised to keep his work to himself till it is completed, because no one can readily help him or advise him with it . . . but the scientist is wiser not to withhold a single finding or a single conjecture from publicity.

Essay on Experimentation

Man errs, while his struggle lasts.[1]

*Faust [1808–1832], pt. I
Prologue in Heaven*

Dear friend, theory is all gray,
And the golden tree of life is green.

Ib. Apprentice Scene

As soon as you trust yourself, you will know how to live.   *Ib.*

He who wishes to uphold the truth and has but one tongue, he will uphold it indeed.   *Ib. Street Scene*

Two souls dwell, alas! in my breast.

Ib. Before the Gate

I am the spirit that always denies.[2]

Ib. Study

My peace is gone,
My heart is heavy.[3]

Ib. Gretchen at the Spinning Wheel

Who can think of something stupid,
Who can think of anything smart
That prior ages haven't thought of? [4]

Ib. pt. II. The Gothic Chamber

Who strives always to the utmost, him can we save.[5]   *Ib.*

He only earns his freedom and existence who daily conquers them anew.[6]

Ib.

I was fair, too, and that was my undoing.   *Ib.*

The Eternal Feminine draws us on.[7]

Ib., last line

[1] Es irrt der Mensch, so lang er strebt.
[2] Ich bin der Geist der stets verneint.
[3] Meine Ruh' ist hin,
    Mein Herz ist schwer.
[4] See *Ecclesiastes 1:9, p. 27a.*
[5] Wer immer strebend sich bemüht,
    Den können wir erlösen.
[6] Nur der verdient sich Freiheit wie das Leben
    der täglich sie erobern muss.
[7] Das Ewig-Weibliche zieht uns hinan.

Do you wish to roam farther and far-
ther?
See! The Good lies so near.
Only learn to seize good fortune,
For good fortune's always here.
                              Erinnerung

In limitations he first shows himself the
    master,
And the law can only bring us free-
    dom.   *Was wir Bringen* [1802]

Create, artist! Do not talk!
                                Saying

Everything in the world can be borne
Except for a series of beautiful days.
                        Proverb collection

There is peace
O'er all the peaks,
In all the treetops
You feel scarce a breath.
The little birds are silent in the forest.
Just wait, soon
You too will rest.
            Wanderers Nachtlied II

America, you have it better than our
continent, the old one.[1]
        Wendts Musen-Almanach [1831]

Without haste, but without rest.
                                Motto

More light!   *Last words*

PIERRE SIMON DE LAPLACE
1749–1827

Given for one instant an intelligence
which could comprehend all the forces
by which nature is animated and the
respective positions of the beings which
compose it, if moreover this intelligence
were vast enough to submit these data
to analysis, it would embrace in the
same formula both the movements of
the largest bodies in the universe and
those of the lightest atom; to it nothing

[1] Amerika, du hast es besser — als unser
Kontinent, das alte.

would be uncertain, and the future as
the past would be present to its eyes.
        *Oeuvres, vol. VII, Théorie Ana-
        lytique des Probabilités* [1812–
        1820], *introduction*

The theory of probabilities is at bottom nothing but common sense reduced to calculus.   *Ib.*

Sire, I have no need of that hypothesis.[1]
        From ERIC TEMPLE BELL, *Men
        of Mathematics* [1937]

HONORÉ GABRIEL DE RIQUETTI, COMTE DE MIRABEAU
1749–1791

Go and tell those who have sent you
that we are here by the will of the nation and that we shall not leave save at
the point of bayonets.
        Speech in the États-Généraux
        [*June 23, 1789*]

LADY ANNE BARNARD
1750–1825

When the sheep are in the fauld, and
    the kye's come hame,
And a' the weary warld to rest are
    gone.
        Auld Robin Gray [1771], *st. 1*

JOHN PHILPOT CURRAN
1750–1817

The condition upon which God hath
given liberty to man is eternal vigilance;[2] which condition if he break,

[1] Reply to Napoleon Bonaparte's remark upon
receiving a copy of Laplace's *Mécanique Céleste:*
"You have written this huge book on the system
of the world without once mentioning the author
of the universe."
[2] Commonly quoted: Eternal vigilance is the
price of liberty. Attributed also to Jefferson.
  There is one safeguard known generally to
the wise, which is an advantage and security to
all, but especially to democracies as against
despots. What is it? Distrust. — DEMOSTHENES
[c. 385–322 B.C.], *Philippic 2, sec. 24*

servitude is at once the consequence of his crime and the punishment of his guilt.

Speech Upon the Right of Election of Lord Mayor of Dublin [July 10, 1790]

JOHN TRUMBULL
1750–1831

But optics sharp it needs, I ween,
To see what is not to be seen.
McFingal [1782], *canto I, l. 67*

JAMES MADISON
1751–1836

By a faction, understand a number of citizens, whether amounting to a majority or minority of the whole, who are united and actuated by some common impulse of passion, or of interest, adverse to the rights of other citizens, or to the permanent and aggregate interests of the community.
The Federalist [1787], *no. 10*

The latent causes of faction are thus sown in the nature of man; and we see them everywhere brought into different degrees of activity, according to the different circumstances of civil society. A zeal for different opinions concerning religion, concerning government, and many other points, as well of speculation as of practice; an attachment of different leaders ambitiously contending for pre-eminence and power; or to persons of other descriptions whose fortunes have been interesting to the human passions, have, in turn, divided mankind into parties, inflamed them with mutual animosity, and rendered them much more disposed to vex and oppress each other than to cooperate for their common good. . . . But the most common and durable source of factions has been the various and unequal distribution of property. *Ib.*

To secure the public good, and private rights, against the danger of . . .

faction, and at the same time to preserve the spirit and form of popular government, is then the great object to which our inquiries are directed.
The Federalist, no. 10

I believe there are more instances of the abridgment of the freedom of the people by gradual and silent encroachments of those in power than by violent and sudden usurpations.
Speech in the Virginia Convention [June 16, 1788]

RICHARD BRINSLEY SHERIDAN
1751–1816

Mrs. Malaprop: Illiterate him, I say, quite from your memory.
The Rivals [1775], *act I, sc. 2*

'Tis safest in matrimony to begin with a little aversion. *Ib.*

A circulating library in a town is as an evergreen tree of diabolical knowledge! It blossoms through the year!
Ib.

A progeny of learning. *Ib.*

Never say more than is necessary.
Ib. II, 1

I know you are laughing in your sleeve. *Ib.*

He is the very pineapple of politeness! *Ib. III, 3*

If I reprehend anything in this world, it is the use of my oracular tongue, and a nice derangement of epitaphs! *Ib.*

As headstrong as an allegory on the banks of the Nile. *Ib.*

Too civil by half. *Ib. 4*

Our ancestors are very good kind of folks; but they are the last people I should choose to have a visiting acquaintance with. *Ib. IV, 1*

No caparisons, miss, if you please. Caparisons don't become a young woman. *Ib. 2*

You are not like Cerberus, three gentlemen at once, are you?
The Rivals, act IV, sc. 2

The quarrel is a very pretty quarrel as it stands; we should only spoil it by trying to explain it. *Ib. 3*

My valor is certainly going! — it is sneaking off! I feel it oozing out, as it were, at the palm of my hands!
Ib. V, 3

I own the soft impeachment. *Ib.*

Through all the drama — whether damned or not —
Love gilds the scene, and women guide the plot. *Ib. Epilogue*

An apothecary should never be out of spirits.
St. Patrick's Day [1775], *act I, sc. 1*

Death's a debt; his mandamus binds all alike — no bail, no demurrer.
Ib. II, 4

I ne'er could any luster see
In eyes that would not look on me.
The Duenna [1775], *act I, sc. 2*

I loved him for himself alone.
Ib. 3

I was struck all of a heap.
Ib. II, 2

A bumper of good liquor
Will end a contest quicker
Than justice, judge, or vicar.[1] *Ib. 3*

Conscience has no more to do with gallantry than it has with politics.
Ib. 4

Tale-bearers are as bad as the tale-makers.
The School for Scandal [1777],
act I, sc. 1

You shall see them on a beautiful quarto page, where a neat rivulet of text shall meander through a meadow of margin. *Ib.*

You had no taste when you married me.
The School for Scandal,
act I, sc. 2

Here's to the maiden of bashful fifteen;
Here's to the widow of fifty;
Here's to the flaunting, extravagant quean,
And here's to the housewife that's thrifty.
    Let the toast pass —
    Drink to the lass;
I'll warrant she'll prove an excuse for the glass. *Ib. III, 3*

An unforgiving eye, and a damned disinheriting countenance.
Ib. IV, 1

Be just before you're generous.
Ib.

There is not a passion so strongly rooted in the human heart as envy.
The Critic [1779], *act I, sc. 1*

The newspapers! Sir, they are the most villainous — licentious — abominable — infernal — Not that I ever read them — no — I make it a rule never to look into a newspaper. *Ib.*

Egad, I think the interpreter is the hardest to be understood of the two!
Ib. 2

A practitioner in panegyric, or, to speak more plainly, a professor of the art of puffing. *Ib.*

The number of those who undergo the fatigue of judging for themselves is very small indeed.[1] *Ib.*

Certainly nothing is unnatural that is not physically impossible. *Ib. II, 1*

I wish, sir, you would practice this without me. I can't stay dying here all night. *Ib. III, 1*

An oyster may be crossed in love.[2]
Ib.

The right honorable gentleman is in-

[1] The government of a nation is often decided over a cup of coffee, or the fate of empires changed by an extra bottle of Johannisberg. — G. P. R. JAMES, *Richelieu* [1829], *ch. 16*

[1] See J. R. Lowell, p. 694b, and Bryce, p. 778a.
[2] From the interpolated tragedy, *The Spanish Armada.*

debted to his memory for his jests, and
to his imagination for his facts.[1]
> *Sheridaniana. Speech in Reply*
> *to Mr. Dundas*

You write with ease to show your breeding,
But easy writing's curst hard reading.
> *Clio's Protest*

JOHANN HEINRICH
VOSS
1751–1826

Who does not love wine, women, and
    song
Remains a fool his whole life long.[2]
> *Attributed*

THOMAS CHATTERTON [3]
1752–1770

Mie love ys dedde,
Gon to hys death-bedde,
Al under the wyllowe-tree.
> *Mynstrelles Songe* [4]

PHILIP FRENEAU
1752–1832

An age employed in edging steel
Can no poetic raptures feel . . .
No shaded stream, no quiet grove
Can this fantastic century move.
> *Poems* [1795]. *To an Author, st.* 6

In spite of all the learned have said,
    I still my old opinion keep;
The posture that we give the dead
    Points out the soul's eternal sleep.
> *The Indian Burying Ground*
> [1788], *st.* 1

---

[1] See Le Sage, p. 391a.
[2] Wer nicht liebt Wein, Weib und Gesang,
  Der bleibt ein Narr sein Leben lang.
  The couplet has also been attributed to Luther,
apparently on no better authority than an
eighteenth-century jingle in which "Luther" is
needed to rhyme with "Futter." REDLICH ascribes
it to Voss in *Die poetischen Beiträge zum Wauds-
becker Bothen* [1871].
[3] See Wordsworth, p. 511b.
[4] This is from the poems of "Thomas Rowley," an imaginary fifteenth-century Bristol
poet invented by Chatterton. Editions of the
poems appeared in 1778 and 1782, and were
exposed in 1777–8 by Thomas Tyrwhitt.

Then rushed to meet the insulting foe;
They took the spear — but left the
shield.[1]
> *To the Memory of the Brave*
> *Americans who Fell at Eutaw*
> *Springs, S.C. September 8,*
> *1781* [1786], *st.* 5

FRIEDRICH
MAXIMILIAN
VON KLINGER
1752–1831

Sturm und Drang [Storm and
stress].
> *Title of a Play* [1776]

LEONARD McNALLY
1752–1820

On Richmond Hill there lives a lass
    More bright than Mayday morn;
Whose charms all other maids' sur-
    pass, —
A rose without a thorn.
> *The Lass of Richmond Hill,*[2] *st.* 1

JOSEPH DE MAISTRE
1753–1821

Every nation has the government it
deserves.   *Letter to X* [1811]

The sword of justice has no scabbard.
> *Les Soirées de Saint-Petersbourg*
> [1821]. *Premier Entretien*

ANTOINE DE RIVAROL
1753–1801

What is not clear is not French.
> *Discours sur l'universalité de la*
> *langue française* [1784]

---

[1] When Prussia hurried to the field,
  And snatched the spear, but left the shield.
      SCOTT, *Marmion* [1808], *canto III,*
                                introduction
[2] Also attributed to J. UPTON [1670–1749] and
W. HUDSON.

JOEL BARLOW
1754–1813

I sing the sweets I know, the charms I
    feel,
My morning incense, and my evening
    meal —
The sweets of Hasty Pudding.
    The Hasty Pudding [1792], *canto I*

E'en in thy native regions, how I blush
To hear the Pennsylvanians call thee
    Mush!   **Ib.**

GEORGE CRABBE[1]
1754–1832

What is a church? — Our honest sex-
    ton tells,
'Tis a tall building, with a tower and
    bells.
    The Borough [1810]. *Letter 2,*
                The Church

Habit with him was all the test of
    truth,
"It must be right: I've done it from my
    youth."   *Ib. 3, The Vicar*

Books cannot always please, however
    good;
Minds are not ever craving for their
    food.   *Ib. 24, Schools*

In idle wishes fools supinely stay;
Be there a will, and wisdom finds a
    way.   *The Birth of Flattery*

Cut and come again.
    Tales [1812]. VII, *The Widow's*
                Tale

And took for truth the test of ridicule.[2]
    Tales of the Hall [1819],
      bk. VIII, The Sisters

[1] See Byron, p. 555a.
[2] How comes it to pass, then, that we appear
such cowards in reasoning, and are so afraid to
stand the test of ridicule? — ANTHONY COOPER,
EARL OF SHAFTESBURY [1671–1713], *Characteristics:
A Letter Concerning Enthusiam, sec. 2*
    Truth, 'tis supposed, may bear all lights; and
one of those principal lights or natural mediums
by which things are to be viewed in order to a
thorough recognition is ridicule itself. —
SHAFTESBURY, *Essay on the Freedom of Wit and
Humor, sec. 1*
    'Twas the saying of an ancient sage (Gorgias

The ring, so worn as you behold,
So thin, so pale, is yet of gold.
    His Mother's Wedding Ring

WILLIAM DRENNAN
1754–1820

Nor one feeling of vengeance presume
    to defile
The cause, or the men, of the Emerald
    Isle.[1]   *Erin* [1795], *st. 3*

JOSEPH JOUBERT
1754–1824

I had to grow old to learn what I
wanted to know, and I should need to
be young to say well what I know.
    Pensées [1842]

Ask the young: they know everything!   **Ib.**

To teach is to learn twice.   **Ib.**

JEANNE MANON
ROLAND
1754–1793

O liberty! O liberty! What crimes
are committed in thy name!
    *Last words, before her death on
    the guillotine. From* LAMARTINE,
    Histoire des Girondins [1847]

CHARLES MAURICE DE
TALLEYRAND-
PÉRIGORD
1754–1838

Black as the devil,
Hot as hell,
Pure as an angel,
Sweet as love.[2]   *Recipe for coffee*

Leontinus, *apud* Aristotle's *Rhetoric,* that humor was the only test of gravity, and gravity
of humor. For a subject which would not bear
raillery was suspicious; and a jest which would
not bear a serious examination was certainly
false wit. — *Ib. 5*
    [1] The first known use of this appellation for
Ireland.
    [2] Noir comme le diable,
        Chaud comme l'enfer,

[Of the Bourbons] They have learned nothing, and forgotten nothing.[1]

> From CHEVALIER DE PANAT, letter to Mallet du Pan [January 1796]

[Of the battle of Borodino, 1812] It is the beginning of the end.[2]

> From EDOUARD FOURNIER, L'Esprit dans l'Histoire [1857]

The United States has thirty-two religions but only one dish.

> *Attributed*

Women sometimes forgive a man who forces the opportunity, but never a man who misses one. *Attributed*

[To a young diplomat] Don't be eager![3]

> From SAINT-BEUVE, Portraits de Femmes: Madame de Staël

BENJAMIN WATERHOUSE
1754–1846

Tobacco is a filthy weed,
That from the devil does proceed;
It drains your purse, it burns your clothes,
And makes a chimney of your nose.

> From DR. OLIVER WENDELL HOLMES [1809–1894], *who was vaccinated by Dr. Waterhouse*

BERTRAND BARÈRE DE VIEUZAC
1755–1841

The tree of liberty only grows when watered by the blood of tyrants.[4]

> *Speech in the National Convention* [1792]

It is only the dead who do not return. *Speech* [1794]

ANTHELME BRILLAT-SAVARIN
1755–1826

Tell me what you eat, and I will tell you what you are.

> *Physiologie du Goût* [1825], *ch.* 4

A dessert without cheese is like a beautiful woman with only one eye.

> *Ib.* 14

One can become a cook, but one is born a roaster of meat. *Ib.* 15

A meal without wine is like a day without sunshine. *Ib.*

NATHAN HALE
1755–1776

I only regret that I have but one life to lose for my country.[1]

> *Last words, before being hanged by the British as a spy* [September 22, 1776]

ALEXANDER HAMILTON
1755–1804

A national debt, if it is not excessive, will be to us a national blessing.[2]

> *Letter to Robert Morris* [April 30, 1781]

I believe the British government forms the best model the world ever produced. . . . This government has for its object public strength and individual security.

> *Federal Convention Debates* [June 18, 1787]

All communities divide themselves into the few and the many. The first are the rich and wellborn, the other the mass of the people. . . . The people are

---

Pur comme un ange,
Doux comme l'amour.

This appears as an inscription on many old coffeepots.

[1] Ils n'ont rien appris, ni rien oublié.

[2] Voilà le commencement de la fin.

[3] Pas de zèle!

[4] See Tertullian, p. 143b, and Jefferson, p. 471b.

---

[1] See Addison, p. 393b.

[2] At the time we were funding our national debt, we heard much about "a public debt being a public blessing." — THOMAS JEFFERSON, *Letter to John W. Epps* [November 6, 1813]

See Daniel Webster, p. 547a.

turbulent and changing; they seldom judge or determine right. Give therefore to the first class a distinct, permanent share in the government. They will check the unsteadiness of the second, and as they cannot receive any advantage by a change, they therefore will ever maintain good government.
Federal Convention Debates

We are now forming a republican government. Real liberty is neither found in despotism or the extremes of democracy, but in moderate governments. *Ib. [June 26, 1787]*

Let Americans disdain to be the instruments of European greatness. Let the thirteen States, bound together in a strict and indissoluble Union, concur in erecting one great American system, superior to the control of all transatlantic force or influence, and able to dictate the terms of the connection between the old and the new world!
The Federalist [1787–1788], no. 11

Government implies the power of making laws. It is essential to the idea of a law, that it be attended with a sanction; or, in other words, a penalty or punishment for disobedience.
Ib. 15

Why has government been instituted at all? Because the passions of men will not conform to the dictates of reason and justice, without constraint. *Ib.*

Every power vested in a government is in its nature sovereign, and includes by force of the term a right to employ all the means requisite . . . to the attainment of the ends of such power.
Opinion on the Constitutionality of the Bank [February 23, 1791]

If the end be clearly comprehended within any of the specified powers, and if the measure have an obvious relation to that end, and is not forbidden by any particular provision of the Constitution, it may safely be deemed to come within the compass of the national authority.
Opinion on the Constitutionality of the Bank

LOUIS XVIII
1755–1824

Punctuality is the politeness of kings.[1] *A favorite saying*

JOHN MARSHALL
1755–1835

It is emphatically the province and duty of the judicial department to say what the law is. . . . If two laws conflict with each other, the courts must decide on the operation of each. . . . This is of the very essence of judicial duty.
Marbury v. Madison, 1 Cranch, 1317 [1803]

We must never forget that it is a *constitution* we are expounding.
McCulloch v. Maryland, 4 Wheaton 316, 407 [1819]

This provision is made in a constitution, intended to endure for ages to come, and consequently, to be adapted to the various *crises* of human affairs.
Ib. 415

Let the end be legitimate, let it be within the scope of the constitution, and all means which are appropriate, which are plainly adapted to that end, which are not prohibited, but consist with the letter and spirit of the constitution, are constitutional. *Ib. 421*

The power to tax involves the power to destroy.[2] *Ib. 431*

The people made the Constitution, and the people can unmake it. It is the creature of their own will, and lives only by their will.
Cohens v. Virginia, 6 Wheaton (19 U.S.) 264, 389 [1821]

[1] L'exactitude est la politesse des rois.
[2] See Oliver Wendell Holmes, Jr., p. 788b.

MARTIN JOSEPH ROUTH
1755–1854

You will find it a very good practice always to verify your references, sir.

From J. W. Burgon, *Memoir of Dr. Routh, Quarterly Review* [*July 1878*]

HENRY LEE
[LIGHT-HORSE HARRY]
1756–1818

To the memory of the Man, first in war, first in peace, and first in the hearts of his countrymen.

Resolutions presented to the House of Representatives on the death of Washington [*December 1799*]

WILLIAM BLAKE[1]
1757–1827

How sweet I roam'd from field to field,
  And tasted all the summer's pride,
Till I the prince of love beheld
  Who in the sunny beams did glide.
        Poetical Sketches [1783]. *Song, st. 1*

He loves to sit and hear me sing,
  Then, laughing, sports and plays with me;
Then stretches out my golden wing,
  And mocks my loss of liberty.
        Ib. st. 4

My silks and fine array,
  My smiles and languish'd air,
By love are driv'n away;
  And mournful lean Despair
Brings me yew to deck my grave:
Such end true lovers have.
        Ib. Song, st. 1

Like a fiend in a cloud,
  With howling woe,
After night I do crowd,
  And with night will go;
I turn my back to the east,
From whence comforts have increas'd;

[1] *Poetry and Prose of William Blake,* Geoffrey Keynes, ed. [*1927*]

For light doth seize my brain
With frantic pain.
        Poetical Sketches. Mad Song, st. 3

How have you left the ancient love
  That bards of old enjoy'd in you!
The languid strings do scarcely move!
  The sound is forc'd, the notes are few!   *Ib. To the Muses, st. 4*

Does the Eagle know what is in the pit?
  Or wilt thou go ask the Mole?
Can Wisdom be put in a silver rod?
  Or Love in a golden bowl?
        The Book of Thel [1789].
        Thel's Motto

Piping down the valleys wild,
Piping songs of pleasant glee,
On a cloud I saw a child,
And he laughing said to me:
"Pipe a song about a Lamb!"
        Songs of Innocence [1789].
        Introduction, st. 1, 2

And I made a rural pen,
And I stain'd the water clear,
And I wrote my happy songs
Every child may joy to hear.
        Ib. st. 5

Sing louder around
To the bells' cheerful sound,
While our sports shall be seen
On the echoing green.
        Ib. The Echoing Green, st. 1

Little Lamb, who made thee?
Dost thou know who made thee?
Gave thee life, and bid thee feed
By the stream and o'er the mead;
Gave thee clothing of delight,
Softest clothing, wooly, bright.
        Ib. The Lamb, st. 1

My mother bore me in the southern wild,
And I am black, but O! my soul is white;
White as an angel is the English child,
But I am black, as if bereav'd of light.
        Ib. The Little Black Boy, st. 1

"And we are put on earth a little space,

That we may learn to bear the beams of
    love;
And these black bodies and this sun-
    burnt face
Is but a cloud, and like a shady grove."
      Songs of Innocence. The
        Little Black Boy, st. 4

I'll shade him from the heat, till he can
    bear
To lean in joy upon our father's knee;
And then I'll stand and stroke his silver
    hair,
And be like him, and he will then love
    me.   *Ib. st. 7*

When my mother died I was very
    young,
And my father sold me while yet my
    tongue
Could scarcely cry " 'weep! 'weep!
    'weep! 'weep!"
So your chimneys I sweep, and in soot I
    sleep.
      Ib. The Chimney Sweeper, st. 1

To Mercy, Pity, Peace, and Love
All pray in their distress;
And to these virtues of delight
Return their thankfulness.
      Ib. The Divine Image, st. 1

For Mercy has a human heart,
Pity a human face,
And Love, the human form divine,[1]
And Peace, the human dress.[2]
            Ib. st. 3

The moon like a flower
In heaven's high bower,
With silent delight
Sits and smiles on the night.
         Ib. Night, st. 1

And there the lion's ruddy eyes
Shall flow with tears of gold,
And pitying the tender cries,
And walking round the fold,
Saying "Wrath, by his meekness,
And by his health, sickness,
Is driven away
From our immortal day."   *Ib. st. 5*

"For, wash'd in life's river,
My bright mane forever

[1] See Milton, p. 344b.
[2] See *A Divine Image*, p. 489b.

Shall shine like the gold
As I guard o'er the fold."
    Songs of Innocence. Night, st. 6

When the voices of children are heard
    on the green
And laughing is heard on the hill,
My heart is at rest within my breast
    And everything else is still.
        Ib. Nurse's Song, st. 1

Can I see another's woe,
And not be in sorrow too?
Can I see another's grief,
And not seek for kind relief?
      Ib. On Another's Sorrow, st. 1

Rintrah roars and shakes his fires in the
    burden'd air;
Hungry clouds swag on the deep.
    The Marriage of Heaven and
      Hell [c. 1793]. The Argument

The reason Milton wrote in fetters
when he wrote of Angels and God, and
at liberty when of Devils and Hell, is
because he was a true poet and of the
Devil's party without knowing it.
    Ib. The Voice of the Devil, note

The busy bee has no time for sorrow.   *Ib. Proverbs of Hell*

No bird soars too high, if he soars
with his own wings.   *Ib.*

The pride of the peacock is the glory
of God.
    The lust of the goat is the bounty of
God.
    The wrath of the lion is the wisdom
of God.
    The nakedness of woman is the work
of God.   *Ib.*

The cistern contains: the fountain
overflows.   *Ib.*

Think in the morning. Act in the
noon. Eat in the evening. Sleep in the
night.   *Ib.*

You never know what is enough unless you know what is more than
enough.   *Ib.*

Improvement makes straight roads;
but the crooked roads without improvement are roads of genius.   *Ib.*

Truth can never be told so as to be understood, and not be believ'd.
The Marriage of Heaven and Hell. Proverbs of Hell

Enough! or Too Much. *Ib.*

Never seek to tell thy love
Love that never told can be;
For the gentle wind does move
Silently, invisibly.

I told my love, I told my love,
I told her all my heart,
Trembling, cold, in ghastly fears —
Ah, she doth depart.

Soon as she was gone from me
A traveler came by
Silently, invisibly —
O, was no deny.
Miscellaneous Poems and Fragments [1793–1818]. Poem

I asked a thief to steal me a peach:
He turned up his eyes.
I ask'd a lithe lady to lie her down:
Holy and meek she cries.

As soon as I went an angel came:
He wink'd at the thief
And smil'd at the dame,
And without one word spoke
Had a peach from the tree,
And 'twixt earnest and joke
Enjoy'd the Lady. *Ib. Poem*

Sleep, Sleep, beauty bright
Dreaming o'er the joys of night.
Sleep, Sleep: in thy sleep
Little sorrows sit and weep.
Ib. A Cradle Song, st. 1

Why art thou silent and invisible,
Father of Jealousy?
Ib. To Nobodaddy

Love to faults is always blind,
Always is to joy inclin'd,
Lawless, wing'd, and unconfin'd,
And breaks all chains from every
mind. *Ib. Poem*

The sword sung on the barren heath,
The sickle in the fruitful field:

The sword he sung a song of death,
But could not make the sickle yield.
Miscellaneous Poems and Fragments. Poem

Abstinence sows sand all over
The ruddy limbs and flaming hair,
But Desire Gratified
Plants fruits of life and beauty there.
Ib. Poem

If you trap the moment before it's
ripe,[1]
The tears of repentance you'll certainly
wipe;
But if once you let the ripe moment
go
You can never wipe off the tears of
woe. *Ib. Poem*

He who binds to himself a joy
Does the winged life destroy;
But he who kisses the joy as it flies
Lives in eternity's sunrise.
Ib. Eternity

What is it men in women do require?
The lineaments of Gratified Desire.
What is it women do in men require?
The lineaments of Gratified Desire.
Ib. The Question Answer'd

The look of love alarms
Because 'tis fill'd with fire;
But the look of soft deceit
Shall win the lover's hire. *Ib. Poem*

Hear the voice of the Bard!
Who Present, Past, and Future, sees;
Whose ears have heard
The Holy Word
That walk'd among the ancient trees.
*Songs of Experience [1794].
Introduction, st. 1*

"Turn away no more;
Why wilt thou turn away?
The starry floor,
The wat'ry shore,
Is giv'n thee till the break of day."[2]
Ib. st. 4

"Love seeketh not itself to please,
Nor for itself hath any care,

[1] See Shakespeare, *II Henry IV, IV, v, 95,* p. 242b.
[2] See Milton, p. 336a.

But for another gives its ease,
And builds a Heaven in Hell's de-
spair."
*Songs of Experience. The
Clod and the Pebble,
st. 1*

"Love seeketh only self to please,
To bind another to its delight,
Joys in another's loss of ease,
And builds a Hell in Heaven's de-
spite." *Ib. st. 3*

O Rose, thou art sick!
The invisible worm
That flies in the night,
In the howling storm,

Has found out thy bed
Of crimson joy,
And his dark secret love
Does thy life destroy.
Ib. The Sick Rose.

Little Fly,
Thy summer's play
My thoughtless hand
Has brush'd away.

Am not I
A fly like thee?
Or art not thou
A man like me?

For I dance,
And drink, and sing,
Till some blind hand
Shall brush my wing.
Ib. The Fly

Tiger! Tiger! burning bright
In the forests of the night,
What immortal hand or eye
Could frame thy fearful symmetry?

In what distant deeps or skies
Burnt the fire of thine eyes?
On what wings dare he aspire?
What the hand dare seize the fire?
Ib. The Tiger, st. 1, 2

What the hammer? what the chain?
In what furnace was thy brain?
What the anvil? what dread grasp
Dare its deadly terrors clasp?

When the stars threw down their
spears,
And water'd heaven with their tears,
Did he smile his work to see?

Did he who made the Lamb make
thee?
*Songs of Experience. The
Tiger, st. 4, 5*

In every cry of every man,
In every infant's cry of fear,
In every voice, in every ban,
The mind-forg'd manacles I hear.
Ib. London, st. 2

But most thro' midnight streets I hear
How the youthful harlot's curse
Blasts the newborn infant's tear,
And blights with plagues the marriage
hearse. *Ib. st. 4*

My mother groan'd! my father wept.
Into the dangerous world I leapt:
Helpless, naked, piping loud:
Like a fiend hid in a cloud.
Ib. Infant Sorrow, st. 1

I was angry with my friend:
I told my wrath, my wrath did end.
I was angry with my foe:
I told it not, my wrath did grow.
Ib. A Poison Tree, st. 1

Cruelty has a human heart,
And Jealousy a human face;
Terror the human form divine,[1]
And Secrecy the human dress.[2]
Ib. A Divine Image, st. 1

My specter around me night and day
Like a wild beast guards my way.
My emanation far within
Weeps incessantly for my sin.
*Poems from MSS [c. 1800–
1803]. Poem, st. 1*

And throughout all eternity
I forgive you, you forgive me.
Ib. st. 14

Mock on, mock on,[3] Voltaire, Rous-
seau:
Mock on, mock on: 'tis all in vain!
You throw the sand against the wind,
And the wind blows it back again.
Ib. Poem, st. 1

Terror in the house does roar,
But Pity stands before the door.
Ib. Fragment

[1] See Milton, p. 344b.
[2] See *The Divine Image*, p. 487a.
[3] See *Job 21:3*, p. 15b.

There is a smile of love,
And there is a smile of deceit,
And there is a smile of smiles
In which these two smiles meet.
                    Poems from MSS. The
                            Smile, st. 1

The cabinet is formed of gold
And pearl and crystal shining bright,
And within it opens into a world
And a little lovely moony night.
            Ib. The Crystal Cabinet, st. 2

For a tear is an intellectual thing,
And a sigh is the sword of an Angel
        King,
And the bitter groan of the martyr's
        woe
Is an arrow from the Almighty's bow.[1]
            Ib The Grey Monk, st. 8

To see a world in a grain of sand
And a heaven in a wild flower,
Hold infinity in the palm of your hand
And eternity in an hour.
            Ib. Auguries of Innocence, l. 1

A robin redbreast in a cage
Puts all Heaven in a rage.   *Ib. l. 5*

A dog starv'd at his master's gate
Predicts the ruin of the state.
                            Ib. l. 9

He who shall hurt the little wren
Shall never be belov'd by men.
                            Ib. l. 29

A truth that's told with bad intent
Beats all the lies you can invent.
                            Ib. l. 53

Every tear from every eye
Becomes a babe in eternity.   *Ib. l. 67*

He who shall teach the child to doubt
The rotting grave shall ne'er get out.
                            Ib. l. 77

He who doubts from what he sees
Will ne'er believe, do what you please.
If the sun and moon should doubt,
They'd immediately go out.   *Ib. l. 97*

The harlot's cry from street to street
Shall weave old England's winding
        sheet.   *Ib. l. 105*

[1] Also in *Jerusalem III, preface* [1804–1820]

Some are born to sweet delight.
Some are born to endless night.
            Poems from MSS. Auguries
                    of Innocence, l. 113

And did those feet in ancient time
Walk   upon   England's   mountains
        green?
And was the holy Lamb of God
On England's pleasant pastures seen?

And did the countenance divine
Shine forth upon our clouded hills?
And was Jerusalem builded here
Among those dark Satanic mills?

Bring me my bow of burning gold:
Bring me my arrows of desire:
Bring me my spear: O clouds unfold!
Bring me my chariot of fire.

I will not cease from mental fight,
Nor shall my sword sleep in my hand
Till we have built Jerusalem
In England's green and pleasant land.
        Milton [1804–1808]. *Preface, poem*

Great things are done when men and
        mountains meet;
This is not done by jostling in the
        street.   *Epigrams* [1808–1811]

If you have form'd a circle to go into,
Go into it yourself and see how you
        would do.   *Ib. To God*

Degrade first the arts if you'd mankind
        degrade.
Hire idiots to paint with cold light and
        hot shade.
            Annotations to Sir Joshua Reyn-
                olds's Discourses [c. 1808]

    To generalize is to be an idiot. To
particularize is the alone distinction of
merit. General knowledges are those
knowledges that idiots possess.   *Ib.*

The Angel that presided o'er my birth
Said, "Little creature, form'd of joy and
        mirth,
Go, love without the help of any thing
        on earth."
            Poems from MSS [c. 1810]

Grown old in love from seven till seven
        times seven,
I oft have wish'd for Hell for ease from
        Heaven.   *Ib.*

The vision of Christ that thou dost see
Is my vision's greatest enemy:
Thine has a great hook nose like thine,
Mine has a snub nose like to mine.
The Everlasting Gospel [*c. 1818*]

Both read the Bible day and night,
But thou read'st black where I read
   white.   *Ib.*

This life's dim windows of the soul
Distorts the heavens from pole to pole
And leads you to believe a lie
When you see with, not thro', the eye [1]
                               Ib.

I am sure this Jesus will not do
Either for Englishman or Jew.   *Ib.*

Poetry fettered fetters the human
race. Nations are destroyed or flourish
in proportion as their poetry, painting,
and music are destroyed or flourish.
     Jerusalem [*1804–1820*], *ch. 1,*
                     preface

He who would do good to another must
   do it in minute particulars:
General good is the plea of the scoundrel, hypocrite and flatterer,
For art and science cannot exist but in
   minutely organized particulars.
                Ib. 3, sec. 55

England! awake! awake! awake!
Jerusalem thy sister calls!
Why wilt thou sleep the sleep of death
   And close her from thy ancient
   walls?   *Ib. 4, sec. 77, st. 1*

JAMES GILLRAY
1757–1815

The Old Lady of Threadneedle
Street.[2]   *Title of cartoon* [*1797*]

JOHN PHILIP KEMBLE
1757–1823

Perhaps it was right to dissemble your
   love,

But — why did you kick me down
  stairs?   *The Panel,*[1] *act I, sc. 1*

ROYALL TYLER
1757–1826

Why should our thoughts to distant
   countries roam,
When each refinement may be found
   at home?   *The Contrast* [*1787*], *prologue*

Since General Shays [2] has sneaked
off and given us the bag to hold.
                Ib. act II, sc. 2

I am at the end of my tether.
                  Ib. III, 1

FISHER AMES
1758–1808

A monarchy is a merchantman which
sails well, but will sometimes strike on a
rock, and go to the bottom; a republic
is a raft which will never sink, but then
your feet are always in the water.
    Speech in the House of Repre-
           sentatives [*1795*]

JAMES MONROE
1758–1831

National honor is national property
of the highest value.
    First Inaugural Address
         [*March 4, 1817*]

The American continents . . . are
henceforth not to be considered as subjects for future colonization by any European powers.
    Annual Message to Congress
    [*December 2, 1823*]; *the Mon-*
    roe Doctrine

In the wars of the European powers
in matters relating to themselves we
have never taken any part, nor does it
comport with our policy so to do.
                       Ib.

---

[1] We are led to believe a lie
  When we see not thro' the eye.
        Auguries of Innocence, l. 112
[2] The Bank of England.

[1] An adaptation of Isaac Bickerstaffe's *'Tis
Well 'Tis No Worse.*
[2] Tyler was involved in suppressing Shays's
Rebellion.

We owe it, therefore, to candor, and to the amicable relations existing between the United States and those powers to declare that we should consider any attempt on their part to extend their system to any portion of this hemisphere as dangerous to our peace and safety. With the existing colonies or dependencies of any European power we . . . shall not interfere. But with the governments . . . whose independence we have . . . acknowledged, we could not view any interposition for the purpose of oppressing them, or controlling, in any other manner, their destiny, by any European power, in any other light than as a manifestation of an unfriendly disposition towards the United States.

> *Annual Message to Congress; the Monroe Doctrine*

HORATIO NELSON
1758–1805

Westminster Abbey, or victory!
> *At the Battle of Cape St. Vincent [February 14, 1797]. From* SOUTHEY, *Life of Nelson [1813], ch. 4*

I have only one eye, I have a right to be blind sometimes . . . I really do not see the signal.
> *At the Battle of Copenhagen [1801]. Ib. 9*

Something must be left to chance; nothing is sure in a sea fight beyond all others.
> *Memorandum to the fleet, off Cadiz [October 9, 1805]*

But, in case signals can neither be seen or perfectly understood, no captain can do very wrong if he places his ship alongside that of the enemy. *Ib.*

England expects every man will do his duty.[1]
> *At the Battle of Trafalgar [October 21, 1805]. From* SOUTHEY, *Life of Nelson [1813], ch. 9*

[1] This famous sentence is thus first reported: "Say to the fleet, England confides that every

Thank God, I have done my duty.
> *At the Battle of Trafalgar. From* SOUTHEY, *Life of Nelson, ch. 9*

Kiss me, Hardy. *Ib.*

ROBERT BURNS
1759–1796

Wee, sleekit, cow'rin, tim'rous beastie,
O, what a panic's in thy breastie!
Thou need na start awa sae hasty,
 Wi' bickering brattle!
> *To a Mouse [1785], st. 1*

I'm truly sorry man's dominion
Has broken Nature's social union.
> *Ib. st. 2*

The best laid schemes o' mice and men
Gang aft a-gley.[1] *Ib. st. 7*

 Nature's law,
That man was made to mourn.
> *Man Was Made to Mourn [1786], st. 4*

Man's inhumanity to man.[2]
Makes countless thousands mourn!
> *Ib. st. 7*

He wales a portion with judicious care;
And "Let us worship God" he says,
 with solemn air.
> *The Cotter's Saturday Night [1786], st. 12*

From scenes like these, old Scotia's grandeur springs,
That makes her loved at home, revered abroad:
Princes and lords are but the breath of kings,[3]
"An honest man's the noblest work of God." [4] *Ib. st. 19*

man will do his duty." Captain Pasco, Nelson's flag lieutenant, suggested substituting "expects" for "confides," which was adopted. Captain Blackwood, who commanded the *Euryalus*, says that the correction suggested was from "Nelson expects" to "England expects."
[1] See Ihara Saikaku, p. 379a.
[2] See Pliny, p. 132b, and Wordsworth, p. 508b.
[3] See Goldsmith, p. 449a.
[4] See Pope, p. 409b.

Gie me ae spark o' Nature's fire,
That's a' the learning I desire.
> *First Epistle to J. Lapraik*
> [1786], *st. 13*

The social, friendly, honest man,
  Whate'er he be,
'Tis he fulfills great Nature's plan,
  And none but he!
> *Second Epistle to J. Lapraik*
> [1786], *st. 15*

On ev'ry hand it will allow'd be,
He's just — nae better than he should
be.
> *A Dedication to Gavin Hamilton*
> [1786]

It's hardly in a body's pow'r,
To keep, at times, frae being sour.
> *Epistle to Davie* [1786], *st. 2*

Misled by fancy's meteor ray,
  By passion driven;
But yet the light that led astray
  Was light from heaven.
> *The Vision* [1786], II, *st. 18*

His lockèd, lettered, braw brass collar
Showed him the gentleman an'
  scholar.
> *The Twa Dogs* [1786], *st. 3*

An' there began a lang digression
About the lords o' the creation.
> *Ib. st. 6*

Oh wad some power the giftie gie us
To see oursels as others see us!
It wad frae monie a blunder free us,
  An' foolish notion.
> *To a Louse* [1786], *st. 8*

Wee, modest, crimson-tippèd flow'r,
Thou's met me in an evil hour;
For I maun crush amang the stoure
  Thy slender stem:
To spare thee now is past my pow'r,
  Thou bonie gem.
> *To a Mountain Daisy* [1786], *st. 1*

Stern Ruin's plowshare drives elate,
Full on thy bloom.[1]   *Ib. st. 9*

[1] See Edward Young, p. 399b.

O life! thou art a galling load,
Along a rough, a weary road,
  To wretches such as I!
> *Despondency* [1786], *st. 1*

Perhaps it may turn out a sang,
Perhaps turn out a sermon.
> *Epistle to a Young Friend*
> [1786], *st. 1*

I waive the quantum o' the sin,
The hazard of concealing;
But, och! it hardens a' within,
And petrifies the feeling!   *Ib. st. 6*

An atheist-laugh's a poor exchange
For Deity offended.   *Ib. st. 9*

There's nought but care on ev'ry han',
In every hour that passes, O:
What signifies the life o' man,
An' 't were nae for the lasses, O.
> *Green Grow the Rashes, O*
> [1787], *st. 1*

Auld Nature swears, the lovely dears
Her noblest work she classes, O:
Her prentice han' she try'd on man,
An' then she made the lasses, O.
> *Ib. st. 5*

Green grow the rashes, O;
Green grow the rashes, O;
The sweetest hours that e'er I spend
Are spent among the lasses, O.
> *Ib. chorus*

I wasna fou, but just had plenty.
> *Death and Dr. Hornbook*
> [1787], *st. 3*

John Barleycorn got up again,
And sore surpris'd them all.
> *John Barleycorn* [1787], *st. 3*

The heart benevolent and kind
The most resembles God.
> *A Winter Night* [1787]

Ye're aiblins nae temptation.
> *Address to the Unco Guid*
> [1787], *st. 6*

Then gently scan your brother man,
Still gentler sister woman;
Tho' they may gang a kennin wrang,
To step aside is human.   *Ib. st. 7*

O, my Luve is like a red, red rose,
That's newly sprung in June.
O, my Luve is like the melodie,
That's sweetly play'd in tune.
          Johnson's Musical Museum
          [1787–1796]. *A Red, Red*
          Rose, st. 1

Contented wi' little and cantie wi'
mair.
          Ib. Contented wi' Little, st. 1

Ye banks and braes o' bonny Doon,
How can ye bloom sae fresh and fair?
How can ye chant, ye little birds,
And I sae weary fu' o' care!
Thou'll break my heart, thou warbling
     bird,
That wantons thro' the flowering
     thorn!
Thou minds me o' departed joys,
Departed never to return.
          Ib. The Banks o' Doon, st. 1

Chords that vibrate sweetest pleasure
Thrill the deepest notes of woe.
          Ib. Sensibility How Charming, st. 4

Ae fond kiss, and then we sever;
Ae farewell and then forever!
          Ib. Ae Fond Kiss, st. 1

But to see her was to love her,
Love but her, and love forever.[1]
Had we never lov'd sae kindly,
Had we never lov'd sae blindly,
Never met — or never parted —
We had ne'er been broken-hearted.
          Ib. st. 2

It was a' for our rightfu' King
We left fair Scotland's strand.
          Ib. It Was A' for Our Rightfu'
          King, st. 1

Now a' is done that men can do,
And a' is done in vain.   *Ib. st. 2*

He turn'd him right and round about
Upon the Irish shore;
And gae his bridle reins a shake,
With adieu forevermore,
          My dear —
And adieu forevermore!   *Ib. st. 3*

[1] See Halleck, p. 565b, and Tennyson, p. 647a.

John Anderson my jo, John,
When we were first acquent,
Your locks were like the raven,
Your bonie brow was brent;
But now your brow is beld, John,
Your locks are like the snaw,
But blessings on your frosty pow,
John Anderson my jo!

John Anderson my jo, John,
We clamb the hill thegither,
And mony a cantie day, John,
We've had wi' ane anither;
Now we maun totter down, John,
And hand in hand we'll go,
And sleep thegither at the foot,
John Anderson, my jo!
          Johnson's Musical Museum.
          John Anderson My Jo, st.
          1, 2

Farewell to the Highlands, farewell to
     the North,
The birthplace of valor, the country of
     worth!
Wherever I wander, wherever I rove,
The hills of the Highlands for ever I
     love.
          Ib. My Heart's in the Highlands,
          st. 1

My heart's in the Highlands, my heart is
     not here,
My heart's in the Highlands a-chasing
     the deer;
A-chasing the wild deer, and following
     the roe,
My heart's in the Highlands wherever
     I go.   *Ib. chorus*

O whistle, and I'll come to you, my
     lad:
Tho' father and mither and a' should
     gae mad,
O whistle, and I'll come to you, my
     lad.
          Whistle, and I'll Come to You,
          My Lad

Should auld acquaintance be forgot,
And never brought to mind?
Should auld acquaintance be forgot,
And auld lang syne!
          Auld Lang Syne [1788], *st. 1*

For auld lang syne, my dear,
For auld lang syne,
We'll tak a cup o' kindness yet
For auld lang syne!
> *Auld Lang Syne, chorus*

Flow gently, sweet Afton, among thy green braes,
Flow gently, I'll sing thee a song in thy praise.
My Mary's asleep by thy murmuring stream,
Flow gently, sweet Afton, disturb not her dream.
> *Afton Water* [1789,] *st.* 1

This day Time winds th' exhausted chain,
To run the twelvemonth's length again.
> *New Year's Day* [1791], *st.* 1

The voice of Nature loudly cries,
And many a message from the skies,
That something in us never dies.
> *Ib. st.* 3

When Nature her great masterpiece design'd,
And fram'd her last, best work, the human mind,
Her eye intent on all the wondrous plan,
She form'd of various stuff the various Man.
> *To Robert Graham* [1791], *st.* 1

She is a winsome wee thing,
She is a handsome wee thing,
She is a lo'esome wee thing,
This sweet wee wife o' mine.
> *My Wife's a Winsome Wee Thing* [1792], *chorus*

The golden hours on angel wings
Flew o'er me and my dearie;
For dear to me as light and life
Was my sweet Highland Mary.
> *Highland Mary* [1792], *st.* 2

But, oh! fell death's untimely frost,
That nipt my flower sae early.
> *Ib. st.* 3

If there's a hole in a' your coats,
I rede you tent it;

A chield's amang you takin' notes,
And faith he'll prent it.
> *On the Late Captain Grose's Peregrinations Thro' Scotland* [1793], *st.* 1

Some hae meat and canna eat,
And some wad eat that want it;
But we hae meat, and we can eat,
And sae the Lord be thankit.
> *The Selkirk Grace* [1793] *(attributed)*

O Mary, at thy window be!
It is the wish'd, the trysted hour.
> *Mary Morison* [1793], *st.* 1

The lovely Mary Morison!   *Ib.*

Whare sits our sulky, sullen dame,
Gathering her brows like gathering storm,
Nursing her wrath to keep it warm.
> *Tam o' Shanter* [1793], *l.* 10

Ah, gentle dames! it gars me greet
To think how monie counsels sweet,
How monie lengthened, sage advices,
The husband frae the wife despises.
> *Ib. l.* 33

His ancient, trusty, drouthy crony;
Tam lo'ed him like a vera brither —
They had been fou for weeks thegither.
> *Ib. l.* 43

Kings may be blest, but Tam was glorious,
O'er a' the ills o' life victorious.
> *Ib. l.* 57

But pleasures are like poppies spread —
You seize the flow'r, its bloom is shed;
Or like the snow falls in the river —
A moment white — then melts forever.
> *Ib. l.* 59

That hour, o' night's black arch the keystane.   *Ib. l.* 69

Inspiring bold John Barleycorn!
What dangers thou canst make us scorn!
Wi' tippenny, we fear nae evil;
Wi' usquebae, we'll face the devil!
> *Ib. l.* 105

As Tammie glow'red, amazed, and curious,
The mirth and fun grew fast and furious.   *Tam o' Shanter, l. 143*

Her cutty sark, o' Paisley harn,
That while a lassie she had worn,
In longitude tho' sorely scanty,
It was her best, and she was vauntie.
      Ib. l. 171

"Weel done, Cutty Sark!"[1]
      Ib. l. 189

Ah, Tam! Ah! Tam! Thou'll get thy
fairin'!
In hell they'll roast you like a herrin'!
      Ib. l. 201

Scots wha hae wi' Wallace bled,
Scots wham Bruce has aften led,
Welcome to your gory bed
    Or to victorie.

Now's the day, and now's the hour;
See the front o' battle lour!
See approach proud Edward's pow-
    er —
    Chains and slaverie!
      Scots Wha Hae [1794], *st. 1, 2*

Lay the proud usurpers low!
Tyrants fall in every foe!
Liberty's in every blow!
    Let us do or die![2]   *Ib. st. 6*

The rank is but the guinea's stamp,
The man's the gowd for a' that.
      For A' That and A' That [1795],
            st. 1

A prince can mak a belted knight,
A marquis, duke, and a' that;
But an honest man's aboon his might,
Guid faith, he mauna fa' that.
      Ib. st. 4

For a' that, and a' that,
An' twice as muckle 's a' that,
I've lost but ane, I've twa behin',
I've wife eneugh for a' that.
      Posthumous Pieces [1799].
      The Jolly Beggars, chorus

[1] The famous tea clipper *Cutty Sark,* designed
by Hercules Linton and built in 1869, had the
story of Tam o' Shanter carved upon her bow
and counter. Nannie, with flying locks and scanty
shift, was the figurehead.
[2] See Fletcher, p. 313b.

God knows, I'm no the thing I should
be,
Nor am I even the thing I could be.
      *Posthumous Pieces. To the Rev-
      erend John M'Math, st. 8*

If there's another world, he lives in
bliss;
If there is none, he made the best of
this.
      Ib. Epitaph on William Muir

In durance vile here must I wake and
weep,
And all my frowsy couch in sorrow
steep.
      Ib. Epistle from Esopus to Maria

It's guid to be merry and wise,
It's guid to be honest and true,
It's guid to support Caledonia's cause
And bide by the buff and the blue.
      *Ib. Here's a Health to Them
            That's Awa', st. 1*

GEORGES JACQUES DANTON
1759–1794

Everything belongs to the fatherland
when the fatherland is in danger.
      *Speech to the Legislative As-
      sembly* [August 28, 1792]

We must dare, and dare again, and
go on daring.[1]
      Ib. [September 2, 1792]

Show my head to the people, it is
worth seeing.
      *Last words, addressed to the
            executioner*

WILLIAM PITT
1759–1806

Necessity is the plea for every in-
fringement of human freedom. It is the
argument of tyrants; it is the creed of
slaves.[2]
      Speech, House of Commons
            [November 18, 1783]

[1] Il nous faut de l'audace, encore de l'audace,
toujours de l'audace.
See Spenser. p. 200b, and note.
[2] See Publilius Syrus, p. 126b.

JOHANN CHRISTOPH FRIEDRICH VON SCHILLER
1759–1805

I feel an army in my fist.
> *Die Räuber (The Robbers)*
> *[1781], act II, end*

The lemonade is weak, like your soul.
> *Kabala und Liebe* [1784], *act V,*
> *sc. 7*

Joy, thou spark from Heav'n immortal,
Daughter of Elysium!
Drunk with fire, toward Heaven advancing
Goddess, to thy shrine we come.
Thy sweet magic brings together
What stern Custom spreads afar;
All mankind knows all men brothers
Where thy happy wing-beats are.[1]
> *An die Freude (Ode to Joy)*
> [1785],[2] *st. 1*

O embrace now all you millions,
With one kiss for all the world.
Brothers, high beyond all stars
Surely dwells a loving Father.
> *Ib. st. 5*

There are three lessons I would write,
Three words as with a burning pen,
In tracings of eternal light
Upon the hearts of men.
> *Hope, Faith, and Love* [c. 1786],
> *st. 1*

Thus grave these lessons on thy soul —
Hope, faith, and love; and thou shalt find

---

[1] Alle Menschen werden Brüder,
Wo dein sanfter Flügel weilt.
[2] Translated by THEODORE SPENCER for the Boston Symphony Orchestra, for the performance of Beethoven's Ninth Symphony.
   It was during his student days in Bonn that Beethoven fastened upon Schiller's poem. . . . The heady sense of liberation in the verses must have appealed to him as they appealed to every German. They were in the spirit of the times, the spirit that had swept Europe and America, and Beethoven belonged to his time. — JOHN N. BURK, *program notes for the Boston Symphony Orchestra* [October 1, 1965]

Strength when life's surges rudest roll,
Light when thou else wert blind!
> *Hope, Faith, and Love, st. 5*

World history is the world's court.[1]
> *Resignation* [1786]

What one refuses in a minute
No eternity will return.   *Ib.*

O who knows what slumbers in the background of the times?
> *Don Carlos* [1787], *act I, sc. 1*

O the idea was childish, but divinely beautiful.   *Ib. 2*

Great souls suffer in silence.   *Ib. 4*

A moment lived in paradise
Is not atoned for too dearly by death.
> *Ib. 5*

The richest monarch in the Christian world;
The sun in my own dominions never sets.[2]   *Ib. 6*

Honor women! They wreathe and weave
Heavenly roses into earthly life.
> *Würde der Frauen (The Wonder of Women)* [1795], *l. 186*

What the inner voice says
Will not disappoint the hoping soul.
> *Hope, last stanza* [1797]

If you want to know yourself,
Just look how others do it;
If you want to understand others,
Look into your own heart.
> *Tabulae Votivae* [1797]

Man is created free, and is free,
Though he be born in chains.[3]
> *Die Worte des Glaubens (The Word of the Faithful)* [1797],
> *st. 2*

Virtue is no empty echo.   *Ib. st. 3*

---

[1] Die Weltgeschichte ist das Weltgericht.
[2] See Scott, p. 522a, and Daniel Webster, p. 548a.
[3] See Rousseau, p. 435b, and Bliss, p. 468b.

Posterity weaves no garlands for imitators.

> *Wallensteins Lager* (*Wallenstein's Camp*) [1798], prologue

He who has done his best for his own time has lived for all times. *Ib.*

Life is earnest, art is gay. *Ib.*

Whatever is not forbidden is permitted. *Ib. sc. 6*

Live and let live.[1] *Ib.*

The peasant is also human — in a manner of speaking. *Ib. sc. 10*

Man is made of ordinary things, and habit is his nurse.

> *Wallensteins Tod* (*Wallenstein's Death*) [1798], act I, sc. 4

I have only an office here, and no opinion. *Ib. 5*

What is life without the radiance of love? *Ib. IV, 12*

Time is man's angel. *Ib. V, 11*

What is the short meaning of the long speech?

> *Piccolomini* [1799], act I, sc. 2

In thy breast are the stars of thy fate. *Ib. II, 6*

You say it as you understand it. *Ib.*

When the wine goes in, strange things come out. *Ib. 12*

The dictates of the heart are the voice of fate. *Ib. III, 8*

O tender yearning, sweet hoping!
The golden time of first love!
The eye sees the open heaven,
The heart is intoxicated with bliss;
O that the beautiful time of young love
Could remain green forever.

> *The Song of the Bell* [1799]

Appearance should never attain reality,
And if nature conquers, then must art retire.

> *To Goethe, when he put Voltaire's Mahomet on the stage* [1800]

Life is only error,
And death is knowledge.

> *Cassandra* [1802]

I am better than my reputation.

> *Maria Stuart* [1801], act III, sc. 4

For this should the singer accompany the king:
Both dwell on the heights of mankind.

> *Die Jungfrau von Orleans* (*Joan of Arc*) [1801], act I, sc. 2

Against stupidity the very gods
Themselves contend in vain.[1]

> *Ib. III, 6*

Pain is short, and joy is eternal.

> *Ib. last lines*

What are hopes, what are plans?

> *Die Braut von Messina* (*The Bride of Messina*) [1803], act III, sc. 5

Don't let your heart depend on things
That ornament life in a fleeting way!
He who possesses, let him learn to lose,
He who is fortunate, let him learn pain. *Ib. IV, 4*

On the mountains there is freedom!
The world is perfect everywhere,
Save where man comes with his torment. *Ib. IV, 7*

Who reflects too much will accomplish little.

> *Wilhelm Tell* [1804], act III, sc. 1

This feat of Tell, the archer, will be told
While yonder mountains stand upon their base.
By Heaven! The apple's cleft right through the core. *Ib. 3*

---

[1] Also attributed to Wieland in the Goethe-Zelter correspondence.

Quoted in GOETHE, *Faust*, prologue [1808], and in SWINBURNE, *Félise* [1866], st. 59.

[1] Against boredom even the gods themselves struggle in vain. — NIETZSCHE [1844–1900], *The Antichrist, 48*

The most pious man can't stay in peace
If it doesn't please his evil neighbor.
Wilhelm Tell, act IV, sc. 3

MASON LOCKE WEEMS
1759–1825

"George," said his father, "do you know who killed that beautiful little cherry tree yonder in the garden?" . . . Looking at his father with the sweet face of youth brightened with the inexpressible charm of all-conquering truth, he bravely cried out. "I can't tell a lie. I did cut it with my hatchet." [1]
The Life of George Washington: With Curious Anecdotes, Equally Honorable to Himself and Exemplary to His Young Countrymen [1800]

JOSEPH ROUGET DE LISLE
1760–1836

Allons, enfants de la patrie,
Le jour de gloire est arrivé! . . .
Aux armes, citoyens!
Formez vos bataillons!
Marchons! Marchons! Qu'un sang impur
Abreuve nos sillons!
The Marseillaise [2] [1792]

AUGUST FRIEDRICH FERDINAND VON KOTZEBUE
1761–1819

There is another and a better world.
The Stranger [1798], *act I, sc. 1*

---

[1] See George Washington, p. 462a.
[2] Forward, sons of France, the day of glory has come! . . . To arms, citizens! Line up in battalions! Let us march on! And let the impure blood [of our enemies] drench our fields.
Composed in the garrison at Strasbourg and originally called *Chant de guerre de l'armée du Rhin*, the *Marseillaise* took its name from the patriots of Marseilles, who first made it known in Paris.

ANTOINE BOULAY DE LA MEURTHE
1761–1840

It is worse than a crime, it is a blunder.[1]
On the execution of the Duc d'Enghien [1804]

WILLIAM LISLE BOWLES [2]
1762–1850

The cause of Freedom is the cause of God! *Edmund Burke, l. 78*

ANDREW CHERRY
1762–1812

Loud roar'd the dreadful thunder,
The rain a deluge show'rd.
The Bay of Biscay

Till next day,
There she lay,
In the Bay of Biscay, O! *Ib.*

GEORGE COLMAN THE YOUNGER
1762–1836

Tell 'em Queen Anne's dead.[3]
The Heir-at-Law [1797],
act I, sc. 1

Not to be sneezed at. *Ib. II, 1*

Like two single gentlemen rolled into one.
Lodgings for Single Gentlemen

When taken,
To be well shaken.
The Newcastle Apothecary

O Miss Bailey!
Unfortunate Miss Bailey!
*Love Laughs at Locksmiths,
act II, song*

Says he, "I am a handsome man, but I'm a gay deceiver." *Ib.*

---

[1] C'est pire qu'un crime, c'est une faute.
Attributed also to TALLEYRAND and FOUCHÉ. SAINTE-BEUVE attributes it to DE LA MEURTHE.
[2] See Simonides, *Fragment 92*, p. 70b.
[3] The phrase became proverbial for telling what everybody knows.

His heart runs away with his head.
Who Wants a Guinea?, act I, sc. 1

I had a soul above buttons.
Sylvester Daggerwood; or, New Hay at the Old Market, sc. 1

Mynheer Vandunck, though he never was drunk,
Sipped brandy and water gaily.
Mynheer Vandunck

John Bull,[1] or An Englishman's Fireside. *Title of play* [1803]

DOROTHEA JORDAN
1762–1816

"Oh where, and Oh! where is your Highland laddie gone?"
"He's gone to fight the French, for King George upon the throne,
And it's Oh! in my heart, how I wish him safe at home!"
The Blue Bells of Scotland

JOSEPH FOUCHÉ
1763–1820

Death is an eternal sleep.[2]
Inscription placed by his orders on cemetery gates [1794]

JOHANN PAUL FRIEDRICH RICHTER [JEAN PAUL]
1763–1825

Weltschmerz.[3]
Selena, oder Über die Unsterblichkeit [or Above Immortality], 2

Providence has given to the French the empire of the land; to the English that of the sea; to the Germans that of — the air!
From CARLYLE, *Critical and Miscellaneous Essays. Richter* [1827]

[1] The origin of the supposed type of the British character.
[2] See Catullus, p. 114b.
[3] Literally, world pain.

SAMUEL ROGERS
1763–1855

Think nothing done while aught remains to do.
Human Life, l. 49

Never less alone than when alone.[1]
Ib. l. 756

By many a temple half as old as Time.[2]
Italy. A Farewell

Mine be a cot beside the hill;
A beehive's hum shall soothe my ear;
A willowy brook that turns a mill,
With many a fall shall linger near.[3]
A Wish, st. 1

Go! you may call it madness, folly;
You shall not chase my gloom away!
There's such a charm in melancholy
I would not if I could be gay.
To —— [1814], st. 1

It doesn't much signify whom one marries, for one is sure to find next morning that it was someone else.
Table Talk

Ward has no heart, they say, but I deny it;
He has a heart, and gets his speeches by it. *Epigram*

JOHANN GOTTFRIED SEUME
1763–1810

You can relax peacefully wherever there is singing
Without fear of what is thought in the land;
No man is robbed where there is singing,
For scoundrels have no songs.
Songs [1804], first strophe

ROBERT HALL
1764–1831

Call things by their right names. . . . Glass of brandy and water! That is the current but not the appropriate

[1] See Cicero, p. 111b.
[2] See John William Burgon, p. 675b.
[3] See Yeats, p. 879b.

name: ask for a glass of liquid fire and distilled damnation.

> *From* OLINTHUS GREGORY, *Brief Memoir of the Life of Hall*

GASTON PIERRE MARC, DUC DE LÉVIS
1764–1830

Noblesse oblige.[1]

> *Maxims and Reflections* [1808]

THOMAS MORTON
1764–1838

Push on — keep moving.

> *A Cure for the Heartache* [1797], act II, sc. 1

Approbation from Sir Hubert Stanley is praise indeed. *Ib.* V, 2

What will Mrs. Grundy say? What will Mrs. Grundy think? [2]

> *Speed the Plow* [1798], act I, sc. 1

ANN RADCLIFFE
1764–1823

Fate sits on these dark battlements and frowns,
And as the portal opens to receive me,
A voice in hollow murmurs through the courts
Tells of a nameless deed.[3]

> *The Mysteries of Udolpho* [1794], motto

CATHERINE MARIA FANSHAWE
1765–1834

'Twas whisper'd in heaven, 'twas mutter'd in hell,
And echo caught faintly the sound as it fell;
On the confines of earth 'twas permitted to rest,
And the depths of the ocean its presence confess'd.

> *Enigma: The Letter H*

---

[1] See Sophocles, p. 81a, and Euripides, p. 85b.
[2] See Spencer, p. 706a, and Locker-Hampson, p. 710a.
[3] See Shakespeare, *Macbeth IV, i, 49*, p. 285b.

ROBERT GOODLOE HARPER
1765–1825

Millions for defense, but not one cent for tribute.[1]

> *Toast at banquet for John Marshall* [June 18, 1798]

MARY LAMB
1765–1847

Thou straggler into loving arms,
Young climber-up of knees.

> *A Child, st. 3*

SIR JAMES MACKINTOSH
1765–1832

Diffused knowledge immortalizes itself. *Vindiciae Gallicae* [1791]

The Commons, faithful to their system, remained in a wise and masterly inactivity. *Ib.*

The frivolous work of polished idleness.

> *Dissertation on Ethical Philosophy* [1830]. *Remarks on Thomas Brown*

Disciplined inaction.

> *History of the Revolution in England in 1688* [1834], ch. 7

ISAAC D'ISRAELI
1766–1848

Whatever is felicitously expressed risks being worse expressed: it is a wretched taste to be gratified with mediocrity when the excellent lies before us.

> *Curiosities of Literature* [1834]. *On Quotation*

---

[1] In 1797 a secret agent from Talleyrand told Charles Cotesworth Pinckney, Minister to the French Republic, that the American Commissioners in Paris to protest French attacks on U.S. shipping would be received only if they paid a $50,000 bribe and made a large loan to the French government. Pinckney's reply was: "Not a sixpence, sir." Later, Harper's remark was attributed to him.

THOMAS ROBERT MALTHUS
1766–1834

Population, when unchecked, increases in a geometrical ratio. Subsistence increases only in an arithmetical ratio. A slight acquaintance with numbers will show the immensity of the first power in comparison of the second.

An Essay on the Principle of Population [1798]

ERNST F. MÜNSTER[1]
1766–1839

Absolutism tempered by assassination.

Description of the Russian Constitution

CAROLINA, BARONESS NAIRNE
1766–1845

Will ye no come back again?
Better lo'ed ye canna be,
Will ye no come back again?

Life and Songs [1869]. *Bonnie Charlie's Now Awa'. Also attributed to* JAMES HOGG [1770–1835]

Charlie is my darling, the young Chevalier.

Ib. Charlie Is My Darling (also attributed to Hogg)

Wi' a hundred pipers an' a', an' a',
We'll up an' gie them a blaw, a blaw,
Wi' a hundred pipers an' a', an' a'.

Ib. The Hundred Pipers

Gude nicht, and joy be wi' you a'.

Ib. Gude Nicht

A penniless lass wi' a lang pedigree.

Ib. The Laird o' Cockpen

I'm wearin' awa'
To the land o' the leal.

Ib. The Land o' the Leal

There's nae sorrow there, John,
There's neither cauld nor care, John,
The day is aye fair,
In the land o' the leal.

Life and Songs. The Land o' the Leal

MADAME DE STAËL [GERMAINE, BARONNE DE STAËL-HOLSTEIN]
1766–1817

Love is the whole history of a woman's life, it is but an episode in a man's.[1]

De l'Influence des Passions [1796]

A man must know how to defy opinion; a woman how to submit to it.

Delphine [1802]

The sight of such a monument is like a continuous and stationary music.[2]

Corinne [1807], *bk. IV, ch. 3*

To understand everything makes one tolerant.[3]

Ib. XVIII, 5

I would gladly give half of the wit with which I am credited for half of the beauty you possess.

Letter to Madame Récamier

JOHN QUINCY ADAMS
1767–1848

Think of your forefathers! Think of your posterity![4]

Speech at Plymouth [December 22, 1802]

In charity to all mankind, bearing no malice or ill-will to any human being, and even compassionating those who

---

[1] Hanoverian envoy at St. Petersburg.

---

[1] L'amour est l'histoire de la vie des femmes, c'est un episode dans celle des hommes.
[2] See Goethe, p. 478a.
[3] Tout comprendre rend très indulgent.
Attributed to Madame de Staël are similar phrases: Comprendre c'est pardonner [To understand is to forgive]. Tout comprendre c'est tout pardonner [To know everything is to forgive everything].
[4] Et maiores vestros et posteros cogitate. — TACITUS [*c.* A.D. 55–117], *Agricola 32, 26*

hold in bondage their fellow men, not knowing what they do.[1]

> *Letter to A. Bronson*
> *[July 30, 1838]*

My wants are many, and, if told,
Would muster many a score;
And were each wish a mint of gold,
I still should long for more.

> *The Wants of Man* [1841], *st. 1*

This is the last of earth! I am content.

> *Last words [February 21, 1848]*

ANDREW JACKSON[2]
1767–1845

The individual who refuses to defend his rights when called by his Government, deserves to be a slave, and must be punished as an enemy of his country and friend to her foe.

> *Proclamation to the people of Louisiana from Mobile [September 21, 1814]*

The brave man inattentive to his duty, is worth little more to his country, than the coward who deserts her in the hour of danger.

> *To troops who had abandoned their lines during the battle of New Orleans [January 8, 1815]*

Our Federal Union! it must be preserved!

> *Toast at Jefferson Birthday Celebration* [1830]

Every man is equally entitled to protection by law; but when the laws undertake to add . . . artificial distinctions, to grant titles, gratuities, and exclusive privileges, to make the rich richer and the potent more powerful, the humble members of society — the farmers, mechanics, and laborers — who have neither the time nor the means of securing like favors to them-

selves, have a right to complain of the injustice of their government.

> *Veto of the Bank Bill*
> *[July 10, 1832]*

There are no necessary evils in government. Its evils exist only in its abuses. If it would confine itself to equal protection, and, as Heaven does its rains, shower its favors alike on the high and the low, the rich and the poor, it would be an unqualified blessing.   *Ib.*

One man with courage makes a majority.   *Saying*

FRANÇOIS RENÉ DE CHATEAUBRIAND
1768–1848

[On his conversion to Christianity] I wept and I believed.[1]

> *Le Génie du Christianisme* [1802]

Achilles exists only through Homer. Take away the art of writing from this world, and you will probably take away its glory.[2]

> *Les Natchez* [1826], *preface*

ERNST MORITZ ARNDT
1769–1860

The God who made iron grow
Wanted no slaves.

> *Vaterlandslied* [1812]

What is the German Fatherland?
Wherever the German tongue is heard.

> *Was Ist Des Deutschen Vaterland* [1813]

The Rhine: Germany's river, but not Germany's border.

> *Title of a work* [1813]

---

[1] See Abraham Lincoln, p. 640b.
[2] He was the most American of Americans — an embodied Declaration of Independence — the Fourth of July incarnate. — JAMES PARTON, *Life of Andrew Jackson* [1859]

[1] J'ai pleuré et j'ai cru.
[2] See Pindar, p. 79b, and Alexander the Great, p. 102a.

NAPOLEON I
[NAPOLEON BONAPARTE]
1769–1821

Soldiers, from the summit of yonder pyramids forty centuries look down upon you.

In Egypt [July 21, 1798]

Go, sir, gallop, and don't forget that the world was made in six days. You can ask me for anything you like, except time.

To an aide [1803]. From R. M. JOHNSTON, The Corsican

A form of government that is not the result of a long sequence of shared experiences, efforts, and endeavors can never take root.

[1803] From J. CHRISTOPHER HEROLD, The Mind of Napoleon [1955]

From the sublime to the ridiculous is but a step.[1]

To the Abbé du Pradt, on the return from Russia [1812], referring to the retreat from Moscow

You write to me that it's impossible; the word is not French.

Letter to General Lemarois [July 9, 1813]

What is the throne? — a bit of wood gilded and covered with velvet. I am the state[2] — I alone am here the representative of the people. Even if I had done wrong you should not have reproached me in public — people wash their dirty linen at home.[3] France has more need of me than I of France.

To the Senate [1814]

France is invaded; I am leaving to take command of my troops, and, with God's help and their valor, I hope soon to drive the enemy beyond the frontier.

At Paris [January 23, 1814]

The bullet that will kill me is not yet cast.

At Montereau [February 17, 1814]

The Allied Powers having proclaimed that the Emperor Napoleon is the sole obstacle to the re-establishment of peace in Europe, he, faithful to his oath, declares that he is ready to descend from the throne, to quit France, and even to relinquish life, for the good of his country.

Act of Abdication [April 4, 1814]

Unite for the public safety, if you would remain an independent nation.

Proclamation to the French People [June 22, 1815]

Wherever wood can swim, there I am sure to find this flag of England.

At Rochefort [July 1815]

Whatever shall we do in that remote spot? Well, we will write our memoirs. Work is the scythe of time.

On board H. M. S. Bellerophon [August 1815]

[Of his relations with the Empress Josephine] I generally had to give in.

On St. Helena [May 19, 1816]

My maxim was, *la carrière est ouverte aux talents,* without distinction of birth or fortune.[1]

Ib. [March 3, 1817]

Our hour is marked, and no one can claim a moment of life beyond what fate has predestined.

To Dr. Arnott [April 1821]

Two o'clock in the morning courage: I mean unprepared courage.[2]

[December 4, 5, 1815] From LAS CASES, Mémorial de Ste-Hélène [1823]

---

[1] Du sublime au ridicule il n'y a qu'un pas. The saying has been attributed also to Talleyrand.

See Paine, p. 467b.

[2] See Louis XIV, p. 378a.

[3] Il faut laver son linge sale en famille [One should wash one's dirty linen at home]. — *Saying current since about 1720*

[1] See Carlyle, p. 575b.

[2] Le courage de l'improviste.

The three o'clock in the morning courage, which Bonaparte thought was the rarest. — THOREAU, *Walden [1854],* ch. 4, Sounds

See F. Scott Fitzgerald, p. 1036b.

Madame Montholon having inquired what troops he considered the best, "Those which are victorious, Madame," replied the Emperor.
From BOURRIENNE, *Memoirs* [1829]

A silk stocking filled with mud.
Description of Talleyrand; attributed by SAINTE-BEUVE

An army marches on its stomach.
Attributed

Every French soldier carries a marshal's baton in his knapsack.[1]
Attributed

Perfidious Albion.[2]   *Attributed*

Chief of the Army.[3]   *Last words*

IVAN KRYLOV
1769–1844

The tricksome little monkey,
The goat with tangled hair,
The donkey,
And the clumsy-fingered bear
A great quartet had planned to start;
They got the notes, viola, fiddles, bass,
And sat beneath a lime tree, on the grass,
To charm creation with their art.
Fables [1809],[4] *The Quartet*

It can't go right like that; you don't know how to sit!   *Ib.*

We'll play to quite another tune
And make the hills and forest dance for glee.   *Ib.*

I'm sure we'll make it go
By sitting in a row.   *Ib.*

---

[1] Tout soldat français porte dans sa giberne le bâton de maréchal de France.

[2] L'Angleterre, ah! la perfide Angleterre. — JACQUES BÉNIGNE BOSSUET [1627–1704], *Sermon sur la Circoncision*

Napoleon used the phrase in 1803, and it became widespread during the French Revolution.

[B] Tête d'armée.

[4] Translated by SIR BERNARD PARES.

We've notes, we've instruments; do tell us how to sit!
The nightingale replies: To sit is not enough.   *Fables, The Quartet*

Then change your seats, and fiddles too:
For chamber music's not for you!   *Ib.*

When partners can't agree
Their business fares disastrously.
Ib. Swan, Pike and Crab

One day, the pike, the crab, the swan
Set out to drag a truck along the road,
All three together harnessed to the load.   *Ib.*

It was not that their load was difficult to move;
But upward strained the swan, toward the skies above,
The crab kept stepping back, the pike was for the pond.
And which was right or wrong, I neither know nor care:
I only know the truck's still there.   *Ib.*

You think I've got the time to count your crimes, you pup?
Your guilt consists in this: I want to eat you up!   *Ib. Wolf and Lamb* [1]

The weak against the strong,
Is always in the wrong.   *Ib.*

What good from you yourselves has come?
Why, yes, our ancestors in Rome.
Ib. Geese

Than that old cat there's no one stronger.   *Ib. Mouse and Rat*

And why not raise the lid? He never tried that way!
This was a box that opened of itself.
Ib. A Little Box

Heaven save you from a foolish friend;
The too officious fool is worse than any foe.   *Ib. Hermit and Bear*

---

[1] See La Fontaine, *Bk. I, Fable 10*, p. 359a.

ARTHUR WELLESLEY, DUKE OF WELLINGTON
1769–1852

Nothing except a battle lost can be half so melancholy as a battle won.
Dispatch [1815]

I used to say of him [Napoleon] that his presence on the field made the difference of forty thousand men.
[November 2, 1831] From STAN-HOPE, *Notes of Conversations with the Duke of Wellington [1888]*

The only thing I am afraid of is fear.[1]   *Ib. [November 3, 1831]*

Ours [our army] is composed of the scum of the earth — the mere scum of the earth.   ***Ib.***

My rule always was to do the business of the day in the day.
Ib. [November 2, 1835]

They wanted this iron fist to command them.
Ib. [November 8, 1840]; of troops sent by Wellington to the Canadian frontier in the war with America

There is no mistake; there has been no mistake; and there shall be no mistake.   *Wellingtoniana [1832]*

I don't care a twopenny damn what becomes of the ashes of Napoleon Buonaparte.   *Attributed*

The battle of Waterloo was won on the playing fields of Eton.
From FRASER, *Words on Wellington [1889]*

Publish and be damned.
Attributed; when his mistress threatened to publish her diary and his letters

[1] See Montaigne, p. 189b, and note.

LUDWIG VAN BEETHOVEN
1770–1827

Art! Who comprehends her? With whom can one consult concerning this great goddess?
Letter to Bettina von Arnim [August 11, 1810]

The world is a king, and, like a king, desires flattery in return for favor; but true art is selfish and perverse — it will not submit to the mold of flattery.
Conversations [March 1820]

GEORGE CANNING
1770–1827

When our perils are past, shall our gratitude sleep?
No — here's to the pilot that weathered the storm.
Song for the Inauguration of the Pitt Club [May 25, 1802]

I give thee sixpence! I will see thee damned first.
The Anti-Jacobin, no. 11 [1797]. The Friend of Humanity and the Knife-Grinder, st. 9

I think of those companions true
Who studied with me at the U--niversity of Göttingen.
Ib. no. 30 [1798]. The Rovers, song, st. 1

A steady patriot of the world alone,
The friend of every country but his own.[1]
Ib. no 36 [1798]. New Morality, l. 113

And finds, with keen, discriminating sight,
Black's not so black — nor white so very white.   *Ib. l. 199*

Give me the avowed, erect, and manly foe,
Firm I can meet, perhaps return the blow;

[1] This refers to the Jacobin.
See Overbury, p. 315b, and note.

But of all plagues, good Heaven, thy
 wrath can send,
Save, save, oh save me from the candid
 friend! [1]
> *The Anti-Jacobin, no. 36. New
> Morality, l. 207*

In matters of commerce the fault of the
 Dutch
Is offering too little and asking too
 much.
> *Dispatch to Sir Charles Bagot,
> British Minister at The Hague
> [January 31, 1826]*

I called the New World into existence to redress the balance of the Old.
> *The King's Message [December
> 12, 1826]*

DAVID EVERETT
1770–1813

You'd scarce expect one of my age
To speak in public on the stage;
And if I chance to fall below
Demosthenes or Cicero,
Don't view me with a critic's eye,
But pass my imperfections by.
Large streams from little fountains
 flow,
Tall oaks from little acorns grow.[2]
> *Written for a school declama-
> tion for Ephraim H. Farrar,
> aged seven, New Ipswich, New
> Hampshire [1791]*

GEORG WILHELM
FRIEDRICH HEGEL
1770–1831

What is reasonable is real; that
which is real is reasonable.
> *Philosophy of Right [1821]*

What experience and history teach is
this — that people and governments
never have learned anything from history, or acted on principles deduced
from it.
> *Philosophy of History [1832],[1]
> introduction*

Amid the pressure of great events, a
general principle gives no help.   *Ib.*

To him who looks upon the world
rationally, the world in its turn presents
a rational aspect. The relation is mutual.   *Ib.*

The history of the world is none
other than the progress of the consciousness of freedom.   *Ib.*

We may affirm absolutely that nothing great in the world has been accomplished without passion.   *Ib.*

It is easier to discover a deficiency in
individuals, in states, and in Providence, than to see their real import and
value.   *Ib.*

Life has a value only when it has
something valuable as its object.   *Ib.*

Serious occupation is labor that has
reference to some want.
> *Ib. pt. I, sec. 2, ch. 1*

It is a matter of perfect indifference
where a thing originated; the only question is: "Is it true in and for itself?"
> *Ib. III, 3, 2*

The Few assume to be the *deputies*,
but they are often only the *despoilers* of
the Many.   *Ib. IV, 3, 3*

JAMES HOGG [2]
1770–1835

We'll o'er the water, we'll o'er the sea,
We'll o'er the water to Charlie;
Come weal, come woe, we'll gather and
 go,
And live and die wi' Charlie.
> *O'er the Water to Charlie*

---

[1] Defend me from my friends; I can defend
myself from my enemies. — *Attributed to Maréchal Villars, when taking leave of Louis XIV*
[2] The lofty oak from a small acorn grows.
— LEWIS DUNCOMBE [1711–1730], *De Minimis
Maxima* (translation)
See Anonymous, p. 151a.

[1] Translated by J. SIBREE. Quoted by G. B.
Shaw in *The Revolutionist's Handbook.*
[2] The Ettrick Shepherd.

For Kilmeny had been she knew not
  where,
And Kilmeny had seen what she could
  not declare.   *Kilmeny, l. 38*

Love is like a dizziness,
It winna let a poor body
Gang about his bizziness.
     Love Is Like a Dizziness, st. 1

PIERRE JACQUES ÉTIENNE, COUNT CAMBRONNE
1770–1842

The Guards die, but never surrender.[1]   *Attributed*

JOSEPH HOPKINSON
1770–1842

Hail, Columbia! happy land!
Hail, ye heroes! heaven-born band!
Who fought and bled in Freedom's
  cause.   *Hail, Columbia,[2] st. 1*

Let independence be our boast,
Ever mindful what it cost;
Ever grateful for the prize,
Let its altar reach the skies.   *Ib.*

WILLIAM ROBERT SPENCER
1770–1834

Oh! where does faithful Gêlert roam,
  The flow'r of all his race?
So true, so brave; a lamb at home,
  A lion in the chase!
     Beth-Gêlert, st. 4

JOHN TOBIN
1770–1804

The man that lays his hand upon a
  woman,

Save in the way of kindness, is a
  wretch
Whom 'twere gross flattery to name a
  coward.
     The Honeymoon [1805], *act II,
     sc. 1*

WILLIAM WORDSWORTH[1]
1770–1850

And homeless near a thousand homes I
  stood,
And near a thousand tables pined and
  wanted food.
     Guilt and Sorrow [written 1791–
     1794], *pt. II, st. 41*

A simple child,
That lightly draws its breath,
And feels its life in every limb,
What should it know of death?
     We Are Seven [1798], *st. 1*

O Reader! had you in your mind
Such stores as silent thought can
  bring,
O gentle Reader! you would find
A tale in everything.
     Simon Lee [1798], *st. 9*

In that sweet mood when pleasant
  thoughts
Bring sad thoughts to the mind.
     Lines Written in Early Spring
     [1798], *st. 1*

And 'tis my faith, that every flower
Enjoys the air it breathes.   *Ib. st. 3*

Have I not reason to lament
What man has made of man?[2]
     Ib. st. 6

Nor less I deem that there are Powers
Which of themselves our minds im-
  press;
That we can feed this mind of ours
In a wise passiveness.
     Expostulation and Reply [1798],
     st. 6

---

[1] La Garde meurt, mais ne se rend pas.
Cambronne denied having said this phrase,
which was invented by Rougemont after the
battle of Waterloo, in the *Indépendant.* —
FOURNIER, *L'Esprit dans l'Histoire* [1857]

[2] The music, generally attributed to Philip
Phile, was Washington's inaugural march. Hopkinson supplied verses at a singer's request, and
the song won instant acclaim.

[1] Coleridge said to Wordsworth, "Since Milton,
I know of no poet with so many *felicities* and
unforgettable lines and stanzas as you."
HENRY NELSON COLERIDGE, *Memoir* [1847]

[2] See Burns, p. 492b.

Up! up! my friend, and quit your
    books;
Or surely you'll grow double:
Up! up! my friend, and clear your
    looks;
Why all this toil and trouble?
        The Tables Turned [1798], *st. 1*

Come forth into the light of things,
Let Nature be your teacher.
                    Ib. st. 4

One impulse from a vernal wood
May teach you more of man,
Of moral evil and of good,
Than all the sages can.[1]   *Ib. st. 6*

These hedgerows, hardly hedgerows, lit-
    tle lines
Of sportive wood run wild.
        Lines Composed a Few Miles
        Above Tintern Abbey [1798],
        l. 15

        Sensations sweet,
Felt in the blood, and felt along the
    heart.   *Ib. l. 27*

That best portion of a good man's life,
His little, nameless, unremembered acts
Of kindness and of love.   *Ib. l. 33*

        Blessed mood,
In which the burthen of the mystery,
In which the heavy and the weary weight
Of all this unintelligible world,
Is lightened.   *Ib. l. 41*

While with an eye made quiet by the
    power
Of harmony, and the deep power of joy
We see into the life of things.
                    Ib. l. 47

      The sounding cataract
Haunted me like a passion; the tall
    rock,
The mountain, and the deep and
    gloomy wood,
Their colors and their forms, were then
    to me
An appetite; a feeling and a love,
That had no need of a remoter charm,
By thoughts supplied, nor any interest
Unborrowed from the eye.   *Ib. l. 76*

[1] See St. Bernard, p. 154a, and Shakespeare,
pp. 247b and 249b.

      I have learned
To look on nature, not as in the hour
Of thoughtless youth; but hearing
    oftentimes
The still, sad music of humanity,
Nor harsh nor grating, though of ample
    power
To chasten and subdue. And I have felt
A presence that disturbs me with the
    joy
Of elevated thoughts; a sense sublime
Of something far more deeply inter-
    fused,
Whose dwelling is the light of setting
    suns,
And the round ocean and the living
    air,
And the blue sky, and in the mind of
    man;
A motion and a spirit, that impels
All thinking things, all objects of all
    thought,
And rolls through all things.[1]
        Lines Composed a Few Miles
        Above Tintern Abbey, l. 88

      All the mighty world
Of eye and ear, both what they half
    create,
And what perceive.   *Ib. l. 105*

Knowing that Nature never did betray
The heart that loved her.   *Ib. l. 122*

Full twenty times was Peter feared,
For once that Peter was respected.
        Peter Bell [*written 1798*], *pt. I,*
                        st. 3

A primrose by a river's brim
A yellow primrose was to him,
And it was nothing more.   *Ib. st. 12*

The soft blue sky did never melt
Into his heart; he never felt
The witchery of the soft blue sky!
                    Ib. st. 15

Fair seedtime had my soul, and I grew
    up
Fostered alike by beauty and by fear.
        The Prelude [*written 1799–*
        1805], *bk. I, l. 301*

[1] See Shelley, p. 568a.

With what strange utterance did the
   loud dry wind
Blow through my ear! the sky seemed
   not a sky
Of earth — and with what motion
   moved the clouds!
     The Prelude, bk. I, l. 337

Dust as we are, the immortal spirit
   grows
Like harmony in music; there is a dark
Inscrutable workmanship that recon-
   ciles
Discordant elements, makes them cling
   together
In one society.   *Ib. l.* 340

     The grim shape
Towered up between me and the stars,
   and still,
For so it seemed, with purpose of its
   own
And measured motion like a living
   thing,
Strode after me.   *Ib. l.* 381

     Where the statue stood
Of Newton with his prism and silent
   face,
The marble index of a mind forever
Voyaging through strange seas of
   thought, alone.   *Ib. III, l.* 61

When from our better selves we have
   too long
Been parted by the hurrying world, and
   droop,
Sick of its business, of its pleasures
   tired,
How gracious, how benign, is Solitude.
     Ib. IV, l. 354

     Brothers all
In honor, as in one community,
Scholars and gentlemen.
     Ib. IX, l. 227

Bliss was it in that dawn to be alive,
But to be young was very heaven! [1]
     Ib. XI, l. 108

    There is
One great society alone on earth:
The noble Living and the noble Dead.
     Ib. XI, l. 393

[1] Also in *French Revolution as It Appears to
Enthusiasts* [1804].

One of those heavenly days that cannot
   die.   *Nutting* [1799], *l.* 3

What fond and wayward thoughts will
   slide
Into a lover's head!
"O mercy!" to myself I cried,
  "If Lucy should be dead!"
    *Strange Fits of Passion Have I
      Known* [1799], *st.* 1

She dwelt among the untrodden ways
   Beside the springs of Dove,
A maid whom there were none to
   praise
   And very few to love.[1]

A violet by a mossy stone
   Half hidden from the eye!
— Fair as a star, when only one
   Is shining in the sky.

She lived unknown, and few could
   know
   When Lucy ceased to be;
But she is in her grave, and, oh,
   The difference to me!
    *Lucy: She Dwelt Among the Un-
      trodden Ways* [1799]

Three years she grew in sun and
   shower,
Then Nature said, "A lovelier flower
   On earth was never sown;
This Child I to myself will take;
She shall be mine, and I will make
   A Lady of my own."
    *Lucy: Three Years She Grew in
      Sun and Shower* [1799], *st.* 1

I traveled among unknown men,
   In lands beyond the sea;
Nor England! did I know till then
   What love I bore to thee.
    *I Traveled Among Unknown
      Men* [1799], *st.* 1

[1] He lived amidst th' untrodden ways
    To Rydal Lake that lead;
  A bard whom there were none to praise,
    And very few to read.
  Unread his works — his "Milk White Doe"
    With dust is dark and dim;
  It's still in Longmans' shop, and oh!
    The difference to him!
    — Parody by Hartley Coleridge
      [1796–1849]

A slumber did my spirit seal;
  I had no human fears:
She seemed a thing that could not feel
  The touch of earthly years.

No motion has she now, no force;
  She neither hears nor sees;
Rolled round in earth's diurnal course,
  With rocks, and stones, and trees.
       A Slumber Did My Spirit Seal
                       [1799]

     A fingering slave,
One that would peep and botanize
Upon his mother's grave.
     A Poet's Epitaph [1799], *st. 5*

A reasoning, self-sufficing thing,
An intellectual All-in-all!   *Ib. st. 8*

And you must love him, ere to you
He will seem worthy of your love.
                    Ib. st. 11

The harvest of a quiet eye.   *Ib. st. 13*

The sweetest thing that ever grew
Beside a human door.
       Lucy Gray [1799], *st. 2*

And sings a solitary song
That whistles in the wind.
                    Ib. st. 16

     A youth to whom was given
So much of earth — so much of heaven,
And such impetuous blood.
         Ruth [1799], *st. 21*

Poetry is the breath and finer spirit
of all knowledge; it is the impassioned
expression which is in the countenance
of all Science.
     Lyrical Ballads [2nd ed., 1800],
                          preface

   In spite of difference of soil and climate, of language and manners, of laws
and customs — in spite of things silently gone out of mind, and things
violently destroyed, the Poet binds
together by passion and knowledge the
vast empire of human society, as it is
spread over the whole earth, and over
all time.   *Ib.*

   I have said that poetry is the spontaneous overflow of powerful feelings: it
takes its origin from emotion recollected in tranquillity.
         Lyrical Ballads, preface

Something between a hindrance and a
  help.   *Michael* [1800], *l. 189*

Drink, pretty creature, drink!
         The Pet Lamb [1800], *st. 1*

May no rude hand deface it,
And its forlorn *hic jacet!*
        Ellen Irwin [1800], *st. 7*

She gave me eyes, she gave me ears;
And humble cares and delicate fears;
A heart, the fountain of sweet tears;
  And love, and thought, and joy.
      The Sparrows' Nest [1801], *st. 2*

My heart leaps up when I behold
  A rainbow in the sky:
So was it when my life began;
So is it now I am a man;
So be it when I shall grow old.
  Or let me die!
The Child is father of the Man; [1]
And I could wish my days to be
Bound each to each by natural piety.
     My Heart Leaps Up When I
                 Behold [1802]

Sweet childish days, that were as long
As twenty days are now.
     To a Butterfly [1802]. *pt. II,*
     I've Watched You Now a Full
     Half-Hour, st. 2

Pleasures newly found are sweet
When they lie about our feet.
     To the Small Celandine [1802],
                         st. 1

I thought of Chatterton, the marvelous
  boy,
The sleepless soul that perished in his
  pride;
Of him who walked in glory and in joy
Following his plow, along the moun-
  tainside:
By our own spirits are we deified:
We Poets in our youth begin in glad-
  ness;

[1] See Milton, p. 348b.

But thereof come in the end despondency and madness.[1]
Resolution and Independence
[1802], st. 7

That heareth not the loud winds when
they call;
And moveth all together, if it move at
all.   *Ib. st. 11*

Choice word and measured phrase,
above the reach
Of ordinary men.   *Ib. st. 14*

And mighty poets in their misery dead.
Ib. st. 17

Earth has not anything to show more
fair:
Dull would he be of soul who could
pass by
A sight so touching in its majesty.
Composed Upon Westminster
Bridge [September 3, 1802], l. 1

Ne'er saw I, never felt, a calm so deep!
The river glideth at his own sweet will;
Dear God! the very houses seem
asleep;
And all that mighty heart is lying still!
Ib. l. 11

Plain living and high thinking are no
more:
The homely beauty of the good old
cause
Is gone; our peace, our fearful inno-
cence,
And pure religion breathing household
laws.
Written in London
[September 1802]

It is a beauteous evening, calm and
free,
The holy time is quiet as a nun
Breathless with adoration.
It Is a Beauteous Evening
[1802], l. 1

Thou liest in Abraham's bosom all the
year;
And worship'st at the Temple's inner
shrine,
God being with thee when we know it
not.   *Ib. l. 12*

[1] See Robert Lowell, p. 1075b.

Once did she hold the gorgeous east in
fee:
And was the safeguard of the west.
On the Extinction of the Vene-
tian Republic [1802], l. 1

And, when she took unto herself a
mate,
She must espouse the everlasting sea.
Ib. l. 7

Men are we, and must grieve when
even the shade
Of that which once was great, is passed
away.   *Ib. l. 11*

Thou hast great allies;
Thy friends are exultations, agonies,
And love, and man's unconquerable
mind.   *To Toussaint L'Ouverture*
[1802], l. 11

Milton! thou should'st be living at this
hour:
England hath need of thee; she is a
fen
Of stagnant waters.
London [1802], l. 1

Thy soul was like a star, and dwelt
apart;
Thou hadst a voice whose sound was
like the sea:
Pure as the naked heavens, majestic,
free,
So didst thou travel on life's common
way,
In cheerful godliness.   *Ib. l. 8*

We must be free or die, who speak the
tongue
That Shakespeare spake; the faith and
morals hold
Which Milton held.
It Is Not To Be Thought Of
[1802], l. 11

Thou unassuming commonplace
Of Nature.
To the Same Flower [1802], st. 1

Oft on the dappled turf at ease
I sit, and play with similes,
Loose types of things through all de-
grees.   *Ib. st. 2*

And stepping westward seemed to be
A kind of heavenly destiny.
    Stepping Westward [1803], *st. 2*

    Old, unhappy, far-off things,
And battles long ago.
    The Solitary Reaper [1803], *st. 3*

The music in my heart I bore
Long after it was heard no more.
                        Ib. st. 4

        The good old rule
Sufficeth them, the simple plan,
That they should take, who have the
    power,
And they should keep who can.
    Rob Roy's Grave [1803], *st. 9*

A brotherhood of venerable trees.
    Sonnet Composed at —— Castle
                        [1803], *l. 6*

O for a single hour of that Dundee
Who on that day the word of onset
    gave!
    In the Pass of Killicranky
                        [1803], *l. 11*

There was a time when meadow, grove,
    and stream,
The earth, and every common sight,
    To me did seem
    Appareled in celestial light,
The glory and the freshness of a
    dream.
It is not now as it hath been of
    yore —
    Turn wheresoe'er I may,
    By night or day,
The things which I have seen I now can
    see no more.
    Ode (Intimations of Immortality
    from Recollections of Early
    Childhood [1]) [1803–1806], *st. 1*

The Rainbow comes and goes,
And lovely is the Rose.   *Ib. st. 2*

    The sunshine is a glorious birth;
    But yet I know, where'er I go,
That there hath passed away a glory
    from the earth.   *Ib.*

---

[1] The *Ode on Immortality* is the high water
mark which the intellect has reached in this
age. — EMERSON, *English Traits* [1856]

Whither is fled the visionary gleam?
Where is it now, the glory and the
    dream?
    Ode (Intimations of Immor-
                tality, st. 4

Our birth is but a sleep and a forget-
    ting:
The soul that rises with us, our life's
    star,
    Hath had elsewhere its setting,
    And cometh from afar:
    Not in entire forgetfulness,
    And not in utter nakedness,
But trailing clouds of glory do we
    come
    From God, who is our home:
Heaven lies about us in our infancy! [1]
Shades of the prison-house begin to
    close
Upon the growing boy.   *Ib. st. 5*

The youth, who daily farther from the
    east
    Must travel, still is Nature's priest,
    And by the vision splendid
    Is on his way attended;
At length the man perceives it die
    away,
And fade into the light of common
    day.   *Ib.*

As if his whole vocation
Were endless imitation.   *Ib. st. 7*

O joy! that in our embers
Is something that doth live,
That nature yet remembers
What was so fugitive!   *Ib. st. 9*

High instincts before which our mortal
    nature
Did tremble like a guilty thing sur-
    prised.   *Ib.*

        Truths that wake,
To perish never.   *Ib.*

        Though inland far we be,
Our souls have sight of that immortal
    sea
Which brought us hither.   *Ib.*

---

[1] See Lowell, p. 692a.

Though nothing can bring back the hour
Of splendor in the grass, of glory in the flower.
            Ode (Intimations of Immortality), *st.* 10

In years that bring the philosophic mind.   *Ib.*

The clouds that gather round the setting sun
Do take a sober coloring from an eye
That hath kept watch o'er man's mortality;
Another race hath been, and other palms are won.
Thanks to the human heart by which we live,
Thanks to its tenderness, its joys, and fears,
To me the meanest flower that blows can give
Thoughts that do often lie too deep for tears.   *Ib. st. 11*

O blithe newcomer! I have heard,
I hear thee and rejoice.
O Cuckoo! shall I call thee bird,
Or but a wandering voice?
            To the Cuckoo [1804], *st. 1*

No bird, but an invisible thing,
A voice, a mystery.   *Ib. st. 4*

She was a phantom of delight
When first she gleamed upon my sight;
A lovely apparition, sent
To be a moment's ornament.
            She Was a Phantom of Delight
            [1804], *st. 1*

A spirit, yet a woman too!   *Ib. st. 2*

And now I see with eye serene
The very pulse of the machine.
            Ib. st. 3

A perfect woman, nobly planned,
To warn, to comfort, and command.
            Ib.

I wandered lonely as a cloud
That floats on high o'er vales and hills,

When all at once I saw a crowd,
A host, of golden daffodils.
            I Wandered Lonely as a Cloud
            [1804], *st. 1*

Continuous as the stars that shine
And twinkle on the milky way.
            Ib. st. 2

Ten thousand saw I at a glance,
Tossing their heads in sprightly dance.
            Ib.

A poet could not but be gay,
In such a jocund company.   *Ib. st. 3*

            That inward eye
Which is the bliss of solitude.
            Ib. st. 4

Stern Daughter of the Voice of God! [1]
            Ode to Duty [1805], *st. 1*

            A light to guide, a rod
To check the erring, and reprove.
            Ib.

Me this uncharterd freedom tires;
I feel the weight of chance-desires;
My hopes no more must change their name,
I long for a repose that ever is the same.   *Ib. st. 5*

Stern Lawgiver!   *Ib. st. 7*

Thou dost preserve the stars from wrong;
And the most ancient heavens, through Thee, are fresh and strong.
            Ib.

The light that never was, on sea or land;
The consecration, and the Poet's dream.
            Suggested by a Picture of Peele
            Castle in a Storm [1805], *st. 4*

Dear Child of Nature, let them rail!
            To a Young Lady [1805], *st. 1*

Thou, while thy babes around thee cling,
Shalt show us how divine a thing
A woman may be made.
            Ib. st. 2

[1] See Milton, p. 347b.

But an old age serene and bright,
And lovely as a Lapland night,
Shall lead thee to thy grave.
To a Young Lady, st. 3

Who is the happy Warrior? Who is
he
That every man in arms would wish to
be?
Character of the Happy Warrior
[1806], l. 1

Who, doomed to go in company with
pain,
And fear, and bloodshed, miserable
train!
Turns his necessity to glorious gain.
Ib. l. 12

More skillful in self-knowledge, even
more pure,
As tempted more; more able to endure,
As more exposed to suffering and distress.   *Ib. l. 23*

But who, if he be called upon to face
Some awful moment to which Heaven
has joined
Great issues, good or bad for human-
kind,
Is happy as a lover.   *Ib. l. 48*

And, through the heat of conflict, keeps
the law
In calmness made, and sees what he
foresaw.   *Ib. l. 53*

Whom neither shape of danger can dismay,
Nor thought of tender happiness betray.   *Ib. l. 77*

Like — but oh how different!
Yes, It Was the Mountain Echo
[1806], st. 2

Nuns fret not at their convent's narrow
room.
Nuns Fret Not [1806], l. 1

The world is too much with us; late
and soon,

Getting and spending, we lay waste our
powers:
Little we see in Nature that is ours;
We have given our hearts away, a sor-
did boon!
The World Is Too Much With
Us [1806], l. 1

Great God! I'd rather be
A Pagan suckled in a creed outworn;
So might I, standing on this pleasant
lea,
Have glimpses that would make me less
forlorn;
Have sight of Proteus rising from the
sea;
Or hear old Triton blow his wreathed
horn.   *Ib. l. 9*

Where lies the land to which yon Ship
must go? [1]
Fresh as a lark mounting at break of
day,
Festively she puts forth in trim array.
Where Lies the Land
[1806], l. 1

Blessed barrier between day and day.
To Sleep [1806], II, A Flock of
Sheep, l. 13

Maidens withering on the stalk.[2]
Personal Talk [1806], Sonnet 1

Dreams, books, are each a world; and
books, we know,
Are a substantial world, both pure and
good.
Round these, with tendrils strong as
flesh and blood,
Our pastime and our happiness will
grow.   *Ib. 3*

A power is passing from the earth.
Lines on the Expected Dissolu-
tion of Mr. Fox [1806], st. 5

[1] Where lies the land to which the ship would
go?
Far, far ahead, is all her seamen know.
ARTHUR HUGH CLOUGH [1819–1861],
Songs of Absence
[2] See Shakespeare, *A Midsummer-Night's*
Dream I, i, 77, p. 228b.

Two voices are there: one is of the sea,[1]
One of the mountains; each a mighty
voice.
> *Thought of a Briton on the Subjugation of Switzerland* [1807],
> *l. 1*

The silence that is in the starry sky,
The sleep that is among the lonely
hills.
> *Song at the Feast of Brougham Castle* [1807] *l. 163*

Every great and original writer, in
proportion as he is great or original,
must himself create the taste by which
he is to be relished.
> *Letter to Lady Beaumont* [*May 21, 1807*]

A few strong instincts, and a few plain
rules.
> *Alas! What Boots the Long Laborious Quest?* [1809]

Surprised by joy — impatient as the
wind.
> *Surprised by Joy* [1812], *l. 1*

Strongest minds
Are often those of whom the noisy
world
Hears least.
> *The Excursion* [2] [1814], *bk. I*

The imperfect offices of prayer and
praise. *Ib.*

The good die first,[3]
And they whose hearts are dry as summer dust
Burn to the socket. *Ib.*

Wrongs unredressed, or insults unavenged. *Ib. III*

Society became my glittering bride.
Ib.

There is a luxury in self-dispraise;
And inward self-disparagement affords
To meditative spleen a grateful feast.
> *The Excursion, bk. IV*

I have seen
A curious child, who dwelt upon a
tract
Of inland ground, applying to his ear
The convolutions of a smooth-lipped
shell,
To which, in silence hushed, his very
soul
Listened intensely; and his countenance
soon
Brightened with joy, for from within
were heard
Murmurings, whereby the monitor expressed
Mysterious union with its native sea.[1]
Ib.

One in whom persuasion and belief
Had ripened into faith, and faith become
A passionate intuition. *Ib.*

Spires whose "silent finger points to
heaven." [2] *Ib. VI*

A man he seems of cheerful yesterdays
And confident tomorrows. *Ib. VII*

The gods approve
The depth, and not the tumult, of the
soul. *Laodamia* [1814], *st. 13*

An ampler ether, a diviner air.
Ib. st. 18

And beauty, for confiding youth,
Those shocks of passion can prepare
That kill the bloom before its time;

---

[1] Two voices are there: one is of the deep;
And one is of an old half-witted sheep
Which bleats articulate monotony,
And indicates that two and one are three.
And, Wordsworth, both art thine.
> JAMES KENNETH STEPHEN, *Sonnet,
> Wordsworth* [1891]

[2] This will never do. — FRANCIS JEFFREY,
Opening sentence, review of WORDSWORTH'S *Excursion, Edinburgh Review* [1814]

[3] See Menander, p. 102a, and note.

[1] See Landor, p. 536a.
Upon a mountain height, far from the sea,
   I found a shell,
And to my listening ear the lonely thing
Ever a song of ocean seemed to sing,
   Ever a tale of ocean seemed to tell.
> EUGENE FIELD [1850–1895],
> *The Wanderer, st. 1*

[2] An instinctive taste teaches men to build
their churches in flat countries with spire
steeples, which, as they cannot be referred to any
other object, point as with silent finger to the
sky and stars. — COLERIDGE, *The Friend* [1809],
no. 14

And blanch, without the owner's crime,
The most resplendent hair.
　　Lament of Mary Queen of Scots
　　　　　　　[1817], st. 6

Enough, if something from our hands have power
To live, and act, and serve the future hour.
　　The River Duddon, Sonnet:
　　Afterthought [1820], l. 10

We feel that we are greater than we know.　　*Ib., l. 14*

Habit rules the unreflecting herd.
　　Ecclesiastical Sonnets [1822],
　　　　　　　pt. II, 28

　　The feather, whence the pen
Was shaped that traced the lives of these good men,
Dropped from an angel's wing.[1]
　　Ib. III, 5. Walton's Book of Lives

Give all thou canst; high Heaven rejects the lore
Of nicely calculated less or more.
　　Ib. 43. Inside of King's College
　　　　Chapel, Cambridge

But hushed be every thought that springs
From out the bitterness of things.
　　Elegiac Stanzas, Addressed to
　　Sir G. H. B. [1824], st. 7

Ethereal minstrel! pilgrim of the sky!
　　To a Skylark [1825], l. 1

Type of the wise who soar, but never roam,
True to the kindred points of heaven and home!　　*Ib.*

Scorn not the sonnet. Critic, you have frowned,
Mindless of its just honors; with this key
Shakespeare unlocked his heart.[2]
　　Scorn Not the Sonnet [1827], l. 1

---

[1] The pen wherewith thou dost so heavenly sing
Made of a quill from an angel's wing.
　　HENRY CONSTABLE [1562–1613], *Sonnet*

[2] See Browning, p. 668a.

Small service is true service while it lasts:
Of humblest friends, bright creature! scorn not one:
The daisy, by the shadow that it casts,
Protects the lingering dewdrop from the sun.
　　To a Child, written in her album
　　　　　　　[1834]

How does the meadow flower its bloom unfold?
Because the lovely little flower is free
Down to its root, and, in that freedom, bold.
　　A Poet! — He Hath Put His
　　Heart to School [1842], l. 9

Minds that have nothing to confer
Find little to perceive.
　　Yes, Thou Art Fair [1845], st. 2

MARIE FRANÇOIS XAVIER BICHAT
1771–1802

Life is the totality of those functions which resist death.
　　Physiological Researches Upon
　　Life and Death [1800]

THOMAS DIBDIN
1771–1841

Oh, it's a snug little island!
A right little, tight little island.
　　The Snug Little Island

WILLIAM PITT
d. 1840

A strong nor'wester's blowing, Bill,
Hark! Don't ye hear it roar, now?
Lord help 'em, how I pities all
Unhappy folks on shore now!
　　The Sailor's Consolation, st. 1

JAMES MONTGOMERY
1771–1854

Tomorrow — oh, 'twill never be,
If we should live a thousand years!
Our time is all today, today.[1]　　*Today*

---

[1] See Sydney Smith, p. 523b.

Give me the hand that is honest and
  hearty,
Free as the breeze and unshackled by
  party.   *Give Me Thy Hand, st. 2*

Who, that hath ever been,
  Could bear to be no more?
Yet who would tread again the scene
  He trod through life before?
           The Falling Leaf, st. 7

Here in the body pent,
  Absent from Him I roam,
Yet nightly pitch my moving tent
  A day's march nearer home.
           At Home in Heaven

Prayer is the soul's sincere desire,
  Uttered or unexpressed;
The motion of a hidden fire
  That trembles in the breast.
           What Is Prayer? st. 1

Prayer is the burden of a sigh,
  The falling of a tear;
The upward glancing of an eye,
  When none but God is near.
           Ib. st. 2

SIR WALTER SCOTT
1771–1832

The way was long, the wind was cold,
The Minstrel was infirm and old;
His withered cheek, and tresses gray,
Seem'd to have known a better day.
     The Lay of the Last Minstrel
     [1805], introduction

The unpremeditated lay.   *Ib.*

Such is the custom of Branksome Hall.
           Ib. canto I, st. 7

What shall be the maiden's fate?
Who shall be the maiden's mate?
           Ib. st. 16

Steady of heart, and stout of hand.
           Ib. st. 21

If thou would'st view fair Melrose
  aright,
Go visit it by the pale moonlight.
           Ib. II, st. 1

I cannot tell how the truth may be;
I say the tale as 'twas said to me.
     The Lay of the Last Minstrel,
           canto II, st. 22

In peace, Love tunes the shepherd's
  reed;
In war, he mounts the warrior's steed;
In halls, in gay attire is seen;
In hamlets, dances on the green.
Love rules the court, the camp, the
  grove,
And men below, and saints above;
For love is heaven, and heaven is love.
           Ib. III, st. 2

    For ne'er
Was flattery lost on poet's ear:
A simple race! they waste their toil
For the vain tribute of a smile.
           Ib. IV, conclusion

Call it not vain; they do not err
Who say, that when the Poet dies,
Mute Nature mourns her worshipper,
And celebrates his obsequies.
           Ib. V, st. 1

True love's the gift which God has
  given
To man alone beneath the heaven:
It is not fantasy's hot fire,
  Whose wishes, soon as granted, fly;
It liveth not in fierce desire,
  With dead desire it doth not die;
It is the secret sympathy,
The silver link, the silken tie,
Which heart to heart and mind to
  mind
In body and in soul can bind.
           Ib. st. 13

Breathes there the man, with soul so
  dead,
Who never to himself hath said,
  This is my own, my native land!
Whose heart hath ne'er within him
  burn'd [1]
As home his footsteps he hath turn'd
  From wandering on a foreign strand!
If such there breathe, go, mark him
  well;
For him no Minstrel raptures swell;

[1] See *Luke 24:32*, p. 47b.

High though his titles, proud his
name,
Boundless his wealth as wish can
claim;
Despite those titles, power, and pelf,
The wretch, concentered all in self,
Living, shall forfeit fair renown,
And, doubly dying, shall go down
To the vile dust, from whence he
sprung,
Unwept, unhonor'd, and unsung.[1]
The Lay of the Last Minstrel,
canto VI, st. 1

O Caledonia! stern and wild,
Meet nurse for a poetic child!
Land of brown heath and shaggy
wood;
Land of the mountain and the flood!
Ib. st. 2

That day of wrath, that dreadful day,
When heaven and earth shall pass
away.[2]   *Ib. st. 31*

November's sky is chill and drear,
November's leaf is red and sear.
Marmion [1808], *canto I, intro-*
duction, st. 1

Stood for his country's glory fast,
And nail'd her colors to the mast!
Ib. st. 10

But search the land of living men,
Where wilt thou find their like again?
Ib. st. 11

Just at the age 'twixt boy and youth,
When thought is speech, and speech is
truth.
Ib. II, introduction, st. 4

And come he slow, or come he fast,
It is but Death who comes at last.
Ib. st. 30

Oh, young Lochinvar is come out of
the West,
Through all the wide Border his steed
was the best.
Ib. V, st. 12 [*Lochinvar, st. 1*]

So faithful in love, and so dauntless in
war,

There never was knight like the young
Lochinvar.
Marmion, canto V, st. 12
[*Lochinvar, st. 1*]

For a laggard in love, and a dastard in
war,
Was to wed the fair Ellen of brave
Lochinvar.
Ib. [*Lochinvar, st. 2*]

With a smile on her lips, and a tear in
her eye.   *Ib.* [*Lochinvar, st. 5*]

Heap on more wood! — the wind is
chill;
But let it whistle as it will,
We'll keep our Christmas merry still.
Ib. VI, introduction, st. 1

England was merry England, when
Old Christmas brought his sports
again.
'Twas Christmas broach'd the mightiest
ale;
'Twas Christmas told the merriest
tale;
A Christmas gambol oft could cheer
The poor man's heart through half the
year.   *Ib. st. 4*

And dar'st thou, then,
To beard the lion in his den,
The Douglas in his hall?   *Ib. st. 14*

Oh, what a tangled web we weave,
When first we practice to deceive!
Ib. st. 17

O Woman! in our hours of ease,
Uncertain, coy, and hard to please,
And variable as the shade [1]
By the light quivering aspen made;
When pain and anguish wring the
brow,
A ministering angel thou! [2]
Ib. st. 30

"Charge, Chester, charge! On, Stanley,
on!"
Were the last words of Marmion.
Ib. st. 32

To all, to each, a fair goodnight,
And pleasing dreams, and slumbers
light!   *Ib. L'Envoy*

---

[1] See Homer, p. 64b, and note.
[2] See Tommaso di Celano, p. 157b.

[1] See Virgil, p. 118b.
[2] See Shakespeare, p. 266a.

The stag at eve had drunk his fill,
Where danced the moon on Monan's
    rill,
And deep his midnight lair had made
In lone Glenartney's hazel shade.
    The Lady of the Lake [1810],
        canto I, st. 1

In listening mood she seemed to stand,
The guardian Naiad of the strand.
        Ib. st. 17

Forward and frolic glee was there,
The will to do, the soul to dare.
        Ib. st. 21

Soldier, rest! thy warfare o'er,
Sleep the sleep that knows not break-
    ing,
Dream of battled fields no more,
Days of danger, nights of waking.
        Ib. st. 31

Hail to the Chief who in triumph ad-
    vances! [1]   *Ib. II, st. 19*

Some feelings are to mortals given,
With less of earth in them than
    heaven.   *Ib. st. 22*

Like the dew on the mountain,
    Like the foam on the river,
Like the bubble on the fountain,
    Thou art gone, and forever!
    Ib. III, st. 16 [*Coronach, st. 3*]

And, Saxon, I am Roderick Dhu!
        Ib. V, st. 9

Come one, come all! this rock shall fly
From its firm base as soon as I.
        Ib. st. 10

Respect was mingled with surprise,
And the stern joy which warriors feel
In foemen worthy of their steel.   *Ib*

Where, where was Roderick then!
One blast upon his bugle horn
Were worth a thousand men!
        Ib. VI, st. 18

But answer came there none.
    The Bridal of Triermain [1813],
        canto III, st. 10

---

[1] The verses beginning with this line were
set to music by JAMES SANDERSON [1769–c. 1841].
The march has become traditionally attached
to the President of the United States.

Still are the thoughts to memory dear.
    Rokeby [1813], *canto I, st. 33*

A mother's pride, a father's joy.
        Ib. III, st. 15

Oh, Brignall banks are wild and fair,
    And Greta woods are green,
And you may gather garlands there
    Would grace a summer's queen.
        Ib. st. 16

O! many a shaft at random sent
Finds mark the archer little meant!
And many a word, at random spoken,
May soothe or wound a heart that's
    broken!
    The Lord of the Isles [1815],
        canto V, st. 18

Randolph, thy wreath has lost a rose.[1]
        Ib. VI, st. 18

There was — and O! how many sor-
    rows crowd
Into these two brief words!
        Ib. conclusion

A lawyer without history or literature
is a mechanic, a mere working mason; if
he possesses some knowledge of these,
he may venture to call himself an architect.   *Guy Mannering* [1815], *ch. 37*

Bluid is thicker than water.[2]
        Ib. 38

It's no fish ye're buying, it's men's
lives.[3]   *The Antiquary* [1816], *ch. 11*

Come as the winds come, when
    Forests are rended,
Come as the waves come, when
    Navies are stranded.
    Pibroch of Donald Dhu [1816],
        st. 4

Time will rust the sharpest sword,
Time will consume the strongest cord;

---

[1] Robert Bruce's censure of Randolph for permitting a body of English cavalry to pass his
flank on the day before the battle of Bannock-
burn [June 24, 1314].
[2] This proverb is found as early as the
seventeenth century.
[3] See Thomas Hood, p. 592b.

That which molders hemp and steel,
Mortal arm and nerve must feel.
> *Harold the Dauntless* [1817],
> *canto I, st. 4*

Sea of upturned faces.
> *Rob Roy* [1817], *ch. 20*

Lochow and the adjacent districts formed the original seat of the Camp-bells. The expression of "a far cry to Lochow" was proverbial.
> *Ib. 29, note*

There's a gude time coming.
> *Ib. 32*

My foot is on my native heath, and my name is MacGregor.   *Ib. 34*

Jock, when ye hae naething else to do, ye may be ay sticking in a tree; it will be growing, Jock, when ye're sleep-ing.[1]
> *The Heart of Midlothian* [1818],
> *ch. 8*

Vacant heart, and hand, and eye,
Easy live and quiet die.
> *The Bride of Lammermoor*
> [1819], *ch. 3. Lucy Ashton's*
> *Song*

There is a Southern proverb — fine words butter no parsnips.
> *The Legend of Montrose*
> [1819], *ch. 3*

The happy combination of fortuitous circumstances.[2]
> *The Monastery* [1820]. *Answer*
> *of the Author of Waverley to*
> *the Letter of Captain Clutter-*
> *buck*

Within that awful volume [3] lies
The mystery of mysteries!   *Ib. ch. 12*

And better had they ne'er been born,
Who read to doubt, or read to scorn.
> *Ib.*

[1] The dying words of a Highland laird to his son.
[2] See Daniel Webster, p. 547b.
Fortuitous combination of circumstances. — DICKENS, *Our Mutual Friend* [1864–1865], *vol. II, ch. 7*
[3] The Bible.

When we are handfasted, as we term it, we are man and wife for a year and day; that space gone by, each may choose another mate, or, at their pleas-ure, may call the priest to marry them for life; and this we call handfasting.[1]
> *The Monastery. Answer of the*
> *Author of Waverley to the Let-*
> *ter of Captain Clutterbuck 25*

Spur not an unbroken horse; put not your plowshare too deep into new land.   *Ib.*

Oh, poverty parts good company.
> *The Abbot* [1820], *ch. 7*

Ah! County Guy, the hour is nigh,
The sun has left the lea.
The orange flower perfumes the bower,
The breeze is on the sea.
> *Quentin Durward* [1823], *ch. 4*

Tell that to the marines — the sail-ors won't believe it.[2]
> *Redgauntlet* [1824], *vol. II, ch. 7*

Too much rest is rust.[3]
> *The Betrothed* [1825], *ch. 13*

The playbill, which is said to have announced the tragedy of Hamlet, the character of the Prince of Denmark be-ing left out.
> *The Talisman* [1825], *introduction*

Rouse the lion from his lair.
> *Ib. heading, ch. 6*

Recollect that the Almighty, who gave the dog to be companion of our pleasures and our toils, hath invested him with a nature noble and incapable of deceit.   *Ib. 24*

[1] This custom of handfasting actually prevailed in the upland days. It arose partly from the want of priests. While the convents subsisted, monks were detached on regular circuits through the wilder districts, to marry those who had lived in this species of connection. —ANDREW LANG, *Note in his edition of The Monastery*
[2] "Right," quoth Ben, "that will do for the marines." — BYRON, *The Island* [1823], *canto II, last line*
"That will do for the marines, but the sailors won't believe it" is an old saying.
[3] German proverb: Rast ich, so rost ich [When I rest, I rust].

If you keep a thing seven years, you are sure to find a use for it.
Woodstock [1826], *ch. 28*

The sun never sets on the immense empire of Charles V.[1]
Life of Napoleon [1827]

Come fill up my cup, come fill up my can,
Come saddle your horses, and call up your men;
Come open the West Port, and let me gang free,
And it's room for the bonnets of Bonny Dundee!
The Doom of Devorgoil [1830].
Bonny Dundee, chorus

One hour of life, crowded to the full with glorious action, and filled with noble risks, is worth whole years of those mean observances of paltry decorum.[2]
Count Robert of Paris [1832],
ch. 25

Heaven knows its time; the bullet has its billet.   *Ib.*

SYDNEY SMITH
1771–1845

The schoolboy whips his taxed top; the beardless youth manages his taxed horse with a taxed bridle on a taxed road; and the dying Englishman, pouring his medicine, which has paid seven per cent, into a spoon that has paid fifteen per cent, flings himself back upon his chintz bed which has paid twenty-two per cent, and expires in the arms of an apothecary who has paid a license of a hundred pounds for the privilege of putting him to death.
Review of SEYBERT, *Annals of the United States* [1820]

If you choose to represent the various parts in life by holes upon a table, of different shapes — some circular, some triangular, some square, some oblong — and the persons acting these parts by bits of wood of similar shapes, we shall generally find that the triangular person has got into the square hole, the oblong into the triangular, and a square person has squeezed himself into the round hole. The officer and the office, the doer and the thing done, seldom fit so exactly that we can say they were almost made for each other.[1]
Sketches of Moral Philosophy
[1850]

That knuckle-end of England — that land of Calvin, oatcakes, and sulphur.
Lady Holland's Memoir [1855],
vol. I, ch. 2

No one minds what Jeffrey says:
. . . it is not more than a week ago that I heard him speak disrespectfully of the equator.   *Ib.*

Preaching has become a byword for long and dull conversation of any kind; and whoever wishes to imply, in any piece of writing, the absence of everything agreeable and inviting, calls it a sermon.   *Ib. 3*

Avoid shame, but do not seek glory, — nothing so expensive as glory.
Ib. 4

Take short views, hope for the best, and trust in God.   *Ib. 6*

Looked as if she had walked straight out of the ark.   *Ib. 7*

No furniture so charming as books.
Ib. 9

Not body enough to cover his mind decently with; his intellect is improperly exposed.   *Ib.*

---

[1] Why should the brave Spanish soldier brag the sun never sets in the Spanish dominions, but ever shineth on one part or other we have conquered for our king? — CAPTAIN JOHN SMITH, *Advertisements for the Unexperienced, &c.* [1631]

It may be said of them [the Hollanders] as of the Spaniards, that the sun never sets on their dominions. — GAGE, *New Survey of the West Indies* [1648], *Epistle Dedicatory*

See Schiller, p. 497b, and Daniel Webster, p. 548a.

[2] See Mordaunt, p. 455b.

[1] Generally accepted as the origin of the phrase "A square peg in a round hole."

He has spent all his life in letting down empty buckets into empty wells; and he is frittering away his age in trying to draw them up again.[1]
Lady Holland's Memoir, vol. I, ch. 9

Ah, you flavor everything; you are the vanilla of society.   *Ib.*

As the French say, there are three sexes — men, women, and clergymen.[2]   *Ib.*

My living in Yorkshire was so far out of the way, that it was actually twelve miles from a lemon.   *Ib.*

Praise is the best diet for us, after all.   *Ib.*

Daniel Webster struck me much like a steam engine in trousers.   *Ib.*

"Heat, ma'am!" I said; "it was so dreadful here, that I found there was nothing left for it but to take off my flesh and sit in my bones."   *Ib.*

Live always in the best company when you read.   *Ib. 10*

Never give way to melancholy; resist it steadily, for the habit will encroach.   *Ib.*

He was a one-book man. Some men have only one book in them; others, a library.   *Ib. 11*

Marriage resembles a pair of shears, so joined that they can not be separated; often moving in opposite directions, yet always punishing anyone who comes between them.[3]   *Ib.*

Macaulay is like a book in breeches . . . He has occasional flashes of silence, that make his conversation perfectly delightful.   *Ib.*

Let onion atoms lurk within the bowl
And, half suspected, animate the whole.   *Ib. Recipe for Salad*

---

[1] See Cowper, p. 458a.
[2] See Lady Mary Wortley Montagu, p. 414a.
[3] We are the two halves of a pair of scissors, when apart, Pecksniff, but together we are something. — DICKENS, *Martin Chuzzlewit* [1843-1844], *ch. 11*

Serenely full, the epicure would say,
Fate cannot harm me, I have dined today.[1]
Lady Holland's Memoir, Recipe for Salad

What you don't know would make a great book.   *Ib.*

In composing, as a general rule, run your pen through every other word you have written; you have no idea what vigor it will give your style.[2]   *Ib.*

Thank God for tea! What would the world do without tea? — how did it exist? I am glad I was not born before tea.   *Ib.*

That sign of old age, extolling the past at the expense of the present.   *Ib.*

We know nothing of tomorrow; our business is to be good and happy today.[3]   *Ib. 12*

SAMUEL TAYLOR COLERIDGE
1772–1834

Poor little Foal of an oppressed race!
I love the languid patience of thy face.
To a Young Ass [1794], *l. 1*

Blest hour! it was a luxury — to be!
Reflections on Having Left a Place of Retirement [1795], *l. 43*

This Lime Tree Bower My Prison.
Title of poem [1797]

In Xanadu did Kubla Khan
A stately pleasure dome decree:
Where Alph, the sacred river, ran
Through caverns measureless to man
Down to a sunless sea.
So twice five miles of fertile ground
With walls and towers were girdled round.   *Kubla Khan* [1798]

A savage place! as holy and enchanted
As e'er beneath a waning moon was haunted
By woman wailing for her demon-lover!   *Ib.*

---

[1] See Horace, p. 122a, and note.
[2] See Samuel Johnson, p. 431b.
[3] See James Montgomery, p. 517b.

Five miles meandering with a mazy motion.   *Kubla Khan*

Ancestral voices prophesying war!
Ib.

It was a miracle of rare device,
A sunny pleasure dome with caves of
    ice!   *Ib.*

A damsel with a dulcimer
In a vision once I saw:
It was an Abyssinian maid,
And on her dulcimer she played,
Singing of Mount Abora.   *Ib.*

That sunny dome! those caves of ice!
And all who heard should see them
    there,
And all should cry, Beware! Beware!
His flashing eyes, his floating hair!
Weave a circle round him thrice,
And close your eyes with holy dread,
For he on honeydew hath fed,[1]
And drunk the milk of Paradise.
Ib.

Sir Leoline, the Baron rich,
Hath a toothless mastiff bitch.
Christabel [1797–1800],
pt. I, l. 6

And the spring comes slowly up this
    way.   *Ib. l. 22*

The one red leaf, the last of its clan,
That dances as often as dance it can.
Ib. l. 49

And what can ail the mastiff bitch?
Ib. l. 149

Her gentle limbs did she undress,
And lay down in her loveliness.
Ib. l. 237

A sight to dream of, not to tell!
Ib. l. 252

Saints will aid if men will call:
For the blue sky bends over all!
Ib. l. 330

And constancy lives in realms above;
And life is thorny; and youth is vain;
And to be wroth with one we love
Doth work like madness in the brain.
Ib. II, l. 410

[1] See Hesiod, p. 67a.

It is an ancient Mariner,
And he stoppeth one of three.
"By thy long gray beard and glittering
    eye,
Now wherefore stopp'st thou me?"
The Ancient Mariner [1798],
pt. I, st. 1

The guests are met, the feast is set:
May'st hear the merry din.   *Ib. st. 2*

He holds him with his glittering eye —
The Wedding Guest stood still,
And listens like a three years' child:
The Mariner hath his will.   *Ib. st. 4*

The ship was cheered, the harbor
    cleared,
Merrily did we drop
Below the kirk, below the hill,
Below the lighthouse top.   *Ib. st. 6*

The Wedding Guest here beat his
    breast,
For he heard the loud bassoon.
Ib. st. 8

The bride hath paced into the hall,
Red as a rose is she.   *Ib. st. 9*

And now there came both mist and
    snow,
And it grew wondrous cold:
And ice, mast-high, came floating by,
As green as emerald.   *Ib. st. 13*

The ice was here, the ice was there,
The ice was all around:
It cracked and growled, and roared and
    howled,
Like noises in a swound!   *Ib. st. 15*

"God save thee, ancient Mariner!
From the fiends, that plague thee
    thus! —
Why look'st thou so?" — "With my
    crossbow
I shot the Albatross."   *Ib. st. 20*

The fair breeze blew, the white foam
    flew,
The furrows followed free;
We were the first that ever burst
Into that silent sea.   *Ib. II, st. 5*

As idle as a painted ship
Upon a painted ocean.   *Ib. st. 8*

Water, water, everywhere,
Nor any drop to drink.
    The Ancient Mariner, pt. II, st. 9

The very deep did rot: O Christ!
That ever this should be!
Yea, slimy things did crawl with legs
Upon the slimy sea.   *Ib. st. 10*

About, about, in reel and rout
The death-fires danced at night.
    Ib. st. 11

I bit my arm, I sucked the blood,
And cried, A sail! a sail!
    Ib. III, st. 4

Her lips were red, her looks were free,
Her locks were yellow as gold:
Her skin was white as leprosy,
The nightmare Life-in-Death was she,
Who thicks man's blood with cold.
    Ib. st. 11

"The game is done! I've won, I've won!"
Quoth she, and whistles thrice.
    Ib. st. 12

The sun's rim dips, the stars rush out:
At one stride comes the dark;
With far-heard whisper o'er the sea
Off shot the specter-bark.   *Ib. st. 13*

We listened and looked sideways up!
Fear at my heart, as at a cup,
My lifeblood seemed to sip.
    Ib. st. 14

The hornèd Moon, with one bright star
Within the nether tip.   *Ib.*

Each turned his face with a ghastly pang,
And cursed me with his eye.
    Ib. st. 15

I fear thee, ancient Mariner!
I fear thy skinny hand!
And thou art long, and lank, and brown,
As is the ribbed sea-sand.[1]
    Ib. IV, st. 1

[1] A note by Coleridge in *Sibylline Leaves* [1817] says: "For [these] lines I am indebted to Mr. Wordsworth."

Alone, alone, all, all alone;
Alone on a wide, wide sea.
    The Ancient Mariner, pt. IV, st. 3

The moving moon went up the sky,
And nowhere did abide;
Softly she was going up,
And a star or two beside.   *Ib. st. 10*

Her beams bemocked the sultry main,
Like April hoarfrost spread;
But where the ship's huge shadow lay,
The charmed water burnt alway
A still and awful red.   *Ib. st. 11*

A spring of love gushed from my heart,
And I blessed them unaware.
    Ib. st. 14

Oh sleep! it is a gentle thing,
Beloved from pole to pole.
    Ib. V, st. 1

We were a ghastly crew.   *Ib. st. 11*

A noise like of a hidden brook
In the leafy month of June,
That to the sleeping woods all night
Singeth a quiet tune.   *Ib. st. 17*

    The man hath penance done,
And penance more will do.
    Ib. st. 25

Like one that on a lonesome road
Doth walk in fear and dread,
And having once turned round walks on,
And turns no more his head;
Because he knows a frightful fiend
Doth close behind him tread.
    Ib. VI, st. 10

Is this the hill? is this the kirk?
Is this mine own countree?
    Ib. st. 14

No voice; but oh! the silence sank
Like music on my heart.   *Ib. st. 22*

And the owlet whoops to the wolf below,
That eats the she-wolf's young.
    Ib. VII, st. 5

"Ha! ha!" quoth he, "full plain I see,
The Devil knows how to row."
    Ib. st. 12

"O shrieve me, shrieve me, holy man!"
   The Ancient Mariner, pt. VII,
                   st. 14

O Wedding Guest! This soul hath
   been
Alone on a wide wide sea:
So lonely 'twas, that God himself
Scarce seemèd there to be.
                   Ib. st. 19

He prayeth well who loveth well
Both man and bird and beast.
                   Ib. st. 22

He prayeth best who loveth best
All things both great and small;
For the dear God who loveth us,
He made and loveth all.[1]   *Ib. st. 23*

A sadder and a wiser man
He rose the morrow morn.
                   Ib. st. 25

With what deep worship I have still
   adored
The spirit of divinest Liberty.
       France: An Ode [1798], *st. 1*

The frost performs its secret ministry,
Unhelped by any wind.
     Frost at Midnight [1798], *l. 1*

Therefore all seasons shall be sweet to
   thee,
Whether the summer clothe the general earth
With greenness, or the redbreast sit
   and sing
Betwixt the tufts of snow on the bare
   branch.   *Ib. l. 65*

Or if the secret ministry of frost
Shall hang them up in silent icicles,
Quietly shining to the quiet moon.
                   Ib. l. 72

Forth from his dark and lonely hiding
   place
(Portentous sight!) the owlet Atheism,
Sailing on obscene wings athwart the
   noon,
Drops his blue-fringèd lids, and holds
   them close,

[1] See Alexander, p. 684b.

And hooting at the glorious sun in
   Heaven,
Cries out, "Where is it?"
       Fears in Solitude [1798], *l. 81*

And the Devil did grin, for his darling
   sin
Is pride that apes humility.[1]
       The Devil's Thoughts [2] [1799],
                   st. 6

Strongly it bears us along in swelling
   and limitless billows,
Nothing before and nothing behind but
   the sky and the ocean.
     The Homeric Hexameter (*trans-
     lated from Schiller*) [1799?]

In the hexameter rises the fountain's
   silvery column;
In the pentameter aye falling in melody
   back.
       The Ovidian Elegiac Metre
        (*from Schiller*) [1799]

All thoughts, all passions, all delights,
Whatever stirs this mortal frame,
All are but ministers of Love,
And feed his sacred flame.
            Love [1799], *st. 1*

Tranquillity! thou better name
Than all the family of Fame!
    Ode to Tranquillity [1801], *st. 1*

Aloof with hermit-eye I scan
The present works of present man —
A wild and dream-like trade of blood
   and guile,
Too foolish for a tear, too wicked for a
   smile!   *Ib. st. 4*

Hast thou a charm to stay the morning
   star
In his steep course?
    Hymn in the Vale of Chamouni
               [1802], *l. 1*

Earth, with her thousand voices, praises
   God.   *Ib.*

[1] See Robert Burton, p. 311a.
[2] This poem was written in collaboration with Southey, who also imitated it in *The Devil's Walk*, p. 533a.

What is an Epigram? A dwarfish whole,
Its body brevity, and wit its soul.[1]
An Epigram [1802]

I see, not feel, how beautiful they are!
Dejection: An Ode [1802], *st.* 2

O Lady! we receive but what we give
And in our life alone does Nature live.
Ib. st. 4

A light, a glory, a fair luminous cloud
Enveloping the Earth. *Ib.*

Joy is the sweet voice, Joy the luminous cloud —
We in ourselves rejoice!
And thence flows all that charms or ear or sight,
All melodies the echoes of that voice,
All colors a suffusion from that light.
Ib. st. 5

How seldom, friend! a good great man inherits
Honor or wealth, with all his worth and pains!
It sounds like stories from the land of spirits
If any man obtain that which he merits,
Or any merit that which he obtains.
The Good Great Man [1802]

Trochee trips from long to short;
From long to long in solemn sort
Slow Spondee stalks.
Metrical Feet [1806]

The Knight's bones are dust,
And his good sword rust;
His soul is with the saints, I trust.
The Knight's Tomb [c. 1817]

With Donne, whose muse on dromedary trots,
Wreathe iron pokers into true-love knots.
On Donne's Poetry [c. 1818]

The Eighth Commandment was not made for bards.
The Reproof and Reply [1823]

[1] See Shakespeare, *Hamlet II, ii, 90,* p. 260b.

Nought cared this body for wind or weather,
When youth and I lived in 't together.
Youth and Age [1823–1832], *st.* 1

Flowers are lovely; love is flower-like;
Friendship is a sheltering tree;
Oh the joys that came down shower-like,
Of friendship, love, and liberty,
Ere I was old! *Ib. st. 2*

All Nature seems at work. Slugs leave their lair —
The bees are stirring — birds are on the wing —
And Winter slumbering in the open air,
Wears on his smiling face a dream of Spring!
And I the while, the sole unbusy thing,
Nor honey make, nor pair, nor build, nor sing.
Work Without Hope [*February 21, 1825*]

Work without Hope draws nectar in a sieve,
And Hope without an object cannot live. *Ib.*

In many ways doth the full heart reveal
The presence of the love it would conceal.
Poems Written in Later Life [1826], *motto*

I counted two-and-seventy stenches,
All well defined, and several stinks.
Cologne [1828]

The river Rhine, it is well known,
Doth wash your city of Cologne;
But tell me, nymphs! what power divine
Shall henceforth wash the river Rhine?
Ib.

Poetry is not the proper antithesis to prose, but to science. Poetry is opposed to science, and prose to metre. The proper and immediate object of science is the acquirement, or communication, of truth; the proper and immediate object of poetry is the communication of immediate pleasure.

Definitions of Poetry [1811]

Reviewers are usually people who would have been poets, historians, biographers, etc., if they could; they have tried their talents at one or at the other, and have failed; therefore they turn critics.[1]

Lectures on Shakespeare and Milton [1811–1812]

The last speech [Iago's soliloquy], the motive-hunting of a motiveless malignity — how awful!

Notes on Shakespeare [c. 1812]

Taste is the intermediate faculty which connects the active with the passive powers of our nature, the intellect with the senses; and its appointed function is to elevate the *images* of the latter, while it realizes the *ideas* of the former.

On the Principles of Genial Criticism [1814]

The most general definition of beauty . . . Multeity in Unity. *Ib.*

The Good consists in the congruity of a thing with the laws of the reason and the nature of the will, and in its fitness to determine the latter to actualize the former: and it is always discursive. The Beautiful arises from the perceived harmony of an object, whether sight or sound, with the inborn and constitutive rules of the judgment and imagination: and it is always intuitive. *Ib.*

The imagination . . . that reconciling and mediatory power, which incorporating the reason in images of the sense and organizing (as it were) the flux of the senses by the permanence and self-circling energies of the reason, gives birth to a system of symbols, har-

[1] Reviewers, with some rare exceptions, are a most stupid and malignant race. As a bankrupt thief turns thief-taker in despair, so an unsuccessful author turns critic. — SHELLEY, *Fragments of Adonais* [1821]

See Disraeli, p. 612b, and Lowell, p. 692b.

monious in themselves, and consubstantial with the truths of which they are the conductors.

The Statesman's Manual [1816]

Not the poem which we have *read*, but that to which we *return*, with the greatest pleasure, possesses the genuine power, and claims the name of *essential poetry*.[1]

Biographia Literaria [1817], ch. 1

Experience informs us that the first defense of weak minds is to recriminate. *Ib. 2*

Indignation at literary wrongs I leave to men born under happier stars. I cannot afford it. *Ib.*

Milton had a highly imaginative, Cowley a very fanciful mind. *Ib. 4*

An idea, in the highest sense of that word, cannot be conveyed but by a symbol. *Ib. 9*

Veracity does not consist in saying, but in the intention of communicating truth. *Ib.*

Never pursue literature as a trade. *Ib. 11*

Until you understand a writer's ignorance, presume yourself ignorant of his understanding. *Ib. 12*

During the act of knowledge itself, the objective and subjective are so instantly united, that we cannot determine to which of the two the priority belongs. *Ib.*

The primary imagination I hold to be the living power and prime agent of all human perception, and as a repetition in the finite mind of the eternal act of creation in the infinite I Am. *Ib. 13*

The secondary imagination . . . dissolves, diffuses, dissipates, in order to re-create; or where this process is rendered impossible, yet still at all events it struggles to idealize and to unify. It is

[1] See Robert Frost, pp. 929b and 930a.

essentially vital, even as all objects (*as objects*) are essentially fixed and dead.
Biographia Literaria, ch. 13

The fancy is indeed no other than a mode of memory emancipated from the order of time and space.   *Ib.*

The two cardinal points of poetry, the power of exciting the sympathy of the reader by a faithful adherence to the truth of nature, and the power of giving the interest of novelty by the modifying colors of imagination.
Ib. 14

That willing suspension of disbelief for the moment, which constitutes poetic faith.   *Ib.*

The poet, described in *ideal* perfection, brings the whole soul of man into activity, with the subordination of its faculties to each other, according to their relative worth and dignity. He diffuses a tone and spirit of unity, that blends, and (as it were) *fuses*, each into each, by that synthetic and magical power . . . imagination.   *Ib.*

[Imagination] reveals itself in the balance or reconciliation of opposite or discordant qualities: of sameness, with difference; of the general, with the concrete; the idea, with the image; the individual, with the representative; the sense of novelty and freshness, with old and familiar objects; a more than usual state of emotion, with more than usual order; judgment ever awake and steady self-possession, with enthusiasm and feeling profound or vehement; and while it blends and harmonizes the natural and the artificial, still subordinates art to nature; the manner to the matter; and our admiration of the poet to our sympathy with the poetry.
Ib.

No man was ever yet a great poet, without being at the same time a profound philosopher.   *Ib.* 15

While [Shakespeare] darts himself forth and passes into all the forms of human character and passion, the one Proteus of the fire and the flood, [Milton] attracts all forms and things to himself, into the unity of his own *Ideal*. All things and modes of action shape themselves anew in the being of Milton; while Shakespeare becomes all things, yet ever remaining himself.
Biographia Literaria, ch. 15

Our myriad-minded Shakespeare.[1]
Ib.

The best part of human language, properly so called, is derived from reflection on the acts of the mind itself.[2]
Ib. 17

The organic form, on the other hand, is innate; it shapes, as it develops, itself from within, and the fullness of its development is one and the same with the perfection of its outward form.
Shakespeare's Judgment Equal to His Genius [1818]

Now Art, used collectively for painting, sculpture, architecture and music, is the mediatress between, and reconciler of, nature and man. It is, therefore, the power of humanizing nature, of infusing the thoughts and passions of man into everything which is the object of his contemplation.
On Poesy or Art [1818]

The artist must imitate that which is within the thing, that which is active through form and figure, and discourses to us by symbols.   *Ib.*

The heart should have fed upon the truth, as insects on a leaf, till it be tinged with the color, and show its food in every . . . minutest fiber.   *Ib.*

Schiller has the material sublime.
Table Talk [*December 29, 1822*]

---

[1] A phrase which I have borrowed from a Greek monk, who applies it to a patriarch of Constantinople. [Coleridge's footnote.]
[2] The poem of the act of the mind. — WALLACE STEVENS [1879–1965], *Collected Poems. Of Modern Poetry*

I wish our clever young poets would remember my homely definitions of prose and poetry; that is, prose = words in their best order; poetry = the best words in their best order.

Table Talk [*July 12, 1827*]

The man's desire is for the woman; but the woman's desire is rarely other than for the desire of the man.

Ib. [*July 23, 1827*]

Poetry is certainly something more than good sense, but it must be good sense at all events; just as a palace is more than a house, but it must be a house, at least. *Ib.* [*May 9, 1830*]

That passage is what I call the sublime dashed to pieces by cutting too close with the fiery four-in-hand round the corner of nonsense. *Ib.*

The happiness of life is made up of minute fractions — the little soon forgotten charities of a kiss or smile, a kind look, a heartfelt compliment, and the countless infinitesimals of pleasurable and genial feeling.

The Friend. The Improvisatore [*1828*]

Beneath this sod
A poet lies, or that which once seemed he —
Oh, lift a thought in prayer for S.T.C.!
That he, who many a year, with toil of breath,
Found death in life, may here find life in death.

Epitaph written for himself [*1833*]

JOSIAH QUINCY, JR.
1772–1864

If this bill [for the admission of Orleans Territory as a State] passes, I am compelled to declare it as my deliberate opinion that the bonds of this Union are virtually dissolved; that the States which compose it are free from their moral obligations; and that, as it will be the right of all, so it will be the duty of some, to prepare definitely for a separation — amicably if they can; violently if they must.[1]

Speech in the U. S. House of Representatives [*January 14, 1811*]

WILLIAM BARNES RHODES
1772–1826

Bombastes: So have I heard on Afric's burning shore
A hungry lion give a grievous roar;
The grievous roar echoed along the shore.
Artaxaminous: So have I heard on Afric's burning shore
Another lion give a grievous roar;
And the first lion thought the last a bore.

Bombastes Furioso [*1810*], *act I, sc. 4*

DAVID RICARDO
1772–1823

Labor, like all other things which are purchased and sold, and which may be increased or diminished in quantity, has its natural and its market price. The natural price of labor is that price which is necessary to enable the laborers, one with another, to subsist and perpetuate their race, without either increase or diminution.

On the Principles of Political Economy and Taxation [*1817*]

FRIEDRICH SCHLEGEL
1772–1829

The historian is a prophet in reverse. *Athenaeum* [*1798–1800*]

---

[1] The gentleman [Quincy] cannot have forgotten his own sentiment, uttered even on the floor of this House, "Peaceably if we can, forcibly if we must." — HENRY CLAY, *Speech* [*January 8, 1813*]

FRANÇOIS HORACE BASTIEN SÉBASTIANI
1772–1851

Order reigns in Warsaw.[1]
Announcement of the fall of Warsaw [1831]

ÉTIENNE DE GRELLET
1773–1855

I expect to pass through this world but once; any good thing therefore that I can do, or any kindness that I can show to any fellow creature, let me do it now; let me not defer or neglect it, for I shall not pass this way again.[2]
Attributed

WILLIAM HENRY HARRISON
1773–1841

We admit of no government by divine right . . . the only legitimate right to govern is an express grant of power from the governed.
Inaugural Address [March 4, 1841]

Never with my consent shall an officer of the people, compensated for his services out of their pockets, become the pliant instrument of the Executive will.
Ib.

A decent and manly examination of the acts of government should be not only tolerated, but encouraged.
Inaugural Address

JOHN RANDOLPH
1773–1833

The surest way to prevent war is not to fear it.
Speech, U.S. House of Representatives [March 5, 1806]

He is a man of splendid abilities, but utterly corrupt. He shines and stinks like rotten mackerel by moonlight.[1]
Of Edward Livingston; from W. CABELL BRUCE, *John Randolph of Roanoke [1923], vol. II, p. 197*

He rowed to his object with muffled oars.   *Of Martin Van Buren*

ROBERT SOUTHEY
1774–1843

"You are old, Father William," the young man cried,
"The few locks which are left you are gray;
You are hale, Father William — a hearty old man:
Now tell me the reason, I pray."
The Old Man's Comforts and How He Gained Them,[2] st. 1

"In the days of my youth, I remembered my God,
And he hath not forgotten my age."
Ib. st. 6

And in at the windows, and in at the door,
And through the walls by thousands they pour;
And down from the ceiling and up through the floor,
From the right and the left, from behind and before,
From within and without, from above and below —

---

[1] 'Tis vain for present fame to wish.
Our persons first must be forgotten;
For poets are like stinking fish,
They never shine until they're rotten.
MCDONALD CLARKE [1798–1842], *Epigram*

[2] Of several parodies of this poem, the one by Lewis Carroll is probably better known than the original. See p. 543b.
"You are old, Father William, and though one would think
All the veins in your body were dry,
Yet the end of your nose is red as a pink;
I beg your indulgence, but why?"
LEE O. HARRIS and JAMES WHITCOMB RILEY, *Father William, st. 1*

---

[1] Des lettres que je reçois de Pologne m'annoncent que la tranquillité règne à Varsovie. — DUMAS [1802–1870], *Mémoires [2nd series], vol. IV, ch. 3*
[2] This is not found in any of Grellet's writings, and has been attributed to many others. See Addison, p. 394a.

And all at once to the Bishop they go.
*God's Judgment on a Wicked
Bishop,*[1] *st. 17*

It was a summer evening;
Old Kaspar's work was done,
And he before his cottage door
Was sitting in the sun;
And by him sported on the green
His little grandchild Wilhelmine.
The Battle of Blenheim [1798],
st. 1

He came to ask what he had found,
That was so large, and smooth, and
round. *Ib. st. 2*

" 'Tis some poor fellow's skull," said
he,
"Who fell in the great victory."
Ib. st. 3

But what they fought each other for,
I could not well make out. *Ib. st. 6*

"And everybody praised the Duke,
Who this great fight did win."
"But what good came of it at last?"
Quoth little Peterkin.
"Why, that I cannot tell," said he;
"But 'twas a famous victory."
Ib. st. 11

Blue, darkly, deeply, beautifully blue.[2]
Madoc in Wales [1805], *pt. I, 5*

What will not woman, gentle woman
dare,
When strong affection stirs her spirit
up? *Ib. II, 2*

And last of all an Admiral came,
A terrible man with a terrible name —
A name which you all know by sight
very well,

---

[1] Hatto, in the time of the great famine of
914, when he saw the poor exceedingly oppressed
by famine, assembled a great company of them
together into a barn at Kaub and burnt them
. . . because he thought the famine would
sooner cease if those poor folks were dispatched
out of the world. . . . But God . . . sent against
him a plague of mice . . . and the prelate retreated to a tower in the Rhine . . . but the
mice chased him continually . . . and at last
he was most miserably devoured. — THOMAS
CORYAT, *Crudities* [1611]

[2] See Byron, p. 561a.

But which no one can speak, and no
one can spell.
The March to Moscow, st. 8

Curses are like young chickens, they always come home to roost.
The Curse of Kehama [1810],
motto

They sin who tell us love can die;
With life all other passions fly,
All others are but vanity.
Ib. canto X, st. 10

Thou hast been called, O sleep! the
friend of woe;
But 'tis the happy that have called thee
so. *Ib. XV, st. 12*

No stir in the air, no stir in the sea,
The ship was still as she could be.
The Inchcape Rock,[1] *st. 1*

And then they knew the perilous
Rock,
And blessed the Abbot of Aberbrothok.
Ib. st. 4

Till the vessel strikes with a shivering
shock —
"O Christ! It is the Inchcape Rock."
Ib. st. 15

My days among the dead are past;
Around me I behold,
Where'er these casual eyes are cast,
The mighty minds of old.
*My Days Among the Dead Are
Past* [1818], *st. 1*

Yet leaving here a name, I trust,
That will not perish in the dust.
Ib. st. 4

Agreed to differ.
Life of Wesley [1820]

The Satanic school.
Vision of Judgment [1821],
original preface

So I told them in rhyme,
For of rhymes I had store.
The Cataract of Lodore

---

[1] A rock in the North Sea, off the Firth of Tay,
Scotland, dangerous to navigators because it is
covered with every tide. There is a tradition
that a warning bell was fixed on the rock by the
Abbot of Aberbrothok, which was stolen by a
sea pirate, who perished on the rock a year later.

From his brimstone bed, at break of
day,
A-walking the Devil is gone,
To look at his little snug farm of the
World,
And see how his stock went on.
The Devil's Walk, st. 1

How then was the Devil dressed?
O, he was in his Sunday's best;
His coat was red, and his breeches were
blue,
And there was a hole where his tail
came through.   *Ib. st. 3*

He passed a cottage with a double
coach-house —
A cottage of gentility;
  And he owned with a grin,
  That his favorite sin
Is pride that apes humility.[1]
Ib. st. 8

The arts babblative and scribblative.
*Colloquies on the Progress and
Prospects of Society* [1829],
no. 1, pt. 2

The march of Intellect.   *Ib. 14*

As frozen as charity.[2]
The Soldier's Wife, st. 4

JANE AUSTEN
1775–1817

It is a truth universally acknowledged, that a single man in possession
of a good fortune, must be in want of a
wife.
Pride and Prejudice [1813], *ch. 1*

She [Mrs. Bennet] was a woman of
mean understanding, little information,
and uncertain temper.   *Ib.*

A lady's imagination is very rapid; it
jumps from admiration to love, from
love to matrimony in a moment.
Ib. 6

Mr. Collins had only to change from
Jane to Elizabeth — and it was soon
done — done while Mrs. Bennet was
stirring the fire.   *Ib. 15*

---

[1] See Coleridge, p. 526b, and note.
[2] See Hood, p. 593a, and O'Reilly, p. 807a.

You have delighted us long enough.
Pride and Prejudice, ch. 18

Mrs. Bennet was restored to her
usual querulous serenity.   *Ib. 42*

You ought certainly to forgive them,
as a Christian, but never to admit them
in your sight, or allow their names to be
mentioned in your hearing.   *Ib. 57*

For what do we live, but to make
sport for our neighbors, and laugh at
them in our turn?   *Ib.*

I have been a selfish being all my life,
in practice, though not in principle.
Ib. 58

One half of the world cannot understand the pleasures of the other.
Emma [1815], *ch. 9*

It was a delightful visit — perfect, in
being much too short.   *Ib. 13*

Nobody who has not been in the
interior of a family can say what the
difficulties of any individual of that
family may be.   *Ib. 18*

Business, you know, may bring
money, but friendship hardly ever does.
Ib. 34

"Only a novel" . . . in short, only
some work in which the greatest powers
of the mind are displayed, in which the
most thorough knowledge of human
nature, the happiest delineation of its
varieties, the liveliest effusions of wit
and humor are conveyed to the world in
the best chosen language.
Northanger Abbey [1818], *ch. 5*

What dreadful hot weather we have!
It keeps me in a continual state of
inelegance.
Letters. To her sister Cassandra
[September 18, 1796]

I do not want people to be very
agreeable, as it saves me the trouble of
liking them a great deal.
Ib. [December 24, 1798]

The little bit (two inches wide) of
ivory on which I work with so fine a

brush as produces little effect after much labor.[1]

> *Letters. To J. Edward Austen*
> *[December 16, 1816]*

CHARLES LAMB
1775–1834

I have something more to do than feel.

> *Letter to Coleridge after the death of Lamb's mother* [1796]

The not unpeaceful evening of a day
Made black by morning storms.

> *Poem-letter to Coleridge* [1797]

I have had playmates, I have had companions,
In my days of childhood, in my joyful school-days —
All, all are gone, the old familiar faces.

> *Old Familiar Faces* [1798]

For God's sake (I never was more serious) don't make me ridiculous any more by terming me gentle-hearted in print [2] . . . substitute drunken dog, ragged head, seld-shaven, odd-eyed, stuttering, or any other epithet which truly and properly belongs to the gentleman in question.

> *Letter to Coleridge* [August 1800]

Separate from the pleasure of your company, I don't much care if I never see a mountain in my life.

> *Letter to Wordsworth* [1801]

The man must have a rare recipe for

---

[1] [Miss Austen] had a talent for describing the involvements and feelings and characters of ordinary life which is to me the most wonderful I ever met with. The Big Bow-Wow strain I can do myself like any now going; but the exquisite touch, which renders ordinary commonplace things and characters interesting, from the truth of the description and the sentiment, is denied to me. — Scott, *Journal* [March 14, 1826]

[2] For thee, my gentle-hearted Charles, to whom No sound is dissonant which tells of life.
Coleridge, *This Lime Tree Bower My Prison* [1797]

melancholy, who can be dull in Fleet Street.

> *Letter to Thomas Manning*
> *[February 15, 1802]*

Nursed amid her [London's] noise, her crowds, her beloved smoke — what have I been doing all my life, if I have not lent out my heart with usury to such scenes?   *Ib.*

Gone before
To that unknown and silent shore.

> *Hester* [1803], st. 7

A good-natured woman, which is as much as you can expect from a friend's wife, whom you got acquainted with a bachelor.   *Letter to Hazlitt* [1805]

Neat, not gaudy.

> *Letter to Wordsworth* [1806]

This very night I am going to leave off tobacco! Surely there must be some other world in which this unconquerable purpose shall be realized.

> *Letter to Thomas Manning* [1815]

Anything awful makes me laugh. I misbehaved once at a funeral.

> *Letter to Southey* [1815]

[Of Coleridge] An archangel a little damaged.

> *Letter to Wordsworth* [1816]

Fanny Kelly's divine plain face.

> *Letter to Mrs. Wordsworth* [1818]

The red-letter days, now become, to all intents and purposes, dead-letter days.

> *Essays of Elia* [1823]. *Oxford in the Vacation* [1]

The human species, according to the best theory I can form of it, is composed of two distinct races, the men who borrow, and the men who lend.

> *Ib. The Two Races of Men*

Your borrowers of books — those mutilators of collections, spoilers of the

---

[1] Which, it has been pointed out, was actually written at Cambridge. See E. V. Lucas, *Lamb and the Universities.*

symmetry of shelves, and creators of odd volumes.

> *Essays of Elia. The Two Races of Men*

Of all sound of all bells (bells, the music nighest bordering upon heaven) most solemn and touching is the peal which rings out the Old Year.

> *Ib. New Year's Eve*

A clear fire, a clean hearth, and the rigor of the game.

> *Ib. Mrs. Battle's Opinions on Whist*

I have no ear.

> *Ib. A Chapter on Ears*

Sentimentally I am disposed to harmony; but organically I am incapable of a tune. *Ib.*

Credulity is the man's weakness, but the child's strength.

> *Ib. Witches, and Other Night Fears*

Not many sounds in life, and I include all urban and all rural sounds, exceed in interest a knock at the door.[1] *Ib. Valentine's Day*

The custom of saying grace at meals had, probably, its origin in the early times of the world, and the hunter-state of man, when dinners were precarious things, and a full meal was something more than a common blessing!

> *Ib. Grace Before Meat*

Presents, I often say, endear absents.

> *Ib. A Dissertation Upon Roast Pig*

Nothing is to me more distasteful than that entire complacency and satisfaction which beam in the countenances of a new-married couple.

> *Ib. The Behavior of Married People*

I came home forever!

> *Letter to Bernard Barton* [1825], *on leaving his "33 years' desk" at the East India House*

[1] Doorbells are like a magic game,
  Or the grab bag at a fair —
You never know when you hear one ring
  Who may be waiting there.
  RACHEL FIELD [1894–1942], *Doorbells*

Who first invented work, and bound
   the free
And holiday-rejoicing spirit down?

> *Work*

Riddle of destiny, who can show
What thy short visit meant, or
   know
What thy errand here below?

> *On an Infant Dying as Soon as Born* [1827]

Martin, if dirt was trumps, what hands you would hold!

> *Lamb's Suppers. From* LEIGH HUNT, *Lord Byron and His Contemporaries* [1828]

Some cry up Haydn, some Mozart,
Just as the whim bites. For my part,
I do not care a farthing candle
For either of them, nor for Handel.[1]

> *Letter to Mrs. William Hazlitt* [1830]

For thy sake, Tobacco, I
Would do anything but die.

> *A Farewell to Tobacco*

A poor relation — is the most irrelevant thing in nature.

> *Last Essays of Elia* [1833]. *Poor Relations*

I love to lose myself in other men's minds.

> *Ib. Detached Thoughts on Books and Reading*

Books think for me. *Ib.*

Books which are no books. *Ib.*

Newspapers always excite curiosity. No one ever lays one down without a feeling of disappointment. *Ib.*

How sickness enlarges the dimensions of a man's self to himself.

> *Ib. The Convalescent*

Your absence of mind we have borne, till your presence of body came to be called in question by it.

> *Ib. Amicus Redivivus*

[1] See John Byrom, p. 415a.

A pun is a pistol let off at the ear; not a feather to tickle the intellect.
> *Last Essays of Elia. Popular Fallacies: IX, That the Worst Puns are the Best*

A presentation copy . . . is a copy of a book which does not sell, sent you by the author, with his foolish autograph at the beginning of it; for which, if a stranger, he only demands your friendship; if a brother author, he expects from you a book of yours, which does not sell, in return.
> *Ib. XI, That We Must Not Look a Gift Horse in the Mouth*

The good things of life are not to be had singly, but come to us with a mixture.
> *Ib. XIII, That You Must Love Me and Love My Dog*

The greatest pleasure I know is to do a good action by stealth, and to have it found out by accident.
> *Table Talk. In the Athenaeum* [1834]

WALTER SAVAGE LANDOR
1775–1864

But I have sinuous shells of pearly hue . . .
Shake one, and it awakens; then apply
Its polished lips to your attentive ear,
And it remembers its august abodes,
And murmurs as the ocean murmurs there.[1]   *Gebir, bk. I* [1798]

Ah what avails the sceptered race,
Ah what the form divine!
> *Rose Aylmer* [1806]

Rose Aylmer, whom these wakeful eyes
May weep, but never see,
A night of memories and of sighs
I consecrate to thee.   *Ib.*

[1] See Wordsworth, p. 516b.

There are no fields of amaranth on this side of the grave: there are no voices, O Rhodopè! that are not soon mute, however tuneful: there is no name, with whatever emphasis of passionate love repeated, of which the echo is not faint at last.
> *Imaginary Conversations* [1824–1829]. *Aesop and Rhodopè, I*

Of all failures, to fail in a witticism is the worst, and the mishap is the more calamitous in a drawn out and detailed one.   *Ib. Chesterfield and Chatham*

'Tis verse that gives
Immortal youth to mortal maids.
> *Verse*

Around the child bend all the three
Sweet Graces; Faith, Hope, Charity.
Around the man bend other faces;
Pride, Envy, Malice, are his Graces.
> *Around the Child*

When we play the fool, how wide
The theatre expands! beside,
How long the audience sits before us!
How many prompters! what a chorus!
> *Plays* [1846], *st. 2*

There is delight in singing, though none hear
Beside the singer.
> *To Robert Browning* [1846]

Shakespeare is not our poet, but the world's,
Therefore on him no speech! and brief for thee,
Browning! Since Chaucer was alive and hale,
No man hath walked along our roads with step
So active, so inquiring eye, or tongue
So varied in discourse.   *Ib.*

I strove with none, for none was worth my strife;
Nature I loved; and next to Nature, Art.
I warm'd both hands before the fire of life;
It sinks, and I am ready to depart.
> *I Strove with None* [1853]

HIRATA ATSUTANE[1]
1776–1843

It was the gods who formed all the lands of the world at the Creation, and these gods were without exception born in Japan. Japan is thus the homeland of the gods, and that is why we call it the Land of the Gods.
Summary of the Ancient Way

With their scientific instruments the Dutch attempt to determine the properties of things. Unlike China, Holland is a splendid country where they do not rely on superficial conjectures. *Ib.*

The ancient Japanese all constantly and correctly practiced what the Chinese called humanity, righteousness, the five cardinal virtues and the rest, without having any need to name them or to teach them. In China . . . there were evil customs from the very outset, and human behavior . . . was extremely licentious. That is the reason why so many sages appeared in ancient times to guide and instruct the Chinese.
Indignant Discussion of Chinese Books [c. 1810]

The art of medicine, though introduced to Japan from abroad, appears originally to have been taught to foreign countries by our own great gods.
Shizu No Iwaya [1811]

THOMAS CAMPBELL
1777–1844

'Tis distance lends enchantment to the view,
And robes the mountain in its azure hue.[2]
Pleasures of Hope [1799], pt. I, l. 7

Hope, for a season, bade the world farewell,

And Freedom shriek'd — as Kosciusko fell!
Pleasures of Hope, pt. I, l. 381

Who hath not own'd, with rapture-smitten frame,
The power of grace, the magic of a name?　　*Ib.* II, l. 5

And muse on Nature with a poet's eye.
Ib. l. 98

Cease, every joy, to glimmer on my mind,
But leave, oh! leave the light of Hope behind!
What though my wingèd hours of bliss have been
Like angel visits, few and far between?[1]　　*Ib.* l. 375

On the green banks of Shannon, when Sheelah was nigh,
No blithe Irish lad was so happy as I;
No harp like my own could so cheerily play,
And wherever I went was my poor dog Tray.[2]　*The Harper* [1799], *st. 1*

Ye mariners of England,
That guard our native seas;
Whose flag has braved, a thousand years,
The battle and the breeze!
Ye Mariners of England [1800], *st. 1*

While the battle rages loud and long, and the stormy winds do blow. *Ib.*

Britannia needs no bulwarks,
No towers along the steep;
Her march is o'er the mountain waves,
Her home is on the deep.　　*Ib. st. 3*

The meteor flag of England
Shall yet terrific burn,
Till danger's troubled night depart,
And the star of peace return. *Ib. st. 4*

Oh! once the harp of Innisfail
Was strung full high to notes of gladness;

---

[1] From *Sources of Japanese Tradition*, edited by William Theodore de Bary [1960].
[2] The mountains too, at a distance, appear airy masses and smooth, but seen near at hand they are rough. — DIOGENES LAERTIUS [c. A.D. 200], *Pyrrho, sec. 9*

[1] See John Norris, p. 385a.
[2] My Old Dog Tray. — *Title of song by* STEPHEN C. FOSTER [1826–1864]

But yet it often told a tale
Of more prevailing sadness.
O'Connor's Child, st. 1

'Tis the sunset of life gives me mystical
lore,
And coming events cast their shadows
before.[1]
Lochiel's Warning [1802]

The combat deepens. On, ye brave,
Who rush to glory or the grave!
Wave, Munich! all thy banners wave,
And charge with all thy chivalry!

Few, few shall part where many meet!
The snow shall be their winding sheet
And every turf beneath their feet
Shall be a soldier's sepulcher.
Hohenlinden [1802], st. 7, 8

There was silence deep as death,
And the boldest held his breath,
For a time.
Battle of the Baltic [1805], st. 2

Ye are brothers! ye are men!
And we conquer but to save.
Ib. st. 5

Star that bringest home the bee,
And sett'st the weary laborer free!
*Song to the Evening Star
[1822], st. 1*

Oh, how hard it is to find
The one just suited to our mind!
Song, st. 1

To live in hearts we leave behind
Is not to die.[2]
Hallowed Ground, st. 6

Oh leave this barren spot to me!
Spare, woodman, spare the beechen
tree![3]
The Beech Tree's Petition, st. 1

[1] See Cicero, p. 111a; Shakespeare, p. 268a;
Shelley, p. 573a; and H. G. Wells, p. 888b.
Often do the spirits
Of great events stride on before the events,
And in today already walks tomorrow.
COLERIDGE, *Wallenstein* [1799–1800], *pt.
II, act V, sc. 1*

[2] They are not dead who live
In hearts they leave behind.
HUGH ROBERT ORR [b. 1887], *They
Softly Walk, st. 1*

[3] See George Pope Morris, p. 600a.

A stoic of the woods — a man without
a tear.
*Gertrude of Wyoming [1809],
pt. I, st. 23*

HENRY CLAY
1777–1852

How often are we forced to charge
fortune with partiality towards the unjust! *Letter [December 4, 1801]*

If you wish to avoid foreign collision,
you had better abandon the ocean.
*Speech, U.S. House of Repre-
sentatives [January 22, 1812]*

Government is a trust, and the officers of the government are trustees; and
both the trust and the trustees are created for the benefit of the people.[1]
*Speech at Ashland, Kentucky
[March 1829]*

The arts of power and its minions are
the same in all countries and in all ages.
It marks its victim; denounces it; and
excites the public odium and the public
hatred, to conceal its own abuses and
encroachments.
*Speech, U.S. Senate [March 14,
1834]*

Precedents deliberately established by
wise men are entitled to great weight.
They are evidence of truth, but *only*
evidence. . . . But a solitary precedent . . . which has never been re-
examined, cannot be conclusive.
*Speech, U.S. Senate [February
18, 1835]*

I have heard something said about
allegiance to the South. I know no
South, no North, no East, no West, to
which I owe any allegiance. The Union,
sir, is my country. *Speech [1848]*

The Constitution of the United
States was made not merely for the

[1] See Mathew Henry, p. 386b; Burke, p. 454b;
Jefferson, p. 472b; Calhoun, p. 545b; and Cleveland, p. 771a.
Our government is the potent, the omnipresent teacher. — LOUIS D. BRANDEIS, *Olmstead
v. U.S.* [1928]

generation that then existed, but for posterity — unlimited, undefined, endless, perpetual posterity.

Speech in the Senate
[January 29, 1850]

Sir, I would rather be right than be President.[1]   *Speech [1850]*

LORENZO DOW
1777–1834

You will be damned if you do. — And you will be damned if you don't [definition of Calvinism].

Reflections on the Love of God
[1836]

CARL FRIEDRICH GAUSS
1777–1855

It may be true that people who are *merely* mathematicians have certain specific shortcomings; however, that is not the fault of mathematics, but is true of every exclusive occupation.

Letter to H. C. Schumacher [1845]

Mathematics is the queen of the sciences.

From SARTORIUS VON WALTERSHAUSEN, *Gauss zum Gedächtniss*
[1856]

VALENTINE BLACKER
1778–1823

Put your trust in God, my boys, and keep your powder dry!

From HAYES, *Ballads of Ireland, Col. Oliver's Advice*

WILLIAM HAZLITT
1778–1830

One of the pleasantest things in the world is going a journey; but I like to go by myself.

Table Talk [1821–1822].
On Going a Journey

When I am in the country I wish to vegetate like the country.   *Ib.*

[1] Said when told that his defense of the Compromise would endanger his chances for the Presidency.

The soul of a journey is liberty, perfect liberty, to think, feel, do just as one pleases.

Table Talk. On Going a Journey

Give me a clear blue sky over my head, and the green turf beneath my feet, a winding road before me, and a three hours' march to dinner — and then to thinking! It is hard if I cannot start some game on these lone heaths.   *Ib.*

Oh! it is great to shake off the trammels of the world and of public opinion — to lose our importunate, tormenting, everlasting personal identity and become the creature of the moment, clear of all ties . . . to be known by no other title than *the gentleman in the parlor!*   *Ib.*

What I mean by living to one's self is living in the world, as in it, not of it. . . . It is to be a silent spectator of the mighty scene of things; . . . to take a thoughtful, anxious interest or curiosity in what is passing in the world, but not to feel the slightest inclination to make or meddle with it.

Ib. On Living to One's Self

Even in the common affairs of life, in love, friendship, and marriage, how little security have we when we trust our happiness in the hands of others!   *Ib.*

There is not a more mean, stupid, dastardly, pitiful, selfish, spiteful, envious, ungrateful animal than the Public. It is the greatest of cowards, for it is afraid of itself.   *Ib.*

When a man is dead, they put money in his coffin, erect monuments to his memory, and celebrate the anniversary of his birthday in set speeches. Would they take any notice of him if he were living? No![1]   *Ib.*

Horus non numero nisi serenas[2] is the motto of a sundial near Venice. There is a softness and a harmony in

[1] See Martial, p. 135a, and Thayer, p. 949a.
[2] I count only the sunny hours.

the words and in the thought unparalleled.   *Table Talk. On a Sundial*

No young man believes he shall ever die.

Ib. The Feeling of Immortality in Youth

The young are prodigal of life from a superabundance of it; the old are tenacious on the same score, because they have little left, and cannot enjoy even what remains of it.   *Ib.*

As we advance in life, we acquire a keener sense of the value of time. Nothing else, indeed, seems of any consequence; and we become misers in this respect.   *Ib.*

The love of liberty is the love of others; the love of power is the love of ourselves.

Political Essays. The Times Newspaper

We never do anything well till we cease to think about the manner of doing it.

Sketches and Essay. On Prejudice

It is better to be able neither to read nor write than to be able to do nothing else.

On the Ignorance of the Learned

Men of genius do not excel in any profession because they labor in it, but they labor in it because they excel.

Characteristics

We are not hypocrites in our sleep.
On Dreams

HENRY PETER, LORD BROUGHAM
1778–1868

What is valuable is not new, and what is new is not valuable.[1]

From The Edinburgh Review [c. 1802], The Work of Thomas Young

[1] See Daniel Webster, p. 548b.

The schoolmaster is abroad,[1] and I trust to him, armed with his primer, against the soldier in full military array.

Speech, Opening of Parliament [January 29, 1828]

In my mind, he was guilty of no error he — was chargeable with no exaggeration — he was betrayed by his fancy into no metaphor, who once said that all we see about us, Kings, Lords, and Commons, the whole machinery of the State, all the apparatus of the system, and its varied workings, end in simply bringing twelve good men into a box.

Present State of the Law [February 7, 1828]

Pursuit of Knowledge Under Difficulties.   *Title of book [1830]*

Education makes a people easy to lead, but difficult to drive; easy to govern but impossible to enslave.

Attributed

The great Unwashed.   *Attributed*

THOMAS, LORD DENMAN
1779–1854

Trial by jury, instead of being a security to persons who are accused, will be a delusion, a mockery, and a snare.

O'Connell v. The Queen [September 4, 1844]

FRANCIS SCOTT KEY
1779–1843

Oh, say, can you see by the dawn's early light,
What so proudly we hailed at the twilight's last gleaming?

[1] At the first meeting of the London Mechanics' Institution, 1825, John Reynolds, head of a school in Clerkenwell, acted as secretary of the meeting. Lord Brougham, who spoke at this meeting, said in the course of his remarks, "Look out, gentlemen, the schoolmaster is abroad." The phrase attracted little attention at that time, but when used in a speech three years later, it at once became popular.

Whose broad stripes and bright stars,
    through the perilous fight,
O'er the ramparts we watched were so
    gallantly streaming?
And the rockets' red glare, the bombs
    bursting in air,
Gave proof through the night that our
    flag was still there.
Oh, say, does that star-spangled banner
    yet wave
O'er the land of the free and the home
    of the brave?
            The Star-Spangled Banner [September 14, 1814], st. 1

Then conquer we must, for our cause it
    is just —
And this be our motto, "In God is our
    trust!"   *Ib. st. 4*

WILLIAM LAMB, VISCOUNT MELBOURNE
1779–1848

I wish I was as cocksure of anything
as Tom Macaulay is of everything.
            From Cowper, *Melbourne's Papers* [1889], *preface*

CLEMENT CLARKE MOORE
1779–1863

'Twas the night before Christmas,
    when all through the house
Not a creature was stirring — not even
    a mouse; [1]
The stockings were hung by the chimney with care,
In hopes that St. Nicholas soon would
    be there.
            A Visit from St. Nicholas [December 1823]

"Happy Christmas to all, and to all a
    goodnight!"   *Ib.*

THOMAS MOORE
1779–1852

Faintly as tolls the evening chime,

Our voices keep tune and our oars keep
    time.[1]
            Poems Relating to America. A Canadian Boat Song, st. 1

Row, brothers, row, the stream runs
    fast,
The rapids are near, and the daylight's
    past.   *Ib.*

Go where glory waits thee!
But while fame elates thee,
    Oh, still remember me!
            Irish Melodies [1807–1834]. Go Where Glory Waits Thee, st. 1

Oh, breathe not his name! let it sleep
    in the shade,
Where cold and unhonor'd his relics
    are laid.
            Ib. Oh Breathe Not His Name, st. 1

And the tear that we shed, though in
    secret it rolls,
Shall long keep his memory green in
    our souls.[2]   *Ib. st. 2*

The harp that once through Tara's
    halls
The soul of music shed,
Now hangs as mute on Tara's walls
As if that soul were fled.
            Ib. The Harp That Once Through Tara's Halls, st. 1

And the heart that is soonest awake to
    the flowers
Is always the first to be touch'd by the
    thorns.
            Ib. Oh, Think Not My Spirits Are Always as Light, st. 1

Rich and rare were the gems she wore,
And a bright gold ring on her wand she
    bore.
            Ib. Rich and Rare Were the Gems She Wore, st. 1

Ah! little they think who delight in her
    strains,
How the heart of the Minstrel is breaking.
            Ib. She Is Far from the Land, st. 2

[1] See Shakespeare, *Hamlet I, i, 10*, p. 256b.   [2] See Shakespeare, *Hamlet I, ii, 2*, p. 257a.

Believe me, if all those endearing young
   charms
Which I gaze on so fondly today,
Were to change by tomorrow and fleet
   in my arms,
Like fairy gifts fading away,
Thou would'st still be adored as this
   moment thou art,
Let thy loveliness fade as it will,
And around the dear ruin each wish of
   my heart
Would entwine itself verdantly still.
      Irish Melodies. Believe Me,
      If All Those Endearing Young
      Charms, st. 1

No, the heart that has truly lov'd never
   forgets,
But as truly loves on to the close;
As the sunflower turns on her god,
   when he sets,
The same look which she turn'd when
   he rose.   *Ib. st. 2*

But there's nothing half so sweet in
   life
As love's young dream.
      Ib. Love's Young Dream, st. 1

Eyes of unholy blue.
      Ib. By That Lake Whose
      Gloomy Shore, st. 2

'Tis the last rose of summer,
   Left blooming alone;
All her lovely companions
   Are faded and gone.
      Ib. The Last Rose of Summer, st. 1

The Minstrel Boy to the war is gone,
In the ranks of death you'll find him.
His father's sword he has girded on,
And his wild harp slung behind him.
      Ib. The Minstrel Boy, st. 1

Then awake! the heavens look bright,
   my dear;
'Tis never too late for delight, my dear;
   And the best of all ways
   To lengthen our days
Is to steal a few hours from the night,
   my dear.
      Ib. The Young May Moon, st. 1

You may break, you may shatter the
   vase, if you will,

But the scent of the roses will hang
   round it still.[1]
      Irish Melodies. Farewell!
      But Whenever, st. 3

No eye to watch, and no tongue to
   wound us,
All earth forgot, and all heaven around
   us.
      Ib. Come O'er the Sea, st. 2

The light that lies
In woman's eyes,
Has been my heart's undoing.
      Ib. The Time I've Lost in
      Wooing, st. 1

My only books
Were woman's looks,
And folly's all they've taught me.
      Ib.

A Persian's heaven is easily made:
'Tis but black eyes and lemonade.
      Intercepted Letters; or, The
      Two-Penny Post Bag [1813],
      VI

Oft in the stilly night,
Ere Slumber's chain has bound me,
Fond Memory brings the light
Of other days around me;
   The smiles, the tears,
   Of boyhood's years,
The words of love then spoken;
   The eyes that shone
   Now dimmed and gone,
The cheerful hearts now broken.
      National Airs [1815]. Oft in the
      Stilly Night, st. 1

I feel like one,
   Who treads alone
Some banquet hall deserted,
   Whose lights are fled,

---

[1] The jar will long keep the fragrance of
what it was once steeped in when new. —
HORACE [65–8 B.C.], *Epistles 1, 2, 69*
   That flavor, absorbed when new, remains. —
QUINTILIAN [A.D. 42–118]
   But, somehow of other, though you fill it
with water, the jar retains the odor which it
acquired when first used. — ST. JEROME [A.D.
342–420]
   The image was frequently used in the classical period; unglazed ware is more absorbent
than glazed.

Whose garlands dead,
And all but he departed.
*National Airs. Oft in the
Stilly Night, st. 2*

What though youth gave love and
roses,
Age still leaves us friends and wine.
Ib. Spring and Autumn, st. 1

Sound the loud timbrel o'er Egypt's
dark sea!
Jehovah has triumph'd — his people
are free.
*Sacred Songs. Sound the Loud
Timbrel, st. 1*

There was a little Man, and he had a
little Soul;
And he said, "Little Soul, let us try, try,
try!"
*Satirical and Humorous Poems.
Little Man and Little Soul, st. 1*

Oh, call it by some better name,
For friendship sounds too cold.
*Ballads and Songs. Oh, Call It
by Some Better Name, st. 1*

There's a bower of roses by Bendemeer's stream,
And the nightingale sings round it all
the day long.[1]
Lalla Rookh [1817], *pt. II*

One morn a Peri at the gate
Of Eden stood disconsolate. *Ib. IV*

Some flow'rets of Eden ye still inherit,
But the trail of the serpent is over them
all. *Ib.*

Oh! ever thus, from childhood's hour,
I've seen my fondest hope decay;
I never loved a tree or flower,
But 'twas the first to fade away.
I never nurs'd a dear gazelle
To glad me with its soft black eye,
But when it came to know me well,
And love me, it was sure to die.
Ib. V

Like Dead Sea fruits, that tempt the
eye,
But turn to ashes on the lips.[1]
Lalla Rookh [1817], *pt. V*

Paradise itself were dim
And joyless, if not shared with him!
Ib. VI

HORACE [HORATIO] SMITH
1779–1849

Thinking is but an idle waste of
thought,
And nought is everything, and every-
thing is nought.
Rejected Addresses [1812]. *Cui
Bono?, st. 8*

In the name of the Prophet — figs.
Johnson's Ghost

And hast thou walk'd about (how
strange a story!)
In Thebes's streets three thousand years
ago,
When the Memnonium was in all its
glory?
*Address to the Mummy at Bel-
zoni's Exhibition, st. 13*

JOSEPH STORY
1779–1849

I will not say with Lord Hale, that
"The Law will admit of no rival" . . .
but I will say that it is a jealous mistress, and requires a long and constant
courtship. It is not to be won by trifling
favors, but by lavish homage.[2]
*The Value and Importance of
Legal Studies* [3] [*August 5, 1829*]

WILLIAM ELLERY CHANNING
1780–1842

We do, then, with all earnestness,
though without reproaching our brethren, protest against the irrational and

---

[1] As I recall them the roses bloom again, and
the nightingales sing by the calm Bendemeer.
— THACKERAY, *The Newcomes* [1853–1855], *ch.
1*

[1] See Byron, p. 556a.
[2] See Emerson, p. 609a.
[3] Inaugural address as Dane Professor of Law
at Harvard University.

unscriptural doctrine of the Trinity. "To us," as to the Apostle and the primitive Christians, "there is one God, even the Father." With Jesus, we worship the Father, as the only living and true God. We are astonished, that any man can read the New Testament, and avoid the conviction, that the Father alone is God.

Unitarian Christianity
[Baltimore, 1819]

I see the marks of God in the heavens and the earth, but how much more in a liberal intellect, in magnanimity, in unconquerable rectitude, in a philanthropy which forgives every wrong, and which never despairs of the cause of Christ and human virtue! I do and I must reverence human nature.[1] . . . I bless it for its kind affections, for its strong and tender love. I honor it for its struggles against oppression . . . for its achievements in science and art, and still more for its examples of heroic and saintly virtue. These are marks of a divine origin and the pledges of a celestial inheritance; and I thank God that my own lot is bound up with that of the human race.[2]

Likeness to God [Providence,
Rhode Island, 1828]

There are seasons, in human affairs, of inward and outward revolution, when new depths seem to be broken up in the soul, when new wants are unfolded in multitudes, and a new and undefined good is thirsted for. There are periods when the principles of experience need to be modified, when hope and trust and instinct claim a share with prudence in the guidance of affairs, when, in truth, *to dare*, is the highest wisdom.[3]

Complete Works [1879].
The Union [1829]

It is chiefly through books that we

[1] See Albert Schweitzer, p. 939a.
[2] Inscription on Channing Memorial, Public Garden, Boston.
[3] See Spenser, p. 200b, and Danton, p. 496b.

enjoy intercourse with superior minds. . . . In the best books, great men talk to us, give us their most precious thoughts, and pour their souls into ours. God be thanked for books. They are the voices of the distant and the dead, and make us heirs of the spiritual life of past ages. Books are true levelers. They give to all, who will faithfully use them, the society, the spiritual presence, of the best and greatest of our race.

Self-Culture [Boston, September
1838]

The mind, in proportion as it is cut off from free communication with nature, with revelation, with God, with itself, loses its life, just as the body droops when debarred from the air and the cheering light from heaven.

Remarks on the Character and
Writings of Fénelon [1843]

I call that mind free which jealously guards its intellectual rights and powers, which calls no man master, which does not content itself with a passive or hereditary faith, which opens itself to light whencesoever it may come, which receives new truth as an angel from Heaven.

Spiritual Freedom

The office of government is not to confer happiness, but to give men opportunity to work out happiness for themselves.

The Life and Character of
Napoleon Bonaparte

KARL VON CLAUSEWITZ
1780–1831

War is not merely a political act, but also a political instrument, a continuation of political relations, a carrying out of the same by other means.[1]

Vom Kriege [1833]

[1] See Mao Tse-Tung, p. 1027b.

CHARLES CALEB COLTON
1780–1832

When you have nothing to say, say nothing.
> *Lacon* [1820–1822], *vol. I, no. 183*

Imitation is the sincerest of flattery.
> *Ib. 217*

The debt which cancels all others.
> *Ib. II, 66*

CHARLES MINER
1780–1865

When I see a merchant over-polite to his customers, begging them to taste a little brandy and throwing half his goods on the counter — thinks I, that man has an ax to grind.
> *Essays from the Desk of Poor Robert the Scribe* [1815]. *Who'll Turn Grindstones* [1]

ADELBERT VON CHAMISSO
1781–1838

Peter Schlemihl.
> *From the title: Peter Schlemihls wundersame Geschichte* [1804]

EBENEZER ELLIOTT
1781–1849

Not kings and lords, but nations!
Not thrones and crowns, but men!
> *Corn Law Rhymes* [1828]. *When Wilt Thou Save the People? st. 1*

God save the people!
> *Ib.*

What is a communist? One who hath yearnings
For equal division of unequal earnings.
> *Poetical Works* [1846]. *Epigram*

[1] First published in *Luzerne Federalist* [September 7, 1810]. Because of the similarity of the title to *Poor Richard*, the phrase "an ax to grind" has often been attributed to Franklin.

CAPTAIN JAMES LAWRENCE
1781–1813

Tell the men to fire faster and not to give up the ship; fight her till she sinks.[1]
> *On board the U.S. frigate Chesapeake* [June 1, 1813]

THOMAS HART BENTON
1782–1858

This new page opened in the book of our public expenditures, and this new departure taken, which leads into the bottomless gulf of civil pensions and family gratuities.
> *Speech in the U.S. Senate against a grant to President Harrison's widow* [April 1841]

JOHN C. CALHOUN
1782–1850

Protection and patriotism are reciprocal.
> *Speech, U.S. House of Representatives* [December 12, 1811]

The very essence of a free government consists in considering offices as public trusts,[2] bestowed for the good of the country, and not for the benefit of an individual or a party.
> *Speech* [February 13, 1835]

A power has risen up in the government greater than the people themselves, consisting of many and various and powerful interests, combined into one mass, and held together by the cohesive power of the vast surplus in the banks.[3] *Speech* [May 27, 1836]

[1] Usually quoted as "Don't give up the ship"; Lawrence's final order as he was carried below fatally wounded, before capture of his ship by the British frigate *Shannon*.
[2] See Henry, p. 386b; Burke, p. 454b; Jefferson, p. 472b; Clay, p. 538b; and Cleveland, p. 771a.
[3] From this speech comes the phrase "Cohesive power of public plunder."

The surrender of life is nothing to sinking down into acknowledgment of inferiority.
> *Speech, U.S. Senate [February 19, 1847]*

It is harder to preserve than to obtain liberty.[1]
> *Speech, U.S. Senate [January 1848]*

ANN TAYLOR
1782–1866

JANE TAYLOR
1783–1824

Who ran to help me when I fell,
And would some pretty story tell,
Or kiss the place to make it well?
My mother.
> *Original Poems for Infant Minds* [1804]. *My Mother [by* ANN TAYLOR], *st. 6*

Twinkle, twinkle, little star,
How I wonder what you are,
Up above the world so high,
Like a diamond in the sky![2]
> *Rhymes for the Nursery* [1806]. *The Star, st. 1*

I like little Pussy, her coat is so warm;
And if I don't hurt her she'll do me no harm.
> *Ib. I Like Little Pussy [by* JANE TAYLOR], *st. 1*

I thank the goodness and the grace
  Which on my birth have smiled,
And made me, in these Christian days,
  A happy English child.
> *Hymns for Infant Minds* [1810]. *A Child's Hymn of Praise, st. 1*

Oh, that it were my chief delight
  To do the things I ought!
Then let me try with all my might
  To mind what I am taught.
> *Ib. For a Very Little Child*

And willful waste, depend upon 't,
Brings, almost always, woeful want!
> *Ib. The Pin [by* ANN TAYLOR], *st. 6*

[1] See S. E. Morison, p. 997b.
[2] See Lewis Carroll, p. 744a.

DANIEL WEBSTER
1782–1852

It is, sir, as I have said, a small college, and yet there are those who love it.
> *Dartmouth College Case* [1818]

Whatever makes men good Christians, makes them good citizens.
> *Speech at Plymouth, Massachusetts* [1] *[December 22, 1820]*

Labor in this country is independent and proud. It has not to ask the patronage of capital, but capital solicits the aid of labor.[2]
> *Speech [April 2, 1824]*

We wish that this column, rising towards heaven among the pointed spires of so many temples dedicated to God, may contribute also to produce in all minds a pious feeling of dependence and gratitude. We wish, finally, that the last object to the sight of him who leaves his native shore, and the first to gladden his who revisits it, may be something which shall remind him of the liberty and the glory of his country.
> *Address on Laying the Corner-Stone of the Bunker Hill Monument [June 17, 1825]*

Mind is the great lever of all things; human thought is the process by which human ends are ultimately answered.
> *Ib.*

Knowledge, in truth, is the great sun in the firmament. Life and power are scattered with all its beams. *Ib.*

Let our object be our country, our whole country, and nothing but our country. *Ib.*

Sink or swim, live or die, survive or

[1] This oration will be read five hundred years hence with as much rapture as it was heard. It ought to be read at the end of every century, and indeed at the end of every year, forever and ever. — JOHN ADAMS, *Letter to Webster* [December 23, 1821]
[2] See Lincoln, p. 637b.

perish, I give my hand and my heart to this vote.[1]

Discourse in Commemoration of Adams and Jefferson, Faneuil Hall, Boston [August 2, 1826]

It is my living sentiment, and by the blessing of God it shall be my dying sentiment — Independence now and Independence forever.[2] *Ib.*

Washington is in the clear upper sky. *Ib.*

The gentleman has not seen how to reply to this, otherwise than by supposing me to have advanced the doctrine that a national debt is a national blessing.[3]

Second Speech on Foote's Resolution [January 26, 1830]

I shall enter on no encomium upon Massachusetts; she needs none. There she is.[4] Behold her, and judge for yourselves. There is her history; the world knows it by heart. The past, at least, is secure. There is Boston and Concord and Lexington and Bunker Hill; and there they will remain forever. *Ib.*

The people's government, made for the people, made by the people, and answerable to the people.[5] *Ib.*

When my eyes shall be turned to behold for the last time the sun in heaven, may I not see him shining on the broken and dishonored fragments of a once glorious Union; on States dissevered, discordant, belligerent; on a

---

[1] See John Adams, p. 463a.
Live or die, sink or swim. — GEORGE PEELE, *Edward I* [c. 1584]
[2] On the day of his [John Adams's] death, hearing the noise of bells and cannon, he asked the occasion. On being reminded that it was "Independent Day," he replied, "Independence forever." — DANIEL WEBSTER, *Works* [1903], *vol. I, p. 150*
[3] See Hamilton, p. 484b.
[4] Generally misquoted as "Massachusetts, there she stands."
[5] Our sovereign, the people. — CHARLES JAMES FOX, toast [1798], for which his name was erased from the Privy Council.
See Wycliffe, p. 163b; Garrison, p. 616a; Lincoln, p. 639a; and Theodore Parker, p. 657b.

---

land rent with civil feuds, or drenched, it may be, in fraternal blood.

Second Speech on Foote's Resolution

Liberty and Union, now and forever, one and inseparable. *Ib.*

There is no refuge from confession but suicide; and suicide is confession.

Argument on the murder of Captain White [April 6, 1830]

There is nothing so powerful as truth — and often nothing so strange.[1] *Ib.*

Fearful concatenation of circumstances.[2] *Ib.*

A sense of duty pursues us ever. It is omnipresent, like the Deity. If we take to ourselves the wings of the morning, and dwell in the uttermost parts of the sea, duty performed or duty violated is still with us, for our happiness or our misery. If we say the darkness shall cover us, in the darkness as in the light our obligations are yet with us.[3] *Ib.*

He smote the rock of the national resources, and abundant streams of revenue gushed forth. He touched the dead corpse of Public Credit, and it sprung upon its feet.[4]

Speech on Hamilton [March 10, 1831]

On this question of principle, while actual suffering was yet afar off, they [the Colonies] raised their flag against a power to which, for purposes of foreign conquest and subjugation, Rome in the height of her glory is not to be compared — a power which has dotted over the surface of the whole globe with

---

[1] See Byron, p. 562a.
[2] See Scott, p. 521a.
[3] See *Psalm 139:9*, p. 23a.
[4] And Moses lifted up his hand, and with his rod he smote the rock twice; and the water came out abundantly. — *Numbers 20:11*
He it was that first gave to the law the air of a science. He found it a skeleton, and clothed it with life, color, and complexion; he embraced the cold statue, and by his touch it grew into youth, health, and beauty. — BARRY YELVERTON, LORD AVONMORE [1736–1805], *On Blackstone*

her possessions and military posts, whose morning drumbeat, following the sun,[1] and keeping company with the hours, circles the earth with one continuous and unbroken strain of the martial airs of England.
Speech [May 7, 1834]

God grants liberty only to those who love it, and are always ready to guard and defend it.
Speech [June 3, 1834]

One country, one constitution, one destiny.   *Speech [March 15, 1837]*

There are persons who constantly clamor. They complain of oppression, speculation, and pernicious influence of wealth. They cry out loudly against all banks and corporations, and a means by which small capitalists become united in order to produce important and beneficial results. They carry on mad hostility against all established institutions. They would choke the fountain of industry and dry all streams.
Speech, U.S. Senate [March 12, 1838]

When tillage begins, other arts follow. The farmers therefore are the founders of human civilization.
On Agriculture [January 13, 1840]

America has furnished to the world the character of Washington. And if our American institutions had done nothing else, that alone would have entitled them to the respect of mankind.
On the Completion of Bunker Hill Monument [June 17, 1843]

Thank God! I — I also — am an American!   *Ib.*

Justice, sir, is the great interest of man on earth.
On Mr. Justice Story [September 12, 1845]

Inconsistencies of opinion, arising

---

[1] See Schiller, p. 497b, and Scott, p. 522a.

from changes of circumstances, are often justifiable.[1]
Speech [July 25 and 27, 1846]

Liberty exists in proportion to wholesome restraint.
Speech at the Charleston Bar Dinner [May 10, 1847]

The law: It has honored us; may we honor it.   *Ib.*

I have read their platform, and though I think there are some unsound places in it, I can stand upon it pretty well. But I see nothing in it both new and valuable. "What is valuable is not new, and what is new is not valuable." [2]
Speech at Marshfield, Massachusetts [September 1, 1848]

I was born an American; I will live an American; I shall die an American.
Speech [July 17, 1850]

Faneuil Hall, the cradle of American liberty.   *Letter [April 1851]*

Men hang out their signs indicative of their respective trades: shoemakers hang out a gigantic shoe; jewelers, a monster watch; and the dentist hangs out a gold tooth; but up in the mountains of New Hampshire, God Almighty has hung out a sign to show that there He makes men.
On the Old Man of the Mountain; [3] *attributed*

I still live.
Last words [October 24, 1852]

SIMÓN BOLÍVAR
1783–1830

A state too extensive in itself, or by virtue of its dependencies, ultimately falls into decay; its free government is transformed into a tyranny; it disre-

---

[1] L'homme absurde est celui qui ne change jamais [The absurd man is he who never changes]. — AUGUSTE MARSEILLE BARTHÉLEMY, *Ma Justification* [1832]
[2] See Lord Brougham, p. 540a.
[3] Natural rock formation in the shape of a human profile, in the Presidential Range of the White Mountains. It gave Hawthorne the theme of his story *The Great Stone Face.*

gards the principles which it should preserve, and finally degenerates into despotism. The distinguishing characteristic of small republics is stability: the character of large republics is mutability. *Letter from Jamaica*

Among the popular and representative systems of government I do not approve of the federal system: it is too perfect; and it requires virtues and political talents much superior to our own. *Ib.*

Let us give to our republic a fourth power with authority over the youth, the hearts of men, public spirit, habits, and republican morality. Let us establish this Areopagus to watch over the education of the children, to supervise national education, to purify whatever may be corrupt in the republic, to denounce ingratitude, coldness in the country's service, egotism, sloth, idleness, and to pass judgment upon the first signs of corruption and pernicious example.
Address to the Congress of Angostura

Those who have served the cause of the revolution have plowed the sea.
Attributed

The three greatest dolts in the world: Jesus Christ, Don Quixote, and I.
Attributed

REGINALD HEBER
1783–1826

Brightest and best of the sons of the morning,
Dawn on our darkness, and lend us thine aid.
Hymns. Epiphany, st. 1

By cool Siloam's shady rill
How sweet the lily grows!
Ib. First Sunday after Epiphany, no. 2

The Son of God goes forth to war,
A kingly crown to gain;

His blood-red banner streams afar;
Who follows in His train?
Hymns. The Son of God Goes Forth to War, st. 1

From Greenland's icy mountains,
From India's coral strand,
Where Afric's sunny fountains
Roll down their golden sand.
Ib. Missionary Hymn, st. 1

Though every prospect pleases,
And only man is vile. *Ib. st. 2*

The heathen in his blindness
Bows down to wood and stone. *Ib.*

Holy, Holy, Holy! Lord God Almighty!
Early in the morning our song shall rise to Thee:
Holy, Holy, Holy! Merciful and Mighty!
God in Three Persons, Blessed Trinity.
Ib. Holy, Holy, Holy!

WASHINGTON IRVING
1783–1859

How convenient it would be to many of our great men and great families of doubtful origin, could they have the privilege of the heroes of yore, who, whenever their origin was involved in obscurity, modestly announced themselves descended from a god.
Knickerbocker's History of New York [1809], *bk. II, ch. 3*

His wife "ruled the roast," and in governing the governor, governed the province, which might thus be said to be under petticoat government.[1]
Ib. IV, 4

They claim to be the first inventors of those recondite beverages, cocktail, stonefence, and sherry cobbler.[2]
Ib. 241

There is in every true woman's heart a spark of heavenly fire, which lies dormant in the broad daylight of prosperity; but which kindles up, and

[1] See Themistocles, p. 77b.
[2] See Browning, p. 666b.

beams and blazes in the dark hour of adversity.
The Sketch-Book [1819–1820].
The Wife

Those men are most apt to be obsequious and conciliating abroad, who are under the discipline of shrews at home.   *Ib. Rip Van Winkle* [1]

A sharp tongue is the only edge tool that grows keener with constant use.
Ib.

That happy age when a man can be idle with impunity.   *Ib.*

A woman's whole life is a history of the affections.
Ib. The Broken Heart

Language gradually varies, and with it fade away the writings of authors who have flourished their allotted time.
Ib. The Mutabilities of Literature

There rise authors now and then, who seem proof against the mutability of language, because they have rooted themselves in the unchanging principles of human nature.   *Ib.*

His [the author's] renown has been purchased, not by deeds of violence and blood, but by the diligent dispensation of pleasure.
Ib. Westminster Abbey [*The Poets' Corner*]

The sorrow for the dead is the only sorrow from which we refuse to be divorced.   *Ib. Rural Funerals*

Whenever a man's friends begin to compliment him about looking young, he may be sure that they think he is growing old.
Bracebridge Hall [1822]. *Bachelors*

[1] The theme of Irving's story derives from DIOGENES LAERTIUS, *Epimenides* [c. A.D. 200]. Epimenides was sent by his father into the field to look for a sheep, turned out of the road at midday and lay down in a certain cave and fell asleep, and slept there fifty-seven years; and after that, when awake, he went on looking for the sheep, thinking that he had been taking a short nap.

I am always at a loss to know how much to believe of my own stories.
Tales of a Traveler [1824]. *To the Reader*

The almighty dollar,[1] that great object of universal devotion throughout our land, seems to have no genuine devotees in these peculiar villages.
Wolfert's Roost [1855]. *The Creole Village*

STENDHAL
[HENRI BEYLE]
1783–1842

I call "crystallization" that action of the mind that discovers fresh perfections in its beloved at every turn of events.   *De l'Amour* [1822], *ch.* 1

A wise woman never yields by appointment. It should always be an unforeseen happiness.   *Ib.* 60

One can acquire everything in solitude — except character.
Ib. Fragments

Prudery is a kind of avarice, the worst of all.   *Ib.*

In matters of sentiment, the public has very crude ideas; and the most shocking fault of women is that they make the public the supreme judge of their lives.   *Ib.*

There is no such thing as "natural law": this expression is nothing but old nonsense. Prior to laws, what is natural is only the strength of the lion, or the need of the creature suffering from hunger or cold, in short, need.
The Red and the Black [1831]

I see but one rule: to be clear. If I am not clear, all my world crumbles to nothing.
Reply to Balzac [October 30, 1840] [2]

Wit lasts no more than two centuries.   *Ib.*

[1] See Jonson, p. 303a.
[2] In reference to *La Chartreuse de Parme* [1839].

It is the nobility of their style which will make our writers of 1840 unreadable forty years from now.
Manuscript note [1840]

Love has always been the most important business in my life, I should say the only one.
La Vie d'Henri Brulard [1890]

ALLAN CUNNINGHAM
1784–1842

A wet sheet and a flowing sea,
 A wind that follows fast,
And fills the white and rustling sail,
 And bends the gallant mast.
The Songs of Scotland [1825].
A Wet Sheet and a Flowing Sea,
st. 1

The hollow oak our palace is,
Our heritage the sea. *Ib. st. 3*

It's hame and it's hame, hame fain wad
 I be —
O, hame, hame, hame to my ain countree!
Ib It's Hame and It's Hame,
refrain

LEIGH HUNT
1784–1859

This Adonis in loveliness was a corpulent man of fifty.[1]
The Examiner [March 22, 1812]

Where the light woods go seaward from the town.
The Story of Rimini [1816],
canto I, l. 18

But most he loved a happy human face. *Ib. canto III, l. 110*

The world was all forgot, the struggle o'er,
Desperate the joy. — That day they read no more.[2] *Ib. l. 607*

[1] For this reference to the Prince Regent, Hunt was imprisoned. But he was allowed to redecorate the walls of his prison with a trellis of roses, had his family with him, and visitors were freely admitted — Byron, indeed, gave a dinner party in his honor at the jail.
[2] See Dante, p. 160a.

Green little vaulter in the sunny grass.
To the Grasshopper and the
Cricket [1817]

Abou Ben Adhem (may his tribe increase!)
Awoke one night from a deep dream of peace.
Abou Ben Adhem [1838]

An angel writing in a book of gold.
Ib.

Write me as one that loves his fellow men. *Ib.*

And show'd the names whom love of God had bless'd,
And lo! Ben Adhem's name led all the rest. *Ib.*

Jenny kissed me when we met,
Jumping from the chair she sat in;
Time, you thief, who love to get
Sweets into your list, put that in:
Say I'm weary, say I'm sad,
Say that health and wealth have missed me,
Say I'm growing old, but add,
Jenny kissed me.[1] *Rondeau* [1838]

Stolen sweets are always sweeter,
Stolen kisses much completer,
Stolen looks are nice in chapels,
Stolen, stolen, be your apples.
Song of Fairies Robbing an
Orchard

A Venus grown fat!
Blue-Stocking Revels

"No love," quoth he, "but vanity, sets love a task like that."
The Glove and the Lions, [2] *st. 4*

Learn the right
Of coining words in the quick mint of joy.
A Rustic Walk and Dinner, l. 33

A fireside is a great opiate.
A Few Thoughts on Sleep

It has been said of ladies when they write letters, that they put their minds

[1] Jenny was Jane Welsh Carlyle, who kissed Hunt when he brought Carlyle good news.
[2] Schiller wrote a poem on the same theme, and Browning's *The Glove* [1845] is a later version of the familiar legend.

in their postscripts — let out the real objects of their writing, as if it were a second thought, or a thing comparatively indifferent.   *Anacreon*

ZACHARY TAYLOR
1784–1850

Hurrah for Old Kentuck! That's the way to do it. Give 'em hell, damn 'em.
> *Shouted to the 2nd Kentucky Regiment on seeing them rally in battle [Buena Vista, Mexico, February 23, 1847]*

A little more grape, Captain Bragg.
> *Attributed [Ib.]*

Tell him to go to hell.[1]
> *Reply to Santa Anna's demand for surrender [Ib.]*

THOMAS DE QUINCEY
1785–1859

The burden of the incommunicable.
> *Confessions of an English Opium-Eater [1822–1856], pt. I*

Call for the grandest of all earthly spectacles, what is that? It is the sun going to his rest. Call for the grandest of all human sentiments, what is that? It is that man should forget his anger before he lies down to sleep.[2]   *Ib.*

So, then, Oxford Street, stony-hearted stepmother, thou that listenest to the sighs of orphans, and drinkest the tears of children, at length I was dismissed from thee.   *Ib.*

Everlasting farewells! and again, and yet again reverberated — everlasting farewells!   *Ib. III*

Dyspepsy is the ruin of most things: empires, expeditions, and everything else.   *Letter to Hessey [1823]*

If once a man indulges himself in murder, very soon he comes to think little of robbing; and from robbing he

[1] See McAuliffe, p. 1042b.
[2] See *Ephesians 4:26*, p. 54a.

comes next to drinking and Sabbath-breaking, and from that to incivility and procrastination.
> *Murder Considered as One of the Fine Arts [1827]*

LADY CAROLINE LAMB
1785–1828

[Of Byron] Mad, bad, and dangerous to know.   *Journal*

THOMAS LOVE PEACOCK
1785–1866

A heeltap! a heeltap! I never could bear it!
So fill me a bumper, a bumper of claret!
> *Headlong Hall [1816], ch. 5, song*

Not drunk is he who from the floor
Can rise alone and still drink more;
But drunk is he who prostrate lies,
Without the power to drink or rise.
> *The Misfortunes of Elphin [1829], ch. 3, heading, translated from the Welsh*

The mountain sheep are sweeter,
But the valley sheep are fatter;
We therefore deemed it meeter
To carry off the latter.   *Ib. 11*

Ancient sculpture is the true school of modesty. But where the Greeks had modesty, we have cant; where they had poetry, we have cant; where they had patriotism, we have cant; where they had anything that exalts, delights, or adorns humanity, we have nothing but cant, cant, cant.
> *Crotchet Castle [1831], ch. 7*

A book that furnishes no quotations is, *me judice*, no book — it is a plaything.   *Ib. 9*

He remembered too late, on his thorny green bed,
Much that well may be thought cannot wisely be said.
> *Ib. The Priest and the Mulberry Tree, st. 5*

Gotham's three wise men we be.
Whither in your bowl so free?
To rake the moon from out the sea.
The bowl goes trim. The moon doth
    shine.
And our ballast is old wine.
                 Three Men of Gotham [1837],
                                st. 1

OLIVER HAZARD PERRY
1785–1819

We have met the enemy, and they
are ours.
    *Dispatch to General William
    Henry Harrison, announcing
    his victory at the battle of
    Lake Erie [United States Brig
    Niagara, September 10, 1813,
    4 P.M.]*

SAMUEL WOODWORTH
1785–1842

How dear to this heart are the scenes of
    my childhood,
When fond recollection presents them
    to view!
                 The Old Oaken Bucket

The old oaken bucket, the iron-bound
    bucket,
The moss-covered bucket which hung
    in the well.   *Ib.*

Pickaxe, shovel, spade, crowbar, hoe,
    and barrow,
Better not invade, Yankees have the
    marrow.
                 The Patriotic Diggers [1814], *st. 1*

We'll show him that Kentucky boys
Are Alligator-horses.
                 The Hunters of Kentucky,[1] *st. 2*

[1] This ballad has the subtitle *Half Horse and
Half Alligator* and celebrates the participation
of Kentuckians, under the command of General
John Coffee, in the Battle of New Orleans
[January 8, 1815]. It was published as a broad-
side in Boston and in 1826 collected in *Melodies,
Duets, Trios, Songs, and Ballads*, by JAMES M.
CAMPBELL.

LUDWIG BÖRNE
1786–1837

Like buttered bread, state ministers
usually fall on the good side.[1]
                 Collected Works, pt. III

DAVID CROCKETT
1786–1836

I leave this rule for others when I'm
    dead,
Be always sure you're right — then go
    ahead.[2]   *Autobiography* [1834]

Don't shoot, Colonel, I'll come
down: I know I'm a gone coon.[3]
                 *Story told by Crockett of a treed
                                raccoon*

WILLIAM LEARNED MARCY
1786–1857

They see nothing wrong in the rule
that to the victor belong the spoils of
the enemy.
                 Speech, U.S. Senate [January
                                1832]

WINFIELD SCOTT
1786–1866

The enemy say that Americans are
good at a long shot, but cannot stand
the cold iron. I call upon you instantly
to give a lie to the slander. Charge!
                 *Address to the 11th Infantry
                 Regiment* [Chippewa, Canada,
                 June 5, 1814]

Say to the seceded States, "Wayward
sisters, depart in peace."
                 Letter to W. H. Seward
                                [March 3, 1861]

[1] I never had a piece of toast
    Particularly long and wide
    But fell upon the sanded floor,
    And always on the buttered side.
                        JAMES PAYN [1884]
[2] Crockett's motto in the War of 1812.
[3] The expression "gone coon" was current
during the Revolutionary War, originating in
the plea of a spy, dressed in raccoon skins, to
his discoverer, an English rifleman. — *Century
Cyclopedia of Names*

BARRY CORNWALL
[BRYAN WALLER PROCTER]
1787–1874

The sea! the sea! the open sea!
The blue, the fresh, the ever free
Without a mark, without a bound,
It runneth the earth's wide regions
    round.   *The Sea, st. 1*

FRANÇOIS GUIZOT
1787–1874

Enrich yourselves! [1]
     Speech [March 1, 1843]

JOHANN LUDWIG UHLAND
1787–1862

Let him sing to whom song is given.
     Des Sängers Fluch [1814]

EMMA WILLARD
1787–1870

Rocked in the cradle of the deep.
     The Cradle of the Deep [1831]

RICHARD HARRIS BARHAM
1788–1845

The Lady Jane was tall and slim,
The Lady Jane was fair.
     Ingoldsby Legends [1840]. The Knight and the Lady

The Devil must be in that little
Jackdaw!
     Ib. The Jackdaw of Rheims

GEORGE NOEL GORDON, LORD BYRON
1788–1824

Friendship is Love without his wings.
     L'Amitié Est l'Amour sans Ailes [1806]

[1] Enrichissez-vous!

I only know we loved in vain;
I only feel — farewell! farewell!
     Farewell! If Ever Fondest Prayer [1808], st. 2

When we two parted
  In silence and tears,
Half broken-hearted,
  To sever for years.
     When We Two Parted [1808], st. 1

Near this spot are deposited the remains of one who possessed Beauty without Vanity, Strength without Insolence, Courage without Ferocity, and all the Virtues of Man, without his Vices. This Praise, which would be unmeaning Flattery if inscribed over human ashes, is but a just tribute to the Memory of Boatswain, a Dog.
     Inscription on the monument of a Newfoundland dog [1808]

The poor dog, in life the firmest friend,
The first to welcome, foremost to
  defend.   *Ib.*

I'll publish right or wrong:
Fools are my theme, let satire be my
  song.
     English Bards and Scotch Reviewers [1809], l. 5

'Tis pleasant, sure, to see one's name in
  print;
A book's a book, although there's nothing in 't.   *Ib. l. 51*

A man must serve his time to every
  trade
Save censure — critics all are ready
  made.   *Ib. l. 63*

With just enough of learning to misquote.   *Ib. l. 66*

  As soon
Seek roses in December, ice in June;
Hope constancy in wind, or corn in
  chaff;
Believe a woman or an epitaph,
Or any other thing that's false, before
You trust in critics.   *Ib. l. 75*

Better to err with Pope, than shine with
  Pye.   *Ib. l. 102*

'Twas thine own genius gave the final
    blow,
And help'd to plant the wound that
    laid thee low:
So the struck eagle, stretch'd upon the
    plain,
No more through rolling clouds to soar
    again,
View'd his own feather on the fatal
    dart,
And wing'd the shaft that quiver'd in
    his heart.[1]
          *English Bards and Scotch
           Reviewers, l. 826*

Though Nature's sternest painter, yet
    the best.[2]   *Ib. l. 839*

Maid of Athens, ere we part,
Give, oh give me back my heart!
        Maid of Athens [1810], *st. 1*

Vex'd with mirth the drowsy ear of
    night.
      *Childe Harold's Pilgrimage,
        canto I* [1812], *st. 2*

Had sigh'd to many, though he loved
    but one.   *Ib. st. 5*

Maidens, like moths, are ever caught by
    glare,
And Mammon wins his way where ser-
    aphs might despair.   *Ib. st. 9*

Might shake the saintship of an an-
    chorite.   *Ib. st. 11*

Adieu! adieu! my native shore
Fades o'er the waters blue.
          Ib. st. 13 [*song*]

My native land, good night!   *Ib.*

Still from the fount of joy's delicious
    springs
Some bitter o'er the flowers its bub-
    bling venom flings.[3]   *Ib. st. 82*

War, war is still the cry, "War even to
    the knife!" [4]   *Ib. st. 86*

[1] See Aesop, p. 766.
[2] Crabbe.
[3] See Lucretius, p. 114a.
[4] "War even to the knife" was the reply of
Palafox, governor of Saragossa, when summoned
to surrender by the French, who besieged that
city in 1808.

Gone — glimmering   through   the
    dream of things that were.
      *Childe Harold's Pilgrimage,
        canto II* [1812], *st. 2*

A schoolboy's tale, the wonder of an an
    hour!   *Ib.*

The dome of thought, the palace of the
    soul.[1]   *Ib. st. 6*

Fair Greece! sad relic of departed
    worth!
Immortal, though no more; though
    fallen, great!   *Ib. st. 73*

Where'er we tread 'tis haunted, holy
    ground.   *Ib. st. 88*

What is the worst of woes that wait on
    age?
What stamps the wrinkle deeper on the
    brow?
To view each loved one blotted from
    life's page,
And be alone on earth, as I am now.
            Ib. st. 98

Once more upon the waters, yet once
    more!
And the waves bound beneath me as a
    steed
That knows his rider!
       Ib. canto III [1816], *st. 2*

        Years steal
Fire from the mind as vigor from the
    limb;
And life's enchanted cup but sparkles
    near the brim.   *Ib. st. 8*

And Harold stands upon this place of
    skulls.   *Ib. st. 18*

There was a sound of revelry by night,
And Belgium's capital had gather'd
    then
Her beauty and her chivalry, and
    bright
The lamps shone o'er fair women and
    brave men.
A thousand hearts beat happily; and
    when
Music arose with its voluptuous swell,
Soft eyes look'd love to eyes which
    spake again,

[1] See Waller, p. 333a.

And all went merry as a marriage bell.
But hush! hark! a deep sound strikes
like a rising knell!
*Childe Harold's Pilgrimage,
canto III, st. 21*

Did ye not hear it? — No! 'twas but
the wind,
Or the car rattling o'er the stony
street.
On with the dance! let joy be uncon-
fined;
No sleep till morn, when Youth and
Pleasure meet
To chase the glowing hours with flying
feet.   *Ib. st. 22*

Arm! Arm! it is — it is — the cannon's
opening roar!   *Ib.*

And there was mounting in hot haste.
Ib. st. 25

Or whispering, with white lips, "The
foe. They come! they come!"
Ib.

Battle's magnificently stern array!
Ib. st. 28

Like to the apples on the Dead Sea's
shore,
All ashes to the taste.[1]   *Ib. st. 34*

  Thou fatal Waterloo.
Millions of tongues record thee, and
anew
Their children's lips shall echo them,
and say —
"Here, where the sword united nations
drew,
Our countrymen were warring on that
day!"
And this is much, and all which will
not pass away.[2]   *Ib. st. 35*

He who ascends to mountaintops, shall
find
The loftiest peaks most wrapt in clouds
and snow;

[1] See Thomas Moore, p. 543b.
[2] This was the passage Sir Winston Churchill
quoted to President Franklin D. Roosevelt when
both agreed to substitute the term United
Nations for Associated Powers in the pact that
the two leaders wished all the free nations to
sign. [In a conference at the White House,
December 1941.]

He who surpasses or subdues mankind
Must look down on the hate of those
below.
*Childe Harold's Pilgrimage,
canto III, st. 45*

All tenantless, save to the crannying
wind.   *Ib. st. 47*

History's purchased page to call them
great.   *Ib. st. 48*

The castled crag of Drachenfels
Frowns o'er the wide and winding
Rhine.   *Ib. st. 55*

To fly from, need not be to hate, mankind.   *Ib. st. 69*

By the blue rushing of the arrowy
Rhone.   *Ib. st. 71*

I live not in myself, but I become
Portion of that around me: [1] and to
me
High mountains are a feeling, but the
hum
Of human cities torture.   *Ib. st. 72*

Sapping a solemn creed with solemn
sneer.   *Ib. st. 107*

Fame is the thirst of youth.
Ib. st. 112

I have not loved the world, nor the
world me; [2]
I have not flatter'd its rank breath, nor
bow'd
To its idolatries a patient knee.
Ib. st. 113

    I stood
Among them, but not of them; in a
shroud
Of thoughts which were not their
thoughts.   *Ib.*

I stood in Venice on the Bridge of
Sighs,
A palace and a prison on each hand.
Ib. canto IV [1818], st. 1

Where Venice sate in state, throned on
her hundred isles.   *Ib.*

[1] I am a part of all that I have met. — TENNY-
SON, *Ulysses* [1842]
[2] See Johnson, p. 433b, and Emerson, p. 601b.

She looks a sea Cybele, fresh from ocean,
Rising with her tiara of proud towers
At airy distance, with majestic motion,
A ruler of the waters and their powers.
Childe Harold's Pilgrimage,
canto IV, st. 2

'Tis solitude should teach us how to die;
It hath no flatterers; vanity can give
No hollow aid; alone — man with his
God must strive. *Ib. st. 33*

The Ariosto of the North.[1] *Ib. st. 40*

Italia! O Italia! thou who hast
The fatal gift of beauty.[2] *Ib. st. 42*

Let these describe the undescribable.
Ib. st. 53

The starry Galileo, with his woes.
Ib. st. 54

The poetry of speech. *Ib. st. 58*

Then farewell, Horace; whom I hated so,
Not for thy faults, but mine.
Ib. st. 77

O Rome! my country! city of the soul!
Ib. st. 78

The Niobe of nations! there she stands,
Childless and crownless, in her voiceless
woe. *Ib. st. 79*

Yet, Freedom! yet thy banner, torn, but flying,
Streams like the thunderstorm against
the wind. *Ib. st. 98*

Alas! our young affections run to waste,
Or water but the desert. *Ib. st. 120*

Of its own beauty is the mind diseased.
Ib. st. 122

Time, the avenger! unto thee I lift
My hands, and eyes, and heart, and
crave of thee a gift. *Ib. st. 130*

Butcher'd to make a Roman holiday!
Ib. st. 141

[1] Sir Walter Scott
[2] Based on the famous sonnet of VINCENZO DA FILICAJA [1642–1707]: Italia, Italia! O tu cui feo la sorte.

"While stands the Coliseum, Rome shall stand;
When falls the Coliseum, Rome shall fall;
And when Rome falls — the world." [1]
Childe Harold's Pilgrimage,
canto IV, st. 145

Oh! that the desert were my dwelling-place.[2] *Ib. st. 177*

There is a pleasure in the pathless woods,
There is a rapture on the lonely shore,
There is society, where none intrudes,
By the deep sea, and music in its roar:
I love not man the less, but Nature
more. *Ib. st. 178*

Roll on, thou deep and dark blue ocean — roll!
Ten thousand fleets sweep over thee in vain;
Man marks the earth with ruin — his control
Stops with the shore. *Ib. st. 179*

He sinks into thy depths with bubbling groan,
Without a grave, unknell'd, uncoffin'd,
and unknown.[3] *Ib.*

Time writes no wrinkle on thine azure brow —
Such as creation's dawn beheld, thou
rollest now.[4] *Ib. st. 182*

Thou glorious mirror, where the Almighty's form
Glasses itself in tempests.
Ib. st. 183

Dark-heaving — boundless, endless, and sublime —
The image of Eternity. *Ib.*

And I have loved thee, Ocean! and my joy

[1] The saying of the ancient pilgrims, quoted from BEDE by GIBBON, *The Decline and Fall of the Roman Empire* [1781], ch. 71.
[2] See *Jeremiah* 9:2, p. 34a, and Cowper, p. 457b.
[3] See Homer, p. 64b; Horace, p. 122b; and Scott, p. 519a.
[4] And thou vast ocean, on whose awful face Time's iron feet can print no ruin-trace.
ROBERT MONTGOMERY, *The Omnipresence of the Deity* [1830]

Of youthful sports was on thy breast to
  be
Borne, like thy bubbles, onward: from a
  boy
I wanton'd with thy breakers.
> *Childe Harold's Pilgrimage,*
> *canto IV, st. 184*

And trusted to thy billows far and
  near,
And laid my hand upon thy mane,[1] —
  as I do here.   *Ib.*

I awoke one morning and found myself famous.
> *Entry in Memoranda after pub-*
> *lication of first two cantos of*
> *Childe Harold's Pilgrimage.*
> *From* THOMAS MOORE, *Life of*
> *Byron* [1830], *ch. 14*

Clime of the unforgotten brave!
> *The Giaour* [1813], *l. 103*

And lovelier things have mercy shown
To every failing but their own;
And every woe a tear can claim,
Except an erring sister's shame.
> *Ib. l. 418*

I die — but first I have possess'd,
And come what may, I have been
  bless'd.   *Ib. l. 1114*

Know ye the land where the cypress
  and myrtle
Are emblems of deeds that are done in
  their clime? [2]
Where the rage of the vulture, the love
  of the turtle,
Now melt into sorrow, now madden to
  crime.
> *The Bride of Abydos* [1813],
> *canto I, st. 1*

Where the virgins are soft as the roses
  they twine,
And all, save the spirit of man, is divine?   *Ib.*

Mark! where his carnage and his conquests cease!

He makes a solitude, and calls it
  — peace! [1]
> *The Bride of Abydos, canto*
> *II, st. 20*

The fatal facility of the octosyllabic
verse.
> *The Corsair* [1814]. *Dedication*

Such hath it been — shall be — beneath the sun
The many still must labor for the one.
> *Ib. canto I, st. 8*

He left a corsair's name to other times,
Link'd with one virtue, and a thousand
  crimes.   *Ib. canto III, st. 24*

The Cincinnatus of the West,
Whom envy dared not hate,
Bequeathed the name of Washington
To make man blush there was but
  one! [2]
> *Ode to Napoleon Bonaparte*
> [1814], *II*

Lord of himself — that heritage of
woe.
> *Lara* [1814], *canto I, st. 2*

She walks in beauty, like the night
  Of cloudless climes and starry skies;
And all that's best of dark and bright
  Meet in her aspect and her eyes:
Thus mellow'd to that tender light
  Which heaven to gaudy day denies.
> *Hebrew Melodies* [1815]. *She*
> *Walks in Beauty, st. 1*

The Assyrian came down like the wolf
  on the fold,
And his cohorts were gleaming in purple and gold;
And the sheen of their spears was like
  stars on the sea,
When the blue wave rolls nightly on
  deep Galilee.
> *Ib. The Destruction of*
> *Sennacherib,*[3] *st. 1*

---

[1] He laid his hand upon "the Ocean's mane,"
And played familiar with his hoary locks.
> ROBERT POLLOK [1798–1827], *The*
> *Course of Time, bk. IV, l. 689*

[2] See Goethe, p. 477a.

[1] See Tacitus, p. 140b.

[2] See *Don Juan*, p. 561b, and *The Age of Bronze*, p. 563a.

[3] And it came to pass that night, that the angel of the Lord went out, and smote in the camp of the Assyrians an hundred fourscore and five thousand: and when they arose early in the morning, behold, they were all dead corpses. — *II Kings 19:35*

For the Angel of Death spread his
wings on the blast.
> *Hebrew Melodies. The Destruc-
> tion of Sennacherib, st. 3*

And the might of the Gentile, unsmote
by the sword,
Hath melted like snow in the glance of
the Lord! *Ib. st. 6*

The Glory and the Nothing of a
name. *Churchill's Grave, l. 43*

For years fleet away with the wings of
the dove.
> *The First Kiss of Love, st. 7*

Fare thee well! and if forever,
Still forever, fare thee well.
> *Fare Thee Well [1816], st. 1*

Sighing that Nature form'd but one
such man,
And broke the die, in molding Sheridan.[1]
> *Monody on the Death of
> Sheridan [1816], l. 117*

My hair is gray, but not with years,
　Nor grew it white
　In a single night,
As men's have grown from sudden
　fears.
> *The Prisoner of Chillon [1816],
> st. 1*

O God! it is a fearful thing
To see the human soul take wing
In any shape, in any mood. *Ib. st. 8*

A light broke in upon my brain —
　It was the carol of a bird;
It ceased, and then it came again,
　The sweetest song ear ever heard.
> *Ib. st. 10*

There be none of Beauty's daughters
　With a magic like thee;
And like music on the waters
　Is thy sweet voice to me.
> *Stanzas for music [1816], st. 1*

I had a dream which was not all a
dream. *Darkness [1816]*

Though the day of my destiny's over,
And the star of my fate hath declined.
> *Stanzas to Augusta [1816], st. 1*

[1] See Ariosto, p. 178a.

My boat is on the shore,
　And my bark is on the sea;
But, before I go, Tom Moore,
　Here's a double health to thee!

Here's a sigh to those who love me,
　And a smile to those who hate;
And, whatever sky's above me,
　Here's a heart for every fate.[1]
> *To Thomas Moore [1817], st. 1, 2*

So we'll go no more a-roving
　So late into the night,
Though the heart be still as loving,
　And the moon be still as bright.

For the sword outwears its sheath,
　And the soul wears out the breast,
And the heart must pause to breathe,
　And love itself have rest.

Though the night was made for loving,
　And the day returns too soon,
Yet we'll go no more a-roving
　By the light of the moon.
> *So, We'll Go No More A-Roving
> [1817]*

Mont Blanc is the monarch of moun-
tains;
　They crowned him long ago
On a throne of rocks, in a robe of
　clouds,
　With a diadem of snow.
> *Manfred [1817], act I, sc. 1*

His heart was one of those which most
enamor us,
Wax to receive, and marble to retain.[2]
> *Beppo [1818], st. 34*

Besides, they always smell of bread and
butter. *Ib. st. 39*

I love the language, that soft bastard
Latin,
Which melts like kisses from a female
mouth. *Ib. st. 44*

I wish he[3] would explain his explanation.
> *Don Juan. Dedication [written
> 1818], st. 2*

[1] See Longfellow, p. 620b.
[2] See Cervantes, p. 197b.
[3] Coleridge.

In virtues nothing earthly could surpass her,
Save thine "incomparable oil," Macassar!
> *Don Juan, canto I, st. 17*

But — Oh! ye lords of ladies intellectual,
Inform us truly, have they not henpeck'd you all? [1]   *Ib. st. 22*

Her stature tall — I hate a dumpy woman.   *Ib. st. 61*

What men call gallantry, and gods adultery,
Is much more common where the climate's sultry.   *Ib. st. 63*

Christians have burnt each other, quite persuaded
That all the Apostles would have done as they did.   *Ib. st. 83*

A little still she strove, and much repented,
And whispering "I will ne'er consent" — consented.   *Ib. st. 117*

'Tis sweet to hear the watchdog's honest bark
Bay deep-mouth'd welcome as we draw near home;
'Tis sweet to know there is an eye will mark
Our coming, and look brighter when we come.   *Ib. st. 123*

Sweet is revenge — especially to women.[2]   *Ib. st. 124*

Pleasure's a sin, and sometimes sin's a pleasure.   *Ib. st. 133*

Man's love is of man's life a thing apart,
'Tis woman's whole existence.
> *Ib. st. 194*

There's nought, no doubt, so much the spirit calms
As rum and true religion.
> *Ib. canto II [1819], st. 34*

A solitary shriek, the bubbling cry

[1] See Addison, p. 395a.
[2] See Shakespeare, *Coriolanus V, iii, 44*, p. 290a.

Of some strong swimmer in his agony.
> *Don Juan, canto II, st. 53*

If this be true, indeed,
Some Christians have a comfortable creed.   *Ib. st. 86*

Let us have wine and women, mirth and laughter,
Sermons and soda water the day after.[1]
> *Ib. st. 178*

In her first passion woman loves her lover,
In all the others, all she loves is love.[2]
> *Ib. canto III [1821], st. 3*

Think you, if Laura had been Petrarch's wife,
He would have written sonnets all his life?   *Ib. st. 7*

He was the mildest-manner'd man
That ever scuttled ship or cut a throat.
> *Ib. st. 41*

Even good men like to make the public stare.   *Ib. st. 81*

The isles of Greece, the isles of Greece! [3]
Where burning Sappho loved and sung.   *Ib. st. 86 [song, st. 1]*

Eternal summer gilds them yet,
But all, except their sun, is set.   *Ib.*

The mountains look on Marathon,
And Marathon looks on the sea;
And musing there an hour alone,
I dreamed that Greece might still be free.   *Ib. [st. 3]*

And where are they? and where art thou,
My country? On thy voiceless shore
The heroic lay is tuneless now —
The heroic bosom beats no more!
And must thy lyre, so long divine,
Degenerate into hands like mine?
> *Ib. [st. 5]*

[1] See Dickens, p. 670a, and George Ade, p. 886b.
[2] See La Rochefoucauld, p. 356b.
[3] From isles of Greece
The princes orgulous, their high blood chaf'd,
Have to the port of Athens sent their ships.
    SHAKESPEARE, *Troilus and Cressida*
    [1601–1603], *Prologue*

Earth! render back from out thy breast
A remnant of our Spartan dead!
Of the three hundred grant but three,
To make a new Thermopylae.
    Don Juan, canto III [*st. 7*]

You have the Pyrrhic dance as yet,
Where is the Pyrrhic phalanx gone?
Of two such lessons, why forget
The nobler and the manlier one?
You have the letters Cadmus gave —
Think ye he meant them for a slave?
    Ib. [*st. 10*]

Fill high the bowl with Samian wine!
    Ib. [*st. 11*]

Place me on Sunium's marble steep,
Where nothing save the waves and I
May hear our mutual murmurs sweep;
There, swan-like, let me sing and die.[1]
A land of slaves shall ne'er be mine —
Dash down yon cup of Samian wine!
    Ib. [*st. 16*]

Milton's the prince of poets — so we say;
A little heavy, but no less divine.
    Ib. st. 91

And if I laugh at any mortal thing,
'Tis that I may not weep.[2]
    Ib. canto IV [*1821*], *st. 4*

    These two hated with a hate
Found only on the stage.   *Ib. st. 93*

"Arcades ambo" — *id est*, blackguards
both.   *Ib.*

    I've stood upon Achilles' tomb,
And heard Troy doubted; time will
doubt of Rome.   *Ib. st. 101*

Oh! "darkly, deeply, beautifully blue," [3]
As someone somewhere sings about the
sky.   *Ib. st. 110*

There's not a sea the passenger e'er
pukes in,
Turns up more dangerous breakers than
the Euxine.
    Ib. canto V [*1821*], *st. 5*

[1] See Plato, p. 93b, and note.
[2] See Beaumarchais, p. 460a, and Lincoln,
p. 638a.
[3] See Southey, p. 532a.

And put himself upon his good behavior.
    Don Juan, canto V, st. 47

That all-softening, overpowering knell,
The tocsin of the soul — the dinner
bell.   *Ib. st. 49*

The women pardon'd all except her
face.   *Ib. st. 113*

Polygamy may well be held in dread,
Not only as a sin, but as a bore.
    Ib. canto VI [*1823*], *st. 12*

A lady of "a certain age," which means
Certainly aged.   *Ib. st. 69*

The drying up a single tear has more
Of honest fame than shedding seas of
gore.
    Ib. canto VIII [*1823*], *st. 3*

Not so Leonidas and Washington,
Whose every battlefield is holy ground,
Which breathes of nations saved, not
worlds undone.[1]   *Ib. st. 5*

Half-pay for life makes mankind worth
destroying.   *Ib. st. 14*

George Washington had thanks and
nought beside,
Except the all-cloudless glory (which
few men's is)
To free his country.[1]
    Ib. canto IX [*1823*], *st. 8*

"Gentlemen farmers" — a race worn
out quite.   *Ib. st. 32*

When Bishop Berkeley said "there was
no matter,"
And proved it — 'twas no matter what
he said.
    Ib. canto XI [*1823*], *st. 1*

And, after all, what is a lie? 'Tis but
The truth in masquerade.   *Ib. st. 37*

'Tis strange the mind, that very fiery
particle,

[1] See *Ode to Napoleon*, p. 558b, and *The Age
of Bronze*, p. 563a.

Should let itself be snuff'd out by an article.
> *Don Juan, canto XI, st.*
> *60 [of John Keats* [1]*]*

Ready money is Aladdin's lamp.
> *Ib. canto XII* [1823]*, st. 12*

Cervantes smil'd Spain's chivalry away.
> *Ib. canto XIII* [1823]*, st. 11*

The English winter — ending in July,
To recommence in August.
> *Ib. st. 42*

Society is now one polish'd horde,
Formed of two mighty tribes, the Bores and Bored. *Ib. st. 95*

> All human history attests
> That happiness for man — the hungry sinner! —
> Since Eve ate apples, much depends on dinner.[2] *Ib. st. 99*

Of all the horrid, hideous notes of woe,
Sadder than owl songs or the midnight blast,
Is that portentous phrase, "I told you so."
> *Ib. canto XIV* [1823]*, st. 50*

'Tis strange — but true; for truth is always strange;
Stranger than fiction.[3] *Ib. st. 101*

The Devil hath not, in all his quiver's choice,
An arrow for the heart like a sweet voice.
> *Ib. canto XV* [1824]*, st. 13*

A lovely being, scarcely form'd or molded,
A rose with all its sweetest leaves yet folded. *Ib. st. 43*

---

[1] See Byron, *John Keats,* p. 562b, and Shelley, p. 571a.

[2] For a man seldom thinks with more earnestness of anything than he does of his dinner. — JOHNSON, from MRS. PIOZZI, *Anecdotes of Samuel Johnson* [1786]
See Fanny Fern, p. 658a.

[3] Le vrai peut quelquefois n'être pas vraisemblable [Truth may sometimes be improbable]. — BOILEAU [1636–1711], *L'Art Poétique, III, l. 48*
See Daniel Webster, p. 547b.
Truth is stranger than fiction, but not so popular. — *Anonymous*

The antique Persians taught three useful things —
To draw the bow, to ride, and speak the truth.
> *Don Juan, canto XVI*
> [1824]*, st. 1*

In truth he was a noble steed.
> *Mazeppa* [1819]*, st. 9*

Oh, talk not to me of a name great in story;
The days of our youth are the days of our glory;
And the myrtle and ivy of sweet two-and-twenty
Are worth all your laurels, though ever so plenty.
> *Stanzas written on the Road*
> *Between Florence and Pisa*
> [1821]*, st. 1*

All farewells should be sudden.
> *Sardanapalus* [1821]*, act V*

> The best of prophets of the future is the past. *Journal* [*January 28, 1821*]

The world is a bundle of hay,
> Mankind are the asses that pull,
Each tugs in a different way —
> And the greatest of all is John Bull!
> *Letter to Thomas Moore*
> [*June 22, 1821*]

> Because
He is all-powerful, must all-good, too, follow?
I judge but by the fruits — and they are bitter —
Which I must feed on for a fault not mine. *Cain* [1821]*, act I, sc. 1*

Who killed John Keats?
"I," says the Quarterly,
So savage and Tartarly;
" 'Twas one of my feats." [1]
> *John Keats* [*c. 1821*]

> He seems
To have seen better days, as who has not
Who has seen yesterday?
> *Werner* [1822]*, act I, sc. 1*

---

[1] See *Don Juan,* p. 562a, and Shelley, p. 571a.

The "good old times" — all times
  when old are good —
Are gone.
> *The Age of Bronze* [1823], *st.* 1

Whose [1] game was empires and whose
  stakes were thrones,
Whose table earth — whose dice were
  human bones.   *Ib. st.* 3

While Franklin's quiet memory climbs
  to heaven,
Calming the lightning which he thence
  had riven,
Or drawing from the no less kindled
  earth
Freedom and peace to that which
  boasts his birth; [2]
While Washington's a watchword,
  such as ne'er
Shall sink while there's an echo left to
  air. [3]   *Ib. st.* 5

Sublime tobacco! which from east to
  west
Cheers the tar's labor or the Turkman's
  rest. [4]
> *The Island* [1823], *canto II, st.* 19

What's drinking?
A mere pause from thinking!
> *The Deformed Transformed*
> [1824], *act III, sc.* 1

My days are in the yellow leaf; [5]
The flowers and fruits of love are gone;
The worm, the canker, and the grief
  Are mine alone!
> *On My Thirty-sixth Year* [1824],
> *st.* 2

Seek out — less often sought than
  found —
A soldier's grave, for thee the best;

Then look around, and choose thy
  ground,
And take thy rest.
> *On My Thirty-sixth Year, st.* 10

Now Barabbas was a publisher.
> *Alleged alteration in the Bible,*
> *John* 18:40 [1]

SARAH JOSEPHA HALE
1788–1879

Mary had a little lamb,
  Its fleece was white as snow,
And everywhere that Mary went,
  The lamb was sure to go.

He followed her to school one day;
  That was against the rule;
It made the children laugh and play,
  To see a lamb at school.
> *Mary's Lamb* [2] [*in The Juvenile*
> *Miscellany, September* 1830], *st.*
> 1, 2

"What makes the lamb love Mary so?"
  The eager children cry.
"Oh, Mary loves the lamb, you know,"
  The teacher did reply.
> *Ib. st.* 5

ARTHUR
SCHOPENHAUER
1788–1860

Hatred comes from the heart; contempt from the head; and neither feeling is quite within our control.
> *Studies in Pessimism.* [3] *Psychological Observations*

Every man takes the limits of his own field of vision for the limits of the world.   *Ib.*

Every parting gives a foretaste of death; [4] every coming together again a foretaste of the resurrection.   *Ib.*

---

[1] Napoleon.

[2] See Franklin, p. 421a, note 1.

[3] See *Ode to Napoleon*, p. 558b, and *Don Juan*, p. 561b.

[4] Let Aristotle and all your philosophers say what they like, there is nothing to be compared with tobacco. — MOLIÈRE [1622–1673], *Don Juan; or, Le Festin de Pierre* [1665], act I, sc. 1. Translated by CURTIS HIDDEN PAGE.
See Anonymous, p. 1085b.

[5] See Shakespeare, pp. 286a and 292b.

[1] The publisher John Murray sent Byron a lavish copy of the Bible in acknowledgment of a favor, and the poet returned it with the word "robber" changed to "publisher."

[2] The first three stanzas are also attributed to John Roulstone [1805–1822], of Sterling, Mass.

[3] Translated by T. BAILEY SAUNDERS.

[4] Partir c'est mourir un peu [To part is to die a little]. — *French proverb*
See Haraucourt, p. 835a.

The fundamental fault of the female character is that it has no sense of justice.

Studies in Pessimism. On Women

Dissimulation is innate in woman, and almost as much a quality of the stupid as of the clever. *Ib.*

Noise is the most impertinent of all forms of interruption. It is not only an interruption, but also a disruption of thought. *Ib. On Noise*

The most general survey shows us that the two foes of human happiness are pain and boredom.

Essays. Personality; or, What a Man Is

A man who has no mental needs, because his intellect is of the narrow and normal amount, is, in the strict sense of the word, what is called a philistine.[1]
Ib.

Intellect is invisible to the man who has none.[2]

Ib. Our Relation to Others, sec. 23

There is no more mistaken path to happiness than worldliness, revelry, high life.

Ib. Our Relation to Ourselves, sec. 24

Do not shorten the morning by getting up late; look upon it as the quintessence of life, as to a certain extent sacred.

Counsels and Maxims, ch. 2

JAMES FENIMORE COOPER
1789–1851

Few men exhibit greater diversity, or, if we may so express it, greater antithesis of character than the native warrior of North America. In war, he is daring, boastful, cunning, ruthless, self-denying, and self-devoted; in peace, just, generous, hospitable, revengeful,

---

[1] See Matthew Arnold, p. 713b.
[2] See La Rochefoucauld, *Maxim 375*, p. 356a.

superstitious, modest, and commonly chaste.

The Last of the Mohicans [1826]

'Tis grand! 'tis solemn! 'tis an education of itself to look upon!

The Deerslayer [1841], *ch. 2*

Those families, you know, are our upper crust — not upper ten thousand.[1]

The Ways of the Hour [1850], *ch. 6*

WILLIAM KNOX
1789–1825

Oh why should the spirit of mortal be proud?

Songs of Israel [1824]. *Mortality, st. 1*

PETER MERE LATHAM
1789–1875

The practice of physic is jostled by quacks on the one side, and by science on the other.

Collected Works, bk. I, ch. 25

There is nothing so captivating as *new* knowledge. *Ib. 51*

Truth in all its kinds is most difficult to win; and truth in medicine is the most difficult of all. *Ib. 60*

Beware of language, for it is often a great cheat. *Ib. 138*

The diagnosis of disease is often easy, often difficult, and often impossible.
Ib. 173

We should always presume the disease to be curable, until its own nature prove it otherwise. *Ib. 174*

Fortunate, indeed, is the man who takes exactly the right measure of himself, and holds a just balance between what he can acquire and what he can use, be it great or be it small!
Ib. II, 11

A bad book is generally a very easy book, having been composed by its au-

---

[1] See Sam Slick, p. 587b.

thor with no labor of mind whatever; whereas a good book, though it be not necessarily a hard one, yet, since it contains important facts, duly arranged, and reasoned upon with care, must require from the reader some portion of the same attention and study to comprehend and profit by it, as it required from the writer to compose it.

Collected Works, bk. II, ch. 43

The way of death is often smoother than the path of life; and great bodily anguish (there is reason to believe) does not often enter largely into the process of dissolution. *Ib.* 91

Common sense is in medicine the master workman. *Ib.* 389

It takes as much time and trouble to pull down a falsehood as to build up a truth. *Ib.* 398

Remedies are our great analyzers of disease. *Ib.* 406

Faith and knowledge lean largely upon each other in the practice of medicine. *Ib.* 408

It is no easy task to pick one's way from truth to truth through besetting errors. *Ib.* 415

Perfect health, like perfect beauty, is a rare thing; and so, it seems, is perfect disease. *Ib.* 443

It would be a great thing to understand pain in all its meanings.
Ib. 474

It is the great mystery of life itself which is at the bottom of all the mysterious language we are obliged to employ concerning it. *Ib.* 494

People in general have no notion of the sort and amount of evidence often needed to prove the simplest matter of fact. *Ib.* 525

FITZ-GREENE HALLECK
1790–1867

Green be the turf above thee,
Friend of my better days!

None knew thee but to love thee,[1]
Nor named thee but to praise.
On the Death of Joseph Rodman Drake [1820], *st.* 1

Strike — till the last armed foe expires,
Strike — for your altars and your fires;
Strike — for the green graves of your sires;
God — and your native land!
Marco Bozzaris [2] [1855], *st.* 3

But to the hero, when his sword
Has won the battle for the free,
Thy voice sounds like a prophet's word,
And in its hollow tones are heard
The thanks of millions yet to be.
Ib. st. 6

One of the few, the immortal names
That were not born to die. *Ib. st.* 7

ALPHONSE DE LAMARTINE
1790–1869

O time, arrest your flight! and you, propitious hours, arrest your course! Let us savor the fleeting delights of our most beautiful days! [3]
The Lake [1820], *st.* 6

I say to this night: "Pass more slowly"; and the dawn will come to dispel the night.[4] *Ib. st.* 8

Limited in his nature, infinite in his desires, man is a fallen god [5] who remembers the heavens.
Méditations Poétiques [1820]. *Sermon* 2

[1] See Burns, p. 494a, and Tennyson, p. 647a.
[2] A Greek patriot, born about 1788, killed in a night attack against the Turks, near Missolonghi, Greece [August 20, 1823].
[3] O temps, suspends ton vol! et vous, heures propices,
Suspendez votre cours!
Laissez-nous savourer les rapides délices
Des plus beaux de nos jours!
[4] Je dis à cette nuit: "Sois plus lente"; et l'aurore
Va dissiper la nuit.
[5] See Emerson, p. 605a.

What is our life but a succession of preludes to that unknown song whose first solemn note is sounded by Death? [1]
Méditations Poétiques. 2nd series. Sermon 15

Experience is the only prophecy of wise men.   *Speech at Mâcon* [1847]

To love for the sake of being loved is human, but to love for the sake of loving is angelic.
Graziella [1849], *pt. IV, ch. 5*

The more I see of the representatives of the people, the more I admire my dogs.
From Count d'Orsay, *Letter to John Forster* [1850]

FERDINAND RAIMUND
1790–1836

No matter how fair the sun shines,
Still it must set.
Das Mädchen aus der Feenwelt (The Maiden from Fairyland) [1826]

SAMUEL GILMAN
1791–1858

Fair Harvard! Thy sons to thy Jubilee throng.
Ode, Bicentennial, Harvard University [September 8, 1836], *st. 1*

First flower of their wilderness, star of their night,
Calm rising through change and through storm.   *Ib.*

HENRY HART MILMAN
1791–1868

And the cold marble leaped to life a god.   *The Belvedere Apollo*

Ride on! ride on in majesty!
In lowly pomp ride on to die.
Hymns. Ride On!

[1] This passage was used by Liszt as a heading for his tone poem *Les Préludes.*

LYDIA HUNTLEY SIGOURNEY
1791–1865

Ye say they all have passed away,
That noble race and brave.
Indian Names, st. 1

But their name is on your waters [1] —
Ye may not wash it out.   *Ib.*

To evil habit's earliest wile
Lend neither ear, nor glance, nor smile —
Choke the dark fountain ere it flows,
Nor e'en admit the camel's nose.
The Camel's Nose, st. 4

CHARLES SPRAGUE
1791–1875

Here lived and loved another race of beings. Beneath the same sun that rolls over your heads the Indian hunter pursued the panting deer. . . . The Indian of falcon glance and lion bearing, the theme of the touching ballad, the hero of the pathetic tale, is gone.
The American Indian

CHARLES WOLFE
1791–1823

Not a drum was heard, not a funeral note,
As his corse to the rampart we hurried.
The Burial of Sir John Moore at Corunna [1817], *st. 1*

But he lay like a warrior taking his rest,
With his martial cloak around him.
Ib. st. 3

We carved not a line, and we raised not a stone —
But we left him alone with his glory.
Ib. st. 8

[1] We will give the names of our fearless race
To each bright river whose course we trace.
Felicia D. Hemans [1793–1835], *Song of Emigration*

JOHN BOWRING
1792–1872

Watchman, tell us of the night,[1]
What its signs of promise are.
Hymn [1825]

VICTOR COUSIN
1792–1867

We need religion for religion's sake, morality for morality's sake, art for art's sake. *Cours de Philosophie* [1818]

JOHN FREDERICK WILLIAM HERSCHEL
1792–1871

Science is the knowledge of many, orderly and methodically digested and arranged, so as to become attainable by one. The knowledge of reasons and their conclusions constitutes *abstract*, that of causes and their effects, and of the laws of nature, *natural science*.
A Preliminary Discourse on the Study of Natural Philosophy [1830]

JOHN KEBLE
1792–1866

The trivial round, the common task,
Would furnish all we ought to ask.
The Christian Year [1827]. *Morning, st. 10*

Abide with me! Fast falls the eventide;
The darkness deepens: Lord, with me abide!
When other helpers fail, and comforts flee,
Help of the helpless, O abide with me! *Ib. Evening, st. 1*

Abide with me from morn till eve,
For without Thee I cannot live;
Abide with me when night is nigh,
For without Thee I dare not die.
Ib. st. 4

[1] See *Isaiah 21:11*, p. 31b.

The voice that breath'd o'er Eden
That earliest wedding day.
Poems [1869]. *Holy Matrimony, st. 1*

FREDERICK MARRYAT
1792–1848

All zeal, Mr. Easy.
Midshipman Easy [1836], *ch. 9*

I haven't the gift of the gab, my sons — because I'm bred to the sea. *The Old Navy, st. 1*

It's just six of one and half-a-dozen of the other. *The Pirate, ch. 4*

Every man paddle his own canoe.
Settlers in Canada [1844], *ch. 8*

JOHN HOWARD PAYNE
1792–1852

'Mid pleasures and palaces though we may roam,
Be it ever so humble, there's no place like home.[1]
Home, Sweet Home. From the opera Clari, the Maid of Milan [1823]

LORD JOHN RUSSELL
1792–1878

If peace cannot be maintained with honor, it is no longer peace.[2]
Speech, Greenock [*September 19, 1853*]

Among the defects of the bill, which were numerous, one provision was conspicuous by its presence and another by its absence.[3]
Speech to the electors of the City of London [*April 1859*]

PERCY BYSSHE SHELLEY
1792–1822

Once, early in the morning,
Beelzebub arose,

[1] Home is home, be it never so homely. — *English proverb* [c. 1300]
[2] See Disraeli, p. 613a, and Neville Chamberlain, p. 897a.
[3] See Tacitus, p. 140a.

With care his sweet person adorning,
He put on his Sunday clothes.[1]
>> *The Devil's Walk* [1812], *st. 1*

How wonderful is Death,
Death and his brother Sleep! [2]
>> *Queen Mab* [1813], I

Power, like a desolating pestilence,
Pollutes whate'er it touches; and obedience,
Bane of all genius, virtue, freedom, truth,
Makes slaves of men, and, of the human frame,
A mechanized automation. *Ib. III*

The awful shadow of some unseen Power
Floats though unseen among us [3] — visiting
This various world with as inconstant wing
As summer winds that creep from flower to flower.
>> *Hymn to Intellectual Beauty* [1816], *st. 1*

Spirit of Beauty, that dost consecrate
With thine own hues all thou dost shine upon
Of human thought or form.
>> *Ib. st. 2*

Some say that gleams of a remoter world
Visit the soul in sleep — that death is slumber,
And that its shapes the busy thoughts outnumber
Of those who wake and live.
>> *Mont Blanc* [1816], *st. 3*

Man's yesterday may ne'er be like his morrow;
Nought may endure but Mutability.[4]
>> *Mutability* [1816], I, *st. 4*

I met a traveler from an antique land
Who said: "Two vast and trunkless legs of stone
Stand in the desert. Near them, on the sand,

---

[1] See Southey, p. 533a, and note.
[2] See Homer, p. 64a, and note.
[3] See Wordsworth, p. 509b.
[4] See Heraclitus, p. 77b.

Half sunk, a shattered visage lies, whose frown,
And wrinkled lip, and sneer of cold command,
Tell that its sculptor well those passions read." *Ozymandias* [1817]

"My name is Ozymandias, king of kings:
Look on my works, ye Mighty, and despair!"
Nothing beside remains. Round the decay
Of that colossal wreck, boundless and bare,
The lone and level sands stretch far away. *Ib.*

With hue like that when some great painter dips
His pencil in the gloom of earthquake and eclipse.
>> *The Revolt of Islam* [1817], *canto V, st. 23*

Lift not the painted veil which those who live
Call Life. *Sonnet* [1818]

I could lie down like a tired child,
And weep away the life of care
Which I have borne and yet must bear,
Till death like sleep might steal on me.
>> *Stanzas Written in Dejection near Naples* [1818], *st. 4*

The good want power, but to weep barren tears.
The powerful goodness want: worse need for them.
The wise want love; and those who love want wisdom;
And all best things are thus confused with ill.
>> *Prometheus Unbound* [1818–1819], *act I, l. 625*

Peace is in the grave.
The grave hides all things beautiful and good:
I am a God and cannot find it there.
>> *Ib. l. 638*

From the dust of creeds outworn.
>> *Ib. l. 697*

kry

SHELLEY

a

Forms more real than living man,
Nurslings of immortality!
Prometheus Unbound,
act I, l. 748

To know nor faith, nor love nor law; to
be
Omnipotent but friendless is to reign.
Ib. act II, sc. iv, l. 47

All love is sweet,
Given or returned. Common as light is
love,
And its familiar voice wearies not
ever. . . .
They who inspire it most are fortunate,
As I am now; but those who feel it
most
Are happier still.[1]   *Ib. II, v, 39*

Death is the veil which those who live
call life:
They sleep, and it is lifted.
Ib. III, iii, 113

Nor yet exempt, though ruling them
like slaves,
From chance, and death, and mutabil-
ity,
The clogs of that which else might
overscar
The loftiest star of unascended heaven,
Pinnacled dim in the intense inane.
Ib. III, iv, 200

Familiar acts are beautiful through
love.   *Ib. act IV, l. 403*

Man, who wert once a despot and a
slave;
A dupe and a deceiver; a decay;
A traveler from the cradle to the grave
Through the dim light of this immortal
day.   *Ib. l. 549*

Good, great and joyous, beautiful and
free;
This is alone Life, Joy, Empire, and
Victory.   *Ib. closing lines*

I love all waste
And solitary places; where we taste
The pleasure of believing what we see
Is boundless, as we wish our souls to
be.
Julian and Maddalo [1819], *l. 14*

[1] See La Rochefoucauld, p. 356a.

b

Thou Paradise of exiles, Italy!
Julian and Maddalo, l. 57

It is our will
That thus enchains us to permitted
ill —
We might be otherwise — we might be
all
We dream of happy, high majestical.
Where is the love, beauty and truth we
seek,
But in our mind?   *Ib. l. 170*

Me — who am as a nerve o'er which do
creep
The else unfelt oppressions of this
earth.   *Ib. l. 449*

Most wretched men
Are cradled into poetry by wrong;
They learn in suffering what they teach
in song.[1]   *Ib. l. 543*

Chameleons feed on light and air:
Poets' food is love and fame.
An Exhortation [1819], *st. 1*

O wild West Wind, thou breath of
Autumn's being,
Thou, from whose unseen presence the
leaves dead
Are driven, like ghosts from an enchant-
er fleeing,
Yellow, and black, and pale, and hectic
red,
Pestilence-stricken multitudes.
Ode to the West Wind [1819], *l. 1*

Wild Spirit, which art moving every-
where;
Destroyer and preserver; hear, oh, hear!
Ib. l. 13

Thou dirge
Of the dying year, to which this closing
night
Will be the dome of a vast sepulcher.
Ib. l. 23

Oh, lift me as a wave, a leaf, a cloud!
I fall upon the thorns of life! I bleed!
Ib. l. 44

Make me thy lyre, even as the forest
is:
What if my leaves are falling like its
own!

[1] See Butler, p. 353b.

569

The tumult of thy mighty harmonies
Will take from both a deep, autumnal
    tone,
Sweet though in sadness. Be thou,
    Spirit fierce,
My spirit! Be thou me, impetuous one!
    Ode to the West Wind, l. 57

The trumpet of a prophecy! O Wind,
If winter comes, can spring be far behind?   *Ib. l.* 69

Men of England, wherefore plow
For the lords who lay ye low?
    Song to the Men of England
              [1819], st. 1

Nothing in the world is single,
All things by a law divine
In one spirit meet and mingle.
    Love's Philosophy [1819], *st.* 1

I arise from dreams of thee
In the first sweet sleep of night,
When the winds are breathing low,
And the stars are shining bright.
    The Indian Serenade [1819], *st.* 1

Hell is a city much like London —
A populous and smoky city.
    Peter Bell the Third [1819],
              pt. III, st. 1

    Teas,
Where small talk dies in agonies.
              Ib. st. 12

An old, mad, blind, despised and dying
king.[1]
    England in 1819 [*written*
              1819], *l.* 1

I met Murder on the way —
He had a mask like Castlereagh.
    The Mask of Anarchy [*written*
              1819], *st.* 2

    One by one, and two by two,
He toss'd them human hearts to chew.
              Ib. st. 3

A lovely lady, garmented in light
From her own beauty.
    The Witch of Atlas [1820], *st.* 5

A Sensitive Plant in a garden grew.
    The Sensitive Plant [1820],
              pt. I, st. 1

[1] George III.

I bring fresh showers for the thirsting
    flowers,
From the seas and the streams.
         The Cloud [1820], *st.* 1

I am the daughter of Earth and Water,
And the nursling of the Sky;
I pass through the pores of the ocean
    and shores,
I change, but I cannot die.   *Ib. st.* 6

Hail to thee, blithe spirit!
    Bird thou never wert,
That from Heaven, or near it,
    Pourest thy full heart
In profuse strains of unpremeditated
    art.   *To a Skylark* [1821], *st.* 1

And singing still dost soar, and soaring
    ever singest.   *Ib. st.* 2

Thou art unseen — but yet I hear thy
    shrill delight.   *Ib. st.* 4

We look before and after,
    And pine for what is not;
Our sincerest laughter
    With some pain is fraught;
Our sweetest songs are those that tell of
    saddest thought.   *Ib. st.* 18

Teach me half the gladness
    That thy brain must know,
Such harmonious madness
    From my lips would flow,
The world should listen then, as I am
    listening now.   *Ib. st.* 21

Kings are like stars — they rise and set,
    they have
The worship of the world, but no re-
    pose.[1]   *Hellas* [1821], *l.* 195

The world's great age begins anew,
    The golden years return,[2]
The earth doth like a snake renew
    Her winter weeds outworn.
              Ib. l. 1060

The world is weary of the past,
Oh, might it die or rest at last!
            Ib. final chorus

[1] See Bacon, p. 208b.
[2] See Virgil, p. 116b.

What! alive, and so bold, O earth?
*Written on Hearing the News of
the Death of Napoleon* [1821],
st. 1

The fields of immortality.
Epipsychidion [1821], *l.* 133

I never was attached to that great
sect,
Whose doctrine is, that each one
should select
Out of the crowd a mistress or a
friend,
And all the rest, though fair and wise,
commend
To cold oblivion, though 'tis in the
code
Of modern morals, and the beaten
road
Which those poor slaves with weary
footsteps tread
Who travel to their home among the
dead
By the broad highway of the world,
and so
With one chained friend, perhaps a
jealous foe,
The dreariest and the longest journey
go.
Ib. l. 149

I weep for Adonais [1] — he is dead!
Oh, weep for Adonais! though our
tears
Thaw not the frost which binds so dear
a head! *Adonais* [1821], *st. 1*

Till the Future dares
Forget the Past, his fate and fame shall
be
An echo and a light unto eternity!
Ib.

Most musical of mourners, weep
again! *Ib. st. 4*

To that high Capital, where kingly
Death
Keeps his pale court in beauty and de-
cay,
He came. *Ib. st. 7*

Lost Angel of a ruined Paradise!

[1] John Keats.
See Byron, p. 562a-b.

She knew not 't was her own; as with
no stain
She faded, like a cloud which had out-
wept the rain.
Adonais, st. 10

Desires and Adorations,
Winged Persuasions and veiled Desti-
nies,
Splendors, and Glooms, and glimmer-
ing Incarnations
Of hopes and fears, and twilight Fan-
tasies;
And Sorrow, with her family of Sighs,
And Pleasure, blind with tears, led by
the gleam
Of her own dying smile instead of eyes,
Came in slow pomp. *Ib. st.* 13

Ah woe is me! Winter is come and
gone,
But grief returns with the revolving
year. *Ib. st.* 18

The intense atom glows
A moment, then is quenched in a most
cold repose. *Ib. st.* 20

Alas! that all we loved of him should
be,
But for our grief, as if it had not been,
And grief itself be mortal! *Ib. st.* 21

As long as skies are blue, and fields are
green,
Evening must usher night, night urge
the morrow,
Month follow month with woe, and
year wake year to sorrow. *Ib.*

Why didst thou leave the trodden
paths of men
Too soon, and with weak hands though
mighty heart
Dare the unpastured dragon in his den?
Defenseless as thou wert, oh, where was
then
Wisdom the mirrored shield, or scorn
the spear? *Ib. st.* 27

The Pilgrim of Eternity,[1] whose fame
Over his living head like Heaven is
bent,
An early but enduring monument,
[1] Byron.

Came, veiling all the lightnings of his
song
In sorrow.   *Adonais, st. 30*

A pard-like spirit, beautiful and swift.
                        Ib. st. 32

In mockery of monumental stone.
                        Ib. st. 35

He wakes or sleeps with the enduring
dead;
Thou canst not soar where he is sitting
now —
Dust to the dust! but the pure spirit
shall flow
Back to the burning fountain whence it
came,
A portion of the Eternal.   *Ib. st. 38*

He hath awakened from the dream of
life.   *Ib. st. 39*

He has outsoared the shadow of our
night;
Envy and calumny and hate and pain,
And that unrest which men miscall de-
light
Can touch him not and torture not
again;
From the contagion of the world's slow
stain
He is secure, and now can never mourn
A heart grown cold, a head grown gray
in vain.   *Ib. st. 40*

He lives, he wakes — 'tis Death is dead,
not he.   *Ib. st. 41*

He is made one with Nature: there is
heard
His voice in all her music, from the
moan
Of thunder to the song of night's sweet
bird.   *Ib. st. 42*

He is a portion of the loveliness
Which once he made more lovely.
                        Ib. st. 43

The One remains, the many change
and pass;
Heaven's light forever shines, Earth's
shadows fly;
Life, like a dome of many-colored glass,
Stains the white radiance of Eternity,
Until Death tramples it to fragments.
                        Ib. st. 52

The soul of Adonais, like a star,
Beacons from the abode where the
Eternal are.   *Adonais, st. 55*

Music, when soft voices die,
Vibrates in the memory;
Odors, when sweet violets sicken,
Live within the sense they quicken.

Rose leaves, when the rose is dead,
Are heaped for the beloved's bed;
And so thy thoughts, when thou art
gone,
Love itself shall slumber on.
        To ——: Music, When Soft
                Voices Die [1821]

One word is too often profaned
For me to profane it,
One feeling too falsely disdained
For thee to disdain it.
        To ——: One Word Is Too
            Often Profaned [1821], *st. 1*

The desire of the moth for the star,
    Of the night for the morrow,
The devotion to something afar
    From the sphere of our sorrow.
                        Ib. st. 2

Swiftly walk o'er the western wave,
    Spirit of Night!
                To Night [1821], *st. 1*

I ask of thee, beloved Night —
Swift be thine approaching flight,
    Come soon, soon!   *Ib. st. 5*

Rarely, rarely, comest thou,
Spirit of Delight!
        Song: Rarely, Rarely, Comest
                Thou [1821], *st. 1*

I love tranquil solitude
And such society
As is quiet, wise, and good.   *Ib. st. 7*

There is no sport in hate when all the
    rage
Is on one side.
            Lines to a Reviewer [1821]

When the lamp is shattered
The light in the dust lies dead —
When the cloud is scattered
The rainbow's glory is shed.
        When the Lamp Is Shattered
                [1822], *st. 1*

Best and brightest, come away!
> *To Jane: An Invitation* [1822]

Away, away, from men and towns,
To the wild wood and the downs. *Ib.*

I am gone into the fields
To take what this sweet hour yields —
Reflection, you may come tomorrow,
Sit by the fireside with Sorrow. —
You with the unpaid bill, Despair —
You, tiresome verse-reciter, Care —
I will pay you in the grave. *Ib.*

Poets are the hierophants of an un-apprehended inspiration; the mirrors of the gigantic shadows which futurity casts upon the present.[1]
> *A Defense of Poetry* [1821]

Poetry is the record of the best and happiest moments of the happiest and best minds. *Ib.*

Poets are the unacknowledged legislators of the world. *Ib.*

PETER VYAZEMSKY
1792–1878

He lives in haste and hurries to feel.[2]
> *First Snow*

JOHN CLARE
1793–1864

I am! yet what I am who cares, or knows?
My friends forsake me like a memory lost. *I Am*

Untroubling and untroubled where I lie —
The grass below — above the vaulted sky. *Ib.*

The wind and clouds, now here, now there,
Hold no such strange dominion
As woman's cold, perverted will,
And soon estranged opinion.
> *When Lovers Part*

[1] See Cicero, p. 111a; Shakespeare, p. 268a; and Campbell, p. 538a, and note.
[2] Quoted by Pushkin as epigraph to *Eugene Onegin.*

Till kicked and torn and beaten out he lies
And leaves his hold and cackles, groans, and dies. *Badger*

If life had a second edition, how I would correct the proofs.[1]
> *Letter to a friend. From* J. W.
> AND ANNE TIBBLE, *John Clare:*
> *A Life* [1932]

FELICIA DOROTHEA
HEMANS
1793–1835

The stately homes of England!
How beautiful they stand,
Amidst their tall ancestral trees,
O'er all the pleasant land! [2]
> *The Homes of England, st.* 1

The breaking waves dashed high
On a stern and rock-bound coast,
And the woods, against a stormy sky,
Their giant branches tossed.
> *The Landing of the Pilgrim*
> *Fathers, st.* 1

A band of exiles moored their bark
On a wild New England shore.
> *Ib. st.* 2

Ay, call it holy ground,
The soil where first they trod!
They have left unstained what there they found —
Freedom to worship God.
> *Ib. st.* 10

The boy [3] stood on the burning deck,

[1] See Benjamin Franklin, p. 421a-b.
[2] Those comfortably padded lunatic asylums, which are known, euphemistically, as the stately homes of England. — VIRGINIA WOOLF [1882–1941], *The Common Reader: Lady Dorothy Nevill*

> The stately homes of England,
> How beautiful they stood
> Before their recent owners
> Relinquished them for good.
> E. V. KNOX [1881–   ], *The*
> *Stately Homes*

[3] Giacomo Casablanca, whose father, Louis, at the battle of the Nile, 1798, commanded the flagship *Orient.* It took fire and blew up, the commander was mortally wounded, and when most of the crew fled, Giacomo remained aboard, in an effort to help his gallant father.

Whence all but he had fled.
> *Casabianca, st.* 1

The flames rolled on; he would not go
Without his father's word.
> *Ib. st.* 3

There came a burst of thunder sound;
The boy — oh! where was he?
> *Ib. st.* 9

Come to the sunset tree!
The day is past and gone.
> *Tyrolese Evening Song, st.* 1

Leaves have their time to fall,
And flowers to wither at the north-
wind's breath,
And stars to set — but all,
Thou hast *all* seasons for thine own, O
Death!
> *The Hour of Death, st.* 1

In the busy haunts of men.
> *Tale of the Secret Tribunal, pt.* I

Oh, call my brother back to me!
I cannot play alone:
The summer comes with flower and
bee —
Where is my brother gone?
> *The Child's First Grief, st.* 1

He never smiled again.
> *Title and refrain of poem*

WILLIAM CULLEN BRYANT
1794–1878

To him who in the love of Nature
holds
Communion with her visible forms, she
speaks
A various language.
> *Thanatopsis* [1817–1821], *l.* 1

Go forth, under the open sky, and list
To Nature's teachings. *Ib. l.* 14

The hills,
Rock-ribbed, and ancient as the sun.
> *Ib. l.* 37

Old ocean's gray and melancholy waste.
> *Ib. l.* 43

So live, that when thy summons comes
to join

The innumerable caravan which moves
To that mysterious realm, where each
shall take
His chamber in the silent halls of
death,
Thou go not, like the quarry-slave at
night,
Scourged to his dungeon, but, sustained
and soothed
By an unfaltering trust, approach thy
grave,
Like one that wraps the drapery of his
couch
About him, and lies down to pleasant
dreams.[1] *Thanatopsis, l.* 73

He who, from zone to zone,
Guides through the boundless sky thy
certain flight,
In the long way that I must tread
alone,
Will lead my steps aright.
> *To a Waterfowl* [1818], *st.* 8

The groves were God's first temples.
> *A Forest Hymn*

The melancholy days are come, the
saddest of the year,
Of wailing winds, and naked woods,
and meadows brown and sere.
> *The Death of the Flowers*
> [1832], *st.* 1

Loveliest of lovely things are they,
On earth, that soonest pass away.
The rose that lives its little hour
Is prized beyond the sculptured flower.
> *A Scene on the Banks of the*
> *Hudson, st.* 3

These are the gardens of the Desert,
these
The unshorn fields, boundless and
beautiful,
For which the speech of England has
no name —
The Prairies. *The Prairies*

Truth, crushed to earth, shall rise
again;
The eternal years of God are hers;
But Error, wounded, writhes in pain,
And dies among his worshippers.
> *The Battlefield, st.* 9

[1] See Lucretius, p. 113b, and Horace, p. 120b.

EDWARD EVERETT [1]
1794–1865

The days of palmy prosperity are not those most favorable to the display of public virtue or the influence of wise and good men. In hard, doubtful, unprosperous, and dangerous times, the disinterested and patriotic find their way, by a species of public instinct, unopposed, joyfully welcomed, to the control of affairs.

Mount Vernon Papers, no. 14

WILLIAM WHEWELL
1794–1866

And so no force however great can stretch a cord however fine into an horizontal line which is accurately straight.[2]

Elementary Treatise on Mechanics [1819]. The Equilibrium of Forces on a Point

NARCISSE ACHILLE, COMTE DE SALVANDY
1795–1856

We are dancing on a volcano.

At a fête given by the Duc d'Orléans to the King of Naples [1830]

THOMAS CARLYLE
1795–1881

A well-written Life is almost as rare as a well-spent one.

Critical and Miscellaneous Essays. Richter [1827]

The great law of culture is: Let each become all that he was created capable of being.   *Ib.*

The three great elements of modern

civilization, gunpowder, printing, and the Protestant religion.

Critical and Miscellaneous Essays. The State of German Literature [1827]

Literary men are . . . a perpetual priesthood.   *Ib.*

In every man's writings, the character of the writer must lie recorded.
                          Ib. Goethe [1828]

A poet without love were a physical and metaphysical impossibility.
                          Ib. Burns [1828]

There is no heroic poem in the world but is at bottom a biography, the life of a man; also, it may be said, there is no life of a man, faithfully recorded, but is a heroic poem of its sort, rhymed or unrhymed.

Ib. Sir Walter Scott [1838]

To the very last, he [Napoleon] had a kind of idea; that, namely, of *La carrière ouverte aux talents*, The tools to him that can handle them.   *Ib.*

No man lives without jostling and being jostled; in all ways he has to elbow himself through the world, giving and receiving offense.   *Ib.*

All greatness is unconscious, or it is little and naught.   *Ib.*

The uttered part of a man's life, let us always repeat, bears to the unuttered, unconscious part a small unknown proportion. He himself never knows it, much less do others.   *Ib.*

It can be said of him, when he departed he took a Man's life along with him. No sounder piece of British manhood was put together in that eighteenth century of Time.   *Ib.*

Nothing that was worthy in the past departs; no truth or goodness realized by man ever dies, or can die.   *Ib.*

The barrenest of all mortals is the sentimentalist.   *Ib.*

Aesop's Fly, sitting on the axle of the

---

[1] His best-known wartime oration was delivered at the dedication of the national cemetery at Gettysburg [November 19, 1863], the same occasion on which Lincoln made his famous address.

[2] In a slightly altered form ("line that shall be absolutey straight"), this was reputed to be an example of unconscious but perfect rhyme.

chariot, has been much laughed at for exclaiming: What a dust I do raise!
On Boswell's Life of Johnson [1832]

Whoso belongs only to his own age, and reverences only its gilt Popinjays or soot-smeared Mumbojumbos, must needs die with it.[1] *Ib.*

The stupendous Fourth Estate, whose wide world-embracing influences what eye can take in? [2] *Ib.*

All work is as seed sown; it grows and spreads, and sows itself anew. *Ib.*

No man who has once heartily and wholly laughed can be altogether irreclaimably bad.[3]
Sartor Resartus [1833–1834], *bk. I, ch. 4*

He who first shortened the labor of copyists by device of movable types was disbanding hired armies, and cashiering most kings and senates, and creating a whole new democratic world: he had invented the art of printing. *Ib. 5*

Man is a tool-using animal. . . . Without tools he is nothing, with tools he is all. *Ib.*

The everlasting No.
Ib. 7 (chapter title)

Be not the slave of Words. *Ib. 8*

The everlasting Yea.
Ib. 9 (chapter title)

Man's unhappiness, as I construe, comes of his greatness; it is because there is an Infinite in him, which with all his cunning he cannot quite bury under the Finite. *Ib.*

Close thy Byron; open thy Goethe. *Ib.*

Wonder is the basis of worship. *Ib. 10*

What you see, yet can not see over, is as good as infinite. *Ib. II, 1*

Sarcasm I now see to be, in general,

the language of the Devil; for which reason I have, long since, as good as renounced it.
Sartor Resartus, bk. II, ch. 4

To consume your own choler, as some chimneys consume their own smoke;[1] to keep a whole Satanic School spouting, if it must spout, inaudibly, is a negative yet no slight virtue, nor one of the commonest in these times. *Ib. 6*

Alas! the fearful Unbelief is unbelief in yourself. *Ib. 7*

As the Swiss inscription says: *Sprechen ist silbern, Schweigen ist golden* — "Speech is silvern, Silence is golden"; or, as I might rather express it, speech is of time, silence is of eternity.[2]
Ib. III, 3

Trust not the heart of that man for whom old clothes are not venerable. *Ib. 6*

The Public is an old woman. Let her maunder and mumble.
Journal [1835]

It is now almost my sole rule of life to clear myself of cants [3] and formulas, as of poisonous Nessus shirts.
Letter to His Wife [1835]

No lie you can speak or act but it will come, after longer or shorter circulation, like a bill drawn on Nature's Reality, and be presented there for payment — with the answer, No effects.
The French Revolution [1837], *pt. I, bk. III, ch. 1*

To a shower of gold most things are penetrable. *Ib. 7*

---

[1] See *Heroes and Hero-Worship*, p. 577b.
Consume your own smoke. — BROWNING, *Pacchiarotto* [1876], 25
Would that he consumed his own smoke. — MELVILLE, *Moby Dick* [1851], *ch. 96*
See Osler, p. 817b.
[2] Silence is deep as Eternity; speech is shallow as Time. — CARLYLE, *Sir Walter Scott* [1838]
[3] See Johnson, p. 433b.

---

[1] See Voltaire, p. 418a.
[2] See *Heroes and Hero-Worship*, p. 577b, and Thackeray, p. 660a.
[3] See W. C. Fields, p. 951b.

"The people may eat grass": [1] hasty words, which fly abroad irrevocable — and will send back tidings.
The French Revolution, pt. I, bk. III, ch. 9

A whiff of grapeshot.   *Ib.* V, 3

O poor mortals, how ye make this earth bitter for each other.   *Ib.* 5

Battles, in these ages, are transacted by mechanism; with the slightest possible development of human individuality or spontaneity; men now even die, and kill one another, in an artificial manner.   *Ib.* VII, 4

The difference between Orthodoxy or My-doxy and Heterodoxy or Thy-doxy.[2]
Ib. pt. II, bk. IV, ch. 2

Aristocracy of the Moneybag.
Ib. VII, 7

Democracy is, by the nature of it, a self-canceling business; and gives in the long run a net result of zero.
Chartism [1839]. *Ch.* 6, *Laissez-Faire*

No sadder proof can be given by a man of his own littleness than disbelief in great men.
Heroes and Hero-Worship [1841]. *The Hero as Divinity*

The history of the world is but the biography of great men.[3]   *Ib.*

We must get rid of fear.   *Ib.*

A vein of poetry exists in the hearts of all men.   *Ib. The Hero as Poet*

The Age of Miracles is forever here!
Ib. The Hero as Priest

In books lies the soul of the whole Past Time; the articulate audible voice of the Past, when the body and ma-terial substance of it has altogether vanished like a dream.
Heroes and Hero-Worship. The Hero as Man of Letters

All that mankind has done, thought, gained or been: it is lying as in magic preservation in the pages of books.
Ib.

The true university of these days is a collection of books.   *Ib.*

Burke said there were Three Estates in Parliament; but, in the Reporters' Gallery yonder, there sat a Fourth Estate more important far than they all. It is not a figure of speech, or witty saying; it is a literal fact — very momentous to us in these times.[1]   *Ib.*

The suffering man ought really to consume his own smoke; there is no good in emitting smoke till you have made it into fire.[2]   *Ib.*

Adversity is sometimes hard upon a man; but for one man who can stand prosperity, there are a hundred that will stand adversity.[3]   *Ib.*

"A fair day's wages for a fair day's work": it is as just a demand as governed men ever made of governing. It is the everlasting right of man.
Past and Present [1843], *bk. I, ch.* 3

Fire is the best of servants; but what a master! [4]   *Ib.* II, 9

All work, even cotton-spinning, is noble; work is alone noble. . . . A life of ease is not for any man, nor for any god.   *Ib.* III, 4

Every noble crown is, and on earth will forever be, a crown of thorns.
Ib. 7

---

[1] The remark of Foullon, when his finance scheme raised the question: What will the people do?

[2] See William Warburton, p. 419a, note.

[3] History is the essence of innumerable biographies. — *On History* [1830]
See Emerson, p. 605b.

[1] The gallery in which the reporters sit has become a fourth estate of the realm. — MACAULAY, *On Hallam's Constitutional History* [1828]
See *On Boswell's Life of Johnson,* p. 576a.

[2] See *Sartor Resartus,* p. 576b.

[3] See Samuel Butler, p. 755b.

[4] Mammon is like fire: the usefulest of all servants, if the frightfulest of all masters! — *Ib. IV, 7*

Blessed is he who has found his work; let him ask no other blessedness.
Past and Present, bk. III, ch. 4

Captains of Industry.
Ib. IV, 4 (chapter title)

There is endless merit in a man's knowing when to have done.
Francia [1845]

He that works and *does* some Poem, not he that merely *says* one, is worthy of the name of Poet.
Introduction to Cromwell's Letters and Speeches [1845]

Respectable Professors of the Dismal Science.[1]
Latter Day Pamphlets, no. 1 [1850]

A Parliament speaking through reporters to Buncombe and the twenty-seven millions, mostly fools. *Ib. 6*

A healthy hatred of scoundrels.
Ib. 12

"Genius" (which means transcendent capacity of taking trouble, first of all).[2]
Life of Frederick the Great [1858–1865], *bk. IV, ch. 3*

Happy the people whose annals are blank in history books! [3] *Ib. XVI, 1*

So here hath been dawning
Another blue day:
Think, wilt thou let it
Slip useless away? *Today*

My whinstone house my castle is;
I have my own four walls.
My Own Four Walls

Lord Bacon could as easily have created the planets as he could have written Hamlet. *Remark in discussion*

[1] Referring to political economy and social science, Carlyle also in his *Occasional Discourse on the Negro Question* [1849] speaks of "What we might call, by way of Eminence, the Dismal Science."
[2] See Buffon, p. 423b, and note.
[3] Carlyle identifies this as "Montesquieu's aphorism."
See George Eliot, p. 689b.

JOSEPH RODMAN DRAKE
1795–1820

When Freedom from her mountain height,
Unfurled her standard to the air,
She tore the azure robe of night,
And set the stars of glory there;
She mingled with its gorgeous dyes
The milky baldric of the skies,
And striped its pure, celestial white
With streakings of the morning light.
Then from his mansion in the sun
She called her eagle bearer down,
And gave into his mighty hand
The symbol of her chosen land.
The American Flag [1819], *st. 1*

JOHN WOODCOCK GRAVES
1795–1886

D' ye ken John Peel with his coat so gay?
D' ye ken John Peel at the break of day?
D' ye ken John Peel when he's far far away
With his hounds and his horn in the morning?

'Twas the sound of his horn brought me from my bed,
And the cry of his hounds, has me oft-times led;
For Peel's view-hollo would waken the dead,
Or the fox from his lair in the morning. *John Peel* [1832]

ALEXANDER GRIBOYEDOV
1795–1829

The houses are new, but prejudices are old.
Wit Works Woe [1822–1824], *act II, sc. 5*

I'll seek me out a nook for the heart that's tried too sore. *Ib. IV, 15*

And what will Princess Marya
Aleksevna say? [1]
> *Wit Works Woe, act II, sc. 15*

JOHN KEATS
1795–1821

I stood tiptoe upon a little hill.
> *Poems* [1817]. *I Stood Tiptoe, l. 1*

And then there crept
A little noiseless noise among the
    leaves,
Born of the very sigh that silence
    heaves.   *Ib. l. 10*

Open afresh your round of starry folds,
Ye ardent marigolds!   *Ib. l. 47*

Where swarms of minnows show their
    little heads,
Staying their wavy bodies 'gainst the
    streams.   *Ib. l. 72*

Sometimes goldfinches one by one will
    drop
From low hung branches; little space
    they stop;
But sip, and twitter, and their feathers
    sleek;
Then off at once, as in a wanton freak:
Or perhaps, to show their black, and
    golden wings,
Pausing upon their yellow flutterings.
>   *Ib. l. 87*

Woman! when I behold thee flippant,
    vain,
Inconstant, childish, proud, and full of
    fancies.
> *Ib. Woman! When I Behold*
> *Thee Flippant, Vain*

To one who has been long in city
    pent,[2]
'Tis very sweet to look into the fair
And open face of heaven.
> *Sonnets* [1816–1817]. *To One*
> *Who Has Been Long in City*
> *Pent*

E'en like the passage of an angel's tear
That falls through the clear ether si-
    lently.   *Ib.*

Much have I travel'd in the realms of
    gold,
And many goodly states and kingdoms
    seen;
Round many western islands have I
    been
Which bards in fealty to Apollo hold.
> *Sonnets. On First Looking*
> *into Chapman's Homer*

Then felt I like some watcher of the
    skies
When a new planet swims into his ken;
Or like stout Cortez when with eagle
    eyes
He star'd at the Pacific — and all his
    men
Look'd at each other with a wild sur-
    mise —
Silent, upon a peak in Darien.   *Ib.*

    Hear ye not the hum
Of mighty workings? —
Listen awhile ye nations, and be dumb.
> *Ib. Addressed to Haydon*

The poetry of earth is never dead.
> *Ib. On the Grasshopper and the*
> *Cricket*

My spirit is too weak — mortality
Weighs heavily on me like unwilling
    sleep,
And each imagin'd pinnacle and steep
Of godlike hardship, tells me I must
    die
Like a sick Eagle looking at the sky.
> *Ib. On Seeing the Elgin Marbles*

It keeps eternal whisperings around
Desolate shores, and with its mighty
    swell
Gluts twice ten thousand caverns.
> *Ib. On the Sea*

    Life is but a day;
A fragile dewdrop on its perilous way
From a tree's summit.
> *Sleep and Poetry* [1817], *l. 85*

O for ten years, that I may overwhelm
Myself in poesy; so I may do the deed
That my own soul has to itself decreed.
> *Ib. l. 96*

---

[1] Name used as a symbol for idle gossip.
[2] See Milton, p. 347b.

A drainless shower
Of light is poesy; 'tis the supreme of
    power;
'Tis might half slumb'ring on its own
    right arm.
        Sleep and Poetry, l. 235

But strength alone though of the Muses
    born
Is like a fallen angel: trees uptorn,
Darkness, and worms, and shrouds, and
    sepulchers
Delight it; for it feeds upon the burrs
And thorns of life; forgetting the great
    end
Of poesy, that it should be a friend
To soothe the cares, and lift the
    thoughts of man.   *Ib. l. 241*

In a drear-nighted December
  Too happy, happy tree,
Thy branches ne'er remember
  Their green felicity.
        Stanzas [written 1817]

But were there ever any
Writh'd not at passing joy?   *Ib.*

Shed no tear — O shed no tear!
The flower will bloom another year.
Weep no more — O weep no more!
Young buds sleep in the root's white
    core.
        Faery Songs, I [written 1818]

There is not a fiercer hell than the
failure in a great object.
        Endymion [1818], preface

The imagination of a boy is healthy,
and the mature imagination of a man is
healthy; but there is a space of life between, in which the soul is in a fer-
ment, the character undecided, the way
of life uncertain, the ambition thick-
sighted: thence proceeds mawkishness,
and the thousand bitters which those
men I speak of must necessarily taste in
going over the following pages.   *Ib.*

A thing of beauty is a joy forever:
Its loveliness increases; it will never
Pass into nothingness; but still will keep
A bower quiet for us, and a sleep
Full of sweet dreams, and health, and
    quiet breathing.   *Ib. bk. I, l. 1*

    The grandeur of the dooms
We have imagined for the mighty
    dead.   *Endymion, bk. I, l. 20*

O magic sleep! O comfortable bird,
That broodest o'er the troubled sea of
    the mind
Till it is hush'd and smooth!
        Ib. l. 453

    Time, that aged nurse,
Rock'd me to patience.   *Ib. l. 705*

Wherein lies happiness? In that which
    becks
Our ready minds to fellowship divine,
A fellowship with essence; till we
    shine,
Full alchemiz'd, and free of space. Be-
    hold
The clear religion of heaven!
        Ib. l. 777

    The crown of these
Is made of love and friendship, and sits
    high
Upon the forehead of humanity.
        Ib. l. 800

A hope beyond the shadow of a dream.
        Ib. l. 857

Pleasure is oft a visitant; but pain
Clings cruelly to us.   *Ib. l. 906*

    'Tis the pest
Of love, that fairest joys give most un-
    rest.   *Ib. II, l. 365*

  To sorrow,
    I bade good-morrow,
And thought to leave her far away be-
    hind;
  But cheerly, cheerly,
    She loves me dearly;
She is so constant to me, and so kind.
        Ib. IV, l. 173

    "For cruel 'tis," said she,
"To steal my Basil-pot away from me."
    Isabella; or, The Pot of Basil
        [1818], st. 62

Blue! Gentle cousin of the forest-green,
Married to green in all the sweetest
    flowers —

Forget-me-not — the blue bell — and that Queen
Of secrecy, the violet.
                    Sonnets [*1818–1819*]. *Blue*

When I have fears that I may cease to be
Before my pen has glean'd my teeming brain.   *Ib. When I Have Fears*

When I behold, upon the night's starr'd face,
Huge cloudy symbols of a high romance.   *Ib.*

          Then on the shore
Of the wide world I stand alone, and think
Till love and fame to nothingness do sink.   *Ib.*

Bright star, would I were steadfast as thou art —
Not in lone splendor hung aloft the night
And watching, with eternal lids apart,
Like nature's patient, sleepless Eremite,
The moving waters at their priest-like task
Of pure ablution round earth's human shores.   *Ib. Bright Star*

The day is gone, and all its sweets are gone!
Sweet voice, sweet lips, soft hand, and softer breast.
                    Ib. The Day Is Gone

O what can ail thee, knight at arms,
Alone and palely loitering?
The sedge has withered from the lake,
And no birds sing!
La Belle Dame Sans Merci [1] [*first version, 1819*], *st. 1*

I met a lady in the meads
  Full beautiful, a faery's child;
Her hair was long, her foot was light,
  And her eyes were wild.   *Ib. st. 4*

She looked at me as she did love,
And made sweet moan.   *Ib. st. 5*

      "La belle dame sans merci
Thee hath in thrall!"   *Ib. st. 10*

[1] The title of a French poem by ALAIN CHARTIER [C. 1385 – C. 1433]

This living hand, now warm and capable
Of earnest grasping, would, if it were cold
And in the icy silence of the tomb,
So haunt thy days and chill thy dreaming nights
That thou would wish thine own heart dry of blood
So in my veins red life might stream again,
And thou be conscience-calm'd — see here it is —
I hold it towards you.
        Lines Supposed to Have Been
        Addressed to Fanny Brawne
        [*1819*]

Love in a hut, with water and a crust,
Is — Love, forgive us! — cinders, ashes, dust.
        Poems [*1820*]. *Lamia, pt. II, l. 1*

There was an awful rainbow once in heaven:
We know her woof, her texture; she is given
In the dull catalogue of common things.
Philosophy will clip an angel's wings.
                    Ib. l. 231

St. Agnes' Eve — Ah, bitter chill it was!
The owl, for all his feathers, was a-cold.
The hare limp'd trembling through the frozen grass,
And silent was the flock in wooly fold
            Ib. The Eve of St. Agnes, st. 1

The silver, snarling trumpets 'gan to chide.   *Ib. st. 4*

The music, yearning like a God in pain.
                    Ib. st. 7

She sigh'd for Agnes' dreams, the sweetest of the year.   *Ib.*

Asleep in lap of legends old.
                    Ib. st. 15

Sudden a thought came like a full-blown rose,
Flushing his brow, and in his pained heart
Made purple riot.   *Ib. st. 16*

A poor, weak, palsy-stricken, churchyard thing.
Poems. The Eve of St. Agnes,
st. 18

As though a tongueless nightingale
should swell
Her throat in vain, and die, heart-stifled
in her dell. *Ib. st. 23*

Full on this casement shone the wintry
moon,
And threw warm gules on Madeline's
fair breast. *Ib. st. 25*

Unclasps her warmed jewels one by
one;
Loosens her fragrant bodice; by degrees
Her rich attire creeps rustling to her
knees. *Ib. st. 26*

And still she slept an azure-lidded sleep.
Ib. st. 30

And the long carpets rose along the
gusty floor. *Ib. st. 40*

And they are gone: aye, ages long ago
These lovers fled away into the storm.
Ib. st. 42

My heart aches, and a drowsy numbness pains
My sense, as though of hemlock I had
drunk,
Or emptied some dull opiate to the
drains
One minute past, and Lethe-wards had
sunk.[1]
Ib. Ode to a Nightingale, st. 1

That thou, light-winged Dryad of the
trees,
In some melodious plot
Of beechen green, and shadows num-
berless,
Singest of summer in full-throated ease.
Ib.

O, for a draught of vintage! that hath
been
Cool'd a long age in the deep-delved
earth,
Tasting of Flora and the country green,
Dance, and Provençal song, and sunburnt mirth!

[1] See Horace, p. 120b.

O, for a beaker full of the warm South,
Full of the true, the blushful Hippo-
crene,
With beaded bubbles winking at the
brim,
And purple-stained mouth.
Poems. Ode to a Nightingale,
st. 2

Fade far away, dissolve, and quite for-
get
What thou among the leaves hast never
known,
The weariness, the fever, and the fret
Here, where men sit and hear each
other groan;
Where palsy shakes a few, sad, last gray
hairs,
Where youth grows pale, and specter-
thin, and dies;
Where but to think is to be full of
sorrow
And leaden-eyed despairs.
Ib. st. 3

Already with thee! tender is the night.
Ib. st. 4

I cannot see what flowers are at my
feet,
Nor what soft incense hangs upon the
boughs,
But, in embalmed darkness, guess each
sweet. *Ib. st. 5*

The murmurous haunt of flies on summer eves. *Ib.*

Darkling I listen; and, for many a time
I have been half in love with easeful
Death,
Call'd him soft names in many a mused
rhyme,
To take into the air my quiet breath;
Now more than ever seems it rich to
die,
To cease upon the midnight with no
pain,
While thou art pouring forth thy soul
abroad
In such an ecstasy!
Still wouldst thou sing, and I have ears
in vain —
To thy high requiem become a sod.
Ib. st. 6

Thou wast not born for death, immortal Bird!
No hungry generations tread thee down;
The voice I hear this passing night was heard
In ancient days by emperor and clown:
Perhaps the self-same song that found a path
Through the sad heart of Ruth, when, sick for home,
She stood in tears amid the alien corn;
    The same that oft-times hath
Charm'd magic casements, opening on the foam
Of perilous seas, in faery lands forlorn.
    Poems. Ode to a Nightingale,
                     st. 7

Forlorn! the very word is like a bell
To toll me back from thee to my sole self!   *Ib. st. 8*

Was it a vision, or a waking dream?
Fled is that music: — Do I wake or sleep?   *Ib.*

Thou still unravish'd bride of quietness,
Thou foster-child of silence and slow time,
Sylvan historian, who canst thus express
A flowery tale more sweetly than our rhyme:
What leaf-fring'd legend haunts about thy shape?
    Ib. Ode on a Grecian Urn, st. 1

What men or gods are these? What maidens loth?
What mad pursuit? What struggle to escape?
What pipes and timbrels? What wild ecstasy?   *Ib.*

Heard melodies are sweet, but those unheard
Are sweeter.   *Ib. st. 2*

Forever wilt thou love, and she be fair!
                   Ib.

Forever piping songs forever new.
             Ib. st. 3

Who are these coming to the sacrifice?
To what green altar, O mysterious priest,

Lead'st thou that heifer lowing at the skies,
And all her silken flanks with garlands drest?
    Poems. Ode on a Grecian
                 Urn, st. 4

O Attic shape! Fair attitude!
               Ib. st. 5

"Beauty is truth, truth beauty," [1] — that is all
Ye know on earth, and all ye need to know.   *Ib.*

    To make delicious moan
Upon the midnight hours.
    Ib. Ode to Psyche, st. 3

A bright torch, and a casement ope at night,
To let the warm Love in!   *Ib. st. 5*

Ever let the fancy roam,
Pleasure never is at home.
         Ib. Fancy, l. 1

Bards of Passion and of Mirth,
Ye have left your souls on earth!
Have ye souls in heaven too?
    Ib. Ode written on the blank
    page before BEAUMONT AND
    FLETCHER, *The Fair Maid of*
    the Inn

Souls of Poets dead and gone,
What Elysium have ye known,
Happy field or mossy cavern,
Choicer than the Mermaid Tavern?
Have ye tippled drink more fine
Than mine host's Canary wine?
    Ib. Lines on the Mermaid Tavern

Season of mists and mellow fruitfulness,

---

[1] See Herbert, p. 323a.

If asked who said "Beauty is truth, truth beauty!" a great many readers would answer "Keats." But Keats said nothing of the sort. It is what he said the Grecian Urn said, his description and criticism of a certain kind of work of art, the kind from which the evils and problems of this life, the "heart high sorrowful and cloyed," are deliberately excluded. The Urn, for example, depicts, among other beautiful sights, the citadel of a hill town; it does not depict warfare, the evil which makes the citadel necessary. — W. H. AUDEN, *The Dyer's Hand* [*1962*]. *Robert Frost*

Close bosom-friend of the maturing sun.
> *Poems. To Autumn, st. 1*

Who hath not seen thee oft amid thy store?
Sometimes whoever seeks abroad may find
Thee sitting careless on a granary floor,
Thy hair soft-lifted by the winnowing wind;
Or on a half-reap'd furrow sound asleep,
Drows'd with the fume of poppies while thy hook
Spares the next swath and all its twined flowers. *Ib. st. 2*

Then in a wailful choir the small gnats mourn
Among the river sallows. *Ib. st. 3*

No, no, go not to Lethe, neither twist
Wolf's-bane, tight-rooted, for its poisonous wine.
> *Ib. Ode on Melancholy, st. 1*

Nor let the beetle, nor the death-moth be
Your mournful Psyche. *Ib.*

Then glut thy sorrow on a morning rose. *Ib. st. 2*

She dwells with Beauty — Beauty that must die. *Ib. st. 3*

Ay, in the very temple of Delight
Veil'd Melancholy has her sovran shrine,
Though seen of none save him whose strenuous tongue
Can burst Joy's grape against his palate fine;
His soul shall taste the sadness of her might,
And be among her cloudy trophies hung. *Ib.*

Deep in the shady sadness of a vale
Far sunken from the healthy breath of morn,
Far from the fiery noon, and eve's one star,
Sat gray-hair'd Saturn, quiet as a stone.
> *Ib. Hyperion, bk. I, l. 1*

That large utterance of the early Gods!
> *Ib. l. 51*

As when, upon a tranced summer-night,
Those green-rob'd senators of mighty woods,
Tall oaks, branch-charmed by the earnest stars,
Dream, and so dream all night without a stir.
> *Poems. Hyperion, bk I, l. 72*

For to bear all naked truths,
And to envisage circumstance, all calm,
That is the top of sovereignty.
> *Ib. II, l. 203*

Knowledge enormous makes a God of me. *Ib. III, l. 113*

I am certain of nothing but the holiness of the heart's affections and the truth of imagination — what the imagination seizes as beauty must be truth — whether it existed before or not.
> *Letter to Benjamin Bailey*
> *[November 22, 1817]*

The imagination may be compared to Adam's dream — he awoke and found it truth. *Ib.*

O for a life of Sensations rather than of Thoughts! *Ib.*

I scarcely remember counting upon happiness — I look not for it if it be not in the present hour — nothing startles me beyond the moment. The setting sun will always set me to rights — or if a sparrow come before my window I take part in its existence and pick about the gravel. *Ib.*

At once it struck me what quality went to form a man of achievement, especially in literature, and which Shakespeare possessed so enormously — I mean *negative capability*, that is, when a man is capable of being in uncertainties, mysteries, doubts, without any irritable reaching after fact and reason.
> *Letter to George and Thomas*
> *Keats [December 22, 1817]*

We hate poetry that has a palpable design upon us — and if we do not agree, seems to put its hand in its breeches pocket. Poetry should be great and unobtrusive, a thing which enters into one's soul, and does not startle or amaze with itself, but with its subject.

Letter to John Hamilton Reynolds [February 3, 1818]

Poetry should surprise by a fine excess, and not by singularity. It should strike the reader as a wording of his own highest thoughts, and appear almost as a remembrance.

Letter to John Taylor [February 27, 1818]

If poetry comes not as naturally as leaves to a tree it had better not come at all. ***Ib.***

Scenery is fine — but human nature is finer.

Letter to Benjamin Bailey [March 13, 1818]

Axioms in philosophy are not axioms until they are proved upon our pulses: we read fine things but never feel them to the full until we have gone the same steps as the author.

Letter to John Hamilton Reynolds [May 3, 1818]

I compare human life to a large mansion of many apartments, two of which I can only describe, the doors of the rest being as yet shut upon me. ***Ib.***

There is an awful warmth about my heart like a load of immortality.

Letter to John Hamilton Reynolds [September 22, 1818]

I begin to get a little acquainted with my own strength and weakness. Praise or blame has but a momentary effect on the man whose love of beauty in the abstract makes him a severe critic on his own works.

Letter to James Hessey [October 9, 1818]

The genius of poetry must work out its own salvation in a man; it cannot be matured by law and precept, but by sensation and watchfulness in itself. That which is creative must create itself —

In *Endymion*, I leaped headlong into the sea, and thereby have become better acquainted with the soundings, the quicksands, and the rocks, than if I had stayed upon the green shore, and piped a silly pipe, and took tea and comfortable advice.

Letter to James Hessey

I would sooner fail than not be among the greatest. ***Ib.***

I think I shall be among the English Poets after my death.

Letter to George and Georgiana Keats [October 14, 1818]

The poetical character . . . is not itself — it has no self — it is everything and nothing. . . . It has as much delight in conceiving an Iago as an Imogen.

Letter to Richard Woodhouse [October 27, 1818]

A poet is the most unpoetical of anything in existence; because he has no identity — he is continually infor[ming] — and filling some other body. ***Ib.***

A man's life of any worth is a continual allegory — and very few eyes can see the mystery of his life — a life like the Scriptures, figurative. . . . Lord Byron cuts a figure, but he is not figurative. Shakespeare led a life of allegory: his works are the comments on it.

Letter to George and Georgiana Keats [February 14–May 3, 1819]

Nothing ever becomes real till it is experienced — Even a proverb is no proverb to you till your Life has illustrated it. ***Ib.***

I myself am pursuing the same instinctive course as the veriest human animal you can think of — I am, however young, writing at random — straining at particles of light in the midst of a great darkness — without knowing the bearing of any one assertion, of any one opinion. Yet may I not in this be free from sin?

***Ib.** [March 19, 1819]*

Call the world if you please "The vale of soul-making."

***Ib.** [April 21, 1819]*

I have two luxuries to brood over in my walks, your loveliness and the hour of my death. O that I could have possession of them both in the same minute.
To Fanny Brawne [*July 25, 1819*]

"If I should die," said I to myself, "I have left no immortal work behind me — nothing to make my friends proud of my memory — but I have lov'd the principle of beauty in all things, and if I had had time I would have made myself remember'd."
Ib. [*c. February 1820*]

You might curb your magnanimity, and be more of an artist, and load every rift of your subject with ore.
Letter to Shelley [*August 1820*]

I can scarcely bid you good-bye, even in a letter. I always made an awkward bow. God bless you!
Letter to Charles Armitage Brown; Keats's last letter [*November 30, 1820*]

Here lies one whose name was writ in water.[1] *Epitaph for himself* [*1821*]

LEOPOLD VON RANKE
1795–1886

You have reckoned that history ought to judge the past and to instruct the contemporary world as to the future. The present attempt does not yield to that high office. It will merely tell how it actually happened.[2]
Geschichten der Romanischen und Germanischen Völker (*History of the Romanic and Germanic Peoples*) *von 1492 bis 1535* [*1824*], *preface*

[1] Among the many things he has requested of me tonight, this is the principal — that on his gravestone shall be this inscription. — *Letter from Severn, in* RICHARD MONCKTON MILNES, *Life, Letters, and Literary Remains of John Keats* [1848]
See Sophocles, p. 83a, and note.
[2] Wie es eigentlich gewesen.
See Thucydides, p. 89a.

FRIEDRICH WILHELM IV
1795–1861

I love an opposition that has convictions. *Speech* [*April 11, 1847*]

Henceforth Prussia goes forward as part of Germany.
Proclamation: To My People, to the German Nation [*March 21, 1848*]

ALFRED BUNN
1796–1860

I dreamt that I dwelt in marble halls, With vassals and serfs at my side.
The Bohemian Girl [*1843*], *act II, song*

HARTLEY COLERIDGE
1796–1849

The soul of man is larger than the sky, Deeper than ocean, or the abysmal dark Of the unfathomed center.
To Shakespeare

She is not fair to outward view
As many maidens be;
Her loveliness I never knew
Until she smiled on me:
Oh! then I saw her eye was bright,
A well of love, a spring of light.
Song, She Is Not Fair

Her very frowns are fairer far
Than smiles of other maidens are.
Ib.

HORACE MANN
1796–1859

Lost, yesterday, somewhere between sunrise and sunset, two golden hours, each set with sixty diamond minutes. No reward is offered, for they are gone forever. *Aphorism*

Be ashamed to die until you have won some victory for humanity.
Commencement Address, Antioch College [*1859*]

JAMES ROBINSON PLANCHÉ
1796–1880

It would have made a cat laugh.
>*The Queen of the Frogs* [1879],
>   *act I, sc. 4*

WILLIAM HICKLING PRESCOTT
1796–1859

What, then, must have been the emotions of the Spaniards, when, after working their toilsome way into the upper air, the cloudy tabernacle parted before their eyes, and they beheld these fair scenes [the valley and city of Mexico] in all their pristine magnificence and beauty! It was like the spectacle which greeted the eyes of Moses from the summit of Pisgah, and, in the warm glow of their feelings, they cried out, "It is the promised land!"
>*The Conquest of Mexico* [1843],
>   *bk. III, ch. 8*

The surest test of the civilization of a people — at least, as sure as any — afforded by mechanical art is to be found in their architecture, which presents so noble a field for the display of the grand and the beautiful, and which, at the same time, is so intimately connected with the essential comforts of life.
>*The Conquest of Peru* [1847],
>   *bk. I, ch. 5*

Drawing his sword he [Pizarro] traced a line with it on the sand from East to West. Then, turning towards the South, "Friends and comrades!" he said, "on that side are toil, hunger, nakedness, the drenching storm, desertion, and death; on this side ease and pleasure.[1] There lies Peru with its riches here, Panama and its poverty. Choose, each man, what best becomes a brave Castilian. For my part, I go to the South." So saying, he stepped across the line.
>   *Ib. II, 4*

[1] See Garibaldi, p. 620a, and Churchill, p. 920b.

SAM SLICK
[THOMAS CHANDLER HALIBURTON]
1796–1865

I want you to see Peel, Stanley, Graham, Shiel, Russell, Macaulay, Old Joe, and so on. These men are all upper crust here.[1]
>*Sam Slick in England*
>*[1843 – 1844]*,[2] *ch. 24*

Circumstances alter cases.
>*The Old Judge* [1849], *ch. 15*

JOSEPH AUGUSTINE WADE
1796–1845

Meet Me by Moonlight Alone.
>   *Title of poem*

THOMAS HAYNES BAYLY
1797–1839

I'd be a butterfly; living a rover,
Dying when fair things are fading away!
>*I'd Be a Butterfly, st. 3*

Oh no! we never mention her —
Her name is never heard;
My lips are now forbid to speak
That once familiar word.
>*Oh No! We Never Mention Her*

Why don't the men propose, Mamma?
Why don't the men propose?
>*Why Don't the Men Propose?*

She wore a wreath of roses
The night that first we met.
>*She Wore a Wreath*

Friends depart, and memory takes them
To her caverns, pure and deep.
>*Teach Me to Forget*

[1] See James Fenimore Cooper, p. 564b.
[2] The "Sam Slick" papers first appeared in a weekly paper in Nova Scotia in 1836.

Tell me the tales that to me were so
    dear,
Long, long ago, long, long ago.
                  Long, Long Ago [1]

Oh pilot, 'tis a fearful night!
There's danger on the deep.
                  The Pilot

Absence makes the heart grow fonder: [2]
Isle of Beauty, fare thee well!
                Isle of Beauty

I'm Saddest When I Sing. [3]
                Title of poem

HEINRICH HEINE [4]
1797–1856

Toward France there journeyed two
grenadiers.
      Nach Frankreich Zogen Zwei
              Grenadier', st. 1

From grief too great to banish
Come songs, my lyric minions. [5]
        Aus Meinen Grossen
             Schmerzen, st. 1

I know not why it should be that I
am so sad; there is a fairy tale of olden
days that I cannot get out of my head. [6]
             Die Lorelei, st. 1

You are like a flower,
So sweet and pure and fair. [7]
    Du Bist Wie eine Blume, st. 1

[1] A popular temperance song, *Where Are the
Friends That to Me Were So Dear?* was set to
the tune of *Long, Long Ago.*
[2] Distance sometimes endears friendship, and
absence sweeteneth it. — JAMES HOWELL, *Familiar Letters* [1650], *bk. I, sec. 1, no. 6*
[3] See Artemus Ward, p. 750b.
[4] Therefore a secret unrest
    Tortured thee, brilliant and bold.
      MATTHEW ARNOLD, *Heine's Grave*
                    [1867]
[5] Out of my own great woe
    I make my little songs.
        Translated by ELIZABETH BARRETT
                        BROWNING
[6] Ich weiss nicht, was soll es bedeuten,
    Dass ich so traurig bin;
    Ein Märchen aus alten Zeiten,
    Das kommt mir nicht aus dem Sinn.
[7] Du bist wie eine Blume,
    So hold und schön und rein.

At first I was almost about to despair,
I thought I never could bear it — but I
did bear it. The question remains:
how?   *An Karl von U.*

Don't make a fool of me, my pretty
child, don't greet me under the lindens;
after we get back home, everything will
be learned.   *Poem*

A knight of the holy spirit.
                Harzreise

Good Luck is a giddy maid,
Fickle and restless as a fawn;
She smooths your hair; and then the
    jade
Kisses you quickly, and is gone. [1]
    Das Glück Ist eine Leichte Dirne,
                    st. 1

But Madame Bad Luck scorns all this,
She shows no eagerness for flitting;
But with a long and fervent kiss
Sits by your bed — and brings her
    knitting.   *Ib. st. 2*

For Sleep is good, but Death is better
    still —
The best is never to be born at all. [2]
    Gross Ist die Ähnlichkeit der
             beiden schönen

If one has no heart, one cannot write
for the masses.
        Letter to Julius Campe
          [March 18, 1840]

No talent, but a character.
      Atta Troll [1843], *ch. 24*

Ordinarily he is insane, but he has
lucid moments when he is only stupid.
    Of Savoye, appointed ambassador to Frankfurt by Lamartine
    [1848]

[1] See Dryden, p. 369b.
Good Luck is the gayest of all gay girls,
    Long in one place she will not stay,
Back from your brow she strokes the curls,
    Kisses you quick and flies away.
But Madame Bad Luck soberly comes . . .
    And sits by your bed, and brings her knitting.
      JOHN HAY [1838–1905], *Good and Bad*
                   Luck (after Heine)
[2] See Theognis, p. 77a, and note.

SAMUEL LOVER
1797–1868

Reproof on her lip, but a smile in her
eye.
Rory O'More [1836], st. 1

For dhrames always go by contrairies,
my dear. *Ib. st. 2*

"For there's luck in odd numbers," says
Rory O'More.[1] *Ib. st. 3*

When first I saw sweet Peggy
'Twas on a market day;
A low-backed car she rode, and sat
Upon a tuft of hay.
The Low-Backed Car, st. 1

WILLIAM MOTHERWELL
1797–1835

I've wandered east, I've wandered west,
Through many a weary way;
But never, never can forget
The love o' life's young day!
Jeannie Morrison, st. 1

MARY WOLLSTONECRAFT SHELLEY
1797–1851

I beheld the wretch — the miserable
monster whom I had created.
Frankenstein [1818], *ch. 5*

ALFRED DE VIGNY
1797–1863

I love the sound of the horn, at
night, in the depth of the woods.[2]
Le Cor [1826]

God! how sad is the sound of the
horn deep in the woods![3] *Ib.*

I [Nature] am called a mother, but I
am a grave.
La Maison du Berger [1864]

Love that which will never be seen
twice. *Ib.*

Silence alone is great; all else is weakness. *La Mort du Loup* [1864]

WILHELM I
1797–1888

In Germany, Prussia must make
moral conquests through legislation.
Speech to the Cabinet
[November 8, 1858]

The Prussian army is the people in
arms. *As Prince Regent* [1860]

I now have no time to be tired.
On his deathbed [March 8, 1888]

AUGUSTE COMTE
1798–1857

Love our principle, order our foundation, progress our goal.
Système de Politique Positive
[1851–1854]

Nothing at bottom is real except humanity.[1] *Ib.*

The dead govern the living.
Catéchisme Positiviste [1852]

HOFFMANN VON FALLERSLEBEN
1798–1874

Deutschland, Deutschland über al-
les.
Title of poem [September 1, 1841]

GEORGE LINLEY
1798–1865

Among our ancient mountains,
And from our lovely vales,
Oh, let the prayer re-echo:
"God bless the Prince of Wales!"
God Bless the Prince of Wales,
st. 1

---

[1] See Pliny, p. 133a, and Shakespeare, p. 267b.
[2] J'aime le son du cor, le soir, au fond des bois.
[3] Dieu! que le son du cor est triste au fond
des bois!

[1] Il n'y a, au fond, de réel que l'humanité.

Though lost to sight, to memory dear
Thou ever wilt remain.[1]
Song (attributed)

JULES MICHELET
1798–1874

England is an empire, Germany is a
nation, a race, France is a person.
Histoire de France [1833–1867]

What is the first part of politics?
Education. The second? Education.
And the third? Education.
Le Peuple [1846]

DAVID MACBETH MOIR
1798–1851

From the lone sheiling of the misty is-
land
Mountains divide us, and the waste of
seas —
Yet still the blood is strong, the heart is
Highland,
And we in dreams behold the Hebrides.[2]
Canadian Boat Song

ROBERT POLLOK
1798–1827

Sorrows remembered sweeten present
joy.[3]
The Course of Time, bk. I, l. 464

[1] Absent or dead, still let a friend be dear. —
ALEXANDER POPE, *Epistle to Robert, Earl of Oxford and Mortimer* [1721]
[2] This poem, now generally called *The Lone
Sheiling*, appeared anonymously in Blackwood's
Edinburgh Magazine in September 1829, in a
section called Noctes Ambrosianae, edited by
John Wilson ("Christopher North"). The poem
has been attributed to him, to John Galt, John
Lockart, Scott, David Macbeth Moir, a Scottish
physician and friend of Galt's, and others. Edward MacCurdy in *A Literary Enigma* [1935]
and G. H. Needler in *The Lone Sheiling* [1941]
produce convincing evidence that establish Moir
as the author.
[3] See Virgil, *Aeneid I, 203*, p. 117b.

AMOS BRONSON ALCOTT
1799–1888

One must be a wise reader to quote
wisely and well.
Table Talk. Quotation

To be ignorant of one's ignorance is
the malady of the ignorant.
Ib. Discourse

Why are we not within?
*Outside the Courthouse, Boston,
during the abortive attempt to
free Anthony Burns* [May 26,
1854]. *From* THOMAS WENT-
WORTH HIGGINSON, *Cheerful
Yesterdays* [1899]

The true teacher defends his pupils
against his own personal influence. He
inspires self-trust. He guides their eyes
from himself to the spirit that quickens
him. He will have no disciple.
Orphic Sayings [1840]. *The
Teacher*

Who loves a garden still his Eden
keeps,
Perennial pleasures plants, and wholesome harvests reaps.
Tablets [1868]

I press thee to my heart as Duty's faithful child.
Sonnet to Louisa May Alcott
[1822]

HONORÉ DE BALZAC
1799–1850

It is easier to be a lover than a husband for the simple reason that it is
more difficult to be witty every day
than to say pretty things from time to
time.
Physiologie du Mariage [1829]

I am a galley slave to pen and ink.
Lettres [1832]

Fame is the sun of the dead.
La Recherche de l'Absolu [1834]

I believe in the incomprehensibility of God.

Letter to Madame de Hanska
[1837]

Those sweetly smiling angels with pensive looks, innocent faces, and cash-boxes for hearts.

Cousin Bette [1846], *ch. 15*

RUFUS CHOATE
1799–1859

The courage of New England was the "courage of conscience." It did not rise to that insane and awful passion, the love of war for itself.

Address at Ipswich Centennial
[1834]

The final end of government is not to exert restraint but to do good.

Speech, U.S. Senate [*July* 2, 1841]

There was a state without king or nobles; there was a church without a bishop; [1] there was a people governed by grave magistrates which it had selected, and by equal laws which it had framed.

Speech before the New England Society [*December* 22, 1843]

We join ourselves to no party that does not carry the flag and keep step to the music of the Union.

Letter to the Whig Convention,
Worcester [*October* 1, 1855]

Its constitution the glittering and sounding generalities [2] of natural right

[1] See Junius, p. 1091b.
It [Calvinism] established a religion without a prelate, a government without a king. — GEORGE BANCROFT, *History of the United States* [1834–1876], *vol. III, ch. 6*
Oh, we are weary pilgrims; to this wilderness we bring
A church without a bishop, a state without a king.
The Puritan's Mistake [1844]; *anonymous*
[2] Six years earlier, Choate gave a lecture in Providence, a review of which, by FRANKLIN J. DICKMAN, appeared in the *Journal* of December 14, 1849. Dickman wrote: "We fear that the

which make up the Declaration of Independence.

Letter to the Maine Whig Committee [1856]

EUGÈNE DELACROIX
1799–1863

O young artist, you search for a subject — everything is a subject. Your subject is yourself, your impressions, your emotions in the presence of nature.

Oeuvres Littéraires

The first virtue of a painting is to be a feast for the eyes.

Journal [1893–1895]

Painting is only a bridge linking the painter's mind with that of the viewer.

Ib.

THOMAS HOOD
1799–1845

Ben Battle was a soldier bold,
  And used to war's alarms;
But a cannonball took off his legs,
  So he laid down his arms.

Faithless Nellie Gray [1826], *st. 1*

His death, which happened in his berth,
  At forty-odd befell:
They went and told the sexton, and
  The sexton tolled the bell.

Faithless Sally Brown [1826], *st. 17*

There is a silence where hath been no sound,
There is a silence where no sound may be,
In the cold grave — under the deep, deep sea,
Or in wide desert where no life is found.   *Silence* [1827]

I remember, I remember
The house where I was born,

glittering generalities of the speaker have left an impression more delightful than permanent." It would seem that Dickman must have the credit of inventing the phrase "glittering generalities," unless his report was merely echoing words used by Choate in the lecture.

The little window where the sun
Came peeping in at morn.
                    I Remember, I Remember
                    [1827], *st. 1*

I remember, I remember
The fir-trees dark and high;
I used to think their slender tops
Were close against the sky:
It was a childish ignorance,
But now 'tis little joy
To know I'm farther off from heaven
Than when I was a boy.   *Ib. st. 4*

She stood breast-high amid the corn.[1]
                    Ruth [1827], *st. 1*

And there is even a happiness
That makes the heart afraid.
                    Ode to Melancholy [1827]

There's not a string attuned to mirth
But has its chord in melancholy.   *Ib.*

But evil is wrought by want of thought,
As well as want of heart.
                    The Lady's Dream [1827], *st. 16*

I saw old Autumn in the misty morn
Stand shadowless like silence, listening
To silence.   *Autumn* [1827], *st. 1*

Straight down the Crooked Lane,
And all round the Square.
                    A Plain Direction, st. 1

Two stern-faced men set out from Lynn
    Through the cold and heavy mist,
And Eugene Aram walked between,
    With gyves upon his wrist.
                    The Dream of Eugene Aram
                    [1829], *st. 36*

Never go to France
    Unless you know the lingo,
If you do, like me,
    You will repent, by jingo.
                    French and English [1839], *st. 1*

No warmth, no cheerfulness, no health-
    ful ease,
No comfortable feel in any member —
No shade, no shine, no butterflies, no
    bees,
No fruits, no flowers, no leaves, no
    birds,
November!   No

[1] See Keats, p. 583a.

Seem'd washing his hands with invisible
    soap
In imperceptible water.
                    *Miss Kilmansegg and Her Pre-
                    cious Leg* [1841–1843]. *Her
                    Christening, st. 10*

O bed! O bed! delicious bed!
That heaven upon earth to the weary
    head.   *Ib. Her Dream, st. 7*

Homemade dishes that drive one from
    home.   *Ib. Her Misery, st. 1*

Another tumble! — that's his precious
    nose!
                    *Parental Ode to My Infant Son,
                    st. 3*

With fingers weary and worn,
    With eyelids heavy and red,
A woman sat in unwomanly rags
    Plying her needle and thread —
        Stitch! stitch! stitch!
In poverty, hunger, and dirt.
                    The Song of the Shirt [1843], *st. 1*

She sang the Song of the Shirt.   *Ib.*

Work! work! work!   *Ib. st. 2*

O men, with sisters dear!
    O men, with mothers and wives!
It is not linen you're wearing out,
    But human creatures' lives! [1]
                            Ib. st. 4

O God! that bread should be so dear,
And flesh and blood so cheap!
                            Ib. st. 5

A wife who preaches in her gown,
And lectures in her nightdress.
                    The Surplice Question, st. 2

One more unfortunate,
    Weary of breath,
Rashly importunate,
    Gone to her death!

Take her up tenderly,
    Lift her with care;
Fashioned so slenderly,
    Young, and so fair!
                    The Bridge of Sighs [1844], *st. 1, 2*

[1] See Scott, p. 520b.

Alas for the rarity
Of Christian charity
   Under the sun! [1]
    The Bridge of Sighs, st. 9

O'er the earth there comes a bloom;
Sunny light for sullen gloom;
Warm perfume for vapor cold —
I smell the rose above the mold!
    Farewell, Life [1845]*, st. 2*

MARY HOWITT
1799–1888

"Will you walk into my parlor?" said
  the spider to the fly;
" 'Tis the prettiest little parlor that
  ever you did spy."
    The Spider and the Fly

Oh! poverty is a weary thing, 'tis full of
  grief and pain;
It keepeth down the soul of man, as
  with an iron chain;
It maketh even the little child with
  heavy sighs complain.
    The Pet Lamb

THOMAS NOEL
1799–1861

Rattle his bones over the stones!
He's only a pauper, whom nobody
  owns!
    The Pauper's Drive, st. 1

ALEXANDER PUSHKIN
1799–1837

The mind's dispassionate notations,
The heart's asides, inscribed in tears.
    Eugene Onegin [2] [1823]*,*
    dedication

For he possessed the happy gift
Of unaffected conversation:
To skim one topic here, one there,
Keep silent with an expert's air
In too exacting disputation.
    Ib. ch. 1, st. 5

Contented ever with his life,
Himself, his dinner, and his wife.
    Ib. st. 12

Rousseau — please pardon this digres-
  sion —
Could not conceive how solemn Grimm
Dared clean his nails in front of him.
    Eugene Onegin, ch. 1, st. 24

Custom is lord of all mankind.
    Ib. st. 25

A malady to whose causation
We have, alas, as yet no clues,
Known as the Spleen to Albion's na-
  tion,
In our parlance just: The Blues.
    Ib. st. 38

Habit is Heaven's own redress:
It takes the place of happiness.[1]
    Ib. 2, st. 31

Pimen [*writing by lamplight*]: One
  more, the final record, and my
  annals
Are ended, and fulfilled the duty laid
By God on me, a sinner. Not in vain
Hath God appointed me for many years
A witness, teaching me the art of let-
  ters;
A day will come when some laborious
  monk
Will bring to light my zealous, name-
  less toil,
Kindle, as I, his lamp, and from the
  parchment
Shaking the dust of ages, will transcribe
My chronicles.
    Boris Godunov [2]
    [*written 1825*]

Like to some magistrate grown gray in
  office
Calmly he contemplates alike the just
And unjust, with indifference he notes
Evil and good, and knows not wrath
  nor pity.   *Ib.*

Ah! heavy art thou, crown of Mo-
  nomakh!   *Ib.*

  Mosalsky: Good folk! Maria Godu-
nov and her son Feodor have poisoned
themselves. We have seen their dead
bodies. [*The people are silent with horror.*] Why are you silent? Cry, Long live
Czar Dimitry Ivanovich! [*The people
are speechless.*]   *Ib.*

---

[1] See Southey, p. 533a, and O'Reilly, p. 807a.
[2] Translated by WALTER AINDT.

[1] See Burke, p. 452a.
[2] Translated by ALFRED HAYES.

And thus he mused: "From here, indeed
Shall we strike terror in the Swede;
And here a city, by our labor
Founded, shall gall our haughty neighbor;
"Here cut" — so Nature gives command —
"Your window through on Europe: [1]
stand
Firm-footed by the sea, unchanging!"
The Bronze Horseman [written 1833]

JOHN BROWN
1800–1859

Had I so interfered in behalf of the rich, the powerful, the intelligent, the so-called great, or in behalf of any of their friends . . . every man in this court would have deemed it an act worthy of reward rather than punishment.
Last Speech to the Court [November 2, 1859]

I am yet too young to understand that God is any respecter of persons. [2] I believe that to have interfered as I have done . . . in behalf of His despised poor, was not wrong, but right. Now, if it is deemed necessary that I should forfeit my life for the furtherance of the ends of justice, and mingle my blood further with the blood of my children, and with the blood of millions in this slave country whose rights are disregarded by wicked, cruel, and unjust enactments, I submit: so let it be done!
Ib.

[1] Algarotti has somewhere said: Pétersbourg est la fênetre, par laquelle la Russie regarde en Europe. — AUTHOR'S NOTE, *The Bronze Horseman*
I am at length going to give you some account of this new city, of the great window lately opened in the North, through which Russia looks into Europe. — FRANCESCO ALGAROTTI, *Letters About Russia* [June 30, 1739]
[2] See *Acts 10:34*, p. 50a.
The Father, who without respect of persons judgeth according to every man's work. — *I Peter 1:17*

This *is* a beautiful country.
Remark as he rode to the gallows, seated on his coffin [December 2, 1859]

JULIA CRAWFORD
1800–1885

Kathleen Mavourneen! the gray dawn is breaking,
The horn of the hunter is heard on the hill.
Kathleen Mavourneen [1835], *st. 1*

Oh! hast thou forgotten this day we must part?
It may be for years, and it may be forever;
Then why art thou silent, thou voice of my heart?
Ib.

THOMAS BABINGTON, LORD MACAULAY
1800–1859

That is the best government which desires to make the people happy, and knows how to make them happy.
On Mitford's History of Greece [1824]

Free trade, one of the greatest blessings which a government can confer on a people, is in almost every country unpopular.
Ib.

Press where ye see my white plume shine, amidst the ranks of war,
And be your oriflamme today the helmet of Navarre.
Ivry [1824], *l. 29*

Nobles by the right of an earlier creation, and priests by the imposition of a mightier hand.
On Milton [1825]

The dust and silence of the upper shelf.
Ib.

As civilization advances, poetry almost necessarily declines.
Ib.

Perhaps no person can be a poet, or even can enjoy poetry, without a certain unsoundness of mind.
Ib.

Nothing is so useless as a general maxim.
On Niccolò de Machiavelli [1827]

The English Bible — a book which if everything else in our language should perish, would alone suffice to show the whole extent of its beauty and power.
On John Dryden [1828]

His imagination resembled the wings of an ostrich. It enabled him to run, though not to soar.   *Ib.*

Ye diners-out from whom we guard our spoons.[1]   *Political Georgics*

Men are never so likely to settle a question rightly as when they discuss it freely.   *Southey's Colloquies* [1830]

A single breaker may recede; but the tide is evidently coming in.[2]   *Ib.*

We know no spectacle so ridiculous as the British public in one of its periodical fits of morality.
On Moore's Life of Lord Byron [1831]

From the poetry of Lord Byron they drew a system of ethics compounded of misanthropy and voluptuousness — a system in which the two great commandments were to hate your neighbor and to love your neighbor's wife. *Ib.*

Boswell is the first of biographers.[3]
On Boswell's Life of Johnson [1831]

That wonderful book, while it obtains admiration from the most fastidious critics, is loved by those who are too simple to admire it.
On Bunyan's Pilgrim's Progress [1831]

Reform, that you may preserve.
Debate on the First Reform Bill [March 2, 1831]

The conformation of his mind was such that whatever was little seemed to him great, and whatever was great seemed to him little.
On Horace Walpole [1833]

Such night in England ne'er had been, nor ne'er again shall be.
The Armada [1833], *l.* 34

An acre in Middlesex is better than a principality in Utopia.[1]
On Lord Bacon [1837]

Every schoolboy knows who imprisoned Montezuma, and who strangled Atahualpa. *On Lord Clive* [1840]

She [the Roman Catholic Church] may still exist in undiminished vigor when some traveler from New Zealand shall, in the midst of a vast solitude, take his stand on a broken arch of London Bridge to sketch the ruins of St. Paul's.[2]
On Ranke's History of the Popes [1840]

She [the Catholic Church] thoroughly understands what no other Church has ever understood, how to deal with enthusiasts. *Ib.*

[1] See Tennyson, p. 647b.
[2] Macaulay used a similar image in his review [1824] of MITFORD, *Greece,* and in his review [1829] of MILL, *Essay on Government.*
Who knows but that hereafter some traveler like myself will sit down upon the banks of the Seine, the Thames, or the Zuyder Zee, where now, in the tumult of enjoyment, the heart and the eyes are too slow to take in the multitude of sensations? Who knows but he will sit down solitary amid silent ruins, and weep a people inurned and their greatness changed into an empty name? — CONSTANTIN DE VOLNEY [1757–1820], *Ruins, ch. 11*
See Horace Walpole, p. 442a-b.
In the firm expectation that when London shall be a habitation of bitterns, when St. Paul and Westminster Abbey shall stand shapeless and nameless ruins in the midst of an unpeopled marsh, when the piers of Waterloo Bridge shall become the nuclei of islets of reeds and osiers, and cast the jagged shadows of their broken arches on the solitary stream, some transatlantic commentator will be weighing in the scales of some new and now unimagined system of criticism the respective merits of the Bells and the Fudges and their historians. — SHELLEY, *Peter Bell the Third* [1819], *dedication*

[1] The louder he talked of his honor, the faster we counted our spoons. — EMERSON, *Conduct of Life* [1860], *Worship*
[2] See Arthur Hugh Clough, p. 688b.
[3] See p. 429b note 2.

The Chief Justice was rich, quiet, and infamous.

On Warren Hastings [1841]

I shall not be satisfied unless I produce something which shall for a few days supersede the last fashionable novel on the tables of young ladies.

Letter to Macvey Napier
[November 5, 1841]

In order that he might rob a neighbor whom he had promised to defend, black men fought on the coast of Coromandel and red men scalped each other by the great lakes of North America. *On Frederick the Great* [1842]

We hardly know an instance of the strength and weakness of human nature so striking and so grotesque as the character of this haughty, vigilant, resolute, sagacious blue-stocking, half Mithridates and half Trissotin, bearing up against a world in arms, with an ounce of poison in one pocket and a quire of bad verses in the other. *Ib.*

Lars Porsena of Clusium
By the Nine Gods he swore
That the great house of Tarquin
Should suffer wrong no more.
By the Nine Gods he swore it,
And named a trysting day,
And bade his messengers ride forth
East and west and south and north,
To summon his array.

Lays of Ancient Rome [1842].
Horatius, st. 1

To every man upon this earth
Death cometh soon or late;
And how can man die better
Than facing fearful odds
For the ashes of his fathers,
And the temples of his gods?

Ib. st. 27

Those behind cried "Forward!"
And those before cried "Back!"

Ib. st. 50

Oh, Tiber! father Tiber!
To whom the Romans pray,
A Roman's life, a Roman's arms,
Take thou in charge this day.

Ib. st. 59

And even the ranks of Tuscany
Could scarce forbear to cheer.

Horatius, st. 60

A man who has never looked on Niagara has but a faint idea of a cataract; and he who has not read Barère's *Memoirs* may be said not to know what it is to lie.

*Review of Mémoires de
Bertrand Barère* [1843]

The highest proof of virtue is to possess boundless power without abusing it.

Review of AIKIN, *Life of
Addison* [1843]

He [Richard Steele] was a rake among scholars, and a scholar among rakes. *Ib.*

There you sit,[1] doing penance for the disingenuousness of years.

Speech, House of Commons
[April 14, 1845]

Forget all feuds, and shed one English tear
O'er English dust. A broken heart lies here.

Epitaph on a Jacobite [1845]

Those who compare the age in which their lot has fallen with a golden age [2] which exists only in imagination, may talk of degeneracy and decay; but no man who is correctly informed as to the past will be disposed to take a morose or desponding view of the present.

History of England [1849–1861],
vol. I, ch. 1

I shall cheerfully bear the reproach of having descended below the dignity of history if I can succeed in placing before the English of the nineteenth century a true picture of the life of their ancestors. *Ib.*

The Puritan hated bear-baiting, not because it gave pain to the bear, but because it gave pleasure to the spectators.[3] *Ib. 2*

[1] Sir Robert Peel.
[2] See Horace, p. 122b.
[3] Even bear-baiting was esteemed heathenish and unchristian: the sport of it, not the inhumanity, gave offense. — HUME, *History of England* [1754–1757], *vol. I, ch. 62*

There were gentlemen and there were seamen in the navy of Charles II. But the seamen were not gentlemen, and the gentlemen were not seamen.
History of England
vol. I, ch. 3

The ambassador [of Russia] and the grandees who accompanied him were so gorgeous that all London crowded to stare at them, and so filthy that nobody dared to touch them. They came to the court balls dropping pearls and vermin.
Ib. V, 23

Your Constitution is all sail and no anchor.
Letter to H. S. Randall, author of a Life of Thomas Jefferson
[May 23, 1857]

Soon fades the spell, soon comes the night;
Say will it not be then the same,
Whether we played the black or white,
Whether we lost or won the game?
Sermon in a Churchyard, st. 8

HELMUTH VON MOLTKE
1800–1891

First ponder, then dare.[1]
Attributed aphorism

The fate of every nation rests in its own power.
To the German Reichstag
[March 1, 1880]

A war, even the most victorious, is a national misfortune.   *Letter [1880]*

RICHARD BETHELL,
LORD WESTBURY
1800–1873

Take a note of that; his Lordship says he will turn it over in what he is pleased to call his mind.[2]
Nash, *Life of Lord Westbury*
[1888], vol. I, p. 158

[1] Erst wägen, dann wagen.
[2] Reported to have been spoken in an audible whisper, from the barristers' table, in reference to a presiding judge. According to Nash, Lord Westbury always disclaimed invention of the mot.

DAVID GLASGOW
FARRAGUT
1801–1870

Damn the torpedoes — full speed ahead![1]
At the Battle of Mobile Bay
[August 5, 1864]

JOHN HENRY,
CARDINAL NEWMAN
1801–1890

Time hath a taming hand.
Persecution [1832], st. 3

Lead, kindly Light, amid the encircling gloom;
Lead thou me on!
The night is dark, and I am far from home;
Lead thou me on!
Keep thou my feet: I do not ask to see
The distant scene; one step enough for me.
The Pillar of Cloud [1833].
Lead Kindly Light, st. 1

And with the morn, those angel faces smile
Which I have loved long since, and lost awhile.   *Ib. st. 3*

Growth is the only evidence of life.
Apologia pro Vita Sua [1864]

It is thy very energy of thought
Which keeps thee from thy God.
Dream of Gerontius [1866],
pt. III

Who lets his feelings run
In soft luxurious flow,
Shrinks when hard service must be done,
And faints at every woe.
Flowers Without Fruit [1868]

Living Nature, not dull Art
Shall plan my ways and rule my heart.
Nature and Art [1868], st. 12

[1] This is the most famous version. The "torpedoes" were mines anchored by the Confederates in Mobile Bay.

O Lord, support us all the day long, until the shadows lengthen and the evening comes, and the busy world is hushed, and the fever of life is over, and our work is done. Then in thy mercy grant us a safe lodging, and a holy rest, and peace at the last.

> *Sermon [1834]; included in the Book of Common Prayer, p. 571*

It is almost a definition of a gentleman to say he is one who never inflicts pain.

> *Idea of a University [1873]. The Man of the World*

A great memory does not make a philosopher, any more than a dictionary can be called a grammar.[1]

> *Ib. Knowledge in Relation to Learning*

Ex umbris et imaginibus in veritatem [From shadows and symbols into the truth]!

> *His Own Epitaph at Edgbaston*

BRIGHAM YOUNG
1801–1877

This is the place!

> *On first seeing the valley of the Great Salt Lake [2] [July 24, 1847]*

LYDIA MARIA CHILD
1802–1880

Over the river and through the wood,
To grandfather's house we'll go;
    The horse knows the way
    To carry the sleigh,
Through the white and drifted snow.

> *Thanksgiving Day, st. 1*

[1] See Confucius, p. 71a; Lao Tzu, p. 75b; and Heraclitus, p. 77b.

[2] Brigham Young and 142 men, three women and two children were the vanguard of Mormon pioneers who explored westward from Nebraska. Mahonri M. Young, noted sculptor and grandson of Brigham Young, designed the "This Is the Place Monument," dedicated July 24, 1947.

DAVID CHRISTY
1802 – c. 1868

Cotton is King; or, The Economical Relations of Slavery.

> *Title of book [1855] [1]*

ALEXANDRE DUMAS
THE ELDER
1802–1870

All for one, one for all, that is our device.[2]

> *The Three Musketeers [1844], ch. 9*

Nothing succeeds like success.[3]

> *Ange Pitou [1854], vol. I, p. 72*

Let us look for the woman.[4]

> *The Mohicans of Paris [1854–1855], vol. III, ch. 10, 11*

VICTOR HUGO
1802–1885

These two halves of God, the Pope and the emperor.

> *Hernani [1830], act IV, sc. 2*

God became a man, granted. The devil became a woman.[5]

> *Ruy Blas [1838], act II, sc. 5*

Popularity? It is glory's small change.

> *Ib. III, 5*

Greater than the tread of mighty armies is an idea whose time has come.[6]

> *Histoire d'un Crime [written 1852], conclusion*

[1] Take away *time is money,* and what is left of England? take away *cotton is king,* and what is left of America? — VICTOR HUGO, *Les Misérables* [1862]. *Marius, bk. IV, ch. 4*

[2] See Shakespeare, p. 220a.

[3] Rien ne réussit comme le succès. — *French proverb*

[4] The phrase "Cherchez la femme" is attributed to JOSEPH FOUCHÉ [1763–1820].

[5] Dieu s'est fait homme; soit. Le diable s'est fait femme.

[6] On résiste à l'invasion des armées; on ne résiste pas à l'invasion des idées. (Literally, one can resist the invasion of armies, but not the invasion of ideas.)

Waterloo! Waterloo! Waterloo! Dismal plain! [1]
> *Les Châtiments* [1853],
> *L'Expiation*

The eye was in the tomb and stared at Cain. *La Conscience* [1859]

You have created a new thrill.[2]
> *Letter to Baudelaire* [October 6, 1859]

The supreme happiness of life is the conviction that we are loved.
> *Les Misérables* [3] [1862].
> *Fantine, bk. V, ch. 4*

Great grief is a divine and terrible radiance which transfigures the wretched. *Ib. 13*

Napoleon . . . mighty somnambulist of a vanished dream.
> *Ib. Cosette, bk. I, ch. 13*

Waterloo is a battle of the first rank won by a captain of the second.
> *Ib. 16*

Would you realize what Revolution is, call it Progress; and would you realize what Progress is, call it Tomorrow. *Ib. 17*

What is that to the Infinite?
> *Ib. 18*

Great blunders are often made, like large ropes, of a multitude of fibers.
> *Ib. V, 10*

Upon the first goblet he read this inscription, *monkey wine;* upon the second, *lion wine;* upon the third, *sheep wine;* upon the fourth, *swine wine.* These four inscriptions expressed the four descending degrees of drunkenness: the first, that which enlivens; the second, that which irritates; the third, that which stupefies; finally the last, that which brutalizes.[4] *Ib. VI, 9*

A man is not idle because he is absorbed in thought. There is a visible labor and there is an invisible labor.
> *Le Misérables. Cosette,*
> *bk. VII, ch. 8*

No one ever keeps a secret so well as a child. *Ib. VIII, 8*

The peculiarity of prudery is to multiply sentinels, in proportion as the fortress is less threatened.[1]
> *Ib. Marius, bk. II, ch. 8*

He had the appearance of a caryatid on vacation; he was supporting nothing but his reverie. *Ib. IV, 2*

Social prosperity means man happy, the citizen free, the nation great.
> *Ib. Saint Denis, bk. I, ch. 4*

Nothing is more dangerous than discontinued labor; it is habit lost. A habit easy to abandon, difficult to resume.
> *Ib. II, 1*

Thought is the labor of the intellect, reverie is its pleasure. *Ib.*

Where the telescope ends, the microscope begins. Which of the two has the grander view? *Ib. III, 3*

A compliment is something like a kiss through a veil. *Ib. VIII, 1*

Great perils have this beauty, that they bring to light the fraternity of strangers. *Ib. XII, 4*

Philosophy is the microscope of thought.
> *Ib. Jean Valjean, bk. II, ch. 2*

The sublimest song to be heard on earth is the lisping of the human soul on the lips of children.
> *Ninety-Three* [1879], *pt. III,*
> *bk. III, ch. 1*

To rise at six, to dine at ten,
To sup at six, to sleep at ten,
Makes a man live for ten times ten.
> *Inscription over the door of*
> *Hugo's study*

---

[1] Waterloo! Waterloo! Waterloo! Morne plaine!
[2] Vous créez un frisson nouveau.
[3] Translated by CHARLES E. WILBOUR.
[4] See George Herbert, p. 322b.

[1] That is the refuge of all old coquettes; it is hard for them to be deserted by the gallants, and from such a desertion, in their spite, they take refuge in the trade of a prude. — MOLIÈRE, *Tartuffe* [1667], *act I, sc. 1*

I represent a party which does not yet exist: the party of revolution, civilization.

This party will make the twentieth century.

There will issue from it first the United States of Europe, then the United States of the World.
On the wall of the room in which Hugo died, Place des Vosges, Paris

LETITIA ELIZABETH LANDON
1802–1838

Few, save the poor, feel for the poor.
The Poor

Were it not better to forget
Than but remember and regret?
Despondency

GEORGE POPE MORRIS
1802–1864

Woodman, spare that tree!
 Touch not a single bough! [1]
In youth it sheltered me,
 And I'll protect it now.
Woodman, Spare That Tree [1830], st. 1

The iron-armed soldier, the true-hearted soldier,
The gallant old soldier of Tippecanoe.[2]
Campaign song for William Henry Harrison [1840]

A song for our banner! The watchword recall
Which gave the Republic her station:
"United we stand, divided we fall!" [3]
It made and preserves us a nation! [4]
The Flag of Our Union

[1] See Campbell, p. 538a.
[2] Morris's words, sung to the tune of *The Old Oaken Bucket*, were immensely popular. — BEN PERLEY POORE, *Reminiscences* [1886]
[3] See John Dickinson, p. 460b.
[4] Bless'd with victory and peace, may our Heaven-rescued land
 Praise the Power that hath made and preserved us a nation.
 FRANCIS SCOTT KEY, *The Star-Spangled Banner* [1814], st. 4

WINTHROP MACKWORTH PRAED
1802–1839

His talk was like a stream, which runs
With rapid change from rocks to roses;
It slipped from politics to puns;
It passed from Mahomet to Moses.
The Vicar, st. 5

Dame Fortune is a fickle gipsy,
And always blind, and often tipsy;
Sometimes for years and years together,
She'll bless you with the sunniest weather,
Bestowing honor, pudding, pence,
You can't imagine why or whence;
Then in a moment — Presto, pass! —
Your joys are withered like the grass.
The Haunted Tree

FRIEDRICH JULIUS STAHL
1802–1861

Authority, not majority.
Speech before the Erfurt Parliament [April 11, 1850]

WILLIAM ALLEN
1803–1879

Fifty-four forty, or fight! [1]
Speech, U.S. Senate [1844]

THOMAS LOVELL BEDDOES
1803–1849

The anchor heaves, the ship swings free,
The sails swell full. To sea, to sea!
Sailor's Song, st. 2

If there were dreams to sell,
 What would you buy?

[1] Phrase adopted as the slogan of the war party in the presidential election of 1844. At the time, war with England over the Oregon question seemed imminent. The Democratic convention of 1844 demanded the reoccupation of the whole of Oregon up to 54°40′, but the new President, James K. Polk, compomised with Great Britain on the forty-ninth parallel.

Some cost a passing-bell;
  Some a light sigh.
                    Dream Pedlary

If thou wilt ease thine heart
Of love and all its smart,
Then sleep, dear, sleep.

But wilt thou cure thy heart
Of love and all its smart,
Then die, dear, die.
            Death's Jest Book [1850]

GEORGE BORROW
1803–1881

There's night and day, brother, both
sweet things; sun, moon, and stars,
brother, all sweet things; there's likewise a wind on the heath. Life is very
sweet, brother; who would wish to die?
            Lavengro [1851], *ch. 25*

I learned . . . to fear God, and to
take my own part.   *Ib. 86*

Youth is the only season for enjoyment, and the first twenty-five years of
one's life are worth all the rest of the
longest life of man, even though those
five-and-twenty be spent in penury and
contempt, and the rest in the possession
of wealth, honors, respectability.
        The Romany Rye [1857], *ch. 30*

EDWARD
BULWER-LYTTON
1803–1873

A good heart is better than all the
heads in the world.
            The Disowned [1828], *ch. 33*

The easiest person to deceive is one's
own self.   *Ib. 42*

Rank is a great beautifier.
        The Lady of Lyons [1838],
                    act II, sc. 1

Love, like Death,
Levels all ranks, and lays the shepherd's
  crook
Beside the scepter.   *Ib. III, 2*

Beneath the rule of men entirely great,
The pen is mightier than the sword.[1]
        Richelieu [1839], *act II, sc. 2*

In the lexicon of youth, which fate
  reserves
For a bright manhood, there is no such
  word
As — *fail*.   *Ib.*

Out-babying Wordsworth and out-
glittering Keats.[2]
        The New Timon [1846], *pt. I*

In science, read, by preference, the
newest works; in literature, the oldest.
The classic literature is always modern.
        *Caxtonia. Hints on Mental
                    Culture*

In science, address the few, in literature the many. In science, the few must
dictate opinion to the many; in literature, the many, sooner or later, force
their judgment on the few.
        Ib. Readers and Writers

WILLIAM DRIVER
1803–1886

I name thee Old Glory.
        *As the flag was hoisted to the
            masthead of his brig* [3]

RALPH WALDO
EMERSON
1803–1882

Good-bye, proud world! I'm going
  home;
Thou art not my friend and I'm not
  thine.[4]
        Poems [1847]. *Good-bye, st. 1*

For what are they all in their high conceit,

[1] See Cervantes, p. 195b, and Burton, p. 311a.
Eloquence a hundred times has turned the
scale of war and peace at will. — EMERSON,
Progress of Culture [1867]
[2] Tennyson.
[3] On August 10, 1831, a large American flag
was presented to Driver, captain of the *Charles
Doggett*, by a band of women in recognition of
his bringing the British mutineers of the ship
Bounty from Tahiti back to their former home,
Pitcairn Island. The flag is now in the Smith-
sonian Institution, Washington, D.C.
[4] See Johnson, p. 433b, and Byron, p. 556b.

When man in the bush with God may
    meet?   *Poems. Good-bye, st.* 4

Nor knowest thou what argument
Thy life to thy neighbor's creed has
    lent.
All are needed by each one;
Nothing is fair or good alone.
           Ib. Each and All, st. 1

I wiped away the weeds and foam,
I fetched my sea-born treasures home;
But the poor, unsightly, noisome
    things
Had left their beauty on the shore,
With the sun and the sand and the
    wild uproar.   *Ib. st.* 3

I like a church; I like a cowl;
I love a prophet of the soul;
And on my heart monastic aisles
Fall like sweet strains or pensive smiles;
Yet not for all his faith can see
Would I that cowlèd churchman be.
           Ib. The Problem, st. 1

Not from a vain or shallow thought
His awful Jove young Phidias brought.
           Ib. st. 2

The hand that rounded Peter's dome,
And groined the aisles of Christian
    Rome,
Wrought in a sad sincerity;
Himself from God he could not free;
He builded better than he knew; —
The conscious stone to beauty grew.
           Ib.

Earth proudly wears the Parthenon
As the best gem upon her zone.
           Ib. st. 3

The passive Master lent his hand
To the vast soul that o'er him planned.[1]
           Ib.

Announced by all the trumpets of the
    sky,
Arrives the snow.   *Ib. The Snowstorm*
      Enclosed
In a tumultuous privacy of storm.
           Ib.

[1] This couplet is inscibed on the boulder
marking Emerson's grave in Sleepy Hollow
Cemetery, Concord, Massachusetts.

The frolic architecture of the snow.
      Poems. The Snowstorm

Life is too short to waste
In critic peep or cynic bark,
Quarrel or reprimand:
'Twill soon be dark;
Up! mind thine own aim, and
God speed the mark!   *Ib. To J.W.*

There's no rood has not a star above
    it.   *Ib. Musketaquid*

    All sorts of things and weather
Must be taken in together,
To make up a year
And a Sphere.
    *Ib. Fable, The Mountain and the
              Squirrel*

In May, when sea winds pierced our
    solitudes,
I found the fresh Rhodora in the
    woods.   *Ib. The Rhodora*

Rhodora! if the sages ask thee why
This charm is wasted on the earth and
    sky,
Tell them, dear, that if eyes were made
    for seeing,
Then Beauty is its own excuse for
    being.   *Ib.*

For Nature beats in perfect tune,
And rounds with rhyme her every rune,
Whether she work in land or sea,
Or hide underground her alchemy.
Thou canst not wave thy staff in air,
Or dip thy paddle in the lake,
But it carves the bow of beauty there,
And the ripples in rhymes the oar for-
    sake.   *Ib. Woodnotes II*

Things are in the saddle,
And ride mankind.
        *Ib. Ode Inscribed to
        W. H. Channing*

There are two laws discrete,
Not reconciled —
Law for man, and law for thing.   *Ib.*

Olympian bards who sung
    Divine ideas below,

Which always find us young,
  And always keep us so.
                  Poems. Ode to Beauty

Give all to love;
Obey thy heart;
Friends, kindred, days,
Estate, good fame,
Plans, credit and the Muse,
Nothing refuse.
          Ib. Give All to Love, st. 1

Heartily know,
When half-gods go,
The gods arrive.   *Ib. st. 4*

Love not the flower they pluck, and
    know it not,
And all their botany is Latin names.
                  Ib. Blight

By the rude bridge that arched the
    flood,
Their flag to April's breeze unfurled,
Here once the embattled farmers stood,
And fired the shot heard round the
    world.
          *Ib. Hymn Sung at the Com-
          pletion of the Battle Monu-
          ment, Concord [July 4, 1837],
          st. 1*

Hast thou named all the birds without
    a gun? [1]
Loved the wood-rose, and left it on its
    stalk? [2]   *Ib. Forbearance*

"Pass in, pass in," the angels say,
"In to the upper doors,
Nor count compartments of the floors,
But mount to paradise
By the stairway of surprise."
                  Ib. Merlin I

God said, I am tired of kings,
I suffer them no more;
Up to my ear the morning brings
The outrage of the poor.
          *May-Day and Other Pieces
          [1867]. Boston Hymn,[3] st. 2*

[1] See S. W. Foss, p. 846a.
[2] See Lytton, p. 741b.
[3] Read at a celebration in Boston of Emancipation Day, January 1, 1863.

Today unbind the captive,
So only are ye unbound;
Lift up a people from the dust,
Trump of their rescue, sound!
          *May-Day and Other Pieces.
          Boston Hymn, st. 17*

Oh, tenderly the haughty day
Fills his blue urn with fire.
                  Ib. Ode, st. 1

Go put your creed into your deed,
Nor speak with double tongue.
                  Ib. st. 5

I think no virtue goes with size.
                  Ib. The Titmouse

So nigh is grandeur to our dust,
  So near is God to man,
When Duty whispers low, *Thou must,*
  The youth replies, *I can.*
                  Ib. Voluntaries, III

Nor sequent centuries could hit
Orbit and sum of Shakespeare's wit.
                  Ib. Solution

Born for success he seemed,
With grace to win, with heart to hold,
With shining gifts that took all eyes.
                  Ib. In Memoriam E.B.E.

Nor mourn the unalterable Days
That Genius goes and Folly stays.
                  Ib.

Fear not, then, thou child infirm,
There's no god dare wrong a worm.
                  Ib. Compensation, I

He thought it happier to be dead,
To die for Beauty, than live for bread.
                  Ib. Beauty

Wilt thou seal up the avenues of ill?
Pay every debt, as if God wrote the bill.
                  Ib. "Suum Cuique"

Too busied with the crowded hour to
    fear to live or die.   *Ib. Nature*

Daughters of Time, the hypocritic
    Days,
Muffled and dumb like barefoot
    dervishes,
And marching single in an endless file,
Bring diadems and fagots in their
    hands.   *Ib. Days*

I, too late,
Under her solemn fillet saw the scorn.
May-Day and Other Pieces.
Days

It is time to be old,
To take in sail.   *Ib. Terminus*

Obey the voice at eve obeyed at prime.
Ib.

Though love repine, and reason chafe,
There came a voice without reply —
" 'Tis man's perdition to be safe,
When for the truth he ought to
        die."   *Ib. Sacrifice*

For what avail the plow or sail,
Or land or life, if freedom fail?
        Ib. Boston, st. 5

If the red slayer think he slays,
    Or if the slain think he is slain,
They know not well the subtle ways
    I keep, and pass, and turn again.[1]
            Ib. Brahma

They reckon ill who leave me out;
    When me they fly, I am the wings;
I am the doubter and the doubt,
    And I the hymn the Brahmin sings.
                Ib.

That book is good
Which puts me in a working mood.
Unless to Thought is added Will,
Apollo is an imbecile.
    Ib. Fragments on the Poetic Gift

In the vaunted works of Art
The master stroke is Nature's part.[2]
        Ib. Art

I am the owner of the sphere,
Of the seven stars and the solar year,
Of Caesar's hand, and Plato's brain,
Of Lord Christ's heart, and Shake-
    speare's strain.   *Ib. History*

Ever from one who comes tomorrow
Men wait their good and truth to bor-
    row.   *Ib. Merlin's Song*

[1] See *The Upanishads*, p. 62a.
[2] Nature paints the best part of a picture, carves the best part of the statue, builds the best part of the house, and speaks the best part of the oration. — *Society and Solitude* [1870], *Art*

The music that can deepest reach,
And cure all ill, is cordial speech.
        May-Day and Other Pieces.
        Merlin's Song

Some of your hurts you have cured,
And the sharpest you still have sur-
    vived,
But what torments of grief you en-
    dured
From evils which never arrived! [1]
    Ib. Borrowing [from the French]

A ruddy drop of manly blood
    The surging sea outweighs,
The world uncertain comes and goes,
    The lover rooted stays.
            Ib. Friendship

To different minds, the same world is
a hell, and a heaven.
        Journal [December 20, 1822]

Four snakes gliding up and down a
hollow for no purpose that I could see
— not to eat, not for love, but only
gliding.   *Ib. [April 11, 1834]*

I wish to write such rhymes as shall
not suggest a restraint, but contrariwise
the wildest freedom.
        Ib. [June 27, 1839]

You shall have joy, or you shall have
power, said God; you shall not have
both.   *Ib. [October 1842]*

The sky is the daily bread of the
eyes.   *Ib. [May 25, 1843]*

Poetry must be as new as foam, and
as old as the rock.   *Ib. [March 1845]*

I hate quotations. Tell me what you
know.   *Ib. [May 1849]*

Blessed are those who have no talent!
        Ib. [February 1850]

The word *liberty* in the mouth of
Mr. Webster sounds like the word *love*
in the mouth of a courtesan.
        Ib. [February 12 (?), 1851]

[1] Let us be of good cheer, however, remembering that the misfortunes hardest to bear are
those which never come. — JAMES RUSSELL LOW-
ELL, *Democracy and Addresses* [1884]

I trust a good deal to common fame, as we all must. If a man has good corn, or wood, or boards, or pigs, to sell, or can make better chairs or knives, crucibles or church organs, than anybody else, you will find a broad hard-beaten road to his house, though it be in the woods.[1]

Journal [February 1855]

The blazing evidence of immortality is our dissatisfaction with any other solution.   *Ib. [July 1855]*

Undoubtedly we have no questions to ask which are unanswerable. We must trust the perfection of the creation so far as to believe that whatever curiosity the order of things has awakened in our minds, the order of things can satisfy.

Nature [1836], introduction

Nature never wears a mean appearance. Neither does the wisest man extort her secret and lose his curiosity by finding out all her perfection.   *Ib. sec. 1*

Give me health and a day and I will make the pomp of emperors ridiculous.
Ib. sec. 3

Every natural fact is a symbol of some spiritual fact.   *Ib. sec. 4*

We are like Nebuchadnezzar, dethroned, bereft of reason, and eating grass like an ox.   *Ib. sec. 8*

A man is a god in ruins.[2]   *Ib.*

He who has mastered any law in his private thoughts, is master to that extent of all men whose language he speaks, and of all into whose language his own can be translated.

The American Scholar [1837], sec. 3

Wherever Macdonald sits, there is the head of the table.[1]   *Ib.*

What would we really know the meaning of? The meal in the firkin; the milk in the pan; the ballad in the street; the news of the boat.   *Ib.*

If the single man plant himself indomitably on his instincts, and there abide, the huge world will come round to him.[2]   *Ib.*

Men grind and grind in the mill of a truism, and nothing comes out but what was put in. But the moment they desert the tradition for a spontaneous thought, then poetry, wit, hope, virtue, learning, anecdote, all flock to their aid.

Literary Ethics [1838]

Time dissipates to shining ether the solid angularity of facts.

Essays: First Series [1841]. History

There is properly no history; only biography.[3]   *Ib.*

Nature is a mutable cloud, which is always and never the same.   *Ib.*

It is the fault of our rhetoric that we cannot strongly state one fact without seeming to belie some other.   *Ib.*

To believe your own thought, to believe that what is true for you in your private heart is true for all men — that is genius.   *Ib. Self-Reliance*

---

[1] The editors, E. W. EMERSON and W. E. FORBES, appended a footnote: "There has been much inquiry in the newspapers recently as to whether Mr. Emerson wrote a sentence very like the above which has been attributed to him in print. The Editors do not find the latter in his works, but there can be little doubt that it was a memory quotation by some hearer, or, quite probably, correctly reported from one of his lectures, the same image in differing words."

If a man can write a better book, preach a better sermon, or make a better mousetrap than his neighbor, though he builds his house in the woods the world will make a beaten path to his door. — SARAH S. B. YULE AND MARY S. KEENE, *Borrowings* [1889], *reported by Mrs. Yule as having been used by Emerson in an address*

[2] See Lamartine, p. 565b.

[1] Emerson's sentence is usually quoted with the substitution of "Macgregor" for "Macdonald."

[2] See Disraeli, p. 612a.

All things come round to him who will but wait. — LONGFELLOW, *Tales of a Wayside Inn, The Student's Tale* [1863]

[3] See Carlyle, p. 577a.

We but half express ourselves, and are ashamed of that divine idea which each of us represents.

Essays: First Series.
Self Reliance

Accept the place the divine providence has found for you, the society of your contemporaries. the connection of events. *Ib.*

Society everywhere is in conspiracy against the manhood of every one of its members. . . . The virtue in most request is conformity. Self-reliance is its aversion. It loves not realities and creators, but names and customs. *Ib.*

Whoso would be a man must be a nonconformist. *Ib.*

The doctrine of hatred must be preached, as the counteraction of the doctrine of love, when that pules and whines. I shun father and mother and wife and brother when my genius calls me. *Ib.*

It is easy in the world to live after the world's opinion; it is easy in solitude to live after our own; but the great man is he who in the midst of the crowd keeps with perfect sweetness the independence of solitude. *Ib.*

A foolish consistency is the hobgoblin of little minds adored by little statesmen and philosophers and divines.[1] *Ib.*

To be great is to be misunderstood. *Ib.*

An institution is the lengthened shadow of one man. *Ib.*

I like the silent church before the service begins, better than any preaching. *Ib.*

Discontent is the want of self-reliance: it is infirmity of will. *Ib.*

Traveling is a fool's paradise. . . . My giant goes with me wherever I go. *Ib.*

[1] See William Allen White, p. 896b.

For every Stoic was a Stoic; but in Christendom where is the Christian? [1]

Essays: First Series.
Self Reliance

Nothing can bring you peace but yourself. *Ib.*

Every sweet has its sour; every evil its good. *Ib. Compensation*

For every thing you have missed, you have gained something else; and for every thing you gain, you lose something else. *Ib.*

Everything in Nature contains all the powers of Nature. Everything is made of one hidden stuff. *Ib.*

It is as impossible for a man to be cheated by anyone but himself, as for a thing to be, and not to be, at the same time. *Ib.*

All mankind love a lover.
Ib. Love

Thou art to me a delicious torment.
Ib. Friendship

Almost all people descend to meet.[2] *Ib.*

Happy is the house that shelters a friend. *Ib.*

A friend is a person with whom I may be sincere. Before him, I may think aloud. *Ib.*

A friend may well be reckoned the masterpiece of Nature. *Ib.*

Two may talk and one may hear, but three cannot take part in a conversation of the most sincere and searching sort. *Ib.*

The only reward of virtue is virtue; the only way to have a friend is to be one. *Ib.*

I do then with my friends as I do with my books. I would have them where I can find them, but I seldom use them. *Ib.*

[1] See Melville, p. 695b.
[2] Men descend to meet. — EMERSON, *Essays. First Series. The Over-Soul*

In skating over thin ice our safety is in our speed.

> *Essays: First Series. Prudence*

Heroism feels and never reasons and therefore is always right.

> *Ib. Heroism*

Beware when the great God lets loose a thinker on this planet.   *Ib. Circles*

One man's justice is another's injustice; one man's beauty another's ugliness; one man's wisdom another's folly.

> *Ib.*

Nature abhors the old, and old age seems the only disease;[1] all others run into this one.   *Ib.*

Nothing great was ever achieved without enthusiasm.   *Ib.*

Nothing astonishes men so much as common sense and plain dealing.

> *Ib. Art*

Beauty will not come at the call of a legislature, nor will it repeat in England or America its history in Greece. It will come, as always, unannounced, and spring up between the feet of brave and earnest men.   *Ib.*

I fancy I need more than another to speak (rather than write), with such a formidable tendency to the lapidary style. I build my house of boulders.

> *Letter to Carlyle* [October 30, 1841]

A man may love a paradox without either losing his wit or his honesty.

> *Walter Savage Landor* [*Dial*, 1841], XII

Literature is the effort of man to indemnify himself for the wrongs of his condition.   *Ib.*

There is always a certain meanness in the argument of conservatism, joined with a certain superiority in its fact.

> *The Conservative* [1842]

For it is not meters, but a meter-making argument that makes a

poem — a thought so passionate and alive that like the spirit of a plant or an animal it has an architecture of its own, and adorns nature with a new thing.

> *Essays: Second Series* [1844]. *The Poet*

Nature and books belong to the eyes that see them.   *Ib. Experience*

Of what use is genius, if the organ is too convex or too concave and cannot find a focal distance within the actual horizon of human life?   *Ib.*

The only gift is a portion of thyself.[1]

> *Ib. Gifts*

The less government we have, the better — the fewer laws, and the less confided power.   *Ib. Politics*

We think our civilization near its meridian, but we are yet only at the cock-crowing and the morning star. In our barbarous society the influence of character is in its infancy.   *Ib.*

Money, which represents the prose of life, and which is hardly spoken of in parlors without an apology, is, in its effects and laws, as beautiful as roses.

> *Ib. Nominalist and Realist*

Every man is wanted, and no man is wanted much.   *Ib.*

The reward of a thing well done, is to have done it.   *Ib.*

He is great who is what he is from Nature, and who never reminds us of others.

> *Representative Men* [1850]. *Uses of Great Men*

When nature removes a great man, people explore the horizon for a successor; but none comes, and none will. His class is extinguished with him. In some other and quite different field, the next man will appear.   *Ib.*

Every hero becomes a bore at last.

> *Ib.*

---

[1] Old age is an incurable disease. — SENECA, *Epistulae ad Lucilium, no. 108*

[1] See Lowell, p. 692b, and Whitman, p. 700b.

Great geniuses have the shortest biographies.
Representative Men. Plato; or, The Philosopher

Things added to things, as statistics, civil history, are inventories. Things used as language are inexhaustibly attractive. *Ib.*

Keep cool: it will be all one a hundred years hence.[1]
Ib. Montaigne; or, The Skeptic

Is not marriage an open question, when it is alleged, from the beginning of the world, that such as are in the institution wish to get out, and such as are out wish to get in? [2] *Ib.*

The Pilgrims came to Plymouth in 1620. The plays of Shakespeare were not published until three years later. Had they been published earlier, our forefathers, or the most poetical among them, might have stayed at home to read them. *Ib. Shakespeare*

Self-reliance, the height and perfection of man, is reliance on God.
The Fugitive Slave Law [1854]

Classics which at home are drowsily read have a strange charm in a country inn, or in the transom of a merchant brig. *English Traits* [1856]

Men are what their mothers made them.
Conduct of Life [1860]. *Fate*

Coal is a portable climate.
Ib. Wealth

The world is his, who has money to go over it. *Ib.*

Art is a jealous mistress.[3] *Ib.*

All educated Americans, first or last, go to Europe. *Ib. Culture*

Solitude, the safeguard of mediocrity, is to genius the stern friend. *Ib.*

There is always a best way of doing everything, if it be to boil an egg. Manners are the happy ways of doing things.
Conduct of Life. Behavior

Fine manners need the support of fine manners in others. *Ib.*

The highest compact we can make with our fellow is — "Let there be truth between us two forevermore."
Ib.

Shallow men believe in luck.[1]
Ib. Worship

Our chief want in life is somebody who shall make us do what we can.
Ib. Considerations by the Way

Make yourself necessary to somebody. *Ib.*

Beauty without grace is the hook without the bait. *Ib. Beauty*

Never read any book that is not a year old. *Ib. In Praise of Books*

The key to the period appeared to be that the mind had become aware of itself. . . . The young men were born with knives in their brain, a tendency to introversion, self-dissection, anatomizing of motives.
Life and Letters in New England [1867]

God may forgive sins, he said, but awkwardness has no forgiveness in heaven or earth.
Society and Solitude [1870], *Society and Solitude*

The most advanced nations are always those who navigate the most.
Ib. Civilization

Hitch your wagon to a star.[2] *Ib.*

The true test of civilization is, not the census, nor the size of cities, nor the crops — no, but the kind of man the country turns out. *Ib.*

[1] What matters what anybody thinks? "It will be all the same a hundred years hence." That is the most sensible proverb ever invented. — GEORGE DU MAURIER, *Peter Ibbetson* [1891]
[2] See Montaigne, p. 190b, and note.
[3] See Story, p. 543b.

[1] Luck is infatuated with the efficient. — *Persian proverb*
[2] See Carl Schurz, p. 733a.

Every genuine work of art has as much reason for being as the earth and the sun.
Society and Solitude. Art

A masterpiece of art has in the mind a fixed place in the chain of being, as much as a plant or a crystal. *Ib.*

We boil at different degrees.
Ib. Eloquence

The best university that can be recommended to a man of ideas is the gauntlet of the mobs. *Ib.*

The ornament of a house is the friends who frequent it.
Ib. Domestic Life

Can anybody remember when the times were not hard and money not scarce? *Ib. Works and Days*

'Tis the good reader that makes the good book; in every book he finds passages which seem confidences or asides hidden from all else and unmistakably meant for his ear; the profit of books is according to the sensibility of the reader; the profoundest thought or passion sleeps as in a mine, until it is discovered by an equal mind and heart. *Ib. Success*

We do not count a man's years until he has nothing else to count.
Ib. Old Age

A mollusk is a cheap edition [of man] with a suppression of the costlier illustrations, designed for dingy circulation, for shelving in an oyster-bank or among the seaweed.
Power and Laws of Thought
[c. 1870]

Poetry teaches the enormous force of a few words, and, in proportion to the inspiration, checks loquacity.
Parnassus [1874]. Preface

There are two classes of poets — the poets by education and practice, these we respect; and poets by nature, these we love. *Ib.*

Life is not so short but that there is always time enough for courtesy.
Letters and Social Aims [1876].
Social Aims

I have heard with admiring submission the experience of the lady who declared that the sense of being perfectly well-dressed gives a feeling of inward tranquillity which religion is powerless to bestow. *Ib.*

Do not say things. What you are stands over you the while, and thunders so that I cannot hear what you say to the contrary. *Ib.*

Great men are they who see that spiritual is stronger than any material force, that thoughts rule the world.
Ib. Progress and Culture, Phi Beta Kappa Address [July 18, 1876]

Next to the originator of a good sentence is the first quoter of it.[1]
Ib. Quotation and Originality

When Shakespeare is charged with debts to his authors, Landor replies, "Yet he was more original than his originals. He breathed upon dead bodies and brought them into life."
Ib.

By necessity, by proclivity, and by delight, we all quote. *Ib.*

A good symbol is the best argument, and is a missionary to persuade thousands. *Ib. Poetry and Imagination*

Wit makes its own welcome, and levels all distinctions.
Ib. The Comic

The perception of the comic is a tie of sympathy with other men. *Ib.*

---

[1] There is not less wit nor less invention in applying rightly a thought one finds in a book, than in being the first author of that thought. — BAYLE, *Dictionnaire Historique et Critique* [1697–1702]
> Though old the thought and oft exprest,
> 'Tis his at last who says it best.
JAMES RUSSELL LOWELL, *For an Autograph* [1868]

What is a weed? A plant whose virtues have not yet been discovered.[1]
Fortune of the Republic [1878]

To live without duties is obscene.
Lectures and Biographical Sketches [1883]. *Aristocracy*

Speak the affirmative; emphasize your choice by utter ignoring of all that you reject.   *Ib. The Preacher*

Genius has no taste for weaving sand.   *Ib. The Scholar*

A poet in verse or prose must have a sensuous eye, but an intellectual coperception.   *Ib. Plutarch*

All thoughts of a turtle are turtles, and of a rabbit, rabbits.
The Natural History of Intellect [1893]

When you strike at a king, you must kill him.
Recollected by OLIVER WENDELL HOLMES, JR. *From* MAX LERNER, *The Mind and Faith of Justice Holmes* [1943]

ROBERT STEPHEN HAWKER
1803–1875

And shall Trelawny die?
Here's twenty thousand Cornish men
Will know the reason why.
The Song of the Western Men [1825],[2] *st. 1*

---

[1] A weed is no more than a flower in disguise. — JAMES RUSSELL LOWELL, *A Fable for Critics* [1848]
A weed is but an unloved flower! — ELLA WHEELER WILCOX [1850–1919], *The Weed, st. 1*
[2] "And shall Trelawny die?" has been a popular phrase throughout Cornwall since the imprisonment in the Tower of London, in 1688, of Sir Jonathan Trelawny [1650–1721] with six other prelates for refusing to recognize the Declaration of Indulgence issued by James II.

RICHARD HENRY HENGIST HORNE
1803–1884

'Tis always morning somewhere in the world.[1]
Orion [1843], *bk. III, canto 2*

DOUGLAS JERROLD
1803–1857

He is one of those wise philanthropists who in a time of famine would vote for nothing but a supply of toothpicks.
Wit and Opinions of Douglas Jerrold [1859]

Dogmatism is puppyism come to its full growth.   *Ib.*

That fellow would vulgarize the day of judgment.   *Ib. A Comic Author*

The best thing I know between France and England is — the sea.
Ib. The Anglo-French Alliance

Some people are so fond of ill-luck that they run halfway to meet it.
Ib. Meeting Troubles Halfway

Earth is here [Australia] so kind, that just tickle her with a hoe and she laughs with a harvest.
Ib. A Land of Plenty

The ugliest of trades have their moments of pleasure. Now, if I were a gravedigger, or even a hangman, there are some people I could work for with a great deal of enjoyment.
Ib. Ugly Trades

He was so good he would pour rosewater on a toad.
Ib. A Charitable Man

Talk to him of Jacob's ladder, and he would ask the number of the steps.
Ib. A Matter-of-fact Man

---

[1] See Longfellow, p. 625a.

ROBERT SMITH SURTEES
1803–1864

Full o' beans and benevolence.
Handley Cross [1843], *ch. 27*

Three things I never lends — my 'oss, my wife, and my name.
Hillingdon Hall [1845], *ch. 33*

More people are flattered into virtue than bullied out of vice.
The Analysis of the Hunting Field [1846], *ch. 1*

Better be killed than frightened to death.
Mr. Facey Romford's Hounds [1864], *ch. 32*

FEDOR TIUTCHEV
1803–1873

A thought, once uttered, is a lie.
Silentium [1830]

Like first love, the heart of Russia will not forget you.
Tribute to Pushkin [*January 29, 1837*]

Homeland of patience, land of the Russian people.
These Poor Villages [1855]

BENJAMIN DISRAELI, EARL OF BEACONSFIELD
1804–1881

The microcosm of a public school.
Vivian Grey [1826], *bk. I, ch. 2*

I hate definitions.　　*Ib. II, 6*

Experience is the child of Thought, and Thought is the child of Action. We cannot learn men from books.
Ib. V, 1

Variety is the mother of Enjoyment.
Ib. 4

There is moderation even in excess.
Ib. VI, 1

I repeat . . . that all power is a trust; that we are accountable for its exercise; that, from the people, and for the people, all springs, and all must exist.[1]　　*Vivian Grey bk. VI, ch. 7*

Man is not the creature of circumstances. Circumstances are the creatures of men.　　*Ib.*

A *dark* horse, which had never been thought of, and which the careless St. James had never even observed in the list, rushed past the grandstand in sweeping triumph.
The Young Duke [1831], *bk. I, ch. 5*

Yes, I am a Jew, and when the ancestors of the right honorable gentleman were brutal savages in an unknown island, mine were priests in the temple of Solomon.[2]
Reply to a taunt by Daniel O'Connell

What we anticipate seldom occurs; what we least expected generally happens.
Henrietta Temple [1837], *bk. II, ch. 4*

Though I sit down now, the time will come when you will hear me.[3]
Maiden speech in the House of Commons [1837]

Free trade is not a principle, it is an expedient.[4]
Speech on import duties [*April 25, 1843*]

The noble lord [5] is the Rupert of Parliamentary discussion.
Speech [*April 1844*]

---

[1] See Wycliffe, p. 163b, and note.
[2] The gentleman will please remember that when his half-civilized ancestors were hunting the wild boar in the forests of Silesia, mine were the princes of the earth. — JUDAH P. BENJAMIN [1811–1884], *reply to a Senator; from* BEN PERLEY POORE, *Reminiscences of Sixty Years in the National Metropolis* [1886]
[3] See Garrison, p. 615b.
[4] See Grover Cleveland, p. 771a.
[5] Lord Stanley.

Youth is a blunder; manhood a struggle; old age a regret.
Coningsby [*1844*], *bk. III, ch. 1*

Property has its duties as well as its rights.[1] *Sybil* [*1845*], *bk. II, ch. 11*

Little things affect little minds.
Ib. III, 2

We all of us live too much in a circle.[2] *Ib. 7*

Mr. Kremlin was distinguished for ignorance; for he had only one idea — and that was wrong.[3] *Ib. IV, 5*

I was told that the privileged and the people formed two nations. *Ib. 8*

The right honorable gentleman [4] caught the Whigs bathing and walked away with their clothes.
Speech, House of Commons [*February 28, 1845*]

A conservative government is an organized hypocrisy.
Speech on Agricultural Interests [*March 17, 1845*]

He was fresh and full of faith that "something would turn up." [5]
Tancred [*1847*], *bk. III, ch. 6*

Everything comes if a man will only wait.[6] *Ib. IV, 8*

A precedent embalms a principle.
Speech on the expenditures of the country [*February 22, 1848*]

Justice is truth in action.
Speech [*February 11, 1851*]

This shows how much easier it is to be critical than to be correct.
Speech [*January 24, 1860*]

[1] Property has its duties as well as its rights. — CAPTAIN THOMAS DRUMMOND (inventor of the Drummond light), *Letter to the Landlords of Tipperary* [May 22, 1838]
[2] The life of man is a self-evolving circle. — EMERSON, *Essays* [*1st series*, 1841], *Circles*
[3] See Johnson, p. 431a.
[4] Sir Robert Peel.
[5] See Dickens, p. 671a.
[6] See Emerson, p. 605b.

The characteristic of the present age is craving credulity.
Speech at Oxford Diocesan Conference [*November 25, 1864*]

Is man an ape or an angel? [1] I, my lord, I am on the side of the angels. I repudiate with indignation and abhorrence those newfangled theories. *Ib.*

In the character of the victim [Lincoln], and even in the accessories of his last moments, there is something so homely and innocent that it takes the question, as it were, out of all the pomp of history and the ceremonial of diplomacy — it touches the heart of nations and appeals to the domestic sentiment of mankind.
Speech, House of Commons [*May 1, 1865*]

Ignorance never settles a question.
Ib. [*May 14, 1866*]

Individualities may form communities, but it is institutions alone that can create a nation.
Speech at Manchester [*1866*]

However gradual may be the growth of confidence, that of credit requires still more time to arrive at maturity.
Speech [*November 9, 1867*]

When a man fell into his anecdotage, it was a sign for him to retire.
Lothair [*1870*], *ch. 28*

Every woman should marry — and no man. *Ib. 30*

You know who the critics are? The men who have failed in literature and art.[2] *Ib. 35*

"My idea of an agreeable person," said Hugo Bohun, "is a person who agrees with me." *Ib.*

Increased means and increased leisure are the two civilizers of man.
Speech to the Conservatives of Manchester [*April 3, 1872*]

The secret of success is constancy to purpose. *Speech* [*June 24, 1872*]

[1] See rascal, p. 363b, and Charles Darwin, p. 628a.
[2] See Coleridge, p. 528a, and Lowell, p. 692b.

A university should be a place of light, of liberty, and of learning.
Speech, House of Commons
[March 11, 1873]

The author who speaks about his own books is almost as bad as a mother who talks about her own children.
Speech [November 19, 1873]

The health of the people is really the foundation upon which all their happiness and all their powers as a state depend.   *Speech [July 24, 1877]*

Lord Salisbury and myself have brought you back peace — but a peace I hope with honor.[1]
Speech, House of Commons
[July 16, 1878]

A series of congratulatory regrets.[2]
Speech, Knightsbridge [July 27, 1878]

A sophistical rhetorician [Gladstone], inebriated with the exuberance of his own verbosity, and gifted with an egotistical imagination that can at all times command an interminable and inconsistent series of arguments to malign an opponent and to glorify himself.   *Ib.*

The harebrained chatter of irresponsible frivolity.
Speech, Guildhall, London
[November 9, 1878]

His Christianity was muscular.
Endymion [1880], ch. 14

The Athanasian Creed is the most splendid ecclesiastical lyric ever poured forth by the genius of man.   *Ib. 52*

"As for that," said Waldershare, "sensible men are all of the same religion." "And pray, what is that?" inquired the prince. "Sensible men never tell."   *Ib. 81*

[1] See Russell, p. 567b, and Chamberlain, p. 897a.
[2] Lord Hartington's Resolution on the Berlin Treaty.

NATHANIEL HAWTHORNE
1804–1864

Amid the seeming confusion of our mysterious world, individuals are so nicely adjusted to a system, and systems to one another and to a whole, that, by stepping aside for a moment, a man exposes himself to a fearful risk of losing his place forever.
Wakefield [1835]

His hour is one of darkness, and adversity, and peril. But should domestic tyranny oppress us, or the invader's step pollute our soil, still may the Gray Champion come, for he is the type of New England's hereditary spirit; and his shadowy march, on the eve of danger, must ever be the pledge, that New England's sons will vindicate their ancestry.
The Gray Champion [1835]

By the sympathy of your human hearts for sin ye shall scent out all the places — whether in church, bedchamber, street, field, or forest — where crime has been committed, and shall exult to behold the whole earth one stain of guilt, one mighty blood spot.
Young Goodman Brown [1835]

As the moral gloom of the world overpowers all systematic gaiety, even so was their home of wild mirth made desolate amid the sad forest.
The Maypole of Merrymount [1836]

"What is the Unpardonable Sin?" asked the lime-burner. . . .
"It is a sin that grew within my own breast," replied Ethan Brand. . . . The sin of an intellect that triumphed over the sense of brotherhood with man and reverence for God."
Ethan Brand [1850]

On the breast of her gown, in red cloth, surrounded with an elaborate embroidery and fantastic flourishes of gold thread, appeared the letter A.
The Scarlet Letter [1850], ch. 2

There is a fatality, a feeling so irresistible and inevitable that it has the force of doom, which almost invariably compels human beings to linger around and haunt, ghostlike, the spot where some great and marked event has given the color to their lifetime; and still the more irresistibly, the darker the tinge that saddens it.

The Scarlet Letter, ch. 5

Wherever there is a heart and an intellect, the diseases of the physical frame are tinged with the peculiarities of these. *Ib.* 9

Let men tremble to win the hand of woman, unless they win along with it the utmost passion of her heart.

Ib. 15

"Never, never!" whispered she. "What we did had a consecration of its own." *Ib.* 17

The scarlet letter was her passport into regions where other women dared not tread. Shame, Despair, Solitude! These had been her teachers — stern and wild ones — and they had made her strong, but taught her much amiss.

Ib. 18

No man, for any considerable period, can wear one face to himself, and another to the multitude, without finally getting bewildered as to which may be the true. *Ib.* 20

Among many morals which press upon us from the poor minister's miserable experience, we put only this into a sentence: "Be true! Be true! Show freely to the world, if not your worst, yet some trait whereby the worst may be inferred." *Ib.* 24

The book, if you would see anything in it, requires to be read in the clear, brown, twilight atmosphere in which it was written; if opened in the sunshine, it is apt to look exceedingly like a volume of blank pages.

Twice-Told Tales [1851],
preface

Not to be deficient in this particular, the author has provided himself with a moral — the truth, namely, that the wrongdoing of one generation lives into the successive ones.

*The House of the Seven
Gables* [1851], *preface*

God will give him blood to drink!

Ib. ch. 1

Life is made up of marble and mud.
Ib. 2

What other dungeon is so dark as one's own heart! What jailer so inexorable as one's self! *Ib.* 11

Of all the events which constitute a person's biography, there is scarcely one . . . to which the world so easily reconciles itself as to his death.

Ib. 21

The greatest obstacle to being heroic is the doubt whether one may not be going to prove one's self a fool; the truest heroism is, to resist the doubt; and the profoundest wisdom, to know when it ought to be resisted, and when to be obeyed.

The Blithedale Romance
[1852], *ch.* 2

I am a woman, with every fault, it may be, that a woman ever had — weak, vain, unprincipled (like most of my sex; for our virtues, when we have any, are merely impulsive and intuitive). *Ib.* 25

It is because the spirit is inestimable that the lifeless body is so little valued.
Ib. 28

In youth men are apt to write more wisely than they really know or feel; and the remainder of life may be not idly spent in realizing and convincing themselves of the wisdom they uttered long ago.

The Snow Image [1852], *preface*

No author, without a trial, can conceive of the difficulty of writing a romance about a country where there is no shadow, no antiquity, no mystery, no picturesque and gloomy wrong, nor anything but a commonplace prosperity, in broad and simple daylight, as is happily the case with my dear native land. . . . Romance and poetry, ivy, lichens and wallflowers need ruin to make them grow.

The Marble Faun [1860], *preface*

This greatest mortal consolation, which we derive from the transitoriness of all things — from the right of saying, in every conjuncture, "This, too, will pass away."[1]   *Ib. ch. 16*

Nobody, I think, ought to read poetry, or look at pictures or statues, who cannot find a great deal more in them than the poet or artist has actually expressed.[2]   *Ib. 41*

Mountains are earth's undecaying monuments.

Sketches from Memory [1868]. *The Notch of the White Mountains*

CHARLES AUGUSTIN SAINTE-BEUVE
1804–1869

Vigny, more secret,
As if in his tower of ivory, retired before noon.[3]

Pensées d'Août, à M. Villemain [1837], *st. 3*

Silence is the sovereign contempt.[4]
Mes Poisons

---

[1] See Lincoln, p. 636b.

[2] Every book is written with a constant secret reference to the few intelligent persons whom the writer believes to exist in the million. . . . The artist has always the masters in his eye. — EMERSON, *Progress of Culture* [1867]

[3]   Vigny, plus secret,
Comme en sa tour d'ivoire, avant midi, rentrait.

The poet, retired in his Tower of Ivory, isolated, according to his desire, from the world of man, resembles, whether he so wishes or not, another solitary figure, the watcher enclosed for months at a time in a lighthouse at the head of a cliff. — JULES DE GAULTIER [b. 1858], *La Guerre et les Destinées de l'Art*

[4] Le silence seul est le souverain mépris.

SARAH FLOWER ADAMS
1805–1848

Yet in my dreams I'd be
Nearer, my God, to Thee,
Nearer to Thee.
Nearer, My God, to Thee, st. 2

He sendeth sun, He sendeth shower.
Hymn, first line and title

WILLIAM LLOYD GARRISON
1805–1879

Our country is the world — our countrymen are all mankind.[1]
Motto of the Liberator [1831]

Let Southern oppressors tremble — let their secret abettors tremble — let their Northern apologists tremble — let all the enemies of the persecuted blacks tremble.

The Liberator, no. 1 *[January 1, 1831]*

I will be as harsh as truth and as uncompromising as justice. On this subject I do not wish to think, or speak, or write, with moderation. No! No! Tell a man whose house is on fire to give a moderate alarm; tell him to moderately rescue his wife from the hands of the ravisher; tell the mother to gradually extricate her babe from the fire into which it has fallen; but urge me not to use moderation.[2]   *Ib.*

I am in earnest — I will not equivocate — I will not excuse — I will not retreat a single inch; and I will be heard![3]   *Ib.*

The compact which exists between the North and the South is a covenant with death and an agreement with hell.[4]

Resolution adopted by the Anti-Slavery Society [January 27, 1843]

---

[1] See Socrates, p. 87b, and note.

[2] See Paine, p. 467b.

[3] See Disraeli, p. 611b.

[4] See *Isaiah 28:15*, p. 32a.

With reasonable men, I will reason; with humane men I will plead; but to tyrants I will give no quarter, nor waste arguments where they will certainly be lost.

W. P. AND F. J. T. GARRISON, *William Lloyd Garrison* [1885–1889], *vol. I, p. 188*

Since the creation of the world there has been no tyrant like Intemperance, and no slaves so cruelly treated as his.
Ib. p. 268

We may be personally defeated, but our principles never.   *Ib. p. 402*

Wherever there is a human being, I see God-given rights inherent in that being, whatever may be the sex or complexion.   *Ib. III, p. 390*

You cannot possibly have a broader basis for any government than that which includes all the people, with all their rights in their hands, and with an equal power to maintain their rights.[1]
Ib. IV, p. 224

COLONEL
SIDNEY SHERMAN
1805–1873

Remember the Alamo![2]
Battle cry, San Jacinto [April 21, 1836]; attributed

ALEXIS
DE TOCQUEVILLE
1805–1859

I know of no country, indeed, where the love of money has taken stronger hold on the affections of men and where a profounder contempt is ex-

---

[1] See Wycliffe, p. 163b; Webster, p. 547a; Lincoln, p. 639a; and Parker, p. 657b.

[2] On March 6, 1836, five days after Texas declared her independence from Mexico, President Antonio López de Santa Anna attacked the Alamo, the fortified mission at San Antonio; captured it after every Texan had been killed or wounded; and put the wounded to death. He was defeated and captured at San Jacinto [April 21, 1836] by the Texas army under Commander in Chief Samuel Houston.

pressed for the theory of the permanent equality of property.
Democracy in America,[1] pt. I [1835], ch. 3

Within these limits the power vested in the American courts of justice of pronouncing a statute to be unconstitutional forms one of the most powerful barriers that have ever been devised against the tyranny of political assemblies.   *Ib. 6*

I have never been more struck by the good sense and the practical judgment of the Americans than in the manner in which they elude the numberless difficulties resulting from their Federal Constitution.   *Ib. 8*

In this question, therefore, there is no medium between servitude and license; in order to enjoy the inestimable benefits that the liberty of the press ensures, it is necessary to submit to the inevitable evils that it creates.   *Ib. 9*

They [the Americans] have all a lively faith in the perfectibility of man, they judge that the diffusion of knowledge must necessarily be advantageous, and the consequences of ignorance fatal; they all consider society as a body in a state of improvement, humanity as a changing scene, in which nothing is, or ought to be, permanent; and they admit that what appears to them today to be good, may be superseded by something better tomorrow.   *Ib. 18*

America is a land of wonders, in which everything is in constant motion and every change seems an improvement. The idea of novelty is there indissolubly connected with the idea of amelioration. No natural boundary seems to be set to the efforts of man; and in his eyes what is not yet done is only what he has not yet attempted to do.   *Ib.*

Democratic nations care but little for what has been, but they are haunted by

---

[1] The Henry Reeve text, as revised by Francis Bowen, corrected and edited by Phillips Bradley [1945].

visions of what will be; in this direction their unbounded imagination grows and dilates beyond all measure. . . . Democracy, which shuts the past against the poet, opens the future before him.
Democracy in America, pt. II
[1840], bk. I, ch. 17

Thus not only does democracy make every man forget his ancestors, but it hides his descendants and separates his contemporaries from him; it throws him back forever upon himself alone and threatens in the end to confine him entirely within the solitude of his own heart.   *Ib. bk. II, ch. 2*

If I were asked . . . to what the singular prosperity and growing strength of that people [the Americans] ought mainly to be attributed, I should reply: To the superiority of their women.   *Ib. bk. III, ch. 12*

The love of wealth is therefore to be traced, as either a principal or accessory motive, at the bottom of all that the Americans do; this gives to all their passions a sort of family likeness. . . . It may be said that it is the vehemence of their desires that makes the Americans so methodical; it perturbs their minds, but it disciplines their lives.
Ib. 17

SAMUEL WILBERFORCE[1]
1805–1873

If I were a cassowary
    On the plains of Timbuctoo,
I would eat a missionary,
    Cassock, band,[2] and hymnbook,
    too.   *Impromptu*

ELIZABETH BARRETT BROWNING
1806–1861

Thou large-brained woman and large-hearted man.
To George Sand, A Desire
[1844]

---

[1] Bishop of Oxford, and later of Winchester — nicknamed "Soapy Sam."
[2] Variant: Skin and bones.

Or from Browning some "Pomegranate," which, if cut deep down the middle,
Shows a heart within blood-tinctured of a veined humanity.
Lady Geraldine's Courtship
[1844], st. 41

Life treads on life, and heart on heart;
We press too close in church and mart
To keep a dream or grave apart.
A *Vision of Poets* [1844],
conclusion, l. 1

Knowledge by suffering entereth,
And life is perfected by death.
Ib. last lines

And I smiled to think God's greatness
    flowed around our incomplete-
    ness —
Round our restlessness, His rest.
Rime of the Duchess May
[1844], conclusion, st. 11

Do ye hear the children weeping, O my
    brothers,
Ere the sorrow comes with years?
The Cry of the Children [1844],
st. 1

The child's sob in the silence curses
    deeper
Than the strong man in his wrath.
Ib. st. 13

I tell you hopeless grief is passionless.
Grief [1844], *l. 1*

Therefore to this dog will I,
Tenderly not scornfully,
    Render praise and favor:
With my hand upon his head,
Is my benediction said
    Therefore and forever.
To Flush, My Dog [1844], *st. 14*

And lips say "God be pitiful,"
Who ne'er said "God be praised."
The Cry of the Human [1844],
st. 1

And kings crept out again to feel the sun.
Crowned and Buried [1844],
st. 11

"Yes," I answered you last night;
  "No," this morning, sir, I say:
Colors seen by candlelight
  Will not look the same by day.[1]
      The Lady's "Yes" [1844], *st. 1*

By thunders of white silence overthrown.
      Hiram Power's Greek Slave
        [1850], *last line*

Unless you can muse in a crowd all
  day
On the absent face that fixed you;
Unless you can love, as the angels
  may,
With the breadth of heaven betwixt
  you;
Unless you can dream that his faith is
  fast,
Through behoving and unbehoving;
Unless you can die when the dream is
  past —
Oh, never call it loving!
      A Woman's Shortcomings
        [1850], *st. 5*

"Guess now who holds thee?" —
  "Death," I said. But there
The silver answer rang — "Not Death,
  but Love."
      Sonnets from the Portuguese
        [1850], *no. 1*

Go from me. Yet I feel that I shall
  stand
Henceforward in thy shadow.   *Ib. 6*

If thou must love me, let it be for
  naught
Except for love's sake only.   *Ib. 14*

When our two souls stand up erect and
  strong,
Face to face, silent, drawing nigh and
  nigher.   *Ib. 22*

[1] To say why gals acts so or so,
  Or don't, 'ould be presumin';
Mebby to mean *yes* an' say *no*
Comes nateral to women.
    JAMES RUSSELL LOWELL, *The Biglow*
        Papers, series II [1867], *st. 18*
And if I loved you Wednesday,
Well, what is that to you?
I do not love you Thursday —
So much is true.
    EDNA ST. VINCENT MILLAY [1892–1950],
               Thursday

God only, who made us rich, can make
  us poor.
      Sonnets from the Portuguese,
          no. 24

Because God's gifts put man's best
  dreams to shame.   *Ib. 26*

How do I love thee? Let me count the
  ways.
I love thee to the depth and breadth
  and height
My soul can reach, when feeling out of
  sight
For the ends of Being and ideal Grace.
            Ib. 43

I love thee with a love I seemed to
  lose
With my lost saints — I love thee with
  the breath,
Smiles, tears, of all my life! — and, if
  God choose,
I shall but love thee better after death.
            Ib.

    Life, struck sharp on death,
Makes awful lightning.
    Aurora Leigh [1] [1857], *bk. I, l. 210*

As sings the lark when sucked up out of
  sight
In vortices of glory and blue air.
           Ib. l. 1055

I should not dare to call my soul my
  own.   *Ib. II, l. 786*

God answers sharp and sudden on some
  prayers,
And thrusts the thing we have prayed
  for in our face,
A gauntlet with a gift in 't.
          Ib. l. 952

How many desolate creatures on the
  earth
Have learnt the simple dues of fellowship
And social comfort, in a hospital.
        Ib. III, l. 1122

A little sunburnt by the glare of life.
        Ib. IV, l. 1140

Since when was genius found respectable?   *Ib. VI, l. 275*

[1] See Edward Fitzgerald, p. 631a.

Earth's crammed with heaven,
And every common bush afire with
God;
But only he who sees takes off his
shoes;
The rest sit round it and pluck black-
berries.
Aurora Leigh, bk. VII, l. 820

What was he doing, the great god Pan,
Down in the reeds by the river?
Spreading ruin and scattering ban,
Splashing and paddling with hoofs of a
goat,
And breaking the golden lilies afloat
With the dragonfly on the river.
A Musical Instrument [1860]

Grief may be joy misunderstood;
Only the Good discerns the good.
De Profundis [1862], *st.* 21

FRIEDRICH HALM
[ELIGIUS FRANZ
JOSEF VON MÜNCH-
BELLINGHAUSEN]
1806–1871

Two souls with but a single thought,
Two hearts that beat as one.[1]
Der Sohn der Wildness [1842],
act II

JOHN STUART MILL
1806–1873

The sole end for which mankind are
warranted, individually or collectively,
in interfering with the liberty of action of any of their number is self-
protection.
Liberty [1859], *introduction*

If all mankind minus one, were of
one opinion, and only one person were
of the contrary opinion, mankind
would be no more justified in silencing
that one person, than he, if he had the
power, would be justified in silencing
mankind.
Ib. ch. 2

[1] Zwei Sellen und en Gedanke,
Zwei Herzen und ein Schlag!
Translated by MARIA LOVELL.

We can never be sure that the opinion we are endeavoring to stifle is a false
opinion; and if we were sure, stifling it
would be an evil still.
Liberty, ch. 2

The liberty of the individual must be
thus far limited; he must not make
himself a nuisance to other people.
Ib. 3

All good things which exist are the
fruits of originality.
Ib.

Liberty consists in doing what one
desires.
Ib. 5

The worth of a state, in the long run,
is the worth of the individuals composing it.
Ib.

Unearned increment.
Dissertations and Discussions
[1859]

It is better to be Socrates dissatisfied
than a pig satisfied.
Utilitarianism [1863]

Ask yourself whether you are happy,
and you cease to be so.
Autobiography [1873], *ch.* 5

JOHANN BERNHARD
GRAF VON RECHBERG
1806–1899

Guarantees which are not worth the
paper they are written on.
In a dispatch concerning the
recognition of Italy [1861]

NATHANIEL PARKER
WILLIS
1806–1867

The sin forgiven by Christ in Heaven
By man is cursed alway.
Unseen Spirits, st. 5

CHARLES FRANCIS
ADAMS
1807–1886

It would be superfluous in me to
point out to your Lordship that this is
war.
Dispatch to Earl Russell
[*September* 5, 1863]

JEAN LOUIS RODOLPHE AGASSIZ
1807–1873

The world has arisen in some way or another. How it originated is the great question, and Darwin's theory, like all other attempts to explain the origin of life, is thus far merely conjectural. I believe he has not even made the best conjecture possible in the present state of our knowledge.

Evolution and Permanence of Type [1874]

GIUSEPPE GARIBALDI
1807–1882

I offer neither pay, nor quarters, nor provisions; I offer hunger, thirst, forced marches, battles and death. Let him who loves his country in his heart, and not with his lips only, follow me.[1]

From G. M. TREVELYAN, *Garibaldi's Defense of the Roman Republic* [1907–1911].

ROBERT EDWARD LEE
1807–1870

It is well that war is so terrible, or we should get too fond of it.[2]

On seeing a Federal charge repulsed at Fredericksburg [December 1862]

Duty is the sublimest word in our language. Do your duty in all things. You cannot do more. You should never wish to do less.

Inscribed beneath his bust in the Hall of Fame

Let the tent be struck.

Last words [October 12, 1870]

HENRY WADSWORTH LONGFELLOW
1807–1882

Music is the universal language of mankind — poetry their universal pastime and delight.

Outre-Mer [1833–1834]

[1] See Prescott, p. 587a, and Churchill, p. 920b.

[2] See William T. Sherman, p. 705a.

I heard the trailing garments of the Night
Sweep through her marble halls.

Hymn to Night [1839], *st.* 1

Tell me not, in mournful numbers,
Life is but an empty dream!
For the soul is dead that slumbers,
And things are not what they seem.[1]
Life is real! Life is earnest!
And the grave is not its goal;
Dust thou art, to dust returnest,
Was not spoken of the soul.

A Psalm of Life [1839], *st.* 1, 2

Art is long, and Time is fleeting,[2]
And our hearts, though stout and brave,
Still, like muffled drums, are beating
Funeral marches to the grave.[3]

Ib. st. 4

Trust no Future, howe'er pleasant!
Let the dead Past bury its dead! [4]
Act — act in the living present!
Heart within, and God o'erhead!

Lives of great men all remind us
We can make our lives sublime,
And, departing, leave behind us
Footprints on the sands of time.

Ib. st. 6, 7

Let us, then, be up and doing,
With a heart for any fate; [5]
Still achieving, still pursuing,
Learn to labor and to wait. *Ib. st. 9*

There is a Reaper whose name is Death,
And, with his sickle keen,
He reaps the bearded grain at a breath,
And the flowers that grow between.

The Reaper and the Flowers [1839], *st.* 1

The hooded clouds, like friars,
Tell their beads in drops of rain.

Midnight Mass for the Dying Year [1839], *st. 4*

[1] See Phaedrus, p. 129b, and W. S. Gilbert, p. 766a.

[2] See Hippocrates, p. 88b, and Goethe, p. 477b.

[3] Our lives are but our marches to the grave.
— BEAUMONT AND FLETCHER, *The Humorous Lieutenant* [1619], act III, sc. 5

[4] See *Matthew 8:22*, p. 41b.

[5] See Byron, p. 559b.

Who ne'er his bread in sorrow ate,
Who ne'er the mournful midnight
   hours
Weeping upon his bed has sate,
He knows you not, ye Heavenly Pow-
   ers.[1]
> *Hyperion* [1839], *bk. I, motto*

Look not mournfully into the Past. It
comes not back again. Wisely improve
the Present. It is thine. Go forth to
meet the shadowy Future, without fear,
and with a manly heart.[2] *Ib. IV, ch. 8*

Skoal! to the Northland! skoal!
Thus the tale ended.
> *The Skeleton in Armor*
> [1841], *st. 20*

It was the schooner Hesperus,
   That sailed the wintry sea;
And the skipper had taken his little
   daughter,
To bear him company.
> *The Wreck of the Hesperus*
> [1842], *st. 1*

But the father answered never a word,
   A frozen corpse was he.   *Ib. st. 12*

Christ save us all from a death like this,
   On the reef of Norman's Woe!
> *Ib. st. 22*

Under the spreading chestnut tree
   The village smithy stands;
The smith a mighty man is he
   With large and sinewy hands.
And the muscles of his brawny arms
   Are strong as iron bands.
> *The Village Blacksmith* [1842],
> *st. 1*

His brow is wet with honest sweat,
   He earns whate'er he can,

---

[1] Wer nie sein Brod mit Tränen ass,
Wer nie die kummervollen Nächte
Auf seinem Bette weinend sass,
Der kennt euch nicht, ihr himmlischen
   Mächte.
> GOETHE, *Wilhelm Meister's Apprentice-*
> *ship* [1786–1830], *bk. II, ch. 13*

See Goethe, p. 477a.

[2] Blicke nicht trauernd in die Vergangenheit,
Sie kommt nicht wieder, nutze weise die
   Gegenwart,
Sie ist dein, der düsteren Zukunft geh ohne
   Furcht mit männliche Sinne entgegen.
> *Inscription, Chapel of St. Gilgen, near*
> *Salzburg*

And looks the whole world in the face,
   For he owes not any man.
> *The Village Blacksmith, st. 2*

Something attempted, something done,
Has earned a night's repose.   *Ib. st. 7*

No one is so accursed by fate,
No one so utterly desolate,
But some heart, though unknown,
Responds unto his own.
> *Endymion* [1842], *st. 8*

Into each life some rain must fall,
Some days must be dark and dreary.
> *The Rainy Day* [1842], *st. 3*

I like that ancient Saxon phrase, which
   calls
The burial ground God's Acre!
> *God's Acre* [1842], *st. 1*

Standing with reluctant feet,
Where the brook and river meet,
Womanhood and childhood fleet!
> *Maidenhood* [1842], *st. 3*

A banner with the strange device,
   Excelsior!   *Excelsior* [1842], *st. 1*

Stars of the summer night!
   Far in yon azure deeps,
Hide, hide your golden light!
   She sleeps!
My lady sleeps!
   Sleeps!
> *The Spanish Student* [1843],
> *act I, sc. 3* [*serenade*]

She floats upon the river of his
   thoughts.   *Ib. II, 3*

I stood on the bridge at midnight,
   As the clocks were striking the hour.
> *The Bridge* [1845]

The day is done, and the darkness
   Falls from the wings of Night,
As a feather is wafted downward
   From an eagle in his flight.
> *The Day Is Done* [1845], *st. 1*

A feeling of sadness and longing,
   That is not akin to pain,
And resembles sorrow only
   As the mist resembles the rain.
> *Ib. st. 3*

Some simple and heartfelt lay.
The Day Is Done, st. 4

The bards sublime,
Whose distant footsteps echo
  Through the corridors of Time.
Ib. st. 5

And the night shall be filled with
  music,
  And the cares, that infest the day,
Shall fold their tents, like the Arabs,
  And as silently steal away. *Ib. st. 11*

The horologe of Eternity
Sayeth this incessantly —
  "Forever — never!
  Never — forever!"
The Old Clock on the Stairs
[1845], st. 9

I shot an arrow into the air,
It fell to earth, I knew not where.
The Arrow and the Song [1845],
st. 1

And the song, from beginning to end,
I found in the heart of a friend.
Ib. st. 3

This is the forest primeval. The murmuring   pines   and   the   hemlocks . . .
Stand like Druids of old.
Evangeline [1847], l. 1

Alike were they free from
Fear, that reigns with the tyrant, and
  envy, the vice of republics.
Ib. pt. I, sec. 1

When she had passed, it seemed like
  the ceasing of exquisite music.
Ib.

Silently one by one, in the infinite
  meadows of heaven
Blossomed the lovely stars, the forget-
  me-nots of the angels.   *Ib. 3*

Talk not of wasted affection! affection
  never was wasted;
If it enrich not the heart of another, its
  waters, returning
Back to their springs, like the rain, shall
  fill them full of refreshment:

That which the fountain sends forth returns again to the fountain.
Evangeline, pt. II, sec. 1

Give what you have. To someone, it
may be better than you dare to think.
Kavanagh [1849]

Build me straight, O worthy Master!
Staunch and strong, a goodly vessel,
That shall laugh at all disaster,
And with wave and whirlwind wrestle!
The Building of the Ship
[1849], l. 1

And see! she stirs!
She starts — she moves — she seems to
  feel
The thrill of life along her keel.
Ib. l. 349

Sail on, O Ship of State!
Sail on, O Union, strong and great!
Humanity with all its fears,
With all the hopes of future years,
Is hanging breathless on thy fate!
Ib. l. 378

Our hearts, our hopes, are all with thee,
Our hearts, our hopes, our prayers, our
  tears,
Our faith triumphant o'er our fears,
Are all with thee — are all with thee!
Ib. l. 396

There is no fireside, howsoe'er de-
  fended,
But has one vacant chair!
Resignation [1849], st. 1

There is no Death! What seems so is
  transition;
  This life of mortal breath
Is but a suburb of the life elysian,
  Whose portal we call Death.
Ib. st. 5

Nothing useless is, or low;
  Each thing in its place is best;
And what seems but idle show
  Strengthens and supports the rest.
The Builders [1849], st. 2

God sent his Singers upon earth
With songs of sadness and of mirth.
The Singers [1849], st. 1

But the great Master said, "I see
No best in kind, but in degree;
I gave a various gift to each,
To charm, to strengthen, and to
    teach."   *The Singers, st. 6*

All your strength is in your union.
All your danger is in discord;
Therefore be at peace henceforward,
And as brothers live together.
    The Song of Hiawatha [1855],
        pt. I

By the shores of Gitche Gumee,
By the shining Big-Sea-Water,
Stood the wigwam of Nokomis,
Daughter of the Moon, Nokomis.
    Ib. III

From the waterfall he named her,
Minnehaha, Laughing Water.
    Ib. IV

As unto the bow the cord is,
So unto the man is woman,
Though she bends him, she obeys him,
Though she draws him, yet she fol-
    lows,
Useless each without the other!
    Ib. X

If we could read the secret history of
our enemies, we should find in each
man's life sorrow and suffering enough
to disarm all hostility.
    Driftwood [1857]

If I am not worth the wooing, I surely
    am not worth the winning.
    The Courtship of Miles Standish
        [1858], *pt. III*

"Why don't you speak for yourself,
John?" [1]   *Ib.*

Saint Augustine! well hast thou said,
    That of our vices we can frame
A ladder, if we will but tread
    Beneath our feet each deed of
    shame.[2]
    The Ladder of St. Augustine
        [1858], *st. 1*

The heights by great men reached and
    kept

[1] See Shakespeare, p. 246a.
[2] See St. Augustine, p. 147a, and Tennyson,
p. 649b.

Were not attained by sudden flight,
But they, while their companions slept,
Were toiling upward in the night.
    The Ladder of St. Augustine,
        st. 10

The long mysterious Exodus of death.
    The Jewish Cemetery at New-
        port [1858], *st. 1*

A boy's will is the wind's will,
And the thoughts of youth are long,
    long thoughts.
    My Lost Youth [1858], *refrain*

A Lady with a Lamp [1] shall stand
In the great history of the land,
A noble type of good,
Heroic womanhood.
    Santa Filomena [1858], *st. 10*

Ye are better than all the ballads
    That ever were sung or said;
For ye are living poems,
    And all the rest are dead.
    Children [1858], *st. 9*

Between the dark and the daylight,
When the night is beginning to
    lower,
Comes a pause in the day's occupa-
    tions,
That is known as the Children's
    Hour.
    The Children's Hour [1860],
        st. 1

I hear in the chamber above me
The patter of little feet.   *Ib. st. 2*

Grave Alice, and laughing Allegra,
And Edith with golden hair.
    Ib. st. 3

Listen, my children, and you shall
    hear,
Of the midnight ride of Paul Revere,
On the eighteenth of April, in Seventy-
    five;
Hardly a man is now alive
Who remembers that famous day and
    year.
    Tales of a Wayside Inn [1863–
      1874], *pt. I, The Landlord's*
      Tale: Paul Revere's Ride, st. 1

[1] Florence Nightingale [1820–1910].

One if by land, and two if by sea; [1]
And I on the opposite shore will be,
Ready to ride and spread the alarm
Through every Middlesex village and
farm.
> *Tales of a Wayside Inn, pt. I,*
> *Paul Revere's Ride, st. 2*

The fate of a nation was riding that
night.   *Ib. st. 8*

He seemed the incarnate "Well, I told
you so!"
> *Ib. The Poet's Tale: The Birds*
> *of Killingworth, st. 9*

Ships that pass in the night, and speak
each other in passing,
Only a signal shown and a distant voice
in the darkness;
So on the ocean of life we pass and
speak one another,[2]
Only a look and a voice; then darkness
again and a silence.
> *Ib. pt. III, The Theologian's*
> *Tale: Elizabeth, IV*

Time has laid his hand
Upon my heart, gently, not smiting it,
But as a harper lays his open palm
Upon his harp to deaden its vibra-
tions.
> *The Golden Legend* [1872],
> *pt. IV, The Cloisters*

The grave itself is but a covered bridge
Leading from light to light, through a
brief darkness.[3]
> *Ib. V, A Covered Bridge at*
> *Lucerne*

Don't cross the bridge till you come to
it,

---

[1] See Paul Revere, p. 464b.
[2] And soon, too soon, we part with pain,
    To sail o'er silent seas again.
       THOMAS MOORE [1779–1852], *Meeting*
                   of the Ships
    Two lives that once part are as ships that
divide. — EDWARD BULWER-LYTTON [1803–1873],
A Lament
    As vessels starting from ports thousands of
miles apart pass close to each other in the naked
breadths of the ocean, nay, sometimes even touch
in the dark. — OLIVER WENDELL HOLMES, *Professor at the Breakfast Table* [1860]
    [3] Death seems but a covered way
    Which opens into light.
       WHITTIER [1807–1892], *My Psalm, st. 14*

Is a proverb old, and of excellent wit.
> *The Golden Legend, pt. VI,*
> *The School of Salerno*

Let him not boast who puts his armor
on
As he who puts if off, the battle done.
> *Morituri Salutamus* [1875],
> *st. 9*

Ye, against whose familiar names not
yet
The fatal asterisk of death is set.
> *Ib. st. 11*

The love of learning, the sequestered
nooks,
And all the sweet serenity of books.
> *Ib. st. 21*

Ah, nothing is too late,
Till the tired heart shall cease to palpitate.   *Ib. st. 22*

For age is opportunity no less
Than youth itself.   *Ib. st. 24*

Not in the clamor of the crowded
street,
Not in the shouts and plaudits of the
throng,
But in ourselves, are triumph and defeat.   *The Poets*

Nothing that is can pause or stay;
The moon will wax, the moon will
wane,
The mist and cloud will turn to rain,
The rain to mist and cloud again,
Tomorrow be today.
> *Kéramos* [1878]

Three silences there are: the first of
speech,
The second of desire, the third of
thought;
This is the lore a Spanish monk, distraught
With dreams and visions, was the first
to teach.
> *The Three Silences of Molinos* [1]

In the long, sleepless watches of the
night.
> *The Cross of Snow* [1879]

---

[1] Miguel Molinos [1640–1696], Spanish mystic,
one of the early Quietists.

The holiest of all holidays are those
Kept by ourselves in silence and apart;
The secret anniversaries of the heart.
Holidays

Your silent tents of green [1]
  We deck with fragrant flowers;
Yours has the suffering been,
  The memory shall be ours.
      Decoration Day, st. 6

Great is the art of beginning, but
    greater the art is of ending;
Many a poem is marred by a superflu-
    ous verse.
        Elegiac Verse, st. 14

  There was a little girl
  Who had a little curl
Right in the middle of her forehead;
  And when she was good
  She was very, very good,
But when she was bad she was horrid.
      There Was a Little Girl [2]

Out of the shadows of night
The world rolls into light;
It is daybreak everywhere.[3]
    The Bells of San Blas,[4] *st. 11*

ROBERT MONTGOMERY
1807–1855

The soul aspiring pants its source to
    mount,
As streams meander level with their
    fount.[5]
    The Omnipresence of the Deity
        [1828], *pt. I*

---

[1]   The low green tent
  Whose curtain never outward swings.
        WHITTIER, *Snowbound* [1866]
[2] BLANCHE ROOSEVELT TUCKER, in *The Home
Life of Henry W. Longfellow* [1882], states that
these lines were written by the poet for his
children on a day when Edith did not want to
have her hair curled.
[3] See Horne, p. 610b.
[4] The last poem written by Longfellow, dated
March 15, 1882. He died March 24.
[5] We take this to be, on the whole, the worst
similitude in the world. In the first place, no
stream meanders or can possibly meander level
with the fount. In the next place, if streams did
meander level with their founts, no two motions

JOHN GREENLEAF WHITTIER
1807–1892

No fetters in the Bay State — no slave
  upon our land!
    Massachusetts to Virginia
        [1843], *st. 24*

What calls back the past, like the rich
  pumpkin pie?
      The Pumpkin [1844], *st. 3*

The Present, the Present is all thou
    hast
  For thy sure possessing;
Like the patriarch's angel hold it fast
  Till it gives its blessing.[1]
      My Soul and I [1847], *st. 34*

The Night is mother of the Day,
  The Winter of the Spring,
And ever upon old Decay
  The greenest mosses cling.
    A Dream of Summer [1847], *st. 4*

So fallen! so lost! the light withdrawn
  Which once he wore!
The glory from his gray hairs gone
  Forevermore!
      Ichabod [2] [1850], *st. 1*

  From those great eyes
  The soul has fled:
When faith is lost, when honor dies,
  The man is dead!   *Ib. st. 8*

---

can be less like each other than that of
meandering level and that of mounting upwards.
— MACAULAY, *Review of Montgomery's Poems*
[1830]
  These lines were omitted in the subsequent
edition of the poem.
[1] See *Genesis 32:26*, p. 7b, and Cotton, p.
421a.
[2] This poem was the outcome of the surprise
and grief and forecast of evil consequences
which I felt on reading the seventh of March
speech of Daniel Webster in support of the
"compromise," and the Fugitive Slave Law. No
partisan or personal enmity dictated it. On the
contrary my admiration of the splendid personality and intellectual power of the great senator
was never stronger than when I laid down his
speech, and, in one of the saddest moments of
my life, penned my protest. — WHITTIER's *Note*
  And she named the child Ichabod, saying,
The glory is departed from Israel. — *I Samuel
4:21*

Search thine own heart. What paineth thee
In others in thyself may be.
The Chapel of the Hermits
[1853], *st. 85*

Blessings on thee, little man,
Barefoot boy, with cheek of tan!
The Barefoot Boy [1856], *st. 1*

Health that mocks the doctor's rules,
Knowledge never learned of schools.
Ib. st. 2

The age is dull and mean. Men creep,
Not walk.
Lines Inscribed to Friends under Arrest for Treason Against the Slave Power [1856], *st. 1*

Nature speaks in symbols and in signs.
To Charles Sumner

For of all sad words of tongue or pen,
The saddest are these: "It might have been!"
Maud Muller [1856], *st. 53*

Old Floyd Ireson, for his hard heart,
Tarred and feathered and carried in a cart
By the women of Marblehead.
Skipper Ireson's Ride [1860], *st. 1*

Round the silver domes of Lucknow,
Moslem mosque and Pagan shrine,
Breathed the air to Britons dearest,
The air of Auld Lang Syne.[1]
The Pipes at Lucknow, st. 9

The windows of my soul I throw
Wide open to the sun.
My Psalm, st. 2

Up from the meadows rich with corn,
Clear in the cool September morn,
Barbara Frietchie [1864], *st. 1*

The clustered spires of Frederick stand
Green-walled by the hills of Maryland.
Ib. st. 2

[1] See Burns, p. 494b.
It was the pipes of the Highlanders,
And now they played "Auld Lang Syne."
ROBERT TRAILL SPENCE LOWELL [1816–1891], *The Relief of Lucknow* [September 25, 1857]

"Shoot, if you must, this old gray head,
But spare your country's flag," she said.
Barbara Frietchie, st. 18

"Who touches a hair of yon gray head
Dies like a dog! March on!" he said.
Ib. st. 21

The sun that brief December day
Rose cheerless over hills of gray,
And, darkly circled, gave at noon
A sadder light than waning moon.
Snowbound [1866], *l. 1*

Shut in from all the world without,
We sat the clean-winged hearth about.
Ib. l. 155

Angel of the backward look.
Ib. l. 714

I know not where His islands lift
Their fronded palms in air;
I only know I cannot drift
Beyond His love and care.
The Eternal Goodness [1867], *st. 20*

Dear Lord and Father of mankind,
Forgive our foolish ways!
Reclothe us in our rightful mind,
In purer lives Thy service find,
In deeper reverence, praise.
The Brewing of Soma [1872]

God is and all is well.[1]
My Birthday, st. 2

He brings cool dew in his little bill,
And lets it fall on the souls of sin:
You can see the mark on his red breast still
Of fires that scorch as he drops it in.[2] *The Robin, st. 4*

[1] See Browning, p. 661b.
[2] Far, far away, is a land of woe and darkness, spirits of evil and fire. Day after day a little bird flies there, bearing in his bill a drop of water to quench the flame. So near the burning stream does he fly that his feathers are scorched by it, and hence he is named "Bron-rhuddyn" — breast-burned. — *Carmarthenshire legend of the robin*

Sweet Robin, I have heard them say
That thou wert there upon the day
That Christ was crowned in cruel scorn,
And bore away one bleeding thorn;
That so the blush upon thy breast

SALMON PORTLAND CHASE
1808–1873

The only way to resumption is to resume.

> *Letter to Horace Greeley*
> *[March 17, 1866]*

The Constitution, in all its provisions, looks to an indestructible Union composed of indestructible States.

> *Decision in Texas v. White, 7*
> *Wallace 725 [1868]*

ANDREW JOHNSON
1808–1875

We are swinging round the circle.

> *On the Presidential Reconstruction Tour [August 1866]*

ALPHONSE KARR
1808–1890

The more things change, the more they remain the same.[1]

> *Les Guêpes [Janvier, 1849]*

MAURICE DE MACMAHON
1808–1893

Here I am, and here I stay.[2]

> *At Sevastopol [September 1855]*

THOMAS MILLER
1808–1874

Christmas comes but once a year.

> *Title of poem*

In shameful sorrow was imprest,
And thence thy genial sympathy
With our redeemed humanity.
  WILLIAM CROSWELL DOANE [1832–1913],
        Robin Redbreast

[1] Plus ça change, plus c'est la même chose.
[2] J'y suis, j'y reste.
Reply to the commander in chief, from the trenches before Malakoff, in the siege of Sevastopol, when warned to beware of an explosion which might follow the retreat of the Russians.

CAROLINE SHERIDAN NORTON
1808–1877

Love not! love not! ye hapless sons of clay;
Hope's gayest wreaths are made of earthly flowers.

> *Love Not, st. 1*

A soldier of the Legion lay dying in Algiers;
There was lack of woman's nursing, there was dearth of woman's tears.

> *Bingen on the Rhine, st. 1*

GEORGE WASHINGTON PATTEN
1808–1882

If we must perish in the fight,
Oh! let us die like men.

> *Oh! Let Us Die Like Men, st. 4*

SAMUEL FRANCIS SMITH
1808–1895

My country, 'tis of thee,
Sweet land of liberty,
  Of thee I sing:
Land where my fathers died,
Land of the pilgrims' pride,
From every mountainside
  Let freedom ring.

> *America [1831], st. 1*

Long may our land be bright
With freedom's holy light;
Protect us by thy might,
  Great God, our King!   *Ib. st. 4*

CHARLES ROBERT DARWIN
1809–1882

I have called this principle, by which each slight variation, if useful, is preserved, by the term Natural Selection.

> *The Origin of Species [1859],*
> *ch. 3*

The expression often used by Mr. Herbert Spencer, of the Survival of the

Fittest, is more accurate, and is sometimes equally convenient.[1]

The Origin of Species, ch. 3

We will now discuss in a little more detail the Struggle for Existence.[2]

Ib.

It is interesting to contemplate an entangled bank, clothed with many plants of many kinds, with birds singing on the bushes, with various insects flitting about, and with worms crawling through the damp earth, and to reflect that these elaborately constructed forms, so different from each other, and dependent on each other in so complex a manner, have all been produced by laws acting around us.   *Ib.*

The highest possible stage in moral culture is when we recognize that we ought to control our thoughts.

The Descent of Man [1871], *ch. 4*

The presence of a body of well-instructed men, who have not to labor for their daily bread, is important to a degree which cannot be overestimated; as all high intellectual work is carried on by them, and on such work material progress of all kinds mainly depends, not to mention other and higher advantages.   *Ib. 5*

Progress has been much more general than retrogression.   *Ib.*

The Simiadae then branched off into two great stems, the New World and Old World monkeys; and from the latter at a remote period, Man, the wonder and the glory of the universe, proceeded.[3]   *Ib. 6*

---

[1] This survival of the fittest which I have here sought to express in mechanical terms, is that which Mr. Darwin has called "natural selection, or the preservation of favored races in the struggle for life." — HERBERT SPENCER, *Principles of Biology* [1864–1867], *Indirect Equilibration*

[2] The perpetual struggle for room and food. — MALTHUS, *On Population* [1798], *ch. 3*

[3] I confess freely to you, I could never look long upon a monkey, without very mortifying reflections. — CONGREVE, *Letter to Dennis* [1695] See Disraeli, p. 612b.

Man scans with scrupulous care the character and pedigree of his horses, cattle, and dogs before he matches them; but when he comes to his own marriage he rarely, or never, takes any such care.

The Descent of Man, ch. 21

For my own part I would as soon be descended from that heroic little monkey, who braved his dreaded enemy in order to save the life of his keeper; or from that old baboon, who, descending from the mountains, carried away in triumph his young comrade from a crowd of astonished dogs — as from a savage who delights to torture his enemies, offers up bloody sacrifices, practices infanticide without remorse, treats his wives like slaves, knows no decency, and is haunted by the grossest superstitions.   *Ib.*

The plow is one of the most ancient and most valuable of man's inventions; but long before he existed the land was in fact regularly plowed, and still continues to be thus plowed by earthworms. It may be doubted whether there are many other animals which have played so important a part in the history of the world, as have these lowly organized creatures.

The Formation of Vegetable Mold Through the Action of Worms [1881], *ch. 7*

Physiological experiment on animals is justifiable for real investigation, but not for mere damnable and detestable curiosity.

Letter to E. Ray Lankester

As for a future life, every man must judge for himself between conflicting vague probabilities.

From Life and Letters of Charles Darwin, edited by FRANCIS DARWIN [1887]

I love fools' experiments. I am always making them.   *Ib.*

Believing as I do that man in the distant future will be a far more perfect creature than he now is, it is an intolerable thought that he and all other sentient beings are doomed to complete annihilation after such long-continued slow progress. To those who fully admit the immortality of the human soul, the destruction of our world will not appear so dreadful.

> *From Life and Letters*
> *of Charles Darwin*

EDWARD FITZGERALD
1809–1883

Wake! For the Sun who scatter'd into flight
The Stars before him from the Field of night,
Drives Night along with them from Heav'n and strikes
The Sultan's Turret with a Shaft of Light.

> *The Rubáiyát of Omar*
> *Khayyám,*[1] *st. 1*

Awake! for Morning in the Bowl of Night
Has flung the Stone that puts the Stars to flight:
And Lo! the Hunter of the East has caught
The Sultan's Turret in a Noose of Light. *Ib.* [*first ed.*]

Now the New Year reviving old Desires,
The thoughtful Soul to Solitude retires. *Ib. st. 4*

Iram indeed is gone with all his Rose. *Ib. st. 5*

Come, fill the Cup, and in the fire of Spring
The Winter garment of Repentance fling:
The Bird of Time has but a little way
To fly — and Lo! the Bird is on the Wing. *Ib. st. 7* [*first ed.*]

The Leaves of Life keep falling one by one. *Ib. st. 8*

---

[1] Translated in four editions, 1859, 1868, 1872, and 1879. The fourth edition is used here, unless otherwise stated.

Each Morn a thousand Roses brings, you say:
Yes, but where leaves the Rose of Yesterday?

> *The Rubáiyát of Omar*
> *Khayyám, st. 9*

A Book of Verses underneath the Bough,
A Jug of Wine, a Loaf of Bread — and Thou
Beside me singing in the Wilderness —
Oh, Wilderness were Paradise enow! *Ib. st. 12*

Ah, take the Cash, and let the Credit go,
Nor heed the rumble of a distant Drum! *Ib. st. 13*

The Worldly Hope men set their Hearts upon
Turns Ashes — or it prospers; and anon,
Like Snow upon the Desert's dusty Face,
Lighting a little hour or two — is gone. *Ib. st. 16*

Think, in this batter'd Caravanserai
Whose Portals are alternate Night and Day,
How Sultan after Sultan with his Pomp
Abode his destin'd Hour, and went his way. *Ib. st. 17*

They say the Lion and the Lizard keep
The Courts where Jamshyd gloried and drank deep:
And Bahram, that great Hunter — the Wild Ass
Stamps o'er his Head, but cannot break his sleep. *Ib. st. 18*

I sometimes think that never blows so red
The Rose as where some buried Caesar bled;
That every Hyacinth the Garden wears
Dropt in her Lap from some once lovely Head.[1] *Ib. st. 19*

---

[1] See Shakespeare, p. 266a, and Tennyson, p. 650a.

Ah, my Belovèd, fill the Cup that clears
Today of past Regrets and future
   Fears:
Tomorrow! — Why, Tomorrow I may
   be
Myself with Yesterday's Sev'n thousand
   Years.[1]
       The Rubáiyát of Omar
         Khayyám, st. 21

For some we loved, the loveliest and
   the best
That from his Vintage rolling Time
   hath prest.   *Ib. st.* 22

Ah, make the most of what we yet may
   spend,
Before we too into the Dust descend;
Dust into Dust, and under Dust, to
   lie,
Sans Wine, sans Song, sans Singer,
   and — sans End!   *Ib. st.* 24

Myself when young did eagerly frequent
Doctor and Saint, and heard great
   argument
About it and about: but evermore
Came out by the same door wherein I
   went.   *Ib. st.* 27

And this was all the Harvest that I
   reap'd —
"I came like Water, and like Wind I
   go."   *Ib. st.* 28

There was the Door to which I found
   no Key;
There was the Veil through which I
   might not see.
Some little talk awhile of Me and
   Thee
There was — and then no more of
   Thee and Me.   *Ib. st.* 32

    "While you live,
Drink! — for, once dead, you never
   shall return."   *Ib. st.* 35

And fear not lest Existence closing
   your
Account, and mine, should know the
   like no more;
The Eternal Saki from that Bowl has
   pour'd

[1] See Euripides, p. 84a.

Millions of Bubbles like us, and will
   pour.[1]
       The Rubáiyát of Omar
         Khayyám, st. 46

'Tis all a Checkerboard of Nights and
   Days
Where Destiny with Men for Pieces
   plays:
Hither and thither moves, and mates,
   and slays,
·And one by one back in the Closet
   lays.   *Ib. st.* 49 [*first ed.*]

    Striking from the Calendar
Unborn Tomorrow and dead Yesterday.   *Ib. st.* 57

The Moving Finger writes; and, having
   writ,
Moves on: nor all your Piety nor Wit
Shall lure it back to cancel half a Line,
Nor all your Tears wash out a Word of
   it.   *Ib. st.* 71

   That inverted Bowl we call The Sky,
Whereunder crawling coop'd we live
   and die.   *Ib. st.* 72 [*first ed.*]

Ah, Moon of my Delight who know'st
   no wane.   *Ib. st.* 74 [*first ed.*]

One Flash of it within the Tavern
   caught
Better than in the Temple lost outright.   *Ib. st.* 77

And He that with his hand the Vessel
   made
Will surely not in after Wrath destroy.   *Ib. st.* 85

After a momentary silence spake
Some Vessel of a more ungainly Make;
"They sneer at me for leaning all
   awry:
What! did the Hand then of the Potter
   shake?"   *Ib. st.* 86

Who *is* the Potter, pray, and who the
   Pot?   *Ib. st.* 87

Indeed the Idols I have loved so long
Have done my credit in this World
   much wrong:
Have drown'd my Glory in a shallow
   Cup,

[1] See Tennyson, p. 644b.

And sold my Reputation for a Song.
The Rubáiyát of Omar
Khayyám, st. 93

I wonder often what the Vintners buy
One half so precious as the stuff they
sell. *Ib. st. 95*

Yet Ah, that Spring should vanish with
the Rose!
That Youth's sweet-scented manuscript
should close! *Ib. st. 96*

Ah Love! could you and I with Him
conspire
To grasp this Sorry Scheme of Things
entire,
Would not we shatter it to bits — and
then
Remold it nearer to the Heart's Desire!
Ib. st. 99

And when like her, O Saki, you shall
pass
Among the Guests Star-scatter'd on the
Grass,
And in your joyous errand reach the
spot
Where I made One — turn down an
empty Glass! *Ib. st. 101*

The King in a carriage may ride,
And the Beggar may crawl at his side;
But in the general race,
They are traveling all the same pace.
Chronomoros

Mrs. Browning's death was rather a
relief to me, I must say; no more Aurora Leighs, thank God!
Letter [July 15, 1861] [1]

Taste is the feminine of genius.
Letter to James Russell Lowell
[October 1877]

---

[1] Aye, dead! and were yourself alive, good Fitz,
How to return your thanks would pass my
wits.
Kicking you seems the common lot of curs,
While more appropriate greeting lends you
grace.
Surely to spit there glorifies your face,
Spitting with lips once sanctified by Hers.
ROBERT BROWNING in *The Athenaeum*
[July 13, 1889]

WILLIAM EWART GLADSTONE
1809–1898

Decision by majorities is as much an
expedient as lighting by gas.
Speech, House of Commons
[1858]

You cannot fight against the future.
Time is on our side.
Speech on the Reform Bill [1866]

[The Turks] one and all, bag and
baggage, shall, I hope, clear out from
the province they have desolated and
profaned.
Speech, House of Commons
[May 7, 1877]

The disease of an evil conscience is
beyond the practice of all the physicians of all the countries in the world.
Speech, Plumstead [1878]

National injustice is the surest road
to national downfall. *Ib.*

Out of the range of practical politics.
Speech, Dalkeith [November 26,
1879]

The resources of civilization are not
yet exhausted.
Speech, Leeds [October 7, 1881]

All the world over, I will back the
masses against the classes.
Speech, Liverpool [June 28, 1886]

I have always regarded that Constitution as the most remarkable work
known to me in modern times to have
been produced by the human intellect,
at a single stroke (so to speak), in its
application to political affairs. [1]
Letter to the committee in
charge of the celebration of
the centennial anniversary
of the American Constitu-
tion [July 20, 1887]

---

[1] As the British Constitution is the most subtle
organism which has proceeded from progressive
history, so the American Constitution is the
most wonderful work ever struck off at a given
time by the brain and purpose of man. — GLAD-
STONE, *Kin Beyond the Sea [North American
Review,* September, 1878]

Selfishness is the greatest curse of the human race.

Speech, Hawarden [May 28, 1890]

NIKOLAI GOGOL
1809–1852

It is dreary to live in this world, gentlemen!

> The Tale of How Ivan Ivanovich Quarreled with Ivan Nikiforovich [1835]

It is no use to blame the looking glass if your face is awry.

> *The Inspector-General [1836], epigraph*

Of course, Alexander the Great was a hero, but why smash the chairs?　　*Ib.*

The more destruction there is everywhere, the more it shows the activity of town authorities.　　*Ib. act I, sc. 1*

I tell everyone very plainly that I take bribes, but what kind of bribes? Why, greyhound puppies. That's a totally different matter.　　*Ib.*

The sergeant's widow told you a lie when she said I flogged her. I never flogged her. She flogged herself.

> *Ib. IV, 15*

What are you laughing at? You are laughing at yourselves!　　*Ib. V, 8*

And for a long time yet, led by some wondrous power, I am fated to journey hand in hand with my strange heroes and to survey the surging immensity of life, to survey it through the laughter that all can see and through the tears unseen and unknown by anyone.

Dead Souls [1842], vol. I, ch. 11

Rus! Rus! I see you, from my lovely enchanted remoteness I see you: a country of dinginess, and bleakness and dispersal; no arrogant wonders of nature crowned by the arrogant wonders of art appear within you to delight or terrify the eyes. . . . So what is the incomprehensible secret force driving me towards you? Why do I constantly hear the echo of your mournful song as it is carried from sea to sea through your entire expanse? . . . And since you are without end yourself, is it not within you that a boundless thought will be born? [1]

Dead Souls, vol. I, ch. 12

Oh troika, winged troika, tell me who invented you? Surely, nowhere but among a nimble nation could you have been born: in a country which has taken itself in earnest and has evenly spread far and wide over half of the globe, so that once you start counting the milestones you may count on till a speckled haze dances before your eyes. . . .

Rus, are you not similar in your headlong motion to one of those nimble troikas that none can overtake? The flying road turns into smoke under you, bridges thunder and pass, all falls back and is left behind! . . . And what does this awesome motion mean? What is the passing strange force contained in these passing strange steeds? Steeds, steeds, what steeds! Has the whirlwind a home in your manes? . . . Rus, whither are you speeding so? Answer me. No answer. The middle bell trills out in a dream its liquid soliloquy; the roaring air is torn to pieces and becomes wind; all things on earth fly by and other nations and states gaze askance as they step aside and give her the right of way.[1]

Ib. vol. I, concluding paragraphs

In the course of the reading he [Pushkin] became more and more melancholy and finally became completely gloomy. When the reading was over he uttered in a voice full of sorrow: "Goodness, how sad is our Russia!"

> *Four Letters Concerning Dead Souls [1843]*

I shall laugh my bitter laugh.

> *Epitaph on Gogol's tombstone*

[1] Translated by VLADIMIR NABOKOV in *Nikolai Gogol* [1944].

OLIVER WENDELL HOLMES[1]
1809–1894

Ay, tear her tattered ensign down!
Long has it waved on high,
And many an eye has danced to see
That banner in the sky;
Beneath it rung the battle shout,
And burst the cannon's roar —
The meteor of the ocean air
Shall sweep the clouds no more.
       Old Ironsides [2] [1830], *st. 1*

One sad, ungathered rose
On my ancestral tree.
       My Aunt, st. 6

And silence, like a poultice, comes
To heal the blows of sound.
       The Music Grinders, st. 10

And since, I never dare to write
As funny as I can.
       The Height of the Ridiculous,
       st. 8

When the last reader reads no more.
       The Last Reader

Age, like distance, lends a double charm.[3]
       A Rhymed Lesson. Urania

And when you stick on conversation's burrs,
Don't strew your pathway with those dreadful *urs*.   *Ib.*

Learn the sweet magic of a cheerful face;
Not always smiling, but at least serene.
       The Morning Visit

One flag, one land, one heart, one hand,
One Nation, evermore!
       Voyage of the Good Ship Union,
       st. 12

---

[1] The most successful combination the world has ever seen, of physician and man of letters. — SIR WILLIAM OSLER. *From* HARVEY CUSHING, *Life of Sir William Osler* [1925], *vol. I, ch. 15*

[2] This poem roused such popular feeling that it is generally credited with saving the frigate *Constitution* from being destroyed as unfit for service.

[3] See Campbell, p. 537a, and note.

Where we love is home,
Home that our feet may leave, but not our hearts.
       Homesick in Heaven, st. 5

There is no time like the old time, when you and I were young.[1]
       No Time Like the Old Time.
       st. 1

Lean, hungry, savage, anti-everythings.
       A Modest Request. The Speech

A thought is often original, though you have uttered it a hundred times.
       The Autocrat of the Breakfast
       Table [1858], *ch. 1*

Everybody likes and respects self-made men. It is a great deal better to be made in that way than not to be made at all.   *Ib.*

Insanity is often the logic of an accurate mind overtaxed.   *Ib. 2*

Man has his will — but woman has her way!   *Ib.*

Put not your trust in money, but put your money in trust.   *Ib.*

I find the great thing in this world is not so much where we stand, as in what direction we are moving: To reach the port of heaven, we must sail sometimes with the wind and sometimes against it — but we must sail, and not drift, nor lie at anchor.   *Ib. 4*

Build thee more stately mansions, O my soul,
As the swift seasons roll!
Leave thy low-vaulted past!
Let each new temple, nobler than the last,
Shut thee from heaven with a dome more vast,
Till thou at length art free,

---

[1] The good old times, the grand old times, the great old times! — DICKENS, *The Chimes* [1844], *First Quarter*
There are no days like the good old days,
The days when we were youthful!
       EUGENE FIELD [1850–1895], *Old Times,*
       Old Friends, Old Love

Leaving thine outgrown shell by life's
    unresting sea!
    *The Autocrat of the Breakfast
    Table, [The Chambered Nauti-
    lus, st. 5]*

Sin has many tools, but a lie is the
handle which fits them all.   *Ib.* 6

There is that glorious Epicurean paradox uttered by my friend the Historian,[1] in one of his flashing moments:
"Give us the luxuries of life, and we
will dispense with its necessaries."[2]
    Ib.

Boston State-House is the hub of the
solar system. You couldn't pry that out
of a Boston man, if you had the tire of
all creation straightened out for a crowbar.   *Ib.*

The axis of the earth sticks out visibly through the center of each and
every town or city.   *Ib.*

The world's great men have not
commonly been great scholars, nor its
great scholars great men.   *Ib.*

Knowledge and timber shouldn't be
much used till they are seasoned.
    Ib.

The hat is the *ultimum moriens* of
respectability.   *Ib.* 8

Have you heard of the wonderful one-
    hoss shay,
That was built in such a logical way
It ran a hundred years to a day?
    Ib. 11. [*The Deacon's Master-
    piece, st.* 1]

End of the wonderful one-hoss shay.
Logic is logic. That's all I say.
    Ib. [*st.* 12]

Little I ask; my wants are few,
    I only wish a hut of stone,
(A *very plain* brown stone will do,)
    That I may call my own.[3]
    Ib. [*Contentment, st.* 1]

[1] John Lothrop Motley [1814–1877].
[2] Said Scopas of Thessaly, "We rich men count
our felicity and happiness to lie in these super-
fluities, and not in those necessary things." —
PLUTARCH [A.D. 46–120], *On the Love of Wealth*
[3] See Edward Young, p. 339a, and Goldsmith,
p. 448a.

He comes of the Brahmin caste of
New England. This is the harmless, inoffensive, untitled aristocracy.
    *The Brahmin Caste of New
    England* [1860]

Science is a first-rate piece of furniture for a man's upper chamber, if he
has common sense on the ground floor.
    *The Poet at the Breakfast Table
    * [1872], *ch.* 5

And if I should live to be
The last leaf upon the tree
    In the spring,
Let them smile, as I do now,
At the old forsaken bough
    Where I cling.
    The Last Leaf, st. 8

RICHARD MONCKTON
MILNES, BARON
HOUGHTON
1809–1885

But the beating of my own heart
Was all the sound I heard.
    The Brookside, st. 1

A fair little girl sat under a tree,
Sewing as long as her eyes could see;
Then smoothed her work, and folded it
    right,
And said, "Dear work, good night,
    good night."
    *Good Night and Good Morning,
    st.* 1

Lady Moon, Lady Moon, where are you
    roving?
Over the sea.
Lady Moon, Lady Moon, whom are
    you loving?
All that love me!   *A Child's Song*

ABRAHAM LINCOLN
1809–1865

If the good people, in their wisdom,
shall see fit to keep me in the background, I have been too familiar with
disappointments to be very much cha-
grined.

    *Address, New Salem, Illinois
    * [*March 9, 1832*]

I go for all sharing the privileges of the government who assist in bearing its burdens.

> *Letter to Editor, Sangamon Journal, New Salem, Illinois [June 13, 1836]*

If destruction be our lot we must ourselves be its author and finisher. As a nation of freemen we must live through all time, or die by suicide.

> *Address, Young Men's Lyceum, Springfield, Illinois [January 27, 1838]*

There is no grievance that is a fit object of redress by mob law.   *Ib.*

Towering genius disdains a beaten path. It seeks regions hitherto unexplored.   *Ib.*

No man is good enough to govern another man without that other's consent.

> *Speech, Peoria, Illinois [October 16, 1854]*

I am not a Know-Nothing; that is certain. How could I be? How can anyone who abhors the oppression of Negroes be in favor of degrading classes of white people? Our progress in degeneracy appears to me to be pretty rapid. As a nation we began by declaring that "all men are created equal." We now practically read it "all men are created equal, except Negroes." When the Know-Nothings get control, it will read "all men are created equal, except Negroes and foreigners and Catholics." When it comes to this, I shall prefer emigrating to some country where they make no pretense of loving liberty — to Russia, for instance, where despotism can be taken pure, and without the base alloy of hypocrisy.

> *Letter to Joshua F. Speed [August 24, 1855]*

The ballot is stronger than the bullet.

> *Speech, Bloomington, Illinois [May 19, 1856]*

"A house divided against itself cannot stand." [1] I believe this government cannot endure permanently half slave and half free. I do not expect the Union to be dissolved — I do not expect the house to fall — but I do expect it will cease to be divided. It will become all one thing, or all the other. Either the opponents of slavery will arrest the further spread of it, and place it where the public mind shall rest in the belief that it is in the course of ultimate extinction; or its advocates will push it forward till it shall become alike lawful in all the states, old as well as new, North as well as South.

> *Speech, Republican State Convention, Springfield, Illinois [June 16, 1858]*

Nobody has ever expected me to be President. In my poor, lean, lank face nobody has ever seen that any cabbages were sprouting out.

> *Second campaign speech against Douglas,[2] Springfield, Illinois [July 17, 1858]*

As I would not be a *slave*, so I would not be a *master*. This expresses my idea of democracy. Whatever differs from this, to the extent of the difference, is no democracy.[3]

> *Fragment [August 1, 1858?]. From* Roy P. Basler, *The Collected Works of Abraham Lincoln [1953], vol. II, p. 532*

When . . . you have succeeded in dehumanizing the Negro; when you have put him down and made it impossible for him to be but as the beasts of the field; when you have extinguished his soul in this world and placed him where the ray of hope is blown out as in the darkness of the damned, are you quite sure that the demon you have

---

[1] See *Mark 3:25*, p. 45a.

[2] They have seen in his [Douglas's] round, jolly, fruitful face, post offices, land offices, marshalships and cabinet appointments, chargéships and foreign missions, bursting and sprouting out in wonderful exuberance, ready to be laid hold of by their greedy hands. — *Ib.*

[3] See *Address to Indiana Regiment*, p. 640b.

roused will not turn and rend you? What constitutes the bulwark of our own liberty and independence? It is not our frowning battlements, our bristling sea coasts, our army and our navy. These are not our reliance against tyranny. All of those may be turned against us without making us weaker for the struggle. Our reliance is in the love of liberty which God has planted in us. Our defense is in the spirit which prized liberty as the heritage of all men, in all lands everywhere. Destroy this spirit and you have planted the seeds of despotism at your own doors. Familiarize yourselves with the chains of bondage and you prepare your own limbs to wear them. Accustomed to trample on the rights of others, you have lost the genius of your own independence and become the fit subjects of the first cunning tyrant who rises among you.[1]

Speech, Edwardsville, Illinois
[September 11, 1858]

That is the issue that will continue in this country when these poor tongues of Judge Douglas and myself shall be silent. It is the eternal struggle between these two principles — right and wrong — throughout the world. They are the two principles that have stood face to face from the beginning of time; and will ever continue to struggle. The one is the common right of humanity, and the other the divine right of kings. It is the same principle in whatever shape it develops itself. It is the same spirit that says, "You toil and work and earn bread, and I'll eat it." No matter in what shape it comes, whether from the mouth of a king who seeks to bestride the people of his own nation and live by the fruit of their labor, or from one race of men as an apology for enslaving another race, it is the same tyrannical principle.

Reply, seventh and last joint debate, Alton, Illinois [October 15, 1858]

This is a world of compensation; and

he who would be no slave must consent to have no slave. Those who deny freedom to others deserve it not for themselves, and, under a just God, cannot long retain it.

Letter to H. L. Pierce and others
[April 6, 1859]

It is said an Eastern monarch once charged his wise men to invent him a sentence to be ever in view, and which should be true and appropriate in all times and situations. They presented him the words: "And this, too, shall pass away." [1] How much it expresses! How chastening in the hour of pride! How consoling in the depths of affliction!

Address, Wisconsin State Agricultural Society, Milwaukee
[September 30, 1859]

What is conservatism? Is it not adherence to the old and tried, against the new and untried?

Address, Cooper Union, New York [February 27, 1860]

Let us have faith that right makes might, and in that faith let us to the end dare to do our duty as we understand it. *Ib.*

No one, not in my situation, can appreciate my feeling of sadness at this parting. To this place, and the kindness of these people, I owe everything. Here I have lived a quarter of a century, and have passed from a young to an old man. Here my children have been born, and one is buried. I now leave, not knowing when or whether ever I may return, with a task before me greater than that which rested upon Washington. Without the assistance of that Divine Being who ever attended him, I cannot succeed. With that assistance I cannot fail. Trusting in Him who can go with me, and remain with you, and be everywhere for good, let us confidently hope that all will yet be well.

Farewell Address, Springfield, Illinois [February 11, 1861]

[1] See Einstein, p. 951a.

[1] See Hawthorne, p. 615a.

If we do not make common cause to save the good old ship of the Union on this voyage, nobody will have a chance to pilot her on another voyage.

> Address, Cleveland, Ohio [February 15, 1861]

I have never had a feeling, politically, that did not spring from the sentiments embodied in the Declaration of Independence. . . . I have often inquired of myself what great principle or idea it was that kept this Confederacy so long together. It was not the mere matter of separation of the colonies from the motherland, but that sentiment in the Declaration of Independence which gave liberty not alone to the people of this country, but hope to all the world, for all future time. It was that which gave promise that in due time the weights would be lifted from the shoulders of all men, and that all should have an equal chance. This is the sentiment embodied in the Declaration of Independence. . . . I would rather be assassinated on this spot than surrender it.

> Speech, Independence Hall, Philadelphia [February 22, 1861]

It is safe to assert that no government proper ever had a provision in its organic law for its own termination.

> First Inaugural Address [March 4, 1861]

If by the mere force of numbers a majority should deprive a minority of any clearly written constitutional right, it might, in a moral point of view, justify revolution — certainly would if such a right were a vital one. ***Ib.***

This country, with its institutions, belongs to the people who inhabit it. Whenever they shall grow weary of the existing government, they can exercise their constitutional right of amending it, or their revolutionary right to dismember or overthrow it. ***Ib.***

Why should there not be a patient confidence in the ultimate justice of the people? Is there any better or equal hope in the world?

> First Inaugural Address

While the people retain their virtue and vigilance, no administration, by any extreme of wickedness or folly, can very seriously injure the government in the short space of four years. ***Ib.***

We are not enemies, but friends. We must not be enemies. Though passion may have strained, it must not break, our bonds of affection. The mystic chords of memory, stretching from every battlefield and patriot grave to every living heart and hearthstone all over this broad land, will yet swell the chorus of the Union when again touched, as surely they will be, by the better angels of our nature. ***Ib.***

I think the necessity of being *ready* increases. Look to it.

> Letter (*this is the whole message*) to Governor Andrew G. Curtin of Pennsylvania [April 8, 1861]

Labor is prior to, and independent of, capital. Capital is only the fruit of labor, and could never have existed if labor had not first existed. Labor is the superior of capital, and deserves much the higher consideration. Capital has its rights, which are as worthy of protection as any other rights.[1]

> First Annual Message to Congress [December 3, 1861]

It is difficult to make a man miserable while he feels he is worthy of himself and claims kindred to the great God who made him.

> Address on colonization to a Negro deputation at Washington [August 14, 1862]

My paramount object in this struggle is to save the Union, and is not either to save or to destroy slavery. If I could save the Union without freeing any slave, I would do it; and if I could save it by freeing all the slaves, I would do

[1] See Webster, p. 546b.

it; and if I could do it by freeing some and leaving others alone, I would also do that.

Letter to Horace Greeley
[August 22, 1862]

I shall try to correct errors when shown to be errors; and I shall adopt new views so fast as they shall appear to be true views. . . . I intend no modification of my oft-expressed personal wish that all men, everywhere, could be free.   ***Ib.***

On the first day of January in the year of our Lord, one thousand eight hundred and sixty-three, all persons held as slaves within any state, or designated part of a state, the people whereof shall then be in rebellion against the United States shall be then, thenceforward, and forever free.

Preliminary [1] *Emancipation Proclamation [September 22, 1862]*

The President takes the result of the New York elections [2] philosophically, and will, doubtless, profit by the lesson. When Colonel Forney inquired of him how he felt about New York, he replied: "Somewhat like the boy in Kentucky, who stubbed his toe while running to see his sweetheart. The boy said he was too big to cry, and far too badly hurt to laugh."

Frank Leslie's Illustrated Weekly
[November 22, 1862]

A nation may be said to consist of its territory, its people, and its laws. The territory is the only part which is of certain durability.

Second Annual Message to Congress [December 1, 1862]

If there ever could be a proper time for mere catch arguments, that time surely is not now. In times like the

present, men should utter nothing for which they would not willingly be responsible through time and in eternity.

Second Annual Message
to Congress

The dogmas of the quiet past are inadequate to the stormy present. The occasion is piled high with difficulty, and we must rise with the occasion. As our case is new, so we must think anew and act anew. We must disenthrall ourselves, and then we shall save our country.

Fellow citizens, we cannot escape history. We of this Congress and this administration will be remembered in spite of ourselves. No personal significance or insignificance can spare one or another of us. The fiery trial through which we pass will light us down in honor or dishonor to the last generation. We say we are for the Union. The world will not forget that we say this. We know how to save the Union. The world knows we do know how to save it. We, even we here, hold the power and bear the responsibility. In giving freedom to the slave, we assure freedom to the free — honorable alike in what we give and what we preserve. We shall nobly save or meanly lose the last, best hope of earth. Other means may succeed; this could not fail. The way is plain, peaceful, generous, just — a way which if followed the world will forever applaud and God must forever bless.

Ib.

Beware of rashness, but with energy and sleepless vigilance go forward and give us victories.

Letter to Major General Joseph Hooker [January 26, 1863]

The Father of Waters again goes unvexed to the sea.

Letter to James C. Conkling
[August 26, 1863]

I have endured a great deal of ridicule without much malice; and have received a great deal of kindness, not

---

[1] The Emancipation Proclamation was issued one hundred days later, on January 1, 1863.

[2] The election was a victory for Horatio Seymour, Democratic candidate for governor of New York. Moreover, throughout the North the Democrats picked up a number of congressional seats and won a number of state elections.

quite free from ridicule. I am used to it.

Letter to James H. Hackett
[November 2, 1863]

Fourscore and seven years ago our fathers brought forth on this continent, a new nation, conceived in Liberty, and dedicated to the proposition that all men are created equal.

Now we are engaged in a great civil war, testing whether that nation or any nation so conceived and so dedicated can long endure. We are met on a great battlefield of that war. We have come to dedicate a portion of that field, as a final resting place for those who here gave their lives that that nation might live. It is altogether fitting and proper that we should do this.

But, in a larger sense, we cannot dedicate — we cannot consecrate — we cannot hallow — this ground. The brave men, living and dead, who struggled here, have consecrated it far above our poor power to add or detract. The world will little note nor long remember what we say here, but it can never forget what they did here. It is for us, the living, rather to be dedicated here to the unfinished work which they who fought here have thus far so nobly advanced. It is rather for us to be here dedicated to the great task remaining before us — that from these honored dead we take increased devotion to that cause for which they gave the last full measure of devotion; that we here highly resolve that these dead shall not have died in vain; that this nation, under God, shall have a new birth of freedom; and that government of the people, by the people, for the people, shall not perish from the earth.[1]

Address at Gettysburg [November 19, 1863]

The President last night had a dream. He was in a party of plain people and as it became known who he was they began to comment on his appear-

[1] See Wycliffe, p. 163b; Webster, p. 547a; Garrison, p. 616a; and Theodore Parker, p. 657b.

ance. One of them said, "He is a common-looking man." The President replied, "Common-looking people are the best in the world: that is the reason the Lord makes so many of them."

From Letters of John Hay and Extracts from His Diary, edited by C. L. Hay [December 23, 1863]

I claim not to have controlled events, but confess plainly that events have controlled me.

Letter to A. G. Hodges
[April 4, 1864]

The world has never had a good definition of the word liberty. And the American people just now are much in want of one. We all declare for liberty; but in using the same word we do not mean the same thing. With some, the word liberty may mean for each man to do as he pleases with himself and the product of his labor; while with others the same word may mean for some men to do as they please with other men and the product of other men's labor. Here are two, not only different, but incompatible things, called by the same name, liberty. And it follows that each of the things is by the respective parties called by two different and incompatible names, liberty and tyranny.

The shepherd drives the wolf from the sheep's throat, for which the sheep thanks the shepherd as his liberator, while the wolf denounces him for the same act. . . . Plainly the sheep and the wolf are not agreed upon a definition of liberty.

Address, Sanitary Fair, Baltimore [April 18, 1864]

I do not allow myself to suppose that either the convention or the League have concluded to decide that I am either the greatest or best man in America, but rather they have concluded that it is not best to swap horses while crossing the river, and have further concluded that I am not so poor a horse that they might not make a botch of it in trying to swap.

Reply to the National Union League [June 9, 1864]

Truth is generally the best vindication against slander.

Letter to Secretary Stanton, refusing to dismiss Postmaster-General Montgomery Blair [July 18, 1864]

It has long been a grave question whether any government, not too strong for the liberties of its people, can be strong enough to maintain its existence in great emergencies.

Response to a serenade [November 10, 1864]

Human nature will not change. In any future great national trial, compared with the men of this, we shall have as weak and as strong, as silly and as wise, as bad and as good. *Ib.*

I desire so to conduct the affairs of this administration that if at the end, when I come to lay down the reins of power, I have lost every other friend on earth, I shall at least have one friend left, and that friend shall be down inside me.

Reply to Missouri Committee of Seventy [1864]

Dear Madam, I have been shown in the files of the War Department a statement of the Adjutant-General of Massachusetts that you are the mother of five [1] sons who have died gloriously on the field of battle. I feel how weak and fruitless must be any words of mine which should attempt to beguile you from the grief of a loss so overwhelming. But I cannot refrain from tendering to you the consolation that may be found in the thanks of the Republic they died to save. I pray that our heavenly Father may assuage the anguish of your bereavement, and leave you only the cherished memory of the loved and lost, and the solemn pride that must be

yours to have laid so costly a sacrifice upon the altar of freedom.

Letter to Mrs. Bixby [November 21, 1864]

It may seem strange that any men should dare to ask a just God's assistance in wringing their bread from the sweat of other men's faces,[1] but let us judge not, that we be not judged.[2]

Second Inaugural Address [March 4, 1865]

The Almighty has His own purposes. *Ib.*

Fondly do we hope, fervently do we pray, that this mighty scourge of war may speedily pass away. Yet, if God wills that it continue until all the wealth piled by the bondsman's two hundred and fifty years of unrequited toil shall be sunk, and until every drop of blood drawn with the lash shall be paid by another drawn with the sword, as was said three thousand years ago, so still it must be said, "The judgments of the Lord are true and righteous altogether." [3]

With malice toward none, with charity for all, with firmness in the right as God gives us to see the right,[4] let us strive on to finish the work we are in, to bind up the nation's wounds, to care for him who shall have borne the battle and for his widow and his orphan, to do all which may achieve and cherish a just and lasting peace among ourselves and with all nations. *Ib.*

I have always thought that all men should be free; but if any should be slaves, it should be first those who desire it for themselves, and secondly those who desire it for others. Whenever I hear anyone arguing for slavery, I feel a strong impulse to see it tried on him personally.[5]

Address to an Indiana Regiment [March 17, 1865]

[1] See *Genesis 3:19*, p. 6a.
[2] See *Matthew 7:1*, p. 41a.
[3] See *Psalms 19:9*, p. 17b.
[4] See John Quincy Adams, p. 503a.
[5] See *Fragment*, p. 635b.

[1] Later, the records were revised; the correct number was two.

Important principles may and must be inflexible.

> *Last public address, Washington*
> *[April 11, 1865]*

If you once forfeit the confidence of your fellow citizens, you can never regain their respect and esteem. It is true that you may fool all the people some of the time; you can even fool some of the people all the time; but you can't fool all of the people all the time.

> *To a caller at the White House.*
> *From* Alexander K. McClure,
> *Lincoln's Yarns and Stories*
> [1904], *p.* 124

If I were to try to read, much less answer, all the attacks made on me, this shop might as well be closed for any other business. I do the very best I know how — the very best I can; and I mean to keep doing so until the end. If the end brings me out all right, what is said against me won't amount to anything. If the end brings me out wrong, ten angels swearing I was right would make no difference.

> *Conversation at the White*
> *House. From* Francis B. Carpenter, *Six Months at the*
> *White House with Abraham*
> *Lincoln* [1866]

EDGAR ALLAN POE [1]
1809–1849

O, human love! thou spirit given,
On Earth, of all we hope in Heaven!
> *Tamerlane* [1827]

All that we see or seem
Is but a dream within a dream.
> *A Dream Within a Dream* [1827]

The happiest day — the happiest hour
 My sear'd and blighted heart hath
  known,
The highest hope of pride and power,
 I feel hath flown.
> *The Happiest Day — The*
> *Happiest Hour* [1827]

[1] See James Russell Lowell, p. 692b.

From childhood's hour I have not been
As others were — I have not seen
As others saw.
> *Alone* [1827]

And the cloud that took the form
When the rest of Heaven was blue
Of a demon in my view.
> *Ib.*

Hast thou not torn the Naiad from her
  flood,
The Elfin from the green grass, and
  from me
The summer dream beneath the tamarind tree?
> *Sonnet: To Science* [1827]

Sound loves to revel in a summer
  night. *Al Aaraaf* [1829], *pt.* II

It is with literature as with law or empire — an established name is an estate in tenure, or a throne in possession.
> *Poems* [1831]. *Preface, Letter to*
> *Mr. B——*

Helen, thy beauty is to me
 Like those Nicean barks of yore,
That gently, o'er a perfumed sea,
 The weary, wayworn wanderer bore
 To his own native shore.

On desperate seas long wont to roam,
 Thy hyacinth hair, thy classic face,
Thy Naiad airs have brought me home
 To the glory that was Greece,
 And the grandeur that was Rome.
> *To Helen* [1831], *st.* 1, 2

If I could dwell
Where Israfel
 Hath dwelt, and he where I,
He might not sing so wildly well
 A mortal melody,
While a bolder note than this might
  swell
From my lyre within the sky.
> *Israfel* [1] [1831], *st.* 8

Lo! Death has reared himself a throne
In a strange city.
> *The City in the Sea* [1831], *st.* 1

[1] And the angel Israfel, whose heartstrings are a lute, and who has the sweetest voice of all God's creatures. — *The Koran*

The viol, the violet, and the vine.
> *The City in the Sea, st. 2*

While from a proud tower in the town
Death looks gigantically down.[1]
> *Ib. st. 3*

And, Guy De Vere, hast *thou* no
tear? — weep now or never more!
> *Lenore* [1831], *st. 1*

A dirge for her the doubly dead in that
she died so young.   *Ib.*

Vastness! and Age! and Memories of
Eld!
Silence! and Desolation! and dim
Night!
> *The Coliseum* [1833], *st. 1*

Thou wast that all to me, love,
For which my soul did pine —
A green isle in the sea, love,
A fountain and a shrine,
All wreathed with fairy fruits and flow-
ers,
And all the flowers were mine.
> *To One in Paradise* [1834], *st. 1*

And all my days are trances,
And all my nightly dreams
Are where thy gray eye glances,
And where thy footstep gleams —
In what ethereal dances,
By what eternal streams.   *Ib. st. 4*

During the whole of a dull, dark, and
soundless day in the autumn of the
year, when the clouds hung oppressively
low in the heavens, I had been passing
alone, on horseback, through a singularly dreary tract of country, and at
length found myself, as the shades of
evening drew on, within view of the
melancholy House of Usher.
> *The Fall of the House of Usher*
> [1838]

Those who dream by day are cogni-
zant of many things which escape those
who dream only by night.
> *Eleonora* [1841]

[1] See Hart Crane, p. 1043b.

And much of Madness, and more of
Sin,
And Horror the soul of the plot.
> *The Conqueror Worm* [1843],
> *st. 3*

While the angels, all pallid and wan,
Uprising, unveiling, affirm
That the play is the tragedy, "Man,"
And its hero, the Conqueror Worm.
> *Ib. st. 5*

There is something in the unselfish
and self-sacrificing love of a brute,
which goes directly to the heart of him
who has had frequent occasion to test
the paltry friendship and gossamer
fidelity of mere Man.
> *The Black Cat* [1843]

Perverseness is one of the primitive
impulses of the human heart.   *Ib.*

The boundaries which divide Life
from Death are at best shadowy and
vague. Who shall say where the one
ends, and where the other begins?
> *The Premature Burial* [1844]

With me poetry has been not a purpose, but a passion; and the passions
should be held in reverence: they must
not — they cannot at will be excited,
with an eye to the paltry compensations, or the more paltry commenda-
tions, of mankind.
> *The Raven and Other Poems*
> [1845], *preface*

Once upon a midnight dreary, while I
pondered, weak and weary,
Over many a quaint and curious volume of forgotten lore —
While I nodded, nearly napping, suddenly there came a tapping,
As of some one gently rapping, rapping
at my chamber door.
> *The Raven* [1845], *st. 1*

Ah, distinctly I remember it was in the
bleak December;
And each separate dying ember
wrought its ghost upon the floor.
Eagerly I wished the morrow; vainly I
had sought to borrow

From my books surcease of sorrow —
    sorrow for the lost Lenore —
For the rare and radiant maiden whom
    the angels name Lenore —
Nameless *here* for evermore.
             The Raven, st. 2

The silken sad uncertain rustling of
each purple curtain.   *Ib. st. 3*

Deep into that darkness peering, long
    I stood there, wondering, fearing,
Doubting, dreaming dreams no mortal
    ever dared to dream before.
                Ib. st. 5

"Ghastly grim and ancient Raven wan-
    dering from the Nightly shore —
Tell me what thy lordly name is on the
    Night's Plutonian shore!"
Quoth the Raven, "Nevermore."
                Ib. st. 8

    Whom unmerciful Disaster
Followed fast and followed faster.
                Ib. st. 11

"Prophet!" said I, "thing of evil! —
    prophet still, if bird or devil!"
                Ib. st. 16

"Take thy beak from out my heart, and
    take thy form from off my door!"
Quoth the Raven, "Nevermore."
                Ib. st. 17

And the Raven, never flitting, still is
    sitting, *still* is sitting
On the pallid bust of Pallas just above
    my chamber door;
And his eyes have all the seeming of a
    demon's that is dreaming,
And the lamplight o'er him streaming
    throws his shadow on the floor;
And my soul from out that shadow that
    lies floating on the floor
Shall be lifted — nevermore!
                Ib. st. 18

From a wild weird clime that lieth, sub-
    lime,
Out of Space — out of Time.
        Dreamland [1845], *st. 1*

The Imp of the Perverse.
        Title of story [1845]

The object Truth, or the satisfaction
of the intellect, and the object Passion,
or the excitement of the heart, are, although attainable, to a certain extent,
in poetry, far more readily attainable in
prose.
    The Philosophy of Composition
                    [1846]

I asked myself — "Of all melancholy
topics, what, according to the universal
understanding of mankind, is the most
melancholy?" Death — was the obvious
reply. "And when," I said, "is this most
melancholy of topics most poetical?"
. . . The answer . . . is obvious —
"When it most closely allies itself to
Beauty: the death, then, of a beautiful
woman is, unquestionably, the most
poetical topic in the world — and
equally is it beyond doubt that the lips
best suited for such topic are those of
a bereaved lover."   *Ib.*

The skies they were ashen and sober;
    The leaves they were crispèd and
        sere —
    The leaves they were withering and
        sere;
It was night in the lonesome October
    Of my most immemorial year.
        Ulalume [1847], *st. 1*

It was down by the dank tarn of
    Auber,
In the ghoul-haunted woodland of
    Weir.   *Ib.*

Here once, through an alley Titanic,
    Of cypress, I roamed with my
        soul —
    Of cypress, with Psyche, my soul.
                Ib. st. 2

Thus I pacified Psyche and kissed her,
And tempted her out of her gloom.
                Ib. st. 8

Can it be fancied that Deity ever vin-
    dictively
Made in his image a mannikin merely
    to madden it? [1]
    The Rationale of Verse [1848]

[1] What! out of senseless Nothing to provoke
A conscious Something to resent the yoke.
      Fitzgerald, *The Rubáiyát of Omar
      Khayyám* [1859–1879], *st. 78*

A Quixotic sense of the honorable
— of the chivalrous.
Letter to Mrs. Whitman
[*October 18, 1848*]

"Over the Mountains
Of the Moon,
Down the Valley of the Shadow,
Ride, boldly ride,"
The shade replied —
"If you seek for Eldorado!"
Eldorado [1849], *st. 4*

And the fever called "Living"
Is conquered at last.
For Annie [1849]

And this maiden she lived with no
other thought
Than to love and be loved by me.

She was a child and *I* was a child,
In this kingdom by the sea,
But we loved with a love that was more
than love —
I and my Annabel Lee —
With a love that the wingèd seraphs
of Heaven
Coveted her and me.
Annabel Lee [1849], *st. 1, 2*

And neither the angels in Heaven
above
Nor the demons down under the
sea,
Can ever dissever my soul from the
soul
Of the beautiful Annabel Lee.
Ib. st. 5

In her sepulcher there by the sea —
In her tomb by the side of the sea.
Ib. st. 6

Keeping time, time, time,
In sort of Runic rhyme,
To the tintinnabulation that so musi-
cally wells
From the bells, bells, bells, bells,
Bells, bells, bells.
The Bells [1849], *st. 1*

Hear the loud alarum bells —
Brazen bells!
What a tale of terror, now, their tur-
bulency tells! *Ib. st. 3*

I would define, in brief, the Poetry of
words as the Rhythmical Creation of
Beauty. Its sole arbiter is Taste.
The Poetic Principle [1850]

**PIERRE JOSEPH
PROUDHON**
1809–1865

Property is theft.
Qu'est-ce que la Propriété?

**ALFRED,
LORD TENNYSON**
1809–1892

Dower'd with the hate of hate, the
scorn of scorn,
The love of love.
The Poet [1830], *st. 1*

For it was in the golden prime
Of good Haroun Alraschid.
*Recollections of the Arabian
Nights* [1830], *st. 2*

She said, "I am aweary, aweary,
I would that I were dead!"
Mariana [1] [1830], *refrain*

A still small voice [2] spake unto me,
"Thou art so full of misery,
Were it not better not to be?"
The Two Voices [1832], *st. 1*

This truth within thy mind rehearse,
That in a boundless universe
Is boundless better, boundless worse.
Ib. st. 9

Though thou wert scattered to the
wind,
Yet is there plenty of the kind. [3]
Ib. st. 11

I know that age to age succeeds,
Blowing a noise of tongues and deeds,
A dust of systems and of creeds.
Ib. st. 69

Like glimpses of forgotten dreams.
Ib. st. 127

No life that breathes with human
breath

[1] See Shakespeare, p. 271b.
[2] See *I Kings 19:12*, p. 13b.
[3] See Fitzgerald, p. 630b.

Has ever truly longed for death.
> *The Two Voices, st. 132*

In after-dinner talk,
Across the walnuts and the wine.
> *The Miller's Daughter* [1832],
> *st. 4*

O mother Ida, many-fountained Ida,
Dear mother Ida, hearken ere I die.
> *Oenone* [1832], *l. 22*

Self-reverence, self-knowledge, self-control,
These three alone lead life to sovereign
power.
> *Ib. l. 142*

I built my soul a lordly pleasure-house,
Wherein at ease for aye to dwell.
> *The Palace of Art* [1832], *st. 1*

The daughter of a hundred Earls,
You are not one to be desired.
> *Lady Clara Vere de Vere* [1832],
> *st. 1*

A simple maiden in her flower
Is worth a hundred coats-of-arms.
> *Ib. st. 2*

The lion on your old stone gates
Is not more cold to you than I.
> *Ib. st. 3*

The gardener Adam and his wife
Smile at the claims of long descent.
> *Ib. st. 7*

'Tis only noble to be good.
Kind hearts are more than coronets,
And simple faith than Norman blood.
> *Ib.*

Oh! teach the orphan boy to read,
Or teach the orphan girl to sew.
> *Ib. st. 9*

You must wake and call me early, call
me early, mother dear;
Tomorrow 'ill be the happiest time of
all the glad New Year;
Of all the glad New Year, mother, the
maddest, merriest day;
For I'm to be Queen o' the May,
mother, I'm to be Queen o' the
May.
> *The May Queen* [1832], *st. 1*

Music that gentlier on the spirit lies,
Than tir'd eyelids upon tir'd eyes.
> *The Lotos-Eaters* [1832]. *Choric*
> *Song, st. 1*

There is no joy but calm!
> *Ib. st. 2*

Ah, why
Should life all labor be?
> *Ib. st. 4*

Let us alone. Time driveth onward
fast,
And in a little while our lips are dumb.
Let us alone. What is it that will last?
All things are taken from us, and become
Portions and parcels of the dreadful
Past.
> *Ib.*

Give us long rest or death, dark death
or dreamful ease.
> *Ib.*

Live and lie reclined
On the hills like Gods together, careless
of mankind.
> *Ib. st. 8*

Dan Chaucer, the first warbler, whose
sweet breath
Preluded those melodious bursts that
fill
The spacious times of great Elizabeth
With sounds that echo still.
> *A Dream of Fair Women* [1832]

A daughter of the gods, divinely tall,
And most divinely fair.
> *Ib. st. 22*

Willows whiten, aspens quiver,
Little breezes dusk and shiver.
> *The Lady of Shalott* [1832],
> *pt. I, st. 2*

But who hath seen her wave her hand?
Or at the casement seen her stand?
Or is she known in all the land,
The Lady of Shalott?
> *Ib. st. 3*

All in the blue unclouded weather.
> *Ib. III, st. 3*

"Tirra lirra," by the river
Sang Sir Lancelot.
> *Ib. st. 4*

She left the web, she left the loom,
She made three paces thro' the room,
She saw the water lily bloom,
She saw the helmet and the plume,
She look'd down to Camelot.

Out flew the web and floated wide;
The mirror cracked from side to side.
"The curse has come upon me," cried
   The Lady of Shalott.
> *The Lady of Shalott,*
> *pt. III, st. 5*

But Lancelot mused a little space;
He said, "She has a lovely face;
God in his mercy lend her grace,
   The Lady of Shalott."
> *Ib. IV, st. 6*

God gives us love. Something to love
   He lends us; but when love is grown
To ripeness, that on which it throve
Falls off, and love is left alone.
> *To J.S.* [1842], *st. 4*

More black than ashbuds in the front
   of March.
> *The Gardener's Daughter*
> [1842], *l. 28*

Half light, half shade,
She stood, a sight to make an old man
   young.   *Ib. l. 139*

The long mechanic pacings to and fro,
The set gray life, and apathetic end.
> *Love and Duty* [1842], *l. 17*

Ah! when shall all men's good
Be each man's rule, and universal
   peace
Lie like a shaft of light across the land,
And like a lane of beams athwart the
   sea,
Through all the circle of the golden
   year?
> *The Golden Year* [1842], *l. 47*

It little profits that an idle king,
By this still hearth, among these barren
   crags,
Match'd with an aged wife, I mete and
   dole
Unequal laws unto a savage race.
> *Ulysses* [1842], *l. 1*

I will drink
Life to the lees.   *Ib. l. 6*

Much have I seen and known; cities of
   men
And manners, climates, councils, governments,

Myself not least, but honor'd of them
   all;
And drunk delight of battle with my
   peers,
Far on the ringing plains of windy
   Troy.
I am a part of all that I have met;
Yet all experience is an arch where-
   through
Gleams that untravel'd world.[1]
> *Ulysses, l.* 13

How dull it is to pause, to make an
   end,
To rust unburnished, not to shine in
   use,
As though to breathe were life!
> *Ib. l. 22*

And this gray spirit yearning in desire
To follow knowledge like a sinking
   star,
Beyond the utmost bound of human
   thought.   *Ib. l. 30*

This is my son, mine own Telemachus.
> *Ib. l. 33*

Death closes all: but something ere the
   end,
Some work of noble note, may yet be
   done,
Not unbecoming men that strove with
   gods.   *Ib. l. 51*

The deep
Moans round with many voices. Come,
   my friends,
'Tis not too late to seek a newer world.
Push off, and sitting well in order
   smite
The sounding furrows, for my purpose
   holds
To sail beyond the sunset, and the
   baths
Of all the western stars, until I die.
It may be that the gulfs will wash us
   down;
It may be we shall touch the Happy
   Isles,
And see the great Achilles, whom we
   knew.   *Ib. l. 55*

[1] See Henry Adams, p. 776b.

To strive, to seek, to find, and not to
  yield.[1]   *Ulysses, l.* 70

Comrades, leave me here a little, while
  as yet 'tis early morn:
Leave me here, and when you want me,
  sound upon the bugle horn.
          Locksley Hall [1842], *l.* 1

In the spring a young man's fancy
  lightly turns to thoughts of love.
          Ib. l. 19

He will hold thee, when his passion
  shall have spent its novel force,
Something better than his dog, a little
  dearer than his horse.   *Ib. l.* 49

The many-winter'd crow that leads the
  clanging rookery home.
          Ib. l. 68

Such a one do I remember, whom to
  look at was to love.[2]   *Ib. l.* 72

          This is the truth the poet sings,
That a sorrow's crown of sorrow is remembering happier things.[3]
          Ib. l. 75

Like a dog, he hunts in dreams.
          Ib. l. 79

With a little hoard of maxims preaching down a daughter's heart.
          Ib. l. 94

But the jingling of the guinea helps the
  hurt that Honor feels.
          Ib. l. 105

For I dipp'd into the future, far as human eye could see,
Saw the Vision of the world, and all the
  wonder that would be;
Saw the heavens fill with commerce,
  argosies of magic sails,
Pilots of the purple twilight, dropping
  down with costly bales;
Heard the heavens fill with shouting,
  and there rain'd a ghastly dew
From the nations' airy navies grappling
  in the central blue.   *Ib. l.* 119

[1] Inscribed on the memorial cross erected to
the memory of Captain Robert Falcon Scott
[1868–1912] and his men at Hut Point in the
Antarctic.
[2] See Burns, p. 494a, and Halleck, p. 565b.
[3] See Pindar, p. 79b, and note.

Till the war drum throbbed no longer
  and the battle flags were furled
In the Parliament of Man, the Federation of the world.
          Locksley Hall, l. 127

And the kindly earth shall slumber,
  lapp'd in universal law.
          Ib. l. 130

Yet I doubt not through the ages one
  increasing purpose runs,
And the thoughts of men are widened
  with the process of the suns.
          Ib. l. 137

Knowledge comes, but wisdom lingers.
          Ib. l. 141

Woman is the lesser man, and all thy
  passions, match'd with mine,
Are as moonlight unto sunlight, and as
  water unto wine.   *Ib. l.* 151

I will take some savage woman, she
  shall rear my dusky race.
          Ib. l. 168

I the heir of all the ages, in the foremost files of time.   *Ib. l.* 178

Let the great world spin forever down
  the ringing grooves of change.
          Ib. l. 182

Better fifty years of Europe than a cycle
  of Cathay.   *Ib. l.* 184

This proverb flashes through his head,
"The many fail, the one suceeds."
          The Day Dream [1842]. *The
          Arrival, st.* 2

And on her lover's arm she leant,
And round her waist she felt it fold,
And far across the hills they went
In that new world which is the old.
          Ib. The Departure, st. 1

And is there any moral shut
Within the bosom of the rose?
          Ib. Moral, st. 1

My strength is as the strength of ten,
Because my heart is pure.
          Sir Galahad [1842], *st.* 1

Or that eternal lack of pence,
Which vexes public men.
          *Will Waterproof's Lyrical Mon-
          ologue, st.* 6

Cophetua sware a royal oath;
"This beggar maid shall be my
queen!" [1]
> *The Beggar Maid* [1842], *st. 2*

Break, break, break,
On thy cold gray stones, O Sea!
And I would that my tongue could
utter
The thoughts that arise in me.

O well for the fisherman's boy,
That he shouts with his sister at
play!
O well for the sailor lad,
That he sings in his boat on the bay!

And the stately ships go on
To their haven under the hill;
But O for the touch of a vanish'd
hand,
And the sound of a voice that is still!
> *Break, Break, Break* [1842], *st. 1–3*

But the tender grace of a day that is
dead
Will never come back to me.
> *Ib. st. 4*

With prudes for proctors, dowagers for
deans,
And sweet girl-graduates in their golden
hair.
> *The Princess* [1847]. *Prologue,*
> *l. 141*

A rosebud set with little willful thorns,
And sweet as English air could make
her, she.   *Ib. l. 153*

When we fall out with those we love
And kiss again with tears!
> *Ib. pt. II [song, As Through the*
> *Land, l. 8]*

And quoted odes, and jewels five-words-
long
That on the stretched forefinger of all
Time
Sparkle forever.   *Ib. l. 355*

Sweet and low, sweet and low,
Wind of the western sea,
Low, low, breathe and blow,
Wind of the western sea!
Over the rolling waters go,

[1] See Shakespeare, p. 223a, and *Ballads*, p.
1087b.

Come from the dying moon, and
blow,
Blow him again to me;
While my little one, while my pretty
one, sleeps.
> *The Princess, pt. III [song,*
> *Sweet and Low, st. 1]*

The splendor falls on castle walls
And snowy summits old in story:
The long light shakes across the lakes,
And the wild cataract leaps in glory.
Blow, bugle, blow, set the wild echoes
flying,
Blow, bugle; answer, echoes, dying, dy-
ing, dying.
> *Ib. IV [song, The Splendor Falls,*
> *st. 1]*

The horns of Elfland faintly blowing.
> *Ib. [st. 2]*

O Love, they die in yon rich sky,
They faint on hill or field or river:
Our echoes roll from soul to soul,
And grow forever and forever.
> *Ib. [st. 3]*

Tears, idle tears, I know not what they
mean,
Tears from the depth of some divine
despair
Rise in the heart, and gather to the
eyes,
In looking on the happy autumn fields,
And thinking of the days that are no
more.
> *Ib. [song, Tears, Idle Tears, st. 1]*

Dear as remember'd kisses after death,
And sweet as those by hopeless fancy
feign'd
On lips that are for others; deep as love,
Deep as first love, and wild with all re-
gret;
O Death in Life, the days that are no
more.   *Ib. [st. 4]*

O Swallow, Swallow, flying, flying
South,
Fly to her, and fall upon her gilded
eaves,
And tell her, tell her, what I tell to
thee.
> *Ib. [song, O Swallow, st. 1]*

Man is the hunter; woman is his game.
          The Princess, pt. V, *l.* 147

Man for the field and woman for the
     hearth:
Man for the sword and for the needle
     she:
Man with the head and woman with
     the heart:
Man to command and woman to obey;
All else confusion.   *Ib. l.* 427

Home they brought her warrior dead.
     She nor swoon'd nor utter'd cry:
All her maidens, watching, said,
     "She must weep or she will die."
               Ib. VI [*song, Home They
               Brought Her Warrior,
               st.* 1]

     The woman is so hard
Upon the woman.   *Ib. l.* 205

Ask me no more: thy fate and mine are
     seal'd:
I strove against the stream and all in
     vain:
Let the great river take me to the main:
No more, dear love, for at a touch I
     yield;
Ask me no more.
          Ib. VII [*song, Ask Me No More,
                              st.* 3]

Now sleeps the crimson petal, now the
     white;
Nor waves the cypress in the palace
     walk;
Nor winks the gold fin in the porphyry
     font:
The firefly wakens: waken thou with
     me.
          Ib. [*song, Now Sleeps the Crim-
                    son Petal, st.* 1]

Now lies the Earth all Danaë to the
     stars,
And all thy heart lies open unto me.
               Ib. [*st.* 3]

     Sweet is every sound,
Sweeter thy voice, but every sound is
     sweet;
Myriads of rivulets hurrying through
     the lawn,

The moan of doves in immemorial
     elms,
And murmuring of innumerable bees.
          The Princess, pt. VII, *l.* 203

     Happy he
With such a mother! faith in woman-
     kind
Beats with his blood, and trust in all
     things high
Comes easy to him; and though he trip
     and fall,
He shall not blind his soul with clay.
               Ib. l. 308

Some sense of duty, something of a
     faith,
Some reverence for the laws ourselves
     have made,
Some patient force to change them
     when we will,
Some civic manhood firm against the
     crowd.   *Ib. Conclusion, l.* 54

Believing where we cannot prove.
          In Memoriam [1850]. *Prologue,
                                   st. 1*

Our little systems have their day.
               Ib. st. 5

Let knowledge grow from more to
     more,
     But more of reverence in us dwell;
     That mind and soul, according well,
May make one music as before.
               Ib. st. 7

I held it truth, with him who sings
     To one clear harp in divers tones,
     That men may rise on stepping-
          stones
Of their dead selves to higher things.[1]
               Ib. 1, *st.* 1

I sometimes hold it half a sin
     To put in words the grief I feel;
     For words, like Nature, half reveal
And half conceal the Soul within.
               Ib. 5, *st.* 2

But, for the unquiet heart and brain
     A use in measured language lies;
     The sad mechanic exercise,

[1] See St. Augustine, p. 147a, and Longfellow,
p. 623a.

Like dull narcotics numbing pain.
In Memoriam, 5, st. 2

Never morning wore
To evening, but some heart did break.
Ib. 6, st. 2

And from his ashes may be made
The violet of his native land.[1]
Ib. 18, st. 1

I do but sing because I must,
And pipe but as the linnets sing.[2]
Ib. 21, st. 6

Who keeps the keys of all the creeds.
Ib. 23, st. 2

And Thought leap'd out to wed with
Thought
Ere Thought could wed itself with
Speech. *Ib. st. 4*

'Tis better to have loved and lost
Than never to have loved at all.[3]
Ib. 27, st. 4

Her eyes are homes of silent prayer.
Ib. 32, st. 1

Short swallow-flights of song, that dip
Their wings in tears, and skim away.
Ib. 48, st. 4

Be near me when my light is low.
Ib. 50, st. 1

And Time, a maniac scattering dust,
And Life, a Fury slinging flame.
Ib. st. 2

Do we indeed desire the dead
Should still be near us at our side?
Ib. 51, st. 1

---

[1] See Shakespeare, p. 266a, and Fitzgerald, p. 629b.

[2] Ich singe, wie der Vogel singt
Der in den Zweigen wohnet.
GOETHE, *Wilhelm Meister's Apprentice-ship* [1786–1830], bk. *II, ch. 11*

[3] Say what you will, 'tis better to be left than never to have been loved. — CONGREVE, *The Way of the World* [1700], act *II, sc. 6*
Better to love amiss than nothing to have loved. — CRABBE, *Tales* [1812], *XIV, The Struggles of Conscience*
What voice did on my spirit fall,
Peschiera, when thy bridge I crost?
'Tis better to have fought and lost
Than never to have fought at all.
ARTHUR HUGH CLOUGH [1819–1861],
Peschiera

Hold thou the good; define it well;
For fear divine Philosophy
Should push beyond her mark, and be
Procuress to the Lords of Hell.
In Memoriam, 53, st. 4

Oh yet we trust that somehow good
Will be the final goal of ill.
Ib. 54, st. 1

But what am I?
An infant crying in the night:
An infant crying for the light:
And with no language but a cry.[1]
Ib. st. 5

So careful of the type she seems,
So careless of the single life.
Ib. 55, st. 2

The great world's altar-stairs,
That slope through darkness up to
God. *Ib. st. 4*

Nature, red in tooth and claw.
Ib. 56, st. 4

The sweetest soul
That ever look'd with human eyes.
Ib. 57, st. 3

Who breaks his birth's invidious bar,
And grasps the skirts of happy chance,
And breasts the blows of circumstance.
Ib. 64, st. 2

So many worlds, so much to do,
So little done, such things to be.[2]
Ib. 73, st. 1

O last regret, regret can die!
Ib. 78, st. 5

God's finger touch'd him, and he slept.
Ib. 85, st. 5

Fresh from brawling courts
And dusty purlieus of the law.
Ib. 89, st. 3

---

[1] See Pliny, p. 132a–b.

[2] How little I have gained,
How vast the unattained.
WHITTIER [1807–1892], *My Triumph, st. 7*

There lives more faith in honest doubt,[1]
Believe me, than in half the creeds.
>> *In Memoriam, 96, st. 3*

He seems so near, and yet so far.
>> *Ib. 97, st. 6*

Ring out, wild bells, to the wild sky!
>> *Ib. 106, st. 1*

Ring out the old, ring in the new,
>> Ring, happy bells, across the snow:
>> The year is going, let him go;
Ring out the false, ring in the true.
>> *Ib. st. 2*

Ring in the nobler modes of life,
With sweeter manners, purer laws.
>> *Ib. st. 4*

Ring out old shapes of foul disease,
>> Ring out the narrowing lust of gold;
>> Ring out the thousand wars of old,
Ring in the thousand years of peace.

Ring in the valiant man and free,
>> The larger heart, the kindlier hand;
>> Ring out the darkness of the land,
Ring in the Christ that is to be.
>> *Ib. st. 7, 8*

The blind hysterics of the Celt.
>> *Ib. 109, st. 4*

And thus he bore without abuse
>> The grand old name of gentleman,
>> Defamed by every charlatan,
And soiled with all ignoble use.
>> *Ib. 111, st. 6*

>> Wearing all that weight
Of learning lightly like a flower.
>> *Ib. Conclusion, st. 10*

One God, one law, one element,
And one far-off divine event,
To which the whole creation moves.
>> *Ib. st. 36*

He clasps the crag with crooked hands;
Close to the sun in lonely lands,
Ring'd with the azure world he stands.

---

[1] Who never doubted never half believed.
Where doubt there truth is — 'tis her shadow.
>> **P. J. BAILEY** [1816–1902], *Festus: A Country Town*

The wrinkled sea beneath him crawls;
He watches from his mountain walls,
And like a thunderbolt he falls.
>> *The Eagle* [1851]

This laurel greener from the brows
Of him that utter'd nothing base.[1]
>> *To the Queen* [1851], *st. 2*

Broad-based upon her people's will,
And compass'd by the inviolate sea.
>> *Ib. st. 9*

Bury the Great Duke
With an empire's lamentation.
>> *Ode on the Death of the Duke of Wellington* [1852], *st. 1*

The last great Englishman is low.
>> *Ib. st. 3*

Rich in saving common sense,
And, as the greatest only are,
In his simplicity sublime.
O good gray head which all men knew!
>> *Ib. st. 4*

O iron nerve to true occasion true,
O fall'n at length, that tower of strength
Which stood four-square to all the winds that blew.
>> *Ib.*

Not once or twice in our rough island story
The path of duty was the way to glory.
>> *Ib. st. 8*

Speak no more of his renown.
Lay your earthly fancies down,
And in the vast cathedral leave him.
God accept him, Christ receive him.
>> *Ib. st. 9*

And yet, my Lords, not well: there is a higher law.
>> *The Third of February, 1852, st. 2*

We are not cotton-spinners all.
>> *Ib. st. 8*

Half a league, half a league,
>> Half a league onward,

---

[1] Wordsworth, Tennyson's predecessor as poet laureate.

All in the valley of death
  Rode the six hundred.
      The Charge of the Light Brigade
        [1854],[1] *st. 1*

"Forward, the Light Brigade!"
Was there a man dismay'd?
                Ib. st. 2

  Someone had blundered:
Theirs not to make reply,
Theirs not to reason why,
Theirs but to do and die.   *Ib.*

Cannon to right of them,
Cannon to left of them,
Cannon in front of them
  Volley'd and thunder'd.   *Ib. st. 3*

Into the jaws of death,
Into the mouth of hell
  Rode the six hundred.   *Ib.*

I come from haunts of coot and hern,
  I make a sudden sally
And sparkle out among the fern,
  To bicker down a valley.
      The Brook [1855], *song, st. 1*

For men may come and men may go,
But I go on forever.   *Ib. st. 6*

Faultily faultless, icily regular, splendidly null,
Dead perfection, no more.
        Maud [1855], *pt. I, sec. ii*

That jeweled mass of millinery,
That oiled and curled Assyrian Bull.
                Ib. vi, st. 6

One still strong man in a blatant land.
                Ib. x, st. 5

And ah for a man to arise in me,
That the man I am may cease to be!
                Ib. st. 6

Gorgonized me from head to foot,
With a stony British stare.
                Ib. xiii, st. 2

Come into the garden, Maud,
  For the black bat, night, has flown,
Come into the garden, Maud,
  I am here at the gate alone.
                Ib. xxii, st. 1

[1] See Bosquet, p. 655b.

For a breeze of morning moves,
  And the planet of Love is on high,
Beginning to faint in the light that she loves
On a bed of daffodil sky.
        Maud, pt. I, sec. xxii, st. 2

All night have the roses heard
  The flute, violin, bassoon;
All night has the casement jessamine stirr'd
  To the dancers dancing in tune;
Till a silence fell with the waking bird,
  And a hush with the setting moon.
                Ib. st. 3

Queen rose of the rosebud garden of girls.   *Ib. st. 9*

There has fallen a splendid tear
  From the passion-flower at the gate.
She is coming, my dove, my dear;
  She is coming, my life, my fate;
The red rose cries, "She is near, she is near";
  And the white rose weeps, "She is late";
The larkspur listens, "I hear, I hear";
  And the lily whispers, "I wait."

She is coming, my own, my sweet;
  Were it ever so airy a tread,
My heart would hear her and beat,
  Were it earth in an earthy bed;
My dust would hear her and beat,
  Had I lain for a century dead;
Would start and tremble under her feet,
  And blossom in purple and red.
                Ib. st. 10, 11

Ah Christ, that it were possible
  For one short hour to see
The souls we loved, that they might tell us
  What and where they be.
                Ib. II, iv, st. 3

And after many a summer dies the swan.   *Tithonus* [1860], *l. 4*

Here at the quiet limit of the world.
                Ib. l. 7

Wearing the white flower of a blameless life,

Before a thousand peering littlenesses,
In that fierce light which beats upon a
　　throne,
And blackens every blot.
　　　　Idylls of the King [1859–1885],
　　　　　　　　dedication, *l.* 24

Man's word is God in man.
　　　Ib. The Coming of Arthur, l. 132

Large divine and comfortable words.[1]
　　　　　　　　　Ib. l. 267

Clothed in white samite, mystic, won-
　　derful.[2]　　　　　*Ib. l.* 284

Live pure, speak true, right wrong, fol-
　　low the King —
Else, wherefore born?
　　　Ib. Gareth and Lynette, l. 117

　　Lightly was her slender nose
Tip-tilted like the petal of a flower.
　　　　　　　　　Ib. l. 574

Our hoard is little, but our hearts are
　　great.
　　　　Ib. The Marriage of Geraint,
　　　　　　　　　　l. 352

For man is man and master of his
　　fate.[3]　　　　　*Ib. l.* 355

The useful trouble of the rain.
　　　　Ib. Geraint and Enid, l. 770

It is the little rift within the lute,
That by and by will make the music
　　mute,
And ever widening slowly silence all.
　　　Ib. Merlin and Vivien, l. 386

　　Blind and naked Ignorance
Delivers　brawling　judgments,　un-
　　ashamed,
On all things all day long.　*Ib. l.* 662

For men at most differ as Heaven and
　　Earth,
But women, worst and best, as Heaven
　　and Hell.　　　　*Ib. l.* 812

Elaine the fair, Elaine the lovable,
Elaine, the lily maid of Astolat.
　　　Ib. Lancelot and Elaine, l. 1

---

[1] Hear what comfortable words our Saviour
Christ saith unto all who truly turn to him. —
Book of Common Prayer, Holy Communion
[2] Also *The Passing of Arthur, l.* 199.
[3] See Sallust, p. 116a, and note.

　　But, friend, to me
He is all fault who hath no fault at
　　all.
For who loves me must have a touch of
　　earth.
　　　　*Idylls of the King, Lancelot
　　　　　　and Elaine, l.* 131

　　In me there dwells
No greatness, save it be some far-off
　　touch
Of greatness to know well I am not
　　great.　　　　　*Ib. l.* 447

The shackles of an old love straitened
　　him,
His honor rooted in dishonor stood,
And faith unfaithful kept him falsely
　　true.　　　　　*Ib. l.* 870

Sweet is true love though given in vain,
　　in vain;
And sweet is death who puts an end to
　　pain.　　　　　*Ib. l.* 1000

He makes no friend who never made a
　　foe.　　　　　*Ib. l.* 1082

Figs out of thistles.[1]
　　　Ib. The Last Tournament, l. 356

The greater man the greater courtesy.
　　　　　　　　　Ib. l. 628

The vow that binds too strictly snaps
　　itself.　　　　　*Ib. l.* 652

For courtesy wins woman all as well
As valor may.　　　*Ib. l.* 702

For manners are not idle, but the fruit
Of loyal nature and of noble mind.
　　　　Ib. Guinevere, l. 333

To love one maiden only, cleave to her,
And worship her by years of golden
　　deeds.　　　　　*Ib. l.* 472

　　No more subtle master under Heaven
Than is the maiden passion for a
　　maid,
Not only to keep down the base in
　　man,
But teach high thought, and amiable
　　words
And courtliness, and the desire of fame,

---

[1] Ye shall know them by their fruits. Do
men gather grapes of thorns, or figs of thistles?
— *Matthew 7:16*

And love of truth, and all that makes a
man.
> *Idylls of the King,*
> *Guinevere, l. 475*

Let no man dream but that I love thee
still.   *Ib. l. 557*

The days will grow to weeks, the weeks
to months,
The months will add themselves and
make the years,
The years will roll into the centuries,
And mine will ever be a name of scorn.
> *Ib. l. 619*

To where beyond these voices there is
peace.   *Ib. l. 692*

I found Him in the shining of the stars,
I mark'd Him in the flowering of His
fields,
But in His ways with men I find Him
not.
> *Ib. The Passing of Arthur, l. 9*

For why is all around us here
As if some lesser god had made the
world,
But had not force to shape it as he
would?   *Ib. l. 13*

And slowly answer'd Arthur from the
barge:
The old order changeth, yielding place
to new;
And God fulfills himself in many ways,
Lest one good custom should corrupt
the world.[1]   *Ib. l. 407*

More things are wrought by prayer
Than this world dreams of. Wherefore,
let thy voice
Rise like a fountain for me night and
day.[1]   *Ib. l. 414*

From the great deep to the great deep
he goes.   *Ib. l. 445*

Cast all your cares on God; that anchor
holds.
> *Enoch Arden [1864], l. 222*

Insipid as the queen upon a card.
> *Aylmer's Field [1864], l. 28*

The worst is yet to come.[2]
> *Sea Dreams [1864], l. 301*

[1] Also in *Morte d'Arthur* [*1842*].
[2] See Browning, p. 666a.

He said likewise
That a lie which is half a truth is ever
the blackest of lies,
That a lie which is all a lie may be met
and fought with outright,
But a lie which is part a truth is a
harder matter to fight.
> *The Grandmother [1864], st. 8*

Dosn't thou 'ear my 'erse's legs, as they
canters awaäy?
Proputty, proputty, proputty — that's
what I 'ears 'em saäy.
> *Northern Farmer: New Style*
> *[1869], st. 1*

Doänt thou marry for munny, but
goä wheer munny is!   *Ib. st. 5*

Speak to Him thou for He hears, and
Spirit with Spirit can meet —
Closer is He than breathing, and nearer
than hands and feet.
> *The Higher Pantheism [1869],*
> *st. 6*

Flower in the crannied wall,
I pluck you out of the crannies,
I hold you here, root and all, in my
hand,
Little flower — but if I could under-
stand
What you are, root and all, and all in
all,
I should know what God and man is.
> *Flower in the Crannied Wall*
> *[1869]*

At Flores in the Azores Sir Richard
Grenville lay,
And a pinnace, like a flutter'd bird,
came flying from far away;
"Spanish ships of war at sea! we have
sighted fifty-three!"
> *The Revenge [1878], st. 1*

I should count myself the coward if I
left them, my Lord Howard,
To these Inquisition dogs and the
devildoms of Spain.   *Ib. st. 2*

The little *Revenge* ran on sheer into
the heart of the foe.   *Ib. st. 5*

All the charm of all the Muses often
flowering in a lonely word.
> *To Virgil [1882], st. 3*

Cleave ever to the sunnier side of
    doubt.
        The Ancient Sage [1885], *l. 68*

That man's the best Cosmopolite
Who loves his native country best.
        Hands All Round [1885], *l. 3*

After it, follow it,
Follow the Gleam.[1]
        Merlin and the Gleam [1889], *st. 9*

Sunset and evening star,
    And one clear call for me!
And may there be no moaning of the
    bar,
    When I put out to sea,[2]

But such a tide as moving seems
    asleep,
Too full for sound and foam,
When that which drew from out the
    boundless deep
Turns again home.
        Crossing the Bar [1889], *st. 1, 2*

Twilight and evening bell,
And after that the dark.   *Ib. st. 3*

I hope to see my Pilot face to face
When I have crossed the bar.
                        Ib. st. 4

ROBERT CHARLES
WINTHROP
1809–1894

Our Country — whether bounded by
the St. John's and the Sabine, or however otherwise bounded [3] or described,

---

[1] The Gleam . . . signifies in my poem the
higher poetic imagination. — *From* HALLAM
TENNYSON, *Alfred, Lord Tennyson, A Memoir*
[1897], *vol. II, p. 366*
        Follow, follow, follow the gleam,
        Banners unfurled o'er all the world.
        Follow, follow, follow the gleam
        Of the chalice that is the Grail.
                SALLIE HUME DOUGLAS [1923],
                        Follow the Gleam, refrain
[2] See Ennius, p. 106b.
[3] The United States — bounded on the north
by the Aurora Borealis, on the south by the
precession of the equinoxes, on the east by the
primeval chaos, and on the west by the Day of
Judgment. — JOHN FISKE [1842–1901], *Bounding
the United States*

---

and be the measurements more or less
— still our Country, to be cherished in
all our hearts, to be defended by all our
hands.
        *Toast at Faneuil Hall [Fourth of
                July, 1845]*

A star for every State, and a State for
every star.
        Address on Boston Common [1862]

SAMUEL DODGE
fl. 1868

People Will Talk.   *Title of poem*

HENRY ALFORD
1810–1871

Come, ye thankful people, come,
Raise the song of Harvest-home;
All is safely gathered in,
Ere the winter storms begin.
        *Come, Ye Thankful People,
                Come* [1844]

PHINEAS TAYLOR
BARNUM
1810–1891

There's a sucker born every minute.
                        Attributed

PIERRE BOSQUET
1810–1861

It is magnificent, but it is not war.[1]
        *On the charge of the Light
        Brigade at Balaklava [October
        25, 1854]*

WILLIAM HENRY
CHANNING
1810–1884

To live content with small means; to
seek elegance rather than luxury, and
refinement rather than fashion; to be
worthy, not respectable, and wealthy,
not rich; to study hard, think quietly,
talk gently, act frankly; to listen to stars

---

[1] C'est magnifique, mais ce n'est pas la guerre.
See Tennyson, p. 652a.

and birds, to babes and sages, with open heart; to bear all cheerfully, do all bravely, await occasions, hurry never. In a word, to let the spiritual, unbidden and unconscious, grow up through the common. This is to be my symphony.

My Symphony

SIR FRANCIS HASTINGS DOYLE
1810–1888

Last night, among his fellow roughs,
  He jested, quaffed, and swore;
A drunken private of the Buffs,
  Who never looked before.
Today, beneath the foeman's frown,
  He stands in Elgin's place,
Ambassador from Britain's crown,
  And type of all her race.
The Private of the Buffs, st. 1

Ay, tear his body limb from limb,
  Bring cord, or axe, or flame,
He only knows that not through him
  Shall England come to shame.
Ib. st. 2

FERDINAND FREILIGRATH
1810–1876

Oh love, as long as you can love.[1]
Der Liebe Dauer [1830]

MARGARET FULLER
1810–1850

I myself am more divine than any I see.
Letter to Emerson [March 1, 1838]

It does not follow because many books are written by persons born in America that there exists an American literature. Books which imitate or represent the thoughts and life of Europe do not constitute an American literature. Before such can exist, an original idea must animate this nation and fresh

[1] See Anonymous, *Pervigilium Veneris*, p. 150a.

currents of life must call into life fresh thoughts along its shores.
In the New York Tribune [1846]

For precocity some great price is always demanded sooner or later in life.
Diary. From THOMAS WENTWORTH HIGGINSON, *Life of Margaret Fuller Ossoli* [1884], *ch. 18*

Genius will live and thrive without training, but it does not the less reward the watering pot and pruning knife.
Ib.

I accept the universe.[1]   *Attributed*

ELIZABETH CLEGHORN GASKELL
1810–1865

A man is *so* in the way in the house.
Cranford [1851–1853], *ch. 1*

A little credulity helps one on through life very smoothly.
Ib. ch. 11

I'll not listen to reason. . . . Reason always means what someone else has got to say.   *Ib. ch. 14*

JAMES SLOAN GIBBONS
1810–1892

We are coming, Father Abraham, three hundred thousand more.
Three Hundred Thousand More [1862],[2] *st. 1*

POPE LEO XIII [GIOACCHINO PECCI]
1810–1903

Every man has by nature the right to possess property as his own.
Rerum Novarum [*encyclical letter on the condition of labor, May 15, 1891*]

[1] By God! she'd better. — CARLYLE's *reported comment*
[2] Song to help raise volunteers for the Union Army.

It is impossible to reduce human society to one level.
Rerum Novarum

It is one thing to have a right to the possession of money, and another to have a right to use money as one pleases.   *Ib.*

WILLIAM MILLER
1810–1872

Wee Willie Winkie rins through the town,
Upstairs and downstairs, in his nicht-gown,
Tirlin' at the window, cryin' at the lock,
"Are the weans in their bed? for it's now ten o'clock."
Willie Winkie

ALFRED DE MUSSET
1810–1857

Doubt, if you will, the being who loves you,
Woman or dog, but never doubt love itself.
Premières Poésies [1829–1835],
La Coupe et les Lèvres

I have come too late into a century too old.
Poésies Nouvelles [1835–1852],
Rolla

The most despairing songs are the loveliest of all,
I know immortal ones composed only of tears.   *Ib. La Nuit de Mai*

Do not trifle with love.[1]
Title of a comedy [1834]

How glorious it is — and also how painful — to be an exception.
Le Merle Blanc. I

THEODORE PARKER
1810–1860

Truth never yet fell dead in the streets; it has such affinity with the soul

[1] On ne badine pas avec l'amour.

of man, the seed however broadcast will catch somewhere and produce its hundredfold.
A Discourse of Matters Pertaining to Religion [1842]

Truth stood on one side and Ease on the other; it has often been so.   *Ib.*

Man never falls so low that he can see nothing higher than himself.
Essay, A Lesson for the Day

All men desire to be immortal.
A Sermon on the Immortal Life
[September 20, 1846]

A democracy — that is a government of all the people, by all the people, for all the people;[1] of course, a government of the principles of eternal justice, the unchanging law of God; for shortness' sake I will call it the idea of Freedom.   *The American Idea*[2] [1850]

EDMUND HAMILTON SEARS
1810–1876

It came upon the midnight clear,
That glorious song of old,
From Angels bending near the earth
To touch their harps of gold;
"Peace on the earth, good will to men
From Heaven's all gracious King."
The world in solemn stillness lay
To hear the angels sing.
The Angel's Song [1850], st. 1

[1] See Wycliffe, p. 163b; Webster, p. 547a; Garrison, p. 616a; and Lincoln, p. 639a.
Parker used the same phrase in a speech delivered in Boston [May 31, 1854] and in a sermon in Music Hall, Boston [July 4, 1858]. William H. Herndon visited Boston and on his return to Springfield, Illinois, took with him some of Parker's sermons and addresses. In his *Abraham Lincoln, vol. II, p. 65*, Herndon says that Lincoln marked with pencil the portion of the Music Hall address, "Democracy is direct self-government, over all the people, by all the people, for all the people."
[2] Speech at the New England Anti-Slavery Convention, Boston [May 29, 1850].

MARTIN FARQUHAR TUPPER
1810–1889

Error is a hardy plant: it flourisheth in every soil.
> *Proverbial Philosophy* [*1838–1842*]. *Of Truth in Things False*

Well-timed silence hath more eloquence than speech.
> *Ib. Of Discretion*

A good book is the best of friends, the same today and forever.
> *Ib. Of Reading*

Nature's own Nobleman, friendly and frank,
Is a man with his heart in his hand!
> *Nature's Nobleman* [*1844*], *st. 1*

JOHN BRIGHT
1811–1889

The Angel of Death has been abroad throughout the land; you may almost hear the beating of his wings.
> *Speech, House of Commons* [*February 23, 1855*]

Force is not a remedy.
> *Speech, Birmingham* [*November 16, 1880*]

My opinion is that the Northern States will manage somehow to muddle through.
> *Said during the American Civil War. From* JUSTIN MCCARTHY, *Reminiscences* [*1899*]

FANNY FERN
[SARA PAYSON PARTON]
1811–1872

The way to a man's heart is through his stomach.[1]   *Willis Parton*

THÉOPHILE GAUTIER
1811–1872

Everything passes. Robust art alone is eternal. The bust outlasts the citadel.[2]   *L'Art* [*1832*]

[1] See Byron, p. 562a.
[2] Tout passe. L'art robuste
Seul a l'éternité;

HORACE GREELEY
1811–1872

A widow of doubtful age will marry almost any sort of a white man.
> *Letter to Dr. Rufus Wilmot Griswold*

If, on a full and final review, my life and practice shall be found unworthy of my principles, let due infamy be heaped on my memory; but let none be thereby led to distrust the principles to which I proved recreant, nor yet the ability of some to adorn them by a suitable life and conversation. To unerring time be all this committed.
> *Statement* [*1846*]. *From* JAMES PARTON, *Life of Horace Greeley* [*1855*]

The best business you can go into you will find on your father's farm or in his workshop. If you have no family or friends to aid you, and no prospect opened to you there, turn your face to the great West,[1] and there build up a home and fortune.
> *To Aspiring Young Men. Ib.*

The illusion that times that were are better than those that are, has probably pervaded all ages.
> *The American Conflict* [*1864–1866*]

Wisdom is never dear, provided the article be genuine.
> *Address on Agriculture, Houston, Texas* [*May 23, 1871*]

WENDELL PHILLIPS
1811–1884

We live under a government of men and morning newspapers.
> *Speech* [*January 28, 1852*]

Revolutions are not made; they come. A revolution is as natural a

Le buste
Survit à la cité.
See Dobson, p. 782b.
[1] See J. B. L. Soule, p. 678b.

growth as an oak. It comes out of the past. Its foundations are laid far back.
Speech [January 8, 1852]

The best use of laws is to teach men to trample bad laws under their feet.
Speech [April 12, 1852]

What the Puritans gave the world was not thought, but action.
Speech [December 21, 1855]

The rock underlies all America; it only crops out here.   *Ib.*

One on God's side is a majority.[1]
Speech [November 1, 1859]

Every man meets his Waterloo at last.   *Ib.*

Truth is one forever absolute, but opinion is truth filtered through the moods, the blood, the disposition of the spectator.   *Idols [October 4, 1859]*

Difference of religion breeds more quarrels than difference of politics.
Speech [November 7, 1860]

Revolutions never go backward.[2]
Speech [February 17, 1861]

Aristocracy is always cruel.
Address on Toussaint L'Ouverture [1861]

HARRIET BEECHER STOWE[3]
1811–1896

Eliza made her desperate retreat across the river just in the dusk of twilight. The gray mist of evening, rising slowly from the river, enveloped her as she disappeared up the bank, and the swollen current and floundering masses

[1] See Knox, p. 186b.
[2] I know, and all the world knows, that revolutions never go backward. — WILLIAM HENRY SEWARD, *Speech at Rochester on the Irrepressible Conflict* [October 1858]
[3] We have seen an American woman write a novel of which a million copies were sold in all languages, and which had one merit, of speaking to the universal heart, and was read with equal interest to three audiences, namely, in the parlor, in the kitchen, and in the nursery of every house. — EMERSON, *Society and Solitude* [1870]. *Success*

of ice presented a hopeless barrier between her and her pursuer.
Uncle Tom's Cabin [1852], ch. 8

I [Topsy] 'spect I growed. Don't think nobody never made me.
Ib. ch. 20

I's wicked — I is. I's mighty wicked, anyhow. I can't help it.   *Ib.*

CHARLES SUMNER
1811–1874

There is the National flag. He must be cold, indeed, who can look upon its folds rippling in the breeze without pride of country. If in a foreign land, the flag is companionship, and country itself, with all its endearments.
Are We a Nation? [November 19, 1867]

The phrase, "public office is a public trust," has of late become common property.[1]
Speech, U.S. Senate [May 31, 1872]

WILLIAM MAKEPEACE THACKERAY
1811–1863

This I set down as a positive truth. A woman with fair opportunities, and without a positive hump, may marry whom she likes.[2]
Vanity Fair [1847–1848], vol. I, ch. 4

Them's my sentiments.   *Ib. 21*

Everybody in Vanity Fair must have remarked how well those live who are comfortably and thoroughly in debt;

[1] See Matthew Henry, p. 386b, and note.
[2] I should like to see any kind of a man, distinguishable from a gorilla, that some good and even pretty woman could not shape a husband out of. — OLIVER WENDELL HOLMES, *The Professor at the Breakfast-Table* [1860]
The whole world is strewn with snares, traps, gins and pitfalls for the capture of men by women. — BERNARD SHAW, *Man and Superman* [1903], *Epistle Dedicatory*

how they deny themselves nothing; how jolly and easy they are in their minds.
Vanity Fair, vol. I, ch. 22

How to Live Well on Nothing a Year. *Ib. 36 [title]*

I think I could be a good woman if I had five thousand a year.[1] *Ib. II, 1*

Ah! *Vanitas vanitatum!* Which of us is happy in this world? Which of us has his desire? or, having it, is satisfied? — Come, children, let us shut up the box and the puppets, for our play is played out. *Ib. 27*

He who meanly admires mean things is a Snob.
The Book of Snobs [1848], ch. 2

Rake's Progress.[2]
Pendennis [1848–1850], ch. 19 [title]

Yes, I am a fatal man, Madame Fribsbi. To inspire hopeless passion is my destiny. *Ib. 23*

Remember, it's as easy to marry a rich woman as a poor woman. *Ib. 28*

Of the Corporation of the Goose-quill — of the Press . . . of the fourth estate.[3] . . . There she is — the great engine — she never sleeps. She has her ambassadors in every quarter of the world — her courtiers upon every road. Her officers march along with armies, and her envoys walk into statesmen's cabinets. They are ubiquitous. *Ib. 30*

'Tis not the dying for a faith that's so hard, Master Harry — every man of every nation has done that — 'tis the living up to it that's difficult.[4]
Henry Esmond [1852], bk. I, ch. 6

'Tis strange what a man may do, and a woman yet think him an angel.
Ib. 7

The wicked are wicked, no doubt, and they go astray and they fall, and

[1] See Huxley, p. 725a.
[2] *The Rake's Progress* is the title of one of the famous series of paintings and engravings by William Hogarth [1697–1764].
[3] See Carlyle, p. 576a.
[4] See Adlai E. Stevenson, p. 1048b.

they come by their deserts; but who can tell the mischief which the very virtuous do?
The Newcomes [1853–1855], ch. 20

This Bouillabaisse a noble dish is —
A sort of soup, or broth, or brew.
Ballads [1855]. The Ballad of Bouillabaisse, st. 2

Christmas is here:
Winds whistle shrill,
Icy and chill.
Little care we;
Little we fear
Weather without,
Sheltered about
The Mahogany Tree.
Ib. The Mahogany Tree, st. 1

Away from the world and its toils and its cares,
I've a snug little kingdom up four pair of stairs.
Ib. The Cane-Bottom'd Chair, st. 1

I sit here,
Alone and merry at forty year,
Dipping my nose in the Gascon wine.
Ib. The Age of Wisdom, st. 6

Werther had a love for Charlotte
Such as words could never utter;
Would you know how first he met her?
She was cutting bread and butter.[1]
Ib. Sorrows of Werther, st. 1

There lived a sage in days of yore,
And he a handsome pigtail wore;
But wondered much and sorrowed more
Because it hung behind him.
Ib. A Tragic Story (from Adelbert von Chamisso), st. 1

There were three sailors of Bristol City
Who took a boat and went to sea.
But first with beef and captain's biscuits
And pickled pork they loaded she.
Ib. Little Billee, st. 1

[1] Charlotte held a brown loaf in her hand, and was cutting slices for the little ones all round in proportion to their age and appetite. — GOETHE, *The Sorrows of Werther* [1774]

And the youngest he was little Billee.
Ballads. Little Billee, st. 2

To gorging Jack says guzzling Jimmy,
"We've nothing left, us must eat we."
Ib. st. 3

A pedigree reaching as far back as
the Deluge.
The Rose and the Ring [1855],
ch. 2

The book of female logic is blotted
all over with tears, and Justice in their
courts is forever in a passion.
The Virginians [1857–1859],
ch. 4

Women like not only to conquer,
but to be conquered.   **Ib.**

Next to the very young, I suppose
the very old are the most selfish.
Ib. 61

Through all the doubt and darkness,
the danger and long tempest of the
war, I think it was only the American
leader's [1] indomitable soul that remained entirely steady.   *Ib.* 90

To endure is greater than to dare; to
tire out hostile fortune; to be daunted
by no difficulty; to keep heart when all
have lost it; to go through intrigue spotless; to forego even ambition when the
end is gained — who can say this is not
greatness?   *Ib.* 92

Bravery never goes out of fashion.
The Four Georges [1860],
George II

ROBERT BROWNING
1812–1889

Sun-treader,[2] life and light be thine
forever!   *Pauline* [1833]

I go to prove my soul!
I see my way as birds their trackless
way.   *Paracelsus* [1835], *pt.* I

In some time, his good time, I shall
arrive:
He guides me and the bird. In his good
time!   **Ib.**

---

[1] George Washington.
[2] Shelley.

Measure your mind's height by the
shade it casts!   *Paracelsus, pt.* III

     Every joy is gain
And gain is gain, however small.
Ib. IV

Over the sea our galleys went.   **Ib.**

I give the fight up: let there be an end,
A privacy, an obscure nook for me.
I want to be forgotten even by God.
Ib. V

Sidney's self, the starry paladin.
Sordello [1] [1840], *pt.* I

Would you have your songs endure?
Build on the human heart.   *Ib.* II

     Any nose
May ravage with impunity a rose.
Ib. VI

Day!
Faster and more fast,
O'er night's brim, day boils at last.
Pippa Passes [1841], *introduction*

The year's at the spring
And day's at the morn;
Morning's at seven;
The hillside's dew-pearled;
The lark's on the wing;
The snail's on the thorn:
God's in his heaven —
All's right with the world.[2]   *Ib. pt.* I

Some unsuspected isle in far-off seas.
Ib. II

In the morning of the world,
When earth was nigher heaven than
now.   *Ib.* III

All service ranks the same with God:
With God, whose puppets, best and
worst,
Are we; there is no last nor first.
Ib. IV

There's a woman like a dewdrop, she's
so purer than the purest.
A Blot in the 'Scutcheon
[1842], *act* I, *st.* 3

---

[1] See Lombroso, p. 770a, note.
[2] See Voltaire, p. 417a, and Whittier, p. 626b.

When is man strong until he feels alone? [1]
>> *Colombe's Birthday* [1842], act III

You know, we French stormed Ratisbon.
>> *Incident of the French Camp* [1842], st. 1

"You're wounded!" "Nay," the soldier's pride
Touched to the quick, he said:
"I'm killed, Sire!" And his chief beside,
Smiling the boy fell dead.
>> *Ib. st. 5*

That's my last Duchess painted on the wall.
>> *My Last Duchess* [1842], l. 1

She had
A heart — how shall I say? — too soon made glad.
>> *Ib. l. 21*

The lie was dead,
And damned, and truth stood up instead.
>> *Count Gismond* [1842], st. 13

Marching along, fifty-score strong,
Great-hearted gentlemen, singing this song.
>> *Cavalier Tunes* [1842], *Marching Along*, st. 1

Boot, saddle, to horse, and away!
>> *Ib. Boot and Saddle, refrain*

Morning, evening, noon and night,
"Praise God!" sang Theocrite.
>> *The Boy and the Angel* [1845], st. 1

Just my vengeance complete,
The man sprang to his feet,
Stood erect, caught at God's skirts, and prayed!
— So, I was afraid!
>> *Instans Tyrannus* [1845], st. 7

Hamelin Town's in Brunswick,
By famous Hanover city.
>> *The Pied Piper of Hamelin* [1845], st. 1

[1] See Ibsen, p. 729b.

Rats!
They fought the dogs and killed the cats,
And bit the babies in the cradles,
And ate the cheeses out of the vats,
And licked the soup from the cooks' own ladles.
>> *The Pied Piper of Hamelin,* st. 2

With shrieking and squeaking
In fifty different sharps and flats.
>> *Ib.*

When the liquor's out, why clink the cannikin?
>> *The Flight of the Duchess* [1845], st. 16

It's a long lane that knows no turnings.
>> *Ib. st. 17*

Just for a handful of silver he left us,
Just for a riband to stick in his coat.
>> *The Lost Leader* [1] [1845], st. 1

We that had loved him so, followed him, honored him,
Lived in his mild and magnificent eye,
Learned his great language, caught his clear accents,
Made him our pattern to live and to die!
>> *Ib.*

Shakespeare was of us, Milton was for us,
Burns, Shelley, were with us — they watch from their graves!
>> *Ib.*

One more devils'-triumph and sorrow for angels,
One more wrong to man, one more insult to God!
>> *Ib. st. 2*

Let him never come back to us!
There would be doubt, hesitation and pain,
Forced praise on our part — the glimmer of twilight,
Never glad confident morning again!
>> *Ib.*

It was roses, roses all the way.
>> *The Patriot* [1845], st. 1

I sprang to the stirrup, and Joris, and he;

[1] Often assumed to refer to Wordsworth.

I galloped, Dirck galloped, we galloped
   all three.
> *How They Brought the Good*
> *News from Ghent to Aix* [*1845*],
> *st. 1*

And into the midnight we galloped
   abreast.   **Ib.**

The gray sea and the long black land;
And the yellow half-moon large and
   low.
> *Meeting at Night* [*1845*], *st. 1*

Then a mile of warm, sea-scented
   beach.   **Ib. st. 2**

Round the cape of a sudden came the
   sea,
And the sun looked over the mountain's rim:
And straight was a path of gold for
   him,
And the need of a world of men for
   me.   *Parting at Morning* [*1845*]

Oh, to be in England now that April's
   there,
And whoever wakes in England sees,
   some morning, unaware,
That the lowest boughs and the brush-
   wood sheaf
Round the elm-tree bole are in tiny
   leaf,
While the chaffinch sings on the
   orchard bough
In England — now!
> *Home Thoughts, from Abroad*
> [*1845*], *l. 1*

That's the wise thrush; he sings each
   song twice over,
Lest you should think he never could
   recapture
The first fine careless rapture!
                Ib. l. 12

Nobly, nobly Cape St. Vincent to the
   northwest died away;
Sunset ran, one glorious blood-red,
   reeking into Cadiz Bay.
> *Home Thoughts, from the Sea*
> [*1845*], *l. 1*

Let's contend no more, Love,
   Strive nor weep:

All be as before, Love,
   — Only sleep!
> *A Woman's Last Word* [*1855*],
> *st. 1*

Where the apple reddens
   Never pry —
Lest we lose our Edens,
   Eve and I.   **Ib. st. 5**

Beautiful Evelyn Hope is dead!
> *Evelyn Hope* [*1855*], *st. 1*

You will wake, and remember, and understand.   **Ib. st. 7**

Where the quiet-colored end of evening
   smiles.
> *Love Among the Ruins* [*1855*],
> *st. 1*

Earth's returns
For whole centuries of folly, noise and
   sin!   **Ib. st. 7**

This world, and the wrong it does.
> *Old Pictures in Florence* [*1855*],
> *st. 7*

What's come to perfection perishes.
Things learned on earth, we shall practice in heaven:
Works done least rapidly, Art most
   cherishes.   **Ib. st. 17**

Your ghost will walk, you lover of trees,
   (If our loves remain)
In an English lane.
> *De Gustibus* [*1855*], *st. 1*

Open my heart, and you will see
Graved inside of it, "Italy." [1]
             Ib. st. 2

How well I know what I mean to do
When the long dark autumn evenings
   come.   *By the Fireside* [*1855*], *st. 1*

O woman-country! [2] wooed not wed.
           Ib. st. 6

Oh, the little more, and how much it
   is!
And the little less, and what worlds
   away!   **Ib. st. 39**

[1] See Mary Tudor, p. 187b.
[2] Italy.

If two lives join, there is oft a scar.
They are one and one, with a shadowy
    third;
One near one is too far.
                    By the Fireside, st. 46

    Only I discern
Infinite passion, and the pain
Of finite hearts that yearn.
            Two in the Campagna [1855],
                            st. 12

This is a spray the Bird clung to,
Making it blossom with pleasure.
            Misconceptions [1855], *st. 1*

Escape me?
Never —
Beloved!
While I am I, and you are you.
            Life in a Love [1855], *st. 1*

To dry one's eyes and laugh at a fall,
And baffled, get up and begin again.
                        Ib. st. 2

Ah, did you once see Shelley plain,
    And did he stop and speak to you,
And did you speak to him again?
    How strange it seems, and new! [1]
            Memorabilia [1855], *st. 1*

Who knows but the world may end to-
    night?
    The Last Ride Together [1855],
                        st. 2

Fail I alone, in words and deeds?
Why, all men strive, and who succeeds?
                        Ib. st. 5

Sing, riding's a joy! For me I ride.
                        Ib. st. 7

The instant made eternity —
And heaven just prove that I and she
Ride, ride together, forever ride?
                        Ib. st. 10

That low man seeks a little thing to
    do,
    Sees it and does it;

This high man, with a great thing to
    pursue,
    Dies ere he knows it.
That low man goes on adding one to
    one,
    His hundred's soon hit;
This high man, aiming at a million,
    Misses an unit.
That, has the world here — should he
    need the next,
    Let the world mind him!
This, throws himself on God, and un-
    perplexed
    Seeking shall find Him.
        A Grammarian's Funeral [1855],
                            l. 113

And inasmuch as feeling, the East's
    gift,
Is quick and transient — comes, and lo,
    is gone —
While Northern thought is slow and
    durable.   *Luria* [1855], *act V*

Less is more.[1]
            Andrea del Sarto [1855], *l. 78*

Ah, but a man's reach should exceed
    his grasp,
Or what's a heaven for?   *Ib. l. 97*

Again the cousin's whistle! Go, my
    love.   *Ib. last line*

    How I shall lie through centuries,
And hear the blessed mutter of the
    mass,
And see God made and eaten all day
    long,
And feel the steady candle-flame, and
    taste
Good strong thick stupefying incense
    smoke!
        *The Bishop Orders His Tomb at
        Saint Praxed's Church* [1855],
        l. 80

    Truth that peeps
Over the glass's edge when dinner's
    done,

---

[1] And did you once find Browning plain?
    And did he really seem quite clear?
    And did you read the book again?
    How strange it seems, and queer.
        CHARLES WILLIAM STUBBS [1845–1912],
                            Parody

[1] See Hesiod, p. 67b.
    Not so honest would be more honest. — G. E.
LESSING, *Emilia Galotti* [1722], *act I, sc. 4*
    A popular aphorism with the architect Lud-
wig Mies van der Rohe.

And body gets its sop and holds its
noise
And leaves soul free a little.
Bishop Blougram's Apology
[1855], *l. 17*

Just when we are safest, there's a sun-
set-touch,
A fancy from a flower-bell, someone's
death,
A chorus-ending from Euripides.
Ib. l. 183

One wise man's verdict outweighs all
the fools'. *Ib. l. 373*

Our interest's on the dangerous edge of
things.
The honest thief, the tender murderer,
The superstitious atheist, demirep
That loves and saves her soul in new
French books. *Ib. l. 396*

You call for faith:
I show you doubt, to prove that faith
exists.
The more of doubt, the stronger faith,
I say,
If faith o'ercomes doubt. *Ib. l. 601*

When the fight begins within himself,
A man's worth something.
Ib. l. 793

What of soul was left, I wonder, when
the kissing had to stop?
A Toccata of Galuppi's [1855],
st. 14

Dear dead women, with such hair, too
— what's become of all the gold
Used to hang and brush their bosoms?
I feel chilly and grown old.
Ib. st. 15

The sin I impute to each frustrate ghost
Is — the unlit lamp and the ungirt
loin.
The Statue and the Bust [1855],
st. 82, 83

How good is man's life, the mere living!
how fit to employ
All the heart and the soul and the
senses forever in joy!
Saul [1855], *st. 9*

All's love, yet all's law. *Ib. st. 17*

'Tis not what man does which exalts
him, but what man would do!
Saul, st. 18

The sprinkled isles,
Lily on lily, that o'erlace the sea.
Cleon [1855], *l. 1*

And I have written three books on the
soul,
Proving absurd all written hitherto,
And putting us to ignorance again.
Ib. l. 57

Rafael made a century of sonnets.
One Word More [1855], 2

Does he paint? he fain would write a
poem —
Does he write? he fain would paint a
picture. *Ib. 8*

Where my heart lies, let my brain lie
also. *Ib. 14*

God be thanked, the meanest of his
creatures
Boasts two soul-sides, one to face the
world with,
One to show a woman when he loves
her.[1] *Ib. 17*

Oh, their Rafael of the dear Madonnas,
Oh, their Dante of the dread Inferno,
Wrote one song — and in my brain I
sing it,
Drew one angel — borne, see, on my
bosom! *Ib. 19*

That out of three sounds he frame, not
a fourth sound, but a star.
Abt Vogler [1864],[2] *st. 7*

On the earth the broken arcs; in the
heaven, a perfect round.
Ib. st. 9

The high that proved too high, the
heroic for earth too hard,
The passion that left the ground to lose
itself in the sky. *Ib. st. 10*

Sorrow is hard to bear, and doubt is
slow to clear,
Each sufferer says his say, his scheme of
the weal and woe:

[1] See Mark Twain, p. 763a.
[2] The Abt or Abbé George Joseph Vogler
[1749–1824] was a composer, professor, Kapell-
meister, and writer on music.

But God has a few of us whom he whispers in the ear;
The rest may reason and welcome; 'tis we musicians know.
Abt Vogler, st. 11

The C Major of this life. *Ib. st.* 12

Grow old along with me!
The best is yet to be,
The last of life, for which the first was made.
Our times are in his hand.
Rabbi Ben Ezra [1864], *st.* 1

Irks care the crop-full bird? Frets doubt the maw-crammed beast?
Ib. st. 4

Then welcome each rebuff
That turns earth's smoothness rough,
Each sting that bids nor sit nor stand, but go!
Be our joys three parts pain!
Strive, and hold cheap the strain;
Learn, nor account the pang; dare, never grudge the throe! *Ib. st.* 6

What I aspired to be,
And was not, comforts me. *Ib. st.* 7

Therefore I summon age
To grant youth's heritage. *Ib. st.* 13

Look not thou down but up!
Ib. st. 30

Such ever was love's way; to rise, it stoops.
A Death in the Desert [1864], *l.* 134

Progress, man's distinctive mark alone,
Not God's, and not the beasts': God is, they are;
Man partly is, and wholly hopes to be.
Ib. l. 586

Letting the rank tongue blossom into speech.
Caliban upon Setebos [1864], *l.* 23

How sad and bad and mad it was [1] —
But then, how it was sweet!
Confessions [1864], *st.* 9

[1] See Swinburne, p. 776a.

Fear death? — to feel the fog in my throat,
The mist in my face.
Prospice [1864], *l.* 1

No! let me taste the whole of it, fare like my peers,
The heroes of old,
Bear the brunt, in a minute pay glad life's arrears
Of pain, darkness, and cold.
Ib. l. 17

Hold me but safe again within the bond
Of one immortal look.
Eurydice to Orpheus [1864], *l.* 5

This could but have happened once —
And we missed it, lost it forever.
Youth and Art [1864], *st.* 17

All that I own is a print,
An etching, a mezzotint.
A Likeness [1864], *st.* 4

He never saw, never before today,
What was able to take his breath away.
A face to lose youth for, to occupy age
With the dream of, meet death with.[1]
Ib. st. 6

We find great things are made of little things,
And little things go lessening till at last
Comes God behind them.
Mr. Sludge, "The Medium" [1864], *l.* 1112

'Tis because stiffish cock-tail, taken in time,
Is better for a bruise than arnica.[2]
Ib. l. 1478

Boston's a hole, the herring-pond is wide,
V-notes are something, liberty still more.
Beside, is he the only fool in the world?
Ib. l. 1523

It's wiser being good than bad;
It's safer being meek than fierce;
It's fitter being sane than mad.

[1] A face that a man might die for. — Sir Arthur Conan Doyle, *The Adventures of Sherlock Holmes: A Scandal in Bohemia* [1892]
[2] See Irving, p. 549b.

My own hope is, a sun will pierce
The thickest cloud earth ever stretched;
That, after Last, returns the First,
Though a wide compass round be
     fetched;
That what began best can't end worst,
Nor what God blessed once, prove
     accurs'd.
                    Apparent Failure [1864], *st. 7*

O Lyric Love, half angel and half bird,
And all a wonder and a wild desire.
          The Ring and the Book [1868–
                         1869], *pt. I*

The truth was felt by instinct here,
— Process which saves a world of trou-
     ble and time.
               Ib. IV, Tertium Quid

'Twas a thief said the last kind word to
     Christ:
Christ took the kindness and forgave
     the theft.
          Ib. VI, Giuseppe Caponsacchi

All poetry is difficult to read,
— The sense of it is, anyhow.
                    Ib. VII, Pompilia

No work begun shall ever pause for
     death!   *Ib.*

Faultless to a fault.
          *Ib. IX, Juris Doctor Johannes-
                    Baptista Bottinius*

     The curious crime, the fine
Felicity and flower of wickedness.
                    Ib. X, The Pope

     What I call God,
And fools call Nature.[1]   *Ib.*

Why comes temptation, but for man
     to meet
And master and make crouch beneath
     his foot,
And so be pedestaled in triumph?
                                    Ib.

White shall not neutralize the black,
     nor good

[1] Some call it Evolution,
    And others call it God. . . .
    Some of us call it Autumn,
    And others call it God.
          W. H. CARRUTH [1859–1924], *Each in
                         His Own Tongue*

Compensate bad in man, absolve him
     so:
Life's business being just the terrible
     choice.
               *The Ring and the Book,
                    pt. X, The Pope*

You never know what life means till
     you die:
Even throughout life, 'tis death that
     makes life live,
Gives it whatever the significance.
                    Ib. XI, Guido

Save the squadron, honor France, love
     thy wife the Belle Aurore!
               Hervé Riel [1871], *st. 11*

A man in armor is his armor's slave.
                    Herakles [1871]

     In God's good time,
Which does not always fall on Satur-
     day
When the world looks for wages.[1]
                                    Ib.

So absolutely good is truth, truth never
     hurts
The teller.
          Fifine at the Fair [1872], *st. 32*

     That far land we dream about,
Where every man is his own architect.
          Red Cotton Nightcap Country
                         [1873], *II*

     A secret's safe
'Twixt you, me, and the gatepost!
               The Inn Album [1875], *II*

Ignorance is not innocence but sin.
                                    Ib. V

Have you found your life distasteful?
     My life did and does smack sweet.
Was your youth of pleasure wasteful?
     Mine I saved and hold complete.
Do your joys with age diminish?
     When mine fail me, I'll complain.
Must in death your daylight finish?
     My sun sets to rise again.
          At the "Mermaid" [1876], *st. 10*

[1] The old Tuscan proverb, *Iddio non paga
sabato* [God does not pay Saturdays]. — *Life in
Letters of William Dean Howells* [1928], *vol.
II, p. 169, letter to Mrs. James T. Fields*
[February 23, 1903]

I find earth not gray but rosy,
  Heaven not grim but fair of hue.
Do I stoop? I pluck a posy.
  Do I stand and stare? [1] All's blue.
        At the "Mermaid," st. 12

    "With this same key
Shakespeare unlocked his heart" [2] once
    more!
Did Shakespeare? If so, the less
  Shakespeare he!
        House [1876], *st. 10*

Because a man has shop to mind
In time and place, since flesh must live,
Needs spirit lack all life behind,
All stray thoughts, fancies fugitive,
All loves except what trade can give?
        Shop [1876], *st. 20*

Good, to forgive;
  Best, to forget!
Living, we fret;
Dying, we live.
    La Saisiaz [1877]. *Introduction,*
        st. 1

Sky — what a scowl of cloud
  Till, near and far,
Ray on ray split the shroud:
  Splendid, a star!
    The Two Poets of Croisic [1878].
        Introduction, st. 2

    As if true pride
Were not also humble!
    Lines written in an album [1882]

Wanting is — what?
  Summer redundant,
  Blueness abundant,
  — Where is the blot?
    Wanting Is — What? [3] [1883]

Out of the wreck I rise.
        Ixion [1883]

[1] What is this life if, full of care,
  We have no time to stand and stare?
    WILLIAM HENRY DAVIES [1871–1940],
        Leisure
[2] See Wordsworth, p. 517a.
[3] Browning is — what?
  Riddle redundant,
  Baldness abundant,
  Sense, who can spot?
    ANONYMOUS, in *Punch* [April 21, 1883]

Never the time and the place
And the loved one all together!
    Never the Time and the Place
        [1883]

Help me with knowledge — for Life's
  Old — Death's New!
    *Epitaph on Levi Lincoln
        Thaxter, 1824–1884*

A minute's success pays the failure of
  years.
    Apollo and the Fates [1886], *st. 42*

One who never turned his back but
    marched breast forward,
Never doubted clouds would break,
Never dreamed though right were
    worsted, wrong would triumph,
Held we fall to rise, are baffled to fight
    better,
Sleep to wake.
    Asolando [1889]. *Epilogue, st. 3*

SAMUEL DICKINSON BURCHARD
1812–1891

We are Republicans, and don't propose to leave our party and identify
ourselves with the party whose ante-
cedents have been Rum, Romanism,
and Rebellion.
    *Speaking for a deputation of
    clergymen calling upon James
    G. Blaine, the Republican
    Presidential candidate, New
    York* [October 29, 1884]

CHARLES DICKENS
1812–1870

A smattering of everything, and a
knowledge of nothing.
    Sketches by Boz [1836–1837].
        Tales, ch. 3

He had used the word [humbug] in
its Pickwickian sense.
    Pickwick Papers [1836–1837],
        ch. 1

"An observer of human nature, sir,"
said Mr. Pickwick.   *Ib. 2*

"It wasn't the wine," murmured Mr. Snodgrass, in a broken voice. "It was the salmon."

Pickwick Papers, ch. 8

I wants to make your flesh creep.

Ib.

Can I unmoved see thee dying
    On a log
    Expiring frog!   *Ib. 15*

Tongue; well that's a wery good thing when it an't a woman's.   *Ib. 19*

Mr. Weller's knowledge of London was extensive and peculiar.   *Ib. 20*

Be wery careful o' vidders all your life.   *Ib.*

The wictim o' connubiality, as Blue Beard's domestic chaplain said, with a tear of pity, ven he buried him.   *Ib.*

Dumb as a drum vith a hole in it, sir.   *Ib. 25*

Eccentricities of genius.   *Ib. 30*

Keep yourself *to* yourself.   *Ib. 32*

Poetry's unnat'ral; no man ever talked poetry 'cept a beadle on Boxin' Day.   *Ib. 33*

She knows wot's wot, she does.

Ib. 37

They don't mind it; it's a regular holiday to them — all porter and skittles.[1]   *Ib. 41*

Anythin' for a quiet life, as the man said wen he took the sitivation at the lighthouse.   *Ib. 43*

Oliver Twist has asked for more!
Oliver Twist [1837–1838], *ch. 2*

"The artful Dodger."   *Ib. 8*

"Hard," replied the Dodger. "As nails," added Charley Bates.   *Ib. 9*

There is a passion for hunting something deeply implanted in the human breast.   *Ib. 10*

I'll eat my head.   *Ib.*

[1] Life ain't all beer and skittles, and more's the pity. — GEORGE DU MAURIER, *Trilby* [1894], *pt. I.* See Hughes, p. 718a.

I only know two sorts of boys. Mealy boys, and beef-faced boys.

Oliver Twist, ch. 10

There's light enough for wot I've got to do.   *Ib. 47*

"If the law supposes that," said Mr. Bumble . . . "the law is a ass, a idiot."   *Ib. 51*

He had but one eye, and the popular prejudice runs in favor of two.
Nicholas Nickleby [1838–1839], *ch. 4*

Subdue your appetites, my dears, and you've conquered human natur. *Ib. 5*

There are only two styles of portrait painting; the serious and the smirk.

Ib. 10

Oh! they're too beautiful to live, much too beautiful!   *Ib. 14*

I pity his ignorance and despise him.

Ib. 15

The unities, sir . . . are a completeness — a kind of universal dovetailedness with regard to place and time.   *Ib. 24*

The two countesses had no outlines at all, and the dowager's was a demd outline.   *Ib. 34*

A demd, damp, moist, unpleasant body!   *Ib.*

Bring in the bottled lightning, a clean tumbler, and a corkscrew.

Ib. 49

All is gas and gaiters.   *Ib.*

My life is one demd horrid grind.

Ib. 64

He has gone to the demnition bowwows.   *Ib.*

What is the odds so long as the fire of soul is kindled at the taper of conwiviality, and the wing of friendship never moults a feather!
The Old Curiosity Shop [1841], *ch. 2*

She's the ornament of her sex.
The Old Curiosity Shop, ch. 5

In love of home, the love of country has its rise. *Ib.* 38

That vague kind of penitence which holidays awaken next morning.
Ib. 40

"Did you ever taste beer?" "I had a sip of it once," said the small servant. "Here's a state of things!" cried Mr. Swiveller. . . . "She *never* tasted it — it can't be tasted in a sip!"
Ib. 57

It was a maxim with Foxey — our revered father, gentlemen — "Always suspect everybody." *Ib.* 66

Rather a tough customer in argyment.
Barnaby Rudge [1841], *ch.* 1

"There are strings," said Mr. Tappertit, ". . . in the human heart that had better not be wibrated."
Ib. 22

Oh gracious, why wasn't I born old and ugly? *Ib.* 70

Any man may be in good spirits and good temper when he's well dressed. There an't much credit in that.
Martin Chuzzlewit [1843–1844], *ch.* 5

With affection beaming in one eye, and calculation shining out of the other. *Ib.* 8

"Do not repine, my friends," said Mr. Pecksniff, tenderly. "Do not weep for me. It is chronic." *Ib.* 9

Keep up appearances whatever you do. *Ib.* 11

"Do other men for they would do you." That's the true business precept.
Ib.

Buy an annuity cheap, and make your life interesting to yourself and everybody else that watches the speculation. *Ib.* 18

Leave the bottle on the chimleypiece, and don't ask me to take none, but let me put my lips to it when I am so dispoged.
Martin Chuzzlewit, ch. 19

"She's the sort of woman now," said Mould . . . "one would almost feel disposed to bury for nothing: and do it neatly, too!" *Ib.* 25

He'd make a lovely corpse. *Ib.*

Our fellow-countryman is a model of a man, quite fresh from Natur's mold!
Ib. 34

Oh Sairey, Sairey, little do we know wot lays afore us! *Ib.* 40

I don't believe there's no sich a person! *Ib.* 49

The words she spoke of Mrs. Harris, lambs could not forgive . . . nor worms forget. *Ib.*

Marley was dead, to begin with. There is no doubt whatever about that. The register of his burial was signed by the clergyman, the clerk, the undertaker, and the chief mourner. Scrooge signed it. And Scrooge's name was good upon 'Change for anything he chose to put his hand to.
Old Marley was as dead as a doornail.
A Christmas Carol [1843], *stave* I

Secret, and self-contained, and solitary as an oyster. *Ib.*

I wear the chain I forged in life.
Ib.

In came a fiddler — and tuned like fifty stomachaches. In came Mrs. Fezziwig, one vast substantial smile.
Ib. stave II

Let's have the shutters up . . . before a man can say Jack Robinson.[1]
Ib.

As good as gold. *Ib. stave* III

[1] I'd do it as soon as say Jack Robinson. — FANNY BURNEY, *Evelina* [1778], *letter 82*
I'd get her off before you could say Jack Robinson. — MARIA EDGEWORTH, *The Absentee* [1812], *ch.* 2

"God bless us every one!" said Tiny Tim, the last of all.
A Christmas Carol, stave III

It *was* a turkey! He could never have stood upon his legs, that bird! He would have snapped 'em off short in a minute, like sticks of sealing wax.
Ib. stave V

O let us love our occupations,
Bless the squire and his relations,
Live upon our daily rations,
And always know our proper stations.
The Chimes [1844], *second quarter*

He's tough, ma'am, tough, is J.B. Tough and devilish sly!
Dombey and Son [1848], *ch. 7*

I want to know what it says. . . . The sea, Floy, what it is that it keeps on saying.[1]
Ib. 8

"Wal'r, my boy," replied the Captain, "in the Proverbs of Solomon you will find the following words, 'May we never want a friend in need, nor a bottle to give him!' When found, make a note of."
Ib. 15

Cows are my passion.
Ib. 21

The bearings of this observation lays in the application on it.
Ib. 23

You'll find us rough, sir, but you'll find us ready.
David Copperfield [1849–1850], *ch. 3*

I am a lone lorn creetur . . . and everythink goes contrairy with me.
Ib.

Barkis is willin'.
Ib. 5

Experientia does it [2] — as Papa used to say.
Ib. 11

"In case anything turned up," which was his [Mr. Micawber's] favorite expression.[3]
Ib.

I never will desert Mr. Micawber.
David Copperfield, ch. 12

Annual income twenty pounds, annual expenditure nineteen nineteen six, result happiness. Annual income twenty pounds, annual expenditure twenty pounds ought and six, result misery.
Ib.

It's a mad world. Mad as Bedlam.
Ib. 14

I'm a very umble person.[1]
Ib. 16

The mistake was made of putting some of the trouble out of King Charles's head into my head.[2]
Ib. 17

I only ask for information.
Ib. 20

It was as true . . . as turnips is. It was as true . . . as taxes is. And nothing's truer than them.
Ib. 21

What a world of gammon and spinach it is, though, ain't it!
Ib. 22

Nobody's enemy but his own.
Ib. 25

Accidents will occur in the best-regulated families.
Ib. 28

Ride on! Rough-shod if need be, smooth-shod if that will do, but ride on! Ride on over all obstacles, and win the race!
Ib.

A long pull, and a strong pull, and a pull all together.
Ib. 30

He's a-going out with the tide.[3]
Ib.

There wasn't room to swing a cat there.
Ib. 35

I ate umble pie with an appetite.
Ib. 39

---

[1] See Carpenter, p. 675b.

[2] A pun on Experientia docet [Experience teaches] — TACITUS [c. 55–c. 117], *History, bk. V, ch. 6*

[3] See Disraeli, p. 612a.

[1] Not only humble but umble, which I look upon to be the comparative, or, indeed, superlative degree. — ANTHONY TROLLOPE, *Doctor Thorne* [1858], *ch. 4*

[2] "King Charles's head" has passed into common use in the English language as a phrase meaning some whimsical obsession. — G. B. STERN [1890–   ], *Monogram*

[3] See Sir James Frazer, p. 829a.

Let sleeping dogs lie — who wants to rouse 'em?
David Copperfield, ch. 39

Skewered through and through with office pens, and bound hand and foot with red tape.   *Ib. 43*

It's only my child-wife.   *Ib. 44*

A man must take the fat with the lean.   *Ib. 51*

Trifles make the sum of life.
Ib. 53

The seamen said it blew great guns.
Ib. 55

This is a London particular. . . . A fog, miss.
Bleak House [1852–1853], ch. 3

Not to put too fine a point upon it.
Ib. 11

Whatever was required to be done, the Circumlocution Office was beforehand with all the public departments in the art of perceiving — HOW NOT TO DO IT.
Little Dorrit [1857–1858], bk. I, ch. 10

Papa, potatoes, poultry, prunes, and prism, are all very good words for the lips: especially prunes and prism.
Ib. II, 5

Once a gentleman, and always a gentleman.   *Ib. 28*

It was the best of times, it was the worst of times.
A Tale of Two Cities [1859], bk. I, ch. 1

A wonderful fact to reflect upon, that every human creature is constituted to be that profound secret and mystery to every other.   *Ib. 3*

It is a far, far better thing that I do, than I have ever done; it is a far, far better rest that I go to, than I have ever known.   *Ib. III, 15*

In the little world in which children have their existence, whosoever brings them up, there is nothing so finely per-

ceived and so finely felt, as injustice.
Great Expectations [1860–1861], ch. 9

Professionally he declines and falls, and as a friend he drops into poetry [Mr. Boffin on Silas Wegg].
Our Mutual Friend [1864–1865], bk. I, ch. 5

My best of wishes for your merry Christmases and your happy New Years, your long lives and your true prosperities. Worth twenty pound good if they are delivered as I send them. Remember? Here's a final prescription added, "To be taken for life."
Doctor Marigold's Prescriptions [1865], ch. 1

IVAN GONCHAROV
1812–1891

"And he was as intelligent as other people, his soul was pure and clear as crystal; he was noble and affectionate — and yet he did nothing!"
"But why? What was the reason?"
"The reason . . . what reason was there? Oblomovism!" [1]
Oblomov [1859], pt. IV, ch. 12

EDWARD LEAR
1812–1888

There was an Old Man with a beard,
Who said: "It is just as I feared!
 Two owls and a hen,
 Four larks and a wren
Have all built their nests in my beard."
Book of Nonsense [1846]. Limerick

How pleasant to know Mr. Lear!
 Who has written such volumes of stuff!

[1] That word is Oblomovism.
Now, when I hear a country squire talking about the rights of man and urging the necessity of developing personality, I know from the first word he utters that he is an Oblomov.
When I hear a government official complaining that the system of administration is too complicated and cumbersome, I know that he is an Oblomov. — NIKOLAI DOBROLIUBOV, *What Is Oblomovism?* [1859]

Some think him ill-tempered and queer,
But a few think him pleasant
enough.
    Nonsense Songs [1871]. *Preface,*
            st. 1

His body is perfectly spherical,
He weareth a runcible hat.   *Ib. st. 5*

The Owl and the Pussycat went to sea
  In a beautiful pea-green boat,
They took some honey, and plenty of
  money,
Wrapped up in a five-pound note.
The Owl looked up to the stars above,
  And sang to a small guitar,
"O lovely Pussy! O Pussy, my love,
What a beautiful Pussy you are."
    The Owl and the Pussycat
          [1871], *st. 1*

Pussy said to the Owl, "You elegant
  fowl!
How charmingly sweet you sing!
O let us be married! too long we have
  tarried:
But what shall we do for a ring?"
They sailed away, for a year and a day,
  To the land where the Bong-tree
  grows
And there in a wood a Piggy-wig stood
  With a ring at the end of his nose.
                  Ib. st. 2

"Dear Pig, are you willing to sell for
  one shilling
Your ring?" Said the Piggy, "I will."
                  Ib. st. 3

They dined on mince, and slices of
  quince,
Which they ate with a runcible
  spoon;
And hand in hand, on the edge of the
  sand,
  They danced by the light of the
  moon.   *Ib.*

Far and few, far and few,
  Are the lands where the Jumblies
  live;
Their heads are green, and their hands
  are blue,
  And they went to sea in a sieve.
      The Jumblies [1871], *st. 1*

Calico Pie,
  The little Birds fly
Down to the calico tree,
  Their wings were blue,
  And they sang "Tilly-loo!"
Till away they flew —
And they never came back to me!
      Calico Pie [1871], *st. 1*

Calico Jam,
  The little Fish swam,
Over the syllabub sea.   *Ib. st. 2*

Who, or why, or which, or what,
Is the Akond of Swat?
    The Akond of Swat [1] [1873], *l. 1*

She sate upon her Dobie,
  To watch the Evening Star,
And all the Punkahs as they passed,
  Cried, "My! how fair you are!"
    The Cummerbund [1874], *st. 1*

On the top of the Crumpetty Tree
  The Quangle Wangle sat,
But his face you could not see,
  On account of his Beaver Hat.
    The Quangle Wangle's Hat
          [1877], *st. 1*

On the coast of Coromandel
  Where the early pumpkins blow,
  In the middle of the woods
Lived the Yonghy-Bonghy-Bò.
Two old chairs, and half a candle,
One old jug without a handle —
  These were all his worldly goods.
    The Courtship of the Yonghy-
      Bongy-Bò [1877], *st. 1*

There he heard a Lady talking,
To some milk-white Hens of Dork-
  ing —
'Tis the Lady Jingly Jones!
               Ib. st. 2

"I would be your wife most gladly!"
(Here she twirled her fingers madly),
  "But in England I've a mate!"
               Ib. st. 5

[1] Now the Ahkoond of Swat is a vague sort of
man
Who lives in a country far over the sea;
Pray tell me, good reader, if tell me you can,
What's the Ahkoond of Swat to you folks or to
me?
    EUGENE FIELD, *The Ahkoond of Swat*
          [1884]

When awful darkness and silence
reign
Over the great Gromboolian plain,
  Through the long, long wintry
  nights.
          *The Dong with the Luminous
                    Nose* [1877], *st. 1*

When storm-clouds brood on the
towering heights
Of the hills of the Chankly Bore.
                                  Ib.

The Pobble who has no toes
Had once as many as we;
When they said, "Some day you may
  lose them all" —
He replied, "Fish fiddle de-dee!"
          The Pobble Who Has No Toes
                    [1877], *st. 1*

Ploffskin, Pluffskin, Pelican jee!
We think no Birds so happy as we!
Plumpskin, Ploshkin, Pelican jill!
We think so then, and we thought so
  still.
          The Pelican Chorus [1877],
                              chorus

SAMUEL SMILES
1812–1904

The spirit of self-help is the root of
all genuine growth in the individual;
and, exhibited in the lives of many, it
constitutes the true source of national
vigor and strength. Help from without
is often enfeebling in its effects, but
help from within invariably invigorates.
                    Self-Help [1859]

WILLIAM
EDMONDSTOUNE
AYTOUN
1813–1865

News of battle! — news of battle!
  Hark! 'tis ringing down the street;
And the archways and the pavement
  Bear the clang of hurrying feet.
          Edinburgh after Flodden [1849],
                              st. 1

Nowhere beats the heart so kindly
As beneath the tartan plaid!
          *Charles Edward at Versailles on
          the Anniversary of Culloden*
          [1849], *l. 219*

They bore within their breasts the grief
  That fame can never heal —
The deep, unutterable woe
  Which none save exiles feel.
          The Island of the Scots [1849],
                              st. 12

HENRY WARD
BEECHER
1813–1887

A thoughtful mind, when it sees a
nation's flag, sees not the flag only, but
the nation itself; and whatever may be
its symbols, its insignia, he reads chiefly
in the flag the government, the principles, the truths, the history which belongs to the nation that sets it forth.
                    The American Flag

Where is human nature so weak as
in the bookstore!
          Star Papers [1855]. *Subtleties of
                              Book Buyers*

Now comes the mystery.
          Last words [*March 8, 1887*]

CLAUDE BERNARD
1813–1878

Great men may be compared to
torches shining at long intervals, to
guide the advance of science. They
light up their time, either by discovering unexpected and fertile phenomena
which open up new paths and reveal
unknown horizons, or by generalizing
acquired scientific facts and disclosing
truths which their predecessors had not
perceived.
          *Introduction à l' Étude de
          la Médecine Expérimentale
          [1865]* [1]

[1] *An Introduction to the Study of Experimental Medicine*, translated by HENRY COPLEY
GREENE [1926].

We may, of course, strike a balance between what a living organism takes in as nourishment and what it gives out in excretions; but the results would be mere statistics incapable of throwing light on the inmost phenomena of nutrition in living beings. According to a Dutch chemist's phrase, this would be like trying to tell what happens inside a house by watching what goes in by the door and what comes out by the chimney.

> *Introduction à l'Étude de la Médecine Expérimentale*

Observation is a passive science, experimentation an active science.
> *Ib.*

The science of life is a superb and dazzlingly lighted hall which may be reached only by passing through a long and ghastly kitchen.   *Ib.*

Science repulses the indefinite.
> *Ib.*

The stability of the *internal medium* is a primary condition for the freedom and independence of certain living bodies in relation to the environment surrounding them.

> *Leçons sur les Phénomènes de la Vie Communs aux Animaux et aux Végétaux* [1878–1879] [1]

All the vital mechanisms, varied as they are, have only one object, that of preserving constant the conditions of life in the internal environment.   *Ib.*

True science teaches us to doubt and to abstain from ignorance.

> *From Bulletin of New York Academy of Medicine, vol. IV* [1928], *p. 997*

Science increases our power in proportion as it lowers our pride.   *Ib.*

If I had to define life in a word, it would be: Life is creation.   *Ib.*

A modern poet has characterized the personality of art and the impersonality of science as follows: Art is I: Science is We.   *Ib.*

[1] *Lessons on Reactions Common to Animals and Plants*, translated by J. M. D. OLMSTEAD.

Man can learn nothing unless he proceeds from the known to the unknown.

> *From Bulletin of New York Academy of Medicine, vol. IV, p. 997*

We must never make experiments to confirm our ideas, but simply to control them.   *Ib.*

GEORG BÜCHNER
1813–1837

The Revolution is like Saturn — it eats its own children.
> *Danton's Death* [1835]

The people are like children; they must smash everything to see what is inside.   *Ib.*

JOHN WILLIAM BURGON
1813–1860

A rose-red city half as old as time.[1]
> *Petra* [*Newdigate Prize Poem, 1845*]

JOSEPH EDWARDS CARPENTER
1813–1885

What are the wild waves saying,[2]
Sister, the whole day long?
> *What Are the Wild Waves Saying?* st. 1

JOHN SULLIVAN DWIGHT
1813–1893

Work, and thou wilt bless the day
    Ere the toil be done;
They that work not, cannot pray,
    Cannot feel the sun.
God is living, working still,
    All things work and move;
Work, or lose the power to will,
    Lose the power to love.   *Working*

[1] By many a temple half as old as Time. — SAMUEL ROGERS [1763–1855], *Italy* [1822–1828], *A Farewell*
[2] See Dickens, p. 671a.

SÖREN KIERKEGAARD
1813–1855

Life can only be understood backwards; but it must be lived forwards.
Life

All essential knowledge relates to existence, or only such knowledge as has an essential relationship to existence is essential knowledge.
Concluding Unscientific Postscript

The absurd . . . the fact that with God all things are possible. The absurd is not one of the factors which can be discriminated within the proper compass of the understanding: it is not identical with the improbable, the unexpected, the unforeseen.
Fear and Trembling [1843]. *Problemata: Preliminary Expectoration*

JOHN LOUIS O'SULLIVAN
1813–1895

Our manifest destiny is to overspread the continent allotted by Providence for the free development of our yearly multiplying millions.[1]
United States Magazine and Democratic Review [July–August 1845]

EPES SARGENT
1813–1880

A life on the ocean wave,
A home on the rolling deep;
Where the scattered waters rave,
And the winds their revels keep!
A Life on the Ocean Wave [1847], *st.* 1

RICHARD WAGNER
1813–1883

Say, where didst thou tarry so long?
Tannhäuser [1845]

[1] See Josh Billings, p. 685a.

O thou, my gracious evening star.
Tannhäuser

To be German means to carry on a matter for its own sake.
Deutsche Kunst und Deutsche Politik [1] [1867]

Ride of the Valkyries.
Die Walküre [1876]

The pure fool. *Parsifal* [1882]

HENRY STEVENSON WASHBURN
1813–1903

We shall meet, but we shall miss him,
There will be one vacant chair.
The Vacant Chair, st. 1

THOMAS OSBORNE DAVIS
1814–1845

Come in the evening, or come in the morning,
Come when you're looked for, or come without warning.
The Welcome, st. 1

Sheep without a Shepherd, when the snow shuts out the sky —
Oh, why did you leave us, Owen? Why did you die?
Lament for the Death of Eoghan Ruadh O'Neill, st. 7

FREDERICK WILLIAM FABER
1814–1863

Hark! Hark! my soul, angelic songs are swelling
O'er earth's green fields, and ocean's wave-beat shore;
How sweet the truth those blessed strains are telling
Of that new life when sin shall be no more!
Oratory Hymns. Pilgrims of the Night

[1] *German Art and German Politics*

O Paradise! O Paradise!
Who doth not crave for rest?
Oratory Hymns. Paradise

Faith of our fathers! holy faith!
We will be true to thee till death.
Ib. A Pledge of Faithfulness

MIKHAIL LERMONTOV
1814–1841

A *Hero of Our Time*, gentlemen, is indeed a portrait, but not of a single individual; it is a portrait composed of all the vices of our generation in the fullness of their development.
A Hero of Our Time [1840],
Author's Introduction

CHARLES MACKAY
1814–1889

There's a good time coming, boys!
A good time coming.
The Good Time Coming, st. 1

Old Tubal Cain was a man of might,
In the days when earth was young.
Tubal Cain, st. 1

Not alone for the blade was the bright steel made,
And he fashioned the first plowshare.[1]
Ib. st. 4

EDWIN McMASTERS STANTON
1814–1869

Now he [Lincoln] belongs to the ages.
On the death of Lincoln
[April 15, 1865]

OTTO VON BISMARCK
1815–1898

The great questions of the time are not decided by speeches and majority decisions — that was the error of 1848 and 1849 — but by iron and blood.[1]
Speech to the Prussian Diet
[September 30, 1862]

A newspaper writer is one who has failed in his calling.
Derived from speech [November 10, 1862]

Politics is not an exact science.[2]
Speech to the Herrenhaus
[December 13, 1863]

The glass house of German statecraft.
Concerning Austro-German power, to a commission of the Prussian Landtag [1864]

Only a completely ready state can permit the luxury of a liberal government.
Speech [1866]

Let us put Germany in the saddle, so to speak — it already knows how to ride.
Speech to the North German Reichstag [*March* 11, 1867]

A conquering army on the border will not be halted by the power of eloquence.
Ib. [*September 24, 1867*]

He who has his thumb on the purse has the power.
Ib. [*May 21, 1869*]

The luxury of one's own opinion.
Speech to the Prussian Diet
[December 17, 1873]

The right people in the right jobs.
Speech to the North German Reichstag [1875]

Politics ruins the character.
Reported by Bernhard Brigl in the Berlin Tägliche Rundschau [1881]

We Germans fear God, but nothing else in the world.
Speech to the Reichstag [*February 6, 1888*]

[1] See *Isaiah 2:4*, p. 30a.
Tubal fashioned the hand-flung spears
And showed his neighbors peace.
KIPLING [1865–1936], *Jubal and Tubal Cain, st. 3*

[1] Eisen und Blut.

[2] Politics is not a science . . . but an art. — *Speech* [March 15, 1884]

RICHARD HENRY DANA
1815–1882

Six days shalt thou labor and do all thou art able,
And on the seventh — holystone the decks and scrape the cable.
Two Years Before the Mast
[1840], ch. 3

He seldom went up to town without coming down "three sheets in the wind." *Ib. 20*

Everything was "shipshape and Bristol fashion." *Ib. 22*

DAVID DAVIS
1815–1886

The Constitution of the United States is a law for rulers and people, equally in war and in peace, and covers with the shield of its protection all classes of men, at all times, and under all circumstances. No doctrine, involving more pernicious consequences, was ever invented by the wit of man than that any of its provisions can be suspended during any of the great exigencies of government.
Ex Parte Milligan, 4 Wallace 2,
120–121 [1866]

DANIEL DECATUR EMMETT
1815–1904

I wish I was in de land ob cotton,
Old times dar am not forgotten.
Look away, look away,
Look away, Dixie Land.
Dixie [1] *[1859], st. 1*

[1] Originally this word [Dixie] applied only to New Orleans; not until the Civil War, when D. D. Emmett's famous song . . . became the favorite battle song of the Confederacy, was it in general use to designate the entire South. It came about in this fashion:
A few years after Louisiana became a part of the United States . . . one of the New Orleans banks began issuing ten-dollar notes, one side of which was printed in English and the other in French. On the latter, in large letters, was the French word for ten, *dix*. . . .

In Dixie's land, we'll took our stand,
To lib an' die in Dixie!
Dixie, st. 3

JOHN BABSONE LANE SOULE
1815–1891

Go west, young man.[1]
Article in the Terre Haute,
Indiana, Express [1851]

ANTHONY TROLLOPE
1815–1882

The tenth Muse who now governs the periodical press.
The Warden [1855], ch. 14

In these days a man is nobody unless his biography is kept so far posted up that it may be ready for the national breakfast table on the morning after his demise.
Doctor Thorne [1858], ch. 25

Those who offend us are generally punished for the offense they give; but we so frequently miss the satisfaction of knowing that we are avenged!
The Small House at Allington
[1864], ch. 50

She understood how much louder a cock can crow in its own farmyard than elsewhere.
The Last Chronicle of Barset
[1867], vol. I, ch. 17

Always remember that when you go into an attorney's office door, you will have to pay for it, first or last.
Ib. 20

One of these notes was known simply as a dix; collectively they were dixies, a name which was soon applied to the city of issue as well. — HERBERT ASBURY, *The French Quarter* [1936], *ch. 3*
[1] Horace Greeley [1811–1872] used the expression in an editorial in *The New York Tribune* (see Greeley, p. 658b). As the saying "Go west, young man, and grow up with the country" gained popularity, Greeley printed Soule's article, to show the source of his inspiration.
Many men have stated that the advice was given to them by Greeley, among them William S. Verity [1837–1930], who said Greeley had given it to him in 1859.

It is a comfortable feeling to know that you stand on your own ground. Land is about the only thing that can't fly away.
The Last Chronicle of Barset, vol. II, ch. 58

It's dogged as does it.   *Ib. 61*

Nothing reopens the springs of love so fully as absence, and no absence so thoroughly as that which must needs be endless.   *Ib. 67*

PHILIP JAMES BAILEY
1816–1902

Let each man think himself an act of God,
His mind a thought, his life a breath of God;
And let each try, by great thoughts and good deeds,
To show the most of Heaven he hath in him.   *Festus [1839]. Proem*

It matters not how long we live, but how.   *Ib. Wood and Water*

We live in deeds, not years; in thoughts, not breaths;
In feelings, not in figures on a dial.
We should count time by heart-throbs. He most lives
Who thinks most — feels the noblest — acts the best.
          Ib. A Country Town

Envy's a coal comes hissing hot from hell.   *Ib.*

The sole equality on earth is death.
          Ib.

America, thou half-brother of the world;
With something good and bad of every land.   *Ib. The Surface*

There is no disappointment we endure One half so great as that we are to ourselves.[1]   *Ib. The Sun*

[1] Every really able man, if you talk sincerely with him, considers his work, however much admired, as far short of what it should be. — EMERSON, *Immortality* [1875]

CHARLOTTE BRONTË
1816–1855

Life, believe, is not a dream
So dark as sages say; [1]
Oft a little morning rain
Foretells a pleasant day.
          Life [1846], st. 1

The human heart has hidden treasures,
In secret kept, in silence sealed.
          Evening Solace [1846], st. 1

Reader, I married him.
          Jane Eyre [1847], ch. 38

An abundant shower of curates has fallen upon the north of England.
          Shirley [1849], ch. 1

JAMES THOMAS FIELDS
1816–1881

"We are lost!" the captain shouted,
As he staggered down the stairs.
          The Captain's Daughter; or, The Ballad of the Tempest [1858], st. 4

But his little daughter whispered,
As she took his icy hand,
"Isn't God upon the ocean,
Just the same as on the land?" [2]
          Ib. st. 5

How sweet and gracious, even in common speech,
Is that fine sense which men call Courtesy!   *Courtesy*

"I'm an owl; you're another. Sir Critic, good day!"
And the barber kept on shaving.
          The Owl-Critic, last lines and refrain

GUSTAV FREYTAG
1816–1895

Madness of the Caesars.
          Die Verlorene Handschrift [1864], concerning the proposition that power is evil per se

[1] See Longfellow, p. 620b.
[2] See Sir Humphrey Gilbert, p. 192a.

ELLEN STURGIS HOOPER
1816–1841

I slept and dreamed that life was beauty.
I woke — and found that life was duty.
Beauty and Duty

EUGÈNE POTTIER
1816–1887

Arise, ye prisoners of starvation,
　Arise, ye wretched of the earth,
For justice thunders condemnation —
　A better world's in birth.
L'Internationale [1871] [1]

JOHN GODFREY SAXE
1816–1887

In battle or business, whatever the
　game,
In law or in love, it is ever the same;
In the struggle for power, or the scramble for pelf,
Let this be your motto — Rely on yourself!
For, whether the prize be a ribbon or
　throne,
The victor is he who can go it alone! [2]
The Game of Life, st. 7

"God bless the man who first invented
　sleep!"
So Sancho Panza said, and so say I.
Early Rising, st. 1

It was six men of Indostan
　To learning much inclined,
Who went to see the Elephant
　(Though all of them were blind),
That each by observation
　Might satisfy his mind.
The Blind Men and the Elephant, st. 1

'Tis wise to learn; 'tis God-like to create.　　　*The Library*

[1] Adolphe Degeyter wrote the music for the *International*, which was adopted as the rallying song of Communism.
[2] He travels the fastest who travels alone. — KIPLING [1865–1936], *The Winners*

GEORG HERWEGH
1817–1875

The poor human heart must break piecemeal.
Strophen aus der Fremde [1840], *in Rückert's Musenalmanach*

TOM TAYLOR
1817–1880

You lay a wreath on murdered Lincoln's bier,
You, who with mocking pencil wont to trace,
Broad for the self-complacent British sneer,
His length of shambling limb, his furrowed face.
Abraham Lincoln Foully Assassinated,[1] *st. 1*

HENRY DAVID THOREAU
1817–1862

I am a parcel of vain strivings tied
By a chance bond together.
Sic Vita [1841], *st. 1*

Great God, I ask thee for no meaner
　pelf
Than that I may not disappoint myself,
That in my action I may soar as high
As I can now discern with this clear
　eye.　　　*A Prayer* [1842], *st. 1*

　Talk of mysteries! Think of our life in nature — daily to be shown matter, to come in contact with it — rocks, trees, wind on our cheeks! the *solid* earth! the *actual* world! the *common sense*! *Contact*! *Contact*! *Who* are we? *where* are we?
The Maine Woods, Ktaadn [1848]

　I think that we should be men first, and subjects afterward. It is not desir-

[1] Printed in *Punch*, London [May 6, 1865]. Taylor became editor of *Punch* in 1874. It was at a performance of Taylor's play, *Our American Cousin*, that Lincoln was shot.

able to cultivate a respect for the law, so much as for the right.
Civil Disobedience [1849]

How does it become a man to behave toward this American government to-day? I answered that he cannot without disgrace be associated with it. **Ib.**

When a sixth of the population of a nation which has undertaken to be the refuge of liberty are slaves, and a whole country [1] is unjustly overrun and conquered by a foreign army, and subjected to military law, I think that it is not too soon for honest men to rebel and revolutionize. What makes this duty the more urgent is the fact that the country so overrun is not our own, but ours is the invading army. **Ib.**

A wise man will not leave the right to the mercy of chance, nor wish it to prevail through the power of the majority. There is but little virtue in the action of masses of men. **Ib.**

I came into this world, not chiefly to make this a good place to live in, but to live in it, be it good or bad. **Ib.**

Any man more right than his neighbors constitutes a majority of one.
Ib.

Under a government which imprisons any unjustly, the true place for a just man is also a prison . . . the only house in a slave State in which a free man can abide with honor. **Ib.**

I saw that the State was half-witted, that it was timid as a lone woman with her silver spoons, and that it did not know its friends from its foes, and I lost all my remaining respect for it, and pitied it. **Ib.**

My life is like a stroll upon the beach,
As near the ocean's edge as I can go.
My Life Is Like a Stroll Upon the Beach [1849], st. 1

Methinks my own soul must be a bright invisible green.
A Week on the Concord and Merrimack Rivers [1849]. *Wednesday*

It takes two to speak the truth — one to speak, and another to hear.
Ib.

This world is but canvas to our imaginations. **Ib.**

Dreams are the touchstones of our characters. **Ib.**

Go where we will on the *surface* of things, men have been there before us.
Ib. *Thursday*

The frontiers are not east or west, north or south, but wherever a man *fronts* a fact. **Ib.**

A true account of the actual is the rarest poetry, for common sense always takes a hasty and superficial view.
Ib.

As if our birth had at first sundered things, and we had been thrust up through into nature like a wedge, and not till the wound heals and the scar disappears, do we begin to discover where we are, and that nature is one and continuous everywhere.
Ib. *Friday*

What are the earth and all its interests beside the deep surmise which pierces and scatters them? **Ib.**

It is so rare to meet with a man outdoors who cherishes a worthy thought in his mind, which is independent of the labor of his hands. **Ib.**

The eye may see for the hand, but not for the mind. **Ib.**

Nothing is so much to be feared as fear.[1] *Journal* [September 7, 1851]

The bluebird carries the sky on his back. **Ib.** [April 3, 1852]

The perception of beauty is a moral test. **Ib.** [June 21, 1852]

---

[1] Mexico.

[1] See Montaigne, p. 189b, and note.

The youth gets together his materials to build a bridge to the moon, or, perchance, a palace or temple on the earth, and, at length, the middle-aged man concludes to build a woodshed with them.
Journal [*July 14, 1852*]

Fire is the most tolerable third party.
Ib. [*January 2, 1853*]

Some circumstantial evidence is very strong, as when you find a trout in the milk. *Ib.* [*November 11, 1854*]

That man is the richest whose pleasures are the cheapest.
Ib. [*March 11, 1856*]

The savage in man is never quite eradicated.
Ib. [*September 26, 1859*]

The fate of the country . . . does not depend on what kind of paper you drop into the ballot box once a year, but on what kind of man you drop from your chamber into the street every morning.
Slavery in Massachusetts [*1854*]

I should not talk so much about myself if there were anybody else whom I knew as well.
Walden [*1854*],[1] *1, Economy*

I have traveled a good deal in Concord. *Ib.*

Public opinion is a weak tyrant compared with our own private opinion. What a man thinks of himself, that is which determines, or rather, indicates, his fate. *Ib.*

As if you could kill time without injuring eternity. *Ib.*

The mass of men lead lives of quiet desperation. *Ib.*

[1] *Walden* is the only book I own, although there are some others unclaimed on my shelves. Every man, I think, reads one book in his life, and this one is mine. It is not the best book I ever encountered, perhaps, but it is for me the handiest, and I keep it about me in much the same way one carries a handkerchief — for relief in moments of defluxion or despair. — E. B. WHITE, *The New Yorker* [*May 23, 1953*]

It is characteristic of wisdom not to do desperate things.
Walden, 1, Economy

Age is no better, hardly so well, qualified for an instructor as youth, for it has not profited so much as it has lost. *Ib.*

Most of the luxuries, and many of the so-called comforts, of life are not only not indispensable, but positive hindrances to the elevation of mankind. *Ib.*

To be a philosopher is not merely to have subtle thoughts, nor even to found a school, but so to love wisdom as to live accordingly to its dictates, a life of simplicity, independence, magnanimity, and trust. *Ib.*

Beware of all enterprises that require new clothes. *Ib.*

Our moulting season, like that of the fowls, must be a crisis in our lives. *Ib.*

In the long run men hit only what they aim at. *Ib.*

The swiftest traveler is he that goes afoot. *Ib.*

It is not necessary that a man should earn his living by the sweat of his brow [1] unless he sweats easier than I do. *Ib.*

The man who goes alone can start today; but he who travels with another must wait till that other is ready. *Ib.*

When a man dies he kicks the dust. *Ib.*

As for doing good, that is one of the professions which are full. *Ib.*

There is no odor so bad as that which arises from goodness tainted.[2] *Ib.*

There are a thousand hacking at the branches of evil to one who is striking at the root. *Ib.*

[1] See *Genesis 3:19*, p. 6a.
[2] See Shakespeare, p. 293a.

Philanthropy is almost the only virtue which is sufficiently appreciated by mankind. *Walden, 1, Economy*

A man is rich in proportion to the number of things which he can afford to let alone.

Ib. 2, Where I Lived, and What I Lived For

To him whose elastic and vigorous thought keeps pace with the sun, the day is a perpetual morning. *Ib.*

To be awake is to be alive. *Ib.*

I know of no more encouraging fact than the unquestionable ability of man to elevate his life by a conscious endeavor. *Ib.*

I went to the woods because I wished to live deliberately, to front only the essential facts of life, and see if I could not learn what it had to teach, and not, when I came to die, discover that I had not lived. *Ib.*

Our life is frittered away by detail . . . Simplify, simplify. *Ib.*

We do not ride on the railroad; it rides upon us. *Ib.*

Time is but the stream I go a-fishing in. *Ib.*

Books must be read as deliberately and reservedly as they are written.

Ib. 3, Reading

What is called eloquence in the forum is commonly found to be rhetoric in the study. *Ib.*

The works of the great poets have never yet been read by mankind, for only great poets can read them. *Ib.*

It is not all books that are as dull as their readers. *Ib.*

How many a man has dated a new era in his life from the reading of a book. *Ib.*

I love a broad margin to my life.

Ib. 4, Sounds

Our horizon is never quite at our elbows. *Ib. 5, Solitude*

I never found the companion that was so companionable as solitude. We are for the most part more lonely when we go abroad among men than when we stay in our chambers. A man thinking or working is always alone, let him be where he will.

Walden 5, Solitude

I had three chairs in my house: one for solitude, two for friendship, three for society. *Ib. 6, Visitors*

Ministers who spoke of God as if they enjoyed a monopoly of the subject. *Ib.*

I was determined to know beans.

Ib. 7, The Beanfield

Through want of enterprise and faith men are where they are, buying and selling, and spending their lives like serfs. *Ib. 10, Baker Farm*

There is never an instant's truce between virtue and vice. Goodness is the only investment that never fails.

Ib. 11, Higher Laws

Heaven is under our feet as well as over our heads.

Ib. 16, The Pond in Winter

While men believe in the infinite, some ponds will be thought to be bottomless. *Ib.*

What is man but a mass of thawing clay? *Ib. 17, Spring*

Through our own recovered innocence we discern the innocence of our neighbors. *Ib.*

As if there were safety in stupidity alone. *Ib. 18, Conclusion*

If one advances confidently in the direction of his dreams, and endeavors to live the life which he has imagined, he will meet with a success unexpected in common hours. *Ib.*

If a man does not keep pace with his companions, perhaps it is because he hears a different drummer. Let him step to the music which he hears, however measured or far away. *Ib.*

Love your life, poor as it is. You may perhaps have some pleasant, thrilling, glorious hours, even in a poorhouse. The setting sun is reflected from the windows of the almshouse as brightly as from the rich man's abode,
Walden 18, Conclusion

It is life near the bone where it is sweetest.   *Ib.*

Rather than love, than money, than fame, give me truth.   *Ib.*

He would have left a Greek accent slanting the wrong way, and righted up a falling man.
A Plea for Captain John Brown
[1859]

I hear many condemn these men because they were so few. When were the good and the brave ever in a majority?
Ib.

It was his peculiar doctrine that a man has a perfect right to interfere by force with the slaveholder, in order to rescue the slave. I agree with him. They who are continually shocked by slavery have some right to be shocked by the violent death of the slaveholder, but no others.   *Ib.*

I speak for the slave when I say that I prefer the philanthropy of Captain Brown to that philanthropy which neither shoots me nor liberates me.
Ib.

So we defend ourselves and our hen-roosts, and maintain slavery.   *Ib.*

He is not Old Brown any longer; he is an angel of light.   *Ib.*

Men will lie on their backs, talking about the fall of man, and never make an effort to get up.
Life Without Principle [1863]

ALEXEI KONSTANTINOVICH TOLSTOI
1817–1875

His pen is breathing revenge.
Vaska Shibanov [1855–1865]

No one can encompass the unencompassable.
Kosma Prutkov [1884] [1]

If thou hast a fountain, shut it up: let even a fountain have a rest.   *Ib.*

Many men are like unto sausages: whatever you stuff them with, that they will bear in them.   *Ib.*

Should you read, upon an enclosure with an elephant, a sign saying *Buffalo*, believe not your eyes.   *Ib.*

If you want to be happy, be.   *Ib.*

CECIL FRANCES ALEXANDER
1818–1895

All things bright and beautiful,
All creatures great and small,
All things wise and wonderful,
The Lord God made them all.[2]
All Things Bright and Beautiful
[1848], st. 1

The rich man in his castle,
The poor man at his gate,
God made them, high or lowly,
And ordered their estate.   *Ib. st. 3*

There is a green hill far away,
Without a city wall,
Where the dear Lord was crucified,
Who died to save us all.
There Is a Green Hill [1848], st. 1

Once in royal David's city
Stood a lowly cattle shed,
Where a Mother laid her Baby
In a manger for his bed:
Mary was that Mother mild,
Jesus Christ her little Child.
Once in Royal David's City
[1848], st. 1

[1] Kosma Prutkov, a pompous and platitudinous clerk who dabbled in the muses, was invented by Tolstoi and the brothers Zhemchuzhnikov, who supplied him with a biography, a portrait, and *Collected Works*, published in 1884. Individual satirical pieces had been appearing under his name since 1851. He became a classic of Russian satirical humor.
Translated by B. G. GURNEY.
[2] See Coleridge, p. 526a.

JOSH BILLINGS
[HENRY WHEELER SHAW]
1818–1885

A sekret ceases tew be a sekret if it iz once confided — it iz like a dollar bill, once broken, it iz never a dollar agin.
Affurisms [1] [1865]

Love iz like the meazles; we kant have it bad but onst, and the later in life we have it the tuffer it goes with us.   *Ib.*

Put an Englishman into the garden of Eden, and he would find fault with the whole blarsted consarn; put a Yankee in, and he would see where he could alter it to advantage; put an Irishman in, and he would want tew boss the thing; put a Dutchman in, and he would proceed tew plant it.   *Ib.*

Better make a weak man your enemy than your friend.   *Ib.*

Nature never makes any blunders; when she makes a fool she means it.
Ib.

I don't care how much a man talks, if he only says it in a few words.
Ib.

As scarce as truth is, the supply has always been in excess of the demand.
Ib.

I never knu a man trubbled with melankolly, who had plenty to dew, and did it.   *Ib.*

Poverty iz the stepmother ov genius.
Ib.

Manifest destiny iz the science ov going tew bust, or enny other place before yu git thare.[2]   *Manifest Destiny*

The wheel that squeaks the loudest
Is the one that gets the grease.
The Kicker

[1] From *Josh Billings: His Sayings.*
[2] See O'Sullivan, p. 676a.

It is better to know nothing than to know what ain't so.[1]   *Proverb* [1874]

EMILY BRONTË
1818–1848

Sleep not, dream not; this bright day
Will not, cannot last for aye;
Bliss like thine is bought by years
Dark with torment and with tears.
Sleep Not [1846], *st. 1*

Cold in the earth — and fifteen wild Decembers
From those brown hills have melted into spring.
Remembrance [1846], *st. 3*

Once drinking deep of that divinest anguish,
How could I seek the empty world again?   *Ib. st. 8*

No coward soul is mine,
No trembler in the world's storm-troubled sphere:
I see Heaven's glories shine,
And faith shines equal, arming me from fear.   *Last Lines* [1846], *st. 1*

There is not room for Death.[2]
Ib. st. 7

I lingered round them, under that benign sky: watched the moths fluttering among the heath and harebells; listened to the soft wind breathing through the grass; and wondered how anyone could ever imagine unquiet slumbers for the sleepers in that quiet earth.
Wuthering Heights [1847], *last words*

WILLIAM ELLERY CHANNING
1818–1901

Habitant of castle gray,
Creeping thing in sober way,

[1] Better know nothing than half-know many things. — NIETZSCHE, *Thus Spake Zarathustra* [1883–1891], *pt. IV, 64*
[2] See Dylan Thomas, p. 1070a.

Visible sage mechanician,
Skillfulest arithmetician.
The Spider

I laugh, for hope hath happy place with
me —
If my bark sinks, 'tis to another sea.
A Poet's Hope

Most joyful let the Poet be;
It is through him that all men see.
*The Poet of the Old and New
Times*

The hills are reared, the seas are
scooped in vain
If learning's altar vanish from the plain.
Inscription for the Alcott house [1]

ELIZA COOK
1818–1889

I love it, I love it; and who shall dare
To chide me for loving that old armchair?   *The Old Armchair*

Better build schoolrooms for "the boy"
Than cells and gibbets for "the
man." [2]
*A Song for the Ragged Schools,
st. 12*

How busy we are on Tom Tiddler's
ground
Looking for gold and silver. [3]
Tom Tiddler's Ground, st. 1

GEORGE DUFFIELD
1818–1888

Stand up! — stand up for Jesus!
Hymn

WILLIAM MAXWELL
EVARTS
1818–1901

The pious ones of Plymouth, who,
reaching the Rock, first fell upon their

own knees and then upon the aborigi-
nes. [1]
From HENRY WATTERSON *in
The Louisville Courier-
Journal [July 4, 1913]*

JOHN JAMES ROBERT
MANNERS, DUKE
OF RUTLAND
1818–1906

Let wealth and commerce, laws and
learning die,
But leave us still our old nobility.
England's Trust, pt. III, l. 231

KARL MARX
1818–1883

Religion . . . is the opium of the
people.
*Critique of the Hegelian Phi-
losophy of Right [1844], introduction*

It is not the consciousness of men
that determines their existence, but on
the contrary their social existence determines their consciousness.
*Critique of Political Econ-
omy [1859], preface*

The history of all hitherto existing
society is the history of class struggles.
*Manifesto of the Communist
Party* [2] *[1848], sec. 1*

Of all the classes that stand face to
face with the bourgeoisie today the
proletariat alone is a really revolutionary class. The other classes decay and
finally disappear in the race of modern
industry; the proletariat is its special
and essential product. [3]   *Ib.*

---

[1] This pun has also been attributed to Oliver
Wendell Holmes, Bill Nye, and George Frisbie
Hoar.
[2] Written in collaboration with FRIEDRICH
ENGELS. Translated by SAMUEL MOORE.
[3] By bourgeoisie is meant the class of modern
capitalists, owners of the means of social production and employers of wage labor. By proletariat, the class of modern wage laborers who,
having no means of production of their own,
are reduced to selling their labor power in
order to live. — FRIEDRICH ENGELS [1820–1895],
footnote to Manifesto of the Communist Party

---

[1] This couplet is painted over the mantel of
the Alcott house, Concord, Massachusetts.
[2] Give them a chance — if you stint them
now, tomorrow you'll have to pay
A larger bill for a darker ill.
       DENIS A. MCCARTHY [1870–1931], *Give
           Them a Place to Play, st. 4*
[3] Here we are on Tom Tiddler's ground,
picking up gold and silver. — *Children's game*

In proportion as the antagonism between classes within the nation vanishes, the hostility of one nation to another will come to an end.
Manifesto of the Communist Party, sec. 2

The ruling ideas of each age have ever been the ideas of its ruling class.
Ib.

The workers have nothing to lose but their chains. They have a world to win. Workers of the world, unite!   *Ib. 4*

Nothing can have value without being an object of utility. If it be useless, the labor contained in it is useless, cannot be reckoned as labor, and cannot therefore create value.
Capital [1] [*1867–1883*], *pt. II, ch. 3*

The intellectual desolation, artificially produced by converting immature human beings into mere machines.
Ib. 10

Capitalist production begets, with the inexorability of a law of nature, its own negation.   *Ib. 15*

When commercial capital occupies a position of unquestioned ascendancy, it everywhere constitutes a system of plunder.   *Ib. 21*

From each according to his abilities, to each according to his needs.
Critique of the Gotha Program [2]
[*1875*]

[1] Abridged edition prepared by JULIAN BORCHARDT, translated by STEPHEN L. TRASK.
[2] This phrase is in quotation marks, and it is believed that Marx is quoting or paraphrasing either Louis Blanc, or the obscure tutor Morelly.
Let each produce according to his aptitudes and his force; let each consume according to his need. — LOUIS BLANC, *Organisation du Travail* [*1840*]
Nothing in society will belong to anyone, either as a personal possession or as capital goods, except the things for which the person has immediate use, for either his needs, his pleasures, or his daily work. Every citizen will make his particular contribution according to the activities of the community according to his capacity, his talent and his age; it is on this basis that his duties will be determined,

JOHN MASON NEALE
1818–1866

Good King Wenceslas looked out
  On the feast of Stephen,
When the snow lay round about,
  Deep and crisp and even.
Good King Wenceslas, st. 1

In his master's steps he trod,
  Where the snow lay dinted;
Heat was in the very sod
  Which the Saint had printed.
Wherefore, Christian men, be sure,
  Wealth or rank possessing,
Ye who now do bless the poor
  Shall yourselves find blessing.
Ib. st. 5

O come, O come, Emmanuel,
And ransom captive Israel.
O Come, O Come, Emmanuel; translated from the Latin, Veni, Veni, Emmanuel

Jerusalem the golden, with milk and
  honey blest,
Beneath thy contemplation sink heart
  and voice oppressed.
Hymn; translated from the Latin of ST. BERNARD OF CLUNY [*c. 1145*]

Brief life is here our portion.   *Ib.*

FRANCIS EDWARD SMEDLEY
1818–1864

You are looking as fresh as paint.
Frank Fairlegh [*1850*]

IVAN SERGEYEVICH TURGENEV
1818–1883

The Diary of a Superfluous Man.[1]
Title of a story [*1851*]

in conformity with the distributive laws. — MORELLY, *Code de Nature* [*c. 1773*]
And distribution was made unto every man according as he had need. — *Acts 4:35*
[1] The phrase is from Pushkin's *Eugene Onegin.*

A nihilist [1] is a man who does not bow to any authorities, who does not take any principle on trust, no matter with what respect that principle is surrounded.

> *Fathers and Sons* [2] [1862], *ch. 5*

That vague, crepuscular time, the time of regrets that resemble hopes, of hopes that resemble regrets, when youth has passed, but old age has not yet arrived. *Ib. 7*

I share no man's opinions; I have my own. *Ib. 13*

The courage not to believe in anything. *Ib. 14*

A picture shows me at a glance what it takes dozens of pages of a book to expound.[3] *Ib. 16*

Whatever a man prays for, he prays for a miracle. Every prayer reduces itself to this: "Great God, grant that twice two be not four." *Prayer*

In days of doubt, in days of sad brooding on my country's fate, thou alone art my rod and my staff — mighty, true, free Russian speech! But for thee, how not to fall into despair, seeing all that happens at home? Yet who can think that such a tongue is not given to a great people?

> *Senilia* [1882]

ARTHUR HUGH CLOUGH
1819–1861

Grace is given of God, but knowledge is bought in the market.

> *The Bothie of Tober-na-Vuolich* [1848], *pt. IV*

---

[1] Nihilism was first encountered in 1829 in Nadazhdin's article against Pushkin. It was used throughout the 1830's with a variety of meanings, but the meaning which became central was applied by Turgenev to the psychology of the men of the 1860's in *Fathers and Sons*. It was also used by Katknov in the magazine which published *Fathers and Sons* four months before the book appeared.

[2] Translated by HARRY STEVENS.

[3] See Anonymous, p. 149b.

A world where nothing is had for nothing.

> *The Bothie of Toberna-Vuolich, pt. VIII*

As ships, becalmed at eve, that lay
With canvas drooping, side by side,
Two towers of sail, at dawn of day
Are scarce long leagues apart descried.

> *Qua Cursum Ventus* [1849],
> *st. 1*

It fortifies my soul to know
That, though I perish, Truth is so:
That, howsoe'er I stray and range,
Whate'er I do, Thou dost not change.
I steadier step when I recall
That, if I slip, Thou dost not fall.

> *"With Whom Is No Variableness"* [1] [1862]

And almost everyone when age,
Disease, or sorrows strike him,
Inclines to think there is a God,
Or something very like Him.

> *Dipsychus* [1862], *pt. I, sc. 5*

How pleasant it is to have money!

> *Ib.*

That out of sight is out of mind [2]
Is true of most we leave behind.

> *Songs of Absence* [1862]

Say not the struggle naught availeth,
The labor and the wounds are vain,
The enemy faints not, nor faileth,
And as things have been they remain.

> *Say Not the Struggle Naught Availeth* [1862], *st. 1*

For while the tired waves, vainly breaking,
Seem here no painful inch to gain,
Far back, through creeks and inlets making,
Comes silent flooding in, the main.[3]

And not by eastern windows only,
When daylight comes, comes in the light;

---

[1] See *James 1:17*, p. 56a.

[2] See Thomas à Kempis, p. 170b, and note.

[3] See Macaulay, p. 595a.

In front, the sun climbs slow, how
slowly,
But westward, look, the land is bright.[1]
Say Not the Struggle Naught
Availeth, st. 3, 4

Thou shalt not kill; but needst not
strive
Officiously to keep alive.
The Latest Decalogue

GEORGE ELIOT
[MARIAN EVANS CROSS]
1819–1880

'Tis God gives skill,
But not without men's hands: He could
not make
Antonio Stradivari's violins
Without Antonio. *Stradivarius*

O may I join the choir invisible
Of those immortal dead who live again
In minds made better by their presence.
O May I Join the Choir Invisible

Any coward can fight a battle when
he's sure of winning; but give me the
man who has pluck to fight when he's
sure of losing. That's my way, sir; and
there are many victories worse than a
defeat.
Janet's Repentance [1857], *ch. 6*

Opposition may become sweet to a
man when he has christened it persecution. *Ib. 8*

It's but little good you'll do a-water-
ing the last year's crops.
Adam Bede [1859], *ch. 18*

It was a pity he couldna be hatched
o'er again, an' hatched different.
Ib.

A patronizing disposition always has
its meaner side. *Ib. 28*

It's them that take advantage that
get advantage i' this world. *Ib. 32*

He was like a cock who thought the
sun had risen to hear him crow.
Ib. 33

[1] Both Sir Winston Churchill and John F.
Kennedy liked to quote this line.

We hand folks over to God's mercy,
and show none ourselves.
Adam Bede, ch. 42

I'm not denyin' the women are foolish; God Almighty made 'em to match
the men. *Ib. 53*

The law's made to take care o'
raskills.
The Mill on the Floss [1860],
bk. III, ch. 4

In natural science, I have understood, there is nothing petty to the
mind that has a large vision of relations, and to which every single object
suggests a vast sum of conditions. It is
surely the same with the observation of
human life. *Ib. IV, 1*

I've never any pity for conceited people, because I think they carry their
comfort about with them.[1] *Ib. V, 4*

The happiest women, like the happiest nations, have no history.[2]
Ib. VI, 3

Nothing is so good as it seems beforehand.
Silas Marner [1861], *ch. 18*

In our springtime every day has its
hidden growth in the mind, as it has in
the earth when the little folded blades
are getting ready to pierce the ground.
Felix Holt, the Radical [1866],
ch. 18

One way of getting an idea of our
fellow-countrymen's miseries is to go
and look at their pleasures. *Ib. 28*

Prophecy is the most gratuitous form
of error.
Middlemarch [1871–1872], *ch. 10*

If we had a keen vision of all that is
ordinary in human life, it would be like
hearing the grass grow or the squirrel's

[1] There is not enough of love and goodness
in the world to throw any of it away on conceited
people. — NIETZSCHE [1844–1900], *Human, All
Too Human, 129*
[2] See Carlyle, p. 578a, and note.

heart beat, and we should die of that roar which is the other side of silence.
Middlemarch, ch. 22

Hostesses who entertain much must make up their parties as ministers make up their cabinets, on grounds other than personal liking.
Daniel Deronda [1876], *bk. I, ch. 5*

A difference of taste in jokes is a great strain on the affections.
Ib. II, 15

Men's men: gentle or simple, they're much of a muchness.   *Ib. IV, 31*

Blessed is the man who, having nothing to say, abstains from giving in words evidence of the fact.
Impressions of Theophrastus Such [1879]

THOMAS DUNN ENGLISH
1819–1902

Oh! don't you remember sweet Alice, Ben Bolt?
Sweet Alice, whose hair was so brown,
Who wept with delight when you gave her a smile,
And trembled with fear at your frown?
Ben Bolt [1]

JOSIAH GILBERT HOLLAND
1819–1881

Heaven is not reached at a single bound;
But we build the ladder by which we rise
From the lowly earth to the vaulted skies,
And we mount to its summit round by round.[2]   *Gradatim* [1872], *st. 1*

[1] First published in the *New York Mirror*, September 2, 1843. It was set to music, an adaptation of an old German melody, by NELSON KNEASS, and sung in the play *The Battle of Buena Vista*. In 1894 GEORGE DU MAURIER used the song in his novel *Trilby* and it at once became popular.

[2] Step after step the ladder is ascended. — GEORGE HERBERT, *Jacula Prudentum* [1640]

God give us men! A time like this demands
Strong minds, great hearts, true faith, and ready hands;
Men whom the lust of office does not kill;
Men whom the spoils of office cannot buy;
Men who possess opinions and a will;
Men who have honor; men who will not lie.   *Wanted* [1872], *l. 1*

JULIA WARD HOWE
1819–1910

Mine eyes have seen the glory of the coming of the Lord;
He is trampling out the vintage where the grapes of wrath are stored; [1]
He hath loosed the fateful lightning of His terrible, swift sword;
His truth is marching on.
Battle Hymn of the Republic [1862], *st. 1*

In the beauty of the lilies Christ was born across the sea,
With a glory in His bosom that transfigures you and me;
As He died to make men holy, let us die to make men free.   *Ib. st. 5*

CHARLES KINGSLEY
1819–1875

Oh! that we two were Maying.
The Saint's Tragedy [1848], *act II, sc. 9*

Oh Mary, go and call the cattle home . . .
Across the sands of Dee.
The Sands of Dee, st. 1

The cruel crawling foam.   *Ib. st. 4*

For men must work, and women must weep,
And there's little to earn and many to keep,
Though the harbor bar be moaning.
The Three Fishers, st. 1

[1] See *Isaiah 63:3*, p. 33b.
He treadeth the winepress of the fierceness and wrath of Almighty God. — *Revelation 19:15*

And the sooner it's over, the sooner to
sleep;
And good-bye to the bar and its moaning.   *The Three Fishers, st. 3*

Be good, sweet maid, and let who will
be clever;
Do noble things, not dream them, all
day long;
And so make Life, and Death, and
that For Ever
One grand sweet song.
          A Farewell, st. 3

In the light of fuller day,
Of purer science, holier laws.
          *On the Death of a Certain
          Journal* [1] *[1848–1849], st. 5*

More ways of killing a cat than choking her with cream.
          Westward Ho [1855], ch. 20

Clear and cool, clear and cool,
By laughing shallow, and dreaming
pool.
          *Water Babies [1863]. Song I,
          st. 1*

When all the world is young, lad,
And all the trees are green;
And every goose a swan, lad,
And every lass a queen;
Then hey for boot and horse, lad,
And round the world away:
Young blood must have its course, lad,
And every dog his day.[2]
          Ib. Song II, st. 1

When all the world is old, lad,
And all the trees are brown;
And all the sport is stale, lad,
And all the wheels run down.
          Ib. st. 2

God grant you find one face there
You loved when all was young!   *Ib.*

I once had a sweet little doll, dears,
The prettiest doll in the world;
Her cheeks were so red and so white,
dears,
And her hair was so charmingly curled.
          Ib. Song IV, st. 1

[1] *The Christian Socialist.*
[2] See Shakespeare, *Hamlet V, i, 313,* p. 266a.

The loveliest fairy in the world; and
her name is Mrs. Doasyouwouldbedoneby.   *Water Babies, ch. 5*

To be discontented with the divine
discontent, and to be ashamed with the
noble shame, is the very germ and first
upgrowth of all virtue.
          *Health and Education [1874].
          The Science of Health*

Some say that the age of chivalry is
past, that the spirit of romance is dead.
The age of chivalry is never past, so
long as there is a wrong left unredressed
on earth.   *Life [1879], vol. II, ch. 28*

JAMES RUSSELL
LOWELL
1819–1891

Be noble! and the nobleness that lies
In other men, sleeping, but never dead,
Will rise in majesty to meet thine own.
          Sonnet IV [1840]

No man is born into the world whose
work
Is not born with him; there is always
work,
And tools to work withal, for those who
will;
And blessèd are the horny hands of
toil!
          A *Glance Behind the Curtain
          [1843]*

They are slaves who fear to speak
For the fallen and the weak.
          Stanzas on Freedom [1843], st. 4

They are slaves who dare not be
In the right with two or three.   *Ib.*

The nurse of full-grown souls is solitude.   *Columbus [1844]*

Once to every man and nation comes
the moment to decide,
In the strife of Truth with Falsehood,
for the good or evil side.
          The Present Crisis [1844], st. 5

Truth forever on the scaffold, Wrong
    forever on the throne [1] —
Yet that scaffold sways the future, and,
    behind the dim unknown,
Standeth God within the shadow, keep-
    ing watch above his own.
            The Present Crisis, st. 8

Then to side with Truth is noble when
    we share her wretched crust.
                Ib. st. 11

New occasions teach new duties; time
    makes ancient good uncouth;
They must upward still, and onward,
    who would keep abreast of Truth.
                Ib. st. 18

I first drew in New England's air, and
    from her hardy breast
Sucked in the tyrant-hating milk that
    will not let me rest;
And if my words seem treason to the
    dullard and the tame,
'Tis but my Bay State dialect — our fa-
    thers spake the same.
         On the Capture of Fugitive
         Slaves Near Washington
         [1845], st. 2

The birch, most shy and ladylike of
    trees.
         An Indian Summer Reverie
               [1846], st. 8

Not only around our infancy
Doth heaven with all its splendors lie;
Daily, with souls that cringe and plot,
We Sinais climb and know it not.[2]
         The Vision of Sir Launfal
         [1848], prelude to pt. I,
         st. 2

For a cap and bells our lives we pay,
Bubbles we buy with a whole soul's
    tasking:
'Tis heaven alone that is given away,
'Tis only God may be had for the ask-
    ing.   *Ib. st. 4*

And what is so rare as a day in June?
Then, if ever, come perfect days;

Then Heaven tries the earth if it be in
    tune,
And over it softly her warm ear lays.
         The Vision of Sir Launfal,
            prelude to pt. I, st. 5

He gives only the worthless gold
Who gives from a sense of duty.
              Ib. pt. I, st. 6

Not what we give, but what we
    share —
For the gift without the giver is bare; [1]
Who gives himself with his alms feeds
    three —
Himself, his hungering neighbor, and
    me.   *Ib. pt. II, st. 8*

In creating, the only hard thing's to be-
    gin;
A grass-blade's no easier to make than
    an oak.
         A Fable for Critics [1848]

For though he builds glorious temples,
    'tis odd
He leaves never a doorway to get in a
    god.   *Ib. [of Emerson]*

And I honor the man who is willing to
    sink
Half his present repute for the freedom
    to think,
And, when he has thought, be his cause
    strong or weak,
Will risk t' other half for the freedom
    to speak.   *Ib.*

There comes Poe, with his raven, like
    Barnaby Rudge,
Three fifths of him genius and two
    fifths sheer fudge.   *Ib.*

Nature fits all her children with some-
    thing to do,
He who would write and can't write,
    can surely review.[2]   *Ib.*

Ez fer war, I call it murder —
    There you hev it plain an' flat;
I don't want to go no furder
    Than my Testyment fer that.
         The Biglow Papers. Series I
         [1848], no. 1, st. 5

---

[1] Worth on foot, and rascals in the coach. —
DRYDEN, *Art of Poetry* [1685], *l. 376*
Wrong rules the land, and waiting Justice
sleeps! — J. G. HOLLAND [1819–1881], *Wanted*
[2] See Wordsworth, p. 513b.

---

[1] See Emerson, p. 607b, and Whitman, p.
700b.
[2] See Coleridge, p. 528a, and Disraeli, p. 612b.

You've gut to git up airly
Ef you want to take in God.
> *The Bigelow Papers. Series I,*
> *no. 1, st. 5*

This goin' ware glory waits ye haint one
agreeable feetur.[1]   *Ib. 2, st. 6*

But John P.
Robinson, he
Sez they didn't know everythin' down
in Judee.   *Ib. 3, st. 8*

A marciful Providunce fashioned us
holler
O' purpose thet we might our principles
swaller.   *Ib. 4, st. 2*

I should like to shoot
The holl gang, by the gret horn spoon!
> *Ib. 5, st. 2*

I du believe with all my soul
   In the gret Press's freedom,
To pint the people to the goal
   An' in the traces lead 'em.
> *Ib. 6, st. 7*

I *don't* believe in princerple,
But oh I *du* in interest.   *Ib. st. 9*

It ain't by princerples nor men
   My preudunt course is steadied —
I scent wich pays the best, an' then
   Go into it baldheaded.   *Ib. st. 10*

Of my merit
On thet pint you yourself may jedge;
All is, I never drink no sperit,
   Nor I haint never signed no pledge.
> *Ib. 7, st. 9*

Ez to my princerples, I glory
In hevin' nothin' o' the sort.
> *Ib. st. 10*

God makes sech nights, all white an'
   still,
   Fur'z you can look or listen,
Moonshine an' snow on field an' hill,
   All silence an' all glisten.
> *Ib. Series II* [1866]. *The*
> *Courtin', st. 1*

His heart kep' goin' pity-pat,
But hern went pity-Zekle.   *Ib. st. 15*

My gran'ther's rule was safer 'n 'tis to
crow:

---

[1] See Thomas Moore, p. 541b.

Don't never prophesy — onless ye
know.
> *The Biglow Papers. Series II.*
> *The Courtin', No. 2*

It's 'most enough to make a deacon
swear.   *Ib.*

Folks never understand the folks they
hate.   *Ib.*

Ef you want peace, the thing you've gut
tu du
Is jes' to show you're up to fightin',
tu.[1]   *Ib.*

Bad work follers ye ez long's ye live.
> *Ib.*

The surest plan to make a Man
Is, think him so.   *Ib.*

Our papers don't purtend to print on'y
   wut Guv'ment choose,
An' thet insures us all to git the very
   best o' noose.   *Ib. 3*

No, never say nothin' without you're
   compelled tu,
An' then don't say nothin' thet you can
   be held tu.   *Ib. 5*

They came three thousand miles, and
   died,
To keep the Past upon its throne;
Unheard, beyond the ocean tide,
Their English mother made her moan.[2]
> *Graves of Two English Sol-*
> *diers on Concord Battle-*
> *ground* [1849], *st. 3*

The snow had begun in the gloaming,
   And busily all the night
Had been heaping field and highway
   With a silence deep and white.
> *The First Snowfall*
> [1849], *st. 1*

There is nothing so desperately
monotonous as the sea, and I no longer
wonder at the cruelty of pirates.
> *Fireside Travels* [1864]. *At Sea*

It is by presence of mind in untried
emergencies that the native metal of a
man is tested.

> *Abraham Lincoln* [1864]

---

[1] See Vegetius, p. 146b, and note.
[2] Inscribed on the memorial to the two British
soldiers, Concord, Massachusetts.

What men call treasure and the gods call dross.
> *Ode Recited at the Harvard Commemoration* [1865], 4

They come transfigured back,
Secure from change in their high-hearted ways,
Beautiful evermore, and with the rays
Of morn on their white Shields of Expectation! [1]   *Ib. 8*

When I was a beggarly boy,
  And lived in a cellar damp,
I had not a friend nor a toy,
  But I had Aladdin's lamp.
> *Aladdin* [1868], *st. 1*

Safe in the hallowed quiets of the past.
> *The Cathedral* [2] [1869], *st. 9*

The wisest man could ask no more of Fate
Than to be simple, modest, manly, true,
Safe from the many, honored by the few;
To count as naught in world, or church, or state;
But inwardly in secret to be great.
> *Sonnet, Jeffries Wyman* [1874]

For me Fate gave, whate'er she else denied,
A nature sloping to the southern side;
I thank her for it, though when clouds arise
Such natures double-darken gloomy skies.
> *Epistle to George William Curtis* [1874]. *Postscript*

The maple puts her corals on in May.
> *The Maple* [1875]

The soil out of which such men as he are made is good to be born on, good to live on, good to die for and to be buried in.
> *Garfield* [*September 24, 1881*]

There is no good in arguing with the inevitable. The only argument avail-able with an east wind is to put on your overcoat.
> *Democracy* [*October 6, 1884*]

In vain we call old notions fudge,
And bend our conscience to our dealing;
The Ten Commandments will not budge,
And stealing *will* continue stealing.[1]
> *International Copyright* [*November 20, 1885*]

These pearls of thought in Persian gulfs were bred,
Each softly lucent as a rounded moon;
The diver Omar plucked them from their bed,
Fitzgerald strung them on an English thread.
> *In a Copy of Omar Khayyám* [1888], *st. 1*

As life runs on, the road grows strange
With faces new, and near the end
The milestones into headstones change,
'Neath every one a friend.
> *Sixty-eighth Birthday* [1889]

Things always seem fairer when we look back at them, and it is out of that inaccessible tower of the past that Longing leans and beckons.
> *Literary Essays, vol. I* [1864–1890], *A Few Bits of Roman Mosaic*

Mishaps are like knives, that either serve us or cut us, as we grasp them by the blade or the handle.
> *Ib. Cambridge Thirty Years Ago*

What a sense of security in an old book which Time has criticized for us!
> *Ib. A Library of Old Authors*

It is curious how tyrannical the habit of reading is, and what shifts we make to escape thinking.[2] There is no bore we dread being left alone with so much as our own minds.
> *Ib. A Moosehead Journal*

---

[1] See Masefield, p. 947b–948a.
[2] Chartres.

[1] Motto of the American Copyright League.
[2] See Sheridan, p. 481b, and Bryce, p. 778a.

Truly there is a tide in the affairs of men,[1] but there is no gulf stream setting forever in one direction.

> *Literary Essays, vol. II* [1870–1890], *New England Two Centuries Ago*

There is no better ballast for keeping the mind steady on its keel, and saving it from all risk of crankiness, than business.   *Ib.*

Puritanism, believing itself quick with the seed of religious liberty, laid, without knowing it, the egg of democracy.   *Ib.*

It was in making education not only common to all, but in some sense compulsory on all, that the destiny of the free republics of America was practically settled.   *Ib.*

Talent is that which is in a man's power; genius is that in whose power a man is.

> *Ib. Rousseau and the Sentimentalists*

Every man feels instinctively that all the beautiful sentiments in the world weigh less than a single lovely action.
                                              Ib.

An umbrella is of no avail against a Scotch mist.

> *Ib. III* [1870–1890], *On a Certain Condescension in Foreigners*

Solitude is as needful to the imagination as society is wholesome for the character.   *Ib. Dryden*

A wise skepticism is the first attribute of a good critic.

> *Ib. Shakespeare Once More*

HERMAN MELVILLE
1819–1891

You must have plenty of sea-room to tell the Truth in.

Hawthorne and His Mosses [1850]

Genius all over the world stands hand in hand, and one shock of recognition runs the whole circle round.

> *Hawthorne and His Mosses*

Many sensible things banished from high life find an asylum among the mob.   *White Jacket* [1850], *ch. 7*

Oh, give me again the rover's life — the joy, the thrill, the whirl! Let me feel thee again, old sea! let me leap into thy saddle once more. I am sick of these terra-firma toils and cares; sick of the dust and reek of towns. Let me hear the clatter of hailstones on icebergs, and not the dull tramp of these plodders, plodding their dull way from their cradles to their graves. Let me snuff thee up, sea breeze! and whinny in thy spray. Forbid it, sea gods! intercede for me with Neptune, O sweet Amphitrite,[1] that no dull clod may fall on my coffin! Be mine the tomb that swallowed up Pharaoh and all his hosts; let me lie down with Drake where he sleeps in the sea.   *Ib. 19*

Familiarity with danger makes a brave man braver, but less daring. Thus with seamen: he who goes the oftenest round Cape Horn goes the most circumspectly.   *Ib. 23*

In time of peril, like the needle to the lodestone, obedience, irrespective of rank, generally flies to him who is best fitted to command.   *Ib. 27*

Are there no Moravians in the Moon, that not a missionary has yet visited this poor pagan planet of ours, to civilize civilization and christianize Christendom? [2]   *Ib. 64*

Call me Ishmael.

> *Moby-Dick* [1851], *ch. 1*

Yes, as everyone knows, meditation and water are wedded forever . . . Why did the old Persians hold the sea holy? Why did the Greeks give it a separate deity, and own brother of Jove? Surely all this is not without meaning.

---

[1] See Shakespeare, *Julius Caesar IV, iii, 217,* p. 256a.

[1] Wife of Neptune.
[2] See Emerson, p. 606b.

And still deeper the meaning of that story of Narcissus, who because he could not grasp the tormenting, mild image he saw in the fountain, plunged into it and was drowned. But that same image, we ourselves see in all rivers and oceans. It is the image of the ungraspable phantom of life; and this is the key to it all.   *Moby-Dick, ch.* 1

But oh! shipmates! on the starboard hand of every woe, there is a sure delight; and higher the top of that delight, than the bottom of the woe is deep. Is not the main-truck higher than the kelson is low? Delight is to him — a far, far upward, and inward delight — who against the proud gods and commodores of this earth, ever stands forth his own inexorable self.   *Ib.* 9

And eternal delight and deliciousness will be his, who coming to lay him down, can say with his final breath — O Father! — chiefly known to me by Thy rod — mortal or immortal, here I die. I have striven to be Thine, more than to be this world's, or mine own. Yet this is nothing; I leave eternity to Thee; for what is man that he should live out the lifetime of his God?   *Ib.*

With the landless gull, that at sunset folds her wings and is rocked to sleep between billows; so at nightfall, the Nantucketer, out of sight of land, furls his sails, and lays him to his rest, while under his very pillow rush herds of walruses and whales.   *Ib.* 14

But when a man's religion becomes really frantic; when it is a positive torment to him; and, in fine, makes this earth of ours an uncomfortable inn to lodge in; then I think it high time to take that individual aside and argue the point with him.   *Ib.* 17

In one word, Queequeg, said I, rather digressively; hell is an idea first born on an undigested apple dumpling;

and since then perpetuated through the hereditary dyspepsias nurtured by Ramadans.   *Moby-Dick, ch.* 17

If, at my death, my executors, or more properly my creditors, find any precious MSS. in my desk, then here I prospectively ascribe all the honor and the glory to whaling; for a whaleship was my Yale College and my Harvard.   *Ib.* 24

That immaculate manliness we feel within ourselves, so far within us, that it remains intact though all the outer character seem gone; bleeds with keenest anguish at the undraped spectacle of a valor-ruined man.   *Ib.* 26

Thou great democratic God! who didst not refuse to the swart convict, Bunyan, the pale poetic pearl; Thou who didst clothe with doubly hammered leaves of finest gold, the stumped and paupered arm of old Cervantes; Thou who didst pick up Andrew Jackson from the pebbles; who didst hurl him upon a warhorse; who didst thunder him higher than a throne! Thou who, in all Thy mighty, earthly marchings, ever cullest thy selectest champions from the kingly commons!   *Ib.*

This it is, that forever keeps God's true princes of the Empire from the world's hustings; and leaves the highest honors that this air can give, to those men who become famous more through their infinite inferiority to the choice hidden handful of the Divine Inert, than through their undoubted superiority over the dead level of the mass.   *Ib.* 33

All that most maddens and torments; all that stirs up the lees of things; all truth with malice in it; all that cracks the sinews and cakes the brain; all the subtle demonisms of life and thought; all evil, to crazy Ahab, were visibly personified, and made practically assailable in Moby Dick. He piled upon the whale's white hump the sum of all the general rage and hate felt by his whole race from Adam down; and then, as if

his chest had been a mortar, he burst his hot heart's shell upon it.
Moby-Dick, ch. 41

For as this appalling ocean surrounds the verdant land, so in the soul of man there lies one insular Tahiti, full of peace and joy, but encompassed by all the horrors of the half known life.
Ib. 58

O Nature, and O soul of man! how far beyond all utterance are your linked analogies! not the smallest atom stirs or lives on matter, but has its cunning duplicate in mind. *Ib. 70*

So, therefore, that mortal man who hath more of joy than sorrow in him, that mortal man cannot be true — not true, or undeveloped. With books the same. The truest of all men was the Man of Sorrows, and the truest of all books is Solomon's and Ecclesiastes is the fine hammered steel of woe.
Ib. 96

Give me a condor's quill! Give me Vesuvius' crater for an inkstand! . . . To produce a mighty book, you must choose a mighty theme. *Ib. 104*

Seat thyself sultanically among the moons of Saturn, and take high abstracted man alone; and he seems a wonder, a grandeur, and a woe. But from the same point, take mankind in mass, and for the most part, they seem a mob of unnecessary duplicates, both contemporary and hereditary.
Ib. 107

There is, one knows not what sweet mystery about this sea, whose gently awful stirrings seem to speak of some hidden soul beneath; like those fabled undulations of the Ephesian sod over the buried Evangelist St. John. And meet it is, that over these sea pastures, wide-rolling watery prairies and Potters' Fields of all four continents, the waves should rise and fall, and ebb and flow unceasingly; for here, millions of mixed shades and shadows, drowned dreams, somnambulisms, reveries; all that we call lives and souls, lie dreaming,

dreaming, still; tossing like slumberers in their beds; the ever-rolling waves but made so by their restlessness.
Moby-Dick, ch. 111

There is no steady unretracing progress in this life; we do not advance through fixed gradations, and at the last one pause: through infancy's unconscious spell, boyhood's thoughtless faith, adolescence' doubt (the common doom), then skepticism, then disbelief, resting at last in manhood's pondering repose of If. But once gone through, we trace the round again; and are infants, boys, and men, and Ifs eternally. Where lies the final harbor, whence we unmoor no more?
Ib. 114

But if the great sun move not of himself; but is as an errand boy in heaven; nor one single star can revolve, but by some invisible power; how then can this one small heart beat; this one small brain think thoughts; unless God does that beating, does that thinking, does that living, and not I. By heaven, man, we are turned round and round in this world, like yonder windlass, and Fate is the handspike. *Ib. 132*

An old, old sight, and yet somehow so young; aye, and not changed a wink since I first saw it, a boy, from the sandhills of Nantucket! The same! — the same! — the same to Noah as to me. There's a soft shower to leeward. Such lovely leewardings! They must lead somewhere — to something else than common land, more palmy than the palms. *Ib.*

Now small fowls flew screaming over the yet yawning gulf; a sullen white surf beat against its steep sides; then all collapsed, and the great shroud of the sea rolled on as it rolled five thousand years ago. *Ib.*

What we take to be our strongest tower of delight, only stands at the caprice of the minutest event — the falling of a leaf, the hearing of a voice, or the receipt of one little bit of paper scratched over with a few small characters by a sharpened feather.

Pierre [1852], bk. IV

One trembles to think of that mysterious thing in the soul, which seems to acknowledge no human jurisdiction, but in spite of the individual's own innocent self, will still dream horrid dreams, and mutter unmentionable thoughts.　　　　　　　　　　*Ib.*

A smile is the chosen vehicle for all ambiguities.　　　　　　　　　　*Ib.*

Say what some poets will, Nature is not so much her own ever-sweet interpreter, as the mere supplier of that cunning alphabet, whereby selecting and combining as he pleases, each man reads his own peculiar lesson according to his own peculiar mind and mood.

Ib. XXV

But me they'll lash in hammock, drop me deep.
Fathoms down, fathoms down, how I'll dream fast asleep.
I feel it stealing now. Sentry, are you there?
Just ease these darbies [1] at the wrist,
And roll me over fair.
I am sleepy, and the oozy weeds about me twist.

Billy Budd, Foretopman [published 1924], Billy in the Darbies [1]

THOMAS WILLIAM PARSONS
1819–1892

Sorrow and the scarlet leaf,
　Sad thoughts and sunny weather;
Ah me, this glory and this grief
　Agree not well together!

A Song for September

JOHN RUSKIN
1819–1900

He is the greatest artist who has embodied, in the sum of his works, the greatest number of the greatest ideas.

Modern Painters, vol. I [1843], pt. I, ch. 2

[1] Manacles.

A falseness in all our impressions of external things, which I would generally characterize as the "Pathetic Fallacy."

Modern Painters, vol. III [1856], pt. IV, ch. 12

In order that people may be happy in their work, these three things are needed: They must be fit for it. They must not do too much of it. And they must have a sense of success in it.

Pre-Raphaelitism [1851]

Remember that the most beautiful things in the world are the most useless; peacocks and lilies for instance.

The Stones of Venice [1851–1853], vol. I, ch. 2

Blue color is everlastingly appointed by the Deity to be a source of delight.

Lectures on Architecture and Painting [1853], I

There is no wealth but life.

Unto This Last [1862], sec. 77

That country is the richest which nourishes the greatest number of noble and happy human beings; that man is richest who, having perfected the functions of his own life to the utmost, has also the widest helpful influence, both personal, and by means of his possessions, over the lives of others.　　*Ib.*

Life being very short, and the quiet hours of it few, we ought to waste none of them in reading valueless books.

Sesame and Lilies [1865], preface

All books are divisible into two classes: the books of the hour, and the books of all time.

Ib. Of Kings' Treasuries, sec. 8

Borrowers are nearly always ill-spenders, and it is with lent money that all evil is mainly done, and all unjust war protracted.

The Crown of Wild Olive [1866]. Work, sec. 34

Give a little love to a child, and you get a great deal back.　　　　*Ib.* 49

There's no music in a "rest," Katie, that I know of: but there's the making

of music in it. And people are always missing that part of the life-melody.
　　Ethics of the Dust [1866].
　　Lecture 4, The Crystal Orders

Life without industry is guilt, industry without art is brutality.
　　Lectures on Art [1870]. *III, The Relation of Art to Morals*

Trust thou thy Love: if she be proud, is she not sweet?
Trust thou thy Love: if she be mute, is she not pure?
Lay thou thy soul full in her hands, low at her feet;
Fail, Sun and Breath! — yet, for thy peace, she shall endure.
　　Trust Thou Thy Love

MAX SCHNECKENBURGER
1819–1849

Dear Fatherland, no fear be thine,
Firm stands thy guard along the Rhine.
　　The Watch on the Rhine,[1] *st. 4*

WILLIAM WETMORE STORY
1819–1895

Of every noble work the silent part is best,
Of all expression that which cannot be expressed.　　*The Unexpressed*

QUEEN VICTORIA
1819–1901

We are not interested in the possibilities of defeat.
　　To A. J. Balfour [December 1899]

We are not amused.
　　Upon seeing an imitation of herself by the Honorable Alexander Grantham Yorke, groom-in-waiting to the Queen. From Notebooks of a Spinster Lady [January 2, 1900]

[1] Die Wacht am Rhein.

WILLIAM ROSS WALLACE
1819–1881

The hand that rocks the cradle is the hand that rules the world.
　　The Hand That Rules the World, st. 1

WALT WHITMAN
1819–1892

The United States themselves are essentially the greatest poem. . . . Here at last is something in the doings of man that corresponds with the broadcast doings of the day and night.
　　Preface to first edition of Leaves of Grass [1855]

The proof of a poet is that his country absorbs him as affectionately as he has absorbed it.　　*Ib.*

Me imperturbe, standing at ease in nature.
　　Leaves of Grass [1855–1892] [1]

I hear America singing, the varied carols I hear.
　　Ib. I Hear America Singing

I will put in my poems that with you is heroism upon land and sea,
And I will report all heroism from an American point of view.
　　Ib. Starting from Paumanok, 7

I say the whole earth and all the stars in the sky are for religion's sake.
　　Ib. 8

I say the real and permanent grandeur of these States must be their religion.　　*Ib.*

[1] The first edition of *Leaves of Grass* consisted of 94 quarto pages and included the preface which set forth Whitman's faith and his poetic theory. Enlarged and revised editions followed. The tenth edition (from which the text used here is taken) was the last edition supervised by Whitman himself, literally from his death-bed, and hence it is sometimes called the "Deathbed Edition." Whitman wrote of it, "as there are now several editions of *Leaves of Grass,* different texts and dates, I wish to say that I prefer and recommend this present one."

Nothing can happen more beautiful than death.[1]
> *Leaves of Grass. Starting from Paumanok, 12*

I celebrate myself and sing myself,
And what I assume you shall assume.
> *Ib. Song of Myself, 1*

I loafe and invite my soul. *Ib.*

Urge and urge and urge,
Always the procreant urge of the world.
> *Ib. 3*

A kelson of the creation is love.
> *Ib. 5*

A child said *What is the grass?* fetching it to me with full hands. *Ib. 6*

Or I guess it is the handkerchief of the Lord. *Ib.*

And now it seems to me the beautiful uncut hair of graves. *Ib.*

Has anyone supposed it lucky to be born?
I hasten to inform him or her, it is just as lucky to die, and I know it.
> *Ib. 7*

I am he that walks with the tender and growing night,
I call to the earth and sea half-held by the night.
Press close bare-bosom'd night — press close magnetic nourishing night!
Night of south winds! night of the large few stars!
Still nodding night! mad naked summer night. *Ib. 21*

Walt Whitman am I, a Kosmos, of mighty Manhattan the son,
Turbulent, fleshy and sensual, eating, drinking and breeding;

[1] Why fear death? Death is only a beautiful adventure. — CHARLES FROHMAN [1860–1915], last words to a group of friends as the *Lusitania* was sinking [May 7, 1915]
> Why should I fear Death's call? Can there e'er be
> In life more beautiful adventure than
> To re-embark upon that unknown sea?
> JAMES TERRY WHITE [1845–1920], *Why Fear?* st. 1

No sentimentalist — no stander above men and women, or apart from them;
No more modest than immodest.
> *Leaves of Grass. Song of Myself, 24*

I dote on myself, there is that lot of me and all so luscious. *Ib.*

I hear the violoncello, ('tis the young man's heart's complaint).
> *Ib. 26*

I believe a leaf of grass is no less than the journey-work of the stars.
> *Ib. 31*

I think I could turn and live with animals, they are so placid and self-contain'd,
I stand and look at them long and long.
They do not sweat and whine about their condition,
They do not lie awake in the dark and weep for their sins,
They do not make me sick discussing their duty to God,
Not one is dissatisfied, not one is demented with the mania of owning things,
Not one kneels to another, nor to his kind that lived thousands of years ago,
Not one is respectable or unhappy over the whole earth. *Ib. 32*

Behold! I do not give lectures or a little charity,
When I give I give myself.[1] *Ib. 40*

I have said that the soul is not more than the body,
And I have said that the body is not more than the soul,
And nothing, not God, is greater to one than one's self is. *Ib. 48*

In the faces of men and women I see God. *Ib.*

Do I contradict myself?
Very well then I contradict myself,
(I am large, I contain multitudes.)
> *Ib. 51*

[1] See Emerson, p. 607b, and Lowell, p. 692b.

I sound my barbaric yawp over the roofs of the world.
> *Leaves of Grass. Song of Myself,* 52

I bequeathe myself to the dirt, to grow from the grass I love;
If you want me again, look for me under your boot-soles.   *Ib.*

A woman waits for me, she contains all, nothing is lacking.
> *Ib. A Woman Waits For Me*

If anything is sacred the human body is sacred.
> *Ib. I Sing the Body Electric,* 8

I hear it was charged against me that I sought to destroy institutions,
But really I am neither for nor against institutions.
> *Ib. I Hear It Was Charged Against Me*

When I peruse the conquer'd fame of heroes and the victories of mighty generals, I do not envy the generals.
> *Ib. When I Peruse the Conquer'd Fame*

Afoot and light-hearted I take to the open road,
Healthy, free, the world before me,
The long brown path before me, leading wherever I choose.
> *Ib. Song of the Open Road,* 1

Henceforth I ask not good-fortune, I myself am good-fortune.   *Ib.*

The earth, that is sufficient,
I do not want the constellations any nearer,
I know they are very well where they are,
I know they suffice for those who belong to them.   *Ib.*

A great city is that which has the greatest men and women.
> *Ib. Song of the Broad-Axe,* 4

Youth, large, lusty, loving — Youth, full of grace, force, fascination,

Do you know that Old Age may come after you, with equal grace, force, fascination?
> *Leaves of Grass. Youth, Day, Old Age and Night*

Come, my tan-faced children,
Follow well in order, get your weapons ready;
Have you your pistols? have you your sharp-edged axes?
> *Ib. Pioneers! O Pioneers!* 1

Through the battle, through defeat, moving yet and never stopping,
Pioneers! O pioneers!   *Ib.* 13

Out of the cradle endlessly rocking,
Out of the mocking-bird's throat, the musical shuttle,
Out of the Ninth-month midnight.
> *Ib. Out of the Cradle Endlessly Rocking*

Whereto answering, the sea,
Delaying not, hurrying not,
Whisper'd me through the night, and very plainly before daybreak,
Lisp'd to me the low and delicious word death.   *Ib.*

Aboard, at a ship's helm,
A young steersman, steering with care.
> *Ib. Aboard, at a Ship's Helm*

But O the ship, the immortal ship! O ship aboard the ship!
O ship of the body — ship of the soul — voyaging, voyaging, voyaging.
> *Ib.*

Silent and amazed, even when a little boy,
I remember I heard the preacher every Sunday put God in his statements,
As contending against some being or influence.   *Ib. A Child's Amaze*

Give me the splendid silent sun, with all his beams full-dazzling!
> *Ib. Give Me the Splendid Silent Sun,* 1

Word over all, beautiful as the sky!
Beautiful that war and all its deeds of carnage must in time be utterly lost,

That the hands of the sisters Death and Night incessantly softly wash again, and ever again, this soil'd world;
For my enemy is dead, a man divine as myself is dead.
Leaves of Grass. Reconciliation

When lilacs last in the dooryard bloom'd,
And the great star early droop'd in the western sky in the night,
I mourn'd — and yet shall mourn with ever-returning spring.
Ib. When Lilacs Last in the Dooryard Bloom'd, 1

O sane and sacred death. *Ib. 7*

Come lovely and soothing death,[1]
Undulate round the world, serenely arriving, arriving,
In the day, in the night, to all, to each,
Sooner or later, delicate death.
Ib. 14

Prais'd be the fathomless universe,
For life and joy, and for objects and knowledge curious,
And for love, sweet love — But praise! praise! praise!
For the sure-enwinding arms of cool-enfolding death. *Ib.*

O Captain! my Captain! our fearful trip is done!
The ship has weather'd every rack, the prize we sought is won,
The port is near, the bells I hear, the people all exulting.
Ib. O Captain! My Captain! 1

Exult O shores, and ring O bells!
But I with mournful tread,
Walk the deck my Captain lies,
Fallen cold and dead. *Ib. 3*

This dust was once the man,
Gentle, plain, just and resolute, under whose cautious hand,
Against the foulest crime in history known in any land or age,
Was saved the Union of these States.
Ib. This Dust Was Once the Man

[1] See Shakespeare, p. 236b

The whole theory of the universe is directed unerringly to one single individual — namely to You.
Leaves of Grass. By Blue Ontario's Shore, 15

Liberty is to be subserved whatever occurs.
Ib. To a Foil'd European Revolutionaire, 1

What do you suppose will satisfy the soul, except to walk free and own no superior?
Ib. Laws for Creations, 3

Not till the sun excludes you do I exclude you.
Ib. To a Common Prostitute

O we can wait no longer,
We too take ship O soul,
Joyous we too launch out on trackless seas,
Fearless for unknown shores.
Ib. Passage to India, 8

Passage, immediate passage! the blood burns in my veins!
Away, O soul! hoist instantly the anchor!
Cut the hawsers — haul out — shake out every sail!
Have we not stood here like trees in the ground long enough?
Have we not grovel'd here long enough, eating and drinking like mere brutes? *Ib. 9*

Darest thou now O soul,
Walk out with me toward the unknown region
Where neither ground is for the feet nor any path to follow?
Ib. Darest Thou Now O Soul

To me every hour of the light and dark is a miracle,
Every cubic inch of space is a miracle.
Ib. Miracles, 2

Today a rude brief recitative,
Of ships sailing the seas, each with its special flag or ship-signal.
Ib. Song for All Seas, All Ships, 1

Of sea captains young or old, and the mates — and of all intrepid sailors . . .

Pick'd sparingly, without noise, by thee, old Ocean — chosen by thee,
Thou Sea, that pickest and cullest the race, in time, and unitest nations!
Suckled by thee, old husky nurse — embodying thee!
Indomitable, untamed as thee.
Leaves of Grass. Song for All Seas, All Ships, 1

Our life is closed — our life begins,
The long, long anchorage we leave,
The ship is clear at last — she leaps!
She swiftly courses from the shore,
Joy! shipmate — joy.
Ib. Joy, Shipmate, Joy!

Camerado, this is no book,
Who touches this touches a man.
Ib. So Long!

The world, the race, the soul — in space and time the universes,
All bound as is befitting each — all surely going somewhere.
Ib. Going Somewhere

Political democracy, as it exists and practically works in America, with all its threatening evils, supplies a training school for making first-class men. It is life's gymnasium, not of good only, but of all. *Democratic Vistas* [1871]

It is native personality, and that alone, that endows a man to stand before presidents or generals, or in any distinguish'd collection, with *aplomb* — and *not* culture, or any knowledge or intellect whatever. *Ib.*

I never see that man [Lincoln] without feeling that he is one to become personally attach'd to, for his combination of purest, heartiest tenderness, and native western form of manliness.
Specimen Days [1882]. *The Inauguration* [March 4, 1865]

He leaves for America's history and biography, so far, not only its most dramatic reminiscence — he leaves, in my opinion, the greatest, best, most characteristic, artistic, moral personality.
Ib. Death of President Lincoln [April 16, 1865]

The real war will never get in the books. *Ib. The Real War*

After you have exhausted what there is in business, politics, conviviality, and so on — have found that none of these finally satisfy, or permanently wear — what remains? Nature remains.
Specimen Days. New Themes Entered Upon

Hast Thou, pellucid, in Thy azure depths, medicine for case like mine?
Ib. The Sky [October 20, 1876]

You must not know too much, or be too precise or scientific about birds and trees and flowers and watercraft; a certain free margin, and even vagueness — perhaps ignorance, credulity — helps your enjoyment of these things.
Ib. Birds [May 14, 1881]

To have great poets, there must be great audiences, too.
Notes Left Over. Ventures on an Old Theme

No really great song can ever attain full purport till long after the death of its singer — till it has accrued and incorporated the many passions, many joys and sorrows, it has itself aroused.
November Boughs [1888]. *The Bible as Poetry*

No one will ever get at my verses who insists upon viewing them as a literary performance.
A Backward Glance O'er Travel'd Roads [1888]

Concluding with two items for the imaginative genius of the West, when it worthily rises — First, what Herder taught to the young Goethe, that really great poetry is always (like the Homeric or Biblical canticles) the result of a national spirit, and not the privilege of a polish'd and select few; Second, that the strongest and sweetest songs yet remain to be sung. *Ib.*

There is no week nor day nor hour, when tyranny may not enter upon this country, if the people lose their roughness and spirit of defiance — Tyranny may always enter — there is no charm,

no bar against it — the only bar against it is a large resolute breed of men.
> *Notes for Lecturers on Democracy and "Adhesiveness." From* C. J. FURNESS, *Walt Whitman's Workshop* [1928]

ALICE CARY
1820–1871

Work, and your house shall be duly fed:
Work, and rest shall be won;
I hold that a man had better be dead
Than alive when his work is done.
> *Work*

LUCRETIA PEABODY HALE
1820–1900

At last Elizabeth Eliza said, "They say that the lady from Philadelphia, who is staying in town, is very wise. Suppose I go and ask her what is best to be done."
> *The Peterkin Papers* [1880]

JEAN INGELOW
1820–1897

But two are walking apart forever,
And wave their hands for a mute farewell.
> *Divided. VI, st. 5*

A sweeter woman ne'er drew breath
Than my son's wife, Elizabeth.
> *High Tide on the Coast of Lincolnshire, 1571, st. 11*

There's no dew left on the daisies and clover,
There's no rain left in heaven:
I've said my "seven times" over and over,
Seven times one are seven.
> *Songs of Seven. Seven Times One, st. 1*

O columbine, open your folded wrapper,
Where two twin turtledoves dwell!
O cuckoopint, toll me the purple clapper
That hangs in your clear green bell!
> *Ib. st. 6*

O land where all the men are stones,
Or all the stones are men.
> *A Land That Living Warmth Disowns*

THEODORE O'HARA
1820–1867

On Fame's eternal camping ground
Their silent tents are spread,
And Glory guards, with solemn round,
The bivouac of the dead.
> *The Bivouac of the Dead* [1] [1847], *st. 1*

Sons of the Dark and Bloody ground.[2]
> *Ib. st. 9*

GEORGE FREDERICK ROOT
1820–1895

Tramp! Tramp! Tramp! the boys are marching,
Cheer up, comrades, they will come,
And beneath the starry flag
We shall breathe the air again
Of the free land in our own beloved home.
> *Tramp! Tramp! Tramp!* [1862]

Yes, we'll rally round the flag, boys, we'll rally once again,
Shouting the battle cry of Freedom,
We will rally from the hillside, we'll gather from the plain,
Shouting the battle cry of Freedom.
> *The Battle Cry of Freedom* [1863]

SIR WILLIAM HOWARD RUSSELL
1820–1907

The Russians dashed on towards that thin red-line streak tipped with a line of steel.[3]
> *To The Times of London from the Crimea, describing the British infantry at Balaklava* [October 25, 1854]

[1] Written to commemorate Americans slain in the battle of Buena Vista, February 22-23, 1847.
[2] Translation of the Indian name Kentucky.
[3] Soon the men of the column began to see that though the scarlet line was slender, it was

WILLIAM TECUMSEH SHERMAN
1820–1891

You cannot qualify war in harsher terms than I will. War is cruelty, and you cannot refine it.
> *Letter [September 12, 1864] to James M. Calhoun, Mayor of Atlanta, and others*

Hold the fort! I am coming! [1]
> *Signal from Kenesaw Mountain to General John Murray Corse in Altoona [October 5, 1864]*

The legitimate object of war is a more perfect peace.
> *Speech [St. Louis, July 20, 1865]*

I am tired and sick of war. Its glory is all moonshine. It is only those who have neither fired a shot nor heard the shrieks and groans of the wounded who cry aloud for blood, more vengeance, more desolation. War is hell.[2]
> *Attributed to a graduation address at Michigan Military Academy [June 19, 1879]; from the National Tribune, Washington, D.C. [November 26, 1914]*

I will not accept if nominated and will not serve if elected.[3]
> *Message to Republican National Convention [June 5, 1884]*

JOHN TYNDALL
1820–1893

Heat Considered as a Mode of Motion.   *Title of treatise [1863]*

Life is a wave, which in no two consecutive moments of its existence is composed of the same particles.[1]
> *Fragments of Science, vol. II, Vitality*

The mind of man may be compared to a musical instrument with a certain range of notes, beyond which in both directions we have an infinitude of silence.   *Ib. Matter and Force*

The brightest flashes in the world of thought are incomplete until they have been proved to have their counterparts in the world of fact.
> *Ib. Scientific Materialism*

It is as fatal as it is cowardly to blink facts because they are not to our taste.   *Ib. Science and Man*

Charles Darwin, the Abraham of scientific men — a searcher as obedient to the command of truth as was the patriarch to the command of God.   *Ib.*

Superstition may be defined as constructive religion which has grown incongruous with intelligence.   *Ib.*

Religious feeling is as much a verity as any other part of human consciousness; and against it, on the subjective side, the waves of science beat in vain.
> *Ib. Professor Virchow and Evolution*

HERBERT SPENCER
1820–1903

Progress, therefore, is not an accident, but a necessity. . . . It is a part of nature.
> *Social Statics [1851], pt. I, ch. 2*

Education has for its object the formation of character.   *Ib. 17*

Opinion is ultimately determined by the feelings, and not by the intellect.   *Ib. IV, 30*

Morality knows nothing of geographical boundaries or distinctions of race.   *Ib.*

---

very rigid and exact. — A. W. KINGLAKE [1809–1891], *Invasion of the Crimea, vol. III, p. 455*

It's "Thin red line of 'eroes" when the drums begin to roll. — KIPLING [1865–1936], *Tommy, st. 3*

[1] He actually said: Hold out. Relief is coming. General Corse replied: I am short a cheekbone and an ear, but am able to whip all hell yet. See Philip Bliss, p. 777b.

[2] See Robert E. Lee, p. 620a.

[3] The familiar version is: If nominated I will not run; if elected I will not serve.

[1] See Heraclitus, p. 77a.

No one can be perfectly free till all are free; no one can be perfectly moral till all are moral; no one can be perfectly happy till all are happy.

> *Social Statics, pt. IV, ch. 30*

Architecture, sculpture, painting, music, and poetry, may truly be called the efflorescence of civilized life.

> *Essays on Education* [1861]. *Education: What Knowledge Is of Most Worth?*

Every cause produces more than one effect.

> *Ib. On Progress: Its Law and Cause*

The tyranny of Mrs. Grundy [1] is worse than any other tyranny we suffer under.

> *Ib. On Manners and Fashion*

Old forms of government finally grow so oppressive that they must be thrown off even at the risk of reigns of terror.   *Ib.*

Music must take rank as the highest of the fine arts — as the one which, more than any other, ministers to human welfare.

> *Ib. On the Origin and Function of Music*

We too often forget that not only is there "a soul of goodness in things evil," [2] but very generally a soul of truth in things erroneous.

> *First Principles* [1861]

The fact disclosed by a survey of the past that majorities have been wrong must not blind us to the complementary fact that majorities have usually not been entirely wrong.   *Ib.*

Volumes might be written upon the impiety of the pious.   *Ib.*

We have unmistakable proof that throughout all past time, there has been a ceaseless devouring of the weak by the strong.   *Ib.*

[1] See Thomas Morton, p. 501a, and Locker-Hampson, p. 710a.
[2] See Shakespeare, *Henry V, IV, i, 4*, p. 244b.

This survival of the fittest.

> *Principles of Biology* [1864–1867], *pt. III, ch. 12*

The Republican form of government is the highest form of government: but because of this it requires the highest type of human nature — a type nowhere at present existing.

> *Essays* [1891]. *The Americans*

The ultimate result of shielding men from the effects of folly is to fill the world with fools.

> *Ib. State Tamperings with Money Banks*

HENRI-FRÉDÉRIC AMIEL
1821–1881

Truth is the secret of eloquence and of virtue, the basis of moral authority; it is the highest summit of art and of life.   *Journal* [1883]

An error is the more dangerous the more truth it contains.   *Ib.*

Doing easily what others find difficult is talent; doing what is impossible for talent is genius.   *Ib.*

If ignorance and passion are the foes of popular morality, it must be confessed that moral indifference is the malady of the cultivated classes.   *Ib.*

Pure truth cannot be assimilated by the crowd; it must be communicated by contagion.   *Ib.*

CHARLES BAUDELAIRE [1]
1821–1867

Hypocrite reader — my fellow man — my brother! [2]

> *Les Fleurs du Mal* [1861]

[1] Baudelaire is the foremost seer, king of poets, a *true* God. Even so, he lived in too artistic a milieu; his so highly praised form is meager. Ventures into the unknown demand new forms. — ARTHUR RIMBAUD [1854–1891], *Lettre à Paul Demeny* [*May 15, 1871*]
[2] Hypocrite lecteur — mon semblable — mon frère! (Quoted by T. S. ELIOT in *The Waste Land.*)

The poet is like the prince of the clouds who haunts the tempest and laughs at the archer; exiled on the ground in the midst of jeers, his giant wings prevent him from walking.[1]
Les Fleurs du Mal.
L'Albatros, st. 4

Perfumes, colors and sounds echo one another.   *Ib. Correspondances*

Mother of memories, mistress of mistresses.[2]   *Ib. Le Balcon, st. 1*

There, everything is order and beauty, richness, quiet and pleasure.[3]
Ib. L'Invitation au Voyage, refrain

I have more memories than if I were a thousand years old.[4]
Ib. Spleen, l. 1

I am the wound and the knife!
I am the blow and the cheek!
I am the limbs and the wheel —
The victim and the executioner! [5]
Ib. L'Héautontimoroumenos

O Death, old captain, it is time! raise the anchor!
Ib. Le Voyage, VIII

What do I care that you are good? Be beautiful! and be sad! [6]
Nouvelles Fleurs du Mal [1866–1868]. *Madrigal Triste, st. 1*

There can be no progress (real, that is, moral) except in the individual and by the individual himself.
Mon Coeur Mis à Nu [1887], XV

There are in every man, at every hour, two simultaneous postulations, one towards God, the other towards Satan.   *Ib. XIX*

---

[1] Le Poète est semblable au prince des nuées
Qui hante la tempête et se rit de l'archer;
Exilé sur le sol au milieu des huées,
Ses ailes de géant l'empêchent de marcher.
[2] Mère des souvenirs, maîtresse des maîtresses.
[3] Là, tout n'est qu'ordre et beauté,
Luxe, calme et volupté.
[4] J'ai plus de souvenirs que si j'avais mille ans.
[5] Je suis la plaie et le couteau!
Je suis le soufflet et la joute!
Je suis les membres et la roue,
Et la victime et le bourreau!
[6] Que m'importe que tu sois sage?
Sois belle! et sois triste!

There exist only three beings worthy of respect: the priest, the soldier, the poet. To know, to kill, to create.
Mon Coeur Mis à Nu XXII

To be a great man and a saint for oneself, that is the one important thing.   *Ib. LII*

Theory of the true civilization. It is not to be found in gas or steam or table turning. It consists in the diminution of the traces of original sin.   *Ib. LIX*

SIR RICHARD FRANCIS BURTON
1821–1890

Why meet we on the bridge of Time to 'change one greeting and to part?
The Kasidah of Haji Abdu El-Yazdi, I, 11

Indeed he knows not how to know who knows not also how to un-know.
Ib. VI, 18

Do what thy manhood bids thee do, from none but self expect applause;
He noblest lives and noblest dies who makes and keeps his self-made laws.   *Ib. VIII, 37*

FËDOR MIKHAILOVICH DOSTOEVSKI
1821–1881

Man is a pliable animal, a being who gets accustomed to everything!
The House of the Dead (Prison Life in Siberia) [1861–1862], *pt. I, ch. 2*

He [Turgenev] said that he was writing a long article against the Russophiles and Slavophiles. I advised him to order a telescope from Paris for his better convenience. "What do you mean?" he asked. "The distance is somewhat great," I replied; "direct the telescope on Russia, and then you will be able to observe us; otherwise you can't really see anything at all."
Letter to Apollon Maikov
[August 16 (28), 1867]

I want to tell you now about the insects to whom God gave "sensual lust." . . . I am that insect, brother, and it is said of me especially. All we Karamazovs are such insects, and, angel as you are, that insect lives in you too, and will stir a tempest in your blood. Tempests, because sensual lust is a tempest — worse than a tempest! Beauty is a terrible and awful thing! It is terrible because it has not been fathomed, for God sets us nothing but riddles.[1] Here the boundaries meet and all contradictions exist side by side. . . .

Yes, man is broad, too broad, indeed. I'd have him narrower. The devil only knows what to make of it! What to the mind is shameful is beauty and nothing else to the heart. Is there beauty in Sodom? Believe me, that for the immense mass of mankind beauty is found in Sodom. Did you know that secret? The awful thing is that beauty is mysterious as well as terrible. God and devil are fighting there, and the battlefield is the heart of man.

The Brothers Karamazov[2] *[1879–1880], bk. III, ch. 3*

And if that is so, if they dare not forgive, what becomes of harmony? Is there in the whole world a being who would have the right to forgive and could forgive? I don't want harmony. From love of humanity I don't want it. I would rather be left with unavenged suffering. I would rather remain with my unavenged suffering and unsatisfied indignation, *even if I were wrong*. Besides, too high a price is asked for harmony; it's beyond our means to pay so much to enter on it. And so I hasten to give back my entrance ticket, and if I am an honest man I am bound to give it back as soon as possible. And that I am doing. It's not God that I don't accept, Alyosha, only I most respectfully return Him the ticket. *Ib. V, 4*

We have corrected Thy work and have founded it upon *miracle, mystery* and *authority*. And men rejoiced that they were again led like sheep, and that the terrible gift that brought them such suffering, was, at last, lifted from their hearts.

The Brothers Karamazov,
bk. V, ch. 5

"How will you escape it? By what will you escape it? That's impossible with your ideas."

"In the Karamazov way, again."

" 'Everything is lawful,' you mean?"
Ib.

Men reject their prophets and slay them, but they love their martyrs and honor those whom they have slain.
Ib. VI, 3

That was a sign to me at that moment. It's for the babe I'm going. Because we are responsible for all.
Ib. XI, 4

Who doesn't desire his father's death? *Ib. XII, 5*

Our fatal troika dashes on in her headlong flight perhaps to destruction, and in all Russia for long past men have stretched out imploring hands and called a halt to its furious reckless course. And if other nations stand aside from that troika that may be not from respect, as the poet would fain believe, but simply from horror. And well it is that they stand aside, but maybe they will cease one day to do so and will form a firm wall confronting the hurrying apparition and will check the frenzied rush of our lawlessness, for the sake of their own safety, enlightenment and civilization. *Ib. 9*

They have their Hamlets, but we still have our Karamazovs! *Ib.*

But profound as psychology is, it's a knife that cuts both ways.
Ib. 10

For a moment the lie becomes truth. *Ib. Epilogue, ch. 2*

We have all come out of Gogol's *Overcoat.*[1]

Attributed to Dostoevski

[1] This statement, traditionally attributed to Dostoevski, and quoted by most writers on Dostoevski and on Russian realism, appears in

---

[1] See Einstein, p. 951a.
[2] Translated by CONSTANCE GARNETT.

MARY BAKER EDDY
1821–1910

Jesus of Nazareth was the most scientific man that ever trod the globe. He plunged beneath the material surface of things, and found the spiritual cause.
Science and Health with Key to the Scriptures [1875], *p. 313*

Spirit is the real and eternal; matter is the unreal and temporal.
Ib. p. 468

Sickness, sin and death, being inharmonious, do not originate in God nor belong to His government.
Ib. p. 472

How would you define Christian Science?
As the law of God, the law of good, interpreting and demonstrating the divine Principle and rule of universal harmony.
Rudimental Divine Science [1891], *p. 1*

GUSTAVE FLAUBERT
1821–1880

One must not always think that feeling is everything. Art is nothing without form.
Letter to Madame Louise Colet [August 12, 1846]

What a horrible invention, the bourgeois, don't you think? [1]
Ib. [September 22, 1846]

Eugène Melchior, vicomte de Vogüé [*1848–1910*], *Le Roman Russe* [*1886*], ch. 3: The more I read the Russians, the more I understand the observation one of them made to me . . . "We have all come out of Gogol's *Overcoat.*" We see further how evident the connection is with Dostoevski: the formidable novelist is all in his first book, *Poor People,* and *Poor People* has its origin in the *Overcoat.*
De Vogüé reiterated this statement in the speech he made on the occasion of unveiling a centennial monument to Gogol in Moscow in 1909.
[1] Il faut épater le bourgeois [You must shock the bourgeois]. — BAUDELAIRE

One becomes a critic when one cannot be an artist, just as a man becomes a stool pigeon when he cannot be a soldier.
Letter to Madame Louise Colet [October 22, 1846]

Axiom: hatred of the bourgeois is the beginning of wisdom. [1]
Letter to George Sand, May 10, 1867

I call a bourgeois anyone whose thinking is vulgar. [1]
Quoted by Maupassant

What is beautiful is moral, that is all there is to it.
Letter to Maupassant [October 26, 1880]

NATHAN BEDFORD FORREST
1821–1872

Get there first with the most men. [2]
Statement reported by General Basil Duke and General Richard Taylor

HERMANN LUDWIG FERDINAND VON HELMHOLTZ
1821–1894

Nature as a whole possesses a store of force which cannot in any way be either increased or diminished . . . therefore, the quantity of force in Nature is just as eternal and unalterable as the quantity of matter. . . . I have named [this] general law "The Principle of the Conservation of Force." [3]
Über die Erhaltung der Kraft [1847]

Whoever, in the pursuit of science, seeks after immediate practical utility, may generally rest assured that he will

---

[1] See note 1 in left column.
[2] Erroneous version usually rendered: Git thar fustest with the mostest.
[3] Translated by E. ATKINSON.
Helmholtz's "force" is equivalent to the modern physicist's "energy."

seek in vain. All that science can achieve is a perfect knowledge and a perfect understanding of the action of natural and moral forces.
Academic discourse, Heidelberg [1862]

FREDERICK LOCKER-LAMPSON
1821–1895

The world's as ugly, ay, as Sin —
And almost as delightful.
The Jester's Plea

And many are afraid of God —
And more of Mrs. Grundy.[1]   *Ib.*

GEORGE JOHN WHYTE-MELVILLE
1821–1878

In the choice of a horse and a wife, a man must please himself, ignoring the opinion and advice of friends.
Riding Recollections [1878]

NIKOLAI NEKRASOV
1821–1877

You do not have to be a poet, but you are obliged to be a citizen.
Poet and Citizen

Wretched and abundant,
Oppressed and powerful,
Weak and mighty,
Mother Russia!
Who Is Happy in Russia?
[1873–1876]

WILLIAM HENRY VANDERBILT
1821–1885

The public be damned.
Reply to a newspaper reporter
[October 2, 1882]

[1] See Thomas Morton, p. 501a, and Herbert Spencer, p. 706a.

RUDOLF VIRCHOW
1821–1902

I formulate the doctrine of pathological generation . . . in simple terms: *omnis cellula a cellula.*[1]
Cellular Pathology [1858].[2]
Disease, Life and Man

MATTHEW ARNOLD
1822–1888

Be his [3]
My special thanks, whose even-balanced soul,
From first youth tested up to extreme old age,
Business could not make dull, nor passion wild:
Who saw life steadily and saw it whole.   *To a Friend* [1849]

Others abide our question. Thou art free.
We ask and ask: Thou smilest and art still,
Out-topping knowledge.
Shakespeare [1849]

Strong is the soul, and wise, and beautiful:
The seeds of godlike power are in us still:
Gods are we, bards, saints, heroes, if we will.
Written in Emerson's Essays [1849]

Come, dear children, let us away;
Down and away below!
Now my brothers call from the bay,
Now the great winds shorewards blow,
Now the salt tides seawards flow;
Now the wild white horses play,
Champ and chafe and toss in the spray.
The Forsaken Merman [1849],
st. 1

Sand-strewn caverns, cool and deep,
Where the winds are all asleep.
Ib. st. 4

[1] All cells come from [pre-existing] cells.
[2] Essays translated by LELLAND J. RATHER [1958].
[3] Sophocles.

Where great whales come sailing by,
Sail and sail, with unshut eye,
Round the world forever and aye.
The Forsaken Merman, st. 4

Down, down, down!
Down to the depth of the sea!
She sits at her wheel in the humming
town,
Singing most joyfully. *Ib. st.* 7

Fate gave, what Chance shall not con-
trol,
His sad lucidity of soul.
Resignation [1849]

We cannot kindle when we will
The fire that in the heart resides,
The spirit bloweth and is still,
In mystery our soul abides.
Morality [1852], *st.* 1

Calm Soul of all things! make it mine
To feel, amid the city's jar,
That there abides a peace of thine,
Man did not make, and can not
mar.
*Lines Written in Kensington
Gardens* [1852], *st.* 10

Goethe in Weimar sleeps, and Greece,
Long since, saw Byron's struggle cease,
But one such death remained to come;
The last poetic voice is dumb —
We stand today by Wordsworth's
tomb.

When Byron's eyes were shut in
death,
We bowed our head and held our
breath.
He taught us little; but our soul
Had *felt* him like the thunder's roll.
Memorial Verses, April 1850
[1852], *st.* 1, 2

Physician of the Iron Age,
Goethe has done his pilgrimage.
He took the suffering human race,
He read each wound, each weakness
clear;
And struck his finger on the place,
And said: Thou ailest here, and here!
Ib. st. 3

But where will Europe's latter hour
Again find Wordsworth's healing
power?
Others will teach us how to dare,
And against fear our breast to steel;
Others will strengthen us to bear —
But who, ah! who will make us feel?
The cloud of mortal destiny,
Others will front it fearlessly —
But who, like him, will put it by?
Memorial Verses, st. 5

Hither and thither spins
The windborne, mirroring soul;
A thousand glimpses wins,
And never sees a whole.
Empedocles on Etna [1852],
act I, sc. ii, l. 82

Be neither saint- nor sophist-led, but be
a man! *Ib. l.* 136

We do not what we ought;
What we ought not, we do; [1]
And lean upon the thought
That chance will bring us through.
Ib. l. 237

Nature, with equal mind,
Sees all her sons at play;
Sees man control the wind,
The wind sweep man away.
Ib. l. 257

Is it so small a thing
To have enjoyed the sun,
To have lived light in the spring,
To have loved, to have thought, to have
done;
To have advanced true friends, and
beat down baffling foes?
Ib. II, l. 397

The day in its hotness,
The strife with the palm;
The night in her silence,
The stars in their calm. *Ib. l.* 465

The same heart beats in every human
breast.
The Buried Life [1852], *st.* 2

But often in the world's most crowded
streets,
But often, in the din of strife,

[1] See *Book of Common Prayer,* p. 59b.

There rises an unspeakable desire
After the knowledge of our buried life.
    The Buried Life, st. 6

What actions are the most excellent? Those, certainly, which most powerfully appeal to the great primary human affections: to those elementary feelings which subsist permanently in the race, and which are independent of time. These feelings are permanent and the same; that which interests them is permanent and the same also.
    Preface to Poems [1853]

Go, for they call you, Shepherd, from the hill.
    The Scholar Gypsy [1853], *st. 1*

Crossing the stripling Thames at Bab-lock-hithe,
Trailing in the cool stream thy fingers wet,
As the slow punt swings round.
    Ib. st. 8

Thou waitest for the spark from heaven: and we,
Light half-believers of our casual creeds,
Who never deeply felt, nor clearly willed . . .
Who hesitate and falter life away,
And lose tomorrow the ground won to-day —
Ah! do not we, wanderer! await it too?
    Ib. st. 18

    And amongst us one
Who most has suffered, takes dejectedly
His seat upon the intellectual throne.
    Ib. st. 19

This strange disease of modern life.
    Ib. st. 21

Still nursing the unconquerable hope,
Still clutching the inviolable shade.
    Ib. st. 22

Strew on her roses, roses,
    And never a spray of yew!
In quiet she reposes;
    Ah, would that I did too!
    Requiescat [1853], *st. 1*

Her cabined, ample spirit,
    It fluttered and failed for breath.
Tonight it doth inherit
    The vasty hall of death.
    Requiescat, st. 4

Hark! ah, the nightingale —
The tawny-throated!
    Philomela [1853], *st. 1*

Eternal passion!
Eternal pain!   *Ib. st. 3*

What shelter to grow ripe is ours?
What leisure to grow wise?
    Stanzas in Memory of the Author of "Obermann" [1] [1853], *st. 18*

Truth sits upon the lips of dying men.
    Sohrab and Rustum [1853], *l. 656*

Sanity — that is the great virtue of the ancient literature; the want of that is the great defect of the modern, in spite of its variety and power.
    Preface to Poems [1854]

Wandering between two worlds, one dead,
The other powerless to be born.
    Stanzas from the Grande Chartreuse [1855], *st. 15*

And we forget because we must
And not because we will.
    Absence [1857], *st. 3*

Peace, peace is what I seek, and public calm;
Endless extinction of unhappy hates.
    Merope [1858], *l. 100*

With women the heart argues, not the mind.   *Ib. l. 341*

The translator of Homer should above all be penetrated by a sense of four qualities of his author: that he is eminently rapid; that he is eminently plain and direct, both in the evolution of his thought and in the expression of it, that is, both in his syntax and in his words; that he is eminently plain and

---

[1] Étienne Pivert de Sénancour [1770–1846], French author. His most notable work, *Obermann*, was published in 1804.

direct in the substance of his thought, that is, in his matter and ideas; and, finally, that he is eminently noble.
On Translating Homer [1861]

The Iliad has a great master's genuine stamp, and that stamp is *the grand style*.   *Ib.*

Of these two literatures [France and Germany], as of the intellect of Europe in general, the main effort, for now many years, has been a *critical* effort; the endeavor, in all branches of knowledge — theology, philosophy, history, art, science — to see the object as in itself it really is.   *Ib.*

The grand style arises in poetry, when a noble nature, poetically gifted, treats with simplicity or with severity a serious subject.   *Ib.*

Nations are not truly great solely because the individuals composing them are numerous, free, and active; but they are great when these numbers, this freedom, and this activity are employed in the service of an ideal higher than that of an ordinary man, taken by himself.   *Democracy* [1861]

It is a very great thing to be able to think as you like; but, after all, an important question remains: *what* you think.   *Ib.*

The critical power . . . tends to make an intellectual situation of which the creative power can profitably avail itself . . . to make the best ideas prevail.
The Function of Criticism at the Present Time [1864]

Ideas cannot be too much prized in and for themselves, cannot be too much lived with.   *Ib.*

There is the world of ideas and the world of practice; the French are often for suppressing the one and the English the other; but neither is to be suppressed.   *Ib.*

Burke is so great because, almost alone in England, he brings thought to bear upon politics, he saturates politics with thought.
The Function of Criticism at the Present Time

His [Burke's] greatness is that he lived in a world which neither English Liberalism nor English Toryism is apt to enter — the world of ideas.   *Ib.*

The notion of the free play of the mind upon all subjects being a pleasure in itself, being an object of desire, being an essential provider of elements without which a nation's spirit, whatever compensations it may have for them, must, in the long run, die of inanition, hardly enters into an Englishman's thoughts.   *Ib.*

I am bound by my own definition of criticism: a disinterested endeavor to learn and propagate the best that is known and thought in the world.
Ib.

Whispering from her [1] towers the last enchantments of the Middle Age . . . Home of lost causes, and forsaken beliefs, and unpopular names, and impossible loyalties!
Essays in Criticism, first series [1865], *preface*

Poetry is simply the most beautiful, impressive and wisely effective mode of saying things, and hence its importance.   *Ib. Heinrich Heine*

Philistine must have originally meant, in the mind of those who invented the nickname, a strong, dogged, unenlightened opponent of the children of the light.   *Ib.*

On the breast of that huge Mississippi of falsehood called *History*, a foam-bell more or less is no consequence.[2]
Ib. Literary Influence of Academies [1864]

[1] Oxford.
[2] This passage appeared only in the first appearance of the essay in *Cornhill Magazine* [August 1864].
History never embraces more than a small

The great apostle of the Philistines,
Lord Macaulay.

> *Essays in Criticism, first
> series, Joubert*

Are ye too changed, ye hills?
See, 'tis no foot of unfamiliar men
Tonight from Oxford up your pathway
strays!
Here came I often, often, in old days —
Thyrsis [1] and I; we still had Thyrsis
then.   *Thyrsis [1866], st. 1*

That sweet city [2] with her dreaming
spires.   *Ib. st. 2*

He went; his piping took a troubled
sound
Of storms that rage outside our happy
ground;
He could not wait their passing; he is
dead.   *Ib. st. 5*

The bloom is gone, and with the bloom
go I.   *Ib. st. 6*

Yes, thou art gone! and round me too
the night
In ever-nearing circle weaves her shade.
I see her veil draw soft across the day,
I feel her slowly chilling breath invade
The cheek grown thin, the brown hair
sprent with gray;
I feel her finger light
Laid pausefully upon life's headlong
train —
The foot less prompt to meet the morn-
ing dew,
The heart less bounding at emotion
new,
And hope, once crushed, less quick to
spring again.   *Ib. st. 14*

---

part of reality. — LA ROCHEFOUCAULD [1613–
1680], *Paul Sabatier*
> How oft we sigh
> **When histories charm to think
> that histories lie!**
> THOMAS MOORE [1780–1852], *The
> Skeptic*

History is nothing more than the belief in
the senses, the belief in falsehood. — NIETZSCHE
[1844–1900], *The Twilight of the Idols, "Reason"
in Philosophy, I*

History is more or less bunk. — HENRY
FORD [1863–1947], interview with Charles N.
Wheeler, *Chicago Tribune* [May 25, 1916]

[1] Arthur Hugh Clough [1819–1861].
[2] Oxford.

Hear it, O Thyrsis, still our tree is
there! —
Ah, vain! These English fields, this
upland dim,
These brambles pale with mist engar-
landed,
That lone, sky-pointing tree, are not
for him;
To a boon southern country he is fled,
And now in happier air,
Wandering with the great Mother's
train divine . . .
Within a folding of the Apennine.
        Thyrsis, st. 18

Why faintest thou? I wandered till I
died.
Roam on! The light we sought is shining still,
Dost thou ask proof? Our tree yet
crowns the hill,
Our scholar travels yet the loved hillside.   *Ib. st. 24*

The sea is calm tonight.
The tide is full, the moon lies fair
Upon the straits.
      Dover Beach [1867], st. 1

Begin, and cease, and then again begin,
With tremulous cadence slow, and
bring
The eternal note of sadness in.   *Ib.*

Sophocles long ago
Heard it on the Aegean.   *Ib. st. 2*

The sea of faith
Was once, too, at the full, and round
earth's shore
Lay like the folds of a bright girdle
furled;
But now I only hear
Its melancholy, long, withdrawing
roar,
Retreating, to the breath
Of the night wind down the vast edges
drear
And naked shingles of the world.

Ah, love, let us be true
To one another! for the world, which
seems
To lie before us like a land of dreams,

So various, so beautiful, so new,
Hath really neither joy, nor love, nor
light,
Nor certitude, nor peace, nor help for
pain;
And we are here as on a darkling plain
Swept with confused alarms of struggle
and flight,
Where ignorant armies clash by night.
Dover Beach, st. 3, 4

It is — last stage of all —
When we are frozen up within, and
quite
The phantom of ourselves,
To hear the world applaud the hollow
ghost
Which blamed the living man.
Growing Old [1867], *st. 7*

Creep into thy narrow bed,
Creep, and let no more be said!
The Last Word [1867], *st. 1*

Let the long contention cease!
Geese are swans, and swans are geese.[1]
Ib. st. 2

Charge once more, then, and be
dumb!
Let the victors, when they come,
When the forts of folly fall,
Find thy body by the wall.
Ib. st. 4

Cruel, but composed and bland,
Dumb, inscrutable and grand,
So Tiberius might have sat,
Had Tiberius been a cat.
Poor Matthias [1867]

Coldly, sadly descends
The autumn evening. The field
Strewn with its dank yellow drifts
Of withered leaves, and the elms,
Fade into dimness apace,
Silent; hardly a shout
From a few boys late at their play!
Rugby Chapel [2] [1867], *st. 1*

O strong soul, by what shore
Tarriest thou now? For that force,

Surely, has not been left vain!
Somewhere, surely, afar,
In the sounding labor-house vast
Of being, is practiced that strength,
Zealous, beneficent, firm!
Rugby Chapel, st. 4

Most men eddy about
Here and there, eat and drink,
Chatter and love and hate,
Gather and squander, are raised
Aloft, are hurled in the dust,
Striving blindly, achieving
Nothing; and then they die.
Ib. st. 6

Friends who set forth at our side
Falter, are lost in the storm!
We, we only, are left! *Ib. st. 8*

Then, in such hour of need
Of your fainting, dispirited race,
Ye, like angels, appear,
Radiant with ardor divine.
Beacons of hope, ye appear!
Languor is not in your heart,
Weakness is not in your word,
Weariness not on your brow.
Ib. st. 13

Herein lies the reason for giving boys
more of Latin composition than of
Greek, superior though the Greek literature be to the Latin; but the power of
the Latin classic is in *character*, that of
the Greek is in *beauty*. Now character
is capable of being taught, learnt, and
assimilated; beauty hardly.
*Schools and Universities on the
Continent* [1868]

Our society distributes itself into
Barbarians, Philistines, and Populace;
and America is just ourselves, with the
Barbarians quite left out, and the Populace nearly.
Culture and Anarchy [1869],
preface

America, that chosen home of newspapers. *Ib.*

I am a Liberal, yet I am a Liberal
tempered by experience, reflection, and
renouncement, and I am, above all, a
believer in culture. *Ib. Introduction*

[1] See Burton, p. 311a.
[2] Arnold's father, Thomas Arnold, the great
headmaster of Rugby, is buried in Rugby
Chapel.

Culture is then properly described not as having its origin in curiosity, but as having its origin in the love of perfection; it is *a study of perfection.*

Culture and Anarchy,
Sweetness and Light

Not a having and a resting, but a growing and a becoming is the character of perfection as culture conceives it. *Ib.*

The pursuit of perfection, then, is the pursuit of sweetness and light.[1] . . . He who works for sweetness and light united, works to make reason and the will of God prevail. *Ib.*

The men of culture are the true apostles of equality. *Ib.*

The governing idea of Hellenism is spirit of consciousness, that of Hebraism, strictness of conscience.

Ib. Hebraism and Hellenism

Below the surface stream, shallow and
    light,
Of what we say and feel — below the
    stream,
As light, of what we think we feel,
    there flows
With noiseless current, strong, obscure
    and deep,
The central stream of what we feel in-
    deed.

St. Paul and Protestantism [1870]

Culture, the acquainting ourselves with the best that has been known and said in the world.

Literature and Dogma [1873],
preface

Conduct is three-fourths of our life and its largest concern. *Ib. ch.* 1

Choose equality.

Mixed Essays [1879]. *Equality*

We have the religion of inequality.
Ib.

To be humanized is to comply with the true law of our human nature; *servare modum, finemque tenere, Naturamque sequi,* says Lucan; "to keep our

[1] See Swift, p. 388b.

measure, and to hold fast our end, and to follow Nature."

Mixed Essays. Equality

Inequality has the natural and necessary effect, under the present circumstances, of materializing our upper class, vulgarizing our middle class, and brutalizing our lower class. *Ib.*

For poetry the idea is everything; the rest is a world of illusion, of divine illusion. Poetry attaches its emotion to the idea; the idea *is* the fact. The strongest part of our religion today is its unconscious poetry.

Introduction to WARD, *English*
Poets [1880]

Eutrapelia. "A happy and gracious flexibility," Pericles calls this quality of the Athenians . . . lucidity of thought, clearness and propriety of language, freedom from prejudice and freedom from stiffness, openness of mind, amiability of manners, all these seem to go along with a certain happy flexibility of nature, and to depend upon it.

Irish Essays [1882]. *A Speech at*
Eton

English civilization — the humanizing, the bringing into one harmonious and truly humane life, of the whole body of English society — that is what interests me.

Ib. Ecce, Convertimur ad Gentes

That which in England we call the middle class is in America virtually the nation.

A Word About America [1882]

The American Philistine was a livelier sort of Philistine than ours.

A Word More About America
[1885]

What really dissatisfies in American civilization is the want of the *interesting,* a want due chiefly to the want of those two great elements of the interesting, which are elevation and beauty.

Civilization in the United States
[1888]

Coleridge, poet and philosopher wrecked in a mist of opium.

> *Essays in Criticism, second series*
> *[1888]. Byron*

A beautiful and ineffectual angel,[1] beating in the void his luminous wings in vain.   *Ib.*

ULYSSES S. GRANT
1822–1885

The art of war is simple enough. Find out where your enemy is. Get at him as soon as you can. Strike at him as hard as you can and as often as you can, and keep moving on.[2]

> *On the art of war*

No terms except an unconditional and immediate surrender can be accepted. I propose to move immediately upon your works.

> *To General S. B. Buckner, Fort*
> *Donelson [February 16, 1862]*

I propose to fight it out on this line, if it takes all summer.

> *Dispatch to Washington, before*
> *Spottsylvania Court House*
> *[May 11, 1864]*

Wherever the enemy goes let our troops go also.

> *Dispatch to General Henry W.*
> *Halleck from City Point, Vir-*
> *ginia [August 1, 1864]*

The war is over — the rebels are our countrymen again.

> *Upon stopping his men from*
> *cheering after Lee's surrender*
> *at Appomattox Court House*
> *[April 9, 1865]*

Let us have peace.

> *Accepting nomination for the*
> *Presidency [May 29, 1868]*

I know no method to secure the repeal of bad or obnoxious laws so effective as their stringent execution.

> *Inaugural Address [March 4,*
> *1869]*

[1] Shelley.
[2] See Halsey, p. 968a.

Let no guilty man escape, if it can be avoided. No personal considerations should stand in the way of performing a public duty.

> *Indorsement of a letter relating*
> *to the Whiskey Ring [July 29,*
> *1875]*

Leave the matter of religion to the family altar, the church, and the private school, supported entirely by private contributions. Keep the church and the State forever separate.

> *Speech at Des Moines, Iowa*
> *[1875]*

Labor disgraces no man; unfortunately you occasionally find men disgrace labor.

> *Speech at Midland International*
> *Arbitration Union, Birmingham,*
> *England [1877]*

They [the Pilgrim Fathers] fell upon an ungenial climate, where there were nine months of winter and three months of cold weather, and that called out the best energies of the men, and of the women too, to get a mere subsistence out of the soil, with such a climate. In their efforts to do that they cultivated industry and frugality at the same time — which is the real foundation of the greatness of the Pilgrims.

> *Speech at New England Society*
> *Dinner [December 22, 1880]*

EDWARD EVERETT HALE
1822–1909

I am only one,
But still I am one.
I cannot do everything,
But still I can do something;
And because I cannot do everything
I will not refuse to do the something
that I can do.

> *For the Lend-a-Hand Society*

Behind all these men you have to do with, behind officers, and government, and people even, there is the country herself, your country, and . . . you be-

long to her as you belong to your own mother. Stand by her, boy, as you would stand by your mother.
The Man Without a Country
[1863]

He loved his country as no other man has loved her, but no man deserved less at her hands.
Ib. Epitaph of Philip Nolan

It is not necessary to finish your sentences in a crowd, but by a sort of mumble, omitting sibilants and dentals. This, indeed, if your words fail you, answers even in public extempore speech, but better where other talking is going on.
My Double and How He Undid Me [1868]

To look up and not down,
To look forward and not back,
To look out and not in, and
To lend a hand.[1]
Ten Times One Is Ten [1870]

RUTHERFORD BIRCHARD HAYES
1822–1893

He serves his party best who serves the country best.
Inaugural Address [March 5, 1877]

THOMAS HUGHES
1822–1896

Life isn't all beer and skittles;[2] but beer and skittles, or something better of the same sort, must form a good part of every Englishman's education.
Tom Brown's Schooldays [1857], pt. I, ch. 2

He never wants anything but what's right and fair; only when you come to settle what's right and fair, it's everything that he wants and nothing that you want.
Ib. II, 2

[1] Rule of the Harry Wadsworth Club.
[2] See Dickens, p. 669a.

WILLIAM PORCHER MILES
1822–1899

"Vote early and vote often," the advice openly displayed on the election banners in one of our northern cities.
Speech, House of Representatives [March 31, 1858]

LOUIS PASTEUR
1822–1895

No, a thousand times no; there does not exist a category of science to which one can give the name applied science. There are science and the applications of science, bound together as the fruit to the tree which bears it.[1]
Pourquoi la France n'a pas trouvé d'hommes supérieurs au moment du péril [Revue Scientifique, 1871]

In the fields of observation, chance favors only the mind that is prepared.
Quoted by RENÉ VALLERY-RADOT *in The Life of Pasteur* [1927]

THOMAS BUCHANAN READ
1822–1872

The terrible grumble, and rumble, and roar,
Telling the battle was on once more,
And Sheridan twenty miles away.
Sheridan's Ride, st. 1

HEINRICH SCHLIEMANN
1822–1890

I have gazed on the face of Agamemnon.
Telegram to the King of Greece, upon excavating the fifth and last grave at Mycenae [August 1876]

[1] Translated by I. BERNARD COHEN

THEODORE DE BANVILLE
1823–1891

We'll to the woods no more,
The laurels all are cut.[1]
> *Nous n'irons plus aux bois*

BERNARD ELLIOTT BEE
1823–1861

There is Jackson, standing like a stone wall!
> *Of General T. J. Jackson at the Battle of Bull Run* [2] *[July 21, 1861]*

GEORGE HENRY BOKER
1823–1890

Lay him low, lay him low,
In the clover or the snow!
What cares he? he cannot know:
Lay him low.
> *Dirge for a Soldier,*[3] *st. 1*

MATTHEW BROWNE [WILLIAM BRIGHTY RANDS]
1823–1882

Never do today what you can
Put off till tomorrow.[4]
> *Lilliput Levee*

Great wide, beautiful, wonderful world,
With the wonderful waters round you curled,
And the wonderful grass upon your breast,
World, you are beautifully dressed.
> *The Child's World, st. 1*

[1] Nous n'irons plus aux bois, les lauriers sont coupés.
From an old nursery rhyme. Translated by A. E. HOUSMAN, *Last Poems* [*1922*], *epigraph*
[2] Bee was killed in this battle.
[3] General Philip Kearny, killed near Chantilly, Virginia [September 1, 1862].
[4] No idleness, no laziness, no procrastination; never put off till tomorrow what you can do today. — LORD CHESTERFIELD, *Letters* [December 26, 1749]

JULIA A. FLETCHER CARNEY
1823–1908

Little drops of water,
Little grains of sand,
Make the mighty ocean
And the pleasant land.
> *Little Things* [*1845*], *st. 1*

Little deeds of kindness,
Little words of love,
Help to make earth happy
Like the heaven above.
> *Ib. st. 4*

WILLIAM JOHNSON CORY
1823–1892

All beauteous things for which we live
By laws of time and space decay.
But oh, the very reason why
I clasp them, is because they die.
> *Mimnermus in Church, st. 4*

They told me, Heraclitus, they told me you were dead;
They brought me bitter news to hear and bitter tears to shed.
I wept, as I remembered how often you and I
Had tired the sun with talking and sent him down the sky.
And now that thou art lying, my dear old Carian guest,
A handful of gray ashes, long long ago at rest,
Still are thy pleasant voices, thy Nightingales,[1] awake,
For Death, he taketh all away, but them he cannot take.
> *Heraclitus. Paraphrase from Callimachus* [2]

BARTHOLOMEW DOWLING
1823–1863

Then stand to your glasses steady!
We drink in our comrades' eyes:

[1] *The Nightingales* was the title of the poems left by Heraclitus. See p. 77a-b.
[2] See Callimachus, p. 104b.

One cup to the dead already —
Hurrah for the next that dies!
The Revel,[1] *st.* 1

THOMAS WENTWORTH
HIGGINSON
1823–1911

When a thought takes one's breath
away, a lesson on grammar seems an
impertinence.
Preface to EMILY DICKINSON'S
Poems, first series [1890]

An easy thing, O Power Divine,
To thank Thee for these gifts of
  Thine,
For summer's sunshine, winter's snow,
For hearts that kindle, thoughts that
  glow;
But when shall I attain to this —
To thank Thee for the things I miss?
The Things I Miss

JOHN KELLS INGRAM
1823–1907

Who fears to speak of Ninety-eight?[2]
  Who blushes at the name?
When cowards mock the patriot's
  fate,
  Who hangs his head for shame?
The Memory of the Dead,[3] *st.* 1

LEOPOLD KRONECKER
1823–1891

God made integers, all else is the
work of man.
*Jahresberichte der Deutschen
Mathematiker Vereinigung,
bk.* 2

---

[1] Commemorating the victims of a cholera
epidemic in India.
[2] Struggle for Irish independence led by Wolfe
Tone, Napper Tandy and others.
[3] First published anonymously in the *Dublin
Nation* [April 1, 1843].

GEORGE MARTIN
LANE
1823–1897

The waiter roars it through the hall:
"We don't give bread with one fish
  ball!"
Lay of the Lone Fish Ball[1]
[1855], *st.* 10

CAROLINE ATHERTON
BRIGGS MASON
1823–1890

Do they miss me at home — do they
  miss me?
'Twould be an assurance most dear,
To know that this moment some loved
  one
Were saying, "I wish he were here."
Do They Miss Me at Home? st. 1

FRANCIS PARKMAN
1823–1893

The growth of New England was a
result of the aggregate efforts of a busy
multitude, each in his narrow circle toiling for himself, to gather competence
or wealth. The expansion of New
France was the achievement of a gigantic ambition striving to grasp a continent. It was a vain attempt.
*Pioneers of France in the New
World* [1865], *introduction*

A boundless vision grows upon us; an
untamed continent; vast wastes of forest verdure; mountains silent in primeval
sleep; river, lake, and glimmering pool;
wilderness oceans mingling with the
sky. Such was the domain which France
conquered for civilization. Plumed hel-
mets gleamed in the shade of its forests,
priestly vestments in its dens and fastnesses of ancient barbarism. Men
steeped in antique learning, pale with
the close breath of the cloister, here
spent the noon and evening of their
lives, ruled savage hordes with a mild,

---

[1] Lane was professor of Latin at Harvard; the
embarrassment of the "lone fish ball" was an
actual experience.

parental sway, and stood serene before the direst shapes of death. Men of courtly nurture, heirs to the polish of a far-reaching ancestry, here, with their dauntless hardihood, put to shame the boldest sons of toil.

> *Pioneers of France in the New World, introduction*

Faithfulness to the truth of history involves far more than a research, however patient and scrupulous, into special facts. Such facts may be detailed with the most minute exactness, and yet the narrative, taken as a whole, may be unmeaning or untrue. The narrator must seek to imbue himself with the life and spirit of the time. He must study events in their bearings near and remote; in the character, habits, and manners of those who took part in them. He must himself be, as it were, a sharer or a spectator of the action he describes.

> *Ib.*

If any pale student, glued to his desk, here seek an apology for a way of life whose natural fruit is that pallid and emasculate scholarship of which New England has had too many examples, it will be far better that this sketch had not been written. For the student there is, in its season, no better place than the saddle, and no better companion than the rifle or the oar.

> *Autobiography* [1868] [1]

The most momentous and far-reaching question ever brought to issue on this continent was: Shall France remain here or shall she not?

> *Montcalm and Wolfe* [1884], *introduction*

Versailles was a gulf into which the labor of France poured its earnings, and it was never full.   *Ib. ch. 1*

The [French] Revolution began at the top — in the world of fashion, birth, and intellect — and propagated itself downwards.   *Ib.*

[1] Published in *Proceedings of the Massachusetts Historical Society, vol. VIII, p. 353.*

France built its best colony on a principle of exclusion, and failed: England reversed the system, and succeeded.

> *Montcalm and Wolfe, ch. 1*

COVENTRY PATMORE
1823–1896

Ah, wasteful woman! she who may
On her sweet self set her own price,
Knowing man cannot choose but pay,
How has she cheapened Paradise!
How given for nought her priceless gift,
How spoiled the bread and spilled the wine,
Which, spent with due respective thrift,
Had made brutes men and men divine!

> *The Angel in the House* [1854–1856], *bk. I, canto 3. Prelude 3, Unthrift*

A Woman is a foreign land,
Of which, though there he settle young,
A man will ne'er quite understand
The customs, politics, and tongue.

> *Ib. canto 9. Prelude 2, Woman*

Why, having won her, do I woo?
Because her spirit's vestal grace
Provokes me always to pursue,
But, spirit-like, eludes embrace.

> *Ib. II, canto 12. Prelude 1, The Married Lover*

His mother, who was patient, being dead.

> *The Unknown Eros* [1877], *bk. I, canto 10. The Toys, l. 6*

He had put, within his reach,
A box of counters and a red-veined stone,
A piece of glass abraded by the beach,
And six or seven shells,
A bottle with bluebells,
And two French copper coins, ranged there with careful art,
To comfort his sad heart.   *Ib. l. 15*

For want of me the world's course will
   not fail:
When all its work is done, the lie shall
   rot;
The truth is great, and shall prevail,[1]
When none cares whether it prevail or
   not.
> *The Unknown Eros, bk. I, canto
> 12. Magna est Veritas*

If I were dead, you'd sometimes say,
   "Poor child!"
> *Ib. canto 14. If I Were Dead*

EDWARD POLLOCK
1823–1858

The one who goes is happier
Than those he leaves behind.
> *The Parting Hour*

ERNEST RENAN
1823–1892

The whole of history is incomprehensible without the Christ.
> *La Vie de Jésus* [1863]

O Lord, if there is a Lord, save my
soul, if I have a soul.
> *Prière d'un Sceptique*

Religion is not a popular error; it is a
great instinctive truth, sensed by the
people, expressed by the people.
> *Les Apôtres* [1866]

An immense river of oblivion is
sweeping us away into a nameless
abyss.
> *Souvenirs d'Enfance et de
> Jeunesse* [1883]

Immortality is to labor at an eternal
task.
> *L'Avenir de la Science* [1890],
> *preface*

Nothing great is achieved without
chimeras.   *Ib. ch. 19*

---

[1] See *I Esdras 4:14*, p. 36b.
  For great is truth, and shall prevail [Magna
est Veritas et praevalebit]. — THOMAS BROOKS,
The Crown and Glory of Christianity [*1662*]

JOHN SHERMAN
1823–1900

I have come home to look after my
fences.[1]
> *Speech to his neighbors,
> Mansfield, Ohio*

WILLIAM MARCY
TWEED
1823–1878

As long as I count the votes, what are
you going to do about it?
> *Statement by the "Boss" of
> Tammany Hall on the bal-
> lot in New York City* [*No-
> vember 1871*]

PHOEBE CARY
1824–1871

Sometimes, I think, the things we see
Are shadows of the things to be;
   That what we plan we build;
That every hope that hath been crossed,
And every dream we thought was lost,
   In heaven shall be fulfilled.
> *Dreams and Realities, st. 7*

And though hard be the task,
"Keep a stiff upper lip."
> *Keep a Stiff Upper Lip*

One sweetly solemn thought
   Comes to me o'er and o'er;
I am nearer home today
   Than I ever have been before.
> *Nearer Home, st. 1*

For of all the hard things to bear and
   grin,
The hardest is being taken in.
> *Kate Ketcham* (parody of
> WHITTIER's *Maud Muller*

GEORGE WILLIAM
CURTIS
1824–1892

While we read history we make history.   *The Call of Freedom*

---

[1] Senator Sherman referred to the fences
around his farm. Said to be the origin of the
political phrase often rendered "to mend
fences."

Every great crisis of human history is a pass of Thermopylae, and there is always a Leonidas and his three hundred to die in it, if they cannot conquer.
The Call of Freedom

ALEXANDRE DUMAS THE YOUNGER
1824–1895

Business? It's quite simple. It's other people's money.
La Question d'Argent [1857], act II, sc. vii

THOMAS JONATHAN [STONEWALL] JACKSON[1]
1824–1863

My duty is to obey orders.
A favorite aphorism

Let us cross over the river, and rest under the trees.
Last words [May 10, 1863]

WILLIAM THOMSON, LORD KELVIN
1824–1907

When you can measure what you are speaking about, and express it in numbers, you know something about it; but when you cannot measure it, when you cannot express it in numbers, your knowledge is of a meager and unsatisfactory kind: it may be the beginning of knowledge, but you have scarcely, in your thoughts, advanced to the stage of *science*.
Popular Lectures and Addresses [1891–1894]

GUSTAV ROBERT KIRCHOFF
1824–1887

The highest object at which the natural sciences are constrained to aim, but which they will never reach, is the determination of the forces which are present in nature, and of the state of

[1] See Bee, p. 719a.

matter at any given moment — in one word, the reduction of all the phenomena of nature to mechanics.[1]
Über das Ziel der Naturwissenschaften [1865]

CHARLES GODFREY LELAND
1824–1903

Hans Breitmann gife a barty —
Where ish dat barty now?
Hans Breitmann's Barty [1857], st. 6

GEORGE MACDONALD
1824–1905

Corage. God mend al.
His anagram motto

Alas! how easily things go wrong!
A sigh too much or a kiss too long,
And there follows a mist and a weeping rain,
And life is never the same again.
Phantastes [1858]. *Song*

Where did you come from, baby dear?
Out of the everywhere into the here.
At the Back of the North Wind.
Baby, st. 1, 2

They were all looking for a king
To slay their foes and lift them high;
Thou cam'st, a little baby thing
That made a woman cry.
That Holy Thing, st. 1

Said the Wind to the Moon, "I will blow you out!"
The Wind and the Moon, st. 1

There is no feeling in a human heart which exists in that heart alone — which is not, in some form or degree, in every heart.
Unspoken Sermons, second series [1885]

You will be dead so long as you refuse to die.
What's Mine's Mine [1886], ch. 31

[1] Translated by J. B. STALLO.

The world and my being, its life and mine, were one. The microcosm and macrocosm were at length atoned, at length in harmony. I lived in everything; everything entered and lived in me.

Lilith [1895], *ch.* 45

JOHN WHITTAKER WATSON
1824–1890

Oh! the snow, the beautiful snow,
Filling the sky and the earth below.

Beautiful Snow [1869], *st.* 1

HENRY DE LAFAYETTE WEBSTER
1824–1896

The years creep slowly by, Lorena,
The snow is on the grass again.

Lorena, st. 1

WILLIAM ALLEN BUTLER
1825–1902

This same Miss McFlimsey of Madison Square,
The last time we met was in utter despair,
Because she had nothing whatever to wear!

Nothing to Wear [1857], *st.* 3

THOMAS HENRY HUXLEY
1825–1895

I cannot but think that he who finds a certain proportion of pain and evil inseparably woven up in the life of the very worms, will bear his own share with more courage and submission.

On the Educational Value of the Natural History Sciences [1854]

To a person uninstructed in natural history, his country or seaside stroll is a walk through a gallery filled with wonderful works of art, nine-tenths of which have their faces turned to the wall.

On the Educational Value of the Natural History Sciences

Extinguished theologians lie about the cradle of every science as the strangled snakes beside that of Hercules.

Darwiniana. The Origin of Species [1860]

The method of scientific investigation is nothing but the expression of the necessary mode of working of the human mind.

Our Knowledge of the Causes of the Phenomena of Organic Nature [1863]

Let us have "sweet girl graduates" by all means. They will be none the less sweet for a little wisdom; and the "golden hair" will not curl less gracefully outside the head by reason of there being brains within.

Emancipation — Black and White [1865]

For every man the world is as fresh as it was at the first day, and as full of untold novelties for him who has the eyes to see them.

A Liberal Education [1868]

The chess board is the world, the pieces are the phenomena of the universe, the rules of the game are what we call the laws of Nature. The player on the other side is hidden from us. We know that his play is always fair, just, and patient. But also we know, to our cost, that he never overlooks a mistake, or makes the smallest allowance for ignorance. *Ib.*

M. Comte's philosophy in practice might be compendiously described as Catholicism *minus* Christianity.

On the Physical Basis of Life [1868]

If some great Power would agree to make me always think what is true and do what is right, on condition of being turned into a sort of clock and wound up every morning before I got out of bed, I should instantly close with the offer.

> *On Descartes' Discourse on Method [1870]. Method and Results*

There is the greatest practical benefit in making a few failures early in life.

> *On Medical Education* [1870]

That mysterious independent variable of political calculation, Public Opinion.

> *Universities, Actual and Ideal [1874]*

Veracity is the heart of morality.

> *Ib.*

Becky Sharp's acute remark that it is not difficult to be virtuous on ten thousand a year [1] has its application to nations; and it is futile to expect a hungry and squalid population to be anything but violent and gross.

> *Joseph Priestley* [1874]

Logical consequences are the scarecrows of fools and the beacons of wise men. *Animal Automatism* [1874]

Size is not grandeur, and territory does not make a nation.

> *On University Education* [1876]

Perhaps the most valuable result of all education is the ability to make yourself do the thing you have to do, when it ought to be done, whether you like it or not; it is the first lesson that ought to be learned; and however early a man's training begins, it is probably the last lesson that he learns thoroughly.

> *Technical Education* [1877]

The great end of life is not knowledge but action. *Ib.*

If a little knowledge is dangerous, where is the man who has so much as to be out of danger?

> *On Elemental Instruction in Physiology* [1877]

[1] See Thackeray, p. 66a.

Irrationally held truths may be more harmful than reasoned errors.

> *The Coming of Age of The Origin of Species* [1880]

It is the customary fate of new truths to begin as heresies and to end as superstitions. *Ib.*

I asserted — and I repeat — that a man has no reason to be ashamed of having an ape for his grandfather. If there were an ancestor whom I should feel shame in recalling it would rather be a man — a man of restless and versatile intellect — who, not content with an equivocal success in his own sphere of activity, plunges into scientific questions with which he has no real acquaintance, only to obscure them by an aimless rhetoric, and distract the attention of his hearers from the real point at issue by eloquent digressions and skilled appeals to religious prejudice.

> *Reply to Wilberforces's question.[1] From* LEONARD HUXLEY, *Life and Letters of Thomas Henry Huxley* [1900], *vol. I*

GEORGE EDWARD PICKETT
1825–1875

Up, men, and to your posts! Don't forget today that you are from Old Virginia.

> *Command at the beginning of his division's charge at Gettysburg [July 3, 1863]*

ADELAIDE ANNE PROCTER
1825–1864

Seated one day at the organ,
  I was weary and ill at ease,
And my fingers wandered idly
  Over the noisy keys.

> *A Lost Chord, st. 1*

[1] If anyone were to be willing to trace his descent through an ape as his *grandfather,* would he be willing to trace his descent similarly on the side of his *grandmother?* — BISHOP SAMUEL WILBERFORCE [1805–1873], at the British Association for the Advancement of Science [1860]

But I struck one chord of music
Like the sound of a great Amen.
A Lost Chord, st. 2

BAYARD TAYLOR
1825–1878

Till the sun grows cold,
And the stars are old,
And the leaves of the Judgment Book
unfold.
Bedouin Song, refrain

They sang of love, and not of fame;
  Forgot was Britain's glory;
Each heart recalled a different name,
  But all sang "Annie Laurie."
The Song of the Camp, st. 5

WILLIAM WHITING
1825–1878

Eternal Father, strong to save,
Whose arm doth bind the restless
  wave,
Who bidd'st the mighty ocean deep
Its own appointed limits keep,
O, hear us when we cry to Thee
For those in peril on the sea!
*The Hymn of the U.S. Navy
[1860], Eternal Father, Strong
to Save, st. 1*

CHARLES HAMILTON
AÏDÉ
1826–1906

I sit beside my lonely fire
  And pray for wisdom yet:
For calmness to remember
  Or courage to forget.
Remember or Forget

GROSS HERZOG
FRIEDRICH VON BADEN
1826–1907

Unity makes strength, and, since we
must be strong, we must also be one.
*On German unity under Prus-
sian hegemony, Versailles [Janu-
ary 18, 1871]*

WALTER BAGEHOT
1826–1877

To a great experience one thing is
essential — an experiencing nature.
Literary Studies. Shakespeare
[1853]

The reason why so few good books
are written is, that so few people that
can write know anything. In general an
author has always lived in a room, has
read books, has cultivated science, is acquainted with the style and sentiments
of the best authors, but he is out of the
way of employing his own eyes and
ears. He has nothing to hear and nothing to see. His life is a vacuum.   *Ib.*

A constitutional statesman is in general a man of common opinions and
uncommon abilities.
*Biographical Studies. The Char-
acter of Sir Robert Peel [1856]*

It is good to be without vices, but it
is not good to be without temptations.
Ib. Sir George Cornewall Lewis
[1863]

[Of Guizot] A Puritan born in
France by mistake.
Ib. M. Guizot [1874]

One of the greatest pains to human
nature is the pain of a new idea.
Physics and Politics [1869], ch. 5

An inability to stay quiet . . . is one
of the most conspicuous failings of
mankind.[1]   *Ib.*

The most melancholy of human reflections, perhaps, is that on the whole
it is a question whether the benevolence
of mankind does most good or harm.
Ib.

The best reason why monarchy is a
strong government is, that it is an intelligible government: the mass of mankind understand it, and they hardly
anywhere in the world understand any
other.
*The English Constitution
[1872]. The Monarchy*

[1] See Pascal, p. 363b; quoted by Bagehot in
the same chapter.

But of all nations in the world, the English are perhaps the least a nation of pure philosophers.

> *The English Constitution.*
> *The Monarchy*

G. W. HUNT
fl. 1878

We don't want to fight, but, by jingo, if we do,
We've got the ships, we've got the men, we've got the money, too.
We've fought the Bear before, and while Britons shall be true,
The Russians shall not have Constantinople.   *Song* [1] *[1878]*

DINAH MARIA MULOCK CRAIK
1826–1887

Douglas, Douglas, tender and true!
> *Douglas, Tender and True,* [2]
> *refrain*

Oh, my son's my son till he gets him a wife,
But my daughter's my daughter all her life.   *Young and Old*

JOHN ELLERTON
1826–1893

Now the laborer's task is o'er;
Now the battle day is past;
Now upon the farther shore
Lands the voyager at last.
> *Hymn, st. 1*

Father, in Thy gracious keeping
Leave we now Thy servant sleeping.
> *Ib. refrain*

---

[1] Sung by Gilbert Hastings Macdermott (Farrell) [1845–1901], "the great Macdermott." The song gave the terms "jingo" and "jingoism" to the political vocabulary, though the phrase "by jingo" had been used earlier by Goldsmith and Thomas Hood.

[2] O Douglas, O Douglas!
Tendir and trewe!
> Sir Richard Holland, *The Buke of the Howlat* [c. 1450], *st. 31*

STEPHEN COLLINS FOSTER
1826–1864

Weep no more, my lady,
Oh! weep no more today!
We will sing one song for the old Kentucky home,
For the old Kentucky home far away.
> *My Old Kentucky Home, chorus*

Way down upon the Swanee River,
Far, far away,
There's where my heart is turning ever;
There's where the old folks stay.
> *The Old Folks at Home, st. 1*

All the world is sad and dreary
Ev'rywhere I roam,
Oh! darkies, how my heart grows weary,
Far from the old folks at home.
> *Ib. chorus*

Down in de cornfield
Hear dat mournful sound:
All de darkies am a-weeping —
Massa's in de cold, cold ground.
> *Massa's in de Cold, Cold*
> *Ground, st. 1*

He's gone whar de good niggers go.
> *Uncle Ned, last stanza*

I'm coming, I'm coming, for my head is bending low;
I hear those gentle voices calling, "Old Black Joe."
> *Old Black Joe, st. 3*

O, Susanna! O, don't you cry for me,
I've come from Alabama, wid my banjo on my knee.
> *O, Susanna,* [1] *chorus*

Gwine to run all night!
Gwine to run all day!
I'll bet my money on de bobtail nag —
Somebody bet on de bay.
> *Camptown Races, chorus*

I dream of Jeanie with the light brown hair,

---

[1] Sung for the first time by Nelson Kneass in Andrews' Eagle Ice Cream Saloon, Pittsburgh, Pennsylvania [September 11, 1847]. It shortly became a world-wide hit.

Floating, like a vapor, on the soft summer air.
> *Jeanie with the Light Brown*
> *Hair, st. 1*

Beautiful dreamer, wake unto me,
Starlight and dewdrop are waiting for
thee.
> *Beautiful Dreamer, st. 1*

GEORGE BRINTON McCLELLAN
1826–1885

All quiet along the Potomac.[1]
> *Frequent report from his Union*
> *headquarters* [1861]

EDWARD STUYVESANT BRAGG
1827–1912

They love him most for the enemies
he has made.[2]
> *Speech seconding presidential*
> *nomination of Grover Cleveland*
> [*July 9, 1884*]

MORTIMER COLLINS
1827–1876

A man is as old as he's feeling,
A woman as old as she looks.
> *The Unknown Quantity*

ALICE HAWTHORNE [SEPTIMUS WINNER]
1827–1902

Listen to the mockingbird, listen to the
mockingbird,
Still singing where the weeping willows
wave.
> *Listen to the Mockingbird* [1855]

[1] All quiet along the Potomac tonight,
No sound save the rush of the river,
While soft falls the dew on the face of the
dead —
The picket's off duty forever.
ETHEL LYNN BEERS [1827–1879], *The
Picket Guard* [1861], *st. 6*
[2] An adaptation of Governor Bragg's expres-
sion became a Cleveland campaign slogan: "We
love him for the enemies he has made."

CHARLES ELIOT NORTON
1827–1908

I think that a knowledge of Greek
thought and life, and of the arts in
which the Greeks expressed their
thought and sentiment, is essential to
high culture. A man may know everything else, but without this knowledge
he remains ignorant of the best intellectual and moral achievements of his own
race.   *Letter to F. A. Tupper* [1885]

Whatever your occupation may be
and however crowded your hours with
affairs, do not fail to secure at least a
few minutes every day for refreshment
of your inner life with a bit of poetry.
> *Used by a Boston newspaper as*
> *a heading for a column of re-*
> *printed poems*

The voice of protest, of warning, of
appeal is never more needed than when
the clamor of fife and drum, echoed by
the press and too often by the pulpit, is
bidding all men fall in and keep step
and obey in silence the tyrannous word
of command. Then, more than ever, it
is the duty of the good citizen not to be
silent.   *True Patriotism* [1898]

The old America, the America of our
hopes and our dreams, has come to an
end, and a new America is entering on
the false course which has been tried so
often and which has often led to calamity. This war will in the long run result
in far more evil to the United States
than to Spain. We shall nominally win,
but at the cost of what infinite loss!
> *Letter to Edward Lee-Childe*
> [1898]

LEW [LEWIS] WALLACE
1827–1905

A man is never so on trial as in
the moment of excessive good fortune.
> *Ben Hur: A Tale of the Christ*
> [1880], *bk. V, ch. 7*

Would you hurt a man keenest,
strike at his self-love.   *Ib. VI, 2*

Beauty is altogether in the eye of the beholder.[1]

> *The Prince of India* [1893],
> *bk. III, ch. 6*

WILLIAM ALLINGHAM
1828–1889

Up the airy mountain,
  Down the rushy glen,
We daren't go a-hunting
  For fear of little men.

> *The Fairies, st. 1*

Four ducks on a pond,
A grass bank beyond,
A blue sky of spring,
White clouds on the wing;
What a little thing
To remember for years —
To remember with tears!

> *Four Ducks on a Pond*

HENRIK IBSEN
1828–1906

All or nothing.   *Brand* [1866]

Out yonder under the skies, men have a common saying: "Man, to thyself be true!" But here, 'mongst Trolls, "Troll, to thyself be — enough!" it runs.

> *Peer Gynt* [1867], *act I*

Go round about, Peer! Room enough on the mountain.   *Ib.*

Look into any man's heart you please, and you will always find, in every one, at least one black spot which he has to keep concealed.

> *Pillars of Society* [1877], *act III*

The spirit of truth and the spirit of freedom — they are the pillars of society.   *Ib. IV*

There can be no freedom or beauty about a home life that depends on borrowing and debt.

> *A Doll's House* [1879], *act I*

To crave for happiness in this world is simply to be possessed by a spirit of revolt. What right have we to happiness?   *Ghosts* [1881], *act I*

I am half inclined to think we are all ghosts, Mr. Manders. It is not only what we have inherited from our fathers that exists again in us, but all sorts of old dead ideas and all kinds of old dead beliefs and things of that kind. They are not actually alive in us; but there they are dormant, all the same, and we can never be rid of them. Whenever I take up a newspaper and read it, I fancy I see ghosts creeping between the lines. There must be ghosts all over the world. They must be as countless as grains of the sands, it seems to me. And we are so miserably afraid of the light, all of us.   *Ib. II*

Mother, give me the sun.   *Ib. III*

I hold that man is in the right who is most closely in league with the future.

> *Letter to Georg Brandes* [*January 3, 1882*]

A community is like a ship; everyone ought to be prepared to take the helm.

> *An Enemy of the People* [1882],
> *act I*

The minority is always right.   *Ib. IV*

You should never wear your best trousers when you go out to fight for freedom and truth.   *Ib. V*

The strongest man in the world is he who stands most alone.[1]   *Ib.*

Rob the average man of his life illusion, and you rob him of his happiness at the same stroke.

> *The Wild Duck* [1884], *act V*

Vine leaves in his hair.

> *Hedda Gabler* [1890], *act II*

The younger generation will come knocking at my door.

> *The Master Builder* [1892], *act I*

---

[1] See Hume, p. 434b, and Hungerford, p. 831b.

[1] See Browning, p. 662a.

GEORGE MEREDITH
1828–1909

I expect that Woman will be the last thing civilized by Man.
> *The Ordeal of Richard Feverel*
> [1859], *ch. 1*

Who rises from prayer a better man, his prayer is answered. *Ib. 12*

The sun is coming down to earth, and the fields and the waters shout to him golden shouts. *Ib. 19*

Kissing don't last; cookery do!
> *Ib. 28*

See ye not, courtesy
Is the true alchemy,
Turning to gold all it touches and tries?
> *The Song of Courtesy*
> [1859], *IV*

I've studied men from my topsy-turvy
  Close, and, I reckon, rather true.
Some are fine fellows: some, right scurvy:
Most, a dash between the two.
> *Juggling Jerry* [1859], *VII*

Two of a trade, lass, never agree.[1]
> *Ib. IX*

Not till the fire is dying in the grate,
Look we for any kinship with the stars.
Oh, wisdom never comes when it is gold,
And the great price we pay for it full worth;
We have it only when we are half earth.
> *Modern Love* [1862], *IV*

And if I drink oblivion of a day,
So shorten I the stature of my soul.
> *Ib. XII*

That rarest gift
To Beauty, common sense.
> *Ib. XXXII*

In tragic life, God wot,
No villain need be! Passions spin the plot:
We are betrayed by what is false within. *Ib. XLIII*

[1] See Hesiod, p. 67b.

Their sense is with their senses all mixed in,
Destroyed by subtleties these women are! *Modern Love, XLVIII*

Ah, what a dusty answer gets the soul
When hot for certainties in this our life! *Ib. L*

Into the breast that gives the rose
Shall I with shuddering fall?
> *The Spirit of Earth in Autumn*
> [1862], *st. 1*

Cynicism is intellectual dandyism.
> *The Egoist* [1879], *ch. 7*

In . . . the book of Egoism, it is written, possession without obligation to the object possessed approaches felicity. *Ib. 14*

On a starred night Prince Lucifer uprose.
Tired of his dark dominion swung the fiend.
> *Lucifer in Starlight* [1883]

Around the ancient track marched, rank on rank,
The army of unalterable law. *Ib.*

Enter these enchanted woods,
You who dare.
> *The Woods of Westermain*
> [1883], *st. 1*

She whom I love is hard to catch and conquer,
Hard, but O the glory of the winning were she won!
> *Love in the Valley* [1883], *st. 2*

Darker grows the valley, more and more forgetting:
So were it with me if forgetting could be willed.
Tell the grassy hollow that holds the bubbling well-spring,
Tell it to forget the source that keeps it filled. *Ib. st. 5*

Love that so desires would fain keep her changeless;
Fain would fling the net, and fain have her free. *Ib. st. 6*

Thence had he the laugh . . .
Broad as ten thousand beeves
At pasture.
　　　The Spirit of Shakespeare [1883]

Civil limitation daunts
His utterance never; the nymphs blush,
　　not he.
　　　An Orson of the Muse [*Walt*
　　　　　Whitman] [1883]

A witty woman is a treasure; a witty
beauty is a power.
　　　Diana of the Crossways [1885],
　　　　　　　　ch. 1

The well of true wit is truth itself.
　　　　　　　　　Ib.

Ireland gives England her soldiers,
her generals too.　　　　　*Ib. 2*

With patient inattention hear him
prate.
　　　Bellerophon [1887], *st. 4*

Full lasting is the song, though he,
The singer, passes.
　　　The Thrush in February [1888],
　　　　　　　　st. 17

Cannon his name,
Cannon his voice, he came.
　　　Napoléon [1891], *I*

DANTE GABRIEL ROSSETTI
1828–1882

The blessed damozel leaned out
　From the gold bar of Heaven;
Her eyes were deeper than the depth
　Of waters stilled at even;
She had three lilies in her hand,
And the stars in her hair were seven.
　　　The Blessed Damozel [1850],
　　　　　　　　st. 1

And the souls mounting up to God
Went by her like thin flames.
　　　　　　　　Ib. st. 7

The Stealthy School of Criticism.
　　Letter to the Athenaeum [1871]

I have been here before,
　But when or how I cannot tell;
I know the grass beyond the door,

The sweet keen smell,
The sighing sound, the lights around
　the shore.
　　　Sudden Light [1881], *st. 1*

Still we say as we go —
　"Strange to think by the way,
Whatever there is to know,
　That shall we know one day."
　　　The Cloud Confines [1881], *st. 1*

Was it a friend or foe that spread these
　lies?
Nay, who but infants question in such
　wise?
'Twas one of my most intimate ene-
　mies.　　　*Fragment* [1881]

A　sonnet　is　a　moment's　monu-
　ment —
Memorial from the soul's eternity
To one dead deathless hour.
　　　Sonnets from the House of
　　　　　Life [1881]. *Proem*

And though thy soul sail leagues and
　leagues beyond —
Still, leagues beyond those leagues,
　there is more sea.
　　　Ib. no. 73. The Choice — III

My name is Might-have-been;
I am also called No-more, Too-late,
　Farewell.
　　　Ib. no. 97. A Superscription

LEO NIKOLAEVICH TOLSTOI[1]
1828–1910

"What's this? am I falling? my legs
are giving way under me," he thought,
and fell on his back. He opened his
eyes, hoping to see how the struggle of
the French soldiers with the artilleryman was ending, and eager to know

[1] Of course you have read Tolstoi's *War and
Peace* and *Anna Karenina*. I never had that
exquisite felicity before the summer, and now
I feel as if I knew the *perfection* in the representation of human life. Life indeed seems less
real than his tale of it. Such infallible veracity!
The impression haunts me as nothing literary
ever haunted me before. — WILLIAM JAMES,
letter to Henry James [1872], *Letters of William
James, vol. II* [1896], *p. 48*

whether the red-haired artilleryman was killed or not, whether the cannons had been taken or saved. But he saw nothing of all that. Above him there was nothing but the sky — the lofty sky, not clear, but still immeasurably lofty, with gray clouds creeping quietly over it.

War and Peace [1865–1869],[1]
pt. III, ch. 16

Three days afterwards the little princess was buried, and Prince Andrey went to the steps of the tomb to take his last farewell of her. Even in the coffin the face was the same, though the eyes were closed. "Ah, what have you done to me?" it still seemed to say.   *Ib. IV, 9*

In historical events great men — so called — are but the labels that serve to give a name to an event, and like labels, they have the least possible connection with the event itself. Every action of theirs, that seems to them an act of their own free will, is in an historical sense not free at all, but in bondage to the whole course of previous history, and predestined from all eternity.

Ib. IX, 1

He [Platon Karataev] did not understand, and could not grasp the significance of words taken apart from the sentence. Every word and every action of his was the expression of a force uncomprehended by him, which was his life.   *Ib. XII, 13*

For us, with the rule of right and wrong given us by Christ, there is nothing for which we have no standard. And there is no greatness where there is not simplicity, goodness, and truth.

Ib. XIV, 18

The subject of history is the life of peoples and of humanity. To catch and pin down in words — that is, to describe directly the life, not only of hu-

manity, but even of a single people, appears to be impossible.[1]

War and Peace, epilogue,
pt. II, ch. 1

Happy families are all alike; every unhappy family is unhappy in its own way.

Anna Karenina [1875–1877],
pt. I, ch. 1

Ivan Ilych's life had been most simple and most ordinary and therefore most terrible.

The Death of Ivan Ilych [2]
[1886]

Ivan Ilych saw that he was dying, and he was in continuous despair.

In the depth of his heart he knew he was dying, but not only was he not accustomed to the thought, he simply did not and could not grasp it.

The syllogism he had learned from Kiezewetter's Logic: "Caius is a man, men are mortal, therefore Caius is mortal," had always seemed to him correct as applied to Caius, but certainly not as applied to himself. That Caius — man in the abstract — was mortal, was perfectly correct, but he was not Caius, not an abstract man, but a creature quite, quite separate from all others.

Ib.

Six feet of land was all that he needed.

How Much Land Does a Man
Need? [1886]

The more is given the less the people will work for themselves, and the less they work the more their poverty will increase.[3]

Help for the Starving, pt. III
[January 1892]

Art is a human activity having for its purpose the transmission to others of the highest and best feelings to which men have risen.

What Is Art? [1898], *ch. 8*

---

[1] See Francis Parkman, p. 721a.
[2] Translated by AYLMER MAUDE.
[3] If you stop supporting that crowd, it will support itself. — SENECA [8 B.C.–A.D. 65], *Epistle*
20, 7

---

[1] Translated by CONSTANCE GARNETT.

ROSCOE CONKLING
1829–1888

He will hew to the line of right, let the chips fall where they may.

> *Speech nominating General Grant for a third term as President, Chicago [June 5, 1880]*

CARL SCHURZ
1829–1906

Ideals are like stars; you will not succeed in touching them with your hands. But like the seafaring man on the desert of waters, you choose them as your guides, and following them you will reach your destiny.[1]

> *Address, Faneuil Hall, Boston [April 18, 1859]*

I will make a prophecy that may now sound peculiar. In fifty years Lincoln's name will be inscribed close to Washington's on this Republic's roll of honor.

> *Letter to Theodore Petrasch [October 12, 1864]*

Our country, right or wrong.[2] When right, to be kept right; when wrong, to be put right.

> *Address, Anti-Imperialistic Conference, Chicago [October 17, 1899]*

CHARLES DUDLEY WARNER[3]
1829–1900

To own a bit of ground, to scratch it with a hoe, to plant seeds, and watch the renewal of life — this is the commonest delight of the race, the most satisfactory thing a man can do.

> *My Summer in a Garden [1870]. Preliminary*

Broad acres are a patent of nobility; and no man but feels more of a man in the world if he have a bit of ground that he can call his own. However small it is on the surface, it is four thousand miles deep; and that is a very handsome property.

> *My Summer in a Garden. Preliminary*

What a man needs in gardening is a cast-iron back, with a hinge in it.

> *Ib. Third Week*

The toad, without which no garden would be complete.

> *Ib. Thirteenth Week*

Politics makes strange bedfellows.

> *Ib. Fifteenth Week*

What small potatoes we all are, compared with what we might be! *Ib.*

Public opinion is stronger than the legislature, and nearly as strong as the Ten Commandments.

> *Ib. Sixteenth Week*

The thing generally raised on city land is taxes. *Ib.*

Everybody talks about the weather, but nobody does anything about it.[1]

> *Editorial, The Hartford Courant [August 24, 1897]*

CHARLOTTE ALINGTON BARNARD ["CLARIBEL"]
1830–1869

I cannot sing the old songs I sang long years ago.

> *I Cannot Sing the Old Songs [2]*

Take back the heart that thou gavest,
What is my anguish to thee?
Take back the freedom thou cravest,
Leaving the fetters to me.

> *Take Back the Heart*

---

[1] See Emerson, p. 608b.

[2] See Charles Churchill, p. 456a.

[3] Warner collaborated with Mark Twain on *The Gilded Age*. See p. 759a.

[1] The phrase is commonly attributed to Mark Twain, but the *Hartford Courant* has the exact statement in the aforementioned editorial, which is of course unsigned. Warner was associate editor of the paper (1867–1900). See Mark Twain, p. 759b.

[2] I cannot sing the old songs now!
It is not that I deem them low;
'Tis that I can't remember how
They go.
> C. S. CALVERLEY [1831–1884], *Changed*

THOMAS EDWARD BROWN
1830–1897

A Garden is a lovesome thing, God wot!
My Garden

Not God! in Gardens! when the eve is
cool?
Nay, but I have a sign:
'Tis very sure God walks in mine.
Ib.

PORFIRIO DÍAZ
1830–1915

Poor Mexico, so far from God and so
close to the United States.
Attributed

EMILY DICKINSON[1]
1830–1886

I never lost as much but twice,
And that was in the sod.
Twice have I stood a beggar
Before the door of God!

Angels – twice descending
Reimbursed my store –
Burglar! Banker! – Father!
I am poor once more!
No. 49 [*c. 1858*]

Surgeons must be very careful
When they take the knife!
Underneath their fine incisions
Stirs the Culprit – *Life!*
No. 108 [*c. 1859*]

Our share of night to bear –
Our share of morning –
Our blank in bliss to fill
Our blank in scorning –

Here a star, and there a star,
Some lose their way!
Here a mist, and there a mist,
Afterwards – Day!
No. 113 [*c. 1859*]

For each ecstatic instant
We must an anguish pay

[1] *The Complete Poems of Emily Dickinson*,
edited by Thomas H. Johnson [1960]. Dates are
of composition, not publication.

In keen and quivering ratio
To the ecstasy.
No. 125 [*c. 1859*], *st. 1*

To fight aloud, is very brave —
But *gallanter,* I know
Who charge within the bosom
The Cavalry of Woe –
No. 126 [*c. 1859*], *st. 1*

Who counts the wampum of the night
To see that none is due?
No. 128 [*c. 1859*], *st. 3*

These are the days when Birds come
back –
A very few – a Bird or two –
To take a backward look.

These are the days when skies resume
The old – old sophistries of June –
A blue and gold mistake.
No. 130 [*c. 1859*], *st. 1, 2*

Oh Sacrament of summer days,
Oh Last Communion in the Haze –
Permit a child to join.

Thy sacred emblems to partake –
Thy consecrated bread to take
And thine immortal wine!
Ib. st. 5, 6

Besides the Autumn poets sing
A few prosaic days
A little this side of the snow
And that side of the Haze –
No. 131 [*c. 1859*], *st. 1*

Just lost when I was saved!
Just felt the world go by!
Just girt me for the onset with Eternity,
When breath blew back,
And on the other side
I heard recede the disappointed tide!
No. 160 [*c. 1860*], *st. 1*

The thought beneath so slight a film –
Is more distinctly seen –
As laces just reveal the surge –
Or Mists – the Apennine –
No. 210 [*c. 1860*]

I taste a liquor never brewed,
From Tankards scooped in Pearl –
No. 214 [*c. 1860*], *st. 1*

Inebriate of Air – am I –
And Debauchee of Dew –
Reeling – through endless summer days –
From inns of Molten Blue –
         No. 214, st. 2

Till Seraphs swing their snowy Hats –
And Saints – to windows run –
To see the little Tippler
Leaning against the – Sun –
         Ib. st. 4

"Hope" is the thing with feathers –
That perches in the soul –
And sings the tune without the words –
And never stops – at all –
         No. 254 [c. 1861], st. 1

There's a certain Slant of light,
Winter Afternoons –
That oppresses, like the Heft
Of Cathedral Tunes –
         No. 258 [c. 1861], st. 1

I'm Nobody! Who are you?
Are you – Nobody – too?
Then there's a pair of us!
Don't tell! they'd advertise – you know!

How dreary – to be – Somebody!
How public – like a Frog –
To tell one's name – the livelong June –
To an admiring Bog!
         No. 288 [c. 1861]

I tasted – careless – then –
I did not know the Wine
Came once a World – Did you?
Oh, had you told me so –
This Thirst would blister – easier – now –
         No. 296 [c. 1861], st. 3

The Soul selects her own Society –
Then – shuts the Door –
To her divine Majority –
Present no more –
         No. 303 [c. 1862], st. 1

I'll tell you how the Sun rose –
A Ribbon at a time –

The Steeples swam in Amethyst –
The news, like Squirrels, ran.
         No. 318 [1862]

Some keep the Sabbath going to Church –
I keep it, staying at Home –
With a bobolink for a Chorister –
And an Orchard, for a Dome –
         No. 324 [1862], st. 1

So instead of getting to Heaven, at last –
I'm going, all along.   *Ib. st. 3*

After great pain, a formal feeling comes.
         No. 341 [c. 1862], st. 1

Of Course – I prayed –
And did God Care?
He cared as much as on the Air
A Bird – had stamped her foot –
And cried "Give Me" –
         No. 376 [c. 1862]

No Rack can torture me –
My Soul – at Liberty –
Behind this mortal Bone
There knits a bolder One –
         No. 384 [c. 1862], st. 1

Except Thyself may be
Thine Enemy –
Captivity is Consciousness –
So's Liberty.   *Ib. st. 4*

Much Madness is divinest Sense –
To a discerning Eye –
Much Sense – the starkest Madness –
'Tis the Majority
In this, as All, prevail –
Assent – and you are sane –
Demur – you're straightway dangerous –
And handled with a Chain.
         No. 435 [c. 1862]

The Wind – tapped like a tired Man.
         No. 436 [c. 1862], st. 1

This is my letter to the World
That never wrote to Me –
The simple News that Nature told –
With tender Majesty.
         No. 441 [c. 1862], st. 1

I died for Beauty – but was scarce
Adjusted in the Tomb
When One who died for Truth, was
      lain
In an adjoining Room –
            No. 449 [*c. 1862*], *st. 1*

And so, as Kinsmen, met a Night –
We talked between the Rooms –
Until the Moss had reached our lips –
And covered up – our names –
                  Ib. st. 3

It was not Death, for I stood up,
And all the Dead, lie down –
            No. 510 [*c. 1862*], *st. 1*

It was not Frost, for on my Flesh
I felt Siroccos – crawl –   *Ib. st. 2*

I reckon – when I count at all –
First – Poets – Then the Sun –
Then Summer – Then the Heaven of
      God –
And then – the List is done –

But, looking back – the First so seems
To Comprehend the Whole –
The Others look a needless Show –
So I write – Poets – All –
            No. 569 [*c. 1862*], *st. 1, 2*

I like to see it lap the Miles –
And lick the Valleys up –
            No. 585 [*c. 1862*], *st. 1*

And neigh like Boanerges –
Then punctual as a Star
Stop – docile and omnipotent
At its own stable door –   *Ib. st. 4*

Afraid! Of whom am I afraid?
Not Death – for who is He?
The Porter of my Father's Lodge
As much abasheth me!
            No. 608 [*c. 1862*], *st. 1*

I asked no other thing –
No other – was denied –
I offered Being – for it –
The Mighty Merchant sneered —

Brazil? He twirled a Button –
Without a glance my way –
"But – Madam – is there nothing else –
That We can show – Today?"
            No. 621 [*c. 1862*]

The Brain – is wider than the Sky –
For – put them side by side –
The one the other will contain
With ease – and You – beside.
            No. 632 [*1862*], *st. 1*

I cannot live with You –
It would be Life –
And Life is over there –
Behind the Shelf.
            No. 640 [*c. 1862*], *st. 1*

And that White Sustenance –
Despair –   *Ib. st. 12*

Pain – has an Element of Blank –
It cannot recollect
When it begun – or if there were
A time when it was not –
            No. 650 [*c. 1862*], *st. 1*

I dwell in Possibility –
A fairer House than Prose –
More numerous of Windows –
Superior – for Doors.
            No. 657 [*c. 1862*], *st. 1*

The Soul unto itself
Is an imperial friend –
Or the most agonizing Spy –
An Enemy – could send –
            No. 683 [*c. 1862*], *st. 1*

Because I could not stop for Death,
He kindly stopped for me –
The Carriage held but just Ourselves
And Immortality.
            No. 712 [*c. 1863*], *st. 1*

Alter! When the Hills do –
Falter! When the Sun
Question if His Glory
Be the Perfect One –

Surfeit! When the Daffodil
Doth of the Dew –
Even as Herself – Sir –
I will – of You –   *No. 729* [*c. 1863*]

God gave a Loaf to every Bird –
But just a Crumb – to Me –
            No. 791 [*c. 1863*], *st. 1*

This quiet Dust was Gentlemen and
      Ladies
And Lads and Girls – [1]

[1] See Shakespeare, p. 291a.

Was laughter and ability and Sighing,
And Frocks and Curls.
        No. 813 [c. 1864], st. 1

Adventure most unto itself
The Soul condemned to be –
Attended by a single Hound
Its own identity.
        No. 822 [c. 1864], st. 4

Dying! To be afraid of thee
One must to thine Artillery
Have left exposed a Friend –
Than thine old Arrow is a Shot
Delivered straighter to the Heart
The leaving Love behind.
        No. 831 [c. 1864], st. 1

Truth – is as old as God –
His Twin identity
And will endure as long as He
A Co-Eternity –
        No. 836 [c. 1864], st. 1

The Poets light but Lamps –
Themselves – go out –
The Wicks they stimulate –
If vital Light

Inhere as do the Suns –
Each Age a Lens
Disseminating their
Circumference –   *No. 883 [c. 1864]*

Love – is anterior to Life –
Posterior – to Death –
Initial of Creation, and
The Exponent of Earth.
        No. 917 [c. 1864]

If I can stop one Heart from breaking
I shall not live in vain
If I can ease one Life the Aching
Or cool one Pain

Or help one fainting Robin
Unto his Nest again
I shall not live in Vain.
        No. 919 [c. 1864]

Partake as doth the Bee
Abstemiously.
The Rose is an Estate –
In Sicily.   *No. 994 [c. 1865]*

Too scanty 'twas to die for you,
The merest Greek could that.

The living, Sweet, is costlier –
I offer even that –

The Dying, is a trifle, past
But living, this include
The dying multifold – without
The Respite to be dead.
        No. 1013 [c. 1865]

'Twas my one Glory –
Let it be
Remembered
I was owned of Thee –
        No. 1028 [c. 1865]

I never saw a Moor –
I never saw the Sea –
Yet know I how the Heather looks
And what a Billow be.

I never spoke with God
Nor visited in Heaven –
Yet certain am I of the spot
As if the Checks were given –
        No. 1052 [c. 1865]

Not to discover weakness is
The Artifice of strength –
        No. 1054 [c. 1865], st. 1

Experiment to me
Is every one I meet
If it contain a Kernel?
The Figure of a Nut

Presents upon a Tree
Equally plausibly,
But Meat within, is requisite
To Squirrels, and to Me.
        No. 1073 [c. 1865]

Nature, like Us is sometimes caught
Without her Diadem.
        No. 1075 [c. 1866], st. 2

The Sweeping up the Heart,
And putting Love away
We shall not want to use again
Until Eternity.
        No. 1078 [c. 1866], st. 2

We never know how high we are
Till we are called to rise
And then, if we are true to plan
Our statures touch the skies.[1]
        No. 1176 [c. 1870], st. 1

[1] See William James, p. 792b.

A word is dead
When it is said,
Some say.
I say it just
Begins to live
That day.   No. 1212 [c. 1872]

There is no Frigate like a Book
To take us Lands away
Nor any Coursers like a Page
Of prancing Poetry –
This Traverse may the poorest take
Without oppress of Toll –
How frugal is the Chariot
That bears the Human Soul!   No. 1263 [c. 1873]

I thought that nature was enough
Till Human nature came
But that the other did absorb
As Parallax a Flame –   No. 1286 [c. 1873], st. 1

Until the Desert knows
That Water grows
His Sands suffice
But let him once suspect
That Caspian Fact
Sahara dies.   No. 1291 [c. 1873], st. 1

Not with a Club, the Heart is broken
Nor with a Stone –
A Whip so small you could not see it
I've known
To lash the Magic Creature
Till it fell.   No. 1304 [c. 1874], st. 1

That short – potential stir
That each can make but once –
That Bustle so illustrious
'Tis almost Consequence –

Is the éclat of Death.
Oh, thou unknown Renown
That not a Beggar would accept
Had he the power to spurn –   No. 1307 [c. 1874]

A little Madness in the Spring
Is wholesome even for the King.   No. 1333 [c. 1875]

Love's stricken "why"
Is all that love can speak –

Built of but just a syllable
The hugest hearts that break.   No. 1368 [c. 1876]

Bees are Black, with Gilt Surcingles –
Buccaneers of Buzz.   No. 1405 [c. 1877], st. 1

A Route of Evanescence
With a revolving Wheel –
A Resonance of Emerald –
A Rush of Cochineal –
And every Blossom on the Bush
Adjusts its tumbled Head –
The mail from Tunis, probably,
An easy Morning's ride.   No. 1463 [c. 1879]

He ate and drank the precious Words –
His Spirit grew robust –
He knew no more that he was poor,
Nor that his frame was Dust –

He danced along the dingy Days
And this Request of Wings
Was but a Book – What Liberty
A loosened spirit brings –   No. 1587 [c. 1883]

The Pedigree of Honey
Does not concern the Bee –
A Clover, any time, to him,
Is Aristocracy.   No. 1627 [c. 1884], version II

A Drunkard cannot meet a Cork
Without a Revery –
And so encountering a Fly
This January Day
Jamaicas of Remembrance stir
That send me reeling in.   No. 1628 [c. 1884]

Beauty crowds me till I die
Beauty mercy have on me
But if I expire today
Let it be in sight of thee –   No. 1654 [n.d.]

Eden is that old-fashioned House
We dwell in every day
Without suspecting our abode
Until we drive away.   No. 1657 [n.d.], st. 1

Glory is that bright tragic thing
That for an instant
Means Dominion –
Warms some poor name
That never felt the Sun,
Gently replacing
In oblivion –   *No. 1660 [n.d.]*

I took one Draught of Life –
I'll tell you what I paid –
Precisely an existence –
The market price, they said.

They weighed me, Dust by Dust –
They balanced Film with Film,
Then handed me my Being's worth –
A single Dram of Heaven!
     No. 1725 [n.d.]

My life closed twice before its close –
It yet remains to see
If Immortality unveil
A third event to me

So huge, so hopeless to conceive
As these that twice befell.
Parting is all we know of heaven,
And all we need of hell.
     No. 1732 [n.d.]

That it will never come again
Is what makes life so sweet.
     No. 1741 [n.d.], st. 1

To make a prairie it takes a clover and
    one bee,
One clover, and a bee,
And revery.
The revery alone will do,
If bees are few.   *No. 1755 [n.d.]*

Elysium is as far as to
The very nearest Room
If in that Room a Friend await
Felicity or Doom –

What Fortitude the Soul contains,
That it can so endure
The accent of a coming Foot –
The opening of a Door –
     No. 1760 [n.d.]

That Love is all there is,
Is all we know of Love;

It is enough, the freight should be
Proportioned to the groove.
     No. 1765 [n.d.]

If I read a book and it makes my
whole body so cold no fire can ever
warm me, I know that is poetry. If I
feel physically as if the top of my head
were taken off, I know that is poetry.
These are the only ways I know it. Is
there any other way?
     From Martha Gilbert Dick-
inson Bianchi, *Life and Letters
of Emily Dickinson* [1924]

CHRISTINA GEORGINA ROSSETTI
1830–1894

Who has seen the wind?
   Neither you nor I:
But when the trees bow down their
   heads,
   The wind is passing by.
     Who Has Seen the Wind?, st. 2

Does the road wind up-hill all the
   way?
Yes, to the very end.
Will the day's journey take the whole
   long day?
From morn to night, my friend.
     Up-Hill [1861], st. 1

My heart is like a singing bird.
     A Birthday [1861], st. 1

The birthday of my life
Is come, my love is come to me.
     Ib. st. 2

When I am dead, my dearest,
   Sing no sad songs for me;
Plant thou no roses at my head,
   Nor shady cypress tree.
Be the green grass above me
   With showers and dewdrops wet;
And if thou wilt, remember
   And if thou wilt, forget.
     Song [1862], st. 1

Remember me when I am gone away,
Gone far away into the silent land.
     Remember [1862], l. 1

Better by far you should forget and
    smile
Than that you should remember and be
    sad.   *Remember, l. 13*

For there is no friend like a sister
In calm or stormy weather;
To cheer one on the tedious way,
To fetch one if one goes astray,
To lift one if one totters down,
To strengthen whilst one stands.
        Goblin Market [1862], *last lines*

In the bleak mid-winter
    Frosty wind made moan,
Earth stood hard as iron,
    Water like a stone;
Snow had fallen, snow on snow,
    Snow on snow,
In the bleak mid-winter,
    Long ago.   *Mid-Winter*

YOSHIDA SHOIN[1]
1830–1859

To consider oneself different from
ordinary men is wrong, but it is right to
hope that one will not remain like ordinary men.
    Yoshida Shoin Zenshu, vol. II

The mind of the superior man is like
Heaven. When it is resentful or angry,
it thunders forth its indignation. But
once having loosed its feelings, it is like
a sunny day with a clear sky: within the
heart there remains not the trace of a
cloud. Such is the beauty of true manliness.   *Ib. III*

Neither the lords nor the shogun can
be depended upon [to save the coun-
try], and so our only hope lies in grass-
roots heroes.   *Ib. V*

ALEXANDER SMITH
1830–1867

In winter, when the dismal rain
Came down in slanting lines,

[1] From *Sources of Japanese Tradition*, edited
by William de Bary [1960].

And Wind, that grand old harper,
    smote
His thunder-harp of pines.
        A Life Drama [1853], *sc. 2*

It is not of so much consequence
what you say, as how you say it. Memorable sentences are memorable on account of some single irradiating word.
        Dreamthorp [1863]. *On the
            Writing of Essays*

Death is the ugly fact which Nature
has to hide, and she hides it well.
        *Ib. Of Death and the Fear
            of Dying*

CHARLES STUART
CALVERLEY
1831–1884

I have a liking old
For thee, though manifold
Stories, I know, are told,
    Not to thy credit!
        Ode to Tobacco, st. 2

The farmer's daughter hath soft brown
    hair
(*Butter and eggs and a pound of
    cheese*)
And I met with a ballad, I can't say
    where,
That wholly consisted of lines like
    these.
        *Ballad, after William Morris
        [The Auld Wife], pt. I, st. 6*

And this song is considered a perfect
    gem,
And as to the meaning, it's what you
    please.   *Ib. II, st. 4*

MARY MAPES DODGE
1831–1905

Life is a mystery as deep as ever death
    can be;
Yet oh, how sweet it is to us, this life
    we live and see!
        The Two Mysteries, st. 3

And as life is to the living, so death is
    to the dead.   *Ib. st. 5*

JAMES ABRAM GARFIELD
1831–1881

Fellow citizens! God reigns, and the Government at Washington still lives!
Speech on assassination of Lincoln, New York [April 15, 1865]

For mere vengeance I would do nothing. This nation is too great to look for mere revenge. But for the security of the future I would do everything.
Ib.

I am not willing that this discussion should close without mention of the value of a true teacher. Give me a log hut, with only a simple bench, Mark Hopkins [1] on one end and I on the other, and you may have all the buildings, apparatus and libraries without him.
Address to Williams College Alumni, New York [December 28, 1871] [2]

HELEN HUNT JACKSON
1831–1885

O suns and skies and clouds of June,
And flowers of June together,
Ye cannot rival for one hour
October's bright blue weather.
October's Bright Blue Weather, st. 1

Find me the men on earth who care
Enough for faith or creed today
To seek a barren wilderness
For simple liberty to pray.
The Pilgrim Forefathers, st. 5

[1] Mark Hopkins [1802–1887], president of Williams College [1836–1872], and president of the American Board of Commissioners for Foreign Missions [1857–1881].
  For Education is Making Men;
  So is it now, so was it when
  Mark Hopkins sat on one end of a log
  And James Garfield sat on the other.
      ARTHUR GUITERMAN [1871–1943], *Education*
[2] In BURKE A. HINSDALE, *President Garfield and Education* [1882], *p. 43.*

Oh, write of me, not "Died in bitter pains,"
But "Emigrated to another star!"
Emigravit

EDWARD ROBERT BULWER-LYTTON, EARL OF LYTTON [OWEN MEREDITH]
1831–1891

Love thou the rose, yet leave it on its stem.[1]
The Wanderer [1857]. Prologue, pt. I, 19

We may live without poetry, music and art;
We may live without conscience, and live without heart;
We may live without friends; we may live without books;
But civilized man cannot live without cooks.
Lucile [2] [1860], pt. I, canto 2, st. 19

Genius does what it must, and talent does what it can.
Last Words of a Sensitive Second-Rate Poet

JAMES CLERK MAXWELL
1831–1879

For the sake of persons of . . . different types, scientific truth should be presented in different forms, and should be regarded as equally scientific, whether it appears in the robust form and the vivid coloring of a physical illustration, or in the tenuity and paleness of a symbolic expression.
Address to the Mathematics and Physics Section, British Association for the Advancement of Science [1870]

[1] See Emerson, p. 603a.
[2] Lord Lytton, the Viceroy, who still lives in the literary hall of fame as the author of *Lucile* — a vast, stale Victorian piece of poetry. — WILLIAM E. WOODWARD, *Meet General Grant* [1928], *pt. IV, ch. 30*

When at last this little instrument appeared, consisting, as it does, of parts every one of which is familiar to us, and capable of being put together by an amateur, the disappointment arising from its humble appearance was only partially relieved on finding that it was really able to talk.

The Telephone [1878]

PHILIP HENRY SHERIDAN
1831–1888

The only good Indians I ever saw were dead.[1]

Remark at Fort Cobb, Indian Territory [*January* 1869]

LOUISA MAY ALCOTT
1832–1888

Christmas won't be Christmas without any presents.

Little Women [1868], *ch. 1*

A little kingdom I possess,
  Where thoughts and feelings dwell;
And very hard the task I find
  Of governing it well.

From EDNAH D. CHENEY, *Louisa May Alcott, Her Life, Letters, and Journals* [1889], *ch. 3* [*My Kingdom*,[2] *st. 1*]

Resolved to take Fate by the throat and shake a living out of her. *Ib. 5*

Above man's aims his nature rose.
The wisdom of a just content
Made one small spot a continent,
And tuned to poetry Life's prose.[3]

Ib. 7. [*Thoreau's Flute*,[4] *st. 2*]

---

[1] EDWARD SYLVESTER ELLIS [1840–1916] reported that after Custer's fight with Black Kettle's band of Cheyenne Indians, the Comanche Chief Toch-a-way (Turtle Dove) was presented to General Sheridan. The Indian said: "Me Toch-a-way, me good Indian." The General's reply, as reported by Ellis, is given in the text; the phrase is more often heard in the version: The only good Indian is a dead Indian.

[2] Written at the age of thirteen.

[3] The word "tuned" is frequently misprinted as "turned."

[4] In *The Atlantic Monthly* [September 1863].

My definition [of a philosopher] is of a man up in a balloon, with his family and friends holding the ropes which confine him to earth and trying to haul him down.

Life, Letters, and Journals, ch. 10

ELIZABETH AKERS ALLEN
1832–1911

Backward, turn backward, O Time, in your flight,
Make me a child again just for tonight!

Rock Me to Sleep [1860], *st. 1*

SIR EDWIN ARNOLD
1832–1904

Shall any gazer see with mortal eyes,
Or any searcher know by mortal mind?
Veil after veil will lift — but there must be
Veil upon veil behind.

The Light of Asia [1879], *bk. VIII*

Nor ever once ashamed
So we be named
Pressmen; Slaves of the Lamp; Servants of Light.

The Tenth Muse, st. 18

WILHELM BUSCH
1832–1908

Diogenes the wise crept into his vat
And spoke: "Yes, yes, this comes from that."

Diogenes und die bösen Buben von Korinth [1856]

This thesis remains firm: Good is the Evil which is permitted.

Fromme Helene [1872]

In general his principle is this:
Whatever is popular is permitted.

Julchen [1877]

To become a father is not hard,
To be a father is, however. *Ib.*

Temperance is the pleasure
In things we can't get.
Thus live moderately and think intelli-
   gently —
He has enough who uses nothing.
               Julchen

A true painter, smart and busy,
Always carries a sharp pencil with him.
     Maler Klecksel [1884]

WILLIAM CROSWELL DOANE
1832–1913

Ancient of Days, who sittest throned in
   glory,
To thee all knees are bent, all voices
   pray.   *Hymn* [1886], *st. 1*

LEWIS CARROLL [CHARLES LUTWIDGE DODGSON]
1832–1898

All in the golden afternoon
   Full leisurely we glide,
For both our oars with little skill
   By little arms are plied
While little hands make vain pretense
   Our wanderings to guide.
     *Alice's Adventures in Wonder-
     land* [1865], *introduction, st. 1*

"What is the use of a book,"
thought Alice, "without pictures or
conversations?"   *Ib. ch. 1*

Do cats eat bats? . . . Do bats eat
cats?   *Ib.*

Curiouser and curiouser!   *Ib. 2*

How doth the little crocodile
Improve his shining tail,
And pour the waters of the Nile
On every golden scale! [1]

How cheerfully he seems to grin,
How neatly spreads his claws,
And welcomes little fishes in
With gently smiling jaws!
                   Ib.

"I'll be judge, I'll be jury," said cunning old Fury; "I'll try the whole cause,
and condemn you to death."
     *Alice's Adventures in Wonder-
              land. ch. 3*

Oh my fur and whiskers!   *Ib. 4*

"I can't explain *myself*, I'm afraid,
sir," said Alice, "because I'm not myself, you see."
"I don't see," said the Caterpillar.
                   Ib. 5

"You are old, Father William," the
   young man said,
"And your hair has become very white;
And yet you incessantly stand on your
   head —
Do you think, at your age, it is right?" [1]
     Ib. [*You are old, Father
             William, st. 1*]

"In my youth," said his father, "I took
   to the law,
And argued each case with my wife;
And the muscular strength, which it
   gave to my jaw,
Has lasted the rest of my life."
               Ib. [*st. 6*]

"I have answered three questions, and
   that is enough,"
Said his father. "Don't give yourself
   airs!
Do you think I can listen all day to
   such stuff?
Be off, or I'll kick you downstairs!"
               Ib. [*st. 8*]

"I shall sit here," he said, "on and
off, for days and days."   *Ib. 6*

"If everybody minded their own
business," said the Duchess in a hoarse
growl, "the world would go round a
deal faster than it does."   *Ib.*

"Talking of axes," said the Duchess,
"chop off her head!"   *Ib.*

Speak roughly to your little boy,
   And beat him when he sneezes:
He only does it to annoy,
   Because he knows it teases.
                   Ib.

---

[1] See Isaac Watts, p. 396b.

[1] See Southey, p. 531b.

"All right," said the [Cheshire] Cat; and this time it vanished quite slowly, beginning with the end of the tail, and ending with the grin, which remained some time after the rest of it had gone.

Alice's Adventures in Wonderland, ch. 6

"Then you should say what you mean," the March Hare went on.

"I do," Alice hastily replied; "at least — at least I mean what I say — that's the same thing, you know."

"Not the same thing a bit!" said the Hatter. "Why, you might just as well say that 'I see what I eat' is the same thing as 'I eat what I see'!"   *Ib.* 7

"It was the *best* butter," the March Hare meekly replied.   *Ib.*

Twinkle, twinkle, little bat!
How I wonder what you're at!
Up above the world you fly,
Like a teatray in the sky.[1]

         Ib.

"Take some more tea," the March Hare said to Alice, very earnestly.

"I've had nothing yet," Alice replied in an offended tone: "so I can't take more."

"You mean you can't take *less*," said the Hatter: "it's very easy to take *more* than nothing."   *Ib.*

They drew all manner of things — everything that begins with an M . . . such as mousetraps, and the moon, and memory, and muchness — you know you say things are "much of a muchness."   *Ib.*

The Queen turned crimson with fury, and after glaring at her for a moment like a wild beast, began screaming, "Off with her head![1] Off with — "   *Ib.* 8

"Tut, tut, child," said the Duchess. "Everything's got a moral if only you can find it."   *Ib.* 9

[1] See Ann and Jane Taylor, p. 546a.
[2] See Shakespeare, p. 217b, and Cibber, p. 392b.

And the moral of that is — "Oh, 'tis love, 'tis love, that makes the world go round!" [1]

Alice's Adventures in Wonderland, ch. 9

Take care of the sense and the sounds will take care of themselves.

         Ib.

"We called him Tortoise because he taught us," said the Mock Turtle angrily. "Really you are very dull!"

         Ib.

"Reeling and Writhing, of course, to begin with," the Mock Turtle replied, "and the different branches of Arithmetic — Ambition, Distraction, Uglification, and Derision."   *Ib.*

"Will you walk a little faster?" said a
    whiting to a snail,
"There's a porpoise close behind us,
    and he's treading on my tail."
   Ib. 10 [*The Lobster-Quadrillle,*
                    st. 1]

Will you, won't you, will you, won't you, will you, will you join the dance?
         Ib.

The further off from England the
    nearer is to France —
Then turn not pale, beloved snail, but
    come and join the dance.
         Ib. [*st.* 3]

'Tis the voice of the Lobster: I heard
    him declare
"You have baked me too brown, I must
    sugar my hair." [2]
     Ib. [*'Tis the Voice of the
                   Lobster*]

Soup of the evening, beautiful soup!
     Ib. [*Turtle Soup*]

Sentence first — verdict afterwards.
         Ib. 12

Child of the pure, unclouded brow
    And dreaming eyes of wonder!
Though time be fleet and I and thou
    Are half a life asunder,

[1] See W. S. Gilbert, p. 768a, and Anonymous, p. 1105b.
[2] See Isaac Watts, p. 396b.

Thy loving smile will surely hail
The love-gift of a fairy tale.

> *Through the Looking-Glass*
> [*1872*], *introduction, st. 1*

"The horror of that moment," the King went on, "I shall never, *never* forget!"

"You will, though," the Queen said, "if you don't make a memorandum of it."   *Ib. ch. 1*

'Twas brillig, and the slithy toves
  Did gyre and gimble in the wabe;
All mimsy were the borogoves,
  And the mome raths outgrabe.

Beware the Jabberwock, my son!
  The jaws that bite, the claws that catch!
Beware the Jubjub bird, and shun
  The frumious Bandersnatch!

> *Ib.* [*Jabberwocky, st. 1, 2*]

And, as in uffish thought he stood,
  The Jabberwock, with eyes of flame,
Came whiffling through the tulgey wood,
  And burbled as it came!

One, two! One, two! And through and through
  The vorpal blade went snicker-snack!
He left it dead, and with its head
  He went galumphing back.

"And hast thou slain the Jabberwock?
  Come to my arms, my beamish boy!
O frabjous day! Callooh! Callay!"
  He chortled in his joy.

> *Ib.* [*st. 4–6*]

Curtsy while you're thinking what to say. It saves time.   *Ib. 2*

"Now! Now!" cried the Queen. "Faster! Faster!"   *Ib.*

"A slow sort of country!" said the Queen. "Now, *here*, you see, it takes all the running you can do, to keep in the same place. If you want to get somewhere else, you must run at least twice as fast as that!"   *Ib.*

Speak in French when you can't think of the English for a thing — turn out your toes when you walk — and remember who you are!

> *Through the Looking-Glass, ch. 2*

"If you think we're waxworks," he said, "you ought to pay, you know. Waxworks weren't made to be looked at for nothing. Nohow!"   *Ib. 4*

"Contrariwise," continued Tweedledee, "if it was so, it might be; and if it were so, it would be; but as it isn't, it ain't. That's logic."   *Ib.*

The sun was shining on the sea,
  Shining with all his might:
He did his very best to make
  The billows smooth and bright —
And this was odd, because it was
  The middle of the night.

> *Ib.* [*The Walrus and the Carpenter, st. 1*]

The Walrus and the Carpenter
  Were walking close at hand:
They wept like anything to see
  Such quantities of sand:
"If this were only cleared away,"
  They said, "it would be grand!"

"If seven maids with seven mops
  Swept it for half a year,
Do you suppose," the Walrus said,
  "That they could get it clear?"
"I doubt it," said the Carpenter,
  And shed a bitter tear.

> *Ib.* [*st. 4, 5*]

"O Oysters, come and walk with us!"
  The Walrus did beseech.
"A pleasant walk, a pleasant talk,
  Along the briny beach."

> *Ib.* [*st. 6*]

And thick and fast they came at last,
  And more, and more, and more —
All hopping through the frothy waves,
  And scrambling to the shore.

> *Ib.* [*st. 9*]

"The time has come," the Walrus said,
  "To talk of many things:
Of shoes — and ships — and sealing-wax —

Of cabbages — and kings —
And why the sea is boiling hot —
   And whether pigs have wings."
      Through the Looking-Glass,
      ch. 4 [The Walrus and the Car-
      penter, st. 11]

"But wait a bit," the Oysters cried,
   "Before we have our chat;
For some of us are out of breath,
   And all of us are fat!"   *Ib. [st. 12]*

The Carpenter said nothing but
   "The butter's spread too thick!"
      Ib. [st. 16]

"I weep for you," the Walrus said:
   "I deeply sympathize."
With sobs and tears he sorted out
   Those of the largest size,
Holding his pocket-handkerchief
   Before his streaming eyes.
      Ib. [st. 17]

But answer came there none —
And this was scarcely odd, because
   They'd eaten every one.
      Ib. [st. 18]

Twopence a week, and jam every
other day.   *Ib. 5*

"The rule is, jam tomorrow, and jam
yesterday — but never jam today."
   "It must come sometimes to 'jam today,'" Alice objected.
   "No, it can't," said the Queen. "It's
jam every other day: today isn't any
other day, you know."   *Ib.*

"It's a poor sort of memory that only
works backwards," the Queen remarked.   *Ib.*

Consider anything, only don't cry!
      Ib.

"There's no use trying," she said:
"one *can't* believe impossible things."
   "I daresay you haven't had much
practice," said the Queen. "When I
was your age, I always did it for half-an-
hour a day. Why, sometimes I've believed as many as six impossible things
before breakfast."   *Ib.*

They gave it me — for an unbirthday
present.   *Ib. 6*

"But 'glory' doesn't mean 'a nice
knockdown argument,'" Alice objected.
   "When *I* use a word," Humpty
Dumpty said, in rather a scornful tone,
"it means just what I choose it to
mean — neither more nor less."
   "The question is," said Alice,
"whether you *can* make words mean so
many different things."
   "The question is," said Humpty
Dumpty, "which is to be master —
that's all."
      Through the Looking-Glass,
      ch. 6

It's as large as life and twice as natural.   *Ib. 7*

His answer trickled through my head,
Like water through a sieve.   *Ib. 8*

What's the French for fiddle-de-
dee?   *Ib. 9*

It isn't etiquette to cut anyone
you've been introduced to. Remove the
joint!   *Ib.*

He would answer to "Hi!" or to any
      loud cry
Such as "Fry me!" or "Fritter my
      wig!"
To "What-you-may-call-um!" or
      "What-was-his-name!"
But especially "Thing-um-a-jig!"
      The Hunting of the Snark
      [1876]. Fit I, st. 9

"What's the good of Mercator's North
      Poles and Equators,
Tropics, Zones and Meridian Lines?"
So the Bellman would cry: and the
      crew would reply,
"They are merely conventional signs!"
      Ib. Fit II, st. 3

It frequently breakfasts at five-o'clock
      tea,
And dines on the following day.
      Ib. st. 17

There was silence supreme! Not a
      shriek, not a scream,
Scarcely even a howl or a groan,

As the man they called "Ho!" told his
  story of woe
In an antediluvian tone.
  The Hunting of the Snark.
  Fit III, st. 3

It is this, it is this that oppresses my
  soul. *Ib. st. 11*

And my heart is like nothing so much
  as a bowl
Brimming over with quivering curds.
  Ib.

You may charge me with murder — or
  want of sense —
(We are all of us weak at times):
But the slightest approach to a false
  pretense
Was never among my crimes!
  Ib. Fit IV, st. 4

They sought it with thimbles, they
  sought it with care;
They pursued it with forks and hope;
They threatened its life with a railway
  share;
They charmed it with smiles and soap.
  Ib. Fit V, st. 1

For the Snark *was* a Boojum, you see.
  Ib. Fit VIII, st. 9

He thought he saw an Elephant,
  That practiced on a fife:
He looked again, and found it was
  A letter from his wife.
"At length I realize," he said,
  "The bitterness of Life!"
  Sylvie and Bruno [1889], *ch. 5*

He thought he saw a Buffalo
  Upon the chimneypiece:
He looked again, and found it was
  His sister's husband's niece.
  Ib. 6

He thought he saw an Albatross
  That fluttered round the lamp:
He looked again, and found it was
  A penny postage stamp.
"You'd best be getting home," he said,
  "The nights are very damp."
  Ib. 12

BENJAMIN HARVEY HILL
1832–1882

He was a foe without hate, a friend
without treachery, a soldier without
cruelty, and a victim without murmuring. He was a public officer without
vices, a private citizen without wrong, a
neighbor without reproach, a Christian
without hypocrisy, and a man without
guile. He was a Caesar without his ambition, a Frederick without his tyranny,
a Napoleon without his selfishness, and
a Washington without his reward.
  Tribute to Robert E. Lee; from
  THOMAS NELSON PAGE, *Robert*
  E. Lee [1911]

JUAN MONTALVO
1832–1889

Old age is an island surrounded by
death. *On Beauty*

Beauty is harmony, grace is melody.
  Ib.

The soul does not hunger for flesh, it
is horrified by it; it does not thirst for
wine, it is killed by it. *On Genius*

Sensibility is most strong among our
young nations who outdistance the
older ones in science and culture by
means of their imagination.
  Chapters Forgotten by Cer-
  vantes. Epilogue

There is nothing harder than the
softness of indifference. *Ib.*

HENRY CLAY WORK
1832–1884

Father, dear father, come home with
  me now,
The clock in the belfry strikes one;
You said you were coming right home
  from the shop
As soon as your day's work was done.
  Come Home, Father [1864], *st. 1*

Bring the good old bugle, boys, we'll
  sing another song;

Sing it with a spirit that will start the
world along,
Sing it as we used to sing it — fifty
thousand strong,
While we were marching through
Georgia.
> *Marching Through Georgia*
> *[1865], st. 1*

"Hurrah! hurrah! we bring the Jubilee!
Hurrah! Hurrah! the flag that makes
you free!"
So we sang the chorus from Atlanta to
the sea,
While we were marching through
Georgia.   *Ib. chorus*

ISAAC HILL BROMLEY
1833–1898

Conductor, when you receive a fare,
Punch in the presence of the passen-
jare! . . .
Punch, brothers! Punch with care!
Punch in the presence of the passen-
jare!
> *Punch, Brother, Punch* [1] *[1875]*

MARY ABIGAIL
DODGE
[GAIL HAMILTON]
1833–1896

Whatever an author puts between
the two covers of his book is public
property; whatever of himself he does
not put there is his private property, as
much as if he had never written a
word.
> *Country Living and Country*
> *Thinking [1862], preface*

What's virtue in man can't be vice in a
cat.   *Both Sides*

ADAM LINDSAY GORDON
1833–1870

A little season of love and laughter,
Of light and life, and pleasure and
pain,

---

[1] Based on a New York streetcar sign. Erroneously attributed to Mark Twain, who wrote
about the verse in *A Literary Nightmare [1876]*.

And a horror of outer darkness after,
And dust returneth to dust again.[1]
> *The Swimmer*

JOHN MARSHALL
HARLAN
1833–1911

In view of the Constitution, in the
eye of the law, there is in this country
no superior, dominant, ruling class of
citizens. There is no caste here. Our
Constitution is color-blind, and neither
knows nor tolerates classes among citizens. In respect of civil rights, all citizens
are equal before the law. The humblest
is the peer of the most powerful.
> *Dissenting opinion, Plessy v.*
> *Ferguson 163 U.S. 537, 559*
> *[1896]*

JOHN JAMES INGALLS
1833–1900

Every man is the center of a circle,
whose fatal circumference he cannot
pass.
> *Eulogy on Benjamin Hill, U.S.*
> *Senate [January 23, 1882]*

The purification of politics is an iridescent dream. Government is force.
> *Article in the New York World*
> *[1890]*

Next in profusion to the divine profusion of water, light and air, those
three physical facts which render existence possible, may be reckoned the universal beneficence of grass.
> *Blue Grass*

I knock unbidden once at every gate!
If sleeping, wake; if feasting, rise be-
fore
I turn away. It is the hour of fate.
> *Opportunity [1891]*

---

[1] See Du Maurier, p. 751b, and Marston, p.
821b.

ROBERT GREEN INGERSOLL
1833–1899

Like an armed warrior, like a plumed knight, James G. Blaine marched down the halls of the American Congress and threw his shining lance full and fair against the brazen forehead of every traitor to his country and every maligner of his fair reputation.

> *Speech nominating Blaine for President, National Republican Convention [June 15, 1876]*

I am the inferior of any man whose rights I trample under foot. Men are not superior by reason of the accidents of race or color. They are superior who have the best heart — the best brain.

> *Liberty*

The superior man is the providence of the inferior. He is eyes for the blind, strength for the weak, and a shield for the defenseless. He stands erect by bending above the fallen. He rises by lifting others.

> *Ib.*

Every cradle asks us, "Whence?" and every coffin, "Whither?" The poor barbarian, weeping above his dead, can answer these questions as intelligently as the robed priest of the most authentic creed.

> *Address at a child's grave*

We, too, have our religion, and it is this: Help for the living, hope for the dead.

> *Ib.*

Few rich men own their own property. The property owns them.[1]

> *Address to the McKinley League, New York [October 29, 1896]*

An honest God is the noblest work of man.

> *The Gods [1876]*

In nature there are neither rewards nor punishments — there are consequences.

> *Some Reasons Why [1896]*

Justice is the only worship.
Love is the only priest.
Ignorance is the only slavery.

[1] See Bion, p. 104b.

Happiness is the only good.
The time to be happy is now,
The place to be happy is here,
The way to be happy is to make others so.

> *Creed*

PETROLEUM V. NASBY [DAVID ROSS LOCKE]
1833–1888

The contract 'twixt Hannah, God and me,
Was not for one or twenty years, but for eternity.

> *Hannah Jane [1871], st. 29*

EDMUND CLARENCE STEDMAN
1833–1908

Prison mate and dockyard fellow,
    Blades to Meg and Molly dear,
Off to capture Porto Bello
    Sailed with Morgan the Buccaneer!

> *Morgan,[1] st. 1*

JULIA LOUISE MATILDA WOODRUFF
1833–1909

Out of the strain of the Doing,
Into the peace of the Done.

> *Harvest Home [1910]*

JOHN EMERICH EDWARD DALBERG-ACTON, LORD ACTON
1834–1902

There is no error so monstrous that it fails to find defenders among the ablest men. Imagine a congress of eminent celebrities such as More, Bacon, Grotius, Pascal, Cromwell, Bossuet, Montesquieu, Jefferson, Napoleon, Pitt, etc. The result would be an Encyclopedia of Error.

> *Letter to Mary Gladstone [April 24, 1881]*

[1] The old bold mate of Henry Morgan. — JOHN MASEFIELD [1878–1967], *Captain Stratton's Fancy*

Power tends to corrupt and absolute power corrupts absolutely.
> Letter to Bishop Mandell Creighton [April 5, 1887]

Advice to Persons About to Write History — Don't.   Ib. postscript

Liberty is not a means to a higher political end. It is itself the highest political end.
> The History of Freedom and Other Essays [1907], ch. 1

It was from America that the plain ideas that men ought to mind their business, and that the nation is responsible to Heaven for the acts of the State — ideas long locked in the breast of solitary thinkers, and hidden among Latin folios — burst forth like a conqueror upon the world they were destined to transform, under the title of the Rights of Man . . . and the principle gained ground, that a nation can never abandon its fate to an authority it cannot control.   Ib. 2

The one pervading evil of democracy is the tyranny of the majority, or rather of that party, not always the majority, that succeeds, by force or fraud, in carrying elections.   Ib. 3

Truth is the only merit that gives dignity and worth to history.   Ib. 4

Writers the most learned, the most accurate in details, and the soundest in tendency, frequently fall into a habit which can neither be cured nor pardoned — the habit of making history into the proof of their theories.
>   Ib. 8

GEORGE ARNOLD
1834–1865

Life for the living, and rest for the dead!
> The Jolly Old Pedagogue, st. 2

The living need charity more than the dead.   Ib. st. 3

SABINE BARING-GOULD
1834–1924

Onward, Christian soldiers,
  Marching as to war,
With the Cross of Jesus
  Going on before!
> Onward, Christian Soldiers [1864], st. 1

Now the day is over,
  Night is drawing nigh;
Shadows of the evening
  Steal across the sky.
> Now the Day Is Over [1865], st. 1

Through the night of doubt and sorrow
  Onward goes the pilgrim band,
Singing songs of expectation,
  Marching to the promised land.
> Through the Night of Doubt and Sorrow, st. 1; translated [1867] from the Danish of B. S. INGEMANN [1825]

CHARLES FARRAR BROWNE
[ARTEMUS WARD]
1834–1867

I now bid you a welcome adoo.
> Artemus Ward, His Book [1862]

My pollertics, like my religion, being of an exceedin' accommodatin' character.   Ib. The Crisis

N.B. This is rote sarcastikul.
> Ib. A Visit to Brigham Young

The female woman is one of the greatest institooshuns of which this land can boste.
> Ib. Woman's Rights

I am not a politician, and my other habits are good.
> Fourth of July Oration

The prevailin' weakness of most public men is to Slop over. G. Washington never slopt over.   Ib.

I can't sing. As a singist I am not a success. I am saddest when I sing. So are those who hear me. They are sadder even than I am.[1]

Artemus Ward, His Travels [1865].
Lecture

Did you ever have the measels, and if so, how many?   *Ib. The Census*

The Puritans nobly fled from a land of despotism to a land of freedim, where they could not only enjoy their own religion, but could prevent everybody else from enjoyin *his.*

London Punch Letters,[2] *no. 5*
[1866]

Why is this thus? What is the reason of this thusness?   *Moses, the Sassy*

He [Brigham Young] is dreadfully married. He's the most married man I ever saw in my life.   *Ib.*

Let us all be happy and live within our means, even if we have to borrow the money to do it with.

Natural History

The sun has a right to "set" where it wants to, and so, I may add, has a hen.   *A Mormon Romance, ch. 4*

They cherish his mem'ry, and them as sell picturs of his birthplace, etc., make it prof'tible cherishin' it.

At the Tomb of Shakespeare

GEORGE LOUIS PALMELLA BUSSON DU MAURIER
1834–1896

The wretcheder one is, the more one smokes; and the more one smokes, the wretcheder one gets — a vicious circle!
Peter Ibbetson [1891]

Songs without words are best.   *Ib.*

All will be well for us all, and of such a kind that all who do not sigh for the moon will be well content.   *Ib.*

[1] See T. H. Bayly, p. 588a.
[2] The Puritan's idea of Hell is a place where everybody has to mind his own business. — *Attributed to* WENDELL PHILLIPS [1811–1884]

Lovely female shapes are terrible complicators of the difficulties and dangers of this earthly life, especially for their owner.   *Trilby* [1894], *pt. I*

That is the worst of those dear people who have charm; they are so terrible to do without, when once you have got accustomed to them and all their ways.
Ib. V

A little work, a little play,
To keep us going — and so, good day!

A little warmth, a little light,
Of love's bestowing — and so, good night! [1]

A little fun, to match the sorrow
Of each day's growing — and so, good morrow!

A little trust that when we die
We reap our sowing! and so — goodby!
Ib. VIII

CHARLES WILLIAM ELIOT
1834–1926

In the modern world the intelligence of public opinion is the one indispensable condition of social progress.
Inaugural address as president of Harvard [1869]

Enter to grow in wisdom.
Depart better to serve thy country and mankind.
Inscriptions on the 1890 Gate to Harvard Yard

To the Fifty-fourth Regiment of Massachusetts Infantry:

[1] La vie est vaine:
    Un peu d'amour,
    Un peu de haine . . .
      Et puis — bonjour!

La vie est brève,
    Un peu d'espoir,
    Un peu de rêve
      Et puis — bonsoir!
      LEON MONTENAEKEN [b. 1859], *Peu de Chose*

See A. L. Gordon, p. 748b, and Marston, p. 821b.

The white officers, taking life and honor in their hands, cast in their lot with men of a despised race unproved in war, and risked death as inciters of servile insurrection if taken prisoners, besides encountering all the common perils of camp march and battle.

The black rank and file volunteered when disaster clouded the Union cause, served without pay for eighteen months till given that of white troops, faced threatened enslavement if captured, were brave in action, patient under heavy and dangerous labors, and cheerful amid hardships and privations.

Together they gave to the nation and the world undying proof that Americans of African descent possess the pride, courage, and devotion of the patriot soldier. One hundred and eighty thousand such Americans enlisted under the Union flag in 1863–1865.

> *Inscription on the back of the Robert Gould Shaw Monument, Boston Common* [1897] [1]

Carrier of news and knowledge, instrument of trade and commerce, promoter of mutual acquaintance among men and nations and hence of peace and good will.

Carrier of love and sympathy, messenger of friendship, consoler of the lonely, servant of the scattered family, enlarger of the public life.

> *Inscriptions for the East and West Pavilions, Post Office, Washington, D.C.* [2]

FUKUZAWA YUKICHI [3]
1834–1901

The final purpose of all my work was to create in Japan a civilized nation as

[1] See Robert Lowell, p. 1076b.

[2] These inscriptions were edited by Woodrow Wilson, to read:

Carrier of news and knowledge, instrument of trade and promoter of mutual acquaintance, of peace and good will among men and nations.

Messenger of sympathy and love, servant of parted friends, consoler of the lonely, bond of the scattered family, enlarger of the common life.

[3] From *Sources of Japanese Tradition*, edited by William Theodore de Bary [1960].

well equipped in both the arts of war and peace as those of the Western world. *Autobiography* [1898]

As long as I remain in private life, I can watch and laugh. But joining the government would draw me into the practice of those ridiculous pretensions which I cannot allow myself to do.
> *Ib.*

ERNST HEINRICH HAECKEL
1834–1919

Ontogenesis, or the development of the individual, is a short and quick recapitulation of phylogenesis,[1] or the development of the tribe to which it belongs, determined by the laws of inheritance and adaptation.
> *The History of Creation* [2] [1868]

The general theory of evolution . . . assumes that in nature there is a great, unital, continuous and everlasting process of development, and that all natural phenomena without exception, from the motion of the celestial bodies and the fall of the rolling stone up to the growth of the plant and the consciousness of man, are subject to the same great law of causation — that they are ultimately to be reduced to atomic mechanics.
> *Freie Wissenschaft und Freie Lehre* [1878] [3]

WALTER KITTREDGE
1834–1905

We're tenting tonight on the old campground,
Give us a song to cheer
Our weary hearts, a song of home
And friends we love so dear.
> *Tenting Tonight*, st. 1

[1] Frequently quoted as "Ontogeny recapitulates phylogeny."
See Freud, p. 833b.
[2] Translated by E. R. LANKESTER.
[3] Translated by J. B. STALLO.

WILLIAM MORRIS
1834–1896

I know a little garden close,
Set thick with lily and red rose,
Where I would wander if I might
From dewy morn to dewy night.
> *The Life and Death of Jason*
> [*1867*]. *A Garden by the Sea,*
> *st. 1*

The idle singer of an empty day.
> *The Earthly Paradise* [*1868–*
> *1870*]. *An Apology, st. 1*

Dreamer of dreams, born out of my due
time,
Why should I strive to set the crooked
straight?   *Ib. st. 4*

Love is enough, though the world be a-
waning,
And the woods have no voice but the
voice of complaining.
> *Love Is Enough* [*1872*]

If you want a golden rule that will
fit everybody, this is it: Have nothing
in your houses that you do not know
to be useful, or believe to be beautiful.
> *The Beauty of Life* [*1880*]

What I mean by Socialism is a condition of society in which there should
be neither rich nor poor, neither master
nor master's man, neither idle nor over-
worked, neither brain-sick brain workers nor heart-sick hand workers, in a
word, in which all men would be living in equality of condition, and would
manage their affairs unwastefully, and
with the full consciousness that harm
to one would mean harm to all — the
realization at last of the meaning of
the word *commonwealth.*
> *Written for "Justice"* [*1884*]

FRANK RICHARD
STOCKTON
1834–1902

He could open either door he
pleased. . . . If he opened the one,
there came out of it a hungry tiger, the
fiercest and most cruel that could be
procured, which immediately sprang
upon him, and tore him to pieces, as a
punishment for his guilt. . . . But if
the accused person opened the other
door, there came forth from it a lady,
the most suitable to his years and station that his Majesty could select
among his fair subjects. . . . So I leave
it with all of you: Which came out of
the opened door — the lady or the
tiger?
> *The Lady or the Tiger?* [*1884*]

The board money is in the ginger jar
and our conscience is clear.
> *The Casting Away of Mrs. Lecks*
> *and Mrs. Aleshine* [*1886*]

JAMES THOMSON
1834–1882

Give a man a pipe he can smoke,
Give ,a man a book he can read:
And his home is bright with a calm
delight,
Though the room be poor indeed.
> *Sunday Up the River* [*1869*],
> *XV, st. 2*

The City is of Night; perchance of
Death,
But certainly of Night.
> *The City of Dreadful Night*
> [*1874*]. *Proem*

CHARLES HENRY
WEBB
1834–1905

Friends I have had both old and
young,
And ale we drank and songs we sung:
Enough you know when this is said,
That, one and all — they died in bed.
In bed they died and I'll not go
Where all my friends have perished so.
> *Dum Vivimus Vigilamus, st. 1*

That 'tis well to be off with the old
love
Before one is on with the new
Has somehow passed into a proverb,[1]

[1] It's gude to be merry and wise,
   It's gude to be honest and true;

But who follows its teaching may rue.
Proverbum Sap, st. 1

Were the proverb not wiser if mended,
And the fickle and wavering told
To be sure that they're on with the new
love
Before being off with the old?
Ib. st. 3

JAMES McNEILL WHISTLER
1834–1903

Two and two continue to make four,
in spite of the whine of the amateur for
three, or the cry of the critic for five.
Whistler v. Ruskin [1] [1878]

The rare few, who, early in life, have
rid themselves of the friendship of the
many.
*The Gentle Art of Making
Enemies* [1890], *dedication*

To say of a picture, as is often said in
its praise, that it shows great and earnest labor, is to say that it is incomplete
and unfit for view.
Ib. Propositions, 2

Industry in art is a necessity — not a
virtue — and any evidence of the same,
in the production, is a blemish, not a
quality; a proof, not of achievement,
but of absolutely insufficient work, for
work alone will efface the footsteps of
work. [2]
Ib.

The masterpiece should appear as the
flower to the painter — perfect in its
bud as in its bloom — with no reason

to explain its presence — no mission to
fulfill — a joy to the artist, a delusion
to the philanthropist — a puzzle to the
botanist — an accident of sentiment
and alliteration to the literary man.
*The Gentle Art of Making
Enemies, Propositions, 2*

Art should be independent of all
claptrap — should stand alone, and appeal to the artistic sense of eye and ear,
without confounding this with emotions entirely foreign to it, as devotion,
pity, love, patriotism, and the like. All
these have no kind of concern with it.
Ib.

The imitator is a poor kind of creature. If the man who paints only the
tree, or flower, or other surface he sees
before him were an artist, the king of
artists would be the photographer. It is
for the artist to do something beyond
this: in portrait painting to put on canvas something more than the face the
model wears for that one day; to paint
the man, in short, as well as his features.
Ib.

One cannot continually disappoint a
Continent. [1]
Ib.

I am not arguing with you — I am
telling you.
Ib.

Wilde: I wish I'd said that.
Whistler: You will, Oscar, you will.
*From L. C. INGLEBY, Oscar
Wilde* [1907]

"I only know of two painters in the
world," said a newly introduced femi-
nine enthusiast to Whistler, "yourself
and Velasquez." "Why," answered
Whistler in dulcet tones, "why drag in
Velasquez?"
*From D. C. SEITZ, Whistler
Stories* [1913]

ALFRED AUSTIN
1835–1913

An earl by right, by courtesy a man.
The Season

It's gude to be off with the old love,
Before you are on with the new.
ANONYMOUS [1816]. Quoted by AN-
THONY TROLLOPE in *Barchester
Towers* [1857], *ch. 46.*
See G. B. Shaw, p. 836a.
[1] In Whistler's lawsuit for libel. Ruskin had
written of Whistler's *Nocturne in Black and
Gold,* "I have seen, and heard, much of Cockney
impudence before now; but never expected to
hear a coxcomb ask two hundred guineas for
flinging a pot of paint in the public's face." —
JOHN RUSKIN, *Fors Clavigera, Letter 79* [1877]
[2] Ars est celare artem [Art lies in concealing
art]. — *Latin proverb*

[1] Referring to a contemplated visit to the
United States.

THOMAS BRIGHAM BISHOP
1835–1905

John Brown's body lies a-moldering in
    the grave,
His soul is marching on.
> *John Brown's Body, st. 1*

Shoo, fly! don't bodder me! I belong to
    Company G,
I feel like a morning star.
> *Shoo, Fly. Refrain*

PHILLIPS BROOKS
1835–1893

O little town of Bethlehem!
    How still we see thee lie;
Above thy deep and dreamless sleep
    The silent stars go by;
Yet in thy dark streets shineth
    The everlasting Light;
The hopes and fears of all the years
    Are met in thee tonight.
> *O Little Town of Bethlehem*
> *[1867], st. 1*

Life comes before literature, as the
material always comes before the work.
The hills are full of marble before the
world blooms with statues.
> *Literature and Life*

Do not pray for easy lives. Pray to be
stronger men! Do not pray for tasks
equal to your powers. Pray for powers
equal to your tasks.
> *Sermons. Going up to Jerusalem*

Greatness after all, in spite of its
name, appears to be not so much a certain size as a certain quality in human
lives. It may be present in lives whose
range is very small.
> *Ib. Purpose and Use of Comfort*

SAMUEL BUTLER
1835–1902

The man who lets himself be bored
is even more contemptible than the
bore.
> *The Fair Haven* [1873]. *Memoir,*
> *ch. 3*

A hen is only an egg's way of making
another egg.
> *Life and Habit* [1877], *ch. 8*

Stowed away in a Montreal lumber
    room
The Discobolus standeth and turneth
    his face to the wall;
Dusty, cobweb-covered, maimed and
    set at naught,
Beauty crieth in an attic and no man
    regardeth.
O God! O Montreal!
> *A Psalm of Montreal* [1884],
> *st. 1*

The Discobolus is put here because he
    is vulgar —
He has neither vest nor pants with
    which to cover his limbs;
I, Sir, am a person of most respectable
    connections —
My brother-in-law is haberdasher to
    Mr. Spurgeon.
O God! O Montreal!   *Ib. st. 5*

It is far safer to know too little than
too much. People will condemn the
one, though they will resent being
called upon to exert themselves to follow the other.
> *The Way of All Flesh* [1] [1903],
> *ch. 5*

Adversity, if a man is set down to it
by degrees, is more supportable with
equanimity by most people than any
great prosperity arrived at in a single
lifetime.[2]   *Ib.*

It is our less conscious thoughts and
our less conscious actions which mainly
mold our lives and the lives of those
who spring from us.   *Ib.*

To me it seems that youth is like
spring, an over-praised season — delightful if it happen to be a favored
one, but in practice very rarely favored
and more remarkable, as a general rule,
for biting east winds than genial
breezes.   *Ib. 6*

---

[1] See John Webster, p. 314b.
[2] See Carlyle, p. 577b.

Taking numbers into account, I should think more mental suffering had been undergone in the streets leading from St. George's, Hanover Square, than in the condemned cells of Newgate.

The Way of All Flesh, 13

Every man's work, whether it be literature or music or pictures or architecture or anything else, is always a portrait of himself. *Ib.* 14

One great reason why clergymen's households are generally unhappy is because the clergyman is so much at home and close about the house.

Ib. 24

The advantage of doing one's praising for oneself is that one can lay it on so thick and exactly in the right places.

Ib. 34

The best liar is he who makes the smallest amount of lying go the longest way. *Ib.* 39

An empty house is like a stray dog or a body from which life has departed.[1]

Ib. 72

A man's friendships are, like his will, invalidated by marriage — but they are also no less invalidated by the marriage of his friends. *Ib.* 75

Life is the art of drawing sufficient conclusions from insufficient premises.

Notebooks [1912]. *Life*

All progress is based upon a universal innate desire on the part of every organism to live beyond its income.

Ib.

[1] I suppose I've passed it a hundred times,
but I always stop for a minute
And look at the house, the tragic house, the house with nobody in it.
JOYCE KILMER [1886–1918], *The House With Nobody In It*

Though analogy is often misleading, it is the least misleading thing we have.

Notebooks. Music, Pictures, and Books

The phrase "unconscious humor" is the one contribution I have made to the current literature of the day.

Ib. Homo Unius Libri

Ideas and opinions, like living organisms, have a normal rate of growth which cannot be either checked or forced beyond a certain point. The more unpopular an opinion is, the more necessary is it that the holder should be somewhat punctilious in his observance of conventionalities generally.

Ib. The Art of Propagating Opinion

Genius . . . has been defined as a supreme capacity for taking trouble.[1] . . . It might be more fitly described as a supreme capacity for getting its possessors into trouble of all kinds and keeping them therein so long as the genius remains. *Ib. Genius*

I am the *enfant terrible* of literature and science.

Ib. Enfant Terrible: Myself

An apology for the Devil: It must be remembered that we have only heard one side of the case. God has written all the books.

Ib. Higgledy-Piggledy: An Apology for the Devil

God is Love — I dare say. But what a mischievous devil Love is!

Ib. God Is Love

To live is like to love — all reason is against it, and all healthy instinct for it. *Ib. Life and Love*

The Ancient Mariner would not have taken so well if it had been called *The Old Sailor*. *Ib. Titles and Subjects*

The public buys its opinions as it buys its meat, or takes in its milk, on the principle that it is cheaper to do

[1] See Buffon, p. 423b, and note.

this than to keep a cow. So it is, but the milk is more likely to be watered.

> *Notebooks. Sequel to "Alps and Sanctuaries"*

I do not mind lying, but I hate inaccuracy.

> *Ib. Truth and Convenience: Falsehood*

ANDREW CARNEGIE
1835–1919

The problem of our age is the proper administration of wealth, so that the ties of brotherhood may still bind together the rich and poor in harmonious relationship.

> *Wealth* [*North American Review, June 1889*]

While the law [of competition] may be sometimes hard for the individual, it is best for the race, because it insures the survival of the fittest in every department. We accept and welcome, therefore, as conditions to which we must accommodate ourselves, great inequality of environment, the concentration of business, industrial and commercial, in the hands of a few, and the law of competition between these, as being not only beneficial, but essential for the future progress of the race.

> *Ib.*

Upon the sacredness of property civilization itself depends — the right of the laborer to his hundred dollars in the savings bank, and equally the legal right of the millionaire to his millions.

> *Ib.*

Surplus wealth is a sacred trust which its possessor is bound to administer in his lifetime for the good of the community.

> *Ib.*

Those who would administer wisely must, indeed, be wise, for one of the serious obstacles to the improvement of our race is indiscriminate charity.

> *Ib.*

Thus is the problem of Rich and Poor to be solved. The law of accumulation will be left free; the laws of distribution free. Individualism will continue, but the millionaire will be but a trustee of the poor; entrusted for a season with a great part of the increased wealth of the community, but administering it for the community far better than it could or would have done for itself.[1]

> *Wealth*

The man who dies . . . rich dies disgraced.

> *Ib.*

Such, in my opinion, is the true Gospel concerning Wealth, obedience to which is destined some day to solve the problem of the Rich and the Poor, and to bring "Peace on earth, among men Good Will."

> *Ib.*

Three generations from shirtsleeves to shirtsleeves.[2]

> *Attributed*

RICHARD GARNETT
1835–1906

Man and woman may only enter Paradise hand in hand. Together, the myth tells us, they left it and together must they return.

> *De Flagello Myrteo* [1905], *preface, 12*

Perfect love casts out prudery together with fear.

> *Ib. 59*

When Silence speaks for Love she has much to say.

> *Ib. 99*

Sweet are the words of Love, sweeter his thoughts:
Sweetest of all what Love nor says nor thinks.

> *Ib. 250*

Ascend above the restrictions and conventions of the world, but not so high as to lose sight of them.

> *Ib. 333*

---

[1] See Maimonides, p. 155b; Spinoza, p. 374a; and Johnson, p. 431a.

[2] There's nobbut three generations atween clog and clog. — *Lancashire proverb*, which Carnegie liked to quote.

JOHN LUCKEY McCREERY
1835–1906

There is no death! The stars go down
  To rise upon some other shore,
And bright in heaven's jeweled crown
  They shine forevermore.
    There Is No Death [1863], *st. 1*

ADAH ISAACS MENKEN
1835–1868

Where is the promise of my years,
  Once written on my brow?
Ere errors, agonies, and fears
Brought with them all that speaks in
    tears,
Ere I had sunk beneath my peers —
  Where sleeps that promise now?
    El Suspiro (Infelix) [1868]

LOUISE CHANDLER MOULTON
1835–1908

Bend low, O dusky Night,
  And give my spirit rest,
  Hold me to your deep breast,
And put old cares to flight.
Give back the lost delight
  That once my soul possessed,
  When Love was loveliest.
    Tonight

I hied me off to Arcady —
  The month it was the month of
    May,
  And all along the pleasant way
The morning birds were mad with
    glee,
And all the flowers sprang up to see,
As I went on to Arcady.   *Arcady*

BISHOP HENRY CODMAN POTTER
1835–1908

We have exchanged the Washingtonian dignity for the Jeffersonian simplicity, which was in truth only another name for the Jacksonian vulgarity.
    Address at the Washington Centennial Service in St. Paul's Chapel, New York [April 30, 1889]

HARRIET PRESCOTT SPOFFORD
1835–1921

The awful phantom of the hungry
poor.   *A Winter's Night*

CELIA LAIGHTON THAXTER
1835–1894

Sad soul, take comfort, nor forget
That sunrise never failed us yet.
    *The Sunrise Never Failed Us
      Yet, st. 4*

Across the narrow beach we flit,
One little sandpiper and I;
And fast I gather, bit by bit,
The scattered driftwood, bleached and
    dry.
The wild waves reach their hands for
    it,
The wild wind raves, the tide runs
    high,
As up and down the beach we flit,
One little sandpiper and I.
    The Sandpiper, st. 1

MARK TWAIN[1] [SAMUEL LANGHORNE CLEMENS]
1835–1910

I'll resk forty dollars that he can outjump any frog in Calaveras county.
    The Celebrated Jumping Frog
      [1865]

I don't see no p'ints about that frog that's any better'n any other frog.
    Ib.

[1] I was a fresh, new journalist, and needed a *nom de guerre;* so I confiscated the ancient mariner's discarded one ["Mark Twain"], and have done my best to make it remain what it was in his hands — a sign and symbol and warrant that whatever is found in its company may be gambled on as being the petrified truth. — *Life on the Mississippi* [1883], *ch. 50.* The earlier use of the pen name was by Captain Isaiah Sellers, in *The New Orleans Picayune.*
The phrase "mark twain," meaning "two fathoms deep," was employed in making soundings on the Mississippi riverboats.

Soap and education are not as sudden as a massacre, but they are more deadly in the long run.

The Facts Concerning the Recent Resignation [1867]

Tomorrow night I appear for the first time before a Boston audience — 4000 critics.

Letter to Pamela Clemens Moffet [November 9, 1869]

They spell it Vinci and pronounce it Vinchy; foreigners always spell better than they pronounce.

The Innocents Abroad [1869], *ch. 19*

I do not want Michael Angelo for breakfast — for luncheon — for dinner — for tea — for supper — for between meals. *Ib. 27*

Lump the whole thing! say that the Creator made Italy from designs by Michael Angelo! *Ib.*

Guides cannot master the subtleties of the American joke. *Ib.*

There's millions in it!

The Gilded Age [1] [1873]

Barring that natural expression of villainy which we all have, the man looked honest enough.

A Mysterious Visit [1875]

This poor little one-horse town.

The Undertaker's Chat [1875]

Tom appeared on the sidewalk with a bucket of whitewash and a long-handled brush. He surveyed the fence, and all gladness left him and a deep melancholy settled down upon his spirit. Thirty yards of board fence nine feet high. Life to him seemed hollow, and existence but a burden.

The Adventures of Tom Sawyer [1876], *ch. 2*

Work consists of whatever a body is *obliged* to do . . . Play consists of whatever a body is not obliged to do. *Ib.*

[1] Written in collaboration with CHARLES DUDLEY WARNER.

The minister gave out his text and droned along monotonously through an argument that was so prosy that many a head by and by began to nod — and yet it was an argument that dealt in limitless fire and brimstone and thinned the predestined elect down to a company so small as to be hardly worth the saving.

The Adventures of Tom Sawyer, ch. 5

There was no getting around the stubborn fact that taking sweetmeats was only "hooking," while taking bacon and hams and such valuables was plain simple *stealing* — and there was a command against that in the Bible. So they inwardly resolved that so long as they remained in the business, their piracies should not again be sullied with the crime of stealing. *Ib. 13*

To promise not to do a thing is the surest way in the world to make a body want to go and do that very thing. *Ib. 22*

She makes me wash, they comb me all to thunder . . . The widder eats by a bell; she goes to bed by a bell; she gits up by a bell — everything's so awful reg'lar a body can't stand it. *Ib. 35*

A baby is an inestimable blessing and bother.

Letter to Annie Webster [September 1, 1876]

There is a sumptuous variety about the New England weather that compels the stranger's admiration — and regret. The weather is always doing something there; always attending strictly to business; always getting up new designs and trying them on people to see how they will go. But it gets through more business in spring than in any other season. In the spring I have counted one hundred and thirty-six different kinds of weather inside of twenty-four hours.[1]

New England Weather. Speech to the New England Society [December 22, 1876]

[1] See Charles Dudley Warner, p. 733b.

Probable nor'east to sou'west winds, varying to the southard and westard and eastard and points between; high and low barometer, sweeping round from place to place; probable areas of rain, snow, hail, and drought, succeeded or preceded by earthquakes with thunder and lightning.

> *New England Weather. Speech to the New England Society*

We haven't all had the good fortune to be ladies; we haven't all been generals, or poets, or statesmen; but when the toast works down to the babies, we stand on common ground.

> *Answering a toast "To the babies," at a banquet in honor of General U.S. Grant [November 14, 1879]*

Among the three or four million cradles now rocking in the land are some which this nation would preserve for ages as sacred things, if we could know which ones they are. *Ib.*

It is the longest river in the world — four thousand three hundred miles. . . . It is also the crookedest river in the world, since in one part of its journey it uses up one thousand three hundred miles to cover the same ground that the crow would fly over in six hundred and seventy-five.

> *Life on the Mississippi* [1883], *ch. 1*

The world and the books are so accustomed to use, and over-use, the word "new" in connection with our country, that we early get and permanently retain the impression that there is nothing old about it. *Ib.*

Sired by a hurricane, dam'd by an earthquake. *Ib. 3*

When I'm playful I use the meridians of longitude and parallels of latitude for a seine, and drag the Atlantic Ocean for whales. I scratch my head with the lightning and purr myself to sleep with the thunder. *Ib.*

The Child of Calamity. *Ib.*

I was gratified to be able to answer promptly, and I did. I said I didn't know. *Life on the Mississippi, ch. 6*

Your true pilot cares nothing about anything on earth but the river, and his pride in his occupation surpasses the pride of kings. *Ib. 7*

By the Shadow of Death, but he's a lightning pilot! *Ib.*

A limb of Satan.[1] *Ib. 8*

I'll learn him or kill him. *Ib.*

Give an Irishman lager for a month, and he's a dead man. An Irishman is lined with copper, and the beer corrodes it. But whiskey polishes the copper and is the saving of him. *Ib. 23*

All the modern inconveniences. *Ib. 43*

The educated Southerner has no use for an *r*, except at the beginning of a word. *Ib. 44*

In the South the war is what A.D. is elsewhere; they date from it. *Ib. 45*

War talk by men who have been in a war is always interesting; whereas moon talk by a poet who has not been in the moon is likely to be dull. *Ib.*

Sir Walter [Scott] had so large a hand in making Southern character as it existed before the war that he is in great measure responsible for the war. *Ib. 46*

It was without a compeer among swindles. It was perfect, it was rounded, symmetrical, complete, colossal. *Ib. 52*

Persons attempting to find a motive in this narrative will be prosecuted; persons attempting to find a moral in it will be banished; persons attempting to find a plot in it will be shot.

> By Order of the Author.
> *Adventures of Huckleberry Finn* [1884]. *Notice*

You don't know about me without you have read a book by the name of

---

[1] Also in *The Prince and the Pauper, ch. 13.*

The Adventures of Tom Sawyer; but that ain't no matter. That book was made by Mr. Mark Twain, and he told the truth, mainly. There was things which he stretched, but mainly he told the truth.
Adventures of Huckleberry Finn, ch. 1

Jim was most ruined for a servant, because he got stuck up on account of having seen the devil and been rode by witches. *Ib. 2*

We catched fish and talked, and we took a swim now and then to keep off sleepiness. It was kind of solemn, drifting down the big, still river, laying on our backs looking up at the stars, and we didn't ever feel like talking loud, and it warn't often that we laughed — only a little kind of a low chuckle. We had mighty good weather as a general thing, and nothing ever happened to us at all. *Ib. 12*

It most froze me to hear such talk. . . . Thinks I, this is what comes of my not thinking. Here was this nigger, which I had as good as helped to run away, coming right out flat-footed and saying he would steal his children — children that belonged to a man I didn't even know, a man that hadn't ever done me no harm. *Ib. 16*

Pilgrim's Progress, about a man that left his family, it didn't say why. I read considerable in it now and then. The statements was interesting but tough.
Ib. 17

There warn't anybody at the church, except maybe a hog or two, for there warn't any lock on the door, and hogs likes a puncheon floor in summertime because it's cool. If you notice, most folks don't go to church only when they've got to; but a hog is different.
Ib. 18

We said there warn't no home like a raft, after all. Other places do seem so cramped up and smothery, but a raft don't. You feel mighty free and easy and comfortable on a raft. *Ib.*

A monstrous big river.
Adventures of Huckleberry Finn. ch. 19

Hain't we got all the fools in town on our side? And ain't that a big enough majority in any town? [1]
Ib. 26

I was trying to make my mouth *say* I would do the right thing and the clean thing, and go and write to that nigger's owner and tell where he was; but deep down in me I knowed it was a lie, and He knowed it. You can't pray a lie — I found that out. *Ib. 31*

I was a-trembling because I'd got to decide forever betwixt two things, and I knowed it. I studied for a minute, sort of holding my breath, and then says to myself, "All right, then, I'll go to hell." *Ib.*

An experienced, industrious, ambitious, and often quite picturesque liar.
The Private History of a Campaign That Failed [1885]

He is now fast rising from affluence to poverty.
Henry Ward Beecher's Farm [1885]

He [George Washington Cable] has taught me to abhor and detest the Sabbath day and hunt up new and troublesome ways to dishonor it.
Letter to William Dean Howells [*February 27, 1885*]

Whenever the literary German dives into a sentence, that is the last you are going to see of him till he emerges on the other side of his Atlantic with his verb in his mouth.
A Connecticut Yankee at King Arthur's Court [1889], *ch. 22*

Weather is a literary speciality, and no untrained hand can turn out a good article on it.
The American Claimant [1892], *foreword*

[1] See *Pudd'nhead Wilson's New Calendar,* p. 763a.

Tell the truth or trump — but get the trick.

> *Pudd'nhead Wilson* [1894].
> *Pudd'nhead Wilson's Calendar, ch. 1*

Adam was but human — this explains it all. He did not want the apple for the apple's sake, he wanted it only because it was forbidden.   *Ib. 2*

Whoever has lived long enough to find out what life is, knows how deep a debt of gratitude we owe to Adam, the first great benefactor of our race. He brought death into the world.   *Ib. 3*

Training is everything. The peach was once a bitter almond; cauliflower is nothing but cabbage with a college education.   *Ib. 5*

Habit is habit, and not to be flung out of the window by any man, but coaxed downstairs a step at a time.
        Ib. 6

One of the most striking differences between a cat and a lie is that a cat has only nine lives.   *Ib. 7*

The holy passion of Friendship is of so sweet and steady and loyal and enduring a nature that it will last through a whole lifetime, if not asked to lend money.   *Ib. 8*

Why is it that we rejoice at a birth and grieve at a funeral? It is because we are not the person involved.   *Ib. 9*

All say, "How hard it is that we have to die" — a strange complaint to come from the mouths of people who have had to live.   *Ib. 10*

When angry, count four; when very angry, swear.[1]   *Ib.*

Courage is resistance to fear, mastery of fear — not absence of fear.
        Ib. 12

Nothing so needs reforming as other people's habits.   *Ib. 15*

Put all your eggs in the one basket and — WATCH THAT BASKET.   *Ib.*

---

[1] See Jefferson, p. 474a.

If you pick up a starving dog and make him prosperous, he will not bite you. This is the principal difference between a dog and a man.

> *Pudd'nhead Wilson. Pudd'n-head Wilson's Calendar, ch. 16*

Few things are harder to put up with than the annoyance of a good example.   *Ib. 19*

It were not best that we should all think alike; it is difference of opinion that makes horse races.   *Ib.*

Be good and you will be lonesome.

> *Following the Equator* [1897].
> *Caption for author's photograph on shipboard, frontispiece of first edition*

When in doubt tell the truth.
> *Ib. vol. I, Pudd'nhead Wilson's New Calendar, ch. 2*

Truth is the most valuable thing we have. Let us economize it.   *Ib. 7*

It could probably be shown by facts and figures that there is no distinctly native American criminal class except Congress.   *Ib. 8*

Everything human is pathetic. The secret source of Humor itself is not joy but sorrow. There is no humor in heaven.   *Ib. 10*

We should be careful to get out of an experience only the wisdom that is in it — and stop there; lest we be like the cat that sits down on a hot stove lid. She will never sit down on a hot stove lid again — and that is well; but also she will never sit down on a cold one any more.   *Ib. 11*

We can secure other people's approval, if we do right and try hard; but our own is worth a hundred of it, and no way has been found out of securing that.   *Ib. 14*

It is easier to stay out than get out.
        Ib. 18

Pity is for the living, envy is for the dead.   *Ib. 19*

It is by the goodness of God that in our country we have those three unspeakably precious things: freedom of speech, freedom of conscience, and the prudence never to practice either of them.

> *Following the Equator, vol. I, Pudd'nhead Wilson's New Calendar, ch. 20*

"Classic." A book which people praise and don't read. *Ib. 25*

Man is the only animal that blushes. Or needs to. *Ib. 27*

Let us be thankful for the fools. But for them the rest of us could not succeed.[1] *Ib. 28*

There are several good protections against temptations, but the surest is cowardice.[2] *Ib. 36*

There is an old-time toast which is golden for its beauty. "When you ascend the hill of prosperity may you not meet a friend." *Ib. II, 5*

Each person is born to one possession which outvalues all his others — his last breath. *Ib. 6*

It takes your enemy and your friend, working together, to hurt you to the heart; the one to slander you and the other to get the news to you. *Ib. 9*

Grief can take care of itself, but to get the full value of a joy you must have somebody to divide it with. *Ib. 12*

In statesmanship get the formalities right, never mind about the moralities. *Ib. 29*

Everyone is a moon, and has a dark side which he never shows to anybody.[3] *Ib. 30*

The reports of my death are greatly exaggerated.

> *Cable from London to the Associated Press [1897]*

[1] See *Huckleberry Finn*, p. 761b.
[2] See *Wilde*, p. 839a.
[3] See Robert Browning, p. 665b.

A round man cannot be expected to fit in a square hole right away. He must have time to modify his shape.

> *More Tramps Abroad [1897]*

In Boston they ask, How much does he know? In New York, How much is he worth? In Philadelphia, Who were his parents?

> *What Paul Bourget Thinks of Us [1899]*

The silent colossal National Lie that is the support and confederate of all the tyrannies and shams and inequalities and unfairnesses that afflict the peoples — that is the one to throw bricks and sermons at.

> *My First Lie, and How I Got Out of It [1900]*

The blessings-of-civilization trust, wisely and cautiously administered, is a daisy. There is more money in it, more territory, more sovereignty, and other kinds of emolument, than there is in any other game that is played. But Christendom . . . has been so eager to get every stake that appeared on the green cloth, that the people who sit in darkness[1] have noticed it . . . and have become suspicious of the blessings of civilization.

> *To the Person Sitting in Darkness [1901]*

Always do right. This will gratify some people, and astonish the rest.[2]

> *To the Young People's Society, Greenpoint Presbyterian Church, Brooklyn [February 16, 1901]*

A powerful agent is the right word. Whenever we come upon one of those intensely right words in a book or a newspaper the resulting effect is physical as well as spiritual, and electrically prompt.

> *Essay on William Dean Howells [1906]*

[1] See *Psalms 107:10*, p. 21b.
The people which sat in darkness saw great light. — *Matthew 4:16*
[2] President Truman kept this saying on his desk in the White House.

It may be called the Master Passion, the hunger for self-approval.
What Is Man? [1906], *ch.* 6

The fact that man knows right from wrong proves his *intellectual* superiority to the other creatures; but the fact that he can *do* wrong proves his *moral* inferiority to any creature that *cannot.*
Ib.

Thunder is good, thunder is impressive; but it is lightning that does the work.
Letter to an Unidentified Person [1908]

As out of place as a Presbyterian in Hell.
From ALBERT BIGELOW PAINE, *Mark Twain* [1912]

You tell me whar a man gits his corn pone, en I'll tell you what his 'pinions is.
Europe and Elsewhere [1925]. *Corn Pone Opinions*

Its name is Public Opinion. It is held in reverence. It settles everything. Some think it is the voice of God. *Ib.*

Biographies are but the clothes and buttons of the man — the biography of the man himself cannot be written.
Autobiography [1924], *vol. I, p.* 2

Of all the creatures that were made he [man] is the most detestable. Of the entire brood he is the only one — the solitary one — that possesses malice. That is the basest of all instincts, passions, vices — the most hateful. . . . He is the only creature that inflicts pain for sport, knowing it to *be* pain. . . . Also — in all the list he is the only creature that has a nasty mind. *Ib. II, p.* 7

The trade of critic, in literature, music, and the drama, is the most degraded of all trades. *Ib. p.* 69

I believe that our Heavenly Father invented man because he was disappointed in the monkey.
From BERNARD DE VOTO, *Mark Twain in Eruption* [1940]

Familiarity breeds contempt — and children.[1] *Notebooks*

Good breeding consists in concealing how much we think of ourselves and how little we think of the other person. *Ib.*

Death, the only immortal who treats us all alike, whose pity and whose peace and whose refuge are for all — the soiled and the pure, the rich and the poor, the loved and the unloved.
Ib. Memorandum written on his deathbed

Loyalty to petrified opinion never yet broke a chain or freed a human soul.
Inscription beneath his bust in the Hall of Fame

The calm confidence of a Christian with four aces. *Attributed*

THOMAS BAILEY ALDRICH
1836–1907

"Root Beer Sold Here." It seemed to me the perfection of pith and poetry.
The Story of a Bad Boy [1870]

Somewhere — in desolate windswept space —
In Twilight land — in No-man's land —
Two hurrying Shapes met face to face,
And bade each other stand.

"And who are you?" cried one agape,
Shuddering in the gloaming light.
"I know not," said the second Shape,
"I only died last night!"
Identity [1877]

We knew it would rain, for the poplars showed
The white of their leaves.
Before the Rain, st. 3

Some weep because they part,
And languish brokenhearted,
And others — O my heart! —
Because they never parted.
The Difference

[1] See Aesop, p. 76a.

My mind lets go a thousand things,
Like dates of wars and deaths of kings.
Memory

It was very pleasant to me to get a letter from you the other day. Perhaps I should have found it pleasanter if I had been able to decipher it. I don't think that I mastered anything beyond the date (which I knew) and the signature (which I guessed at). There's a singular and a perpetual charm in a letter of yours; it never grows old, it never loses its novelty. . . . Other letters are read and thrown away and forgotten, but yours are kept forever — unread. One of them will last a reasonable man a lifetime.
Letter to Edward Sylvester Morse

So take him, Earth, and this his mortal part
With that shrewd alchemy thou hast, transmute
To flower and leaf in thine unending springs!
Inscription on his gravestone

ISABELLA MARY BEETON
1836–1865

A place for everything and everything in its place.
The Book of Household Management [1861]

Clear as you go.   *Ib.*

EDWARD ERNEST BOWEN
1836–1901

Forty years on, when afar and asunder
Parted are those who are singing today.
Forty Years On, Harrow football song [1872]

JOSEPH CHAMBERLAIN
1836–1914

I never like being hit without striking back.
Speech on tariff reform, Greenock, Scotland [October 7, 1903]

Provided that the City of London remains as it is at present, the clearing-house of the world.
Speech, Guildhall, London [January 19, 1904]

The day of small nations has long passed away. The day of Empires has come.
Speech, Birmingham [May 12, 1904]

WILLIAM SCHWENCK GILBERT[1]
1836–1911

Of all the ships upon the blue,
No ship contain'd a better crew
Than that of worthy Captain Reece,
Commanding of the Mantelpiece.
The "Bab" Ballads [1866–1871]. *Captain Reece, st. 1*

The *Times* and *Saturday Review*
Beguiled the leisure of the crew.
Ib. st. 7

I write the pretty mottoes which you find inside the crackers.
Ib. Ferdinando and Elvira

And down in fathoms many went the captain and the crew;
Down went the owners — greedy men whom hope of gain allured:
Oh, dry the starting tear, for they were heavily insured.
Ib. Etiquette, st. 1

Oh, I am a cook and a captain bold
And the mate of the *Nancy* brig,
And a bo'sun tight, and a midshipmite,
And the crew of the captain's gig.
The "Bab" Ballads. The Yarn of the "Nancy Bell," st. 3

As innocent as a new-laid egg.
Engaged [1877], *act I*

I'm called Little Buttercup — dear little Buttercup,
Though I could never tell why.
H.M.S. Pinafore [1878], *act I*

[1] His foe was folly and his weapon wit. — ANTHONY HOPE HAWKINS, *inscription on Gilbert Memorial, Victoria Embankment, London*

I am the Captain of the *Pinafore;*
And a right good captain too!
        H.M.S. Pinafore, act I

And I'm never, never sick at sea!
  What, never?
  No, never!
  What, *never?*
  Hardly ever!
He's hardly ever sick at sea!
Then give three cheers, and one cheer
  more
For the hardy Captain of the *Pinafore!*
        Ib.

I never never use a big, big D.   *Ib*

And so do his sisters, and his cousins,
  and his aunts!
His sisters and his cousins,
Whom he reckons up by dozens,
And his aunts!   *Ib.*

When I was a lad I served a term
As office boy to an Attorney's firm.
I cleaned the windows and I swept the
  floor
And I polished up the handle of the big
  front door.
I polished up that handle so carefullee
That now I am the Ruler of the
  Queen's Navee!   *Ib.*

Stick close to your desks and *never go
  to sea,*
And you all may be Rulers of the
  Queen's Navee!   *Ib.*

Things are seldom what they seem,
Skim milk masquerades as cream.[1]
        Ib. II

He is an Englishman!
  For he himself has said it,
  And it's greatly to his credit,
That he is an Englishman!   *Ib.*

  For he might have been a Roosian,
  A French or Turk or Proosian,
Or perhaps Itali-an.
  But in spite of all temptations
  To belong to other nations,
He remains an Englishman.   *Ib.*

[1] See Phaedrus, p. 129b, and Longfellow, p. 620b.

It is, it is a glorious thing
To be a Pirate King.
      Pirates of Penzance [1879], *act I*

I am the very model of a modern Major-
  General.   *Ib.*

I know the Kings of England, and I
  quote the fights historical,
From Marathon to Waterloo, in order
  categorical.   *Ib.*

When the foeman bares his steel,
  Tarantara, tarantara!
We uncomfortable feel,
  Tarantara.   *Ib. II*

When constabulary duty's to be done,
The policeman's lot is not a happy
  one.   *Ib.*

Come, friends, who plow the sea,
  Truce to navigation,
  Take another station;
Let's vary piracee
With a little burglaree.[1]   *Ib.*

Twenty love-sick maidens we,
Love-sick all against our will.
        Patience [1881], *act I*

You must lie upon the daisies and discourse in novel phrases of your
  complicated state of mind,
The meaning doesn't matter if it's only
  idle chatter of a transcendental
  kind.
And everyone will say,
As you walk your mystic way,
"If this young man expresses himself in
  terms too deep for *me,*
Why, what a very singularly deep young
  man this deep young man must
  be!"   *Ib.*

Then a sentimental passion of a vegetable fashion must excite your languid spleen,
An attachment à la Plato for a bashful
  young potato, or a not too French
  French bean!
Though the Philistines may jostle, you
  will rank as an apostle in the high
  aesthetic band,

[1] The roistering chorus "Hail, hail, the gang's all here" is sung to Sir Arthur Sullivan's music for these lines.

If you walk down Piccadilly with a
  poppy or a lily in your medieval
  hand.
And everyone will say,
As you walk your flowery way,
"If he's content with a vegetable love,
  which would certainly not suit *me*,
Why, what a most particularly pure
  young man this pure young man
  must be!"   *Patience, act I*

Prithee, pretty maiden, will you marry
  me?
(Hey, but I'm hopeful, willow, willow,
  waly!)   *Ib.*

While this magnetic,
Peripatetic
Lover, he lived to learn,
By no endeavor,
Can magnet ever
Attract a silver churn!   *Ib. II*

Sing "Hey to you — good day to
  you" —
Sing "Bah to you — ha! ha! to
  you" —
Sing "Booh to you — pooh, pooh to
  you."   *Ib.*

Francesca di Rimini, miminy, piminy,
Je-ne-sais-quoi young man!   *Ib.*

A greenery-yallery, Grosvenor Gallery,
Foot-in-the-grave young man!   *Ib.*

I see no objection to stoutness, in moderation.   *Iolanthe* [1882], *act I*

None shall part us from each other,
  One in life and death are we:
All in all to one another —
  I to thee and thou to me!
Thou the tree and I the flower —
  Thou the idol; I the throng —
Thou the day and I the hour —
  Thou the singer; I the song!   *Ib.*

Bow, bow, ye lower middle classes!
Bow, bow, ye tradesmen, bow, ye
  masses.   *Ib.*

The Law is the true embodiment
Of everything that's excellent.
It has no kind of fault or flaw,
And I, my Lords, embody the Law.
                                   Ib.

Pretty young wards in Chancery.
                        Iolanthe, act I

A pleasant occupation for
A rather susceptible Chancellor!   *Ib.*

For I'm not so old, and not so plain,
And I'm quite prepared to marry
  again.   *Ib.*

Spurn not the nobly born
  With love affected,
Nor treat with virtuous scorn
  The well-connected.   *Ib.*

Hearts just as pure and fair
May beat in Belgrave Square
As in the lowly air
  Of Seven Dials.   *Ib.*

Here's a pretty kettle of fish!   *Ib. II*

When I went to the Bar as a very
  young man
(Said I to myself, said I).   *Ib.*

I am an intellectual chap,
And think of things that would aston-
  ish you.
I often think it's comical
  How nature always does contrive
That every boy and every gal,
  That's born into the world alive,
Is either a little Liberal,
  Or else a little Conservative!   *Ib.*

The House of Peers, throughout the
  war,
Did nothing in particular,
  And did it very well.   *Ib.*

Oh, Captain Shaw!
Type of true love kept under!
  Could thy Brigade
  With cold cascade
Quench my great love, I wonder!
                                   Ib.

When you're lying awake with a dismal
  headache, and repose is tabooed by
  anxiety,
I conceive you may use any language
  you choose to indulge in, without
  impropriety.   *Ib.*

For you dream you are crossing the
  Channel, and tossing about in a
  steamer from Harwich —
Which is something between a large

bathing machine and a very small
second class carriage.
Iolanthe, act II

Faint heart never won fair lady!
Nothing venture, nothing win [1] —
Blood is thick, but water's thin —
In for a penny, in for a pound —
It's Love that makes the world go
     round! [2]   *Ib.*

Politics we bar,
     They are not our bent:
On the whole we are
     Not intelligent.
Princess Ida [1884], *act I*

I love my fellow creatures — I do all
     the good I can —
Yet everybody says I'm such a disagree-
able man!
And I can't think why!   *Ib.*

Darwinian Man, though well-behaved,
At best is only a monkey shaved!
     Ib. II

A wandering minstrel I —
     A thing of shreds and patches,
     Of ballads, songs and snatches,
And dreamy lullaby!
The Mikado [1885], *act I*

I can't help it. I was born sneering.
     Ib.

As some day it may happen that a victim must be found,
I've got a little list — I've got a little
list.
Of society offenders who might well be
underground,
And who never would be missed —
who never would be missed.   *Ib.*

The idiot who praises, with enthusiastic
tone,
All centuries but this, and every country but his own.[3]   *Ib.*

Three little maids from school are we,
Pert as a schoolgirl well can be,
Filled to the brim with girlish glee.
     Ib.

[1] See Heywood, p. 184b.
[2] See Lewis Carroll, p. 744b, and Anonymous.
p. 1105b.
[3] See Overbury, p. 315b, and Canning, p.
506b.

Ah, pray make no mistake,
     We are not shy;
We're very wide awake,
     The moon and I!
The Mikado, act I

Here's a pretty state of things!
Here's a pretty how-de-do.   *Ib.*

My object all sublime
I shall achieve in time —
To make the punishment fit the crime.
     Ib. II

A source of innocent merriment!   *Ib.*

     On a cloth untrue
     With a twisted cue
And elliptical billiard balls.   *Ib.*

I drew my snickersnee!   *Ib.*

The flowers that bloom in the spring,
     tra la,
Have nothing to do with the case.
     Ib.

On a tree by a river a little tomtit
Sang "Willow, titwillow, titwillow!"
And I said to him, "Dicky-bird, why do
     you sit
Singing 'Willow, titwillow, titwillow!'
"Is it weakness of intellect, birdie?" I
     cried,
"Or a rather tough worm in your little
     inside?"
With a shake of his poor little head he
     replied,
"Oh, willow, titwillow, titwillow!"
     Ib.

     There's a fascination frantic
     In a ruin that's romantic;
Do you think you are sufficiently de-
cayed?   *Ib.*

He uses language that would make
your hair curl.
Ruddigore [1887], *act I*

For you are such a smart little craft —
Such a neat little, sweet little craft,
Such a bright little, tight little,
Slight little, light little
Trim little, prim little craft!   *Ib. II*

I have a song to sing O!
Sing me your song, O!
The Yeomen of the Guard
[1888], *act I*

It's a song of a merryman, moping
    mum,
Whose soul was sad, and whose glance
    was glum,
Who sipped no sup, and who craved no
    crumb,
As he sighed for the love of a lady.
        The Yeoman of the
          Guard, act I

He led his regiment from behind —
He found it less exciting.
        The Gondoliers [1889], *act I*

That celebrated,
Cultivated,
Underrated nobleman,
The Duke of Plaza Toro!   *Ib.*

No soldier in that gallant band
    Hid half as well as he did.
He lay concealed throughout the war,
    And this preserved his gore, O!
                         Ib.

Of that there is no manner of
    doubt —
No probable, possible shadow of
    doubt —
No possible doubt whatever.   *Ib.*

Life's a pudding full of plums;
Care's a canker that benumbs,
Wherefore waste our elocution
On impossible solution?
Life's a pleasant institution,
Let us take it as it comes!   *Ib.*

Life's perhaps the only riddle
That we shrink from giving up. *Ib.*

The gratifying feeling that our duty has
    been done.   *Ib.*

Take a pair of sparkling eyes.   *Ib.*

When everyone is somebodee,
Then no one's anybody.   *Ib.*

The world has joked incessantly for
    over fifty centuries,
And every joke that's possible has long
    ago been made.
    His Excellency: The Played-Out
        Humorist [1894]

Humor is a drug which it's the fashion
    to abuse.   *Ib.*

BRET HARTE [FRANCIS BRETT HARTE]
1836–1902

A smile lit the eyes of the expiring
Kentuck. "Dying!" he repeated. "He's
a-taking me with him — tell the boys
I've got the Luck with me now"; and
the strong man, clinging to the frail
babe as a drowning man is said to cling
to a straw, drifted away into the shadowy river that flows forever to the unknown sea.
    The Luck of Roaring Camp [1868]

At the head of the gulch, on one
of the largest pine trees, they found
the deuce of clubs pinned to the bark
with a bowie knife. It bore the following, written in pencil in a firm hand:
"Beneath this tree lies the body of
JOHN OAKHURST, who struck a streak
of bad luck on the 23rd of November,
1850, and handed in his checks on the
7th of December, 1850."
    The Outcasts of Poker Flat
             [1858]

Which I wish to remark,
    And my language is plain,
That for ways that are dark
    And for tricks that are vain,
The heathen Chinee is peculiar.
    Plain Language from Truthful
        James [1870], *st. 1*

Ah Sin was his name.   *Ib. st. 2*

With the smile that was childlike and
    bland.   *Ib. st. 4*

We are ruined by Chinese cheap
    labor.   *Ib. st. 7*

And on that grave where English oak
    and holly
And laurel wreaths entwine,
Deem it not all a too presumptuous
    folly,
This spray of Western pine!
    Dickens in Camp [1870], *st. 10*

I reside at Table Mountain, and my
    name is Truthful James;

I am not up to small deceit, or any
   sinful games.
     The Society Upon the Stanislaus,
                st. 1

And he smiled a kind of sickly smile,
   and curled up on the floor,
And the subsequent proceedings interested him no more.   *Ib. st. 7*

For there be women, fair as she,
Whose verbs and nouns do more
   agree.   *Mrs. Judge Jenkins, st. 19*

Oh, yer's yer good old whiskey,
Drink it down.
     Two Men of Sandy Bar [1876],
                act IV

One big vice in a man is apt to keep
out a great many smaller ones.   *Ib.*

Give me a man that is capable of a
devotion to anything, rather than a cold,
calculating average of all the virtues!
                           Ib.

JANE ELLICE HOPKINS
1836–1904

Genius is an infinite capacity for taking pains.[1]
     Work Amongst Working Men
                      [1870]

CESARE LOMBROSO
1836–1909

Klopstock was questioned regarding
the meaning of a passage in his poem.
He replied, "God and I both knew
what it meant once; now God alone
knows." [2]
    The Man of Genius, pt. I, ch. 2

The appearance of a single great
genius is more than equivalent to the
birth of a hundred mediocrities.
                     Ib. II, 2

"Lawsuit mania" . . . a continual
craving to go to law against others,
while considering themselves the injured party.   *Ib. III, 3*

[1] See Buffon, p. 423b, and note.
[2] Also attributed to Browning, apropos of his
Sordello.

The ignorant man always adores
what he cannot understand.
        The Man of Genius,
               pt. III, ch. 3

Men in general, but more particularly the insane, love to speak of themselves, and on this theme they even become eloquent.   *Ib. IV, 1*

FITZHUGH LUDLOW
1836–1870

While we wait for the napkin, the soup
   gets cold,
While the bonnet is trimming, the face
   grows old,
When we've matched our buttons, the
   pattern is sold,
And everything comes too late — too
   late.   *Too Late, st. 2*

JOHN BURROUGHS
1837–1921

Serene, I fold my hands and wait,
   Nor care for wind, nor tide, nor sea;
I rave no more 'gainst time or fate,
   For lo! my own shall come to me.
               Waiting, st. 1

I was born with a chronic anxiety
about the weather.
         Is It Going to Rain?

Literature is an investment of genius
which pays dividends to all subsequent
times.   *Literary Fame*

It is always easier to believe than to
deny. Our minds are naturally affirmative.
    The Light of Day. The Modern
                   Skeptic

Time does not become sacred to us
until we have lived it.
        The Spell of the Past

Nature teaches more than she
preaches. There are no sermons in
stones. It is easier to get a spark out of
a stone than a moral.
    Time and Change. The Gospel
                 of Nature

Life is a struggle, but not a warfare.
     The Summit of the Years

GROVER CLEVELAND
1837–1908

Public officers are the servants and agents of the people, to execute the laws which the people have made.
> *Letter accepting the nomination for Governor of New York [October 1882]*

Your every voter, as surely as your chief magistrate, exercises a public trust.[1]
> *Inaugural Address [March 4, 1885]*

However plenty silver dollars may become, they will not be distributed as gifts among the people.
> *First Annual Message [December 8, 1885]*

The so-called debtor class . . . are not dishonest because they are in debt.
> *Ib.*

After an existence of nearly twenty years of almost innocuous desuetude these laws are brought forth.
> *Message [March 1, 1886]*

When more of the people's sustenance is exacted through the form of taxation than is necessary to meet the just obligations of government and expenses of its economical administration, such exaction becomes ruthless extortion and a violation of the fundamental principles of a free government.
> *Second Annual Message [December 1886]*

It is a condition which confronts us — not a theory.[2]
> *Third Annual Message [December 6, 1887]*

The lessons of paternalism ought to be unlearned and the better lesson taught that while the people should patriotically and cheerfully support their government, its functions do not include the support of the people.
> *Inaugural Address [March 4, 1893]*

I have tried so hard to do the right.
> *Last words*

ADMIRAL GEORGE DEWEY
1837–1917

You may fire when you are ready, Gridley.
> *To the captain of Dewey's flagship at the Battle of Manila Bay [May 1, 1898]*

WILLIAM DEAN HOWELLS
1837–1920

We live, but a world has passed away
With the years that perished to make us men. *The Mulberries*

Lord, for the erring thought
Not into evil wrought:
Lord, for the wicked will
Betrayed and baffled still:
For the heart from itself kept,
Our thanksgiving accept.
> *A Thanksgiving*

Though I move with leaden feet,
Light itself is not so fleet;
And before you know me gone
Eternity and I are one. *Time*

He who sleeps in continual noise is wakened by silence.
> *Pordenone, IV*

See how today's achievement is only tomorrow's confusion;
See how possession always cheapens the thing that was precious. *Ib.*

The wrecks of slavery are fast growing a fungus crop of sentiment.
> *Their Wedding Journey [1872]*

They were Americans, and they knew how to worship a woman.
> *The Lady of the Aroostook [1879]*

---

[1] "Public office is a public trust" was used by the Cleveland administration as its motto. See Matthew Henry, p. 386b; Burke, p. 454b; Jefferson, p. 472b; Clay, p. 538b; and Calhoun, p. 545b.

[2] See Disraeli, p. 611b.

The Bostonian who leaves Boston ought to be condemned to perpetual exile.
The Rise of Silas Lapham
[1885], *ch. 5*

The man of letters must make up his mind that in the United States the fate of a book is in the hands of the women.   *Literature and Life* [1902]

Does it afflict you to find your books wearing out? I mean literally. . . . The mortality of all inanimate things is terrible to me, but that of books most of all.
Letter to Charles Eliot Norton
[*April 6, 1903*]

I am not sorry for having wrought in common, crude material so much; that is the right American stuff; and perhaps hereafter, when my din is done, if anyone is curious to know what that noise was, it will be found to have proceeded from a small insect which was scraping about on the surface of our life and trying to get into its meaning for the sake of the other insects larger or smaller. That is, such has been my unconscious work; consciously, I was always, as I still am, trying to fashion a piece of literature out of the life next at hand.
Ib. [*April 26, 1903*]

Clemens was sole, incomparable, the Lincoln of our literature.
My Mark Twain

Some people can stay longer in an hour than others can in a week.
Attributed

HORACE PORTER
1837–1921

A mugwump is a person educated beyond his intellect.
A slogan of the Cleveland-Blaine campaign [1884]

INNES RANDOLPH
1837–1887

Oh, I'm a good old rebel, that's what I am,

And for this land of freedom, I do not give a damn.
I'm glad I fought agin her, I only wish we'd won,
And I ain't axed any pardon for anything I've done.
A Good Old Rebel [*c. 1870*],
st. 1

I won't be reconstructed, and I don't give a damn.
Ib. st. 4

ALGERNON CHARLES
SWINBURNE
1837–1909

Maiden and mistress of the months and stars
Now folded in the flowerless fields of heaven.
Atalanta in Calydon [1865], *l. 1*

When the hounds of spring are on winter's traces,
The mother of months in meadow or plain
Fills the shadows and windy places
With lisp of leaves and ripple of rain;
And the brown bright nightingale amorous
Is half assuaged for Itylus,
For the Thracian ships and the foreign faces,
The tongueless vigil, and all the pain.
Ib. chorus, st. 1

Come with bows bent and with emptying of quivers,
Maiden most perfect, lady of light,
With a noise of winds and many rivers,
With a clamor of waters, and with might;
Bind on thy sandals, O thou most fleet,
Over the splendor and speed of thy feet,
For the faint east quickens, the wan west shivers,
Round the feet of the day and the feet of the night.   *Ib. st. 2*

For winter's rains and ruins are over,
And all the season of snows and sins;

The days dividing lover and lover,
The light that loses, the night that
    wins;
And time remembered is grief forgot-
    ten,
And frosts are slain and flowers begot-
    ten,
And in green underwood and cover
Blossom by blossom the spring begins.
    Atalanta in Calydon, chorus, st. 4

Before the beginning of years
There came to the making of man
Time, with a gift of tears;
Grief, with a glass that ran;
Pleasure, with pain for leaven;
Summer, with flowers that fell;
Remembrance fallen from heaven,
And madness risen from hell;
Strength without hands to smite;
Love that endures for a breath;
Night, the shadow of light,
And life, the shadow of death.
    Ib. chorus, st. 1

Eyesight and speech they wrought
For the veils of the soul therein,
A time for labor and thought,
A time to serve and to sin; [1]
They gave him light in his ways,
And love, and a space for delight,
And beauty and length of days,
And night, and sleep in the night.
His speech is a burning fire;
With his lips he travaileth;
In his heart is a blind desire,
In his eyes foreknowledge of death;
He weaves, and is clothed with deri-
    sion;
Sows, and he shall not reap;
His life is a watch or a vision
Between a sleep and a sleep.
    Ib. st. 3

We have seen thee, O Love, thou art
    fair; thou art goodly, O Love.
    Ib. chorus

For words divide and rend;
But silence is most noble till the end.
    Ib.

[1] See *Ecclesiastes 3:2*, p. 27b.

O wise among women, and wisest,
Our Lady of Pain.
    Dolores [1866], *st. 5*

    Change in a trice
The lilies and languors of virtue
For the raptures and roses of vice.
    Ib. st. 9

O splendid and sterile Dolores,
Our Lady of Pain.   *Ib.*

Ah beautiful passionate body
That never has ached with a heart!
    Ib. st. 11

The delight that consumes the desire,
The desire that outruns the delight.
    Ib. st. 14

Despair the twin-born of devotion.
    Ib.

I have passed from the outermost
    portal
To the shrine where a sin is a prayer.
    Ib. st. 17

For the crown of our life as it closes
Is darkness, the fruit there of dust;
No thorns go as deep as a rose's,
And love is more cruel than lust.
Time turns the old days to derision,
Our loves into corpses or wives;
And marriage and death and division
Make barren our lives.   *Ib. st. 20*

What ailed us, O gods, to desert you
For creeds that refuse and restrain?
Come down and redeem us from vir-
    tue,
Our Lady of Pain.   *Ib. st. 35*

Lo, this is she that was the world's de-
    light.
    Laus Veneris [1866], *st. 3*

Ah, yet would God this flesh of mine
    might be
Where air might wash and long leaves
    cover me;
Where tides of grass break into foam of
    flowers,
Or where the wind's feet shine along
    the sea.   *Ib. st. 14*

O sad kissed mouth, how sorrowful
    it is!   *Ib. st. 79*

To have known love, how bitter a thing
    it is.   *Laus Veneris, st. 103*

There will no man do for your sake, I
    think,
What I would have done for the least
    word said.
I had wrung life dry for your lips to
    drink,
Broken it up for your daily bread.
    The Triumph of Time [1866],
                   st. 12

At the door of life, by the gate of breath,
There are worse things waiting for men
    than death.   *Ib. st. 20*

I will go back to the great sweet mother,
Mother and lover of men, the sea.
                  Ib. st. 33

I shall never be friends again with
    roses;
I shall loathe sweet tunes.   *Ib. st. 45*

Marvelous mercies and infinite love.
    Les Noyades [1866], *st. 1*

I am sick of singing; the bays burn deep
    and chafe: I am fain
To rest a little from praise and grievous
    pleasure and pain.
    *Hymn to Proserpine: After the
    Proclamation in Rome of the
    Christian Faith* [1866]

Thou hast conquered, O pale Galilean; [1]
    the world has grown gray from thy
    breath;
We have drunken of things Lethean,
    and fed on the fullness of death.
Laurel is green for a season, and love is
    sweet for a day;
But love grows bitter with treason, and
    laurel outlives not May.
Sleep, shall we sleep after all? for the
    world is not sweet in the end;
For the old faiths loosen and fall, the
    new years ruin and rend.   *Ib.*

I shall die as my fathers died, and sleep
    as they sleep; even so.
For the glass of the years is brittle
    wherein we gaze for a span.   *Ib.*

[1] See Julian, p. 144b.

For there is no God found stronger
    than death; and death is a sleep.
         Hymn to Proserpine

If you loved me ever so little,
    I could bear the bonds that gall,
I could dream the bonds were brittle;
    You do not love me at all.
    Satia Te Sanguine [1866], *st. 1*

While he lives let a man be glad,
For none hath joy of his death.
    A Lamentation [1866]. I, *st. 4*

If love were what the rose is,
    And I were like the leaf,
Our lives would grow together
In sad or singing weather.
    A Match [1866], *st. 1*

If you were April's lady,
    And I were lord in May.   *Ib. st. 5*

If you were queen of pleasure,
    And I were king of pain,
We'd hunt down love together,
Pluck out his flying feather,
And teach his feet a measure,
    And find his mouth a rein.
                  Ib. st. 6

For in the time we know not of
    Did fate begin
Weaving the web of days that wove
    Your doom, Faustine.
    Faustine [1866], *st. 24*

Take hand and part with laughter;
    Touch lips and part with tears;
Once more and no more after,
    Whatever comes with years.
    Rococo [1866], *st. 1*

Forget that I remember,
    And dream that I forget.   *Ib. st. 2*

The burden of long living. Thou shalt
    fear
Waking, and sleeping mourn upon thy
    bed;
And say at night "Would God the day
    were here,"
And say at dawn "Would God the day
    were dead." [1]
    A Ballad of Burdens [1866], *st. 4*

[1] See *Deuteronomy 28:67*, p. 10b.

For life is sweet, but after life is death.
This is the end of every man's desire.
            A Ballad of Burdens. L'Envoy

I shall remember while the light lives
      yet
And in the nighttime I shall not for-
      get.   *Erotion* [1866]

Here, where the world is quiet;
   Here, where all trouble seems
Dead winds' and spent waves' riot
   In doubtful dreams of dreams.
            The Garden of Proserpine
               [1866], *st. 1*

I am tired of tears and laughter,
   And men that laugh and weep;
Of what may come hereafter
   For men that sow and reap:
I am weary of days and hours,
Blown buds of barren flowers,
Desires and dreams and powers
   And everything but sleep.
                  Ib. st. 2

We are not sure of sorrow,
   And joy was never sure.   *Ib. st. 10*

From too much love of living,
   From hope and fear set free,
We thank with brief thanksgiving
   Whatever gods may be
That no life lives forever;
That dead men rise up never;
That even the weariest river
   Winds somewhere safe to sea.[1]
                  Ib. st. 11

Ah that such sweet things should be
      fleet,
Such fleet things sweet!
            Félise [1866], *st. 22*

Those eyes the greenest of things blue,
The bluest of things gray.   *Ib. st. 24*

I remember the way we parted,
   The day and the way we met;
You hoped we were both broken-
      hearted
   And knew we should both forget.
         An Interlude [1866], *st. 11*

[1] No matter how long the river, the river will
reach the sea. — EUGENE FITCH WARE ("IRON-
QUILL") [1841–1911], *The Blizzard*

And the best and the worst of this is
   That neither is most to blame,
If you have forgotten my kisses
   And I have forgotten your name.
            An Interlude, st. 14

And through the trumpet of a child of
      Rome
Rang the pure music of the flutes of
      Greece.
      *Song for the Centenary of
      Walter Savage Landor* [1866],
      st. 17

I am that which began;
   Out of me the years roll;
Out of me God and man;
   I am equal and whole;
God changes, and man, and the form
   of them bodily; I am the soul.
            Hertha [1871], *st. 1*

Before ever land was,
   Before ever the sea,
Or soft hair of the grass,
   Or fair limbs of the tree,
Or the flesh-colored fruit of my
   branches, I was, and thy soul was
   in me.   *Ib. st. 2*

A creed is a rod,
   And a crown is of night;
But this thing is God,
   To be man with thy might,
To grow straight in the strength of thy
   spirit, and to live out thy life as
   the light.   *Ib. st. 15*

In the gray beginning of years, in the
      twilight of things that began,
The word of the earth in the ears of
      the world, was it God? was it
      man?   *Hymn of Man* [1871]

Ask nothing more of me, sweet,
All I can give you I give;
Heart of my heart, were it more,
More would be laid at your feet:
Love that should help you to live,
Song that should spur you to soar.
            The Oblation [1871], *st. 1*

It is long since Mr. Carlyle expressed
his opinion that if any poet or other
literary creature could really be "killed

off by one critique" or many, the
sooner he was so dispatched the better;
a sentiment in which I for one humbly
but heartily concur.
Under the Microscope [1872]

A blatant Bassarid of Boston, a
rampant Maenad of Massachusetts.[1]
Ib.

To wipe off the froth of falsehood
from the foaming lips of inebriated virtue, when fresh from the sexless orgies
of morality and reeling from the deliri-
ous riot of religion, may doubtless be a
charitable office.   *Ib.*

The tadpole poet will never grow
into anything bigger than a frog; not
though in that stage of development he
should puff and blow himself till he
bursts with windy adulation at the heels
of the laureled ox.   *Ib.*

Poor splendid wings so frayed and
   soiled and torn!
      A Ballad of François Villon
                  [1878], *st. 3*

Villon, our sad bad glad mad brother's
name.[2]   *Ib. refrain*

In a coign of the cliff between lowland
   and highland,
At the sea-down's edge between wind-
   ward and lee,
Walled round with rocks as an inland
   island,
The ghost of a garden fronts the sea.
   A Forsaken Garden [1878], *st. 1*

Sleep; and if life was bitter to thee, par-
   don,
If sweet, give thanks; thou hast no
   more to live;
And to give thanks is good, and to for-
   give.
   *Ave atque Vale: In Memory of
   Charles Baudelaire* [1878], *st. 17*

[1] Harriet Beecher Stowe, whose accusations
against Byron in "The True Story of Lady
Byron's Life" [*Atlantic Monthly*, September
1869] and in *Lady Byron Vindicated* [1870]
aroused strong protests in England.
[2] See Browning, p. 666a.

Body and spirit are twins: God only
   knows which is which.
   *The Higher Pantheism in a Nut-
         shell* [1880], *st. 7*

God, whom we see not, is: and God,
   who is not, we see:
Fiddle, we know, is diddle: and diddle,
   we take it, is dee.   *Ib. st. 12*

HENRY BROOKS ADAMS
1838–1918

Accident counts for much in companionship as in marriage.
   The Education of Henry Adams
                  [1907], *ch. 4*

Women have, commonly, a very
positive moral sense; that which they
will, is right; that which they reject, is
wrong; and their will, in most cases,
ends by settling the moral.   *Ib. 6*

All experience is an arch, to build
upon.[1]   *Ib.*

Only on the edge of the grave can
man conclude anything.   *Ib.*

Although the Senate is much given
to admiring in its members a superiority
less obvious or quite invisible to outsid-
ers, one Senator seldom proclaims his
own inferiority to another, and still
more seldom likes to be told of it.
                        Ib. 7

Friends are born, not made.   *Ib.*

A friend in power is a friend lost.[2]
                        Ib.

The effect of power and publicity on
all men is the aggravation of self, a sort
of tumor that ends by killing the victim's sympathies.   *Ib. 10*

Young men have a passion for regarding their elders as senile.   *Ib. 11*

Knowledge of human nature is the
beginning and end of political education.   *Ib. 12*

These questions of taste, of feeling,
of inheritance, need no settlement.

[1] See Tennyson, p. 646b.
[2] See *ch. 28*, p. 777b.

Everyone carries his own inch-rule of taste, and amuses himself by applying it, triumphantly, wherever he travels.
The Education of Henry Adams, ch. 12

Intimates are predestined.   *Ib.* 13

Chaos often breeds life, when order breeds habit.   *Ib.*

At best, the renewal of broken relations is a nervous matter.   *Ib.*

Sumner's [1] mind had reached the calm of water which receives and reflects images without absorbing them; it contained nothing but itself.   *Ib.*

The difference is slight, to the influence of an author, whether he is read by five hundred readers, or by five hundred thousand; if he can select the five hundred, he reaches the five hundred thousand.   *Ib.* 17

The newspaperman is, more than most men, a double personality; and his person feels best satisfied in its double instincts when writing in one sense and thinking in another.   *Ib.*

A teacher affects eternity; he can never tell where his influence stops.
Ib. 20

One friend in a lifetime is much; two are many; three are hardly possible. Friendship needs a certain parallelism of life, a community of thought, a rivalry of aim.   *Ib.*

What one knows is, in youth, of little moment; they know enough who know how to learn.   *Ib.* 21

He had often noticed that six months' oblivion amounts to newspaper death, and that resurrection is rare. Nothing is easier, if a man wants it, than rest, profound as the grave.
Ib. 22

Morality is a private and costly luxury.   *Ib.*

Practical politics consists in ignoring facts.   *Ib.*

[1] Charles Sumner [1811–1874].

Nothing in education is so astonishing as the amount of ignorance it accumulates in the form of inert facts.
The Education of Henry Adams, ch. 25

Power when wielded by abnormal energy is the most serious of facts.
Ib. 28

Those who seek education in the paths of duty are always deceived by the illusion that power in the hands of friends is an advantage to them.[1]   *Ib.*

A certain chronic irritability — a sort of Bostonitis — which, in its primitive Puritan forms, seemed due to knowing too much of his neighbors and thinking too much of himself.   *Ib.*

Modern politics is, at bottom, a struggle not of men but of forces.
Ib.

We combat obstacles in order to get repose, and, when got, the repose is insupportable.   *Ib.* 29

Simplicity is the most deceitful mistress that ever betrayed man.   *Ib.* 30

No one means all he says, and yet very few say all they mean, for words are slippery and thought is viscous.
Ib. 31

Even in America, the Indian summer of life should be a little sunny and a little sad, like the season, and infinite in wealth and depth of tone — but never hustled.   *Ib.* 35

PHILIP PAUL BLISS
1838–1876

Hold the fort, for I am coming! [2]
Gospel Songs [1874], *Hold the Fort, refrain*

[1] See *ch.* 7, p. 776b.
[2] Popular version of what General William Tecumseh Sherman signaled to General John Murray Corse from Kenesaw Mountain when Corse was attacked at Allatoona Pass [October 5, 1864]: "Hold out; relief is coming."
See Sherman, p. 705a.

JOHN WILKES BOOTH
1838–1865

Sic semper tyrannis! [1] The South is avenged!

His words after shooting President Lincoln [April 14, 1865]

JAMES BRYCE
1838–1922

Law will never be strong or respected unless it has the sentiment of the people behind it. If the people of a state make bad laws, they will suffer for it. They will be the first to suffer. Suffering, and nothing else, will implant that sentiment of responsibility which is the first step to reform.

The American Commonwealth [1888], vol. I, p. 352

To the vast majority of mankind nothing is more agreeable than to escape the need for mental exertion. . . . To most people nothing is more troublesome than the effort of thinking.[2]

Studies in History and Jurisprudence [1901]. Obedience

The greatest liberty that man has taken with Nature.[3]

South America [1912]

Medicine, the only profession that labors incessantly to destroy the reason for its own existence.

Address at dinner for General W. C. Gorgas [March 23, 1914]

GEORGE COOPER
1838–1927

Sweet Genevieve,
The days may come, the days may go,
But still the hands of memory weave
The blissful dreams of long ago.

Sweet Genevieve [c. 1877]

[1] Thus always to tyrants. — *Motto of Virginia*
[2] See R. B. Sheridan, p. 481b, and note.
[3] The Panama Canal.

JOHN MILTON HAY
1838–1905

A keerless man in his talk was Jim,
And an awkward hand in a row,
He never flunked, and he never lied —
I reckon he never knowed how.

Jim Bludso, st. 2

I'll hold her nozzle agin the bank
Till the last galoot's ashore.

Ib. 5

And they all had trust in his cussedness,
And knowed he would keep his word.

Ib. 6

He seen his duty, a dead-sure thing —
And went for it thar and then;
And Christ ain't a-going to be too hard
On a man that died for men.

Ib. 7

I don't go much on religion,
I never ain't had no show;
But I've got a middlin' tight grip, sir,
On the handful o' things I know.
I don't pan out on the prophets
And free will, and that sort of thing —
But I b'lieve in God and the angels
Ever since one night last spring.

Little Breeches, st. 1

And I think that saving a little child,
And fotching him to his own,
Is a derned sight better business
Than loafing around The Throne.

Ib. last stanza

There are three species of creatures who when they seem coming are going,
When they seem going they come:
Diplomats, women, and crabs.

Distichs, no. 2

Who would succeed in the world should be wise in the use of his pronouns.
Utter the You twenty times, where you once utter the I.

Ib. 13

True luck consists not in holding the best of the cards at the table:

Luckiest he who knows just when to rise and go home.
Distichs, no. 15

The open door.
To the cabinet regarding completion of negotiations for the "open door" in China [January 2, 1900]

GEORGE WASHINGTON JOHNSON
1838–1917

And now we are aged and gray, Maggie,
The trials of life nearly done,
Let us sing of the days that are gone, Maggie,
When you and I were young.
When You and I Were Young, Maggie [1866], refrain

WILLIAM EDWARD HARTPOLE LECKY
1838–1903

Offspring of an idle hour,
Whence has come thy lasting power?
On an old song

The stately ship is seen no more,
The fragile skiff attains the shore;
And while the great and wise decay,
And all their trophies pass away,
Some sudden thought, some careless rhyme,
Still floats above the wrecks of Time.
Ib.

ERNST MACH
1838–1916

Physics is experience, arranged in economical order.
The Economical Nature of Physical Inquiry [1882]

Intelligible as it is . . . that the efforts of thinkers have always been bent upon the "reduction of all physical processes to the motions of atoms," it must yet be affirmed that this is a chimerical ideal. This ideal has often

played an effective part in popular lectures, but in the workshop of the serious inquirer it has discharged scarcely the least function.
On the Principle of the Conservation of Energy [1894]

JOHN, VISCOUNT MORLEY OF BLACKBURN
1838–1923

Evolution is not a force but a process; not a cause but a law.
On Compromise [1874]

Those who would treat politics and morality apart will never understand the one or the other.
Rousseau [1876]

You cannot demonstrate an emotion or prove an aspiration. *Ib.*

It is not enough to do good; one must do it the right way. *Ib.*

You have not converted a man because you have silenced him. *Ib.*

A great interpreter of life ought not himself to need interpretation.
Emerson [1884]

The great business of life is to be, to do, to do without, and to depart.
Address on Aphorisms [1887]

Simplicity of character is no hindrance to subtlety of intellect.
Life of Gladstone [1903]

No man can climb out beyond the limitations of his own character.
Critical Miscellanies [1908], Robespierre

There are some books which cannot be adequately reviewed for twenty or thirty years after they come out.
Recollections [1917], vol. I, bk. 2, ch. 8

The proper memory for a politician is one that knows what to remember and what to forget. *Ib. II, 4, 2*

In my creed, waste of public money is like the sin against the Holy Ghost.
Ib. 5, 3

Success depends on three things: who says it, what he says, how he says it; and of these three things, what he says is the least important.

Recollections, vol. I, bk. 5, ch. 4

Excess of severity is not the path to order. On the contrary, it is the path to the bomb. ***Ib.***

MARGARET ELIZABETH SANGSTER
1838–1912

Never yet was a springtime,
  Late though lingered the snow,
That the sap stirred not at the whisper
  Of the southwind, sweet and low;
Never yet was a springtime
  When the buds forgot to blow.
Awakening

PHILIPPE AUGUSTE VILLIERS DE L'ISLE-ADAM
1838–1889

Living? We'll leave that to the servants.[1] *Axel* [1890]

I have thought too much to stoop to action. ***Ib.***

GEORGE LEYBOURNE
d. 1884

He flies through the air with the greatest of ease,
This daring young man on the flying trapeze;
His figure is handsome, all girls he can please,
And my love he purloined her away!
The Man on the Flying Trapeze [1860]

PAUL CÉZANNE
1839–1906

Treat nature in terms of the cylinder, the sphere, the cone, all in perspective.
From EMILE BERNARD, *Paul Cézanne* [1925]

[1] Vivre? Les serviteurs feront cela pour nous.

There's a minute of life passing! Paint it in its reality and forget everything to do that! Become it itself . . . give the image of what we actually see, forgetting everything that has appeared before us.

From JOACHIM GASQUET, *Paul Cézanne* [1926]

FRANCIS PHARCELLUS CHURCH
1839–1906

Virginia, your little friends are wrong. They have been affected by the skepticism of a skeptical age. They do not believe except they see. They think that nothing can be which is not comprehensible by their little minds. All minds, Virginia, whether they be men's or children's, are little. In this great universe of ours man is a mere insect, an ant, in his intellect, as compared with the boundless world about him, as measured by the intelligence capable of grasping the whole of truth and knowledge.

Editorial: Is There a Santa Claus? [1]

Not believe in Santa Claus? You might as well not believe in fairies. . . . No Santa Claus! Thank God, he lives, and he lives forever. A thousand years from now, Virginia, nay, ten times ten thousand years from now, he will continue to make glad the heart of childhood. ***Ib.***

HENRY GEORGE
1839–1897

So long as all the increased wealth which modern progress brings goes but to build up great fortunes, to increase luxury and make sharper the contrast between the House of Have and the House of Want, progress is not real and cannot be permanent.
Progress and Poverty [1879]. *Introductory: The Problem*

[1] First published in the *New York Sun* [September 21, 1897] in reply to an inquiry from Virginia O'Hanlon.

WALTER PATER
1839–1894

Every intellectual product must be judged from the point of view of the age and the people in which it was produced.

> *The Renaissance* [1873].
> *Mirandola*

That sweet look of devotion which men have never been able altogether to love, and which still makes the born saint an object almost of suspicion to his earthly brethren.   *Ib. Botticelli*

Hers is the head upon which all "the ends of the world are come," and the eyelids are a little weary. It is a beauty wrought out from within upon the flesh, the deposit, little cell by cell, of strange thoughts and fantastic reveries and exquisite passions. Set it for a moment beside one of those white Greek goddesses or beautiful women of antiquity, and how would they be troubled by this beauty, into which the soul with all its maladies has passed?

> *Ib. Leonardo de Vinci*
> *[Mona Lisa]*

She is older than the rocks among which she sits; like the vampire, she has been dead many times, and learned the secrets of the grave; and has been a diver in deep seas, and keeps their fallen day about her; and trafficked for strange webs with Eastern merchants: and as Leda, was the mother of Helen of Troy, and, as Saint Anne, the mother of Mary; and all this has been to her but as the sound of lyres and flutes, and lives only in the delicacy with which it has molded the changing lineaments, and tinged the eyelids and the hands.   *Ib.*

All art constantly aspires towards the condition of music.

> *Ib. The School of Giorgione*

To burn always with this hard, gemlike flame, to maintain this ecstasy, is success in life.   *Ib. Conclusion*

What we have to do is to be forever curiously testing new opinions and courting new impressions.

> *The Renaissance. Conclusion*

Art comes to you proposing frankly to give nothing but the highest quality to your moments as they pass.   *Ib.*

A book, like a person, has its fortunes with one; is lucky or unlucky in the precise moment of its falling in our way, and often by some happy accident counts with us for something more than its independent value.

> *Marius the Epicurean* [1885],
> *ch. 6*

To know when one's self is interested, is the first condition of interesting other people.   *Ib.*

We need some imaginative stimulus, some not impossible ideal such as may shape vague hope, and transform it into effective desire, to carry us year after year, without disgust, through the routine work which is so large a part of life.   *Ib. 25*

JAMES RYDER RANDALL
1839–1908

Hark to an exiled son's appeal,
Maryland, my Maryland!
My Mother State to thee I kneel.

> *Maryland, My Maryland* [1861],
> *st. 2*

WILFRID SCAWEN BLUNT
1840–1922

He who has once been happy is for aye
Out of destruction's reach.

> *With Esther*

Ay, this is the famed rock, which Hercules
And Goth and Moor bequeathed us. At this door
England stands sentry.   *Gibraltar*

HENRY BURTON
1840–1930

Have you had a kindness shown?
Pass it on.　　　　*Pass It On, st. 1*

TIMOTHY J. CAMPBELL
1840–1904

What's the Constitution between
friends?[1]　　　　*Attributed [c. 1885]*

HENRY AUSTIN DOBSON
1840–1921

Once at the Angelus
(Ere I was dead),
Angels all glorious
　　Came to my bed.
　　　"Good Night, Babette!" st. 1

Time goes, you say? Ah no!
Alas, Time stays, *we* go.
　　　The Paradox of Time, st. 1

The ladies of St. James's!
　They're painted to the eyes;
Their white it stays forever,
　Their red it never dies:
But Phyllida, my Phyllida!
　Her color comes and goes;
It trembles to a lily —
　It wavers to a rose.
　　　The Ladies of St. James's, st. 4

Ah, would but one might lay his lance
　in rest,
And charge in earnest — were it but a
　mill!　　　*Don Quixote*

Form is the cage and sense the bird.
The poet twirls them in his mind,
And wins the trick with both com-
　bined.　　　*The Toyman*

He praised the thing he understood;
'Twere well if every critic would.
　　　The 'Squire at Vauxhall. Moral 2

I intended an ode,
　And it turned to a sonnet.
It began à la mode,
I intended an ode;

---

[1] Reported comment to President Cleveland,
who refused to support a bill on the grounds
that it was unconstitutional.

But Rose crossed the road
　In her latest new bonnet;
I intended an ode;
　And it turned to a sonnet.
　　　　Urceus Exit

All passes. Art alone
　Enduring stays to us;
The bust outlasts the throne —
　The coin, Tiberius.[1]
　　　　Ars Victrix, st. 8

Fame is a food that dead men eat —
I have no stomach for such meat.
　　　*Fame Is a Food That Dead
　　　　Men Eat, st. 1*

THOMAS HARDY
1840–1928

These purblind Doomsters had as
　readily strown
Blisses about my pilgrimage as pain.
　　　　Hap [1866]

When I set out for Lyonnesse,
　A hundred miles away,
The rime was on the spray,
And starlight lit my lonesomeness.
　　*When I Set Out for Lyonnesse
　　　[1870], st. 1*

Good, but not religious-good.
　　*Under the Greenwood Tree
　　　[1872], ch. 2*

The kingly brilliance of Sirius pierced
the eye with a steely glitter, the star
called Capella was yellow, Aldebaran
and Betelgueux shone with a fiery red.
To persons standing alone on a hill during a clear midnight such as this, the
roll of the world eastward is almost a
palpable movement.
　　*Far from the Madding Crowd
　　　[1874], ch. 2*

Like the British Constitution, she
owes her success in practice to her inconsistencies in principle.
　　The Hand of Ethelberta [1876]

A lover without indiscretion is no
lover at all.　　　　*Ib.*

---

[1] See Théophile Gautier, p. 658a.

In fact, precisely at this transitional point of its nightly roll into darkness the great and particular glory of the Egdon waste began, and nobody could be said to understand the heath who had not been there at such a time. It could best be felt when it could not clearly be seen.

The Return of the Native
[1878], ch. 1

The place became full of a watchful intentness now; for when other things sank brooding to sleep the heath appeared slowly to awake and listen.

Ib.

The great inviolate place had an ancient permanence which the sea cannot claim. Who can say of a particular sea that it is old? Distilled by the sun, kneaded by the moon, it is renewed in a year, in a day, or in an hour. The sea changed, the fields changed, the rivers, the villages, and the people changed, yet Egdon remained. *Ib.*

That cold accretion called the world, which, so terrible in the mass, is so unformidable, even pitiable, in its units.

Tess of the D'Urbervilles [1891],
ch. 13

That shabby corner of God's allotment where He lets the nettles grow, and where all unbaptized infants, notorious drunkards, suicides, and others of the conjecturally damned are laid. *Ib. 14*

The chronic melancholy which is taking hold of the civilized races with the decline of belief in a beneficent power.
Ib. 18

The debatable land between predilection and love. *Ib. 20*

Patience, that blending of moral courage with physical timidity.

Ib. 43

"Justice" was done, and the President of the Immortals (in Aeschylean phrase) had ended his sport with Tess.

Ib. 59

William Dewy, Tranter Reuben,
   Farmer Ledlow late at plow,
Robert's kin, and John's and Ned's,
And the Squire, and Lady Susan, lie in
   Mellstock churchyard now! [1]

Friends Beyond [1898], st. 1

I leant upon a coppice gate
When Frost was specter-gray,
And Winter's dregs made desolate
The weakening eye of day.

The Darkling Thrush [1900], st. 1

An aged thrush, frail, gaunt, and
   small,
In blast-beruffled plume.   *Ib. st. 3*

So little cause for carolings
Of such ecstatic sound
Was written on terrestrial things
Afar or nigh around,
That I could think there trembled
   through
His happy good-night air
Some blessed hope, whereof he knew
And I was unaware.   *Ib. st. 4*

Yes; quaint and curious war is!
You shoot a fellow down
You'd treat if met where any bar is,
Or help to half-a-crown.

The Man He Killed [1902], st. 5

What of the Immanent Will and its
   designs?
It works unconsciously as heretofore,
External artistries in circumstance.

The Dynasts [1904–1908], pt. I,
forescene

A local cult called Christianity.

Ib. Spirit of the Years, sc. vi

Ere systemed suns were globed and
   lit
The slaughters of the race were writ.

Ib. II, v, semichorus

My argument is that War makes rattling good history; but Peace is poor reading.   *Ib. Spirit Sinister*

---

[1] From the aisles each window smiles on grave
   and grass and yew-tree bough —
While Tranter Reuben, Gordon Selfridge,
   Edna Best and Thomas Hardy lie in Mellstock Churchyard now.

JOHN BETJEMAN, *Dorset* [1937], *st. 3*

A star looks down at me,
And says: "Here I and you
Stand, each in our degree:
What do you mean to do?"
Waiting Both, st. 1

We two kept house, the Past and I,
   The Past and I;
I tended while it hovered nigh,
Leaving me never alone.
The Ghost of the Past, st. 1

I seem but a dead man held on end
To sink down soon. . . . O you could
      not know
   That such swift fleeing
   No soul foreseeing —
Not even I — would undo me so!
The Going [1912], *st. 6*

Woman much missed, how you call to
   me, call to me,
Saying that now you are not as you
   were
When you had changed from the one
   who was all to me,
But as at first, when our day was fair.
The Voice [1912], *st 1*

What of the faith and fire within us
   Men who march away
   Ere the barn cocks say
   Night is growing gray,
Leaving all that here can win us?
Men Who March Away
[1914], *st. 1*

That night your great guns, unawares,
Shook all our coffins as we lay,
And broke the chancel window-
   squares,
We thought it was the Judgment Day.
Channel Firing [1914], *st. 1*

Only a man harrowing clods
In a slow silent walk
With an old horse that stumbles and
   nods
Half asleep as they stalk.

Only thin smoke without flame
From the heaps of couch grass:
Yet this will go onward the same
Though dynasties pass.

Yonder a maid and her wight
Come whispering by;
War's annals will cloud into night
Ere their story die.
*In Time of "The Breaking of
Nations"* [1915]

When the Present has latched its
   postern behind my tremulous
   stay,
And the May month flaps its glad green
   leaves like wings,
Delicate-filmed as new-spun silk, will
   the neighbors say,
"He was a man who used to notice
   such things"?   *Afterwards, st. 1*

Ah, no; the years O!
Down their chiseled names the rain-
   drop plows.
During Wind and Rain, st. 4

This is the weather the shepherd shuns,
   And so do I;
When beeches drip in browns and
   duns,
   And thresh, and ply;
And hill-hid tides throb, throe on
   throe,
And meadow rivulets overflow,
And drops on gate bars hang in a row,
And rooks in families homeward go,
   And so do I.   *Weathers* [1922], *st. 2*

ROSSITER JOHNSON
1840–1931

O for a lodge in a garden of cucum-
   bers! [1]
O for an iceberg or two at control!
O for a vale which at midday the dew
   cumbers!
O for a pleasure trip up to the Pole!
Ninety-nine in the Shade, st. 1

**ALFRED THAYER
MAHAN**
1840–1914

   The world has never seen a more impressive demonstration of the influence

[1] See *Isaiah 1:8,* p. 30a.

of sea power upon its history. Those far distant, storm-beaten ships, upon which the Grand Army never looked, stood between it and the dominion of the world.[1]

> *The Influence of Sea Power Upon the French Revolution and Empire, 1793–1812* [1892], *vol. II, p. 118*

Whether they will or no, Americans must begin to look outward.

> *The Interest of America in Sea Power* [1897]

ROSSITER WORTHINGTON RAYMOND
1840–1918

Life is eternal; and love is immortal; and death is only a horizon; and a horizon is nothing save the limit of our sight.   *A Commendatory Prayer*

WILLIAM GRAHAM SUMNER
1840–1910

The Forgotten Man [2] . . . delving away in patient industry, supporting his family, paying his taxes, casting his vote, supporting the church and the school . . . but he is the only one for whom there is no provision in the great scramble and the big divide. Such is the Forgotten Man. He works, he votes, generally he prays — but his chief business in life is to pay. . . . Who and

---

[1] Apart from the accidents of weather and the tides and currents, about which he admits he could not obtain trustworthy information, Julius Caesar saw no difficulty in invading the Island. There was not then that far-off line of storm-beaten ships which about two thousand years later stood between the great Corsican conqueror and the dominion of the world. — Sir Winston S. Churchill, *A History of the English-Speaking Peoples. The Birth of Britain* [1956], *p. 5*

Also quoted by Churchill in the same work under *The Age of Revolution, p. 300.*

See Themistocles, p. 78a.

[2] See Franklin D. Roosevelt, p. 970b.

where is the Forgotten Man in this case, who will have to pay for it all?

> *Speech: The Forgotten Man* [1883]

JOHN ADDINGTON SYMONDS
1840–1893

No seed shall perish which the soul hath sown.

> *Sonnet: Versöhnung, A Belief*

Gods fade; but God abides and in man's heart
Speaks with the clear unconquerable cry
Of energies and hopes that cannot die.

> *Sonnet: On the Sacro Monte*

She smiled, and the shadows departed;
  She shone, and the snows were rain;
And he who was frozen-hearted
  Bloomed up into love again.

> *Eyebright*

These things shall be — a loftier race
Than e'er the world hath known shall rise
With flame of freedom in their souls,
And light of knowledge in their eyes.

> *The Days That Are to Be*

HENRY WATTERSON
1840–1921

Things have come to a helluva pass
When a man can't cudgel his own jackass.

> *Reply when rebuked for criticizing the Governor of Kentucky*

ELIZABETH WORDSWORTH
1840–1932

If all the good people were clever,
  And all clever people were good,
The world would be nicer than ever
  We thought that it possibly could.

> *The Clever and the Good* [1890]

ÉMILE ZOLA
1840–1902

I am little concerned with beauty or perfection. I don't care for the great centuries. All I care about is life, struggle, intensity. I am at ease in my generation.
Mes Haines [1866]

My own art is a negation of society, an affirmation of the individual, outside all rules and demands of society.
Ib.

Truth is on the march and nothing can stop it.
Article in Le Figaro
[November 25, 1897]

J'accuse.
Title of letter to the President of the République, L'Aurore [January 13, 1898]

JOHN WILSON[1]
d. 1889

Oh for a book and a shady nook, either in door or out.
For a catalogue of secondhand books

ROBERT BUCHANAN
1841–1901

The Fleshly School of Poetry.
Title of article [1871]

The sweet post-prandial cigar.
De Berny

GEORGES CLEMENCEAU
1841–1929

War is much too serious a matter to be entrusted to the military.[2]
From G. Suarez, Clemenceau [1886]

The good Lord had only ten.
In reference to Wilson's Fourteen Points [3]

[1] A London bookseller, friend of Austin Dobson.
[2] La guerre! c'est une chose trop grave pour la confier à des militaires.
[3] See Wilson, p. 842b.

America is the only nation in history which miraculously has gone directly from barbarism to degeneration without the usual interval of civilization.
Attributed

There is nothing harder for the human spirit to bear than being cold-shouldered.
Quoted by Charles de Gaulle, *Le Fil de l' Epée* [1932], *ch. 2*

OLIVER WENDELL HOLMES, JR.
1841–1935

The life of the law has not been logic: it has been experience.
The Common Law [1881]

The law embodies the story of a nation's development through many centuries, and it cannot be dealt with as if it contained only the axioms and corollaries of a book of mathematics. *Ib.*

I think that, as life is action and passion, it is required of a man that he should share the passion and action of his time at peril of being judged not to have lived.
Memorial Day Address [1884]

Through our great good fortune, in our youth our hearts were touched with fire. *Ib.*

The Law, wherein, as in a magic mirror, we see reflected not only our own lives, but the lives of all men that have been! When I think on this majestic theme, my eyes dazzle.[1]
To the Suffolk Bar Association [1885]

I say to you in all sadness of conviction, that to think great thoughts you must be heroes as well as idealists.
The Profession of the Law [1886]

Thus only can you gain the secret isolated joy of the thinker, who knows that, a hundred years after he is dead and forgotten, men who never heard of

[1] See John Webster, p. 315a.

him will be moving to the measure of his thought — the subtle rapture of a postponed power, which the world knows not because it has no external trappings, but which to his prophetic vision is more real than that which commands an army.
The Profession of the Law

The prophecies of what the courts will do in fact, and nothing more pretentious, are what I mean by the law.
The Path of the Law [1897]

Certainty generally is illusion, and repose is not the destiny of man.   *Ib.*

The remoter and more general aspects of the law are those which give it universal interest. It is through them that you not only become a great master in your calling, but connect your subject with the universe and catch an echo of the infinite, a glimpse of its unfathomable process, a hint of the universal law.   *Ib.*

The rule of joy and the law of duty seem to me all one.
Speech at Bar Association Dinner, Boston [1900]

Life is an end in itself, and the only question as to whether it is worth living is whether you have enough of it.[1] *Ib.*

A great man represents a great ganglion in the nerves of society, or, to vary the figure, a strategic point in the campaign of history, and part of his greatness consists in his being *there*.
John Marshall [1901]

Taxes are what we pay for civilized society.
Compañia de Tabacos v. Collector, 275 U.S. 87, 100 [1904]

Great cases like hard cases make bad law.
Northern Securities Co. v. United States, 193 U.S. 197, 400 [1904]

[1] See William James, p. 794a.

The Fourteenth Amendment does not enact Mr. Herbert Spencer's *Social Statics.*
Lochner v. New York, 198 U.S. 45, 75 [1905]

General propositions do not decide concrete cases. The decision will depend on a judgment or intuition more subtle than any articulate major premise.   *Ib. 78*

The great act of faith is when man decides that he is not God.
Letter to William James [1907]

Life is painting a picture, not doing a sum.
The Class of '61 [*Speeches*, 1913]

I learned in the regiment and in the class the conclusion, at least, of what I think the best service that we can do for our country and for ourselves: To see so far as one may, and to feel the great forces that are behind every detail . . . to hammer out as compact and solid a piece of work as one can, to try to make it first rate, and to leave it unadvertised.   *Ib.*

The only prize much cared for by the powerful is power. The prize of the general is not a bigger tent, but command.   *Law and the Court* [1913]

Judges are apt to be naïf, simple-minded men, and they need something of Mephistopheles. We too need education in the obvious — to learn to transcend our own convictions and to leave room for much that we hold dear to be done away with short of revolution by the orderly change of law.
Ib.

I do not think the United States would come to an end if we lost our power to declare an Act of Congress void. I do think the Union would be imperiled if we could not make that declaration as to the laws of the several states.   *Ib.*

The attacks upon the Court are merely an expression of the unrest that seems to wonder vaguely whether law and order pay. When the ignorant are taught to doubt, they do not know what they safely may believe.

Law and the Court

I do not think we need trouble ourselves with the thought that my view depends upon differences of degree. The whole law does so as soon as it is civilized.

LeRoy Fibre Co. v. C., M. & St. P. Ry., 232 U.S. 340, 354 [1914]

I recognize without hesitation that judges do and must legislate, but they can do so only interstitially; they are confined from molar to molecular motions.

Southern Pacific Co. v. Jensen, 244 U.S. 205, 221, [1917]

The common law is not a brooding omnipresence in the sky but the articulate voice of some sovereign or quasi-sovereign that can be identified.

Ib. 222

Certitude is not the test of certainty.   *Natural Law [1918]*

The most stringent protection of free speech would not protect a man in falsely shouting fire in a theater and causing a panic. . . . The question in every case is whether the words used are used in such circumstances and are of such a nature as to create a clear and present danger that they will bring about the substantive evils that Congress has a right to prevent.

Schenck v. United States, 249 U.S. 47 [1919]

When men have realized that time has upset many fighting faiths, they may come to believe even more than they believe the very foundations of their own conduct that the ultimate good desired is better reached by free trade in ideas — that the best test of truth is the power of the thought to get itself accepted in the competition of the market, and that truth is the only ground upon which their wishes safely

can be carried out. That at any rate is the theory of our Constitution. It is an experiment, as all life is an experiment.

Abrams v. United States, 250 U.S. 616, 630 [1919]

I dare say that I have worked off my fundamental formula on you that the chief end of man is to frame general propositions and that no general proposition is worth a damn.

Letter to Sir Frederick Pollock [1920]

Upon this point a page of history is worth a volume of logic.

New York Trust Co. v. Eisner, 256 U.S. 345, 349 [1921]

It is said that this manifesto is more than a theory, that it was an incitement. Every idea is an incitement.

Gitlow v. New York, 268 U.S. 652, 673 [1925]

Three generations of imbeciles are enough.

Buck v. Bell, 274 U.S. 200, 207 [1927]

But if we are to yield to fashionable conventions, it seems to me that theaters are as much devoted to public use as anything well can be. We have not that respect for art that is one of the glories of France. But to many the superfluous is the necessary,[1] and it seems to me that Government does not go beyond its sphere in attempting to make life livable for them.

Tyson & Bro. v. Banton, 273 U.S. 418, 447 [1927]

The power to tax is not the power to destroy while this Court sits.[2]

Panhandle Oil Co. v. Knox, 277 U.S. 223 [1928]

For my part I think it a less evil that some criminals should escape than that the government should play an ignoble part. . . . If the existing code does not permit district attorneys to have a hand in such dirty business, it does not permit

[1] See Voltaire, p. 416b.
[2] See John Marshall, p. 485b.

the judge to allow such iniquities to succeed.

> *Olmstead v. United States, 277 U.S. 438, 470 [1928]*

If there is any principle of the Constitution that more imperatively calls for attachment than any other it is the principle of free thought — not free thought for those who agree with us but freedom for the thought that we hate.

> *United States v. Schwimmer, 279 U.S. 644, 653 [1928]*

The riders in a race do not stop short when they reach the goal. There is a little finishing canter before coming to a standstill. There is time to hear the kind voice of friends and to say to one's self: "The work is done." But just as one says that, the answer comes: "The race is over, but the work never is done while the power to work remains." The canter that brings you to a standstill need not be only coming to rest. It cannot be, while you still live. For to live is to function. That is all there is in living.

> *Radio address on his ninetieth birthday [March 8, 1931]*

Life seems to me like a Japanese picture which our imagination does not allow to end with the margin. We aim at the infinite and when our arrow falls to earth it is in flames.

> *Message to the Federal Bar Association [February 29, 1932]*

WILLIAM HENRY HUDSON
1841–1922

You cannot fly like an eagle with the wings of a wren.

> *Afoot in England [1909], ch. 6*

MARY ARTEMISIA LATHBURY
1841–1913

Children of yesterday, heirs of tomorrow,

What are you weaving? Labor and sorrow?
Look to your looms again; faster and faster
Fly the great shuttles prepared by the Master.
Life's in the loom! Room for it, room!

> *Song of Hope, st. 1*

JOAQUIN[1] [CINCINNATUS HINER or HEINE] MILLER
c. 1841–1913

That man who lives for self alone
Lives for the meanest mortal known.

> *Walker in Nicaragua. Chant I, st. 1*

I do not question school nor creed
Of Christian, Protestant, or Priest;
I only know that creeds to me
Are but new names for mystery,
That good is good from east to east,
And more I do not know nor need
To know, to love my neighbor well.

> *The Tale of the Tall Alcalde*

In men whom men condemn as ill
I find so much of goodness still,[2]
In men whom men pronounce divine
I find so much of sin and blot,
I do not dare to draw a line
Between the two, where God has not.[3]

> *Byron*

The bravest battle that ever was fought;

[1] In a paper, *How I Came to Be a Writer of Books* [*Lippincott's Magazine*, 1886], quoted in STUART P. SHERMAN's introduction to *The Poetical Works of Joaquin Miller* [1923], Miller explains that his first writing was a public letter in defense of Joaquin Murietta, the outlaw. A Sacramento newspaper banteringly identified him with the outlaw and the name Joaquin clung to him. Miller accepted it and used it in the title of his first book and thereafter.

[2] See Shakespeare, *Henry V, IV, i, 4*, p. 244b.

[3] There is so much good in the worst of us,
And so much bad in the best of us,
That it hardly behooves any of us
To talk about the rest of us.

First printed in the *Marion* (Kansas) *Record*, owned by Governor Edward Wallis Hoch [1849–1925]; assumed to have been written by him

Shall I tell you where and when?
On the maps of the world you will find
    it not;
It was fought by the mothers of men.
                    The Bravest Battle, st. 1

The soul that feeds on books alone —
I count that soul exceeding small
That lives alone by book and creed —
A soul that has not learned to read.
                    The Larger College, st. 10

The biggest dog has been a pup.
            William Brown of Oregon, st. 5

Behind him lay the gray Azores,
    Behind the Gates of Hercules;
Before him not the ghost of shores,
    Before him only shoreless seas.
                    Columbus, st. 1

He gained a world; he gave that world
Its grandest lesson: "On! sail on!" [1]
                    Ib. st. 5

The Lightning reached a fiery rod,
And on Death's fearful forehead wrote
The autograph of God.
            With Love to You and Yours,
                    pt. I, canto 3

PIERRE AUGUSTE RENOIR
1841–1919

I have a predilection for painting
that lends joyousness to a wall.
            From AMBROISE VOLLARD,
                    Renoir [1919]

In a few generations you can breed
a racehorse. The recipe for making a
man like Delacroix is less well known.
            From JEAN RENOIR, *Renoir My*
                    Father [1958]

M·INOT JUDSON SAVAGE
1841–1918

There comes an hour of sadness
    With the setting of the sun,

---

[1] Actually, it was Martín Alonso Pinzón who
said, "Adelante, adelante, I can't hold with
turning back without sighting land."
    See Columbus, p. 171b.

Not for the sins committed,
    But the things I have not done.
                    Things Not Done

A man's truest monument must be a
    man.
        The Song of a Man [*Phillips*
                Brooks], *st. 8*

CLEMENT WILLIAM SCOTT
1841–1904

Oh, promise me that some day you
    and I
Will take our love together to some
    sky
Where we can be alone and faith re-
    new,
And find the hollows where those flow-
    ers grew.
            Oh, Promise Me [1888] [1]

EDWARD ROWLAND SILL
1841–1887

At the punch bowl's brink
Let the thirsty think
    What they say in Japan:
"First the man takes a drink,
Then the drink takes a drink,
    Then the drink takes the man!" [2]
            An Adage from the Orient

No pity, Lord, could change the heart
From red with wrong to white as wool;
The rod must heal the sin: but Lord,
Be merciful to me, a fool!
                    The Fool's Prayer

'Tis by our follies that so long
We hold the earth from heaven away.
                    Ib.

The ill-timed truth we might have
    kept —
Who knows how sharp it pierced and
    stung?

---

[1] Reginald De Koven wrote the music for
Scott's ballad, which was first sung in Chicago
at the second performance of his opera *Robin
Hood*, by the famous contralto Jessie Bartlett
Davis [June 10, 1890].
    [2] See Herbert, p. 322b, and Swift, p. 389a.

The word we had not sense to say —
Who knows how grandly it had rung?
The Fool's Prayer

Earth bears no balsam for mistakes;
Men crown the knave, and scourge the
tool
That did his will.[1]   *Ib.*

SIR HENRY MORTON STANLEY
1841–1904

Doctor Livingstone, I presume?
*On meeting David Livingstone
in Ujiji, Central Africa* [*November 10, 1871*]

IRONQUILL
[EUGENE FITCH WARE]
1841–1911

Human hopes and human creeds
Have their root in human needs.
The Rhymes of Ironquill, preface

O Dewey was the morning
Upon the first of May,
And Dewey was the Admiral
Down in Manila Bay;
And Dewey were the Regent's eyes,
"Them" orbs of royal blue!
And Dewey feel discouraged?
I Dew not think we Dew.
*In the Topeka (Kansas) Daily
Capital* [*May 3, 1898*]

Work brings its own relief;
He who most idle is
Has most of grief.   *Today*

No evil deed live oN.
The Palindrome

[1] The law locks up both man and woman
Who steals the goose from off the common,
But lets the greater felon loose
Who steals the common from the goose.
    ANONYMOUS. *From* EDWARD POTTS
    CHEYNEY, *Social and Industrial
History of England* [1901], *introduction*

AMBROSE BIERCE[1]
1842–c. 1914

Mark how my fame rings out from zone
to zone:
A thousand critics shouting: "He's unknown!"   *Couplet*

Cynic, perforce, from study of mankind
In the false volume of his single mind,
He damned his fellows for his own unworth,
And, bad himself, thought nothing
good on earth.
He yearned to squander what he lived
to save
And did not, for he could not, cheat
the grave.   *An Epitaph*

Peyton Farquhar was dead; his body,
with a broken neck, swung gently from
side to side beneath the timbers of the
Owl Creek bridge.
    In the Midst of Life[2] [*1891*],
    *An Occurrence at Owl Creek
    Bridge*

To men a man is but a mind. Who
cares
What face he carries or what form he
wears?
But woman's body is the woman. O
Stay thou, my sweetheart, and do never
go.
    The Devil's Dictionary[3] [*1906*]

Achievement, n. the death of endeavor and the birth of disgust.   *Ib.*

Advice, n. the smallest current coin.
    Ib.

Bore, n. a person who talks when you
wish him to listen.   *Ib.*

Cynic, n. a blackguard whose faulty
vision sees things as they are, not as
they ought to be.   *Ib.*

Edible, adj. good to eat, and wholesome to digest, as a worm to a toad, a

[1] In 1913 Bierce wearied of American civilization and disappeared into Mexico, to seek
"the good, kind darkness."
[2] First published as *Tales of Soldiers and
Civilians*, retitled in 1892.
[3] First published as *The Cynic's Word Book*,
retitled in 1911.

toad to a snake, a snake to a pig, a pig
to a man, and a man to a worm.[1]
The Devil's Dictionary

Habit, n. a shackle for the free.
Ib.

Labor, *n.* one of the processes by
which A acquires property for B.
Ib.

Lawsuit, *n.* a machine which you go
into as a pig and come out as a sau-
sage.   *Ib.*

Marriage, *n.* a community consisting
of a master, a mistress, and two slaves,
making in all, two.   *Ib.*

Prejudice, *n.* a vagrant opinion without visible means of support.   *Ib.*

Saint, *n.* a dead sinner revised and
edited.   *Ib.*

Woman would be more charming if
one could fall into her arms without
falling into her hands.   *Epigrams*

You are not permitted to kill a
woman who has wronged you, but nothing forbids you to reflect that she is
growing older every minute. You are
avenged 1440 times a day.   *Ib.*

Self-denial is indulgence of a propensity to forego.   *Ib.*

CHARLES EDWARD
CARRYL
1842–1920

A capital ship for an ocean trip
Was the *Walloping Window Blind* —
No gale that blew dismayed her crew
Or troubled the captain's mind.
The man at the wheel was taught to
      feel
Contempt for the wildest blow,
And it often appeared, when the
      weather had cleared,
That he'd been in his bunk below.
*Davy and the Goblin: A
Nautical Ballad, st. 1*

[1] See Wallace Stevens, p. 955b.

WILLIAM JAMES
1842–1910

I have often thought that the best
way to define a man's character would
be to seek out the particular mental or
moral attitude in which, when it came
upon him, he felt himself most deeply
and intensely active and alive. At such
moments there is a voice inside which
speaks and says: "This is the real me!"
*The Letters of William James,
vol. I, p. 199, to Mrs. James
[1878]*

Nothing so fatiguing as the eternal
hanging on of an uncompleted task.
*Ib. p. 249, to Carl Stumpf
[January 1, 1886]*

The difference between the first- and
second-best things in art absolutely
seems to escape verbal definition — it is
a matter of a hair, a shade, an inward
quiver of some kind — yet what miles
away in the point of preciousness!
*Ib. II, p. 87, to Henry Rutgers
Marshall [February 7, 1899]*

Most people live, whether physically,
intellectually or morally, in a very restricted circle of their potential being.
They *make use* of a very small portion
of their possible consciousness, and of
their soul's resources in general, much
like a man who, out of his whole bodily
organism, should get into a habit of
using and moving only his little finger.
Great emergencies and crises show us
how much greater our vital resources
are than we had supposed.[1]
*Ib. p. 253, to W. Lutoslawski
[May 6, 1906]*

The moral flabbiness born of the exclusive worship of the bitch-goddess
SUCCESS. That — with the squalid cash
interpretation put on the word success
— is our national disease.
*Ib. Letter to H. G. Wells [Sep-
tember 11, 1906]*

Habit is . . . the enormous flywheel
of society, its most precious conserva-

[1] See Emily Dickinson, p. 737b.

tive agent. It alone is what keeps us all within the bounds of ordinance.

> *The Principles of Psychology*
> [1890], *ch. 4*

There is no more miserable human being than one in whom nothing is habitual but indecision. *Ib.*

Keep the faculty of effort alive in you by a little gratuitous exercise every day. That is, be systematically ascetic or heroic in little unnecessary points, do every day or two something for no other reason than that you would rather not do it, so that when the hour of dire need draws nigh, it may find you not unnerved and untrained to stand the test. *Ib.*

The hell to be endured hereafter, of which theology tells, is no worse than the hell we make for ourselves in this world by habitually fashioning our characters in the wrong way. *Ib.*

We are spinning our own fates, good or evil, and never to be undone. Every smallest stroke of virtue or of vice leaves its never so little scar . . . Nothing we ever do is, in strict scientific literalness, wiped out. *Ib.*

Consciousness . . . does not appear to itself chopped up in bits. . . . A "river" or a "stream" are the metaphors by which it is most naturally described. In talking of it hereafter, let us call it the stream of thought, of consciousness, or of subjective life. *Ib. 9*

As we take, in fact, a general view of the wonderful stream of our consciousness, what strikes us first is this different pace of its parts. Like a bird's life, it seems to be made of an alternation of flights and perchings. *Ib.*

As the brain changes are continuous, so do all these consciousnesses melt into each other like dissolving views. Properly they are but one protracted consciousness, one unbroken stream. *Ib.*

The last peculiarity of consciousness to which attention is to be drawn in this first rough description of its stream is that . . . it is always interested more in one part of its object [thought] than in another, and welcomes and rejects, or chooses, all the while it thinks.

> *The Principles of Psychology, ch. 4*

An act has no ethical quality whatever unless it be chosen out of several all equally possible. *Ib.*

In its widest possible sense, however, a man's Self is the sum total of all that he *can* call his, not only his body and his psychic powers, but his clothes and his house, his wife and children, his ancestors and friends, his reputation and works, his lands and horses, and yacht and bank account. All these things give him the same emotions. If they wax and prosper, he feels triumphant; if they dwindle and die away, he feels cast down. *Ib. 10*

So our self-feeling in this world depends entirely on what we *back* ourselves to be and do. *Ib.*

Creatures extremely low in the intellectual scale may have conception. All that is required is that they should recognize the same experience again. A polyp would be a conceptual thinker if a feeling of "Hello! thingumbob again!" ever flitted through its mind. *Ib. 12*

Let anyone try, I will not say to arrest, but to notice or attend to, the *present* moment of time. One of the most baffling experiences occurs. Where is it, this present? It has melted in our grasp, fled ere we could touch it, gone in the instant of becoming. *Ib. 15*

Genius . . . means little more than the faculty of perceiving in an unhabitual way. *Ib. 19*

The impulse to take life strivingly is indestructible in the race. *Ib. 21*

The art of being wise is the art of knowing what to overlook. *Ib. 22*

The more rational statement is that we feel sorry because we cry, angry because we strike, afraid because we tremble, and not that we cry, strike, or tremble, because we are sorry, angry, or fearful, as the case may be. Without the bodily states following on the perception, the latter would be purely cognitive in form, pale, colorless, destitute of emotional warmth.

> *The Principles of Psychology, ch.* 25

A purely disembodied human emotion is a nonentity. *Ib.*

A thing is important if anyone *think* it important. *Ib. 28, note*

In the deepest heart of all of us there is a corner in which the ultimate mystery of things works sadly.

> *The Will to Believe* [1897]. *Is Life Worth Living?*

Need and struggle are what excite and inspire us; our hour of triumph is what brings the void. Not the Jews of the captivity, but those of the days of Solomon's glory are those from whom the pessimistic utterances in our Bible come. *Ib.*

It is only by risking our persons from one hour to another that we live at all. And often enough our faith beforehand in an uncertified result is the only thing that makes the result come true.

> *Ib.*

This life is worth living, we can say, since it is what we make it, from the moral point of view.[1] *Ib.*

If this life be not a real fight, in which something is eternally gained for the universe by success, it is no better than a game of private theatricals from which one may withdraw at will. But it *feels* like a real fight. *Ib.*

Be not afraid of life. Believe that life *is* worth living, and your belief will help create the fact. *Ib. p. 62*

Man's chief difference from the brutes lies in the exuberant excess of

[1] See Oliver Wendell Holmes, Jr., p. 787a, and Santayana, p. 867a.

his subjective propensities — his preeminence over them simply and solely in the number and in the fantastic and unnecessary character of his wants, physical, moral, aesthetic, and intellectual. Had his whole life not been a quest for the superfluous, he would never have established himself as inexpugnably as he has done in the necessary.

> *The Will to Believe. Reflex Action and Theism*

All the higher, more penetrating ideals are revolutionary. They present themselves far less in the guise of effects of past experience than in that of probable causes of future experience.

> *Ib. The Moral Philosopher and the Moral Life*

There is but one unconditional commandment, which is that we should seek incessantly, with fear and trembling, so to vote and to act as to bring about the very largest total universe of good which we can see. *Ib.*

An unlearned carpenter of my acquaintance once said in my hearing: "There is very little difference between one man and another; but what little there is, is very important." This distinction seems to me to go to the root of the matter.

> *Ib. The Importance of Individuals*

Wherever you are it is your own friends who make your world.

> *From* RALPH BARTON PERRY, *The Thought and Character of William James* [1935], *vol. II* [1899], *ch.* 91, *conclusion*

Tell him to live by yes and no — yes to everything good, no to everything bad. *Ib.*

Religion . . . shall mean for us the feelings, acts, and experiences of individual men in their solitude.

> *The Varieties of Religious Experience* [1902]. *Lecture* 2

Religion . . . is a man's total reaction upon life. *Ib.*

We can act *as if* there were a God; feel *as if* we were free; consider Nature *as if* she were full of special designs; lay plans *as if* we were to be immortal; and we find then that these words do make a genuine difference in our moral life.

The Varieties of Religious Experience. Lecture 3

There is no worse lie than a truth misunderstood by those who hear it.

Ib. Lectures 14 and 15

The philosophy which is so important in each of us is not a technical matter; it is our more or less dumb sense of what life honestly and deeply means. It is only partly got from books; it is our individual way of just seeing and feeling the total push and pressure of the cosmos.

Pragmatism [1907]. *Lecture 1*

I myself believe that the evidence for God lies primarily in inner personal experiences. *Ib. Lecture 3*

Our minds thus grow in spots; and like grease spots, the spots spread. But we let them spread as little as possible: we keep unaltered as much of our old knowledge, as many of our old prejudices and beliefs, as we can. We patch and tinker more than we renew. The novelty soaks in; it stains the ancient mass; but it is also tinged by what absorbs it. *Ib. Lecture 5*

Truth *happens* to an idea. It *becomes* true, is *made* true by events. Its verity *is* in fact an event, a process: the process namely of its verifying itself, its veri-*fication*. Its validity is the process of its valid-*ation*. *Ib. Lecture 6*

Pluralism lets things really exist in the each-form or distributively. Monism thinks that the all-form or collective-unit form is the only form that is rational.

A Pluralistic Universe [1909]. *Lecture 8*

What we really need the poet's and orator's help to keep alive in us is not . . . the common and gregarious

courage which Robert Shaw showed when he marched with you, men of the Seventh Regiment. It is that more lonely courage which he showed when he dropped his warm commission in the glorious Second to head your dubious fortunes, Negroes of the Fifty-fourth. That lonely kind of courage (civic courage, as we call it in times of peace) is the kind of valor to which the monuments of nations should most of all be reared.[1]

Memories and Studies [1911]. *Robert Gould Shaw: Oration Upon the Unveiling of the Shaw Monument* [*May 31, 1897*]

The deadliest enemies of nations are not their foreign foes; they always dwell within their borders. And from these internal enemies civilization is always in need of being saved. The nation blessed above all nations is she in whom the civic genius of the people does the saving day by day, by acts without external picturesqueness; by speaking, writing, voting reasonably; by smiting corruption swiftly; by good temper between parties; by the people knowing true men when they see them, and preferring them as leaders to rabid partisans or empty quacks. *Ib.*

Democracy is still upon its trial. The civic genius of our people is its only bulwark. *Ib.*

So long as antimilitarists propose no substitute for war's disciplinary function, no *moral equivalent* of war, analogous, as one might say, to the mechanical equivalent of heat, so long they fail to realize the full inwardness of the situation.

Ib. The Moral Equivalent of War

Our colleges ought to have lit up in us a lasting relish for the better kind of man, a loss of appetite for mediocrities.

Ib. The Social Value of the College-Bred

[1] See Robert Lowell, p. 1076b.

Real culture lives by sympathies and admirations, not by dislikes and disdains; under all misleading wrappings it pounces unerringly upon the human core.
> *Memories and Studies. The Social Value of the College-Bred*

The "through-and-through" universe seems to suffocate me with its infallible impeccable all-pervasiveness. . . . It seems too buttoned-up and white-chokered and clean-shaven a thing to speak for the vast slow-breathing unconscious Kosmos with its dread abysses and its unknown tides.
> *Essays in Radical Empiricism* [1912], *ch.* 12, *Absolutism and Empiricism*

The union of the mathematician with the poet, fervor with measure, passion with correctness, this surely is the ideal.
> *Collected Essays and Reviews* [1920], *ch.* 11, *Clifford's "Lectures and Essays"* [1879]

I wished, by treating Psychology *like* a natural science, to help her to become one.
> *Ib. A Plea for Psychology as a Natural Science* [1892]

JOHN ALEXANDER JOYCE
1842–1915

I shall love you in December
With the love I gave in May! [1]
> *Question and Answer, st. 8*

PRINCE PËTR ALEKSEEVICH KROPOTKIN
1842–1921

Sociability is as much a law of nature as mutual struggle . . . mutual aid is as much a law of animal life as mutual struggle.   *Mutual Aid* [1902]

[1] Will you love me in December as you do in May? — JAMES J. WALKER; set to music by ERNEST R. BALL [1905]

SIDNEY LANIER
1842–1881

And the sun is a-wait at the ponderous gate of the West.
> *The Marshes of Glynn*
> [1877], *l.* 22

Ye marshes, how candid and simple
    and nothing-withholding and free
Ye publish yourselves to the sky and
    offer yourselves to the sea!
> *Ib. l.* 65

As the marsh hen secretly builds on the
    watery sod,
Behold I will build me a nest on the
    greatness of God:
I will fly in the greatness of God as the
    marsh hen flies
In the freedom that fills all the space
    'twixt the marsh and the skies:
By so many roots as the marsh grass
    sends in the sod
I will heartily lay me a-hold on the
    greatness of God:
Oh, like to the greatness of God is the
    greatness within
The range of the marshes, the liberal
    marshes of Glynn.   *Ib. l.* 71

Out of the hills of Habersham,
Down the valleys of Hall.
> *Song of the Chattahoochee*
> [1877], *st.* 1

Downward the voices of Duty call —
Downward, to toil and be mixed with
    the main.
The dry fields burn, and the mills are to
    turn.   *Ib. st.* 5

The incalculable Up-and-Down of
    Time.   *Clover* [1877]

Into the woods my Master went,
Clean forspent, forspent.
Into the woods my Master came,
Forspent with love and shame.
> *A Ballad of Trees and the Master*
> [1877], *st.* 1

'Twas on a tree they slew Him — last
When out of the woods He came.
> *Ib. st.* 2

STÉPHANE MALLARMÉ
1842–1898

The flesh is sad, alas, and I have read all the books.[1]

> *Poésies. Brise Marine*

Such as into himself at last Eternity has changed him.[2]

> *Ib. Le Tombeau d'Edgar Poe*

A throw of the dice will never abolish chance.[3]   *Ib. Title of poem*

To *name* an object is to take away three-fourths of the pleasure given by a poem. This pleasure consists in guessing little by little: to *suggest* it, that is the ideal.

> *Réponse à une enquête sur l'évolution littéraire* [1891]

You don't make a poem with ideas, but with words.[4]

> *From* PAUL VALÉRY, *Degas, Danse, Dessin*

DAVID LAW PROUDFIT
[PELEG ARKWRIGHT]
1842–1897

A man sat on a rock and sought
   Refreshment from his thumb;
A dinotherium wandered by
   And scared him some.
His name was Smith. The kind of rock
   He sat upon was shale.
One feature quite distinguished him —
   He had a tail.   *Prehistoric Smith*

Nature abhors imperfect work
   And on it lays her ban;
And all creation must despise
   A tailless man.   *Ib.*

HUGH ANTOINE D'ARCY
1843–1925

"Say, boys! if you give me just another
   whiskey I'll be glad,

And I'll draw right here a picture of the
   face that drove me mad.
Give me that piece of chalk with which
   you mark the baseball score,
You shall see the lovely Madeleine
   upon the bar-room floor."
> *The Face Upon the Floor* [1887] [1]

With chalk in hand the vagabond began
To sketch a face that well might buy
   the soul of any man.
Then as he placed another lock upon
   the shapely head,
With a fearful shriek he leaped and fell
   across the picture — dead!   *Ib.*

SARAH DOUDNEY
1843–1926

Oh, the wasted hours of life
   That have drifted by!
Oh, the good that might have been,
   Lost without a sigh!
> *The Lesson of the Water Mill* [1864]

But the waiting time, my brothers,
Is the hardest time of all.
> *Psalms of Life. The Hardest Time of All*

HENRY JAMES[2]
1843–1916

The face of nature and civilization in this our country is to a certain point a very sufficient literary field. But it will yield its secrets only to a really *grasping*

[1] La chair est triste, hélas! et j'ai lu tous les livres.

[2] Tel qu'en Lui-Même enfin l'éternité le change.

[3] Un coup de dés n'abolira jamais le hasard.

[4] Ce n'est point avec des idées que l'on fait des vers, c'est avec des mots.

[1] Often called "The Face on the Barroom Floor."

[2] You know how opposed your whole "third manner" of execution is to the literary ideals which animate my crude and Orson-like breast, mine being to say a thing in one sentence as straight and explicit as it can be made, and then to drop it forever; yours being to avoid naming it straight, but by dint of breathing and sighing all round and round it, to arouse in the reader who may have had a similar perception already . . . the illusion of a solid object, made . . . wholly out of impalpable materials, air, and the prismatic interference of light, ingeniously focused by mirrors upon empty space. But you *do* it, that's the queerness! — WILLIAM JAMES, *letter to his brother Henry James* [1907]
See Guedalla, p. 1011b.

imagination. . . . To write well and worthily of American things one need even more than elsewhere to be a *master.*

> *Letter to Charles Eliot Norton*
> *[January 16, 1871]*

It's a complex fate, being an American, and one of the responsibilities it entails is fighting against a superstitious valuation of Europe.

> *Letter [1872] quoted in* PERCY LUBBOCK, *Letters of Henry James* [1920], *vol. I, Biographical note*

It takes a great deal of history to produce a little literature.

> *Hawthorne* [1879], *ch. 1*

Whatever question there may be of his [Thoreau's] talent, there can be none, I think, of his genius. It was a slim and crooked one, but it was eminently personal. He was unperfect, unfinished, inartistic; he was worse than provincial — he was parochial. *Ib. 4*

Cats and monkeys, monkeys and cats — all human life is there.

> *The Madonna of the Future* *[1879]*

There are few hours in life more agreeable than the hour dedicated to the ceremony known as afternoon tea.

> *The Portrait of a Lady* [1881]

The real offense, as she ultimately perceived, was her having a mind of her own at all. Her mind was to be his — attached to his own like a small garden plot to a deer park. *Ib.*

You were ground in the very mill of the conventional! *Ib.*

The only reason for the existence of a novel is that it does attempt to represent life. *The Art of Fiction* [1888]

The only obligation to which in advance we may hold a novel, without incurring the accusation of being arbitrary, is that it be interesting. *Ib.*

The advantage, the luxury, as well as the torment and responsibility of the novelist, is that there is no limit to what he may attempt as an executant — no limit to his possible experiments, efforts, discoveries, successes.

> *The Art of Fiction*

The power to guess the unseen from the seen, to trace the implications of things, to judge the whole piece by the pattern, the condition of feeling life in general so completely that you are well on your way to knowing any particular corner of it — this cluster of gifts may almost be said to constitute experience. . . . If experience consists of impressions, it may be said that impressions *are* experience. . . . Therefore, if I should certainly say to a novice, "Write from experience and experience only," I should feel that this was rather a tantalizing monition if I were not careful immediately to add, "Try to be one of the people on whom nothing is lost." *Ib.*

We must grant the artist his subject, his idea, his *donnée:* our criticism is applied only to what he makes of it. . . . If we pretend to respect the artist at all, we must allow him his freedom of choice, in the face, in particular cases, of innumerable presumptions that the choice will not fructify. Art derives a considerable part of its beneficial exercise from flying in the face of presumptions. *Ib.*

There are few things more exciting to me . . . than a psychological reason. *Ib.*

The practice of "reviewing" . . . in general has nothing in common with the art of criticism.

> *Criticism* [1893]

The critical sense is so far from frequent that it is absolutely rare, and the possession of the cluster of qualities that minister to it is one of the highest distinctions. . . . In this light one sees the critic as the real helper of the artist, a torchbearing outrider, the interpreter, the brother. . . . Just in proportion as he is sentient and restless, just in proportion as he reacts and reciprocates and penetrates, is the critic a valuable instrument.   *Criticism*

However incumbent it may be on most of us to do our duty, there is, in spite of a thousand narrow dogmatisms, nothing in the world that anyone is under the least obligation to *like* — not even (one braces one's self to risk the declaration) a particular kind of writing.   *Flaubert* [1893]

The time-honored bread sauce of the happy ending.
    Theatricals: Second Series [1895]

I caught him, yes, I held him — it may be imagined with what passion; but at the end of a minute I began to feel what it truly was that I held. We were alone with the quiet day, and his little heart, dispossessed, had stopped.
        The Turn of the Screw
        [1898], *ending*

Live all you can; it's a mistake not to. It doesn't so much matter what you do in particular, so long as you have had your life. If you haven't had that what *have* you had? . . . What one loses one loses; make no mistake about that. . . . The right time is *any* time that one is still so lucky as to have. . . . Live!
        The Ambassadors [1903], *bk.* V,
        ch. 2

Really, universally, relations stop nowhere, and the exquisite problem of the artist is eternally but to draw, by a geometry of his own, the circle within which they shall happily *appear* to do so.
        Prefaces [1907–1909]. *Roderick*
        Hudson

There is, I think, no more nutritive or suggestive truth . . . than that of the perfect dependence of the "moral" sense of a work of art on the amount of felt life concerned in producing it. The question comes back thus, obviously, to the kind and the degree of the artist's

prime sensibility, which is the soil out of which his subject springs.
        Prefaces. The Portrait
        of a Lady

To see deep difficulty braved is at any time, for the really addicted artist, to feel almost even as a pang the beautiful incentive, and to feel it verily in such sort as to wish the danger intensified. The difficulty most worth tackling can only be for him, in these conditions, the greatest the case permits of.
        Ib.

Life being all inclusion and confusion, and art being all discrimination and selection, the latter, in search of the hard latent *value* with which it alone is concerned, sniffs round the mass as instinctively and unerringly as a dog suspicious of some buried bone.
        Ib. The Spoils of Poynton

The fatal futility of Fact.   *Ib.*

No themes are so human as those that reflect for us, out of the confusion of life, the close connection of bliss and bale, of the things that help with the things that hurt, so dangling before us forever that bright hard medal, of so strange an alloy, one face of which is somebody's right and ease and the other somebody's pain and wrong.
        Ib. What Maisie Knew

The effort really to see and really to represent is no idle business in face of the *constant* force that makes for muddlement. The great thing is indeed that the muddled state too is one of the very sharpest of the realities, that it also has color and form and character, has often in fact a broad and rich comicality.
        Ib.

To criticize is to appreciate, to appropriate, to take intellectual possession, to establish in fine a relation with the criticized thing and to make it one's own.   *Ib.*

The historian, essentially, wants more documents than he can really use;

the dramatist only wants more liberties
than he can really take.
Prefaces. The Aspern Papers

The ever importunate murmur,
"Dramatize it, dramatize it!"
Ib. The Altar of the Dead

In art economy is always beauty.
Ib.

The terrible *fluidity* of self-revelation.
Ib. The Ambassadors

The anomalous fact is that the
theater, so called, can flourish in barbarism, but that any *drama* worth speaking
of can develop but in the air of civilization.
Letter to C. E. Wheeler
[April 9, 1911]

I'm glad you like adverbs — I adore
them; they are the only qualifications I
really much respect.
*Letter to Miss M. Betham
Edwards [January 5, 1912]*

We must know, as much as possible,
in our beautiful art . . . what we are
talking about — and the only way to
know is to have lived and loved and
cursed and floundered and enjoyed and
suffered. I think I don't regret a single
"excess" of my responsive youth — I
only regret, in my chilled age, certain
occasions and possibilities I didn't embrace.
*Letter to Hugh Walpole
[August 21, 1913]*

I still, in presence of life . . . have
reactions — as many as possible. . . .
It's, I suppose, because I am that queer
monster, the artist, an obstinate
finality, an inexhaustible sensibility.
Hence the reactions — appearances,
memories, many things, go on playing
upon it with consequences that I note
and "enjoy" (grim word!) noting. It all
takes doing — and I *do.* I believe I
shall do yet again — it is still an act of
life.
*Letter to Henry Adams
[March 21, 1914]*

The effect, if not the prime office, of
criticism is to make our absorption and
our enjoyment of the things that feed
the mind as aware of itself as possible,
since that awareness quickens the mental demand, which thus in turn wanders
further and further for pasture. This
action on the part of the mind practically amounts to a reaching out for
the reasons of its interest, as only by its
ascertaining them can the interest grow
more various. This is the very education
of our imaginative life.
The New Novel [1914]

It is art that *makes* life, makes interest, makes importance, for our consideration and application of these things,
and I know of no substitute whatever
for the force and beauty of its process.
*Letter to H. G. Wells
[July 10, 1915]*

The full, the monstrous demonstration that Tennyson was not Tenny-
sonian.
The Middle Years [1917], *ch. 6*

Summer afternoon — summer afternoon; to me those have always been the
two most beautiful words in the English
language.
Quoted by EDITH WHARTON
in A Backward Glance [1934],
ch. 10

To take what there *is,* and use it,
without waiting forever in vain for the
preconceived — to dig deep into the actual and get something out of *that*
— this doubtless is the right way to
live. *Notebooks* [1948]

FREDERIC WILLIAM
HENRY MYERS
1843–1901
Coldly sublime, intolerably just.
Saint Paul

ROBERT BRIDGES
1844–1930
When first we met we did not guess
That Love would prove so hard a mas-
ter.

Of more than common friendliness
When first we met we did not guess.
> *Shorter Poems*, bk. I [1873],
> no. 16, l. 1

For beauty being the best of all we
know
Sums up the unsearchable and secret
aims
Of nature.
> *The Growth of Love* [1876].
> *Sonnet 8*

Whither, O splendid ship, thy white
sails crowding,
Leaning across the bosom of the urgent
West,
That fearest nor sea rising, nor sky
clouding,
Whither away, fair rover, and what thy
quest?
> *Shorter Poems*, bk. II [1879],
> no. 2 (A Passer-By), st. 1

I have loved flowers that fade,
Within whose magic tents
Rich hues have marriage made
With sweet unmemoried scents.
> *Ib. no. 13, st. 1*

Perfect little body, without fault or
stain on thee,
With promise of strength and manhood full and fair!
> *Ib. III [1880–1884], no. 4*
> *(On a Dead Child), st. 1*

So sweet love seemed that April morn,
When first we kissed beside the thorn,
So strangely sweet, it was not strange
We thought that love could never
change.
> *Ib. V [1893], no. 5, st. 1*

My delight and thy delight
Walking, like two angels white,
In the gardens of the night.
> *New Poems* [1899] *no. 9*

Gird on thy sword, O man, thy
strength endue,
In fair desire thine earth-born joy renew.
Live thou thy life beneath the making
sun

Till Beauty, Truth, and Love in thee
are one.
> *Later Poems* [1913], *no. 19 (A*
> *Hymn of Nature), VII, st. 1*

Wisdom will repudiate thee, if thou
think to inquire
why things are as they are or whence
they came: thy task
is first to learn what is, and in pursuant
knowledge
pure intellect will find pure pleasure
and the only ground
for a philosophy comformable to truth.
> *The Testament of Beauty* [1929]

Man, in the unsearchable darkness,
knoweth one thing
That as he is, so was he made.   *Ib.*

ROBERT JONES BURDETTE
1844–1914

There are two days in the week about
which and upon which I never worry.
Two carefree days, kept sacredly free
from fear and apprehension. One of
these days is Yesterday. . . . And the
other day I do not worry about is Tomorrow.   *The Golden Day*

It isn't the experience of today that
drives men mad. It is the remorse for
something that happened yesterday,
and the dread of what tomorrow may
disclose.   *Ib.*

ANATOLE FRANCE [JACQUES ANATOLE FRANÇOIS THIBAULT]
1844–1924

I do not know any reading more easy,
more fascinating, more delightful than
a catalogue.
> *The Crime of Sylvestre Bon-*
> *nard* [1] [1881]. *The Log, De-*
> *cember 24, 1849*

All the historical books which contain no lies are extremely tedious.
>   *Ib.*

---

[1] Translated by LAFCADIO HEARN.

Lovers who love truly do not write down their happiness.

> The Crime of Sylvestre Bon-
> nard. November 30, 1859

To know is nothing at all; to imagine is everything.   *Ib. pt. II, ch. 2*

He flattered himself on being a man without any prejudices; and this pretension itself is a very great prejudice.
> *Ib. 4*

Those who have given themselves the most concern about the happiness of peoples have made their neighbors very miserable.   *Ib.*

Man is so made that he can only find relaxation from one kind of labor by taking up another.   *Ib.*

People who have no weaknesses are terrible; there is no way of taking advantage of them.   *Ib.*

The whole art of teaching is only the art of awakening the natural curiosity of young minds for the purpose of satisfying it afterwards.   *Ib.*

The good critic is one who tells of his mind's adventures among masterpieces.
> *La Vie Littéraire [1888], preface*

We reproach people for talking about themselves; but it is the subject they treat best.
> *Ib. Journal des Goncourt*

Chance is perhaps the pseudonym of God when He did not want to sign.[1]
> *Le Jardin d'Epicure [1894]*

The law, in its majestic equality, forbids the rich as well as the poor to sleep under bridges, to beg in the streets, and to steal bread.   *Le Lys Rouge[1894]*

We have medicines to make women speak; we have none to make them keep silence.
> *The Man Who Married a Dumb
> Wife [1912],[2] act II, sc. iv*

[1] See Einstein, p. 950b.
[2] Translated by CURTIS HIDDEN PAGE.

A tale without love is like beef without mustard: an insipid dish.
> *La Révolte des Anges [1914], ch. 8*

RICHARD WATSON GILDER
1844–1909

What is a sonnet? 'Tis a pearly shell
That murmurs of the far-off murmuring sea;
A precious jewel carved most curiously;
It is a little picture painted well.
> *The Sonnet*

GERARD MANLEY HOPKINS[1]
1844–1889

And I have asked to be
  Where no storms come,
Where the green swell is in the havens dumb,
  And out of the swing of the sea.
> *Poems,[2] no. 20, Heaven-
> Haven, st. 2*

Elected Silence, sing to me
And beat upon my whorlèd ear,
Pipe me to pastures still and be
The music that I care to hear.
> *No. 24, The Habit of
> Perfection, st. 1*

  Thou mastering me
    God! giver of breath and bread;
  World's strand, sway of the sea;
    Lord of living and dead;
Thou hast bound bones and veins in me, fastened me flesh,
And after it almost unmade, what with dread,
  Thy doing: and dost thou touch me afresh?
Over again I feel thy finger and find thee.
> *No. 28, The Wreck of the
> Deutschland, st. 1*

[1] He has left us only ninety poems — but so essential that they will color and convert the development of English poetry for many decades to come. — HERBERT READ [1893–] in *The Criterion*, April, 1931
[2] First published in 1918, edited by Robert Bridges. Poem numbers are from the third edition [1948], edited by W. H. Gardner.

The world is charged with the grandeur of God.
> No. 31, *God's Grandeur, l. 1*

Look at the stars! look, look up at the skies!
O look at all the fire-folk sitting in the air!
> No. 32, *The Starlight Night, l. 1*

I caught this morning morning's minion, king-
dom of daylight's dauphin, dapple-
dawn-drawn Falcon, in his riding
Of the rolling level underneath him steady air, and striding
High there, how he rung upon the rein of a wimpling wing
In his ecstasy!
> No. 36, *The Windhover, l. 1*

The achieve of, the mastery of the thing!   *Ib. l. 8*

Brute beauty and valor and act, oh, air, pride, plume, here
Buckle!   *Ib. l. 9*

Glory be to God for dappled things.
> No. 37, *Pied Beauty, l. 1*

All things counter, original, spare, strange;
Whatever is fickle, freckled (who knows how?)
With swift, slow; sweet, sour; adazzle, dim;
He fathers-forth whose beauty is past change:
Praise him.   *Ib. l. 7*

Summer ends now; now, barbarous in beauty, the stooks arise
Around; up above, what wind-walks! what lovely behavior
Of silk-sack clouds! Has wilder, willful-wavier
Meal-drift molded ever and melted across skies?
> No. 38, *Hurrahing in Harvest, st. 1*

Felix Randal the farrier, O is he dead then? My duty all ended,
Who have watched his mold of man, big-boned and hardy-handsome,
Pining, pining.
> No. 53, *Felix Randal, st. 1*

When thou at the random grim forge, powerful amidst peers,
Didst fettle for the great gray drayhorse his bright and battering sandal!
> No. 53, *Felix Randal, st. 4*

Margaret, are you grieving
Over Goldengrove unleaving?
> No. 55, *Spring and Fall, l. 1*

Nor mouth had, no nor mind, ex-pressed
What heart heard of, ghost guessed:
It is the blight man was born for,
It is Margaret you mourn for.
> *Ib. l. 12*

As kingfishers catch fire, dragonflies draw flame.   No. 57, *l. 1*

How to keep — is there any any, is there none such, nowhere known some, bow or brooch or braid or brace, lace, latch or catch or key to keep
Back beauty, keep it, beauty, beauty, beauty . . . from vanishing away?
> No. 59, *The Leaden Echo and the Golden Echo, l. 1*

I say that we are wound
With mercy round and round
As if with air.
> No. 60, *The Blessed Virgin Compared to the Air We Breathe, l. 34*

World-mothering air, air wild,
Wound with thee, in thee isled,
Fold home, fast fold thy child.
> *Ib. l. 124*

Not, I'll not, carrion comfort, Despair, not feast on thee;
Not untwist — slack they may be — these last strands of man
In me or, most weary, cry *I can no more*. I can;
Can something, hope, wish day come, not choose not to be.
> No. 64, *Carrion Comfort, l. 1*

That night, that year
Of now done darkness I wretch lay wrestling with (my God!) my God.   *Ib. l. 13*

No worst, there is none. Pitched past
   pitch of grief,
More pangs will, schooled at forepangs,
   wilder wring.   *No. 65, l. 1*

O the mind, mind has mountains; cliffs
   of fall
Frightful, sheer, no-man-fathomed.
                 Ib. l. 9

I wake and feel the fell of dark, not day.
What hours, O what black hours we
   have spent
This night.   *No. 69, l. 1*

I am gall, I am heartburn.   *Ib. l. 9*

I am all at once what Christ is, since he
   was what I am, and
This Jack, joke, poor potsherd, patch,
   matchwood, immortal diamond,
Is immortal diamond.
     No. 72, That Nature Is a Hera-
     clitean Fire and of the Comfort
     of the Resurrection, last lines

No doubt my poetry errs on the side
of oddness. I hope in time to have a
more balanced and Miltonic style. But
as air, melody, is what strikes me most
of all in music, and design in painting,
so design, pattern, or what I am in the
habit of calling *inscape* is what I above
all aim at in poetry. Now it is the virtue
of design, pattern, or inscape to be distinctive, and it is the vice of distinctiveness to become queer. This vice I
cannot have escaped.
     Letter to Robert Bridges
     [February 15, 1879]

The poetical language of an age
should be the current language heightened, to any degree heightened and unlike itself, but not . . . an obsolete
one.   *Ib. [August 14, 1879]*

ANDREW LANG
1844–1912

You can cover a great deal of country in
   books.
     To the Gentle Reader, st. 5

Why, why are rhymes so rare to *love?*
     Ballade of Difficult Rhymes

There's a joy without canker or cark,
There's a pleasure eternally new,
'Tis to gloat on the glaze and the mark
Of China that's ancient and blue.
     Ballade of Blue China, st. 1

The surge and thunder of the Odyssey.
     Sonnet, The Odyssey

JAMES HILARY
MULLIGAN
1844–1916

The moonlight is the softest, in Ken-
   tucky,
Summer days come oftest, in Kentucky,
   Friendship is the strongest,
   Love's fires glow the longest,
   Yet a wrong is always wrongest,
     In Kentucky.
     In Kentucky, st. 1

Songbirds are sweetest, in Kentucky,
Thoroughbreds the fleetest, in Ken-
   tucky;
   The mountains tower proudest,
   Thunder peals the loudest,
   The landscape is the grandest,
   And politics the damnedest,
     In Kentucky.   *Ib. st. 7*

FRIEDRICH WILHELM
NIETZSCHE
1844–1900

Our destiny exercises its influence
over us even when, as yet, we have not
learned its nature: it is our future that
lays down the law of our today.
     Human, All Too Human [1]
     [1878], 7

One must have a good memory to be
able to keep the promises one makes.
                 Ib. 59

One will rarely err if extreme actions
be ascribed to vanity, ordinary actions
to habit, and mean actions to fear.
                 Ib. 74

Every tradition grows ever more
venerable — the more remote is its
origin, the more confused that origin is.
The reverence due to it increases from

[1] Translated by ALEXANDER HARVEY.

generation to generation. The tradition finally becomes holy and inspires awe.
Human, All Too Human, 96

I teach you the Superman. Man is something that is to be surpassed.
Thus Spake Zarathustra [1] [1883–1891], *prologue, ch. 3*

Man is a rope stretched between the animal and the Superman — a rope over an abyss. *Ib. 4*

I want to teach men the sense of their existence, which is the Superman, the lightning out of the dark cloud man. *Ib. 7*

This is the hardest of all: to close the open hand out of love, and keep modest as a giver. *Ib. pt. II, ch. 23*

Distrust all in whom the impulse to punish is powerful. *Ib. 29*

We ought to learn from the kine one thing: ruminating. *Ib. IV, 68*

If ye would go up high, then use your own legs! Do not get yourselves *carried* aloft; do not seat yourselves on other people's backs and heads! *Ib. 73*

It is certainly not the least charm of a theory that it is refutable.
Beyond Good and Evil [2] [1885–1886], *I, 18*

No one is such a liar as the indignant man. *Ib. II, 26*

It is not the strength but the duration of great sentiments that makes great men. *Ib. IV, 72*

In revenge and in love woman is more barbarous than man. *Ib. 139*

The thought of suicide is a great consolation: [3] by means of it one gets successfully through many a bad night.
Ib. 157

[1] Translated by THOMAS COMMON.
[2] Translated by HELEN ZIMMERN.
[3] We are in the power of no calamity while death is in our own. — SIR THOMAS BROWNE, *Religio Medici* [1642] (Everyman ed.), *p. 50*

Blessed are the forgetful: for they get the better even of their blunders.
Beyond Good and Evil VII, 217

Is not life a hundred times too short for us to bore ourselves? *Ib. 227*

One does not know — cannot know — the best that is in one.
Ib. VIII, 249

The melancholia of everything completed! *Ib. IX, 277*

The masters have been done away with; the morality of the common man has triumphed.
Genealogy of Morals [1887], *essay 1, aphorism 9*

At the core of all these aristocratic races the beast of prey is not to be mistaken, the magnificent *blond beast*, avidly rampant for spoil and victory.
Ib. 11

The broad effects which can be obtained by punishment in man and beast are the increase of fear, the sharpening of the sense of cunning, the mastery of the desires; so it is that punishment tames man, but does not make him "better." *Ib. 2, 15*

The sick are the greatest danger for the healthy; it is not from the strongest that harm comes to the strong, but from the weakest. *Ib. 3, 14*

A strong and well-constituted man digests his experiences (deeds and misdeeds all included) just as he digests his meats, even when he has some tough morsels to swallow. *Ib. 16*

Two great European narcotics, alcohol and Christianity.
The Twilight of the Idols [1888]. *Things the Germans Lack, 2*

What is it: is man only a blunder of God, or God only a blunder of man?
—— *Ib.*

If a man have a strong faith he can indulge in the luxury of skepticism.
Ib. 12

Liberal institutions straightway cease

from being liberal the moment they are soundly established: once this is attained no more grievous and more thorough enemies of freedom exist than liberal institutions.

The Twilight of the Idols.
Things the Germans Lack,
38

It is my ambition to say in ten sentences what everyone else says in a whole book — what everyone else does *not* say in a whole book. *Ib.* 51

Love is the state in which man sees things most widely different from what they are. The force of illusion reaches its zenith here, as likewise the sweetening and transfiguring power. When a man is in love he endures more than at other times; he submits to everything.

The Antichrist [1] [1888],
aphorism 23

God created woman. And boredom did indeed cease from that moment — but many other things ceased as well! Woman was God's *second* mistake. *Ib.* 48

Life always gets harder toward the summit — the cold increases, responsibility increases. *Ib.* 57

I call Christianity the one great curse, the one enormous and innermost perversion, the one great instinct of revenge, for which no means are too venomous, too underhand, too underground and too petty — I call it the one immortal blemish of mankind.

Ib. 62

My doctrine is: Live that thou mayest desire to live again — that is thy duty — for in any case thou wilt live again! *Eternal Recurrence,*[1] 27

Even a thought, even a possibility, can shatter us and transform us.

Ib. 30

Nothing on earth consumes a man more quickly than the passion of resentment. *Ecce Homo* [1] [1888]

I believe only in French culture, and regard everything else in Europe which

[1] Translated by ANTHONY M. LUDOVICI.

calls itself "culture" as a misunderstanding. I do not even take the German kind into consideration.

Ecce Homo

Wherever Germany extends her sway, she ruins culture. *Ib.*

As an artist, a man has no home in Europe save in Paris. *Ib.*

Simply by being compelled to keep constantly on his guard, a man may grow so weak as to be unable any longer to defend himself. *Ib.*

My time has not yet come either; some are born posthumously. *Ib.*

No one can draw more out of things, books included, than he already knows. A man has no ears for that to which experience has given him no access.

Ib.

The Germans are like women, you can scarcely ever fathom their depths — they haven't any.[1] *Ib.*

All prejudices may be traced back to the intestines. A sedentary life is the real sin against the Holy Ghost.[2] *Ib.*

One must separate from anything that forces one to repeat No again and again. *Ib.*

JOHN BOYLE O'REILLY
1844–1890

They who see the Flying Dutchman never, never reach the shore.
The Flying Dutchman

Doubt is brother-devil to Despair.
Prometheus

The world is large when weary leagues two loving hearts divide
But the world is small when your enemy is loose on the other side.
Distance

The red rose whispers of passion
And the white rose breathes of love;

[1] Man thinks woman profound — why? Because he can never fathom her depths. Woman is not even shallow. — *The Twilight of the Idols, Maxims and Missiles, 27*

[2] Translated by CLIFTON P. FADIMAN.

O, the red rose is a falcon,
 And the white rose is a dove.
     A White Rose, st. 1

You may grind their souls in the self-
 same mill,
You may bind them, heart and brow;
But the poet will follow the rainbow
 still,
And his brother will follow the plow.
   The Rainbow's Treasure, st. 5

Be silent and safe — silence never betrays you.   *Ib.*

This truth keep in sight — every man
 on the planet
Has just as much right as yourself to
 the road.   *Ib.*

The organized charity, scrimped and
 iced,
In the name of a cautious, statistical
 Christ.[1] *In Bohemia, st. 5*

Well blest is he who has a dear one
 dead;
A friend he has whose face will never
 change —
A dear communion that will not grow
 strange;
The anchor of a love is death.
      Forever, st. 3

ARTHUR WILLIAM
EDGAR
O'SHAUGHNESSY
1844–1881

We are the music-makers,
 And we are the dreamers of dreams,
Wandering by lone sea breakers,
 And sitting by desolate streams;
World-losers and world-forsakers,
 On whom the pale moon gleams:
Yet we are the movers and shakers
 Of the world forever, it seems.
      Ode, st. 1

One man with a dream, at pleasure,
 Shall go forth and conquer a crown;

[1] See Southey, p. 533a, and Hood, p. 593a.

And three with a new song's measure
Can trample an empire down.
      Ode, st. 2

For each age is a dream that is dying,
Or one that is coming to birth.
      Ib. st. 3

WILLIAM ARCHIBALD
SPOONER[1]
1844–1930

Kinquering Congs their titles take.
 *Announcing the hymn in college
      chapel*

You have deliberately tasted two
worms and you can leave Oxford by the
next town drain.
 Dismissing a student (attributed)

This audience of beery wenches.
    At a woman's college

I remember your name perfectly, but
I just can't think of your face.
      A greeting

PAUL VERLAINE
1844–1896

I often have this strange and moving
 dream
Of an unknown woman, whom I love
 and who loves me.
 Poèmes Saturniens [1866]. *Mon
      Rêve Familier*

The long sobbings
Of the violins
Of autumn
Wound my heart
With monotonous
Languor.[2] *Ib. Chanson d'Automne*

[1] Canon Spooner, for many years warden of New College, Oxford, was famous for unintentional transposition of (usually initial) word sounds, giving rise to the term "spoonerism."

[2] Les sanglots longs
 Des violons
 De l'automne
 Blessent mon coeur
 D'une langueur
 Monotone.

There is weeping in my heart
Like the rain falling on the city.[1]
    Romances sans Paroles [1874], III

Here are fruits, flowers, leaves and
    branches,
And here is my heart which beats only
    for you.[2]   *Ib. Green*

What have you done, you there
    Weeping without cease,
Tell me, yes you, what have you done
    With all your youth?[3]
      Sagesse [1881], III, st. 6

Music above all, and for this
Prefer an uneven rhythm.[4]
    Jadis et Naguère [1884]. *L'Art*
              Poetique

Take eloquence and wring its neck!
                  Ib.

And all else is literature.   *Ib.*

BREWSTER HIGLEY
fl. 1873

Oh, give me a home where the buffalo
    roam,
Where the deer and the antelope play,
Where seldom is heard a discouraging
    word
And the skies are not cloudy all day.
    Home on the Range [1873]

R. L. SHARPE
fl. 1890

Each is given a bag of tools,
A shapeless mass and a book of rules;

[1] Il pleure dans mon coeur
  Comme il pleut sur la ville.
  See Rimbaud, p. 830b.
[2] Voici des fruits, des fleurs, des feuilles et
    des branches,
  Et puis voici mon coeur qui ne bat que pour
    vous.
[3] Qu'as-tu fait, O toi que voilà
    Pleurant sans cesse,
  Dis, qu'as-tu fait, toi que voilà
    De ta jeunesse?
[4] De la musique avant toute chose,
  Et pour cela préfère l'Impair.

And each must make, ere life is flown,
A stumblingblock or a steppingstone.
    Stumblingblock or Stepping-
              stone, st. 2

JOHN B. BOGART[1]
1845–1921

When a dog bites a man, that is not
news, because it happens so often. But
if a man bites a dog, that is news.
    From FRANK M. O'BRIEN, *The*
    Story of The [New York] *Sun*
    [1918]

WILL CARLETON
1845–1912

Worm or beetle — drought or tempest
    — on a farmer's land may fall,
Each is loaded full o' ruin, but a
    mortgage beats 'em all.
          The Tramp's Story

Not a log in this buildin' but its memo-
    ries has got,
And not a nail in this old floor but
    touches a tender spot.
    Out of the Old House, Nancy,
              st. 17

Draw up the papers, lawyer, and make
    'em good and stout,
For things at home are crossways, and
    Betsey and I are out.
    Betsey and I Are Out, st. 1

So I have talked with Betsey, and
    Betsey has talked with me,
And so we've agreed together that we
    can't never agree.   *Ib. st. 3*

Betsey, like all good women, had a
    temper of her own.   *Ib. st. 4*

The more we arg'ed the question the
    more we didn't agree.   *Ib. st. 5*

    To appreciate heaven well
'Tis good for a man to have some fif-
    teen minutes of hell.
    Gone with a Handsomer Man,
              st. 20

[1] City editor of *The Sun*, New York, 1873–1890.

Over the hill to the poorhouse I'm
trudgin' my weary way.
> *Over the Hill to the Poorhouse,*
> *st. 1*

WILLIAM KINGDON
CLIFFORD
1845–1879

Remember, then, that it [science] is
the guide of action; that the truth
which it arrives at is not that which we
can ideally contemplate without error,
but that which we may act upon without fear; and you cannot fail to see that
scientific thought is not an accompani-
ment or condition of human progress,
but human progress itself.
> *Aims and Instruments of Scien-*
> *tific Thought* [1872]

CHARLES FLETCHER
DOLE
1845–1927

Good will is the mightiest practical
force in the universe.
> *Cleveland Address*

Democracy is on trial in the world,
on a more colossal scale than ever before.   *The Spirit of Democracy*

EDWARD HARRIGAN
1845–1911

The drums and fifes, how sweetly they
did play,
As we marched, marched, marched in
the Mulligan Guard.
> *The Mulligan Guard* [1873]

DANIEL WEBSTER
HOYT
1845–1936

If you have a friend worth loving,
Love him. Yes, and let him know
That you love him, ere life's evening

Tinge his brow with sunset glow.
Why should good words ne'er be said
Of a friend till he is dead?
> *A Sermon in Rhyme* [1878], *st. 1*

GEORGE KENNAN
1845–1924

Heroism, the Caucasian mountain-
eers say, is endurance for one moment
more.
> *Letter to Henry Munroe Rogers*
> [*July 25, 1921*]

EUGENE
LEE-HAMILTON
1845–1907

Things bygone are the only things that
last:
The present is mere grass, quick-mown
away;
The past is stone, and stands forever
fast.   *Roman Baths*

HAMILTON WRIGHT
MABIE
1845–1916

The peculiarity of the New England
hermit has not been his desire to get
near to God, but his anxiety to get
away from man.
> *Backgrounds of Literature.*
> *Emerson and Concord*

GEORGE SAINTSBURY
1845–1933

I have never tried to be in the fashion for the sake of being in it, and seldom, I think, to be out of it for the
sake of being out of it.
> *Notes on a Cellar Book* [1920],
> *preface*

I have never yet given a secondhand
opinion of any thing, or book, or person.   *Ib.*

CHARLES WILLIAM STUBBS
1845–1912

To sit alone with my conscience
Will be judgment enough for me.[1]
Conscience and Future Judgment [1876]

JOHN BANISTER TABB
1845–1909

Out of the dusk a shadow,
  Then a spark;
Out of the clouds a silence,
  Then a lark;
Out of the heart a rapture,
  Then a pain;
Out of the dead, cold ashes,
  Life again.   *Evolution*

PUNCH

Advice to persons about to marry.
— "Don't."   *Vol. VIII, p. 1* [1845]

You pays your money and you takes your choice.   *X, 16* [1846]

What is Matter? — Never mind.
What is Mind? — No matter.
          XXIX, 19 [1855]

It ain't the 'unting as 'urts 'un, it's the 'ammer, 'ammer, 'ammer along the 'ard 'igh road.   *XXX, 218* [1856]

It appears the Americans have taken umbrage.
The deuce they have! Whereabouts is that?   *LXIII, 189* [1872]

Go directly — see what she's doing, and tell her she mustn't.
          Ib. 202 [1872]

There was an old owl liv'd in an oak,
The more he heard, the less he spoke;
The less he spoke, the more he heard,
O, if men were all like that wise bird!
          LXVIII, 155 [1875]

[1] There's just ae thing I cannae bear,
  An' that's my conscience.
      R. L. STEVENSON [1850–1894], *In Scots,
      XIV, My Conscience*

It's worse than wicked, my dear, it's vulgar.   *Almanac* [1876]

Don't look at me, sir, with — ah — in that tone of voice.
          XCVII, 38 [1884]

I'm afraid you've got a bad egg, Mr. Jones.
Oh no, my Lord, I assure you! Parts of it are excellent!   *CIX, 222* [1895]

Look here, Steward, if this is coffee, I want tea; but if this is tea, then I wish for coffee.   *CXXIII, 44* [1902]

CHARLES DUPEE BLAKE
1846–1903

Rock-a-bye-baby on the tree top,
When the wind blows the cradle will rock,
When the bough breaks the cradle will fall,
And down will come baby, cradle and all.   *Attributed*

JOSEPH IGNATIUS CONSTANTINE CLARKE
1846–1925

"Well, here's to good honest fighting blood!"
Said Kelly and Burke and Shea.
          The Fighting Race, st. 4

"Oh, the fighting races don't die out,
If they seldom die in bed."   *Ib. st. 5*

DANIEL HUDSON BURNHAM
1846–1912

Make no little plans; they have no magic to stir men's blood.
          Attributed [1]

[1] This quotation is now doubted. See HENRY M. SAYLOR, *"Make No Little Plans": Daniel Burnham Thought It but Did He Say It?," Journal of the American Institute of Architects, vol. XXVII, p. 3* [1957]

ALEXANDER MacGREGOR ROSE
1846–1898

Der Kaiser auf der Vaterland
Und Gott on high, all dings gom-
   mand,
Ve two, ach, don'd you understandt?
   Meinself — und Gott.
       Hoch! Der Kaiser (Kaiser &
         Co.) [1] *[1897], st. 1*

Gott pulls mit me, und I mit him.
       Ib. st. 16

CHARLES PRESTWICK SCOTT
1846–1932

The primary office of a newspaper is
the gathering of news . . . comment is
free, but facts are sacred.
    In the Manchester Guardian
       [May 6, 1926] [2]

HENRYK SIENKIEWICZ
1846–1916

The greater philosopher a man is, the
more difficult it is for him to answer the
foolish questions of common people.
    Quo Vadis? *[1896]* [3] *ch. 19*

EDWARD NOYES WESTCOTT
1846–1898

Do unto the other feller the way he'd
like to do unto you an' do it fust.
      David Harum [1898], *ch. 20*

They say a reasonable number of
fleas is good fer a dog — keeps him
from broodin' over *bein'* a dog.
       Ib. 32

The' ain't nothin' truer in the Bible
'n that sayin' thet them that has gits.
       Ib. 35

[1] These verses caused an international incident
when recited by Captain Joseph Bullock Coghlan
[1844–1908] at a dinner given in his honor at the
Union League Club, New York [April 21, 1899].
[2] Its one-hundredth anniversary.
[3] Translated by Jeremiah Curtin [1838–1906].

JOHN PETER ALTGELD [1]
1847–1902

In writing *Progress and Poverty,*
he dipped his pen into the tears of the
human race, and with celestial clearness
wrote down what he conceived to be
eternal truths.
    Memorial Address on Henry
       George [1897]

ALEXANDER GRAHAM BELL
1847–1922

Mr. Watson, come here, I want
you.
    To his assistant [March 10,
    1876]; the first intelligible
    words transmitted by tele-
    phone

THOMAS ALVA EDISON
1847–1931

There is no substitute for hard
work.   *Life [1932], ch. 24*

Genius is one per cent inspiration
and ninety-nine per cent perspiration.
       Ib

EDGAR FAWCETT
1847–1904

At some glad moment was it nature's
   choice
To dower a scrap of sunset with a
   voice?   *To an Oriole, st. 2*

WALTER LEARNED
1847–1915

A lure more strong, a wish more faint,
Makes one a monster, one a saint.
    On the flyleaf of Manon Lescaut

JOHN LOCKE
1847–1889

O Ireland, isn't it grand you look —
Like a bride in her rich adornin'?

[1] See Vachel Lindsay, p. 952b, *The Eagle
That Is Forgotten* and note 1.

And with all the pent-up love of my
    heart
I bid you the top o' the mornin'!
        *The Exile's Return [Th' an'am
        an Dhia: My Soul to God], st. 1*

ALICE MEYNELL
1847–1922

She walks — the lady of my delight —
A shepherdess of sheep.
Her flocks are thoughts. She keeps
    them white;
She guards them from the steep.
        The Shepherdess, st. 1

I must not think of thee; and, tired yet
    strong,
I shun the thought that lurks in all
    delight —
The thought of thee — and in the blue
    heaven's height
And in the sweetest passage of a song.
        Sonnet, Renouncement

With the first dream that comes with
    the first sleep
I run, I run, I am gathered to thy
    heart.   *Ib.*

LLOYD MIFFLIN
1847–1921

Inscrutable, colossal, and alone.
        Sesostris

JULIA A. MOORE[1]
1847–1920

And now, kind friends, what I have
    wrote
I hope you will pass o'er,
And not criticize as some have done
Hitherto herebefore.
        To My Friends and Critics

"Lord Byron" was an Englishman,
    A poet I believe
His first works in old England
    Was poorly received.

---

[1] "The Sweet Singer of Michigan," of whom
Mark Twain wrote: "The one and unfailing
great quality which distinguishes her poetry
from Shakespeare's and makes it precious to us
is its stern and simple irrelevancy." — *Following
the Equator* [1897], *vol. II, ch. 8*

Perhaps it was "Lord Byron's" fault
    And perhaps it was not.
His life was full of misfortunes,
    Ah, strange was his lot.
        A Sketch of Lord Byron's Life

Leave off the agony, leave off style,
Unless you've got money by you all the
    while.
If you look about you you'll often have
    to smile
To see so many poor people putting on
    style.
        Leave Off the Agony in Style

MILTON NOBLES
1847–1924

The villain still pursued her.
        The Phoenix [1875], act I, sc. iii

WILLIAM EDWARD
NORRIS
1847–1925

If your lips would keep from slips,
    Five things observe with care:
To whom you speak; of whom you
    speak;
    And how, and when, and where.
        Quoted in Thirlby Hall

JAMES JEFFREY ROCHE
1847–1908

I'd rather be handsome than homely;
    I'd rather be youthful than old;
If I can't have a bushel of silver
    I'll do with a barrel of gold.
        Contentment

All loved Art in a seemly way
With an earnest soul and a capital A.
        The V-A-S-E

ARCHIBALD PHILIP
PRIMROSE,
EARL OF ROSEBERY
1847–1929

It is beginning to be hinted that we
are a nation of amateurs.
        *Rectorial Address, Glasgow
        [November 16, 1900]*

GEORGE ROBERT SIMS
1847–1922

It was Christmas Day in the work-house.
> *Christmas Day in the Work-house, st. 1*

MARY DOW BRINE
fl. 1878

She's somebody's mother, boys, you know,
For all she's aged and poor and slow.
> *Somebody's Mother* [1878]

ARTHUR JAMES BALFOUR
1848–1930

The energies of our system will decay, the glory of the sun will be dimmed, and the earth, tideless and inert, will no longer tolerate the race which has for a moment disturbed its solitude. Man will go down into the pit, and all his thoughts will perish.
> *The Foundations of Belief* [1895], *pt. I, ch. 1*

Biography should be written by an acute enemy.
> *Quoted by* S. K. RATCLIFFE *in the London Observer* [January 30, 1927]

JOHN VANCE CHENEY
1848–1922

Who drives the horses of the sun
Shall lord it but a day;
Better the lowly deed were done,
And kept the humble way.
> *The Happiest Heart, st. 1*

The happiest heart that ever beat
Was in some quiet breast
That found the common daylight sweet,
And left to Heaven the rest.
> *Ib. st. 3*

JOHN CHURTON COLLINS
1848–1908

Truth is the object of philosophy, but not always of philosophers.
> *From* LOGAN PEARSALL SMITH, *A Treasury of English Aphorisms*

Mistrust a subordinate who never finds fault with his superior.   *Ib.*

The secret of success in life is known only to those who have not succeeded.
> *Ib.*

If men were as unselfish as women, women would very soon become more selfish than men.   *Ib.*

SIR FRANCIS DARWIN
1848–1925

But in science the credit goes to the man who convinces the world, not to the man to whom the idea first occurs.[1]
> *First Galton Lecture before the Eugenics Society* [1914]

DIGBY MACKWORTH DOLBEN
1848–1867

The world is young today:
Forget the gods are old,
Forget the years of gold
When all the months were May.
> *A Song*

SAMUEL MILLER HAGEMAN
1848–1905

Every sound shall end in silence, but the silence never dies.
> *Silence* [1876], *st. 10*

Earth is but the frozen echo of the silent voice of God.   *Ib. st. 19*

JOEL CHANDLER HARRIS
1848–1908

How many po' sinners'll be kotched out late

---

[1] See Zinsser, p. 949a, and Fleming, p. 963a.

En fin' no latch ter de golden gate?
No use fer ter wait twell ter-morrer,
De sun mus'n't set on yo' sorrer —
Sin's ez sharp ez a bamboo-brier, —
O Lord! fetch de mo'ners up higher!
Uncle Remus: His Songs and
His Sayings [1881]

Hit look lak sparrer-grass, hit feel lak sparrer-grass, hit tas'e lak sparrer-grass, en I bless ef 'taint sparrer-grass.
Nights with Uncle Remus
[1883], *ch. 27*

No 'pollygy aint gwine ter make h'ar come back whar de b'iling water hit.
Ib. 45

Tar-baby ain't sayin' nuthin', en Brer Fox, he lay low.
Uncle Remus and His Friends
[1892]

Ez soshubble ez a baskit er kittens.
Ib.

Bred en bawn in a brier-patch, Brer Fox. *Ib.*

You do de pullin', Sis Cow, en I'll do de gruntin'. *Ib.*

W'en ole man Rabbit say "scoot," dey scooted, en w'en old Miss Rabbit say "scat," dey scatted. *Ib.*

Lazy fokes' stummucks don't git tired.
Uncle Remus: Plantation Proverbs

Jaybird don't rob his own nes'.
Ib.

Licker talks mighty loud w'en it gits loose fum de jug. *Ib.*

Hongry rooster don't cackle w'en he fine a wum. *Ib.*

Youk'n hide de fier, but w'at you gwine do wid de smoke? *Ib.*

Watch out w'en youer gittin' all you want. Fattenin' hogs ain't in luck.
Ib.

Hop light, ladies,
Oh, Miss Loo!
Oh, swing dat yaller gal!
Do, boys, do!
Plantation Play Song

When you've got a thing to say,
Say it! Don't take half a day.
When your tale's got little in it,
Crowd the whole thing in a minute!
Life is short — a fleeting vapor —
Don't you fill the whole blamed paper
With a tale which, at a pinch,
Could be cornered in an inch!
Boil her down until she simmers,
Polish her until she glimmers.
Advice to Writers for the Daily
Press

JORIS KARL HUYSMANS
1848–1907

The loveliest tune imaginable becomes vulgar and insupportable as soon as the public begins to hum it and the hurdygurdies make it their own.
Against the Grain,[1] *ch. 9*

Perfumes, in fact, rarely come from the flowers whose names they bear . . . with the exception of the inimitable jasmine, which it is impossible to counterfeit. *Ib. 10*

Art is the only clean thing on earth, except holiness.
Les Foules de Lourdes [1906]

RICHARD JEFFERIES
1848–1887

It is eternity now. I am in the midst of it. It is about me in the sunshine; I am in it, as the butterfly in the light-laden air. Nothing has to come; it is now. Now is eternity; now is the immortal life.
The Story of My Heart [1883]

VILFREDO PARETO
1848–1923

Give me a fruitful error any time, full of seeds, bursting with its own corrections. You can keep your sterile truth for yourself.
Comment on Kepler

[1] Translated by JOHN HOWARD.

EBEN EUGENE REXFORD
1848–1916

Darling, I am growing old,
Silver threads among the gold
Shine upon my brow today;
Life is fading fast away.
Silver Threads Among the Gold
[1873], st. 1

HENRY AUGUSTUS ROWLAND
1848–1901

American science is a thing of the future, and not of the present or past; and the proper course of one in my position is to consider what must be done to create a science of physics in the country, rather than to call telegrams, electric lights, and such conveniences by the name of science.
Address before the American
Association for the Advancement of Science [1883]

FREDERIC EDWARD WEATHERLY
1848–1929

Always the same, Darby, my own,
Always the same to your old wife Joan.
Darby and Joan,[1] refrain

The sailor's wife the sailor's star shall be. *Nancy Lee, refrain*

BERNHARD VON BÜLOW
1849–1929

A place in the sun.
A Promise for Germany. Speech
before the Reichstag [December
6, 1897]

The king in Prussia — forward; Prussia in Germany — forward; Germany in the world — forward! *Ib.*

[1] Old Darby with Joan by his side,
  You've often regarded with wonder;
  He's dropsical, she is sore-ey'd,
  Yet they're ever uneasy asunder.
    HENRY WOODFALL, *The Gentleman's*
      Magazine [March 1735]

LORD RANDOLPH SPENCER CHURCHILL
1849–1895

The old gang [members of the Conservative government].
Speech, House of Commons
[March 7, 1878]

Ulster will fight; Ulster will be right.
Letter [May 7, 1886]

All great men make mistakes. Napoleon forgot Blücher, I forgot Goschen.[1]
Quoted by LADY DOROTHY
NEVILL, *notebooks*

EDMUND GOSSE
1849–1928

The Past is like a funeral gone by,
The Future comes like an unwelcome guest. *May Day*

I do not hunger for a well-stored mind,
I only wish to live my life, and find
My heart in unison with all mankind.
Lying in the Grass

WILLIAM ERNEST HENLEY
1849–1903

Far in the stillness a cat
Languishes loudly.
In Hospital [1888]. VII, Vigil

Bland as a Jesuit, sober as a hymn.
Ib. XVI, House Surgeon

Valiant in velvet, light in ragged luck,
Most vain, most generous, sternly critical,
Buffoon and poet, lover and sensualist:
A deal of Ariel, just a streak of Puck,
Much Antony, of Hamlet most of all,
And something of the Shorter-Catechist.
Ib. XXV, Apparition [Robert
Louis Stevenson]

[1] George Joachim Goschen [1831–1907], British statesman who helped form the Liberal Unionist party [1886].

As dust that drives, as straws that blow,
Into the night go one and all.
>   *Ballade of Dead Actors* [1888]

Out of the night that covers me,
Black as the Pit from pole to pole,
I thank whatever gods may be
For my unconquerable soul.

In the fell clutch of circumstance,
I have not winced nor cried aloud;
Under the bludgeonings of chance
My head is bloody, but unbowed.
>   *Echoes* [1888]. *IV, In Memo-
>   riam R. T. Hamilton Bruce*
>   [*"Invictus"*], *st. 1, 2*

It matters not how strait the gate,
How charged with punishments the
>   scroll,
I am the master of my fate;
I am the captain of my soul.[1]
>   *Ib. st. 4*

Night with her train of stars
And her great gift of sleep.
>   *Ib. XXXV, In Memoriam
>   Margaritae Sororis, st. 2*

Or ever the knightly years were gone
>   With the old world to the grave,
I was a King in Babylon
And you were a Christian Slave.
>   *Ib. XXXVII, To W. A., st. 1*

>   These poor Might-Have-Beens,
These fatuous, ineffectual Yesterdays!
>   *To James McNeill Whistler* [1892]

What have I done for you,
>   England, my England?
What is there I would not do,
>   England, my own?
>   *For England's Sake. Pro Rege
>   Nostro* [1892], *st. 1*

SARAH ORNE JEWETT
1849–1909

A harbor, even if it is a little harbor, is a good thing, since adventures
come into it as well as go out, and the
life in it grows strong, because it takes

---

[1] See Sallust, p. 116a, and note.

---

something from the world and has
something to give in return.
>   *Country Byways. River
>   Driftwood*

Captain Littlepage had overset his
mind with too much reading.
>   *The Country of the Pointed
>   Firs* [1896], *ch. 5*

The old poets little knew what comfort they could be to man.   *Ib.*

Wrecked on the lee shore of age.
>   *Ib. 7*

We were standing where there was a
fine view of the harbor and its long
stretches of shore all covered by the
great army of the pointed firs, darkly
cloaked and standing as if they waited
to embark. As we looked far seaward
among the outer islands, the trees
seemed to march seaward still, going
steadily over the heights and down to the
water's edge.   *Ib.*

Tact is after all a kind of mind-
reading.   *Ib. 10*

Yes'm, old friends is always best, 'less
you can catch a new one that's fit to
make an old one out of.   *Ib. 12*

In the life of each of us, I said to
myself, there is a place remote and islanded, and given to endless regret or
secret happiness.   *Ib. 15*

'Tain't worthwhile to wear a day all
out before it comes.   *Ib. 16*

The road was new to me, as roads
always are, going back.   *Ib. 19*

So we die before our own eyes; so we
see some chapters of our lives come to
their natural end.   *Ib.*

The thing that teases the mind over
and over for years, and at last gets itself
put down rightly on paper — whether
little or great, it belongs to Literature.
>   *Letter to Willa Cather. Quoted
>   in preface to The Country of the
>   Pointed Firs and Other Stories*
>   [1925]

EMMA LAZARUS
1849–1887

Give me your tired, your poor,
Your huddled masses yearning to
breathe free,
The wretched refuse of your teeming
shore,
Send these, the homeless, tempest-
tossed, to me:
I lift my lamp beside the golden door.
*The New Colossus: Inscription
for the Statue of Liberty, New
York Harbor*

SIR WILLIAM OSLER
1849–1919

The greater the ignorance the greater
the dogmatism.
Montreal Medical Journal [1902]

The philosophies of one age have become the absurdities of the next, and
the foolishness of yesterday has become
the wisdom of tomorrow.   *Ib.*

The natural man has only two primal
passions, to get and to beget.
Science and Immortality
[1904], *ch. 2*

Tact is the saving virtue without
which no woman can be a success.
*Commencement address to
nurses, Johns Hopkins University* [*May 7, 1913*]

Speck in cornea, 50¢.
*Entry in his account book, first
fee as a practicing physician.
From* HARVEY CUSHING, *Life of
Sir William Osler* [1925], *vol. I,
ch. 6*

The desire to take medicine is perhaps the greatest feature which distinguishes man from animals.   *Ib. 14*

This is yet the childhood of the
world, and a supine credulity is still the
most charming characteristic of man.
Ib.

We are here to add what we can *to*,
not to get what we can *from*, Life.[1]
From HARVEY CUSHING, *Life of
Sir William Osler, vol. I, ch.
14*

Humanity has but three great enemies: fever, famine and war; of these by
far the greatest, by far the most terrible, is fever.   *Ib.*

The master word [work] . . . is the
open sesame to every portal, the great
equalizer in the world, the true philosopher's stone which transmutes all the
base metal of humanity into gold.[2]
Ib. 22

Things cannot always go your way.
Learn to accept in silence the minor
aggravations, cultivate the gift of
taciturnity and consume your own
smoke [3] with an extra draught of hard
work, so that those about you may not
be annoyed with the dust and soot of
your complaints.   *Ib.*

Take the sum of human achievement
in action, in science, in art, in literature
— subtract the work of the men above
forty, and while we should miss great
treasures, even priceless treasures, we
would practically be where we are
today. . . . The effective, moving, vitalizing work of the world is done between the ages of twenty-five and
forty.[4]   *Ib. 24* [*The Fixed Period*]

My second fixed idea is the uselessness of men above sixty years of age,
and the incalculable benefit it would be
in commercial, political, and in professional life, if as a matter of course, men
stopped work at this age.[5]   *Ib.*

[1] Also in *Doctor and Nurse,* in *Aequanimitas
and Other Addresses* [1904].
[2] Lecture, *The Master Word in Medicine,*
Toronto [October 1, 1903]; also in *Aequanimitas.*
[3] See Carlyle, p. 576b, and note.
[4] Address at Johns Hopkins University,
Baltimore, February 22, 1905.
[5] This valedictory address caused much discussion and misquotation. It was headlined in
the press OSLER RECOMMENDS CHLOROFORM AT

Nothing will sustain you more potently than the power to recognize in your humdrum routine, as perhaps it may be thought, the true poetry of life — the poetry of the commonplace, of the ordinary man, of the plain, toil-worn woman, with their loves and their joys, their sorrows and their griefs.

From HARVEY CUSHING, *Life of Sir William Osler*, vol. I, ch. 24 [*The Student Life*]

I have three personal ideals. One, to do the day's work well and not to bother about tomorrow. . . . The second ideal has been to act the Golden Rule, as far as in me lay, toward my professional brethren and toward the patients committed to my care. And the third has been to cultivate such a measure of equanimity as would enable me to bear success with humility, the affection of my friends without pride, and to be ready when the day of sorrow and grief came to meet it with the courage befitting a man.

Ib. [*Farewell Dinner, May 2, 1905*]

Throw all the beer and spirits into the Irish Channel, the English Channel, and the North Sea for a year, and people in England would be infinitely better. It would certainly solve all the problems with which the philanthropists, the physicians, and the politicians have to deal.[1]   *Ib. II, 26*

No man is really happy or safe without a hobby, and it makes precious little difference what the outside interest may be — botany, beetles or butterflies, roses, tulips or irises; fishing, mountaineering or antiquities — anything will do so long as he straddles a hobby and rides it hard.[2]   *Ib. 29*

SIXTY, and occasioned many columns of letters, caustic cartoons, and the like, until to "Oslerize" became a byword.

[1] Address at Working Men's College, Camden Town [November 17, 1906].

[2] Address, Medical Library Association, Belfast [July 28, 1909].

Nothing in life is more wonderful than faith — the one great moving force which we can neither weigh in the balance nor test in the crucible.

From HARVEY CUSHING, *Life of Sir William Osler, vol. II, ch. 30*

In the life of a young man the most essential thing for happiness is the gift of friendship.   *Ib. 31*

No bubble is so iridescent or floats longer than that blown by the successful teacher.   *Ib.*

The quest for righteousness is Oriental, the quest for knowledge, Occidental.[1]   *Ib. 34*

Save the fleeting minute; learn gracefully to dodge the bore.

From W. S. THAYER, *Osler the Teacher, Johns Hopkins Hospital Bulletin* 30:198 [1919]

IVAN PETROVICH PAVLOV
1849–1936

What can I wish to the youth of my country who devote themselves to science?

Firstly, gradualness. About this most important condition of fruitful scientific work I never can speak without emotion. Gradualness, gradualness and gradualness. From the very beginning of your work, school yourselves to severe gradualness in the accumulation of knowledge.

Learn the ABC of science before you try to ascend to its summit.

Bequest to the Academic Youth of Soviet Russia [1936]

Learn, compare, collect the facts!   *Ib.*

Secondly, modesty. Never think that you already know all. However highly

---

[1] Address, Jewish Historical Society of England [April 27, 1914].

you are appraised, always have the courage to say to yourself — I am ignorant.

Bequest to the Academic Youth of Soviet Russia

Thirdly, passion. Remember that science claims a man's whole life. Had he two lives they would not suffice. Science demands an undivided allegiance from its followers. In your work and in your research there must always be passion. *Ib.*

JAMES WHITCOMB RILEY
1849–1916

O'er folded blooms
  On swirls of musk,
The beetle booms adown the glooms
  And bumps along the dusk.
The Beetle, st. 7

The ripest peach is highest on the tree.
The Ripest Peach, st. 1

An' all us other children, when the supper things is done,
We set around the kitchen fire an' has the mostest fun
A-list'nin' to the witch-tales 'at Annie tells about,
An' the Gobble-uns 'at gits you
  Ef you
    Don't
      Watch
        Out!
Little Orphant Annie, st. 1

It hain't no use to grumble and complain,
  It's jest as easy to rejoice;
When God sorts out the weather and sends rain,
  Why rain's my choice.
Wet Weather Talk

Heaven holds all for which you sigh —
There! little girl; don't cry!
A Life Lesson, st. 3

"As surely as the vine
Grew 'round the stump," she loved me
  — that old sweetheart of mine.
An Old Sweetheart of Mine, st. 12

Tell you what I like the best —
'Long about knee-deep in June,
'Bout the time strawberries melts
On the vine — some afternoon
Like to jes' git out and rest,
And not work at nothin' else.
Knee-Deep in June, st. 1

Oh! the old swimmin' hole! When I last saw the place,
The scenes was all changed, like the change in my face.
The Old Swimmin' Hole, st. 5

Work is the least o' my idees
When the green, you know, gits back in the trees!
When the Green Gits Back in the Trees, st. 1

O, the Raggedy Man! He works fer Pa;
An' he's the goodest man ever you saw!
The Raggedy Man, st. 1

O, it sets my heart a-clickin' like the tickin' of a clock,
When the frost is on the punkin and the fodder's in the shock.
When the Frost Is on the Punkin, st. 3

EDWARD BELLAMY[1]
1850–1898

Your system was liable to periodical convulsions, overwhelming alike the wise and unwise, the successful cutthroat as well as his victim. I refer to the business crises at intervals of five to ten years, which wrecked the industries of the nation.
Looking Backward [1887]

AUGUSTINE BIRRELL
1850–1933

Libraries are not made; they grow.
Obiter Dicta. Book Buying

Good as it is to inherit a library, it is better to collect one. *Ib.*

[1] There is at least a fair chance that another fifty years will confirm Edward Bellamy's position as one of the most authentic prophets of our age. — HEYWOOD BROUN [1931]

That great dust heap called "history."
    Obiter Dicta. Carlyle

EUGENE FIELD
1850–1895

I feel a sort of yearnin' 'nd a chokin' in
  my throat
When I think of Red Hoss Mountain
  'nd of Casey's tabble dote!
    Casey's Table d'Hôte, st. 1

He could whip his weight in wildcats.
    Modjesky as Cameel, st. 10

No matter what conditions
  Dyspeptic come to feaze,
The best of all physicians
  Is apple pie and cheese!
    Apple Pie and Cheese, st. 5

I'm sure no human heart goes wrong
That's told "Good-by — God bless
  you!"
    "Good-by — God Bless You!",
    st. 2

I never lost a little fish — yes, I am free
  to say
It always was the biggest fish I caught
  that got away.
    Our Biggest Fish, st. 2

How gracious those dews of solace that
  over my senses fall
At the clink of the ice in the pitcher
  the boy brings up the hall!
    The Clink of the Ice, st. 1

When one's all right, he's prone to
  spite
The doctor's peaceful mission;
But when he's sick, it's loud and quick
He bawls for a physician.[1]
    Doctors, st. 2

When I demanded of my friend what
  viands he preferred,

---

[1] Three faces wears the doctor: when first
  sought
  An angel's; and a god's the cure half-
  wrought;
  But when, the cure complete, he seeks his fee,
  The Devil looks less terrible than he.
    ANONYMOUS

He quoth: "A large cold bottle, and a
  small hot bird!"
    The Bottle and the Bird, st. 1

Have you ever heard of the Sugarplum
  Tree?
'Tis a marvel of great renown!
It blooms on the shore of the Lollipop
  Sea
In the garden of Shuteye Town.
    The Sugarplum Tree, st. 1

Wynken, Blynken, and Nod one night
Sailed off in a wooden shoe —
Sailed on a river of crystal light
Into a sea of dew.
    Wynken, Blynken, and Nod, st. 1

The little toy dog is covered with dust,
  But sturdy and staunch he stands;
And the little toy soldier is red with
  rust,
  And his musket molds in his hands;
Time was when the little toy dog was
  new,
  And the soldier was passing fair;
And that was the time when our Little
  Boy Blue
  Kissed them and put them there.
    Little Boy Blue, st. 1

The Rock-a-Bye Lady from Hushaby
  street
Comes stealing; comes creeping.
    The Rock-a-Bye Lady, st. 1

Have you ever heard the wind go
  "Yooooo"?
'Tis a pitiful sound to hear!
It seems to chill you through and
  through
  With a strange and speechless fear.
    The Night Wind, st. 1

The Dinkey Bird goes singing
In the amfalula tree!
    The Dinkey Bird, st. 1

The gingham dog went "Bow-wow-
  wow!"
And the calico cat replied "Mee-ow!"
The air was littered, an hour or so,
With bits of gingham and calico.
    The Duel, st. 2

Father calls me William, sister calls me
  Will,

Mother calls me Willie, but the fellers
   call me Bill!
Jest 'Fore Christmas, st. 1

'Most all the time, the whole year
   round, there ain't no flies on me,
But jest 'fore Christmas I'm as good as
   I kin be!   *Ib.*

FRED GILBERT
1850–1903

The Man Who Broke the Bank at
Monte Carlo.   *Title of song* [1892]

SAMUEL GOMPERS
1850–1924

The trade unions are the legitimate
outgrowth of modern societary and industrial conditions. . . . They were
born of the necessity of workers to protect and defend themselves from encroachment, injustice and wrong. . . .
To protect the workers in their inalienable rights to a higher and better life;
to protect them, not only as equals before the law, but also in their health,
their homes, their firesides, their liberties as men, as workers, and as citizens;
to overcome and conquer prejudices
and antagonism; to secure to them the
right to life, and the opportunity to
maintain that life; the right to be full
sharers in the abundance which is the
result of their brain and brawn, and the
civilization of which they are the founders and the mainstay; to this the workers
are entitled. . . . The attainment of
these is the glorious mission of the
trade unions.   *Speech* [1898]

JOHN CHEEVER
GOODWIN
1850–1912

For that elephant ate all night,
   And that elephant ate all day;
Do what he could to furnish him food,
   The cry was still *more hay.*
Wang: The Man with an Ele-
phant on His Hands [1891]

HENRY CABOT LODGE
1850–1924

Let every man honor and love the
land of his birth and the race from
which he springs and keep their memory green. It is a pious and honorable
duty. But let us have done with British-
Americans and Irish-Americans and
German-Americans, and so on, and all
be Americans. . . . If a man is going
to be an American at all let him be so
without any qualifying adjectives; and
if he is going to be something else, let
him drop the word American from his
personal description.
The Day We Celebrate [Fore-
fathers' Day]. Address, New Eng-
land Society of Brooklyn [De-
cember 21, 1888]

It is the flag just as much of the man
who was naturalized yesterday as of the
man whose people have been here many
generations.   *Address* [1915]

He was a great patriot, a great man;
above all, a great American. His country was the ruling, mastering passion of
his life from the beginning even unto
the end.
Theodore Roosevelt: Address Be-
fore Congress [February 9, 1919]

PHILIP BOURKE
MARSTON
1850–1887

A little time for laughter,
   A little time to sing,
   A little time to kiss and cling,
And no more kissing after.[1]
After, st. 1

LAURA ELIZABETH
RICHARDS
1850–1943

Be you clown or be you King,
Still your singing is the thing.
Tirra Lirra [1930], *dedication, l. 1*

[1] See A. L. Gordon, p. 748b, and Du Maurier
p. 751b.

Every little wave had its nightcap on.
Song for Hal, refrain

Once there was an elephant
Who tried to use the telephant —
No! No! I mean an elephone
Who tried to use the telephone.
Eletelephony, l. 1

ROBERT RICHARDSON
1850–1901

Warm summer sun, shine friendly
here;
Warm western wind, blow kindly here;
Green sod above, rest light, rest
light —
Good night, Annette! Sweetheart, good
night.[1]　　　　*To Annette*

ROBERT LOUIS STEVENSON[2]
1850–1894

Mankind was never so happily inspired as when it made a cathedral.
An Inland Voyage [1878]. *Noyon*

Every man is his own doctor of divinity, in the last resort.　　*Ib.*

For my part, I travel not to go anywhere, but to go. I travel for travel's
sake. The great affair is to move.
Travels with a Donkey [1878]

Marriage is like life in this — that it
is a field of battle, and not a bed of
roses.
Virginibus Puerisque [1881], I,
ch. 1

Times are changed with him who
marries; there are no more bypath

meadows, where you may innocently
linger, but the road lies long and
straight and dusty to the grave.
Virginibus Puerisque, I, ch. 2

Man is a creature who lives not upon
bread alone but principally by catch-
words.　　　　*Ib.*

The cruelest lies are often told in silence.　　*Ib. 4, Truth of Intercourse*

Old and young, we are all on our last
cruise.
Ib. II, Crabbed Age and Youth

It is better to be a fool than to be
dead.　　　　*Ib.*

Give me the young man who has
brains enough to make a fool of him·
self!　　　　*Ib.*

Books are good enough in their own
way, but they are a mighty bloodless
substitute for life.
Ib. III, An Apology for Idlers

Perpetual devotion to what a man
calls his business, is only to be sustained
by perpetual neglect of many other
things.　　　　*Ib.*

There is no duty we so much under-
rate as the duty of being happy.　*Ib.*

To travel hopefully is a better thing
than to arrive.　*Ib. VI, El Dorado*

To be what we are, and to become
what we are capable of becoming, is the
only end of life.
*Familiar Studies of Men and
Books* [1882]

I am in the habit of looking not so
much to the nature of a gift as to the
spirit in which it is offered.
New Arabian Nights [1882].
The Suicide Club

Fifteen men on the Dead Man's
Chest — [1]

---

[1] Mark Twain adapted this verse by the
Australian poet Richardson for the stone mark-
ing the grave of his daughter Olivia Susan
Clemens, who died August 18, 1896, aged twenty-
four:
　Warm summer sun, shine kindly here;
　Warm southern wind, blow softly here;
　Green sod above, lie light, lie light —
　Good night, dear heart, good night, good
　　night.
　See Euripides, p. 83b; Anonymous Latin, p.
151b; and Beaumont and Fletcher, p. 316b.

[2] See Henley, p. 815b.

[1] *Treasure Island* came out of Kingsley's *At
Last*, where I got the Dead Man's Chest — and
that was the seed. — R. L. STEVENSON, *Letter
to Sidney Colvin*
　We were crawling slowly along, looking out
for Virgin Garda; the first of those numberless
isles which Columbus, so goes the tale, discovered

Yo-ho-ho, and a bottle of rum!
Drink and the devil had done for the
    rest —
Yo-ho-ho, and a bottle of rum!
                Treasure Island [1883], *ch. 1*

Doctors is all swabs.
                Ib. 3 [*Billy Bones*]

Many's the long night I've dreamed
of cheese — toasted, mostly.
                Ib. 15 [*Ben Gunn*]

In winter I get up at night
And dress by yellow candlelight.
In summer, quite the other way,
I have to go to bed by day.

I have to go to bed and see
The birds still hopping on the tree,
Or hear the grown-up people's feet
Still going past me on the street.
    A Child's Garden of Verses
    [1885]. *Bed in Summer, st. 1, 2*

A child should always say what's true
And speak when he is spoken to,
And behave mannerly at table;
At least as far as he is able.
        Ib. Whole Duty of Children

Whenever the moon and stars are set,
Whenever the wind is high,
All night long in the dark and wet,
A man goes riding by.
Late in the night when the fires are
    out,
Why does he gallop and gallop about?
            Ib. Windy Nights, st. 1

Dark brown is the river,
    Golden is the sand,
It flows along forever,
    With trees on either hand.
        Ib. Where Go the Boats, st. 1

The pleasant land of counterpane.
    Ib. The Land of Counterpane, st. 4

---

on St. Ursula's day, and named them after the
saint and her eleven thousand mythical virgins.
Unfortunately, English buccaneers have since
given to most of them less poetic names. The
Dutchman's Cap, Broken Jerusalem, The Dead
Man's Chest, Rum Island, and so forth, mark
a time and race more prosaic. — CHARLES KINGS-
LEY, *At Last* [1870], *ch. 1*

I have a little shadow that goes in and
    out with me,
And what can be the use of him is more
    than I can see.
He is very, very like me from the heels
    up to the head;
And I see him jump before me, when I
    jump into my bed.
        A Child's Garden of Verses.
                My Shadow, st. 1

The friendly cow all red and white,
    I love with all my heart:
She gives me cream with all her might,
    To eat with apple tart.
                Ib. The Cow, st. 1

The world is so full of a number of
    things,
I'm sure we should all be as happy as
    kings.   *Ib. Happy Thought*

Little Indian, Sioux or Crow,
Little frosty Eskimo,
Little Turk or Japanee,
O! don't you wish that you were me?
                Ib. Foreign Children

Am I no a bonny fighter?
        Kidnapped [1886], *ch. 10*
                [*Alan Breck*]

Of all my verse, like not a single line;
But like my title, for it is not mine.
That title from a better man[1] I stole:
Ah, how much better, had I stol'n the
    whole!
        Underwoods [1887], *foreword*

Life is over, life was gay:
We have come the primrose way.
                Ib. Envoy

Dear Andrew, with the brindled hair.[2]
            Ib. To Andrew Lang

Under the wide and starry sky,
Dig the grave and let me lie.
Glad did I live and gladly die,
    And I laid me down with a will.

This be the verse you grave for me:
Here he lies where he longed to be;

---

[1] Ben Jonson.
[2] Dear Louis of the awful cheek!
    Who told you it was right to speak,
    Where all the world might hear and stare,
    Of other fellows' "brindled hair"?
        ANDREW LANG [1844–1912], *To R. L. S.*

Home is the sailor, home from sea,
And the hunter home from the hill.
Underwoods. Requiem

If I have faltered more or less
In my great task of happiness.
Ib. The Celestial Surgeon

Yet, O stricken heart, remember, O remember
How of human days he lived the better part.
April came to bloom and never dim December
Breathed its killing chills upon the head or heart.
Ib. In Memoriam F. A. Stilwell [1] [1881]

Let first the onion flourish there,
Rose among roots, the maiden-fair
Wine-scented and poetic soul
Of the capacious salad bowl.
Ib. To a Gardener

My body, which my dungeon is,
And yet my parks and palaces.
Ib. XXXVII

I have thus played the sedulous ape to Hazlitt, to Lamb, to Wordsworth, to Sir Thomas Browne, to Defoe, to Hawthorne, to Montaigne, to Baudelaire and to Obermann.
Memories and Portraits [1887]. *A College Magazine*

A Penny Plain and Twopence Colored.
Ib. Essay About Skelt's Juvenile Drama

Wealth I ask not, hope nor love,
Nor a friend to know me;
All I ask, the heaven above
And the road below me.
Songs of Travel. The Vagabond, st. 4

The untented Kosmos my abode,
I pass, a willful stranger;
My mistress still the open road
And the bright eyes of danger.
Ib. Youth and Love

[1] Lady Colvin's son by her first marriage; he died at the age of eighteen.

I will make you brooches and toys for your delight
Of birdsong at morning and starshine at night.
Songs of Travel. Romance, st. 1

God, if this were enough,
That I see things bare to the buff.
Ib. If This Were Faith

Bright is the ring of words
When the right man rings them.
Ib. XIV

In the highlands, in the country places,
Where the old plain men have rosy faces,
And the young fair maidens
Quiet eyes. *Ib. XV*

Trusty, dusky, vivid, true,
With eyes of gold and bramble dew,
Steel-true and blade-straight
The great artificer
Made my mate.
Ib. XXV, To My Wife, st. 1

Be it granted me to behold you again in dying,
Hills of home!
Ib. XLV, To S. R. Crockett

Not every man is so great a coward as he thinks he is — nor yet so good a Christian.
The Master of Ballantrae [1889]. *Mr. Mackellar's Journey*

Nothing like a little judicious levity.
The Wrong Box [1889], *ch.* 7

Do you know what the Governor of South Carolina said to the Governor of North Carolina? It's a long time between drinks, observed that powerful thinker.[1] *Ib.* 8

[1] Of the several traditions relating to the origin of this remark, the most reasonable one traces it to John Motley Morehead [1796–1866], who was Governor of North Carolina 1841–1845. He was visited by James H. Hammond [1807–1864], who was Governor of South Carolina 1842–1844. They engaged in discussion and argument, and when the latter waxed hot, Governor Morehead was reported by a servant to have exclaimed: "It's a long time between drinks." — JOHN MOTLEY MOREHEAD, *letter* [November 21, 1934]

So long as we love we serve; so long as we are loved by others, I would almost say that we are indispensable; and no man is useless while he has a friend.

Across the Plains [1892].
Lay Morals

To be honest, to be kind — to earn a little and spend a little less, to make upon the whole a family happier for his presence, to renounce when that shall be necessary and not to be embittered, to keep a few friends, but these without capitulation — above all, on the same grim condition, to keep friends with himself — here is a task for all that a man has of fortitude and delicacy.

A Christmas Sermon

If your morals make you dreary, depend upon it, they are wrong. I do not say give them up, for they may be all you have, but conceal them like a vice lest they should spoil the lives of better and simpler people. *Ib.*

Here lies one who meant well, tried a little, failed much: — surely that may be his epitaph of which he need not be ashamed. *Ib.*

Ice and iron cannot be welded.
Weir of Hermiston [1896]

Give us grace and strength to forbear and to persevere. Give us courage and gaiety and the quiet mind, spare to us our friends, soften to us our enemies.
Prayer [1]

Youth is wholly experimental.
Letter to a Young Gentleman

ROSE HARTWICK THORPE
1850–1939

She breathed the husky whisper —
"Curfew must not ring tonight."
Curfew Must Not Ring Tonight
[1882], *st. 2*

[1] On the bronze memorial to Stevenson in St. Giles Cathedral, Edinburgh, Scotland.

Long, long years I've rung the curfew
from that gloomy, shadowed tower;
Every evening, just at sunset, it has tolled the twilight hour;
I have done my duty ever, tried to do it just and right,
Now I'm old, I will not miss it. Curfew bell must ring tonight!
Curfew Must Not Ring Tonight,
st. 3

Out she swung — far out; the city seemed a speck of light below,
There 'twixt heaven and earth suspended as the bell swung to and fro. *Ib. st. 7*

ELLA WHEELER WILCOX
1850–1919

Talk happiness. The world is sad enough
Without your woe. No path is wholly rough. *Speech, st. 1*

Talk faith. The world is better off without
Your uttered ignorance and morbid doubt. *Ib. st. 2*

One ship drives east and another drives west
With the selfsame winds that blow.
'Tis the set of sails and not the gales
Which tells us the way to go.
Winds of Fate

No! the two kinds of people on earth that I mean
Are the people who lift and the people who lean. *To Lift or to Lean*

It ever has been since time began,
And ever will be, till time lose breath,
That love is a mood — no more — to man,
And love to woman is life or death.[1]
Blind, st. 1

Laugh, and the world laughs with you;
Weep, and you weep alone;

[1] See Byron, p. 560a.

For the sad old earth must borrow its
  mirth,
But has trouble enough of its own.
                    Solitude, st. 1

So many gods, so many creeds,
  So many paths that wind and wind,
  When just the art of being kind
Is all this sad world needs.
                    The World's Need

No question is ever settled
Until it is settled right.
                Settle the Question Right

FERDINAND FOCH
1851–1929

My center is giving way, my right is
pushed back, situation excellent, I am
attacking.[1]
  *Said at the Second Battle of the
  Marne* [1918]. *From* B. H. LID-
  DELL HART, *Reputations Ten
  Years After* [1928]

EDWARD SMITH
UFFORD
1851–1929

Throw out the lifeline across the dark
  wave,
There is a brother whom someone
  should save.
              Throw Out the Lifeline
                      [1884], *st. 1*

Throw out the lifeline, throw out the
  lifeline,
Someone is sinking today.
                      Ib. refrain

FRANCIS WILLIAM
BOURDILLON
1852–1921

The night has a thousand eyes,[2]
  And the day but one;
Yet the light of the bright world dies
  With the dying sun.

  [1] Mon centre cède, ma droite recule, situation
excellente, j'attaque.
  [2] On the stars thou gazest, my star; would I
were heaven to look at thee with many eyes. —
Greek Anthology, pt. VIII, no. 7. Translated by
J. W. MACKAIL.
  See Lyly, p. 203a.

The mind has a thousand eyes,
  And the heart but one;
Yet the light of a whole life dies
  When love is done.
            The Night Has a Thousand Eyes

ROBERT BONTINE
CUNNINGHAME-
GRAHAM
1852–1936

Success, which touches nothing that
it does not vulgarize, should be its own
reward . . . the odium of success is
hard enough to bear, without the added
ignominy of popular applause.
                    Success [1902]

God forbid that I should go to any
heaven in which there are no horses.
        Letter to Theodore Roosevelt
                          [1917]

EDWIN MARKHAM
1852–1940

Bowed by the weight of centuries he
  leans
Upon his hoe and gazes on the
  ground,
The emptiness of ages in his face,
And on his back the burden of the
  world.
        The Man with the Hoe [1] [1899],
                          st. 1

O masters, lords and rulers in all lands,
Is this the handiwork you give to God?
                      Ib. st. 3

Here was a man to hold against the
  world,
A man to match the mountains [2] and
  the sea.
        Lincoln, the Man of the People
                      [1901], *st. 1*

  [1] Inspired by Millet's painting.
  [2] A man to match his mountains, not to
creep
Dwarfed and abased below them.
          WHITTIER, *Among the Hills* [1869],
                          prelude
  Bring me men to match my mountains. —
SAM WALTER FOSS [1858–1911], *The Coming
American*

The color of the ground was in him,
  the red earth,
The smack and tang of elemental
  things.
> *Lincoln, the Man of the*
> *People, st. 2*

He went down
As when a lordly cedar, green with
  boughs,
Goes down with a great shout upon the
  hills,
And leaves a lonesome place against the
  sky.   *Ib. st. 4*

He drew a circle that shut me out —
Heretic, rebel, a thing to flout.
But Love and I had the wit to win:
We drew a circle that took him in.
> *Outwitted*

ALBERT ABRAHAM MICHELSON
1852–1931

The more important fundamental laws and facts of physical science have all been discovered, and these are now so firmly established that the possibility of their ever being supplanted in consequence of new discoveries is exceedingly remote . . . Our future discoveries must be looked for in the sixth place of decimals.
> *Address, dedication ceremony,*
> *Ryerson Physical Laboratory,*
> *University of Chicago* [1894]

GEORGE MOORE
1852–1933

After all there is but one race — humanity.
> *The Bending of the Bough*
> [1900], *act III*

The difficulty in life is the choice.
> *Ib. IV*

The wrong way always seems the more reasonable.   *Ib.*

English, Scotchmen, Jews, do well in Ireland — Irishmen never; even the patriot has to leave Ireland to get a hearing.   *Ave* [1911]. *Overture*

A man travels the world over in search of what he needs and returns home to find it.
> *The Brook Kerith* [1916], *ch. 11*

HENRY VAN DYKE
1852–1933

If all the skies were sunshine,
  Our faces would be fain
To feel once more upon them
  The cooling plash of rain.
> *If All the Skies, st. 1*

Raise the stone, and thou shalt find me; cleave the wood and there am I.[1]
> *The Toiling of Felix* [1900],
> *pt. I, prelude*

So it's home again, and home again, America for me.
My heart is turning home again, and there I long to be.
> *America for Me, st. 2*

Oh, London is a man's town, there's power in the air;
And Paris is a woman's town, with flowers in her hair.   *Ib. st. 3*

Not to the swift, the race:
Not to the strong, the fight:[2]
Not to the righteous, perfect grace:
Not to the wise, the light.
> *Reliance, st. 1*

The lintel low enough to keep out pomp and pride:
The threshold high enough to turn deceit aside.
> *For the Friends at Hurstmont.*
> *The Door*

Self is the only prison that can ever bind the soul.
> *The Prison and the Angel*

[1] *Oxyrhynchus Logia Agrapha, The Unwritten Sayings of Jesus, Fifth Logion.*
Raise ye the stone or cleave the wood to make a path more fair or flat;
Lo, it is black already with blood some Son of Martha spilled for that.
> RUDYARD KIPLING [1865–1936]. *The Sons of Martha*

[2] See *Ecclesiastes 9:11*, p. 28b, and John Davidson, p. 844b.

It is with rivers as it is with people: the greatest are not always the most agreeable nor the best to live with.
Little Rivers, ch. 2

The first day of spring is one thing, and the first spring day is another. The difference between them is sometimes as great as a month.
Fisherman's Luck, ch. 5

EDGAR WATSON HOWE
1853–1937

A really busy person never knows how much he weighs.
Country Town Sayings [1911]

What people say behind your back is your standing in the community.   *Ib.*

There is nothing so well known as that we should not expect something for nothing — but we all do and call it Hope.   *Ib.*

JOSÉ MARTÍ
1853–1895

A knowledge of different literatures is the best way to free one's self from the tyranny of any of them.
On Oscar Wilde [1882]

To beautify life is to give it an object.   *Ib.*

Terrible times in which priests no longer merit the praise of poets and in which poets have not yet begun to be priests.
On "El Poema de Niágara" of Pérez Bonalde [1883]

This is the age in which hills can look down upon the mountains.   *Ib.*

Only those who hate the Negro see hatred in the Negro.
Manifesto of Montecristi [1895]

The spirit of a government must be that of the country. The form of a government must come from the makeup of the country. Government is nothing but the balance of the natural elements of a country.   *Our America* [1891]

I have lived in the monster [the United States] and I know its insides; and my sling is the sling of David.
Letter to Manuel Mercado [1895]

CECIL JOHN RHODES
1853–1902

I desire to encourage and foster an appreciation of the advantages which will result from the union of the English-speaking peoples throughout the world, and to encourage in the students from the United States of America an attachment to the country from which they have sprung without I hope withdrawing them or their sympathies from the land of their adoption or birth.
Will, establishing the Rhodes Scholarships

Educational relations make the strongest tie.   *Ib.*

So little done — so much to do.
Last words

IRWIN RUSSELL
1853–1879

De man what keeps pullin' de grapevine shakes down a few bunches at leas'.
Precepts at Parting [1888], *st. 3*

You mus' reason with a mule.
Nebuchadnezzar [1888], *st. 3*

JAMES A. BLAND
1854–1911

Carry me back to old Virginny,
There's where the cotton and the corn and taters grow;
There's where the birds warble sweet in the springtime,
There's where this old darky's heart am long'd to go.
Carry Me Back to Old Virginny [1875], *st. 1*

SIR JAMES GEORGE FRAZER
1854–1941

Dwellers by the sea cannot fail to be impressed by the sight of its ceaseless ebb and flow, and are apt, on the principles of that rude philosophy of sympathy and resemblance . . . to trace a subtle relation, a secret harmony, between its tides and the life of man. . . . The belief that most deaths happen at ebb tide is said to be held along the east coast of England from Northumberland to Kent.[1]
The Golden Bough,[2] *ch. 3*

The heaviest calamity in English history, the breach with America, might never have occurred if George the Third had not been an honest dullard.
Ib.

By religion, then, I understand a propitiation or conciliation of powers superior to man which are believed to direct and control the course of nature and of human life.   *Ib. 4*

It is a common rule with primitive people not to waken a sleeper, because his soul is away and might not have time to get back.   *Ib. 18*

The awe and dread with which the untutored savage contemplates his mother-in-law are amongst the most familiar facts of anthropology.   *Ib.*

The world cannot live at the level of its great men.   *Ib. 37*

THOMAS RILEY MARSHALL
1854–1925

What this country needs is a good five-cent cigar.[3]
Remark to John Crockett, Chief Clerk of the United States Senate

[1] See Shakespeare, *Henry V, II, iii, 11, p.* 243b, and Dickens, p. 671b.
[2] Abridged one-volume edition [1922]. The original appeared in twelve volumes from 1890 to 1915.
[3] What this country needs is a good five-cent nickel. — FRANKLIN P. ADAMS [1932]

BENJAMIN PIERCE
1854–1914

Mathematics is the science which draws necessary conclusions.
Linear Associative Algebra. In the American Journal of Mathematics, vol. IV [1881], *p. 97*

JULES HENRI POINCARÉ
1854–1912

The advance of science is not comparable to the changes of a city, where old edifices are pitilessly torn down to give place to new, but to the continuous evolution of zoologic types which develop ceaselessly and end by becoming unrecognizable to the common sight, but where an expert eye finds always traces of the prior work of the past centuries.
Valeur de la Science [1] [1904]

Science is built up with facts, as a house is with stones. But a collection of facts is no more a science than a heap of stones is a house.
La Science et l'Hypothèse [1] [1908]

ARTHUR RIMBAUD
1854–1891

I went out under the sky, Muse! and I was your vassal.
Ma Bohème. Fantaisie

My tavern was the Big Bear. — My stars in the sky rustled softly.
Ib.

My sad heart foams at the stern.
Le Coeur Volé

Lighter than a cork I danced on the waves.   *Le Bateau Ivre* [1871]

Sweeter than apples to children
The green water spurted through my wooden hull.   *Ib.*

I have bathed in the poem of the sea . . .
Devouring the green azures.   *Ib.*

[1] Translated by G. B. HALSTED.

Sometimes I saw what men have only dreamed of seeing.

Le Bateau Ivre

I have seen the sunset, stained with mystic wonders,
Illumine the rolling waves with long purple forms,
Like actors in ancient plays. *Ib.*

I long for Europe of the ancient parapets. *Ib.*

I have seen starry archipelagoes! and islands
Whose heavens are opened to the voyager:
Is it in these bottomless nights that you sleep, in exile,
A million golden birds, O future Vigor?

Ib.

Black A, white E, red I, green U, blue O: vowels,
Someday I shall recount your latent births.[1] *Voyelles* [1871]

It is found again.
What? Eternity.
It is the sea
Gone with the sun.

L'Éternité [1872]

O seasons, O châteaux,
What soul is without flaws? [2]

Bonheur, refrain

One evening, I sat Beauty in my lap.
— And I found her bitter. — And I cursed her.

Une Saison en Enfer (1873)

I found I could extinguish all human hope from my soul. *Ib.*

Baptism enslaved me.

Ib. Nuit de L'Enfer

I am the master of fantasy. *Ib.*

Old poetics played a large part in my alchemy of the word. *Ib.*

---

[1] I devised colors for the vowels! — A black, E white, I red, O yellow, U green. — *Une Saison en Enfer* [1873], *Délires II, Alchimie de Verbe*
[2] O saisons, O châteaux
Quelle âme est sans défauts?

I! I who fashioned myself a sorcerer or an angel, who dispensed with all morality, I have come back to the earth.

Une Saison en Enfer. Adieu

One must be absolutely modern.

Ib.

I have embraced the summer dawn.

Illuminations [1874]. *Aube*

It rains softly on the town.[1]

From a lost poem

I say one must be a *seer*, make oneself a *seer*.
The poet makes himself a *seer* by an immense, long, deliberate derangement of all the senses.[2]

Lettre à Paul Demeny [May 15, 1871]

EDITH MATILDA THOMAS
1854–1925

The God of Music dwelleth out of doors. *Music*

WILLARD DUNCAN VANDIVER
1854–1932

I come from a state that raises corn and cotton and cockleburs and Democrats, and frothy eloquence neither convinces nor satisfies me. I am from Missouri. You have got to show me.

Speech at a naval banquet in Philadelphia [1899]

GERALD BRENNAN
fl. 1899

Th' mem'ry comes like a banshee meself an' me wealth between,
An' I long for a mornin's mornin' in Shanahan's ould shebeen.

Shanahan's Ould Shebeen [1899], *st. 4*

---

[1] Il pleut doucement sur la ville.
Verlaine used this as an epigraph for his *Ariettes Oubliées*, III. See Verlaine, p. 808a.
[2] Déréglement de tous les sens.
See Baudelaire, footnote [1], p. 706b.

If you couldn't afford good whiskey,
he'd take you on trust for beer.
Shanahan's Ould Shebeen, st. 5

WILLIAM COWPER
BRANN [1]
1855–1898

Boston runs to brains as well as to
beans and brown bread. But she is
cursed with an army of cranks whom
nothing short of a straitjacket or a
swamp elm club will ever control.
From The Iconoclast. Beans and
Blood

No man can be a patriot on an
empty stomach.
Ib. Old Glory [July 4, 1893]

It has the subtle flavor of an old pair
of socks. *Ib. Godey's Magazine*

The Lydian notes of Andrew Carnegie as he warbles a riant roundelay in
praise of poverty, or laments in pathetic
spondees the woes of the man with
spondulix. *Ib. Our American Czars*

HENRY CUYLER
BUNNER
1855–1896

Off with your hat as the flag goes by!
And let the heart have its say;
You're man enough for a tear in your
eye
That you will not wipe away.
The Old Flag, st. 1

I have a bookcase, which is what
Many much better men have not.
There are no books inside, for books,
I am afraid, might spoil its looks.
But I've three busts, all secondhand,
Upon the top. You understand
I could not put them underneath —
Shake, Mulleary and Go-ethe.
Shake, Mulleary and Go-ethe,
st. 1

[1] Known as "The Iconoclast" from the name
of his paper, first published in Austin, Texas,
and later in Waco.

EUGENE VICTOR DEBS
1855–1926

While there is a lower class I am in
it, while there is a criminal element I
am of it; while there is a soul in prison,
I am not free. *On labor and freedom*

The savings of many in the hands of
one. *On wealth*

MARGARET WOLFE
HUNGERFORD
1855–1897

Beauty is in the eye of the beholder.[1]
Molly Bawn [1878]

FRANK FRANKFORT
MOORE
1855–1931

He knew that to offer a man friendship when love is in his heart is like
giving a loaf of bread to one who is
dying of thirst.
The Jessamy Bride, ch. 9

To strike at a serpent that hisses may
only cause it to spring. *Ib. 19*

WALTER HINES PAGE
1855–1918

There is one thing better than good
government, and that is government in
which all the people have a part.
Life and Letters [1922–1925],
vol. III, p. 31

SIR ARTHUR WING
PINERO
1855–1934

From forty till fifty a man is at heart
either a stoic or a satyr.
The Second Mrs. Tanqueray
[1893], act I

[1] See Hume, p. 434b, and Wallace, p. 729b.

OLIVE SCHREINER
[RALPH IRON]
1855–1920

The barb in the arrow of childhood suffering is this: its intense loneliness, its intense ignorance.
The Story of an African Farm
[1884], ch. 1

There never was a man who said one word for woman but he said two for man and three for the whole human race.   *Ib. 4*

FIONA MACLEOD
[WILLIAM SHARP]
1855–1905

My heart is a lonely hunter that hunts on a lonely hill.
The Lonely Hunter, st. 6

CY WARMAN
1855–1914

Every daisy in the dell knows my secret, knows it well,
And yet I dare not tell, sweet Marie.
Sweet Marie [1893], st. 1

GEORGE EDWARD
WOODBERRY
1855–1930

She from old fountains doth new judgment draw,
Till, word by word, the ancient order swerves
To the true course more nigh; in every age
A little she creates, but more preserves.
My Country

JOSEPH TABRAR
fl. 1892

I've got a little cat,
And I'm very fond of that,
But I'd rather have a bow-wow, wow.
Daddy Wouldn't Buy Me a Bow-
Wow [1892]

LYMAN FRANK BAUM
1856–1919

The Wonderful Wizard of Oz.
Title of book [1900]

FRANCIS BELLAMY
1856–1931

I pledge allegiance to the flag of the United States of America and to the republic for which it stands, one nation, under God, indivisible, with liberty and justice for all.[1]
The Pledge of Allegiance to the
Flag [1892]

THEOBALD VON
BETHMANN-HOLLWEG
1856–1921

Just for a word — "neutrality," a word which in wartime has so often been disregarded, just for a scrap of paper — Great Britain is going to make war.
To Sir Edward Goschen [August
4, 1914]; dispatch from Goschen
to the British Foreign Office

LOUIS D. BRANDEIS
1856–1941

Those who won our independence believed that the final end of the State was to make men free to develop their faculties; and that in its government the deliberative forces should prevail over the arbitrary. They valued liberty both as an end and as a means. They believed liberty to be the secret of happiness and courage to be the secret of liberty.[2]
Whitney v. California, 274 U.S.
357, 375 [1927]

Fear of serious injury cannot alone justify suppression of free speech and assembly. Men feared witches and burned women. It is the function of speech to free men from the bondage of irrational fears.   *Ib. 376*

[1] In 1888 JAMES B. UPHAM [1845–1905] wrote a rough draft of the pledge which Bellamy, as chairman of a committee for a national school program to celebrate the four-hundredth anniversary of the discovery of America, helped to put into its final form.

The phrase "under God" was added by a joint resolution of Congress approved by the President, June 14, 1954.

[2] See Thucydides, p. 90a.

They [the makers of the Constitution] conferred, as against the Government, the right to be let alone — the most comprehensive of rights and the right most valued by civilized men.

> *Olmstead v. United States,*
> *277 U.S. 438, 478* [1928]

The greatest dangers to liberty lurk in insidious encroachment by men of zeal, well-meaning but without understanding.

> *Ib. 479*

Our Government is the potent, the omnipresent teacher. For good or for ill, it teaches the whole people by its example.   *Ib. 485*

If we would guide by the light of reason, we must let our minds be bold.

> *New State Ice Co. v. Liebmann,*
> *285 U.S. 262, 311* [1932]

Stare decisis is usually the wise policy, because in most matters it is more important that the applicable rule of law be settled than that it be settled right. . . . But in cases involving the Federal Constitution, where correction through legislative action is practically impossible, this Court has often overruled its earlier decisions. The Court bows to the lessons of experience and the force of better reasoning, recognizing that the process of trial and error, so fruitful in the physical sciences, is appropriate also in the judicial function.

> *Burnet v. Coronado Oil and Gas*
> *Co., 285 U.S. 393, 406* [1932]

There is in most Americans some spark of idealism, which can be fanned into a flame. It takes sometimes a divining rod to find what it is; but when found, and that means often, when disclosed to the owners, the results are often extraordinary.

> *The Words of Justice Brandeis*
> [1953]

KENYON COX
1856–1919

Work thou for pleasure — paint, or sing, or carve
The thing thou lovest, though the body starve —
Who works for glory misses oft the goal;
Who works for money coins his very soul.
Work for the work's sake, then, and it may be
That these things shall be added unto thee.

> *The Gospel of Art* [1895]

SIGMUND FREUD[1]
1856–1939

Being entirely honest with oneself is a good exercise.

> *Origins of Psychoanalysis. Letter*
> *to Fliess* [October 15, 1897]

No one who, like me, conjures up the most evil of those half-tamed demons that inhabit the human breast, and seeks to wrestle with them, can expect to come through the struggle unscathed.

> *Complete Psychological Works.*
> *Dora* [1905]

Conscience is the internal perception of the rejection of a particular wish operating within us.

> *Ib. Totem and Taboo* [1912–1913]

At bottom God is nothing more than an exalted father.   *Ib.*

The psychic development of the individual is a short repetition of the course of development of the race.[2]

> *Leonardo da Vinci* [1916]

When the wayfarer whistles in the dark, he may be disavowing his timidity, but he does not see any the more clearly for doing so.

> *The Problem of Anxiety* [1925]

---

[1] See Auden, p. 1060a, and Whitehead, p. 861b.

[2] See Haeckel, p. 752b.

The poets and philosophers before me discovered the unconscious; what I discovered was the scientific method by which the unconscious can be studied.
On his seventieth birthday [1926]; from LIONEL TRILLING, The Liberal Imagination

The voice of the intellect is a soft one, but it does not rest until it has gained a hearing. Ultimately, after endlessly repeated rebuffs, it succeeds. This is one of the few points in which one may be optimistic about the future of mankind, but in itself it signifies not a little.   Future of an Illusion [1928]

Analogies prove nothing, that is quite true, but they can make one feel more at home.
New Introductory Lectures on Psychoanalysis [1932]

One might compare the relation of the ego to the id with that between a rider and his horse. The horse provides the locomotor energy, and the rider has the prerogative of determining the goal and of guiding the movements of his powerful mount towards it. But all too often in the relations between the ego and the id we find a picture of the less ideal situation in which the rider is obliged to guide his horse in the direction in which it itself wants to go.
Ib. The Anatomy of the Mental Personality (Lecture 31)

The poor ego has a still harder time of it; it has to serve three harsh masters, and has to do its best to reconcile the claims and demands of all three. . . . The three tyrants are the external world, the superego and the id.   Ib.

Where id was, there shall ego be.
Ib.

Thinking is an experimental dealing with small quantities of energy, just as a general moves miniature figures over a map before setting his troops in action.
Ib. Anxiety and Instinctual Life (Lecture 32)

If one wishes to form a true estimate of the full grandeur of religion, one must keep in mind what it undertakes to do for men. It gives them information about the source and origin of the universe, it assures them of protection and final happiness amid the changing vicissitudes of life, and it guides their thoughts and motions by means of precepts which are backed by the whole force of its authority.
New Introductory Lectures on Psychoanalysis. A Philosophy of Life (Lecture 35)

Religion is an attempt to get control over the sensory world, in which we are placed, by means of the wish-world, which we have developed inside us as a result of biological and psychological necessities.   Ib.

Religion is an illusion and it derives its strength from the fact that it falls in with our instinctual desires.   Ib.

The Mosaic religion had been a Father religion; Christianity became a Son religion. The old God, the Father, took second place; Christ, the Son, stood in His stead, just as in those dark times every son had longed to do.
Moses and Monotheism [1938]

Man found that he was faced with the acceptance of "spiritual" forces, that is to say such forces as cannot be apprehended by the senses, particularly not by sight, and yet having undoubted, even extremely strong, effects. If we may trust to language, it was the movement of the air that provided the image of spirituality, since the spirit borrows its name from the breath of wind (animus, spiritus, Hebrew: ruach = smoke). The idea of the soul was thus born as the spiritual principle in the individual. . . . Now the realm of spirits had opened for man, and he was ready to endow everything in nature with the soul he had discovered in himself.   Ib.

A man who has been the indisputable favorite of his mother keeps for life the feeling of a conqueror, that confidence of success that often induces real success.

> From ERNEST JONES, *Life and Works of Sigmund Freud, vol. I* [1953], *ch. 1*

The great question . . . which I have not been able to answer, despite my thirty years of research into the feminine soul, is "What does a woman want?"

> Quoted in CHARLES ROLO, *Psychiatry in American Life* [1963]

EDMOND HARAUCOURT
1856–1941

To leave is to die a little;
To die to what we love.
We leave behind a bit of ourselves
Wherever we have been.[1]

> *Choix de Poésies* [1891]. *Rondel de l'Adieu*

ELBERT HUBBARD
1856–1915

It is not book learning young men need, nor instruction about this and that, but a stiffening of the vertebrae which will cause them to be loyal to a trust, to act promptly, concentrate their energies, do a thing — "carry a message to Garcia." [2]

> *A Message to Garcia* [March 1899]

The man who is anybody and who does anything is surely going to be criticized, vilified, and misunderstood. This is a part of the penalty for greatness, and every great man understands it;

[1] Partir, c'est mourir un peu;
C'est mourir à ce qu'on aime.
On laisse un peu de soi-même
En toute heure et dans tout lieu.
Translated by NORBERT GUTERMAN.
See Schopenhauer, p. 563b.

[2] After the declaration of the Spanish-American War, Andrew Summers Rowan, then Lieutenant, United States Bureau of Military Intelligence, was sent to communicate with General Calixto Garcia. He landed in an open boat near Turquino Peak, April 24, 1898, executed the mission, and brought back information regarding the insurgent army.

and understands, too, that it is no proof of greatness. The final proof of greatness lies in being able to endure contumely without resentment.

> *Get Out or Get in Line*

This will never be a civilized country until we expend more money for books than we do for chewing gum.

> From *The Philistine* [1895–1915]

The path of civilization is paved with tin cans. **Ib.**

EDWARD SANDFORD MARTIN
1856–1939

A Little Brother of the Rich.

> *Title of poem*

ROBERT EDWIN PEARY
1856–1920

The Eskimo, Ootah, had his own explanation. Said he: "The devil is asleep or having trouble with his wife, or we should never have come back so easily."

> *The North Pole* [1910]

HENRI PHILIPPE PÉTAIN
1856–1951

They shall not pass.[1]

> *Attributed. Verdun* [February 26, 1916]

LIZETTE WOODWORTH REESE
1856–1935

When I consider life and its few years —
A wisp of fog betwixt us and the sun;

[1] Ils ne passeront pas.
The first official record of the expression appears in General Nivelle's Order of the Day [June 23, 1916] to his troops at the height of battle: *Vous ne les laisserez pas passer* [You will not let them pass]! — ALAN HORNE, *New York Times Magazine* [February 20, 1966]
The inscription on the Verdun medal is: **On ne passe pas.**

A call to battle, and the battle
   done . . .
I wonder at the idleness of tears.
Tears

The burst of music down an unlisten-
   ing street.   *Ib.*

Creeds grow so thick along the way,
Their boughs hide God.   *Doubt*

GEORGE BERNARD SHAW
1856–1950

My method is to take the utmost
trouble to find the right thing to say,
and then to say it with the utmost
levity.   *Answers to Nine Questions*

It's well to be off with the Old
Woman before you're on with the
New.[1]
The Philanderer [1893], *act II*

The fickleness of the women I love is
only equaled by the infernal constancy
of the women who love me.[2]   *Ib.*

The test of a man or woman's breeding is how they behave in a quarrel.
Ib. IV

People are always blaming their circumstances for what they are. I don't
believe in circumstances. The people
who get on in this world are the people
who get up and look for the circumstances they want, and, if they can't
find them, make them.
Mrs. Warren's Profession
[1893], *act II*

There are no secrets better kept than
the secrets that everybody guesses.
Ib. III

A great devotee of the Gospel of
Getting On.   *Ib. IV*

We have no more right to consume
happiness without producing it than to
consume wealth without producing it.
Candida [1898], *act I*

I'm only a beer teetotaler, not a
champagne teetotaler.   *Ib. III*

---

[1] See C. H. Webb, p. 753b.
[2] See Cervantes, p. 194b.

We don't bother much about dress
and manners in England, because as a
nation we don't dress well and we've no
manners.
You Never Can Tell [1898],
act I

The great advantage of a hotel is
that it's a refuge from home life.
Ib. II

There is only one religion, though
there are a hundred versions of it.
Plays Pleasant and Unpleasant
[1898], *vol. II, preface*

You're not a man, you're a machine.
Arms and the Man [1898], *act III*

The worst sin towards our fellow
creatures is not to hate them, but to be
indifferent to them: that's the essence
of inhumanity.
The Devil's Disciple [1901], *act II*

This is the true joy in life, the being
used for a purpose recognized by yourself as a mighty one; the being thoroughly worn out before you are thrown
on the scrap heap; the being a force of
nature instead of a feverish selfish little
clod of ailments and grievances complaining that the world will not devote
itself to making you happy.
Man and Superman [1903],
epistle dedicatory

A lifetime of happiness! No man
alive could bear it: it would be hell on
earth.   *Ib. act I*

The more things a man is ashamed
of, the more respectable he is.   *Ib.*

Marry Ann; and at the end of a week
you'll find no more inspiration in her
than in a plate of muffins.   *Ib. II*

An Englishman thinks he is moral
when he is only uncomfortable.
Ib. III

The golden rule is that there is no
golden rule.
Ib. Maxims for Revolutionists

He who can, does. He who cannot,
teaches.   *Ib.*

Marriage is popular because it combines the maximum of temptation with the maximum of opportunity.
Man and Superman, Maxims for Revolutionists

If you strike a child, take care that you strike it in anger, even at the risk of maiming it for life. A blow in cold blood neither can nor should be forgiven. *Ib.*

Virtue consists, not in abstaining from vice, but in not desiring it. *Ib.*

Lack of money is the root of all evil.[1] *Ib.*

The greatest of evils and the worst of crimes is poverty.
Major Barbara [1907], *preface*

I can't talk religion to a man with bodily hunger in his eyes.[2]
Ib. act II

Blood and fire! *Ib.*

Home life as we understand it is no more natural to us than a cage is natural to a cockatoo.
Getting Married [1908], *preface*

When two people are under the influence of the most violent, most insane, most delusive, and most transient of passions, they are required to swear that they will remain in that excited, abnormal, and exhausting condition continuously until death do them part. *Ib.*

A man is like a phonograph with half-a-dozen records. You soon get tired of them all; and yet you have to sit at table whilst he reels them off to every new visitor. *Ib. (The Play)*

The whole strength of England lies in the fact that the enormous majority of the English people are snobs. *Ib.*

You don't learn to hold your own in the world by standing on guard, but by attacking, and getting well hammered yourself. *Ib.*

Religion is a great force — the only real motive force in the world; but what you fellows don't understand is that you must get at a man through his own religion and not through yours.
Getting Married

I like a bit of a mongrel myself, whether it's a man or a dog; they're the best for every day.
Misalliance [1910], *episode I*

If parents would only realize how they bore their children! *Ib.*

He's a gentleman: look at his boots.
Pygmalion [1912], *act I*

Women upset everything. When you let them into your life, you find that the woman is driving at one thing and you're driving at another. *Ib. II*

Not bloody likely. *Ib. III*

I have to live for others and not for myself; that's middle-class morality.
Ib. V

Independence? That's middle-class blasphemy. We are all dependent on one another, every soul of us on earth. *Ib.*

All great truths begin as blasphemies.
Annajanska [1919]

The nauseous sham goodfellowship our democratic public men get up for shop use.
Back to Methuselah [1921]. *Gospel of the Brothers Barnabas*

Everything happens to everybody sooner or later if there is time enough.
Ib. As Far As Thought Can Reach

Silence is the most perfect expression of scorn. *Ib.*

The worst cliques are those which consist of one man. *Ib.*

Assassination is the extreme form of censorship.
The Rejected Statement, pt. I

The Jews generally give value. They make you pay; but they deliver the

---

[1] See *I Timothy* 6:10, p. 55b.
[2] See Conrad, p. 843b.

goods. In my experience the men who want something for nothing are invariably Christians.
Saint Joan [1923], *sc. iv*

One man that has a mind and knows it can always beat ten men who haven't and don't.
The Apple Cart [1929], *act I*

I have defined the hundred per cent American as ninety-nine per cent an idiot.
Remarks on Sinclair Lewis receiving the Nobel Prize [1930]

An American has no sense of privacy. He does not know what it means. There is no such thing in the country.
Speech, New York [April 11, 1933]

You in America should trust to that volcanic political instinct which I have divined in you.   *Ib.*

LOUIS HENRI SULLIVAN
1856–1924

Form ever follows function.
The Tall Office Building Artistically Considered, Lippincott's Magazine [March 1896]

JOSEPH JOHN THOMSON
1856–1940

From the point of view of the physicist, a theory of matter is a policy rather than a creed; its object is to connect or coordinate apparently diverse phenomena, and above all to suggest, stimulate and direct experiment.
The Corpuscular Theory of Matter [1907]

BOOKER TALIAFERRO WASHINGTON
1856–1915

No race can prosper till it learns that there is as much dignity in tilling a field as in writing a poem.
Up from Slavery [1901]

OSCAR FINGAL O'FLAHERTIE WILLS WILDE
1854–1900

Tread lightly, she is near
  Under the snow,
Speak gently, she can hear
  The daisies grow.
Requiescat, st. 1

    And yet, and yet,
These Christs that die upon the barricades,
God knows it I am with them, in some things.
Sonnet to Liberty: Not That I Love Thy Children

And down the long and silent street,
The dawn, with silver-sandaled feet,
Crept like a frightened girl.
The Harlot's House

    Lo! with a little rod
I did but touch the honey[1] of romance —
And must I lose a soul's inheritance?
Hélas [1881], *l. 12*

A poet can survive everything but a misprint.
The Children of the Poets

As for borrowing Mr. Whistler's ideas about art, the only thoroughly original ideas I have ever heard him express have had reference to his own superiority as a painter over painters greater than himself.
Reply to an attack by James McNeill Whistler. In Truth [January 9, 1890]

Meredith is a prose Browning, and so is Browning. He used poetry as a medium for writing in prose.
The Critic as Artist [1891], *pt. I*

It is through art, and through art only, that we can realize our perfection; through art and art only that we can shield ourselves from the sordid perils of actual existence.   *Ib. II*

[1] See *I Samuel 14:27*, p. 12a.

As long as war is regarded as wicked, it will always have its fascination. When it is looked upon as vulgar, it will cease to be popular.
The Critic as Artist, pt. II

There is no sin except stupidity.[1]
Ib.

There is no such thing as a moral or an immoral book. Books are well written, or badly written. That is all.
The Picture of Dorian Gray [1891], *preface*

All art is quite useless.   *Ib.*

There is only one thing in the world worse than being talked about, and that is not being talked about.   *Ib. ch. 1*

Conscience and cowardice are really the same things.[2]   *Ib.*

A man cannot be too careful in the choice of his enemies.[3]   *Ib.*

The only way to get rid of a temptation is to yield to it.   *Ib. 2*

He knew the precise psychological moment [4] when to say nothing.   *Ib.*

The only difference between a caprice and a lifelong passion is that the caprice lasts a little longer.   *Ib.*

Children begin by loving their parents; as they grow older they judge them; sometimes they forgive them.
Ib. 5

Conscience makes egotists of us all.[5]   *Ib. 8*

[1] See Marlowe, p. 212b.
[2] See Mark Twain, p. 763a.
[3] See Conrad, p. 843a.
[4] In all considerations the psychological momentum or factor must be allowed to play a prominent part, for without its cooperation there is little to be hoped from the work of the artillery. — *Neue Preussische Kreuzzeitung* [December 16, 1870], commenting upon the siege of Paris.
    An error in translation gave us "psychological moment" (i.e. the critical moment). The Parisians ridiculed the phrase as an example of German pedantry, but it speedily became universal.
[5] See Shakespeare, p. 262a.

When a woman marries again it is because she detested her first husband. When a man marries again, it is because he adored his first wife.[1] Women try their luck; men risk theirs.
The Picture of Dorian Gray, ch. 15

Over the piano was printed a notice: Please do not shoot the pianist. He is doing his best.
Impressions of America. Leadville

Nowadays we are all of us so hard up that the only pleasant things to pay are compliments. They're the only things we *can* pay.
Lady Windermere's Fan [1892], *act I*

I can resist everything except temptation.   *Ib.*

We are all in the gutter, but some of us are looking at the stars.   *Ib. III*

In this world there are only two tragedies. One is not getting what one wants, and the other is getting it.
Ib.

What is a cynic? A man who knows the price of everything, and the value of nothing.   *Ib.*

Experience is the name everyone gives to their mistakes.   *Ib.*

I have never admitted that I am more than twenty-nine, or thirty at the most. Twenty-nine when there are pink shades, thirty when there are not.[2]
Ib. IV

Mrs. Allonby: They say, Lady Hunstanton, that when good Americans die they go to Paris.[3]
Lady Hunstanton: Indeed? And

[1] See Samuel Johnson, p. 431a.
[2] When you come to write my epitaph, Charles, let it be in these delicious words, "She had a long twenty-nine." — JAMES M. BARRIE [1860–1937], *Rosalind*
[3] Good Americans, when they die, go to Paris. — THOMAS GOLD APPLETON [1812–1884]; *from* OLIVER WENDELL HOLMES, *The Autocrat of the Breakfast Table* [1858]

when bad Americans die, where do they go to?

Lord Illingworth: Oh, they go to America.

A Woman of No Importance
[1893], act I

The youth of America is their oldest tradition. It has been going on now for three hundred years. *Ib.*

Lord Illingworth: The Book of Life begins with a man and a woman in a garden.

Mrs. Allonby: It ends with Revelations. *Ib.*

I suppose society is wonderfully delightful. To be in it is merely a bore. But to be out of it simply a tragedy.
Ib. III

Really, if the lower orders don't set us a good example, what on earth is the use of them?

The Importance of Being
Earnest [1895], act I

I have invented an invaluable permanent invalid called Bunbury, in order that I may be able to go down into the country whenever I choose. *Ib.*

Of course the music is a great difficulty. You see, if one plays good music, people don't listen, and if one plays bad music people don't talk. *Ib.*

To lose one parent . . . may be regarded as a misfortune; to lose both looks like carelessness. *Ib.*

Relations are simply a tedious pack of people, who haven't got the remotest knowledge of how to live, nor the smallest instinct about when to die.
Ib.

I never travel without my diary. One should always have something sensational to read in the train. *Ib. II*

No woman should ever be quite accurate about her age. It looks so calculating. *Ib. III*

Democracy means simply the bludgeoning of the people by the people for the people.[1]

The Soul of Man Under
Socialism [1895]

The fact is, that civilization requires slaves. The Greeks were quite right there. Unless there are slaves to do the ugly, horrible, uninteresting work, culture and contemplation become almost impossible. Human slavery is wrong, insecure, and demoralizing. On mechanical slavery, on the slavery of the machine, the future of the world depends.[2] *Ib.*

Charity creates a multitude of sins.
Ib.

Art is the most intense mode of individualism that the world has known.
Ib.

Now art should never try to be popular. The public should try to make itself artistic. *Ib.*

The only thing that one really knows about human nature is that it changes. Change is the one quality we can predicate on it.[3] *Ib.*

Anybody can make history. Only a great man can write it. *Aphorisms*

I never saw a man who looked
  With such a wistful eye
Upon that little tent of blue
  Which prisoners call the sky.
The Ballad of Reading Gaol
[1898], pt. I, st. 3

When a voice behind me whispered low,
  "That fellow's got to swing."
Ib. st. 4

Yet each man kills the thing he loves,[4]
  By each let this be heard,
Some do it with a bitter look,
  Some with a flattering word.

[1] See Lincoln, p. 851a.
[2] See Havelock Ellis, p. 639a.
[3] See Heraclitus, p. 77b.
[4] See Shakespeare, p. 234a.

The coward does it with a kiss,
The brave man with a sword!
The Ballad of Reading Gaol,
pt. I, st. 7

It is sweet to dance to violins
When Love and Life are fair:
To dance to flutes, to dance to lutes
Is delicate and rare:
But it is not sweet with nimble feet
To dance upon the air!
Ib. II, st. 9

Something was dead in each of us,
And what was dead was Hope.
Ib. st. 31

And the wild regrets, and the bloody
sweats,
None knew so well as I:
For he who lives more lives than one
More deaths than one must die.
Ib. st. 37

I know not whether laws be right,
Or whether laws be wrong;
All that we know who lie in gaol
Is that the wall is strong;
And that each day is like a year,
A year whose days are long.
Ib. V, st. 1

The vilest deeds like poison weeds
Bloom well in prison air:
It is only what is good in man
That wastes and withers there:
Pale Anguish keeps the heavy gate
And the Warder is Despair.
Ib. st. 5

How else but through a broken heart
May Lord Christ enter in?
Ib. st. 14

Where there is sorrow there is holy
ground. *De Profundis* [1905]

WOODROW WILSON
1856–1924

The United States must be neutral in
fact as well as in name. . . . We must
be impartial in thought as well as in
action.
Message to the U.S. Senate
[August 19, 1914]

You deal in the raw material of opinion, and, if my convictions have any
validity, opinion ultimately governs the
world.
Address to the Associated Press
[April 20, 1915]

There is such a thing as a man being
too proud to fight.
Address to Foreign-Born Citizens
[May 10, 1915]

[The Civil War] created in this
country what had never existed before
— a national consciousness. It was not
the salvation of the Union; it was the
rebirth of the Union.
Memorial Day Address [1915]

The things that the flag stands for
were created by the experiences of a
great people. Everything that it stands
for was written by their lives. The flag
is the embodiment, not of sentiment,
but of history. It represents the experiences made by men and women, the
experiences of those who do and live
under that flag.
Address [June 14, 1915]

We have stood apart, studiously
neutral.
Message to Congress [Decem-
ber 7, 1915]

America cannot be an ostrich with its
head in the sand.
Speech, Des Moines [Feb-
ruary 1, 1916]

There must be, not a balance of
power, but a community of power; not
organized rivalries, but an organized
common peace.
Address to the U.S. Senate
[January 22, 1917]

It must be a peace without victory.
. . . Victory would mean peace forced
upon the loser, a victor's terms imposed
upon the vanquished. It would be accepted in humiliation, under duress, at
an intolerable sacrifice, and would leave
a sting, a resentment, a bitter memory
upon which terms of peace would rest,

not permanently, but only as upon quicksand. Only a peace between equals can last.

Address to the U.S. Senate

A little group of willful men, representing no opinion but their own, have rendered the great Government of the United States helpless and contemptible.

Statement made in reference to certain members of the Senate [1] [March 4, 1917]

Armed neutrality is ineffectual enough at best.

Address to Congress, asking for a declaration of war [April 2, 1917]

The world must be made safe for democracy.[2] *Ib.*

It is a fearful thing to lead this great peaceful people into war, into the most terrible and disastrous of all wars, civilization itself seeming to be in the balance. But the right is more precious than peace, and we shall fight for the things which we have always carried nearest our hearts — for democracy, for the right of those who submit to authority to have a voice in their own governments, for the rights and liberties of small nations, for a universal dominion of right by such a concert of free peoples as shall bring peace and safety to all nations and make the world itself at last free. To such a task we can dedicate our lives and our fortunes, everything that we are and everything that we have, with the pride of those who know that the day has come when America is privileged to spend her blood and her might for the principles that gave her birth and happiness and the peace which she has treasured. God helping her, she can do no other.

Ib.

---

[1] Eleven Senators had conducted a filibuster against a bill authorizing the arming of American merchant vessels.

[2] See James Harvey Robinson, p. 866b.

1. Open covenants of peace, openly arrived at.

2. Absolute freedom of navigation upon the seas.

5. A free, open-minded, and absolutely impartial adjustment of all colonial claims.

Address to Congress (The Fourteen Points) [1] [January 8, 1918]

14. A general association of nations must be formed . . . for the purpose of affording mutual guarantees of political independence and territorial integrity to great and small states alike. *Ib.*

Sometimes people call me an idealist. Well, that is the way I know I am an American. America is the only idealistic nation in the world.

Address at Sioux Falls [September 8, 1919]

The highest and best form of efficiency is the spontaneous cooperation of a free people.

From BERNARD BARUCH, *American Industry at War: A Report of the War Industries Board [March 1921]*

EDWARD FRANCIS ALBEE
1857–1930

Never give a sucker an even break.[2]
Remark

ALICE BROWN
1857–1948

Praise not the critic, lest he think
You crave the shelter of his ink;
But pray his halo, when he dies,
May tip the steelyards of the skies.
The Critic

---

[1] See Clemenceau, p. 786a.

[2] Often attributed to W. C. Fields.

JOSEPH CONRAD
1857–1924

A work that aspires, however humbly, to the condition of art should carry its justification in every line.

The Nigger of the Narcissus
[1898], preface

But the artist appeals to that part of our being which is not dependent on wisdom; to that in us which is a gift and not an acquisition — and, therefore, more permanently enduring. He speaks to our capacity for delight and wonder, to the sense of mystery surrounding our lives: to our sense of pity, and beauty, and pain. *Ib.*

The ship, a fragment detached from the earth, went on lonely and swift like a small planet. *Ib. ch. 2*

Goodbye, brothers! You were a good crowd. As good a crowd as ever fisted with wild cries the beating canvas of a heavy foresail; or tossing aloft, invisible in the night, gave back yell for yell to a westerly gale. *Ib. 5*

I am a great foe of favoritism in public life, in private life, and even in the delicate relationship of an author to his works.

Lord Jim [1900], author's note

There is a weird power in a spoken word. . . . And a word carries far — very far — deals destruction through time as the bullets go flying through space. *Ib. ch. 15*

That faculty of beholding at a hint the face of his desire and the shape of his dream, without which the earth would know no lover and no adventurer. *Ib. 16*

You shall judge of a man by his foes as well as by his friends.[1] *Ib. 34*

Vanity plays lurid tricks with our memory. *Ib. 41*

Only a moment; a moment of strength, of romance, of glamour — of

[1] See Wilde, p. 839a.

youth! . . . A flick of sunshine upon a strange shore, the time to remember; the time for a sigh, and — goodbye! — Night — Goodbye . . . !

Youth [1902]

She strode like a grenadier, was strong and upright like an obelisk, had a beautiful face, a candid brow, pure eyes, and not a thought of her own in her head.

Tales of Unrest [1902]. The Return

Running all over the sea trying to get behind the weather.

Typhoon [1902], ch. 2

The sea never changes and its works, for all the talk of men, are wrapped in mystery. *Ib.*

We live, as we dream — alone.
Heart of Darkness [1902],[1] I

I don't like work — no man does — but I like what is in work — the chance to find yourself. Your own reality — for yourself, not for others — what no other man can ever know. *Ib.*

The mind of man is capable of anything — because everything is in it, all the past as well as all the future. *Ib. II*

No fear can stand up to hunger, no patience can wear it out, disgust simply does not exist where hunger is; and as to superstition, beliefs, and what you may call principles, they are less than chaff in a breeze.[2] *Ib.*

[1] "Heart of Darkness" is experience . . . but it is experience pushed a little (and only very little) beyond the actual facts of the case for the perfectly legitimate, I believe, purpose of bringing it home to the minds and bosoms of the readers. . . . That somber theme had to be given a sinister resonance, a tonality of its own, a continued vibration that, I hoped, would hang in the air and dwell on the ear after the last note had been struck. — CONRAD, *Youth: A Narrative, and Two Other Stories, author's preface*
[2] See G. B. Shaw, p. 837a.

Exterminate all the brutes! [1]
> *Heart of Darkness II*

The horror! The horror! *Ib.*

Mistah Kurtz — he dead.[2] *Ib.*

The air of the New World seems favorable to the art of declamation.
> *Nostromo* [1904], *ch. 6*

Efficiency of a practically flawless kind may be reached naturally in the struggle for bread. But there is something beyond — a higher point, a subtle and unmistakable touch of love and pride beyond mere skill; almost an inspiration which gives to all work that finish which is almost art — which *is* art.
> *The Mirror of the Sea* [1906].
> *The Fine Art*

A man's real life is that accorded to him in the thoughts of other men by reason of respect or natural love.
> *Under Western Eyes* [1911], *pt. I*

Let a fool be made serviceable according to his folly. *Ib. 3*

The belief in a supernatural source of evil is not necessary; men alone are quite capable of every wickedness.
> *Ib. II, 4*

All ambitions are lawful except those which climb upward on the miseries or credulities of mankind.
> *A Personal Record* [1912],
> *preface*

Only in men's imagination does every truth find an effective and undeniable existence. Imagination, not invention, is the supreme master of art as of life. *Ib. ch. 1*

---

[1] For two hundred years, the Judges of England sat on the Bench, condemning to the penalty of death every man, woman, and child who stole property to the value of five shillings; and, during all that time, not one Judge ever remonstrated against the law. We English are a nation of brutes, and ought to be exterminated to the last man. — JOHN BRIGHT [1888]; quoted by Henry Adams, *The Education of Henry Adams* [1907], *ch. 12*

[2] Used by T. S. Eliot as an epigraph for *The Hollow Men* [1925]

In plucking the fruit of memory one runs the risk of spoiling its bloom.
> *The Arrow of Gold* [1919],
> *author's note*

Historian of fine consciences.
> *Notes on Life and Letters* [1921]. *Henry James, An Appreciation*

ÉMILE COUÉ
1857–1926

Every day, in every way, I'm getting better and better.
> *Formula of his faith cures*

CLARENCE SEWARD DARROW
1857–1938

I do not consider it an insult, but rather a compliment to be called an agnostic. I do not pretend to know where many ignorant men are sure — that is all that agnosticism means.
> *Scopes trial, Dayton, Tennessee*
> [*July 13, 1925*]

I don't believe in God because I don't believe in Mother Goose.
> *Speech, Toronto* [1930]

There is no such thing as justice — in or out of court.
> *Interview, Chicago* [*April 1936*]

JOHN DAVIDSON
1857–1909

My feet are heavy now but on I go,
My head erect beneath the tragic years.
> *I Felt the World A-Spinning*

In anguish we uplift
A new unhallowed song:
The race is to the swift;
The battle to the strong.[1]
> *War Song, st. 1*

---

[1] See *Ecclesiastes 9:11*, p. 28b, and Van Dyke, p. 827b.

And blood in torrents pour
In vain — always in vain,
For war breeds war again.
War Song, st. 7

BENJAMIN FRANKLIN KING, JR.
1857–1894

Nothing to do but work,
Nothing to eat but food,
Nothing to wear but clothes
To keep one from going nude.
The Pessimist, st. 1

Nowhere to go but out,
Nowhere to come but back.
Ib. st. 4

KARL PEARSON
1857–1936

Modern science, as training the mind
to an exact and impartial analysis of
facts, is an education specially fitted to
promote sound citizenship.
The Grammar of Science [1892]

EDGAR SMITH
1857–1938

You may tempt the upper classes
With your villainous demitasses,
But Heaven will protect the working
girl.
*Heaven Will Protect the
Working Girl* [1]

FRANK LEBBY STANTON
1857–1927

Jest a-wearyin' fer you —
All the time a-feelin' blue;
Wishin' fer you — wonderin' when
You'll be comin' home again.
Wearyin' for You, st. 1

Sweetes' li'l' feller —
  Everybody knows;

[1] Sung by Marie Dressler [1873–1934] in *Til-
lie's Nightmare.*

Dunno what ter call 'im,
  But he's mighty lak' a rose!
Mighty Lak' a Rose, st. 1

THORSTEIN VEBLEN
1857–1929

Conspicuous consumption of valuable goods is a means of reputability to
the gentleman of leisure.
The Theory of the Leisure Class
[1899], *ch. 4*

With the exception of the instinct of
self-preservation, the propensity for
emulation is probably the strongest and
most alert and persistent of the economic motives proper.   *Ib. 5*

The requirement of conspicuous
wastefulness is not commonly present,
consciously, in our canons of taste, but
it is none the less present as a constrain-
ing norm selectively shaping and sus-
taining our sense of what is beautiful,
and guiding our discrimination with
respect to what may legitimately be
approved as beautiful and what may
not.   *Ib. 6*

Priestly vestments show, in accentu-
ated form, all the features that have
been shown to be evidence of a servile
status and a vicarious life.   *Ib. 7*

The dog . . . commends himself to
our favor by affording play to our propensity for mastery, and as he is also an
item of expense, and commonly serves
no industrial purpose, he holds a well-
assured place in men's regard as a thing
of good repute.   *Ib.*

The adoption of the cap and gown
is one of the striking atavistic features
of modern college life.   *Ib. 14*

The classics have scarcely lost in absolute value as a voucher of scholastic
respectability, since for this purpose it
is only necessary that the scholar should
be able to put in evidence some learning which is conventionally recognized
as evidence of wasted time.   *Ib.*

OWEN HALL
[JAMES DAVIS]
d. 1907

O tell me, pretty maiden, are there
any more at home like you?
> *Floradora* [1900], *act II*

JOHN BURNS
1858–1943

The St. Lawrence is water, and the
Mississippi is muddy water; but that,
sir, is liquid history.
> *Said on the terrace of the House
> of Commons, to transatlantic
> visitors who belittled the size of
> the Thames*

SAM WALTER FOSS
1858–1911

And men two centuries and a half
Trod in the footsteps of that calf.
> *The Calf-Path,*[1] *st. 6*

A rodless Walton of the brooks,
A bloodless sportsman, I.[2]
> *The Bloodless Sportsman*

The woods are made for the hunters of
dreams,
The brooks for the fishers of song;
To the hunters who hunt for the gun-
less game
The streams and the woods belong.
> *Ib.*

Let me live in my house by the side of
the road
Where the race of men go by;
They are good, they are bad, they are
weak, they are strong,
Wise, foolish — so am I.
Then why should I sit in the scorner's
seat,
Or hurl the cynic's ban?
Let me live in my house by the side of
the road
And be a friend of man.
> *The House by the Side of the
> Road,*[3] *st. 5*

[1] The reference is to the streets of Boston.
[2] See Emerson, p. 603a.
[3] He held his seat; a friend to human race.
Fast by the road, his ever-open door

REMY DE GOURMONT
1858–1915

Aesthetic emotion puts man in a
state favorable to the reception of erotic
emotion. Art is the accomplice of love.
Take love away and there is no longer
art.
> *Décadence* [1]

It is because peoples do not know
each other that they hate each other so
little.
> *Ib.*

There are too few obscure writers in
French. We accustom ourselves like
cowards to love only writing that is easy
and that will soon be elementary.
> *Ib.*

Man is a successful animal, that's
all.
> *Promenades Philosophiques*

JOHN TROTWOOD
MOORE
1858–1929

Only the gamefish swims upstream.[2]
> *The Unafraid*

ADOLPH S. OCHS
1858–1935

All the news that's fit to print.
> *Motto of the New York Times* [3]

MAX PLANCK
1858–1947

We have no right to assume that any
physical laws exist, or if they have ex-

Obliged the wealthy, and relieved the poor.
> POPE, translation of HOMER's *Iliad,*
> *bk. VI, l. 18*

[1] Translated by W. A. BRADLEY.
[2] Quoted by GRANTLAND RICE [1880–1954] in
The Ballade of the Gamefish and *Expanding the
Theme.*
> Only the gamefish swims upstream,
> But the sensible fish swims down.
> OGDEN NASH [b. 1902], *When You Say
> That, Smile*

[3] When Adolph Ochs bought the *New York
Times* in 1896 he adopted this motto, which has
been printed in every issue since.
It is hard to think of any group of seven words
that have aroused more newspaper controversy.
— GERALD W. JOHNSON, *An Honorable Titan*
[1946]

isted up to now, that they will continue to exist in a similar manner in the future.

The Universe in the Light of Modern Physics [1931]

Anybody who has been seriously engaged in scientific work of any kind realizes that over the entrance to the gates of the temple of science are written the words: *Ye must have faith.* It is a quality which the scientist cannot dispense with.

Where Is Science Going? [1932]

An important scientific innovation rarely makes its way by gradually winning over and converting its opponents: it rarely happens that Saul becomes Paul. What does happen is that its opponents gradually die out and that the growing generation is familiarized with the idea from the beginning.

The Philosophy of Physics [1936]

THEODORE ROOSEVELT
1858–1919

I wish to preach, not the doctrine of ignoble ease,[1] but the doctrine of the strenuous life.

Speech before the Hamilton Club, Chicago [*April 10, 1899*]

Far better it is to dare mighty things, to win glorious triumphs, even though checkered by failure, than to take rank with those poor spirits who neither enjoy much nor suffer much, because they live in the gray twilight that knows not victory nor defeat. *Ib.*

We must remember not to judge any public servant by any one act, and especially should we beware of attacking the men who are merely the occasions and not the causes of disaster. *Ib.*

[1] Me . . . dulcis alebat
Parthenope, studiis florentem ignobilis otii.
[Sweet Parthenope nourished me, flourishing in studies of ignoble ease.]
VIRGIL [70–19 B.C.]. *Georgics, bk. IV, l. 563*
Parthenope: ancient name of Naples.

Death is always and under all circumstances a tragedy, for if it is not, then it means that life itself has become one.

Letter to Cecil Spring-Rice [*March 12, 1900*]

I am as strong as a bull moose and you can use me to the limit.

Letter to Mark Hanna [*June 27, 1900*]

No man is justified in doing evil on the ground of expediency.

The Strenuous Life [1900]

If we seek merely swollen, slothful ease and ignoble peace, if we shrink from the hard contests where men must win at the hazard of their lives and at the risk of all they hold dear, then bolder and stronger peoples will pass us by, and will win for themselves the domination of the world. *Ib.*

There is a homely adage which runs, "Speak softly and carry a big stick; you will go far." If the American nation will speak softly and yet build and keep at a pitch of the highest training a thoroughly efficient navy, the Monroe Doctrine will go far.

Speech at Minnesota State Fair [*September 2, 1901*]

The first requisite of a good citizen in this Republic of ours is that he shall be able and willing to pull his weight.

Speech, New York [*November 11, 1902*]

A man who is good enough to shed his blood for his country is good enough to be given a square deal afterwards. More than that no man is entitled to, and less than that no man shall have.

Speech at Springfield, Illinois [*July 4, 1903*]

No man is above the law and no man is below it; nor do we ask any man's permission when we require him to obey it. Obedience to the law is demanded as a right; not asked as a favor.

Third Annual Message [December 7, 1903]

In the Western Hemisphere the adherence of the United States to the Monroe Doctrine may force the United States, however reluctantly, in flagrant cases of such wrongdoing or impotence, to the exercise of an international police power.

Annual Message to Congress: Corollary to the Monroe Doctrine [December 6, 1904]

Men with the muckrake are often indispensable to the well-being of society, but only if they know when to stop raking the muck.[1]

Address, laying of the cornerstone, House Office Building, Washington [April 14, 1906]

Malefactors of great wealth.

Speech at Provincetown, Massachusetts [August 20, 1907]

Nature-faker.

Everybody's Magazine [September 1907]

To waste, to destroy, our natural resources, to skin and exhaust the land instead of using it so as to increase its usefulness, will result in undermining in the days of our children the very prosperity which we ought by right to hand down to them amplified and developed.

Message to Congress [December 3, 1907]

The object of government is the welfare of the people. The material progress and prosperity of a nation are desirable chiefly so far as they lead to the moral and material welfare of all good citizens.

The New Nationalism [1910]

Every man holds his property subject to the general right of the community

[1] See John Bunyan, p. 366a.

to regulate its use to whatever degree the public welfare may require it.

Speech, Osawatomie [August 31, 1910]

The lunatic fringe in all reform movements. *Autobiography [1913]*

We demand that big business give the people a square deal; in return we must insist that when anyone engaged in big business honestly endeavors to do right he shall himself be given a square deal. *Ib.*

We stand equally against government by a plutocracy and government by a mob. There is something to be said for government by a great aristocracy which has furnished leaders to the nation in peace and war for generations; even a democrat like myself must admit this. But there is absolutely nothing to be said for government by a plutocracy, for government by men very powerful in certain lines and gifted with "the money touch," but with ideals which in their essence are merely those of so many glorified pawnbrokers.

Letter to Sir Edward Grey [November 15, 1913]

There is no room in this country for hyphenated Americanism. . . . The one absolutely certain way of bringing this nation to ruin, of preventing all possibility of its continuing to be a nation at all, would be to permit it to become a tangle of squabbling nationalities.

Speech before the Knights of Columbus, New York [October 12, 1915]

Put out the light.

Last words [January 6, 1919]

LANGDON SMITH
1858–1908

When you were a tadpole and I was a fish,
In the Paleozoic time.

Evolution [1895], st. 1

SIR WILLIAM WATSON
1858–1935

April, April,
Laugh thy girlish laughter;
Then, the moment after,
Weep thy girlish tears.   *Song*

To dress, to call, to dine, to break
  No canon of the social code,
The little laws that lackeys make,
  The futile decalogue of Mode —
How many a soul for these things lives,
  With pious passion, grave intent!
While Nature careless-handed gives
  The things that are more excellent.
     *The Things That Are More
     Excellent, st. 6*

The sense of greatness keeps a nation
  great.   *Our Eastern Treasure*

KATHARINE LEE BATES
1859–1929

O beautiful for spacious skies,
  For amber waves of grain,
For purple mountain majesties
  Above the fruited plain!
America! America!
  God shed his grace on thee
And crown thy good with brotherhood
  From sea to shining sea!
     America the Beautiful [1893],
     st. 1

O beautiful for patriot dream
  That sees beyond the years
Thine alabaster cities gleam
  Undimmed by human tears!
     Ib. st. 4

HENRI BERGSON
1859–1941

We are free when our actions emanate from our total personality, when they express it, when they resemble it in the indefinable way a work of art sometimes does the artist.
     *Essai sur les Données Immédiates
     de la Conscience* [1889]

The present contains nothing more than the past, and what is found in the effect was already in the cause.
     L'Evolution Créatrice [1907] [1]

Intelligence . . . is the faculty of making artificial objects, especially tools to make tools.   *Ib.*

L'élan vital [the vital spirit].   *Ib.*

HAROLD EDWIN BOULTON
1859–1935

Speed, bonnie boat, like a bird on the
  wing;
Onward, the sailors cry:
Carry the lad that's born to be king
Over the sea to Skye.
     Skye Boat Song, st. 1

SIR ARTHUR CONAN DOYLE
1859–1930

London, that great cesspool into which all the loungers of the Empire are irresistibly drained.
     A Study in Scarlet [1887]

When you have eliminated the impossible, whatever remains, *however improbable*, must be the truth.
     The Sign of Four [1890], *ch. 6*

The Baker Street irregulars.   *Ib.*

It is my belief, Watson, founded upon my experience, that the lowest and vilest alleys of London do not present a more dreadful record of sin than does the smiling and beautiful countryside.
     *The Adventures of Sherlock
     Holmes* [1891]. *Copper
     Beeches*

To Sherlock Holmes she is always *the woman.*   *Ib. A Scandal in Bohemia*

[1] O my Bergson, you are a magician, and your book is a marvel, a real wonder in the history of philosophy. . . . In finishing it I found . . . such a flavor of persistent *euphony,* as of a rich river that never foamed or ran thin, but steadily and firmly proceeded with its banks full to the brim. — WILLIAM JAMES, *The Letters of William James, vol. II, p. 290 [1907]*

". . . the curious incident of the dog in the nighttime."

"The dog did nothing in the nighttime."

"That was the curious incident," remarked Sherlock Holmes.
    *The Memoirs of Sherlock
    Holmes* [1894]. *Silver Blaze*

You know my methods, Watson.
    Ib. The Crooked Man

"Excellent!" I [Watson] cried. "Elementary," said he [Holmes].
    Ib.

They were the footprints of a gigantic hound!
    The Hound of the Baskervilles
    [1902], *ch. 2*

Come, Watson, come! The game is afoot.[1]
    The Return of Sherlock Holmes
    [1904]. *The Adventure of the
    Abbey Grange*

The fair sex is your department.
    Ib. The Second Stain

It is a great thing to start life with a small number of really good books which are your very own.
    Through the Magic Door [1908]

Mediocrity knows nothing higher than itself, but talent instantly recognizes genius.
    The Valley of Fear [1914]

The bow was made in England:
Of true wood, of yew wood,
The wood of English bows.
    The Song of the Bow, st. 1

HAVELOCK ELLIS
1859–1939

To be a leader of men one must turn one's back on men.
    Introduction to HUYSMANS,
    Against the Grain

The text of the Bible is but a feeble symbol of the Revelation held in the text of Men and Women.
    Impressions and Comments

[1] See Shakespeare, *Henry V, III, i, 32,* p. 244a.

God is an Unutterable Sigh in the Human Heart, said the old German mystic.[1] And therefore said the last word.   *Impressions and Comments*

Without an element of the obscene there can be no true and deep aesthetic or moral conception of life. . . . It is only the great men who are truly obscene. If they had not dared to be obscene they could never have dared to be great.   *Ib.*

The omnipresent process of sex, as it is woven into the whole texture of our man's or woman's body, is the pattern of all the process of our life.
    The New Spirit

Every artist writes his own autobiography.   *Ib.*

If men and women are to understand each other, to enter into each other's nature with mutual sympathy, and to become capable of genuine comradeship, the foundation must be laid in youth.
    The Task of Social Hygiene, ch. 1

There are few among us who have not suffered from too early familiarity with the Bible and the conceptions of religion.   *Ib. 7*

There has never been any country at every moment so virtuous and so wise that it has not sometimes needed to be saved from itself.   *Ib. 10*

The family only represents one aspect, however important an aspect, of a human being's functions and activities. . . . A life is beautiful and ideal, or the reverse, only when we have taken into our consideration the social as well as the family relationship.
    *Little Essays of Love and
    Virtue* [1922], *ch. 1*

One can know nothing of giving aught that is worthy to give unless one also knows how to take.   *Ib.*

[1] God is an unutterable sigh, planted in the depths of the soul. — JEAN PAUL RICHTER [1763–1825]

The byproduct is sometimes more valuable than the product.
Little Essays of Love and Virtue, ch. 3

All civilization has from time to time become a thin crust over a volcano of revolution.   *Ib. 7*

The greatest task before civilization at present is to make machines what they ought to be, the slaves, instead of the masters of men.[1]   *Ib.*

The art of dancing stands at the source of all the arts that express themselves first in the human person. The art of building, or architecture, is the beginning of all the arts that lie outside the person; and in the end they unite.
The Dance of Life [1923], *ch. 2*

Dancing is the loftiest, the most moving, the most beautiful of the arts, because it is no mere translation or abstraction from life; it is life itself.
Ib.

The place where optimism most flourishes is the lunatic asylum.
Ib. 3

Thinking in its lower grades is comparable to paper money, and in its higher forms it is a kind of poetry.
Ib.

In philosophy, it is not the attainment of the goal that matters, it is the things that are met with by the way.
Ib.

The mathematician has reached the highest rung on the ladder of human thought.   *Ib.*

A man must not swallow more beliefs than he can digest.   *Ib. 5*

The Promised Land always lies on the other side of a wilderness.   *Ib.*

What we call "morals" is simply blind obedience to words of command.
Ib. 6

The sun and the moon and the stars would have disappeared long ago . . .

[1] See Oscar Wilde, p. 840b.

had they happened to be within the reach of predatory human hands.
The Dance of Life, ch. 7

Had there been a lunatic asylum in the suburbs of Jerusalem, Jesus Christ would infallibly have been shut up in it at the outset of his public career. That interview with Satan on a pinnacle of the Temple would alone have damned him, and everything that happened after could but have confirmed the diagnosis.
Impressions and Comments, series 3

H. W. FOWLER
1859–1933
AND
F. G. FOWLER
1871–1918

Prefer geniality to grammar.
The King's English [1906], *ch. 2*

HACKNEYED PHRASES. . . . The purpose with which these phrases are introduced is for the most part that of giving a fillip to a passage that might be humdrum without them . . . but their true use when they come into the writer's mind is as danger signals; he should take warning that when they suggest themselves it is because what he is writing is bad stuff, or it would not need such help; let him see to the substance of his cake instead of decorating with sugarplums.
A Dictionary of Modern English Usage[1] [1926]

QUOTATION. . . . A writer expresses himself in words that have been used before because they give his meaning better than he can give it himself, or because they are beautiful or witty, or because he expects them to touch a chord of association in his reader, or because he wishes to show that he is learned and well read. Quotations due to the last motive are invariably ill-advised; the discerning reader detects it and is contemptuous; the undiscern-

[1] Written by H. W. Fowler.

ing is perhaps impressed, but even then is at the same time repelled, pretentious quotations being the surest road to tedium.

A *Dictionary of Modern English Usage*

KENNETH GRAHAME
1859–1932

As a rule, indeed, grown-up people are fairly correct on matters of fact; it is in the higher gift of imagination that they are so sadly to seek.

The Golden Age [1895]. *The Finding of the Princess*

Monkeys, who very sensibly refrain from speech, lest they should be set to earn their livings. *Ib. "Lusisti Satis"*

There is nothing — absolutely nothing — half so much worth doing as simply messing about in boats . . . or with boats. . . . In or out of 'em, it doesn't matter.

The Wind in the Willows [1908], *ch. 1*

"Glorious, stirring sight!" murmured Toad . . . "The poetry of motion! The *real* way to travel! The *only* way to travel! Here today — in next week tomorrow! Villages skipped, towns and cities jumped — always somebody else's horizons! O bliss! O poop-poop! O my! O my!" *Ib. 2*

ALFRED EDWARD HOUSMAN [1]
1859–1936

From Clee to heaven the beacon burns,
The shires have seen it plain.
    A Shropshire Lad [1896] *1, st. 1*

Oh, God will save her, fear you not:
  Be you the men you've been,
Get you the sons your fathers got,
  And God will save the Queen.
    Ib. st. 8

[1] I am not a pessimist but a pejorist (as George Eliot said she was not an optimist but a meliorist); and that philosophy is founded on my observation of the world, not on anything so trivial and irrelevant as personal history. — *Autobiographical note written for a French translation of his poems*

Loveliest of trees, the cherry now
Is hung with bloom along the bough.
    A Shropshire Lad 2, st. 1

Now, of my threescore years and ten,
Twenty will not come again,
And take from seventy springs a score,
It only leaves me fifty more.

And since to look at things in bloom
Fifty springs are little room,
About the woodlands I will go
To see the cherry hung with snow.
    Ib. st. 2, 3

Clay lies still, but blood's a rover;
  Breath's a ware that will not keep.
Up, lad: when the journey's over
  There'll be time enough to sleep.
    Ib. 4 (Reveille)

Lovers lying two and two
Ask not whom they sleep beside,
And the bridegroom all night through
Never turns him to the bride. *Ib. 12*

When I was one-and-twenty
  I heard a wise man say,
"Give crowns and pounds and guineas
  But not your heart away;
Give pearls away and rubies
  But keep your fancy free."
But I was one-and-twenty,
  No use to talk to me.

When I was one-and-twenty
  I heard him say again,
"The heart out of the bosom
  Was never given in vain;
'Tis paid with sighs aplenty
  And sold for endless rue."
And I am two-and-twenty,
  And Oh, 'tis true, 'tis true. *Ib. 13*

His folly has not fellow
  Beneath the blue of day
That gives to man or woman
  His heart and soul away. *Ib. 14*

Oh, when I was in love with you,
  Then I was clean and brave,
And miles around the wonder grew
  How well I did behave.

And now the fancy passes by,
  And nothing will remain,

And miles around they'll say that I
  Am quite myself again.
              A Shropshire Lad 18

And silence sounds no worse than
    cheers
After earth has stopped the ears.
        Ib. 19 (*To an Athlete Dying
              Young*), st. 4

The bells they sound on Bredon,
  And still the steeples hum.
"Come all to church, good people" —
Oh, noisy bells, be dumb;
I hear you, I will come.
                Ib. 21, *st.* 7

The lads that will die in their glory and
    never be old.   *Ib.* 23, *st.* 4

The goal stands up, the keeper
  Stands up to keep the goal.
                Ib. 27, *st.* 4

And fire and ice within me fight
Beneath the suffocating night.[1]
                Ib. 30, *st.* 4

There, like the wind through woods in
    riot,
Through him the gale of life blew high;
The tree of man was never quiet:
Then 'twas the Roman, now 'tis I.
                Ib. 31, *st.* 4

Oh tarnish late on Wenlock Edge,
Gold that I never see.
                Ib. 39, *st.* 3

Into my heart an air that kills
  From yon far country blows:
What are those blue remembered hills,
  What spires, what farms are those?

That is the land of lost content,
  I see it shining plain,
The happy highways where I went
  And cannot come again.   *Ib.* 40

Earth and high heaven are fixed of old
    and founded strong.
                Ib. 48, *st.* 1

Far in a western brookland
  That bred me long ago

[1] See Dante, p. 159b, and Frost, p. 927a.

The poplars stand and tremble
  By pools I used to know.
              A Shropshire Lad 52, *st.* 1

There, by the starlit fences,
  The wanderer halts and hears
My soul that lingers sighing
  About the glimmering weirs.
                Ib. st. 4

With rue my heart is laden
  For golden friends I had,
For many a rose-lipped maiden
  And many a lightfoot lad.
                Ib. 54, *st.* 1

By brooks too broad for leaping
The lightfoot boys are laid.   *Ib. st.* 2

Now hollow fires burn out to black,
  And lights are guttering low:
Square your shoulders, lift your pack,
  And leave your friends and go.

Oh never fear, man, nought's to dread,
  Look not left nor right:
In all the endless road you tread
  There's nothing but the night.
                Ib. 60

Oh many a peer of England brews
Livelier liquor than the Muse,
And malt does more than Milton can
To justify God's ways to man.[1]
Ale, man, ale's the stuff to drink
For fellows whom it hurts to think.
                Ib. 62

Mithridates, he died old.[2]   *Ib.*

Pass me the can, lad; there's an end of
    May.   *Last Poems* 9, *st.* 1

The troubles of our proud and angry
    dust
Are from eternity, and shall not fail.
Bear them we can, and if we can we
    must.
Shoulder the sky, my lad, and drink
    your ale.   *Ib. st.* 7

[1] See Milton, p. 341b.
[2] Housman's passage is based on the belief of
the ancients that Mithridates the Great [c. 135–
63 B.C.] had so saturated his body with poisons
that none could injure him. When captured by
the Romans he tried in vain to poison himself,
then ordered a Gallic mercenary to kill him.

But men at whiles are sober
  And think by fits and starts.
And if they think, they fasten
  Their hands upon their hearts.
        Last Poems 10, *st.* 2

The laws of God, the laws of man,
He may keep that will and can;
Not I: let God and man decree
  Laws for themselves and not for me.
        Ib. 12

And how am I to face the odds
Of man's bedevilment and God's?
I, a stranger and afraid
In a world I never made.   *Ib.*

He stood, and heard the steeple
Sprinkle the quarters on the morning
  town.
One, two, three, four, to marketplace
  and people
It tossed them down.

Strapped, noosed, nighing his hour,
He stood and counted them and cursed
  his luck;
And then the clock collected in the
  tower
Its strength, and struck.
        Ib. 15 (*Eight O'Clock*)

Happy bridegroom, Hesper brings
All desired and timely things.
All whom morning sends to roam,
Hesper loves to lead them home.
Home return who him behold,
Child to mother, sheep to fold,
Bird to nest from wandering wide: [1]
Happy bridegroom, seek your bride.
        Ib. 24 (*Epithalamium*), *st.* 3

These, in the day when heaven was fall-
  ing,
The hour when earth's foundations
  fled,
Followed their mercenary calling
And took their wages and are dead.
        Ib. 37 (*Epitaph on an Army of
        Mercenaries*),[2] *st.* 1

---

[1] See Sappho, p. 69b; and Meleager, p. 110a.
[2] The British regulars who made the retreat
from Mons, beginning August 24, 1914.

What God abandoned, these defended.
        Last Poems 37, *st.* 2

Tell me not here, it needs not saying,
  What tune the enchantress plays
In aftermaths of soft September
  Or under blanching mays,
For she and I were long acquainted
  And I knew all her ways.
        Ib. 40, *st.* 1

They say my verse is sad: no wonder;
  Its narrow measure spans
Tears of eternity, and sorrow,
  Not mine, but man's.
        More Poems [1936], *foreword*

I to my perils
  Of cheat and charmer
  Came clad in armor
By stars benign.
Hope lies to mortals
  And most believe her,
  But man's deceiver
Was never mine.   *Ib.* 6, *st.* 1

The rainy Pleiads wester,
  Orion plunges prone,
And midnight strikes and hastens,
  And I lie down alone.[1]
        Ib. 11, *st.* 1

My kind and foolish comrade
That breathes all night for me.
        Ib. 13, *st.* 3

Life, to be sure, is nothing much to
  lose,
But young men think it is, and we were
  young.   *Ib.* 36

We now to peace and darkness
  And earth and thee restore
Thy creature that thou madest
  And wilt cast forth no more.
        Ib. 47 (*For My Funeral*), *st.* 3

Good night; ensured release,
Imperishable peace,
  Have these for yours.[2]

---

[1] See Sappho, p. 69b.
[2] These three lines are on the tablet over Housman's grave in the parish church at Ludlow,
Shropshire.

While sky and sea and land
And earth's foundations stand
    And heaven endures.
        More Poems 48 (Alta Quies),
            st. 1

Oh they're taking him to prison for the
    color of his hair.
        Additional Poems [1937], *18, st. 1*

Good literature continually read for
pleasure must, let us hope, do some
good to the reader: must quicken his
perception though dull, and sharpen his
discrimination though blunt, and mellow the rawness of his personal opinions.
        The Name and Nature of Poetry [1]

Experience has taught me, when I
am shaving of a morning, to keep
watch over my thoughts, because, if a
line of poetry strays into my memory,
my skin bristles so that the razor ceases
to act. . . . The seat of this sensation
is the pit of the stomach.   *Ib.*

JEROME KLAPKA JEROME
1859–1927

Let your boat of life be light, packed
with only what you need — a homely
home and simple pleasures, one or two
friends, worth the name, someone to
love and someone to love you,[2] a cat, a
dog, and a pipe or two, enough to eat
and enough to wear, and a little more
than enough to drink; for thirst is a
dangerous thing.
        Three Men in a Boat [1889],
            ch. 3

It is impossible to enjoy idling thoroughly unless one has plenty of work to
do.
        Idle Thoughts of an Idle Fellow
        [1889]. *On Being Idle*

[1] The Leslie Stephen Lecture, Cambridge University [May 9, 1933].
[2] Find someone to love . . . and, oh, someone
to love you. — SACHA GUITRY, *Deburau* [1918]

Love is like the measles; we all have
to go through it.
        *Idle Thoughts of an Idle Fel-
            low. On Being in Love*

"Nothing, so it seems to me," said
the stranger, "is more beautiful than
the love that has weathered the storms
of life. . . . The love of the young for
the young, that is the beginning of life.
But the love of the old for the old,
that is the beginning of — of things
longer."
        *The Passing of the Third Floor
            Back* [1908]

WILLIAM JAMES LAMPTON
1859–1917

Same old slippers,
    Same old rice,
Same old glimpse of
    Paradise.   *June Weddings, st. 10*

Where the corn is full of kernels
And the colonels full of corn.
            Kentucky

TSUBOUCHI SHOYO [1]
1859–1935

The writers of popular fiction seem
to have taken as their guiding principle
the dictum that the essence of the
novel lies in the expression of the approved moral sentiments. They accordingly erect a framework of morality into
which they attempt to force their
plots.
        The Essence of the Novel [1885]

The indiscriminate readers throughout the country also must shoulder
their share of the blame. It has long
been the custom in Japan to consider
the novel as an instrument of education . . . In actual practice, however,
only stories of bloodthirsty cruelty or
else of pornography are welcomed.
            Ib.

[1] From *Modern Japanese Literature,* edited by
Donald Keene [1960].

CHARLES E. STANTON[1]
1859–1933

Lafayette, we are here.[2]
> *Address at the Tomb of Lafayette, Picpus Cemetery, Paris [July 4, 1917]*

JAMES KENNETH STEPHEN[3]
1859–1892

When the Rudyards cease from Kipling
And the Haggards ride no more.
> *Lapsus Calami. To R. K.*

Of sentences that stir my bile,
  Of phrases I detest,
There's one beyond all others vile:
  "He did it for the best."
> *Ib. The Malefactor's Plea, st. 1*

FRANCIS THOMPSON
1859–1907

The fairest things have fleetest end,
  Their scent survives their close:
But the rose's scent is bitterness
  To him that loved the rose.
> *Daisy [1893], st. 10*

She went her unremembering way,
  She went and left in me
The pang of all the partings gone,
  And partings yet to be.
> *Ib. st. 12*

Nothing begins, and nothing ends,
  That is not paid with moan;

---

[1] Chief disbursing officer of the American Expeditionary Forces in France [1917], deputed by General Pershing to speak on behalf of the A.E.F. on this occasion. He used the phrase again on July 14.

[2] The remark has also been attributed to General Pershing, who in *My Experiences in the World War* [1931] says he cannot remember having said "anything so splendid." However Naboth Hedin, one of the uniformed American correspondents present upon the July 4, 1917, occasion, states that he heard Pershing pronounce the phrase three weeks earlier, on June 14, his second day in Paris:
"Pershing stepped up to it [Lafayette's grave] and saluted in his best manner and then said in a loud voice, 'Lafayette, we are here.' I was about twenty feet away" [*letter from Naboth Hedrin to Samuel Eliot Morison, June 21, 1954*].

[3] See Wordsworth, note 1, p. 516a.

For we are born in other's pain,
  And perish in our own.
> *Daisy, st. 15*

Look for me in the nurseries of Heaven.[1]
> *To My Godchild*

The innocent moon, which nothing does but shine,
Moves all the laboring surges of the world.
> *Sister Songs, pt. II*

I fled Him, down the nights and down the days;
I fled Him, down the arches of the years;
I fled Him, down the labyrinthine ways
Of my own mind; and in the mist of tears
I hid from Him, and under running laughter.
> *The Hound of Heaven [1893], l. 1*

But with unhurrying chase,
And unperturbèd pace,
Deliberate speed, majestic instancy,
They beat — and a Voice beat
More instant than the Feet —
"All things betray thee, who betrayest Me."
> *Ib. l. 10*

Across the margent of the world I fled,
And troubled the gold gateways of the stars.
> *Ib. l. 25*

I said to dawn, Be sudden; to eve, Be soon.
> *Ib. l. 30*

My days have crackled and gone up in smoke.
> *Ib. l. 122*

All which I took from thee I did but take,
Not for thy harms,
But just that thou might'st seek it in My arms.
> *Ib. l. 171*

There is no expeditious road
To pack and label men for God,
And save them by the barrel load.
> *A Judgment in Heaven, epilogue*

Thou canst not stir a flower
Without troubling of a star.
> *The Mistress of Vision*

---

[1] This line is inscribed on Thompson's tombstone in Kensal Green.

O world invisible, we view thee,
O world intangible, we touch thee,
O world unknowable, we know thee.
> *The Kingdom of God ("In No
> Strange Land")* [1913], *st. 1*

The drift of pinions, would we
hearken,
Beats at our own clay-shuttered doors.
> *Ib. st. 3*

The angels keep their ancient places;
Turn but a stone, and start a wing!
'Tis ye, 'tis your estrangèd faces,
That miss the many-splendored thing.
> *Ib. st. 4*

Upon thy so sore loss
Shall shine the traffic of Jacob's ladder
Pitched betwixt Heaven and Charing
Cross. *Ib. st. 5*

Short arm needs man to reach to
Heaven
So ready is Heaven to stoop to him.
> *Grace of the Way, st. 6*

Know you what it is to be a child? It
is to be something very different from
the man of today. It is to have a spirit
yet streaming from the waters of baptism; it is to believe in love, to believe
in loveliness, to believe in belief; it is to
be so little that the elves can reach to
whisper in your ear; it is to turn pumpkins into coaches, and mice into horses,
lowness into loftiness, and nothing into
everything, for each child has its fairy
godmother in its soul.
> *Shelley. In The Dublin Review
> [July 1908]*

Few poets were so mated before, and
no poet was so mated afterwards, until
Browning stooped and picked up a fair-
coined soul that lay rusting in a pool of
tears. *Ib.*

SIDNEY WEBB
[LORD PASSFIELD]
1859–1947
AND
BEATRICE WEBB
1858–1943

The inevitability of gradualness.
> *Presidential address, British La-
> bour Party Congress* [1923]

JANE ADDAMS
1860–1935

Private beneficence is totally inadequate to deal with the vast numbers of
the city's disinherited.
> *Twenty Years at Hull House* [1910]

The common stock of intellectual enjoyment should not be difficult of access because of the economic position
of him who would approach it. *Ib.*

JAMES MATTHEW
BARRIE
1860–1937

The most gladsome thing in the
world is that few of us fall very low; the
saddest that, with such capabilities, we
seldom rise high.
> *The Little Minister* [1891], *ch. 3*

It's a weary warld, and nobody bides
in't. *Ib. 4*

You canna expect to be baith grand
and comfortable. *Ib. 10*

Let no one who loves be called altogether unhappy. Even love unreturned
has its rainbow. *Ib. 24*

Them that has china plates themsels
is the maist careful no to break the
china plates of others. *Ib. 26*

We never understand how little we
need in this world until we know the
loss of it.
> *Margaret Ogilvy* [1896], *ch. 8*

In dinner talk it is perhaps allowable
to fling on any fagot rather than let the
fire go out.
> *Tommy and Grizel* [1900], *ch. 3*

Shall we make a new rule of life from
tonight: always to try to be a little
kinder than is necessary?
> *The Little White Bird* [1902],
> *ch. 4*

His lordship may compel us to be
equal upstairs, but there will never be
equality in the servants' hall.
> *The Admirable Crichton
> [1903], act 1*

When the first baby laughed for the first time, the laugh broke into a thousand pieces and they all went skipping about, and that was the beginning of fairies.   *Peter Pan* [1904], *act I*

Every time a child says "I don't believe in fairies" there is a little fairy somewhere that falls down dead.   *Ib.*

Do you believe in fairies? . . . If you believe, clap your hands!   *Ib. IV*

It's a sort of bloom on a woman. If you have it [charm], you don't need to have anything else, and if you don't have it, it doesn't much matter what else you have. Some women, the few, have charm for all; and most have charm for one. But some have charm for none.[1]
What Every Woman Knows [1908], *act I*

The tragedy of a man who has found himself out.   *Ib. IV*

One's religion is whatever he is most interested in, and yours is Success.
The Twelve-Pound Look [1910]

JOHN COLLINS BOSSIDY
1860–1928

And this is good old Boston,
 The home of the bean and the cod,
Where the Lowells talk to the Cabots
And the Cabots talk only to God.[2]
*Toast, Holy Cross Alumni
Dinner* [1910]

[1] What is charm? It is what the violet has and the camellia has not. — MARION CRAWFORD [1854–1909], *Children of the King, ch. 5*
"Charm" — which means the power to effect work without employing brute force — is indispensable to women. Charm is a woman's strength just as strength is a man's charm. — HAVELOCK ELLIS [1859–1939], *The Task of Social Hygiene, ch. 3*
[2] Patterned on the toast given at the twenty-fifth anniversary dinner of the Harvard Class of 1880, by a Westerner.
 Here's to old Massachusetts,
  The home of the sacred cod,
 Where the Adamses vote for Douglas,
  And the Cabots walk with God.

WILLIAM JENNINGS BRYAN
1860–1925

The humblest citizen of all the land, when clad in the armor of a righteous cause, is stronger than all the hosts of Error.
Speech at the National Democratic Convention, Chicago [1896]

You shall not press down upon the brow of labor this crown of thorns. You shall not crucify mankind upon a cross of gold.[1]   *Ib.*

ANTON PAVLOVICH CHEKHOV
1860–1904

I feel more contented when I remember that I have two professions, and not one. Medicine is my lawful wife and literature my mistress. When I am bored with one I spend the night with the other. Though this is irregular, it is not monotonous, and besides neither really loses anything through my infidelity.
Letter to A. S. Suvorin [*August 29, 1888*]

We shall rest! We shall hear the angels, we shall see the whole sky all diamonds, we shall see how all earthly evil, all our sufferings are drowned in the mercy that will fill the whole world. And our life will grow peaceful, tender, sweet as a caress. I believe, I do believe.   *Uncle Vanya* [1897], *act IV*

To Moscow, to Moscow, to Moscow!
Three Sisters [1901], *act II*

All I wanted was to say honestly to people: "Have a look at yourselves and see how bad and dreary your lives are!"   *Letter to Alexander Tikhonov*

[1] I shall not help crucify mankind upon a cross of gold. I shall not aid in pressing down upon the bleeding brow of labor this crown of thorns. — WILLIAM JENNINGS BRYAN, *speech, House of Representatives* [*December 22, 1894*]

CHARLES TOWNSEND COPELAND
1860–1952

If I had not been there I should have been very much bored.[1]
> *Comment on a tea party. From* WALTER LIPPMANN, *William Bolitho: A Memoir*

HARRY MICAJAH DAUGHERTY
1860–1941

In a smoke-filled room in some hotel.[2]
> *Republican National Convention, Chicago [June 1920]*

HAMLIN GARLAND
1860–1940

A Son of the Middle Border
> *Title of autobiographical narrative [1917]*

CHARLOTTE PERKINS STETSON GILMAN
1860–1935

Cried all, "Before such things can come,
You idiotic child,
You must alter human nature!"
And they all sat back and smiled.
> *Similar Cases*

"I do not want to be a fly!
I want to be a worm!"
> *A Conservative, st. 6*

---

[1] I quite agree with Alexander Dumas who, when asked how he had enjoyed a fearfully dull party, said, "I should not have enjoyed it if *I* had not been there." — LAURA TENNANT, *letter to Sidney Colvin* [December 1884]; from E. V. Lucas, *The Colvins and Their Friends*

[2] Daugherty, presidential campaign manager for Senator Warren G. Harding, predicted that the convention would be deadlocked and would be decided by a group of men who "will sit down about two o'clock in the morning around a table in a smoke-filled room." The room was in the suite occupied by George Harvey, rooms 804–805 in the Blackstone Hotel.

I ran against a Prejudice
That quite cut off the view.
> *An Obstacle, st. 1*

There's a whining at the threshold —
There's a scratching at the floor —
To work! To work! In Heaven's name!
The wolf is at the door.
> *The Wolf at the Door, st. 6*

The people people have for friends
Your common sense appall,
But the people people marry
Are the queerest folk of all.
> *Queer People*

WILLIAM RALPH INGE
1860–1954

Literature flourishes best when it is half a trade and half an art.
> *The Victorian Age [1922]*

A man may build himself a throne of bayonets, but he cannot sit on it.
> *From Wit and Wisdom of Dean Inge, edited by* MARCHANT, *no. 108*

JAMES BALL NAYLOR
1860–1945

King David and King Solomon
Led merry, merry lives,
With many, many lady friends
And many, many wives;
But when old age crept over them —
With many, many qualms,
King Solomon wrote the Proverbs
And King David wrote the Psalms.
> *Ancient Authors*

OWEN WISTER
1860–1938

When you call me that, *smile!*
> *The Virginian [1902], ch. 2*

WILLIAM BLISS CARMAN
1861–1929

An open hand, an easy shoe,
And a hope to make the day go through.
> *The Joys of the Road, st. 8*

No fidget and no reformer, just
A calm observer of ought and must.
       The Joys of the Road, st. 22

The scarlet of the maples can shake me
   like a cry
Of bugles going by.
       A Vagabond Song, st. 2

There is something in October sets the
   gypsy blood astir.   *Ib. st. 3*

I took a day to search for God,
And found Him not. But as I trod
By rocky ledge, through woods un-
   tamed,
Just where one scarlet lily flamed,
I saw His footprint in the sod.
       Vestigia, st. 1

LOUISE IMOGEN GUINEY
1861–1920

He has done with roofs and men,
Open, Time, and let him pass.
       Ballad of Kenelm

A short life in the saddle, Lord!
Not long life by the fire.
       The Knight Errant, st. 2

I hear in my heart, I hear in its ominous
   pulses
All day, on the road, the hoofs of invisible horses,
All night, from their stalls, the importunate pawing and neighing.
       The Wild Ride, st. 1 and 6

Quotations (such as have point and
lack triteness) from the great old authors are an act of filial reverence on
the part of the quoter, and a blessing to
a public grown superficial and external.[1]
       In Scribner's Magazine [January 1911]

JOHN LUTHER LONG
1861–1927

To die with honor when one can no
longer live with honor.[2]
       *Madame Butterfly [1897] (in-
       scription on Samurai blade)*

[1] See Kipling, p. 874a, and note.
[2] One should die proudly when it is no longer
possible to live proudly. — NIETZSCHE [1844–

EDWARD MacDOWELL
1861–1908

A house of Dreams untold
That looks out over the whispering
   treetops
And faces the setting sun.
       House of Dreams [1]

BYRON RUFUS NEWTON
1861–1938

Vulgar of manner, overfed,
Overdressed and underbred;
Heartless, Godless, hell's delight,
Rude by day and lewd by night.
       Owed to New York [1906]

Purple-robed and pauper-clad,
Raving, rotting, money-mad;
A squirming herd in Mammon's mesh,
A wilderness of human flesh;
Crazed with avarice, lust, and rum,
New York, thy name's Delirium.
       Ib.

ALBERT BIGELOW PAINE
1861–1937

The Great White Way.[2]
       Title of novel [1901]

SIR WALTER RALEIGH
1861–1922

I wish I loved the human race;
I wish I loved its silly face;
I wish I liked the way it walks;
I wish I liked the way it talks;
And when I'm introduced to one
I wish I thought, *What jolly fun!*
       *Wishes of an Elderly Man;
       wished at a garden party
       [June 1914]*

RABINDRANATH TAGORE
1861–1941

When one knows thee, then alien
there is none, then no door is shut. Oh,

1900], *The Twilight of the Idols, Skirmishes in
a War with the Age, 36*
[1] Preface to his composition *From a Log Cabin,*
and inscribed on the memorial tablet near his
grave.
[2] Later a name for Broadway.

grant me my prayer that I may never lose the touch of the one in the play of the many. *Gitanjali* [1913]

When I bring you colored toys, my child, I understand why there is such a play of colors on clouds, on water, and why flowers are painted in tints.
The Crescent Moon [1913].
When and Why

I do not love him because he is good, but because he is my little child.
Ib. The Judge

ALFRED NORTH WHITEHEAD
1861–1947

The study of mathematics is apt to commence in disappointment. . . . We are told that by its aid the stars are weighed and the billions of molecules in a drop of water are counted. Yet, like the ghost of Hamlet's father, this great science eludes the efforts of our mental weapons to grasp it.
An Introduction to Mathematics [1911]

All the world over and at all times there have been practical men, absorbed in irreducible and stubborn facts; all the world over and at all times there have been men of philosophic temperament, who have been absorbed in the weaving of general principles.
Science and the Modern World [1925]

The science of pure mathematics, in its modern developments, may claim to be the most original creation of the human spirit. *Ib.*

The greatest invention of the nineteenth century was the invention of the method of invention. *Ib.*

The human body is an instrument for the production of art in the life of the human soul.
Adventures of Ideas [1933], *ch. 18*

A general definition of civilization: a civilized society is exhibiting the five qualities of truth, beauty, adventure, art, peace.
Adventures of Ideas, ch. 19

The deliberate aim at Peace very easily passes into its bastard substitute, Anesthesia. *Ib. 20*

There are no whole truths; all truths are half-truths. It is trying to treat them as whole truths that plays the devil.
Dialogues of Alfred North Whitehead [1953],[1] *p. 16*

The vitality of thought is in adventure. *Ideas won't keep.* Something must be done about them. When the idea is new, its custodians have fervor, live for it, and, if need be, die for it.
Ib. p. 100

Intelligence is quickness to apprehend as distinct from ability, which is capacity to act wisely on the thing apprehended. *Ib. p. 135*

Our minds are finite, and yet even in these circumstances of finitude we are surrounded by possibilities that are infinite, and the purpose of human life is to grasp as much as we can out of that infinitude. *Ib. p. 163*

A culture is in its finest flower before it begins to analyze itself. *Ib. p. 169*

The ideas of Freud [2] were popularized by people who only imperfectly understood them, who were incapable of the great effort required to grasp them in their relationship to larger truths, and who therefore assigned to them a prominence out of all proportion to their true importance. *Ib. p. 211*

Art is the imposing of a pattern on experience, and our aesthetic enjoyment in recognition of the pattern.
Ib. p. 228

A philosopher of imposing stature doesn't think in a vacuum. Even his most abstract ideas are, to some extent, conditioned by what is or is not known in the time when he lives. *Ib. p. 229*

With the sense of sight, the idea communicates the emotion, whereas,

[1] As recorded by LUCIEN PRICE.
[2] See Freud, p. 833b.

with sound, the emotion communicates the idea, which is more direct and therefore more powerful.

Dialogues of Alfred North Whitehead, p. 231

Intellect is to emotion as our clothes are to our bodies: we could not very well have civilized life without clothes, but we would be in a poor way if we had only clothes without bodies.

Ib. p. 232

No period of history has ever been great or ever can be that does not act on some sort of high, idealistic motives, and idealism in our time has been shoved aside, and we are paying the penalty for it. *Ib. p. 276*

The English never abolish anything. They put it in cold storage.

Ib. p. 309

Shakespeare wrote better poetry for not knowing too much; Milton, I think, knew too much finally for the good of his poetry. *Ib. p. 369*

JOHN KENDRICK BANGS
1862–1922

I think mankind by thee would be less bored
If only thou wert not thine own reward. *A Hint to Virtue*

ARTHUR CHRISTOPHER BENSON
1862–1925

Land of hope and glory, mother of the free,
How shall we extol thee, who are born of thee?
Wider still and wider shall thy bounds be set;
God, who made thee mighty, make thee mightier yet.

Land of Hope and Glory, chorus

ALBERT JEREMIAH BEVERIDGE
1862–1927

This party comes from the grass roots. It has grown from the soil of the people's hard necessities.

Address as temporary chairman of the Bull Moose Convention, Chicago [August 5, 1912]

JAMES W. BLAKE
1862–1935

East Side, West Side, all around the town,
The tots sang "Ring-a-rosie," "London Bridge is falling down";
Boys and girls together, me and Mamie O'Rourke,
Tripped the light fantastic on the sidewalks of New York.

The Sidewalks of New York [1]
[1894]

CARRIE JACOBS BOND
1862–1946

Well, this is the end of a perfect day,
Near the end of a journey, too.

A Perfect Day, st. 2

For mem'ry has painted this perfect day
With colors that never fade,
And we find at the end of a perfect day
The soul of a friend we've made.

Ib.

NICHOLAS MURRAY BUTLER
1862–1947

An expert is one who knows more and more about less and less.

Commencement address, Columbia University

[1] The music of the song was composed by Charles B. Lawlor [1852–1925].

JOHN JAY CHAPMAN
1862–1933

The New Testament, and to a very large extent the Old, *is* the soul of man. You cannot criticize it. It criticizes you.
Letter [March 26, 1898]

The present in New York is so powerful that the past is lost.   *Ib.* [1909]

People who love soft words and hate iniquity forget this, that reform consists in taking a bone away from a dog. Philosophy will not do this.   *Saying*

GOLDSWORTHY LOWES DICKINSON
1862–1932

Dissatisfaction with the world in which we live and determination to realize one that shall be better, are the prevailing characteristics of the modern spirit.
The Greek View of Life [1898], *ch. 5*

Chinese poetry is of all poetry I know the most human and the least symbolic or romantic. It contemplates life just as it presents itself, without any veil of ideas, any rhetoric or sentiment; it simply clears away the obstruction which habit has built up between us and the beauty of things.
An Essay on the Civilizations of India, China, and Japan [1914]

The United States of America — the greatest potential force, material, moral, and spiritual, in the world.
The Choice Before Us [1917], *ch. 1*

Government is everywhere to a great extent controlled by powerful minorities, with an interest distinct from that of the mass of the people.   *Ib. 4*

LUDWIG FULDA
1862–1939

You remain the King — even in your underwear.   *Der Talisman* [1893]

EDWARD, VISCOUNT GREY OF FALLODON
1862–1933

The lamps are going out all over Europe; we shall not see them lit again in our lifetime.
Comment [August 3, 1914],[1] standing at the windows of his room in the Foreign Office, London, as the lamplighters were turning on the lights in St. James Park

O. HENRY
[WILLIAM SYDNEY PORTER]
1862–1910

If men knew how women pass the time when they are alone, they'd never marry.
The Four Million [1906]. *Memoirs of a Yellow Dog*

What a woman wants is what you're out of. She wants more of a thing when it's scarce.
Heart of the West [1907]. *Cupid à la Carte*

Perhaps there is no happiness in life so perfect as the martyr's.
The Trimmed Lamp [1907]. *The Country of Elusion*

Bohemia is nothing more than the little country in which you do not live.   *Ib.*

You're the goods.
The Voice of the City [1908]. *From Each According to His Ability*

It was beautiful and simple as all truly great swindles are.
The Gentle Grafter [1908]. *The Octopus Marooned*

There are two times when you can never tell what is going to happen. One is when a man takes his first drink; and the other is when a woman takes her latest.   *Ib.*

[1] War was declared 11 P.M. August 4, 1914.

Busy as a one-armed man with the nettle-rash pasting on wallpaper.
The Gentle Grafter.
The Ethics of Pig

Bagdad-on-the-Subway.[1]
Roads of Destiny [1909]. *The Discounters of Money*

History is bright and fiction dull with homely men who have charmed women.
Ib. Next to Reading Matter

You can't appreciate home till you've left it, money till it's spent, your wife till she's joined a woman's club, nor Old Glory till you see it hanging on a broomstick on the shanty of a consul in a foreign town.
Ib. The Fourth in Salvador

She plucked from my lapel the invisible strand of lint (the universal act of woman to proclaim ownership).
Strictly Business [1910]. *A Ramble in Aphasia*

East is East, and West is San Francisco, according to Californians. Californians are a race of people; they are not merely inhabitants of a State.
Ib. A Municipal Report

Take of London fog 30 parts; malaria 10 parts; gas leaks 20 parts; dewdrops gathered in a brickyard at sunrise 25 parts; odor of honeysuckle 15 parts. Mix. The mixture will give you an approximate conception of a Nashville drizzle.
Ib.

It couldn't have happened anywhere but in little old New York.[2]
Whirligigs [1910]. *A Little Local Color*

I was made by a Dago and presented to the American people on behalf of the French Government for the purpose of welcomin' Irish immigrants into the Dutch city of New York.
Sixes and Sevens [1911]. *The Lady Higher Up* [1]

A straw vote only shows which way the hot air blows.
Rolling Stones [1913]. *A Ruler of Men*

Take it from me — he's got the goods.
The Unprofitable Servant

Turn up the lights — I don't want to go home in the dark.[2]
Last Words [*June 5, 1910*]

CHARLES EVANS HUGHES
1862–1948

We are under a Constitution, but the Constitution is what the judges say it is, and the judiciary is the safeguard of our liberty and of our property under the Constitution.
Speech at Elmira, New York [May 3, 1907]

How amazing it is that, in the midst of controversies on every conceivable subject, one should expect unanimity of opinion upon difficult legal questions! In the highest ranges of thought, in theology, philosophy and science, we find differences of view on the part of the most distinguished experts — theologians, philosophers and scientists. The history of scholarship is a record of disagreements. And when we deal with questions relating to principles of law and their applications, we do not suddenly rise into a stratosphere of icy certainty.
Speech to the American Law Institute [May 7, 1936]

The greater the importance of safeguarding the community from incitements to the overthrow of our institutions by force and violence, the more imperative is the need to preserve inviolate the constitutional rights of free

---

[1] Also in *A Madison Square Arabian Night, A Night in New Arabia,* and *What You Want.*
[2] Also in *A Midsummer Knight's Dream, Past One at Rooney's* and *The Rubber Plant's Story.*

[1] The Statue of Liberty.
[2] The reference is to a popular song of the day, "I'm Afraid to Go Home in the Dark."

speech, free press and free assembly in order to maintain the opportunity for free political discussion, to the end that government may be responsive to the will of the people and that changes, if desired, may be obtained by peaceful means. Therein lies the security of the Republic, the very foundation of constitutional government.

DeJonge v. Oregon, 299 U.S. 353, 365 [1937]

MAURICE MAETERLINCK
1862–1949

It is always a mistake not to close one's eyes, whether to forgive or to look better into oneself.

Pelléas et Mélisande [1892]

There are no dead.

The Blue Bird [1909], *act IV, sc. 2*

SIR HENRY NEWBOLT
1862–1938

To set the cause above renown,
To love the game beyond the prize,
To honor, while you strike him down,
The foe that comes with fearless eyes;
To count the life of battle good
And dear the land that gave you birth,
And dearer yet the brotherhood
That binds the brave of all the earth.

The Island Race. Clifton Chapel, st. 2

Qui procul hinc, the legend's writ,
The frontier grave is far away —
Qui ante diem periit:
Sed miles, sed pro patria.[1]   *Ib. st. 4*

Take my drum to England, hang et by the shore,
Strike et when your powder's runnin' low;
If the Dons sight Devon, I'll quit the port o' Heaven,
An' drum them up the Channel as we drummed them long ago.

Drake's Drum, st. 2

[1] Who died far away, before his time: but as a soldier, for his country.

Drake he's in his hammock till the great Armadas come.
(Capten, art tha sleepin' there below?)   *Drake's Drum, st. 3*

Now the sunset breezes shiver,
And she's fading down the river,
But in England's song forever
She's the Fighting Téméraire.

The Fighting Téméraire, st. 6

Play up! play up! and play the game!

Vitaï Lampada

EDEN PHILLPOTTS
1862–1960

His father's sister had bats in the belfry and was put away.

Peacock House

ROBERT CAMERON ROGERS
1862–1912

The hours I spent with thee, dear heart,
Are as a string of pearls to me;
I count them over, every one apart,
My rosary, my rosary.   *My Rosary*

EDITH WHARTON
1862–1937

There are two ways of spreading light: to be
The candle or the mirror that reflects it.   *Vesalius in Zante*

Mrs. Ballinger is one of the ladies who pursue Culture in bands, as though it were dangerous to meet it alone.   *Xingu* [1916]

I was never allowed to read the popular American children's books of my day because, as my mother said, the children spoke bad English *without the author's knowing it.*

A Backward Glance [1934], *ch. 3*

To [Henry] James's intimates, however, these elaborate hesitancies, far from being an obstacle, were like a cobweb bridge flung from his mind to theirs, an invisible passage over which one knew that silver-footed ironies, veiled jokes, tiptoe malices, were stealing to explode a huge laugh at one's feet. *A Backward Glance, ch. 8*

REVEREND E. J. HARDY
fl. 1910

How To Be Happy Though Married. *Title of book* [1910]

HENRY HOLCOMB BENNETT
1863–1924

Hats off!
Along the street there comes
A blare of bugles, a ruffle of drums,
A flash of color beneath the sky:
Hats off!
The flag is passing by.
The Flag Goes By, st. 1

GAMALIEL BRADFORD
1863–1932

I sometimes wish that God were back
In this dark world and wide;[1]
For though some virtues he might lack,
He had his pleasant side.
Exit God

DAVID LLOYD GEORGE, EARL OF DWYFOR
1863–1945

What is our task? To make Britain a fit country for heroes to live in.
Speech, Queen's Hall, London [September 19, 1914]

OLIVER HERFORD
1863–1935

Children, behold the Chimpanzee:
He sits on the ancestral tree
From which we sprang in ages gone.
I'm glad we sprang: had we held on,

[1] See Milton, p. 341a.

We might, for aught that I can say,
Be horrid Chimpanzees today.
The Chimpanzee

Ermined and minked and Persian-lambed,
Be-puffed (be-painted, too, alas!)
Be-decked, be-diamonded — be-damned!
The women of the better class.
The Women of the Better Class, st. 4

SIR ARTHUR THOMAS QUILLER-COUCH
1863–1944

Literature is not an abstract science, to which exact definitions can be applied. It is an art, the success of which depends on personal persuasiveness, on the author's skill to give as on ours to receive.
Inaugural Lecture at Cambridge University [1913]

JAMES HARVEY ROBINSON
1863–1935

Political campaigns are designedly made into emotional orgies which endeavor to distract attention from the real issues involved, and they actually paralyze what slight powers of cerebration man can normally muster.
The Human Comedy [1937], *ch. 9*

With supreme irony, the war to "make the world safe for democracy" [1] ended by leaving democracy more unsafe in the world than at any time since the collapse of the revolutions of 1848.
Ib.

GEORGE SANTAYANA
1863–1952

O World, thou choosest not the better part!
It is not wisdom to be only wise,
And on the inward vision close the eyes,

[1] See Woodrow Wilson, p. 842a.

But it is wisdom to believe the heart.
Columbus found a world, and had no
   chart,
Save one that faith deciphered in the
   skies;
To trust the soul's invincible surmise
Was all his science and his only art.
        O World, Thou Choosest Not
                     [*1894*]

Beauty as we feel it is something indescribable: what it is or what it means
can never be said.
        The Sense of Beauty [*1896*].
                  Expression

Beauty is a pledge of the possible
conformity between the soul and nature, and consequently a ground of
faith in the supremacy of the good.
                     Ib.

That life is worth living is the most
necessary of assumptions, and, were it
not assumed, the most impossible of
conclusions.[1]
        The Life of Reason [*1905–*
                1906], *vol. I*

Fanaticism consists in redoubling
your efforts when you have forgotten
your aim.   *Ib.*

Those who cannot remember the past
are condemned to repeat it.   *Ib.*

The highest form of vanity is love of
fame.   *Ib. II*

The human race, in its intellectual life, is organized like the bees: the
masculine soul is a worker, sexually
atrophied, and essentially dedicated to
impersonal and universal arts; the feminine is a queen, infinitely fertile, omnipresent in its brooding industry, but
passive and abounding in intuitions
without method and passions without
justice.   *Ib.*

Let a man once overcome his selfish
terror at his own finitude, and his finitude is, in one sense, overcome.
        The Ethics of Spinoza [*1910*],
                  introduction

[1] See William James, p. 794a.

Perhaps the only true dignity of man
is his capacity to despise himself.
        The Ethics of Spinoza,
                  introduction

Miracles are propitious accidents, the
natural causes of which are too complicated to be readily understood.   *Ib.*

The Bible is literature, not dogma.
                     Ib.

American life is a powerful solvent.
It seems to neutralize every intellectual
element, however tough and alien it
may be, and to fuse it in the native
good will, complacency, thoughtless-
ness, and optimism.
        *Character and Opinion in the
              United States* [*1920*]

All his life he [the American] jumps
into the train after it has started and
jumps out before it has stopped; and he
never once gets left behind, or breaks a
leg.   *Ib.*

England is the paradise of individuality, eccentricity, heresy, anomalies,
hobbies, and humors.
        Soliloquies in England [*1922*].
             The British Character

The world is a perpetual caricature of
itself; at every moment it is the mockery and the contradiction of what it is
pretending to be.   *Ib. Dickens*

There is no cure for birth and death
save to enjoy the interval.
                Ib. War Shrines

I like to walk about amidst the beautiful things that adorn the world; but
private wealth I should decline, or any
sort of personal possessions, because
they would take away my liberty.
        Ib. The Irony of Liberalism

My atheism, like that of Spinoza, is
true piety towards the universe and
denies only gods fashioned by men in
their own image, to be servants of their
human interests.
        Ib. On My Friendly Critics

The young man who has not wept is
a savage, and the old man who will not
laugh is a fool.
        Dialogues in Limbo [*1925*], *III*

There is nothing impossible in the existence of the supernatural: its existence seems to me decidedly probable.

The Genteel Tradition at Bay
[*1931*]

ERNEST LAWRENCE THAYER
1863–1940

There was ease in Casey's manner as he
stepped into his place,
There was pride in Casey's bearing, and
a smile on Casey's face,
And when, responding to the cheers, he
lightly doffed his hat,
No stranger in the crowd could doubt
'twas Casey at the bat.

Casey at the Bat,[1] *st. 6*

Oh! somewhere in this favored land the
sun is shining bright;
The band is playing somewhere, and
somewhere hearts are light;
And somewhere men are laughing and
somewhere children shout,
But there is no joy in Mudville —
mighty Casey has struck out.

Ib. st. 13

HARRY BRAISTED
fl. 1896

You're Not the Only Pebble on the
Beach.   *Title of song* [1896]

JOSEPH HAYDEN
fl. 1896

There'll be a hot time in the old town
tonight.

A Hot Time in the Old Town[2]
[1896]

---

[1] First printed in the *San Francisco Examiner*
[June 3, 1888].
> Yet I'd take my chance with fame,
> Calmly let it go at that,
> With the right to sign my name
> Under "Casey at the Bat."
> GRANTLAND RICE [1880–1954], *The Masterpiece*

[2] Hayden's text for a march, *A Hot Time in the Old Town Tonight* [1886], by Theodore August Metz [1848–1936], later a favorite of Theodore Roosevelt's Rough Riders in Cuba, and still later Roosevelt's campaign song.

SIR ROGER CASEMENT
1864–1916

Where all your rights become only an accumulated wrong; where men must beg with bated breath for leave to subsist in their own land, to think their own thoughts, to sing their own songs, to garner the fruits of their own labors . . . then surely it is braver, a saner and truer thing, to be a rebel in act and deed against such circumstances as these than tamely to accept it as the natural lot of men.

Statement from prison
[*June 29, 1916*]

RICHARD HOVEY
1864–1900

For it's always fair weather
When good fellows get together
With a stein on the table and a good
song ringing clear.

A Stein Song [1898], *st. 1*

I do not know beneath what sky
Nor on what seas shall be thy fate:
I only know it shall be high,
I only know it shall be great.

Unmanifest Destiny [1898], *st. 7*

O, Eleazer Wheelock was a very pious
man;
He went into the wilderness to teach
the Indian,
With a *Gradus ad Parnassum*, a Bible,
and a drum,
And five hundred gallons of New England rum. . . .
Eleazar was the faculty, and the whole
curriculum
Was five hundred gallons of New England rum.

Eleazer Wheelock [*Dartmouth
College song*], *st. 1*

MARK ANTONY
DE WOLFE HOWE
1864–1960

Now, thieving Time, take what you
must —
Quickness to hear, to move, to see;

When dust is drawing near to dust
Such diminutions needs must be.
Yet leave, O leave exempt from plunder
My curiosity, my wonder!
Thieving Time [1951]

ROBERT LOVEMAN
1864–1923

It is not raining rain to me,
  It's raining daffodils;
In every dimpled drop I see
  Wildflowers on the hills.
April Rain [1901], *st. 1*

A health unto the happy!
  A fig for him who frets! —
It is not raining rain to me,
  It's raining violets.   *Ib. st. 4*

ANDREW BARTON
[BANJO] PATERSON
1864–1941

Once a jolly swagman camped by a billabong,
Under the shade of a coolibar tree,
And he sang as he sat and waited for
  his billy-boil,
"You'll come a-waltzing, Matilda, with
  me." [1]
*Waltzing Matilda (Australian
soldiers' marching song)*

STEPHEN PHILLIPS
1864–1915

A man not old, but mellow, like good
  wine.   *Ulysses, act III, sc. i*

JULES RENARD
1864–1910

To succeed you must add water to
your wine, until there is no more wine.
Journal

There are moments when everything
goes well; don't be frightened, it won't
last.   *Ib.*

[1] Swagman: tramp. Billabong: pool. Coolibar:
gum tree. Billy: tin container used for brewing
tea.

I am not sincere even when I am
saying that I am not sincere.
Journal

We don't understand life any better
at forty than at twenty, but we know it
and admit it.   *Ib.*

MIGUEL DE UNAMUNO
1864–1936

The man of flesh and blood; the one
who is born, suffers and dies — above
all, who dies; the man who eats and
drinks and plays and sleeps and thinks
and wills; the man who is seen and is
heard; the brother, the real brother.
The Tragic Sense of Life [1913],
ch. 1

Man, by the very fact of being
man, by possessing consciousness, is, in
comparison with the ass or the crab, a
diseased animal. Consciousness is a disease.   *Ib.*

Pantheism is said . . . to be merely
atheism in disguise.   *Ib. 5*

Science is a cemetery of dead ideas,
even though life may issue from them.
Ib.

True science teaches, above all, to
doubt and be ignorant.   *Ib.*

To believe in God is to yearn for His
existence and, furthermore, it is to act
as if He did exist.   *Ib. 8*

Martyrs create faith, faith does not
create martyrs.[1]   *Ib. 9*

To fall into a habit is to begin to
cease to be.   *Ib.*

The intellectual world is divided into
two classes — dilettantes, on the one
hand, and pedants, on the other.
Ib. 11

Warmth, warmth, more warmth! for
we are dying of cold and not of darkness. It is not the night that kills, but
the frost.   *Ib. Conclusion*

The devil is an angel too.
Two Mothers

[1] See Tertullian, p. 143b, and Suarès, p. 896a.

There are pretenses which are very sincere, and marriage is their school.
                    Two Mothers

And killing time is perhaps the essence of comedy, just as the essence of tragedy is killing eternity.
                    San Manuel Bueno, prologue

I would say that teleology is theology, and that God is not a "because," but rather an "in order to."   *Ib.*

Let us go on committing suicide by working among our people, and let them dream life just as the lake dreams the sky.   *Ib.*

One of those leaders of what they call the social revolution has said that religion is the opiate of the people.[1] Opium . . . opium . . . opium, yes. Let us give them opium so that they can sleep and dream.   *Ib.*

Use harms and even destroys beauty. The noblest function of an object is to be contemplated.   *Mist* [1914]

In Homeric times people and things had two names: the one given them by men and the one given by the gods. I wonder what God calls me?   *Ib.*

Isolation is the worst possible counselor.   *Civilization Is Civilism*

Every peasant has a lawyer inside of him, just as every lawyer, no matter how urbane he may be, carries a peasant within himself.   *Ib.*

It is sad not to be loved, but it is much sadder not to be able to love.
                    To a Young Writer

These terrible sociologists, who are the astrologers and alchemists of our twentieth century.
                    Fanatical Skepticism

Faith which does not doubt is dead faith.   *The Agony of Christianity*

We never know, believe me, when we have succeeded best.
                    Essays and Soliloquies

[1] See Marx, p. 686b.

ISRAEL ZANGWILL
1864–1926

Scratch the Christian and you find the pagan — spoiled.
                    Children of the Ghetto [1892]

America is God's crucible, the great melting pot where all the races of Europe are melting and re-forming!
                    The Melting Pot [1908], *act I*

FRANK MOORE COLBY
1865–1925

Men will confess to treason, murder, arson, false teeth, or a wig. How many of them will own up to a lack of humor?
                    The Colby Essays [1926], *vol. I*

Nobody can describe a fool to the life, without much patient self-inspection.   *Ib.*

A new movement is not a stampede to some new object, but a stampede away from some old person.   *Ib. II*

Were it not for the presence of the unwashed [1] and the half-educated, the formless, queer and incomplete, the unreasonable and absurd, the infinite shapes of the delightful human tadpole, the horizon would not wear so wide a grin.   *Imaginary Obligations*

HERBERT ALBERT LAURENS FISHER
1865–1940

All political decisions are taken under great pressure, and if a treaty serves its turn for ten or twenty years, the wisdom of its framers is sufficiently confirmed.[2]   *Political Prophecies* [1918]

It is easier for eight or nine elderly men to feel their way towards unanimity if they are not compelled to conduct their converging maneuvers under the microscopes and telescopes of the press,

[1] See Brougham, p. 540b.
[2] Thirty years is the life of most great treaties. — R. B. MOWAT, *A History of Great Britain* [1922]

but are permitted to shuffle about a little in slippers.

> *An International Experiment* [1]
> [1921]

Purity of race does not exist. Europe is a continent of energetic mongrels.

> *A History of Europe* [1934], *ch. 1*

Politics is the art of human happiness.

> *Ib. 31*

KING GEORGE V
1865–1936

How is the Empire?

> *Last words* [*January 21, 1936*]

FREDERIC WILLIAM GOUDY
1865–1947

I am the voice of today, the herald of tomorrow. . . . I coin for you the enchanting tale, the philosopher's moralizing, and the poet's visions. . . . I am the leaden army that conquers the world — I am TYPE.

> *The Type Speaks*

LAURENCE HOPE [ADELA FLORENCE CORY NICOLSON]
1865–1904

Less than the dust beneath thy chariot wheel,
Less than the rust that never stains thy sword.

> *Indian Love Lyrics. Less Than the Dust, st. 1*

Less than the weed that grows beside thy door.

> *Ib. st. 2*

For this is wisdom: to love, to live,
To take what Fate, or the Gods, may give.

> *Ib. The Teak Forest*

To have — to hold — and — in time — let go!

> *Ib.*

Pale hands I loved beside the Shalimar,

[1] The League of Nations.

Where are you now? Who lies beneath your spell?

> *Indian Love Lyrics. Kashmiri Song, st. 1*

RUDYARD KIPLING
1865–1936

I have eaten your bread and salt.
I have drunk your water and wine.
The deaths ye died I have watched beside
And the lives ye led were mine.

> *Departmental Ditties* [1886].
> *Prelude, st. 1*

Little Tin Gods on Wheels.

> *Ib. Public Waste, st. 4*

The blush that flies at seventeen
Is fixed at forty-nine.

> *Ib. My Rival, st. 2*

The toad beneath the harrow knows
Exactly where each tooth point goes;
The butterfly upon the road
Preaches contentment to that toad.

> *Ib. Pagett, M.P., prelude*

Cross that rules the Southern Sky!
Stars that sweep, and turn, and fly,
Hear the Lovers' Litany:
"Love like ours can never die!"

> *Ib. The Lovers' Litany, st. 2*

And a woman is only a woman, but a good cigar is a smoke.

> *Ib. The Betrothed, st. 25*

You'll never plumb the Oriental mind,
And if you did, it isn't worth the toil.

> *Ib. One Viceroy Resigns*

It takes a great deal of Christianity to wipe out uncivilized Eastern instincts, such as falling in love at first sight.

> *Plain Tales from the Hills*
> [1888]. *Lispeth*

Never praise a sister to a sister, in the hope of your compliments reaching the proper ears.

> *Ib. False Dawn*

Many religious people are deeply suspicious. They seem — for purely religious purposes, of course — to know

more about iniquity than the unregen-
erate.
> *Plain Tales from the Hills.*
> *Watches of the Night*

She was as immutable as the hills.
But not quite so green.
> *Ib. Venus Annodomini*

Youth had been a habit of hers for so
long that she could not part with it.
> *Ib.*

Everyone is more or less mad on one
point.[1]
> *Ib. On the Strength of a Likeness*

The silliest woman can manage a
clever man; but it needs a very clever
woman to manage a fool!
> *Ib. Three and — an Extra*

Lalah is a member of the most ancient profession in the world.
> *In Black and White* [1888].
> *On the City Wall*

Steady the Buffs.
> *Soldiers Three* [1888]

Being kissed by a man who didn't
wax his moustache was — like eating
an egg without salt.
> *The Story of the Gadsbys*
> [1888]. *Poor Dear Mamma*

Down to Gehenna or up to the
  Throne,
He travels the fastest who travels
  alone.[2]
> *Ib. The Winners (L' Envoi:*
> *What Is the Moral?), st. 1*

More men are killed by overwork
than the importance of the world justi-
fies.
> *The Phantom 'Rickshaw* [1888]

[1] Semel insanivimus omnes [We have all once
been mad]. — JOHANNES BAPTISTA MANTUANUS
[1448–1516], *Eclogues, no. I*
[2] He may well win the race that runs by himself. — BENJAMIN FRANKLIN, *Poor Richard's Almanac* [1757]
Who travels alone, without lover or friend,
But hurries from nothing, to nought at the end.
> ELLA WHEELER WILCOX, *Reply to*
> *Rudyard Kipling's Poem*

He became an officer *and* a gentleman, which is an enviable thing.
> *Under the Deodars* [1888].
> *Only a Subaltern*

Tea fights.[1]
> *Ib.*

Oh, East is East, and West is West,
  and never the twain shall meet,
Till Earth and Sky stand presently at
  God's great Judgment Seat;
But there is neither East nor West,
  border, nor breed, nor birth,
When two strong men stand face to
  face, though they come from the
  ends of the earth!
> *The Ballad of East and West*
> [1889]

For all we take we must pay, but the
price is cruel high.
> *The Courting of Dinah Shadd,*
> [1890]

If I were damned of body and soul,
I know whose prayers would make me
  whole,
Mother o' mine, O mother o' mine.
> *Mother o' Mine* [1891]

And the end of the fight is a tombstone
  white with the name of the late
  deceased,
And the epitaph drear: "A Fool lies
  here who tried to hustle the
  East."
> *The Naulahka* [1892], ch. 5

When Earth's last picture is painted,
  and the tubes are twisted and
  dried,
When the oldest colors have faded, and
  the youngest critic has died,
We shall rest, and, faith, we shall need
  it — lie down for an eon or two,
Till the Master of All Good Workmen
  shall put us to work anew.
> *When Earth's Last Picture Is*
> *Painted* [1892], st. 1

Ever the wide world over, lass,
  Ever the trail held true,

[1] Giggle, gabble, gobble, git. — OLIVER WEN-
DELL HOLMES [1809–1894], *description of a tea
party*

Over the world and under the world,
And back at the last to you.
> *The Gipsy Trail* [1892], *st.* 2

They rise to their feet as He passes by,
gentlemen unafraid.
> *Ballads and Barrack Room Ballads* [1892, 1893]. *Dedication, st.* 5

"What are the bugles blowin' for?"
said Files-on-Parade.
"To turn you out, to turn you out," the
Color-Sergeant said.
> *Ib. Danny Deever, st.* 1

They've taken of his buttons off an' cut
his stripes away,
An' they're hangin' Danny Deever in
the mornin'.   *Ib.*

We aren't no thin red 'eroes.[1]
> *Ib. Tommy, st.* 4

Single men in barricks don't grow into
plaster saints.   *Ib.*

For it's Tommy this, an' Tommy that,
an' "Chuck 'im out, the brute!"
But it's "Savior of 'is country" when
the guns begin to shoot.
> *Ib. st.* 5

So 'ere's *to* you, Fuzzy-Wuzzy, at your
'ome in the Soudan;
You're a pore benighted 'eathen but a
first-class fightin' man.
> *Ib. Fuzzy-Wuzzy, st.* 1

The uniform 'e wore
Was nothin' much before,
An' rather less than 'arf o' that be'ind.
> *Ib. Gunga Din, st.* 2

An' for all 'is dirty 'ide
'E was white, clear white, inside
When 'e went to tend the wounded
under fire!   *Ib. st.* 3

Though I've belted you an' flayed you,
By the livin' Gawd that made you,
You're a better man than I am, Gunga
Din!   *Ib. st.* 5

'Ave you 'eard o' the Widow at Windsor
With a hairy gold crown on 'er 'ead?
> *Ib. The Widow at Windsor, st.* 1

[1] See Sir W. H. Russell, p. 704b.

By the old Moulmein Pagoda, lookin'
eastward to the sea,
There's a Burma girl a-settin', and I
know she thinks o' me;
For the wind is in the palm trees, and
the temple bells they say:
"Come you back, you British soldier;
come you back to Mandalay!"
Come you back to Mandalay,
Where the old Flotilla lay;
Can't you 'ear their paddles chunkin'
from Rangoon to Mandalay?
On the road to Mandalay,
Where the flyin' fishes play,
An' the dawn comes up like thunder
outer China 'crost the Bay!
> *Ballads and Barrack Room Ballads. Mandalay, st.* 1

I've a neater, sweeter maiden in a
cleaner, greener land.   *Ib. st.* 5

Ship me somewheres east of Suez,
where the best is like the worst,
Where there aren't no Ten Commandments,
an' a man can raise a
thirst.   *Ib. st.* 6

The Devil whispered behind the leaves,
"It's pretty, but is it Art?"
> *Ib. The Conundrum of the Workshops, st.* 1

To the legion of the lost ones, to the
cohort of the damned.
> *Ib. Gentlemen Rankers, st.* 1

We're poor little lambs who've lost our
way,
Baa! Baa! Baa!
We're little black sheep who've gone
astray,
Baa — aa — aa!
Gentlemen rankers out on the spree,
Damned from here to Eternity,
God ha' mercy on such as we,
Baa! Yah! Baa!
> *Ib. refrain*

We have done with Hope and Honor,
we are lost to Love and Truth,
We are dropping down the ladder rung
by rung;
And the measure of our torment is the
measure of our youth.

God help us, for we knew the worst too
   young!
> Ballads and Barrack Room Bal-
> lads. Gentlemen Rankers, st. 4

And what should they know of England
   who only England know?
> Ib. The English Flag, st. 1

And the naked soul of Tomlinson grew
   white as a rain-washed bone.
> Ib. Tomlinson, l. 10

The sin ye do by two and two ye must
   pay for one by one.   Ib. l. 60

There's a legion that never was 'listed,
That carries no colors or crest.
> Ib. The Lost Legion, st. 1

To go and find out and be damned
(Dear boys!).   Ib.

There are nine and sixty ways of constructing tribal lays,
And every single one of them is right.
> Ib. In the Neolithic Age, st. 5

There be triple ways to take, of the
   eagle or the snake,
   Or the way of a man with a maid;[1]
But the sweetest way to me is a ship's
   upon the sea
   In the heel of the Northeast Trade.
> Ib. The Long Trail, st. 5

He wrapped himself in quotations[2]
— as a beggar would enfold himself in
the purple of emperors.
> Many Inventions [1893]. The
> Finest Story in the World

But, spite all modern notions, I've
   found her first and best —
The only certain packet for the Islands
   of the Blest.
> The Three-Decker [1894], st. 1

They copied all they could follow, but
   they couldn't copy my mind.
> The Mary Gloster [1894], l. 59

When 'Omer smote 'is bloomin' lyre,
He'd 'eard men sing by land an' sea;

[1] See Proverbs 30:19, p. 26b.
[2] In literature quotation is good only when
the writer whom I follow goes my way, and,
being better mounted than I, gives me a cast.
— EMERSON, Quotation and Originality [1876]
  See Louise Imogen Guiney, p. 860a.

An' what he thought 'e might require,
'E went an' took — the same as me!
> When 'Omer Smote 'Is Bloomin'
> Lyre [1894], st. 1

Back to the Army again, sergeant,
   Back to the Army again.
Out o' the cold an' the rain.
> Back to the Army Again
> [1894], refrain

For to admire an' for to see,
For to be'old this world so wide —
It never done no good to me
But I can't drop it if I tried!
> For to Admire [1894], refrain

We be of one blood, ye and I.
> The Jungle Book [1894].
> Kaa's Hunting

Brother, thy tail hangs down behind.
> Ib. Road Song of the Bandar-Log,
> refrain

When Pack meets with Pack in the
   Jungle, and neither will go from
   the trail,
Lie down till the leaders have spoken
   — it may be fair words shall prevail.
> The Second Jungle Book [1895].
> The Law of the Jungle, st. 6

Now these are the Laws of the Jungle,
   and many and mighty are they;
But the head and the hoof of the Law
   and the haunch and the hump
   is — Obey!
> Ib. st. 19

He who rebukes the world is rebuked
by the world.
> Ib. The Undertakers

They change their skies above them,
But not their hearts that roam.[1]
> The Nativeborn [1895], st. 2

The Liner she's a lady, an' she never
   looks nor 'eeds —
The Man-o'-War's 'er 'usband, an' 'e
   gives 'er all she needs,
But, oh, the little cargo boats that sail
   the wet seas roun',

[1] See Horace, p. 123b.

They're just the same as you an' me
a-plyin' up and down!
The Liner She's a Lady
[1895], st. 1

I've taken my fun where I've found it.
The Ladies [1895], st. 1

An' I learned about women from 'er.
Ib. refrain

For the Colonel's Lady an' Judy
O'Grady
Are sisters under their skins!
Ib. st. 8

Though there's never a wave of all her
waves
But marks our English dead.
The Song of the Dead
[1896], II, st. 1

If blood be the price of admiralty,
Lord God, we ha' paid in full!   *Ib.*

'E's a sort of a bloomin' cosmopolouse
— soldier an' sailor too.
Soldier an' Sailor Too
[1896], st. 2

A fool there was and he made his
prayer
(Even as you and I!)
To a rag and a bone and a hank of
hair
(We called her the woman who did not
care)
But the fool he called her his lady
fair —
(Even as you and I!)
The Vampire [1897], st. 1

Make ye no truce with Adam-zad —
the Bear that walks like a Man! [1]
The Truce of the Bear
[1898], st. 2

Daughter am I in my mother's house;
But mistress in my own.
Our Lady of the Snows [2]
[1898], st. 1

God of our fathers, known of old,
Lord of our far-flung battle line,
Beneath whose awful Hand we hold
Dominion over palm and pine —

[1] Russia.
[2] The Dominion of Canada.

Lord God of Hosts, be with us yet,
Lest we forget — lest we forget!
Recessional [1899], st. 1

The tumult and the shouting dies;
The captains and the kings depart:
Still stands Thine ancient sacrifice,
An humble and a contrite heart.
Ib. st. 2

Lo, all our pomp of yesterday
Is one with Nineveh and Tyre!
Ib. st. 3

Lesser breeds without the Law.
Ib. st. 4

For heathen heart that puts her trust
In reeking tube and iron shard,
All valiant dust that builds on dust,
And guarding, calls not Thee to guard,
For frantic boast and foolish word —
Thy mercy on Thy People, Lord!
Ib. st. 5

He's an absent-minded beggar, but he
heard his country call,
And his reg'ment didn't need to send to
find him!
The Absent-Minded Beggar
[1899], st. 3

Take up the White Man's burden.[1]
The White Man's Burden
[1899], st. 1

Your new-caught, sullen peoples,
Half devil and half child.   *Ib.*

We have had a jolly good lesson, and it
serves us jolly well right!
The Lesson [1901], st. 2

We have forty million reasons for failure, but not a single excuse.
Ib. st. 8

Little Friend of All the World.
Kim [1901], ch. 1

Then ye returned to your trinkets; then
ye contented your souls
With the flanneled fools at the wicket
or the muddied oafs at the goals.
The Islanders [1902], l. 31

[1] Pile on the brown man's burden
To satisfy your greed.
London Truth; reprinted in *Middle-*
bury [Vermont] Register [March 17,
1899]

When the ship goes *wop* (with a wiggle between)
And the steward falls into the soup tureen . . .
Why, then you will know (if you haven't guessed)
You're "Fifty north and forty west!"
> *The Just-So Stories* [1902].
> *How the Whale Got Its Throat*

We get the hump —
Cameelious hump —
The hump that is black and blue!
> *Ib. How the Camel Got His Hump*

I keep six honest serving men
(They taught me all I knew);
Their names are What and Why and When
And How and Where and Who.
> *Ib. The Elephant's Child*

The great gray-green, greasy Limpopo River, all set about with fever-trees. *Ib.*

Yes, weekly from Southampton,
Great steamers, white and gold,
Go rolling down to Rio
(Roll down — roll down to Rio!)
And I'd like to roll to Rio
Some day before I'm old!
> *Ib. The Beginning of the Armadilloes, st. 4*

The Cat. He walked by himself, and all places were alike to him.
> *Ib. The Cat That Walked By Himself*

He went through the wet wild woods, waving his wild tail, and walking by his wild lone. But he never told anybody. *Ib.*

Who hath desired the sea? — the sight of salt water unbounded.
The Sea and the Hills [1903], *st.* 1

So and no otherwise — hillmen desire their hills! *Ib.*

Something hidden. Go and find it. Go and look behind the Ranges —

Something lost behind the Ranges.
Lost and waiting for you. Go! [1]
> *The Explorer* [1903], *st.* 2

Creation's cry goes up on high
From age to cheated age:
"Send us the men who do the work
For which they draw the wage!"
> *The Wage Slaves* [1903], *st.* 3

Boots — boots — boots — boots —
movin' up and down again!
There's no discharge in the war! [2]
> *Boots* [1903], *st.* 1

If England was what England seems,
An' not the England of our dreams,
But only putty, brass, an' paint,
'Ow quick we'd drop 'er! But she ain't.
> *The Return* [1903], *refrain*

'Tisn't beauty, so to speak, nor good talk necessarily. It's just It. Some women'll stay in a man's memory if they once walked down a street.
> *Traffics and Discoveries* [1904].
> *Mrs. Bathurst*

If once you have paid him the Dane-geld
You never get rid of the Dane.
> *Ib. What Dane-Geld Means, st.* 4

What say the reeds at Runnymede?
> *Ib. The Reeds of Runnymede, st.* 1

When crew and captain understand each other to the core,
It takes a gale and more than a gale to put their ship ashore.
> *Ib. Together, st.* 2

Of all the trees that grow so fair,
Old England to adorn,
Greater are none beneath the Sun,
Than oak, and ash, and thorn.[3]
> *Puck of Pook's Hill* [1906]. A *Tree Song, st.* 1

---

[1] Because it is there. — GEORGE LEIGH MALLORY [1886–1924], *when asked why he wanted to climb Mt. Everest*
[2] See *Ecclesiastes 8:8,* p. 28a.
[3] See *Glasgerion,* p. 1088a.

Land of our birth, we pledge to thee
Our love and toil in the years to be.
>   *Puck of Pook's Hill. The
>   Children's Song, st. 1*

Teach us delight in simple things,
And mirth that has no bitter springs.
>   *Ib. st. 7*

Enough work to do, and strength
enough to do the work.
>   *A Doctor's Work. Address at
>   Middlesex Hospital* [1] *[October
>   1908]*

Brothers and Sisters, I bid you beware
Of giving your heart to a dog to tear.
>   *The Power of the Dog* [1909]

Take of English earth as much
As either hand may rightly clutch.
In the taking of it breathe
Prayer for all who lie beneath.
>   *Rewards and Fairies* [2] *[1910].
>   A Charm, st. 1*

If you can meet with Triumph and
        Disaster
And treat those two impostors just the
        same.   *Ib. If, st. 2*

If you can talk with crowds and keep
        your virtue,
Or walk with Kings — nor lose the
        common touch.   *Ib. st. 4*

Yours is the Earth and everything
        that's in it,
And — which is more — you'll be a
        Man, my son!   *Ib.*

One man in a thousand, Solomon says,
Will stick more close than a brother. [3]
>   *Ib. The Thousandth Man, st. 1*

But the Thousandth Man will stand by
        your side
To the gallows foot — and after!
>   *Ib. st. 4*

The female of the species is more
        deadly than the male.
>   *The Female of the Species
>   [1911], st. 1*

Our England is a garden, and such gardens are not made

By singing "Oh, how beautiful!" and
        sitting in the shade.
>   *The Glory of the Garden
>   [1911], st. 5*

Oh, Adam was a gardener, [1] and God
        who made him sees
That half a proper gardener's work is
        done upon his knees.
>   *Ib. st. 8*

For all we have and are,
        For all our children's fate,
Stand up and take the war.
        The Hun is at the gate!
>   *For All We Have and Are
>   [1914], st. 1*

There is but one task for all —
        One life for each to give.
What stands if Freedom fall?
Who dies if England live?
>   *Ib. st. 4*

That packet of assorted miseries
which we call a Ship.
>   *The First Sailor* [1918]

Hot and bothered.
>   *Independence. Rectorial Ad-
>   dress, St. Andrew's [October
>   10, 1923]*

Never again will I spend another
winter in this accursed bucketshop of a
refrigerator called England.
>   *Letter to Sidney Colvin. From
>   E. V. Lucas, The Colvins and
>   Their Friends [1928], p. 294*

When your Daemon is in charge, do
not try to think consciously. Drift, wait,
and obey.
>   *Something of Myself for My
>   Friends Known and Unknown
>   [1937], ch. 8*

LOGAN PEARSALL
SMITH [2]
1865–1946

What a bore it is, waking up in the
morning always the same person. I wish

---

[1] Where Kipling died in 1936.
[2] See Corbet, p. 315b.
[3] See *Ecclesiastes 7:28*, p. 28a.

[1] See Shakespeare, p. 215a.
[2] Two weeks before his death, a friend asked
him half jokingly if he had discovered any
meaning in life. "Yes," he replied, "there is

I were unflinching and emphatic, and had big, bushy eyebrows and a Message for the Age. I wish I were a deep Thinker, or a great Ventriloquist.
Trivia [1902]. *Green Ivory*

There are two things to aim at in life: first, to get what you want; and, after that, to enjoy it. Only the wisest of mankind achieve the second.
Afterthoughts [1931]

Happiness is a wine of the rarest vintage, and seems insipid to a vulgar taste. *Ib.*

How awful to reflect that what people say of us is true! *Ib.*

Solvency is entirely a matter of temperament and not of income.
Ib.

It is almost always worth while to be cheated; people's little frauds have an interest which more than repays what they cost us. *Ib.*

When they come downstairs from their Ivory Towers, idealists are apt to walk straight into the gutter. *Ib.*

The indefatigable pursuit of an unattainable perfection, even though it consist in nothing more than in the pounding of an old piano, is what alone gives a meaning to our life on this unavailing star. *Ib.*

Eat with the rich, but go to the play with the poor, who are capable of joy.
Ib.

A best seller is the gilded tomb of a mediocre talent. *Ib.*

What I like in a good author is not what he says, but what he whispers.
Ib.

People say that life is the thing, but I prefer reading. *Ib.*

a meaning; at least, for me, there is one thing that matters — to set a chime of words tinkling in the minds of a few fastidious people."
— CYRIL CONNOLLY [b. 1903], *A Tribute to Logan Pearsall Smith*, in *The New Statesman*

Thank heavens, the sun has gone in, and I don't have to go out and enjoy it. *Afterthoughts*

ARTHUR SYMONS
1865–1945

Twitched strings, the clang of metal, beaten drums,
Dull, shrill, continuous, disquieting;
And now the stealthy dancer comes
Undulantly with catlike steps that cling. *Javanese Dancers* [1889]

And I would have, now love is over,
An end to all, an end:
I cannot, having been your lover,
Stoop to become your friend!
After Love [1892], *st. 3*

Life is a dream in the night, a fear among fears,
A naked runner lost in a storm of spears.
In the Wood of Finvara [1896], *st. 1*

My life is like a music hall.
Prologue [1895]

The gray-green stretch of sandy grass,
Indefinitely desolate;
A sea of lead, a sky of slate;
Already autumn in the air, alas!

One stark monotony of stone,
The long hotel, acutely white,
Against the after-sunset light
Withers gray-green, and takes the grass's tone.
Color Studies [1895]. *At Dieppe*

My soul is like this cloudy, flaming opal ring. *Opals* [1896]

I broider the world upon a loom,
I broider with dreams my tapestry;
Here in a little lonely room
I am master of earth and sea,
And the planets come to me.
The Loom of Dreams [1900], *st. 1*

He knew that the whole mystery of beauty can never be comprehended by the crowd, and that while clearness is a virtue of style, perfect explicitness is not a necessary virtue.

> *The Symbolist Movement in Literature* [1899]. *Gérard de Nerval*

Without charm there can be no fine literature, as there can be no perfect flower without fragrance.

> *Ib. Stéphane Mallarmé*

The mystic too full of God to speak intelligibly to the world.

> *Ib. Arthur Rimbaud*

Many excellent writers, very many painters, and most musicians are so tedious on any subject but their own.

> *Ib.*

Criticism is properly the rod of divination: a hazel switch for the discovery of buried treasure, not a birch twig for the castigation of offenders.

> *An Introduction to the Study of Browning* [1906], *preface*

The great things in poetry are song at the core, but externally mere speech.

> *Dramatis Personae* [1923]. *Sir William Watson*

HERBERT TRENCH
1865–1923

A circumnavigator of the soul.

> *Shakespeare, st. 4*

WILLIAM BUTLER YEATS[1]
1865–1939

Down by the salley gardens my love and
    I did meet;
She passed the salley gardens with little
    snow-white feet.
She bid me take love easy, as the leaves
    grow on the tree;

---

[1] Yeats was the greatest poet of our times . . . certainly the greatest in this language, and so far as I am able to judge, in any language. — T. S. ELIOT

See W. H. Auden, p. 1060a.

But I, being young and foolish, with
    her would not agree.

> *Down by the Salley Gardens* [1889]

She bid me take life easy, as the grass
    grows on the weirs;
But I was young and foolish, and now
    am full of tears.   *Ib.*

The years like great black oxen tread
    the world
And God, the herdsman, goads them
    on behind.

> *The Countess Cathleen* [1892]

Red Rose, proud Rose, sad Rose of all
    my days!
Come near me, while I sing the ancient
    ways.

> *To the Rose Upon the Rood of Time* [1893], *st. 1*

When you are old and gray and full of
    sleep,
And nodding by the fire, take down this
    book.[1]

> *When You Are Old* [1893]

How many loved your moments of glad
    grace,
And loved your beauty, with love false
    or true,
But one man loved the pilgrim soul in
    you,
And loved the sorrows of your changing
    face.   *Ib.*

I will arise and go now, and go to Innis-
    free,
And a small cabin build there, of clay
    and wattles made:
Nine bean-rows will I have there, a hive
    for the honeybee,
And live alone in the bee-loud glade.

And I shall have some peace there, for
    peace comes dropping slow,
Dropping from the veils of the morning
    to where the cricket sings;
There midnight's all a glimmer, and
    noon a purple glow,
And evening full of the linnet's wings.

> *The Lake Isle of Innisfree* [2] [1893], *st. 1, 2*

---

[1] See Ronsard, p. 187b.

[2] I had still the ambition, formed in Sligo in my teens, of living in imitation of Thoreau on

I hear it in the deep heart's core.
The Lake Isle of Innisfree, st. 3

A pity beyond all telling
Is hid in the heart of love.
The Pity of Love [1893]

The brawling of a sparrow in the eaves,
The brilliant moon and all the milky sky,
And all that famous harmony of leaves,
Had blotted out man's image and his cry.
The Sorrow of Love [1893],
st. 1

The land of faery,
Where nobody gets old and godly and grave,
Where nobody gets old and crafty and wise,
Where nobody gets old and bitter of tongue.
The Land of Heart's Desire 1
[1894]

Land of Heart's Desire,
Where beauty has no ebb, decay no flood,
But joy is wisdom, time an endless song.   *Ib.*

And God stands winding His lonely horn,
And time and the world are ever in flight.
Into the Twilight [1899]

And pluck till time and times are done
The silver apples of the moon,
The golden apples of the sun.
The Song of Wandering Aengus
[1899], *st. 3*

All things uncomely and broken, all things worn out and old,
The cry of a child by the roadway, the creak of a lumbering cart,
The heavy steps of the plowman, splashing the wintry mold,
Are wronging your image that blossoms a rose in the deeps of my heart.
The Lover Tells of the Rose in
His Heart [1899], *st. 1*

Had I the heavens' embroidered cloths,
Enwrought with gold and silver light.
He Wishes for the Cloths of
Heaven [1899]

But I, being poor, have only my dreams;
I have spread my dreams under your feet;
Tread softly because you tread on my dreams.   *Ib.*

When I play on my fiddle in Dooney,
Folk dance like a wave of the sea.
The Fiddler of Dooney [1899],
st. 1

O heart! O heart! if she'd but turn her head,
You'd know the folly of being comforted.
The Folly of Being Comforted
[1904]

Never give all the heart, for love
Will hardly seem worth thinking of
To passionate women if it seem
Certain, and they never dream
That it fades out from kiss to kiss;
For everything that's lovely is
But a brief, dreamy kind of delight.
Never Give All the Heart [1904]

Better go down upon your marrow-bones
And scrub a kitchen pavement, or break stones
Like an old pauper, in all kinds of weather;
For to articulate sweet sounds together
Is to work harder than all these, and yet
Be thought an idler by the noisy set

Innisfree, a little island in Lough Gill, and when walking through Fleet Street very homesick I heard a little tinkle of water and saw a fountain in a shop window which balanced a little ball upon its jet, and began to remember lake water. From the sudden remembrance came my poem Innisfree. — *The Trembling of the Veil* [1926]

See Samuel Rogers, p. 500b.

1 Excluded by Yeats from his *Collected Poems* [*1933*]

Of bankers, schoolmasters, and clergy-
men
The martyrs call the world.
Adam's Curse [1904], *st. 2*

It's certain there is no fine thing
Since Adam's fall but needs much laboring. *Ib. st. 4*

I heard the old, old men say,
"All that's beautiful drifts away
Like the waters."
*The Old Men Admiring Them-
selves in the Water* [1904]

Why, what could she have done, being
what she is?
Was there another Troy for her to
burn? *No Second Troy* [1910]

The fascination of what's difficult
Has dried the sap out of my veins, and
rent
Spontaneous joy and natural content
Out of my heart.
*The Fascination of What's
Difficult* [1910]

Wine comes in at the mouth
And love comes in at the eye;
That's all we shall know for truth
Before we grow old and die.
A Drinking Song [1910]

Though leaves are many, the root is
one;
Through all the lying days of my youth
I swayed my leaves and flowers in the
sun;
Now I may wither into the truth.
*The Coming of Wisdom with
Time* [1910]

In dreams begins responsibility.[1]
*Old Play. Epigraph, Responsi-
bilities* [1914]

Was it for this the wild geese spread
The gray wing upon every tide;
For this that all that blood was shed,
For this Edward Fitzgerald died,
And Robert Emmet and Wolfe Tone,
All that delirium of the brave?

[1] In Dreams Begin Responsibilities. — DEL-
MORE SCHWARTZ, *title of book of poems* [1938]

Romantic Ireland's dead and gone,
It's with O'Leary in the grave.
September 1913 [1914]

Be secret and exult,
Because of all things known
That is most difficult.
*To a Friend Whose Work Has
Come to Nothing* [1914]

I made my song a coat
Covered with embroideries
Out of old mythologies
From heel to throat;
But the fools caught it,
Wore it in the world's eyes
As though they'd wrought it.
Song, let them take it,
For there's more enterprise
In walking naked. *A Coat* [1914]

I know that I shall meet my fate
Somewhere among the clouds above;
Those that I fight I do not hate,
Those that I guard I do not love;
My country is Kiltartan Cross,
My countrymen Kiltartan's poor.
*An Irish Airman Foresees His
Death* [1919]

Nor law, nor duty bade me fight,
Nor public men, nor cheering crowds,
A lonely impulse of delight
Drove to this tumult in the clouds.
Ib.

And I may dine at journey's end
With Landor and with Donne.
To a Young Beauty [1919],
st. 3

Lord, what would they say
Did their Catullus walk that way?
The Scholars [1919], *st. 2*

All the wild witches, those most noble
ladies,
For all their broomsticks and their
tears,
Their angry tears, are gone.
Lines Written in Dejection [1919]

I knew a phoenix in my youth, so let
them have their day.
His Phoenix [1919]

Bring the balloon of the mind
That bellies and drags in the wind
Into its narrow shed.
The Balloon of the Mind [1919]

We have lit upon the gentle, sensitive
mind
And lost the old nonchalance of the
hand;
Whether we have chosen chisel, pen or
brush,
We are but critics, or but half create.
Ego Dominus Tuus [1919]

All changed, changed utterly:
A terrible beauty is born.
Easter 1916 [1921]

Nothing that we love overmuch
Is ponderable to our touch.
Towards Break of Day [1921],
st. 3

Turning and turning in the widening
gyre
The falcon cannot hear the falconer;
Things fall apart; the center cannot
hold;
Mere anarchy is loosed upon the
world,
The blood-dimmed tide is loosed, and
everywhere
The ceremony of innocence is
drowned;
The best lack all conviction, while the
worst
Are full of passionate intensity.
The Second Coming [1921],
st. 1

And what rough beast, its hour come
round at last,
Slouches towards Bethlehem to be
born? *Ib. st. 2*

Imagining in excited reverie
That the future years had come,
Dancing to a frenzied drum,
Out of the murderous innocence of the
sea.
A Prayer for My Daughter
[1921], st. 2

For such,
Being made beautiful overmuch,
Consider beauty a sufficient end,

Lose natural kindness and maybe
The heart-revealing intimacy
That chooses right, and never find a
friend.
A Prayer for My Daughter,
st. 3

It's certain that fine women eat
A crazy salad with their meat.
Ib. st. 4

In courtesy I'd have her chiefly learned;
Hearts are not had as a gift but hearts
are earned. *Ib. st. 5*

And many a poor man that has roved,
Loved and thought himself beloved,
From a glad kindness cannot take his
eyes. *Ib.*

If there's no hatred in a mind
Assault and battery of the wind
Can never tear the linnet from the
leaf. *Ib. st. 7*

An intellectual hatred is the worst,
So let her think opinions are accursed.
Have I not seen the loveliest woman
born
Out of the mouth of Plenty's horn,
Because of her opinionated mind
Barter that horn and every good
By quiet natures understood
For an old bellows full of angry wind?
Ib. st. 8

That is no country for old men. The
young
In one another's arms, birds in the
trees
— Those dying generations — at their
song,
The salmon-falls, the mackerel-crowded
seas,
Fish, flesh, or fowl, commend all sum-
mer long
Whatever is begotten, born, and dies.
Caught in that sensual music all neg-
lect
Monuments of unaging intellect.
Sailing to Byzantium [1928], st. 1

An aged man is but a paltry thing,
A tattered coat upon a stick, unless
Soul clap its hands and sing, and louder
sing
For every tatter in its mortal dress.
Ib. st. 2

Consume my heart away; sick with de-
sire
And fastened to a dying animal
It knows not what it is; and gather
me
Into the artifice of eternity.
Sailing to Byzantium, st. 3

Once out of nature I shall never take
My bodily form from any natural thing,
But such a form as Grecian goldsmiths
make
Of hammered gold and gold enameling
To keep a drowsy Emperor awake;
Or set upon a golden bough to sing
To lords and ladies of Byzantium
Of what is past, or passing, or to
come.[1] *Ib. st. 4*

What shall I do with this absurdity —
O heart, O troubled heart — this cari-
cature,
Decrepit age that has been tied to
me
As to a dog's tail?
Never had I more
Excited, passionate, fantastical
Imagination, nor an ear and eye
That more expected the impossible.
The Tower [1928], I

Does the imagination dwell the most
Upon a woman won or a woman lost?
Ib. II, st. 13

Come let us mock at the great
That had such burdens on the mind
And toiled so hard and late
To leave some monument behind,
Nor thought of the leveling wind.
*Nineteen Hundred and Nine-
teen* [1928], V

Mock mockers after that
That would not lift a hand maybe
To help good, wise or great
To bar that foul storm out, for we
Traffic in mockery. *Ib.*

Much did I rage when young,
Being by the world oppressed,
But now with flattering tongue
It speeds the parting guest.
Youth and Age [1928]

[1] I have read somewhere that in the Emperor's
palace at Byzantium was a tree made of gold and
silver, and artificial birds that sang. — YEATS's
note

Everything that man esteems
Endures a moment or a day.
Love's pleasure drives his love away,
The painter's brush consumes his
dreams.
Two Songs from a Play [1928],
II, *st. 2*

Whatever flames upon the night
Man's own resinous heart has fed.
Ib.

A shudder in the loins engenders
there
The broken wall, the burning roof and
tower
And Agamemnon dead.
Leda and the Swan [1928]

O chestnut tree, great rooted blos-
somer,
Are you the leaf, the blossom or the
bole?
O body swayed to music, O brightening glance,
How can we know the dancer from the
dance?
Among School Children [1928],
st. 8

Never to have lived is best, ancient
writers say;
Never to have drawn the breath of life,
never to have looked into the eye
of day
The second best's a gay goodnight and
quickly turn away.[1]
From "Oedipus at Colonus,"
st. 3

The innocent and the beautiful
Have no enemy but time.
*In Memory of Eva Gore-booth
and Con Markiewicz* [1933]

My Self: A living man is blind and
drinks his drop.
What matter if the ditches are impure?
What matter if I live it all once more?
Endure that toil of growing up;
The ignominy of boyhood; the distress
Of boyhood changing into man;
The unfinished man and his pain

[1] See Theognis, p. 77a, and note.

Brought face to face with his own clumsiness.
A Dialogue of Self and Soul
[1933], *II, st. 1*

I am content to live it all again
And yet again, if it be life to pitch
Into the frog-spawn of a blind man's
ditch. *Ib. st. 3*

When such as I cast out remorse
So great a sweetness flows into the
breast
We must laugh and we must sing,
We are blest by everything,
Everything we look upon is blest.
Ib. st. 4

But what is Whiggery?
A leveling, rancorous, rational sort of
mind
That never looked out of the eye of a
saint
Or out of a drunkard's eye.
The Seven Sages [1933]

No man has ever lived that had enough
Of children's gratitude or woman's
love. *Vacillation* [1933], *st. 3*

Swift has sailed into his rest;
Savage indignation there
Cannot lacerate his breast,
Imitate him if you dare,
World-besotted traveler; he
Served human liberty.
Swift's Epitaph [1] [1933]

The intellect of man is forced to
choose
Perfection of the life, or of the work,
And if it take the second must refuse
A heavenly mansion, raging in the
dark. *The Choice* [1933], *st. 1*

But Love has pitched his mansion in
The place of excrement.
*Crazy Jane Talks with the
Bishop* [1933], *st. 3*

What were all the world's alarms
To mighty Paris when he found
Sleep upon a golden bed
That first dawn in Helen's arms?
Words for Music Perhaps
[1933]. *Lullaby, st. 1*

[1] See Swift, p. 391a, and note.

Speech after long silence; it is right,
All other lovers being estranged or
dead . . .
That we descant and yet again descant
Upon the supreme theme of Art and
Song:
Bodily decrepitude is wisdom; young
We loved each other and were ig-
norant.
*Words for Music Perhaps.
After Long Silence*

I carry the sun in a golden cup,
The moon in a silver bag.
*Ib. Those Dancing Days Are
Gone, refrain*

I gave what other women gave
That stepped out of their clothes,
But when this soul, its body off,
Naked to naked goes,
He it has found shall find therein
What none other knows.
A Woman Young and Old
[1933]. *A Last Confession,
st. 3*

He that sings a lasting song
Thinks in a marrowbone.
A Prayer for Old Age [1935], *st. 1*

I pray — for fashion's word is out
And prayer comes round again —
That I may seem, though I die old,
A foolish, passionate man. *Ib. st. 3*

All perform their tragic play,
There struts Hamlet, there is Lear.
Lapis Lazuli [1936–1939]

Heaven blazing into the head:
Tragedy wrought to its uttermost.
Though Hamlet rambles and Lear
rages,
And all the drop-scenes drop at once
Upon a hundred thousand stages,
It cannot grow by an inch or an ounce.
Ib.

If soul may look and body touch,
Which is the more blest?
The Lady's Second Song [1936–
1939], *st. 3*

My temptation is quiet.
Here at life's end
Neither loose imagination,

Nor the mill of the mind
Consuming its rat and bone,
Can make the truth known.
        An Acre of Grass [1936–1939],
                                st. 2

Grant me an old man's frenzy,
Myself must I remake
Till I am Timon and Lear
Or that William Blake
Who beat upon the wall
Till Truth obeyed his call.   *Ib. st. 3*

Hurrah for revolution and more can-
        non-shot!
A beggar upon horseback lashes a beg-
        gar on foot.
                The Great Day [1936–
                        1939], *l. 1*

You think it horrible that lust and
        rage
Should dance attention upon my old
        age;
They were not such a plague when I
        was young;
What else have I to spur me into
        song?   *The Spur* [1936–1939]

Down the mountain walls
From where Pan's cavern is
Intolerable music falls.
Foul goat-head, brutal arm appear,
Belly, shoulder, bum,
Flash fishlike; nymphs and satyrs
Copulate in the foam.
        News for the Delphic Oracle
                [1936–1939], *st. 3*

What shall I do for pretty girls
Now my old bawd is dead?
        *John Kinsella's Lament for
        Mrs. Mary Moore* [1936–
        1939], *refrain*

Irish poets, learn your trade,
Sing whatever is well made.
        Under Ben Bulben [1936–
                        1939], *V*

Under bare Ben Bulben's head
In Drumcliff churchyard Yeats is laid.
                        Ib. VI

On limestone quarried near the spot
By his command these words are cut:

Cast a cold eye
On life, on death.
Horseman, pass by! [1]
        Under Ben Bulben, V

The friends that have it I do wrong
When ever I remake a song
Should know what issue is at stake,
It is myself that I remake.
        *Variorum Edition of the Poems
                of W. B. Yeats*

I am still of opinion that only two
topics can be of the least interest to a
serious and studious mood — sex and
the dead.
        The Letters of W. B. Yeats

If a poet interprets a poem of his
own he limits its suggestibility.   *Ib.*

We poets would die of loneliness but
for women, and we choose our men
friends that we may have somebody to
talk about women with.
        Ib. Letter to Olivia Shakespeare
                                [1936]

In life courtesy and self-possession,
and in the arts style, are the sensible
impressions of the free mind, for both
arise out of a deliberate shaping of all
things and from never being swept
away, whatever the emotion, into confusion or dullness.
        Essays and Introductions
        [1961]. *Poetry and The
        Tradition*

HARRY DACRE
fl. 1892

Daisy, Daisy, give me your answer, do!
I'm half crazy, all for the love of you!
    It won't be a stylish marriage,
    I can't afford a carriage,
But you'll look sweet upon the seat
Of a bicycle built for two!
                Daisy Bell [1892]

[1] The last three lines are inscribed on Yeats's
grave.

HENRY J. SAYERS
d. 1932

Ta-ra-ra-boom-de-ay!
> *Title of minstrel show number
> [1891], made famous by Lottie
> Collins in 1892*

GEORGE W. YOUNG
fl. 1900

The lips that touch liquor must never
touch mine!
> *The Lips That Touch Liquor,
> st. 5*

GEORGE ADE[1]
1866–1944

A good folly is worth what you pay
for it.
> *Fables in Slang [1899]. A Lot
> for Three Dollars*

In uplifting, get underneath.
> *Ib. The Good Fairy*

He had been kicked in the head by a
mule when young and believed everything he read in the Sunday papers.
> *Ib. The Slim Girl*

Only the more rugged mortals should
attempt to keep up with current literature.
> *Ib. Didn't Care for Storybooks*

Never put off until tomorrow what
should have been done early in the Seventies.
> *Forty Modern Fables [1901].
> The Third and Last Call*

To insure peace of mind ignore the
rules and regulations.
> *Ib. The Crustacean*

If it were not for the presents, an
elopement would be preferable.
> *Ib. The General Manager of the
> Love Affair*

[1] Somehow I always like to think
Of *Georgeade* as a summer drink,
Sparkling and cool, with just a tang
Of pleasant effervescent slang.
OLIVER HERFORD [1863–1935], *Celebrities
I Have Never Met*

Stay with the procession or you will
never catch up.
> *Forty Modern Fables. The
> Old-Time Pedagogue*

The time to enjoy a European trip is
about three weeks after unpacking.
> *Ib. The Hungry Man*

Draw your salary before spending it.
> *Ib. The People's Choice*

The man was a pinhead in a good
many respects, but he was wise as a
serpent. > *Ib. The Wise Piker*

For parlor use the vague generality is
a life-saver. > *Ib.*

Last night at twelve I felt immense,
But now I feel like thirty cents.
> *The Sultan of Sulu [1902].
> Remorse*

But, R – e – m – o – r – s – e!
The water-wagon is the place for me;
It is no time for mirth and laughter,
The cold, gray dawn of the morning
after! [1] > *Ib.*

TRISTAN BERNARD
1866–1947

Men are always sincere. They change
sincerities, that's all.
> *Ce que l'on dit aux femmes*

To live happily with other people one
should only ask of them what they can
give. > *L'Enfant prodigue du Vesinet*

HENRY BLOSSOM
1866–1919

I Want What I Want When I
Want It.
> *Mademoiselle Modiste [1905].
> Title of song*

GELETT BURGESS
1866–1951

I never saw a purple cow,
  I never hope to see one;

[1] See Byron, p. 560b, and Dickens, p. 670a.

886

But I can tell you, anyhow,
  I'd rather see than be one.
                    The Purple Cow [1895]

Ah, yes, I wrote the "Purple Cow" —
  I'm sorry, now, I wrote it!
But I can tell you, anyhow,
  I'll kill you if you quote it.
                    Cinq Ans Après

EDMUND VANCE COOKE
1866–1932

The woman tempted me — and tempts
    me still!
Lord God, I pray You that she ever will!
                    Adam

And it isn't the fact that you're hurt
    that counts,
But only how did you take it.
                    How Did You Die? st. 1

PHILANDER JOHNSON
1866–1939

The world would sleep if things were
    run
By men who say, "It can't be done!"
                    It Can't Be Done

Cheer up, the worst is yet to come.[1]
                    Shooting Stars

RICHARD LE GALLIENNE
1866–1947

The cry of the Little Peoples goes up to
    God in vain,
For the world is given over to the cruel
    sons of Cain.
                    The Cry of the Little Peoples

WALTER MALONE
1866–1915

And if a lowly singer dries one tear,
Or soothes one humble human heart in
    pain,
Be sure his homely verse to God is
    dear,
And not one stanza has been sung in
    vain.
                    The Humbler Poets, st. 3

[1] See Tennyson, p. 654a.

THOMAS L. MASSON
1866–1934

Obey That Impulse.
                    Subscription slogan, Life

A Safe and Sane Fourth.   *Slogan*

GEORGE BARR McCUTCHEON
1866–1928

"You brute!" hissed the Countess.
                    Graustark [1901], *ch. 16*

BEATRIX POTTER
1866–1943

Once upon a time there were four
little Rabbits, and their names were
— Flopsy, Mopsy, Cottontail, and Peter.
  They lived with their Mother in a
sandbank underneath the root of a very
big fir tree.
                    The Tale of Peter Rabbit

But don't go into Mr. McGregor's
garden.   *Ib.*

The water was all slippy-sloppy in the
larder and the back passage. But Mr.
Jeremy liked getting his feet wet; nobody ever scolded him, and he never
caught a cold.
                    The Tale of Mr. Jeremy Fisher

No more twist!
                    The Tailor of Gloucester

LINCOLN STEFFENS
1866–1936

"So you've been over into Russia?"
said Bernard Baruch, and I answered
very literally, "I have been over into the
future, and it works." [1]
                    Autobiography [1931], *ch. 18*

BERT LESTON TAYLOR
1866–1921

When men are calling names and mak-
    ing faces,

[1] On Steffens's return from the Bullitt mission, 1919.

And all the world's ajangle and ajar,
I meditate on interstellar spaces
And smoke a mild seegar.
Canopus

A bore is a man who, when you ask
him how he is, tells you.
The So-Called Human Race [1922]

HERBERT GEORGE
WELLS
1866–1946

The Time Machine.
Title of book [1895]

The past is but the beginning of a
beginning, and all that is and has been
is but the twilight of the dawn.
The Discovery of the Future
[1901]

Nothing could have been more obvious to the people of the early twentieth
century than the rapidity with which
war was becoming impossible. And as
certainly they did not see it. They did
not see it until the atomic bombs burst
in their fumbling hands.
The World Set Free [1914]

The catastrophe of the atomic bombs
which shook men out of cities and businesses and economic relations, shook
them also out of their old-established
habits of thought, and out of the
lightly held beliefs and prejudices that
came down to them from the past.
Ib.

The War That Will End War.
Title of book [1914]

The professional military mind is by
necessity an inferior and unimaginative
mind; no man of high intellectual quality would willingly imprison his gifts in
such a calling.
The Outline of History [1920],
ch. 40

The Great War and the Petty
Peace. *Ib.*

Human history is in essence a history
of ideas.
The Outline of History, ch. 40

Every one of these hundreds of millions of human beings is in some form
seeking happiness. . . . Not one is altogether noble nor altogether trustworthy nor altogether consistent; and
not one is altogether vile. . . . Not a
single one but has at some time wept.
Ib.

Our true nationality is mankind.
Ib. ch. 41

Human history becomes more and
more a race between education and
catastrophe. *Ib.*

Life begins perpetually. Gathered together at last under the leadership of
man . . . unified, disciplined, armed
with the secret powers of the atom and
with knowledge as yet beyond dreaming, Life, forever dying to be born
afresh, forever young and eager, will
presently stand upon this earth as upon
a footstool, and stretch out its realm
amidst the stars.[1] *Ib.*

An artist who theorizes about his
work is no longer artist but critic.
The Temptation of Harringay

In England we have come to rely
upon a comfortable time lag of fifty
years or a century intervening between
the perception that something ought to
be done and a serious attempt to do
it.
*The Work, Wealth and Happi-
ness of Mankind* [1931], *ch.* 11

The Shape of Things to Come.[2]
Title of book [1933]

SUN YAT-SEN[3]
1866–1925

It is only after mature deliberation
and thorough preparation that I have

[1] See *Matthew 5:34–35,* p. 40b; Pope, p. 408a
and Clarence Day, p. 925b.
[2] See Cicero, p. 111a; Shakespeare, *Troilus and
Cressida I, iii, 334,* p. 268a; and Campbell, p.
538a, and note.
[3] From *Sources of Chinese Tradition,* edited by
William Theodore de Bary [1960].

decided upon the Program of Revolution and defined the procedure of the revolution in three stages. The first is the period of military government; the second, the period of political tutelage; and the third, the period of constitutional government.

> *The Three Phases of National Reconstruction* [1918]

The Chinese people have only family and clan solidarity; they do not have national spirit . . . they are just a heap of loose sand. . . . Other men are the carving knife and serving dish; we are the fish and the meat.

> *China As a Heap of Loose Sand* [1924]

China is now suffering from poverty, not from unequal distribution of wealth. Where there are inequalities of wealth, the methods of Marx can, of course, be used; a class war can be advocated to destroy the inequalities. But in China, where industry is not yet developed, Marx's class war and dictatorship of the proletariat are impracticable.   *Capital and the State* [1924]

In the construction of a country it is not the practical workers but the idealists and planners that are difficult to find.

> *Chung-shan Ch'üan-shu, vol. II*

STANLEY BALDWIN
1867–1947

When you think about the defense of England you no longer think of the chalk cliffs of Dover. You think of the Rhine. That is where our frontier lies today.

> *Speech in the House of Commons* [July 30, 1934]

ENOCH ARNOLD
BENNETT
1867–1931

The Old Wives' Tale.[1]

> *Title of novel* [1908]

[1] But refuse profane and old wives' fables, and exercise rather unto godliness. — *I Timothy* 4:7

Being a husband is a whole-time job.   *The Title* [1918], *act I*

Pessimism, when you get used to it, is just as agreeable as optimism.

> *Things That Have Interested Me* [1918]

The price of justice is eternal publicity.   *Ib. Second Series* [1923]

VICENTE
BLASCO-IBÁÑEZ
1867–1928

It was the roar of the real, the only beast [the crowd in the arena].

> *Blood and Sand* [1908]

WILLIAM CECIL
DAMPIER-WHETHAM
1867–1952

Beyond the bright searchlights of science,
Out of sight of the windows of sense,
Old riddles still bid us defiance,
Old questions of Why and of Whence.

> *The Recent Development of Physical Science* [1904]

ERNEST DOWSON
1867–1900

They saw the glory of the world displayed;
They saw the bitter of it, and the sweet;
They knew the roses of the world should fade,
And be trod under by the hurrying feet.

> *Nuns of the Perpetual Adoration* [1891], *st. 5*

Last night, ah, yesternight, betwixt her lips and mine
There fell thy shadow,[1] Cynara! thy breath was shed

A fool he is to believe the tales of an old wife. — ALEXANDER BARCLAY, *The Ship of Fools* [1508]
Old wives' foolish tales of Robin Hood. — NICHOLAS UDALL [1542]
[1] See T. S. Eliot, p. 1003a.

Upon my soul between the kisses and
   the wine;
And I was desolate and sick of an old
   passion,
Yea, I was desolate and bowed my
   head:
I have been faithful to thee, Cynara! in
   my fashion.
> *Non Sum Qualis Eram Bonae
> Sub Regno Cynarae* [1] [1896],
> st. 1

I have forgot much, Cynara! gone with
   the wind,[2]
Flung roses, roses riotously with the
   throng.   *Ib. st. 3*

I cried for madder music and for
   stronger wine,
But when the feast is finished and the
   lamps expire,
Then falls thy shadow, Cynara! the
   night is thine.   *Ib. st. 4*

They are not long, the weeping and the
   laughter,
Love and desire and hate:
I think they have no portion in us
   after
We pass the gate.

They are not long, the days of wine and
   roses;
Out of a misty dream
Our path emerges for a while, then
   closes
Within a dream.
> *Vitae Summa Brevis Spem Nos
> Vetat Incohare Longam* [3] [1896]

Because I am idolatrous and have be-
   sought,
With grievous supplication and consuming prayer,
The admirable image that my dreams
   have wrought
Out of her swan's neck and her dark,
   abundant hair:
The jealous gods, who brook no worship save their own,
Turned my live idol marble and her
   heart to stone.   *Epigram* [1896]

---

[1] See Horace, *Odes IV, i, 3,* p. 122b.
[2] See Rutebeuf, p. 158a.
[3] See Horace, p. 120b.

From troublous sights and sounds set
   free;
In such a twilight hour of breath,
Shall one retrace his life, or see,
Through shadows, the true face of
   death?
> *Extreme Unction* [1896], st. 3

MR. DOOLEY
[FINLEY PETER DUNNE]
1867–1936

Life'd not be worth livin' if we didn't
keep our inimies.
> *Mr. Dooley in Peace and in War*
> [1898]. *On New Year's Resolu-*
> *tions*

Th' dead ar-re always pop'lar. I
knowed a society wanst to vote a mony-
ment to a man an' refuse to help his
fam'ly, all in wan night.
> *Ib. On Charity*

"I think," said Mr. Dooley, "that if
th' Christyan Scientists had some science an' th' doctors more Christianity,
it wudden't make anny diff'rence which
ye called in — if ye had a good nurse."
> *Mr. Dooley's Opinions* [1900].
> *Christian Science*

No matther whether th' constitution
follows th' flag or not, th' supreme
coort follows th' iliction returns.
> *Ib. The Supreme Court's*
> *Decisions*

I think a lie with a purpose is wan iv
th' worst kind an' th' mos' profitable.
> *Ib. On Lying*

Th' dimmycratic party ain't on
speakin' terms with itsilf.
> *Ib. Mr. Dooley Discusses Party*
> *Politics*

Th' raypublican party broke ye, but
now that ye're down we'll not turn a
cold shoulder to ye. Come in an' we'll
keep ye — broke.   *Ib.*

Hogan's r-right whin he says: "Justice is blind." Blind she is, an' deef an'
dumb an' has a wooden leg.
> *Ib. Cross-Examinations*

No wan cares to hear what Hogan calls "Th' short an' simple scandals iv th' poor."

Mr. Dooley's Opinions. Cross-Examinations

'Twas founded be th' Puritans to give thanks f'r bein' presarved fr'm th' Indyans, an' . . . we keep it to give thanks we are presarved fr'm th' Puritans. *Ib. Thanksgiving*

Vice . . . is a creature of such heejous mien . . . that th' more ye see it th' betther ye like it.

Ib. The Crusade Against Vice

Glory be, whin business gets above sellin' tinpinny nails in a brown paper cornucopy, 't is hard to tell it fr'm murther. *Ib. On Wall Street*

"D' ye think th' colledges has much to do with th' progress iv th' wurruld?" asked Mr. Hennessy.

"D' ye think," said Mr. Dooley, " 'tis th' mill that makes th' wather run?" *Ib.*

" 'Twill civilize th' Chinnymen," said Mr. Hennessy.

" 'Twill civilize thim stiff," said Mr. Dooley.

Ib. The Future of China (on German intervention in China)

If ye live enough befure thirty ye won't care to live at all afther fifty.

Ib. Casual Observations

Among men, Hinnissy, wet eye manes dhry heart. *Ib.*

A fanatic is a man that does what he thinks th' Lord wud do if He knew th' facts iv th' case. *Ib.*

A vote on th' tallysheet is worth two in the box. *Ib.*

'Tis as hard f'r a rich man to enther th' kingdom iv Hiven as it is f'r a poor man to get out iv Purgatory. *Ib.*

Thrust ivrybody, but cut th' ca-ards. *Ib.*

A man that'd expict to thrain lobsters to fly in a year is called a loonytic; but a man that thinks men can be tu-rrned into angels be an iliction is called a rayformer an' remains at large.

Mr. Dooley's Opinions. Casual Observations

Miracles are laughed at be a nation that r-reads thirty millyon newspapers a day an' supports Wall sthreet. *Ib.*

Th' flag [1] floats free an' well guarded over th' govermint offices, an' th' cheery people go an' come on their errands — go out alone an' come back with th' throops. Iverywhere happiness, contint, love iv th' shtep-mother counthry, excipt in places where there ar-re people.

Observations by Mr. Dooley [1902]. The Philippine Peace

A reg'lar pollytician can't give away an alley without blushin', but a businessman who is in pollytics jus' to see that th' civil sarvice law gets thurly enfoorced, will give Lincoln Park an' th' public libr'y to th' beef thrust, charge an admission price to th' lake front an' make it a felony f'r annywan to buy stove polish outside iv his store, an' have it all put down to public improvemints with a pitcher iv him in th' cornerstone. *Ib.*

If a man is wise, he gets rich, an' if he gets rich, he gets foolish, or his wife does. That's what keeps the money movin' around. *Ib. Newport*

"Oh, well," said Mr. Hennessy, "we are as th' Lord made us."

"No," said Mr. Dooley, "lave us be fair. Lave us take some iv th' blame oursilves." *Ib.*

But th' best thing about a little judicyous swearin' is that it keeps th' temper. 'Twas intinded as a compromise between runnin' away an' fightin'. Befure it was invinted they was on'y th' two ways out iv an argymint.

Ib. Swearing

I don't think we injye other people's sufferin', Hinnissy. It isn't acshally injyement. But we feel betther f'r it.

Ib. Enjoyment

[1] The American flag in the Philippines.

"Ye know a lot about [raising children]," said Mr. Hennessy.

"I do," said Mr. Dooley. "Not bein' an author, I'm a gr-reat critic."

Dissertations by Mr. Dooley [1906]. The Bringing Up of Children

Th' old story iv th' ant an' th' grasshopper — th' ant that ye can step on an' th' grasshopper ye can't catch.

Ib. The Labor Troubles

"If ye had a boy wud ye sind him to colledge?" asked Mr. Hennessy.

"Well," said Mr. Dooley, "at th' age whin a boy is fit to be in colledge I wudden't have him around th' house."

Ib. The Intellectual Life

Th' prisidincy is th' highest office in th' gift iv th' people. Th' vice-prisidincy is th' next highest an' th' lowest. It isn't a crime exactly. Ye can't be sint to jail f'r it, but it's a kind iv a disgrace. It's like writin' anonymous letters.

Ib. The Vice-President

It is his jooty to rigorously enforce th' rules iv th' Sinit. There ar-re none. Th' Sinit is ruled be courtesy, like th' longshoreman's union.   *Ib.*

Slug-ye'er-spouse is an internaytional spoort that has niver become pop'lar on our side iv th' wather. An American lady is not th' person that anny man but a thrained athlete wud care to raise his hand again' save be way iv smoothin' her hair.

Ib. Corporal Punishment

Won't [public flogging] be fine? Th' govermint gives us too little amusemint nowadays. Th' fav'rite pastime iv civilized man is croolty to other civilized man.   *Ib.*

"Spare th' rod an' spile th' child," said Mr. Hennessy.

"Yes," said Mr. Dooley, "but don't spare th' rod an' ye spile th' rod, th' child, an' th' child's father."   *Ib.*

This home iv opporchunity where ivry man is th' equal iv ivry other man befure th' law if he isn't careful.

Dissertations by Mr. Dooley. The Food We Eat

"Ye ra-aly do think dhrink is a nicissry evil?" said Mr. Hennessy.

"Well," said Mr. Dooley, "if it's an evil to a man, it's not nicissry, an' if it's nicissry it's an evil."   *Ib. The Bar*

"He made [money]," said Mr. Dooley, "because he honestly loved it with an innocint affiction. He was thrue to it. Th' reason ye have no money is because ye don't love it f'r itsilf alone. Money won't iver surrinder to such a flirt."

Mr. Dooley on Making a Will and Other Evil Necessities [1919]. On Making a Will

JOHN GALSWORTHY
1867–1933

Justice is a machine that, when someone has once given it the starting push, rolls on of itself.

Justice [1910], act II

Public opinion's always in advance of the law.   *Windows [1922], act I*

The value of a sentiment is the amount of sacrifice you are prepared to make for it.   *Ib. II*

By the cigars they smoke, and the composers they love, ye shall know the texture of men's souls.

Indian Summer of a Forsyte [1920], ch. 1

He ordered himself a dozen oysters; but, suddenly remembering that the month contained no *r*, changed them to a fried sole.[1]

The White Monkey [1924], pt. III, ch. 7

---

[1] It is unseasonable and unwholesome in all months that have not an *r* in their name to eat an oyster. — WILLIAM BUTLER, *Dyet's Dry Dinner* [1599]

Let's sing a song of glory to Themistocles O'Shea,

If you do not think about the future, you cannot have one.
Swan Song [1928], *pt. II, ch. 6*

A man of action forced into a state of thought is unhappy until he can get out of it.
Maid in Waiting [1931], *ch. 3*

There's just one rule for politicians all over the world: Don't say in Power what you say in Opposition; if you do, you only have to carry out what the other fellows have found impossible.
Ib. 7

One's eyes are what one is, one's mouth what one becomes.
Flowering Wilderness [1932], *ch. 2*

The beginnings and endings of all human undertakings are untidy, the building of a house, the writing of a novel, the demolition of a bridge, and, eminently, the finish of a voyage.
Over the River [1933], *ch. 1*

How to save the old that's worth saving, whether in landscape, houses, manners, institutions, or human types, is one of our greatest problems, and the one that we bother least about.
Over the River, ch. 39

LIONEL JOHNSON
1867–1902

The saddest of all kings
Crown'd, and again discrown'd.
By the Statue of King Charles at Charing Cross, st. 2

Vanquished in life, his death
By beauty made amends.   *Ib. st. 8*

I know you: solitary griefs,
Desolate passions, aching hours!
The Precept of Silence, st. 1

Who ate a dozen oysters on the second day of May.
    Stoddard King [1889–1933], *The Man Who Dared*

CHARLES EDWARD MONTAGUE
1867–1928

I was born below par to th' extent of two whiskies.
Fiery Particles [1923]

"A.E." [GEORGE WILLIAM RUSSELL]
1867–1935

Our hearts were drunk with a beauty
Our eyes could never see.
The Unknown God

Twilight, a timid fawn, went glimmering by,
And Night, the dark-blue hunter, followed fast.   *Refuge*

HENRY LEWIS STIMSON
1867–1950

The only way to make a man trustworthy is to trust him; and the surest way to make him untrustworthy is to distrust him and show your distrust.
The Bomb and the Opportunity [*March 1946*]

The only deadly sin I know is cynicism.
On Active Service in Peace and War [1948], *introduction*

HARRY LEON WILSON
1867–1939

I can be pushed just so far.
Ruggles of Red Gap [1915]

ALAIN
[ÉMILE CHARTIER]
1868–1951

To think is to say *no.*
Le Citoyen contre les Pouvoirs

Nothing is more dangerous than an idea, when it's the only one we have.
Système des Beaux-Arts

PAUL CLAUDEL
1868–1955

You explain nothing, O poet, but thanks to you all things become explicable.   *La Ville* [1892]

The words I use
Are everyday words and yet are not the same!
You will find no rhymes in my verse, no magic.
There are your very own phrases.
     La Muse Qui Est la Grace [1910]

When man tries to imagine Paradise on earth, the immediate result is a very respectable Hell.
     Conversations dans le Loir-et-Cher [1929]

NORMAN DOUGLAS
1868–1952

You can tell the ideals of a nation by its advertisements.
     South Wind [1917], *ch.* 7

Men have lost sight of distant horizons. Nobody writes for humanity, for civilization; they write for their country, their sect; to amuse their friends or annoy their enemies.
     Ib. 8

No one can expect a majority to be stirred by motives other than ignoble.
     Ib. 10

No great man is ever born too soon or too late. When we say that the time is not ripe for this or that celebrity, we confess by implication that this very man, and no other, is required.
     Ib. 13

For three consecutive months they could barely afford the most unnecessary luxuries of life.   *Ib.* 20

Many a man who thinks to found a home discovers that he has merely opened a tavern for his friends.
     Ib. 24

WILLIAM EDWARD BURGHARDT DuBOIS
1868–1963

Herein lies the tragedy of the age: not that men are poor — all men know something of poverty; not that men are wicked — who is good? Not that men are ignorant — what is truth? Nay, but that men know so little of men.
     The Souls of Black Folk [1903]

It is a peculiar sensation, this double-consciousness, this sense of always looking at one's self through the eyes of others. . . . One feels his two-ness — an American, a Negro; two souls, two thoughts, two unreconciled strivings; two warring ideals in one dark body, whose dogged strength alone keeps it from being torn asunder.
     Ib.

MAXIM GORKI [1]
[ALEKSEI MAKSIMOVICH PESHKOV]
1868–1936

The brave man's folly — that is life's wisdom.
     The Song of the Falcon [1895]

Former people [Creatures that once were men].   *Title of story* [1897]

Let the storm rage ever stronger! [2]
     Song of a Stormy Petrel [1901]

Lies — there you have the religion of slaves and taskmasters.[3]
     The Lower Depths [1903]

How marvelous is Man! How proud the word rings — Man!   *Ib.*

The proletarian state must bring up thousands of excellent "mechanics of culture," "engineers of the soul." [4]
     Speech at the Writers' Congress [1934]

[1] Gorki, "the bitter one," was the writer's pseudonym for his first sketch in a Tiflis newspaper [1892].
[2] This became a rallying cry of the revolutionaries.
[3] The censor forbade this line to be spoken on the stage.
[4] Attributed to Stalin in conversation with Gorki [October 26, 1934]. See Stalin, p. 954b.

Life, as asserted by socialist realism, is deeds, creativeness, the aim of which is the uninterrupted development of the priceless individual qualities of man.
Speech at the Writers' Congress

The basic hero of our books should be labor; that is, man organized by the processes of labor. **Ib.**

ABE MARTIN
[FRANK McKINNEY
"KIN" HUBBARD]
1868–1930

Miss Fawn Lippincut says she wouldn' marry th' best man on earth, but we supposed she wuz much younger.
Abe Martin's Sayings and Sketches [1915]

It's no disgrace t' be poor, but it might as well be. **Ib.**

He was a power politically fer years, but he never got prominent enough t' have his speeches garbled. **Ib.**

When a fellow says it hain't the money but the principle o' the thing, it's th' money.
Hoss Sense and Nonsense [1926]

Nobuddy ever fergits where he buried a hatchet.
Abe Martin's Broadcast [1930]

If capital an' labor ever do git t'gether it's good night fer th' rest of us. *Saying*

Knowin' all about baseball is just about as profitable as bein' a good whittler. **Ib.**

Now and then an innocent man is sent to the legislature. **Ib.**

EDWARD VERRALL
LUCAS
1868–1938

The French never allow a distinguished son of France to lack a statue.
Wanderings and Diversions [1926]. *Zigzags in France*

Americans are people who prefer the Continent to their own country, but refuse to learn its languages.
Wanderings and Diversions. The Continental Dictionary

Ticket collector — the man who never wants to see your ticket unless you are asleep. **Ib.**

People in hotels strike no roots. The French phrase for chronic hotel guests even says so: they are called dwellers *sur la branche.* **Ib. To Be Let or Sold**

There can be no defense like elaborate courtesy.
Reading, Writing and Remembering [1932]

WILLIAM TYLER PAGE
1868–1942

I believe in the United States of America as a Government of the people, by the people, for the people; whose just powers are derived from the consent of the governed; a democracy in a republic, a sovereign Nation of many sovereign States; a perfect Union one and inseparable; established upon those principles of freedom, equality, justice and humanity for which American patriots sacrificed their lives and fortunes. I therefore believe it is my duty to my country to love it, to support its Constitution, to obey its laws, to respect its flag, and to defend it against all enemies.
The American's Creed [1]

EDMOND ROSTAND
1868–1918

A great nose indicates a great man —
Genial, courteous, intellectual,
Virile, courageous.
Cyrano de Bergerac [2] [1897], *act I*

Free fighters, free lovers, free spenders —

[1] Adopted by the House of Representatives [April 3, 1918].
[2] Translated by BRIAN HOOKER.

The Cadets of Gascoyne — the defenders
Of old homes, old names, and old splendors.
Cyrano de Bergerac, act II

I fall back dazzled at beholding myself all rosy red,
At having, I myself, caused the sun to rise.
Chantecler [1907], act II, sc. iii

It is at night that faith in light is admirable. *Ib.*

ROBERT FALCON SCOTT
1868–1912

Had we lived, I should have had a tale to tell of the hardihood, endurance, and courage of my companions which would have stirred the heart of every Englishman. These rough notes and our dead bodies must tell the tale.[1]
Journal.[2] *Message to the Public*

ANDRÉ SUARÈS
1868–1948

Heresy is the lifeblood of religions. It is faith that begets heretics. There are no heresies in a dead religion.[3]
Péguy

WILLIAM ALLEN WHITE
1868–1944

What's the Matter with Kansas?
Title of editorial, Emporia Gazette [August 15, 1896]

Tinhorn politicians.
Emporia Gazette [October 25, 1901]

All dressed up, with nowhere to go.
Of the Progressive Party in 1916, after Theodore Roosevelt retired from Presidential competition

Put fear out of your heart. This nation will survive, this state will prosper, the orderly business of life will go forward if only men can speak in whatever way given them to utter what their hearts hold — by voice, by posted card, by letter, or by press. Reason never has failed men. Only force and oppression have made the wrecks in the world.
Emporia Gazette [July 27, 1922]

Consistency is a paste jewel that only cheap men cherish.[1]
Ib. [November 17, 1923]

The talent of a meat-packer, the morals of a moneychanger and the manners of an undertaker.
Obituary of Frank A. Munsey [December 23, 1925]

LAURENCE BINYON
1869–1943

They shall grow not old, as we that are left grow old:
Age shall not weary them, nor the years condemn.
At the going down of the sun and in the morning
We will remember them.
For the Fallen, st. 4

ELLIS PARKER BUTLER
1869–1937

Pigs is Pigs. *Title of story [1906]*

NEVILLE CHAMBERLAIN
1869–1940

For the second time in our history, a British Prime Minister has returned

---

[1] Inscribed on the memorial to Captain Scott and his companions, Waterloo Place, London.
[2] Found by searching party, November 1912.
[3] See Tertullian, p. 143b, and Unamuno, p. 869b.

[1] Commenting on an item in the Topeka *Capital:* "The *Emporia Gazette* is the best-loved paper in Kansas because its editor never looks in yesterday's files to see if what he proposes to write today is consistent."
See Emerson, p. 606a.

from Germany bringing peace with honor. I believe it is peace for our time. . . . Go home and get a nice quiet sleep.[1]

> *Address from 10 Downing Street, London [September 30, 1938] after returning from the Munich Conference*

Hitler has missed the bus.

> *Speech in the House of Commons [April 4, 1940]*

MOHANDAS KARAMCHAND [MAHATMA] GANDHI[2]
1869–1948

Nonviolence is the first article of my faith. It is also the last article of my creed.

> *Defense against charge of sedition [March 23, 1922]*

The term *Satyagraha* was coined by me . . . in order to distinguish it from the movement then going on . . . under the name of Passive Resistance. Its root meaning is "holding on to truth," hence "force of righteousness." I have also called it love force or soul force. In the application of *Satyagraha*, I discovered in the earliest stages that pursuit of truth did not permit violence being inflicted on one's opponent, but that he must be weaned from error by patience and sympathy. For what appears truth to the one may appear to be error to the other. And patience means self-suffering. So the doctrine came to mean vindication of truth, not by the infliction of suffering on the opponent, but on one's self.[3]   *Ib.*

Nonviolence and truth (*Satya*) are inseparable and presuppose one an-

other. There is no god higher than truth.

> *True Patriotism: Some Sayings of Mahatma Gandhi [1939]* [1]

ANDRÉ GIDE
1869–1951

Families! I hate you! Shut-in homes, closed doors, jealous possessions of happiness.

> *Les Nourritures Terrestres [1897]*

What another would have done as well as you, do not do it. What another would have said as well as you, do not say it; written as well, do not write it. Be faithful to that which exists nowhere but in yourself — and thus make yourself indispensable.   *Ib. Envoi*

Sin is whatever obscures the soul.

> *La Symphonie Pastorale [1919]*

The most decisive actions of our life . . . are most often unconsidered actions.

> *Les Faux Monnayeurs [1925]*

Art begins with resistance — at the point where resistance is overcome. No human masterpiece has ever been created without great labor.   *Poétique*

It is with noble sentiments that bad literature gets written.[2]

> *Letter to François Mauriac [1928]*

STRICKLAND GILLILAN
1869–1954

Bilin' down 's repoort, wuz Finnigin!
An' he writed this here: "Musther Flannigan —
Off agin, on agin,
Gone agin. — FINNIGIN."

> *Finnigin to Flannigan, st. 6*

Adam
Had 'em.

> *Lines on the Antiquity of Microbes* [3]

[1] While we endeavor to maintain peace, I certainly should be the last to forget that if peace cannot be maintained with honor, it is no longer peace. — LORD JOHN RUSSELL, *Speech at Greenock, Scotland [September 19, 1853]*
See Disraeli, p. 613a.
[2] Mahatma — Great Soul.
[3] See Martin Luther King, p. 1082b.

[1] Edited by S. Hobhouse.
[2] C'est avec de beaux sentiments qu'on fait de la mauvaise littérature.
[3] Said to be the shortest poem in the language.

FREDERIC LAWRENCE KNOWLES
1869–1905

Each little lyrical
Grave or satirical
Musical miracle!
> *On a flyleaf of Burns's songs*

Joy is a partnership,
  Grief weeps alone;
Many guests had Cana,
  Gethsemane had one.
> *Grief and Joy*

STEPHEN BUTLER LEACOCK
1869–1944

He flung himself from the room, flung himself upon his horse and rode madly off in all directions.
> *Gertrude the Governess* [1911]

The general idea, of course, in any first-class laundry, is to see that no shirt or collar ever comes back twice.
> *Winnowed Wisdom* [1926], ch. 6

By American literature in the proper sense we ought to mean literature written in an American way, with an American turn of language and an American cast of thought. The test is that it couldn't have been written anywhere else.
> *Mark Twain as National Asset* [1932]

EDGAR LEE MASTERS
1869–1950

All, all, are sleeping on the hill.
> *Spoon River Anthology* [1915].
> *The Hill, refrain*

Seeds in a dry pod, tick, tick, tick,
Tick, tick, tick, what little iambics,
While Homer and Whitman roar in
  the pines! *Ib. Petit, the Poet*

Degenerate sons and daughters,
Life is too strong for you —
It takes life to love life.
> *Ib. Lucinda Matlock*

Out of me unworthy and unknown
The vibrations of deathless music.
> *Spoon River Anthology.*
> *Anne Rutledge*

I am Anne Rutledge who sleep beneath
  these weeds,
Beloved in life of Abraham Lincoln.
> *Ib.*

Immortality is not a gift,
Immortality is an achievement;
And only those who strive mightily
Shall possess it.
> *Ib. The Village Atheist*

HENRI MATISSE
1869–1954

I want to reach that state of condensation of sensations which constitutes a picture.
> *Notes d'un Peintre* [1908]

What interests me most is neither still life nor landscape, but the human figure. It is through it that I best succeed in expressing the almost religious feeling I have towards life. *Ib.*

WILLIAM VAUGHN MOODY
1869–1910

This earth is not the steadfast place
We landsmen build upon;
From deep to deep she varies pace,
And while she comes is gone.
> *Gloucester Moors* [1901], st. 4

To be out of the moiling street
With its swelter and its sin!
Who has given to me this sweet,
And given my brother dust to eat?
And when will his wage come in?
> *Ib. st. 8*

Then not to kneel, almost
Seemed like a vulgar boast.
> *Good Friday* [1901], st. 9

Gigantic, willful, young,
Chicago sitteth at the northwest gates,

With restless violent hands and casual
     tongue
Molding her mighty fates.
          An Ode in Time of Hesitation
                    [*1901*], *st. 3*

Now limb doth mingle with dissolvèd
     limb [1]
In nature's busy old democracy.
                    Ib. st. 6

          The spring-laden breeze
Out of the gladdening west is sinister
With sounds of nameless battle over-
     seas.[2]   *Ib. st. 7*

Our fluent men of place and conse-
     quence
Fumble and fill their mouths with hol-
     low phrase,
Or for the end-all of deep arguments
Intone their dull commercial liturgies.
                              Ib.

          O ye who lead,
Take heed!
Blindness we may forgive, but baseness
     we will smite.   *Ib. st. 9*

EDWIN ARLINGTON
ROBINSON
1869–1935

We cannot know how much we learn
From those who never will return,
Until a flash of unforeseen
Remembrance falls on what has been.
                         Flammonde

          To shake the tree
Of life itself and bring down fruit
unheard-of.
          *Ben Jonson Entertains a Man
                    from Stratford*

I would have rid the earth of him
Once, in my pride. . . .
I never knew the worth of him
Until he died.   *An Old Story*

[1] The reference is to the battlefield grave of
Colonel Robert Gould Shaw and the men of the
54th Massachusetts Regiment (the first enlisted
Negro regiment of the Civil War) who fell at
Fort Wagner [July 18, 1863].
[2] The war in the Philippines.

Life is the game that must be played:
This truth at least, good friends, we
     know;
So live and laugh, nor be dismayed
As one by one the phantoms go.
               Ballade by the Fire. Envoy

The songs of one who strove to play
The broken flutes of Arcady.
               Ballade of Broken Flutes

There be two men of all mankind
That I'm forever thinking on:
They chase me everywhere I go —
Melchizedek, Ucalegon.   *Two Men*

Like dead, remembered footsteps on
     old floors.
               The Pity of the Leaves

          And thus we die,
Still searching, like poor old astrono-
     mers
Who totter off to bed and go to sleep
To dream of untriangulated stars.
                         Octaves, XI

The saddest among kings of earth,
Bowed with a galling crown, this
     man
Met rancor with a cryptic mirth,
Laconic — and Olympian.
               The Master: Lincoln

Wearing upon his forehead, with no
     fear,
The laurel of approved iniquity.
                    Uncle Ananias

Miniver Cheevy, child of scorn,
Grew lean while he assailed the sea-
     sons;
He wept that he was ever born,
And he had reasons.
          Miniver Cheevy [*1910*], *st. 1*

Miniver loved the Medici,
Albeit he had never seen one;
He would have sinned incessantly
Could he have been one.   *Ib. st. 5*

Miniver Cheevy, born too late,
Scratched his head and kept on think-
     ing;
Miniver coughed and called it fate,
And kept on drinking.   *Ib. st. 8*

Who of us, being what he is,
May scoff at others' ecstasies?
However we may shine today,
More-shining ones are on the way.
Atherton's Gambit

I shall have more to say when I am
dead.   *John Brown*

Art's long hazard, where no man may
choose
Whether he play to win, or toil to
lose.   *Caput Mortuum*

Love that's wise
Will not say all it means.
Tristram [1927], *pt.* VII

Love must have wings to fly away from
love,
And to fly back again.   *Ib.* VIII

Here where the wind is always north-
northeast
And children learn to walk on frozen
toes.   *New England*

Are you to pay for all you have
With all you are?   *Cassandra, st.* 12

He glittered when he walked.
Richard Cory, st. 2

So on we worked, and waited for the
light,
And went without the meat, and cursed
the bread;
And Richard Cory, one calm summer
night,
Went home and put a bullet through
his head.   *Ib.* 4

"Drink to the bird." He raised up to
the light
The jug that he had gone so far to fill,
And answered huskily: "Well, Mr.
Flood,
Since you propose it, I believe I will."
Mr. Flood's Party, st. 2

GEORGE STERLING
1869–1926

Thou art the star for which all evening
waits.   *Aldebaran at Dusk*

WILLIAM STRUNK, JR.
1869–1935

Vigorous writing is concise. A sentence should contain no unnecessary
words, a paragraph no unnecessary sentences, for the same reason that a drawing should have no unnecessary lines
and a machine no unnecessary parts.
This requires not that the writer make
all his sentences short, or that he avoid
all detail and treat his subjects only in
outline, but that every word tell.
The Elements of Style [1918],
ch. 2, *sec.* 13

BOOTH TARKINGTON
1869–1946

There are two things that will be believed of any man whatsoever, and one
of them is that he has taken to drink.
Penrod [1914], *ch.* 10

They were upon their great theme:
"When I get to be a man!" Being
human, though boys, they considered
their present estate too commonplace
to be dwelt upon. So, when the old
men gather, they say: "When I was a
boy!" It really is the land of nowadays
that we never discover.   *Ib.* 26

FRANK LLOYD
WRIGHT
1869–1959

No house should ever be *on* any hill
or on anything. It should be *of* the hill,
belonging to it, so hill and house could
live together each the happier for the
other.   *An Autobiography* [1932]

BERNARD MANNES
BARUCH
1870–1965

America has never forgotten — and
will never forget — the nobler things
that brought her into being and that
light her path — the path that was en-

tered upon only one hundred and fifty years ago. . . . How young she is! It will be centuries before she will adopt that maturity of custom — the clothing of the grave — that some people believe she is already fitted for.

Address on accepting The Churchman Award, New York [May 23, 1944]

We are here to make a choice between the quick and the dead. That is our business. Behind the black portent of the new atomic age lies a hope which, seized upon with faith, can work out salvation. If we fail, then we have damned every man to be the slave of fear. Let us not deceive ourselves: we must elect world peace or world destruction.

Address to the United Nations Atomic Energy Commission [June 14, 1946]

We are in the midst of a cold war [1] which is getting warmer.

Speech before the Senate Committee [1948]

The role of government and its relationship to the individual has been changed so radically that today government is involved in almost every aspect of our lives.

Political, economic and racial forces have developed which we have not yet learned to understand or control. If we are ever to master these forces, make certain that government will belong to the people, not the people to the government, and provide for the future better than the past, we must somehow learn from the experiences of the past.

Speech on presenting his papers to Princeton University [May 11, 1964]

HILAIRE BELLOC
1870–1953

Child! do not throw this book about;
Refrain from the unholy pleasure

[1] The phrase was first used by Baruch in 1947.

Of cutting all the pictures out!
Preserve it as your chiefest treasure.

A Bad Child's Book of Beasts [1896], dedication

When people call this beast to mind,
They marvel more and more
At such a little tail behind,
So large a trunk before.

Ib. The Elephant

I shoot the Hippopotamus
With bullets made of platinum,
Because if I use leaden ones
His hide is sure to flatten 'em.

Ib. The Hippopotamus

The Whale that wanders round the Pole
Is not a table fish.
You cannot bake or boil him whole
Nor serve him in a dish.

Ib. The Whale

Here richly, with ridiculous display,
The Politician's corpse was laid away.
While all of his acquaintance sneered and slanged,
I wept; for I had longed to see him hanged.

Epitaph on the Politician Himself

A smell of burning fills the startled air —
The Electrician is no longer there!

Newdigate Poem

Oh, he didn't believe in Adam and Eve —
He put no faith therein;
His doubts began with the fall of man,
And he laughed at original sin.

Song of the Pelagian Heresy

How slow the shadow creeps: but when 'tis past
How fast the shadows fall. How fast! How fast!   *For a Sundial*

Loss and Possession, death and life are one,
There falls no shadow where there shines no sun.   *Ib.*

And the men that were boys when I
    was a boy
Shall sit and drink with me.
           The South Country, st. 10

Of courtesy, it is much less
Than courage of heart or holiness,
Yet in my walks it seems to me
That the Grace of God is in courtesy.
                Courtesy

Do you remember an inn,
Miranda?   *Tarantella*

And the fleas that tease in the High
    Pyrenees,
And the wine that tasted of the tar?
                  Ib.

I said to Heart, "How goes it?" Heart
    replied:
"Right as a Ribstone Pippin!" But it
    lied.   *The False Heart*

Now just imagine how it feels
When first your toes and then your
    heels,
And then by gradual degrees,
Your shins and ankles, calves and
    knees,
Are slowly eaten, bit by bit.
No wonder Jim detested it!
        Cautionary Tales [1907]. *Jim*

The chief defect of Henry King
Was chewing little bits of string.
           Ib. Henry King

"Oh, my friends, be warned by me,
That breakfast, dinner, lunch and tea
Are all the human frame requires . . ."
With that the wretched child expires.
                  Ib.

Matilda told such dreadful lies,
It made one gasp and stretch one's
    eyes;
Her aunt, who, from her earliest youth,
Had kept a strict regard for truth,
Attempted to believe Matilda:
The effort very nearly killed her.
           Ib. Matilda

It happened that a few weeks later
Her aunt was off to the theater
To see that interesting play
The Second Mrs. Tanqueray.   *Ib.*

For every time she shouted "Fire!"
They only answered "Little liar!"
And therefore when her aunt returned,
Matilda, and the house, were burned.
        Cautionary Tales. Matilda

The nicest child I ever knew
Was Charles Augustus Fortescue.
    Ib. Charles Augustus Fortescue

Pale Ebenezer thought it wrong to fight,
But Roaring Bill (who killed him)
    thought it right.   *The Pacifist*

When I am dead, I hope it may be
    said:
"His sins were scarlet, but his books
    were read."   *On His Books*

BENJAMIN NATHAN CARDOZO
1870–1938

What has once been settled by a
precedent will not be unsettled over-
night, for certainty and uniformity are
gains not lightly to be sacrificed.
Above all is this true when honest men
have shaped their conduct on the faith
of the pronouncement.
        *The Paradoxes of Legal
             Science* [1928]

As I search the archives of my memory, I seem to discern six types or methods [of judicial writing] which divide
themselves from one another with
measurable distinctness. There is the
type magisterial or imperative; the type
laconic or sententious; the type conver-
sational or homely; the type refined or
artificial, smelling of the lamp,[1] verging
at times upon preciosity or euphuism;
the type demonstrative or persuasive;
and finally the type tonsorial or agglutinative, so called from the shears
and the pastepot which are its imple-
ments and emblem.
        Law and Literature [1931]

[The Constitution] was framed
upon the theory that the peoples of the
several states must sink or swim together, and that in the long run pros-

[1] See Pytheas, p. 101b.

perity and salvation are in union and not division.

Baldwin v. Seelig, 294 U.S. 511, 523 [1935]

Freedom of expression is the matrix, the indispensable condition, of nearly every other form of freedom.

Palko v. Connecticut, 302 U.S. 319, 327 [1937]

ARTHUR J. LAMB
1870–1928

Her beauty was sold for an old man's gold,
She's a bird in a gilded cage.

A Bird in a Gilded Cage [1900]

SIR HARRY LAUDER
1870–1950

Oh, it's nice to get up in the mornin',
But it's nicer to lie in bed. Song

Just a wee doch-an'-dorris
Before we gang awa' . . .
If y' can say
It's a braw brecht moonlecht necht,
Yer a' recht, that's a'. Song

Roamin' in the gloamin'. Song

I Love a Lassie. Title of song

NIKOLAI LENIN
[VLADIMIR ILICH ULYANOV]
1870–1924

Political institutions are a superstructure resting on an economic foundation.

The Three Sources and Three Constituent Parts of Marxism [1] [1913]

Every cook has to learn how to govern the state.

Will the Bolsheviks Retain Government Power [1917]

The war is relentless: it puts the alternative in a ruthless relief: either to perish, or to catch up with the ad-

[1] Translated by MAX EASTMAN.

vanced countries and outdistance them, too, in economic matters.[1]

The Impending Catastrophe and How to Fight It [1917]

Communism is Soviet government plus the electrification of the whole country.

New External and Internal Position and the Problems of the Party [1920]

When we say "the state," the state it is we, it is the proletariat, it is the advanced guard of the working class.

Speech [May 27, 1922]

It is true that liberty is precious — so precious that it must be rationed.

Attributed. Quoted by SIDNEY AND BEATRICE WEBB in Soviet Communism: A New Civilization? [1936], p. 1036

ROSCOE POUND
1870–1964

The law must be stable, but it must not stand still.

Introduction to the Philosophy of Law [1922]

SAKI
[HECTOR HUGH MUNRO]
1870–1916

The cook was a good cook, as cooks go; and as cooks go she went.

Reginald [1904]. Reginald on Besetting Sins

[1] We have caught up with and outdistanced the advanced countries politically by having built the proletarian dictatorship. But this is not enough. We have to catch up with and outdistance the advanced countries also economically. — JOSEPH STALIN, Speech [November 19, 1928]
When we sent the first Sputniks into cosmos . . . the whole world saw that the Soviet Union has by far outdistanced the United States of America in important branches of science and technology. Even President John Kennedy was forced to admit that the United States are confronted by the difficult problem of catching up with the Soviet Union in this field. As you see, the expression "catch up with" has appeared in the American vocabulary too. — NIKITA KHRUSHCHEV, Report to the XXII Congress of the Party [October 17, 1961]

Women and elephants never forget an injury.
>*Reginald. Reginald on Besetting Sins*

I might have been a goldfish in a glass bowl for all the privacy I got.
>*Ib. The Innocence of Reginald*

The Western custom of one wife and hardly any mistresses.
>*Reginald in Russia* [1910]. *A Young Turkish Catastrophe*

Hating anything in the way of ill-natured gossip ourselves, we are always grateful to those who do it for us and do it well.
>*Ib. The Soul of Laploshka*

Poverty keeps together more homes than it breaks up.
>*The Chronicles of Clovis* [1911]. *Esmé*

"After all, it's not my Axminster," was Tobermory's rejoinder.
>*Ib. Tobermory*

Sredni Vashtar went forth,
His thoughts were red thoughts and his teeth were white.
His enemies called for peace, but he brought them death.
Sredni Vashtar the Beautiful.
>*Ib. Sredni Vashtar*

His socks compelled one's attention without losing one's respect.
>*Ib. Ministers of Grace*

Sherard Blaw, the dramatist who had discovered himself, and who had given so ungrudgingly of his discovery to the world.
>*The Unbearable Bassington* [1912]

The sacrifices of friendship were beautiful in her eyes as long as she was not asked to make them.
>*Beasts and Super-Beasts* [1914]. *Fur*

"The man is a common murderer."
"A common murderer, possibly, but a very uncommon cook."
>*Ib. The Blind Spot*

Waldo is one of those people who would be enormously improved by death.
>*Beasts and Super-Beasts. The Feast of Nemesis*

Children with Hyacinth's temperament don't know better as they grow older; they merely know more.
>*The Toys of Peace* [1919]. *Hyacinth*

In baiting a mousetrap with cheese, always leave room for the mouse.
>*The Square Egg* [1924]. *The Infernal Parliament*

A little inaccuracy sometimes saves tons of explanation.
>*Ib. The Comments of Moung Ka*

T. LAURENCE SEIBERT
fl. 1900

Casey Jones! Orders in his hand.
Casey Jones! Mounted to the cabin,
Took his farewell journey to that promised land.
>*Casey Jones* [1900]; *adapted from verses by* WALLACE SAUNDERS,[1] *set to music by* EDDIE NEWTON

STEPHEN CRANE
1871–1900

They were going to look at war, the red animal — war, the blood-swollen god.
>*The Red Badge of Courage* [1895], *ch.* 3

[1] Of the many versions of this traditional ballad, the most familiar is printed in CARL SANDBURG'S *The American Songbag* [1927]. It begins:
>Come all you rounders, for I want you to hear
>The story of a brave engineer.
>Casey Jones was the rounder's name,
>On a big eight-wheeler of a mighty fame.

To the memory of the locomotive engineer whose name as "Casey Jones" became a part of folklore and the American language. "For I'm going to run till she leaves the rail—or make it on time with the southbound mail."—*Inscription on monument to* JOHN LUTHER JONES [*1864–1900*], *in Calvary Cemetery, Jackson, Tennessee*

It was surprising that Nature had gone tranquilly on with her golden process in the midst of so much devilment.
The Red Badge of Courage, ch. 5

At times he regarded the wounded soldiers in an envious way. He conceived persons with torn bodies to be peculiarly happy. He wished that he, too, had a wound, a red badge of courage. *Ib. 9*

The red sun was pasted in the sky like a wafer. *Ib.*

He had fought like a pagan who defends his religion. *Ib. 17*

He had been to touch the great death, and found that, after all, it was but the great death. He was a man.
Ib. 24

None of them knew the color of the sky. *The Open Boat [1898]*

When it came night, the white waves paced to and fro in the moonlight, and the wind brought the sound of the great sea's voice to the men on shore, and they felt that they could then be interpreters. *Ib. Last line*

A man said to the universe:
"Sir, I exist!"
"However," replied the universe,
"The fact has not created in me
A sense of obligation."
War Is Kind [1899]. Fragment

THOMAS AUGUSTINE DALY
1871–1948

Sing clear, O throstle,
Thou golden-tongued apostle
And little brown-frocked brother
Of the loved Assisian! *To a Thrush*

WILLIAM HENRY DAVIES
1871–1940

What is this life if, full of care,
We have no time to stand and stare? [1]
Leisure

[1] See Browning, p. 668a.

THEODORE DREISER
1871–1945

Our civilization is still in a middle stage, scarcely beast, in that it is no longer wholly guided by instinct; scarcely human, in that it is not yet wholly guided by reason.
Sister Carrie [1900]

I acknowledge the Furies, I believe in them, I have heard the disastrous beating of their wings.
To Grant Richards [1911]

Oh, the moon is fair tonight along the Wabash,
From the fields there comes the breath of new-mown hay;
Through the sycamores the candle lights are gleaming
On the banks of the Wabash, far away.
On the Banks of the Wabash, chorus [1]

ARTHUR GUITERMAN
1871–1943

The finest thing in London is the Bobby; [2]
Benignant information is his hobby.
The Lyric Baedeker. London

Amoebas at the start
Were not complex;
They tore themselves apart
And started Sex. *Sex, st. 1*

Of all cold words of tongue or pen
The worst are these: "I knew him when — " [3]
Prophets in Their Own Country

RALPH HODGSON
1871–1962

'Twould ring the bells of Heaven
The wildest peal for years,

[1] Dreiser's brother, Paul Dreiser, is credited with writing the song, but according to H. L. Mencken, Dreiser wrote the chorus.
[2] The constable with lifted hand
Conducting the orchestral Strand.
STEPHEN PHILLIPS [1864–1915],
The Wife
[3] See Whittier, p. 626a.

If Parson lost his senses
And people came to theirs,
And he and they together
Knelt down with angry prayers
For tamed and shabby tigers
And dancing dogs and bears,
And wretched, blind pit ponies,
And little hunted hares.
                    The Bells of Heaven

But oh, the den of wild things in
The darkness of her eyes!
                    The Gypsy Girl

God loves an idle rainbow
No less than laboring seas.
                    A Wood Song

Time, you old gypsy man,
Will you not stay,
Put up your caravan
Just for one day?
        Time, You Old Gypsy Man, st. 1

Pity him, this fallen chief,
All his splendor, all his strength,
All his beauty's breadth and length
Dwindled down with shame and grief,
Half the bull he was before,
Bones and leather, nothing more.
                    The Bull

Oh, had our simple Eve
Seen through the make-believe!
Had she but known the
Pretender he was!
Out of the boughs he came,
Whispering still her name,
Tumbling in twenty rings
Into the grass.   *Eve, st. 5*

How they all pitied
Poor motherless Eve!   *Ib.*

I climbed the hill as light fell short,
And rooks came home in scramble
    sort.   *The Song of Honor*

I stood upon that silent hill
And stared into the sky until
My eyes were blind with stars and still
I stared into the sky.   *Ib.*

Reason has moons, but moons not
    hers
Lie mirrored on her sea,
Confounding her astronomers,
But O! delighting me.   *Reason*

I saw with open eyes
Singing birds sweet
Sold in the shops
For the people to eat,
Sold in the shops of
Stupidity Street.

I saw in vision
The worm in the wheat,
And in the shops nothing
For people to eat;
Nothing for sale in
Stupidity Street.   *Stupidity Street*

JAMES WELDON JOHNSON
1871–1938

We have come over a way that with
    tears has been watered,
We have come, treading our path
    through the blood of the slaugh-
    tered.
        Lift Every Voice and Sing
                [1900], st. 2

O black and unknown bards of long
    ago,
How came your lips to touch the sacred
    fire?
How, in your darkness, did you come to
    know
The power and beauty of the minstrel's
    lyre?
        O Black and Unknown Bards,
                st. 1

And God stepped out on space,
And He looked around and said,
"I'm lonely —
I'll make me a world."
        God's Trombones [1927]. The
                Creation, st. 1

And God smiled again,
And the rainbow appeared,
And curled itself around his shoulder.
                Ib. st. 7

With his head in his hands,
God thought and thought,
Till he thought: I'll make me a man!
                Ib. st. 10

        Find Sister Caroline . . .
And she's tired —

She's weary —
Go down, Death, and bring her to me.
God's Trombones. Go Down,
Death, st. 5

CHARLES RANN KENNEDY
1871–1950

A peculiar kind of fear they call
courage.
The Terrible Meek [1912]

The meek, the terrible meek, the
fierce agonizing meek, are about to enter into their inheritance.   *Ib.*

WILBUR DICK NESBIT
1871–1927

Each page of them Quotations that
    this Bartlett man got out
Is sure to have old Ibid's prose or
    poems strung about.
Old Ibid, st. 2

HERBERT GEORGE PONTING
1871–1935

On the outside grows the furside, on
    the inside grows the skinside;
So the furside is the outside, and the
    skinside is the inside.[1]
The Sleeping Bag [2]

MARCEL PROUST
1871–1922

When from a long distant past nothing subsists, after the people are dead,

[1] When he killed the Mudjokivis,
    Of the skin he made him mittens,
    Made them with the fur side inside,
    Made them with the skin side outside,
    He, to get the warm side inside,
    Put the inside skin side outside;
    He, to get the cold side outside,
    Put the warm side fur side inside.
    That's why he put the fur side inside,
    Why he put the skin side outside,
    Why he turned them inside outside —
      Anonymous, The Modern Hiawatha
[2] For *The South Polar Times*, Midwinter Day
[June 22, 1911], prepared by the men of Captain
Robert Falcon Scott's last Antarctic expedition.

after the things are broken and scattered, still, alone, more fragile, but with
more vitality, more unsubstantial, more
persistent, more faithful, the smell and
taste of things remain poised a long
time, like souls, ready to remind us,
waiting and hoping for their moment,
amid the ruins of all the rest; and bear
unfaltering, in the tiny and almost impalpable drop of their essence, the vast
structure of recollection.
Remembrance of Things Past [1]
[1913–1926]. Swann's Way

In his younger days a man dreams of
possessing the heart of the woman
whom he loves; later, the feeling that
he possesses the heart of a woman may
be enough to make him fall in love with
her.   *Ib.*

What artists call posterity is the posterity of the work of art.
Ib. Within a Budding Grove,
pt. I

Not only does one not retain all at
once the truly rare works, but even within such works it is the least precious parts
that one perceives first. Less deceptive
than life, these great masterpieces do
not give us their best at the beginning.[2]
Ib.

The time which we have at our dis-
posal every day is elastic; the passions
that we feel expand it, those that we
inspire contract it; and habit fills up
what remains.   *Ib.*

Like everybody who is not in love, he
imagined that one chose the person
whom one loved after endless delibera-
tions and on the strength of various
qualities and advantages.
Ib. Cities of the Plain, pt. I

We passionately long that there may
be another life in which we shall be
similar to what we are here below. But

Ponting was the photographer for the Scott
expedition.
[1] *À la Recherche du Temps Perdu*, translated
by C. K. SCOTT MONCRIEFF, except the last
section, *The Past Recaptured*, which was translated by FREDERICK A. BLOSSOM.
[2] See Daniel Gregory Mason, p. 915b.

we do not pause to reflect that, even without waiting for that other life, in this life, after a few years we are unfaithful to what we have been, to what we wished to remain immortally.

Remembrance of Things Past.
Cities of the Plain, pt. II

It is often simply from want of the creative spirit that we do not go to the full extent of suffering. And the most terrible reality brings us, with our suffering, the joy of a great discovery, because it merely gives a new and clear form to what we have long been ruminating without suspecting it.   *Ib.*

The bonds that unite another person to ourself exist only in our mind. Memory as it grows fainter relaxes them, and notwithstanding the illusion by which we would fain be cheated and with which, out of love, friendship, politeness, deference, duty, we cheat other people, we exist alone. Man is the creature that cannot emerge from himself, that knows his fellows only in himself; when he asserts the contrary, he is lying.   *Ib. The Sweet Cheat Gone*

We do not succeed in changing things according to our desire, but gradually our desire changes. The situation that we hoped to change because it was intolerable becomes unimportant. We have not managed to surmount the obstacle, as we were absolutely determined to do, but life has taken us round it, led us past it, and then if we turn round to gaze at the remote past, we can barely catch sight of it, so imperceptible has it become.   *Ib.*

There is not a woman in the world the possession of whom is as precious as that of the truths which she reveals to us by causing us to suffer.   *Ib.*

We are healed of a suffering only by experiencing it to the full.   *Ib.*

Happiness is beneficial for the body but it is grief that develops the powers of the mind.

Ib. The Past Recaptured

Only through art can we get outside of ourselves and know another's view of the universe which is not the same as ours and see landscapes which would otherwise have remained unknown to us like the landscapes of the moon. Thanks to art, instead of seeing a single world, our own, we see it multiply until we have before us as many worlds as there are original artists. . . . And many centuries after their core, whether we call it Rembrandt or Vermeer, is extinguished, they continue to send us their special rays.

The Maxims of Marcel Proust [1]

ERNEST RUTHERFORD
1871–1937

We cannot control atomic energy to an extent which would be of any value commercially, and I believe we are not likely ever to be able to do so.

Speech to the British Association
for the Advancement of Science
[1933]

JOHN MILLINGTON SYNGE
1871–1909

What is the price of a thousand horses against a son where there is one son only?   *Riders to the Sea* [1904]

When I was writing *The Shadow of the Glen* I got more aid than any learning could have given me from a chink in the floor of the old Wicklow house where I was staying, that let me hear what was being said by the servant girls in the kitchen.

The Playboy of the Western
World [1907], *preface*

Drink a health to the wonders of the Western world, the pirates, preachers, poteen-makers, with the jobbing jockies; parching peelers, and the juries fill their stomachs selling judgments of the English law.   *Ib. act II*

[1] Edited and translated by JUSTIN O'BRIEN [1948].

May I meet him with one tooth and it aching, and one eye to be seeing seven and seventy divils in the twists of the road, and one old timber leg on him to limp into the scalding grave. There he is now crossing the strands, and that the Lord God would send a high wave to wash him from the world.[1]

The Playboy of the Western World, act II

Aid me for to win her, and I'll be asking God to stretch a hand to you in the hour of death, and lead you short cuts through the Meadows of Ease, and up the floor of Heaven to the Footstool of the Virgin's Son. *Ib.*

They're cheering a young lad, the champion playboy of the Western World. *Ib. III*

A man who is not afraid of the sea will soon be drowned, he said, for he will be going out on a day he shouldn't. But we do be afraid of the sea, and we do only be drownded now and again.

The Aran Islands [1907]

There is no language like the Irish for soothing and quieting. *Ib.*

A translation is no translation, he said, unless it will give you the music of a poem along with the words of it. *Ib.*

I knew the stars, the flowers, and the birds,
The gray and wintry sides of many glens,
And did but half remember human words,
In converse with the mountains, moors, and fens. *Prelude* [1910]

[1] May the grass grow at your door and the fox build his nest on your hearthstone. May the light fade from your eyes, so you never see what you love. May your own blood rise against you, and the sweetest drink you take be the bitterest cup of sorrow. May you die without benefit of clergy; may there be none to shed a tear at your grave, and may the hearthstone of hell be your best bed forever. — *Traditional Wexford curse*

PAUL VALÉRY
1871–1945

The folly of mistaking a paradox for a discovery, a metaphor for a proof, a torrent of verbiage for a spring of capital truths, and oneself for an oracle, is inborn in us.

Introduction to the Method of Leonardo da Vinci [1] [1895]

Collect all the facts that can be collected about the life of Racine and you will never learn from them the art of his verse. All criticism is dominated by the outworn theory that the man is the cause of the work as in the eyes of the law the criminal is the cause of the crime. Far rather are they both the effects. *Ib.*

The sea, the ever renewing sea! [2]

Charmes [1922]. *Le Cimitière Marin*

The wind is rising . . . we must attempt to live.[3] *Ib.*

Poetry is simply literature reduced to the essence of its active principle. It is purged of idols of every kind, of realistic illusions, of any conceivable equivocation between the language of "truth" and the language of "creation."

Littérature [1930]

An intelligent woman is a woman with whom one can be as stupid as one wants.

Mauvaises Pensées et Autres [1941]

The painter should not paint what he sees, but what will be seen. *Ib.*

That which has always been accepted by everyone, everywhere, is almost certain to be false. *Tel Quel* [1943]

God created man, and finding him not sufficiently alone, gave him a female companion so that he might feel his solitude more acutely. *Ib.*

[1] Translated by THOMAS McGREEVY.
[2] La mer, la mer toujours recommence!
[3] Le vent se leve . . . il faut tenter de vivre.

The purpose of psychology is to give us a completely different idea of the things we know best. *Tel Quel*

WILBUR WRIGHT
1867–1912
AND
ORVILLE WRIGHT
1871–1948

Success/ four flights Thursday morning/ all against twenty-one-mile wind/ started from level with engine power alone/ average speed through air thirty-one miles/ longest fifty-nine seconds/ inform press/ home Christmas.

Telegram to the Reverend Milton Wright, from Kitty Hawk, N.C. [December 17, 1903]

EVERARD JACK APPLETON
1872–1931

Somewhere she waits to make you win,
Your soul in her firm white hands;
Somewhere the gods have made for you
The woman who understands.
The Woman Who Understands

SIR MAX BEERBOHM
1872–1956

Most women are not so young as they are painted.
A Defense of Cosmetics

Zuleika, on a desert island, would have spent most of her time in looking for a man's footprint.
Zuleika Dobson [1911], ch. 2

She was hardly more affable than a cameo. *Ib. 3*

The dullard's envy of brilliant men is always assuaged by the suspicion that they will come to a bad end. *Ib. 4*

Ordinary saints grow faint to posterity; whilst quite ordinary sinners pass vividly down the ages. *Ib. 6*

She was one of the people who say "I don't know anything about music really, but I know what I like." [1]
Zuleika Dobson, ch. 9

Of all the objects of hatred, a woman once loved is the most hateful.
Ib. 13

I have known no man of genius who had not to pay, in some affliction or defect either physical or spiritual, for what the gods had given him.
No. 2. The Pines

It seems to be a law of nature that no man ever is loth to sit for his portrait. A man may be old, he may be ugly, he may be burdened with grave responsibilities to the nation, and that nation be at a crisis of its history; but none of these considerations, nor all of them together, will deter him from sitting for his portrait.
Quia Imperfectum

To say that a man is vain means merely that he is pleased with the effect he produces on other people. A conceited man is satisfied with the effect he produces on himself. *Ib.*

Strange, when you come to think of it, that of all the countless folk who have lived before our time on this planet not one is known in history or in legend as having died of laughter.
Laughter

The past is a work of art, free of irrelevancies and loose ends.
Comment

LÉON BLUM
1872–1950

Life does not give itself to one who tries to keep all its advantages at once. I

[1] Bromide no. 1. — GELETT BURGESS, *Are You a Bromide?* [1906]
In art I pull no highbrow stuff,
I know what I like, and that's enough.
WILLIAM W. WOOLLCOTT [1877–1949], *I Am a One Hundred Percent American, st. 3*

have often thought morality may perhaps consist solely in the courage of making a choice. *On Marriage*

No government can remain stable in an unstable society and an unstable world.

À l'Échelle Humaine [1945]

JAMES BONE
1872–1962

The mighty fleet of Wren, with their topgallants and mainsails of stone.

The London Perambulator [1925]

PATRICK REGINALD CHALMERS
1872–1942

"I find," said 'e, "things very much as 'ow I've always found,
For mostly they goes up and down or else goes round and round."

Roundabouts and Swings, st. 2

What's lost upon the roundabouts we pulls up on the swings! *Ib.*

CALVIN COOLIDGE
1872–1933

There is no right to strike against the public safety by anybody, anywhere, any time.

Telegram to Samuel Gompers, president of the American Federation of Labor, on the Boston police strike [September 14, 1919]

One with the law is a majority.
Speech [July 27, 1920]

Inflation is repudiation.
Speech, Chicago [January 11, 1922]

The business of America is business.
Speech to the Society of American Newspaper Editors [January 17, 1925]

They hired the money, didn't they?
Referring to the European war debts [1925]

I do not choose to run for President in 1928.
Statement to reporters [August 2, 1927]

I love Vermont because of her hills and valleys, her scenery and invigorating climate, but most of all because of her indomitable people.
Address from train platform, Bennington, Vermont [September 21, 1928]

If you don't say anything, you won't be called on to repeat it. *Saying*

He said he was against it.
On being asked what a clergyman preaching on sin had said

PAUL LAURENCE DUNBAR
1872–1906

Folks ain't got no right to censuah otha folks about dey habits;
Him dat giv' de squir'ls de bushtails made de bobtails fu' de rabbits.

Accountability

It's easy 'nough to titter w'en de stew is smokin' hot,
But hit's mighty ha'd to giggle w'en dey's nuffin' in de pot.

Philosophy

LEARNED HAND
1872–1961

You may ask what then will become of the fundamental principles of equity and fair play which our constitutions enshrine; and whether I seriously believe that unsupported they will serve merely as counsels of moderation. I do not think that anyone can say what will be left of those principles; I do not know whether they will serve only as counsels; but this much I think I do know — that a society so riven that the spirit of moderation is gone, no court *can* save; that a society where that spirit flourishes, no court *need* save; that in a society which evades its responsibility by thrusting upon the courts the nurture of that spirit, that spirit in the end will perish.

> *The Contribution of an Independent Judiciary to Civilization* [1942]

Justice, I think, is the tolerable accommodation of the conflicting interests of society, and I don't believe there is any royal road to attain such accommodations concretely.

> *From* PHILIP HAMBURGER, *The Great Judge* [1946]

"I beseech ye in the bowels of Christ, think that ye may be mistaken." [1] I should like to have that written over the portals of every church, every school, and every courthouse, and, may I say, of every legislative body in the United States. I should like to have every court begin, "I beseech ye in the bowels of Christ, think that we may be mistaken."

> *Morals in Public Life* [1951]

I had rather take my chance that some traitors will escape detection than spread abroad a spirit of general suspicion and distrust, which accepts rumor and gossip in place of undismayed and unintimidated inquiry.

> *Speech to the Board of Regents, University of the State of New York* [October 24, 1952]

That community is already in the process of dissolution where each man begins to eye his neighbor as a possible enemy, where nonconformity with the accepted creed, political as well as religious, is a mark of disaffection; where denunciation, without specification or backing, takes the place of evidence; where orthodoxy chokes freedom of dissent; where faith in the eventual supremacy of reason has become so timid that we dare not enter our convictions in the open lists, to win or lose.   *Ib.*

[1] See Oliver Cromwell, p. 328a.

The mutual confidence on which all else depends can be maintained only by an open mind and a brave reliance upon free discussion.

> *Speech to the Board of Regents, University of the State of New York*

JOHN McCRAE
1872–1918

In Flanders fields the poppies blow
Between the crosses, row on row.
> *In Flanders Fields* [1915], *st.* 1

Take up our quarrel with the foe:
To you from failing hands we throw
The torch; be yours to hold it high.
If ye break faith with us who die
We shall not sleep, though poppies grow
In Flanders fields.   *Ib. st. 3*

PATRICK F. O'KEEFE
1872–1934

Say It with Flowers.[1]
> *Slogan for the Society of American Florists* [1917]

JOSÉ ENRIQUE RODÓ
1872–1917

To govern is to populate, assimilating in the beginning, then educating and selecting.   *Ariel*

BERTRAND RUSSELL
1872–1970

Thus mathematics may be defined as the subject in which we never know what we are talking about, nor whether what we are saying is true.

> *Recent Work on the Principles of Mathematics* [1901], *in International Monthly, vol. 4, p. 84*

Mathematics, rightly viewed, posesses not only truth, but supreme beauty — a beauty cold and austere, like that of

[1] Say It with Music. — *Title of song by* IRVING BERLIN [1921]

sculpture, without appeal to any part of our weaker nature, without the gorgeous trappings of painting or music, yet sublimely pure, and capable of a stern perfection such as only the greatest art can show.[1]

The Study of Mathematics [1902]

Mathematics takes us still further from what is human, into the region of absolute necessity, to which not only the actual world, but every possible world, must conform. *Ib.*

It is preoccupation with possession, more than anything else, that prevents men from living freely and nobly.

Principles of Social Reconstruction [1917]

The psychology of adultery has been falsified by conventional morals, which assume, in monogamous countries, that attraction to one person cannot coexist with a serious affection for another. Everybody knows that this is untrue.

Marriage and Morals [1929], *ch. 16*

To fear love is to fear life, and those who fear life are already three parts dead. *Ib.*

A good society is a means to a good life for those who compose it; not something having a kind of excellence on its own account.

Authority and the Individual [1949]

Fear is the main source of superstition, and one of the main sources of cruelty. To conquer fear is the beginning of wisdom.

An Outline of Intellectual Rubbish [1950]

ELLERY SEDGWICK
1872–1960

Autobiographies ought to begin with Chapter Two.

The Happy Profession [1946], *ch. 1*

In America, getting on in the world means getting out of the world we have known before. *Ib.*

[1] See Millay, p. 1023b.

ALBERT PAYSON TERHUNE
1872–1942

He was red-gold-and-snow of coat, a big slender youngster, with the true "look of eagles" in his deepset dark eyes.

The Heart of a Dog [1924], *ch. 8*

CARL LOTUS BECKER
1873–1945

Economic distress will teach men, if anything can, that realities are less dangerous than fancies, that fact-finding is more effective than fault-finding.

Progress and Power [1935]

The significance of man is that he is that part of the universe that asks the question, What is the significance of Man? He alone can stand apart imaginatively and, regarding himself and the universe in their eternal aspects, pronounce a judgment: The significance of man is that he is insignificant and is aware of it. *Ib.*

Those of us who think that we are a nation of starry-eyed idealists [1] who have been twice tricked by the British into a European war in order to pull their chestnuts out of the fire [2] have read the history of this country to little purpose. . . . The truth is rather that the existence and friendliness of the British Empire and the power of the British Fleet have for more than a century enabled us to roast our own chestnuts at leisure and eat them in security. *Ib.*

GEORGE BENNARD
1873–

I will cling to the old rugged cross,
And exchange it some day for a crown.

The Old Rugged Cross [1913] *refrain*

[1] See Henry Agard Wallace, p. 1010b.
[2] See Molière, p. 360b.

GUY WETMORE CARRYL
1873–1904

Thank God for peace! Thank God for peace, when the great gray ships come in!
When the Great Gray Ships Come In [New York Harbor, August 20, 1898], st. 4

ARTHUR CHAPMAN
1873–1935

Out where the handclasp's a little stronger,
Out where the smile dwells a little longer,
That's where the West begins.
Out Where the West Begins, st. 1

Out where the skies are a trifle bluer,
Out where friendship's a little truer.
Ib. st. 2

Where there's more of singing and less of sighing,
Where there's more of giving and less of buying,
And a man makes friends without half trying.
Ib. st. 3

SIDONIE-GABRIELLE COLETTE
1873–1954

Those pleasures so lightly called physical.
Mélanges

Whether you are dealing with an animal or a child, to convince is to weaken.
Le Pur et l'Impur

WALTER DE LA MARE
1873–1956

Slowly, silently, now the moon
Walks the night in her silver shoon.
Silver

Here lies a most beautiful lady,
Light of step and heart was she;
I think she was the most beautiful lady
That ever was in the West Country.
An Epitaph

"Is there anybody there?" said the Traveler,
Knocking on the moonlit door;
And his horse in the silence champed the grasses
Of the forest's ferny floor.
The Listeners

"Tell them that I came, and no one answered,
That I kept my word," he said.
Ib.

Look thy last on all things lovely,
Every hour — let no night
Seal thy sense in deathly slumber
Till to delight
Thou hast paid thy utmost blessing;
Since that all things thou wouldst praise
Beauty took from those who loved them
In other days.
Fare Well, st. 3

Nought but vast sorrow was there —
The sweet cheat gone.
The Ghost

Who said "Peacock Pie"?
The old king to the sparrow:
Who said "Crops are ripe"?
Rust to the harrow.
The Song of the Mad Prince

Who said, "Ay, mum's the word"?
Ib.

Life's troubled bubble broken.
Ib.

No lovelier hills than thine have laid
My tired thoughts to rest:
No peace of lovelier valleys made
Like peace within my breast.
England, st. 1

Poor Jim Jay
Got stuck fast
In Yesterday.
Jim Jay

It's a very odd thing —
As odd as can be —
That whatever Miss T. eats
Turns into Miss T.
Miss T.

Three jolly gentlemen,
In coats of red,
Rode their horses
Up to bed.
The Huntsmen

Be not too wildly amorous of the far,
Nor lure thy fantasy to its utmost
　scope.
　　　　　　　The Imagination's Pride

Bang! Now the animal
Is dead and dumb and done.
Nevermore to peep again, creep again,
　leap again,
Eat or sleep or drink again, oh, what
　fun!
　　　　　　　　　　　　　Hi!

MARK FENDERSON
1873–1944

What's the use? Yesterday an egg,
tomorrow a feather duster.
　　　　*Caption of cartoon: The
　　　　　　　Dejected Rooster*

FORD MADOX
[HUEFFER] FORD
1873–1939

This is the saddest story I have ever
heard.
　　　　The Good Soldier [1915],
　　　　　　　　　　first line

Only two classes of books are of universal appeal: the very best and the very
worst.　　　　*Joseph Conrad* [1924]

WILLIAM GREEN
1873–1952

The labor union is an elemental response to the human instinct for group
action in dealing with group problems.
　　　　　　　　Speech [1925]

PERCY HAMMOND
1873–1936

The female knee is a joint and not an
entertainment.　　　*Dramatic review*

ALFRED JARRY
1873–1907

Mother Ubu, you're very ugly today.
Is it because we have company?
　　　　　　　Ubu Roi [1896]

O the despair of Pygmalion, who
might have created a statue and only
made a woman!
　　　　　L'Amour Absolu [1899]

DANIEL GREGORY
MASON
1873–1953

The ideal of independence requires
resistance to the herd spirit now so
widespread, to our worship of quantity
and indifference to quality, to our unthinking devotion to organization,
standardization, propaganda, and advertising.　　　*Artistic Ideals* [1927]

Art of any profundity can be appreciated only slowly, gradually, in
leisurely contemplation.[1]　　　*Ib.*

GEORGE EDWARD
MOORE
1873–1958

It appears to me that in Ethics, as
in all other philosophical studies, the
difficulties and disagreements, of which
history is full, are mainly due to a very
simple cause: namely to the attempt to
answer questions, without first discovering precisely *what* question it is which
you desire to answer.
　　　Principia Ethica [1903], *preface*

DWIGHT WHITNEY
MORROW
1873–1931

Any party which takes credit for the
rain must not be surprised if its opponents blame it for the drought.
　　　　　　　　　　Saying

ALBERT JAY NOCK
1873–1945

All Souls College, Oxford, planned
better than it knew when it limited the
number of its undergraduates to four;
four is exactly the right number for any

[1] See Proust, p. 907b.

college which is really intent on getting results.
Memoirs of a Superfluous Man [1943], III, ch. 3

Money does not pay for anything, never has, never will. It is an economic axiom as old as the hills that goods and services can be paid for only with goods and services. *Ib. 13*

As sheer casual reading matter, I still find the English dictionary the most interesting book in our language.
Ib. IV, ch. 1

CHARLES PÉGUY
1873–1914

It's a nuisance, God said. When those French are gone,
No one will be left to understand certain things I do.
Les Sept Contre Paris

Surrender is essentially an operation by means of which we set about explaining instead of acting.
Les Cahiers de la Quinzaine [1905]

Homer is new and fresh this morning, and nothing, perhaps, is as old and tired as today's newspaper.
Note sur M. Bergson et la Philosophie Bergsonienne [1914]

Freedom is a system based on courage.
From HALÉVY, *Life of Charles Péguy*

SIME SILVERMAN[1]
1873–1933

Wall Street Lays An Egg.
Headline announcing stock market crash [October 1929]

[1] Silverman, who founded and edited the famous theatrical trade paper *Variety* [1905], had perhaps more influence on American slang than any man of his time.

Sticks Nix Hicks Pix.
Headline, meaning that rural audiences do not care for moving pictures dealing with country themes

ALFRED EMANUEL SMITH[1]
1873–1944

The kiss of death.
Alluding to Hearst's support of Ogden Mills, Smith's unsuccessful opponent for Governor of New York State [1926]

Let's look at the record.
Campaign speeches [1928]

The Governor of New York State does not have to be an acrobat.
Speech in behalf of Franklin D. Roosevelt [1928]

Nobody shoots at Santa Claus.
Campaign speeches [1936]

No matter how thin you slice it, it's still baloney. *Ib.*

HENRY MAJOR TOMLINSON
1873–1958

The sea is at its best at London, near midnight, when you are within the arms of a capacious chair, before a glowing fire, selecting phases of the voyages you will never make.
The Sea and the Jungle [1912]

The reader who is illuminated is, in a real sense, the poem.
Between the Lines [1930]

Bad and indifferent criticism of books is just as serious as a city's careless drainage. *Ib.*

[1] He is the Happy Warrior of the political battlefield. — FRANKLIN D. ROOSEVELT, *Nominating speech, Democratic National Convention* [June 26, 1924]. See Wordsworth, p. 515a.
Al Smith knew as much as any living man of the art of democratic government. — ELLERY SEDGWICK, *The Happy Profession* [1946], *ch. 17*

LENA GUILBERT FORD
d. 1915

Keep the home fires burning,
While your hearts are yearning;
Though your lads are far away
They dream of home.
There's a silver lining
Through the dark cloud shining;
Turn the dark cloud inside out,
Till the boys come home.
> *Keep the Home Fires Burning*
> *[1915]*

SIR NORMAN ANGELL
1874–1967

The Great Illusion.
> *Title of book [1910] on the*
> *futility of war*

MAURICE BARING
1874–1945

All theories of what a good play is, or how a good play should be written, are futile. A good play is a play which when acted upon the boards makes an audience interested and pleased. A play that fails in this is a bad play.
> *Have You Anything to Declare?*

CHARLES AUSTIN BEARD
1874–1948
AND
MARY RITTER BEARD
1876–1958

At no time, at no place, in solemn convention assembled, through no chosen agents, had the American people officially proclaimed the United States to be a democracy. The Constitution did not contain the word or any word lending countenance to it, except possibly the mention of "We, the people," in the preamble . . . When the Constitution was framed no respecta-ble person called himself or herself a democrat.
> *America in Midpassage* [1939],
> *ch. 17*

GORDON BOTTOMLEY
1874–1948

Many deaths have place in men
Before they come to die;
Joys must be used and spent, and then
Abandoned and passed by.
> *New Year's Eve, 1913*

When you destroy a blade of grass
You poison England at her roots.
> *To Ironfounders and Others*

Your worship is your furnaces,
Which, like old idols, lost obscenes,
Have molten bowels; your vision is
Machines for making more machines.
> *Ib.*

ANNA HEMPSTEAD BRANCH
1874–1937

Order is a lovely thing;
On disarray it lays its wing,
Teaching simplicity to sing.
> *The Monk in the Kitchen*

His screaming stallions maned with
whistling wind.
> *Nimrod Wars with the Angels*

God wove a web of loveliness,
Of clouds and stars and birds,
But made not anything at all
So beautiful as words.
> *Songs for My Mother: Her*
> *Words, st. 5*

ARTHUR HENRY REGINALD BULLER
1874–1944

There was a young lady named Bright,
Whose speed was far faster than light;
She set out one day
In a relative way,
And returned home the previous night.
> *Limerick* [1]

[1] *Punch,* December 19, 1923.

GILBERT KEITH
CHESTERTON
1874–1936

Likelier the barricades shall blare
Slaughter below and smoke above,
And death and hate and hell declare
That men have found a thing to love.
The Napoleon of Notting Hill
[1906]

"The Christian ideal," it is said, "has not been tried and found wanting; it has been found difficult and left untried."
What's Wrong with the World
[1910], pt. I, ch. 5

Nothing sublimely artistic has ever arisen out of mere art, any more than anything essentially reasonable has ever arisen out of pure reason. There must always be a rich moral soil for any great aesthetic growth.
A Defense of Nonsense [1911]

For the great Gaels of Ireland
Are the men that God made mad,
For all their wars are merry,
And all their songs are sad.[1]
The Ballad of the White Horse
[1911], bk. II

And if ever ye ride in Ireland,
The jest may yet be said,
There is the land of broken hearts,
And the land of broken heads.
Ib. V

Every great literature has always been allegorical — allegorical of some view of the whole universe. *Ib.*

The whole difference between construction and creation is exactly this: that a thing constructed can only be loved after it is constructed; but a thing created is loved before it exists.
Preface to DICKENS, *Pickwick*
Papers

[1] For the Young Gaels of Ireland
Are the lads that drive me mad;
For half their words need footnotes,
And half their rhymes are bad.
ARTHUR GUITERMAN [1871–1943], *The Young Celtic Poets, st. 2*

A good joke is the one ultimate and sacred thing which cannot be criticized. Our relations with a good joke are direct and even divine relations.
Preface to DICKENS, *Pickwick*
Papers

The world will never starve for wonders; but only for want of wonder.
Inscription, General Motors Building, Century of Progress Exposition, Chicago

But they that fought for England,
Following a fallen star,
Alas, alas for England
They have their graves afar.
Elegy in a Country Churchyard

Strong gongs groaning as the guns boom far
(Don John of Austria is going to the war);
Stiff flags straining in the night blasts cold
In the gloom black-purple, in the glint old gold;
Torchlight crimson on the copper kettledrums,
Then the tuckets, then the trumpets, then the cannon, and he comes.
Lepanto [1915]

Cervantes on his galley sets the sword back in the sheath
(Don John of Austria rides homeward with a wreath).
And he sees across a weary land a straggling road in Spain,
Up which a lean and foolish knight forever rides in vain. *Ib.*

To an open house in the evening
Home shall men come,
To an older place than Eden
And a taller town than Rome.
The House of Christmas

Burn from my brain and from my breast
Sloth, and the cowardice that clings,
And stiffness and the soul's arrest:
And feed my brain with better things.
A Ballade of a Book Reviewer

The strangest whim has seized me
. . . After all
I think I will not hang myself today.
     A Ballade of Suicide

Don't ever take a fence down until
you know the reason why it was put
up.[1]
     *Ascribed to Chesterton by John
F. Kennedy in a 1945 notebook*

The face of Father Brown . . .
could shine with ignorance as well as
with knowledge.
     The Scandal of Father Brown
     [1935]

St. George he was for England,
And before he killed the dragon
He drank a pint of English ale
Out of an English flagon.
     The Englishman

Step softly, under snow or rain,
To find the place where men can pray;
The way is all so very plain
That we may lose the way.
     The Wise Men

And Noah he often said to his wife
     when he sat down to dine,
"I don't care where the water goes if it
     doesn't get into the wine."
     Wine and Water

Before the Roman came to Rye or out
     to Severn strode,
The rolling English drunkard made the
     rolling English road.
     The Rolling English Road

Tea, although an Oriental,
Is a gentleman at least;
Cocoa is a cad and coward,
Cocoa is a vulgar beast.
     The Song of Right and Wrong

I also had my hour;
One far fierce hour and sweet:
There was a shout about my ears,
And palms before my feet.
     The Donkey

The Yankee is a dab at electricity and
     crime,

[1] See Robert Frost, p. 926a.

He tells you how he hustles and it takes
     him quite a time,
I like his hospitality that's cordial and
     frank,
I do not mind his money but I do not
     like his swank.
     A Song of Self-Esteem

SIR WINSTON SPENCER CHURCHILL[1]
1874–1965

I pass with relief from the tossing sea
of Cause and Theory to the firm
ground of Result and Fact.
     The Malakand Field Force [1898]

It is better to be making the news
than taking it; to be an actor rather
than a critic.   *Ib.*

Nothing in life is so exhilarating as
to be shot at without result.   *Ib.*

There are men in the world who derive as stern an exaltation from the
proximity of disaster and ruin, as others
from success.   *Ib.*

Victory is the beautiful, bright-
colored flower. Transport is the stem
without which it could never have
blossomed.   *The River War* [1899]

Terminological inexactitude.
     Speech, House of Commons
     [*February 22, 1906*]

The maxim of the British people is
"Business as usual."
     Speech, Guildhall [*November 9,
     1914*]

Politics are almost as exciting as war,
and quite as dangerous. In war you can
only be killed once, but in politics
many times.   *Remark* [1920]

By being so long in the lowest form
[at Harrow] I gained an immense advantage over the cleverer boys. . . . I
got into my bones the essential structure of the ordinary British sentence
— which is a noble thing. Naturally I

[1] He mobilized the English language and sent
it into battle. — JOHN F. KENNEDY, on conferring
honorary citizenship on Churchill [April 9, 1963]
     See Roosevelt and Churchill, p. 974.

am biased in favor of boys learning English; I would make them all learn English: and then I would let the clever ones learn Latin as an honor, and Greek as a treat.

Roving Commission: My Early Life [1930]

It is a good thing for an uneducated man to read books of quotations. Bartlett's *Familiar Quotations* is an admirable work, and I studied it intently. The quotations when engraved upon the memory give you good thoughts. They also make you anxious to read the authors and look for more. *Ib.*

Come on now, all you young men, all over the world. You are needed more than ever now to fill the gap of a generation shorn by the war. You have not an hour to lose. You must take your places in life's fighting line. Twenty to twenty-five! These are the years! Don't be content with things as they are. "The earth is yours and the fullness thereof." Enter upon your inheritance, accept your responsibilities. Raise the glorious flags again, advance them upon the new enemies, who constantly gather upon the front of the human army, and have only to be assaulted to be overthrown. Don't take no for an answer, never submit to failure. Do not be fobbed off with mere personal success or acceptance. You will make all kinds of mistakes; but as long as you are generous and true, and also fierce, you cannot hurt the world or even seriously distress her. She was made to be wooed and won by youth. *Ib.*

Decided only to be undecided, resolved to be irresolute, adamant for drift, solid for fluidity, all-powerful to be impotent.[1]

While England Slept [1936]

Dictators ride to and fro upon tigers which they dare not dismount. And the tigers are getting hungry.[2] *Ib.*

[1] Of Stanley Baldwin's policies.
[2] He who rides a tiger is afraid to dismount. — WILLIAM SCARBOROUGH, *Chinese Proverbs* [1875], *no. 2082*
See Truman, p. 983a.

I have watched this famous island descending incontinently, fecklessly, the stairway which leads to a dark gulf. It is a fine broad stairway at the beginning, but after a bit the carpet ends. A little farther on there are only flagstones, and a little farther on still these break beneath your feet.

While England Slept

The German dictator, instead of snatching the victuals from the table, has been content to have them served to him course by course.

Speech on the Munich agreement, House of Commons [*October 5, 1938*]

That long [Canadian] frontier from the Atlantic to the Pacific Oceans, guarded only by neighborly respect and honorable obligations, is an example to every country and a pattern for the future of the world.

Speech in honor of R. B. Bennett, Canada Club, London [*April 20, 1939*]

I cannot forecast to you the action of Russia. It is a riddle wrapped in a mystery inside an enigma.

Radio broadcast [*October 1, 1939*]

For each and for all, as for the Royal Navy, the watchword should be, "Carry on, and dread nought."

Speech on traffic at sea, House of Commons [*December 6, 1939*]

I have nothing to offer but blood, toil, tears and sweat.[1]

First Statement as Prime Minister, House of Commons [*May 13, 1940*]

[1] Mollify it with thy tears, or sweat, or blood. — JOHN DONNE, *An Anatomy of the World* [1611], *I, 430–431*
    Year after year they voted cent per cent, Blood, sweat, and tear-wrung millions — why? for rent!
        BYRON, *The Age of Bronze* [1823], *XIV*
See Prescott, p. 587a, and Garibaldi, p. 620a.
It [poetry] is forged slowly and patiently, link by link, with sweat and blood and tears. —

Victory at all costs, victory in spite of all terror, victory however long and hard the road may be; for without victory there is no survival.

> *First Statement as Prime Minister, House of Commons*

We shall not flag or fail. We shall go on to the end. We shall fight in France, we shall fight on the seas and oceans, we shall fight with growing confidence and growing strength in the air, we shall defend our island, whatever the cost may be, we shall fight on the beaches, we shall fight on the landing grounds, we shall fight in the fields and in the streets, we shall fight in the hills; we shall never surrender.

> *Speech on Dunkirk, House of Commons [June 4, 1940]*

If we open a quarrel between the past and the present, we shall find that we have lost the future.

> *Speech, House of Commons [June 18, 1940]*

Upon this battle [of Britain] depends the survival of Christian civilization. Upon it depends our own British life, and the long continuity of our institutions and our Empire. The whole fury and might of the enemy must very soon be turned on us. Hitler knows that he will have to break us in this island or lose the war. If we can stand up to him, all Europe may be free and the life of the world may move forward into broad, sunlit uplands. But if we fail, then the whole world, including the United States, including all that we have known and cared for, will sink into the abyss of a new Dark Age made more sinister, perhaps more protracted, by the lights of perverted science. Let

us therefore brace ourselves to our duties, and so bear ourselves that, if the British Empire and its Commonwealth last for a thousand years, men will still say: "This was their finest hour."

> *Speech, House of Commons*

We shall defend every village, every town and every city. The vast mass of London itself, fought street by street, could easily devour an entire hostile army; and we would rather see London laid in ruins and ashes than that it should be tamely and abjectly enslaved.

> *Radio broadcast [July 14, 1940]*

Never in the field of human conflict was so much owed by so many to so few.

> *Tribute to the Royal Air Force, House of Commons [August 20, 1940]*

The British Empire and the United States will have to be somewhat mixed up together in some of their affairs for mutual and general advantage. For my own part, looking out upon the future, I do not view the process with any misgivings. I could not stop it if I wished; no one can stop it. Like the Mississippi, it just keeps rolling along.[1] Let it roll. Let it roll on full flood, inexorable, irresistible, benignant, to broader lands and better days. *Ib.*

This wicked man Hitler, the repository and embodiment of many forms of soul-destroying hatred, this monstrous product of former wrongs and shame.

> *Radio broadcast [September 11, 1940]*

Death and sorrow will be the companions of our journey; hardship our garment; constancy and valor our only shield. We must be united, we must be undaunted, we must be inflexible.

> *Report on the war, House of Commons [October 8, 1940]*

LORD ALFRED DOUGLAS, *Collected Poems* [1919]
 Their sweat, their tears, their blood bedewed the endless plain. — WINSTON S. CHURCHILL, *The Unknown War* [1931], referring to the armies of the Czar before the Russian Revolution
 Churchill referred to his promise of blood, toil, tears and sweat in subsequent speeches on October 8, 1940, May 7 and December 2, 1941, and January 27 and November 10, 1942.

[1] Ol' Man River [Mississippi] . . . he keeps on rollin' along. — OSCAR HAMMERSTEIN 2ND [1927], *music by* JEROME KERN

We are waiting for the long-promised invasion. So are the fishes.

Radio broadcast to the French people [October 21, 1940]

History with its flickering lamp stumbles along the trail of the past, trying to reconstruct its scenes, to revive its echoes, and kindle with pale gleams the passion of former days. What is the worth of all this? The only guide to a man is his conscience; the only shield to his memory is the rectitude and sincerity of his actions. It is very imprudent to walk through life without this shield, because we are so often mocked by the failure of our hopes and the upsetting of our calculations; but with this shield, however the fates may play, we march always in the ranks of honor.

Tribute to Neville Chamberlain, House of Commons [November 12, 1940]

To die at the height of a man's career, the highest moment of his effort here in this world, universally honored and admired, to die while great issues are still commanding the whole of his interest, to be taken from us at a moment when he could already see ultimate success in view — is not the most unenviable of fates.[1]

Report on the war, House of Commons [December 19, 1940]

I do not resent criticism, even when, for the sake of emphasis, it parts for the time with reality.

Speech, House of Commons [January 22, 1941]

Here is the answer which I will give to President Roosevelt. . . . Give us the tools, and we will finish the job.

Radio broadcast [February 9, 1941]

[1] Lord Lothian, British Ambassador to the United States, died in Washington, December 12, 1940.

See Lord Lothian, p. 969b.

This is one of those cases in which the imagination is baffled by the facts.

Remark in the House of Commons following the parachute descent in Scotland of Rudolf Hess [May 13, 1941]

The British nation is unique in this respect. They are the only people who like to be told how bad things are, who like to be told the worst.

Report on the war, House of Commons [June 10, 1941]

A vile race of quislings[1] — to use the new word which will carry the scorn of mankind down the centuries.

Speech at St. James's Palace, London [June 12, 1941]

The destiny of mankind is not decided by material computation. When great causes are on the move in the world . . . we learn that we are spirits, not animals, and that something is going on in space and time, and beyond space and time, which, whether we like it or not, spells duty.

Radio broadcast to America on receiving an honorary degree of Doctor of Laws from the University of Rochester, New York [June 16, 1941]

Hitler is a monster of wickedness, insatiable in his lust for blood and plunder. Not content with having all Europe under his heel, or else terrorized into various forms of abject submission, he must now carry his work of butchery and desolation among the vast multitudes of Russia and of Asia. The terrible military machine, which we and the rest of the civilized world so foolishly, so supinely, so insensately allowed the Nazi gangsters to build up year by year from almost nothing, cannot stand idle lest it rust or fall to pieces. It must be in continual motion, grinding up

[1] Vidkun Quisling, head of the Nasjonal Samling party in Norway, who cooperated and collaborated with the Nazis when Germany invaded Norway [April 9, 1940]. Quisling was executed [October 23, 1945].

human lives and trampling down the homes and the rights of hundreds of millions of men. Moreover it must be fed, not only with flesh but with oil. So now this bloodthirsty guttersnipe must launch his mechanized armies upon new fields of slaughter, pillage and devastation.
> Radio broadcast on the German invasion of Russia [June 22, 1941]

We will have no truce or parley with you [Hitler], or the grisly gang who work your wicked will. You do your worst — and we will do our best.
> Speech, London County Council [July 14, 1941]

The V sign is the symbol of the unconquerable will of the occupied territories, and a portent of the fate awaiting the Nazi tyranny.
> Message to the people of Europe on launching the V for Victory propaganda campaign [July 20, 1941]

Nothing is more dangerous in wartime than to live in the temperamental atmosphere of a Gallup Poll,[1] always feeling one's pulse and taking one's temperature.
> Report on the war, House of Commons [September 30, 1941]

Do not let us speak of darker days; let us speak rather of sterner days. These are not dark days: these are great days — the greatest days our country has ever lived; and we must all thank God that we have been allowed, each of us according to our stations, to play a part in making these days memorable in the history of our race.
> Address, Harrow School [October 29, 1941]

In the past we have had a light which flickered, in the present we have a light which flames, and in the future

there will be a light which shines over all the land and sea.
> Speech on war with Japan, House of Commons [December 8, 1941]

What kind of people do they [the Japanese] think we are?
> Speech to United States Congress [December 26, 1941]

We have not journeyed all this way across the centuries, across the oceans, across the mountains, across the prairies, because we are made of sugar candy.
> Speech to the Canadian Senate and House of Commons, Ottawa [December 30, 1941]

This is no time to speak of the hopes of the future, or the broader world which lies beyond our struggles and our victory. We have to win that world for which lies beyond our struggles and our sacrifices. We have not won it yet. The crisis is upon us. . . . In this strange, terrible world war there is a place for everyone, man and woman, old and young, hale and halt; service in a thousand forms is open. There is no room now for the dilettante, the weakling, for the shirker, or the sluggard. The mine, the factory, the dockyard, the salt sea waves, the fields to till, the home, the hospital, the chair of the scientist, the pulpit of the preacher — from the highest to the humblest tasks, all are of equal honor; all have their part to play.
> *Ib.*

When I warned [the French] that Britain would fight on alone whatever they did, their generals told their prime minister and his divided cabinet, "In three weeks England will have her neck wrung like a chicken." Some chicken; some neck. *Ib.*

The late M. Venizelos[1] observed that in all her wars England — he

---

[1] Dr. George H. Gallup founded the British Institute of Public Opinion in 1936.

[1] Eleutherios Venizelos [1864–1936], Greek statesman.

should have said Britain, of course — always wins one battle — the last.

Speech at the Lord Mayor's Day Luncheon, London [November 10, 1942]

Now this is not the end. It is not even the beginning of the end.[1] But it is, perhaps, the end of the beginning.

Ib.

I have not become the King's First Minister in order to preside over the liquidation of the British Empire.

Ib.

The soft underbelly of the Axis.

Report on the war, House of Commons [November 11, 1942]

The proud German Army has once again proved the truth of the saying, "The Hun is always either at your throat or at your feet."

Speech to United States Congress [May 19, 1943]

There was a man who sold a hyena skin while the beast still lived and who was killed in hunting it.

Speech on Allied war gains, House of Commons [August 2, 1944]

"Not in vain" may be the pride of those who survived and the epitaph of those who fell.[2]

Speech, House of Commons [September 28, 1944]

The United States is a land of free speech. Nowhere is speech freer — not even here where we sedulously cultivate it even in its most repulsive form.

Ib.

He [President Franklin D. Roosevelt] died in harness, and we may well

say in battle harness, like his soldiers, sailors and airmen who died side by side with ours and carrying out their tasks to the end all over the world. What an enviable death was his.

Speech, House of Commons [April 17, 1945]

In Franklin Roosevelt there died the greatest American friend we have ever known — and the greatest champion of freedom who has ever brought help and comfort from the New World to the Old.

Ib.

I think "No comment" is a splendid expression. I am using it again and again. I got it from Sumner Welles.

To reporters at Washington airport, after conferring with President Truman at the White House [February 12, 1946]

From Stettin in the Baltic to Trieste in the Adriatic an iron curtain[1] has descended across the Continent.

Address, Westminster College, Fulton, Missouri [March 5, 1946]

This address to which I have given the title, "The Sinews of Peace."

Ib.

---

[1] Between them [Germany] and me there is now a bloody iron curtain which has descended forever! — QUEEN ELIZABETH OF BELGIUM [1874–1965], in 1914. Though German-born, she stood staunchly by her adopted country in World War I.

France . . . a nation of forty millions with a deep-rooted grievance and an iron curtain at its frontier. — GEORGE WASHINGTON CRILE, *A Mechanistic View of War and Peace* [1915]

With a rumble and a roar, an iron curtain is descending on Russian history. — VASILY ROZANOV, *Apocalypse of our Time* [1918]

We were behind the "iron curtain" at last. — ETHEL ANNAKIN SNOWDEN, *Through Bolshevik Russia* [1920]

The Nazi Minister of Enlightenment and Propaganda, Dr. Josef Goebbels [1897–1945], used the phrase "iron curtain" in reference to the U.S.S.R. in *Das Reich* [February 23, 1945]. Hitler's Minister of Finance, Count Lutz Schwerin von Krosigk, also used it [May 2, 1945].

Churchill used it — not publicly — in a top-secret telegram to President Truman [May 12, 1945].

---

[1] See Talleyrand, p. 484a.

[2] The eight thousand paratroopers of the First British Airborne Division who landed in Arnhem, Holland, behind the German lines in September 1944 and held the area for nine days and nights, with a loss of six thousand. Major General R. E. Urquhart, the division commander, radioed to Field Marshal Bernard Montgomery: All will be ordered to break out rather than surrender.

In War: Resolution. In Defeat: Defiance. In Victory: Magnanimity. In Peace: Good Will.
> *The Second World War: Moral of the Work, vol. I, The Gathering Storm* [1948]

No one can guarantee success in war, but only deserve it.
> *Ib. II, Their Finest Hour* [1949]

When you have to kill a man it costs nothing to be polite.
> *Ib. III, The Grand Alliance* [1950]

[Clement] Attlee is a very modest man. And with reason.
> *On Clement Attlee, the Labor Prime Minister*

Everyone has his day and some days last longer than others.
> *House of Commons* [*January* 1952]

A fanatic is one who can't change his mind and won't change the subject.
> *Saying*

The inherent vice of capitalism is the unequal sharing of blessings; the inherent virtue of socialism is the equal sharing of miseries.   *Ib.*

Short words are best and the old words when short are best of all.   *Ib.*

It is hard, if not impossible, to snub a beautiful woman — they remain beautiful and the rebuke recoils.   *Ib.*

This is the sort of English up with which I will not put.[1]   *Attributed*

CLARENCE DAY
1874–1935

When eras die, their legacies
Are left to strange police.
Professors in New England guard
The glory that was Greece.
> *Thoughts Without Words*

The parting injunctions
Of mothers and wives

Are one of those functions
That poison their lives.
> *Scenes from the Mesozoic*

It is possible that our race may be an accident, in a meaningless universe, living its brief life uncared for, on this dark, cooling star: but even so — and all the more — what marvelous creatures we are! What fairy story, what tale from the Arabian Nights of the jinns, is a hundredth part as wonderful as this true fairy story of simians! It is so much more heartening, too, than the tales we invent. A universe capable of giving birth to many such accidents is — blind or not — a good world to live in, a promising universe. . . . We once thought we lived on God's footstool; it may be a throne.[1]
> *This Simian World* [1920]. XIX

Father declared he was going to buy a new plot in the cemetery, a plot all for himself. "And I'll buy one on a corner," he added triumphantly, "where I can get out!"
Mother looked at him, startled but admiring, and whispered to me, "I almost believe he could do it."
> *Life with Father* [1935]

ROBERT FROST
1874–1963

I'm going out to clean the pasture spring;
I'll only stop to rake the leaves away
(And wait to watch the water clear, I may):
I shan't be gone long. — You come too.   *The Pasture, st. 1*

They would not find me changed from him they knew —
Only more sure of all I thought was true.
> *Into My Own* [1913], *st. 4*

Ah, when to the heart of man
Was it ever less than a treason
To go with the drift of things,
To yield with a grace to reason,

---

[1] See Wolcott Gibbs, p. 1050b.

[1] See *Matthew 5:34*, p. 40b; Pope, p. 408a; and H. G. Wells, p. 888b.

And bow and accept the end
Of a love or a season? [1]
Reluctance [1913], *st. 4*

Something there is that doesn't love a
wall.   *Mending Wall* [1914]

My apple trees will never get across
And eat the cones under his pines, I tell
him.
He only says, "Good fences make good
neighbors."   *Ib.*

Before I built a wall I'd ask to know
What I was walling in or walling out. [2]
Ib.

And nothing to look backward to with
pride,
And nothing to look forward to with
hope.
The Death of the Hired Man
[1914]

Home is the place where, when you
have to go there,
They have to take you in.   *Ib.*

The nearest friends can go
With anyone to death, comes so far
short
They might as well not try to go at
all.   *Home Burial* [1914]

Most of the change we think we see in
life
Is due to truths being in and out of
favor.
The Black Cottage [1914]

The blue's but a mist from the breath
of the wind,
A tarnish that goes at a touch of the
hand.   *Blueberries* [1914]

The best way out is always through.
A Servant to Servants [1914]

This sleep of mine, whatever sleep it is.
Were he not gone,
The woodchuck could say whether it's
like his
Long sleep, as I describe its coming on,
Or just some human sleep.
After Apple-Picking [1914]

[1] See Pope, p. 412b.
[2] See Chesterton, p. 919a.

Pressed into service means pressed out
of shape.
The Self-Seeker [1914]

I shall be telling this with a sigh
Somewhere ages and ages hence:
Two roads diverged in a wood, and
I —
I took the one less traveled by,
And that has made all the difference.
The Road Not Taken [1916], *st. 4*

The Hyla breed
That shouted in the mist a month ago,
Like ghost of sleighbells in a ghost of
snow.   *Hyla Brook* [1916]

We love the things we love for what
they are.   *Ib.*

I'd like to get away from earth awhile
And then come back to it and begin
over.
May no fate willfully misunderstand
me
And half grant what I wish and snatch
me away
Not to return. Earth's the right place
for love:
I don't know where it's likely to go better.   *Birches* [1916]

One could do worse than be a swinger
of birches.   *Ib.*

I wonder about the trees:
Why do we wish to bear
Forever the noise of these
More than another noise
So close to our dwelling place?
The Sound of the Trees [1916]

I shall set forth for somewhere,
I shall make the reckless choice
Some say when they are in voice
And tossing so as to scare
The white clouds over them on.
I shall have less to say,
But I shall be gone.   *Ib.*

I met a Californian who would
Talk California — a state so blessed,
He said, in climate, none had ever died
there
A natural death.
New Hampshire [1923]

Do you know,
Considering the market, there are more
Poems produced than any other thing?
No wonder poets sometimes have to seem
So much more businesslike than businessmen.
Their wares are so much harder to get rid of.   *New Hampshire*

Anything I can say about New Hampshire
Will serve almost as well about Vermont,
Excepting that they differ in their mountains.
The Vermont mountains stretch extended straight;
New Hampshire mountains curl up in a coil.   *Ib.*

The snake stood up for evil in the Garden.   *The Ax-Helve* [1923]

Why make so much of fragmentary blue
In here and there a bird, or butterfly,
Or flower, or wearing-stone, or open eye,
When heaven presents in sheets the solid hue?
  Fragmentary Blue [1923], *st. 1*

Some say the world will end in fire,
Some say in ice.
From what I've tasted of desire
I hold with those who favor fire.
But if it had to perish twice,
I think I know enough of hate
To say that for destruction ice
Is also great
And would suffice.
  Fire and Ice [1] [1923]

The way a crow
Shook down on me
The dust of snow
From a hemlock tree

Has given my heart
A change of mood

---

[1] See Dante, p. 159b, and Housman, p. 853a.

And saved some part
Of a day I had rued.
  Dust of Snow [1923]

We heard the miniature thunder where he fled.   *The Runaway* [1923]

Whose woods these are I think I know.
His house is in the village though;
He will not see me stopping here
To watch his woods fill up with snow.
  Stopping by Woods on a Snowy Evening [1923], *st. 1*

My little horse must think it queer
To stop without a farmhouse near.
  Ib. st. 2

He gives his harness bells a shake
To ask if there is some mistake.
  Ib. st. 3

The woods are lovely, dark and deep.
But I have promises to keep,
And miles to go before I sleep.[1]
  Ib. st. 4

Love at the lips was touch
As sweet as I could bear;
And once that seemed too much;
I lived on air.
  To Earthward [1923], *st. 1*

Now no joy but lacks salt
That is not dashed with pain
And weariness and fault;
I crave the stain

Of tears, the aftermark
Of almost too much love,
The sweet of bitter bark
And burning clove.   *Ib. st. 5, 6*

Keep cold, young orchard. Goodbye and keep cold.
Dread fifty above more than fifty below.
  Goodbye and Keep Cold [1923]

Heaven gives its glimpses only to those
Not in position to look too close.
  A Passing Glimpse [1928]

---

[1] The stars look very cold about the sky,
And I have many miles on foot to fare.
  KEATS, *Keen, fitful gusts are whispering here and there* [*1817*]

Tree at my window, window tree,
My sash is lowered when night comes
    on;
But let there never be curtain drawn
Between you and me.
         Tree at My Window [1928], *st. 1*

That day she put our heads together,
Fate had her imagination about her,
Your head so much concerned with
    outer,
Mine with inner, weather.   *Ib. st. 4*

It looked as if a night of dark intent
Was coming, and not only a night, an
    age.
Someone had better be prepared for
    rage.
There would be more than ocean-water
    broken
Before God's last *Put out the Light* was
    spoken.
         Once by the Pacific [1928]

I have been one acquainted with the
    night.
    Acquainted with the Night [1928]

If, as they say, some dust thrown in my
    eyes
Will keep my talk from getting over-
    wise,
I'm not the one for putting off the
    proof.
Let it be overwhelming.
         Dust in the Eyes [1928]

Don't join too many gangs. Join few if
    any.
Join the United States and join the
    family —
But not much in between unless a col-
    lege.   *Build Soil* [1932]

The sun was warm but the wind was
    chill.
You know how it is with an April day
When the sun is out and the wind is
    still,
You're one month on in the middle of
    May.
But if you so much as dare to speak,
A cloud comes over the sunlit arch,
A wind comes off a frozen peak,

And you're two months back in the
    middle of March.
        Two Tramps in Mud Time
               [1936], *st. 3*

But yield who will to their separation,
My object in living is to unite
My avocation and my vocation
As my two eyes make one in sight.
Only where love and need are one,
And the work is play for mortal stakes,
Is the deed ever really done
For Heaven and the future's sakes.
                 Ib. st. 9

No memory of having starred
Atones for later disregard,
Or keeps the end from being hard.

Better to go down dignified
With boughten friendship by your side
Than none at all. Provide, provide! [1]
        Provide, Provide, st. 6, 7

I never dared be radical when young
For fear it would make me conservative
    when old.   *Precaution* [1936]

Never ask of money spent
Where the spender thinks it went.
Nobody was ever meant
To remember or invent
What he did with every cent.
        The Hardship of Accounting
                 [1936]

The land was ours before we were the
    land's.
She was our land more than a hundred
    years
Before we were her people.
        The Gift Outright [1941] [2]

    Happiness Makes Up in Height for
What It Lacks in Length.
        Title of poem [1942]

Far in the pillared dark
Thrush music went —
Almost like a call to come in
To the dark and lament.

[1] See Samuel Johnson, p. 432b.
[2] Read first before the Phi Beta Kappa Society
at William and Mary College [December 5, 1941],
later at the inauguration of President John
F. Kennedy [January 20, 1961].

But no, I was out for stars:
I would not come in.
I meant not even if asked,
And I hadn't been.
Come In [1942], *st. 4, 5*

And were an epitaph to be my story
I'd have a short one ready for my own.
I would have written of me on my
stone:
I had a lover's quarrel with the world.
The Lesson for Today [1942]

We dance round in a ring and suppose,
But the Secret sits in the middle and
knows.   *The Secret Sits* [1945]

Here are your waters and your watering
place.
Drink and be whole again beyond confusion.
Directive [1947]

Any eye is an evil eye
That looks in on to a mood apart.
A Mood Apart [1947]

It asks a little of us here.
It asks of us a certain height,
So when at times the mob is swayed
To carry praise or blame too far,
We may take something like a star
To stay our minds on and be staid.
Take Something Like a Star [1949]

Forgive, O Lord, my little jokes on
Thee
And I'll forgive Thy great big one on
me.
From In the Clearing [1962]

Have I not walked without an upward
look
Of caution under stars that very well
Might not have missed me when they
shot and fell?
It was a risk I had to take — and took.
Bravado [1962]

I am assured at any rate
Man's practically inexterminate.
Someday I must go into that.
There's always been an Ararat
Where someone someone else begat
To start the world all over at.
A-Wishing Well [1962]

It takes all sorts of in and outdoor
schooling
To get adapted to my kind of fooling.
It Takes All Sorts [1962]

Unless I'm wrong
I but obey
The urge of a song:
I'm — bound — away! [1]

And I may return
If dissatisfied
With what I learn
From having died.
Away! [1962], *st. 5, 6*

It is absurd to think that the only
way to tell if a poem is lasting is to wait
and see if it lasts. The right reader of a
good poem can tell the moment it
strikes him that he has taken an immortal wound — that he will never get
over it. [2]
The Poetry of Amy Lowell.
From the Christian Science
Monitor [May 16, 1925]

A poem . . . begins as a lump in the
throat, a sense of wrong, a homesickness,
a lovesickness. . . . It finds the thought
and the thought finds the words.
Letter to Louis Untermeyer
[January 1, 1916]

Everything written is as good as it is
dramatic. It need not declare itself in
form, but it is drama or nothing.
A Way Out [1929], *preface*

It should be of the pleasure of a poem
itself to tell how it can. The figure a
poem makes. It begins in delight and
ends in wisdom. The figure is the same
for love.
The Figure a Poem Makes,
preface to Collected Poems
[1939]

No tears in the writer, no tears in the
reader. [3]   *Ib.*

Like a piece of ice on a hot stove
the poem must ride on its own melt-

---

[1] See *Shenandoah* (chantey), p. 1101a.
[2] See Coleridge, p. 528b; also see *The Figure a Poem Makes,* this column.
[3] See Charles Churchill, p. 456a, and note.

ing. . . . Read it a hundred times; it will forever keep its freshness as a metal keeps its fragrance. It can never lose its sense of a meaning that once unfolded by surprise as it went.[1]
The Figure a Poem Makes, preface to Collected Poems

How many times it thundered before Franklin took the hint! How many apples fell on Newton's head before he took the hint! Nature is always hinting at us. It hints over and over again. And suddenly we take the hint.
Comment

It is only a moment here and a moment there that the greatest writer has. *Ib.*

Love is an irresistible desire to be irresistibly desired. *Ib.*

Poetry is a way of taking life by the throat. *Ib.*

Talking is a hydrant in the yard and writing is a faucet upstairs in the house. Opening the first takes all the pressure off the second. *Ib.*

The greatest thing in family life is to take a hint when a hint is intended — and not to take a hint when a hint isn't intended. *Ib.*

Always fall in with what you're asked to accept. Take what is given, and make it over your way. My aim in life has always been to hold my own with whatever's going. Not against: with.
Ib.

There's absolutely no reason for being rushed along with the rush. Everybody should be free to go very slow. . . . What you want, what you're hanging around in the world waiting for, is for something to occur to you. *[March 21, 1954]*

Education is . . . hanging around until you've caught on.
[January 30, 1963]

[1] See Coleridge, p. 528b, and Frost, *The Poetry of Amy Lowell,* p. 929b.

ELLEN GLASGOW
1874–1945

Preserve, within a wild sanctuary, an inaccessible valley of reveries.
A Certain Measure [1943]

Tilling the fertile soil of man's vanity. *Ib.*

HARRY GRAHAM
1874–1936

Billy, in one of his nice new sashes,
Fell in the fire and was burnt to ashes;
Now, although the room grows chilly,
I haven't the heart to poke poor Billy.
Ruthless Rhymes for Heartless Homes [1899]. *Tenderheartedness*

HERBERT CLARK HOOVER
1874–1964

I do not favor the repeal of the Eighteenth Amendment. . . . Our country has deliberately undertaken a great social and economic experiment,[1] noble in motive, far-reaching in purpose. *Speech [August 1928]*

The American system of rugged individualism.[2]
Campaign speech, New York [October 22, 1928]

Conditions are fundamentally sound.
Speech [December 1929]

The fundamental strength of the nation's economy is unimpaired.
Message to Congress [December 2, 1930]

[1] Hoover used the phrase also in a letter to Senator William E. Borah [February 28, 1928].
[2] While I can make no claim for having introduced the term "rugged individualism," I should be proud to have invented it. It has been used by American leaders for over a half-century in eulogy of those God-fearing men and women of honesty whose stamina and character and fearless assertion of rights led them to make their own way in life. — HOOVER, *The Challenge to Liberty* [1934]*, ch. 5*

The grass will grow in the streets of a hundred cities.

> *Speech [October 31, 1932]*

A good many things go around in the dark besides Santa Claus.

> *Address, John Marshall Republican Club, St. Louis, Missouri [December 16, 1935]*

Older men declare war. But it is youth that must fight and die. And it is youth who must inherit the tribulation, the sorrow, and the triumphs that are the aftermath of war.[1]

> *Speech, Republican National Convention, Chicago [June 27, 1944]*

HAROLD L. ICKES
1874–1952

I am against government by crony.

> *On resigning as Secretary of the Interior [February 1946]*

HEWLETT JOHNSON
1874–1966

Nothing is better calculated to drive men to desperation than when, in attempting to carry out beneficial reform, they find the whole world aligned against them. The more especially so if amongst those so aligned they discover men who had preached the same ideal, but now dreaded its concrete realization.

> *The Soviet Power: The Socialist Sixth of the World [1940], bk. II, ch. 3*

W. L. MACKENZIE KING[2]
1874–1950

Labor can do nothing without capital, capital nothing without labor, and neither labor nor capital can do anything without the guiding genius of management; and management, how-

---

[1] See Grantland Rice, p. 962a.
[2] See Truman, Joint Declaration, p. 982b.

ever wise its genius may be, can do nothing without the privileges which the community affords.

> *Canadian Club Speech, Montreal [March 17, 1919]*

Government, in the last analysis, is organized opinion. Where there is little or no public opinion, there is likely to be bad government, which sooner or later becomes autocratic government.

> *Message of the Carillon [1927]*

AMY LOWELL
1874–1925

A pattern called a war.
Christ! What are patterns for?

> *Patterns*

Sappho would speak, I think, quite openly,
And Mrs. Browning guard a careful silence,
But Emily would set doors ajar and slam them
And love you for your speed of observation.   *The Sisters*

You are beautiful and faded,
Like an old opera tune
Played upon a harpsichord.   *A Lady*

Heart-leaves of lilac all over New England,[1]
Roots of lilac under all the soil of New England,
Lilac in me because I am New England.   *Lilacs*

WILLIAM SOMERSET MAUGHAM
1874–1965

Like all weak men he laid an exaggerated stress on not changing one's mind.

> *Of Human Bondage [1915], ch. 39*

People ask you for criticism, but they only want praise.   *Ib. 50*

---

[1] Stands the lilac bush tall-growing with heart-shaped leaves of rich green.
WALT WHITMAN, *When Lilacs Last in the Dooryard Bloomed* [1865–1866]

There is nothing so degrading as the constant anxiety about one's means of livelihood. . . . Money is like a sixth sense without which you cannot make a complete use of the other five.
Of Human Bondage, ch. 51

The mystic sees the ineffable, and the psychopathologist the unspeakable.
The Moon and Sixpence [1919], *ch. 1*

I forget who it was that recommended men for their soul's good to do each day two things they disliked [1] . . . it is a precept that I have followed scrupulously; for every day I have got up and I have gone to bed. *Ib. 2*

Impropriety is the soul of wit.[2]
Ib. 4

Conscience is the guardian in the individual of the rules which the community has evolved for its own preservation. *Ib. 14*

Do you know that conversation is one of the greatest pleasures in life? But it wants leisure.
The Trembling of a Leaf [1921], *ch. 3*

The tragedy of love is indifference.
Ib. 4

I would sooner read a timetable or a catalogue than nothing at all. They are much more entertaining than half the novels that are written.
The Summing Up [1938]

If a nation values anything more than freedom, it will lose its freedom; and the irony of it is that if it is comfort or money that it values more, it will lose that too.
Strictly Personal [1941], *ch. 31*

As mean as cat's meat.
From THOMAS F. BRADY, *The Eighty Years of Mr. Maugham, New York Times Magazine* [*January 24, 1954*]

[1] See William James, p. 793a, and T. H. Huxley, p. 725a.
[2] See Shakespeare, p. 260b.

As far as I can judge, with women it is all take and no give. There must be some women who are not liars.
From Time [*October 17, 1960*]

ALICE DUER MILLER
1874–1942

The white cliffs of Dover, I saw rising steeply
Out of the sea that once made her [England] secure.
The White Cliffs [1940]

I am American bred,
I have seen much to hate here — much to forgive,
But in a world where England is finished and dead,
I do not wish to live. *Ib.*

PAUL RICHARD
1874–

The vagabond, when rich, is called a tourist.
The Scourge of Christ [1929]

JOHN DAVISON ROCKEFELLER, JR.
1874–1960

I believe that every right implies a responsibility; every opportunity, an obligation; every possession, a duty.
Ten Principles: Address in behalf of United Service Organizations, New York [*July 8, 1941*]

ROBERT WILLIAM SERVICE
1874–1958

This is the Law of the Yukon, that only the strong shall thrive;
That surely the weak shall perish, and only the fit survive.[1]
Dissolute, damned and despairful, crippled and palsied and slain,

[1] Now this is the Law of the Jungle — as old and as true as the sky;
And the Wolf that shall keep it may prosper, but the Wolf that shall break it must die.
KIPLING, *The Law of the Jungle* [1895]

This is the Will of the Yukon — Lo,
how she makes it plain!
  The Law of the Yukon

Back of the bar, in a solo game, sat
Dangerous Dan McGrew,
And watching his luck was his light-o'-
love, the lady that's known as
Lou.
  The Shooting of Dan McGrew,
  st. 1

The Northern Lights have seen queer
sights,
But the queerest they ever did see
Was that night on the marge of Lake
Lebarge
I cremated Sam McGee.
  The Cremation of Sam McGee,
  st. 1

A promise made is a debt unpaid.
  Ib. st. 8

Fate has written a tragedy; its name is
"The Human Heart."
The theater is the house of life,
Woman the mummer's part;
The Devil enters the prompter's box
and the play is ready to start.
  The Harpy, st. 12

When we, the workers, all demand:
"What are we fighting for?" . . .
Then, then we'll end that stupid crime,
that devil's madness — War.
  Michael

GERTRUDE STEIN
1874–1946

Rose is a rose is a rose is a rose.
  Sacred Emily [written 1913]

You are all a lost generation.[1]
  Used by Ernest Hemingway as
  an epigraph for The Sun Also
  Rises [1926]

Pigeons on the grass alas.
  Four Saints in Three Acts
  [written 1927]

[1] Hemingway states that the remark was originally made by a garage owner in the Midi to
Gertrude Stein in reference to his young mechanics, who were "une génération perdue."

Before the Flowers of Friendship
Faded Friendship Faded.
  Title [written 1930]

Remarks are not literature [said to
Hemingway].
  The Autobiography of Alice B.
  Toklas [written 1930]

America is my country and Paris is
my home town and it is as it has come
to be. After all anybody is as their land
and air is. Anybody is as the sky is low
or high, the air heavy or clear and anybody is as there is wind or no wind
there. It is that which makes them and
the arts they make and the work they
do and the way they eat and the way
they drink and the way they learn and
everything.
And so I am an American and I have
lived half my life in Paris, not the half
that made me but the half in which I
made what I made.
  An American and France [1936]

In the United States there is more
space where nobody is than where anybody is.
This is what makes America what it
is.
  The Geographical History of
  America [1936]

What is the answer? [*I was silent.*]
In that case, what is the question?
  Last words. From ALICE B.
  TOKLAS, *What Is Remem-*
  bered [1963]

TRUMBULL STICKNEY
1874–1904

Be still. The Hanging Gardens were a
  dream.   *Be Still [1905]*

It's autumn in the country I remember.
  Mnemosyne

The swallows veering skimmed the
  golden grain
At midday with a wing aslant and
  limber;
And yellow cattle browsed upon the
  plain.   *Ib.*

We sang together in the woods at
night. *Mnemosyne*

HARRY WILLIAMS
1874-1924

It's a long way to Tipperary, it's a long
way to go;
It's a long way to Tipperary, to the
sweetest girl I know!
Goodbye, Piccadilly, farewell, Leicester
Square,
It's a long, long way to Tipperary, but
my heart's right there!
Tipperary [1908] [1]

In the Shade of the Old Apple
Tree. *Title of song* [1]

EDMUND CLERIHEW [2]
BENTLEY
1875-1956

Sir Christopher Wren
Said "I am going to dine with some
men.
If anybody calls
Say I am designing St. Paul's."
*Biography for Beginners. Sir
Christopher Wren*

John Stuart Mill
By a mighty effort of will
Overcame his natural bonhomie
And wrote *Principles of Political Econ-
omy.* *Ib. John Stuart Mill*

George the Third
Ought never to have occurred.
One can only wonder
At so grotesque a blunder.[3]
Ib. George III

[1] Set to music by JACK JUDGE [1878-1938]
[2] A quatrain in the form Bentley popularized
is known as a clerihew.
[3] George the First was always reckoned
Vile, but viler George the Second;
And what mortal ever heard
Any good of George the Third?
When from earth the Fourth descended
God be praised, the Georges ended!
WALTER SAVAGE LANDOR, *Epigram after
hearing* THACKERAY'S *lectures on the four
Georges* [1855]

What I like about Clive
Is that he is no longer alive.
There is a great deal to be said
For being dead.
Biography for Beginners. Clive

JOHN BUCHAN,
LORD TWEEDSMUIR
1875-1940

We can only pay our debt to the past
by putting the future in debt to ourselves.
*Address to the people of Canada,
on the coronation of George VI
[May 12, 1937]*

He [Raymond Asquith] disliked
emotion, not because he felt lightly but
because he felt deeply. He most sincerely loved his country, but he loved
her too much to identify her with the
pasteboard goddess of the music halls
and the hustings. . . . Austerely self-
respecting, he had been used to hide his
devotions under a mask of indifference,
and would never reveal them except in
deeds.
Our roll of honor is long, but it holds
no nobler figure. He will stand to those
of us who are left as an incarnation of
the spirit of the land he loved. . . .
He loved his youth, and his youth has
become eternal.
Pilgrim's Way [1940]

Democracy — the essential thing as
distinguished from this or that democratic government — was primarily an
attitude of mind, a spiritual testament,
and not an economic structure or a
political machine. The testament involved certain basic beliefs — that the
personality was sacrosanct, which was
the meaning of liberty; that policy
should be settled by free discussion;
that normally a minority should be
ready to yield to a majority, which in
turn should respect a minority's sacred
things.
Public life is regarded as the crown of
a career, and to young men it is the
worthiest ambition. Politics is still the
greatest and the most honorable adventure. *Ib.*

ZANE GREY
1875–1939

We'll use a signal I have tried and found far-reaching and easy to yell. Waa-hoo!

The Last of the Plainsmen, ch. 4

CARL GUSTAV JUNG
1875–1961

The dynamic principle of fantasy is play, which belongs also to the child, and as such it appears to be inconsistent with the principle of serious work. But without this playing with fantasy no creative work has ever yet come to birth. The debt we owe to the play of imagination is incalculable.

Psychological Types [1923], *ch. 1, p. 82*

The great problems of life — sexuality, of course, among others — are always related to the primordial images of the collective unconscious. These images are really balancing or compensating factors which correspond with the problems life presents in actuality. This is not to be marveled at, since these images are deposits representing the accumulated experience of thousands of years of struggle for adaptation and existence.   *Ib. ch. 5, p. 271*

We should not pretend to understand the world only by the intellect; we apprehend it just as much by feeling. Therefore the judgment of the intellect is, at best, only the half of truth, and must, if it be honest, also come to an understanding of its inadequacy.   *Ib. conclusion, p. 628*

The woman is increasingly aware that love alone can give her her full stature, just as the man begins to discern that spirit alone can endow his life with its highest meaning. Fundamentally, therefore, both seek a psychic relation one to the other, because love needs the spirit, and the spirit love, for their fulfillment.

Contributions to Analytical Psychology [1928], *p. 185*

Seldom, or perhaps never, does a marriage develop into an individual relationship smoothly and without crises; there is no coming to consciousness without pain.

Contributions to Analytical Psychology, p. 193

In studying the history of the human mind one is impressed again and again by the fact that the growth of the mind is the widening of the range of consciousness, and that each step forward has been a most painful and laborious achievement.   *Ib. p. 340*

The meeting of two personalities is like the contact of two chemical substances: if there is any reaction, both are transformed.

Modern Man in Search of a Soul [1933], *p. 57*

The great decisions of human life have as a rule far more to do with the instincts and other mysterious unconscious factors than with conscious will and well-meaning reasonableness. The shoe that fits one person pinches another; there is no recipe for living that suits all cases. Each of us carries his own life-form — an indeterminable form which cannot be superseded by any other.   *Ib. p. 69*

Aging people should know that their lives are not mounting and unfolding but that an inexorable inner process forces the contraction of life. For a young person it is almost a sin — and certainly a danger — to be too much occupied with himself; but for the aging person it is a duty and a necessity to give serious attention to himself.

Ib. p. 125

All ages before ours believed in gods in some form or other. Only an unparalleled impoverishment in symbolism could enable us to rediscover the gods as psychic factors, which is to say, as archetypes of the unconscious. No doubt this discovery is hardly credible as yet.

The Integration of the Personality [1939], *p. 72*

If there is anything that we wish to change in the child, we should first examine it and see whether it is not something that could better be changed in ourselves.

The Integration of the Personality, p. 285

The conscious mind allows itself to be trained like a parrot, but the unconscious does not — which is why St. Augustine thanked God for not making him responsible for his dreams.

Psychology and Alchemy [1953], *p. 51*

The unconscious is not just evil by nature, it is also the source of the highest good: not only dark but also light, not only bestial, semihuman, and demonic but superhuman, spiritual, and, in the classical sense of the word, "divine."

The Practice of Psychotherapy [1953], *p. 364*

The little world of childhood with its familiar surroundings is a model of the greater world. The more intensively the family has stamped its character upon the child, the more it will tend to feel and see its earlier miniature world again in the bigger world of adult life. Naturally this is not a conscious, intellectual process.

From Psychological Reflections: A Jung Anthology [1] [1953], *p. 83: Collected Works, vol. 4 The Theory of Psychoanalysis* [1913]

This whole creation is essentially subjective, and the dream is the theater where the dreamer is at once scene, actor, prompter, stage manager, author, audience, and critic.

Ib. p. 58: vol. 8, General Aspects of Dream Psychology [1928]

The dream is the small hidden door in the deepest and most intimate sanctum of the soul, which opens into that primeval cosmic night that was soul long before there was a conscious

[1] Edited by Jolande Jacobi.

ego and will be soul far beyond what a conscious ego could ever reach.

From Psychological Reflections: A Jung Anthology, p. 46: vol. 10, The Meaning of Psychology for Modern Man [1934]

Emotion is the chief source of all becoming-conscious. There can be no transforming of darkness into light and of apathy into movement without emotion.

Ib. p. 32: vol. 9, Psychological Aspects of the Modern Archetype [1938]

No one can flatter himself that he is immune to the spirit of his own epoch, or even that he possesses a full understanding of it. Irrespective of our conscious convictions, each one of us, without exception, being a particle of the general mass, is somewhere attached to, colored by, or even undermined by the spirit which goes through the mass. Freedom stretches only as far as the limits of our consciousness.

Ib. p. 143: vol. 15, Paracelsus the Physician [1942]

Where love rules, there is no will to power; and where power predominates, there love is lacking. The one is the shadow of the other.

Ib. p. 87: vol. 7, The Psychology of the Unconscious [1943]

The erotic instinct is something questionable, and will always be so whatever a future set of laws may have to say on the matter. It belongs, on the one hand, to the original animal nature of man, which will exist as long as man has an animal body. On the other hand, it is connected with the highest forms of the spirit. But it blooms only when spirit and instinct are in true harmony. If one or the other aspect is missing, then an injury occurs, or at least there is a one-sided lack of balance which easily slips into the pathological. Too much of the animal disfigures the civilized human being, too much culture makes a sick animal.

Ib. p. 93

THOMAS MANN
1875–1955

We are most likely to get angry and excited in our opposition to some idea when we ourselves are not quite certain of our own position, and are inwardly tempted to take the other side.

Buddenbrooks [1903], *pt. VIII, ch. 2*

Beauty can pierce one like a pain.
Ib. XI, 2

Space, like time, engenders forgetfulness; but it does so by setting us bodily free from our surroundings and giving us back our primitive, unattached state. . . . Time, we say, is Lethe; but change of air is a similar draught, and, if it works less thoroughly, does so more quickly.

The Magic Mountain [1924],[1] *ch. 1*

A man lives not only his personal life, as an individual, but also, consciously or unconsciously, the life of his epoch and his contemporaries. *Ib. 2*

The only religious way to think of death is as part and parcel of life; to regard it, with the understanding and the emotions, as the inviolable condition of life. *Ib. 5*

Time has no divisions to mark its passage, there is never a thunderstorm or blare of trumpets to announce the beginning of a new month or year. Even when a new century begins it is only we mortals who ring bells and fire off pistols. *Ib.*

Order and simplification are the first steps toward the mastery of a subject — the actual enemy is the unknown. *Ib.*

Human reason needs only to will more strongly than fate, and she *is* fate. *Ib. 6*

Opinions cannot survive if one has no chance to fight for them. *Ib.*

[1] Translated by H. T. LOWE-PORTER.

All interest in disease and death is only another expression of interest in life.
The Magic Mountain, ch. 6

The invention of printing and the Reformation are and remain the two outstanding services of central Europe to the cause of humanity. *Ib.*

Speech is civilization itself. The word, even the most contradictory word, preserves contact — it is silence which isolates. *Ib.*

A man's dying is more the survivors' affair than his own. *Ib.*

What we call mourning for our dead is perhaps not so much grief at not being able to call them back as it is grief at not being able to want to do so. *Ib. 7*

Time cools, time clarifies; no mood can be maintained quite unaltered through the course of hours. *Ib.*

Seven is a good handy figure in its way, picturesque, with a savor of the mythical; one might say that it is more filling to the spirit than a dull academic half-dozen. *Ib.*

In the Word is involved the unity of humanity, the wholeness of the human problem, which permits nobody to separate the intellectual and artistic from the political and social, and to isolate himself within the ivory tower of the "cultural" proper.

Letter [1] to the dean of the Philosophical Faculty, Bonn University [January 1937]

Hold fast the time! Guard it, watch over it, every hour, every minute! Unregarded it slips away, like a lizard, smooth, slippery, faithless, a pixy wife. Hold every moment sacred. Give each clarity and meaning, each the weight of thine awareness, each its true and due fulfillment.

The Beloved Returns [1939]

[1] Mann, who had left Germany in 1933, wrote from Zurich, after being informed that his name had been struck off the list of Honorary Doctors.

HUGHES MEARNS
1875–1965

As I was going up the stair
I met a man who wasn't there.
He wasn't there again today.
I wish, I wish he'd stay away.

The Psychoed

HASEGAWA NYOZEKAN [1]
1875–

We must direct our efforts towards turning in the reverse direction the cultural nature of the Japanese, which hitherto has had a propensity for the intuitive, until it shows instead a propensity for the intellectual.

The Lost Japan [1952]

The war was started as the result of a mistaken intuitive "calculation" which transcended mathematics. We believed with a blind fervor that we could triumph over scientific weapons and tactics by means of our mystic will. . . . The characteristic reliance on intuition by Japanese had blocked the objective cognition of the modern world.   *Ib.*

FRANK WARD O'MALLEY
1875–1932

Life is just one damned thing after another.[2]

Attributed. (Also attributed to Elbert Hubbard)

RAINER MARIA RILKE
1875–1926

Her smile was not meant to be seen by anyone and served its whole purpose in being smiled.

The Journal of My Other Self [3]

He was a poet and hated the approximate.   *Ib.*

Love consists in this, that two solitudes protect and touch and greet each other.

Letters to a Young Poet [1]

The future enters into us, in order to transform itself in us, long before it happens.   *Ib.*

We're never single-minded, unperplexed, like migratory birds.

The Duino Elegies, 4

The most visible joy can only reveal itself to us when we've transformed it, within.   *Ib. 7*

Death is the side of life which is turned away from us.

Letter to W. von Hulewicz

A good marriage is that in which each appoints the other guardian of his solitude.   *Letters* [2]

Once the realization is accepted that even between the *closest* human beings infinite distances continue to exist, a wonderful living side by side can grow up, if they succeed in loving the distance between them which makes it possible for each to see the other whole against the sky.   *Ib.*

In the difficult are the friendly forces, the hands that work on us.   *Ib.*

Works of art are indeed always products of having been in danger, of having gone to the very end in an experience, to where man can go no further.   *Ib.*

RAFAEL SABATINI
1875–1950

Born with the gift of laughter and the sense that the world was mad,[3] and that was his only patrimony.

Scaramouche, ch. 1

[1] Translated by M. D. HERTER NORTON [1934].
[2] Translated by JANE BARNARD GREENE and M. D. HERTER NORTON.
[3] Inscribed over a door in the Hall of Graduate Studies, Yale University. The architect, John Donald Tuttle, explained in a letter in *The New Yorker* [December 8, 1934] his recoiling from

[1] From *Sources of Japanese Tradition*, edited by William Theodore de Bary [1960].
[2] The phrase probably precedes both O'Malley and Hubbard.
[3] Translated by JOHN LINTON [1930].

ALBERT SCHWEITZER
1875–1965

Late on the third day, at the very moment when, at sunset, we were making our way through a herd of hippopotamuses, there flashed upon my mind, unforeseen and unsought, the phrase, "Reverence for Life." [1] . . . Now I had found my way to the idea in which affirmation of the world and ethics are contained side by side; now I knew that the ethical acceptance of the world and of life, together with the ideals of civilization contained in this concept, has a foundation in thought.
Out of My Life and Thought [1949]

Affirmation of life is the spiritual act by which man ceases to live unreflectively and begins to devote himself to his life with reverence in order to raise it to its true value. To affirm life is to deepen, to make more inward, and to exalt the will to live. *Ib.*

Truth has no special time of its own. Its hour is now — always. *Ib.*

You don't live in a world all alone. Your brothers are here too.
On Receiving the Nobel Prize [1952]

JOEL ELIAS SPINGARN
1875–1939

The gibe of European scholars that there are three sexes in America — men, women, and professors.
Creative Criticism and Other Essays [1931]

RIDGELY TORRENCE
1875–1950

Of all the languages of earth in which the human kind confer

The Master Speaker is the Tear: it is the Great Interpreter.
The House of a Hundred Lights. The Conclusion of the Whole Matter

SHERWOOD ANDERSON
1876–1941

Everyone in the world is Christ and they are all crucified.
Winesburg, Ohio [1919]. *The Philosopher*

I am a lover and have not found my thing to love. *Ib. Tandy*

WILLA SIBERT CATHER
1876–1947

No one can build his security upon the nobleness of another person.
Alexander's Bridge [1912], *ch. 8*

There are only two or three human stories, and they go on repeating themselves as fiercely as if they had never happened before.
O Pioneers! [1913], *pt. II, ch. 4*

The history of every country begins in the heart of a man or a woman. *Ib.*

I like trees because they seem more resigned to the way they have to live than other things do. *Ib. 8*

I tell you there is such a thing as creative hate!
The Song of the Lark [1915], *pt. I*

Artistic growth is, more than it is anything else, a refining of the sense of truthfulness. The stupid believe that to be truthful is easy; only the artist, the great artist, knows how difficult it is. *Ib. VI*

That is happiness; to be dissolved into something complete and great.[1]
My Antonia [2] [1918], *bk. I, ch. 2*

---

collegiate Gothic, "a type of architecture that had been designed expressly . . . to enable yeomen to pour molten lead through slots on their enemies below. As a propitiatory gift to my gods . . . and to make them forget by appealing to their senses of humor, I carved the inscription over the door."

[1] See W. E. Channing, p. 544a.

[1] Inscribed on Willa Cather's grave in Jaffrey, New Hampshire.

[2] It lifts me to all my superlatives. — OLIVER WENDELL HOLMES, JR., *letter to Ferris Greenslet*

Winter lies too long in country towns; hangs on until it is stale and shabby, old and sullen.

> *My Antonia, bk. II, ch. 7*

Art, it seems to me, should simplify. That, indeed, is very nearly the whole of the higher artistic process; finding what conventions of form and what detail one can do without and yet preserve the spirit of the whole — so that all that one has suppressed and cut away is there to the reader's consciousness as much as if it were in type on the page.

> *On the Art of Fiction [1920]*

That irregular and intimate quality of things made entirely by the human hand.

> *Death Comes for the Archbishop [1927], bk. I, ch. 3*

In New Mexico he always awoke a young man. . . . He had noticed that this peculiar quality in the air of new countries vanished after they were tamed by man and made to bear harvests . . . that lightness, that dry aromatic odor . . . one could breathe that only on the bright edges of the world, on the great grass plains or the sagebrush desert. . . . Something soft and wild and free; something that whispered to the ear on the pillow, lightened the heart, softly, softly picked the lock, slid the bolts, and released the prisoned spirit of man into the wind, into the blue and gold, into the morning, into the morning! [1]

> *Ib. IX, 3*

Only solitary men know the full joys of friendship. Others have their family; but to a solitary and an exile his friends are everything.

> *Shadows on the Rock [1931], bk. III, ch. 5*

[1] The moment I saw the brilliant proud morning shine high up over the deserts of Santa Fe, something stood still in my soul, and I started to attend. . . . In the magnificent fierce morning of New Mexico one sprang awake, a new part of the soul woke up suddenly, and the old world gave way to a new. — D. H. LAWRENCE, *New Mexico [Survey Graphic, 1931]*

SARAH NORCLIFFE CLEGHORN
1876–1959

The golf links lie so near the mill
That almost every day
The laboring children can look out
And watch the men at play.

> *Quatrain [1915]*

IRVIN SHREWSBURY COBB
1876–1944

I hope it's nothing trivial.

> *Upon hearing that his boss, Charles S. Chapin of the New York World, was ill [c. 1910]*

It smells like gangrene starting in a mildewed silo, it tastes like the wrath to come, and when you absorb a deep swig of it you have all the sensations of having swallowed a lighted kerosene lamp. A sudden, violent jolt of it has been known to stop the victim's watch, snap his suspenders and crack his glass eye right across.

> *Definition of "corn licker" given to the Distillers' Code Authority, NRA*

CHARLES FRANKLIN KETTERING
1876–1958

A man must have a certain amount of intelligent ignorance to get anywhere.

> *On his seventieth birthday [August 29, 1946]*

We should all be concerned about the future because we will have to spend the rest of our lives there.

> *Seed for Thought [1949]*

MAXIM MAXIMOVICH LITVINOV
1876–1951

To strengthen the League of Nations is to abide by the principle of collective

security . . . to abide by the principle that peace is indivisible.[1]
> *Speech, League of Nations, Geneva, condemning Italian aggression in Ethiopia [July 1, 1936]*

WILSON MIZNER
1876–1933

No opium-smoking in the elevators.
> *Sign in Hotel Rand, New York, which Mizner managed [1907]*

Carry out your own dead.   *Ib.*

Life's a tough proposition, and the first hundred years are the hardest.
> *Saying*

Be nice to people on your way up because you'll meet 'em on your way down.
> *Ib. (Also attributed to Jimmy Durante)*

When you steal from one author, it's plagiarism; if you steal from many, it's research.   *Ib.*

Treat a whore like a lady and a lady like a whore.   *Ib.*

A good listener is not only popular everywhere, but after a while he gets to know something.   *Ib.*

It's a trip through a sewer in a glass-bottomed boat.[2]
> *Comment on Hollywood*

You sparkle with larceny.   *Remark*

You're a mouse studying to be a rat.
> *Ib.*

Why should I talk to you? I've just been talking to your boss.
> *On his deathbed, to a priest [1933]*

[1] In an earlier speech at the League [September 5, 1935] during the Italian preparations for the invasion, Litvinov used a similar phrase: "The thesis of the indivisibility of peace. . . . It has now become clear to the whole world that each war is the creation of a preceding war and the generator of new present or future wars."
See Haile Selassie, p. 1020a, and Wendell Willkie, p. 1025a.

[2] This was later adapted by Mayor James J. Walker as "A reformer is a guy who rides through a sewer in a glass-bottomed boat."

POPE PIUS XII
[EUGENIO PACELLI]
1876–1958

Private property is a natural fruit of labor, a product of intense activity of man, acquired through his energetic determination to ensure and develop with his own strength his own existence and that of his family, and to create for himself and his own an existence of just freedom, not only economic, but also political, cultural and religious.
> *Radio broadcast [September 1, 1944]*

If a worker is deprived of hope to acquire some personal property, what other natural stimulus can be offered him that will inspire him to hard work, labor, saving and sobriety today, when so many nations and men have lost everything and all they have left is their capacity for work?   *Ib.*

A. S. W. ROSENBACH
1876–1952

After love, book collecting is the most exhilarating sport of all.
> *A Book Hunter's Holiday [1936]*

GEORGE MACAULAY
TREVELYAN
1876–1962

A man and what he loves and builds have but a day and then disappear; nature cares not — and renews the annual round untired. It is the old law, sad but not bitter. Only when man destroys the life and beauty of nature, there is the outrage.
> *Grey of Fallodon [1937], bk. I, ch. 3*

Disinterested intellectual curiosity is the lifeblood of real civilization.
> *English Social History [1942], preface*

Education . . . has produced a vast population able to read but unable to distinguish what is worth reading.
> *Ib. ch. 18*

GRACE NOLL CROWELL
1877–1969

God wrote His loveliest poem on the
    day
He made the first tall silver poplar tree.
Silver Poplars, st. 1

ANTHONY EUWER
1877–

As a beauty I'm not a great star.
There are others more handsome, by
    far,
    But my face — I don't mind it
    For I am behind it;
It's the people in front get the jar.
Limeratomy [1]

ROSE FYLEMAN
1877–1957

There are fairies at the bottom of our
    garden!   *The Fairies, st. 1*

The Queen — now can you guess who
    that could be
(She's a little girl by day, but at night
    she steals away)?
Well — it's me!   *Ib. st. 3*

GODFREY HAROLD
HARDY
1877–1947

A mathematician, like a painter or a
poet, is a maker of patterns. If his patterns are more permanent than theirs,
it is because they are made with ideas.
A Mathematician's Apology
[1940]

SIR JAMES HOPWOOD
JEANS
1877–1946

Taking a very gloomy view of the future of the human race, let us suppose
that it can only expect to survive for
two thousand million years longer, a period about equal to the past age of the
earth. Then, regarded as a being des-

[1] Often quoted by Woodrow Wilson.

tined to live for threescore years and
ten, humanity, although it has been
born in a house seventy years old, is
itself only three days old.
The Wilder Aspects of
Cosmogony [1928]

All the pictures which science now
draws of nature and which alone seem
capable of according with observational
fact are mathematical pictures. . . .
From the intrinsic evidence of his creation, the Great Architect of the Universe now begins to appear as a pure
mathematician.
The Mysterious Universe [1930]

Physics tries to discover the pattern
of events which controls the phenomena we observe. But we can never know
what this pattern means or how it origi-
nates; and even if some superior intelligence were to tell us, we should find the
explanation unintelligible.
Physics and Philosophy [1942]

RICHARD R. KIRK
1877–

Thrice blessed are our friends: they
    come, they stay,
And presently they go away.
Thrice Blessed

A book's an inn whose patrons' praise
Depends on seasons and on days,
On dispositions, and — in fine —
Not wholly on the landlord's wine.
A Book's an Inn

DOUGLAS MALLOCH
1877–1938

If it's your Mississippi in dry time,
If it's yours, Uncle Sam, when it's wet,
If it's your Mississippi in fly time,
In flood time it's your Mississippi yet.
Uncle Sam's River, st. 6

Courage is to feel
The daily daggers of relentless steel
And keep on living.   *Courage, st. 2*

ANGELO PATRI
1877–1965

In one sense there is no death. The life of a soul on earth lasts beyond his departure. You will always feel that life touching yours, that voice speaking to you, that spirit looking out of other eyes, talking to you in the familiar things he touched, worked with, loved as familiar friends. He lives on in your life and in the lives of all others that knew him.[1]

> *Keep Children from Funerals*
> *[November 30, 1938]*

CHARLES HANSON TOWNE
1877–1949

Youth, there are countless stories spread
By gentlemen whose hair is gray.
Believe them not, but me instead—
The Nineties were not really gay.
> *Ballade of Gentle Denial*

WILLIAM W. WOOLLCOTT
1877–1949

I am a One Hundred Percent American;
I am a superpatriot.
> *I Am a One Hundred Percent*
> *American, st. 1*

EMILIANO ZAPATA
c. 1877–1919

Men of the South! It is better to die on your feet than to live on your knees![2]   *Attributed*

McLANDBURGH WILSON
fl. 1915

'Twixt the optimist and pessimist
The difference is droll:

[1] Even the death of friends will inspire us as much as their lives. . . . Their memories will be incrusted over with sublime and pleasing thoughts, as their monuments are overgrown with moss. — THOREAU, *A Week on the Concord and Merrimack Rivers* [1849], *Concord River*
[2] See Roosevelt, p. 973a, and note.

The optimist sees the doughnut
But the pessimist sees the hole.
> *Optimist and Pessimist*

YOSANO AKIKO
1878–1942

Because my songs are brief,
People think I hoarded words.
I have spared nothing in my songs.
There is nothing I can add.
Unlike a fish, my soul swims without gills.
I sing on one breath.   *My Songs*[1]

LOUIS KAUFMAN ANSPACHER
1878–1947

Marriage is that relation between man and woman in which the independence is equal, the dependence mutual, and the obligation reciprocal.
> *Address, Boston [December 30,*
> *1934]*

KARLE WILSON BAKER
1878–

Let me grow lovely, growing old —
So many fine things do:
Laces, and ivory, and gold,
And silks need not be new.
> *Old Lace: Let Me Grow Lovely*

Today I have grown taller from walking with the trees.   *Good Company*

AMELIA JOSEPHINE BURR
1878–

As one who looks on a face through a window, through life I have looked on God.
Because I have loved life, I shall have no sorrow to die.
> *A Song of Living, st. 3*

[1] From *Modern Japanese Literature*, edited by Donald Keene [1960].

HENRY SEIDEL CANBY
1878–1961

We can put our children on wheels to see the world, but we cannot give them the kind of home that any town provided in the Nineties, not at any price.
The Age of Confidence, ch. 14

Skunk cabbages! a thousand sonnets died in that misnomer.
Meditations in the Woods

GEORGE MICHAEL COHAN
1878–1942

Always Leave Them Laughing When You Say Goodbye.   *Title of song*

Give my regards to Broadway,
  Remember me to Herald Square,
Tell all the gang at Forty-second Street
  That I will soon be there.
Give My Regards to Broadway
[1904]

     The Yanks are coming,
The drums rum-tumming everywhere.
Over There [1917]

And we won't come back till it's over
  over there.   *Ib.*

   What's all the shootin' for?
The Tavern [1920]

GRACE HAZARD CONKLING
1878–1958

I have an understanding with the hills
At evening when the slanted radiance fills
  Their hollows, and the great winds let
    them be,
And they are quiet and look down at
  me.   *After Sunset*

Invisible beauty has a word so brief
A flower can say it or a shaken leaf,
But few may ever snare it in a song.
               Ib.

To build the trout a crystal stair.
The Whole Duty of
Berkshire Brooks

He who gives a passion flower
Always asks it back.   *Tampico*

ALFRED EDGAR COPPARD
1878–1957

Adam and Eve and Pinch Me.
Title of story [1921]

Truth is truth and love is love,
Give us grace to taste thereof;
But if truth offend my sweet,
Then I will have none of it.
Mendacity, st. 1

Ere this trick of truth undo me,
Little love, my love, come to me.
Ib. st. 3

ADELAIDE CRAPSEY
1878–1914

These be
Three silent things:
The falling snow . . . the hour
Before the dawn . . . the mouth of
  one
Just dead.   *Cinquain: Triad*

EDWARD JOHN MORETON DRAX PLUNKETT, LORD DUNSANY
1878–1957

A new thing came and they could not
  see,
A new wind blew and they would not
  feel it.
In His Own Country, st. 1

May you go safe, my friend, across that
  dizzy way
No wider than a hair, by which your
  people go
From earth to Paradise; may you go safe
  today
With stars and space above, and time
  and stars below.
May You Go Safe: On the
Death of a Mohammedan
Friend, st. 1

HARRY EMERSON FOSDICK
1878–1969

The Sea of Galilee and the Dead Sea
are made of the same water. It flows
down, clear and cool, from the heights
of Hermon and the roots of the cedars
of Lebanon. The Sea of Galilee makes
beauty of it, for the Sea of Galilee has
an outlet. It gets to give. It gathers in
its riches that it may pour them out
again to fertilize the Jordan plain. But
the Dead Sea with the same water
makes horror. For the Dead Sea has no
outlet. It gets to keep.

The Meaning of Service [1920]

WILFRID WILSON GIBSON
1878–1962

One song leads on to another,
One friend to another friend,
So I'll travel along
With a friend and a song.

The Empty Purse, st. 1

All life moving to one measure —
Daily bread.

All Life Moving to One Measure

Just what it meant to smile and smile
And let my son go cheerily —
My son . . . and wondering all the
   while
What stranger would come back to me.

The Return, st. 2

OLIVER ST. JOHN GOGARTY
1878–1957

Only the lion and the cock,
As Galen says, withstand love's shock.[1]
So, dearest, do not think me rude
If I yield now to lassitude,
But sympathize with me. I know
You would not have me roar, or crow.

After Galen

If only gladiators died,
Or heroes, death would be his pride;

[1] See Donne, p. 307a.

But have not little maidens gone,
And Lesbia's sparrow,[1] all alone?

Per Iter Tenebricosum

DONALD ROBERT PERRY MARQUIS
1878–1937

My heart hath followed all my days
Something I cannot name.

The Name, st. 1

The saddest ones are those that wear
The jester's motley garb.

The Tavern of Despair

The world hath just one tale to tell,
   and it is very old,
A little tale — a simple tale — a tale
   that's easy told:
"There was a youth in Babylon who
   greatly loved a maid!"

News from Babylon

And similar goddamned phrases.

Ballade of Goddamned Phrases [2]

I pray Thee make my column read,
And give me thus my daily bread.

Prayer

I love you as New Englanders love pie!

Sonnets to a Red-Haired Lady
[1922], XII

One boob may die, but deathless is
   The royal race of hicks —
When Ahab went to Askelon
   They sold him gilded bricks.

Boob Ballad

There will be no beans in the Almost
Perfect State.[3]

The Almost Perfect State [1927]

dedicated to babs
   with babs knows what
   and babs knows why

archy [4] *and mehitabel* [1927]
dedication

[1] See Catullus, p. 114a.
[2] Inspired by a protest from General Ian
Hamilton, Commander of the Mediterranean
Expeditionary Force [1915], against turning his
cables into hackneyed phrases.
[3] See Robert Burton, p. 310b.
[4] archy a cockroach is unable to use the shift
key on the typewriter for capitals and punctua-
tion

oh i should worry and fret
death and i will coquette
there is a dance in the old dame yet
toujours gai toujours gai
   archy and mehitabel the song
      of mehitabel

procrastination is the
art of keeping
up with yesterday
   ib certain maxims of archy

an optimist is a guy that has never had
  much experience   *ib*

what in hell
have i done to deserve all these kittens
  ib mehitabel and her kittens

dance mehitabel dance
caper and shake a leg
what little blood is left
will fizz like wine in a keg
  ib mehitabel dances with boreas

i have noticed that when chickens
quit quarreling over their food they
often find that there is enough for all
of them i wonder if it might not be the
same with the human race
  archy's life of mehitabel [1933]
   random thoughts by archy

 so unlucky
that he runs into accidents
which started out to happen
to somebody else *ib archy says*

theres life in the old dame yet
  ib the retreat from hollywood

it is a cheering thought to think
that god is on the side of the best digestion [1]
  archy does his part [1935]
   the big bad wolf

there is bound to be a certain amount
 of
trouble running any country
if you are president the trouble happens
 to you

---

[1] Give me a good digestion, Lord,
 And also something to digest.
 ANONYMOUS, *A Pilgrim's Grace, st. 1*

but if you are a tyrant you can arrange
 things so
that most of the trouble happens to
 other people
    archy's newest deal

there is always
a comforting thought
in time of trouble when
it is not our trouble
   ib comforting thoughts

too many creatures
both insects and humans
estimate their own value
by the amount of minor irritation
they are able to cause
to greater personalities than themselves
     ib pride

the females of all species are most
dangerous when they appear to retreat
    ib a farewell

To stroke a platitude until it purrs
like an epigram. *The Sun Dial*

Publishing a volume of verse is like
dropping a rose petal down the Grand
Canyon and waiting for the echo.
       Ib.

JOHN MASEFIELD
1878–1967

I must down to the seas again, to the
 lonely sea and the sky,
And all I ask is a tall ship and a star to
 steer her by,
And the wheel's kick and the wind's
 song and the white sail's shaking,
And a gray mist on the sea's face and a
 gray dawn breaking.
   Sea Fever [1902], *st. 1*

I must down to the seas again, for the
 call of the running tide
Is a wild call and a clear call that may
 not be denied.   *Ib. st. 2*

I must down to the seas again, to the
 vagrant gypsy life,
To the gull's way and the whale's way
 where the wind's like a whetted
 knife;

And all I ask is a merry yarn from a
laughing fellow rover,
And quiet sleep and a sweet dream
when the long trick's over.
Sea Fever, st. 3

It's a warm wind, the west wind, full of
birds' cries.
The West Wind [1902], *st. 1*

One road leads to London,
One road runs to Wales,
My road leads me seawards
To the white dipping sails.
Roadways, st. 1

The schooners and the merry crews are
laid away to rest,
A little south the sunset in the Islands
of the Blest.
A Ballad of John Silver
[*1902*], *st. 6*

To get the whole world out of bed
And washed, and dressed, and warmed,
and fed,
To work, and back to bed again,
Believe me, Saul, costs worlds of pain.
The Everlasting Mercy [1911]

And he who gives a child a treat
Makes joy-bells ring in Heaven's street,
And he who gives a child a home
Builds palaces in Kingdom come.
Ib.

O Christ, the plow, O Christ, the
laughter
Of holy white birds flying after.   *Ib.*

The days that make us happy make us
wise.   *Biography*

Quinquireme of Nineveh from distant
Ophir,
Rowing home to haven in sunny Pales-
tine,
With a cargo of ivory,
And apes and peacocks,[1]
Sandalwood, cedarwood, and sweet
white wine.   *Cargoes, st. 1*

Dirty British coaster with a salt-caked
smokestack,
Butting through the Channel in the
mad March days,
With a cargo of Tyne coal,

[1] See *I Kings 10:22*, p. 13a.

Road rail, pig lead,
Firewood, ironware, and cheap tin
trays.   *Cargoes, st. 3*

Oh London Town's a fine town, and
London sights are rare,
And London ale is right ale, and brisk's
the London air.
London Town, st. 1

When Life knocks at the door no one
can wait,
When Death makes his arrest we have
to go.[1]
The Widow in the Bye Street
[*1912*], *pt. 2*

What good can painting do to anyone?
I don't say never do it; far from that —
No harm in sometimes painting just for
fun.
Keep it for fun, and stick to what
you're at.
Dauber [1913], *pt. II*

Spit brown, my son, and get a hairy
breast.   *Ib.*

What am I, Life? A thing of watery
salt
Held in cohesion by unresting cells,
Which work they know not why, which
never halt,
Myself unwitting where their Master
dwells?   *Sonnets, 14*

Bitter it is, indeed, in human Fate
When Life's supreme temptation
comes too late.
The Woman Speaks

When custom presses on the souls
apart,
Who seek a God not worshiped by the
herd,
Forth, to the wilderness, the chosen
start
Content with ruin, having but the
Word.
*Lines on the Tercentenary of
Harvard College* [1936]

But he has gone,
A nation's memory and veneration,
Among the radiant, ever venturing on,

[1] See Shakespeare, *Hamlet V, ii 350*, p. 266b.

Somewhere, with morning, as such spirits will.[1]
> *On the Finish of the Sailing Ship*
> *Race Lisbon to Manhattan*
> *[July 1964]*

PAUL REYNAUD
1878–1966

We shall win because we are the
stronger.[2]
> *Radio Speech [September 10,*
> *1939]*

CARL SANDBURG
1878–1967

I am the people — the mob — the
crowd — the mass.
Do you know that all the great work of
the world is done through me?
> *I Am the People, the Mob*
> *[1916]*

Hog butcher for the world,
Tool maker, stacker of wheat,
Player with railroads and the nation's
freight handler;
Stormy, husky, brawling,
City of the big shoulders.
> *Chicago [1916]*

The fog comes
on little cat feet.
It sits looking
over the harbor and city
on silent haunches
and then moves on. *Fog [1916]*

Pile the bodies high at Austerlitz and
Waterloo.
Shovel them under and let me work —
I am the grass; I cover all.

And pile them high at Gettysburg
And pile them high at Ypres and Ver-
dun.
Shovel them under and let me work.

[1] The reference is to the death of John F.
Kennedy [November 22, 1963].
See James Russell Lowell, p. 694a.
[2] Nous vaincrons parce que nous sommes les
plus forts.
The phrase became a war slogan.

Two years, ten years, and passengers
ask the conductor:
What place is this?
Where are we now?

I am the grass.
Let me work. *Grass [1918]*
I tell you the past is a bucket of ashes.
> *Prairie*

The republic is a dream.
Nothing happens unless first a dream.
> *Washington Monument by Night*

When Abraham Lincoln was shoveled
into the tombs, he forgot the copperheads and the assassin . . . in
the dust, in the cool tombs.
> *Cool Tombs [1918]*

Take any streetful of people buying
clothes and groceries, cheering a
hero or throwing confetti and
blowing tin horns . . . tell me if
the lovers are losers . . . tell me
if any get more than the lovers
. . . in the dust . . . in the cool
tombs. *Ib.*

Lay me on an anvil, O God.
Beat me and hammer me into a crow-
bar.
Let me pry loose old walls.
Let me lift and loosen old foundations.
> *Prayers of Steel [1920]*

Drum on your drums, batter on your
banjos, sob on the long cool winding saxophones.
Go to it, O jazzmen.
> *Jazz Fantasia [1920]*

Look out how you use proud words.
When you let proud words go, it is not
easy to call them back.
They wear long boots, hard boots.
> *Primer Lesson*

Man is a long time coming.
Man will yet win.
Brother may yet line up with brother:
This old anvil laughs at many broken
hammers.
There are men who can't be bought.
> *The People Will Live On [1936]*

Time is a great teacher.
Who can live without hope?
In the darkness with a great bundle of
grief the people march.
The People Will Live On

LOUIS EDWIN THAYER
1878–

I fancy when I go to rest someone will
bring to light
Some kindly word or goodly act long
buried out of sight;
But, if it's all the same to you, just give
to me, instead,
The bouquets while I'm living and the
knocking when I'm dead.[1]
Of Post-Mortem Praises, st. 1

EDWARD THOMAS
1878–1917

As poetry is a criticism of life by livers, so the epigram is a criticism of life
by those who have not lived.
Oxford [1903], *p. 195*

JOHN BROADUS WATSON
1878–1958

Give me a dozen healthy infants,
well-formed, and my own specified
world to bring them up in and I'll guarantee to take any one at random and
train him to become any type of spe-
cialist I might select — doctor, lawyer,
artist, merchant chief and, yes, even
beggarman and thief, regardless of his
talents, penchants, tendencies, abilities,
vocations, and race of his ancestors.
Behaviorism [1925], *p. 104*

HANS ZINSSER
1878–1940

The scientist takes off from the manifold observations of predecessors, and
shows his intelligence, if any, by his
ability to discriminate between the important and the negligible, by selecting
here and there the significant steppingstones that will lead across the difficul-

[1] See Martial, p. 135a, and Hazlitt, p. 539b.

ties to new understanding. The one
who places the last stone and steps
across to the terra firma of accomplished discovery gets all the credit.
Only the initiated know and honor
those whose patient integrity and devotion to exact observation have made the
last step possible.[1]
As I Remember Him
[1940], *ch. 20*

ETHEL BARRYMORE
1879–1959

That's all there is, there isn't any
more.

*Added, with the permission of
author* THOMAS RACEWARD, *as
the curtain line of his play
Sunday* [1906], *starring Miss
Barrymore*

SIR WILLIAM HENRY BEVERIDGE
1879–1963

Simple effluxion of time.[2]
Social Insurance [1942]

The object of government in peace
and in war is not the glory of rulers or
of races, but the happiness of the common man. *Ib.*

JAMES BRANCH CABELL
1879–1958

I shall marry in haste, and repeat at
leisure.[3] *Jurgen* [1919], *ch. 38*

There is no faith stronger than that
of a bad-tempered woman in her own
infallibility. *Ib. 39*

The optimist proclaims that we live
in the best of all possible worlds; and
the pessimist fears this is true.
The Silver Stallion [1926], *ch. 26*

[1] See Sir Francis Darwin, p. 813b, and Sir
Alexander Fleming, p. 963a.
[2] The *Oxford English Dictionary* traces the
phrase "effluxion of time" to JOHN MOLLE, *The
Living Library* [1621].
[3] See Shakespeare, p. 219a, and Congreve,
p. 391b.

No lady is ever a gentleman.
Something About Eve [1927]

LEE WILSON DODD
1879–1933

Much that I sought, I could not find;
Much that I found, I could not bind;
Much that I bound, I could not free;
Much that I freed returned to me.
Ronde Macabre

ALBERT EINSTEIN
1879–1955

$E = mc^2$
*Statement of the mass-energy
equivalence relationship* [1]

The most beautiful thing we can experience is the mysterious. It is the source of all true art and science.
*"What I Believe," in Forum
[October 1930]*

It is not enough that you should understand about applied science in order that your work may increase man's blessings. Concern for man himself and his fate must always form the chief interest of all technical endeavors, concern for the great unsolved problems of the organization of labor and the distribution of goods — in order that the creations of our mind shall be a blessing and not a curse to mankind. Never forget this in the midst of your diagrams and equations.
*Address, California Institute of
Technology* [1931]

The whole of science is nothing more than a refinement of everyday thinking.
Physics and Reality [1936]

Physical concepts are free creations of the human mind, and are not, however it may seem, uniquely determined by the external world.
Evolution of Physics [1938]

[1] Energy equals mass times the speed of light squared.
The original statement is: If a body gives off the energy L in the form of radiation, its mass diminishes by L/c²." — *Ist die Tragheit eines Korpers von seinem Energieghalt abhangig?*
[*1905*]

Some recent work by E. Fermi and L. Szilard, which has been communicated to me in manuscript, leads me to expect that the element uranium may be turned into a new and important source of energy in the immediate future. Certain aspects of the situation which has arisen seem to call for watchfulness and, if necessary, quick action on the part of the Administration.
*Letter to President Franklin D.
Roosevelt* [*August 2, 1939*] (*the
letter which resulted in assignment of government funds for
development of the atom bomb*)

This new phenomena [atomic energy] would also lead to the construction of bombs. . . . A single bomb of this type, carried by boat and exploded in a port, might very well destroy the whole port, together with some of the surrounding territory. However, such bombs might very well prove to be too heavy for transportation by air.   *Ib.*

As long as there are sovereign nations possessing great power, war is inevitable.
*Einstein on the Atomic Bomb
[Atlantic Monthly, November
1945]*

I do not believe that civilization will be wiped out in a war fought with the atomic bomb. Perhaps two thirds of the people of the earth might be killed, but enough men capable of thinking, and enough books, would be left to start again, and civilization could be restored.   *Ib.*

Since I do not foresee that atomic energy is to be a great boon for a long time, I have to say that for the present it is a menace. Perhaps it is well that it should be. It may intimidate the human race into bringing order into its international affairs, which, without the pressure of fear, it would not do.   *Ib.*

I shall never believe that God plays dice with the world.[1]
From PHILIPP FRANK, *Einstein,
His Life and Times* [1947]

[1] See Anatole France, p. 802a.

The Lord God is subtle, but malicious he is not.[1]
Inscription in Fine Hall, Princeton University

Every intellectual who is called before one of the committees ought to refuse to testify, i.e., he must be prepared . . . for the sacrifice of his personal welfare in the interest of the cultural welfare of his country. . . . This kind of inquisition violates the spirit of the Constitution.

If enough people are ready to take this grave step they will be successful. If not, then the intellectuals of this country deserve nothing better than the slavery which is intended for them.
Letter to William Frauenglass [2]
[*May 16, 1953*]

The unleashed power of the atom has changed everything save our modes of thinking, and we thus drift toward unparalleled catastrophes.
From RALPH E. LAPP, *The Einstein Letter That Started It All* [*New York Times Magazine, August 2, 1964*]

Our defense is not in armaments, nor in science, nor in going underground. Our defense is in law and order.[3]   *Ib.*

Something deeply hidden had to be behind things.
Ib. [*autobiographical handwritten note*]

JOHN ERSKINE
1879–1951

The Moral Obligation to Be Intelligent.   *Title of book* [*1915*]

[1] Raffiniert ist der Herr Gott, aber Boshaft ist er nicht.
See Dostoevski, p. 708a.
[2] Einstein's letter was published in the *New York Times* [June 12, 1953]. Mr. Frauenglass had been subpoenaed to testify before the Senate Internal Security Subcommittee.
[3] See Lincoln, p. 636a.

W. C. FIELDS
1879–1946

It ain't a fit night out for man or beast.   *The Fatal Glass of Beer*

Anyone who hates children and dogs can't be all bad.   *Attributed*

On the whole, I'd rather be in Philadelphia.   *His own epitaph*

EDWARD MORGAN FORSTER
1879–1970

When the book of life is opening, our readings are secret.
The Longest Journey [*1907*]

Nonsense and beauty have close connections.   *Ib.*

Railway termini . . . are our gates to the glorious and the unknown. Through them we pass out into adventure and sunshine, to them, alas! we return. In Paddington all Cornwall is latent and the remoter west; down the inclines of Liverpool Street lie fenlands and the illimitable Broads; Scotland is through the plyons of Euston; Wessex behind the poised chaos of Waterloo.
Howards End [*1910*], *ch. 2*

It will be generally admitted that Beethoven's Fifth Symphony is the most sublime noise that has ever penetrated into the ear of man.   *Ib. 5*

Only connect! That was the whole of her sermon. Only connect the prose and the passion, and both will be exalted, and human love will be seen at its height. Live in fragments no longer. Only connect, and the beast and the monk, robbed of the isolation that is life to either, will die.   *Ib. 22*

The echo began in some indescribable way to undermine her hold on life. Coming at a moment when she chanced to be fatigued, it had managed to murmur, "Pathos, piety, courage — they exist, but are identical, and so is filth. Everything exists, nothing has value." If one had spoken vileness in that place,

or quoted lofty poetry, the [echo's] comment would have been the same —
"Ou-boum."

A *Passage to India* [1924]

The historian must have some conception of how men who are not historians behave.

Abinger Harvest [1936]. *Captain Edward Gibbon*

How rare, how precious is frivolity! How few writers can prostitute all their powers! They are always implying, "I am capable of higher things."

Notes on English Character. Ronald Firbank

EDMUND L. GRUBER
1879–1941

Over hill, over dale,[1] we have hit the
    dusty trail
And those caissons go rolling along.
Countermarch! Right about! hear those
    wagon soldiers shout
While those caissons go rolling along.
Oh, it's hi-hi-yee! for the field artilleree,
Shout out your numbers loud and
    strong,
And where'er we go, you will always
    know
That those caissons are rolling along.

The Caisson Song [2] [1908]

JOHN HAYNES HOLMES
1879–1964

If Christians were Christians, there would be no anti-Semitism. Jesus was a Jew. There is nothing that the ordinary Christian so dislikes to remember as this awkward historical fact. But it happens, none the less, to be true.

The Sensible Man's View of Religion [1933]

[1] See Shakespeare, p. 229a.
[2] In April 1908 the 1st Battalion of the 5th Field Artillery relieved the 2nd Battalion in the Philippines. Gruber, then a lieutenant in the 5th, was asked to write a song that would symbolize the spirit of the reunited regiment. There are many variant wordings.

Priests are no more necessary to religion than politicians to patriotism.

The Sensible Man's View of Religion

The universe is not hostile, nor yet is it friendly. It is simply indifferent.

Ib.

The life of humanity upon this planet may yet come to an end, and a very terrible end. But I would have you notice that this end is threatened in our time not by anything that the universe may do to us, but only by what man may do to himself.   *Ib.*

VACHEL LINDSAY
1879–1931

Booth died blind and still by faith he
    trod,
Eyes still dazzled by the ways of God.

General William Booth Enters into Heaven [1913]

Sleep softly . . . eagle forgotten . . .
    under the stone,
Time has its way with you there, and
    the clay has its own.
Sleep on, O brave-hearted, O wise man,
    that kindled the flame —
To live in mankind is far more than to
    live in a name.

The Eagle That Is Forgotten [1]
[1913], *st. 5*

Factory windows are always broken.
Somebody's always throwing bricks,
Somebody's always heaving cinders,
Playing ugly Yahoo tricks.

Factory Windows, st. 1

Fat black bucks in a wine-barrel room,
Barrel-house kings; with feet unstable,
Sagged and reeled and pounded on the
    table,
Pounded on the table,

[1] John Peter Altgeld [1847–1902; Governor of Illinois 1893–1897], widely criticized for pardoning, in June 1893, the anarchists who had been serving life terms since the Haymarket riot in Chicago, May 4, 1886. Altgeld, in pardoning them, declared that "the judge conducted the trial with malicious ferocity."

Beat an empty barrel with the handle of a broom.
> *The Congo* [1914], *pt. I*

Then I saw the Congo, creeping through the black,
Cutting through the forest with a golden track.   *Ib.*

Be careful what you do,
Or Mumbo-Jumbo, God of the Congo,
And all of the other
Gods of the Congo,
Mumbo-Jumbo will hoo-doo you.
> *Ib.*

A bronzed, lank man! His suit of ancient black,
A famous high top-hat and plain worn shawl
Make him the quaint great figure that men love,
The prairie-lawyer, master of us all.
> *Abraham Lincoln Walks at Midnight* [1914], *st. 3*

They spoke, I think, of perils past.
They spoke, I think, of peace at last.
One thing I remember:
Spring came on forever,
Spring came on forever,
Said the Chinese nightingale.
> *The Chinese Nightingale*
> [1917], *end*

Planting the trees that would march and train
On, in his name to the great Pacific,
Like Birnam Wood to Dunsinane,[1]
Johnny Appleseed[2] swept on.
> *In Praise of Johnny Appleseed*

The more probable chance for me will come in some little row where strikers are being shot down. . . . I would be with the fool strikers, right or wrong.
> *Letter to Eleanor Dougherty*
> [*October 12, 1918*]

[1] See Shakespeare, p. 285b.
[2] John Chapman [1774–1847].
Remember Johnny Appleseed,
All ye who love the apple;
He served his kind by word and deed,
In God's grand greenwood chapel.
WILLIAM HENRY VENABLE [1836–1918], *Johnny Appleseed, st. 25*

ST. JOHN LUCAS
1879–1934

The curate thinks you have no soul;
I know that he has none.[1]   *My Dog*

GEORGE WASHINGTON LYON
1879–

Worry, the interest paid by those who borrow trouble.
> *In Judge* [*March 1, 1924*]

DIXON LANIER MERRITT
1879–

A wonderful bird is the pelican,
His bill will hold more than his belican.
He can take in his beak
Food enough for a week,
But I'm damned if I see how the helican.   *The Pelican* [1910]

HAROLD MONRO
1879–1932

How lonely we shall be!
What shall we do,
You without me,
I without you?
> *Midnight Lamentation, st. 1*

They are better than stars or water,
Better than voices of winds that sing,
Better than any man's fair daughter,
Your green glass beads on a silver ring.
> *Overheard on a Saltmarsh*

A long, dim ecstasy holds her life;
Her world is an infinite shapeless white,
Till her tongue has curled the last holy drop,
Then she sinks back into the night.
> *Milk for the Cat, st. 8*

FELIX RIESENBERG
1879–1939

The sea has always been a seducer, a careless lying fellow, not feminine, as

[1] There are things that even the youngest curate cannot explain. — LEONARD MERRICK, *One Man's View* [1897]

many writers imagine, but strongly masculine in its allurement. The king of the sea, with his whiskers of weed and his trident and dolphins, truly represents the main and gives it character. The sea, like a great sultan, supports thousands of ships, his lawful wives. These he caresses and chastises as the case may be. This explains the feminine gender of all proper vessels.

Vignettes of the Sea

WILL ROGERS
1879–1935

All I know is just what I read in the papers. *Prefatory remark*

I tell you folks, all politics is applesauce. *The Illiterate Digest* [1924], *p. 30*

Everything is funny as long as it is happening to somebody else.
Ib. p. 131

More men have been elected between sundown and sunup than ever were elected between sunup and sundown.
Ib. p. 152

I never met a man I didn't like.
Address, Boston [June 1930]

A comedian can only last till he either takes himself serious or his audience takes him serious.
Syndicated newspaper article [June 28, 1931]

I not only "don't choose to run"[1] [for President] but I don't even want to leave a loophole in case I am drafted, so I won't "choose." I will say "won't run" no matter how bad the country will need a comedian by that time.
Ib.

Politics has got so expensive that it takes lots of money to even get beat with. *Ib.*

My forefathers didn't come over on the *Mayflower*, but they met the boat.[2] *Remark*

[1] See Calvin Coolidge, p. 911b.
[2] Rogers was of Indian descent.

JOSEPH STALIN [IOSIF VISSARIONOVICH DZHUGASHVILI]
1879–1953

Print is the sharpest and the strongest weapon of our party.
Speech [April 19, 1923]

Dizziness from success.
Speech [March 2, 1930]

The most remarkable thing about socialist competition is that it creates a basic change in people's view of labor, since it changes the labor from a shameful and heavy burden into a matter of honor, matter of fame, matter of valor and heroism.
Speech [June 27, 1930]

The Hitlerite blackguards have covered Europe with gallows and concentration camps. . . . They have turned Europe into a prison of nations,[1] and this they call the new order in Europe.
Address to the Moscow Soviet [November 6, 1942]

You cannot make a revolution with silk gloves.
From JOHN GUNTHER, *Soviet Russia Today*

The writer is an engineer of the human soul.[2] *Ib.*

A single death is a tragedy, a million deaths is a statistic.
Quoted statement

The inevitability of wars between capitalist countries remains in force.
Last public statement [1952]

WALLACE STEVENS
1879–1955

I heard them cry — the peacocks.
Was it a cry against the twilight
Or against the leaves themselves
Turning in the wind,

[1] . . . The saying that Russia is a prison of nations. — V. I. LENIN, *On the Question of National Policy* (and elsewhere)
The expression originated in *La Russie en 1839* by ADOLPHE DE CUSTINE [1790–1857].
[2] See Gorki, p. 894b.

Turning as the flames
Turned in the fire,
Turning as the tails of the peacocks
Turned in the loud fire,
Loud as the hemlocks
Full of the cry of the peacocks?
Or was it a cry against the hemlocks?
          Domination of Black [1923]

Twenty men crossing a bridge,
Into a village,
Are twenty men crossing twenty
     bridges,
Into twenty villages,
Or one man
Crossing a single bridge into a village.
     Metaphors of a Magnifico [1923]

Poetry is the supreme fiction, madame.
     A High-toned Old Christian
                    Woman [1923]

Let be be the finale of seem.
The only emperor is the emperor of ice
     cream.
     The Emperor of Ice Cream [1923]

Only, here and there, an old sailor,
Drunk and asleep in his boots,
Catches tigers
In red weather.
     Disillusionment of Ten O'clock
                         [1923]
Complacencies of the peignoir, and late
Coffee and oranges in a sunny chair.
          Sunday Morning [1923], st. 1

We live in an old chaos of the sun,
Or old dependency of day and night,
Or island solitude, unsponsored, free,
Of that wide water, inescapable.
Deer walk upon our mountains, and the
     quail
Whistle about us their spontaneous
     cries;
Sweet berries ripen in the wilderness;
And, in the isolation of the sky,
At evening, casual flocks of pigeons
     make
Ambiguous undulations as they sink,
Downward to darkness, on extended
     wings.   *Ib.* st. 8

Chieftain Iffucan of Azcan in caftan
Of tan with henna hackles, halt!
          Bantams in Pine Woods [1923]

Damned universal cock, as if the sun
Was blackamoor to bear your blazing
     tail.   *Bantams in Pine Woods*

I placed a jar in Tennessee,
And round it was, upon a hill.
It made the slovenly wilderness
Surround that hill.
          Anecdote of the Jar [1923], *st.* 1

     Frogs Eat Butterflies. Snakes Eat
Frogs. Hogs Eat Snakes. Men Eat
Hogs.[1]   *Title of poem* [1923]

I had as lief be embraced by the porter
     at the hotel
As to get no more from the moonlight
Than your moist hand.
          Two Figures in Dense Violet
                         Night [1923]

Just as my fingers on these keys
Make music, so the self-same sounds
On my spirit make a music, too.
          Peter Quince at the Clavier
                         [1923], 1

Beauty is momentary in the mind —
The fitful tracing of a portal;
But in the flesh it is immortal.
The body dies; the body's beauty lives.
                         Ib. 4

Susanna's music touched the bawdy
     strings
Of those white elders; but, escaping,
Left only Death's ironic scraping.
Now, in its immortality, it plays
On the clear viol of her memory,
And makes a constant sacrament of
     praise.   *Ib.*

I do not know which to prefer,
The beauty of inflections
Or the beauty of innuendoes,
The blackbird whistling
Or just after.
          Thirteen Ways of Looking at a
                Blackbird [1923], *st.* 5

The gongs rang loudly as the windy
     booms
Hoo-hooed it in the darkened ocean-
     booms
          Sea Surface Full of Clouds
                         [1923], II

[1] See Ambrose Bierce, p. 791b-792a.

Then the sea
And heaven rolled as one and from the
two
Came fresh transfigurings of freshest
blue.
Sea Surface Full of Clouds, V

She sang beyond the genius of the sea,
The water never formed to mind or
voice,
Like a body wholly body, fluttering
Its empty sleeves; and yet its mimic
motion
Made constant cry, caused constantly a
cry,
That was not ours although we under-
stood,
Inhuman, of the veritable ocean.
The Idea of Order at Key West
[1936], st. 1

Oh! Blessed rage for order, pale Ra-
món,
The maker's rage to order words of the
sea,
Words of the fragrant portals, dimly
starred,
And of ourselves and of our origins,
In ghostlier demarcations, keener
sounds.　　　　　　　*Ib. st. 7*

Poetry is the subject of the poem.
The Man with the Blue Guitar
[1937], *XXII*

I am a native in this world
And think in it as a native thinks.
Ib. XXVIII

The prologues are over. It is question,
now,
Of final belief. So, say that final belief
Must be in a fiction. It is time to
choose.
Asides on the Oboe [1942], *st. 1*

Light
Is the lion that comes down to drink.
The Glass of Water [1942], *st. 2*

A. A violent order is disorder; and
B. A great disorder is an order. These
Two things are one.
Connoisseur of Chaos [1942], *st. 1*

One's grand flights, one's Sunday
baths,

One's tootings at the weddings of the
soul
Occur as they occur.
*The Sense of the Sleight-of-
Hand Man* [1942], *st. 1*

The motive for metaphor, shrinking
from
The weight of primary noon,
The ABC of being,

The ruddy temper, the hammer
Of red and blue, the hard sound —
Steel against intimation — the sharp
flash,
The vital, arrogant, fatal, dominant X.
The Motive for Metaphor, st. 4, 5

To get at the thing
Without gestures is to get at it as
Idea.
*So-and-So Reclining on Her
Couch* [1947], *st. 6*

The President ordains the bee to be
Immortal.
*The President Ordains the Bee
to Be* [1947], *st. 1*

The inconceivable idea of the sun.
Notes Toward a Supreme Fiction
[1947], *I*

You must become an ignorant man
again
And see the sun again with an ignorant
eye
And see it clearly in the idea of it.
Ib.

The death of one god is the death of
all.　　　　　　　*Ib.*

There is a project for the sun. The sun
Must bear no name, gold flourisher, but
be
In the difficulty of what it is to be.
Ib.

The monastic man is an artist. The philosopher
Appoints man's place in music, say, today.
But the priest desires. The philosopher
desires.
And not to have is the beginning of
desire.　　　　　　　*Ib. II*

We keep coming back and coming back
To the real: to the hotel instead of the
   hymns
That fall upon it out of the wind.
> *An Ordinary Evening in New*
> *Haven* [1950], IX

The essential gaudiness of poetry.
> *Stevens's note to The Emperor*
> *of Ice Cream*

The essential thing in form is to be
free in whatever form is used. A free
form does not assure freedom. As a
form, it is just one more form. So that
it comes to this, I suppose, that I believe in freedom regardless of form.
> *A Note on Poetry* [1937]

What makes the poet the potent figure that he is, or was, or ought to be, is
that he creates the world to which we
turn incessantly and without knowing it
and that he gives to life the supreme
fictions without which we are unable to
conceive of it.
> *The Noble Rider and the Sound*
> *of Words* [1942]

Each man resembles all other men,
each woman resembles all other
women, this year resembles last year.
The beginning of time will, no doubt,
resemble the end of time. One world is
said to resemble another.
> *Three Academic Pieces* [1947]

Poetry is poetry, and one's objective
as a poet is to achieve poetry precisely
as one's objective in music is to achieve
music. There are poets who would regard that as a scandal and who would
say that a poem which had no importance except its importance as poetry
had no importance at all, and that a
poet who had no objective except to
achieve poetry was a fribble and something less than a man of reason.
> *On Selecting Domination of*
> *Black as his best poem*

Sentimentality is a failure of feeling.
> *Opus Posthumous* [1957].
> *Adagia*

A poem should be part of one's sense
of life.   *Ib.*

A poet looks at the world as a man
looks at a woman.
> *Opus Posthumous. Adagia*

All history is modern history.   *Ib.*

Poetry is the sum of its attributes.
> *Ib.*

In the world of words, the imagination is one of the forces of nature.
> *Ib.*

God is in me or else is not at all
(does not exist).   *Ib.*

The world is a force, not a presence.
> *Ib.*

Poetry is a search for the inexplicable.   *Ib.*

SIMEON STRUNSKY
1879–1948

No colonization without misrepresentation.
> *No Mean City* [1944], *ch.* 1

Famous remarks are very seldom
quoted correctly.   *Ib.* 38

LEON TROTSKY
1879–1940

The literary "fellow travelers" of the
Revolution.
> *Literature and Revolution*
> [1923], *ch.* 2

The dictatorship of the Communist
Party is maintained by recourse to every
form of violence.
> *Terrorism and Communism*
> [1924], *p.* 71

CH'EN TU-HSIU [1]
1879–1942

The pulse of modern life is economic
and the fundamental principle of economic production is individual independence.
> *The New Youth* [December
> 1916]

[1] From *Sources of Chinese Tradition*, edited
by William Theodore de Bary [1960]. Ch'en was
the founder [1921] of the Chinese Communist
Party.

All religions, laws, moral and political systems are but necessary means to preserve social order. They are not the individual's original purpose of enjoyment in life and can be changed in accordance with the circumstances of the time.

Man's happiness in life is the result of man's own effort and is neither the gift of God nor a spontaneous natural product.

> *The New Youth* [*February* 1918]

During his lifetime, an individual should devote his efforts to create happiness and to enjoy it, and also to keep it in store in society so that individuals of the future may also enjoy it. ***Ib.***

GEORGE ASAF
[GEORGE H. POWELL]
1880–1951

What's the use of worrying?
It never was worthwhile,
So, pack up your troubles in your old
     kit-bag,
And smile, smile, smile.
> *Pack Up Your Troubles in Your Old Kit-Bag* [1915]

ALEXANDER BLOK
1880–1921

On they march with sovereign tread,
With a starving dog behind,
With a blood-red flag ahead —
In a storm where none can see,
From the rifle bullets free,
Gently walking in the snow,
Where like pearls the snowflakes glow,
Marches rose-crowned in the van
Jesus Christ, the son of man.
> *The Twelve* [1918]

Yes, we are Scythians, yes, we are
     Asians. *Scythians* [1918]

JOSEPH CLARK GREW
1880–1965

This [sartorial convention] is a real problem with which I shall have to wrestle during the next few days, for of such stuff is diplomacy made.[1]
> *Ten Years in Japan* [1944]
> [*July 20, 1932*]

We have a phrase in English, "straight from the horse's mouth."
> *Ib.* [*October 19, 1939*]. *Address, America–Japan Society*

ROBERT BROWNING
HAMILTON
1880–

I walked a mile with Pleasure.
     She chattered all the way,
But left me none the wiser
     For all she had to say.

I walked a mile with Sorrow,
     And ne'er a word said she;
But, oh, the things I learned from her
     When Sorrow walked with me!
> *Along the Road*

BRIAN HOOKER
1880–1946

O youth foregone, foregoing!
O dream unseen, unsought!
God give you joy of knowing
What life your death has bought.[2]
> *A.D. 1919, st.* 5

HELEN KELLER
1880–1968

Literature is my Utopia. Here I am not disfranchised. No barrier of the senses shuts me out from the sweet, gracious discourse of my book friends. They talk to me without embarrassment or awkwardness.
> *The Story of My Life* [1902]

[1] In a diplomat's soul you may find iron ore, but it is usually oil — and in a whale of a diplomat you'll find the whole equipment — the blubber of charity, the whalebone of flexibility, the oil of commodity. A great diplomat is a regular Moby Dick. — FRANCIS HACKETT, *Review of* ROGER B. MERRIMAN, *Suleiman the Magnificent, New York Times* [January 4, 1945]

[2] On a tablet at Yale University commemorating the Yale men who died in the First World War.

DOUGLAS MacARTHUR
1880–1964

The unfailing formula for production of morale is patriotism, self-respect, discipline, and self-confidence within a military unit, joined with fair treatment and merited appreciation from without. It cannot be produced by pampering or coddling an army, and is not necessarily destroyed by hardship, danger, or even calamity. Though it can survive and develop in adversity that comes as an inescapable incident of service, it will quickly wither and die if soldiers come to believe themselves the victims of indifference or injustice on the part of their government, or of ignorance, personal ambition, or ineptitude on the part of their military leaders.

> *Annual Report of the Chief of Staff, United States Army, for the Fiscal Year Ending June 30, 1933*

I shall return.

> *On leaving Corregidor for Australia [March 11, 1942]*

I have returned. By the grace of Almighty God, our forces stand again on Philippine soil.

> *Upon landing on Leyte [October 20, 1944]*

I see that the old flagpole still stands. Have your troops hoist the colors to its peak, and let no enemy ever haul them down.

> *To Colonel George M. Jones and 503rd Regimental Combat Team, who recaptured Corregidor [March 2, 1945]*

In war there is no substitute for victory.

> *Address, Joint Meeting of Congress [April 19, 1951]*

I still remember the refrain of one of the most popular barracks ballads of that day, which proclaimed most proudly that old soldiers never die; they just fade away. I now close my military career and just fade away.[1]   *Ib.*

[1] See Anonymous, p. 1103a.

It is fatal to enter any war without the will to win it.

> *Speech, Republican National Convention [July 7, 1952]*

GEORGE CATLETT MARSHALL
1880–1959

The refusal of the British and Russian peoples to accept what appeared to be inevitable defeat was the great factor in the salvage of our civilization.

> *Biennial Report of the Chief of Staff, United States Army [September 1, 1945]*

If man does find the solution for world peace it will be the most revolutionary reversal of his record we have ever known.   *Ib.*

Our policy is directed not against any country or doctrine but against hunger, poverty, desperation and chaos. Its purpose should be the revival of a working economy in the world so as to permit the emergence of political and social conditions in which free institutions can exist.

> *Address, Harvard University [June 5, 1947], embodying the European Recovery Plan (Marshall Plan)*

You can have all of the materiel in the world, but without morale it is largely ineffective.

> *Military Review [October 1948]*

It is not enough to fight. It is the spirit which we bring to the fight that decides the issue. It is morale that wins the victory.   *Ib.*

Morale is the state of mind. It is steadfastness and courage and hope. It is confidence and zeal and loyalty. It is *élan, esprit de corps* and determination.   *Ib.*

HENRY LOUIS MENCKEN
1880–1956

The virulence of the national appetite for bogus revelation.
A Book of Prefaces [1917], *ch. 1*

To the man with an ear for verbal delicacies — the man who searches painfully for the perfect word, and puts the way of saying a thing above the thing said — there is in writing the constant joy of sudden discovery, of happy accident. *Ib. 2*

Poverty is a soft pedal upon all branches of human activity, not excepting the spiritual. *Ib. 4*

Formalism is the hallmark of the national culture. *Ib.*

Time is a great legalizer, even in the field of morals. *Ib.*

The prophesying business is like writing fugues; it is fatal to everyone save the man of absolute genius.
Prejudices, First Series [1919], *ch. 2*

The public . . . demands certainties; it must be told definitely and a bit raucously that this is true and that is false. But there *are* no certainties.
Ib. 3

All successful newspapers are ceaselessly querulous and bellicose. They never defend anyone or anything if they can help it; if the job is forced upon them, they tackle it by denouncing someone or something else. *Ib. 13*

The great artists of the world are never Puritans, and seldom even ordinarily respectable. *Ib. 16*

To be in love is merely to be in a state of perceptual anesthesia — to mistake an ordinary young man for a Greek god or an ordinary young woman for a goddess. *Ib.*

All the more pretentious American authors try to write chastely and elegantly; the typical literary product of the country is still a refined essay in the *Atlantic Monthly*, perhaps gently jocose but never rough — by Emerson, so to speak, out of Charles Lamb.
The American Language [1919]

Philadelphia is the most pecksniffian of American cities, and thus probably leads the world. *Ib.*

It is the dull man who is always sure, and the sure man who is always dull.
Prejudices, Second Series [1920], *ch. 1*

If, after I depart this vale, you ever remember me and have thought to please my ghost, forgive some sinner and wink your eye at some homely girl.
Epitaph. From Smart Set [*December* 1921]

There are no mute, inglorious Miltons,[1] save in the hallucinations of poets. The one sound test of a Milton is that he functions as a Milton.
Prejudices, Third Series [1922], *ch. 3*

Nine times out of ten, in the arts as in life, there is actually no truth to be discovered; there is only error to be exposed. *Ib.*

Injustice is relatively easy to bear; what stings is justice. *Ib.*

The older I grow the more I distrust the familiar doctrine that age brings wisdom. *Ib.*

Faith may be defined briefly as an illogical belief in the occurrence of the improbable. *Ib. 14*

To be happy one must be (*a*) well fed, unhounded by sordid cares, at ease in Zion, (*b*) full of a comfortable feeling of superiority to the masses of one's fellow men, and (*c*) delicately and unceasingly amused according to one's taste. It is my contention that, if this definition be accepted, there is no country in the world wherein a man constituted as I am — a man of my peculiar weakness, vanities, appetites, and aversions — can be so happy as he can be in the United States. Going further, I lay down the doctrine that it is a

[1] See Gray, p. 440b.

sheer physical impossibility for such a man to live in the United States and *not* be happy.

On Being an American [1922]

The difference between a moral man and a man of honor is that the latter regrets a discreditable act, even when it has worked and he has not been caught.

Prejudices, Fourth Series [1924], *ch. 11*

Nothing can come out of an artist that is not in the man.

Ib. Fifth Series [1926], *ch. 5*

Christian endeavor is notoriously hard on female pulchritude.

The Aesthetic Recoil

The learned are seldom pretty fellows, and in many cases their appearance tends to discourage a love of study in the young.

The New Webster International Dictionary [1934]

The Gaseous Vertebrata who own, operate and afflict the universe have treated me with excessive politeness.

Happy Days [1940], *preface*

When A annoys or injures B on the pretense of saving or improving X, A is a scoundrel.

Newspaper Days: 1899–1906 [1941]

I've made it a rule never to drink by daylight and never to refuse a drink after dark.

From the New York Post [*September 18, 1945*]

Conscience is the inner voice that warns us somebody may be looking.

A Mencken Chrestomathy [1949]

There are some people who read too much: the bibliobibuli. I know some who are constantly drunk on books, as other men are drunk on whiskey or religion. They wander through this most diverting and stimulating of worlds in a haze, seeing nothing and hearing nothing.

Minority Report: H. L. Mencken's Notebooks [1956]

The booboisie. *Passim*

ALFRED NOYES
1880–1958

Forty singing seamen, who was puzzled for to know
If the grog they dreamed they swallowed made them dream of all that followed.

Forty Singing Seamen

Go down to Kew in lilac time (it isn't far from London!)
And you shall wander hand in hand with love in summer's wonderland.

Barrel Organ, st. 5

The wind was a torrent of darkness among the gusty trees,
The moon was a ghostly galleon tossed upon cloudy seas,
The road was a ribbon of moonlight over the purple moor,
And the highwayman came riding —
Riding — riding —
The highwayman came riding, up to the old inn-door.

The Highwayman

The landlord's black-eyed daughter,
Bess, the landlord's daughter,
Plaiting a dark red love knot into her long black hair. *Ib.*

I'll come to thee by moonlight, though hell should bar the way. *Ib.*

Calling as he used to call, faint and far away,
In Sherwood, in Sherwood, about the break of day. *Sherwood*

GRANTLAND RICE
1880–1954

When the One Great Scorer comes to write against your name —
He marks — not that you won or lost — but how you played the game.[1]

Alumnus Football

[1] But just this line ye grave for me:
"He played the game."
ROBERT WILLIAM SERVICE [1874–1958],
The Lost Master

All wars are planned by old men
  In council rooms apart,
Who plan for greater armament
  And map the battle chart.[1]
            Two Sides of War, st. 1

I've noticed nearly all the dead
  Were hardly more than boys.
                Ib. st. 4

RICHARD HENRY TAWNEY
1880–1962

Industrialized communities neglect
the very objects for which it is worth
while to acquire riches in their feverish
preoccupation with the means by which
riches can be acquired.
      The Acquisitive Society [1920]

MARGARET WIDDEMER
1880–

I have shut my little sister in from life
    and light
(For a rose, for a ribbon, for a wreath
    across my hair).
        The Factories [1915], *st. 1*

Round my path they cry to me, little
    souls unborn —
God of Life! Creator! It was I! It was I!
                Ib. st. 3

THOMAS RUSSELL YBARRA
1880–

A Christian is a man who feels
    Repentance on a Sunday
For what he did on Saturday
    And is going to do on Monday.
                The Christian

ALBERT JAY COOK
fl. 1917

It's Heaven, Hell or Hoboken[2] before
    next Christmas Day.
        Heaven, Hell or Hoboken

[1] See Herbert Hoover, p. 931a.
[2] Port of embarkation and return for the
American Expeditionary Forces during World
War I.

FRANKLIN PIERCE ADAMS [F.P.A.]
1881–1960

Christmas is over and Business is
Business.   *For the Other 364 Days*

Up, to the office . . . and so to bed.
    A Ballade of Mr. Samuel Pepys.
                Refrain

Ruthlessly pricking our gonfalon bub-
    ble,
Making a Giant hit into a double,
Words that are weighty with nothing
    but trouble:
"Tinker to Evers to Chance."
        Baseball's Sad Lexicon

The rich man has his motor car,
  His country and his town estate.
He smokes a fifty-cent cigar
  And jeers at Fate.
            The Rich Man, st. 1

The best you get is an even break.[1]
        Ballade of Schopenhauer's
                Philosophy

I shot a poem into the air,
It was reprinted everywhere
From Bangor to the Rocky Range
And always credited to — Exchange.
                Frequently

O bards of rhyme and meter free,
My gratitude goes out to ye
For all your deathless lines — ahem!
Let's see now . . . What *is* one of
    them?   *To a Vers Librist*

Of making many books there is no
    end —
So Sancho Panza said, and so say I.
Thou wert my guide, philosopher and
    friend
When only one is shining in the sky.
      Lines on and from Bartlett's
            Familiar Quotations

Go, lovely Rose that lives its little hour!
Go, little booke! and let who will be
    clever!
Roll on! From yonder ivy-mantled tow-
    er

[1] See Albee, p. 842b.

The moon and I could keep this up forever.
Lines on and from Bartlett's Familiar Quotations

MARY ANTIN
1881–1949

So at last I was going to America! Really, really going, at last! The boundaries burst. The arch of heaven soared. A million suns shone out for every star. The winds rushed in from outer space, roaring in my ears, "America! America!"   *The Promised Land* [1912]

JOSEPH CAMPBELL
1881–1944

As a white candle
In a holy place,
So is the beauty
Of an aged face.
            The Old Woman, st. 1

SIR ALEXANDER FLEMING
1881–1955

It is the lone worker who makes the first advance in a subject: the details may be worked out by a team, but the prime idea is due to the enterprise, thought and perception of an individual.[1]
    Address, Edinburgh University [1951]

PADRAIC COLUM
1881–1972

Years hence, in rustic speech, a phrase,
As in wild earth a Grecian vase!
      A Poor Scholar of the Forties

O woman shapely as a swan.
        I Shall Not Die for Thee

And I am praying God on high,
And I am praying Him night and day,

[1] See Sir Francis Darwin, p. 813b, and Hans Zinsser, p. 949b.

For a little house — a house of my own —
Out of the wind's and the rain's way.
       An Old Woman of the Roads,
                   st. 6

JOHN FREEMAN
1881–1929

Who may regret what was, since it has made
Himself himself? All that I was I am,
And the old childish joy now lives in me
At sight of a green field or a green tree.
        All That I Was I Am

EDGAR ALBERT GUEST
1881–1959

Somebody said that it couldn't be done,
But he with a chuckle replied
That maybe it couldn't, but he would be one
Who wouldn't say so till he'd tried.
       It Couldn't Be Done

It takes a heap o' livin' in a house t' make it home,
A heap o' sun an' shadder, an' ye sometimes have t' roam
Afore ye really 'preciate the things ye lef' behind,
An' hunger fer 'em somehow, with 'em allus on yer mind.   *Home*

Let me be a little kinder,
Let me be a little blinder
To the faults of those around me,
Let me praise a little more.   *A Creed*

I'd rather see a sermon than hear one any day;
I'd rather one should walk with me than merely tell the way.
           Sermons We See

In this bright little package, now isn't it odd?
You've a dime's worth of something known only to God!
        The Package of Seeds

JOHN EDWARD HAZARD
1881–1935

Ain't It Awful, Mabel!
Title of book

POPE JOHN XXIII
[ANGELO GIUSEPPE
RONCALLI]
1881–1963

The social progress, order, security and peace of each country are necessarily connected with the social progress, order, security and peace of all other countries.

At the present day no political community is able to pursue its own interests and develop itself in isolation, because the degree of its prosperity and development is a reflection and a component part of the degree of prosperity and development of all other political communities.

Pacem in Terris
[Encyclical letter,
April 11, 1963]

There exists an intrinsic connection between the common good on the one hand and the structure and function of public authority on the other. The moral order, which needs public authority in order to promote the common good in human society, requires also that the authority be effective in attaining that end. . . .

Today the universal common good poses problems of world-wide dimensions, which cannot be adequately tackled or solved except by the efforts of public authorities endowed with a wideness of power, structure and means of the same proportions: that is, of public authorities which are in a position to operate in an effective manner on a world-wide basis. The moral order itself, therefore, demands that such a form of public authority be established. *Ib.*

An act of the highest importance performed by the United Nations Organization was the universal Declaration of Human Rights, approved in the General Assembly of December 10, 1948. . . . The document represents an important step on the path towards the juridical-political organization of the world community. For in it, in most solemn form, the dignity of a person is acknowledged to all human beings; and as a consequence there is proclaimed, as a fundamental right, the right of free movement in search for truth and in the attainment of moral good and of justice, and also the right to a dignified life.

Pacem in Terris

The representative of the highest spiritual authority of the earth is glad, indeed boasts, of being the son of a humble but robust and honest laborer.

Remark to the Mayor of Fleury-sur-Loire. From Wit and Wisdom of Good Pope John, collected by Henri Fesquet [1963]

PABLO PICASSO
1881–1973

For me, a painting is a dramatic action in the course of which reality finds itself split apart. For me, that dramatic action takes precedence over all other considerations. The pure plastic act is only secondary as far as I'm concerned. What counts is the drama of that plastic act, the moment at which the universe comes out of itself and meets its own destruction.

From FRANÇOISE GILOT AND CARLTON LAKE, *Life With Picasso* [1964], *pt. I*

When I was a child, my mother said to me, "If you become a soldier you'll be a general. If you become a monk you'll end up as the Pope." Instead I became a painter and wound up as Picasso. *Ib.*

Painting isn't an aesthetic operation; it's a form of magic designed as a mediator between this strange hostile world and us, a way of seizing the power by giving form to our terrors as well as our desires. *Ib. VI*

I am only a public entertainer who has understood his time. *Remark*

WILLIAM TEMPLE
1881–1944

There is no structural organization of society which can bring about the coming of the Kingdom of God on earth, since all systems can be perverted by the selfishness of man.
The Malvern Manifesto [1]

Human status ought not to depend upon the changing demands of the economic process. *Ib.*

PIERRE TEILHARD DE CHARDIN [2]
1881–1955

If there were no internal propensity to unite, even at a prodigiously rudimentary level — indeed in the molecule itself — it would be physically impossible for love to appear higher up, with us, in "hominized" form. . . . Driven by the forces of love, the fragments of the world seek each other so that the world may come into being.
The Phenomenon of Man [1955],
bk. IV, ch. 2, sec. 2

Love alone is capable of uniting living beings in such a way as to complete and fulfill them, for it alone takes them and joins them by what is deepest in themselves. . . . Does not love every instant achieve all around us, in the couple or the team, the magic feat . . . of "personalizing" by totalizing? And if that is what it can achieve daily on a small scale, why should it not repeat this one day on world-wide dimensions? *Ib.*

The end of the world: the wholesale internal introversion upon itself of the noosphere, which has simultaneously reached the uttermost limit of its com-

plexity and its centrality . . . the overthrow of equilibrium, detaching the mind, fulfilled at last, from its material matrix, so that it will henceforth rest with all its weight on God-Omega . . . critical point simultaneously of emergence and emersion, of maturation and evasion.
*The Phenomenon of Man, bk. IV,
ch. 3, sec. 3*

We have only to believe. And the more threatening and irreducible reality appears, the more firmly and desperately must we believe. Then, little by little, we shall see the universal horror unbend, and then smile upon us, and then take us in its more than human arms.
The Divine Milieu [1957],
pt. III, ch. 3, sec. B

PELHAM GRENVILLE WODEHOUSE
1881–1975

He spoke with a certain what-is-it in his voice, and I could see that, if not actually disgruntled, he was far from being gruntled.
The Code of the Woosters

REGINALD ARKELL
1882–1959

Actual evidence I have none,
But my aunt's charwoman's sister's son
Heard a policeman, on his beat,
Say to a housemaid in Downing Street
That he had a brother, who had a friend,
Who knew when the war was going to end. *All the Rumors* [1916]

BERTON BRALEY
1882–1966

The grammar has a rule absurd
Which I would call an outworn myth:
"A preposition is a word
You mustn't end a sentence with!" [1]
No Rule to Be Afraid Of, st. 1

---

[1] Drawn up by a Conference of the Province of York, January 10, 1941; signed for the Conference by Temple, then Archbishop of York (later Archbishop of Canterbury).

[2] Translated by BERNARD WALL.

[1] See Churchill, p. 925a.

And so they sailed away, these three,
　　Mencken,
　　　　　Nathan
　　And God.[1]
　　　　　　　Three Minus One, st. 1

Back of the beating hammer
　By which the steel is wrought,
Back of the workshop's clamor
　The seeker may find the thought.
　　　　　　　The Thinker, st. 1

Back of the job — the dreamer
Who's making the dream come true!
　　　　　　　Ib. st. 4

GEORGES BRAQUE
1882–1963

Art upsets, science reassures.
　　　　　　　Pensées sur l'Art

　Truth exists, only falsehood has to be invented.　　　　　　　*Ib.*

PERCY WILLIAMS
BRIDGMAN
1882–1961

　To find the length of an object, we have to perform certain physical operations. The concept of length is therefore fixed when the operations by which length is measured are fixed: that is, the concept of length involves as much as and nothing more than the set of operations by which length is determined.
　　　　The Logic of Modern Physics
　　　　　　　　　　　　[1927]

EDWARD ARTHUR
BURROUGHS,
BISHOP OF RIPON
1882–1934

　After all we could get on very happily if aviation, wireless, television and the like advanced no further than at present. . . . Dare I even suggest, at the risk of being lynched by some of my hearers, that the sum of human happiness would not necessarily be reduced if for ten years every physical and chemi-

[1] See Eugene Field, p. 820b.

cal laboratory were closed and the patient and resourceful energy displayed in them transferred to the lost art of getting on together and finding the formula for making both ends meet in the scale of human life. Much, of course, we should lose by this universal scientific holiday . . . but human happiness would not necessarily suffer.
　　　Sermon, to the British Association for the Advancement of Science [Leeds, September 4, 1927]

JOHN DRINKWATER
1882–1937

This be my pilgrimage and goal,
　Daily to march and find
The secret phrases of the soul,
　The evangels of the mind.
　　　　　　　Vocation

And not a girl goes walking
　Along the Cotswold lanes
But knows men's eyes in April
　Are quicker than their brains.
　　　　　　　Cotswold Love

Grant us the will to fashion as we feel,
Grant us the strength to labor as we
　know,
Grant us the purpose, ribbed and edged
　with steel,
To strike the blow.　　　*A Prayer, st. 9*

SIR ARTHUR STANLEY
EDDINGTON
1882–1944

　It is one thing for the human mind to extract from the phenomena of nature the laws which it has itself put into them; it may be a far harder thing to extract laws over which it has no control. It is even possible that laws which have not their origin in the mind may be irrational, and we can never succeed in formulating them.
　　　Space, Time, and Gravitation
　　　　　　　　　　　　[1920]

　We have found that where science has progressed the farthest, the mind has but regained from nature that which the mind put into nature.

We have found a strange footprint on the shores of the unknown. We have devised profound theories, one after another, to account for its origin. At last we have succeeded in reconstructing the creature that made the footprint. And lo! it is our own.

Space, Time, and Gravitation

FELIX FRANKFURTER
1882–1965

The [Fifteenth] Amendment nullifies sophisticated as well as simple-minded modes of discrimination.

Lane v. Wilson, 307 U.S. 268,
275 [1939]

The history of liberty has largely been the history of the observance of procedural safeguards.

McNabb v. United States, 318
U.S. 332, 347 [1943]

One who belongs to the most vilified and persecuted minority in history is not likely to be insensible to the freedoms guaranteed by our Constitution. . . . But as judges we are neither Jew nor Gentile, neither Catholic nor agnostic.

Flag Salute Cases, 319 U.S. 624,
646 [1943]

Courts ought not to enter this political thicket.

Colegrove v. Green, 328 U.S.
549, 556 [1946]

After all, this is the Nation's ultimate judicial tribunal, not a super-legal-aid bureau.

Uveges v. Pennsylvania, 335 U.S.
437, 449 [1948]

In a democratic society like ours, relief must come through an aroused popular conscience that sears the conscience of the people's representatives.

Baker v. Carr, 369 U.S. 186, 270
[1962]

I know of no title that I deem more honorable than that of Professor of the Harvard Law School.

Of Law and Life and Other
Things [1965]

JEAN GIRAUDOUX
1882–1944

There are truths which can kill a nation.   *Electra*

Faithful women are all alike, they think only of their fidelity, never of their husbands.

Amphitryon 38 [1929]

SAMUEL GOLDWYN
1882–

Include me out.   *Saying*

In two words: im-possible.

From ALVA JOHNSTON,
The Great Goldwyn

A verbal contract isn't worth the paper it's written on.   *Ib.*

I read part of it all the way through.
Ib.

I would be sticking my head in a moose.   *Ib.*

If you can't give me your word of honor, will you give me your promise?
Ib.

HERMANN HAGEDORN
1882–1964

The bomb that fell on Hiroshima fell on America too.
It fell on no city, no munition plants, no docks.
It erased no church, vaporized no public buildings, reduced no man to his atomic elements.
But it fell, it fell.
It burst. It shook the land.
God have mercy on our children.
God have mercy on America.

The Bomb That Fell on America

WILLIAM FREDERICK HALSEY, JR.
1882–1959

Attack — Repeat — Attack.
> *Dispatch to the South Pacific Force (October 26, 1942) before the Battle of Santa Cruz Islands*

Hit hard, hit fast, hit often.[1]
> *Formula for waging war*

Send them our latitude and longitude.
> *Retort to the enemy's question, "Where is the American Fleet?" [October 1944]*

Our ships have been salvaged and are retiring at high speed toward the Japanese fleet.
> *Radio message [October 1944] after Japanese claims that most of the U.S. Third Fleet had either been sunk or had retired*

JAMES JOYCE
1882–1941

He was outcast from life's feast.
> *Dubliners* [1916]. *A Painful Case*

Snow was general all over Ireland. It was falling on every part of the dark central plain, on the treeless hills, falling softly upon the Bog of Allen and, farther westward, softly falling into the dark mutinous Shannon waves. It was falling, too, upon every part of the lonely churchyard on the hill where Michael Furey lay buried. It lay thickly drifted on the crooked crosses and headstones, on the spears of the little gate, on the barren thorns. His soul swooned slowly as he heard the snow falling faintly through the universe and faintly falling, like the descent of their last end, upon all the living and the dead.   *Ib. The Dead*

Pity is the feeling which arrests the mind in the presence of whatsoever is

[1] See Grant, p. 717a.

grave and constant in human sufferings and unites it with the human sufferer.
> *A Portrait of the Artist as a Young Man* [1916], *ch. 5*

Welcome, O life! I go to encounter for the millionth time the reality of experience and to forge in the smithy of my soul the uncreated conscience of my race.

Old father, old artificer, stand me now and ever in good stead.
> *Ib. Concluding words of Stephen Dedalus*

My patience are exhausted [Molly Bloom].   *Ulysses* [1] [1922]

A man of genius makes no mistakes. His errors are volitional and are the portals of discovery.   *Ib.*

And yes I said yes I will Yes.
> *Ib. Last words*

Can't hear with bawk of bats, all thim liffeying waters of. Ho, talk save us! My foos won't moos. I feel as old as yonder elm. A tale told of Shaun or Shem? All Livia's daughter-sons. Dark hawks hear us. Night! Night! My ho head halls. I feel as heavy as yonder stone. Tell me of John or Shaun? Who were Shem and Shaun the living sons or daughters of? Night now! Tell me, tell me, tell me, elm! Night night! Telmetale of stem or stone. Beside the rivering waters of, hitherandthithering waters of. Night!
> *Finnegans Wake* [1939], *pt. I (end)*

I am passing out. O bitter ending! I'll slip away before they're up. They'll never see. Nor know. Nor miss me. And it's old and old it's sad and old it's sad and weary I go back to you, my cold father, my cold mad father, my cold

[1] In respect of the recurrent emergence of the theme of sex in the minds of his characters, it must always be remembered that his locale was Celtic and his season spring . . . whilst in many places the effect of *Ulysses* on the reader undoubtedly is somewhat emetic, nowhere does it tend to be an aphrodisiac. *Ulysses* may, therefore, be admitted into the United States. — JUDGE JOHN M. WOOLSEY, *U.S. v. One Book Called "Ulysses," 5 Federal Supplement 182, 184 [1933]*

mad feary father, till the near sight of the mere size of him, the moyles and moyles of it, moananoaning, makes me seasilt saltsick and I rush, my only, into your arms, I see them rising! Save me from those therrble prongs! Two more. Onetwo moremens more. So. Avelaval. My leaves have drifted from me. All. But one clings still. I'll bear it on me. To remind me of. Lff! So soft this morning, ours. Yes. Carry me along, taddy, like you done through the toy fair! If I seen him bearing down on me now under whitespread wings like he'd come from Arkangels, I sink I'd die down over his feet, humbly dumbly, only to washup. Yes, tid. There's where. First. We pass through grass behush the bush to. Whish! A gull. Gulls. Far calls. Coming, far! End here. Us then. Finn, again! Take. Bussoftlhee, mememormee! Till thousendsthee. Lps. The keys to. Given! A way a lone a last a loved a long the
Finnegans Wake, pt. IV

FIORELLO H. LAGUARDIA
1882–1947

Ticker tape ain't spaghetti.
Speech, United Nations Relief and Rehabilitation Administration [March 29, 1946]

WINIFRED MARY LETTS
1882–

I saw the spires of Oxford
  As I was passing by,
The gray spires of Oxford
  Against a pearl-gray sky.
My heart was with the Oxford men
  Who went abroad to die.
    The Spires of Oxford, st. 1

That God once loved a garden
We learn in Holy writ.
And seeing gardens in the spring
I well can credit it.
    Stephen's Green, st. 1

PHILIP HENRY KERR, MARQUESS OF LOTHIAN [1]
1882–1940

A limitation of armaments by political appeasement.[2]
    Letter to The Times (London)
    [May 1934]

JACQUES MARITAIN
1882–1973

In the modern social order, the *person* is sacrificed to the *individual*. The individual is given universal suffrage, equality of rights, freedom of opinion; while the person, isolated, naked, with no social armor to sustain and protect him, is left to the mercy of all the devouring forces which threaten the life of the soul, exposed to relentless actions and reactions of conflicting interests and appetites. . . . It is a homicidal civilization.   *Three Reformers [1925]*

ALAN ALEXANDER MILNE
1882–1956

Hush! Hush! Whisper who dares!
Christopher Robin is saying his prayers.
    When We Were Very Young
    [1924]. Vespers

They're changing guard at Buckingham
  Palace —
Christopher Robin went down with
  Alice.   *Ib. Buckingham Palace*

The King asked
The Queen, and
The Queen asked
The Dairymaid:
"Could we have some butter for
The Royal slice of bread?"
    Ib. The King's Breakfast

Nobody, my darling,
Could call me
A fussy man —
  BUT

---

[1] See Winston Churchill, p. 922a.
[2] One of the most portentous slogans of the period was coined here. — KONRAD HEIDEN, *Der Führer* [1944], *p. 714*

I do like a little bit of butter to my
  bread!
     When We Were Very Young.
       The King's Breakfast

What shall I call my dear little
  dormouse?
His eyes are small, but his tail is e-nor-
  mouse.   *Ib. The Christening*

Christopher Robin goes
Hoppity, hoppity,
Hoppity, hoppity, hop.
Whenever I tell him
Politely to stop it, he
Says he can't possibly stop.
           Ib. Hoppity

James James
Morrison Morrison
Weatherby George Dupree
Took great
Care of his Mother
Though he was only three.
James James
Said to his Mother,
"Mother," he said, said he:
"You must never go down to the end of
   the town, if you don't go down
   with me."   *Ib. Disobedience*

I am a Bear of Very Little Brain, and
long words Bother me.
    Winnie-the-Pooh [1926], *ch. 4*

Time for a little something.   *Ib. 6*

Christopher Robin
Had wheezles
And sneezles.
   Now We Are Six [1927]. *Sneezles*

If I were a bear,
  And a big bear, too,
I shouldn't much care
  If it froze or snew.   *Ib. Furry Bear*

FRANCES PERKINS
1882–1965

Call me Madame.
   On being asked how she pre-
   ferred to be addressed when
   she joined the Cabinet [1933]

SAM RAYBURN
1882–1961

I like to make running water walk.
   On Conversation. From VALTON
   J. YOUNG, *The Speaker's Agent*
   [1956]

The greatest domestic problem facing our country is saving our soil and
water. Our soil belongs also to unborn
generations.   *Ib.*

The one thing besides people that I
claim to know is land.   *Ib.*

FRANKLIN DELANO
ROOSEVELT
1882–1945

There is nothing I love as much as a
good fight.
   Interview, New York Times
      [*January 22, 1911*]

These unhappy times call for the
building of plans . . . that build from
the bottom up and not from the top
down, that put their faith once more in
the forgotten man [1] at the bottom of
the economic pyramid.
   Radio address [*April 7, 1932*]

The country needs and, unless I mistake its temper, the country demands
bold, persistent experimentation. It is
common sense to take a method and try
it. If it fails, admit it frankly and try
another. But above all, try something.
   Address, Oglethorpe University
       [*May 22, 1932*]

I pledge you, I pledge myself, to a
new deal for the American people.
   Speech accepting the Demo-
   cratic nomination for the Presi-
   dency, Chicago [*July 2, 1932*]

There is no indispensable man.
   Campaign speech, New York
      [*November 3, 1932*]

[1] See William Graham Sumner, p. 785a.

All honor to the one that in this hour
Cries to the world as from a lighted tower —
Cries for the Man Forgotten.
   EDWIN MARKHAM [1852–1940], *The*
               Forgotten Man

The only thing we have to fear is fear itself.[1]
> *First Inaugural Address*
> *[March 4, 1933]*

The moneychangers have fled from their high seats in the temple of our civilization.[2]   *Ib.*

In the field of world policy I would dedicate this nation to the policy of the good neighbor.[3]   *Ib.*

If I were asked to state the great objective which Church and State are both demanding for the sake of every man and woman and child in this country, I would say that that great objective is "a more abundant life."
> *Address, Federal Council of Churches of Christ [December 6, 1933]*

I am not for a return to that definition of liberty under which for many years a free people were being gradually regimented into the service of the privileged few. I prefer and I am sure you prefer that broader definition of liberty under which we are moving forward to greater freedom, to greater security for the average man than he has ever known before in the history of America.
> *Fireside Chat [September 30, 1934]*

We have earned the hatred of entrenched greed.
> *Message to Congress [January 3, 1936]*

The truth is found when men are free to pursue it.
> *Address, Temple University [February 22, 1936]*

Out of this modern civilization economic royalists carved new dynasties. . . . The royalists of the economic order have conceded that political freedom was the business of the Govern-

ment, but they have maintained that economic slavery was nobody's business.
> *Speech accepting renomination [June 27, 1936]*

This generation of Americans has a rendezvous with destiny.   *Ib.*

I have seen war. . . . I hate war.
> *Address, Chautauqua [August 14, 1936]*

I have not sought, I do not seek, I repudiate the support of any advocate of Communism or of any other alien "ism" which would by fair means or foul change our American democracy.
> *Address, Syracuse [September 29, 1936]*

I should like to have it said of my first Administration that in it the forces of selfishness and of lust for power met their match. I should like to have it said of my second Administration that in it these forces met their master.
> *Speech, Madison Square Garden [October 31, 1936]*

Men with a passion for anonymity.
> *Report of President's Committee on Administrative Management [January 12, 1937]*

We have always known that heedless self-interest was bad morals; we know now that it is bad economics.
> *Second Inaugural Address [January 20, 1937]*

I see one-third of a nation ill-housed, ill-clad, ill-nourished.   *Ib.*

The test of our progress is not whether we add more to the abundance of those who have much; it is whether we provide enough for those who have too little.   *Ib.*

The epidemic of world lawlessness is spreading. When an epidemic of physical disease starts to spread, the community approves and joins in a quarantine of the patients in order to protect the health of the community against the spread of the disease. . . . The will for peace on the part of peace-loving na-

[1] See Montaigne, p. 189b, and note.
[2] See *Matthew 21:12–13*, p. 43b.
[3] I am as desirous of being a good neighbor as I am of being a bad subject. — THOREAU, *Civil Disobedience* [1849]

tions must express itself to the end that nations that may be tempted to violate their agreements and the rights of others will desist from such a course. There must be positive endeavors to preserve peace.

Speech, Chicago [1] *[October 5, 1937]*

War is a contagion. *Ib.*

History proves that dictatorships do not grow out of strong and successful governments, but out of weak and helpless ones. If by democratic methods people get a government strong enough to protect them from fear and starvation, their democracy succeeds; but if they do not, they grow impatient. Therefore, the only sure bulwark of continuing liberty is a government strong enough to protect the interests of the people, and a people strong enough and well enough informed to maintain its sovereign control over its government.

Fireside Chat [April 14, 1938]

Remember, remember always that all of us, and you and I especially, are descended from immigrants and revolutionists.[2]

Address, Daughters of the American Revolution [April 21, 1938]

A program whose basic thesis is not that the system of free private enterprise for profit has failed in this generation, but that it has not yet been tried.

Message on Concentration of Economic Power [April 29, 1938]

The Democratic Party will live and continue to receive the support of the majority of Americans just so long as it remains a liberal party.

Address, Denton, Maryland [September 5, 1938]

But the future lies with those wise political leaders who realize that the great public is interested more in Government than in politics.

Address, Jackson Day Dinner [January 8, 1940]

The Soviet Union, as everybody who has the courage to face the fact knows, is run by a dictatorship as absolute as any other dictatorship in the world.

Address, American Youth Congress [February 10, 1940]

On this tenth day of June 1940 the hand that held the dagger has struck it into the back of its neighbor.[1]

Address, University of Virginia, Charlottesville [June 10, 1940]

Eternal truths will be neither true nor eternal unless they have fresh meaning for every new social situation.

Address, University of Pennsylvania [September 20, 1940]

And while I am talking to you mothers and fathers, I give you one more assurance. I have said this before, but I shall say it again and again and again: Your boys are not going to be sent into any foreign wars.

Campaign speech, Boston [October 30, 1940]

That great historic trio . . . Martin, Barton and Fish.[2] *Ib.*

It is an unfortunate human failing that a full pocketbook often groans more loudly than an empty stomach.

Speech, Brooklyn [November 1, 1940]

We must be the great arsenal of democracy.

Fireside Chat [December 29, 1940]

In the future days, which we seek to make secure, we look forward to a world founded upon four essential human freedoms. The first is freedom of speech and expression — everywhere

---

[1] The "Quarantine the aggressors" speech.
[2] See *Campaign Speech, Boston,* p. 973b-974a.

[1] Italian Foreign Minister Count Galeazzo Ciano had just notified the French Ambassador that Italy considered herself at war with France beginning June 11.
[2] Joseph Martin, Bruce Barton, and Hamilton Fish.

in the world. The second is freedom of every person to worship God in his own way — everywhere in the world. The third is freedom from want . . . everywhere in the world. The fourth is freedom from fear . . . anywhere in the world.[1]

> *Message to Congress [January 6, 1941]*

One great difference which has characterized this division [between liberal and conservative parties] has been that the liberal party — no matter what its particular name was at the time — believed in the wisdom and efficacy of the will of the great majority of the people, as distinguished from the judgment of a small minority. . . . The other great difference between the two parties has been this: The liberal party is a party which believes that, as new conditions and problems arise beyond the power of men and women to meet as individuals, it becomes the duty of the Government itself to find new remedies with which to meet them. The liberal party insists that the Government has the definite duty to use all its power and resources to meet new social problems with new social controls — to insure to the average person the right to his own economic and political life, liberty, and the pursuit of happiness.

> *Public Papers and Addresses, 1938 Volume [1941], introduction*

We, too, born to freedom, and believing in freedom, are willing to fight to maintain freedom. We, and all others who believe as deeply as we do, would rather die on our feet than live on our knees.[2]

> *On receiving the degree of Doctor of Civil Law from Oxford University [June 19, 1941]*

[1] See *Atlantic Charter,* p. 974a-b.
[2] See Zapata, p. 943a.
The phrase was a watchword with the Republican forces in the Spanish Civil War, 1936–1939, and is especially identified with the celebrated woman leader La Pasionara.

When you see a rattlesnake poised to strike, you do not wait until he has struck before you crush him.

> *Fireside Chat [September 11, 1941]*

Yesterday, December 7, 1941 — a date which will live in infamy — the United States of America was suddenly and deliberately attacked by naval and air forces of the Empire of Japan.

> *War Message to Congress [December 8, 1941]*

Never before have we had so little time in which to do so much.[1]

> *Fireside Chat [February 23, 1942]*

We all know that books burn — yet we have the greater knowledge that books cannot be killed by fire. People die, but books never die. No man and no force can abolish memory. . . . In this war, we know, books are weapons.

> *Message, American Booksellers Association [April 23, 1942]*

It is not a tax bill but a tax relief bill providing relief not for the needy but for the greedy.

> *Tax bill veto message [February 22, 1944]*

These Republican leaders have not been content with attacks on me, or my wife, or on my sons. No, not content with that, they now include my little dog, Fala. Well, of course, I don't resent attacks . . . but Fala *does* resent them. . . . I think I have a right to resent, to object to libelous statements about my dog.[2]

> *Speech, Teamsters' Dinner, Washington [September 23, 1944]*

All of our people all over the country — except the pure-blooded Indians

[1] See Churchill, p. 921b.
[2] It had been charged that the President, at a cost of several million dollars to the taxpayers, had sent a destroyer to the Aleutian Islands to fetch his Scottie, Fala, allegedly stranded there. When Fala heard these baseless stories of government extravagance on his account, "his Scotch soul was furious. He has not been the same dog since."

— are immigrants or descendants of immigrants, including even those who came over here on the Mayflower.[1]

Campaign speech, Boston
[November 4, 1944]

The American people are quite competent to judge a political party that works both sides of a street. *Ib.*

Perfectionism, no less than isolationism or imperialism or power politics, may obstruct the paths to international peace.

State of the Union Message
[January 6, 1945]

We have learned that we cannot live alone, at peace; that our own well-being is dependent on the well-being of other nations, far away. We have learned that we must live as men, and not as ostriches, nor as dogs in the manger. We have learned to be citizens of the world, members of the human community.

Fourth Inaugural Address
[January 20, 1945]

More than an end to war, we want an end to the beginnings of all wars.

Address written for Jefferson Day
[April 13, 1945] broadcast [2]

The only limit to our realization of tomorrow will be our doubts of today. Let us move forward with strong and active faith. *Ib.*

FRANKLIN D. ROOSEVELT AND WINSTON CHURCHILL

First, their countries seek no aggrandizement, territorial or other.

Second, they desire to see no territorial changes that do not accord with

[1] See *Address to D.A.R.*, p. 972a.
[2] President Roosevelt died April 12, at Warm Springs, Georgia.

the freely expressed wishes of the peoples concerned.

Atlantic Charter, drawn up
aboard U.S.S. Augusta in Argentia Harbor, Newfoundland
[issued August 14, 1941]

Sixth, after the final destruction of the Nazi tyranny, they hope to see established a peace which will afford to all nations the means of dwelling in safety within their own boundaries, and which will afford assurance that all the men in all the lands may live out their lives in freedom from fear and want.[1]

Ib.

Eighth, they believe that all of the nations of the world, for realistic as well as spiritual reasons, must come to the abandonment of the use of force. Since no future peace can be maintained if land, sea or air armaments continue to be employed by nations which threaten, or may threaten, aggression outside of their frontiers, they believe, pending the establishment of a wider and permanent system of general security, that the disarmament of such nations is essential. *Ib.*

JAMES STEPHENS
1882–1950

I hear a sudden cry of pain!
There is a rabbit in a snare.

The Snare

Forgive us all our trespasses,
Little creatures, everywhere!

Little Things, st. 5

In cloud and clod to sing
Of everything and anything.

The Pit of Bliss

I heard a bird at dawn
Singing sweetly on a tree,
That the dew was on the lawn,
And the wind was on the lea;
But I didn't listen to him,
For he didn't sing to me.

The Rivals, st. 1

[1] See Roosevelt, *Message to Congress, January 6, 1941*, p. 972b-973a.

They fell out over pigs, let them fall in over pigs.
> *In the Land of Youth* [1924]

Women are wiser than men because they know less and understand more.
> *The Crock of Gold* [1930], *ch. 2*

The bad poet is superabundant in all anthologies of verse.
> *Preface to A Trophy of Arms* [1936], *by* RUTH PITTER

VIRGINIA WOOLF[1]
1882–1941

In people's eyes, in the swing, tramp, and trudge; in the bellow and uproar; the carriages, motor cars, omnibuses, vans, sandwich men shuffling and swinging; brass bands; barrel organs; in the triumph and the jingle and the strange high singing of some aeroplane overhead was what she loved; life; London; this moment in June.
> *Mrs. Dalloway* [1925]

Those comfortably padded lunatic asylums which are known, euphemistically, as the stately homes of England.[2]
> *The Common Reader* [1925]. *Lady Dorothy Nevill*

Trivial personalities decomposing in the eternity of print.
> *Ib. The Modern Essay*

There is no room for the impurities of literature in an essay.   *Ib.*

That complete statement which is literature.
> *Ib. How It Strikes a Contemporary*

The word-coining genius, as if thought plunged into a sea of words and came up dripping.
> *Ib. An Elizabethan Play*

The beauty of the world has two edges, one of laughter, one of anguish, cutting the heart asunder.
> *A Room of One's Own* [1929]

[1] The talent of this generation which is most certain of survival. — REBECCA WEST, *Ending in Earnest* [1931]
[2] See Felicia D. Hemans, p. 573b.

Women have served all these centuries as looking-glasses possessing the magic and delicious power of reflecting the figure of man at twice its natural size.   *A Room of One's Own*

Surely it was time someone invented a new plot, or that the author came out from the bushes.
> *Between the Acts* [1941]

SIR ANDREW BROWNE CUNNINGHAM
1883–1963

We are so outnumbered there's only one thing to do. We must attack.[1]
> *Before attacking the Italian fleet,* *Taranto* [November 1940]

MAX EASTMAN
1883–1969

I don't know why it is we are in such a hurry to get up when we fall down. You might think we would lie there and rest awhile.
> *The Enjoyment of Laughter* [1936], *pt. III, ch. 4*

KAHLIL GIBRAN
1883–1931

Let there be spaces in your togetherness.[2]
> *The Prophet* [1923]. *On Marriage*

You may give them your love but not your thoughts,
For they have their own thoughts.
You may house their bodies but not their souls,
For their souls dwell in the house of tomorrow, which you cannot visit, not even in your dreams.
You may strive to be like them, but seek not to make them like you,
For life goes not backward nor tarries with yesterday.

[1] Quoted in *British Commanders,* published by *British Information Services* [1945].
[2] See Rilke, p. 938b.

You are the bows from which your children as living arrows are sent forth.
The Prophet. On Children

You give but little when you give of your possessions. It is when you give of yourself that you truly give.[1]
Ib. On Giving

Work is love made visible. And if you cannot work with love but only with distaste, it is better that you should leave your work and sit at the gate of the temple and take alms of those who work with joy.
Ib. On Work

You pray in your distress and in your need; would that you might pray also in the fullness of your joy and in your days of abundance.   *Ib. On Prayer*

He who wears his morality but as his best garment were better naked.
Ib. On Religion

I have learned silence from the talkative, toleration from the intolerant, and kindness from the unkind; yet strange, I am ungrateful to those teachers.
Sand and Foam [1926]

We shall never understand one another until we reduce the language to seven words.[2]   *Ib.*

JOHN CEREDIGION JONES
1883–1947

All's well, for over there among his peers
A happy warrior sleeps.[3]
The Returning Man, st. 4

---

[1] See Emerson, p. 607b; James Russell Lowell, p. 692b, and Whitman, p. 700b.
[2] If we go on explaining we shall cease to understand one another. — TALLEYRAND [1754–1838], quoted by B. BERENSON, *Aesthetics and History*
[3] These lines are inscribed over the archway of the Memorial Chamber in the Peace Tower, Parliament Buildings, Ottawa.
See Wordsworth, p. 515a.

HARRY KEMP
1883–1960

I pitied him in his blindness;
But can I boast, "I see"?
Perhaps there walks a spirit
Close by, who pities me.   *Blind, st. 2*

JOHN MAYNARD KEYNES
1883–1946

He [Clemenceau] had one illusion — France; and one disillusion — mankind, including Frenchmen.
Economic Consequences of the Peace [1919], ch. 3

Watching the company, with six or seven senses not available to ordinary men, judging character, motive, and subconscious impulse, perceiving what each was thinking and even what each was going to say next, and compounding with telepathic instinct the argument or appeal best suited to the vanity, weakness, or self-interest of his immediate auditor.[1]   *Ib.*

He [Woodrow Wilson] could write Notes from Sinai or Olympus; he could remain unapproachable in the White House or even in the Council of Ten and be safe. But if he once stepped down to the intimate quality of the Four, the game was evidently up.   *Ib.*

To make the defeated Central Empires into good neighbors.   *Ib. 6*

We have been moved already beyond endurance, and need rest.   *Ib. 7*

Marxian Socialism must always remain a portent to the historians of opinion — how a doctrine so illogical and so dull can have exercised so powerful and enduring an influence over the minds of men, and, through them, the events of history.
The End of Laissez-Faire [1925], ch. 3

Thrift may be the handmaid and nurse of Enterprise. But equally she

---

[1] Lloyd George.

may not. . . . For the engine which drives Enterprise is not Thrift, but Profit.   *A Treatise on Money* [1930]

The love of money as a possession — as distinguished from the love of money as a means to the enjoyments and realities of life — will be recognized for what it is, a somewhat disgusting morbidity, one of those semi-criminal, semi-pathological propensities which one hands over with a shudder to the specialists in mental disease.
Essays in Persuasion [1931], *pt.* V

In the United States, it is almost inconceivable what rubbish a public man has to utter today if he is to keep respectable.
In the Atlantic Monthly [*May 1932*]

Words ought to be a little wild for they are the assault of thoughts on the unthinking.
In the New Statesman and Nation [*July 15, 1933*]

His [Newton's] peculiar gift was the power of holding continuously in his mind a purely mental problem until he had seen through it. . . . Anyone who has ever attempted a pure scientific or philosophical thought knows how one can hold a problem momentarily in one's mind and apply all one's power of concentration to piercing through it, and how it will dissolve and escape and you find that what you are surveying is a blank.   *Essays in Biography* [1933]

There is no harm in being sometimes wrong — especially if one is promptly found out.   *Ib.*

Practical men, who believe themselves to be quite exempt from any intellectual influences, are usually the slaves of some defunct economist. . . . It is ideas, not vested interests, which are dangerous for good or evil.
The General Theory of Employment, Interest and Money [1936]

BENITO MUSSOLINI
1883–1945

The Italian proletariat needs a blood bath for its force to be renewed.
Editorial, Popolo d'Italia [1920]

War alone brings up to its highest tension all human energy and puts the stamp of nobility upon the peoples who have the courage to face it.
Written for The Italian Encyclopedia. From GEORGE SELDES, *Sawdust Caesar* [1935]

Fortunately the Italian people is not yet accustomed to eating several times per day.
Speech [*December 1930*]; *ib.*

We have buried the putrid corpse of liberty.
Speech. From MAURICE PARMELEE, *Bolshevism, Fascism and the Liberal-Democratic State* [1934]

The Italian race is a race of sheep.
From the Ciano Diaries [*January 29, 1940*]

To make a people great it is necessary to send them to battle even if you have to kick them in the pants.
Ib. [*April 11, 1940*]

JOSÉ ORTEGA Y GASSET
1883–1955

Rancor is an outpouring of a feeling of inferiority.
Meditations on Quixote [1911]

I am myself and what is around me, and if I do not save it, it shall not save me.   *Ib.*

The Mediterraneans, who do not think clearly, do see clearly.   *Ib.*

Culture is not life in its entirety, but just the moment of security, strength, and clarity.   *Ib.*

Nations are formed and are kept alive by the fact that they have a program for tomorrow.
Invertebrate Spain [1922], *ch.* 2

A society without an aristocracy, without an elite minority, is not a society.   *Invertebrate Spain, ch.* 4

Conversation is the socializing instrument par excellence, and in its style one can see reflected the capacities of a race.   *Ib.* 7

Man was formed by his struggle with exterior forces and it is only easy for him to discern things which are outside of himself.
     The Modern Theme [1923], *ch.* 2

Rationalism, in order to save truth, renounces life.   *Ib.* 3

The choice of a point of view is the initial act of a culture.   *Ib.* 7

To define is to exclude and negate.
          Ib. appendix

Order is not pressure which is imposed on society from without, but an equilibrium which is set up from within.
     Mirabeau and Politics [1927]

Europe is really a swarm: many bees on a single course.
     The Revolt of the Masses
          [1930], *prologue*

America, far from being the future, was in truth a remote past because it was primitivism.   *Ib.*

Minorities are individuals or groups of individuals especially qualified. The masses are the collection of people not specially qualified.   *Ib. ch.* 1

Physical space and time are the absolute stupidity of the universe.   *Ib.* 4

Our life is at all times and before anything else the consciousness of what we can do.   *Ib.*

A revolution only lasts fifteen years, a period which coincides with the effectiveness of a generation.   *Ib.* 10

War is not an instinct but an invention.   *Ib. epilogue*

It is not the material of life which makes up Dostoevski's "realism," but rather the shape of life.
     Notes on the Novel [1948]

The person portrayed and the portrait are two entirely different things.
     The Dehumanization of Art [1948]

The masses feel that it is easy to flee from reality, when it is the most difficult thing in the world.   *Ib.*

The metaphor is probably the most fertile power possessed by man.   *Ib.*

I am a Spaniard, that is to say, a man without imagination.
          Esthetic Essays [1956]

Primitive man is by definition tactile man.   *Ib.*

TAKAMURA KOTARO[1]
1883–1956

Cheekbones protruding, lips thick, eyes
     triangular,
Face like a netsuke[2] carved by the
     great Shuzan,
Expression vacant as though the soul
     were removed,
Ignorant of himself, jumpy,
Cheap-lived,
Show-off,
Small-minded, self-satisfied,
Monkey-like,   fox-like,   squirrel-like,
     gudgeon-like, minnow-like, potsherd-like, gargoyle-faced Japanese!
          The Land of Netsuke

HOWARD ARNOLD
WALTER
1883–1918

I would be true, for there are those who
     trust me;
I would be pure, for there are those
     who care;
I would be strong, for there is much to
     suffer;

[1] From *Modern Japanese Literature*, edited by Donald Keene [1960].
[2] A carved button.

I would be brave, for there is much to
dare.
My Creed

ANGELA MORGAN
d. 1957

Work!
Thank God for the swing of it,
For the clamoring, hammering ring of
it,
Passion of labor daily hurled
On the mighty anvils of the world.
Work: A Song of Triumph

WILLIAM CARLOS
WILLIAMS
1883–1963

No wreaths please —
especially no hothouse flowers.
Some common memento is better,
something he prized and is known by:
his old clothes — a few books perhaps.
Tract [*1917*]

Hell take curtains! Go with some show
of inconvenience; sit openly —
to the weather as to grief.
Or do you think you can shut grief in?
Ib.

so much depends
upon

a red wheel
barrow

glazed with rain
water

beside the white
chickens
Spring and All [*1923*], *no. XXI*

Mothlike in mists, scintillant in the
minute
brilliance of cloudless days, with broad
bellying sails
they glide to the wind tossing green
water
from their sharp prows while over them
the crew crawls.
The Yachts [*1935*], *st. 1, 2*

It's the anarchy of poverty
delights me.
The Poor [*1938*], *st. 1*

THESE
are the desolate, dark weeks
when nature in its barrenness
equals the stupidity of man.[1]

The year plunges into night
and the heart plunges
lower than night.
These [*1938*], *st. 1, 2*

ERNEST BEVIN
1884–1951

There has never been a war yet
which, if the facts had been put calmly
before the ordinary folk, could not have
been prevented. The common man is
the greatest protection against war.
Speech, House of Commons
[*November 1945*]

ÉDOUARD DALADIER
1884–1970

If French and German blood is now
to be spilled, as it was twenty-five years
ago . . . then each of the two peoples
will fight confident of its own victory.
But surely Destruction and Barbarism
will be the real victors.
Letter to Adolf Hitler
[*August 26, 1939*]

The weakness of democracies is that
once a general has been built up in public opinion it becomes impossible to remove him.
From PERTINAX [ANDRÉ GÉ-
RAUD], *Gravediggers of France*
[*1944*]

A phrase has spread from civilians to
soldiers and back again: "This is a
phony war." [2]
Ib. [*Speech to the Deputies, December 22, 1939*]

[1] See William Cullen Bryant. p. 574b.
[2] Une drôle de guerre.

JAMES ELROY FLECKER
1884–1915

West of these out to seas colder than
  the Hebrides
I must go
Where the fleet of stars is anchored
  and the young
Star captains glow.
The Dying Patriot

We who with songs beguile your pilgrimage
And swear that Beauty lives though
  lilies die,
We Poets of the proud old lineage
Who sing to find your hearts, we know
  not why.
The Golden Journey to Samar-
kand [1913], *prologue*

When even lovers find their peace at
  last,
And Earth is but a star, that once had
  shone.   *Ib.*

I have seen old ships sail like swans
  asleep.   *The Old Ships* [1915]

A ship, an isle, a sickle moon —
With few but with how splendid stars.[1]
A Ship, An Isle, A Sickle Moon

TEXAS GUINAN
1884–1933

Hello, sucker!
Greeting to night club patrons

A big butter-and-egg man.[2]
Describing a lavish spender or
theatrical "angel"

FRANZ KAFKA
1884–1924

"This village belongs to the Castle,
and whoever lives here or passes the
night here does so in a manner of
speaking in the Castle itself. Nobody
may do that without the Count's permission."
The Castle [3] [1926]

[1] See Whitman, p. 700a.
[2] Title of play by George S. Kaufman [1925].
[3] Translated by EDWIN and WILLA MUIR.

The true way goes over a rope which
is not stretched at any great height but
just above the ground. It seems more
designed to make people stumble than
to be walked upon.
The Great Wall of China.
Reflections

You do not need to leave your room.
Remain sitting at your table and listen.
Do not even listen, simply wait. Do not
even wait, be quite still and solitary.
The world will freely offer itself to you
to be unmasked, it has no choice, it will
roll in ecstasy at your feet.   *Ib.*

Only our concept of time makes it
possible for us to speak of the Day of
Judgment by that name; in reality it is
a summary court in perpetual session.
Letters. Quoted in MAX BROD,
Franz Kafka

All human error is impatience, a pre-
mature renunciation of method, a delusive pinning down of a delusion.   *Ib.*

There are two cardinal sins from
which all the others spring: impatience
and laziness.   *Ib.*

BRONISLAW MALINOWSKI
1884–1942

Is war a biological necessity? As regards the earliest cultures the answer is
emphatically negative. The blow of the
poisonous dart from behind a bush, to
murder a woman or a child in their
sleep, is not pugnacity. Nor is head-
hunting, body-snatching, or killing for
food instinctive or natural.
Address, Phi Beta Kappa, Har-
vard University [*September* 17,
1936]

The hero of the next war, the man
who from the air destroys a whole
peaceful township in its sleep with
poison gas, is not expressing any biological characteristics of his organism, or
showing any moral virtues.   *Ib.*

SEAN O'CASEY
1884–1964

The whole world is in a state of chassis.

> *Juno and the Paycock* [1] [1924]

One minute with him is all I ask; one minute alone with him, while you're runnin' for th' priest an' th' doctor.

> *The Plow and the Stars* [1926], act II

A few hundhred scrawls o' chaps with a couple o' guns and Rosary beads, again' a hundhred thousand thrained men with horse, fut an' artillery . . . an' he wants us to fight fair!

> *Ib. IV*

A sober black shawl hides her body entirely,
Touch'd be th' sun an' th' salt spray of th' sea;
But deep in th' darkness a slim hand, so lovely,
Carries a rich bunch of red roses for me!

> *Red Roses for Me* [1942], act IV

CHARLES LEO O'DONNELL
1884–1934

I have never been able to school my eyes
Against young April's blue surprise.

> *Wonder*

KEITH PRESTON
1884–1927

Among our literary scenes,
  Saddest this sight to me,
The graves of little magazines
  That died to make verse free.

> *The Liberators*

I am the captain of my soul; [2]
  I rule it with stern joy;
And yet I think I had more fun
  When I was a cabin boy.

> *An Awful Responsibility*

[1] See Aesop, p. 76a.
[2] See Sallust, p. 116a, and note.

ANNA ELEANOR ROOSEVELT [1]
1884–1962

No one can make you feel inferior without your consent.

> *This Is My Story* [1937]

You gain strength, courage and confidence by every experience in which you really stop to look fear in the face. You are able to say to yourself, "I lived through this horror. I can take the next thing that comes along." . . . You must do the thing you think you cannot do.

> *You Learn by Living* [1960]

Life was meant to be lived, and curiosity must be kept alive. One must never, for whatever reason, turn his back on life.

> *The Autobiography of Eleanor Roosevelt* [1961]

GEORGE SARTON
1884–1956

Scientific activity is the only one which is obviously and undoubtedly cumulative and progressive.

> *The History of Science and the History of Civilization* [1930]

SARA TEASDALE
1884–1933

When I am dead and over me bright April
Shakes out her rain-drenched hair,
Though you should lean above me broken-hearted,
I shall not care.

> *I Shall Not Care*, st. 1

Strephon's kiss was lost in jest,
  Robin's lost in play,
But the kiss in Colin's eyes
  Haunts me night and day.

> *The Look*, st. 2

[1] I have lost more than a friend, I have lost an inspiration. She would rather light candles than curse the darkness and her glow has warmed the world. — ADLAI E. STEVENSON [November 7, 1962]
It is better to light one candle than curse the darkness. — *Motto of the Christopher Society*

Alone in the night
  On a dark hill
With pines around me
  Spicy and still.
                    Stars [1921], *st. 1*

Let it be forgotten, as a flower is forgotten,
Forgotten as a fire that once was singing gold,
Let it be forgotten forever and ever,
Time is a kind friend, he will make us
  old.
          Let It Be Forgotten [1921], *st. 1*

Oh better than the minting
  Of a gold-crowned king
Is the safe-kept memory
  Of a lovely thing.
                    The Coin [1921]

O beauty, are you not enough?
Why am I crying after love?
                    Spring Night

HARRY S. TRUMAN
1884–1972

When they told me yesterday what
had happened, I felt like the moon, the
stars and all the planets had fallen on
me.
          *To reporters the day after his
          accession to the Presidency*
          [*April 13, 1945*]

The responsibility of the great states
is to serve and not to dominate the
world.
          First Message to Congress
          [*April 16, 1945*]

When Kansas and Colorado have a
quarrel over the water in the Arkansas
River they don't call out the National
Guard in each state and go to war over
it. They bring a suit in the Supreme
Court of the United States and abide
by the decision. There isn't a reason in
the world why we cannot do that inter-
nationally.
          Speech, Kansas City [*April 1945*]

You members of the conference are
to be the architects of the better world.
In your hands rests our future. By your
labors at this conference we shall know
if suffering humanity is to achieve a
just and lasting peace.
          *Radio address to delegates
          at the opening session of the
          United Nations conference,
          San Francisco* [*April 23, 1945*]

We must build a new world, a far
better world — one in which the eternal dignity of man is respected.   *Ib.*

Sixteen hours ago an American airplane dropped one bomb on Hiroshima. . . . It is a harnessing of the
basic power of the universe. The force
from which the sun draws its power has
been loosed against those who brought
war to the Far East.
          *First announcement of the
          atomic bomb* [*August 6,
          1945*]

The release of atomic energy constitutes a new force too revolutionary to
consider in the framework of old
ideas.
          *Message to Congress on atomic
          energy* [*October 3, 1945*]

Means of destruction hitherto unknown, against which there can be no
adequate military defense, and in the
employment of which no single nation
can in fact have a monopoly.
          *Declaration on Atomic Energy
          by President Truman and Prime
          Ministers Clement Attlee and
          W. L. Mackenzie King* [*No-
          vember 15, 1945*]

Effective, reciprocal, and enforceable
safeguards acceptable to all nations.
                                        Ib.

We must embark on a bold new program for making the benefits of our scientific advances and industrial progress
available for the improvement and
growth of underdeveloped areas. More
than half the people of the world are
living in conditions approaching misery.
Their food is inadequate. They are the
victims of disease. Their economic life
is primitive and stagnant. Their poverty

is a handicap and a threat both to them and to more prosperous areas.

Inaugural Address (Point Four Program) [January 20, 1949]

If you can't stand the heat, get out of the kitchen.   *Saying* [1]

There is enough in the world for everyone to have plenty to live on happily and to be at peace with his neighbors.

Memoirs [1955], vol. I, Year of Decisions, preface

Being a President is like riding a tiger. A man has to keep on riding or be swallowed.[2]

Ib. II, Years of Trial and Hope, ch. 1

A President either is constantly on top of events or, if he hesitates, events will soon be on top of him. I never felt that I could let up for a single moment.   *Ib.*

No one who has not had the responsibility can really understand what it is like to be President, not even his closest aides or members of his immediate family. There is no end to the chain of responsibility that binds him, and he is never allowed to forget that he is President.   *Ib.*

Once a decision was made, I did not worry about it afterward.   *Ib.*

Most of the problems a President has to face have their roots in the past.   *Ib.*

The Marshall Plan will go down in history as one of America's greatest contributions to the peace of the world.   *Ib. 8*

[1] President Truman has used variations of the aphorism . . . for many years, both orally and in his writings. For instance, in his book *Mr. Citizen [1960]* in the chapter entitled "Some Thoughts on the Presidency," he states, "Some men can make decisions and some cannot. Some men fret and delay under criticism. I used to have a saying that applies here, and I note that some people have picked it up." — *Letter to editor from* Philip D. Lagerquist, Harry S. Truman Library, Independence, Missouri [February 11, 1966]

[2] See Churchill, p. 920a, and note.

To me, party platforms are contracts with the people.

Memoirs, vol. II, Years of Trial and Hope, ch. 13

Polk was a positive man . . . and settled every issue before his term of office expired.   *Ib. 14*

A man who is influenced by the polls or is afraid to make decisions which may make him unpopular is not a man to represent the welfare of the country.   *Ib.*

A President cannot always be popular.   *Ib.*

Every great President in our history had a policy of his own, which eventually won the people's support.   *Ib.*

Popularity and glamor are only part of the factors involved in winning presidential elections. One of the most important of all is luck. In my own case, luck was always with me, though there was never any intention on my part to make things work my way. If a man starts out to make himself President, he hardly ever arrives.   *Ib.*

A President needs political understanding to *run* the government, but he may be *elected* without it.   *Ib.*

The convention system has its faults, of course, but I do not know of a better method for choosing a presidential nominee.   *Ib.*

The Point Four program . . . was created and designed to operate on a continuing basis to point the way to better living for more and more of the world's people — and thus the way to a more lasting peace.   *Ib. 16*

All my life I have fought against prejudice and intolerance.   *Ib. 19*

I have little patience with people who take the Bill of Rights for granted. The Bill of Rights, contained in the first ten amendments to the Constitution, is every American's guarantee of freedom.   *Ib.*

It [General Douglas MacArthur's statement on Korea, March 24, 1951] was in open defiance of my orders as President and as Commander in Chief. This was a challenge to the authority of the President under the Constitution. It also flouted the policy of the United Nations. . . . I was deeply shocked.
Memoirs, vol. II, Years of Trial and Hope, ch. 19

If there is one basic element in our Constitution, it is civilian control of the military.   *Ib.*

There is a right kind and wrong kind of victory, just as there are wars for the right thing and wars that are wrong from every standpoint. . . . The kind of victory MacArthur had in mind — victory by the bombing of Chinese cities, victory by expanding the conflict to all of China — would have been the wrong kind of victory.   *Ib.*

The buck stops here.
Sign on Truman's desk as President. From ALFRED STEINBERG, *The Man from Missouri* [1962]

SOPHIE TUCKER[1]
1884–1966

From birth to age eighteen, a girl needs good parents. From eighteen to thirty-five, she needs good looks. From thirty-five to fifty-five, she needs a good personality. From fifty-five on, she needs good cash.

Said at sixty-nine

NIELS BOHR
1885–1962

In our description of nature the purpose is not to disclose the real essence of the phenomena but only to track down, so far as it is possible, relations

[1] Known as "The Last of the Red-Hot Mamas" from the title of a song by JACK YELLEN [1892–   ] which she introduced in 1928.

between the manifold aspects of our experience.
Atomic Theory and the Description of Nature [1934]

ARTHUR WALLACE CALHOUN
1885–

Gentlemen of the old régime in the South would say, "A woman's name should appear in print but twice — when she marries and when she dies."
Social History of the American Family [1918], *citing* MYRTA LOCKETT AVARY, *Dixie After the War* [1906]

ZECHARIAH CHAFEE, JR.
1885–1957

The press is a sort of wild animal in our midst — restless, gigantic, always seeking new ways to use its strength. . . . The sovereign press for the most part acknowledges accountability to no one except its owners and publishers.
The Press Under Pressure [Nieman Reports, April 1948]

Freedom from something is not enough. It should also be freedom for something. Freedom is not safety but opportunity. Freedom ought to be a means to enable the press to serve the proper functions of communication in a free society.   *Ib.*

ISAK DINESEN
[KAREN BLIXEN]
1885–1962

What is man, when you come to think upon him, but a minutely set, ingenious machine for turning, with infinite artfulness, the red wine of Shiraz into urine?
Seven Gothic Tales [1934]

I had seen a herd of elephant traveling through dense native forest . . . pacing along as if they had an appointment at the end of the world.
Out of Africa [1937], *pt. I, ch. 1*

The giraffe, in their queer, inimitable, vegetative gracefulness, as if it were not a herd of animals but a family of rare, long-stemmed, speckled gigantic flowers slowly advancing.
Out of Africa, pt. I, ch. 1

If I know a song of Africa — I thought — of the giraffe, and the African new moon lying on her back, of the plows in the fields, and the sweaty faces of the coffee-pickers, does Africa know a song of me? Would the air over the plain quiver with a color that I had had on, or the children invent a game in which my name was, or the full moon throw a shadow over the gravel of the drive that was like me, or would the eagles of Ngong look out for me?
Ib. 4

I have before seen other countries, in the same manner, give themselves to you when you are about to leave them.
Ib. V, 1

WILL DURANT
1885–

A statesman cannot afford to be a moralist.   *What Is Civilization?*

The finger that turns the dial rules the air.   *Ib.*

The health of nations is more important than the wealth of nations.   *Ib.*

SACHA GUITRY
1885–1957

The little I know, I owe to my ignorance.   *Toutes Réflexions Faites*

KAREN HORNEY
1885–1952

Fortunately [psycho]analysis is not the only way to resolve inner conflicts. Life itself still remains a very effective therapist.
Our Inner Conflicts [1945]

ISHIKAWA TAKUBOKU[1]
1885–1912

Like a kite
Cut from the string,
Lightly the soul of my youth
Has taken flight.
Song of My Youth

Sickness is the only way we have to obtain peace of mind.
The Romaji Diary

RING LARDNER
1885–1933

A good many young writers make the mistake of enclosing a stamped, self-addressed envelope, big enough for the manuscript to come back in. This is too much of a temptation to the editor.
How to Write Short Stories
[1924]

"Are you lost, daddy?" I arsked tenderly.
"Shut up," he explained.
The Young Immigrunts

DAVID HERBERT LAWRENCE
1885–1930

You love me so much, you want to put me in your pocket. And I should die there smothered.
Sons and Lovers [1913], *ch. 15*

So now it is vain for the singer to burst
into clamor
With the great black piano appassionato. The glamor
Of childish days is upon me, my manhood is cast
Down in the flood of remembrance, I weep like a child for the past.
Piano [1916], *st. 3*

Not I, not I, but the wind that blows through me!
A fine wind is blowing the new direction of Time.
Song of a Man Who Has Come Through [1920]

[1] From *Modern Japanese Literature* edited by Donald Keene [1960].

I never saw a wild thing
Sorry for itself.   *Self-Pity* [1923]

A snake came to my water trough
On a hot, hot day, and I in pajamas for
    the heat,
To drink there.   *Snake* [1923]

For he seemed to me again like a king,
Like a king in exile, uncrowned in the
    underworld,
Now due to be crowned again.   *Ib.*

Necessary, forever necessary, to burn
out false shames and smelt the heaviest
ore of the body into purity.
          Lady Chatterley's Lover [1928]

How beastly the bourgeois is
especially the male of the species.
          How Beastly the Bourgeois Is
          [1929]

Now in November nearer comes the
    sun
down the abandoned heaven.
          November by the Sea [1929]

Reach me a gentian, give me a torch!
Let me guide myself with the blue,
    forked torch of a flower
Down the darker and darker stairs,
    where blue is darkened on blueness
Down the way Persephone goes, just
    now, in first-frosted September.
          Bavarian Gentians [written 1929]

Beauty is a mystery. You can neither
eat it nor make flannel out of it.
          Sex Versus Loveliness [1930]

Sex and beauty are inseparable, like
life and consciousness. And the intelligence which goes with sex and beauty,
and arises out of sex and beauty, is intuition.   *Ib.*

How the horse dominated the mind
of the early races, especially of the
Mediterranean! You were a lord if you
had a horse. Far back, far back in our
dark soul the horse prances. . . . The
horse, the horse! The symbol of surging
potency and power of movement, of
action, in man.   *Apocalypse* [1931]

For man, the vast marvel is to be
alive. . . . We ought to dance with

rapture that we should be alive and in
the flesh, and part of the living, incarnate cosmos. I am part of the sun as my
eye is part of me. That I am part of the
earth my feet know perfectly, and my
blood is part of the sea. My soul knows
that I am part of the human race, my
soul is an organic part of the great human race, as my spirit is part of my nation. In my own very self, I am part of
my family.   *Apocalypse*

Oh build your ship of death. Oh build
    it!
For you will need it.
For the voyage of oblivion awaits you.
          The Ship of Death [1933]

SINCLAIR LEWIS
1885–1951

His name was George F. Babbitt,
and . . . he was nimble in the calling
of selling houses for more than people
could afford to pay.
          Babbitt [1922], *ch. 1*

A sensational event was changing
from the brown suit to the gray the
contents of his pockets. He was earnest
about these objects. They were of eternal importance, like baseball or the Republican Party.   *Ib.*

Every compulsion is put upon writers
to become safe, polite, obedient, and
sterile. In protest, I declined election to
the National Institute of Arts and Letters some years ago, and now I must
decline the Pulitzer Prize.[1]
          Letter declining the Pulitzer
          Prize for his novel Arrow-
          smith [1926]

To a true-blue professor of literature
in an American university, literature is
not something that a plain human
being, living today, painfully sits down
to produce. No; it is something dead.
          The American Fear of Literature,
          address, Stockholm, on receiving
          the Nobel Prize for Literature
          [December 12, 1930]

[1] Lewis became a member of the National
Institute in 1935.

Our American professors like their literature clear and cold and pure and very dead.

> *The American Fear of Literature, address, Stockholm, on receiving the Nobel Prize for Literature*

It Can't Happen Here.

> *Title of book* [*1935*]

ANDRÉ MAUROIS
1885–1967

The minds of different generations are as impenetrable one by the other as are the monads of Leibniz.

> *Ariel* [1] [*1924*], *ch. 12*

Modesty and unselfishness — these are virtues which men praise — and pass by.

> *Ib. 24*

There are certain persons for whom pure truth is a poison.

> *Ib. 29*

CHESTER WILLIAM NIMITZ
1885–1966

A ship is always referred to as "she" because it costs so much to keep one in paint and powder.

> *Speech, Society of Sponsors of the United States Navy* [*February 13, 1940*]

Uncommon valor was a common virtue.

> *Of the Marines at Iwo Jima* [*February–May, 1945*]

GEORGE SMITH PATTON [2]
1885–1945

Wars may be fought with weapons, but they are won by men. It is the spirit of the men who follow and of the man who leads that gains the victory.

> *In the Cavalry Journal* [*September 1933*]

To be a successful soldier you must know history. . . . What you must

[1] Translated by ELLA D'ARCY.
[2] Old Blood and Guts.

know is how man reacts. Weapons change but man who uses them changes not at all. To win battles you do not beat weapons — you beat the soul of man of the enemy man.

> *Letter to Cadet George S. Patton IV* [*June 6, 1944*]

Take calculated risks. That is quite different from being rash.

> *Ib.*

The most vital quality a soldier can possess is self-confidence, utter, complete and bumptious.

> *Ib.*

Never tell people *how* to do things. Tell them *what* to do and they will surprise you with their ingenuity.

> *War As I Knew It* [*1947*], *p. 357*

In war nothing is impossible, provided you use audacity.

> *Ib. p. 358*

A pint of sweat will save a gallon of blood.

> *Ib. p. 405*

EZRA POUND
1885–1972

Your mind and you are our Sargasso Sea.

> *Portrait d'une Femme* [*1916*]

Haie! Haie!
> These were the swift to harry;

These the keen-scented;
These were the souls of blood.
Slow on the leash,
> pallid the leash-men!

> *The Return* [*1916*]

Tree you are,
Moss you are,
You are violets with wind above them.
A child — so high — you are;
And all this is folly to the world.

> *A Girl*

The apparition of these faces in the crowd;
Petals on a wet, black bough.

> *In a Station of the Metro* [*1916*]

Winter is icumen in,
Lhude sing Goddamm,

Raineth drop and staineth slop,
And how the wind doth ramm!
  Sing: Goddamm.[1]   *Ancient Music*

The leaves fall early this autumn, in
  wind.
The paired butterflies are already yellow
  with August
Over the grass in the West garden;
They hurt me. I grow older.
      The River Merchant's Wife:
      A Letter (After Rihaku)

For three years, out of key with his
  time,
He strove to resuscitate the dead art
Of poetry; to maintain "the sublime"
In the old sense. Wrong from the
  start —
No, hardly, but seeing he had been
  · born
In a half savage country, out of date.
      Hugh   Selwyn   Mauberley.
      E.P. Ode pour l'élection de
      son sepulchre [1920], *I*

His true Penelope was Flaubert,
He fished by obstinate isles.   *Ib.*

The age demanded an image
Of its accelerated grimace,
Something for the modern stage,
Not, at any rate, an Attic grace.
                                  Ib. II

Better mendacities
Than the classics in paraphrase!   *Ib.*

Some quick to arm,
some for adventure,
some from fear of weakness,
some from fear of censure,
some for love of slaughter, in imagination,
learning later . . .
some in fear, learning love of slaughter;
Died some, pro patria,
    non "dulce" non "et decor" . . .
walked eye-deep in hell
believing in old men's lies, the unbeliev-
  ing
came home, home to a lie.   *Ib. IV*

hysterias, trench confessions,
laughter out of dead bellies.   *Ib.*

[1] See Anonymous, p. 1083b.

There died a myriad,
And of the best, among them,
For an old bitch gone in the teeth,
For a botched civilization.

Charm, smiling at the good mouth,
Quick eyes gone under earth's lid,

For two gross of broken statues,
For a few thousand battered books.
      Hugh Selwyn Mauberley. E. P.
      Ode pour l'élection de son sep-
      ulchre, V

    As for literature
It gives no man a sinecure.
And no one knows, at sight, a master-
  piece.
And give up verse, my boy,
There's nothing in it.
                  Ib. IX. Mr. Nixon [1]

Hang it all, Robert Browning,
there can but be the one "Sordello".
          Cantos [1925–1959], *II*

And the betrayers of language
  ......n and the press gang
And those who had lied for hire;
The perverts, the perverters of language, the perverts, who have set
  money-lust
Before the pleasures of the senses;
howling, as of a hen-yard in a printing-
  house, the clatter of presses,
the blowing of dry dust and stray paper,
foetor, sweat, the stench of stale oranges.   *Ib. XIV*

With *Usura*
With usura hath no man a house of
  good stone
each block cut smooth and well fitting.
                                  Ib. XLV

No picture is made to endure nor to
  live with
but it is made to sell and sell quickly
with usura, sin against nature,
is thy bread ever more of stale rags
is thy bread dry as paper.   *Ib.*

Usura slayeth the child in the womb
It stayeth the young man's courting
It hath brought palsey to bed, lyeth

[1] Arnold Bennett.

between the young bride and her bridegroom
CONTRA NATURAM
Cantos, XLV

What thou lovest well remains,
the rest is dross
What thou lov'st well shall not be reft
from thee
What thou lov'st well is thy true heritage
Whose world, or mine or theirs
or is it of none?
First came the seen, then thus the palpable
Elysium, though it were in the
halls of hell.
What thou lovest well is thy true heritage. *Ib. LXXXI*

The ant's a centaur in his dragon
world.
Pull down thy vanity, it is not man
Made courage, or made order, or made
grace,
Pull down thy vanity, I say pull
down.
Learn of the green world what can be
thy place
In scaled invention or true artistry,
Pull down thy vanity,
Paquin pull down!
The green casque has outdone your elegance. *Ib.*

The history of an art is the history of
masterwork, not of failures, or mediocrity.
The Spirit of Romance [1910]

Poetry must be as well written as
prose.
Letter to Harriet Monroe
[January 1915]

Objectivity and again objectivity, and
expression: no hindside-before-ness, no
straddled adjectives (as "addled mosses
dank"), no Tennysonianness of speech;
nothing — nothing that you couldn't,
in some circumstance, in the stress of
some emotion, actually say. *Ib.*

Literature is language charged with
meaning.
ABC of Reading [1934], *ch. 2*

Literature is news that *stays* news.
ABC of Reading, ch. 2

Genius . . . is the capacity to see
ten things where the ordinary man sees
one, and where the man of talent sees
two or three, *plus* the ability to register
that multiple perception in the material
of his art.
Jefferson and/or Mussolini [1935]

America, my country, is almost a
continent and hardly yet a nation.
Patria Mia

CHARLES SEYMOUR
1885–1963

We seek the truth, and will endure
the consequences.
*Statement made while president
of Yale University* [1937–1950]

LOUIS UNTERMEYER
1885–

God, if You wish for our love,
Fling us a handful of stars!
*Caliban in the Coal Mines,
st. 4*

His are the triumphs till the day
There's no more grass to cut away
And, weary of labor, weary of play,

Having exhausted every whim,
He stretches out each conquering limb.
And then the small grass covers him.
Long Feud, st. 5, 6

CARL VAN DOREN
1885–1950

The first writers are first and the rest,
in the long run, nowhere but in anthologies.
What Is American Literature?

HAROLD TUCKER
WEBSTER
1885–1952

Caspar Milquetoast: The Timid
Soul. *Character in series of cartoons*

The Thrill that Comes Once in a
Lifetime.   *Title of series of cartoons*

HUMBERT WOLFE
1885–1940

Like a small gray
coffee pot
sits the squirrel.
        The Gray Squirrel [1924], st. 1

Clean as a lady,
cool as glass,
fresh without fragrance
the tulip was.
                Tulip [1924], st. 1

Listen! the wind is rising,
    and the air is wild with leaves,
We have had our summer evenings,
    now for October eves!
            Autumn (Resignation)
                [1926], st. 2

ELINOR HOYT WYLIE
1885–1928

We shall walk in velvet shoes:
    Wherever we go
Silence will fall like dews
    On white silence below.
        Velvet Shoes [1921], st. 4

Avoid the reeking herd,
    Shun the polluted flock,
Live like that stoic bird
    The eagle of the rock.
        The Eagle and the Mole [1921],
                st. 1

If you would keep your soul
    From spotted sight or sound,
Live like the velvet mole;
    Go burrow underground.   *Ib. st. 5*

Say not of Beauty she is good,
Or aught but beautiful.
            Beauty [1921]

Enshrine her and she dies, who had
The hard heart of a child.   *Ib.*

Down to the Puritan marrow of my
    bones
There's something in this richness that
    I hate.

I love the look, austere, immaculate,
Of landscapes drawn in pearly mono-
    tones.
        Wild Peaches [1921], st. 4

I was, being human, born alone;
I am, being woman, hard beset;
I live by squeezing from a stone
The little nourishment I get.

In masks outrageous and austere
The years go by in single file;
But none has merited my fear,
And none has quite escaped my smile.
        Let No Charitable Hope [1923],
                st. 2, 3

My soul, be not disturbed
By planetary war;
Remain securely orbed
In this contracted star.
        Address to My Soul [1928], st. 1

A subtle spirit has my path attended,
In likeness not a lion but a pard;
And when the arrows flew like hail, and
    hard,
He licked my wounds, and all my
    wounds were mended.
        One Person [1928]. Sonnet 9

My late discovered earth and early sky.
            Ib. Sonnet 17

If any have a stone to throw
It is not I, ever or now.   *The Pebble*

The worst and best are both inclined
To snap like vixens at the truth;
But, O, beware the middle mind
That purrs and never shows a tooth!
            Nonsense Rhyme, st. 2

    Honeyed words like bees,
Gilded and sticky, with a little sting.
                Pretty Words

Hail, element of earth, receive thy own,
And cherish, at thy charitable breast,
This man, this mongrel beast:
He plows the sand, and, at his hardest
    need,
He sows himself for seed.
        Hymn to Earth [1929], st. 6

ZOË AKINS
1886–1958

The Greeks Had a Word For It.
>   *Title of play* [*1930*]

KARL BARTH
1886–1968

Conscience is the perfect interpreter of life.
>   *The Word of God and the Word of Man* [*1957*]

We have before us the fiendishness of business competition and the world war, passion and wrongdoing, antagonism between classes and moral depravity within them, economic tyranny above and the slave spirit below.   *Ib.*

WILLIAM ROSE BENÉT
1886–1950

Rain, with a silver flail;
  Sun, with a golden ball;
Ocean, wherein the whale
  Swims minnow-small.
>   *Whale, st. 1*

And now there is merely silence, silence, silence, saying
All we did not know.   *Sagacity*

HUGO LAFAYETTE BLACK
1886–1971

No higher duty, or more solemn responsibility, rests upon this Court than that of translating into living law and maintaining this constitutional shield deliberately planned and inscribed for the benefit of every human being subject to our Constitution — of whatever race, creed or persuasion.
>   *Chambers v. Florida,* 309 *U.S.* 227 [*1938*]

The First Amendment has erected a wall between church and state. That wall must be kept high and impregnable. We could not approve the slightest breach.
>   *Everson v. Board of Education,* 330 *U.S.* 1 [*1947*]

It is my belief that there *are* "absolutes" in our Bill of Rights, and that they were put there on purpose by men who knew what words meant and meant their prohibitions to be "absolutes."
>   *Interview Before the American Jewish Congress* [*April 14, 1962*]

My view is, without deviation, without exception, without any ifs, buts, or whereases, that freedom of speech means that you shall not do something to people either for the views they have or the views they express or the words they speak or write.   *Ib.*

I am for the First Amendment from the first word to the last. I believe it means what it says.   *Ib.*

An unconditional right to say what one pleases about public affairs is what I consider to be the minimum guarantee of the First Amendment.
>   *New York Times Company v. Sullivan,* 376 *U.S.* 254 [*1964*]

VAN WYCK BROOKS
1886–1963

His wife not only edited his works but edited him.
>   *The Ordeal of Mark Twain* [*1920*], *ch. 5*

FRANCES CORNFORD
1886–1960

Magnificently unprepared
For the long littleness of life.
>   *Rupert Brooke* [*1915*]

O why do you walk through the fields in gloves,
Missing so much and so much?
O fat white woman whom nobody loves,
Why do you walk through the fields in gloves
When the grass is as soft as the breast of doves
And shivering-sweet to the touch?
>   *To a Fat Lady Seen from the Train* [*1915*]

AL JOLSON
1886–1950

You ain't heard nothin' yet, folks.
Ad lib remark introduced in the first talking motion picture, The Jazz Singer [July 1927]

JOYCE KILMER
1886–1918

I think that I shall never see
A poem lovely as a tree.
A tree whose hungry mouth is pressed
Against the earth's sweet flowing breast.
Trees [1] *[1913]*

Poems are made by fools like me,
But only God can make a tree.   *Ib.*

DAVID MORTON
1886–1957

Who walks with Beauty has no need of fear;
The sun and moon and stars keep pace with him;
Invisible hands restore the ruined year,
And time, itself, grows beautifully dim.
Who Walks with Beauty

SHAEMAS O'SHEEL
1886–1954

They went forth to battle, but they always fell; [2]
Their eyes were fixed above the sullen shields;
Nobly they fought and bravely, but not well,
And sank heart-wounded by a subtle spell.
They Went Forth to Battle, st. 1

SIEGFRIED SASSOON
1886–1967

Soldiers are citizens of death's gray land.   *Dreamers*

[1] See Heywood Broun, p. 1000a, and Ogden Nash, p. 1051b.
[2] They came forth to battle, but they always fell. — JAMES MACPHERSON [1736–1796], *Poems of Ossian, Cath-Loda, Duan Second*

Soldiers are dreamers; when the guns begin
They think of firelit homes, clean beds, and wives.   *Dreamers*

And when the war is done and youth stone dead
I'd toddle safely home and die — in bed.   *Base Details*

Who will remember, passing through this gate,
The unheroic dead who fed the guns?
Who shall absolve the foulness of their fate —
Those doomed, conscripted, unvictorious ones?
On Passing the New Menin Gate

TANIZAKI JUNICHIRO
1886–

The Chinese love jade. That strange lump of stone with its faintly muddy light, like the crystallized air of the centuries, melting dimly, dully back, deeper and deeper — are not we Orientals the only ones who know its charm? We cannot say ourselves what it is that we find in this stone. It quite lacks the brightness of a ruby or an emerald or the glitter of a diamond. But this much we can say: when we see that shadowy surface, we think how Chinese it is, we seem to find in cloudiness the accumulated sediment of the long Chinese past, we think how appropriate it is that the Chinese should admire that surface and that shadow.
In Praise of Shadows [1934] [1]

We do not dislike everything that shines, but we prefer a pensive shadow to a thin transparence.   *Ib.*

We Orientals . . . find beauty not only in the thing itself but in the pattern of shadows, the light and the darkness, which that thing produces. A phosphorescent jewel gives off its glow

[1] From Edward Seidensticker's adaptation, *Atlantic Monthly* Supplement. *Perspective of Japan [January 1955].*

and color in the dark and loses its beauty in the light of day . . .

Our ancestors cut off the brightness on the land from above and created a world of shadows, and far in the depths of it they placed woman, making her the whitest of beings.
In Praise of Shadows

I would call back at least for literature this world of shadows we are losing. In the mansion called literature I would have the eaves deep and the walls dark, I would push back into the shadows the things that come forward too clearly, I would strip away the useless decoration. I do not ask that this be done everywhere, but perhaps we may be allowed at least one mansion where we can turn off the electric lights and see how it is without them.   *Ib.*

ED WYNN
1886–1966

Every radish I ever pulled up seemed to have a mortgage attached to it.
Explaining Why He Sold His Farm

BRUCE BAIRNSFATHER
1887–1959

Well, if you knows of a better 'ole,[1] go to it.
Fragments from France [1915].
Caption of cartoon

RUPERT BROOKE[2]
1887–1915

Breathless, we flung us on the windy hill,
Laughed in the sun, and kissed the lovely grass.   *The Hill* [1910]

And then you suddenly cried, and turned away.   *Ib.*

Unkempt about those hedges blows
An English unofficial rose.
The Old Vicarage, Grant-chester [1912]

[1] A trench.
[2] See Frances Cornford, p. 991b.

Curates, long dust, will come and go
On lissom, clerical, printless toe.
The Old Vicarage, Grant-chester

England's the one land, I know,
Where men with Splendid Hearts may go;
And Cambridgeshire, of all England,
The shire for Men who Understand.   *Ib.*

For Cambridge people rarely smile,
Being urban, squat, and packed with guile.   *Ib.*

Oh! yet
Stands the church clock at ten to three?
And is there honey still for tea?   *Ib.*

Fish say, they have their stream and pond;
But is there anything beyond?
Heaven [1913]

But somewhere, beyond Space and Time,
Is wetter water, slimier slime!   *Ib.*

And in that Heaven of all their wish,
There shall be no more land, say fish.
Ib.

But there's wisdom in women, of more than they have known,
And thoughts go blowing through them, are wiser than their own.
There's Wisdom in Women [1913]

These I have loved:
White plates and cups, clean-gleaming.   *The Great Lover* [1914]

Then, the cool kindliness of sheets, that soon
Smooth away trouble; and the rough male kiss
Of blankets; grainy wood; live hair that is
Shining and free; blue-massing clouds; the keen
Unpassioned beauty of a great machine;
The benison of hot water; furs to touch;
The good smell of old clothes,   *Ib.*

If I should die, think only this of me:
That there's some corner of a foreign
field
That is forever England.
The Soldier [1914]

And think, this heart, all evil shed
away,
A pulse in the eternal mind, no less
Gives somewhere back the thoughts by
England given.   *Ib.*

Now, God be thanked, Who has
matched us with His hour,
And caught our youth, and wakened us
from sleeping.   *Peace*

The worst friend and enemy is but
Death.   *Ib.*

Blow out, you bugles, over the rich
dead!
There's none of these so lonely and
poor of old,
But, dying, has made us rarer gifts than
gold.   *The Dead* [1914], I

Honor has come back, as a king, to
earth,
And paid his subjects with a royal wage;
And Nobleness walks in our ways again;
And we have come into our heritage.
Ib.

ISAAC GOLDBERG
1887–1938

Diplomacy is to do and say
The nastiest thing in the nicest way.
The Reflex

SIDNEY HILLMAN
1887–1946

Politics is the science of how who
gets what, when and why.
*Political Primer for All
Americans* [1944]

EARNEST A. HOOTON
1887–1954

Up from the Ape.
Title of book [1931]

Why Men Behave Like Apes, and
Vice Versa.   *Title of book* [1940]

ROBINSON JEFFERS
1887–1962

You make haste on decay: not blameworthy; life is good, be it stub-
bornly long or suddenly
A mortal splendor; meteors are not
needed less than mountains: shine,
perishing republic.
Shine, Perishing Republic
[1924], *st. 3*

Lend me the stone strength of the past
and I will lend you
The wings of the future, for I have
them.
*To the Rock That Will be a
Cornerstone* [1924]

The deep dark-shining
Pacific leans on the land,
Feeling his cold strength
To the outmost margins.
Night [1925]

A creature progressively
Thirsty for life will be for death too.
Age in Prospect [1926]

Happy people die whole, they are all
dissolved in a moment, they have
had what they wanted,
No hard gifts; the unhappy
Linger a space, but pain is a thing that
is glad to be forgotten; but one
who has given
His heart to a cause or a country,
His ghost may spaniel it a while, disconsolate to watch it.
Post Mortem [1926]

The world's God is treacherous and full
of unreason.   *Birth-Dues* [1928]

I'd sooner, except the penalties, kill a
man than a hawk.
Hurt Hawks [1928]

I have grown to believe
A stone is a better pillow than many
visions.
Clouds of Evening [1930]

The strong lean upon death as on a
rock. *Gale in April* [1930]

Give Your Heart to the Hawks.
Title of poem [1933]

I hate my verses, every line, every word.
Love the Wild Swan

Does it matter whether you hate your
. . . self? At least
Love your eyes that can see, your mind
that can
Hear the music, the thunder of the
wings. Love the wild swan. *Ib.*

Well: the day is a poem but too much
Like one of Jeffers's, crusted with blood
and barbaric omens,
Painful to excess, inhuman as a hawk's
cry. *The Day Is a Poem (September
19, 1939)* [1941]

We shall have to perceive that battle is
a burning flower or like a huge
music, and the dive-bomber's
screaming orgasm
As beautiful as other passions; and that
death and life are not serious alter-
natives. *May–June, 1940, st. 2*

If millions are born millions must die,
If England goes down and Germany up
The stronger dog will still be on top.
Ib. st. 3

As for me, I would rather
Be a worm in a wild apple than a son of
man. *Original Sin* [1948]

CHIANG KAI-SHEK [1]
1887–1975

The general psychology of our people
today can be described as spiritless.
What manifests itself in behavior is
this: lack of discrimination between
good and evil, between what is public
and what is private, and between what
is primary and what is secondary.
*Speech, Nanchang [September
1934]*

[1] From *Sources of Chinese Tradition*, edited by
William Theodore de Bary [1960].

The main object of the New Life
Movement [1] is to substitute a rational
life for the irrational.
Speech, Nanchang

The life of our people will be elevated if we live artistically; we will become wealthy if we live productively;
and we will be safe if we lead a military
way of life. When we do this, we will
have a rational life. . . . If we can
achieve [a rational life], we will have revolutionized the daily life of our people
and laid the foundation for the rehabilitation of our nation. *Ib.*

LE CORBUSIER
[CHARLES ÉDOUARD
JEANNERET]
1887–1965

A house is a machine for living in.[2]
Vers une Architecture [1923]

EMILIO MOLA
1887–1937

Fifth column.[3]
Phrase, Spanish Civil War
[1936–1939]

SIR BERNARD
MONTGOMERY
[VISCOUNT
MONTGOMERY OF
ALAMEIN]
1887–1976

To us is given the honor of striking a
blow for freedom which will live in history, and in the better days that lie
ahead men will speak with pride of our
doings. *Message to his troops [June 5,
1944] on the eve of the Allied
invasion of Europe*

[1] The New Life Movement, whose beginning
is marked by this speech, was intended to "rally
the . . . people against the Communists," and
further to "tighten discipline and build up morale in the Kuomintang and nation as a whole."
[2] Une maison est une machine-à-habiter.
[3] Mola, one of Franco's generals, boasted that
he had four columns of troops to lead against
Madrid, and a fifth column of sympathizers
inside Madrid.

I am not a bit anxious about my battles. If I am anxious I don't fight them. I wait until I am ready.

> *From British Information Services publication British Commanders* [1945]

MARIANNE MOORE
1887–1972

I, too, dislike it: there are things that are important beyond all this fiddle.   *Poetry* [1935], *st. 1*

nor till the poets among us can be
    "literalists of
the imagination" — above
    insolence and triviality and can present
for inspection, imaginary gardens with
    real toads in them,
    shall we have
it.   *Ib. st. 4, 5*

There is a great amount of poetry in unconscious fastidiousness.
          Critics and Connoisseurs [1935]

Literature is a phase of life. If
    one is afraid of it, the situation is
    irremediable; if
one approaches it familiarly
    what one says of it is worthless.
          Picking and Choosing [1935]

I wonder what Adam and Eve
think of it by this time.
          Marriage [1935]

But one would not be he who has nothing but plenty.[1]
          The Jerboa [1935]

My father used to say,
"Superior people never make long visits,"
Have to be shown Longfellow's grave
or the glass flowers at Harvard.
          Silence [1935] [2]

The deepest feeling always shows itself
    in silence;
not in silence, but restraint.
Nor was he insincere in saying, "Make
    my house your inn."
Inns are not residences.   *Silence*

What is our innocence,
what is our guilt? All are
naked, none is safe.
          What Are Years? [1941]

I am troubled, I'm dissatisfied, I'm Irish.
          Spenser's Ireland [1941],
                              last line

Among animals, one has a sense of humor.
Humor saves a few steps, it saves years.
          The Pangolin [1941], *st. 8*

        As contagion
    of sickness makes sickness,
contagion of trust can make trust.
          In Distrust of Merits [1941]

they're fighting that I
may yet recover from the disease, My
Self; some have it lightly; some will die. "Man
        wolf to man"; yes. We devour
        ourselves.   *Ib.*

O small dust of the earth
that walks so arrogantly,
    trust begets power and faith is
an affectionate thing.   *Ib.*

Hate-hardened heart, O heart of iron,
    iron is iron till it is rust.
There never was a war that was not
    inward; I must
fight till I have conquered in myself
    what
causes war, but I would not believe it.
    I inwardly did nothing.
    O Iscariotlike crime!

---

[1] I Got Plenty o' Nuttin. — IRA GERSHWIN, *Porgy and Bess* [1935], title and refrain of song.
[2] The author's footnote for *Silence:* "My father used to say, 'Superior people never make long visits. When I am visiting, I like to go

about by myself. I never had to be shown Longfellow's grave or the glass flowers at Harvard.' " Miss A. M. Homans. Edmund Burke, in *Burke's Life,* by Prior: "Throw yourself into a coach," said he. "Come down and make my house your inn."

Beauty is everlasting
And dust is for a time.
> *In Distrust of Merits, st.* 8

O to be a dragon
a symbol of the power of Heaven — of
　silkworm
size or immense; at times invisible.
Felicitous phenomenon!
> *O To Be a Dragon* [1959]

To wear the arctic fox
you have to kill it.
> *The Arctic Ox (Or Goat)* [1959]

Camels are snobbish
and sheep, unintelligent;
　water buffaloes, neurasthenic —
even murderous.
Reindeer seem over-serious.　　*Ib.*

SAMUEL ELIOT
MORISON
1887–1976

A tough but nervous, tenacious but
restless race [the Yankees]; materially
ambitious, yet prone to introspection,
and subject to waves of religious emotion. . . . A race whose typical member is eternally torn between a passion
for righteousness and a desire to get on
in the world.
> *Maritime History of Massachu-*
> *setts* [1921], *ch.* 2

He [Columbus] enjoyed long
stretches of pure delight such as only a
seaman may know, and moments of
high, proud exultation that only a discoverer can experience.
> *Admiral of the Ocean Sea*
> [1942], *ch.* 49

A few hints as to literary craftsmanship may be useful to budding historians. First and foremost, *get writing!*
> *History as a Literary Art. Old*
> *South Leaflets, ser. II, No.* 1
> [1946]

Franklin may . . . be considered
one of the founding fathers of Ameri-

can democracy, since no democratic
government can last long without conciliation and compromise.
> *The Wisdom of Benjamin*
> *Franklin* [1961]

An historian should yield himself to
his subject, become immersed in the
place and period of his choice, standing
apart from it now and then for a fresh
view.
> *Vistas of History* [1964]. *The*
> *Experiences and Principles of an*
> *Historian*

If the European discovery had been
delayed for a century or two, it is possible that the Aztec in Mexico or the
Iroquois in North America would have
established strong native states capable
of adopting European war tactics and
maintaining their independence to this
day, as Japan kept her independence
from China.
> *The Oxford History of the*
> *American People* [1965], *ch.* 1

America was discovered accidentally
by a great seaman who was looking for
something else; when discovered it was
not wanted; and most of the exploration for the next fifty years was done in
the hope of getting through or around
it. America was named after a man who
discovered no part of the New World.
History is like that, very chancy.
> *Ib.* 2

But sea power has never led to despotism. The nations that have enjoyed
sea power even for a brief period —
Athens, Scandinavia, the Netherlands,
England, the United States — are
those that have preserved freedom for
themselves and have given it to others.
Of the despotism to which unrestrained
military power leads we have plenty of
examples from Alexander to Mao.
> *Ib.* 3

Make no mistake; the American Revolution was not fought to *obtain* freedom, but to *preserve* the liberties that
Americans already had as colonials. In-

dependence was no conscious goal, secretly nurtured in cellar or jungle by bearded conspirators, but a reluctant last resort, to preserve "life, liberty and the pursuit of happiness."

> *The Oxford History of the American People, ch.* 12

The freedmen were not really free in 1865, nor are most of their descendants really free in 1965. Slavery was but one aspect of a race and color problem that is still far from solution here, or anywhere. In America particularly, the grapes of wrath have not yet yielded all their bitter vintage. *Ib.* 33

These clipper ships of the early 1850's were built of wood in shipyards from Rockland in Maine to Baltimore. These architects, like poets who transmute nature's message into song, obeyed what wind and wave had taught them, to create the noblest of all sailing vessels, and the most beautiful creations of man in America. With no extraneous ornament except a figurehead, a bit of carving and a few lines of gold leaf, their one purpose of speed over the great ocean routes was achieved by perfect balance of spars and sails to the curving lines of the smooth black hull; and this harmony of mass, form and color was practiced to the music of dancing waves and of brave winds whistling in the rigging. These were our Gothic cathedrals, our Parthenon; but monuments carved from snow. For a few brief years they flashed their splendor around the world, then disappeared with the finality of the wild pigeon.[1] *Ib.* 36

No big modern war has been won without preponderant sea power; and, conversely, very few rebellions of maritime provinces have succeeded without acquiring sea power.[2] *Ib.* 40

[1] A shorter version of this passage appeared in *Maritime History of Massachusetts [1921], ch.* 23.

[2] See Themistocles, p. 78a; Bacon, p. 209b; and Mahan, p. 785b.

FAIRFIELD OSBORN
1887–1969

We do not live to extenuate the miseries of the past nor to accept as incurable those of the present.

> *The Limits of the Earth, ch.* 10

H. I. PHILLIPS
1887–1965

Horse-sense in an atmosphere of
Pomp and glory,
Self-effacement in a generation
Of self-salesmanship,
A Vermont Yankee in
King Ballyhoo's Court!

> *Calvin Coolidge*

JOHN REED
1887–1920

Ten Days That Shook the World.
> *Title of firsthand account of the outbreak of the Bolshevik Revolution* [1919]

DAME EDITH SITWELL
1887–1964

Remember only this of our hopeless
love
That never till Time is done
Will the fire of the heart and the fire of
the mind be one.

> *Heart and Mind*

Still falls the Rain —
Dark as the world of man, black as our
loss —
Blind as the nineteen hundred and
forty nails
Upon the Cross.

> *Still Falls the Rain* [1940]

My poems are hymns of praise to the glory of life.

> *Collected Poems* [1957]. *Some Notes on My Poetry*

Rhythm is one of the principal translators between dream and reality. Rhythm might be described as, to the world of sound, what light is to the world of sight. It shapes and gives new meaning. Rhythm was described by Schopenhauer as melody deprived of its pitch. *Taken Care Of* [1965], *ch. 14*

ALEXANDER WOOLLCOTT
1887–1943

The two oldest professions in the world — ruined by amateurs.
> *The Knock at the Stage Door. The Actor and the Streetwalker*

Ladies, just a little more virginity, if you don't mind.
> *Capsule Criticism. Beerbohm Tree to the Extras*

There is less in this than meets the eye.
> *A companion's comment at a Maeterlinck play (attributed to* TALLULAH BANKHEAD)

I must get out of these wet clothes and into a dry Martini.
> *From Reader's Digest*

Babies in silk hats playing with dynamite.
> *Of diplomats. From* SAMUEL HOPKINS ADAMS, *A. Woollcott* [1945]

Germany was the cause of Hitler just as much as Chicago is responsible for the Chicago *Tribune.*
> *Last words before the microphone* [January 23, 1943], *on People's Platform program*

ROLAND YOUNG
1887–1953

And here's the happy bounding flea —
You cannot tell the he from she.
The sexes look alike, you see;
But she can tell, and so can he.
> *The Flea*

SAM M. LEWIS AND JOE YOUNG
fl. 1919

How You Gonna Keep 'Em Down on the Farm After They've Seen Paree?
> *Title and refrain of song* [1919]

MAXWELL ANDERSON
1888–1959

What Price Glory?
> *Title of play* [1924] *with* LAWRENCE STALLINGS [1894–1968]

IRVING BERLIN
1888–

You've got to get up, you've got to get up,
You've got to get up this morning!
> *Oh! How I Hate to Get Up in the Morning* [1918]

There's No Business Like Show Business.
> *Composition* [1946]

HENRY BESTON
(1888–1968)

The neon glow of the age of comfort and violence.
> *Review of John Burroughs's America, in The Freeman* [February 11, 1952]

For a moment of night we have a glimpse of ourselves and of our world islanded in its stream of stars — pilgrims of mortality, voyaging between horizons across the eternal seas of space and time.
> *The Outermost House: A Year of Life on the Great Beach of Cape Cod* [1928]

HEYWOOD BROUN
1888–1939

In the march up to the heights of fame there comes a spot close to the summit in which man reads "nothing but detective stories."
> *G.K.C.* [1922]

"Trees" (if I have the name right) is one of the most annoying pieces of verse within my knowledge. The other one is Kipling's "If," with third place reserved for Henley's "Invictus."

"Trees" maddens me, because it contains the most insincere line ever written by mortal man. Surely the Kilmer tongue must have been not far from the Kilmer cheek when he wrote, "Poems are made by fools like me."

> *It Seems to Me* [1935]. *"Trees," "If," and "Invictus"*

Life is a copycat and can be bullied into following the master artist who bids it come to heel.

> *Ib. Nature the Copycat*

I have known people to stop and buy an apple on the corner and then walk away as if they had solved the whole unemployment problem.

> *Ib. Chummy Charlie*

The swaggering underemphasis of New England.

> *Heywood Broun: Collected Edition* [1941]

DALE CARNEGIE
1888–1955

How to Win Friends and Influence People. *Title of book* [1938]

RAYMOND CHANDLER
1888–1959

The Big Sleep.[1]

> *Title of novel* [1939]

J. FRANK DOBIE
1888–1964

The average Ph.D. thesis is nothing but a transference of bones from one graveyard to another.

> *A Texan in England* [1945], *ch. 1*

Conform and be dull.

> *The Voice of the Coyote* [1949], *introduction*

[1] A synonym for death.

Putting on the spectacles of science in expectation of finding the answer to everything looked at signifies inner blindness.

> *The Voice of the Coyote, introduction*

JOHN FOSTER DULLES
1888–1959

Local defense will always be important. But there is no local defense which alone will contain the mighty land power of the Communist world. Local defense must be reinforced by the further deterrent of massive retaliatory power.

> *Address to the Council on Foreign Relations* [January 12, 1954]

You have to take chances for peace, just as you must take chances in war. . . . The ability to get to the verge without getting into the war is the necessary art. If you try to run away from it, if you are scared to go to the brink,[1] you are lost.

> *From* JAMES SHEPLEY, *How Dulles Averted War, in Life* [January 16, 1956]

THOMAS STEARNS ELIOT
1888–1965

Let us go then, you and I,
When the evening is spread out against the sky
Like a patient etherized upon a table.

> *The Love Song of J. Alfred Prufrock* [1917]

In the room the women come and go
Talking of Michelangelo. *Ib.*

There will be time to murder and create. *Ib.*

And indeed there will be time
To wonder, "Do I dare?" and, "Do I dare?" *Ib.*

I have measured out my life with coffee spoons. *Ib.*

[1] From the phrase "to the brink" developed "brinkmanship."

I should have been a pair of ragged
claws
Scuttling across the floors of silent seas.
The Love Song of J. Alfred
Prufrock

Should I, after tea and cakes and ices,
Have the strength to force the moment
to its crisis? *Ib.*

I have seen the moment of my greatness flicker,
And I have seen the eternal Footman
hold my coat, and snicker,
And in short, I was afraid. *Ib.*

No! I am not Prince Hamlet, nor was
meant to be;
Am an attendant lord, one that will do
To swell a progress, start a scene or
two,
Advise the prince; no doubt, an easy
tool,
Deferential, glad to be of use,
Politic, cautious, and meticulous;
Full of high sentence, but a bit obtuse;
At times, indeed, almost ridiculous —
Almost, at times, the Fool. *Ib.*

I grow old . . . I grow old . . .
I shall wear the bottoms of my trousers
rolled. *Ib.*

Shall I part my hair behind? Do I dare
to eat a peach?
I shall wear white flannel trousers, and
walk upon the beach.
I have heard the mermaids singing,[1]
each to each.

I do not think that they will sing to
me. *Ib.*

Till human voices wake us, and we
drown. *Ib.*

We have been, let us say, to hear the
latest Pole
Transmit the Preludes, through his hair
and fingertips.
Portrait of a Lady [1917], I

And I must borrow every changing
shape
To find expression. *Ib. III*

One thinks of all the hands
That are raising dingy shades
In a thousand furnished rooms.
Preludes [1917], II

Twelve o'clock.
Along the reaches of the street
Held in a lunar synthesis.
Rhapsody on a Windy Night
[1917]

I am aware of the damp souls of house-
maids
Sprouting despondently at area gates.
Morning at the Window [1917]

The readers of the *Boston Evening
Transcript*
Sway in the wind like a field of ripe
corn.
The Boston Evening Transcript
[1917]

Upon the glazen shelves kept watch
Matthew and Waldo, guardians of the
faith,
The army of unalterable law.[1]
Cousin Nancy [1917]

His laughter tinkled among the tea-
cups. *Mr. Apollinax* [1917]

He laughed like an irresponsible foetus.
Ib.

Stand on the highest pavement of the
stair —
Lean on a garden urn —
Weave, weave the sunlight in your hair.
La Figlia Che Piange [1917]

Simple and faithless as a smile and
shake of the hand. *Ib.*

Here I am, an old man in a dry month,
Being read to by a boy, waiting for rain.
Gerontion [1920]

After such knowledge, what forgiveness? Think now
History has many cunning passages,
contrived corridors
And issues, deceives with whispering
ambitions,
Guides us by vanities. *Ib.*

Paint me the bold anfractuous rocks
Faced by the snarled and yelping seas.
Sweeney Erect [1920], st. 1

This oval O cropped out with teeth.
Sweeney Erect, st. 4

The broad-backed hippopotamus
Rests on his belly in the mud;
Although he seems so firm to us
He is merely flesh and blood.
The Hippopotamus [1920], *st. 1*

Webster was much possessed by death
And saw the skull beneath the skin.
Whispers of Immortality [1920],
st. 1

He knew the anguish of the marrow
The ague of the skeleton;
No contact possible to flesh
Allayed the fever of the bone.
Ib. st. 4 [*of Donne*]

Uncorseted, her friendly bust
Gives promise of pneumatic bliss.
Ib. st. 5

Reorganized upon the floor
She yawns and draws a stocking up.
*Sweeney Among the Nightin-
gales* [1920], *st. 4*

And sang within the bloody wood
When Agamemnon cried aloud,
And let their liquid siftings fall
To stain the stiff dishonored shroud.
Ib. st. 10

April is the cruelest month, breeding
Lilacs out of the dead land, mixing
Memory and desire, stirring
Dull roots with spring rain.
The Waste Land [1922]. *I, The
Burial of the Dead*

You know only
A heap of broken images, where the sun
beats,
And the dead tree gives no shelter, the
cricket no relief,
And the dry stone no sound of water.
Only
There is shadow under this red rock,
(Come in under the shadow of this red
rock),
And I will show you something differ-
ent from either
Your shadow at morning striding be-
hind you

Or your shadow at evening rising to
meet you;
I will show you fear in a handful of
dust.
*The Waste Land. I, The
Burial of the Dead*

I had not thought death had undone so
many.[1]
Sighs, short and infrequent, were ex-
haled.[2]
Ib.

I think we are in rats' alley
Where the dead men lost their bones.
Ib. II, The Game of Chess

O O O O that Shakespeherian Rag —
It's so elegant
So intelligent.
Ib.

Hurry up please its time.
Ib.

But at my back from time to time I
hear[3]
The sound of horns and motors, which
shall bring
Sweeney to Mrs. Porter in the spring.
O the moon shone bright on Mrs. Porter
And on her daughter
They wash their feet in soda water.
Ib. III, The Fire Sermon

At the violet hour, when the eyes and
back
Turn upward from the desk, when the
human engine waits
Like a taxi throbbing waiting,
I Tiresias, though blind, throbbing be-
tween two lives.[4]
Ib.

When lovely woman stoops to folly[5]
and
Paces about her room again, alone,
She smooths her hair with automatic
hand,
And puts a record on the gramophone.
Ib.

Phlebas the Phoenician, a fortnight
dead,

[1] DANTE. *Inferno, canto III, ll. 55–57.*
[2] DANTE, *Inferno, canto IV, ll. 25–27.*
[3] See Marvell, p. 360a.
[4] See Matthew Arnold, p. 712b.
[5] See Goldsmith, p. 448b.

Forgot the cry of gulls, and the deep
    sea swell
And the profit and loss.
      The Waste Land. IV, Death
                by Water

Here is no water but only rock.
    Ib. V, What the Thunder Said

Who is the third who walks always be-
    side you?   *Ib.*

And voices singing out of empty cis-
    terns and exhausted wells.   *Ib.*

Dayadhvam: I have heard the key
Turn in the door once and turn once
    only
We think of the key, each in his prison
Thinking of the key, each confirms a
    prison.   *Ib.*

These fragments I have shored against
    my ruins.   *Ib.*

We are the hollow men
We are the stuffed men
Leaning together
Headpiece filled with straw. Alas!
      The Hollow Men [1925], I

Shape without form, shade without
    color,
Paralyzed force, gesture without mo-
    tion;

    Those who have crossed
With direct eyes, to death's other
    Kingdom
Remember us — if at all — not as lost
Violent souls, but only
As the hollow men
The stuffed men.   *Ib.*

Between the idea
And the reality
Between the motion
And the act
Falls the Shadow.[1]   *Ib. V*

This is the way the world ends
Not with a bang but a whimper. *Ib.*

A cold coming we had of it,
Just the worst time of the year.
    Journey of the Magi [1927]

[1] See Dowson, p. 889b.

Because I do not hope to turn again [1]
Because I do not hope
Because I do not hope to turn.
      Ash-Wednesday [1930], I

Because these wings are no longer wings
    to fly
But merely vans to beat the air
The air which is now thoroughly small
    and dry
Smaller and dryer than the will
Teach us to care and not to care
Teach us to sit still.   *Ib.*

Lady, three white leopards sat under a
    juniper tree.   *Ib. II*

Terminate torment
Of love unsatisfied
The greater torment
Of love satisfied.   *Ib.*

Blown hair is sweet, brown hair over
    the mouth blown,
Lilac and brown hair;
Distraction, music of the flute, stops
    and steps of the mind over the
    third stair,
Fading, fading; strength beyond hope
    and despair
Climbing the third stair.   *Ib. III*

    Redeem
The time. Redeem
The unread vision in the higher dream
While jeweled unicorns draw by the
    gilded hearse.   *Ib. IV*

Against the Word the unstilled world
    still whirled
About the center of the silent Word.

    O my people, what have I done unto
    thee.

Where shall the word be found, where
    will the word
Resound? Not here, there is not enough
    silence.   *Ib. V*

Wavering between the profit and the
    loss
In this brief transit where the dreams
    cross

[1] GUIDO CAVALCANTI, *Perch' Io Non Spero.*

The dreamcrossed twilight between
   birth and dying.
              Ash-Wednesday, V

The white sails still fly seaward, seaward
   flying
Unbroken wings.

And the lost heart stiffens and rejoices
In the lost lilac and the lost sea voices
And the weak spirit quickens to rebel
For the bent goldenrod and the lost sea
   smell.   *Ib.*

Even among these rocks,
Our peace in His will.[1]   *Ib.*

What seas what shores what gray rocks
   and what islands
What water lapping the bow
And scent of pine and the woodthrush
   singing through the fog
What images return
O my daughter.   *Marina* [1930]

   I'll convert *you!*
Into a stew.
A nice little, white little, missionary
   stew!   *Sweeney Agonistes*

Birth, and copulation, and death.
That's all the facts when you come to
   brass tacks.   *Ib.*

Two live as one
One live as two
Two live as three
Under the bam
Under the boo
Under the bamboo tree.   *Ib.*

Stone, bronze, stone, steel, stone, oak-
   leaves, horses' heels
Over the paving.
    Coriolan I. Triumphal March

O hidden under the dove's wing, hid-
   den in the turtle's breast,
Under the palmtree at noon, under the
   running water
At the still point of the turning world.
   O hidden.   *Ib.*

How unpleasant to meet Mr. Eliot! [2]
With his features of clerical cut,

[1] See Dante, p. 161b.
[2] See Edward Lear, p. 672b.

And his brow so grim
And his mouth so prim.
      Five-Finger Exercises, V

All our knowledge brings us nearer to
   our ignorance,
All our ignorance brings us nearer to
   death,
But nearness to death no nearer to
   God.
Where is the Life we have lost in liv-
   ing?
Where is the wisdom we have lost in
   knowledge?
Where is the knowledge we have lost in
   information?
The cycles of Heaven in twenty cen-
   turies
Bring us farther from God and nearer
   to the Dust.
        The Rock [1934], I

Yet we have gone on living,
Living and partly living.
   Murder in the Cathedral [1935],
                  pt. I

They know and do not know, what it is
   to act or suffer.
They know and do not know, that acting is suffering.   *Ib.*

Saint and Martyr rule from the tomb.
                   Ib.

The last temptation is the greatest treason:
To do the right deed for the wrong reason.   *Ib.*

Human kind cannot bear very much reality.[1]   *Ib. II*

Time present and time past
Are both perhaps present in time fu-
   ture,
And time future contained in time past.
   Four Quartets. Burnt Norton
                 [1935], I

Footfalls echo in the memory
Down the passage which we did not
   take
Towards the door we never opened
Into the rose garden.   *Ib.*

[1] Also in *Four Quartets, Burnt Norton, pt. I.*

Shall we follow
The deception of the thrush? Into our
first world.
Four Quartets. Burnt Norton, I

Garlic and sapphires in the mud
Clot the bedded axle-tree.
The trilling wire in the blood
Sings below inveterate scars
And reconciles forgotten wars.
Ib. II

At the still point of the turning world.
Neither flesh nor fleshless.   *Ib.*

Except for the point, the still point,
There would be no dance, and there is
only the dance.   *Ib.*

Only through time time is conquered.
Ib.

Sudden in a shaft of sunlight
Even while the dust moves
There rises the hidden laughter
Of children in the foliage
Quick now, here, now, always —
Ridiculous the waste sad time
Stretching before and after.   *Ib. V*

In my beginning is my end.
Ib. East Coker [1940], *I*

Keeping time,
Keeping the rhythm in their dancing
As in their living in the living seasons
The time of the seasons and the con-
stellations
The time of milking and the time of
harvest
The time of the coupling of man and
woman
And that of beasts. Feet rising and fall-
ing.
Eating and drinking. Dung and death.
Ib.

What is the late November doing
With the disturbance of the spring.
Ib. II

A periphrastic study in a worn-out
poetical fashion,
Leaving one still with the intolerable
wrestle
With words and meanings. The poetry
does not matter.   *Ib.*

The only wisdom we can hope to acquire
Is the wisdom of humility: humility is
endless.
Four Quartets. East Coker, II

The houses are all gone under the sea.
Ib.

The dancers are all gone under the hill.
Ib.

O dark dark dark.[1] They all go into the
dark,
The vacant interstellar spaces, the vacant into the vacant.   *Ib.*

And we all go with them, into the silent
funeral,
Nobody's funeral, for there is no one to
bury.

I said to my soul, be still, and let the
dark come upon you
Which shall be the darkness of God.
Ib.

To arrive where you are, to get from
where you are not,
You must go by a way wherein there is
no ecstasy.
In order to arrive at what you do not
know
You must go by the way which is the
way of ignorance.   *Ib.*

The whole earth is our hospital
Endowed by the ruined millionaire.
Ib.

We call this Friday good.   *Ib.*

And so each venture
Is a new beginning, a raid on the inar-
ticulate
With shabby equipment always deteri-
orating
In the general mess of imprecision of
feeling,
Undisciplined squads of emotion.
Ib. V

For us, there is only the trying. The
rest is not our business.   *Ib.*

Home is where one starts from. As we
grow older

[1] See Milton, p. 349a.

The world becomes stranger, the pattern more complicated
Of dead and living. Not the intense moment
Isolated, with no before and after,
But a lifetime burning in every moment
And not the lifetime of one man only
But of old stones that cannot be deciphered.
> *Four Quartets. East Coker, V*

Love is most nearly itself
When here and now cease to matter.
Old men ought to be explorers [1]
Here and there does not matter
We must be still and still moving
Into another intensity
For a further union, a deeper communion
Through the dark cold and the empty desolation,
The wave cry, the wind cry, the vast waters
Of the petrel and the porpoise. In my end is my beginning.[2]   *Ib.*

I do not know much about gods; but I think that the river
Is a strong brown god — sullen, untamed and intractable.
> *Ib. The Dry Salvages* [1941], I

The sea is the land's edge also, the granite
Into which it reaches, the beaches where it tosses
Its hints of earlier and other creation:
The starfish, the hermit crab, the whale's backbone;
The pools where it offers to our curiosity
The more delicate algae and the sea anemone.
It tosses up our losses, the torn seine,
The shattered lobsterpot, the broken oar
And the gear of foreign dead men. The sea has many voices.[3]   *Ib.*

There is no end of it, the voiceless wailing,

[1] See Roethke, p. 1065b.
[2] See Mary, Queen of Scots, p. 192b.
[3] See Tennyson, p. 646b.

No end to the withering of withered flowers.
> *Four Quartets. The Dry Salvages, II*

Only the hardly, barely prayable
Prayer of the one Annunciation.   *Ib.*

The backward look behind the assurance
Of recorded history, the backward half-look
Over the shoulder, towards the primitive terror.   *Ib.*

Not fare well,
But fare forward, voyagers.   *Ib. III*

Music heard so deeply
That it is not heard at all, but you are the music
While the music lasts.   *Ib. V*

Only undefeated
Because we have gone on trying;
We, content at the last
If our temporal reversion nourish
(Not too far from the yew tree)
The life of significant soil.   *Ib.*

What the dead had no speech for, when living,
They can tell you, being dead: the communication
Of the dead is tongued with fire beyond the language of the living.
> *Ib. Little Gidding* [1942], I

Water and fire shall rot
The marred foundations we forgot,
Of sanctuary and choir.
This is the death of water and fire.
> *Ib. II*

In the uncertain hour before the morning
Near the ending of interminable night
At the recurrent end of the unending
After the dark dove with the flickering tongue
Had passed below the horizon of his homing.   *Ib.*

Since our concern was speech, and speech impelled us
To purify the dialect of the tribe.[1]
> *Ib.*

[1] Donner un sens plus pur aux mots de la tribu. — STÉPHANE MALLARMÉ [*1842–1898*], *Le Tombeau d'Edgar Poe*

Who then devised the torment? Love.
Love is the unfamiliar Name
Behind the hands that wove
The intolerable shirt of flame
Which human power cannot remove.
We only live, only suspire
Consumed by either fire or fire.
> *Four Quartets. Little*
> *Gidding, IV*

So, while the light fails
On a winter's afternoon, in a secluded
    chapel
History is now and England.   *Ib. V*

We shall not cease from exploration
And the end of all our exploring
Will be to arrive where we started
And know the place for the first time.
> *Ib.*

A condition of complete simplicity
(Costing not less than everything)
And all shall be well and
All manner of thing shall be well
When the tongues of flame are in-
    folded
Into the crowned knot of fire
And the fire and the rose are one.
> *Ib.*

By the delicate, invisible web you
    wove —
The inexplicable mystery of sound.
> *To Walter de la Mare* [1948]

What is hell? Hell is oneself,
Hell is alone, the other figures in it
Merely projections.[1]
> *The Cocktail Party* [1950]

It [tradition] cannot be inherited,
and if you want it you must obtain it
by great labor.
> *Tradition and the Individual*
> *Talent* [1919]

The progress of an artist is a continual self-sacrifice, a continual extinction
of personality.   *Ib.*

Poetry is not a turning loose of emotion, but an escape from emotion; it is
not the expression of personality, but
an escape from personality. But, of
course, only those who have personality

[1] See Virgil, p. 119a; and Marlowe, p. 213a,
and note.

and emotions know what it means to
want to escape from these things.
> *Tradition and the Individual*
> *Talent*

The only way of expressing emotion
in the form of art is by finding an "objective correlative"; in other words, a
set of objects, a situation, a chain of
events which shall be the formula of
that *particular* emotion.
> *Hamlet and His Problems* [1919]

Immature poets imitate; mature
poets steal.
> *Philip Massinger* [1920]

Every vital development in language
is a development of feeling as well.
> *Ib.*

In the seventeenth century a dissociation of sensibility set in, from which
we have never recovered; and this
dissociation, as is natural, was aggra-
vated by the influence of the two most
powerful poets of the century, Milton
and Dryden.
> *The Metaphysical Poets* [1921]

Poets in our civilization, as it exists at
present, must be *difficult*. . . . The
poet must become more and more comprehensive, more allusive, more indirect, in order to force, to dislocate if
necessary, language into its meaning.
> *Ib.*

Humility is the most difficult of all
virtues to achieve; nothing dies harder
than the desire to think well of oneself.
> *Shakespeare and the Stoicism of*
> *Seneca* [1927]

The great poet, in writing himself,
writes his time.[1]   *Ib.*

We know too much, and are convinced of too little. Our literature is a
substitute for religion, and so is our religion.
> *A Dialogue on Dramatic Poetry*
> [1928]

[1] In a footnote, Eliot writes: "Rémy de Gour-
mont said much the same thing, in speaking
of Flaubert."

If I ask myself . . . why I prefer the poetry of Dante to that of Shakespeare, I should have to say, because it seems to me to illustrate a saner attitude towards the mystery of life.

> *The Sacred Wood, introduction*
> [1928]

The general point of view may be described as classicist in literature, royalist in politics, and Anglo-Catholic in religion.

> For *Lancelot Andrews* [1928],
> *preface*

We fight for lost causes because we know that our defeat and dismay may be the preface to our successors' victory, though that victory itself will be temporary; we fight rather to keep something alive than in the expectation that anything will triumph.

> *Ib. Francis Herbert Bradley*

The great weakness of Pragmatism is that it ends by being of no *use* to anybody. *Ib.*

Genuine poetry can communicate before it is understood.

> *Dante* [1929]

More can be learned about how to write poetry from Dante than from any English poet. . . . The language of each great English poet is his own language; the language of Dante is the perfection of a common language.

> *Ib.*

Shakespeare gives the greatest width of human passion; Dante the greatest altitude and greatest depth. *Ib.*

Sometimes, however, to be a "ruined man" is itself a vocation.

> *The Use of Poetry and the Use*
> *of Criticism* [1933]. *Words-*
> *worth and Coleridge*

As things are, and as fundamentally they must always be, poetry is not a career, but a mug's game. No honest poet can ever feel quite sure of the permanent value of what he has writ-

ten: he may have wasted his time and messed up his life for nothing.

> *The Use of Poetry and the Use*
> *of Criticism. Conclusion*

Tradition by itself is not enough; it must be perpetually criticized and brought up to date under the supervision of what I call orthodoxy.

> *After Strange Gods* [1934]

WILLIAM L. LAURENCE
1888–

[On the first atom bomb explosion [1]] A great ball of fire about a mile in diameter, changing colors as it kept shooting upward, from deep purple to orange, expanding, growing bigger, rising as it was expanding, an elemental force freed from its bonds after being chained for billions of years.

> *In the New York Times* [*Sep-*
> *tember 26, 1945*]

At first it was a giant column that soon took the shape of a supramundane mushroom. *Ib.*

T. E. LAWRENCE [2]
1888–1935

I loved you, so I drew these tides of
> men into my hands and wrote my
> will across the sky in stars.
To earn you Freedom, the seven-pil-
> lared worthy house, that your eyes
> might be shining for me
When we came.
> *Seven Pillars of Wisdom* [3]
> [1926], *dedication*

There could be no honor in a sure success, but much might be wrested from a sure defeat.

> *Revolt in the Desert* [1927],
> *ch. 19*

---

[1] At Alamogordo, New Mexico, July 16, 1945.
[2] Lawrence changed his name to T. E. Shaw in 1927.
[3] See *Proverbs 9:1*, p. 23b.

EUGENE O'NEILL
1888–1953

Dat ole davil, sea.
Anna Christie [1922], *act I*

We's all poor nuts and things happen, and we yust get mixed in wrong, that's all. *Ib. IV*

For de little stealin' dey gits you in jail soon or late. For de big stealin' dey makes you emperor and puts you in de Hall o' Fame when you croaks. If dey's one thing I learns in ten years on de Pullman cars listenin' to de white quality talk, it's dat same fact.
The Emperor Jones [1920], *sc. 1*

Poverty — that most deadly and prevalent of all diseases. *Ib.*

Yank: Sure! Lock me up! Put me in a cage! Dat's de on'y answer yuh know. G'wan, lock me up!
Policeman: What you been doin'?
Yank: Enough to gimme life for! I was born, see? Sure, dat's de charge. Write it in de blotter. I was born, get me! *The Hairy Ape* [1922]

Desire Under the Elms.
Title of play [1924]

He couldn't design a cathedral without it looking like the First Supernatural Bank!
The Great God Brown [1926]

Our lives are merely strange dark interludes in the electrical display of God the Father!
Strange Interlude [1928]

Mourning Becomes Electra.
Title of dramatic trilogy [1931]

A Long Day's Journey into Night.
Title of play [1956]

JOHN CROWE RANSOM
1888–

Two evils, monstrous either one apart,
Possessed me, and were long and loath
　　at going:
A cry of Absence, Absence, in the
　　heart,

And in the wood the furious winter
　　blowing. *Winter Remembered*

Hands hold much of heat in little storage. *They Hail the Sunrise*

The lazy geese, like a snow cloud
Dripping their snow on the green grass,
Tricking and stopping, sleepy and
　　proud,
Who cried in goose, Alas.
*Bells for John Whiteside's
　　Daughter*

Here lies a lady of beauty and high degree.
Of chills and fever she died, of fever
　　and chills,
The delight of her husband, her aunts,
　　an infant of three,
And of medicos marveling sweetly on
　　her ills. *Here Lies a Lady*

God have mercy on the sinner
Who must write with no dinner,
No gravy and no grub,
No pewter and no pub,
No belly and no bowels,
Only consonants and vowels.
Survey of Literature

Captain Carpenter rose up in his prime
Put on his pistols and went riding out.
Captain Carpenter, st. 1

ROBERT EMMONS ROGERS
1888–1941

Marry the boss's daughter.
*Advice to the Class of 1929,
Massachusetts Institute of Technology*

ALAN SEEGER
1888–1916

I have a rendezvous with Death
At some disputed barricade,
When spring comes back with rustling
　　shade
And apple blossoms fill the air.
I Have a Rendezvous with Death

When spring trips north again this
　　year,

And I to my pledged word am true,
I shall not fail that rendezvous.
            I Have a Rendezvous with Death

BARTOLOMEO VANZETTI
1888–1927

I found myself compelled to fight back from my eyes the tears, and quanch my heart trobling to my throat to not weep before him. But Sacco's name will live in the hearts of the people when your name, your laws, institutions and your false god are but a dim rememoring of a cursed past in which man was wolf to the man.
            Last Speech to the Court [1]

HENRY AGARD WALLACE [2]
1888–1965

Unemployed   purchasing   power means unemployed labor and unemployed labor means human want in the midst of plenty. This is the most challenging paradox of modern times.
            Address [1934]

The object of this war is to make sure that everybody in the world has the privilege of drinking a quart of milk a day.[3]
            Address, The Price of Free World Victory [May 8, 1942]

The century on which we are entering can be and must be the century of the common man.   *Ib.*

The hair goes with the hide.
            When asked why he had not mentioned Franklin D. Roosevelt's running mate, Harry S. Truman, in his campaign speech in Madison Square Garden, New York [September 21, 1944]

[1] Vanzetti and Nicolo Sacco, Italian anarchists, were executed August 23, 1927, by the Commonwealth of Massachusetts on charges, never conclusively proved, of murder and robbery.
[2] See Clare Boothe Luce, p. 1053b.
[3] This statement became twisted into the purported slogan "Milk for Hottentots."

The people who are fighting against me know that they are not fighting a starry-eyed liberal or mystic. If they really thought that, they wouldn't be worried.[1]
            Speech at testimonial dinner [January 29, 1945]

CONRAD AIKEN
1889–1973

Music I heard with you was more than music,
And bread I broke with you was more than bread.
Now that I am without you, all is desolate;
All that was once so beautiful is dead.
            Bread and Music [1914]

Stars in the purple dusk above the rooftops
Pale in a saffron mist and seem to die,
And I myself on a swiftly tilting planet
Stand before a glass and tie my tie.
            Senlin. Morning Song

One by one in the moonlight there,
Neighing far off on the haunted air,
The unicorns come down to the sea.
            Ib. Evening Song

Rock meeting rock can know love better
Than eyes that stare or lips that touch.
All that we know in love is bitter,
And it is not much.
            Annihilation, st. 8

All lovely things will have an ending,
All lovely things will fade and die,
And youth, that's now so bravely spending,
Will beg a penny by and by.
            All Lovely Things Will Have an Ending

The hiss was now becoming a roar — the whole world was a vast moving screen of snow — but even now it said peace, it said remoteness, it said cold, it said sleep.
            Silent Snow, Secret Snow [1932]

[1] See C. L. Becker, p. 913b.

O Altitudo in the bloodstream swims.[1]
And in the Human Heart
[1940]. *Sonnet 6*

Ice is the silent language of the peak;
and fire the silent language of the star.
Ib. 10

For brief as water falling will be death,
and brief as flower falling, or a leaf,
brief as the taking, and the giving,
    breath;
thus natural, thus brief, my love, is
    grief.   *Ib. 18*

ROBERT CHARLES BENCHLEY
1889–1945

I haven't been abroad in so long that
I almost speak English without an accent.   *The Old Sea Rover Speaks*

An Austrian scientist has come out
with the announcement that there is no
such thing as a hundred per cent male
or a hundred per cent female. If this is
true, it is really a big step forward.
Ib. A Talk to Young Men: Grad-
uation Address, The Decline of
Sex

Tell us your phobias and we will tell
you what you are afraid of.   *Phobias*

It took me fifteen years to discover
that I had no talent for writing, but I
couldn't give it up because by that time
I was too famous.   *Remark*

CHRISTOPHER DAWSON
1889–

As soon as men decide that all means
are permitted to fight an evil, then their
good becomes indistinguishable from
the evil that they set out to destroy.
The Judgment of the Nations
[1942]

[1] See Sir Thomas Browne, p. 329b.

PHILIP GUEDALLA
1889–1944

Biography, like big game hunting, is
one of the recognized forms of sport,
and it is as unfair as only sport can
be.   *Supers and Supermen* [1920]

The work of Henry James has always
seemed divisible by a simple dynastic
arrangement into three reigns: James I,
James II, and the Old Pretender.[1]   *Ib.*

Strange that pre-eminence in Germany has more than once been indi-
cated by an eccentric pattern in the
hair upon the upper lip.
The Hundred Years [1936]

The true history of the United States
is the history of transportation . . . in
which the names of railroad presidents
are more significant than those of Presidents of the United States.   *Ib.*

There is no plant in the whole world
of more cautious growth than Anglo-
American negotiation.
Mr. Churchill [1942] *(apropos*
the wedding of Mr. Churchill's
parents)

ADOLF HITLER
1889–1945

My adversaries . . . applied the one
means that wins the easiest victory over
reason: terror and force.
Mein Kampf [1933],[2] *vol. I,*
ch. 2

A majority can never replace the
man. . . . Just as a hundred fools do
not make one wise man, an heroic decision is not likely to come from a hundred cowards.   *Ib. 3*

Mankind has grown strong in eternal
struggles and it will only perish through
eternal peace.   *Ib. 4*

Strength lies not in defense but in
attack.   *Ib.*

All propaganda has to be popular
and has to adapt its spiritual level to

[1] See Henry James, p. 797b.
[2] *My Battle.*

the perception of the least intelligent of those towards whom it intends to direct itself. *Mein Kampf vol. I, ch. 6*

The great masses of the people . . . will more easily fall victims to a big lie than to a small one. *Ib.* 10

If an idea is right in itself, and if thus armed it embarks on the struggle in this world, it is invincible and every persecution will lead to its inner strengthening. *Ib.* 12

Germany will be either a world power or will not be at all.
Ib. II, 14

Never tolerate the establishment of two continental powers in Europe.
Ib.

The Sudetenland is the last territorial claim I have to make in Europe.
Address, at Sports Palast, Berlin [September 26, 1938]

After fifteen years of work I have achieved, as a common German soldier and merely with my fanatical will power, the unity of the German nation, and have freed it from the death sentence of Versailles.[1]
Proclamation to the troops on taking over the leadership of the German armed forces [December 21, 1941]

This war no longer bears the characteristics of former inter-European conflicts. It is one of those elemental conflicts which usher in a new millennium and which shake the world once in a thousand years.
Speech to the Reichstag [April 26, 1942]

Whomsoever England allies herself with, she will see her allies stronger

[1] The Allied and Associated Governments affirm and Germany accepts the responsibility of Germany and her Allies for causing all the loss and damage to which the Allied and Associated Governments and their nationals have been subjected as a consequence of the war imposed upon them by the aggression of Germany and her Allies. — *Article 231 (the "war guilt clause"), Treaty of Versailles* [June 28, 1919]

than she is herself at the end of this war. *Speech to the Reichstag*

If the German people despair, they will deserve no better than they get. If they despair, I will not be sorry for them if God lets them down.
Speech at Munich on the twentieth anniversary of the Munich beer hall putsch [broadcast November 8, 1943]

Is Paris burning?[1]
Asked while at the Oberkommando der Wehrmacht, Rastenburg, Germany [August 25, 1944]

GEORGE S. KAUFMAN
1889–1961

You Can't Take It With You.[2]
Title of play [1936]

Satire is what closes Saturday night.
Saying

STODDARD KING
1889–1933

There's a long, long trail a-winding
Into the land of my dreams,
Where the nightingales are singing
And a white moon beams.
The Long, Long Trail [1913]

WALTER LIPPMANN
1889–1974

Surely the task of statesmanship is more difficult today than ever before in history. . . . The distance between what we know and what we need to know appears to be greater than ever. . . . Nor can we keep to the problem within our borders. Whether we wish it or not we are involved in the world's problems, and all the winds of heaven blow through our land.
A Preface to Politics [1913], *ch. 4*

[1] Brennt Paris?
[2] Lo, no man taketh his goods with him. — *Song of the Harp-Player* [c. 2100 B.C.]

The principles of liberalism . . . are older than all existing constitutions and are more deeply rooted than any formulation of them that can be put into words. . . .

The liberal philosophy holds that enduring governments must be accountable to someone beside themselves; that a government responsible only to its own conscience is not for long tolerable. It holds that since any government is liable to fail, there is needed a method of changing the governors without wrecking the state. It holds that unless there is a method, be it through elections or otherwise, by which the governed can make their views effective in some proportion to their weight, the nation is at the mercy of violence in the form of terrorism, assassination, conspiracy, mass compulsion, and civil war.

In Defense of Liberalism [Vanity
Fair, November 1934]

The denial that men may be arbitrary in human transactions *is* the higher law. . . . By this higher law all formal laws and all political behavior are judged in civilized societies. . . . If the sovereign himself may not act willfully, arbitrarily, by personal prerogative, then no one may. His ministers may not. The legislature may not. Majorities may not. Individuals may not. Crowds may not. The national state may not. This law which is the spirit of law is the opposite of an accumulation of old precedents and new fiats. By this higher law, that men must not be arbitrary, the old law is continually tested and the new law reviewed.

The Good Society [1937], ch. 15

In foreign relations, as in all other relations, a policy has been formed only when commitments and power have been brought into balance.

U. S. Foreign Policy [1943]

The final test of a leader is that he leaves behind him in other men the conviction and the will to carry on. . . . The genius of a good leader is to leave behind him a situation which

common sense, without the grace of genius, can deal with successfully.

Roosevelt Has Gone
[April 14, 1945]

The world state is inherent in the United Nations as an oak tree is in an acorn.   *One World or None [1946]*

A regime, an established order, is rarely overthrown by a revolutionary movement; usually a regime collapses of its own weakness and corruption and then a revolutionary movement enters among the ruins and takes over the powers that have become vacant.

For Charles de Gaulle [Today
and Tomorrow, June 5, 1958]

I don't care about the word isolationism, and I don't care about the word appeasement. I'm interested in the rights and needs and responsibilities of the United States. We are not the policeman of mankind. We are not able to run the world, and we shouldn't pretend that we can. Let us tend to our own business, which is great enough as it is. It's very great. We have neglected our own affairs. Our education is inadequate, our cities are badly built, our social arrangements are unsatisfactory. We can't wait another generation. Unless we can surmount this crisis, and work and get going onto the path of a settlement in Asia, and a settlement in Europe, all of these plans of the Great Society here at home, all the plans for the rebuilding of backward countries in other continents will all be put on the shelf, because war interrupts everything like that.

Conversations with Walter Lipp-
mann [1965]. Lippmann and
Eric Sevareid, February 22, 1965

A free press is not a privilege but an organic necessity in a great society. . . . A great society is simply a big and complicated urban society.[1]

Address, International Press Insti-
tute Assembly, London [May 27,
1965]

[1] See Lyndon Johnson, p. 1064a.

Without criticism and reliable and intelligent reporting, the government cannot govern.

> *Address, International Press Institute Assembly, London*

Responsible journalism is journalism responsible in the last analysis to the editor's own conviction of what, whether interesting or only important, is in the public interest. *Ib.*

As the free press develops, the paramount point is whether the journalist, like the scientist or scholar, puts truth in the first place or in the second.

> *Ib.*

KATHERINE MANSFIELD
1889–1923

Whenever I prepare for a journey I prepare as though for death. Should I never return, all is in order. This is what life has taught me.

> *Journal* [1922]

I want, by understanding myself, to understand others. I want to be all that I am capable of becoming. . . . This all sounds very strenuous and serious. But now that I have wrestled with it, it's no longer so. I feel happy — deep down. *All is well.*

> *Ib.* (*end of her journal*)

JAWAHARLAL NEHRU
1889–1964

The French Revolution of a hundred and fifty years ago gradually ushered in an age of political equality, but the times have changed, and that by itself is not enough today. The boundaries of democracy have to be widened now so as to include economic equality also. This is the great revolution through which we are all passing.

> *Glimpses of World History* [1939]

The basic fact of today is the tremendous pace of change in human life.

> *Credo* [*reprinted in the New York Times, September 7, 1958*]

Democracy and socialism are means to an end, not the end itself. *Ib.*

The forces of a capitalist society, if left unchecked, tend to make the rich richer and the poor poorer. *Ib.*

I want nothing to do with any religion concerned with keeping the masses satisfied to live in hunger, filth, and ignorance. I want nothing to do with any order, religious or otherwise, which does not teach people that they are capable of becoming happier and more civilized, on this earth, capable of becoming true *man*, master of his fate and captain of his soul.[1]

> *From* EDGAR SNOW, *Journey to the Beginning* [1958]

ANNA AKHMATOVA
1889–1966

Oh, how good the snapping and the
    crackle
Of the frost that daily grows more
    keen!
Laden with its dazzling icy roses,
The white-flaming bush is forced to
    lean.

> *Oh, How Good* [1940], *st.* 1

What hangs in the balance is nowise in
    doubt;
We know the event and we brave what
    we know;
Our clocks are all striking the hour of
    courage.   *Courage* [1942]

O great language we love:
It is you, Russian tongue, we must save,
    and we swear
We will give you unstained to the sons
    of our sons;
You shall live on our lips, and we promise you — never
A prison shall know you, but you shall
    be free
Forever.   *Ib.*

[1] See Sallust, p. 116a, and note.

VANNEVAR BUSH
1890–

Science: The Endless Frontier.
Title of book [1945]

The scene changes but the aspirations of men of good will persist.
Modern Arms and Free Men
[1949], *foreword*

If democracy loses its touch, then no great war will be needed to overwhelm it. If it keeps and enhances its strength, no great war need come again.
Ib. Conclusion

Fear cannot be banished, but it can be calm and without panic; and it can be mitigated by reason and evaluation.
Ib.

KAREL ČAPEK
1890–1938

Rossum's Universal Robots.[1]
R.U.R. [1920]

MARCUS COOK CONNELLY
1890–

Gangway for de Lawd God Jehovah!
The Green Pastures [2]
[1930]

God: I'll jest r'ar back an' pass a miracle.
Ib.

Gabriel: How about cleanin' up de whole mess of 'em and sta'tin' all over ag'in wid some new kind of animal?
God: An' admit I'm licked?
Ib.

Even bein' Gawd ain't a bed of roses.
Ib.

ELMER DAVIS
1890–1958

Atomic warfare is bad enough; biological warfare would be worse; but there is something that is worse than

---

[1] The term "robot" came into English through Čapek's play.
[2] Suggested by Roark Bradford's stories, *Ol' Man Adam an' His Chillun.*

either. The French can tell you what it is; or the Czechs, or the Greeks, or the Norwegians, or the Filipinos; it is subjection to an alien oppressor.
No World, If Necessary [*in Saturday Review of Literature, March 30, 1946*]

One world or none, say the atomic scientists. Has it occurred to them that if their one world turned out to be totalitarian and obscurantist, we might better have no world at all? *Ib.*

The republic was not established by cowards, and cowards will not preserve it.
Phi Beta Kappa Oration, Harvard [1953]

With a great price our ancestors obtained this freedom, but we were born free . . . But that freedom can be retained only by the eternal vigilance which has always been its price.
But We Were Born Free
[1954], *ch. 1*

The first and great commandment is, Don't let them scare you. *Ib.*

I believe it [the nation] will endure, but only if we stand up for it. *Ib.*

This will remain the land of the free only so long as it is the home of the brave. *Ib.*

What makes Western civilization worth saving is the freedom of the mind, now under heavy attack from the primitives . . . who have persisted among us. If we have not the courage to defend that faith, it won't matter much whether we are saved or not.
Ib. 6

CHARLES ANDRÉ JOSEPH MARIE DE GAULLE
1890–1970

The sword is the axis of the world, and grandeur is indivisible.
Le Fil de l'Épée [1934]

The perfection preached in the Gospels never yet built up an empire. Every man of action has a strong dose of egotism, pride, hardness, and cunning. But all those things will be forgiven him, indeed, they will be regarded as high qualities, if he can make of them the means to achieve great ends.

Le Fil de l'Épée

Nothing great will ever be achieved without great men, and men are great only if they are determined to be so.

Ib.

France has lost a battle. But France has not lost the war.

Broadcast from London to the French people after the fall of France [June 18, 1940]

Since those whose duty it was to hold the sword of France have let it fall, I have picked up its broken point.

Radio address [July 13, 1940]

Then, at the sight of those bewildered people and of those soldiers in rout . . . I felt myself borne up by a limitless fury. Ah! It's too stupid! The war is beginning as badly as it could. Therefore it must go on. For that, the world is wide. If I live, I will fight, wherever I must, as long as I must, until the enemy is defeated and the national stain washed clean. All I have managed to do since was resolved upon that day.

Les Mémoires de Guerre, vol. I [1954]

At this moment, the worst in her history [the fall of France], it was for me to assume the burden of France.   *Ib.*

But there is no France without a sword.   *Ib.*

France cannot be France without greatness.   *Ib.*

I always thought I was Jeanne d'Arc and Bonaparte. How little one knows oneself.

Reply to speaker who compared him to Robespierre; from Figaro Littéraire [1958]

DWIGHT DAVID EISENHOWER
1890–1969

People of Western Europe: A landing was made this morning on the coast of France by troops of the Allied Expeditionary Force. This landing is part of the concerted United Nations plan for the liberation of Europe, made in conjunction with our great Russian allies. . . . I call upon all who love freedom to stand with us now. Together we shall achieve victory.

Broadcast [June 6, 1944 — D-Day]

Humility must always be the portion of any man who receives acclaim earned in the blood of his followers and the sacrifices of his friends.

Address at Guildhall, London [July 12, 1945]

Nothing is easy in war. Mistakes are always paid for in casualties and troops are quick to sense any blunder made by their commanders.

Infantry School Quarterly [April 1953]

This conjunction of an immense military establishment and a large arms industry is new in the American experience. . . . We recognize the imperative need for this development. Yet we must not fail to comprehend its grave implications. . . . In the councils of government, we must guard against the acquisition of unwarranted influence, whether sought or unsought, by the military-industrial complex. The potential for the disastrous rise of misplaced power exists and will persist.

Farewell Radio and Television Address to the American People [January 17, 1961]

SIR ALAN PATRICK HERBERT
1890–1971

I'm not a jealous woman, but I *can't* see what he sees in her,

I can't see *what* he sees in her, I can't
see what he *sees* in her!
*I Can't Think What He Sees
in Her*

Holy Deadlock.[1]
Title of novel [1934] *satirizing
the paradoxes of British divorce
law*

The Common Law of England has
been laboriously built upon a mythical
figure — the figure of "The Reasonable
Man."
Uncommon Law [1935], *p. 1*

The critical period in matrimony is
breakfast-time.   *Ib. p. 98*

An Act of God was defined as something which no reasonable man could
have expected.   *Ib. p. 316*

SAMUEL HOFFENSTEIN
1890–1947

Babies haven't any hair;
Old men's heads are just as bare;
Between the cradle and the grave
Lies a haircut and a shave.
*Songs of Faith in the Year after
Next, VIII*

The heart's dead
Are never buried.   *Summer Day*

GERALD WHITE
JOHNSON
1890–

A man who has tried to play Mozart,
and failed, through that vain effort
comes into position better to understand the man who tried to paint the
Sistine Madonna, and did.
A Little Night-Music [1937]

Nothing changes more constantly
than the past; for the past that influences our lives does not consist of what
actually happened, but of what men believe happened.
*American Heroes and Hero-
Worship* [1943], *ch. 1*

[1] Monagony — the state of being married to
one person. — BROOKS BECK [1963]

Heroes are created by popular de-
mand, sometimes out of the scantiest
materials . . . such as the apple that
William Tell never shot, the ride that
Paul Revere never finished, the flag that
Barbara Frietchie never waved.
*American Heroes and Hero-
Worship, ch. 1*

In all the world there is nothing
more timorous than a million dollars,
except ten million. In revolutionary
times the rich are always the people
who are most afraid.
*American Freedom and the
Press* [1958]

ROBERT LEY
1890–1945

Strength through joy.[1]
*Instruction for the German La-
bor Front* [*December 2, 1933*]

CHRISTOPHER MORLEY
1890–1957

And of all man's felicities
The very subtlest one, say I,
Is when for the first time he sees
His hearthfire smoke against the sky.
A Hallowe'en Memory, st. 5

If you have to keep reminding yourself of a thing, perhaps it isn't so.
Thunder on the Left
[1925], *ch. 9*

April prepares her green traffic light
and the world thinks Go.
John Mistletoe [1931], 8

A human being; an ingenious assembly of portable plumbing.
Human Being [1932], *ch. 11*

The enemies of the Future are always
the very nicest people.
Kitty Foyle [1939], *ch. 5*

Dancing is wonderful training for
girls, it's the first way you learn to guess
what a man is going to do before he
does it.   *Ib. 11*

[1] Kraft durch Freude.

There was so much handwriting on the
    wall
That even the wall fell down.
          Around the Clock [1943]

Chattering voltage like a broken wire
The wild cicada cried, Six weeks to
    frost!   *End of August*

Why do they put the Gideon Bibles
only in the bedrooms, where it's usually
too late, and not in the barroom downstairs?
   Contribution to a Contribution

ALLAN NEVINS
1890–1971

Too little and too late.
          Current History [1935]

BORIS PASTERNAK
1890–1960

I cherish this, Thy rigorous conception,
And I consent to play this part therein;
But another play is running at this mo-
    ment,
So, for the present, release me from the
    cast.

And yet, the order of the acts has been
    schemed and plotted,
And nothing can avert the final cur-
    tain's fall.
I stand alone. All else is swamped by
    Pharisaism.
To live life to the end is not a childish
    task.
      Doctor Zhivago [1958]. *The
      Poems of Yurii Zhivago,*[1] *Ham-
      let, st. 3, 4*

It snowed and snowed, the whole world
    over,
Snow swept the world from end to end.
A candle burned on the table;
A candle burned.
        Ib. Winter Night, st. 1

A corner draft fluttered the flame
And the white fever of temptation

[1] Translated by BERNARD GUILBERT GUERNEY.

Upswept its angel wings that cast
A cruciform shadow.
      *Doctor Zhivago. The Poems of
      Yurii Zhivago, Winter Night,
      st. 7*

GEORGE SELDES
1890–1970

Sawdust Caesar.[1]
         Title of book [1932]

FRED M. VINSON
1890–1953

Wars are not "acts of God." They
are caused by man, by man-made institutions, by the way in which man has
organized his society. What man has
made, man can change.
      *Speech, Arlington National
      Cemetery* [*Memorial Day,
      1945*]

"RED" ROWLEY
fl. 1915

Mademoiselle from Armenteers,
Hasn't been kissed in forty years,
    Hinky dinky, parley-voo.
    Mademoiselle from Armentières [2]

Mademoiselle from St. Nazaire,
She never heard of underwear.   *Ib.*

AGATHA CHRISTIE
1891–1976

It is completely unimportant. That is
why it is so interesting.
    The Murder of Roger Ackroyd
                    [1926]

JEAN COCTEAU
1891–1963

Mirrors should reflect a little before
throwing back images.
          Des Beaux-Arts

[1] Mussolini.
[2] Soldier song of World War I, with innumerable versions. The tune and verse structure were
based on a British Army song composed by
Alfred James Walden ["Harry Wincott," 1867–
1947].

ELY CULBERTSON
1891–1955

The bizarre world of cards . . . a world of pure power politics where rewards and punishments were meted out immediately. A deck of cards was built like the purest of hierarchies, with every card a master to those below it, a lackey to those above it. And there were "masses" — long suits — which always asserted themselves in the end, triumphing over the kings and aces.

Total Peace [1943], *ch. 1*

Power politics is the diplomatic name for the law of the jungle.

Must We Fight Russia? [1946], *ch. 2*

We must conquer war, or war will conquer us. *Ib.*

God and the politicians willing, the United States can declare peace upon the world, and win it. *Ib. 5*

KARL KEICHNER DARROW
1891–

One of the things which distinguishes ours from all earlier generations is this, that we have seen our atoms.

The Renaissance of Physics [1936]

HU SHIH[1]
1891–1962

We in China today have not reached the point where we can take concrete steps to create a new literature, and there is no need of talking theoretically about the techniques of creation. Let us first devote our efforts to the first . . . steps of preparatory work.

La Jeunesse Nouvelle [April 1918]

Only when we realize that there is no eternal, unchanging truth or absolute

[1] From *Sources of Chinese Tradition*, edited by William Theodore de Bary [1960].

truth can we arouse in ourselves a sense of intellectual responsibility.

La Jeunesse Nouvelle [April 1919]

The Chinese people's philosophy of life has not yet been brought face to face with science. At this moment we painfully feel that science has not been sufficiently promoted, that scientific education has not been developed.

Ib. Hu Shih wen ts'un

At present the most unfounded and most harmful distortion is to ridicule Western civilization as materialistic and worship Eastern civilization as spiritual. . . . Modern civilization of the West, built on the foundation of the search for human happiness, not only has definitely increased material enjoyment to no small degree, but can also definitely satisfy the spiritual demands of mankind. *Ib.*

The most outstanding characteristic of Eastern civilization is to know contentment, whereas that of Western civilization is not to know contentment. Contented Easterners are satisfied with their simple life and therefore do not seek to increase their material enjoyment. . . . They are satisfied with their present lot and environment and therefore do not want to conquer nature but merely be at home with nature and at peace with their lot. *Ib.*

The civilization under which people are restricted and controlled by a material environment from which they cannot escape, and under which they cannot utilize human thought and intellectual power to change environment and improve conditions, is the civilization of a lazy and nonprogressive people. It is a truly materialistic civilization. *Ib.*

DAVID LOW
1891–1963

I have never met anybody who wasn't against war. Even Hitler and

Mussolini were, according to themselves.

> *In the New York Times*
> *[February 10, 1946]*

OSIP MANDELSTAM
1891 – 1938

On every still suburban street
The gatekeepers are shoveling snow.
> *On Every Still Suburban*
> *Street [1916], st. 1*

In teahouses and in home alike
The samovars' red roses glow.
> *Ib. st. 2*

ELLIOT PAUL
1891–1958

The last time I see Paris will be on the day I die. The city was inexhaustible, and so is its memory.
> *The Last Time I Saw Paris* [1]
> *[1942], pt. II, 23*

HAILIE SELASSIE
1891–1975

Outside the kingdom of the Lord there is no nation which is greater than any other. God and history will remember your judgment.
> *Speech, the League of Nations* [2]
> *[1936]*

ARTHUR HAYS
SULZBERGER
1891–1968

Obviously, a man's judgment cannot be better than the information on which he has based it. Give him the truth and he may still go wrong when he has the chance to be right, but give him no news or present him only with distorted and incomplete data, with ig-

---

[1] The last time I saw Paris, her heart was warm and gay,
I heard the laughter of her heart in every street café.
OSCAR HAMMERSTEIN II [1895–1960],
The Last Time I Saw Paris
[2] He sought sanctions against Italy, which had invaded Ethiopia.

---

norant, sloppy or biased reporting, with propaganda and deliberate falsehoods, and you destroy his whole reasoning processes, and make him something less than a man.
> *Address, New York State Publishers Association [August 30, 1948]*

Freedom cannot be trifled with. You cannot surrender it for security unless in a state of war, and then you must guard carefully the methods of so doing.
> *Upon receiving the Columbia College award for distinguished service [1952]*

There has been dropped upon utterance and thought a smoke screen of intimidation that dims essential thought and essential talk and begets a fog through which we wander uncertainly. Nor is it the superzealots who bother me so much in all this — it is the lack of plain old-fashioned guts on the part of those who capitulate to them. *Ib.*

There is more fear in this country than the facts warrant. Beset by doubt, the nation listens to those who seem to offer a cure, even though the medicine be more harmful than the disease. Once more we are met upon a battlefield testing whether this nation or any nation similarly dedicated can long endure.[1] *Ib.*

The vital measure of a newspaper is not its size but its spirit — that is its responsibility to report the news fully, accurately and fairly.
> *On accepting an award to the New York Times by Temple Israel, Boston [May 9, 1956]*

EARL WARREN
1891–1974

To separate [Negro children] from others of similar age and qualifications solely because of their race generates a feeling of inferiority as to their status in

---

[1] See Lincoln, p. 639a.

the community that may affect their hearts and minds in a way unlikely ever to be undone. . . . We conclude that in the field of public education the doctrine of "separate but equal"[1] has no place. Separate educational facilities are inherently unequal.

> Brown v. Board of Education of Topeka, 347 U.S. 483 [1954][2]

HERBERT V. WILEY
1891–1954

Stand by to crash.
> Last command to the crew of the falling U.S. Navy dirigible Akron [April 4, 1933]

STELLA BENSON
1892–1933

Call no man foe, but never love a stranger.   To the Unborn, st. 3

PEARL S. BUCK
1892–1973

I feel no need for any other faith than my faith in human beings. Like Confucius of old, I am so absorbed in the wonder of earth and the life upon it that I cannot think of heaven and the angels. I have enough for this life. If there is no other life, then this one has been enough to make it worth being born, myself a human being.
> I Believe [1939]

JOHN BURDON SANDERSON HALDANE
1892–1964

Now, my suspicion is that the universe is not only queerer than we sup-

[1] All railway companies carrying passengers in their coaches in the state shall provide equal but separate accommodations for the white and colored races. — *Louisiana Acts of 1890, no. 111, p. 152;* quoted by Mr. Justice HENRY B. BROWN in *Plessy v. Ferguson, 163 U.S. 537 [1896]*
[2] In a later implementation of the same case (*349 U.S. 294 [1955]*) the Supreme Court asked that desegregation proceed "with all deliberate speed."

pose, but queerer than we *can* suppose. . . . I suspect that there are more things in heaven and earth than are dreamed of, in any philosophy.[1] That is the reason why I have no philosophy myself, and must be my excuse for dreaming.   Possible Worlds [1927]

ROBERT HOUGHWOUT JACKSON
1892–1954

If there is any fixed star in our constitutional constellation, it is that no official, high or petty, can prescribe what shall be orthodox in politics, nationalism, religion, or other matters of opinion or force citizens to confess by word or act their faith therein.
> Minersville School District v. Gobitis, 319 U.S. 624, 642 [1940]

The first trial in history for crimes against the peace of the world imposes a grave responsibility. The wrongs which we seek to condemn and punish have been so calculated, so malignant and so devastating that civilization cannot tolerate their being ignored because it cannot survive their being repeated.
> Opening address before the International Military Tribunal, Nuremberg [1945]

If it is interstate commerce that feels the pinch, it does not matter how local the operation which applies the squeeze.
> U.S. v. Women's Sportswear Manufacturers Association 336 U.S. 460, 464 [1949]

There is danger that, if the Court does not temper its doctrinaire logic with a little practical wisdom, it will convert the constitutional Bill of Rights into a suicide pact.
> Terminiello v. Chicago, 337 U.S. 1, 37 [1949]

It is not the function of our Government to keep the citizen from falling into error; it is the function of the citi-

[1] See Shakespeare, p. 260a.

zen to keep the Government from falling into error.

> American Communications Association v. Douds, 339 U.S. 382, 442 [1950]

The day that this country ceases to be free for irreligion, it will cease to be free for religion.

> Dissenting opinion, Zorach v. Clausor, 343 U.S. 306, 325 [1952]

HOWARD MUMFORD JONES
1892–

They say the forties are the dangerous
ages.   The Forties [1937]

A few unrepentant old sinners wonder
if Marx
Also explains the unsocialized pairs in
the parks.   Ib. 32

ARCHIBALD MacLEISH
1892–

Sometimes within the brain's old ghost-
ly house,
I hear, far off, at some forgotten door,
A music and an eerie faint carouse,
And stir of echoes down the creaking
floor.
> Chambers of Imagery, st. 1

Beauty is that Medusa's head
Which men go armed to seek and
sever.
It is most deadly when most dead,
And dead will stare and sting forever.
> Beauty

A poem should not mean
But be.   Ars Poetica [1926]

There with vast wings across the canceled skies,
There in the sudden blackness the
black pall
Of nothing, nothing, nothing — nothing at all.
> The End of the World [1926]

The world was always yours: you would
not take it.
> Speech to a Crowd

And here face downward in the sun
To feel how swift how secretly
The shadow of the night comes on.
> You, Andrew Marvell [1930]

Christ but this earth goes over to the
squall of time!
Hi but she heels to it — rail down: ribs
down: rolling
Dakotas under her hull! And the night
climbing
Sucking the green from the ferns by
these Berkshire boulders!
> The Sunset Piece

We were the first that found that fa-
mous country:
We marched by a king's name: we
crossed the sierras:
Unknown hardships we suffered . . .
We were lords of it all.
> Conquistador [1932]. Bernal
> Diaz' Preface

She lies on her left side her flank gold-
en:
Her hair is burned black with the
strong sun:
The scent of her hair is of rain in the
dust on her shoulders:
She has brown breasts and the mouth
of no other country.
> Frescoes for Mr. Rockefeller's
> City [1933]. Landscape as a
> Nude

America was promises . . .
It was Man who had been promised.
> America Was Promises [1939]

EDWARD POWYS MATHERS
1892–

A love-sick heart dies when the heart is
whole,
For all the heart's health is to be sick
with love.
> Fard. Translation from the
> Hindustani of MIYAN JAGNU
> [eighteenth century]

EDNA ST. VINCENT MILLAY
1892–1950

All I could see from where I stood
Was three long mountains and a wood.
Renascence [1912] *l. 1*

The world stands out on either side
No wider than the heart is wide;
Above the world is stretched the sky, —
No higher than the soul is high.[1]
The heart can push the sea and land
Farther away on either hand;
The soul can split the sky in two,
And let the face of God shine through.
But East and West will pinch the heart
That cannot keep them pushed apart;
And he whose soul is flat — the sky
Will cave in on him by and by.
Ib. last lines

O world, I cannot hold thee close
enough!
God's World [1917], *st. 1*

Lord, I do fear
Thou'st made the world too beautiful
this year.
My soul is all but out of me — let fall
No burning leaf; prithee, let no bird
call. *Ib. st. 2*

I will be the gladdest thing under the
sun!
I will touch a hundred flowers and not
pick one.
Afternoon on a Hill [1917], *st. 1*

Life goes on forever like the gnawing of
a mouse.
Ashes of Life [1917], *st. 3*

My candle burns at both ends;
It will not last the night;
But, ah, my foes, and, oh, my friends —
It gives a lovely light.[2]
A Few Figs from Thistles.
[1920]. *First Fig*

Safe upon the solid rock the ugly
houses stand:

[1] See Hartley Coleridge, p. 586b.
[2] I burned my candle at both ends,
And now have neither foes nor friends.
SAMUEL HOFFENSTEIN [1890–1947],
Songs of Fairly Utter Despair, 8

Come and see my shining palace built
upon the sand!
A Few Figs from Thistles.
Second Fig

I had a little Sorrow,
Born of a little Sin.
Ib. The Penitent, st. 1

Whether or not we find what we are
seeking
Is idle, biologically speaking.
Ib. I Shall Forget You
Presently, l. 13

Death devours all lovely things;
Lesbia with her sparrow
Shares the darkness — presently
Every bed is narrow.
Passer Mortuus Est [1921], *st. 1*

My heart is warm with the friends I
make,
And better friends I'll not be knowing;
Yet there isn't a train I wouldn't take,
No matter where it's going.
Travel [1921], *st. 3*

I know I am but summer to your heart,
And not the full four seasons of the
year.
I Know I Am But Summer
[1923], *l. 1*

I drank at every vine.
The last was like the first.
I came upon no wine
So wonderful as thirst.
Feast [1923], *st. 1*

I only know that summer sang in me
A little while, that in me sings no more.
What Lips My Lips Have Kissed
[1923], *l. 13*

Pity me that the heart is slow to learn
What the swift mind beholds at every
turn.
Pity Me Not [1923], *l. 13*

Euclid alone
Has looked on Beauty bare.[1] Fortunate
they
Who, though once only and then but
far away,

[1] See Russell, p. 913a.

Have heard her massive sandal set on
stone.
> *Euclid Alone Has Looked on*
> *Beauty Bare* [1923], *l. 11*

If ever I said, in grief or pride,
I tired of honest things, I lied.
> *The Goose Girl* [1923], *l. 5*

Music my rampart, and my only one.
> *On Hearing a Symphony of*
> *Beethoven* [1928], *l. 14*

I am not resigned to the shutting away
of loving hearts in the hard
ground.
So it is, and so it will be, for so it has
been, time out of mind:
Into the darkness they go, the wise and
the lovely. Crowned
With lilies and with laurel they go; but
I am not resigned.
> *Dirge Without Music* [1928], *st. 1*

Love is not all: it is not meat nor drink
Nor slumber nor a roof against the rain;
Nor yet a floating spar to men that
sink.
> *Love Is Not All* [1931], *l. 1*

REINHOLD NIEBUHR
1892–1971

O God, give us serenity to accept
what cannot be changed, courage to
change what should be changed, and
wisdom to distinguish the one from the
other. *Prayer* [1934] [1]

[1] This prayer was composed . . . when Niebuhr preached occasionally in the small church
near his summer home in Heath, Massachusetts.
After the service, Howard Chandler Robbins, a
summer neighbor, asked for a copy. He is reported to have been handed the original, with
words to the following effect: "Here, take the
prayer. I have no further use for it." Other
people, it is clear, have felt differently. Robbins
published it as part of a pamphlet the following
year. Since then it has been adopted as the motto
of Alcoholics Anonymous; the U.S.O. distributed millions of copies to servicemen during
World War II; the National Council of Churches
has reprinted it; and even today it is used commercially on Christmas cards. — JUNE BINGHAM,
*Courage to Change: An Introduction to the Life
and Thought of Reinhold Niebuhr* [1961]

Goodness, armed with power, is corrupted; and pure love without power is
destroyed. *Beyond Tragedy* [1938]

Man's capacity for justice makes
democracy possible, but man's inclination to injustice makes democracy necessary.
> *The Children of Light and the*
> *Children of Darkness* [1944]

Life has no meaning except in terms
of responsibility.
> *Faith and History* [1949]

Nothing worth doing is completed in
our lifetime; therefore, we must be
saved by hope. Nothing true or beautiful or good makes complete sense in
any immediate context of history;
therefore, we must be saved by faith.
Nothing we do, however virtuous, can
be accomplished alone; therefore, we
are saved by love. No virtuous act is
quite as virtuous from the standpoint of
our friend or foe as from our standpoint. Therefore, we must be saved by
the final form of love which is forgiveness.
> *The Irony of American History*
> [1952]

BASIL O'CONNOR
1892–1972

The world cannot continue to wage
war like physical giants and to seek
peace like intellectual pygmies.
> *Address, National Conference of*
> *Christians and Jews* [1945]

HAROLD WALLACE
ROSS
1892–1951

The New Yorker will not be edited
for the old lady from Dubuque.[1]
> *Upon founding The New Yorker*
> [1925]

[1] Later this became "the little old lady from
Dubuque."

JOHN RONALD REUEL TOLKIEN
1892–1973

In a hole in the ground there lived a hobbit. Not a nasty, dirty, wet hole, filled with the ends of worms and an oozy smell, nor yet a dry, bare, sandy hole with nothing in it to sit down on or to eat: it was a hobbit-hole, and that means comfort.

The Hobbit; or There and Back Again [1937], *ch. 1*

WENDELL LEWIS WILLKIE
1892–1944

Freedom is an indivisible word.[1] If we want to enjoy it, and fight for it, we must be prepared to extend it to everyone, whether they are rich or poor, whether they agree with us or not, no matter what their race or the color of their skin. *One World, ch. 13*

The Constitution does not provide for first and second class citizens.

An American Program [1944], *ch. 2*

I believe in America because in it we are free —
free to choose our government, to speak our minds,
to observe our different religions.
Because we are generous with our freedom, we share
our rights with those who disagree with us.
Because we hate no people and covet no people's lands.
Because we are blessed with a natural and varied abundance.
Because we have great dreams and because we have the
opportunity to make those dreams come true.

His creed, inscribed on a marker by his grave in Rushville, Indiana

[1] See Litvinov, p. 941a.

DEAN ACHESON
1893–1971

Whatever the outcome of the appeal, I do not intend to turn my back on Alger Hiss.

Statement [*Time, February 6, 1950*]

MORRIS BISHOP
1893–

After the day is over
    And the passers-by are rare
The lights burn low in the barber-shop
    And the shades are drawn with care
To hide the haughty barbers
    Cutting each other's hair.

The Tales the Barbers Tell

OMAR BRADLEY
1893–

We have grasped the mystery of the atom and rejected the Sermon on the Mount.

Address [*Armistice Day, 1948*]

But it [Pearl Harbor], and the subsequent lessons we learned, day by day, until September 1945, should have taught all military men that our military forces are one team — in the game to win regardless of who carries the ball. This is no time for "fancy dans" who won't hit the line with all they have on every play, unless they can call the signals. Each player on this team — whether he shines in the spotlight of the backfield or eats dirt in the line — must be an All-American.

Testimony, Committee on Armed Services, House of Representatives [*October 19, 1949*]

In war there is no second prize for the runner-up.

In the Military Review [*February 1950*]

Red China is not the powerful nation seeking to dominate the world. Frankly, in the opinion of the Joint Chiefs of Staff, this strategy would involve us in the wrong war, at the wrong place, at the wrong time, and with the wrong enemy.

> *Testimony, Committee on Armed Services and Committee on Foreign Affairs, U.S. Senate [May 15, 1951]*

Only one military organization can hold and gain ground in war — a ground army supported by tactical aviation with supply lines guarded by the navy.

> *In the Military Review [September 1951]*

JAMES BRYANT CONANT
1893–

He who enters a university walks on hallowed ground.

> *Notes on the Harvard Tercentenary [1936]*

Each honest calling, each walk of life, has its own elite, its own aristocracy based on excellence of performance.

> *Our Fighting Faith. "In This Country There Are No Classes"* [1]

Liberty like charity must begin at home.

> *Ib. Our Unique Heritage* [2]

The primary concern of American education today is not the development of the appreciation of the "good life" in young gentlemen born to the purple. . . . Our purpose is to cultivate in the largest possible number of our future citizens an appreciation of both the responsibilities and the benefits which come to them because they are Americans and are free.

> *Annual Report to the Board of Overseers, Harvard University* [3] *[January 11, 1943]*

[1] Baccalaureate sermon [June 16, 1940]. The title is taken from a statement in an address by JAMES A. GARFIELD [1831–1881], *The Future of the Republic: Its Dangers and its Hopes* [1873].

[2] Address, opening of the first wartime summer term, Harvard College [June 30, 1942].

[3] Describing his purpose, as president of Harvard University, in appointing a University Com-

There is only one proved method of assisting the advancement of pure science — that of picking men of genius, backing them heavily, and leaving them to direct themselves.

> *Letter to the New York Times [August 13, 1945]*

The stumbling way in which even the ablest of the scientists in every generation have had to fight through thickets of erroneous observations, misleading generalizations, inadequate formulations, and unconscious prejudice is rarely appreciated by those who obtain their scientific knowledge from textbooks.

> *Science and Common Sense [1951]*

JIMMY DURANTE
1893–

Goodnight, Mrs. Calabash, wherever you are. *Saying*

Dese are de conditions dat prevail. *Saying*

HANS FALLADA
[RUDOLF DITZEN]
1893–1947

Little Man, What Now?

> *Title of novel [1932]*

HERMANN GOERING
1893–1946

Shoot first and inquire afterwards, and if you make mistakes, I will protect you.

> *Instruction for the Prussian police [1933]*

Guns will make us powerful; butter will only make us fat. [1]

> *Broadcast [1936]*

When I hear anyone talk of culture, I reach for my revolver. *Attributed*

mittee on the Objectives of a General Education in a Free Society. The committee's report was published [1945] under the title *General Education in a Free Society.*

[1] See Goebbels, p. 1040a.

HAROLD JOSEPH LASKI
1893–1950

We live under a system by which the many are exploited by the few, and war is the ultimate sanction of that exploitation.

Plan or Perish [1945]

We must plan our civilization or we must perish. **Ib.**

It would be madness to let the purposes or the methods of private enterprise set the habits of the age of atomic energy. **Ib.**

ANITA LOOS
1893–

Gentlemen always seem to remember blondes.

Gentlemen Prefer Blondes [1925], *ch. 1*

She always believed in the old adage, "Leave them while you're looking good." **Ib.**

A girl never really looks as well as she does on board a steamship, or even a yacht. **Ib.**

Kissing your hand may make you feel very, very good, but a diamond and sapphire bracelet lasts forever. **Ib. 4**

JOHN PHILLIPS
MARQUAND
1893–1960

It is worthwhile for anyone to have behind him a few generations of honest, hard-working ancestry.

The Late George Apley [1937], *ch. 3*

His father watched him across the gulf of years and pathos which always must divide a father from his son. **Ib. 10**

Marriage . . . is a damnably serious business, particularly around Boston. **Ib. 11**

There is a certain phase in the life of the aged when the warmth of the heart seems to increase in direct proportion with the years. This is a time of life when a solicitous family does well to watch affectionately over the vagaries of its unattached relatives, particularly of those who are comfortably off.

The Late George Apley, ch. 23

MAO TSE-TUNG
1893–1976

The contradiction between imperialism and the Chinese nation, and the contradiction between feudalism and the great masses of the people, are the principal contradictions in modern Chinese society. . . . The great revolutions of modern and contemporary China have emerged and developed on the basis of these fundamental contradictions.

Selected Works,[1] *III, pp. 81–82*

Armament is an important factor in war, but not the decisive factor. . . . Man, not material, forms the decisive factor.[2] *Lecture* [1938]

War cannot be divorced from politics for a single moment.[3] **Ib.**

The people are like water and the army is like fish.

Aspects of China's Anti-Japanese Struggle [1948]

"Let a hundred flowers blossom" and "let a hundred schools of thought contend."

Speech, Peking [*February 27, 1957*]

The policy of letting a hundred flowers blossom and a hundred schools of thought contend is designed to promote the flourishing of the arts and the progress of science; it is designed to en-

[1] From *Sources of Chinese Tradition*, edited by William Theodore de Bary [1960].
[2] There is still one absolute weapon. . . . That weapon is man himself. — MATTHEW B. RIDGWAY, *Address, Cleveland, Ohio* [November 10, 1953]
[3] See von Clausewitz, p. 544b.

able a socialist culture to thrive in our land. Different forms and styles in art can develop freely, and different schools in science can develop freely, and different schools in science can contend freely. We think that it is harmful to the growth of art and science if administrative measures are used to impose one particular style of art or school of thought and to ban another.

Speech, Peking

When the majority of the people have clear-cut criteria to go by, criticism and self-criticism can be conducted along proper lines, and these criteria can be applied to people's words and actions to determine whether they are fragrant flowers or poisonous weeds.

Ib.

VLADIMIR MAYAKOVSKY
1893–1930

If you wish,
I shall be irreproachably tender:
Not a man, but a cloud in pants!
Cloud in Pants [1914–1915]

Citizen!
Consider my traveling expenses:
Poetry —
    all of it —
        is a trip into the unknown.
Conversation with a Tax Collector about Poetry [1926]

Then there is amortization,
                the worst of all:
amortization of heart and soul.   *Ib.*

ALBERT SZENT-GYÖRGYI VON NAGYRAPOLT
1893–

The real scientist . . . is ready to bear privation and, if need be, starvation rather than let anyone dictate to him which direction his work must take.

Science Needs Freedom [*World Digest,* 1943]

WILFRED OWEN
1893–1918

Above all, this book is not concerned
    with Poetry,
The subject of it is War, and the pity
    of War.
The Poetry is in the pity.
All a poet can do is warn.[1]
Preface to the Poems [*published 1920*]

What passing bells for these who die
    as cattle?
Only the monstrous anger of the guns.
Only the stuttering rifles' rapid rattle
Can patter out their hasty orisons.
The Anthem for Doomed Youth, st. 1

And bugles calling for them from sad
    shires.   *Ib.*

What candles may be held to speed
    them all?
Not in the hands of boys, but in their
    eyes
Shall shine the holy glimmers of good-
    byes.   *Ib.*

And each slow dusk a drawing-down of
    blinds.   *Ib.*

If anything might rouse him now
The kind old sun will know.
Futility, st. 1

— Oh what made fatuous sunbeams
    toil
To break earth's sleep at all?   *Ib. st. 2*

Red lips are not so red
As the stained stones kissed by the Eng-
    lish dead.
Kindness of wooed and wooer
Seems shame to their love pure.
Greater Love

Courage was mine, and I had mystery,
Wisdom was mine, and I had mastery;
To miss the march of this retreating
    world
Into vain citadels that are not walled.
Strange Meeting

[1] The last three lines serve as the motto for Benjamin Britten's *War Requiem* (*Op. 66*), which uses the Latin text of the Mass for the Dead and some of the poems of Wilfred Owen.

DOROTHY PARKER
1893–1967

Where's the man could ease a heart
Like a satin gown?
The Satin Dress, st. 1

Four be the things I am wiser to know:
Idleness, sorrow, a friend, and a foe.
Inventory, st. 1

Four be the things I'd been better
without:
Love, curiosity, freckles, and doubt.
Ib. st. 2

Scratch a lover, and find a foe.
Ballade of a Great Weariness,
st. 1

Men seldom make passes
At girls who wear glasses.
News Item

Guns aren't lawful;
Nooses give;
Gas smells awful;
You might as well live.   *Résumé*

Why is it no one ever sent me yet
One perfect limousine, do you suppose?
Ah no, it's always just my luck to get
One perfect rose.
One Perfect Rose, st. 3

He lies below, correct in cypress wood,
And entertains the most exclusive
worms.
Epitaph for a Very Rich Man

There was nothing more fun than a
man!
The Little Old Lady in
Lavender Silk, st. 3

Excuse my dust.
Epitaph, suggested by herself

Wit has truth in it; wisecracking is
simply calisthenics with words.
In Paris Review [Summer 1956]

SIR HERBERT READ
1893–1968

Poetry can never again become a
popular art until the poet gives himself
wholly to "the cadence of consenting
feet." [1]
Phases of English Poetry [1928]

The no-man's-years between the wars
[1919–1939].
Annals of Innocence and
Experience [1940]

JOACHIM
VON RIBBENTROP
1893–1945

The Führer is always right.
Address, Königsberg [August 24,
1939]

ROBERT LEROY RIPLEY
1893–1949

Believe It or Not.
Title of syndicated newspaper
feature

HAROLD CLAYTON UREY
1893–

We need first of all to be thoroughly
frightened.
Speech on the atomic bomb
[December 3, 1945]

The most dangerous situation that
humanity has ever faced in all history.
One World or None [1946], ch. 2

MAE WEST
1893–

Come up and see me sometime.
Diamond Lil [2] [1932]

Beulah, peel me a grape.
I'm No Angel [1933]

FRED ALLEN
1894–1956

Hollywood is a great place if you're
an orange.   *Saying*

---

[1] The quotation is from FRANCIS BARTON
GUMMERE, *The Beginnings of Poetry* [1901].
[2] The play was later made into a movie, *She
Done Him Wrong.*

To a newspaperman a human being is an item with the skin wrapped around it. *Saying*

DON BLANDING
1894–1957

It's more than just an easy word for casual goodbye;
It's gayer than a greeting, and it's sadder than a sigh.
Aloha Oe: Its Meaning

It's said a hundred different ways, in sadness and in joy,
Aloha means "I love you." So I say "Aloha Oe." *Ib.*

EDWARD ESTLIN
CUMMINGS[1]
1894–1962

All in green went my love riding
on a great horse of gold
into the silver dawn.
All in green went my love riding
[1923]

four lean hounds crouched low and smiling
my heart fell dead before. *Ib.*

in Just-
spring when the world is mud-
luscious the little
lame balloonman
whistles far and wee
Chansons Innocentes [1923], 1

when the world is puddle-wonderful
Ib.

Buffalo Bill's
defunct
    who used to
    ride a watersmooth-silver
                        stallion
and break onetwothreefourfive pigeons-
    justlikethat
            Jesus
he was a handsome man
    and what i want to know is

how do you like your blueeyed boy
Mister Death   *Portraits* [1923], 8

the Cambridge ladies who live in furnished souls
are unbeautiful and have comfortable minds.
Sonnets — Realities [1923], I

Humanity i love you because
when you're hard up you pawn your
intelligence to buy a drink.
Humanity i love you [1925]

i spill my bright incalculable soul.
Sonnets [1925], II

take it from me kiddo
believe me
my country, 'tis of

you, land of the Cluett
Shirt Boston Garter and Spearmint
Girl With The Wrigley Eyes (of you
land of the Arrow Ide
and Earl &
Wilson
Collars) of you i
sing: land of Abraham Lincoln and
    Lydia E. Pinkham,
land above all of Just Add Hot Water
    And Serve —
from every B.V.D.

let freedom ring

amen.
            Poem, Or Beauty Hurts
            Mr. Vinal [1926]

    Turn Your Shirttails Into
Drawers and If It Isn't An Eastman It
    Isn't A
Kodak   *Ib.*

    And there're a
hun-dred-mil-lion-oth-ers, like
all of you successfully if
delicately gelded(or spaded)
gentlemen(and ladies)   *Ib.*

a tiny violetflavored nuisance   *Ib.*

next to of course god america i

[1] The terror of typesetters, an enigma to book reviewers, and the special target of all the world's literary philistines. — *Publisher's note, Modern Library edition of The Enormous Room*

love you land of the pilgrims' and so
    forth
        next to of course god america i
            [1926]

thy sons acclaim your glorious name by
    gorry
by jingo by gee by gosh by gum   *Ib.*

for life's not a paragraph
And death i think is no parenthesis.
        since feeling is first [1926]

lady through whose profound and frag-
    ile lips
the sweet small clumsy feet of April
    came
into the ragged meadow of my soul.
        if i have made, my lady,
            intricate [1926]

i sing of Olaf glad and big
whose warmest heart recoiled at war
    i sing of Olaf glad and big [1931]

"I will not kiss your f.ing flag"   *Ib.*

"there is some s. I will not eat"   *Ib.*

unless statistics lie he was
more brave than me:more blond than
    you.   *Ib.*

somewhere i have never travelled, gladly
    beyond
any experience, your eyes have their
    silence.
        somewhere I have never
            travelled [1931]

nobody, not even the rain, has such
    small hands   *Ib.*

King Christ, this world is all aleak;
and lifepreservers there are none:
and waves which only He may walk
Who dares to call Himself a man.
    Jehovah buried, Satan dead [1935]

    Always the beautiful answer who asks
a more beautiful question.
        Collected Poems [1938],
            introduction

as freedom is a breakfastfood
or truth can live with right and wrong
or molehills are from mountains made

— long enough and just so long
will being pay the rent of seem
and genius please the talentgang
and water most encourage flame
        as freedom is a breakfastfood
            [1940]

worms are the words but joy's the voice
                                        Ib.

anyone lived in a pretty how town
(with up so floating many bells down)
spring summer autumn winter
he sang his didn't he danced his did.
        anyone lived in a pretty how
            town [1940]

my father moved through dooms of
    love
through sames of am through haves of
    give,
singing each morning out of each night
my father moved through depths of
    height
        my father moved through dooms
            of love [1940]

though dull were all we taste as bright,
bitter all utterly things sweet,
maggoty minus and dumb death
all we inherit, all bequeath   *Ib.*

and nothing quite so least as truth
— i say though hate were why men
    breathe —
because my father lived his soul
love is the whole and more than all
                                        Ib.

a politician is an arse upon
which everyone has sat except a man
        One Times One [1944], 10

mr u will not be missed
who as an anthologist
sold the many on the few
not excluding mr u   *Ib.* 11

pity this busy monster, manunkind,
not. Progress is a comfortable disease.
                                Ib. 14

    A world of made
is not a world of born   *Ib.*

We doctors know
a hopeless case if — listen: there's a
   hell
of a good universe next door; let's go
                    One Times One, 14

what if a much of a which of a wind
gives the truth to summer's lie.
                              Ib. 20

— when skies are hanged and oceans
   drowned,
the single secret will still be man   *Ib.*

all ignorance toboggans into know
and trudges up to ignorance again
                              Ib. 39

ALDOUS LEONARD HUXLEY
1894–1963

There are not enough *bon mots* in
existence to provide any industrious
conversationalist with a new stock for
every social occasion.
     Point Counter Point [1928], *ch. 7*

A bad book is as much of a labor to
write as a good one; it comes as sincerely from the author's soul.   *Ib. 13*

There is no substitute for talent. Industry and all the virtues are of no
avail.   *Ib.*

Parodies and caricatures are the most
penetrating of criticisms.   *Ib. 28*

Blood of the world, time staunchless
   flows;
The wound is mortal and is mine.
                            Seasons

Over her the swan shook slowly free
The folded glory of his wings, and
   made
A white-walled tent of soft and
   luminous shade.   *Leda*

A poor degenerate from the ape,
Whose hands are four, whose tail's a
   limb,
I contemplate my flaccid shape

And know I may not rival him
Save with my mind.
              First Philosopher's Song

NIKITA SERGEYEVICH KHRUSHCHEV
1894–1971

Cult of personality.
       *Special Report to Twentieth
       Party   Congress   [February
       1956]*

About the capitalist states, it doesn't
depend on you whether or not we exist.
If you don't like us, don't accept our
invitations, and don't invite us to come
and see you. Whether you like it or
not, history is on our side. We will bury
you.[1]

       *Reported statement at reception
       for Wladyslaw Gomulka at the
       Polish Embassy, Moscow [No-
       vember 18, 1956]*

Life is short; live it up.
       *Quoted by the New York Times
       Magazine [August 3, 1958]*

WESTBROOK PEGLER
1894–1969

The Era of Wonderful Nonsense.[2]
              Mr. Gump Himself

I am a reactionary, that is what I am,
and I would like to see a political reaction get off to a good start in our largest
city.
       *In the New York World-
       Telegram [October 31, 1941]*

I am a member of the rabble in good
standing.   *The Lynching Story*

[1] Neither the original nor the translation of
the last two sentences appeared in either *Pravda*
or the *New York Times* which carried the rest
of the text. Another possible translation of the
last sentence is "We shall be present at your
funeral," i.e., we shall outlive you; but the
above is the familiar version.
[2] The period of spending and speculation during the "Coolidge prosperity."

KENNETH CLAIBORNE ROYALL
1894–1971

A "brass hat" is an officer of at least one rank higher than you whom you don't like and who doesn't like you.[1]
> *Speech, Chamber of Commerce, Wilson, North Carolina [February 15, 1946]*

GENEVIEVE TAGGARD
1894–1948

Try tropic for your balm,
Try storm,
And after storm, calm.
Try snow of heaven, heavy, soft, and slow,
Brilliant and warm.
Nothing will help, and nothing do much harm.
> *Of the Properties of Nature for Healing an Illness, st. 1*

JAMES THURBER
1894–1961

Well, if I called the wrong number, why did you answer the 'phone?
> *Caption for cartoon (The New Yorker)*

I love the idea of there being two sexes, don't you?   *Ib.*

He knows all about art, but he doesn't know what he likes.   *Ib.*

It's a naive domestic Burgundy without any breeding, but I think you'll be amused by its presumption.   *Ib.*

The War Between Men and Women.
> *Series of cartoons*

Is Sex Necessary?
> *Title of book [1929] written with E. B. WHITE*

Let Your Mind Alone.
> *Title of book [1937]*

[1] Some big brass hat from the War Office. — JAMES HILTON, *Goodbye, Mr. Chips* [1934], *ch. 14*

Early to rise and early to bed makes a male healthy and wealthy and dead.
> *Fables for Our Time [1940]. The Shrike and the Chipmunks*

You might as well fall flat on your face as lean over too far backward.
> *Ib. The Bear Who Let It Alone*

Don't count your boobies until they're hatched.
> *Ib. The Unicorn in the Garden*

It is better to know some of the questions than all of the answers.
> *Saying*

MARK VAN DOREN
1894–1972

Wit is the only wall
Between us and the dark.   *Wit, st. 1*

He talked, and as he talked
  Wallpaper came alive;
Suddenly ghosts walked
  And four doors were five.
> *The Storyteller, st. 1*

Grass nibbling inward
Like green fire.
> *Former Barn Lot, st. 3*

NORBERT WIENER
1894–1964

We have decided to call the entire field of control and communication theory, whether in the machine or in the animal, by the name of Cybernetics, which we form from the Greek [for] steersman.   *Cybernetics [1948]*

This new development [automation] has unbounded possibilities for good and for evil.   *Ib.*

The independent scientist who is worth the slightest consideration as a scientist has a consecration which comes entirely from within himself: a vocation which demands the possibility of supreme self-sacrifice.
> *The Human Use of Human Beings [1950]*

DUKE OF WINDSOR [KING EDWARD VIII] 1894–1972

I have found it impossible to carry the heavy burden of responsibility and to discharge my duties as King as I would wish to do without the help and support of the woman I love.

Farewell broadcast after abdication [December 11, 1936]

RICHARD BUCKMINSTER FULLER 1895–

We must think of our whole economics in terms of a preventive pathology instead of a curative pathology.

Don't oppose forces; use them.

God is a verb,

Not a noun.

No More Secondhand God

Nature has . . . some sort of arithmetical-geometrical coordinate system, because nature has all kinds of models. What we experience of nature is in models, and all of nature's models are so beautiful. It struck me that nature's system must be a real beauty, because in chemistry we find that the associations are always in beautiful whole numbers — there are no fractions.

From In the Outlaw Area; profile by CALVIN TOMKINS, *The New Yorker [January 8, 1966]*

All nature's structuring, associating, and patterning must be based on triangles, because there is no structural validity otherwise. This is nature's basic structure, and it is modelable. **Ib.**

Either war is obsolete or men are. **Ib.**

ROBERT GRAVES 1895–

As you are woman, so be lovely:
As you are lovely, so be various,

Merciful as constant, constant as various,
So be mine, as I yours for ever.
Pygmalion to Galatea

Hate is a fear, and fear is rot
That cankers root and fruit alike:
Fight cleanly then, hate not, fear not,
Strike with no madness when you
  strike. *Hate Not, Fear Not*

"How is your trade, Aquarius,
This frosty night?"
"Complaints is many and various,
And my feet are cold," says Aquarius.
Star Talk, st. 5

I do not love the Sabbath,
  The soapsuds and the starch,
The troops of solemn people
  Who to Salvation march.
The Boy Out of Church

"Blonde or dark, sir?" says enough
Whether of women, drink, or snuff.
Blonde or Dark?

Goodbye to All That.
Title of autobiography [1929]

A well-chosen anthology is a complete dispensary of medicine for the more common mental disorders, and may be used as much for prevention as cure. *On English Poetry, 29*

The reason why the hairs stand on end, the eyes water, the throat is constricted, the skin crawls and a shiver runs down the spine when one writes or reads a true poem is that a true poem is necessarily an invocation of the White Goddess, or Muse, the Mother of All Living, the ancient power of fright and lust — the female spider or the queen bee whose embrace is death.[1]
The White Goddess [1948], ch. 1

ROBERT HILLYER 1895–1961

Ah, could we know what vogue will be
  tomorrow,
What plumes of Paradise our pens
  could borrow!
A Letter to Robert Frost [1937]

[1] See Sophocles, p. 83a.

Blest be thy name, O Vogue, that canst embalm
A minor poet with a potted palm;
Make me immortal in thy exegesis —
Or failing that, at least a Doctor's thesis.
                    A *Letter to Robert Frost*

BASIL HENRY LIDDELL HART
1895–1972

Keep strong, if possible. In any case, keep cool. Have unlimited patience. Never corner an opponent, and always assist him to save his face. Put yourself in his shoes — so as to see things through his eyes. Avoid self-righteousness like the devil — nothing so self-blinding.
          Deterrent or Defense [1960].
                    Advice to Statesmen

GROUCHO MARX
1895–1977

I never forget a face, but in your case I'll make an exception.   *Saying*

LEWIS MUMFORD
1895–

People have hesitated to call Whitman's poems poetry; it is useless to deny that they belong to sacred literature.   *The Golden Day* [1926], 5

Layer upon layer, past times preserve themselves in the city until life itself is finally threatened with suffocation; then, in sheer defense, modern man invents the museum.
          The Culture of Cities [1938]

EDWARD E. PARAMORE, JR.
1895–

Oh, the North Countree is a hard countree
That mothers a bloody brood;
And its icy arms hold hidden charms

For the greedy, the sinful and lewd.
And strong men rust, from the gold and the lust
That sears the Northland soul.
          The Ballad of Yukon Jake [1921]

Oh, tough as a steak was Yukon Jake —
Hard-boiled as a picnic egg.   *Ib.*

EDMUND WILSON
1895–1972

As for the aims and ideals of Marxism, there is one feature of them that is now rightly suspect. The taking-over by the state of the means of production and the dictatorship in the interests of the proletariat can by themselves never guarantee the happiness of anybody but the dictators themselves. Marx and Engles, coming out of authoritarian Germany, tended to imagine socialism in authoritarian terms; and Lenin and Trotsky after them, forced as they were to make a beginning among a people who had known nothing but autocracy, also emphasized this side of socialism and founded a dictatorship which perpetuated itself as an autocracy.
          To the Finland Station [1940].
                    Summary as of 1940

I have derived a good deal more benefit of the civilizing as well as of the inspirational kind [of tradition] from the admirable American bathroom than I have from the cathedrals of Europe. . . . I have had a good many more uplifting thoughts, creative and expansive visions — while soaking in comfortable baths or drying myself after bracing showers — in well-equipped American bathrooms than I have ever had in any cathedral.
          A Piece of My Mind [1956], *ch.* 4

I attribute such success as I have had to the use of the periodic sentence.
          An Interview with Edmund Wilson [1962]

JOHN RODERIGO DOS PASSOS
1896–1970

The chilly December day [1]
two shivering bicycle mechanics from
    Dayton, Ohio,[2]
first felt their homemade contraption
whittled out of hickory sticks,
gummed together with Arnstein's bicy-
    cle cement,
stretched with muslin they'd sewn on
    their sister's sewingmachine in
    their own backyard on Hawthorn
    Street in Dayton, Ohio,
soar into the air
above the dunes and the wide beach
at Kitty Hawk.
> *The Big Money* [1936]. *The*
> *Campers at Kitty Hawk*

EDMUND BLUNDEN
1896–

I am for the woods against the world,
But are the woods for me?
> *The Kiss*

Then is not Death at watch
    Within those secret waters?
What wants he but to catch
    Earth's heedless sons and daughters?
With but a crystal parapet
Between, he has his engines set.
> *The Midnight Skaters*

Dance on this ball-floor thin and wan,
    Use him as though you love him;[3]
Court him, elude him, reel and pass,
And let him hate you through the glass.
> *Ib.*

FRANCIS SCOTT FITZGERALD
1896–1940

The victor belongs to the spoils.
> *The Beautiful and Damned* [1922]

Then wear the gold hat, if that will
    move her;

---

[1] December 17, 1903.
[2] See Wilbur and Orville Wright, p. 910a.
[3] See Izaak Walton, p. 326b.

If you can bounce high, bounce for her
    too,
Till she cry "Lover, gold-hatted, high-
    bouncing lover,
I must have you!"
> *The Great Gatsby* [1925], *epigraph*

Everyone suspects himself of at least
one of the cardinal virtues, and this is
mine: I am one of the few honest people that I have ever known.
> *Ib. ch. 3*

Her voice is full of money. *Ib. 7*

Thirty — the promise of a decade of
loneliness, a thinning list of single men
to know, a thinning briefcase of enthusiasm, thinning hair. *Ib.*

They were careless people, Tom and
Daisy — they smashed up things and
creatures and then retreated back into
their money or their vast carelessness, or
whatever it was that kept them together, and let other people clean up
the mess they had made. *Ib. 9*

So we beat on, boats against the current, borne back ceaselessly into the
past. *Ib. last line*

One writes of scars healed, a loose
parallel to the pathology of the skin,
but there is no such thing in the life of
an individual. There are open wounds,
shrunk sometimes to the size of a pin-
prick, but wounds still. The marks of
suffering are more comparable to the
loss of a finger, or of the sight of an
eye. We may not miss them, either, for
one minute in a year, but if we should
there is nothing to be done about it.
> *Tender Is the Night* [1933],
> *bk. III, ch. 13*

The test of a first-rate intelligence is
the ability to hold two opposed ideas in
the mind at the same time, and still
retain the ability to function.
> *The Crack-up* [1936]

In a real dark night of the soul it is
always three o'clock in the morning.[1]
> *Ib.*

---

[1] See Napoleon, p. 504b, and note.

It was about then [1920] that I wrote a line which certain people will not let me forget: "She was a faded but still lovely woman of twenty-seven."

Early Success [1937]

Egyptian Proverb: The worst things:
To be in bed and sleep not,
To want for one who comes not,
To try to please and please not.

Notebooks [1]

Show me a hero and I will write you a tragedy.   *Ib.*

Draw your chair up close to the edge of the precipice and I'll tell you a story.   *Ib.*

It is in the thirties that we want friends. In the forties we know they won't save us any more than love did.   *Ib.*

The hangover became a part of the day as well allowed-for as the Spanish siesta.   *My Lost City* [1]

All good writing is swimming under water and holding your breath.

Undated letter

HAROLD N. GILBERT
1896–1966

Keep 'em flying.
Slogan of the Air Forces, poster caption, World War II

GRAHAM LEE HEMMINGER
1896–1949

Tobacco is a dirty weed. I like it.
It satisfies no normal need. I like it.
It makes you thin, it makes you lean,
It takes the hair right off your bean.[2]

[1] In *The Crack-up,* edited by Edmund Wilson [1945].
[2] Caution: Cigarette smoking may be hazardous to your health. — *Warning on cigarette packages, required by federal legislation* [July 27, 1965]

It's the worst darn stuff I've ever seen. I like it.   *Tobacco* [1] [1915]

JOE JACOBS
1896–1940

We was robbed!
After the heavyweight title fight between Max Schmeling and Jack Sharkey [June 21, 1932], Jacobs, Schmeling's manager, shouted into the microphone this protest against the decision.

I should of stood in bed.
After leaving a sickbed to attend the World's Series in Detroit [October 1935] and betting on the loser

ROBERT EMMET SHERWOOD
1896–1955

The trouble with me is, I belong to a vanishing race. I'm one of the intellectuals.   *The Petrified Forest* [1934]

Poor, dear God. Playing Idiot's Delight. The game that never means anything, and never ends.

Idiot's Delight [1936]

LUTHER W. YOUNGDAHL
1896–

When public excitement runs high as to alien ideologies, is the time when we must be particularly alert not to impair the ancient landmarks set up in the Bill of Rights.
United States v. Lattimore, 112 F. Supp. 507, 518 [May 2, 1953]

JOSEPH AUSLANDER
1897–1965

So there are no more words and all is ended;

[1] See Anonymous, p. 1085b.

The timbrel is stilled, the clarion laid
away;
And Love with streaming hair goes un-
attended
Back to the loneliness of yesterday.
So There Are No More Words
[1924]

LOUISE BOGAN
1897–1970

I burned my life that I might find
A passion wholly of the mind,
Thought divorced from eye and bone,
Ecstasy come to breath alone.
The Alchemist

I had found unmysterious flesh —
Not the mind's avid substance — still
Passionate beyond the will. *Ib.*

Women have no wilderness in them,
They are provident instead,
Content in the tight hot cell of their
hearts
To eat dusty bread. *Women*

BERNARD DE VOTO
1897–1955

New England is a finished place. Its
destiny is that of Florence or Venice,
not Milan, while the American empire
careens onward toward its unpredicted
end. . . . It is the first American section to be finished, to achieve stability
in the conditions of its life. It is the
first old civilization, the first permanent
civilization in America.
*New England: There She Stands.
In Harper's Magazine* [March
1932]

The West begins where the average
annual rainfall drops below twenty
inches. When you reach the line which
marks that drop — for convenience, the
one hundredth meridian — you have
reached the West.
*The Plundered Province. In
Harper's Magazine* [August
1934]

Pessimism is only the name that men
of weak nerves give to wisdom.
*Mark Twain: The Ink of His-
tory. Address, University of Missouri* [December 1935]

Art is the terms of an armistice
signed with fate.
Mark Twain at Work [1942]

The achieved West had given the
United States something that no people
had ever had before, an internal, domestic empire.
The Year of Decision [1943]

Between the amateur and the professional . . . there is a difference not
only in degree but in kind. The skillful
man is, within the function of his skill,
a different integration, a different nervous and muscular and psychological
organization. . . . A tennis player or a
watchmaker or an airplane pilot is an
automatism but he is also criticism and
wisdom.
Across the Wide Missouri [1947]

You can no more keep a martini in
the refrigerator than you can keep a kiss
there. The proper union of gin and vermouth is a great and sudden glory; it is
one of the happiest marriages on earth
and one of the shortest-lived.
The Hour [1951]

The water of life was given to us to
make us see for a while that we are
more nearly men and women, more
nearly kind and gentle and generous,
pleasanter and stronger, than without
its vision there is any evidence we are.
Ib.

One of the facts which define the
United States is that its national and its
imperial boundaries are the same. Another is that it is a political unit which
occupies a remarkably coherent geographical unit of continental extent.
The Course of Empire
[1952], *preface*

History abhors determinism but cannot tolerate chance. *Ib.*

a   DE VOTO — FAULKNER   *b*
The dawn of knowledge is usually the false dawn.

The Course of Empire, ch. 2

SIR ANTHONY EDEN
1897–

Every succeeding scientific discovery makes greater nonsense of old-time conceptions of sovereignty.

Speech, House of Commons
[November 22, 1945]

WILLIAM FAULKNER
1897–1962

Time is dead as long as it is being clicked off by little wheels; only when the clock stops does time come to life.

The Sound and the Fury
[1929], June Second 1910

I've seed de first en de last. . . . I seed de beginnin, en now I sees de endin.   *Ib. April Eighth 1928*

Because no battle is ever won he said. They are not even fought. The field only reveals to man his own folly and despair, and victory is an illusion of philosophers and fools.   *Ib.*

They [the Negroes] will endure. They are better than we are. Stronger than we are. Their vices are vices aped from white men or that white men and bondage have taught them: improvidence and intemperance and evasion — not laziness: evasion: of what white men had set them to, not for their aggrandizement or even comfort but his own. . . . And their virtues. . . . Endurance . . . and pity and tolerance and forbearance and fidelity and love of children . . . whether their own or not or black or not.

The Bear [1932], *pt. IV*

Poor man. Poor mankind.

Light in August [1932], *ch.* 4

Too much happens. . . . Man performs, engenders, so much more than he can or should have to bear. That's

how he finds that he can bear anything. . . . That's what's so terrible.

Light in August, ch. 13

My, my. A body does get around. Here we aint been coming from Alabama but two months, and now it's already Tennessee.   *Ib.* 21

It's not when you realize that nothing can help you — religion, pride, anything — it's when you realize that you don't need any aid.   *Ib.*

Gettysburg.[1] . . . You cant understand it. You would have to be born there.

Absalom, Absalom! [1936], *ch.* 9

Why do you hate the South? I dont hate it. . . . I dont hate it. . . . *I dont hate it* he thought, panting in the cold air, the iron New England dark; *I dont. I dont! I dont hate it! I dont hate it!*   *Ib.*

He [the writer] must teach himself that the basest of all things is to be afraid; and, teaching himself that, forget it forever, leaving no room in his workshop for anything but the old verities and truths of the heart, the old universal truths lacking which any story is ephemeral and doomed — love and honor and pity and pride and compassion and sacrifice.

Speech upon receiving the Nobel
Prize [December 10, 1950]

I decline to accept the end of man.
          Ib.

I believe that man will not merely endure: he will prevail.   *Ib.*

It is the writer's privilege to help man endure by lifting his heart.   *Ib.*

JEFFERSON, YOKNAPATAWPHA CO., Mississippi. Area, 2400 Square Miles. Population, Whites, 6298; Negroes, 9313. WILLIAM FAULKNER, Sole Owner & Proprietor.

Caption for map drawn by
author [1951]

[1] Representing, in context, the South.

1039

The writer's only responsibility is to his art. He will be completely ruthless if he is a good one. He has a dream. It anguishes him so much he must get rid of it. He has no peace until then. Everything goes by the board: honor, pride, decency, security, happiness, all, to get the book written. If a writer has to rob his mother, he will not hesitate; the "Ode on a Grecian Urn" is worth any number of old ladies.

> *From an interview with* FAULK-NER [*New York City*, 1956] *by* JEAN STEIN. *From Writers at Work: The Paris Review Interviews* [1959]

Really the writer doesn't want success. . . . He knows he has a short span of life, that the day will come when he must pass through the wall of oblivion, and he wants to leave a scratch on that wall — Kilroy was here [1] — that somebody a hundred, or a thousand years later will see.

> *Faulkner in the University* [1959], *Session 8*

PAUL JOSEPH GOEBBELS
1897–1945

We can do without butter, but, despite all our love of peace, not without arms. One cannot shoot with butter but with guns.[2]

> *Address, Berlin* [*January 17*, 1936]

DAVID McCORD
1897–

A handful of sand is an anthology of the universe.

> *Once and for All* [1929], *introduction*

Call home the child, whose credulous first hours
Burn at the heart of living, and surprise
The better reason with unbidden truth.

> *A Bucket of Bees* [1934]

[1] See Anonymous, p. 1103b.
[2] Probably the origin of the slogan "Guns or butter." See Goering, p. 1026b.

March is outside the door
Flaming some old desire
As man turns uneasily from his fire.

> *The Crows* [1934]

By and by
God caught his eye.

> *Epitaphs: The Waiter*

Still for us where Cottons mather
In the spring the Willas cather
As of yore.

> *And What's More: On Stopping at a New Hampshire Inn* [1941]

The decent docent doesn't doze;
He teaches standing on his toes.
His student dassn't doze and does,
And that's what teaching is and was.

> *What Cheer* [1945]

But man must light for man
The fires no other can,
And find in his own eye
Where the strange crossroads lie.

> *Communion* [1950]

Life is the garment we continually alter, but which never seems to fit.

> *Whereas to Mr. Franklin* [1956]

Your life will be rich for others only as it is rich for you.

> *On the Frontiers of Understanding* [1959]

ERICH MARIA REMARQUE
1897–1970

Monotonously the lorries sway, monotously come the calls, monotonously falls the rain. It falls on our heads and on the heads of the dead up the line, on the body of the little recruit with the wound that is so much too big for his hip; it falls on Kemmerich's grave; it falls in our hearts.

> *All Quiet on the Western Front* [1] [1929]

[1] Im Westen Nichts Neues.

THORNTON NIVEN WILDER
1897–

Even memory is not necessary for love. There is a land of the living and a land of the dead and the bridge is love, the only survival, the only meaning.
The Bridge of San Luis Rey [1927], *last lines*

A man looks pretty small at a wedding, George. All those good women standing shoulder to shoulder, making sure that the knot's tied in a mighty public way.   *Our Town* [1938]

The dead don't stay interested in us living people for very long. Gradually, gradually, they let go hold of the earth . . . and the ambitions they had . . . and the pleasures they had . . . and the things they suffered . . . and the people they loved. They get weaned away from earth — that's the way I put it, weaned away.   *Ib.*

That's what it was to be alive. To move about in a cloud of ignorance; to go up and down trampling on the feelings of those about you. To spend and waste time as though you had a million years. To be always at the mercy of one self-centered passion, or another. Now you know — that's the happy existence you wanted to go back to.   *Ib.*

I hold that we cannot be said to be aware of our minds save under responsibility.   *The Ides of March* [1948]

STEPHEN VINCENT BENÉT
1898–1943

I died in my boots like a pioneer
With the whole wide sky above me.
The Ballad of William Sycamore

He could fiddle all the bugs off a sweet potato vine.
The Mountain Whippoorwill
[1923], *st. 22*

Oh, Georgia booze is mighty fine booze,

The best yuh ever poured yuh,
But it eats the soles right offen yore shoes,
For Hell's broke loose in Georgia.
The Mountain Whippoorwill,
st. 48

I have fallen in love with American names,
The sharp names that never get fat,
The snakeskin titles of mining claims,
The plumed war bonnet of Medicine Hat,
Tucson and Deadwood and Lost Mule Flat.
American Names [1927], *st. 1*

Bury my heart at Wounded Knee.
Ib. st. 7

American Muse, whose strong and diverse heart
So many men have tried to understand
But only made it smaller with their art,
Because you are as various as your land.
John Brown's Body [1928],
invocation

And Thames and all the rivers of the kings
Ran into Mississippi and were drowned.
Ib.

Broad-streeted Richmond . . .
The trees in the streets are old trees used to living with people,
Family trees that remember your grandfather's name.
Ib. bk. IV

Stonewall Jackson, wrapped in his beard and his silence.   *Ib.*

A great victor, in defeat as great,
No more, no less, always himself in both.   *Ib.*

The ant finds kingdoms in a foot of ground.   *Ib.*

But all of them are sure they know God's will.
I am the only man who does not know it.   *Ib. V*

Sherman's buzzin' along to de sea,
Like Moses ridin' on a bumblebee.
Ib. VIII

We thought we were done with these things but we were wrong.
We thought, because we had power, we had wisdom.
Litany for Dictatorships [1936]

Our fathers and ourselves sowed dragon's teeth.
Our children know and suffer the armed men.   **Ib.**

If two New Hampshiremen aren't a match for the devil, we might as well give the country back to the Indians.
The Devil and Daniel Webster [1936]

Even the damned may salute the eloquence of Mr. Webster.   **Ib.**

They were half of the first families in Virginia.
Well, where do you start, when you start counting F.F.V.s?
Western Star [1943], bk. I

HORACE GREGORY
1898–

My boyhood saw
Greek islands floating over Harvard Square.[1]
Chorus for Survival [1935], 14

CLIVE STAPLES LEWIS
1898–1963

The safest road to Hell is the gradual one — the gentle slope, soft underfoot, without sudden turnings, without milestones, without signposts.
The Screwtape Letters [1941], 12

The Future is something which everyone reaches at the rate of sixty minutes an hour, whatever he does, whoever he is.   *Ib.* 25

The long, dull, monotonous years of middle-aged prosperity or middle-aged adversity are excellent campaigning weather [for the Devil].   *Ib.* 28

[1] The speaker in the poem is Emerson.

ANTHONY CLEMENT McAULIFFE
1898–

Nuts!
Reply [December 23, 1944] *to a German demand for surrender of the* 101st *Airborne Division, which had been trapped for seven days at Bastogne*

DONALD CULROSS PEATTIE
1898–1964

The time to hear bird music is between four and six in the morning. Seven o'clock is not too late, but by eight the fine rapture is over, due, I suspect, to the contentment of the inner man that comes with breakfast; a poet should always be hungry or have a lost love.
An Almanac for Moderns [1935]. *April* 22

AMELIA EARHART PUTNAM
1898–1937

Courage is the price that life exacts for granting peace.
The soul that knows it not, knows no release
From little things;
Knows not the livid loneliness of fear,
Nor mountain heights where bitter joy can hear
The sound of wings.   *Courage*

DOROTHY E. REID

A goosegirl ermined is a goosegirl still
And geese will gabble everywhere she goes.   *Not in Andersen*

YOKOMITSU RIICHI[1]
1898–1947

Pleasure — indeed there is nothing to compare with the gaiety and trans-

[1] From *Modern Japanese Literature*, edited by Donald Keene [1960]

parency of the pleasure before death.
The heart begins to choke from its extremity of pleasure, as if it were licking
some luscious piece of fruit.
Jikan [Time] [1931]

NOEL COWARD
1899–1973

Mad dogs and Englishmen go out in
the midday sun;
The Japanese don't care to, the Chi-
nese wouldn't dare to;
Hindus and Argentines sleep firmly
from twelve to one,
But Englishmen detest a siesta.
Mad Dogs and Englishmen

Dance, dance, dance, little lady,
Life is fleeting
To the rhythm beating
In your mind.
*Dance, Dance, Dance, Little
Lady [1928]*

I'll see you again,
Whenever spring breaks through again.
Bittersweet [1929], act I sc. 1

Certain women should be struck
regularly, like gongs.
Private Lives [1930], act III

I've got those weary Twentieth-Century Blues.
Cavalcade [1931], pt. 3, sc. 2

Don't Let's be Beastly to the Germans.　*Title of song*

HART CRANE
1899–1932

And yet this great wink of eternity,
Of rimless floods, unfettered leewardings.　*Voyages [1926], II*

Adagios of islands, O my Prodigal.
Ib.

Bind us in time, O seasons clear, and
awe.
O minstrel galleons of Carib fire,
Bequeath us to no earthly shore until
Is answered in the vortex of our grave

The seal's wide spindrift gaze toward
paradise.　*Voyages, II*

It was a kind and northern face
That mingled in such exile guise
The everlasting eyes of Pierrot
And, of Gargantua, the laughter.
*Praise for an Urn: In Memoriam
Ernest Nelson [1926]*

Damp tonnage and alluvial march of
days . . .
Tortured with history, its one will —
flow.
*The Bridge [1930]. The River
(Mississippi)*

The swift red flesh, a winter king —
Who squired the glacier woman down
the sky?
She ran the neighing canyons all the
spring;
She spouted arms; she rose with maize
— to die.　*Ib. The Dance*

Bunched in mutual glee
The bearings glint — O murmurless
and shined
In oilrinsed circles of blind ecstasy!
Ib. Power: Cape Hatteras

And why do I often meet your visage
here,
Your eyes like agate lanterns — on and
on
Below the toothpaste and the dandruff
ads?
And did their riding eyes right through
your side,
And did their eyes like unwashed plat-
ters ride?
And Death, aloft — gigantically down [1]
Probing through you toward me, O
evermore!
Ib. The Tunnel

Compass, quadrant and sextant con-
trive
No farther tides . . . High in the
azure steeps
Monody shall not wake the mariner.
This fabulous shadow only the sea
keeps.
At Melville's Tomb [1933]

[1] See Poe, p. 642a.

ERNEST HEMINGWAY
1899–1961

You and me, we've made a separate peace.

> *In Our Time* [1924]. *A Very Short Story*

It makes one feel rather good deciding not to be a bitch. . . . It's sort of what we have instead of God.

> *The Sun Also Rises* [1926], *ch. 19*

"Oh, Jake," Brett said, "we could have had such a damned good time together." . . .

"Yes," I said. "Isn't it pretty to think so?"   *Ib. last lines*

I was always embarrassed by the words sacred, glorious, and sacrifice and the expression in vain. We had heard them, sometimes standing in the rain almost out of earshot, so that only the shouted words came through . . . now for a long time, and I had seen nothing sacred, and the things that were glorious had no glory and the sacrifices were like the stockyards at Chicago if nothing was done with the meat except to bury it . . . Abstract words such as glory, honor, courage, or hallow were obscene.

> *A Farewell to Arms* [1929], *ch. 27*

If people bring so much courage to this world the world has to kill them to break them, so of course it kills them. The world breaks everyone and afterward many are strong at the broken places. But those that will not break it kills. It kills the very good and the very gentle and the very brave impartially. If you are none of these you can be sure that it will kill you too but there will be no special hurry.   *Ib. 34*

That was what you did. You died. You did not know what it was about. You never had time to learn. They threw you in and told you the rules and the first time they caught you off base they killed you.   *Ib. 41*

It was like saying goodbye to a statue. After a while I went out and left the hospital and walked back to the hotel in the rain.

> *A Farewell to Arms, ch. 27*

Grace under pressure.

> *Definition of "guts" in The New Yorker* [November 30, 1929]

I know only that what is moral is what you feel good after and what is immoral is what you feel bad after.

> *Death in the Afternoon* [1932], *ch. 1*

I was trying to write then and I found the greatest difficulty, aside from knowing truly what you really felt, rather than what you were supposed to feel, and had been taught to feel, was to put down what really happened in action; what the actual things were which produced the emotion that you experienced . . . the real thing, the sequence of motion and fact which made the emotion and which would be as valid in a year or in ten years or, with luck and if you stated it purely enough, always.   *Ib.*

If he wrote it he could get rid of it. He had gotten rid of many things by writing them.

> *Winner Take Nothing* [1933]. *Fathers and Sons*

All good books are alike in that they are truer than if they had really happened and after you are finished reading one you will feel that all that happened to you and afterwards it all belongs to you: the good and the bad, the ecstasy, the remorse and sorrow, the people and the places and how the weather was. If you can get so that you can give that to people, then you are a writer.

> *Old Newsman Writes* [*Esquire, December 1934*]

All modern American literature comes from one book by Mark Twain called *Huckleberry Finn.*

> *Green Hills of Africa* [1935], *ch. 1*

The rich were dull and they drank too much. . . . He remembered poor Julian [1] and his romantic awe of them and how he had started a story once that began, "The very rich are different from you and me." And how someone [2] had said to Julian, "Yes, they have more money."

The Snows of Kilimanjaro
[1936]

Kilimanjaro is a snow-covered mountain 19,710 feet high, and is said to be the highest mountain in Africa. Its western summit is called the Masai "Ngàje Ngài," the House of God. Close to the western summit there is the dried and frozen carcass of a leopard. No one has explained what the leopard was seeking at that altitude.

Ib. epigraph

Ezra [Pound] was right half the time, and when he was wrong, he was so wrong you were never in any doubt about it. Gertrude [Stein] was always right.

To John Peale Bishop; quoted in his Homage to Hemingway, New Republic [November 11, 1936]

No matter how a man alone ain't got no bloody f — ing chance.

To Have and Have Not [1937], *ch. 23*

If we win here we will win everywhere. The world is a fine place and worth the fighting for and I hate very much to leave it.

For Whom the Bell Tolls
[1940], *ch. 43*

Cowardice, as distinguished from panic, is almost always simply a lack of ability to suspend the functioning of the imagination.

Men at War [1942], *introduction*

Time is the least thing we have of.

*From The New Yorker,
Profile by* LILLIAN ROSS
[*May 13, 1950*] [3]

[1] F. Scott Fitzgerald.
[2] Hemingway.
[3] Reprinted in book form, *Portrait of Hemingway* [1961].

A man can be destroyed but not defeated.

The Old Man and the Sea [1952]

If it is any use to know it, I always try to write on the principle of the iceberg. There is seven-eighths of it under water for every part that shows. Anything you know you can eliminate and it only strengthens your iceberg. It is the part that doesn't show. If a writer omits something because he does not know it then there is a hole in the story.

Interview, Paris Review
[*Spring 1958*]

If you are lucky enough to have lived in Paris as a young man, then wherever you go for the rest of your life, it stays with you, for Paris is a movable feast.

A Movable Feast [1964], *epigraph*

ROBERT MAYNARD HUTCHINS
1899–

Democracy . . . is the only form of government that is founded on the dignity of man, not the dignity of some men, of rich men, of educated men or of white men, but of all men. Its sanction is not the sanction of force, but the sanction of human nature. Equality and justice, the two great distinguishing characteristics of democracy, follow inevitably from the conception of men, all men, as rational and spiritual beings.

Democracy and Human Nature

The death of democracy is not likely to be an assassination from ambush. It will be a slow extinction from apathy, indifference, and undernourishment.

Great Books [1954]

CHARLES W. MORTON
1899–1967

It was around two decades ago, in the city room of the Boston *Evening Transcript*, that I first became aware of the elongated-yellow-fruit school of writing. The phrase turned up in a story

. . . about some fugitive monkeys and the efforts of police to recapture them by using bananas as bait.
> *The Elongated Yellow Fruit*
> [1954]

VLADIMIR NABOKOV
1899–1977

Lolita, light of my life, fire of my loins. My sin, my soul. Lo-lee-ta.
> *Lolita* [1955], *pt. I, ch. 1*

LELAND STOWE
1899–

An American will tinker with anything he can put his hands on. But how rarely can he be persuaded to tinker with an abstract idea.
> *They Shall Not Sleep* [1944]

E. B. WHITE[1]
1899–

All poets who, when reading from their own works, experience a choked feeling, are major. For that matter, all poets who read from their own works are major, whether they choke or not.
> *How to Tell a Major Poet from a Minor Poet*

"It's broccoli, dear."
"I say it's spinach, and I say the hell with it."
> *Caption for cartoon by Carl Rose in The New Yorker*

Commuter — one who spends his life
In riding to and from his wife;
A man who shaves and takes a train
And then rides back to shave again.
> *Commuter*

It is easier for a man to be loyal to his club than to his planet; the bylaws are shorter, and he is personally acquainted with the other members.
> *One Man's Meat* [1944]

The future . . . seems to me no unified dream but a mince pie, long in the baking, never quite done. *Ib.*

[1] See Thoreau, *Walden*, footnote, p. 682a.
See James Thurber, p. 1033a.

Democracy is the recurrent suspicion that more than half of the people are right more than half of the time.
> *The Wild Flag. In The New Yorker* [July 3, 1943]

When Mrs. Frederick C. Little's second son was born, everybody noticed that he was not much bigger than a mouse. The truth of the matter was, the baby looked very much like a mouse in every way. He was only two inches high; and he had a mouse's sharp nose, a mouse's tail, a mouse's whiskers, and the pleasant, shy manner of a mouse. Before he was many days old he was not only looking like a mouse but acting like one, too — wearing a gray hat and carrying a small cane.
> *Stuart Little* [1945], *ch. 1*

"My name is Margalo," said the bird, softly, in a musical voice. "I come from fields once tall with wheat, from pastures deep in fern and thistle; I come from vales of meadowsweet, and I love to whistle." *Ib. 8*

It was the best place to be, thought Wilbur, this warm delicious cellar, with the garrulous geese, the changing seasons, the heat of the sun, the passage of swallows, the nearness of rats, the sameness of sheep, the love of spiders, the smell of manure, and the glory of everything.
> *Charlotte's Web* [1952], *ch. 22*

LOUIS ARMSTRONG
1900–1971

If you have to ask what jazz is, you'll never know. *Saying*

HUMPHREY BOGART
1900–1957

Tennis, anyone?
> *His sole line in his first play*

DENIS WILLIAM BROGAN
1900–

The Englishman is interested in contemporary America. It evokes no response to tell him that Boston is like an English town. He has seen quite enough English towns and would rather hear about New York or Chicago, which are not like English towns.

The English People [1943]

American social fences have to be continually repaired; in England they are like wild hedges; they grow if left alone. *Ib.*

A people that has licked a more formidable enemy than Germany or Japan, primitive North America . . . a country whose national motto has been "root, hog, or die."

The American Character [1944]

Any well-established village in New England or the northern Middle West could afford a town drunkard, a town atheist, and a few Democrats. *Ib.*

JOHN MASON BROWN
1900–1969

Brutus seemed no more than a resounding set of vocal cords wrapped up in a toga. *Two on the Aisle* [1938]

To many people dramatic criticism must seem like an attempt to tattoo soap bubbles.

Broadway in Review [1940]

Part of the American myth is that people who are handed the skin of a dead sheep at graduation time think that it will keep their minds alive forever. *Remark*

HERBERT BUTTERFIELD
1900–

It [the scientific revolution] outshines everything since the rise of Christianity and reduces the Renaissance and Reformation to the rank of mere episodes, mere internal displacements, within the system of medieval Christendom. . . . It looms so large as the real origin of the modern world and of the modern mentality that our cus-

tomary periodization of European history has become an anachronism and an encumbrance.

The Origins of Modern Science
[1949]

ELIZABETH, QUEEN MOTHER OF ENGLAND
1900–

The children will not leave unless I do. I shall not leave unless their father does, and the King will not leave the country in any circumstances whatever.

Reported reply as to whether the Princesses would leave England after the bombing of Buckingham Palace [1940]

JAMES HILTON
1900–1954

Anno domini — that's the most fatal complaint of all in the end.

Goodbye, Mr. Chips [1934], *ch. 1*

The austere serenity of Shangri-La. Its forsaken courts and pale pavilions shimmered in repose from which all the fret of existence had ebbed away, leaving a hush as if moments hardly dared to pass. *Lost Horizon* [1933], *ch. 5*

When the High Lama asked him whether Shangri-La was not unique in his experience, and if the Western world could offer anything in the least like it, he answered with a smile: "Well, yes — to be quite frank it reminds me very slightly of Oxford." *Ib. 9*

Memory put a red star in the corner like pictures in a gallery that get sold.

Time and Time Again [1953]

If you forgive people enough you belong to them, and they to you, whether either person likes it or not — squatter's rights of the heart. *Ib.*

MARTHA OSTENSO
1900–1963

Pity the Unicorn,
Pity the Hippogriff,

Souls that were never born
Out of the land of If!
The Unicorn and the Hippogriff,
st. 1

LEROY [SATCHEL] PAIGE
c. 1900–

Don't look back. Something may be gaining on you.
How to Keep Young [1953]

ERNIE PYLE
1900–1945

I write from the worm's-eye point of view.   *Here Is Your War* [1943]

If you go long enough without a bath even the fleas will let you alone.   *Ib.*

ANTOINE DE
SAINT-EXUPÉRY
1900–1944

Although human life is priceless, we always act as if something had an even greater price than life. . . . But what is that something?   *Vol de Nuit*

Freedom and constraint are two aspects of the same necessity which is to be what one is and no other.
La Citadelle

ADLAI STEVENSON
1900–1965

More important than winning the election, is governing the nation. That is the test of a political party — the acid, final test.
Speech accepting Democratic
presidential nomination [July 26, 1952]

Let's talk sense to the American people. Let's tell them the truth, that there are no gains without pains.   *Ib.*

What do we mean by patriotism in the context of our times? . . . A patriotism that puts country ahead of self; a patriotism which is not short,

frenzied outbursts of emotion, but the tranquil and steady dedication of a lifetime. There are words that are easy to utter, but this is a mighty assignment. For it is often easier to fight for principles than to live up to them.[1]
Speech, New York City
[*August 27, 1952*]

When an American says that he loves his country, he means not only that he loves the New England hills, the prairies glistening in the sun, the wide and rising plains, the great mountains, and the sea. He means that he loves an inner air, an inner light in which freedom lives and in which a man can draw the breath of self-respect.
Ib.

A hungry man is not a free man.[2]
Speech, Kasson, Minnesota
[*September 6, 1952*]

A wise man does not try to hurry history.
Speech, San Francisco
[*September 9, 1952*]

The time to stop a revolution is at the beginning, not the end.   *Ib.*

Your public servants serve you right.
Speech, Los Angeles [*September 11, 1952*]

This is the first time I have ever heard of a party going into battle under the slogan, "Throw the rascals in."
Speech, Phoenix, Arizona,
[*September 12, 1952*]

Those who corrupt the public mind are just as evil as those who steal from the public purse.
Speech, Albuquerque, New Mexico [*September 12, 1952*]

Nature is neutral. Man has wrested from nature the power to make the world a desert or to make the deserts bloom. There is no evil in the atom; only in men's souls.[3]
Speech, Hartford, Connecticut
[*September 18, 1952*]

[1] See Thackeray, p. 660a.
[2] See Cato, 107a, and note.
[3] See J. Robert Oppenheimer, p. 1055a-b.

Government [in a democracy] cannot be stronger or more tough-minded than its people. It cannot be more inflexibly committed to the task than they. It cannot be wiser than the people.

Speech, Chicago [September 29, 1952]

As citizens of this democracy, you are the rulers and the ruled, the lawgivers and the law-abiding, the beginning and the end. *Ib.*

Africa for the Africans means Africa for the Africans and not Africa as a hunting ground for alien ambitions.

Speech, United Nations [February 18, 1961]

If total isolationism is no answer, total interventionism is no answer, either. In fact, the clear, quick, definable, measurable answers are ruled out. In this twilight of power, there is no quick path to a convenient light switch.[1]

Speech, Harvard University [June 17, 1965]

The art of government has grown from its seeds in the tiny city-states of Greece to become the political mode of half the world. So let us dream of a world in which all states, great and small, work together for the peaceful flowering of the republic of man. *Ib.*

VIOLET ALLEYN STOREY
1900–

I have a small-town soul.
It makes me want to know
Wee, unimportant things
About the folks that go
Past on swift journeyings. *Ironical*

WILLIAM LINDSAY WHITE
1900–1973

They Were Expendable.
Title of book [1942]

THOMAS WOLFE
1900–1938

A stone, a leaf, an unfound door.
Look Homeward, Angel! [1] [1929],
foreword

Which of us has known his brother? Which of us has looked into his father's heart? Which of us has not remained forever prison-pent? Which of us is not forever a stranger and alone? *Ib.*

O lost, and by the wind grieved, ghost, come back again. *Ib.*

Most of the time we think we're sick, it's all in the mind. *Ib. pt. I, ch. 1*

Making the world safe for hypocrisy.
Ib. III, 36

The young men of this land are not, as they are often called, a "lost" race — they are a race that never yet has been discovered. And the whole secret, power, and knowledge of their own discovery is locked within them — they know it, feel it, have the whole thing in them — and they cannot utter it.

The Web and the Rock [1939], ch. 13

If a man has a talent and cannot use it, he has failed. If he has a talent and uses only half of it, he has partly failed. If he has a talent and learns somehow to use the whole of it, he has gloriously succeeded, and won a satisfaction and a triumph few men ever know. *Ib. 30*

You Can't Go Home Again.
Title of novel [1940]

ROY CAMPBELL
1901–1957

You praise the firm restraint with
which they write —
I'm with you there, of course.
They use the snaffle and the curb all
right,
But where's the bloody horse?
On Some South African Novelists

---

[1] See John F. Kennedy, p. 1073a.

[1] See Milton, p. 339a.

The sap is the music, the stem is the
flute,
And the leaves are the wings of the
seraph I shape
Who dances, who springs in a golden
escape,
Out of the dust and the drought of the
plain,
To sing with the silver hosannas of
rain.
The Palm [1928]

JAMES MICHAEL
KIERAN, JR.
1901–1952

The brains trust.
*In conversation with Franklin
D. Roosevelt [August 1932], re-
ferring to the professors and
other such advisers who served
Roosevelt in his first campaign.
The phrase later became "brain
trust."*

LINUS CARL PAULING
1901–

Science is the search for truth — it is
not a game in which one tries to beat
his opponent, to do harm to others.
We need to have the spirit of science in
international affairs, to make the conduct of international affairs the effort to
find the right solution, the just solution
of international problems, not the effort
by each nation to get the better of
other nations, to do harm to them
when it is possible.
No More War! [1958]

CORNELIA OTIS
SKINNER
1901–

Woman's virtue is man's greatest invention. *Paris '90*

THOMAS EDMUND
DEWEY
1902–1971

That's why it's time for a change.[1]
*Campaign speech, San Francisco
[September 21, 1944]*

STELLA GIBBONS
1902–

The farm was crouched on a bleak
hillside, whence its fields, fanged with
flints, dropped steeply to the village of
Howling a mile away.
Cold Comfort Farm [1932],
ch. 3

Something nasty in the woodshed.
Ib. 8

WOLCOTT GIBBS
1902–1958

Backward ran sentences until reeled
the mind.[2]
More in Sorrow [1958]. *Time
. . . Fortune . . . Life . . .
Luce*

Where it will all end, knows God!
Ib.

Generally speaking, the American
theater is the aspirin of the middle
classes.[3]
*Ib. Shakespeare, Here's Your
Hat*

LANGSTON HUGHES
1902–1967

I swear to the Lord
I still can't see
Why Democracy means
Everybody but me.
The Black Man Speaks

I am the people, humble, hungry,
mean —
Hungry yet today despite the dream.
Beaten yet today — O Pioneers![4]
I am the man who never got ahead,

[1] The phrase was used extensively in the
campaigns of 1944, 1948, and 1952.
[2] See Winston Churchill, p. 925a.
[3] See Marx, p. 686b.
[4] See Whitman, p. 701b.

The poorest worker bartered through the years.
> *Let America Be America Again* [1938]

O, let America be America again —
The land that never has been yet —
And yet must be.   *Ib.*

Negro blood is sure powerful — because just *one* drop of black blood makes a colored man. *One* drop — you are a Negro! . . . Black is powerful.
> *Simple Takes a Wife* [1953]

CHARLES AUGUSTUS LINDBERGH[1]

1902–

We (that's my ship and I) took off rather suddenly. We had a report somewhere around 4 o'clock in the afternoon before that the weather would be fine, so we thought we would try it.
> *Lindbergh's Own Story. In the New York Times* [May 23, 1927]

I saw a fleet of fishing boats. . . . I flew down almost touching the craft and yelled at them, asking if I was on the right road to Ireland.
They just stared. Maybe they didn't hear me. Maybe I didn't hear them. Or maybe they thought I was just a crazy fool. An hour later I saw land.   *Ib.*

OGDEN NASH

(1902–1971)

O money, money, money, I'm not
  necessarily one of those who think
  thee holy,
But I often stop to wonder how thou
  canst go out so fast when thou
  comest in so slowly.
> *Hymn to the Thing That Makes the Wolf Go* [January 1934]

[1] In the spring of '27, something bright and alien flashed across the sky. A young Minnesotan who seemed to have had nothing to do with his generation did a heroic thing, and for a moment people set down their glasses in country clubs and speakeasies and thought of their old best dreams. — F. SCOTT FITZGERALD [*of Lindbergh*]

There are two kinds of people who
  blow through life like a breeze,
And one kind is gossipers, and the other
  kind is gossipees.
> *I'm a Stranger Here Myself* [1938]. *I Have It on Good Authority*

Bankers Are Just Like Anybody Else, Except Richer.
> *Ib. Title of poem*

Dogs display reluctance and wrath
If you try to give them a bath.
They bury bones in hideaways
And half the time they trot sideaways.
> *Ib. An Introduction to Dogs, st. 4*

Barmaids Are Diviner Than Mermaids.
> *Ib. Title of poem*

There was a young belle of old Natchez
Whose garments were always in
  patchez.
When comment arose
On the state of her clothes,
She drawled, When Ah itchez, Ah
  scratchez!   *Ib. Requiem*

There is only one way to achieve happiness on this terrestrial ball,
And that is to have either a clear conscience, or none at all.
> *Ib. Inter-Office Memorandum*

Women would rather be right than reasonable.
> *Good Intentions* [1942]. *Frailty, Thy Name Is a Misnomer*

Candy
Is dandy
But liquor
Is quicker.
> *Many Long Years Ago* [1945]. *Reflections on Ice-Breaking*

I think that I shall never see
A billboard lovely as a tree.
Indeed, unless the billboards fall
I'll never see a tree at all.[1]
> *Ib. Song of the Open Road*

One would be in less danger
From the wiles of the stranger

[1] See Joyce Kilmer, p. 1051b.

If one's own kin and kith
Were more fun to be with.
> *Many Long Years Ago.*
> *Family Court*

The turtle lives 'twixt plated decks
Which practically conceal its sex.
I think it clever of the turtle
In such a fix to be so fertile.
> *Ib. The Turtle*

A bit of talcum
Is always walcum.
> *Ib. Reflection on Babies*

The old men know when an old man
dies. *Ib. Old Men*

There is something about a Martini,
A tingle remarkably pleasant;
A yellow, a mellow Martini;
I wish that I had one at present.
There is something about a Martini,
Ere the dining and dancing begin,
And to tell you the truth,
It is not the vermouth —
I think that perhaps it's the gin.
> *Ib. A Drink with Something in It*

Middle age is when you've met so many
people that every new person you
meet reminds you of someone else.
> *Versus* [1949]. *Let's Not*
> *Climb the Washington*
> *Monument Tonight*

I believe a little incompatibility is the
spice of life, particularly if he has
income and she is pattable.
> *Ib. I Do, I Will, I Have*

My garden will never make me famous,
I'm a horticultural ignoramus,
I can't tell a stringbean from a soybean,
Or even a girl bean from a boy bean.
> *Ib. He Digs, He Dug, He Has Dug*

When I remember bygone days
I think how evening follows morn;
So many I loved were not yet dead,
So many I love were not yet born.
> *Ib. The Middle*

He tells you when you've got on too
much lipstick,
And helps you with your girdle when
your hips stick.
> *Ib. The Perfect Husband*

A door is what a dog is perpetually on
the wrong side of.
> *The Private Dining Room*
> [1953]. *A Dog's Best Friend*
> *Is His Illiteracy*

GEORGE GAYLORD SIMPSON
1902–

The present chaotic stage of humanity is not, as some wishfully maintain,
caused by a lack of faith but by too
much unreasoning faith and too many
conflicting faiths within these boundaries where such faith should have no
place. The chaos is one that only responsible human knowledge can reduce
to order.
> *The Meaning of Evolution* [1949]

THEODORE SPENCER
1902–1949

Eunuchs, abortive Platonists and priests
Speak always very wisely about love.
> *An Act of Life* [1944]

JOHN ERNST STEINBECK
1902–1968

Man, unlike any other thing organic
or inorganic in the universe, grows beyond his work, walks up the stairs of his
concepts, emerges ahead of his accomplishments.
> *The Grapes of Wrath* [1939],
> *ch. 14*

Okie use' ta mean you was from
Oklahoma. Now it means you're scum.
Don't mean nothing itself, it's the way
they say it. *Ib. 18*

ERSKINE CALDWELL
1903–

Tobacco Road.
> *Title of novel* [1] [1932]

[1] The play [1933], adapted by JACK KIRKLAND,
[1903–1969] had one of the longest runs in
American stage history.

COUNT GALEAZZO CIANO
1903–1944

As always, victory finds a hundred fathers but defeat is an orphan.[1]
> *The Ciano Diaries 1939–1943*
> [1946]. [September 9, 1942]

CYRIL CONNOLLY [PALINURUS]
1903–1974

There is no fury like a woman searching for a new lover.
> *The Unquiet Grave* [1945], *pt. I*

Obesity is a mental state, a disease brought on by boredom and disappointment.   *Ib.*

Imprisoned in every fat man a thin one is wildly signaling to be let out.
> *Ib. II*

COUNTEE CULLEN
1903–1946

One three centuries removed
From the scenes his fathers loved,
Spicy grove, cinnamon tree,
What is Africa to me?
> *Heritage* [1925]

WILLIAM THOMAS CUMMINGS[2]
1903–1944

There are no atheists in the foxholes.
> *Field sermon, Bataan* [1942].
> From CARLOS P. ROMULO, *I Saw the Fall of the Philippines* [1942]

[1] There's an old saying that victory has a hundred fathers and defeat is an orphan. — JOHN F. KENNEDY, *after the debacle at the Bay of Pigs, Cuba, April 21, 1961*
[2] Father Cummings, a chaplain, was aboard an unmarked Japanese ship transporting prisoners from the Philippines to Japan which was sunk by an American submarine [December 15, 1944].

CLARE BOOTHE LUCE
1903–

Much of what Mr. Wallace[1] calls his global thinking is, no matter how you slice it, still Globaloney.
> *Speech, House of Representatives* [February 9, 1943]

GEORGE ORWELL [ERIC BLAIR]
1903–1950

All animals are equal, but some animals are more equal than others.
> *Animal Farm* [1945], *ch. 10*

Big Brother is watching you.
> *1984* [1948]

BENJAMIN SPOCK
1903–

The more people have studied different methods of bringing up children the more they have come to the conclusion that what good mothers and fathers instinctively feel like doing for their babies is the best after all.
> *The Common Sense Book of Baby and Child Care* [1946], *ch. 1*

EVELYN WAUGH
1903–1966

That's the public school system all over. They may kick you out, but they never let you down.
> *Decline and Fall* [1929]

PETER ARNO
1904–1968

I consider your conduct unethical and lousy.   *Caption for cartoon*

RICHARD EBERHART
1904–

But the year had lost its meaning,
And in intellectual chains

[1] Vice-President Henry Wallace.

I lost both love and loathing,
Mured up in the wall of wisdom.
Collected Poems 1930–1960
[1960]. The Groundhog

I stood there in the whirling summer,
My hand capped a withered heart,
And thought of China and of Greece,
Of Alexander in his tent;
Of Montaigne in his tower,
Of Saint Theresa in her wild lament.
Ib.

It is what man does not know of God
Composes the visible poem of the
world.   *Ib. On a Squirrel*

This fevers me, this sun on green,
On green glowing, this young spring.
Ib. A Bravery of Earth

Not God he'll catch, in the mystery of
space.
He flaunts his own outcast state
As he throws his imperfections outward
bound.
*Ib. On Shooting Particles
Beyond the World*

CLIFTON FADIMAN
1904–

When you reread a classic you do
not see more in the book than you did
before; you see more in *you* than there
was before.
Any Number Can Play [1957]

MARGARET FISHBACK
1904–

The same old charitable lie
Repeated as the years scoot by
Perpetually makes a hit —
"You really haven't changed a bit!"
The Lie of the Land

GRAHAM GREENE
1904–

That whiskey priest, I wish we had
never had him in the house.
The Power and the Glory [1940]

Have you seen a room from which
faith has gone? . . . Like a marriage
from which love has gone. . . . And
patience, patience everywhere like a
fog.   *The Potting Shed* [1957]

Catholics and Communists have
committed great crimes, but at least
they have not stood aside, like an established society, and been indifferent. I
would rather have blood on my hands
than water like Pilate . . . if you have
abandoned one faith, do not abandon
all faith. There is always an alternative
to the faith we lose. Or is it the same
faith under another name?
The Comedians [1966]

CHRISTOPHER WILLIAM BRADSHAW ISHERWOOD
1904–

I am a camera with its shutter open,
quite passive, recording, not thinking.
Recording the man shaving at the window opposite and the woman in the
kimono washing her hair. Some day, all
this will have to be developed, carefully
printed, fixed.
The Berlin Stories [1945].
Goodbye to Berlin [1939],
A Berlin Diary [Autumn
1930]

GEORGE F. KENNAN
1904–

Something which is vitally important
but which, I think, is often lost sight of
in the United States . . . is the fact
that international life normally has in
it strong competitive elements. It did
not take the challenge of Communism
to produce this situation. Just as there
is no uncomplicated personal relationship between individuals, so, I think,
there is no international relationship
between sovereign states which is without its elements of antagonism, its
competitive aspects. Many of the
present relationships of international
life are only the eroded remnants of
ones which, at one time, were relation-

ships of uncompromising hostility. Every government is in some respects a problem for every other government, and it will always be this way so long as the sovereign state, with its supremely self-centered rationale, remains the basis of international life.

> *Russia and the West under Lenin and Stalin* [1961], ch. 25

If we are to regard ourselves as a grown-up nation — and anything else will henceforth be mortally dangerous — then we must, as the Biblical phrase goes, put away childish things; and among these childish things the first to go, in my opinion, should be self-idealization and the search for absolutes in world affairs: for absolute security, absolute amity, absolute harmony.

> *Ib.*

CECIL DAY LEWIS
1904–1971

Tempt me no more; for I
Have known the lightning's hour,
The poet's inward pride,
The certainty of power.

> *Tempt Me No More, st. 1*

And if our blood alone
Will melt this iron earth,
Take it. It is well spent
Easing a savior's birth.　　*Ib. st. 7*

Rest from loving and be living.
Fallen is fallen past retrieving.

> *Rest from Loving*

Make us a wind to shake the world!

> *The Magnetic Mountain* [1933], 31

J. ROBERT OPPENHEIMER[1]
1904–1967

In some sort of crude sense which no vulgarity, no humor, no overstatement

[1] For the passage quoted by Oppenheimer at the explosion of the first atom bomb [Alamogordo, New Mexico, July 16, 1945], see *Bhagavad Gita*, p. 106b. He also quoted Vishnu from the *Gita:* I am become death, the destroyer of worlds.

can quite extinguish, the physicists have known sin; and this is a knowledge which they cannot lose.

> *Physics in the Contemporary World, lecture at Massachusetts Institute of Technology* [November 25, 1947]

The open society, the unrestricted access to knowledge, the unplanned and uninhibited association of men for its furtherance — these are what may make a vast, complex, ever growing, ever changing, ever more specialized and expert technological world, nevertheless a world of human community.

> *Science and the Common Understanding* [1953]

JAMES WILLIAM FULBRIGHT
1905–

There is an inevitable divergence, attributable to the imperfections of the human mind, between the world as it is and the world as men perceive it.

> *Speech in the Senate* [March 27, 1964]

We are handicapped by [foreign] policies based on old myths rather than current realities.　　*Ib.*

The character of the cold war has been profoundly altered . . . by the implicit repudiation by both sides of a policy of total victory. . . . The effect has been to commit us to a policy that can be accurately, though perhaps not prudently, defined as one of "peaceful coexistence."　　*Ib.*

There is much cant in American moralism and not a little inconsistency.
　　Ib.

We are inclined to confuse freedom and democracy, which we regard as moral principles, with the way in which these are practiced in America — with capitalism, federalism and the two-party system, which are not moral principles, but simply the accepted practices of the American people.　　*Ib.*

The master myth of the cold war is that the Communist bloc is a monolith, composed of governments which are not really governments at all, but organized conspiracies . . . all equally resolute and implacable in their determination to destroy the free world.

Speech in the Senate

We must dare to think "unthinkable" thoughts. We must learn to explore all the options and possibilities that confront us in a complex and rapidly changing world. We must learn to welcome and not to fear the voices of dissent. We must dare to think about "unthinkable things" because when things become unthinkable, thinking stops and action becomes mindless. *Ib.*

GRETA GARBO
1905–

I want to be alone.[1] *Attributed*

DAG HAMMARSKJÖLD
1905–1961

Smiling, sincere, incorruptible —
His body disciplined and limber.
A man who had become what he could,
And was what he was —
Ready at any moment to gather everything
Into one simple sacrifice.

Markings [1964]

Never look down to test the ground before taking your next step: only he who keeps his eye fixed on the far horizon will find his right road. *Ib.*

We carry our nemesis within us: yesterday's self-admiration is the legitimate father of today's feeling of guilt. *Ib.*

What gives life its value you can find — and lose. But never possess. This

[1] Garbo maintains that her most famous remark has always been misquoted. . . . "I only said, 'I want to be *let* alone!'" — JOHN BAINBRIDGE, in *Life* [January 24, 1955]

holds good above all for "the Truth about Life." *Markings*

The longest journey[1]
Is the journey inwards
Of him who has chosen his destiny,
Who has started upon his quest
For the source of his being
(Is there a source?). *Ib.*

So! *That* is the way in which you are tempted to overcome your loneliness — by making the ultimate escape from life. — No! It may be that death is to be your ultimate gift to life: it must not be an act of treachery against it. *Ib.*

In the last analysis, what does the word "sacrifice" mean? Or even the word "gift"? He who has nothing can give nothing. The gift is God's — to God. *Ib.*

STANLEY KUNITZ
1905–

Awake!
      My whirling hands stay at the noon,
Each cell within my body holds a heart
And all my hearts in unison strike twelve.
The Science of the Night

When the light falls, it falls on her
In whose rose-gilded chamber
A music strained through mind
Turns everything to measure.
When the Light Falls

Doomsday is the eighth day of the week.
Foreign Affairs

O Magus with the leathern hand,
The wasted heart, the trailing star,
Time is your madness, which I share,
Blowing next winter into mind . . .
And love herself not there, not there.
The Man Upstairs, st. 4

[1] See Shelley, p. 571a.

On the royal road to Thebes
I had my luck, I met a lovely monster,
And the story's this: I made the monster me.
The Approach to Thebes

We learn, as the thread plays out, that we belong
Less to what flatters us than to what scars,
So, freshly turning, as the turn condones,
For her I killed the propitiatory bird,
Kissing her down. Peace to her bitter bones,
Who taught me the serpent's word, but yet the word.
The Dark and the Fair

A fine Italian hand,
With its mimosa touch, has made me feel
Blind-skinned, indelicate, a fool Americano
Touring a culture like a grand museum,
People and statues interchangeable shows,
Perception blunted as one's syntax fails.
The Thief

I recognize the gods' capricious hand
And write this poem for money, rage, and love.   *Ib.*

I stand on the terrible threshold, and I see
The end and the beginning in each other's arms.
Open the Gates, st. 3

An agitation of the air,
A perturbation of the light
Admonished me the unloved year
Would turn on its hinge that night.
End of Summer, st. 1

Already the iron door of the north
Clangs open: birds, leaves, snows
Order their populations forth,
And a cruel wind blows.   *Ib. st. 4*

Now, while the antler of the eaves
Liquefies, drop by drop, I brood

On a Christian thing: unless the leaves
Perish, the tree is not renewed.

If all our perishable stuff
Be nourished to its rot, we clean
Our trunk of death, and in our tough
And final growth are evergreen.
Deciduous Branch, st. 4, 5

I wept for my youth, sweet passionate young thought,
And cozy women dead that by my side
Once lay: I wept with bitter longing, not
Remembering how in my youth I cried.
I Dreamed That I Was Old, st. 3

The thing that eats the heart is mostly heart.
The Thing That Eats the Heart, last line

Cities shall suffer siege and some shall fall,
But man's not taken. What the deep heart means,
Its message of the big, round, childish hand,
Its wonder, its simple lonely cry,
The bloodied envelope addressed to you,
Is history, that wide and mortal pang.
Night Letter

When young I scribbled, boasting, on my wall,
No Love, No Property, No Wages.
In youth's good time I somehow bought them all,
And cheap, you'd think, for maybe a hundred pages.
Now in my prime, disburdened of my gear,
My trophies ransomed, broken, lost,
I carve again on the lintel of the year
My sign: *Mobility* — and damn the cost!   *The Summing-Up*

If I must build a church,
Though I do not really want one,
Let it be in the wilderness
Out of nothing but nail-holes.
Revolving Meditation

LIU SHAO·CH'I[1]
1905–

Our ethics are great precisely because they are the ethics of Communism and of the proletariat. Such ethics are not built upon the backward basis of safeguarding the interests of individuals or a small number of exploiters. They are built, on the contrary, upon the progressive basis of . . . saving the world from destruction and of building a happy and beautiful Communist world.[2]

How To Be a Good Communist

Inside the Party we must cultivate the practice of submitting to reason.[3]

On Inner-Party Struggle

PHYLLIS McGINLEY
1905–

Meek-eyed parents hasten down the ramps
To greet their offspring, terrible from camps.

Ode to the End of Summer

Always on Monday morning the press reports
God as revealed to His vicars in various guises —
Benevolent, stormy, patient, or out of sorts.
God knows which God is the God God recognizes.

The Day After Sunday

Prince, I warn you, under the rose,
Time is the thief you cannot banish.
These are my daughters, I suppose.
But where in the world did the children vanish?

Ballade of Lost Objects

[1] From *Sources of Chinese Tradition*, edited by William Theodore de Bary [1960].
[2] *Note from the text: How to Be a Good Communist* is a basic text of indoctrination for party members, delivered first as a series of lectures in July 1939 at the Institute of Marxism-Leninism in Yenan. — W. T. DE BARY
[3] *Note from the text:* This essay, delivered by Liu Shao-ch'i in July 1941 as a series of lectures to a Party school is a kind of sequel to *How To Be a Good Communist.* — W. T. DE BARY

JEAN PAUL SARTRE
1905–

Everything is gratuitous, this garden, this city and myself. When you suddenly realize it, it makes you feel sick and everything begins to drift . . . that's nausea.   *La Nausée* [1938]

Man is not the sum of what he has but the totality of what he does not yet have, of what he might have.

Situations [1939], I

This freedom should not be seen as a metaphysical power of human "nature," nor as the right to do whatever one pleases. . . . We do not do what we want and yet we are responsible for what we are — that is the fact.

Ib. II

Because the Nazi venom worked its way even into our thoughts, every accurate thought was a conquest; because an all-powerful police sought to force us into silence, every word became as precious as a declaration of principle; because we were persecuted, each of our gestures carried the weight of a commitment.   *Les Mouches* [1942]

Man can will nothing unless he has first understood that he must count on no one but himself; that he is alone, abandoned on earth in the midst of his infinite responsibilities, without help, with no other aim than the one he sets himself, with no other destiny than the one he forges for himself on this earth.

Le Être et le Néant [1943]

Hell is — other people! [1]

Huis-Clos [1944]

CHARLES PERCY SNOW
1905–

Literary intellectuals at one pole — at the other scientists. . . . Between the two a gulf of mutual incomprehension.

The Two Cultures and the Scientific Revolution [1959]

[1] See Virgil, p. 119a; and Marlowe, p. 213a, and note.

Scientists have it within them to know what a future-directed society feels like, for science itself, in its human aspect, is just that.

Science and Government [1960]

No one is fit to be trusted with power. . . . No one. . . . Any man who has lived at all knows the follies and wickedness he's capable of. If he does not know it, he is not fit to govern others. And if he does know it, he knows also that neither he nor any man ought to be allowed to decide a single human fate.

The Light and the Dark [1961]

Corridors of Power.

Title of novel [1965]

JOHN BETJEMAN
1906–

He rose, and he put down The Yellow
    Book.
He staggered — and, terrible-eyed,
He brushed past the palms on the stair-
    case
And was helped to a hansom outside.

*The Arrest of Oscar Wilde
    at the Cadogan Hotel* [1937],
    st. 9

Gracious Lord, oh bomb the Germans.
Spare their women for Thy Sake,
And if that is not too easy
We will pardon Thy Mistake.
But, gracious Lord, whate'er shall be,
Don't let anyone bomb me.

In Westminster Abbey [1940]

The sort of girl I like to see
Smiles down from her great height at
    me. *The Olympic Girl* [1954]

Oh! would I were her racket pressed
With hard excitement to her breast.

Ib.

Summoned by Bells.

Title of book [1960]

LEO DUROCHER
1906–

Nice guys finish last. *Remark*

WYSTAN HUGH AUDEN
1907–1973

Let us honor if we can
The vertical man
Though we value none
But the horizontal one.

Epigraph for Poems [1930]

If we really want to live, we'd better
    start at once to try;
If we don't it doesn't matter, we'd bet-
    ter start to die.

If We Really Want to Live
    [1930]

Sir, no man's enemy, forgiving all
But will his negative inversion, be
    prodigal.

Sir, No Man's Enemy [1930]

Harrow the house of the dead; look
    shining at
New styles of architecture, a change of
    heart. *Ib.*

The greater the love, the more false to
    its object,
    Not to be born is the best for man; [1]
After the kiss comes the impulse to
    throttle,
    Break the embraces, dance while you
    can.

O Who Can Ever Gaze His Fill
    [1937]

The stars are dead. The animals will
    not look.
We are left alone with our day, and the
    time short, and History to the de-
    feated
May say Alas but cannot help nor
    pardon. *Spain* [1937]

About suffering they were never wrong,
The old masters.

Musée des Beaux Arts [1940]

O plunge your hands in water,
    Plunge them in up to the wrist;
Stare, stare in the basin
    And wonder what you've missed.

The glacier knocks in the cupboard,
    The desert sighs in the bed,

[1] See Sophocles, p. 83a.

And the crack in the tea cup opens
A lane to the land of the dead.
    As I Walked Out One Evening
        [1940], *st. 10, 11*

You were silly like us: your gift survived
    it all;
The parish of rich women, physical de-
    cay,
Yourself; mad Ireland hurt you into
    poetry.
        In Memory of W. B. Yeats
            [1940]

To us he is no more a person
Now but a whole climate of opinion.
        In Memory of Sigmund Freud
            [1940]

One rational voice is dumb: over a
    grave
The household of Impulse mourns one
    dearly loved.
    Sad is Eros, builder of cities,
    And weeping anarchic Aphrodite.
                        Ib.

Lay your sleeping head, my love,
Human on my faithless arm.
        Lay Your Sleeping Head, My
                Love [1940]

At Dirty Dick's and Sloppy Joe's
    We drank our liquor straight,
Some went upstairs with Margery,
    And some, alas, with Kate.
        The Sea and the Mirror [1944].
            Master and Boatswain

And children swarmed to him like set-
    tlers. He became a land.
        Edward Lear [1945]

Sob, heavy world,
Sob as you spin,
Mantled in mist, remote from the
    happy.
        The Age of Anxiety [1947]

She looked over his shoulder
    For vines and olive trees,
Marble, well-governed cities
    And ships upon wine-dark seas;
But there on the shining metal
    His hands had put instead

An artificial wilderness
    And a sky like lead.
        The Shield of Achilles [1955],
                        st. 1

The mass and majesty of this world,
    all
That carries weight and always
    weighs the same,
Lay in the hands of others; they were
    small
And could not hope for help, and no
    help came;
What their foes liked to do was
    done, their shame
Was all the worst could wish: they lost
    their pride
And died as men before their bodies
    died.   *Ib. st. 6*

Our researchers into Public Opinion are
    content
That he held the proper opinions for
    the time of year;
When there was peace, he was for
    peace; when there was war, he
    went.
        The Unknown Citizen (*To
        JS/07/M/378 This Marble
        Monument Is Erected by
        the State*)

Was he free? Was he happy? The
    question is absurd:
Had anything been wrong, we should
    certainly have heard.   *Ib.*

A culture is no better than its woods.
        Bucolics. Woods

When a just man dies,
Lamentation and praise,
Sorrow and joy, are one.
        Elegy for John F. Kennedy
            [1963]

Some thirty inches from my nose
The frontier of my Person goes,
And all the untilled air between
Is private *pagus* or demesne.
Stranger, unless with bedroom eyes
I beckon you to fraternize,
Beware of rudely crossing it:
I have no gun, but I can spit.
        About the House [1965]

Some books are undeservedly forgotten; none are undeservedly remembered.

The Dyer's Hand [1] [1962]. *Pt. I, Reading*

It takes little talent to see clearly what lies under one's nose, a good deal of it to know in which direction to point that organ. *Ib. Writing*

The old lady, quoted by E. M. Forster — "How can I know what I think till I see what I say?" *Ib.*

Speaking for myself, the questions which interest me most when reading a poem are two. The first is technical: "Here is a verbal contraption. How does it work?" The second is, in the broadest sense, moral: "What kind of a guy inhabits this poem? What is his notion of the good life or the good place? His notion of the Evil One? What does he conceal from the reader? What does he conceal even from himself?"

Ib. II, Making, Knowing and Judging

Whatever its actual content and overt interest, every poem is rooted in imaginative awe. Poetry can do a hundred and one things, delight, sadden, disturb, amuse, instruct — it may express every possible shade of emotion, and describe every conceivable kind of event, but there is only one thing that all poetry must do; it must praise all it can for being and for happening.

Ib.

RACHEL LOUISE CARSON
1907–1964

The sea lies all around us. The commerce of all lands must cross it. The very winds that move over the lands have been cradled on its broad expanse and seek ever to return to it. The continents themselves dissolve and pass to the sea, in grain after grain of eroded land. . . . In its mysterious past it encompasses all the dim origins of life and

[1] See Shakespeare, *Sonnet III*, p. 294a.

receives in the end, after, it may be, many transmutations, the dead husks of that same life. For all at last returns to the sea — the beginning and the end.

The Sea Around Us [1951]

Over increasingly large areas of the United States, spring now comes unheralded by the return of the birds, and the early mornings are strangely silent where once they were filled with the beauty of bird song.

Silent Spring [1962]

As crude a weapon as the cave man's club, the chemical barrage has been hurled against the fabric of life. *Ib.*

CHRISTOPHER FRY
1907–

I travel light; as light,
That is, as a man can travel who will
Still carry his body around because
Of its sentimental value.

The Lady's Not for Burning
[1950], *act I*

Religion
Has made an honest woman of the
     supernatural,
And we won't have it kicking over the
     traces again. *Ib. II*

Where in this small-talking world can I
     find
A longitude with no platitude?
Ib. III

The moon is nothing
But a circumambulatory aphrodisiac
Divinely subsidized to provoke the
     world
Into a rising birth rate. *Ib.*

Try thinking of love or something.
Amor vincit insomnia. [1]
A Sleep of Prisoners [1951]

ANNE MORROW LINDBERGH
1907–

The wave of the future is coming and there is no fighting it.

The Wave of the Future [1940]

[1] See Virgil, p. 117a.

LOUIS MacNEICE
1907–1963

Holidays should be like this,
Free from overemphasis,
Time for soul to stretch and spit
Before the world comes back on it.
Epilogue, for W. H. Auden
[1936]

It's no go my honey love, it's no go my
    poppet;
Work your hands from day to day, the
    winds will blow the profit.
The glass is falling hour by hour, the
    glass will fall forever,
But if you break the bloody glass you
    won't hold up the weather.
Bagpipe Music, last stanza

The sunlight on the garden
Hardens and grows cold,
We cannot cage the minute
Within its net of gold,
When all is told
We cannot beg for pardon.
The Sunlight on the Garden,
st. 1

PAUL ENGLE
1908–

Wisdom is knowing when you can't be
    wise.   *Poems in Praise* [1959]

HOWELL M. FORGY
1908–

Praise the Lord and pass the ammunition.[1]
Said at Pearl Harbor
[December 7, 1941]

JOHN KENNETH GALBRAITH
1908–

It is told that such are the aerodynamics and wing-loading of the bumblebee that, in principle, it cannot fly. . . . If all this be true . . . life

[1] Forgy was serving as chaplain on a cruiser at the time of the Japanese attack; the words were said to a chain of men handling ammunition. They were used as the title of a song by Frank Loesser [September 1942].

among bumblebees must bear a remarkable resemblance to life in the United States.
American Capitalism: The Concept of Countervailing Power
[1952]

Historians and novelists always have known that tragedy wonderfully reveals the nature of man. But, while they have made rich use of war, revolution, and poverty, they have been singularly neglectful of financial panics. And one can relish the varied idiocy of human action during a panic to the full, for, while it is a time of great tragedy, nothing is being lost but money.
The Great Crash, 1929 [1955],
ch. 1

Perhaps it was worth being poor for a long time to be so rich for just a little while.   *Ib. 3*

The end had come, but it was not yet in sight.   *Ib. 5*

The stock market is but a mirror which, perhaps as in this instance, somewhat belatedly, provides an image of the underlying or *fundamental* economic situation. Cause and effect run from the economy to the stock market, never the reverse. In 1929 the economy was headed for trouble. Eventually that trouble was violently reflected in Wall Street.   *Ib. 6*

Men have been swindled by other men on many occasions. The autumn of 1929 was, perhaps, the first occasion when men succeeded on a large scale in swindling themselves.   *Ib. 7*

At any given time there exists an inventory of undiscovered embezzlement in — or more precisely not in — the country's businesses and banks. This inventory — it should perhaps be called the bezzle — amounts at any moment to many millions of dollars. It also varies in size with the business cycle. In good times people are relaxed, trusting, and money is plentiful. But even though money is plentiful, there are always many people who need more. Under these circumstances the rate of embezzlement grows, the rate of discovery falls off, and bezzle increases rapidly. In depression all this is reversed. Money is watched with a narrow, suspicious eye. The man who handles it is assumed to be dishonest until he proves himself otherwise. Audits are penetrating and meticulous. Commercial morality is enormously improved. The bezzle shrinks.

> *The Great Crash, 1929, ch. 8*

Illusion is a comprehensive ill. The rich man who deludes himself into behaving like a mendicant may conserve his fortune although he will not be very happy. The affluent country which conducts its affairs in accordance with rules of another and poorer age also foregoes opportunities. And in misunderstanding itself it will, in any time of difficulty, implacably prescribe for itself the wrong remedies.

> *The Affluent Society* [1958],
> *ch. 1*

. . . the myth that military power is a function of economic output. If peace and survival are to be achieved, the search must almost certainly go beyond the effort to find a balance in thermonuclear terror.   *Ib. 12*

The family which takes its mauve and cerise, air-conditioned, power-steered, and power-braked automobile out for a tour passes through cities that are badly paved, made hideous by litter, blighted buildings, billboards, and posts for wires that should long since have been put underground. They pass on into a countryside that has been rendered largely invisible by commercial art. . . . They picnic on exquisitely packaged food from a portable icebox by a polluted stream and go on to spend the night at a park which is a menace to public health and morals. Just before dozing off on an air mattress, beneath a nylon tent, amid the stench of decaying refuse, they may re-flect vaguely on the curious unevenness of their blessings. Is this, indeed, the American genius?

> *The Affluent Society, ch. 18*

In a community where public services have failed to keep abreast of private consumption things are very different. Here, in an atmosphere of private opulence and public squalor, the private goods have full sway.   *Ib.*

Nothing so weakens government as persistent inflation.   *Ib.*

People are the common denominator of progress. So . . . no improvement is possible with unimproved people, and advance is certain when people are liberated and educated. It would be wrong to dismiss the importance of roads, railroads, power plants, mills, and the other familiar furniture of economic development. . . . But we are coming to realize . . . that there is a certain sterility in economic monuments that stand alone in a sea of illiteracy. Conquest of illiteracy comes first.

> *Economic Development*
> [*1964*], *ch. 2*

LYNDON BAINES JOHNSON
1908–1973

All I have I would have given gladly not to be standing here today.

> *First address to Congress as President* [*November 27, 1963*]

We have talked long enough in this country about equal rights. We have talked for a hundred years or more. It is time now to write the next chapter — and to write in the books of law.
>   *Ib.*

Unfortunately many Americans live on the outskirts of hope — some because of their poverty, some because of their color, and all too many because of both. Our task is to help replace their despair with opportunity.[1]

> *First State of the Union Message*
> *[January 8, 1964]*

The challenge of the next half century is whether we have the wisdom to use [our] wealth to enrich and elevate our national life — and to advance the quality of American civilization — for in your time we have the opportunity to move not only toward the rich society and the powerful society but upward to the Great Society.[2]

> *Speech, University of Michigan*
> *[May 22, 1964]*

This nation, this generation, in this hour has man's first chance to build a Great Society, a place where the meaning of man's life matches the marvels of man's labor.

> *Address, accepting the Presidential nomination [August 1964]*

EDWARD ROSCOE MURROW
1908–1965

I am entirely persuaded that the American public is more reasonable, restrained and mature than most of the broadcast industry's planners believe. Their fear of controversy is not warranted by the evidence.

> *Speech, Radio and Television News Directors Convention, Chicago [October 15, 1958]*

In order to progress, radio need only go backward, to the time when singing commercials were not allowed on news reports, when there was no middle commercial on a news report, when radio was rather proud, alert and fast.
> *Ib.*

THEODORE ROETHKE
1908–1963

For something is amiss or out of place
When mice with wings can wear a
   human face.   *The Bat* [1941]

[1] See Michael Harrington, p. 1082a.
[2] See Lippmann, p. 1013b.

My secrets cry aloud.
I have no need for tongue.
My heart keeps open house,
My doors are widely flung.
> *Open House* [1941]

The veins within our hands betrayed
   our fear.
What we had hoped for had not come
   to pass.   *Interlude* [1941]

Thought does not crush to stone.
The great sledge drops in vain.
Truth never is undone;
His shafts remain.
> *The Adamant* [1941]

This urge, wrestle, resurrection of dry
   sticks,
Cut stems struggling to put down feet,
What saint strained so much,
Rose on such lopped limbs to a new
   life?   *Cuttings* [1948]

I study the lives on a leaf: the little
Sleepers, numb nudgers in cold dimensions,
Beetles in caves, newts, stone-deaf
   fishes,
Lice tethered to long limp subterranean
   weeds,
Squirmers in bogs,
And bacterial creepers.
> *The Minimal* [1948]

Once upon a tree
I came across a time.
> *Where Knock Is Open Wide*
> *[1951]*

At Woodlawn I heard the dead cry;
I was lulled by the slamming of iron,
A slow drip over stones,
Toads brooding in wells.
All the leaves stuck out their tongues;
I shook the softening chalk of my
   bones,
Saying,
Snail, snail, glister me forward,
Bird, soft-sigh me home.
Worm, be with me.
This is my hard time.
> *The Lost Son* [1951], 1

I feel the slime of a wet nest.
  Beware Mother Mildew.
Nibble again, fish nerves.
                    The Lost Son, 2

A lively understandable spirit
Once entertained you.
It will come again.
Be still.
Wait.   *Ib. 5*

And the new plants, still awkward in
    their soil,
The lovely diminutives.
                    A Field of Light [1951]

I could watch! I could watch!
I saw the separateness of all things!
                    Ib.

My meat eats me. Who waits at the
    gate?
Mother of quartz, your words writhe
    into my ear.
                    The Shape of the Fire [1951], 2

To follow the drops sliding from a lifted
    oar,
Head up, while the rower breathes,
  And the small boat drifts quietly
    Shoreward;
To know that light falls and fills,
    Often without our knowing.
                    Ib. 5

I remember the neckcurls, limp and
    damp as tendrils,
And her quick look a sidelong pickerel
    smile.
                    Elegy for Jane [1951–1953]

I take this cadence from a man named
    Yeats;
I take it, and I give it back again.
                    Four for Sir John Davies [1951–
                        1953]. I, *The Dance*

Who rise from flesh to spirit know the
    fall:
The word outleaps the world, and light
    is all.   *Ib. 4*

I wake to sleep, and take my waking
    slow.
I feel my fate in what I cannot fear.
I learn by going where I have to go.
                    The Waking [1953]

I knew a woman, lovely in her bones,
When small birds sighed, she would
    sigh back at them;
Ah, when she moved, she moved more
    ways than one:
The shapes a bright container can con-
    tain!   *I Knew a Woman* [1959]

I long for the imperishable quiet at the
    heart of form.
                    The Longing [1964]

Old men should be explorers? [1]
I'll be an Indian.
Iroquois.   *Ib.*

Now, in this waning of light,
I rock with the motion of morning;
In the cradle of all that is,
I'm lulled into half-sleep
By the lapping of water,
Cries of the sandpiper.
Water's my will, and my way,
And the spirit runs, intermittently,
In and out of the small waves,
Runs with the intrepid shorebirds —
How graceful the small before danger!

In the first of the moon,
All's a scattering,
A shining.
                    Meditation at Oyster River
                        [1964], IV

What I love is near at hand,
Always, in earth and air.
                    The Far Field [1964], III

All finite things reveal infinitude.
                    Ib. IV

O what could be more nice
Than her ways with a man?
                    Light Listened [1964]

She sang a final song;
Light listened when she sang.   *Ib.*

I am most immoderately married:
The Lord God has taken my heaviness
    away;
I have merged, like the bird, with the
    bright air,
And my thought flies to the place by
    the bo-tree.

[1] See T. S. Eliot, p. 1006a.

Being, not doing, is my first joy.
The Abyss [1964], V

We end in joy.
The Moment [1964], *last line*

In a dark time, the eye begins to see.
In a Dark Time [1964], *st.* 1

A steady storm of correspondences!
A night flowing with birds, a ragged moon,
And in broad day the midnight come again! *Ib. st.* 3

Was I too glib about eternal things,
An intimate of air and all its songs?

Pure aimlessness pursued and yet pursued
And all wild longings of the insatiate blood
Brought me down to my knees. O who can be
Both moth and flame? The weak moth blundering by.

Whom do we love? I thought I knew the truth;
Of grief I died, but no one knew my death. *The Sequel* [1964], I

The soul has many motions, body one.
The Motion [1964], I

Love begets love. This torment is my joy. *Ib. II*

Rising or falling's all one discipline!
The line of my horizon's growing thin!
Which is the way? I cry to the dread black,
The shifting shade, the cinders at my back.
Which is the way? I ask, and turn to go,
As a man turns to face on-coming snow. *The Decision* [1964], II

What's the worst portion in this mortal life?
A pensive mistress, and a yelping wife.
The Marrow [1964], I

Brooding on God, I may become a man.
Pain wanders through my bones like a lost fire;
What burns me now? Desire, desire, desire. *Ib. II*

Lord, hear me out, and hear me out this day:
From me to Thee's a long and terrible way. *The Marrow, III*

Yea, I have slain my will, and still I live;
I would be near; I shut my eyes to see;
I bleed my bones, their marrow to bestow
Upon that God who knows what I would know. *Ib. IV*

The present falls, the present falls away;
How pure the motion of the rising day,
The white sea widening on a farther shore.
The bird, the beating bird, extending wings —
Thus I endure this last pure stretch of joy,
The dire dimension of a final thing.
The Tree, the Bird [1964]

Let others probe the mystery if they can.
Time-harried prisoners of *Shall* and *Will* —
The right thing happens to the happy man.

The bird flies out, the bird flies back again;
The hill becomes the valley, and is still;
Let others delve that mystery if they can.
The Right Thing [1964], *st.* 1, 2

Now I adore my life
With the Bird, the abiding Leaf,
With the Fish, the questing Snail,
And the Eye altering all;
And I dance with William Blake
For love, for Love's sake.
Once More, the Round [1964]

WILLIAM SAROYAN
1908–

The Time of Your Life.
Title of play [1939]

If you give to a thief he cannot steal from you, and he is then no longer a thief.
The Human Comedy [1943], *ch. 4*

RICHARD WRIGHT
1908–1960

Goddammit, look! We live here and they live there. We black and they white. They got things and we ain't. They do things and we can't. It's just like living in jail.   *Native Son* [1940]

Who knows when some slight shock, disturbing the delicate balance between social order and thirsty aspiration, shall send the skyscrapers in our cities toppling?   *Ib.*

JAMES AGEE
1909–1955

Now is the night one blue dew.
A Death in the Family [1957],
Knoxville: Summer 1915

Sleep, soft smiling, draws me unto her: and those receive me, who quietly treat me, as one familiar and well-beloved in that home: but will not, oh, will not, not now, not ever; but will not ever tell me who I am.   *Ib.*

DAZAI OSAMU
1909–1948

It is true, I suppose, that nobody finds it exactly pleasant to be criticized or shouted at, but I see in the face of the human being raging at me a wild animal in its true colors, one more horrible than any lion. . . . Anger makes them reveal in a flash human nature in all its horror.
No Longer Human [1958] [1]

My definition of a "respected" man was one who had succeeded almost completely in hoodwinking people, but who was finally seen through by some

[1] Translated by DONALD KEENE.

omniscient, omnipotent person who ruined him and made him suffer a shame worse than death.
No Longer Human

My unhappiness was the unhappiness of a person who could not say no.
Ib.

STEPHEN SPENDER
1909–

I think continually of those who were truly great —
The names of those who in their lives fought for life,
Who wore at their hearts the fire's center.
I Think Continually of Those

Born of the sun they traveled a short while towards the sun,
And left the vivid air signed with their honor.   *Ib.*

GEORGE CASPAR HOMANS
1910–

Liberty is a beloved discipline.
The Human Group [1950], *ch. 12*

DON K. PRICE
1910–

Science . . . cannot exist on the basis of a treaty of strict nonaggression with the rest of society; from either side, there is no defensible frontier.
Science and Government [1954]

ELIZABETH BISHOP
1911–

Think of the storm roaming the sky uneasily
like a dog looking for a place to sleep in,
listen to it growling.   *Little Exercise*

This iceberg cuts its facets from within.
Like jewelry from a grave
It saves itself perpetually and adorns
Only itself.
The Imaginary Iceberg
[1946], *st. 3*

Icebergs behoove the soul
(Both being self-made from elements
    least visible)
To see them so: fleshed, fair, erected,
    indivisible.
          The Imaginary Iceberg, st. 3

WILLIAM GOLDING
1911–

"Fancy thinking the Beast was something you could hunt and kill!" said the head. For a moment or two the forest and all the other dimly appreciated places echoed with the parody of laughter. "You knew, didn't you? I'm part of you? Close, close, close! I'm the reason why it's no go? Why things are what they are?"
          The Lord of the Flies [1954], *ch. 8*

CLARK KERR
1911–

The university has become the multiversity and the nature of the presidency has followed this change. . . . The president of the multiversity is leader, educator, wielder of power, pump; he is also officeholder, caretaker, inheritor, consensus seeker, persuader, bottleneck. But he is mostly a mediator.
          The Uses of the University [*The Godkin lectures at Harvard University, 1963*]

GEORGE BARKER
1913–

Fiend behind the fiend behind the fiend
    behind the
Fiend. Mastodon with mastery, monster
    with an ache
At the tooth of the ego, the dead
    drunk judge:
Wheresoever Thou art our agony will
    find Thee
Enthroned on the darkest altar of our
    heartbreak
Perfect. Beast, brute, bastard. O dog
    my God!
          Sacred Elegy V [1943], *iv*

My joy, my jockey, my Gabriel
Who bares his horns above my sleep
Is sleeping now.
          First Cycle of Love Poems
          [1947], V

ALBERT CAMUS
1913–1960

Mother died today, or maybe it was yesterday.   *L'Étranger* [1942], I

For the first time, the first, I laid my heart open to the benign indifference of the universe. To feel it so like myself, indeed, so brotherly, made me realize that I'd been happy, and that I was happy still.   *Ib.* IV

The absurd is essentially a divorce. It is in neither one nor the other of the compared elements. It is born of their confrontation.
          Le Mythe de Sisyphe [1942]

The absurd is the essential concept and the first truth.   *Ib.*

It is not rebellion itself which is noble but the demands it makes upon us.   *La Peste* [1947]

Can one be a saint if God does not exist? That is the only concrete problem I know of today.   *Ib.*

In the midst of winter, I finally learned that there was in me an invincible summer.
          Actuelles [*January 6, 1960*]

I shall tell you a great secret, my friend. Do not wait for the last judgment. It takes place every day.
          La Chute [1956]

Freedom of the press is perhaps the freedom that has suffered the most from the gradual degradation of the idea of liberty.
          Resistance, Rebellion, and
          Death [1] [1960]

A free press can of course be good or bad, but, most certainly, without free-

[1] Translated by JUSTIN O'BRIEN from selected essays in *Actuelles* [1950, 1953, 1958].

dom it will never be anything but bad.
. . . Freedom is nothing else but a
chance to be better, whereas enslavement is a certainty of the worse.
Resistance, Rebellion, and Death

NATHALIA CRANE
1913–

Oh, I'm in love with the janitor's boy,
  And the janitor's boy loves me;
He's going to hunt for a desert isle
  In our geography.
    The Janitor's Boy [1924], *st. 1*

I linger on the flathouse roof, the
  moonlight is divine.
But my heart is all aflutter like the
  washing on the line.
    The Flathouse Roof, st. 1

DONALD FRANCIS
MASON
1913–

Sighted sub, sank same.
    *Radio message to U. S. Navy
    Base* [*January 28, 1942*]

MURIEL RUKEYSER
1913–

Fly down, Death: Call me:
I have become a lost name.
    Madboy's Song, refrain

DELMORE SCHWARTZ[1]
1913–1966

Time is the school in which we learn,
Time is the fire in which we burn.
    For Rhoda [1938]

That inescapable animal walks with me,
Has followed me since the black womb
  held,
Moves where I move, distorting my
  gesture,

[1] See Robert Lowell, p. 1075b.

A caricature, a swollen shadow,
A stupid clown of the spirit's motive,
Perplexes and affronts with his own
  darkness,
The secret life of belly and bone.
    *The Heavy Bear Who Goes
    with Me, st. 3*

KARL SHAPIRO
1913–

Haul up the flag, you mourners,
Not half-mast but all the way;
The funeral is done and disbanded;
The devil's had the final say.
    Elegy for Two Banjos, st. 1 and 14

JOHN HERSEY
1914–

There was no sound of planes. The
morning was still; the place was cool
and pleasant.
  Then a tremendous flash of light cut
across the sky. Mr. Tanimoto has a distinct recollection that it traveled from
east to west, from the city toward the
hills. It seemed a sheet of sun. Both he
and Mr. Matsuo reacted in terror.
. . . Under what seemed to be a local
dust cloud, the day grew darker and
darker.   *Hiroshima* [1946], *ch. 1*

There, in the tin factory, in the first
moment of the atomic age, a human
being was crushed by books.   *Ib.*

ROSS PARKER
1914–
AND
HUGHIE CHARLES
1907–

There'll always be an England
  While there's a busy street,
Wherever there's a turning wheel,
  A million marching feet.
    *There'll Always Be an
    England* [1939]

DYLAN THOMAS[1]
1914–1953

The force that through the green fuse
drives the flower
Drives my green age; that blasts the
roots of trees
Is my destroyer.
And I am dumb to tell the crooked rose
My youth is bent by the same wintry
fever.
> *The Force That Through the
> Green Fuse Drives the Flower*
> [*1934*]

Light breaks where no sun shines;
Where no sea runs, the waters of the
heart
Push in their tides.
> *Light Breaks Where No
> Sun Shines* [*1934*]

The hand that signed the paper felled a
city;
Five sovereign fingers taxed the breath,
Doubled the globe of dead and halved a
country;
These five kings did a king to death.
> *The Hand That Signed the
> Paper* [*1936*]

When all my five and country senses
see,
The fingers will forget green thumbs
and mark
How, through the halfmoon's vegetable
eye,
Husk of young stars and handfull zo-
diac,
Love in the frost is pared and wintered
by.
> *When All My Five and Country
> Senses See* [*1939*]

And death shall have no dominion.[2]
> *Title and refrain of poem* [*1943*]

After the first death there is no other.
> *A Refusal to Mourn the Death,
> by Fire, of a Child in London*
> [*1946*]

[1] The poetry excerpts are from *Collected Poems*
[*1953*].
[2] See *Romans 6:9*, p. 50b, and Emily Brontë,
p. 685b.

Forgotten mornings when he walked
with his mother
Through the parables
Of sunlight
And the legend of the green chapels.
> *Poem in October* [*1946*]

Now as I was young and easy under the
apple boughs
About the lilting house and happy as
the grass was green.
> *Fern Hill, st. 1* [*1946*]

And the sabbath rang slowly
In the pebbles of the holy streams.
> *Ib. st. 2*

In the sun that is young once only,
Time let me play and be
Golden in the mercy of his means.
> *Ib.*

And honored among foxes and pheas-
ants by the gay house
Under the new-made clouds and happy
as the heart was long,
In the sun born over and over,
I ran my heedless ways.
> *Ib. st. 5*

Time held me green and dying
Though I sang in my chains like the
sea. *Ib. st. 6*

Do not go gentle into that good night,
Old age should burn and rave at close
of day;
Rage, rage against the dying of the
light.
> *Do Not Go Gentle into That
> Good Night* [*1952*]

One Christmas was so much like
another, in those years around the seatown corner now and out of all sound
except the distant speaking of the voices
I sometimes hear a moment before
sleep, that I can never remember
whether it snowed for six days and six
nights when I was twelve or whether it
snowed for twelve days and twelve
nights when I was six.
> *Quite Early One Morning*
> [*1954*]. *A Child's Christ-
> mas in Wales*

It is spring, moonless night in the small town, starless and bible-black.
Under Milk Wood [1954]

You can tear a poem apart to see what makes it technically tick. . . . You're back with the mystery of having been moved by words. The best craftsmanship always leaves holes and gaps in the works of the poem so that something that is *not* in the poem can creep, crawl, flash, or thunder in.

The joy and function of poetry is, and was, the celebration of man, which is also the celebration of man.
Dylan Thomas's Poetic Manifesto. In the Texas Quarterly [*Winter 1961*]

HAROLD ADAMSON

Comin' in on a Wing and a Prayer.
Title of song [1943]

JEROME SEYMOUR BRUNER

1915–

The shrewd guess, the fertile hypothesis, the courageous leap to a tentative conclusion — these are the most valuable coin of the thinker at work. But in most schools guessing is heavily penalized and is associated somehow with laziness.
The Process of Education [1960]

ARTHUR MILLER

1915–

I don't say he's a great man. Willy Loman never made a lot of money. His name was never in the paper. He's not the finest character that ever lived. But he's a human being, and a terrible thing is happening to him. So attention must be paid. He's not to be allowed to fall into his grave like an old dog. Attention, attention must be finally paid to such a person.
Death of a Salesman [1949], *act I*

Willy was a salesman. And for a salesman, there is no rock bottom to the life. He don't put a bolt to a nut, he don't tell you the law or give you medicine. He's a man way out there in the blue, riding on a smile and a shoeshine. And when they start not smiling back — that's an earthquake. And then you get yourself a couple of spots on your hat, and you're finished. Nobody dast blame this man. A salesman is got to dream, boy. It comes with the territory.
Death of a Salesman, Requiem

RICHARD ROVERE

1915–

It is now of course conceded by most fair-minded and objective authorities that there is an establishment in America, a more or less closed and self-sustaining institution that holds a preponderance of power in our more or less open society.
The American Establishment [1962]

The Establishment is a general term for those people in finance, business and the professions, mostly from the Northeast, who hold the principal measure of power and influence in this country, regardless of what administration occupies the White House.   *Ib.*

The Establishment has very nearly unchallenged power in deciding what is and what is not respectable opinion in this country.   *Ib.*

ROBERT CONQUEST

1917–

Pure joy of knowledge rides as high as art.
The whole heart cannot keep alive on either.
Wills as of Drake and Shakespeare strike together;
Cultures turn rotten when they part.
True frontiers march with those in the mind's eye:

— The white sound rising now to fury
In efflux from the hot venturi
As Earth's close down, give us the end-
less sky.[1]

For the 1956 Opposition of Mars
[1961]

JOHN FITZGERALD KENNEDY
1917–1963

It was involuntary. They sank my
boat.

Remark when asked how he be-
came a hero. Quoted in ARTHUR
M. SCHLESINGER, JR., A *Thou-*
sand Days [1965], *ch. 4*

For without belittling the courage
with which men have died, we should
not forget those acts of courage with
which men . . . have *lived*. The courage of life is often a less dramatic spectacle than the courage of a final moment; but it is no less a magnificent
mixture of triumph and tragedy. A man
does what he must — in spite of personal consequences, in spite of obstacles
and dangers and pressures — and that is
the basis of all human morality.

Profiles in Courage [1956], *ch. 11*

It is time for a new generation of
leadership, to cope with new problems
and new opportunities. For there is a
new world to be won.

Television address [July 4, 1960]

The New Frontier of which I speak
is not a set of promises — it is a set of
challenges. It sums up not what I intend to offer the American people, but
what I intend to ask of them.

Speech accepting Democratic
presidential nomination [July
15, 1960]

Today, the eyes of all people are
truly upon us, and our governments, in
every branch, at every level, national,

state, and local, must be as a city upon
a hill,[1] constructed and inhabited by
men aware of their grave trust and their
great responsibilities.

Speech, Massachusetts State
Legislature [January 9, 1961]

For of those to whom much is given,
much is required.[2] And when at some
future date the high court of history sits
in judgment on each of us, recording
whether in our brief span of service we
fulfilled our responsibilities to the state,
our success or failure, in whatever office
we hold, will be measured by the answers to four questions: First, were we
truly men of courage . . . Second,
were we truly men of judgment . . .
Third, were we truly men of integrity
. . . Finally, were we truly men of dedication?   *Ib.*

We observe today not a victory of
party but a celebration of freedom,
symbolizing an end as well as a beginning, signifying renewal as well as
change.

Inaugural address [January 20,
1961]

Let the word go forth from this time
and place, to friend and foe alike, that
the torch has been passed to a new generation of Americans, born in this century, tempered by war, disciplined by a
hard and bitter peace, proud of our ancient heritage, and unwilling to witness
or permit the slow undoing of those
human rights to which this nation has
always been committed, and to which
we are committed today at home and
around the world.

Let every nation know, whether it
wishes us well or ill, that we shall pay
any price, bear any burden, meet any
hardship, support any friend, oppose
any foe to assure the survival and the
success of liberty.   *Ib.*

If a free society cannot help the
many who are poor, it cannot save the
few who are rich.   *Ib.*

---

[1] These lines were used in the Pacific Science
Center at the Seattle World's Fair in 1962 to
epitomize the interdependence of science and the
humanities.

[1] See John Winthrop, p. 318a, whom Kennedy
quoted in the preceding passage, and note.
[2] See *Luke 12:48*, p. 47a.

Let us never negotiate out of fear, but let us never fear to negotiate.
Inaugural address

All this will not be finished in the first one hundred days. Nor will it be finished in the first one thousand days, nor in the life of this Administration, nor even perhaps in our lifetime on this planet. But let us begin. *Ib.*

Now the trumpet summons us again — not as a call to bear arms, though arms we need; not as a call to battle, though embattled we are; but a call to bear the burden of a long twilight struggle,[1] year in and year out, "rejoicing in hope, patient in tribulation," a struggle against the common enemies of man: tyranny, poverty, disease and war itself. *Ib.*

The energy, the faith, the devotion which we bring to this endeavor will light our country and all who serve it, and the glow from that fire can truly light the world. *Ib.*

And so, my fellow Americans, ask not what your country can do for you; ask what you can do for your country.[2] *Ib.*

---

[1] See Stevenson, p. 1049a.

[2] For, stripped of the temporary associations which gave rise to it, it is now the moment when by common consent we pause to become conscious of our national life and to rejoice in it, to recall what our country has done for each of us, and to ask ourselves what we can do for our country in return. — OLIVER WENDELL HOLMES, JR. *Address Before John Sedwick Post No. 4, Grand Army of the Republic* [May 30, 1884]
As has often been said, the youth who loves his Alma Mater will always ask, not "What can she do for me?" but "What can I do for her?" — LE BARON RUSSELL BRIGGS, *Routine and Ideals* [1904]. *College Life*
In the great fulfillment we must have a citizenship less concerned about what the government can do for it and more anxious about what it can do for the nation. — WARREN GAMALIEL HARDING, *Republican National Convention, Chicago* [June 7, 1916]
This thought had lain in Kennedy's mind for a long time. As far back as 1945 he had noted down in a looseleaf notebook a quotation from Rousseau: "As soon as any man says of the affairs of the state, What does it matter to

It is our task in our time and in our generation to hand down undiminished to those who come after us, as was handed down to us by those who went before, the natural wealth and beauty which is ours.
Address, dedication ceremonies of the National Wildlife Federation Building [March 3, 1961]

For in the development of this organization [the United Nations] rests the only true alternative to war, and war appeals no longer as a rational alternative. Unconditional war can no longer lead to unconditional victory. It can no longer serve to settle disputes. It can no longer be of concern to great powers alone. For a nuclear disaster, spread by winds and waters and fear, could well engulf the great and the small, the rich and the poor, the committed and the uncommitted alike. Mankind must put an end to war or war will put an end to mankind. So let us resolve that Dag Hammarskjöld did not live, or die, in vain. Let us call a truce to terror.
Address, United Nations [September 25, 1961]

However close we sometimes seem to that dark and final abyss, let no man of peace and freedom despair. For he does not stand alone. If we all can persevere, if we can in every land and office look beyond our own shores and ambitions, then surely the age will dawn in which the strong are just and the weak secure and the peace preserved. *Ib.*

Those who make peaceful revolution impossible will make violent revolution inevitable.
Address to Latin American diplomats, the White House [March 12, 1962]

No one can doubt that the wave of the future is not the conquest of the world by a single dogmatic creed but

---

me? the state may be given up as lost." — ARTHUR M. SCHLESINGER, JR. *A Thousand Days* [1965], *prologue, footnote*

the liberation of the diverse energies of free nations and free men.
>*Address, University of California, Berkeley [March 23, 1962]*

I think this is the most extraordinary collection of talent, of human knowledge, that has ever been gathered together at the White House, with the possible exception of when Thomas Jefferson dined alone.
>*Address, White House dinner and reception honoring Nobel Prize winners [April 1962]*

Let us not be blind to our differences — but let us also direct attention to our common interests and the means by which those differences can be resolved. And if we cannot end now our differences, at least we can help make the world safe for diversity.
>*Address, American University, Washington, D.C. [June 10, 1963]*

Every American ought to have the right to be treated as he would wish to be treated, as one would wish his children to be treated. This is not the case.
>*Television address on civil rights, after the registration of two Negroes at the University of Alabama [June 12, 1963]*

We are confronted primarily with a moral issue. It is as old as the Scriptures and is as clear as the American Constitution.   *Ib.*

No one has been barred on account of his race from fighting or dying for America — there are no "white" or "colored" signs on the foxholes or graveyards of battle.
>*Message to Congress on proposed civil rights bill [June 19, 1963]*

All free men, wherever they may live, are citizens of Berlin. And therefore, as a free man, I take pride in the words "Ich bin ein Berliner."
>*Address at City Hall, West Berlin [June 26, 1963]*

Yesterday, a shaft of light cut into the darkness. . . . For the first time, an agreement has been reached on bringing the forces of nuclear destruction under international control. . . . It offers to all the world a welcome sign of hope. . . . But the achievement of this goal is not a victory for one side; it is a victory for mankind.
>*Television address, Washington [July 26, 1963]* [1]

When power leads man toward arrogance, poetry reminds him of his limitations. When power narrows the areas of man's concern, poetry reminds him of the richness and diversity of his existence. When power corrupts,[2] poetry cleanses, for art establishes the basic human truths which must serve as the touchstone of our judgment.
>*Address, Amherst College [October 26, 1963]*

I look forward to a great future for America, a future in which our country will match its military strength with our moral restraint, its wealth with our wisdom, its power with our purpose. I look forward to an America which will not be afraid of grace and beauty, which will protect the beauty of our natural environment . . . an America which will reward achievement in the arts as we reward achievement in business or statecraft. . . . I look forward to an America which commands respect throughout the world not only for its strength but for its civilization as well. And I look forward to a world which will be safe not only for democracy and diversity but also for personal distinction.   *Ib.*

Washington is a city of southern efficiency and northern charm.
>*Remark quoted in* ARTHUR M. SCHLESINGER, JR., *A Thousand Days* [1965], *ch. 25*

---

[1] In Moscow on July 25 Averell Harriman, Lord Hailsham, and Chairman Khrushchev initialed the nuclear test ban treaty.
[2] See Lord Acton, p. 750a.

ROBERT TRAILL SPENCE LOWELL
1917–1977

I will catch Christ with a greased
  worm.
> *The Drunken Fisherman*
> [1946], *st. 5*

I saw the spiders marching through air,
Swimming from tree to tree that mil-
  dewed day
In latter August when the hay
Came creaking to the barn.[1]
> *Mr. Edwards and the Spider*
> [1946], *st. 1*

On Windsor Marsh, I saw the spider
  die
When thrown into the bowels of fierce
  fire:
  There's no long struggle, no desire
  To get up on its feet and fly —
  It stretches out its feet
And dies. This is the sinner's last re-
  treat;
Yes, and no strength exerted on the
  heat
Then sinews the abolished will, when
  sick
And full of burning, it will whistle on a
  brick.   *Ib. st. 4*

This is the Black Widow, death.
> *Ib. st. 5*

Christ walks on the black water. In
  Black Mud
Darts the kingfisher. On Corpus Christi,
  heart,
Over the drum-beat of St. Stephen's
  choir
I hear him, *Stupor Mundi*, and the
  mud
Flies from his hunching wings and
  beak — my heart,
The blue kingfisher dives on you in fire.
> *Colloquy in Black Rock*
> [1946], *st. 5*

---

[1] Jonathan Edwards [1703–1758], the Calvin-
ist theologian, wrote at the age of twelve a series
of scientific observations on the spider. One of
his most famous sermons was "Sinners in the
Hands of an Angry God."

Our Lady of Babylon, go by, go by,
I was once the apple of your eye;
Flies, flies are on the plane tree, on the
  streets.
> *As a Plane Tree by the Water*
> [1946], *st. 1*

I saw the sky descending, black and
  white,
Not blue, on Boston.
> *Where the Rainbow Ends*
> [1946], *st. 1*

Now Paris, our black classic, breaking
  up
like killer kings on an Etruscan cup.
> *Beyond the Alps* [1959]

Your *Good Soldier*
the best French novel in the language.[1]
> *Ford Madox Ford* [1959]

O divorced, divorced
from the whale-fat of postwar London!
  Boomed,
cut, plucked and booted! In Provence,
  New York . . .
marrying, blowing . . . nearly dying
at Boulder, when the altitude
pressed the world on your heart.   *Ib.*

Fiction! I'm selling short
your lies that made the great your
  equals. Ford,
you were a kind man and you died in
  want.   *Ib.*

There is no God and Mary is His
  Mother.
> *For George Santayana* [1959]

You said:
"We poets in our youth begin in sadness;
thereof in the end come despondency
  and madness." [2]
> *To Delmore Schwartz (Cam-*
> *bridge 1946)* [1959]

Who asks for me, the Shelley of my
  age,
must lay his heart out for my bed and
  board.
> *Words for Hart Crane* [1959]

---

[1] See Ford Madox Ford, p. 915a.
[2] See Wordsworth, pp. 511b-512a.

I doodle handlebar
moustaches on the last Russian Czar.
                Grandparents [1959]

We are old-timers,
each of us holds a locked razor.
                Waking in the Blue [1959]

I keep no rank nor station.
Cured, I am frizzled, stale and small.
                *Home After Three Months
                Away* [1959]

Only teaching on Tuesdays, bookworm-
        ing
in pajamas fresh from the washer each
        morning,
I hog a whole house on Boston's
"hardly passionate Marlborough
        Street." [1]
                *Memories of West Street and
                Lepke* [1959]

These are the tranquillized *Fifties*,
and I am forty. Ought I to regret my
        seedtime?
I was a fire-breathing Catholic C.O.,
and made my manic statement,
telling off the state and president, and
        then
sat waiting sentence in the bull pen
beside a Negro boy with curlicues
of marijuana in his hair.   *Ib.*

Flabby, bald, lobotomized,
he drifted in a sheepish calm,
where no agonizing reappraisal
jarred his concentration on the electric
        chair —
hanging like an oasis in his air
of lost connections.   *Ib.*

Tamed by *Miltown*, we lie on Mother's
        bed.   *Man and Wife* [1959]

        Oh my *Petite*,
clearest of all God's creatures, still all
        air and nerve.   *Ib.*

your old-fashioned tirade —
loving, rapid, merciless —
breaks like the Atlantic Ocean on my
        head.   *Ib.*

[1] The quotation is from Henry James.

Gored by the climacteric of his want,
he stalls above me like an elephant.
        *"To Speak of Woe That Is in
                Marriage"* [1959]

My mind's not right.

A car radio bleats,
"Love, O careless Love. . . ." I hear
my ill-spirit sob in each blood cell,
as if my hand were at its throat. . . .
I myself am hell; [1]
nobody's here.
        Skunk Hour [1959], *st.* 5, 6

My old flame, my wife!
Remember our lists of birds?
        The Old Flame [1964], *st.* 1

Father, forgive me
my injuries,
as I forgive
those I
have injured!

You never climbed
Mount Sion, yet left
dinosaur
death-steps on the crust,
where I must walk.
        Middle Age [1964], *st.* 3, 4

We are like a lot of wild
spiders crying together,
but without tears.
        Fall 1961 [1964], *st.* 4

I am tired. Everyone's tired of my
        turmoil.
        Eye and Tooth [1964], *st.* 9

Two months after marching through
        Boston,
half the regiment was dead;
at the dedication,
William James could almost hear the
        bronze Negroes [2] breathe.

[1] See Virgil, p. 119a; and Marlowe, p. 213a,
and note.
[2] On the Saint-Gaudens monument to Colonel
Robert Gould Shaw and the 54th Massachusetts
Regiment.
        There on foot go the dark outcasts, so true
to nature that one can almost hear them breathing as they march. — WILLIAM JAMES, *Oration
at Dedication of the Monument* [May 31, 1897]
        See Charles W. Eliot, p. 752a, and Moody,
p. 899a.

Their monument sticks like a fishbone
in the city's throat.
Its Colonel is as lean
as a compass needle.

He has an angry wrenlike vigilance,
a greyhound's gentle tautness;
he seems to wince at pleasure,
and suffocate for privacy.
                        For the Union Dead
                        [1964], st. 7–9

on Boylston Street, a commercial
    photograph
shows Hiroshima boiling.   *Ib. st.* 14

When I crouch to my television set,
the drained faces of Negro school chil-
    dren rise like balloons. *Ib. st.* 15

The Aquarium is gone. Everywhere,
giant finned cars nose forward like fish;
a savage servility
slides by on grease.   *Ib. st.* 17

We beg delinquents for our life.
        *Central Park. In the New York
        Review [October 1965]*

ARTHUR MEIER
SCHLESINGER, JR.
1917–

Above all he [John F. Kennedy]
gave the world for an imperishable moment the vision of a leader who greatly
understood the terror and the hope, the
diversity and the possibility, of life on
this planet and who made people look
beyond nation and race to the future of
humanity.
        A Thousand Days [1] *[1965], ch.* 37

HARLAN CLEVELAND
1918–

The Revolution of Rising Expectations. [2]

        *Title of speech, Colgate
        University [1949]*

[1] See John F. Kennedy, p. 1073a-b, and
1074b.
[2] Almost fifteen years ago, when I was working
for Paul Hoffman in the Marshall Plan, I had to
substitute for him in making a speech at Col-

EDWIN O'CONNOR
1918–1968

The Last Hurrah.
        Title of novel [1956]

STEWART LEE UDALL
1920–

The most common trait of all primitive peoples is a reverence for the life-
giving earth, and the native American
shared this elemental ethic: the land
was alive to his loving touch, and he, its
son, was brother to all creatures. His
feelings were made visible in medicine
bundles and dance rhythms for rain,
and all of his religious rites and land
attitudes savored the inseparable world
of nature and God, the master of Life.
During the long Indian tenure the land
remained undefiled save for scars no
deeper than the scratches of cornfield
clearings or the farming canals of the
Hohokams on the Arizona desert.
        The Quiet Crisis [1] *[1963], ch.* 1

A land ethic for tomorrow should be
as honest as Thoreau's *Walden*, and as
comprehensive as the sensitive science
of ecology. It should stress the oneness
of our resources and the live-and-help-
live logic of the great chain of life. If,
in our haste to "progress," the economics of ecology are disregarded by citizens and policy makers alike, the result
will be an ugly America.   *Ib.* 14

gate University. Remembering Edmund Burke's
famous commentary on the turbulence of
his time, I called this speech "Reflections on the
Revolution of Rising Expectations." The phrase
has since been attributed to nearly every literate
American of our time, but I think this was the
first time that phrase saw the light of day. —
HARLAN CLEVELAND, *The Evolution of Rising
Responsibility, address before the U.N. [Decem-
ber 13, 1964]*
[1] The race between education and erosion,
between wisdom and waste has not run its course.
. . . The nation's battle to preserve the common
estate is far from won. . . . The crisis may be
quiet, but it is urgent. — JOHN F. KENNEDY,
introduction to The Quiet Crisis

JEROME DAVID SALINGER

1919–

I keep picturing all these little kids in this big field of rye. . . . If they're running and they don't look where they're going I have to come out from somewhere and catch them. That's all I'd do all day. I'd just be the catcher in the rye and all. I know it's crazy.
The Catcher in the Rye [1951]

There isn't anyone *any*where that isn't Seymour's Fat Lady. Don't you know that? Don't you know that goddam secret yet? And don't you know — *listen* to me, now — *don't you know who that Fat Lady really is?* . . . Ah, buddy. It's Christ Himself. Christ Himself, buddy.
Franny and Zooey [1961]

MAY SWENSON

1919–

Body my house
my horse my hound
what will I do
when you are fallen   *Question* [1963]

Where can I go
without my mount
all eager and quick
How will I know
in thicket ahead
is danger or treasure
when Body my good
bright dog is dead   *Ib.*

SLOAN WILSON

1920–

The Man in the Gray Flannel Suit.
Title of novel [1955]

RICHARD PURDY WILBUR

1921–

We respect
Some scholars' stutters.
Grace [1947], *st. 5*

The beautiful changes as a forest is changed
By a chameleon's tuning his skin to it.
The Beautiful Changes
[1947], *st. 2*

I dreamt the past was never past redeeming:
But whether this was false or honest dreaming
I beg death's pardon now. And mourn the dead.
The Pardon [1950], *last stanza*

We milk the cow of the world, and as we do
We whisper in her ear, "You are not true."   *Epistemology* [1950], *II*

I never knew the road
From which the whole earth didn't call away,
With wild birds rounding the hill crowns,
Haling out of the heart an old dismay.
The Sirens [1950], *st. 1*

He rocked his only world, and everyone's.
Forgive the hero, you who would have died
Gladly with all you knew; he rode that tide
To Ararat: all men are Noah's sons.
Still, Citizen Sparrow [1950],
last stanza

Ho-hum. I am for wit and wakefulness,
And love this feigning lady by Bazille.
What's lightly hid is deepest understood,
And when with social smile and formal dress
She teaches leaves to curtsy and quadrille,
I think there are most tigers in the wood.   *Ceremony* [1950], *st. 3*

The eyes open to a cry of pulleys,
And spirited from sleep, the astounded soul
Hangs for a moment bodiless and simple.
as false dawn.

Outside the open window
The morning air is all awash with
    angels.
*Love Calls Us to the Things of
This World* [1956]

The soul shrinks
From all that it is about to remember,
From the punctual rape of every blessèd
    day,
And cries,
    "Oh, let there be nothing on earth
    but laundry,
Nothing but rosy hands in the rising
    steam
And clear dances done in the sight of
    heaven.   *Ib.*

Neither pale nor bright,
The turkey-cock parades
Through radiant squalors, darkly auspi-
    cious as
The ace of spades,

Himself his own cortège
And puffed with the pomp of death,
Rehearsing over and over with strangled
    râle
His latest breath.
    A Black November Turkey
        [1956], *st. 3, 4*

Mind in its purest play is like some bat
That beats about in caverns all alone,
Contriving by a kind of senseless wit
Not to conclude against a wall of stone.

It has no need to falter or explore;
Darkly it knows what obstacles are
    there,
And so may weave and flitter, dip and
    soar
In perfect courses through the blackest
    air.

And has this simile a like perfection?
The mind is like a bat. Precisely. Save
That in the very happiest intellection
A graceful error may correct the cave.
        Mind [1956]

Dear God, let it be with these donkeys
    that I come,
And let it be that angels lead us in
    peace

To leafy streams where cherries tremble
    in air,
Sleek as the laughing flesh of girls; and
    there
In that haven of souls let it be that,
    leaning above
Your divine waters, I shall resemble
    these donkeys,
Whose humble and sweet poverty will
    appear
Clear in the clearness of your eternal
    love.
    *Francis Jammes: A Prayer to Go
    to Paradise with the Donkeys*
    [1956]

The werewolf's painful change. Turn-
    ing his head away
On the sweaty bolster, he tries to re-
    member
The mood of manhood,

But lies at last, as always,
Letting it happen, the fierce fur soft
    to his face,
Hearing with sharper ears.
        Beasts [1956], *st. 3, 4*

What is our praise or pride
But to imagine excellence, and try to
    make it?
What does it say over the door of
    Heaven
But *homo fecit?*
    *For the New Railway Station in
    Rome* [1956], *last stanza*

When you come, as you soon must, to
    the streets of our city,
Mad-eyed from stating the obvious,
Not proclaiming our fall but begging
    us
In God's name to have self-pity,

Spare us all word of the weapons, their
    force and range,
The long numbers that rocket the
    mind;
Our slow, unreckoning hearts will be
    left behind,
Unable to fear what is too strange.

Nor shall you scare us with talk of the
    death of the race.

How should we dream of this place
    without us? —
The sun mere fire, the leaves untrou-
    bled about us,
A stone look on the stone's face?
        Advice to a Prophet [1961], *st.* 3

Ask us, prophet, how we shall call
Our natures forth when that live
    tongue is all
Dispelled, that glass obscured or broken

In which we have said the rose of our
    love and the clean
Horse of our courage, in which beheld
The singing locust of the soul un-
    shelled,
And all we mean or wish to mean.
        Ib. st. 7, 8

Duke, keep your coin. All men are born
    distraught,
And will not for the world be satisfied.
Whether we live in fact, or but in
    thought,
We die of thirst, here at the fountain-
    side.
        *Ballade for the Duke of Or-
        léans* [1] [1961], *who offered a
        prize at Blois* [c. 1457] *for the
        best ballade employing the line
        "Je meurs de soif auprès de la
        fontaine."*

All bitter things conduce to sweet,
    As this example shows;
Without the little spirochete
We'd have no chocolate to eat,
Nor would tobacco's fragrance greet
    The European nose.
        *Pangloss's Song: A Comic
        Opera Lyric* [1961]

What can I do but move
From folly to defeat,
And call that sorrow sweet
That teaches us to see
The final face of love
In what we cannot be?
        *Someone Talking to Himself
        [1961], last stanza*

[1] See Charles d'Orléans, p. 170b.

WILLIAM H. MAULDIN
1921–

I feel like a fugitive from th' law of
averages.
        Up Front [1944]. *Caption
        for cartoon*

Look at an infantryman's eyes and
you can tell how much war he has seen.
        Ib.

He's right, Joe, when we ain't fightin' we should ack like sojers.   *Ib.*

JACK KEROUAC
1922–1969

The beat generation.   *Remark*

But then they danced down the
street like dingledodies, and I shambled
after as I've been doing all my life after
people who interest me, because the
only people for me are the mad ones,
the ones who are mad to live, mad to
talk, mad to be saved, desirous of everything at the same time, the ones who
never yawn or say a commonplace
thing, but burn, burn, burn like fabulous yellow roman candles exploding
like spiders across the stars and in the
middle you see the blue centerlight pop
and everybody goes "Awww!"
        On the Road [1957]

PHILIP LARKIN
1922–

Only one ship is seeking us, a black-
Sailed unfamiliar, towing at her back
A huge and birdless silence. In her wake
No waters breed or break.
        Next, Please [1955]

JAMES DICKEY
1923–

All families lie together, though some
    are burned alive.
The others try to feel
For them. Some can, it is often said.
        The Firebombing [1965]

There,
In the other wood,

The uncornered animal's, running off
Upon instinct. Sails spread, fox wings
Lift him alive over gullies,
Hair tips all over him lightly

Touched with the moon's red silver,
  Back-hearing around
The stream of his body the tongue of
    hounds
  Feather him. In his own animal sun
Made of human moonlight,

He flies like a bolt running home.
              Fox Blood [1965]

JAMES BALDWIN
1924–

[The Negro past] of rope, fire, torture, castration, infanticide, rape; death and humiliation; fear by day and night, fear as deep as the marrow of the bone; doubt that he was worthy of life, since everyone around him denied it; sorrow for his women, for his kinfolk, for his children, who needed his protection, and whom he could not protect; rage, hatred and murder, hatred for white men so deep that it often turned against him and his own, and made all love, all trust, all joy impossible.
      The Fire Next Time [1963] [1]

TRUMAN CAPOTE
1924–

Other Voices, Other Rooms.
          Title of book [1948]

I didn't want to harm the man. I thought he was a very nice gentleman. Soft-spoken. I thought so right up to the moment I cut his throat.
         In Cold Blood [1966]

[1] Originally published in *The New Yorker* as *Letter from a Region of My Mind* [November 1962]

See Anonymous, Spiritual, p. 1101a.

MISHIMA YUKIO
1925–1970

My solitude grew more and more obese, like a pig.
   Temple of the Golden Pavilion [1]
                 [1959]

The first real problem I faced in my life was that of beauty.   *Ib.*

What made her ugly was — hope. Incurable hope, like an obstinate case of scabies, which lodges, damp and reddish, in the infected skin, producing a constant itching, and refusing to yield to any outer force.   *Ib.*

ALLEN GINSBERG
1926–

I saw the best minds of my generation
  destroyed by madness, starving
  hysterical naked,
dragging themselves through the negro
  streets at dawn looking for an
  angry fix
angelheaded hipsters burning for the
  ancient heavenly connection to the
  starry dynamo in the machinery of
  night.   *Howl* [1956]

WILLIAM D. SNODGRASS
1926–

It was the nature of the thing:
No moon outlives its leaving night,
No sun its day. And I went on
Rich in the loss of all I sing
To the threshold of waking light,
To larksong and the live, gray dawn.
So night by night, my life has gone.
           Orpheus [1959]

Pale soul, consumed by fear
of the living world you haunt,
have you learned what habits lead you
to hunt what you do not want;
learned who does not need you;
learned you are no one here?
        Home Town [1959]

Though trees turn bare and girls turn
  wives,

[1] Translated by IVAN MORRIS.

We shall afford our costly seasons;
There is a gentleness survives
That will outspeak and has its reasons.
There is a loveliness exists,
Preserves us, not for specialists.
April Inventory [1959]

MICHAEL HARRINGTON
1928–

The millions who are poor in the United States tend to become increasingly invisible. . . . It takes an effort of the intellect and will even to see them.
The Other America: Poverty in the United States [1962], *ch.* 1

The other America, the America of poverty, is hidden today in a way that it never was before. Its millions are socially invisible to the rest of us. . . . The very development of American society is creating a new kind of blindness about poverty. The poor are increasingly slipping out of the very experience and consciousness of the nation. *Ib.*

That the poor are invisible is one of the most important things about them. They are not simply neglected . . . they are not seen. *Ib.*

For the urban poor the police are those who arrest you. In almost any slum there is a vast conspiracy against the forces of law and order. *Ib.*

ANNE SEXTON
1928–

You, Doctor Martin, walk
from breakfast to madness. Late August,
I speed through the antiseptic tunnel
    where the moving dead still talk
of pushing their bones against the
    thrust
of cure. And I am queen of this summer hotel
    or the laughing bee on a stalk
of death.
You, Doctor Martin [1960], *st.* 1

And we are magic talking to itself,
noisy and alone. I am queen of all my
sins

forgotten. Am I still lost?
Once I was beautiful. Now I am myself,
counting this row and that row of
moccasins
    waiting on the silent shelf.
You, Doctor Martin, last stanza

MARTIN LUTHER KING, JR.
1929–1968

Injustice anywhere is a threat to justice everywhere.
Letter from the Birmingham jail. In the Atlantic Monthly [*August 1963*]

Unearned suffering is redemptive. *Ib.*

Nonviolence is the answer to the crucial political and moral questions of our time; the need for man to overcome oppression and violence without resorting to oppression and violence.
Man must evolve for all human conflict a method which rejects revenge, aggression and retaliation. The foundation of such a method is love.[1]
Speech accepting Nobel Peace Prize [*December 11, 1964*]

The tortuous road which has led from Montgomery to Oslo is a road over which millions of Negroes are traveling to find a new sense of dignity. It will, I am convinced, be widened into a superhighway of justice. *Ib.*

I accept this award with an abiding faith in America and an audacious faith in the future of mankind. I refuse to accept the idea that the "isness" of man's present nature makes him morally incapable of reaching up for the "oughtness" that forever confronts him. *Ib.*

I refuse to accept the cynical notion that nation after nation must spiral down a militaristic stairway into the hell of nuclear destruction. I believe that unarmed truth and unconditional love will have the final word in reality. *Ib.*

[1] See Gandhi, p. 897a.

Nonviolent action, the Negro saw, was the way to supplement, not replace, the process of change. It was the way to divest himself of passivity without arraying himself in vindictive force.
　　　　　Why We Can't Wait [1964]

The Negro was willing to risk martyrdom in order to move and stir the social conscience of his community and the nation . . . he would force his oppressor to commit his brutality openly, with the rest of the world looking on . . . Nonviolent resistance paralyzed and confused the power structures against which it was directed.
　　　　　　　　　　　　　Ib.

YEVGENY ALEXANDROVICH YEVTUSHENKO
1933–

There is no Jewish blood in my veins,
But I am hated with a scabby hatred
By all the anti-Semites,
　　　like a Jew.
And therefore
　　　I am a true Russian.
　　　　　　　Babi Yar [1961]

ANDREI VOZNESENSKY
1933–

I am Goya
of the bare field, by the enemy's beak
　　　gouged
till the craters of my eyes gape
I am grief

I am the tongue
of war, the embers of cities

on the snows of the year 1941
I am hunger
　　　I Am Goya [1] [1960], *st. 1, 2*

The urge to kill, like the urge to beget,
Is blind and sinister. Its craving is set
Today on the flesh of a hare: tomorrow
　　　it can
Howl the same way for the flesh of a
　　　man.
　　　Hunting a Hare [2] [1964], *st. 5*

Does each cell have a soul within it?
If so, fling open all your little doors,
And all your souls shall flutter like the
　　　linnet
In the cages of my pores.
　　　　Dead Still [3] [1965], *st. 4*

　　I am myself
Among the avalanches, like the Abominable
Snowman, absolutely elusive.
　　　Who Are We? [4] [1959], *st. 7*

Along a parabola life like a rocket flies,
Mainly in darkness, now and then on a
　　　rainbow.
　　　　Parabolic Ballad [5] [1960]

Worms come through holes and bold
　　　men on parabolas.　　　*Ib.*

[1] A good example of his use of assonance: *Ya Goya . . . nagoye . . . ya gore . . . ya golos . . . goda . . . ya golod . . . ya gorlo . . . goloi.* — P. BLAKE and M. HAYWARD, eds., *Antiworlds: Poetry by Andrei Voznesensky* [1966]
　　Translated by STANLEY KUNITZ.
[2] Translated by W. H. AUDEN.
[3] Translated by RICHARD WILBUR.
[4] Translated by STANLEY MOSS.
[5] Translated by W. H. AUDEN.

ANONYMOUS [1]

ANONYMOUS
1250–1700

Sumer is icumen in,
　Lhude sing cuccu!
Groweth sed, and bloweth med,
　And springth the wude nu —
Sing cuccu! [2]　*Cuckoo Song* [c. 1250]

[1] See also p. 149.
[2] See Vogelweide, p. 156a, and Pound, p. 987b-988a.

Ich am of Irlonde
Ant of the holy lande
　Of Irlonde.
Gode sire, pray ich the,
For of saynte charite,
Come ant dance wyth me
　In Irlonde.
　　　Ich Am of Irlonde

When Adam delved and Eve span
Who was then a gentleman?
> *Text used by* JOHN BALL *for his*
> *speech at Blackheath to the men*
> *in Wat Tyler's Rebellion* [1381]

I sing of a maiden
  That is makeless;
King of all kings
  To her son she ches.
> *Carol. I Sing of a Maiden* [15th
> century]

For in my mind, of all mankind
I love but you alone.
> *The Nut-Brown Maid* [15th
> century], *refrain*

For I must to the greenwood go,
Alone, a banished man.   *Ib.*

No burial this pretty pair
  Of any man receives,
Till Robin Redbreast piously
  Did cover them with leaves.
> *The Children in the Wood,*
> st. 16

A fool's paradise.
> *Paston Letters* [1462], *no.* 457

Everyman, I will go with thee, and be
  thy guide,
In thy most need to go by thy side.
> *Everyman* [before 1500], *act I,*
> *l.* 522

O Western wind, when wilt thou blow,
  That the small rain down can rain?
Christ, that my love were in my arms
  And I in my bed again!   [*c.* 1530]

Why fearest thou thy outward foe,
  When thou thyself thy harm dost
  feed?
Of grief, or hurt, of pain, or woe,
  Within each thing is sown the seed.
> *From* TOTTEL'S MISCELLANY,
> *Songs and Sonnets* [1557]

Crabbed age and youth cannot live together.
Youth is full of pleasance, age is full of
  care.
> *The Passionate Pilgrim* [1] [1599]

[1] Often attributed to Shakespeare.

Love me little, love me long,
Is the burden of my song.[1]
> *Love Me Little* [1569–1570],
> *refrain*

Multiplication is vexation,
Division is as bad;
The rule of three doth puzzle me,
And practice drives me mad.
> *Elizabethan MS* [1570]

Greensleeves was all my joy,
  Greensleeves was my delight;
Greensleeves was my heart of gold,
  And who but Lady Greensleeves.

Alas, my Love! ye do me wrong
  To cast me off discourteously:
And I have loved you so long,
  Delighting in your company.
> *From A Handful of Pleasant*
> *Delights* [1584], *refrain and st.* 1

Shall I bid her go? What, and if I do?
Shall I bid her go, and spare not?
O no, no, no, I dare not.[2]
> *Corydon's Farewell to Phillis,*
> st. 2

Where griping griefs the heart would
  wound
And doleful dumps the mind oppress,
There music with her silver sound
With speed is wont to send redress.[3]
> *A Song to the Lute in Musicke,*
> st. 1

The blinded boy that shoots so trim,[4]
From heaven down did hie.
> *King Cophetua and the Beggar*
> *Maid,* st. 2

It was a friar of orders gray [5]
Walked forth to tell his beads.
> *The Friar of Orders Gray,*[6] *st.* 1

[1] See Shakespeare, *Romeo and Juliet* II, *vi,*
14, p. 224b and Herrick, p. 320a.
[2] Paraphrased by Shakespeare in *Twelfth-*
Night [1598–1600], *act II, sc. iii.*
[3] Another version is used by Shakespeare in
Romeo and Juliet [1594–1595], *act IV, sc. v.*
[4] See Shakespeare, *Romeo and Juliet* II, *i, 13,*
p. 223b.
[5] See Shakespeare, *The Taming of the Shrew*
IV, *i, 148,* p. 219b.
[6] THOMAS PERCY [1728–1811] composed this
ballad from various fragments of ancient
ballads found in Shakespeare's plays. It appeared

Our joys as wingèd dreams do fly;
  Why then should sorrow last?
Since grief but aggravates thy loss,
  Grieve not for what is past.
          The Friar of Orders Gray, st. 13

King Stephen was a worthy peer,
His breeches cost him but a crown.
          *Take Thy Old Cloak About
              Thee,*[1] *st.* 7

It's pride that puts this country down;
Man, take thine old cloak about thee.
                              Ib.

A fool and his money are soon parted.
          Saying current since the 16*th
                          century*

April is in my mistress' face,
And July in her eyes hath place,
Within her bosom is September,
But in her heart a cold December.
          From THOMAS MORLEY, *Madri-
          gals to Four Voices . . . the
          First Book* [1594]

Lo here a new Aurora!
          From THOMAS MORLEY, *The
          First Book of Canzonets*
          [1595]

Kill then, and bliss me,
But first come kiss me.
          From THOMAS MORLEY, *The
          First Book of Ballets* [1595]

Shoot, false Love, I care not.
Spend thy shafts and spare not.   *Ib.*

I was more true to Love than Love to
  me.
          From JOHN DOWLAND, *The
          First Book of Songs or Airs*
          [1597]

Thulé, the period of cosmography,
  Doth vaunt of Hecla, whose sulphur-
      eous fire
Doth melt the frozen clime and thaw
      the sky;
  Trinacrian Aetna's flames ascend not
      higher.

These things seem wondrous, yet more
  wondrous I,
Whose heart with fear doth freeze, with
  love doth fry.
          From THOMAS WEELKES, *Mad-
          rigals of Six Parts* [1600]

Jerusalem, my happy home,
  When shall I come to thee?
When shall my sorrows have an end?
  Thy joys when shall I see?
          The Song of Mary [1601]

What poor astronomers are they
Take women's eyes for stars!
          From JOHN DOWLAND, *The
          Third and Last Book of Songs
          or Airs* [1603]

O what a plague is love! How shall I
  bear it?
She will inconstant prove, I greatly fear
  it.
          Phillida Flouts Me, st. 1

And let all women strive to be
As constant as Penelope.
          Constant Penelope, st. 18

Fain would I change that note
To which fond Love hath charmed me.
          From TOBIAS HUME, *Musical
                      Humors* [1605]

Turn again Whittington,
Lord Mayor of London.[1]
          *Refrain of Bow Bells heard by
          Dick Whittington* [c. 1605]

O metaphysical tobacco,
Fetched as far as from Morocco,
    Thy searching fume
    Exhales the rheum,
O metaphysical tobacco.[2]
          From MICHAEL EAST, *The
          Second Set of Madrigals*
          [1606]

From the hag and hungry goblin
That into rags would rend ye,
And the spirit that stands by the naked
  man
In the book of Moons defend ye!
          Tom o' Bedlam [17*th century*],
                              st. 1

in his *Reliques of Ancient English Poetry*
[1765].
  [1] Quoted in Shakespeare, *Othello II, iii,* 93.

  [1] Richard Whittington, son of a London
mercer, rose to be mayor of London three times
before his death in 1423.
  [2] See Byron, p. 563a, and note.

With an host of furious fancies
Whereof I am commander,
With a burning spear, and a horse of
    air,
To the wilderness I wander.
By a knight of ghosts and shadows
I summoned am to tourney
Ten leagues beyond the wide world's
    end.
Methinks it is no journey.
                Tom o' Bedlam, st. 8

There is a lady sweet and kind,
Was never face so pleased my mind;
I did but see her passing by,
And yet I love her till I die.
        From THOMAS FORD, *Music of*
        Sundry Kinds [1607], *st. 1*

Cupid is wingèd and doth range,
Her country so my love doth change;
But change she earth, or change she sky,
Yet will I love her till I die.   *Ib. st. 6*

Four arms, two necks, one wreathing;
Two pairs of lips, one breathing;
Two hearts that multiply
Sighs interchangeably.
        From THOMAS WEELKES, *Airs*
        or Fantastic Spirits [1608]

Love not me for comely grace,
For my pleasing eye or face,
Nor for any outward part,
No, nor for a constant heart.
        From JOHN WILBYE, *Second Set*
        of Madrigals [1608]

The silver swan, who living had no note,
When death approached unlocked her
    silent throat;
Leaning her breast against the reedy
    shore,
Thus sung her first and last, and sung
    no more:
Farewell, all joys; O death, come close
    mine eyes;
More geese than swans now live, more
    fools than wise.
        From ORLANDO GIBBONS, *The*
        First Set of Madrigals and Mo-
        tets [1612], *I*

Laïs now old, that erst attempting lass,
To goddess Venus consecrates her glass;
For she herself hath now no use of one,

No dimpled cheeks hath she to gaze
    upon.
She cannot see her springtime damask
    grace,
Nor dare she look upon her winter face.[1]
        From ORLANDO GIBBONS, *The*
        First Set of Madrigals and Mo-
        tets, XIII

Stay, O sweet, and do not rise!
The light that shines comes from thine
    eyes;
The day breaks not: it is my heart,
Because that you and I must part.
    Stay, or else my joys will die,
    And perish in their infancy.[2]
        JOHN DOWLAND, *A Pilgrim's*
        Solace [1612]

If there is a paradise on the face of the
    earth,
It is this, oh! it is this, oh! it is this.[3]
        Mogul Inscription in the Red
        Fort at Delhi [1640]

And when with envy Time, transported,
Shall think to rob us of our joys,
You'll in your girls again be courted,
And I'll go wooing in my boys.
                Winifreda, st. 8

But in vain she did conjure him
To depart her presence so;
Having a thousand tongues to allure
    him,
And but one to bid him go.
              Dulcina,[4] *st. 2*

Over the mountains and over the waves,
Under the fountains and under the
    graves;
Under floods that are deepest, which
    Neptune obey,
Over rocks that are steepest, Love will
    find out the way.
    Love Will Find Out the Way, st. 1

Begone, dull Care! I prithee begone
    from me!

[1] Imitated from the Greek of Plato, *The
Greek Anthology.*
See Prior, p. 388a.

[2] Attributed also to John Donne, and included
in a variant in the seventh edition of his poems
[1669].

[3] The translation is from Persian in Murray's
Guide to India.

[4] This song is mentioned by IZAAK WALTON
in *The Compleat Angler* [1653]. It has been
ascribed to Raleigh, on very doubtful authority.

Begone, dull Care! Thou and I shall
  never agree.
> *From* JOHN PLAYFORD, *Musical*
>   *Companion* [1687]

Though little, I'll work as hard as a
  Turk,
If you'll give me employ,
To plow and sow, and reap and mow,
And be a farmer's boy.
> *The Farmer's Boy* [before
>   1689], *st.* 2

Carriages without horses shall go,
And accidents fill the world with woe.
> *Prophecy attributed to Mother*
>   *Shipton* [1] [*17th century*]

Around the world thoughts shall fly
In the twinkling of an eye.   *Ib.*

Under water men shall walk,
Shall ride, shall sleep, and talk;
In the air men shall be seen
In white, in black, and in green.   *Ib.*

Iron in the water shall float
As easy as a wooden boat.   *Ib.*

A swarm of bees in May
Is worth a load of hay;
A swarm of bees in June
Is worth a silver spoon;
A swarm of bees in July
Is not worth a fly.
> *Old English saying*

When poverty comes in at the door,
loves flies out the window.
> *Saying current since the 17th*
>   *century*

Please to remember the fifth of November,
Gunpowder treason and plot.
> *Guy Fawkes's Rhyme, tradi-*
>   *tional in England since the*
>   *17th century*

BALLADS

The king sits in Dunfermline town
Drinking the blude-red wine.
> *Sir Patrick Spens, st.* 1

[1] Most of the prophecies attributed to Mother
Shipton — a witch and prophetess, according to
tradition, who lived in Yorkshire in Tudor
times — are fabrications of the seventeenth century and later.

To Noroway, to Noroway,
To Noroway o'er the faem;
The king's daughter o' Noroway,
'Tis thou must bring her hame.

The first word that Sir Patrick read
So loud, loud laughed he;
The neist word that Sir Patrick read
The tear blinded his e'e.   *Ib. st. 4, 5*

I saw the new moon late yestreen
Wi' the auld moon in her arm;
And if we gang to sea, master,
I fear we'll come to harm.   *Ib. st. 10*

O laith, laith were our gude Scots lords
To wet their cork-heel'd shoon;
But lang or a' the play was play'd
They wat their hats aboon.
> *Ib. st. 15*

Half owre, half owre to Aberdour,
'Tis fifty fathoms deep;
And there lies gude Sir Patrick Spens,
Wi' the Scots lords at his feet!
> *Ib. st. 19*

"And what will ye leave to your ain
  mither dear,
Edward, Edward?"
> *Edward, Edward, st. 7*

"The curse of hell frae me sall ye bear,
Sic counsels ye give to me, O!"   *Ib.*

Fight on, my merry men all;
For why, my life is at an end.[1]
> *Chevy Chase*

A fairer lady there never was seen
Than the blind beggar's daughter of
  Bethnal Green.
> *The Beggar's Daughter of Beth-*
>   *nal Green,* [2] *st. 33*

When captains courageous, whom
  death could not daunt,

[1] Says Johnnie, "Fight on, my merry men all,
I'm a little wounded, but I am not slain;
I will lay me down for to bleed a while,
Then I'll rise and fight with you again."
> *Johnnie Armstrong's Last Goodnight,*
>   *st. 18; from* DRYDEN'S *Miscellanies*
>   [1702]

[2] This very house was built by the blind
beggar of Bednall Green, so much talked of
and sung in ballads. — SAMUEL PEPYS, *Diary*
[June 26, 1663]

Did march to the siege of the city of
   Gaunt,
They mustered their soldiers by two and
   by three,
And the foremost in battle was Mary
   Ambree.   *Mary Ambree,*[1] *st. 1*

Then let Jane Shore with sorrow sing,
That was belovèd of a king.
              Jane Shore, st. 1

"I'll rest," said he, "but thou shalt
   walk";
   So doth this wandering Jew
From place to place, but cannot rest
   For seeing countries new.
          The Wandering Jew, st. 9

For thirty pence our Savior was sold[2]
Among the false Jews, as I have been
   told;
And twenty-nine is the worth of thee,
For I think thou art one penny worser
   than he.
        King John and the Abbot of
               Canterbury, st. 21

Glasgerion swore a full great oath,
By oak, and ash and thorn.[3]
            Glasgerion, st. 19

In Scarlet town, where I was born,
There was a fair maid dwellin',
Made every youth cry Well-a-way!
   Her name was Barbara Allen.

All in the merry month of May,
When green buds they were swellin',
Young Jemmy Grove on his deathbed
   lay,
For love of Barbara Allen.
        Barbara Allen's Cruelty, st. 1, 2

So slowly, slowly rase she up,
And slowly she came nigh him,
And when she drew the curtain by —
"Young man, I think you're dyin'."
                 Ib. st. 4

True Thomas lay on Huntlie Bank;
A ferlie he spied wi' his e'e;

And there he saw a lady bright
Come riding down by the Eildon Tree.
         Thomas the Rhymer, st. 1

"A bed, a bed," Clerk Saunders said,
"A bed for you and me!"
"Fye na, fye na," said may Margaret,
"Till anes we married be!"
            Clerk Saunders, st. 2

There were twa sisters sat in a bour;
   Binnorie, O Binnorie!
There came a knight to be their wooer,
   By the bonnie milldams o' Binnorie.
                Binnorie, st. 1

There were three ravens sat on a tree,
They were as black as they might be.

The one of them said to his make,
"Where shall we our breakfast take?"
          The Three Ravens, st. 1, 2

Down there came a fallow doe
As great with young as she might go.
                 Ib. st. 6

She buried him before the prime,
She was dead herself ere evensong time.

God send every gentleman
Such hounds, such hawks, and such a
   leman.   *Ib. st. 9, 10*

Mony a one for him maks mane,
But nane sall ken where he is gane:
O'er his white banes, when they are
   bare,
The wind sall blaw for evermair.
          The Twa Corbies, st. 5

Ye Highlands and ye Lawlands,
O where hae ye been?
They hae slain the Earl of Murray,
And hae laid him on the green.
        The Bonny Earl of Murray, st. 1

O waly, waly, up the bank,
And waly, waly, doun the brae,
And waly, waly, yon burnside,
Where I and my Love wont to gae!
            Waly, Waly, st. 1

O waly, waly, gin love be bonnie,
A little time while it is new!
But when 'tis auld it waxeth cauld,
And fades awa' like morning dew.
                 Ib. st. 2

---

[1] Ben Jonson calls any virago Mary Ambree, and John Fletcher alludes to Mary Ambree in *The Scornful Lady* [1616].
[2] See George Herbert, p. 322b.
[3] See Kipling, p. 876b.

But had I wist, before I kist,
That love had been sae ill to win,
I had lock'd my heart in a case o' gowd,
And pinn'd it wi' a siller pin.
Waly, Waly, st. 5

"What gat ye to your dinner, Lord
   Randal, my son?
What gat ye to your dinner, my hand-
   some young man?"
"I gat eels boil'd in broo'; mother, make
   my bed soon,
For I'm weary wi' hunting, and fain
   wald lie down."   *Lord Randal*

A ship I have got in the North Country
And she goes by the name of the
   "Golden Vanity,"
O, I fear she will be taken by a Spanish
   Gal-la-lee,
As she sails by the Lowlands low.
The Golden Vanity, st. 1

THE NEW ENGLAND PRIMER[1]

In Adam's fall
We sinned all.

My Book and Heart
Must never part.

Young Obadias,
David, Josias —
All were pious.

Peter denied
His Lord, and cried.

Young Timothy
Learnt sin to fly.

Xerxes did die,
And so must I.

Zaccheus he
Did climb the tree
Our Lord to see.

Our days begin with trouble here,
Our life is but a span,[2]

[1] As early as 1691, Benjamin Harris of Boston
advertised the forthcoming second impression of
the *New England Primer*. The oldest known
copy extant is dated 1737.
[2] See Bacon, p. 209b-210a.

And cruel death is always near,
So frail a thing is man.

Now I lay me down to sleep,[1]
I pray the Lord my soul to keep;
If I should die before I wake,
I pray the Lord my soul to take.

ANONYMOUS
18th century

Sabina has a thousand charms
   To captivate my heart;
Her lovely eyes are Cupid's arms,
   And every look a dart:
But when the beauteous idiot speaks,
   She cures me of my pain;
Her tongue the servile fetters breaks
   And frees her slave again.
From Amphion Anglicus [1700]

Who will change old lamps for new?
The Arabian Nights [European
Version, c. 1700], *The History
of Aladdin*

Open sesame!
Ib. The History of Ali Baba

Drive a coach and six through an Act
of Parliament.
*Credited to Sir Stephen Rice
[1637–1715], Chief Baron of
the Exchequer, by* MACAULAY *in
History of England* [1849–1861],
ch. 12

The Campbells are comin', oho, oho.
Song [c. 1715]

For without money, George,
   A man is but a beast:
But bringing money, thou shalt be
   Always my welcome guest.
George Barnwell,[2] II, st. 25

[1] The first record of this prayer is found in
the *Enchiridion Leonis* [A.D. 1160]. The early
editions of the *Primer* give the first line of the
prayer as: "Now I lay me down to take my
sleep." The familiar version of the line appeared in the edition of 1784. In the edition of
1814 the second line reads, "I pray thee, Lord,
my soul to keep."
[2] Inspired by GEORGE LILLO's play, *The London Merchant; or, The History of George
Barnwell*, first acted in 1731.

The Girl I Left Behind Me.
　　　　　Title of song [1759]

The united voice of all His Majesty's free and loyal subjects in America —liberty and property, and no stamps.
　　　Motto of various American colonial newspapers [1765–1766]

Yankee Doodle came to town
　Upon a little pony,
He stuck a feather in his hat
　And called it macaroni.

Yankee Doodle, keep it up,
　Yankee Doodle dandy,
Mind the music and the step,
　And with the girls be handy.
　　　Yankee Doodle,[1] *st. 1, chorus*

It's all in the day's work.
　　　Current since the 18th century

Man may work from sun to sun,
But woman's work is never done.
　　　　　　　　　Old saying

Count that day lost whose low descending sun
Views from thy hand no worthy action done.[2]　　　*Old saying*

In good king Charles's golden days,
When loyalty no harm meant;
A furious High-Churchman I was,
And so I gain'd preferment.
Unto my flock I daily preach'd,
Kings are by God appointed,

---

[1] This version was sufficiently popular in America in 1767 to be used in the ballad opera *The Disappointment; or, The Force of Credulity* by ANDREW BARTON.
　　Father and I went up to camp,
　　　Along with Captain Goodwin;
　　And there we saw the men and boys,
　　　As thick as hasty pudding.
　　　　Yankee doodle do.
　　　　Version used by ROYALL TYLER,
　　　　　in The Contrast [1790]
The origin of *Yankee Doodle* remains as mysterious as ever, unless it be deemed a positive result to have eliminated definitely every theory thus far advanced. — OSCAR GEORGE THEODORE SONNECK, *Report on the Star-Spangled Banner, Hail Columbia, America, Yankee Doodle* [1909]

[2] An earlier version (signed by JAMES BOBART, December 8, 1697) begins "Think" rather than "Count."

And damned are those who dare resist,
Or touch the Lord's Anointed.
And this is law, I will maintain,
Unto my dying day, sir,
That whatsoever king shall reign,
I will be the Vicar of Bray, sir!
　　　The Vicar of Bray [1734],
　　　　　st. 1 and chorus

Don't tread on me.
　　　Motto of the first official American flag; first raised by Lieutenant John Paul Jones in Commodore Esek Hopkins's flagship Alfred [December 3, 1775]

Rebellion to tyrants is obedience to God.[1]
　　　Motto on Thomas Jefferson's seal [c. 1776]

Lost is our old simplicity of times,
The world abounds with laws, and teems with crimes.
　　　On the Proceedings Against America,[2] *st. 1*

Our cargoes of meat, drink, and clothes beat the Dutch.
　　　　Siege of Boston [1775]

There is nothing new except what is forgotten.
　　　Attributed to Mademoiselle Bertin, milliner to Marie Antoinette [c. 1785]

O Paddy dear, an' did ye hear the news that's goin' round?
The shamrock is by law forbid to grow on Irish ground!
No more St. Patrick's Day we'll keep, his color can't be seen,
For there's a cruel law agin the wearin' o' the Green!
　　　The Wearing o' the Green; or,
　　　　　The Shan-von-Voght

---

[1] The motto of one, I believe, of the regicides of Charles I. — *Letter from Jefferson to Edward Everett* [February 24, 1823]
Jefferson's reference probably is to John Bradshaw [1602–1659].
[2] In the *Pennsylvania Gazette* [February 8, 1775], "from a late London Magazine."

For they're hangin' men an' women
there for wearin' o' the Green.
The Wearing o' the Green; or,
The Shan-von-Voght

JUNIUS[1]

One precedent creates another. They
soon accumulate and constitute law.
What yesterday was fact, today is doctrine.
The Letters of Junius [1769–
1771]. *Dedication to the Eng-*
lish Nation

The liberty of the press is the palla-
dium of all the civil, political, and religious rights of an Englishman.   *Ib.*

These are the gloomy companions of
a disturbed imagination; the melancholy madness of poetry, without the
inspiration.
Ib. 7, to Sir William Draper
[*March 3, 1769*]

There are some hereditary strokes of
character by which a family may be as
clearly distinguished as by the blackest
features of the human face.
Ib. 12, to the Duke of Grafton
[*May 30, 1769*]

I believe there is yet a spirit of resistance in this country, which will not
submit to be oppressed; but I am sure
there is a fund of good sense in this
country, which cannot be deceived.
Ib. 16, to the Printer of the
Public Advertiser (*H. S.*
Woodfall) [*July 19, 1769*]

We owe it to our ancestors to preserve entire those rights, which they
have delivered to our care: we owe it to
our posterity, not to suffer their dearest
inheritance to be destroyed.
Ib. 20, to the Printer of the
Public Advertiser [*August 8,*
1769]

When the constitution is openly invaded, when the first original right of
the people, from which all laws derive
their authority, is directly attacked, inferior grievances naturally lose their
force, and are suffered to pass by without punishment or observation.
The Letters of Junius. 30, to
the Printer of the Public Adver-
tiser [*October 17, 1769*]

There is a moment of difficulty and
danger at which flattery and falsehood
can no longer deceive, and simplicity
itself can no longer be misled.
Ib. 35,[1] to the Printer of the
Public Advertiser [*December 19,*
1769]

They [the Americans] equally detest
the pageantry of a king, and the super-
cilious hypocrisy of a bishop.[2]   *Ib.*

There is a holy mistaken zeal in politics as well as in religion. By persuading
others, we convince ourselves.   *Ib.*

The least considerable man among us
has an interest equal to the proudest
nobleman, in the laws and constitution
of his country, and is equally called
upon to make a generous contribution
in support of them — whether it be the
heart to conceive, the understanding to
direct, or the hand to execute.[3]
Ib. 37, to the Printer of the
Public Advertiser [*March 19,*
1770]

We lament the mistakes of a good
man, and do not begin to detest him
until he affects to renounce his principles.
Ib. 41, to Lord Mansfield [*No-*
vember 14, 1770]

The injustice done to an individual is
sometimes of service to the public.

[1] Pseudonym of the author of a series of letters
in the London *Public Advertiser* 1769–1771 published in book form in 1772. They have been
attributed to, among others, Sir Philip Francis,
Lord Shelburne, Lord George Sackville, and
Lord Temple.

[1] This letter is of great significance in the
history of freedom of the press. The publisher
was prosecuted for seditious libel, and the jury
brought in a verdict of "guilty of printing and
publishing only." After a second trial, Woodfall
was freed on payment of costs.
[2] See Rufus Choate, p. 591a.
[3] See Gibbon, p. 466a.

Facts are apt to alarm us more than the most dangerous principles.
The Letters of Junius, 41, to Lord Mansfield

An honest man, like the true religion, appeals to the understanding, or modestly confides in the internal evidence of his conscience. The impostor employs force instead of argument, imposes silence where he cannot convince, and propagates his character by the sword.
Ib.

If individuals have no virtues, their vices may be of use to us.
Ib. 59, to the Printer of the Public Advertiser [October 5, 1771]

The temple of fame is the shortest passage to riches and preferment.
Ib.

NURSERY RHYMES[1]

A man of words and not of deeds
Is like a garden full of weeds.
A Man of Words and Not of Deeds

It's like a lion at the door;
And when the door begins to crack,
It's like a stick across your back;
And when your back begins to smart,
It's like a penknife in your heart;
And when your heart begins to bleed,
You're dead, and dead, and dead, indeed.   *Ib.*

Cock a doodle doo!
My dame has lost her shoe;
My master's lost his fiddle stick,
And knows not what to do.
Cock a Doodle Doo

[1] The rhymes of Mother Goose originated with *Mother Goose Tales* as *Contes de ma mère l'Oye* [1697] by CHARLES PERRAULT [1628–1703]. The *Tales* were first translated in 1729, the rhymes as *Mother Goose's Melody* in 1781 by ROBERT SAMBER, and published in London by John Newbery [1713–1767], who originated the publication of children's books. There are many other collections and versions of the rhymes, like *Gammer Gurton's Garland* [1784], which also included older rhymes of English origin.

Three blind mice, see how they run!
They all ran after the farmer's wife,
She cut off their tails with a carving-knife,
Did you ever see such a sight in your life,
As three blind mice?
Three Blind Mice

A frog he would a-wooing go.
Sing heigh-ho says Rowley.
A Frog He Would A-Wooing Go

With a rowley powley gammon and spinach,
Heigh-ho says Anthony Rowley.
Ib. chorus

Old King Cole
Was a merry old soul,
And a merry old soul was he,
He called for his pipe,
And he called for his bowl,
And he called for his fiddlers three.
Old King Cole

The King of France went up the hill
With forty thousand men;
The King of France came down the hill
And ne'er went up again.
The King of France

Jack Sprat could eat no fat,
His wife could eat no lean;
And so betwixt them both,
They licked the platter clean.
Jack Sprat

Rain, rain, go away,
Come again another day.
Rain, Rain

Pat-a-cake, pat-a-cake, baker's man,
Bake me a cake as fast as you can;
Pat it and prick it, and mark it with B,
Put it in the oven for baby and me.
Pat-a-Cake

The lion and the unicorn
Were fighting for the crown;
The lion beat the unicorn
All round about the town.
Some gave them white bread,
And some gave them brown;

Some gave them plum cake,
And sent them out of town.
         The Lion and the Unicorn

Little Jack Horner sat in the corner,
Eating a Christmas pie.
He put in his thumb, and pulled out a
    plum,
And said, "What a good boy am I!"
         Little Jack Horner

London Bridge is broken down,
My fair lady.   *London Bridge*

Tell tale tit,
Your tongue shall be slit,
And all the dogs in our town
Shall have a bit.
         Tell Tale Tit

As I was going to St. Ives,
I met a man with seven wives,
Each wife had seven sacks,
Each sack had seven cats,
Each cat had seven kits:
Kits, cats, sacks, and wives,
How many were there going to St. Ives?
         As I Was Going to St. Ives

The man in the wilderness asked of me
How many strawberries grew in the
    sea.
I answered him as I thought good,
"As many as red herrings grow in the
    wood."
         The Man in the Wilderness

Ladybug, ladybug, fly away home,
Your house is on fire, and your children
    will burn.   *Ladybug, Ladybug*

Hickory dickory dock,
The mouse ran up the clock,
The clock struck one,
The mouse ran down;
Hickory dickory dock.
         Hickory Dickory Dock

Baa, baa, black sheep,
Have you any wool?
Yes, sir, yes, sir,
Three bags full:
One for my master,
And one for my dame,
And one for the little boy
Who lives down the lane.
         Baa, Baa, Black Sheep

Mary, Mary, quite contrary,
How does your garden grow?
With silver bells, and cockleshells,
And pretty maids all in a row.
      Mary, Mary, Quite Contrary

Oranges and lemons,
Say the bells of St. Clement's.
When will you pay me?
Say the bells of Old Bailey.
When I grow rich,
Say the bells of Shoreditch.
         Oranges and Lemons

Here comes a candle to light you to
    bed,
Here comes a chopper to chop off your
    head.   *Ib.*

"Who killed Cock Robin?"
"I," said the sparrow,
"With my bow and arrow,
I killed Cock Robin." [1]
      Who Killed Cock Robin?

"Who saw him die?"
"I," said the fly,
"With my little eye,
I saw him die."   *Ib.*

This little pig went to market;
This little pig stayed home;
This little pig had roast beef;
This little pig had none;
And this little pig cried, Wee, wee,
    wee!
All the way home.   *This Little Pig*

Little boy blue, come blow your horn,
The sheep's in the meadow, the cow's
    in the corn;
But where is the boy who looks after
    the sheep?
He's under the haystack fast asleep.
Will you wake him? No, not I,
For if I do, he'll be sure to cry.
         Little Boy Blue

Simple Simon met a pieman
Going to the fair:
Says Simple Simon to the pieman,
"Let me taste your ware."
         Simple Simon

Ding dong bell,
The cat is in the well.

[1] See Byron, p. 562b.

Who put her in?
Little Johnny Green.

Plato's Song

Little Tom Tucker
Sings for his supper;
What shall he eat?
White bread and butter.
How will he cut it
Without e'er a knife?
How will he be married
Without e'er a wife?

Little Tom Tucker

Crosspatch, draw the latch,
Set by the fire and spin:
Take a cup and drink it up,
Then call your neighbors in.

Cross Patch

High diddle diddle
The cat and the fiddle,
The cow jumped over the moon;
The little dog laughed
To see such craft
And the dish ran away with the spoon.

High Diddle Diddle

Three wise men of Gotham
Went to sea in a bowl:
And if the bowl had been stronger,
My song had been longer.

Three Wise Men of Gotham

Jack and Jill went up the hill
To fetch a pail of water;
Jack fell down and broke his crown,
And Jill came tumbling after.

Jack and Jill

Seesaw, Margery Daw,
Jacky shall have a new master;
Jacky must have but a penny a day,
Because he can work no faster.

Seesaw, Margery Daw

Taffy was a Welshman, Taffy was a
thief;
Taffy came to my house and stole a
piece of beef.
I went to Taffy's house, Taffy wasn't in;
Taffy came to my house and stole a
marrowbone.

Taffy Was a Welshman

The Queen of Hearts
She made some tarts,

All on a summer's day;
The Knave of Hearts
He stole the tarts,
And took them clean away.

The Queen of Hearts

Bye baby bunting,
Daddy's gone a-hunting,
Gone to get a rabbit skin
To wrap the baby bunting in.

Bye Baby Bunting

Come, let's to bed,
Says Sleepyhead;
Tarry awhile, says Slow;
Put on the pot,
Says Greedy-gut,
We'll sup before we go.

Let's to Bed

Four and twenty tailors went to kill a
snail,
The best man among them durst not
touch her tail.
She put out her horns like a little Kyloe
cow,
Run, tailors, run, or she'll kill you all
e'en now.

Four and Twenty Tailors

Goosey goosey gander,
Whither shall I wander?
Upstairs and downstairs,
And in my lady's chamber;
There I met an old man who wouldn't
say his prayers;
I took him by the left leg
And threw him down the stairs.

Goosey Goosey Gander

Sing a song of sixpence,
A pocket full of rye,
Four and twenty blackbirds,
Baked in a pie;
When the pie was opened,
The birds began to sing;
Wasn't that a dainty dish
To set before a king?

The king was in his countinghouse
Counting out his money;
The queen was in the parlor
Eating bread and honey;
The maid was in the garden
Hanging out the clothes,

Along came a blackbird,
  And snipped off her nose.
                    Sing a Song of Sixpence

There was an old woman who lived in a
  shoe,
She had so many children she didn't
  know what to do;
She gave them some broth without any
  bread,
She whipped them all soundly and put
  them to bed.
              There Was an Old Woman

Ride a cockhorse to Banbury Cross,
To see a fine lady upon a white horse;
Rings on her fingers and bells on her
  toes,
She shall have music wherever she goes.
                    Ride a Cockhorse

Tom, Tom, the piper's son,
He learned to play when he was young.
But all the tune that he could play
Was "Over the hills and far away." [1]
              Tom, Tom, the Piper's Son

Tom, Tom, the piper's son,
Stole a pig, and away he run;
The pig was eat, and Tom was beat,
And Tom went howling down the
  street.   *Ib.*

"Where are you going to, my pretty
  maid?"
"I'm going a-milking, sir," she said.
          *Where Are You Going To, My
                          Pretty Maid?*

"My face is my fortune, sir," she said.
                              Ib.

"Nobody asked you, sir," she said.
                              Ib.

One a penny, two a penny, hot cross
  buns;
If you have no daughters, give them to
  your sons.   *Hot Cross Buns*

Pease-porridge hot, pease-porridge cold,
Pease-porridge in the pot, nine days old.
                    Pease-Porridge Hot

Curlylocks, Curlylocks,
Wilt thou be mine?
Thou shalt not wash dishes

[1] See D'Urfey, p. 384a, and Gay, p. 401b.

Nor yet feed the swine,
But sit on a cushion
And sew a fine seam,
And feed upon strawberries,
Sugar and cream.   *Curlylocks*

I had a little nut tree, nothing would it
  bear
But a silver nutmeg and a golden pear;
The king of Spain's daughter came to
  visit me,
And all for the sake of my little nut
  tree.   *I Had a Little Nut Tree*

Humpty Dumpty sat on a wall,
Humpty Dumpty had a great fall;
All the king's horses
And all the king's men
Couldn't put Humpty Dumpty to-
  gether again.   *Humpty Dumpty*

Little Bo-peep has lost her sheep,
And cannot tell where to find them;
Leave them alone, and they'll come
  home,
And bring their tails behind them.
                      Little Bo-peep

Little Polly Flinders
Sat among the cinders,
Warming her pretty little toes.
Her mother came and caught her,
And whipped her little daughter
For spoiling her nice new clothes.
                  Little Polly Flinders

There was an old woman tossed in a
  blanket,
Seventeen times as high as the moon;
But where she was going no mortal
  could tell,
For under her arm she carried a broom.
Old woman, old woman, old woman,
  said I,
Whither, ah whither, ah whither so
  high?
To sweep the cobwebs from the sky,
And I'll be with you by and by.
              There Was an Old Woman

The north wind doth blow,
And we shall have snow,
And what will poor robin do then,
      Poor thing?
He'll sit in a barn,
To keep himself warm,

And hide his head under his wing,
   Poor thing!
      The North Wind Doth Blow

Old mother Hubbard
Went to the cupboard,
To fetch her poor dog a bone;
But when she came there
The cupboard was bare,
And so the poor dog had none.
      Old Mother Hubbard

Pussy cat, pussy cat, where have you
   been?
I've been to London to look at the
   queen.
Pussy cat, pussy cat, what did you
   there?
I frightened a little mouse under the
   chair.   *Pussy Cat*

Peter Piper picked a peck of pickled
   peppers;
A peck of pickled peppers Peter Piper
   picked.
If Peter Piper picked a peck of pickled
   peppers,
Where's the peck of pickled peppers
   Peter Piper picked?
      Peter Piper

Monday's child is fair of face,
Tuesday's child is full of grace,
Wednesday's child is full of woe,
Thursday's child has far to go,
Friday's child is loving and giving,
Saturday's child has to work for its liv-
   ing,
But a child that's born on the Sabbath
   day
Is fair and wise and good and gay.
   Monday's Child Is Fair of Face

Solomon Grundy,
Born on a Monday,
Christened on Tuesday,
Married on Wednesday,
Took ill on Thursday,
Worse on Friday,
Died on Saturday,
Buried on Sunday:
This is the end
Of Solomon Grundy.
      Solomon Grundy

What are little boys made of?
Snips and snails, and puppy dogs' tails;
That's what little boys are made of.
   What Are Little Boys Made Of?

What are little girls made of?
Sugar and spice, and everything nice;
That's what little girls are made of.
      Ib.

Hickety pickety, my black hen,
She lays eggs for gentlemen.
Gentlemen come every day
To see what my black hen doth lay.
      Hickety Pickety

Little Miss Muffet
Sat on a tuffet,
Eating some curds and whey.
Along came a spider,
And sat down beside her,
And frightened Miss Muffet away.
      Little Miss Muffet

Peter, Peter Pumpkin-Eater,
Had a wife and couldn't keep her.
He put her in a pumpkin shell,
And there he kept her very well.
   Peter, Peter Pumpkin-Eater

Jack, be nimble,
Jack, be quick,
Jack, jump over the candlestick.
      Jack Be Nimble

There was a crooked man, and he went
   a crooked mile,
He found a crooked sixpence against a
   crooked stile;
He bought a crooked cat, which caught
   a crooked mouse,
And they all lived together in a little
   crooked house.
      There Was a Crooked Man

Diddle diddle dumpling, my son John,
He went to bed with his stockings on;
One shoe off, one shoe on;
Diddle diddle dumpling, my son John.
      Diddle Diddle Dumpling

Rub-a-dub-dub,
Three men in a tub,
And who do you think they be?
The butcher, the baker,

The candlestick-maker;
Turn 'em out, knaves all three!
                    Rub-a-Dub-Dub

I saw three ships come sailing by,
Come sailing by, come sailing by,
I saw three ships come sailing by,
On New Year's Day in the morning.
                    I Saw Three Ships

In fir tar is,
In oak none is.
In mud eel is,
In clay none is.
Goats eat ivy.
Mares eat oats.   *In Fir Tar Is*

Lucy Locket lost her pocket,
Kitty Fisher found it;
There was not a penny in it,
But a ribbon round it.   *Lucy Locket*

There were three jolly huntsmen,
As I have heard them say,
And they would go a-hunting
Upon St. David's Day.
                    *There Were Three Jolly
                              Huntsmen*

All day they hunted,
And nothing did they find,
But a ship a-sailing,
A-sailing with the wind.   *Ib.*

O do you know the muffin man,
The muffin man, the muffin man,
O do you know the muffin man,
That lives in Drury Lane?
                    The Muffin Man

To market, to market, to buy a fat pig,
Home again, home again, jiggety-jig.
                    To Market, To Market

Doctor Foster went to Gloucester
In a shower of rain;
He stepped in a puddle, up to his mid-
    dle,
And never went there again.
                    Doctor Foster

There was an old woman
Lived under a hill;
And if she's not gone,
She lives there still.
              There Was an Old Woman

There was a little man, and he had a
    little gun,
And his bullets were made of lead, lead,
    lead;
He went to the brook, and saw a little
    duck,
And shot it through the head, head,
    head.
              There Was a Little Man

Lavender's blue, dilly dilly, lavender's
    green;
When I am king, dilly dilly, you shall
    be queen.   *Lavender's Blue*

A dillar, a dollar,
A ten o'clock scholar,
What makes you come so soon?
You used to come at ten o'clock,
And now you come at noon.
                    A Dillar, a Dollar

I had a little pony,
His name was Dapple Gray;
I lent him to a lady
To ride a mile away.
She whipped him, she slashed him,
She rode him through the mire;
I would not lend my pony now
For all the lady's hire.
                    I Had a Little Pony

Polly, put the kettle on,
Polly, put the kettle on,
Polly, put the kettle on,
We'll all have tea.

Sukey, take it off again,
Sukey, take it off again,
Sukey, take it off again,
They've all gone away.
                    Polly, Put the Kettle On

Little Tommy Tittlemouse
Lived in a little house;
He caught fishes
In other men's ditches.
              Little Tommy Tittlemouse

The farmer in the dell, the farmer in
    the dell,
Heigho! the derry oh, the farmer in the
    dell.   *The Farmer in the Dell*

Hark! Hark! The dogs do bark,
The beggars are coming to town;

Some in rags, some in tags,
And some in velvet gowns.
                    Hark! Hark!

Ten little Indians standing in a line —
One went home, and then there were
    nine.   *Ten Little Indians*

When good King Arthur ruled this
    land,
He was a goodly king,
He bought three pecks of barley meal,
To make a bag pudding.
                    Good King Arthur

One misty, moisty morning,
When cloudy was the weather,
I chanced to meet an old man
Clothed all in leather;
He began to compliment,
And I began to grin —
"How do you do?" and "How do you
    do?"
And "How do you do?" again!
              One Misty, Moisty Morning

Bobby Shaftoe's gone to sea,
Silver buckles on his knee;
He'll come back and marry me,
Pretty Bobby Shaftoe.

Bobby Shaftoe's fat and fair,
Combing down his yellow hair;
He's my love forevermore,
Pretty Bobby Shaftoe.
                    Bobby Shaftoe

Fe fi fo fum!
I smell the blood of an Englishman;
Be he alive or be he dead,
I'll grind his bones to make my bread.
                    Fe Fi Fo Fum

Sing, sing! What shall I sing?
The cat's run away with the pudding-
    bag string.
              Sing, Sing! What Shall I Sing?

Shoe the horse, shoe the mare,
But let the little colt go bare.
                    Shoe the Horse

There was a man in our town,
And he was wondrous wise;
He jumped into a bramble bush
And scratched out both his eyes.
              There Was a Man in Our Town

There were two blackbirds,
Sitting on a hill,
The one named Jack,
The other named Jill;
Fly away, Jack! Fly away, Jill!
Come again, Jack! Come again, Jill!
                    Two Blackbirds

This is the farmer sowing the corn,
That kept the cock that crowed in the
    morn,
That waked the priest all shaven and
    shorn,
That married the man all tattered and
    torn,
That kissed the maiden all forlorn,
That milked the cow with the crumpled
    horn,
That tossed the dog
That worried the cat
That killed the rat
That ate the malt
That lay in the house that Jack built.
              The House That Jack Built

ANONYMOUS
1800–

Christmas is coming, the geese are get-
    ting fat,
Please to put a penny in the old man's
    hat;
If you haven't got a penny, a ha'penny
    will do,
If you haven't got a ha'penny, God
    bless you!   *Beggar's rhyme*

From ghoulies and ghosties and long-
    leggety beasties
And things that go bump in the night,
    Good Lord, deliver us!
                    Scottish prayer

Rest and be thankful.
        *Inscription on stone seat in the
        Scottish Highlands, and title of
        one of Wordsworth's poems*

The wisdom of many and the wit of
one.   *Definition of a proverb* [1]

[1] Probably based on the definition of a proverb
which Lord John Russell gave one morning at
breakfast at Mardock's: "One man's wit, and all
men's wisdom." — *Memoirs of Sir James Mack-
intosh* [1765–1832], *vol. I, p. 473*

Sister Anne, do you see any one coming?

> *The anxious cry of Fatima, one of the wives of Bluebeard*

The woods are full of them.

> Quoted by ALEXANDER WILSON, *American Ornithology* [1808], *preface*

The cunning seldom gain their ends;
The wise are never without friends.

> *The Fox and the Hen, moral. From* JOHN PIERPONT, *Young Reader* [1843]

Oh, ye'll tak' the high road an' I'll tak' the low road,
An' I'll be in Scotland before ye;
But I and my true love will never meet again,
On the bonnie, bonnie banks o' Loch Lomond.

> *Loch Lomond, refrain*

Went out to milk and I didn't know how,
I milked the goat instead of the cow;
A monkey sittin' on a pile of straw
A-winkin' at his mother-in-law.
Turkey in the straw, turkey in the hay,
Roll 'em up and twist 'em up a high tuckahaw,
And hit 'em up a tune called Turkey in the Straw.

> *Turkey in the Straw,*[1] *st. 1 and refrain*

Sugar in the gourd and honey in the horn,
I never was so happy since the hour I was born. *Ib. st. 6*

God rest you merry, gentlemen,
Let nothing you dismay;
Remember Christ our Savior,
Was born on Christmas Day. *Carol*

The holly and the ivy,
When they are both full grown,
Of all the trees that are in the wood,
The holly bears the crown:

[1] The classical American rural tune . . . steps around like an apple-faced farmhand . . . as American as Andrew Jackson, Johnny Appleseed, and Corn on the Cob. — CARL SANDBURG, *The American Songbag* [1927]

The rising of the sun
And the running of the deer,
The playing of the merry organ,
Sweet singing in the choir.

> *Carol. The Holly and the Ivy, st. 1 and refrain*

With drums and guns, and guns and drums
The enemy nearly slew ye.
My darling dear, you look so queer,
Oh, Johnny, I hardly knew ye.

> *Irish folk song, st. 1*

Where are the legs with which you run,
When you went to carry a gun?
Indeed your dancing days are done —
Oh, Johnny, I hardly knew ye.

> *Ib. st. 3*

The press lives by disclosures.

> *The London Times* [1851]

Women and children first.

> *The Birkenhead Drill*[1] [February 26, 1852]

Up and down the City Road,
In and out the Eagle,
That's the way the money goes —
Pop goes the weasel!

> *Pop Goes the Weasel*[2] [c. 1853]

It is a newspaper's duty to print the news and raise hell.

> *The Chicago Times* [1861]

Free soil, free men, free speech, Frémont.[3]

> *Republican party rallying cry* [1856]

Dirty work at the crossroads.

> *Attributed*[4] *to* WALTER MELVILLE'S *melodrama The Girl Who Took the Wrong Turning; or, No Wedding Bells for Him*

[1] The women and children were the first to be removed from the sinking ship *Birkenhead*.
[2] The weasel was a hatter's tool, and "pop" was a term meaning to pawn or "hock." The Eagle was a music hall in the City Road. The song is attributed to W. R. MANDALE.
[3] John Charles Frémont [1813–1890] was the party's candidate for President.
[4] In *Notes and Queries* (London).

The goose hangs high.[1]
Common saying

All I want of you is a little seevility, and that of the commonest goddamnedest kind.[2]
The New Bedford Classic, as reported in ZEPHANIAH W. PEASE, *The History of New Bedford* [1918]. *Supposed to be said by the mate of a whaler to his illhumored captain*

You-all means a race or section,
Family, party, tribe, or clan;
You-all means the whole connection
Of the individual man.
You-All; from The Richmond Times-Dispatch

Some talk of Alexander, and some of Hercules;
Of Hector, and Lysander, and such great names as these;
But of all the world's brave heroes, there's none that can compare
With a tow, row, row, row, row, row for the British Grenadier.
The British Grenadiers

From the halls of Montezuma,
To the shores of Tripoli,
We fight our country's battles
On the land as on the sea.
U.S. Marines' Song, st. 1

There is a tavern in the town,
And there my true love sits him down,
And drinks his wine with laughter and with glee,
And never, never thinks of me.
There Is a Tavern in the Town, st. 1

Adieu, adieu, kind friends, adieu, adieu, adieu,
I can no longer stay with you.

I'll hang my harp on a weeping willow-tree,[1]
And may the world go well with thee.
There Is a Tavern in the Town, refrain

I belong to that highly respectable tribe
Which is known as the Shabby Genteel . . .
Too proud to beg, too honest to steal.
The Shabby Genteel; sung by Sol Smith Russell [1848–1901] *in A Poor Relation*

The sons of the prophet are brave men and bold,
And quite unaccustomed to fear,
But the bravest by far in the ranks of the Shah
Was Abdullah Bulbul Amir.
Abdullah Bulbul Amir, st. 1

Now the heroes were plenty and well known to fame
In the troops that were led by the Czar,
And the bravest of these was a man by the name
Of Ivan Petrofski Skevar. *Ib. st. 3*

Is that Mr. Reilly, can anyone tell?
Is that Mr. Reilly that owns the hotel?
Well, if that's Mr. Reilly, they speak of so highly,
Upon me soul, Reilly, you're doin' quite well.
Is That Mr. Reilly? [2] [1882], *chorus*

Sow a thought, and you reap an act;
Sow an act, and you reap a habit;
Sow a habit, and you reap a character;
Sow a character, and you reap a destiny.
Quoted by SAMUEL SMILES [1812–1904], *Life and Labor* [1887]

Now is the time for all good men to come to the aid of the party.
Practice sentence used in typewriting [3]

---

[1] Originally, perhaps, "the goose *honks* high" — it cries and flies high. Wild geese fly higher when the weather is fine or promises to be fine. Hence, the prospects are bright; everything is favorable. — *Century Dictionary*

[2] Another traditional version, repudiated by New Bedford authority, is that the skipper said: "All I want out of you is silence, and damn little of that."

[1] See *Psalm 137*, p. 22b.

[2] Assumed to be the origin of "the life of Riley," meaning an easy time.

[3] Charles Weller, a court reporter, originated this expression in . . . 1867 to test the efficiency

The quick brown fox jumps over the lazy dog.
> *Practice sentence used in typewriting*

As Maine goes, so goes the nation.[1]
> *American political maxim* [c. 1888]

Slide, Kelly, Slide.
> *Title of song by* J. W. KELLY [1889]

Oh, Shenandoah, I long to hear you.
Away, you rolling river,
Oh Shenandoah, I long to hear you.
Away, I'm bound away
'Cross the wide Missouri.[2]   *Chantey*

Swing low, sweet chariot,
Comin' for to carry me home;
I looked over Jordan, an' what did I see?
A band of angels coming after me,
Comin' for to carry me home.
> *Negro spiritual*

God gave Noah the rainbow sign.
No more water, the fire next time! [3]
> *Negro spiritual*

Ladling the butter from adjacent tubs,
Stubbs butters Freeman, Freeman butters Stubbs.
> *Variously quoted* [c. 1890], *alluding to the mutual praise of two Oxford historians*

Lizzie Borden took an ax
And gave her mother forty whacks;
When she saw what she had done
She gave her father forty-one!
> *Rhyme popular after the murder trial of Lizzie Borden, Fall River, Massachusetts* [June 1893]

The little cares that fretted me,
I lost them yesterday,

Among the fields above the sea,
Among the winds at play.
> *Out in the Fields* [1]

Out in the fields with God!   *Ib.*

Remember the Maine! [2]
> *Slogan, Spanish-American War* [1898]

Frankie and Johnny were lovers, my gawd, how they could love,
Swore to be true to each other, true as the stars above;
He was her man, but he done her wrong.
> *Frankie and Johnny,*[3] *st.* 1

The halls of fame are open wide
And they are always full;
Some go in by the door called "push,"
And some by the door called "pull."
> *Quoted by Stanley Baldwin* [1867–1947] *in a speech in the House of Commons*

The codfish lays ten thousand eggs,
The homely hen lays one.
The codfish never cackles
To tell you what she's done.
And so we scorn the codfish,
While the humble hen we prize,
Which only goes to show you
That it pays to advertise.
> *It Pays to Advertise*

One white foot — try him,
Two white feet — buy him,
Three white feet — look well about him;
Four white feet — go without him.[4]
> *Rhyme for a horse-buyer*

[1] Published in the Boston *Sunday Globe* April 30, 1899, credited to *St. Paul's Magazine* but not discovered there. Erroneously attributed to E. B. Browning and Imogen Guiney.

[2] On February 15, 1898, the American battleship *Maine* was blown up in Havana harbor, Cuba.

[3] Traditional ballad; there are innumerable versions and verses.
See Shakespeare, p. 220b, and note.

[4] Three white feet and a white nose,
Rip off his skin and throw him to the crows.
> *New Hampshire version of last two lines*

---

of the first practical typewriter which his friend Christopher Sholes had constructed. — *Life* [April 11, 1955]

[1] As Maine goes, so goes Vermont. — JAMES FARLEY, *statement to press* [November 4, 1936] *after predicting that Roosevelt would carry 46 states in the presidential election.*

[2] See Robert Frost, p. 929b.

[3] See James Baldwin, p. 1081a.

An apple a day keeps the doctor away.
Current since the 19th century

Time is of the essence.   *Saying*

The three most beautiful things in the world: a full-rigged ship, a woman with child, and a full moon.   *Saying*

All the world is queer save me and thee; and sometimes I think thee is a little queer.
Attributed to a Quaker, speaking to his wife

Everyone has at least one sermon in him.   *Saying*

Man is the only animal that eats when he is not hungry, drinks when he is not thirsty, and makes love at all seasons.   *Remark*

You can always tell a Harvard man, but you can't tell him much.
Attributed to JAMES BARNES [1866–1936]

I seen my duty and I done it.
Current since the 19th century

Keeping up with the Joneses.
Popular saying

Paying through the nose.[1]
Popular phrase for excessive payment

Doesn't amount to Hannah Cook.[2]
Saying common in Maine and on Cape Cod

Hit's a lot worse to be soul-hungry than to be body-hungry.
A Kentucky mountain woman asking for her granddaughter to be admitted to Berea College high school [c. 1900]. Quoted by CARL R. WOODWARD *in The Wonderful World of Books, edited by Alfred Stefferud* [1953]

There ain't no such animal.
Comment of a New Jersey farmer looking at a dromedary at a circus: cartoon in Life, November 7, 1907, credited to Everybody's Magazine

How old is Ann?
Popular saying in the early 20th century [1]

The Pyramids first, which in Egypt were laid;
Next Babylon's Garden, for Amytis made;
Then Mausolos' Tomb of affection and guilt;
Fourth, the Temple of Dian in Ephesus built;
The Colossus of Rhodes, cast in brass, to the Sun;
Sixth, Jupiter's Statue, by Phidias done;
The Pharos of Egypt comes last, we are told,
Or the Palace of Cyrus, cemented with gold.
Seven Wonders of the Ancient World

Use it up, wear it out;
Make it do, or do without.
New England maxim

Earned a precarious living by taking in one another's washing.
Saying

Something old, something new,
Something borrowed, something blue,
And a lucky sixpence in her shoe.[2]
Wedding rhyme

God looks after fools, drunkards, and the United States.   *Epigram*

Oh, why don't you work
Like other men do?
How the hell can I work
When there's no work to do?
Hallelujah, I'm a Bum [c. 1907]

---

[1] Grimm says that Odin had a poll tax which was called in Sweden a nose tax; it was a penny per nose, or poll. — *Deutsche Rechts Alterthümer*

[2] Variously explained as a character who once lived on Campobello Island; a corruption of a phrase in Indian dialect; and a comparison with the worthlessness (for navigation) of a cook on board ship.

[1] This question became well known when *The New York Press*, October 16, 1903, printed the problem: "Mary is 24 years old. She is twice as old as Ann was when Mary was as old as Ann is now. How old is Ann?" The answer is that Ann is 18.

[2] There are variants for the less familiar last line, such as "And a silver sixpence in each shoe."

Old soldiers never die;
They only fade away! [1]
> *War song, British Army*
> [1914–1918]

She was poor but she was honest,
And her parents was the same,
Till she met a city feller,
And she lost her honest name.
> *War song* [1914–1918]

It's the same the whole world over,
It's the poor wot gets the blame,
It's the rich wot gets the pleasure,
Ain't it all a bloomin' shame?
> *Ib. chorus*

Fifty million Frenchmen can't be wrong.[2]
> *Saying popular with American soldiers during World War I* [1917–1918]

Don't sell America short.[3]
> *Popular American saying* [1925–1929]

Lord, through this hour
Be Thou our Guide,
So by Thy power
No foot shall slide.
> *Westminster Chimes*

Climb high
Climb far
Your goal the sky
Your aim the star.
> *Inscription on Hopkins Memorial Steps, Williams College, Williamstown, Massachusetts*

Mother, may I go out to swim?
Yes, my darling daughter:
Hang your clothes on a hickory limb
And don't go near the water.
> *Rhyme*

See the happy moron,
He doesn't give a damn.
I wish I were a moron —
My God, perhaps I am!
> *Rhyme*

Work and pray, live on hay,
You'll get pie in the sky when you die.
> *The Preacher and the Slave* [1]

The difficult we do immediately. The impossible takes a little longer.
> *Slogan of United States Army Service Forces*

Kilroy was here.[2]
> *Army saying, World War II*

Hurry up and wait.
> *Ib.*

SNAFU (Situation Normal All Fouled Up).
> *Ib.*

G.I. Joe.
> *World War II term for infantryman* [3]

And when he goes to heaven
To Saint Peter he will tell:
Another Marine reporting, sir;
I've served my time in hell!
> *Epitaph on grave of Pfc. Cameron of the Marine Corps, Guadalcanal* [1942]

Stay with me, God. The night is dark,
The night is cold: my little spark
Of courage dies. The night is long;
Be with me, God, and make me strong.
> *A Soldier — His Prayer,*[4] *st. 1*

---

[1] See Douglas MacArthur, p. 959a.

[2] Sometimes "forty" or "thirty" is heard instead of "fifty." When Texas Guinan and her troupe were refused entry into France in 1931, she was quoted as saying: "It goes to show that fifty million Frenchmen *can* be wrong." She promptly renamed her show *Too Hot for Paris*, and toured the United States with it.

[3] The phrase may have stemmed from "Never be a bear on the United States," attributed variously to JUNIUS S. MORGAN [1813–1890] and J. P. MORGAN [1837–1913].

[1] Attributed to Joe Hill in the 1927 edition of *I.W.W. Songs*.

[2] See Faulkner, p. 1040a.

[3] This name, chosen for the soldier in Lieutenant DAVE BREGER's comic strip for *Yank*, the Army weekly, first appeared in the issue of June 17, 1942. Writing in *Time* [February 26, 1945], Lieutenant Breger said: "I decided on 'G.I. Joe,' the 'G.I.' [Government Issue] because of its prevalence in Army talk, and the 'Joe' for the alliterative effect."

[4] This poem, found on a scrap of paper in a slit trench in Tunisia during the battle of El Agheila, was printed in *Poems from the Desert*, by members of the British Eighth Army [1944].

We sure liberated the hell out of this place.

> *American soldier in the ruins of a French village, 1944; quoted by* MAX MILLER, *The Far Shore* [1945]

Spartan simplicity must be observed. Nothing will be done merely because it contributes to beauty, convenience, comfort, or prestige.

> *From the Office of the Chief Signal Officer, U.S. Army* [*May 29, 1945*]

Soldiers who wish to be a hero
Are practically zero,
But those who wish to be civilians,
Jesus, they run into the millions.

> *Army latrine inscription. Quoted by* NORMAN ROSTEN, *The Big Road* [1945]

We, the peoples of the United Nations, determined to save succeeding generations from the scourge of war, which twice in our lifetime has brought untold sorrow to mankind, and to reaffirm faith in fundamental human rights, in the dignity and worth of the human person, in the equal right of men and women and of nations large and small . . .
And for these ends to practice tolerance and live together in peace with one another as good neighbors . . .
Have resolved to combine these efforts to accomplish our aims.

> *Charter of the United Nations* [*June 1945*], *preamble* [1]

Since wars begin in the minds of men, it is in the minds of men that the defenses of peace must be constructed.

> *Constitution of the United Nations Educational, Scientific and Cultural Organization* [1946]

We are not dealing simply with a military or scientific problem but with a

problem in statecraft and the ways of the human spirit.

> *Report on the International Control of Atomic Energy* [1] [*March 16, 1946*]

Relief from the terrible fear which can do so much to engender the very thing feared.   *Ib.*

Education is what you have left over after you have forgotten everything you have learned.   *Saying*

Till Hell freezes over.   *Saying*

A club is a place where twenty men pay for the pleasure of one.   *Saying*

One man, one vote.

> *Civil rights slogan*

We shall overcome, we shall overcome,
We shall overcome some day
Oh, deep in my heart I do believe
We shall overcome some day.

> *Civil rights song* [1960] [2]

EPITAPHS

A zealous locksmith died of late,
And did arrive at heaven gate,
He stood without and would not knock,
Because he meant to pick the lock.

> *Epitaph upon a Puritanical Locksmith; from* WILLIAM CAMDEN, *Remains Concerning Britain* [1637]

All the brothers were valiant, and all the sisters virtuous.

> *From the inscription on the tomb of the Duchess of Newcastle in Westminster Abbey* [1673]

---

[1] The preamble is based on a draft by JAN CHRISTIAN SMUTS [1870–1950].

[1] Prepared for the U.S. Department of State by a board of consultants: Chester I. Barnard, J. Robert Oppenheimer, Charles A. Thomas, Harry A. Winne, and David E. Lilienthal, chairman.

[2] The song originated on slave plantations in pre-Civil War days. It became a formal Baptist hymn around 1900, called "I'll Overcome Some Day" by the adapter, C. Albert Tindley. It became a protest theme when used by colored workers in 1946 on picket lines in Charleston, S.C.

A house she hath, 'tis made of such good fashion,
The tenant ne'er shall pay for reparation,
Nor will the landlord ever raise her rent
Or turn her out of doors for nonpayment;
From chimney tax this cell is free,
To such a house who would not tenant be?
>*For Rebecca Bogess, Folkestone [August 22, 1688]*

It is so soon that I am done for,
I wonder what I was begun for.
>*For a child aged three weeks, Cheltenham Churchyard*

Here lie I, Martin Elginbrodde:
Ha'e mercy o' my soul, Lord God,
As I wad do, were I Lord God
And ye were Martin Elginbrodde.
>*Aberdeen Churchyard. From* GEORGE MACDONALD, *David Elginbrod* [1862], *ch. 13*

Immaturus obi: sed tu felicior annos
Vive meos, Bona Republica! Vive tuos.
[I died young; but thou, O Good Republic, be more fortunate,
Live out my years! Live your own.]
>*Inscription furnished by Nathaniel Cross, classics professor at the University of Nashville, on the tomb of explorer Meriwether Lewis* [1774–1809]

This is the grave of Mike O'Day
Who died maintaining his right of way.

His right was clear, his will was strong,
But he's just as dead as if he'd been wrong.
>*20th century*

FRENCH

Revenons à nos moutons [Let us return to our sheep — i.e., subject].
>*Maître Patnelin (15th century farce)*

Il ne faut pas être plus royaliste que le roi [One must not be more royalist than the king].
>*Saying from the time of Louis XVI*

Ça ira, ça tiendra [That will be, that will last].
>*Revolutionary song, based on a phrase of Benjamin Franklin's*

Liberté! Egalité! Fraternité! [Liberty! Equality! Fraternity!]
>*Phrase dating from before the French Revolution, officially adopted in 1793*

Tout passe, tout casse, tout lasse [Everything passes, everything perishes, everything palls].
>*Proverb*

Ah, les bons vieux temps où nous étions si malheureux! [Oh, the good old times when we were so unhappy!]
>*Saying*

L'amour, l'amour fait tourner le monde [It's love, it's love that makes the world go round].
>*Song*

Index of Authors

INDEX OF AUTHORS

Index

INDEX

Entries are arranged alphabetically, with hyphenated words indexed as one word. Spelling is in general in accordance with Webster, with dialect spellings indexed in both dialect and standard forms.

The order for possessives and plurals of identical spelling is: *author's, authors, authors'*.

The letter *a* after the page number indicates the left column of the text page referred to; the letter *b* indicates the right column.

For fuller discussion of the index, see the section on the index (pages xvi–xviii) in the *Guide to the Use of* FAMILIAR QUOTATIONS in the front of the book.

Age, old a. lacking neither honor nor lyre, 121a
old a. not yet arrived, 688a
old a. only disease, 607a
old a. play's last act, 112a
old a. serene and bright, 515a
old a. should burn, 1070b
old a. time of spending, 351b
olives of endless a., 293b
or grief or sickness, 321a
outworn buried a., 292b
pays us with a. and dust, 199b
perform promises of youth, 428a
philosophies of one a., 817a
physician of Iron A., 711a
prayers which are a. his alms, 204b
preferable to youth, 395b
regret in chilled a., 800a
returns the Golden A., 116b
scarce expect one of my a., 507a
shakes rooted folly of a., 377b
shall be clearer than noonday, 15a
Shelley of my a., 1075b
sign of old a., 523b
smack of a. in you, 241b
soon comes a., 200a
soul of the a., 303b
spirit of a., 418a
tested to extreme old a., 710b
the a. is dull and mean, 626a
the harbor of all ills, 104b
therefore summon a., 666a
think at your a. it is right, 743b
thinks better of gilded fool, 301b
thou hast nor youth nor a., 271a
'tis well an old a. is out, 372a
to age succeeds, 644b
to cheated age, 876b
too late or cold climate, 347b
toys of a., 409a
tragedy of the a., 894b
'twixt boy and youth, 519a
vastness and a., 642a
veracity with old a., 356b
very staff of my a., 232b
view a. of poverty, 235a
war dearth a. agues, 307b
weak evils a. and hunger, 248b
when a. in wit out, 246b
when old a. crept over, 859b
when Thule no more ultimate, 131a
with stealing steps, 187a
without a name, 455b
wives companions for middle a., 208a
world's great a. begins, 570b
worst of woes wait on a., 555b
young whom a. doth chill, 351a
youth and a. equally a burden, 93b
youth passed a. not arrived, 688a

Aged and gray Maggie, 779a
and poor and slow, 813a
beauty of a. face, 963a
certain age means a., 561b
later times more a. than earlier, 206b
man paltry thing, 882b
matched with a. wife, 646a
thrush frail gaunt, 783b

Aged, youth becomes as a., 271a
Agent, actions work good of a., 373b
free a. thou wast before, 142b
imagination a. of perception, 528b
thus the poor a. despised, 269b
trust no a., 246a
Agents, public officers a., 771a
Age's, poison for a. tooth, 236a
Ages, all a. believed in gods, 935b
and a. hence, 926b
before history, 459b
cycle of the a. renewed, 116b
emptiness of a. in face, 826b
famous to all a., 340a
forties the dangerous a., 1022a
God our help in a. past, 396b
gone a. long ago, 582a
heir of all a., 647b
how many a. hence, 255a
now he belongs to the a., 677a
pass vividly down a., 910a
prior a. haven't thought of, 478b
rock of A., 469a
seven a., 249a
thousand a. in Thy sight, 396b
three poets in three a., 370b
through a. one purpose, 647b
value from esteem of a., 366b
ye unborn a., 442a
Agglomeration called Holy Roman Empire, 417a
Agglutinative, tonsorial or a. type, 902b
Aggrandizement, no a. territorial or other, 974a
Aggravate, I will a. my voice, 229a
Aggravation of self, 776b
Aggravations, accept minor a., 817b
Aggregate efforts of busy multitude, 720b
interests of community, 480a
Aggression of Germany, 1012a
threaten a., 974b
Aggressions, when a. require war, 472b
Aggressors, quarantine the a., 972a
Agin, off a. on a., 897b
Agincourt, affright air at A., 243a
Aging people in contraction of life, 935b
person give attention to self, 935b
Agitation of the air, 1057a
A-gley, gang aft a., 492b
Aglow, all a. is the work, 117b
Agnes, world dear A. is strange, 360b
Agnes', St. A. Eve, 581b
Agnosco veteris vestigia flammae, 118b
Agnostic, compliment to be called a., 844b
judges neither Catholic nor a., 967a
Agnosticism, that's all a. means, 844b
Agnus Dei, 59a
A-going out with tide, 671b
Agonies, errors a. and fears, 758a
exultations a., 512b
small talk dies in a., 570a
Agonizing, fierce a. meek, 907a

Agonizing, most a. spy, 736b
reappraisal, 1076a
Agony, charm a. with words, 247a
leave off a., 812b
strong swimmer in a., 560b
will find Thee, 1068a
Agree, agreed we can't never a., 808b
all things differ all a., 405a
birds in little nests a., 396b
free thought for those who a., 789a
how a. kettle and pot, 38a
let mankind a., 372a
music and poetry a., 309a
people have good sense a. with us, 356a
the more we didn't a., 808b
two of a trade never a., 401b, 730a
verbs and nouns more a., 770a
when partners can't a., 505b
whether they a. or not, 1025a
with her would not a., 879b
Agreeable, do not want people a., 533b
greatest not most a., 828a
haint one a. feetur, 693a
in conversation, 394b
person agrees with me, 612b
to escape mental exertion, 778a
what is more a. than home, 111a
Agreeably, affect you a. in reading, 469b
Agreed, except they be a., 35b
to differ, 532b
together we can't agree, 808b
Agreement, living in a. with nature, 103b
love is a., 211a
on nuclear control, 1074b
who does not forget old a., 72a
with hell, 615b
with hell are we at a., 32a
Agreements, nations tempted to violate a., 972a
Agrees, agreeable person a., 612b
large style a. not with purse, 214b
Agricultural men the bravest, 133a
Agriculture, all taxes fall upon a., 465b
navigation commerce a., 463a
Ague of skeleton, 1002a
Ague's privilege, 227a
Agues, praise doth nourish a., 240a
war dearth age a., 307b
Ah Sin was his name, 769b
Ahab, all evil to crazy A., 696b
he ran before A., 13b
when A. went to Askelon, 945b
Ahead, man who never got a., 1050b
of the world, 75a
sure you're right go a., 553b
Ahkoond of Swat, 673b
A-hunting, daddy's gone a., 1094b
daren't go a., 729a
upon St. David's Day, 1097a
we will go, 424a
Aid, alliteration's artful a., 456a
and comfort, 474a
come to a. of party, 1100b
expletives feeble a. join, 403a

Amiss or out of place, 1064a
thou shalt never do a., 37b
Amittuntur, non a. sed praemittuntur, 130a
Amity, absolute a., 1055a
'Ammer along 'ard 'igh road,
810a
Ammiral, mast of some great a.,
342a
Ammunition, pass a., 1062a
Amo amas, 476a
odi et a., 115a
Amoebas at start not complex,
905b
Among them but not of them,
556b
Amor, and after A. vincit omnia,
166a
batallas de a. campo de pluma,
128b
l'a. che muove il sole e l'altre
stelle, 162a
omnia vincit a., 117a
vincit insomnia, 1061b
Amorous descant sung, 345b
excite my a. propensities, 429b
from a. causes springs, 404a
nightingale a., 772b
not too a. of far, 915a
of their strokes, 287b
sweet reluctant a. delay, 345a
tangled in a. nets, 348b
Amorphous, all was vague and a.,
110a
Amortization of heart and soul,
1028a
Amount to Hannah Cook, 1102a
Amour, doux comme l'a., 484a
l'a. fait tourner le monde,
1105b
l'a. l'histoire de la vie des
femmes, 502b
on ne badine pas avec l'a., 657a
un peu d'a., 751b
Amphibious ill-born mob, 385a
Amphitrite, O sweet A., 695b
Amphitryon, I am the true A.,
371a
true A. gives dinners, 361b
Ample, cabined a. spirit, 712b
knowledge her a. page, 440b
room and verge enough, 441b
Ampler ether, 516b
Amplification vice of oratory,
473b
Amplified, hand prosperity down
a., 848a
Amuck, too discreet to run a.,
411b
Amurath, not A. an A. succeeds,
242b
Amuse his riper stage, 409a
you with stories, 452b
Amused according to taste,
960b
by its presumption, 1033a
delicately and unceasingly a.,
960b
we are not a., 699a
Amusement, let early education
be a., 94b
Amusements, great friend to public a., 431a
Amusing with numerous errors,
448a
Amyntas, what if A. is dark, 116b
Amytis, for A. made, 1102a
Anachronism, periodization of
history a., 1047b

Analogies, linked a., 697a
make one more at home, 834a
prove nothing, 834a
Analogy least misleading thing,
756b
Analysis, last point reached by a.,
474b
submit data to a., 479a
Analyze, culture a. itself, 861b
Anarch, thy hand great A., 414a
Anarchic, weeping a. Aphrodite,
1060a
Anarchy, digest of a., 454a
freedom cure of a., 453a
mere a. loosed on world, 882a
of poverty, 979b
show me greater evil, 82a
wild a. of drink, 304a
Anathema Maranatha, 53a
Anatomizing of motives, 608b
Anatomy, learn a. from dissections, 312b
Pinch a mere a., 218b
Ancestor I feel shame in recalling,
725b
Ancestors created world of shadows, 993a
cut off brightness, 993a
democracy makes man forget a.,
617a
glory belongs to our a., 137a
in Rome, 505b
look backward to a., 454a
no need of a., 417a
of honorable gentleman, 611b
owe it to a., 1091a
part of self, 793b
true picture of a., 596b
turned savage wilderness, 453b
very good kind of folks, 480b
wisdom of our a., 452a
Ancestral, amidst tall a. trees,
573b
happy man works a. acres, 120b
in a. Jove Troy's sons rejoice,
119b
on my a. tree, 633a
sits on a. tree, 866a
voices prophesying war, 524b
Ancestry, heirs to polish of a.,
721a
honest hand-working a., 1027a
pride of a., 454a
Anchor, all sail no a., 597a
heaves ship free, 600b
hoist instantly a., 702b
holding a. lost, 216b
it is time raise a., 707a
of love is death, 807a
that a. holds, 654a
Anchorage, long a. we leave, 703a
Anchored, fleet of stars a., 980a
Anchoring, yond tall a. bark,
279b
Anchorite, saintship of an a., 555a
Anchors, moor bark with two a.,
125a
sons a. of mother's life, 83a
weigh thine a., 105a
Ancient, according to a. custom,
391b
account a. ordine retrogrado,
206b
and fish-like smell, 297a
and honorable, 31a
and natural strength, 444b
angels keep a. places, 857a
around a. track, 730b
close her from a. walls, 491a

Ancient, Europe of a. parapets,
830a
fear thee a. mariner, 525a
feed fat the a. grudge, 232a
feel spark of that a. flame, 118b
feet in a. time, 490b
gentlemen, 265b
good uncouth, 692a
heavenly connection, 1081b
heavens fresh and strong, 514b
hills as sun, 574a
how left the a. love, 486b
landmark, 25b
landmarks in Bill of Rights,
1037b
like actors in a. plays, 830a
mariner, 524b, 525a
Mariner called Old Sailor, 756b
marry a. people, 333b
models perpetuated, 148a
most a. profession, 872a
of a. race by birth, 368b
of days, 35a, 743a
order swerves, 832a
power of fright, 1034b
praise of a. authors, 318a
raven, 643a
recognize signals of a. flame,
161b
remove not the a. landmark,
25b
sacrifice, 875b
sanity in a. literature, 712b
simplicity is gone, 379a
sing a. ways, 879b
suit of a. black, 953a
these times are a. times, 206b
trusty drouthy crony, 495b
walked among a. trees, 488b
with the a. is wisdom, 15a
writers say, 883b
Ancients, speak of a. without idolatry, 415b
we are a. of the earth, 206b
wisdom of the a., 452a
Andalusia, weather like April in
A., 172a
Anderson, John A. my jo John,
494b
Andrew with brindled hair, 823b
Andrey, Prince A. went to tomb,
732a
Ane, I've lost but a., 496a
Anecdotage, fell into a., 612b
Anemone, delicate algae and sea
a., 1006a
Anesthesia bastard substitute,
861b
perceptual a., 960a
Anew, ruined love when built a.,
294a
think a. act a., 638b
Anfractuous rocks, 1001b
Ange, pur comme un a., 484a
Angel and archangel join, 412a
ape or a., 612b
appear to each lover, 398a
as you are insect in you, 708a
beautiful ineffectual a., 717a
consideration like a. came, 243a
curse his better a., 276a
devil an a. too, 869b
drew one a., 665b
ended and in Adam's ear, 347a
faces smile, 597b
golden hours on a. wings, 495a
good and bad a., 310b
half a. half bird, 667a
he is a. of light, 684a

Ascend into the hill of the Lord, 18a
  muse of fire a., 242b
Ascendancy, capital in a. system of plunder, 687a
Ascended, bright pomp a. jubilant, 347a
  into heaven, 60a
Ascending, angels a. and descending, 7a, 48a
  my voice a. high, 396b
Ascends to mountaintops, 556a
Ascent, no a. too steep for mortals, 120b
Ascetic in unnecessary points, 793a
  systematically a., 793a
Asclepius, I swear by A., 88a
  owe a cock to A., 88a
Ash, oak a. and thorn, 876b, 1088a
Ashamed, epitaph of which not a., 825a
  more a. more respectable, 836b
  naked and were not a., 5b
  never a. to own wrong, 413a
  no reason to be a. of ape, 725b
  nor ever a. so we be named, 742b
  not a. to fail, 427a
  of death, 329b
  of divine idea, 666a
  of having been in love, 355a
  shame is a. to sit, 225a
  to be seen with him, 376a
  to defend a friend, 38a
  to die, 586b
  to look upon one another, 326a
  with noble shame, 691b
  workman that needeth not to be a., 55b
Ashbuds, more black than a., 646a
Ashen, skies a. and sober, 643b
Ashes, all a. to taste, 556a
  am I and dust, 152b
  beauty for a., 33b
  cinders a. dust, 581b
  e'en in our a. live, 441a
  fell in fire burned to a., 930b
  from his a. made, 650a
  handful of gray a. at rest, 719b
  heaven and earth in a., 157a
  in a. olde is fyr yreke, 167b
  in a. rather than enslaved, 921b
  into a. all my lust, 360a
  new-create another heir, 299b
  of his fathers, 596a
  of Napoleon Bonaparte, 506a
  out of a. life again, 810a
  past a bucket of a., 948b
  put on sackcloth with a., 14a
  speak to your silent a., 115b
  splendid in a., 331a
  to ashes, 61b
  turn to a. on lips, 543b
  turns a. or prospers, 629b
  well-wrought urn becomes greatest a., 305a
  yesterday embryo tomorrow a., 142a
Ashore, put their ship a., 876b
  till last galoot's a., 778b
Asia and Africa expelled freedom, 466b
  settlement in A., 1013b
  seven churches in A., 57b
  vast multitudes of A., 922b
Asians, yes we are A., 958a

Aside, in life many things draw us a., 138a
  not idly stand a., 90a
  to step a. is human, 493b
Asides, heart's a. in tears, 593a
Asinorum, pons a., 103b
Ask, all I a. is merry yarn, 947a
  all I a. is tall ship, 946b
  and it shall be given, 41a
  and ye shall receive, 49a
  cease to a. what morrow will bring, 121a
  don't a. me to take none, 670b
  dost thou a. proof, 714b
  drink divine, 303a
  for anything except time, 504a
  for me tomorrow, 225a
  for no meaner pelf, 680a
  for the old paths, 34a
  how he is he tells you, 888a
  I do not a. you much, 237b
  if there is some mistake, 927b
  little I a., 634a
  me blessing, 280a
  me no more, 649a
  me no more where Jove bestows, 326b
  me no questions, 450b
  never a. of money spent, 928b
  never a. refuse resign office, 423b
  not a dinner to a. a man to, 431a
  not a. for what you wish you had not, 130b
  not offer to people but a., 1072a
  not what country can do for you, 1073a
  not whom sleep beside, 852b
  nothing more of me sweet, 775b
  nothing want nothing, 156a
  of him will they a. more, 47a
  of thee forgiveness, 280a
  only a. for information, 671b
  only what they can give, 886b
  the beasts, 15a
  the young, 483b
  us prophet, 1080a
  we a. and a., 710b
  wealth I a. not, 824a
  what you can do for country, 1073a
  where a. is have, 444a
  why I have no statue, 107a
  wilt thou go a. the mole, 486b
Asked a lithe lady, 488a
  for it Georges Dandin, 361b
  how pearls did grow, 320a
  no other thing, 736a
  not come even if a., 929a
  Oliver a. for more, 669a
  one another the reason, 250b
  thief to steal me peach, 488a
  to be where no storms, 802b
Askelon, publish it not in the streets of A., 12a
  when Ahab went to A., 945b
Asking, only God had for a., 692a
  too much, 507a
Asks a little of us here, 929a
  gives passion flower a. back, 944b
  if this be joy, 450a
  of us certain height, 929a
Asleep, athwart noses as they lie a., 223a
  devil is a., 835b

Asleep, drunk and a. in boots, 955a
  half a. as they stalk, 784a
  in lap of legends, 581b
  is in world of his own, 137a
  keep it quiet till it falls a., 366b
  lips of those that are a. to speak, 29b
  my Mary's a., 495a
  not see ticket unless a., 895b
  on furrow sound a., 584a
  sail like swans a., 980a
  sucks the nurse a., 289a
  tide moving seems a., 655a
  under haystack a., 1093b
  very houses seem a., 512a
  where winds all a., 710b
A-sorrowing, goeth a., 188a
Aspect, lend the eye terrible a., 243b
  meet in her a. and eyes, 558b
  sweet a. of princes, 298b
Aspects, relations between a. of experience, 984b
Aspen, as a. leef gan to quake, 164b
  light quivering a., 519b
Aspens quiver, 645b
Aspics' tongues, 275a
Aspiration, cannot prove an a., 779b
  social order and thirsty a., 1067a
Aspirations of men of good will, 1015a
Aspire, by due steps a., 336a
  light and will a., 220a
  mind a. to higher things, 203b
  on what wings dare he a., 489a
  smile we would a. to, 298b
Aspired to be and was not, 666a
Aspires, art a. to condition of music, 781a
  each of us a. to worth, 198a
Aspirin of middle classes, 1050b
Aspiring, all to have a. minds, 212a
  to be gods, 408a
  youth that fired Ephesian dome, 331a
Ass, covet thy neighbor's a., 9a
  egregiously an a., 273b
  enamored of an a., 230a
  idle to play lyre for a., 145a
  jawbone of an a., 11b
  knoweth his master's crib, 30a
  law a., 669b
  opened the mouth of the a., 10a
  recover and prove an a., 231a
  riding upon an a., 36a
  sinned against my brother the a., 157b
  thinks he may kick him, 476b
  wild a. stamps o'er head, 629b
  will carry load, 197a
  write me down an a., 247a
Assail, ills scholar's life a., 427a
Assailed seasons, 899b
Assails, all he reads a., 404a
Assassin, forgot copperheads and a., 948b
Assassinated, rather be a. than surrender, 637a
Assassination, absolutism tempered by a., 502a
  extreme censorship, 837b
  trammel up consequence, 282a

Atrocious crime of being young man, 425b
Atrophied, sexually a., 867a
Attach golden chain from heaven, 63b
Attachée, à sa proie a., 378b
Attachment à la Plato, 766b
to government, 453a-b
Attack all the more boldly, 118b
first to a. neighbors, 360b
is the reaction, 431b
lawless a. upon liberty, 444a
prompt in a., 453a
repeat a., 968a
so outnumbered we a., 975b
strength in a., 1011b
Attacked, rather a. than unnoticed, 432b
United States a., 973b
Attacking and getting hammered, 837a
situation excellent I am a., 826a
Attacks on me my wife my sons, 973b
try to answer a., 641a
Attain, old experience do a., 336a
Attainable, truth a. in poetry, 643b
Attainment, Zeus grant a. of sweet delight, 79b
Attains upmost round, 254a
Attempt and not the deed, 283b
fearing to a., 270a
literary a. unfortunate, 434b
no limit to what novelist a., 798b
perception and a., 888b
the end, 320b
wind rising a. to live, 909b
Attempted, not done is not a., 616b
something a. done, 621b
Attend men and not women, 95b
shooting stars a. thee, 320b
to history of Rasselas, 428a
Attendance, dance a., 299b
Attendant, am an a. lord, 1001a
bark a. sail, 410a
Attended, is on his way a., 513b
Attending, captive good a. captain ill, 292b
softest music to a. ears, 224a
Attendre, j'ai failli a., 378a
Attention, dance a. on old age, 885a
like deep harmony, 226b
must be paid, 1071a
socks compelled a., 904
tongues of dying enforce a., 226b
Attentive eyes, 429a
sit a. to own applause, 411a
Attic, beauty crieth in a., 755b
bird, 348b
not an A. grace, 988a
seasoned with A. salt, 362a
shape, 583b
Atticus, if A. were he, 411a
Attire comely not costly, 202b
in halls in gay a., 518b
man's a., 38a
rich a. creeps rustling, 582a
Attitude, democracy a. of mind, 934b
fair a., 583b
in which most alive, 792b
towards mystery of life, 1008a
Attitudenize, don't a., 433b

Attlee modest man with reason, 925a
Attorney, Hocus an old cunning a., 414b
Attorney's, go to a. office pay for it, 678b
office boy to a. firm, 766a
Attract silver churn, 767a
Attracted, those far off are a., 72a
Attraction and affection, 913a
Attractive, sweet a. grace, 314b, 345a
Attracts envy of world, 452b
Attribute, no a. of superior man greater, 99b
to awe and majesty, 234b
Attributes, God and a. of God eternal, 373a
poetry sum of a., 957b
Auber, dank tarn of A., 643b
Auburn, sweet A., 449a
Audace, de l'a. encore de l'a., 496b
Audacia certe laus erit, 127b
Audacibus annue coeptis, 117a
Audacity, nothing impossible provided you use a., 987b
Audentes fortuna iuvat, 119b
Audi partem alteram, 147a
Audible, ill-bred as a. laughter, 449b
Audience, Boston a. critics, 759a
dreamer a. of dream, 936a
for sake of crowded a., 88b
good play a. pleased, 917a
how long a. sits, 536b
never fail to laugh, 91b
of beery wenches, 807b
takes him serious, 954a
Audiences, addressing popular a., 98b
great poets great a., 703b
Auditor, appeal best suited to a., 976b
Audits penetrating, 1063a
Aught that I could ever read, 228b
Augur misgovernment, 453a
Augurs mock their own presage, 293b
Augury, defy a., 266b
his powers of a., 62b
single best a. is to fight, 63b
August, day in latter A., 1075a
winter recommence in A., 562a
yellow with A., 988a
Augustan, next A. age will dawn, 442a
Augustine, Saint A. well said, 623a
why St. A. thanked God, 936a
Auld, air of A. Lang Syne, 626a
lang syne, 494b, 495a
moon in her arm, 1087b
should a. acquaintance, 494b
when a. waxeth cauld, 1088b
Aunt kept regard for truth, 902a
Aunt's charwoman's sister's son, 965b
Aunts, delight of husband a. infant, 1009b
sisters cousins and a., 766a
Auream quisquis mediocritatem diliget, 121b
Aurora, new A., 1085a
Aurora Borealis, bounded on north by A., 655a
Aurora Leighs, no more A. thank God, 631a

Aurore, Belle A., 667b
Auspicious as ace of spades, 1079a
one a. eye, 257a
Austere beauty of mathematics, 913a
look a. of landscapes, 990b
masks outrageous and a., 990b
Austerlitz, pile bodies at A., 948a
Austria, Don John of A., 918b
outlive eagle of A., 466a
Authentic, when a. watch is shown, 350a
Author acquainted with authors, 726b
and finisher of our faith, 56a
choose a. as choose friend, 374b
dreamer a. of dream, 936a
he was the a., 129b
Holy A. of that religion, 387a
leaves of any a., 329b
not bein' a. gr-reat critic, 892a
of peace, 60a
ourselves a. and finisher, 635a
out from bushes, 975b
read by five hundred, 777a
relationship of a. to works, 843a
revised and corrected by A., 421b
same steps as a., 585a
select five hundred readers, 777a
sent by a. with autograph, 536a
shrimp of an a., 442a
steal from one a. plagiarism, 941a
thou art my master and a., 159b
time the a. of authors, 206b
unsuccessful a. turns critic, 528a
what good a. whispers, 878a
what I like in good a., 878a
whatever a. puts in book, 748a
when man of rank an a., 433b
where any a. teaches such beauty, 222a
who speaks of own books, 613a
worst thing do to a., 432b
Authoritarian Germany, 1035b
socialism in a. terms, 1035b
Authorities, destruction shows activity of a., 632a
nihilist not bow to a., 688a
world-wide public a., 964a
Authority, adduces a. uses not intellect, 174a
age in virtuous carries a., 395b
and place try tempers of men, 136b
and show of truth, 246b
base a. from others' books, 221a
by whose a. do you act, 468a
challenge to a. of President, 984a
common good and public a., 964a
compass of national a., 485b
every shadow of a., 453b
fit for public a., 82a
highest spiritual a., 964b
little brief a., 270b
miracle mystery a., 708a
nation cannot control, 750a
not majority, 600b
obedient to whomsoever in a., 89b
of Church moved me, 147a
precepts backed by a., 834b
tongue-tied by a., 292b
truth basis of moral a., 706b

Bad, he is writing b. stuff, 851b
herdsmen ruin flocks, 66b
himself thought nothing good, 791b
I have b. dreams, 261a
immoral what you feel b. after, 1044b
keep no b. company, 450a
laws bring about worse, 436a
leaves aside good and b., 455b
mad b. and dangerous, 552b
Madame B. Luck, 588b
man who brings b. news, 82a
man's refuge, 74b
means and b. men, 467a
meaning good or b., 369a
men as b. and as good, 640a
men live that they may eat, 87b
moral character, 423a
neighbor is misfortune, 67b
never b. man good service, 453b
never good to bring b. news, 288a
never good war or b. peace, 422b
no benefit in gifts of b. man, 84a
no man who laughed b., 576a
no to everything b., 794b
nothing either good or b., 261a
obstinacy in b. cause, 329b, 437b
or obnoxious laws, 717a
persecution b. way to plant religion, 329b
pious fraud as with b. action, 467a
play not please audience, 917a
poet in anthologies, 975a
prosperity comes to a b. man, 77a
provide b. examples, 355b
rhyming a disease, 412b
sad and mad and b., 666a
sad b. brother's name, 776a
so much b. in best of us, 789b
start assuming that men are b., 177b
streak of b. luck, 769b
the b. affright, 439b
they are good they are b., 846a
things ill got had b. success, 215b
truth told with b. intent, 490a
two nations good b., 360a
war never slays b. man, 82b
when b. she was horrid, 625a
when b. men combine, 452a
wiser being good than b., 666b
work follers ye, 693b
world is grown so b., 217a
Badge, mercy nobility's true b., 218b
of all our tribe, 232a
red b. of courage, 905a
Badine, on ne b. pas avec l'amour, 657a
Badly, when things going b., 417a
Badness you can get easily, 67b
Bad-tempered, infallibility of b. woman, 949b
Baffled get up begin again, 664a
imagination b. by facts, 922b
to fight better, 668b
Baffling, beat down b. foes, 711b
Bag and baggage, 249b, 631b
bagworm separated from b., 380a
empty b. cannot stand, 422a
given us b. to hold, 491b

Bag, moon in silver b., 884b
sealed b. of ducats, 233a
to make b. pudding, 1098a
your old kit b., 958a
Bagdad-on-the-Subway, 864a
Baggage, bag and b., 249b, 631b
Bags, three b. full, 1093a
two sealed b. of ducats, 233a
Bagworm separated from bag, 380a
Bah to you ha ha to you, 767a
Bahamas, arrived at island of B., 172a
Bahram that great hunter, 629b
Bail, no b. no demurrer, 481a
Bailey, bells of Old B., 1093b
unfortunate Miss B., 499b
Bait, as a swallowed b., 294b
hook well, 246a
hook without b., 608b
melancholy b., 231b
your b. of falsehood, 260a
Baited like eagles, 240a
with dragon's tail, 332a
Baiting mousetrap with cheese, 904b
Baits, good news b., 350a
Bake, cannot b. or boil whole, 901b
me a cake, 1092b
Baked, funeral b. meats, 258a
in a pie, 1094b
me too brown, 744b
Baker, butcher b. candlestick-maker, 1096b-1097a
Baker Street irregulars, 849b
Baker's man, 1092b
Baking, long b. never done, 1046a
Balance between nourishment and excretion, 675a
between order and aspiration, 1067a
between what acquire and use, 564b
civilization in b., 842a
commitments and power b., 1013a
in thermonuclear terror, 1063a
not weigh faith in b., 818b
of power, 397b, 841b
or reconciliation of opposite, 529a
redress b. of the Old, 507a
small dust of the b., 32b
uncertain b. of proud time, 206a
what hangs in b., 1014b
Balanced and Miltonic style, 804a
film with film, 739a
Balances, weighed in the b., 35a
Balbec, editions of B. and Palmyra, 442b
Bald, old b. cheater Time, 302b
wish b. eagle not chosen, 423a
Baldheaded, go into it b., 693a
Baldness abundant, 668a
Baldric, milky b. of skies, 578b
Bale, bliss and b., 799b
Bales, down with costly b., 647a
Ball, balm scepter and b., 244b
earthly b. a peopled garden, 477b
great b. of fire, 1008b
one fish b., 720b
regardless who carries b., 1025b
sun with golden b., 991a
terrestrial b., 1051b
Ballad, I love a b. in print, 295b
in street, 605b

Ballad, met with b. I can't say where, 740b
to mistress' eyebrow, 249a
Balladmongers, meter b., 239b
Ballads, better than all b., 623b
permitted to make all b., 384b
songs and snatches, 768a
stuck about wall, 326a
Ballast is old wine, 553a
more sail than b., 381a
no better b. than business, 695a
Ball-floor thin and wan, 1036a
Balloon of the mind, 882a
philosopher man in b., 742b
Balloonman, little lame b., 1030a
Balloons, faces rise like b., 1077a
Ballot, paper you drop in b. box, 682a
stronger than bullet, 635a
Balls, elliptical billiard b., 768b
Ballyhoo's, King B. Court, 998b
Balm in Gilead, 34a
not the b. the scepter, 244b
of hurt minds, 283b
sleep b. of bruised heart, 210b
the hydroptic earth hath drunk, 306a
tropic for your b., 1033a
wash b. from anointed king, 227a
Balmy sleep, 398b
spring brings back b. warmth, 114b
Baloney, it's still b., 916b
Balsam, no b. for mistakes, 791a
Bam, under the b., 1004a
Bamboo, sin's sharp ez b. brier, 814a
under the b. tree, 1004a
Ban, hurl cynic's b., 846a
in every voice every b., 489b
spreading ruin scattering b., 619a
'Ban 'Ban Ca-Caliban, 297a
Bananas as bait, 1046a
Banbury Cross, 1095a
Band, heaven-born b., 508a
high aesthetic b., 766b
no soldier in gallant b., 769a
of angels, 1101a
of brothers, 245a
pilgrim b., 750b
playing somewhere, 868a
Bandersnatch, frumious B., 745a
Bandits, kingdoms destroyed by b., 379a
Bands, brass b. and barrel organs, 975a
dissolve political b., 470b
drew them with b. of love, 35b
end of life cancels b., 240a
her hands as b., 28a
iron b., 621a
loose the b. of Orion, 16a
pursue culture in b., 865b
Bandusian, O fount B., 122a
Bane of all genius, 568a
precious b., 343a
suspicion b. of good society, 466b
Baneful spirit of party, 461b
Banes, o'er his white b., 1088b
Bang, not with b. but whimper, 1003a
now animal is dead, 915a
Banish all the world, 239b
grief too great to b., 588a
pleasures b. pain, 397a
plump Jack, 239b

Banish, thief you cannot b., 1058a
  think not king did b. thee, 226a
  understanding from his mind, 86a
  wisdom, 101b
  with night we b. sorrow, 301b
Banished, alone a b. man, 1084a
  fear cannot be b., 1015a
  find moral in narrative b., 760b
  for my willful crime b., 348b
  yet true-born Englishman, 226b
Banishing for hours, 457a
Banishment, bitter bread of b., 227a
Banjo on my knee, 727b
Banjos, batter on your b., 948b
Bank and shoal of time, 282a
  breathes upon b. of violets, 251a
  broke b. at Monte Carlo, 821a
  contemplate entangled b., 628a
  First Supernatural B., 1009a
  grass b. beyond, 729a
  moonlight sleeps upon this b., 235a
  waly up the b., 1088b
  whereon wild thyme blows, 229b
Banker, Burglar B. Father, 734a
Bankers just like anybody, 1051b
  schoolmates clergymen, 881a
Bankrupt of life, 368a
Banks, allegory on b. of Nile, 480b
  and braes o' bonny Doon, 494a
  Brignall b., 520b
  o' Loch Lomond, 1099a
  of Wabash far away, 905a
  Tiber trembled underneath b., 253a
  vast surplus in b., 545a
Banner, blood-red b. streams, 549b
  over me was love, 29a
  royal b. and all quality, 275a
  song for our b., 600a
  that b. in sky, 633a
  torn but flying, 557a
  with strange device, 621b
  yet freedom yet thy b., 557a
Banners, all thy b. wave, 538a
  confusion on thy b. wait, 441b
  flout the sky, 281a
  hang b. on outward walls, 286b
  terrible as an army with b., 29b
  unfurled o'er world, 655a
Banquet, behave in life as at b., 138b
  hall deserted, 542a
  partaken in anxiety, 76a
  sated with b. of life, 113b
Banqueting upon borrowing, 38a
Banshee, memory comes like b., 830b
Baptism enslaved me, 830a
  spirit streaming from b., 857a
Baptist's, John B. head in a charger, 42b
Baptizing in name of Father, 45a
Bar against tyranny resolute men, 703b-704a
  back of b. in solo game, 933a
  birth's invidious b., 650b
  crossed the b., 655a
  foul storm out, 883a
  gold b. of heaven, 731a
  harbor b. moaning, 690b
  no moaning of b., 655a
  politics we b., 768a

Bar, to b. as very young man, 767b
Barabbas a publisher, 563b
  stock of B., 235a
  was a robber, 49b
Barb in arrow of childhood, 832a
Barbara, name was B. Allen, 1088a
Barbarian Scythian bond nor free, 54b
  weeping above dead, 749a
Barbarians, if superior man dwelt among b., 72a
  Philistines populace, 715b
Barbaric omens, 995a
  pearl and gold, 343a
  yawp, 701a
Barbarism and despotism, 473b
  destruction and b. victors, 979b
  fanaticism to b. one step, 437a
  fastnesses of ancient b., 720b
  from b. to degeneration, 786b
  my native land prey to b., 145a
  theater flourish in b., 800a
Barbarous dissonance, 337a
  in beauty stooks arise, 803a
  multitude, 233a
  triumph o'er her b. foes, 426b
  woman more b. than man, 805a
Barber, imprudently married b., 442b
  kept on shaving, 679b
Barbers, hide the haughty b., 1025a
Barbershop, lights burn low in b., 1025b
Bard, hear voice of the b., 488b
  here dwelt, 420a
  is envious of bard, 67b
  old or modern b., 336b
  whom none to praise, 510b
Bards, black and unknown b., 906b
  eighth commandment not for b., 527a
  have a share of honor, 66a
  in fealty to Apollo, 579b
  name me among lyric b., 120b
  of old enjoyed in you, 486b
  of passion, 583b
  of rhyme free, 962b
  Olympian b., 602b
  saints heroes, 710b
  sublime, 622a
Bare, back and side go b., 188b
  Ben Bulben's head, 885a
  bodkin, 262a
  cupboard was b., 1096a
  gift without giver b., 692b
  Goya of the b. field, 1083a
  imagination of feast, 226a
  let little colt go b., 1098a
  looked on Beauty b., 1023b
  old men's heads b., 1017a
  on b. earth he lies, 371b
  poor b. forked animal, 278b
  ruined choirs, 292b
  to the buff, 824b
  trees turn b., 1081b
Bare-bosomed night, 700a
Barefaced poverty drove me to verses, 124a
Barefoot boy, 626a
  dance b. on wedding day, 219a
  dervishes, 603b
  him that makes shoes go b., 184b
Barère's, not read B. Memoirs, 596b

Bares, foeman b. steel tarantara, 766b
  his horns above sleep, 1068b
Bargain catch cold and starve, 290b
  in the way of b., 239b
  necessity never good b., 421b
  never better b. driven, 203b
Barge, Arthur from the b., 654a
  drag the slow b., 459b
  like burnished throne, 287b
Bark and bite, 396a
  attendant sail, 410a
  band of exiles moored b., 573b
  bitter b. burning clove, 927b
  cynic b., 602b
  fatal and perfidious b., 338b
  hark dogs do b., 1097b
  if my b. sinks, 686a
  is on the sea, 559b
  let no dog b., 231b
  moor b. with two anchors, 125a
  off shot the specter b., 525a
  puts from native bay, 232b
  see they b. at me, 279a
  star to every wandering b., 294a
  watchdog's honest b., 560a
  worse than bite, 325b
  yond tall anchoring b., 279b
Barking, crowing of cocks and b. of dogs, 75a
Barkis is willin', 671a
Barks, Hylax b. in doorway, 116b
  Nicean b. of yore, 641b
  sail upstream, 4a
Barley, land of wheat and b., 10a
Barleycorn, inspiring bold John B., 495b
  John B. got up again, 493b
Barmaids diviner than mermaids, 1051b
Barn, hay creaking to b., 1075a
  sit in a b., 1095b
  stack or the b. door, 334b
Barnaby, like B. Rudge, 692b
Barns, neither reap nor gather into b., 41a
Barometer, high and low b., 760a
  sweeping around, 760a
Baron, Sir Leoline the b. rich, 524a
Barracks, single men in b., 873a
Barrage, chemical b. against life, 1061b
Barred on account of race, 1074a
  recognize good but be b., 79b
Barrel, beat an empty b., 953a
  do with b. of gold, 812b
  of meal wasted not, 13a
  organs, 975a
  save them by b. load, 856b
Barrel-house kings, 952b
Barren, acre of b. ground, 296a
  after summer b. winter, 214b
  among b. crags, 646a
  bosom starves birth, 439b
  bride, 406b
  buds of b. flowers, 775a
  imagination cold and b., 452b
  leave this b. spot, 538a
  live a b. sister all your life, 228b
  make b. our lives, 773b
  small model of b. earth, 227b
  superfluity of words, 385b
  sword sung on b. heath, 488b
  'tis all b., 438b
  weep b. tears, 568b

Bearing burdens of government, 635a
  on excellence of character, 98a
  precious seed, 22b
  seen him b. down on me, 969a
Bearings glint, 1043b
  lays in application, 671a
Bears all its sons away, 397a
  and lions growl, 396a
  dancing dogs and b., 906a
  each b. his own Hell, 119a
  first born are shapeless, 133a
  greatest honors, 349b
  his blushing honors, 298b
  in itself causes of destruction, 435b
  it out to edge of doom, 294a
  sorrows with steadfast spirit, 67a
  stamp of human condition, 190b
  strongly it b. us, 526b
  time b. away all things, 116b
Beast, a very gentle b., 230b
  blond b., 805b
  brute bastard, 1068a
  call this b. to mind, 901b
  civilization scarcely b., 905b
  cocoa a vulgar b., 919a
  cursed above every b., 6a
  deem himself god or b., 408b
  either a b. or god, 98a
  every b. of the forest is mine, 19a
  fist b. like a lion, 57b
  fit night for man or b., 951b
  fourth b. like a flying eagle, 57b
  in view, 372a
  like wild b. guards way, 489b
  little better than b., 232a
  making b. with two backs, 272b
  man and bird and b., 526a
  man neither angel nor b., 363b
  mark or name of the b., 58b
  maw-crammed b., 666a
  more subtile than any b., 5b
  multitude b. of many heads, 123a
  no b. so fierce but knows pity, 216b
  no more, 264b
  of prey in aristocratic races, 805b
  only b. in arena the crowd, 889b
  only connect b. and monk, 951b
  owest b. no hide, 278b
  Pellinore followed questing b., 175a
  people a many-headed b., 123a
  people resemble wild b., 177b
  righteous man regardeth the life of his b., 14a
  second b. like a calf, 57b
  serpent subtlest b., 347b
  something you could hunt, 1068a
  strangest b. ever he saw, 175a
  that wants discourse of reason, 257b
  third b. had a face as a man, 57b
  what rough b., 882a
  with many heads butts me, 289b
  without money man b., 1089b
  would act angel acts b., 363b
Beastie, tim'rous b., 492b
Beasties, long-leggety b., 1098b

Beastly, how b. bourgeois is, 986a
  to the Germans, 1043a
Beast's, man's life cheap as b., 277b
Beasts, ape vilest of b., 107a
  ask the b., 15a
  coupling of b., 1005a
  fly to wilderness, 100a
  four b. had six wings, 57b
  judgment fled to b., 255b
  man lived with birds and b., 101a
  nature teaches b. to know friends, 289b
  of all wild b. preserve me from tyrant, 302b
  of the forest creep forth, 21b
  pair of very strange b., 250b
  shall be at peace with thee, 14b
  small and great b., 21b
  transform ourselves into b., 274a
Beasts', not God's not b., 666a
Beat an empty barrel, 953a
  Blake b. on wall, 885a
  down baffling foes, 711b
  downward b. thy wings, 113b
  earth with unfettered foot, 121a
  generation, 1080b
  gold to airy thinness b., 306a
  heart hear her and b., 652b
  him when he sneezes, 743b
  his breast, 524b
  in Belgrave Square, 767b
  me and hammer me, 948b
  my people to pieces, 30a
  on wall till Truth obeyed, 885a
  so we b. on, 1036b
  soul of enemy man, 987b
  sound trumpet b. drums, 420b
  sound trumpets b. drums, 371a
  swords into plowshares, 30a
  the bush, 182b, 318b
  the Dutch, 1090b
  the ground, 336b
  they b. and Voice b., 856b
  to win not b. weapons, 987b
  Turk b. a Venetian, 276b
  upon whorled ear, 802b
  water they b., 287b
  waves of science b. in vain, 705b
  with fist instead of stick, 351b
  you b. your pate, 407b
Beaten at all points, 90b
  genius disdains b. path, 635a
  poop was b. gold, 287b
  till they know, 352b
  with his own rod, 182a
  yet today, 1050b
Beatific, enjoyed in vision b., 343a
Beating bird extending wings, 1066b
  disastrous b. of wings, 905b
  in void luminous wings, 717a
  living thinking, 697b
  of my own heart, 634b
Beatrice a light between truth and intellect, 161a
Beats about in caverns, 1079a
  all lies you can invent, 490a
  at clay-shuttered doors, 857a
  back envious siege, 227a
  light b. on throne, 653a
  them on his anvil, 351b
  upon high shore of world, 244b
  with his blood, 649b

Beaumont, bid B. lie a little further, 303b
  rare B., 319a
Beauteous bright creation, 152a
  commands the b. files, 363b
  dear b. death, 363a
  evening calm and free, 512a
  eye of heaven to garnish, 237a
  idiot speaks, 1089b
  kindness not b. looks, 219b
  pearls in b. ladies' eyes, 221a
  prove a b. flower, 224a
  things for which we live, 719b
Beauties, in small proportions b. see, 304a
  meaner b. of the night, 300b
  not his own, 413b
  unripened b. of north, 393b
Beautifier, rank great b., 601a
Beautiful a fairy's child, 581a
  all b. and accessible, 173a
  all b. drifts away, 881a
  all b. sentiments in world, 695a
  all once so b. is dead, 1010b
  all things bright and b., 684b
  always the b. answer, 1031a
  and ineffectual angel, 717a
  and therefore to be wooed, 214b
  as other passions, 995a
  as the sky, 701b
  as words, 917b
  be b. and be sad, 707a
  beauty making b. old rhyme, 293b
  beauty not good or aught but b., 990a
  changes as forest, 1078b
  childish but divinely b., 497b
  dancing most b. art, 851a
  death b. adventure, 700a
  death of b. woman, 643b
  dreamer, 728a
  Evelyn Hope, 663b
  evermore, 694a
  face candid brow, 843b
  find b. human soul, 475a
  for spacious skies, 849a
  from perceived harmony, 528a
  how b. they are, 527a
  how b. they stand, 573b
  how b. they stood, 573b
  innocent and b., 883b
  joyous b. and free, 569a
  life b. or reverse, 850b
  most b. among gods, 67b
  most b. lady, 914a
  most b. most useless, 698b
  most b. mouth in world, 416a
  most b. thing is mysterious, 950a
  nature's models b., 1034a
  nothing b. makes complete sense, 1024b
  nothing in house not b., 753a
  nothing more b. than death, 700a
  once I was b., 1082b
  overmuch, 882a
  palace B., 365b
  passionate body, 773b
  pea-green boat, 673a
  poetry most b. mode, 713b
  pussy you are, 673a
  quarto page, 481a
  question, 1031a
  sacrifices of friendship b., 904a
  scorn looks b., 252b
  series of b. days, 479a
  singing Oh how b., 877b

Believed, against hope b. in hope, 50b
  always everywhere by all, 147b
  because he b. in his God, 35a
  everything in papers, 886a
  I wept and I b., 503b
  juggling fiends no more b., 287a
  not seen yet b., 49b
  to be b. because absurd, 143b
  truth never understood and not b., 488a
  what we least know, 190a
Believer, above all a b. in culture, 715b
Believers, half b. of casual creeds, 712a
  take precautions against enemies, 149a
Believes, atheist half b. God, 399a
  each b. his own, 402b
  he who b. nothing, 471a
  what each wishes he b., 99a
Believeth, he that b. shall live, 48b
  liveth and b., 49a
  neither b. that it is sound of the trumpet, 16b
  whosoever b. in him, 48a
Believing, be not faithless but b., 49b
  in old men's lies, 988a
  to b. souls gives light, 214b
  where cannot prove, 649b
Bell book and candle, 236b
  book b. and candle, 175b
  clear green b., 704a
  curfew b. must ring tonight, 825b
  ding dong b., 1093b
  eats and goes to bed by b., 759b
  fancy from flower b., 665a
  foam b. no consequence, 713b
  for whom the b. tolls, 308b
  hear the surly sullen b., 292b
  heart sound as b., 246a
  in cowslip's b. I lie, 297b
  invites me, 283a
  merry as marriage b., 556a
  middle b. trills out, 632b
  sexton tolled a b., 591b
  silence that dreadful b., 273b
  some cost passing b., 601a
  strikes one, 399a
  swung to and fro, 825b
  the cat, 76a, 169b
  tocsin the dinner b., 561b
  tongue sounds as sullen b., 241a
  twilight and evening b., 655a
  very word like b., 583a
  who will b. cat, 76a, 169b
Belle Aurore, 667b
  dame sans merci, 581a
  of old Natchez, 1051b
  sois b. et sois triste, 707A
  vain to be a b., 434a
Bellicose, newspapers querulous and b., 960a
Bellies and drags in wind, 882a
  cold comfort to fill hungry b., 319a
  fills their b., 73b
  laughter out of dead b., 988a
Bellies', for b. sake creep, 338b
Bellman, fatal b., 283a
  would cry crew reply, 746b
Bellow, in b. and uproar, 975a
Bellows full of angry wind, 882b

Bellows like sea combated by winds, 159b
Bells and bonfires, 463b
  bells bells bells, 644a
  brazen b., 644a
  building with tower and b., 483a
  cap and b., 692a
  floating many b. down, 1031b
  for those who die, 1028b
  gives harness b. shake, 927b
  I hear, 702a
  in your parlors, 273a
  knolled to church, 248b
  loud alarum b., 644a
  merits of B. and Fudges, 595b
  music nighest heaven, 535a
  noisy b. be dumb, 853a
  of Old Bailey, 1093b
  of Shoreditch, 1093b
  of St. Clement's, 1093b
  on her toes, 1095a
  ring b. for new century, 937a
  ring b. of heaven, 905b
  ring O b., 702a
  ring out wild b., 651a
  ring out your b., 203b
  silver b. cockleshells, 1093b
  sound on Bredon, 853a
  summoned by b., 1059a
  sweet b. jangled, 262b
  temple b. they say, 873b
Bells', to b. cheerful sound, 486b
Belly, eye bigger than b., 325b
  fill his b. with east wind, 15a
  God send thee good ale, 188b
  hard to argue with b., 107a
  has no ears, 107a
  he who does not mind his b., 430b
  if it is well with your b., 123b
  increasing b., 241b
  injured by hunger, 100b
  Jonah was in the b. of the fish, 35b
  justice in fair round b., 249a
  like a heap of wheat, 29b
  men's only God their b., 145a
  no b. no bowels, 1009b
  noise in the beast's b., 175a
  rests on b. in mud, 1002a
  secret life of b., 1069b
  shoulder bum, 885a
  spent under b., 313b
  upon thy b. shalt thou go, 6a
  wears his wit in his b., 268a
  whose God is their b., 54b
Bellyful of fighting, 290b
Bellying, broad b. sails, 979a
Belong less to what flatters, 1057a
  secret things b. unto the Lord, 10b
  suffice for who b. to them, 701a
  to Company G, 755a
  to sacred literature, 1035a
  to vanishing race, 1037b
Belongs, now he b. to ages, 677a
Beloved, ah my b. fill cup, 630a
  creature that is b., 252a
  escape me never b., 664a
  from pole to pole, 525b
  he giveth his b. sleep, 22b
  let my b. come into his garden, 29b
  liberty a b. discipline, 1067a
  never be b. by men, 490a
  of a king, 1088a
  of Abraham Lincoln, 898b
  our own b. home, 704b

Beloved Pan, 92b
  perfection in b., 550b
  physician, 54b
  so is my b. among the sons, 29a
  Son, 39b
  this is my b., 29b
  thought himself b., 882b
Beloved's, heaped for b. bed, 572b
  I am my b., 30a
Below, down and away b., 710b
  from above and b., 531b
  joy to pass to world b., 118b
  my thoughts remain b., 264a
  no safety here b., 179b
  slave spirit b., 991a
  thy element's b., 277b
  what we are here b., 907b
Belshazzar made a great feast, 35a
Belted, prince can make b. knight, 496a
  you and flayed you, 873a
Belua multorum es capitum, 123a
Bemocked, beams b. sultry main, 525b
Bemused, parson much b. in beer, 410a
Ben Adhem's name led rest, 551b
  Battle soldier bold, 591b
  Bolt, 690a
  Bulben's head, 885a
  Jonson his best poetry, 302b
  O rare B. Jonson, 302a
Bench, log hut with simple b., 741a
Bend, grass must b. when wind blows, 72a
  I b. but do not break, 359a
  if I cannot b. Heaven, 119b
  low O dusky night, 758a
  shall I b. low, 232a
  soften rocks or b. oak, 392a
Bended, on b. arm doglike, 78b
Bendemeer's stream, 543a
Bending sickle's compass, 294a
  to your wool, 187b
Bends, blue sky b. over all, 524a
  gallant mast, 551a
  though she b. him, 623a
  to the grave, 449a
  with remover to remove, 294a
Beneath, at once above b. around, 444a
  rung battle shout, 633a
Benedick the married man, 245b
Benediction, face like a b., 194a
  therefore and forever, 617b
Benefaction, calling to mind previous b., 88b
Benefactor, less to blame than b., 355b
Beneficence of grass, 748b
  private b. inadequate, 857b
Beneficent, belief in b. power, 783a
  zealous b. firm, 715b
Benefit, find man to b. kingdom, 99b
  God made for b. of men, 366b
  government for common b., 446a
  he receives hope who recognizes b., 148b
  human b. and enjoyment, 453a
  if men stop work at sixty, 817b
  no b. in gifts of bad man, 84a
  of clergy, 909a
  of ill, 294a
  practical b. in failures, 725a

Bicycle mechanics from Dayton, 1036a

Bid, come between b. us part, 420a
farewell to every fear, 397a
gave thee life b. thee feed, 486b
me discourse, 219b
me Good morning, 470a
me to live, 319b
not serve God if devil b., 272a
shall I b. her go, 1084b
soul of Orpheus sing, 336a
them wash their faces, 289b
time return, 227a
you a welcome adoo, 750b
you top o' the mornin', 812a

Bidding, thousands at his b. speed, 341a

Bide by the buff and the blue, 496b

Bides, weary warld nobody b. in, 857b

Bids, do what manhood b., 707b
expectation rise, 447a
it break, 285b
it come to heel, 1000a
remembrance rise, 447a

Bier, murdered Lincoln's b., 680b

Big big D, 766a
Brother watching you, 1053b
bushy eyebrows, 878a
business give square deal, 848b
butter-and-egg man, 980a
carry b. stick, 847b
city of b. shoulders, 948a
lie, 1012a
monstrous b. river, 761b
my tavern the B. Bear, 829b
round childish hand, 1057b
sleep, 1000a
stealin' makes you emperor, 1009a
this too would become b., 67b
words always punished, 82b

Big-boned and hardy-handsome, 803a

Bigger, eye b. than belly, 325b
no b. than agate stone, 223a
seems no b. than his head, 279b

Biggest dog has been pup, 790a
fish got away, 820a

Bigness, world in b. as star, 344a

Bigotry, gives b. no sanction, 461b

Big-Sea-Water, shining B., 623a

Bile, sentences that stir b., 856a

Bill, as if God wrote b., 603b
cool dew in b., 626b
fellers call me B., 821a
hold more than belican, 953b
larger b. for darker ill, 686a
Roaring B. who killed him, 902b
tax relief b., 973a
unpaid b. Despair, 573a

Bill of Rights, absolutes in B., 991b
guarantee of freedom, 983b
into suicide pact, 1021b
landmarks in B., 1037b
take B. for granted, 983b

Billabong, camped by b., 869a

Billboard lovely as tree, 1051b

Billboards, unless b. fall, 1051b

Billee, youngest little B., 661a

Billet, bullet has its b., 383a, 522a

Billiard, elliptical b. balls, 768b

Billions, chained for b. of years, 1008b

Billow, what a b. be, 737b

Billows, rocked to sleep between b., 696a
smooth and bright, 745b
swelling and limitless b., 526b
thy b. far and near, 558a

Bill's, Buffalo B. defunct, 1030a

Bills of rights, 446a

Billy in one of new sashes, 930b

Billy-boil, waited for b., 869a

Bind another to its delight, 489a
arm b. restless wave, 726a
fast b. fast find, 182b
in body and in soul b., 518b
much found I could not b., 950a
on thy sandals, 772b
safe b. safe find, 182b
shall my joyful temples b., 332b
the sweet influences of Pleiades, 16a
them heart and brow, 807a
us in time, 1043a
up my wounds, 217b
up nation's wounds, 640b

Binding Nature fast in fate, 412b

Binds brave of all earth, 865a
he who b. to himself a joy, 488b
so dear a head, 571a
vow b. too strictly, 653b

Binnorie, milldams o' B., 1088b

Biographers, Boswell first of b., 429b
reviewers would have been b., 528a

Biographies clothes and buttons, 764a
geniuses shortest b., 608a
history innumerable b., 577a

Biography, heroic poem a b., 575b
history of world b., 577a
like big game hunting, 1011b
no history only b., 605b
of man cannot be written, 764a
ready morning after demise, 678b
recognized sport, 1011b
written by acute enemy, 813a

Biological, is war b. necessity, 980b
not expressing b. characteristics, 980b
warfare, 1015a

Biologically, idle b. speaking, 1023b

Biped, divide b. class, 96b

Birch most shy ladylike, 692a
Tom B. brisk as a bee, 429b
twig for castigation, 879a

Birches, swinger of b., 926b

Bird, a very few a b. or two, 734b
as b. endearment tries, 449b
Attic b., 348b
beat bush another take b., 182b
beating b. extending wings, 1066b
change me to winged b., 84b
crop-full b., 666a
cuckoo shall I call thee b., 514a
day after day b. flies, 626b
Dinkey B. goes singing, 820b
divine b. of Zeus, 79a
drink to the b., 900a
flee as a b., 17a
flies out, 1066b

Bird, forgets dying b., 467b
form is cage and sense b., 782a
foul b. that filleth own nest, 176a
guides me and b., 661a
half angel half b., 667a
hath made his pendent bed, 282a
heard b. at dawn, 974b
heart like singing b., 739b
here and there b. or butterfly, 927a
if men like wise b., 810a
immortal b., 583a
in gilded cage, 903a
in hand worth two in bush, 137a
is in the sky, 364b
is on the wing, 629a
it was carol of b., 559a
Jubjub b., 745a
let no b. call, 1023a
like b. on wing, 849b
live like stoic b., 990a
loaf to every b., 736b
man and b. and beast, 526a
merged like the b., 1065b
music, 1042b
night's sweet b., 572a
no b. but invisible thing, 514a
no b. soars too high, 487b
no further than wanton's b., 224a
O comfortable b., 580b
of bad moral character, 423a
of dawning, 257a
of night did sit, 254a
of wonder dies, 299b
or devil, 643a
pinnace like fluttered b., 654b
propitiatory b., 1057a
rare b. on earth, 139a
rise up at the voice of the b., 29a
said b. in musical voice, 1046b
shall carry the voice, 28b
silence with waking b., 652b
small hot b., 820b
soft-sigh me home, 1064b
soul of grandam inhabit b., 234a
spray b. clung to, 664a
stamped foot, 735b
swift as b. or thought, 65b
that shunnest noise of folly, 335b
this her solemn b., 345b
thou never wert, 570b
thou warbling b., 494a
to nest from wandering, 854a
to others flew, 318b
turkey a more respectable b., 423a
with b. the abiding leaf, 1066b
wonderful b. is pelican, 953b

Birdcage, like summer b. in garden, 191a

Birdless silence, 1080b

Bird's, consciousness like b. life, 793a
sweet b. throat, 248a

Birds, all the tribes of b. sang, 156b
babes and sages, 656a
bees stirring b. on wing, 527b
began to sing, 1094b
blossoms b. and bowers, 319b
chant ye little b., 494a
charm of earliest b., 345b

Black, burn out to b., 853b
  burned b. with sun, 1022b
  but comely, 29a
  by morning storms, 534a
  creeping through the b., 953a
  devil damn thee b., 286a
  drop of b. blood, 1051a
  eyes and lemonade, 542b
  fat b. bucks, 952b
  from b. to red turn, 353a
  Hecate's summons, 284b
  hump b. and blue, 876a
  hung be heavens with b., 214a
  I am b. but O my soul is white,
    486b
  in B. Mud kingfisher, 1075a
  let the devil wear b., 263a
  little b. sheep, 873b
  long b. land, 663a
  love of children whether b. or
    not, 1039a
  men are pearls, 221a
  men fought on Coromandel,
    596a
  more b. than ashbuds, 646a
  my b. hen, 1096b
  night's b. arch, 495b
  no b. raiment when I am gone,
    107a
  Old B. Joe, 727b
  pall of nothing, 1022a
  piano appassionato, 985b
  played b. or white, 597a
  portent of atomic age, 901a
  pot calls kettle b., 197a
  powerful, 1051a
  ram tupping your ewe, 272a
  rank and file, 752a
  secret b. midnight hags, 285a
  shawl hides her body, 981a
  since b. womb held, 1069a
  spirits and white, 314a
  spot to keep concealed, 729a
  suit of ancient b., 953a
  suits of solemn b., 257b
  swan rare bird, 139a
  these b. bodies, 487a
  thou readest b., 491a
  we b. and they white, 1067a
  wet b. bough, 987b
  white not neutralize b., 667a
  who art b. as hell, 294b
  Widow death, 1075a
  wings one b. other white, 349b
  wires grow on her head, 294b
  with gilt surcingles, 738b
  years like great b. oxen, 879b
  yellow b. pale hectic red, 569b
Blackamoor, as if sun b., 955b
Blackberries, reasons as plenty as
    b., 239a
  sit round it pluck b., 619a
Blackbird snipped off nose, 1095a
  than b. 'tis to whistle, 352a
  whistling or just after, 955b
Blackbirds, four and twenty b.,
    1094b
  sitting on a hill, 1098b
Blackens every blot, 653a
  skuttle fish b. water, 395a
Blackest, Cerberus and b. mid-
    night, 334b
  perfect through b. air, 1079a
Black-eyed, landlord's b. daugh-
    ter, 961b
Blackguard whose faulty vision,
    791b
Blackguards both, 561a
  Hitlerite b., 954b

Blackness, faces as b. of a kettle,
    35b
  faces all gather b., 35b
  in sudden b. the pall, 1022a
  of darkness, 57a
  of death, 113b
Black-purple, in gloom b., 918b
Black's not so black, 506b
Blacks, enemies of persecuted b.,
    615b
Black-sailed unfamiliar, 1080b
Bladder, blows man up like a b.,
    239a
Bladders, boys that swim on b.,
    298b
  of philosophy, 382b
Blade, destroy b. of grass, 917b
  first b. then ear, 45a
  grasp by b. or handle, 694b
  knife without a b., 470a
  of grass, 311a
  steel not alone for b., 677a
  trenchant b. Toledo trusty,
    352b
  vorpal b., 745a
Blade's, grass b. no easier than
    oak, 692b
Blades to Meg and Molly dear,
    749b
  two b. of grass grow, 389b
  which b. bears better temper,
    214a
Blade-straight, steel-true and b.,
    824b
Blaine marched down halls, 749a
Blaize, lament for Madame B.,
    447a
Blake, dance with William B.,
    1066b
  William B. beat on wall, 885a
Blame, alike reserved to b., 411a
  bloody full of b., 294a
  needless to b. things past, 71a
  neither is most to b., 775b
  no dispraise or b., 350a
  no reason to b. Trojans, 63a
  or b. it too much, 451a
  poor wot gets b., 1103a
  praise at morning b. at night,
    403b
  praise nor b. writings, 403b
  praise or b. momentary, 585a
  praise or b. too far, 929a
  readers share b., 855b
  secret thoughts without b., 318a
  take some iv th' b. ourselves,
    891b
  ungrateful man less to b., 355b
  yet not afraid to b., 404a
Blamed living man, 715a
Blameless life, 652b
  vestal's lot, 405b
Blameworthy, least b. was Confu-
    cius, 455b
  the other strife is b., 67b
Blaming, always b. circumstances,
    836a
  mortals are b. the gods, 65a
Blanch, Tray B. and Sweetheart,
    279a
  without owner's crime, 517a
Blanching, under b. mays, 854b
Bland as a Jesuit, 815b
  childlike and b., 769b
  cruel composed b., 715a
Blandishing persuasion, 64a
Blandishments not fascinate us,
    475a
Blank, a b. my lord, 252a

Blank, bumbast out b. verse,
    206a
  our b. in bliss to fill, 734a
  pain has element of b., 736b
  surveying a b., 977a
  universal b., 344b
Blanket of the dark, 282a
  old woman tossed in b., 1095b
  sleeping is a wool b., 92a
Blankets, rough male kiss of b.,
    993b
Blare, barricades b., 918a
  of bugles ruffle of drums, 866a
Blasphemies, great truths begin as
    b., 837b
Blasphemy, in soldier is flat b.,
    271a
  Mass the greatest b., 179b
  middle-class b., 837b
Blast, contrary b. proclaims, 349b
  drives wicked spirits, 159b-160a
  midnight b., 562a
  of no b. he died, 367b
  of war blows in our ears, 243b
  one b. upon bugle horn, 520a
  spread wings on b., 559a
  stormy b., 396b
  striding the b., 282b
Blast-beruffled plume, 783b
Blasted with antiquity, 241b
  with excess of light, 441b
  with the east wind, 7b
Blastments, contagious b. immi-
    nent, 258b
Blasts, hollow b. of wind, 401a
  newborn infant's tear, 489b
  night b. cold, 918b
  roots of trees, 1070a
  sunk to silence, 105a
Blatant Bassarid of Boston, 776a
  land, 652a
Blaw, Sherard B. the dramatist,
    904a
  up an' gie them a b., 502a
  wind sall b., 1088b
Blaze, burst out into sudden b.,
    338b
  dark amid b. of noon, 349a
  heavens b. forth, 254b
  the sapphire b., 441b
Blazing evidence of immortality,
    605a
  heaven b. into head, 884b
  no more b. hearth, 440a
  potentates b. in the heavens,
    78b
  tail, 955b
Blazon of sweet beauty's best,
    293b
Blazoning, quirks of b. pens, 273a
Bleached, driftwood b. and dry,
    758b
Bleak December, 642b
  in b. midwinter frosty wind,
    740a
Bleakness, country of b., 632a
Bleat the one at the other, 295a
Bleats articulate monotony, 51a
Bled, buried Caesar b., 629b
  in freedom's cause, 508a
  Scots wha hae wi' Wallace b.,
    496a
Bleed awhile, 1087b
  carcasses b. at sight of murder-
    er, 169a
  heart begins to b., 1092a
  I fall upon thorns I b., 569b
  if you prick us do we not b.,
    233b

Breaking waves dashed high, 573b
  wrestled until b. of day, 7b
Breaks, bough b. cradle fall, 810b
  butterfly upon wheel, 411a
  chains from every mind, 488a
  jest b. no bones, 433b
  lance of justice b., 279b
  light through yonder window b., 223b
  like Atlantic Ocean, 1076a
  my pate across, 261b
  rider that b. youth, 325a
  sorrow b. seasons, 217a
  sun b. through darkest clouds, 219b
  world b. everyone, 1044a
Breast, against fear our b. steel, 711b
  arm the obdured b., 344a
  burn from brain and b., 918b
  cherish at charitable b., 990b
  crude Orson-like b., 797b
  deep in her b. like silent wound, 118b
  earth's sweet flowing b., 992a
  from her hardy b., 692a
  Hampden with dauntless b., 440b
  heart at rest within b., 487b
  heart in some quiet b., 813a
  hold me to your deep b., 758a
  hope springs in human b., 408a
  in thy b. stars of fate, 498a
  lacerate his b., 884a
  love lodged in woman's b., 300b
  Madeline's fair b., 582a
  marble of her snowy b., 332b
  marched b. forward, 668b
  mark on red b., 626b
  master passion in b., 409a
  my baby at my b., 289a
  Nature's learned b., 193b
  nunnery of thy chaste b., 358b
  of huge Mississippi, 713b
  one thought in b. another on tongue, 115b
  peace within my b., 914b
  pressed with excitement to b., 1059a
  sail upon her patient b., 267b
  same heart in every b., 711b
  soft as b. of doves, 991b
  soft hand softer b., 581a
  soothe a savage b., 391b
  soul wears out b., 559b
  spit brown get hairy b., 947b
  sweetness flows into b., 884a
  tamer of human b., 439b
  that gives rose, 730b
  thy b. encloseth my heart, 217a
  trembles in the b., 518a
  truth hath a quiet b., 226a
  turtle's b., 1004a
  two souls dwell in my b., 478b
  wail or knock the b., 350a
  weariness toss him to my b., 323b
  Wedding Guest beat b., 524b
  what his b. forges, 289b
Breast-burned, named B., 626b
Breastie, panic's in thy b., 492b
Breastplate of faith, 55a
  what stronger b. than heart, 215a
Breasts blows of circumstance, 650b
  brown b., 1022b
  come to my woman's b., 282a
  her b. are dun, 294b

Breasts like two young roes, 29b
  Sestos and Abydos of her b., 307a
  that feed France, 206a
Breath, a b. thou art, 271a
  a little flesh a little b., 141b
  able to take b. away, 666b
  bated b. and whispering humbleness, 232b
  boldest held his b., 538a
  bowed head held b., 711a
  breathes with human b., 644b
  brief as giving b., 1011a
  by the gate of b., 774a
  call the fleeting b., 440b
  Chaucer whose sweet b., 645b
  draw thy b. in pain, 266b
  dulcet and harmonious b., 229a
  ecstasy come to b., 1038a
  everything that hath b., 23a
  fail sun and b., 699a
  fancied life in others' b., 409b
  flattered its rank b., 556b
  fluttered failed for b., 712b
  fly away b., 252a
  from one mother both draw b., 79b
  give hautboys b. he comes, 371a
  giver of b. and bread, 802b
  he giveth b., 50a
  healthy b. of morn, 584a
  heaven's b. smells wooingly, 282a
  hot and cold with same b., 76a
  I sing on one b., 943b
  if b. terrible as terminations, 246a
  in treetops scarce b., 479a
  is in his nostrils, 30a
  kept b. to cool his pottage, 68a
  last b. most valued, 763a
  last gasp of love's latest b., 211b
  life of mortal b., 622b
  lightly draws its b., 508b
  love endures for b., 773a
  make them as breath made, 449a
  mist from b. of wind, 926a
  mouth-honor b., 286a
  my quiet b., 582b
  never drawn b. of life, 883b
  no b. at all, 280b
  of autumn's being, 569b
  of life, 5b, 883b
  of new-mown hay, 905b
  of self-respect, 1048b
  of the night wind, 714b
  of vernal shower, 442a
  poetry b. of knowledge, 511a
  princes but b. of kings, 492b
  rehearsing latest b., 1079a
  rides on posting winds, 291a
  say with final b., 696a
  slowly chilling b., 714a
  some of us out of b., 746a
  summer's ripening b., 224a
  sweet is the b. of morn, 345b
  sweeter ne'er drew b., 704a
  thought takes b. away, 720a
  thy b. was shed, 889b
  to cool pottage, 68a
  to last moment of b., 447a
  toil of b., 530a
  twilight hour of b., 890b
  utter sweet b., 230b
  want of words lack of b., 349b
  weary of b., 592b
  when b. blew back, 734b
  will be till time lose b., 825b

Breath, world gray from thy b., 774a
  writing is holding your b., 1037a
Breathe air again, 704b
  and blow, 648a
  as though to b. life, 646b
  hate were why men b., 1031b
  hear bronze Negroes b., 1076b
  heart pause to b., 559b
  his native air, 402a
  if such there b., 518b
  not his name, 541b
  prayer for all beneath, 877a
  slaves cannot b. in England, 457b
  thou thereon didst only b., 303b
  thoughts that b., 441b
  yearning to b. free, 817a
  you but knock b. shine, 308a
Breathed, first true gentleman that b., 302a
  killing chills, 824a
  still b. in sighs, 405b
Breathes all night for me, 854b
  enjoys air it b., 508b
  hell itself b. out, 263b
  of nations saved, 561b
  there the man, 518b
  upon bank of violets, 251a
  with human breath, 644b
Breathing and sighing round it, 797b
  closer He than b., 654b
  health and quiet b., 580a
  household laws, 512a
  music b. from her face, 358b
  revenge, 684a
  talking coeval with b., 391b
  two pairs of lips one b., 1086a
  whether b. is eating, 92a
Breathless, hanging b. on fate, 622b
  we flung us on hill, 993a
  with adoration, 512a
Breath's a ware that will not keep, 852b
Bred, dainties b. of a book, 221b
  en bawn in brier patch, 814a
  I am American b., 932b
  me long ago, 853a
  where is fancy b., 233b
Bredon, bells sound on B., 853a
Breeches Bible, 5b
  coat red b. blue, 533a
  cost a crown, 1085a
  hand in b. pocket, 584b
  Macaulay a book in b., 523a
  women wear the b., 310b
Breed and haunt, 282a
  border nor b. nor birth, 872b
  careful of b. of horses, 381a
  feared by their b., 226b
  happy b. of men, 226b
  Hyla b., 926b
  if sun b. maggots, 260b
  no waters b. nor break, 1080b
  or England b. again, 211a
  resolute b. of men, 704a
  use doth b. habit, 221a
Breeding, bad b. and vulgar manner, 91a
  Burgundy without b.,-1033a
  eating drinking b., 700a
  good b. is concealing, 764b
  lilacs out of dead land, 1002a
  test of man's b., 836a
  write with ease to show b., 482a

Broken it up for daily bread,
774a
  land of b. hearts b. heads, 918a
  laughs at b. hammers, 948b
  life's bubble b., 914b
  more than ocean water b., 928a
  Nature's social union, 492b
  not with club heart b., 738a
  oar and gear of dead men,
1006a
  on earth b. arcs, 665b
  picked up b. point, 1016a
  pitcher b. at the fountain, 29a
  ransomed for b. lost, 1057b
  renewal of b. relations, 777a
  resting upon b. staff, 461a
  staff of this b. reed, 32b
  things b. and scattered, 907b
  things uncomely and b., 880b
  two gross b. statues, 988b
  unto the ground, 31b
  wall burning tower, 883b
  wheel b. at the cistern, 29a
  with storms of state, 299a
  wound heart that's b., 520b
Brokenhearted, half b., 554b
  hoped we were b., 775a
  languish b., 764b
  lean above b., 981b
  we had ne'er been b., 494a
Bromide number one, 910b
Bronze, hear b. Negroes breathe,
1076b
  mangled by the b. spear, 64b
  monument more lasting than
b., 122b
  stone b. stone steel, 1004a
  work with breathing b., 119a
Bronzed lank man, 953a
Brooch, bow or b. or braid,
803b
  of gold ful sheene, 166a
Brooches, make you b. and toys,
824b
Brood like decrepit herons, 80b
  mothers a bloody b., 1035a
  of Folly, 335b
  on Christian thing, 1057a-b
Broodest o'er troubled sea, 580b
Broodin' over bein' a dog, 811a
Brooding, birds sit b. in snow,
223a
  on country's fate, 688a
  on God, 1066a
  toads b. in wells, 1064b
Broods, darkness b., 4a
Brook, dwelt by the b. Cherith,
13a
  many can b. the weather, 222a
  noise like hidden b., 525b
  smooth water where b. deep,
199a
  went to the b., 1097b
  where b. and river meet, 621b
  willowy b. that turns mill, 500b
Brookland, far in western b., 853a
Brooks, as b. make rivers, 372a
  as hart panteth after water b.,
19a
  books in running b., 247b
  for fishers of song, 846a
  golden sands crystal b., 306a
  I sing of b., 319b
  shallow b. and rivers wide, 334b
  strow b. in Vallombrosa, 342a
  too broad for leaping, 853b
Broom, beat barrel with b., 953a
  new b. sweepeth clean, 184b
  under arm carried b., 1095b
Brooms, new b. sweep well, 158b

Broomstick, Old Glory on b., 864a
  write finely upon b., 389a
Broomsticks, all their b. and
tears, 881b
Broth without any bread, 1095a
Brother, am I not man and b.,
456a
  and companion in tribulation,
57a
  be my b. or I kill you, 469a
  Big B. watching, 1053b
  brown-frocked b., 905a
  came with subtilty, 7a
  critic b. of artist, 798b
  Death and b. Sleep, 568a
  death's b. sleep, 119a
  devil to Despair, 806b
  every one said to his b., 33a
  every sword against his b., 35a
  far off, 26b
  fight against his b., 31b
  follow the plow, 807a
  gently scan b. man, 493b
  given b. dust to eat, 898b
  had b. who had friend, 965b
  half b. of world, 679a
  I am that insect b., 708a
  lawless linsey-woolsey b., 352b
  life sweet b., 601a
  little b. of rich, 835b
  loved him like a b., 495b
  man and b., 456a
  more close than b., 877a
  my fellow man my b., 706b
  no b. near the throne, 410b
  of loved Assisian, 905a
  of the Angle, 325b
  offended is harder to be won,
25a
  Remus and his b. knew this
life, 117b
  safety for my son b. shipmates,
174a
  shall be my b., 245a
  sinned against my b. the ass,
157b
  sleep death's twin b., 64a
  sleep the b. of death, 64a,
210b
  sticketh closer than a b., 25a
  still to my b. turns, 447b
  Sun who brings us day, 157a
  the b. the real b., 869b
  thy tail hangs down, 874b
  to all creatures, 1077b
  to dragons, 16a
  where is my b. gone, 574b
  which of us known b., 1049b
  whom someone should save,
826a
  would brother cheat, 156b
  yet line up with brother, 948b
Brotherhood bind rich and poor,
757a
  crown good with b., 849a
  intellect triumphed over b.,
613b
  love the b., 56b
  of venerable trees, 513a
  that binds brave, 865a
Brother-in-law haberdasher, 755b
Brotherly, feel it so b., 1068b
  love, 51a, 56a
Brother's, called b. father dad,
236a
  keeper, 6a
  mote in b. eye, 41a
  murder, 263b
  sad mad b. name, 776a
  voice of thy b. blood, 6a

Brothers all in honor, 510a
  all the b. too, 252b
  and sisters beware, 877a
  are evil, 3a
  as b. live together, 623a
  band of b., 245a
  call from bay, 710b
  forty thousand b., 266a
  good-bye b., 843a
  high beyond all stars, 497a
  linsey-woolsey b., 413b
  mankind knows men b., 497a
  sons kindred slain, 410b
  valiant sisters virtuous, 1104b
  waiting time my b., 797b
  ye are b. ye are men, 538a
Brought, Antony b. drunken
forth, 289a
  before the mountains were b.
forth, 20a
  daughters of music b. low, 29a
  death into the world, 341b
  forth on this continent, 639a
  me down to knees, 1066a
  me home to glory, 641b
  mouse will be b. forth, 124a
  never b. to mind, 494b
  nothing into this world, 55a
  over vast and furious ocean,
319a
  palsy to bed, 988b
  ravens b. him bread, 13a
  up in this city, 50b
  which b. us hither, 513b
Brought'st Thy sweets along with
Thee, 322a
Brow, athlete crowned in sweat of
b., 145a
  bind them heart and b., 807a
  bonny b. was brent, 494b
  candid b., 843b
  dangerous b. by night, 254b
  flushing his b., 581b
  forty winters besiege thy b.,
291b
  grace seated on this b., 264a
  Helen's beauty in b. of Egypt,
230b
  no wrinkle on azure b., 557b
  now your b. is beld John, 494b
  of labor, 858b
  of lip of eye of b., 293b
  pain and anguish wring b.,
519b
  parallels in beauty's b., 292b
  promise written on my b., 758a
  pure unclouded b., 744b
  shine upon b. today, 815a
  so grim mouth so prim, 1004a
  sweat of b., 682b
  tinge b. with sunset glow, 809b
  upon his b. shame ashamed,
225a
  view with wrinkled b., 235a
  weariness not on b., 715b
  wet with honest sweat, 621a
  where he got that high b., 139a
  wrinkle deeper on b., 555b
Brown, baked me too b., 744b
  bread and the Gospel, 386b
  breasts, 1022b
  bright nightingale, 772b
  changing from b. suit to gray,
986b
  dark b. is river, 823a
  Father B., 919a
  hair and speaks small, 266a
  hair over mouth, 1003b
  hair sprent with gray, 714a
  heath and shaggy wood, 519a

Busy old fool unruly Sun, 305a
  on Tom Tiddler's ground, 686a
  really b. person, 828a
  riches make one b., 176b
  the stop to b. fools, 362a
  till night, 375b
  while there's a b. street, 1069b
  whisper circling round, 449b
Busybodies, tattlers and b., 55a
Butcher baker candlestick-maker,
  1096b-1097a
  his father was a b., 365a
  hog b. for world, 948a
Butchered to make Roman holiday, 557a
Butchers, gentle with these b.,
  255a
Butchery, work of b. and desolation, 922b
Butt and very sea-mark, 276a
  fixed as an aim or b., 243a
  knocks you with b. end, 451b
Butter, cutting bread and b.,
  660b
  eggs pound of cheese, 740b
  for royal slice of bread, 969b
  guns or b., 1040a
  in a lordly dish, 11a
  it was the best b., 744a
  ladling b. from tubs, 1101a
  little bit of b., 970a
  not melt in her mouth, 183b
  only make us fat, 1026b
  quarrel with bread and b., 390b
  smell of bread and b., 559b
  white bread and b., 1094a
  words b. no parsnips, 521a
  words smoother than b., 19b
Butter-and-egg man, 980a
Buttercup, called Little B., 765b
Buttered, always on b. side, 553b
  bread fall on good side, 553b
  on which side bread b., 185b
Butterflies are already yellow,
  988a
  botany beetles b., 818a
  frogs eat b., 955b
  laugh at gilded b., 280a
  no b. no bees, 592a
Butterfly, blue in b., 927a
  breaks b. upon wheel, 411a
  dreaming I was a b., 101a
  I'd be a b., 587b
  in eternity as b. in air, 814b
  upon road, 871b
Butter's spread too thick, 746a
Butters, Stubbs b. Freeman, 1101a
Butting through the Channel,
  947a
Button, Brazil he twirled b., 736a
  little b. at top, 442b
  pray you undo this b., 280b
Buttoned-up and white-chokered,
  796a
Buttonhole, take you a b. lower,
  222b
Buttons be disclosed, 258b
  biographies clothes and b., 764a
  matched b. pattern sold, 770b
  soul above b., 500a
  taken of b. off, 873a
Buttress nor coign of vantage,
  282a
Butts, beast with many heads b.
  me, 289b
Buxom blithe and debonair, 334b
Buy a fat pig, 1097a
  a world of happy days, 217a
  annuity cheap, 670a
  apple on corner, 1000a

Buy, bubbles we b., 692a
  cherries which none may b.,
  300a
  costly as purse can b., 258b
  decline to b. repentance, 99a
  dispraise thing you desire to b.,
  269a
  full and fair ones come and b.,
  319b
  I will b. with you, 232a
  lose it that b. it with care, 231a
  no man might b. or sell, 58a
  nor can b. tomorrow, 302a
  pawn intelligence to b. drink,
  1030b
  spoils of office not b., 690b
  tomorrow, 302a
  two white feet b. him, 1101b
  what would you b., 600b
  what you do not want, 474a
Buyer, city to perish if it finds b.,
  116a
  it is naught saith the b., 25a
  let b. beware, 150a
  needs a hundred eyes, 324b
Buying and selling, 683b
  it's no fish ye're b., 520b
  more giving less b., 914a
Buys, who b. a minute's mirth,
  220a
Buzz, buccaneers of b., 738b
  crowd b. and murmurings, 357b
  the witty and fair annoys, 411a
B.V.D., from every B., 1030b
By and by easily said, 263b
  and by God caught eye, 1040b
Bye baby bunting, 1094b
Bygone days, 1052a
  only things b. last, 809b
Byproduct more valuable than
  product, 851a
Byron, close thy B., 576a
  cuts a figure, 585b
  from poetry of B. ethics, 595a
  Lord B. was Englishman, 812a
  mad bad dangerous to know,
  552b
Byron's eyes shut in death, 711a
  perhaps Lord B. fault, 812b
  struggle cease, 711a
Byway to heaven, 385b
Byword, proverb and a b., 13a
  story and b. through world,
  318a
  thou shalt become a b., 10b
Byzantium, lords and ladies of B.,
  883a

C

C major of this life, 666a
Ça ira ça tiendra, 1105b
Cabbage, cut a c. leaf, 442b
  with college education, 762a
Cabbages and kings, 746a
  death seize me whilst setting c.,
  189b
  happy those who plant c., 181a
  no c. sprouting out, 635b
  skunk c., 944a
Cabin, enter Logan's c. hungry,
  445b
  more fun when c. boy, 981a
  mounted to his c., 904b
  small c. build there, 879b
  willow c. at gate, 251b
Cabined ample spirit, 712b

Cabined cribbed confined, 284b
  from her c. loophole peep, 336b
Cabinet is formed of gold, 490a
  post offices and c. appointments, 635b
Cabinets, make parties as ministers c., 690a
Cable broke anchor lost, 216b
  no c. draw forcibly as love,
  312a
  on seventh day scrape c., 678a
  that in storm ne'er broke, 332a
Cabots talk only to God, 858a
Cackle, don't c. w'en fin' wum,
  814a
Cackles, codfish never c., 1101b
  groans and dies, 573b
Cad, cocoa c. and coward, 919a
Cadence from man named Yeats,
  1065a
  harsh c. of rugged line, 369b
  of consenting feet, 1029b
  to his verse a smooth c., 377a
  tremulous c. slow, 714b
Cadets of Gascoyne, 896a
Cadiz, reeking into C. Bay, 663a
Cadmean victory, 86b
Cadmus, letters C. gave, 561a
Caeli, fiat iustitia ruant c., 330b
Caelum, quid si nunc c. ruat,
  108b
  ruat c. fiat voluntas tua, 330b
Caesar, appeal unto C., 50b
  buried C. bled, 629b
  carry C. in your boat, 112b
  every wound of C., 256a
  great C. fell, 255b
  had his Brutus, 464b
  I come to bury C., 255a
  imperious C. dead, 266a
  not that I loved C. less, 255a
  O mighty C., 255a
  poor cried C. wept 255b
  render unto C., 43b
  sawdust C., 1018b
  upon what meat C. feed, 253b
  with senate at heels, 409b
  without ambition, 747b
  word of C. stood, 255b
Caesar's, all is C., 354a
  dead C. trencher, 288a
  hand Plato's brain, 604a
  self is God's, 354a
  wife must be above suspicion,
  112a
Caesars, madness of the C., 679b
Café, every street c., 1020a
Caftan of tan with henna, 955a
Cage, form c. sense bird, 782a
  gilded c., 903a
  minute within net of gold,
  1062a
  nor iron bars a c., 358b
  put me in a c., 1009a
  robin redbreast in c., 490a
  sing like birds i' the c., 280a
Cages, marriage as with c., 190b
  of my pores, 1083b
Cain, cruel sons of C., 887a
  eye stared at C., 599a
  set a mark upon C., 6a
  Tubal C. man of might, 677a
  was tiller of the ground, 6a
  went out from presence of the
  Lord, 6a
Caissons go rolling along, 952a
Caius is a man, 732b
Cake, bake c. fast as can, 1092b
  eat c. and have it, 185b
  heaven's sugar c., 381b

Cause, calledst me dog before c., 234a
cannot cross c. why born, 222a
common c. decays, 89b
common c. to save Union, 637a
died in virtue's c., 218b
do not kill or c. to kill, 80b
effect defective comes by c., 260b
effect whose c. is God, 459a
evolution not c. but law, 779b
final c. produces motion, 97b
found spiritual c., 709a
full c. of weeping, 278a
Germany the c. of Hitler, 999a
given his heart to c., 994b
good old c. is gone, 512a
Great First C., 459b
griefs we c. ourselves, 81b
hear me for my c., 255a
hidden but result well known, 128b
idea of oneself as c., 373b
if any man show just c., 61a
if astray c. is in you, 161b
is there any c. in nature, 279a
it is just, 541a
laws or kings c. or cure, 428a
little grace my c., 272b
magnificent and awful c., 458a
not a field but a c., 467a
not be judge in own c., 126a
not jealous for the c., 275b
nothing comes without c., 420b
obstinacy in bad c., 329b, 437b
of freedom cause of God, 499b
of this effect, 260b
or men of Emerald Isle, 483b
perseverance in good c., 437b
produces more than one effect, 706a
report me and my c., 266b, 706a
sea of c. and theory, 919b
set c. above renown, 865a
support Caledonia's c., 496b
tenacious of purpose in rightful c., 121b
try to condemn to death, 743b
turn him to c. of policy, 243a
watercolors to impaint c., 240b
what in effect already in c., 849b
wherein tongue confuted, 333b
wit in other men, 241b
Zeus first c., 78b
Caused the widow's heart to sing, 15b
Causes célèbres, 396a
flowers as in c. sleep, 327a
from amorous c. springs, 404a
great c. on move, 922b
happy man who could search out c., 117a
home of lost c., 713b
investigation of hidden c., 192b
lost c. preface victory, 1008a
of destruction, 435b
of disaster, 847a
which impel separation, 470b
why and wherefore, 245a
Caution in refusing benefits, 374a
scars of others teach c., 145b
upward look of c., 929a
Cautious, plant of c. growth, 1011b
politic c. and meticulous, 1001a
seldom err, 71b
statistical Christ, 807a
under whose c. hand, 702a
Cavalry of woe, 734b

Cave, courts thee in some pleasant c., 120b
error correct c., 1079a
idols of the c., 207a
shadows on opposite wall of c., 94b
sky will c. in on him, 1023a
Stygian c. forlorn, 334b
vacant interlunar c., 349a
Cave ab homine unius libri, 158b
canem, 150a
Caveat emptor, 150a
Cavern, mossy c., 583b
Pan's c., 885a
Caverns cool and deep, 710b
in c. all alone, 1079a
measureless to man, 523b
pure and deep, 587b
sand-strewn c., 710b
twice ten thousand c., 579b
Caves, beetles in c., 1064b
dark unfathomed c., 440b
of ice, 524a
Caviar to the general, 261a
Cavil on ninth part of hair, 239b
Cawdor, Glamis thou art and C., 281b
I am Thane of C., 281a
shall sleep no more, 283b
Cease and then again begin, 714b
Byron's struggle c., 711a
Catullus you should c. folly, 114b
day and night shall not c., 6b
efforts to find where last rose lingers, 121b
every joy, 537b
fears that I may c., 581a
from mental fight, 490b
from thine own wisdom, 25b
grinders c., 28b
hatreds never c. by hatred, 80a
long contention c., 715a
man I am c. to be, 652a
not c. from exploration, 1007a
poor shall never c., 10b
sing or c. to sing, 412b
the wicked c. from troubling, 14b
time c. and midnight never come, 213b
to ask what morrow will bring, 121a
to be free for religion, 1022a
upon the midnight, 582b
weeping without c., 808a
ye from man, 30a
Ceased, God created woman boredom c., 806a
when Lucy c. to be, 510b
Ceaseless devouring of weak by strong, 706a
thoughts of roaming, 380a
turns with c. pain, 447b
Ceases, forbearance c. to be virtue, 452a
happiness c. like dream, 328b
to be free for irreligion, 1022a
Ceasing, O swiftness never c., 204b
of exquisite music, 622a
pray without c., 55a
Cedant arma togae, 111b
Cedar, as c. tall and slender, 476a
grow like a c. in Lebanon, 21a
lordly c. green with boughs, 827a
Cedars of Lebanon, 21b
roots of c. of Lebanon, 945a
Cedarwood, sandalwood c., 947a

Ceiling, down from the c., 531b
Célébrait, Ronsard me c., 187b
Celebrate, I c. myself, 700a
not c. funeral with weeping, 106b
Celebrated cultivated Duke of Plaza Toro, 769a
Saviour's birth c., 257a
Celebrates his obsequies, 518b
pale Hecate's offerings, 283a
Celebration of freedom, 1072b
of man, 1071a
Célèbres, causes c., 396a
Celebrities, congress of c., 749b
Celeriter, sat c. fieri satis bene, 124b
Celerity never more admired, 288a
Celestial, apparelled in c. light, 513a
pattern of c. peace, 214b
sate itself in c. bed, 259b
so c. article as freedom, 467a
wisdom calms the mind, 427b
with c. clearness wrote, 811b
Celia, come my C., 302b
has undone me, 439a
Celibacy has no pleasures, 428a
Cell, deposit little c. by c., 781a
does c. have soul, 1083b
dwell on rock or in c., 199a
ill-spirit sob in each c., 1076b
in body holds heart, 1056b
in narrow c. forever laid, 440a
thine eternal c., 266b
tight hot c., 1038a
Cellar, born in a c., 442b
lived in c. damp, 694a
secretly nurtured in c., 998a
warm delicious c., 1046b
Cells, all c. from pre-existing c., 710b
better schoolrooms than c., 686a
condemned c. of Newgate, 756a
held in cohesion by c., 947b
unresting c., 947b
Cellula, omnis c. a c., 710b
Celt, blind hysterics of C., 651a
Celtic, locale was C., 968b
Cement glue and lime of love, 319b
gummed with bicycle c., 1036b
Cemetery, father buy plot in c., 925b
of dead ideas, 869b
Censorship, assassination extreme c., 837b
if c. reigns, 460a
Censure, careless of c., 404a
durst not c., 426b
every trade save c., 554b
fear of c., 988a
folks no right to c., 911b
freely who have written well, 402b
mankind c. injustice, 94a
pardons raven, 139a
take each man's c., 258a
tax for being eminent, 389a
Census, test of civilization not c., 608b
Cent, not one c. for tribute, 501b
what did with every c., 928b
Centaur, cloud that looked like c., 91a
in dragon world, 98a
Center cannot hold, 882a
intention stabs the c., 295a
man c. of circle, 748b
many lines in dial's c., 243a
my c. giving way, 826a

Chicken, she's no c., 390b
  some c. some neck, 923b
Chickens, all my pretty c., 285b
  as hen gathereth c., 43b
  beside white c., 979a
  count c. before hatched, 75b
  quit quarreling over food, 946a
Chide, fall out and c. and fight, 396b
  God for countenance, 250a
  me for loving armchair, 686a
  trumpets 'gan to c., 558b
Chides, at fifty c. delay, 399a
Chiding, better a little c., 267b
Chief, a c. a rod, 409b
  defect of Henry King, 902a
  good and market, 264b
  hail to the C., 520a
  his c. beside, 662a
  Justice was rich quiet, 596a
  nourisher in life's feast, 283b
  of the Army, 505a
  pity him fallen c., 906a
  sinners of whom I am c., 55a
  society's c. joys, 457a
  train anyone to be merchant c., 949a
Chiefest treasure, 901b
Chief's, vain the c. pride, 412b
Chieftain Iffucan of Azcan, 955a
Chield's amang you takin' notes, 495b
Child, a simple c., 508b
  again just for tonight, 742b
  always say what's true, 823a
  and the child's father, 892a
  anything we change in c., 936a
  around c. bend all three, 536b
  as yet a c., 410b
  beautiful a fairy's c., 581a
  behold the c., 409a
  better is a poor and wise c., 27b
  bring c. back to its mother, 69b
  burnt c. fire dreadeth, 184b
  call home the c., 1040a
  christom c., 243b
  cry of c. by roadway, 880b
  dear C. of Nature, 514b
  do not throw book, 901a
  duty's faithful c., 590b
  Eros Zeus's c., 84b
  every c. may joy to hear, 486b
  family stamped character on c., 936a
  fast fold thy c., 803b
  father of the man, 511b
  foster c. of silence, 583a
  get with c. mandrake root, 304b
  give a little love to c., 698b
  gives a c. a treat, 947a
  great with c. longing for prunes, 270b
  half devil half c., 875b
  happy English c., 546a
  hard heart of c., 990a
  has fairy godmother, 857a
  heard one calling C., 323b
  Heaven-born c., 334a
  her innocence a c., 369b
  here a little c. I stand, 321a
  I spake as a c., 52b
  idiotic c., 859a
  if you strike a c., 837a
  in simplicity a c., 369b
  infirm, 603b
  is father of the man, 511b
  is known by his doings, 25a
  Jesus Christ her little C., 684b
  keeps secret well, 599b
  know what it is to be c., 857a

Child, lie down like tired c., 568b
  life like froward c., 366b
  like three years' c., 524b
  little c. shall lead them, 31a
  look upon a little c., 425b
  love him because my c., 861a
  meet nurse for poetic c., 519a
  Monday's c. fair, 1096a
  more hideous in a c., 277b
  my c. wife, 672a
  ne'er spend fury on c., 216b
  nicest c. I ever knew, 902b
  of calamity, 760a
  of my right hand, 302b
  of our grandmother Eve, 221b
  of pure unclouded brow, 744b
  of scorn, 899b
  old man twice a c., 261a
  on a cloud I saw a c., 486b
  on parent knees newborn c., 476a
  painted c. of dirt, 411a
  permit c. to join, 734b
  room of absent c., 236b
  Rowland to dark tower, 278b
  said What is grass, 700a
  saving little c., 778b
  seemed a small ungainly c., 69b
  seen a curious c., 516b
  Shakespeare Fancy's c., 335a
  shall play on hole of the asp, 31a
  she was a c., 644a
  slayeth c. in womb, 988b
  so high you are, 987b
  sometimes say Poor c., 722a
  spare rod and spoil c., 102b, 353a
  teach c. to doubt, 490a
  thankless c., 277b
  there is a man c. conceived, 14b
  this c. to myself take, 510b
  thought as a c., 52b
  to mother sheep to fold, 854a
  train up a c. in the way, 25b
  trumpet of c. of Rome, 775b
  tyrant is c. of pride, 81b
  understood as a c., 52b
  unto us a c. is born, 31a
  virgin shall be with c., 39a
  warble c., 221b
  weep like c. for past, 985b
  what will c. learn sooner, 412a
  when I was a c., 52b
  white as angel English c., 486b
  wise father knows own c., 232b
  with sighs complain, 593a
  woman with c., 1102a
  wretched c. expires, 902a
  young c. with Mary, 39b
Childhood, barb in arrow of c., 832a
  eye of c., 263b
  in my days of c., 534a
  little world of c., 936a
  make glad heart of c., 780b
  manhood and decrepit age, 322a
  model of greater world, 936a
  scenes of my c., 553a
  shows the man, 348b
  this is c. of world, 817a
Childhood's hour, 543a, 641b
Childish but divinely beautiful, 497b
  glamour of c. days, 985b
  hand, 1057b
  inconstant c. proud, 579a
  live life not c. task, 1018a

Childish, practice c. ways, 65a
  put away c. things, 1055a
  religion but a c. toy, 212b
  sweet c. days, 511b
  things, 52b
  treble, 249a
Childishly, sucked on pleasures c., 304a
Childishness, second c., 249a
Childless and crownless, 557a
Childlike, smile c. and bland, 769b
Children, an' all us other c., 819a
  and fools cannot lie, 184b
  and fools want everything, 376a
  as c. fear in darkness, 113b
  as he would wish c. treated, 1074a
  become as little c., 43a
  begin by loving parents, 839a
  behold chimpanzee, 866a
  belonged to man I didn't know, 761a
  books c. of brain, 388b
  blood on us and on our c., 45a
  breed of horses dogs c., 381a
  bring forth c. in sorrow, 6a
  bringing up c., 1053b
  can c. of bridechamber mourn, 41b
  come dear c. let us away, 710b
  drinkest tears of c., 552a
  even c. followed, 449b
  familiarity breeds c., 764b
  fear death as c. fear dark, 208a
  give c. right to study painting, 463a
  God have mercy on c., 967b
  had so many c., 1095a
  hates c. and dogs can't be all bad, 951b
  her c. arise up, 27a
  here my c. born, 636b
  in days of our c., 848a
  in peace c. inter parents, 86b
  in the foliage, 1005a
  in the wood, 1084a
  indifferent c. of earth, 261a
  iniquity of the fathers upon the c., 9a
  invent a game, 985a
  king over c. of pride, 16b
  know and suffer, 1042a
  laboring c. look out, 940b
  lisping on lips of c., 599b
  listen my c., 623b
  living arrows, 976a
  love of c. whether black or not, 1039a
  made c. laugh and play, 563b
  nature fits c., 692b
  Negro school c., 1077a
  nigger saying he would steal his c., 761a
  no longer any c., 362a
  nor do c. prattle about his knees, 63a
  not leave unless I do, 1047b
  of an idle brain, 223a
  of kingdom cast out, 41b
  of larger growth, 415b
  of light, 47a, 713b
  of light and day, 55a
  of men full of wiles, 91a
  of the day, 55a
  of this world wiser, 47a
  of yesterday, 789a
  old men are c., 91a
  parents bore their c., 837b
  people are like c., 675b

Children, provoke not c. to anger, 54b
put c. on wheels, 944a
Rachel weeping for her c., 39b
return ye c. of men, 20a
Revolution eats own c., 675b
second wife hateful to c., 83b
shall wander in the wilderness, 9b
sins of fathers upon c., 86a
so act toward c. so toward wife, 138b
so are c. of the youth, 22b
suffer armed men, 1042a
suffer little c., 45b
swarmed like settlers, 1060a
sweeter than apples to c., 829b
tale which holdeth c. from play, 203b
tan-faced c., 701b
teach them diligently unto thy c., 10a
their country their c., 116a
they shall be called c. of God, 40a
walk on frozen toes, 900a
weeping O brothers, 617b
were all thy c. kind, 243b
when voices of c., 487b
where did c. vanish, 1058a
who needed his protection, 1081a
wife and c. impediments, 208a
wife and c. stand afraid, 330a
will burn, 1093a
win world for c., 923b
wisdom exalteth her c., 37b
wisdom justified of c., 42a
with Hyacinth's temperament, 904b
women and c. first, 1099b
Children's, all our c. fate, 877b
books of my day, 865b
gratitude woman's love, 884a
hour, 623b
lips shall echo, 556a
teeth set on edge, 34b
Child's amang you takin' notes, 495b
credulity c. strength, 535a
no c. pley to take wyf, 168b
not lose his c. heart, 100a
sob curses deeper, 617b
Child's-heart, not lose his c., 100a
Chill and drear, 519a
bitter c. it was, 581b
in wintry age feel no c., 459a
mantle of wind and c. and rain, 170b
penury, 440b
sun was warm wind c., 928a
thy dreaming nights, 581b
wind is c., 519b
you through and through, 820b
young whom age doth c., 351a
Chilling, slowly c. breath invade, 714a
Chills, breathed killing c., 824a
of c. and fever died, 1009b
winter lingering c. May, 447b
Chilly, although room c., 930b
December day, 1036a
I feel c. and old, 665a
Chime, faintly as tolls evening c., 541a
higher than the sphery c., 338a
hours to which heaven c., 362b
set c. of words tinkling, 878a
to guide their c., 360b
Chimera, what a c. is man, 364a

Chimeras, nothing great without c., 722a
Chimerical, reduction to atoms c. ideal, 779a
Chimes at midnight, 242a
little jingle little c., 400b
Chimleypiece, bottle on c., 670b
Chimney, as c. sweepers come to dust, 291a
from c. tax cell free, 1105a
hung by c. with care, 541a
little c. hot in moment, 219a
made c. in my father's house, 215b
makes c. of your nose, 484a
old men from c. corner, 203b
watching what comes out c., 675a
Chimneypiece, buffalo upon c., 747a
Chimney's, stretched out c. length, 335a
Chimneys consume own smoke, 576b
your c. I sweep, 487a
Chimpanzee, children behold c., 866a
Chimpanzees, might be c. today, 866b
Chin, close-buttoned to the c., 459a
dogs shame the gray c., 64b
new-reaped, 238a
China, behavior in C. licentious, 537a
break c. plates of others, 857b
crost the bay, 873b
great revolutions of C., 1027b
how troublesome a country C., 419a
mankind from C. to Peru, 427a
not seeking to dominate world, 1025b
suffering poverty, 889a
that's ancient and blue, 804b
though c. fall, 407a
thought of C. and Greece, 1054a
we in C. today, 1019a
Chinee, heathen C. peculiar, 769b
Chinese, bombing of C. cities, 984a
cheap labor, 769b
contradiction between imperialism and C., 1027b
contradictions in C. society, 1027b
love jade, 992b
nightingale, 953a
people have solidarity, 889a
people's philosophy, 1019b
poetry most human, 863a
sages to guide C., 537a
sediment of long C. past, 992b
wouldn't dare to, 1043a
Chink, importunate c., 454b
in floor of Wicklow house, 908b
Chinks of her sickness-broken body, 333a
that Time has made, 333a
Chinnymen, civilize th' C., 891a
Chip of old block, 453b
Chips, let c. fall where may, 733a
Chisel, whether c. pen or brush, 882a
Chiseled, down c. names raindrop, 784b
Chivalrous, proud and c. spirit, 99a
quixotic sense of c., 644a
Chivalry, age of c. past, 691b

Chivalry, charge with all thy c., 538a
her beauty and her c., 555b
herein c. courtesy humanity, 174b
smiled c. away, 562a
Chloe, what can C. want, 406b
Chocolate, no c. to eat, 1080a
Choice and master spirits, 255a
between quick and dead, 901a
brave man's c. is danger, 85a
careful in c. of enemies, 839a
courage of making c., 911a
difficulty in life is c., 827a
grain into this wilderness, 372b
hidden handful of inert, 696b
Hobson's c., 312b
in the worth and c., 302a
life's business c., 667b
of horse and wife, 710a
of point of view, 978a
pays money takes c., 810a
reckless c., 926b
small c. in rotten apples, 219a
word measured phrase, 512a
Choir, full-voiced c. below, 336a
invisible, 68ga
of saints, 308a
sanctuary and c., 1006b
singing in the c., 1099b
St. Stephen's c., 1075a
wailful c., 584a
Choirs, bare ruined c., 292b
Choix, le c. fait les amis, 468a
Choke fountain of industry, 548a
heart c. from pleasure, 1043a
them amid flowers, 114a
Choked with ambition of meaner sort, 214a
Chokes, error c. windows of mind, 301a
Choking to death with cream, 691a
Choler, consume own c., 576b
Choleric, captain's c. word, 271a
who subdued passion, 469b
Choose, any language you c., 767b
author as you c. friend, 374b
do not c. to run, 911b
don't c. to run, 954a
equality, 716a
firm cloud, 406b
fool multitude c. by show, 233a
free to c. government, 1025a
ground and take thy rest, 563b
if you dare, 331b
intellect forced to c., 884a
it is time to c., 956a
let's c. executors, 227b
likely man in preference to rich, 78a
multitude that c. by show, 233a
not alone proper mate, 459b
not c. not to be, 803b
on'y wut guv'ment c., 693b
path leading where I c., 701a
slavery or death, 393b
therefore c. life, 10b
thine own time, 470a
to live without friends, 98a
Venus here c. dwelling, 371a
we c. our friends, 468a
what becomes Castilian, 587a
Choosers, beggars should be no c., 184a
Chooses, consciousness c. object, 793a-b
intimacy that c. right, 882b
Choosest not better part, 866b

Cottage, hides not visage from our c., 295b
  modest looks c. adorn, 450b
  of gentility, 533a
  poor man in mean c., 38b
  poorest man in his c., 426b
  soul's dark c., 333a
Cottages, poor men's c. palaces, 231b
Cotton, corn and c. and cockleburs, 830b
  is king, 598b
  land of c., 678a
  spinning noble, 577b
  where c. and taters grow, 828b
Cottons mather, 1040b
Cottontail and Peter, 887b
Couch, frowsy c. in sorrow steep, 496b
  when owls do cry, 297b
  wraps drapery of c., 574b
Cough, love and a c., 324a
Coughed and called it fate, 899b
Coughing drowns parson's saw, 223a
Could, if youth but knew and old age c., 188b
  nor even thing I c. be, 496b
Council, outcome of words is in the c., 64a
  unapproachable in C. of Ten, 976b
  Zeus god of c., 62b
Councilor ought not to sleep, 62b
Councils, takes wisdom from c., 453b
Counsel, fitter for execution than c., 209a
  good c. cheap, 311b
  how hard for women to keep c., 254b
  if this c. be of men, 49b
  love overwhelms wise c., 67b
  man who c. can bestow, 404a
  of thine own heart, 38b
  princely c. in his face, 343b
  sometimes c. take, 404b
  spirit of c. and might, 31a
  three keep c. if two away, 185a
  took sweet c. together, 19b
  two may keep c., 185a
  walketh not in c. of ungodly, 16b
  who darkeneth c. by words, 16a
Counseled ignoble ease, 343b
Counselor, isolation worst c., 870a
  name shall be called C., 31a
Counselors, good c. lack no clients, 270a
  kings and c. of the earth, 14b
  multitude of c., 24a
  wisest of c. Time, 80b
Counsels, close designs crooked c., 368a
  excellent things in c., 25b
  hate c. not in such quality, 233b
  how monie c. sweet, 495b
  of moderation, 911b
  principles serve as c., 911b
  sic c. ye give, 1087b
Count, as long as I c. votes, 722b
  as naught in world, 694a
  chickens before hatched, 75b
  don't c. your boobies, 1033b
  let me c. the ways, 618b
  let us c. our spoons, 430b
  milestones till haze dances, 632b
  myself in nothing else so happy, 227a

Count myself king of space, 261a
  only sunny hours, 539b
  that day lost, 1090a
  them over every one apart, 865b
  time by heartthrobs, 679a
  time to c. your crimes, 505b
  until nothing else to c., 609a
  when angry c. ten, 474a
Counted as the small dust, 32b
  them and cursed luck, 854a
  two and seventy stenches, 527b
Countenance, bright c. of truth, 339b
  cannot lie, 314b
  chide God for c., 250a
  damned disinheriting c., 481b
  did the c. divine, 490b
  heart changeth his c., 32b
  his c. like richest alchemy, 254a
  human c. composed of ten parts, 132b
  lift up his c. upon thee, 9b
  lift up the light of thy c., 17a
  like lightning, 45a
  merry heart maketh a cheerful c., 24b
  more in sorrow than anger, 258a
  of all science, 511a
  soon brightened, 516b
  tyrant's threatening c., 122a
Counter original spare strange, 803a
Counteracts Devil who is Death, 444b
Countercheck quarrelsome, 251a
Counterfeit a gloom, 335b
  jasmine impossible to c., 814b
  Jove's dread clamors c., 275a
  sleep death's c., 284a
Counterfeited, laughed with c. glee, 449b
Countermarch right about, 952a
Counterpane, land of c., 823a
Counterparts in world of fact, 705b
Counters, box of c. red-veined stone, 721b
  wise men's c., 317b
Countess, hissed the c., 887b
Countesses had no outlines, 669b
Counteth, sitteth and c. cost, 47a
Counting this row, 1082b
Countinghouse, king in c., 1094b
Countless infinitesimals of feeling, 530a
  thousands mourn, 492b
Countree, hame to my ain c., 551a
  is this mine own c., 525b
  North C. hard c., 1035a
Countries, air in new c., 940a
  churches in flat c., 516b
  give themselves to you, 985a
  our country source of other c., 455b
  outdistance advanced c., 903a-b
  peace of all c. connected, 964a
  preferreth all c. before his own, 315b
  seek no aggrandizement, 974a
  tamed and made to bear, 940a
  to distant c. roam, 491b
  wandering through many c., 115b
  wars between capitalist c., 954a
Country, abroad for good of c., 398a
  absorbs poet, 699b

Country, affluent c., 1063a
  all places all airs one c., 330a
  America my c., 933b, 989b
  American says he loves c., 1048b
  anything for good of c., 398a
  as soldier for c., 865a
  ask not what c. do for you, 1073a
  behind people your c., 717b
  belongs to people, 637a
  best c. is at home, 447b
  best service for c., 787b
  Bohemia little c., 863b
  boon southern c., 714b
  ceases to be free for irreligion, 1022a
  cherished in hearts, 655b
  construction of c., 889a
  cover c. in books, 804a
  defended by our hands, 655b
  departed into their own c., 39b
  devotion will light our c., 1073a
  die but once to serve c., 393b
  die in defense of his c., 64a
  disable benefits of your c., 250a
  disenthrall selves save c., 638b
  diversion, 392a
  dreary tract of c., 642a
  duty to c. love it, 895b
  essential service to c., 389b
  every c. but his own, 768a
  every c. hath its Machiavel, 176b
  fame noised throughout c., 11a
  fate of c. not in ballot, 682a
  father of your c., 460b
  fight for one's c., 63b
  fight to set c. free, 467a
  five and c. senses, 1070a
  Flora and c. green, 582a
  for heroes to live in, 866a
  foreign troop in my c., 426a
  fornication but in another c., 212b
  found that famous c., 1022b
  friend of every c. but own, 506b
  from yon far c. blows, 853a
  genius is of no c., 456a
  give c. to Indians, 1042a
  given heart to cause or c., 994b
  glory to free his c., 561b
  God made the c., 457b
  good news from a far c., 26a
  governed by despot, 432b
  government spirit of c., 828a
  grow up with c., 678b
  half savage c., 988a
  hame to my ain c., 551a
  his ruling passion, 821b
  history of c. begins in heart, 939b
  honorable to die for one's c., 121b
  I loathe the c., 392a
  I tremble for my c., 471a
  if my c. require my life, 463a
  in c. you praise city, 120b
  in highlands in c. places, 824b
  in town, 135b
  is this mine own c., 525b
  it's autumn in c., 933b
  king will not leave c., 1047b
  know something of own c., 438a
  leaving c. for country's sake, 398a
  let me have free c., 463a
  love c. and be poor, 413a
  love home love c., 670a
  loved c. as no other man, 718a

Curate thinks you have no soul, 953b
Curates long dust, 993b
  shower of c., 679b
  will come and go, 993b
Curative, economics c. pathology, 1034a
Curb, care's check and c., 362a
  use snaffle and c. all right, 1049b
  your magnanimity, 586a
Curd, white c. of ass's milk, 411a
Curdied by frost from snow, 290a
Curds and whey, 1096b
  quivering c., 747a
Cure, absence c. of love, 195a
  disease kill patient, 209a
  freedom c. of anarchy, 453a
  laws or kings cause or c., 428a
  no c. for birth and death, 867b
  not worth the pain, 125b
  on exercise depend, 372a
  past c. I am, 294b
  past hope past c. past help, 225b
  seem to offer c., 1020b
  tale would c. deafness, 296a
  thrust of c., 1082a
Cured I am frizzled stale, 1076a
  I treated him God c. him, 187b
  more than Galen c., 324b
  of every folly but vanity, 436a
  some hurts you c., 604b
Cures, endure neither evils nor c., 125a
  me of my pain, 1089b
  to fear worst c. worse, 268b
Curfew bell must ring tonight, 825b
  far-off c. sound, 335b
  must not ring tonight, 825a
  tolls knell, 439b
Curiosity, culture origin not in c., 716a
  damnable detestable c., 628b
  do well in closet by way of c., 415b
  intellectual c., 941b
  love c. freckles doubt, 1029a
  must be kept alive, 981b
  my c. my wonder, 869a
  natural c. of young, 802a
  newspapers excite c., 535b
  offers to our c., 1006a
  order awakened c., 605a
  permanent and certain, 427b
Curious, amazed and c., 496a
  busy c. thirsty fly, 418b
  crime, 667a
  in unnecessary matters, 37a
  incident of dog, 850a
  objects and knowledge c., 702a
  quaint and c. war is, 783b
  seen a c. child, 516b
  volume of forgotten lore, 642b
Curiouser and curiouser, 743a
Curl, had a little c., 625a
  make your hair c., 768b
  New Hampshire mountains c., 927a
  not c. less gracefully, 724b
Curled Assyrian Bull, 652a
  hair so charmingly c., 691a
  last holy drop, 953b
  rainbow c. around shoulder, 906b
  up on the floor, 770a
  wealthy c. darlings, 272b
  wonderful waters c., 719a

Curlicues of marijuana, 1076a
Curls, frocks and c., 737a
  Hyperion's c., 264a
  natural c., 134a
Curlylocks wilt be mine, 1095a
Curr, let me c. to quercine shades, 110b
Current, genial c. of soul, 440b
  icy c. compulsive course, 275a
  noiseless c. strong, 716a
  swollen c. masses of ice, 659a-b
  take c. when it serves, 256a
  time a river of strong c., 142a
Currents, fresh c. of life, 656a-b
  turn awry, 262a
Curriculum was rum, 868b
Curried, short horse soon c., 183b
Currite, lente c. noctis equi, 213b
Curs, mouths sentence as c. bone, 456a
  of low degree, 448b
Curse, began to c., 44b
  bless them that c. you, 40b
  Christianity one great c., 806a
  creations of mind blessing not c., 950a
  God and die, 14a
  has come upon me, 646a
  his better angel, 276a
  I know how to c., 296a
  O c. of marriage, 274b
  of hell frae me, 1087b
  on his virtues, 393b
  primal eldest c., 263b
  selfishness greatest c., 632a
  the darkness, 981b
  with book bell and candle, 175b
  youthful harlot's c., 489b
Cursed above all cattle, 6a
  be he that moves my bones, 299b
  be man trusteth in man, 34a
  be my tribe, 232a
  be the verse, 411a
  Beauty in lap and c. her, 830a
  Boston c. with cranks, 831a
  bread, 900a
  by man c. alway, 619b
  counted and c. luck, 854a
  Fate has c. you, 84a
  floundered enjoyed, 800a
  hard reading, 482a
  me with his eye, 525a
  name to all ages c., 368a
  O c. spite, 260a
  past, 1010a
  plagues with which mankind c., 385b
  sat Beauty and I c. her, 830a
  thoughts, 283a
Curses all Eve's daughters, 267a
  deeper than strong man, 617b
  like young chickens, 532b
  not loud but deep, 286a
  of the firmament, 373a
  rigged with c. dark, 338b
Cursing, blessing and c., 10b
Cursores vitae lampada tradunt, 113b
Curtain, Anarch lets c. fall, 414a
  close his eyes and draw c., 215a
  iron c., 924b
  never c. between you and me, 928a
  never outward swings, 625a
  Priam's c., 241a
  purple c., 643a
  when she drew c. by, 1088a

Curtained, dreams abuse c. sleep, 283a
Curtain's fall, 1018a
Curtains, for whom your c. drawn, 319b
  fringed c. of thine eye, 296b
  hell take c., 979a
  let fall the c., 458a
  of Solomon, 29a
  spread canopy or c. spun, 381a
  through c. call on us, 305a
Curtius Rufus seems descended from himself, 96a
Curtsied when you have, 296a
Curtsy, customs c. to great kings, 245b
  leaves c. and quadrille, 1078b
  while you're thinking, 745a
Cushion, sit on a c., 1095b
Cussedness, trust in his c., 778b
Custodians, new c. have fervor, 861b
Custom, age cannot wither nor c. stale, 287b
  almost second nature, 221a
  conform to tyrant c., 193b
  follow c. of church where you are, 144b
  Fortune more kind than her c., 234b
  gods' c. to bring low greatness, 87a
  guide of human life, 434b
  in all line of order, 267b
  lord of mankind, 593b
  made property of easiness, 265b
  make it their perch, 270b
  maturity of c., 901a
  more honored in breach, 259a
  nature her c. holds, 265b
  of Branksome Hall, 518a
  old c. made life sweet, 247b
  one good c. corrupt, 654a
  public use and c., 188b
  reconciles to everything, 452a
  sitting at receipt of c., 41b
  stern c. spreads afar, 497a
  to whom c. due, 51b
  when c. presses, 947b
Customary fate of new truths, 725b
  suits of solemn black, 257b
Customer, tough c., 670a
Customers, empire for raising c., 445a
  sign brings c., 359b
Customs curtsy to great kings, 245b
  evil c. in China, 357a
  language manners laws c., 511a
  politics and tongue, 721b
Cut, all one c. away in reader's consciousness, 940a
  and come again, 483a
  anyone introduced to, 746b
  diamond c. diamond, 317b
  features of clerical c., 1004a
  hawsers haul out, 702b
  him out in little stars, 225a
  if thy hand offend thee c. it off, 40a
  in the evening it is c. down, 20a
  is branch that might have grown, 213b
  it is soon c. off and we fly away, 20b
  it without any knife, 1094a
  kite c. from string, 985b
  knives that serve or c., 694b

Cut, laurels all c., 719a
  like a flower and is c. down,
    15a
  moment I c. his throat, 1081a
  my coat after my cloth, 183a
  no more grass to c. away, 989b
  off in blosoms of sin, 259b
  off tails, 1092b
  short c. to everything, 429a
  stems struggling, 1064b
  stripes away, 873a
  unkindest c. of all, 255b
  ways of men c. off, 344b
  where were the righteous c. off,
    14b
  with beard of formal c., 249a
Cuts off what we possessed, 367b
  psychology c. both ways, 708b
Cutthroat dog, 232a
Cutting all pictures out, 901b
  bread and butter, 66ob
  corner of nonsense, 530a
  each other's hair, 1025b
  through the forest, 953b
Cutty sark o' Paisley harn, 496a
  weel done C. Sark, 496a
Cybele, sea C. fresh from ocean,
    557a
Cybernetics from Greek steersman, 1033b
Cycle of Cathay, 647b
  of the ages renewed, 116b
Cycles of heaven, 1004b
Cygnet to this pale swan, 237a
Cylinder, nature in terms of c.,
    780a
Cymbal, tinkling c., 52b
Cymbals, played before the Lord
  on c., 121b
Cynara, faithful to thee C., 890a
  falls thy shadow C., 890a
  fell thy shadow C., 889b
Cynic bark, 602b
  from study of mankind, 791b
  knows price of everything, 839b
  sees things as they are, 791b
Cynicism deadly sin, 893b
  intellectual dandyism, 730b
Cynic's, hurl c. ban, 846a
Cynosure of neighboring eyes,
    335a
Cynthia of this minute, 406b
  regent of night, 464a
Cypress, alley of c., 643b
  and myrtle, 558a
  correct in c. wood, 1029a
  in palace walk, 649a
  sad c., 252a
  shady c. tree, 739b
Cyprian, forsake her C. groves,
    371a
Cyrus, Palace of C., 1102b
Czar, I am a c. a slave, 470a
  last Russian C., 1076a
  long live c., 593b
  troops led by the C., 1100b
Czechs Greeks or Norwegians,
    1015b

D

D, never use big big D, 766a
Da da da iti, 62a
  mi basia mille, 114b
Dab at an index, 447a
  at electricity and crime, 919a
Dad, called brother's father d.,
    236a

Daddy, are you lost d., 985b
Daddy's gone a-hunting, 1094b
Daemon, when your d. in charge,
    877b
Daffodil doth of the dew, 736b
  sky, 652b
  surfeit when d., 736b
Daffodils, fair d. we weep to see,
    320b
  host of golden d., 514b
  raining d., 869a
  that come before swallow, 295b
Dagger, air-drawn d., 285a
  into back of neighbor, 972b
  is this a d. which I see, 283a
  of the mind, 283a
  wear not my d. in my mouth,
    291a
Daggers, daily d. of steel, 942b
  give me the d., 283b
  speak d. to her, 263b
Dago, made by a D., 864a
Daily beauty in his life, 276a
  before us lies in d. life, 347a
  bread, 945a
  die d., 330a
  duly and d. serving him, 444b
  give me thus my d. bread, 945b
  give us our d. bread, 40b
  revolutionized d. life, 995b
  wealth small aid for d. glad-
    ness, 85a
  with souls that cringe, 692a
Dainties bred of a book, 221b
  such d. to them, 451a
Daintiest last to make end sweet,
    226a
Dainty dish, 1094b
Dairymaid, queen asked d., 969b
Daisies and clover, 704a
  lie upon the d., 766b
  meadows trim with d. pied,
    334b
  pied and violets blue, 222b
  she can hear d. grow, 838b
  such as men callen d., 165b
Daisy, blessings-of-civilization trust
  a d., 763b
  by shadow it casts, 517b
  every d. in dell, 832a
  give me answer do, 885b
  there's a d., 265a
Dakotas under her hull, 1022b
Dale, haunted spring and d., 334a
  hawthorn in the d., 334b
  over hill over d., 229a, 952a
Dalliance, not give d. rein, 297a
  primrose path of d., 258b
  silken d., 243b
Dallies with innocence of love,
    252a
Dam, all my chickens and their
  d., 285b
Damaged, archangel a little d.,
    534b
Damask, feed on her d. cheek,
    252b
  springtime d. grace, 1086b
Dam'd by earthquake, 760a
Dame, dance in old d. yet, 946a
  has lost shoe, 1092a
  la belle d. sans merci, 581a
  life in old d. yet, 946a
  one for my d., 1093a
  our sulky sullen d., 495b
  smiled at the d., 488a
Dames, ah gentle d., 495b
  struts his d. before, 334b
  that squire of d., 200a

Damn authors they never read,
    456a
  cost, 1057b
  devil d. thee black, 286a
  doesn't give a d., 1109b
  don't care twopenny d., 506a
  don't give a d., 772b
  for land of freedom not give
    a d., 772b
  no general proposition worth
    d., 788b
  such, 469b
  torpedoes, 597b
  with faint praise, 411a
Damnable deceitful woman, 383b
  detestable curiosity, 628b
  iteration, 238a
Damnably, marriage d. serious
  business, 1027a
Damnation, deal d. round land,
    412b
  deep d. of his taking off, 282b
  distilled d., 501a
  marriage bed to this d., 308b
  two fingers' breadth of d., 69a
Damned, another d. thick book,
    470a
  at certain revolutions all the d.,
    344a
  be d. dear boys, 874a
  be him that first cries Hold,
    287a
  better d. than not mentioned,
    468b
  born by dying and being d.,
    180a
  cohort of the d., 873b
  conjecturally d., 783a
  could have had d. good time,
    1044a
  darkness of d., 635b
  dear d. distracting town, 405b
  devilish and d. tobacco, 311b
  disinheriting countenance, 481b
  dissolute d. despairful, 932b
  drama whether d. or not, 481a
  every man to be slave, 901a
  Faustus must be d., 213b
  forever d. with Lucifer, 213a
  from here to eternity, 873b
  his fellows for his own un-
    worth, 791b
  I will see thee d. first, 506b
  if goats cannot be d., 308a
  if I see how helican, 953b
  if you do or don't, 539a
  in fair wife, 272a
  lie dead and d., 662a
  many an old host d., 239b
  of body and soul, 872b
  one d. thing after another, 938a
  one hour then d. perpetually,
    213b
  out d. spot, 286a
  perpetually, 213b
  public be d., 710a
  publish and be d., 506a
  salute eloquence, 1042a
  smiling d. villain, 26oa
  those who dare resist, 1090b
  to everlasting fame, 410a
  to fame, 419a
  universal cock, 955b
  what d. minutes tells he, 274a
Damning those they have no
  mind to, 352a
Damozel, blessed d., 731a
Damp, demd d. moist unpleasant
  body, 669b

Damp, lived in cellar d., 694a
  nights are very d., 747a
  souls of housemaids, 1001b
  tonnage, 1043b
  years d. my intended wing,
    347b
Damsel lay deploring, 401a
  to every man a d. or two, 11a
  with dulcimer, 524a
Damyata datta dayadhvamiti, 62a
Dan, Dangerous D. McGrew, 933a
  from D. to Beersheba, 116, 438b
  senior-junior D. Cupid, 221b
Danaë to the stars, 649a
Danaos, timeo D. et dona ferentis,
    118a
Dance, a god has given the d.,
    63b
  and drink and sing, 489a
  and Provençal song, 582a
  antic hay, 212b
  as often as d. it can, 524a
  attendance, 299b
  attention on old age, 885a
  barefoot on wedding day, 219a
  dancer from d., 883b
  in old dame yet, 946a
  join the d., 744b
  like wave of sea, 880b
  little lady, 1043a
  maids d. in a ring, 300b
  make hills and forest d., 505a
  mehitabel dance, 946a
  move easiest who learned to d.,
    403b
  on this ball-floor, 1036a
  on with the d., 556a
  Pyrrhic d. as yet, 561a
  rhythms for rain, 1077b
  round in ring and suppose, 929a
  rouses him up to d., 66b
  sweet to d. to violins, 184a
  the antic hay, 212b
  there is only the d., 1005a
  time to d., 27b
  tipsy d. and jollity, 336b
  to flutes dance to lutes, 841a
  tossing heads in sprightly d.,
    514b
  upon the air, 841a
  walk before they d., 412a
  when you do d., 295b
  while you can, 1059b
  with rapture that we alive,
    986a-b
  with William Blake, 1066b
  wyth me in Irlonde, 1083b
Danced along dingy days, 738b
  by light of moon, 673a
  daughter of Herodias d., 42b
  David d. before the Lord, 12b
  death-fires d., 525a
  his did, 1031b
  lighter than cork, 829b
  like dinglebodies, 1080b
  moon on Monan's rill, 520a
  star d., 246a
  till doomsday, 391b
  to see that banner, 633a
Dancer from the dance, 883b
  stealthy d. comes, 878b
Dancers all gone under hill, 1005b
  dancing in tune, 652b
Dances as often as dance it can,
    524a
  he capers he d., 267a
  in golden escape, 1050a
  in hamlets d. on green, 518b
  in sight of heaven, 1079a

Dances, in what ethereal d., 642a
  lulled with d. and delight, 229b
  oh she d. such a way, 350b
  when she d. in the wind, 369b
Dancing and architecture, 851a
  dancers d. in tune, 652b
  days are done, 223a, 1099b
  dining and d. begin, 1052a
  dogs and bears, 906a
  emptier ever d. in air, 228a
  in the checkered shade, 335a
  is life itself, 851a
  keeping rhythm in d., 1005a
  loftiest of arts, 851a
  music of d. waves, 998a
  on volcano, 575a
  past our d. days, 223a
  source of arts, 851a
  to frenzied drum, 882a
  very merry d. drinking, 372a
  wonderful training, 1017b
Dandin, asked for it Georges D.,
    361b
Dandruff, toothpaste and d. ads,
    1043b
Dandy, candy is d., 1051b
  Yankee Doodle D., 1090a
Dandyism, intellectual d., 730b
Dane, more antique Roman than
    D., 266b
  never rid of D., 876b
Danegeld, once paid him D., 876b
Danger, above noise and d., 363a
  and tempest of war, 661a
  brave man's choice is d., 85a
  bright eyes of d., 824a
  clear and present d., 788a-b
  days of d., 520a
  difficulty and d., 1091b
  familiarity with d., 695b
  feared no d. knew no sin, 370a
  foretold that d. lurks within,
    216a
  glory and d. alike, 89b
  graceful the small before d.,
    1065b
  hackneyed phrases d. signals,
    851a
  in view of d. give up life, 72a
  is in discord, 623a
  less d. from stranger, 1051b
  morale not destroyed by d., 959a
  neither shape of d. dismay, 515a
  nettle d., 239a
  of faction, 480a-b
  of violent death, 318a
  on the deep, 588a
  or treasure, 1078a
  pleased with d., 368a
  when fatherland in d., 496b
  where is man out of d., 725a
Dangerous brow by night, 524
  Dan McGrew, 933a
  delays d. in war, 202b, 214a
  delays have d. ends, 214a
  demur you're d., 735b
  edge of things, 665a
  forties the d. ages, 1022a
  guiled shore to d. sea, 233b
  have in me something d., 266a
  idea d. when only one, 893b
  ideas d. for good or evil, 977a
  if a little knowledge d., 725a
  into d. world I leaped, 489b
  little learning d., 402b
  mad bad d. to know, 552b
  most d. situation humanity has
    faced, 1029b
  politics as d. as war, 919b

Dangerous, realities less d.
    than fancies, 913b
  say nothing in d. times, 317b
  such men are d., 253b
  temptation in gay colors, 299b
  thirst d. thing, 855a
  to be of no church d., 428b
  to meet culture alone, 865b
  to our peace and safety, 492a
  when appear to retreat, 946b
  who make no noise are d., 359b
Danger's troubled night, 537b
Dangers, defend us from d. of
    night, 60b
  delays breed d., 202b
  greatest d. to liberty, 833a
  in what great d. ye spend little
    span, 113b
  no d. fright him, 427a
  of the seas, 328b
  she loved me for the d., 273a
  thorns and d. of world, 237a
  what d. thou make us scorn,
    495b
  with d. compassed round, 346b
Daniel, cast D. into the den of
    lions, 35a
  come to judgment, 234b
  had convicted them, 39a
  second D., 235a
Dank, addled mosses d., 989a
  tarn of Auber, 643b
Danny, hangin' D. Deever, 873a
Dans, no time for fancy d., 1025b
Dante greatest depth of passion,
    1008a
  language of D. common lan-
    guage, 1008a
  more learned from D., 1008a
  of dread Inferno, 665b
  saner attitude towards life,
    1008a
Daphnis, my songs draw D. home,
    116b
Dapple, name was D. Gray, 1097b
Dappled things, 803a
  turf at ease, 512b
Dapple-dawn-drawn Falcon, 803a
Darbies, ease d. at wrist, 698a
Darby, always same D. my own,
    815a
Dare and dare again, 496b
  ask just God's assistance, 640b
  bear to live or d. to die, 409b
  call soul my own, 618b
  choose if you d., 331b
  deadly terrors clasp, 489a
  do duty as understand it, 636b
  endure greater than d., 661a
  enter you who d., 730b
  first ponder then d., 597a
  heart would deny and d. not,
    286a
  I d. do all, 282b
  I d. yet may not, 192b
  if they d. not forgive, 708a
  imitate him if you d., 884a
  is highest wisdom, 544a
  letting I d. not, 282b
  love that and say so too, 305a
  mighty things, 847a
  more as I grow older, 190b
  never d. utter untruth, 110b
  never grudge throe, 666a
  no no no I d. not, 1084b
  none d. call it treason, 210a
  O what men d. do, 246b
  on what wings d. he aspire,
    489a

Dissolve, all which it inherit d., 297b
and quite forget, 582b
me into ecstasies, 336a
political bands, 470b
wish to d. Union, 472a
Dissolved in a moment, 994b
into something great, 939b
mingle with d. limb, 899a
ought to be totally d., 460b
Union not to be d., 635b
Union virtually d., 530a
Dissolves diffuses dissipates, 528b
when all the world d., 213a
Dissonance, barbarous d., 337a
Dissonant, no sound d., 534a
Distance, airy d., 557a
augur misgovernment at d., 453a
endears friendship, 588a
just that d. from death, 69a
lends enchantment, 537a
Distances, infinite d. between humans, 938a
Distant deeps or skies, 489a
dull prospect of d. good, 370b
from heaven alike, 311b
in what d. deeps, 489a
misery, 466a
Ophir, 947a
religion of which rewards d., 428b
speaking of voices, 1070b
to d. countries roam, 491b
ye d. spires, 439a
Distasteful, found life d., 667b
nothing more d. than complacency, 535a
Distastes, prosperity not without d., 208a
Distemper, of no d. died, 367b
Distill, would men d. goodness out, 244b
Distilled almost to jelly, 258a
damnation, 501a
earthlier happy is rose d., 228b
from limbecks foul, 294a
Distills, love d. desire, 84b
Distinction between virtue and vice, 430b
make no d. between Trojan and Tyrian, 118a
safe for personal d., 1074b
without difference, 424b
Distinctions between gentlemen and common people, 101a
by means of ceremony, 101a
of race, 705b
Distinctive, man's d. mark, 666a
Distinctiveness, vice of d. to become queer, 804a
Distinctly I remember, 642b
Distinguish, he could d. and divide, 352a
read but not d. what worth it, 941b
true from false, 373a
wisdom to d., 1024a
Distinguished for ignorance, 612a
no two men who cannot be d., 132b
Distorted incomplete data, 1020a
Distorting my gesture, 1069a
Distorts the heavens, 491a
Distract attention from issues, 866a
Distracted, seat in this d. globe, 260a

Distracting, dear damned d. town, 405b
my d. grief, 445a
Distraction music of flute, 1003b
to mankind, 313a
uglification, 744b
Distraught, all men born d., 1080a
with dreams visions, 624b
Distress, all pray in their d., 487a
economic d. will teach, 913b
exposed to suffering and d., 515a
greatest d. is poverty, 379a
mean man always full of d., 71b
needy in d., 31b
of boyhood into man, 883b
pray in your d. and need, 976a
reality of d., 467b
time removes d., 108b
Distressed by his want of ability, 72b
town like place d., 375b
vacant mind d., 457a
we commend those who are d., 60a
Distresses of our friends, 356b
Distressful bread, 244b
Distributed, good sense equally d., 327a
Distribution according to need, 687b
laws of d., 757b
unequal d. of property, 480a
Distributive, economy d. virtue, 455a
Distributively, pluralism lets exist d., 795a
Distrust all in whom impulse to punish, 805a
doctrine that age brings wisdom, 960b
fear and d. the people, 473b
here all d. left behind, 159b
is safeguard, 479b
spirit of suspicion and d., 912a
to make man untrustworthy d. him, 893b
Distrusting, heart d. asks, 450a
Distrusts, him who d. self, 355a
Disturb not her dream, 495a
Disturbance of the spring, 1005a
Disturbed by planetary war, 990b
Disturbing delicate balance, 1067a
Disturbs, presence that d. me, 509b
Disuse, iron rusts from d., 174a
of any organ, 475a
Ditch, blind man's d., 884a
both fall into d., 43a
die in the last d., 383a
Ditch-delivered by a drab, 285a
Ditchers, gardeners d. and gravemakers, 265b
Ditches impure, 883b
other men's d., 1097b
Diurnal, earth's d. course, 511a
Dive, heaven's great lamps d., 300a
into bottom of deep, 238b
Dive-bomber's screaming orgasm, 995a
Diver in deep seas, 781a
Omar plucked them, 694b
Diverb, as the d. goes, 312a
Diverged, two roads d., 926b
Divers, state of man in d. functions, 243a
why d. send out oil, 132a

Diverse, strong and d. heart, 1041b
Diversion or improvement of country, 394a
walking 'tis a country d., 392a
Diversity, universal quality is d., 190b
world safe for d., 1074a
Diverter of sadness, 326a
Divest, deprive or d. posterity, 446a
Divide and rule, 150b
biped class, 96b
distinguish and d., 352a
et impera, 150b
great scramble and big d., 785a
life from death, 642b
mountains d. us, 590a
never d. upon opinion, 329b
not d. Sunday from week, 256b
sense from thought d., 368a
therefore doth heaven d., 243a
thin partitions their bounds d., 368a
two almost d. the kind, 406b
two loving hearts d., 806b
words d. and rend, 773a
Divided an inheritance with him, 469b
duty, 273a
fair d. excellence, 236a
Gaul d. into three parts, 112a
have they not d. the prey, 11a
house d. against itself, 45a, 635b
in death they were not d., 12b
mankind into parties, 480a
thy kingdom is d., 35a
we fall, 600a
with but half a heart, 321b
Dividends, literature pays d., 770b
Dividing asunder of soul and spirit, 55b
by d. we fall, 460b
lover and lover, 773a
your sweet d. throat, 327a
Divina natura dedit agros, 209b
Divination, criticism rod of d., 879a
Divine, against thy D. Majesty, 61a
all save man d., 558a
all things by law d., 570a
and terrible radiance, 599a
ardor d., 715b
ask a drink d., 303a
Athens d. city, 79b
bird of Zeus, 79a
comfortable words, 653a
countenance d. shine forth, 490b
despair, 648b
discontent, 691b
discovery of d. truths, 397b
drink d., 303a
event, 651a
fear of some d. powers, 312a
fellowship d., 580b
God the Father a school d., 412a
good amiable or sweet, 348a
Hand that made us is d., 393a
heavy but no less d., 561a
how d. a thing woman, 514b
human face d., 344b
human form d., 487a, 489b
I myself more d., 656a
idea which each represents, 606a
ideas below, 602b
illusion, 716b

Divine Inert, 696b
  Love the human form d., 487a
  love which graybeards call d., 216b
  lyre so long d., 560b
  made brutes men men d., 721b
  majority, 735a
  makes drudgery d., 324a
  man d. as myself dead, 702a
  marks of a d. origin, 544a
  men whom men pronounce d., 789b
  Milton's no less d., 561a
  moonlight is d., 1069a
  no government by d. right, 531a
  nor glimpse d., 414a
  philosophy, 337a, 650b
  plain face, 534b
  principle and rule of harmony, 709a
  profane no d. ordinances, 450a
  profusion, 748b
  relations with good joke, 918b
  reliance on d. providence, 471a
  right d. of kings, 413b
  right of kings, 636a
  sign indicates future, 87b
  superhuman spiritual and d., 936a
  tale of Troy d., 336a
  terror human form d., 489b
  thought thinks of itself, 97b
  to forgive d., 403b
  tobacco d. nothing equal, 563a
  tobacco d. rare, 311b
  train d., 714b
  truth is precious and d., 353a
  what the form d., 536a
  whatever poet writes with d. inspiration, 88a
Divinely, childish but d. beautiful, 497b
  in the wrong, 398b
  subsidized, 1061b
  tall, 645b
Divineness, in poesy participation of d., 206b-207a
Diviner air, 516b
  barmaids d. than mermaids, 1051b
Diviner's, glad d. theme, 368b
Divinest anguish, 685b
  madness d. sense, 735b
  Melancholy, 335b
Divining, takes d. rod to find, 833a
Divinities, new d. of his own, 93a
Divinity, all the d. I understand, 196b
  doth hedge a king, 265a
  dry volumes of d., 470b
  gives wealth even to wicked man, 77a
  gossip a kind of d., 68a
  in odd numbers, 267b
  lectures of ethics or d., 383a
  man own doctor of d., 822a
  piece of d. in us, 330b
  stirs within us, 393b
  that shapes our ends, 266a
  wingy mysteries in d., 329b
Divisa, Gallia est omnis d. in partes tres, 112a
Division, equal d. of unequal earnings, 545a
  is as bad, 1084b
  marriage death and d., 773b
  mirth the music of d., 199b

Division, salvation not in d., 903a
  same as creation, 101a
  saw d. grow together, 267b
Divorce, absurd essentially a d., 1068b
  long d. of steel, 298a
Divorced divorced, 1075b
  from eye and bone, 1038a
  from whale-fat, 1075b
  sorrow from which not d., 550a
  war not d. from politics, 1027b
Divulge, I will never d. such things, 88a-b
Dixie Land, 678a
  live and die in D., 678b
Dixit, ipse d., 151a
Dizziness from success, 954b
  love like a d., 508a
Dizzy, across that d. way, 944a
  how fearful and d., 279a
Do, a' is done that men can d., 494a
  all the good you can, 421a
  as chapmen do, 269a
  as I say not as I do, 317b
  as you would be done by, 415a
  boys do, 814a
  damned if you d., 539a
  decided on what they will not d., 100a
  each day two things disliked, 92a
  enough work to d., 877a
  go and d. likewise, 46b
  great right little wrong, 234b
  his arms might d. what this has done, 332b
  how not to d. it, 672a
  I d. it more natural, 251b
  I dare d. all, 282b
  if to d. as easy as to know, 231b
  it after high Roman fashion, 288b
  it as for thee, 324a
  it with thy might, 28b
  just as one pleases, 539b
  justly and love mercy, 35b
  know not what they d., 47b
  know what he ought to d., 158b
  let us d. or die, 496a
  make it d. or d. without, 1102b
  nastiest thing in nicest way, 994a
  never d. today what can put off, 719a
  never tell how to d. things, 987b
  no one knows what he can d., 127a
  noble things not dream, 691a
  not as some pastors, 258b
  not do what we want, 1058b
  not choose to run, 911b
  not d. what another d. as well, 897b
  not do thing they most do show, 293a
  not do to others, 72b
  not go gentle, 1070b
  not we wanderer await, 712a
  not what we ought, 711b
  nothing we d. wiped out, 793a
  now I'll d. it, 263b
  O what men dare d., 246b
  or die, 313b, 496a
  other men for they d. you, 670a
  reckless what I d., 284b
  seeks little thing to d., 664a
  she can d. no other, 842a

Do, so much to d., 650b, 828b
  that thou doest d. quickly, 49a
  the evil I d., 51a
  the very best I can, 641a
  theirs but to d. and die, 652a
  they d. things we can't, 1067a
  they know not what they d., 47b
  thing I was born to d., 211a
  thing that ends other deeds, 288b
  thing think you cannot, 981b
  thing you have to, 725a
  things worth writing, 421b
  this in remembrance, 47b
  this one thing I d., 54a
  this will never d., 516a
  thou but thine, 347a
  to be to d. to d. without, 779b
  to will and to d. his pleasure, 54a
  two things is to do neither, 125a
  unto other feller fust, 811a
  what country d. for you, 1073a
  what d. about it, 722b
  what d. when you fallen, 1078a
  what d. you mean to d., 784a
  what have you or I to d. with it, 437b
  what he may, 266a
  what I will with mine, 43b
  what man may d. to himself, 952b
  what man would d. exalts, 665b
  what manhood bids, 707b
  what then thou would'st, 349b
  what thou wilt, 181a
  what we back ourselves to d., 793b
  what you can d. for country, 1073a
  what you d. still betters what is done, 295b
  whatsoever thy hand findeth to d., 28b
  will to d., 520a
  without being commanded, 97a
  write what men d., 207a
  ye even so unto them, 41a
Doasyouwouldbedoneby, Mrs. D., 691b
Dobie, sate upon her d., 673b
Docent, decent d., 1040b
Doch-an'-dorris, wee d., 903a
Docile and omnipotent, 736a
Dockyard fellow, 749b
  mine factory d., 923b
Doctor and saint, 630a
  apple keeps d. away, 1102a
  Diet Quiet Merryman, 390b
  every man own d. of divinity, 822a
  fee d. for nauseous draught, 372a
  Foster went to Gloucester, 1097a
  kills more than general, 382a
  Livingstone I presume, 791a
  silent d. shook his head, 401a
  three faces wears d., 820a
  train anyone to be a d., 949a
  while runnin' for d., 981a
Doctor's, failing that D. thesis, 1035a
  outlived the d. pill, 401b
  peaceful mission, 820a
Doctors, best d. in the world, 390b
  is all swabs, 823a

Down

Dwelt

Dust, heap of d. alone remains, 406a
hear her and beat, 652b
hearts dry as summer d., 516a
I shall lie in the d., 64b
if as they say some d., 928a
in the d. the cool tombs, 948b
is for a time, 997a
kicks d., 682b
lay mightily in whirl of d., 64a
less than the d., 871a
lick the d., 20a
light in d. lies, 572b
limns on water writes in d., 210a
love reachest but to d., 203b
make d. of all things, 331a
make d. our paper, 227b
maniac scattering d., 650a
marry my body to that d., 321a
mouth filled with d., 308b-309a
much learned d., 458a
mysteries beyond thy d., 363a
name not perish in d., 532b
noble d. of Alexander, 266a
nor that frame was d., 738b
not without d. and heat, 340a
of creeds outworn, 568b
of snow, 927a
of systems and creeds, 644b
on marble pavement d. grows, 110a
pays us with age and d., 199b
plummets to d. of hope, 81b
pride that licks the d., 411b
proud and angry d., 853b
quaint honor turn to d., 360a
quintessence of d., 261a
rain in d. on her shoulders, 1022b
raised aloft hurled in d., 715b
return to the earth, 29a
returneth to d. again, 748b
seemed to be local d. cloud, 1069b
shake off d. of your feet, 42a
shalt thou eat, 6a
silent d., 440b
small d. of earth, 996b
small d. of the balance, 32b
so nigh grandeur to d., 603b
tear o'er English d., 596b
that is a little gilt, 269a
that is blown away, 37a
this d. once the man, 702a
this quiet d., 736b
thou art to dust returneth, 620b
thou art unto dust return, 6a
thrown in my eyes, 928a
to dust ashes to ashes, 61b
to dust pure spirit flow, 572a
toy dog covered with d., 820b
unto d. and under d., 630a
unto d. return, 6a
valiant d., 245b
valiant d. builds on d., 875b
vile d. whence he sprung, 519a
was gentlemen and ladies, 736b
we are but d. and shadow, 122b
we too into d. descend, 630a
weighed me d. by d., 739a
what a d. I raise, 576a
what is pomp but earth and d., 216b
with d. is dark and dim, 510b
write good in d., 178b
you are not worth the d., 279a
Duster, tomorrow feather d., 915a
Dusty answer, 730b

Dusty cobweb-covered maimed, 755b
eat d. bread, 1038a
grated to d. nothing, 268b
hit the d. trail, 952a
purlieus of law, 650b
road long and d. to grave, 822b
way to d. death, 286b
Dutch, beat the D., 1090b
city of New York, 864b
determine properties, 537a
fault of the D., 507a
Dutchman in Eden would plant it, 685a
see Flying D., 806b
Dutchman's, icicle on D. beard, 252b
Duties, brace ourselves to d., 921b
live without d. obscene, 610a
new occasions new d., 692a
property has d., 612a
Duty, astray from d. and interest, 461b
better one's own d., 106a
book you read from d., 430b
brave man inattentive to d., 503a
constabulary d., 766b
dare do d. as we understand it, 636b
dead then my d. ended, 803a
devoting himself to d., 363a
discussing d. to God, 700b
divided d., 273a
do d. in all things, 620a
do your d., 331b
done my d. and no more, 424a
done my d. ever, 825b
essence of judicial d., 485b
every man to do d., 492a
faithful below he did his d., 475b
gives from sense of d., 692b
gratifying d. done, 769a
knowledge of their d., 90a
laid on me a sinner, 593b
lies in what is near, 100a
limping with d., 101a
lively sense of filial d., 470a
love is then our d., 401b
my d. to obey orders, 723a
neatness a d., 421a
not law nor d. bade fight, 881b
not to be silent, 728b
of being happy, 822b
of judicial department, 485b
out of d. cheat others, 908a
path of d. way to glory, 651b
performed or d. violated, 547b
picket's off d. forever, 728a
possession implies d., 932b
public d., 717b
seen d. and done it, 1102a
seen d. dead-sure thing, 778b
sense of d. pursues us, 547b
some sense of d., 649b
subject's d. is king's, 244b
sublimest word, 620a
such d. as subject owes, 219b
thank God I have done d., 492b
to love those who wrong him, 142b
to my country to love it, 895b
transforms obedience into d., 435b
trespasses against d., 452a
voices of d. call, 796b
we all did our d., 468a
we owe Creator, 465b

Duty whispers low, 603b
whole d. of man, 29a
woke found life d., 680a
Duty's, constabulary d. to be done, 766b
faithful child, 590b
Dux femina facti, 117b
O vitae philosophia d., 111b
vitae animus est, 116a
Dwarf on shoulders of giant, 310a
sees farther than giant, 134a
Dwarfed and abased below, 826b
whole, 527a
Dwell a weeping hermit, 443a
at ease for aye d., 645a
better to d. in a corner, 25b
critic d. on excellencies, 394b
heart place devils d. in, 330a
house we d. in every day, 738b
in house of the Lord, 18a
in midst of people of unclean lips, 30b
in possibility, 736b
in the tents of wickedness, 20a
in the uttermost parts of the sea, 23a
not d. in temples, 364a
nothing ill d. in such a temple, 296b
on heights of mankind, 498b
peace and rest never d., 341b-342a
shall I like a hermit d., 199a
such as d. in tents, 6a
to perdition there to d., 341b
together in unity, 22b
twin turtledoves d., 704a
two souls d. in my breast, 478b
where Israfel, 641b
where thoughts and feelings d., 742a
who shall d. in thy holy hill, 17a
with vilest worms to d., 292b
world and they that d. therein, 18a
Dwelled, Abram d. in Canaan, 6b-7a
Lot d. in the cities, 7a
Dwellers by the sea, 829a
sur la branche, 895b
Dwelleth in the secret place, 20b
not in temples, 50a
Dwellin', fair maid d., 1088a
Dwelling, desert my d. place, 557b
in tents, 7a
much on right, 377b
of the blest, 119a
single soul d. in two bodies, 97a
so close to d. place, 926b
thou hast been our d. place, 20a
Venus here choose d., 371a
whose d. is light of suns, 509b
Dwells, in me d. no greatness, 653b
surely d. loving Father, 497a
unwitting where Master d., 947b
water d. in lowly places, 73b
wherever Roman conquers he d., 131a
with beauty, 584a
with gods above, 268b
Dwelt among untrodden ways, 510b
by the brook Cherith, 13a
child who d. upon tract, 516b

Earth, more things in heaven
   and e., 260a, 1021b
my footstool e., 408a
new heaven and new e., 58b
new heavens and a new e., 33b
niggard e., 439b
nigher heaven than now, 661b
nightly to listening e., 393a
no less kindled e., 563a
no more a mother, 132a
not gray but rosy, 668a
not sky of e., 510a
not steadfast place, 898b
nothing but hath bound in e.,
   218a
nothing on e. but laundry,
   1079a
of all languages of e., 939a
of the e. earthy, 53a
on bare e. he lies, 371b
on confines of e., 501a
on e. broken arcs, 665b
on e. no sure happiness, 200b
on e. peace and good will, 46a
on e. peace to men, 59a
one mighty blood spot, 613b
only when we are half e., 730a
or air, 257a
or ever thou hadst formed the
   e., 20a
paradise on e., 894a
peace on e. good will, 657b
peace on e. mercy mild, 425b
peopling e. waters and sky,
   377a
pleasant country's e., 227b
plowed before man, 628b
poetry of e. never dead, 579b
power passing from the e.,
   515b
proudly wears Parthenon, 602a
put on e. a little space, 486b
puts forth sweet flowers, 112b
rain was upon the e., 6b
raises man from e. to God, 178a
receive her King, 397a
render back from breast, 561a
replenish the e., 5a
rest lightly on you, 151b
reverence for e., 1077b
rich stone in bowels of e., 309b
rid e. of him in my pride, 899a
room on e. for honest men,
   467a
sad old e. borrow mirth, 826a
saddest among kings of e., 899b
salt of the e., 40a
scum of the e., 506a
sepulcher of famous men, 90a
shall be full of knowledge, 31a
shall not perish from e., 639a
since e. began to exist, 459b
sing ye heavens e. reply, 425a
sleepers in quiet e., 685b
small dust of e., 996b
small model of barren e., 227b
so much of e., 511a
solid e. actual world, 680b
speak to the e., 15a
spirit given on e., 641a
stand at Judgment Seat, 872b
stand on e. as footstool, 888b
stood hard as iron, 740a
suffered to crawl upon e., 389b
sufficient, 701a
summer clothe general e., 526a
sun is lost and the e., 307b
sure and firm-set e., 283a
swear not by heaven nor e., 40b

Earth, table e. dice human bones,
   563a
take him e., 765a
that bears thee dead, 241a
the e. that is sufficient, 701a
their proper element, 319a
they shall inherit the e., 40a
thirsty e. soaks up rain, 357b
this blessed plot this e., 226b
this e. of majesty, 226b
this goodly frame the e., 261a
this is the last of e., 503a
those who labor in e., 471a
though the e. be removed, 19a
thy will be done in e., 40b
tideless and inert, 813a
till heaven and e. pass, 40a
to e. and thee restore, 854b
to earth, 61b
touch of e., 653b
tries e. if it in tune, 692b
truth crushed to e., 574b
two kinds of people on e., 825b
unfolds both heaven and e.,
   228b
upon e. not his like, 16b
walk the earth unseen, 345b
was without form, 5a
weaned away from e., 1041a
what e. and its interests, 681b
what is pomp but e. and dust,
   216b
when I am laid in e., 383b
when I laid the foundations of
   the e., 16a
when religion makes e. uncomfortable, 696a
whether in e. or air, 257a
which made heaven and e., 22a
while the e. remaineth, 6b
whole e. and all time, 511a
whole e. for religion's sake,
   699b
whole e. grows rich, 378b
whole e. our hospital, 1005b
with her thousand voices, 526b
wonder of e. and life, 1021a
word of e. in ears of world,
   775b
words are daughters of e., 427b
would know no adventurer,
   843a
wretched of e., 680a
write sorrow on bosom of the
   e., 227b
yours and fullness thereof, 920a
yours is the e., 877a
Earthborn joy renew, 801a
Earthen, kettle and e. pot, 38a
Earthlier happy is rose distilled,
   228b
Earthly ball a peopled garden,
   477b
dignities, 298b
fancies, 651b
godfathers of heaven's lights,
   221a
mighty e. marchings, 696b
nothing e. surpass her, 560a
paragon, 291a
power then likest God's, 234b
roses into e. life, 497b
sum of e. bliss, 347a
sweet fruition of e. crown, 212a
things heavenly or things e.,
   365b
this wisdom is e., 56b
thoughts of e. men, 67a
touch of e. years, 511a

Earthly, very honey of all e. joy,
   357b
who mind e. things, 54b
Earthquake, dam'd by e., 760a
gloom of e. and eclipse, 568b
Lord was not in the e., 13b
when not smiling back, 1071b
Earthquakes with thunder lightning, 760a
Earth's, ablution round e. shores,
   581a
as e. close down, 1072a
break e. sleep, 1028b
crammed with heaven, 619a
diurnal course, 511a
foundations fled, 854a
foundations stand, 855a
green fields, 676b
heedless sons, 1036a
human shores, 581a
last picture painted, 872b
lid, 988b
returns, 663b
right place for love, 926b
round e. imagined corners, 307b
round e. shore, 714b
shadows fly, 572a
smoothness rough, 666a
sweet flowing breast, 992a
wide regions round, 554a
Earthworm, feeble e., 364b
Earthworms, earth plowed by e.,
   628b
Earthy and cold hand of death,
   241a
earth in e. bed, 652b
of the earth e., 53a
Ease after war, 200a
an age of e., 449a
and speed not give work beauty, 168b
at e. for aye dwell, 645a
at e. in nature, 699b
at e. in own generation, 786a
but for another gives e., 489a
careless e., 398a
dappled turf at e., 512b
darbies at wrist, 698a
death or dreamful e., 645b
done with so much e., 368a
equal e. unto my pain, 327a
for e. from heaven, 490b
full-throated e., 582a
gives happiness or leaves e.,
   412b
good pleasure e. content, 409b
greater e. than hogs eat, 352a
heart like satin gown, 1029a
ignoble e., 847a
ignoble e. and peaceful sloth,
   343b
joys in another's loss of e., 489a
life of e. not for man, 577b
live at home at e., 328b
live with e., 410b
Meadows of E., 909a
Nature bent to e. us, 356b
never desire worldly e., 420b
no healthful e., 592a
one life the aching, 737a
poet's dignity and e., 411a
prodigal of e., 368a
rots in e. on Lethe wharf, 259b
slothful e., 847b
some come to take their e.,
   299b
somebody's right and e., 799b
take mine e. in mine inn, 183a
take thine e., 46b

Education makes people easy to lead, 540b
  most valuable result of e., 725a
  not only common but compulsory, 695a
  novel is instrument of e., 855b
  of a liberal e., 194b
  of imaginative life, 800b
  of itself to look upon, 564b
  only ignorant despise e., 126b
  our e. inadequate, 1013b
  produced population able to read, 941b
  respect poets by e., 609a
  root of honesty in good e., 137a
  science e. for citizenship, 845a
  scientific e., 1019b
  seek e. in paths of duty, 777b
  soap and e. deadly, 759a
  soul takes nothing but e. and culture, 93b
  supervise national e., 549a
  to love her is liberal e., 395b
  travel part of e., 208b
  treatise of natural e., 436a
  what left over, 1104b
Educational relations strongest tie, 828b
  separate e. facilities, 1021a
Educator wielder of power, 1068a
Edward Edward, 1087b
  sons of E. sleep, 217b
Edward's, proud E. power, 496a
  winding-sheet of E. race, 441b
Eel, in mud e. is, 1097a
Eels boiled in broo', 1089a
Eerie faint carouse, 1022a
Effaced, forget when image e., 95b
Effect, cause and e. from economy, 1062b
  cause has more than one e., 706a
  cause of this e., 260b
  defective comes by cause, 260b
  ek gret e. write in place lite, 165a
  little e. much labor, 534a
  man e. of work, 909b
  nature but name for e., 459a
  nothing exists without e., 373a
  peace between e. and it, 282a
  what in e. already in cause, 849b
Effective, governed make views e., 1013a
  life a very e. therapist, 985a
  poetry most wisely e. mode, 713b
  reciprocal safeguards, 982b
  simplicity makes uneducated e., 98b
Effects, baneful e. of party, 461b
  dire e. from civil discord, 394a
  no e., 576b
Effectual fervent prayer, 56b
Efficiency, highest best form of e., 842b
  in struggle for bread, 844a
  southern e., 1074b
Efflorescence of civilized life, 706a
Efflux from hot venturi, 1072a
Effluxion of time, 94b
Effort, critical e., 713a
  dignity in e. of patriots, 462b
  happiness result of man's e., 958a
  keep faculty of e. alive, 793a
  nearly killed her, 902a
  of intellect to see poor, 1082a

Effort to get up, 684a
  to see and represent, 799b
Efforts, no human e. deliver them, 461a
  noble e. in last war, 426a
  of busy multitude, 720b
  redoubling e., 867a
  to create happiness, 958a
Effund your albid hausts, 110b
Effusion, foils foe by e. of ink, 444b
Effusions, liveliest e. of wit, 533b
Égalité, liberté é. fraternité, 1105b
Egdon, glory of E. waste, 783a
Egg, as one e. like another, 181b
  best way to boil e., 608b
  egg's way of making e., 755b
  from the e., 124a
  full of quarrels as e. full of meat, 224b
  good to keep nest e., 196a
  hard-boiled as picnic e., 1035b
  heaven like e. earth like yolk, 141a
  innocent as new-laid e., 765b
  of democracy, 695a
  puritanism laid e. of democracy, 695a
  serpent's e., 254a
  Wall Street lays e., 916a
  without salt, 872a
  yesterday e. tomorrow duster, 915a
  you've got a bad e., 810b
Egg's way of making egg, 755b
Eggs, all e. in one basket, 195a, 762a
  as like as e., 181b
  as the partridge sitteth on e., 34b
  as weasel sucks e., 248a
  butter e. pound of cheese, 740b
  codfish ten thousand e., 1101b
  goose with golden e., 76b
  lays e. for gentlemen, 1096b
  set house on fire to roast e., 209a
  silent when e. hatched, 333b
  walk on e., 301b
Eglantine, sweet musk roses and e., 229b
Ego non flocci pendere, 109a
  serves three masters, 834a
  soul beyond e. reach, 936b
  sum rex Romanus, 362a
  to id as rider to horse, 834a
  tooth of the e., 1068a
  where id was there e. be, 834a
Egoism, book of e., 730b
Egotism sloth idleness, 549a
  strong dose of e., 1016a
Egotists, conscience makes e., 839a
Egregiously an ass, 273b
Egypt, came out from E., 8b
  carry me out of E., 7b
  great cry in E., 8b
  Helen's beauty in brow of E., 230b
  I am dying E. dying, 288b
  I will pass through the land of E., 8b
  in E. pyramids laid, 1102b
  one more plague upon E., 8a
  out of E. called my son, 39b
  Pharos of E., 1102b
Egypt's dark sea, 543a
Eheu fugaces Postume Postume, 121b

Eigentlich, wie es e. gewesen, 586a
Eight or nine elderly men, 870b
  victories over Syracusans, 86a-b
Eighteen, from birth to age e., 984a
  from e. to thirty-five, 984a
Eighteenth Amendment, 930b
  of April, 623b
Eighth commandment not for bards, 527a
  day of week, 1056b
Eight-wheeler of mighty fame, 904b
Eildon, riding by E. Tree, 1088b
Ein' feste burg, 179b
Eisen und Blut, 677b
Elaborately constructed forms, 628a
Elaine the fair, 653a
Élan and determination, 959b
  vital, 849b
Elastic and vigorous thought, 683a
  time is e., 907a
Elate, Ruin's plowshare drives e., 493a
Elbow, soul hath e. room, 237a
  through world, 575b
Elbows, our horizon never at our e., 683a
Eld, beg alms of palsied e., 271a
  memories of e., 642a
Elder, more e. than thy looks, 234b
  sun is e. by a year, 305b
  take e. than herself, 252a
Elderly, eight or nine e. men, 870b
Elders, discourse of the e., 37b
  regarding e. as senile, 776b
  strings of white e., 955b
  when he sitteth among e., 27a
Eldest, primal e. curse, 263b
Eldorado, seek for E., 644a
Eleazer faculty, 868b
Elect, predestined e. thinned down, 759b
Elected between sundown and sunup, 954a
  if e. I will not serve, 705a
  silence sing to me, 802b
  without political understanding, 983b
Election, declined e. some years ago, 986b
  supreme court follows e., 890b
  tub told of his e., 178b
  turned into angels by e., 891b
Elections end slavery begins, 463b
  factors in winning presidential e., 983b
  succeeds in carrying e., 750a
  takes e. philosophically, 638a
Electra, mourning becomes E., 1009a
Electric chair hanging like oasis, 1076a
  lights not science, 815a
Electrical, air pump or e. machine, 462a
  display of God, 1009a
Electrically prompt, 763b
Electrician no longer there, 901b
Electricity and crime, 919a
Electrification of whole country, 903b
Elegance of female friendship, 428a

Evil, never suffer e. in future,
66b
news fly faster than good, 137a
news rides post, 350a
no e. can happen to good man,
93a
no e. deed live on, 791a
no e. for one who commits
none, 80b
no e. in atom, 1048b
not into e. wrought, 771b
notion of E. One, 1061a
obscures the show of e., 233b
of moral e. and of good, 509a
on grounds of expediency, 847b
one e. ignorance, 87b
one that eschewed e., 14a
overcome e. with good, 51b
partial e. universal good, 408b
pervading e. of democracy, 750a
plan is most harmful to planner, 67b
please his e. neighbor, 499a
possibilities for good and e.,
1033b
punish world for their e., 31a-b
rash hand in e. hour, 347b
recognition of e., 73b
recompense no e. for e., 51a
religion potent in persuading to
e., 112b
resist not e., 40b
return good for e., 388a
rewarded e. for good, 7b
rewardeth e. for good, 25a
root of all e., 55b
see e. drowned in mercy, 858b
show me a greater e., 82a
snake stood for e. in Garden,
927a
Socrates a doer of e., 93a
spinning fates good or e., 793a
stifling opinion is e., 619b
stubborn heart shall fare e., 37b
submit to present e., 129b
sufficient unto day is e., 41a
supernatural source of e., 844a
that men do lives after them,
255a
the e. I do, 51a
them that call e. good, 30b
thing of e., 643a
think not lightly of e., 80a
to depart from e. is understanding, 15b
to him who evil thinks, 163a
tongue an unruly e., 56b
tree of knowledge of good and
e., 5b
unconscious not only e. but
good, 936a
vanish like e. spirits, 473a
vice lost half its e., 454a
what e. I intend to do, 84b
whether it be good or e., 29a
wi' tippenny fear nae e., 495b
with indifference notes e., 593b
with lent money e. done, 698b
withstand in the e. day, 54a
write e. in marble, 178b
wrought by want of thought,
592a
Evildoers, seeing e. taken to execution, 186b
Evildoing, greatest penalty of e.,
96a
pleasantness waits upon e., 145a
Evil's, believe no evil till e. done,
359a

Evils, all e. equal when extreme,
331b
avoided powers exercised, 138b
cities no rest from e., 94a-b
compel philosophy to inquire
about e., 111b
Congress has right to prevent,
788b
draw men together, 98b
endure neither e. nor cures,
125a
greatest of e. is poverty, 837a
knowledgeable of e., 78a
least of the e., 97b
least of two e., 64a
most preferable of e., 64a
no necessary e. in government,
503b
one of e. and another of blessings, 65a
philosophy triumphs over past
e., 355a
present e. triumph over philosophy, 355a
suffering e. of long peace, 139b
they say e. come from us, 65a
three great e., 417a
two e. monstrous either one,
1009a
weak e. age and hunger, 248b
when e. most free, 254b
which never arrived, 604b
yield not to e., 118b
Evolution, advance of science an
e., 829b
general theory of e., 752b
not a force but a process, 779b
of thought, 712b
some call it e., 667a
Ewe, lilting at e. milking, 446b
tupping your white e., 272a
Ewes, milk my e. and weep, 295b
Ewig-Weibliche, das E. zieht uns
hinan, 478b
Ex pede Herculem, 86b
ungue leonem, 150b
Exact, devotion to e. observation,
949b
equal and e. justice, 472a
knowledge of the past, 89a
set e. wealth of states, 240a
timing is e., 88b
writing maketh an e. man, 209b
Exaction becomes extortion, 771a
Exactitude, l'e. la politesse des
rois, 485b
Exactness, facts detailed with e.,
721a
write life with e., 431a
Exaggerated, reports of death e.,
763a
stress on not changing mind,
931b
Exaggeration, chargeable with no
e., 540b
Exalt him above all, 39a
himself shall be abased, 43b
will to live, 939a
Exaltation from proximity of disaster, 919b
in chanting of Muses, 84a
Exalted, both will be e., 951b
every valley shall be e., 32b
God an e. father, 833b
no very e. opinion, 452b
Satan e. sat, 343a
them of low degree, 45b
whoso humble himself be e.,
43b

Exalteth, righteousness e. a nation, 24b
wisdom e. her children, 37b
Exalts, not what man does e.,
665b
Examination, decent and manly
e., 531a
of acts of government, 531a
Examine, I pause I e., 191b
turn inwards and e., 71b
Example, annoyance of good e.,
762b
bear patiently results of own e.,
129b
from others take e., 109b
government teaches by e., 833a
is school of mankind, 455a
lower orders set e., 840a
more efficacious than precept,
428a
profit by their e., 464b
salutary influence of e., 428b
Examples from Alexander to
Mao, 997b
no longer able to provide bad
e., 355b
Exceed, flies worms e. me still,
396b
never e. your rights, 435b
reach e. grasp, 664b
Exceedeth, thy wisdom and prosperity e. the fame, 13a
Exceeding, gave e. delight by his
verse, 90b
grind e. small, 329a
honest e. poor man, 232b
wise fair-spoken, 299b
Exceeds, far e. all earthly bliss,
192a
man's might, 268b
Excel, arts in which wise e., 382b
bees for government, 193a
discredit what they do not e.
in, 101b
not e. because they labor, 540a
teach who themselves e., 402b
thou shalt not e., 8a
useless to e., 434a
Excellence, activity in accordance
with e., 98a
bearing on e. of character, 98a
elite based on e., 1026a
fair divided e., 236a
fame of her e., 67a
imagine e., 1079b
in front of e. gods put sweat,
67b
is nobly to die, 70b
long time to bring e. to maturity, 127a
mental e. a splendid possession,
115b
not exchange e. for riches, 68b
stewards of their e., 293a
to few men comes e., 77a
Excellencies, smaller e. of conversation, 469a
true critic dwell on e., 394b
Excellent angler now with God,
326a
dumb discourse, 297a
everything that's e., 767a
fancy, 265b
first e. second good, 177b
foppery of the world, 277a
hard to be truly e., 70b
how e. is thy lovingkindness,
18b
how e. is thy name, 17a

Existence determines consciousness, 686b
  earns freedom and e., 478b
  essential relation to e., 676a
  fret of e., 1047b
  life hollow e. burden, 759a
  nature owes me another e., 478a
  of supernatural probable, 868a
  precisely an e., 739a
  saw him spurn reign, 426b
  sordid perils of actual e.,
    838b
  sorrow of human e., 455b
  struggle for e., 628a, 935a
  teach men sense of e., 805a
  truth find e., 844a
  woman's whole e., 560a
  you wanted to go back to,
    1041a
Exists, everything e. nothing has
  value, 951b
  nowhere but in yourself, 897b
Exit pursued by a bear, 295a
  wheresoever called to make e.,
    475a
Exits and their entrances, 249a
  doors for men to take their e.,
    315a
Exodus, mysterious e. of death,
  623b
Expanding conflict to all China,
  984a
Expansion, not a breach but an
  e., 306a
Expatiate free o'er scene of man,
  407a
Expect Saint Martin's summer,
  214a
  something for nothing, 828a
Expectation, better bettered e.,
  245b
  makes a blessing dear, 350b
  oft e. fails, 269b
  rise, 447a
  shields of e., 694a
  songs of e., 750b
  whirls me round, 268a
Expectations, revolution of rising
  e., 1077a
  rising e., 1077a
Expected, least e. happens, 611b
  no reasonable man e., 1017a
Expects, blessed he who e. nothing, 407b
  England e., 492a
  from you a book, 536a
Expediency, evil on grounds of e.,
  847b
Expedient, all things not e., 52a
  as lighting by gas, 631b
  free trade e., 611b
  that one die, 49a
Expedition, so ended Sicilian e.,
  90b
Expeditionary, Allied E. Force,
  1016b
Expeditions, dyspepsy ruin of e.,
  552a
Expeditious, no e. road, 856b
Expelled, Asia and Africa e. freedom, 466b
Expendable, they were e., 1049a
Expende Hannibalem, 139b
Expenditures, book of public e.,
  545b
Expense, dog item of e., 845b
  great e. may be essential, 455a
  of spirit in waste of shame,
    294a

Expenses, consider my traveling
  e., 1028a
Expensive, nothing so e. as glory,
  522b
  politics e., 954a
Experience, accumulated e., 935a
  an arch wherethrough, 646b
  arch to build upon, 776b
  arranged in order, 779a
  art pattern on e., 861b
  believe one who has e., 119b
  causes of future e., 794b
  child of thought, 611a
  cluster of gifts e., 798b
  court bows to e., 833a
  effects of past e., 794b
  encounter reality of e., 968b
  essential to great e., 726b
  get out of e. only wisdom in it,
    762b
  gladly beyond any e., 1031a
  gone to end in e., 938b
  has given no access, 806b
  home where small e. grows,
    219a
  ignorant in spite of e., 426a
  keeps dear school, 422a
  knowledge not personal e., 94a
  lamp of e., 465a
  Liberal tempered by e., 715b
  life of law, 786b
  make me sad, 250a
  mother of sciences, 194b
  name for mistakes, 839b
  no knowledge beyond e., 372b
  of this sweet life, 162a
  Old Age and E., 382b
  old e. do attain, 336a
  optimist never had much e.,
    946a
  periods when e. modified, 544a
  prophecy of wise men, 566a
  pushed beyond facts, 843b
  recognize same e., 793b
  relations between aspects of e.,
    984b
  tells in every soil, 448a
  travel part of e., 208b
  treacherous, 88b
  triumph of hope over e., 431a
  what e. and history teach, 507b
  wisdom acting upon e., 429a
  write only from e., 798b
Experienced industrious liar, 761b
  not real till e., 585b
Experiences, evidence for God in
  inner e., 795a
  flag represents e., 841b
  in solitude, 794b
  shared e., 504a
  strong man digests e., 805b
Experiencing nature, 726b
  suffering to full, 908a
Experientia docet, 671a
  does it, 671a
Experiment as all life is e., 788b
  convinced of imbecility by e.,
    428b
  entrusted to America, 461b
  every e. like weapon, 180b
  great social e., 930b
  on animals, 628b
  so great an e. as dying, 332a
  social and economic e., 930b
  stimulate and direct e., 838a
  to me every one I meet, 737b
Experimental philosophy, 379b
  thinking is e. dealing, 834a
  youth is wholly e., 825a

Experimentation active science,
  675a
  bold persistent e., 970b
Experiments, eclipses of moon
  and other e., 173b
  I love fools' e., 628b
  sure e. and demonstrated argu-
    ments, 192b
  to control ideas, 675b
Expert, believe an e., 119b
  knows more about less, 862b
Experto credite, 119b
Experts, differences among e.,
  864b
Expire, if I e. today, 738b
  lamps e., 890a
Expires in arms of apothecary,
  522a
  last armed foe e., 565b
  unawares Morality e., 414a
  wretched child e., 902a
Expiring frog, 669a
Explain, can't e. myself said
  Alice, 743b
  his explanation, 559b
  spoil it by trying to e., 481a
  till all men doubt, 413b
  time will e. all, 85b
  you e. nothing O poet, 894a
Explained, shut up he e., 985b
Explaining, go on e. cease to understand, 976a
  surrender e. not acting, 916a
Explanation, explain his e., 559b
  inaccuracy saves e., 904b
  unintelligible, 942b
Expletives their feeble aid do
  join, 403a
Explicable, thanks to poet things
  e., 894a
Explicitness not necessary virtue,
  879a
Explode huge laugh at feet, 866a
Exploitation, ultimate sanction of
  e., 1027a
Exploited, many e. by few, 1027a
Exploiters, interests of e., 1058a
Exploits, fond of relating own e.,
  373b
Exploration, not cease from e.,
  1007a
Explore all options, 1056a
  falter or e., 1079a
  happy Nature to e., 409a
Explorers, old men ought to be e.,
  1006a
  old men should be e., 1065b
Exploring, end of e. to arrive,
  1007a
Exponent of earth, 737a
Exposed, intellect improperly e.,
  522b
  left e. a friend, 737a
  more e. to suffering, 515a
  on bare earth e. he lies, 371b
Exposition of sleep upon me, 230a
Expounding, it is a constitution
  we are e., 485b
Express flowery tale, 583a
  it in numbers, 723a
  speech not to e. but conceal,
    376b
  we half e. ourselves, 606a
Expressed even such a beauty,
  293b
  find more than poet e., 615a
  monitor e., 516b
  ne'er so well e., 403a
  not e. in fancy, 258b

God, my G. Father and Friend, 374b
my G. have mercy, 191b
my G. look not so fierce, 213b
my G. why hast thou forsaken me, 17b, 45a
my soul thirsteth for G., 19a
nakedness of woman work of G., 487b
name of G. upon lips, 436a
name called the mighty G., 31a
Nature and Nature's G., 397b
nature is the art of G., 329b
Nature's G., 397b, 410a
nearer my G. to thee, 615b
nearer to church further from G., 183a
ne'er said G. be praised, 617b
nest on greatness of G., 796b
never made work for man to mend, 372a
never spoke with G., 737b
next to G. of course g., 1030b
no G. and Mary His Mother, 1075b
no G. but He most merciful, 149a
no g. higher than truth, 897b
no g. stronger than death, 774b
no g. wrong worm, 603b
no man hath seen G., 48a
no more Aurora Leighs thank G., 631a
no nearer to G., 1004b
no society bring kingdom of G., 965a
noblest work of G., 409b, 492b
none but G. is near, 518a
none other but the house of G., 7a
nor what G. blessed accursed, 667a
not alone G. is within, 138a
not G. for father if not Church for mother, 144a
not G. he'll catch, 1054a
not G. in gardens, 734a
not G. of dead, 47b
not pay Saturdays, 667b
not serve G. if devil bid, 272a
not to get near G., 809b
not willing to do everything, 177b
not worshiped by herd, 947b
nothing not G. greater than self, 700b
now G. alone knows, 770a
O dog my G., 1068a
O G. O Montreal, 755b
O G. that bread so dear, 592b
O G. that it were possible, 301b
O Lamb of G., 59a
O sole G., 4a
obligeth no man to more than ability, 149a
of battles, 245a
of Clotilda grant victory, 147b
of fathers known of old, 875a
of God, 60a
of Life Creator, 962a
of music out of doors, 830b
of my idolatry, 224a
of Nature, 323b
of Nature placed in power, 465a
of such is kingdom of G., 45b
of the Congo, 953a
of truth, 10b
Omega, 765b

God, on right hand of G., 60a
on seventh day G. ended his work, 5a
on side of best digestion, 946a
on side of big squadrons, 357a
once loved a garden, 969a
one G. even the Father, 544a
one g. greatest among gods, 70b
one G. law element, 651a
one G. one principle of being, 142b
one nation under G., 832b
one that feared G., 14a
only G. and angels lookers-on, 207a
only G. can make tree, 992a
only G. had for asking, 692a
only knows which is which, 776b
or Mother Goose, 844b
others call it G., 667a
our help in ages past, 396b
out in fields with G., 1101b
out of me G. and man, 775b
owe G. a death, 242b
pairs off like with like, 66b
patriarch obedient to G., 705b
peace of G. passeth understanding, 54b
perfect blessedness vision of G., 158b
plays dice with world, 950b
pleased G. to visit us with death, 319a
poor dear G., 1037b
poverty in hand of G., 4b
praise G. sang Theocrite, 662a
presume not G. to scan, 408b
pride of peacock glory of G., 487b
pseudonym of G., 802a
purlieu of g. of love, 306b
put G. in his statements, 701b
put hand to ark of G., 458a
reason in man like G. in world, 158b
rebellion obedience to G., 1090b
reflect that G. is just, 471a
register of G., 331a
reigns government lives, 741a
render unto G., 43b
rest you merry, 1099a
rib which Lord G. had taken, 5b
round fat oily man of G., 420a
sacrifice to G. of devil's leavings, 413a
said I am tired, 603a
said Let Newton be, 412b
said Let there be light, 5a
said Let us make man, 5a
saint if G. does not exist, 1068b
save the king, 12a, 401a
save the king say amen, 228a
save the mark, 238b
save the people, 545a
save thee Ancient Mariner, 524b
saw that it was good, 5a
say first of G. above, 407b
says there is no G., 436a
Scourge of G., 212a
sea of infinite substance, 152a
secluded from sight of G., 308b
see G. made and eaten, 664b
seen G. face to face, 7b
sees G. in clouds, 408a
self-reliance is reliance on G., 608a

God send every gentleman, 1088b
sends meat Devil sends cooks, 183a
servant of G. well done, 346b
servant of living G., 444b
served my G. with half the zeal, 299a
service greater than the g., 268a
sets nothing but riddles, 708a
setteth the solitary in families, 19b
shall any teach G., 15b
shall smite thee, 50b
shall wipe away tears, 58b
she for G. in him, 345a
shed grace on thee, 849a
shield us, 230a
sigh in heart, 850b
smiled again, 906b
so commanded, 347b
so loved the world, 48a
so near G. to man, 603b
some lesser g. made world, 654a
something known only to G., 963b
sometimes wish G. back, 866a
Son of G. goes forth, 549a
Son of the living G., 43a
sons of G. shouted for joy, 16a
sons of the living G., 35a
souls are in the hand of G., 36b
souls mounting up to G., 731a
speed the mark, 602b
Spirit of G. descending, 39b
spirit shall return unto G., 29a
standeth G. within shadow, 692a
stands winding horn, 880a
stay with me G., 1103b
stepped out on space, 906b
stern daughter of voice of G., 514b
strong brown g., 1006a
subject to G. and Justice, 155a
take in G., 693a
tempers wind, 188b, 438b
temple of G. is holy, 52a
thank G. for peace, 914a
thank G. for tea, 523b
thank G. I have done duty, 492b
the Father a school divine, 412a
the Father in second place, 834b
the first garden made, 358a
the herdsman goads, 879b
the most resembles G., 493b
the unknown g., 50a
the word spake it, 189a
these old men, 83b
they shall be called children of G., 40a
they shall see G., 40a
think himself act of G., 679a
think not G. at all, 349a
think public opinion voice of G., 764a
this is the finger of G., 8a
this nation under G., 639a
this thing is G., 775b
those G. loves do not live long, 102a
those whom G. hath joined together, 61b
thou art the Son of G., 42b
thought and thought, 906b
three-personed G., 308a
through darkness up to G., 650b

God, through life looked on G., 943b
  throws himself on G., 664b
  thy G. shall be my G., 11b
  'tis G. gives skill, 689a
  to the greater glory of G., 186a
  too full of G. to speak, 879a
  took day to search for G., 860a
  toward G. and toward Satan, 707a
  trust in G. hope for best, 522b
  trust in G. keep powder dry, 539a
  truth as old as G., 737a
  two halves of G., 598b
  unchanging law of G., 657b
  unless G. does that beating living thinking, 697b
  unutterable sigh, 850b
  up to Nature's G., 410a
  very G. of very G., 60a
  voice of people is voice of G., 152b
  walk humbly with thy G., 35b
  wants nothing of a g. but eternity, 290a
  war blood-swollen g., 904b
  was it G. was it man, 775b
  was the holy Lamb of G., 490b
  ways of G. justifiable, 349a
  ways of G. to man, 407b
  ways of G. to men, 341b
  were I Lord G., 1105a
  what G. hath joined, 43a
  what hath G. wrought, 10a
  what I call G., 667a
  what is G. everything, 80a
  what kind of g. art thou, 244b
  what man not know of G., 1054a
  what we have instead of G., 1044a
  when G. sorts out weather, 819a
  where end knows G., 1050b
  where G. built church, 179b
  who brought over ocean, 319a
  who G. doth late and early pray, 300b
  who gave life gave liberty, 470b
  who is able to prevail, 325b
  who is not we see, 776b
  who is our home, 513b
  who knows what I would, 1066b
  who made him sees, 877b
  who made rich make poor, 618b
  who made thee mighty, 862a
  who make iron grow, 503b
  whole armor of G., 54a
  whom we see not is, 776b
  whose puppets are we, 661b
  why St. Augustine thanked G., 936a
  will of G. prevail, 716a
  will provide himself a lamb, 7a
  will put an end to these, 117b
  will save her, 852a
  wills it, 150b
  wills us free, 468b
  winepress of wrath of G., 690b
  wisheth none wreck, 303a
  with G. nothing impossible, 45b
  with strongest battalions, 435a
  with thousand voices praises G., 526b
  with us, 39a
  without me G. cannot live, 364b
  wonder what G. calls me, 870a
  word of G. is quick, 55b

God, word of our G. shall stand, 32b
  Word was with G., 47b
  worketh in you, 54a
  world of nature and G., 1077b
  world's G. is treacherous, 994b
  worship G. in own way, 973a
  would G. this flesh might be, 773b
  would have three sides, 414b
  wove web of loveliness, 917b
  wrath of G., 690b
  wrath of lion wisdom of G., 487b
  wrote loveliest poem, 942a
  wrote of angels and G., 487b
  yearning like g., 581b
  your false g. dim rememoring, 1010a
  your G. is one G., 149a
  Zion city of our G., 446a
Goddamm, lhude sing G., 987b
Goddamned, similar g. phrases, 945b
Goddamnedest, seevility of commonest g. kind, 1100a
Goddess, bitch g. Success, 792b
  consult concerning great g., 506b
  Demeter or Earth, 85a
  excellently bright, 302a
  mistake young woman for g., 960a
  moves a g., 405a
  night sable g., 399a
  of Grecian woes O g. sing, 405a
  of the silver lake, 337b
  pasteboard g. of hustings, 934b
  to thy shrine we come, 497a
  walk revealed her as true g., 118a
  White G., 1034b
  write about it G., 413b
Goddesses, even if g. too should be looking, 65b
  take hold ye gods and g., 63b
Godfathers of heaven's lights, 221a
God-given rights, 616a
God-intoxicated man, 373a
Godless hell's delight, 860b
Godlike, capability and g. reason, 264b
  erect, 345a
  power in us still, 710b
  to create, 680a
Godliness, cheerful g., 512b
  cleanliness next to g., 421a
Godly, old and g. and grave, 880a
  thou art fair thou art g., 773b
Godmother, fairy g. in soul, 857a
God's above all, 273b
  abusing of G. patience, 267a
  acre, 621b
  allotment, 783a
  arrest, 381b
  Caesar's self is G., 354a
  crucible, 870b
  dare ask just G., 640b
  Devil is ever G. ape, 179b
  do deed without G. knowledge, 79a
  earthly power then likest G., 234b
  finger touched, 650b
  first creature light, 344b
  first temples, 574b
  footstool may be throne, 925b
  for G. sake sit upon ground, 227b

God's, gift is G. to God, 1056b
  gifts put dreams to shame, 618b
  great Judgment Seat, 872b
  greatness flowed, 617b
  greenwood chapel, 953a
  hand folks over to G. mercy, 689b
  heaven is G. throne, 40b
  help and their valor, 504b
  here is G. plenty, 372a
  I'm under G. arrest, 381b
  in his heaven, 661b
  issue is in G. hands, 79a
  justify G. ways to men, 853b
  last Put out the light, 928a
  light G. eldest daughter, 333b
  man's bedevilment and G., 854a
  mill grinds slow, 325a
  mouth knows not falsehood,78b
  my spirit in G. hand, 364b
  not G. not beasts', 666a
  one on G. side majority, 659a
  preaching of G. sacred Word, 5a
  reason G. crowning gift, 82a
  skirts, 662a
  spies, 280a
  sure they know G. will, 1041b
  things which are G., 43b
  thy country's thy G. and truth's, 299a
  true princes of empire, 696b
  voice of G. creatures, 641b
  ways to man, 853b
  we are in G. hand, 244a
  will be done, 468b
  woman G. second mistake, 806a
  ye are G. husbandry, 52a
Gods, all ages believed in g., 935b
  all men have need of g., 65a
  angels would be g., 408a
  approve the depth, 516b
  are just, 280b
  are on side of stronger, 140a
  are we, 710b
  arrive, 603a
  as flies to boys we to g., 279a
  as psychic factors, 935b
  aspiring to be g., 408a
  believe in g. of state, 93a
  built against will of g., 63b
  by Nine G. he swore, 596a
  call the g. to witness, 290a
  contend in vain, 498b
  convenient that there be g., 128b
  darling of men and g., 112b
  daughter of g., 645b
  dish fit for g., 254b
  do not give all men gifts, 65b
  dwells with g. above, 268b
  even if g. should be looking, 65b
  execute judgment against g. of Egypt, 8b
  fade God abides, 785b
  fashioned by men, 867b
  fault of angels and g., 406a
  fight against necessity, 68b
  forbid it sea g., 695b
  forget g. are old, 813b
  formed world at creation, 537a
  glorious gifts of the g., 62b
  go in various disguises, 66b
  good g. how he will talk, 384b
  grant me this, 115a
  graven images of her g., 31b
  happy who knows rural g., 117a-b
  have neither age nor death, 83a

Good

Good boy am I, 1093a
  bringeth thee into a g. land, 10a
  but not religious-good, 782b
  by evil and g. report, 53b
  by quiet natures understood, 882b
  call this Friday g., 1005b
  cannot come to g., 257b
  captive g. attending captain ill, 292b
  charm to make bad g., 272a
  cheer is best physician, 79b
  chief g. and market, 264b
  cigar is a smoke, 871b
  club assembly of g. fellows, 427b
  commodity of g. names, 238a
  common g. and public authority, 964a
  communicated more abundant, 346a
  company good discourse, 326a
  constituted for practice of g., 100b
  corn wood boards to sell, 605a
  counselors lack no clients, 270a
  crown g. with brotherhood, 849a
  day's work, 423b
  deed in naughty world, 235b
  deed to say well, 298a
  demean selves as g. citizens, 461b
  deny us for our g., 287b
  depart from evil and do g., 18b
  desires be for what is g., 72a
  devil have all g. tunes, 475a
  die early bad late, 385b
  die first, 516a
  digestion wait on appetite, 284b
  dinner and feasting, 375b
  do after g. leave evil, 175a
  do all the g. I can, 768a
  do all the g. you can, 421a
  do g. the right way, 779b
  do g. to them that hate you, 40b
  doing g. one of professions full, 682b
  end of government to do g., 591a
  enough to shed blood, 847b
  Epicurus set forth highest g., 114a
  errors of g. men, 351a
  every creature of God is g., 55a
  every evil has g., 606b
  every g. gift, 56a
  everything in world g. for something, 369a
  evil be thou my g., 345a
  evil which is permitted, 742b
  fair and learned and g. as she, 319b
  fair is by nature g., 201b
  faith toward nations, 461b
  familiar creature, 274a
  fell into g. ground, 42b
  fellows get together, 868b
  fences make good neighbors, 926a
  fight of faith, 55b
  filches my g. name, 274a
  finds g. in everything, 247b
  five-cent cigar, 829a
  for a man that he bear the yoke, 34b
  for sore eyes, 390b

Good fortune is god among men, 79a
  fortune may be short-lived, 318b
  fortune to be born human, 379a
  fought a g. fight, 55b
  free press g. or bad, 1068b
  friend for Jesus' sake, 299b
  full of g. nature as egg of meat, 224b
  general g. is plea of scoundrel, 491a
  gentle beast of a g. conscience, 230b
  gentle into that g. night, 1070b
  glad of other men's g., 249b
  go please the gentle and g., 165b
  go with me like g. angels, 298a
  God saw that it was g., 5a
  gods do not give all men g. looks, 65b
  gray head all knew, 651b
  gods how he will talk, 384b
  great and joyous, 569a
  great man inherits, 527a
  great poet so g. friend, 371b
  half so g. a grace, 270b
  hand that made you g., 271b
  hanging too g. for him, 365b
  happiness the only g., 749b
  hard beginning g. ending, 183a
  Haroun Alraschid, 644b
  have no need of advocate, 96b
  hay sweet hay, 230a
  he our g. will sever, 302b
  he who would do g., 491a
  hearkeners seldom hear g., 386b
  hell full of g. intentions, 154b
  hell full of g. meanings, 324b
  hell paved with g. intentions, 154b, 324b
  help g. wise great, 883a
  highest g., 111b, 114a
  him that bringeth g. tidings, 33a
  hold fast that which is g., 55a
  hold thou the g., 650b
  honest painful sermon, 375a
  how few know own g., 371a
  how g. and how pleasant, 22b
  how g. man's life, 665a
  I am the g. shepherd, 48b
  I have g. eye uncle, 245b
  if all g. people clever, 785b
  if g. why do I yield, 281a
  if he had not been born, 44b
  ill wind blows no man g., 185b
  in everything, 247b
  in which mind at rest, 161b
  is good east to east, 789b
  it is not nor cannot come to g., 257b
  jest forever, 238b
  joke cannot be criticized, 918b
  jolly g. lesson, 875b
  judge men by g. fortune, 355b
  keep g. tongue in head, 297a
  King Arthur, 1098a
  King Charles's golden days, 1090a
  King Wenceslas, 687b
  kissing carrion, 260b
  know g. as g., 73a
  know what were g. to do, 231b
  knowing g. and evil, 5b
  lad of mettle a g. boy, 239a
  largest universe of g., 794b

Good, law commands that which is g., 462b
  law is g., 55a
  law is good order, 98b
  law of God law of g., 709a
  laws lead to better, 436a
  laws where state armed, 177a
  leave while looking g., 1027a
  leaves aside g. and bad, 455b
  left country for country's g., 398a
  life is g., 994b
  life of battle g., 865a
  life or g. place, 1061a
  listener popular, 941a
  literature must do g., 855a
  live in world g. or bad, 681a
  Lord deliver us, 60b, 1098b
  Lord is g., 21a
  lose g. we oft might win, 270a
  love as much as g. fight, 970b
  love g. pursue the worst, 129a
  love sought is g., 252b
  loves what he is g. at, 380a
  luck gayest, 588b
  luck giddy maid, 588b
  luck in odd numbers, 267a-b
  luxury was doing g., 386a
  maintain g. government, 485a
  make g. thing too common, 241b
  maketh sun rise on evil and g., 40b
  man and a just, 47b
  man does not argue, 75a
  man's fortune, 277b
  man's love, 250a
  man's sin, 438a
  man's treasure, 74b
  many g. men are poor, 68b
  marriage, 938b
  Master of All G. Workmen, 872b
  meaning g. or bad, 369a
  meaning in saying he is a g. man, 232a
  men and true, 246b
  men desire the g., 98a
  men eat that they may live, 87b
  men of g. will, 46a, 59a, 1015a
  men of ill judgment ignore g., 81a
  men to do nothing, 454b
  mingled yarn g. and ill, 269b
  moral what you feel g. after, 1044b
  morrow to our waking souls, 304b
  mothers and fathers, 1053b
  mouth-filling oath, 240a
  music g. to melancholy, 374a
  must associate, 452a
  my g. vain hope of gain, 205a
  my religion is to do g., 467b
  name better than precious ointment, 28a
  name better than riches, 125a
  name in man and woman, 274a
  name is rather to be chosen, 25b
  name like precious ointment, 208a
  nature in conversation, 394b
  neighbor is great blessing, 67b
  neighbor policy, 971a
  neighbors, 1104a
  neither honesty nor g. fellowship, 238a
  never bad man g. service, 453b

H

Hang themselves in hope one will cut halter, 333b
there like fruit my soul, 291a
together or hang separately, 423a
up philosophy, 225a
upon his penthouse lid, 281a
us every mother's son, 229a
when icicles h. by the wall, 222b
yellow leaves do h., 29b
Hanged, house of a man h., 195a
I'll be h., 238b
knows he is to be h., 432b
longed to see him h., 901b
millstone h. about neck, 47a
my poor fool is h., 280b
our harps upon willows, 22b
that horses not be stolen, 376b
they h. Haman, 14a
when skies are h., 1032a
Hangin' Danny Deever, 873a
men and women there, 1091a
Hanging and wiving by destiny, 182b
around in world, 930a
around till you've caught on, 930a
breathless on thy fate, 622b
Danny Deever, 873a
Gardens were dream, 933b
in a golden chain, 344a
likewise destiny, 182b
men and women there, 1091a
not deserve h., 191a
too good for him, 365b
worst use for man, 301a
Hangman, if I were a h., 610b
Hangman's, fear of hell's a h. whip, 312a
Hangover became part of day, 1037a
Hangs as mute on Tara's walls, 541b
blossom that h. on bough, 297b
bodiless as false dawn, 1078b
goose h. high, 1100a
he h. between in doubt, 408b
head for shame, 720a
in clear green bell, 704a
in uncertain balance, 206a
on Dian's temple, 290a
on princes' favors, 298b
tail h. down behind, 874b
thereby h. a tale, 181b, 219b, 248b
upon cheek of night, 223a
what h. in balance nowise in doubt, 1014b
Hank of hair, 875a
Hannah, amount to H. Cook, 1102a
God and me, 749b
Hannibal is at the gates, 151a
know how to win victory H., 106a
put H. in the scales, 139b
Hanover, famous H. city, 662a
St. George's H. Square, 756a
Hans Breitman gife a barty, 723b
Hansom, helped to h. outside, 1059a
Hap, from better h. to worse, 210b
my hope my h. my love, 193b
Ha'penny will do, 1098b
Hapless sons of clay, 627b
Haply I think on thee, 292a

Happen, accidents which started to h. to somebody else, 946a
cannot tell what will h., 863b
it can't h. here, 987a
lies at last letting it h., 1079b
things you do not hope h., 106a
we's nuts and things h., 1009a
Happened, good book h. to you, 1044b
history tell how it h., 386a
nothing ever h. at all, 761a
put down what really h., 1044b
this could have h. once 666b
what men believe h., 1017a
Happening, being and h., 1061a
funny if h. to somebody else, 954a
Happens, future in us before it h., 938b
nothing h. unless first a dream, 948b
too much h., 1039a
trouble h. to others, 946b
trouble h. to you, 946a
truth h. to idea, 795a
unexpected always h., 106a
whatever h. h. as it should, 141b
Happier air, 714b
envy of less h. lands, 226b
family h. for his presence, 825a
I am h. than I know, 347a
in passion we feel, 356a
people capable of being h., 1014b
remembering h. things, 647a
the one who goes is h., 722a
those who feel love most are h., 569a
to be dead, 603b
Happiest conversation no competition, 431b
day happiest hour, 641a
heart that ever beat, 813a
intellection, 1079a
martini one of h. marriages, 1038b
nations no history, 689b
of mortals, 417a
time of New Year, 645a
treatise of natural education, 436a
women have no history, 689b
Happily, plenty to live on h., 983a
Happiness activity in accordance with excellence, 98a
avarice and h., 421b
being's end and aim, 409b
beneficial for body, 908a
care of life and h., 472b
ceases like dream, 328b
consume h., 836a
counting upon h., 584b
depends less on exterior things, 456b
efforts to create h., 958a
envy no man's h., 249b
eternal h. above in heaven, 5a
every human seeking h., 888b
freedom secret of h., 90a
friendship essential for h., 818b
great task of h., 824a
greatest degree of h., 446a
greatest h. for greatest numbers, 416b
habit takes place of h., 593b
hairbreadth missings of h., 424b

Happiness, health foundation of h., 613a
hope for h. beyond life, 467b
in hands of others, 539b
in married estate, 333b
is of retired nature, 394a
ivrywhere excipt where people, 891b
jealous possessions of h., 897b
keep h. in store for society, 958a
liberty secret of h., 832b
lifetime of h. hell, 836b
look into h. through another's eyes, 250b
made of minute fractions, 530a
make ourselves worthy of h., 445b
makes up in height, 928b
mistaken path to h., 564a
no h. perfect as martyr's, 863b
no h. where no wisdom, 82b
no man bear lifetime of h., 836b
not in multitude of friends, 302a
not suffer from scientific holiday, 966a
not write down h., 802a
object of government h., 949b
of common man, 949b
of human race, 453b
of nobody but dictators, 1035b
of peoples, 802a
of society end of government, 463b
on earth no sure h., 200b
on terrestrial ball, 1051b
pastime and our h., 515b
politics art of human h., 871a
principles to effect h., 470b
produced by good tavern, 432a
pursuing and obtaining h., 446a
pursuit of h., 470b, 973a
regret or secret h., 816b
religion assures final h., 834b
result h., 671b
result of man's effort, 958a
rhyming gives men h., 412b
rob of illusion rob of h., 729a
search for human h., 1019b
secret of h. freedom, 90a
she does not find, 427b
sum of human h., 966a
supreme h. of life, 599a
talk h., 825b
tender h. betray, 515a
that makes heart afraid, 592a
the only good, 749b
thirst after h., 436b
to be dissolved into something great, 939b
to crave h. is revolt, 729a-b
too swiftly flies, 439b
two foes of human h., 564a
what right have we to h., 729a
wherein lies h., 580b
wine of rarest vintage, 878a
work out h. for selves, 544b
Happy a health unto the h., 869a
a man as any in world, 375a
accident, 314a, 960a
age when idle with impunity, 550a
alchemy of mind, 418b
and I wrote my h. songs, 486b
as a lover, 515a
as grass was green, 1070b
as heart was long, 1070b

Happy as kings, 823b
  as we imagine, 355a
  ask yourself whether h., 619b
  autumn fields, 648b
  be and have immortal bliss, 200a
  be good and h. today, 523b
  best government desires to make people h., 594b
  blesseth with two h. hands, 201b
  bounding flea, 999a
  bread sauce of h. ending, 799a
  breed of men, 226b
  bridegroom Hesper brings, 854a
  call that man h., 78b
  Christmas to all, 541a
  combination of circumstances, 521a
  convents, 414a
  days that make us h., 947a
  deep down, 1014a
  description of h. state, 373a
  duty of being h., 822b
  earthlier h. is rose distilled, 228b
  ending, 799a
  English child, 546a
  families alike, 732b
  fault, 59a
  few, 245a
  field mossy cavern, 583b
  fool h. he knows no more, 409a
  for son whose father went to hell, 215b
  good government when those near made h., 72b
  good-night air, 783b
  hail Columbia h. land, 508a
  he of calm and h. nature, 93b
  he who has once been h., 781b
  he with such mother, 649b
  heart that sighed, 210b
  high majestical, 569b
  highways where I went, 853a
  horse to bear Antony, 287a
  hour wherein man might be h., 325b
  house shelters friend, 606b
  how h. he who crowns, 449a
  how h. vestal's lot, 405b
  how h. with either, 402a
  how we make ourselves h., 445a
  if ever wife h. in man, 351b
  if you want to be h. be, 684b
  illusion which makes me h., 462a
  in arms of chambermaid, 432b
  in nothing else so h., 227a
  in work three things needed, 698b
  is he born and taught, 300b
  Isles, 646b
  Jerusalem h. home, 1085b
  laugh before we are h., 381b
  let a lord once own the h. lines, 403b
  let us be h. as we can, 433a
  liking what they do, 438b
  little h. if say how much, 246a
  little needed to make h. life, 142b
  lucid intervals and h. pauses, 207b
  make earth h., 719b
  make fellow creatures h., 467b
  make two lovers h., 407b
  man be his dole, 182b
  man happy dole, 182b

Happy man that hath his quiver full, 22b
  man who could search out causes, 117a
  man who works ancestral acres, 120b
  man's without a shirt, 182a
  master of himself a h. man, 122a
  mindful of h. time in misery, 160a
  moron, 1103b
  Nature to explore, 409a
  never was so h., 1099a
  no lad so h. as I, 537b
  no lot is altogether h., 121b
  no man h. who does not think so, 126b
  no man h. without hobby, 818a
  no one h. till all h., 706a
  noble h. human beings, 698b
  old man, 116a
  pair, 345b
  people die whole, 994b
  people whose annals blank, 578a
  persons with torn bodies h., 905a
  place green groves of blest, 119a
  place to be h. here, 749b
  place with me, 686a
  policeman's lot not h., 766b
  ports and h. havens, 226a
  prologues to swelling act, 281a
  prospects more pleasing than fruition, 140b
  rage outside h. ground, 714a
  rarely find a h. life, 120a
  realize I'd been happy, 1068b
  remote from the h., 1060a
  rich h. in plenty, 409a
  right happens to h. man, 1066b
  ring h. bells, 651a
  so h. as America, 467a
  that we are not over happy, 261a
  the h. that have called thee so, 532b
  the man and h. he alone, 369b
  the man who void of care, 397a
  the man whose wish, 402a
  they h. are and love, 332b
  thing to be father to many sons, 216a
  this h. country, 444a
  this the h. morn, 333b
  those early days when I, 362b
  those who plant cabbages, 181a
  those whose walls already rise, 118a
  though married, 866a
  time to be h. is now, 749b
  to be h. be well fed, 960b
  to be h. make others so, 749b
  to have been h. most unhappy, 148a
  too h. tree, 580a
  'twere now to be most h., 273b
  until dead not call man h., 69a
  Warrior, 515a
  warrior of politics, 916b
  warrior sleeps, 976a
  was he free was he h., 1060b
  where one is h. there's homeland, 151b
  where h. wing-beats are, 497a
  which of us h. in world, 660a
  who hath this only, 68b
  who in verse steer, 376b

Happy who knows rural gods, 117a-b
  who uses blessings with wisdom, 122b
  whom unbroken bond unites, 121a
  world not making you h., 836b
  world of h. days, 217a
  yet h. pair, 345b
Harangue, telling nothing in great h., 361a
Harbinger, evening star love's h., 348a
Harbingers are come, 323b
  to heaven, 333a
Harbor, age the h. of all ills, 104b
  arrived in a good h., 318b
  bar be moaning, 690b
  cleared, 524b
  even a little h. is good, 816a
  final h., 697b
  I tarried not in any h., 172b
  in life did h. give, 303a
  looking over h. and city, 948a
  run into a safe h., 69a
  ship comes into the h., 319a
  ship of state safely to h., 81b
  takes and gives something, 816a-b
  whence unmoor no more, 697b
Harbors I by sweating blood won, 174a
Hard as a piece of nether millstone, 16b
  as nails, 66a
  beginning good ending, 183a
  cause that makes these h. hearts, 279a
  Christ ain't going to be too hard, 778b
  cursed h. reading, 482a
  dealing teaches them suspect, 232b
  doubtful dangerous times, 575a
  for women to keep counsel, 254b
  gemlike flame, 781a
  heart of child, 990a
  heroic for earth too h., 665b
  hit h. fast often, 968a
  stairs, 162a
  how h. the way up another's
  it is well I die h., 462a
  it shall go h., 233b
  keeps end from being h., 928b
  latent value, 799b
  long boots h. boots, 948b
  no h. gifts, 994b
  not think what is h. is impossible, 142b
  nothing's so h. but search will find, 320b
  prove him with h. questions, 13a
  sloth finds down pillow h., 291a
  solid massy h. particles, 379b
  things that are too h. for thee, 37a
  things to bear, 722b
  this is my h. time, 1064b
  to argue with belly, 107a
  to be a father, 742b
  to catch and conquer, 730b
  to kick against pricks, 49b
  to please everybody, 127a
  very hard is my fare, 401a
  was their lodging, 385b
  way of transgressors is h., 24a

Heart, heathen h. that puts trust, 875b
help by lifting his h., 1039b
here is my h., 808a
hid in h. of love, 880a
hide what false h. know, 283a
high as my h., 249b
high-erected thoughts in h. of courtesy, 203a
history begins in h. of man or woman, 939b
hold me in thy h., 266b
hope deferred maketh h. sick, 24a
hot within me, 18b
how but through broken h., 841a
how dear to this h., 553a
how h. grows weary, 727b
how this small h. beat, 697b
human h. by which we live, 514a
humble and contrite h., 875b
I am sick at h., 256b
I have h. of a king, 189a
I told her all my h., 488a
idol marble h. stone, 890a
if h. fails climb not, 199a
if h. just frank kindly, 361a
if one has no h., 588b
imagination of man's h., 6b
in h. a little heaven, 387b
in h. blind desire, 773a
in h. cold December, 1085a
in his pained h., 581b
in my h. of h., 263a
in the h. or in the head, 233b
in unison with mankind, 815b
into h. air that kills, 853a
intoxicated with bliss, 498a
is a lonely hunter, 832a
is deceitful, 34b
is harder than stone, 67a
is Highland, 590a
is in Highlands, 494b
is lying still, 512a
is slow to learn, 1023b
is wounded within me, 21b
keep h. when all lost, 661a
keep thy h. with all diligence, 23b
keeps open house, 1064b
kep' goin' pity-pat, 693a
kindness makes h. run over, 469a
knock at my ribs, 281b
know truth by the h., 363b
knoweth own bitterness, 24a-b
laid h. open to indifference, 1068b
language of the h., 411b
languor not in your h., 715b
large wealth larger h., 368b
larger h. kindlier hand, 651a
lay h. out for my board, 1075b
leaps up, 511b
lent out h. with usury, 534b
less bounding, 714a
let h. have its say, 831a
let no man's h. fail, 12a
let not h. be troubled, 49a
level in her husband's h., 252a
lies open unto me, 649a
light of step and h., 914a
like bowl brimming, 747a
like music on my h., 525b
like singing bird, 739b
little body mighty h., 243b

Heart, live without h., 741b
loaves when h. joyous, 4b
locked my h., 1089a
logic of h. absurd, 460b
lonely hunter, 832a
look in thy h. and write, 203b
look into your h., 497b
looked into father's h., 1049b
Lord Christ's h., 604a
Lord looketh on the h., 12a
lost h. stiffens, 1004a
love cow with all my h., 823b
love gushed from my h., 525b
love the Lord with all thine h., 10a
love-sick h. dies, 1022b
make glad h. of childhood, 780b
man after his own h., 12a
man's own resinous h. fed, 883b
May when lusty h. blossom, 175a
meditation of my h., 17b
meet mutual h., 420a
mend the h., 404b
Mercy has a human h., 487a
merry h. doeth good, 25a
merry h. goes all day, 295b
merry h. maketh cheerful countenance, 24b
mind is dupe of the h., 355b
mind lives on the h., 355b
mind thousand eyes h. one, 826b
mine with my h. in it, 297a
mortality touches h., 118a
moved more than with trumpet, 203b
music in h. I bore, 513a
must break piecemeal, 680b
must pause to breathe, 559b
my crown is in my h., 215b
my h. aches, 582a
my h. consumed in fire, 153a
my h. in my mouth, 133b
my h. is at rest, 487b
my h. is heavy, 478b
my h. is not here, 494b
my h. is pure, 647b
my h. is wax, 197b
my h. leaps up, 511b
my h. shall not fear, 18a
my h. with Oxford men, 969a
my sad h. foams at stern, 829b
my true-love hath my h., 203b
naughtiness of thine h., 12a
ne'er within him burned, 518b
never ached with h., 773b
never give all h., 880b
never given in vain, 852b
never say I was false of h., 293b
new-opened, 298b
no feeling in h. not in every h., 723b
no human h. goes wrong, 820a
no island but continent, 208b
no matter from the h., 269b
no nor for constant h., 1086a
no pity could change h., 790b
no wider than h. wide, 1023a
nook for h. tried sore, 578b
nor h. to report, 230b
not a cloud in heart, 740a
not keep alive on either, 1071b
not lose his child's h., 100a
not with club h. broken, 738a
not your h. away, 852b
now cracks a noble h., 266b
nowhere beats so kindly, 674b
O h. if she'd but turn, 880b

Heart, O h. O troubled h., 883a
O stricken h. remember, 824a
obey thy h., 603a
o'erfraught h., 285b
of a king, 189a
of a lion, 149b
of form, 1065b
of hearts, 263a
of iron, 996b
of lead, 413b
of man changeth countenance, 38a
of man depressed, 401b
of man place devils dwell, 330a
of minstrel breaking, 541b
of my heart were it more, 775b
of my mystery, 263b
of oak our ships, 439a
of Russia not forget, 611a
old darky's h., 828b
once woman has given h., 388a
one jot of h. or hope, 341a
open my h. and see, 663b
open unto me, 649a
out of h. rapture, 810a
penknife in your h., 1092a
pent-up love of h., 812a
Pharaoh's h., 8a
physical tinged with h., 614a
plunges lower than night, 979b
poor h. would fain deny, 286a
possessing h. of woman, 907b
pourest thy full h., 570b
preaching down daughter's h., 647a
press thee to my h., 590b
prithee send back my h., 350b
put fear out of h., 896b
put them in thy h., 4b
quanch my h. trobling, 1010a
razors to my wounded h., 218b
recoiled at war, 1031a
recover old h., 100b
recovered greenness, 323b
red-leaved table of my h., 301b
replies, 459a
revolting and rebellious h., 34a
rise in the h., 648b
room my h. keeps, 321a-b
rose in deeps of h., 880b
rule my h., 597b
runs away with head, 500a
sad h. of Ruth, 583a
said to h. How goes it, 902a
same h. in every breast, 711b
savage indignation tear h., 391a
seal upon thine h., 30a
search thine own h., 626a
seared and blighted h., 641a
season priketh every gentil h., 167a
secret anniversaries of h., 625a
secret of freedom a brave h., 90a
set my poor h. free, 271b
set not h. upon goods, 37b
sets my h. a-clickin', 819b
sets my h. to fluttering, 69b
shaft that quivered in h., 555a
Shakespeare unlocked h., 517a, 668a
she wants a h., 406b
sheer into h. of foe, 654b
shot straighter to h., 737a
sick at h., 256b
sky melt into his h., 509b
some h. did break, 650a
some h. responds, 621b

Heart soonest awake to flowers, 541b
soothes humble h., 887a
sound as bell, 246a
soured kindness in my h., 281b
squatter's rights of h., 1047b
squirrel's h. beat, 689b-690a
steady of h., 518a
stick the h. of falsehood, 268b
stirred h. of Englishman, 896a
stop h. from breaking, 737a
strike mine eyes but not my h., 302b
strong and diverse h., 1041b
stubborn h. shall fare evil, 37b
stuff which weighs upon h., 286b
subject of Japanese poetry, 419a
summer to your h., 1023b
superior have best h., 749a
sweeping up the h., 737b
take back h. thou gavest, 733b
take beak from out my h., 643a
that has truly loved, 542a
that loveth nought in May, 164a
there will your h. be also, 40b
there's where h. turning, 727b
thing that eats h., 1057b
thinks tongue speaks, 246a
though h. still as loving, 559b
thou'll break my h., 494a
through fire for kind h., 267a
thy breast encloseth my h., 217a
tiger's h. in player's hide, 206a
tiger's h. in woman's hide, 215b
Time laid hand on my h., 624a
tired h. cease to palpitate, 624b
to conceive, 1091b
to dog to tear, 877a
to heart, 518b
to hold, 603b
to mind shameful to h. beauty, 708a
to poke poor Billy, 930b
to resolve, 466a
too soon made glad, 662a
too tender or too firm h., 406a
tragedy The Human H., 933a
trusteth in his own h., 26b
turned to stone, 275b
turning home again, 827b
unfortified, 257b
unquiet h. and brain, 649b
untraveled turns to thee, 447b
vacant h. hand eye, 521a
veracity h. of morality, 725a
verities and truths of h., 1039b
visit my sad h., 254b
want of thought and h., 592a
war in his h., 19b
ward has no h. they say, 500b
warm and gay, 1020a
warm h. within, 459a
warm h. with friends, 1023b
was one which most enamor, 559b
wasted h., 1056b
waters of the h., 1070a
way to h. through stomach, 658a
weak hands mighty h., 571b
weaned h. from low desires, 178a
wear h. upon my sleeve, 272a
weeping in my h., 808a
wet eye dhry h., 891a
what deep h. means, 1057b

Heart, what dungeon dark as h., 614b
what female h. gold despise, 439b
what stronger breastplate than h., 215a
when my h. hath 'scaped, 293a
when to h. of man, 925b
where h. lies brain lie, 665b
which beats only for you, 808a
whole h. is faint, 30a
wine that maketh glad the h., 21b
wisdom to believe h., 867a
wise and understanding h., 13a
with but half a h., 321b
with fear freeze, 1085b
with h. in hand, 658a
with love fry, 1085b
with my whole h., 34b
with rue h. laden, 853b
withered h., 1054a
within blood-tinctured, 617b
within God o'erhead, 620b
woman whose h. is snares, 28a
woman with the h., 649a
world no wider than h., 1023a
words shall be in thine h., 10a
wound h. that's broken, 520b
wound h. with languor, 807a
wounded is wounding h., 354b
Heartache, by sleep we end h., 261b
Heartbreak, altar of our h., 1068a
better chiding than h., 267b
Heartburn, I am h., 804a
Heartfelt, simple and h. lay, 622a
Hearth, by this still h., 646a
clean-winged h., 626b
clear fire clean h., 535a
cricket on the h., 335b
no more blazing h., 440a
woman for the h., 649a
Hearthfire smoke against sky, 1017b
Hearths, their country their h., 116a
Hearthstone, every h. over land, 637b
fox build on h., 909a
of hell best bed, 909a
Heartiest, purest h. tenderness, 703a
Heartily know when half-gods go, 603a
Heart-leaves of lilac, 931b
Heartless Godless hell's delight, 860b
Heart-revealing intimacy, 882b
Heart's affections, 584b
asides in tears, 593a
at liberty, 359a
dead never buried, 1017a
deep h. core, 880a
desire, 17b, 631a, 880a
desires be with you, 247a
health to be sick, 1022b
his h. his mouth, 289b
hot h. shell, 697a
my h. in the Highlands, 494b
my h. right there, 934a
my h. undoing, 542b
supreme ambition, 434a
wear him in my h. core, 263a
young man's h. complaint, 700b
Hearts, affect h. and minds, 1021a
all that human h. endure, 428a
apply our h. unto wisdom, 20b
are earned, 882b

Hearts, as much love as if giving h., 173a
as pure and fair, 767b
blind h., 113b
cashboxes for h., 591a
cause that makes hard h., 279a
cheerful h. now broken, 542b
cherish h. that hate thee, 299a
cleanse thoughts of our h., 60b
come not to steal away h., 255b
country cherished in h., 655b
daystar arise in your h., 57a
drunk with beauty, 893b
dry as summer dust, 516a
ennobled our h., 392a
ensanguined h., 458b
fasten hands upon h., 854a
feet leave but not h., 633b
finite h. that yearn, 664a
first in h. of countrymen, 486a
given our h. away, 515b
high in people's h., 254a
hoard little h. great, 653a
hope men set h. upon, 629b
hugest h. that break, 738b
human h. to chew, 570a
in imagination of their h., 45b
in love use own tongues, 245b
in retiring draw h., 348b
in unison strike twelve, 1056b
itch grows old in sick h., 139b
keep your h. and minds, 54b
keeps their h. vacuous, 73b
kind h. more than coronets, 645a
Knave of H., 1094b
land of broken h., 918a
Lord dwelt in people's h., 364a
Lord searcheth all h., 14a
men with Splendid H., 993b
mercy enthroned in h. of kings, 234b
neither have h. to stay, 353b
new heraldry hands not h., 275a
not had as gift, 882b
not their h. that roam, 874b
O blind h., 113b
of controversy, 253b
of oak, 181b
of the noble may be turned, 64a
our h. all with thee, 622b
pluck their h. from them, 245a
Queen of H., 1094b
rain falls in h., 1040b
shutting away of loving h., 1024a
sing to find your h., 980a
slow unreckoning h., 1079b
somewhere h. are light, 868a
steel my soldiers' h., 245a
strong minds great h., 690b
that beat as one, 619a
that kindle, 720a
that roam, 874b
they leave behind, 538a
though stout and brave, 620b
thousand h. beat happily, 555b
tight hot cell of h., 1038a
touched with fire, 786b
true plain h., 304b
two h. multiply, 1086a
two loving h. divide, 806b
union of hands and h., 356b
unto whom all h. are open, 60b
utter what h. hold, 896b
we leave behind, 538a

Hedge, divinity doth h. a king, 265a
over h. before stile, 194b
pull not down your h., 324a
Hedgehog knows one great thing, 68a
Hedgehogs, thorny h., 229b
Hedgerows, these h. little lines, 509a
Hedges grow if left alone, 1047a
social fences like h., 1047a
unkempt about those h., 993a
Heed, I will take h. to my ways, 18b
rumble of distant drum, 629b
take h. lest he fall, 52a
take h. of loving me, 306b
ye who lead take h., 899a
Heedless, earth's h. sons, 1036a
ran my h. ways, 1070b
self-interest bad economics, 971b
unwise to be h. while giving advice, 129b
Heejous, creature of h. mien, 891a
Heel, bids it come to h., 1000a
coat from h. to throat, 881b
Europe under his h., 922b
of courtier, 265b
of Northeast Trade, 874a
thou shalt bruise his h., 6a
tread each other's h., 265a
Heels, at his h. a stone, 265a
first toes then h., 902a
follow truth too near h., 199b
fortune grow out at h., 277b
from h. up to head, 823b
gunpowder out at h., 443a
hi but she h. to it, 1022b
horses' h. over paving, 1004a
out at h., 267a
over head and h., 114b
repose with h. higher than head, 191b
took to my h., 109a
Heeltap I never could bear it, 552b
Heft of cathedral tunes, 735a
Heifer, if ye had not plowed with my h., 11b
lowing at skies, 583b
Heifer's, false as wolf to h. calf, 268b
Height, asks of us certain h., 929a
blue heaven's h., 812a
depths of h., 1031b
happiness makes up in h., 928b
measure h. by shade, 661b
my soul can reach, 618b
nor depth, 51a
objects in an airy h., 387a
of man equal to tips of hands, 132b
smiles from h. at me, 1059a
street wide as h. of houses, 174b
worth's unknown though h. taken, 294b
Heights by great men reached, 623a
dwell on h. of mankind, 498b
march up h. of fame, 999b
towering h. of hills, 674a
Heir as great in admiration as herself, 299b
grandchild h. of the first, 304a
great h. of fame, 334a
of all the ages, 647b
of mongrel bitch, 277b

Heir, that flesh is h. to, 261b
yourself sole h. of world, 377b
Heirs, joint h. with Christ, 51a
of all eternity, 221a
of God, 51a
of spiritual life, 544b
of tomorrow, 789a
Helen brought her dowry destruction, 78b
did not board the ships, 69a
Leda mother of H., 781a
like another H., 371b
sweet H. make me immortal, 213a
thy beauty is to me, 641b
Helen's beauty in brow of Egypt, 230b
dawn in H. arms, 884a
dust hath closed H. eye, 300b
Helican, damned if I see how h., 953b
Helicon, muses of H., 67a
shepherding below holy H., 67a
watered our horses in H., 205b
Hell, agreement with h., 615b
all h. broke loose, 346a
all h. stir for this, 245a
all right then I'll go to h., 761b
all we need of h., 739a
better to reign in h., 342a
black as h., 294b
born on undigested dumpling, 696a
characters of h. to trace, 441b
city much like London, 570a
cunning livery of h., 271a
curse of h. frae me, 1087b
death hate and h., 918a
differ as heaven and h., 653a
each bears his own h., 119a
easy to go down into h., 118b
England h. of horses, 201b, 312a
entertained great scorn of h., 160b
failure in great object, 580a
father for hoarding went to h., 215b
fifteen minutes of h., 808b
followed with him, 58a
full of good intentions, 154b
full of good meanings, 324b
gates of h. not prevail, 43a
give 'em h., 552a
halls of h., 989a
has no fury, 392a
hath no limits, 213a
hearthstone of h. best bed, 909a
heaven h. or Hoboken, 962a
heaven that leads men to h., 294b
hissing hot from h., 679a
hot as h., 483b
I myself am h., 1076b
I oft wished for h., 490b
I shall move h., 119b
I suffer seems a heaven, 345a
in h. roast like herrin, 496a
in heaven's despite, 489a
injured lover's h., 346a
into mouth of h., 652a
is alone, 1007a
is oneself, 1007a
is other people, 1058b
Italy h. for women, 312a
itself breathes out, 263b
keys of h. and death, 57b

Hell, lead apes in h., 219a
liberated the h. out of place, 1104a
limbecks foul as h., 294a
madness risen from h., 773a
make a heaven of h., 342a
make my bed in h., 23a
milk of concord into h., 285b
more devils than h. hold, 230b
muttered in h., 501a
myself am h., 345a, 1076b
never married that's his h., 311a
nor h. a fury like woman scorned, 392a
of a good universe, 1032a
of nuclear destruction, 1082b
old age is woman's h., 359a
on earth, 836b
out of h. leads to light, 343b
passage broad to h., 104b
paved with good intentions, 154b, 324b
Presbyterian in h., 764a
print news and raise h., 1099b
procuress to lords of h., 650b
Puritan's idea of h., 751a
rebellious h., 264a
reign in h., 342a
riches grow in h., 343a
road to h. gradual, 1042a
same world h. heaven, 604b
served my time in h., 1103b
spinach and the h. with it, 1046a
summons thee to heaven or h., 283a
take curtains, 979a
tell him to go to h., 552a
this is h. nor am I out, 213a
though h. bar way, 961b
till h. freezes, 1104b
tyranny like h., 466b
very respectable h., 894a
walked eye-deep in h., 988a
war is h., 705a
way I fly is h., 345a
we make ourselves, 793a
wedlock forced a h., 214b
what h. in suing long, 201a
what in h. have i done, 946a
what is h., 1007a
where h. is there must we be, 213a
where we are is h., 213a
whip all h. yet, 705a
whole body not be cast into h., 40a
with h. are we at agreement, 32a
within him, 344b
within myself, 330a
wrote of devils and h., 487b
Hellas, all H. monument of Euripides, 90b
confounded H., 90b
Hellenes, boy is most powerful of H., 77b
Hellenism, governing idea of H., 716a
spirit of consciousness, 716a
Hellespont, Propontic and H., 275a
Hell-kite, O h., 285b
Hello sucker, 980a
thingumbob again, 793b
Hell's broke loose in Georgia, 1041b
broken loose, 206a

History, uninstructed in natural
h., 724a
very chancy, 997b
war makes good h., 783b
what's her h., 252a
while we read h. we make h.,
722b
wide and mortal pang, 1057b
wise man does not hurry h.,
1048b
with its flickering lamp, 922a
witness to passing time, 110b
world h. is world's court, 497b
History's purchased page, 556b
Hit, a very palpable h., 266b
dusty trail, 952a
hard hit fast hit often, 968a
hard it rebounds, 431b
nail on head, 186a
only what aim at, 682b
without striking back, 765a
Hitch wagon to star, 608b
Hither and thither moves, 630b
and thither spins, 711b
come h., 248a
even as their coming h., 280a
let him come h., 366a
thither downward upward, 160a
Hitherandthithering waters, 968b
Hitherto herebefore, 812a
shalt thou come but no further,
16a
Hitler break island or lose war,
921a
even H. against war, 1019b
Germany the cause of H., 999a
missed bus, 897a
monster, 922b
wicked man H., 921b
Hitlerite blackguards, 954b
Hive for the honeybee, 879b
helmet now h. for bees, 204b
this great h. the city, 357b
Hiven, rich man enther H., 891a
Ho everyone that thirsteth, 33a
man they called H., 747a
my h. head halls, 968b
talk save us, 968b
with a hey and a h., 250b
Hoard, little h. of maxims, 647a
little hearts great, 653a
up our true liberty, 190a
Hoarded, beauty must not be h.,
337b
people think I h. words, 943b
Hoarding, father for h. went to
hell, 215b
Hoarfrost, like April h. spread,
525b
Hoarse, raven himself is h., 281b
unchanged to h. or mute, 346b
Hoary, as I in h. winter night,
210b
head a crown of glory, 24b
my days dull and h., 362b
sage replied, 429a
Hobbes clearly proves, 390a
Hobbies and humors, 867b
Hobbit, in hole in ground lived
h., 1025a
Hobby, benignant information h.,
905b
no man safe without h., 818a
Hobbyhorse, rides h. peaceably,
437b
Hobgoblin of little minds, 606a
Hoboken, heaven hell or H.,
962a
Hobson's choice, 312b

Hoc erat in votis, 120a
genus omne, 120a
volo sic iubeo, 139b
Hockcarts, maypoles h. wassails,
319b
Hocus an old cunning attorney,
414b
Hocus-pocus, law a h. science,
414b
Hoe, crowbar h. and barrow, 553a
leans upon h. and gazes, 826b
scratch it with a h., 733a
tickle earth with h., 610b
Hog butcher for world, 948a
is different, 761a
of Epicurus' herd, 123a
root h. or die, 1047a
whole house, 1076a
Hogan's right, 890b
Hogs eat acorns, 352a
eat snakes, 955b
fattenin' h. ain't in luck, 814a
like puncheon floor, 761a
men eat h., 955b
Hohokams on Arizona desert,
1077b
Ho-hum I am for wit, 1078b
Hoist colors to peak, 959a
instantly anchor, 702b
with his own petar, 264b
Hold, affection cannot h. bent,
252a
aloof to gain reputation, 95b
bag, 491b
candle to my shames, 233a
cannot h. mortality's hand,
237a
cannot h. thee close enough,
1023a
center cannot h., 882a
cry H. h., 282a
damned that cries H. enough,
287a
dominion over palm and pine,
875a
each thing his turn does h.,
320b
eternal Footman h. my coat,
1001a
faith h. which Milton held,
512b
farthing candle to sun, 312a
fast our end, 716b
fast that which is good, 55a
fast the time, 937b
fast till gives blessing, 625b
fire in his hand, 226a
fleet angel fast, 421a
fort I am coming, 705a, 777b
given us bag to h., 491b
glimmering tapers to sun, 312a
gorgeous east in fee, 512b
how take firm h., 100b
I h. it toward you, 581b
infinity in palm of hand, 490a
makes nice of no vile h., 236b
me but safe again, 666b
me in thy heart, 266b
me to your deep breast, 758a
mirror up to nature, 262b
more devils than hell can h.,
230b
net to h. the wind, 315b
nozzle agin the bank, 778b
opinion with Pythagoras, 234a
out relief is coming, 705a
own with whatever's going,
930a
poison in the hand, 80a

Hold, speak or forever h. his
peace, 61a
that you know it, 71a
thou the good, 650b
thy right hand shall h. me, 23a
to have and to h., 61b
to have to h. and let go, 871a
to one despise other, 41a
up Adam's profession, 265b
water, 392b
with hare run with hound,
183b
world but as world, 231a
world wide enough to h. both,
437b
you as thing enskyed, 270a
you here root and all, 654b
your hand victorious, 85b
your own by attacking, 837a
your tongue and let me love,
305a
yours to h. it high, 912b
Hold-fast the only dog, 243b
Holding mental problem in mind,
977a
pocket handkerchief, 746a
writing is h. your breath, 1037a
Holds, guess now who h. thee,
618a
him with glittering eye, 524b
in perfection but moment, 291b
nature her custom h., 265b
that anchor h., 654a
Hole, better h., 993b
Boston's a h., 666b
child shall play on h. of the
asp, 31a
entrusts life to one h., 105b
hobbit h., 1025a
in a' your coats, 495a
in the story, 1045b
mouse that hath one hole, 105b
not a nasty dirty wet h., 1025a
old swimmin' h., 819b
pessimist sees h., 943b
poisoned rat in h., 390a
put in his hand by the h. of
the door, 29b
round man in square h., 763b
stop h. to keep wind away,
266a
where tail came through, 533a
Holes, foxes have h., 41b
of different shapes, 522b
worms come through h., 1083b
Holiday, he speaks h., 267a
regular to them, 669a
Roman h., 557a
sunshine h., 335a
universal scientific h., 966b
Holiday-rejoicing spirit, 535b
Holidays free from overemphasis,
1062a
holiest of all h., 625a
if year playing h., 238a
Holier laws, 691a
richer man held to be h., 145a
than thou, 33b
Holiest of all holidays, 625a
Holiness, art only clean thing except h., 814b
courage or h., 902a
in the beauty of h., 18a
of heart's affections, 584b
Holla your name to hills, 251b
Hollaing and singing of anthems,
241b
Holland splendid country, 537a
where H. lies, 447b

Honor, accompany old age as h., 286a
action faithful h. clear, 407a
all lost save h., 180b
all men, 56b
all tasks of equal h., 923b
and greatness of his name, 299b
as valiant I h. him, 255a
bards have a share of h., 66a
before h. is humility, 24b
bestowing h. pudding pence, 600b
better h. than shameful wealth, 169b
bright, 268b
brothers all in h., 510a
but an empty bubble, 371b
by h. and dishonor, 53b
can h. set a leg, 240b
can't give word of h. give promise, 967b
changes labor from burden to h., 954b
chastity of h., 454a
clear, 407a
comes from Zeus, 62b
comes a pilgrim gray, 443a
dearer than life, 195a
depends on opinion of mob, 374a
desirous of h. and glory, 374a-b
die with h., 860a
done with hope and h., 873b
duty is word of great h., 468a
favor well bestowed an h., 395b
foe while you strike, 865a
free man abide with h., 681a
friend who prospered, 78b
from books of h. razed, 291b
full of days riches and h., 14a
giving h. unto the wife, 57a
good death does h. to whole life, 163a
has come back, 994a
his memory, 304a
hurt that h. feels, 647a
if peace not with h., 897a
if we can vertical man, 1059b
in her left hand riches and h., 23a
inherits h. or wealth, 527a
is a mere scutcheon, 240b
jealous in h., 249a
lacking neither h. nor lyre, 121a
life and h. in hands, 752a
like an island, 377b
louder talked of h., 595a
love in excess brings nor h., 84a
loved I not h. more, 358b
make one vessel unto h., 51a
man of h. regrets discreditable act, 961a
man willing to sink, 692b
map of h. in thy face, 215a
march in ranks of h., 922a
may we h. law, 548b
meaning and import, 468a
men who have a sense of h., 64a
men who have h., 690b
mine h. is my life, 226a
national h. national property, 491b
naught in hate all in h., 276b
neither property nor h. touched, 177b
new-made h. doth forget, 236a

Honor, no h. in sure success, 1008b
no longer live with h., 860a
not least in h. or applause, 201a
not pay h. with tears, 106b
of striking blow for freedom, 995b
or dishonor to last generation, 638b
our sacred h., 471a
peace with h., 613a, 897a
peace with justice and h., 107b
peace without h. not peace, 567b
peasants carry h. in their hands, 316a
peereth in meanest habit, 219b
perseverance keeps h. bright, 268b
physician, 38b
pluck bright h. from moon, 238b
pluck up drowned h., 238b
post of h. is private station, 393b
pricks me on, 240b
prophet not without h., 42b
purchased by merit, 233a
quaint h. turn to dust, 360a
Republic's roll of h., 733a
roll of h. holds no nobler figure, 934b
rooted in dishonor, 653b
sacred h., 471a
sense of h. in action, 90a
set h. in one eye, 253b
shall uphold the humble, 26b
signed with their h., 1067b
sin to covet h., 245a
sin to prefer life to h., 139b
sinks, 447b
so long shall your h. endure, 118a
stain in thine h., 38b
strength and h. are her clothing, 27a
subject of my story, 253b
take h. from me and life done, 226a
that h. would thee do, 243b
the king, 56b
those they have slain, 708b
through his h. I conquered him, 316b
thy father and mother, 9a
to whom honor due, 51b
travels in strait so narrow, 268b
truth above friends, 97b
voyage not for gain h. wealth, 174a
what is h. a word, 240b
what is left when h. lost, 125b
when faith lost h. dies, 625b
whom king delighteth to h., 14a
with native h. clad, 345a
women, 497b
words such as h. obscene, 1044a
Honorable, all h. men, 255b
ancient and h., 31a
and glorious, 461a
Brutus is an h. man, 255b
conquests, 453b
designs were strictly h., 424b
get loose from h. engagement, 452a
have that which is truly h., 100b
intentions h., 460a

Honorable murderer, 276b
no title more h., 967b
not h. to tell lies, 83a
object only of war h., 467a
politics most h. adventure, 934b
quixotic sense of h., 644a
retreat, 249b
style of Christian, 329b
to die for one's country, 121b
true and h. wife, 254b
yet write verse badly, 361a
Honored among foxes, 1070b
bones, 334a
by strangers h., 406a
by the few, 694a
custom more h. in breach, 259a
die h. and admired, 922a
followed him h. him, 662b
how loved how h. once, 406a
in their generations, 38b
of them all, 646b
these h. dead, 639a
Honorificabilitudinitatibus, 222b
Honoring, not so much h. thee, 303a
Honor's, can h. voice provoke, 440b
listen for dear h. sake, 337b
when h. at the stake, 265a
Honors acquired by unrighteousness, 71b
bears his blushing h., 298b
beauties wits, 305b
gave his h. to the world, 299a
highest h. this air give, 696b
mindless of its just h., 517a
people I cannot win with h., 364b
Hood, him that wears a h., 188b
more than a h. to make monk, 150a
Hooded clouds like friars, 620b
Hoodoo, Mumbo-Jumbo will h. you, 953a
Hoodwinking, respected succeeded in h., 1067a
Hoof, head and h. of Law, 874b
whatsoever parteth the h., 9b
Hoofs of invisible horses, 860a
of swinish multitude, 454a
Hoohooed it in ocean-booms, 955b
Hook, bait the h. well, 246a
baited with dragon's tail, 332a
by h. or by crook, 163b
draw out leviathan with a h., 16b
spares next swath, 584a
thine has great h. nose, 491a
without bait, 608b
Hooking, taking sweetmeats only h., 759b
Hook-nosed fellow of Rome, 242b
Hooks, silver h., 306a
Hoops, grapple with h. of steel, 258b
Hooting and shrieking, 254a
at glorious sun, 526b
Hoots, owl that nightly h., 229b
Hop, hoppity hoppity h., 970a
lets it h. a little, 224a
light ladies, 814a
Hope a waking dream, 97a
Admiral cheered them holding out h., 172a
against h. believed in h., 50b
all h. abandon who enter here, 159b
all I have am and h., 463a

Humble, ne'er ebb to h. love,
  275a
  out of pride, 190b
  pie, 671b
  soft meek patient h., 301b
  son of h. laborer, 964b
  station of private citizen, 472b
  the greater the more h., 37a
  very h. person, 671b
  wisdom is h., 459a
Humbleness, whispering h., 232b
Humbler heaven, 408a
Humblest citizen of land, 858b
  friends, 517b
  highest to h. tasks, 923b
  peer of powerful, 748b
Humbly beseech you of pardon,
  274b
  dumbly, 969a
  walk h. with thy God, 35b
Humdrum, passage might be h.,
  851b
  routine poetry of life, 818a
Humiliation, Negro past of h.,
  1081a
  peace accepted in h., 841b
  valley of H., 365b
Humility a thing commendable,
  183b
  a virtue all preach, 317a
  angling like virtue of h., 326a
  bear success with h., 818a
  before honor is h., 24b
  for acclaim earned in blood,
  1016b
  is endless, 1005b
  modest stillness and h., 243b
  most difficult virtue, 1007b
  pride that apes h., 526b, 533a
  proud in h., 311a
  sense of reverence, 85b
  where there is h., 157a
Humming town, 711a
Humor, according as man is you
  must h. him, 109b
  awe man from career of his h.,
  246a
  call it h. when they gibe, 390a
  is a drug, 76a
  most when she obeys, 407a
  no h. in heaven, 762b
  one has sense of h., 996b
  only test of gravity, 483b
  own up to lack of h., 870b
  saves few steps, 996b
  source of h. sorrow, 762b
  that's the h. of it, 243b
  third glass for good h., 394b
  unconscious h., 756b
  unyoked h. of idleness, 238a
  woman in this h. wooed, 217a
Humored, played with and h.,
  366b
Humorous sadness, 250a
  very beadle to h. sigh, 221b
Humors, gather h. of men daily,
  365a
  grave or mellow, 394a
  hobbies and h., 867b
Hump, cameelious h., 876a
  haunch and h. is Obey, 874b
  that is black and blue, 876a
  whale's white h., 696b
  without a positive h., 659b
Humpty Dumpty, 1095b
  when I use word said H., 746b
Hums, beetle with drowsy h., 284b
Hun at throat or feet, 924a
  is at the gate, 877b

Huncamunca O, 402a
Hunching wings and beak, 1075a
Hundred, a few h. scrawls, 981a
  at three h. pence ointment
  prize, 322b
  buyer needs a h. eyes, 324b
  daughter of h. earls, 645a
  father more than h. schoolmasters, 325a
  first h. days, 1073a
  first h. years hardest, 941a
  flowers blossom, 1027b
  fourteen h. years ago nailed,
  237b
  had I a h. tongues, 119a
  if very angry count h., 474a
  of three h. grant three, 561a
  one h. percent American, 838a,
  943a
  one h. years hence, 608a
  ran a h. years to a day, 634a
  rode the six h., 652a
  said h. different ways, 1030a
  schools of thought, 1027b
  ten jokes a h. enemies, 437b
  thousand thrained men, 981a
  thousand to that h., 320a
  to that twenty add h. more,
  320a
  touch a h. flowers, 1023a
  victory finds a h. fathers,
  1053a
  while one might tell a h.,
  258a
  wi' a h. pipers an' a', 502a
Hundredfold, brought forth fruit
  h., 42b
Hun-dred-mil-lion-oth-ers, 1030b
Hundred's soon hit, 664b
Hundredth part of members in
  arms, 465a
Hung aloft the night, 581a
  among cloudy trophies h., 584a
  be heavens with black, 214a
  because it h. behind him, 660b
  here h. those lips, 265b
  with bloom along bough, 852b
Hunger and thirst after righteousness, 40a
  bodily h. in eyes, 837a
  fer 'em somehow, 963b
  filth and ignorance, 1014b
  for self-approval, 764a
  for well-stored mind, 815b
  I am h., 1083b
  I offer h. thirst battles, 620a
  mouth and belly injured by h.,
  100b
  no fear stand up to h., 843b
  no patience wear h. out, 843b
  no sauce like h., 196a
  our policy against h., 959b
  they shall h. no more, 58a
  toil h. nakedness, 587a
  weak evils age and h., 248b
  when done with h. rich and
  poor as one, 85a
Hungered and ye gave meat, 44a
Hungering neighbor and me,
  692b
Hungry and he gave him meat,
  445b
  as grave, 419b
  ate when we were not h.,
  389b
  clouds swag, 487b
  cloy h. edge of appetite, 226a
  cold comfort to fill h. bellies,
  319a

Hungry despite the dream, 1050b
  generations, 583a
  hag and h. goblin, 1085b
  he hath filled h., 46a
  if thine enemy be h., 26a
  judges the sentence sign, 404b
  lean and h. look, 253b
  makes h. where most satisfies,
  287b
  man eats when not h., 1102a
  man not free, 1048b
  ocean gain advantage, 292b
  Pinch a h. lean-faced villain,
  218b
  poet should be h., 1042b
  poor, 758b
  rich when he is h., 96b
  sheep look up, 338b
  sleep is meat to h., 197a
  soul, 26b
  squalid population, 725a
  stomach cannot hear, 359b
  tigers getting h., 920a
Hungry-looking, fear pale and h.
  men, 112b
Hunt, beast something you could
  h., 1068a
  for a desert isle, 1069a
  gunless game, 846a
  in fields for health, 371b
  it in the dark, 457a
  love down together, 774b
  what you do not want, 1081b
Hunted, freedom h. round globe,
  466b
  little h. hares, 906a
  past reason h., 294b
Hunter, Bahram that great h.,
  629b
  Esau was a cunning h., 7a
  heart lonely h., 832a
  home from hill, 824a
  lo h. of east caught, 629a
  man is the h., 649a
  night dark-blue h., 893b
  Nimrod the mighty h., 6b
Hunters who hunt gunless game,
  846a
  woods for h. of dreams, 846a
Hunter-state of man, 535a
Hunting, ain't 'unting as 'urts 'un,
  810a
  biography like big game h.,
  1011b
  daddy's gone a-h., 1094b
  daren't go a-h., 729a
  ground for ambitions, 1049a
  passion for h. something, 669a
  upon St. David's Day, 1097a
  we will go, 424a
  weary wi' h., 1089a
Huntlie, true Thomas on H.
  Bank, 1088a
Huntress, queen and h., 302a
Hunts in dreams, 647a
  on a lonely hill, 832a
Huntsman, as h. his pack, 451a
  winds his horn, 424a
Huntsmen are up in America,
  331a
  three jolly h., 1097a
  three jovial h., 424a
Hurdygurdies make tune their
  own, 814b
Hurl cynic's ban, 846a
Hurled headlong flaming, 341b
  in ruin and confusion h., 393a
  into ruin h., 408a
  world and her train h., 362b

I

Imperfections of human mind, 1055b
on my head, 260a
outward bound, 1054a
pass my i. by, 507a
Imperial, act of the i. theme, 281a
ensign full high advanced, 342b
friend, 736b
man's i. race ensnare, 404b
national and i. boundaries the same, 1038b
sword mace crown i., 244b
Tom Jones outlive i. eagle, 466a
votaress passed on, 229a
Imperialism and Chinese, 1027b
obstruct peace, 974a
Imperiled, Union would be i., 787b
Imperious Caesar dead, 266a
Imperishable peace, 854b
quiet, 1065b
Impersonality of science, 675a
Impertinence, lesson on grammar i., 720a
Imperturbe, me i., 699b
Impetuous, be thou me i. one, 570a
such i. blood, 511a
Impiety of pious, 706a
Impious, course of i. stubbornness, 257b
men bear sway, 393b
Implacable Charybdis guards left, 234a
in hate, 368b
Implausible already said by philosopher, 327b
Implications, trace i. of things, 798b
Implore, I adore thee i. thee, 192b
Implores passing tribute of sigh, 441a
Import, honor meaning and i., 468a
Importance, art makes life and i., 800b
eternal i. like baseball, 986b
hence i. of poetry, 713b
no human thing of i., 95a
poem no i. except as poetry, 957a
Important, beginning most i. part, 94a
beyond this fiddle, 996a
discriminate between i. and negligible, 949a
if anyone think it important, 794a
people most i. element, 100b
principles inflexible, 641a
question is what you think, 713a
timing is most i. factor, 68a
Importunate chink, 454b
pawing and neighing, 860a
rashly i., 592b
Importune, I here i. death, 288b
too proud to i., 442a
Impose, fates i. that men abide, 216a
one style of art, 1028a
Imposition, reputation a false i., 273b
Impossibility, begotten upon i., 360a
likely i. preferable, 99a

Impossibility, physical and metaphysical, i., 575b
Impossible, can't believe i. things, 746a
carry out the i., 893a
certain because i., 143b
doing what is i. genius, 706b
ear and eye expected i., 883a
eliminate i. truth remains, 849b
in two words i., 967b
in war nothing i., 987b
looked on as i. until effected, 132b
loyalties, 713b
most i. of conclusions, 867a
not think what is hard is i., 142b
nothing i. in supernatural, 868a
nothing i. to willing heart, 183a
nothing unnatural that is not i., 481b
takes longer, 1103b
that not i. she, 354a
these i. women, 91b
to be cheated, 606b
to be silent, 454a
to live pleasurably without living wisely, 103a
to love and be wise, 125a
to please all the world, 359a
to reduce society to level, 657a
to write history i., 732a-b
with God nothing i., 45b
word i. not French, 504a
Im-possible, in two words i., 967b
Impostor employs force, 1092a
Impostors, sages all i., 455b
treat two i. same, 877a
Impotent, all-powerful to be i., 920a
lame and i. conclusion, 273b
Impotently great, 405a
Impoverished stock of harmless pleasure, 428b
Impoverishment in symbolism, 935b
Imprecision of feeling, 1005b
Impregnable, seas for fence i., 216a
Impress, themselves our minds i., 508b
Impressed, line in which force i., 379b
Impression as from seal of ring, 95b
be not swept off feet by i., 138b
Impressions, did not trust my own i., 89a
early i. hard to eradicate, 146a
falseness in i. of external, 698b
forever courting new i., 781b
of free mind, 885b
Impressive, poetry most i. mode, 713b
thunder i., 764a
Imprinted, remember what is i., 95b
Imprison gifts in such calling, 888a
Imprisoned in every fat man, 1053a
in viewless winds, 271b
Montezuma, 595b
Imprisonment, age ache penury and i., 271b
Improbable, absurd not the i., 676a
truth sometimes i., 562a
what remains however i., 849b

Impropriety, indulge in without i., 767b
soul of wit, 932a
Improve each shining hour, 396b
shining tail, 743a
Improved by death, 904b
for literary conversation, 310a
Improvement, diversion or i. of country, 394a
learned with view to i., 72a
makes straight roads, 487b
of underdeveloped areas, 982b
Improvements by generation, 459b
Improves, love i. a woman, 398a
Improving, middle age time of i., 351b
Improviste, le courage de l'i., 504b
Imprudently married barber, 442b
Impudence, Cockney i., 754a
Impulse, blot out pomp check i., 143a
faction united by common i., 480a
household of I. mourns, 1060a
lonely i. of delight, 881b
obey that i., 887b
one i. from vernal wood, 509a
to see it tried, 640b
to take life strivingly, 793b
Impulses, primitive i. of heart, 642b
Impulsive, our virtues are i., 614b
Impunity, no one provokes me with i., 151a
ravage with i. rose, 661b
Impure, although it passes among i., 96b
ditches i., 883b
Impurities, no room for i. in essay, 975a
Impute, sin I i. to ghost, 665a
In and out the Eagle, 1099b
birds without despair to get i., 190b
look out not i., 718a
those i. wish to get out, 608a
when age i. wit out, 246b
who's i. who's out, 280a
Inability to stay quiet, 726b
Inaccessible, desert i., 248b
tower of past, 694b
valley of reveries, 930b
Inaccuracy, not mind lying hate i., 757a
saves explanation, 904b
Inaction, disciplined i., 501b
moment not of action or i., 106a
saps vigors of mind, 174a
Inactivity, wise and masterly i., 501b
Inadequacy, intellect understand its i., 935a
Inadequate formulations, 1026b
their food is i., 982b
Inadvertently said some evil thing, 96b
Inane, intense i., 569a
Inanimate, mortality of i. things, 772a
Inanition, spirit die of i., 713b
Inarticulate, raid on i., 1005b
Inartistic, Thoreau i., 798a
Inattention, patient i., 731a
Inattentive, brave man i. to duty, 503a

Inhumanity, indifferent is essence of i., 836b
man's i. to man, 492b
Inimies, livin' without i., 890b
Inimitable vegetative gracefulness, 985a
Iniquities, judge allow i., 789a
Iniquity, approved i., 899b
bond of i., 49b
draw i. with cords of vanity, 30b
gray i., 239b
him that doeth i., 3a
I was shapen in i., 19a
is pardoned, 32b
love soft words hate i., 863a
of oblivion, 331a
punish wicked for their i., 31b
reaped i., 35b
religious know more about i., 871b-872a
visiting the i. of the fathers, 9a
Initial of creation, 737a
Iniuria, volenti non fit i., 152a
Injunctions, parting i., 925a
Injure, to benefit and not i., 75b
Injured, forgiveness to i. does belong, 130b
lover's hell, 346a
minds i. by hunger and thirst, 100b
no one i. save by himself, 144b
party, 770a
those I have i., 1076b
whom they have i. they hate, 130b
Injures, never pardons those he i., 130b
Injuries, forgive me my i., 1076b
saints in your i., 273a
Injuring, at expense of i. their virtue, 72b
kill time without i. eternity, 682a
rarely escapes i. own hands, 75a
restrain men from i., 472a
Injurious, beauty though i., 349b
Injury, add insult to i., 129b, 435b
engraved in metal, 179a
fear of i., 832b
greatest service or greatest i., 93b
never forget i., 904a
never use treatment with view to i., 88a
recompense i. with justice, 72b
sooner than insult, 415a
such i. vex a saint, 219a
violence and i. to humanity, 100a
violence and i. to willow, 100a
where i. let me sow pardon, 157a
Injustice, bear with patience i., 361a
complain of i. of government, 503b
conscience with i. corrupted, 215a
easy to bear, 960b
extreme justice extreme i., 151b
extreme justice often i., 108b
extreme law is extreme i., 108b
fear of suffering i., 355a
inclination to i., 1024b
jealousy i., 400a
makes democracy necessary, 1024b

Injustice, mankind censure i., 94a
no i. to person who consents, 152a
nothing so felt as i., 672a-b
on part of government, 959a
one man's justice another's i., 607a
road to downfall, 631b
sometimes public service, 1091b
threat to justice, 1082b
Injye other people's sufferin', 891b
Ink, crave shelter of i., 842b
effusion of i., 444b
essential in painting, 153a
every drop of i. ran cold, 442a
gall enough in thy i., 253a
galley slave to i., 590b
hath not drunk i., 222a
never saw pen and i., 253a
seated livelong day before i. slab, 162a
Inkstand, Vesuvius' crater for i., 697a
Inky, not alone my i. cloak, 257b
Inlaid with patines of bright gold, 235b
Inland island, 776a
though i. far we be, 513b
tract of i. ground, 516b
Inlets, through creeks and i. making, 688b
Inn, book's an i., 942b
classics have charm in i., 608a
gain timely i., 284b
happiness produced by i., 432a
make my house your i., 996b
no room in the i., 46a
remember i. Miranda, 902a
take mine ease in mine i., 183a
up to old i. door, 961b
warmest welcome at an i., 432a
world not i. but hospital, 330a
Inner air i. light, 1048b
blindness, 1000b
man, 54a
mine with i. weather, 928a
resolve i. conflicts, 985a
temple's i. shrine, 512a
weather, 928a
what i. voice says, 497b
Innisfail, harp of I., 537b
Innisfree, go to I., 879b
Innocence and health, 449a
ceremony of i., 882a
changed i. for i., 295a
closing up his eyes, 211b
confession next thing to i., 127b
fearful i., 512a
has nothing to dread, 378b
her i. a child, 369b
ignorance not i., 667b
murderous i. of sea, 882a
never blossom into license, 378b
of love, 252a
of our neighbors, 683b
our peace our i., 512a
recovered i., 683b
silence often of pure i., 295a
what is our i., 996b
Innocent and beautiful, 883b
armed without i. within, 412a
as new-laid egg, 765b
calm quiet i. recreation, 326b
children's souls not i., 146b
condemn an i. person, 417a
coursed down his i. nose, 247b
he that maketh haste to be rich not i., 26a

Innocent, look like i. flower, 282a
man sent to legislature, 895a
merriment, 768b
minds i. and quiet, 358b
moon, 856b
no i. wit be suppressed, 469a
of the blood, 45a
officious i. sincere, 433b
skin of i. lamb parchment, 215a
sleep, 283b
than one i. suffer, 444b
who perished being i., 14b
women i. and pure, 296b
Innocently, live i. God here, 425a
Innocuous desuetude, 771a
Innovation, opponents of i. die out, 847a
scientific i. rarely converts opponents, 847a
Inns not residences, 996b
of molten blue, 735a
Innuendoes, beauty of i., 955b
Innumerable bees, 649b
caravan which moves, 574b
things creeping i., 21b
Inoffensive, smooth easy i. down to Hell, 104b
untitled aristocracy, 634b
Inquire, shoot first i. afterwards, 1026b
why things as they are, 801b
Inquirer, workshop of serious i., 779b
Inquiries, suspended religious i., 466a
Inquiring eye or tongue, 536b
Inquiry thought to aim at some good, 97b
undismayed unintimidated i., 912a
Inquisition, committee i., 951a
dogs, 654b
Inquisitive, acute i. dexterous, 453a
Insane love to speak of selves, 770b
most i. of passions, 837a
ordinarily he is i., 588b
root, 281a
Insanity often logic, 633b
Insatiate blood, 1066a
to pursue war with heaven, 343a
Inscape is what I aim at, 804a
Inscription, altar with i., 793a
Inscriptions, lapidary i., 431b
Inscrutable colossal and alone, 812a
dark i. workmanship, 510a
dumb i. grand, 715a
jest unseen i., 220b
Insect carries impress of Maker, 383a
I am that i. brother, 708a
man mere i., 780b
scraping on surface of life, 772a
vile i. that has risen up, 420b
Insects, creatures both i. and humans, 946b
get meaning for other i., 772a
loud and troublesome i., 454b
of the hour, 454b
to whom God gave lust, 708a
Insensate care of mortals, 113b
Insensibility, stark i., 429b
Insensible, honor i. then, 240b
to freedoms of Constitution, 967a
Inseparable, nonviolence and truth i., 897a

Kennel, truth's a dog must to k., 277b
Kennin', gang a k. wrang, 493b
Kennst du das Land, 477a
Kentuck, hurrah for old K., 552a
smile lit eyes of K., 769b
Kentucky boys alligator-horses, 553a
moonlight softest in K., 804b
old K. home, 727b
Kept breath to cool his pottage, 68a
by transgressing k. law, 340b
easier k. than recovered, 467a
falling oars k. time, 360b
I have not k. my square, 287b
I k. my word he said, 914b
the faith, 55b
watch Matthew and Waldo, 1001b
when no proportion k., 228a
Kernel, if it contain k., 737b
Kernels, corn full of k., 855b
Kettle, faces as blackness of a k., 35b
how agree the k. and pot, 38a
of fish, 767b
Polly put k. on, 1097b
pot calls k. black, 197a
Kettledrums, copper k., 918b
Kew, his Highness' dog at K., 412b
in lilac time, 961b
Key, door to which no k., 630a
golden k., 336a
I have heard k., 1003a
in a bondman's k., 232a
out of k. with his time, 988a
think of k. each in prison, 1003a
this is the k. to it all, 696a
to keep back beauty, 803b
under thy own life's k., 269b
used k. always bright, 422a
with this k. Shakespeare, 517a, 668a
you shall keep the k., 259a
Keys, fingers on these k., 955b
of all the creeds, 650a
of hell and death, 57b
of kingdom of heaven, 43a
over the noisy k., 725b
the k. to, 969a
two massy k. he bore, 338b
Keystone, night's black arch the k., 495b
Kibe, galls his k., 265b
Kick against pricks, 49b, 78b
ass thinks he may k., 476b
out but not let down, 1053b
them in the pants, 977b
wheel's k., 946b
why k. me downstairs, 491b
you downstairs, 743b
Kicked and torn and beaten out, 573b
in head by mule, 886a
until they can feel, 352b
waxed fat and k., 10b
Kicks dust, 682b
Kid, leopard shall lie down with the k., 31a
Kiddo, take it from me k., 1030b
Kidney, man of my k., 267a
Kids in big field of rye, 1078a
Kilimanjaro highest mountain, 1045a
Kill admiral from time to time, 417a

Kill, almost k. man as k. book, 340a
and bliss me, 1085a
basilisk is sure to k., 402a
be my brother or I k. you, 469a
beast something you could k., 1068a
bloom before its time, 516b
bullet that will k. me, 504a
cankers in musk rose buds, 229b
care k. a cat, 247a
cure disease k. patient, 209a
do not k. or cause to k., 80b
flea though he k. none, 308b
hates thing he would not k., 234a
him in the shell, 254a
in artificial manner, 577a
joys with love, 225b
kill kill kill kill, 280a
learn him or k. him, 760b
let's k. all the lawyers, 215a
lust of office not k., 690b
nor yet canst thou k. me, 308a
not k. but needst not keep alive, 689a
princes privileged to k., 460a
sooner k. man than hawk, 994b
strike at king k. him, 610a
things they do not love, 234a
thou shalt not k., 9a
thy physician, 277a
time injuring eternity, 682a
time to k., 27b
to know to k. to create, 707b
to wear fox have to k. it, 997a
truths which can k. nation, 967b
urge to k., 1083b
us for their sport, 279a
when you have to k., 925a
wife with kindness, 219b
willingly k. a fly, 219a
world has to k. people, 1044a
you if you quote it, 887a
Killed, before he k. dragon, 919a
books not k. by fire, 973b
by overwork, 872a
calf in high style, 365a
care k. a cat, 247a
effort nearly k. her, 902a
fought dogs k. cats, 662b
hawked at and k., 284a
hunting hyena, 924a
if poet could be k., 775b
I'm k. sire, 662a
little cherry tree, 499a
many times in politics, 919b
more k. by suppers, 324b
only once in war, 919b
propitiatory bird, 1057a
Roaring Bill who k. him, 902b
scotched snake not k. it, 284b
some sleeping k., 227b
soul k. by wine, 747b
than frightened to death, 611a
the rat, 1098b
two thirds of people k., 950b
who k. Cock Robin, 1093b
who k. John Keats, 562b
you first time off base, 1044a
Killer kings on Etruscan cup, 1075a
Killeth, letter k., 53a
wrath k. the foolish man, 14b
Killing as canker to rose, 338a
breathed k. chills, 824a
eternity essence of tragedy, 870a

Killing for food not natural, 980b
frost, 298b
more ways of k. cat, 691a
time essence of comedy, 870a
why use k. at all, 72a
Kills, air that k., 853a
destroys book k. reason, 340a
doctor k. more, 382a
gout k. more rich than poor, 364b
not night that k., 869b
shadow k. the growth, 304a
six or seven dozen Scots, 239a
the very good, 1044a
thing he loves, 840b
world k. the good, 1044a
Kilmeny been she knew not where, 508a
Kilmer tongue not far from cheek, 1000a
Kilroy was here, 1040a, 1103b
Kiltartan, my country K. Cross, 881b
Kiltartan's poor, 881b
Kimono, woman in k., 1054b
Kin, little more than k., 257a
makes whole world k., 269a
one's own k. and kith, 1052a
Kind, adieu k. friends, 1100a
adieu k. friends, 1100a
and foolish comrade, 854b
and northern face, 1043b
art of being k., 826a
as kings upon coronation, 370a
be k. to my remains, 371a
be to her virtues k., 387a
blundering k. of melody, 369a
charity is k., 52b
cruel only to be k., 264b
enjoy her while she's k., 369b
Fortune more k. than her custom, 234b
had it been early had been k., 429b
heart benevolent and k., 493b
hearts more than coronets, 645a, 700b
his k. that lived years ago, human k. not bear much reality, 1004b
I am a k. of burr, 272a
kindness not therefore k., 406a
lady sweet and k., 1086a
less than k., 257a
love is k., 52b
man and died in want, 1075a
more nearly k. and gentle, 1038b
no best in k. but degree, 623a
not seek for k. relief, 487b
old sun will know, 1028b
plenty of the k., 644b
so constant and so k., 580b
thief said last k. word, 667a
through fire for k. heart, 267a
time is a k. friend, 982a
to be honest to be k., 825a
too k. to be k. enough, 402a
two almost divide the k., 406b
were all thy children k., 243b
yet he was k., 449b
Kinder, a little k. than necessary, 857b
let me be a little k., 963b
Kindle, cannot k. when will, 711a
hearts that k., 720a
passion of former days, 922a
soft desire, 371b
Kindled, anger of Lord k., 458a

L

Lawful, guns aren't l., 1029a
is it not l., 43b
without some l. recreation, 195b
Lawfully, if a man use it l., 55a
Lawgiver, stern L., 514b
Lawgivers and law-abiding, 1049a
Lawlands, ye Highlands and L., 1088b
Lawless attack upon liberty, 444a
linsey-woolsey brother, 352b
winged unconfined, 488a
Lawlessness, rush of our l., 708b
world l., 971b
Lawn, dew was on l., 974b
rivulets through l., 649a
white as driven snow, 295b
Lawns, like satyrs grazing on the l., 212b
Law's delay, 262a
in l. grave study six, 198b
to take care o' raskills, 689b
Laws, abhor makers and their l. approve, 370b
abounds with l. teems with crimes, 1090b
acting around us, 628a
after desuetude, 771a
and arms foundations of states, 177a
and constitution of country, 1091b
and learning die, 686b
and regulations like spider's web, 321a
are like cobwebs, 388b
are like spiders' webs, 68b
bad l. bring about worse, 436a
bad or obnoxious l., 717a
base l. of servitude, 367a
best l. teach to trample bad l., 659a
breathing household l., 512a
conflict courts decide, 485b
Constitution and l. of U.S., 474a
devise l. for blood, 231b
doing what l. permit, 414b
end tyranny begins, 426a
for themselves not me, 854a
forms all produced by l., 628a
found state and give it l., 177b
France mother of l., 187b
give little Senate l., 411a
good l. lead to better, 436a
government free where l. rule, 380b
government of l. not men, 463b
grind the poor, 448a
holier l., 691a
human mind put in nature, 966b
judges of facts not l., 399b
know not whether l. right, 841a
language manners l. customs, 511a
little l. lackeys make, 849a
love knoweth no l., 183a
nation territory people l., 638a
nature and nature's l. hid, 412b
necessary to preserve order, 958a
not assume physical l. exist, 846b
not care who make l., 384b
not good l. where not armed, 177a
obedient to their l. we lie, 70b
obey l. respect flag, 895b

Laws of distribution, 757b
of God l. of man, 854a
of nature and nature's God, 470b
of the jungle, 874b
or kings cause or cure, 428a
ought not to remain unaltered, 98a
people make bad l. then suffer, 778a
physical l. all discovered, 827a
power of making l., 485a
right from which l. derive 1091b
rules of game l. of nature, 724b
self-made l., 707b
submit thoughts and actions to l., 191a
sweeps a room as for thy l., 324a
the more l. are made prominent, 74b
three l. of righteousness, 78a
to execute l. royal office, 454b
true friendship's l., 405b
two l. discrete, 602b
unequal l. to savage race, 646a
useless l. weaken necessary l., 414b
which ran like drinking songs, 90b
Lawsuit machine you go into, 792a
mania, 770a
Lawsuits, win l. and are happy, 90b
Lawyer, deceive not thy l., 324a
draw up the papers l., 808b
has peasant inside, 870a
nor for every quarrel to l., 324b
not what l. tells me, 453a
peasant has l. inside, 870a
prairie l. master of all, 953a
skull of a l., 265b
train anyone to be l., 949a
without history a mechanic, 520b
Lawyers, charge prepared l. met, 402a
let's kill all the l., 215a
no l. among them, 178b
Lay aside long-cherished love, 115a
cleric before and l. behind, 352b
Doric l., 339a
down in her loveliness, 524a
down life for friends, 49a
dying in Algiers, 627b
down reins of power, 640a
earthly fancies down, 651b
enough to l. up, 400b
field to field, 30b
heart out for my board, 1075b
her in the earth, 266a
heroic l. tuneless, 560b
him low lay him low, 719a
his weary bones among ye, 299a
hold on eternal life, 55b
it on thick, 756a
like folds of bright girdle, 714b
like warrior taking rest, 566b
me down in peace, 17a
me down to bleed, 1087b
me down to sleep, 1089b
me on anvil O God, 948b
nature's l. idiot, 307a
not flattering unction, 264a

Lay not up treasures, 40b
on Macduff, 287a
Pelion on Ossa, 66a
proud usurpers low, 496a
simple heartfelt l., 622a
sleeping head my love, 1060a
them down in their dens, 21b
till next day there she l., 499b
unpremeditated l., 518a
up treasures in heaven, 40b
upon thy lips, 288b
waste our powers, 515b
Layer upon layer city, 1035a
Layer-up, ill l. of beauty, 245a
Layeth beams of his chambers, 21a
Lays, constructing tribal l., 874a
eggs for gentlemen, 1096b
Laziness, evasion not l., 1039a
impatience and l., 980b
no l. no procrastination, 719a
Lazy dog, 1101a
fokes' stummucks, 814a
geese like snow cloud, 1009b
leaden-stepping Hours, 339a
look for something to do, 439a
nonprogressive people, 1019b
Scheldt or wandering Po, 447b
Lea, slowly o'er the l., 440a
standing on pleasant l., 515b
sun has left the l., 521b
wind was on l., 974b
Lead apes in hell, 219a
bullets made of l., 1097b
but not master them, 73b
but to grave, 440a
easy to l., 540b
from death to immortality, 62a
heart of l., 413b
in traces l. 'em, 693b
kindly Light, 597b
lapped in l., 309a
little child shall l. them, 31a
me from darkness to light, 62a
me from unreal to real, 62a
me to rock higher than I, 19b
me Zeus and Fate, 103b
my steps aright, 574b
road rail pig l., 947b
sea of l. sky of slate, 878b
sky like l., 1060b
take l. in all things, 63b
tears scald like molten l., 280a
thee to thy grave, 515a
there shall thy hand l. me, 23a
these graces to grave, 251b
those that are with young, 32a
to more than common land, 697b
us not into temptation, 40b
wild-goose chase, 194b
ye who l. take heed, 899a
Leaden army conquers world, 871a
death, 405a
feet, 771b
if I use l. ones, 901b
scepter, 399a
Leaden-eyed despairs, 582b
Leaden-stepping, lazy l. Hours, 339a
Leader and commander to people, 33a
because of not daring to be ahead, 75a
educator wielder of power, 1068a
leaves conviction in others, 1013a

Line, lives along the l., 103a
  Marlowe's mighty l., 303b
  most insincere l. written, 1000a
  not a day without a l., 102a
  of horizon's growing thin, 1066a
  second l. sublime third bombast, 144a
  Shakespeare never blotted l., 304a
  stepped across l., 587a
  thin red l. of 'eroes, 705a
  thin red-l. streak, 704b
  uniform motion in right l., 379b
  upon line, 32a
  will l. stretch out, 285b
  write a living l., 303b
Linea, nulla dies sine l., 102a
Lineage, proud old l., 980a
Lineaments, molded changing l., 781a
  of Gospel books, 314b
  of gratified desire, 488b
Lined himself with hope, 241b
Linen, not l. wearing out, 592b
  old l. wash whitest, 314b
  wash dirty l. at home, 504a
Liner she's a lady, 874b
Lines are fallen unto me, 17a
  as l. so loves oblique, 360a
  deathless l. ahem, 962b
  desert of a thousand l., 412a
  drawing no unnecessary l., 900b
  let lord once own happy l., 403b
  many l. in dial's center, 243a
  my l. and life are free, 323a
  paint shadows in imaginary l., 210b
  rain in slanting l., 740a
  silken l. silver hooks, 306a
  supply l. guarded by navy, 1026a
  these hedgerows little l., 509a
  town crier spoke my l., 262b
  silver l. on the night, 336b
  wholly consisted of l. like these, 740b
  zones and meridian l., 746b
Linge, laver son l. sale, 504a
Linger, do not live but l., 310b
  many a fall l. near, 500b
  on flathouse roof, 1069a
  out a purposed overthrow, 293a
  unhappy l. a space, 994b
Lingered under benign sky, 685b
Lingering bays, 426b
  dewdrop, 517b
  hoping l. flying, 404a
  I alone sit l. here, 362b
  longing l. look behind, 441a
  winter l. chills May, 447b
Lingers, borrowing only l. it out, 241b
  find where last rose l., 121b
  no falsehood l. to old age, 83a
  one who l. behind, 63b
  soul that l. sighing, 853b
  wisdom l., 647b
Lingo, unless you know l., 592a
Lining, silver l., 917a
  silver l. on the night, 336b
Link, I feel the l. of nature, 348a
  silver l. silken tie, 518b
Linked analogies, 697a
  sweetness long drawn out, 335a
  to radiant angel l., 259b
  with one virtue, 558b

Links, golf l. lie so near mill, 940b
Linnet, flutter like the l., 1083b
  never tear l. from leaf, 882b
Linnet's, evening full of l. wings, 879b
Linnets, pipe but as l., 650a
Linsey-woolsey brother, 352b
Linsey-woolsey brothers, 413b
Lint, invisible strand of l., 864a
Lintel low to keep out pride, 827b
  of the year, 1057b
Lion among ladies, 230a
  and cock, 945a
  and fatling together, 31a
  and lizard keep, 629b
  and unicorn, 1092b
  as l. woos his brides, 445a
  at the door, 1092a
  be l. to frighten wolves, 177b
  beard l. in his den, 519b
  devil as roaring l., 57a
  every l. cometh forth, 3b
  first beast like a l., 57b
  first l. thought last a bore, 530b
  from his toenail a l., 150b
  he has heart of a l., 149b
  honey in the carcass of the l., 11b
  hungry l. grievous roar, 530b
  in the way, 26a
  in thy house, 37b
  Indian of l. bearing, 566b
  is in the streets, 26a
  lamb at home l. in chase, 508a
  light is the l. that comes to drink, 956a
  living dog better than dead l., 28b
  mated by the l., 269b
  more horrible than l., 1067a
  not l. but pard, 990b
  not more fearful wildfowl than l., 230a
  not so fierce as they paint him, 324b
  now the old l. is dead, 476b
  on old stone gates, 645a
  only l. and cock, 945a
  prince imitate fox and l., 177b
  prince must be l., 136b
  righteous are bold as a l., 26b
  rouse l. from his lair, 521b
  rouse l. than start hare, 238b
  shall eat straw, 31a
  thou shalt tread upon the l., 20b
  vapor like bear or l., 288b
  well roared L., 230b
  when l. fawns upon lamb, 216b
  wine, 599a
  wrath of l. wisdom of God, 487b
  young l. and the dragon, 20b
Lion's, hardy as Nemean l. nerve, 259b
  patch l. skin with fox's, 136b
  saw l. shadow ere himself, 235a
  there the l. ruddy eyes, 487a
  thou wear l. hide, 236a
Lions, bears and l. growl, 396a
  cast Daniel into the den of l., 35a
  cocks and l. jocund be, 306b
  if l. had hands, 70b
  my darling from the l., 18b
  no compacts between l. and men, 64b

Lions, plucks dead l. by beard, 236a
  stronger than l., 12b
  young l. roar after prey, 21b
Lip, between cup and l., 311b
  contempt and anger of l., 252b
  coral l. admires, 327a
  hair on upper l., 1011b
  language in her l., 269a
  not l. or eye beauty call, 403a
  of hand of foot of l., 293b
  reproof on her l., 589a
  stiff upper l., 722b
  vermeil-tinctured l., 337b
Lips, apply polished l. to ear, 536a
  are dumb, 645b
  betwixt her l. and mine, 889b
  causing l. of those asleep to speak, 29b
  closed l. hurt no one, 137a
  coral more red than l., 294b
  crimson in l. and cheeks, 225b
  eternity was in our l., 287a
  fitted in thy l., 25b
  flattereth with his l., 25b
  forbid to speak, 587b
  had I a hundred l., 119a
  her l. suck forth my soul, 213b
  here hung those l., 265b
  his swords are, 205a
  keep from slips, 812b
  keep thy l. from speaking guile, 18b
  kiss my soul through my l., 213b
  lay upon thy l., 288b
  love at the l., 927b
  man of unclean l., 30b
  names of God upon l., 436a
  of a strange woman drop as honeycomb, 23b
  of bereaved lover, 643b
  of dying men, 712b
  of inebriated virtue, 776a
  oh that l. had language, 459b
  once sanctified by hers, 631a
  open thou my l., 19a
  people of unclean l., 30b
  persuasion hung upon l., 437b
  poverty to the very l., 275b
  profound and fragile l., 1031a
  put l. to it when dispoged, 670b
  red l. not so red, 1028b
  rosy l. and cheeks, 294a
  say God be pitiful, 617b
  slughorn to my l. I set, 278b
  smile on l. tear in eye, 519b
  sweet voice sweet l., 581a
  take O take those l. away, 271b
  talk of the l. tendeth to penury, 24b
  that are for others, 648b
  that touch, 1010b
  that touch liquor, 886a
  thick eyes triangular, 978b
  touch l. part with tears, 774b
  touch sacred fire, 906b
  truth from his l., 449b
  two pairs of l., 1086a
  until moss reached l., 736a
  weary l. I close, 442a
  were red looks free, 525a
  when I ope my l., 231b
  where my Julia's l. smile, 320a
  whispering with white l., 556a
  with l. he travaileth, 773a
  wrung life dry for your l., 774a

Lips, you shall live on our l., 1014b
Lipstick, too much l., 1052a
Liquefaction of her clothes, 321a
Liquefies drop by drop, 1057a
Liquid, bedewed with l. odors, 120b
dew of youth, 258b
fire, 501a
history, 846a
inventing l. wine, 85a
lapse of murmuring streams, 347a
notes close eye of day, 339b
siftings fall, 1002a
Liquidation of British Empire, 924a
Liquor, bumper of good l., 481a
claret the l. for boys, 433a
corn l. stop victim's watch, 940b
drank l. straight, 1060a
good l., 450b
is quicker, 1051b
lips that touch l., 886a
livelier l. than Muse, 853b
never brewed, 734b
talks mighty loud, 814a
Liquor's out why clink cannikin 62b
Liquors, hot and rebellious l., 247b
Lisp and wear strange suits, 250a
of leaves, 772b
Lisped, I l. in numbers, 410b
somewhat he l., 166a
to me low delicious word, 701b
Lisping of human soul, 599b
Lissom clerical printless toe, 993b
List, I've got a little l., 768a
then the l. is done, 736a
thinning l. of single men, 1036b
'Listed, legion never was 'l., 874a
Listen all day to such stuff, 743b
and save, 337b
as I am listening now, 570b
awhile ye nations, 579b
darkling I l., 582b
didn't l. to him, 974b
do not l. simply wait, 980b
for dear honor's sake, 337b
fur'z you look or l., 693a
go and l. as thou goest, 161a
gods to him particularly l., 62b
good music people don't l., 840a
heath slowly awake and l., 783a
my children, 623b
not l. to reason, 656b
remain sitting and l., 980b
there's a hell of good universe, 1032a
to it and do not hear, 74a
to it growling, 1067b
to little bird's voice, 91a
to the mockingbird, 728a
where thou art sitting, 337b
wind is rising, 990a
wish him to l., 791b
Listened and looked sideways up, 525a
light l., 1065b
soul l. intensely, 516b
Listener, good l. gets to know something, 941a
speak to unwilling l., 145b
Listening, and to my l. ear, 516b
disease of not l., 241b
mood seemed to stand, 520a

Listening, nightly to l. earth, 393a
planets in stations l., 347a
to himself appears, 404a
Listens, he l. well who takes notes, 160b
larkspur l., 652b
like three years' child, 524b
Listeth, wind bloweth where it l., 48a
Lit upon gentle sensitive mind, 882a
Litany, Lovers' L., 871b.
Literalists of the imagination, 996a
Literary, among our l. scenes, 981a
attempt unfortunate, 434b
craftsmanship, 997a
fellow travelers, 957b
German dives into sentence, 761b
ideals animate my breast, 797b
improved for l. conversation, 310a
indignation at l. wrongs, 528b
intellectuals at one pole, 1058b
men a priesthood, 575b
nature and civilization l. field, 797b
parole of l. men, 433b
performance, 703b
weather l. speciality, 761b
Literature a phase of life, 996a
all else is l., 808a
belong to sacred l., 1035a
best half trade half art, 859b
Bible l. not dogma, 867b
books not American l., 656a
classicist in l., 1008a
clear and cold, 987a
Clemens was Lincoln of l., 772a
complete statement l., 975a
create new l., 1019a
current l. of day, 756b
defect of modern l., 712b
effort to indemnify, 607a
enfant terrible of l., 756b
for l. call back world of shadows, 993a
gives no man sinecure, 988b
good l. must do good, 855a
great l. allegorical, 918a
impurities of l., 975a
in l. read oldest, 601b
investment of genius, 770b
is something dead, 986b
keep up with current l., 886a
language charged with meaning, 989a
life before l., 755a
little or great l., 816b
modern American l. from one book, 1044b
my mistress, 858b
my utopia, 958b
never pursue l. as trade, 528b
news that stays news, 989b
noble sentiments in bad l., 897b
not abstract science, 866b
out of life, 772a
patronize polite l., 462a
reduced to essence, 909b
remarks are not l., 933b
sanity in ancient l., 712b
substitute for religion, 1007b
to produce a little l., 798a
true-blue professor of l., 986b
with l. as with law, 641b
without charm no l., 879a

Literature written in American way, 898a
Literatures, effort of l. critical 713a
knowledge of different l., 828a
Lithe, I asked a l. lady, 488a
Litigious terms fat contentions, 340a
Litter, cities hideous by l., 1063a
Littérature, beaux sentiments de la l., 897b
Little, a l. I can read, 287a
a l. more than kin, 257a
advantages every day, 423b
ah l. they think, 541b
all minds are l., 780b
better is l. with the fear of the Lord, 24b
better than one of wicked, 238a
black sheep, 873b
body with mighty heart, 243b
Bo-peep, 1095b
boy blue, 1093b
Boy Blue kissed them, 820b
boys made of, 1096b
breezes shiver, 645b
brother of rich, 835b
but l. at a time, 390a
candle throws beams, 235b
care we, 660b
cares that fretted, 1101a
cargo boats, 874b
child shall lead them, 31a
creature formed of joy, 490b
creatures everywhere, 974b
dear l. Buttercup, 765b
deeds of kindness, 719b
do great right l. wrong, 234b
dogs and all, 279a
drops of water, 719b
earn a l. spend a l. less, 825a
every l. makes a mickle, 196a
fall by l. and l., 38a
fire quickly trodden out, 216a
fly, 489a
foxes that spoil the vines, 29b
friend of all the world, 875b
gain l. patch of ground, 264b
girl don't cry, 819a
girls made of, 1096b
go l. book, 165b, 962b
goodness in l. finger, 390b
graves in l. magazines, 981a
great empire and l. minds, 453b
great love goes here with l. gift, 104a
great ones eat up l. ones, 290b
group of willful men, 842a
happy if say how much, 246a
have and seek no more, 192a
having been a l. chastised, 36b
heads so l. no room for wit, 333b
here a l. and there a l., 32a
here a l. child I stand, 321a
hills like lambs, 22a
hoard l. hearts great, 653a
horse think it queer, 927b
how l. gained, 650b
how l. one knows oneself, 1016a
how l. room we take in death, 327b
how l. we think of other, 764b
hunted hares, 906a
I ask my wants are few, 634a
I know owe to ignorance, 985a
if thou have but a l., 36b
Indian Sioux or Crow, 823b
infinite riches in l. room, 212b

Lord God is subtle, 951a
 God made them all, 684b
 God of Hosts, 875b
 God planted a garden, 5b
 God send high wave, 909a
 God walking in garden, 5b
 God we paid in full, 875a
 good L. deliver us, 60b, 1098b
 good L. had only ten, 786a
 Gracious L. bomb Germans,
  1059a
 great and dreadful day of the
  L., 36a
 handkerchief of L., 700a
 hath chosen thee, 10a
 hath taken away, 14a
 have mercy on us, 59a, 300b
 hear me out, 1066b
 hear word of the L., 34b
 help 'em how I pities all, 517b
 holy is the L. of hosts, 30b
 how discourse is of death, 375b
 how long, 30b
 how world given to lying, 241a
 I believe, 45b
 I heard the voice of the L., 30b
 I replied My L., 323b
 I were l. in May, 774b
 I will sing unto the L., 8b
 if you had horse, 986a
 in glance of the L., 559a
 in the morning hear, 396b
 is a man of war, 8b
 is come, 397a
 is good, 21a
 is in his holy temple, 36a
 is in this place, 7a
 is it I, 44b
 is my helper, 56a
 is my light, 18a
 is my rock, 12b
 is my shepherd, 17b
 is my strength and shield, 18a
 is my strength and song, 8b
 is nigh unto them that call, 23a
 is risen, 59b
 is the strength of my life, 18a
 is thy keeper, 22a
 is thy shade, 22a
 is with thee, 45b
 it but a day, 813a
 Jehovah Jove or L., 421b
 kingdoms of our L., 58a
 king's our only l., 211a
 know ye that the L. he is God,
  21a
 land which the L. giveth thee,
  9a
 lendeth unto the L., 25a
 lift up his countenance, 9b
 looketh on the heart, 12a
 love the L. with all thine heart,
  10a
 made all to prosper, 7b
 make a joyful noise unto the
  L., 21a
 make his face shine upon thee,
  9b
 make me an instrument, 157a
 make my enemies ridiculous,
  417b
 Mayor of London, 1085b
 mercy on Thy people L., 875b
 methought what pain to drown,
  217a
 my help cometh from the L.,
  22a
 my soul doth magnify L., 45b
 name of the L. in vain, 9a

Lord neat and trimly dressed,
  238a
 not everyone that saith L., 41b
 not tempt the L. your God, 10a
 O L. if there is a L., 722a
 O L. my God I have trusted,
  192b
 of all yet prey to all, 409a
 of far-flung battle line, 875a
 of folded arms, 221b
 of heaven and earth, 50a
 of himself, 300b, 558b
 of hosts he is the King of glory,
  18a
 of living and dead, 802b
 of lords, 58b
 of the ocean, 84b
 of yourself, 371b
 once own happy lines, 403b
 patient unto coming of L., 56b
 praise L. pass ammunition,
  1062a
 pray L. soul to keep, 1089b
 precious in the sight of the L.,
  22a
 prepare way of L., 32b, 39b
 preserve thee, 22a
 preserve thy going and coming,
  22a
 raise me up I trust, 199b
 reason L. makes so many, 639b
 reigneth, 21a
 replied O L. Thou art, 444a
 rib which L. God had taken, 5b
 Savior which is Christ the L.,
  46a
 searcheth all hearts, 14a
 secret things belong unto the
  L., 10b
 seeth not as man, 12a
 servant in love l. in marriage,
  16ga
 servant not above l., 42a
 serve the L. with gladness, 21a
 set a mark upon Cain, 6a
 short life in saddle L., 860a
 showed me so I did see, 364a
 sitting upon a throne, 30b
 sole l. taking captive, 3b
 Spirit of the L. shall rest upon
  him, 31a
 support us all day long, 598a
 swear to L., 1050b
 sword of the L. and of Gideon,
  11a
 taste and see that the L. is
  good, 18b
 through this hour, 1103a
 thy God is with thee, 10b
 wait upon the L., 32b
 was not in the wind the earthquake the fire, 13b
 watch between me and thee,
  7a-b
 we are as L. made us, 891b
 went before them, 8b
 what fools these mortals be,
  230a
 what would they say, 881b
 where dear L. crucified, 684b
 whom the L. loveth he chasteneth, 56a
 whose hope the L. is, 34a
 will wipe away tears, 31b
 with me abide, 567a
 woman that feareth the L., 27a
 word of the L. endureth, 56b
 worship the L. in beauty of holiness, 18a

Lordly, butter in a l. dish, 11a
 cedar green with boughs, 827a
 name is, 643a
Lord's Anointed, 1090b
 anointed temple, 284a
 earth is the L., 18a, 52a
 it is the L. passover, 8b
 name is to be praised, 22a
 sing the L. song, 22b
 who is on the L. side, 9a
Lords and ladies of Byzantium,
  883a
 and owners of their faces, 293a
 but breath of kings, 492b
 gude Scots l., 1087b
Lord of l., 58b
 masters l. and rulers, 826b
 neither l. nor shogun, 740a
 not kings and l., 545a
 o' the creation, 493a
 of hell, 650b
 of humankind pass by, 447b
 of it all, 1022b
 of ladies intellectual, 560a
 princes and l., 449a
 Scots l. at his feet, 1087b
 seemed l. of all, 345a
 who lay ye low, 570a
 wit among l., 430a
 women who love their l., 445a
Lordships', dance attendance on l.
  pleasures, 299b
Lore, admire virtue follow not
  her l., 348b
 Christ's l. and his apostles
  twelve, 166b
 gives me mystical l., 538a
 Heaven rejects the l., 517a
 volume of forgotten l., 642b
Lorena, years creep slowly L.,
  724a
Lorn, lone l. creetur, 671a
Lorries, monotonously l. sway,
  1040b
Lose and neglect creeping hours,
  248b
 comfort or money too, 932a
 convictions to win or l., 912a
 freedom if value something
  more, 932a
 gain world l. soul, 43a
 good we oft might win, 270a
 has no wits to l., 455a
 having nothing nothing l., 216a
 he that findeth life shall l. it,
  42a
 he who doesn't l. wits, 455a
 his child's-heart, 100a
 I would not l. you, 233b
 if once we l. this light, 302b
 it in moment you detect, 406a
 it that buy it with care, 231a
 itself in sky, 665b
 knife ill-used l. edge, 293a
 lest we l. Edens, 663b
 life nothing much to l., 854b
 myself in a mystery, 329b
 myself in other minds, 535b
 name of action, 262a
 natural kindness, 882b
 never l. touch of the one, 861a
 nobly save meanly l., 638b
 nor l. common touch, 877a
 nothing to but chains, 687a
 one life to l. for country, 484b
 our ventures, 256a
 play to win toil to l., 900a
 some day l. them all, 674a
 some l. their way, 734a

Love, harmony is pure l., 211a
hate one and l. other, 41a
hate traitors treason l., 370b
hath so long possessed me, 159a
hatred as well as l., 436b
he bore to learning, 449b
he was all for l., 475b
he will then l. me, 487a
he's my l. forevermore, 1098a
hearts in l. use own tongues, 245b
heaven is l., 518b
her till I die, 1086a
herself not there, 1056b
hid in heart of l., 880a
Highlands forever I l., 494b
him and let him know, 809a
him because my child, 861a
him most for enemies, 728a
him who in l. of nature, 574a
his banner over me was l., 29a
history of woman's life, 502b
hold your tongue and let me l., 305a
hope faith and l., 497a
hope nor l. nor friend, 824a
hopeth all things, 52b
hot and cold fareth l., 175b
how do I l. thee, 618b
how left the ancient l., 486b
how should I true l. know, 265a
how they could l., 1101b
how vast a memory has L., 402b
human l. seen at its height, 951b
humanity i l. you, 1030b
hunt l. down together, 774b
I am sick of l., 29a
I and my true l., 1099a
I both l. and do not l., 70a
I hate and I l., 115a
I l. a lass, 476a
I l. a lassie, 903a
I l. broad margin to life, 683a
I l. everything old, 450b
I loathe that I did l., 187a
I seemed to lose, 618b
I taught thee to l., 307a
I told my l., 488a
idea of two sexes, 1033a
if ever thou shalt l., 252a
if I l. you what business of yours, 477b
if l. were what rose is, 774b
if music food of l., 251a
if no l. is what feel I so, 164b
if she l. me this believe, 318b
if she will not l., 350a
if thou must l. me, 618a
if world and l. were young, 198b
if You wish for our l., 989b
I'm in l. with janitor's boy, 1069a
in a golden bowl, 486b
in a hut, 581b
in idleness, 229b
in it was l. and desire, 64a
in l. illusion reaches zenith, 806a
in l. things different, 806a
in l. two solitudes touch, 938b
in l. with American names, 1041b
in l. with loving, 146b
in law and l. same, 680a
in my bosom like a bee, 204b
in others they l. l., 356b

Love, in our will to l. or not, 346b
in spite of darkness, 305b
in summer's wonderland, 961b
in the frost, 1070a
inestimable l., 60b
infinite l., 774a
innocence of l., 252a
irresistible desire, 930a
is a boy, 353a
is a mood to man, 825b
is a sickness full of woes, 211a
is agreement, 211a
is all there is, 739a
is blind, 168b, 233a
is dead, 203b
is enough, 753a
is flowerlike, 527b
is fulfilling of law, 51b
is heaven, 518b
is intercourse between tyrants and slaves, 448b
is kind, 52b
is left alone, 646a
is like measles, 685a, 855b
is most beautiful among gods, 67a
is most nearly itself, 1006a
is not all, 1024a
is not love which alters, 294a
is only meaning, 1041a
is strong as death, 30a
is the whole, 1031b
is then our duty, 401b
it and who shall dare, 686a
it would conceal, 527b
itself have rest, 559b
itself slumber on, 572b
jealousy born with l., 356a
joy and l. triumphing, 344b
joy nor l. nor light, 715a
joy of l. too short, 175a
jumps from admiration to l., 533a
keep corner in thing I l., 274b
kelson of creation l., 700a
kill things they do not l., 234a
kill your joys with l., 225b
kindled by virtue, 161b
kindness shall win my l., 219b
King without woman I l., 1034a
know the l. betwixt us, 358a
knoweth no laws, 183a
known l. how bitter, 774a
knows nothing of order, 145a
labor of l., 54b
laggard in l., 519b
last not least in l., 255a
law to itself, 148a
lay aside long-cherished l., 115a
learn to bear beams of l., 487a
lease of my true l., 293b
least that let men know, 220b
leave me O L., 203b
leaving l. behind, 737a
lest thy l. prove variable, 224a
let l. who never loved, 150a
let me l. river and woodland, 117a
let thy l. be younger, 252a
let us be true, 714b
let us live and l., 114b, 300a
let us surrender to l., 117a
let warm l. in, 583b
life eternal l. immortal, 785a
light dies when l. done, 826b
light l. life, 475a
like a dizziness, 508a
like death levels, 601a

Love, like everybody not in l., 907b
like measles, 685a, 855b
like ours never die, 871b
liken l. to summer and winter, 175b
little l. come to me, 944b
little words of l., 719b
live and l. in God's light, 178a
live with me and be my l., 212a, 306a
live with thee and be thy l., 198b
lodged in woman's breast, 300b
long l. doth so, 224b
long life better than figs, 287b
look at enemies with l., 375a
look at was to l., 647a
look of l. alarms, 488b
looked as she did l., 581a
looks not with eyes, 228b
lose power to l., 675b
lose thy l. lose all, 405b
lost l. and loathing, 1054a
lost to l. and truth, 873b
lover, 606b
lovers who l. do not write, 802a
lovers' quarrels renewal of l., 108a
loving all that l. me, 634b
lyric l. half angel, 667a
makes l. at all seasons, 1102a
makes world go round, 744b, 768a, 1105b
makes young, 351a
man in l. endures more, 806a
mankind except American, 432b
man's l. apart from life, 560a
many waters cannot quench l., 30a
marriage from which l. gone, 1054b
marriage without l., 421b
martyrs honor slain, 708b
May never month of l., 210a
may perfectly l. thee, 60b
me in December, 796a
me little love me long, 320a, 1084b
me not for grace, 1086a
me sure to die, 543a
medicines to make me l. him, 238b
men died but not for l., 250a
men hope and l., 477a
Mercy Pity Peace and L., 487a
met you not with my true l., 198b
mie l. ys dedde, 482a
mighty pain to l., 357b
ministers of l., 526b
mischievous devil, 756b
mistress to the man I l., 405b
moderately, 224b
money rage and l., 1057a
money the sinew of l., 104b
moody food of l., 288a
more cruel than lust, 773b
more l. less we flatter, 361a
more libertines than l., 436a
more than l., 644a
more true than l. to me, 1085a
most important business, 551a
music food of l., 251a, 288a
music thing I l. most, 375b
must have wings, 900a
my home of l., 293b
my hope my hap my l., 193b
my hope my l., 332b

Means and leisure civilizers, 612b
appliances and m. to boot, 242a
bad m. and bad men, 467a
by all the m. you can, 421a
by any m. get wealth, 412a
by fair m. if you can, 123a
changes by peaceful m., 865a
content with small m., 655b
dumb sense of what life m.,
  795a
end must justify the m., 387b
fair m. or foul, 971b
find m. of evil, 342a
First Amendment m. what it
  says, 991b
for every man alive, 270a
game that never m. anything,
  1037b
give enemies m. of our destruction, 76b
God placed in our power, 465a
heaven finds m. to kill joys,
  225b
if all m. permitted to fight evil,
  1011a
it m. mischief, 263a
justifying m. by the end, 145a
liberty as end and m., 832b
live within m., 751a
love not say all it m., 900a
love of money as m., 977a
make money by any m., 123a
mercy of his m., 1070b
not but blunders round meaning, 410b
of destruction hitherto unknown, 982b
of production, 686b
requisite to ends, 485a
take m. whereby I live, 235a
thanks for m. of grace. 60b
that wins easiest victory, 1011b
to achieve great ends, 1016a
to do ill deeds, 237a
to make us one, 306b
war political relations by other
  m., 544b
what beauty m., 867a
what deep heart m., 1057b
what I choose it to mean, 746b
Meant, more m. than meets ear,
  336a
well tried a little, 825a
Measles and if so how many, 751a
love is like m., 685a, 855b
Measure every wandering planet's
  course, 212a
fervor with m., 796a
keep our m., 716a-b
last full m. of devotion, 639a
life moving to one m., 945a
man is m. of all things, 87a
mind's height, 661b
my judgment approves m., 463a
narrow m. spans, 854a
observe due m., 68a
of my days, 18b
of torment measure of youth,
  873b
shrunk to this little m., 255a
takes right m. of self, 564b
teach his feet a m., 774b
there is m. in all things, 120a
three with new song's m., 807b
turns everything to m., 1056b
what you are speaking about,
  723a
with what m. ye mete, 41a
Measured by my soul, 396a

Measured, choice word m.
  phrase, 512a
it shall be m. to you, 41a
language, 649b
motion, 510a
out my life with coffee spoons,
  1000b
Measureless, caverns m. to man,
  523b
rhythms m. and wild, 84b
shut up in m. content, 283a
Measures, in short m. life perfect
  be, 304a
Lydian m., 371b
not men, 415a, 449a
not men but m., 452a
to impose one style, 1028a
Measuring earth and heaven, 95b
Meat, as egg is full of m., 224b
born a roaster of m., 484b
buys opinions like m., 756b
cannot eat but little m., 188b
crazy salad with m., 882b
dined upon cold m., 375b
drink and cloth to us, 181b
flowers in garden m. in hall,
  165b
God sends m. Devil sends cooks,
  183a
hungered and ye gave m., 44a
hungry and he gave him in.,
  445b
in due season, 21b
is not life more than m., 41a
made worms' m. of me, 225a
mean as cat's m., 932a
mock m. it feeds on, 274a
my m. eats me, 1065a
no stomach for such m., 782b
not m. but appetite, 350b
not m. nor drink, 1024a
on our m. and on us all, 321a
one appointed to buy m., 317b
one man's poison another's m.,
  114a
out of the eater came m., 11b
outdid the m., 320b
provideth her m. in the summer, 23b
seek their m. from God, 21b
sendeth mouth sendeth m., 183a
sit down and taste my m., 324a
sleep is m. to hungry, 197a
snewed of m. and drynke, 166b
some hae m. canna eat, 495b
strong m. to them of full age,
  55b
this dish of m. too good, 326b
upon what m. Caesar feed, 253b
was locusts and wild honey, 39b
we are fish and m., 889a
we hae m. we can eat, 495b
went without the m., 900a
within requisite, 737b
Meatpacker, talent of m., 896b
Meats, funeral baked m., 258a
of all m. soonest cloy, 357b
Mecca, turn thy face towards M.,
  148b
Mechanic, lawyer without history
  a m., 520b
long m. pacings, 646a
made poetry m. art, 456b
mere m. operation, 353b
sad m. exercise, 649b
Mechanical equivalent of heat,
  795b
slavery future of world, 840b
Mechanician, visible sage m., 686a

Mechanics, bicycle m. from Dayton, 1036a
farmers m. and laborers, 503a
of culture, 894b
reduced to atomic m., 752b
reduction of nature to m., 723b
Mechanism, battles by m., 577a
Mechanisms, vital m. have object,
  675a
Mechanized armies, 923a
automation, 568a
Med, bloweth m., 1083a
Medal, bright hard m., 799b
Med'cinable gum, 276b
Meddle, inclination to m., 539b
not with him that flattereth,
  25b
wise men m. in commonwealth,
  178b
Meddles with cold iron, 200a
Meddling, every fool will be m.,
  25a
Mede, of all the floures in the m.,
  165b
Medea gathered enchanted herbs,
  235a
Medes, crushed the gold-bearing
  M., 70b
law of the M. and Persians, 35a
Mediator, painting m. between
  world and us, 964b
president mostly a m., 1068a
Mediatory, reconciling m. power,
  528a
Mediatress, art m. between nature
  and man, 529b
Medici, Miniver loved M., 899b
Medicinable gum, 276b
some griefs are m., 290b
Medicine bundles, 1077b
desire to take m. distinguishes
  man from animals, 817a
doeth good like m., 25a
faith and knowledge in m.,
  565a
for case like mine, 703b
for life which has fled, 70a
for mental disorders, 1034b
for misery, 85a
has to examine disease, 136b-
  137a
in m. common sense master,
  565a
in m. sins of commission
  mortal, 434a
labors to destroy own existence,
  778a
live by m. live horribly, 425a
more harmful than disease,
  1020b
my lawful wife, 858b
no m. but hope, 271a
of life, 37b
paid seven percent, 522a
taught by gods, 537a
thee to sweet sleep, 274b
truth in m. difficult, 564b
worse than malady, 125b
Medicine Hat, war bonnet of M.,
  1041b
Medicines to make me love him,
  238b
to make women speak, 802a
Medicos marveling sweetly, 1009b
Medieval hand, 767a
Medio tutissimus ibis, 128b
Mediocre, if you are m. and grovel, 460a
minds, 356a

Men, fifteen m. on Dead Man's Chest, 822b
find me m. who care, 741a
finds too late m. betray, 448b
first subjects afterward, 680b
fishers of m., 39b
flourish only for a moment, 67a
foolery wise·m. have, 247a
fools laugh at m. of sense, 381b
foot of unfamiliar m., 714a
forty thousand m., 1092b
fought by mothers of m., 790a
free m. free speech, 1099b
gear of foreign dead m., 1006a
get and give, 477a
get there first with most m., 709b
give place to better m., 328a
go armed to seek, 1022a
God give us m., 690b
God justifiable to m., 349a
God made mad, 918a
God these old m., 83b
gods fashioned by m., 867b
gods in likeness of m., 50a
goeth on to meet the armed m., 16b
good m. and true, 246b
good m. eat that they may live, 87b
good m. to do nothing, 454b
good will to m., 657b
good will toward m., 46a
Gotham's three wise m., 553a
government of laws not m., 463b
government of m. and newspapers, 658b
great city greatest m., 701a
great m. are not always wise, 16a
great m. contending with adversity, 311a
great m. light up time, 674b
great m. like torches, 674b
great m. make mistakes, 815b
great m. not scholars. 634a
group of willful m., 842a
grow into likeness of bad m., 96a
hanged that horses may not be stolen, 376b
hangin' m. and women, 1091a
happy breed of m., 226b
have died from time to time, 250a
have found thing to love, 918a
have lost their reason, 255b
have their price, 397b
heard old old m. say, 881a
heart of oak our m., 439a
heaven that leads m. to hell, 294b
His ways with m., 654a
history biography of great m., 577a
hit only what they aim at, 682b
hollow m., 1003a
homely m. charmed women, 864a
honest m. revolutionize, 681a
honest m. shaped conduct, 902b
honest m. with understanding, 472b
honor all m., 56b
hope and love, 477a
if all m. were just, 92a
if God punish m. according to what they deserve, 149a

Men, if m. are destroyed, 80b
if m. knew how women pass time, 863b
if m. like that wise bird, 810a
if m. unselfish as women, 813b
in catalogue ye go for m., 284a
in m. we various passions find, 406b
infants boys m. Ifs, 697b
keeping m. off keep them on, 401b
knocking around with m., 477a
know so little of m., 894b
label m. for God, 856b
labels that give name to event, 732a
land where m. are stones, 704b
laws not m., 463b
lead lives of desperation, 682a
let us die like m., 627b
let us praise famous m., 38b
let your light shine before m., 40a
light upon hearts of m., 497a
like m. undergo fatigue, 467a
like satyrs grazing, 212b
little group of willful m., 842a
live as m. not ostriches, 974a
live at level of great m., 829a
lived like fishes, 290b
lives of great m. remind us, 620b
lodging place of wayfaring m., 34a
looks quite through deeds of m., 253b
lost sight of horizons, 894a
love to speak of selves, 770b
made brutes m. m. divine, 721b
made m. and not made them well, 263a
made spectacle to m., 52a
make the city, 90b
makes m. mad, 276a
man that died for m., 778b
many deaths in m., 917b
masters of their fates, 253b
may come men may go, 652a
may read strange matters, 282a
measures not m., 415a, 449a
melancholy m. eat beans, 310b
melancholy m. most witty, 311a
men's m., 690a
merriest when from home, 243b
merry m. all, 1087b
met with erected look, 369b
mice and m., 492b
mighty m. of valor, 10b
mighty m. which were of old, 6b
mocks married m., 222b
more lonely among m., 683b
more m. killed by overwork, 872a
more nearly m. and women, 1038b
most m. eddy about, 715b
must be decided, 100a
must be taught, 403b
must endure their going, 280a
must work women weep, 690b
my m. like satyrs grazing, 212b
naturally in two parties, 473b
need of world of m., 663a
never be beloved by m., 590a
no compacts between lions and m., 64b
no country for old m., 882b

Men, no stander above m. and women, 700b
no two m. cannot be distinguished, 132b
no worse than best of m., 287b
nor blame the writings but the m., 403b
not fit that m. be compared with gods, 115a
not m. but laws, 463b
not m. but manners, 424a
not m. but measures, 452a
not m. you took them for, 246b
not similar are gods and m., 63a
not three good m. unhanged, 239a
nothing great without great m., 1016a
O miserable minds of m., 113b
O what m. dare do, 246b
of Athens, 50a
of courtly nurture, 721a
of culture true apostles, 716a
of despised race, 752a
of England wherefore plow, 570a
of few words best, 244a
of good will, 46a, 59a, 1015a
of ill judgment ignore good, 81a
of less value than gold, 178b
of like passions, 50a
of other minds, 447b
of philosophic temperament, 861a
of place and consequence, 899a
of polite learning, 386b
of renown, 6b
of stones, 280b
of the South, 943a
of weak nerves, 1038b
old m. are children, 91a
old m. from chimney corner, 203b
old m. garrulous by nature, 112a
old m. have rosy faces, 824b
old m. know when old man dies, 1052a
old m. know young m. fools, 205a
old m. ought to be explorers, 1006a
old m. should be explorers, 1065b
old m. shall dream dreams, 35b
older m. declare war, 931a
on shore interpreters, 905a
only great m. obscene, 850b
ought to mind business, 750a
our democratic public m., 837b
Oxford m. who went abroad to die, 969a
parole of literary m., 433b
persuade eyes of m. without orator, 220a
place where m. can pray, 919a
port liquor for m., 433a
practical m. absorbed in facts, 861a
practical m. usually slaves, 977a
praise famous m., 38b
preached as to dying m., 357a
princerples or m., 693a
private m. enjoy, 244b
prize the thing ungained, 267b
proper m. as ever trod, 253a
proud m. in old age, 82b

Men put enemy in their mouths, 274a
quit you like m., 53a
quit yourselves like m., 12a
rational spiritual beings, 1045b
ready booted and spurred, 362a
reason never failed m., 896b
reject prophets, 708b
rich m. rule the law, 448a
rise on steppingstones, 649b
rivalship of wisest m., 395b
roll of common m., 239b
room for honest m., 467a
sailors but m., 232a
saints aid if m. call, 524a
sandwich m. shuffling, 975a
savage m. uncouth manners, 452b
schemes of mice and m., 492b
school for making first-class m., 703a
search land of living m., 519a
see m. as trees walking, 45b
seldom make passes, 1029a
send m. who do work, 876b
sensible conscientious m., 430b
sensible m. never tell, 613a
sent not corn for rich m. only, 289b
shire for M. who Understand, 993b
should be what they seem, 274a
shut doors against setting sun, 290a
sing by land an' sea, 874a
single m. in barracks, 873a
sit and hear each other groan, 582b
six m. of Industan, 680a
slain a thousand m. with jawbone, 11b
slave to fate chance desperate m., 308a
sleek-headed m., 253b
small m. afraid of writings, 460b
small things make base m. proud, 215a
so many m. so many opinions, 109a
some m. love not a pig, 234a
some to pleasure take, 406b
sons of m. and angels say, 425a
speak with tongues of m., 52a
speech given to wise m., 376b
spirit of m. who follow, 987a
spirits of just m., 56a
strange that m. fear, 254b
strength of twenty m., 225b
strong m. shall bow themselves, 28b
studied m. from topsy-turvy close, 730a
such as sleep o' nights, 253b
such m. as dangerous, 253b
suffer the armed m., 1042a
swindled by other m., 1062b
take best they can get, 432b
talk of crabbed old m., 114b
talking of fall of man, 684a
text of m. and women, 850a
that are ruined, 454b
that hazard all, 233a
that laugh and weep, 775a
that sow and reap, 775a
that strove with gods, 646b
that were boys when I was a boy, 902a
there before us, 681b

Men, there He makes m., 548b
think all m. mortal but themselves, 399a
thoughts of m. decay, 201a
thoughts of m. widened, 647b
thousand m. that fishes gnaw, 217a
tide in affairs of m., 256a
tides of m., 1008b
to be leader of m., 850a
to m. a man is a mind, 791b
to match mountains, 826b
tongues of m. and of angels, 52a
touched by heaven's virtue, 378b
traced lives of good m., 517a
traveled among unknown m., 510b
truest of m. Man of Sorrows, 697a
trust ears less than eyes, 86b
truth on lips of dying m., 712b
truths not for all m., 417b
turn one's back on m., 850a
twelve honest m., 399b
twenty m. crossing bridge, 955a
two m. of all mankind, 899b
two m. went up to pray, 354a
two strong m. face to face, 872b
upon the hearts of m., 497a
uselessness of m. above sixty, 817b
vexes public m., 647b
waken and stand, 4a
war between m. and women, 1033a
wars planned by old m., 962a
wars won by m., 987a
waster of rich m., 82a
watch the m. at play, 940b
ways of God to m., 341b
we are m. my liege, 284a
we are the stuffed m., 1003a
we petty m., 253b
we will die free m., 475a
were deceivers ever, 246a
we've got the m., 727a
what is it m. in women require, 488b
what m. call treasure, 694a
what m. or gods these, 583a
what mothers made them, 608a
what you and other m. think, 253b
whatever you stuff m. with they bear, 684b
whatsoever ye would m. do, 41a
when bad m. combine, 452a
when force subdues men, 99b
when good m. die, 85b
when m. and mountains meet, 490b
when m. drink they are rich, 90b
when old m. gather, 900b
where dead m. lost bones, 1002b
where race of m. go by, 846a
which ordinary m. fit for, 277a
who are not historians, 952a
who borrow men who lend, 534b
who can't be bought, 948b
who do the work, 876b
who drown, 430a
who have a sense of honor, 64a
who know much say little, 436a
who march away, 784a

Men who possess opinions, 690b
who say It can't be done, 887a
whom lust of office not kill, 690b
whom men condemn as ill, 789b
whose heads do grow beneath their shoulders, 272b
whose visages do cream, 231a
why don't m. propose, 587b
why men behave like apes, 994b
willful m., 842a
willingly believe what they wish, 112a
wise m. from the east, 39a
wise m. in great struggle, 464b
wise m. meddle in commonwealth, 178b
wise m. of Gotham, 1094a
wise m. profit more from fools, 107a
wise m. shun mistakes of fools, 107a
wisest m. have erred, 349a
wish m. everywhere free, 638b
with firebrand in hand, 172a
with knives in brains, 608b
with mothers and wives, 592b
with muckrake, 848a
with passion for anonymity, 971b
with sisters dear, 592b
with Splendid Hearts, 993b
women and clergymen, 523a
women and Herveys, 414a
women and professors, 939a
women better or worse than m., 382a
women foolish to match m., 689b
women try luck m. risk it, 839b
women wiser than m., 975a
won by m. with courage, 90a
wonder m. trust selves with m., 290a
words are women deeds m., 325a
worth a thousand m., 520a
would be angels, 408a
write what m. do not what they ought, 207a
ye are brothers ye are m., 538a
ye m. of Athens, 50a
ye shall die like m., 20a
years perished to make us m., 771b
you are m. of stones, 280b
young m. all over world, 920a
young m. fitter to invent, 209a
young m. need stiffening, 835a
young m. regard elders as senile, 776b
young m. shall see visions, 35b
young m. think it is, 854b
young m. think old m. fools, 205a
youngsters read m. understand, 195b
Menace, atomic energy a m., 950b
Menaces, insolent m. of villains, 464b
Mencken Nathan and God, 966a
Mend anger and m. not, 412a
fences, 722b
it or be rid on it, 284b
knock breathe seek to m., 308a
never made for man to m., 372a
nor yet too vain to m., 404a
the heart, 404b
your speech a little, 276b

Moderator of passions, 326a
  reasonable m. Death, 329b
Modern, all history m., 957b
  American literature from one
    book, 1044b
  born empty into m. age, 378b
  characteristics of m. spirit, 863a
  disease of m. life, 712a
  inconveniences, 760b
  life economic, 957b
  man invents museum, 1035a
  old or m. bard, 336b
  one must be absolutely m., 830b
  origin of m. world, 1047a
  something for m. stage, 988a
  spite all m. notions, 874a
  wise saws and m. instances,
    249a
Moderns, speak of m. without
  contempt, 415b
Modes, for m. of faith, 409b
Modest and commonly chaste,
    564b
  coy submission m. pride, 345a
  doubt, 268a
  front of this small floor, 354b
  in speech, 72b
  keep m. as giver, 805a
  looks cottage adorn, 450b
  man with reason, 925a
  no more m. than immodest,
    700b
  quip m., 251a
  simple m. manly true, 694a
  stillness and humility, 243b
  the m. near to virtue, 72a
  wee m. crimson-tipped, 493a
  woman dressed in finery, 450b
Modesty a species of nobility,
    373b
  ancient sculpture true m., 552b
  and unselfishness, 987a
  maids in m. say No., 220b
  mine is blushing m., 128a
  overstep not m. of nature, 262b
  secondly m., 818b
  speaks without m., 72a
Modification, bad plan admits no
  m., 126a
Modify, time to m. shape, 763b
Modifying colors of imagination,
    529a
Modo liceat vivere est spes, 108b
Modum, servare m. finemque tenere, 716a
Modus, est m. in rebus, 120a
Moi, l'état c'est m., 378a
Moiling street, 898b
Moist, cold and hot m. and dry,
    369b
  eye dry hand, 241b
  hot cold m. and dry, 344a
  no more than m. hand, 955b
  star upon whose influence, 257a
  unpleasant body, 669b
Moisty morning, 1098a
Molar to molecular motions, 788a
Mold, emperors and cobblers in
  same m., 190a
  fresh from natur's m., 670b
  made him and then broke m.,
    178a
  of form, 262b
  rose above m., 593a
  splashing wintry m., 880b
Molded, best men m. of faults,
    272a
  changing lineaments, 781a
  heart m. as she pleases, 197b

Molded, scarcely formed or m.,
    562a
  two berries m. on one stem,
    230a
Moldering, a-m. in grave, 755a
Molders hemp and steel, 521a
Molding mighty fates, 899a
  wine jar when m. began, 124a
Molds, crack nature's m., 278a
  musket m. in his hands, 820b
Mole, live like velvet m., 990a
  wilt thou go ask the m., 486b
Molecular motions, 788a
Molecule, propensity to unite
  even in m., 965a
Molecules, by mathematics m.
  counted, 861a
  simple and indivisible m., 474b
Molehills from mountains made,
    1031a
Moles, cast his idols to m., 30a
Molle atque facetum, 120a
Mollify it with tears, 920b
Mollusk cheap edition of man,
    609a
Molly Stark a widow, 451b
Moloch sceptered king, 343a
Molten bowels, 917b
  inns of m. blue, 735a
  tears scald like m. lead, 280a
Mome raths outgrabe, 745a
Moment, courage of final m.,
    1072a
  culture m. of clarity, 977b
  dissolved in a m., 994b
  endurance for m. more, 809b
  endures m. or day, 883b
  eternity was in that m., 391b
  face some awful m., 515a
  first m. of atomic age, 1069b
  force m. to its crisis, 1001a
  great pith and m., 262a
  hide thyself for a little m., 32a
  hold every m. sacred, 937b
  I cut his throat, 1081a
  in a m. of time, 46b
  intense m. isolated, 1006a
  knew m. to say nothing, 839a
  lifetime burning in m., 1006a
  lived in paradise, 497b
  loyal and neutral in m., 284a
  men flourish only for a m., 67a
  never let up for single m., 983a
  not of action or inaction, 106a
  nothing startles beyond m.,
    584b
  of difficulty and danger, 1091b
  of greatness flicker, 1001a
  of strength of romance, 843a
  once let ripe m. go, 488b
  only a m., 843a
  only m. here and m. there,
    930a
  perfection but m., 291b
  precise m. to say nothing, 839a
  psychological m., 839a
  this m. in June, 975a
  this which you deem of no m.,
    96a
  time of death every m., 106a
  to decide, 691b
  trap m. before ripe, 488b
  work of a m., 194a
  worst m. in history of France,
    1016a
Momentary, beauty m. in mind,
    955b
Moment's monument, 731b
  sent to be m. ornament, 514a

Moments, art gives quality to m.,
    781b
  best and happiest m., 573a
  hardly dared pass, 1047b
  lucid m., 588b
  no two m. the same, 705b
  of glad grace, 879b
  of high exultation, 997a
  when everything goes well, 869a
Momentum, psychological m.,
    839a
Monads of Leibniz, 987a
Monagony being married to one
  person, 1017a
Monan's, moon on M. rill, 520a
Monarch, becomes throned m.
  better than crown, 234b
  hears, 371a
  love teach m. to be wise, 439b
  merry m. scandalous and poor,
    382a
  morsel for a m., 287b
  of all I survey, 457b
  of mountains, 559b
  of the vine, 288a
  richest m. in world, 497b
Monarchs, fate summons m. obey,
    369a
  perplexes m., 342b
Monarchy intelligible government,
    726b
  is a merchantman, 491b
  universal m. of wit, 326b
  why m. strong government,
    726b
Monastic aisles, 602a
  man artist, 956b
Monday, betwixt Saturday and
  M., 401a
  born on a M., 1096a
  going to do on M., 962a
  morning press reports, 1058a
  snatched on M. night, 237b
Monday's child fair of face, 1096a
Monde, l'amour fait tourner le
  m., 1105b
Mondes, le meilleur des m. possibles, 417a
Mo'ners, Lord fetch m. up higher, 814a
Money, a little wanton m., 178b
  alone preserves life, 379a
  answereth all things, 28b
  ask of m. spent, 928b
  beautiful in laws, 607b
  bet my m. on bobtail nag, 727b
  blessing m. cannot buy, 326b
  board m. in ginger jar, 753b
  bringing m. be welcome, 1089b
  business may bring m., 533b
  business other people's m., 723a
  by you all the while, 812b
  counting out m., 1094b
  disease called lack of m., 181a
  doänt marry for m., 654b
  fool and his m., 1085a
  friendship last lifetime if not
    asked for m., 762a
  go where m. is, 654b
  government consists in taking
    m., 417b
  hain't the m. but the principle,
    895a
  having more credit than m.,
    477a
  hired m. didn't they, 911a
  honey and plenty of m., 673a
  how painful to keep m., 376a
  how pleasant to have m., 688b

Morning of the world, 661b
  our share of m., 734a
  penitence next m., 670a
  praise at m. blame at night, 403b
  quintessence of life, 564a
  shadow at m. striding, 1002a
  shining m. face, 249a
  singing each m., 1031b
  so soft this m., 969a
  some m. unaware, 663a
  somewhere with m., 948a
  son of the m., 31b
  sons of the m., 549a
  sorrow makes night m., 217a
  sow thy seed in the m., 28b
  stars sang together, 16a
  they that watch for m., 22b
  think in the m., 487b
  this m. came home cloak, 375a
  top o' the m., 812a
  two o'clock in m. courage, 504b
  uncertain hour before m., 1006b
  veils of m., 879b
  wings of the m., 23a
  woe to them that rise early in m., 30b
  womb of m. dew, 200a
  would God it were m., 10b
Morning's at seven, 661b
  easy m. ride, 738b
  minion, 803a
  mornin', 830b
Mornings, forgotten m., 1070b
  savor of m. great delight, 171b
  strangely silent, 1061b
Morocco, far as from M., 1085b
Moron, happy m., 1103b
Morose, obstinate pliant merry m., 135b
  view of present, 596b
Morrison Morrison, 970a
Morrow, a little fun and good m., 751b
  cease to ask what m. will bring, 121a
  desire of night for the m., 572b
  good m. to our waking souls, 304b
  good night till it be m., 224b
  man's yesterday ne'er like m., 568a
  misty m. a myrie someris day, 164b
  night urge the m., 571b
  put not trust in the m., 121a
  rainy m., 293a
  rash who reckons on m., 82b
  rose the m. morn, 526a
  take no thought for m., 41a
  wished the m., 642b
Mors, nil igitur m. est ad nos, 113b
  ultima ratio, 151a
Morsel for a monarch, 287b
  I found you as a m., 288a
  under tongue sweet m., 386a
Morsels, tough m. to swallow, 805b
Mort, que la m. me trouve plantant mes choux, 189b
Mortal and may err, 327b
  arm and nerve feel, 521a
  behind m. bone, 735b
  cloud of m. destiny, 711b
  coil, 262a
  dreams no m. dared, 643a
  every tatter in m. dress, 882b

Mortal frame, 526b
  genius and m. instruments, 254a
  grief itself be m., 571b
  grows on m. soil, 338b
  I sing with m. voice, 346b
  immortal death has taken m. life, 113b
  immortal youth to m. maids, 536b
  knew my son was m., 92b
  laugh at m. thing, 561a
  locked up from m. eye, 354a
  man who hath more joy, 697a
  meanest m. known, 789b
  melody, 641b
  moon eclipse endured, 293b
  nature did tremble, 513b
  nature of mind m., 113b
  no m. could vie with Zeus, 65a
  not m. what you desire, 128b
  O you m. engines, 275a
  or immortal here I die, 696a
  purest treasure m. times afford, 226a
  put on immortality, 53a
  quit this m. frame, 404a
  raised a m. to the skies, 371b
  shall m. man be more just, 14b
  shuffled off this m. coil, 262a
  sins of commission m., 434a
  spirit of m. be proud, 564b
  splendor, 994b
  stakes, 928b
  struck a deep m. blow, 78b
  sufferest m. griefs, 244b
  temples of king, 227b
  tend on m. thoughts, 281b
  therefore Caius is m., 732b
  things doth sway, 200b
  think all men m. but themselves, 399a
  think m. thoughts, 84a
  this his m. part, 765a
  tree whose m. taste, 341b
  what m. heard good of George the Third, 934a
  wide and m. pang, 1057b
  wound is m. and is mine, 1032a
Mortalem vitam mors cum immortalis, 113b
Mortality, nothing serious in m., 284a
  of inanimate things, 772a
  pilgrims of m., 999b
  to frail m. trust, 210a
  touches the heart, 118a
  watch o'er man's m., 514a
  weighs on me like sleep, 579b
Mortality's strong hand, 237a
  too weak to bear them, 385a
Mortals are blaming the gods, 65a
  changeful mind of m., 80a
  happiest of m., 417a
  Hope lies to m., 854b
  make earth bitter, 577a
  miserable m. like leaves, 64b
  more rugged m., 886a
  no ascent too steep for m., 120b
  not in m. to command success, 393a
  some feelings to m. given, 520a
  what all m. may correct, 390a
  what fools these m. be, 129b, 230a
  when to mischief m. bend, 404b
Mortar, his chest as a m., 697a
Mortgage beats 'em all, 808b

Mortgage, every radish had a m., 993a
Mortification, live in continual m., 420b
Mortify a wit, 412b
Mortifying reflections, 628a
Mortis, timor m. conturbat me, 176a
Mosaic religion a father religion, 834b
Moscow, to M. to M., 858b
Moses, greeted M. from Pisgah, 587a
  hid his face, 8a
  Mahomet to M., 600b
  ridin' on bumblebee, 1041b
  smote rock twice, 547b
  was there forty days, 9b
Moslem mosque and pagan shrine, 626a
Mosquitoes, lets big m. through, 321a
Moss, rolling stone gathers no m., 126a
  until m. reached lips, 736a
  you are, 987b
Moss-covered bucket, 553a
Mosses, addled m. dank, 989a
  greenest m. cling, 625b
Mossy cavern, 583b
  violet by m. stone, 510b
Most enjoy contented least, 292a
  fails where m. it promises, 269b
  make the m. of it, 464b
  may err grossly as few, 368b
  thing they m. do show, 293a
  who is it that says m., 293a
Mostest, git thar fustest with m., 709b
Mote in thy brother's eye, 41a
Motes that people sunbeams, 335b
  thick as m. in sonne-beem, 168a
Moth and rust doth corrupt, 40b
  blundering by, 1066a
  both m. and flame, 1066a
  desire of m. for star, 572b
Mother accursed the night she bore me, 84a
  and lover the sea, 774a
  arose a m. in Israel, 11a
  as m. so her daughter, 34b
  blessed m. of us all, 474a
  bring child back to its m., 69b
  call me early m., 645a
  calls me Willie, 821a
  came and caught her, 1095b
  Charybdis your m., 234a
  child to m. sheep to fold, 854a
  Church, 143b
  cruel m. of sweet loves, 122b
  despise not thy m., 26a
  died today, 1068b
  diligence m. of good fortune, 197a
  earth no more a m., 132a
  English m. made moan, 693b
  experience m. of sciences, 194b
  fairer daughter of fair m., 121a
  father and m. gae mad, 494b
  foolish son the heaviness of his m., 24a
  France m. of arts, 187b
  from one m. both draw breath, 79b
  gave m. forty whacks, 1101a
  give me the sun, 729b
  Goose, 844b
  happy with such a m., 649b

Music, like a huge m., 995a
like harmony in m., 510a
like m. on the waters, 559a
live without m., 741b
madder m., 890a
mads me, 228b
make m. mute, 653a
make merry by means of m., 101a
make one m. as before, 649b
makes sweet m. with stones, 220b
making of m. in rest, 698b-699a
man that has taste of m., 394b
man that hath no m., 235b
man's place in m., 956b
mind that can hear m., 995a
ministers to human welfare, 706a
mirth the m. of division, 199b
moody food, 288a
must investigate discord, 137a
my life like m. hall, 878b
my rampart, 1024a
never merry when hear sweet m., 235b
night filled with m., 622a
no m. in a rest Katie, 698b
no m. in nightingale, 220b
not for doctrine but m., 403a
not listen to good m., 840a
of dancing waves, 998a
of flute, 1003b
of flutes of Greece, 775b
of men's lives, 228a
of poem as well as words, 909a
of the spheres, 252b, 330a
of the Union, 591a
oft hath such a charm, 272a
on spirit make m. too, 955b
one chord of m., 726a
painting m. poetry, 706a
pasteboard goddess of m. halls, 934b
poetry painting and m., 491a
raise and quell, 370a
reasonable good ear in m., 230a
sap is the m., 1050a
say it with m., 912b
setting sun and m. at close, 226b
shall untune the sky, 370a
silence sank like m., 525b
softest m. to attending ears, 224a
soul of m. shed, 541b
sphere-descended maid, 443b
step to the m. he hears, 683b
still sad m. of humanity, 509b
strained through mind, 1056b
Susanna's m., 955b
sweet compulsion in m. lie, 334b
that deepest reach, 604b
that gentlier lies, 645b
thing I love most, 375b
thrush m. went, 928b
time to hear bird m., 1042b
to hear sea-maid's m., 229a
universal language, 620a
untune the sky, 370a
vibrations of deathless m., 898b
when soft voices die, 572b
wherever she goes, 1095a
wherever there is harmony, 330a
why hearest thou m. sadly, 291b
with silver sound, 1084b

Music yearning like a god, 581b
you are m. while m. lasts, 1006b
Musical as bright Apollo's lute, 222a
as is Apollo's lute, 337a
mind like m. instrument, 705b
miracle, 898a
most m. most melancholy, 335b
most m. of mourners, 571a
Shakespeare and the m. glasses, 448a
shuttle, 701b
so m. a discord, 230a
Musically, so m. wells, 644a
Musicians tedious on other subjects, 879a
we m. know, 666a
Music-makers, we are the m., 807a
Music's, chamber m. not for you, 505b
melting fall, 442a
power obey, 370a
Musing there an hour alone, 560b
while I was m. the fire burned, 18b
Musique, de la m. avant toute chose, 808a
Musk, cankers in m. rose buds, 229b
sweet m. roses and eglantine, 229b
swirls of m., 819a
Musket molds in his hands, 820b
Muslin, stretched with m., 1036a
Mussolini, even M. against war, 1019b-1020a
Must, die we m., 216b
if we can we m., 853b
shoot if you m., 626b
thou m., 603b
to greenwood go, 1084a
Mustard, beef without m., 802b
heaven like to m. seed, 42b
Johnson's conversation was m., 468b
Muster many a score, 503a
Mutabile, varium et m. femina, 118b
Mutability, chance death and m., 569a
in large republics, 549a
naught endure but m., 568a
of language, 550a
Mutable cloud, 605b
rank-scented many, 289b
Mute, by and by music m., 653a
farewell, 704a
hangs as m., 541b
if m. is she not pure, 699a
inglorious Milton, 440b
law stands m. in midst of arms, 110b
Nature mourns worshiper, 518b
soon m. however tuneful, 536b
unchanged to hoarse or m., 346b
Mutilators of collections, 534b
Mutine in matron's bones, 264a
Mutinous and quarrelsome, 423b
Shannon waves, 968a
Mutiny, move stones of Rome to m., 256a
Mutter, blessed m. of Mass, 664b
unmentionable thoughts, 698a
Muttered in hell, 501a
Mutual aid law of animal life, 796a

Mutual and partaken bliss, 337b
bunched in m. glee, 1043b
confidence, 912b
envy of the living, 318a
guarantees of independence, 842b
incomprehension, 1058b
inflamed with m. animosity, 480a
meet m. heart, 420a
prevention of m. crime, 98b
My-doxy, orthodoxy m., 577a
Myriad laughter of ocean waves, 78a
there died a m., 988b
Myriad-minded Shakespeare, 529b
Myriads of rivulets hurrying, 649a
Myrrh, gold and frankincense and m., 39b
Myrtle and ivy of two-and-twenty, 562b
land where cypress and m., 558a
laurel and m. and rose, 477a
Myrtles brown, 338a
once more ye m., 338a
which a grove of m. made, 309a
Myself, all by m., 170b
am hell, 345a
awe of such thing as m., 253b
coming down shift for m., 179a
commanded by boy's mother, 77b
feel it so like m., 1068b
first glass for m., 394b
garden city and m., 1058b
hell within m., 330a
his only son m., 445a
I am m. and what is around me, 977b
I celebrate m., 700a
I contradict m., 700b
I live not in m., 556b
I m. am hell, 1076b
I owe my fame to m., 332a
I pray for no man but m., 290a
it is m. I remake, 885b
know all except m., 171b
must I remake, 885a
no greater monster than m., 191b
not disappoint m., 680b
not least honored of all, 646b
not talk so much about m., 682a
quite m. again, 853a
that favorite subject m., 468b
this man shall be m., 436b
unwitting where Master dwells, 947b
when I give I give m., 700b
when young, 630a
with yesterday's years, 630a
Mysteries are revealed unto the meek, 37a
lie beyond thy dust, 363a
love's m. in souls grow, 306b
mystery of m., 521a
power in m. of thought, 84a
talk of m., 680b
wingy m. in divinity, 329b
Mysterious, beauty m. and terrible, 708a
by this love, 305a
God moves in m. way, 456b
independent variable, 725a
law true source, 346a
O m. priest, 583a
past of sea, 1061a

Ocean, tomorrow we sail the O.
Sea, 121a
vast and furious o., 319a
vast o. on whose face, 557b
veritable o., 956a
where broad o. leans, 447b
wherein the whale, 991a
Ocean's, as near o. edge as can,
681a
gray melancholy waste, 574a
in o. bosom unespied, 360a
Oceans drowned, 1032a
fight on seas and o., 921a
same image in o., 696a
wilderness o., 720b
O'clock, it's now ten o., 657a
says wisely it is ten o., 248a
two o. in morning courage,
504b
October, falls with leaf in O.,
312b
lonesome O., 643b
March July O. May, 187a
now for O. eves, 990a
something in O., 860a
October's bright blue weather,
741a
Octopus, adopt character of o.,
77a
Octosyllabic verse, 558b
O'Day, grave of Mike O., 1105a
Odd, and this was o., 745b
as can be, 914b
divinity in o. numbers, 267b
good luck in o. numbers,
267a-b
he never leaves doorway, 692b
luck in o. numbers, 589a
numbers are most effectual,
133a
old ends stolen of holy writ,
217a
people's voice o., 412a
this was scarcely o., 746a
volumes, 535a
Odd-eyed, seld-shaven o., 534a
Oddness, my poetry on side of o.,
804a
Odds, all Caesar's and what o.,
354a
almost at o. with morning,
285a
facing fearful o., 596a
is gone, 288b
life, 387a
of man's bedevilment, 854a
what is the o., 669b
Ode, I intended an o., 782a,b
Oderint dum metuant, 109b
Odes, quoted o. and jewels, 648a
Odiet amo, 115a
profanum vulgus, 358a
Odious, comparisons are o., 171a
she and comparisons o., 307a
vermin, 389b
Odium of success, 826b
Odor, dry aromatic o., 940a
no o. so bad as goodness tainted, 682b
of honeysuckle, 864a
stealing and giving o., 251a
Odorous, amber scent of o. perfume, 349b
Odors, bedewed with liquid o.,
120b
crushed sweeter still, 208a
of ointments more durable,
208a-b
virtue like precious o., 208a

Odors when violets sicken, 572b
Odysseus, soon as he had seen O.,
66b
Odyssey, thunder of the O., 804b
Oedipus, I am Davos not O., 108a
O'ercast, sun's o. with blood, 236a
O'erdoing Termagant, 262b
O'erdusted, more laud than gilt
o., 269a
O'erfraught heart, 285b
O'er-informed tenement of clay,
368a
O'erleaps, ambition which o. itself, 282b
O'erthrown, noble mind here o.,
262b
O'ertrip, fearfully o. the dew,
235a
O'erwhelm, though all earth o.
them, 258a
Off agin on agin, 897b
put o. thy shoes, 8a
with her head, 744a
with his head, 217b, 392b
with old love, 753b, 754a
off with Old Woman, 836a
with you where you want to go,
165b
you lendings, 278b
Offend, averse to flatter or o.,
404a
if thy right hand o. thee, 40a
if truth o. my sweet, 944b
not o. you by speaking truth,
177b
those who o. punished, 678b
Offended, brother o. is harder to
be won, 25a
Deity o., 493b
devils being o., 273a
him have I o., 255a
if we shadows have o., 231a
this hath not o. king, 179a
with his estate, 148a
Offender, hugged o. forgave offense, 372a
love o. detest offense, 372a
never pardons, 130b
Offenders, mercy on us miserable
o., 59b
society o., 768a
Offending Adam, 243a
most o. soul alive, 245a
Offends me to the soul, 262b
no law is king indeed, 205b
Offense, conscience void of o., 50b
dire o. from amorous causes,
404a
giving and receiving o., 575b
hugged offender forgave o.,
372a
love offender detest o., 372a
my o. is rank, 263b
pardon one o. encourage many,
127a
real o. was having mind, 798a
rock of o., 31a
scorn to take o., 403b
would appear o. in us, 254a
Offenses, enemies for small o.,
310a
old o. of affections new, 294a
Offer, I o. even that, 737b
I o. hunger thirst battles, 620a
instantly close with o., 725a
itself to be unmasked, 980b
not o. to people but ask, 1072a
nothing to o. but blood, 920b
yourselves to sea, 796b

Offered, I o. Being for it,
736a
Offering, a lamb for a burnt o.,
7a
too little asking too much,
507a
Offerings, knowledge of God
more than burnt o., 35b
pale Hecate's o., 283a
Office and affairs of love, 245b
and custom, 267b
boy to attorney's firm, 766a
cast longing eye on o., 471b
Circumlocution O., 672a
due participation of o., 472b
have only o. no opinion, 498a
heaven about to confer great o.,
100b
I shall return to the o., 395a
insolence of o., 262a
lust of o., 690b
never ask refuse resign o., 423b
public o. public trust, 659b,
771a
scribe skillful in o., 4b
serves it in o. of a wall, 226b
so act toward o. so toward
wealth, 138b
so clear in his great o., 282b
spoils of o., 690b
to execute laws royal o., 454b
to o. and so to bed, 962b
unfit to hold an o., 105a
which false man does easy, 284a
Officeholder, president is o.,
1068a
Officer and gentleman, 872b
at least one rank higher, 1033a
fear each bush an o., 216b
Officers, behind o. government
people, 717b
her o. march with armies, 660a
make o. but not scholars, 311a
public o. servants, 771a
white o. cast lot, 752a
Offices acceptable as elsewhere,
471b
estates degrees and o., 233a
imperfect o. of prayer, 516a
people I cannot win with o.,
364b
post o. and cabinet appointments, 635b
Official, no o. high or petty,
1021b
Officious fool worse than foe,
505b
innocent sincere, 433b
Officiously to keep alive, 689a
Offspring of heaven firstborn,
344b
of idle hour, 779a
tempt its new-fledged o., 449b
terrible from camps, 1058a
time's noblest o., 400a
true source of human o., 346a
we are also his o., 50a, 104a
we are your o., 103b
Oft in the stilly night, 542b
Often, hit o., 968a
strike o. as you can, 717a
O'Grady, colonel's lady an' Judy
O., 875a
Oil, everything soothed by o.,
132a
for its own wheels, 457a
her mouth is smoother than o.,
23b
in diplomat's soul, 958b

Peril, those in p. on sea, 726a
  woods more free from p., 247b
Perilous, cleanse bosom of p.
    stuff, 286b
  dewdrop on p. way, 579b
  fight, 541a
  nothing more p. than new
    order, 176b-177a
  seas in faery lands forlorn,
    583a
  stuffed bosom of p. stuff, 286b
  thought without learning is p.,
    71a
  turns to p. waters, 159a
  unsifted in p. circumstance,
    259a
Perils, avoid p. by united forces,
    374a
  bring fraternity, 599b
  defend us from all p., 60b
  how many p. do enfold, 200a
  I to my p., 854b
  of actual existence, 838b
  of camp march and battle, 752a
  of cheat and charmer, 854b
  spoke I think of p. past, 953a
  when our p. are past, 506b
Period, immersed in place and
    p., 997b
  of effectiveness of generation,
    978a
Periodic, success to p. sentence,
    1035b
Periodization of European history,
    1047b
Peripatetic lover, 767a
Periphrastic study, 1005a
Perish, all man's thoughts p.,
    813a
  city to p. if it finds buyer, 116a
  drink unto him that is ready to
    p., 26b
  fame of her excellence will
    never p., 67a
  hero p. or sparrow fall, 408a
  if it had to p. twice, 927a
  if we must p. in fight, 627b
  in our own, 856b
  in their infancy, 1086b
  in this wilderness, 319a
  justice done though world p.,
    186a
  let the day p., 14b
  may they p. who used our
    words, 151a
  name not p. in dust, 532b
  no seed shall p., 785b
  or catch up, 903a
  plan civilization or p., 1027a
  shall not p. from earth, 639a
  should not p., 48a
  so p. all who do the like, 405a
  spirit of moderation p., 911b-
    912a
  surely weak p., 932b
  survive or p., 546b-547a
  survive or p. with country, 463a
  that one of thy members should
    p., 40a
  the thought, 392b
  their goodness does not p., 85b
  though I p. truth is so, 688b
  thy money p., 49b
  truths wake to p. never, 513b
  twice, 927a
  unless leaves p. tree not re-
    newed, 1057a
  weakly p. at another moment,
    64b

Perish, where no vision the people
    p., 26b
  with the sword, 44b
Perishable stuff, 1057b
Perished as they had never been,
    39a
  by own follies they p., 65a
  in his pride, 511b
  not go where friends p., 753b
  swine p. in waters, 41b
  the weapons of war p., 12b
  who p. being innocent, 14b
  years p. to make us men, 771b
Perishes, come to perfection p.,
    663b
  everything p., 1105b
Perishing, shine p. republic, 994b
Periuria ridet amantum Iupiter,
    128a
Periwig, new p. make a great
    show, 376a
Periwig-pated, robustious p. fel-
    low, 262b
Perjured, gloriously p., 122a
  murderous bloody, 294a
Perjuries, at lovers' p. Jove
    laughs, 223b
  of lovers, 128a
Perked up in glistering grief,
    298a
Permanence sea cannot claim,
    783a
Permanent alliances, 461b
  and certain characteristics, 427b
  and the same, 712a
  disuse of any organ, 475a
  feelings p. and the same, 712a
  grandeur of States, 699b
  interests of community, 480a
  nothing ought to be p., 616b
  share in government, 485a
  system of security, 974b
Permission, nobody without
    Count's p., 980a
Permit base contagious clouds,
    238a
  child to join, 734b
  doing what laws p., 414b
  how long p. to Heaven, 348a
  Nature to take her way, 191b
Permitte divis cetera, 121a
Permitted, good evil p., 742b
  not forbidden is p., 498a
  to shuffle in slippers, 871a
  'twas p. to rest, 501a
  whatever popular is p., 742b
Pernicious consequences, 678a
  love of flattery, 395b
  race of odious vermin, 389b
  weed, 457a
Perpetual, court in p. session,
    980b
  desire a p. rack, 310b
  devotion to business, 822b
  feast of nectared sweets, 337a
  kingdom of p. night, 217a
  neglect of other things, 822b
  night, 302b
  quarrel, 453a
  scoured with p. motion, 241b
  work us a p. peace, 334a
Perpetually, life begins p., 888b
  nation p. to be conquered, 452b
  one hour then damned p., 213b
  saves itself p., 1067b
Perpetuated through hereditary
    dyspeptics, 696b
Perpetuity, merit of p., 331a
Perplexed in the extreme, 276b

Perplexed labyrinthical soul, 308b
  to have plenty is to be p., 74a
Perplexes and affronts, 1069b
  monarchs, 342b
Persecute, despitefully use and p.
    you, 40b
Persecuted church of God, 52b
  for righteousness' sake, 40a
  most p. minority, 967a
Persecutes the mind, 370a
Persecutest, why p. thou me, 49b
Persecution bad way to plant reli-
    gion, 329b
  gives p. no assistance, 461b
  opposition christened p., 689a
  religious p. shield itself, 453b
  strengthen idea, 1012a
Persecutions have made Church
    grow, 143b
Persecutor, single zealot com-
    mence p., 471a
Persepolis, ride in triumph
    through P., 212a
Persephone, the way P. goes, 986a
Persever in obstinate condole-
    ment, 257b
Perseverance and soothing lan-
    guage, 471b
  fortitude and p., 444a
  in good cause, 437b
  keeps honor bright, 268b
  more prevailing than violence,
    136b
Persevere, forbear and p., 825a
  if we all p., 1073b
Persia, past first sleep in P., 331a
Persian, how can anyone be P.,
    414b
  luxury I hate, 121a
  pearls of thought in P. gulfs
    bred, 694b
Persian-lambed, minked and P.,
    866b
Persian's heaven easily made,
    542b
Persians accustomed to deliberate
    when drunk, 86b
  law of the Medes and P., 35a
  old P. hold sea holy, 695b
  taught three things, 562b
Persicos odi puer apparatus, 121a
Persistent, unsubstantial p. faith-
    ful, 907b
Person, aging p. give attention to
    self, 935b
  agreeable p. agrees, 612b
  arts outside p., 851a
  arts that express in p., 851a
  attention must be paid to p.,
    1071a
  average p. right to live, 973a
  beggared all description, 287b
  blood of this just p., 45a
  bore waking up same p., 877b
  dignity and worth of p., 1104a
  dignity of p., 964b
  don't believe no sich p., 670a
  France a p., 590a
  freedom of p., 472a
  frontier of my P., 1060b
  new p. you meet, 1052a
  no more a p. but climate of
    opinion, 1060a
  no p. must have to, 455a
  no sich p., 670b
  noble p. attracts noble, 477b
  of contrary opinion, 619a
  of head root of family, 99b
  portrayed and portrait, 978b

Pilot, great p. sail with canvas rent, 130a
in calm sea every man p., 366a
lightning p., 760b
lives our p. still, 216b
no chance to p. another, 637a
of the Galilean lake, 338b
see P. face to face, 655a
that weathered storm, 506b
'tis fearful night, 588a
unstable p. steers leaking ship, 145a
Pilots of purple twilight, 647a
Pimples warts and everything, 328a
Pin, pinned it wi' siller p., 1089a
with a little p., 227b
Pinafore, captain of the P., 766a
Pinch, Adam and Eve and p. me, 944b
death as lover's p., 289a
East and West will p. heart, 1023a
hungry lean-faced villain, 218b
interstate commerce feels p., 1021b
necessity's sharp p., 277b
Pinches, none tell where shoe p. me, 136b
shoe fits one p. another, 935b
Pinching, paddling palms and p. fingers, 295a
Pine, against blue a p. tree, 384a
because they lost virtue, 133b
dwindle peak and p., 281a
for what is not, 570b
for which soul did p., 642a
into waves p. needles, 380b
palm and p., 875a
scent of p. and woodthrush, 1004a
shadows of p. boughs, 386a
shall I ever sigh and p., 323a
spray of Western p., 769b
tallest p., 342a
they p. I live, 192a
with fear and sorrow, 201a
Pineapple of politeness, 480b
Pined and wanted food, 508b
she p. in thought, 252b
Pines around me, 982a
cones under his p., 926a
murmuring p. hemlocks, 622a
roar in the p., 898a
thunder harp of p., 740b
Pinhead in many respects, 886b
Pining pining, 803a
Pinions, drift of p., 857a
of great deeds, 477b
'Pinions, tell you what his 'p. is, 764a
Pink, Bacchus with p. eyne, 288a
of courtesy, 196a, 224b
of perfection, 450b
twenty-nine when p. shades, 839b
Pinkham, land of Lydia E. P., 1030b
Pinks that grow, 271b
Pinnace like fluttered bird, 654b
Pinnacle, imagined p. and steep, 579b
Pinnacled dim in inane, 569a
Pinned it wi' siller pin, 1089a
Pinning down of delusion, 980b
Pin's, set life at p. fee, 259b
Pint, come within p. of wine, 395b
of sweat save blood, 987b

P'int people to goal, 693a
Pioneer, died in boots like p., 1041a
Pioneers, O p. I never got ahead, 1050b
O pioneers, 701b
Pious action sugar o'er, 261b
all were p., 1089a
Eleazer Wheelock p., 868b
feeling of gratitude, 546b
fool that raised it, 331a
fraud as with bad action, 467b
frauds of friendship, 424b
impiety of p., 706a
love is p., 170b
man can't stay in peace, 499a
man not less a man, 360b
not p. longer than rod behind, 179b
ones of Plymouth, 686a
passion grave intent, 849a
thoughts as harbingers, 333a
times ere priestcraft, 368a
Pipe but as linnets, 650a
called for p., 1092b
cat dog p. or two, 855a
easier played on than p., 263b
for fortune's finger, 263a
he can smoke, 753b
me to pastures still, 802b
piped silly p., 585b
rumor is a p., 241a
song about a Lamb, 486b
Piped silly pipe, 585b
Piper, pay the p., 391b
Peter P. picked peck, 1096a
Piper's son, 1095a
Pipers, wi' a hundred p. an' a', 502a
Pipes and timbrels, 583a
and whistles in his sound, 249a
Piping, cicadas pour out their p. voices, 63a
down valleys wild, 486b
helpless naked p. loud, 489b
songs forever new, 583a
songs of pleasant glee, 486b
took troubled sound, 714a
weak p. time of peace, 216b
Pippin, right as Ribstone P., 902a
Pippins, old p. toothsomest, 314b
Piracee, vary p., 766b
Piracies not sullied with stealing, 759b
Piracy, let's vary p., 766b
Pirate king, 766b
Pirates preachers poteen-makers, 908b
wonder at cruelty of p., 693b
Pire qu'un crime c'est une faute, 499b
Pis, tant p. and tant mieux, 438b
Piscem natare doces, 151b
Pisgah, greeted Moses from P., 587a
Pistol, if his p. misses fire, 451b
pun a p. not feather, 536a
Pistols, fire p. for new century, 937a
have you your p., 701b
put on p. went riding, 1009b
Pit, black as the p., 816a
eagle know what is in p., 486b
man will go down into p., 813a
many-headed monster of p., 412b
ponies, 906a
whoso diggeth a p., 26a

Pitch, daubed with slime and p., 8a
into frog-spawn, 884a
melody deprived of p., 999a
nightly p. moving tent, 518a
pitched past p. of grief, 804a
they that touch p. defiled, 246b
what validity and p., 251a
which hawks flies higher p., 214a
Pitch-black, night p. upon the deep, 117b
Pitched, as mind p. ear pleased, 458b
betwixt heaven and Charing Cross, 857a
his tent toward Sodom, 7a
love p. mansion, 884a
past pitch of grief, 804a
Pitcher, as wheel runs why water p., 124a
boy brings up hall, 820a
broken at the fountain, 29a
Pitchers, small p. have wide ears, 185a
Pitchfork, clothes thrown on with p., 390b
drive out Nature with p., 123b
Piteous, coursed down in p. chase, 247b
thing among wretched mortals, 64b
Pitfalls, snares traps gins p., 659b
Pith and poetry, 764b
enterprises of great p., 262a
Pitiable, world p. in units, 783a
Pitied, better envied than p., 86b
him in blindness, 976a
how they p. Eve, 906a
lost respect and p. it, 681a
pity and be p., 248b
Pities, Lord help 'em how I p. all, 517b
plumage, 467b
spirit who p. me, 976b
Pitiful, lips say God be p., 617b
longsuffering and very p., 37a
selfish Public, 539b
sound to hear, 820b
tender eye of p. day, 284b
'twas wondrous p., 273a
Pitiless, pelting of p. storm, 278b
Pitt, celebrities such as P., 749b
Pity a human face, 487a
akin to love, 313a
beyond all telling, 880a
deserveth double p., 199a
feeling which arrests mind, 968a
for living envy for dead, 762b
from blust'ring wind, 359a
gave ere charity began, 449b
hid in heart of love, 880a
him fallen chief, 906a
hippogriff, 1047b
his ignorance, 669b
know what 'tis to p., 248b
knows not wrath nor p., 593b
like naked newborn babe, 282b
loved her that she did p., 273a
me that heart is slow, 1023b
melts mind to love, 313a
Mercy P. Peace and Love, 487a
my simplicity, 425b
no beast but knows touch of p., 216b
no concern with art, 754b
no p. Lord change heart, 790b
no p. sitting in clouds, 225a

Press acknowledges accountability to no one, 984b
close bare-bosomed night, 700a
corporation of p., 66oa
enable p. to serve communication, 984b
fell dead-born from p., 434b
free p. good or bad, 1068b
free p. necessity, 1013b
free speech p. assembly, 864b-865a
freedom of p. bulwark of liberty, 446a
freedom of p. has suffered most, 1068b
freedom of p. religion person, 472a
freedom of speech or of p., 474a
inform p. home Christmas, 910a
liberty of p., 616b, 1091a
lives by disclosures, 1099b
microscopes and telescopes of p., 870b
Monday p. reports, 1058a
not falling man, 298b
not p. upon brow of labor, 858b
sort of wild animal, 984b
tenth Muse governs p., 678b
toward the mark, 54a
where ye see plume, 594b
with vigor on, 420a
Pressed into service out of shape, 926b
love though p. with ill, 459a
tree whose mouth is p., 992a
Presses, clatter of p., 988b
Presseth, thy hand p. me sore, 18b
Pressmen, so we be named p., 742b
Press's, gret p. freedom, 693a
Pressure, form and p., 263a
grace under p., 1044b
hardly feel p. of age, 93b
of cosmos, 795a
opening first p. off second, 930a
Prestige, convenience comfort p., 1104a
Presto, in moment p. pass, 600b
Presume, Dr. Livingstone I p., 791a
not God to scan, 408b
yourself ignorant, 528b
Presuming on changeful potency, 269a
Presumption, amused by its p., 1033a
in wisdom, 452b
Presumptions, art flies in face of p., 798b
Presumptuous, not too p. folly, 769b
Pretend to know when you do not, 75a
Pretender, God bless the P., 414b
had she known p. he was, 906a
James I James II and Old P., 1011b
who P. or who King, 415a
Pretense, false p., 747a
for a p. make prayers, 45b
no p. of liberty, 635a
to faint meaning make p., 369a
undivulged p., 284a
Pretenses to break known rules by, 328a
which are sincere, 870a

Pretension, this p. a prejudice, 802a
Pretensions, government draw into p., 752b
Pretentious American authors, 960a
Prettier, pebble or p. shell, 379b
Prettiest doll in world, 691a
Pretty, all my p. ones, 285b
Babe all burning bright, 210b
birds do sing, 300b
Bobby Shaftoe, 1098a
but is it art, 873b
drink p. creature, 511b
everything that p. is, 290b
Fanny's way, 398a
feet like snails, 320b
follies themselves commit, 233a
foot gift of nature, 478a
how town, 1031b
how-de-do, 768b
in amber to observe, 410b
kettle of fish, 767b
learned seldom p., 961a
little toes, 1095b
maids all in row, 1093b
my p. maid, 1095a
no burial this p. pair, 1084a
only p. ring time, 250b
pleasures might me move, 198b
poem Mr. Pope, 386a
puts on his p. looks, 236b
state of things, 768b
tell me p. maiden, 846a
to see what money will do, 376a
to think so, 1044b
what do for p. girls, 885a
young wards, 767b
Preudunt course steadied, 693a
Prevail, conditions dat p., 1026b
evening shades p., 393a
fair words p., 874b
gates of hell not p., 43a
God who is able to p., 325b
his rising fogs p., 369a
make best ideas p., 713a
man will p., 1039b
necessity knows no law except p., 126b
none cares whether it p., 722a
'tis the majority p., 735b
truth great shall p., 722a
will looking ill p., 350a
Prevailed, David p. over the Philistine, 12a
the dragon p. not, 58a
with double sway, 449b
Prevails, when vice p., 393b
where commerce long p., 447b
Prevalent, poverty most p. of diseases, 1009a
religion most p., 453a
Prevarication, last dike of p., 454a
Prevent, enjoy religion p. others, 751a
faults it has not strength to p., 448b
lower from getting more, 98a
me from carrying you up, 83b
surest way to p. war, 531a
Prevented, war could have been p., 979b
Preventing angels met it, 370b
Prevention, anthology used for p., 1034b
of mutual crime, 98b
Preventive, economics p. pathology, 1034a
Prevents our being natural, 356b

Previous, returned home p. night, 917b
Prey at fortune, 274b
beast of p. in aristocratic races, 805b
expects his evening p., 441b
fear birds of p., 270b
greater p. upon less, 418b
have they not divided the p., 11a
of rich on poor, 471b
on garbage, 259b
people easily becomes p., 178a
smaller fleas on him p., 390a
great lord yet p. to all, 409a
to dumb forgetfulness a p., 441a
to hastening ills a p., 449a
universal p., 268a
Venus fastened to p., 378b
where eagles dare not perch, 217a
young lions roar after p., 21b
Preys, brain p. on self, 456a
Priam's curtain, 241a
Priapus, I. P. of the harbor, 105a
made of marble, 116b
Price, abatement and low p., 251a
blood p. of admiralty, 875a
cruel high, 872b
existence market p., 739a
for precocity p. demanded, 656b
freedom with great p., 1015b
great p. for wisdom, 730a
greater p. than life, 1048a
greet cheep holde at litel p., 168a
heaven put p. on goods, 466b
is far above rubies, 27a
life exacts for peace, 1042b
market p. they said, 739a
men have their p., 397b
natural and market p., 530b
of everything, 839b
of justice eternal publicity, 889b
of liberty, 479b
of thousand horses, 908b
of wisdom is above rubies, 15b
on sweet self set p., 721b
pay any p., 1072b
pearl of great p., 42b
too high p. for harmony, 708a
weighed for my p., 36a
what p. glory, 999b
will fall, 209a
Priceless, human life p., 1048a
Prick and sting her, 260a
if you p. us do we not bleed, 233b
it mark it with B., 1092b
sides of my intent, 282b
Pricking, gentle knight p. on plain, 200a
gonfalon bubble, 962b
of my thumbs, 285a
Pricks, honor p. me on, 240b
kick against the p., 49b, 78b
to subsequent volumes, 268a
Pride, age that will p. deflower, 200a
aiming at blessed abodes, 408a
all the p. cruelty and ambition, 199b
and conceit original sin, 391a
and courage of patriot, 752a
as if p. not humble, 668a
bear affection without p., 818a

R

Remain sitting at your table, 980b
  smell and taste r., 907b
  thou ever wilt r., 590a
  until death do part, 837a
  wished to r. immortally, 908a
  with unavenged suffering, 708a
Remained to pray, 449b
Remaineth, while the earth r., 6b
Remains, be kind to my r., 371a
  heap of dust alone r., 406a
  nature r., 703b
  nothing done while aught r., 500b
  the One r., 572a
  what r. is bestial, 273b
  what r. Nature r., 703b
  what thou lovest well r., 989a
Remake, myself I must r., 885a
  myself that I r., 885b
  song, 885b
Remark, Frenchman's r. shrewd, 457a
  which I wish to r., 769b
Remarkable, nothing r. beneath moon, 288b
Remarks are not literature, 933b
  seldom quoted correctly, 957b
Rembrandt, whether R. or Vermeer, 908b
Remedies, all r. refusing, 211a
  analyzers of disease, 565a
  die of r. not illnesses, 362a
  new conditions new r., 973a
  worse than disease, 125b
Remedy against consumption of purse, 241b
  cannot r. folly of people, 178b
  force not r., 658a
  found out the r., 270b
  God wounds r. follow, 176b
  is to inform discretion, 473b
  patience best r. for trouble, 105b
  sought the r., 250b
  things without all r., 284b
  tobacco sovereign r., 311b
  too strong for disease, 83a
  true r. for superstition, 453a
  worse than disease, 125b
Remember Alamo, 616a
  all it is about to r., 1079a
  and be sad, 740a
  and regret, 600a
  and understand, 663b
  branches ne'er r., 580a
  bygone days, 1052a
  calmness to r., 726a
  can't r. how they go, 733b
  Christ our Savior, 1099a
  distinctly I r., 642b
  do you r. inn, 902a
  fifth of November, 1087a
  fir trees dark high, 592a
  for years r. with tears, 729a
  forget that I r., 774b
  gentlemen r. blondes, 1027a
  God and history r., 1020a
  half r. human words, 909a
  heart r. O r., 824a
  house where I was born, 591b
  I heard preacher, 701b
  if I do not r. thee, 22b-23a
  if thou wilt r., 739b
  in sweet pangs r. me, 252a
  inn Miranda, 902a
  lists of birds, 1076b
  little note nor r., 639a
  Lot's wife, 47a
  me to Herald Square, 944a

Remember me when I am gone, 739b
  me when in thy kingdom, 47b
  not r. what I must be, 227b
  now thy Creator, 28b
  o remember, 824a
  oh still r. me, 541b
  only this, 998b
  pleasant to r. even this, 117b
  politician knows what to r., 779b
  such a one I r., 647a
  sweet Alice Ben Bolt, 690a
  that we die all, 37b
  the end, 37b
  the Maine, 1101b
  the neckcurls, 1065a
  the sabbath day, 9a
  thee, 260a
  things that were precious, 286a
  this day ye came out, 8b
  those who cannot r. past, 867a
  time to r., 843b
  to pay the debt, 88a
  to r. or invent, 928b
  us if at all not as lost, 1003a
  way we parted, 775a
  we will r. them, 896b
  what is imprinted, 95b
  what we say here, 639a
  while light lives yet, 775a
  who commended yellow stockings, 252b
  who will r. unheroic dead, 992b
  who you are, 745b
Remembered, be all my sins r., 262a
  blue r. hills, 853a
  dead r. footsteps, 899b
  he shall be no more r., 15b
  how often you and I, 719b
  I was owned of thee, 737b
  in spite of ourselves, 638b
  kisses after death, 648b
  knolling departing friend, 241b
  my God, 531b
  no books undeservedly r., 1061a
  not r. in thy epitaph, 241a
  poor Julian, 1045a
  sorrows r., 590a
  thy sweet love r., 292a
  time r., 773a
  when we r. Zion, 22b
  would have made self r., 586a
Rememberest not slightest folly, 248a
Remembering happier things, 647a
  soul r. my good friends, 227a
  this he wept bitterly, 64b
Remembers all that he wrought, 66b
  its august abodes, 536a
  me his gracious parts, 236b
  nature yet r., 513b
  who r. famous day, 623b
Remembrance, absence doth breed continual r., 170b
  and reflection allied, 368a
  bids r. rise, 447a
  fallen from heaven, 773a
  falls on what been, 899a
  flood of r., 985b
  Jamaicas of r., 738b
  let his r. rest, 38b
  makes r. dear, 270a
  of a guest, 37a
  of former things, 27a

Remembrance of prosperity, 38a
  of them is grievous, 61a
  of things past, 292a
  of things to come, 27a
  poetry almost r., 585a
  rosemary for r., 265a
  sweet r. of just, 327b
  this do in r. of me, 47b
  writ in r., 226b
Remembrances, burden our r., 297b
Rememoring, false god dim r., 1010a
Remind him of glory of country, 546b
  lives of great men r. us, 620b
  things poised to r. us, 907b
  to r. me of Lff, 969a
Reminding yourself of a thing, 1017b
Reminds you of someone else, 1052a
Reminiscence, most dramatic r., 703a
Remission, shed for r. of sins, 44b
  without shedding of blood no r., 56a
Remnant of Spartan dead, 561a
  show r. of their fires, 377a
  waste not r. of life in imaginations, 141b
Remnants, deal in r. of r., 392a
Remold it nearer to heart's desire, 631a
R-e-m-o-r-s-e, 886b
Remorse, access and passage to r., 281b
  disjoins r. from power, 254a
  farewell r., 345a
  for yesterday, 801b
  sleeps, 436b
  such as I cast r., 884a
Remorseful, gaudy blabbing r. day, 215a
  pardon, 270a
Remote, do in that r. spot, 504b
  from the happy, 1060a
  from wrangling world, 467a
  is virtue a thing r., 71b
  man seeks for what is r., 100a
  place r. and islanded, 816b
  sound of thunder heard r., 343b
  unfriended melancholy, 447b
  where r. Bermudas ride, 360a
Remoteness, snow said r., 1010b
Remoter aspects of law, 787a
  no need of r. charm, 509a
Remove, bends with remover to r., 294a
  not landmark, 4b
  not the ancient landmark, 25b
  shirt human power not r., 1007a
  the joint, 746b
  things which elemented it, 306a
  till Birnam wood r., 285b
Removed, though the earth be r., 19a
  three centuries r., 1053a
Remover, bends with r. to remove, 294a
Removes, three r. as bad as fire, 422a
Remuneration Latin word for three farthings, 221b
Remus knew this life, 117b
Renaissance mere episode, 1047a
Rend, la Garde meurt mais ne se r. pas, 508a

Sacred, time not s. until lived, 770b
  to departed spirit, 150b
  to oblivion, 309b
  two most s. names, 358b
  veils her s. fires, 414a
Sacredness of property, 757a
Sacrifice, ancient s., 875b
  coming to s., 583a
  make one sweet s., 298a
  mercy and not s., 35b
  of devil's leavings, 413a
  one simple s., 1056a
  peace accepted at s., 841b
  ready at hour of s., 463a
  so costly a s., 640b
  to the muses, 69a
  unpitied s., 452a
  what does s. mean, 1056b
  you make for sentiment, 892b
Sacrificed, person s. to individual, 969b
Sacrifices it to your opinion, 452b
  like stockyards, 1044a
  of friends, 1016b
  of friendship, 904a
  such s. my Cordelia, 280b
  win world by s., 923b
  with such s. God is pleased, 56a
Sacrilegious murder hath broke ope, 284a
Sacrosanct, personality s. meaning of liberty, 934b
Sacrum, oblivioni s., 309b
Sad, a little sunny a little s., 777b
  all their songs s., 918a
  all world s. dreary, 727b
  and mad and bad, 666a
  and weary I go back, 968b
  as angels, 438a
  augurs mock own presage, 293b
  bad brother's name, 776a
  be beautiful and be s., 707a
  bring s. thoughts to mind, 508b
  brooding on country's fate, 688a
  companion dull-eyed melan-choly, 290b
  cypress, 252a
  did world become s. for me alone, 149b
  experience make me s., 250a
  flesh is s. alas, 797a
  heart foams at stern, 829b
  heart of Ruth, 583a
  how s. our Russia, 632b
  is Eros builder of cities, 1060a
  kissed mouth, 773b
  know not why s., 588a
  last gray hairs, 582b
  lucidity of soul, 711a
  make man look s., 231a
  mechanic exercise, 649b
  mine a s. one, 231a
  my verse s. no wonder, 854b
  name forever s., 405b
  no s. songs for me, 739b
  not to be loved, 870a
  of itself, 384a
  old earth borrow mirth, 826a
  old law s. not bitter, 941b
  or singing weather, 774b
  remember and be s., 740a
  rose of all my days, 879b
  say I'm s., 551b
  soul s. glance glum, 769a
  soul take comfort, 758b
  sound of horn, 589a
  still s. music of humanity, 509b
  stories of death of kings, 227b

Sad, sullen and s., 419b
  tale's best for winter, 295a
  thing s. of itself, 384a
  thoughts sunny weather, 698a
  tires in a mile-a, 295b
  to see s. sights moves, 220b
  'twas s. by fits, 443b
  uncertain rustling, 643a
  vicissitude of things, 437a
  visit my s. heart, 254b
  votarist in palmer's weed, 336b
  weight of this s. time, 280b
  when one says it is s., 384a
  words of tongue or pen, 626a
  world is s. enough, 825b
Sadder and wiser man, 526a
  light than waning moon, 626b
  not to be able to love, 870a
  than a sigh, 1030a
  than owl songs, 562a
  those who hear s. than I, 751a
Saddest among kings of earth, 899b
  are these, 626a
  of all kings, 893a
  of the year, 574b
  ones wear jester's garb, 945b
  story ever heard, 915a
  sweetest songs s. thought, 570b
  thing in world, 857b
  this sight to me, 981a
  when I sing, 588a, 750b
Saddle, boot s. to horse, 662a
  come s. your horses, 522a
  leap into thy s. once more, 695b
  no better place than s., 721a
  put Germany in s., 677b
  short life in s., 86oa
  things are in s., 602b
Saddled, millions s. and bridled, 362a
Sadly descends autumn, 715a
  part we s. in troublous world, 216b
  why hearest thou music s., 291b
Sadness, begin in s., 1075b
  comes an hour of s., 790a
  diverter of s., 326a
  eternal note of s., 714b
  feeling of s. longing, 621b
  humorous s., 250a
  more prevailing s., 538a
  of a vale, 584a
  of conviction, 786b
  of her might, 584a
  songs of s. and mirth, 622b
  sweet though in s., 570a
  unmannerly s. in youth, 231b
  where s. let me sow joy, 157b
  with setting of sun, 790a
  wraps me in humorous s., 250a
Sado, over S. the Milky Way, 380b
Safe and sane Fourth, 887b
  be silent and s., 807a
  bind safe find, 182b
  compulsion to become s., 986b
  depository of public interests, 473b
  direct and honest not s., 275a
  for democracy, 866b
  for hypocrisy, 1049b
  from the many, 694a
  hold me but s., 666b
  if military way of life, 995b
  may you go s. my friend, 944b
  no man s. without hobby, 818a
  none is s., 996b
  perdition to be s., 604a

Safe, run into a s. harbor, 69a
  see me s. up, 179a
  shall wooden wall continue, 77b
  upon solid rock, 1023a
  weariest river s. to sea, 775a
  wish him s. at home, 500a
  world s. for democracy, 842a
  world s. for diversity, 1074a
Safeguard, judiciary s. of liberty, 864b
  of the west, 512b
Safeguarding community from in-citements, 864b
Safeguards acceptable to all na-tions, 982b
  history of procedural s., 967a
Safe-kept memory, 982a
Safely, but to be s. thus, 284b
  Judah and Israel dwelt s., 13a
  ship of state s. to harbor, 81b
  toddle s. home, 992b
Safer being meek than fierce, 666b
  to be feared than loved, 177a
Safest, home is s. refuge, 198a
  in the middle, 128b
  just when s. sunset touch, 665a
  road to hell, 1042a
Safety, as if s. in stupidity, 683b
  dangerous to peace and s., 492a
  enlightenment civilization, 708b
  fame for ale and s., 244a
  for my son brother shipmates, 174a
  freedom not s. but opportunity, 984b
  greatest degree of s., 446a
  in multitude of counselors, 24a
  in s. within boundaries, 974b
  in seas and ourselves s. lies, 216a
  in skating s. speed, 607a
  neither liberty nor s., 422b
  no s. here below, 179b
  no strike against public s., 911a
  obtaining happiness and s., 446a
  peace liberty and s., 472b
  people's s. is highest law, 151b
  pluck this flower s., 239a
  principles to effect s., 470b
  to hope not safety, 118a
  unite for public s., 504b
  with which error tolerated, 472a
Saffron mist, 1010b
Sagacious bluestocking, 596a
  bold and turbulent of wit, 368a
  how s. the mouse, 105b
Sagacity, no s. no powers, 455a
Sage, by saint by savage by s., 412b
  daughters of Muses, 79b
  does not accumulate, 75b
  government of the s., 73b
  hoary s. replied, 429a
  hold tongue pass for s., 127a
  Homer's rule best, 411b
  in days of yore, 660b
  knows without going about, 74b
  lengthened s. advices, 495b
  mechanician, 686a
  Milton's wormwood words, 339b
  never strives for the great, 74a
  que m'importe que tu sois s., 707a
  way of s. is to act, 75b
Sagebrush desert, 940a
Sager sort deeds reprove, 300a
Sage's, vain the s. pride, 412b

Saw, last time I s. Paris, 1020a
  life steadily saw it whole, 710b
  man clothed with rags, 365b
  manners in face, 429a
  ne'er s. I never felt, 512a
  never s. a moor, 737b
  never s. a man who looked,
    840b
  never s. never before today,
    666b
  never s. purple cow, 886b
  no sound of s., 458b
  not seen as others s., 641b
  on a cloud I s. a child, 486b
  skull beneath skin, 1002a
  spiders marching, 1075a
  spires of Oxford, 969a
  then I s. the Congo, 953a
  three ships, 1097a
  water lily bloom, 645b
  what men dreamed of seeing,
    820a
  with open eyes, 906b
  young Harry with beaver on,
    240a
Sawdust Caesar, 1018b
Saws, full of wise s., 249a
Sawyer, Adventures of Tom S.,
    761a
Saxa, in spatio pertundere s., 113a
Saxon, ancient S. phrase, 621b
  I am Roderick Dhu, 520a
Saxophones, long cool winding s.,
    948b
Say a thing straight, 797b
  all she had to s., 958b
  canst not s. I did it, 285a
  defend right to s. it, 418a
  disapprove of what you s., 418a
  do as I s. not as I do, 317b
  do not s. things, 609b
  don't s. anything, 911b
  find right thing to s., 836a
  first of God above, 407b
  good deed to s. well, 298a
  good night till it be morrow,
    224b
  got a thing to s., 814a
  I don't s. never do it, 947b
  I s. it's spinach, 1046a
  I shall have less to s., 926b
  it as you understand it, 498a
  it don't take half day, 814b
  it with flowers, 912b
  it with utmost levity, 836a
  know much s. little, 436a
  light stream of what we s., 716a
  Lord what would they s., 881b
  love not s. all it means, 900a
  man may s. what he likes, 140a
  more to s. when dead, 900a
  nastiest thing in nicest way,
    994a
  need to be young to s., 483b
  never s. I was false 293b
  never s. more than necessary,
    480b
  not of Beauty, 990a
  not struggle naught availeth,
    688b
  not what we ought to s., 280b
  not what you s. but how, 740b
  nothin' without compelled,
    693b
  nothin' you can be held to,
    693b
  nothing but what said, 310a
  nothing to s., 690a
  nothing to s. s. nothing, 545a

Say, nothing you couldn't actually
    s., 989a
  person who could not s. no,
    1067b
  reeds at Runnymede, 876b
  remember what we s. here, 639a
  right to s. what one pleases,
    991b
  secure within can s., 369b
  see what I s., 1061a
  shall my little bark, 410a
  shame s. what it will, 265b
  shudder to s. it, 118a
  silence has much to s., 757b
  so long as we can s., 279a
  some s. world end in fire, 927a
  sometimes s. Poor child, 722a
  still we s. as we go, 731b
  tale as said to me, 518b
  temple bells they s., 873b
  that's all I s., 634a
  there is no more to s., 269b
  they s. my verse sad, 854b
  thing to s. s. it, 814b
  this with presence of mind,
    109a
  though I s. it that should not,
    316b
  to all the world, 256b
  to the fleet, 492a
  too late to s. anything not said,
    381b
  way they s. it, 1052b
  wet mind and s. something
    clever, 91a
  what everyone else does not s.,
    806a
  what law is, 485b
  what others s. of them, 363b
  what people s. behind back,
    828a
  what s. they let them s., 202a
  what will Mrs. Grundy s., 501a
  what you mean, 744a
  which can s. more, 293a
  which grain will grow, 281a
  will it not be the same, 597a
  wouldn't s. so till tried, 963b
Saying all we did not know, 991a
  for loving and for s. so, 305a
  good-bye to statue, 1044a
  is one thing, 190b
  mode of s., 713b
  reputed wise for s. nothing,
    231b
  sea what is it s., 671a
  thoughtless s. of princess, 436b
  way of s. above thing said, 960a
  what are wild waves s., 675b
  wise and old, 200b
  Wrath by his meekness, 487a
Sayings, incline ears to my s., 4a
Says a lot in vain refusing, 477b
  First Amendment means what
    it s., 991b
  love nor s. nor thinks, 757b
  no one means all he s., 777b
  she speaks yet s. nothing, 223b
  what he s. least important, 780a
  who is it that s. most, 293a
  who s. it what he s., 780a
Scab of churches, 301a
Scabbard, sword of justice has no
    s., 482b
  sword within the s. keep, 372a
Scabby, hated with s. hatred,
    1083a
Scabies, disputandi pruritus ec-
    clesiarum s., 301a

Scabies, incurable hope like
    s., 1081b
Scaffold sways the future, 692a
  truth forever on s., 692a
Scaffoldage, 'twixt footing and s.,
    268a
Scald, tears s. like molten lead,
    280a
Scalding grave, 909a
Scale, every golden s., 743a
  he by geometric s., 352a
  in equal s. weighing, 257a
  Justice with lifted s., 413b
  so shall you s. the stars, 119b
Scaled invention or artistry, 989a
Scales, device of pair of s., 190a
  father held out golden s., 64b
  fell from his eyes, 49b
  put Hannibal in the s., 139b
Scallop shell of quiet, 199a
Scalped each other, 596a
Scan, faults to s., 449b
  gently s. brother man, 493b
  presume not God to s., 408b
Scandal, greatest s. waits on great-
    est state, 220b
  love and s., 424b
  poets who regard that as s.,
    957a
  public s. is wicked, 360b
  tea and s., 391b
Scandalous and poor, 382a
Scandals of the poor, 891a
  short and simple s., 891a
Scant, if store of crowns be s.,
    309a
Scanted, what s. in hair given in
    wit, 218a
Scanter of your maiden presence,
    259a
Scanty, in longitude though s.,
    496a
  too s. to die for you, 737a
'Scape, who should 's. whipping,
    261b
'Scaped, heart 's. this sorrow,
    293a
Scapegoat, let him go for a s.,
    9b
'Scapes, hair-breadth 's., 272b
Scar, two lives join oft s., 664a
  virtue or vice leaves s., 793a
  wound heals s. disappears, 681b
Scarce, woman wants s. thing,
    863b
Scarcely greet me with that sun,
    292a
Scarceness, eat bread without s.,
    10a
Scarcity, on first s. will turn, 455a
Scare, don't let them s. you,
    1015b
  nor shall you s. with talk,
    1079b
  white clouds on, 926b
Scarecrow, not make s. of law,
    270a
Scarecrows of fools, 725a
Scared, diontherium s. him some,
    797a
  to go to brink, 1000b
Scarf up tender eye of day, 284b
Scarfed bark puts from her bay,
    232b
Scarfs garters gold, 409a
Scarlet, in S. town, 1088a
  letter her passport, 614a
  lily flamed, 86oa
  of maples shake me, 860a

Season, bringeth forth his fruit in s., 16b
each thing that in s. grows, 221a
end of love or s., 926a
ever 'gainst that s., 257a
little s. of love laughter, 748a
love no s. knows, 305a
meat in due s., 21b
moulting s. crisis, 682b
my scope had not this s., 299a
no s. such delight can bring, 319b
of love and laughter, 748a
of mists, 583b
of snows and sin, 772b
overpraised s., 755b
proportion s. form, 267b
shock of corn cometh in s., 14b
tale out of s., 38a
things by s. seasoned, 235b
to come and go, 412b
to every thing there is a s., 27b
word spoken in due s., 24b
your admiration, 258a
youth's s. for joys, 401b
Seasoned, speech s. with salt, 54a
things by season s., 235b
timber never gives, 323a
with a gracious voice, 233b
with Attic salt, 362a
Seasoning of all enjoyments, 361a
sharp s. of truth, 145a
Seasons, afford costly s., 1082a
all s. sweet to thee, 526a
all s. thine O Death, 574a
all times are his s., 308b
appointeth moon for s., 21b
as swift s. roll, 633b
assailed the s., 899b
defend you from s., 278b
depends on s. and days, 942b
he makes s. by months, 3b
joys abound as s. fleet, 214b
lovers' s. run, 305a
man for all s., 179a
mercy s. justice, 234b
not the full four s., 1023b
O s. clear, 1043a
O s. O châteaux, 830a
sorrow breaks s., 217a
time of s. and constellations, 1005a
vernal s. of year, 340a
with the year s. return, 344b
yin and yang became four s., 110a
Seat, castle hath pleasant s., 282a
God's great Judgment S., 872b
of desolation, 342a
of Mars, 226b
of pleasures and loves, 371a
of sensation stomach, 855a
proud s. of Lucifer, 348a
sit in scorner's s., 846a
sitteth in the s. of the scornful, 16b
thy s. is up on high, 228b
thyself sultanically, 697a
upon intellectual throne, 712a
while memory holds a s., 260a
wild sequestered s., 443b
Seated, all s. on the ground, 384a
grace s. on this brow, 264a
heart knock at my ribs, 281b
in thy silver chair, 302a
one day at organ, 725b
Seatown, years around s. corner, 1070b

Seats, change s. and fiddles, 505b
high s. in temple of civilization, 971a
put down mighty from s., 45b
Seaward flying unbroken wings, 1004a
from the town, 551a
looked s. among islands, 816b
trees seemed to march s., 816b
Seawards, my road leads s., 947a
salt tides s. flow, 710b
Secluded chapel, 1007a
eternally from God, 308b
Second, appointed for my s. race, 362b
best to go back quickly, 83a
best's gay goodnight, 883b
childishness, 249a
children for s. time, 91a
class citizens, 1025a
custom almost s. nature, 221a
Daniel, 235a
first among these than s. in Rome, 112a
friend is a s. self, 111b
great nature's s. course, 283b
in war no s. prize, 1025b
is frugality, 75a
mads him, 251b
Mrs. Tanqueray, 902a
no dishonor to halt at s. place, 111a
Theseus a s. Hercules, 136a
thoughts are best, 84b
wife hateful to children, 83b
Secondary, between primary and s., 995a
imagination, 528b
Seconded with will and power, 268a
Secondhand, never give s. opinion, 809b
three busts all s., 831a
Secrecy, for s. no lady closer, 239a
nature's infinite book of s., 287a
queen of s. violet, 581a
the human dress, 489b
Secret aims of nature, 801a
and his dark s. love, 489a
anniversaries of heart, 625a
as grave, 197a
be s. and exult, 881b
black midnight hags, 285a
book with s. reference, 615a
bread eaten in s., 24a
cleanse me from s. faults, 17b
courage s. of liberty, 832b
death a s. of Nature, 141b
dwelleth in s. place, 20b
every creature s. to other, 672a
every daisy knows my s., 832a
extort s. lose curiosity, 605a
guilt by silence betrayed, 370b
inwardly in s. great, 694a
isolated joy of thinker, 786b
keeps s. well as child, 599b
liberty s. of happiness, 832b
life of belly and bone, 1069b
locked within them, 1049b
ministry, 526a
not s. if confided, 685a
nothing is s., 46b
of being a bore, 416b
of freedom a brave heart, 90a
of happiness freedom, 90a
of success constancy, 612b
of success in life, 813b
of their own discovery, 1049b

Secret, open rebuke better than s. love, 26b
our readings s., 951b
phrases of soul, 966b
powers of atom, 888b
self-contained solitary, 670b
single s. will still be man, 1032a
sits in middle and knows, 929a
source of humor, 762b
sympathy, 518b
tell you a great s., 1068b
things belong unto the Lord, 10b
though s. it rolls, 541b
thoughts run over all things, 318a
three keep s. if two dead, 421b
treasures in s. kept, 679b
waters, 1036a
whence this s. dread, 393b
whispers of other's watch, 244a
with every s. thing, 29a
Secretary of Nature, 326b
Secretly, how swift how s., 1022b
nurtured in cellar, 998a
Secret's safe 'twixt you and me, 667b
Secrets cry aloud, 1064b
everybody guesses, 836a
from whom no s. are hid, 60b
holding such things to be holy s., 88b
learned s. of grave, 781a
reveal no s., 450a
trust not him with s., 469b
Sect, know neither s. nor idolatry, 173a
never attached to that s., 571a
slave to no s., 410a
write for country for s., 894a
Section, you-all means s., 1100a
Sects, vicissitude of s. and religions, 209b
Seculo, alteri s., 107b
Secure a few minutes for poetry, 728b
amidst falling world, 393a
and now never mourn, 572a
approval if try hard, 762b
blessings of liberty, 474a
friends by doing favors, 90a
from change, 694a
he who s. within can say, 369b
repeal of bad laws, 717a
strong just weak s., 1073b
you count many friends, 129a
Secured against maladministration, 446a
Securely founded, 477b
orbed, 990b
Security, absolute s., 1055a
against future violations, 426a
collective s., 940b-941a
culture moment of s., 977b
for average man, 971a
for the future, 426a
how little s. we have, 539b
in old book, 694b
no s. in nobleness of another, 939b
of all countries connected, 964a
of future, 741a
of people, 446a
of the Republic, 865a
order s. and peace, 964a
public strength individual s., 484b
system of general s., 974b

Six hundred pounds a year, 411b
impossible things before breakfast, 746a
men of Industan, 680a
of one half-dozen other, 567b
or seven dozen Scots, 239a
Richmonds in the field, 218a
rode the s. hundred, 652a
sette world on s. and sevene, 165a
snowed for s. days and s. night, 1070b
weeks to frost, 1018a
Sixes, things go at s. and sevens, 165a
Sixpence, found crooked s., 1096b
I give thee s., 506b
in her shoe, 315b, 1102b
not a s. sir, 501b
song of s., 1094b
Sixteen hours ago Hiroshima, 982b
Sixth of population slaves, 681a
Sixty minutes an hour, 1042a
uselessness of men above s., 817b
Sixtyfold, brought forth fruit s., 42b
Size, near sight of mere s. of him, 969a
no virtue with s., 603b
not grandeur, 725a
not s. but spirit, 1020b
silkworm s. or immense, 997a
take s. of pots of ale, 352a
those of largest s., 746a
Skating, in s. safety is speed, 607a
Skeleton, ague of s., 1002a
found s. and clothed it, 547b
Skeptic, too much knowledge for s., 408b
Skepticism, luxury of s., 805b
of skeptical age, 780b
then s. then disbelief, 697b
wise s. in good critic, 695a
Sketch ruins of St. Paul's, 595b
Skevar, Ivan Petrofski S., 1100b
Skewered with office pens, 672a
Skies a trifle bluer, 914a
are hanged, 1032a
as long as s. are blue, 571b
ashen and sober, 643b
change s. above them, 874b
cloudless climes starry s., 558b
common people of the s., 300b
common sun air s., 441a
distant deeps or s., 489a
double-darken gloomy s., 694a
earth to vaulted s., 690a
faith deciphered in s., 867a
fear can see more in s., 194b
forehead of frowning s., 193a
heifer owing at s., 583b
if all s. sunshine, 827b
join triumph of the s., 425b
ladder to s., 201a
let its altar reach s., 508a
look look up at s., 803a
looks commercing with the s., 335b
mansions in the s., 397a
many a message from s., 495a
molded and melted across s., 803a
moon climbest s., 203b
my canopy the s., 408a
not cloudy all day, 808a
raised mortal to the s., 371b

Skies, rend the affrighted s., 404b
resume sophistries of June, 734b
rush into the s., 408a
spacious s., 849a
statures touch s., 737b
steelyards of s., 842b
suns s. clouds of June, 741a
tempt offspring to s., 449b
watcher of the s., 579b
wings across canceled s., 1022a
Skiff, fragile s. attains shore, 779a
Skill, a little s. in antiquity, 280b
author's s. to give, 866b
constructed with s., 434a
force has no place for s., 86b
honor hath no s. in surgery, 240b
oars plied with little s., 743a
pass days in that where s. greatest, 127b
sharpens s., 454b
simple truth his utmost s., 300b
'tis God gives s., 689a
to conceal skill, 355b
to him that can get it, 366a
Skilled in works of both languages, 122a
orator a good man s. in speaking, 107b
poet through natural gift, 79a
Skillful, all s. in the wars, 363a
man a different integration, 1038b
more s. in self-knowledge, 515a
scribe s. in office, 4b
Skillfulest arithmetician, 686a
Skillfully, play s. with a loud noise, 18b
Skim, dip wings and s. away, 650a
in airy rings s. heath, 405a
milk masquerades, 766a
one topic here there, 593a
Skimble-skamble stuff, 239b
Skimmed, swallows s. golden grain, 933b
Skin, after my s. worms destroy, 15b
and bones and hymnbook, 617a
beauty's but s. deep, 299b
calf's s. on recreant limbs, 236a
can the Ethiopian change his s., 34a
chameleon's tuning s., 1078b
color loves and s., 305a
come off with whole s., 194b
deep, 299b
for skin, 14a
item with s. wrapped around, 1030a
man who sold hyena s., 924a
no matter color of s., 1025a
of dead sheep, 1047a
of innocent lamb parchment, 215a
patch lion's s. with fox's, 136b
rip off s., 1101b
side outside, 907a
since soul dead save s., 155a
skull beneath the s., 1002a
snake throws enameled s., 229b
squeeze orange throw away s., 417a
white as leprosy, 525a
with the s. of my teeth, 15a
Skinny, fear thy s. hand, 525a
Skins, sisters under s., 875a
Skinside is inside, 907a

Skipped, mountains s. like rams, 22a
Skipper had taken daughter, 621a
Skirmish of wit, 245b
Skirt, sound of her silk s., 110a
Skirts, God's s., 662a
of happy chance, 650b
Skittish, unstaid and s. in motions, 252a
Skittles, beer and s., 669a, 718a
porter and s., 669a
Skoal to the Northland, 621a
Skugg, here S. lies, 422b
Skull beneath the skin, 1002a
of a lawyer, 265b
place of s., 45a
some poor fellow's s., 532a
Skulls, place of s., 555b
Skunk cabbages, 944a
Sky, above the vaulted s., 573a
above world stretched the s., 1023a
admitted to that equal s., 408a
against pearl-gray s., 969a
all the milky s., 880a
and sea and land, 855a
anybody as s. low or high, 933b
banners flout the s., 281a
beautiful as the s., 701b
believe power and goodness in s., 173a
believe these ships from s., 173a
bird is in the s., 364b
blue ethereal s., 393a
blue s. bends over all, 524a
blue s. of spring, 729a
blue s. over my head, 539b
bluebird carries s., 681b
brain wider than s., 736b
bridal of earth and s., 323a
bright reversion in s., 406a
change she earth or s., 1086a
changes when wives, 250b 871b
daffodil s., 652b
daily bread of eyes, 604b
descending black and white, 1075b
dusky night rides down s., 424a
eagle looking at s., 579b
earth and all stars in s., 699b
equal s., 408a
ethereal s., 341b
fair weather for s. is red, 43a
flash of color beneath s., 866a
forehead of morning s., 339a
give us endless s., 1072a
go forth under open s., 574a
goal the s., 1103a
guides through s. thy flight, 574b
hearthfire smoke against s., 1017b
horizons of the s., 3b
immeasurably lofty, 732a
in yon rich s., 648b
inverted bowl we call s., 630b
isolation of s., 955a
late discovered early s., 990b
like lead, 1060b
lingered under benign s., 685b
living air and blue s., 509b
lonely sea and s., 946b
lonesome place against s., 827a
lord believing Christians from s., 172b
lose itself in s., 665b
lyre within s., 641b

Speak daggers to her, 263b
did he stop s. to you, 664a
disrespectfully of equator, 522b
don't s. well of self, 363a
each other in passing, 624a
English without accent, 1011a
for yourself John, 623a
free to s. our minds, 1025a
free to think s. write, 473b
freedom to s., 692b
friends absent s., 307a
gently she can hear, 838b
grief that does not s., 285b
hands for me, 254b
have mouths but s. not, 22a
how to s. true things, 67a
I must s. in passion, 239a
I only s. right on, 255b
I will s. to thee, 259a
if any s., 255a
ill of the dead, 68b
in monstrous little voice, 229a
in public on the stage, 507a
in whatever way given, 896b
less than thou knowest, 277b
let no one s. ill of absent, 128a
let not God s. with us, 9a
let us not s. of them, 159b
liars when they s. truth, 97a
lips forbid to s., 587b
live pure s. true, 653a
Lord for thy servant heareth, 11b
low if you speak love, 245b
masters of things they s., 317a
men love to s. of selves, 770b
more in minute, 224b
name which no one can s., 532a-b
needless to s. about things done, 71a
no man s. to him, 373a
no more of his renown, 651b
not loud or long, 201b
of comfort no man s., 227a
of me as I am, 276b
of moderns without contempt, 415b
of one that loved, 276b
one to s. another hear, 681b
or forever hold his peace, 61a
power to s., 373b
rather of sterner days, 923a
rather s. ill of selves, 355b
Reilly they s. of so highly, 1100b
roughly to little boy, 743b
Sappho would s. openly, 931b
slaves who fear to s., 691b
slow to s., 56a
softly carry big stick, 847b
Spanish to God, 163b
suffer me that I may s., 15b
tears that s., 358a
the affirmative, 610a
the speech I pray you, 262b
the tongue Shakespeare spake, 512b
time to s., 27b
to be silent better than to s., 137a
to God as if men listening, 130a
to him again, 664a
to Him for He hears, 654b
to it Horatio, 256b
to me as to thy thinkings, 274a
to s. and purpose not, 277a
to s. and s. well are two things, 304a

Speak, to s. dishonorably is pardonable, 83a
to the earth, 15a
to whom do I s. today, 3a
to whom s. of whom s., 812b
to your silent ashes, 115b
too full of God to s., 879a
trees known to s., 285a
truth and shame Devil, 181b
we s. not what we mean, 271a
what we feel, 280b
when I s. they are for war, 22a
when I think I s., 249b
when spoken to, 823a
who knows does not s., 74b
with pride of our doings, 995b
with tongues of men, 52a
woe when men s. well, 46b
you s. like a green girl, 259a
Speaker, master s. is the tear, 939b
of words and doer, 63b
Speakest, think before thou s., 195a
wiser than thou art ware, 248a
Speaketh, out of abundance of the heart mouth s., 42b
Speakin' terms with itself, 890b
Speaking, distant s. of voices, 1070b
God loveth not s. ill, 149a
hears you nearby sweetly s., 69b
idle biologically s., 1023b
in s. for myself, 272b
keep thy lips from s. guile, 18b
lies in hypocrisy, 55a
measure what s. about, 723a
orator a good man skilled in s., 107b
persuades when s. fails, 295a
prose without knowing it, 361b
terms with itself, 890b
things which they ought not, 55a
writing voting reasonably, 795b
Speaks a new scene, 322a
according to his actions, 71a
acts before he s., 71a
as man s. so is he, 127b
heart thinks tongue s., 246a
her foot s., 269a
hides one thing and s. another, 63b
holiday, 267a
infinite deal of nothing, 231b
needs no questioning before he s., 85b
poetry is painting that s., 70b
priest that to her s., 201b
she s. poniards, 246a
she s. yet says nothing, 223b
small like a woman, 266b
when he s. air is still, 243a
when Love s., 222a
who s. does not know, 74b
wise man s., 304a
without modesty, 72a
Spear, bring me my s., 490b
burning s. horse of air, 1086a
idle s. and shield, 334a
mangled by the bronze s., 64b
to equal tallest pine, 342a
to thrust club to strike, 180b
took s. but left shield, 482b
where scorn the s., 571b
Spearmint Girl, 1030b
Spears, hand-flung s., 677a
into pruninghooks, 30a
lost in storm of s., 878b
sheen of their s., 558b

Spears, stars threw down s., 489a
Special flag or ship signal, 702b
people unto himself, 10a
providence, 266b
Specialists in mental disease, 977a
preserves us not for s., 1082a
Specialty, weather literary s., 761b
Species, especially male of s., 986a
female of s., 877a
not individual but s., 424a
one s. of superstition, 434b
Specified, my own s. world, 949a
Specious, murder takes s. name, 398b
Speck in cornea fifty cents, 817a
Speckled gigantic flowers, 985a
Spectacle unto the world, 52a
Spectacles, finest s. in nature, 422b
grandest of earthly s., 552a
of books, 367a
of science, 1000b
on nose pouch on side, 249a
Spectator, blood and disposition of s., 659a
live in world as s., 394a
of action he describes, 721a
of mankind, 394a
of mighty scene, 539b
Spectators, pleasure to s., 596b
some must be s., 304a
Spectatum veniunt veniunt spectentur, 128b
Specter bark, 525a
my s. around me, 489b
Specter-gray, when frost was s., 783b
Specter-thin, pale and s., 582b
Speculating, theologian not born by s., 180a
Speculation, everybody watches s., 670a
Speculators, philosophical s., 192b
Speech, abridging freedom of s., 474b
after long silence, 884b
be alway with grace, 54b
be craftsman in s., 3a
burning fire, 773a
cordial s., 604b
day unto day uttereth s., 17b
dead had no s. for, 1006b
ere thought wed with s., 650a
externally mere s., 879a
eyesight and s. wrought, 773a
finely framed, 39a
first silence of s., 624b
free men from bondage, 832b
free s. Frémont, 1099b
free s. in repulsive form, 924a
free s. press assembly, 864b-865a
freedom of s., 763a
freedom of s. and expression, 972b
freedom of s. means, 991b
freedom of s. taken, 461a
given to communicate, 376b
gracious in common s., 679b
great s. impassioned, 101a
I am slow of s., 8a
I wrote in a garret, 426a
impelled us, 1006b
in substaunce ys but air, 163b-164a
is civilization, 937b
is image of actions, 68b
is like tapestries, 78a
is truth, 519a
let thy s. be short, 38b

Task, long day's t. is done, 288b
my t. is smoothly done, 337b
of fortitude and delicacy, 825a
of pure ablution, 581a
one t. for all, 877b
remaining before us, 639a
sore t., 256b
there's the rub the t., 118b
though hard be t., 722b
trivial round common t., 567a
uncompleted t., 792b
what he reads as t., 430b
worldly t. hast done, 291a
Tasking, whole soul's t., 692a
Taskmaster's, my great T. eye, 334b
Taskmasters, lies religion of t., 894b
Tasks, highest to humblest t., 923b
not t. equal to powers, 755a
Tassel-gentle, lure this t. back, 224a
Taste, all ashes to the t., 556a
and see that the Lord is good, 18b
arbiter of t., 140a
by which relished, 516a
connects active with passive, 528a
dull were all we t., 1031b
feminine of genius, 631a
from fountain wells up bitter t., 114a
good strong thick smoke, 664b
inch rule of t., 777a
last t. of sweets, 226b
liquor never brewed, 734b
loathe in t. of sweetness, 240a
man's hand not able to t., 230b
never t. who always drink, 304a
no t. when you married me, 481b
not Pierian spring, 403a
of death but once, 254b
of your quality, 261a
prosperity with more t., 391a
questions of t. and feeling, 776b
sans t. sans everything, 249b
sit down and t. my meat, 324a
smell and t. of things, 907a
sole arbiter is t., 644b
things sweet to t. prove sour, 226a
touch not t. not, 54b
tree whose mortal t., 341b
whole joys, 307b
whole of it, 666b
wild vicissitudes of t., 427a
wretched t., 501b
your ware, 1093b
Tasted all the summer's pride, 486a
can't be t. in sip, 670a
eternal joys of Heaven, 213a
I t. careless then, 735a
of desire, 927a
some books to be t., 209b
two worms, 807b
Tasteless, this age how t., 114b
Tastes like wrath to come, 940b
no accounting for t., 150b
runs against popular t., 380b
wit ne'er t., 411b
woman ruin meets, 402a
Tasting of Flora and country, 582a
Tat, tit for t., 185a

Taters, corn and t. grow, 828b
Tatter in mortal dress, 882b
Tattered coat upon stick, 882b
married man t. and torn, 1098b
through t. clothes, 279b
Tatters, tear a passion to t., 262b
Tattlers and busybodies, 55a
Tattoo soap bubbles, 1047a
Taught as if you taught them not, 403b
character t. learned, 715b
dream t. me this wisdom, 328b
first he wroghte afterward t., 166b
folly's all they t. me, 542b
genius never can be t., 371a
happy is he born and t., 300b
her dazzling fence, 337b
I t. thee to love, 307a
it hath t. me to rhyme, 222a
man never flogged never t., 102a
me all I knew, 876a
me serpent's world, 1057a
mind what I am t., 546a
obeyed what wind had t., 998a
rather be t. than teach, 171b
three useful things, 562b
tortoise because he t. us, 744b
us how to live, 400b
us little but our soul, 711a
wise words t. in numbers, 201a
you t. me language, 296a
Tautness, greyhound's gentle t., 1077a
Tavern, happiness produced by t., 432a
I am come to t. alone, 395a
in the town, 1100a
intend to die in t., 155b
let me in t. die, 154b
Mermaid T., 583b
my t. the Big Bear, 829b
one flash in t. caught, 630b
opened t. for friends, 894a
sweeter wine in t. than bishop decanted, 154b
Taverns, knew t. wel in every toun, 166a
Tawny-throated, nightingale t., 712b
Tax for being eminent, 389a
from chimney t. free, 1105a
heavier than kings, 422b
I t. you not you elements, 278a
just man will pay more income t., 94a
not t. bill but t. relief bill, 973b
power to t. not power to destroy, 788b
power to t. power to destroy, 485b
where no revenue found, 452a
Taxation, more t. than necessary, 771a
without representation, 446a
Taxed, never t. for speech, 269b
schoolboy whips t. top, 522a
without consent, 446b
Taxes, all t. fall upon agriculture, 465b
death and t., 423a
generally raised on city land, 733b
pay for civilized society, 787a
true as t., 671b
war certain to increase t., 467a
Taxi throbbing waiting, 1002b

Te spectem te teneam, 128a
Tea, after t. and cakes and ices, 1001a
although Oriental, 919a
and comfortable advice, 585b
and scandal, 391b
and sometimes t., 404b
breakfast dinner lunch t., 902a
breakfasts at five-o'clock t., 746b
ceremony known as afternoon t., 798a
destruction of t. so bold, 462b
fights, 872b
glad not born before t., 523b
honey still for t., 993b
hot water remain upon t., 328b
if this t. I want coffee, 810b
Michelangelo for t., 759a
sweeteners of t., 424b
take some more t., 744a
thank God for t., 523b
without stratagem, 398b
Teach act of order to kingdom, 243a
aim of oratory to t., 111a
beasts shall t. thee, 15a
charm strengthen and t., 623a
child to doubt, 490b
crab to walk straight, 91a
delight in simple things, 877a
gladly lerne and gladly t., 166b
go and t. all nations, 45a
he who shall t. child, 490a
high thought, 653b
him to tell my story, 273a
himself to be afraid, 1039b
his feet a measure, 774b
I t. you Superman, 805a
learn from those who can t., 82a
learn suffering t. in song, 569b
learn what it had to t., 683a
learning does not t. intelligence, 77b
let such t. others, 402b
me half the gladness, 570b
me my God and King, 323a
me to feel another's woe, 412b
me to hear mermaids singing, 304b
me to live, 377b
men sense of existence, 805a
new occasions t. duties, 692a
noble negligences t., 387b
nothing but to name tools, 352a
order to peopled kingdom, 243a
orphan boy to read, 645a
others t. how to dare, 711b
pleased to t., 404a
rather be taught than t., 171b
same prayer doth t. us all, 234b
shall any t. God, 15b
still pleased to t., 404a
the earth shall t. thee, 15a
them diligently unto thy children, 10a
thy necessity to reason, 226a
to t. is to learn twice, 483b
trees and stones will t. you, 154a
us good Lord to serve Thee, 180b
us how to die, 557a
us to care, 1003b
us to have aspiring minds, 212a
us to number our days, 20b
us to sit still, 1003b
villainy you t. me, 233b

Touched be th' sun, 981a
chord in unison t., 458b-459a
God's finger t. him, 650b
nothing he did not adorn, 432a
spirits not finely t., 270a
things he t. worked with, 943a
to the quick, 662a
with fire, 786b
with moon's red silver, 1081a
Touches, mortality t. the heart, 118a
of sweet harmony, 235b
who t. this t. a man, 703a
Touching, not succeed in t. ideals, 733a
sight so t. in majesty, 512a
Touchstone by which we try services, 472b
calamity man's true t., 316b
panics t. of sincerity, 467a
Touchstones, dreams t. of characters, 681b
Touchy, pacify t. tribe of poets, 124a
testy pleasant fellow, 394a
Tough and devilish sly, 671a
and final growth, 1057b
as a steak, 1035b
but nervous, 997a
customer, 670a
interesting but t., 761a
life t. proposition, 941a
rack of this t. world, 280b
wedge for tough log, 127a
worm in little inside, 768b
Tough-minded, government not more t., 1049a
Toujours gai, 946a
Touring culture like museum, 1057a
Tourist, rich vagabond called t., 932b
Tourney, summoned am to t., 1086a
Tout comprendre t. pardonner, 502b
est pour le mieux, 417a
milieu entire rien et t., 363b
passe, 658a
passe casse lasse, 1105b
perdu fors l'honneur, 180b
rire de t., 460a
Toves, slithy t., 745a
Tower and bells, 483a
burning roof and t., 883b
clock collected in t., 854a
cries as from lighted t., 970b
gloomy shadowed t., 825b
inaccessible t. of past, 694b
intending to build t., 47a
ivory t., 615a
ivory t. of cultural, 937b
ivy-mantled t., 440b, 962b
king's name a t. of strength, 217b
Montaigne in his t., 1054a
neck is as a t. of ivory, 29b
of ivory, 615a
of strength, 651b
proud t., 642a
stand like a firm t., 161a
strongest t. of delight, 697b
to dark t. came, 278b
Trojans sitting on the t., 63a
yonder ivy-mantled t., 440a
Towered citadel pendant rock, 288b
cities please us then, 335a
grim shape t. up, 510a

Towering confidence of twenty-one, 430a
hopes like t. falcons, 387a
in her pride of place, 284a
Towers and battlements it sees, 334b
cloud-capped t., 297b
death overtake you though in lofty t., 149a
elephants endorsed with t., 348b
ivory t., 878a
no t. along the steep, 537b
proud t., 557a
topless t. of Ilium, 213a
two t. of sail, 688b
walls and t. girdled round, 523b
whispering from her t., 713b
ye antique t., 439a
Town, all around the t., 862b
all round t., 1092b
atheist, 1047a
consul in foreign t., 864a
country in t., 135b
crier spoke my lines, 262b
dear damned distracting t., 405b
defend village t. city, 921b
distressed and forsaken, 375b
drunkard, 1047a
end of the t., 970a
follies of t. crept slowly, 450b
hot time in old t., 868a
humming t., 711a
in Scarlet t., 1088a
is lighter than vanity, 365b
it rains softly on t., 830b
leave by t. drain, 807b
little t. of Bethlehem, 755a
London a man's t., 827b
London Town's fine t., 947b
man in our t., 1098a
man made the t., 457b
many ways meet in one t., 243a
never go down to t., 970a
one-horse t., 759a
Paris a woman's t., 827b
Paris my home t., 933b
pretty how t., 1031b
proud tower in t., 642a
sent them out of t., 1093a
Shuteye T., 820b
sprinkle quarters on t., 854a
taller t. than Rome, 918b
tavern in the t., 1100a
what common talk of t. is, 375a
woods go seaward from t., 551a
Yankee Doodle to t., 1090a
Town's, London T. fine town, 947b
Towns, away away from t., 573a
dust and reek of t., 695b
seen enough English t., 1047a
seven t. contend for Homer, 301b
taken t. with words, 311a
winter too long in country t., 940a
Township, destroys t. in sleep, 980b
Toy dog covered with dust, 820b
foolish thing but a t., 253a
had not friend nor t., 694a
like through t. fair, 969a
religion but a childish t., 212b
sells eternity to get t., 220a
soldier red with rust, 820b
Toyed and kissed, 401b
Toys, all is but t., 84a

Toys, bring you colored t., 861a
brooches and t. for delight, 824b
enemies for t., 310a
for your delight, 824b
love and all his pleasures t., 300a
of age, 409a
Trace, boding tremblers learned to t. 449b
characters of hell to t., 441a
misery still delights to t., 459b
noble dust of Alexander, 266a
on dark theme t. verses of light, 113a
painters cannot t., 397a
Traced lives of good men, 517a
Traces, in the t. lead 'em, 693a
of original sin, 707b
winter's t., 772b
Tracing, fitful t. of portal, 955b
Tracings of eternal light, 497a
Track, around ancient t., 730b
down relations of aspects of experience, 984a-b
golden t. 953a
narrow t. to highest good, 114a
Trackless, launch on t. seas, 702b
way, 661a
Tract of inland ground, 516b
Trade, commonly called slave t., 420b
dreadful t., 279b
except what t. give, 668a
food of us that t. in love, 288a
free t., 594b
free t. in ideas, 788a
free t. not principle, 611b
heel of Northeast T., 874a
homely slighted shepherd's t., 338a
how is your t. Aquarius, 1034b
instrument of t., 752a
Irish poets learn t., 885a
literature half t. half art, 859b
love t. thou hast learned, 142a
mission of t. unions, 821a
never pursue literature as t., 528b
no nation ruined by t., 423a
nothing to do but t., 467a
of blood and guile, 526b
serve time to every t., 554b
slave t., 420b
two of a t. never agree, 401b, 730a
unions outgrowth of conditions, 821a
Trades, critic most degraded of t., 764a
ugliest t. have pleasure, 610b
Tradesmen, bow ye t., 767a
lying becomes none but t., 295b
Tradition becomes holy, 805a
cannot be inherited, 1007a
desert t., 605b
finally inspires awe, 805a
for three hundred years, 840a
grows more venerable, 804b
not enough, 1008b
reverence due t. increases, 804b
youth of America oldest t., 840a
Traduced the state, 276b
Traffic, green t. light, 1017b
in mockery, 883a
no kind of t., 296b
of Jacob's ladder, 857a
Trafficked for strange webs, 781a
Trafficking, sail to all thy t., 105a

Walking round the fold, 487a
  taller from w. with trees, 943b
  two w. apart forever, 704a
  up and down in it, 14a
Walks, bear that w. like man, 875a
  biggest rascal that w., 140b
  eye Nature's w., 407b
  God w. in mine, 734a
  having once turned w. on, 525b
  in beauty, 558b
  in w. it seems to me, 902a
  lards lean earth as he w., 238b
  night in silver shoon, 914a
  Nobleness w. our ways, 994a
  o'er dew on eastern hill, 257a
  on hallowed ground, 1026a
  she w. lady of delight, 812a
  so arrogantly, 996b
  third who w. beside you, 1003a
  thy spirit w. abroad, 256b
  two luxuries in w., 586a
  up and down with me, 236b
  up stairs of concepts, 1052b
  who w. with Beauty, 992a
  wish I liked way it w., 860b
  with tender growing night, 700a
Wall, ballads stuck about w., 326a
  before I built a w., 926a
  between church and state, 991a
  Blake beat upon w., 885a
  boasting on my w., 1057b
  bores through his castle w., 227b
  broken w. burning tower, 883b
  close w. up with English dead, 243b
  confronting apparition, 708b
  crannied w., 654b
  doesn't love a w., 926a
  even w. fell down, 1018a
  faces turned to w., 724b
  fell down flat, 11a
  find thy body by w., 715a
  Humpty Dumpty sat on w., 1095b
  Jackson like stone w., 719a
  know the w. is strong, 841a
  must be kept high, 991a
  not conclude against w. of stone, 1079a
  of oblivion, 1040a
  of wisdom, 1054a
  painting lends joy to w., 790a
  serves it in office of a w., 226b
  shadows on opposite w. of cave, 94b
  stone shall cry out of w., 283a
  thou whited w., 50b
  waters were a w., 8b
  weakest goes to w., 195b
  when icicles hang by the w., 222b
  whitewashed w., 450a
  wit is the only w., 1033b
  without a city w., 684b
  wooden w. is your ships, 77b
  your concern when neighbor's w. on fire, 123b
Wall Street, economy reflected in W., 1062b
  lays egg, 916a
  nation that supports W., 891b
Wallace, what W. calls global, 1053b
  wi' W. bled, 496a
Walled round with rocks, 776a
  vain citadels not w., 1028b

Walled, wear out in a w. prison, 280a
Wallet at his back, 268b
  for alms a pilgrim's w., 380b
Walling in or w. out, 926a
Walloping Window Blind, 792a
Wallow naked in December snow, 226a
Wallpaper came alive, 1033b
  one-armed man with w., 864a
Walls and towers girdled round, 523b
  are nothing, 81a
  close her from ancient w., 491a
  down the mountain w., 885a
  falls on castle w., 648b
  hang banners on outward w., 286b
  happy those whose w. already rise, 118a
  have ears, 167a
  I have my own four w., 578a
  of Cumnor Hall, 464a
  peace be within thy w., 22b
  prison w. cannot control, 359a
  pry loose old w., 948b
  stone w. not prison make, 358b
  through w. by thousands pour, 531b
  Troilus mounted Troyan w., 235a
  Troy w. famed in battle, 118a
  watches from mountain w., 651b
Walnuts and wine, 645a
Walrus and the Carpenter, 745b
  weep for you W. said, 746a
Walruses, herds of w. and whales, 696a
Walsinghame, holy land of W., 198b
Walt Whitman am I, 700a
Walter, Sir W. responsible for war, 760b
Walton, rodless W., 846a
Waltzes, Congress doesn't run it w., 464a
Waltzing Matilda, 869a
Waly waly up the bank, 1088b
Wampum of the night, 734b
Wan, angels pallid and w., 642b
  how silently with how w. face, 203b
  so w. with care, 237b
  west shivers, 772b
  why so pale and w., 350a
Wander, children shall w. in the wilderness, 9b
  forth sons of Belial, 342b
  hand in hand, 961b
  if I might, 753a
  thoughts that w. through eternity, 343b
  where'er I w. boast of this, 226b
  wherever I w. wherever I rove, 494b
  whither shall I w., 1094b
Wandered east w. west, 589a
  fingers w. idly, 725b
  lonely as cloud, 514a
  till I died, 714b
Wanderer, ah do not we w., 712a
  halts and hears, 853b
  merry w. of the night, 229a
  weary wayworn w., 641b
Wandering about from house to house, 55a
  between two worlds, 712b
  bird or w. voice, 514a

Wandering by lone sea breakers, 807a
  from nightly shore, 643a
  in w. mazes lost, 344a
  Jew, 1088a
  lazy Scheldt or w. Po, 447b
  minstrel I, 768a
  moon, 335b
  on foreign strand, 518b
  planet's course, 212a
  star to every w. bark, 294a
  stars, 57a
  steps and slow, 348b
  through many countries, 115b
  to nest from w. wide, 854a
  with great Mother's train, 714b
Wanderings, errors w. mists and tempests, 113a
  to guide, 73a
Wane, constellations when they w., 78b
  moon who knowest no w., 630b
  moon will wax w., 624b
Waneth, youth w. by increasing, 204b
Wangle, quangle w., 673b
Waning, beneath w. moon haunted, 523b
  in this w. of light, 1065b
  sadder than w. moon, 626b
Want, buy what you do not w., 474a
  climacteric of his w., 1076b
  covetous man ever in w., 123a
  died in w., 1075b
  for one who comes not, 1037a
  for w. of me, 722a
  for w. of nail shoe lost, 324b, 422a
  freedom from w., 973a, 974b
  get what you w., 878a
  House of W., 780b
  I shall not w., 17b
  if you w. me again, 701a
  in midst of plenty, 1010a
  it most like it least, 415b
  labor with reference to w., 507b
  no man will supply thy w., 309a
  nothing you w., 718a
  of coincidence between accounts, 89a
  of decency want of sense, 374b
  only w. and discontent, 353b
  progress from w. to w., 432a
  thy w. as an armed man, 23b
  to be alone, 1056a
  to be forgotten, 661b
  to spend to give to w., 201a
  toil envy w., 427a
  we do not do what we w., 1058b
  weariness vice and w., 417a
  what I w. when I w., 886b
  woeful w., 546a
Wanted, every man is w., 607b
  never w. a good word, 447a
  one immortal song, 368b
  when discovered not w., 997b
Wanting is what, 668a
  not w. what is stolen, 274b
  perfect and entire w. nothing, 56a
  that which is w. cannot be numbered, 27b
  tried and found w., 918a
  weighed in the balances and found w., 35a
  words once my stock w., 371b

War, quaint and curious w. is, 783b
ready for w. to avoid it, 383a
real w. never in books, 703a
red animal, 904b
regarded as wicked, 839a
relentless, 903a
result of mistaken calculation, 938a
same reason causes w., 190a
Scott responsible for w., 760b
scourge for w., 640b, 1104a
seldom enters but where wealth allures, 370b
sentence is for open w., 343a
silent w. of lilies, 220a
sinews of w., 104b, 181a
some slain in w., 227b
Son of God goes forth to w., 549a
Spanish ships of w., 654D
spares not the brave, 70a
stand up and take w., 877b
strange terrible world w., 923b
study politics and w., 463a
stupid crime, 933a
subject of it is W., 1028b
sweets with sweet w. not, 291b
sword of w. or of law, 473a
talk by men who have been in w., 760b
tempered by w., 1072b
that will end war, 888a
the w. is over, 717a
there was w. in heaven, 58a
this is w., 619b
this w. elemental conflict, 1012a
those who brought w. to Far East, 982b
though w. should rise against me, 18a
Thucydides wrote history of w., 89a
time of w. time of peace, 27b
tired and sick of w., 705a
to make world safe, 866b
to prevent w. not fear it, 531a
to w. and arms I fly, 358b
tongue of w., 1083a
too serious for military, 786a
train of circumstances, 467a
tricked into European w., 913b
ultimate sanction of exploitation, 1027a
unconditional w., 1073b
United Nations alternative to w., 1073b
unjust peace before just w., 422b
unjust w. protracted, 698b
unsuccessful or successful w., 457b
vain w. with heaven, 343a
wage w. like physical giants, 1024b
want an end to w., 974a
warmest heart recoiled at war, 1031a
weapons of w. perished, 12b
well that w. so terrible, 620a
what A.D. is elsewhere, 760b
when aggressions require w., 472b
when I speak they are for w., 22a
when w. he went, 1060b
when w. is done, 992b
who desires peace prepare for w., 146b

War, will to win w., 959b
with reremice, 229b
with rights of mankind, 471b
woman cause of ten years' w., 383b
wrong w. at wrong time, 1025b-1026a
Warble child, 221b
native wood-notes wild, 335a
sweet in springtime, 828b
Warbled to the string, 336a
Warbler, Dan Chaucer first w., 645b
Warblest at eve, 339b
Warbling his Doric lay, 339a
thou w. bird, 494a
Warbonnet of Medicine Hat, 1041b
Ward has no heart they say, 500b
Warder is Despair, 841a
memory the w. of brain, 283a
Wardrobe, dalliance in w. lies, 243b
Wards in Chancery, 767b
pretty young w., 767b
Ware, ill w. is never cheap, 324a
pleasing w. is half sold, 324a
taste your w., 1093b
that will not keep, 852b
wiser than thou art w., 248a
Wares harder to get rid of, 927a
Warfare, atomic w. bad enough, 1015a
biological w. worse, 1015a
is accomplished, 32b
life struggle not w., 770b
love a kind of w., 128b
thy w. o'er, 520a
War-horse, hurl Jackson on w., 696b
Warld, a' the weary w., 479b
it's a weary w., 857b
Warlike, people numerous and w., 173b
Warling, young man's w., 185b
Warm and capable of grasping, 581b
cheek and rising bosom, 441b
heart within, 459a
her coat is so w., 546a
into the w. sun, 185a
keeper of w. lights, 82a
keeps w. her note, 327a
let out to w. air, 389b
man whose blood is w., 231a
now w. in love, 405b
nursing wrath to keep it w., 495b
precincts of cheerful day, 441a
ruddy drops that w. heart, 254b
sea-scented beach, 663a
side inside, 907a
so cold no fire w., 739b
summer sun shine friendly, 822a
sun was w. wind chill, 928a
this sensible w. motion, 271a
virtue keep me w., 369b
weather in bed, 388b
wind the west wind, 947a
with friends I make, 1023b
without heating, 399b
Warm-blooded animals from one filament, 459b
Warmed, glow has w. the world, 981b
hands before fire of life, 536b
unclasps w. jewels, 582a
washed dressed w. fed, 947a

Warmest heart recoiled at war, 1031a
welcome at an inn, 432a
Warming pretty little toes, 1095b
Warmly, in numbers w. pure, 443b
Warms some poor name, 739a
Warmth, a little w. a little light, 751b
about my heart, 585a
no w. no cheerfulness, 592a
of heart increase with years, 1027b
spring brings back balmy w., 114b
warmth more warmth, 869b
Warn, all poet can do is w., 1028b
to comfort and command, 514a
Warned, friends be w. by me, 902a
in a dream, 39b
Warning, come without w., 676b
give w. to world, 292b
steal away give little w., 470a
voice of w. needed, 728b
Warp, weave the w., 441b
Warrant him heart-whole, 250a
she'll prove an excuse, 481b
truth shall be thy w., 199a
Warred for Homer dead, 301b
Warring within breasts, 212a
Warrior, British w. queen, 459a
every lover a w., 128b
happy w. of politics, 916b
happy w. sleeps, 976a
home brought her w., 649a
lay like w. taking rest, 566b
like an armed w., 749a
of North America, 564a
painful w. famoused for fight, 291b
who is the happy W., 515a
Warrior's, in war mounts w. steed, 518b
Warriors, female w., 417b
stern joy w. feel, 520a
War's a game, 458b
annals cloud into night, 784b
disciplinary functions, 795b
glorious art, 398b
used to w. alarms, 591b
Wars, all skillful in the w., 363a
all their w. merry, 918a
and alarums unto nations, 200b
and rumors of wars, 43b
begin in minds, 1104a
boys not sent into foreign w., 972b
brought nothing about, 372a
caused by man, 1018b
chronicle the w. of kites, 350a
dates of w., 765a
disciplines of w., 244a
end to beginnings of w., 974a
fierce w. and faithful loves, 200a
for right thing, 984a
forgotten w., 1005a
inevitability of w., 954b
more pangs than w. or women, 298b
most terrible of all w., 842a
not acts of God, 1018b
of European powers, 491b
planned by old men, 962a
that make ambition virtue, 275a
thousand w. of old, 651a

White radiance stretches above
  it, 65b
raiment w. as snow, 45a
red thoughts teeth w., 904a
rose breathes of love, 806b
rose is a dove, 807a
rose weeps She is late, 652b
roses and w. lilies grow, 300a
sails still fly seaward, 1004a
samite, 175a, 653a
scare w. clouds on, 926b
sea widening, 1066b
seas show w. when rocks near,
  315a
shields of expectation, 694a
silence, 618a, 990a
silence deep and w., 693b
silken turbans wreathed, 348b
singe my w. head, 278a
sins shall be w. as snow, 30a
sound rising to fury, 1072a
steamers w. and gold, 876a
striped pure celestial w., 578b
sullen w. surf, 697b
superfluity comes by w. hairs,
  231b
sustenance despair, 736b
sweet w. wine, 947a
three w. leopards, 1003b
thunders of w. silence, 618a
tupping your w. ewe, 272a
we black and they w., 1067a
wear w. flannel trousers, 1001a
whale's w. hump, 696b
wild w. horses play, 710b
wings one black other w., 349b
White House, unapproachable in
  W., 976b
White-chokered and clean-shaven,
  796a
Whited sepulchers, 43b
  thou w. wall, 50b
White-flaming bush, 1014b
Whiten, willows w., 645b
Whiteness, restore to w. wool
  dyed purple, 146a
Whiter, I shall be w. than snow,
  19a
Whites of their eyes, 435a, 446b
Whitespread wings, 969a
Whitest, old linen wash w., 314b
  woman w. of beings, 993a
White-walled tent, 1032a
Whitewash and a long-handled
  brush, 759a
Whitewashed wall, 450a
Whither away fair rover, 801a
  coffin asks w., 749a
  fled visionary gleam, 513b
  goest thou, 49a
  shall I go from thy spirit, 23a
  so high, 1095b
  thou goest I will go, 11b
Whithersoever, with thee w. thou
  goest, 10b
Whiting to a snail, 744b
Whitman, Homer and W. roar in
  pines, 898a
Walt W. am I, 700a
Whitman's poems poetry, 1035a
Whittington, turn again W.,
  1085b
Whittled out of hickory, 1036a
Whittler, bein' a good w., 895a
Who ah who will make us feel,
  711b
  are these coming, 583a
  are we where are we, 680b
  are you cried one agape, 764b

Who breaks birth's bar, 650b
  can hold fire in his hand, 226a
  doesn't desire father's death,
    708b
  doth ambition shun, 248a
  ever got out of winding sheet,
    308b
  ever loved not at first sight,
    212b
  fears to speak of Ninety-eight,
    720a
  follows in His train, 549b
  gained by it, 110b
  has seen the wind, 739b
  hath desired sea, 876a
  hath known mind of Lord, 51a
  hath seen her wave, 645b
  How and Where and W., 876a
  how w. gets what, 994a
  I'm nobody w. are you, 735a
  is in who's out, 280a
  is master who's man, 391a
  is Silvia what is she, 221a
  is the happy Warrior, 515a
  is the third, 1003a
  is this King of glory, 18a
  killed Cock Robin, 1093b
  killed John Keats, 562b
  knows but world may end, 664a
  loses and who wins, 280a
  night and silence w. is here,
    229b
  of us being what he is, 900a
  ran to help me, 546a
  said Peacock pie, 914b
  shall ascend into the hill of the
    Lord, 18a
  shall deliver me, 51a
  shall stand in his holy place,
    18a
  should 'scape whipping, 261b
  then devised torment, 1007a
  to himself law no law doth
    need, 205b
  touches a hair, 626b
  walks with Beauty, 992a
  why which what, 673b
  will bell cat, 76a, 169b
  would have thought so much
    blood, 286a
Whoe'er has traveled, 432a
  she be, 354a
  thou art behold master, 418a
Whoever wishes to attain English
  style, 428a
Whole America nothing less, 452b
  armor of God, 54a
  beautiful w. numbers, 1034a
  better had I stolen w., 823b
  by sample we judge w., 194a
  climate of opinion, 1060a
  dies when heart is w., 1022b
  drink and be w. again, 929a
  duty of man, 29a
  earth for religion's sake, 699b
  earth is sepulcher of famous
    men, 90a
  earth our hospital, 1005b
  first comprehend w., 736a
  general joy of w. table, 285a
  happy people die w., 994b
  has beginning middle and end,
    99a
  how much more is half than w.,
    67b
  I am equal and w., 775b
  indictment against w. people,
    453a
  love is the w., 1031b

Whole, makes w. world kin, 269a
  my w. course of love, 272b
  need not physician, 41b
  never sees a w., 711b
  one stupendous w., 408b
  prayers make me w., 872b
  saw life w., 710b
  soul's tasking, 692a
  taste w. of it, 666b
  tribe of fops, 277a
  volumes in folio, 221b
  wide sky above me, 1041a
  willing to know w. truth, 465a
Wholeness of human problem,
  937b
Wholesome even for king, 738a
  harvests reaps, 590b
  nights are w., 257a
Wholesomest, old wine w., 314b
Wholly, I shall not w. die, 122b
Whom shall I fear, 18a
  they fear they hate, 107a
Whooping, out of all w., 249b
Whoops, owlet w. to wolf below,
  525b
Whore, pity she's a w., 317b
  posture of a w., 289a
  the woman's a w., 431b
  treat w. like lady, 941a
Whore's oath, 279a
Whores, till all w. burned alive,
  387b
Whorled ear, 802b
Who's in who's out, 280a
  master who's man, 391a
Whose world or mine or theirs,
  989a
Why, causes w. and wherefore,
  245a
  don't you speak for yourself,
    623a
  every w. hath a wherefore, 218a
  how who gets what when w.,
    994a
  I can't say w. I don't like you,
    135a
  I can't think w., 768a
  is plain as way to church, 248a
  is this thus, 751a
  love's stricken w., 738a
  man of morals tell me w., 357b
  men fell out knew not w., 351b
  persecutest thou me, 49b
  though I could never tell w.,
    765b
  What and W. and When, 876a
  who w. which what, 673b
Wibrated, strings better not w.,
  670a
Wicked are w. no doubt, 660a
  deceitful and desperately w.,
    34b
  dreams abuse sleep, 283a
  flee when no man pursueth,
    26b
  forsake his way, 33b
  God help the w., 239b
  I have seen the w. in great
    power, 18b
  intents w. or charitable, 259a
  I's w. I is, 659b
  little better than one of w.,
    238a
  man Hitler, 921b
  men are w. who is good, 894b
  men from out thee go, 358a
  name of the w. shall rot, 24a
  no peace unto the w., 33a
  public scandal is w., 360b

X

Y

Z